A BIBLIOGRAPHY OF
ENGLISH HISTORY
TO 1485

A BIBLIOGRAPHY OF
ENGLISH HISTORY
TO 1485

BASED ON

*The Sources and Literature of English History
from the earliest times to about 1485*

BY

CHARLES GROSS

EDITED BY

EDGAR B. GRAVES

*Professor of History, Emeritus
Hamilton College*

AND ISSUED UNDER THE SPONSORSHIP OF
THE ROYAL HISTORICAL SOCIETY
THE AMERICAN HISTORICAL ASSOCIATION
AND
THE MEDIAEVAL ACADEMY OF AMERICA

OXFORD
AT THE CLARENDON PRESS
1975

Oxford University Press, Ely House, London W. 1

GLASGOW NEW YORK TORONTO MELBOURNE WELLINGTON
CAPE TOWN IBADAN NAIROBI DAR ES SALAAM LUSAKA ADDIS ABABA
DELHI BOMBAY CALCUTTA MADRAS KARACHI LAHORE DACCA
KUALA LUMPUR SINGAPORE HONG KONG TOKYO

ISBN 0 19 822391 9

© *Oxford University Press 1975*

*Printed in Great Britain
at the University Press, Oxford
by Vivian Ridler
Printer to the University*

PREFACE

THIS bibliography is basically a revision of *The Sources and Literature of English History from the earliest times to about 1485* by Charles Gross. The first edition of that remarkable work, which appeared in 1900, was designed as 'a systematic survey of the printed materials relating to the political, constitutional, legal, social, and economic history of England, Wales and Ireland' down to 1485. It was 'the outcome of an annual course of lectures on the sources and literature of English history delivered at Harvard University from 1890 to 1899'. From the time of its publication Gross steadily collected material for a contemplated second edition; but his death on 3 December 1909 forestalled its realization under Gross's guidance.

The publication of the second edition, revised and enlarged, in 1915 was supervised by a committee of Gross's colleagues at Harvard, with financial assistance from the Gross family.

Charles Gross (1857–1909), a native of Troy, New York, graduated from Williams College in 1878. Shortly thereafter, he spent several years of study at the universities of Leipzig, Berlin, Paris, and Göttingen. From Göttingen he received a doctorate in 1883 with a dissertation which was later expanded into two volumes as *The Gild Merchant* (no. 5364 below). In 1888 Gross became an instructor in history at Harvard University and spent the rest of his academic life there.

In 1897 he published his well-founded *Bibliography of British Municipal History*, for the reissue (1966) of which Geoffrey Martin wrote an appreciation of the significance and permanence of Gross's work in British municipal history. Gross's publications for the Selden Society and on other subjects are cited under his name in the index below. The work for which Gross's name has been most widely and most deservedly acclaimed is *The Sources and Literature of English History . . . to about 1485*. A pioneer-work in assembling in an organized fashion the printed sources and modern commentaries of medieval English history, it has served several generations of scholars as an 'indispensable instrument of investigation'. Anyone who has closely examined it must have been impressed with its judiciousness in selection and its accuracy in detail. Tributes by his colleagues to Gross's scholarship and influence may be found in *The Dictionary of American Biography* and in *The Proceedings of the Massachusetts Historical Society*, xlix (1916), 161–6.

Within two decades of the publication of the 1915 edition of *Sources and Literature*, the preparation of a third edition was proposed. In March of 1935 Professor F. M. Powicke, President of the Royal Historical Society, invited the Mediaeval Academy of America to collaborate in the preparation of a revised edition. The Mediaeval Academy accepted the invitation; and an editorial board consisting of N. S. B. Gras, C. H. McIlwain, F. M. Powicke, F. M. Stenton, and W. E. Lunt, as editor, was appointed. Collaborating scholars were solicited for undertaking topical sections.

Attempts to secure sufficient funds for the project were not entirely successful. Contributions were made by the Royal Historical Society, The British Academy, The Public Archives of Canada, and the American Council of Learned Societies, and by nine of the American colleges and universities represented by collaborating scholars. With the coming of the Second World War and with financial support insufficient, work on the revision was postponed. The project was revived in the spring of 1949, with strong support from the Royal Historical Society. Professor Lunt collected several trays of cards of relevant entries, and conducted a considerable correspondence with collaborators, especially with Professor Powicke. However, in 1951 Professor Lunt requested to be released from the editorship. For some time an Anglo-American committee, headed by Dr. Stanley Pargellis, sought a sufficiently large subsidy to make feasible the preparation of a complete series of bibliographies of British history. The quest was successful when in early 1956 the American Historical Association received a grant from the Ford Foundation 'to enable the Association, in co-operation with the British Academy, the Mediaeval Academy of America, and the Royal Historical Society, to revise and complete a planned series of British bibliographies'. The co-operating societies appointed the Anglo-American Committee for British Bibliographies to select editors for specific volumes and to give a general supervision to the project.

For the revision of Gross's *Sources*, I was invited to become editor-in-chief in June of 1956. Clearly I could not embark on the task of revising such a monumental work without the assurance of full assistance from many scholars. With that assurance in hand, I accepted the editorship; and I must say immediately that I have not been disappointed through lack of support. In November of 1956 Mr. Charles Miller, the Executive Secretary of the Mediaeval Academy of America, informed me that 'the editorial board for the new Gross bibliography now consists of Sir Maurice Powicke, Sir Frank Stenton, Professor Charles H. McIlwain, Professor Sidney Painter, Professor William H. Dunham, Jr., and Edgar B. Graves, chairman and editor-in-chief'.

An extensive correspondence with Sir Maurice Powicke produced long letters which, once deciphered, provided informative answers to questions which arose in the preliminary stages on my work. I lost his counsel with his death in May of 1963. Similarly, Sidney Painter's death in January 1960 had cut off the help which he had previously given. In the spring of

1960 Professor the Revd. M.D. Knowles and Professor J. G. (later Sir Goronwy) Edwards accepted appointment to the Advisory Committee. Subsequently they were joined by Professor Richard W. Southern, Professor Christopher N. L. Brooke, and Professor James C. Holt. These five British scholars and Professor William H. Dunham, Jr., of Yale University have constituted the generously active committee during the productive stages of this revision.

The general principles on which this present bibliography has been fashioned are broadly those set forth by Charles Gross. However, the extension of knowledge, particularly in the fields of economic and cultural history, has necessitated some rearrangement for the pre-Norman period and considerable reorganization for the subsequent period.

Local History has been assigned its own chapter (VII), with an introduction on pages 211–12; and sections on the Structure of Society and on Learning and Literature have been developed. The new section listing the articles in *Festschriften* and Collected Works obviates the need for repeating the book's title when reference is made to an article therein. Studies on the Palatinates, the Forests, and the Jews have been gathered together under the heading of Special Jurisdictions. New chapters have been created under the titles Land Tenures and Estates (XVIII), Agrarian Society (XIX), Urban Society (XX), The Church (XXI–XXII), and Intellectual Interests (XXIII). Chapter XVIII draws together feudal tenures, inquests, charters, deeds, wills, family records, household books, and estate management. Chapters XIX, XX, and XXI separate out the component parts of Section 57: Local Records and Local Annals in Gross's arrangement. Some miscellaneous entries, scattered in the 1915 edition, are subsumed under Intellectual Interests. It has seemed advisable throughout to enter the secondary accounts in as close a juxtaposition to the sources as feasible.

This edition is a bibliography of English history; and in that respect it differs from the subsequent volumes in the series published by the Clarendon Press. Like previous editions, it includes for the pre-Norman period some fundamental studies on Welsh and Irish history; but it comprises for the period from 1066 to 1485 only those studies about non-English areas which relate directly to England. *The Bibliography of the History of Wales* with its supplements (No. 10) and the commentary on the sources provided by R. Ian Jack in *Mediaeval Wales* (No. 22) serve as sufficient guides. A full-length bibliography of Irish history is being prepared by Irish scholars (No. 23); meanwhile the older compilations of Kenney (No. 23) and O'Curry (No. 30) can be reinforced by the citations given by Asplin (No. 4030), Byrne (No. 35), Eager (No. 16), Hughes (No. 22), and Otway-Ruthven (Nos. 35 and 1203). No attempt has been made to include Scottish history; but the index under 'Scotland' refers to such bibliographical aids as exist for Scottish medieval history.

The terminal date for subject-matter in this edition is 1485, thereby coinciding with the terminal date set by Gross and the commencing date used by Conyers Read in the volume following in this series. This selection is not intended to maintain the now often discarded periodization in which 1485 marks a watershed between the Middle Ages and the New Monarchy. The subject-matter stretches back into prehistory, to which the scant selection given here can serve as only the barest introduction.

The terminal date for entries is December 1969 for the period before the Norman Conquest, and December 1970 for the period from 1066 to 1485. A bibliography is, of course, out of date as soon as the proofs are returned to the printer. Numerous noteworthy studies have appeared since the terminal dates cited above; a few of them have been squeezed in where space could be found in the proofs without disturbing the pagination.

The mass of publications over the past six decades relevant to this bibliography has required the rigorous selection of entries. In broad terms the criteria of selection have restricted inclusion to (*a*) editions of sources and direct commentaries thereon, (*b*) older standard or seminal studies in books and articles, and (*c*) recent writings, especially those which set forth new or controversial interpretations or include modern specialized bibliographies. Virtually all the entries fitting the first two categories which appear in the 1915 edition have been repeated in this edition. Often the language of the previous edition has been retained; but, where necessary, it has been revised and brought up to date by both omission and addition. Like earlier editions, this edition concentrates on the source material in print; accordingly an attempt has been made to include the publications of source material since 1910. Specialists in narrower fields of research will, of course, turn to more specialized bibliographies, many of which are catalogued below (see the index under 'Bibliography'). Throughout we have tried to keep in mind the audience to which Charles Gross addressed himself in his course for graduate students at Harvard University; accordingly the auxiliaries to the study of history and the aids to historical research have been given special attention. Although these have been the general principles of selection, deviations from them have occasionally seemed warranted.

My obligations to scholars who have provided information and advice are extensive. As I express my sincere gratitude to each of them, I absolve them, of course, from responsibility for any errors or shortcomings which remain. Liability for deficiencies in this edition must rest entirely with me.

Mere acknowledgement insufficiently expresses my debt to those scholars who examined sections of my tentative typescript in my presence, and normally line by line. At Newnham College, Cambridge, Professor Dorothy Whitelock and Dr. Kathleen Hughes criticized sections on

Anglo-Saxon and early Irish history. At the British Museum Dr. Godfrey R. C. Davis remoulded my lists of illuminated manuscripts and facsimiles. In Cambridge, Professor Christopher Cheney discussed the entries for diplomatic and gave some general advice; and Professor Philip Grierson amended my suggestions for numismatics. At the Bodleian, Dr. Richard Hunt discussed palaeography and illuminated manuscripts. At the Public Record Office, Mr. H. C. Johnson, then Keeper of the Public Records, and Dr. Patricia Barnes criticized my lists concerning exchequer records. At the Institute of Historical Research, Professor Ralph B. Pugh provided much information on local history and particularly on the Victoria County History. Professor Geoffrey Martin allowed me to see some of the proofs for his forthcoming bibliography of municipal history, from which I copied a couple of items.

Other scholars have examined sections, or answered inquiries, by correspondence. The first drafts dealing with archaeology, architecture, and palaeography benefited from the criticism of Professor Grahame Clark, President T. S. R. Boase, and Dr. Neil Ker respectively; but they have since been completely redrawn. Professor Ruth J. Dean examined the section on the Anglo-Norman Language; and Professor Brian Tierney commented on an early draft concerning canon law. Professor Alec R. Myers wrote to me at length on some of the chroniclers of the later middle ages, particularly the foreign chroniclers. Dr. J. J. N. Palmer divulged his conclusions on the authorships of the *Chronique de la Traison* (No. 2841) and associated chronicles, which will be substantiated in his forthcoming edition of the *Chronique de la Traison*. With keen eyes the members of the Graduate Centre of Medieval Studies at Reading University uncovered numerous typographical errors, particularly in the smaller print; for their painstaking scrutiny I offer especial thanks.

Among my immediate colleagues, I must mention Professor Peter Marcy of Kirkland College who interrupted his research in England to provide some citations in local journals; to Professor Stephen Bonta of Hamilton College who steered me in the preparation of the brief section on late medieval music; and Dr. Michael Haltzel who eliminated many mistakes in my citations of Russian works.

But most of all I must express my deepest appreciation to the members of my Advisory Committee. In conferences and in correspondence they have given information, advice, and criticism. They enlisted the co-operation of most of the scholars mentioned in the preceding paragraphs. Each of them has reviewed those pages both of the manuscript and of the printer's proofs which were most pertinent to his immediate interests. Finally we acknowledge most gratefully our obligation to Professor Christopher Brooke who has not only served as co-ordinator and reporter for the Committee in England, but also has unflinchingly read, with a censor's pencil in hand, nearly all of the pages in typescript, in galley-proof, and in page-proof.

If the dozen or more libraries on both sides of the Atlantic Ocean which have graciously opened their facilities to me during my work on this project are not named individually, their services were none the less deeply appreciated. I should, however, make special reference to the searchers in the Research Libraries of the New York Public Library and to the Librarian and Staff of the Hamilton College Library.

The not inconsiderable expenses of this enterprise have been met, in large measure, by various subsidies. Office expenses, stenographic costs, and compensation for temporary search-assistance have been paid from the aforementioned subsidies from the Ford Foundation and from the unused balance of the pre-war contributions administered by the Mediaeval Academy of America. Substantial portions of the expenditures on the editor's three trips to England have been defrayed by grants from the American Philosophical Society of Philadelphia, the National Foundation for the Humanities, and the Trustees of Hamilton College. To each of these institutions, I offer my thanks.

Finally, suffice it in this place to express my gratitude to my wife, Beatrice Palmer Graves, for her material contribution in collecting data and in sorting thousands of cards, as well as for her understanding and forbearance over nearly half a century.

In an undertaking of this scope, the possibility, indeed the likelihood, of error is large; accordingly we shall be grateful for the reader's corrections along with his indulgence.

EDGAR B. GRAVES

Hamilton College
Clinton, New York
18 March 1974

CONTENTS

CORRIGENDA   xxii
LIST OF ABBREVIATIONS   xxiii
LIST OF SYMBOLS   xxiv

PART ONE
GENERAL WORKS AND AUXILIARY SCIENCES

I. BIBLIOGRAPHICAL GUIDES   1

  A. GENERAL BIBLIOGRAPHIES   1
    1. Bibliographies of Bibliographies   1
    2. Guides to Reprints   2
  B. BIBLIOGRAPHIES OF BRITISH HISTORY   2
  C. FOREIGN BIBLIOGRAPHIES   7
  D. PRINTED CATALOGUES OF BOOKS   11
    1. General Catalogues   11
    2. Catalogues of Important Libraries   11

II. JOURNALS OF MORE THAN LOCAL SCOPE   13

  A. BIBLIOGRAPHY OF JOURNALS   13
  B. GUIDES TO PERIODICAL LITERATURE   14
  C. GENERAL HISTORICAL JOURNALS   16
    1. British Journals   16
    2. Foreign Journals   20
  D. PUBLICATIONS OF SOCIETIES   22
    1. England   23
      a. Proceedings, transactions, etc.   23
      b. Record series of societies   25
    2. Wales: Record Publications of Societies   26
    3. Scotland: Record Publications of Societies   27
    4. Ireland   28
      a. Record publications of societies   28
      b. Serials devoted primarily to Ireland   29

III. AUXILIARIES TO HISTORICAL STUDY   30

  A. PHILOSOPHY AND METHODOLOGY OF HISTORY   30
  B. PHILOLOGY   34
    1. English   34
    2. French: Anglo-Norman   37
    3. Latin   38
    4. Celtic Languages   40
    5. Runic Inscriptions   44

C. CHRONOLOGY   45

D. PALAEOGRAPHY AND DIPLOMATIC   47
    1. Palaeography: Guides and Manuals   47
    2. Abbreviations and Writing Materials   49
    3. Diplomatic: Codicology   50
    4. Incipits   53
    5. Facsimiles   53

E. SEALS AND HERALDRY   57
    1. The Study of Seals   57
    2. Heraldry   59
      a. General treatises   59
      b. Armorial bearings, rolls of arms, etc.   61

F. BIOGRAPHY AND GENEALOGY   62
    1. Journals and Guides   63
    2. Dictionaries and Reference Works   65
    3. Family History   66
      a. Royalty   66
      b. Titles of honour and pedigrees   67
    4. Personal Names: Guides and Indexes   70

G. GEOGRAPHY AND PLACE-NAMES   71
    1. Dictionaries, Gazetteers, and Maps   72
    2. Treatises   74
    3. Place-names   75

H. NUMISMATICS   78
    1. Bibliography and Journals   78
    2. Particular Periods   79
      a. Pre-Roman   79
      b. Roman   79
      c. From Roman to Tudor times   80
      d. Important articles on numismatics, 1066–1485   84

I. ARCHAEOLOGY   84
    1. Bibliographical Guides and Journals   85
    2. Inventories   87
    3. General Techniques and Interpretations   88
    4. Air Photography   89
    5. General Treatises on Archaeology   90

J. ART   92
    1. Bibliographical Guides and Journals   92
    2. General Treatises on Architecture and Art   93
    3. Domestic Architecture   96
    4. Castles   97
    5. Treatises on Sculpture, Painting, and Minor Arts   98
    6. Illuminated Manuscripts   101
      a. General books   101
      b. Studies on groups   101
    7. Costume, Armour, and Weapons   103

PART TWO

ARCHIVES, SOURCE COLLECTIONS, AND MODERN NARRATIVES

IV. ARCHIVES AND LIBRARIES   107

  A. BIBLIOGRAPHICAL GUIDES   107

  B. REPOSITORIES   108

    1. British Archives   108

      a. General Works   110

      b. Public Record Office   111

    2. English Libraries   118

      a. Catalogues and accounts of general manuscript collections   118

      b. British Museum   120

      c. Other important repositories in London   122

      d. Important English repositories outside London   124

      e. The larger cathedral libraries   127

    3. Welsh Repositories   129

    4. Scottish Repositories   130

      a. Archives   130

      b. Catalogues of MSS. in Scottish libraries   131

    5. Irish Repositories   131

      a. Archives   131

      b. Catalogues of MSS. in Irish libraries   133

V. PRINTED COLLECTIONS OF SOURCES   134

  A. PUBLICATIONS OF THE BRITISH GOVERNMENT   135

  B. COLLECTIONS PRIVATELY EDITED   136

    1. Chronicles, etc.   136

    2. Church History: General Sources   144

    3. Church History: Monasticism: Sources   147

    4. Church History: *Acta Sanctorum*   148

VI. COMPREHENSIVE MODERN NARRATIVES   152

  A. GENERAL NARRATIVES IN SERIES   152

    1. Series Relating to Britain   152

    2. General Narratives for Ireland   155

  B. CONSTITUTIONAL HISTORY   155

  C. LEGAL HISTORY   159

  D. HISTORIES OF THE CHURCH   164

    1. General Bibliography   164

    2. Modern Treatises   165

    3. Studies on Monasticism   167

    4. Studies on Canon Law   168

    5. Service Books, Liturgy, Ritual, etc.   170

    6. The Coronation Service   173

E. COMMENTARIES ON THE STRUCTURE OF SOCIETY   174
    1. General Treatises   175
    2. Borough and Town   177
F. LITERATURE AND LEARNING   179
G. *FESTSCHRIFTEN* AND COLLECTED WORKS   183
    1. *Festschriften* Analysed   183
    2. Collected Works Analysed   194

VII. LOCAL HISTORY   211
  A. GENERAL BIBLIOGRAPHY   211
  B. COUNTY HISTORY   215
    1. Victoria County History   215
    2. England: County by County Alphabetically   219
    3. Wales: County by County   250
    4. Isle of Man and Channel Islands   254

PART THREE

FROM PREHISTORY TO ANGLO-SAXON CONQUEST

VIII. PREHISTORIC AND CELTIC TIMES   256
  A. PRE-ROMAN AGE IN BRITAIN   256
    1. Bibliography, Journals, and Guides   256
    2. General Treatises on the Prehistoric Age   257

IX. THE ROMAN OCCUPATION   261
  A. BIBLIOGRAPHY, JOURNALS, AND GUIDES   262
  B. ANCIENT SOURCES   263
    1. Greek and Roman Literary Sources   263
    2. Other Ancient Sources   266
  C. MODERN WRITERS   268
    1. Comprehensive Accounts   268
    2. Special Sites   271
    3. Special Topics   273
      a. The Roman Army   274
      b. Art and buildings   274
      c. Roman mining   274
      d. Roman pottery   275
      e. Religion   275
      f. Roman roads   275
      g. Roman walls   275
      h. Frontiers: Wales and Scotland   276
  D. THE END OF THE ROMAN OCCUPATION: ROMAN SURVIVALS   277

X. CELTIC BRITAIN AFTER THE ROMAN
    OCCUPATION   279

PART FOUR

THE ANGLO-SAXON PERIOD

XI. ANGLO-SAXONS AND CELTS: SOURCES 283

A. CHRONICLES AND ANNALS 283

B. ADMINISTRATIVE SOURCES 299

  1. Anglo-Saxon 299
    a. Anglo-Saxon laws 300
    b. Latin law-books 301
    c. Charters, writs, wills, etc. 303
    d. Isolated pieces 307
    e. Studies on Anglo-Saxon charters 309
  2. Laws of the Celtic Areas 310
    a. Wales 310
    b. Ireland 312

C. CHURCH SOURCES 314

  1. Canons, Penitentials, etc. 314
  2. Homilies 316
  3. Monastic Rules 317
  4. Lives and Letters of Saints and Scholars 319
    a. Anglo-Saxon 319
      i. General commentaries 319
      ii. Collections of sources 319
      iii. Individual saints and scholars 320
    b. Celtic saints 333

D. LITERATURE AND LEARNING 339

  1. Anglo-Saxon 339
    a. Sources 340
    b. Modern commentaries 343
    c. Scientific Writings 344
  2. Celtic Literature 346
    a. Sources 346
    b. Modern studies on Celtic literature 350
  3. Scandinavian Literature 351
    a. Bibliographical guides 352
    b. Principal collective editions 353
    c. Particular sagas 354
    d. Modern commentaries in English 356

E. NON-LITERARY SOURCES 357

XII. MODERN COMMENTARIES ON THE ANGLO-SAXON PERIOD   360

  A. GENERAL COMPREHENSIVE SURVEYS   360

  B. ANGLO-SAXON INVASIONS AND SETTLEMENTS   362
    1. The Anglo-Saxon Invaders in their Continental Homelands   362
    2. The Anglo-Saxon Invasions and Settlements to *c.* A.D. 871   364
    3. Alfred to the Norman Invasion   368

  C. ANGLO-SAXON ADMINISTRATION AND LAW   372

  D. STRUCTURE OF SOCIETY IN ANGLO-SAXON TIMES   374
    1. Rural Society   375

  E. THE CHURCH IN ANGLO-SAXON TIMES   378
    1. Survivals of Paganism   378
    2. The Celtic Church   379
    3. Anglo-Saxon Church   382
      a. From Augustine to Bede   382
      b. From the death of Bede to Norman Conquest   383

PART FIVE

FROM NORMANS TO TUDORS

XIII. CHRONICLES AND ROYAL BIOGRAPHIES   386
  A. INTRODUCTORY COMMENTS   386
  B. GENERAL COLLECTIONS OF CHRONICLES   392
  C. ALPHABETICAL TABLE OF CHRONICLES   395

XIV. LAW TRACTS   454
  A. PRINCIPAL TREATISES   455
  B. TRACTS, LARGELY ON PROCEDURE   459

XV. PUBLIC ADMINISTRATIVE RECORDS   462
  A. EXCHEQUER RECORDS   462
    1. General Documents: Dialogus and Exchequer Books   462
    2. Domesday Book and its Satellites   463
      a. Domesday Book   463
      b. Satellites   464
      c. Domesday Book by counties   465
      d. Modern commentaries on Domesday Book   468
    3. Local Inquests and Surveys 1066–1200   471
    4. Pipe Rolls   473
      a. General collections   474
      b. Pipe Rolls by counties   475
    5. Receipt and Issue Rolls   477
    6. Household: Wardrobe and Chamber   479
      a. Household ordinances and accounts   479
      b. Modern commentaries   482

7. Subsidy Rolls and Taxation   483
   a. General collections   483
   b. Taxation by counties   484
8. Memoranda and Originalia Rolls   491
9. Miscellaneous: Various Classes   493
10. Selected Commentaries on the Exchequer and Taxation   495

B. KING AND COUNCIL   499
   1. Royal Prerogatives   500
   2. Charters of Liberty: Magna Carta, etc.   501
   3. Council Documents   502
   4. Modern works on the King's Council   502

C. PARLIAMENT   503
   1. Parliamentary Records   503
      a. General records   503
      b. Statutes: collections and individual   506
   2. Modus Tenendi Parliamentum   509
   3. Modern Studies on Parliament   510
      a. Surveys of recent interpretations   511
      b. General descriptions of early development   514
      c. Articles on specific developments   517
      d. Articles on specific parliaments   518
      e. Officers and meeting-places   520
      f. Elections and attendance   520
      g. Representation: general studies and returns   521
      h. Parliamentary representation by counties, alphabetically   522
      i. The clergy in parliament   524

D. THE CENTRAL COURTS   524
   1. Introduction   524
   2. Records of Central Courts   525
   3. Law Records of Particular Counties   533
   4. Year Books   545
   5. Modern Treatises on Law Courts   548
      a. General   548
      b. Personnel   551
      c. Procedure   552
      d. Law of treason   553
      e. Equity   554
   6. The County Court and Local Administration   555

E. CHANCERY ENROLMENTS AND RECORDS   557
   1. Introductory Comments   557
   2. General Rolls, Registers, etc. for England   559
   3. Records for Wales, Scotland, Ireland, Channel Isles   565
   4. Continental Affairs: Chancery and Foreign Documents   568
   5. Specialized Studies on Administrative History   572

F. SPECIAL JURISDICTIONS   574
1. Palatinate of Chester   574
2. Palatinate of Durham   576
3. Duchy of Lancaster   578
4. The Forests   580
   a. Primary sources   580
   b. Secondary works   582
5. The Jews   584

VOLUME TWO

XVI. MODERN POLITICAL NARRATIVES   589
A. WILLIAM I TO STEPHEN 1066–1154   589
B. HENRY II TO JOHN 1154–1216   593
C. THE THIRTEENTH CENTURY 1216–1307   597
1. Domestic Politics   597
2. Anglo-Scottish Relations   599
3. Relations with the Continent   601
D. THE FOURTEENTH CENTURY 1307–1399   603
1. Domestic Politics   603
2. Peasants' Revolt of 1381   606
3. Relations with the Continent   608
   a. Comprehensive narratives   608
   b. The Hundred Years War: First phase   609
E. THE FIFTEENTH CENTURY 1399–1485   612
1. Domestic Politics   612
2. Relations with the Continent   616

XVII. MILITARY AND NAVAL HISTORY   619
A. SOURCES   619
B. SECONDARY WORKS   623
1. Army   623
2. Navy   625

XVIII. LAND TENURE AND ESTATES   627
A. GENERAL PUBLIC RECORDS   627
B. RECORDS BY COUNTY   630
C. CHARTERS, DEEDS, AND WILLS   636
1. Collections and Catalogues   636
2. Charters and Deeds by County   638
3. Wills   647
   a. Indexes and aids   647
   b. Collections of wills   648
   c. Wills by county   649
D. SOME FAMILIES AND THEIR RECORDS   654
E. HOUSEHOLD BOOKS AND LETTERS   657
F. ESTATE MANAGEMENT   659
G. FEUDAL TENURES   661

XIX. AGRARIAN SOCIETY   666
- A. SOURCES FOR MANORIAL HISTORY   666
  1. Bibliographical Aids   667
  2. Collected Sources   668
  3. Manorial Sources by County   669
- B. MODERN DESCRIPTIONS OF AGRARIAN SOCIETY   691
  1. Manor and Village   691
  2. Agriculture and Husbandry   696

XX. URBAN SOCIETY   700
- A. URBAN RECORDS   700
  1. Comprehensive Urban Records   700
  2. Urban Records by County   701
  3. Cinque Ports   729
  4. Commercial Records   730
- B. MODERN STUDIES OF BOROUGHS AND TOWNS   733
  1. Comprehensive Accounts   733
  2. Gilds and Livery Companies   734
- C. STUDIES ON COMMERCE AND TRADE   735
  1. General Accounts   735
  2. Wool and Woollens   738
  3. Alien Merchants   740
- D. MISCELLANEOUS STUDIES ON SOCIETY   742
  1. Comprehensive Studies   742
  2. Population Problems   744
  3. Wages and Prices   746
  4. Money, Banking, and Industry   747
  5. Fairs, Markets, and Inland Transportation   749

XXI. THE CHURCH, 1066–1485   750
- A. PAPAL LETTERS CONCERNING ENGLAND   751
  1. Vatican Archives   751
  2. Papal Letters   752
- B. GENERAL COUNCILS AND ENGLAND   754
- C. DIOCESAN RECORDS AND HISTORIES   755
  1. General Introduction   755
  2. English Dioceses: Bishops and Chapters   758
  3. Welsh Dioceses   790
- D. MONASTIC RECORDS AND HISTORIES   792
  1. General Information   792
  2. The Monastic Orders   795
     a. Monks and nuns   795
     b. Regular canons   799
     c. Friars   800
     d. Military orders   807
     e. Secular colleges   809
     f. Hospitals   810
  3. Religious Houses, by County   810

E. CANON LAW IN ENGLAND, 1066-1485   846
   1. General Studies on Canon Law in England   846
   2. Judicial Relations with the Papacy   850
   3. Ecclesiastical Courts in England   851
   4. Becket and his Contemporaries   853
     a. The Becket controversy   853
     b. Some participants in the Becket controversy   856

F. SCHOLARS, MYSTICS, AND THEIR WORKS   858
   1. Individual Scholars   858
   2. Mystics, Anchorites, and their Writings   875
   3. Devotional Writings and Sermons   877

XXII. MODERN STUDIES OF THE MEDIEVAL ENGLISH CHURCH   880

A. THE PAPACY AND PAPAL ADMINISTRATION   880
   1. General Histories of the Papacy   880
   2. England and the Papacy, 1066-1485   882
     a. General studies   882
     b. Legates and envoys   883
     c. Nominations to benefices   885
     d. Papal taxation of the clergy   886

B. ADMINISTRATION OF THE CHURCH IN ENGLAND   888
   1. General Histories   888
   2. Convocation and Synod   891
   3. Clerical Subsidies   892
   4. Church Life and the Lower Clergy   893
   5. Heresy and the Lollards   896

XXIII. INTELLECTUAL INTERESTS 1066-1485   898

A. LEARNING: PHILOSOPHY AND SCIENCE   898
   1. General References   898
   2. Studies on English Learning 1066-1300   900
   3. Studies on English Learning 1300-1485   902
   4. Science in the Late Middle Ages   903

B. LITERATURE   907
   1. Middle English Literature   907
   2. History and Literature   909
     a. Particular writers   909
     b. Political poems; literature of dissent   914

C. EDUCATIONAL INSTITUTIONS   916
   1. Universities and Colleges   916
     a. Sources   916
       i. Cambridge   917
       ii. Oxford   917

Contents

    b. Modern Accounts   919
       i. General references   920
      ii. Cambridge   921
     iii. Oxford   922
  2. Schools   924
  3. Inns of Court   925
  4. Medieval Libraries   927
  5. Music of the later Middle Ages   929
  6. Printing   933

APPENDIX   934

INDEX   937

CORRIGENDA

Page 30, line 14 from bottom. *For* history of philosophy *read* philosophy of history
46, line 10 (No. 367). *For* christiana *read* cristiana
51, line 9 (No. 412). *For* Jordan, 1.+ *read* Jordan. 1+.
53, line 6. *For* Nöel *read* Noël
66, line 9 from bottom (No. 542). *For* CYMREIGHYD *read* CYMREIG HYD
70, line 11 from bottom (No. 579). *For* des *read* der
107, line 16 (No. 929). *For* Soc. of Amer. *read* Society of American
107, line 20 (end of line). *For* series *read* series of reports
107, line 21 (end of line). *For* publication *read* publications supple-
141, line 20. *For* Oesterreichen *read* Oesterreichische
144, line 22. *For* in volume ii *read* below pp. 750–880
164, line 12. *For* 880 *read* 898
167, lines 7–8. *Delete* in volume ii
169, line 8. *Delete* in volume ii
174, line 3 from bottom. *For* volume ii *read* chapters xix–xx
211, line 16 from bottom. *For* volume ii *read* chapters xviii–xx
212, line 13. *For* Gouldesborough *read* Gouldesbrough
235, line 16. *For* 'Borough and Town in volume ii' *read* Urban Records pp. 712–18
283, line 6. *For* of little value *read* of uneven value
320, line 9 (No. 2286). *For* Wulker *read* Wülker
329, line 9 from bottom. *For* 1866 *read* 1886
383, bottom line. *For* vigour in *read* vigour only in
384, line 23. *Add* See Barlow, No. 2709.
389, line 11. *For* provides not only *read* not only provides
495, line 26. *Add* 735–8
495, line 28. *Add* 886–8
569, line 8. *For* as keeper as *read* as keeper of
572, line 1 (No. 3832). *For* cartulairer *read* cartulaires
589, line 6. *For* vol. i *read* above
596, line 30 (No. 4038). *For* Isabella *read* Isabelle
608, line 2 from bottom. *For* Loviette *read* Loirette
628, line 29. *For* receptable *read* receptacle
647, line 8 from bottom. *For* locatio *read* location
666, line 6 from bottom. *Add* 636–8
691, line 9. *For* vol. i *read* above
691, lines 10–11. *For* pp. 2645–52 *read* pp. 374–8
756, line 26. *For* vol. i *read* above
756, line 38 (No. 5575). *For* vol. i *read* above
846, line 5 from bottom. *For* in vol. i *read* above on
927, line 19. *For* in vol. i. *read* above.

ABBREVIATIONS

A.A.S.R.P.	Associated Architectural Societies Reports and Papers; No. 171
A.H.R.	*American Historical Review*; No. 144
Anal. Boll.	*Analecta Bollandiana*; No. 145
Année Philol.	*L'Année philologique*; No. 266
Antiq. Jour.	*Antiquaries Journal*; No. 107
app.	appendix
Archaeol.	Archaeological
Archaeol.	*Archaeologia*
Archaeol. Camb.	*Archaeologia Cambrensis*; No. 109
Archit.	Architecture
B.B.C.S.	*Bulletin of the Board of Celtic Studies*; No. 111
Bibl. Celt.	*Bibliotheca Celtica*; No. 110
B.I.H.R.	*Bulletin of the Institute of Historical Research*; No. 112
B.J.R.L.	*Bulletin of John Rylands Library*; No. 129
B.M.	British Museum
Bonser, A.-S.C.B.	Wilfrid Bonser, *An Anglo-Saxon and Celtic Bibliography*; No. 12
Bonser, R.-B.B.	Wilfrid Bonser, *Romano-British Bibliography*; No. 13
Bull.	*Bulletin*
Cambr.	Cambridge, England
C.B.E.L.	*Cambridge Bibliography of English Literature*; No. 14
Cambr. Med. H.	*Cambridge Medieval History*; No. 1176
Collingwood–Myres	*Roman Britain and the English Settlements*; No. 1189
Comm.	Commission
comp.	compiler
D.N.B.	*Dictionary of National Biography*
Eccles.	Ecclesiastical
Econ. H.R.	*Economic History Review*; No. 119
ed.	editor or edited
Edin.	Edinburgh
edn.	edition
Eng. Hist. Docs.	*English Historical Documents*; No. 17
E.E.T.S.	Early English Text Society; No. 187
E.H.R.	*English Historical Review*; No. 121
Emden, Cambr.	*Biographical Register of the University of Cambridge to 1500.* Cambr. 1963. No. 532
Emden, Oxf.	*Biographical Register of the University of Oxford to 1500.* Oxf. 1957–9. No. 533
Hardy, Cat.	T. D. Hardy, *Descriptive Catalogue of Materials*; No. 21
History	*History*: the quarterly journal of the Historical Association; No. 125
I.B.O.H.S.	*International Bibliography of Historical Sciences*; No. 53
Jacob, Fifteenth Cent.	E. F. Jacob, *The Fifteenth Century 1399–1485*; No. 1189

Jour.	Journal
J.E.G.P.	*Journal of English and German Philology*
J.E.H.	*Journal of Ecclesiastical History*; No. 130
Kenney	J. F. Kenney, *The Sources for the Early History of Ireland*; No. 23
Lond.	London, England
McKisack	M. McKisack, *The Fourteenth Century*; No. 1189
M.I.O.G.	Mitteilungen des Instituts der österreichische Geschichtsforschung
M.G.H.	Monumenta Germaniae Historica; No. 1114
Mullins, *Guide* (also MG)	*Guide to the Historical Publications of the Societies of England and Wales, 1901–33*; No. 28
Mullins, *Texts*	E. L. C. Mullins, *Texts and Calendars*; No. 29
N.Y.	New York, U.S.A.
Oxf.	Oxford, England
pb.	Paperback edition
P.B.A.	*Proceedings of the British Academy*; No. 172
Philol.	Philology, *philologique*
Poole, *Domesday*	A. L. Poole, *Domesday Book to Magna Carta*; No. 1189
Potthast	A. Potthast, *Bibliotheca Historica*; No. 62
Powicke, *Thir. Cent.*	F. M. Powicke, *The Thirteenth Century*; No. 1189
P.R.O.	Public Record Office, London
Procs.	Proceedings
pt., pts.	part, parts
pubn., pubns.	publication, publications
Read	C. Read, *Bibliography of . . . Tudor period*; No. 32
Rec.	Record
Repert. Font.	*Repertorium Fontium Historiae Medii Aevi*; No. 64
Rev.	Review or Revue
R.H.E.	*Revue d'histoire ecclésiastique*; No. 166
Scot. H.R.	*Scottish Historical Review*; No. 139
Ser.	Series
Soc.	Society
Stenton, *A.-S. Eng.*	F. M. Stenton, *Anglo-Saxon England*; No. 1186
Trans.	Transactions
T.R.H.S.	*Transactions of Royal Historical Society*; No. 177
vol., vols.	volume, volumes
Writings 1901–33	*Writings on British History 1901–33*; No. 38
Writings 1934–45	*Writings on British History 1934–45*; No. 39

SYMBOLS

★	reprint listed in *Guide to Reprints*; No. 5
†	microfilm edition listed in *Guide to Microforms*; No. 4
+	regular series publication
(in progress)	irregular but anticipated series publication

PART ONE

GENERAL WORKS AND AUXILIARY SCIENCES

PART ONE consists of three chapters, to wit: I. Bibliographical Guides; II. Journals of more than Local Scope; and III. Auxiliaries to Historical Study. The selection of items has been limited to those standard works and more recent publications which are most serviceable to historians of pre-Tudor England.

I. BIBLIOGRAPHICAL GUIDES

The principal retrospective bibliographies dealing specifically with British history before 1485 are followed by foreign bibliographies which contain items germane to British history. The fourth section of this chapter lists the catalogues of the principal libraries; the subject-catalogues are particularly useful for the development of a bibliography.

Current bibliographies are to be found in periodicals, which are listed on pages 16–29 below. Those journals which provide the fullest bibliographical information within their sphere are *Antiquaries Journal* (No. 107), *Economic History Review* (No. 119), *English Historical Review* (No. 121), *Irish Historical Studies* (No. 128), *Scottish Historical Review* (No. 139), *Welsh History Review* (No. 142), *Cahiers de civilisation mediévale* (No. 151), *Revue d'histoire ecclésiastique* (No. 166), and *Traditio* (No. 169). The annual, but not current, *International Bibliography of Historical Sciences* (No. 53) should be consulted. The *Annual Bulletin of Historical Literature* (No. 7) and the *International Medieval Bibliography* (No. 54) provide references expeditiously.

A. GENERAL BIBLIOGRAPHIES

1. *Bibliographies of Bibliographies*

1 BESTERMAN (THEODORE). A world bibliography of bibliographies and of bibliographical catalogues. 2 vols. Lond. 1939–40. 3rd edn., 4 vols. Geneva, 1955–6. 4th edn., 5 vols. Lausanne. 1965–6.

In this listing of about 85,000 bibliographies for all subjects and all countries, the arrangement is topical, embracing subjects, persons, and places. British county and local bibliographies are well represented; catalogues of manuscripts are included. Vol. iv of the 3rd edn. is an index of authors, libraries, and archives.

2 COULTER (EDITH M.) and GERSTENFELD (MELANIE). Historical bibliographies: a systematic and annotated guide. Berkeley (Calif.). 1935. *

Also Norman E. Binns, *An introduction to historical bibliography*: with a preface by Arundell Esdaile (Lond. 1953).

3 WALFORD (ALBERT J.), ed. Guide to reference material. The Library Association. Lond. 1959. Supplement. 1963. 2nd edn. 1968.

A serviceable annotated compilation for all subjects, particularly strong on British matters; it records, *inter alia*, references on general bibliography, on the auxiliaries to history, and on the national and local histories of all the British Isles.

Its American counterpart is Constance M. Winchell, *Guide to reference books*, 7th edn. (Chicago, 1951), with three supplements, 1954–60; 8th edn. (Chicago, 1967).

2. *Guides to Reprints*

The developments in the photo-offset process of printing have made feasible the reproduction of texts without the re-setting of type. Similarly the developments in micro-photography permit the reproduction of periodicals and the publications in series as microfilms, microcards, and microfiches in economical and space-saving forms. Thousands of serials and out-of-print texts have been thus reproduced, particularly in the 1960s. Convenient guides to these reprints are given here.

Some reprints are reissues from the original plates. Less frequently the type is re-set, except in the production of paperback editions.

4 GUIDE TO MICROFORMS IN PRINT. Ed. by Albert J. Diaz. Washington, D.C. 1961+.

An annual, cumulative guide to books, journals, etc. which are available on microfilm, micro-opaque cards, or microfiches and are offered for sale by some fifty-odd publishers in the United States.

5 GUIDE TO REPRINTS. Ed. by Carol Wade. NCR (National Cash Register Company): Microcards editions. Washington, D.C. 1967+.

An annual list of reprints by photo-offset process from some 250 publishers, American and foreign. The *1970 Guide* lists about 35,000 items.

The *Guide* is supplemented by *Announced Reprints* (Washington, 1969+), a quarterly catalogue of forthcoming reprints. The issue for August 1969 lists about 10,000 items, largely individual volumes.

B. BIBLIOGRAPHIES OF BRITISH HISTORY

6 ANDERSON (JOHN P.). The book of British topography: a classified catalogue of the topographical works in the library of the British Museum relating to Great Britain and Ireland. Lond. 1881. *

7 ANNUAL BULLETIN OF HISTORICAL LITERATURE. The Historical Association. Lond. 1911+*. Index of vols. i–xii (1911–22), 1923.

Briefly annotated lists of new editions of the principal sources and secondary books and articles for all centuries and all areas. The medieval sections have been well done for many years.

8 BALE (JOHN). Illustrium majoris Britanniae scriptorum summarium. Ipswich. 1548. 2nd edn. 2 pts. Basel, 1557–9. Another version (arranged alpha-

betically, compiled *c.* 1549–57): Index Britanniae Scriptorum. Ed. by R. L. Poole and Mary Bateson. Oxf. 1902.

The earliest detailed account of the medieval writers of England: useful, but disfigured by inaccuracies and misrepresentations. Based on John Leland's manuscript notes, subsequently published as *Commentarii de scriptoribus Britannicis*, by Anthony Hall, 2 vols. (Oxf. 1709). On John Bale, see Jesse W. Harris, *John Bale, a study in the minor literature of the Reformation* (Urbana, Ill. 1940), and W. T. Davies, 'A bibliography of John Bale', *Oxford Bibliographical Soc. Procs.* iv for 1939 (1940), 201–79. Cf. J. H. Baxter, Charles Johnson, and J. F. Willard, 'An index of British and Irish Latin writers, 400–1520', *Bulletin Du Cange*, vii (1932), 110–219.

9   BEST (RICHARD I.). A bibliography of Irish philology and of printed Irish literature. Dublin. 1913. Idem, A bibliography of Irish philology and manuscript literature, 1913–1941. Dublin. 1942.

A fundamental bibliography for Irish historical annals, law materials, saints' lives, etc.

10   A BIBLIOGRAPHY OF THE HISTORY OF WALES. Prepared by the History and Law Committee of the Board of Celtic Studies of the University of Wales. Cardiff. 1962.

The second edition of a similar title edited by Robert T. Jenkins and William Rees (Cardiff), 1931. Supplements in *B.B.C.S.* xx (1963), 126–64; ibid. xxii (1966), 49–70; ibid. xxiii (1969), 263–83.

11   BLACK (GEORGE F.). List of works relating to Scotland. New York Public Library. N.Y. 1916.

Most of it can be found in *Bull. N.Y. Pub. Lib.* xviii (1914).

12   BONSER (WILFRID). An Anglo-Saxon and Celtic bibliography (450–1087). 2 vols. Oxf. 1957.

In vol. i there are more than 12,000 entries drawn from 376 British and foreign periodicals and 46 collective works. It 'covers all aspects of the period, as pertaining to the whole of the British Isles', with the exception of purely literary and linguistic materials and the source material which can be found in Gross and Kenney. It is indispensable for tracking down articles. Vol. ii contains a full index.

13   BONSER (WILFRID). A Romano-British bibliography (55 B.C.–A.D. 449) 2 vols. Oxf. 1964.

14   CAMBRIDGE BIBLIOGRAPHY OF ENGLISH LITERATURE. Ed. by F. W. Bateson. 4 vols. Cambr. 1940. Vol. v, Supplement: A.D. 600–1900. Ed. by George Watson. Cambr. 1957.

A catalogue of titles without annotation; includes many topics ancillary to literature. Vol. i for the period A.D. 600–1660 has helpful sections on the writings in Latin.

15   CONFERENCE ON BRITISH STUDIES BIBLIOGRAPHICAL HANDBOOKS. General editor: J. Jean Hecht. (In progress.)

The first handbook dealing with medieval England in this series is Michael Altschul's *Anglo-Norman England 1066–1154* (Cambr. 1969), which lists, generally with concise annotations, 1,838 books and articles under topical arrangement. By including items which cannot find a place in the bibliography at hand, Altschul's handbook supplements this present work for the period from 1066 to 1154.

16   EAGER (ALAN R.). A guide to Irish bibliographical material, being a bibliography of Irish bibliographies and some sources of information. Lond. 1964.

This is a stop-gap, but useful, listing for Irish history, pending the publication of 'A Guide to the study of medieval Irish history'. See No. 23; and P. W. A. Asplin, *Medieval Ireland, c.* 1170–1495 (No. 4030).

17   ENGLISH HISTORICAL DOCUMENTS. General editor: David C. Douglas. Lond. 1953+.

This series of twelve stout volumes will provide sources in English for the study of English history from *c.* 500 to 1914. Of the four volumes scheduled for the period before 1485, three have been published, namely: vol. i, *c.* 500–1042, edited by Dorothy Whitelock (1955); vol. ii, 1042–1189, edited by David C. Douglas and George W. Greenaway (1953); and vol. iv, 1327–1485, edited by A. R. Myers (1969). Each volume furnishes translations of numerous extracts from chronicles and records, with masterly introductions and critical commentaries.

18   FURBER (ELIZABETH C.), ed. Changing views on British history: essays on historical writing since 1939. Cambr. (Mass.). 1966.

This volume reprints valuable narrative essays which assess, in a thumb-nail fashion, the significance of each of the works listed. On pages 1–57 Bryce Lyon, 'From Hengist and Horsa to Edward of Caernarvon: recent writings on English history (1939–62)', is reprinted from *Tijdschrift voor Geschiedenis*, lxxvi (1963), 377–422; and on pages 58–100 is reprinted Margaret Hastings, 'High history or hack history: England in the later middle ages', from *Speculum*, xxxvi (1961), 225–53.

19   HALL (HUBERT). A select bibliography for the study, sources, and literature of English medieval economic history. Lond. 1914. *

Broader in scope than the title indicates; lists 3,199 titles; succinct introductory comments on the sources. Cf. E. A. Kosminsky, 'Russian work on English economic history', *Econ. H.R.* i (1928), 199–233. Margaret F. Moore, 'Bibliography of manorial and agrarian history' in her *Two select bibliographies of medieval historical study* (Lond. 1912), pp. 71–185. *
   (Cf. Nos. 4691–2, 4695.)

20   HANCOCK (P. D.). A bibliography of works relating to Scotland 1916–1950. 2 pts. Edin. 1959.

A more comprehensive supplement to Mitchell and Cash (No. 27).

21   HARDY (THOMAS D.). Descriptive catalogue of materials relating to the history of Great Britain and Ireland (to 1327). Rolls Series. 3 vols. in 4 pts. Lond. 1862–71. * N.Y. 1963.

A mine of useful information, particularly on the chronicles. The appendix of vol. i contains a list of the printed materials: publications of societies, collections of records and chroniclers, etc. The body of the work is mainly a catalogue of MSS. The over-all review of the chroniclers, given in the nineteenth-century general accounts (e.g. by Bernhard Ten Brink, James Gairdner, Samuel R. Gardiner, and James B. Mullinger) needs revisions in details; for the latter, see the individual chroniclers cited below (pp. 283–99 and 386–454).

22   HUGHES (KATHLEEN). Early Christian Ireland. An introduction to the sources (to *c.* 1200). Lond. and Ithaca (N.Y.). 1972. R. IAN JACK. Medieval Wales (*c.* 400–1542). Ibid. 1972. See Elton (No. 256).

23 KENNEY (JAMES F.). The sources for the early history of Ireland: an introduction and guide. Vol. i: Ecclesiastical. Columbia Univ.: Records of Civilization. N.Y. 1929 (no more published). Corrected reprint with preface, addenda, and corrigenda by Ludwig Bieler. Shannon. 1966.

A heavily documented, annotated bibliography, with learned commentaries, on sources for Irish ecclesiastical history and biography from earliest times to the twelfth century. The Irish MSS. Comm. has in preparation a 'Guide to the study of medieval Irish history', under the editorship of the late Eric St. John Brooks, Aubrey Gwynn, and A. Jocelyn Otway-Ruthven. Its contemplated coverage is described in Irish MSS. Comm. *Catalogue of publications* (1962), pp. 83–4. See E. St. John Brooks, 'The sources for medieval Anglo-Irish history', *Historical Studies* (No. 124), ii (1958), 86–92; and Aubrey Gwynn, 'Bibliographical note on medieval Anglo-Irish history', ibid. pp. 93–9.

24 LANCASTER (JOAN C.). Bibliography of historical works issued in the United Kingdom 1946–56. University of London, Institute of Historical Research. Lond. 1957. Continued under like title for 1957–60 and for 1961–5 by William Kellaway. Lond. 1962 and 1967.

These well-arranged lists of books were compiled for the Anglo-American Conference of Historians of July 1957, July 1962, and July 1967.

25 LIST OF ABBREVIATED TITLES OF THE PRINTED SOURCES OF SCOTTISH HISTORY TO 1560. Supplement to the *Scottish Historical Review* for October 1963, pp. i–xxxi.

Designed to establish a standard system of reference to the printed sources, this list provides the titles of the important sources.

26 MARWICK (W. H.). 'A bibliography of Scottish economic history'. *Econ. H.R.* iii (1931), 117–37; and a Supplement as 'A bibliography of works on Scottish economic history published during the last twenty years', in ibid. 2nd Ser. iv (1952), 376–82. Idem, 'A bibliography of Scottish economic history, 1951–62', ibid. 2nd Ser. xvi (1963), 149–54; '1963–70', ibid. xxiv (1971), 469–79.

27 MITCHELL (ARTHUR) and CASH (CALEB G.). A contribution to the bibliography of Scottish topography. Scot. Hist. Soc. Pubns. 2nd Ser. xiv–xv. 2 vols. Edin. 1917.

Vol. i, an extensive, uncritical bibliography of local history, arranged by counties. Vol. ii, topical and on pp. 483–8 a list of Scottish bibliographies.

28 MULLINS (EDWARD L. C.), compiler. A guide to the historical and archaeological publications of societies in England and Wales 1901–1933. The Institute of Historical Research. Lond. 1968.

This large volume of 850 pages in double columns of small print lists and indexes articles in the journals of more than 400 local and national societies. It is complementary to *Writings . . . 1901–1933* (No. 38).

29 MULLINS (EDWARD L. C.). Texts and calendars: an analytical guide to serial publications. R.H.S. Guides and Handbooks No. 7. Lond. 1958.

Lists of the publications of records by official bodies, national societies, English local societies, and Welsh societies, arranged under the name of the publishing body. P.R.O. calendars, Rolls Series, and other volumes issued by various commissions are included.

There is an analytical index. These lists were to be continued in *B.I.H.R.* (No. 112) where the first supplementary list was printed in xxxiii (1960), 133–4. See also *Handbook of record publications* (No. 933).

30 O'CURRY (EUGENE). Lectures on the manuscript materials of ancient Irish history. Dublin. 1861. Reprinted, 1873. *

The principal older works on the Irish chroniclers are: James Ware, *De scriptoribus Hiberniae* (Dublin, 1639 *); trans. by Walter Harris, *History of the writers of Ireland* (Dublin, 1764); William Nicolson, *The Irish historical library* (Dublin, 1724); Tanner (No. 33); Edward O'Reilly, *An account of nearly four hundred Irishwriters* (Dublin, 1820) *.

31 OXFORD HISTORY OF ENGLAND. Ed. by G. N. Clark. 15 vols. Oxf. 1936–65.

See No. 1189 for Collingwood and Myres; Stenton; Poole; Powicke; McKisack; Jacob. Each volume contains an excellent annotated selective bibliography of sources and secondary works for its period, as well as numerous footnotes which are not repeated in the bibliography.

32 READ (CONYERS). Bibliography of British history. Tudor period, 1485–1603. Oxf. 1933. 2nd edn. 1959.

Tabulates some general materials which are useful for the pre-Tudor period and are not repeated in this medieval bibliography.

33 TANNER (THOMAS). Bibliotheca Britannico-Hibernica sive de scriptoribus, etc. By David Wilkins. Lond. 1748. Reprinted, Tucson (Ariz.) and N.Y. 1965.

A dictionary of writers, containing much valuable historical material, and in large part superseding the older works of Leland, Bale, Pits, Ware, Cave, and Nicolson. See Hardy, *Catalogue of materials* (No. 21), vol. i, pp. 36–42.

34 TERRY (CHARLES S.). A catalogue of the publications of Scottish historical and kindred clubs and societies, and of the volumes relative to Scottish history issued by H.M. Stationery Office, 1780–1908. Glasgow. 1909.

Continued in Cyril Matheson's catalogue of similar title for the years 1908–27, which includes the reports of the Royal Commission on Historical Manuscripts (Aberdeen, 1928).

35 THIRTY YEARS' WORK IN IRISH HISTORY. *Irish Hist. Stud.* xv–xvi (1968): Francis J. Byrne, 'Ireland before the Norman invasion', xvi (1968), 1–14; J. Otway-Ruthven, 'Medieval Ireland, 1169–1485', xv (1968), 359–65. Reprinted in *Irish Historiography*, Ed. by T. W. Moody. Dublin. 1971.

36 TRAUTZ (FRITZ). 'Literaturbericht über die Geschichte Englands im Mittelalter, Veröffentlichungen 1945 bis 1962/63'. *Historische Zeitschrift:* Sonderheft ii. Munich. 1965, pp. 108–259.

Trautz's report is followed on pp. 260–76 by Ludwig Bieler's report: 'Irland: Lateinische Kultur im Mittelalter'.

37 WATT (ROBERT). Bibliotheca Britannica. 4 vols. Edin. 1834. *

Vols. i–ii, Authors; vols. iii–iv, Subjects. A general index of British and foreign literature, medicine, law, classical literature, etc. with useful references to older studies.

38 WRITINGS ON BRITISH HISTORY 1901–1933: A bibliography of books and articles on the history of Great Britain from about 400 A.D. to 1914, published during the years 1901–1933 inclusive, with an appendix containing a select list of publications in these years on British history since 1914. General editor H. Hale Bellot. Royal Hist. Soc. 5 vols. in 7 pts. Lond. 1968–70.

Vol. i—Auxiliary sciences and general works (1968). Vol. ii—The Middle Ages 450–1485 (1968). Vol. iii—The Tudor and Stuart periods 1485–1714 (1968). These volumes do not, with few exceptions, repeat the entries in Mullins, *Guide* (No. 28), Terry, *Catalogue* (No. 34), and Matheson, *Catalogue* (No. 34).

39 WRITINGS ON BRITISH HISTORY (1934–1945). Ed. by A. Taylor Milne. Royal Hist. Soc. 8 vols. Lond. 1937–60.

Annual volumes appeared for the years 1934, 1935, 1936, 1937, 1938, 1939; for the years 1940–45, two inclusive volumes were published in 1960. A continuation is being compiled currently (1971) under the auspices of The Institute of Historical Research.

C. FOREIGN BIBLIOGRAPHIES

40 THE AMERICAN HISTORICAL ASSOCIATION. Guide to Historical Literature. By a Board of Editors, George F. Howe, Chairman. N.Y. 1961.

A revision of *A guide to historical literature*, edited by George M. Dutcher, *et al.* (N.Y. 1931. New impressions, 1937 and 1949).

41 BIBLIOGRAPHIE ANNUELLE DE L'HISTOIRE DE FRANCE DU Vᵉ SIÈCLE À 1939. Paris. 1956+.

The first volume covers the year 1955. Cf. No. 63.

42 BIBLIOGRAPHIE GÉNÉRALE DES TRAVAUX HISTORIQUES ET ARCHÉOLOGIQUES PUBLIÉS PAR LES SOCIÉTÉS SAVANTES DE LA FRANCE, 1886–1900. 6 vols. Paris. 1888–1918.

Continued as *Bibliographie annuelle des travaux . . .*, *1900–10* (Paris, 1904–14). Continued as René Gandilhon and Charles Samaran, *Bibliographie générale . . .*, *1910–1940* (Paris, 1944+). In progress (vols. i–v, 1944–61).

43 BOSSUAT (ROBERT). Manuel bibliographique de la littérature française du moyen âge. Melun. 1951.* Supplements for 1949–53 and 1954–60. Paris. 1955, 1961.

44 BRUNET (JACQUES-CHARLES). Manuel du libraire. 1st edn. Paris. 1809. 5th edn. 6 vols. Paris. 1860–5. † Supplément, 2 vols. 1878–80. Reprinted, Berlin. 1922.

Lists old editions, with annotations.

45 CALMETTE (JOSEPH L. A.). Le Monde féodal. Clio, introduction aux études historiques, iv. Paris. 1934. New edn. 1951. Idem, L'Élaboration du monde moderne. Ibid. v. Paris. 1934. 3rd edn. 1949.

Historical outline, chapter by chapter, followed by annotated lists of sources, modern works, and the current state of matters at issue. Of high value. A new series, Nouvelle Clio, entitled L'histoire et ses problèmes, directed by Robert Boutruche et Paul Lemerle, is in progress (1971).

46　CHEVALIER (CYR ULYSSE J.). Répertoire des sources historiques du moyen âge. Bio-bibliographie. (Issued in parts.) Paris. 1877–86. Supplement. 1888. New edn. 2 vols. 9 pts. 1905 (1903)–7. *

An elaborate list or encyclopedia of medieval writers, statesmen, etc., with bibliographical references.

47　CHEVALIER (CYR ULYSSE J.). Topo-bibliographie. 2 vols. 6 pts. Montbéliard. 1894–1903. *

The second part of the preceding work. It contains bibliographical references arranged under the names of places and subjects: see under 'Angleterre', etc. The article on 'Angleterre' was also separately printed (Montbéliard, 1893). The *Topo-bibliographie*, like the *Bio-bibliographie*, though very useful, contains much obsolete rubbish and omits many valuable works. Lawrence H. Cottineau, *Répertoire topo-bibliographique des abbayes et prieurés* (2 vols., Mâcon, 1935–7), is only slightly useful for Great Britain.

48　DAHLMANN–WAITZ. Quellenkunde der deutschen Geschichte. 1st and 2nd edns. by F. C. Dahlmann. 1830–8. 3rd, 4th, and 5th edns. by Georg Waitz. 1869–83. 6th edn. by Ernst Steindorff. Göttingen. 1894. 7th edn. by Erich Brandenburg. Leipzig. 1906. Supplement. 1907. 8th edn. by Paul Herre, Leipzig. 1912. 9th edn. by Hermann Häring. 2 vols. Leipzig. 1931–2. 10th edn. by Hermann Heimpel and Herbert Geuss. Stuttgart. 1965 (in progress).

This is supplemented by the periodical bibliography in Nos. 153 and 154.

49　DE BRIE (G. A.), ed. Bibliographia philosophica 1934–45. Vol. i: Bibliographia historiae philosophiae. Brussels. 1950. Vol. ii: Bibliographia philosophiae. Antwerp. 1954.

It was planned to publish a retrospective continuation every five years. Section iii of vol. i, entitled 'Historia philosophiae patristicae et medii aevi' (4,106 items) is very useful for biographies and works of authors; and section xv of vol. ii lists 488 items on the philosophy of history. Also helpful for topics ancillary to history are *Bibliographie de la philosophie* (Paris, 1937+) and *Répertoire bibliographique de la philosophie publié sous les auspices de l'institut international de philosophie avec le patronage de l'UNESCO* (Louvain, 1949+). This last is the successor to *Revue philosophique de Louvain* (1946–8), which continued the *Répertoire bibliographique* of the *Revue néoscolastique de philosophie* (Louvain, 1934–40).

50　ERICHSEN (BALDER V. A.) and KRARUP (ALFRED). Dansk historisk bibliografi. 3 vols. Copenhagen. 1917–27.

A new bibliographical series is planned by the Danish Historical Assoc. Its first volume, *Dansk historisk bibliografi, 1943–47*, compiled by Henry Bruun was published in Copenhagen in 1956. H. Bruun has also projected a six-volume *Dansk historisk bibliografi 1913 til 1942*, the first volume of which appeared in 1966.

51　FABRICIUS (JOHANN A.). Bibliotheca Latina mediae et infimae aetatis. 6 vols. Hamburg. 1734–46. Revised edn. by J. D. Mansi. 6 vols. in 3. Padua. 1754. New edn. Florence. 1858–9.

52　FARRAR (CLARISSA P.) and EVANS (AUSTIN P.). Bibliography of English translations from medieval sources. Columbia Univ. Records of Civilization, No. 39. N.Y. 1946.

Cf. *The literature of the world in English translation: a bibliography*, ed. by George B. Parks and Ruth Z. Temple. Vol. i: *Greek and Latin literatures* (N.Y. 1968). (Latin 450–1450 by R. W. Emery, pp. 269–335.)

53 INTERNATIONAL BIBLIOGRAPHY OF HISTORICAL SCIENCES.
Edited for the International Committee of Historical Sciences. Paris, etc. Vols.
i–xiv. 1926 (1930)–39; xvi+. 1947+.

> Selective, topical annual comprehending the whole field of historical sciences for the
> world. Vol. xv for 1940–6 has not yet appeared; but material collected for it has been
> separately published in Louis B. Frewer, *Bibliography of historical writings published in
> Great Britain and the empire, 1940–45* (Oxf. 1947).

54 INTERNATIONAL MEDIEVAL BIBLIOGRAPHY. Prepared under
the direction of Robert S. Hoyt and Peter H. Sawyer. Minneapolis. 1967+;
then Minneapolis and Leeds.

> This comprehensive inventory of articles in learned journals on the whole range of
> medieval studies was first issued quarterly on 3 in. × 5 in. cards, beginning with the first
> quarter of 1967; and a quarterly subject guide to these cards was provided on letter-sized
> paper. After 1 January 1969, *I.M.B.* was issued in book form only, available in quarterly
> instalments with an annual cumulation. Each instalment contains both author and
> subject indexes.

55 LANGLOIS (CHARLES V.). Manuel de bibliographie historique. Pt. i.
Paris. 1896. Revised, edn. 2 pts. 1901–4. Reprinted, Graz. 1966.

> Pt. i, *Instruments bibliographiques*, is an admirable little book, containing an account of
> the principal bibliographical aids for the study of the history of the various European
> nations at the end of the nineteenth century. A similar précis is Louis Halphen, *Initiation
> aux études d'histoire du moyen âge*, 3rd edn., revised by Yves Renouard (Paris, 1952).

56 MANITIUS (MAX). Geschichte der lateinischen Literatur des Mittelalters. 3 vols. Munich. 1911–31. *

> This standard survey extends from Justinian to about 1200.

57 MOLINIER (AUGUSTE). Les Sources de l'histoire de France [to 1494].
6 vols. Vol. vi is an index. Paris. 1901–6. * A revised edition is in preparation.

> An excellent work which gives much space to English chroniclers, and, of course, to
> French chroniclers who touch upon English affairs.

58 MONOD (GABRIEL). Bibliographie de l'histoire de France. Paris. 1888. *

> The best nineteenth-century bibliography of French history, now out of date. It must
> be supplemented by the various volumes in the Clio series (No. 45) and by reference to
> *Répertoire bibliographique* (No. 63), and *Bibliographie annuelle* (No. 41). Modern biblio-
> graphies for Normandy and Gascony will be found in Nos. 3978, 4013, 4164 and 4262.

59 PAETOW (LOUIS J.). A guide to the study of medieval history. Berkeley
(Calif.). 1917. Revised edn. by Gray C. Boyce. N.Y. 1931. *

60 PETTERSEN (HJALMAR). Bibliotheca norvegica. 4 vols. in 5. Christiania. 1899–1924.

> See for 1919–44 W. P. Sommerfeldt, *Norsk bibliografisk bibliothek*, iii (Oslo, 1944). For
> current bibliography, see *Bibliografi til Norges historie: Utgitt av den Norske historiske
> forening* (Oslo, 1927+), issued as annual supplements to *Historisk tidsskrift*.

61 PIRENNE (HENRI). Bibliographie de l'histoire de Belgique. Ghent. 1893.
3rd edn. with collaboration of Henri Nowé and Henri Obreen. Brussels. 1931.

> See also Martinus Nijhoff, *Bibliotheca Historico-Neerlandica* (The Hague, 1899).

62 POTTHAST (AUGUST). Bibliotheca historica medii aevi: Wegweiser durch die Geschichtswerke des europäischen Mittelalters bis 1500. One vol. and Supplement. Berlin. 1862–8. 2nd edn. 2 vols. 1896. Reprint of 1896 edn. Graz. 1955.

Potthast lists editions, translations, and some manuscripts of chronicles and other writings. A replacement rather than a revision is being prepared by an International Committee; for the first volumes, see *Repert. Font.* (No. 64).

63 RÉPERTOIRE BIBLIOGRAPHIQUE DE L'HISTOIRE DE FRANCE. By Pierre Caron and Henri Stein. 6 vols. for 1920–31. Paris. 1923–38.

Caron–Stein is now continued from 1955 on by *Bibliographie annuelle de l'histoire de France du Ve siècle à 1939*, prepared by Comité français des sciences historiques (Paris, 1956+).

64 REPERTORIUM FONTIUM HISTORIAE MEDII AEVI primum ab Augusto Potthast digestum, nunc cura collegii historicorum e pluribus nationibus emendatum et auctum. i: Series collectionum. Rome. 1962. ii: Fontes, A–B. 1967. iii: Fontes, C. 1970. In progress.

65 SETTERWALL (NILS KRISTIAN). Svensk historisk bibliografi, 1771–1920. 3 vols. Skrifter utgivna av Svenska Historiska Föreningen, ii–iv. Uppsala and Stockholm. 1907–37. Supplement 1921–35 by Paul Sjörgren, Skrifter . . . Föreningen, v (1956). Supplements published annually for *Svenska Historiska Föreningen* by Percy Elfstrand.

66 WATTENBACH (WILHELM). Deutschlands Geschichtsquellen im Mittelalter bis zur Mitte des dreizehnten Jahrhunderts. Berlin. 1858. 6th edn. 2 vols. 1893–4. 7th edn. by Ernst Dümmler. Stuttgart etc. 1904. The eighth edition is a co-operative work being published in parts:

Vol. i. Pt. i. Die Vorzeit von den Anfangen bis zur Herrschaft der Karolinger. Ed. by Wilhelm Levison and Heinz Loewe. Weimar. 1952.

Pt. ii. Die Karolinger vom Anfang des 8. Jahrhunderts bis zum Tode Karls des Grossen. Ed. by Wilhelm Levison and Heinz Loewe. Weimar. 1953.

Pt. iii. Die Karolinger vom Tode Karls des Grossen bis zum Vertrag von Verdun. Ed. by Heinz Loewe. Weimar. 1957.

Pt. iv. Die Karolinger vom Vertrag von Verdun bis zum Herrschaftsantritt der Herrscher aus dem sächsischen Hause. Ed. by Heinz Loewe. Weimar. 1963.

Vol. ii. Die Zeit der Sachsen und Salier.

Pt. i. Das Zeitalter des ottonischen Staats (900–1050). Ed. by Robert Holtzmann and Franz-Jos. Schmale. Cologne. 1967.

Pt. ii. Das Zeitalter des Investiturstreits (1050–1125). Ed. by Holtzmann and Schmale. Cologne. 1967.

Beiheft: Die Rechtsquellen. Ed. by Rudolf Buchner. Weimar. 1953.

For additions, see reviews by L. Wallach in *Speculum*, xxix (1954), 131 and 820; xxx (1955), 93; xxxiv (1959), 343. Refer also to Ottokar Lorenz, *Deutschlands Geschichtsquellen im Mittelalter seit der Mitte des dreizehnten Jahrhunderts* (Berlin, 1870; 3rd edn. 2 vols. 1886–7).

D. PRINTED CATALOGUES OF BOOKS

1. *General Catalogues*

67 BRITISH BOOKS IN PRINT: The reference catalogue of current literature. J. Whitaker & Sons. Lond. 1965+.

An annual which supersedes *The reference catalogue of current literature* (Lond. 1874–1961).

68 THE BRITISH NATIONAL BIBLIOGRAPHY. Council of the British National Bibliography, Ltd. Lond. 1950+.

A subject list with author index of new British books, published weekly, quarterly, and cumulatively annually.

69 THE ENGLISH CATALOGUE OF BOOKS PUBLISHED FROM 1835. Lond. 1864+. Catalogue of books published from 1801 to 1836. 1 vol. Lond. 1914. * (1801–1951).

Annual. The appendices contain lists (incomplete) of the publications of learned societies and printing clubs. Four index volumes (subject indexes) for the years 1837–89 (Lond. 1858–93).

70 PEDDIE (ROBERT A.). Subject index of books published before 1880. 4 vols. Lond. 1933–48.

Published as 1st Ser. (1933) and 2nd Ser. (1935), 3rd Ser. (1939); new Ser. (1948); the 3rd Ser. has cross-references to 1st and 2nd Ser. For books published after 1880, consult the British Museum *Subject index* (No. 77). R. R. Bowker Co. (Lond. and N.Y.) publishes *Subject guide to books in print* annually.

71 POLLARD (ALFRED W.) and REDGRAVE (GILBERT R.), comp. A short-title catalogue of books printed in England, Scotland and Ireland, and of English books printed abroad 1475–1640. Lond. 1926. Reprinted 1946 and 1969.* Continued by D. G. Wing. Short title catalogue . . . 1641–1700. 3 vols. Lond. 1945–51. For supplements see Read (No. 32).

72 THE UNITED STATES CATALOG. 4th edn. New York. 1928. Supplement: Cumulative book index: a world list of books in the English language. 1928+. (H. W. Wilson Co.). N.Y. 1933+.

73 WHITAKER'S CUMULATIVE BOOK LIST. Lond. 1924+.

A record of titles issued or reissued each year; it appears quarterly and annually.

2. *Catalogues of Important Libraries*

74 BIBLIOTHÈQUE NATIONALE. Catalogue général des livres imprimés de la Bibliothèque Nationale. Paris. 1897. (In progress.)

75 BODLEIAN LIBRARY. Catalogus librorum impressorum Bibliothecae Bodleianae. 4 vols. Oxf. 1843–51.

76 BRITISH MUSEUM. Catalogue of books printed in the fifteenth century. Pts. i–viii. Lond. 1908–49. Lithographic reprint. Lond. 1963.

77   BRITISH MUSEUM. Catalogue of printed books (95 vols.). Lond. 1881–
1900. Reprinted (57 vols.). Ann Arbor (Mich.). 1946. Supplement (13 vols.).
Lond. 1900–5. Reprinted (10 vols.). Ann Arbor. 1950.

This is supplemented by the following works, which contain subject indexes:

Catalogue of books in the galleries in the Reading Room. 1886.

List of bibliographical works in the Reading Room. 2nd edn. 1889.

List of books of reference in the Reading Room. 3rd edn. 1889. 4th edn.
2 vols. 1910 (vol. ii is list of subjects).

Subject index of modern works added to the library of the British Museum (in
1880–95). By G. K. Fortescue. 3 vols. 1886–97; of works added in 1881–1900.
3 vols. 1902–3; of works added in 1901–5. 1 vol. 1906; of works added in
1906–10. 1 vol. 1911; of works added in 1911–15. 1 vol. 1918; of works
added in 1916–20 (excluding European war). 1 vol. 1922; of works added in
1921–5. 1 vol. 1927; of works added in 1926–30. 1 vol. 1933; of works added
in 1931–5. 2 vols. 1937; of works added in 1936–40. 2 vols. 1944; of works
added 1941–5. 1 vol. 1953; of works added 1946–50. 4 vols. 1961; of works
added 1951–5 (in progress); of works added 1956–60. 6 vols. 1965–6.
[Subject indexes 1880–1940, reprinted 1967–8.]

See also No. 78. F. C. Francis, 'The catalogues of the Museum: Printed Books'. *Journal
of Documentation*, iv (1948), 13–40.

78   BRITISH MUSEUM. General catalogue of printed books. Photolitho-
graphic edition to 1955. Lond. 1959–66. Ten Year Supplement, 1956–1965.
Lond. 1968. Five Year Supplement, 1965–70. Lond. 1971. In progress.

This indispensable edition is a copy of the working catalogue in use in the Reading Room.
Vols. lxii–lxvi bear the subtitle 'England' and vols. clxxxiv–clxxxvii comprise 'Periodical
Publications'.

79   FACULTY OF ADVOCATES LIBRARY, EDINBURGH. Catalogue of
printed books. 7 vols. Edin. etc. 1867 (1863)–79.

The Edinburgh University Library supplements its *Catalogue of the printed books . . .* by
F. C. Nicholson, 3 vols. (Edin. 1918–23), with an annual *List of additions*, 1920+.

80   JOHN RYLANDS LIBRARY. Catalogue of the printed books and manuscripts in the John Rylands Library. 3 vols. Manchester. 1899. *

81   A LONDON BIBLIOGRAPHY OF THE SOCIAL SCIENCES, being
the subject catalogue of the British Library of Political and Economic Science at
the School of Economics, the Goldsmiths' Library of Economic Literature at the
University of London, the libraries of the Royal Statistical Society and the Royal
Anthropological Institute, and certain special collections at University College,
London, and elsewhere. By B. M. Headicar, C. Fuller, and others. 14 vols. in 15.
Lond. 1931–68. *(1931–7). Supplement, 1962–8. Vols. xv–xxii. Lond. 1970.

Basically a subject-catalogue of the library of the London School of Economics, which
has a good collection on medieval English history. The first four volumes appeared in
1931–2; supplements have since been added, bringing the entries down to 1968.

82   LONDON LIBRARY. Catalogue of the London Library, St. James
Square, London. By Charles H. Wright and C. J. Purnell. 2 vols. Lond. 1913–14.

Supplement, 1913–20. Lond. 1920; 1920–8. Lond. 1929; 1928–50. Lond. 1953. *(1913–50).

83 LONDON LIBRARY. Subject-index of the London Library. By C. H. Wright and C. J. Purnell. 4 vols. Lond. 1909–55. *(1909–55).

84 NEW YORK UNIVERSITY. A catalogue of the law collection at New York University with selected annotations. By Julius J. Marke. N.Y. 1953.
The annotations are fuller than usual.

85 U.S. LIBRARY OF CONGRESS. A catalog of books represented by Library of Congress printed cards issued from August 1898 to July 31, 1942. 167 vols. Ann Arbor (Mich.). 1942–6. Supplement, Aug. 1, 1942–Dec. 31, 1947. 42 vols. Ann Arbor. 1948. The Library of Congress author catalog: a cumulative list of works represented by Library of Congress printed cards, 1948–52. 24 vols. Ann Arbor. 1953. National Union Catalog: A cumulative list of works represented by Library of Congress printed cards. Books: Authors, 1952–5. 30 vols. Ann Arbor. 1954–6. National Union Catalog: a cumulative author index list 1953–7. 28 vols. Ann Arbor. 1958. Reprints of all of the preceding catalogs are available.

All of the preceding catalogues of the Library of Congress will eventually be replaced by the *National Union Catalog*: the pre-1956 imprints (No. 86 (*a*)).

86 U.S. LIBRARY OF CONGRESS. National Union Catalog: a cumulative author list representing Library of Congress printed cards and titles reported by other American libraries. Compiled and edited with the co-operation of the Library of Congress and the National Union Subcommittee of . . . American Library Association.
(*a*) The pre-1956 imprints. Lond. 1968 (in progress). A comprehensive retrospective catalog.
(*b*) Cumulative author list 1958 (1956)–1962. 54 vols. N.Y. 1963.
(*c*) Cumulative author list 1963–7. 72 vols. Ann Arbor 1969.
(*d*) Then continued monthly and quarterly and annually. Ann Arbor. 1968+.

87 U.S. LIBRARY OF CONGRESS. Library of Congress catalog. A cumulative list of works represented by Library of Congress printed cards. Books: Subjects, 1950–4. 20 vols. Ann Arbor. 1955. Subjects, 1955–9. 22 vols. Ann Arbor. 1960. Subjects, 1960–4. 25 vols. Ann Arbor. 1965. Then quarterly and annually.

II. JOURNALS OF MORE THAN LOCAL SCOPE

For local journals, see Chapter VII, Sect. B, county by county. Bonser's bibliographies (Nos. 12 and 13) list several hundred periodicals bearing on British history from Roman to Anglo-Saxon times.

A. BIBLIOGRAPHY OF JOURNALS

88 BOEHM (ERIC H.) and ADOLPHUS (LALIT), eds. Historical periodicals: an annotated world list of historical and related serial publications. Santa Barbara (Calif.) and Munich. 1961.
For Great Britian, pp. 216–44.

89   BRITISH UNION-CATALOGUE OF PERIODICALS. A record of the periodicals of the world, from the seventeenth century to the present day, in British libraries. Edited for the Council of the British Union-Catalogue of Periodicals by James D. Stewart with Muriel E. Hammond and Erwin Saenger. 4 vols. Lond. and N.Y. 1955–8. Supplement to 1960. Lond. and N.Y. 1962.

Vol. i, A–C (1955); vol. ii, D–K (1956); vol. iii, L–R (1957); vol. iv, S–Z (1958). Supersedes *Union catalogue of the periodical publications in the university libraries of the British Isles* . . . compiled . . . by Marion G. Roupell (Lond. 1937); and Kenneth A. Mallaber and Philip M. De Paris, *The London union list of periodicals: Holdings of the municipal and county libraries of Greater London* (Lond. 1951). The Institute of Advanced Legal Studies (Univ. of London) published in 1949 *A survey of legal periodicals held in British libraries* (Lond. 1949).

90   CARON (PIERRE) and JARYC (MARC). World list of historical periodicals and bibliographies. International Committee of Historical Sciences. Oxf. 1939.

Alphabetical list of periodicals. See also Eliza Jeffries Davis and Eva G. R. Taylor, *Guide to periodicals and bibliographies dealing with geography, archaeology, and history.* Hist. Assoc. Pamphlet No. 110 (1938). Unusually useful and clearly arranged is *Catalogo delle pubblicazioni periodiche esistenti in varie biblioteche di Roma e Firenze* (Vatican City, 1955).

91   KIRBY (JOHN L.). Guide to historical periodicals in the English language. Helps for students of history. Historical Assoc. London, no. 80. Lond. 1970.

92   UNION LIST OF SERIALS IN LIBRARIES OF THE UNITED STATES AND CANADA. Ed. by Winifred Gregory. (H. W. Wilson Co.). N.Y. 1943. Supplement 1941–43, and 1944–49. Third edn. by Edna B. Titus, under the sponsorship of the joint committee of the Union list of serials. 5 vols. N.Y. 1965. Supplements. 1966+.

For serials which began publication after 31 December 1949 and which were received by the Library of Congress and a number of co-operating libraries, see *New Serials Titles: a Union List of Serials* . . . *prepared under the sponsorship of the joint committee on the Union List of Serials* 3rd edn. 1950–60, 2 vols. Library of Congress, 1961. Ibid. 1961–5 Accumulation. Library of Congress, 1966. Ibid. 1966 Accumulation. Library of Congress, 1967. Ibid. In progress, monthly issues.

B. GUIDES TO PERIODICAL LITERATURE

Before the last quarter of the nineteenth century there were few journals devoted exclusively to historical studies. Until then historical articles were published largely in archaeological and antiquarian magazines and in the proceedings and transactions of local societies. A few such articles find places in Poole's *Index* (No. 100); a considerable number in Gomme's *Index* (No. 717) and in the index to *Archaeologia* (No. 108). For fuller references, the journals and local publications must be individually searched. The *British humanities index* (No. 93) and its predecessor, *Subject index to Periodicals* (No. 102), analyse the most extensive issues of journals, national and regional, germane to English medieval history. They form basic tools for general and local British history. The publications of local societies are entered under Local History in Chapter VII below; and additional references to archaeological and antiquarian magazines are given on pages 85–7.

Many journals periodically carry lists of current articles which appear elsewhere; convenient examples are *American Historical Review, Economic History Review, English Historical Review, Revue d'histoire ecclésiastique,* and *Speculum.* The *International Bibliography of Historical Sciences* (No. 53) analyses some 1,500 journals. See also Bonser (Nos. 12; 13); *Writings* (Nos. 38; 39); and de Brie (No. 49).

93 BRITISH HUMANITIES INDEX. Lond. 1963+.

Supersedes *The subject index to periodicals* (No. 102). The quarterly issues of *British humanities index* are by subject only; the annual issues have subject and author sections. The Regional Lists, for England county by county, are essential for local history.

94 HASKELL (DANIEL C.). A check list of cumulative indexes to individual periodicals in the New York Public Library. N.Y. 1942.

95 INDEX OF ECONOMIC ARTICLES IN JOURNALS AND COLLECTIVE SOURCES. Prepared under the auspices of the American Economic Association. Homewood (Ill.). 1961+.

Vol. i covers the period 1886–1924; vol. ii, 1925–39; and so forth until vol. viii for 1966 alone was published in 1969.

96 INDEX TO LEGAL PERIODICALS. By American Association of Law Libraries. N.Y. etc. 1909+.

97 INDEX TO RELIGIOUS PERIODICAL LITERATURE. By American Theological Association. 1949/52+. Chicago. 1953+.

98 INTERNATIONAL INDEX TO PERIODICALS, devoted chiefly to the humanities and science. . . . A cumulative author and subject index to a selected list of the periodicals of the world. N.Y. 1916–65. Thereafter THE SOCIAL SCIENCES AND HUMANITIES INDEX. N.Y. 1965+.

This started as a supplement to Readers' Guide, with vol. i for the period 1907–15 (1916).

99 KRAMM (HEINRICH). Bibliographie historischer Zeitschriften, 1939–1951. Marburg. 1952–4.

Fascicle ii (1953), pp. 79 ff. deals with Great Britain and Ireland.

100 POOLE'S INDEX TO PERIODICAL LITERATURE. 6 vols. Boston etc. 1882–1908.

101 ROUSE (RICHARD H.) *et al.* Serial bibliographies for medieval studies. Pubns. Center for Medieval–Renaissance Stud. no. 3. Berkeley and Los Angeles. 1969.

A convenient descriptive list of nearly 300 serials which provide current bibliographies.

102 THE SUBJECT INDEX TO PERIODICALS, 1915–61. Library Assoc. Lond. 1919+. Published quarterly and annually; after 1947 limited to British periodicals. Superseded by British Humanities Index (No. 93).

The *Subject Index* was entitled *Athenaeum subject index* 1915–19. The *Subject index* and its successor, *British humanities index,* form the most valuable guides to periodicals and the publications of local societies from 1915 on.

103   SUBJECT INDEX TO WELSH PERIODICALS. Ed. by Arthur ap
Gwynn and Idwal Lewis. Library Assoc. Wales and Monmouthshire Branch. i+
(1931+). Cardiff. 1934+.

> Vol. vi for 1941–5 appeared in 1957; vol. vii for 1946–55 appeared 1964 (Swansea, 1964).
> For bibliographical references on Wales and the Celts in periodicals, see *National Library
> of Wales Journal* (No. 134), and *Bibliotheca Celtica* (No. 110).

C. GENERAL HISTORICAL JOURNALS

The general historical journals listed here are (1) the principal reviews published
in Great Britain, and (2) the foreign periodicals which give attention to British
history. The journals which are devoted to specialized subjects are catalogued
under those subjects; and the periodicals dealing with English local history
appear in Chapter VII, pp. 211–50 below, county by county. Journals concerned
primarily with archaeological subjects are listed under Archaeology, pp. 85–7.

1. *British Journals*

104   ABERDEEN UNIVERSITY REVIEW. Aberdeen. 1913+.*

105   ABERYSTWYTH STUDIES. By members of the University College of
Wales. Vols. i–xiv. Aberystwyth. 1912–36.

106   AGRICULTURAL HISTORY REVIEW. Journal of the British Agricultural History Society. Reading and Welwyn. 1953+.

107   ANTIQUARIES JOURNAL. Journal of the Society of Antiquaries of
London. Lond. 1921+. Index of vols. i–x (1921–30). 1934.

> Replaces *Procs.* of Soc. 1843+ (Lond. 1849–1920); for which, index of first series,
> 1859; of second series, vols. i–xx (1859–1905), 1908; xxi–xxxii (1906–20), 1938. General
> index, 1959.
>   Since 1921 each quarterly issue has contained a long section of periodical literature.
> The articles on history and its auxiliaries appearing in British national journals, in the
> transactions of local societies, and in foreign periodicals are listed, not by topic, but
> under the title of each periodical. Cf. No. 723.

108   ARCHAEOLOGIA, or miscellaneous tracts relating to antiquity. Published by the Society of Antiquaries of London. Lond. 1770+. Index of vols. i–l
(1770–1887), 1889. *(index). Index of vols. li–c (1888–1966), 1970.

109   ARCHAEOLOGIA CAMBRENSIS. Published by Cambrian Archaeological Assoc. Lond. 1846+. Index of the first four series (1846–83), 1892; of the
fifth series (1884–1900), 1902. Index (1846–1900) compiled by Lily F. Chitty,
revised by Elizabeth Edwards. Cardiff. 1964.

> *Archaeologia Cambrensis* lists the periodicals of Wales and the articles therein.

110   BIBLIOTHECA CELTICA: a register of publications relating to Wales
and the Celtic peoples and languages. National Library of Wales. Aberystwyth.
1910+.

> First series, 1909–28 (1910–34); second series, 1929–38 (1939–52); third series, 1953+
> (1954+). Although this annual includes Celtic materials for Ireland and Scotland, it is
> fullest on Welsh aspects.

111 BOARD OF CELTIC STUDIES. University of Wales. Bulletin. Lond. 1921+. Also History and law series. Cardiff. 1929+.

The *Bulletin* includes, *inter alia*, tabulated lists of excavations and a bibliography of Welsh archaeology and art since 1914; it has printed many important documents *in extenso*. The History and law series is listed in *Repert. Font.* (No. 64), i. 756.

112 BULLETIN OF THE INSTITUTE OF HISTORICAL RESEARCH. University of London. 1923+. Lond. 1925+. * Alphabetical table of contents of vols. i–xxv (1923–52), 1952. Supplements 1–13 (1930–1948). Special Supplements 1–6 (1932–67). Theses Supplements.

The *Bulletin* proper is a rich quarry of historical information. Besides articles, select documents, and historical news, it has printed corrections to the *D.N.B.*, lists of historical manuscript accessions to British depositories, and migrations thereof elsewhere. Of the occasional summaries entitled 'Bibliographical aids to research', those on 'Indexes to periodicals' (xi (1934), 165–80) and on 'General lists of books printed in England' (xii (1935), 164–74) are most helpful for our purposes.

The Supplements 1–13 form a *Guide to the historical publications of the societies of England and Wales from 1929 to 1946*. Articles in periodicals were not listed. These supplements are largely superseded by Mullins, *Texts* (No. 29) and Milne, *Writings 1934–45* (No. 39).

Special Supplements 1 (1932) and 2 (1934) print a *Guide to the accessibility of local records of England and Wales*. Special Supplement 3 (1936) is Russell's *Dictionary* (No. 541). Special Supplement 6 (1967) is Jane Sayers's *Original papal documents* (No. 1009). The annual Theses Supplements have the sub-title 'Historical Research for University Degrees in the United Kingdom'. Previously research in progress was indicated; currently only completed theses are listed.

113 CAMBRIDGE HISTORICAL JOURNAL. Lond. 1923–57. * Continued as: The historical journal. Vol. i+, 1958+.

After 1956, primarily a journal of modern history.

114 CHURCH QUARTERLY REVIEW. Lond. 1875–1968. Index of vols. i–lix (1875–1905), 1906. *(1875–1906).

115 COLLECTANEA TOPOGRAPHICA ET GENEALOGICA. By John Gough Nichols. 8 vols. Lond. 1834–43. Continued as The Topographer and Genealogist. 3 vols. Lond. 1846–58. Later Nichols edited the Herald and Genealogist. 8 vols. Lond. 1863–74.

116 DOWNSIDE REVIEW: A quarterly of catholic thought. Lond. (1880+), 1882+. *(1880–1915).

Articles on Church history, published under the auspices of the Downside Abbey, near Bath.

117 DUBLIN REVIEW. Lond. 1836+. * Index by subject, 1836–63, 1864; index by vol. 1836–1936, 1936; index of articles, vols. i–cxviii (1836–96), in cxviii. 467–520.

Deals especially with church history.

118 DURHAM UNIVERSITY JOURNAL. Durham. 1876+.

119 ECONOMIC HISTORY REVIEW. Published for the Economic History Society. Lond. and Welwyn. 1927+. *(1927–67).

> 1st Ser. i–xviii (1927–48), 2nd Ser. 1+ (1948+). Prints annually, in the April issue, an extensive, unannotated list of books and articles on the economic history of Great Britain and Ireland. Index for Ser. i, vols. i–xviii (1927–48), by Jean Brotherhood and R. M. Hartwell (Utrecht (n.d.)).

120 ECONOMIC JOURNAL: the journal of the Royal Economic Society. Lond. 1891+. *† Indexes of every ten volumes, 1901, 1911, 1922, 1934. * Supplement: Economic history. Ser. i, 1926–9; then Economic history, ii–iv, 1930–40.

121 ENGLISH HISTORICAL REVIEW. Lond. 1886+. *(1886–1905). †(1886–1961). Index of vols. i–xx (1886–1905), 1906; thereafter, every ten volumes, 1916, 1927, 1938; and for vols. li–lxx (1936–55), 1963.

> The foremost British journal on history. In addition to articles and reviews it has printed since 1924 annually, in the July issue, a selected annotated list of articles on history.

122 GENTLEMAN'S MAGAZINE. 303 vols. Lond. 1731–1907. *†. Indexes for the years 1731–1818. 4 vols. 1789–1821. Another edn. of vols. i–ii (1731–86). 1818.

> Before 1868 this magazine devoted much attention to historical and antiquarian subjects, including archaeology and topography. There is a classified collection of the chief contents, from 1731 to 1868, in the *Gentleman's magazine library*, ed. by G. L. Gomme, 30 vols. Lond. 1883–1905.

123 HISTORICAL SOCIETY OF THE CHURCH IN WALES. Journal. Cardiff. 1947+.

124 HISTORICAL STUDIES: being papers read before the Irish conference of historians. Lond. 1958+.

> N.B. A different journal is *History Studies*. Oxford. 1968+.

125 HISTORY: THE QUARTERLY JOURNAL OF THE HISTORICAL ASSOCIATION. New Ser. Lond. 1916+.

> Superseded *History: a quarterly magazine for the student and the expert*. Vols. i–iv (1912–15), by Harold F. B. Wheeler. *A journal of high quality whose scholarly articles are frequently of broad scope.

126 HONOURABLE SOCIETY OF CYMMRODORION. Y Cymmrodor. Lond. 1877+. Index, vols. i–xxiii (1877–1912). Lond. 1913. Transactions. Lond. (1892/3), 1894+. Index to Transactions. 1892/3–1911/12. Lond. 1913. Record Series (No. 202).

> Called Honourable Society of Cymmrodorion since 1878. R. T. Jenkins and Helen Ramage, *A history of the Honourable Society of Cymmrodorion* (Lond. 1951).

127 INNES REVIEW. Scottish Catholic historical studies. Glasgow. 1950+.

128 IRISH HISTORICAL STUDIES. The joint journal of the Irish Historical Society and the Ulster Society for Irish Historical Studies. Dublin. 1938+.

Supplement i (1968), pp. 8–80: Index to *I.H.S.* vols. i–xv (1938–67); and pp. 81–124: List of bibliographical abbreviations and short titles, which serves as a brief guide to materials on Irish history.

> Contains comprehensive annual bibliographies of writings on Irish history and reports on research on Irish history in British, American, and Irish universities.

129   JOHN RYLANDS LIBRARY. Bulletin. Manchester. 1903+. *(1903–50). Index of vols. i–xxv (1903–41) in xxv. 189–233.

130   JOURNAL OF ECCLESIASTICAL HISTORY. Lond. 1950+. *(1950–65). With volume xvii (1966), it came into the ownership of the Cambridge University Press.

131   JURIDICAL REVIEW. The law journal of Scottish universities. Edin. 1889+. *Index of vols. i–xlvi.

132   LAW QUARTERLY REVIEW. Lond. 1885+. *(1885–1954). †(1885–1906). Index of vols. i–x (1885–94) in x; thereafter, every fifth volume, 1899, etc.; also vols. i. 1 (1895–1934); vols. li–lv; and lvi–lxiv. Index for vols. i–lxxii by Peter Allsop. Lond. 1957; and vols. i–lxxx (1885–1964) by Peter Allsop. Lond. 1965.

133   MEDIAEVAL AND RENAISSANCE STUDIES. Warburg Institute. Lond. 1941+.

134   NATIONAL LIBRARY OF WALES. Journal. Aberystwyth. 1939+.

135   NORTHERN HISTORY. A review of the history of the north of England. Leeds. 1966+.

136   NOTES AND QUERIES. Lond. 1849+. *† Vol. cxcix (1954) became New Ser. i. Periodical general indexes.

137   NOTTINGHAM MEDIAEVAL STUDIES. University of Nottingham. 1957+.

138   PAST AND PRESENT. A journal of historical studies. Oxf. 1952+.

139   SCOTTISH HISTORICAL REVIEW. Glasgow. 1903/4–28, Edin. 1947+. *(1903–28). Index of vols. i–xii (1903–16), 1918; vols. xiii–xxv (1916–28), 1933.

> A semi-annual, scholarly journal devoted to Scottish history; it is a continuation of *Northern notes and queries . . . (1886–90)* and the *Scottish antiquary . . . (1891–1903)*. Discontinued from 1928 to 1947. Beginning with vol. xxxix (1960), it includes a list of articles on Scottish history published during the previous year.

140   UNIVERSITY OF BIRMINGHAM HISTORICAL JOURNAL. Birmingham. 1947–70. Replaced by MIDLAND HISTORY. Birmingham. 1971+.

141   WELSH BIBLIOGRAPHICAL SOCIETY. Journal. Carmarthen. 1910+.

142 THE WELSH HISTORY REVIEW (Cylchgrawn Hanes Cymru). Cardiff. 1960+.

It includes summaries of articles in Welsh county society publications and in other Welsh periodicals. It lists articles elsewhere relating to the history of Wales.

2. *Foreign Journals*

143 AGRICULTURAL HISTORY. Agricultural History Society. Chicago, Baltimore, Champaign. 1927+. *

Deals almost exclusively with American agricultural history.

144 AMERICAN HISTORICAL REVIEW. N.Y. 1895+. * Indexes vols. i–x (1895–1905), 1906; xi–xx (1905–15), 1916; xxi–xxx (1915–25), 1926; xxxi–xl (1925–35), 1939; xli–lx (1935–55), 1962; lxi–lxx (1955–65), 1968.

Cf. Franklin D. Scott and Elaine Teigler, eds. *Guide to the American Historical Review, 1895–1945*, Annual Report of the American Historical Association, 1944, vol. i, pt. ii, pp. 65–292 (Washington, 1945).

145 ANALECTA BOLLANDIANA. Société des Bollandistes. Paris and Brussels. 1882+. †(1882–1943). Indexes of vols. i–xx (1882–1901), 1904; xxi–xl (1902–22), 1931. Table générale des articles publiés en 80 ans, 1882–1961. Brussels. 1962.

146 ANNALES D'HISTOIRE ÉCONOMIQUE ET SOCIALE. 10 vols. Paris. 1929–38. Continued under the title, Annales d'histoire sociale, 3 vols. 1939–41; then Mélanges d'histoire sociale, 6 vols. 1942–4; then, Annales d'histoire sociale, 2 vols. 1945; then, Annales, économies, sociétés, civilisations, 1946+. Index ('Table') of vols. i–x (1929–38), in x. 528–44.

147 ANNALES DU MIDI. Revue de la France méridionale. Toulouse. 1889+. *(1889–1914). Indexes ('Tables') of vols. i–xxx (1889–1918), 1918; Supplément, 1934; xxxi–xl (1919–28), in 1939/40, pp. 507–32; xli–l (1929–38) in 1950, pp. 419–47.

148 ARCHIV FÜR DAS STUDIUM DER NEUEREN SPRACHEN UND LITERATUREN. Berlin and Hamburg. 1846+. *(1846–72).

148A THE BRITISH STUDIES MONITOR. Published at Bowdoin College by the Anglo-American Associates. Brunswick (Maine). 1970+.

Includes items on societies, projects, and persons.

149 BIBLIOTHÈQUE DE L'ÉCOLE DES CHARTES. Revue d'érudition publiée par la Société de l'École des Chartes. Paris. 1839/40+. *(1839–69). Indexes ('Tables') of vols. i–lxxxv (1839–1924), 7 vols. 1849, 1862, 1870, 1888, 1903, 1911, 1926.

150 BULLETIN DE THÉOLOGIE ANCIENNE ET MÉDIÉVALE. Abbaye du Mont–César. Louvain. 1933+.

See also *Recherches de théologie ancienne et médiévale*. Louvain, 1929+.

151 CAHIERS DE CIVILISATION MÉDIÉVALE: xᵉ–xiiᵉ siecles. Université de Poitiers. 1958+.

The bibliography, arranged alphabetically, is strong on periodical literature.

152 CLASSICA ET MEDIAEVALIA. Copenhagen. 1938+. *

153 DEUTSCHE ZEITSCHRIFT FÜR GESCHICHTSWISSEN-SCHAFT. 14 vols. Freiburg im Breisgau. 1889–98. Continued under the title, Historische Vierteljahrschrift. 31 vols. Leipzig. 1898–1939.

Contains a good periodical bibliography of works relating to German history. Vols. i–viii (1889–92) contain valuable articles by F. Liebermann, entitled 'Neuere Literatur zur Geschichte Englands im Mittelalter', covering the publications of about 1886–91.

154 DEUTSCHES ARCHIV FÜR ERFORSCHUNG DES MITTEL-ALTERS: namens der Monumenta Germaniae Historica. Weimar, Cologne, Graz. 1937+. *(1937–66).

Deutsches Archiv analyses articles from the principal journals and prints the annual report on the progress of the *M.G.H.* It is the successor of *Neues Archiv für ältere deutsche Geschichtskunde*, Hannover and Berlin, i–l (1876–1935).

155 HARVARD LAW REVIEW. Cambr. (Mass.). 1887+. Index of vols. i–l (1887–1937), 1938.

Recent numbers are but rarely concerned with medieval English history.

156 HISTORISCHE ZEITSCHRIFT. Munich. 1859–1942*; 1959+. *(1859–1942). Indexes ('Register') of vols. i–lvi (1859–1886), 1888; lvii–xcvi (1887–1906), 1906; xcvii–cxxx (1906–24), 1925.

In recent years it has printed little on medieval English history.

157 JAHRESBERICHTE DER GESCHICHTSWISSENSCHAFT im Auftrage der historischen Gesellschaft zu Berlin. Berlin. 1880–1916.

Annual. Contained a survey of the historical works published in the various countries of Europe. Medieval England was dealt with in vols. xi–xiii, xxvii–xxviii only, covering the publications of the years 1888–90, 1904–5. The reports for 1904–5, by Miss Bateson, were excellent. Continued as *Jahresberichte der deutschen Geschichte*, i–vii, 1918–24 (Breslau, 1920–6); i–xvi, 1925–40 (Leipzig, 1927–42); and *Neue Folge*, i+, 1949+ (Berlin, 1952+). The continuations are not useful for British medieval history.

158 JOURNAL OF BRITISH STUDIES. Conference on British Studies. Hartford (Conn.). 1961+. Proceedings, *Albion* (Seattle, Elmira). 1969+.

159 JOURNAL OF ECONOMIC HISTORY. N.Y. 1941+. *

160 MEDIAEVAL SCANDINAVIA. Odense. 1968+.

Articles, principally in English, on medieval research in Scandinavian countries.

161 MEDIEVALIA ET HUMANISTICA. An American journal for the Middle Ages and Renaissance. Boulder (Colo.). 1943–68 and Cleveland (Ohio). 1969+.

162 MEDIAEVAL STUDIES. Pontifical Institute of Medieval Studies, Toronto. Lond. and N.Y. 1939+. *

163 MÉLANGES D'ARCHÉOLOGIE ET D'HISTOIRE. École française de Rome. Rome and Paris. 1881+. Indexes ('Tables') of vols. i–xx (1881–1900), in vol. xx; xxi–xxxviii (1901–20), (Paris, 1921).

164 LE MOYEN AGE. Paris. 1888+. *

Occasional bibliographies of publications on the history of the middle ages.

165 REVUE DES QUESTIONS HISTORIQUES. Paris. 1866–1914; 1922–39. Indexes ('Tables') of vols. i–xx (1866–76), 1887; xxi–xl (1877–86), 1889; xli–lx (1887–96), 1897; lxi–lxxx (1897–1906), 1925; lxxxi–ci (1907–24), 1928.

Not published between 1914 and 1922.

166 REVUE D'HISTOIRE ECCLÉSIASTIQUE. Louvain. 1900+. * Index ('Table') of vols. i–xxii (1900–26), 1928. *

The *chronique* on historical activities and the full bibliographies are very valuable and constitute one of the most helpful guides to many topics of medieval history.

167 REVUE HISTORIQUE. Paris. 1876+. *

Especially valuable are the critical summaries of current publications on medieval England, prepared every few years by Charles Bémont until 1936 and subsequently by Édouard Perroy; e.g. ccviii (1952), 255–73; ccix (1953), 65–84; ccxiv (1955), 282–321; ccxx (1958), 111–55.

168 SPECULUM: a journal of mediaeval studies. Published by the Mediaeval Academy of America. Cambr. (Mass.). 1926+.

169 TRADITIO. Studies in ancient and mediaeval history, thought and religion. N.Y. 1943+.

In addition to articles on a broad range of subjects, *Traditio* included the bulletin of the Institute of Medieval Canon Law and a select bibliography on Canon Law and its ancillary topics from 1955 to 1970; then the *Bulletin* became separate (No. 6426).

170 VIERTELJAHRSCHRIFT FÜR SOZIAL- UND WIRTSCHAFTS-GESCHICHTE. Leipzig, Stuttgart. 1903+. * Index ('Register') of vols. i–xx (1903–28), 1930. *

D. PUBLICATIONS OF SOCIETIES

Learned societies whose interests transcend the county of their origin provide two types of material of use to the historian, (1) the papers and lectures published in proceedings, transactions, or journals, and (2) the records printed under their auspices. The latter form source collections indispensable to the student. The Anglia Christiana Society, the Caxton Society, and the English Historical Society accomplished some good work in the second quarter of the nineteenth century, but perished from lack of support. The Surtees Society, established in 1834, and the Camden Society, established in 1838 and merged with the Royal Historical Society in 1897, have published, and continue to publish, many important volumes of diverse sources. Other societies, such as the Pipe Roll

Society, founded 1883, the Selden Society, founded 1887, and the Canterbury and York Society, founded 1904, have specialized in particular classes of documents, financial, legal, episcopal, etc.

Various local record societies have fostered the publication of local sources, many of which have much wider than local relevance and utility. The local societies are listed, county by county, below in Chapter VII.

Complete lists of the publications prior to March 1957 of the important record societies of England and Wales are given in Mullins, *Texts* (No. 29); and publications (1901–33) of many societies in Mullins, *Guide* (No. 28). The medieval records printed by the more important English, Irish, Scottish, and Welsh societies are catalogued in *Repert. Font.* (No. 64). The older publications of societies are listed in Hardy's *Catalogue* (No. 21), and up to 1900, in the older British Museum Catalogue under 'Academies'. In the most recent B.M. Catalogue (No. 78) publications of societies are listed in the volumes 'Periodical Publications' (Vols. clxxxiv–clxxxvii) under the geographical place of publication. A useful inventory is Robert Somerville, *Handlist of record publications (England)*, Brit. Records Assoc. Publication Pamphlet No. 3 (Lond. 1951) (No. 933), with periodic supplements in *Archives* (No. 1504).

For Scottish societies, refer to Terry and Matheson (No. 34), and for Scottish and Welsh societies, *Handlist of Scottish and Welsh record publications*, the Scottish section by Peter Gouldesbrough and A. P. Kup; the Welsh section by Idwal Lewis, British Records Assoc. Publication Pamphlet, No. 4 (Lond. 1954).

Information on the addresses, officers, and current publications of British societies can be found in the annual volume, *Yearbook of the scientific and learned societies of Great Britain* (Lond. 1884–1939 and 1951+). Since 1951 these volumes have been published by the British Council. The names and addresses of the principal societies are also listed in *Whitaker's Almanack* (Lond. 1868+) and *The world of learning* (Lond.). The fullest list of the names and addresses of societies is to be found in Sara E. Harcup's *Historical, archaeological and kindred societies in the British Isles* (No. 1512).

1. *England*

(*a*) Proceedings, transactions, etc.

171   ASSOCIATED ARCHITECTURAL SOCIETIES. Reports and papers. Lond. [1851]–1937. Thereafter, Architectural and Archaeological Society of the County of Lincoln. New Series. 1938+. Indexes of vols. i–xxv. 4 vols. Lincoln. 1905; xxvi–xxxvi (1901–22), 1929 (includes index of articles in vols. i–xxv).

Contain papers (many of which relate to other subjects besides architecture) read at the meetings of the following societies:

Archit. and Arch. Soc. of the Counties of Lincoln and Nottingham. Beds. Archit. and Arch. Soc. Leics. Archit. and Arch. Soc. St. Albans Archit. and Arch. Soc. Sheffield Archit. and Arch. Soc. Worcester Diocesan Archit. and Arch. Soc. Various architectural societies.

The association was dissolved in 1936. Cf. No. 1717.

172 BRITISH ACADEMY. Proceedings. Lond. 1903/4+. Index of vols. i–x (1901–34), 1937. Supplemental papers. 6 vols. 1911–31.

Important lectures by fellows of the academy and others; and informative obituary notices of fellows.

173 BRITISH ARCHAEOLOGICAL ASSOCIATION. Journal. Lond. 1845–6+. †(1846–1955). Indexes of vols. i–xxx (1845–74), 1875; xxxi–xlii (1875–86), 1887; xliii–lii (1887–96), 1915; New Ser. i–xxv (1895–1919), 1924.

This society also published *Collectanea archaeologica*, 2 vols. 1861–71, and proceedings or transactions of meetings held at Canterbury, Gloucester, Winchester, and Worcester, 4 vols. 1845–51; contents included in the general index, 1887 (mentioned above).

174 ECCLESIASTICAL HISTORY SOCIETY. Studies in church history. Lond. 1964+. [Later published at Leiden and Cambr.].

Publishes papers read at meetings of the society.

175 HISTORICAL ASSOCIATION (London). Annual Bulletin of Historical Literature (No. 7). History (No. 125).

Helps for Students of History, vols. lii+ (1950+). Vols. 1–li (1918–24) were sponsored by S.P.C.K.). The Association also publishes several series of pamphlets, entitled Historical Association leaflets, i–xcvii (1907–34); then Historical Association pamphlets, xcviii–cxxx (1934–44); then Publications, cxxxi+ (1944+). Other publications are Association Pamphlets: General Series G. i+ (1945+); and Special Series S. i+ (1945+).

176 JEWISH HISTORICAL SOCIETY OF ENGLAND. Transactions. Lond. 1895+. Index of vols. i–xii (1893–1928/31), in Miscellanies, pt. ii, pp. 107–12. Miscellanies. Lond. 1925+.

Consult Mullins, *Guide* (No. 28), pp. 206–8.

177 ROYAL HISTORICAL SOCIETY. Transactions. Lond. 1872+. Centenary guide to the publications of the Royal Historical Society, 1868–1968, and of the former Camden Society 1838–97. Ed. by A. Taylor Milne. Lond. 1968.

Milne's *Guide* supersedes that by Hubert Hall, published in 1925. When the Society was founded in 1868, it was called the Historical Society of Great Britain, and the title of volume i is *Transactions of the Historical Society*; in 1872 the name was changed to Royal Historical Society. See R. A. Humphreys, *The Royal Historical Society, 1868–1968* (Lond. 1969). Besides the *Transactions*, a few separate works have been published by the Society, e.g. Guides and Handbooks (Nos. 29, 371, 372, 2219). In 1897 the publications of the Camden Society became the Camden Series of the Royal Historical Society (No. 184).

178 SOCIETY OF ANTIQUARIES OF LONDON. *Archaeologia* (No. 108). Also Proceedings. Lond. 1849–1920, which became *Antiquaries Journal* 1921+ (No. 107). General index to Proceedings, 2nd Ser. i–xx (1859–1905), 1908; xxi–xxxii (1906–20), 1938. General index of *Antiquaries Journal* i–x (1921–30), 1934.

Listed in Mullins, *Guide*, pp. 385–93. This society has also published *Vetusta monumenta* (No. 742), and several other works.

179 SOUTH-EASTERN UNION OF SCIENTIFIC SOCIETIES. The south-eastern naturalist and antiquary (earlier title varies). Lond. 1896+. Index to the transactions of the preceding works, i–xl (1896–1935), 1935.

Listed in Mullins, *Guide*, pp. 416–17.

(*b*) Record series of societies

See Mullins, *Texts* (No. 29), and *Repert. Font.* (No. 64).

180 ANGLIA CHRISTIANA SOCIETY. Publications. 3 vols. Lond. 1846–48.

Cf. *Repert. Font.* i. 35.

181 BRITISH ACADEMY. Records of the social and economic history of England and Wales. 9 vols. Lond. 1914–35. (Listed in Mullins, *Texts*, pp. 102–3; in *Repert. Font.* i. 107.)

182 BRITISH RECORD SOCIETY. Index library. Lond. 1890+. *(Listed in Mullins, *Texts*, pp. 104–14.)

In 1890 this society absorbed the Index Library (Lond. 1888+) and the Index Society. Contains mainly indexes of names in records of the sixteenth and seventeenth centuries; but includes some wills and inquisitions, and some pleas from King's Bench rolls for the pre-Tudor period.

183 BRITISH SOCIETY OF FRANCISCAN STUDIES. Publications. vols. i–xix, Aberdeen, Manchester, Oxf. 1908–37. Extra Ser. * i–iii, 1912–32. * (Listed in Mullins, *Texts*, pp. 115–18.)

184 CAMDEN SOCIETY. Publications, 1st Ser. 105 vols. (1838–72) *†; 2nd Ser. 62 vols. (1871–1901); 3rd Ser. 1900+. Descriptive catalogue of the first series by J. G. Nichols. Lond. 1862; 2nd edn. 1872. List and index of the publications of the Royal Hist. Soc. 1871–1924, and of the Camden Soc. 1840–97, ed. by Hubert Hall, 1925. (Listed in Mullins, *Texts*, pp. 239–75; in *Repert. Font.* i. 117–20; 629–31.) These lists are superseded by Milne's *Centenary guide* (No. 177). F. J. Levy, 'The founding of the Camden Society'. *Victorian Studies*, vii (1964), 295–305. The Third and Fourth Series are published under the auspices of the Royal Historical Society.

185 CANTERBURY AND YORK SOCIETY. Publications. Lond. 1905+. * (Listed in Mullins, *Texts*, pp. 119–25; in *Repert. Font.* i. 121–3.)

Publishes archiepiscopal and episcopal registers.

186 CAXTON SOCIETY. Publications. 16 vols. Lond. 1844–54. * (Listed in Mullins, *Texts*, pp. 140–2; in *Repert. Font.* i. 125.)

Printed chronicles and similar works.

187 EARLY ENGLISH TEXT SOCIETY. Publications. Lond. 1864+. † Extra Ser. vols. i–cxxvi (1867–1935). † List of publications (i, Classified survey; ii, Order of publications), 1931. (Listed in *Repert. Font.* i. 239–48.)

188 ENGLISH HISTORICAL SOCIETY. Publications. 29 vols. Lond. 1838–56. * (Listed in Mullins, *Texts*, pp. 143–5; in *Repert. Font.* i. 251–2.)

Printed chronicles.

189 ENGLISH PLACE-NAME SOCIETY (No. 623). (Listed in Mullins, *Texts*, pp. 146–7.)

190 HARLEIAN SOCIETY. Publications. Lond. 1869+. (Listed in Mullins, *Texts*, pp. 179–89.) Registers. Lond. 1877+. (Listed in Mullins, *Texts*, pp. 190–7.)

Its principal interests are genealogy and heraldry.

191 HENRY BRADSHAW SOCIETY. Publications. Lond. 1891+. (Listed in Mullins, *Texts*, pp. 198–207; in *Repert. Font.* i. 322–3.)

Prints liturgical manuscripts and service books.

192 MANORIAL SOCIETY. Monographs. i–ii, iv. Lond. 1907–10. Continued as Publications. iii, v–xvi. Lond. 1909–29.

Merged in British Rec. Soc. in 1929. Includes *Lists of manor court rolls in private hands*, ed. by A. L. Hardy (Nos. i, pp. 21; ii, pp. 25; iv, pp. 23; 2nd edn. of pt. i, 1913); E. Margaret Thompson, *A descriptive catalogue of manorial rolls belonging to Sir H. F. Burke* (Pubns. xi, xii, 1922); T. F. Hobson, *A catalogue of manorial documents preserved in the muniment room of New College, Oxford* (Pubn. xvi, 1929).

193 PIPE ROLL SOCIETY, for the publication of the Pipe Rolls and other documents. Pipe Rolls, etc. Lond. 1884+. * (Listed in Mullins, *Texts*, pp. 232–8; in *Repert. Font.* i. 579–80.)

194 ROXBURGHE CLUB. Publications. Lond. (and elsewhere). 1814+. (Listed in *Repert. Font.* i. 625–9.)

Issues well-printed editions of rare works.

195 SELDEN SOCIETY. Publications. Lond. 1888+. (Listed in Mullins, *Texts*, pp. 276–85; in *Repert. Font.* i. 679–81.)

Prints sources for the history of the early common law. Founded in 1887 to encourage the study and advance the knowledge of the history of English law. A detailed and indexed summary of the contents of the Introductions to volumes i–lxxix is given in *General guide to the Society's publications*, compiled by A. K. R. Kiralfy and Gareth H. Jones (Lond. 1960).

196 SURTEES SOCIETY. Publications. Lond. etc., 1835+. (Listed in Mullins, *Texts*, pp. 309–31; in *Repert. Font.* i. 726–9.)

Publishes records of the north-east from the Humber to the Forth.

2. *Wales: Record Publications of Societies*

197 BOARD OF CELTIC STUDIES. University of Wales. History and Law Ser. Cardiff. 1929+. (Listed in *Repert. Font.* i. 756.)

198 CAERNARVONSHIRE HISTORICAL SOCIETY. Record Series. 1951+. (Listed in Mullins, *Texts*, p. 530.)

199 FLINTSHIRE HISTORICAL SOCIETY. Record Series. 1929+. (Listed in Mullins, *Texts*, p. 531.)

200 HISTORICAL SOCIETY OF THE CHURCH IN WALES (No. 123 above). 1946+. (Listed in Mullins, *Texts*, pp. 520–2.)

201 HISTORICAL SOCIETY OF WEST WALES: WEST WALES HISTORICAL RECORDS. 14 vols. 1912–29. (Listed in Mullins, *Texts*, pp. 523–7.)

This society was dissolved in 1931.

202 HONOURABLE SOCIETY OF CYMMRODORION. Record Series. Lond. 1892+. (Listed in Mullins, *Texts*, pp. 517–19 and *Repert. Font*. i. 332–3.) Cf. No. 126.

203 SOCIETY FOR THE PUBLICATION OF ANCIENT WELSH MANUSCRIPTS. Publications. 9 vols. Llandovery. 1840–74. (Listed in *Repert. Font*. i. 703.)

204 SOUTH WALES AND MONMOUTH RECORD SOCIETY. Cardiff. 1949+. (Listed in Mullins, *Texts*, pp. 528–9.)

3. *Scotland: Record Publications of Societies*

205 ABBOTSFORD CLUB. Miscellany. 1 vol. Edin. 1837. Publications. 35 vols. Edin. 1835–66. (Listed in *Repert. Font*. i. 1 and in Terry (No. 34).)

206 ABERDEEN UNIVERSITY STUDIES. (Listed in *Titles in Series*, iii. 1179–83.)

207 BANNATYNE CLUB. Publications. 120 vols. Edin. 1823–67. * (Listed in *Repert. Font*. i. 54–5 and in Terry (No. 34).)

208 DUMFRIESSHIRE AND GALLOWAY NATURAL HISTORY AND ANTIQUARIAN SOCIETY (Dumfries). Publications. Edin. 1862/3–1867/8, 1876+.

209 GRAMPIAN CLUB. Publications. 23 vols. Lond. and Edin. 1869–91.

210 MAITLAND CLUB. Publications. 75 vols. Glasgow. 1829–59. * Miscellany . . . 4 vols. Pubns. vols. xxv, li, lvii, lxvii. 1840–7. * (Listed in *Repert. Font*. i. 400–1.)

211 SCOTTISH BURGH RECORD SOCIETY. Publications. 26 vols. Edin. 1868–1911.

212 SCOTTISH GAELIC TEXT SOCIETY. Scottish Gaelic Texts. Vols. i–iii. Edin. 1937–9. (Listed in *Repert. Font*. i. 661.)

213 SCOTTISH HISTORY SOCIETY. Publications. Edin. 1887+. (Listed in *Repert. Font*. i. 662.)

214 SCOTTISH RECORD SOCIETY. Publications. Edin. 1898+.

215 SCOTTISH TEXT SOCIETY. Publications. Edin. 1884+. * (Listed in *Repert. Font*. i. 662–3.)

216 SOCIETY OF ANTIQUARIES OF SCOTLAND. Archaeologia Scotica (also Transactions of the Society . . .). 5 vols. Edin. 1792–1890. Then merged in the Proceedings; index i–iii, in iii. Proceedings. Edin. 1851+. Index of vols. i–xxiv (1851–90), 1892; vols. xxv–xlviii (1890–1914), 1936.

217 SPALDING CLUB. Publications. 38 vols. Aberdeen. 1841–71. * New Spalding Club. Publications. 43 vols. 1887–1924. Third Spalding Club. Miscellany. 1935+. Publications. 1929+. (Listed in *Repert. Font.* i. 709–10.)

218 SPOTTISWOODE SOCIETY. Miscellany: a collection of original papers and tracts, illustrative chiefly of the civil and ecclesiastical history of Scotland. Ed. by James Maidment. 2 vols. Edin. 1944–5.

219 STAIR SOCIETY. Publications. Edin. 1936+.

> Are making accessible the materials for a history of the law in Scotland, such as
> Regiam majestatem;
> Register of brieves;
> Survey of sources;
> Introduction to legal history.

220 VIKING SOCIETY FOR NORTHERN RESEARCH. Old-lore series. Lond. 1907+. Caithness and Sutherland records. i, 1909–28. Orkney and Shetland miscellany. i, 1907–8. Continued as, Old-lore miscellany of Orkney, Shetland, Caithness and Sutherland. ii+, 1909+. Orkney and Shetland records. i+, 1907+.

> See *Saga Book* (No. 2466), the most important publication of the Viking Society.

4. Ireland

(a) Record publications of societies

For series on Irish literature, see pp. 347–8. Cf. Irish Repositories, pp. 131–4.

221 ANALECTA HIBERNICA. Published by the Irish MSS. Comm. Dublin. 1930+.

> This serial for publication of documents, reports of MSS., etc. is analysed in Irish MSS. Comm. *Catalogue of publications.*

222 ARCHIVIUM HIBERNICUM: Irish historical records. Catholic Record Soc. of Ireland. Maynooth. 1912–21. New Ser. 1941+.

223 CELTIC SOCIETY. Publications. 6 vols. Dublin. 1847–55. (Merged in the Irish Archaeological Society in 1853.) (Listed in *Repert. Font.* i. 125–6.)

224 INSTITUTE OF ADVANCED STUDIES OF DUBLIN. Scriptores latini Hiberniae. Dublin. 1955+. (Listed in *Repert. Font.* i. 233.)

225 IRISH ARCHAEOLOGICAL SOCIETY. Publications. 15 vols. Dublin. 1841–52. Continued as Publications of the Irish Archaeological and Celtic Society. 6 vols. Dublin. 1855–69. (Listed in *Repert. Font.* i. 340–1.)

226 IRISH MANUSCRIPT COMMISSION. Publications. 1931+. (Listed in *Repert. Font.* i. 145–6.)

227 IRISH RECORD COMMISSIONERS. Publications. 1826–1901. (Listed in *Repert. Font.* i. 341.)

228 IRISH RECORD OFFICE. Publications. 1905+. (Listed in *Repert. Font.* i. 341.)

229 ROYAL IRISH ACADEMY (Dublin). Publications. 1870+. (Listed in *Repert. Font.* i. 631.)

(b) Serials devoted primarily to Ireland

230 CELTICA. Dublin Institute for Advanced Studies. Dublin. 1946+.

231 ÉIGSE. A journal of Irish studies. National University of Ireland. Dublin. 1939+.

232 ÉRIU. The journal of the school of Irish learning. Dublin. 1904+. Index of vols. i–x (1904–28), in x.

233 IRISH ECCLESIASTICAL RECORD. Dublin. 1864–76; 1880–1968. Index, 1864–1922, and P. J. C. Hamell, 'Index to the Irish Ecclesiastical Record 1864–1917: Documents', *Irish Eccles. Rec.* xcii (1959), 1–44; idem, '1918–63', ibid. cii (1964), 297–344.

234 IRISH HISTORICAL STUDIES. Dublin. 1938+. (See No. 128 above).

235 IRISH THEOLOGICAL QUARTERLY. Maynooth. i–xvii (1906–22). New Ser. 1951+.

235A REPERTORIUM NOVUM. Dublin Diocesan Historical Record. Dublin. 1955+.

236 ROYAL IRISH ACADEMY. Transactions. 33 vols. Dublin. 1787–1907. Proceedings. Section C: Archaeology, Linguistic, and Literature. Dublin. 1837+. List of papers published in the Transactions etc. 1786–1886. Dublin. 1887. Index to the serial publications, 1786–1906. Dublin etc. 1912. Index . . . 1907–32. Dublin. 1934.

See No. 229.

237 ROYAL SOCIETY OF ANTIQUARIES OF IRELAND. Journal. 1892+. Dublin. 1892+.

The successor to *Trans. Kilkenny Archaeol. Soc.* Dublin, 1850–4; then *Procs. and Trans. of the Kilkenny and Southeast Ireland Archaeol. Soc.* 1854–5; then *Journal* (of same), 1856–67, Dublin, 1858–71; then *Journal of Historical and Archaeol. Assoc. of Ireland*, 1868–90, Dublin, 1873–90; then *Procs. and Papers of Royal Soc. of Antiquaries of Ireland*, 1890–1, Dublin, 1892; then *Journal* as above. Index of vols. i–xix (1849–89), Dublin, 1902; vols. xxi–xl (1891–1910), Dublin, 1915; vols. xli–lx (1911–30), Dublin, 1933.

238 STUDIA HIBERNICA. St. Patrick's Training College. Dublin. 1961+.

239 STUDIES. An Irish quarterly review of letters, philosophy, and science. Dublin. 1912+. General index of vols. i–l (1912–61) compiled by Father Aloysius O'Rahilly.

III. AUXILIARIES TO HISTORICAL STUDY

Those correlative disciplines which are particularly useful to the historian are normally described as 'auxiliaries to historical study'. In some areas, however, they form the very bases of historical information and, in others, they complement the written sources. Accordingly, they cannot be neglected. Their relationship to history is explained in many works on historical method, e.g. Bernheim (No. 251) and Samaran (No. 265).

Each of these ancillary fields of inquiry has its own specialized bibliographical tools, which are recorded in the appropriate sections below. In this volume palaeography and diplomatic are assigned to Chapter III, sect. D (pp. 47–56). For auxiliaries as a whole, older references can be found in such works as Bernheim (No. 251), Dahlmann–Waitz (No. 48), and Monod (No. 58). For studies published between 1901 and 1933, see *Writings . . . 1901–33* (No. 38), vol. i; and for 1934–45, see Milne, *Writings* (No. 39). For recent studies, turn to Lancaster and Kellaway (No. 24). Current bibliographies are given in *Internat. Bibliog. Hist. Sci.* (No. 53) and in *R.H.E.* (No. 166). For palaeography and numismatics, *L'Année philologique* (No. 266) is helpful, as are the topical bibliographies on pages 47 and 78–9.

A. PHILOSOPHY AND METHODOLOGY OF HISTORY

From the extensive and rapidly growing literature on the philosophy of history, a few tractates by philosophers, which are generally commended, will illustrate the issues and provide guidance to further reading. Retrospective bibliography can be found in Ronald Thompson, 'Selective reading lists on historiography and philosophy of history', *Social Science Research Council* (New York) *Bulletin*, liv (1946), 141–63; and John C. Rule's *Bibliography* and its supplements (No. 246). For current literature, comprehensive lists are given in the bibliographies of philosophy, such as *Bibliographie de la philosophie* (Paris, 1937+) and *Répertoire bibliographique de la philosophie* (Louvain, 1949+). The journal *History and Theory* (No. 245) is one of the most important periodicals devoted to the studies in the history of philosophy and includes lengthy review articles. The philosophy of history, however, has rarely been a formal concern of practising historians of medieval English history; for them, methodology and historiography have had a stronger pragmatic appeal.

For methodology and historiography, a few general expositions, written by historians and applicable to medieval English history, must serve for the numerous manuals of instruction. The treatises by Bernheim and by Langlois and Seignobos, which exemplify research in archives, formed and still form basic handbooks for students approaching research among documents. The often expressed criticism that this methodology based on archives circumscribed history too closely and left too little room for interpretations, comparisons, and analyses, led to the several schools of historiography which are described in the works cited below. The broad approach, advocated by Marc Bloch and Lucien Febvre in the *Annales* (No. 249) and exemplified in their writings, has had its influence in recent years on some English medieval historians, particularly in the areas of economic and agrarian history. For this school, history is the science of human societies and not a chain of events or persons; accordingly, historians, having formulated the most pertinent questions, must utilize all the techniques of the several ancillary disciplines in seeking answers. On other fronts, too, the historiography of medieval England has been vastly expanded in the twentieth century; but the methodology is predominantly research based on archives.

The student contemplating research among medieval records in England might well turn to Galbraith's studies (Nos. 258, 949) and to Elton's survey of sources (No. 256), where the quantities, complexities, limitations, and some of the pitfalls are described. Other helpful manuals are listed below; considerable sections on methodology and historiography are included in the American Historical Association's *Guide* (No. 40), in the annual volumes of the *International Bibliography of Historical Sciences* (No. 53), and in the quarterly issues of *Historical Abstracts*, 1775–1945, edited by Eric H. Boehm (N.Y. 1955+).

240   CARR (EDWARD H.). What is history? G. M. Trevelyan Lectures, 1961. Lond. and N.Y. 1962.

These contentious lectures wherein history is regarded as 'a continuous process of interaction between the historian and his facts' criticize the 'fetish of facts' and documents, since it is the historian's interpretation of a fact which makes it a historical fact. Carr's propositions have excited strongly divergent assessments; compare Boyd Shafer's review in *A.H.R.* lxvii (1962), 676–7, with Trevor-Roper in *Encounter*, xviii (1962), 69–77; J. M. Price in *History and Theory*, iii (1963), 136–45; and Elton, *Practice* (No. 257).

241   COLLINGWOOD (ROBIN G.). The idea of history. Ed. by T. M. Knox. Oxf. 1946. Reprinted several times.

This esteemed work, published posthumously from materials left by the philosopher-historian, holds that not documents or books but the mind of the historian creates history. For the many commentaries and further references on Collingwood's work, see Alan Donagan, *The later philosophy of R. G. Collingwood* (Lond. 1957); Louis O. Mink in *History and Theory*, vii (1968), 3–37; and Leon J. Goldstein, ibid. ix (1970), 1–36.

242   DANTO (ARTHUR C.). Analytical philosophy of history. Lond. 1965.

243   DRAY (WILLIAM H.). Philosophy of history. Englewood Cliffs (N.J.). 1964.

Dray also edited articles by thirteen modern writers in *Philosophical analysis and history* (N.Y. and Lond. 1966).

244   GARDINER (PATRICK). The nature of historical explanation. Lond. 1952.

Gardiner also made a collection from writings of various authors in *Theories of history from classical and contemporary sources* (Glencoe, Ill. 1959) and added a bibliography thereto. Among other anthologies are Hans Meyerhoff, *The philosophy of history in our time*, with a bibliography (N.Y. 1959); and Fritz Stern, *The varieties of history from Voltaire to the present* (N.Y. and Cleveland, 1956; and several reprints).

245   HISTORY AND THEORY: Studies in the philosophy of history. The Hague and Wesleyan University Press. 1960+.

246 RULE (JOHN C.). Bibliography of works in the philosophy of history, 1945–1957, in *History and Theory*, Beiheft i (1961). Supplements, 1958–1961 by M. Nowicki, ibid. Beiheft iii (1964), and 1962–5 by L. D. Wurgaft, ibid. Beiheft vii (1967).

247 WALSH (WILLIAM H.). An introduction to philosophy of history. Hutchinson University Library. Lond. 1951. 3rd edn. 1967.

An important, systematic exposition for philosophers by a philosopher, from which historians can take much profit. The third edition includes two appendices, one on 'The limits of scientific history', and the other on 'Historical causation'.

248 WHITE (MORTON). Foundations of historical knowledge. N.Y. and Lond. 1965.

See review by Rudolph H. Weingartner in *History and Theory*, vii (1968), 240–56.

249 ANNALES: ÉCONOMIES, SOCIÉTÉS, CIVILISATIONS. Paris. 1946+. Supersedes Annales d'histoire économique et sociale. Paris. 1929–39.

250 APPROACHES TO HISTORY: A SYMPOSIUM. Ed. by Herbert P. R. Finberg. Lond. 1962.

A series of brief papers by various authors on different areas of historical study: political, economic, social, archaeological, etc.

251 BERNHEIM (ERNST). Lehrbuch der historischen Methode. Mit Nachweis der wichtigsten Quellen und Hülfsmittel zum Studium der Geschichte. Leipzig. 1889. 5th edn.: Lehrbuch der historischen Methode und der Geschichtsphilosophie. Leipzig. 5th and 6th edns. 1908 and 1914. *

A nineteenth-century classic, still important for the study of documentary sources. See also Wilhelm Bauer, *Einführung in das Studium der Geschichte* (Tübingen, 1921; 2nd edn. 1928).

252 BLOCH (MARC L. B.). Apologie pour l'histoire; ou Métier d'historien. Paris. 1949. Trans. by Peter Putnam as The historian's craft. N.Y. 1953. Manchester. 1954.

Bloch advocated a broad programme involving team-work linking all disciplines in the service of history and the comparisons and contrasts of societies. See his 'A contribution towards a comparative history of European societies', in *Land and work in medieval Europe: selected papers by Marc Bloch*, translated by J. E. Anderson (Berkeley and Los Angeles, 1967), pp. 44–81. This contribution originally appeared in *Revue de Synthèse Historique*, xlvi (1928), 15–50. For other works by Marc Bloch see below, No. 4951. Many appreciations of Bloch's stimulating, seminal works have been written. See, for example, Charles E. Perrin, 'L'œuvre historique de Marc Bloch', *Revue Historique*, cxcix (1948), 161–88; J. Ambrose Raftis, 'Marc Bloch's comparative method and the rural history of mediaeval England', *Mediaeval Studies*, xxiv (1962), 349–65; R. R. Davies in *History*, lii (1967), 265–82; and W. H. Sewell, Jr. in *History and Theory*, vi (1967), 208–18.

253 BUTTERFIELD (HERBERT). The Englishman and his history. Cambr. 1944. * Idem, Christianity and history. Lond. 1949. Idem, Man on his past: the study of the history of historical scholarship. Cambr. 1955. Idem, Present state of historical scholarship. Lond. 1965.

254 CHANGING VIEWS ON BRITISH HISTORY. Essays on historical
writing since 1939. Ed. by Elizabeth C. Furber. Cambr. (Mass.). 1966. See
No. 18.

255 CRUMP (CHARLES G.). History and historical research. Lond. 1928.

256 ELTON (GEOFFREY R.). England, 1200–1640. The sources of history:
studies in the uses of historical evidence. Ithaca (N.Y.) and Lond. 1969.

257 ELTON (GEOFFREY R.). The practice of history. Lond., Sydney and
N.Y. 1967.

This strong statement that 'the study and writing of history are justified in themselves'
provides a large measure of practical advice on the purpose, research, writing, and teaching of history, heavily salted with pungent criticism of some modern practitioners of
historical studies. For the graduate student, Sherman Kent's *Writing history* (2nd edn.
N.Y. 1967) is full of good sense.

258 GALBRAITH (VIVIAN H.). An introduction to the study of history.
Lond. 1964.

Three sections: (*a*) The historian at work; (*b*) Historical research and the preservation
of the past; (*c*) Who wrote Asser's *Life of Alfred*?

259 HALPHEN (LOUIS). Initiation aux études d'histoire du moyen âge.
Paris. 1940. 3rd edn. revised and enlarged by Yves Renouard. 1952.*

260 HELPS FOR STUDENTS OF HISTORY. Ed. by Charles Johnson and
James P. Whitney. 51 vols. S.P.C.K. Lond. and N.Y. 1918–24*; vols. 52+.
Historical Association, London. 1951+.

A series of small, useful handbooks.

261 HISTORICAL STUDY IN THE WEST; France, Great Britain,
Western Germany, The United States. With an introduction by Boyd C. Shafer.
N.Y. 1968.

This work describes the organization of historical studies in each of the named countries.
The chapter on Great Britain (pp. 129–71) is by A. Taylor Milne.

262 KNOWLES (DAVID). Great historical enterprises and problems in early
monastic history. Edin. 1963.

The Great Historical Enterprises were presidential addresses to the Royal Historical
Society and were printed in *T.R.H.S.* from 1957 to 1960. They were entitled 'The
Bollandists', 'The Maurists', 'The Monumenta Germaniae Historica', and 'The Rolls
Series'. The Problems were the Birkbeck Lectures for 1962.

263 LANGLOIS (CHARLES V.) and SEIGNOBOS (CHARLES). Introduc-
tion aux études historiques. Paris. 1898. 4th edn. 1909. Trans. by G. G. Berry as
Introduction to the study of history. Lond. 1898. New edn. 1912. Reprinted
N.Y. 1932 and 1966. *

An influential summary of nineteenth-century methodology, emphasizing the study of
documentary sources. For criticism, see *History and Theory*, vi (1967), 236–41. Now
consult Samaran (No. 265).

263A McKISACK (MAY). Medieval history in the Tudor age. Oxf. 1971.

Chapters on Leland and Bale, Matthew Parker and his circle, archivists and record-searchers, local historians, etc. See also F. J. Levy, *Tudor historical thought* (San Marino, Calif. 1967), and Kendrick, *British Antiquity* (No. 1476).

264 MARROU (HENRI-IRÉNÉE). 'La méthodologie historique', *Revue historique*, ccix (1953), 256–70; ccxvii (1957), 270–89.

265 SAMARAN (CHARLES), ed. L'Histoire et ses méthodes. Recherche, conservation et critique des témoignages. Paris. 1961.

These surveys of methodology and auxiliaries by various scholars serve to replace or modernize the manual by Langlois and Seignobos. Although the subject coverage is very broad, it is heavily French in orientation. A brief bibliography follows each chapter.

B. PHILOLOGY

This section seeks to list the guides to philology most useful to the historian of medieval England. It concentrates, therefore, on the most important dictionaries, general philological treatises, and bibliographical tools, including journals. The indispensable *Cambridge Bibliography of English Literature* (No. 14) includes British writers in Latin and other subjects kindred to English literature. The brief glossaries appended to editions of texts and to specialized studies sometimes supply translations of unusual words. Annual bibliographies on philological and literary topics, including medieval Latin as well as modern languages, can be conveniently found in the following publications.

266 L'ANNÉE PHILOLOGIQUE: bibliographie critique et analytique de l'antiquité gréco-latine. Paris. 1928+. See No. 2014.

267 MEDIUM AEVUM. Society for the Study of Medieval Languages and Literature. Oxf. 1932+. *(1932–65).

268 PUBLICATIONS OF THE MODERN LANGUAGE ASSOCIATION OF AMERICA. Baltimore. 1884/5+. * Index, vols. i–l (1884–1935). Menasha (Wis.). 1936. vols. li–lv (1936–40), in lv. 1534–46.

From 1919 to 1956 the annual bibliography was limited to American writers of books and articles; subsequently the intention has been to 'strive for international coverage'.

269 THE YEAR'S WORK IN MODERN LANGUAGE STUDIES Modern Humanities Research Association. Lond. 1929/30+. *(1930–58).

1. *English*

For restrospective bibliography, consult *Cambr. Bibliog. Eng. Lit.* (No. 14), and Kennedy (No. 273). For current bibliography, turn to Nos. 272 and 276, and *PMLA* (No. 268). Good summary treatises, with bibliographical notes, are Albert C. Baugh, *A history of the English language* (Lond. and N.Y. 1935) and Otto Jespersen, *Growth and structure of the English language* (Leipzig and N.Y. 1905; 9th edn. Oxf. 1948). Mary S. Serjeantson lists, among others, Celtic, Scandinavian, and French loan-words, in *A history of foreign words in English* (Lond. 1935).

270 ANGLIA. Zeitschrift für englische Philologie . . . Halle etc. 1877+
*†(1879–1913). Index ('Register') of vols. i–l (1878–1926), 1930.

The monthly *Beiblatt: Mitteilungen aus dem gesamten Gebiete der englischen Sprache und Literatur*, begun in April 1890, contains notices and reviews of books and lists of articles in periodicals. The normally annual supplementary volume entitled *Übersicht* . . . *der englischen Philologie*, starting with volume iv for 1877–9, is a mine of bibliographical notices.

271 ANGLISTISCHE FORSCHUNGEN. Heidelberg. 1900+. *(1900–67).

272 ANNUAL BIBLIOGRAPHY OF ENGLISH LANGUAGE AND LITERATURE. Edited for the Modern Humanities Research Association. Cambr. 1920+. *(1920–58).

The volume xlii for 1967 appeared in 1969. It lists articles and books, with references to reviews of the latter; and the publications of the Early Eng. Text Soc., English Place-name Soc., Early English MSS. in Facsimile. It treats all periods from Old English to the twentieth century and is useful to the historian on many subjects.

273 KENNEDY (ARTHUR G.). A bibliography of writings on the English language from the beginning of printing to the end of 1922. Cambr. and New Haven (Conn.). 1927.

Comprehensive and basic. See also his *A concise bibliography for students of English*, Palo Alto (Calif.), 1940; revised edn. 1954; 4th edn. by Donald B. Sands, 1960.

274 THE REVIEW OF ENGLISH STUDIES. A quarterly journal of English literature and English language. Lond. 1925+. *(1925–63).

275 WELLS (JOHN E.). A manual of writings in Middle English, 1050–1400. New Haven (Conn.) and Lond. 1916. Supplements. 1919+.

Index in original volume, and cumulative index for Supplements 1–8 in 8th Supplement; 9th Supplement published in 1952. The first volume covering 'Romances' and edited by J. Burke Severs, begins a new edition sponsored by Modern Language Assoc. (New Haven (Conn.), 1967); the second volume appeared in 1970.

276 THE YEAR'S WORK IN ENGLISH STUDIES. Edited for the English Association (London). Lond. 1919/21+. *(1921–53).

Brief critical analyses of the principal publications, including a few outstanding works on historical background.

277 BOSWORTH (JOSEPH). An Anglo-Saxon dictionary, based on the manuscript collections of Joseph Bosworth. Ed. by Thomas N. Toller. Oxf. 1882–[98]. Supplements, issued in 3 parts, 1908–21.

The best Anglo-Saxon dictionary; it replaces Bosworth's *Dictionary of the Anglo-Saxon Language* (London, 1838), which is untrustworthy.

278 EKWALL (EILERT). Contributions to the history of Old English dialects. Lunds Universitets Årsskrift, N.F. Bd. 12, No. 6. Lund. 1917.

Cf. Ekwall's bibliography (No. 632).

279 HALL (JOHN R. C.). A concise Anglo-Saxon dictionary for the use of students. Lond. etc. 1894. 3rd edn. rev. and enl. Cambr. and N.Y. 1931. 4th edn. with Supplement by Herbert D. Meritt. Cambr. 1960.

Records some words not in Bosworth–Toller (No. 277).

280 HALLIWELL-PHILLIPS (JAMES O.). A dictionary of archaic and provincial words, obsolete words, proverbs and ancient customs from the fourteenth century. 2 vols. Lond. 1847. 6th edn. in one vol. Lond. 1904. 7th edn. N.Y. 1924.

281 MIDDLE ENGLISH DICTIONARY. Ed. by Hans Kurath, Sherman M. Kuhn, and John Reidy. Ann Arbor, etc. [1952+].

A research project of the University of Michigan, this dictionary had reached the word 'langāğe' in 1971. It is based on a large collection of Middle English quotations.

282 MURRAY (JAMES A. H.) and others, eds. A new English dictionary on historical principles; founded mainly on the materials collected by the Philological Society. 10 vols. in 13. Oxf. 1888–1928. Introduction, Supplement, and Bibliography, by William A. Craigie and Charles T. Onions, Oxf. 1933.

Corrections and additions: *B.I.H.R.* i. 97–8; ii. 28–30; iii. 68–9, 196–7; iv. 186–7; v. 60–1, 188–9; vi. 53–9; vii. 127; x. 204–5.

283 LAURENCE NOWELL'S VOCABULARIUM SAXONICUM. By Albert H. Marckwardt. Ann Arbor. 1952.

Cf. Robin Flower, 'Laurence Nowell and the discovery of England in Tudor times', *P.B.A.* xxi (1935), 47–73.

284 OXFORD DICTIONARY OF ENGLISH ETYMOLOGY. Ed. by C. T. Onions. Oxf. 1966.

285 QUIRK (RANDOLPH) and WRENN (CHARLES L.). An Old English grammar. 2nd edn. Lond. 1958.

286 SKEAT (WALTER W.). An etymological dictionary of the English language arranged on an historical basis. Oxf. 1882. 4th edn. 1910. New impression. 1935.

The classic on the subject. Also provides a useful catalogue of glossaries. See also *An English–Anglo-Saxon vocabulary*, Lond. [1935], centenary (of Skeat's birth) edition limited to 150 copies; originally printed in 1879 for private distribution. There are good bibliographical notes in Henry Sweet's *Anglo-Saxon Reader in Prose and Verse*, revised throughout by Dorothy Whitelock (Oxf. 1967).

287 STRATMANN (FRANZ H.). A dictionary of the Old English language,... Krefeld. [1864–7]. 3rd edn. 1878. New edition, by Henry Bradley: A Middle-English dictionary. Oxf. 1891. Reprinted. 1914.

Bradley's edition is especially valuable.

288 WRIGHT (JOSEPH). The English dialect dictionary. 6 vols. Lond. 1898 [1896]–1905. *

Contains English dialect words which are known to have been in use at any time during the last two hundred years in England, Ireland, Scotland, and Wales. The eighty volumes published by the English Dialect Society between 1873 and 1896 are incorporated in this dictionary. At the end of vol. vi, Wright reprints his *English dialect grammar* (Oxf. 1905*).

2. *French: Anglo-Norman*

The neglect of the study of Anglo-Norman language, of which Skeat complained in his *Principles of English etymology*, 2nd Ser. p. 26 (Lond. 1891), is being rapidly repaired in the twentieth century. Summaries of the status of these studies are presented in Ruth J. Dean, 'Anglo-Norman Studies', *Romanic Rev.* xxx (1939), 3–14; idem, 'A fair field needing folk: Anglo-Norman', *P.M.L.A.* lxix (1954), 965–78; idem, 'What is Anglo-Norman', *Annuale Mediaevale* (Duquesne Univ.), vi (1965), 29–46; A. Ewert, 'Anglo-Norman studies', *Medium Aevum*, vii (1938), 164–6; M. Dominica Legge, 'Anglo-Norman and the historian', *History*, N.S. xxvi (1941–2), 163–75; idem, 'Anglo-Norman studies today', *Revue de linguistique romane*, xvii (1950), 213–22; and M. K. Pope, 'Research in Anglo-Norman', *Mod. Hum. Res. Assoc. Annual Bull.* xix (1948), 11–20. A dictionary of Anglo-Norman is being prepared under the auspices of the Anglo-Norman Text Society; and a glossary of Anglo-Norman terms of law is being compiled, originally under the editorship of the late T. F. T. Plucknett and the late Elsie Shanks, for the Selden Society. For law French, to Maitland's fundamental paper, 'Of the Anglo-French language in the early Year Books', in *Year Book 1–2 Edward II* (Selden Soc. vol. xvii, 1903) introd. pp. xxxiii–lxxxi, and reprinted in *Cambr. Hist. of Eng. Lit.* (No. 1400), vol. i, chap. xx, may be added Theobald Mathew 'Law French' in *Law Quarterly Review*, lix (1938), 358–69; G. E. Woodbine, 'The language of English law', *Speculum*, xviii (1943), 395–436; Samuel J. Stoljar, 'A common lawyer's French', *Law Library Journal*, xlvii (1954), 119–33 and 209–24; R. J. Schoeck, 'Law French: its problems and the status of the scholarship', *Kentucky Foreign Lang. Quart.* vi (1959), 132–9; and the introductions to Year Books series of the Selden Society, vols. lii, liv, and lxx, and especially lxxi (below, No. 291). K. V. Sinclair supplies a comprehensive bibliographical essay, which is devoted to more than the last 20 years, as 'Anglo-Norman Studies: the past twenty years' in *Australian Journal of French Studies*, ii (1965), 113–55, 225–78.

289 ANGLO-NORMAN TEXT SOCIETY. Anglo-Norman texts. Oxf. 1939+. Partially reprinted. *

   The publications are listed in *Repert. Font.* (No. 64), i. 36. These and later volumes relevant to this bibliography are entered below.

290 BLOCH (OSCAR) and WARTBURG (WALTHER von). Dictionnaire étymologique de la langue française. 2 vols. Paris. 1932; 2nd edn. 1950.

291 COLLAS (JOHN P.). 'Problems of language and interpretation' in Year Books of Edward II. 12 Edward II. Year Book series, xxv. Selden Society, lxxi. (1964), pp. xiv–cxxviii.

292 GODEFROY (FRÉDÉRIC). Dictionnaire de l'ancienne langue française et de tous ses dialectes, du IXe au XVe siècle . . . (with supplement). 10 vols. Paris. 1881–1902. *

   This is a well-known work. For a briefer, handy dictionary, see Greimas (A. Julien), *Dictionnaire de l'ancien français jusqu'au milieu du XIVe siècle* (Paris, 1968).

293 LEGGE (MARY DOMINICA). Anglo-Norman in the cloisters: the influence of the orders upon Anglo-Norman literature. Edin. 1950. Cf. No. 1437.

294 LEGGE (MARY DOMINICA). Anglo-Norman literature and its background. Oxf. 1963.

The latter work deals with three centuries of Anglo-Norman literature in its various forms, much more comprehensively than any other book on Anglo-Norman literature. Its footnotes form an extensive bibliography.

295 POPE (MILDRED K.). From Latin to modern French with especial consideration of Anglo-Norman phonology and morphology. Manchester. 1934. 2nd edn. 1952.

This volume includes good bibliographical references. It is fuller and more up to date than the still useful *The Anglo-Norman dialect* by Louis E. Menger (N.Y. and Lond. 1904).

296 SUGGETT (HELEN). 'The use of French in the later middle ages', *T.R.H.S.* 4th Ser. xxviii (1946), 61–83. Reprinted in *R.H.S. Essays*, edited by R. W. Southern (No. 1493).

See also R. M. Wilson, 'English and French in England, 1100–1300', *History*, N.S. xxviii (1943), 37–60; and M. D. Legge in *Studies . . . to Rose Graham* (No. 1437).

297 TOBLER (ADOLF). Altfranzösisches Wörterbuch. Ed. by Erhard Lommatzsch. Berlin and Wiesbaden. 1925+. New edn. Wiesbaden, 1955+.

In progress: vol. vii: P–Pythonique (1969).

298 VISING (JOHAN). Anglo-Norman language and literature. Lond. 1923.

This compendious catalogue of all then known Anglo-Norman writings and the manuscripts in which they are found appears as a deceptively small manual, but it is a basic guide, relying chiefly on printed sources. An expanded revision of this manual, based on an examination of the manuscripts, is in preparation by Ruth J. Dean; the section on legal texts is being prepared by R. J. Schoeck.

299 VORETZSCH (KARL). Einführung in das Studium der altfranzösischen Literatur in Anschluss an die Einführung in das Studium der altfranzösischen Sprache. Halle. 1905. 3rd edn. 1925. Introduction to the study of Old French literature by Karl Voretzsch . . . Authorized translation of the third and last German edition by Francis M. Du Mont. N.Y. 1931.

300 WALBERG (EMMANUEL). Quelques aspects de la littérature anglo-normande. Paris. 1936.

3. *Latin*

The project for a revision of Du Cange's *Glossarium* (No. 305), initiated in 1920 by Union Académique Internationale, resulted in the establishment of national committees charged with the examination of the medieval texts of their respective countries. *Bulletin Du Cange* (No. 303) has published from time to time wordlists submitted by various national committees. The first fascicle of the proposed dictionary, *Novum Glossarium* (No. 311), appeared in 1957. For Britain, the

British Academy appointed two committees, one to co-operate in the above-mentioned project and another to continue the dictionary of non-classical Latin words to later periods. Subsequently the two British committees merged and in 1934 issued a preliminary volume, entitled *Medieval Latin Word-List* (Nos. 301; 308). Current bibliography in No. 269.

301 BAXTER (JAMES H.) and JOHNSON (CHARLES). Medieval Latin word-list from British and Irish sources . . . Oxf. 1934. Revised and expanded by R. E. Latham. Oxf. 1965. (No. 308).

Gives Latin word of non-classical origin or connotation (600–1600), date of its earliest recorded usage, and equivalent English word or phrase.

302 BROWNE (RICHARD A.), ed. British Latin selections, A.D. 500–1400. With introduction, notes, mainly linguistic and literary, and vocabulary of medieval words and meanings. Oxf. 1955.

Good introductory treatise.

303 BULLETIN DU CANGE. Union Académique Internationale. Archivum Latinitatis medii aevi . . . Paris. 1924+. Tables générales . . . vols. i–xxv (1955) include a Table des mots, with references to volume and page.

Has published word-lists prepared by some of the national committees.

304 CATHOLICON ANGLICUM, an English–Latin wordbook, dated 1483. Ed. by S. J. H. Herrtage. E.E.T.S. vol. lxxv. Lond. 1881. The same edition. Camden Soc. N.S. xxx (1882). *

305 DU CANGE (CHARLES DU FRESNE). Glossarium mediae et infimae Latinitatis . . . Ed. by G. A. L. Henschel. 7 vols. Paris. 1840–50. Other edns. 3 vols. Paris. 1678. By Benedictines and Pierre Carpentier. 10 vols. Paris. 1733–66. By Léopold Favre. 10 vols. Niort. 1883–7. Reprinted Paris. 1937–8. *(1954). Petit supplément au Dictionnaire de Du Cange, by Charles Schmidt. Strasbourg. 1906.

Vols. i–viii, A–Z; vol. ix, Glossaire français; vol. x, Indexes. The best and most complete glossary of Low Latin; a rich mine of information concerning the Middle Ages, especially in France. Some of the additions made by Favre are of doubtful value. W. H. Maigne d'Arnis's *Lexicon manuale ad scriptores mediae et infimae Latinitatis* (Paris, 1858, reprinted 1866) is a useful compendium of Du Cange's work, with some additions. See No. 311 for the new dictionary of medieval Latin.

306 ERNOUT (ALFRED) and MEILLET (ANTOINE). Dictionnaire étymologique de la langue latine: histoire des mots. Paris. 1932. 3rd edn. 2 vols. 1951.

307 GLOSSARIA LATINA iussu Academiae Britannicae edita . . . Ed. by Wallace M. Lindsay *et al.* (Part of *Nouvelle Collection de textes et documents.*) 5 vols. Paris. 1926–31.

Cf. Georg Goetz, *Corpus glossariorum Latinorum* (7 vols. Leipzig etc. 1888–1923); vol. vii, fasc. ii contains an Index anglosaxonicus by Gustav Loewe.

308 LATHAM (RONALD E.), ed. Revised medieval Latin word-list from British and Irish sources. British Acad. Lond. 1965. See No. 301.

309 MITTELLATEINISCHES WÖRTERBUCH BIS ZUM AUS-
GEHENDEN 13. JAHRHUNDERT. Issued by Bayerische Akad. der Wissenschaften and Deutsche Akad. der Wissensch. zu Berlin. Munich and Berlin. 1959
(in progress).

310 NIERMEYER (JAN F.). Mediae Latinitatis lexicon minus. A medieval
Latin–French/English dictionary. Leiden. 1954+.

> To be completed in 6–8 fascicles. A scholarly dictionary, less comprehensive than Du
> Cange but more extensive than the word-lists. History and usage of words shown by
> quotations, mostly from sources A.D. 550–1150.

311 NOVUM GLOSSARIUM MEDIAE LATINITATIS ab anno DCCC
usque ad annum MCC edendum curavit Consilium Academiarum Consocia-
tarum. General editors: Franz Blatt *et al.* Copenhagen. 1957+. Index scriptorum
mediae Latinitatis ab anno DCCC usque ad annum MCC, qui afferuntur in Novo
glossario ab Academiis Consociatis iuris publici facto. Copenhagen. 1957.

> When completed, this dictionary of medieval Latin undertaken by the Union Inter-
> nationale des Académies will be an indispensable work of reference. The first fascicle,
> of 232 columns in 116 pages for the letter 'L', appeared in 1957. The completed dictionary
> is expected to comprise about 4,640 pages. The definitions are translated into French.

312 PROMPTORIUM PARVULORUM SIVE CLERICORUM, LEXICON
ANGLO-LATINUM PRINCEPS, auctore fratre Galfrido Grammatico dicto,
A.D. circa 1440. Ed. by Albert Way. Camden Soc. xxv, liv, lxxxix. 3 vols.
Lond. 1843–65. Another edition, by A. L. Mayhew. E.E.T.S. Extra Ser. cii.
Lond. 1908.

> See also Peter Haworth, 'The first Latin–English dictionary: a Bristol University manu-
> script', *Bristol and Glos. Archaeol. Soc. Trans.* xlv (1923–4), 253–75.

313 SOUTER (ALEXANDER). A glossary of later Latin to 600 A.D. Oxf. 1949.

> See J. H. Baxter, 'Notes on Souter's Glossary . . .', *Bull. Du Cange*, xxiii (1953), 7–12;
> xxv (1955), 101–41.

314 STRECKER (KARL). Einführung in das Mittellatein. Berlin. 1928.
English translation and revision, by Robert B. Palmer. Introduction to medieval
Latin. [Berlin. 1957.]

> Authoritative German manual, greatly enlarged in English translation.

315 WRIGHT, THOMAS. A volume of vocabularies. 2 vols. Lond. 1857–73.
2nd edn. by R. P. Wülker. Anglo-Saxon and Old English vocabularies (Latin–
English). 2 vols. Lond. 1884. *

> Vol. i, Vocabularies, Vol. ii, Indexes.

4. *Celtic Languages*

Retrospective bibliography can be found in Bonser, *A.-S.C.B.* (No. 12) and in
Donahue's essay (No. 317). Current bibliography can be traced in *Bibliotheca
Celtica* (No. 110) and the *Subject index to Welsh periodicals* (No. 103).

316 CELTIC REVIEW. Vols. i–x. Edin. etc. 1904–16.

317 DONAHUE (CHARLES). 'Medieval Celtic Literature', on pp. 382–409 of *The medieval literature of western Europe: a review of research, mainly 1930–1960*. Ed. by John H. Fisher. N.Y. and Lond. 1966.

> An annotated bibliographical study. See also Elwyn Davies, ed. *Celtic Studies in Wales: a survey* (for the Second International Congress of Celtic Studies, 1963) (Cardiff, 1963).

318 DOTTIN (GEORGES). Manuel pour servir à l'étude de l'antiquité celtique. Paris. 1906.

> Dottin's general treatise on Celtic philology, with bibliographical material, stands side by side with the older standard history of Victor Tourneur, *Esquisse d'une histoire des études celtiques* (Liège, 1905).

319 HOLDER (ALFRED). Alt-celtischer Sprachschatz. 2 vols. and 2 pts. Leipzig. 1896 (1891)–1908. Supplement (A–Cor). 1908–13. (No more published.)

> Issued in parts. A dictionary of the earliest Celtic, including continental languages and British. 'There is a good deal in Holder which Celticists now know to be mistaken' (Kenneth Jackson). Jackson's article in *Jour. Roman Stud.* xxxviii (1948), 54–8, 'On some Romano-British place-names', is a short list of addenda and corrigenda to Holder.

320 JACKSON (KENNETH). Language and history in early Britain: a chronological survey of the Brittonic languages, first to twelfth centuries. Cambr. and Edin. 1953.

> A work of high importance on the contributions of Brittonic linguistics to history. Also idem, 'Common Gaelic, the evolution of the Goedelic languages', *P.B.A.* xxxvii (1953), 71–97.

321 JOURNAL OF CELTIC STUDIES. Two vols. only. Philadelphia. 1949–58.

322 OGAM. Bulletin des amis de la tradition celtique. Rennes. 1949+.

323 PEDERSEN (HOLGER). Vergleichende Grammatik der keltischen Sprachen. 2 vols. Göttingen. 1909 (1908)–13. Henry Lewis and Holger Pedersen. A concise comparative Celtic grammar. Göttingen. 1937.

324 REVUE CELTIQUE. Vols. i–li. Paris. 1870–1934. Continued under the title, Études celtiques, 1936–9, 1948+. Indexes ('Tables') of vols. i–vi (1870–85), by G. Dottin. Thereafter, every five years, by P. Le Nestour, until xxxi–xlv (1910–28), by J. Vendryes, in xlv, no. 4, pp. 1–102.

325 WEISGERBER (LEO). Die Sprache der Festlandkelten. *Deutsches Arch. inst.* (Röm.-Germ. Komm.), xx. Bericht 1930. Frankfurt. 1931. pp. 147–226.

> Includes a glossary of old Celtic words, pp. 191–214, and a bibliography of 272 items.

326 ZEITSCHRIFT FÜR KELTISCHE PHILOLOGIE UND VOLKS-FORSCHUNG. Halle. 1897–1943. 1953+ Indexes ('Register') of vols. i–v (1896–1905), in v. 588–604; vi–x (1907–15), in x. 456–71; xi–xv (1917–25), in xvi. 469–76.

> Vols. i–xxi as *Zeitsch. f. keltische Philologie.*

327 ZEUSS (JOHANN KASPAR). Grammatica Celtica: e monumentis vetustis tam Hibernicae linguae quam Britannicae dialecti Cambricae Cornicae

Armoricae nec non e Gallicae priscae reliquiis. 2 vols. Leipzig. 1853. Another edn. in 1 vol. Revised by Herman Ebel. Berlin etc. 1871. Indexes, by Bruno Güterbock and Rudolf Thurneysen. Leipzig. 1881.

The foundation of the scientific study of Celtic grammar.

Cornish

328 JENNER (HENRY). A handbook of the Cornish language, chiefly in its latest stages, with some account of its history and literature. Lond. 1904.

329 NANCE (ROBERT MORTON). A new Cornish–English dictionary. St. Ives. 1938. Idem, An English–Cornish dictionary. Marazion. 1952.

330 WILLIAMS (ROBERT). Lexicon Cornu-Britannicum: a dictionary of the ancient Celtic language of Cornwall. Llandovery etc. 1865.

See Joseph Loth, *Remarques et corrections au Lexicon Cornu-Britannicum de Williams* (Paris, 1902).

Scottish Gaelic

331 CALDER (GEORGE). A Gaelic grammar, containing the parts of speech and the general principles of phonology and etymology, with a chapter on proper and place names. Glasgow. [1923].

Scholarly work for the advanced student.

332 CRAIGIE (WILLIAM A.) and AITKEN (A. J.). A dictionary of the older Scottish tongue, from the twelfth century to the end of the seventeenth. Chicago and Lond. 1931+ (in progress). Pts. 1–23 (1931–68).

333 DICTIONARIUM SCOTO-CELTICUM: a dictionary of the Gaelic language. [Ed. by Macintosh Mackay.] Highland Soc. of Scotland. 2 vols. Edin. 1828.

334 SCOTTISH GAELIC STUDIES. By University of Aberdeen, Celtic department. Lond. 1926+.

335 SCOTTISH GAELIC TEXTS. Edin. 1937+.

336 STEWART (ALEXANDER). Elements of Ga[e]lic grammar. Edin. 1801. 3rd edn. 1876.

Based upon Stewart's book is one of the same title by H. Cameron Gillies (Lond. 1896; 2nd edn. 1902).

Welsh

For a descriptive treatise on the Welsh language, see John Rhys, *Lectures on Welsh philology* (Lond. 1877; 2nd edn. 1879). For Welsh legal terms, see Timothy Lewis, *A glossary of Mediaeval Welsh law, based upon the Black Book of Chirk* (Manchester, 1913).

337 GEIRIADUR PRIFYSGOL CYMRU: a dictionary of the Welsh language. Vol. i (A–Ffysun) (1950–67), in progress. Cardiff. 1950+.

A scholarly historical Welsh–English dictionary on the same general pattern as the *Oxford English Dictionary*. See also Daniel Evans, *A dictionary of the Welsh language*, pts. i–v (A–Eiddig) (Carmarthen etc. 1887–1906); and for a vocabulary of the oldest Welsh, Joseph Loth, *Vocabulaire vieux-breton* (Paris, 1884).

338   JONES (JOHN M.). A Welsh grammar, historical and comparative. Oxf. 1913. Idem, An elementary Welsh grammar. Oxf. 1921.

339   PARRY (THOMAS). A history of Welsh literature. Translated from the Welsh by H. Idris Bell. Oxf. 1955.

340   PARRY-WILLIAMS (THOMAS). The English element in Welsh: a study of English loan-words in Welsh. Cymmrodorion Record Series, no. x. Lond. 1923.

     See the essays by Parry-Williams, J. R. R. Tolkien, and B. G. Charles in *Angles and Britons* (Cardiff, 1963).

341   PUGHE (WILLIAM O.). A dictionary of the Welsh language explained in English. 2nd edn. 2 vols. Denbigh. 1832. Earlier edns. 1793, 1803.

     Important in the history of Welsh lexicography, yet should be used with caution.

342   SPURRELL (WILLIAM). Spurrell's English–Welsh dictionary, by J. B. Anwyl. 11th edn. Carmarthen. 1937. Spurrell's Welsh–English dictionary, by J. B. Anwyl. 13th ed. Carmarthen. 1937.

343   STRACHAN (JOHN). An introduction to early Welsh. Manchester. 1909.

     A systematic grammar and reader, and a useful glossary.

Irish

See R. I. Best's *Bibliography* (No. 9)

344   HESSEN'S IRISH LEXICON: a concise dictionary of early Irish by Séamus Coamhánach, Rudolf Hertz, V. E. Hull and Gustav Lehmacher. Vol. i and pts. i, ii of vol. ii. Halle. 1933–8.

345   JONES (JOHN M.). A grammar of Old Irish. Dublin. 1946.

346   LANE (TIMOTHY O'N.). Larger English-Irish dictionary. Rev. edn. Dublin. 1916.

347   McINTOSH (ANGUS) and SAMUELS (M. L.). 'Prolegomena to a study of mediaeval Anglo-Irish'. *Medium Aevum*, xxxvii (1968), 1–11.

348   ROYAL IRISH ACADEMY (Dublin). Dictionary of the Irish language, based mainly on Old and Middle Irish materials. Dublin. 1913+.

     In progress: fascicles D–I, L–TU (1913–66). For A–D see Kuno Meyer, *Contributions to Irish lexicography* (2 vols. Halle and Lond. 1906–7). Pending the completion of the *Dictionary*, the R.I.A. is publishing in parts *Contributions to a dictionary of the Irish language* (1939+).

349   THURNEYSEN (RUDOLF). Handbuch des Alt-Irischen: Grammatik, Texte, und Wörterbuch. 2 vols. Heidelberg. 1909. English trans. rev. and enlarged, by D. A. Binchy and O. Bergin. Dublin. 1946.

     Vol. i, Grammatik. Vol. ii, Texte und Wörterbuch. An authoritative book on early Irish. An elementary survey is Myles Dillon and Donncha O'Cróinin, *Teach yourself Irish* (Lond. 1961).

350 VENDRYES (JOSEPH). Lexique étymologique d'irlandais ancien. Paris and Dublin. 1959–67.

351 WINDISCH (ERNST) and STOKES (WHITLEY). Irische Texte, mit Übersetzungen und Wörterbuch. Series i–iv, 7 pts. in 5 vols. (The 1st series, containing the Wörterbuch, is by Windisch alone.) Leipzig. 1880–1909.

5. Runic Inscriptions

The runic alphabet, presumably the only form of writing known to the Anglo-Saxons before the adoption of Christianity, survives in occasional examples until about A.D. 900. The principal British examples are on the Bewcastle (Cumberland) Cross, the Ruthwell (Dumfries) Cross, and the Franks Casket in the British Museum. For reference to these, consult the index to Bonser, *A.-S.C.B.* (No. 12).

The basic bibliography for runes in general is Helmut Arntz, *Bibliographie der Runenkunde* (Leipzig, 1937); and for Britain in particular, Marquardt's compilation (No. 360). References to runic writings in Britain may also be found in Kennedy (No. 273), entries 2072–2354; Bonser, *A.-S.C.B.* (No. 12), entries 9378–10035; Derolez (No. 354) and Elliott (No. 357).

352 ARNTZ (HELMUT). Handbuch der Runenkunde. Halle. 1935. 2nd edn. 1944.

> See also his *Die einheimischen Runendenkmäler des Festlandes* (Leipzig, 1939). The works of an outstanding authority on the subject.

353 COLLINGWOOD (WILLIAM G.). Northumbrian crosses of the pre-Norman age. Lond. 1927.

> For various crosses, see W. G. Collingwood, 'A pedigree of Anglian crosses', *Antiquity*, vi (1932), 35–54; Eric Mercer, 'The Ruthwell and Bewcastle crosses', ibid. xxxviii (1964), 268–76; Roy. Comm. Hist. Monuments, Scotland (No. 739) (Ruthwell Cross); Fritz Saxl, 'The Ruthwell Cross', *Jour. Warburg and Courtauld Inst.* vi (1943), 1–19; Knut Berg, 'The Gosforth Cross', ibid. xxi (1958), 27–43; R. I. Page, 'The Bewcastle Cross', *Nottingham Mediaeval Stud.* iv (1960), 36–57.

354 DEROLEZ (R.). Runica manuscripta: the English tradition. Rijksuniversiteit te Gent. Werken uitgegeven door de Faculteit van de Wijsbegeerte en Letteren. 118e Aflevering. Bruges. 1954.

> Includes a very valuable bibliography and indexes of manuscripts and inscriptions. See also Joan Blomfield, 'Runes and the Gothic alphabet', *Saga-Book of the Viking Soc.* xii (1941–2), 177–94, 209–31.

355 DIACK (FRANCIS C.). The inscriptions of Pictland: an essay on the sculptured and inscribed stones of the north-east and north of Scotland . . . Ed. by William M. Alexander and John Macdonald. Third Spalding Club. Aberdeen. 1944.

> For criticism see K. Jackson, *P.B.A.* xxxvii (1951), 93–7. Cf. R. A. S. Macalister, 'The inscriptions and language of the Picts', in *Essays and studies presented to E. MacNeill* (No. 1442), 184–226.

356 DICKINS (BRUCE), ed. Runic and heroic poems of the old Teutonic peoples. Cambr. 1915. *

357 ELLIOTT (RALPH W. V.). Runes: an introduction. Manchester. 1959.

An introduction to runic writing, particularly to English runic inscriptions, designed for novices. See Sven F. B. Jansson, *Swedish Vikings in England: the evidence of the rune stones* (Lond. 1966).

358 KERMODE (PHILIP M. C.). Manx crosses; or The inscribed and sculptured monuments of the Isle of Man from about the end of the fifth to the beginning of the thirteenth century. Lond. 1907.

359 MACALISTER (ROBERT A. S.). Corpus inscriptionum insularum celticarum. 2 vols. Irish MSS. Comm. Dublin. 1945–49.

A useful listing of non-Roman inscriptions for Britain and Ireland, omitting the Pictish inscriptions of Scotland. For its inaccuracies in drawings and readings as well as the inadequacy of bibliographical and other documentation, consult Kenneth Jackson's reviews in *Speculum*, xxi (1946), 521–3 and xxiv (1949), 598–601. O. G. S. Crawford's contribution to MacNeill's *Festschrift* (No. 1445), pp. 184–226, lists the Pictish inscriptions of Scotland which were omitted from Macalister's *Corpus*.

360 MARQUARDT (HERTHA). 'Die Runeninschriften der Britischen Inseln.' *Abhandl. Akad. Wissen. in Göttingen*, Phil.-hist. Klasse, dritte Folge, no. 48. Göttingen. 1961.

A full bibliography of 158 pages. There are, for example, about 330 entries on the Ruthwell Cross alone. This work forms the first part of *Bibliographie der Runeninschriften nach Fundorten*.

361 OLSEN (MAGNUS). Runic inscriptions in Great Britain, Ireland and the Isle of Man. Bergen. 1955.

Separately published from Shetelig's *Viking Antiquities* (No. 2483), vi. 152–233.

362 STEPHENS (GEORGE). The old-northern runic monuments of Scandinavia and England . . . 4 vols. Lond. etc. 1866–1901.

363 WESTWOOD (JOHN O.). Lapidarium Walliae: the early inscribed and sculptured stones of Wales. Cambrian Archaeol. Assoc. Oxf. 1876–9.

One hundred and one valuable plates.

C. CHRONOLOGY

The two essential aids to British chronology are the *Handbook of British chronology* (No. 371) which lists rulers, officers of state, bishops, higher nobility 1066–1603, parliaments 1258–1547, church councils, the reckonings of time, saints' days, and legal chronology; and *Handbook of dates* (No. 372) which is a handy guide to calendar variations. Both of these works include bibliographical notes, which should be consulted.

364 L'ART DE VÉRIFIER LES DATES . . . Paris. 1750. 4th edn. by N. V. de Saint-Allais and others. 44 vols. 1818–44.

The best of the older works, the 3rd edn. 3 vols. (1783–7), is more convenient to use than the 4th. Vols. vi–xxiii (1818–19) are pertinent to our period. Enormously detailed, it is especially valuable for continental history.

365 BOND (JOHN J.). Handy-book of rules and tables for verifying dates . . . Lond. 1866. 4th edn. 1889. *

> The parts that deal with general chronology are in need of revision. Contains tables of regnal years.

366 THE BOOK OF SAINTS, compiled by the Benedictine monks of St. Augustine's Abbey, Ramsgate. Lond. 1921.

> A little dictionary of saints, many of post-medieval times.

367 CAPPELLI (ADRIANO). Cronologia e calendario perpetuo; tavole cronografiche e quadri sinottici per verificare le date storiche dal principio dell'era christiana ai giorni nostri. Milan. 1906. 2nd edn. 1930.

368 FRY (EDWARD A.). Almanacks for students of English history . . . Lond. 1915.

> This handy guide is now superseded by Nos. 371, 372.

369 GROTEFEND (HERMANN). Taschenbuch der Zeitrechnung des deutschen Mittelalters und der Neuzeit. 10th edn. Ed. by Th. Ulrich. Hannover. 1960.

370 HAMPSON (ROBERT T.). Medii aevi kalendarium; or dates, charters, and customs of the middle ages . . . 2 vols. Lond. 1841.

> Helpful for facts about festivals and for the texts of calendars.

371 HANDBOOK OF BRITISH CHRONOLOGY. Ed. by Frederick Maurice Powicke with the assistance of Charles Johnson and W. J. Harte. Royal Hist. Soc. Guides and Handbooks, no. 2. Lond. 1939. 2nd edn. by Sir Maurice Powicke and E. B. Fryde. Lond. 1961.

> This work and the one that follows (No. 372) supersede all others on questions of British chronology.

372 HANDBOOK OF DATES FOR STUDENTS OF ENGLISH HISTORY. Ed. by Christopher R. Cheney. Royal Hist. Soc. Guides and Handbooks, no. 4. Lond. 1945. Revised edn. 1970.

373 MAS LATRIE (JACQUES M. J. L. DE). Trésor de chronologie, d'histoire et de géographie pour l'étude et l'emploi des documents du moyen âge. Paris. 1889.

> Most useful for French and for ecclesiastical history, but not always critical or reliable.

374 POOLE (REGINALD LANE). Studies in chronology and history. Ed. by Austin Lane Poole. Oxf. 1934. See No. 1487. Reprinted, 1969.

> See his *Medieval reckonings of time*, Helps for Students of History, no. 3 (Lond. 1918). Reprinted, 1921. Also his *Chronicles and annals*: a brief outline of their origin and growth (Oxf. 1926).

375 SEARLE (WILLIAM G.). Anglo-Saxon bishops, kings and nobles: the succession of the bishops and the pedigrees of the kings and nobles. Cambr. 1899.

> See No. 2161 and R. I. Page's list (No. 2722).

376 WALLIS (JOHN E. W.). English regnal years and titles: hand-lists, Easter dates, etc. Helps for Students of History, no. 40. Lond. 1921.

D. PALAEOGRAPHY AND DIPLOMATIC

Palaeography is the study of the handwriting of former ages. Diplomatic is the study of the construction or constituent parts of records whereby their age, authenticity, and historical value may be determined. Dom Jean Mabillon (1622–1707) was the founder of the science of diplomatic and of palaeography in *De Re Diplomatica* (No. 418); the fathers of English palaeography and diplomatic were George Hickes and Humfrey Wanley. A brief review of the history of the subject is given by Denholm-Young (No. 385).

For retrospective bibliography, consult Denholm-Young, and Moore (No. 19); for particular periods or subjects, such works as Ker's Catalogue (No. 977). Current research may be followed in *Scriptorium* (No. 381) where each fascicle, beginning with vol. xiii (1959), includes as 'Bulletin Codicologique' an analysis or list of publications about manuscripts. Reports by C. Perrat, B. Bischoff, and Gaines Post are printed in *Relazioni del X Congresso Internazionale di Scienze Storiche* (Florence, 1955).

Good, brief chapters on handwriting are those by E. A. Lowe in *The legacy of the Middle Ages* (No. 1479), pp. 197–226, reprinted separately (1969), and by V. H. Galbraith in *Medieval England* (No. 1485), pp. 541–58. Pierre Chaplais discusses 'the study of palaeography and sigillography in England' in *Jenkinson essays* (No. 1440). Kathleen Major's 'The teaching and study of diplomatic in England', *Archives*, viii, no. 39 (1968), 114–18, is followed by a report on the discussion of the subject at the annual conference of the British Records Association. Christopher Brooke prints a paper on 'The teaching of diplomatic' in *Jour. Soc. Archivists*, iv, no. 1 (1970). Consult also the studies on the practices of the royal chancery (pp. 572–4, and Nos. 3763 and 7223–4).

1. *Palaeography: Guides and Manuals*

377 CATALOGUE OF WORKS DEALING WITH THE STUDY OF WESTERN PALAEOGRAPHY in the libraries of the University of London at its central buildings and at University College and King's College. By John Wilks and A. D. Lacey. Lond. 1921.

378 HASELDEN (REGINALD B.). Scientific aids for the study of manuscripts. *Bibliographical Soc. Trans.* Supplement no. 10. Oxf. 1935.

379 PUBLICATIONS DE L'INSTITUT DE RECHERCHE ET D'HISTOIRE DE TEXTES. i+ (1952). Paris. 1953+.

380 RECORD (PETER D.). 'The bibliography of palaeography'. *Jour. of Documentation*, vi (1950), 1–5.

381 SCRIPTORIUM. Revue internationale des études relatives aux manuscrits. Antwerp and Brussels. 1946+ *. Les publications de Scriptorium. Vol. i. Brussels. 1947.

382 ASTLE (THOMAS). The origin and progress of writing. Lond. 1784. 2nd edn. 1803. Reprinted. 1876. *

Devotes particular attention to Anglo-Saxon and Irish scripts. This is one of the more important of the older palaeographical works written in England.

383 BATTELLI (GIULIO). Lezioni di paleografia. Vatican City. 1936. 3rd edn. 1949.

An excellent handbook with bibliographies based on up-to-date research.

384 BISCHOFF (BERNHARD). Paläographie. 2nd edn. Berlin. 1956.

A survey by a master-hand.

384A BISHOP (TERENCE A. M.). English Caroline minuscule. Oxford Palaeographic Handbooks. Lond. 1971.

385 DENHOLM-YOUNG (NOËL). Handwriting in England and Wales. Cardiff. 1954.

A succinct manual for beginners, with good bibliography and 31 plates.

386 HECTOR (LEONARD C.). The handwriting of English documents. Lond. and N.Y. 1958.

387 JENKINSON (HILARY). Palaeography and the practical study of the court hand. Cambr. 1915. Idem, The later court hands in England. Cambr. 1927. *

388 JOHNSON (CHARLES) and JENKINSON (HILARY). English court hand, A.D. 1066 to 1500, illustrated chiefly from the public records. Pt. i, text. Pt. ii, plates. Oxf. 1915. *

A detailed study of the history of individual letters and abbreviations in documents preserved in the Public Record Office.

389 KELLER (WOLFGANG). 'Angelsächsische Palaeographie'. *Palaestra*, xliii, pt. 1 (1906); pt. 2 (1922).

Cf. 'Angelsächsische Schrift', in *Reallexikon d. germ. Altertumskunde* (Berlin, 1906), Bd. A–E; and particularly the 'Notes on the palaeography' in the introduction to Ker's *Catalogue* (No. 977).

390 KER (NEIL R.). English manuscripts in the century after the Norman Conquest. Lond. 1960.

The Lyell Lectures, 1952–3, accompanied by 29 plates.

391 LINDSAY (WALLACE M.). Early Irish minuscule script. Oxf. 1910.

F. Masai, *Essai sur les origines de la miniature dite irlandaise*, Les publications de Scriptorium, i (Brussels, 1947).

392 LINDSAY (WALLACE M.). Early Welsh script. Oxf. 1912.

393 LINDSAY (WALLACE M.), ed. Palaeographia Latina. St. Andrews Univ. Pubns. vols. i–vi. Lond. 1922–9.

Notes on palaeographical matters by various hands.

394 LOWE (ELIAS A.). Codices latini antiquiores: a palaeographical guide to Latin manuscripts prior to the ninth century. Pts. i–xi. Oxf. 1934–66.

Pt. ii, Great Britain and Ireland, includes a total of 277 entries, each illustrated by a photograph, even if fragmentary. More than 80 items are in the insular script developed in England and Ireland. See also Lowe's *English uncial* (No. 447); and *Lowe's Palaeographical papers, 1907–1965*, ed. by Ludwig Bieler, 2 vols. (Oxf. 1970).

395 PARKES (M. B.). English cursive book hands 1250–1500. Oxford Palaeographic Handbooks. Oxf. 1969.

396 PROU (MAURICE). Manuel de paléographie latine et française du VIᵉ au XVIIᵉ siècle, suivi d'un dictionnaire des abréviations; avec 23 fac-similés. Paris. 1890. 4th edn. with collaboration of Alain de Boüard. Paris. 1924.

This valuable handbook is supplemented by his *Recueil de fac-similés* (Paris, 1892); and *Nouveau Recueil de fac-similés* (1896); and *Recueil de fac-similés du Vᵉ au XVIIᵉ siècle* (1904).

397 STEFFENS (FRANZ). Lateinische Paläographie. . . . Freiburg. 1903–6. With Supplement, pts. i–ii. Trier. 1907–9. 2nd edn. Trier. 1909. 125 plates. French edn. by R. Coulon. Paléographie latine. Trèves etc. 1910. 125 plates.

398 THOMPSON (EDWARD MAUNDE). Handbook of Greek and Latin palaeography. Lond. 1893. 3rd edn. 1906. Enlarged edn. An introduction to Greek and Latin palaeography. Oxf. 1912. *

Thompson's *Introduction* is now somewhat out of date.

399 THOMSON (SAMUEL HARRISON). Latin bookhands of the later middle ages, 1100–1500. Lond. and N.Y. 1969.

400 TRAUBE (LUDWIG). Vorlesungen und Abhandlungen, herausgegeben von Franz Boll. 3 vols. in 2. Munich. 1909–20. *

See T. J. Brown, 'Latin palaeography since Traube' (Inaugural lecture), *Cambr. Bibliog. Soc. Trans.* iii (1963), 361–81. Reprinted in large part in the *Vorlesungen*, iii, 95–119, is Traube's 'Perrona Scottorum: ein Beitrag zur Überlieferungsberichte und zur Palaeographie des Mittelalters', *Bayer. Akad. d. Wissensch. Sitzungsberichte Phil.-hist. Classe* (1900), 469–538. Cf. Louis Gougaud, 'Les scribes monastiques d'Irlande au travail', *R.H.E.* xxvii (1931), 293–306; and K. Hughes, 'The distribution of Irish scriptoria' (No. 2665).

401 WRIGHT (CYRIL E.). English vernacular hands from the twelfth to the fifteenth centuries. Oxford Palaeog. Handbooks. Oxf. 1960.

It includes 24 collotype plates of MSS. of English literature. See also Hilda Grieve, *Examples of English Handwriting, 1150–1750* (Essex County Council, 2nd edn. 1959).

2. *Abbreviations and Writing Materials*

402 CAPPELLI (ADRIANO). Lexicon abbreviaturarum. Milan. 1899. New edn. Leipzig. 1901. 3rd edn. Milan. 1929. Reprinted. 1949.

This standard work is supplemented by Auguste Pelzer, *Abréviations latines médiévales* (Louvain and Paris, 1964).

403 CHASSANT (ALPHONSE). Dictionnaire des abréviations latines et françaises du moyen âge usitées dans les inscriptiones. Paris. 1846. 5th edn. 1884. *

404 LINDSAY (WALLACE M.). Notae Latinae: an account of abbreviation
in Latin MSS. of the early minuscule period (*c.* 700–850). Cambr. 1915.

> Supplements Ludwig Traube, *Nomina sacra* (Quellen und Untersuchungen zur latei-
> nischen Philologie des Mittelalters, II) (Munich, 1907). See also Doris Bains, *A supplement
> to Notae latinae* (abbreviations in Latin MSS. of A.D. 850 to 1050) (Cambr. 1936); E. K.
> Rand, 'A nest of ancient notae', *Speculum*, ii (1927), 160–76.

405 MARTIN (CHARLES T.). The record interpreter: a collection of
abbreviations, Latin words and names used in English historical manuscripts and
records. Lond. 1892. 2nd edn. 1910. Reissued, 1967.

> A handy, convenient guide which includes lists of Latin forms of place-names and sur-
> names.

406 SANTIFALLER (LEO). Beiträge zur Geschichte der Beschriebstoffe im
Mittelalter. Mit besonderer Berücksichtigung der päpstlichen Kanzlei. Teil I:
Untersuchungen. *M.I.O.G.* Erg.-Bd. xvi, Heft i. Graz–Cologne. 1953.

> See also Battelli (No. 383), pp. 26–44.

407 SCHIAPARELLI (LUIGI). Avviamento allo studio delle abbreviature
nel Medioevo. Florence. 1926.

408 THOMPSON (DANIEL V.). The materials of medieval painting. Lond.
1936.

> The materials considered include parchment, inks, etc. See also Thompson's 'Medieval
> parchment making', *The Library*, 4th Ser. xvi, no. 1 (1935), 113–17. Cf. W. Lee Ustick,
> 'Parchment and vellum', ibid. 4th Ser. xvi, no. 4 (1936), 439–43; H. Saxl, 'A note on
> parchment', in Singer, Holmyard, and Hall, *A history of technology*, ii. 187–90 (Lond.
> 1955 in progress).

409 WALTHER (JOHANN L.). Lexicon Diplomaticum, abbreviationes
syllabarum et vocum in diplomatibus et codicibus a seculo viii ad xvi usque
occurrentes exponens . . . 3 pts. Göttingen. 1745–7. Another edn. Ulm. 1756. *

410 WATTENBACH (WILHELM). Das Schriftwesen im Mittelalter.
Leipzig. 1871. 3rd edn. 1896. 4th edn. Graz. 1958.

> Manuals on palaeography include remarks on writing materials, e.g. Prou (No. 396),
> pp. 1–27, Thompson, *Introduction* (No. 398, pp. 8–43). A brief account, with biblio-
> graphical citations, is given by G. S. Ivy, 'The bibliography of the manuscript-book' in
> F. Wormald and C. Wright, *The English library before 1700* (No. 7181), pp. 32–65.

411 WRIGHT (ANDREW). Court-hand restored, or the student's assistant in
reading old deeds, charters, etc. Lond. 1776. 10th edn. by C. Trice Martin.
1912. *

3. *Diplomatic: Codicology*

A comprehensive treatise on English diplomatic has yet to be written. Below are
given the principal treatises on continental diplomatic; and secondly, those concerned specifically with English diplomatic. Numerous studies of particular
problems of English diplomatic are listed elsewhere in this volume. For those of
the Anglo-Saxon period, see the studies on charters (pp. 309–10 below) and
Nos. 2215–21; and for those of the later Middle Ages, refer to the sections on

Chancery and Exchequer, especially Nos. 3751, 3838. For episcopal chanceries, see No. 421. Consult the index under 'diplomatic'; and for the teaching of diplomatic in England, refer to the articles cited on p. 47 above. See also the introduction to Delisle's *Recueil* (No. 3823), Richardson in Pipe Roll Soc. Pubns. (No. 3078), xxi, pp. lix–lxxv; and van Caenegem in Selden Soc. Pubns. (No. 3503), pp. xxxiii–xlix; and the introduction to Davis, *et al. Regesta*, vol. iv.

412 ARCHIV FÜR DIPLOMATIK, SCHRIFTGESCHICHTE, SIEGEL-UND WAPPENKUNDE, hrg. v. E. E. Stengel, in Verbindung mit H. Büttner und K. Jordan, i.+ Münster. 1955.+

413 ARNDT (WILHELM). Schrifttafeln zum Gebrauch bei Vorlesungen. 2 pts. Berlin. 1874–8. 2nd edn. Schrifttafeln zur Erlernung der lateinischen Palaeographie. 2 pts. Berlin. 1887–8. 4th edn. by Michael Tangl. 2 pts. 70 plates. 1904–6. Pt. iii, by M. Tangl. 37 plates. 1903.

414 BOÜARD (ALAIN DE). Manuel de diplomatique française et pontificale. Vol. i. Diplomatique générale. Vol. ii. L'Acte privé. Paris. 1929–48. 1ère Série. Planches I à XVII. 1949. 2ème Série. Planches XVIII à XXXIV. 1952.

415 BRESSLAU (HARRY). Handbuch der Urkundenlehre für Deutschland und Italien. Vol. i. Leipzig, 1889. 2nd edn. 2 vols. (Vol. ii. Ed. by Hans Walter Klewitz.) 1912–31. Reprinted. 2 vols. Berlin. 1958. Index. 1960.

416 CLARK (ALBERT C.). The cursus in mediaeval and vulgar Latin. Oxf. 1910. Cf. Denholm-Young (Nos. 1451, 1467).

417 DÉPREZ (EUGÈNE). Études de diplomatique anglaise . . ., 1272–1485: Le sceau privé, le sceau secret, le signet. [Vol. i.] Paris. 1908.

Deals mainly with documents issued under the privy seal, the secret seal, or one of the various signets.

417A GIRY (ARTHUR). Manuel de diplomatique. Paris. 1894. Reprinted. 2 vols. 1925. *

The English chancery, 794–9; a rather meagre account. This classic should now be used with discretion.

418 MABILLON (JEAN). De re diplomatica libri VI. Paris. 1681. Supplement. 1704. 2nd edn. 1709. 3rd edn. 2 vols. Naples. 1789.

An epoch-making work; it formulates the critical canons of diplomatic study, most of which are still accepted by scholars. For an assessment of Mabillon's work, see Knowles's *Historian and character* (No. 1477), pp. 213–39.

419 MADAN (FALCONER). Books in manuscript: a short introduction to their study and use. Lond. 1893. 2nd edn. 1920. *

A popular handbook. Lists works on illuminations, pp. 178–9. See also idem, 'Tests for localization of manuscripts' in *Poole essays* (No. 1448), pp. 5–29.

420 POOLE (REGINALD LANE). Lectures on the history of the papal chancery down to the time of Innocent III. Cambr. 1915. See No. 1487.

Cf. Christopher R. Cheney, *The study of the medieval papal chancery* (Glasgow, 1965).

421   CHENEY (CHRISTOPHER R.). English bishops' chanceries 1100–1250. Manchester. 1950. Idem, Notaries public in England in the thirteenth and fourteenth centuries. Oxf. 1972.

422   GALBRAITH (VIVIAN H.). Studies in the Public Records. Lond. etc. 1948.

> See Galbraith, 'Monastic foundation charters', *Cambr. Hist. Jour.* iv, no. 3 (1934), 205–22, 296–8. See also Nos. 258, 949; and T. F. T. Plucknett, 'Deeds and Seals', *T.R.H.S.* 4th Ser. xxxii (1950), 141–51.

423   HALL (HUBERT). Studies in English official historical documents. Cambr. 1908. *

> Pt. i: History, classification, etc. of archives. Pt. ii: Diplomatic. Pt. iii. Palaeography. Valuable broad treatment of diplomatic of official documents, but somewhat lacking in lucidity and method. Supplemented by *A formula book of English official historical documents*, pts. i–ii (Cambr. 1908–9). See also Hall's paper, 'The diplomatics of Welsh records', *Hon. Soc. Cymmrodorion Trans.* (1900–1), 40–52 (Lond. 1902).

424   HECTOR (LEONARD C.). Palaeography and medieval forgery. Lond. and York. 1959.

425   HICKES (GEORGE). Linguarum veterum septentrionalium thesaurus grammatico-criticus. . . . 2 vols. Oxf. 1703–5.

> Vol. i. Part i—Institutiones grammaticae Anglo-Saxonicae et Moeso-Gothicae.
>   Part ii—Institutiones grammaticae Franco-Theotiscae.
>   Part iii—Grammaticae Islandicae rudimenta.
>   Part iv—De antiquae litteraturae septentrionalis utilitate sive de linguarum veterum septentrionalium usu dissertatio epistolaris, cum numismatibus Saxonicis.
> Vol. ii. Part v—Antiquae litteraturae septentrionalis liber alter seu Humphredi Wanleii librorum vett. septentrionalium qui in Angliae bibliothecis extant etc. catalogus historico-criticus cum totius thesauri linguarum septentrionalium sex indicibus.
>   Part vi—Addenda et emendanda.
> The classic foundation for the study of English diplomatic. The contents and authors of its various parts are explained in J. A. W. Bennett, 'Hickes' Thesaurus: a study in Oxford book production', *English Studies* (English Assoc.) N.S. i (1948), 28–45. Volume ii is Wanley's important catalogue of Anglo-Saxon manuscripts. 'Since some of the manuscripts were destroyed in the Cottonian fire of 1731, it (Wanley's catalogue) will always retain its value' (Denholm-Young). On Wanley, consult C. E. Wright, 'Humphrey Wanley, Saxonist and library-keeper', *P.B.A.* xlvi (1960), 91–129; reprinted 1961; and Cyril E. and Ruth C. Wright, *The diary of Humfrey Wanley, 1715–26*, The Bibliographical Soc. (Lond. 1966); of this last work the valuable introduction has been reprinted separately.

425A   KANTOROWICZ (ERNST). 'Petrus de Vinea in England'. *M.I.O.G.* li (1937–8), 43–88.

426   [MADOX (THOMAS)]. Formulare Anglicanum: a collection of ancient charters and instruments of divers kinds, from the Norman conquest to the end of the reign of Henry VIII. Lond. 1702.

> An important Dissertation concerning Ancient Charters and Instruments, pp. i–xxxiv. The body of the work contains numerous covenants, royal charters, private grants, concords, releases, wills, etc.

427 FORMULARIES WHICH BEAR ON THE HISTORY OF OXFORD, *c.* 1204–1420. Ed. by H. E. Salter, W. A. Pantin, H. G. Richardson. Oxf. Hist. Soc. N.S. iv and v. 2 vols. Oxf. 1942.

The first part of vol. i, pp. 6–79, is a series of documents from *Liber epistolaris Ricardi de Bury*, of which a complete edition (in part the edited text and in part calendar) was published for the Roxburghe Club by Nöel Denholm-Young in 1950. For *Dictamen*, see W. A. Pantin, 'A medieval treatise on letter writing with examples, from the Rylands Latin MS. 394', *B.J.R.L.* xiii (1929), 326–82. W. A. Pantin, 'English monastic letter-books', in *Tait essays* (No. 1455), pp. 201–22.

428 LEGAL AND MANORIAL FORMULARIES, edited from originals at the British Museum and the Public Record Office, in memory of Julius Parnell Gilson. Oxf. 1933.

429 SNAPPE'S FORMULARY AND OTHER RECORDS. Ed. by H. E. Salter. Oxf. Hist. Soc. lxxx. Oxf. 1924.

4. *Incipits*

430 LITTLE (ANDREW G.). Initia operum Latinorum quae saeculis xiii, xiv, xv attribuuntur. Manchester. 1904. *

Contains incipits of nearly 6,000 writings, many of them anonymous, preserved in English libraries. Cf. Morton W. Bloomfield, 'A preliminary list of incipits of Latin works on the virtues and vices, mainly of the thirteenth, fourteenth, and fifteenth centuries', *Traditio*, xi (1955), 259–379. Refer to the table in the *B.M. Cat. Royal MSS.* (No. 1002).

431 PELZER (AUGUSTE). Répertoires d'incipit pour la littérature latine, philosophique et théologique du moyen âge. Édn. augmentée. Rome. 1951.

First published in *R.H.E.* xliii (1948), 495–512.

432 THORNDIKE (LYNN) and KIBRE (PEARL). A catalogue of incipits of mediaeval scientific writings in Latin. Cambr. (Mass.). 1937. Revised edn. Lond. 1963.

See also their 'More incipits of mediaeval scientific writings in Latin', *Speculum*, xvii (1942), 342–66; L. Thorndike, 'Additional incipits . . .', ibid. xiv (1939), 93–105, and 'Further incipits . . .', ibid. xxvi (1951), 673–95. Pearl Kibre, 'Further addenda and corrigenda to the revised edition' (of the above catalogue), *Speculum*, xliii (1968), 78–114.

5. *Facsimiles*

Reproductions of portions of isolated folios may be found in many of the previously noticed works on palaeography and on illuminated manuscripts (Nos. 386, 387, 394). For preliminary study, the student will find helpful the following works which provide transcriptions of the reproduced documents: for the records of the Public Record Office, Johnson and Jenkinson (No. 388) and Jenkinson (No. 387); for early writs, Bishop and Chaplais (No. 436), which includes 30 plates; see also *Sir Christopher Hatton's Book of Seals* (No. 464), which includes 9 plates; *Hereford Domesday* (No. 3075). For specimen documents and transcriptions of the Bibliothèque Nationale and Archives Nationales, see Prou's *Manuel*

(No. 396) with the sub-title *Recueil de fac-similés d'écritures du* V^e *au* XVIIe *siècle* (Paris, 1904); for those from several French archives, Boüard (No. 414); for Vatican manuscripts and records, refer to *Exempla Scripturarum edita consilio et opera procuratorum bibliothecae et tabularii Vaticani*, 3 fasc. (Rome, 1928–33).

Volume iv of the *Catalogue of the Royal Library in the British Museum* (No. 1002) contains 125 excellent plates, some of them with multiple reproductions. Hardy's *Catalogue* (No. 21), vol. iii, includes 20 plates from manuscripts of Roger Wendover and Matthew Paris. The publications of the Henry Bradshaw Society include reproductions of liturgical texts, and those of the Roxburghe Club several other facsimiles.

Facsimiles of Welsh and Irish manuscripts will be found in the series of Welsh texts (Nos. 2383–6) edited by John Rhys and J. Gwenogvryn Evans (Oxf. 1887+) and in various other books, like the *Book of Leinster* (No. 2394), published by the Royal Irish Academy.

The sets of facsimiles published by the Ordnance Survey Office (No. 448) are marred by inaccuracies; those of the Palaeographical Society and New Palaeographical Society (No. 445) are excellent. A fine series, *Early English manuscripts in facsimile* (No. 441), is being produced in Copenhagen.

For older lists of facsimiles, refer to Denholm-Young (No. 385), pp. 90–2. With the advent of microfilms, many individuals and organizations have undertaken to photograph medieval manuscripts. For such activities among American scholars, one might turn to Loren C. MacKinney, 'Manuscript photoreproductions in classical, mediaeval and renaissance research', *Speculum*, xxi (1946), 244–52; his 'Post-war microfilming of mediaeval research material', ibid. xxxvii (1962), 492–6; and particularly for historical purposes, *The British Manuscripts Project* (No. 438).

433 ALBUM PALÉOGRAPHIQUE. Ed. by Léopold Delisle. Société de l'École des Chartes. Paris. 1887. 50 plates.

434 ANDERSON (JAMES). Selectus diplomatum et numismatum Scotiae thesaurus. Ed. by T. Ruddimann. Edin. 1739. 180 plates.

435 APPENDIX TO REPORTS FROM THE RECORD COMMISSIONERS: engraved facsimiles inserted in the works of the record commission. Lond. 1819. 86 plates.

See No. 964.

436 BISHOP (TERENCE A. M.) and CHAPLAIS (PIERRE), eds. Facsimiles of English royal writs to A.D. 1100 presented to Vivian Hunter Galbraith. Oxf. 1957.

Includes a select bibliography of the publications of V. H. Galbraith, 1911–57, pp. [63]–[68].

437 BISHOP (TERENCE A. M.). Scriptores regis: facsimiles to identify and illustrate the hands of royal scribes in the original charters of Henry I, Stephen, and Henry II. Oxf. 1961.

Seventy-four facsimiles illustrate the hands of forty-eight scribes, with an introduction on chancery practice.

438 BRITISH MANUSCRIPTS PROJECT: A checklist of the microfilms prepared in England and Wales for the American Council of Learned Societies 1941–5. Compiled by Lester K. Born. Library of Congress: photoduplication Service. Washington. 1955.

   2,652 reels of approximately 5,000,000 pages, mostly from MSS.

439 CATALOGUE OF ANCIENT MANUSCRIPTS IN THE BRITISH MUSEUM. Ed. by E. M. Thompson and G. F. Warner. Pt. ii. 61 plates. Lond. 1884.

440 COLLOTYPE FACSIMILES OF IRISH MANUSCRIPTS IN THE BODLEIAN LIBRARY. No. i: Rawlinson B. 502. A collection of pieces in prose and verse in the Irish language. Ed. by Kuno Meyer. Oxf. 1909.

441 EARLY ENGLISH MANUSCRIPTS IN FACSIMILE. Ed. by Bertram Colgrave *et al.* Copenhagen and Baltimore. 1951+.

   Vol. i. The Thorkelin Transcripts of Beowulf. Ed. by Kemp Malone. 1951. (No. 2332.)
   Vol. ii. The Leningrad Bede. Ed. by O. Arngart. 1952. (No. 2148 (*d*)).
   Vol. iii. The Tollemache Orosius. Ed. by Alistair Campbell. 1953.
   Vol. iv. The Peterborough Chronicle. Ed. by Dorothy Whitelock. 1955. (No. 2142 (E)).
   Vol. v. Bald's Leechbook. Ed. by Cyril E. Wright. 1955. (No. 2365.)
   Vol. vi. The Pastoral Care. Ed. by Neil Ker. 1956.
   Vol. vii. Textus Roffensis. Pt. 1. Ed. by Peter Sawyer. 1957. (No. 5794.)
   Vol. viii. The Paris Psalter. Ed. by John Bromwich. 1958.
   Vol. ix. The Moore Bede: Bede's Ecclesiastical History. Ed. by Peter Hunter Blair. 1959. (No. 2148 (*e*).)
   Vol. x. The Blickling Homilies. Ed. by Rudolph Willard. 1960. (No. 2267.)
   Vol. xi. Textus Roffensis Pt. 2. Ed. by Peter Sawyer. 1962. (No. 5794.)
   Vol. xii. The Nowell Codex-Beowulf: B.M. Cotton Vitellius A XV. Ed. by Kemp Malone. 1963. (No. 2333.)
   Vol. xiii. Ælfric's Catholic Homilies. 1st Ser. Ed. by Norman Eliason and Peter Clemoes. 1966. (No. 2292.)
   Vol. xiv. The Vespasian Psalter. Ed. by David H. Wright and Alistair Campbell. 1966.
   Vol. xv. The Rule of St. Benedict: Oxford Bodleian Hatton 48. Ed. by D. H. Farmer. 1968.
   Other volumes are announced for early publication.

442 EARLY ENGLISH TEXT SOCIETY. Facsimiles. 1864+. †

   See *Repert. Font.* i. 239–48.

443 FACSIMILES IN COLLOTYPE OF IRISH MANUSCRIPTS. Irish MSS. Comm. Dublin. 1931+.

   Listed to 1950 in *Repert. Font.* i. 146. See also Nos. 2393–7.

444 FACSIMILES OF ANCIENT CHARTERS IN THE BRITISH MUSEUM. Anglo-Saxon period. Ed. by E. A. Bond. 4 pts. Lond. 1873–8. 144 plates. Facsimiles of royal and other charters in the British Museum. Ed. by G. F. Warner and H. J. Ellis. Vol. i. Wm. I–Richard I. Lond. 1903. 50 plates.

   140 English documents from the seventh to the eleventh century are reproduced in the first-mentioned series; later documents in the second series.

445 FACSIMILES OF MANUSCRIPTS AND INSCRIPTIONS. Ed. by E. A. Bond, E. M. Thompson, and G. F. Warner. Palaeographical Soc. 3 vols.

Lond. 1873–83. 2nd Ser. 2 vols. 1884–94. Indexes. 1901. Facsimiles of ancient manuscripts. Ed. by E. M. Thompson, G. F. Warner, F. G. Kenyon, J. P. Gilson, *et al.* New Palaeographical Soc. 1st Ser. 2 vols. Lond. 1903–12. Indexes. 1st Ser. 1914. 2nd Ser. 2 vols. 1913–30. Indexes 2nd Ser. 1932. New Pal. Soc. *

> The two series published by the Palaeographical Soc. contain 465 plates, embracing writing of all ages and of all regions of Europe. Lindley R. Dean, *An index to facsimiles in the Palaeographical Society publications, arranged as a guide for students in palaeography* (Princeton, 1914), covers the two series published by the Palaeographical Society and the first series published by the New Palaeographical Society. The publications of both series of the New Palaeographical Society are listed in Mullins, *Guide* (No. 28), pp. 263–6.

446 GREG (WALTER W.). Facsimiles of twelve early English MSS. in the library of Trinity College, Cambridge. Edited with transcriptions. Oxf. 1913.

447 LOWE (ELIAS A.). English uncial. Lond. 1960.

> Forty collotype facsimiles from Anglo-Saxon times, with introductions. Cf. David H. Wright, 'Some notes on English uncial', *Traditio*, xvii (1961), 441–56.

448 ORDNANCE SURVEY OFFICE. Facsimiles of national manuscripts (of England), from William the Conqueror to Queen Anne. Ed. by W. B. Sanders. 4 pts. Southampton. 1865–8. 341 facsimiles. Facsimiles of Anglo-Saxon manuscripts. Ed. by W. B. Sanders. 3 pts. Southampton. 1878–84. 121 plates. Domesday Book, or the great survey of William the Conqueror (facsimiles of the parts relating to the various counties). Ed. by W. B. Sanders. 2 vols. and also 33 pts. in 35 vols. Southampton. 1861–4. Facsimiles of national manuscripts of Scotland. Ed. by Cosmo Innes. 3 pts. Southampton. 1867–71. 272 facsimiles. Facsimiles of national manuscripts of Ireland. Ed. by J. T. Gilbert. 4 pts. in 5 vols. Lond. etc. 1874–84. 182 facsimiles.

> In the case of the last mentioned, the introductions were also separately printed: *Account of facsimiles of national MSS. of Ireland* (Lond. 1884).

449 RECUEIL DE FAC-SIMILÉS A L'USAGE DE L'ÉCOLE DES CHARTES. 4 pts. Paris. 1880–(7). 100 plates, containing 185 facsimiles.

450 SALTER (HERBERT E.). Oxford charters. Oxf. 1929.

451 STENTON (FRANK M.), ed. Facsimiles of early charters from Northamptonshire collections. Pubns. of Northamptonshire Record Society, iv. Lincoln etc. 1930.

452 TURNER (CUTHBERT H.), ed. Early Worcester MSS. Fragments of four books and a charter of the eighth century belonging to Worcester Cathedral. Oxf. 1916. 32 plates.

453 WESTWOOD (JOHN O.). Facsimiles of the miniatures and ornaments of Anglo-Saxon and Irish manuscripts. Lond. 1868. 53 plates.

> Benedikt E. H. Zimmerman, *Vorkarolingische Miniaturen* (Berlin, 1916, 341 plates), includes many reproductions of Irish MSS.

E. SEALS AND HERALDRY

I. *The Study of Seals*

The study of seals and their history bears upon several areas of investigation. It sheds light upon the history of art, archaeology, diplomatic, numismatics, and heraldry. The student must accordingly refer to each of these subjects. A general account is provided in Bresslau's *Handbuch* (No. 415), Chap. xix. For the earliest English seals, see, in addition to Bonser (No. 12) items 9362–77, Harmer (No. 2197), pp. 92–105, and Bishop and Chaplais (No. 436), pp. xix ff. For the later period, the writings of Jenkinson (Nos. 460, 469) and of Hunter Blair (No. 458) are particularly important; the footnotes to Jenkinson's *Guide* (No. 460) provide a useful bibliography. On the use of governmental seals in England, much can be found in Tout's *Administrative history* (No. 1223) and Maxwell Lyte's *Great seal* (No. 3844). The quantity of surviving seals is very large: e.g. 'one series (A) alone of the Ancient Deeds at the Public Record Office has proved to contain over 7,300 seals', *Archives*, iii (1957), 29.

454	BIRCH (WALTER DE GRAY). Catalogue of seals in the department of manuscripts in the British Museum. 6 vols. 90 plates. Lond. 1887–1900. On some MSS. and seals relating to Wales in the British Museum, refer to *Archaeologia Cambrensis*, 5th Ser. vi (1889), 273–92.

455	BIRCH (WALTER DE GRAY). History of Scottish seals from the eleventh to the seventeenth century. 2 vols. Stirling. 1905–7. 126 plates.

See also his *Seals* (Connoisseurs' Library) (Lond. 1907). Cf. also Robert Hannay, *The early history of the Scottish signet* (Edin. 1936). See No. 463.

456	BRITISH MUSEUM. Department of British and medieval antiquities. Catalogue of British seal-dies in the British Museum. Ed. by A. B. Tonnochy. Lond. 1952.

457	DOUËT D'ARCQ (LOUIS). Collection de sceaux. France, Archives de l'Empire, Inventaires et Documents. 3 vols. in 2. Paris. 1863–8.

Elements of sphragistics, vol. i, pp. xvii–cix; English seals, i. 110–13, and iii. 261–309.

458	GREENWELL (WILLIAM) and BLAIR (CHARLES HUNTER). Durham seals. *Archaeologia Aeliana*, 3rd Ser. vii–xvii (1911–20).

On the seals of Newcastle, see C. H. Hunter Blair, ibid. 3rd Ser. xix (1922); also idem, 'Fourteenth-century seal from Northumberland', *Antiq. Jour.* xxi, no. 194 (1951); idem, 'The Great Seals of Richard I', *Archaeol. Aeliana*, 4th Ser. xxxi (1953), 95–7; idem, 'Some northern ecclesiastical and commercial seals', ibid. xxvi (1948), 62–85 and plates.

459	HOWARD DE WALDEN (THOMAS E. SCOTT-ELLIS). Some feudal lords and their seals, 1301. Lond. 1904.

Cf. Walter de Gray Birch, *Seals of the earls of Devon* (Lond. 1882); Léopold V. Delisle, *Le sceau de Guillaume le Maréchal* (Paris, 1908); A. R. Wagner, 'A seal of Strongbow in the Huntington Library', *Antiq. Jour.* xxi (1941), 128–32.

460 JENKINSON (CHARLES HILARY). A guide to seals in the Public Record Office. H.M.S.O. Lond. 1954. 2nd edn. 1968.

Cf. idem, 'The study of English seals: illustrated chiefly from examples in the Public Record Office', *Brit. Archaeol. Assoc. Jour.* 3rd Ser. i (1937), 93–127; R. C. Fowler, 'Seals in the Public Record Office', *Archaeologia*, lxx (1925), 103–16.

461 KING (EDWIN J.). The seals of the order of St. John of Jerusalem. Lond. 1932.

Cf. Joseph M. Delaville Le Roulx, 'Mélanges sur les sceaux de l'ordre de S. Jean de Jérusalem', in his *Mélanges sur l'ordre de S. Jean de Jérusalem* (Paris, 1910): Nos. v and vii, 'Des sceaux des prieurs anglais de l'ordre de l'hôpital aux XIIᵉ et XIIIᵉ siècles', originally published in 1882 and 1887.

462 KINGSFORD (HUGH S.). Seals. Helps for Students of History. Lond. 1920.

Cf. also idem, 'The epigraphy of medieval English seals', *Archaeologia*, lxxix, 2nd Ser. xxix (1929), 149–78.

463 LAING (HENRY). Descriptive catalogue of impressions from ancient Scottish seals, royal, baronial, ecclesiastical, and municipal . . . from 1094 to the Commonwealth . . . Maitland Club. Edin. 1850. * Supplement. A.D. 1150 to the eighteenth century. 1866.

Contains 44 valuable plates.

464 LOYD (LEWIS C.) and STENTON (DORIS M.), eds. Sir Christopher Hatton's book of seals. Oxf. 1950. See Nos. 2201A and 4410.

The seals appended to the charters are described.

465 PEDRICK (GALE). Monastic seals of the thirteenth century. Lond. 1902. 50 plates. Idem, Borough seals of the Gothic period. Lond. 1904. 50 plates.

See also C. T. Clay, 'The seals of the religious houses of Yorkshire', *Archaeologia*, lxxviii (1928), 1–36 and plates; H. S. Kingsford, 'The seals of the Franciscans', in *Franciscan history and legend in English mediaeval art*, Brit. Soc. of Franciscan Studies, xix for 1935–6, 79–100 (Manchester, 1937); Francis Wormald, 'Seals of Evesham abbey', *Brit. Museum Quart.* viii (1934), 93–4; Frank Taylor, 'Ecclesiastical, monastic and local seals (15th–17th cent.) from the Hatton Wood MSS. in the John Rylands library', *B.J.R.L.* xxx (1946–7), 247–70.

466 POOLE (REGINALD LANE). 'Seals and documents'. *P.B.A.* ix (1919–20), 319–39. Lond. 1924. Reprinted in *Studies in chronology* (No. 1487), pp. 90–111.

467 STEVENSON (JOHN H.) and WOOD (MARGUERITE). Scottish heraldic seals: royal, official, ecclesiastical, collegiate, burghal, personal. 3 vols. Glasgow. 1940.

Cf. William R. Macdonald, *Scottish armorial seals* (Edin. 1904).

468 VICTORIA AND ALBERT MUSEUM. List of books and pamphlets in the National Art Library . . . illustrating seals. Ed. by Robert H. S. Smith. Lond. 1886.

469 WYON (ALFRED B.) and WYON (ALLAN). The great seals of England, from the earliest period to the present time . . . 55 plates. Lond. 1887.

> Valuable, but the text contains many errors. Cf. W. de G. Birch, 'On the three great seals of King Edward the Confessor', *Trans. Royal Soc. of Lit.* 2nd Ser. x (1874), 613–48; and 'On the great seals of William the Conqueror', ibid. 149–84; and 'The great seals of King Stephen', ibid. xi (1875), 1–29; C. H. Jenkinson, 'The great seal of England: deputed or departmental seals', *Archaeologia*, lxxxv (1936 for 1935), 293–340; 'The great seal of England: some notes and suggestions', *Antiq. Jour.* xvi (1936), 8–28, and 'A new great seal of Henry V', ibid. xviii (1938), 382–90; H. Stanford London, 'King John's seal as lord of Ireland', ibid. xxxv (1955), 224; P. Chaplais, 'The seals and original charters of Henry I', *E.H.R.* lxxv (1960), 260–75.

2. Heraldry

The foremost authorities are Sir Thomas Innes of Learney (Lord Lyon King of Arms in Scotland 1945–69) and Sir Anthony R. Wagner (since 1961 Garter Principal King of Arms of England) (Nos. 478, 483, 484, 499, 527). See also Gatfield (No. 512), Moule (No. 518), and S. Trehearne Cope's *Heraldry, flags and seals*: a select bibliography, with annotations, covering the period 1920 to 1945 (Lond. 1948), which originally appeared in *Journal of Documentation*, iv (1948), 92–146. The Victoria and Albert Museum's *Catalogue of printed books 'Heraldry'* (Lond. 1901) is useful. Consult the section on seals, pp. 57–9 and the section on genealogy, pp. 62–70; *Collectanea topographica* (No. 115); and the bibliography attached to Sir Anthony Wagner's article on Heraldry in *Chambers's Encyclopedia*. *The Coat of Arms* (No. 502) is a useful periodical.

(a) General treatises

470 BARRON (A. OSWALD). 'Heraldry' in *Ency. Brit.* 11th edn. 1910–11.

471 BOUTELL (CHARLES). A manual of heraldry, historical and popular. . . . Lond. 1863. Abridged under the title: English heraldry. Lond. etc. 1867. 11th edn. revised as The handbook to English heraldry, by A. C. Fox-Davies. 1914 (1913). Also Heraldry: ancient and modern. Including Boutell's Heraldry, edited and revised, with additions, by S. T. Aveling. 1891. By C. W. Scott-Giles. 1950, 1954. Boutell's Heraldry, revised by C. W. Scott-Giles and J. P. Brooke-Little. Lond. 1963.

472 DALLAWAY (JAMES). Inquiries into the origin and progress of the science of heraldry in England. Gloucester. 1793.

473 DENHOLM-YOUNG (NOEL). The country gentry in the fourteenth century with special reference to the heraldic rolls of arms. Oxf. 1969.

> It is based on contemporary rolls of arms, particularly four rolls of 1334–6. See reviews by Lawrence Stone in *Speculum*, xlv (1970), 465–7; and by Edward Miller in *Welsh History Rev.* v (1970), 182–3.

474 DENHOLM-YOUNG (NOEL). History and heraldry 1254–1310: a study of the historic value of the Rolls of Arms. Lond. 1965.

> See also Denholm-Young, 'The Song of Carlaverock and the parliamentary Roll of Arms . . .', *P.B.A.* xlvii (1962), 251–62.

475 FOX-DAVIES (ARTHUR C.). The art of heraldry: an encyclopedia of
armory. Lond. 1904. Idem, A complete guide to heraldry. Lond. etc. 1909. New
edn. Edin. 1961.

   The Art of Heraldry has 153 fine plates and 1135 illustrative figures in the text. It is an
   elaborate work based on H. G. Ströhl's *Heraldischer Atlas* (published in parts at Stuttgart, completed 1899). The 1961 edition is illustrated with nearly 800 designs by
   Graham Johnston.

476 GALBREATH (DONALD L.). Manuel du blason. Lausanne. 1942.

477 THE HERALDS' COMMEMORATIVE EXHIBITION 1484–1934
HELD AT THE COLLEGE OF ARMS. Enlarged and illustrated catalogue.
Lond. 1936. Reprinted, 1970.

   Other important catalogues are: *Memorial catalogue heraldic exhibition Edinburgh
   MDCCCXCI* (Edin. 1892); *Illustrated catalogue of the heraldic exhibition Burlington
   House 1894* (Lond. 1896); *City of Birmingham Museum and Art Gallery heraldic ex-
   hibition November–December 1936* (Birmingham, 1936); *Bodleian Library heraldry:
   Catalogue of an exhibition held in connection with the English Heraldry Society, 1967*
   (Oxf. 1967).

478 HOPE (WILLIAM H. ST. J.). A grammar of English heraldry. Cambr.
1913. 2nd edn. rev. by Anthony R. Wagner. 1963. Idem, Heraldry for craftsmen
and designers . . . Artistic crafts series of technical handbooks. Lond. 1913.

   Cf. George W. Eve, *Decorative heraldry: a practical handbook of its artistic treatment*
   (Lond, 1897, 2nd edn. 1908).

479 INNES OF LEARNEY (SIR THOMAS). Scots heraldry: a practical
handbook. The historical principles and modern application of the art and
science. Edin. 1934. 2nd edn. rev. 1956.

   The standard treatise. Cf. G. H. Johnston, *Scottish heraldry made easy* . . . (Edin. etc.
   1904); John Stevenson, *Heraldry in Scotland, including a recension of 'The law and
   practice of heraldry in Scotland' by the late George Seton*, 2 vols. (Glasgow, 1914); Robert
   Stodart, *Scottish arms, being a collection of armorial bearings, A.D. 1370–1678* . . . , 2 vols.
   (Edin. 1881).

480 JONES (EVAN J.), ed. Medieval heraldry: some fourteenth century
heraldic works edited with introduction, English translation of the Welsh text,
arms in colour and notes. . . . Cardiff. 1943.

481 LONDON (HUGH STANFORD). The right road to heraldry. Revised
by C. R. Humphrey-Smith. The Heraldry Soc. Lond. 1960. Idem, 'Some
medieval treatises on English heraldry'. *Antiquaries Jour.* xxxiii (1953), 169–83.
Idem, The Queen's Beasts: an account . . . of the heraldic animals. . . . Lond.
1954. Idem, 'The terminology of heraldry' in *Chambers's Encyclopedia* 1967 edn.
under 'Heraldry'.

482 SCOTT-GILES (CHARLES W.). The romance of heraldry. Lond. 1965.

   This revision of a popular survey by the current Fitzalan Pursuivant of Arms Extraordinary is addressed to those who have no previous knowledge of heraldry.

483 WAGNER (ANTHONY R.). Heralds and heraldry in the Middle Ages:
an inquiry into the growth of the armorial function of heralds. Lond. 1939. 2nd

edn. 1956. Idem, Historic heraldry of Britain: an illustrated series of British historical arms, with notes, glossary, and an introduction to heraldry. Lond. etc. 1939. Idem, The records and collections of the College of Arms. Lond. 1952. See also his chapter on heraldry in *Medieval England* (No. 1485) and the article on heraldry in *Chambers's Encyclopedia*, 1950 edn. 1959 edn. and 1967 edn.; and especially his catalogue (No. 499).

484 WAGNER (SIR ANTHONY). Heralds of England: a history of the Office and College of Arms. H.M.S.O. Lond. 1967.

This large, handsomely produced volume by the current Garter Principal King of Arms traces the development of heralds from their functions at thirteenth-century tournaments to the present. The sections most pertinent to the Middle Ages are on pages 1–71.

485 WHEATLEY (JOSEPH L.). Armorial bearings of Wales. Cardiff. 1902.

486 WOODWARD (JOHN) and BURNETT (GEORGE). A treatise on heraldry, British and foreign. 2 vols. Edin. etc. 1892. New edn. 1896. Reprinted, 1969.

(b) Armorial bearings, rolls of arms, etc.
See Denholm-Young (Nos. 473, 474)

487 BEDFORD (WILLIAM K. R.). The blazon of episcopacy, being the arms borne by . . . the archbishops and bishops of England and Wales. . . . Lond. 1858. 2nd edn. Oxf. 1897.

See also William T. Lyon, *The arms of the Scottish bishoprics* (Selkirk, 1917).

488 BLAIR (CHARLES H. HUNTER). 'Armorials upon English seals from the twelfth to the sixteenth centuries'. *Archaeologia*, lxxxix (1943), 1–26.

489 BROMLEY (JOHN). The armorial bearings of the guilds of London: a record of the heraldry of the surviving companies with historical notes. Lond. and N.Y. (1960), 1961.

490 BURKE (SIR BERNARD). A general armory of England, Scotland, Ireland and Wales: comprising a registry of armorial bearings from the earliest to the present time. Lond. 1884. Reprinted 1962.

Originally published by John and John B. Burke in 1842. Cf. S. M. Collins, 'Some English, Scottish, Welsh and Irish arms in medieval continental rolls', *Antiq. Jour.* xxi (1941), 203–10; and Henry Lawrance, *Heraldry from military monuments before 1350 in England and Wales*, Harleian Soc. xcviii (Lond. 1946).

491 FAIRBAIRN (JAMES). Crests of the families of Great Britain and Ireland. 2 vols. Edin. etc. 1860. New edn. by A. C. Fox-Davies: Book of crests of the families of Great Britain and Ireland. 2 vols. Edin. 1892. 4th edn. 1905. New edn. 1909.

Vol. ii contains 314 plates.

492 FOX-DAVIES (ARTHUR C.) and CROOKES (M. E. B.), eds. The book of public arms: a cyclopaedia of the armorial bearings, heraldic devices, and seals . . . of counties, cities . . . of the United Kingdom. Edin. 1894. 130 plates. A new

edition, containing over 1,300 drawings, by A. C. Fox-Davies: The book of public arms: a complete encyclopaedia of all royal, territorial, municipal, corporate, official, and impersonal arms. Lond. etc. 1915.

493 FRANKLYN (JULIAN) and TANNER (JOHN). An encyclopaedic dictionary of heraldry. Oxf. and Lond. 1970.

An alphabetical list of all terms used, with some indication of medieval origins, etc. Cf. James Parker, *A Glossary of terms used in heraldry* (Oxf. 1894. Reprinted, Newton Abbot, 1970).

494 GALE (ROBERT C.), ed. Index to Powell's Roll, c. 1350. Soc. of Genealogists. Eltham. 1963.

495 JOCELYN (ARTHUR). Awards of honour, the orders, decorations, medals, and awards of Great Britain and the Commonwealth, from Edward III to Elizabeth II. Lond. 1956.

Largely concerned with a later period.

496 LONDON (HUGH STANFORD) and TREMLETT (T. D.). 'Rolls of Arms Henry III'. *Aspilogia, being materials of heraldry*, ii. Lond. 1967.

Harleian Soc. Pubns. cxiii–xiv. Matthew Paris shields, c. 1244–59; Glover's roll, c. 1253–8 and Walford's roll, c. 1273. Additions and corrections to No. 499 by A. R. Wagner.

497 PAPWORTH (JOHN W.). An alphabetical dictionary of coats of arms belonging to families in Great Britain and Ireland: forming an extensive ordinary of British armorial. 2 vols. Lond. (1858)–74. Reprinted, with introductions by G. D. Squibb and A. R. Wagner. 1961.

Lists coats of arms alphabetically under heraldic charges and facilitates their identification.

498 SCOTT-GILES (WILFRID). Civic heraldry of England and Wales. Lond. 1933. 2nd edn. 1953.

499 WAGNER (ANTHONY R.). Catalogue of English medieval rolls of arms. Society of Antiquaries Series. *Aspilogia, being materials of heraldry*, i. Lond. 1950. Also Harleian Soc. vol. c.

In *Aspilogia*, ii (No. 496), are additions and corrections to the Catalogue. Cf. Josiah C. Wedgwood, 'Staffordshire coats of arms, 1272–1327, from rolls of arms in MS. in the British Museum', *William Salt Archaeol. Soc. Collections*, N.S. xvi (1913). See also Denholm-Young (Nos. 473, 474) for references to some printed rolls, e.g. Boroughbridge Roll, Powell's Roll.

500 WOODWARD (JOHN). A treatise on ecclesiastical heraldry. Edin. 1894.

'Comprehensive' on both British and foreign ecclesiastical heraldry.

F. BIOGRAPHY AND GENEALOGY

The standard biographical works of reference are the *Dictionary of national biography* (No. 531) and the *Welsh biographical dictionary* (No. 542). Emden's registers of Oxford and Cambridge (Nos. 532–3) supply detailed references to university men; and the *Handbook of British chronology* (No. 537) lists officials, bishops, and peers. An invaluable work on the peerage is the recent edition of Cokayne (No. 556); and for Scottish peerage, see Paul (No. 568). The critical works of J. H. Round (No. 569), W. Farrer (No. 4498), and C. T. Clay (No. 4499) provide a wealth of details on both legitimate and spurious peerages. Wagner and Sainty (No. 3388) describe the investiture of peers. Most of the longer county histories (below, pp. 219–50) pay considerable attention to genealogies and pedigrees. The topographical sections of the *Victoria County History* (below pp. 215–19) describe the descent of manors and hence include much genealogical material.

The outstanding summary treatise is Sir Anthony Wagner's *English genealogy*, in which Chapter IX constitutes an excellent analytical and descriptive bibliography. For a full listing, see Mrs. Kaminkow's bibliography (No. 516).

1. *Journals and Guides*

501   THE ANCESTOR: a quarterly review of county and family history, heraldry and antiquities. Ed. by Oswald Barron *et al*. 12 vols. Westminster. 1902–5.

502   THE COAT OF ARMS: a journal published by the Heraldry Society. Lond. 1950+.

503   THE GENEALOGIST. Ed. by George W. Marshall *et al*. Vols. i–vii. New Ser. i–xxxviii. And 5 Supplements. Lond. 1877–1922.

504   THE GENEALOGISTS' MAGAZINE, published by the Society of Genealogists. Lond. 1925+. Previously Quarterly Queries of the Society of Genealogists. Nos. 1–31. 1917–25.

505   MISCELLANEA GENEALOGICA ET HERALDICA. Ed. by Joseph J. Howard *et al*. 31 vols. Lond. 1868 (1866)–1938.

506   ADAM (FRANK). The clans, septs and regiments of the Scottish Highlands. Edin. 1908. 4th edn. by Sir Thomas Innes of Learney.
A standard work.

507   ANSCOMBE (ALFRED). Indexes to Old-Welsh genealogies. *Archiv für celtische Lexikographie*, i. 187–212, 513–49; ii. 147–96; iii. 57–103. 1898–1906.
See also his 'Some Old-Welsh pedigrees', *Y Cymmrodor*, xxiv (1913), 74–85.

508   BARTRUM (PETER C.). Early Welsh genealogical tracts. Cardiff. 1966.
See Bartrum, 'Notes on the Welsh genealogical tracts', *Hon. Soc. Cymmrodorion Trans.* 1968, pt. i (1969), 63–98; and R. Bromwich in *Welsh Hist. Rev.* iv (1968–9), 175–80.

509   EDINBURGH PUBLIC LIBRARY. Scottish family histories: a list of books for consultation in the Reference Library, George IV Bridge. Edin. 1951. Supplement. 1953. 2nd edn. 1955. 3rd edn. 1958.

510   FALLEY (MARGARET D.). Irish and Scotch-Irish ancestral records: a guide to the genealogical records, etc. 2 vols. Evanston (Ill.). 1962.

511 GARDNER (DAVID E.) and SMITH (FRANK A.). Genealogical research in England and Wales. 3 vols. Salt Lake City. 1956–65.

512 GATFIELD (GEORGE). Guide to printed books and manuscripts relating to English and foreign heraldry and genealogy. Lond. 1892. Reprinted. N.Y. 1967. *

> A long list, badly arranged; useful for manuscript collections. Cf. *American and English genealogies in the Library of Congress* (Washington, 1910; 2nd edn. 1919).

513 HARRISON (HOWARD G.). A select bibliography of English genealogy, with brief lists for Wales, Scotland and Ireland. Lond. 1937.

> A useful manual for students; arranged by county, now superseded by Marion J. Kaminkow's *Bibliography* (No. 516).

514 JONES (FRANCIS). 'Approach to Welsh Genealogy'. *Trans. Cymmrodorion Soc.* xlix (1948), 303–466.

515 KAMINKOW (MARION J.). Genealogical manuscripts in British libraries: a descriptive guide. With a foreword by Sir Anthony Wagner. Baltimore. 1967.

516 KAMINKOW (MARION J.). A new bibliography of British genealogy with notes. With a foreword by Sir Anthony Wagner. Baltimore. 1965.

517 MARSHALL (GEORGE W.). The genealogist's guide to printed pedigrees. Lond. 1879. 4th edn. Guildford. 1903. Reprinted 1967.

> Supplemented by J. B. Whitmore, *A genealogical guide: an index to British pedigrees*, in continuation of Marshall's *Genealogist's guide* (Lond. 1953). Previously published in Harleian Soc. Pubns. xcix, ci, cii, civ (1947–53); but printed edn. contains additions. See also P. William Filby, *American and British Genealogy and heraldry*, American Library Assoc. (Chicago, 1970).

518 MOULE (THOMAS). Bibliotheca heraldica Magnae Britanniae: an analytical catalogue of books on genealogy, heraldry, nobility, knighthood, and ceremonies. Lond. 1822.

> Still valuable for its details. See C. Bridger, *Index to printed pedigrees contained in county and local histories, the heralds' visitations, and in the more important genealogical collections* (Lond. 1867).

519 NEW YORK PUBLIC LIBRARY. List of works relating to British genealogy and local history. N.Y. 1910.

520 O'HART (JOHN). Irish pedigrees, or the origin and stem of the Irish nation. 2 vols. Dublin. 1876–8. 5th edn. 1892.

521 PHILLIMORE (WILLIAM P. W.). How to write the history of a family: a guide for the genealogist. Lond. 1887. 2nd edn. 1888. Supplement. 1892. 2nd edn. 1900.

> Includes a selective bibliography. Cf. Milton Rubicam, ed. *Genealogical research, methods and sources.* American Soc. of Genealogists (Washington, 1960). Leslie G. Pine, *The genealogists' encyclopedia* (Newton Abbot, 1969).

522 RYE (WALTER). Records and record searching: a guide to the genealogist and topographer. Lond. etc. 1888. 2nd edn. 1897. *

523 SIMS (RICHARD). A manual for the genealogist, topographer, antiquary, and legal professor. . . . Lond. 1856. 2nd edn. 1861. New edn. 1888.

Used manuscript collections in the British Museum. The three editions are printed from the same plates.

524 SOCIETY OF GENEALOGISTS OF LONDON. The genealogists' handbook: being an introduction to the pursuit of genealogy. Lond. 1937. 3rd impression 1948. 4th edn. by Peter Spufford and A. J. Camp. Lond. 1967. 5th edn. 1969.

525 STUART (MARGARET). Scottish family history: a guide to works of reference on the history and genealogy of Scottish families . . . to which is prefixed an essay on how to write the history of a family, by Sir James B. Paul. Edin. etc. 1930.

526 THOMSON (THEODORE R.). A catalogue of British family histories. Lond. 1928. 2nd edn. 1935.

527 WAGNER (ANTHONY R.). English genealogy. Oxf. 1960. 2nd edn. 1971.

A general survey; includes references to source materials and to the methods of genealogists. Pages 277–354 give a description of the sources and literature of genealogical study. A résumé sketching the principal outlines of this important book but lacking its critical apparatus is provided in a paperback: A. R. Wagner, *English ancestry* (Lond. 1961).

2. Dictionaries and Reference Works

528 CALENDARIUM GENEALOGICUM, Henry III–Edward I. Ed. by Charles Roberts. Rolls Series. 2 vols. Lond. 1865.

529 CAMPBELL (JOHN). The lives of the chief justices of England. 3 vols. Lond. 1849–57. 3rd edn. 4 vols. 1874.

530 CAMPBELL (JOHN). The lives of the lord chancellors of England. 8 vols. Lond. 1845–69. 4th edn. 10 vols. 1856–7. *

531 DICTIONARY OF NATIONAL BIOGRAPHY. Ed. by Leslie Stephen and Sidney Lee. 63 vols. Lond. 1885–1900. Supplement. 3 vols. 1901. Index and epitome. 1903. Errata. 1904. New edn. in 22 vols. 1908–9. Second supplement. 3 vols. 1912. Index and epitome. 1913. Reprinted in 24 vols. 1921–7. Supplement. 1912–30. Ed. by H. W. C. Davis and J. R. H. Weaver. 2 vols. 1927–37. Supplement. 1931–40. Ed. by L. G. W. Legg. 1949. Supplement. 1941–50. Ed. by L. G. W. Legg and E. T. Williams. 1959.

For supplementary materials, see *B.I.H.R.* vol. i+. *The concise Dictionary* (*The Dictionary of National Biography*), *part 1, From the beginnings to 1900: being an epitome of the main work and its supplement* (Lond. 1903). Reprinted.

532 EMDEN (ALFRED B.). A biographical register of the university of Cambridge to 1500. Cambr. 1963.

533 EMDEN (ALFRED B.). A biographical register of the university of Oxford to A.D. 1500. 3 vols. Oxf. 1957-9.

Corrections and Additions: *Bodleian Library Record*, vi (1957-61), 668-88; vii (1962-7), 149-64.

534 FOSS (EDWARD). The judges of England. 9 vols. Lond. 1848-64. * Abridged under the title: Biographia juridica, a biographical dictionary of the judges of England, 1066-1870. Lond. 1870. *

For justices of the reigns of Edw. I-III, see Sayles, No. 3510, and for individual justices, Nos. 3685-93.

535 GEORGE (HEREFORD B.). Genealogical tables illustrative of modern history. Oxf. 1874. 6th edn. by J. R. H. Weaver. 1930.

536 GRANT (FRANCIS J.). Court of the Lord Lyon: list of His Majesty's officers of arms and other officials with genealogical notes, 1318-1945. Scottish Record Soc. Edin. 1945.

537 HANDBOOK OF BRITISH CHRONOLOGY. Ed. by Sir Maurice Powicke and E. B. Fryde. 2nd edn. Lond. 1961. (No. 371).

538 HAYDN (JOSEPH). The book of dignities, containing lists of the official personages of the British empire from the earliest periods to the present time. Lond. 1851. 3rd edn. 1894. Reprinted. Bath. 1969.

Better for modern times than for the Middle Ages; superseded by Powicke's *Handbook* (No. 537).

539 O'FLANAGAN (JAMES R.). The lives of the lord chancellors and keepers of the great seal of Ireland. 2 vols. Lond. 1870. *

540 OWEN (WILLIAM). The Cambrian biography: or historical notices of celebrated men among the ancient Britons. Lond. 1803.

541 RUSSELL (JOSIAH C.). Dictionary of writers of thirteenth century England. *B.I.H.R.* Special Supplement 3. Lond. 1936.

For additions and corrections, see No. 6909.

542 (WELSH BIOGRAPHICAL DICTIONARY). Y BYWGRAFFIADUR CYMREIGHYD 1940; paratowyd dan nawdd Anrhydeddus Gymdeithas y Cymmrodorion. Llundain. 1953.

Translated into English as *The dictionary of Welsh biography down to 1940* (Lond. 1959).

543 WRIGHT (THOMAS). Biographia Britannica Literaria. Anglo-Saxon period. Lond. 1842. Reprinted. Anglo-Norman period. Lond. 1846. Reprinted.

3. *Family History*

(*a*) Royalty

544 BARTRUM (PETER C.). 'Pedigrees of the kings and princes of Wales'. *B.B.C.S.* xix (1961), 201-25. Idem, *Nat. Lib. Wales Jour.* xiii (1963), 93-146; xv (1967), 157-66.

545 BURKE (JOHN) and BURKE (JOHN BERNARD). The royal families of England, Scotland, and Wales, with their descendants. 2 vols. Lond. 1848–51. Index by A. G. C. Fane. Lond. 1932.

The genealogical data cannot always be trusted.

546 GREEN (MARY A. E.). Lives of the princesses of England from the Norman Conquest. 6 vols. Lond. 1849–55. Reprinted 1957.

This work displays considerable research.

547 SISAM (KENNETH). 'Anglo-Saxon royal genealogies'. *P.B.A.* xxxix (1953), 287–348.

Sisam's study is of first importance. See also G. H. Wheeler, 'The genealogy of early West Saxon kings', *E.H.R.* xxxvi (1921), 161–71. See Stenton in *Poole essays* (No. 1448).

548 STRICKLAND (AGNES). Lives of the queens of England, from the Norman conquest. 12 vols. Lond. 1840–8. New edn. 8 vols. 1851–2, and 6 vols. 1864–5.

549 WILLIAMS (ROBERT F.). Lives of the princes of Wales . . . Vol. i (to 1376). Lond. 1843.

(b) Titles of honour and pedigrees

550 ANSTIS (JOHN). Register of the Most Noble Order of the Garter. 2 vols. Lond. 1724.

John Anstis, the elder, was Garter King of Arms 1715–50.

551 BANKS (THOMAS C.). The dormant and extinct baronage of England . . . 4 vols. Lond. 1807–37.

This work originally appeared in 3 vols. (1807–9). In 1837 his *Stemmata Anglicana* (1825), which contained some emendations and additions to the *Baronage*, was published as a fourth volume.

552 BELTZ (GEORGE F.). Memorials of the order of the Garter from its foundation to the present time, with biographical notices of the knights of the reigns of Edward III and Richard II. Lond. 1841.

Cf. Edmund H. Fellowes, *The knights of the Garter 1348–1939 with a complete list of the stall-plates in St. George's Chapel* (Lond. 1940). S. L. Ollard is the general editor of a series Historical monographs relating to St. George's Chapel, Windsor Castle.

553 BURKE (JOHN), (JOHN BERNARD), and (ASHWORTH PETER). A genealogical and heraldic dictionary of the peerage and baronetage of the British empire. Lond. 1826. 100th edn. thoroughly revised. 1953. 101st edn. by L. G. Pine, 1956. 104th edn. 1967.

This well-known work, at least in earlier editions, should be used with caution; see Wagner, *Eng. geneal.* (No. 527), pp. 339–43. For the untitled, see John Burke, *A genealogical and heraldic history of the commoners of Great Britain and Ireland*, 4 vols. (Lond. 1833–8; continued as *Burke's genealogical and heraldic history of the landed gentry of Great Britain*), 3 vols. (Lond. 1847–9, and later editions; 17th edn. by L. G. Pine, 1952; Supplement, 1954. 18th edn. 1965 in progress). 18th edn. Vol. i (1965); Vol. ii (1969); Vol. iii to come.

554 CLAY (JOHN W.). The extinct and dormant peerages of the northern counties of England. Lond. 1913.

555 CLEVELAND (DUCHESS OF) C. L. W. ROWLETT. The Battle Abbey roll. 3 vols. Lond. 1889.

> Deals with the pedigrees of many noble families; professes to be a list of the principal followers of William the Conqueror who took part in the battle of Hastings. The original is not extant (it was borrowed from the abbot of Battle by Henry V and was never returned), and the various copies have little historical value.

556 C[OKAYNE] (GEORGE EDWARD). Complete peerage of England, Scotland, Ireland, Great Britain, and United Kingdom, extant, extinct, or dormant. By G. E. C. 8 vols. Lond. 1887–98. New edn. revised and much enlarged, by Vicary Gibbs, H. A. Doubleday, Duncan Warrand, Lord Howard de Walden, Geoffrey H. White. 12 vols. (Vol. xii is in two parts.) Lond. 1910–59. Vol. xiii deals with peerage creations, 1901–38.

> This most comprehensive and scholarly work is important for the medievalist, for biographical information. Of the numerous appendices, the titles of all of which are given in vol. xii, pt. ii, the following deal with subjects more general than a single family:
> *a.* Vol. ii, App. C, pp. 597–602. The battle of Boroughbridge and the Boroughbridge roll.
> *b.* Vol. iv, App. H, pp. 649–760. Earldoms and baronies in history and law, and the doctrine of abeyance.
> *c.* Vol. x, App. F, pp. 47–90. The office of Lord Great Chamberlain of England.
> *d.* Vol. x, App. G, pp. 91–9. Rise of the Marshal.
> *e.* Vol. xi, App. B, pp. 7–38. The battle of Bannockburn.
> *f.* Vol. xi, App. C, pp. 39–104. Heralds of the nobility.
> *g.* Vol. xi, App. D, pp. 105–21. Henry I's illegitimate children.
> *h.* Vol. xii, pt. i, App. L, pp. 35–48. The battle of Hastings and the death of Harold (and Companions of the Conqueror).
> *i.* Vol. xii, pt. ii, App. J, pp. 32–9. The princes in the Tower.
> *j.* Vol. xii, pt. ii, App. K, pp. 40–4. Problems of the Bayeux Tapestry.

557 COLLINS (ARTHUR). The peerage of England. Lond. 1709. New edn. by S. E. Brydges. 9 vols. Lond. 1812. *

> For significance and criticism, see Wagner, *Eng. geneal.* (No. 527), pp. 328–9.

558 DOYLE (JAMES E.). The official baronage of England, showing the succession, dignities, and offices of every peer from 1066 to 1885. . . . 3 vols. Lond. 1886.

> Valuable, but deals only with the higher grades of peerage, giving the offices held by dukes, marquises, earls, and viscounts.

559 DUGDALE (WILLIAM). The baronage of England. 2 vols. Lond. 1675–6.

> Though many of Dugdale's pedigrees are wrong, his work remains of value for its references, especially for the post-Norman periods.

560 ELLIS (ROBERT GEOFFREY). Earldoms in fee: a study in peerage law and history. Lond. 1963.

561 FOSTER (JOSEPH). The peerage, baronetage and knightage of the British Empire. 5 vols. Lond. 1879–83. Idem, Collectanea genealogica. 20 pts. Lond. etc.

1881–5. Idem, Pedigrees of the county families of England. Vol. i, Lancashire. Lond. 1873. Idem, Pedigrees of the county families of Yorkshire. 4 vols. Lond. 1874–5.

562 GRIFFITH (JOHN E.). Pedigrees of Anglesey and Caernarvonshire families with their collateral branches in Denbighshire, Merionethshire and other parts. Horncastle. 1914.

563 HUNTER (JOSEPH), ed. Familiae minorum gentium. Harleian Soc. Pubns. xxxvii–xl. 4 vols. Lond. 1894–96. Hunter's pedigrees, a continuation of Familiae minorum gentium. Ed. by J. W. Walker. ibid. lxxxviii. 1936. Yorkshire pedigrees. Ed. by J. W. Walker. ibid. civ–xcvi. 3 vols. 1942–4. Lincolnshire pedigrees. Ed. by A. R. Maddison. ibid. l, li, lii, lv. 4 vols. 1902–6.

564 LOYD (LEWIS C.). The origins of some Anglo-Norman families. Ed. by C. T. Clay and D. C. Douglas. Harleian Soc. Pubns. ciii. Leeds. 1951.

For bibliography on the subject of the Companions of the Conqueror, see the references cited by J. F. A. Mason in *E.H.R.* lxxi (1956), 61–9; and Wagner (No. 527), pp. 51–83; and the important article by D. C. Douglas, 'Companions of the Conqueror', *History*, xxvii (1943), 129–47. Also Stenton, *Preparatory . . . to A.S. Eng.* (No. 1496), pp. 325–34.

565 MacLYSAGHT (EDWARD). Irish families, their names, arms and origins. Illustrated with arms in colour. 2nd edn. Dublin. 1957. Idem, More Irish families. Galway. 1960. Idem, Supplement to Irish families. Dublin. 1964.

566 MOOR (CHARLES). Knights of Edward I. Harleian Soc. Pubns. lxxx–lxxxiv. 5 vols. 1929–32.

567 O'BRIEN (MICHAEL A.), ed. Corpus genealogiarum Hiberniae. Dublin Inst. Advanced Stud. Dublin. 1962.

See review and commentary by John V. Kelleher, 'The pre-Norman Irish genealogies', *Irish Hist. Stud.* xvi (1968), 138–53.

568 PAUL (JAMES BALFOUR), ed. Scots peerage, founded on Wood's edition of Sir Robert Douglas's Peerage of Scotland: containing an historical and genealogical account of the nobility of that kingdom. Edin. 1904–14.

569 ROUND (JOHN HORACE). Studies in peerage and family history. Westminster. 1901. Idem, Peerage and pedigree; studies in peerage law and family history. 2 vols. Lond. 1910. Idem, Family origins and other studies. Ed. by W. Page. Lond. 1930.

570 SANDERS (IVOR J.). English baronies: a study of their origin and descent: 1086–1327. Oxf. 1960.

A mine of data on the descent of baronies through families; some errors have crept in among the details.

571 SELDEN (JOHN). Titles of honour. Lond. 1614. 3rd edn. 1672. Also printed in *Works of Selden*, vol. iii. Lond. 1726.

Part i deals with titles of kings or rulers; part ii with inferior titles, particularly Chap v, pp. 627–854.

572 SHAW (WILLIAM A.). The knights of England; a complete record from the earliest time to the present day of the knights of all the orders of chivalry in England, Scotland, and Ireland, and of knights bachelors . . . 2 vols. Lond. 1906.

573 SHIRLEY (EVELYN P.). The noble and gentle men of England. Westminster. 1859. 3rd edn. 1866.

574 WALFORD (EDWARD). The county families of the United Kingdom; or the Royal manual of the titled and untitled aristocracy of England, Wales, Scotland, and Ireland . . . Lond. 1860+.

4. *Personal Names: Guides and Indexes*

The most useful general dictionary of surnames is that by Reaney (No. 586).

See *English Place-Name Society Journal* (No. 623).

575 BARBER (HENRY). British family names: their origin and meaning. Lond. 1894. 2nd edn. 1902.

'A mere collection of guesses unsupported by evidence' (Reaney).

576 BLACK (GEORGE F.). The surnames of Scotland: their origin, meaning and history. N.Y. 1946.

This dictionary of Scottish names was first published in *Bull. N.Y. Pub. Library*, vols. xlvii–l (1943–6).

577 EKWALL (EILERT). Early London personal names. Lund. 1947.

578 EWEN (CECIL H. L.). A history of surnames of the British Isles: a concise account of their origin, evolution, etymology and legal status. Lond. 1931. Idem, A guide to the origin of British surnames. Lond. 1938.

Cf. Richard W. Emery, 'A further note on medieval surnames', *Medievalia et Humanistica*, ix (1955), 104–6.

579 FEILITZEN (OLOF VON). The pre-Conquest personal names of Domesday Book. Uppsala. 1937.

Cf. M. Hofmann, *Die Französierung des Personennamenschatzes im Domesday Book des Grafschaften Hampshire und Sussex* (Murnau, 1934). G. F. Jensen, *Scandinavian personal names in Lincolnshire and Yorkshire* (Copenhagen, 1968).

580 FORSSNER (THORVALD). Continental-Germanic personal names in England in old and middle English times. Uppsala. 1916.

581 FRANSSON (GUSTAV). Middle English surnames of occupation, 1100–1350, with an excursus on toponymical surnames. Lund Studies in English, iii. Lund etc. 1935.

Supplements *Onomasticon Anglo-Saxonicum* (No. 589).

582 GENTRY (THOMAS G.). Family names from the Irish, Anglo-Saxon, Anglo-Norman and Scotch considered in relation to their etymology . . . Philadelphia. 1892.

583 KNEEN (JOHN J.). The personal names of the Isle of Man. Lond. 1937.

Cf. Arthur W. Moore, *The surnames and place-names of the Isle of Man* (Lond. 1890. 2nd rev. edn. 1903).

584 LÖFVENBERG (MATTIAS T.). Studies on Middle English local surnames. Lund Studies in English, xi. Lund etc. 1942.

585 LOWER (MARK A.). English surnames: essays on family nomenclature ... Lond. 1842. 4th edn. 2 vols. 1875. Idem, Patronimica Britannica: a dictionary of the family names of the United Kingdom. Lond. 1860.

586 REANEY (PERCY H.). A dictionary of British surnames. Lond. 1958. Idem, The origin of English surnames. Lond. 1967.

587 REDIN (MATS A.). Studies on uncompounded personal names in Old English. Uppsala. [1919].

Cf. Hilmer Ström, *Old English personal names in Bede's History: an etymological-phonological investigation*, Lund Studies in English, viii (Lund, [1939]).

588 ROBINSON (FRED C.). 'The significance of names in Old English literature'. *Anglia*, lxxxvi (1968), 14–58.

589 SEARLE (WILLIAM G.). Onomasticon Anglo-Saxonicum: a list of Anglo-Saxon proper names [i.e. of persons], from the time of Beda to that of King John. Cambr. 1897.

Severely criticized in the *Athenaeum*, 22 Jan. 1898, p. 110; but still useful. Cf. J. M. Kemble, 'The names, surnames, and nicnames of the Anglosaxons', *Royal Archaeol. Institute of Great Britain, Proceedings at Winchester, 1845* (London, 1846), pp. 81–102.

590 TENGVIK (GÖSTA). Old English bynames. Uppsala. 1938.

591 WITHYCOMBE (ELIZABETH G.). The Oxford history of English Christian names. Oxf. 1945. Reprinted, with corrections. 1948.

Cf. Charlotte M. Yonge, *History of Christian names*, 2 vols. (Lond. 1863). New edn. 1 vol. (1884).

G. GEOGRAPHY AND PLACE-NAMES

The fundamental geographical studies are listed in the excellent annotated bibliography by John K. Wright and Elizabeth T. Platt, *Aids to geographical research*, 2nd edn. N.Y. 1947. The most serviceable current bibliography is *Bibliographie géographique internationale* (*1893–1962), beginning in 1891 and now published annually under the auspices of L'Union géographique Internationale (UNESCO), Paris. Both of these works include studies on Great Britain. See also *Handbook for geography teachers*, edited by George J. Cons (Lond. Univ. Institute of Education, Lond. 1955), a later edition of a work first edited in 1932 by Dorothy M. Forsaith.

The principal journals for British geography are:

i. *The Geographical Journal*, including the *Proceedings*, etc. published by the Royal Geographical Society, Lond. 1893+; with general indexes for every twenty volumes published in 1906, 1925, 1930, 1935, and 1951. This journal is the successor to *Journal of the Royal Geographical Society*, 1830–80 (and the Proceedings, 1855–92), with indexes of the *Journal* at the end of each decade.

ii. *The Scottish Geographical Magazine*, published by the Royal Scottish Geographical Society, Edin. 1885+; with index to vols. i–l (1885–1934), 1935.

The three most serviceable general accounts, each for a different viewpoint are Mackinder (No. 619), Demangeon (No. 611), and Sölch (No. 620).

The principal maps drawn in Britain in the Middle Ages are those of Matthew Paris (No. 596), the Gough map in the Bodleian (No. 602), and the World Map at Hereford Cathedral (No. 606).

See also E. J. Davis and E. G. R. Taylor's *Guide to periodicals and bibliographies dealing with geography* (No. 716); and Wright and Platt, op. cit. pp. 186–9.

1. *Dictionaries, Gazetteers, and Maps*

592 BARTHOLOMEW (JOHN), ed. Gazetteer of the British Isles, statistical and topographical. Edin. 1887. New edn. by J. G. Bartholomew: Survey gazetteer of the British Isles . . . Lond. 1904. 9th edn. Edin. 1943. *

593 BAUDRILLART (ALFRED), MEYER (ALBERT DE), AUBERT (R.), and CAUWENBERGH (ÉTIENNE VAN), eds. Dictionnaire d'histoire et de géographie ecclésiastiques. Vols. i–x (A–B). Paris. 1912–38. Vol. xi, fasc. 61–6 (C–Catulensis), 1939–49. Vol. xii, fasc. 67–93 (Catulinus-Ferdinand). 1950–67.

594 BRABNER (JOHN H. F.), ed. The comprehensive gazetteer of England and Wales. 6 vols. Lond. 1893–5.

595 EARLY MAPS OF THE BRITISH ISLES A.D. 1000–1579. Ed. by Gerald R. Crone. Royal Geog. Soc. Lond. 1961.

596 EARLY MAPS OF GREAT BRITAIN. i. The Matthew Paris maps, by J. B. Mitchell. ii. The Gough map, by R. A. Pelham, (cf. No. 602). iii. Aegidius Tschudi's maps, by Edward Heawood. *Geog. Jour.* lxxxi (1933), 27–45.

597 GROOME (FRANCIS H.), ed. Ordnance gazetteer of Scotland: a survey of Scottish topography, statistical, biographical and historical. 3 vols. Edin. 1886. New edn. in 6 vols. Lond. 1895. Another edn. containing all the printed matter of the six-volume edn. with its revisions etc. Edin. 1901.

598 HONEYBOURNE (MARJORIE B.). Sketch map of London under Richard II. Lond. Topographical Soc. Pubn. No. 93. 1960.
See *Lond. Topographical Record*, xxxii (1965), 29–76.

599 INGLIS (HARRY R. G.), MATHIESON (JOHN), and WATSON (C. B. B.). The early maps of Scotland, with an account of the Ordnance Survey. Edin. 1934. 2nd edn. revised. 1936.

600 LEWIS (SAMUEL). A topographical dictionary of England . . . 4 vols. Lond. 1831. 7th edn. 1849. * Idem, A topographical dictionary of Ireland. 2 vols.

Lond. 1837. * 2nd edn. 1842. Idem, A topographical dictionary of Scotland. 2 vols. Lond. 1846. 2nd edn. 1851. Idem, A topographical dictionary of Wales. 2 vols. Lond. 1833. 4th edn. 1849.

Still of use for historical information.

601   LONGNON (AUGUSTE). Atlas historique de la France depuis César (à 1380). Bks. i–iii. Paris. 1885–89.

Invaluable as far as it goes; accompanied by a volume of explanatory text.

602   THE MAP OF GREAT BRITAIN *c.* A.D. 1360, issued by the Bodleian Library in association with the Royal Geographical Society. Oxf. 1958.

A facsimile of the Gough map, the earliest known road map of Britain, with an introductory booklet by E. J. S. Parsons. Cf. No. 596.

603   MILLER (KONRAD). Mappaemundi: die ältesten Weltkarten herausgegeben und erläutert. 6 pts. Stuttgart. 1895–8.

604   ORDNANCE SURVEY MAPS. Printed and published by the Director of the Ordnance Survey. Southampton and Chessington.

Among the numerous Ordnance Survey Maps are four which specify historical antiquities. These are drawn 10 or 16 miles to one inch. Where there are two sheets, the line of division is through the counties of Durham and Westmorland; hence the North Sheet includes Scotland and Northern Ireland. A brief, but authoritative, commentary accompanies each sheet. Professional Papers dealing with historical antiquities and including maps are published under the same authority. See No. 1965. Consult *The historian's guide to Ordnance Survey maps*, by J. B. Harley and C. W. Phillips (Lond. 1964) (reprinted from the *Amateur Historian*).

(*a*) Map of Roman Britain. 3rd edn. 1956.
(*b*) Map of Britain in the dark ages (410–871).
    South Sheet, 1935; new edn. 1939.
    North Sheet, 1938.
(*c*) Ancient Britain: a map of the major visible antiquities older than A.D. 1066.
    South Sheet, 1951.
    North Sheet, 1951.
    Cf. map of Southern Britain in the Iron Age, 1962.
(*d*) Map of Monastic Britain.
    South Sheet (1066–1547), 2nd edn. 1954; prepared by R. N. Hadcock. Maps of the monasteries of England and Wales are attached to Knowles and Hadcock (No. 1299).
    North Sheet (eleventh to sixteenth centuries), 2nd edn. 1955; prepared by D. E. Easson. Maps of the monasteries of Scotland are attached to Easson (No. 1299).

605   POOLE (REGINALD L.), ed. Historical atlas of modern Europe from the decline of the Roman empire . . . Oxf. etc. (1896)–1902. 90 maps.

Roman Britain, by F. J. Haverfield.
England and Wales before 1066, by W. H. Stevenson.
England and Wales in 1086, by James Tait.
England and Wales under Edward I, by T. F. Tout.
Anglia sacra. temp. Edw. I, by C. W. C. Oman.
England and Wales under the house of Lancaster, by James Tait.
Anglia monastica, by A. M. Cooke.
Parliamentary representation, England and Wales, to 1832, by G. W. Prothero.
Early Ireland, by G. H. Orpen.

606 THE WORLD MAP BY RICHARD OF HALDINGHAM IN HERE-
FORD CATHEDRAL, with a memoir by G. R. Crone. Royal Geog. Soc.
Reproductions of Early Manuscript Maps, III. Lond. 1953.

For further comment on this almost full-scale, beautiful reproduction, consult N.
Denholm-Young, 'The Mappamundi of Richard of Haldingham at Hereford', *Speculum*,
xxxii (1957), 307–14.

2. Treatises

607 BERESFORD (MAURICE). The lost villages of England. Lond. 1954.

607A BRITTON (CHARLES E.). A meteorological chronology to A.D. 1450.
Geophysical Memoirs, no. 70. H.M.S.O. 1937.

608 BOWEN (EMRYS G.), ed. Wales: a physical, historical and regional
geography. Lond. 1957.

609 CAMDEN (WILLIAM). Britannia: a chronological description of Great
Britain and Ireland together with the adjacent islands. Lond. 1586. 6th edn. 1607.
Trans. by Edmund Gibson. 2 vols. Lond. 1722; and by Richard Gough. 3 vols.
1789. 2nd edn. 4 vols. 1806. *

Cf. Stuart Piggott, 'William Camden and the Britannia', *P.B.A.* xxxvii (1951), 197–217;
Sir Maurice Powicke, 'William Camden', *Eng. Stud.* (1948), 67–84.

610 DARBY (HENRY C.), ed. An historical geography of England before
1800. Cambr. 1936.

Includes 14 studies, by divers hands; the best brief account. Cf. H. C. Darby, 'Historical
geography of England twenty years after', *Geographical Jour.* cxxvi (1960), 147–59. See
Darby, *Domesday Geography* (No. 1465).

611 DEMANGEON (ALBERT). Les îles britanniques. Géographie Univer-
selle. Ed. by P. Vidal de la Blache and L. Gallois. Vol. i. Paris. 1927. Trans. by
E. D. Laborde: The British Isles. Lond. 1939. 3rd edn. 1952.

612 FLEURE (HERBERT J.). A natural history of man in Britain, conceived
as a study of changing relations between men and environment. Lond. 1951.

613 FOX (CYRIL). The personality of Britain: its influence on inhabitant and
invader in prehistoric and early historic times. 4th edn. Cardiff. 1943.

See No. 1988 and Bonser, *A.–S.C.B.* (No. 12), index under Fox.

614 FREEMAN (EDWARD A.). The historical geography of Europe. 2 vols.
Lond. 1881. 3rd edn. by J. B. Bury. 1903.

615 GENTLEMAN'S MAGAZINE LIBRARY: English topography. Ed. by
George L. Gomme. Lond. 1891–1905.

These are vols. xii–xxix of the total work. For other volumes see Nos. 122; 769.

616 GOUGH (RICHARD). British topography: or, An historical account of
what has been done for illustrating the topographical antiquities of Great Britain
and Ireland. 2 vols. Lond. 1780.

See also No. 115 for *Collectanea topographica*, ed. by J. G. Nichols.

617 HOSKINS (WILLIAM G.). The making of the English landscape. Lond. 1955.

Deals in 240 pages with the historical evolution of the English landscape; strong on the Middle Ages; a scholarly popularization of indoor research and outdoor fieldwork. Forms an introduction to the series on individual counties, entitled *The making of the English landscape,* each volume of which contains numerous illustrations (No. 1517). Cf. *Medieval England* (No. 1485), pp. 1–36.

618 LYSONS (DANIEL) and LYSONS (SAMUEL). Magna Britannia; being a concise topographical account of the several counties of Great Britain. 6 vols. Lond. 1806–22. ★

Excellent in quality, especially the account of Roman remains. Vol. i: Beds. Berks. Bucks.; vol. ii: Cambs. Cheshire; vol. iii: Cornwall; vol. iv: Cumberland; vol. v: Derbyshire; vol. vi: Devonshire.

619 MACKINDER (HALFORD J.). Britain and the British seas. N.Y. 1902. ★

620 SÖLCH (JOHANN). Die Landschaften der Britischen Inseln. Erster Band: England und Wales. Vienna. 1951.

Detailed regional geography; ranks with Mackinder and Demangeon.

621 STAMP (LAURENCE D.). Man and the land. Lond. 1955.

The modifications of the rural landscape from the Ice Age to the present. See also idem, *British structure and scenery,* 2nd edn (Lond. 1947); and Patrick W. Bryan, *Man's adaptation of nature: studies of the cultural landscape* (Lond. 1933).

621A TITOW (J. Z.). 'Evidence of weather in the account rolls of the bishopric of Winchester, 1209–1350', *Econ. Hist. Rev.* 2nd Ser. xii (1960), 360–407. Idem, 'Histoire et climat dans l'évêché de Winchester, 1350–1450', *Annales,* 25e année (1970), 312–50.

See Britton (No. 607A); and H. H. Lamb, *The changing climate* (Lond. 1966).

3. *Place-names*

Over the past four decades, the publications on the study of place-names have been numerous; they are particularly valuable for the Anglo-Saxon period. Extensive bibliographies can be found in Bonser (No. 12), pt. vii, nos. 6283–6953, and in the publications of the English Place-Name Society (No. 623), whose editors along with Eilert Ekwall are the outstanding authorities. Ekwall's *Dictionary* (No. 632) is basic. Extensive selective references are given in the convenient surveys by Cameron (No. 629) and Reaney (No. 635) and in Roberts (No. 625). See also personal names, pp. 70–1. *Onoma,* Journal of International Committee on Onomastic Sciences (Louvain), carries a detailed bibliography annually, country by country.

622 DINNSEANCHAS. Journal of the Irish Place-Name Society. Dublin. 1964+.

623 ENGLISH PLACE-NAME SOCIETY. Publications. General editors: A. Mawer and F. M. Stenton (vols. i–xix), Bruce Dickins (xx–xxii), A. H. Smith (xxiii–xliii), and K. Cameron (xliv+). Cambr. 1924+. Journal i+. 1968/9+.

> The publications are listed in Mullins, *Texts*, pp. 146–7. Subsequent volumes are xxvii–xxix for Derbyshire; xxx–xxxvii for Yorkshire West Riding; xxviii–xli for Gloucestershire; xlii–xliii for Westmorland; xliv for Cheshire. The general volumes are vol. i (two parts), Introduction to the survey of English place-names (1924), and vols. xxv–xxvi, English place-name elements by A. H. Smith (1956). By 1969, twenty-six counties were represented in 45 volumes. The *Journal* includes the annual report, addenda, and corrigenda for previous publications, an annual bibliography of books, articles, and reviews on place-names, and an occasional review.

624 NAMN OCH BYGD. Tidskrift för nordisk ortnamnsforskning. Uppsala. 1913+.

625 ROBERTS (R. J.). 'Bibliography of writings in English place names and personal names' (to 1959). *Onoma*, Journal of International Committee on Onomastic Sciences (Louvain), viii (1958–9), *1–*82.

626 STUDIA NEOPHILOLOGICA: a journal of Germanic and Romanic philology. Uppsala. 1928+.

627 WOOLLEY (JOHN S.). Bibliography for Scottish linguistic studies. Edin. 1954.

> Has a large section on place-name studies. Consult the *Transactions* and *Proceedings* of the Gaelic Society of Inverness, the *Scottish Geographical Magazine* (p. 72), and the *Celtic Rev.* (No. 316) for articles on Scottish place-names.

628 ANDERSON (afterwards ANDERSON-ARNGART) (OLOF S.). The English hundred-names. (Yorks., Lancs., and Midlands.) *Lunds Universitets Årsskrift*, N.F. Avd. i. 30. No. 1. Lund. 1934. Idem, The English hundred-names: the south-western counties. Ibid. 35. No. 5. Lund etc. 1939. Idem, The English hundred-names: the south-eastern counties, with a survey of elements found in hundred-names and a chapter on the origin of the hundred. Ibid. 37. No. 1. Lund etc. 1941.

> The latter includes an index to the hundred-names of all England. Anderson's work 'makes a solid contribution to the history of English governmental divisions and of the hundred court' (Cam).

629 CAMERON (KENNETH). English place-names. Lond. 1961. Reprinted, 1969.

630 COPLEY (GORDON J.). English place-names and their origin. Newton Abbot. 1968. New edn. 1971.

631 DICKINS (BRUCE). 'The progress of English place-name studies since 1901'. *Antiquity*, xxxv (1961), 281–5.

632 EKWALL (EILERT). The concise Oxford dictionary of English place-names. Oxf. 1936. 3rd edn. 1947. 4th edn. 1960.

> The standard dictionary by a foremost authority. Of Ekwall's many works, note the following: *Studies on English place- and personal-names* (Lund, 1931); *Studies on English place-names* (Stockholm, 1936); *Etymological notes on English place-names* (Lund, 1959);

Street names of the City of London (Oxf. 1954); *English river-names* (Oxf. 1928); 'Selected papers', *Lund Stud. in English*, xxxiii (1963). Cf. Olaf von Feilitzen, 'The published writings of Eilert Ekwall: a bibliography', *Lund Stud. in English*, xxx (1962).

633 LINDKVIST (H.). Middle-English place-names of Scandinavian origin. Uppsala. 1912.

634 MAWER (ALLEN). Problems of place-name study: being a course of three lectures delivered at King's College under the auspices of the University of London. Lond. 1929.

Mawer's paper on field-names in Tait essays (No. 1455).

635 REANEY (PERCY H.). The origin of English place-names. Lond. 1960.

636 STENTON (FRANK M.). 'The historical bearing of place-names studies'. *T.R.H.S.* 4th Ser. xxi (1939), 1–19; xxii (1940), 1–22; xxiii (1941), 1–24; xxiv (1942), 1–24; xxv (1943), 1–13; xxvii (1945), 1–12.

i. England in the sixth century; ii. The English occupation of southern Britain; iii. Anglo-Saxon heathenism; iv. The Danish settlement of eastern England; v. The place of women in Anglo-Saxon society; vi. The Scandinavian colonies in England and Normandy. See also John McN. Dodgson, 'The significance of the distribution of the English place-names in -ingas, -inga, in south-east England', *Medieval Archaeology*, x (1966), 1–29.

637 SMITH (ALBERT H.). English place-name elements. English Place-Name Society, xxv, xxvi. Cambr. 1956.

See review by E. Ekwall in *Namn Och Bygd* (No. 624), xlv (1958), 133–46. Cf. A. H. Smith, 'Place-names and the Anglo-Saxon settlement', *P.B.A.* xlii (1956), 67–88.

638 ZACHRISSON (ROBERT E.). Some instances of Latin influence on English place-names. Lund. 1910.

Cf. Bruce Dickins, 'Latin additions to place and parish-names of England and Wales', *Leeds Philos. and Lit. Soc. Procs.* (Lit. and Hist. Section), iii, pt. vi (Leeds, 1935), 334–41.

639 MOORE (ARTHUR W.). The surnames and place-names of the Isle of Man. Lond. 1890. 2nd edn.: Manx names; or, The surnames etc. Lond. 1903.

640 A GAZETTEER OF WELSH PLACE-NAMES. Ed. by Elwyn Davies. Prepared for the Language and Literature Section of the Board of Celtic Studies of the University of Wales. Cardiff. 1957.

The main body of the work is in Welsh (English key to limited vocabulary). See also S. Wales and Monmouth Record Soc. Pubns. ii, for a general account with an alphabetical list of the place-names of Cardiff, ed. by W. Rees and H. J. Randall (Cardiff, 1950). R. J. Thomas, *Enwau afonydd a nentydd Cymru* (Welsh river names) (Cardiff, 1938). Ifor Williams, *Enwau Lleoedd* (Welsh place-names) (Liverpool, 1945). K. Jackson, *Language and history* (No. 320). On Welsh place-names, see Melville Richards in *Études celtiques*, xi (1967), 383–408; and in *Studia Celtica*, ii (1968), 29–90.

641 ALEXANDER (WILLIAM McC.). The place-names of Aberdeenshire. The Third Spalding Club. Aberdeen. 1952.

642 JOHNSON-FERGUSON (EDWARD A. J.). The place-names of Dumfriesshire. Dumfries. 1935.

643 WATSON (WILLIAM J.). History of the Celtic place-names of Scotland. Edin. 1926.

H. NUMISMATICS

Grierson (No. 647) provides a general bibliography to the whole subject of numismatics. Current literature can be traced in *Numismatic Literature* (No. 650) and in the *British Numismatic Journal* (No. 644). The best historical summary of coinage in Roman Britain is given by Sutherland (No. 665); for English coins the standard work is by G. C. Brooke (No. 673). The introductions to the various catalogues of coins in the British Museum (Nos. 661, 668, 672, 677, 678, 689) are valuable. Oman (No. 696) joins numismatics and history for the Anglo-Saxon and subsequent periods. Among recent writers of comprehensive histories of particular periods who have made extensive use of numismatic evidence are Richmond (No. 2049A), Collingwood–Myers (No. 2036), Hunter-Blair (No. 2493), Loyn (No. 2499), and Stenton (No. 2503). For recent research, see especially the numerous articles by R. H. M. Dolley (Nos. 677–79) and the Dolley–Pagan survey (No. 646). The most convenient handbook for beginners is by Seaby (No. 700). For Wales, R. I. Jack, *Medieval Wales* (No. 22), pp. 198–212.

1. *Bibliography and Journals*

644 BRITISH NUMISMATIC JOURNAL. By the British Numismatic Society. Lond. 1903+. Index of vols. i–x (1903–13) in x (1913), 393–402; vols. xi–xx (1915–30) in xx (1930), 397–410. There is an analytical index of articles on British coins by E. Harris in Seaby's *Bulletin* (No. 651) (1963), 95–103.

This most important journal for British numismatics is strong on medieval historical material.

645 CLAIN-STEFANELLI (ELVIRA E.). Select numismatic bibliography. N.Y. 1965.

646 DOLLEY (R. H. M.) and PAGAN (H.). (In) A Survey of numismatic research 1960–1965. International Numismatic Commission. Ed. by K. Skaare and G. C. Miles. ii. 174–202. Copenhagen. 1967.

647 GRIERSON (PHILIP). Bibliographie numismatique. *Cercle d'études numismatiques.* Brussels. 1966.

Grierson here issues a revised and much enlarged edition of his *Coins and medals: a select bibliography.* Helps for students of history, No. 56. Lond. 1954. The *Rapports* of the International Congress(es) of Numismatics include reports on Roman coins and medieval coins. For the Congress at Rome in 1961, H. and H. B. Mattingly and J. P. C. Kent reported on Roman coins and R. H. M. Dolley on British coins. For the Congress at Copenhagen in 1965, A. S. Robertson and M. R. Alföldi reported on Roman coins and R. H. M. Dolley on medieval coins.

648 NUMISMATIC CHRONICLE AND JOURNAL of the Royal Numismatic Society. Lond. 1838+. Index of vols. i–xx (1838–60) in vol. xx; thereafter, every tenth volume from 1870. Analytical index of articles on British coins 1900–61 by E. Harris in Seaby's *Bulletin*, no. 546 (1963), 368–75.

This periodical is a continuation of *Numismatic Journal*, 2 vols. (1836–8), and is a very valuable journal for British numismatics.

649 THE NUMISMATIC CIRCULAR. Lond. 1940+.

Formerly Spink's *Numismatic Circular*, i–xlvii (1892–1939).

650 NUMISMATIC LITERATURE. Published by the American Numismatic Society. N.Y. 1947/9+.

A half-yearly (formerly quarterly) annotated bibliography, valuable for current literature.

651 SEABY'S COIN AND MEDAL BULLETIN. Lond. 1946+.

2. *Particular Periods*

(*a*) Pre-Roman

652 ALLEN (DEREK F.). 'Belgic coins as illustrative of life in the late pre-Roman Iron Age of Britain'. *Procs. Prehistoric Soc.* xxiv (1955), 43–63. Idem, 'The Belgic dynasties of Britain and their coins'. *Archaeologia*, xc (1944), 1–46. Idem, 'The origins of coinage in Britain: a reappraisal'. *Problems of the iron age in southern Britain*. Lond. 1961. pp. 97–308.

653 BROOKE (G. C.). 'The distribution of Gaulish and British coins in Britain'. *Antiquity*, vii (1933), 268–89. Idem, 'The Philippus in the west and the Belgic invasions of Britain'. *Numismatic Chron.* 5th Ser. xiii (1933), 88–138.

654 EVANS (JOHN). The coins of the ancient Britons. Lond. 1864. Supplement. 1890.

The standard treatment.

655 MACK (RICHARD P.). The coinage of ancient Britain. Lond. 1953.

Well-organized summary.

656 MILNE (JOSEPH G.). Finds of Greek coins in the British Isles . . . Lond. 1948.

Notable critical analysis of coin finds.

(*b*) Roman

See Sylloge of Coins (No. 704).

657 COHEN (HENRY). Description historique des monnaies frappées sous l'empire romain . . . 7 vols. Paris. 1859–68. 2nd edn. 8 vols. 1880–92.

The second edition is much the better; but it is superseded by Mattingly and Sydenham (No. 662) so far as the latter has appeared.

658 EVANS (A.). 'Notes on the coinage and silver currency in Roman Britain from Valentinian I to Constantine III'. *Numis. Chron.* 4th Ser. xv (1915), 433–519.

659 LEEDS (EDWARD T.). A hoard of Roman folles from Diocletian's reform (A.D. 296) to Constantine Caesar, found at Fyfield, Berks. Oxf. 1946.

Specialized treatment of coins lacking mint-marks.

660 MACDONALD (GEORGE). 'Roman coins found in Scotland'. *Soc. Antiq. Scot. Procs.* lii (1917/18), 253–76; lviii (1923/4), 325–9.

661 MATTINGLY (HAROLD). Coins of the Roman empire in the British Museum. British Museum: Department of Coins and Medals. 5 vols. Lond. 1923–50. Vol. vi, by Robert A. G. Carson. 1962.

Important introductions.

662 MATTINGLY (HAROLD), SYDENHAM (EDWARD A.), *et al.* Roman imperial coinage. Vols. i–v and ix. Lond. 1923. In progress.

Important introductions.

663 O'NEIL (B. H. St. J.). 'A hoard of late Roman coins from Northamptonshire; its parallels and significance'. *Archaeol. Jour.* xc (1934), 282–305.

A seminal article.

664 ROBERTSON (ANNE S.). 'The numismatic evidence of Romano-British coin hoards', in *Essays in Roman coinage presented to Harold Mattingly.* Ed. by R. A. G. Carson and C. H. V. Sutherland. pp. 262–85. Oxf. 1956.

665 SUTHERLAND (CAROL HUMPHREY V.). Coinage and currency in Roman Britain. Lond. 1937.

The standard work.

666 SUTHERLAND (C. H. V.). Romano-British imitations of bronze coins of Claudius I. Amer. Numis. Soc. Numismatic Notes and Monographs. no. 65. N.Y. 1935.

667 TOYNBEE (JOCELYN M. C.). '"Britannia" on Roman coins of the second century A.D.' *Jour. Roman Stud.* xiv (1924), 142–57.

(c) From Roman to Tudor times
See Bonser's bibliographies, Nos. 12, 13

668 ALLEN (DEREK F.). A catalogue of English coins in the British Museum: the cross-and-crosslets ('Tealby') type of Henry II. Lond. 1951.

669 ANGLO-SAXON COINS. Studies presented to F. M. Stenton . . . Ed. by R. H. M. Dolley. Lond. 1961. (Fifteen papers by various scholars.) See No. 1454.

670 BEARDWOOD (ALICE). 'The royal mints and exchanges', in *The English government at work, 1327–1336* (No. 3836), iii. 35–66.

671 BLUNT (C. E.). 'The Anglo-Saxon coinage and the historian'. *Medieval Archaeology,* iv (1960), 1–15. Blunt *et al.* 'The coinage of southern England, 796–840'. *Brit. Numis. Jour.* xxxvii (1964), 1–74.

672 BROOKE (GEORGE C.). A catalogue of English coins in the British Museum: the Norman kings. 2 vols. Lond. 1916.

673 BROOKE (GEORGE C.). English coins from the seventh century to the present day. Lond. 1932. 3rd edn. revised by C. A. Whitton. 1950.

Authoritative treatise. The third edition is a reprint with a supplement.

674 BURNS (EDWARD). The coinage of Scotland. 3 vols. Edin. 1887.

Full descriptions of all issues.

675 COCHRAN-PATRICK (R. W.). Records of the coinage of Scotland. 2 vols. Edin. 1876.

676 CRAIG (JOHN). The mint. A history of the London mint from A.D. 287 to 1948. Cambr. 1953.

A valuable history with good bibliography, precise metrological data on virtually every English coin. T. F. Reddaway, 'The king's mint and exchange in London 1343–1543', *E.H.R.* lxxxii (1967), 1–23. For administrative malfeasance, see Mavis Mate, 'A mint of trouble, 1279–1307', *Speculum*, xliv (1969), 201–12.

677 DOLLEY (R. H. MICHAEL). 'Coinage' in Poole's *Medieval England* (No. 1485), pp. 264–99. Idem, Some reflections on Hildebrand Type A. of Aethelraed II. Stockholm. 1958. Idem, 'Some late Anglo-Saxon pence'. *British Museum Quarterly*, xix (1954), 59–64. The numerous recent articles by Dolley in *British Museum Quarterly*, *Numismatic Chronicle*, and elsewhere (e.g. Nos. 678, 679) must not be overlooked. For the popular British Museum Publications, Dolley has written *Anglo-Saxon Pennies* (1964) and *Viking Coins of the Danelaw and of Dublin* (1965).

678 DOLLEY (R. H. M.) and MORRISON (K. F.). The Carolingian coins in the British Museum. Lond. 1966.

679 DOLLEY (R. H. M.) and O'SULLIVAN (WILLIAM). 'The chronology of the first Anglo-Irish coinage' in *North Munster Studies: essays in commemoration of Msgr. Michael Moloney*. Ed. by Étienne Rynne. Limerick. 1967. pp. 437–78.

R. H. M. Dolley, 'The Irish mints of Edward I in the light of the coin-hoards from Ireland and Great Britain', *Procs. Royal Irish Acad.* sect. C. lxvi (1968), 235–97. See Anthony Dowle and Patrick Finn, *The guide book to the coinage of Ireland: from 995 A.D. to the present day* (Lond. 1969).

680 ENGEL (ARTHUR) and SERRURE (RAYMOND). Traité de numismatique du moyen âge. 3 vols. Paris. 1891–1905. Reprinted. N.Y. 1967.

This work is essential for the European setting, but its purely English sections have been superseded.

681 FEAVEARYEAR (ALBERT E.). The pound sterling: a history of English money. Oxf. 1931. 2nd edn. by E. Victor Morgan. Lond. 1963.

682 GRIERSON (PHILIP). 'The volume of Anglo-Saxon coinage', *Econ. H.R.* xx (1967), 153–60.

See also Sylloge (No. 704).

683 GRIERSON (PHILIP). 'La fonction sociale de la monnaie en Angleterre aux viie–viiie siècles'. Centro Italiano di Studi sull'alto medioevo: Moneta e scambi . . . Spoleto. 1961. pp. 341–62.

684 GRUEBER (HERBERT A.). Handbook of the coins of Great Britain and Ireland in the British Museum, with sixty-four plates. Lond. 1899.

Useful because it brings in all the British Isles.

685 HAWKINS (EDWARD). The silver coins of England. Lond. 1841. 3rd edn. by R. L. Kenyon. 1887.

Standard for citations of coin-types.

686 HEWLETT (LIONEL M.). Anglo-Gallic coins. Lond. 1920.

687 HILDEBRAND (BROR E.). Anglosachsiska mynt i svenska kongliga myntkabinettet. Stockholm. 1846. New edn. 1881.

Essential, but for some corrections thereto, see G. van der Meer in *Anglo-Saxon Coins* (No. 1454), pp. 169–87.

688 The *De moneta* of Nicholas Oresme, and English mint documents. Ed. and trans. by Charles Johnson. Medieval Classics (No. 1113). Lond. etc. [1956].

Contains 3 sections: (*a*) Introduction on English coinage for three centuries after Conquest; (*b*) Texts on English coinage in thirteenth and fourteenth centuries; (*c*) Oresme's treatise on French currency of *c.* 1356. A boon to numismatists.

689 KEARY (CHARLES F.) and GRUEBER (HERBERT A.). A catalogue of English coins in the British Museum: Anglo-Saxon series. 2 vols. Lond. 1887–93.

Valuable; the introduction to vol. 1 contains a good account of Anglo-Saxon coinage. See *E.H.R.* xi (1896), 759–91 and articles by G. C. Brooke in *Numis. Chron.* (No. 648), (1922–5).

690 KENYON (ROBERT L.). The gold coins of England . . . Lond. 1884.

A study complementary to that by Hawkins (No. 685).

691 LAWRENCE (LAURIE A.). The coinage of Edward III from 1351. Oxf. 1937.

A series of offprints from the *Numis. Chron.* (No. 648).

692 MADOX (THOMAS). The history and antiquities of the exchequer of the kings of England . . . [1066–1327]. Lond. 1711. Cf. No. 3250. 2nd edn. with compleat index. Lond. 1769. *

The Compleat Index to Mr. Madox's History of the Exchequer (Lond. 1741).

693 NOLAN (PATRICK). A monetary history of Ireland. 2 vols. Lond. 1926–8.

694 NORDMAN (CARL A.). Anglo-Saxon coins found in Finland. Helsingfors. 1921.

695   NORTH (JEFFREY J.). English hammered coinage: vol. i. Early Anglo-Saxon to Henry III, *c.* 650–1272. Lond. 1963. Vol. ii. Edward I to Charles II, 1272–1662. Lond. 1960.

Attempts to list every known type of coin struck in England during these periods.

696   OMAN (CHARLES). The coinage of England. Oxf. 1931.

697   PETERSSON (H. BERTIL A.). Anglo-Saxon currency: King Edgar's reform to the Norman Conquest. Bibliotheca Historica Lundensis, xxii. Lund. 1969.

698   REPORT OF THE COMMISSIONERS appointed to inquire into the constitution, etc., of the royal mint. *Parl. Papers.* 1849, vol. xxviii. Lond. 1849.

Contains much information concerning the history of the mint.

699   RUDING (ROGERS). Annals of the coinage of Great Britain. 3 vols. Lond. 1817–19. 3rd edn. 1840.

Based on a remarkable knowledge of the record material. A comprehensive work, with numerous documents, it now needs revision.

700   SEABY (PETER). The story of English coinage. Lond. 1952.

701   SIMON (JAMES). Simon's essay on Irish coins. 2nd edn. Dublin. 1810.

See also William O'Sullivan, 'The earliest Irish coinage', *Royal Soc. Antiq. Ireland. Jour.* lxxix (1949), 190–235.

702   STEWART (IAN H.). The Scottish coinage. Lond. 1955.

A comprehensive work with a good bibliography.

703   SUTHERLAND (CAROL H. V.). Anglo-Saxon gold coinage in the light of the Crondall hoard. Lond. 1948.

Fundamentally a corpus. See Sutherland's paper on coinage of the fifth and sixth centuries in *Dark Age Britain* (No. 1442).

704   SYLLOGE OF COINS OF THE BRITISH ISLES.

This series prints photographs of hundreds of coins and adds brief annotations.

   A. Published by the British Academy:
      1. FITZWILLIAM MUSEUM, CAMBRIDGE. Part i. Ancient British and Anglo-Saxon coins. By Philip Grierson. 1958.
      2. HUNTERIAN AND COATS COLLECTIONS, UNIVERSITY OF GLASGOW. Part i. Anglo-Saxon coins. By Anne S. Robertson. 1961.
      3. The coins of the Coritani. By D. F. Allen. 1963.
      4. ANCIENT BRITISH AND ANGLO-SAXON COINS IN THE ROYAL DANISH COIN CABINET, COPENHAGEN. Part i. By Georg Galster. 1964. (See B immediately below.)
      5. GROSVENOR MUSEUM, CHESTER. Part i. The Willoughby Gardner Collection of coins with the Chester mint signature. By Elizabeth J. E. Pirie. 1964.
      6. NATIONAL MUSEUM OF ANTIQUITIES OF SCOTLAND, EDINBURGH. Part i. Anglo-Saxon coins (with associated foreign coins). By R. B. K. Stevenson. 1966.
      7. ASHMOLEAN MUSEUM, OXFORD. Anglo-Saxon pennies. By J. D. A. Thompson. 1967.
      8. ULSTER MUSEUM, BELFAST. Part i. Anglo-Irish coins: John–Edward III. By Michael Dolley and Wilfred Seaby. 1968.

9. UNIVERSITY COLLECTION, READING. Anglo-Saxon and Norman coins. By C. E. Blunt, Michael Dolley, et al. 1969.

12. ASHMOLEAN MUSEUM, OXFORD. English coins, 1066–1279. By D. M. Metcalf. 1969.

B. Published by the British Academy and the Carlsberg Foundation:

10. ANGLO-SAXON COINS IN THE ROYAL DANISH COIN CABINET, COPENHAGEN. Part ii. By Georg Galster. 1966. (Parts iii and iv in preparation.)

C. Published by the Trustees of the British Museum:

11. HIBERNO-NORSE COINS. By R. H. M. Dolley. 1966.

705 THOMPSON (JAMES D. A.). Inventory of British coin hoards, A.D. 600–1500. Royal Numis. Soc. Special Pubns. No. 1. Oxf. 1956.

An essential survey and analysis of coin hoards, arranged alphabetically. See *Medieval Archaeology* (No. 729), ii (1958), 169–71; and iii (1959), 280–2; and *London and Middlesex Archaeol. Soc. Trans.* xx (1959–61), 37–50.

(d) Important articles on numismatics, 1066–1485

706 BERGHAUS (PETER). 'Die Perioden des Sterlings'. *Hamburger Beiträge zur Numismatik*, i (1947), 34–53.

707 BLUNT (CHRISTOPHER E.) and WHITTON (C. A.). 'The coinages of Edward IV and Henry VI (Restored)'. *Brit. Numis. Jour.* xxv (1945/8), 4–59, 130–82, 291–339.

708 CRUMP (GEORGE C.) and JOHNSON (CHARLES). 'Tables of bullion coined under Edward I, II, and III'. *Numis. Chron.* 4th Ser. xiii (1913), 200–45.

709 FOX (EARLE) and SHIRLEY-FOX (JOHN). 'Numismatic history of the reigns of Edward I, II, and III'. *Brit. Numis. Jour.* vi–x (1908–13).

710 GRIERSON (PHILIP). 'Oboli de Musc'. *E.H.R.* lxvi (1951), 75–81.

711 POTTER (W. J. W.). 'The silver coinage of Edward III (1361–77)'. *Numis. Chron.* 7th Ser. ii (1962), 203–24. Idem, 'The silver coinage of Richard II, Henry IV and Henry V'. *Brit. Numis. Jour.* xxix (1959), 334–52; xxx (1960), 124–50.

712 RIGOLD (STUART E.). 'The trail of the easterlings'. *Brit. Numis. Jour.* xxvi (1949–51), 31–55.

713 STOKES (E.). 'Tables of bullion coined from 1377 to 1550'. *Numis. Chron.* 5th Ser. ix (1929), 27–69.

714 THOMPSON (JAMES D. A.). 'Continental imitations of the rose noble of Edward IV'. *Brit. Numis. Jour.* xxv (1945–8), 183–208.

715 WHITTON (C. A.). 'Some aspects of English currency in the later middle ages'. *Brit. Numis. Jour.* xxiv (1941–4), 36–46.

I. ARCHAEOLOGY

Until the First World War, save for the work of a handful of outstanding pioneers, British archaeological studies were largely the output of amateur antiquarians devoted to local sites. Within the past half-century the subject-matter has been transformed by more formally trained specialists. As a technical science, archaeology has developed its own independent discipline and its extensive and detailed bibliography. For the application of scientific technology to archaeology, reference may be made to *Science in archaeology: a comprehensive survey of progress and research*, edited by Don R. Brothwell and Eric Higgs (Lond. 1963, 2nd edn. 1969); and to *The Scientist and archaeology*, edited by Edward Pyddoke (Lond. 1963). An attempt to present the specialized studies of this technical discipline in a selective bibliography of centuries of British history would be inordinate in length and unserviceable in content. Yet the historian must utilize the findings of the archaeologist; and accordingly the guides and more generalized treatises touching British archaeology must be entered here, even at the risk of misleading inadequacy. The novice might profitably begin with the Ordnance Survey's *Field Archaeology* (No. 748).

For the history of archaeological studies in Britain, one may consult Sir Thomas Kendrick, *British Antiquity* (Lond. 1950); Stuart Piggott, *William Stukeley* (Oxf. 1950); Glyn E. Daniel, *A hundred years of archaeology* (Lond. 1950); Ronald Jessup, *The story of archaeology in Britain* (Lond. 1964); the inaugural lecture of J. G. D. Clark, *The study of pre-history* (Cambr. 1954); and the editorials in the numbers of *Antiquity*.

The principal journals of broad scope which unite archaeology and history are *Antiq. Jour.* (No. 107), *Archaeologia* (No. 108), *Archaeol. Cambrensis* (No. 109), *Medieval Archaeology* (No. 729) (with an annual review of the work done in Great Britain), and *Saga Book* (No. 2466). Some other important but somewhat more exclusively archaeological journals are listed immediately below. For particular periods, turn to Chapter VIII (Prehistoric Times), Chapter IX (Roman Occupation), and Chapter XI (E) (Anglo-Saxon Period).

1. *Bibliographical Guides and Journals*

For brief lists, No. 716; for older works, No. 717. Good bibliographies can be found in Nos. 741, 761. Bibliographies on Art History (below, pp. 92–3) often include references to archaeological studies. Current bibliographies are supplied in Nos. 723, 726, and in *Année philol.* (No. 266) and *Répertoire d'art et d'archéologie* (Paris, 1910+). For bibliography on Welsh antiquities, consult *Bull. Bd. Celtic Stud.* (No. 111).

The Victoria County History and the publications of local societies are often valuable. In the mid twentieth century two new societies were founded with the expectation of publishing archaeological studies: the Society of Archaeological Historians concerns itself with the history of the archaeology of Great Britain, and the Society for Medieval Archaeology deals with the material on England from the end of the Roman occupation to the end of the middle ages. (See No. 729).

716 BRITISH ARCHAEOLOGY: a book-list for teachers. Issued by the Council for British Archaeology. Lond. 1949. New edn. 1960.

Eliza Jeffries Davis and Eva G. R. Taylor, *Guide to periodicals and bibliographies dealing with geography, archaeology, and history*, Hist. Assoc. Pamphlet No. 110 (Lond. 1938). David P. Dymond, *Archaeology for the historian* (Helps for Students of History, No. 71) (Lond. 1967).

717 INDEX OF ARCHAEOLOGICAL PAPERS, 1665–1890. Ed. by George L. Gomme. Published under the direction of the Congress of Archaeological Societies in union with the Society of Antiquaries. Lond. 1907. * (Annual) Index of archaeological papers. *J.B.A.A.* (No. 728), i–xx (1891–1909/10). Compiled by G. L. Gomme, Bernard Gomme, Allan Gomme, and William Martin. Lond. 1892–1914.

More than three score societies are covered in this index.

718 ANCIENT MONUMENTS SOCIETY. Transactions. New Ser. 1+. Lond. 1953+.

719 ANTIQUARIAN MAGAZINE AND BIBLIOGRAPHER. 12 vols. Lond. 1882–7.

In July 1885 the name was changed to *Walford's Antiquarian*.

720 ANTIQUARY. 51 vols. Lond. 1880–1915.

721 ANTIQUITY: a quarterly review of archaeology. Gloucester, then Newbury, then Cambr. 1927+. *(1950–61). Index of vols. i–xxv (1927–51). 1956.

An important, although not highly specialized, journal edited by O. G. S. Crawford from 1927 to 1957 and subsequently by Glyn Daniel.

722 ARCHAEOLOGIA AELIANA. The Society of Antiquaries of Newcastle-upon-Tyne. Newcastle. 1822+.

See Mullins, *Guide*, pp. 398–402.

723 ARCHAEOLOGICAL BULLETIN FOR THE BRITISH ISLES. Council for British Archaeology. 1940–6 to 1949. Lond. 1949. Continued as Archaeological bibliography for Great Britain and Ireland. 1950+. Lond. 1954+.

Before 1940, similar material appeared annually in *Report of the Research Committee of the Congress of Archaeological Societies* (London). Includes current bibliography.

724 ARCHAEOLOGICAL JOURNAL. Published by the Royal Archaeological Institute of Great Britain and Ireland. Lond. 1844+.

Not to be confused with No. 728.

725 ARCHAEOLOGICAL REVIEW. 4 vols. Lond. 1888–90.

An Index of Archaeological Papers is appended to these four volumes. The *Archaeological Review* and the *Folklore Journal* were united in 1890 and continued as *Folklore*.

726 COWA. Surveys and bibliographies. The Council of Old World Archaeology. Cambr. (Mass.). 1958+. Series ii (1960) for the British Isles. In progress.

727 JANSON (SVERKER) and VESSBERG (OLOF). Svenska arkeologiska samfundet. Swedish archaeological bibliography (1939–1948). Stockholm and Uppsala. 1951. Vol. ii (1949–53), edited by Christian Callmer and Wilhelm Holmquist. Stockholm. 1956+.

A survey in English of Swedish archaeological literature, to be continued.

728 JOURNAL OF THE BRITISH ARCHAEOLOGICAL ASSOCIATION. Lond. 1845+. i–l (1845–94); New Ser. i–xli (1895–1936); 3rd Ser. 1+ (1937+).

729 MEDIEVAL ARCHAEOLOGY. The Society of Medieval Archaeology.
Lond. 1957+. Indexes i–x (1957–66).

See also Colin Platt, *Medieval archaeology in England: a guide to historical sources*,
Pinhorns Handbooks (Isle of Wight, 1969).

730 RELIQUARY: quarterly archaeological journal and review. Lond. 1860–
1909.

In January 1895 the title was changed to the *Reliquary and Illustrated Archaeologist*.

731 SOCIETY OF THE ANTIQUARIES OF SCOTLAND. Proceedings.
Edin. 1851+.

Archaeologia Scotica, The Transactions of the Society of the Antiquaries of Scotland.
Edin. 1792–1890; then merged with the proceedings.

2. *Inventories*

The custody of ancient monuments and historic buildings is committed to the
Ministry of Public Building and Works which in 1940 superseded the Commissioners of H.M. Works and Public Buildings. Within the Ministry, separate
inspectorates for England and Scotland exist. The Ministry of Public Building
and Works, or its predecessor, has published (*a*) lists of sites in its care; (*b*) a
series of short pamphlets on individual sites prepared by expert hands, under the
title *Ancient Monuments and Historic Buildings Guides*; (*c*) *Illustrated Regional
Guides* (3 authoritative sketches for England, 2 for Wales, and 1 for Scotland);
(*d*) introductions to castles and religious houses. A complete list of the Guides is
given in H.M.S.O. Sectional List No. 27. In addition to Ministry of Works
Archaeological Reports, the Ministry has published reports on excavations in
established journals; a list of such publications for the period 1939–52 is given
in *Antiquity*, xxvi (1952), 147–8. More extensive, copiously illustrated county
or city inventories have been prepared by Royal Commissions (Nos. 737–9).
The Ordnance Survey maps (No. 604) should be consulted.

732 EVANS (ESTYN). A guide to prehistoric and early Christian Ireland.
Lond. 1966.

733 FEACHEM (RICHARD). A guide to prehistoric Scotland. Lond. 1963.

734 HAWKES (JACQUETTA). A guide to the prehistoric and Roman monuments in England and Wales. Lond. 1951. Idem, History in earth and stone:
prehistoric and Roman monuments in England and Wales. Cambr. (Mass.). 1952.

735 INVENTARIA ARCHAEOLOGICA: an illustrated card-inventory of
important associated finds in archaeology. Founded by M. E. Mariën. Lond.
1955+.

For list, see B.M. *Books in Print and Forthcoming Publications* (Lond. 1968), p. 49.

736 A PRELIMINARY SURVEY OF THE ANCIENT MONUMENTS
OF NORTHERN IRELAND. Ed. for the Ancient Monuments Advisory
Council by D. A. Chart. H.M.S.O. Belfast. 1940.

Supplemented by *Ancient Monuments in Northern Ireland not in State Charge* (H.M.S.O.,
Belfast, 1952).

737 ROYAL COMMISSION ON THE ANCIENT AND HISTORICAL MONUMENTS AND CONSTRUCTIONS OF ENGLAND. Inventories . . . Lond. 1911 etc.

Buckinghamshire, 2 vols. (1912–13); Cambridge, City of, 2 vols. (1959); Cambridge-shire, West (1968); Dorset, West (1952); Essex, 4 vols. (1916–23); Herefordshire, 3 vols. (1931–4); Hertfordshire (1911); Huntingdonshire (1926); London, 5 vols. (1924–30); Middlesex (1937); Oxford, City of (1939); Westmorland (1936); Roman York, vol. i (1962). Dorset vol. ii (1970).

For London, vol. i, Westminster Abbey; vol. ii, West London; vol. iii, Roman London; vol. iv, The City; vol. v, East London.

738 ROYAL COMMISSION ON THE ANCIENT AND HISTORICAL MONUMENTS AND CONSTRUCTIONS IN WALES AND MON-MOUTHSHIRE. Inventories . . . Lond. 1911 etc.

Anglesey (1937); Caernarvonshire, Part i (1956), ii (1960), iii (1964); Carmarthenshire (1917); Denbighshire (1914); Flintshire (1912); Merionethshire (1921); Montgomery-shire (1911); Pembrokeshire (1925); Radnorshire (1913).

739 ROYAL COMMISSION ON THE ANCIENT AND HISTORICAL MONUMENTS AND CONSTRUCTIONS OF SCOTLAND. Reports and inventories . . . Edin. 1909 etc.

Berwick (1909; revised 1915); Caithness (1911); Dumfries (1916); East Lothian (1924); City of Edinburgh (1951); Fife, Kinross, and Clackmannan (1933); Kirkcudbright (1914); Midlothian and West Lothian (1929); Orkney and Shetland, 3 vols. (1946); Outer Hebrides, Skye, and the Small Isles (1928); Peebleshire, 2 vols. (1967); Rox-burghshire, 2 vols. (1956); Selkirk (1957); Stirlingshire (1963); Sutherland (1911); Wigton (1912).

740 SMITH (CHARLES R.). Collectanea antiqua. 7 vols. Lond. 1848–80.

A valuable work, dealing with Celtic, Roman, and Anglo-Saxon remains. Contains many plates.

741 THOMAS (NICHOLAS). A guide to prehistoric England. Lond. 1960.

742 VETUSTA MONUMENTA. Soc. of Antiq. of London. 7 vols. Lond. 1747–1906. Indexes, 2 vols. 1810–97.

A fine series of large plates, including castles, abbeys, tombs, seals, swords, the Bayeux tapestry, etc.

743 WRIGHT (THOMAS) [of Durham]. Louthiana: an introduction to the antiquities of Ireland. 3 pts. Lond. 1748. 2nd edn. 1758.

The plates illustrating early mounds and castles are valuable. See also Thomas Wright [M.A., F.S.A.], *The Celt, the Roman, and the Saxon, illustrated by ancient remains* (Lond. 1852. 4th edn. 1885).

3. General Techniques and Interpretations

744 ARCHAEOLOGY AND THE MICROSCOPE: The scientific examina-tion of archaeological evidence. By Leo Biek with a foreword by Sir Mortimer Wheeler. Lond. 1963.

Fundamentally a treatise on the scientific techniques, such as physics and chemistry, needed by the archaeologist. Adversely reviewed in *Medieval Archaeology*, viii (1964), 316.

745 ATKINSON (RICHARD J. C.). Field archaeology. Lond. 1946. 2nd edn.
1953. Idem, Archaeology, history, and science. Inaugural lecture. 1960. Cardiff.
1965.

746 CHILDE (VERE GORDON). Piecing together the past. Lond. 1956.

747 CLARK (JOHN GRAHAME D.). Archaeology and society. Lond. 1939.
3rd edn. 1957.

748 FIELD ARCHAEOLOGY: Some notes for beginners issued by the
Ordnance Survey. Ordnance Survey Professional Papers. N.S. no. 13. H.M.S.O.
Lond. 1951. Reprinted, 1960.
   Text and topical bibliographies from prehistory to 1688.

749 PIGGOTT (STUART). Approach to archaeology. Lond. 1959.

750 WHEELER (ROBERT E. MORTIMER). Archaeology from the earth.
Lond. 1954.

751 ZEUNER (FRIEDRICH E.). Dating the past: an introduction to geo-
chronology. Lond. 1946. * 3rd edn. 1952.

4. *Air Photography*

Since the First World War, air photography has become an auxiliary of primary
importance to the archaeologist. J. K. St. Joseph's paper, 'Air photography and
archaeology', *Geographical Jour.* cv (1945), 47–61, is an interesting summary. For
a brief survey of the history of archaeology from the air, see O. G. S. Crawford,
'A century of air-photography' in *Antiquity*, xxviii (1954), 206–10; and *General
Index to Antiquity* (No. 721) under 'Air photographs' and 'Air photography'. Air
photographs provide illustrations in numerous recent publications. The Ordnance Survey Department has a collection of photographs taken by the Royal Air
Force, some of which are published in its Professional Papers (cf. The Ordnance
Survey Annual Reports); it has published air photographs for much of south-east
England. Portions of the Cambridge University Collection of Air Photography
are listed in Nos. 752, 755, 756; a well-produced *Guide to an exhibition of air
photographs of archaeological sites, Ashmolean Museum, Oxford, November 1948
to February 1949* appeared in 1948.

752 BERESFORD (MAURICE W.) and ST. JOSEPH (JOHN K. S.).
Medieval England: an aerial survey. Cambridge Air Surveys II. Cambr. 1958.
   117 air photographs on 'the varied pattern of the English landscape', field systems,
   villages, towns, chosen 'as far as possible, . . . to illustrate features of the English rural
   and urban landscape assignable to the period between the Anglo-Saxon settlement and
   the end of the reign of Elizabeth I'.

753 CRAWFORD (OSBERT GUY S.) and KEILLER (ALEXANDER).
Wessex from the air . . . with contributions by R. C. C. Clay . . . Eric Gardner.
Oxf. 1928.
   Cf. O. G. S. Crawford, *Air survey and archaeology . . .*, Ordnance Survey, Professional
   papers, N.S. no. vii (Southampton, 1924; 2nd edn. 1928); *Air photography for archaeo-
   logists*, ibid. N.S. no. xii (Southampton 1929); 'Air reconnaissance of Roman Scotland',
   Antiquity, xiii (1939), 280–92.

754 CURWEN (ELIOT C.). Air-photography and economic history: the evolution of the corn-field. Econ. Hist. Soc. Bibliographies and pamphlets No. 2. Lond. 1929. 2nd edn. Air-photography and the evolution of the corn-field. Lond. 1938.

755 KNOWLES (DAVID) and ST. JOSEPH (JOHN K. S.). Monastic sites from the air. Cambridge Air Surveys. Cambr. 1952.

125 photographs.

756 NORMAN (EDWARD R.) and ST. JOSEPH (JOHN K. S.). The early development of Irish society: The evidence of aerial photography. Cambridge Air Surveys. Cambr. 1969.

757 RICHMOND (I. A.). 'Recent discoveries in Roman Britain from the air and in the field'. *Jour. Roman Stud.* xxxiii (1943), 45–54.

758 ST. JOSEPH (JOHN K. S.). 'Air reconnaissance of north Britain'. *Jour. Roman Stud.* xli (1951), 52–65. Idem, 'Air reconnaissance of southern Britain'. ibid. xliii (1953), 81–97. Idem, 'Air reconnaissance in Britain' (1951–5). ibid. xlv (1955), 82–91; (1955–7), ibid. xlviii (1958), 86–101; (1958–60), ibid. li (1961), 119–35; (1961–4), ibid. lv (1965), 74–89; (1965–8), ibid. lix (1969), 104–28.

759 ST. JOSEPH (JOHN K. S.). 'Air reconnaissance: recent results'. *Antiquity*, xxxviii (1964), 217–18; and nearly every quarterly issue thereafter. Idem, 'Aerial reconnaissance in Wales'. *Antiquity*, xxxv (1961), 263–75. D. N. Riley, 'Aerial reconnaissance in the Fen Basin'. *Antiquity*, xix (1945), 145–53.

760 ST. JOSEPH (JOHN K. S.), ed. The uses of air photography: nature and man in a new perspective. Lond. 1966.

This book includes contributions by several scholars and a hundred plates. For St. Joseph's paper on pioneering in air photography, see Crawford essays (No. 1432).

5. *General Treatises on Archaeology*

Turn to Chapters VIII, IX, and XI for works on particular periods.

761 ANCIENT PEOPLES AND PLACES. Ed. by Glyn Daniel. Lond.

A series, international in scope and of high quality, designed for the general reader. Each volume has 150–75 pages of text and good illustrations. The volumes pertinent to British history which have been published:

S. J. deLaet. *The Low Countries.* 1958.
T. G. E. Powell. *The Celts.* 1958.
M. and L. dePaor. *Early Christian Ireland.* 1958.
J. F. S. Stone. *Wessex before the Celts.* 1958.
R. R. Clarke. *East Anglia.* 1960.
D. M. Wilson. *The Anglo-Saxons.* 1960.
H. Arbman. *The Vikings.* 1961.
N. K. Chadwick. *Celtic Britain.* 1963.
Aileen M. Fox. *South-west England.* 1964.
Isabel Henderson. *The Picts.* 1967.
Stuart Piggott. *The Druids.* 1968.
Ronald Jessup. *South-east England.* 1970.

762 COUNTY ARCHAEOLOGIES. Ed. by Thomas Kendrick. The Methuen series. Lond. 1930 etc.

Harold J. E. Peake. *The archaeology of Berkshire.* 1931.
Hugh O'Neill Hencken. *The archaeology of Cornwall and Scilly.* 1932.
Ronald F. Jessup. *The archaeology of Kent.* 1930.
Colwyn E. Vulliamy. *The archaeology of Middlesex and London.* 1930.
Dina P. Dobson. *The archaeology of Somerset.* 1931.
Donald C. Whimster. *The archaeology of Surrey.* 1931.
Eliot C. Curwen. *The archaeology of Sussex.* 1937. 2nd edn. 1954.
Frank and Harriet W. Elgee. *The archaeology of Yorkshire.* 1933.
L. V. Grinsell. *The archaeology of Wessex.* 1958.

763 CABROL (FERNAND), LECLERCQ (HENRI), *et al.* Dictionnaire d'archéologie chrétienne et de liturgie. 15 vols. Paris. 1903–53. See No. 1265.

The standard encyclopedia for its field.

764 GAY (VICTOR). Glossaire archéologique du moyen âge et de la renaissance. 2 vols. Paris. 1887–1928.

765 ALLCROFT (ARTHUR H.). Earthwork of England: prehistoric, Roman, Saxon, Danish, Norman, and mediaeval. Lond. 1908.

See also his *The circle and the cross: a study in continuity.* 2 vols. (Lond. 1927–30), whose chapters originally appeared in *Archaeol. Jour.* lxxvii–lxxx (1924–7).

766 BRUCE-MITFORD (RUPERT L. S.), ed. Recent archaeological excavations in Britain. Selected excavations 1939–1955. Lond. 1956.

(*a*) J. G. D. Clark, 'Star Carr, a mesolithic site in Yorkshire', pp. 1–20.
(*b*) R. Rainbird Clarke, 'The Smettisham Treasure', pp. 21–42.
(*c*) Sir Mortimer Wheeler, 'The Brigantian fortification at Stanwick, Yorkshire', pp. 43–63.
(*d*) Ian A. Richmond, 'The cult of Mithras and its temple at Carrawburgh on Hadrian's Wall', pp. 65–85.
(*e*) G. W. Meates, 'The Lullingstone Roman villa', pp. 87–109.
(*f*) W. F. Grimes, 'Excavations in the City of London', pp. 111–43.
(*g*) C. W. Phillips, 'The excavation of the Sutton Hoo Ship-burial', pp. 145–66.
(*h*) R. L. S. Bruce-Mitford, 'A Dark-age settlement at Mawgan Porth, Cornwall', pp. 167–96.
(*i*) J. R. C. Hamilton, 'Jarlshof, a prehistoric and Viking settlement site in Shetland', pp. 197–222.
(*j*) Brian Hope-Taylor, 'The Norman motte at Abinger, Surrey, and its wooden castle', pp. 223–49.
(*k*) J. G. Hurst, 'Deserted medieval villages and the excavations at Wharram Percy, Yorkshire', pp. 251–73.
(*l*) J. K. S. St. Joseph, 'Air reconnaissance in Britain: some recent results', pp. 275–96.
(*m*) R. L. S. B.-M., 'Note on the law and practice of Treasure Trove', pp. 297–301.

767 CRAWFORD (OSBERT GUY S.). Archaeology in the field. Lond. 1953 and later impressions.

768 EVANS (JOHN). The ancient bronze implements, weapons, and ornaments of Great Britain. Lond. 1881. Idem, The ancient stone implements, weapons, and ornaments of Great Britain. Lond. 1872. 2nd edn. 1897.

The works of a pioneer.

769 GENTLEMAN'S MAGAZINE LIBRARY. Ed. by George L. Gomme. 30 vols. Lond. 1883–1905. See No. 615.

Archaeology, 2 pts. 1886; Architectural antiquities, 2 pts. 1890–1; Ecclesiology, 1894; Romano-British remains, 2 pts. 1887.

770 GRIMES (WILLIAM F.). The excavation of Roman and mediaeval London. Lond. 1968.

771 THE HERITAGE OF EARLY BRITAIN. Ed. by M. D. Knowles. Lond. 1952.

A series of brief essays by experts, from prehistoric times to about A.D. 1200. The book is dedicated to the memory of Martin P. Charlesworth. Cf. No. 1430.

772 HOARE (RICHARD C.). The ancient history of south (and north) Wiltshire. 2 vols. Lond. 1812–21.

An important landmark, on British and Roman remains.

773 A HUNDRED YEARS OF WELSH ARCHAEOLOGY: centenary volume, 1846–1946. Ed. by V. E. Nash-Williams. Cambrian Archaeol. Assoc. Gloucester. 1949. See R. I. Jack, *Medieval Wales* (No. 22), pp. 163–97.

774 KENDRICK (THOMAS D.) and HAWKES (CHARLES F. CHRISTOPHER). Archaeology in England and Wales, 1914–31. Lond. 1932.

A notable summary of its period, with which the student might well begin. Bruce-Mitford (No. 766) is of more limited scope.

775 MACALISTER (ROBERT A. S.). The archaeology of Ireland. Lond. 1928.

The outstanding survey of prehistoric, early Christian, and medieval archaeology of Ireland, with full bibliographical references.

776 THE PREHISTORIC PEOPLES OF SCOTLAND. Ed. by Stuart Piggott. Studies in Ancient History and Archaeology. Lond. 1962.

Lectures on Scottish archaeology to *c.* A.D. 900 by several specialists.

777 WAINWRIGHT (FREDERICK T.). Archaeology and place-names and history: an essay of the problems of coordination. Lond. 1962.

J. ART

1. *Bibliographical Guides and Journals*

Extensive bibliographies are provided in the *Oxford history of art* (No. 782) and selective lists in the *Pelican history of art* (No. 783). The *Catalog of the Avery Memorial Architectural Library of Columbia University*, 6 vols. (Boston, 1958), contains approximately 250,000 entries. Current bibliographies are supplied in the *Bibliography of the history of British art* (No. 778), *Art index* (No. 778A), and *Répertoire d'art et d'archéologie* (Paris, 1910+).

For works on Anglo-Saxon art, see pp. 357–60 and for surviving monuments, see Nos. 2464, 2472, 2487.

778   ANNUAL BIBLIOGRAPHY OF THE HISTORY OF BRITISH ART.
Courtauld Institute of Art. Vols. i–iv (1934–7). Cambr. etc. 1936–9. Continued
as *Bibliography of the history of British art*. Vol. v (1938–45), published in 2 parts.
1951. Vol. vi (1946–8), 2 parts. Lond. 1956.

> Cf. 'List of bibliographies compiled from material in the Library of the Royal Institute
> of British Architects', *Royal Institute of British Architects Bulletin*, v (May 1951), 2–3.
> See also Howard Colvin, *A guide to the sources of English architectural history*, Pinhorns
> Handbooks. Isle of Wight (1967).

778A   ART INDEX: a cumulative and subject index (from 1929). Edited for
H. W. Wilson Co. N.Y. 1933+. Quarterly and annually.

779   BURLINGTON MAGAZINE FOR CONNOISSEURS. Lond. 1903+.
*(1903–48).

780   JOURNAL OF THE WARBURG AND COURTAULD INSTI-
TUTES. Lond. 1937+. *

2. General Treatises on Architecture and Art

781   THE HISTORY OF THE KING'S WORKS. General editor: H. M.
Colvin. Vols. i and ii, with plates and plans : *The Middle Ages*, by R. Allen
Brown, H. M. Colvin, and A. J. Taylor. H.M.S.O. Lond. 1963.

> These are the first volumes of outstanding scholarship of a series to be completed in five
> volumes on 'the history of building as a government enterprise from Saxon times to the
> year 1851'. The volumes on the middle ages (to 1485) describe the civil, military, and
> ecclesiastical buildings for which the kings of medieval England were responsible and
> the administrative arrangements which were devised to erect and maintain them. The
> work is of great value for the study of royal castles, the king's houses, Westminster
> Palace, and Westminster Abbey. There are also chapters on the king's works in Scot-
> land, in Calais, in Normandy (1415–49), and in royal appanages.

782   THE OXFORD HISTORY OF ENGLISH ART. Ed. by Thomas S. R.
Boase. Oxf. 1949+. Eleven volumes are planned, of which the following have
appeared: vol. ii: David Talbot Rice. *English art, 871–1100* (1952); vol. iii:
Thomas S. R. Boase. *English art, 1100–1216* (1953); vol. iv: Peter H. Brieger
English art, 1216–1307 (1956); vol. v: Joan Evans. *English art, 1307–1461*
(1949). See also Boase in *Medieval England* (No. 1485), pp. 485–513.

783   PELICAN HISTORY OF ART. Ed. by Nikolaus Pevsner. Harmondsworth and Baltimore. A multivolume series, of which the volumes pertinent to
this bibliography are Geoffrey Webb, *Architecture in Britain: the middle ages*
(1956); Lawrence Stone, *Sculpture in Britain: the middle ages* (1955); and
Margaret Rickert, *Painting in Britain: the middle ages* (1954).

> The architecture of England is also treated county by county in the Penguin series,
> entitled *The buildings of England* by Nikolaus Pevsner (Lond. 1951+). Over thirty
> volumes, ranging from about 200 pages to 450 pages have been published. For ecclesias-
> tical architecture, see also Webb in *Medieval England* (No. 1485), pp. 439–84.

784   ATKINSON (THOMAS D.). A glossary of terms used in English architecture. Lond. [1906]. 7th edn. 1948.

785 BILSON (JOHN). 'Durham Cathedral: the chronology of its vaults'. *Archaeol. Jour.* lxxix (1922), 101–60. Idem, 'The architecture of the Cistercians with special reference to some of their earlier churches in England', ibid. lxvi (1909), 185–280.

786 BOND (FRANCIS). Gothic architecture in England: an analysis of the origin and development of English church architecture from the Norman conquest to the dissolution of the monasteries. Lond. 1905. 1,254 illustrations. Idem, Introduction to English church architecture from the eleventh to the sixteenth century. 2 vols. Lond. 1913. About 1,400 illustrations.

787 BONY (JEAN). 'French influences on the origins of English Gothic architecture'. *Jour. Warburg and Courtauld Inst.* xii (1949), 1–15.

788 CLAPHAM (ALFRED W.). English Romanesque architecture. Vol. i. Before the conquest. Vol. ii. After the conquest. Oxf. 1930–4. Reprinted, 1965. Idem, Romanesque architecture in England (brief). Lond. 1950.

789 COLLINS GUIDE TO ENGLISH PARISH CHURCHES. Ed. by John Betjeman. Lond. 1958.

790 COLVIN (HOWARD M.). Building accounts of King Henry III. Oxf. 1971.

791 COOK (GEORGE H.). The English mediaeval parish church. Lond. 1954.

792 COX (JOHN C.). The parish churches of England, edited with additional chapters by Charles B. Ford. Lond. 1935.

793 FISHER (ERNEST A.). The greater Anglo-Saxon churches: an architectural-historical study. Lond. 1962.

794 FLETCHER (BANISTER F.). A history of architecture on the comparative method . . . Lond. 1896. 17th edn. 1961.

One of the most useful general histories of architecture in English.

795 GARDNER (SAMUEL). A guide to English Gothic architecture. Cambr. 1922. 2nd edn. 1925.

796 HARVEY (JOHN H.). The English cathedrals. Lond. etc. 1950. 2nd edn. 1956. 3rd edn. 1961. Idem, Gothic England: a survey of national culture, 1300–1550. Lond. 1947. 2nd edn. Lond. etc. 1948.

797 HARVEY (JOHN H.). English medieval architects; a biographical dictionary down to 1500, including master-masons, carpenters, carvers, building contractors, and others responsible for design . . . With contributions by Arthur Oswald. Lond. 1954.

798 HASTINGS (MAURICE). St. Stephen's Chapel and its place in the development of the perpendicular style in England. Cambr. 1955.

Cf. J. H. Harvey, 'The origin of the perpendicular style', *Studies in Building History*, ed. by E. M. Jope (Lond. 1961), pp. 134–65 (No. 809).

799 KENDRICK (THOMAS D.). Late Saxon and Viking Art. Lond. 1949.

800 KNOOP (DOUGLAS) and JONES (GWILYM P.). The mediaeval mason: an economic history of English stone building in the later middle ages and early modern times. Univ. of Manchester Pubns. ccxxvii; Econ. Hist. Ser. no. 8. Manchester. 1933. 3rd edn. 1967.

See L. R. Shelby, 'The role of the master-mason in mediaeval English building', *Speculum*, xxxix (1964), 387–403.

801 LEASK (HAROLD G.). Irish churches and monastic buildings. 3 vols. Dundalk. 1955–60.

802 LEHMANN-BROCKHAUS (OTTO). Lateinische Schriftquellen zur Kunst in England, Wales und Schottland, vom Jahre 901 bis zum Jahre 1307. 5 vols. Munich. 1955–60.

Vols. i and ii give sources in topographical order. Vol. iii, other sources according to subject. Vols. iv and v, Indexes.

803 LETHABY (WILLIAM R.). Medieval art from the peace of the church to the eve of the renaissance, 312–1350. New edn. David Talbot Rice. Lond. etc. 1949.

804 MacGIBBON (DAVID) and ROSS (THOMAS). The ecclesiastical architecture of Scotland from the earliest Christian times to the seventeenth century. 3 vols. Edin. 1896–7.

805 MARTIN (A. R.). Franciscan architecture in England. British Soc. of Franciscan Studies Pubns. vol. xviii. Manchester 1937.

806 PRIOR (EDWARD S.). A history of Gothic art in England. Lond. 1900.

807 PRIOR (EDWARD S.). Eight chapters on English medieval art: a study in English economics. Cambr. 1922.

A review of church-building in England.

808 ROBERTS (H. ERNEST). Notes on the medieval monasteries and minsters of England and Wales. Lond. 1949.

Annotated list of the remains surviving in 1939. See No. 1435.

809 SALZMAN (LOUIS F.). Building in England, down to 1540: a documentary history. Oxf. 1952. Reprinted, Oxf. and N.Y. 1968.

See E. M. Jope, 'The Saxon building-stone industry in southern and midland England', *Medieval Archaeology*, viii (1965), 91–118. Fourteen essays, largely on Roman and medieval subjects, in recognition of the work of B. H. St. J. O'Neil were printed as *Studies in Building History*, edited by E. M. Jope (Lond. 1961).

810 SAXL (FRITZ) and WITTKOWER (RUDOLF). British art and the Mediterranean. Lond. 1948.

A profusely illustrated commentary on the British debt to Mediterranean lands from prehistoric times to the nineteenth century.

811 TAYLOR (HAROLD M.) and TAYLOR (JOAN). Anglo-Saxon architecture. 2 vols. Lond. 1965.

This magnificently produced work seeks to describe every known surviving Anglo-Saxon edifice. Its inventory is illustrated with numerous plans, diagrams, and photographs. See their 'Architectural sculpture in pre-Norman England', *Jour. Brit. Archaeol. Assoc.* xxix (1966), 3–51.

812 THOMPSON (ALEXANDER HAMILTON). The historical growth of the English parish church. Cambr. 1911. Idem, The ground plan of the English parish church. Cambr. 1911. Idem, The cathedral churches of England. Lond. 1925.

813 WILLIS (ROBERT). The architectural history of Canterbury Cathedral. Lond. 1845.

Willis also wrote good short accounts of the architecture of York Cathedral (1848) and Glastonbury Abbey (1866). He also wrote 'The Architectural history of the conventual buildings of Christ Church, Canterbury', *Arch. Cantiana*, vii (1868), 1–206.

3. *Domestic Architecture*

814 ADDY (SIDNEY O.). The evolution of the English house. Lond. etc. 1898. 2nd edn. by John Summerson. [1933].

See also Alexander Hamilton Thompson, The English house (Hist. Assoc. Pamphlet No. 105) (Lond. 1936).

815 COLVIN (HOWARD M.). 'Domestic architecture and town planning', in *Medieval England* (No. 1485), pp. 37–93 with a bibliography, pp. 93–7.

816 FOX (CYRIL) and SOMERSET (FITZ-ROY RICHARD, Baron Raglan). Monmouthshire houses: a study of building techniques and smaller house-plans in the fifteenth to seventeenth centuries. Part i: Medieval houses, 1415–1560. Part ii: Sub-medieval houses, *c.* 1550–1610. Part iii: Renaissance, *c.* 1500–1714. Cardiff. 1951–4.

See also Iorwerth C. Peate, 'The Welsh house: a study in folk culture', *Y Cymmrodor*, xlvii (Lond. 1940). See No. 1435.

817 GOTCH (JOHN A.). The growth of the English house: a short history of its architectural development from 1100 to 1800. Lond. 1909. 2nd edn rev. and enlarged, N.Y. and Lond. 1928.

818 LLOYD (NATHANIEL). A history of the English house from primitive times to the Victorian period. Lond. etc. 1931.

819 MacGIBBON (DAVID) and ROSS (THOMAS). The castellated and domestic architecture of Scotland from the twelfth to the eighteenth century. 5 vols. Edin. 1887–92.

This is a monumental work on Scottish architecture.

820 TIPPING (HENRY A.). English homes. 9 vols. Lond. 1920–37. Vol. i: Norman and Plantagenet, 1066–1485. 1921.

Large volumes with excellent photographs, handsomely produced by *Country Life*.

821 TURNER (THOMAS H.) [and PARKER (JOHN H.)]. Some account of domestic architecture in England . . . 3 vols. in 4. Oxf. etc. 1851–9.

From the Conquest to Henry VIII.

822 WOOD (MARGARET E.). The English medieval house. Lond. 1965. Idem, 'Thirteenth century domestic architecture in England', *Archaeol. Jour.* cv. Supplement. 1950; Idem, 'Norman domestic architecture', *Archaeol. Jour.* xcii (1935), 167–242. See Pantin in No. 1435.

4. Castles

On motte-and-bailey earthworks and castles, the Victoria County histories (No. 1529) are a fundamental source. W. Douglas Simpson has published numerous articles, scattered in various journals, on Welsh and Scottish castles; for them refer to Nos. 823, 838.

823 ARTICLES ABOUT CASTLES.

Articles of high significance are: G. Neilson, 'The motes of Norman Scotland', *Scottish Rev.* xxxii (1898), 209–38; W. H. St. John Hope, 'English fortresses and castles', *Archaeol. Jour.* lx (1903), 72–90; J. H. Round, 'The castles of the conquest', *Archaeologia*, lviii (1912), 313–40 and 'Castle guard', *Archaeol. Jour.* lix (1902), 144–59; S. Painter 'English castles in the early middle ages: their number, location and legal position', *Speculum*, x (1935), 321–2; C. H. Hunter-Blair, 'The early castles of Northumberland', *Archaeol. Aeliana*, 4th Ser. xxii (1944), 116–70; J. G. Edwards, 'Edward I's castle-building in Wales', *P.B.A.* xxxii (1946), 15–81; A. J. Taylor, 'Master James of St. George builder of Welsh castles', *E.H.R.* lxv (1950), 433–57; R. Allen Brown, 'Royal castle building in England, 1154–1216', ibid. lxx (1955), 353–98, 692; John H. Beeler, 'Castles and strategy in Norman and early Angevin England', *Speculum*, xxxi (1956), 581–601. A. J. Taylor in *Medieval England* (No. 1485), pp. 98–127; Brian K. Davison, 'The origins of the castle in England'. A report of research to Royal Archaeol. Institute, *Archaeol. Jour.* cxxiv (1967), 202–11.

824 ARMITAGE (ELLA S.). The early Norman castles of the British isles. Lond. 1912.

Expanded from papers in the *E.H.R.* (1904–5), the *Antiquary* (1906), etc.

825 BRAUN (HUGH). The English castle. Lond. 1936. 2nd edn. 1943.

826 BROWN (REGINALD A.). English medieval castles. Lond. 1954.

Cf. his 'A list of castles, 1154–1216', *E.H.R.* lxxiv (1959), 249–80; and his 'Royal castle building in England', *E.H.R.* lxx (1955), 353–98.

827 CLARK (GEORGE T.). Mediaeval military architecture in England. 2 vols. Lond. 1884.

This is still an important work, although some of the theories are now generally discredited, especially the theory of pre-Norman origins.

828 CRUDEN (STEWART). The Scottish castle. Edin. 1960.

829 FRAPRIE (FRANK R.). The castles and keeps of Scotland. Boston. 1907. 5th impression. 1932.

830 HARVEY (ALFRED). The castles and walled towns of England. Lond. [1911.] 2nd edn. [1925.]

831   HOGG (A. H. A.) and KING (D. J. C.). 'Early castles in Wales and the Marches'. *Archaeol. Cambrensis*, cxii (1963), 77–124.

832   LEASK (HAROLD G.). Irish castles and castellated houses. Dundalk. 1941. 2nd edn. 1944.

833   MACKENZIE (JAMES D.). The castles of England, their history and structure. 2 vols. Lond. 1897.

834   MACKENZIE (WILLIAM MACKAY). The mediaeval castle in Scotland. Rhind lectures for 1925–6. Lond. [1927.]

835   OMAN (CHARLES W. C.). Castles. The Great Western Railway Series. Lond. 1926.

836   O'NEIL (BRYAN H. St. J.). Castles and cannon: a study of early artillery fortifications in England. Oxf. 1960.

837   RENN (DEREK). Norman castles in Britain (1066–1216). Lond. 1968.
     Largely a descriptive gazetteer of about 800 castles with 70 plates and 220 plans.

838   SIMPSON (WILLIAM D.). Castles from the air. Lond. etc. [1949.] Idem, Castles in England and Wales. Lond. 1969.

839   STENTON (FRANK M.). The development of the castle in England and Wales. Historical Assoc. Pamphlet, No. 22. Lond. 1938.
     Cf. Bryan H. St. John O'Neil, *An introduction to the castles of England and Wales* (H.M.S.O. Lond. 1953), a brief summary of 66 pages, based on the numerous guides published by the Ministry of Works.

840   THOMPSON (ALEXANDER HAMILTON). Military architecture in England during the Middle Ages. Lond. 1912.
     See also Thompson in *Cambridge Medieval History*, vol. vi, pp. 773–84 and 969–70.

841   TOY (SIDNEY). The castles of Great Britain. Lond. 1953.
     Toy revives the now rarely accepted theory that some castles are pre-Norman.

5. *Treatises on Sculpture, Painting, and Minor Arts*

See Oxford History of Art (No. 782) and Pelican History of Art (No. 783); and for the Anglo-Saxon period, pp. 357–60.

842   ANDERSON (MARY D.). The mediaeval carver. Cambr. 1935. Idem, Drama and imagery in English medieval churches. Cambr. 1963.

843   CHRISTIAN ART IN ANCIENT IRELAND: selected objects illustrated and described, edited in behalf of the Government of Irish Free State. Vol. i by Adolf Mahr. Dublin. 1932. Vol. ii by Joseph Raftery. Dublin. 1941.
     There are 130 plates, with some commentary.

844   GARDNER (SAMUEL). English Gothic foliage sculpture. Cambr. 1927.

845 GRANT (MAURICE H.). A dictionary of British sculptors from the 13th century to the 20th. Lond. 1953.

846 HENRY (FRANÇOISE). Irish art in the early Christian period (to A.D. 800). Lond. and Ithaca. 1965. Idem, Irish art during the Viking invasions (A.D. 800–1020). Lond. and Ithaca. 1967. Idem, Irish art in the Romanesque period (A.D. 1020–1170). Lond. and Ithaca. 1970.

> These three volumes are translations with revisions of F. Henry, *L'Art irlandais* (Paris, 1963–4). Cf. F. Henry, *Early Christian Irish Art*, trans. by Maire MacDermott (Dublin, 1954).

847 LITTLE (ANDREW G.), ed. Franciscan history and legend in English mediaeval art. Brit. Soc. of Franciscan Studies. Pubns. xix. Manchester. 1937. *

848 PORTER (ARTHUR K.). The crosses and culture of Ireland. New Haven. 1931.

> For criticism of these attractive, controversial lectures see reviews in *Burlington Magazine*, lxi (1932), 183–4 and in *Speculum*, viii (1933), 104–8.

849 PRIOR (EDWARD S.) and GARDNER (ARTHUR). An account of medieval figure-sculpture in England, with 855 photographs. Cambr. 1912. Idem, Abridged edn. by Arthur Gardner: A handbook of English medieval sculpture. Cambr. 1935. New edn.: English medieval sculpture; the original handbook revised and enlarged. Cambr. 1951.

850 PRITCHARD (V.). English medieval graffiti. Cambr. 1967.

851 REMNANT (G. L.). A catalogue of misericords in Great Britain. With an essay on their iconography by M. D. Anderson. Oxf. and N.Y. 1969.

852 SAUNDERS (O. ELFRIDA). A history of English art in the Middle Ages. Oxford. 1932.

> E. Kitzinger, *Early medieval art in the British Museum*. Lond. 1940. 2nd edn. 1955.

853 SAXL (FRITZ). English sculptures of the twelfth century. Ed. by Hanns Swarzenski. Lond. 1954. Boston. 1955.

854 STONE (LAWRENCE). Sculpture in Britain: the Middle Ages. Baltimore 1955.

855 ZARNECKI (GEORGE). English Romanesque sculpture 1066–1140. 82 plates. Lond. 1951. Idem, Later English Romanesque sculpture 1140–1210. 133 plates. Lond. 1953. Idem, '1066 and architectural sculpture'. *P.B.A.* lii (1966), 87–104 and 24 plates.

856 BORENIUS (TANCRED) and TRISTRAM (ERNEST W.). English medieval painting. Florence and Paris. 1927.

> See also T. Borenius, 'English primitives', *P.B.A.* xi (1924–5), 75–88, and idem, *St. Thomas Becket in art* (Lond. 1932).

857 KENDON (FRANK). Mural paintings in English churches during the middle ages. Lond. 1923.

858 RICKERT (MARGARET J.). Painting in Britain: the middle ages. Pelican History of Art, vol. v. Lond. and Baltimore. 1954.

See also John H. Harvey, 'The Wilton Diptych: a re-examination', *Archaeol.* xcviii (1961), 1–28 and 13 plates; and Maude Clarke, *Fourteenth Century Studies* (No. 1464).

859 TRISTRAM (ERNEST W.). English medieval wall painting. Vol. i. The twelfth century. Vol. ii. The thirteenth century. Lond. and Oxf. 1944–50. Idem, English wall painting of the fourteenth century. Ed. by Eileen Tristram . . . Lond. [1955.]

860 WORMALD (FRANCIS). 'Paintings in Westminster abbey and contemporary paintings', *P.B.A.* xxxv (1949), 161–76, and W. R. Lethaby, 'Medieval paintings at Westminster', ibid. xiii (1927), 123–51.

861 ARNOLD (HUGH). Stained glass of the middle ages in England and France, painted by Lawrence B. Saint . . . Lond. 1913. 2nd edn. 1939. Reprinted N.Y. 1955.

862 HARRISON (FREDERICK). The painted glass of York, an account of the medieval glass of the minster and the parish churches . . . Lond. [1927.]

863 KNOWLES (JOHN A.). Essays in the history of the York school of glass painting. Lond. 1936.

864 RACKHAM (BERNARD). The ancient glass of Canterbury cathedral. Lond. 1949.

21 coloured plates, 82 in monochrome.

865 WOODFORDE (CHRISTOPHER). English stained and painted glass. Oxf. 1954.

Also 'English stained glass and glass-painters in the fourteenth century', *P.B.A.* xxv (1939), 29–49.

866 CHRISTIE (A. GRACE G. I.). English mediaeval embroidery. Oxf. 1938.

See Bayeux Tapestry (No. 4276).

867 CROSSLEY (FRED H.). English church monuments, 1150–1550. An introduction to the study of tombs and effigies in the medieval period. Lond. 1921.

868 EVANS (JOAN). Magical jewels of the Middle Ages and the Renaissance, particularly in England. Oxf. 1922. Anglo-Norman lapidaries. Ed. by Paul Studer and Joan Evans. Paris. 1924. English mediaeval lapidaries. Ed. by Joan Evans and Mary S. Serjeantson. E.E.T.S. Original Ser. No. 190. Lond. 1933 (for 1932).

869 HAINES (HERBERT). A manual of monumental brasses. 2 vols. Oxf. 1861.

870 LONGHURST (MARGARET H.). English ivories. Lond. 1926.

871 OMAN (CHARLES). English church plate 597–1830. Lond. 1957. (597–1548), pp. 3–126.

872 WILSON (DAVID M.). Anglo-Saxon ornamental metalwork, 700–1100, in the British Museum. Lond. 1964.

  A catalogue with an introduction.

6. Illuminated Manuscripts

The volumes by Talbot Rice, Boase, and Brieger in the Oxford History of Art series (No. 782) and by Margaret Rickert (No. 783) treat this subject well and provide detailed bibliographical citations. Some of the works listed under facsimiles (pp. 53–6) are useful; and for the Anglo-Saxon period, items 11,828–11,975 in Bonser (No. 12) may be consulted. The Roxburghe Club (No. 194) has sponsored the publication of several illuminated manuscripts, some of them under the guidance of Montague Rhodes James (e.g. Nos. 892, 893, 895).

(a) General books

873 BIRCH (WALTER DE GRAY) and JENNER (HENRY). Early drawings and illuminations . . . with a dictionary of subjects in the British Museum. Lond. 1879.

874 BRITISH MUSEUM. Illuminated manuscripts in the British Museum: miniatures, borders, and initials, reproduced in gold and colours. With a descriptive text by George F. Warner. Ser. i–iv. 60 plates. Lond. 1899–1903. 2nd edn. of Ser. i. 1904.

875 BRITISH MUSEUM. Reproductions from illuminated manuscripts. Ser. i–iii. 150 plates. 3rd edn. Lond. 1923–5. Ser. iv by Eric G. Millar. 1928. Ser. v by D. H. Turner. 1965.

  Series i and ii had appeared in editions of 1907 and 1910. Series iii in editions of 1908 and 1910. Series iv includes on pp. 21–38 a table of plates and a list of the manuscripts of the first four series.

876 HERBERT (JOHN A.). Illuminated manuscripts. Connoisseur's Library. Lond. 1911. 2nd edn. 1912. 51 plates.

877 MILLAR (ERIC G.). English illuminated manuscripts from the Xth to the XIIIth century. Paris and Brussels. 1926. Idem, English illuminated manuscripts of the XIVth and XVth centuries. Paris and Brussels. 1928.

878 PÄCHT (OTTO) and ALEXANDER (J. J. G.). Illuminated MSS. in the Bodleian Library, Oxford. Oxf. 1970.

879 SAUNDERS (O. ELFRIDA). English illumination. 2 vols. Florence etc. 1928.

(b) Studies on groups of manuscripts or important single manuscripts

880 THE BENEDICTIONAL OF ST. AETHOLWOLD. Facsimile edition by G. F. Warner and H. A. Wilson. Roxburghe Club. Oxf. 1910.

  Cf. *The Benedictional of St. Ethelwold*, with introduction and notes by Francis Wormald (Lond. 1959).

881 THE BOOK OF KELLS. Evangeliorum quattuor Codex Cenannensis. Auctoritate Collegii Sacrosanctae et Individuae Trinitatis juxta Dublin auxilioque Bibliothecae Confederationis Helveticae totius codicis similitudinem accuratissime depicti exprimendam curavit typographeum Urs Graf. Prolegomenis auxerunt viri doctissimi Ernestus Henricus Alton (et) Petrus Meyer. 3 vols. Bern. 1950–1.

Vols. i and ii, reproductions of folios; vol. iii, introduction. See also Edward Sullivan, *The Book of Kells described and illustrated with 24 plates in colours* (Lond. 1914. 5th edn. Studio Pubns. 1952). For general survey, see F. Masai, *Essai sur les origines de la miniature dite irlandaise* (Brussels, 1947); and T. J. Brown in *Anglo-Saxon England*, i (1972), 218–46.

882 THE CAEDMON MANUSCRIPT OF ANGLO-SAXON BIBLICAL POETRY: Junius XI in the Bodleian Library. Introduction by Israel Gollancz. Lond. 1927.

883 COCKERELL (SYDNEY C.). The Gorleston psalter. Lond. 1907.

884 COCKERELL (SYDNEY C.). The work of W. de Brailes, an English illuminator of the thirteenth century. Roxburghe Club. Cambr. 1930.

885 DODWELL (CHARLES R.). The Canterbury school of illumination, 1066–1200. Cambr. etc. 1954. Idem, The great Lambeth Bible. Lond. 1959.

886 EGBERT (DONALD D.). The Tickhill psalter and related manuscripts. N.Y. etc. 1939–40.

887 HASELOFF (GÜNTHER). Die Psalterillustration im 13. Jahrhundert: Studien zur Geschichte der Buchmalerei in England, Frankreich und den Niederlanden. Kiel. 1938.

888 HENDERSON (GEORGE). 'Studies in English manuscript illumination: pt. i, Stylistic sequence and stylistic overlap in thirteenth century manuscripts; pt. ii, The English Apocalypse', *Jour. Warburg-Courtauld Inst.* xxx (1967), 71–137; xxxi (1968), 103–47.

889 HOMBURGER (OTTO). Die Anfänge der Malerschule von Winchester im x. Jahrhundert. Studien über christliche Denkmäler, hrsg. von J. Ficker; N.F. der archäol. Studien, 13. Leipzig. 1912.

890 ILLUSTRATIONS TO THE LIFE OF ST. ALBAN in Trin. Coll. Dublin, MS. E. i. 40, reproduced in collotype facsimile by the care of W. R. L. Lowe and E. F. Jacob, with a description of the illustrations by M. R. James. Oxf. 1924.

891 JAMES (MONTAGUE R.). The apocalypse in art. Lond. 1931.

This study, which was originally a lecture to the British Academy in 1927, is here preceded by a 'prefatory list of Apocalypses, manuscript and other'.

892 JAMES (MONTAGUE R.). The apocalypse in Latin and French (Bodleian MS. 180). Roxburghe Club. Oxf. 1922.

893 JAMES (MONTAGUE R.). The bestiary: being a reproduction in full of the manuscript I. i. 4. 26 in the University Library, Cambridge, with supplementary plates from other manuscripts of English origin, and a preliminary study of the Latin bestiary as current in England. Roxburghe Club. 1928.

894 JAMES (MONTAGUE R.). The Canterbury psalter. Lond. 1935.

895 JAMES (MONTAGUE R.) and MILLAR (ERIC G.). The Bohun manuscripts. Roxburghe Club. 1936.

896 THE LINDISFARNE GOSPELS. Evangeliorum quattuor Codex Lindisfarnensis: Musei Britannici Codex Cottonianus Nero D. IV permissione Musei Britannici totius codicis similitudo expressa. Prolegomenis auxerunt T. D. Kendrick (*et al.*). Lausanne etc. 1956.

> The Lindisfarne gospels: 3 plates in colour and 36 in monochrome from Cotton MS. Nero D. IV, in the British Museum, with pages from two related manuscripts, with introduction by Eric G. Millar (Lond. 1923).

897 MILLAR (ERIC G.). The Luttrell psalter. Lond. 1932.

898 MILLAR (ERIC G.). A thirteenth-century York psalter: a MS. written and illuminated in the diocese of York about A.D. 1250. Roxburghe Club. 1952.

899 OAKESHOTT (WALTER F.). The artists of the Winchester Bible. Lond. 1945.

900 QUEEN MARY'S PSALTER: Miniatures and drawings by an English artist of the fourteenth century. Reproduced from Royal MS. 2 B vii in the British Museum with an introduction by Sir George Warner. Lond. 1912.

901 RICKERT (MARGARET). The reconstructed Carmelite missal. Lond. 1952.

902 THE ST. ALBANS PSALTER. MS. described by Francis Wormald, miniatures by Otto Pächt, initials by C. R. Dodwell, palaeography by Francis Wormald. *Studies of the Warburg Institute*, vol. xxv. Lond. 1960.

903 TWO EAST ANGLIAN PSALTERS AT THE BODLEIAN LIBRARY, OXFORD. The Ormesby Psalter: MS. Douce 366 described by Sidney C. Cockerell. The Bromholm Psalter: MS. Ashmole 1523 described by Montague R. James. Roxburghe Club. 1926.

904 WORMALD (FRANCIS). English drawings of the tenth and eleventh centuries. Lond. 1952. Idem, 'The survival of Anglo-Saxon illumination after the Norman Conquest', *P.B.A.* xxx (1944), 127–45.

7. Costume, Armour, and Weapons

For illustrations of medieval costumes, we are dependent upon the Bayeux Tapestry, sculpture, illuminated manuscripts, embroidery, stained glass, and monumental brasses. Accordingly works on these subjects should be consulted. Writings on the history of the theatre sometimes deal with the development of costumes. Bibliographies are available in Blanch M. Baker, *The theatre and allied arts* (N.Y. 1952), pp. 314–51; Hilaire and Meyer Hiler, *Bibliography of costume, a dictionary catalogue of about eight thousand books and periodicals,* ed. by Helen G. Cushing (N.Y. 1939); and Isabel S. Munro and Dorothy E. Cook, eds. *Costume index,* a subject index to plates and to illustrated text (N.Y. 1937), with a Supplement edited by Isabel S. Munro and Kate M. Munro (N.Y. 1957). Consult also the sections on military history (pp. 619–27, etc.).

For bibliography on arms and armour, see the *Catalogue of European Arms and Armour of the Wallace Collection,* part iii (Lond. 1945). For heraldic devices, coats of arms, armorial bearings, etc. see pp. 59–62 above. Summary chapters on civil costume and on arms and armour appear in *Medieval England* (No. 1485), pp. 300–37.

905 ASHDOWN (CHARLES H.). British and foreign arms and armour, illustrated with 450 engravings in the text and 42 plates, etc. Lond. 1909. Idem, Armour and weapons in the middle ages. Lond. 1925.

The illustrations of the second are not so good as those of the first book.

906 BLAIR (CLAUDE). European Armour circa 1066 to circa 1700. Lond. 1958.

A good textbook.

907 BOEHN (MAX ULRICH von). Die Mode. 8 vols. Munich. 1908–25. Vols. i–iv translated by Joan Joshua: Modes and manners. 4 vols. Lond. 1932–5. *

Vol. i: from the decline of the ancient world to the Renaissance.

908 BRADFIELD (NANCY M.). Historical costumes of England, from the eleventh to the twentieth century. Lond. 1938. 2nd edn. revised. 1958.

909 BRETT (EDWIN J.). A pictorial and descriptive record of the origin and development of arms and armour. Lond. 1894.

133 valuable plates.

910 CALTHROP (DION C.). English costume. 4 vols. Lond. 1906. Reissued in one vol. 1907. 6th reprinting, as English costume from William I to George IV 1066–1830. Lond. 1937.

911 CUNNINGTON (CECIL W.) and (PHILLIS). Handbook of English mediaeval costume. Lond. 1952.

912 DAVIDSON (HILDA R. E.). The sword in Anglo-Saxon England: its archaeology and literature. Oxf. 1962.

913 DRUITT (HERBERT). A manual of costume as illustrated by monumental brasses. Lond. 1906.

914 FAIRHOLT (FREDERICK W.). Costume in England: a history of dress to the end of the eighteenth century. Lond. 1846. 4th edn. by H. A. Dillon. 2 vols. 1896. *(1885 edn.).

Vol. i. History. Vol. ii. Glossary.

915 FFOULKES (CHARLES J.). The armourer and his craft: from the XIth to the XVIth century. Lond. 1912. * See No. 1495 (e).

916 HEWITT (JOHN). Ancient armour and weapons in Europe: from the iron period of the northern nations to the end of the seventeenth century. 3 vols. Oxf. etc. 1855–60. *
This work cites medieval documentary sources.

917 HOLLIS (THOMAS) and (GEORGE). The monumental effigies of Great Britain. Drawn and etched by T. Hollis and G. Hollis. Lond. 1840–2.

918 HOUSTON (MARY G.). 'Medieval costume in England and France: the 13th, 14th, and 15th centuries' (Illustrated). *A technical history of costume,* vol. iii. Lond. 1939. Reprinted (1950).

919 KELLY (FRANCIS M.) and SCHWABE (RANDOLPH). A short history of costume and armour chiefly in England, 1066–1800. 2 vols. Lond. 1931.
Vol. i. 1066–1485.

920 LAKING (GUY F.). A record of European armour and arms through seven centuries. 5 vols. Lond. 1920–2.
The record includes numerous illustrations.

921 LAVER (JAMES). Costumes through the ages. Lond. 1963.

922 MACALISTER (ROBERT A. S.). Ecclesiastical vestments: their development and history. Lond. 1896. *
Also Joseph Braun, *Die liturgische Gewandung im Occident und Orient nach Ursprung und Entwicklung, Verwendung und Symbolik* (Freiburg etc. 1907). Cf. Cabrol and Leclercq, *DACL* (No. 763), vol. xv, *under* 'Vêtement'.

923 NORRIS (HERBERT). Costume and fashion. Vols. i–iii (2 pts.), vi. Lond. etc. 1924–38.
Vol. i: The evolution of European dress through the earlier ages.
Vol. ii: Senlac to Bosworth, 1066–1485.

924 OAKESHOTT (R. EWART). The archaeology of weapons: arms and armour from prehistory to the age of chivalry. Lond. and N.Y. 1966.

925 PLANCHÉ (JAMES R.). A cyclopaedia of costume . . .: a general chronological history of the costumes of the principal countries of Europe, from the commencement of the Christian era to the accession of George the Third (elaborately illustrated). 2 vols. Lond. 1876–9.
Vol. i: Dictionary. Vol. ii: History. Planché also wrote a shorter *History of British costume* (Lond. 1834; 3rd edn. 1874. Reprinted, 1881, 1900, 1907).

926 SHAW (HENRY). Dresses and decorations of the Middle Ages, from the seventh to the seventeenth centuries. 2 vols. Lond. 1843. Reprinted, 1859.
94 valuable coloured plates.

927   STOTHARD (CHARLES A.). The monumental effigies of Great Britain
. . . from the Norman conquest to the reign of Henry the Eighth. Lond. 1817.
New edn. with large additions, by John Hewitt. Lond. 1876.

928   STRUTT (JOSEPH). A complete view of the dress and habits of the
people of England. 2 vols. Lond. 1796–9. New edn. by J. R. Planché. 1842. 143
valuable coloured plates.

  Standard reference work. Vol. i: to the thirteenth century; Vol. ii: to 1800.

928A   STRUTT (J.). Glig-Gamena Angel Deod, or the sports and pastimes
of the people of England, from the earliest period to the present time, illustrated
by engravings selected from ancient paintings. Lond. 1801. New edn. by J. C.
Cox. 1903. Reprinted, Lond. 1969 and N.Y. 1970.

  Still the best book on pastimes. See also C. P. Hargrave, *A history of playing cards and
  a bibliography of cards and gaming* (Boston and N.Y. 1930), and Harold J. R. Murray,
  A history of chess (Oxf. 1913).

PART TWO

ARCHIVES, SOURCE COLLECTIONS, AND MODERN NARRATIVES

IV. ARCHIVES AND LIBRARIES

THE repositories of manuscripts fall into two general categories: (*a*) archives in which public documents or documents of a public nature are stored under official supervision, and (*b*) libraries which, in addition to the accumulation of printed books, have acquired collections of manuscripts. For the study of manuscripts the two correlative disciplines of palaeography, or the study of the handwritten scripts of former ages, and diplomatic, or the study of the textual construction, formulae, etc. of manuscripts, are essential. Archives, libraries possessing manuscripts, palaeography, and diplomatic are interdependent subjects to be treated conjointly. Special bibliographies for these topics are extensive and cannot be reproduced in full here; however, guides to further material are suggested in the introductions to sections in this chapter.

A. BIBLIOGRAPHICAL GUIDES

The most important journal is *Scriptorium*, No. 381. Consult *Bulletin of the National Register* (No. 943), and *List of Accessions* (No. 942).

929 AMERICAN ARCHIVIST. Soc. of Amer. Archivists. Washington. 1938+.

It includes an annual survey of writings on archives and manuscripts.

930 ARCHIVES. The journal of the British Records Association. Lond. 1949+. *

Indispensable for the student of British archives. Contains, *inter alia*, a series of reports on the local archives of Great Britain (No. 1504), and lists of record publications supplementary to the *Handlist of record publications* (No. 933).

931 ARCHIVUM. Revue internationale des archives, published by UNESCO and Conseil international des archives. Paris. 1951+.

Includes Bibliographie analytique internationale des publications relatives à l'archivistique et aux archives. For the United Kingdom, see ii (1952), 212–18; iii (1953), 177–82; iv (1954), 282–6; vii (1957), 212–25; etc.

932 GUIDE INTERNATIONAL DES ARCHIVES: EUROPE. Société des nations: Institut international de coopération intellectuelle. Vol. i (Europe). Rome and Paris. 1934. Supplément. 1935.

Pp. 276–323 Hilary Jenkinson on British archives. Supplement by R. H. Bautier, 'Bibliographie sélective des guides d'archives', *Jour. Documentation*, ix (1953), 1–41.

933 HANDLIST OF RECORD PUBLICATIONS. England. Ed. by Robert Somerville. British Records Assoc. Pamphlet No. 3. Lond. 1951. Scottish section by Peter Gouldesbrough and A. P. Kup; and Welsh section by Idwal Lewis. British Records Assoc. Pamphlet No. 4. Lond. 1954.

934 JOURNAL OF DOCUMENTATION: devoted to the recording, organization, and dissemination of specialized knowledge. Assoc. Spec. Libraries and Information Bureaux. Lond. 1945+. *

935 JOURNAL OF THE SOCIETY OF ARCHIVISTS. Lond. 1955+.

Includes important articles on individual libraries.

936 YEAR'S (FIVE YEARS') WORK IN ARCHIVES. 1933+.

Printed annually from 1933 to 1937, and then periodically from 1938 to 1947 in *The Year's Work in Librarianship* by the Library Association, London. The latter publication has been replaced by *Five Years' Work in Librarianship*, the first volume of which for the period 1951–5 appeared in 1958. The first volume reported the Work in Archives for 1948–55; subsequent reports appeared in the volume for 1956–60 and the volume for 1961–5. Most, if not all, of the reports have been reissued for the British Records Association.

B. REPOSITORIES

1. *British Archives*

The official repositories for the public records of the United Kingdom are the Public Record Office (London), the Scottish Record Office (Edinburgh), and the Public Record Office in Northern Ireland (Belfast). Some public records are also housed in the Public Record Office of the Republic of Ireland (Dublin) and in the National Library of Wales (Aberystwyth). Further public records, including many of importance for the medieval period, may be found in the local record offices which have been established in recent decades in most English and some Welsh counties as well as in a number of boroughs and other places. Brief descriptions of some of the more important of the local record offices are provided in a series entitled Local Archives of Great Britain in the journal, *Archives*, and are listed below on page 213. The list of *Record repositories in Great Britain* (No. 944) and the (annual) *List of accessions to repositories* (No. 942) are essential reference works.

Manuscripts belonging to private families and institutions and to the archives of cities, boroughs, cathedrals, colleges, etc. have been the concern of the Royal Commission on Historical Manuscripts. This commission was established in 1869; its competence was significantly broadened in 1959. It has issued periodic reports since 1870. For its reports and other valuable publications, consult No. 945 below.

In 1945 the National Register of Archives was inaugurated as an activity of the Historical Manuscripts Commission, with the aim of reporting on the collections in all the archives of England and Wales, except those of the state. Its functions are described by Lionel W. Van Kersen in 'The National Register of Archives

(London)', *American Archivist*, xxiii (1960), 319–38. For the reports of the National Register, consult its *Bulletin* (No. 943). The Register also prepares the *List of accessions* (No. 942). The scope of the Register's survey is enormous and the bulk of its reports staggering. Copies of the full reports may be found in the National Register's Office (Quality Court, Chancery Lane, London, W.C. 2), the British Museum, the University Library at Cambridge, the Bodleian Library, the John Rylands Library at Manchester, the National Library of Wales, and the Institute of Historical Research of the University of London. An index to the contents of the reports is being prepared and may be consulted at the National Register's Office. There is also an independent Register of National Archives (Scotland) with its separate organization.

In 1958–9 the Historical Manuscripts Commission had also committed to its care the registers of manorial documents and the sealed (local) copies of instruments of tithe apportionment which had been maintained by the Public Record Office under the direction of the Master of the Rolls since 1926 and 1937 respectively.

For ecclesiastical documents, classified lists of the archives of dioceses, cathedrals, and archdeaconries of both provinces of Canterbury and York appeared in typewritten copies of *A Survey of ecclesiastical archives*, which is the shortened title of *A Survey of the principal collections of archives of the Church of England* (made between 1946 and 1951 under the direction of Miss L. M. Midgley and issued by the Pilgrim Trust). Copies of the survey are deposited in the Bodleian Library, the British Museum, the Institute of Historical Research, the National Register's Office, and the Public Record Office. Appropriate sections are also available in appropriate local archives. Although the survey is still very useful, it is somewhat out of date as a guide to repositories. Some changes are noted by C. E. Welch in 'The preservation of ecclesiastical records', *Archives*, iv, No. 22 (1959), 75–80, where a list of diocesan records as of 1958 is printed. The submission of some diocesan records to county record offices continued in the sixties. *Record repositories in Great Britain* (1968) (No. 944) indicates in summary fashion the location of diocesan records. The principal catalogues of the manuscript collections of ecclesiastical corporations are listed below on pages 127–9. The location of some ecclesiastical records, especially those concerned with wills, is given in Peter Walne, *English wills* (Richmond, Va. 1964); and in Camp. *Wills and their whereabouts* (No. 4506). The most-up-to-date (1970) listing of locations is given in Dorothy Owen, *Records of the established church in England* (British Records Assoc. Archives and the User, No. 1 (1970)). See No. 5574.

The guides to local archives are listed, county by county, in the chapter on Local History, below pp. 215–55. Summary statements are given in Maurice F. Bond, 'Record Offices today', *B.I.H.R.* xxx (1957), 1–16; in F. G. Emmison, 'New sources of British history: the service of the local record office', *History*, xli (1956), 176–83; and especially in Philip Hepworth (No. 940). The *Bulletin of the National Archives* (No. 943) carries a list of County Honorary Secretaries with addresses; and P. H. Hardacre prints 'County record offices in England and Wales: a list of guides and references', in *American Archivist*, xxv (1962), 477–83. However, since changes in the development of local repositories occur with some rapidity, printed lists do not long remain current guides.

(a) General Works

937 CHENEY (CHRISTOPHER R.). The records of medieval England. Inaugural lecture. Cambr. 1956.

938 CLARK (GEORGE S. R. KITSON) and ELTON (GEOFFREY R.). Guide to research facilities in history in the universities of Great Britain and Ireland. Cambr. 1963. 2nd edn. 1965.

939 HALL (HUBERT). A repertory of British archives: pt. i, England. Royal Hist. Soc. Lond. 1920. See No. 952.

940 HEPWORTH (PHILIP). Archives and manuscripts in libraries. Library Assoc. 2nd edn. Lond. 1964.

This work includes a near-forty-page bibliography of catalogues and guides to local collections.

941 JENKINSON (HILARY). A manual of archive administration. Oxf. 1922. 2nd edn. 1937. Reprinted with introduction and bibliography by Roger H. Ellis. 1965.

H. Jenkinson, *The English archivist: a new profession*, being an inaugural lecture for a new course in archive administration (Lond. 1948). Charles Johnson, *The care of documents and management of archives*, Helps for Students of History, No. 5 (Lond. 1919). Henry G. T. Christopher, *Palaeography and archives: a manual for the librarian, archivist and student* (Lond. 1938), which is a textbook summarizing much English material.

942 LIST OF ACCESSIONS TO REPOSITORIES. Hist. MSS. Comm. H.M.S.O. Lond. 1958+.

This annual list covers repositories in England, Wales, Scotland, and Northern Ireland. The lists, which were formerly printed in *B.I.H.R.* (from 1930 to 1951; and then shorter lists), became the responsibility of the Hist. MSS. Comm. in 1954; and until 1957 were published as special numbers of the *Bulletin of the National Register* (No. 943); since, then, although they have continued to be prepared by the Register, they have been published separately and annually.

943 NATIONAL REGISTER OF ARCHIVES, BULLETIN. Published under the direction of the Registrar of the National Register of Archives. Lond. 1948+.

A work of great value for its descriptions of MSS. in private hands. From 1950 to 1957, the *Bulletin* included 'Summaries of Selected Reports'; since 1957 it has concentrated on reports from outstanding archives. Since September 1957, summaries of all reports have been printed as an appendix to the *Hist. MSS. Comm. Reports* (No. 945).

944 RECORD REPOSITORIES IN GREAT BRITAIN. H.M.S.O. Lond. 1964. 2nd edn. 1966. 3rd edn. 1968.

This list was prepared by a joint committee of the Hist. MSS. Comm. and the British Records Assoc. and in the 1966 edition named over 250 repositories. It replaces the *List of record repositories in Great Britain*, which was published by British Records Assoc. Reports from Committee No. 5 (1956). The latter was based on the reports to *Archivum* (No. 931) for an international directory of archives. See *Archivum*, v (1955), 192–218. The British Records Assoc. projects a series of pamphlets, entitled *Archives and the User*, written by specialists; the announced titles give promise of a helpful series.

945 REPORTS OF THE ROYAL COMMISSION ON HISTORICAL MANUSCRIPTS. Lond. 1870+.

These reports relate to MSS. in private libraries and to the archives of cities, boroughs, cathedrals, colleges, etc. The first report appeared in 1870; the twenty-third report covering the years 1946–59 appeared in 1961. The twenty-third report began a series of Reports to the Crown which 'should include in an Appendix summaries of all reports upon MS. collections received (mainly through the National Register of Archives) during the year'. Down to the Fifteenth Report (1899), each report was followed by an elaborate appendix, usually of several parts or volumes which contained valuable extracts or calendars of the documents examined. Since 1899 such calendars have been issued independently. Sectional List No. 17 (H.M.S.O. London) lists the publications of the Hist. MSS. Comm. as does Mullins, *Texts* (No. 29), pp. 61–90. Indexes to the reports have been published as *Part I, Topographical* (Lond. 1914); *Part II, Index of personal names*, edited by Francis Bickley, 2 vols. (Lond. 1935, 1938). *A guide to the reports . . . 1911–1957, part ii: index of persons*, edited by A. C. S. Hall (Lond. H.M.S.O. 1966), is a composite index in three volumes of all persons mentioned in the indexes to the 1911–57 Reports. See No. 4693.

A history of the Commission by Roger H. Ellis and of its more important collections is provided in the catalogue to the commemorative exhibition held at the National Portrait Gallery in 1969 entitled *Manuscripts and Men* (H.M.S.O. 1969). For a general survey, see Roger H. Ellis, 'The Historical Manuscript Commission, 1869–1969 [*sic*]', *Jour. Soc. Archivists*, ii (1960–4), 233–42.

In 1959–60 the Commission initiated a joint publication plan under which material, though selected and prepared by record societies, might become a joint publication of the record society and the *Hist. MSS. Comm.* Part iii of the Missenden cartulary (No. 6094) appeared as Joint Publication No. 1 in 1962; and others have followed.

(b) Public Record Office

The medieval public records of England are more copious and more complete than those of any other European government. Although often subject to neglect and migrations before the middle of the nineteenth century, they have rarely suffered through the invasions and civil wars that have wrought havoc elsewhere. A complete history of the records and their remarkable survival has not yet been written; but the main outlines and particular topics have been described. On these subjects, see Edwards (No. 974) and immediately below Nos. 947, 952, 953, 970, and the bibliography attached to the 1912–19 Reports (No. 966).

The early history of the record repositories is obscure. Some documents required for current business travelled with the itinerant royal household; others were deposited in places of safety such as the royal Treasury at Winchester, subsequently at Westminster. As each function of government emerged as a distinct court or department, so it acquired its own repository. See especially Galbraith (No. 949) and Tout's British Academy lecture (No. 1499) and Tout's Administrative History (No. 1223). There are said to have been more than sixty such repositories in and around London before the reign of Queen Victoria (Hardy's *Langdale* (No. 953), ii. 112 and 143), accommodating past and accruing documents. The largest collections were housed in the Tower of London, the Chapter House at Westminster, the New Temple, the State Paper Office, and the Rolls Chapel in Chancery Lane. A table of records and their former repositories is given in Hall, *Studies* (No. 952), pp. 111–14.

The condition of records in these storehouses had long caused concern. In the seventeenth century Prynne complained in his *Brevia Parliamentaria Rediviva* that records in the Tower 'had for many years past layen buried in one confused chaos under corroding, putrifying cobwebs, dust [and] filth' and that he, their keeper, had proceeded to 'rake up this dung-heap'. In the eighteenth century parliamentary committees complained of the neglect of the public muniments; in 1800 a comprehensive review of the situation was ordered. As a result, the first Record Commission of Great Britain 'to provide for the better arrangement, preservation, and more convenient use of the said records' was appointed; this commission was followed by others appointed in 1806, 1817, 1821, and 1831. Under their direction, some editions of early records were produced; yet little attention was directed to the fundamental care and preservation of the great accumulation. On the Commissions' work, see below, Nos. 963, 964, 965.

Following a spate of criticism and acrimonious personal dissension, a committee of the House of Commons reported in 1836 on the unsafe and squalid condition of many valuable records. The Record Commission was brought to an end in 1837; and in the following year the Public Record Office Act, 1 & 2 Vic. c. 94, was passed 'to establish one Record Office and a better custody, and to allow for the free use of the said records'. The records of the ancient courts, Exchequer and Chancery, Queen's Bench and Common Pleas, Admiralty and some others, were placed in the care of the Master of the Rolls; the Treasury was empowered to provide buildings; and a staff, headed by a Deputy Keeper, was created. The definition of public records was amplified by an Order in Council in 1852 to include 'all records belonging to Her Majesty deposited in any office, court, place or custody', with a few exceptions. Between 1856 and 1859 the contents of most of the former repositories were moved to the new Public Record Office, where the sorting, repair, listing, and publication have been carried on ever since.

These achievements of the nineteenth century laid a firm foundation. In 1910 a Royal Commission was appointed to inquire into and report on the working of the 1838 Act; it was further directed to look into the custody of local records of a public nature, the training of archivists and similar matters. Its first report was issued in 1912; its second in 1914; and its third in 1919. By the middle of the twentieth century, 'it had become clear that existing administrative arrangements were no longer adequate to cope with the immense quantities of documents accumulating in government departments'. A departmental committee under the chairmanship of Sir James Grigg was appointed and reported (Cmd. 9163) in 1954 on the selection and preservation of these masses of documents. As a result, the Public Records Act 1958, 6 & 7 Eliz. II, c. 51, reconstituted the Public Record Office and placed it and all public records, whether legal or departmental, under the general responsibility of the Lord Chancellor, assisted by an Advisory Council under the chairmanship of the Master of the Rolls. The Lord Chancellor was empowered to appoint a Keeper of Public Records to take charge under his direction of the Public Record Office and the records therein.

The records of the various extraordinary, palatine jurisdictions, such as those of Durham, Lancaster, Chester, Cornwall, and Wales, were kept separately at their administrative centres until the middle of the nineteenth century. The records of the palatinate of Ely and the duchy of Cornwall have never been transferred to the Public Record Office. The archives of the palatinate of Chester and of the principality of Wales were removed to the Public Record Office in 1854, but the records of the Courts of Great Sessions were returned to Wales in 1962, to be deposited in the National Library of Wales (K. O. Fox, 'The records of the Courts of Great Sessions', *Jour. Soc. Archivists*, iii. (1966), 177–82). Those of the duchy of Lancaster were brought to the Public Record Office in 1868; on them see R. Somerville, 'Duchy of Lancaster records', *T.R.H.S.* 4th Ser. xi (1928), 17–37. The records of the palatinate of Durham were transferred to the P.R.O. in the same year; but in 1876 those relating to the estates of the bishopric were assigned to the custody of the Ecclesiastical Commissioners, whose successors in 1956 deposited them at the Prior's Kitchen, Durham. J. Conway Davies describes 'Ecclesiastical and Palatinate archives at the Prior's Kitchen, Durham' in *Jour. Soc. Archivists*, i, no. 7 (1958), 185–91.

The Public Record Office stands in Chancery Lane, London, on part of the estate once belonging to the Masters of the Rolls. See Roger H. Ellis in *Jenkinson Essays* (No. 1440) and Charles Johnson in *Jenkinson Studies* (No. 1441). With certain exceptions, all public records are open, thirty years after their creation, to inspection by holders of students' tickets. The comprehensive *Guide* is No. 951. Photographic services now supplement the facilities of the several Search Rooms.

946   [AYLOFFE, (JOSEPH).] Calendars of the ancient charters, with an introduction giving some account of the state of the public records from the [Norman] conquest to the present time. Lond. 1772. Reprinted, 1774, with Ayloffe's name on the title-page.

The introduction, said to have been written by Thomas Astle, contains much material concerning the history of the records. For a later edition, see No. 3750.

947   COOPER (CHARLES P.). An account of the most important public records of Great Britain and the publications of the record commissions . . . Record Comm. 2 vols. Lond. 1832.

See also idem, *A proposal for the erection of a general office* [with remarks on the history of the records], Record Comm. (Lond. 1832). This was remodelled and printed for the convenience of the Record Commission in 1835, under the title, *Papers relative to the project of building a general record office.*

948   EWALD (ALEXANDER C.). Our public records: a brief handbook to the national archives. Lond. 1873.

Contains a brief account of the history of the archives, taken mainly from Thomas's handbook (No. 952); a useful alphabetical list of the records; an essay on the state papers; and a glossary of words found in records. The account of the archives, rewritten, will also be found in his *Paper and parchment* (Lond. 1890), pp. 249–80.

949   GALBRAITH (VIVIAN H.). An introduction to the use of the public records. Oxf. 1934. Idem, Studies in the public records. Lond. etc. 1948. N.Y. 1949.

Charles G. Crump, *Encycl. Brit.* 11th edn. under 'Records'; Hilary Jenkinson, 'The Public Record Office and its work', in Irwin (No. 1006), pp. 55–91; Charles Johnson, *The Public Record Office*, Helps for Students of History, No. 4 (Lond. 1918); Idem, in *Jenkinson Studies* (No. 1441); A. E. Stamp, 'The Public Record Office and the historical student: a retrospect', *T.R.H.S.* 4th Ser. xi (1928), 17–37.

950 GREAT BRITAIN STATIONERY OFFICE. British National Archives : Sectional List No. 24. Formerly, Record Publications : Sectional List No. 24; and List of Record Publications : List Q. H.M.S.O. Lond.

Revised from time to time. An invaluable list of P.R.O. Calendars, Guides, printed Lists and Indexes, Privy Council Registers, and of the Rolls Series, and of the publications of the Record Commissioners, as well as government record publications relating to Scotland, Ireland, and Northern Ireland. It also includes works in facsimile and miscellaneous publications sponsored by the government.

951 GUIDE TO THE CONTENTS OF THE PUBLIC RECORD OFFICE. 2 vols. H.M.S.O. Lond. 1963. Vol. iii: Documents transferred 1960–66. H.M.S.O. 1969.

This indispensable guide is a revision (to 1960) of the work of M. S. Giuseppi entitled *A guide to the manuscripts preserved in the Public Record Office*, 2 vols. (Lond. 1923–4). Vol. i bears the sub-title *Legal Records*, etc. and contains the references to medieval records. The latest *Guide*, like that by Giuseppi, is arranged as a classification of documents by their administrative origin; but it differs from Giuseppi's work not only in the revision of descriptions but also by the addition of the class number for each category. An introduction of 70 pages, prepared by Sir Hilary Jenkinson and published by H.M.S.O. (Lond. 1949) is not included in the 1963 edition.

These editions have superseded Francis S. Thomas, *Handbook to the Public Records* (Lond. 1853), and Samuel R. Scargill-Bird, *A guide to the principal classes of documents preserved in the Public Record Office* (Lond. 1891; 3rd edn. 1908). Scargill-Bird's guide was arranged as a subject-index.

952 HALL (HUBERT). The antiquities and curiosities of the exchequer. Lond. 1891. Reprinted. 1898. * Idem, Studies in English official historical documents. Cambr. 1908. *

The first two chapters of *The antiquities* form an account of the early history of the public archives; pt. i of the *Studies* (pp. 13–52) contains the history, classification, etc. of archives.

953 HARDY (THOMAS D.). Memoirs of the Right Honourable Henry, Lord Langdale. 2 vols. Lond. 1852.

There is a good account of the history of the public records, from 1837 to 1851, in vol. ii, pp. 111–93. The establishment of the present Record Office was due mainly to the efforts of Lord Langdale. See Roger H. Ellis, 'The building of the Public Record Office' in *Jenkinson essays* (No. 1440).

954 LANGLOIS (CHARLES VICTOR) and STEIN (HENRI). Les archives de l'histoire de France. 3 pts. Paris. 1891–3.

Great Britain, pp. 711–41.

955 LISTS AND INDEXES (of records preserved in the Public Record Office). H.M.S.O. Lond. 1892+. A Kraus reprint produced from the reference copy in the P.R.O. with numerous corrections and additions. N.Y. 1963+.

These are the finding-lists prepared for use in the Search Rooms of the P.R.O. Between 1892 and 1936, fifty-five volumes appeared in this valuable series; a complete list is given in *British National Archives* (No. 950). Other lists and indexes prepared for the Search Rooms are being issued in a Supplementary Series, 1964+, and by the List and Index Society founded in 1965. The volumes which appertain to the Middle Ages are:

No. i. Index of ancient petitions of the chancery and the exchequer, Edw. I–Hen. VII: No. 3225. Revised on reissue, 1966.

No. iv. List of plea rolls, 5 Rich. I onward: No. 3496.

Nos. v, viii, xxxiv. List of original ministers' accounts, Edw. I–Hen. VIII. 2 pts. and index to pt. 1 (no. viii): No. 3228.

No. vi. List and index of court rolls, pt. i. Edw. I–Geo. III (1896).

No. ix. List of sheriffs for England and Wales, to 1831: No. 3740.

No. xi. List of foreign [i.e. not sheriffs'] accounts enrolled on the great rolls of the exchequer, Hen. III–Rich. III: No. 3227.

Nos. xii, xvi. pt. ii, xx, xxix, xxxviii. List of early chancery proceedings, mainly 1386–1529, 5 vols.: No. 3496.

No. xiv. List of the records of the duchy of Lancaster, 1066 onward (1901); Supplementary Lists (3 vols.). No. 3879.

No. xv. List of ancient correspondence of the chancery and the exchequer, *circa* Rich. I–Hen. VII: Nos. 3224, 3775. Revised and enlarged edn. 1968–9.

Nos. xvii, xxii. List of inquisitions *ad quod damnum*, Hen. III–Rich. III, 2 pts.: No. 3758.

No. xxv. List of rentals and surveys, Edw. I–Charles II (1908).

No. xxvii. List of chancery rolls, 1 John onward.

No. xxxii. Index of *placita de banco*, 1327–28, 2 pts.: No. 3496.

No. xxxv. List of various accounts formerly preserved in the exchequer, Hen. II–Geo. III (1912); Supplementary Lists, ix: No. 3226.

No. xl. List of records of Chester, Durham, Lancaster, Peveril, and Wales (1914): Nos. 3856, 3878–9.

No. xlix. List of diplomatic and Scottish documents and papal bulls.

955A LISTS AND INDEXES: SUPPLEMENTARY (Not reprints). Kraus Reprint Corporation. 1964+.

    i. Lists of various common law records. 1970. No. 3496.
    ii. List of ministers' accounts. 1967.
    v. Supplementary list of records: Duchy of Lancaster. 3 vols. 1964–5.
    ix. Exchequer records: List of accounts various. 1969. No. 3226.
    xiv. List of rentals and surveys. 1969.
    xv. Index to ancient correspondence of the chancery and the exchequer. 2 vols. 1969.

956 LIST AND INDEX SOCIETY

An independent, private society which supplies to its members copies of unpublished lists and indexes in the Public Record Office. These lists are essential tools for research in the P.R.O. Those bearing on medieval history are analysed below (No. 7222).

957 LYTE (HENRY C. MAXWELL). 'The rolls chapel'. *Deputy Keeper's Reports*, lvii (1896), 19–47.

Cf. W. J. Hardy, '(History of) the rolls house and chapel', *Middlesex and Herts. Notes and Queries*, ii (1896), 49–68; and his popular account of the contents of the Record Office, entitled 'Our public records' in *Notes and Queries* (No. 136), 6 May–15 July 1893.

958 [NICOLAS (NICHOLAS HARRIS)]. Public records: a description of the contents, objects, and uses of the various works published by the Record Commission. Lond. 1831.

959 PALGRAVE (FRANCIS). The antient kalendars and inventories of the treasury of His Majesty's exchequer, with other documents illustrating the history of that repository. Record Comm. 3 vols. Lond. 1836.

Other early inventories are given in 'Inventory of the records in the Tower', *Deputy Keeper's Reports*, ii, app. ii, pp. 1–65; Catalogue of the records in the office of the king's remembrancer of the exchequer (1066–1272), Record Comm. [Lond. 1835]: Adam Martin, *Index to repositories and other records in the court of exchequer* (Lond. 1819); Frank Taylor, 'An early seventeenth century calendar of records preserved in Westminster Palace treasury', *B.J.R.L.* xxiii (1939), 228–341.

960   POWELL (THOMAS). The repertorie of records remaining in the four treasuries of the receipt side at Westminster, the two remembrancers of the exchequer, etc., as also a calendar of the records of the Tower. Lond. 1631.

A large portion of this work was compiled from notes collected by Arthur Agarde, an Elizabethan deputy chamberlain of the exchequer who made transcripts of many documents (see *D.N.B.*).

961   REPORT OF THE LORDS COMMITTEES APPOINTED TO VIEW THE PUBLICK RECORDS, as also in what manner and place the same are now kept. Lond. 1719. Reprinted as The state of the public records of the kingdom. Lond. 1723.

For a summary of reports of commissions 1703–1919, see Hubert Hall, *British Archives . . . World War* (Lond. and New Haven, 1925), pp. 210–44.

962   REPORT FROM THE COMMITTEE APPOINTED TO VIEW THE COTTONIAN LIBRARY AND SUCH OF THE PUBLIC RECORDS OF THIS KINGDOM AS THEY THINK PROPER, and to report to the house the condition thereof. Lond. 1732. Also printed in Reports from Committees of the House of Commons, i. 445–535. Lond. [1773].

Deals with eighteen record repositories in London. App. F contains some valuable documents relating to the history of the records, 14 Edw. II–1712.

963   REPORTS FROM THE SELECT COMMITTEE APPOINTED TO INQUIRE INTO THE STATE OF THE PUBLIC RECORDS OF THE KINGDOM. Reported 4 July 1800. *Reports from Committees of the House of Commons*, vol. xv. Lond. [1803].

Embraces the public record offices, libraries of universities, cathedrals, inns of court, Lambeth Palace, British Museum, etc. Thomas (*Handbook*, p. xx) calls this 'the most important volume on the records of this country that has ever appeared'. Cf. Peter Walne, 'The Record Commissions, 1800–1837', *Jour. Soc. Archivists*, ii, No. 1 (1960), 8–16.

964   REPORTS [First and Second] FROM THE COMMISSIONERS ON THE PUBLIC RECORDS, 1800–1819. 2 vols. *Parl. Papers*, 1819, vol. xx. [Lond.] 1819.

965   GENERAL REPORT FROM THE COMMISSIONERS [1831–37]. *Parl. Papers*. 1837, vol. xxxiv. [Lond.] 1837.

The proceedings of the commissioners from 1819 to 1831 were not printed. The report of 1837 embraces (besides the public record offices) the municipal archives, the libraries of universities, cathedrals, inns of court, Lambeth Palace, British Museum, etc. See also the first report (1912) of the Record Commission appointed in 1910.

See also the following: (1) Report from the select committee appointed to inquire into the affairs of the record commission and the present state of the records of the United Kingdom, *Parl. Papers*, 1836, vol. xvi (Lond. 1836). (2) *Proceedings of his majesty's commissioners on the public records of the kingdom, June, 1832–August, 1833*, ed. C. P. Cooper (Lond. 1833), which contains valuable extracts from the early plea rolls, fines, wardrobe accounts, memoranda rolls, etc.; seemingly only 25 copies were printed, for the use of the commissioners. (3) [Charles Purton Cooper], *A proposal for the erection of a general record office* [with remarks on the history of the records], Record Comm. (Lond. 1832), which was remodelled and printed for the convenience of the Record Commission in 1835, under the title, *Papers relative to the Project of Building a General Record Office.* (4) William Illingworth, *Observations on the public records of the four courts at Westminster* [Lond. 1831], p. 67, of which only 50 copies were printed, for the use of the Record Commission.

For controversial literature, see the following: (5) *Letters from eminent historical writers relating to the publications of the commissioners on the public records* (Lond. 1836). (6) *Papers and documents relating to the evidence of certain witnesses examined before the select committee of the house of commons to inquire into the affairs of the record commission* [Lond.] 1837, which supplements the report of 1836 [above (1)]. (7) Nicholas Harris Nicolas, *Observations on the state of historical literature*, with remarks on the record offices and on the proceedings of the record commissioners (Lond. 1830). (8) Idem, *Refutation of Mr. Palgrave's Remarks*, etc. [below (10)]: additional facts relative to the record commission and record offices (Lond. 1831). (9) Idem, *Record commission: a letter to Lord Brougham on the constitution and proceedings of the commission* (Lond. 1832); cf. his remarks on the public records and the Record Commission, in *Retrospective Review*, ix (1827), 55–76; and *Westminster Review*, x (1829), 393–414. (10) Francis Palgrave, *Remarks in reply to a pamphlet by N. H. Nicolas, entitled Observations on the state of historical literature* [above, (7)] (Lond. 1831); cf. his article on 'Records and registration', *Quarterly Review*, xxxix (1829), 41–73, also in his *Collected Works*, ix, 153–86 (Cambr. 1922).

966 REPORT OF THE ROYAL [Pollock] COMMISSION ON THE PUBLIC RECORDS. 3 vols. and appendices. Lond. 1912–19.

First Report (1912) dealt with records in the Public Record Office. Second Report (1914) dealt with public records outside this office. Third Report (1919) dealt with local records of a public nature. Cf. vol. i, pt. ii, pp. 164–8, for a good bibliography on the history of the public records.

967 REPORTS [Annual] OF THE DEPUTY KEEPER OF THE PUBLIC RECORDS. (Reports 1–120) *Parl. Papers.* Lond. 1840–1958. Index (1840–61) 1865; (1862–78) 1880. The annual reports of the Keeper of Public Records on the work of the Public Record Office and the [first report] of the Advisory Council on Public Records. Lond. 1959+.

The appendixes, especially those of reports i–x and xxiv–l, contain many lists and calendars of records. There is a useful abstract of their contents in some of the Catalogues of Record Publications (No. 950).

968 RETURN OF ALL THE RECORD PUBLICATIONS RELATING TO ENGLAND AND WALES PUBLISHED BY THE LATE RECORD AND STATE-PAPER COMMISSIONERS, or under the Master of the Rolls, up to the end of the year 1866, including the Irish and Scotch records. *Parl. Papers.* 1867–8. Vol. lv. [Lond.] 1867.

For a return of the titles of works left unfinished by the Record Commissioners, see ibid. vol. xxxiv (1842).

969 RYE (WALTER). Records and record-searching: a guide to the genealogist and topographer. Lond. 1888. 2nd edn. 1897. *

970 THOMAS (FRANCIS S.). Notes of materials for the history of public departments. Lond. 1846.

Public Record Office, pp. 111–216; the fullest account of the history of the public records. App. E contains a list of the publications of the various record commissions.

971 VIRGINIA COLONIAL RECORDS PROJECT. The British Public Record Office. Special reports 25–8. Richmond (Va.). 1960.

Report 25 gives a brief history of the P.R.O. and makes suggestions for the student beginning his research there. Report 27 specifies the Search Room catalogues and signalizes some of the lists and indexes, printed and typed, available in the Search Rooms.

2. *English Libraries*

(*a*) Catalogues and accounts of general manuscript collections

For medieval libraries, see below, pp. 927–9; and for the Reports of the Royal Commission on Historical Manuscripts, see No. 945 and Hepworth (No. 940).

972 BERNARD (EDWARD). Catalogi librorum MSS. Angliae et Hiberniae in unum collecti cum indice alphabetico. Oxf. 1697.

This old catalogue includes the Bodleian library, the University Library at Cambridge, the college libraries of Oxford and Cambridge, cathedral, and private libraries. It may be supplemented by reference to columns 777–910 of Gustav Haenel, *Catalogi librorum manuscriptorum qui in bibliothecis Galliae, Helvetiae, Belgii, Britanniae M., Hispaniae, Lusitaniae asservantur, nunc primum editi* (Leipzig, 1830). Cf. Thomas Phillipps, *Catalogus MSS. Magnae Britanniae* (2 pts. Middle Hill, 1850), i, pp. iii–iv, on changes of ownership of some of the libraries catalogued by Bernard.

973 CATALOGUS LIBRORUM MSS. IN BIBLIOTHECA THOMAE PHILLIPPS. 3 pts. Middle Hill, [1824–67].

Cf. Schenkl (No. 984), vols. cxxvi–cxxvii. The Phillipps Library of some sixty thousand MSS. has been widely dispersed. For its history and dispersal, see A. N. L. Munby, *Phillipps Studies*, 5 vols. (Cambr. 1951–60), vol. v for the dispersal to 1946. For subsequent sales and dispersal, see Sotheby's Catalogues; and C. R. Cheney in *Traditio*, xxiii (1967), 512–16; and R. W. Hunt, *Bodleian Lib. Rec.* vi (1957), 348–69.

974 EDWARDS (EDWARD). Memoirs of libraries. 2 vols. Lond. 1859. *
Idem, Libraries and founders of libraries. Lond. etc. 1865. *

The former contains an account of the MSS. in the British Museum, the libraries of Oxford and Cambridge, cathedrals, inns of court, Lambeth Palace, etc. In the latter, the history of the State Paper Office, pp. 178–210; the history of the public records, pp. 211–326; synoptical view of the public records, pp. 459–503.

975 HUNTER (JOSEPH). Three catalogues, describing the contents of the Red Book of the Exchequer, of the Dodsworth manuscripts in the Bodleian Library, and of the manuscripts in the library of the Honourable Society of Lincoln's Inn. Lond. 1838.

976 JAMES (MONTAGUE R.). The wanderings and homes of manuscripts. Helps for Students of History, No. 17. Lond. 1919.

See *B.I.H.R.* i+ (1925+) for 'Migrations of historical manuscripts'; beginning with vol. viii, expanded to include also accessions of manuscripts by British repositories.

977 KER (NEIL R.). Catalogue of manuscripts containing Anglo-Saxon. Oxf. 1957.

'Notes on the palaeography and history of the principal manuscripts', pp. xxiii–liv; bibliography, pp. 485–510. Contains full descriptions of the 200 principal manuscripts and brief description of manuscripts showing notes, glosses, or scribbles in Anglo-Saxon; cartularies and single-sheet documents not included. Manuscripts written on the Continent are included in an appendix. See also N. R. Ker, *Medieval Libraries* (No. 7168).

978 KER (NEIL R.). Medieval manuscripts in British libraries. Vol. i: London. Oxf. 1969.

979 KRISTELLER (PAUL O.). Latin manuscript books before 1600. Part i: a bibliography of the printed catalogues of extant collections. Part ii: a tentative list of unpublished inventories of imperfectly catalogued extant collections. N.Y. 1960. Originally printed in *Traditio*, vi (1948), 227–317; ix (1953), 393–418.

Cf. Blanche B. Boyer, 'Insular contribution to medieval tradition on the continent', *Classical Philology*, xlii (1947), 209–22; xliii (1948), 31–9, which asserts that for Latin MSS. 'on the continent there are preserved more than twice as many Anglo-Saxon and Irish manuscripts as on the British Isles'.

980 RICCI (SEYMOUR DE) and WILSON (WILLIAM J.). Census of medieval and Renaissance manuscripts in the United States and Canada. 3 vols. N.Y. 1935–40. *

981 RICCI (SEYMOUR DE). English collectors of books and manuscripts (1530–1930) and their marks of ownership. Cambr. 1930. *

982 RICHARDSON (ERNEST C.), ed. A union world catalog of manuscript books: preliminary studies in method . . . 6 vols. N.Y. 1935. *

Pertinent volumes are vol. i: *The world's collections of manuscript books: a preliminary survey* (1933) and especially vol. iii: *A list of printed catalogs of manuscript books* (1935), arranged alphabetically by cities, said to be 'indispensable but uncritical and full of errors' (Kristeller).

983 SAXL (FRITZ) and MEIER (HANS). Catalogue of astrological and mythological illuminated manuscripts of the Middle Ages. Vol. iii: Manuscripts in English libraries. Ed. by Harry Bober. Lond. 1953.

MSS. from ninth to early sixteenth centuries in 75 English collections.

984 SCHENKL (HEINRICH). Bibliotheca patrum Latinorum Britannica. *Akademie der Wissensch. Sitzungsberichte, Philos.-hist. Classe*, vols. cxxi, cxxiii, cxxiv, cxxvi, cxxvii, cxxxi, cxxxiii, cxxxvi, cxxxvii, cxxxix, cxliii, cl, clvii. 13 pts. Vienna. 1890–1908.

Includes patristic literature and Latin classical works in the libraries of Great Britain, excepting the University Library at Cambridge, certain series in the Bodleian and college libraries at Oxford, and the British Museum.

985 SINGER (DOROTHEA W.), ANDERSON (ANNIE), and ADDIS (ROBINA). Catalogue of Latin and vernacular alchemical manuscripts in Great Britain and Ireland, dating from before the XVI century. 3 vols. Brussels. 1928–31.

Cf. *Les manuscrits des Îles Britanniques*, décrits par Dorothea Waley Singer avec la collaboration de Annie Anderson et William J. Anderson (Union académique internationale, *Catalogue des manuscrits alchimiques grecs*, ed. by J. Bidez *et al.* (Brussels, 1924+), vol. iii). Mrs. Singer has deposited in the British Museum (Department of MSS.) an inventory of scientific manuscripts in Great Britain and Ireland for the period before 1500; microfilm copies of this inventory are to be found in the Warburg Institute and the Library of Congress in Washington.

986   TALBOT (CHARLES H.). 'A list of Cistercian manuscripts in Great Britain'. *Traditio*, viii (1952), 402–18.

987   TANNER (THOMAS). Bibliotheca Britannico-Hibernica sive de scriptoribus . . . Ed. by David Wilkins. Lond. 1748.

A dictionary of writers, containing much valuable historical material, and in large part superseding the older works of Leland, Bale, Pits, Ware, Cave, and Nicolson. See Hardy, *Catalogue* (No. 21), vol. i, pp. xxxvi–xlii. See also idem, *Notitia monastica: an account of all abbeys*, etc. *in England and Wales* (Lond. 1744; reprinted, with additions by James Nasmith, Cambr. 1787), which contains a brief account of each religious house, with many references to unpublished records; this work is an expansion of his *Notitia monastica* (Oxf. 1695).

(b) British Museum

The largest collection of medieval manuscripts, as distinct from public records, in Great Britain is housed in the British Museum. The first four titles listed below constitute summary guides to the collections. Much information concerning recent important acquisitions can be found in the numbers of the *British Museum Quarterly* (1926+). The printed catalogues of medieval materials (Nos. 992–1005) may be supplemented by unpublished indexes in the Student's Room, Department of MSS. For a list of catalogues, see Skeat (No. 991).

988   EDWARDS (EDWARD). Lives of the founders of the British Museum, with notices of its augmentors and other benefactors, 1570–1870. 2 vols. Lond. etc. 1870. * Cf. No. 974.

989   ESDAILE (ARUNDELL J. K.). The British Museum library, a short history and survey . . . with an introduction by Sir Frederic G. Kenyon. The Library Assoc. series of library manuals. Vol. x. Lond. 1946.

Bibliographical references in notes, pp. 349–75.

990   GILSON (JULIUS P.). A student's guide to the manuscripts of the British Museum. Helps for Students of History, No. 31. Lond. and N.Y. 1920.

991   SKEAT (THEODORE C.), comp. The catalogues of the manuscript collections in the British Museum. The catalogues of the British Museum. Vol. ii. Lond. 1951. Revised edn. 1962.

992   CATALOGUE OF ADDITIONS TO THE MSS. IN 1836–1945. 19 vols. [Lond.] 1843–1970. Index to the Additional and Egerton MSS. acquired in 1783–1835. [Lond.] 1849.* Index to the additions in 1854–75. [Lond.] 1880.

The 'additions' include Additional MSS., Additional Charters and Rolls, Egerton MSS., Egerton Charters and Rolls, etc. See below, Ayscough's *Catalogue of Sloane MSS.* (No. 1000), which described the additional manuscripts to 1782. The Egerton MSS. are a continually growing collection through purchases from Bridgewater and Farnborough Funds. A fuller description of the lists of additions is given in Skeat (No. 991), pp. 5–8.

993   CATALOGUE OF MSS. IN THE BRITISH MUSEUM [Arundel and Burney collections]. 2 vols. and index. Lond. 1834–40.

Arundel collection contains early copies of chroniclers, some ecclesiastical charters and registers, etc.; while Burney collection is composed of Greek and Latin classics.

994   CATALOGUE OF THE MSS. IN THE COTTONIAN LIBRARY. Record Comm. [Lond.] 1802.

See No. 962. This catalogue was compiled by J. Planta, the then principal librarian of the Museum. Since many Cotton manuscripts were destroyed or mutilated by fire in 1731, reference should be made to Thomas Smith, *Catalogus librorum manuscriptorum Bibliothecae Cottonianae* (Oxford, 1696), and to Hickes's *Thesaurus* (No. 425). On the formation of the Cottonian Library, see F. Wormald and C. E. Wright, *The English Library before 1700* (No. 7181), pp. 177–212.

995   CATALOGUE OF MSS. FORMERLY IN THE POSSESSION OF FRANCIS HARGRAVE. Lond. 1818.

About 500 MSS. concentrating on legal history.

996   CATALOGUE OF THE HARLEIAN MSS. IN THE BRITISH MUSEUM. Record Comm. 4 vols. [Lond.] 1808–12.

Collected by Robert and Edward Harley, first and second Earls of Oxford, with the assistance of the great antiquarian, Humphrey Wanley, the Collection was purchased by the Government in 1753. An early catalogue was that compiled by several hands and Wanley. On Wanley, see C. E. Wright and Ruth C. Wright, *Diary of Humfrey Wanley 1715–1726*, 2 vols. (Lond. 1966).

997   CATALOGUE OF IRISH MSS. 3 vols. Lond. 1926–53.

Vol. i was begun by Standish O'Grady in 1886 and largely printed in 1889–92; Robin Flower compiled the rest of the catalogue, with vol. iii revised and published by M. Dillon (1953).

998   CATALOGUE OF THE LANSDOWNE MSS. Record Comm. 2 pts. [Lond.] 1819.

Rather heavily weighted on the post-medieval side.

999   CATALOGUE OF ROMANCES IN THE DEPARTMENT OF MANUSCRIPTS IN THE BRITISH MUSEUM. By H. L. D. Ward. Vols. i–iii (vol. iii by J. A. Herbert). Lond. 1883–1910. Reprinted. 1961–2.

Vol. i contains much about the MSS. of Geoffrey of Monmouth's *Historia Regum* (No. 2166); vol. iii deals with homilies, etc.

1000   CATALOGUE OF THE MANUSCRIPTS PRESERVED IN THE BRITISH MUSEUM, hitherto undescribed . . . including the collections of Hans Sloane, Thomas Birch, etc. [Additional MSS. to no. 5017]. By Samuel Ayscough. 2 vols. Lond. 1782. Index to the Sloane MSS. By E. J. L. Scott. Lond. 1904.

The charters of the Sloane collection are included in the *Index to the Charters and Rolls* (No. 1004).

1001 CATALOGUE OF THE STOWE MSS. [acquired in 1883]. 2 vols. Lond. 1895–6.

The Duke of Buckingham's collection at Stowe House was purchased by the Earl of Ashburnham, after whose death the British Museum bought 996 Stowe MSS. Among them are many charters, 42 of which are Anglo-Saxon.

1002 CATALOGUE OF WESTERN MANUSCRIPTS IN THE OLD ROYAL AND KING'S COLLECTIONS. By George F. Warner and J. P. Gilson. 4 vols. Lond. 1921.

This beautifully printed catalogue includes many plates. Cf. David Casley, *Catalogue of the MSS. of the king's library: an appendix to the catalogue of the Cottonian library . . .* (Lond. 1734, 16 plates); M. R. James, 'The royal manuscripts at the British Museum', *The Library*, ii (1921–2), 193–200.

1003 CATALOGUE OF THE MSS. RELATING TO WALES IN THE BRITISH MUSEUM. By Edward Owen. Soc. Cymmrodorion, Record Ser. No. 4. 4 vols. Lond. 1900–22.

See also Harold Idris Bell, 'The Welsh MSS. in the British Museum collections', *Soc. Cymmrodorion Trans. for 1936* (1937), 15–40; and *Historical MSS. Commission, Report on MSS. in the Welsh language*, vol. ii, pt. iv (Lond. 1910) (*Parl. Papers*, 1910, vol. xxxvi).

1004 INDEX TO THE CHARTERS AND ROLLS IN THE DEPARTMENT OF MANUSCRIPTS. Ed. by Henry J. Ellis and Francis B. Bickley. 2 vols. [Vol. ii. ed. by H. J. Ellis.] Lond. 1900–12. ★

This index covers all charters acquired by the British Museum before 1900. See No. 444 for *Facsimiles of Ancient Charters* and *Facsimiles of Royal and Other Charters*.

1005 INDEX TO THE CONTENTS OF THE COLE MANUSCRIPTS IN THE BRITISH MUSEUM. By George J. Gray. Cambr. 1912.

(c) Other important repositories in London

1006 IRWIN (RAYMOND), ed. The libraries of London . . . Lond. 1949.

Accounts of the Public Record Office, Guildhall, University of London Library, etc.; Supplements Reginald A. Rye, *The libraries of London* (Lond. 1908). 3rd edn. *The students' guide to the libraries of London* (Lond. 1927). See also Leonard M. Harrod, *The libraries of Greater London: a guide* (Lond. 1951).

1007 CATALOGUE OF THE ARUNDEL MSS. IN THE LIBRARY OF THE COLLEGE OF ARMS. By W. H. Black. Lond. 1829.

Of special interest to genealogists. See Report of the Record Commissioners, 1837 (No. 965), 106–10. Cf. Anthony R. Wagner, *The records and collections of the College of Arms* (Lond. 1952).

1008 CATALOGUE OF MSS. IN THE LIBRARY OF LAMBETH PALACE. By H. J. Todd. Lond. 1812. ★

The registers of the archbishops of Canterbury, numerous ancient charters, court rolls of manors, rentals, etc. See also Jane Sayers, *Short catalogue of estate documents at Lambeth Palace Library* (Leicester, 1965). Todd's catalogue is continued as Vol. 2, MSS. 1222–1860, by E. G. W. Bill (Oxf. 1972).

1009 DESCRIPTIVE CATALOGUE OF THE MSS. IN THE LIBRARY OF LAMBETH PALACE. By Montague R. James and Claude Jenkins. 5 pts. Cambr. 1930–2. Reprinted as a single volume, 1955.

Amended from 'The MSS. in the library at Lambeth Palace', *Cambridge Antiq. Soc.* (1900), pp. 64. Cf. Claude Jenkins, 'The historical manuscripts at Lambeth', *T.R.H.S.* 3rd Ser. xi (1917), 185–97. M. R. James, 'The history of Lambeth Palace Library' was printed in *Cambridge Bibliog. Soc. Trans.* iii (1959), 1–31. Dorothy Owen, 'Canterbury archiepiscopal archives in Lambeth Palace Library', *Jour. Soc. Archivists*, ii (1960–4), 140–7. Dorothy M. Owen, *Catalogue of Lambeth manuscripts 889 to 901* (Carte antique et miscellanée) (Lond. 1968). J. E. Sayers, *Original papal documents in the Lambeth Palace Library*, *B.I.H.R.* Supplement, No. 6 (Lond. 1967).

1010 CALENDAR OF THE CAREW MSS. PRESERVED IN THE LIBRARY AT LAMBETH. Ed. by John S. Brewer and William Bullen. (P.R.O. calendars) 6 vols. Lond. 1867–73.

Vol. v contains the texts of the *Book of Howth* and *Thomas Bray's Conquest of Ireland* (Nos. 2799, 2800), together with a calendar of papers relating to Ireland ranging from the reign of Henry II to the close of the sixteenth century. These papers comprise royal letters, grants, proclamations, etc. See No. 1026. Vols. i–iv calendar MSS. 1515–1603; vol. vi, 1603–24.

1011 CATALOGUE OF MSS. IN THE LIBRARY OF LINCOLN'S INN. By Joseph Hunter. Lond. 1838. Also printed in his Three Catalogues. Lond. 1838 (No. 975), and in the Report of the Record Commissioners. 1837 (No. 965), pp. 352–91.

Note particularly the Hale MSS.

1012 CATALOGUE OF MSS. IN THE LIBRARY OF THE SOCIETY OF ANTIQUARIES OF LONDON. Lond. 1816.

The library includes *Liber Winton,* wardrobe accounts, two registers of Peterborough abbey, etc.

1013 CATALOGUE OF THE PRINTED BOOKS AND MSS. IN THE LIBRARY OF THE INNER TEMPLE. Lond. 1833.

Notices *inter alia* of the transcripts of documents in the Tower by William Petyt (d. 1707), for which see *D.N.B.* and Hist. MSS. Comm. Reports.

1014 CATALOGUE OF THE PRINTED BOOKS AND MSS. IN THE LIBRARY OF THE MIDDLE TEMPLE. Lond. 1863. Catalogue of the printed books etc. Ed. by C. E. A. Bedwell. 3 vols. Lond. 1914. Supplement to a catalogue of the printed books in the library . . . of the Middle Temple, 1914–1924. By H. A. C. Sturgess. Lond. [1925].

1015 CATALOGUE OF THE MSS. AND AUTOGRAPH LETTERS IN THE UNIVERSITY LIBRARY AT THE CENTRAL BUILDING OF THE UNIVERSITY OF LONDON, SOUTH KENSINGTON. By Reginald Arthur Rye. Lond. 1921.

Cf. Dorothy K. Coveney, *Descriptive catalogue of manuscripts in the library* [of University College, London]. Lond. 1936.

1016   MANUSCRIPTS OF WESTMINSTER ABBEY. By Joseph Armitage Robinson and Montague Rhodes James. Cambr. 1909.

> Cf. L. E. Tanner, 'The nature and use of the Westminster Abbey muniments', *T.R.H.S.* 4th Ser. xix (1936), 43–80.

(d) Important English repositories outside London

See Nos. 945, 963, 965, 972, 974, 984, and Luxmoore Newcombe, *The university and college libraries of Great Britain and Ireland* . . . (Lond. 1927). For the muniments concerned with the administration of various colleges, see pp. 916–19.

(i) Bodleian Library, Oxford

The best history of the Bodleian is by Macray. Current references can be found in the *Bodleian Library Record*, 1+ (1938+), which supplanted the *Bodleian Quarterly Record*, vols. i–viii (1914–37).

1017   ANECDOTA OXONIENSIA. Medieval and Modern Series. i–xv. Oxf. 1882–1929.

> Texts, etc. chiefly from the Bodleian and other Oxford libraries.

1018   ANNALS OF THE BODLEIAN LIBRARY. By W. D. Macray. Lond. 1868. 2nd edn. Oxf. 1890.

> For briefer history, see Strickland Gibson, *Some Oxford libraries* (Oxf. 1914), and Reginald Lane Poole, *A lecture on the history of the university archives* (Oxf. 1912). Also *Letters of Sir Thomas Bodley to Thomas James, first keeper of the Bodleian library*, ed. by G. W. Wheeler (Oxf. 1926); Frederick S. Boas, 'Sir Thomas Bodley and his library', *Royal Soc. of Lit. of the United Kingdom Trans.* 3rd ser. xxiii (1947), 20–36.

1019   CRASTER (HERBERT H. E.). History of the Bodleian Library, 1845–1945. Oxf. 1952.

> H. H. E. Craster, *The western manuscripts of the Bodleian library*. Helps for Students of History, No. 43 (Lond. 1921).

1020   CALENDAR OF CHARTERS AND ROLLS PRESERVED IN THE BODLEIAN LIBRARY. By H. O. Coxe and W. H. Turner. Oxf. 1878.

> For numerous additions since 1878, there is a manuscript index in the Library itself.

1021   CATALOGUE OF PRINTED BOOKS AND MANUSCRIPTS BEQUEATHED BY FRANCIS DOUCE. Oxf. 1840.

1022   CATALOGI CODICUM MSS. BIBLIOTHECAE BODLEIANAE. 14 pts. in 22. Oxf. 1845–1918.

> This is the quarto series of catalogues, of which the following contain material pertinent to this bibliography:
>
> Pt. ii, Laud MSS. Ed. by H. O. Coxe, 1858–85.
> Pt. iv, Tanner MSS. Ed. by A. Hackman, 1860.
> Pt. v, Rawlinson MSS. Ed. by W. D. Macray, 1892–1900.
> Pt. ix, Digby MSS. Ed. by W. D. Macray, 1883.
> Pt. x, Ashmolean MSS. See No. 1023.
>
> These entries here are not repeated in Summary Catalogue (No. 1028).

1023   A DESCRIPTIVE, ANALYTICAL, AND CRITICAL CATALOGUE
OF THE MSS. BEQUEATHED UNTO THE UNIVERSITY OF OXFORD
BY ELIAS ASHMOLE. By W. H. Black. Oxf. 1845. With an index by W. D.
Macray. 1866.

Forms pt. x of No. 1022.

1024   INDEX OF THE FIRST SEVEN VOLUMES OF THE DODS-
WORTH MSS. Oxf. 1879. Cf. Hunter (No. 975).

1025   INTRODUCTION TO THE STUDY OF SOME OF THE OLDEST
LATIN MUSICAL MANUSCRIPTS IN THE BODLEIAN LIBRARY,
OXFORD. By E. W. B. Nicholson. Lond. 1913.

1026   REPORT TO THE MASTER OF THE ROLLS UPON THE
CARTE AND CAREW PAPERS IN THE BODLEIAN AND LAMBETH
LIBRARIES. [By T. D. Hardy and J. S. Brewer.] Lond. 1864.

1027   A SUMMARY CATALOGUE OF WESTERN MANUSCRIPTS IN
THE BODLEIAN LIBRARY AT OXFORD. By Falconer Madan, H. H. E.
Craster, N. Denholm-Young, R. W. Hunt, and P. D. Record. 7 vols. in 8. Oxf.
1895–1953.

Cf. No. 972. The summary catalogue excludes charters and rolls, for which see above,
No. 1020. Vol. iii appeared in 1895, others at later dates; thus vol. i: *Historical introduc-
tion and conspectus of shelf-marks*, ed. by R. W. Hunt (1953), and vol. vii: *Index*, by P. D.
Record (1953).

(ii) Oxford Colleges

1028   CATALOGUS CODICUM MSS. QUI IN BIBLIOTHECA AEDIS
CHRISTI APUD OXONIENSES ADSERVANTUR. By George W. Kitchin.
Oxf. 1867.

1029   CATALOGUS CODICUM MSS. QUI IN COLLEGIIS AULISQUE
OXONIENSIBUS HODIE ADSERVANTUR. By Henry O. Coxe. 2 pts. Oxf.
1852.

See also Frederick Maurice Powicke, *The medieval books of Merton College* (Oxf. 1931),
not specifically a catalogue of the surviving MSS. at Merton; for this and other catalogues of the medieval libraries, see pp. 927–9.

1030   CATALOGUE OF THE MANUSCRIPTS OF BALLIOL COLLEGE,
OXFORD. Compiled by Roger A. B. Mynors. Oxf. 1963.

(iii) Cambridge

1031   SAYLE (CHARLES). Annals of the Cambridge university library.
Cambr. 1916.

Cf. Harry G. Aldis, *The University Library, Cambridge.* Helps for Students of History,
No. 46 (Lond. 1922): meagre. See with its references *V.C.H. Cambridge*, iii. 312–21.

1032   CATALOGUE OF THE MSS. PRESERVED IN THE LIBRARY OF
THE UNIVERSITY OF CAMBRIDGE. 5 vols. and index. Cambr. 1856–67.

1033   JAMES (MONTAGUE R.). A descriptive catalogue of the manuscripts in the library of [various colleges of Cambridge University]. Cambr. [1895–1925].

The separate catalogues with dates of publication are: Christ's College (1905); Clare College (1905); Corpus Christi College, 2 vols. (1909–12); Emmanuel College (1904); Gonville and Caius College, 3 vols. (1907–14); Jesus College (1895); King's College (1895); Magdalene College (1909); Pembroke College (1905); Peterhouse (1899); Queen's College (1905); Sidney Sussex College (1895); St. Catherine's College (1925); St. John's College (1913); Trinity College, 4 vols. (1900–4); Trinity Hall (1907).

Dr. James has also published: *A descriptive catalogue of the MSS. in the Fitzwilliam Museum* (Cambr. 1895); *A descriptive catalogue of the McClean Collection of MSS. in the Fitzwilliam Museum* (Cambr. 1912); and *Bibliotheca Pepysiana: a descriptive catalogue of the library of Samuel Pepys* (vol. iii: *The Medieval Manuscripts*) (Lond. 1914). See also Richard Vaughan and John Fine, 'A handlist of MSS. in the library of Corpus Christi College, Cambridge, not described by M. R. James', *Cambr. Bibliog. Soc. Trans.* iii (1960), 113–23. R. W. Hunt, 'Medieval inventories of Clare College library', ibid. i (1949–53), 105–25. Francis Wormald and Phyllis M. Giles, 'A handlist of the additional MSS. in the Fitzwilliam Museum (since 1895)', ibid. i (1949–53), 197–207, 297–309, 365–75; ii (1954), 1–13. T. A. M. Bishop, 'Notes on Cambridge MSS.', ibid. (in progress).

(iv) John Rylands Library

1034   GUPPY (HENRY). John Rylands Library, Manchester, 1899–1935. Manchester. 1935.

Cf. *The John Rylands Library, Manchester: a brief historical description of the library and its contents, illustrated* . . . (Manchester, 1914); Frank Taylor, *The charter room in the John Rylands Library* (Manchester, 1947).

1035   DUFF (EDWARD G.), comp. Catalogue of the printed books and manuscripts in the John Rylands Library. 3 vols. Manchester. 1899.

1036   JAMES (MONTAGUE R.). A descriptive catalogue of the Latin manuscripts in the John Rylands Library at Manchester. 2 vols. Manchester. 1921.

For Latin MSS. 1–183 (vol. ii: facsimiles in collotype). See also 'Hand-list of additions to the collection of Latin manuscripts in the John Rylands library, 1908–1920', by Robert Fawtier, *B.J.R.L.* vi (1921), 186–206. For Latin MSS. 184–395, see 'Hand-list of additions . . ., 1908–1928', by Moses Tyson, ibid. xii (1928), 581–604; for MSS. 396–447, Frank Taylor, *Supplementary hand-list of western manuscripts in the John Rylands library* (Manchester, 1937).

1037   HAND-LISTS OF CHARTERS AND DEEDS AND SIMILAR DOCUMENTS IN POSSESSION OF THE JOHN RYLANDS LIBRARY. Vol. i, by Robert Fawtier (1925); vol. ii, by Moses Tyson (1935); vol. iii, by Frank Taylor (1937). Cf. above, No. 1034.

These are reprints from *B.J.R.L.* vols. vii, viii, ix, xvii, xviii. For similar documents, see also 'Hand-list of the Mainwaring manuscripts', by Robert Fawtier, ibid. vii (1922–3), 143–67, 279–89 (Cheshire charters, many before 1485; rolls, first four before 1485); 'Hand-list of the Jodrell manuscripts', by Robert Fawtier, ibid. vii (1923), 290–6 (court rolls, deeds, manorial documents, etc.); Frank Taylor, 'The Hatton Wood manuscripts in the John Rylands library', ibid. xxiv (1940), 353–75; idem, 'Court rolls, rentals, surveys and analogous documents . . .', ibid. xxxi (1948), 345–86; idem, 'Hand-list of the Legh of Booths charters . . .', ibid. xxxii (1950), 229–85 (few are medieval); idem, 'Hand-list of the Crutchley manuscripts . . .', ibid. xxxiii (1950–1), 138–87, 327–72 (largely Derbyshire documents, twelfth century onward, but relatively few medieval).

(v) Leeds University

1038   THE BROTHERTON LIBRARY. A catalogue of ancient manuscripts and early printed books collected by Edward Allen, Baron Brotherton of Wakefield. By J. A. Symington. Leeds. 1931.

(e) The larger cathedral libraries

Miss M. S. G. Hands described a project for a union catalogue of the cathedral libraries of England and Wales in 'The cathedral libraries', *The Library*, 5th Ser. ii (1947), 1–10 (the card index for this venture is now housed in British Museum, North Library). To the above article is appended a list of 'Printed catalogues of books and manuscripts in cathedral libraries: England and Wales', by Margaret S. Smith (pp. 11–13). Cf. Bernard (No. 972), Edwards (No. 974), Leland, *Commentarii* (No. 8), and Schenkl (No. 984). The Historical MSS. Commission's Reports include inventories for all English cathedrals, except Rochester and Durham. Catalogues of medieval libraries will be found below on page 1009. See *A Survey of Ecclesiastical Archives* (p. 109, above) and No. 1009.

1039   READ (E. ANNE). A checklist of books, catalogues and periodical articles relating to the cathedral libraries of England. Oxford Bibliog. Soc. Occasional Pubn. no. 6. Oxf. 1970.

1040   CATALOGUE OF THE BOOKS, both manuscript and printed, which are preserved in the library of Christ Church, Canterbury. By Henry J. Todd. Lond. 1802.

> Also idem, *Some account of the deans of Canterbury . . . to which is added a catalogue of the manuscripts in the church library* (Canterbury, 1793). Cf. *Catalogus librorum bibliothecae ecclesiae Christi Cantuariensis* (Canterbury, 1743).

1041   JAMES (MONTAGUE R.). The ancient libraries of Canterbury and Dover: the catalogues of the libraries of Christ Church priory and St. Augustine's abbey at Canterbury and of St. Martin's priory at Dover. Cambr. 1903.

> Cf. Charles E. Woodruff, *A catalogue of the manuscript books in the library of Christ Church, Canterbury* (Canterbury, 1911).

1042   BIBLIOTHECAE ECCLESIAE CICESTRENSIS LIBRORUM CATALOGUS IN DUAS PARTES DIVISUS . . . By Thomas B. Wilmhurst. Chichester. 1871.

1043   CODICUM MSS. ECCLESIAE CATHEDRALIS DUNELMENSIS CATALOGUS CLASSICUS descriptus a Thoma Rud . . . cum appendice eos codices continente qui post catalogum confectum diversis temporibus comparati sunt. [Edited by J. Raine.] Durham. 1825.

> See also *Catalogi veteres librorum ecclesiae cathedralis Dunelm.: Catalogues of the library of Durham cathedral, at various periods, from the conquest to the dissolution, including catalogues of the library of the abbey of Hulne, and of the MSS. preserved in the library of Bishop Cosin, at Durham.* Ed. by Beriah Botfield. Surtees Soc. Pubns. vol. vii (Lond. 1838). Hubert D. Hughes, *A history of Durham cathedral library* (Durham, 1925).

1044   MYNORS (ROGER A. B.). Durham cathedral manuscripts to the end of the twelfth century. Oxf. 1939. Includes 57 plates.

> W. A. Pantin, Report on the Muniments of the Dean and Chapter of Durham (privately printed, 1939). J. Conway Davies, 'The muniments of the dean and chapter of Durham', *Durham Univ. Jour.* xliv (1952), 77–87; idem, 'Ecclesiastical and palatinate archives at Prior's Kitchen, Durham', *Jour. Soc. Archivists*, i (1958), 185–91; idem, 'Official and private record and manuscript collections in the Prior's Kitchen, Durham', ibid. i, No. 10 (1959), 261–70.

1045   CATALOGUS LIBRORUM QUI IN BIBLIOTHECA CATHE-DRALIS ELIENSIS ADSERVANTUR. Lond. 1815.

1046   A DESCRIPTIVE CATALOGUE OF THE MANUSCRIPTS IN THE HEREFORD CATHEDRAL LIBRARY. By Arthur T. Bannister. Hereford. 1927.

> Cf. Frederick C. Morgan, *Hereford cathedral library . . . its history and contents, with appendix of early printed books* (Hereford, 1952; 2nd edn. 1958), and F. C. and Penelope E. Morgan, *Hereford Cathedral libraries and muniments* (Hereford, 1970).

1047   CATALOGUE OF THE MUNIMENTS AND MSS. BOOKS PERTAINING TO THE DEAN AND CHAPTER OF LICHFIELD. Analysis of the Magnum Registrum Album. Catalogue of the muniments of the Lichfield vicars. By John C. Cox. William Salt Archaeol. Soc. Collections, vol. vi, part ii. Lond. 1886.

> Cf. *A catalogue of the printed books and manuscripts in the library of the cathedral church of Lichfield* (Lond. 1888). N. R. Ker, 'Patrick Young's Catalogue of the MSS. of Lichfield Cathedral', *Medieval and Renaiss. Stud.* ii (1950), 151–68.

1048   CATALOGUE OF THE MANUSCRIPTS OF LINCOLN CATHE-DRAL CHAPTER LIBRARY. By Reginald M. Woolley. Oxf. 1927.

> Cf. George F. Apthorp, *A catalogue of the books and manuscripts in the library of Lincoln cathedral . . .* (Lincoln, 1859); Dorothy M. Williamson, *The muniments of the dean and chapter of Lincoln* (Lincoln Minster Pamphlets, No. 8, Lincoln, 1956).

1049   A HANDLIST OF THE RECORDS OF THE BISHOP OF LIN-COLN AND OF THE ARCHDEACONS OF LINCOLN AND STOW. By Kathleen Major. Lond. etc. 1953.

> See also idem, 'The Lincoln diocesan records', *T.R.H.S.* 4th Ser. xxii (1940), 39–66.

1050   CATALOGUE OF THE LIBRARY OF THE DEAN AND CHAPTER OF NORWICH. Lond. 1819. Also, A catalogue of the library belonging to the dean and chapter of Norwich. Norwich. 1836.

> N. R. Ker, 'Medieval manuscripts from Norwich Cathedral Priory', *Cambr. Bibliog. Soc. Trans.* i (1949), 1–28.

1051   A CATALOGUE OF THE LIBRARY OF THE CATHEDRAL CHURCH OF SALISBURY. MSS. by Edward Maunde Thompson. PRINTED BOOKS by S. M. Lakin. Lond. 1880.

> N. R. Ker, 'Salisbury Cathedral manuscripts and Patrick Young's Catalogue', *Wilts. Archaeol. and Nat. Hist. Magazine*, liii (1949), 153–83.

1052 CATALOGUS LIBRORUM MANUSCRIPTORUM BIBLIO-
THECAE WIGORNIENSIS. Made in 1622–3 by Patrick Young . . . Edited
with an introduction by Ivor Atkins and Neil R. Ker. Cambr. 1944. Also,
Catalogue of manuscripts preserved in the chapter library of Worcester cathedral.
Compiled by J. K. Floyer. Edited by S. G. Hamilton. Worcester Hist. Soc.
Worcester. 1906.

> Cf. C. H. Turner, *Early Worcester MSS. . . . photographically reproduced* (Oxf. 1916).
> H. M. Bannister, 'Bishop Roger of Worcester and the church of Keynsham, with a list of
> vestments and books possibly belonging to Worcester', *E.H.R.* xxxii (1917), 387–93.

3. *Welsh Repositories*

The principal repository of manuscripts in Wales is the National Library of
Wales which was chartered in 1907 and began to function at Aberystwyth in 1909.
The National Library of Wales serves as a Record Office, housing some court,
civil, manorial, and ecclesiastical records. It has acquired important collections
for the study of the Middle Ages, among them the Peniarth Collection and the
Llanstephan Collection, both deposited in 1909. In 1944 the episcopal, diocesan,
and chapter records of Welsh sees began to be deposited in the National Library.
The National Library publishes *Bibliotheca Celtica* (No. 110) and the *Journal of
the National Library of Wales* (No. 134), the latter of which contains articles on
its manuscript collections. Further, the *Journal* has printed serially since 1940
a *Handlist of Manuscripts in the National Library*.

There are, however, medieval records concerned with Welsh affairs in several
P.R.O. (London) classes, e.g. Ministers' Accounts. The later legal records of
the Principality, from Tudor times onwards, were transferred to the P.R.O. in
1854; they are described in Giuseppi (No. 951) and the *Guide to the Public Record
Office* (No. 951), pp. 168–71. In 1962 the bulk of these records, comprising the
records of the Courts of Great Sessions, was returned to Wales and deposited
in the National Library. R. I. Jack, *Medieval Wales* (No. 22), pp. 67–78.

Welsh records are described in the Reports of the Royal Commission on
Public Records (1912–1919) (No. 966).

1053 DAVIES (W. LLEWELYN). The National Library of Wales: a survey
of its history, its contents and its activities. Aberystwyth. 1937.

1054 EVANS (J. GWENOGVRYN). Report on manuscripts in the Welsh
language. Hist. MSS. Comm. 2 vols. in 6 pts. Lond. 1898–1910.

> A mine of information, made before the establishment of the National Library of Wales,
> to which most of the manuscripts have since been transferred.

1055 JONES (EVAN D.). 'The National Library as the national records
depository for Wales', *American Archivist*, xiii (1950), 35–45.

1056 LIST OF RECORDS . . . of the PRINCIPALITY OF WALES.
P.R.O. Lists and Indexes. No. 40. Lond. 1914.

1057   THE NATIONAL LIBRARY OF WALES. *Times* (London) *Literary Supplement*. No. 2684, 10 July 1953, p. 452.

    See also *T.R.H.S.* 4th Ser. ii (1919), 33–7.

1058   ROBERTS (RICHARD A.). 'The public records relating to Wales', *Y Cymmrodor* (No. 126), x (1890), 157–206.

4. Scottish Repositories

(a) Archives

The public records of Scotland are housed in the General Register House in Edinburgh under the supervision of the Keeper of the Records of Scotland. Established in the late eighteenth century, the General Register House antedates the Public Record Office in London. The earlier records were despoiled by Edward I, Cromwell, and the frequent civil wars in Scotland; hence medieval documents have not survived in the vast quantities which England provides. Indeed, the records in England supply much on Scottish history. The state of the records in Scotland in 1800 is described in the *Report of the Record Commissioners* for that year (No. 963), pp. 393–494, and the annual reports of the Deputy Clerk Register for 1806 to 1811 are given in the *1812 Report of the Record Commissioners*, pp. 195–299. For the history of Scottish records, consult Livingstone's introduction (No. 1059) and the articles by Macphail (No. 1059) and Fergusson (No. 1059). The Historical MSS. Commission's Reports (No. 945) contain many references to Scotland, for which see the indexes thereto. A National Register of Archives (Scotland) similar to that for England is being made by the Historical MSS. Commission (see *Scottish Hist. Rev.* xxvi (1947), p. 89); its reports are given in the annual *Report of the Keeper of the Records of Scotland* and in the October issues of the *Scottish Historical Review*. Peter Gouldesbrough describes 'The Record Commissions of Scotland' in *Jour. Soc. Archivists*, iii, No. 3 (1966), 101–7; and Richard F. Dell considers 'Some differences between Scottish and English archives', ibid. iii, no. 7 (1968), 386–97. John Imrie and Grant Simpson report on 'The local and private archives of Scotland' in *Archives* (No. 1504), iii (1958), 137–47, 219–30.

1059   LIVINGSTONE (MATTHEW). A guide to the public records of Scotland deposited in H.M. General Register House, Edinburgh. Edin. 1905.

    Supersedes Millar and Bryce, *Hand-book of records in H.M. General Register House* (Edin. 1885). For list of records acquired since Livingstone's guide was printed, refer to William Angus, 'Accessions of public records to the Register House since 1905', *Scot. Hist. Rev.* xxvi (1947), 26–46; and James Fergusson's listing of additions since 1950 annually in *Scottish Historical Review*, xxxi (1952), and following. For general accounts, see J. H. Stevenson, 'The public records of Scotland', ibid. xx (1922), 1–10; and J. R. N. Macphail, 'The national records of Scotland', ibid. xxiv (1927), 202–11; and Sir James Fergusson, 'The public records of Scotland', *Archives*, No. 8 (1952), 30–8, and No. 9 (1953), 4–10.

1060   TERRY (CHARLES S.). An index to the papers relating to Scotland, described or calendared in the Historical MSS. Commission's Reports. Glasgow. 1908.

    Covers the years 1870–1907; continued to 1927 by Matheson (No. 34).

1061 THOMSON (JOHN M.). The public records of Scotland. Glasgow. 1922.

An archivist deals with the administrative history of medieval Scotland, the surviving records, and their location. Complementary to Livingstone's *Guide* (No. 1059).

(b) Catalogues of MSS. in Scottish libraries

The National Library of Scotland was founded in 1925 when the library of the Faculty of Advocates (the Scottish Bar) was presented to the nation. Over two and a half centuries the Faculty of Advocates had built up a notable collection of books and manuscripts and after 1709 had the privilege of receiving books under the Copyright Act. The earlier catalogues bear the title of the Advocates' Library. See Arundell Esdaile, *National libraries of the world*, 2nd edn. revised by F. J. Hill (Lond. 1957), pp. 28–38. No complete catalogue of manuscripts within the Library has been printed, but a complete list of the printed and unprinted catalogues of the manuscript collections is given by H. W. Meikle in *Scot. Hist. Rev.* xxv (1928), 221–3. For manuscripts acquired 1925–38, see No. 1062. For general description, see John Durkan and Anthony Ross, *Early Scottish Libraries* (Glasgow, 1961), a reprint from the *Innes Rev.* ix (1958), 3–167.

1062 NATIONAL LIBRARY OF SCOTLAND, EDINBURGH. Catalogue of manuscripts acquired since 1925. Vol. i. Edin. 1938.

See also Donald Mackinnon, *A descriptive catalogue of Gaelic manuscripts in the Advocates' library, Edinburgh, and elsewhere in Scotland* (Edin. 1912); and William B. Turnbull, *Catalogue of manuscripts relating to genealogy and heraldry, preserved in* the library of the Faculty of Advocates, at Edinburgh (Lond. 1852); M. R. Dobie, 'The first twenty years of the National Library of Scotland: manuscripts', *Edinburgh Bibliog. Soc. Trans.* ii (1946), 285 ff.

1063 ABERDEEN UNIVERSITY LIBRARY. A catalogue of the medieval manuscripts in Aberdeen university library. By M. R. James. Cambr. 1932.

Includes a reprint of a 1465 catalogue.

1064 EDINBURGH UNIVERSITY LIBRARY. A descriptive catalogue of the western mediaeval manuscripts in Edinburgh university library. By Catherine R. Borland. Edin. 1916.

See especially *Calendar of Laing charters belonging to the University of Edinburgh*, ed. by John Anderson (Edin. 1899).

1065 HUNTERIAN MUSEUM. A catalogue of the manuscripts in the library of the Hunterian museum in the university of Glasgow. By J. Young and P. H. Aitken. Glasgow. 1908.

1066 McROBERTS (DAVID). Catalogue of Scottish medieval liturgical books and fragments. Glasgow. 1953.

Careful inventory of surviving books from sixth to sixteenth century and their dispersion.

5. *Irish Repositories*

(a) Archives

Fire, civil disturbance, and lack of proper care had, over the centuries, taken their toll of Irish records before the holocaust of 1922 destroyed the Public Record

Office in Dublin. The Irish Record Commission was appointed in 1810 and for the following fifteen years published reports, calendared and printed some documents, and compiled lists and indexes of records. No satisfactory repository, however, existed until 1867 when an act of parliament established the Public Record Office of Ireland and provided for the concentration therein of broadly defined public records. The reports of the deputy keeper began anew in 1869 and for the next half-century much was accomplished in sorting, indexing, and abstracting the Irish records. The 1810–25 reports of the Irish Record Commission and the work of the deputy keepers and their colleagues from 1869 to 1922 were to take on additional value after 1922. During the civil war in Ireland in that year, irregulars occupied the Record Office and on 30 June, an explosion followed by a fire destroyed the building and virtually all of its record contents.

The government of the Irish Republic re-established the Public Record Office and in 1928 appointed the Irish Manuscripts Commission under the direction of Eoin MacNeill. This Commission issues *Analecta Hibernica* (No. 1067) and promotes the publication of manuscripts (No. 1069).

The government of Northern Ireland set up its own Record Office at Belfast in 1923.

1067   ANALECTA HIBERNICA. Irish Manuscripts Commission. Dublin. 1930+.

A serial, issued from time to time, includes the annual reports of Irish MSS. Comm. and publication of documents, calendars, lists, etc. The separate issues are analysed in *Catalogue of Publications of Irish MSS. Comm.* (No. 1069); Nos. 5, 9, 13, and 19 are index volumes.

1068   ARCHIVIST. On the history, position, and treatment of the public records of Ireland. By an Irish archivist (J. T. Gilbert). 2nd edn. Lond. 1864.

This is the 2nd edn. of *Record revelations*, etc. (Lond. 1863). It is largely devoted to an attack upon James Morrin's *Calendar of the patent and close rolls*, 3 vols. (Dublin etc. 1861–3). In the preface to vol. i of this Calendar there is a useful account of the history of Irish records and the Irish Record Commission.

1069   IRISH MANUSCRIPTS COMMISSION. Publications. Dublin. 1928+.

Catalogue of publications 1928–62 (Dublin, 1962) describes the contents of each of the publications. The publications are listed in *Repert. Font.* i, 145–6.

1070   IRISH RECORD COMMISSIONERS. Publications. 1826–1901.

Listed in *Repert. Font.* i. 341.

1071   IRISH RECORD OFFICE. Archivum generale Hiberniae. Publications. 1905+.

Listed in *Repert. Font.* i. 341.

1072   KILKENNY ARCHAEOLOGICAL SOCIETY ANNUARY. Dublin. Founded 1849, then 1869–89 Royal Historical and Archaeological Association of Ireland, then 1890+ the Royal Society of Antiquaries of Ireland.

Listed in *Repert. Font.* i. 356.

1073 MANUSCRIPT SOURCES FOR THE HISTORY OF IRISH CIVILIZATION. Ed. by Richard J. Hayes. 11 vols. Boston (Mass.). 1965.

An enumeration of the MSS.; catalogued as persons (vols. i–iv); subjects (vols. v–vi); places in Ireland (vols. vii–viii); dates (vols. ix–x); and lists, locations, etc. (vol. xi).

1074 MURRAY (ROBERT H.). A short guide to the principal classes of documents preserved in the Public Record Office. Dublin. Helps for Students of History. No. 7. Lond. 1919.

Cf. his *Ireland (1494–1829)*, 3 parts in Helps for Students of History, Nos. 33–5 (Lond. 1920).

1075 REPORTS from the commissioners respecting the public records of Ireland. 3 vols. Lond. 1815–25.

These three volumes contain the first fifteen annual reports. The 16th and 17th reports are in *Parliamentary Papers*, 1828, vol. xii; the 18th and 19th, ibid. 1830, vol. xvi. The supplement to the 8th report (1819) contains valuable inventories of plea, pipe, and memoranda rolls, etc.

1076 REPORTS (ANNUAL) OF THE DEPUTY KEEPER OF THE PUBLIC RECORDS, IRELAND. Dublin. 1869 etc.

For an abstract of their contents, see *Catalogue of Record Publications* (No. 1069). The first report gives an account of the contents of the principal repositories of Irish public records. The appendices to the reports include lists and calendars. Continued with consecutive enumeration by the deputy keeper of the Irish Free State or the Irish Republic.

1077 REPORTS (ANNUAL) OF THE DEPUTY-KEEPER OF THE RECORDS OF NORTHERN IRELAND. Belfast. 1924+ (1925+).

D. A. Chart, 'The Public Record Office of Northern Ireland, 1924–36', *Irish Historical Studies*, i (1938), 42–57.

1078 WOOD (HERBERT). A guide to the records deposited in the Public Record Office of Ireland. Dublin. 1919.

Herbert Wood, 'The public records of Ireland before and after 1922', *T.R.H.S.* 4th Ser. xiii (1930), 17–49. David B. Quinn, 'Irish Records, 1920–1933: a survey', *B.I.H.R.* xi (1934), 99–104. Margaret Griffith, 'A short guide to the Public Record Office of Ireland', *Irish Hist. Stud.* vii (1951), 17–38; viii (1952), 45–58. Kenneth Darwin, 'The Irish record situation', *Jour. Soc. Archivists*, ii, No. 8 (1963), 361–6.

(b) Catalogues of MSS. in Irish libraries

See O'Curry (No. 30), Best (No. 9), Kenney (No. 23), especially pp. 84–90.

1079 CATALOGUE OF MANUSCRIPTS IN THE PUBLIC LIBRARY OF ARMAGH. Ed. by James Dean. Dundalk. 1928.

1080 NATIONAL LIBRARY OF IRELAND. Report of the Council of Trustees. 1877+.

Recent reports describe the project, begun in 1945, to microfilm the documents and manuscripts relating to Ireland now in foreign archives and libraries. In 1950 the National Library replaced the Irish MSS. Comm. for the cataloguing of manuscripts in private hands.

1081 ROYAL IRISH ACADEMY, DUBLIN. Catalogue of Irish manuscripts in the Royal Irish Academy. Ed. by T. F. O'Rahilly *et al.* (fascicles i–xxvi in 6 vols.). Dublin. 1926–42. Kathleen Mulchrone and Elizabeth Fitzpatrick. Catalogue of Irish manuscripts in the Royal Irish Academy. Index I. Dublin. 1948.

1082 BIBLIOTHECA MS. STOWENSIS. A descriptive catalogue of the manuscripts in the Stowe library. Ed. by Charles O'Conor. Vol. i. Buckingham. 1818.

> Cf. H.M.C. Reports. Eighth Report (1881), App. 3, pp. 1–110. In 1883 the British government bought the Stowe MSS. and deposited the Irish MSS. in the R.I.A. and the others in the B.M.

1083 TRINITY COLLEGE, DUBLIN. Catalogue of the manuscripts in the library of Trinity College, Dublin. Dublin. 1900. T. K. Abbott and E. J. Gwynn. Catalogue of the Irish manuscripts in the library of Trinity College, Dublin. Dublin. 1921.

> A few manuscripts are described in Robert H. Murray, *Short guide to some MSS. in the Library of Trinity College, Dublin,* Helps for Students of History, No. 32 (Lond. 1920).

V. PRINTED COLLECTIONS OF SOURCES

Many of the most important sources for British medieval history have been edited in series, published either under governmental auspices or through private initiative. Such series, in their inclusiveness or diversity, treat of more than one segment of the Middle Ages and therefore cannot be specifically assigned to a chronological or topical category.

In this section are included the principal collections of chronicles and records.

Collections (below, pp. 136–44) privately printed in the sixteenth, seventeenth, and eighteenth centuries by Parker, Twysden, Savile, Hearne, Wharton, and other editors made texts of English medieval chronicles more accessible to students; but these editions often do not satisfy the modern canons of historical criticism. For commentaries on historical scholarship for this period, see, e.g., David Douglas, *English scholars, 1660–1730* (Lond. 1939; 2nd revised edn. 1951); *English historical scholarship in the sixteenth and seventeenth centuries: A record of the papers delivered . . . to commemorate the tercentenary of the publication of Dugdale's Antiquities of Warwickshire,* ed. by Levi Fox (Dugdale Soc.) (Lond. and N.Y. 1956); Henry B. Walters, *The English antiquaries of the sixteenth, seventeenth and eighteenth centuries* (Lond. 1934); R. J. Schoeck, 'Early Anglo-Saxon studies and legal scholarship in the Renaissance', *Stud. in the Renaissance,* v (1958), 102–10; T. S. Dorsch, 'Two English antiquaries: John Leland and John Stow', *Essays and Studies* (1959), 18–35; C. E. Wright, 'The dispersal of the monastic libraries and the beginning of Anglo-Saxon studies: Matthew Parker and his circle: a preliminary study', *Trans. Cambr. Bibliog. Soc.* i (1949–53), 208–37.

The first large-scale undertaking, subsidized by the Government, for the publication of records produced Rymer's *Foedera* (1704–13) (No. 3765). In the eighteenth century the government also provided for the publication of the *Rolls of Parliament* in 1771 (No. 3322) and *Domesday Book* in 1783 (No. 3009). The temper of that century did not encourage public expenditure for medieval studies. From the beginning of the nineteenth century, however, to the present, governmental subsidies have sustained the publication of six series of medieval documents. These series are (1) the Publications of the Record Commissioners, 1802–37/69 (No. 1085); (2) the appendices to the Reports of the Deputy Keeper of the Public Records, 1840–89 (No. 967); (3) the Rolls Series of Chronicles and Memorials, 1858–96 (No. 1087); (4) the Reports of the Historical Manuscripts Commission, 1870–present (No. 945); (5) the Calendars of rolls etc., 1891–present (No. 1086) (a few calendars of foreign archives were published under the direction of the Master of the Rolls before 1891, see Nos. 3806, 3834); and (6) Lists and Indexes, 1892–1936 (No. 955).

The Record Commission, first appointed in 1800 (cf. pp. 112 ff.), entrusted to Henry Petrie in 1823 the task of editing a new collection of chronicles and other materials of English history extending to the close of Henry VII's reign. After the text of the first volume had been prepared and materials for other volumes gathered, the work was suspended in 1835 by order of the commissioners, and volume one was not published until 1848 (No. 1084). Meanwhile, the Record Commissioners had begun the publication of records, as distinct from chronicles, and this project was continued by the Master of the Rolls for three decades after the expiration of the last commission in 1837 (No. 1085).

Under the authority of the Public Record Office Act of 1838, the Master of the Rolls caused concise calendars of some records to be included periodically in the Deputy Keeper's Reports (No. 967) and in 1857–8 began the series of Chronicles and Memorials (No. 1087). For the latter series commonly known as 'The Rolls Series', each chronicle or collection of documents was to be a separate work complete in itself, confided to a competent editor. The series eventually included most of the prominent chroniclers of England; it was brought to a halt in 1896. For a history and critique of the Rolls Series, Knowles's *Great enterprises* (No. 262), pp. 101–34, may be consulted. Since the 1890s the Master of the Rolls has directed the printing of calendars of the public records in his custody. Periodically, a printed list of record publications under government sponsorship appears (No. 950); those which had already been published are listed in Mullins, *Texts* (No. 29) and in *Repert. Font.* (No. 64).

A. PUBLICATIONS OF THE BRITISH GOVERNMENT

1084 MONUMENTA HISTORICA BRITANNICA. Ed. by Henry Petrie, assisted by John Sharpe. Vol. i. Lond. 1848. *

Contains excerpts from Greek writers, with English translations, and Roman writers; Roman inscriptions; an account of British and Roman coins, with plates; and the following chronicles, or parts thereof, to 1066:

Æthelweard.	Annales Cambriae.
Anglo-Saxon chronicle.	Asser.

Bede.	Gildas.
Brut y Tywysogion.	Guy of Amiens.
Chronologia brevissima.	Henry of Huntingdon.
Florence of Worcester	Nennius.
Gaimar.	Simeon of Durham.
Genealogia regum.	

For the history of Petrie's work, see the preface by T. D. Hardy; and Thomas, *Notes of Materials* (No. 970), pp. 182–4.

1085 PUBLICATIONS OF THE RECORD COMMISSIONERS. Lond. 1802–48. 1869.

Listed in Mullins, *Texts*, pp. 3–15, and in *Repert. Font.* i. 599–602.

1086 PUBLIC RECORD OFFICE (Calendars, texts, state papers, etc.). Lond. 1858+.

Listed in Mullins, *Texts*, pp. 16–36, and in *Repert. Font*, i. 574–6. The publication of the Calendars of medieval records began in 1891.

1087 RERUM BRITANNICARUM MEDII AEVI SCRIPTORES. Lond. 1858–96. *†. Commonly called 'Rolls Series'.

Listed in Mullins, *Texts*, pp. 42–60, and in *Repert. Font.* i. 612–19. Reprint in progress by Kraus Reprint Corporation, New York. The ninety-nine separate works are printed in 251 volumes.

B. COLLECTIONS PRIVATELY EDITED

1. *Chronicles, etc.*

On the collections of chronicles, mentioned below, see the introduction to Petrie's *Monumenta* (No. 1084) and Hardy's *Catalogue* (No. 21), vol. i, pp. xliii–xlvi and appendix. For modern source-books, designed for undergraduate instruction, see especially *English historical documents* (No. 17) and shorter works cited below (Nos. 1204–1209). For Scottish chronicles, see Nos. 1088A, 1088B, and 1103A.

Owing to England's connections with the continent, and especially with France, continental collections include sources pertinent to English history. For the contents of such series, consult Potthast's *Bibliotheca* (No. 62), *Repertorium Fontium* (No. 64), and A. Molinier, *Les sources de l'histoire de France* (Paris, 1901–6). Only the principal continental series are listed here. A new series for Britain, entitled *Auctores Britannici Medii Aevi*, to be sponsored by the British Academy and published by the Clarendon Press, is being prepared.

1088 ACHERY (LUC D'). Veterum scriptorum spicilegium. 13 vols. Paris. 1655–77. New edn. 3 vols. 1723.

Listed in *Repert. Font.* i. 12–14; and Hardy's, *Catalogue*, i. 888–9. Anselm's *Epistolae*; Chrodegang's *Regula canonicorum*; Nicholas Trevet.

1088A ANDERSON (ALAN O.), ed. Early sources of Scottish history A.D. 500 to 1286. 2 vols. Edin. 1922.

Two stout volumes of translations from Irish, Norse, and Scottish sources, preceded by an annotated catalogue of the sources.

1088B ANDERSON (ALAN O.), ed. Scottish annals from English chroniclers
A.D. 500 to 1286. Lond. 1908.

1089 BOHN'S ANTIQUARIAN LIBRARY. 41 vols. Lond. 1847–64.*

A series of translations. Listed in *Repert. Font.* i. 103–4.
Includes *Six Old English Chronicles*, translated by J. A. Giles, namely: Aethelweard,
Asser, Geoffrey of Monmouth, Gildas, Nennius, and Richard of Cirencester.
Other translations of Bede's *Ecclesiastical History*; *Anglo-Saxon Chronicle*; *Chronicles
of the Crusades*; Richard of Devizes; *Itinerary of Richard I*; Florence of Worcester;
Giraldus Cambrensis; Henry of Huntingdon; *Acts of King Stephen*; the so-called
'Ingulf'; Matthew of Westminster; Matthew Paris; Ordericus Vitalis; Roger of Hove-
den; Roger of Wendover; and William of Malmesbury's *Chronicle of the Kings*.
The translations vary in value; some of them have been several times reprinted.

1090 BOUQUET (MARTIN) [*et al.*]. Recueil des historiens des Gaules et de
la France [to 1328]. 24 vols. Paris. 1738–1904. † *

Contains many extracts, arranged chronologically, from English chroniclers. See Hardy,
Catalogue (No. 21), i. 791–2.

1091 BUCHON (JEAN A. C.). Collection des chroniques nationales
françaises écrites en langue vulgaire du treizième au seizième siècle. 47 vols.
Paris. 1824–8.

Listed in *Repert. Font.* i. 109–12.

1092 CAMDEN (WILLIAM). Anglica, Normannica, Hibernica, Cambrica, a
veteribus scripta. Frankfurt. 1602. Another edn. 1603.

Asser.   *Vita Gulielmi Conquestoris* (Anonymous).
Giraldus Cambrensis.   Walsingham.
'Thomas de la More', *Vita Edw. II.*   William of Jumièges.
The texts of these writers are the same in both editions.

1093 COLLECTION DE DOCUMENTS INÉDITS RELATIFS À
L'HISTOIRE DE FRANCE, publiés sous les auspices du Ministère de l'Instruction Publique. Paris. 1835+.

Listed in *Repert. Font.* i. 156–60. Records and cartularies, rather than chronicles.

1094 COLLECTION DE TEXTES POUR SERVIR À L'ÉTUDE ET À
L'ENSEIGNEMENT DE L'HISTOIRE. Paris. 1886+.

Listed in *Repert. Font.* i. 161–3. Over 50 volumes. Chronicles and documents, not
restricted to the history of France, or to the Middle Ages.

1095 [COMMELIN (JEROME).] Rerum Britannicarum . . . scriptores
vetustiores. Heidelberg. 1587.

Listed in *Repert. Font.* i. 169.

Bede.   Gildas.
Froissart (abridged).   William of Newburgh.
Geoffrey of Monmouth.
The first printed collection of English chroniclers.

1096 DUCHESNE (ANDRÉ). Historiae Normannorum scriptores antiqui. Paris. 1619.

Listed in *Repert. Font.* i. 234.

Annalis historia brevis.
Battle abbey roll.
Chronica Normanniae.
Dudo of St. Quentin.
Encomium Emmae.

Gesta Stephani.
Ordericus Vitalis.
William of Jumièges.
William of Poitiers.

See No. 1112.

1097 FAUROUX (MARIE). Recueil des actes des ducs de Normandie de 911 à 1066. *Mémoires de la Société des antiquaires de Normandie*, xxxvi. 4th. Ser. vi. Caen. 1961.

1098 [FULMAN (WILLIAM).] Rerum Anglicarum scriptores. Vol. i. Oxf. 1684.

Listed in *Repert. Font.* i. 277.

Annals of Burton.
Chronicle of Melrose.

'Ingulf'.
Historiae Croylandensis continuatio.

This collection was made under the auspices of Bishop John Fell, and is often ascribed to him. It is usually called vol. i of Gale's collection (Nos. 1099, 1100), although the two works are entirely distinct.

1099 [GALE (THOMAS).] Historiae Anglicanae scriptores quinque. Oxf. 1687.

Listed in *Repert. Font.* i. 278.

Annals of Margam.
Annals of Waverley.
Itinerary of Richard I.

Thomas Wykes.
Walter of Hemingford.

1100 [GALE (THOMAS).] Historiae Britannicae [etc.] scriptores XV. Oxf. 1691.

Listed in *Repert. Font.* i. 278.

Alcuin, *De pontificibus Ebor'.*
Chronicon fani S. Neoti.
Eddi, *Vita S. Wilfridi.*
Fordun, *Scotichronicon.*
Gildas.
Higden.
Historia Eliensis, bks. i–ii.

Historia Ramesiensis.
Nennius.
Ralph de Diceto, *Historia de regibus*
  Britonum.
Wallingford.
William of Malmesbury: *De Glastonia;*
  De pontificibus.

An appendix contains extracts from various Roman writers, etc. Gale calls this collection vol. i and the *Scriptores Quinque*, vol. ii; but the *Scriptores XV* is usually bound up as vol. iii, Fulman's collection (No. 1098) forming vol. i.

1101 [GILES (JOHN A.).] The monkish historians of Great Britain. [Scriptores monastici: a series of translations.] 6 vols. Lond. 1841–5.

Listed in *Repert. Font.* i. 665–6.

Bede's *Works.*
Chronicles of the white rose (temp.
  Edw. IV).
Geoffrey of Monmouth.

Gildas, and Nennius.
Richard of Devizes's *Chronicle*, and
  Richard of Cirencester's *Description*
  of Britain (a forgery).

Giles also translated *Six Old English Chroniclers* and other works for the Bohn Antiquarian Library (No. 1089).

1102   GILES (JOHN A.). Patres ecclesiae Anglicanae. 35 vols. Oxf. etc. 1843–8.

Listed in *Repert. Font.* i. 548–9.

Aldhelm, *Opera,* 1 vol.
Arnulf of Lisieux, *Epistolae,* 1 vol.
Becket, *Epistolae et Vita,* 4 vols.
Bede, *Opera,* 12 vols.
Boniface, *Opera,* 2 vols.

Foliot, *Epistolae,* 2 vols.
Herbert of Bosham, *Opera,* 2 vols.
John of Salisbury, *Opera,* 5 vols.
Lanfranc, *Opera,* 2 vols.
Peter of Blois, *Opera,* 4 vols.

Giles also edited various works for the Caxton Society (No. 186), which are listed in *Repert. Font.* i. 125. These editions of a pioneer now leave much to be desired.

1103   HEARNE (THOMAS). Chronica Angliae. (Chroniclers and records). 20 vols. Oxf. 1709–35.

Adam of Domerham.
Alured of Beverley.
Annals of Dunstable.
Benedict of Peterborough.
Fordun, *Scotichronicon.*
Heming's Chartulary.
Historia vitae Ric. II
History of Glastonbury.
John of Glastonbury.
John of Trokelowe (also Henry of
   Blaneford, and *Vita Edw. II*).
Liber niger scaccarii and William of
   Worcester.
Mannyng, *Langtoft's Chronicle.*

Otterbourne and Whethamstede and
   Blackman, *Vita Hen. VI.*
Robert of Avesbury.
Robert of Gloucester.
Ross, *Historia regum.*
Sprott, *Chronica* and Fragment of
   chronicle of Edw. IV.
Textus Roffensis.
Thomas of Elmham (but see now No. 2877),
   Vita et gesta Hen. V.
Titus Livy, *Vita Hen. V.*
Walter of Hemingford (and *Historia
   Edw. III*).
William of Newburgh.

The appendices of many of these volumes contain much miscellaneous and extraneous material (documents, etc.). For their contents, see Hardy, *Catalogue* (No. 21), i. 807–10.

1103A   HISTORIANS OF SCOTLAND. 10 vols. Edin. 1871–85.

Listed in *Repert. Font.* i. 327–8.

1104   IRISH RECORD COMMISSIONERS. Publications, 1826–1901. Dublin.

Listed in *Repert. Font.* i. 341. See No. 226.

1105   IRISH RECORD OFFICE. Publications 1905+. Dublin.

Listed in *Repert. Font.* i. 341. See No. 227.

1106   LANGEBEK (JACOB). Scriptores rerum Danicarum medii aevi. 9 vols. Copenhagen. 1772–1878. *

Listed in *Repert. Font.* i. 666–71.

Genealogia regum Anglo-Saxonum, i. 6–9.
Vita S. Odonis archiepiscopi Cant. auctore Osberno (Eadmer), ii. 401–11.
Vita S. Elphegi, ii. 439–63.
Sermo Lupi ad Anglos, ii. 463–71.
Encomium Emmae, ii. 472–502.
Svenis Aggonis Historia legum Castrensium Canuti Magni, iii. 139–64.
Chronicon regum Manniae, 1066–1266, iii. 209–44.
Gesta Siwardi ejusque filii Waldevi, iii. 287–302.

1107   LIEBERMANN (FELIX). Ueber Ostenglische Geschichtsquellen in *Neues Archiv,* xviii (1892), 225–67.

1108 LIEBERMANN (FELIX). Ungedruckte anglo-normannische Geschichtsquellen. Strasburg. 1879. *

Annales Anglo-Saxonici, A.D. 935–1202.
Eadmer, *Miracles of St. Anselm.*
Matthew Paris, *Life of Stephen Langton.*
Miracles of St. Edmund.

This valuable little book also contains various brief local annals of Battle Abbey, Bury St.
Edmunds, Chichester, Colchester, Peterborough, Plympton, Reading, St. Albans, and
Winchester, extending from A.D. 1 to 1260. See also Liebermann's 'Annals of Lewes
Priory', *E.H.R.* xvii (1902), 83–9; 'Annalium Angliae Excerpta', edited in M.G.H. SS.
xvi. 480–4; C. W. Previté-Orton, 'Annales Radingenses posteriores, 1135–1264',
E.H.R. xxxvii (1922), 400–3.

1109 MARTÈNE (EDMOND) and DURAND (URSIN). Thesaurus novus
anecdotorum. 5 vols. Paris. 1717. *†

Listed in *Repert. Font.* i. 405–6.

1110 MARTÈNE (EDMOND) and DURAND (URSIN). Veterum scriptorum
et monumentorum amplissima collectio. 9 vols. Paris. 1724–33. *†

Listed in *Repert. Font.* i. 406–8.

These two collections contain many letters and charters relating to England. See Hardy,
Catalogue (No. 21), i. 897–906.

1111 MASERES (FRANCIS). Historiae Anglicanae circa tempus conquestus
Angliae selecta monumenta: excerpta ex Historiae Normannorum scriptoribus
antiquis [No. 1096]. Lond. 1807.

Battle abbey roll.   Ordericus Vitalis (excerpts).
Encomium Emmae.   William of Poitiers.

1112 MICHEL (FRANCISQUE). Chroniques anglo-normandes. 3 vols.
Rouen. 1836–40.

Listed in *Repert. Font.* i. 420.
Benoît de Sainte-Maure (excerpts).   Geoffrey Gaimar (excerpts).
De gestis Herwardi.   Guy of Amiens, *Carmen.*
De inventione S. Crucis Walthamensis. Langtoft (excerpts).
Du roi Guillaume, and *Le dit de*   *Vie de S. Edward* (excerpts).
   Guillaume.   Vita Haroldi.
                                        Vita Waldevi comitis.

1113 MEDIEVAL TEXTS. General editors: V. H. Galbraith, R. A. B.
Mynors, and C. N. L. Brooke. Lond. Edin. etc. 1949–67. Oxf. 1967 (in progress).

This series of literary and historical texts with English translations was published as
Nelson's Medieval Classics or Medieval Texts from 1949 to 1965. Thereafter the series
became the Oxford Medieval Texts published by the Clarendon Press, the first volume
in 1967. Listed in *Repert. Font.* i. 413. The texts directly germane to British history are
listed herewith:

Annales Gandenses.   *Life of Ailred of Rievaulx.*
Dialogus de scaccario.   Nicolas Oresme, *De moneta.*
Gesta Stephani.   Pope Innocent III, *Selected letters.*
Jocelin of Brakelond, *Chronicle.*   *Regularis concordia.*
John of Salisbury, *Historia pontificalis.* *Vita Edwardi Secundi.*
John of Salisbury, *Letters,* i.   William of Malmesbury, *Historia novella.*
Lanfranc, *Monastic constitutions.*

Hugh the Chantor.
St. Hugh of Lincoln, Magna Vita.
Chronicle of Æthelweard.
Life of Edward the Confessor.
Life of Anselm, by Eadmer.
Bury Chronicle.
Chronicle of Richard of Devizes.

Anglo-Scottish Documents.
Glanvill.
Bede's *Ecclesiastical History.*
Ordericus Vitalis (No. 2937).
W. Worcestre, *Itineraries.*
Others in preparation.

1114 MONUMENTA GERMANIAE HISTORICA. Edited by Georg H. Pertz, Georg Waitz, and others; 1947–58 by Friedrich Baethgen, and 1959–70 by H. Grundmann. Hanover, Berlin, or Weimar etc. 1826+. Indices eorum quae Monumentorum Germaniae historicorum tomis hucusque editis continentur. By Oswald Holder-Egger and Karl Zeumer. Hanover and Berlin. 1890. Reprint of Scriptores in folio, vols. i–xxx; of Leges in folio, vols. i–v; of Diplomata in folio, vol. i. ★

Listed in *Repert. Font.* i. 466–79. See M. D. Knowles, 'The Monumenta Germaniae Historica', *T.R.H.S.* 5th Ser. x (1960), 129–50; reprinted (No. 262), pp. 63–97. See Harry Bresslau, *Geschichte der Monumenta Germaniae historica* (Hanover, 1921), and the reports on current progress since 1943 by Friedrich Baethgen and others, recently H. Grundmann, published in *Sitzungsberichte der deutschen Akademie der Wissenschaften zu Berlin, Phil.-hist. Klasse*, 1949+; in *Deutsches Archiv für Erforschung*; and in *Anzeiger d. Oesterreichen Akademie d. Wissenschaften, Phil.-hist. Kl.* Vienna. Under Baethgen, headquarters were set up in Munich. The directors of the *Monumenta* have edited the review *Neues Archiv der Gesellschaft für ältere deutsche Geschichtskunde* . . . 1876–1935; and *Deutsches Archiv für Geschichte des Mittelalters*, 1938–44; continued as *Deutsches Archiv für Erforschung*, each volume of which carries a progress report on M.G.H.

This is a most important collection, in over 200 volumes, of sources for the European Middle Ages; although primarily connected with Germany, it includes some material directly relative to Britain. It comprises five series, to wit: Scriptores, Leges, Epistolae, Diplomata, and Antiquitates. The series Scriptores is split into several sub-series, of which the following contain British material: *Auctores antiquissimi, Scriptores rerum Merovingicarum*, and *Scriptores.*

Vol. xiii (1898) of the *Auctores* contains Theodor Mommsen's editions of Gildas, Nennius, and Bede's *Chronica*; and vol. xv (1913–19), Rudolf Ehwald's edition of Aldhelm's works. Vol. vi (1913) of Scriptores rerum Merovingicarum, edited by Bruno Krusch and Wilhelm Levison, contains the *Life of Bishop Wilfrid* by Eddius Stephanus; vol. vii (1920) includes Alcuin's *Life of St. Willibrord*, and Constantius' *Life of St. Germanus.*

The *Scriptores* contain several lives of saints and extracts from English chroniclers; for the list, see Holder-Egger and Zeumer, *Indices*. The pertinent references are given below, under the appropriate title. However, special attention should be paid to vols. xiii (1881), xxvii (1885), and xxviii (1888), where extracts from the following chronicles are edited by Felix Liebermann and Reinhold Pauli:

Volume xiii

Æthelweard.
Annales Anglo-Saxonici (or *Anglo-Saxon chronicle*).
Asser.
Eadmer.
Florence of Worcester, with continuation.

Henry of Huntingdon.
Northumbrian chronicle.
Simeon of Durham.
William of Malmesbury.

Volume xxvii

Ambrose's *Carmen.*
Annales Burtonenses.
Annales de Margan.
Annales de Southwark.

Annales Dorenses.
Annales Dunstaplenses.
Annales Melrosenses.
Annales Meneviae.

Annales Osneienses.
Annales S. Edmundi.
Annales Stratae Floridae.
Annales Teokesburienses.
Annales Waverleienses.
Annales Wigornienses.
Annales Wintonienses.
Benedict of Peterborough.
Brut y tywysogion.
Chronicon Anglo-Scoticum.
Chronicon Eveshamense.
Gervase of Canterbury.
Gervase of Tilbury.
Gesta Stephani.
Giraldus Cambrensis.
Itinerarium peregrinorum.

Jocelin of Brakelond.
John of Hexham.
John of Salisbury.
Jordan Fantosme.
Lives of Becket.
Lives of Hugh of Lincoln.
Map's *De nugis.*
Ralph Niger.
Ralph de Diceto.
Ralph of Coggeshall.
Richard of Devizes.
Richard of Hexham.
Roger of Hoveden.
Thomas de Wykes.
Walter of Coventry.
William of Newburgh.

Volume xxviii

Abbreviatio chronicorum Angliae.
Annales Angliae et Scotiae, and *Annales regni Scotiae.*
Annales Furnesienses.
Annales Londonienses.
Annales Norwicenses.
Annales S. Pauli Londoniensis.
Annales Stanleienses.
Arnold Fitz-Thedmar.
Bartholomew Cotton.
Chronicon de Bello.
Flores historiarum

John de Tayster.
John of Wallingford.
Matthew Paris.
Opus chronicorum.
Peter of Langtoft.
Rishanger.
Robert of Gloucester.
Roger Bacon.
Roger of Wendover.
Thomas Eccleston.
Vita Stephani [Langton].
Walter of Hemingburgh.

The *Epistolae* include the registers of Gregory I and Gregory VII, the Pertz-Rodenberg catalogue of selected papal letters of the thirteenth century, and letters of Alcuin, Boniface, *et al.*

1115 MONUMENTA HISTORICA NORVEGIAE. Ed. by Gustav Storm. Christiania. 1880.

Listed in *Repert. Font.* i. 485.
Contains the Latin histories of Norway. Theodoric's *Historia de antiquitate regum Norwagiensium* (written *c.* 1180), pp. 1–68; *Historia Norwegiae* (written *c.* 1200), pp. 71–124.

1116 MYVYRIAN ARCHAIOLOGY OF WALES, collected out of ancient manuscripts. Ed. by Owen Jones, Edward Williams, and William Owen Pughe. 3 vols. Lond. 1801–7. Another edn. (with additions). Denbigh. 1870. See No. 2382.

These editions must be treated with caution; for criticism, including charges of forgery, see *Dict. Welsh Biog.* (No. 542), pp. 1033–4, under 'Williams, Edward'.

1117 O'CONOR (CHARLES). Rerum Hibernicarum scriptores veteres. 4 vols. Buckingham. 1814–26.

Listed in *Repert. Font.* i. 531–2.
A collection of Irish chronicles, sometimes inaccurately transcribed. For better, more recent editions, see Nos. 2170, 2778, 2780, 2784, 2786. Vol. i contains extracts from Greek and Roman writers concerning Ireland; vol. ii, *Annals of Boyle, Annals of Innisfallen, Tigernach's Annals*; vol. iii, *Annals of the Four Masters*; vol. iv, *Annals of Ulster.*

1118 PARKER (MATTHEW). Chronicles. 4 vols. Lond. 1567–74.

This collection includes Asser, Matthew Paris, Matthew of Westminster, and Walsingham.

1119 [SAVILE (HENRY).] Rerum Anglicarum scriptores post Bedam. Lond. 1596. Another edn. Frankfurt. 1601. *

Listed in *Repert. Font.* i. 643.
Æthelweard.
Henry of Huntingdon.
'Ingulf'.
Roger of Hoveden.

William of Malmesbury: *De gestis pontificum*; *De gestis regum*; *Historia novella*.

1120 SKENE (WILLIAM F.), ed. Chronicles of the Picts, chronicles of the Scots, and other early memorials of Scottish history. Edin. 1867.

For the Scottish materials in the Paris manuscript, Bib. Nat. Latin 4126, see the article by M. O. Anderson in *Scot. Hist. Rev.* xxviii (1949), 31–42; also 'The lists of kings', ibid. pp. 108–18 and xxix (1950), 13–22. For a better text, plus a translation and commentary of an early Irish poem on Scottish history, see Kenneth Jackson, 'The Duan Albanach' in *Celtica*, iii (1955), 149 ff. and in *Scot. Hist. Rev.* xxxvi (1957), 125–37.

1121 SOCIÉTÉ DE L'HISTOIRE DE FRANCE. [Chronicles, letters, etc.] Paris. 1835+. *

Listed in *Repert. Font.* i. 688–92.
Of more than 450 volumes, about half deal with the Middle Ages. Some early volumes are not well edited, but the editions pertinent to British history, cited below, are competently done.

1122 [SPARKE (JOSEPH).] Historiae Anglicanae scriptores varii. 2 vols. Lond. 1723.

Listed in *Repert. Font.* i. 710.
Contains *Chronicle* attributed without basis to John of Peterborough (No. 2834); Fitzstephen's *Life of Becket*; and histories of Peterborough abbey by Hugh Candidus, Robert Swapham, Walter of Whittlesey, etc. (No. 6268).

1123 STEVENSON (JOSEPH). The church historians of England. [A series of translations.] 5 vols. in 8. Lond. 1853–8.

Listed in *Repert. Font.* i. 129–30.
Vol. i, pt. ii. Historical works of Bede.

Vol. ii, pt. i. *Anglo-Saxon chronicle*; Florence of Worcester.

Vol. ii, pt. ii. Asser; *Book of Hyde*; Æthelweard; Geoffrey Gaimar; 'Ingulf'; John of Wallingford.

Vol. iii, pt. i. William of Malmesbury, *History of the kings*, and *History of his own times*.

Vol. iii, pt. ii. Simeon of Durham, *Historical works*.

Vol. iv, pt. i. *Chronicle of Holyrood*; *Chronicle of Melrose*; *Chronicles of Winchester and Canterbury*.

John and Richard of Hexham; Jordan Fantosme.

Vol. iv, pt. ii. Robert de Monte, *Chronicles*; William of Newburgh.

Vol. v, pt. i. *Acts of king Stephen*; *Chronicle of the Isle of Man*; Gervase of Canterbury, *Archbishops of Canterbury*; Giraldus Cambrensis, *Instruction of princes*; Richard of Devizes; Robert of Gloucester (excerpts); Robert de Monte, *History of Henry I*.

1124 [TWYSDEN (ROGER).] Historiae Anglicanae scriptores x. Lond. 1652.

Aelred of Rievaulx.
Brompton.
Gervase of Canterbury.
John of Hexham.
Knighton.
Ralph de Diceto.

Richard of Hexham.
Simeon of Durham.
Thomas Stubbs, *Chronica pontificum Ebor'*.
William Thorne, *De rebus abbatum Cant'*
(St. Augustine's Abbey).

For a biography of Twysden, see F. W. Jessup, *Sir Roger Twysden, 1597–1672*. Lond. 1965.

1125 [WHARTON (HENRY).] Anglia sacra sive collectio historiarum de archiepiscopis et episcopis Angliae ad annum 1540. 2 vols. Lond. 1691. *

Listed in *Repert. Font.* i. 777.
Contains Giraldus Cambrensis, *Lives of Bishops*; *Historiae Eliensis*; Robert Graystanes, *History of the Church of Durham*; Thomas Rudborne, *History of the Church of Winchester*; and many other works. For a full table of contents, see Hardy, *Catalogue* (No. 21), i, 691–4.

2. *Church History: General Sources*

The principal collections of ecclesiastical sources dealing with the Middle Ages as a whole are grouped together at this point. They are normally useful for both the Anglo-Saxon period and the later Middle Ages. For Dugdale's *Monasticon*, see No. 1147. The section on general collections of sources, above, pp. 135–44, must also be consulted, and the Church sources cited in volume ii.

1126 BARONIUS (CAESAR). Annales ecclesiastici . . . Ed. by J. D. Mansi. 38 vols. Lucca. 1738–59. Another edn. By A. Theiner. 37 vols. Paris. 1864–83.

1127 CORPUS CHRISTIANORUM: Series Latina. Continuatio Mediaevalis. Turnhout. 1954+. (in progress).

Critical editions which replace those of Migne as they appear.

1128 GEE (HENRY) and HARDY (WILLIAM J.). Documents illustrative of English church history (A.D. 314–1700). Lond. etc. 1896. *

Contains forty-five medieval and seventy-nine modern documents (translations only).

1129 HADDAN (ARTHUR W.) and STUBBS (WILLIAM). Councils and ecclesiastical documents relating to Great Britain and Ireland. 3 vols. Oxf. 1869–78. Reprinted. 1965.

A new edition of a part of Wilkins's *Concilia* (No. 1142), and one of the most important collections of materials on early English history. Vol. i deals with the British church, A.D. 200–681, and the church of Wales, A.D. 681–1295; vol. ii with Cumbria and Scotland to 1188, and Ireland to 665; vol. iii with Anglo-Saxon England to 870. The work contains canons, penitentials, records of synods, dooms of Anglo-Saxon kings, extracts from chronicles, letters of popes and prelates, charters, and other documents of general interest for the study of ecclesiastical history, including the relations of church and state. For councils of the thirteenth century, see Powicke–Cheney (No. 6816).

1130 HISTORIANS OF THE CHURCH OF YORK AND ITS ARCHBISHOPS. Ed. by James Raine. Rolls Series. 3 vols. Lond. 1879–94. *

This valuable collection contains Alcuin's *Carmen* (No. 2295); several lives of bishops Oswald and Wilfrid (Nos. 2311, 2313); lives of Bishop John of Beverley, who died in

Printed Collections of Sources

-1135] **Printed Collections of Sources** 145

721; *Chronica Pontificum Ecclesiae Eboracensis*, A.D. 601–1140, written in the first half of the twelfth century; vol. iii: documents relating to the church of York, only three of them before A.D. 1066. The most important biography in vol. ii is the history of four archbishops of York, Thomas I, Gerard, Thomas II, and Thurstan, A.D. 1070–1127 (with additions to 1153), by Hugh the Chantor, or Hugh Sottovagina, precentor of York (see No. 5853): a valuable account of the controversy between the archbishops of Canterbury and York, told by an eyewitness. Vol. ii also contains a letter of Archbishop Ralph to the Pope, 1119, concerning the same controversy; anonymous lives of archbishops Thurstan and William Fitzherbert; several papers relating to Archbishop Scrope and his execution in 1405; the part of *Chron. Pont. Eccles. Ebor.* (A.D. 601–1519) from 1147 to 1373 by Thomas Stubbs, a writer of the fourteenth century; etc. Vol. iii is a collection of letters, wills, and other documents, from 930 to 1522; they are connected with the history of the northern bishoprics, and are taken from the registers of the archbishops of York etc. For Thomas II, see Walter Edward Hodgson, *The life of Thomas II, Archbishop of York* [1108–14] (Nottingham, 1909).

1131 JAFFÉ (PHILIPP). Regesta pontificum romanorum ab condita ecclesia ad annum post Christum datum MCXCVIII. Berlin. 1851. 2nd edn. in 2 vols., under the direction of W. Wattenbach, by S. Loewenfeld, F. Kaltenbrunner, P. Ewald. Leipzig. 1885–8.

For continuation, see Potthast's *Regesta* (No. 1138). For additions to Jaffé–Lowenfeld, consult Kehr's *Regesta* (No. 1132). The second edition of Jaffé is considerably enlarged and is indispensable. It analyses in chronological order the papal letters which were scattered in numerous works at the time of its compilation. Potthast's volumes are similar in content. For papal registers, see below, pp. 752–4.

1132 KEHR (PAUL F.), ed. Regesta pontificum Romanorum (designed to be a complete collection of surviving papal documents to 1198), in *Abhandlungen der Akad. der Wissensch. in Göttingen.*

Italia pontificia. Ed. by P. F. Kehr. 7 vols. (1906–25).
Germania pontificia. Ed. by A. Brackmann.
Papsturkunden in Spanien. Ed. by P. F. Kehr.
Papsturkunden in den Niederlanden. Ed. by J. Ramackers.
Papsturkunden in Frankreich. Ed. by Hermann Meinert and J. Ramackers.
Papsturkunden in Portugal. Ed. by Carl Erdmann.
Papsturkunden in England. Ed. by Walther Holtzmann. 3 vols. (1930–52). See No. 5550.

1133 LIBRARY OF CHRISTIAN CLASSICS. Ed. by John Baillie, John T. McNeill, and Henry P. Van Dusen. 26 vols. Philadelphia, 1953+.

Vol. x: A scholastic miscellany: Anselm to Ockham, ed. by Eugene R. Fairweather. Translations and good bibliographies.

1134 LUNT (WILLIAM E.). Papal revenues in the Middle Ages. Columbia Univ. Records of Civilization, xix. 2 vols. N.Y. 1934. *

Vol. i, pp. 1–136 describe the fiscal administration and each of the various revenues; pp. 139–341 are translations of documents on the fiscal administration. Vol. ii gives translations of documents relating to each of the various revenues.

1135 MIGNE (JACQUES PAUL), ed. Patrologiae cursus completus. Patres . . . ecclesiae latinae. 217 vols. Paris. 1844–55. 4 vols. of tables. 1862–4. Microcard edn., Washington.

A collection of old editions of works of the church fathers, theologians, historians, papal letters, etc., down to the death of Innocent III. Despite inaccuracies in the texts, it remains a fundamental source for consultation. For the contents of the series, see Hardy,

Catalogue (No. 21), i. 845–8; Potthast (No. 62), vol. i, pp. xciv ff.; *Catalogue of the London Library* (1903), pp. 986–95 or (1914), ii. 285–94; and *Repert. Font.* i. 434–54. A supplement is edited by A. Hamman as *Migne, Patrologia Latina Supplementum* (Paris, 1959). In progress; 4 vols. by 1968. For information on revisions of Migne's texts, see P. Glorieux, 'Pour révaloriser Migne: Tables rectificatives', *Mélanges de Science religieuse* (Lille), ix (1952), 1–82.

1136 MIRBT (CARL). Quellen zur Geschichte des Papsttums und des römischen Katholizismus. Freiburg etc. 1895. 5th edn. Tübingen. 1934. 6th edn. in two volumes. Vol. i: Von den Anfängen bis zum Tridentinum by Kurt Aland. Tübingen. 1967.

1137 PONTIFICIA HIBERNICA. Medieval papal chancery documents concerning Ireland, 640–1261. Ed. by Maurice P. Sheehy. 2 vols. Dublin. 1962–5.

A critical edition, with annotations, of about 500 papal letters. Indexes, ii. 350–440.

1138 POTTHAST (AUGUST). Regesta pontificum romanorum inde ab anno post Christum natum MCXCVIII ad annum MCCCIV. 2 vols. Berlin. 1874–5.

1139 PRYNNE (WILLIAM). An exact chronological vindication of our kings' supreme ecclesiastical jurisdiction over all religious affairs [from the establishment of Christianity to the death of Edward I]. 3 vols. in 6. Lond. 1666, 1665–8. Vol. iii, with a new title-page: The history of king John, Henry III, and Edward I. Lond. 1670. Vol. iii, with another title-page: Antiquae constitutiones regni Angliae circa jurisdictionem ecclesiasticam, John–Edward I. Lond. 1672.

Consists largely of extracts from the charter, close, and patent rolls, chroniclers, etc. These three volumes are usually called Prynne's *Records.*

1140 SPELMAN (HENRY). Concilia, decreta, leges, constitutiones in re ecclesiarum orbis Britannici. 2 vols. Lond. 1639–64.

Superseded by Wilkins's collection (No. 1142).

1141 USSHER (JAMES). Veterum epistolarum Hibernicarum sylloge. Dublin 1632. Another edn. in his Works, iv. 384–572. Dublin. 1847.

Contains fifty letters, mainly on church affairs, about A.D. 600–1200.

1142 WILKINS (DAVID). Concilia Magnae Britanniae et Hiberniae, A.D. 446–1718. 4 vols. Lond. 1737. *

See Hardy, *Catalogue* (No. 21), i. 754–62. The earlier portions of Wilkins's work are uncritical and incomplete, and are now superseded (to A.D. 870) by the edition of Haddan and Stubbs (No. 1129), and the later portions need revision. The most nearly complete collection of Concilia, though far from satisfactory, is *Sacrorum conciliorum nova et amplissima collectio,* ed. by J. D. Mansi, 31 vols. (Florence etc. 1759–98); reissued and supplemented by J. B. Martin and L. Petit (Paris 1901+; with Introduction, 1903). See also C. R. Cheney, 'Legislation of the medieval English church', *E.H.R.* i (1935), 193–224, 385–417; E. F. Jacob, 'Wilkins's *Concilia* and the fifteenth century', *T.R.H.S.* 4th Ser. xv (1932), 91–131; Richard Hart, *Ecclesiastical records of England, Ireland, and Scotland, to the reformation* (Cambr. 1836; 2nd edn. 1846, an epitome of Wilkins's *Concilia*). For a critical edition of thirteenth-century texts to replace Wilkins, see Powicke–Cheney (No. 6816).

1143 WILLELMI MALMESBIRIENSIS DE GESTIS PONTIFICUM
ANGLORUM LIBRI QUINQUE. Ed. by N. E. S. A. Hamilton. Rolls Series.
Lond. 1870. * Also in Migne's *Patrologia*, clxxix, 1441–1680. Paris. 1855. An
imperfect text of bks. i–iv is printed in Savile's *Scriptores* (No. 1119), pp. 111–
68. Lond. 1596. Extracts. Ed. by Waitz, in M.G.H. *SS.* (No. 1114), x. 454–7,
notes; and by Pauli, ibid. xiii. 136–9. Hanover. 1852–81.

> Completed A.D. 1125; it contains a valuable account of the bishops and abbots of Eng-
> land, A.D. 601 to the writer's own time. Bk. v (which is also printed in Gale's *Scriptores
> XV* (No. 1100), pp. 337–81, and in Wharton's *Anglia Sacra* (No. 1125), ii. 1–49) is
> devoted to the life of Aldhelm.

3. Church History: Monasticism: Sources

Dugdale (No. 1147) is the fullest authority on the history of particular religious
houses, and Tanner's *Notitia* (No. 1150) is a useful work of reference. Dugdale
is now supplemented by sections in the Victoria County Histories (No. 1529).
For English monasticism subsequent to the tenth century, the works of Knowles
(Nos. 1295, 1297) supersede all previous general accounts, and his lengthy
bibliographical references should be consulted. The vast majority of the sources
of the Middle Ages touch upon various aspects of monasticism; here are entered
the primary collections or histories with an exclusive concern for monasticism.
For a map of monastic Britain, see No. 604.

1144 BACKMUND (NORBERT). Monasticon Praemonstratense: id est
historia circariarum atque canoniarum candidi et canonici ordinis Praemonstratensis. 3 vols. Straubing. 1949–52.

> A history, not a collection of sources.

1145 CANIVEZ (JOSEPH M.). Statuta capitulorum generalium ordinis
Cisterciensis (1116–1789). 8 vols. Biblio. Rev. d'Hist. Eccles. Louvain. 1933.

1146 CORPUS CONSUETUDINUM MONASTICARUM under the
general direction of Kassius Hallinger of the Pontifical Athenaeum of St. Anselm.
Siegburg. 1963. In progress.

> A description and critique of the first five volumes of this project of some twenty-five
> volumes of critical editions of Benedictine customaries is provided in Anselm Stritt-
> matter, 'Corpus consuetudinum monasticarum', *Traditio*, xxv (1969), 431–57. Vol. i:
> *Initia consuetudinis Benedictinae: consuetudines saeculi octavi et noni.* Co-operantibus D.
> Petro Becker, O.S.B., et al. . . . (Siegburg, 1963).
> Vol. ii: *Customary of the Benedictine Abbey of Eynsham in Oxfordshire.* Ed. by Antonia
> Gransden (Siegburg, 1963). Vol. iii: *Decreta Lanfranci monachis Cantuariensibus trans-
> missa.* Ed. by David Knowles (Siegburg, 1967). (A re-edition with additional biblio-
> graphy of his edition of 1951). Vol. iv: *Consuetudines Beccenses.* Ed. by Marie P. Dickson
> (Siegburg, 1967). Vol. v: *Consuetudines et observantiae monasteriorum Sancti Mathiae et
> Sancti Maximini ab Rode Abbate conscriptae.* Ed. by Petrus Becker (Siegburg, 1968).

1147 DUGDALE (WILLIAM). Monasticon Anglicanum. 3 vols. Lond.
1655–73. 2nd edn. of vol. i. 1682. Two additional volumes, by John Stevens.
1772–3. New edition [of the whole work, with many additions], by John Caley,

Henry Ellis, and Bulkeley Bandinel. 6 vols. in 8. Lond. 1817–30. Reprinted. 6 vols. 1846. *

A valuable collection of charters and other records relating to the monastic houses of England and Wales, with an account of the history of each house. English abridgments of the original work were published in 1693 and 1718. A valuable supplement to Dugdale is George Oliver, *Monasticon diocesis Exoniensis: records illustrating the ancient foundations in Cornwall and Devon* (Exeter, 1846; additional supplement, 1854). Cf. David Douglas, 'William Dugdale: the "grand plagiary"', *History*, N.S. xx (1935–6), 193–210; and Lady Stenton in her introduction to *Hatton Seals* (No. 464); Francis Maddison, Dorothy Styles, and Anthony Wood, *Sir William Dugdale 1605–1686: a list of his printed works*, etc. (Warwick, 1953).

1148   JANAUSCHEK (LEOPOLD). Originum Cisterciensium . . . Tomus i. Vienna. 1877.

1149   MABILLON (JEAN). Annales ordinis S. Benedicti occidentalium monachorum patriarchae (to 1157). 6 vols. Paris. 1703–39. New edn. Lucca. 1739–45.

On Mabillon, see David Knowles, *The historian and character* (No. 1477), pp. 213–39.

1150   TANNER (THOMAS). Notitia monastica: an account of all abbeys, etc. in England and Wales. Lond. 1744. Reprinted, with additions by James Nasmith. Cambr. 1787.

Valuable; contains a brief account of each religious house, with many references to unpublished records. This work is the expansion of his *Notitia monastica* (Oxf. 1695).

4. *Church History:* Acta Sanctorum

Although the 'lives' of saints are filled with miracles and incredible stories and are often written at a later period, they form a rich mine of information concerning the life and customs of the people. For some parts of the Anglo-Saxon period, they are almost the only written material at our disposal. For an introduction to hagiography in general, reference may be made to two masterly works. The first is Hippolyte Delehaye, *Les légendes hagiographiques* (Brussels, 1905; 4th edn. 1955), part of which first appeared in *Revue des questions historiques*, lxxiv (1903), 56–122; it was translated by V. M. Crawford as *The legends of the saints, an introduction to hagiography* (Lond. 1907); and newly translated by Donald Attwater (Lond. and N.Y. 1962). The second valuable work is a manual synthesizing in some 400 pages the principal researches of the past three centuries: René Aigrain, *L'hagiographie, ses sources, ses méthodes, son histoire* (Paris, 1953). The latter is described as 'une somme de ce que tout historien doit connaître en matière d'hagiographie' (R. Aubert, in *R.H.E.* xlix (1954), 536).

An elaborate bibliographical list of *acta sanctorum* is given in Potthast's *Bibliotheca* (No. 62), ii. 1131–1646. See also Charles de Smedt's *Introductio generalis ad historiam ecclesiasticam critice tractandam* (Ghent etc. 1876), pp. 111–97. Consult also No. 1153, and for current bibliography see No. 166.

The great work on hagiography has been done by the Bollandists, for which see Hippolyte Delehaye, *A travers trois siècles: l'œuvre des Bollandistes, 1615–1915* (Brussels, 1920; 2nd edn. 1959); translated as *The work of the Bollandists through three centuries 1615–1915* (Princeton, 1922); and Société des Bollandistes, *L'œuvre des Bollandistes de 1837 à 1937* (Brussels, 1937). Cf. Nos. 1152, 1153, 1156, below. For an appreciation, see M. D. Knowles, *Great Historical Enterprises* (No. 262).

For British saints, see Bonser (No. 12), especially items 3911–5128; and Hardy's *Catalogue* (No. 21), vol. i, part i. For Irish saints including those who had relations with Britain, consult, in addition to O'Hanlon (No. 1167) and others, Kenney, *Sources* (No. 23), Ludwig Bieler, 'Recent research in Irish hagiography', *Studies* (No. 239), xxxv (1946), 230–8, 536–44; and the numerous articles by P. Grosjean in *Analecta Bollandiana* and elsewhere which are catalogued in Grosjean's bibliography in *Anal. Boll.* lxxxii (1964), 307–18. For Celtic saints consult also the section on the Celtic Church, below, pp. 379–82. For individual saints, see pp. 333–9.

The principal collections of saints' lives and cognate materials follow:

1151 ACHERY (LUC D') and MABILLON (JEAN). Acta sanctorum ordinis S.Benedicti (A.D. 500–1100). 9 vols. Paris. 1668–1701. Reprinted. 9 vols. Venice. 1733–(40).

> For the parts relating to England, see Hardy, *Catalogue* (No. 21), i. 832–4. Cf. *The book of saints: a biographical dictionary*, compiled by the Benedictine monks of St. Augustine's Abbey, Ramsgate (4th edn. Lond. 1947).

1152 ACTA SANCTORUM QUOTQUOT TOTO URBE COLUNTUR VEL A CATHOLICIS SCRIPTORIBUS CELEBRANTUR, quae ab antiquis monumentis latinis aliarumque gentium collegit digessit notis illustravit J. Bollandus, servata primigenia scriptorum phrasi. Operam et studium contulit G. Henschenius. (66 vols. covering 1 January to 10 November). Antwerp. 1643–1770. Brussels. 1780–1925. In progress. * (1643–1883).

> The most valuable collection of saints' lives, compiled during the past three centuries by the Bollandists, is noted in *Repert. Font.* i. 16–17. In addition to the above cited edition, there are editions published at Venice 1734–70, and at Paris 1863–75. For clarity of citation, 'it is necessary to quote the month, the volume, and the edition'. For more detailed references, consult Potthast, *Bibliotheca* (No. 62), i, pp. xxxii–xxxiv; and for British saints included herein, Hardy's *Catalogue* (No. 21), i. 683–6. The other serial publications of the Bollandists are *Analecta Bollandiana* (No. 1153) and *Subsidia Hagiographica*.

1153 ANALECTA BOLLANDIANA. Ed. by Charles de Smedt, Joseph de Backer, and others. Paris etc. 1882+. Indexes of vols. i–xx (1881–1901), Brussels. 1904; vols. xxi–xl (1902–22), 1931; vols. xli–lx (1923–42), 1944; vols. lxi–lxxx (1943–62), 1964. † (1882–1943).

> A periodical supplement to the *Acta Sanctorum* (No. 1152), including articles, texts, catalogues of hagiographical MSS., and in each number an important 'Bulletin des publications hagiographiques'. In recent years P. Grosjean has contributed a series of notes on Celtic hagiography. The bibliography of Father Grosjean (d. 1964) is given in *Analecta Bollandiana*, lxxxii (1964), 307–18.

1154 ARNOLD-FOSTER (FRANCES). Studies in church dedications, or England's patron saints. 3 vols. Lond. 1899.

1155 BARING-GOULD (SABINE) and FISHER (JOHN). Lives of the British saints (Wales and Cornwall). 4 vols. Soc. of Cymmrodorion. Lond. 1907–13.

'Extensive but uncritical'. Also Baring-Gould, *The lives of the saints*, 15 vols. (Lond. 1872–82); new and revised edition, 16 vols. (Edin. 1914). Alban Butler, *The lives of the fathers, martyrs, and other saints*, 5 vols. (Lond. 1745); another edn. 12 vols. 1812–13, frequently reprinted; illuminated edn. 2 vols. (1883–6); index, (1886): complete edn. revised and supplemented by H. Thurston and D. Attwater, 4 vols. (N.Y. 1956). John H. Newman and others, *Lives of the English saints*, 14 vols. in 5. (Lond. 1844–5).

1156 BIBLIOTHECA HAGIOGRAPHICA LATINA ANTIQUAE ET MEDIAE AETATIS, ed. Socii Bollandiani. 2 vols. Brussels, 1898–1901.

A supplement for the period 1901–11 appeared in 1911. These valuable bibliographies form part of the Bollandists' series Subsidia Hagiographica.

1157 BOND (FRANCIS). Dedications and patron saints of English churches; ecclesiastical symbolism; saints and their emblems. Lond. 1914.

Cf. Christiana Hole, *English Shrines and Sanctuaries* (Lond. 1954).

1158 CAPGRAVE (JOHN). Nova legenda Angliae. Lond. 1516. Reprinted. 1527. New edn. by Carl Horstmann, Nova legenda Angliae: as collected by John of Tynemouth, John Capgrave, and others, and first printed, with new lives, by Wynkyn de Worde, A.D. MDXVI, now re-edited with fresh material from MS. and printed sources. 2 vols. Oxf. 1901.

This collection of abridged lives of saints is based on the *Sanctilogium* of John of Tynemouth, who died about 1348. Horstmann gives a full account of him. See P. J. Lucas, *The Library* (Lond.), 5th Ser. xxv (1970), 1–10.

1159 CATALOGUS SANCTORUM HIBERNIAE, printed in Haddan and Stubbs, *Councils*, ii, pt. ii. 292+.

Cf. Paul Grosjean, 'Édition et commentaire du Catalogus Sanctorum Hiberniae secundum diversa tempora . . .' *Analecta Bollandiana*, lxxiii (1955), 197–213; 289–322.

1160 COLGAN (JOHN). Acta sanctorum veteris Scotiae seu Hiberniae. 2 vols. Louvain. 1645–7.

This is the most elaborate collection of the lives of Irish saints, but it is incomplete. Vol. i embraces the lives of saints in the order of the calendar from 1 January to 31 March; vol. ii deals with Patrick, Brigit, and Columba. See Hardy, *Catalogue* (No. 21), i. 750–2; and L. Bieler, ed. [Colgan's] *Four Latin lives of St. Patrick* (Dublin, 1971).

1161 DOBLE (GILBERT H.). The saints of Cornwall. Ed. by Donald Attwater. 4 pts. Truro. 1960–4. See No. 2666.

1162 GEROULD (GORDON HALL). Saints' legends. Boston etc. 1916.

In a series entitled The types of English literature, ed. by W. A. Neilson.

1163 GROSJEAN (PAUL). 'Notes d'hagiographie celtique.' *Analecta Bollandiana*, lxi (1943), 91–107; lxxi (1963), 251–72.

For a complete list, see Grosjean's bibliography (No. 1153).

1164 HEIST (W. W.). Vitae sanctorum Hiberniae ex codice olim Salmanticensi nunc Bruxellensi. *Subsidia hagiographica*, xxviii. Société des Bollandistes. Brussels. 1965.

1165 HORSTMANN (CARL), ed. The lives of women saints of our countrie of England. Also some other liues of holie women written by some of the auncient fathers (c. 1610–15). E.E.T.S. Orig. Ser. lxxxvi. Lond. 1886.

1166 LE MIRACLE IRLANDAIS. Textes réunis sous la direction de M. Daniel-Rops. Bibliothèque chrétienne d'histoire. Paris. 1956.

> A collection by various hands, including G. Le Bras, 'Les pénitentiels irlandais', pp. 172–90.

1167 O'HANLON (JOHN). Lives of the Irish saints. 10 vols. Dublin, 1875–1903.

1168 PINKERTON (JOHN). Vitae antiquae sanctorum qui habitaverunt in ex parte Britanniae nunc vocata Scotia vel in ejus insulis. Lond. 1789. Pinkerton's Lives of the Scottish saints. Ed. by W. M. Metcalfe. Paisley. 1889.

1169 PLUMMER (CHARLES). Vitae sanctorum Hiberniae. 2 vols. Oxf. 1910. Reprinted, Oxf. 1968.

> See also his *Bethada Náem n'Erenn*, Lives of Irish saints, 2 vols. (Oxf. 1922); and his valuable catalogue, entitled *Miscellanea hagiographica Hibernica vitae adhuc ineditae sanctorum* in Bollandists' *Subsidia hagiographica* xiv (Brussels, 1925).

1170 SMEDT (CHARLES DE) and BACKER (JOSEPH DE). Acta sanctorum Hiberniae ex codice Salmanticensi. Edin. etc. 1888.

1171 STOKES (WHITLEY). Lives of [Irish] saints from the Book of Lismore. Oxf. 1890.

> Irish text and translation; well edited. See also Whitley Stokes, ed. *The Martyrology of Oengus the Culdee*, Henry Bradshaw Soc. xxix (Lond. 1905). (A calendar of saints, composed about A.D. 800.)

1172 VIES DES SAINTS ET DES BIENHEUREUX SELON L'ORDRE DU CALENDRIER AVEC L'HISTOIRE DES FÊTES. By the Benedictines of Paris. 13 vols. Paris. 1935–59.

1173 WADE-EVANS (ARTHUR WADE). Vitae sanctorum Britanniae et genealogiae. Board of Celtic Studies, History and Law Series, No. 9. Cardiff. 1944.

> Text in Latin and Welsh with English translation of most of the text on opposite pages. See also S. M. Harris, 'The Kalendar of the *Vitae Sanctorum Wallensium*', *Jour. Hist. Soc. of the Church in Wales* (No. 123), iii (1953), 3–53; K. Hughes in No. 2670. For a new edition of one saint's life, see *Rhigyfarch's life of St. David; the basic twelfth-century text, with translation*, by J. W. James (Cardiff, 1967).

VI. COMPREHENSIVE MODERN NARRATIVES

A. GENERAL NARRATIVES IN SERIES

1. *Series Relating to Britain*

This section includes comprehensive histories which treat all or most of the period covered by this bibliography. The co-operative series on general history published by French scholars are useful for British topics.

1174 BROOKE (CHRISTOPHER) and SMITH (DENIS M.), eds. A history of England. Nelson Series. 8 vols. Edin. 1960 (in progress).

> i. Peter Hunter Blair. *Roman Britain and early England: 55 B.C.–A.D. 871.* 1963.
> ii. Christopher Brooke. *From Alfred to Henry III: 871–1272.* 1961.
> iii. George Holmes. *The later Middle Ages: 1272–1485.* 1962.

1175 CAMBRIDGE ECONOMIC HISTORY, planned and edited by J. H. Clapham and Eileen Power; later by M. Postan and H. J. Habakkuk. Cambr. 1941 (in progress). See No. 1364.

1176 CAMBRIDGE MEDIEVAL HISTORY. Planned by J. B. Bury, edited by H. M. Gwatkin, J. P. Whitney, J. R. Tanner, C. W. Previté-Orton, Z. N. Brooke. 8 vols. Cambr. etc. 1911–36.

> Each chapter is accompanied by a bibliography at the end of the volume. Charles Previté-Orton, *The shorter Cambridge medieval history* (2 vols. Cambr. 1952), is a scholarly, factual, independent work rather than a summary of the longer *Cambridge Medieval History.*

1177 DOUGLAS (DAVID C.), ed. English historical documents. Lond. 1953+.

> Cf. No. 17. The introduction to each volume provides a general historical summary.

1178 EDINBURGH HISTORY OF SCOTLAND. General editor: Gordon Donaldson. Edin. and N.Y.

> Vols. i and ii in preparation.
> Vol. iii. G. Donaldson, *James V to James VII.* 1965.
> Vol. iv. William Ferguson, *1689 to the present.* 1968.

1179 L'ÉVOLUTION DE L'HUMANITÉ, dirigée par Henri Berr. Paris. 1920+.

> t. xxxi: *La fin du monde antique et les débuts du moyen âge.* F. Lot. (2nd edn. 1951). Trans. Philip Leon and Mariette Leon. Lond. and N.Y. 1931.
> t. xxxiv: *La société féodale.* M. Bloch. 2 vols. 1939–40. Trans. L. A. Manyon. Chicago, 1961.
> t. xli: *La monarchie féodale en France et en Angleterre (X^e–XIIIe siècles).* Ch. Petit-Dutaillis. 1933. Trans. E. D. Hunt. Lond. 1936. *

1180 GREEN (JOHN R.). History of the English people. 4 vols. Lond. 1877–80. Reprinted. 8 vols. 1895–6 and 1905–8.

> An older classic, a general history of England, devoting much attention to the social condition of the people. It is an expansion of his *Short history of the English people* (Lond. 1874; new edn. 4 vols. 1892–4, and various later editions and reprints).

1181 HISTOIRE DE FRANCE DEPUIS LES ORIGINES JUSQU'À LA RÉVOLUTION, publiée sous la direction d' Ernest Lavisse. Paris. 1901–11. *
9 titles in 18 volumes.

1182 HISTOIRE GÉNÉRALE, publiée sous la direction de Gustave Glotz. Paris. 1925+.

Histoire du moyen âge:

t. i: *Les destinées de l'Empire en Occident de 395 à 888.* F. Lot, Ch. Pfister, F.-L. Ganshof. 4 fasc. 1928–34. 2nd edn. 2 vols. 1940–1.

t. ii: *L'Europe occidentale de 888 à 1125.* A. Fliche. 1930.

t. iv: pt. ii: *L'essor des États d'Occident (France, Angleterre, péninsule ibérique).* Ch. Petit-Dutaillis et P. Guinard. 1937.

t. vi: *L'Europe occidentale de 1270 à 1380.* A. Coville et R. Fawtier. 1940–1.

t. vii: *L'Europe occidentale de la fin du XIVᵉ siècle aux guerres d'Italie.* J. Calmette et E. Déprez. 2 vols. 1937–9.

t. viii: *La civilisation occidentale au moyen âge, du XIᵉ au milieu du XVᵉ siècle.* H. Pirenne, G. Cohen, et H. Focillon. 1933.

1183 HUNT (WILLIAM) and POOLE (REGINALD LANE), eds. The political history of England [in twelve volumes]. Lond. etc. 1905+. *

i: *To 1066*, by Thomas Hodgkin.
ii: *1066–1216*, by G. B. Adams.
iii: *1216–1377*, by T. F. Tout.
iv: *1377–1485*, by C. W. C. Oman.

Each volume contains a valuable appendix of authorities. Another series, *A history of England* (in nine volumes) issued by the same press under the editorship of W. N. Medlicott, is projected. Thus far two pre-Tudor volumes have appeared: Frank Barlow, *The feudal kingdom of England, 1042–1216* (Lond. 1955) and Bertie Wilkinson, *The later middle ages* (Lond. 1969).

1184 LAPPENBERG (JOHANN M.) and PAULI (REINHOLD). Geschichte von England [to 1509]. 5 vols. Hamburg. 1834–58.

Vols. i–ii, by Lappenberg, were translated by Benjamin Thorpe: *A history of England under the Anglo-Saxon kings* (2 vols. Lond. 1845 *; new edn. 1881); and *A history of England under the Norman kings . . .* (Oxf. 1857). The five volumes give a good survey of the works of the chroniclers.

1185 LINGARD (JOHN). A history of England to 1688. 8 vols. Lond. 1819–30. 5th edn. [the last edition revised by the author]. 10 vols. 1849. New edn. 10 vols. 1883. Reprinted with addition of vol. xi, covering the period from 1688 to 1910, by Hilaire Belloc. Lond. 1912–15. Several abridgments, the latest [brought down to 1910] by Henry N. Birt. Lond. 1912.

A survey of English history from the Roman Catholic point of view. His account of the fourteenth, fifteenth, and sixteenth centuries is more useful than the earlier portions of the work.

1186 LLOYD (JOHN E.). A history of Wales from the earliest times to the Edwardian conquest. 2 vols. Lond. 1911. 3rd edn. 1939. New impression, 1954. *
The standard account of Welsh history for the period.

1187 LOW (SIDNEY) and PULLING (FREDERICK S.). The dictionary of English history. Lond. 1884. Revised 1896 etc. New edn. revised and enlarged by H. J. C. Hearnshaw, H. M. Chew, and A. C. F. Beales. Lond. etc. 1928.

1188   OMAN (CHARLES W. C.), ed. A history of England. 8 vols. Lond. 1904–34.

> i. C. W. C. Oman. *England before the Norman Conquest.* 1910.
> ii. H. W. C. Davis. *England under the Normans and Angevins.* 1905.
> iii. K. H. Vickers. *England in the later middle ages.* 1914.

1189   THE OXFORD HISTORY OF ENGLAND, ed. G. N. Clark. 15 vols. Oxf. 1936–65.

> i. R. G. Collingwood and J. N. L. Myres. *Roman Britain and the English Settlements.* 1936. 2nd edn. 1937.
> ii. F. M. Stenton. *Anglo-Saxon England* (c. *550–1087*). 1943. 2nd edn. 1947. 3rd edn. 1970.
> iii. A. L. Poole. *From Domesday Book to Magna Carta.* 1951. 2nd edn. 1955.
> iv. Sir Maurice Powicke. *The thirteenth century: 1216–1307.* 1953. 2nd edn. 1962.
> v. May McKisack. *The fourteenth century: 1307–1399.* 1959.
> vi. E. F. Jacob. *The fifteenth century: 1399–1485.* 1961.

1190   PELICAN HISTORY OF ENGLAND. 9 vols. (Penguin Books). Harmondsworth. 1951–65.

> i. Ian A. Richmond. *Roman Britain.* 1955.
> ii. Dorothy Whitelock. *The beginnings of English society.* 1952.
> iii. Doris M. Stenton. *English society in the early middle ages.* 1951/2.
> iv. Alec R. Myers. *England in the late middle ages.* 1952.

1191   PEUPLES ET CIVILISATIONS. Histoire générale, publiée sous la direction de Louis Halphen et Philippe Sagnac. 20 vols. Paris. 1926+.

> *t.* vi: *L'essor de l'Europe, XIe–XIIIe siècles.* Louis Halphen. 1932. 3e edn. revue et augmentée, 1948.
> *t.* vii: *La fin du moyen âge, en deux parties*: i. *La désagrégation du monde médiéval* (*1285–1453*). H. Pirenne, A. Renaudet, E. Perroy, M. Handelsman, L. Halphen. 2 vols. 1931. Many reprints without any changes.

1192   POOLE (AUSTIN LANE), ed. Medieval England. 2 vols. Oxf. 1958.

Summaries of recent scholarship by experts, in a completely rewritten edition of the work *Companion to English history* first published by Francis P. Barnard in 1902 and revised by H. W. C. Davis in 1924. Cf. No. 1485.

1193   RAMSAY (JAMES H.). The foundations of England, or twelve centuries of British history, B.C. 55–A.D. 1154. 2 vols. Lond. 1898. The Angevin empire . . . 1154–1216. Lond. etc. 1903. The dawn of the constitution . . . 1216–1307. Lond. etc. 1908. * Genesis of Lancaster, 1307–99. 2 vols. Oxf. 1913. Lancaster and York . . . 1399–1485. 2 vols. Oxf. 1892.

This useful survey of the main facts of English history, to be employed with some caution, devotes much attention to military and financial operations.

1194   RHYS (JOHN) and BRYNMOR-JONES (DAVID). The Welsh people: their origin, history, laws, language, literature and characteristics. Lond. etc. 1900. 4th edn. Reprinted. 1923.

1195   STEINBERG (SIGFRID H.), ed. A new dictionary of British history. Lond. 1963. New edn. S. H. Steinberg and I. H. Evans. Lond. 1970.

This co-operative work presents clear, succinct accounts of events and definitions of subjects; but omits purely biographical material.

1196 TRAILL (HENRY D.), ed. Social England: a record of the progress of the people in religion, laws, learning, arts, industry, commerce, science, literature, and manners, from the earliest times to the present day, by various writers. 6 vols. Lond. etc. 1894–7. Illustrated edition [revised], by H. D. Traill and J. S. Mann. 6 vols. 1901–4.

Useful, but unequal in value. There is a bibliography at the end of each chapter.

1197 VICTORIA HISTORY OF THE COUNTIES OF ENGLAND. Ed. by H. A. Doubleday, William Page, L. F. Salzman, and R. B. Pugh. Westminster etc. 1900+.

See No. 1529.

1198 WILLIAMS (ALBERT H.). An introduction to the history of Wales. 2 vols. Vol. i: Prehistoric times to 1063 A.D.; Vol. ii: The middle ages, pt. i, 1063–1284. Cardiff. 1940. Vol. i, reprinted 1949.

2. General Narratives for Ireland

A New History of Ireland as a multi-volume series stretching from prehistory to 1945 is projected by a board of editors under the auspices of the Royal Irish Academy; the project is described in *Irish Hist. Stud.* xvi (1969), 241–57.

1199 CURTIS (EDMUND R.). History of medieval Ireland from 1110 to 1513. Lond. 1923. 2nd edn. from 1086 to 1513. Lond. 1938. *

Now consult Dillon–Chadwick (No. 2125) and Otway–Ruthven (No. 1203).

1200 McNALLY (ROBERT E.), ed. Old Ireland. Dublin. 1965.

Papers by various scholars.

1201 MacNEILL (EOIN). Phases of Irish history. Dublin. 1919. New edn. 1968.

1202 MOODY (THEODORE W.) and MARTIN (FRANCIS X.), eds. The course of Irish history. Cork. 1967.

Scholarly résumés of Irish history from prehistoric times to 1966 given by various experts as a series of television broadcasts.

1203 OTWAY-RUTHVEN (ANNETTE JOCELYN). A history of medieval Ireland [to 1495], with an introduction [to c. 1014] by Kathleen Hughes. Lond. etc. 1968.

The best single volume on medieval Ireland. See a review by Aubrey Gwynn in *Studies* (No. 239), lvii (1968), 161–73. J. F. Lydon, *The lordship of Ireland in the middle ages* (*1014–1541*) (Toronto, 1972).

B. CONSTITUTIONAL HISTORY

In the second quarter of the nineteenth century Palgrave and Kemble did much to stimulate studies among the documents, but their investigations related mainly to the Anglo-Saxon period (see Nos. 2201, 2501). In the last quarter of that century Bishop Stubbs produced the paramount exposition of medieval English constitutional history (No. 1221) from which subsequent research has sprung; obviously the massive exploitation of documents and the changes in historical viewpoints within nearly a century necessitate revisions in detail and in theses, yet Stubbs's volumes remain a classic which no student may neglect. Similarly Pollock and Maitland's renowned *History of English law* (No. 1242) and Holdsworth's monumental *History of English law* (No. 1235) are indispensable for topics in constitutional history. T. F. Tout, deeply exploring a field hitherto largely unexamined, created a masterpiece on administrative history (No. 1223). Books cited above under Comprehensive General Narratives, pp. 152–5, often emphasize constitutional developments, e.g. Petit-Dutaillis, *La monarchie féodale.*

Several general collections of documents on constitutional history have been prepared for the use of undergraduates; of these the first and most celebrated is Stubbs's *Select Charters* (No. 1208) which is continued for the period 1307–1485 by Lodge and Thornton (No. 1206) and by Chrimes and Brown (No. 1205). The fullest collections will be found in *English historical documents* (No. 17). For particular topics within the period 1216 to 1485, B. Wilkinson gives translations of many documents with long commentaries in four volumes (Nos. 4071, 4143–4, 4233).

1204   ADAMS (GEORGE B.) and STEPHENS (HENRY M.), eds. Select documents of English constitutional history. Lond. 1902.

> Translations of documents from William I to Victoria; pp. 1–212 for the period before 1485.

1205   CHRIMES (STANLEY B.) and BROWN (ALFRED L.), eds. Select documents of English constitutional history: 1307–1485. Lond. and N.Y. 1961.

> This selection concentrates on the documents touching royal depositions and on proceedings in parliament; accordingly a large percentage of the documents are in Norman French.

1206   LODGE (ELEANOR C.) and THORNTON (GLADYS A.), eds. English constitutional documents, 1307–1485. Cambr. 1935.

> Documents printed in the original languages; each section is preceded by a concise introduction and brief bibliography.

1207   STEPHENSON (CARL) and MARCHAM (FREDERICK G.), eds. Sources of English constitutional history: a selection of documents from A.D. 600 to the present, edited and translated. N.Y. and Lond. 1937.

1208   STUBBS (WILLIAM). Select charters and other illustrations of English constitutional history from the earliest times to the reign of Edward the First. Oxf. 1870. 9th edn. revised throughout by H. W. C. Davis. 1913.

> The extracts are in the original languages; those in Anglo-Saxon and French are also translated.

1209   UNIVERSITY OF LONDON INTERMEDIATE SOURCE-BOOKS OF HISTORY. Lond. etc. 1918+.

Translations of political, constitutional, ecclesiastical, and economic and social documents, by the following editors:

Chambers, R. W. *England before the Norman Conquest,* with a foreword on Roman Britain by M. Cary. Lond. 1926.
Hennings, Margaret A. *England under Henry III.* Lond. 1924.
Hughes, Dorothy. *Illustrations of Chaucer's England.* Lond. 1918.
Flemming, Jessie H. *England under the Lancastrians, 1399–1460.* Lond. 1921.
Thornley, Isobel D. *England under the Yorkists, 1460–1485.* Lond. 1920.

1210   ADAMS (GEORGE B.). Constitutional history of England. N.Y. 1921. Revised by Robert L. Schuyler [1934].

One of the better textbooks; pp. 1–239 relate to the period before 1485.

1211   ADAMS (GEORGE B.). The origin of the English constitution. N.Y. etc. 1912. 2nd edn. 1920.

See also his papers in *Columbia Law Rev.* April 1913, and *Yale Law Jour.* April 1914. Seminal studies on the effect of Anglo-Norman feudalism on constitutional development.

1212   CHRIMES (STANLEY B.). An introduction to the administrative history of medieval England. Oxford Studies in Mediaeval History, vol. vii. Oxf. 1952. 3rd edn. 1966.

A brief, perceptive résumé of modern research.

1213   GNEIST (RUDOLF). Englische Verfassungsgeschichte. Berlin. 1882. Translated by P. A. Ashworth: The history of the English constitution. 2 vols. Lond. 1886. 2nd edn. 1889. Another edn. 1 vol. 1891.

This is a sort of digest of Gneist's more detailed works on English history; it was a standard work before the detailed documentary researches of the twentieth century. It retains an interest as an excellent example of late-nineteenth-century historiography, but has been superseded for the German reader by Julius Hatschek, *Englische Verfassungsgeschichte bis zum Regierungsantritt der Königin Victoria* (Munich etc. 1913).

1214   JOLLIFFE (JOHN E. A.). The constitutional history of medieval England, from the English settlement to 1485. Lond. 1937. 4th edn. 1961.

A provocative and learned study, based on the original authorities, emphasizing the role of the folk and 'the underlying currents behind government'. For critique, see G. Lapsley, 'Mr. Jolliffe's construction of early constitutional history', *History*, N.S. xxiii (1938–9), 1–11.

1215   LYON (BRYCE). A constitutional and legal history of medieval England. N.Y. 1960.

1216   MAITLAND (FREDERIC W.). The constitutional history of England. Cambr. 1908.

Early professorial lectures to law students; often very valuable and original. Printed twenty years after their delivery from a manuscript which Maitland had not intended for publication.

1217 MORRIS (WILLIAM A.). The constitutional history of England to 1216. N.Y. 1930.

1218 RICHARDSON (HENRY G.) and SAYLES (GEORGE O.). The governance of mediaeval England from the Conquest to Magna Carta. Edin. 1963.

> The *Governance* is not a comprehensive, continuous treatment of the constitutional development from the Conquest to Magna Carta; rather it is a series of studies on many facets of that development, sometimes stated contentiously, but none the less with extraordinary erudition. For summaries and criticisms of this stimulating, provocative work, designed as a refutation of Stubbs's fundamental theme and presenting a reconstruction of English institutional history, 1066–1215, see reviews by C. R. Cheney in *History*, xlix (1964), 207–10; by W. H. Dunham, Jr. in *Speculum*, xxxix (1964), 561–5; by J. W. Gray in *Irish Hist. Stud.* xiv (1964), 187–90; by John Le Patourel in *E.H.R.* lxxx (1965), 115–20; by B. Lyon in *Tijdschrift voor Rechtsgeschiedenis*, xxxii (1964), 274–80; by R. L. Schuyler in *Journal of British Studies*, iii (1964), 1–23; by B. Wilkinson in *A.H.R.* lxix (1964), 427–9. Consult C. R. Cheney, 'A recent view of the general interdict in England, 1208–14', *Stud. in Church Hist.* iii (1966), 140–68.

1219 RICHARDSON (HENRY G.) and SAYLES (GEORGE O.). Law and legislation from Aethelberht to Magna Carta. Edin. 1966.

> A series of studies complementary to *The governance* (No. 1218). For critical reviews, see Lady Stenton in *Columbia Law Rev.* lxvii (1967), 1341–4; G. D. G. Hall in *E.H.R.* lxxxiii (1968), 783–4; J. C. Holt in *History*, lv (1970), 232–3; and Gaines Post, *Amer. Jour. Legal Hist.* xii. (1968), 176–80.

1220 SAYLES (GEORGE O.). The medieval foundations of England. Lond. 1948. Revised edn. 1950 and 1966 (paperback).

> From the Anglo-Saxon conquest to *c.* 1300, it seeks to evaluate modern researches on institutional developments.

1221 STUBBS (WILLIAM). The constitutional history of England [to 1485]. 3 vols. Oxf. 1874–8. 5th edn. of vol. i. 1891. Reprinted, 1926. 4th edn. of vol. ii. 1896. Reprinted, 1929. 5th edn. of vol. iii. 1898. Reprinted, 1929. Library edition. 3 vols. 1880. French edition with studies and notes, by Charles Petit-Dutaillis: Histoire constitutionnelle de l'Angleterre. Vols. i–ii. Paris. 1907–13. Studies and notes supplementary to Stubbs' Constitutional history by C. Petit-Dutaillis and Georges Lefebvre, translated by W. E. Rhodes, W. T. Waugh, M. I. E. Robertson, and R. F. Treharne. 3 vols. Manchester. 1908–29. 2nd edn. of vol. i. 1911. *

> The fundamental treatise is based largely on wide reading of the printed sources and the chroniclers, several of whose works Stubbs edited. The twentieth-century detailed investigations of public documents have necessitated changes in viewpoint and in detail. For summary statements of such changes, consult F. M. Stenton, 'Early English history, 1895–1920', *T.R.H.S.* 4th Ser. xxviii (1946), 7–19; H. G. Richardson, 'The Commons and medieval politics', ibid. 21–45; Gaillard Lapsley, 'Some recent advance in English constitutional history (before 1485)', *Cambr. Hist. Jour.* v (1936), 119–61, reprinted in G. T. Lapsley, *Crown, community and parliament* (No. 1478), pp. 1–33; H. M. Cam, 'Stubbs seventy years after', ibid. ix (1948), 129–47; John Goronwy Edwards, *William Stubbs*, Historical Assoc. pamphlet G 22 (Lond. 1952), reprinted in No. 1461; G. Templeman, 'The history of parliament to 1400 in the light of modern research', *Univ. of Birmingham Hist. Jour.* i (1948), 202–31, reprinted in Robert L. Schuyler and Herman Ausubel, *The making of English history* (N.Y. 1952), pp. 109–27. For a disparagement of Stubbs, see Richardson and Sayles, *Governance* (No. 1218), Chap. 1.

1222 TASWELL-LANGMEAD (THOMAS P.). English constitutional history; a text-book for students and others. Lond. 1875. 10th edn. rev. and enl. by T. F. T. Plucknett: English constitutional history, from the Teutonic conquest to the present time. Lond. and Boston. 1946. 11th edn. Lond. 1960.

Plucknett's edition should be used.

1223 TOUT (THOMAS F.). Chapters in the administrative history of medieval England: the wardrobe, the chamber and the small seals. 6 vols. Manchester. 1920–33.

The foundation-stone for the study of medieval administrative history, 1200–1400. Covers in detail the thirteenth and fourteenth centuries. Vol. v includes a chapter on the Queen's Household by Hilda Johnstone and a chapter on the Central Administrative System of Edward, the Black Prince, by Margaret Sharp. Vol. vi comprises appendices, lists of officials, and a full index.

C. LEGAL HISTORY

The authoritative account of legal history to the reign of Edward I is that of Pollock and Maitland (No. 1242). Holdsworth (No. 1235) covers afresh the same period and continues to be valuable for subsequent centuries. Plucknett's *Concise History* (No. 1241) is a scholarly single volume. Blackstone's classic is largely outdated; and Coke (No. 1233) is useful particularly for his references to the year-books. For more specialized studies, see pp. 548–55.

1224 BEALE (JOSEPH H.). A bibliography of early English law books. The Ames Foundation. Cambr. (Mass.). 1926.

Standard for its subject. See also Robert B. Anderson, *A Supplement to Beale's Bibliography* (Cambr. (Mass.), 1943).

1225 A CATALOGUE OF THE LAW COLLECTION AT NEW YORK UNIVERSITY with selected annotations compiled and edited by Julius J. Marke. N.Y. 1953.

A volume of 1,372 pages with a rather full annotation for each entry.

1226 HOLDSWORTH (WILLIAM S.). Sources and literature of English law. Oxf. 1925.

1227 INDEX TO LEGAL PERIODICALS. N.Y. 1909+.

Useful for references not listed elsewhere.

1228 MAXWELL (LESLIE F.). A bibliography of English law. 3 vols. [Vol. i to 1650.] Lond. 1925–33.

The 2nd edn. entitled *English law to 1800, including Wales, the Channel Islands and the Isle of Man*, compiled by W. Harold Maxwell and Leslie F. Maxwell (Lond. 1955), constitutes vol. i of Sweet and Maxwell's *Legal bibliography of the British commonwealth of nations*.

1229 WINFIELD (PERCY H.). The chief sources of English legal history. Cambr. (Mass.). 1925. *

1230 BRUNNER (HEINRICH). Forschungen zur Geschichte des deutschen und französischen Rechtes. Stuttgart. 1894.

> This work throws light on the history of some parts of the English law; for example, Ch. vii deals with the history of attorneys in England; Ch. viii with outlawry; and Ch. x with unintentional misdoing.

1231 BUCKLAND (WILLIAM W.) and McNAIR (ARNOLD D.). Roman law and common law: a comparison in outline. Cambr. 1936.

1232 COHEN (HERMANN J.). A history of the English bar and attornatus to 1450. Lond. etc. 1929.

1233 COKE (EDWARD). Institutes of the laws of England. 4 pts. Lond. 1628–44. Various later editions.

> Pt. i. Commentary on Littleton; Pt. ii. Exposition of statutes; Pt. iii. Pleas of the crown; Pt. iv. Jurisdiction of courts.
>
> The many references to the year-books contained in this 'learned collection of disjointed notes' are helpful, but they are often incorrect. See William Prynne, *Brief animadversions on the fourth part of the Institutes of the laws of England* (Lond. 1669), which contains many extracts from letters patent and close.

1234 FOX (JOHN C.). The history of contempt of court, the form of trial, and the mode of punishment. Oxf. 1927.

1235 HOLDSWORTH (WILLIAM S.). A history of English law. 12 vols. Lond. 1922–38. Vols. i–iii. 3rd edn. rewritten. Tables and index (vols. i–ix) by Edward Patton. Lond. 1932. Vol. i, The judicial system, 7th edn. revised under the general editorship of A. L. Goodhart and H. G. Hanbury, with an introductory essay and additions by S. B. Chrimes. Lond. 1956.

> See also Holdsworth, *An historical introduction to the land law*. Oxf. 1927.

1236 HOLMES (OLIVER W.). The common law. Boston. 1881. Lond. 1882.

> A valuable account of some of the great formative ideas of English law.

1237 JENKS (EDWARD). Law and politics in the Middle Ages. Lond. 1898. 2nd edn. 1913. * Idem, History of the doctrine of consideration. Lond. 1892. [Early history, 161–202] Idem, Short history of English law. Lond. 1912. 3rd edn. 1924.

> *Law and politics* contains a popular and useful account of the origin of various institutions and legal ideas: the state, the village, hundred, shire, courts of justice, property, and contract.

1238 LÉVY-ULLMAN (HENRI). Éléments d'introduction générale à l'étude des sciences juridiques. ii. Le système juridique de l'Angleterre. T. i. Le système traditionnel. Paris. 1928. Trans. by M. Mitchell as The English legal tradition: its sources and history. Ed. by F. M. Goadby. Lond. 1935.

1239 MAINE (HENRY J. S.). Ancient law: its connection with the early history of society and its relation to modern ideas. Lond. 1861. New edn. by Frederick Pollock [1930]. *

> This work, several times reprinted, contains a valuable comparison of English and Roman law, etc. In this work, as also in his *Early history of institutions* (Lond. 1875) and

in his *Early law and custom* (Lond. 1883), Maine connects certain modern institutions with the usages of primitive mankind. His works are valuable for the study of the comparative history of institutions, though some of his theories are untenable.

1240 MAITLAND (FREDERIC W.). Collected papers. Ed. by H. A. L. Fisher. 3 vols. Cambr. 1911. (For details, see No. 1482.)

1241 PLUCKNETT (THEODORE F. T.). A concise history of the common law. Rochester. 1929. 5th edn. revised. Lond. 1956.

The best single volume on the subject.

1242 POLLOCK (FREDERICK) and MAITLAND (FREDERIC W.). The history of English law before the time of Edward I. 2 vols. Cambr. 1895. 2nd edn. 1898. Reprinted several times; and re-issued with a new introduction (pp. xxiii–lxxiii) and select bibliography (pp. lxxv–xci) by S. C. F. Milsom. Cambr. 1968. (pb.)

This classic of the highest order is particularly valuable for the study of English institutions from 1066 to 1272. It is supplemented by Maitland's *Domesday Book* (No. 2636), which deals mainly with Anglo-Saxon times. Maitland's 'Prologue to a history of English law', in *Law Quart. Rev.* xiv (1898), 13–33, is incorporated in the 2nd edition of the *History of English law*, as is Pollock's 'English law before the Norman conquest', ibid. pp. 291–306. See also Maitland's paper in *Encyclopaedia Britannica*, 11th edn. (1910), ix. 600–7; and Pollock, *The land laws* (Lond. 1883; 3rd edn. 1896).

1243 REEVES (JOHN). A history of the English law [to 1509]. 2 vols. Lond. 1783–4. 2nd edn. [to 1558] 4 vols. 1787. * 3rd edn. 1814. Vol. v. Reign of Elizabeth. 1829. New edition [of the whole work], by W. F. Finlason. 3 vols. 1869.

For the period from Edward I to Elizabeth this still remains a useful general history of English law. Finlason's attempt to modernize the treatise was a failure, and his edition cannot be recommended.

1244 SALMOND (JOHN W.). Essays in jurisprudence and legal history. Lond. 1891. Several editions.

Ch. i. History of the law of evidence; Ch. ii. History of law of prescription; Ch. iii. Principles of civil liability; Ch. iv. History of the law of contract. A scholarly work.

1245 SCRUTTON (THOMAS E.). The influence of the Roman law on the law of England. Cambr. 1885.

For recent discussions of this influence, see T. F. T. Plucknett, 'Relations between Roman law and English common law down to the sixteenth century: a general survey', *Univ. Toronto Law Jour.* iii (1939), 24–50; W. Senior, 'Roman law in England before Vacarius', *Law Quart. Rev.* xlvi (1930), 191–206. Van Caenegem, *Royal Writs* (No. 3503), pp. 360–90; Richardson and Sayles, *Law and legislation* (No. 1219), Chap. iv; and the references given below to Bracton (No. 2985), Glanville (No. 2989), and Vacarius (No. 3004).

1246 SELECT ESSAYS IN ANGLO-AMERICAN LEGAL HISTORY. By various authors. Edited by a committee of the Association of American Law Schools. 3 vols. Boston. 1907–9.

History of canon law, by W. Stubbs. i. 248–88.
Five ages of bench and bar, by J. M. Zane. i. 625–729.
Sources of English law, by H. Brunner. ii. 7–52.
Materials for the history of English law, by F. W. Maitland. ii. 53–95.

The year books, by W. S. Holdsworth. ii. 95–122.
History of admiralty jurisdiction, by T. L. Mears. ii. 312–64.
The king's peace, by F. Pollock. ii. 403–17.
Register of original writs, by F. W. Maitland. ii. 549–96.
Early English equity, by O. W. Holmes. ii. 705–21.
Common law in court of chancery, by L. O. Pike. ii. 722–36.
Merchants of the staple, by S. Brodhurst. iii. 16–33.
Early history of negotiable instruments, by Edward Jenks. iii. 51–71.
Early forms of corporateness, by C. T. Carr. iii. 161–82.
Early forms of partnership, by W. Mitchell. iii. 183–94.
History of assumpsit, by J. B. Ames. iii. 259–303.
History of parol contracts prior to assumpsit, by J. B. Ames. iii. 304–19.
History of contract, by J. W. Salmond. iii. 320–38.
History of the beneficiary's action in assumpsit, by C. D. Hening. iii. 339–67.
History of agency, by O. W. Holmes. iii. 368–414.
History of trover, by J. B. Ames. iii. 417–45.
History of the law of defamation, by V. V. Veeder. iii. 446–73.
Responsibility for tortious acts, by J. H. Wigmore. iii. 474–537.
The disseisin of chattels, by J. B. Ames. iii. 541–90.
The mystery of seisin, by F. W. Maitland. iii. 591–610.
The gage of land in medieval England, by H. D. Hazeltine. iii. 646–72.
The medieval law of intestacy, by C. Gross. iii. 723–36.
Executors in early English law, by O. W. Holmes. iii. 737–45.
The executor in England and on the continent, by Robert Caillemer. iii. 746–69.
Rise of the English will, by M. M. Bigelow. iii. 770–81.

1247 VINOGRADOFF (PAUL). Roman law in medieval Europe. Lond. 1909. 2nd edn. Ed. by F. de Zulueta. Oxf. 1929. *

Ch. iv on England.

1248 BRUNNER (HEINRICH). Die Entstehung der Schwurgerichte. Berlin. 1871. 1872. *

In this treatise Brunner sought to demonstrate the Frankish royal, despotic origin of the jury, which was imported into England by the Normans. Brunner's thesis was until recently generally accepted (see, for example, Haskins, *Norman Institutions*, pp. 196–238); but it does not survive current criticism, which tends to look to an English, pre-conquest derivation. Van Caenegem seeks to distinguish between an administrative jury of foreign origin and a judicial jury of Anglo-Saxon origin. This distinction is rejected by Lady Stenton. Van Caenegem, *Royal Writs* (No. 3503), pp. 57–103; D. M. Stenton, *English Justice* (No. 3681), pp. 13–21; Richardson and Sayles, *Law and legislation* (No. 1219), pp. 117–19. For survey see Ralph V. Turner, 'The origins of the medieval English jury: Frankish, English, or Scandinavian', *Jour. British Stud.* vii (1967–8), 1–10.

1249 DUGDALE (WILLIAM). Origines juridiciales, or historical memorials of the English laws, courts of justice, forms of trial, inns of court, etc. Lond. 1666. 3rd edn. 1680.

1250 GOMME (GEORGE L.). Primitive folk-moots, or open-air assemblies in England. Lond. 1880. *

1251 HAZELTINE (HAROLD D.). Die Geschichte des englischen Pfand-rechts. Breslau. 1907.

Deals with the history of distress, mortgages, etc.

1252 KOVALEVSKY (MAXIME M.). Istoriya politseiskoi administratsii, etc. [History of police administration in England to the death of Edward III.] 2 pts. Prague. 1876-7.

Treats of the origin of the frankpledge system, trial by jury, justices of the peace, etc. The appendix contains valuable extracts from patent and manorial court rolls; also an inquiry into the economic results of the Black Death.

1253 LEA (HENRY C.). Superstition and force: essays on the wager of law, the wager of battle, the ordeal, torture. Philadelphia. 1866. 2nd edn. 1870. 4th edn. 1892. *

The best general treatises on the ordeal are Federico Patetta, *Le ordalie* (Turin, 1890), and Hermann Nottarp, 'Gottesurteilsstudien', *Bamberger Abhandlungen und Forschungen* (Munich), ii (1956). George Neilson, *Trial by combat* (Lond. etc. 1890), is also a scholarly work. For general canonical background, see John W. Baldwin, 'The intellectual preparation for the canon of 1215 against ordeals', *Speculum*, xxxvi (1961), 613-36.

1254 MORRIS (WILLIAM A.). The frankpledge system. N.Y. etc. 1910.

The standard monograph on the subject.

1255 PIKE (LUKE OWEN). A history of crime in England . . . 2 vols. Lond. 1873-6. *

1256 PUGH (RALPH B.). Imprisonment in medieval England. Cambr. 1968.

See R. B. Pugh, 'The king's prisons before 1250'. *T.R.H.S.* 5th Ser. v (1955), 1-22.

1257 STEPHEN (JAMES FITZJAMES). A history of the criminal law of England. 3 vols. Lond. 1883. *

An enlarged edition of his *General view of the criminal law* (Lond. 1863. 2nd edn. 1890).

1258 THAYER (JAMES B.). A preliminary treatise on evidence at the common law. Pt. i: Development of trial by jury. Boston. 1896. Reprinted, with pt. ii. A preliminary treatise on evidence. Boston. 1898. *

A standard work on the jury; throws light on the history of this institution, especially since the thirteenth century. For an older work, see William Forsyth, *History of trial by jury* (Lond. 1853; new edn. by J. A. Morgan. N.Y. 1875).

Note that there were two types of sanctuary, ecclesiastical and secular.

1259 COX (JOHN C.). The sanctuaries and sanctuary seekers of medieval England. Lond. 1911.

See his supplementary paper in *Archaeol. Jour.* lxviii (1911), 273-99.

1260 PEGGE (SAMUEL). 'A sketch of the history of the asylum or sanctuary, from its origin to the final abolition of it in the reign of James I.' *Archaeologia*, viii (1787), 1-44.

1261 RÉVILLE (ANDRÉ). 'L'abjuratio regni: histoire d'une institution anglaise.' *Revue Historique*, i (1892), 1-42.

A valuable account of the history of sanctuary.

1262   TRENHOLME (NORMAN M.). The right of sanctuary in England: a study in institutional history. Columbia (Mo.). 1903.

See under 'Asile' in *Dict. d'Hist. et de Géog. Ecclés.* (No. 1266), vol. iv; and *Dict. de droit canonique* (p. 168), vol. i, pp. 1084–1104. Isobel D. Thornley, 'The sanctuary register of Beverley', *E.H.R.* xxxiv (1919), 393–7.

D. HISTORIES OF THE CHURCH

1. *General Bibliography*

The comprehensive works which are cited below cover the history of the Church throughout the Middle Ages. The modern studies on the Church in the British Isles for more limited periods are listed elsewhere; for the Celtic Church, pp. 379–82; for the Anglo-Saxon Church, pp. 382–5; for the Church in England, 1066–1485, pp. 750–880.

Many of the comprehensive works, and particularly the French dictionaries, include excellent references. For current bibliography, *Revue d'histoire ecclésiastique* (No. 166) is essential; and the *International Bibliography of historical sciences* (No. 53) and the *Journal of Ecclesiastical History* (No. 130) are conveniently useful.

1263   A CATHOLIC DICTIONARY OF THEOLOGY. A work projected with the approval of the Catholic hierarchy in England. Lond. Edin. etc. 1962 (in progress).

1264   CROSS (FRANK L.), ed. The Oxford dictionary of the Christian Church. Lond. etc. 1957. Revised edn. 1958.

This useful, single volume is a co-operative work of short articles with selective bibliographies.

1265   DICTIONNAIRE D'ARCHÉOLOGIE CHRÉTIENNE ET DE LITURGIE. Ed. by Fernand Cabrol and Henri Leclercq. 176 fascicules in 15 vols. Paris. 1903–53.

This is the fundamental encyclopedia for liturgy and cognate subjects.

1266   DICTIONNAIRE D'HISTOIRE ET DE GÉOGRAPHIE ECCLÉ-SIASTIQUES. Ed. by Alfred Baudrillart *et al.* Paris. 1912 (in progress).

The biographical articles are often the best available, with good bibliographies.

1267   DICTIONNAIRE DE THÉOLOGIE CATHOLIQUE . . . Ed. by A. Vacant, E. Mangenot, and É. Amann. 15 vols. Paris. 1903–47. Table analytique, tomes i–ix, A–L. 1929. Tables générales, by Bernard Loth and Albert Michel. Paris. 1951 (in progress).

The dictionary contains the best available Roman Catholic exposition of doctrine and practice, with full bibliographies up to the date of printing.

1268   DICTIONARY OF CHRISTIAN BIOGRAPHY, LITERATURE, SECTS AND DOCTRINES to about A.D. 800. Ed. by William Smith and Henry Wace. 4 vols. Lond. 1877–87. Abridged edn. in 1 vol. Ed. by Henry Wace and W. C. Piercy. Lond. 1911.

1269 ENCICLOPEDIA CATTOLICA. 12 vols. Città del Vaticano. 1948–54.

1270 LEXIKON FÜR THEOLOGIE UND KIRCHE. Ed. by M. Buchberger. 10 vols. Freiburg. 1930–8. 2nd edn. Ed. by J. Höfer and K. Rahner. 10 vols. Freiburg. 1957–65.

1271 NEW CATHOLIC ENCYCLOPEDIA. 15 vols. Washington, D.C. 1966–7.

A generally scholarly, although uneven work of articles, each with a selective bibliography. Prepared by an editorial staff at the Catholic University of America.

1272 OLLARD (SIDNEY L.) and CROSSE (GORDON), eds. A dictionary of English church history. Lond. etc. 1912. Third edn. by Ollard, Crosse, and M. F. Bond. Oxf. 1948.

1273 PURVIS (JOHN S.). Dictionary of ecclesiastical terms. Edin. etc. 1962.

See also Frederick G. Lee, *A glossary of liturgical and ecclesiastical terms* (Lond. 1877).

2. Modern Treatises

1274 CORISH (PATRICK J.), ed. A history of Irish catholicism. Dublin and Sidney. 1967 (in progress).

Vol. i:
  fasc. i. Ludwig Bieler, *St. Patrick and the coming of Christianity.* 1967.
Vol. ii:
  fasc. i. Aubrey Gwynn, *The twelfth-century reform.* 1968.
  fasc. iii. Geoffrey Hand, *The church in the English lordship.* 1968.
  fasc. iv. Aubrey Gwynn, *Anglo-Irish church life in the fourteenth and fifteenth century.* 1968.
  fasc. v. Canice Mooney, *The church in Gaelic Ireland.* 1969.

1275 DEANESLY (MARGARET). A history of the medieval church. Lond. 1925. 8th edn. 1965.

1276 AN ECCLESIASTICAL HISTORY OF ENGLAND. General editor, J. C. Dickinson. 5 vols. Lond. and N.Y. 1961 (in progress).

The first volumes of this series to be published were M. Deanesly, *The pre-conquest church* (1961) and Owen Chadwick, *The Victorian church*, 2 pts. (1966–70).

1277 FLICHE (AUGUSTIN) and MARTIN (VICTOR) [later J. B. Duroselle and E. Jarry], eds. Histoire de l'église depuis les origines jusqu'à nos jours. Paris. 1934 (in progress).

This notable history of the church is planned for 24 volumes, of which 15 will relate to the Middle Ages.

1278 FULLER (THOMAS). The church history of Britain (to 1648). 6 pts. Lond. 1655. New edn. by J. S. Brewer. 6 vols. Oxf. 1845. *

1279 HEFELE (CARL JOSEPH VON). Conciliengeschichte. 7 vols. Freiburg. 1855–74. 2nd edn. 6 vols. 1873–90; continued by Joseph Hergenröther as vols. viii–ix. 1887–90. Translated by Henri Leclercq. *Histoire des conciles d'après les documents originaux.* 20 vols. Paris. 1907–38.

Leclercq's edition is recommended.

1280 KNOWLES (DAVID) with OBOLENSKY (DIMITRI). The middle ages. Lond. 1968. Being volume ii of The Christian centuries : a new history of the Catholic Church.

> A short history, political, institutional, and doctrinal of Roman and Orthodox Christendom from 604 to 1500. Cf. Philip Hughes, *A history of the church: an introductory study.* 3 vols. Lond. and N.Y. 1934–47. Revised edn. of vols. i and ii. 1949. Hughes's history is also an excellent modern summary with good bibliographical notes.

1281 LAWRENCE (CLIFFORD H.), ed. The English church and the papacy in the Middle Ages. Lond. 1965.

> This survey of the relations of the Church in England with the papacy comprises a series of chronological essays by expert scholars. They form the best summary of up-to-date researches on the subject.

1282 LEA (HENRY C.). An historical sketch of sacerdotal celibacy in the Christian church. Philadelphia. 1867. 3rd edn. as *History of sacerdotal celibacy* etc. 2 vols. Lond. 1907. *

> A controversial work whose views can be moderated by reference to the articles on the subject in *D.A.C.L.* (No. 1265) and *D.D.C.* (p. 168).

1283 LEA (HENRY C.). A history of auricular confession and indulgences in the Latin church. 3 vols. Philadelphia. 1896. *

> Despite his erudition, Lea's studies tended towards polemics and are now out-dated. See Paulus (No. 1286) and Poschmann (No. 1287).

1284 MAKOWER (FELIX). Die Verfassung der Kirche von England. Berlin. 1894. Translated as *The constitutional history and the constitution of the church of England.* Lond. etc. 1895. *

> This standard work has not yet been superseded.

1285 MOORMAN (JOHN R. H.). History of the church in England. Lond. 1953. N.Y. 1963.

1286 PAULUS (NIKOLAUS). Geschichte des Ablasses im Mittelalter vom Ursprunge bis zur Mitte des 14. Jahrhunderts. 2 vols. Paderborn. 1922–3.

1287 POSCHMANN (BERNHARD). Der Ablass im Licht der Bussgeschichte. Bonn. 1948.

1288 SCHNÜRER (GUSTAV). Kirche und Kultur im Mittelalter. 3 vols. Paderborn. 1924–9. 3rd edn. 1936. French translation: *L'église et la civilisation au moyen âge.* 3 vols. Paris. 1933–8. Volume i is translated by George J. Undreiner, *Church and culture in the Middle Ages.* Paterson (N.J.). 1956.

1289 STEPHENS (WILLIAM R. W.) and HUNT (WILLIAM), eds. A history of the English church. 8 vols. in 9. Lond. 1899–1910. Reissued, 1910–24. *

> i. (To the Norman conquest) by W. Hunt.
> ii. (From 1066 to the close of the thirteenth century) by W. R. W. Stephens.
> iii. (Fourteenth and fifteenth centuries) by W. W. Capes.

3. *Studies on Monasticism*

Good histories of monasticism in general are Ursmer Berlière, *L'ordre monastique des origines au xiie siècle* (Paris, 1912; 3rd edn. 1924), and Edward Cuthbert Butler, *Benedictine monachism: studies in Benedictine life and rule* (Lond. 1919; 2nd edn. 1924; reprinted, Cambr. and N.Y. 1961). On English monasticism, the volumes by Knowles supersede all previous treatises. The studies concerning the new orders to the twelfth and later centuries are to be found below in volume ii, pp. 792–810.

1290 COTTINEAU (LAWRENCE H.). Répertoire topo-bibliographique des abbayes et prieurés. 2 vols. Mâcon. 1935–8. Vol. iii. Paris. 1970.

A repertory of several thousands of monasteries of all countries, alphabetically arranged, with brief bibliography to each entry. Vol. iii is a catalogue of authors. None of these volumes is particularly useful for England.

1291 COULTON (GEORGE G.). Five centuries of religion (1000–1500). 4 vols. Cambr. 1923–50.

1292 DICKINSON (JOHN C.). Monastic life in medieval England. Lond. 1961.

1293 GASQUET (FRANCIS A.). English monastic life. Lond. etc. 1904. 4th edn. 1910. *

1294 GASQUET (FRANCIS A.). Monastic life in the middle ages, with a note on Great Britain and the Holy See, 1792–1806. Lond. 1922.

1295 GWYNN (AUBREY) and HADCOCK (R. NEVILLE). Medieval religious houses: Ireland. With an appendix to early sites. Lond. 1970.

A catalogue from the fifth to the early seventeenth century.

1296 HEIMBUCHER (MAXIMILIAN J.). Die Orden und Kongregationen der katholischen Kirche. 2 vols. 3rd edn. Paderborn. 1933–4.

1297 KAPSNER (OLIVER L.), ed. A Benedictine bibliography: an author-subject union list compiled for . . . American Benedictine Academy. Collegeville (Minn.). 1962. 2nd edn. vol. i: authors. 1962; vol. ii: subject headings and classification schedule. 1962, enlarged 1964.

1298 KNOWLES (DAVID). The monastic order in England: a history of its development from the times of St. Dunstan to the Fourth Lateran Council, 943–1216. Cambr. 1940. New edn. largely reprint, 1963.

1299 KNOWLES (DAVID). The religious houses of medieval England. Lond. 1940; a revised and enlarged edn. by David Knowles and R. Neville Hadcock, *Medieval religious houses: England and Wales.* Lond. and N.Y. 1953. Rev. edn. 1971.

Cf. M. D. Knowles and R. N. Hadcock, 'Additions and corrections to Medieval religious houses: England and Wales', *E.H.R.* lxxii (1957), 60–87. For medieval Scottish houses, see the publication of David Easson, *Medieval religious houses: Scotland* (Lond. 1957).

1300 KNOWLES (DAVID). The religious orders in England. 3 vols. Cambr. 1948–59.

> Vol. i. The old orders, 1216–1340; the friars, 1216–1340; the monasteries and their world.
> Vol. ii. The end of the middle ages.
> Vol. iii. The Tudor age.
> See also Knowles, 'Some developments in English monastic life, 1216–1336', *T.R.H.S.* 4th Ser. xxvi (1944), 37–52; idem, 'English monastic life in the later middle ages', *History*, N.S. xxxix (1954), 26–38; and *Historian and Character* (No. 1477).

1301 POWER (EILEEN E.). Medieval English nunneries: *c.* 1275 to 1535. Cambridge Studies in Medieval Life and Thought. Cambr. 1922. *

1302 REYNER (CLEMENT). Apostolatus Benedictinorum in Anglia sive disceptatio historica de antiquitate ordinis monachorum nigrorum S. Benedicti in regno Angliae. Douai. 1626. Appendix. 1626.

> The appendix of this classic contains many statutes, etc., including the *Regularis Concordia*, Lanfranc's statutes, and others, which are now often available in modern editions (Nos. 2274, 5909).

1302A RYAN (JOHN). Irish monasticism. Dublin. 1931. (No. 2676).

1303 THOMPSON (ALEXANDER HAMILTON). English monasteries. Cambr. 1913. 2nd edn. 1923.

> Other interesting works are: Rotha M. Clay, *The hermits and anchorites of England* (Lond. 1914); David H. S. Cranage, *The home of the monk: an account of English monastic life and buildings in the middle ages* (Cambr. 1926; 3rd edn. 1934); Frederick H. Crossley, *The English abbey, its life and work in the middle ages* (Lond. etc. 1936).

4. *Studies on Canon Law*

For medieval commentators and subjects of the canon law, detailed articles and bibliographies can be found in *Dictionnaire de droit canonique* (*D.D.C.*), edited by A. Amanieu, A. Villien, E. Magnin, and R. Naz, 7 vols. (Paris, 1924–65); for briefer accounts, consult the *New Catholic Encyclopedia* (No. 1271). The principal journals are *Revue de droit canonique* (Strasbourg, 1951+); *Zeitschrift der Savigny-Stiftung für Rechtsgeschichte: Kanonistische Abteilung* (Weimar, 1911+); *Studia Gratiana* (Bologna, 1953+); and *Traditio* (No. 169).

The Institute of Research and Study of Medieval Canon Law, under the leadership of Professor Stephan Kuttner, formerly at Catholic University and at Yale University and currently (1971) at Berkeley, promotes and brings together international research on the canon law. The Institute's journal, *Traditio* (No. 169), carries scholarly articles, reports on current activities, and from 1956 to 1970, an expansive, annotated, normally annual, bibliography on the medieval canon law and ancillary subjects. For the new *Bulletin* see No. 6426. The Institute has projects for the publication of *Monumenta Iuris Canonici* in three series: series A, *Corpus Collectionum*; series B, *Corpus Glossatorum*; series C, *Subsidia*. The Institute has held three international congresses; the first at Louvain in 1958, whose proceedings appear as *Congrès de droit canonique médiéval, Louvain et*

Bruxelles, 22–26 juillet 1958 in *Bibliothèque de la R.H.E.* (Louvain, 1959); the
second congress was held at Boston in 1963, its proceedings form the first volume
of *Subsidia* (No. 1313); and the third congress was held at Strasbourg in 1968. Its
proceedings are printed in series C: *Subsidia*, vol. iv (Vatican City, 1971).

Immediately below are listed indispensable or standard works on the canon
law. The influence of Englishmen on the canon law, the influence of the
canon law in England, specific incidents, and particular cases are allocated to
pp. 846–53 below in volume ii. Summary accounts may be found in Cheney,
From Becket to Langton (No. 6789), Chap. iii; and in Lawrence, *English Church*
(No. 1281).

1304 FEINE (HANS E.). Kirchliche Rechtsgeschichte auf der Grundlage
des Kirchenrechts von Ulrich Stutz. Vol. i. Die katholische Kirche. Weimar.
1950. 4th edn. Cologne and Graz. 1964.

1305 FOURNIER (PAUL) and LE BRAS (GABRIEL). Histoire des collections canoniques en occident depuis les fausses décrétales jusqu'au Décret
de Gratien. 2 vols. Paris. 1931–2.

An outstanding study in which the British material is necessarily scanty.

1306 FRIEDBERG (EMIL). Corpus juris canonici. 2 vols. Leipzig. 1879–81.
Reprinted, 1922–8.

The standard collection which has some shortcomings; see e.g. *Traditio,* xxii (1966),
460; and S. Kuttner in *Apollinaris* (Rome), xxi (1948), 118–28.

1307 HINSCHIUS (PAUL). System des katholischen Kirchenrechts: Das
Kirchenrecht der Katholiken und Protestanten in Deutschland. 6 vols. in 7.
Berlin. 1869–97. Reprinted, 1959.

1308 HOVE (ALPHONSE VAN). Prolegomena (ad codicem juris canonici).
Commentarium Lovaniense in codicem iuris canonici, I. i. Malines. 1928.

2nd edn. Malines and Rome, 1945.

1309 KUTTNER (STEPHAN). Repertorium der Kanonistik, 1140–1234.
Vatican City. 1937. (A new edition is in prospect.)

A scholarly study of the manuscripts of the glosses. Kuttner's masterly Wimmer lecture
of 64 pages is printed as *Harmony from dissonance: an interpretation of medieval canon law*
(Latrobe (Pa.), 1961).

1310 LE BRAS (GABRIEL). Histoire du droit et des institutions de l'église
en occident. Vol. i. Prolégomènes. Paris. 1955.

See Le Bras's summary in *Legacy* (No. 1479).

1311 LE BRAS (GABRIEL), LEFEBVRE (CHARLES), and RAMBAUD
(JACQUELINE). Histoire du droit et des institutions de l'église en occident.
Vol. vii. L'âge classique, 1140–1378: sources et théorie du droit. Paris. 1965.

1312 PLÖCHL (WILLIBALD M.). Geschichte des Kirchenrechts. 3 vols.
Vienna and Munich. 1953–9. 2nd edn. 1960.

1313 PROCEEDINGS OF THE SECOND INTERNATIONAL CONGRESS OF MEDIEVAL CANON LAW. Boston College. 12–16 August 1963. Ed. by Stephan Kuttner and J. Joseph Ryan. *Monumenta Iuris Canonici.* Ser. C: *Subsidia*, vol. i. Vatican City. 1965. Cited as *Boston proceedings.*

The papers dealing directly with England are entered below: Boyle (No. 6436), Cheney (No. 6811), Duggan (No. 6430), Sheehan (No. 6444) and Herde (6452). For third Congress (1968), see Nos. 2261, 2985h, 6457.

1314 STICKLER (ALPHONSUS M.). Historia iuris canonici latini: institutiones academicae. I. Historia fontium. Turin. 1950.

5. *Service Books, Liturgy, Ritual, etc.*

For service books, liturgy, and ritual, consult the dictionaries listed on pp. 164–5, particularly *D.A.C.L.* (No. 1265); and the printed *B.M. Catalogue* (No. 78), vols. cxxxviii–cxxxix under 'Liturgies—Latin Rite', columns 104–608. 'A chronological table shewing the rise and decline of Sarum, Lincoln and other English uses' (A.D. 383–1633), printed in Henry Bradshaw and Christopher Wordsworth, *Lincoln Cathedral statutes* (Cambr. 1897), iii. 824–59, serves as selective bibliographical guide. Valuable liturgical texts have been published by the Henry Bradshaw Society and by the Surtees Society; their titles are listed in Mullins, *Texts* (No. 29), and in *Repert. Font.* (No. 64) and are rarely reprinted below. Some works on ritual are conveniently listed in Harrison's *Music in Medieval Britain* (No. 1336). For lists of Anglo-Saxon pontificals, see *The Pontifical of Egbert* (No. 1316), pp. vii–xi. For Coronation Service, see pp. 173–4. Modern editions of Service Books are mentioned in Knowles, *Lanfranc's Constitutions* (No. 5909), p. xxxii.

1315 ENGLISH FRAGMENTS FROM LATIN MEDIEVAL SERVICE-BOOKS. Ed. by Henry Littlehales, E.E.T.S. Extra Ser. No. xc (1903).

1316 THE PONTIFICAL OF EGBERT, archbishop of York, A.D. 732–766. Ed. by William Greenwell. Surtees Soc. xxvii (1853).

1317 LIBER PONTIFICALIS OF EDMUND LACY, bishop of Exeter, a MS. of the fourteenth century. Ed. by Ralph Barnes. Exeter. 1847.

1318 LIBER REGIE CAPELLE. Ed. by Walter Ullmann. Henry Bradshaw Soc. xcii. London. 1961.

1319 THE MONASTIC BREVIARY OF HYDE ABBEY. Ed by J. B. L. Tolhurst. Henry Bradshaw Soc. 6 vols. 1930–42.

The introduction is excellent.

1320 RITUALE ECCLESIAE DUNELMENSIS. The Durham collectar. A new and revised edition, the Latin text with the interlinear Anglo-Saxon version. Ed. by Uno Lindelöf. Surtees Soc. cxl (1927).

1321 THE SARUM MISSAL. Ed. from three early manuscripts by J. Wickham Legg. Oxf. 1916. Oxford Reprint. 1970. THE SARUM MISSAL IN

ENGLISH. Trans. by Frederick E. Warren. 2 vols. Alcuin Club, Lond. 1913. ORDINALE SARUM SEU DIRECTORIUM SACERDOTUM. Ed. by W. Cooke and C. Wordsworth. 2 vols. Henry Bradshaw Soc. 1901–2.

1322 SPECULUM SACERDOTALE. Ed. by Edward H. Weatherly. E.E.T.S. cc (1936).

1323 ANDRIEU (MICHEL). Le pontifical romain au moyen âge. 4 vols. *Studi e Testi*, lxxxvi–lxxxviii, lxci. Vatican City. 1938–41.

1324 BAUMSTARK (ANTON). Liturgie comparée: principes et méthodes pour l'étude historique des liturgies chrétiennes. 3rd edn. by Bernard Botte. Chevetogne (Belgium). 1953. English trans. by Frank L. Cross. Westminster (Md.). 1953.

1325 BISHOP (EDMUND). Liturgica historica, papers on the liturgy and religious life of the western church. Ed. by R. H. Connolly and K. Sisam. Oxf. 1918.

> For Bishop, see Nigel Abercrombie, *The life and work of Edmund Bishop* (Lond. 1959). For 'Religious sentiment and church design in the later middle ages', see C. N. L. Brooke in *B.J.R.L.* i (1967/8), 13–33.

1326 BRIGHTMAN (FRANK E.). The English rite, being a synopsis of the sources and revisions of the Book of Common Prayer, with an introduction and an appendix. Lond. 1915. *

1327 CABROL (FERNAND). Les livres de la liturgie latine. Paris. 1930. Trans. by The Benedictines of Stanbrook. Lond. and St. Louis. 1932.

1327A CAMBRIDGE HISTORY OF THE BIBLE. 3 vols. Cambr. and N.Y. 1963–70.

> Vol. ii. The West from the Fathers to the Reformation. Ed. by G. W. H. Lampe.

1328 CHAMBERS (JOHN D.). Divine worship in England in the thirteenth and fourteenth centuries. Lond. 1877. New edn. revised, 1877. Supplement, 1886.

> On this subject, see also Christopher Wordsworth, *Notes on medieval services in England* (Lond. 1898); and H. B. Swete, *Church services and service-books before the reformation* (Lond. etc. 1896).

1329 DALMAIS (IRÉNÉE). Introduction to the liturgy. Trans. by Roger Capel. Baltimore and Lond. 1961.

1330 DEANESLY (MARGARET). The Lollard Bible and other medieval biblical versions. Cambr. Stud. in medieval life and thought. Cambr. 1920. New edn. 1966.

> Cf. her Ethel M. Wood Lecture, 'The significance of the Lollard Bible' (Lond. 1951). See also R. L. Atkinson, 'A French Bible in England about the year 1322', *E.H.R.* xxxviii (1923), 248–9.

1331 DIX (GREGORY). The shape of the liturgy. Westminster. 1945.

1332 FORTESCUE (ADRIAN). The Mass: a study of the Roman liturgy. Westminster. 1906. New edn. 1937; and Lond. 1950. *

1333 FRERE (WALTER H.). A collection of his papers on liturgical and historical subjects. Ed. by J. H. Arnold and E. G. P. Wyatt with an introduction by A. S. Duncan-Jones. Alcuin Club. Lond. 1940.

1334 FRERE (WALTER H.), ed. The use of Sarum. 2 vols. Cambr. 1898–1901.

1335 GLUNZ (HANS H.). History of the Vulgate in England from Alcuin to Roger Bacon: being an inquiry into the text of some English manuscripts of the Vulgate Gospels. Cambr. 1933.

1336 HARRISON (FRANK Ll.). Music in medieval Britain. Lond. 1958.

1337 HOARE (HENRY W.). The evolution of the English Bible: an historical sketch of the successive versions from 1382 to 1885. Lond. 1901. 2nd edn. 1902.

See also Francis A. Gasquet, *The old English Bible and other essays.* Lond. 1897. New edn. 1908.

1338 JUNGMANN (JOSEF A.). Missarum sollemnia. Eine genetische Erklärung der römischen Messe. 3rd edn. 2 vols. Freiburg. 1952. Trans. as *The Mass of the Roman rite, its origins and development,* by Francis A. Brunner. N.Y. 1951. Abridged edn. 1959.

1339 KING (ARCHDALE A.). The liturgy of the Roman Church. Lond. and N.Y. 1957.

1340 LEGG (J. WICKHAM). Essays liturgical and historical. Lond. 1917.

1341 MASKELL (WILLIAM). Monumenta ritualia ecclesiae Anglicanae or occasional offices of the church of England. 3 vols. Lond. 1846–7. 2nd edn. Oxf. 1882.* Idem, The ancient liturgy of the church of England, according to the uses of Sarum, Bangor, York, and Hereford, arranged in parallel columns. Lond. 1844. 3rd edn. Oxf. 1882. *

1342 PALMER (WILLIAM). Origines liturgicae or antiquities of the English ritual. 2 vols. Oxf. 1832. 4th edn. Lond. 1845. *

1343 ROCK (DANIEL). The church of our fathers, as seen in St. Osmund's rite for the cathedral of Salisbury. 3 vols. in 4 pts. Lond. 1849–53. New edn. 4 vols. 1903–4. *

Deals with services, vestments, buildings, relics, etc. Vol. iii, pt. ii of the first edition contains St. Osmund's *De Officiis Ecclesiasticis Tractatus*; an ordinal of an unknown Cistercian abbey in Yorkshire; an inventory of ornaments in the church of Salisbury, A.D. 1222; and excerpts from an ordinal of St. Paul's, London.

1344 SMALLEY (BERYL). The study of the Bible in the middle ages. Oxf. 1941. 2nd edn. 1952. pb.

1345 SRAWLEY (JAMES H.). The early history of the liturgy. Cambridge Handbooks of Liturgical Study. 2nd edn. Cambr. 1947.

1346 VAN DIJK (STEPHEN J. P.) and WALKER (JOAN HAZELDEN). The origin of the modern Roman liturgy. The liturgy of the papal court and the Franciscan Order in the thirteenth century. Westminster (Md.) and Lond. 1960.

1347 URE (JAMES M.). The Benedictine office: an Old English text. Edin.
1957.

Cf. Peter Clemoes, 'The Old English Benedictine office: Corpus Christi College, Cambridge, MS. 190 and the relations of Ælfric and Wulfstan: a reconsideration', *Anglia*,
lxxviii (1960), 265–83.

1348 WORDSWORTH   (CHRISTOPHER)   and   LITTLEHALES
(HENRY). The old service-books of the English church. Antiquary's Books.
Lond. 1904. 1910.

1349 WORMALD (FRANCIS). English kalendars before A.D. 1100. Henry
Bradshaw Soc. Pubns. lxxii (1934). Idem, English Benedictine kalendars after
A.D. 1100. 2 vols. Ibid. lxxvii (1939); lxxxi (1946).

6. *The Coronation Service*

The most important book on the history of the English coronation is by Schramm
(No. 1358). In recent years numerous articles on various aspects of the subject
have come from the pens of H. G. Richardson, G. O. Sayles, P. L. Ward, B.
Wilkinson, and R. S. Hoyt; these articles are cited in Robert S. Hoyt, 'The
coronation oath of 1308', *E.H.R.* lxxi (1956), 353–83 (cf. *Traditio*, xi (1955),
235–57); and Bertie Wilkinson, 'Notes on the coronation records of the fourteenth century', *E.H.R.* lxx (1955), 581–600.

1350 ARMSTRONG (CHARLES A. J.). 'The inauguration ceremonies of
the Yorkist kings and their title to the throne.' *T.H.R.S.* 4th Ser. v (1948),
51–73.

J. W. McKenna, 'The coronation oil of the Yorkist kings', *E.H.R.* lxxxii (1967), 102–4.

1351 BIRCH (WALTER DE GRAY). Index of the styles and titles of
sovereigns of England. Index Soc. First Report, pp. 49–72. Lond. 1879.

1352 BOUMAN (CORNELIUS A.). Sacring and crowning: the development
of the Latin ritual for the anointing of kings and the coronation of an emperor
before the eleventh century. Groningen. 1957.

1353 KANTOROWICZ (ERNST H.). Laudes Regiae. A study of liturgical
acclamations and mediaeval ruler worship . . . with a study of the music of the
laudes and musical transcriptions by Manfred F. Bukofzer. Berkeley (Calif.).
1946.

1354 LEGG (LEOPOLD G. WICKHAM). English coronation records. Lond.
1901.

Cf. John Wickham Legg, ed. *Three coronation orders*, Henry Bradshaw Soc. vol. xix
(1900).

1355 LIBER REGALIS SEU ORDO CONSECRANDI REGEM SOLUM.
Ordo consecrandi reginam cum rege. Ordo consecrandi reginam solam. Rubrica
de regis exequiis, e codice Westmonasteriensi editus. Roxburghe Club. Lond.
1870.

The date of the manuscript is about 1350–80.

1356 PASSINGHAM (W. J.). A history of the coronation. Lond. 1957.

1357 RICHARDSON (HENRY G.). 'The Coronation in medieval England', *Traditio*, xvi (1960), 111–202. Idem, 'Coronations and crown-wearings before the conquest'. Richardson and Sayles, *The Governance* (No. 1218), app. i, pp. 397–412.

1358 SCHRAMM (PERCY E.). Geschichte des englischen Königtums im Lichte der Krönung. Weimar 1937. Reprinted 1970. * Translated by Leopold G. Wickham Legg: *A history of the English coronation*. Oxf. 1937.

> The fundamental text is followed by a list of the English *Ordines* (pp. 233–8) and biblio-graphical notes (pp. 239–74). Paul L. Ward, 'An early version of the Anglo-Saxon coronation ceremony', *E.H.R.* lvii (1942), 345–61. See also P. E. Schramm, *Herrschafts-zeichen und Staatssymbolik*, 3 vols. (Stuttgart, 1954–6).

1359 TAYLOR (ARTHUR). The glory of regality: a treatise on the anointing and crowning of the kings and queens of England. Lond. 1820.

E. COMMENTARIES ON THE STRUCTURE OF SOCIETY

The study of medieval economic and social history has been considerably transformed in the twentieth century. Once treated as an appendage to political and constitutional history, it has now achieved a significant place and brought about important revisions in historiography. Its bibliography has become extensive. The articles and bibliographies in the *Cambridge Economic History* (No. 1364) form a point of departure. Presumably these will be reinforced by the studies in the planned first three volumes of the *Agrarian History* (No. 1360). The most useful specialized journals in English are *Agricultural History* (No. 143), *Agricultural History Review* (No. 106), and *Economic History Review* (No. 119). The last of these journals carries annually a list of books and articles on the economic history of Great Britain and Ireland. The *Index of economic articles* (No. 95) directs attention to some pertinent studies. The more comprehensive bibliographies, such as *Writings* (Nos. 38, 39), the Lancaster–Kellaway series (No. 24), and the *Annual Bulletins* (No. 7) record publications in economic and social history.

The seminal studies for the Anglo-Saxon and early Norman periods, such as those of Lennard, Maitland, Seebohm, and Vinogradoff, are registered on pages 376–8 below. The section (pp. 74–5) on Geography includes several works pertinent to this subject, e.g. Darby (No. 610). The commentaries on *Domesday Book* (pp. 468–70) are often helpful. For the pre-conquest period, the principal sources are Anglo-Saxon laws and charters, and for these see *English historical documents* (No. 17), vols. i and ii. The commentaries on feudalism in England have been grouped together on pages 661–6; they are obviously particularly pertinent to the structure of society. Many of the most important revisions, however, rest on the much fuller written sources of the twelfth and subsequent centuries; they are accordingly recorded in volume ii. A few continental studies of relatively similar societies are included here. The school advocating com-parative history is best represented by Marc Bloch and the journal *Annales*

(No. 146). Sylvia L. Thrupp has brought together in translation a series of articles largely by continental scholars in the spirit of comparative history in each of two volumes, entitled *Change in medieval society: Europe north of the Alps, 1050–1500* (N.Y. 1964), and *Early medieval society* (N.Y. 1967).

1. *General Treatises*

1360 THE AGRARIAN HISTORY OF ENGLAND AND WALES. H. P. R. Finberg, general editor. Vol. iv: 1500–1640. Ed. by Joan Thirsk. Cambr. 1967.

Vols. i–iii for the period before 1500 are in preparation. Vol. i, pt. 2 (A.D. 43–1042), 1972.

1361 ASHLEY (WILLIAM J.). An introduction to English economic history and theory. 2 vols. Lond. etc. 1888–93; 4th edn. of vol. i, 1909; of vol. ii, 1906. Reprinted, 1923–5. *

Vol. i deals with the manor, gilds, and economic legislation; vol. ii, with the towns, the crafts, the woollen industry, the agrarian revolution, the relief of the poor, and the canonist doctrine. See also his *Surveys, historic and economic* (Lond. etc. 1900), which deals with the history of the township, boroughs, gilds, etc.; and *The bread of our fore-fathers: an inquiry in economic history* (Oxf. 1928), in which he contends that rye rather than wheat formed the staff of life.

1362 BLAND (ALFRED E.), BROWN (PHILIP A.), and TAWNEY (RICHARD H.), eds. English economic history; selected documents. Part i: 1000–1485. Lond. 1914. 2nd edn. 1915. Reprinted, 1925, 1937. Also paperback edn.

1363 BLOCH (MARC). La société féodale: la formation des liens de dépen-dance. Paris. 1939. Idem, La société féodale: les classes et le gouvernement des hommes. Paris. 1940.

Both volumes were translated by L. A. Manyon, as *Feudal Society* (Lond. 1961, and paperback edn., Chicago, 1964). See No. 252.

1364 THE CAMBRIDGE ECONOMIC HISTORY OF EUROPE FROM THE DECLINE OF THE ROMAN EMPIRE. General editors: J. H. Clap-ham, Eileen Power, M. M. Postan, E. E. Rich.

Each volume prints summary chapters by various scholars, fortified by good biblio-graphies of printed sources and secondary authorities.

vol. i: *The agrarian life of the middle ages.* Ed. by J. H. Clapham. Cambr. 1941. Second revised edition. Ed. by M. M. Postan. Cambr. 1966. (The chapter on English agrarian society in the thirteenth century by Nellie Neilson in the first edition, pp. 448–66, has been completely replaced by a chapter by M. M. Postan in the second edition, pp. 548–632.)

vol. ii: *Trade and industry in the middle ages.* Cambr. 1952.

vol. iii: *Economic organization and policies in the middle ages.* Cambr. 1963.

vol. iv: *The economy of expanding Europe in the sixteenth and seventeenth centuries.* Cambr. 1967.

1365 CLAPHAM (JOHN H.). A concise economic history of Britain, from the earliest times to 1750. Cambr. 1949.

1366 CUNNINGHAM (WILLIAM). The growth of English industry and commerce. 2nd edn. 2 vols. (Vol. i, early and medieval; vol. ii, modern.) Cambr.

1890–2. 1st and 6th edns. of vol. i, 1882, 1915*; 6th edn. of vol. ii, pt. i, 1919, 1921; of vol. ii, pt. ii, 1917, 1921, 1925.

Bibliography, i. 657–81.

1367 DOPSCH (ALFONS). Wirtschaftliche und soziale Grundlagen der europäischen Kulturentwicklung (Caesar to Charlemagne). Vienna. 1918. 2nd edn. 2 vols. 1923–4. * Trans. and condensed by Erna Patzelt. N.Y. 1937.

Critical review by J. E. A. Jolliffe in *E.H.R.* liii (1938), 277–83. Part i, pp. 8–52 of Dopsch summarizes and criticizes the Germanist theories about the Mark and the Markgenossen; on this subject, see Stephenson, 'Problem of the common man' (No. 1497), and the studies cited there. See also Dopsch, 'The agrarian institutions of the Germanic kingdoms from the fifth to the ninth century', *Cambr. Econ. Hist.* (No. 1364), i (1966), 180–204; and Dopsch, *Die freien Marken in Deutschland: Beitrag zur Agrar- und Socialgeschichte des Mittelalters* (Baden, 1933).

1368 DUBY (GEORGES). L'économie rurale et la vie des campagnes dans l'occident mediéval (France, Angleterre, Empire, ix–xv siècles). Essai de synthèse et perspective de recherches. 2 vols. Paris. 1962. Trans. by Cynthia Postan. Lond. 1968.

Useful bibliography, predominantly French.

1369 FUSSELL (GEORGE E.). Farming techniques from prehistoric to modern times. Lond. 1966.

1370 GRAY (HOWARD L.). English field systems. Harvard Historical Studies, xxii. Cambr. (Mass.). 1915.

Cf. Evert Barger, 'The present position of studies in English field-systems', *E.H.R.* liii (1938), 385–411. A. R. H. Baker, 'Howard Levi Gray and English field systems: an evaluation', *Agricultural Hist.* (Champaign), xxxix (1965), 86–91.

1371 LIPSON (EPHRAIM). An introduction to the economic history of England. Vol. i, The middle ages. Vols. ii and iii, The age of mercantilism. Lond. 1915–31. 11th edn. of vol. i. 1959. 6th edn. of vols. ii and iii. 1956.

Placing British medieval economic history in its wider European context, consult Prosper Boissonnade, *Life and work in medieval Europe (fifth to fifteenth centuries)*, translated by Eileen Power (History of Civilization series, ed. C. K. Ogden) (Lond. 1927); Henri Pirenne, *Economic and social history of medieval Europe*, translated by I. E. Clegg (from Henri Pirenne, Gustave Cohen, and Henri Focillon, *Histoire du moyen âge*) (Lond. 1936); Herbert Heaton, *Economic history of Europe* (N.Y. etc. 1936), chaps. ii–xi, from prehistory to *c.* 1500.

1372 MEITZEN (AUGUST). Siedelung und Agrarwesen der Westgermanen und Ostgermanen, der Kelten, Römer, Finnen, und Slawen. 3 vols. and atlas. Berlin. 1895. *

Ireland: i. 174–232; England: ii. 97–140. His system of characteristic settlement of races is not now generally accepted.

1373 ORWIN (CHARLES) and ORWIN (CHRISTABEL). The open fields. Oxf. 1938. 2nd edn. 1954. New edn. with introduction by Joan Thirsk. 1967.

For a critical review, see Beresford in *Antiquity*, xxix (1955), 186–9.

1374 PEAKE (HAROLD). The English village: the origin and decay of its community. Lond. 1922.

Cf. William Page, 'Notes on the types of English villages and their distribution', *Antiquity*, i (1927), 447–68.

1375 PROTHERO (ROWLAND E.) (BARON ERNLE). English farming, past and present. Lond. 1912. 5th edn. by A. D. Hall. 1936. 6th edn. with new introduction. Lond. and Chicago. 1962.

Expanded from a volume entitled *The pioneers and progress of English farming* (Lond. etc. 1888).

1376 ROGERS (JAMES E. THOROLD). A history of agriculture and prices in England, 1259–1793. 7 vols. Oxf. 1866–1902.* Idem, Six centuries of work and wages: the history of English labour. 2 vols. Lond. 1884. 11th edn. 1 vol. 1912. Idem, The economic interpretation of history. Lond. etc. 1888. 7th edn. 1909.

The studies of a pioneer, some of whose views are rejected by more recent authorities. See Index below.

1377 RUSSELL (JOSIAH C.). British medieval population. Albuquerque. 1948. See No. 5481.

1378 SANDYS (CHARLES). Consuetudines Kanciae: a history of gavelkind and other customs in Kent. Lond. 1851.

See No. 2644.

1379 SEEBOHM (MABEL E.). The evolution of the English farm. Cambr. (Mass.). 1927. 2nd revised edn. Lond. 1952. *

1380 SLICHER VAN BATH (BERNARD H.). The agrarian history of Western Europe, A.D. 500–1850. Lond. 1963. N.Y. 1964.

Translated from the Dutch edition of 1960.

1381 USHER (ABBOTT P.). An introduction to the industrial history of England. Boston etc. 1920. *

Broader than its title indicates: Chap. ii, The rise of the craft in antiquity; Chap. iii, Crafts and craft gilds in medieval France; Chap. iv, The population of England 1086–1700; Chap. v, Village and manor; Chap. vi, The traders and towns; Chap. vii, The development of gilds in England; Chap. viii, The woollen industries: 1450–1750.

1382 WRIGHT (THOMAS). A history of domestic manners and sentiments in England, copiously illustrated. Lond. 1862. * New edn. as: The homes of other days, a history of domestic matters, etc. Lond. 1871.

2. Borough and Town

For a century following the publication of Merewether and Stephens (No. 1388) no substantial, broad history of the English medieval town was written, although about the turn of the century studies of various aspects thereof came from the pens of Gross, Maitland, Round, Ballard, and others. This deficiency was in large measure remedied by the appearance in 1933 of Carl Stephenson's *Borough and town* (No. 1389) and in 1936 of James Tait's *The medieval English borough* (No. 1390). Stephenson, applying continental theses to town development in England, particularly those of Pirenne, contended *inter alia* that the Anglo-Saxon borough as late as 1066 was merely 'a military and official centre' remaining largely agrarian in character and lacking the corporate attributes of town and townsmen. His revolutionary theses, based on scholarship of a high order, have provoked much controversy and have not been generally accepted. Tait especially took issue with Stephenson on many points and provided the most widely adopted reconstruction of the origin and constitutional history of the English borough from Anglo-Saxon beginnings to the twelfth century. The issues are discussed in a Historical Revision, stemming from Tait's volume, by R. R. Darlington, 'The early history of English towns', *History*, xxiii (1938), 141–50, and by S. K. Mitchell in his review of Tait's volume in *Speculum*, xiii (1938), 256–9. See also the notes under Nos. 1389, 1390 below. Except for a chapter in Stephenson, little had been done on the topography of medieval English towns; this gap is partially filled by William Savage, *The making of our towns* (Lond. 1952), and in much larger measure by the works of M. Beresford (Nos. 1383, 1384), and in the projected series on Historic Towns edited by M. D. Lobel (No. 1386). On the general subject of towns consult Hoskins (No. 1516) and the works cited below, pp. 700–35.

1383 BERESFORD (MAURICE W.). The lost villages of England. Lond. 1954.

Useful for the topographical nuclei of towns; consult Beresford and St. Joseph (No. 752).

1384 BERESFORD (MAURICE W.). New towns of the middle ages: Town plantation in England, Wales and Gascony. Lond. 1967.

Virtually all of the plantations are post-1066. See No. 5349.

1385 GROSS (CHARLES). The gild merchant: a contribution to British municipal history. 2 vols. Oxf. 1890. Reprinted 1965.

Vol. ii contains many records concerning the municipal history of particular towns. See a review by F. W. Maitland in *Economic Jour.* (1891), reprinted in his *Collected Papers* (No. 1482), ii. 223–31. Cf. F. Liebermann, 'Die englische Gilde im achten Jahrhundert', *Archiv für das Studium der neueren Sprachen*, etc. xcvi (1896), 333–40; and Liebermann, 'Einleitung zum Statut der Londoner Friedensgilde unter Aethelstan', in *Mélanges Fitting* (Montpellier, 1908), ii. 77–103. See also below, vol. ii, Nos. 5360–72.

1386 HISTORIC TOWNS. Maps and plans of towns and cities in the British Isles with historical commentaries from the earliest times to 1800. Ed. by Mary D. Lobel for the British Committee of the International Commission for the Study of Town History. Vol. i. Lond. and Oxf. 1969.

Vol. i is devoted to Banbury, Caernarvon, Glasgow, Gloucester, Hereford, Nottingham, Reading, and Salisbury. Vol. ii will be devoted to Bristol, Cambridge, Coventry, Edinburgh, Winchester, and Windsor. For each of these large, magnificently-produced volumes, there are descriptions of the Romano-British and Saxon town, the thirteenth-century town, etc. with specially drawn maps and plans, medieval street names, parishes and wards, and similar information.

1387 MAITLAND (FREDERIC W.). Townships and borough. Cambr. 1898. Reprinted, 1965.

See his 'The origin of the borough', *E.H.R.* xi (1896), 13–19; reprinted in his *Collected Papers* (No. 1482), iii. 31–42. This essay is expanded in his *Domesday Book* (No. 2636), pp. 172–219. He contends that the special royal peace conferred upon fortified places is the original principle which serves to mark off the borough from the village. See Tait's criticism, in *E.H.R.* xii (1897), 772–7.

1388 MEREWETHER (HENRY A.) and STEPHENS (ARCHIBALD J.). The history of the boroughs and municipal corporations of the United Kingdom. 3 vols. Lond. 1835.

The material in this work is valuable, but many of the general conclusions are untenable.

1389 STEPHENSON (CARL). Borough and town: a study of urban origins in England. Cambr. (Mass.). 1933.

Cf. 'The origin of the English towns', *A.H.R.* xxxii (1926–7), 10–21; 'The Anglo-Saxon borough', *E.H.R.* xlv (1930), 177–207. For critical reviews, see J. Tait in *E.H.R.* xlviii (1933), 642–8; and J. N. L. Myres in *Antiquity*, viii (1934), 359–61; and H. Cam (No. 1462). More laudatory reviews are by W. E. Lunt in *A.H.R.* xxxix (1933), 99–101; Charles Johnson in *E.H.R.* iv (1934), 486–91; C. W. David in *Speculum*, ix (1934), 341–2; and E. Perroy in *Le Moyen Âge*, xlv (1935), 113–19.

1390 TAIT (JAMES). The medieval English borough: studies on its origins and constitutional history. Univ. of Manchester, Pubns. No. 245. Historical Series, No. 70. Manchester, 1936. Reprinted, Manchester and N.Y. 1968.

Critical review by C. Stephenson in *A.H.R.* xliii (1937), 96–9. Laudatory review by H. M. Cam, *E.H.R.* lii (1937), 303–6.

F. LITERATURE AND LEARNING

The intellectual developments in medieval Britain cannot be isolated from the general cultural changes of Western Europe. The flow of ideas and cultural influences across the Channel, in both directions, coupled British culture with that of the Continent. From the vast literature on this subject, only the principal bibliographical guides and the indispensable general treatises are noted here. Commentaries restricted by period or subject arel isted below on pages 343 and 344. *The Cambridge bibliography of English literature* (No. 14), Manitius (No. 56), and the dictionaries and encyclopedias cited on pp. 34–6 provide preliminary guidance. Additional helpful bibliographies can be found in the works listed under Historical Bibliography, especially Nos. 102, 133, 150, 152, 168; and in the section on Philology, especially numbers 267, 268, 269, 272, and 276. For science, see George Sarton, *A guide to the history of science* (Waltham (Mass.), 1952), and for current research consult the periodic 'critical bibliography of the history of science and its cultural influences' in *Isis*, the quarterly journal of the History of Science Society, i+ (1912+), (Nos. 6933–4).

In the accompanying list, general studies of broad topics are grouped together; each group is separated by a space.

1391 HASKINS (CHARLES H.). The renaissance of the twelfth century. Cambr. (Mass.). 1927. 3rd reprinting, 1933. * Paperback.

Cf. Christopher Brooke, *The twelfth century renaissance* (Lond. and N.Y. 1969), which is a broad survey with many illustrations intended for the general reader. Haskins's seminal summary has become a classic account.

1392 LESNE (ÉMILE). Les écoles de la fin du VIIIe siècle à la fin du XIIe. Vol. v of *Histoire de la propriété ecclésiastique en France*. Lille. 1940. *

Cf. Léon A. Maître, *Les écoles épiscopales et monastiques en Occident avant les universités.* (*768–1180*) (Paris, 1866; reprinted, Paris, 1924).

1393 MARROU (HENRI IRÉNÉE). Histoire de l'éducation dans l'antiquité. Paris. 1948. 3rd edn. 1955, which is translated by George Lamb, *A history of education in antiquity*. N.Y. 1956.

Excellent as a background for medieval education.

1394 PARÉ (GÉRARD M.), BRUNET (ADRIEN M.), and TREMBLAY (PIERRE). La renaissance du XIIe siècle: les écoles et l'enseignement. Paris. 1933.

1395 PARRY (ALBERT W.). Education in England in the middle ages. Lond. 1920.

1396 ROGER (MAURICE). L'enseignement des lettres classiques d'Ausone à Alcuin. Paris. 1905.

One of the better books on the Irish schools and the work of Aldhelm, Bede, Boniface, and Alcuin.

1397 SANDYS (JOHN E.). A history of classical scholarship . . . 3 vols. Cambr. 1903–8. 3rd edn. 1931. *

Vol. i covers the period from the end of the sixth century B.C. to the end of the middle ages. See also Sandys, *A short history of classical scholarship* (Cambr. 1915); and R. R. Bolgar, *The classical heritage and its beneficiaries* (Cambr. 1954 and paperback edn. N.Y. 1964).

1398 SOUTHERN (RICHARD W.). The making of the middle ages. Lond. and New. Haven. 1953. Pb. New Haven. 1962.

1399 BAUGH (ALBERT C.), ed. A literary history of England. N.Y. [1948].

1400 CAMBRIDGE HISTORY OF ENGLISH LITERATURE. Ed. by A. W. Ward and A. R. Waller. 15 vols. and index. Cambr. 1907–27. Reprinted, 1920, 1932.

Chapters by various writers cover both the Latin and the vernacular literature of England. Contains bibliographies.

1401 GREENFIELD (STANLEY B.). A critical history of Old English literature. Lond. and N.Y. 1965.

1402 OXFORD HISTORY OF ENGLISH LITERATURE. Ed. by F. P. Wilson and Bonamy Dobrée. [12 vols.] Oxf. 1945 (in progress).

Vol. ii: pt. i, Henry Bennett, *Chaucer and the fifteenth century*, 1947. pt. ii, Edmund K. Chambers, *English literature at the close of the middle ages*, 1945.

1403 BOLTON (WHITNEY F.). A history of Anglo-Latin literature 597–1066. Vol. i, 597–740. Princeton. 1967. Idem, 'Pre-Conquest Anglo-Latin: Perspectives and prospects', *Comparative Literature*, xxiii (1971), 151–66.

1404 MANITIUS (MAX). Geschichte der lateinischen Literatur des Mittelalters. 3 vols. Munich. 1911–31. *

Vol. i, von Justinian bis zur Mitte des zehnten Jahrhunderts; vol. ii, bis zum Ausbruch Kampfes zwischen Kirche und Staat; vol. iii, bis zum ende des zwölften Jahrhunderts. Cf. Joseph de Ghellinck, *Littérature latine au moyen âge*, 2 vols. (Paris, 1939); Frederick A. Wright and Thomas A. Sinclair, *A history of later Latin literature from the middle of the fourth to the end of the seventeenth century* (Lond. and N.Y. 1931).

1405 RABY (FREDERIC J. E.). A history of Christian-Latin poetry from the beginnings to the close of the middle ages. Oxf. 1927. 2nd edn. 1953.

1406 RABY (FREDERIC J. E.). A history of secular Latin poetry in the Middle Ages. 2 vols. Oxf. 1934. 2nd edn. with new material in an Appendix. 1957.

Excellent bibliography.

1407 GILSON (ÉTIENNE). History of Christian philosophy in the middle ages. N.Y. 1955.

Gilson provides a rich mine of bibliographical references.

1408 KNOWLES (DAVID). The evolution of medieval thought. Lond. and Baltimore. 1962. Pb. N.Y. 1964.

1409 ÜBERWEG (FRIEDRICH). Die patristische und scholastische Philosophie. Ed. by Bernhard Geyer. Vol. ii. Grundriss der Geschichte der Philosophie. 11th edn. Berlin. 1928. Reprinted, Basel. 1951.

The standard work.

1410 WULF (MAURICE DE). Histoire de la philosophie médiévale. Louvain. 1900. 5th edn. 2 vols. Louvain. 1924–5. 6th edn. 3 vols. Louvain etc. 1934–47. 3rd edn. translated by P. Coffey: *History of medieval philosophy*. Lond. etc. 1909. Translations by Ernest C. Messenger: of 5th French edn. 2 vols. Lond. etc. 1926; of 6th French edn. 2 vols. 1935–8; definitive translation of 6th French edn. [3 vols.] vol. i. N.Y. 1952.

Gives bibliographies at the end of each section. His *Philosophy and civilization in the middle ages* (Princeton, 1922) is helpful, though less technical.

1411 CARLYLE (ROBERT W.) and CARLYLE (ALEXANDER J.). A history of medieval political theory in the West. 6 vols. Edin. and Lond. 1903–36. 2nd. edn. of vol. i. 1927.

1412 GIERKE (OTTO VON). Das deutsche Genossenschaftsrecht. 4 vols. Berlin. 1868–1913. A section of vol. iii translated by F. W. Maitland: *Political theories of the middle ages*. Cambr. 1900; 1927.

Maitland's edition contains valuable notes and useful list of the works of the major publicists.

1413   KERN (FRITZ). Gottesgnadentum und Widerstandsrecht im früheren Mittelalter; zur Entwicklungsgeschichte der Monarchie. Leipzig. 1914. Revised and translated by S. B. Chrimes: *Kingship and law in the middle ages.* Oxf. 1939.

Of major importance for concepts in the Germanic tradition. Chrimes's work includes a translation of an article entitled 'Recht und Verfassung im Mittelalter' (*Histor. Zeitsch.* 1919) but omits most of the valuable notes in the 1914 publication.

1414   LEWIS (EWART). Medieval political ideas. 2 vols. Lond. 1954.

Includes selections of readings, seventh to fifteenth centuries; useful bibliographical note, vol. ii, 633–48.

1415   McILWAIN (CHARLES H.). The growth of political thought in the West, from the Greeks to the end of the middle ages. N.Y. 1932. *

A masterly work. See also George H. Sabine, *A history of political theory* (N.Y. (1937); revised edn. 1950); Alessandro Passerin d'Entrèves, *The medieval contribution to political thought* . . . (Lond. 1939); Peter N. Riesenberg, *Inalienability of sovereignty in medieval political thought,* Columbia Studies in the Social Sciences, No. 591 (N.Y. etc. 1956); *The social and political ideas of some great medieval thinkers,* ed. by F. J. C. Hearnshaw (London, 1932).

1416   POOLE (REGINALD LANE). Illustrations of the history of medieval thought in the department of theology and ecclesiastical politics. Lond. 1884. 2nd revised edn.: Illustrations of the history of medieval thought and learning. Lond. etc. 1920. * Pb. N.Y. 1960.

1417   ULLMANN (WALTER). The principles of government and politics in the middle ages. Lond. 1966. Idem, A history of political thought: the middle ages (Penguin Books, Harmondsworth. 1965).

1418   CROMBIE (ALISTAIR C.). Augustine to Galileo: the history of science, A.D. 400–1650. Lond. [1953]. 2nd edn. 2 vols. Pb. N.Y. 1959. Lond. 1961.

Includes extensive bibliographies.

1419   HASKINS (CHARLES H.). Studies in the history of medieval science. Harvard Historical Studies, xxvii. Cambr. (Mass.). etc. 1924. 2nd edn. 1927. *

See also his *Studies in mediaeval culture* (Oxf. 1929).

1420   SARTON (GEORGE). Introduction to the history of science. 3 vols. in 5 pts. Baltimore. 1927–48.

Vol. i, from Homer to Omar Khayyam; vol. ii, pt. i, from Rabbi ben Ezra to Ibn Rushd; vol. ii, pt. ii, from Robert Grosseteste to Roger Bacon; vol. iii, pt. i, first half of the fourteenth century; vol. iii, pt. ii, second half of the fourteenth century. See also Pierre Duhem, *Le système du monde: histoire des doctrines cosmologiques de Platon à Copernique,* 5 vols. (Paris, 1913–17) and five posthumous volumes, vi–x (1954–9).

1421   TALBOT (CHARLES H.). Medicine in medieval England. Lond. 1967.

See also his 'Some notes on Anglo-Saxon medicine', *Medical History* (Lond.), ix (1965), 156–69.

1422   TALBOT (CHARLES H.) and HAMMOND (EUGENE A.). The medical practitioners in medieval England: a biographical register. Wellcome Hist. Medical Lib. Pubns. N.S. viii. Lond. 1965.

1423 THORNDIKE (LYNN). A history of magic and experimental science. 8 vols. N.Y. 1923–58. Vols. i and ii, reprinted, 1929.

1424 WHITE (LYNN J.). Medieval technology and social change. Lond. 1962. Also paperback edn. N.Y. 1966.

For criticism, see, e.g., Titow, *Eng. Rural Soc.* (No. 4701), pp. 37–41.

G. *FESTSCHRIFTEN* AND COLLECTED WORKS

Many significant articles by various hands have been printed in *Festschriften* and memorial volumes dedicated to outstanding scholars. Other papers have been published or reprinted in the collected works of an individual scholar. Studies published under these auspices are often difficult to locate; no complete guide exists. Analytical entries are given for some *Festschriften* in No. 1425; they are sometimes recorded in the periodic bibliographies printed in historical journals, e.g. *Econ. Hist. Rev.* The general titles of *Festschriften* without analyses of contents are noted, as they appear, in *Année Philol.* (No. 266) and *I.B.O.H.S.* (No. 53).

Those volumes whose contents relating to Britain fall exclusively within a particular section of his bibliography are recorded in that section. On the other hand those volumes which embody a considerable diversity of subject matter are enumerated with analytical entries immediately below, so that repetition of bibliographical detail may be minimized. Cross-references to many of these entries are made by number in appropriate places.

1. Festschriften *Analysed*

1424A BIBLIOGRAPHIE INTERNATIONALE DES TRAVAUX HISTORIQUES PUBLIÉS DANS LES VOLUMES DE 'MÉLANGES', 1880–1939. Comité internationale des sciences historiques. Paris. 1955. Vol. ii for 1940–50. Paris. 1965.

1425 WILLIAMS (HARRY F.). An index of medieval studies published in Festschriften, 1865–1946, with special reference to Romanic material. Berkeley (Calif.). 1951.

See also Hedwig Schleiffer and Ruth Crandall, *Index to economic history essays in Festschriften* (Cambr., Mass. 1953), covering all periods.

1426 (Bémont) MÉLANGES D'HISTOIRE OFFERTS À M. CHARLES BÉMONT par ses amis et ses élèves à l'occasion de la vingt-cinquième année de son enseignement à l'École pratique des Hautes Études. Paris. 1913.

(a) Ferdinand Lot, Hengist, Horsa, Vortigern: la conquête de la Grand-Bretagne par les Saxons. 1–19. Reprinted in *Recueil des travaux historiques de Ferdinand Lot*, i. 731–49 (Geneva and Paris, 1968).
(b) Felix Liebermann, Ueber die Gesetze Ines von Wessex. 21–42.
(c) Petit-Dutaillis, Ch. Les origines franco-normandes de la 'forêt' anglaise. 59–76.
(d) Charles H. Haskins, The manor of Portswood under Henry I. 77–83.
(e) Louis Halphen, Les entrevues des rois Louis VII et Henri II durant l'exil de Thomas Becket en France. 151–62.
(f) Eugène Déprez, Le Trésor des chartes de Guyenne sous Édouard II. 225–42.

(g) Rod Reuss, La première invasion des 'Anglais' en Alsace, épisode de l'histoire du xive siècle. 281–303.
(h) Gabreille Loviette, Arnaud Amanieu, sire d'Albret, et l'appel des seigneurs gascons en 1368. 317–40.
(i) J. A. Twemlow, The liturgical credentials of a forgotten English saint. 365–71.
(j) Pierre Gautier, De l'état des monastères cisterciens anglais à la fin du XVe siècle. 423–35.

1427 (Birley) BRITAIN AND ROME. Ed. by M. G. Jarrett and B. Dobson (No. 2045).

1428 (Callus) OXFORD STUDIES PRESENTED TO DANIEL CALLUS. Oxf. Hist. Soc. N.S. xvi. 1964 for 1959–1960.

(a) A. B. Emden, Northerners and southerners in the organization of the university to 1509. 1–30.
(b) W. A. Pantin, The halls and schools of medieval Oxford: an attempt at reconstruction. 31–100.
(c) W. A. Hinnebusch, Foreign Dominican students and professors at the Oxford Blackfriars. 101–34.
(d) L. Boyle, The curriculum of the faculty of Canon Law at Oxford in the first half of the fourteenth century. 135–62.
(e) R. W. Hunt, Oxford grammar masters in the middle ages. 163–93.
(f) C. Martin, Walter Burley. 194–230.
(g) J. A. Weisheipl, Roger Swyneshed, O.S.B., logician, natural philosopher, and theologian. 231–52.
(h) B. Smalley, Wyclif's *Postilla* on the Old Testament and his *Principium.* 253–96.
(i) I. Thomas, Medieval aftermath: Oxford logic and logicians of the seventeenth century. 297–311.
(j) Bibliography of the published writings of Daniel Callus. 312–19.

1429 (Chadwick) THE EARLY CULTURES OF NORTH-WEST EUROPE. H. M. Chadwick Memorial Studies. Ed. by Cyril Fox and Bruce Dickins. Cambr. 1950.

22 essays on archaeology, Celtic and Anglo-Saxon subjects, Norse literature, and one on place-names. See review in *E.H.R.* lxviii (1953), 264–5; and *Mod. Lang. Rev.* xlvi (1951), 259–60.
(a) Cyril Fox, The burial ritual and custom in the bronze age. 51–73.
(b) J. M. de Navarro, British Isles and the beginning of the early bronze age. 75–105.
(c) B. R. S. and E. M. Megaw, Norse heritage in the Isle of Man. 141–70.
(d) T. G. E. Powell, The Celtic settlement in Ireland. 172–95.
(e) K. Jackson, Notes on the Ogam inscriptions in southern Britain. 197–213.
(f) P. Hunter Blair, Moore memoranda on Northumbrian history. 243–57.
(g) D. Whitelock, Interpretation of the Seafarer. 259–72.
(h) B. Colgrave, Post-Bedan miracles and translations of St. Cuthbert. 305–32.
(i) F. Harmer, Chipping and Market: a lexicographical investigation. 333–60.
(j) C. E. Wright, Sir Edward Dering: Seventeenth century antiquary and his Saxon Charters. 369–93.
(k) O. K. Schram, Fenland place-names. 427–41.

1430 (Charlesworth) THE HERITAGE OF EARLY BRITAIN. By various members of Cambridge University. Ed. by M. D. Knowles. Lond. 1952.

(a) G. E. Daniel, The peoples of prehistoric Britain. 11–32.
(b) J. G. D. Clark, How the earliest people lived. 32–55.
(c) J. M. de Navarro, The Celts in Britain and their art. 56–82.
(d) M. P. Charlesworth, The Roman occupation. 83–103.

(e) N. K. Chadwick, The Celtic West. 104–27.
(f) P. H. Blair, The foundations of England. 128–52.
(g) Edward Miller, The Norman conquest. 153–73.
(h) M. D. Knowles, The heritage completed. 174–91.

1431 (Childe) No. 1974.

1432 (Crawford) ASPECTS OF ARCHAEOLOGY IN BRITAIN AND BEYOND. Essays presented to O. G. S. Crawford. Ed. by W. F. Grimes. Lond. 1951.

Contributions by 21 British archaeologists, of which the most important specifically on British history are the following:

(a) J. N. L. Myres, The Adventus Saxonum. 221–41.
(b) Stuart Piggott, Stonehenge reviewed. 274–92.
(c) J. K. St. Joseph, A survey of pioneering in air photography. 303–15.
(d) C. E. Stevens, Britain between the (Roman) invasions. 332–44.
(e) p. 382 contains a Bibliography of the published work of O. G. S. Crawford.
(f) For full contents, see *Antiquity*, xxvii (1953), 110–15.

1433 (Dickins) THE ANGLO-SAXONS. Studies in some aspects of their history and culture. Ed. by Peter Clemoes. Lond. 1959.

(a) K. Cameron, An early Mercian boundary in Derbyshire: the place-name evidence. 13–34.
(b) K. H. Jackson, Edinburgh and the Anglian occupation of Lothian. 35–42.
(c) F. M. Stenton, The East Anglian kings of the seventh century. 43–52.
(d) F. T. Wainwright, Æthelflæd Lady of the Mercians. 53–69.
(e) D. Whitelock, The dealings of the kings of England with Northumbria in the tenth and eleventh centuries. 70–88.
(f) F. E. Harmer, A Bromfield and a Coventry writ of King Edward the Confessor. 89–103.
(g) G. Turville-Petre, Legends of England in Icelandic manuscripts. 104–21.
(h) M. Ashdown, An Icelandic account of the survival of Harold Godwinson. 122–36.
(i) H. M. Taylor, Some little-known aspects of English pre-conquest churches. 137–58.
(j) D. M. Wilson, A group of Anglo-Saxon amulet rings. 159–70.
(k) N. K. Chadwick, The monsters and Beowulf. 171–203.
(l) J. I. Young, Two notes on the *Later Genesis*. 204–11.
(m) P. A. M. Clemoes, The chronology of Aelfric's works. 212–47.
(n) G. N. Garmonsway, The development of the colloquy. 248–61.
(o) N. R. Ker, Three old English texts in a Salisbury pontifical, Cotton Tiberius C i. 262–79.
(p) G. L. Brook, The relation between the textual and the linguistic study of Old English. 280–91.
(q) R. M. Wilson, The provenance of the Vespasian Psalter Gloss: The linguisitic evidence. 292–310.
(r) A. H. Smith, Two notes on some West Yorkshire place-names. 311–15.
(s) A biographical note and list of books and papers (of Bruce Dickins). 316–22.

1434 (Dopsch) WIRTSCHAFT UND KULTUR. Festschrift zum 70. Geburtstag von Alfons Dopsch. Baden bei Wien, etc. 1938.

(a) R. Lennard, From Roman Britain to Anglo-Saxon England. 34–73.
(b) F. M. Powicke, Observations on the English freeholder in the thirteenth century. 382–93.
(c) H. M. Cam, The early burgesses of Cambridge in relation to the surrounding countryside (No. 1462).

1435 (Fox) CULTURE AND ENVIRONMENT: essays in honour of Sir Cyril Fox. Ed. by Idris Ll. Foster and Leslie Alcock. Lond. 1963.

(*a*) M. Wheeler, Homage to Sir Cyril Fox. 1–6.

(*b*) G. Daniel, The personality of Wales. 7–24.

(*c*) H. N. Savory, The personality of the southern marches of Wales in the neolithic and early bronze age. 25–52.
(and five other papers on pre-Roman times.)

(*d*) I. A. Richmond, The Cornovii. 251–62.

(*e*) C. A. Gresham, The interpretation of settlement patterns in northwest Wales. 263–80.

(*f*) L. Alcock, Pottery and the settlements in Wales and the March, A.D. 400–700. 281–302.

(*g*) Lord Rennell of Rodd, The land of Lene. 303–26.

(*h*) E. M. Jope, The regional cultures of medieval Britain. 327–50.

(*i*) C. A. R. Radford, The native ecclesiastical architecture of Wales (*c.* 1100–1285): the study of a regional style. 355–72.

(*j*) Lord Raglan, The origin of vernacular architecture. 373–88.

(*k*) J. T. Smith, The long house in Monmouthshire (and similar papers by P. Smith and I. C. Peate). 389–444.

(*l*) W. A. Pantin, Some medieval English town-houses. 445–78.

(*m*) L. J. Lloyd, Bibliography of works of Sir Cyril Fox. 503–12.

For a score of publications by Sir Cyril Fox, see Bonser, *A.-S.C.B.* (No. 12), index, p. 18. *Culture and Environment* includes 111 figures and 26 plates.

1436 (Gay) FACTS AND FACTORS IN ECONOMIC HISTORY. Articles by former students of Edwin F. Gay. Cambr. (Mass.). 1933.

(*a*) H. L. Gray, The first benevolence. 90–113.

(*b*) W. E. Lunt, The consent of the English lower clergy to taxation, 1166–1216. 62–89.

1437 (Graham) MEDIEVAL STUDIES PRESENTED TO ROSE GRAHAM. Ed. by Veronica Ruffer and A. J. Taylor. Oxf. 1950.

(*a*) H. M. Cam, The community of the vill. 1–14.

(*b*) H. M. Colvin, Holme Lacy: an episcopal manor and its tenants in the twelfth and thirteenth centuries. 15–40.

(*c*) J. C. Dickinson, Early suppressions of English houses of Austin canons. 54–77.

(*d*) E. F. Jacob, The disputed election at Fountains Abbey, 1410–16. 78–97.

(*e*) M. D. Knowles, The last abbot of Wigmore (1518–38). 138–45.

(*f*) M. D. Legge, The French language and the English cloister. 146–62.

(*g*) K. Major, The office of chapter clerk at Lincoln in the middle ages. 163–88.

(*h*) W. A. Pantin, Some medieval English treatises on the origins of monasticism. 189–215.

(*i*) A. H. Thompson, William Beverley, archdeacon of Northumberland. 216–32.

(*j*) A. J. Taylor, A bibliography of the published writings of Rose Graham. 233–40.

1438 (Gwynn). MEDIEVAL STUDIES: presented to Aubrey Gwynn, S.J. Ed. by J. A. Watt, J. B. Morrall, and F. X. Martin, O.S.A. Dublin. 1961.

Excellent for Irish church bibliography. Three parts: (i) Ireland, (ii) England, (iii) Europe.
Essays particulary germane to this bibliography are:

(*a*) John Ryan, S.J., The early Irish church and the see of Peter. 3–18.

(*b*) H. G. Richardson, Some Norman monastic foundations in Ireland. 29–43.

(*c*) C. R. Cheney, A group of related synodal statutes of the thirteenth century. 114–32.

(*d*) John A. Watt, English law and the Irish church: the reign of Edward I. 133–67.

(*e*) Mary Donovan O'Sullivan, Italian merchant bankers and the collection of the customs in Ireland, 1275–1311. 168–85.

(*f*) G. O. Sayles, The rebellious first earl of Desmond. 203–29.
(*g*) R. Dudley Edwards, The kings of England and papal provisions in fifteenth century Ireland. 265–96.
(*h*) M. D. Knowles, The English bishops, 1070–1532. 283–96.
(*i*) W. A. Pantin, John of Wales and medieval humanism. 297–319.
(*j*) Helen M. Cam, The religious houses of London and the eyre of 1321. 320–9.
(*k*) M. B. Hackett, William Flete and the 'De remediis contra temptaciones'. 330–48.
(*l*) E. F. Jacob, A note on the English concordat of 1418. 349–58.
(*m*) Walter Ullmann, Eugenius IV, Cardinal Kemp, and Archbishop Chichele. 359–83.
(*n*) Bibliography of Revd. Professor Aubrey Gwynn. 502–9.

1439 (Haskins). ANNIVERSARY ESSAYS IN MEDIAEVAL HISTORY, by students of Charles H. Haskins. Ed. by Charles H. Taylor and John L. LaMonte. Boston etc. 1929.
(*a*) J. S. Beddie, Libraries in the 12th century: their catalogues and contents. 1–23.
(*b*) J. Birdsall, The English manors of La Trinité at Caen. 25–44.
(*c*) C. W. David, The claim of King Henry I to be called learned. 45–56.
(*d*) E. B. Graves, The legal significance of the Statute of Praemunire of 1353. 57–80.
(*e*) H. L. Gray, Greek visitors to England in 1455–6. 81–116.
(*f*) W. E. Lunt, Clerical tenths levied in England by papal authority during the reign of Edward II. 157–82.
(*g*) H. MacKenzie, The anti-foreign movement in England, 1231–2. 183–203.
(*h*) R. A. Newhall, Henry V's policy of conciliation in Normandy, 1417–22. 205–29.
(*i*) S. R. Packard, The Norman communes under Richard and John, 1189–1204. 231–54.
(*j*) J. C. Russell, The canonization of opposition to the king in Angevin England. 279–90.
(*k*) C. Stephenson, Taxation and representation in the middle ages. 291–312. (Eng., Fr., Ger.)
(*l*) G. W. Robinson, Bibliography of Charles H. Haskins. 389–98.

1440 (Jenkinson). ESSAYS IN MEMORY OF SIR HILARY JENKINSON. Edited for the Society of Archivists by Albert E. J. Hollaender. Chichester. 1962.
(*a*) Roger H. Ellis, The building of the Public Record Office. 9–30.
(*b*) F. W. Steer, Some early seals at Arundel Castle. 31–40.
(*c*) Pierre Chaplais, The study of palaeography and sigillography in England: Sir Hilary Jenkinson's contribution. 41–9.
(*d*) Elizabeth Ralph and Felix Hull, The development of the local archive service in England. 57–70.
(*e*) Maurice F. Bond, The British Records Association and the modern archive movement. 71–90.

1441 (Jenkinson). STUDIES PRESENTED TO SIR HILARY JENKINSON. Ed. by J. Conway Davies. Lond. 1957.
(*a*) H. E. Bell, Italian archives. 1–19.
(*b*) H. S. Bennett, Medieval ordination lists in the English episcopal records. 20–34.
(*c*) R. A. Brown, The treasury in the later twelfth century. 35–49.
(*d*) H. M. Cam, The 'private' hundred before the Norman conquest. 50–60.
(*e*) P. Chaplais, The chancery of Guyenne, 1289–1453. 61–96.
(*f*) J. C. Davies, Memoranda rolls to 1307. 97–154.
(*g*) C. Johnson, The Public Record Office. 178–95.
(*h*) K. B. McFarlane, William Worcester. 196–221.
(*i*) C. A. F. Meekings, The Pipe Roll order of 12 Feb. 1270. 222–53.
(*j*) M. H. Mills, The medieval shire house. 254–71.
(*k*) J. H. P. Pafford, Univ. of London Libr. MS. 378, Robert of Gloucester's Chronicle. 309–19.

(*l*) B. Schofield, Wreck rolls of Leiston Abbey. 361–71.
(*m*) R. Somerville, The preparation and issue of instruments under seal in the duchy of Lancaster. 372–89.
(*n*) A. Steel, Collectors of customs of Newcastle on Tyne in the reign of Richard II. 390–413.

1442 (Leeds). DARK AGE BRITAIN: Studies presented to E. T. Leeds with a bibliography of his works. Ed. by D. B. Harden. Lond. 1956.

14 essays, including 36 plates and 58 figures.
I. Roman and Celtic Survival.
(*a*) C. H. V. Sutherland, Coinage in Britain in the fifth and sixth centuries. 3–10.
(*b*) I. A. Richmond. Two Celtic heads in stone from Corbridge, Northumberland. 11–15.
(*c*) J. N. L. Myres, Romano-Saxon pottery. 16–39.
(*d*) H. N. Savory, Some sub-Romano-British brooches from south Wales. 40–58.
(*e*) C. A. R. Radford, Imported pottery found at Tintagel, Cornwall. 59–70.
(*f*) Françoise Henry, Irish enamels of the dark ages. 71–88.
II. The Pagan Saxons.
(*g*) C. F. C. Hawkes, The Jutes of Kent. 91–111. Cf. No. 2545.
(*h*) T. C. Lethbridge, The Anglo-Saxon settlement in eastern England. 112–22.
(*i*) Jean R. Kirk, Anglo-Saxon cremation and inhumation in the upper Thames valley in pagan times. 123–31.
(*j*) D. B. Harden, Glass vessels in Britain and Ireland, A.D. 400–1000. 132–67.
III. The Christian Saxon and the Viking Age.
(*k*) R. L. S. Bruce-Mitford, Late Saxon disc-brooches. 171–201.
(*l*) Cyril Fox, The siting of the monastery of St. Mary and St. Peter in Exeter. 202–17.
(*m*) G. C. Dunning, Trade relations between England and the continent in the late Anglo-Saxon period. 218–33.
(*n*) E. M. Jope, Saxon Oxford and its region. 234–58.

1443 (Lot). MÉLANGES D'HISTOIRE DU MOYEN ÂGE, offerts à M. Ferdinand Lot par ses amis et ses élèves. Paris. 1925.

(*a*) A. E. Levett, Baronial councils and their relation to manorial courts. 421–41.
(*b*) B. Marx, Guillaume de Poitiers et Guillaume de Jumièges. 543–61.
(*c*) F. M. Powicke, Master Simon of Faversham. 649–58.

1444 (McIlwain). ESSAYS IN HISTORY AND POLITICAL THEORY in honor of Charles H. McIlwain. Cambr. (Mass.). 1936.

(*a*) P. Birdsall, 'Non obstante': a study of the dispensing power of English kings. 37–76.
(*b*) D. B. Weske, The attitude of the English clergy in the 13th and 14th centuries toward the obligation of attendance on convocations and parliaments. 77–108.
(*c*) M. H. Maguire, Attack of the common lawyers on the oath *ex officio* as administered in the ecclesiastical courts in England. 199–229.
(*d*) M. A. Shepard, The political and constitutional theory of Sir John Fortescue. 289–319.

1445 (MacNeill). ESSAYS AND STUDIES presented to Professor Eóin MacNeill . . . on the occasion of his seventieth birthday . . . Ed. by John Ryan. Dublin. 1940.

Special studies on the language, literature, and history of early Ireland, listed in Williams (No. 1423), pp. 22–4. The following may be signalized:
(*a*) E. Curtis, Feudal Charters of the DeBurgo lordship of Connacht (1237–1325). 286–95.

(b) R. W. D. Edwards, Magna Carta Hiberniae. 307–18.

(c) L. Gougaud, The remains of ancient Irish monastic libraries. 319–34.

(d) P. Grosjean, Édition du Catalogus praecipuorum sanctorum Hiberniae de Henri Fitzsimon. 335–93.

(e) A. Gwynn, Nicholas Mac Maol Íosa, archbishop of Armagh (1272–1303). 394–405.

(f) J. Hogan, The Uí Briain kingship in Telach Óc. 406–44.

1446   (Pirenne). MÉLANGES D'HISTOIRE offerts à Henri Pirenne par ses anciens élèves et ses amis à l'occasion de sa quarantième année d'enseignement à l'Université de Gand, 1886–1926. 2 vols. Brussels. 1926.

(a) Bibliographie des travaux historiques de Henri Pirenne. 25–39.

(b) H. E. de Sagher, L'immigration des tisserands flamands et brabançons en Angleterre sous Édouard III. 109–26.

(c) J. Huizinga, Koning Eduard IV van Engeland in Ballingschap. 245–56.

(d) L. Leclère, La grande charte de 1215 est-elle une 'illusion'? 279–90.

(e) C. Stephenson, The seignorial tallage in England. 465–74.

(f) T. F. Tout, The English parliament and public opinion, 1376–1388. 545–62.

1447   (Pirenne). ÉTUDES D'HISTOIRE dédiées à la mémoire de Henri Pirenne par ses anciens élèves. Brussels. 1937.

(a) H. Berben, Une guerre économique au moyen âge: l'embargo sur l'exportation des laines anglaises (1270–1274). 1–19.

(b) J. L. Cate, The English mission of Eustace of Flay (1200–1). 67–90.

(c) H. S. Lucas, A document relating to the marriage of Philippa of Hainault in 1327. 199–207.

(d) L. Vercauteren-de-Smet, Étude sur les chatelains comtaux de Flandre, du xie au début du xiiie siècle. 413–24.

1448   (Poole). ESSAYS IN HISTORY PRESENTED TO REGINALD LANE POOLE. Ed. by H. W. C. Davis. Oxf. 1927. Reprinted, 1969.

(a) F. Madan, The localization of manuscripts. 5–29.

(b) C. G. Crump, Eo quod expressa mentio, etc. 30–45.

(c) T. F. Tout, The household of the chancery and its disintegration. 46–85.

(d) C. Oman, Concerning some Gloucestershire boundaries. 86–97.

(e) J. P. Whitney, A note on the work of the Wyclif Society. 98–114.

(f) F. M. Stenton, Lindsey and its kings. 136–50.

(g) J. Tait, An alleged charter of William the Conqueror. 151–67.

(h) H. W. C. Davis, Some documents of the anarchy (Henry, Stephen, Matilda). 168–89.

(i) H. Jenkinson, A money-lender's bonds of the 12th century. 190–210.

(j) Z. N. Brooke, The register of Master David of London and the part he played in the Becket crisis. 227–45.

(k) F. M. Powicke, Alexander of St. Albans, a literary muddle. 246–60.

(l) A. L. Poole, England and Burgundy in the last decade of the 12th century. 261–73.

(m) A. Mercati, La prima relazione del Cardinale Nicolò de Romanis sulla sua legazione in Inghilterra. 274–89.

(n) C. C. J. Webb, Roger Bacon on Alphonse of Poitiers. 290–300.

(o) A. G. Little, Thomas Docking and his relations to Roger Bacon. 301–31.

(p) C. L. Kingsford, John de Benstede and his missions for Edward I. 332–59.

(q) J. G. Edwards, The negotiating of the treaty of Leake, 1318. 360–78.

(r) V. H. Galbraith, The *Historia aurea* of John, vicar of Tynemouth, and the sources of the St. Albans Chronicle (1327–77). 379–98.

(s) C. Johnson, An act of Edward III as Count of Toulouse. 399–404.

(t) H. E. Salter, An Oxford hall in 1424. 421–35.

(u) A. L. Poole, Lists of the published works of Reginald Lane Poole, and his academic and other offices. 466–78.

1449 (Porter). MEDIEVAL STUDIES IN MEMORY OF A. KINGSLEY
PORTER. Ed. by Wilhelm R. W. Koehler. 2 vols. Cambr. (Mass.). 1939.

- (*a*) R. A. S. Macalister, Medieval art in Scandinavia and the British Isles: the sculptured stones of Wales. 577–87.
- (*b*) E. I. Seaver, Some examples of Viking figure representation in Scandinavia and the British Isles. 589–610.
- (*c*) A. Goldschmidt, English influence on medieval art of the continent. 709–28.
- (*d*) Bibliography of the writings of A. Kingsley Porter. xvii–xxiv.
- (*e*) A. M. Friend, Jr., The canon tables of the Book of Kells. 611–66.

1450 (Powicke). STUDIES IN MEDIEVAL HISTORY PRESENTED TO
F. M. POWICKE. Ed. by R. W. Hunt, W. A. Pantin, and R. W. Southern.
Oxf. 1948. Reprinted, 1969.

- (*a*) T. A. M. Bishop, The Norman settlement of Yorkshire. 1–14.
- (*b*) J. Le Patourel, The reports of the trial on Penenden Heath. 15–26.
- (*c*) R. W. Southern, Lanfranc of Bec and Berengar of Tours. 27–48.
- (*d*) N. R. Ker, Hemming's cartulary: a description of the two Worcester cartularies in Cotton Tiberius A. xiii. 49–75.
- (*e*) M. McKisack, London and the succession to the crown during the middle ages. 76–89.
- (*f*) A. L. Poole, Richard the first's alliance with the German princes in 1194. 90–91.
- (*g*) C. R. Cheney, The alleged deposition of King John. 100–16.
- (*h*) J. E. A. Jolliffe, The chamber and the castle treasures under King John. 117–42.
- (*i*) R. W. Hunt, The disputation of Peter of Cornwall against Symon the Jew. 143–56.
- (*j*) N. D. Hurnard, Magna carta, clause 34. 157–79.
- (*k*) D. A. P. Callus, The *Summa theologiae* of Robert Grosseteste. 180–208.
- (*l*) B. Smalley, The *Quaestiones* of Simon of Hinton. 209–22.
- (*m*) R. F. Treharne, The mise of Amiens, 23 January 1264. 223–39.
- (*n*) N. Denholm-Young, The tournament in the 13th century. 240–68.
- (*o*) D. L. Douie, Archbishop Pecham's sermons and collations. 269–82.
- (*p*) V. H. Galbraith, The death of a champion (1287). 283–95.
- (*q*) J. G. Edwards, The treason of Thomas Turberville, 1295. 296–309.
- (*r*) N. B. Lewis, The English forces in Flanders, August–November 1297. 310–18.
- (*s*) H. Rothwell, Edward I and the struggle for the charters, 1297–1305. 319–32.
- (*t*) B. Wilkinson, The negotiations preceding the 'treaty' of Leake, August 1318. 333–53.
- (*u*) G. Mathew, Ideals of knighthood in late fourteenth-century England. 354–62.
- (*v*) W. A. Pantin, Two treaties of Uthred of Boldon on the monastic life. 363–85.
- (*w*) E. F. Jacob, Chichele and Canterbury. 386–404.
- (*x*) K. B. McFarlane, At the death-bed of Cardinal Beaufort. 405–28.
- (*y*) C. A. J. Armstrong, Some examples of the distribution and speed of news at the time of the Wars of the Roses. 429–54.
- (*z*) K. Major, Fifteenth-century presentation deeds in the Lincoln diocesan record office. 455–64.
- (*aa*) R. A. B. Mynors, Some book-markers at Peterhouse. 465–68.
- (*bb*) M. Tyson, A bibliography of the published writings of F. M. Powicke. 469–91.

1451 (Salter). OXFORD ESSAYS IN MEDIEVAL HISTORY presented to
Herbert E. Salter. Oxf. 1934.

- (*a*) J. E. A. Jolliffe, The era of the folk in English history. 1–32.
- (*b*) N. Denholm-Young, The cursus in England. 68–103.
- (*c*) M. D. Lobel, The ecclesiastical banleuca in England. 122–40.
- (*d*) J. G. Edwards, The *plena potestas* of English parliamentary representatives. 141–54.
- (*e*) A. M. Leys, The forfeiture of the lands of the Templars in England. 155–63.
- (*f*) M. V. Clarke, The origin of impeachment. 164–89.

(*g*) J. N. L. Myres, Notes on the history of Butley priory, Suffolk. 190–206.
(*h*) B. J. H. Rowe, The *Grand conseil* under the Duke of Bedford, 1422–35. 207–34.
(*i*) T. A. M. Bishop, A list of the published writings of Herbert E. Salter. 242–5.

1452 (Saxl). FRITZ SAXL, 1890–1948. Knowledge and learning: a volume of memorial essays. Ed. by D. J. Gordon. Lond. and Edin. 1957.

(*a*) M. Deanesly, The implications of the term *sapiens* as applied to Gildas. 53–76.
(*b*) F. Wormald, The Sherborne chartulary. 101–19.
(*c*) F. M. Powicke, King Edward I in fact and fiction. 120–35.
(*d*) V. H. Galbraith, The chronicle of Henry Knighton. 136–48.
(*e*) R. A. B. Mynors, The Latin classics known to Boston of Bury. 199–217.
(*f*) R. Weiss, Humphrey duke of Gloucester and Tito Livio Frulovisi. 218–27.

1453 (D. M. Stenton). A MEDIEVAL MISCELLANY FOR DORIS MARY STENTON. General editors: Patricia M. Barnes and C. F. Slade. Pipe Roll Soc. N.S. xxxvi (1960). Lond. 1962.

The contributors edited 'hitherto unpublished documents within the field of Lady Stenton's interests'.

(*a*) Patricia M. Barnes, The Anstey Case. 1–24.
(*b*) G. Barraclough, Some charters of the earls of Chester. 25–44.
(*c*) C. N. L. Brooke, Episcopal charters for Wix priory. 45–64.
(*d*) R. Allen Brown, Early charters of Sibton abbey, Suffolk. 65–76.
(*e*) F. A. Cazel, Jnr., Norman and Wessex charters of the Roumare family. 77–88.
(*f*) Pierre Chaplais, The original charters of Herbert and Gervase abbots of Westminster (1121–1157). 89–110.
(*g*) R. R. Darlington, Winchcombe annals 1049–1181. 111–38.
(*h*) R. H. C. Davis, Treaty between William earl of Gloucester and Roger earl of Hereford. 139–46.
(*i*) Barbara Dodwell, Some charters relating to the honour of Bacton. 147–66.
(*j*) J. C. Holt, Willoughby deeds. 167–88.
(*k*) Robert S. Hoyt, A pre-Domesday Kentish assessment list. 189–202.
(*l*) Kathleen Major, Blyborough charters. 203–20.
(*m*) Dorothy M. Owen, Some Revesby charters of the Soke of Bolingbroke. 221–34.
(*n*) C. F. Slade, Whitley deeds of the twelfth century. 235–46.
(*o*) David Walker, Some charters relating to St. Peter's abbey, Gloucester. 247–68.
(*p*) A list of the published writings of Doris Mary Stenton. 269–74.

1454 (Sir Frank Stenton). ANGLO-SAXON COINS: Historical studies presented to Sir Frank Stenton on the occasion of his 80th birthday. Ed. by R. H. Michael Dolley. Lond. 1961.

(*a*) J. P. C. Kent, From Roman Britain to Saxon England. 1–22.
(*b*) P. D. Whitting, The Byzantine empire and the coinage of the Anglo-Saxons. 23–38.
(*c*) C. E. Blunt, The coinage of Offa. 39–62.
(*d*) R. H. M. Dolley and K. Skaare, The coinage of Æthelwulf, king of West Saxons, 839–858. 63–76.
(*e*) R. H. M. Dolley and C. E. Blunt, The chronology of the coins of Alfred the Great. 77–95.
(*f*) C. S. S. Lyon and B. H. I. H. Stewart, The Northumbrian Viking coins in the Cuerdale hoard. 96–121.
(*g*) H. R. Loyn, Boroughs and mints 900–1066. 122–35.
(*h*) R. H. M. Dolley and D. M. Metcalfe, The reform of English coinage under Edgar. 136–68.
(*i*) G. van der Meer, Some corrections to and comments on B. E. Hildebrand's Catalogue of Anglo-Saxon coins, 169–87.

(*j*) D. Whitelock, The numismatic interest of an Old English version of the Legend of the Seven Sleepers. 188–94.

(*k*) V. J. Butler, The metrology of the late Anglo-Saxon penny: the reigns of Aethelraed II and Cnut. 195–214.

(*l*) R. H. M. Dolley and F. E. Jones, A new suggestion concerning the so-called Martelets in the arms of St. Edward. 215–26.

(*m*) Joan S. Martin, Some remarks on xviii century numismatic manuscripts and numismatics. 227–40.

(*n*) R. H. M. Dolley and J. Ingold, Viking age coin hoards from Ireland and their relevance to Anglo-Saxon studies. 241–65.

(*o*) Philip Grierson, Sterling. 266–83.

1455 (Tait). HISTORICAL ESSAYS IN HONOUR OF JAMES TAIT. Ed. by J. G. Edwards, V. H. Galbraith, and E. F. Jacob. Manchester. 1933.

(*a*) D. Atkinson, Classis britannica. 1–11.

(*b*) H. M. Cam, Early groups of hundreds. 13–26.

(*c*) M. V. Clarke, Committees of estates and the deposition of Edward II. 27–45.

(*d*) D. C. Douglas, Odo, Lanfranc and the Domesday survey. 47–57.

(*e*) J. G. Edwards, The *Itinerarium Regis Ricardi* and the *Estoire de la Guerre Sainte*. 59–77.

(*f*) E. Ekwall, Names of trades in English place-names. 79–89.

(*g*) E. F. Jacob, The building of All Souls college, 1438–43. 121–43.

(*h*) C. Johnson, Some charters of Henry I. 137–42.

(*i*) H. Johnstone, The Queen's exchequer under the three Edwards. 143–53.

(*j*) J. E. A. Jolliffe, The origin of the hundred in Kent. 155–68.

(*k*) A. Jones, Basingwerk abbey. 169–78.

(*l*) A. G. Little, A royal inquiry into property held by the Mendicant Friars in England in 1349 and 1350. 179–88.

(*m*) A. Mawer, The study of field-names in relation to place-names. 189–200.

(*n*) W. A. Pantin, English monastic letter-books. 201–22.

(*o*) A. F. Pollard, The making of Sir Thomas More's Richard III. 223–38.

(*p*) A. L. Poole, Outlawry as a punishment of criminous clerks. 239–46.

(*q*) F. M. Powicke, Loretta, Countess of Leicester. 247–72.

(*r*) C. W. Previté-Orton, A manuscript of the Chronicon patriarcharum Aquileiensium. 273–81.

(*s*) A. E. Prince, The indenture system under Edward III. 283–97.

(*t*) H. E. Salter, An Oxford mural mansion. 299–303.

(*u*) A. E. Stamp, Some notes on the court and chancery of Henry III. 305–11.

(*v*) F. M. Stenton, Medeshamstede and its colonies. 313–26.

(*w*) A. H. Thompson, Some letters from the register of William Zouche, Archbishop of York. 327–43.

(*x*) G. H. Tupling, Markets and fairs in medieval Lancashire. 345–56.

(*y*) G. J. Turner, Bookland and folkland. 357–86.

(*z*) W. T. Waugh, Joan of Arc in English sources of the 15th century. 387–98.

(*aa*) M. Weinbaum, Das Londoner iter von 1341. 399–404.

(*bb*) B. Wilkinson, The coronation oath of Edward II. 405–16.

(*cc*) J. F. Willard, Taxation boroughs and parliamentary boroughs, 1294–1336. 417–35.

(*dd*) V. H. Galbraith and G. R. Galbraith. A select bibliography of the historical writings of James Tait. 437–49.

1456 (Thompson). ADDRESS PRESENTED TO ALEXANDER HAMILTON THOMPSON, with a bibliography of his writings. Privately printed. Oxf. 1948.

Not a series of essays but a tribute to a prolific scholar of wide interests, centring on medieval ecclesiastical and architectural history. His bibliography included 413 items in 1948.

1457 (Todd). ESSAYS IN BRITISH AND IRISH HISTORY, in honour of James Eadie Todd. Lond. 1949.

(a) H. A. Cronne, The royal forest in the reign of Henry I. 1–23.
(b) I. Megaw, The ecclesiastical policy of Stephen, 1135–39: a reinterpretation. 24–45.
(c) R. R. Betts, Richard Fitz Ralph, archbishop of Armagh, and the doctrine of dominion. 46–60.

1458 (Tout). ESSAYS IN MEDIEVAL HISTORY PRESENTED TO THOMAS FREDERICK TOUT. Ed. by A. G. Little and F. M. Powicke. Manchester. 1925.

(a) M. Deanesly, The familia at Christchurch, Canterbury, 597–832. 1–13.
(b) F. M. Stenton, The south-western element in the Old English Chronicle. 15–24.
(c) F. Liebermann, Nennius the author of the 'Historia Brittonum'. 25–44.
(d) H. W. C. Davis, London lands and liberties of St. Paul's, 1066–1135. 45–59.
(e) R. L. Poole, The early lives of Robert Pullen and Nicholas Breakspear, with notes on other Englishmen at the Papal Court about the middle of the 12th century. 61–70.
(f) C. H. Haskins, Henry II as a patron of literature. 71–7.
(g) J. Tait, Liber Burgus. 79–97.
(h) Ch. Petit-Dutaillis, Querimoniae Normannorum. 99–118.
(i) F. M. Powicke, Some observations on the Baronial Council (1258–1260) and the Provisions of Westminster. 119–34.
(j) C. Johnson, The keeper of papal bulls (Henry III). 135–8.
(k) A. Sandys, The financial and administrative importance of the London Temple in the 13th century. 147–62.
(l) C. Bémont, Le statut 'De justiciis assignatis quod vocatur Rageman'. 163–70.
(m) H. Johnstone, Archbishop Pecham and the Council of Lambeth of 1281. 171–88.
(n) P. Vinogradoff, Ralph of Hengham as Chief Justice of the common pleas (Edw. I). 189–96.
(o) J. G. Edwards, The personnel of the commons in parliament under Edward I and Edward II. 197–214.
(p) J. F. Willard, The memoranda rolls and the remembrancers, 1282–1350. 215–29.
(q) V. H. Galbraith, The Tower as an exchequer record office in the reign of Edward II. 231–47.
(r) A. G. Little, The constitution of provincial chapters in the Minorite order. 249–67.
(s) R. Dunlop, Some notes on Barbour's 'Bruce', Books xiv–xvi and xviii. 277–90.
(t) D. M. Broome, Exchequer migrations to York in the 13th and 14th centuries. 291–300.
(u) E. Déprez, La conférence d'Avignon (1344). L'arbitrage pontifical entre la France et l'Angleterre. 301–20.
(v) M. Sharp (née Tout), The administrative chancery of the Black Prince before 1362. 321–33.
(w) C. G. Crump, What became of Robert Rag, or some chancery blunders (Edw. III). 335–47.
(x) W. T. Waugh, The administration of Normandy, 1420–22. 349–59.
(y) F. M. G. Hingham (née Evans), A note on the pre-Tudor secretary. 361–6.
(z) M. Tout (née Johnstone), A list of the published writings of T. F. Tout. 379–97.
The list of Tout's published writings is completed for the years 1925 to 1929 in *History* xiv (1929–30), 323–4.

1459 (Wilkinson). ESSAYS IN MEDIEVAL HISTORY PRESENTED TO BERTIE WILKINSON. Ed. by T. A. Sandquist and M. R. Powicke. Toronto. 1969.

(a) J. G. Rowe, Hadrian IV, the Byzantine empire, and the Latin orient. 3–16.
(b) G. Constable, An unpublished letter by Abbot Hugh II of Reading concerning Archbishop Hubert Walter. 17–31.

(c) H. Mackinnon, William de Montibus: A medieval teacher. 32–45.
(d) (the late) R. F. Treharne, The constitutional problem in thirteenth century England. 46–78.
(e) C. R. Cheney, Notes on the making of the Dunstable Annals. 79–98.
(f) J. Brückmann, The ordines of the third recension of the medieval English coronation order. 99–115.
(g) J. J. Saunders, Matthew Paris and the Mongols. 116–32.
(h) P. H. Brieger, A statue of Henry of Almain. 133–38.
(i) J. R. O'Donnell, The commentary of Giles of Rome on the *Rhetoric* of Aristotle. 139–56.
(j) B. Lyon, What made a medieval king constitutional? 157–75.
(k) V. H. Galbraith, Statutes of Edward I: Huntington Library MS. H. M. 25782. 176–91.
(l) W. A. Pantin, The letters of John Mason: a fourteenth-century formulary from St. Augustine's, Canterbury. 192–219.
(m) F. D. Blackley, Isabella and the Bishop of Exeter. 220–35.
(n) N. B. Lewis, The summons of the English feudal levy: 5 April 1327. 236–49.
(o) E. B. Fryde, Parliament and the French war, 1336–40. 250–69.
(p) L. J. Daly, Some notes on Walter Burley's commentary on the *Politics*. 270–81.
(q) J. A. Raftis, The structure of commutation in a fourteenth-century village. 282–300.
(r) A. R. Myers, The wealth of Richard Lyons. 301–29.
(s) T. A. Sandquist, The holy oil of St. Thomas of Canterbury. 330–44.
(t) E. F. Jacob, The Canterbury convocation of 1406. 345–53.
(u) B. Tierney, Hermeneutics and history: the problem of Haec sancta. 354–70.
(v) M. R. Powicke, Lancastrian captains. 371–82.
(w) Sir J. G. Edwards, The Huntingdonshire parliamentary election of 1450. 383–95.
(x) Moses Tyson, Bibliography of the published works of Bertie Wilkinson. 396–401.

2. Collected Works Analysed

1460 BIRLEY (ERIC). Roman Britain and the Roman army: collected papers. Kendal. 1953. (No. 2075).

1461 CAM (HELEN M.). Law-finders and law-makers in medieval England. Lond. 1962.

Introduction: the rule of law in English history. 11–21.

(a) The evolution of the medieval English franchise (*Speculum*, xxxii (1957), 427–42). 22–43.
(b) The quality of English feudalism. 44–58.
(c) The 'private' hundred in England before the Norman Conquest (Jenkinson Studies, No. 1441). 59–70.
(d) The community of the vill (Graham, *Studies*, No. 1437). 71–84.
(e) The law-courts of medieval London (*In memoriam Werner Näf*, Berne, 1960–1). 85–94.
(f) Cases of novel disseisin in the eyre of London 1321 (*Études d'histoire du droit privé offertes à Pierre Petot*, Paris, 1959). 95–105.
(g) From witness of the shire to full parliament (*T.R.H.S.* 4th Ser. xxvi (1944), 13–35). 106–31.
(h) The legislators of medieval England (*P.B.A.* xxi (1945), 127–50). 132–58.
(i) The theory and practice of representation in medieval England (*History*, N.S. xxviii (1931), 11–26). 159–75.
(j) The study of English medieval history today. 176–87.
(k) Stubbs seventy years after (*Cambr. Hist. Jour.* ix (1948), 129–47). 188–211.
(l) Maitland—the historian's historian (Introd. to *Selected hist. essays F. W. Maitland*, No. 1484). 212–34.

1462   CAM (HELEN M.). Liberties and communities in medieval England. Collected studies in local administration and topography. Cambr. 1933. Reprinted, 1963.

   Introd. In defence of the study of local history. ix.
   (a) The origin of the borough of Cambridge: a consideration of Professor Carl Stephenson's theories (*Cambr. Antiq. Soc. Communications*, xxxv (1935), 33–53). 1–18.
   (b) The early burgesses of Cambridge in relation to the surrounding countryside (*Wirtschaft und Kultur: Alfons Dopsch*, 1938) (No. 1434), 19–26.
   (c) Cambridgeshire sheriffs in the thirteenth century (*Cambr. Antiq. Soc. Communications*, xxv (1924). 27–48.
   (d) Suitors and scabini (*Speculum*, x (1935), 189–200). 49–63.
   (e) Manerium cum hundredo: the hundred and the hundredal manor (*E.H.R.* xlvii (1932), 353–76). 64–90.
   (f) Early groups of hundreds (*Tait essays*, No. 1455). 91–106.
   (g) The hundred outside the north gate of Oxford (*Oxoniensia*, i (1936), 113–28). 107–23.
   (h) Pedigree of villeins and freemen in the thirteenth century (*Genealogists' Magazine*, 1933). 124–35.
   (i) The marshalsy of Eyre (*Cambr. Hist. Jour.* i (1924), 126–37). 136–49.
   (j) The general eyres of 1329–30 (*E.H.R.* xxxix (1924), 241–52). 150–62.
   (k) Some early inquests before custodes pacis (*E.H.R.* xl (1925), 411–19). 163–72.
   (l) The Quo warranto proceedings under Edward I (*History*, xi (1926), 143–48). 173–82.
   (m) The king's government as administered by the greater abbots of East Anglia (*Cambr. Antiq. Soc. Communications*, xxix, 1928). 183–204.
   (n) The decline and fall of English feudalism (*History*, xxv (1940), 216–33). 205–22.
   (o) The relation of English members of parliament to their constituencies in the fourteenth century (*L'organisation corporative du moyen âge: études présentées*, 1939). 223–35.
   (p) The community of the shire and the payment of its representatives in parliament (*Journées de droit, Dijon*, June 1939). 236–50.

1463   CHADWICK (N. K.), ed. Nos. 2122, 2123, 2665.

1464   CLARKE (MAUDE V.). Fourteenth century studies. Ed. by L. S. Sutherland and M. McKisack. Oxf. 1937.

   (a) Irish parliaments in the reign of Edward II (*T.R.H.S.* 4th Ser. ix (1926), 29–62). 1–35.
   (b) The Lancastrian faction and the wonderful parliament (Read at International Congress at Oslo, 1928). 36–52.
   (c) The deposition of Richard II, by M. V. Clarke and Vivian H. Galbraith (*B.J.R.L.* xiv (1930), 125–81). 53–98.
   (d) The Kirkstall chronicle, 1355–1400, by M. V. Clarke and N. Denholm-Young (*B.J.R.L.* xv (1931), 100–37). 99–114.
   (e) Forfeitures and treason in 1388 (*T.R.H.S.* 4th Ser. xiv (1931), 65–94). 115–45.
   (f) William of Windsor in Ireland, 1369–76 (*Royal Irish Acad. Procs.* Sect C. (1932)). 146–241.
   (g) The origin of impeachment (*Salter essays*, No. 1451). 242–71.
   (h) The Wilton diptych (*Burlington Mag.* lviii (1931), 283–94). 272–92.
   (i) Henry Knighton and the library catalogue of Leicester Abbey (*E.H.R.* xlv (1930), 103–7). 293–9.
   (j) Bibliography. 300–1.

1465   DARBY (HENRY C.), ed. An historical geography of England before 1800: fourteen studies. Cambr. 1936.

   (a) E. G. Bowen, Introductory background: prehistoric south Britain. 1–29.
   (b) E. W. Gilbert, The human geography of Roman Britain. 30–87.

(c) S. W. Wooldridge, The Anglo-Saxon settlement. 88–132.
(d) E. Ekwall, The Scandinavian settlement. 133–64.
(e) H. C. Darby, The economic geography of England A.D. 1000–1250. 165–229.
(f) R. A. Pelham, Fourteenth-century England. 230–65.
(g) D. T. Williams, Medieval foreign trade: western ports. 266–97.
(h) R. A. Pelham, Medieval foreign trade: eastern ports. 298–329.

1466 (Davis). HENRY WILLIAM CARLESS DAVIS, 1874–1928. A memoir by J. R. H. Weaver and a selection of his historical papers. Ed. by J. R. H. Weaver and Austin Lane Poole. Lond. 1933.

Part i: Memoir. 3–60.
Part ii: Historical Papers.
 (a) The study of history (Inaugural lecture as Regius Professor, 1925). 65–80.
 (b) The anarchy of Stephen's reign (*E.H.R.* xviii (1903), 630–41). 81–96.
 (c) England and Rome in the middle ages (*Church Quart. Rev.* lvi (1903), 118–42). 97–122.
 (d) The Canon Law in England (*Zeitschrift der Savigny-Stiftung für Rechtsgeschichte*, xxxiv (1913), Kanon. Abt. iii. 344–63). 123–43.
 (e and f) Two subjects in modern history. 144–202.
 (g) List of the principal writings of H. W. C. Davis. 203–9.

1467 DENHOLM-YOUNG (NOEL). Collected papers on medieval subjects. Oxf. 1946. New edn. with additional papers. Cardiff. 1969.

 (a) Richard de Bury (1287–1345) (*T.R.H.S.* 4th Ser. xx (1937), 135–68). 1–25.
 (b) The cursus in England (*Salter essays*, No. 1451). 26–55.
 (c) Feudal society in the thirteenth century: the knights (*History*, xxix (1944), 107–19). 56–67.
 (d) Who wrote 'Fleta'? (*E.H.R.* lviii (1943), 1–12). 68–79.
 (e) Matthew Cheker (*E.H.R.* lix (1944), 252–7). 80–5.
 (f) The Winchester–Hyde chronicle (*E.H.R.* xlix (1934), 85–93). 86–95.
 (g) Robert Carpenter and the provisions of Westminster (*E.H.R.* l (1935), 22–35). 96–110.
 (h) Documents of the barons' wars (*E.H.R.* xlviii (1933), 558–75). 111–29.
 (i) The paper constitution attributed to 1244 (*E.H.R.* lviii (1943), 401–23). 130–53.
 (j) Eudo Dapifer's honour of Walbrook (*E.H.R.* xlvi (1931), 623–9). 154–61.
 (k) Edward of Windsor and Bermondsey priory (*E.H.R.* xlviii (1933), 431–43). 162–74.
 (l) Reviews.

The new edition adds to the above the following articles:

 (m) Mappa Mundi of Richard of Haldingham at Hereford (*Speculum*, xxxii (1957), 307–14).
 (n) Tournament in the thirteenth century (*Powicke essays*, No. 1450).
 (o) Song of Carlaverock, the parliamentary rolls of arms, and the Galloway roll (*P.B.A.* xlvii (1961), 251–62).
 (p) Walter of Henley (*Medievalia et Humanistica*, xiv (1962), 61–68).
 (q) Authorship of *Vita Edwardi Secundi* (*E.H.R.* lxxi (1956) 189–211).
 (r) Merchants of Cahors (*Medievalia et Humanistica*, iv (1946), 37–44).

1468 ESSAYS IN ECONOMIC HISTORY. Reprints edited for the Economic History Society by E. M. Carus-Wilson. Vol. i. Lond. 1954. Vols. ii and iii. 1962.

Vol. i:
 (a) M. M. Postan, The rise of a money economy (*Econ. H. R.* xiv (1944), 2). 1–12.
 (b) Lord Beveridge, The yield and price of corn in the middle ages (*Econ. H. R.* (1927), 2, with a postscript, July 1953). 13–25.

(*c*) T. A. M. Bishop, Assarting and the growth of the open fields (*Econ. H. R.* vi (1935), 1). 26–40.

(*d*) E. M. Carus-Wilson, An industrial revolution of the 13th century (*Econ. H. R.* xi (1941), with a postscript, 1954). 41–60.

(*e*) M. M. Postan, Credit in medieval trade (*Econ. H. R.* i (1928), 2). 61–87.

Vol. ii:

(*f*) T. A. M. Bishop, The Norman settlement of Yorkshire. 1–11. (No. 1450).

(*g*) J. S. Drew, Manorial accounts of St. Swithun's priory. 12–30. (No. 5815).

(*h*) E. A. Kosminsky, Services and money rents in the thirteenth century. 31–48. (No. 4971).

(*i*) H. S. Lucas, The great European famine of 1315, 1316, and 1317. 49–72. (No. 5003).

(*j*) R. H. Hilton, Peasants' movements in England before 1381. 73–90. (No. 4965).

(*k*) Nora Ritchie (née Kenyon), Labour conditions in Essex in the reign of Richard II. 91–111. (No. 4149).

(*l*) F. G. Davenport, The decay of villeinage in East Anglia. 112–24. (No. 4959).

(*m*) M. K. James, The fluctuations of the Anglo-Gascon trade during the fourteenth century. 125–50. (No. 5395).

(*n*) E. M. Carus-Wilson, Evidences of industrial growth on some fifteenth century manors. 151–67. (No. 4953).

(*o*) E. H. Phelps-Brown and S. V. Hopkins, Seven centuries of building wages. 168–78. (No. 5495).

(*p*) E. H. Phelps-Brown and S. V. Hopkins, Seven centuries of prices of consumables, compared with builders' wages. 179–96. (No. 5495).

(The other articles in volumes ii and iii are post-medieval.)

1469 FINANCE AND TRADE UNDER EDWARD III. By the members of the history school. Ed. by George Unwin. Pubns. Univ. of Manchester, Historical Series, no. 32. Manchester. 1918.*

(*a*) G. Unwin, Social evolution in mediaeval London. 1–18.

(*b*) G. Unwin, London tradesmen and their creditors. 19–34.

(*c*) M. Curtis, The London lay subsidy of 1332. 35–92.

(*d*) E. Russell, The societies of the Bardi and the Peruzzi and their dealings with Edward III, 1327–1345. 93–135.

(*e*) F. R. Barnes, The taxation of wool, 1327–1348. 137–77.

(*f*) G. Unwin, The estate of merchants, 1336–1365. 179–255.

(*g*) F. Sargeant, The wine trade with Gascony. 257–311.

(*h*) D. Greaves, Calais under Edward III. 313–50.

1470 FINBERG (HERBERT P. R.). Lucerna: studies of some problems in the early history of England. Lond. 1964.

(*a*) Continuity or cataclysm. 1–20. (Continuity between Roman Britain and Saxon England.)

(*b*) Roman and Saxon Withington (*Leicester Occasional Papers*, No. 8 (1955)) 21–65. (An example of continuity.)

(*c*) Mercians and Welsh. 66–82.

(*d*) Ynyswitrin. 83–94. (Not identifiable with Glastonbury.)

(*e*) Sherborne, Glastonbury, and the expansion of Wessex (*T.R.H.S.* 5th Ser. iii (1953), 101–24). (Expansion of Wessex.) 95–115.

(*f*) Hyple's Old Land (*Leicester Occasional Papers*, No. 2 (1953)). 116–30. (Celtic survivals in Devon.)

(*g*) The churls of Hurstbourne. 131–43. (An examination of Maitland's argument from a charter.)

(*h*) Charltons and Carltens. 144–160. (Places occupied by groups of ceorls, not independent communities.)

(*i*) The making of a boundary (*Devonshire studies*, ed. Hoskins and Finberg (1952)). 161–80. (Boundary between Devon and Cornwall.)

(*j*) The Domesday plough-team (*E.H.R.* lxv (1951), 67–71). 181–5. (Comment on Lennard's article in *E.H.R.* lx (1945), 217–33.)

(*k*) Childe's tomb (*Devonshire Studies*), 186–203. (Centres on Tavistock Abbey.)

(*l*) Uffculme (*Devonshire Studies*), 204–21. (Possession of the manor up to Stephen's reign.)

1471   GRAHAM (ROSE). English ecclesiastical studies. Lond. 1929.

(*a*) The papal schism of 1378 and the English province of the order of Cluny (*E.H.R.* xxxviii (1923), 481–95). 46–61.

(*b*) The English province of the order of Cluny in the 15th century (*T.R.H.S.* 4th Ser. vii (1924), 98–130). 62–90.

(*c*) The prioyr of La Charité-sur-Loire and the monastery of Bermondsey (*Jour. Brit. Archaeol. Assoc.* N.S. xxxii (1926), 157–91). 91–124.

(*d*) The intellectual influence of English monasticism between the 10th and the 12th centuries (*T.R.H.S.* N.S. xvii (1903), 23–65). 146–87.

(*e*) The monastery of Battle (Wm. I) (*Jour. Brit. Archaeol. Assoc.* N.S. xxx (1924), 55–75). 188–208.

(*f*) The order of Grandmont and its houses in England (*Archaeol.* lxxv, 2nd Ser. xxv (1926), 159–88). 209–46.

(*g*) The finance of Malton priory, 1244–57 (*T.R.H.S.* N.S. xviii (1904), 131–56). 247–70.

(*h*) The taxation of Pope Nicholas IV (*E.H.R.* xxiii (1908), 434–54). 271–301.

(*i*) A petition to Boniface VIII from the clergy of the province of Canterbury in 1297 (*E.H.R.* xxxvii (1922), 35–46). 302–16.

(*j*) An ecclesiastical tenth for national defence in 1298 (*E.H.R.* xxxiv (1919), 200–5). 317–23.

(*k*) An interdict on Dover, 1298–99 (*Archaeol. Jour.* lxxviii (1921), 227–32). 324–9.

(*l*) The metropolitical visitation of the diocese of Worcester by Archbishop Winchelsey in 1301 (*T.R.H.S.* 4th Ser. ii (1919), 59–93). 330–59.

1472   HISTORICAL ESSAYS first published in 1902 in commemoration of the jubilee of the Owens college, Manchester. Ed. by T. F. Tout and James Tait. Pubns. of the Univ. of Manchester, Historical Series, No. vi. Lond. etc. 1902. Reprinted, with an index, Manchester. 1907.

(*a*) M. Tout (Mrs. T. F.), The legend of St. Ursula and the eleven thousand virgins. 17–56.

(*b*) T. F. Tout, Wales and the March during the barons' wars, 1258–67. 76–136.

(*c*) W. E. Rhodes, The Italian bankers in England and their loans to Edward I and Edward II. 137–68.

(*d*) J. Tait, Did Richard II murder the Duke of Gloucester? 193–216.

(*e*) H. W. Clemesha, The borough of Preston and its gild merchant. 217–43.

1473   JACOB (ERNEST F.). Essays in the conciliar epoch. Manchester. 1943. 2nd edn. with two additional chapters. 1953.

The original papers have been thoroughly revised for these editions of essays. Those dealing directly with England are:

(*a*) Englishmen and the general councils of the 15th century (*History*, xxiv (1939–40), 206–19). 44–56.

(*b*) English conciliar activity, 1395–1418 (*B.J.R.L.* xv (1931), 358–94). 57–84.

(*c*) Ockham as a political thinker (*B.J.R.L.* xx (1936), 332–53). 85–105.

(*d*) Sir John Fortescue and the law of nature (*B.J.R.L.* xviii (1934), 359–76). 106–20.

(*e*) Verborum florida venustas (*B.J.R.L.* xvii (1933), 264–90). 185–206.

(*f*) English university clerks in the later middle ages. 207–39:
   1. The problem of maintenance (*B.J.R.L.* xxix (1946), 304–25). 207–22.
   2. Petitions for benefices during the Great Schism (*T.R.H.S.* 4th Ser. xxvii (1945), 41–59). 223–39.
(*g*) Notes and comments on chapters i–x (*a, b, c, d*, above). 240–52.

1474 JACOB (ERNEST F.). Essays in later medieval history. Manchester and N.Y. 1968.

(*a*) Reynold Pecock, bishop of Chichester (*P.B.A.* xxxvii (1951), 121–53). 1–34.
(*b*) Archbishop John Stafford (*T.R.H.S.* 5th Ser. xii (1962), 1–23). 35–57.
(*c*) To and from the Court of Rome in the early fifteenth century (*Studies in French language and medieval literature presented to M. K. Pope* (Manchester, 1939), 161–81). 58–78.
(*d*) One of Swan's cases: the disputed election at Fountains Abbey, 1410–1416 (Graham, *Essays* (No. 1437), 78–97). 79–97.
(*e*) The conciliar movement in recent study (*B.I.R.L.* xli (1958), 26–53). 98–123.
(*f*) Theory and fact in the general councils of the fifteenth century (*Studies in Church Hist.* i (1964), 80–97). 124–40.
(*g*) Huizinga and the autumn of the middle ages (not previously printed). 141–53.
(*h*) Founders and foundations in the later middle ages (*B.I.H.R.* xxxv (1962), 29–46). 154–74.
(*i*) John of Roquetaillade (a Spiritual Franciscan interested in chemistry and the occult, died 1362) (*B.J.R.L.* xxxix (1956), 75–96). 175–94.
(*j*) The Book of St. Albans (*B.J.R.L.* xxviii (1944), 99–118). 195–213.

1475 JOHN (ERIC). Orbis Britanniae and other studies. Leicester. 1966.

(*a*) Orbis Britanniae and the Anglo-Saxon kings. 1–63.
(*b*) Folkland reconsidered. 64–127.
(*c*) English feudalism and the structure of Anglo-Saxon society (*B.J.R.L.* xlvi (1963), 14–41). 128–53.
(*d*) The king and the monks in the tenth century reformation (*B.J.R.L.* xlii (1959), 61–87). 154–80.
(*e*) Some Latin charters of the tenth century reformation (*Rev. Bénédictine*, lxx (1960), 333–59). 181–209.
(*f*) Some alleged charters of King Edgar for Ely. 210–33.
(*g*) St. Oswald and the church of Worcester (*J.E.H.* ix (1958), 159–72). 234–48.
(*h*) The beginning of the Benedictine reform in England (*Rev. Bénédictine*, lxxiii (1963), 74–88). 249–64.
(*i*) Notes on some texts:
   (i) Bede's use of 'facultas'. 265–71.
   (ii) The Newminster charter. 271–5.
   (iii) King Edgar's coronation. 276–89.
   (iv) The 'Vita Oswaldi'. 290–1.
   (v) The battle of Maldon. 292–3.

1476 KENDRICK (THOMAS D.). British antiquity. Lond. 1950.

(*a*) The British history in the middle ages. 1–17.
(*b*) John Rous and William of Worcester. 18–33.
(*c*) The Tudor cult of the British history. 34–44.
(*d*) John Leland. 45–64.
(*e*) The medieval tradition. 65–77.
(*f*) The battle over the British history. 78–98.
(*g*) The eclipse of the British history. 99–133.
(*h*) Britannia, 134–67.

1477 KNOWLES (DOM DAVID). The historian and character and other essays by Dom David Knowles, collected and presented to him by his friends, pupils and colleagues. . . . Cambr. 1963.

Curriculum Vitae by W. A. Pantin. xvii–xxviii.

(*a*) The historian and character (Inaugural lecture, 1954). 1–15.
(*b*) The humanism of the twelfth century (*Studies*, xxx (1941), 43–58). 16–30.
(*c*) Saint Bernard of Clairvaux: 1090–1153 (*Dublin Rev.* ccxxvii (1953), 104–21). 31–49.
(*d*) Cistercians and Cluniacs: the controversy between St. Bernard and Peter the Venerable (Friends of Dr. Williams's Library, 9th Lecture, Lond. 1955). 50–75.
(*e*) The case of St. William of York (*Cambr. Hist. Jour.* v (1936), 162–77, and 212–14). 76–97.
(*f*) Archbishop Thomas Becket: a character study (*P.B.A.* xxxv (1949), 177–205). 98–128.
(*g*) The censured opinions of Uthred of Boldon (*P.B.A.* xxxvii (1951), 305–42). 129–70.
(*h*) The last abbot of Wigmore (Graham, *Essays*, No. 1437). 171–8.
(*i*) The monastic buildings of England. 179–212.
(*j*) Jean Mabillon (*J.E.H.* x (1959), 153–73). 213–39.
(*k*) Cardinal Gasquet as an historian (Creighton lecture, 1956). 240–63.
(*l*) Edward Cuthbert Butler: 1858–1934 (*Downside Rev.* lii (1934), 347–465). 264–362.
(*m*) A bibliography of the writings of Dom David Knowles: 1919–1962. 363–73.

1478 LAPSLEY (GAILLARD T.). Crown, community and parliament in the later middle ages: studies in English constitutional history. Ed. by Helen M. Cam and Geoffrey Barraclough. Studies in medieval history, vi. Oxf. 1951.

(*a*) Some recent advance in English constitutional history (*Cambr. Hist. Jour.* v (1936), 119–46). 1–33.
(*b*) John de Warenne and the *Quo warranto* proceedings in 1279 (ibid. ii (1927), 110–32). 35–62.
(*c*) Buzones (*E.H.R.* xlvii (1932), 177–93, 545–67). 63–110.
(*d*) Knights of the shire in the parliaments of Edward II (ibid. xxxiv (1919), 25–42, 152–71). 111–52.
(*e*) The interpretation of the Statute of York (ibid. lvi (1941), 22–49, 411–46). 153–230.
(*f*) Archbishop Stratford and the parliamentary crisis of 1341 (ibid. xx (1915), 6–18, 193–215). 231–72.
(*g*) The parliamentary title of Henry IV (ibid. xliv (1934), 423–49, 577–606). 273–340.
(*h*) Richard II's 'Last Parliament' (ibid. liii (1938), 53–78). 341–73.
(*i*) The problem of the North (*A.H.R.* v (1900), 440–66). 375–405.

1479 LEGACY OF THE MIDDLE AGES. Ed. by C. G. Crump and E. F. Jacob. Oxf. 1927.

Seventeen essays on various facets of the Middle Ages by distinguished scholars. See Nos. 1310, 1488, and Lowe on p. 47.

1480 LEVETT (ADA E.). Studies in manorial history. Ed. by H. M. Cam, M. Coate, and L. S. Sutherland. Oxf. 1938.

(*a*) Inaugural lecture (1929). 1–20.
(*b*) Baronial councils and their relation to manorial courts (Mélanges . . . à F. Lot, 1925). 21–40.
(*c*) Financial organization of the manor (*Econ. H. R.* i (1927), 65–86). 41–68.
(*d*) Studies in the manorial organization of St. Albans abbey. 69–286.
(*e*) The accounts of St. Mary des Prés. 286–99.

Appendices:

1. Extracts from the Court Books (Halimote of Park 1237–52 and of Kingsbury 1240–49). 300–37.
2. Redditus et consuetudines de Codicote, 1332. 338–68.

Published writings of Professor Ada E. Levett.

1481   McILWAIN (CHARLES H.). Constitutionalism and the changing world: collected papers. N.Y. etc. 1939.

Reprints with some changes and additions.

(a) The historian's part in a changing world (*A.H.R.* xlii (1937), 207–24). 1–25.
(b) Due process of law in Magna Carta (*Columbia Law Rev.* Jan. 1914). 86–126.
(c) Magna carta and common law (in *Magna carta commemoration essays*, Royal Hist. Soc. 1917). 127–77.
(d) The tenure of English judges (*Amer. Pol. Sci. Rev.* vii (1913), 217–29). 294–307.

1482   MAITLAND (FREDERIC W.). Collected papers. Ed. by H. A. L. Fisher. 3 vols. Cambr. 1911.

This edition comprises some 68 papers originally published in various law reviews, *E.H.R.*, and other journals. It includes much of Maitland's best and most original work. A full bibliography of Maitland's publications can be found in Arthur L. Smith's *Frederic William Maitland: two lectures and a bibliography* (Oxf. 1908), and in V. T. H. Delany's *Frederic William Maitland Reader* (N.Y. 1957), pp. 235–42. Some of Maitland's essays have been reprinted in Helen M. Cam's *Selected Historical Essays of F. W. Maitland* (Cambr. 1957). Generous excerpts from various of Maitland's writings are given by Robert L. Schuyler in *Frederic William Maitland, historian: selections* (Berkeley and Los Angeles, 1960).

For biography of Maitland, consult Herbert A. L. Fisher, *Frederic William Maitland* (Cambr. 1910), and C. H. S. Fifoot, ed., *The letters of Frederic William Maitland* (Cambr. Univ. Press and Selden Soc. Supplementary Ser. i, Lond. and Cambr. (Mass.), 1965). For tributes to Maitland, see *Frederic William Maitland 1850–1906* (Selden Soc. Annual Lecture 1953: A memorial address by Henry A. Hollond (Lond. 1953); T. F. T. Plucknett, 'Maitland's view of law and history', *Law Quart. Rev.* lxvii (1951), 179–94; Robert L. Schuyler, 'The historical spirit incarnate: Frederic William Maitland', *A.H.R.* lvii (1952), 303–22; and Helen Cam (No. 1461). Other tributes are referred to in Delaney, op. cit. pp. 9–41; 187–208; 245–57. Henry E. Bell in *Maitland: a critical examination and assessment* (Lond. 1965) sets forth the revisions of Maitland's writings which more recent research seems to indicate. C. H. S. Fifoot, *Frederic W. Maitland: a biography* (Cambr. Mass. 1971).

Vol. i:

(a) A historical sketch of liberty and equality (Submitted as a dissertation for a fellowship at Trinity and privately printed in 1875). 1–161.
(b) The law of real property (*Westminster Rev.* No. 222 (1879), 162–73). 162–201.
(c) The law of Wales—the kindred and the blood feud (*Law Mag. and Rev.* 4th Ser. vi (1881), 344–67). 202–29.
(d) The criminal liability of the hundred (*Law Mag. and Rev.* 4th Ser. vii (1881–2), 367–80). 230–46.
(e) Mr. Herbert Spencer's theory of society (*Mind*, viii (1883), 354–71, 506–24). 247–303.
(f) The early history of malice aforethought. (*Law Mag. and Rev.* 4th Ser. viii (1882–3), 406–26). 304–28.
(g) The seisin of chattels (*Law Quart. Rev.* i (1885), 324–41). 329–57.
(h) The mystery of seisin (*Law Quart. Rev.* ii (1886), 481–96). 358–84.
(i) The deacon and the Jewess: or, apostasy at Common Law (*Law Quart. Rev.* ii (1886), 153–65). 385–406.

(*j*) The beatitude of seisin (*Law Quart. Rev.* iv (1888), 24–39, 286–99). 407–57.

(*k*) The suitors of the county court (*E.H.R.* ii (1888), 417–21). 458–66.

(*l*) The shallows and silences of real life (*The Reflector*, i (1888), 113–17). 467–79.

(*m*) Why the history of English law is not written (The Inaugural Lecture delivered in the Arts School at Cambridge on 13 October 1888). 480–97.

Vol. ii:

(*a*) The materials for English legal history (*Political Sci. Quart.* iv (1889), 496–518, 628–57). 1–60. Reprinted in No. 1246.

(*b*) Possession for year and day (*Law Quart. Rev.* v (1889), 253–64). 61–80.

(*c*) The introduction of English law into Ireland (*E.H.R.* iv (1889), 516–17). 81–3.

(*d*) The surnames of English villages (*The Archaeol. Rev.* iv (1889), 233–40). 84–95.

(*e*) Northumbrian tenures (12th–13th centuries) *E.H.R.* v (1890), 625–32). 96–109.

(*f*) The history of the Register of Original Writs (*Harvard Law Rev.* iii (1889), 97–115, 167–79, 212–25). 110–73.

(*g*) Remainders after conditional fees (*Law Quart. Rev.* vi (1890), 22–6). 174–81.

(*h*) The 'Praerogativa Regis' (*E.H.R.* vi (1891), 367–72). 182–9.

(*i*) A conveyancer in the thirteenth century (*Law Quart. Rev.* vii (1891), 63–9). 190–201.

(*j*) A new point on villain tenure (*Law Quart. Rev.* vii (1891), 174–5). 202–4.

(*k*) Frankalmoign in the twelfth and thirteenth centuries (*Law Quart. Rev.* vii (1891), 354–63). 205–22.

(*l*) Review of 'The Gild Merchant' (*Econ. Jour.* i (1891), 220–4). 223–31.

(*m*) Henry II and the criminous clerks (*E.H.R.* vii (1892), 224–34). 232–50.

(*n*) Tenures in Rousillon and Namur (*E.H.R.* vii (1892), 748–54). 251–65.

(*o*) Glanvill revised (*Harvard Law Rev.* vi (1892), 1–20). 266–89.

(*p*) The Peace of God and the Land–Peace (*E.H.R.* viii (1893), 328–31). 290–7. Review of L. Huberti, *Studien zur Rechtsgeschichte.*

(*q*) History from the Charter Roll (*E.H.R.* viii (1893), 726–33). 298–309.

(*r*) Taltarum's Case (*Law Quart Rev.* ix (1893), 1–2). 310–12.

(*s*) The survival of archaic communities. I. The Malmesbury Case. II. The Aston Case. (*Law Quart. Rev.* ix (1893), 36–50, 211–28). 313–65.

(*t*) The history of the Cambridgeshire Manor (*E.H.R.* ix (1894), 417–39). 366–402.

(*u*) The origin of uses and trusts (*Harvard Law Rev.* viii (1894), 127–37). 403–16.

(*v*) Outlines of English legal history 560–1600 (*Social England*, ed. by H. D. Traill, 1893). 417–96.

Vol. iii:

(*a*) The tribal system in Wales (*Econ. Jour.* v (1895), 589–94). 1–10. Review of Seebohm.

(*b*) The murder of Henry Clement (*E.H.R.* x (1895), 294–7). 11–16.

(*c*) Two chartularies of the Priory of St. Peter at Bath (*E.H.R.* x (1895), 558–60). 17–20. (Review.)

(*d*) The history of marriage, Jewish and Christian (*E.H.R.* x (1895), 755–9). 21–30.

(*e*) The origin of the borough (*E.H.R.* xi (1896), 13–19). 31–42.

(*f*) A song on the death of Simon de Montfort (*E.H.R.* xi (1896), 314–18). 43–9.

(*g*) Wyclif on English and Roman law (*Law Quart. Rev.* xii (1896), 76–8). 50–3.

(*h*) 'Execrabilis' in the Common Pleas (*Law Quart. Rev.* xii (1896), 174–80). 54–64.

(*i*) Canon Law (*Renton's Encyclopedia of the Laws of England* (1897)., ii. 354–9. 65–77. Cf. No. 6437.

(*j*) Records of the Honourable Society of Lincoln's Inn (*E.H.R.* xiii (1898), 576–8 and xv (1900), 170–1). 78–86.

(*k*) Magistri Vacarii Summa de Matrimonio (*Law Quart. Rev.* xiii (1897), 133–43, 270–87). 87–105.

(*l*) Landholding in mediaeval towns (*E.H.R.* xiv (1899), 137–41). 106–14. (Review of G. Des Marez, *Étude*).

(*m*) An unpublished 'Revocation' of Henry II (*E.H.R.* xiv (1899), 135–7). 115–18.

(*n*) Canon MacColl's New Convocation (*Fortnightly Rev.* lxxii (1899), 926–35). 119–36.

(*o*) Canon Law in England (*E.H.R.* xvi (1901), 35–45). 137–56 (A reply to Dr. MacColl.)

(p) Elizabethan gleanings (*E.H.R.* xv (1900), 120–4, 324–30, 530–32, 757–60). 157–209.
(q) The corporation sole (*Law Quart. Rev.* xvi (1900), 335–54). 210–43.
(r) The Crown as corporation (*Law Quart. Rev.* xvii (1901), 131–46). 244–70.
(s) The unincorporate body (Read to the Erasmus Club). 271–84.
(t) The body politic (Read to the Erasmus Club). 285–303.
(u) Moral personality and legal personality (The Sidgwick Lecture for 1903 delivered at Newnham College) (*Jour. Soc. Comparative Legis.* N.S. xiv (1905), 192–200). 304–20.
(v) Trust und Korporation (*Grünhuts Zeitschrift für das Privat- und Öffentliche Recht,* xxxii (1904), 1–76). 321–404.
(w) The teaching of history (*Essays on the Teaching of History,* ed. by W. A. J. Archbold. Cambr. 1901). 405–18.
(x) Law at universities (A paper read to the Cambridge Law Club. 1901). 419–31.
(y) A survey of the century (law) (*The Twentieth Century* (Jan. 1901), 164–9). 432–9.
(z) Lincolnshire court rolls and Yorkshire inquisitions (*E.H.R.* xviii (1903), 780–82). 440–6.
(aa) The laws of the Anglo-Saxons (*Quart. Rev.* cc (1904), 139–57). 447–73. Commentary Liebermann's *Gesetze* and other works.
(bb) The making of the German civil code. A Presidential Address delivered to the Social and Political Education League (*Independent Rev.* x (1906), 211–21). 474–88.
(cc) State trials of the reign of Edward I (*E.H.R.* xxi (1906), 783–6). 489–94. Review of Tout–Johnstone (No. 3519).
(dd) William Stubbs, Bishop of Oxford (*E.H.R.* xvi (1901), 417–26). 495–511.
(ee) Lord Acton (*The Cambr. Rev.* 16 Oct. 1902). 512–21.
(ff) Sir Leslie Stephen (*P.B.A.* (1903–4), 316–20). 522–30.
(gg) Henry Sidgwick (*Henry Sidgwick: A Memoir.* By A. S. and E. M. S. 324–31. Lond. 1906) (*Independent Rev.* ix (1906)). 531–40.
(hh) Mary Bateson (*The Athenaeum,* no. 4128 (8 Dec. 1906), p. 736). 541–3.

1483 MAITLAND (FREDERIC W.). Selected essays. Ed. by H. D. Hazeltine, G. Lapsley, and P. H. Winfield. Cambr. 1936.

(a) Introduction to *Memoranda de parliamento, 1305* (Rolls Ser.) (Abbreviated). 13–72.
(b) The corporation sole (*Collected Papers,* iii. 201–43). 73–103.
(c) The crown as corporation (*Collected Papers,* iii. 244–70). 104–27.
(d) Trust and corporation (*Collected Papers,* iii. 321–404). 144–222.
(e) Moral personality and legal personality (*Collected Papers,* iii. 304–20). 223–39.
(f) The body politic (*Collected Papers,* iii. 285–303). 240–56.

References to recent research have been added by the editors.

1484 MAITLAND (FREDERIC W.). Selected historical essays of F. W. Maitland, chosen and introduced by Helen M. Cam. Cambr. 1957.

(a) Township and borough (Cambr. 1898). 3–15.
(b) The history of a Cambridgeshire manor (*Collected Papers,* ii. 366–402). 16–40.
(c) Leet and tourn (The second selection of his introduction to *Select Pleas in Manorial Courts,* Selden Soc. Pubns. ii (1888)). 41–51.
(d) Introduction to *Memoranda de parliamento, 1305* (*Records of the parliament holden at Westminster . . . in the 33rd year of the reign of King Edward I . . .* (Rolls Ser.), 1893). 52–96. See No. 3319.
(e) History of English law (*Encycl. Brit.* 10th edn. Supplement, 1902, vol. xxviii, 246–53; 11th edn. vol. ix. 600–7). 97–111.
(f) English law, 1307–1600 (*Collected Papers,* ii. 477–96). 122–34.
(g) Round's 'Commune of London' (*The Athenaeum,* 21 Oct. 1899). 259–65.
(h) William Stubbs, bishop of Oxford (*Collected Papers,* iii. 495–511). 266–76.
(i) Mary Bateson (*Collected Papers,* iii. 541–3). 277–8.

References to recent research have been added by the editor.

1485 MEDIEVAL ENGLAND: A new edition rewritten and revised. Ed. by Austin L. Poole. 2 vols. Oxf. 1958.

The successor to F. P. Barnard, *Companion to English history* (Oxf. 1902), and H. W. C. Davis, *Medieval England* (Oxf. 1924). A selected bibliography is appended to each chapter.

Vol. i:

(*a*) W. G. Hoskins, The English landscape. 1–36.
(*b*) H. M. Colvin, Domestic architecture and town-planning. 37–97.
(*c*) A. J. Taylor, Military architecture. 98–127.
(*d*) R. C. Smail, Art of war. 128–67.
(*e*) K. M. E. Murray, Shipping. 168–95.
(*f*) Lady Stenton, Communications. 196–208.
(*g*) E. M. Carus-Wilson, Towns and trade. 209–63.
(*h*) R. H. Dolley, Coinage. 264–99.
(*i*) J. L. Nevison, Civil costume. 300–13.
(*j*) Sir James Mann, Arms and Armour. 314–37.
(*k*) A. R. Wagner, Heraldry. 338–81.

Vol. ii:

(*l*) D. Knowles, Religious life and organization. 382–438.
(*m*) G. F. Webb, Ecclesiastical architecture. 439–84.
(*n*) T. S. R. Boase, Art. 485–514.
(*o*) A. B. Emden, Learning and education. 515–40.
(*p*) V. H. Galbraith, Handwriting. 541–58.
(*q*) S. Gibson, Printed books, the book trade, and libraries. 559–70.
(*r*) A. C. Crombie, Science. 571–604.
(*s*) A. L. Poole, Recreations. 605–32.

1486 PAINTER (SIDNEY). Feudalism and liberty; articles and addresses of Sidney Painter. Ed. by Fred A. Cazel, Jr. Baltimore. 1961.

The most important papers concerning medieval English history are:

(*a*) The houses of Lusignan and Châtellerault, 1150–1250 (*Speculum*, xxx (1955), 374–84). 73–89.
(*b*) To whom were dedicated the *Fables* of Marie de France? (*Modern Lang. Notes*, xlviii (1933), 367–9). 107–10.
(*c*) The sources of Fouke Fitz Warin (*Modern Lang. Notes*, l (1935), 13–15). 111–14.
(*d*) English castles in the early middle ages: their number, location, and legal position (*Speculum*, x (1935), 321–32). 125–43.
(*e*) Castle-guard (*A.H.R.* xl (1935), 450–9). 144–56.
(*f*) The rout of Winchester (*Speculum*, vii (1932), 70–5). 157–64.
(*g*) The marriage of Isabella of Angoulême (*E.H.R.* lxiii (1948), 83–9; ibid. lxvii (1952), 233–5, written in collaboration with F. A. Cazel, Jr.). 165–77.
(*h*) A synthetic charter of Chertsey abbey (*Medievalia et Humanistica*, iii (1945), 81–5). 178–84.
(*i*) Norwich's three Geoffreys (*Speculum*, xxviii (1953), 803–13). 185–94.
(*j*) The family and the feudal system in twelfth-century England (*Speculum*, xxxv (1960), 1–16). 195–219.
(*k*) The earl of Clare: Richard de Clare, earl of Hertford (Not previously published). 220–5.
(*l*) The lands of Ralph Fitz Hubert (Not previously published). 226–9.
(*m*) The house of Quency, 1136–1264 (*Medievalia et Humanistica*, xi (1957), 3–9). 230–9.
(*n*) Who was the mother of Oliver Fitz Roy? (*Medievalia et Humanistica*, viii (1954), 17–19). 240–3.
(*o*) Magna Carta (*A.H.R.* liii (1947), 42–9). 244–53.
(*p*) Bibliography (of Sidney Painter). 274–82.

1487 POOLE (REGINALD LANE). Studies in chronology and history. Ed. by Austin Lane Poole. Oxf. 1934. Reprinted 1969.

(a) The beginning of the year in the middle ages (*P.B.A.* x (1921–3), 113–37). 1–27.
(b) The earliest use of the Easter cycle of Dionysius (*E.H.R.* xxxiii (1918), 56–62, 210–13). 28–37.
(c) The chronology of Bede's *Historia ecclesiastica* and the councils of 679–80 (*Jour. Theological Stud.* xx (1918), 24–40). 38–55.
(d) St. Wilfrid and the see of Ripon (*E.H.R.* xxxiv (1919), 1–24). 56–81.
(e) Monasterium Niridanum (*E.H.R.* xxxvi (1921), 540–5). 82–7.
(f) A stage in the history of the Laudian MS. of Acts (*Jour. Theological Stud.* xxix (1928), 399–400). 88–9.
(g) Seals and documents (*P.B.A.* ix (1919), 319–39). 90–111.
(h) The seal and monogram of Charles the Great (*E.H.R.* xxxiv (1919), 198–200). 112–14.
(i) The Alpine son-in-law of Edward the Elder (*E.H.R.* xxvi (1911), 310–17). 115–22.
(j) The see of Maurienne and the Valley of Susa (*E.H.R.* xxxi (1916), 1–19). 123–43.
(k) Papal chronology in the eleventh century (*E.H.R.* xxxii (1917), 204–14). 144–55.
(l) The names and numbers of medieval popes (*E.H.R.* xxxii (1917), 465–78)). 156–71.
(m) Imperial influences on the forms of papal documents (*P.B.A.* viii (1917–18), 237–49). 172–84.
(n) Benedict IX and Gregory VI (*P.B.A.* viii (1917–18), 199–235). 185–222.
(o) The masters of the schools at Paris and Chartres in John of Salisbury's time (*E.H.R.* xxxv (1920), 321–42). 223–47.
(p) John of Salisbury at the papal court (*E.H.R.* xxxviii (1923), 321–30). 248–58.
(q) The early correspondence of John of Salisbury (*P.B.A.* xi (1924–5), 727–53). 259–86.
(r) The early lives of Robert Pullen and Nicholas Breakspear, with notes on other Englishmen at the papal court about the middle of the 12th century (*Essays to T. F. Tout* (No. 1458)). 287–97.
(s) Two documents concerning Archbishop Roger of York (*Speculum*, iii (1928), 81–4). 298–301.
(t) The dates of Henry II's charters (*E.H.R.* xxiii (1908), 79–83). 302–7.
(u) The publication of Great Charters by the English kings (ibid. xxviii (1913), 444–53). 308–18.
(v) Henry Symeonis (ibid. xxvii (1912), 515–17). 319–21.

1488 POWICKE (FREDERICK M.). The Christian life in the middle ages and other essays. Oxf. 1935.

(a) The Christian life in the middle ages (*Legacy*, No. 1479). 1–30.
(b) Gerald of Wales (*B.J.R.L.* xii (1928), 389–410). 107–29.
(c) Stephen Langton (*Theology, Jour. Hist. Christianity*, xvii (1928), 83–96). 130–46.
(d) Loretta, Countess of Leicester (Tait, *Essays*, No. 1455). 147–68.

1489 POWICKE (FREDERICK M.). Modern historians and the study of history: essays and papers. Lond. etc. 1955.

Part i: Memoirs and notices; Part ii: Historical study.

Part i:

(a) Sir Paul Vinogradoff (*E.H.R.* xli (1926), 236–43). 9–18.
(b) The Manchester history school: T. F. Tout, J. Tait, A. G. Little (adapted from an article on Univ. of Manchester, *History Today*, May 1951). 19–95.
(c) Henri Pirenne (*E.H.R.* li (1936), 78–89). 96–108.
(d) Charles Haskins (ibid. lii (1937), 649–56). 109–17.
(e) H. W. C. Davis (ibid. xliii (1928), 578–84). 118–26.

(*f*) Three Cambridge scholars: C. W. Previté-Orton, Z. N. Brooke, and G. G. Coulton (*Cambr. Hist. Jour.* ix (1947), 106–16). 127–41.
(*g*) Leopold Delisle and Anglo-French history (*Quart. Rev.* (Apr. 1911), latter part of article). 142–9.
(*h*) Sir Charles Firth (*The Oxford Magazine*, 12 March 1936). 150–3.
(*i*) Reginald Lane Poole (*The Times*, 3 Nov. 1939). 154–5.
(*j*) James F. Willard (Extract from a review in *History*, xxvi (1942)). 156–8.

Part ii:

(*k*) Historical study in Oxford (inaugural lecture at Oxford, 8 Feb. 1929). 164–83.
(*l*) The collection and criticism of original texts (*History*, xvii (1932), 1–8). 184–92.
(*m*) Modern methods of medieval research (*T.R.H.S.* 4th Ser. xvi (1933), 45–53). 193–9.
(*n*) Recent work on the origin of the English parliament (address, published by University of Louvain, 1939). 217–24.

1490   POWICKE (FREDERICK M.). Ways of medieval life and thought: essays and addresses. Lond. 1950. Boston. 1951.

Mostly reprints, greatly revised.

(*a*) Ailred of Rievaulx and his biographer Walter Daniel (2nd part from *B.J.R.L.* vi (1921–2), 310–51, 452–521). 7–26.
(*b*) The disappearance of Arthur of Brittany (short version of article in *E.H.R.* xxiv (1909), 659–74). 27–37.
(*c*) The murder of Henry Clement and the pirates of Lundy Island (*History*, xxv (1941), 285–310; revised in *Henry III and the Lord Edward*, ii. 740–59). 38–68.
(*d*) Guy de Montfort (1265–71) (*T.R.H.S.* 4th Ser. xviii (1935), 1–23). 69–88.
(*e*) England and Europe in the 13th century (*Independence, Converging and Borrowing in Institutions, Thought and Art* (Harvard Univ. Press, 1937), 135–50). 115–29.
(*f*) Reflections on the medieval state (*T.R.H.S.* 4th Ser. xix (1936), 1–18). 130–48.
(*g*) Bologna, Paris, Oxford: three *studia generalia* (*Prague Essays*, Oxf. 1949, 29–52). 149–79.
(*h*) Some problems in the history of the medieval university (*T.R.H.S.* 4th Ser. xvii (1934), 1–18). 180–97.
(*i*) The medieval university in church and society. 198–212.
(*j*) Oxford (*Polish Science and Learning*, Dec. 1944, 23–30). 213–29.
(*k*) Master Simon of Faversham (*Mélanges offerts à Ferdinand Lot*, 1925. No. 1443). 230–8.
(*l*) An American scholar: George Lincoln Burr (*Medium Aevum*, xiii (1945)). 249–55.

1491   ROBINSON (JOSEPH ARMITAGE). Somerset historical essays. British Academy. Lond. 1921.

(*a*) William of Malmesbury 'on the antiquity of Glastonbury'. 1–25.
(*b*) The Saxon abbots of Glastonbury. 26–53.
(*c*) The first deans of Wells. 54–72.
(*d*) Early Somerset archdeacons. 73–99.
(*e*) Peter of Blois. 100–40.
(*f*) Bishop Jocelin and the interdict. 141–59.

1492   ROUND (JAMES H.). Family origins and other studies by the late J. Horace Round, ed. with a memoir and bibliography by William Page. Lond. 1930.

Pages xlix–lxxiv contain the enormous bibliography of Round's publications. His books often comprise a series of studies not identifiable under the titles of the books. For his books, see the index below.

1493 ROYAL HISTORICAL SOCIETY. Essays in medieval history, selected from the *Transactions of the Royal Historical Society* (1871–1950) on the occasion of its centenary. Ed. by Richard W. Southern. Lond. 1968.

(a) F. Dvornik, The Kiev State and its relations with western Europe (*T.R.H.S.* 4th Ser. xxix (1947), 27–46). 1–23.

(b) J. M. Hussey, The Byzantine Empire in the eleventh century: some different interpretations (*T.R.H.S.* 4th Ser. xxxii (1950), 71–85). 24–41.

(c) D. Whitelock, Archbishop Wulfstan, homilist and statesman (*T.R.H.S.* 4th Ser. (1942), 25–45). 42–60.

(d) P. Grierson, Relations between England and Flanders before the Norman Conquest (*T.R.H.S.* 4th Ser. xxiii (1941), 71–112). 61–92.

(e) F. M. Stenton, English families and the Norman Conquest (*T.R.H.S.* 4th Ser. xxvi (1944), 1–12). 93–105.

(f) R. W. Hunt, English learning in the late twelfth century (*T.R.H.S.* 4th Ser. xix (1936), 19–42). 106–28.

(g) M. H. Mills, Experiments in exchequer procedure (1200–1232) (*T.R.H.S.* 4th Ser. viii (1925), 151–70). 129–45.

(h) H. G. Richardson, The origins of parliament (*T.R.H.S.* 4th Ser. xi (1928), 137–83). 146–78.
W. Rees, The Black Death in Wales (*T.R.H.S.* 4th Ser. iii (1920), 115–35). 179–99.

(j) N. B. Lewis, The organization of indentured retinues in fourteenth century England (*T.R.H.S.* 4th Ser. xxvii (1945), 29–39). 200–12.

(k) H. Suggett, The use of French in England in the later middle ages (*T.R.H.S.* 4th Ser. xxviii (1946), 61–83). 213–39.

(l) K. B. McFarlane, Parliament and 'bastard feudalism' (*T.R.H.S.* 4th Ser. xxvi (1944), 53–79). 240–63.

1494 SMITH (REGINALD A. L.). Collected papers. With a memoir by D. Knowles. Lond. 1947.

(a) The central financial system of Christ Church, Canterbury, 1186–1512 (*E.H.R.* lv (1940), 353–69). 23–41.

(b) The financial system of Rochester Cathedral Priory (*E.H.R.* lxi (1941), 586–95). 42–53.

(c) The 'regimen scaccarii' in English monasteries (*T.R.H.S.* 4th Ser. xxiv (1942), 73–94). 54–73.

(d) John of Tours, bishop of Bath, 1088–1122 (*Downside Rev.* lx (1942), 132–41). 74–82.

(e) The place of Gundulf in the Anglo-Norman church (*E.H.R.* lviii (1943), 257–72). 83–102.

(f) The Benedictine contribution to mediaeval English agriculture (not previously published). 103–16.

1495 SOCIAL LIFE IN EARLY ENGLAND. Historical Association Essays. Ed. by Geoffrey Barraclough. Lond. 1960.

A reissue with revisions of nine essays, originally published by the Historical Association as individual pamphlets.

(a) J. N. L. Myres, Roman Britain. 1–28.

(b) L. C. Latham, The manor and the village (thoroughly revised). 29–50.

(c) R. Graham, An essay on English monasteries. 51–95.

(d) Sir Frank Stenton, The development of the castle in England and Wales. 96–123.

(e) C. J. Ffoulkes, European Arms and Armour (abridged). 124–38.

(f) A. H. Thompson, The English house. 139–78.

(g) Sir Frank Stenton, Norman London (revised). 179–207.

(h) G. G. Coulton, The meaning of medieval moneys (abridged). 208–23.

(i) J. N. L. Baker, Medieval trade routes. 224–46.

1496 STENTON (F. M.). Preparatory to Anglo-Saxon England: being the collected papers of Frank Merry Stenton. Ed. by Doris Mary Stenton. Oxf. 1970.

(a) 'Godmundeslaech' (*E.H.R.* xx (1905), 697–9). 1–2.
(b) The death of Edward the Elder (*Athenaeum*, 2 Oct. 1905 and 11 Nov. 1905). 3–4.
(c) 'Inwara' and 'Utwara' (*Athenaeum*, 24 June 1905). 5.
(d) Place-names as evidence of female ownership of lands in Anglo-Saxon times (*Academy*, 7 July 1906). 6.
(e) 'Utwara' (*Athenaeum*, 13 July 1907). 7.
(f) Aethelweard's account of the last years of King Alfred's reign (*E.H.R.* xxiv (1909), 79–84). 8–13.
(g) The Danes at Thorney Island in 893 (*E.H.R.* xxvii (1912), 512–13). 14–15.
(h) Frederic Seebohm (*Reading University College Review*, iv (1912), 244–55). 16–22.
(i) Norman London (*Historical Assoc. Leaflet*, 1915; revised 1934 and again 1960. See No. 1495). 23–47.
(j) The supremacy of the Mercian kings (*E.H.R.* xxxiii (1918), 433–52). 48–66.
(k) The English element (*English Place-Name Soc.* i, pt. i, 36–54). 67–83.
(l) Personal names in place-names (Ibid. pp. 165–89). 84–105.
(m) The south-western element in the Old English Chronicle (Tout, *Essays*, No. 1458). 106–15.
(n) The foundations of English history (*T.R.H.S.* 4th Ser. ix (1926), 159–73). 116–26.
(o) Lindsey and its kings (Poole, *Essays*, No. 1448). 127–37.
(p) The Danes in England (*P.B.A.* xiii (1927), 203–46). 136–65.
(q) Acta episcoporum (*Cambr. Hist. Jour.* iii (1929), 1–14). 166–78.
(r) Medeshamstede and its colonies (Tait, *Essays*, No. 1455). 179–92.
(s) Pre-conquest Herefordshire (*R.C.H. Mons. Herefordshire*, iii, pp. lv–lxi). 193–202.
(t) The changing feudalism of the middle ages (*History*, xix (1935), 289–301). 203–13.
(u) Pre-conquest Westmorland (*R.C.H. Mons. Westmorland*, pp. xlviii–lv). 214–23.
(v) St. Frideswide and her times (*Oxoniensia*, i (1936), 103–12). 224–33.
(w) The road system of medieval England (*Econ. Hist. Rev.* vii (1936), 1–21). 234–52.
(x) The historical bearing of place-name studies (*T.R.H.S.* 4th Ser. xxi (1939), 1–19; xxii (1940), 1–22; xxiii (1941), 1–24; xxiv (1942), 1–24; xxv (1943), 1–13). 253–324. See No. 636.
(y) English families and the Norman Conquest (*T.R.H.S.* 4th Ser. xxvi (1945), 1–12). 325–34.
(z) The Scandinavian colonies in England and Normandy (*T.R.H.S.* 4th Ser. xxvii (1945), 1–12). 335–45.
(aa) Early English history, 1895–1920 (*T.R.H.S.* 4th Ser. xxviii (1946), 7–19). 346–56.
(bb) Foreword to Sir Cyril Fox's *Offa's Dyke*, pp. xvii–xxi. 357–63.
(cc) The founding of Southwell Minster (*The Southwell Rev.* v, no. 3 (1956), 1–8). 364–70.
(dd) The Anglo-Saxon coinage and the historian (Hitherto unprinted lecture to British Numismatic Soc. 1958). 371–82.
(ee) The thriving of the Anglo-Saxon ceorl (Hitherto unprinted lecture of 1958). 383–93.
(ff) The East Anglian kings of the seventh century (Dickins, *Essays*, No. 1433). 394–402.
(gg) Review of Anne S. Robertson's 'Sylloge . . . Part i, Anglo-Saxon coins' (No. 704) (*Brit. Numismatic Jour.* xxx, pt. ii (1961), 369–71). 403–6.

1497 STEPHENSON (CARL). Mediaeval institutions: selected essays. Ed. by Bryce D. Lyon. Ithaca (N.Y.). 1954. Pb. rpt. 1967.

(a) The aids of the French towns in the twelfth and thirteenth centuries (*Le Moyen Âge*, 2nd Ser. xxiv (1922), 274–328). 1–40.
(b) The origin and nature of the taille (*La Revue Belge de Philologie et d'Histoire*, v (1926), 801–70). 41–103.
(c) Taxation and representation in the middle ages (Haskins, *Essays* (No. 1439), 291–312). 104–25.

(*d*) The beginnings of representative government in England (*The Constitution Reconsidered* (N.Y. 1938), 25–36). 126–38.

(*e*) The *firma noctis* and the customs of the hundred (*E.H.R.* xxxix (1924), 161–74). 139–55.

(*f*) Commendation and related problems in Domesday (*E.H.R.* lix (1944), 289–310). 156–83.

(*g*) Notes on the composition and interpretation of Domesday Book (*Speculum*, xxii (1947), 1–15). 184–204.

(*h*) The origin and significance of feudalism (*A.H.R.* xlvi (1941), 788–812). 205–33.

(*i*) Feudalism and its antecedents in England (*A.H.R.* xlviii (1943), 245–65). 234–60.

(*j*) The problem of the common man in early mediaeval Europe (*A.H.R.* li (1946), 419–38). 261–84.

(*k*) Writings of Carl Stephenson. 285–9.

1498 STUBBS (WILLIAM). Lectures on early English history. Ed. by Arthur Hassall. Lond. etc. 1906.

(*a*) The Anglo-Saxon constitution. 1–17.

(*b*) Feudalism. 18–36.

(*c*) The laws and legislation of the Norman kings. 37–133.

(*d*) The *Dialogus de scaccario*. 134–42.

(*e*) Leges Henrici Primi. 143–65.

(*f*) The shiremoot and hundredmoot. 166–74.

(*g*) The charters of Stephen. 175–83.

(*h*) The Domesday and later surveys. 184–93.

(*i*) The comparative constitutional history of mediaeval Europe. 194–204.

(*j*) The elements of nationality among European nations. 205–25.

(*k*) The languages of the principal European states. 226–36.

(*l*) The origin and position of the German, Roman, Frank, Celtic and English churches. 237–48.

(*m*) The historical origin of European law. 249–60.

(*n*) System of landholding in mediaeval Europe. 261–72.

(*o*) The early European constitutions. 273–84.

(*p*) The kings and their councils in England, France, and Spain. 285–96.

(*q*) The functions of the national assemblies. 297–309.

(*r*) The growth of the representative principle. 310–22.

(*s*) Early judicial systems. 323–34.

(*t*) The growth of the constitutional principle in the 13th and 14th centuries. 335–53.

(*u*) The beginnings of the foreign policy of England in the middle ages. 354–72.

1499 TOUT (THOMAS F.). The collected papers of Thomas Frederick Tout with a memoir and bibliography. 3 vols. Manchester. 1932–4.

Vol. i:

Miscellaneous papers chiefly on the study of history and the University of Manchester, followed by (pp. 207–13) a select bibliography of the historical writings of T. F. Tout.

Vol. ii:

(*a*) The Welsh shires: a study in constitutional history (*Y Cymmrodor* ix (1888), 201–26). 1–20.

(*b*) Flintshire: its history and records (Flintshire Hist. Soc. Pubn. i, 1911), 21–46.

(*c*) Wales and the March during the Barons' Wars (Hist. Essays, Owens College, 1902). (No. 1472). 47–100.

(*d*) John of Halton, Bishop of Carlisle: an introduction to the Registrum Johannis de Halton (Canterbury and York Soc. Lond. 1913). 101–42.

(*e*) The household of the Chancery and its disintegration (Poole, *Essays* (No. 1448), pp. 46–85). 143–72.

(*f*) The English parliament and public opinion, 1376–1388 (*Mélanges offerts à Henri Pirenne*, 1926). (No. 1446). 173–90.
(*g*) The Fair of Lincoln and the 'Histoire de Guillaume Le Maréchal' (*E.H.R.* xviii (1903), 240–65). 191–220.
(*h*) The tactics of the battles of Boroughbridge and Morlaix (*E.H.R.* xix (1904), 711–15). 221–6.
(*i*) Some neglected fights between Crécy and Poitiers (*E.H.R.* xx (1905), 726–30). 227–32.
(*j*) Firearms in England in the fourteenth century (*E.H.R.* xxvi (1911), 666–702). 233–76.
(*k*) The 'Communitas Bacheleriae Angliae' (*E.H.R.* xvii (1902), 89–95). 277–84.
(*l*) A thirteenth-century phrase (*E.H.R.* xviii (1903), 482–3). 285–8.
(*m*) The Westminster Chronicle attributed to Robert of Reading (*E.H.R.* xxxi (1916), 450–64). 289–304.

Vol. iii:
(*a*) The study of medieval chronicles (*B.J.R.L.* vi (1921–2), 414–38). 1–26.
(*b*) The place of St. Thomas of Canterbury in history: a centenary study (*B.J.R.L.* vi (1921–2), 235–65). 27–58.
(*c*) Mediaeval town planning (*B.J.R.L.* iv (1917–18), 26–58). 59–72.
(*d*) A mediaeval burglary (*B.J.R.L.* ii (1914–15), 348–69). 93–116.
(*e*) Mediaeval forgers and forgeries (*B.J.R.L.* v (1918–20), 208–34). 117–44.
(*f*) The captivity and death of Edward of Carnarvon (*B.J.R.L.* vi (1921–2), 69–114). 145–90.
(*g*) The English civil service in the fourteenth century (*B.J.R.L.* iii (1916–17), 185–214). 191–222.
(*h*) Some conflicting tendencies in English administrative history during the fourteenth century (*B.J.R.L.* viii (1924), 82–106). 223–48.
(*i*) The beginnings of a modern capital: London and Westminster in the fourteenth century (*P.B.A.* x (1921–3), 487–511). 249–75.

1500 (Unwin). STUDIES IN ECONOMIC HISTORY: THE COLLECTED PAPERS OF GEORGE UNWIN. Ed. by R. H. Tawney. Lond. 1927.

Part II:
(*a*) The medieval city: (i) The roots of the city; (ii) Social evolution in mediaeval London. (The latter in *Finance and trade under Edward III* (Manchester, 1918), 1–18). 49–91.
(*b*) Mediaeval gilds and education (in *A Cyclopedia of Education* (N.Y. 1912), vol. iii. 107–10). 92–9.
(*c*) London tradesmen and their creditors (13th century) (in *Finance and trade under Edward III*, 19–34). 100–16.
(*d*) The economic policy of Edward III (Introd. to *Finance and trade*). 117–32.
(*e*) The history of the cloth industry in Suffolk: (i) The old draperies; (ii) The new draperies, wool-combing and spinning (in *Victoria County History*, *Suffolk*, vol. ii. 254–71). 262–301.

1501 (Vinogradoff). THE COLLECTED PAPERS OF PAUL VINOGRADOFF, with a memoir. Ed. by H. A. L. Fisher. 2 vols. Oxf. 1928.

Vol. i: Historical; Vol. ii: Jurisprudence.

Vol. i: Memoir. 1–74.
(*a*) The text of Bracton (*Law Quart. Rev.* i (1885), 189–200). 77–90.
(*b*) Folkland (*E.H.R.* viii (1893), 1–17). 91–111.
(*c*) Agricultural services (*Econ. Jour.* x (1900), 308–22). 112–28.
(*d*) The end of villainage in England, by T. W. Page (*E.H.R.* xv (1900), 774–81). 129–38.

(*e*) An illustration of the continuity of the open field system (*Quart. Jour. Econ.* xxii (1907–8), 62–73). 139–48.

(*f*) Transfer of land in old English law (*Harvard Law Rev.* xx (1907), 532–48). 149–67.

(*g*) Das Buchland (*Mélanges Fitting* (Montpellier, 1908), ii. 499–522). 168–91. (Full title in *Mélanges Fitting* is Romanistische Einflüsse im Angelsächsischen Recht: Das Buchland.)

(*h*) Constitutional history and the Year Books (*Law Quart. Rev.* xxix (1913), 272–84). 192–206.

(*i*) Magna Carta, cl. 39, Nullus liber homo, etc. (*Essays on Magna Carta* (No. 3289), 78–95). 207–21.

(*j*) The Roman elements in Bracton's treatise (*Yale Law Jour.* xxxii (1922–3), 751–6). 237–44.

(*k*) Ralph of Hengham as Chief Justice of the common pleas (Tout, *Essays*, No. 1458, 189–96). 245–52.

(*l*) Frederic W. Maitland (*E.H.R.* xxii (1907), 280–9). 253–64.

(*m*) A master of historical jurisprudence: The collected papers of F. W. Maitland (*The Nation*, 15 July 1911). 265–71.

(*n*) A notebook of Bracton (*The Athenaeum*, 19 July 1884). 297–302.

Vol. ii:

(*o*) Les maximes dans l'ancien droit commun anglais (*Rev. hist. de droit français et étranger*, 4th Ser. ii (1923), 333–43). 239–47.

(*p*) Quelques problèmes d'histoire du droit Anglo-Normand (ibid. iv (1926), 195–212). 423–37.

(*q*) Bibliography. 479–500.

VII. LOCAL HISTORY

A. GENERAL BIBLIOGRAPHY

The principal guides to local history and to the important comprehensive histories of counties are entered here. Studies and records which concentrate on a single locality, borough, town, parish, or manor are frequently useful for more general purposes. Some of the latter are assembled under appropriate counties in volume ii; they may be found by reference to the index, or by scanning the later sections on ecclesiastical history and on the structure of society. The monographs on topography (pp. 74–5) and place-names (pp. 75–8), and the volumes in the series on Domesday geography (No. 3044) contain much of value to the local historian.

A good introduction to the various aspects of local historiography is provided by Hoskins (No. 1516); and a brief guide to local archives can be found in Hepworth (No. 940), and in *Record Repositories* (No. 944). The activities of the British Records Association are described by M. F. Bond in *Jenkinson Essays* (No. 1440), and periodically in its journal, *Archives*. The names and addresses of national and local societies are given in Harcup (No. 1512), and in the *Bulletin of the National Register of Archives* (No. 943). The journal *Archives* (No. 1504) contains a series of report on 'Local Archives of Great Britain' (see p. 213 below); the *Journal of the Society of Archivists* (No. 935) includes articles on individual archives; and the issues of the *Amateur Historian* (1951–68), subsequently the *Local Historian* (1968+), present a series of articles as aids to local research. The Historical Manuscripts Commission Reports (No. 945), the Reports on the National Archives (No. 943), and the reports of the commissions on public records (Nos. 965–6) form rich quarries. See also the *Survey of ecclesiastical archives* (p. 109), and Hall's *Repertory* (No. 939), and page 109 above. The invaluable *Victoria County History* is analysed on pages 215–19 below.

The volumes of *Hist. Monuments of Great Britain* (Nos. 737–9) provide illustrations and commentaries on surviving monuments. The publications of the most important local record societies up to March 1957 are catalogued in Mullins, *Texts* and *Calendars* (No. 29); and the publications of many local societies are listed in the *Catalogue of the London Library* (Nos. 82–3) and for the period 1901–33 in Mullins, *Guide* (No. 28); and in Somerville's *Handlist* (No. 933) and Gouldesborough (No. 933).

The standard older bibliographies are Gross (No. 1511) and Humphreys (No. 1518). Numerous local libraries have printed catalogues of their local collections; for them consult Bestermann (No. 1) under the name of the county or the town, and Hobbs (No. 1515) and Hepworth (No. 940). Among its bibliographical publications, the Library Association issues Regional Guides (No. 93) which are of fundamental value for current publications. Bonser (No. 12) covers extensively the period 450 to 1087; and *Writings 1901–33* (No. 38) and *Writings 1934–45* (No. 39) include sections on local history. The periodic, normally annual, bibliographies in *Econ. H. R.* (No. 119) and in *Antiquaries Jour.* (No. 107) furnish current references.

The Standing Conference for Local History (established in 1948) of the National Council of Social Science (London) has published the following brief pamphlets in its Local History Series: (1) *A plan for the study of local history*, (2) *The compilation of county bibliographies* (1948), (3) *A selection of books on English local history* (1949), (4) *A directory of local historians: national and local organizations, statutory bodies, record offices* (1968).

In the listing below, the general bibliography (pp. 212–15) is followed by a county bibliography, alphabetically county by county (pp. 219–55). Under each county, the three groups of entries—county bibliography, county journals, and county histories—are separated by spaces. Some important local histories of towns, boroughs, villages, and other areas smaller than the county are to be found under agrarian and urban history (pp. 669–73). The publications of local record societies up to March 1957 are listed in Mullins, *Texts* (No. 29), which is referred to below as 'Mullins, *Texts*'; and the transactions and papers presented to local societies during the period 1901 to 1933 are listed in Mullins, *Guide* (No. 28), here abbreviated as 'MG'.

1502   AMATEUR HISTORIAN. National council of social service, London. Lond. 1952–68. Subsequently (Vol. viii, no. 1) LOCAL HISTORIAN. Lond. 1968+.

1503   ANDERSON (JOHN P.). The book of British topography. Lond. 1881.*

A catalogue of topographical works then in the library of the British Museum relating to Great Britain and Ireland. See No. 6.

1504   ARCHIVES: Journal of the British Records Association. Lond. 1949+.*

This journal carries a series entitled 'Local Archives of Great Britain', listed herewith:

i.	1 (1949)	I. The County Record Office at Bedford.
	2 (1949)	II. The Essex Record Office.
	3 (1950)	III. The County Record Office of Glamorgan.
	4 (1950)	IV. The Hertford County Record Office.
	5 (1951)	V. The Birmingham Reference Library.
	6 (1951)	VI. The Lincolnshire Archives Committee.
ii.	7 (1952)	VII. The Lancashire Record Office.
	10 (1953)	VIII. The Norwich Central Library.
	11 (1954)	IX. The Records of the City of London.
	12 (1954)	X. The Warwick County Record Office.
	13 (1955)	XI. The Kent Archives Office.
	14 (1955)	XII. The Guildhall Library (London).
	16 (1956)	XIII. The County of London Record Office.
iii.	18 (1957)	XIV. The City of Bristol Record Office.
	19 (1958)	XV. Local and private records of Scotland, no. 1.
	20 (1958)	XVI. Local and private records of Scotland, no. 2.
iv.	21 (1959)	XVII. The Ipswich and East Suffolk Record Office.
	22 (1959)	XVIII. The Berkshire Record Office.
	24 (1960)	XIX. Record Office work in Staffordshire.
v.	25 (1961)	XX. The Stratford-upon-Avon Record Office.
	26 (1961)	XXI. The Plymouth Archives Department.
	27 (1962)	XXII. Worcestershire County Record Office.
	28 (1962)	XXIII. Newcastle-upon-Tyne City Archives Office.
	29 (1963)	XXIV. The Middlesex County Record Office.
vi.	31 (1964)	XXV. The Gloucestershire Record Office.
	32 (1964)	XXVI. The Gloucester City Library.
vii.	33 (1965)	XXVII. The Caernarvonshire Record Office.
	34 (1965)	XXVIII. The Cumberland, Westmorland, and Carlisle Record Office, 1960–5.
	36 (1966)	XXIX. The Dorset Record Office.
	38 (1967)	XXX. The Norfolk and Norwich Record Office.

1505   BIBLIOTHECA TOPOGRAPHICA BRITANNICA. By John Nichols. and others. 10 vols. Lond. 1780–1800.*

Vol. i: Kent and Sussex.

Vol. ii: Middlesex and Surrey.

Vol. iii: Lincolnshire.

Vol. iv: Varous counties.

Vol. v: Cambridgeshire, Suffolk, and Wales.

Vol. vi: Biography, etc.

Vols. vii–viii: Leicestershire.

Vols. ix–x: Various counties.

This work contains histories of various manors, parishes, abbeys, etc. including many records. See also *Collectanea topographica* (No. 115).

1506   DANIELL (WALTER V.) and NIELD (FREDERICK J.). Manual of British topography: a catalogue of county and local histories, pamphlets, etc. Lond. 1909.

1507   EMMISON (FREDERICK G.). Archives and local history. Lond. 1966.

1508   FINBERG (HERBERT P. R.) and SKIPP (V. H. T.). Local history: objective and pursuit. Newton Abbot. 1967.

1509   A GUIDE TO THE REPORTS ON COLLECTIONS OF MANU-SCRIPTS of private families, corporations and institutions in Great Britain and Ireland issued by the royal commissioners for historical manuscripts, 1870–1911. Pt. i. Topographical. Lond. 1914. Pt. ii. Index of persons, 1870–1911. 2 vols. Lond. 1935, 1938. Guide to reports, II: Index of persons, 1911–57. Ed. by A. C. S. Hall. H.M.S.O. Lond. 1966. See Hist. MSS. Comm. (No. 945).

1510 GOMME (GEORGE L.). The literature of local institutions. Lond. 1886.

Useful, but incomplete. See No. 769.

1511 GROSS (CHARLES). A bibliography of British municipal history, including gilds and parliamentary representation. Harvard Historical Studies. N.Y. 1897. Reprinted, with an introductory essay. Leicester. 1966.

Standard work for publications prior to 1897. G. H. Martin and S. McIntyre have prepared a continuation to include studies published since 1897, now in the press. (Vol. i, Leicester, 1972).

1512 HARCUP (SARA E.). Historical, archaeological and kindred societies in the British Isles: a List. Inst. Hist. Res. Lond. 1965. 2nd edn. 1968.

1513 HARDACRE (PAUL H.). 'County record offices in England and Wales: a list of guides and references.' *Amer. Archivist*, xxv (1962), 477–83.

1514 HISTORICAL ASSOCIATION (London). Local History Committee. English local history handlist: a short bibliography and list of sources for the study of local history and antiquities. Compiled by F. W. Kuhlicke and F. G. Emmison. Helps for Students of History, No. 69. Lond. 1965. Supersedes editions of 1947 and 1952.

Alexander H. Thompson, *A short bibliography of local history* (Lond. 1928); William C. Donkin, *Outline bibliography of the northern region* (Newcastle-upon-Tyne, 1956). The Kuhlicke–Emmison compilation is a general list of works on English history in its many facets, not specifically local.

1515 HOBBS (JOHN L.). Libraries and the materials of local history. Grafton and Lond. 1948. Idem, Local history and the library. Library Assoc. 1962.

1516 HOSKINS (WILLIAM G.). Local history in England. Lond. 1959.

'A book of advice and guidance' designed for the beginner, but useful to more advanced students. Cf. Francis Celoria, *Teach yourself local history* (Teach Yourself Series, Lond. 1959).

1517 HOSKINS (WILLIAM G.). The making of the English landscape. Lond. 1955.

The introductory volume to a series which includes the following: W. G. V. Balchin, *Cornwall* (1954); H. P. R. Finberg, *Gloucester* (1955); R. Millward, *Lancashire* (1955); W. G. Hoskins, *Leicestershire* (1957); C. Taylor, *Dorset* (1970); A. Raistrick, *West Riding of Yorkshire* (1970). See Hoskins in *Medieval England* (No. 1485).

1518 HUMPHREYS (ARTHUR L.). A handbook to county bibliographies, being a bibliography of bibliographies relating to the counties and towns of Great Britain and Ireland. Lond. 1917.

A detailed listing of bibliographies.

1519 LYSONS (DANIEL) and LYSONS (SAMUEL). Magna Britannia: being a concise topographical account of the several counties of Great Britain. 6 vols. Lond. 1806–22.*

Cf. Lewis, *Topographical dictionary* (No. 600).

1520 MEADS (DOROTHY M.). 'Searching local records'. *Rev. Eng. Studies*, iv (1928), 173–90, 301–22.

1521 MUNCEY (RAYMOND W. L.). The romance of parish registers. Lond. 1933.

Lists the printed parish registers. See also John Cox, *How to write the history of a parish* (Lond. 1879; 5th edn. rev. 1909); completely rewritten by Ralph B. Pugh, *How to write a parish history* (Lond. 1954), with excellent bibliographical detail. Also William E. Tate, *The parish chest: a study of the records of parochial administration in England* (Cambr. 1946; 3rd edn. 1950). George W. Marshall, *Parish registers: a list of those printed, or of which MS. copies exist in public collections*, 2 parts (Lond. 1900–4).

1522 NEW SURVEY OF ENGLAND. Lond. 1953.

A projected series, of which R. M. Robbins on Middlesex (1953) and W. G. Hoskins on Devon (1954) have been published.

1523 RECORD REPOSITORIES IN GREAT BRITAIN. 3rd edn. H.M.S.O. Lond. 1968.

1524 REDSTONE (LILIAN J.) and STEER (FRANCIS W.). Local records: their nature and care. Lond. 1953.

1525 REPORT OF THE COMMITTEE appointed to enquire as to the existing arrangements for the collection and custody of local records, and as to further measures which it may be desirable to take for the purpose (with appendices). *Parl. Papers*, 1902, vol. xlix. Lond. 1902.

The appendices print answers to questions on the state of local records.

1526 THIRD REPORT OF THE ROYAL COMMISSION ON PUBLIC RECORDS appointed to inquire into and report on the state of the public records and local records of a public nature of England and Wales (with appendices, minutes of evidence, etc.). Vol. iii (3 pts.). H.C. 1919 (Cmd. 367, Cmd. 368, Cmd. 369), xxviii. I, 53, 189.

1527 THOMPSON (ALEXANDER HAMILTON). Parish history and records. Helps for Students of History. Lond. 1919.

1528 UPCOTT (WILLIAM). A bibliographical account of the principal works relating to English topography. 3 vols. Lond. 1818.*

Still useful for the older publications.

B. COUNTY HISTORY

1. *Victoria County History*

1529 VICTORIA HISTORY OF THE COUNTIES OF ENGLAND. Ed. by H. Arthur Doubleday, William Page, Louis F. Salzman, and Ralph B.

Pugh. Lond. and Westminster. 1900–34; then Institute of Historical Research. Lond. 1935+.

In 1933 the rights to the *V.C.H.* were transferred to the University of London by its proprietor, William Page; and the Institute of Historical Research assumed responsibility for its continuation. Louis F. Salzman was general editor from 1935 to 1949 and was succeeded by Ralph B. Pugh.

The Doubleday–Page *Guide* (to contributors, Lond. 1903) established 'certain general rules which should be scrupulously observed' by contributors, and thus set a pattern. That pattern moulded for each county chapters on Early Man, ancient earthworks, Roman and Anglo-Saxon remains, a commentary and translation of *Domesday Book* and kindred records, ecclesiastical history, religious houses, political, social, and economic history, topographical accounts of parishes and manors which stressed the feudal baronage, family history and heraldry, and natural history.

This pattern was generally followed until the 1950s when the series for Wiltshire showed a more flexible design. The sections on natural history were excluded. More attention was to be devoted to economic, social, and ecclesiastical history. Narrative chapters describe the specific application within the county of national institutions. Thus Wiltshire i, pt. i (1957), deals with the king's government in the Middle Ages, feudal Wiltshire, the commons of Wiltshire in medieval parliaments. Wiltshire ii (1955) is almost exclusively Professor Darlington's commentary on *Domesday Book* and its satellites for Wiltshire. Oxford iii (1954) concerns the university; and Cambridge iii (1959) the city and the university. Occasionally a whole volume is devoted to a single city: Leicester, Chichester, Birmingham, Coventry and Warwick, Hull and York. For editorial policy, see Ralph B. Pugh, 'The structure and aims of the Victoria History of the Counties of England', *B.I.H.R.* xl (1967), 65–73. For a conspectus of the whole history to 1970, see Pugh (No. 1530).

The table below attempts to give a brief analysis of the general contents of each of the volumes of the *Victoria County History* as of 1969. The double dagger indicates that the history for the county is regarded as completed.

‡Bedford   i (1904) Domesday (J. H. Round) and eccles.-religious hist.
                 ii (1908) Social and econ., political, hist. and topography.
                 iii (1912) Topography. Index (1914).

‡Berkshire   i (1906) Domesday (J. H. Round); industries.
                 ii (1907) Ecclesiastical and religious hist.; social, econ., political hist.
                 iii (1923) and iv (1924) Topography. Index (1927).

‡Buckingham   i (1905) Domesday (J. H. Round) and eccles.-religious hist.
                 ii (1908) Social, econ., political hist. and topography.
                 iii (1925) and iv (1927) Political hist. and topography.
                 Index (1928).

Cambridgeshire   i (1938) Domesday and Inquisitio (L. F. Salzman).
and Isle of Ely   ii (1948) Social, econ. hist. (H. C. Darby and L. F. Salzman); polit. hist., A.-S. to Tudors (Darby and E. Miller).
                 iii (1959) City (H. Cam) and university (J. P. C. Roach).
                 iv (1953) Topography. Index i–iv (1960).

Cornwall   i (1906) Industries.
                 ii pt. v (1924); pt. viii (1924) Domesday (L. F. Salzman).

Cumberland   i (1901) Early pipe rolls, Testa de Nevill (J. Wilson).
                 ii (1905) Eccles.-relig. hist.; polit. hist.; industries.

Derby   i (1905) Domesday (F. M. Stenton).
                 ii (1907) Eccles.-relig. hist.; social, econ., polit. hist.; industries.

Devon   i (1906) Domesday (O. J. Reichel).

Dorset   ii (1908) Eccles.-relig. hist.; social, econ., polit. hist.; industries.
                 iii (1968) Domesday (A. Williams).

Durham   i (1905) Boldon Book (G. T. Lapsley).
                ii (1907) Eccles.-relig. hist.; social, econ., polit. hist.; industries.
                iii (1928) Topography.

Essex   i (1903) Domesday (J. H. Round).
                ii (1907) Eccles.-relig. hist.; social, econ., polit. hist.; industries.
                iii (1963) Romano-British antiquities.
                iv (1956) Topography.
                v (1966) Bibliography, ed. W. R. Powell.

Gloucester   ii (1907) Eccles.-relig. hist.; social, econ. hist.; industries.
                vi (1965) Topography.
                viii (1968) Topography.

‡Hampshire and i (1900) Domesday (J. H. Round).
  Isle of Wight ii (1903) Eccles.-relig. hist.; social, econ., etc.
                iii (1908), iv (1911), v (1912) Topography.
                Index (1914).

Hereford   i (1908) Domesday (J. H. Round); polit. hist.

‡Hertford   i (1902) Domesday (J. H. Round).
                ii (1908) Polit. hist.; topography.
                iii (1912) Topography.
                iv (1914) Eccles.-relig. hist.; social, econ. hist.; industries.
                Index (1923).

‡Huntingdon   i (1926) Domesday (F. M. Stenton); eccles.-relig. hist.
                ii (1932) Polit., social, econ. hist.
                iii (1936) Topography.
                Index (1938).

Kent   i (1908) Natural hist.; A.-S. remains; sport; etc.
                ii (1926) Eccles.-relig. hist.
                iii (1932) Romano-British remains; Domesday and Domesday Mon-
                achorum (N. Neilson); social, econ. hist. etc.

‡Lancaster   i (1906) Domesday (from 'Cheshire' and Yorkshire returns: W. Farrer).
                ii (1908) Eccles.-relig. hist.; social, econ. hist.; polit. hist.; and index
                to vols. i and ii.
                iii–viii Topography: iii (1907); iv (1911); v, with index to vols. iii, iv,
                and v (1911); vi (1911); vii, with index to vols. vi and vii (1912);
                viii with index (1914).

Leicester   i (1907) Domesday and Leicestershire Survey (F. M. Stenton), eccles.
                hist.
                ii (1954) Relig. hist.; polit. and agrarian hist.; industries.
                iii (1955) Social, econ. hist.; index for vols. i, ii, iii.
                iv (1958) The city of Leicester.
                v (1964) Topography: Gartree Hundred.

Lincoln   ii (1906) Eccles.-relig. hist.; social, econ., polit. hist.; industries.
London   i (1909) Eccles.-relig. hist.
Middlesex   i (1969) Relig. hist.; Domesday; general subjects.
                ii (1911) Social, econ., polit. hist.; industries, topography.
                iii (1962) Topography.

Norfolk   i (1901) Natural hist.; Romano-British remains; A.-S. remains.
                ii (1906) Domesday (C. Johnson); eccles.-relig. hist.; polit. hist.

Northampton   i (1902) Domesday and Northampton Survey (J. H. Round).
                ii (1906) Eccles.-relig. hist.; industries.
                iii (1930) and iv (1937) Topography.

Nottingham   i (1906) Domesday (F. M. Stenton), polit. hist.
                ii (1910) Eccles.-relig. hist.; social, econ. hist.; industries.

Oxford	i (1939) Domesday (F. M. Stenton), polit. hist. ii (1907) Eccles.-relig. hist.; social, econ. hist.; industries. iii (1954) The University of Oxford. v–ix Topography: v (1957); vi (1959); vii (1962); viii (1964); ix (1969).
‡Rutland	i (1908) Domesday (F. M. Stenton); eccles.-relig. hist.; social, econ., polit. hist.; industries. ii (1935) Topography. Index (1936).
Shropshire	i (1908) Domesday (J. Tait); industries. viii (1968) Topography.
Somerset	i (1906) Domesday (J. H. Round), Geld Inquest. ii (1911) Eccles.-relig. hist.; social, econ., polit. hist.; industries; index to vols. i and ii.
Stafford	i (1908) Social, econ., polit. hist. ii (1967) Industries; index for vols. i and ii. iii (1970) Eccles.-relig. hist. iv (1958) Domesday (C. F. Slade). v (1959) and viii (1963) Topography.
Suffolk	i (1911) Domesday (B. A. Lees), social-econ. hist. ii (1907) Eccles.-relig. hist.; polit. hist.; industries.
‡Surrey	i (1902) Domesday (J. H. Round); polit. hist. ii (1905) Eccles.-relig. hist.; industries. iii (1911) Topography iv (1912) Social, econ. hist.; topography. Index (1914).
Sussex	i (1905) Domesday (J. H. Round); polit. hist. ii (1907) Eccles.-relig. hist.; social, econ. hist.; industries. iii (1935) City of Chichester. iv (1953), vii (1940), and ix (1937) Topography.
Warwick	i (1904) Domesday (J. H. Round). ii (1908) Eccles.-relig. hist.; social, econ., polit. hist.; industries. iii–vi Topography: iii (1945), iv (1947), v (1949), vi (1951); Index for vols. i–vi (1955). vii (1964) City of Birmingham. viii (1969) City of Coventry and borough of Warwick.
Wiltshire	i, pt. i (1957) Archaeological Gazetteer: pre-historic, Roman, and pagan Saxon sites. ii (1955) Domesday and Geld Rolls (R. R. Darlington). iii (1956) Eccles.-relig. hist. iv (1959) Econ. hist.; medieval agriculture, woollen industry, forests. v (1957) King's government in Middle Ages, feudal Wiltshire, the Commons in medieval parliaments, etc. vi–viii Topography: vi (1962), vii (1953), viii (1965).
‡Worcester	i (1901) Domesday and some early Worcestershire surveys (J. H. Round). ii (1906) Eccles.-relig. hist.; polit. hist.; industries. iii (1913) Topography. iv (1924) Social, econ. hist.; topography. Index (1926).
‡Yorkshire (General)	i (1907) ii (1912) Domesday (W. Farrer); industries. iii (1913) Eccles.-relig. hist.; social, econ., polit. hist. Index (1925).

York, East Riding	i (1969) Kingston on Hull.
‡York, North Riding	i (1914) Honour and castle of Richmond. ii (1923) Topography. Index (1925).
‡York, City of	(1961) From Roman times to 1959.

1530 VICTORIA HISTORY OF THE COUNTIES OF ENGLAND. General introduction. Ed. by R. B. Pugh. Lond. 1970.

In 300 pages 'this introduction provides a conspectus of all that has appeared up to and including 1970, with a bibliographical survey, contents of each volume, and indices of the titles of articles and authors'. There is a new edition of the *Handbook for Editors and Authors* by C. R. Elrington (Lond. 1970).

2. *England: County by County Alphabetically*

BEDFORDSHIRE
See Nos. 171, 1504, and *V.C.H.* (No. 1529)

1531 CONISBEE (LEWIS R.). A Bedfordshire bibliography, with some comments and biographical notes. Bedfordshire Hist. Rec. Soc. 1962. Supplement (1961–5). 1967.

1532 COUNTY COUNCIL. County records committee. Guide to the Bedfordshire record office. Bedford. 1957. Idem, A handlist of the Bedfordshire county muniments. Bedford. 1925. 3rd edn. 1938.

The earlier part of the *Guide* calendars official archives, and is comprehensive.

1533 BEDFORDSHIRE ARCHAEOLOGICAL COUNCIL. The Bedfordshire Archaeological Journal. Luton. 1962+.

1534 BEDFORDSHIRE HISTORICAL RECORD SOCIETY. Publications. Aspley Guise, then Bedford. 1913+. Quarto memoirs. 1922+. (Mullins, *Texts*, pp. 289–95; 535.)

1535 BEDFORDSHIRE MAGAZINE (THE). A quarterly miscellany and review of Bedfordshire life and history. Luton. 1947+.

1536 BEDFORDSHIRE NOTES AND QUERIES. Ed. by F. A. Blaydes. 3 vols. Bedford. 1886–93.

1537 FISHER (THOMAS). Collections historical, genealogical, and topographical for Bedfordshire. Lond. 1812–36.

1538 GODBER (JOYCE). History of Bedfordshire, 1066–1888. Bedfordshire County Council. Bedford. 1969. New impression. 1970.

A well-illustrated history based on the publications of the Beds. Hist. Soc., pages 1–170, deal with the period prior to 1530. See also G. H. Fowler, 'The shire of Bedford and the earldom of Huntingdon', *Beds. Hist. Soc. Pubns.* xi (1925).

1539 PARRY (JOHN D.). Select illustrations, historical and topographical, of Bedfordshire. Lond. 1827.

Deals with Bedford, Ampthill, Houghton, Luton, and Chicksands.

BERKSHIRE
See Nos. 762, 1504, and *V.C.H.* (No. 1529)

1540 HULL (FELIX). Guide to the Berkshire record office. County records committee. Reading. 1952.

1541 HUMPHREYS (ARTHUR L.). Berkshire parishes. A year's record in bibliography, 1921–2. Lond. 1923.

1542 READING, PUBLIC LIBRARIES. Local collection catalogue of books and maps relating to Berkshire. Reading. 1958.

1543 BERKSHIRE ARCHAEOLOGICAL AND ARCHITECTURAL SOCIETY. Quarterly journal. 3 vols. Reading. 1889–95. Continued by the Berks., Bucks., and Oxon. archaeological journal, (1895)–1930; then, the Berkshire archaeological journal, 1930+. Index of vols. i–iii (1890–5), Berks archaeological journal and vols. i–xxv (1895–1919), Berks., Bucks., & Oxon. archaeological journal. Oxf. 1924. (Issued as vol. xxviii, no. 2, of the journal.) (MG).

1544 BERKSHIRE NOTES AND QUERIES. Vol. i, pts. i–iii. Lond. 1890–1.

1545 NEWBURY DISTRICT FIELD CLUB. Transactions. Newbury. 1871+. (MG).

1546 ASHMOLE (ELIAS). The history and antiquities of Berkshire, with a description of Windsor. 3 vols. Lond. 1719. 3rd edn. Reading. 1736.

BUCKINGHAMSHIRE
See No. 1529.

1547 A CALENDAR OF DEEDS and other records present in the muniment room at the Museum, Aylesbury. Bucks. Archaeol. Soc., Rec. Branch Pubn. v for 1941 (1944).

1548 GOUGH (HENRY). Bibliotheca Buckinghamiensis. Bucks. Archit. and Arch. Soc. Aylesbury. 1890.

1549 ARCHITECTURAL AND ARCHAEOLOGICAL SOCIETY FOR THE COUNTY OF BUCKINGHAM. Records of Buckinghamshire. Aylesbury for 1854+(1858+). Index of vols. i–x (1854–1916), 1928 (MG). Records branch (Buckingham Rec. Soc.). Publications. High Wycombe. 1937+. (Mullins, *Texts*, pp. 296–7.)

1550 GIBBS (ROBERT). Buckinghamshire, a record of local occurrences, A.D. 1400–1800. 4 vols. Aylesbury. 1878–82.

1551 LIPSCOMB (GEORGE). The history and antiquities of the county of Buckingham. 4 vols. Lond. 1831–47.

A standard work of high quality.

CAMBRIDGESHIRE

See Nos. 1682, 1818, and *V.C.H.* (No. 1529).

1552 BARTHOLOMEW (AUGUSTUS T.). Catalogue of the books and papers, for the most part relating to the university, town, and county of Cambridge, bequeathed to the university by J. W. Clark. Cambr. 1912.

1553 GIFFORD (P. R.). Cambridgeshire: an annotated list of books, maps, prints . . . in the Cambridgeshire County Library Local History Collection. Cambr. 1961.

1554 CAMBRIDGE ANTIQUARIAN SOCIETY. Antiquarian communications. Vols. i–vi. Cambr. 1959–88. Continued as Proceedings. vol. vii+ (N.S. i+), 1893+. Publications. Octavo Ser. 1851+. Quarto Ser. 1840–9, 1908–51. Index (1840–97), 1898 (Octavo pubns. No. 30). Index to Proceedings, vols. ix–xxiv, including subjects and authors of quarto and octavo pubns. (1895–1922), 1927 (Octavo pubns. No. 51). (MG).

1555 CAMBRIDGE BIBLIOGRAPHICAL SOCIETY. Monographs. Cambr. 1951+. Transactions. 1949+.

1556 CAMBRIDGESHIRE AND HUNTINGDONSHIRE ARCHAEOLOGICAL SOCIETY. Transactions. Ely. 1904+. (MG).

1557 BLOMEFIELD (FRANCIS). Collectanea Cantabrigiensia, or collections relating to Cambridge university, town and county. Norwich. 1750.

1558 CARTER (EDMUND). The history of the county of Cambridge, from the earliest account to the present time. Cambr. 1753. New edn. by W. Upcott. Lond. 1819.

1559 CONYBEARE (J. W. EDWARD). History of Cambridgeshire. Lond. 1897.

1560 CUNNINGHAM (WILLIAM). The story of Cambridgeshire as told by itself. Cambr. 1920.

1561 DARBY (HENRY C.), ed. The Cambridge region. Cambr. 1938.

CHESHIRE

See Nos. 1698–1702.

1562 COOKE (JOHN H.). Bibliotheca Cestriensis, a biographical account of books relating to, published in or written by authors resident in Cheshire. Warrington. 1904.

1563 ARCHITECTURAL, ARCHAEOLOGICAL, AND HISTORIC SOCIETY FOR THE COUNTY, CITY AND NEIGHBOURHOOD OF CHESTER. Journal Vols. i–iii. Chester. 1849–85. N.S. 1887+. Subject indexes to the old ser. and the new ser. (i–xviii, 1887–1911). 1912. Subject index and index of authors to vols. xviii–xxviii (1911–29). 1929.

Name of society varies: Chester Archaeological and Historic Society (1887–92); Architectural, Archaeological and Historic Society for Chester and North Wales (1983–1914); Chester and North Wales (Architectural) Archaeological and Historic Society, 1915+. (MG.)

1564   CHESHIRE LOCAL HISTORY COMMITTEE. Chester. 1934+.

1565   CHESHIRE NOTES AND QUERIES. N.S. vols. i–iv. Stockport (1886–9). 3rd Ser. i–ix (1896–1913).

Formerly, Advertiser notes and queries, reprinted from the *Stockport Advertiser*. Vols. i–v. 1881–5.

1566   THE CHESHIRE SHEAF. (Published quarterly for the *Chester Courant*.) 3rd Ser. Chester. 1880+.

1567   THE PALATINE NOTE-BOOK FOR THE COUNTIES OF LANCASTER, CHESTER, ETC. 4 vols. and pp. 1–16 of vol. v. Manchester etc. 1881–5.

1568   WIRRAL NOTES AND QUERIES. 2 vols. Birkenhead. 1893–4.

1569   CHESHIRE HISTORIAN. Chester. 1951+.

1570   BAGLEY (JOHN J.), ed. History of the county-palatine of Chester sponsored by the Cheshire County Council. (13 vols. contemplated). *Roman Cheshire*, by F. H. Thompson (1965) (No. 1577).

1571   BARRACLOUGH (GEOFFREY). 'The earldom and county palatine of Chester'. *Hist. Soc. of Lancs. and Cheshire Trans.* ciii (1951–2), 23–57. Reprinted Oxf. 1953.

A brief survey of 30 pages plus a few documents from the Norman Conquest to 1543, with ample footnote references. Cf. Ronald Stewart-Brown, 'The end of the Norman earldom of Chester', *E.H.R.* xxxv (1920), 26–54; and for the protection granted to a stranger coming to the palatinate, see Ronald Stewart-Brown, 'The Avowries of Cheshire', *E.H.R.* xxix (1914), 41–55; and his 'The exchequer of Chester', published posthumously in *E.H.R.* lvii (1942), 289–97. For other articles by Stewart-Brown, see *Writings 1901–33*, ii, nos. 1632–5.

1572   EARWAKER (JOHN P.). East Cheshire, past and present; or A history of the hundred of Macclesfield. 2 vols. Lond. 1877–80.

1573   HEWITT (HERBERT). Mediaeval Cheshire: an economic and social history of Cheshire in the reigns of the three Edwards. Pubns. Univ. Manchester, No. cxcv in co-operation with Chetham Soc. N.S. lxxxviii. Manchester. 1929.

1574   ORMEROD (GEORGE). The history of the county palatine and city of Chester. 3 vols. Lond. 1819. 2nd edn. by Thomas Helsby. 3 vols. (1875)–82.

Built around family history and manors, but contains a valuable collection of charters and other documents.

1575 REPORT ON THE RECORDS OF THE COUNTY PALATINE OF CHESTER. The Deputy Keeper's Reports, i (1840), 78–122. List of officers of the palatinate of Chester, in the counties of Chester and Flint, and north Wales. Ibid. xxxi (1870), 169–261.

1576 TAIT (JAMES), ed. The Domesday Survey of Cheshire. Chetham Soc. N.S. lxxv. 1916.

See Tait's 'Knight-service in Cheshire', *E.H.R.* lvii (1942), 26–54.

1577 THOMPSON (F. H.). Roman Cheshire. Chester. 1965. See No. 1570.

CORNWALL
See Nos. 762, 1517, 1605, 1610, and *V.C.H.* (No. 1529).

1578 BOASE (GEORGE C.) and COURTNEY (WILLIAM P.). Bibliotheca Cornubiensis, a catalogue ... of works relating to the county of Cornwall. 3 vols. Lond. 1874–82.

1579 CORNISH NOTES AND QUERIES. 1st ser. Vol. i. Lond. etc. 1906.

1580 CORNWALL ARCHAEOLOGICAL SOCIETY. Cornish Archaeology. St. Ives. 1961+.

1581 NATURAL HISTORY AND ANTIQUARIAN SOCIETY OF PENZANCE. Transactions. Penzance. 1851–66, 1880/4–97/8.

1582 ROYAL INSTITUTION OF CORNWALL. Journal and Reports. Truro. 1864–1942, 1951+. General index, 1818–1906, by C. R. Hewitt. 1907. (MG).

1583 WEST CORNWALL FIELD CLUB. Proceedings. 1936–7+.

1584 BOASE (GEORGE C.). Collectanea Cornubiensia: a collection of biographical and topographical notes relating to the county of Cornwall. Truro. 1890.

1585 BORLASE (WILLIAM). Observations on the antiquities, historical and monumental, of the county of Cornwall ... Oxf. 1754. 2nd edn. Lond. 1769.

1586 CAREW (RICHARD). The survey of Cornwall. Lond. 1602. 2nd edn. by Thomas Tonkin. 1811. Another edn. by E. Halliday. 1953.

1587 ELLIOTT-BINNS (LEONARD). Medieval Cornwall. Lond. 1955.

1588 HALLIDAY (FRANK E.). A history of Cornwall. Lond. 1959.

1589 HENDERSON (CHARLES G.). Essays in Cornish history, ed. A. L. Rowse and M. I. Henderson. Oxf. 1935.

1590 MATTHEWS (GORDON F.). The Isles of Scilly: a constitutional, economic and social survey of the development of an island people from early times to 1900. Lond. 1960.

1591 POLWHELE (RICHARD). The history of Cornwall: civil, military, religious, etc. 7 vols. in 2. Falmouth, Exeter, and Lond. 1803–16.

CUMBERLAND
See Nos. 1504, 1771, and *V.C.H.* (No. 1529).

1591A HODGSON (HENRY W.), ed. A bibliography of the history and topography of Cumberland and Westmorland. (Joint Archives Committee for Cumberland, Westmorland and Carlisle: Record Office. Pubn. No. 1). 1968.

1592 HOLTBY (R. T.). 'Carlisle cathedral library and records'. *Cumber.-Westm. A. A. Soc. Trans.* N.S. lxvi (1966), 201–19.

1593 CUMBERLAND AND WESTMORLAND ANTIQUARIAN AND ARCHAEOLOGICAL SOCIETY.

(*a*) Transactions. Vols. i–xvi. Kendal. 1866–1900. New Ser. 1901+. Index of vols. i–xvi, 1901. Index catalogue. N.S. i–xii (1901–12), 1915; xiii–xxv (1913–25), 1928; author and subject index to New Ser. i–xlv, in vol. xlvi. (MG).
(*b*) Extra Series. Lond. 1877–1937. (Mullins, *Texts*, pp. 298–300.)
(*c*) Publications. Chartulary series. Vols. i–iii. Kendal. 1897–1915. Continued as Record series. Vols. iv–viii, 1923–32. (Mullins, *Texts*, pp. 301–2).
(*d*) Tract series, 1882–1915, 1928+. (Mullins, *Texts*, pp. 303–4.)

1594 COLLINGWOOD (WILLIAM G.). Lake district history. Kendal. 1925.

1595 FERGUSON (RICHARD S.). History of Cumberland. Lond. 1890. Chs. ii–vi: Roman period. Ch. xiii: City of Carlisle.

1596 HUTCHINSON (WILLIAM). The history of the county of Cumberland, and some places adjacent . . . 2 vols. Carlisle. 1794.

1597 NICOLSON (JOSEPH) and BURN (RICHARD). The history and antiquities of Westmorland and Cumberland. 2 vols. Lond. 1777. Index, ed. by Henry Hornyold-Strickland. *Cumb. and Westm. Antiq. and Arch. Soc.* Extra series, xvii (1934).

The appendix contains charters granted to towns, priories, etc.

1598 WHELLAN (WILLIAM). The history and topography of the counties of Cumberland and Westmorland. Pontefract. 1860.

Inferior to Hutchinson and Nicolson and Burn.

DERBYSHIRE
See Nos. 1782, and *V.C.H.* (No. 1529).

1599 ORMEROD (JAMES). A select catalogue of books about the county. Derby. 1930.

1600 DERBYSHIRE ARCHAEOLOGICAL AND NATURAL HISTORY SOCIETY. Journal. Lond. 1879–1959. Then the Derbyshire Archaeological Journal. 1960+. Index of cols. i–xxv (1879–1903). Derby. 1912. (MG).

1601 YEATMAN (JOHN PYM). The feudal history of the county of Derby. 5 vols. in 9 pts. Lond. etc. [1886–1907].

Contains translations of extracts from Domesday, the pipe rolls, the Red Book of the Exchequer, Testa de Nevill, Kirkby's Quest, scutages, aids, the subsidy roll of 1 Edward III, charters, hundred rolls, assize roll of Peak forest (36 Hen. III), etc.

DEVONSHIRE
See Nos. 761 (Fox), 1504, 1522, and *V.C.H.* (No. 1529).

1602 BOASE (GEORGE C.). Devonshire bibliography. Lond. 1883.

1603 DAVIDSON (JAMES). Bibliotheca Devoniensis, a catalogue of the printed books relating to the county of Devon. Exeter. 1852. Supplement. [1861].

1604 HARTE (WALTER J.). *A bibliography of Exeter*. Historical Assoc. Leaflet, No. 9. Lond. 1908.

An index of over a million entries of the contents of all books and manuscripts (except names in parish registers) about Devon was compiled by R. B. Morris. The index is housed in Exeter City Reference Library.

1605 DEVON AND CORNWALL RECORD SOCIETY. [Publications.] Exeter. 1906–54; New Ser. 1955+. (Mullins, *Texts*, pp. 305–8.)

1606 DEVON NOTES AND QUERIES. Vols. i–v. Exeter. 1901–9. Continued as Devon and Cornwall notes and queries. A quarterly journal, etc. Vol. vi+. 1910+.

1607 DEVONSHIRE ASSOCIATION FOR THE ADVANCEMENT OF SCIENCE, LITERATURE, AND ART. Transactions. Plymouth. 1863+. Index of vols. i–xvii, 1886; i–xxxx, 1909; Key to vols. i–lx (1862–1928), 1928; lxi–lxx (1938); lxxi–lxxx (1948). [Extra volumes.] 1899+. (MG).

1608 HISTORY OF EXETER RESEARCH GROUP. Monographs. 1923+.

Taken over in 1930 by a Committee of the Senate of University College, Exeter (subsequently the University of Exeter).

1609 NOTES AND GLEANINGS: A MONTHLY MAGAZINE FOR DEVON AND CORNWALL. 5 vols. Exeter. 1883–92.

1610 THE WESTERN ANTIQUARY, OR DEVON AND CORNWALL NOTE-BOOK. 12 vols. and supplement. Plymouth. 1882–95.

1611 HOSKINS (WILLIAM G.) and FINBERG (HERBERT P. R.). Devonshire studies. Lond. 1952.

Partly revised and three studies, including comments on Anglo-Saxon charters added in H. P. R. Finberg, *West Country Historical Studies* (Newton Abbot, 1969). The second part of vol. xvii (1970) of *Agricultural History Rev.* is a series of essays presented to Professor H. P. R. Finberg, and includes a bibliography of Finberg's publications.

1612 MOORE (THOMAS). History of Devon from the earliest period to the present time. 2 vols. Lond. 1829–31.

1613 POLWHELE (RICHARD). A history of Devonshire. 3 vols. Exeter. 1793–1806.

Polwhele's history should be used with caution.

DORSETSHIRE

See Nos. 1504, 1517, and *V.C.H.* (No. 1529).

1614 COX (A. C.). Index to the county records in the record room at the county offices and the shire hall, Dorchester. Dorchester. 1938.

1615 DOUCH (ROBERT). A handbook of local history, Dorset. [Bristol], 1952. New edn. 1962. Well arranged and comprehensive.

1616 MAYO (CHARLES H.). Bibliotheca Dorsetiensis, being a carefully compiled account of printed books and pamphlets relating to the history and topography of the county of Dorset. Lond. 1885.

1617 DORSET NATURAL HISTORY AND ANTIQUARIAN FIELD CLUB. Proceedings. Sherborne. 1877–1950. Indexes of vols. i–xli (1877–1920), in vol. xli, 115–38; i–lv in *Proceedings* for 1941. Occasional publications. Dorchester. 1948+.

In 1928 name was changed to Dorset Natural History and Archaeological Society. (MG).

1618 DORSET RECORD SOCIETY. Dorchester. 1962+.

1619 DORSET RECORDS: indexes, calendars, and abstracts of records. By E. A. Fry and G. S. Fry [Lond.] 1894+.

1620 HUTCHINS (JOHN). The history and antiquities of the county of Dorset. 2 vols. Lond. 1774. 3rd edn. by William Shipp and James W. Hodson. 4 vols. Westminster. 1861–73.

1621 WEINSTOCK (MAUREEN). Studies in Dorset history. Dorchester. 1953. Idem, More Dorset Studies. Dorchester, 1960.

DURHAM

See Nos. 196, 1771, and *V.C.H.* (No. 1529).

No printed bibliography.

1622 GREENSLADE (S. L.). 'The contents of the library of Durham cathedral priory'. *Archit. and Archaeol. Soc. Durham and Northumb. Trans.* xi, pts. 5–6 (1965), 347–69.

See Nos. 1043–4.

1623 ARCHITECTURAL AND ARCHAEOLOGICAL SOCIETY OF DURHAM AND NORTHUMBERLAND. Transactions. Sunderland and Durham. 1962/70+. (MG).

1624 DURHAM COUNTY LOCAL HISTORY SOCIETY. Durham. 1964+.

1625 HUTCHINSON (WILLIAM). The history and antiquities of the county palatine of Durham. 3 vols. Newcastle. 1785–94. New edn. 3 vols. Durham. 1823.

His account of the bishops of Durham is particularly valuable.

1626 LAPSLEY (GAILLARD T.). The county palatine of Durham: a study in constitutional history. N.Y. etc. 1900.

The best history. Idem, 'The problem of the north' (the relations of the central government to the northern border counties), *A.H.R.* v. (1900) 440–66: reprinted in No. 1478 above. C. M. Fraser, 'Edward I of England and the regalian franchise of Durham', *Speculum*, xxxi (1956), 329–42; idem, 'Prerogative and the bishops of Durham, 1267–1376', *E.H.R.* lxxiv (1959), 467–76. Jean Scammel, 'The origin and limitations of the liberty of Durham', ibid. lxxxi (1966), 449–73. See appropriate chapters in biographies of bishops: Scammell, *du Puiset* (No. 5700), Fraser, *Bek* (No. 5689), and Storey, *Langley* (No. 5690).

1627 LIST OF RECORDS OF THE PALATINATES of Chester, Durham and Lancaster, the honour of Peveril and the principality of Wales, preserved in the P.R.O. *P.R.O. Lists and indexes*, No. xl (1914). (No. 955 above.)

1628 RAINE (JAMES). The history and antiquities of North Durham . . . now united to the county of Northumberland. Lond. 1852.

1629 SURTEES (ROBERT). The history and antiquities of the county palatine of Durham. 4 vols. Lond. 1816–40. New edition in progress: 3 vols. Sunderland. 1908–10.

Essex
See Nos. 1504, 1818, and *V.C.H.* (No. 1529).

1630 CUNNINGTON (AUGUSTUS). Catalogue of books, maps and manuscripts, relating to . . . the county of Essex . . . Braintree. 1902.

1631 EMMISON (FREDERICK G.). Guide to the Essex record office. Essex Record Office, Pubns. Nos. 1, 2. 2 pts. in 1 vol. Chelmsford. 1946–8. Revised and enlarged edn. Pubn. No. 51. 1969. Pt. i: Essex quarter sessions and other official records. Pt. ii: Estate, eccles. and other deposited archives. One of the best guides to a local record office, the 1969 edn. covers an extensive collection.

1632 ERITH (E. J.). Essex parish records, 1240–1894. Essex Record Office, Pubns. No. 7. Chelmsford. 1950. 2nd edn. as Catalogue of Essex parish records, 1240–1894, prepared by F. G. Emmison. Chelmsford. 1966.

1633 VICTORIA COUNTY HISTORY. Bibliography (of Essex). Ed. by W. R. Powell. Lond. 1959. A supplement was published separately in 1962.

1634 WARD (GLADYS A.). Essex local history: a short guide to books and manuscripts. Essex. Comm. of the National Register of Archives. Witham. 1950.

1635   ESSEX ARCHAEOLOGICAL SOCIETY. Transactions. Colchester. 1858+. Indexes of vols. i–v (1858–73), and N.S. i–v (1878–95), 1900. N.S. vi–xv (1896–1920), 1926. (MG). Occasional publications. Colchester. 1946+.

1636   ESSEX RECORD OFFICE. Publications. Chelmsford. 1946+.

1637   THE ESSEX REVIEW. Chelmsford. [1892+]. Index of vols. i–xxxvi. (1892–1927), 1930; vols. xxxvii–lxi (1928–52), 1953.

1638   WALTHAMSTOW ANTIQUARIAN SOCIETY. Occasional publications. Lond. 1937+. Monographs. Lond. 1915+. (MG).

1639   MORANT (PHILIP). History and antiquities of the county of Essex. 2 vols. Lond. 1768. Reprinted, Chelmsford. 1816.

> A scholarly work, based on the researches of Thomas Jekyll (d. 1653), William Holman (d. 1730), and Morant.

1640   WRIGHT (THOMAS). History and topography of Essex. 2 vols. Lond. 1836.

> Rather heavily indebted to Morant (No. 1639).

GLOUCESTERSHIRE
See Nos. 1504 (18, 31, 32), 1517, and *V.C.H.* (No. 1529).

1641   AUSTIN (ROLAND). Catalogue of Gloucestershire books collected by Sir Francis Hyett of Painswick. Gloucester. 1949. Idem, Catalogue of the Gloucestershire collection: books, pamphlets and documents in the Gloucester Public Library relating to the county . . . of Gloucestershire. Gloucester. 1928.

> The 1928 catalogue is a large work of 1,236 pages.

1642   HYETT (FRANCIS A.) and BAZELEY (WILLIAM). The bibliographer's manual of Gloucestershire literature. 3 vols. Gloucester. 1895–7. Supplement by F. A. Hyett and R. Austin. 2 vols. Gloucester. 1915–16.

1643   HYETT (FRANCIS A.). CATALOGUE OF MSS. IN THE BRITISH MUSEUM RELATING TO THE COUNTY OF GLOUCESTER AND THE CITY OF BRISTOL. *Bristol and Glos. Archaeol. Soc. Trans.* xx [1897], 161–221.

1644   JAMIESON (ALAN) and SMITH (BRIAN S.). Gloucestershire local handlist. Gloucestershire Community Council. 1968.

1645   BRISTOL AND GLOUCESTERSHIRE ARCHAEOLOGICAL SOCIETY. Transactions. Bristol. 1876+. Indexes of vols. i–xx (1876–97), Gloucester, 1900; xxi–xl (1898–1917), 1919; xli–lx (1918–29), 2 vols. 1930–42. (MG). Records Branch, 1952+. (Mullins, *Texts,* p. 537.)

1646   BRISTOL RECORD SOCIETY. Publications. Bristol. 1930+. (Mullins, *Texts,* pp. 332–4.)

1647   CLIFTON ANTIQUARIAN CLUB. Proceedings. Bristol. 1884–1912. Index of vols. i–vii (1884–1912) in vol. vii, 219–241. (MG).

1648 GLOUCESTERSHIRE NOTES AND QUERIES. 10 vols. Lond. 1881–1914. Discontinued in 1905; resumed in 1913–14.

1649 ATKYNS (ROBERT). The ancient and present state of Gloucestershire. Lond. 1712. 2nd edn. 1768.

1650 BIGLAND (RALPH). Historical, monumental, and genealogical collections relative to the county of Gloucester. 2 vols. Lond. 1786–92.

Devoted mainly to monumental inscriptions, genealogical tables, etc. For an index of the heraldry, by F. Were, see *Bristol. and Glos. Archaeol. Soc. Trans.* xxviii (1905), 147–510.

1651 GLOUCESTER STUDIES. Ed. by H. P. R. Finberg. Leicester. 1957.

A group of papers by various hands; strong on A.-S. and medieval periods; includes E. A. L. Moir, 'The historians of Gloucestershire'.

1652 FOSBROKE (THOMAS D.). Abstracts of records and manuscripts respecting the county of Gloucester. [Half-title: History of Gloucestershire.] 2 vols. Gloucester etc. 1807.

Supersedes Atkyns and Bigland.

1653 [RUDDER (SAMUEL).] A new history of Gloucestershire. Cirencester. 1779.

Contains a facsimile copy of the Domesday for Gloucestershire, and an appendix of documents.

HAMPSHIRE

See *V.C.H.* (No. 1529).

1654 GILBERT (HENRY M.) and GODWIN (GEORGE N.). Bibliotheca Hantoniensis: a list of books relating to Hampshire . . . Southampton. [1891].

1655 SOUTHAMPTON RECORDS. I. Guide to the records of the corporation. Southampton. 1964.

Supplements in No. 1656, iii (1895–8), 303–16; v (1904–6), 127–36, 229–43.

1656 HAMPSHIRE FIELD CLUB [SINCE 1899 CALLED HAMPSHIRE FIELD CLUB AND ARCHAEOLOGICAL SOCIETY]. Papers and proceedings. Southampton. 1887+ [for 1885+]. Index to vols. i–x (1885–1931), 1932. (MG).

1657 HAMPSHIRE NOTES AND QUERIES. 6 vols. Winchester. 1883–98.

1658 HAMPSHIRE RECORD SOCIETY. Publications. 12 vols. Lond. 1889–99. (Mullins, *Texts*, pp. 335–7.)

Winchester Cathedral Records were published by this society.

1659 ISLE OF WIGHT NATURAL HISTORY AND ARCHAEO-LOGICAL SOCIETY. Proceedings. Newport. 1919+.

1660 SOUTHAMPTON ARCHAEOLOGICAL SOCIETY. Southampton. 1961.

1661 SOUTHAMPTON RECORD SOCIETY. Publications. Southampton. 1905+. (Mullins, *Texts*, pp. 338–41.)

1662 SOUTHAMPTON RECORD SERIES. Published by University College (subsequently the University). Southampton. 1951+. (Mullins, *Texts*, p. 342.)

1663 SUMNER (HEYWOOD). Local papers, archaeological and topographical: Hampshire, Dorset, Wiltshire. Lond. 1931.

1664 WOODWARD (BERNARD B.), WILKS (THEODORE C.), and LOCKHART (CHARLES). A general history of Hampshire . . . including the Isle of Wight. 3 vols. Lond. [1861–9].

HEREFORDSHIRE
See *V.C.H.* (No. 1529).

1665 ALLEN (JOHN). Bibliotheca Herefordiensis; or a descriptive catalogue of books, pamphlets, maps . . . relating to the county of Hereford. Hereford. 1821.

  25 copies (privately printed).

1666 BODENHAM (FREDERICK). The bibliographer's manual of Hereford literature. Hereford. 1890.

1667 COUNTY LIBRARY. Herefordshire books: select list of books in the local collection. Hereford. 1955.

1668 CANTILUPE SOCIETY. [Publications.] Hereford. 1908+. (Mullins, *Texts*, p. 343.)

  The Cantilupe Society has published jointly with the Canterbury and York Society the episcopal registers of Hereford.

1669 WOOLHOPE NATURALISTS' FIELD CLUB. Transactions. Hereford. 1852+. Indexes 1866–82, 1895–1911, 1912–35, 1936–54. (MG).

1670 DUNCUMB (JOHN). Collections towards the history and antiquities of the county of Hereford. 3 vols. (vol. iii by William H. Cooke). Hereford etc. 1804–82. Continuation, by W. H. Cooke: Hundred of Grimsworth. Lond. 1886. Continuations, by M. G. Watkins: Hundred of Huntington, and Hundred of Radlow. 2 pts. in 1 vol. Hereford, 1897–1902. Continuation, by J. H. Matthews: Hundred of Wormslow. Upper division, 2 pts. 1912–13; Lower division. 2 pts. Hereford. 1913–15.

HERTFORDSHIRE
See Nos. 171, 1504, and *V.C.H.* (No. 1529).

1671 LE HARDY (WILLIAM). Guide to the Hertfordshire Record Office. Pt. i: Quarter sessions and other records. Hertford. 1961 (in progress).

1672 CATALOGUE OF RECORDS, MAPS, ETC. RELATING TO HERTFORDSHIRE. County Record Office. Hertford. 1957.

1673 EAST HERTFORDSHIRE ARCHAEOLOGICAL SOCIETY. Transactions. Hertford. 1899+. (MG). Joined with No. 1675 to publish *Hertfordshire Archaeology*, 1968+.

1674 HERTFORDSHIRE NATURAL HISTORY SOCIETY AND FIELD CLUB. Transactions. Lond. and Hertford. 1879+. Classified subject index, 1875–1914, in vol. xv, 257–71.

> Society founded in 1875 as Watford Natural History Soc. and Hertfordshire Field Club and reorganized in 1879 under present name.

1675 ST. ALBANS ARCHITECTURAL AND ARCHAEOLOGICAL SOCIETY. Transactions. St. Albans. 1884+. Index (1884–95). 1898.

> Since 1895 called St. Albans and Hertfordshire Architectural and Archaeological Society. (MG.) See No. 1673.

1676 CHAUNCY (HENRY). Historical antiquities of Hertfordshire. Lond. 1700. New edn. 2 vols. 1826.

1677 CLUTTERBUCK (ROBERT). The history and antiquities of the county of Hertford. 3 vols. Lond. 1815–27.

> The appendices of vols. ii–iii contain a survey of the borough of Hertford, 5 Edw. III, and surveys of the manors of Hatfield, Stevenage, Totteridge, Little Hadham, and Kelshall, made in 1277.

1678 CUSSANS (JOHN E.). History of Hertfordshire. 3 vols. Lond. etc. 1870–81.

HUNTINGDONSHIRE
See No. 1556, and *V.C.H.* (No. 1529).

1679 COUNTY LIBRARY. Catalogue of the local history collection [at] Gazeley House, Huntingdon. Huntingdon. 1950. 2nd edn. 1958.

1680 FINDLAY (G. H.). Guide to the Huntingdonshire record office. Huntingdon. 1958.

1681 NORRIS (HERBERT E.). Catalogue of the Huntingdonshire books collected by H. E. Norris. Cirencester. 1895.

1682 FENLAND NOTES AND QUERIES: A QUARTERLY ANTIQUARIAN JOURNAL FOR THE COUNTIES OF HUNTINGDON, CAMBRIDGE, LINCOLN, NORTHAMPTON, NORFOLK, AND SUFFOLK. 7 vols. Peterborough. 1889–1909.

1682A RECORDS OF HUNTINGDONSHIRE. Huntingdonshire Local History Soc. 1965+.

KENT
See Nos. 762 (Jessup), 1504, 1505, and *V.C.H.* (No. 1529).

1683 CHURCHILL (IRENE J.). A handbook to Kent records, containing a summary account of the principal classes of historical documents relating to the county of Kent, and a guide to their chief places of deposit. Kent Archaeol. Soc. *Kent Records*, vol. ii. Lond. 1914.

1684 HULL (FELIX), ed. Guide to the Kent County Archives Office. Maidstone. 1958. Annual accessions are listed in *Archaeol. Cant.* (No. 1689).

1685 JESSUP (FRANK W.). The history of Kent: a bibliography. Maidstone. 1966.

1686 KENT COUNTY LIBRARY. Catalogue of books on local history. Maidstone. 1932. Local history catalogue (1939), 1939.

1687 SMITH (JOHN R.). Bibliotheca Cantiana: a bibliographical account of what has been published on the history, topography, antiquities . . . of the county of Kent. Lond. 1837; 1851.

1851 edition includes Surrey and Sussex.

1688 CANTERBURY ARCHAEOLOGICAL SOCIETY. Occasional papers. Canterbury.

1689 KENT ARCHAEOLOGICAL SOCIETY. Archaeologia Cantiana: transactions of the society. Lond. 1858+. Index of vols. i–xviii (1858–89), issued as vol. xix; xx–xlv (1893–1933), issued as vol. lii, 1940; xlvi–lxiv issued as vol. lxvii, 1954. (MG). Records Branch. Kent records. Canterbury. 1912+. (Mullins, *Texts*, pp. 344–6.)

1690 THE KENTISH NOTE BOOK. 2 vols. Gravesend. 1891–4.

Reprinted from the *Gravesend and Dartford Reporter.*

1691 LEWISHAM ANTIQUARIAN SOCIETY. Publications. 8 vols. Lee. 1888–95. Proceedings. 1899+.

1692 FURLEY (ROBERT). A history of the Weald of Kent, with an outline of the early history of the county. 2 vols. in 3 pts. Ashford etc. 1871–4.

Vol. ii, Ch. ii contains extracts from the assize rolls of 25 and 39 Henry III.

1693 HASTED (EDWARD). The history and topographical survey of Kent. 4 vols. Canterbury. 1778–99. 2nd edn. 12 vols. 1797–1801. New edn. of part i: The Hundred of Blackheath, by H. H. Drake. 1886.

1694 LAMBARDE (WILLIAM). A perambulation of Kent: containing the description, hystorie, and customes of that shyre. Lond. 1576. 2nd edn. 1596. Later edn. 1826.

Customal of Kent, translation and original in alternate lines, pp. 570–85.

LANCASHIRE
See Nos. 1504, 1517, and *V.C.H.* (No. 1529).

1695 FISHWICK (HENRY). The Lancashire library: a bibliographical account of books . . . relating to the county palatine . . . Lond. 1875.

1696 FRANCE (REGINALD SHARPE). Guide to the Lancashire record office. Preston. 1948. 2nd edn. 1962.

1697 SUTTON (ALBERT). Bibliotheca Lancastriensis: a catalogue of books on the topography and genealogy of Lancashire, with an appendix of Cheshire books. Manchester. 1894. 2nd edn. 1898.

1698 CHETHAM SOCIETY. Remains historical and literary connected with the palatine counties of Lancaster and Chester. Vols. i–cxiv. Manchester. 1844–86. N.S. i–cx. 1883–1947. 3rd Ser. i+. 1949+. Indexes of vols. i–cxiv. 2 vols. 1863–93. (Mullins, *Texts*, pp. 360–88.)

1699 HISTORIC SOCIETY OF LANCASHIRE AND CHESHIRE. Proceedings or Transactions. Liverpool. 1849+. Indexes of vols. i–li (1849–1900), 1904; lii–lxi (1900–9), in vol. lxi. [N.S. xxv], 229–30; lxii–lxxi (1910–19), in lxxiv. [N.S. xxxviii], 198–209; lxxii–lxxxv (1920–33), in lxxxvi. 119–36. (MG).

Called Transactions since 1855.

1700 LANCASHIRE AND CHESHIRE ANTIQUARIAN SOCIETY. Transactions. Manchester. 1884+. Indexes every tenth volume, 1893, 1903, etc. (MG).

1701 LANCASHIRE AND CHESHIRE HISTORICAL AND GENEALOGICAL NOTES. 3 vols. Leigh. 1879–83.

1702 RECORD SOCIETY FOR LANCASHIRE AND CHESHIRE. Publications. Lond. 1879+. (Mullins, *Texts*, pp. 347–59.)

1703 UNIVERSITY OF LIVERPOOL, INSTITUTE OF ARCHAEOLOGY. Annals of archaeology and anthropology. Liverpool etc. 1908–48.

1704 UNIVERSITY OF LIVERPOOL, SCHOOL OF LOCAL HISTORY AND RECORDS. Publications. Lond. 1906–35.

Charters in R. Muir and E. M. Platt (No. 5128).

1705 BAINES (EDWARD). The history of the county palatine and duchy of Lancaster. 2 vols. Manchester. 1824. 4 vols. 1836. 2 vols. 1868–70. New edn. by James Croston. 5 vols. Manchester. 1888(1886)–93.*

Baines's *History* is weak on the medieval period.

1706 FISHWICK (HENRY). A history of Lancashire. Lond. 1894.*

1707 SOMERVILLE (ROBERT). History of the duchy of Lancaster, vol. i (1265–1603). Lond. 1953.

For the duchy of Lancaster, see the entries under 'Special Jurisdictions'. Somerville's *History* is a detailed, scholarly study based on the records of the duchy; it includes long lists of officers.

LEICESTERSHIRE
See Nos. 171, 1505, 1517, and *V.C.H.* (No. 1529).

1708 LEE (J. M.). Leicestershire history: a handlist to printed sources in the libraries of Leicester. Leicester. 1958.

This work is not very useful for the medieval period.

1709 LEICESTERSHIRE AND RUTLAND NOTES AND QUERIES. 3 vols. Leicester. 1891[1889]–95.

1710 LEICESTERSHIRE ARCHITECTURAL AND ARCHAEO-LOGICAL SOCIETY. Transactions. Leicester. 1866+. General index, vols. i–xx. (MG).
Title changed to Leicestershire Archaeological Society in 1915.

1711 UNIVERSITY COLLEGE, LEICESTER, DEPARTMENT OF ENGLISH LOCAL HISTORY. Occasional papers. 1952+.

1712 FOX (LEVI). The administration of the honour of Leicester in the fourteenth century. Leicester. 1940.
A brief account, with records, of administration of part of the duchy of Lancaster.

1713 HOSKINS (WILLIAM G.). Essays in Leicestershire history. Liverpool. 1950. Studies in Leicestershire agrarian history. Ed. by W. G. Hoskins. Leicestershire Archaeol. Soc. Leicester. 1948.

1714 NICHOLS (JOHN). The history and antiquities of the county of Leicester. 4 vols. in 8. Lond. 1795–1815.
The following are some of the many records printed in this work:
Rental etc. of Leicester abbey, i, app. 53–108.
Lists of knights' fees, i, pp. ciii–cxxxvi.
Charters, etc., of Belvoir priory, ii, app. 2–39.
Documents relating to Croxton abbey, ii, app. 77–107.
Chartulary of the honour of Segrave (extracts), ii, app. 108–20.
Chartulary of Garendon abbey (extracts), ii, app. 133–8.
See also his 'Antiquities in Leicestershire', etc. in his *Bibliotheca topographica Britannica* (No. 1505), vols. vii–viii (Lond. 1790).

LINCOLNSHIRE
See Nos. 171, 1504, 1505, 1682, and *V.C.H.* (No. 1529).

1715 CORNS (ALBERT R.). Bibliotheca Lincolniensis: a catalogue of the books, pamphlets, etc., relating to the city and county of Lincoln in the City of Lincoln Public Library. Lincoln. 1904.

1716 LINCOLNSHIRE ARCHIVES COMMITTEE. Archivists' reports, nos. [1+]. July 1948+. Annual report on inventory.

1717 ARCHITECTURAL AND ARCHAEOLOGICAL SOCIETY OF THE COUNTY OF LINCOLN: REPORTS AND PAPERS. Lincoln. 1851–1937. New Ser. 1938–65 (MG). Replaced in 1966 by No. 1718.
Superseded No. 171 above.

1718 LINCOLN RECORD SOCIETY. Publications. Lincoln. 1911+. (Mullins, *Texts*, pp. 389–94.)

1719 LINCOLNSHIRE LOCAL HISTORY SOCIETY 1947–65. Lincolnshire Historian. 1947–65. See No. 1720.

1720 LINCOLNSHIRE HISTORICAL AND ARCHAEOLOGICAL SOCIETY. 1966+.

Founded in 1966, it supersedes Nos. 1717 and 1719; and publishes Lincolnshire History and Archaeology. 1966+.

1721 LINCOLNSHIRE MAGAZINE. Lindsey Local History Society. Vols. i–iv. Lincoln. 1932–9. Continued by LINCOLNSHIRE HISTORIAN. Lincolnshire Local History Society. Lincoln. 1947+.

1722 LINCOLNSHIRE NOTES AND QUERIES. 24 vols. Horncastle. 1888–1936.

1723 ALLEN (THOMAS). The history of the county of Lincoln. 2 vols. Lond. 1833–4.

Extent of Boston, 1279, i. 217–19. A cooperative history of Lincolnshire in 12 vols., edited by Joan Thirsk, is in preparation. See No. 6798.

LONDON AND MIDDLESEX

See Nos. 762 (Vulliamy), 1504 (11, 14, 16), 1505, 1522, and *V.C.H.* (No. 1529).

The records and more specialized histories of London will be found in the section entitled 'Borough and Town' in volume ii.

1724 CATALOGUE OF THE GUILDHALL LIBRARY of the city of London with additions to June 1889. Lond. 1889.

1725 LONDON COUNTY COUNCIL, LIBRARY. Members' library catalogue. vol. i. London history and topography. Lond. 1939.

The fullest bibliography, partly annotated.

1726 DARLINGTON (IDA). Guide to the records in the London county record office. pt. i. Lond. 1963. (in progress).

1727 JEAFFRESON (JOHN C.). Middlesex county records. Middlesex County Record Soc. 4 vols. Lond. 1887–1902. (See No. 1738.)

1728 JONES (PHILIP E.) and SMITH (RAYMOND). A guide to the records in the corporation of London Records Office and the Guildhall Library muniment room. Lond. 1951.

1729 SMITH (RAYMOND), comp. The city of London: a select book list. National Book League. Lond. 1951.

Cf. *Bibliography of London*, Historical Assoc. Leaflet, No. 14 (1908). For older works, Gross, *Bibliog. Municipal History* (No. 1511); and Martin (No. 1511).

1730 SMITH (JOHN EDWARD). A catalogue of Westminster records deposited at the town hall. Lond. 1900.

1731 GUILDHALL MISCELLANY. London Corporation Library Committee. 1952+.

1732 HOME COUNTIES MAGAZINE: DEVOTED TO THE TOPO-
GRAPHY OF LONDON, MIDDLESEX, ESSEX, HERTS, BUCKS,
BERKS, SURREY, AND KENT. 14 vols. Lond. 1899–1912. Index of vols.
i–x (1899–1908). 1911.

Supersedes *Middlesex and Hertfordshire Notes and Queries*, 4 vols. (1895–8).

1733 LONDON AND MIDDLESEX ARCHAEOLOGICAL SOCIETY.
Transactions. Vols. i–vi. Lond. 1860–90. New Ser. 1905+ Index of vols. i–vii
in New Ser. i.

Not published between 1891 and 1904.

1734 LONDON AND MIDDLESEX NOTE BOOK. 1 vol. Lond. 1891–2.

1735 LONDON SOCIETY. Journal. Lond. 1913+. Index, 1913–26 (nos.
1–106). 1927.

1736 LONDON RECORD SOCIETY. Founded 1964. Publications. 1965+.

See Nos. 3579A, 3580, 5201, 6225.

1737 LONDON TOPOGRAPHICAL SOCIETY. London topographical
record. Lond. 1899+. Index of vols. i–viii (1900–1912/13), in vol. ix. 57–76.
Publications. 1881+.

1738 MIDDLESEX COUNTY RECORD SOCIETY. Lond. 1886–92.
(Mullins, *Texts*, p. 395.)

1739 ST. PAUL'S ECCLESIOLOGICAL SOCIETY. Transactions. New
Ser. vol. i. Lond. 1879–84+.

Originally *Cambridge Camden Soc. Trans.*, vols. i–iii (1839/41–43/45).

1740 BIRD (RUTH). Turbulent London of Richard II. Lond. 1949.

M. B. Honeybourne, *Sketch map of London under Richard II*, London Topograph. Soc.
Pubn. No. 93 (Lond. 1960).

1741 HARBEN (HENRY A.). A dictionary of London: being notes topographical and historical relating to the streets and principal buildings in the city
of London. Lond. 1918.

An important work on the topography and history of London.

1742 NOORTHOUCK (JOHN). A new history of London, including Westminster and Southwark. Lond. 1773.

The appendix contains a translation of the charters of London, etc.

1743 NORTON (GEORGE). Commentaries on the history, constitution, and
chartered franchises of the city of London. Lond. 1829. 3rd edn. 1869.

Bk. i. Historical account; bk. ii. The charters. Valuable for the constitution and history
of the city.

1744 PAGE (WILLIAM). London: its origin and early development. Lond.
1923.

See also Williams (No. 1748).

1745 SHARPE (REGINALD R.). London and the kingdom: a history derived mainly from the archives at Guildhall . . . 3 vols. Lond. 1894–5.

Deals mainly with the political history of London, i.e. its relations with the king and the kingdom down to 1832.

1746 STENTON (FRANK M.). Norman London: an essay. With a translation of William FitzStephen's description by H. E. Butler and a Map of London under Henry II by Marjorie B. Honeybourne, annotated by E. Jeffries Davis. Historical Assoc. Leaflets, Nos. 93 and 94. Lond. 1934.

For a revised edition of Stenton's essay, see No. 1495–6. For Saxon and Viking London, see Wheeler (No. 2489).

1746A STOW (JOHN). A survey of the cities of London and Westminster and the borough of Southwark. Reprinted from the edition of 1603 with introduction by C. L. Kingsford. 2 vols. Oxf. 1908. (Many earlier editions).

1747 STUDIES IN LONDON HISTORY, presented to Philip Edmund Jones. Ed. by A. E. J. Hollaender and William Kellaway. Lond. 1969. (No. 5177).

1748 WILLIAMS (GWYN A.). Medieval London: from commune to capital. Univ. London Hist. Stud. xi. Lond. 1963. Also pb.

The best modern history of the medieval city. Paperback edn. with corrections (1970). See also Martin Weinbaum, *London unter Eduard I und Eduard II* (Stuttgart, 1933); and Tout, *Collected Papers* (No. 1499), vol. iii.

NORFOLK

See Nos. 1504 (10, 38), 1682, 1818, and *V.C.H.* (No. 1529).

1749 [QUINTON (JOHN).] Bibliotheca Norfolciensis: a catalogue of . . . works relating to . . . Norfolk in the library of J. J. Colman, at Carrow abbey, Norwich. Norwich. 1896.

1750 RYE (WALTER). A handbook to the materials available to students of local history and genealogy. Rye's Norfolk handbooks, N.S. no. 1. Norwich. 1924. Idem, index to Norfolk topography. Index Soc. No. 10. Lond. 1881. Supplement. Norwich. 1896. Idem, Appendix . . . forming an index to . . . books published or written since. Rye's Norfolk handlists. 2nd ser. No. 1. Norwich. 1916. Idem, an index *rerum* to Norfolk antiquities. Norwich. 1899.

See also George Stephen, 'Literature relating to Norfolk archaeology and kindred subjects, 1934', *Norfolk Archaeol.* xxv (1935), 429–48. J. C. Tingey, *A short catalogue of the records of the county of Norfolk* (1904).

1751 WOODWARD (SAMUEL). The Norfolk topographer's manual . . . Revised and augmented by W. C. Ewing. Lond. 1842.

1752 NORFOLK AND NORWICH ARCHAEOLOGICAL SOCIETY. Norfolk Archaeology. Norwich. 1847+. Indexes of vols. i–x (1846–90), 1891; xi–xx (1892–1921), 1928. (MG).

Published *Norfolk records*. Ed. by W. D. Selby and Walter Rye. 2 vols. 1886–92. See No. 4372.

1753   THE NORFOLK ANTIQUARIAN MISCELLANY. 3 vols. Norwich.
1877–87. 2nd Ser. 1906–8+.

1754   NORFOLK RECORD SOCIETY. [Publications.] Fakenham and Lond.
1931+. (Mullins, *Texts*, pp. 396–8.)

1755   ASTLEY (HUGH J. D.). Memorials of old Norfolk. Lond. 1908.

1756   BLOMEFIELD (FRANCIS) and PARKIN (CHARLES). An essay
towards a topographical history of the county of Norfolk . . . 5 vols. Fersfield
etc. 1739–75. Another edn. 11 vols. Lond. 1805–10. Index *nominum*, by J. N.
Chadwick. King's Lynn. 1862. A supplement to Blomefield's *Norfolk*. Ed. by
Clement Ingleby. Lond. 1929.

> Blomefield's history is partly based on the manuscript collections of Peter de Neve
> (d. 1729).

1757   REDSTONE (LILIAN J.). Our East Anglian heritage; or, Between the
Wash and the Stour. Lond. 1939. 3rd edn. 1951.

1758   RYE (WALTER). A history of Norfolk. Lond. 1885.

NORTHAMPTONSHIRE
See No. 1682 and *V.C.H.* (No. 1529).

1759   KING (PATRICK I.). Summary guide to the Northamptonshire record
office. Northampton. 1954.

1760   TAYLOR (JOHN). Bibliotheca Northantoniensis. Northampton [*c.*
1870]. Another edn. 1884.

> A bibliographical account of what has been written or printed relating to the history,
> topography, antiquities . . . of Northamptonshire (original printing limited to six copies).

1761   NORTHAMPTONSHIRE NATURAL HISTORY SOCIETY AND
FIELD CLUB. Journal. Northampton. 1880+. Index to vols. i–x (1880–1900),
[1901]. (MG).

> Society founded 1876 as Northampton Natural History Soc. and Field Club.

1762   NORTHAMPTONSHIRE NOTES AND QUERIES. 6 vols. Northampton. 1884–96. New Ser. 6 vols. 1905–31.

> Suspended 1914–20.

1763   NORTHAMPTONSHIRE RECORD SOCIETY. Northamptonshire
past and present. Northampton. 1948+. Publications. Hereford, etc. 1924+.
(Mullins, *Texts*, pp. 399–402.)

1764   NORTHAMPTON COUNTY MAGAZINE. Northampton. 1928–33.

1765   BAKER (GEORGE). The history and antiquities of the county of
Northampton. 2 vols. Lond. 1822–41.

> Lists incumbents of churches.

1766 BRIDGES (JOHN). The history and antiquities of Northamptonshire, compiled from the manuscript collections of the late antiquary John Bridges. By the Rev. Peter Whalley. 2 vols. Lond. 1791.

NORTHUMBERLAND
See Nos. 196, 1504, 1623, 1628.

1767 ANDERTON (BASIL). Local catalogue of material concerning Newcastle and Northumberland as represented in the central public library. Newcastle-upon-Tyne. 1932.

1768 DONKIN (WINIFRED C.) and PATTERSON (EDWIN F.). Northumberland and Tyneside: a bibliography. Ministry of town and country planning. 1946.

1769 SOCIETY OF ANTIQUARIES OF NEWCASTLE-UPON-TYNE. Archaeologia Aeliana. Newcastle. 1822+. General indexes. 1897 and 1925. (MG). Proceedings. Newcastle. 1855+. General indexes. 1897 and 1925. (MG).

1770 NEWCASTLE UPON TYNE RECORDS COMMITTEE. Publications. 1920+. (Mullins, *Texts*, pp. 403–4.)

1771 NORTHERN NOTES AND QUERIES. Devoted to the antiquities of Northumberland, Cumberland, Westmorland, and Durham. Newcastle-upon-Tyne. 1906+.

1772 A HISTORY OF NORTHUMBERLAND. Issued under the direction of the Northumberland County History Committee. 15 vols. Newcastle etc. 1893–1940.

> A continuation of Hodgson's *History* (No. 1775). A monumental work, comparable to the *Victoria County History*.

1773 BATES (C. J.). The border holds of Northumberland. Vol. i. Soc. of Antiq. of Newcastle. Newcastle. 1891.

1774 HARTSHORNE (C. H.). Feudal and military antiquities of Northumberland and the Scottish borders. Royal Archaeol. Institute of Great Britain. Memoirs of Northumberland, vol. ii. Lond. 1858.

1775 HODGSON (JOHN). A history of Northumberland, in three parts. [Pt. i by J. H. Hinde, 1858.] 7 vols. Newcastle. 1820–58.

> Charters relating to Simonburne parish, pt. iii, vol. i, pp. 1–25.
> Ancient deeds, etc., pt. iii, vol. ii, pp. 1–36.
> Records respecting church institutions, pt. iii, vol. ii, pp. 37–170.
> Pipe rolls, 1129–1272, pt. iii, vol. iii; also printed separately, as Magnus Rotulus Pipae, or the Great Roll of the exchequer for Northumberland, 1130–1272 (Newcastle, 1835).

1776 PAGE (WILLIAM). 'Some remarks on the Northumbrian palatinates and regalities'. *Archaeologia*, li (1888), 143–55.

> Tries to show that the regalian rights enjoyed within the palatinates of Durham and Lancaster, the honours of Richmond, Holderness, Hexham, etc., had their origin in the regality of the ancient kingdom and earldom of Northumbria.

NOTTINGHAMSHIRE

See No. 171 and *V.C.H.* (No. 1529).

1777 BRISCOE (JOHN P.). Nottinghamshire history, topography, antiquities and natural history: a topographical index of papers and notes. Nottinghamshire index series, No. 1. Nottingham. [1919].

1778 COUNTY LIBRARY. Nottinghamshire: a catalogue of . . . the local history collection. Nottingham, 1953. New edn. 1961.

1779 KENNEDY (P. A.). Guide to the Nottinghamshire county record office. Nottingham. 1960.

1780 [WARD (JAMES).] Descriptive catalogue of books relating to Nottinghamshire in the library of James Ward. Nottingham. 1892. Supplementary catalogue etc. Nottingham. 1898.

1781 [WARD (JAMES).] List of books relating to the history, bibliography, and genealogy of Nottinghamshire published under the direction of James Ward. Nottingham. 1904. Another edn. 1913.

1782 NOTTS & DERBYSHIRE NOTES AND QUERIES. 6 vols. Derby. 1892–8.

1783 THOROTON SOCIETY. Transactions. Nottingham. 1898+. Record series. Nottingham. 1903+. (Mullins, *Texts*, pp. 405–7.)

1784 THOROTON (ROBERT). The antiquities of Nottinghamshire. Lond. 1677. 2nd edn. 3 vols. 1790. With additions by John Throsby. 3 vols. 1797.

1785 WOOD (ALFRED C.). A history of Nottinghamshire. Thoroton Soc. Nottingham. 1947. 2nd edn. 1948.

OXFORDSHIRE

See *V.C.H.* (No. 1529).

1786 CORDEAUX (EDWARD H.) and MERRY (DENIS H.), eds. A bibliography of printed works relating to Oxfordshire, excluding the university and city of Oxford. Oxford Historical Soc. [Publications]. New Ser. vol. xi. Oxf. 1955.

Supplement, *Bodleian Library Record*, vi (1957–61), 433–43; 557–71.

1787 MADAN (FALCONER). Oxford books: a bibliography of printed works relating to the university and city of Oxford. 3 vols. Oxf. 1895–1931.

1788 ASHMOLEAN SOCIETY, OXFORD. Proceedings. Vols. i–iii, 1832–58. New Ser. i–v, 1866–8. Continued as Journal of the proceedings. Nos. i–iv, 1879–81.

In 1901 united with Oxfordshire Natural History Soc. to form Ashmolean Natural History Soc. of Oxfordshire.

1789 ARCHAEOLOGICAL SOCIETY OF NORTH OXFORDSHIRE. Title varies: Reports and publications; transactions and papers, etc. Banbury. 1953+. Index, 1853–1915, in Report for 1915, pp. 255–66. (MG).

Called since 1888 the Oxfordshire Archaeological Society.

1790 OXONIENSIA: A JOURNAL DEALING WITH THE ARCHAEO-
LOGY, HISTORY AND ARCHITECTURE OF OXFORD AND ITS
NEIGHBOURHOOD. Oxford Architectural and Historical Society. Oxf.
1936+.

1791 OXFORD BIBLIOGRAPHICAL SOCIETY. Proceedings and papers,
1923+. Oxf. 1928+. (MG).

1792 OXFORD HISTORICAL SOCIETY. Publications. Vols. i–ci. Oxf.
1885–1936. New ser. 1939+. (Mullins, *Texts*, pp. 412–25.)

1793 OXFORDSHIRE RECORD SOCIETY. Oxfordshire Record Series.
Oxf. 1919+. (Mullins, *Texts*, pp. 408–11.)

No scholarly county history, except *V.C.H.* (No. 1529).

Rutlandshire
See No. 1709 and *V.C.H.* (No. 1529).

No important printed bibliography.

1794 RUTLAND ARCHAEOLOGICAL AND NATURAL HISTORY
SOCIETY. 1902+. (MG).

> The first nine reports were published as *The Rutland Magazine and County Historical
> Record*, vols. i–v. Oakham, 1903–12. Thereafter as Reports and Transactions of the
> Society.

1795 WRIGHT (JAMES). History and antiquities of the county of Rutland.
Lond. 1684.

Shropshire
See *V.C.H.* (No. 1529).

1796 HILL (MARY C.). A guide to the Shropshire records. Salop County
Council. Shrewsbury. 1952.

1797 SALOPIAN SHREDS AND PATCHES. 10 vols. Shrewsbury. 1874–91.

1798 SHROPSHIRE ARCHAEOLOGICAL AND NATURAL HISTORY
SOCIETY. Transactions. Shrewsbury. 1878+. Indexes in 2nd Ser. vol. xii,
1900; 3rd Ser. x, 1910; 4th Ser. xii, 1930. (MG).

> From 1923 on, also known as Shropshire Archaeological Society.

1799 SHROPSHIRE NOTES AND QUERIES. 3 vols. Shrewsbury. 1886–7.
Another Ser. 8 vols. 1892–9. 3rd Ser. 13 vols. 1923–35.

1800 ANDERSON (JOHN C.). Shropshire: its early history and antiquities
. . . Lond. 1864.

> Based on Domesday; contains tables of Domesday hundreds.

1801 EYTON (ROBERT W.). Antiquities of Shropshire. 12 vols. Lond. 1853–60.
> Covers 1066–1272 in detail, hence particularly valuable for the twelfth and thirteenth centuries.

SOMERSET
See *V.C.H.* (No. 1529).

1802 GREEN (EMANUEL). Bibliotheca Somersetensis: a catalogue of books, pamphlets, single sheets, and broadsides in some way connected with the county of Somerset. 3 vols. Taunton. 1902.

1803 HUMPHREYS (ARTHUR L.). Somersetshire parishes. 2 vols. Lond. 1906.
> Gives reference to printed and MS. material relating to the various parishes.

1804 KING (JOHN E.). Inventory of parochial documents in the diocese of Bath and Wells and the county of Somerset. Somerset county council: County records committee. Book i. Taunton. 1938.

1805 BATH NATURAL HISTORY AND ANTIQUARIAN FIELD CLUB. Proceedings. 11 vols. Bath. 1867–1909. Index of vols. i–ix (1867–1901), in ix, pp. 317–23. (MG).

1806 NOTES AND QUERIES FOR SOMERSET AND DORSET. Sherborne. 1890+.

1807 SOMERSET RECORD SOCIETY. Collectanea. Vols. i–ii. 1924–8. Publications. Lond. 1887+. Extra Ser. 1931. (Mullins, *Texts*, pp. 426–34.)

1808 SOMERSETSHIRE ARCHAEOLOGICAL AND NATURAL HISTORY SOCIETY. Proceedings. Taunton. 1851+. Indexes of vols. i–xx (1849–74), Bristol, 1876; xxi–xl (1875–94), Taunton, 1898; short index chiefly topographical, i–lxxx (1849–1934), 1937. (MG).

1809 SOMERSETSHIRE ARCHAEOLOGICAL AND NATURAL HISTORY SOCIETY. Bath and District Branch. Proceedings. 8 vols. Bath. 1904–47. (MG).

1810 COLLINSON (JOHN) and RACK (EDMUND). The history and antiquities of the county of Somerset . . . 3 vols. Bath. 1791. An index by Frederic W. Weaver and E. H. Bates. Somers. Archaeol. and Nat. Hist. Soc. Taunton. 1898.

1811 PHELPS (WILLIAM). The history and antiquities of Somersetshire. 2 vols. Lond. 1836–9.

STAFFORDSHIRE
See No. 1504 and *V.C.H.* (No. 1529).

1812 SIMMS (RUPERT). Bibliotheca Staffordiensis: or, a bibliographical account of books and other printed matter relating to . . . the county of Stafford. Lichfield. 1894.

1812A LICHFIELD AND SOUTH STAFFORDSHIRE ARCHAEOLO-GICAL AND HISTORICAL SOCIETY, Transactions. 1959–60+.

1813 NORTH STAFFORDSHIRE FIELD CLUB. Transactions and annual report (title varies). Stafford 1866–1960. Then North Staffordshire Journal of Field Studies. 1961+. Index of vols. i–xxxii in xxxii. (MG).

For the years 1865–96 is called North Staffordshire Naturalists' Field Club and Archaeol. Soc.

1814 THE WILLIAM SALT ARCHAEOLOGICAL SOCIETY. Collections for a history of Staffordshire. Birmingham etc. 1880. Indexes in vols. for the years 1919, 1923, 1925/6, 1928/31, 1933/5, and 1937/40 to contents of previous vols.

In 1936, name changed to Staffordshire Record Society. Ser. 1 (1880–97); Ser. 2 (1898–1909); Ser. 3 (1919–54); Ser. 4 (1957+). (Mullins, *Texts*, pp. 435–50.)

1815 ERDESWICK (SAMPSON). A survey of Staffordshire (with additions and corrections). Ed. by Thomas Harwood. Westminster. 1820. New edn. Lond. 1844.

Erdeswick died in 1603, leaving his work in manuscript. Early editions, 1717, 1723.

1816 SHAW (STEBBING). The history and antiquities of Staffordshire. Vols. i–ii. pt. i. Lond. 1798–1801.

Cf. Conrad Gill, *Studies in midland history* (Oxf. 1930).

1817 WEDGWOOD (JOSIAH C.). 'Early Staffordshire history', in William Salt Archaeol. Soc. Collections (for 1916), 138–208; (for 1919), 134–53, 182–4. Lond. 1918–20.

SUFFOLK

See Nos. 1504, 1505, 1682, and *V.C.H.* (No. 1529).

No first-rate bibliography; but see Copinger (No. 1824).

1818 EAST ANGLIAN, or NOTES AND QUERIES FOR SUFFOLK, CAMBRIDGE, ESSEX, AND NORFOLK. Vols. i–iv. Lowestoft. 1858–71. New Ser. i–xiii. 1885–1910.

1819 EAST ANGLIAN MAGAZINE. Ipswich. 1935+.

1820 SUFFOLK GREEN BOOKS [ed. by S. H. A. Hervey]. 20 vols. Woodbridge. 1894–1929.

1821 SUFFOLK INSTITUTE OF ARCHAEOLOGY AND NATURAL HISTORY. Proceedings. Bury St. Edmunds. 1853+. Indexes of vols. i–ix (1849–98), in ix. Ipswich. x–xvii (1898–1921), in xviii, pp. 80–9. (MG).

1822 SUFFOLK RECORDS SOCIETY. Publications. Ipswich. 1958+.

1823 SUFFOLK REVIEW. Suffolk Local Hist. Council. Ipswich. 1956+.

Supersedes the same title. 8 nos. 1953–6.

1824 COPINGER (WALTER A.). County of Suffolk: its history as disclosed by existing records, being materials for a history of Suffolk gleaned . . . mainly from MSS. . . . 5 vols. Lond. 1904–5.

> Valuable, but not always critical. Cf. H. B. Copinger, *Index nominum et locorum* [viz. those mentioned in the above work] (Manchester, 1907).

1825 DOUGLAS (DAVID C.). The social structure of medieval East Anglia. Oxf. 1927.

> Contributes to the general history of the period. See No. 2628.

1826 SUCKLING (ALFRED). The history and antiquities of the county of Suffolk. 2 vols. Lond. 1846–8.

SURREY

See No. 1505 and *V.C.H.* (No. 1529).

1827 GUIDE TO THE ARCHIVES and other collections of documents relating to Surrey. By C. H. Jenkinson, M. S. Giuseppi, and D. L. Powell. Surrey Record Soc. xxiii (1925), xxiv (1926), xxvi (1927), xxviii (1928), xxix (1929), xxxi (1930), xxxii (1931).

1828 MINET (WILLIAM) and COURTNEY (CHARLES J.). A catalogue of the collection of works relating to the county of Surrey contained in the Minet public library. Aberdeen. 1901. Supplement. 1923.

1829 STEPHENSON (MILL). A catalogue of books in the library of the Surrey archaeological society. *Surrey Archaeol. Collections*, x (1891), 173–204.

1830 GUILDFORD PUBLIC LIBRARY. Catalogue of works in the library relating to the county of Surrey. Guildford. 1957.

1831 SURREY ARCHAEOLOGICAL SOCIETY. Surrey archaeological collections. Lond. 1858+. Indexes of vols. i–xx (1854–1907), 1914; xxi–xxxviii (1908–30), Guildford. 1934. Extra volume, i. 1894. (MG). Local history series. Guildford. 1949+. Research papers. Guildford. 1948+.

1832 SURREY RECORD SOCIETY. [Publications.] Lond. 1913+. (Mullins, *Texts*, pp. 451–4.)

1833 BRAYLEY (EDWARD W.). A topographical history of Surrey. 5 vols. Dorking etc. 1841–8; also Lond. 1850. Another edn. revised by E. Walford. 4 vols. Lond. [1878–81].

1834 MANNING (OWEN). The history and antiquities of the county of Surrey. Continued by William Bray. 3 vols. Lond. 1804–14.

> A good county history which contains a facsimile of Domesday and 13 plates. It is normally cited as Manning and Bray.

SUSSEX
See No. 1505 and *V.C.H.* (No. 1529).

1835 BUTLER (G. SLADE). Topographica Sussexiana: an attempt towards forming a list of the various publications relating to the county of Sussex. [Lewes. 1866].

> Reprinted from Sussex Archaeol. Soc. Collections, xv–xviii (1863–6); continued to 1882 by F. E. Sawyer, ibid. xxxii–xxxiii (1882–3).

1836 EASTBOURNE PUBLIC LIBRARIES. Catalogue of the local collection: comprising books on Eastbourne and Sussex. 1956.

1837 SUSSEX ARCHAEOLOGICAL SOCIETY. Sussex archaeological collections. Lond. 1848+. General index of vols. i–xxv (1848–73), Lewes, 1874; of vols. xxvi–l (1875–1907), Brighton, 1914; brief subject indexes in vols. xli and li. 1898, 1908; general index of vols. li–lxxv of the Collections (1908–34) and vols. i–iv of Notes and Queries (1926–33), Oxf. 1936; and vols. lxxvi–c (1963). (MG).

1838 SUSSEX NOTES AND QUERIES. Lewes. 1926+.

1839 SUSSEX RECORD SOCIETY. [Publications]. Lewes. 1902+. (Mullins, *Texts*, pp. 455–61.)

1840 DALLAWAY (JAMES). A history of the western division of the county of Sussex, including the rapes of Chichester, Arundel and Bramber. 2 vols. in 3 pts. Lond. 1815–30. 2nd edn. of pt. ii of vol. ii. 1832.

1841 HORSFIELD (THOMAS W.). The history, antiquities and topography of the county of Sussex. 2 vols. Lewes etc. 1835.

WARWICKSHIRE
See No. 1504 (5, 12, 25), and *V.C.H.* (No. 1529).

1842 BIRMINGHAM PUBLIC LIBRARIES. A catalogue of the Birmingham collection, ed. Walter Powell and H. M. Cashmore. Birmingham. 1918. Supplement (1918–31). 1931.

1843 WILSON (ROGER B.). A hand-list of books relating to the county of Warwick. Birmingham. 1955.

1844 BIRMINGHAM AND MIDLAND INSTITUTE, ARCHAEOLOGICAL SECTION. Transactions. Birmingham. 1871+. Index of vols. i–xxxi (1870–1905), 1907. (MG).

> Later became independent and name was changed to Birmingham Archaeological Soc.

1845 DUGDALE SOCIETY. Occasional papers. Oxf. 1924+. Publications. Lond. 1921+. (Mullins, *Texts*, pp. 462–4.)

1846 THE MIDLAND ANTIQUARY. 4 vols. Birmingham. 1882–7. Another number (No. 17) was issued in April 1891.

1847 MIDLAND RECORD SOCIETY. Transactions. 6 vols. [Birmingham. 1896/7]. 1902. (MG).

1848 THE WARWICKSHIRE ANTIQUARIAN MAGAZINE. 8 pts. Warwick. 1859–77.

1848A WARWICKSHIRE LOCAL HISTORY SOCIETY. Warwickshire history. Warwick. 1969+.

1849 DUGDALE (WILLIAM). The antiquities of Warwickshire illustrated. Lond. 1656. Reprinted, Coventry. 1765. 2nd edn. by William Thomas. 2 vols. Lond. 1730.

> Dugdale's *Antiquities* is the most outstanding of the older county histories. See also R. H. Hilton, 'Social Structure of rural Warwickshire in the Middle Ages', *Dugdale Soc. Occasional Papers*, No. 9 (1950); H. A. Cronne, 'Warwick in the Middle Ages', ibid. No. 10 (1951).

WESTMORLAND

See Nos. 1504, 1593, 1597, 1598, 1771.

For printed bibliography, see Hodgson (No. 1591A).

1850 CUMBERLAND AND WESTMORLAND ANTIQUARIAN AND ARCHAEOLOGICAL SOCIETY. See No. 1593.

1851 NICOLSON (JOSEPH) and BURN (RICHARD). The history and antiquities of Westmorland and Cumberland. 2 vols. Lond. 1777. Index, by Henry Hornyold-Strickland. Cumb. and Westmor. Antiq. and Archaeol. Soc. Extra Ser. xvii. 1934.

> The appendix contains charters granted to towns, priories, etc. There is a supplement by John F. Curwen, 'The later records relating to north Westmorland or the barony of Appleby', Cumb. and Westmor. Antiq. and Archaeol. Soc. Record Series, 1932.

1852 ROYAL COMMISSION ON HISTORICAL MONUMENTS OF ENGLAND (No. 737). Westmorland. Lond. 1936.

> The introductory sections by Frank M. Stenton form the best account of the early history of Westmorland.

WILTSHIRE

See *V.C.H.* (No. 1529).

1853 GODDARD (EDWARD H.). Wiltshire bibliography: a catalogue of printed books . . . bearing on the history, topography and natural history of the county. Wilts. Education Committee. Trowbridge. 1929.

> 'Wiltshire books, pamphlets, and articles', *Wilts. Archaeol. Mag.* xlvii (1935), 136–60, 299–310.

1854 RATHBONE (MAURICE G.). Guide to the records in the custody of the clerk of the Peace for Wiltshire. Wiltshire County Record Committee. Pts. i (1959) and ii (1961). Trowbridge. (in progress).

1855 RATHBONE (MAURICE G.). 'A list of Wiltshire borough records earlier in date than 1836'. Wiltshire Archaeol. and Nat. Hist. Soc. Records Branch, vol. v. Devizes. 1951.

1856 WILTS RECORD SOCIETY. [Publications.] 3 vols. Salisbury. 1896–1902. (Mullins, *Texts*, p. 465.)

1857 WILTSHIRE ARCHAEOLOGICAL AND NATURAL HISTORY MAGAZINE (WILTSHIRE ARCHAEOL. AND NATURAL HIST. SOC.). Devizes. 1854+. Indexes of vols. i–viii (1853–64), in viii; ix–xvi (1864–76), in xvi; xvii–xxiv (1877–89), in xxiv; xxv–xxxii (1890–1902), in xxxii. (MG).

1858 WILTSHIRE ARCHAEOLOGICAL AND NATURAL HISTORY SOCIETY. Publications. 7 vols. Devizes. 1862–1930. Records Branch. Devizes. 1939+. (Mullins, *Texts*, pp. 466–9.) Name changed to WILTSHIRE RECORD SOCIETY. 1967.

1859 WILTSHIRE NOTES AND QUERIES. 8 vols. Lond. 1893–1916.

1860 AUBREY (JOHN). Collections for the natural and topographical history of Wiltshire. By Thomas Phillipps. 2 vols. Lond. 1821–38. With extensions by John Britton. Lond. 1847. Further extended by J. E. Jackson. Devizes. 1862.

1861 HOARE (RICHARD C.). The modern history of south Wiltshire. [Second title: The history of modern Wiltshire.] 6 vols. Lond. 1822–44.

Contains many charters, inquests post mortem, pleas, etc. Vol. vi contains a good account of the history of the city and bishopric of Salisbury, with a valuable appendix of documents. See No. 772.

WORCESTERSHIRE
See Nos. 171, 1504, and *V.C.H.* (No. 1529).

1862 BURTON (JOHN R.) and PEARSON (F. S.), eds. Bibliography of Worcestershire, pt. ii being a classified catalogue of books, and other printed matter relating to the county of Worcestershire. Worc. Hist. Soc. 3 pts. in 2 vols. Pt. iii on botany by John Humphreys. Oxf. 1898–1907.

Pt. ii is the bibliography.

1863 WOOF (RICHARD). Catalogue of manuscript records and printed books in the library of the corporation of Worcester. Worcester. 1874.

1864 WORCESTERSHIRE ARCHAEOLOGICAL SOCIETY. Transactions. New Ser. Worcester. 1923/4+. (MG).

For 1st Ser., see Associated Archit. Soc. Reports (No. 171).

1865 WORCESTERSHIRE HISTORICAL SOCIETY. [Publications]. Oxf. 1893+. (Mullins, *Texts*, pp. 470–5.)

1866 HABINGTON (THOMAS). A survey of Worcestershire. Ed. by John Amphlett. Worc. Hist. Soc. 2 vols. Oxf. 1895 [1893]–9.

1867 [NASH (TREADWAY R.)]. Collections for the history of Worcestershire. 2 vols. Lond. 1781–2. 2nd edn. and supplement. 1799. Index, by John Amphlett. 2 pts. Worc. Hist. Soc. Oxf. 1894–5.

Valuable; contains many charters and other records. The second edition, 1799, is a reprint of the first. Lists incumbents.

YORKSHIRE
See Nos. 196, 1517, and *V.C.H.* (No. 1529).

1868 BICKLEY (FRANCIS B.). A catalogue of the muniments at Kirklees, in the West Riding in the county of York, from the time of king Richard I to the end of the eighteenth century, in the possession of Sir George John Armytage. Lond. 1900.

Privately printed. Relates to various places in Yorkshire.

1869 BOYNE (WILLIAM). The Yorkshire library: a bibliographical account of books on topography . . . relating to the county of York. Lond. 1869.

1870 DICKENS (ARTHUR G.) and MacMAHON (KENNETH A.). A guide to regional studies on the East Riding of Yorkshire and the city of Hull. Hull. 1956.

1871 KIRK (GEORGE E.), comp. Catalogue of the printed books and pamphlets in the library of the Yorkshire Archaeological Society. 2 vols. Wakefield. 1935–6.

1872 LIST OF BOOKS in the local collection relating to the city and county of York. Public library. York. 1912.

1873 BORTHWICK INSTITUTE OF HISTORICAL RESEARCH. York. St. Anthony's Hall Pubns. 1952–64. Borthwick Papers. 1965+.

See N. K. M. Gurney, 'The Borthwick Institute of Historical Research', *Archives*, vii (1966), 157–62; and J. S. Purvis, 'The archives of York', *Studies in Church Hist.* iv (1967), 1–14.

1874 BRADFORD HISTORICAL AND ANTIQUARIAN SOCIETY. Bradford antiquary. Bradford. 1881+. Index (1881–1910), in N.S. vol. iii. (MG). Local Record Series. Leeds. 1914+. (Mullins, *Texts*, p. 490.)

1875 EAST RIDING ANTIQUARIAN SOCIETY. Transactions. Hull. 1893–1939. 1949+. Index of vols. i–xx (1893–1913), 1919. (MG).

1876 EAST RIDING ARCHAEOLOGICAL SOCIETY. Hull. 1960.

1877 EAST YORKSHIRE LOCAL HISTORY SOCIETY. Local History Series. York. 1950+.

1878 HALIFAX ANTIQUARIAN SOCIETY. Papers, reports, etc. Halifax. 1901–28. Continued as Transaction. 1929+. Index (1901–31), 1932. Record series, vols. i–iii. 1906–17. (MG).

1879 HUNTER ARCHAEOLOGICAL SOCIETY. Transactions. Sheffield. 1914/18+. (MG).

1880 LEEDS STUDIES IN ENGLISH AND KINDRED LANGUAGES (LEEDS UNIVERSITY). 6 vols. Leeds. 1932–7.

1881 NORTH–RIDING RECORD SOCIETY. North-Riding records. 13 vols. Lond. 1884–97. (Mullins, *Texts*, pp. 491–3.)

> In 1897 merged into Yorkshire Archaeol. Soc. For later records, see Yorkshire Archaeol. Soc., Halifax. Record series.

1882 OLD YORKSHIRE. Lond. Vols. i–v (1881–4). 2nd Ser. i. 1885. N.S. i–iii (1889–91).

1883 THORESBY SOCIETY. Publications. Leeds. 1889+. Index of vols. i–xxxviii (1889–1938), 1941; and vols. xxxvii–l (1937–68) in vol. l Supplement. Gen. index of the first six vols. of the 'Miscellanea' (vols. ii, iv, ix, xi, xv, xxii of the Publications), in Pubns. vol. xxii, pp. 409–21. (Mullins, *Texts*, pp. 494–505.)

1884 YORKSHIRE ARCHAEOLOGICAL AND TOPOGRAPHICAL ASSOCIATION: called since 1893 YORKSHIRE ARCHAEOLOGICAL SOCIETY.

> Journal. Lond. 1870+. Index to vols. i–xvii (1870–1903). Leeds. 1904, Index i–xxx. 1939. (MG).
> Extra Series, vols. i–v (1888–1926). (Mullins, *Texts*, p. 476.)
> Record Series. (Worksop, etc.) 1885+. (Mullins, *Texts*, pp. 477–87.)
> Record Series. Extra series. 1914+. (Mullins, *Texts*, pp. 488–9.)
> Roman Antiquities Committee. Roman Malton and district report. York, 1928+. See No. 2069.

1885 YORKSHIRE COUNTY MAGAZINE, WITH WHICH IS INCORPORATED THE YORKSHIRE NOTES AND QUERIES. 4 vols. Bingley. 1891–4.

1886 YORKSHIRE DIALECT SOCIETY. Transactions. Bradford. 1898+. (MG).

1887 YORKSHIRE NOTES AND QUERIES. 2 vols. Bingley. 1888–90.

> Merged in the *Yorkshire County Magazine* in 1890. Another journal with the same name was published at Bradford from 1904 to 1909.

1888 YORKSHIRE PHILOSOPHICAL SOCIETY. Annual report. York. 1822+. (MG). Proceedings. 1847–54.

1889 ALLEN (THOMAS). A new and complete history of the county of York. 3 vols. Lond. 1828–31.

1890 HUNTER (JOSEPH). South Yorkshire: the history and topography of the deanery of Doncaster. 2 vols. Lond. 1828–31.

1891 LANGDALE (THOMAS). A topographical dictionary of Yorkshire. Northallerton. 1809. 2nd edn. 1822.

1892 POULSON (GEORGE). The history and antiquities of the seigniory of Holderness. 2 vols. Hull. 1840–1. Idem, Beverlac (No. 5288).

1893 WHITAKER (THOMAS D.). History and antiquities of the deanery of Craven. Lond. 3rd edn. by A. W. Morant. Leeds. etc. 1878.

Extracts from the accounts of the priory of Bolton, 1290–1325, pp. 448–67.

1894 WHITAKER (THOMAS D.). History of Richmondshire. 2 vols. Lond. 1823.

Lists incumbents.

3. *Wales: County by County*

For Welsh local history, consult *Archaeol. Cambrensis* (No. 109), *Bibliography ... Wales* (No. 10), *Bibliotheca Celtica* (No. 110), *Trans. . . . Soc. Cymmrodorion* (No. 126), *B.B.C.S.* (No. 111), *Y Cymmrodor* (No. 126), *Roy. Comm. Hist. Monuments* (No. 738), and Nos. 197–204; and the annual lists of articles relating to the history of Wales in the *Welsh History Review* (No. 142). For a general view, see Glanmor Williams, 'Local and national history of Wales', *Welsh Hist. Rev.* v (1970), 45–66.

ANGLESEY

1895 ANGLESEY ANTIQUARIAN SOCIETY AND FIELD CLUB (Llangefni). Transactions. 1913+. Index for 1913–38 in 1938 volume. (MG).

1896 LLWYD (ANGHARAD). History of the island of Mona or Anglesey. Ruthin. 1833.

BRECKNOCKSHIRE

1897 BRECKNOCK SOCIETY (Brecon.). Transactions and records, 1928–9. Then journal entitled *Brycheiniog*. 1955+.

1898 JONES (THEOPHILUS). History of the county of Brecknock. 2 vols. Brecon. 1805–9. Reprinted in 1 vol. 1898. Enlarged with notes added. 4 vols. Brecon. 1909–30.

1899 LLOYD (JOHN of Brecon, the younger). Historical memoranda of Breconshire. 2 vols. Brecon. 1903–4.

William Rees, 'The mediaeval lordship of Brecon', *Trans. Soc. Cymmr.* (1915–16), 165–224.

CAERNARVONSHIRE
See No. 1504.

1900 WILLIAMS (WILLIAM O.). Guide to the Caernarvonshire record office. Caernarvon. 1952. Idem, An introduction to the county records. Caernarvon. 1950.

1901 CAERNARVONSHIRE HISTORICAL SOCIETY (Caernarvon). Transactions. 1939+. Idem, Record series (No. 198). 1951+.

1902 LLANDUDNO, COLWYN BAY AND DISTRICT FIELD CLUB. Proceedings. 1906+. (MG).

1902A DODD (ARTHUR H.). History of Caernarvonshire, 1284–1900. Caernarvon. 1969.

1903 OWEN (NICHOLAS). Caernarvonshire: a sketch of its history, antiquities, etc. Lond. 1792.

CARDIGANSHIRE
See No. 201.

1904 CARDIGANSHIRE ANTIQUARIAN SOCIETY (Aberayon). Transactions and archaeological record (1911–15); Transactions (1924–39); *Ceredigion*, 1950+. Index to Transactions. 1953. (MG).

1905 EDWARDS (JOHN GORONWY). 'The early history of the counties of Carmarthen and Cardigan', *E.H.R.* xxxi (1916), 90–8.

1906 LLOYD (JOHN E.). The story of Ceredigion (400–1277). Cardiff. 1937.

1907 MEYRICK (SAMUEL R.). History and antiquities of the county of Cardigan. Lond. 1810. Another edn. 1907.

CARMARTHENSHIRE
See Nos. 201, 1905.

1908 CARMARTHENSHIRE ANTIQUARIAN SOCIETY AND FIELD CLUB (Carmarthen). Transactions. 1905–39. Then Carmarthen Antiquary. 1941+. Index, i–xii. 1928. (MG).

1909 CARMARTHENSHIRE LOCAL HISTORY COUNCIL (Carmarthen). 1955+.

1910 JONES (ARTHUR G. PRYS) or PRYS–JONES (ARTHUR G.). The story of Carmarthenshire. Vol. i: From prehistoric times to . . . sixteenth century. Llandybie. 1959.

1911 LLOYD (JOHN E.), ed. A history of Carmarthenshire. 2 vols. Cardiff. 1935–9.

DENBIGHSHIRE

1912 WILLIAMS (OWEN). Bibliography of the county. Pt. ii: historical and topographical sources. Wrexham. 1937. New edn. Ruthin. 1951.

1913 DENBIGHSHIRE HISTORICAL SOCIETY (Ruthin). Transactions. Conway, then Denbigh. 1952+.

1914 WILLIAMS (ALBERT H.). The early history of Denbighshire: an outline. Cardiff. 1950.

1915 WILLIAMS (JOHN). The medieval history of Denbighshire: records of Denbigh and its lordship. Vol. i. Wrexham. 1860.

FLINTSHIRE

1916 EVANS (MYRDDYN J. BEVAN) or BEVAN–EVANS (MYRDDYN J.). Guide to the Flintshire record office. Mold. 1955.

1917 FLINTSHIRE HISTORICAL SOCIETY (Hawarden). Journal and publications. Prestatyn. 1911–25. Caernarvon. 1952+ Idem, Record series (No. 199). (MG).

1918 WILLIAMS (CYRIL R.), ed. History of Flintshire. Vol. i: from the earliest times to the Act of Union. Denbigh. 1961.

See Thomas F. Tout, *Flintshire: its history and its records.* Flintshire Hist. Soc. (Prestatyn, 1911).

GLAMORGAN
See No. 1504.

1919 CARDIFF PUBLIC LIBRARY. Handlist of early documents (before 1500) in MSS. department of the reference library. 1926.

1920 ABERAFAN AND MARGAM DISTRICT HISTORICAL SOCIETY. Transactions. Vols. i–vi. 1928–34.

1921 CARDIFF NATURALISTS' SOCIETY. Report and Transactions. Cardiff and Penarth. 1867+. General index for vols. i–lxx in vol. lxx (1938), 1941. (MG).

1922 GLAMORGAN HISTORIAN. Ed. by S. Williams. Cowbridge. 1964+.

1923 GLAMORGAN LOCAL HISTORY SOCIETY (Cardiff). Transactions entitled *Morgannwg.* 1957+.

1924 EVANS (CYRIL J. O.). Glamorgan, its history and topography. Cardiff. 1938. 2nd edn. 1944.

1925 JONES (DAVID W.). (Pseudonym = Morganwg, Dafydd). Hanes Morganwg. Aberdâr. 1874.

1926 NICHOLAS (THOMAS). The history and antiquities of Glamorganshire and its families. Lond. 1874.

1927 TATTERSALL (W. M.), ed. Glamorgan county history. 3 vols. Cardiff. 1936–71. Vol. iii. T. B. Pugh, ed. The middle ages. 1971.

MERIONETH

1928 MERIONETH HISTORICAL AND RECORD SOCIETY (several branches). Journal. 1950+.

1929 BOWEN (EMRYS G.) and GRESHAM (COLIN A.). History of Merioneth. Vol. i. From the earliest times to the age of the native princes. Merioneth Hist. and Rec. Soc. Dolgellau. 1967.

MONMOUTHSHIRE
See No. 204.

1930 BAKER (W. H.), ed. Guide to the Monmouth record office. Newport. 1959.

1931 MONMOUTH AND DISTRICT FIELD CLUB AND ANTI-QUARIAN SOCIETY. 1952+.

1932 MONMOUTHSHIRE AND CAERLEON ANTIQUARIAN ASSOCI-ATION. Publications. 1847+. (MG).

1933 MONMOUTHSHIRE LOCAL HISTORY COUNCIL (Newport). 1954+.

1934 BRADNEY (JOSEPH A.). A history of Monmouthshire from the coming of the Normans into Wales down to the present time. 4 vols. 1904/7–1932/3.

1935 CLARK (ARTHUR). The story of Monmouthshire. Vol. i. Llandybie. 1962.

1936 EVANS (CYRIL J. O.). Monmouthshire: its history and topography. Cardiff. 1954.

MONTGOMERYSHIRE

1937 POWYSLAND CLUB. Collections, historical and archaeological, relating to Montgomeryshire and its borders. Lond. 1868–1942. (MG). Idem, Transactions as *Montgomeryshire Collections*. 1943+. (1946+).

Reprinted from the above 'Collections', *Montgomeryshire Records* (1911).

PEMBROKESHIRE
See No. 201.

1938 OWEN (HENRY), ed. A calendar of public records relating to Pembroke-shire. Cymmrodorion Record Series, No. 7. 3 vols. Lond. 1911–18.

1939 PEMBROKESHIRE LOCAL HISTORY SOCIETY (Haverfordwest). Pembrokeshire Historian. 1959+.

1940 PHILLIPS (JAMES D.). The history of Pembrokeshire. Lond. 1909.

RADNORSHIRE

1941 RADNORSHIRE SOCIETY. Llandrindod Wells. Transactions. 1931+.

1942 HOWSE (WILLIAM H.). Radnorshire. Hereford. 1949.

1943 WILLIAMS (JONATHAN). General history of the county of Radnor. Tenby. 1859. 2nd edn. Brecon. 1905.

4. *Isle of Man and Channel Islands*

MAN, ISLE OF

See Nos. 1106, 2132.

1944 CUBBON (WILLIAM). A bibliographical account of the work relating to the Isle of Man. 2 vols. Lond. 1933–9.

1945 ISLE OF MAN NATURAL HISTORY AND ANTIQUARIAN SOCIETY. Proceedings. New Ser. Douglas. 1880–1906. New Ser. 1907+.

1946 MANX MUSEUM. Manx Museum Journal. Douglas. 1924/30+.

Manx Archaeological Survey, 1st–5th Reports (5 vols. in 1) by P. M. Kermode; 6th Report by J. R. Bruce (Douglas, 1966).

1947 MANX SOCIETY. Publications. 33 vols. Douglas. 1859–95. (Mullins, *Texts,* pp. 506–10.)

1948 KINVIG (ROBERT H.). History of the Isle of Man. Lond. and Douglas. 1944. Liverpool. 1950.

1949 MOORE (ARTHUR W.). History of the Isle of Man. 2 vols. Lond. 1900.

1950 THE CHRONICLE OF THE ISLE OF MAN. Trans. by J. Stevenson. *Church Historians,* vol. v.

1951 THE CHRONICLE OF MAN AND THE SUNDREYS. Ed. by P. A. Munch and Rev. Dr. Gross. Manx Society. Douglas. 1874.

THE CHANNEL ISLANDS

No important printed bibliography.

1952 LA SOCIÉTÉ GUERNESIAISE. Report and Transactions. Guernsey. 1922+. Gen. index, 1882–1932 (1934); 1933–6 (1937).

Name of society varies: founded in 1882 as The Guernsey Society of Natural Science; Guernsey Society of Natural Science and Local Research (1889–1921). Reports and Transactions. 1882+.

1953 LA SOCIÉTÉ JERSIAISE POUR L'ÉTUDE DE L'HISTOIRE. Bulletin annual. 1875+. Index, vols. i–xxi, 1875–96. Publications. St. Helier. 1876+. (Mullins, *Texts,* pp. 511–13.)

Includes assizes, extents, petitions, etc.

1954 DUPONT (GUSTAVE). Histoire du Cotentin et de ses îles. 4 vols. Caen. 1870–85.

1955 LE PATOUREL (JOHN H.). The medieval administration of the Channel Islands 1199–1399. Lond. 1937.

1956 LE QUESNE (CHARLES). Constitutional history of Jersey. Lond. 1856.

1957 QUENTEL (PAUL). 'Les noms des îles dites "anglo-normandes".' *Revue internationale d'onomastique*, xxi (1969), 145–54.

1958 TUPPER (FERDINAND B.). History of Guernsey and its bailiwick. Guernsey. 1854. 2nd edn. 1876.

1959 UTTLEY (JOHN). The story of the Channel Islands. Lond. 1966.

A popular history in 200 pages from prehistoric times to the present.

PART III

FROM PREHISTORY TO ANGLO-SAXON CONQUEST

VIII. PREHISTORIC AND CELTIC TIMES

A. THE PRE-ROMAN AGE IN BRITAIN

The materials for the study of prehistoric times are archaeological artifacts. The notable advances in archaeological studies and techniques and the specialized character of this discipline have been noted on pp. 84–5 above. The bibliography is long, the subject-matter complex, and the analysis and interpretation explicable only by the trained expert. Accordingly there are listed only the more serviceable bibliographical guides and general treatises wherein scholars in archaeology unfold a broad view to the inquiring historian.

The general treatises on archaeology which are listed on pages 90–2 above are particularly applicable to prehistoric and early Celtic times. Volumes in the series entitled *Ancient Peoples and Places* (No. 761) form good starting-points. The journals on archaeology are catalogued on pages 85–7 above.

1. *Bibliography, Journals, and Guides*

1960 AMERICAN SCHOOL OF PREHISTORIC RESEARCH. Old World bibliography. Compiled by Hallam L. Movius, Jr. Cambr. (Mass.). 1948+.

Annual bibliography (mimeographed) of prehistory. After 1955 it is continued in *Bibliographie annuelle de l'âge de la pierre taillée*, ed. R. Vaufrey (Paris, 1958). Cf. *COWA* (No. 726).

1961 COUNCIL FOR BRITISH ARCHAEOLOGY. A survey and policy of field research in the archaeology of Great Britain: i. Prehistoric and early historical ages to the seventh century A.D. Institute of Archaeology. Lond. 1948.

1962 EBERT (MAX), ed. Reallexikon der Vorgeschichte . . . 15 vols. in 16. Berlin, 1924–32.

A standard encyclopedia with contributions by specialists.

1963 FIRST INTERNATIONAL CONGRESS OF PREHISTORIC AND PROTOHISTORIC SCIENCES (held in) London. 1932. A handbook of the prehistoric archaeology of Britain. Oxf. 1932. Proceedings. Lond. 1934.

1964 BRITISH MUSEUM GUIDES.

(*a*) A guide to the antiquities of the stone age in the department of British and mediaeval antiquities. Lond. 1902. 3rd edn. 1926.

(*b*) C. H. Read, A guide to the antiquities of the bronze age . . . Oxf. 1904. 2nd edn. 1920.

(*c*) A guide to the antiquities of the early iron age . . . Oxf. 1905. 2nd edn. 1925.

(*d*) J. W. Brailsford, Later prehistoric antiquities of the British Isles. 1953.

1965 ORDNANCE SURVEY.

(*a*) Megalithic survey of England and Wales: The long barrows and stone circles of the Cotswolds and the Welsh Marches (Sheet 8). Professional Paper, 6. Lond. 1922.

(*b*) The long barrows and megalithic monuments of Kent, Surrey and Sussex (Sheet 12). Professional Paper, 8. 1924.

(*c*) Map of Neolithic Wessex (Sheet 11). 1933.

(*d*) Map of the Trent basin: showing the distribution of long barrows, etc. (Sheet 6A). 1933.

(*e*) Map of South Wales, showing the distribution of long barrows and megaliths. Introduction by W. F. Grimes. 1936.

(*f*) Map of Southern Britain in the Iron Age. Chessington. 1962.

See also Osbert Guy Crawford, *The long barrows of the Cotswolds*: a description of long barrows, stone circles and other megalithic remains in the area covered by sheet 8 of the . . . Ordnance Survey . . . (Gloucester, 1925) and W. F. Grimes's article on 'Megalithic monuments of Wales' in *Prehistoric Soc. Procs.* N.S. ii, pt. i (1936), 106–39.

The megalithic survey maps, ¼ mile to inch, show distribution of long barrows, megaliths, dwelling-sites, flint-mines, with lists and explanatory text; the series will be completed in 11 sheets. Ordnance Survey is also bringing out a survey of Celtic earthworks of Salisbury Plain, in six sheets, of which only one has so far been published: *Old Sarum* (Southampton, 1934; revised edn. 1937).

1966 THE PREHISTORIC SOCIETY. Proceedings. Cambr. 1935+. Formerly The Prehistoric Society of East Anglia. Proceedings. Cambr. 1908–34.

The most important British journal devoted exclusively to prehistory; it contains an annual account of excavations in England, Scotland, and Wales during the preceding year.

2. General Treatises on the Prehistoric Age

1967 ABERCROMBY (JOHN). A study of the bronze age pottery of Great Britain and Ireland and its associated grave-goods. 2 vols. Oxf. 1912.

1968 ÅBERG (NILS F.). Bronzezeitliche und früheisenzeitliche Chronologie. 5 vols. Stockholm. 1930–5.

1969 ALCOCK (LESLIE). Dinas Powys: an iron age, dark age and early medieval settlement in Glamorgan. Cardiff. 1963.

1970 ATKINSON (RICHARD J. C.). Stonehenge. Lond. 1956.

See the series of papers by various writers critical of the theories of Gerald S. Hawkins in *Antiquity*, xl (1966), 212–16; 262–76; xli (1967), 91–8, 174–80. By computer calculations Hawkins concluded that Stonehenge was an astronomical observatory.

1971 CHILDE (VERE GORDON). The dawn of European civilization. Lond. 1925. 6th edn. 1957.

This book deals with the mesolithic, neolithic, and early Bronze Age in Britain; its final chapter links Britain with the Continent.

1972 CHILDE (VERE GORDON). Prehistoric communities of the British Isles. Lond. etc. 1940. 2nd edn. 1947.

1973 CHILDE (VERE GORDON). The prehistory of Scotland. Lond. 1935. Idem, Scotland before the Scots. Lond. 1946.

For the prehistoric age in Scotland, see Feachem's *Guide* (No. 733).

1974 CONTRIBUTIONS TO PREHISTORIC ARCHAEOLOGY offered to Professor V. Gordon Childe in honour of his sixty-fifth birthday. Edited by J. G. D. Clarke, assisted by K. P. Oakley and S. Piggott. *Prehistoric Soc. Procs.* (for 1955), N.S. xxi. Gloucester and Cambr. 1956.

1975 CLARK (JOHN GRAHAME D.). Excavations at Star Carr: an early mesolithic site at Seamer near Scarborough, Yorkshire. Cambr. 1954.

1976 CLARK (JOHN GRAHAME D.). Prehistoric England. The British Heritage series. Lond. 1940. 4th edn. 1948. Later edn. 1962.

1977 CLARK (JOHN GRAHAME D.). Prehistoric Europe: the economic basis. Lond. 1952.

See the review in *Econ. H. R.* 2nd Ser. v (1952), 266–76.

1978 CLARK (JOHN GRAHAME D.) and PIGGOTT (STUART). Prehistoric societies. The History of Human Society. Ed. by J. H. Plumb. N.Y. 1965.

1979 CLARKE (DAVID L.). Beaker pottery of Great Britain and Ireland. Gulbenkian Archaeological Series. 2 vols. Cambr. and N.Y. 1969 (1970).

1980 CURWEN (ELIOT C.) and HATT (GUDMUND). Plough and pasture: the early history of farming. N.Y. 1953. Pb. edn. 1961.

Part i, Curwen's portion of the book, was originally published in England in 1946 under the same title. H. Helbaek, 'Early crops in southern England', *Prehistoric Soc. Procs.* N.S. xviii (1952), 194–233; F. G. Payne, 'The plough in ancient Britain', *Archaeol. Jour.* civ (1947), 82–111.

1981 DANIEL (GLYN E.). The prehistoric chamber tombs of England and Wales. Cambr. 1950.

Leslie V. Grinsell, *The ancient burial-mounds of England* (Lond. 1936; new edn. 1953) is 'a kind of barrow-guide'. William Greenwell and George Rolleston, *British barrows* (Oxf. 1877) records the examination of above 230 sepulchral mounds belonging to the period before the occupation of Britain by the Romans.

1982 EVANS (JOHN). The ancient bronze implements, weapons, and ornaments of Great Britain. Lond. 1881. Idem, The ancient stone implements, weapons, and ornaments of Great Britain. Lond. 1872. 2nd edn. 1897.

The work of a pioneer.

1983 FEACHEM (RICHARD). The north Britons: the prehistory of a border people. Lond. 1965.

1984 FOSTER (IDRIS Ll.) and DANIEL (GLYN E.). Prehistoric and early Wales. Lond. 1965.

1985 FOX (CYRIL F.). Archaeology of the Cambridge region: a topographical study of the bronze, early iron, Roman and Anglo-Saxon ages, with an introductory note on the neolithic age. Cambr. 1923.

Idem, 'Reflections on the archaeology of the Cambridge region', *Cambr. Hist. Jour.* ix (1947), 1–21.

1986 FOX (CYRIL F.). Life and death in the bronze age: an archaeologist's field-work. Lond. 1959.

This work is concerned largely with tombs in Wales.

1987 FOX (CYRIL F.). Pattern and purpose: a survey of early Celtic art in Britain. Cardiff. 1958.

Covering the period from *c.* 2500 B.C. to the beginning of the Christian era, it is the best book on the subject.

1988 FOX (CYRIL F.). The personality of Britain (No. 613).

1989 FOX (CYRIL F.) and DICKINS (BRUCE), eds. The early cultures of north-west Europe. H. M. Chadwick Memorial Studies. Cambr. 1950.

Cf. No. 1429.

1990 GARROD (DOROTHY A. E.). The upper palaeolithic age in Britain. Oxf. 1926.

1991 GRIMES (WILLIAM F.). A guide to the collections illustrating the pre-history of Wales. Cardiff, National Museum of Wales. 1939. 2nd enlarged edn.: The prehistory of Wales. Cardiff. 1951.

An exhaustive account which incorporates the advances made since the publication of R. E. Mortimer Wheeler, *Prehistoric and Roman Wales* (Oxf. 1925). See also Grimes, 'Wales and Ireland in prehistoric times: some meditations' (Presidential address), *Archaeol. Cambrensis*, cxiii (1964), 1–15.

1992 HAMILTON (JOHN R. C.). Excavations at Jarlshof, Shetland. Ministry of Works Archaeological Report no. 1. H.M.S.O. Edin. 1956.

This volume including ground and aerial photography deals with a site of prehistoric and Viking settlements preserved by sand inundation.

1993 HAWKES (CHARLES F. CHRISTOPHER). The prehistoric foundations of Europe: to the Mycenean age. Lond. 1940. Idem, 'The ABC of the British iron age', *Antiquity*, xxxiii (1959), 170–82, which is a sequel to his 'Hill Forts', ibid. v (1931), 60–97.

Cf. John Lubbock (Lord Avebury), *Prehistoric times* . . . (Lond. 1865; 7th edn. 1913) and Edward B. Taylor, *Primitive culture* . . . (Lond. 1871; 7th edn. 1924).

1994 HAWKES (C. F. CHRISTOPHER) and DUNNING (GERALD C.). 'The Belgae of Gaul and Britain', *Archaeol. Jour.* lxxxvii (1930), 150–341. Separate reprint, Lond. 1931.

The history of the Belgae is reconstructed from the distribution of certain pottery types; illustrated with a wealth of material both historical and archaeological. See also the articles by M. E. Cunnington, 'Was there a second Belgic invasion?' *Antiq. Jour.* xii (1932), 27–34; and C. F. C. Hawkes and G. C. Dunning, 'The second Belgic invasion', ibid. pp. 411–30; C. Hawkes, 'New thoughts on the Belgae', *Antiquity*, xlii (1968), 6–16; and C. E. Stevens's essay 'Britain between the invasions (B.C. 54–A.D. 43)' (No. 1432).

1995 HAWKES (C. F. C.), MYRES (J. N. L.), and STEVENS (C. G.). St. Catharine's Hill, Winchester. *Hampshire Field Club and Archaeol. Soc. Procs.* xi. Winchester. 1930.

Contains an excursus on the rise and development of hill-fort construction, by Hawkes; cf. his 'Hill-forts', *Antiquity*, v (1931), 60–97; and W. J. Varley, 'The hill-forts of the Welsh Marches', *Archaeol. Jour.* cv (1948), 41–66.

1996 HAWKES (JACQUETTA) and HAWKES (CHRISTOPHER). Prehistoric Britain. Lond. 1943. Revised edn. 1949. J. and C. Hawkes, A work of the same title. Cambr. (Mass.). 1953; 1955. (Penguin Books, 1958.)

1997 HUBERT (HENRI). Les celtes et l'expansion celtique jusqu'à l'époque de la Tène. Paris. 1932. Idem, Les Celtes depuis l'époque de La Tène et la civilisation celtique. Paris. 1932. Translated by M. R. Dobie as respectively: The rise of the Celts *; The greatness and decline of the Celts. Lond. etc. 1934.

1998 JACOBSTHAL (PAUL). Early Celtic art. 2 vols. Oxf. 1944. *

A learned work of reference for the specialist, superbly illustrated. See also Jacobsthal's 'Imagery in early Celtic art', *P.B.A.* xxvii (1941/4), 301–20.

1999 KENDRICK (THOMAS D.). The Druids: a study in Keltic prehistory. Lond. 1927. 2nd edn. 1928. *

See Piggott (No. 761).

2000 KENDRICK (THOMAS D.) and HAWKES (JACQUETTA). The archaeology of the Channel Islands. Vol. i: The bailiwick of Guernsey. Vol. ii: The bailiwick of Jersey. Lond. 1928–39.

Sir Thomas Kendrick is the author of Vol. i, Mrs. Hawkes, of Vol. ii.

2001 LACAILLE (ARMAND D.). The stone age in Scotland. Publications of the Wellcome Historical Medical Museum, N.S. No. 6. Lond. etc. 1954.

2002 LEAKEY (LOUIS S. B.). Adam's ancestors. Lond. 4th edn. 1953.

A popular but useful outline, but not, of course, concerned specifically with the British Isles.

2003 LEEDS (EDWARD T.). Celtic ornament in the British Isles down to A.D. 700. Oxf. 1933.

2004 MOVIUS (HALLAM L., Jr.). Irish stone age: its chronology, development and relationships. Cambr. 1942.

A report on the field-work carried out by one section of the Harvard Irish Survey's archaeological expedition to Ireland (1932–6).

2005 O'RÍORDÁIN (SÉAN PÁDRAIG). Antiquities of the Irish countryside. 3rd edn. rev. Lond. 1953. 4th edn. 1964.

Originally published in 1942 and 1943; for later phases of British prehistoric archaeology.

2006 PIGGOTT (STUART). Ancient Europe. Edin. 1965.

A remarkable treatise on general archaeology of Europe.

2007 PIGGOTT (STUART). 'Ireland and Britain in pre-history: changing perspectives and viewpoints'. *Jour. Cork Hist.-Archaeol. Soc.* lxxi (1966), 5–18.

2008 PIGGOTT (STUART). The neolithic cultures of the British Isles: a study of the stone-using agricultural communities of Britain in the second millennium B.C. Cambr. 1954. *

> See also *British prehistory* (Home Univ. Library, Oxf. 1949); Grahame Clark and Stuart Piggott, 'The age of British flint mines', *Antiquity*, vii (1933), 166–83, includes a bibliography of European flint mines.

2009 PIGGOTT (STUART). Scotland before history. Edin. 1954.

> The development of human habitation in Scotland from earliest times to Roman occupation. To be preferred to No. 1973.

2010 PITT-RIVERS (AUGUSTUS HENRY L. F.). Excavations in Cranborne Chase. 5 vols. with 316 good plates. Lond. 1887–1905.

> The work of a pioneer in scientific excavation. Cf. C. F. C. Hawkes, 'Britons, Romans and Saxons round Salisbury and in Cranborne Chase', *Archaeol. Jour.* civ (1948), 36–42, which interprets General Pitt-Rivers's evidence in the light of more recent archaeological discoveries.

2011 PROBLEMS OF THE IRON AGE IN SOUTHERN BRITAIN. Ed. by S. S. Frere. Papers given at a Council for British Archaeology Conference held at the Institute of Archaeology, 12–14 December 1958. Univ. London Inst. Archaeol. Occasional Paper No. 11 (1961).

> Important papers on period immediately preceding the Roman occupation. On this topic, see also *Ordnance Survey Map of Southern Britain in the Iron Age* (Chessington, 1962); and Hawkes–Dunning (1994); and B. W. Cunliffe, 'Early pre-Roman iron age communities in eastern England', *Antiquaries Jour.* xlviii (1968), 175–91.

2012 THOM (ALEXANDER). Megalithic sites in Britain. Oxf. 1967.

IX. THE ROMAN OCCUPATION

Collections of written sources, including inscriptions, for the study of the Roman occupation of Britain are to be found in Petrie's *Monumenta* (No. 1084), Horsley's *Britannia Romana* (No. 2044), Hübner's *Inscriptiones* (No. 2028), and Collingwood–Wright (No. 2027). The written sources provide, however, only a scanty, if essential, framework; archaeological and numismatic studies constitute the main sources of our knowledge. The progress in these fields, made both through new discoveries and through the scientific study of earlier survivals, particularly during the past half-century, is transforming the recorded history of the period. A notable report on fifty years of archaeological research is provided by I. A. Richmond in The Jubilee (1960) Volume of *The Journal of Roman Studies* (No. 2015). For the succeeding decade progress in the study of Roman Britain has continued at such a pace that current bibliographies must be searched.

The father of modern scholarship on Roman Britain was F. J. Haverfield (1860–1919), among whose outstanding successors were Sir George Macdonald, R. G. Collingwood, and Sir Ian Richmond. An excellent, well-written account of the period was supplied by Collingwood in his 1937 volume of the Oxford

History of England, where annotated lists (pp. 462–78) still furnished a fundamental bibliography of books and periodicals as of 1936; but the considerable
detailed progress that has been made since Collingwood wrote dates his survey.
Thirty years later extensive bibliographies are provided in Bonser, *R.-B.B.* (No.
2013), in Collingwood–Wright, *Roman Inscriptions* (No. 2027), and in Frere's
Britannia (No. 2040). The last two works are indispensable bases for the study
of Roman Britain.

The journals, such as *The Antiquaries Journal* (No. 107), the *Archaeological
Journal* (No. 724), *Archaeologia* (No. 108), and the *Journal of Roman Studies* (No.
2015), and *Britannia* (No. 2015) and treatises cited (pp. 90–2) above are in
many instances germane to the Roman period. The *Ordnance Survey Map* (No.
2022) summarizes recent archaeological information. The chapters on Roman
remains for each county in the *Victoria County History* (No. 1529), noting especially *V.C.H. Essex*, iii, which is entirely devoted to Roman Essex, and the sections
on the Roman period in the better county histories mentioned in Chapter VII
above should be consulted. The inventories of the *Royal Commission on Ancient
and Historical Monuments* (Nos. 737–9) and the *Reports of the Society of Antiquaries of London* (No. 2070) are recent and authoritative. For the important
numismatic evidence, see Nos. 657–67. The study of sites and inscriptions,
including the researches of the Council for British Archaeology, may be kept
current through the annual surveys in *The Journal of Roman Studies* (No. 2015);
and the contributions made by air photography must be kept in view.

A. BIBLIOGRAPHY, JOURNALS, AND GUIDES

2013 BONSER (WILFRID). A Romano-British Bibliography (55 B.C.–A.D.
449). Oxf. 1964.

A classified bibliography of some 9,370 items drawn from 253 periodicals and collective
works down to the end of 1959.

2014 L'ANNÉE PHILOLOGIQUE: bibliographie critique et analytique de
l'antiquité gréco-latine. Paris. 1928+.

Continues *Dix années de bibliographie classique*: bibliographie critique et analytique de
l'antiquité Gréco-Latine pour la période 1914–1924, by Jules Marouzeau (Paris, 1927–8).
This annual detailed listing of books and articles drawn now from some 600 journals
includes much pertaining to the Middle Ages as well as earlier times in Great Britain
and elsewhere. It begins with publications of 1914. For earlier bibliography consult the
following works: Wilhelm Engelmann, *Bibliotheca scriptorum classicorum* (for the years
1700–1878), ed. E. Preuss (8th edn. 2 vols. Leipzig, 1880–2); Rudolf Klussmann, *Bibliotheca scriptorum classicorum et graecorum et latinorum* (for the years 1878–96) (2 vols. in
4 parts, Leipzig, 1909–13); Scarlat Lambrino, *Bibliographie de l'antiquité classique 1896–
1914*. Part i: Auteurs et textes (Paris, 1951).

2015 JOURNAL OF ROMAN STUDIES. Lond. 1911+. Index of vols. i–xx
(1911–30), in vol. xx. 129–227. A numismatic index of vols. i–xl, compiled by
J. R. Jones. Cambr. 1969. BRITANNIA. Lond. 1970.+

Includes (since 1921) an annual detailed survey of archaeological finds, divided into two
sections. i: Sites explored (compiled by M. V. Taylor, I. A. Richmond, D. R. Wilson,
and others); and ii: Inscriptions (1921–36, by R. G. Collingwood; from 1938 on, by
Roman sites. Both journals are published by the Society for the Promotion of Roman
Studies.

2016 NAIRN (JOHN A.). A hand-list of books relating to the classics and classical antiquity. Oxf. 1931. 2nd edn. as: J. A. Nairn's Classical Handlist. Ed. by B. H. Blackwell, Ltd. Oxf. 1939. 3rd edn. 1953.

The last edition which includes reorganized sections on Roman Britain and on Numismatics amounts to a select bibliography for students.

2017 RICHMOND (IAN A.). 'Roman Britain, 1910–1960'. *Jour. Roman Stud.* l (1960), 173–91.

F. J. Haverfield, 'Roman Britain in 1913' and 'Roman Britain in 1914', *Brit. Acad. Supplementary Papers*, ii (1914), and iii (1915). George Macdonald, 'Roman Britain 1914–1928', ibid. vi (1931), which was originally published in the xix *Bericht* (1929) . . . *Römisch-Germanische Kommission . . . Deutsches Archäologisches Institut* (1930), pp. 1–85.

2018 THE YEARS WORK IN CLASSICAL STUDIES. Ed. by W. H. D. Rouse and others, for the years 1906–1945/7. Lond. 1907–20. Bristol. 1921–50.

2019 BRITISH MUSEUM. A guide to the antiquities of Roman Britain in the department of British and medieval antiquities. By Reginald A. Smith. Oxf. 1922. Another edn. 1951.

Useful catalogues for local museums of Roman antiquities are mentioned in Collingwood–Wright (No. 2027), pp. xxxi–xxxiii.

2020 CURLE (JAMES). An inventory of objects of Roman and provincial Roman origin, found on sites in Scotland not definitely associated with Roman constructions. *Soc. of Antiquaries of Scotland Procs.* lxvi (1931–2), 227–397.

Cf. the author's 'Roman drift in Caledonia', *Jour. Roman Stud.* xxii (1932), 73–7.

2021 LAPIDARIUM SEPTENTRIONALE: or a description of the monuments of Roman rule in the north of England. Ed. by J. C. Bruce. Soc. Antiq. Newcastle. Lond. etc. 1875.

The Lapidarium contains many inscriptions.

2022 ORDNANCE SURVEY. Map of Roman Britain: map and text. 3rd edn. Chessington. 1956.

Map (a single sheet for Great Britain, 39½ × 30½ inches) summarizes archaeological knowledge; text (19 pages plus maps and indexes) is also based on the latest scholarship. Figure 1 shows the British Isles according to Ptolemy and Figure 2 the British section of the Antonine Itinerary.

2023 ROMAN REMAINS (papers by various writers). *Archaeol. Review*, vols. i–iv *passim*. Lond. 1888–90.

Mostly lists of publications.

B. ANCIENT SOURCES

1. *Greek and Roman Literary Sources*

No complete collection of the passages in ancient authors dealing with Britain has been made since the publication of *Monumenta Historica Britannica*, vol. i (No. 1084), which has long been out of print and does not, of course, incorporate the work of modern textual criticism and scholarship. Petrie's *Monumenta* is supplemented by the list of classical authors in Hardy's *Catalogue* (No. 21), vol. i, pp. cxv–cxxxiv. For a collection of selected passages, cf. T. S. Cayzer, *Britannia: a collection of the principal passages in Latin authors that refer to this island* (Lond. 1878), and *The Romans in Britain: a selection of Latin texts,* ed. by R. W. Moore (Lond. 1938; 2nd edn. 1939). The most important are translated in M. Cary's 'Foreword on Roman Britain' in R. W. Chambers, *England before the Norman Conquest* (Lond. 1926), pp. 1–48. The fullest references are found in Caesar, Tacitus' *Agricola*, Ammianus, and the unreliable *Historia Augusta*. The following is a list of the chief ancient writers who mention Britain, in standard editions. Loeb editions are published in London and New York, and Teubner editions are published in Leipzig, and now also in Stuttgart. There are, of course, many editions and translations. The current translations and commentaries are listed annually in *L'Année Philologique* (No. 2014).

2024 STEVENS (COURTENAY E.). 'Ancient writers of Britain'. *Antiquity*, i. (1927), 189–96.

2025 ANCIENT AUTHORS

(*a*) Caesar, *de bello Gallico*. Ed. by T. Rice Holmes (Oxf. 1908, 1914); ed. and tr. by H. J. Edwards (Loeb Classical Library, 1917, 1926).

(*b*) Strabo, *Geographica*. Ed. by A. Meineke (Teubner, 1866–77); ed. and tr. by H. L. Jones and J. R. S. Sterrett, 8 vols. (Loeb, 1917–49).

(*c*) Pliny the Elder, *Naturalis historia*. Ed. by C. Mayhoff (Teubner, 1870–98; 3rd edn., vols. i and ii, 1906, 1909); ed. and tr. by H. Rackham, *et al.* 11 vols. (Loeb, 1938–64). Ed. and tr. into French by J. André, A. Ernout, *et al.* (Paris, 1950 (in progress)).

(*d*) Tacitus, *de vita Agricolae*. Ed. by H. Furneaux (Oxf. 1898; 2nd edn. revised by J. G. C. Anderson with contributions by F. Haverfield, 1922; reprinted [1947]). The best edition, with valuable introduction, is by R. M. Ogilvie and Sir Ian Richmond. Lond. 1967.

(*e*) Tacitus, *Annales*. Ed. by Erich Koestermann (Teubner, 1965); ed. by H. Furneaux, 2 vols. (Oxf. 1896–1907); ed. and tr. by J. Jackson (Loeb, 1931–7; 1951–2); tr. by Michael Grant (Lond. 1963); D. R. Dudley (N.Y. 1966). Only partly extant. Commentary by Erich Koestermann, in *Wissenschaftliche Kommentare zu griechischen und lateinischen Schriftstellern* (Heidelberg, 1963, 1965, 1967).

(*f*) Tacitus, *Historiae*. Ed. and tr. by C. H. Moore (Loeb, 1931–7; 1951–2). Extant for A.D. 69–70. Commentary by Heinz Huebner, in *Wissenschaftliche Kommentare zu griechischen und lateinischen Schriftstellern* (Heidelberg, 1963); and Ronald Syme, Tacitus. 2 vols. Oxf. 1958.

Trans. of Histories by K. Wellesley (Penguin Classics, 1964). See also No. 2505 and the pamphlet by F. R. D. Goodyear, *Tacitus*. New Surveys of the Classics, no. 4 (Oxf. 1970).

(*g*) Suetonius, *de vita Caesarum*. Ed. by M. Ihm (Teubner, 1908); ed. and tr. by J. C. Rolfe (Loeb, 1914). Separate lives with commentaries: *Divus Iulius*. Ed. by H. E. Butler and M. Cary (Oxf. 1927); *Divus Vespasianus*. Ed. by A. W. Braithwaite (Oxf. 1927).

(*h*) Ptolemy, *Geographia*. Ed. by C. Müller and C. T. Fischer. Vol. i (Paris, 1883, 1901); *Opera* (Teubner, 1961+); tr. by Edward L. Stevenson (N.Y. 1932).

Henry Bradley, 'Ptolemy's geography of the British Isles', *Archaeologia*, xlviii (1885), 379–96; reprinted in his *Collected Papers* (1928), pp. 59–79. Ian A. Richmond, 'A forgotten exploration of the western isles', *Antiquity*, xiv (1940), 193–5. See Ordnance Survey Map of Roman Britain (No. 2022).

(*i*) Cassius Dio, *Historia Romana*. Ed. by U. P. Boissevain (Berlin, 1895–1931); ed. and tr. by E. Cary, 9 vols. (Loeb, 1914–27).

Cf. Fergus Millar, *A study of Cassius Dio* (Oxf. 1964).

(*j*) Ammianus Marcellinus, *Historiae*. Ed. by C. U. Clark (Berlin, 1910–15); ed. and tr. by J. C. Rolfe, 3 vols. (Loeb, 1935–9 and 1956–8).

E. A. Thompson, *The historical work of Ammianus Marcellinus* (Cambr. 1947); and Sir Ronald Syme, *Ammianus and the Historia Augusta* (Oxf. 1968) (No. 2025 (*m*)).

(*k*) Diodorus Siculus, *Bibliotheca historica*. Ed. by F. Vogel and C. T. Fischer (Teubner, 1888–1906); ed. and tr. by C. H. Oldfather and others (Loeb, 1912+).

(*l*) Herodian, *Ab excessu divi Marci*. Ed. by K. Stavenhagen (Teubner, 1922); tr. by Edward C. Echols, *History of the Roman Empire from the death of Marcus Aurelius to the accession of Gordian III* (Berkeley and Lond. 1961). See *Jour. Roman Stud.* lvi (1966), 92–107 and lvii (1967), 61–4.

(*m*) *Historia Augusta, Scriptores historiae augustae*. Ed. by E. Hohl (Teubner, 1927; rev. edn. 1965); ed. and tr. by David Magie. 3 vols. (Loeb, 1922–32).

For the problems of dating and authorship, see *Fifty years of classical scholarship*, ed. Maurice Platnauer (Oxf. 1954), p. 404 and pp. 411–12. For a study stressing the unreliability of the impostor who wrote *Historia Augusta* about 395, see Sir Ronald Syme, *Ammianus and the Historia Augusta* (Oxf. 1968). Compare Peter White, 'The authorship of the *Historia Augusta*', *Jour. Roman Stud.* lvii (1967), 115–33; Alan D. Cameron's review article in *J.R.S.* lv (1965), 240–50; and his 'Three notes on the *Historia Augusta*', *Classical Review*, xviii (1968), 17–20; and Jacques Schwartz, 'Sur la date de l'Histoire Auguste', *Bonner Historia-Augusta Colloquium*, 1966–7 (1968), 91–9.

(*n*) *Panegyrici Latini*. Ed. by E. Baehrens (Teubner, 1874); ed. by G. Baehrens (Teubner, 1911); ed. by Roger A. B. Mynors (Oxf. Classical Texts, Oxf. 1964).

(*o*) Aurelius Victor, *De viris illustribus* and *Epitome de Caesaribus*. Ed. by F. Pichlmayr (Teubner, 1911; rev. edn. 1961–6).

(*p*) Eutropius, *Breviarium historiae Romanae*. Ed. by F. Ruehl (Teubner, 1887). Cf. *Historia Augusta*.

(*q*) Zosimus, *Historia nova*. Ed. by L. Mendelssohn (Teubner, 1887); trans. by J. J. Buchanan and H. T. Davis (San Antonio, Texas, 1967).

See Thompson (No. 2112).

(*r*) Orosius, *Historiae*. Ed. by C. Zangemeister (Teubner, 1889); tr. by Irving W. Raymond, Columbia Univ. Records of Civilization (N.Y. 1936); and by Roy J. Defarrari, *Seven books of history against the pagans* in Fathers of the Church, vol. 1 (Washington, 1964).

2. *Other Ancient Sources*

Next to Caesar and Tacitus, the *Antonine Itinerary* and the *Notitia Dignitatum* (Nos. 2029, 2030) are of the greatest value. Peutinger's *Tabula* and the *Anonymus Ravennas* (Nos. 2032, 2031) supplement the *Antonine Itinerary*. On these three geographical works, see Horsley (No. 2044) and Henry F. Tozer, *A history of ancient geography* (Cambr. 1897; 2nd edn. with additional notes by M. Cary 1935; reprinted N.Y. 1964). The spurious treatise ascribed to Richard of Cirencester (No. 2026) gives a fictitious itinerary of Britain. The information concerning the laws and government of Britain furnished by the Greek and Roman authors is very meagre. The *Codex Theodosianus* (ed. by Gustav Haenel, Bonn, 1842; new edn. by Theodor Mommsen and P. M. Meyer, *Theodosiani Libri XVI*, etc. Berlin, 1905), lib. xi. tit. vii. § 2 ('De exactionibus') contains a brief rescript of the fifth century relating to Britain, in which the decurion is mentioned. See Nos. 2162, 2167 for the work of Gildas and Nennius.

2026 'CIRENCESTER, RICHARD OF'. The description of Britain, translated from Richard of Cirencester, with the original treatise De situ Britanniae, and a commentary on the Itinerary. [Ed. by Henry Hatcher.] Lond. 1809.

This treatise was first published in C. J. Bertram's *Britannicarum Gentium Historiae Antiquae Scriptores Tres: Ricardus Corinensis, Gildas, Nennius* (Copenhagen, 1757), pp. 1–60. For other editions, and for arguments proving that it could not have been written by Richard of Cirencester in the fourteenth century, but that it was probably fabricated by Bertram, see B. B. Woodward, 'A literary forgery, Richard of Cirencester's Tractate on Britain', in *Gentleman's Magazine*, N.S. (1866), i. 301–8, 617–24; ii. 458–66; and (1867), iv. 443–51; and *Ricardi de Cirencestria Speculum Historiale* (Ed. by J. E. B. Mayor, Rolls Series, 2 vols. 1863–9), vol. ii, pp. xvii–clxiv. Mayor gives a full account of the history of this spurious work; cf. H. J. Randall, 'Splendide mendax', *Antiquity*, vii (1933), 49–60. See Nos. 1089, 1101; and, for Bertram's life, *Dictionary of National Biography* (1885), iv. 412–13.

2027 COLLINGWOOD (ROBIN G.) and WRIGHT (RICHARD P.). The Roman inscriptions of Britain. Vol. i. Lond. 1965.

Vol. i, inscriptions on stone with a drawing of each inscription; notes on its size, its location, its date of discovery; a transcription and translation; and bibliographical references. This first volume of a complete corpus contains 800 pages, 24 plates, and 2,500 illustrations. It supersedes all other works in its field. Vol. ii will catalogue *Instrumentum domesticum*.

2028 INSCRIPTIONES BRITANNIAE LATINAE. Ed. by Emil Hübner. Akademie der Wissensch. zu Berlin, Corpus Inscriptionum Latinarum. Vol. vii. Berlin. 1873.

'Additamenta ad Corporis vol. vii' have been published in the same society's *Ephemeris Epigraphica*, iii. 113–55 and 311–18; iv. 194–212, by Hübner; and vii. 273–354; ix. 510–690, by F. J. Haverfield (Berlin, 1876–1913). British inscriptions discovered since 1888 are also noted year by year in the *Revue Archéologique* (Paris, 1884+) in a section entitled 'Revue des Publications Épigraphiques relatives à l'Antiquité Romaine'. New and re-deciphered inscriptions are noted in the annual survey of Roman Britain published in the *Journal of Roman Studies* since 1921. The completed new corpus of Romano-British inscriptions by Collingwood and Wright (No. 2027) will supersede all others. For other collections of inscriptions, see the following: Petrie's *Monumenta* (No. 1084); John McCaul, *Britanno-Roman inscriptions* (Toronto, etc. 1863); Gordon McN. Rushforth, *Latin historical inscriptions illustrating the history of the early empire* (Oxf.

1893; 2nd edn. Lond. 1930); Andrew R. Burn, *The Romans in Britain: an anthology of inscriptions, with translations and a running commentary* (Oxf. 1932; 2nd edn. 1969). Cf. F. N. Pryce, 'A new diploma for Roman Britain', *Jour. Roman Stud.* xx (1930), 16–23, which lists the diplomas of the Empire for Britain. See also *Lapidarium septentrionale*, ed. Bruce (No. 2021), which contains many inscriptions.

2029 ITINERARIA ROMANA. Vol. i. Itineraria Antonini et Burdigalense. Ed. by Otto Cuntz. Leipzig. 1929.

The *Antonine Itinerary* names the principal stations and towns in the Roman Empire, with the intermediate distances; it is essentially a road-map. It was probably compiled in the second or early third century; but the edition which has come down to us belongs to the time of Diocletian or of Constantine the Great. Other editions: [Ed. by Andreas Schottus] (Cologne, 1600); William Burton, *Commentary on Antoninus his Itinerary* (Lond. 1658); Thomas Gale, *Antonini iter Britanniarum commentariis illustratum: accessit anonymi Ravennatis Britanniae chorographia* (Lond. 1709); Thomas Reynolds, *Iter Britanniarum* (Cambr. 1799); *Itinerarium Antonini Augusti et Hierosolymitanum*, ed. by Gustav Parthey and Moritz Pinder (Berlin, 1848); Konrad Miller, *Itineraria Romana . . .* (Stuttgart, 1916) (unsatisfactory); and Horsley (No. 2044). Cf. [J. J.] Raven, 'The British section of Antonine's Itinerary' (a series of papers in the *Antiquary*, xxxvi–xl (1900–4), *passim*); A. C. Yorke, 'Iter V and Iter IX of Antonine', *Cambr. Antiq. Soc. Procs.* xi (1907) [1903–6], 2–74; the *Catalogue of the British Museum Library*, under 'Antoninus Augustus'; Ivan Margary, *Roman Roads in Britain* (No. 2084); Thomas Codrington, *Roman Roads in Britain* (No. 2084); O. G. S. Crawford, 'A Note on the Peutinger Table and the fifth and ninth iters', *Jour. Roman Stud.* xiv (1924), 137–41; G. H. Wheeler, 'Textual errors in the Itinerary of Antoninus', *E.H.R.* xxxv (1920), 377–82; C. E. Stevens's article cited above (No. 2024); Bonser, *R.–B.B.* (No. 2013), pp. 108–11.

2030 NOTITIA DIGNITATUM. Ed. by Eduard Böcking. 2 vols. in 3, and index. Bonn. 1839–53. Also edited by Otto Seeck. Berlin. 1876 (the better edition, but Böcking gives a more detailed commentary). Translation of extracts by William Fairley. Philadelphia. 1899.

This work is an official register or list of the military and civil dignitaries in both the eastern and the western empire, with the names of the places at which they were stationed, and the number of troops under their command. It was probably compiled under Honorius early in the fifth century. Mommsen (in *Hermes*, xxxvi (1901), 544–7) shows that the date of the last redaction is about 425 A.D. For the editions and literature, see Potthast, *Bibliotheca* (No. 62), ii. 868; and Horsley (No. 2044). Of fundamental importance for understanding the *Notitia* is J. B. Bury's article, 'The *Notitia Dignitatum*', in *Jour. Roman Stud.* x (1920), 131–54, which precipitated extended controversy; cf. Collingwood (No. 2036), pp. 476–7, for bibliography to which may be added: F. S. Salisbury, 'On the date of the "Notitia Dignitatum"', *Jour. Roman Stud.* xvii (1927), 102–6, and 'The *Notitia Dignitatum* and the western mints', ibid. xxiii (1933), 217–20; C. E. Stevens, 'The British sections of the *Notitia Dignitatum*', *Archaeol. Jour.* xcvii (1940), 125–54; Denis van Berchem, 'On some chapters of the *Notitia Dignitatum* relating to the defence of Gaul and Britain', *Amer. Jour. Philol.* lxxvi (1955), 138–47; and the article by J. P. C. Kent on the coin evidence cited under No. 2104; C. E. Stevens's article cited above (No. 2024). See also Arnold H. M. Jones, *Later Roman Empire* (No. 2046), ii. 1417–50.

2031 RAVENNATIS ANONYMI COSMOGRAPHIA ET GUIDONIS GEOGRAPHICA. Ed. by Moritz Pinder and Gustav Parthey. Berlin. 1860. RAVENNATIS ANONYMI COSMOGRAPHIA. Ed. by Joseph Schnetz. 2 vols. Leipzig. 1939–40.

This compilation by a clerk at Ravenna seems, as we have it, to belong to the seventh or eighth century. He enumerated the rivers and the Roman stations; and named over 300

English places. See the edition of Thomas Gale (No. 2029); Horsley (No. 2044); M. A. P. de Avezac-Macaya, *Le Ravennate et son exposé cosmographique* (Rouen, 1888); and for the editions, etc., Potthast, *Bibliotheca* (No. 62), i. 498. Cf. also the article of C. E. Stevens cited above (No. 2024); I. A. Richmond and O. G. S. Crawford, 'The British section of the Ravenna cosmography', *Archaeologia*, xciii (1949), 1–50 (reprinted, Oxf. 1949).

2032   TABULA ITINERARIA PEUTINGERIANA. Edited, with a valuable introduction, by Conrad Mannert. Leipzig. 1824. La Table de Peutinger. Ed. by Ernest Desjardins. Nos. 1–14. Paris. 1869–74.

This chart or map of the world in the time of the Romans is 21 ft. long and 1 ft. wide. The oldest existing copy, now at Vienna, was made by a monk of Colmar in 1265, and belonged to Konrad Peutinger of Augsburg in the first half of the sixteenth century. It traces the lines of the roads throughout the Roman empire, marking the military stations and indicating the distances between them. The part relating to Britain is incomplete. Miller (see below) ascribes the work to a cartographer of Rome called Castorius, who compiled it about A.D. 366; but Mannert adduces strong evidence that it was drawn up in the third century, while Desjardins believes that some portions belong to the age of Augustus and others to the fourth, fifth, and sixth centuries. Other editions: *Peutingeriana tabula itineraria nunc primum arte photographica expressa* (Vienna, 1888); *Die Weltkarte des Castorius genannt die Peutinger'sche Tafel*, ed. by Konrad Miller, 2 vols. (text and atlas) (Ravensburg, 1887–8); Miller, *Die Peutinger'sche Tafel* (Stuttgart, 1962); Horsley (No. 2044). Cf. the article of C. E. Stevens cited above (No. 2024) and that of O. G. S. Crawford (No. 2029).

C. MODERN WRITERS

Of the older authorities, Camden's *Britannia* (No. 609) and Horsley's *Britannia Romana* (No. 2044) should be consulted. The best recent summaries are those of Collingwood (Nos. 2034, 2036–7), Richmond (No. 2049A), Hunter Blair (No. 2033), and Frere (No. 2040). The general, comprehensive accounts which are listed immediately below are followed by some studies of special sites and the latter are followed by a few studies on special topics, grouped under administration, army, art, and buildings, mining, pottery, religion, roads, walls, and frontiers: Wales and Scotland. The end of the Roman occupation is considered on pages 277–9. On all of the subjects, Bonser's *Bibliography* (No. 2013), Collingwood-Wright (No. 2027), and Frere's *Britannia* (No. 2040) cite full references.

1. *Comprehensive Accounts*

2033   BLAIR (PETER HUNTER). Roman Britain and early England 55 B.C.–A.D. 871. Nelson's History of England, i. Edin. etc. 1963.

2034   THE CAMBRIDGE ANCIENT HISTORY. Vols. x, xi, xii. Ed. by S. A. Cook, F. E. Adcock, M. P. Charlesworth, and (vol. xii) N. H. Baynes. Cambr. 1934, 1936, 1939; vol. x reprinted 1952.

Vol. x: The Augustan Empire, 44 B.C.–A.D. 70, Ch. xxiii, pp. 790–802 (R. Syme and R. G. Collingwood); cf. C. E. Stevens, 'Britain between the invasions', in *Aspects of Archaeology*, etc. (No. 1432), 332–44. Vol. xi: The Imperial Peace, A.D. 70–192, Ch. iv. 150–7 (Syme); xiii. 511–25 (Collingwood). Vol. xii: The Imperial Crisis and Recovery, A.D. 193–324, Ch. i. 36–42 (S. N. Miller), Ch. viii. 282–96 (Collingwood). Each volume contains bibliographical lists.

2035 CHARLESWORTH (MARTIN P.). The lost province, or the worth of Britain. Gregynog Lectures, 1948. Cardiff. 1949.

On the causes of the Roman occupation and its benefits for Rome and Britain. Cf. *Heritage* (No. 1430).

2036 COLLINGWOOD (ROBIN G.) and MYRES (JOHN N. L.). Roman Britain and the English settlements. *The Oxford History of England*, vol. i. Oxf. 1936. 2nd edn. 1937.

Collingwood's admirable treatment of Roman Britain needs some revision from recent archaeological evidence; Myres contributed an excellent summary on the English settlements to about A.D. 550. Earlier work of Collingwood, *Roman Britain* (Lond. 1923; 3rd edn. Oxf. 1934).

2037 COLLINGWOOD (ROBIN G.) and RICHMOND (IAN). The archaeology of Roman Britain, with a preface by D. R. Wilson and a chapter on Samian ware by B. R. Hartley. Lond. 1969.

This is essentially a revised and expanded edition of R. G. Collingwood, *The archaeology of Roman Britain* (Lond. 1930). See also Collingwood's contributions to the *Cambridge Ancient History* (No. 2034) and to *An Economic Survey of Ancient Rome* (No. 2039) as well as 'R. G. Collingwood: Bibliography of writings on ancient history and archaeology', *P.B.A.* xxix (1943), 481–5. See S. Applebaum, 'The pattern of settlement in Roman Britain', *Agricultural Hist. Rev.* xi (1963), 1–14.

2038 DUDLEY (DONALD R.) and WEBSTER (GRAHAM). The Roman conquest of Britain, A.D. 43–57. British Battles series. Lond. 1965.

2039 AN ECONOMIC SURVEY OF ANCIENT ROME. Ed. by Tenney Frank. Vol. iii, pt. i: *Roman Britain*, by R. G. Collingwood, pp. 1–118. Baltimore. 1937. Reprinted. 1959.

See also C. E. Stevens, 'Agriculture and rural life in the later Roman Empire', *Cambridge Econ. Hist.* (No. 1175), i (1941), 89–117; 2nd edn. i (1966), 92–124.

2040 FRERE (SHEPPARD). Britannia. A history of the provinces of the Roman Empire, vol. i. Lond. 1967.

Frere's somewhat encyclopaedic history, utilizing the extensive recent research, supersedes previous general accounts. After a summary of the situation before Caesar's invasion, it provides a chronological history as well as chapters on administration, army towns, trade, and culture.

2041 HAVERFIELD (FRANCIS J.). 'The Romanization of Roman Britain'. *P.B.A.* ii (1905–6), 185–217. Printed separately, 1906. 4th edn. by George Macdonald. Oxf. 1923.

2042 HAVERFIELD (FRANCIS J.). The Roman occupation of Britain. Ford Lectures, 1907. Ed. by George Macdonald. Oxf. 1924.

Includes a notice of Haverfield's life and a list of his writings; see also *Jour. Roman Stud.* viii (1918), 184–98 for a bibliography. See his sections on Roman Remains in the *V.C.H.* (No. 1529), and his chapter on Roman Britain in the *Cambridge Med. Hist.* (No. 1176), i (1911), 367–91.

2043 HOLMES (THOMAS RICE E.). Ancient Britain and the invasions of Julius Caesar. Oxf. 1907. 2nd edn. 1935.

Unsatisfactory on the side of prehistoric archaeology. See also H. D. Warburg, 'Caesar's first expedition to Britain', *E.H.R.* xxxviii (1923), 226–40, and C. E. Stevens, '55 B.C. and 54 B.C.', *Antiquity*, xxi (1947), 3–9.

2044 HORSLEY (JOHN). Britannia Romana, or the Roman antiquities of Britain. Lond. 1732.

Bk. i. History of Roman Britain, Roman walls, etc.

Bk. ii. Roman inscriptions and sculptures (76 plates).

Bk. iii. Ptolemy's *Geography*, the *Antonine Itinerary*, *Notitia Dignitatum*, *Anonymus Ravennas*, and Peutinger's *Table*, so far as they relate to Britain, with essays thereon.

The editions of older standard works, such as those of Alexander Gordon, John Leland, Samuel Lysons, William Stukeley are cited in Collingwood–Wright (No. 2027), pp. xxiii–xxxi.

2045 JARRETT (MICHAEL G.) and DOBSON (BRIAN), eds. Britain and Rome. Essays presented to Eric Birley on his sixtieth birthday. Kendal. 1966.

(*a*) L. P. Wenham, The south-west defences of the fortress of Eboracum. 1–26.

(*b*) M. G. Jarrett, The garrison of Maryport and the Roman army in Britain. 27–40.

(*c*) D. Charlesworth, Three sherds of stamped ware from Aldborough. 41–4.

(*d*) A. R. Birley, The origins of Gordian. 56–60.

(*e*) B. Heywood, The vallum: its problems restated. 85–94.

(*f*) B. J. N. Edwards, Roman Lancashire. 95–104.

(*g*) A. P. Detsicas, A Samian bowl from Eccles, Kent. 105–8.

(*h*) J. C. Mann, City foundations in Gaul and Britain. 109–13.

(*i*) J. J. Wilkes, Early fourth-century rebuilding in Hadrian wall-forts. 114–38.

(*j*) J. Morris, Dark Age dates. 145–85.

2046 JONES (ARNOLD H. M.). The later Roman Empire. 284–602: a social, economic and administrative survey. 3 vols. Oxf. 1964.

2047 LIVERSIDGE (JOAN). Britain in the Roman Empire. Lond. 1968.

2048 MOMMSEN (THEODOR). Römische Geschichte, vol. v: Die Provinzen von Caesar bis Diocletian. Berlin. 1885. 5th edn. 1904. Translated by William P. Dickson. 2 vols. Lond. 1886. Reprinted with corrections (by F. J. Haverfield) as *The provinces of the Roman Empire*. 2 vols. Lond. 1909.

2049 RICHMOND (IAN A.). Roman archaeology and art. Ed. by Peter Salway. Lond. 1969.

Richmond's unpublished papers, including his Ford Lectures of 1951, are printed without revision by the author.

2049A RICHMOND (IAN A.). Roman Britain. Pelican History of England, i. Harmondsworth. 1955. Reprinted subsequently.

This work by a foremost scholar includes a select, but fairly extensive, bibliography, particularly of articles in journals. Richmond has another book with the same title in the Britain in Pictures series (Lond. 1947; reprinted).

2050 RIVET (ALBERT L. F.), ed. The Roman villa in Britain. Lond. 1969.

(*a*) H. C. Bowen, The Celtic background. 1–48.

(*b*) Ian Richmond, The plans of Roman villas in England. 49–70.

(*c*) D. J. Smith, The mosaic pavements. 71–126.
(*d*) Joan Liversidge, Furniture and interior decoration. 127–72.
(*e*) A. L. F. Rivet, Social and economic aspects. 173–216.
(*f*) G. Webster, The future of villa studies. 217–49.

2051 RIVET (ALBERT L. F.). Town and country in Roman Britain. Hutchinson University Library. Lond. 1958.

The select bibliography is useful.

2. *Special Sites*
Consult the annual reports of 'Sites Explored' in *Jour. Roman Stud.*

2052 (Aldborough). MYRES (JOHN N. L.), STEER (K. A.), and CHITTY (MRS. A. M. H.). 'The defences of Isurium Brigantum'. *Yorks. Archaeol. Jour.* xl (1959), 1–77.

2052A (Bath). CUNLIFFE (BARRY). Roman Bath discovered. Lond. 1971.

2053 (Chester). THOMPSON (F. H.). Roman Cheshire. A history of Cheshire. Ed. by J. J. Bagley. Vol. ii. Chester. 1965.

2054 (Cirencester). HAVERFIELD (F. J.). 'Roman Cirencester'. *Archaeologia,* lxix (1918), 161–209. J. S. WACHER in *Antiq. Jour.* xli (1961), 63–71; xlii (1962), 3–14; xliii (1963), 15–26; and subsequent issues.

2055 (Colchester). WHEELER (R. E. M.) and LAVER (PHILIP G.). 'Roman Colchester'. *Jour. Roman Stud.* ix (1919), 139–69. M. R. HULL. Roman Colchester. Oxf. 1958 (No. 2070).

2056 (Exeter). FOX (AILEEN). Roman Exeter. Manchester, 1952.

2057 (Fishbourne). CUNLIFFE (BARRY W.). Fishbourne: a Roman palace and its gardens. Lond. 1971.

A volume in the series New Aspects of Antiquity, edited by Sir Mortimer Wheeler.

2058 (Gloucester). LEGGATT (L. E. O. FULLBROOK). Roman Gloucester. 2nd edn. Stroud. 1968.

2059 (Hod Hill). Vol. i: Antiquities from Hod Hill in the Durden Collection. By J. W. Brailsford. Brit. Mus. 1962. Vol. ii: Excavations, 1951–8. By Ian Richmond and others. Brit. Mus. 1968.

2060 (Leicester). HAVERFIELD (F. J.). 'Roman Leicester'. *Archaeol. Jour.* lxxv (1918), 1–46.

2061 (Lincolnshire). VARIOUS CONTRIBUTORS. 'Contributions to the archaeology of Lincolnshire, ii: The Roman occupation'. *Archaeol. Jour.* ciii (1946).

Among the contributions are C. F. C. Hawkes, 'Roman Ancaster, Horncastle and Caistor'; I. A. Richmond, 'The Roman city of Lincoln'; and I. A. Richmond, 'The four *coloniae* of Roman Britain'.

2062 (London). GRIMES (WILLIAM F.). The excavation of Roman and mediaeval London. Lond. 1968.

2063 (London). MERRIFIELD (RALPH). Roman city of London. Lond. 1965.

2064 (London). ROMAN LONDON. Royal Comm. Hist. Monuments: An Inventory of the historical monuments in London. Vol. iii. Lond. 1928.

R. E. M. Wheeler, *London in Roman Times*. London Museum Catalogue, no. 3 (Lond. 1930).

2065 (Lullingstone). MEATES (GEOFFREY W.). Lullingstone Roman villa. Lond. 1955; 1962.

See K. S. Painter in *Brit. Mus. Quart.* xxxiii (1969), 131–50.

2066 (Silchester). BOON (GEORGE C.). Roman Silchester. The archaeology of a Romano-British town. Lond. 1957.

2067 (St. Albans). FRERE (SHEPPARD S.). 'Verulamium, three Roman cities'. *Antiquity*, xxxviii (1964), 103–12. See No. 2070.

2068 (York). EBURACUM: ROMAN YORK. Royal Comm. Hist. Monuments: An inventory of the historical monuments in the city of York. Vol. i. Lond. 1962.

2069 YORKSHIRE ARCHAEOLOGICAL SOCIETY. Roman Malton and District Reports of the Roman Antiquities Committee. Leeds. 1928+.

i: P. Corder, *The Roman pottery at Crambeck, Castle Howard* (1928).
ii: P. Corder, *The defences of the Roman fort at Malton*, with contributions by H. Mattingly and M. R. Hull (1930).
iii: P. Corder, *Roman pottery at Throlam, Holme-on-Spalding Moor, East Yorkshire* (1930).
iv: P. Corder and J. L. Kirk, *A Roman villa at Langton, near Malton* (1932).
v: M. Kitson Clark, *A gazetteer of Roman remains in East Yorkshire* (1935).
vi: I. A. Richmond, *Roman pavements at Rudston, East Riding* (1935).
vii: R. H. Hayes and E. Whitley, *The Roman pottery at Norton, East Yorkshire* (1950). Cf. R. Gilyard-Beer, *The Romano-British baths at Wells* (Yorkshire), Roman Antiquities Committee, Research Report No. 1. Leeds. 1951.

2070 REPORTS OF THE RESEARCH COMMITTEE OF THE SOCIETY OF ANTIQUARIES OF LONDON. Lond. 1913+.

A Classic Series.

i, ii, and iv: J. P. Bushe-Fox, *Excavations on the site of the Roman town at Wroxeter, Shropshire* (1913, 1914, 1916).
iii: J. P. Bushe-Fox, *Excavations at Hengistbury Head, Hampshire* (1915).
v: J. P. Bushe-Fox, *Excavation of the late Celtic urnfield at Swarling, Kent* (1925).
vi, vii, x, and xvi, xxiii: J. P. Bushe-Fox, *Excavation of the Roman fort at Richborough, Kent* (1926, 1928, 1932, 1949, 1968).
viii: W. Whiting, W. Hawley, T. May, *Report on the excavation of the Roman cemetery at Ospringe, Kent* (1931).
ix: R. E. M. and T. V. Wheeler, *Report on the excavation of the prehistoric, Roman, and post-Roman site in Lydney Park, Gloucestershire* (1932).

xi: R. E. M. and T. V. Wheeler, *Verulamium: a Belgic and two Roman cities* (1936); cf. Philip Corder, 'Verulamium, 1930–40', *Antiquity*, xv (1941), 113–24.
xii: R. E. M. Wheeler, *Maiden Castle, Dorset* (1943).
xiii: (Not concerned with Great Britain.)
xiv: C. F. C. Hawkes and M. R. Hull, *Camulodunum: first report on the excavations at Colchester, 1930–9* (1947).
xv: Kathleen M. Kenyon, *Excavations at the Jewry Wall Site, Leicester* (1948).
xvi: Above under vi.
xvii: R. E. M. Wheeler, *The Stanwick fortifications, North Riding of Yorkshire* (1954).
xviii: (Not concerned with Great Britain.)
xix: Sir Mortimer Wheeler and Katherine M. Richardson, *Hill Forts of Northern France* (1957).
xx: M. R. Hull and others, *Roman Colchester* (1958). Introduction by I. A. Richmond.
xxi: M. R. Hull, *Roman Potter's Kilns of Colchester* (1963).
xxii: (Not concerned with Great Britain.)
xxiii: Above under vi.

3. Special Topics

2071 BURN (ANDREW R.). Agricola and Roman Britain. Teach Yourself History Ser. Lond. 1953.

See the following for the expansion of Roman rule in Britain: George Macdonald, 'Agricola in Britain', *Classical Assoc. Procs.* xxix (1932), 7–21; I. A. Richmond, 'Gnaeus Iulius Agricola!', *Jour. Roman Stud.* xxxiv (1944), 34–45; T. D. Pryce, 'The Roman occupation of Britain: its early phase', *Antiq. Jour.* xviii (1938), 29–48; E. Birley, 'Britain under the Flavians: Agricola and his predecessors', *Durham Univ. Jour.* xxxviii (N.S. vii) (1945–6), 79–84 and 'Britain after Agricola, and the end of the ninth legion', ibid. xl (N.S. ix) (1947–8), 78–83; D. Atkinson, 'The governors of Britain from Claudius to Diocletian', *Jour. Roman Stud.* xii (1922), 60–73; George H. Stevenson, *Roman provincial administration till the age of the Antonines* (Oxf. etc. 1939); for a recent assessment of the frontier policy of Agricola, see the contribution of I. A. Richmond to *Carnuntina* (No. 2072).

2072 CARNUNTINA: Ergebnisse der Forschung über die Grenzprovinzen des römischen Reiches. Vorträge beim internationalen Kongress der Altertumsforscher, Carnuntum, 1955 (Römische Forschungen in Niederösterreich, Band III). Ed. by Erich Swoboda. Graz. 1956.

Includes the following contributions on Roman Britain: Eric Birley, 'Hadrianic frontier policy', pp. 25–33; John P. Gillam, 'Roman pottery in the north of Britain', pp. 64–77; J. P. C. Kent, 'Coin evidence for the abandonment of a frontier province', pp. 85–90; V. E. Nash-Williams, 'The Roman town of Venta Silurum (Caerwent) and its defences', pp. 100–16; Ian A. Richmond, 'New evidence upon the achievements of Agricola', pp. 161–7.

2073 THE CIVITAS CAPITALS OF ROMAN BRITAIN; papers given . . . at conference at the University of Leicester, 13–15 December 1963. Ed. by J. S. Wacher. Leicester. 1966.

Brief reports on a series of nine lectures by various scholars on miscellaneous subjects relating to Roman towns.

2074 RURAL SETTLEMENT IN ROMAN BRITAIN: papers read January, 1965. Ed. by Charles Thomas. Council for British Archaeology. Research Report, No. 7. Lond. 1966.

(*a*) The Roman Army

2075 BIRLEY (ERIC). Roman Britain and the Roman Army; collected papers. Kendal. 1953.

Sixteen papers published between 1935 and 1953. Other articles on the Roman army are: M. G. Jarrett, 'Legio II Augusta in Britain', *Archaeol. Cambrensis*, cxiii (1964), 47–63; M. G. Jarrett, 'Septimus Severus and the defences of York', *Yorks. Archaeol. Jour.* xli (1965/7), 516–23; B. R. Hartley, 'Some problems of the Roman military occupation of the north of England', *Northern History*, i (1966), 7–20. See also Simpson (No. 2093). Among the older literature, attention should be given to Emil Hübner, 'Das römische Heer in Britannien', *Hermes: Zeitschrift für classische Philologie*, xvi (1881), 513–84; and his 'Eine römische Annexion', *Deutsche Rundschau*, xv (1878), 221–52, which is translated by Thomas Hodgkin in *Archaeol. Aeliana*, xi (1886), 82–116, and expanded in Hübner's *Römische Heerschaft in Westeuropa* (Berlin, 1890), pp. 3–68.

For the Roman navy, see Donald Atkinson, 'Classis Britannica' in *Tait essays* (No. 1455), pp. 1–11; and Chester G. Starr, jr., *The Roman imperial navy 31 B.C.–A.D. 324* in Cornell Studies in Classical Philology, xxvi (1941).

2076 ROY (WILLIAM). The military antiquities of the Romans in Britain. Soc. of Antiquaries of London. Lond. 1793. *

Includes 51 large plates. 'There is yet in Britain no rival to his great work' (Richmond); cf. I. A. Richmond, 'Roman Britain and Roman military antiquities', *P.B.A.* xli (1955), 297–315; and Richmond's report on 1910–60 research (No. 2017).

(*b*) Art and buildings

2077 LEWIS (MICHAEL J. T.). Temples in Roman Britain. Cambr. 1966.

2078 TOYNBEE (JOCELYN M. C.). Art in Roman Britain. The Society for the Promotion of Roman Studies. 219 pp. and 235 plates. Lond. 1962. Idem, Art in Britain under the Romans. Oxf. 1964.

2079 WARD (JOHN). Romano-British buildings and earthworks. Lond. 1911.

2080 WHEELER (R. E. M.). 'Notes on building construction in Roman Britain', *Jour. Roman Stud.* xxii (1932), 117–34.

See also C. A. F. Berry, 'The dating of Romano-British houses', ibid. xli (1951), 25–31; John E. Price and Frederick G. H. Price, *A description of the remains of Roman buildings at Morton near Brading, Isle of Wight* (Lond. 1881; also *Royal Institute of British Architects Trans.* (1880–1), 125–60); Samuel E. Winbolt, *The Roman villa at Bignor, Sussex, its mosaic pavements described, with a plan of the villa* (Oxf. 1925; new edn. by Winbolt and George Herbert, 1930); Thomas Morgan, *Romano-British mosaic pavements* (with valuable plates) (Lond. 1886); I. A. Richmond and J. P. Gillam, 'Buildings of the first and second centuries north of the granaries at Corbridge', *Archaeol. Aeliana*, xxxi (1953), 205–53; Joan Liversidge, *Furniture in Roman Britain* (Lond. 1955); F. Haverfield and H. Stuart Jones, 'Some representative examples of Romano-British sculpture', *Jour. Roman Stud.* ii (1912), 121–52.

(*c*) Roman Mining

2081 WHITTICK (G. C.). Roman mining in Britain. *Newcomen Soc. Trans.* xii (1931–2), 57–79.

See also F. Haverfield's appendix in J. G. C. Anderson's edition of Tacitus' *Agricola* (No. 2025), pp. 173–82; Oliver Davies, *Roman mines in Europe* (Oxf. 1935), Chap. v. 140–64; Robert J. Forbes, *Metallurgy in antiquity: a notebook for archaeologists and* technologists (Leiden, 1950); John W. Gough, *The mines of Mendip* (Oxf. 1930); G. Webster, 'The lead mining industry in north Wales in Roman times', *Flintshire Hist. Soc. Pubns.* xiii (1952–3), 5–33, and 'A note on the use of coal in Roman Britain', *Antiq. Jour.* xxv (1955), 199–216; Thomas A. Rickard, *Man and metals . . .* 2 vols. (N.Y. etc. 1932).

(d) Roman pottery

2082 ROMANO-BRITISH COARSE POTTERY: a student's guide. Council for British Archaeology, Research Report, No. 6. Lond. 1964.

See also Felix Oswald, *Index of Potters' Stamps on sigillata, Samian ware* (East Bridgford, Notts. 1931); M. R. Hull (No. 2070); and J. P. Gillam in *Carnuntina* (No. 2072). J. P. Gillam, *Types of Roman coarse pottery vessels in Northern Britain* (2nd edn. Newcastle, 1968).

(e) Religion

2083 BARLEY (MAURICE W.) and HANSON (RICHARD P. C.), eds. Christianity in Britain, 300–700. Leicester. 1968.

Papers presented at the conference on Christianity in Roman and sub-Roman Britain held at . . . Nottingham, 1967. For numerous studies on religion in Britain in Roman times, see Bonser, *R.-B.B.* (No. 2013), pp. 80–106.

(f) Roman roads

2084 MARGARY (IVAN D.). Roman roads in Britain. Vol. i: South of the Foss Way–Bristol Channel. Vol. ii: North of the Foss Way–Bristol Channel. Lond. 1955–7. Rev. edn. in one vol. 1967.

See also his earlier work, *Roman ways in the Weald* (Lond. 1948); Thomas Codrington, *Roman roads in Britain* (Lond. 1903; 3rd edn. 1918; repr. 1928); H. Fairhurst, 'The roads of Scotland: I. Roman Roads', *Scottish Geographical Magazine*, lxxi (1955), 77–82.

(g) Roman walls

2085 BRUCE (JOHN C.). The Roman wall: a historical, topographical and descriptive account of the barrier of the lava isthmus, extending from the Tyne to the Solway. Newcastle. 1851. 3rd edn. Lond. 1867.

Contains also an account of coins, inscriptions, and other remains. This book was reproduced by Bruce in a condensed form (No. 2086). For a survey, see *Map of Hadrian's Wall*, The Ordnance Survey (Chessington, 1964). Thomas Hodgkin, 'The literary history of the Roman Wall', *Archaeol. Aeliana*, xviii (1896), 83–108, deals with the notices of the Roman Wall furnished by writers down to the time of Bede. For a history of the problem of the wall, including modern bibliography, see the following: R. G. Collingwood, 'Hadrian's wall: a history of the problem', *Jour. Roman Stud.* xi (1921), 37–66; idem, 'The British frontier in the age of Severus', ibid. xiii (1923), 69–81; idem, 'Hadrian's wall: 1921–30', ibid. xxi (1931), 36–64; idem, 'Hadrian's wall', *History*, N.S. x (1925–6), 193–202; F. G. Simpson and I. A. Richmond, 'The turf wall of Hadrian, 1895–1935', *Jour. Roman Stud.* xxv (1935), 1–18; I. A. Richmond, 'Hadrian's wall, 1939–1949', ibid. xl (1950), 43–56, and idem, 'The Roman frontier land', *History*, xliv (1959), 1–15. For a recent assessment of the frontier policy of Hadrian, see the contribution of Eric Birley to *Carnuntina* (No. 2072) and Eric Birley, *Research on Hadrian's Wall* (Kendal, 1961); C. E. Stevens, 'The building of Hadrian's wall', *Cumbm. and Westm. Antiq. and Archaeol. Soc.* Extra Ser. xx (Kendal, 1966); and Salway, *Frontier People* (No. 2092).

2086 BRUCE (JOHN C.). Handbook to the Roman Wall. 12th edn. By I. A. Richmond. Newcastle-upon-Tyne. 1966.

First published by Bruce as *The Wallet book of the Roman Wall, a guide to pilgrims* (Lond. and Newcastle-upon-Tyne, 1863).

2087 MACDONALD (GEORGE). The Roman wall in Scotland. Glasgow. 1911. 2nd edn. Oxf. 1934.

A definitive work which gives references to earlier literature. I. A. Richmond, 'The Antonine frontier in Scotland', *Jour. Roman Stud.* xxvi (1936), 190–4. Anne S. Robertson, 'The Antonine wall', in *University of Durham: The Congress of Roman Frontier Studies, 1849*, ed. by E. Birley (Durham, 1952), pp. 99–111, reviews recent work and outlines the problems which remain for research. Anne S. Robertson, *The Antonine Wall:* a handbook and a guide to its surviving remains, Glasgow Archaeol. Soc. (Edin., 1960; 3rd edn. Glasgow, 1968). K. A. Steer, 'The Antonine Wall 1934–1959', *Jour. Roman Stud.* l (1960), 84–93. Ordnance Survey, *The Antonine Wall* (H.M.S.O. 1969).

(h) Frontiers: Wales and Scotland

2088 CRAWFORD (OSBERT GUY S.). Topography of Roman Scotland, north of the Antonine Wall. Cambr. 1949.

See the following for the problem of the duration of the first Roman occupation of Scotland: George Macdonald, 'The Agricolan occupation of north Britain', *Jour. Roman Stud.* ix (1919), 111–38; T. D. Pryce and Eric Birley, 'The first Roman occupation of Scotland', ibid. xxv (1935), 59–80; G. Macdonald, 'The dating-value of Samian ware: a rejoinder', ibid. 187–200, and 'Britannia statim omissa', ibid. xxvii (1937), 93–8; Pryce and Birley, 'The fate of Agricola's northern conquests', ibid. xxviii (1938), 141–52; Macdonald, 'Verbum non amplius addam', ibid. xxix (1939), 5–27. For the archaeological advances since 1937 and a review of the present state of knowledge of the Roman occupation from the time of Agricola to that of Septimius Severus, see Kenneth Steer, 'Roman Scotland', *Scottish H. R.* xxiii (1954), 115–28. Cf. E. Birley, 'Some military aspects of Roman Scotland', *Dumfries and Galloway Nat. Hist. and Antiq. Soc. Trans.* 3rd Ser. xxi (1954), 9–21 and Douglas Young, *Romanisation in Scotland: an essay in perspective* (privately printed, 1955); J. Curle's inventory (No. 2020) and Nos. 2090 and 2087.

2089 NASH–WILLIAMS (VICTOR E.). The Roman frontier in Wales. *Board of Celtic Studies.* Cardiff. 1954. 2nd revised edn. by Michael G. Jarrett. Cardiff. 1969.

See also his account of Caerwent, in *Carnuntina* (No. 2072); E. Birley, 'Roman garrisons in Wales', *Archaeol. Cambrensis*, cii (1952), 9–19. Francis J. Haverfield, *Military aspects of Roman Wales* (Lond. 1910); Robert E. Mortimer Wheeler, *Prehistoric and Roman Wales* (Oxf. 1925); Ellis Davies, *The prehistoric and Roman remains of Denbighshire* (Cardiff, 1929); R. E. M. Wheeler, *The Roman fort near Brecon* in *Y Cymmrodor*, xxxvii (1926); W. F. Grimes, *Holt, Denbighshire* in *Y Cymmrodor*, xli (1930), which includes a topographical list of Romano-British pottery sites, with notes and full bibliographical references; Paul Reynolds, *Excavations on the site of the Roman fort of Kanovium at Caerhun, Caernarvonshire* (Cardiff, 1938); V. E. Nash-Williams, *The Roman legionary fortress at Caerleon, Monmouthshire* (Cardiff, 1946); R. E. M. and T. V. Wheeler, 'The Roman amphitheatre at Caerleon, Monmouthshire', *Archaeologia*, lxxviii (2nd Ser. xxviii) (1928), 111–218. For a guide to the Roman monuments of Wales, see No. 1991. Ian A. Richmond on Cornovii (No. 1435 d). See also M. G. Jarrett and J. C. Mann, 'The tribes of Wales' (as recorded by Roman writers), *Welsh Hist. Rev.* iv (1968–9), 161–74.

2090 ROMAN AND NATIVE IN NORTH BRITAIN. Ed. by I. A. Richmond. Nelson's Studies in History and Archaeology. Edin. 1958.

A co-operative work on the Roman penetration into Scotland, as a companion volume to *The Problem of the Picts* (No. 2137). Chapters by Piggott, John Clarke, J. P. Gillam, K. A. Steer, and I. A. Richmond.

2091 THE ROMAN OCCUPATION OF SOUTH-WESTERN SCOTLAND. Being reports of excavations and surveys carried under the auspices of the Glasgow Archaeological Society, by J. Clarke, J. M. Davidson, A. S. Robertson, and J. K. St. Joseph. Edited for the Society with an historical survey by S. N. Miller. Glasgow Univ. Publications, lxxxiii. Glasgow. 1952.

Other excavation reports on Scottish sites have been published by the Glasgow Archaeological Society.

2092 SALWAY (PETER). The frontier people of Roman Britain. Cambridge Classical Stud. Cambr. 1965.

This is an advanced study of the population of the northern frontier.

2093 SIMPSON (GRACE). Britons and the Roman army: a study of Wales and the southern Pennines in the first to third centuries. Lond. 1964.

See G. D. B. Jones, 'The Romans in the north-west', *Northern History*, iii (1968), 1–26.

2094 WILSON (DAVID R.). Roman frontiers of Britain. Regional Archaeologies. Lond. 1967.

This small book by a specialist is in the Heinemann Educational series. On the Roman frontiers of Britain, consult the contributions by six British scholars in *Bonner Jahrbücher* (Cologne), xix (1967), 6–53; and J. P. Gillam and J. C. Mann, 'The northern British frontier (138–217)', *Archaeologia Aeliana*, xlviii (1970), 1–44.

D. THE END OF THE ROMAN OCCUPATION: ROMAN SURVIVALS

The decline of Roman control, the fourth-century raids of Picts, Scots, and Saxons against the Romano-British, and the considerable infiltration of Germanic peoples before the end of the fourth century are described in the general works on Roman Britain (pp. 268–70). The meagre written sources for the late Roman period include the works of Gildas (No. 2162) and Zosimus (No. 2025), the biography of St. Germanus (No. 2108), and oddments from other continental writers. The archaeological evidence is summarized in the appropriate volumes of the Ancient Peoples and Places series, for example the volumes of Clarke, Stone, and Wilson (No. 761), and particularly Chapter 17 of Frere's *Britannia* (No. 2040). The works on Celtic Britain (pp. 279–82) present views on the end of the Roman occupation.

The question of the survival and influence of Roman institutions after the fifth century has evoked much discussion. Seebohm in his *English Village Community* (No. 2646) maintained the continuity of the Roman villa to the Anglo-Saxon village and the manor. Maitland in the chapter on 'The growth of seignorial power' in his *Domesday Book and Beyond* (No. 2636), Vinogradoff in No. 2651, and Round in No. 4004 controverted Seebohm's thesis. Recent archaeological and linguistic researches seem to support the disappearance of the villa; but clear-cut generalizations for all of Britain cannot be drawn. The problem of continuity dovetails with that of the character of the Anglo-Saxon conquest, the free or servile status of the invaders, their settlement sites, and the expulsion or retention of the Romano-British and the Roman introduction of Germans, presumably Franks, to resist the invasions of other Germanic tribes. The issues on the continuity from Roman to Saxon times are sketched by Loyn (No. 2499), pp. 5–22. Studies on the character of the Anglo-Saxon conquest are entered below on pages 364–8.

2095   ALCOCK (LESLIE). 'Roman Britons and pagan Saxons: an archaeological appraisal' (with select bibliography of recent studies). *Welsh Hist. Rev.* iii (1967), 229–49.

2096   CRAWFORD (O. GUY S.). 'Our debt to Rome'. *Antiquity*, ii (1928), 173–88.

2097   DEANESLY (MARGARET). 'Roman traditionalist influences among the Anglo-Saxons'. *E.H.R.* lviii (1943), 129–47.

2098   EVISON (VERA L.). The fifth century invasions south of the Thames. Lond. and N.Y. 1965.

    See reviews in *Medieval Archaeol.* ix (1965), 221–3 and in *E.H.R.* lxxxi (1966), 340–5.

2099   FINBERG (HERBERT P. R.). Roman and Saxon Withington: a study in continuity. Dept. Local Eng. Hist. . . . Leicester, Occasional Paper No. 8. Leicester. 1955. Reprinted in his *Lucerna* (No. 1470) with another paper entitled 'Continuity or cataclysm'.

    Finberg traces the continuity in use of the villa of Withington and cautiously suggests it as a not wholly exceptional example. See the review by F. T. Wainwright in *E.H.R.* lxxii (1957), 144–5.

2100   HAWKES (C. F. CHRISTOPHER). 'Britons, Romans and Saxons round Salisbury and in Cranborne Chase'. *Archaeol. Jour.* civ (1948), 1–48.

2101   HAWKES (SONIA C.) and DUNNING (GERALD C.). 'Soldiers and settlers in Britain fourth and fifth century, with a catalogue of animal-ornamented buckles and related belt-fittings'. *Medieval Archaeol.* v (1961), 1–70.

2102   HUGHES (MICHAEL W.). 'The end of Roman rule in Britain: a defence of Gildas'. *Hon. Soc. Cymmrodorion Trans.* for 1946–47 (1948), 150–87.

    See Gildas (No. 2162).

2103   JONES (GLANVILLE). 'Settlement patterns in Anglo-Saxon England'. *Antiquity*, xxxv (1961), 221–32.

    Jones argues in favour of continuity from Romano-British times.

2104   KENT (JOHN P. C.). 'Coin evidence for the abandonment of a frontier province' in *Carnuntina* (No. 2072). Idem, 'From Roman Britain to Saxon England' in *Anglo-Saxon coins* (No. 1454), pp. 1–22.

2105   LENNARD (REGINALD). 'From Roman Britain to Anglo-Saxon England' in Dopsch, *Festschrift* (No. 1434), pp. 34–73.

2106 MYRES (JOHN N. L.). 'The survival of the Roman villa into the Dark Ages'. *Archaeol. News Letter*, vi (1955), 41–3.

Myres's paper is one of several reports from the Conference on Romano-British villas held in 1955 by the Council for British Archaeology. See Bonser, *R.-B.B.* (No. 2013), p. 47.

2107 MYRES (JOHN N. L.). 'Pelagius and the end of Roman rule in Britain'. *Jour. Roman Stud.* l (1960), 21–36. Idem, 'Archaeology and history: Britons and Saxons in the post-Roman centuries', *Council for Brit. Archaeol. Report*, ii (1961).

2108 ST. GERMANUS, LIFE OF. Ed. by Wilhelm Levison. M.G.H. *Script. Rerum Meroving.* (No. 1114), vol. vii (1920).

This is Constantius's biography of St. Germanus, bishop of Auxerre, who was sent as papal envoy to Britain in 429 to countermine the Pelagian heresy. See J. Evans, 'S. Germanus in Britain', *Archaeol. Cantiana*, lxxx (1965), 175–85; and Chadwick, S.E.B.H. (No. 2122).

2109 SALISBURY (FREDERICK S.). 'The Richborough coins and the end of Roman occupation'. *Antiq. Jour.* vii (1927), 268–81.

2110 SHELDON (GILBERT). The transition from Roman Britain to Christian England, A.D. 368–664. Lond. 1932.

2111 SUTHERLAND (C. H. V.). 'Coinage in Britain in the fifth and sixth centuries', in *Dark Age Britain* (No. 1442), pp. 3–10.

'The Dark Ages have not yet produced a single reliable instance . . . of the association, closely knit, of coins with other forms of mutually corroborative evidence' (p. 4).

2112 THOMPSON (E. A.). 'Zosimus on the end of Roman Britain'. *Antiquity*, xxx (1956), 163–7.

2113 WHITE (DONALD A.). Litus Saxonicum. The British Saxon Shore in scholarship and history. Madison (Wisc.). 1961.

See Frere, *Britannia* (No. 2040), p. 339.

X. CELTIC BRITAIN AFTER THE ROMAN OCCUPATION

For the general works on the early Celts, some of which reach into the period under consideration here, refer to pages 257–61. The most important historical sources for the centuries after the Roman period in the P-Celtic areas are Gildas (No. 2162), Nennius (No. 2167), the *Annales Cambriae* (No. 2144), Saints' Lives (pp. 333–9), and English sources, especially Bede, the *Anglo-Saxon Chronicle*, and Asser's *Life of Alfred* (Nos. 2148, 2141–2, 2147). Additional information can be gathered from the inscribed stones (Nos. 353, 355, 363), from linguistic (pp. 40–4) and archaeological studies (pp. 90–2), genealogies (pp. 62–71), and Welsh poetry (pp. 346–51). For Scotland, Adomnan's *Life of Columba* (No. 2319), the *Senchus Fer nAlban* (No. 2116), and Bede's *Hist. Ecc.* (No. 2148) are the most important works, together with other sources translated by A. O. Anderson (No. 1088A).

Among the modern summaries which can be found in the comprehensive works cited on pages 152–5, attention may be called especially to Kathleen Hughes's introductory chapter in A. J. Otway Ruthven, *A history of medieval Ireland* (No. 1203), and in Wainwright's *Problem of the Picts* (No. 2137).

2114 ANDERSON (MARJORIE O.). 'The lists of kings' (articles on texts concerning Pictish and the earliest Scottish kings). *Scot. H.R.* xxviii (1949), 108–18; xxix (1950), 13–22.

2115 ANSCOMBE (ALFRED). 'Indexes to Old-Welsh genealogies'. *Archiv für celtische Lexikographie*, i (1898), 187–212, 513–49; ii (1904), 147–96; iii (1906–7), 57–103. See No. 507.

2116 BANNERMAN (JOHN). 'Senchus Fer nAlban'. *Celtica*, vii (1967), 142–62; viii (1968), 90–111.

2117 BIELER (LUDWIG). 'The Christianization of the insular Celts during the sub-Roman period and its repercussions on the continent'. *Celtica*, viii (1968), 112–25.

2118 CHADWICK (HECTOR M.). Early Scotland: the Picts, the Scots and the Welsh of Southern Scotland. Cambr. 1949.

> A posthumous collection of essays, broad in scope.

2119 CHADWICK (NORA K.). Celtic Britain. Ancient peoples and places. Lond. 1963.

> 'An introduction to the history and culture of Celtic Britain between the departure of the Romans and the establishment of the Saxon kingdoms.' See also I. C. Peate, 'The Kelts in Britain', *Antiquity*, vi (1932), 156–60.

2120 CHADWICK (NORA K.). 'The colonization of Brittany from Celtic Britain'. *P.B.A.* li (1965), 235–99.

2121 CHADWICK (NORA K.), ed. Studies in the early British church. Cambr. 1958. (Analysed in No. 2665 below.)

2122 CHADWICK (NORA K.), ed. Studies in early British history. Cambr. 1954. *

(a) H. M. Chadwick, The end of Roman Britain. 9–20.
(b) H. M. and N. K. Chadwick, Vortigern. 21–46.
(c) H. M. Chadwick, The foundation of the early British kingdoms. 47–56.
(d) N. K. Chadwick, A note on Constantine, Prince of Devon. 56–60.
(e) Kenneth Jackson, The British language during the period of the English settlements. 61–82.
(f) Rachel Bromwich, The character of the early Welsh tradition. 83–136.
(g) Peter Hunter Blair, The Bernicians and their northern frontier. 137–72.
(h) Owen Chadwick, The evidence of dedications in the early history of the Welsh church. 173–88.
(i) N. K. Chadwick, Intellectual contacts between Britain and Gaul in the fifth century. 189–263.

2123 CHADWICK (NORA K.), ed. Celt and Saxon. Studies in the early British border. Cambr. 1963.

   (*a*) N. K. Chadwick, Introduction. 1–19.
   (*b*) Kenneth Jackson, On the Northern British Section in Nennius. 20–62.
   (*c*) Peter Hunter Blair, Some Observations on the *Historia Regum* attributed to Symeon of Durham. 63–118.
   (*d*) Bertram Colgrave, The Earliest Life of St. Gregory the Great, written by a Whitby Monk. 119–37.
   (*e*) N. K. Chadwick, The Conversion of Northumbria: a comparison of sources. 137–66.
   (*f*) N. K. Chadwick, The Battle of Chester: A study of sources. 167–85.
   (*g*) N. K. Chadwick, Bede, St. Colman and the Irish Abbey of Mayo. 186–205.
      Bruce Dickins, '*Dewi Sant*' (St. David) in Early English Kalendars and Place-
   (*h*) Names. 206–9.
   (*i*) Joan and Harold Taylor, Pre-Norman Churches of the Border. 210–57.
   (*j*) Christopher Brooke, St. Peter of Gloucester and St. Cadoc of Llancarfan. 258–322.
   (*k*) N. K. Chadwick, The Celtic Background of Early Anglo-Saxon England. 323–52.

2124 DAVIES (ELWYN), ed. Celtic studies in Wales: a survey. Cardiff. 1963.

Papers on art and architecture, history, laws, etc. prepared by several scholars for the second meeting of the International Congress of Celtic Studies.

2125 DILLON (MYLES) and CHADWICK (NORA K.). The Celtic realms. Lond. 1967.

An excellent summary of history, geography, religion, literature, and art of Celtic Britain and Ireland.

2126 JACKSON (KENNETH). 'The Britons of Southern Scotland'. *Antiquity*, xxix (1955), 77–88.

A sketch of the period from the end of Roman rule to the eleventh century.

2127 JACKSON (KENNETH). Language and history in early Britain: a chronological survey of the Brittonic languages first to twelfth century A.D. Edin. and Cambr. (Mass.). 1953.

Chap. iii, entitled Britons and Romans under the Empire, deals with Vulgar Latin in Roman Britain; Chap. v studies the early Christian inscriptions; Chap. vi is entitled Britons and Saxons in the fifth to eighth centuries. The rest of the book is linguistic and phonological.

2128 MacNEILL (EOIN). Celtic Ireland. Dublin. 1921. Idem, Phases of Irish history. Dublin, 1919. * See No. 1201.

2129 O'RAHILLY (THOMAS F.). Early Irish history and mythology. Dublin. 1946. * Addenda and Corrigenda in *Celtica*, i (1950), 387–402, 408–9.

'For the most part it confines itself to the history of Ireland previous to the official introduction of Christianity in A.D. 431.' It is a critical but highly controversial examination of early Irish traditions. See reviews by M. Dillon in *Speculum* (1947), K. Jackson in *Zeit. für celt. Philologie* (1954); and J. Vendryes in *Études Celtiques* (1956). See also O'Rahilly's lecture 'The Goidels and their predecessors', *P.B.A.* xx (1935), 342–72.

2130 PIGGOTT (STUART). Celts, Saxons and the early antiquaries. Edin. 1967.

2131 RAFTERY (JOSEPH), ed. The Celts. The Thomas Davis Lectures. Cork. 1964.

Contributions by various scholars.

2132 RHYS (SIR JOHN). Celtic Britain. Lond. etc. 1882. 4th edn. 1908. Idem, Celtic folklore, Welsh and Manx. 2 vols. Oxf. 1901.

2133 RICHARDS (MELVILLE). 'The Irish settlements in south-west Wales' (fifth to sixth centuries). *Royal Soc. Antiq. Ireland Jour.* xc (1960), 133–62.

2134 ROSS (ANNE). Pagan Celtic Britain: studies in iconography and tradition. N.Y. and Lond. 1967. Idem, Everyday life of the pagan Celts. Lond. 1970.

2135 SKENE (WILLIAM F.). Celtic Scotland. 3 vols. Edin. 1876–90.

Cf. James Anderson, 'William Forbes Skene', *Scot. H.R.* xlvi (1967), 140–50.

2136 WADE-EVANS (ARTHUR W.). The emergence of England and Wales. Wetteren, Belgium. 1956. No. 2558.

2137 WAINWRIGHT (FREDERICK T.), ed. The problem of the Picts. Studies in History and Archaeology. Edin. 1955. No. 2488.

2138 WRENN (CHARLES L.). 'Saxons and Celts in southwest Britain'. *Hon. Soc. Cymmrodorion Trans.* (1959), 38–75.

The 1958 O'Donnell Lectures in Celtic Studies at Oxford University. Part i: 'Some Celtic elements in Anglo-Saxon culture'; Part ii: 'Saxon and Celtic factors in Cornwall'.

2139 WILLIAMS (SIR IFOR). 'When did British become Welsh?' *Anglesey Antiq. Soc. and Field Club Trans.* (1939), 27–39. Idem, 'Wales and the North'. *Trans. Cumb. and Westm. Antiq. and Archaeol. Soc.* N.S. li (1951–2), 73–88.

PART FOUR

THE ANGLO-SAXON PERIOD

XI. ANGLO-SAXONS AND CELTS: SOURCES

A. CHRONICLES AND ANNALS

For the events of the fifth and sixth centuries we must rely mainly upon the meagre, but generally plausible, information afforded by Gildas (No. 2162). Nennius (No. 2167), whose work has evoked considerable discussion in recent years, is of little value as a historical authority; and Geoffrey of Monmouth (No. 2166) is romantic.

From 596 we have two principal guides, the two most important authorities mentioned in this section, namely, Bede and the *Anglo-Saxon Chronicle* in its several redactions. It is from them that Æthelweard (No. 2140) and the Latin chroniclers of the twelfth century, notably Florence of Worcester, Simeon of Durham, Henry of Huntingdon, and William of Malmesbury, derive most of their facts regarding Anglo-Saxon history. However, these later writers, especially Simeon of Durham (No. 2157), add some information drawn from sources not now extant. See No. 2168; Petrie's *Monumenta* (No. 1084), pp. 83–92; 522–829; and John Earle's *Two of the Saxon chronicles parallel* (Oxf. 1865), pp. lix–lxvii.

Bede is the foremost exponent of Northumbrian culture, which was unequalled elsewhere in Europe in the seventh and eighth centuries; and his *Historia Ecclesiastica*, with its connected narrative or grouping of facts, represents a type of historical writing quite distinct from the brief chronological memoranda of events contained in the annals or chronicles. The germinating point of the latter is to be sought in contemporary Latin notes or jottings entered in the margins of Easter tables, a practice which began in England probably not long after the coming of Augustine and which was later introduced into the kingdom of the Franks by English missionaries. These chronological notes were soon copied, amplified, and continued as independent works. Consult Reginald Lane Poole, *Chronicles and Annals: a brief outline of the growth and origin* (Oxf. 1926).

In the elaboration of the Easter-table jottings, old popular songs and royal genealogies (No. 2161) were sometimes turned to account. Thus were produced some of the annals that were used in the earlier portions of the *Anglo-Saxon Chronicle*, which originated in southern England. To this category of annalistic works belong also four remnants of Northumbrian historiography, such as the *Annales Lindisfarnenses*, the *Chronologia Brevissima*, the *Continuatio Bedae*, and the lost chronicle (Nos. 2145, 2154, 2156, 2168); also the *Annales Cambriae* and the *Annales of Tigernach* (Nos. 2144, 2170). The last two are the primary authorities for Wales and Ireland respectively; from them later writers derive much of their information regarding this period: they are, indeed, to Welsh and Irish history what the *Anglo-Saxon Chronicle* is to English history. Of these later derivatives the *Brut y Tywysogion*, the *Annals of Ulster*, and the *Chronicon Scotorum* (Nos. 2805, 2786, 2839) deserve particular mention, because, although the first is based partly upon the *Annales Cambriae* and the other two upon Tigernach, they contain additional information concerning the early history of England, Ireland, and Wales.

Another group of sources comprises the monastic histories of Ramsey, Abingdon, Crowland (spurious), Ely, and Hyde (Nos. 2151, 2153, 2163, 2164, 2165), all compiled after the Norman Conquest. They are a combination of chartulary and chronicle, dealing mainly with local ecclesiastical history, but also containing some details as to the general affairs of the kingdom and interesting illustrations of customs and institutions. Simeon's *History of the Church of Durham* (No. 2157 (*a*)) gives some valuable information regarding the secular affairs of northern England in the ninth century. Still more local in their scope are the tract on the siege of Durham and Elmham's work on Canterbury (Nos. 2157, 2158).

Of royal biographies Asser's *Life of Alfred* is the most important. Two others are also worthy of notice, the *Encomium Emmae* and the contemporary *Vita Ædwardi* (Nos. 2159, 2171); these are of some value for the study of political history in the eleventh century. For biographies of prelates, etc., see pp. 320–3.

For the careers of Sweyn, Cnut, and other Danish chieftains who invaded Britain, see Adam of Bremen (No. 2149), the *War of the Gaedhil* (No. 2174), Langebek's *Scriptores* (No. 1106), and the Norse sagas (pp. 351–7).

An enumeration of editions, and other information concerning the chroniclers of the Anglo-Saxon period, will be found in the bibliographies mentioned above on pages 2–10, especially *Cambridge Bibliography of English Literature* (No. 14), Hardy's *Catalogue* (No. 21), Manitius' *Lateinische Literatur* (No. 56), Potthast's *Bibliotheca* (No. 62), and *Repertorium Fontium* (No. 64). On editions and commentaries, special attention should be paid to Dorothy Whitelock in *English Historical Documents* (No. 17), i, pts. i and iii, and to R. W. Chambers in *England before the Norman Conquest* (No. 1209), where each chapter is preceded by Notes on the Sources. For Irish chronicles, Best (No. 9), Kenney (No. 23), and O'Curry (No. 30), should be consulted; and especially K. Hughes (No. 22), Chap. 4.

2140 ÆTHELWEARD (d. 998 ?). (*a*) The chronicle of Æthelweard. Ed. by Alistair Campbell. Medieval Texts. Lond. etc. 1962. (*b*) *Chronicon*. Ed. by Savile (No. 1119), pp. 473–83. (*c*) Edited, from Savile's text, by Petrie (No. 1084), pp. 499–521. (*d*) Brief extracts. Ed. by Pauli in M.G.H. *SS*. (No. 1114), xiii, 122–3. (*e*) Translated by Joseph Stevenson, *Church historians* (No. 1123) by J. A. Giles (No. 1089), and by Alistair Campbell as above. See E. E. Barker, 'The Cottonian fragments of Æthelweard's chronicle'. *B.I.H.R.* xxiv (1951), 45–52.

The author was a West Saxon ealdorman and a descendant of Alfred's brother. His chronicle, which Savile printed in 1596 but of which only fragments survived the Cottonian fire of 1731, is a Latin translation from a copy of the *Anglo-Saxon Chronicle*, which 'was at some points nearer to the original than any extant text (Stenton, *A.-S. England*, pp. 681–2). It is an independent authority from 893 to 975, but chapter-headings in the surviving fragments indicate that the author intended to continue it into the reign of Ethelred.

See Hardy's *Catalogue* (No. 21), i. 571–4; Stenton in *Tout Essays* (No. 1458), in *E.H.R.* xxiv (1909), 79–84, and in *A.-S. England*, pp. 455 and 681–2; K. Sisam in *P.B.A.* xxxix (1953), 320–1; L. Whitbread, 'Aethelweard and the Anglo-Saxon

Chronicle', *E.H.R.* lxxiv (1959), 577–89; E. E. Barker, 'The Anglo-Saxon Chronicle used by Aethelweard', *B.I.H.R.* xl (1967), 74–91; Michael Winterbottom, 'The style of Aethelweard', *Medium Ævum*, xxxvi (1967), 109–18.

2141 THE ANGLO-SAXON CHRONICLE. Ed. by Benjamin Thorpe. 2 vols. Rolls Series. Lond. 1861. The best edition is TWO OF THE SAXON CHRONICLES *PARALLEL*. Ed. by Charles Plummer on the basis of an edition (Oxf. 1865) by John Earle. 2 vols. Oxf. 1892. 1899; Reprinted with a note on the commencement of the year and a bibliographical note by Dorothy Whitelock. 1952.

> In Thorpe's edition, vol. i provides the texts of the six versions A to F, and vol. ii a translation thereof; neither the text nor the translation is deemed entirely satisfactory. In Plummer's edition, vol. i produces a text based largely on A and E as published by Earle; vol. ii contains Plummer's seminal introduction, notes, and index.

2142 THE ANGLO-SAXON CHRONICLE. A revised translation edited by Dorothy Whitelock with David C. Douglas and Susie I. Tucker, with an introduction by Dorothy Whitelock. Lond. 1961.

> This translation is based on those in vols. i and ii of *Eng. Hist. Docs.* (No. 17), and indicates the MS. or MSS. from which each entry is drawn. Among other translations, that by George N. Garmonsway, *The Anglo-Saxon Chronicle* (Everyman's Library, 1953; 2nd edn. 1955), can be especially recommended. The *Anglo-Saxon Chronicle* comprises a series of progressive annals copied and continued at different times and in different places, yet related to one another or derived from common prototypes. None of the archetypes survives; all of the existing versions are copies of texts, now lost. The surviving versions are found in seven MSS. to which a few scattered fragments can be added. The development and complex relationships of the MS. copies and the authorship of the Alfredian compilation are discussed in Plummer's introduction, in Stenton (No. 1189), pp. 679–83; and in *Eng. Hist. Docs.* (No. 17), i. 109–16, 135–6. The MSS. of the surviving versions are referred to by letter.
>
> A. Cambridge Corpus Christi College MS. 173, which is also designated as the Parker Chronicle (60 B.C.–A.D. 1070). The oldest surviving copy, whose entries to 891 were written about 900, was founded on now-vanished annals. Once apparently at Winchester, the MS. came into the possession of Christ Church, Canterbury, in the eleventh century and was left to Corpus Christi College by Archbishop Parker. See Ker (No. 977), No. 39. A collotype facsimile of this MS., including also the laws of Alfred and Ine, is produced in Robin Flower and Albert H. Smith, eds., *The Parker Chronicle and laws* (E.E.T.S., Lond. 1941). A portion of version A, with brief bibliography, is printed in Albert Hugh Smith, *The Parker Chronicle 832–900* (Lond. 1935). For commentary, see W. S. Angus, 'The eighth scribe's dates in the Parker Manuscript of the Anglo-Saxon Chronicle', *Medium Ævum*, x (1941), 130–49; and Richard Vaughan, 'The chronology of the Parker Chronicle 890–970', *E.H.R.* lxix (1954), 59–66.
>
> B. Brit. Mus. Cotton Tiberius A. vi (60 B.C.–A.D. 977). See Ker (No. 977), No. 188. Tiberius A. iii, f. 178, was probably the preface on Royal genealogy to B.
>
> C. Brit. Mus. Cotton Tiberius B. i (60 B.C.–A.D. 1056 and for 1065–6). Probably produced in the mid eleventh century at Abingdon. B and C interpolate the Mercian Annals 902–24. See Ker (No. 977), No. 191. Version C is edited by Harry Rositzke, *The C-text of the Old English Chronicle*, Beiträge zur englischen Philologie, xxxiv (Bochum-Langenteer, 1940). A portion of the text, with translation, for the years 978 to 1017 is given in Ashdown (No. 2437), pp. 38–71 with notes, pp. 90–106.
>
> D. Brit. Mus. Cotton Tiberius B. iv (60 B.C.–A.D. 1079), copied in the twelfth century, sometimes referred to as the Worcester Chronicle. It ends abruptly in the middle of a folio, on the back of which is an entry marked '1080', but apparently for the year 1130.

See Ker (No. 977), No. 192. Printed in Ernest Classen and Florence E. Harmer, *An Anglo-Saxon Chronicle from British Museum MS. Tiberius B. iv* (Manchester, 1926). I. Atkins, 'The origin of the later part of the Saxon Chronicle known as D', *E.H.R.* lv (1940), 8–27.

E. Bodleian Laud MS. Misc. 636 (60 B.C.–A.D. 1154), copied at Peterborough in the early twelfth century and continued there. D and E introduce material on the north of England not found in other versions; their archetype was probably written at York. See Ker (No. 977), No. 346. Produced in facsimile in Dorothy Whitelock, *The Peterborough Chronicle*, Early English MSS. in Facsimile, No. 4 (Copenhagen and Lond. 1955). A portion is printed in Cecily Clark, *Peterborough Chronicle, 1070–1154, edited from MS. Bodley Laud Misc. 636 with introduction, commentary and an appendix*, Oxford English Monograph (Lond. 1958; a new, revised edn. 1970). A translation, with introduction and bibliography, is given in Harry Rositzke, *The Peterborough Chronicle* (N.Y. 1951).

F. Brit. Mus. Cotton Domitian A. viii (60 B.C.–A.D. 1058), an abbreviated English and Latin version produced at Canterbury about 1100; the least important of the versions. See Ker (No. 977), No. 148. Printed in Francis P. Magoun, Jr., *Annales Domitiani Latini: An Edition*, Mediaeval Stud. ix (1947), 235–95.

G. Brit. Mus. Cotton Otho B. xi (60 B.C.–A.D. 1001), largely a copy of version A, made about 1025. Only fragments of the manuscript of G survived the Cottonian fire of 1731, but a transcript had been made by Laurence Nowell and is now B.M. Addit. MS. 43703. See Ker (No. 977), No. 180. Printed before the fire in Abraham Wheloc, *Chronologica Anglo-Saxonica*, pp. 492–962 (Cambr. 1643–4).

H. Fragments: Brit. Mus. Cotton Domitian A. ix, f. 9 (for 1113–14) (see Ker, No. 180), printed in Julius Zupitza, 'Fragment einer englischen Chronik aus den Jahren 1113 und 1114', *Anglia* i (1877), 195–7; and in Plummer, p. 243.

Early editions of the *Anglo-Saxon Chronicle* are listed in *C.B.E.L.* (No. 14), i. 88, and are described by Hardy (No. 21), i. 650–1; and by Plummer, vol. ii, pp. cxxvii ff. Some Latin writers, having access to versions which have not survived, translated segments from Anglo-Saxon into Latin; of these translations the most important are in (*a*) Asser (No. 2147) for the years 851–87; (*b*) Æthelweard (No. 2140) probably closer to an archetype up to 892 than any surviving copy and from 893 to 975 an independent authority; and (*c*) Florence of Worcester's *Chronicle* (No. 3019). For listings of articles on the *Anglo-Saxon Chronicle*, see *Eng. Hist. Docs.* (No. 17), i. 130–1, and the index of Bonser (No. 12).

2143 ANNALES ANGLOSAXONICI BREVES, A.D. 925–1202. Ed. by Felix Liebermann, *Geschichtsquellen* (No. 1108), pp. 1–8. An extract for 1084–1147 is edited by Pertz in M.G.H. *SS.* (No. 1114), xvi (1859), 480–1.

Brief notices or annals relating largely to Christ Church, Canterbury, in Anglo-Saxon 988–1109 and in Latin 1109–1202, from B.M. Cotton Caligula A. xv, ff. 133–9. See Ker (No. 977), No. 139r.

2144 ANNALES CAMBRIAE (A.D. 444–954, with a continuation to 1288). Ed. (in an unsatisfactory manner) by John Williams ab Ithel. Rolls Series. Lond. 1860. (*b*) The part A.D. 444–1066 in Petrie's *Monumenta* (No. 1084), pp. 830–40. (*c*) Well edited by Egerton Phillimore as 'The Annales Cambriae (A.D. 457–954) and Old Welsh genealogies' in *Y Cymmrodor* (No. 126), ix (1888), 143–83. (*d*) Excerpts from the continuation: for 1107–1273 as 'Annales Meneviae' and 'Annales Stratae Floridae'. Ed. by Liebermann in M.G.H. *SS.* xxvii. 442–4; for 1035–93, with two separate texts edited by J. E. Lloyd, 'Wales and the coming of the Normans'. *Hon. Soc. Cymmrodorion Trans.* (No. 126), 1899–1900, pp. 122–79; for 1190–1266 as 'Cronica de Wallia' by Thomas Jones in *Bull. Board of Celtic*

Studies, xii (1948), 27–44. (*e*) Translated by A. W. Wade-Evans, *Nennius* (No. 2167).

One of the best authorities for early Welsh history, this group of annals forms a basis for later chronicles of Wales. The oldest copy (B.M. Harley 3859) dates from about 1100. For the earliest part down to 954, which was probably compiled at St. David's, the edition by Phillimore should be used. There appear to have been two independent continuations, one at St. David's to 1288 and one at the monastery of Strata Florida from *c*. 1203 to 1286. These texts are unfortunately conflated in the editions of Petrie and Williams. For valuable papers on the relationship of *Annales Cambriae* and *Brut y Tywysogion* (No. 2805), see Egerton Phillimore, 'The publication of Welsh historical records', *Y Cymmrodor*, xi (1892), 133–75; and J. E. Lloyd, 'The Welsh Chronicles', *P.B.A.* xiv (1928), 369–91.

2145 ANNALES LINDISFARNENSES (A.D. 532–993) ET ANNALES DUNELMENSES (A.D. 995–1199). (*a*) Ed. by Pertz in M.G.H. *SS.* xix (1866), 502–8. (*b*) Edited by W. Levison, 'Die Annales Lindisfarnenses et Dunelmenses, kritisch untersucht und neu herausgegeben'. *Deutsches Archiv*, xxii (1961), 447–506.

These brief northern annals were discovered by Pertz in Glasgow in 1862. Pertz's view that they were contemporary annals and that they were used by Simeon of Durham is combatted by L. Theopold, *Kritische Untersuchungen über die Quellen zur angelsächsischen Geschichte* (Lemgo, 1872), pp. 71–3. Levison regards them as a Durham compilation made at the end of the eleventh or beginning of the twelfth century: *England and the Continent* (No. 2282), p. 114, and *Deutsches Archiv*, xvii (1961), 447–506.

2146 ANNALS OF IRELAND: three fragments copied from ancient sources by Dubhaltach MacFirbisigh (Irish text with an English translation). Ed. by John O'Donovan. Irish Archaeol. and Celtic Soc. Dublin. 1860.

O'Donovan printed from a copy, now in Brussels, of a copy which Duald MacFirbis made in 1643 of a vellum MS. whose age is not known. The *Three Fragments* extend from A.D. 571 to about 918. They dwell especially upon the military achievements of the princes of the territory of Ossory and Leix. They also give an account of the invasion of Norsemen under Ingimund from Ireland into north-west England in the early tenth century.

A discussion of the historicity of the *Three Fragments* occurs in F. T. Wainwright's 'Ingimund's Invasion', *E.H.R.* lxiii (1948), 145–67; to which is appended on pp. 167–9 a translation by I. L. Foster of that portion of the *Three Fragments* which pertains to Ingimund's invasion.

2147 ASSER (d. *c*. 909). (*a*) Asser's Life of Alfred, together with the Annals of Saint Neots erroneously ascribed to Asser, edited with introduction and commentary by William H. Stevenson. Oxf. 1904. Reprinted, 1959, with an essay on recent work by Dorothy Whitelock. (*b*) *Annales rerum gestarum Aelfredi Magni*. Ed. by Francis Wise. Oxf. 1722; and based on Wise's edition, in Petrie, *Monumenta* (No. 1084). (*c*) Older editions by Parker (No. 1118), 1574, and Camden (No. 1092), 1602. Translations: Albert Cook, *Asser's Life of King Alfred*. N.Y. 1906 (translated from Stevenson's text). L. Cecil Jane, *Asser's Life of King Alfred*. Lond. 1908. Reprinted, 1924 and 1926 (based on Petrie's edition with interpolations in italics). Other translations are in J. A. Giles, *Six Old English Chronicles* (No. 1089), pp. 41–86; J. Stevenson, *Church historians* (No. 1123); and Conybeare (No. 2575). Commentaries: W. H. Stevenson (above) is fundamental. G. H. Wheeler, 'Textual emendations to Asser's Life of Alfred', *E.H.R.* xlvii

(1932), 86–8; Marie Schütt, 'The literary form of Asser's Vita Alfredi', *E.H.R.*
lxxii (1957), 209–20; *Eng. Hist. Docs.* (No. 17), i. 120, and the article on recent
work in the 1959 reprint cited above; and the references to King Alfred given
below, pp. 370–1. V. H. Galbraith in *An Introduction to the Study of history* (No.
258), pp. 85–128, revives the doubts on authorship and suggests Leofric, bishop
of Exeter (d. 1072) as a plausible candidate. This view is challenged and the
authenticity of the work reaffirmed by D. Whitelock, *The genuine Asser* (The
Stenton Lecture). Reading. 1967.

> Asser, a monk of St. David's, went to the court of Alfred about 886 to assist the king in
> his studies, and a few years later he was made bishop of Sherborne. The *Life of Alfred*
> consists of two intertwined accounts: (1) a narrative of events, A.D. 849–87, drawn mainly
> from the *Anglo-Saxon Chronicle*; (2) an account of Alfred's career to 893, based presum-
> ably on the author's personal observations. The only MS. then known to exist was
> destroyed in the Cottonian fire of 1731; but it had already been transcribed by Arch-
> bishop Parker. By separating the genuine Asser from later interpolations, W. H.
> Stevenson established a reliable text and offered proof of the genuineness of the bio-
> graphy.

2148 BEDE (672/3–735). (*a*) Bede's Ecclesiastical History of the English
People. Ed. by Bertram Colgrave and R. A. B. Mynors. Oxford Medieval Texts.
Oxf. 1969. For this edition Colgrave wrote a Historical Introduction, and Mynors
a Textual Introduction. The Latin is printed on the left-hand page and an
English translation on the right-hand page.

(*b*) Baedae Historia Ecclesiastica gentis Anglorum: Venerabilis Baedae opera
historica. Ed. by Charles Plummer. 2 vols. Oxf. 1896. 1 vol. 1946. Plummer's
exemplary edition includes a notable introduction and the text in volume i and
copious notes in volume ii. However, Plummer did not use the Leningrad MS.

(*c*) Venerabilis Bedae historiae ecclesiasticae gentis Anglorum libri quinti. Ed. by
John Smith. Cambr. 1722.

(*d*) Published in facsimile as Leningrad Bede: an eighth-century manuscript of
the Venerable Bede's Historia ecclesiastica gentis Anglorum in the public library,
Leningrad. Ed. by Olof Sigrid Anderson-Arngart. Early English MSS. in Facsimile, no. 2. Copenhagen and Lond. 1952.

(*e*) Also a facsimile edition as the Moore Bede, an eighth-century MS. of the
Venerable Bede's Historia Ecclesiastica gentis Anglorum in Cambridge Univer-
sity Library MS. Kk 5.16. Ed. by Peter Hunter Blair. Early English MSS. in
Facsimile, no. 9. Copenhagen. 1959.

(*f*) Putnam F. Jones, A concordance to the Historia Ecclesiastica of Bede.
Cambr. (Mass.). 1929.

Other editions, based largely on Smith's text: Joseph Stevenson. Eng. Hist. Soc.
Lond. 1838; Giles, *Patres* (No. 1102); Robert Hussey, Oxf. 1846; Petrie,
Monumenta (No. 1084), 103–289; G. H. Moberly. Oxf. 1869. Reprinted 1881;
books iii–iv, J. E. B. Mayor and J. R. Lumby. Cambr. 1878. 3rd edn. 1881;
Alfred Holder. Freiburg. 1882. 2nd edn. 1890; J. E. King, Loeb Classical
Library. 2 vols. with translation. Lond. 1930. König Alfreds Übersetzung von
Beda's Kirchengeschichte. Ed. by Jacob Schipper in Grein's *Bibliothek* (No.
2286), vol. iv. Leipzig. 1899. The old English version of Bede's ecclesiastical

history, with a translation. Ed. by Thomas Miller. E.E.T.S. 2 pts. Lond. 1890–
98. A shortened free translation of books i–ii is given in A middle Irish fragment
of Bede's ecclesiastical history. Ed. by E. G. Cox in *Anecdota from Irish MSS.*,
ed. by O. J. Bergin, Kuno Meyer, and others, iii. 63–76. Halle and Dublin. 1910;
reprinted with introduction and English translation in *Studies in Celebration of
the Seventieth Birthday of J. M. Hart*, pp. 122–78. N.Y. 1910.

Translations: Editions of translations into English of the Ecclesiastical History
which often include the lives of the abbots, the letter to Egbert, and the Life of
St. Cuthbert, are listed in Potthast (No. 62) and in *Repert. Font.* (No. 64), ii
under 'Beda'. The Colgrave–Mynors edition prints an English translation on the
right-hand page; it includes the letter of Cuthbert, future abbot of Jarrow, on
the death of Bede. Thomas Stapelton's Elizabethan translation was re-edited by
Philip Hereford. Oxf. 1930 and Lond. 1935. It formed the basis of King's translation (above). Giles, *Scriptores* (No. 1101); J. Stevenson, *Church historians* (No.
1123); L. C. Jane. Temple Classics. Lond. 1903; A. M. Sellar. Bohn's Antiquarian Library. Lond. 1907, 1912; Vida D. Scudder *et al.* Everyman's Library.
Lond. 1910 and several reprints, the latest in 1954, with an Introduction by
D. Knowles; Leo Sherley-Price. Penguin Classics. Lond. 1955; and revised
by R. E. Latham, 1968. Considerable portions are translated in *Eng. Hist. Docs.*
(No. 17), i. 588–686.

The foremost scholar of Western Europe in his generation and one of the most eminent
historians of the Middle Ages, Bede was born in 672 or 673 at or near Wearmouth, and
spent most of his life in the monastery of Jarrow. Of his many writings the most
important is the *Historia Ecclesiastica*, extending from 55 B.C. to A.D. 731, the date of its
compilation. The brief account of British history to 596 in book i is derived mainly from
Orosius and Gildas. From 597 to 731 the narrative is based upon written documents and
verbal communications; for these years it is the primary source of our knowledge. At
least four eighth-century MS. copies survive; namely the Moore MS. in Cambridge
University Library, the British Museum Cotton MSS. Tiberius A xiv and C ii, and the
Leningrad MS. To these may be added an eighth-century single leaf which fits into
Plummer, i. 198–200 (E. A. Lowe in *E.H.R.* xli (1926), 244–6). For a history of the
texts, see Colgrave–Mynors edition, pages xxxix–lxxvi. The only critical editions are
those by John Smith, Plummer, and Colgrave–Mynors. References to other editions
can be found in Colgrave–Mynors, Plummer, in Hardy's *Catalogue* (No. 21), i. 433–47;
in Potthast (No. 62); in *Repert. Font.* (No. 64), vol. ii; and in *Hand-list of Bede Manuscripts*, by M. L. W. Laistner and H. H. King (Ithaca, 1943).

For discussions as to the beginning of the year in the *Ecclesiastical History*, see R. L.
Poole, *Studies* (No. 1487); W. Levison, *England and the Continent* (No. 2282), app. vi;
C. W. Jones, *Saints' Lives* (No. 2281), and additional references in Bonser (No. 12) and
Eng. Hist. Docs. (No. 17), i. For 'the growth of Bede's reputation and the circulation of
his works in early times, in the generation or two after his death in 735', see Dorothy
Whitelock, *After Bede* (Jarrow Lecture, 1960). Dorothy Whitelock, 'The Old English
Bede', *P.B.A.* xlviii (1962), 57–90. D. P. Kirby, 'Bede and Northumbrian chronology',
E.H.R. lxxviii (1963), 514–27; and 'Bede's native sources for the Historia Ecclesiastica',
B.J.R.L. xlviii (1965–6), 341–71. W. F. Bolton, 'A Bede bibliography, 1935–1960',
Traditio, xviii (1962), 436–45. A. Hamilton Thompson, ed., *Bede, his life, times and
writings; essays in commemoration of the twelfth centenary of his death* (Oxf. 1935)
(No. 2297). For other writings of Bede and additional bibliography, see below, No.
2297 and *Repert. Font.* ii. 469–73.

2149 BREMEN, ADAM OF (d. *c.* 1081–5). Gesta Hammaburgensis ecclesiae
pontificum. Ed. by J. M. Lappenberg in M.G.H. *SS.* (No. 1114), vii. 267–389.

2nd edn. 1876. 3rd edn. in *Scriptores . . . in usum Scholarum* by Bernhard Schmeidler, 1917. Published in photolithography with preface by C. A. Christensen. Copenhagen. 1948. Translated into German by S. Steinberg, *Die Geschichtsschreiber der deutschen Vorzeit*, xiv. Leipzig. 1926. Translated into English by Francis Tschan, *History of the Archbishops of Hamburg–Bremen*. Columbia Univ. Records of Civilization, liii. N.Y. 1959. For editions, see Wattenbach–Holtzmann (No. 66), i. 566–72; Manitius (No. 56), ii. 398–413; and *Repert. Font.* (No. 64), ii. 116–17.

> This remarkable history contains some valuable details regarding the relations of the Danes to England, especially in the eleventh century.

2150 CAITHRÉIM CELLACHÁIN CAISIL: the victorious career of Cellachan of Cashel, or the wars between the Irishmen and the Norsemen in the middle of the 10th century. Ed., with a translation, by Alexander Bugge. Christiania. 1905.

> The foundation of this saga is historical. Cellachan was king of Munster who began his reign *c.* 934 and died *c.* 954. The work was compiled toward the end of the fifteenth century, but was based on an older text, which may have been produced in the early twelfth century (B. Ó Cuív, *P.B.A.* xlix (1963), 240–1). See Hughes (No. 22), pp. 299–300.

2151 CHRONICON ABBATIAE RAMESEIENSIS (circa A.D. 924–1200, in four parts). Ed. by W. D. Macray. Rolls Series. Lond. 1886. Pts. i–iii. Ed. by Gale, *Scriptores XV* (No. 1100), pp. 385–462. Oxf. 1691.

> Probably compiled in 1170, some of the matter in pt. iv having been added later. It is commonly cited as the *Historia Rameseiensis*; the unknown author calls it *Liber Benefactorum Ecclesiae Rameseiensis*. Pts. i–iii, extending to 1066, comprise the story of the foundation of the abbey, the life of St. Oswald, and charters of lands granted to Ramsey, together with some notices of public events. Pt. iv is little more than a register of legal documents; it contains many charters conveying lands to the abbey, A.D. 974 to *c.* 1200. The work affords many illustrations of legal customs. App. iv, pp. 368–417, of Macray's edition also contains a letter-book of Abbot John de Sautre, A.D. 1285–1316, and extracts from a register of the letters of Abbot Simon de Eye, A.D. 1317–32.

2152 CHRONICON FANI SANCTI NEOTI SIVE ANNALES ASSERII (60 B.C.–A.D. 914). Ed. by William H. Stevenson, *Asser's life* (No. 2147). Oxf. 1904. Edited also in Gale, *Scriptores XV* (No. 1100), pp. 141–75.

> These annals (probably compiled in the twelfth century) are in part derived from Asser's *Life of Alfred*, and hence were formerly assigned to Asser. 'Of little value in themselves for history . . . they are of great importance for the criticism of the Anglo-Saxon Chronicle, for, while founded largely on that Chronicle, they have preserved the true chronology, which in all our MSS. is disjointed' (Plummer, *Two Saxon Chronicles* (No. 2141), ii. 103). See Barker under Aethelweard (No. 2140).

2153 CHRONICON MONASTERII DE ABINGDON (A.D. 201–1189). Ed. by Joseph Stevenson. Rolls Series. 2 vols. Lond. 1858.

> The oldest MS. belongs to the first half of the thirteenth century. The earlier and larger portion of the chronicle is mainly a transcript of the title-deeds of the abbey, A.D. 687–1066, with some narrative. After 1066 we find fewer charters and more narrative. The documents embodied in this work illustrate political and ecclesiastical history, institutional life, and the social condition of the people. The narrative portions, though dealing mainly with the monastery, also give some information concerning the general affairs of

the kingdom. App. i is Ælfric's *Life of St. Æthelwold* (No. 2293); App. iii, *De consuetu-dinibus Abbendoniae*, on the receipts, expenditures, rents of the abbey; and App. iv, *De obedientiariis abbatiae*, on the officers thereof. See also F. M. Stenton, *The early history of the abbey of Abingdon* (Oxf. 1913); and M. Biddle, G. Lambrick, and J. N. L. Myres, 'The early history of Abingdon, Berkshire, and its abbey', *Medieval Archaeology*, xii (1968), 26–9, particularly 68–9.

2154 CHRONOLOGIA BREVISSIMA AD NORTHANHYMBROS SPE-CTANS, A.D. 547–737 in Petrie's *Monumenta* (No. 1084), p. 290.

A few lines containing scanty chronological notes, recording the length of the reigns of several Northumbrian kings and the dates of certain other events. Most of the compilation is derived from Bede's *Historia Ecclesiastica*. Petrie believed that it may have been written in 737, but this conclusion was doubted by Hardy in *Catalogue* (No. 21), i. 464.

2155 CIRENCESTER, RICHARD OF (d. c. 1401). Speculum historiale de gestis regum Angliae (A.D. 447–1066). Ed. by J. E. B. Mayor. Rolls Series. 2 vols. Lond. 1863–9.

A careless compilation of little value, derived from Bede, Geoffrey of Monmouth, Roger of Wendover, and other chroniclers. Book iv is devoted to Edward the Confessor. The author was a monk of Westminster. For the forgery entitled *De Situ Britanniae*, attributed to him, see No. 2026.

2156 CONTINUATIO BEDAE. Printed at the end of most of the editions of Bede's *Historia Ecclesiastica* (No. 2148): for example, Smith's, pp. 223–4; Stevenson's, ii. 256–8; Hussey's, pp. 313–15; Petrie's, pp. 288–9; Plummer's, i. 361–3.

This continuation of Bede's *Historia Ecclesiastica*, often called *Appendix ad Bedam*, comprises brief but valuable memoranda, which extend from A.D. 731 to 766 and relate mainly to Northumbrian affairs. The earliest MS. is of the twelfth century; and the text which uses the *Anglo-Saxon Chronicle* cannot have been earlier than late ninth century, even though it may have been based on earlier material. Hahn conjectured, but surely on weak evidence, that the part to 734 had been written by Bede and the rest by Egbert of York. See H. Hahn, 'Die Continuatio Bedae', in *Forschungen zur deutschen Geschichte*, xx (1880), 553–69; and the Colgrave–Mynors edition of Bede (No. 2148).

2157 DURHAM, SIMEON OF (d. after 1129). Symeonis monachi opera omnia. Ed. by Thomas Arnold. 2 vols. Rolls Series. Lond. 1882–5. Also Symeonis Dunelmensis opera et collectanea. Ed. by J. Hodgson Hinde. Surtees Soc. li. 1868. (For the contents of each edition, see Mullins, *Texts* (No. 29), pp. 56 and 316). The historical works of Simeon of Durham, translated by Joseph Stevenson, *Church historians* (No. 1123), vol. iii, pt. ii.

The most important works written by, or once attributed to, Simeon, a monk and then precentor of Durham, are listed herewith. Simeon is accepted as the author of (*a*) *Historia Dunelmensis ecclesiae*; his role in the compilation of (*b*) *Historia regum* is uncertain; but none of the other works cited here is now ascribed to him. For the historians of Durham, see H. S. Offler, *Medieval historians of Durham* (Durham, 1958).

(*a*) Historiae Dunelmensis ecclesiae, A.D. 635–1096, with two continuations to 1154. Arnold, i. 1–169; Twysden, *Scriptores* (No. 1124), pp. 1–68.

Written between 1104 and 1109, it deals mainly with the history of the church of Durham, but also supplies fundamental information on northern England for the ninth to the eleventh centuries. The early portion is derived chiefly from Bede's *Ecclesiastical History* and his *Life of St. Cuthbert*. For its relationship to the lost *Liber Magni Altaris*, see H. H. E. Craster, 'The Red Book of Durham', *E.H.R.* xl (1925), 504–32.

(b) Historia regum (616–1129). Arnold, ii. 1–283; Hinde, pp. 1–131; Twysden's *Scriptores*, pp. 85–256; and to A.D. 957 in Petrie's *Monumenta* (No. 1084), pp. 645–88. Translated in part in *Eng. Hist. Docs.* i. 239–54; cf. ibid. p. 118.

Fundamentally it comprises two overlapping chronicles, one from 731 to 957 and the other from 848 to 1129. The first incorporates lost northern annals for the eighth to tenth centuries (see No. 2168) and material from Asser; the second is derived largely from Asser and then up to 1119 from Florence of Worcester. For a continuation from 1130 to 1150 by John of Hexham, see No. 2893. Consult C. W. David, 'A tract attributed to Simeon of Durham', *E.H.R.* xxxii (1917), 382–7; P. Hunter Blair, 'Some observations on the "Historia Regum"' in *Celt and Saxon* (No. 2123); W. S. Angus, 'The annals for the tenth century in Symeon of Durham's Historia regum', *Durham Univ. Jour.* xxxii (1940), 213–29.

(c) Historia de Sancto Cuthberto. Arnold, i. 196–214; Hinde, pp. 138–52. A translation of a portion in *Eng. Hist. Docs.* i. 261–3.

A mixture of historical statements and land grants, compiled about 1050, but important for the ninth and tenth centuries. See F. T. Wainwright, 'The battles of Corbridge', *Saga Book of the Viking Society*, xiii (1950), 156–73.

(d) Libellus de primo Saxonum adventu sive de eorumdem regibus. Arnold, ii. 365–84; Hinde, pp. 202–15.

Probably written in 1138 or 1139 after Simeon's death. It gives a brief account of Anglo-Saxon kings, together with a sketch of the earls of Northumbria, the archbishops of Canterbury and York, and the bishops of Durham. The portion relating to Northumbria contains particulars not met with elsewhere and probably derived from authorities which no longer exist.

(e) De injusta vexatione Willelmi Episcopi per Willelmum regem filium Willelmi Magni. Arnold, i. 170–95; translated in Stevenson, *Church historians* (No. 1123), iii, pt. ii. 731–50; in Dugdale, *Monasticon* (No. 1147), i. 244–50; and in *Eng. Hist. Docs.* ii. 609–24.

This work concerns the trial of William of St. Calais, bishop of Durham, in the court of the king (1088) for alleged complicity in the revolt on behalf of Odo of Bayeux. Cf. C. W. David (loc. cit.); G. B. Adams (No. 3659), pp. 43–70; and H. S. Offler, 'The tractate De iniusta vexacione Willelmi episcopi primi', *E.H.R.* lxvi (1951), 32–41. Offler argues that the tractate in its present form dated from the second quarter of the twelfth century. R. W. Southern, *St. Anselm* (No. 6535), p. 148, expresses doubts on Offler's case.

(f) De obsessione Dunelmi et de probitate Uchtredi comitis. Arnold, i. 215–20; Hinde, pp. 154–7; Twysden, *Scriptores* (No. 1124), pp. 79–82. Translated in Stevenson, *Church historians* (No. 1123), iii, pt. ii, 765–8.

Although no longer attributed to Simeon, these tracts are valuable for the first half of the eleventh century; they deal with the siege of Durham by the Scots in 1006 and with the earls of Bernicia. See Stenton, *A.S. Eng.* (No. 1189), pp. 412 and 689.

2158 ELMHAM, THOMAS OF (d. *c.* 1428). Historia monasterii S. Augustini Cantuariensis (A.D. 597–1191). Ed. by Charles Hardwick. Rolls Series. Lond. 1858.

Compiled in 1414, probably by Thomas of Elmham, a monk of St. Augustine's. The portion of the work actually completed covers the years 597–806, while the rest of the volume is made up of rough materials for the projected continuation of the history, such as charters and bulls (many of them spurious) relating to the abbey, from about 1066 to 1191. The author passes with facility from the history of St. Augustine's to that of the Anglo-Saxon church in general, and the net result of his labour is little more than a painstaking compilation. He made free use of Bede, William of Malmesbury, and other well-known sources. For other writings attributed to him, see Nos. 2864, 2877. For another Chronicle of St. Augustine's, see William Thorne (No. 2959), of which pp. 2–47 in Davis's translation deal with the Anglo-Saxon period. See below, No. 6181.

2159 ENCOMIUM EMMAE REGINAE. Ed. by Alistair Campbell. R.H.S. Camden. 3rd Ser. lxxii. Lond. 1949. Also carefully edited in M. Cl. Gertz, *Scriptores minores historiae Danicae medii aevi*, ii. 376–426. Copenhagen. 1917–20. Another edition edited in M.G.H. *SS.*, xix. 509–25. Older editions listed in Potthast (No. 62), i. 512–13, under 'Gesta Cnutonis' and in Hardy, *Catalogue* (No. 21), i. 627–30; ii. 1–5. Part of Campbell's translation is reprinted in *Eng. Hist. Docs.* i. 322–4.

> This is a contemporary source by a monk of St. Omer, and covers the years 1012–42. The eulogy is dedicated to Queen Emma, as the wife of Canute; it mentions Ethelred only as a prince. Although it must be used with caution, it is useful for the Danish conquest of England and its aftermath. Campbell's scholarly introduction and appendices are based in part on Scandinavian sources. See also F. Barlow, 'Two notes: Cnut's second pilgrimage and Queen Emma's disgrace in 1043', *E.H.R.* lxxiii (1958), 649–56.

2160 FLANN MAINISTREACH (d. 1056). (*a*) Synchronisms. Photolithographed facsimile of Robert Atkinson's *Book of Ballymote*, pp. 11–14. Royal Irish Academy. Dublin. 1887. (*b*) Idem, Synchronisms from the Book of Ballymote, ed. by B(artholomew) MacCarthy, in The Codex Palatino-Vaticanus. No. 830, pp. 235–332. Royal Irish Academy. Todd Lectures, vol. iii. Dublin. 1892. (Irish text and English translation.) Extracts in W. F. Skene, *Chronicles* (No. 1120), pp. 18–22.

> In this tract, which is written in Irish, the author compares or synchronizes the chronology of Ireland with that of other countries, giving careful lists of Irish kings, together with the names of contemporary monarchs who reigned elsewhere. The work, with its continuation, extends from the creation to 1119. MacCarthy (p. 243) contends that there is no evidence that the work was written by Flann of the Monastery. He says (pp. 247–59) that the *Chronicon Scotorum* (No. 2839) is a compendium of Tigernach (No. 2170) and the pre-Patrician portion of Tigernach was based mainly on the *Synchronisms*. Flann also wrote some historical poems. See O'Curry (No. 30), pp. 53–7.

2161 GENEALOGIA REGUM.

> Royal genealogies of British kings were compiled at least as early as the eighth century. The subject is treated, with full references, by Kenneth Sisam, 'Anglo-Saxon Royal Genealogies', *P.B.A.* xxxix (1953), 287–346. For lists, with supporting references, of kings in Anglo-Saxon times, consult Powicke–Fryde, *Handbook* (No. 371), pp. 6–31.

2162 GILDAS (d. *c.* 570). (*a*) The best edition is De excidio et conquestu Britanniae. Ed. by Theodor Mommsen in M.G.H. *AA.* (No. 1114), xiii (1894), 1–85. (*b*) De excidio Britanniae. Ed. by Joseph Stevenson. Eng. Hist. Soc. Lond. 1838. (*c*) Also in Petrie, *Monumenta* (No. 1084), pp. 1–46; and in Gale, *Scriptores XV* (No. 1100). (*d*) Gildae de excidio Britanniae, liber de paenitentia, accedit et lorica Gildae. Ed. by Hugh Williams in Soc. Cymmrodorion Record Ser. No. 3, pts. i–xi (1899–1901), which reproduces Mommsen's text of *De excidio* with translation and notes. Translated also by Giles, *Historians* (No. 1101) and *Six Chronicles* (No. 1089); and in A. W. Wade-Evans, *Nennius's History* (No. 2167). Other editions are mentioned in Potthast (No. 62), i. 525.

> Part jeremiad, part narrative, valuable on general conditions, but dubious on details. Recent assessments in Bolton, *A.-S. Lit.* (No. 1403), pp. 27–37, with bibliography, pp. 244–8; in Jack, *Medieval Wales* (No. 22), pp. 16–18. Other commentaries are

found in Stenton, *A.S. Eng.*, pp. 2–4; Ferdinand Lot, 'De la valeur historique du *De excidio* . . . de Gildas' in *Medieval Studies in memory of Gertrude Schoepperle Loomis* (Paris and N.Y. 1927), pp. 229–64; reprinted in *Recueil des travaux historiques de Ferdinand Lot*, i. 750–85 (Geneva and Paris, 1968); Ferdinand Lot, 'Bretons et anglais aux vᵉ et viᵉ siècles', *P.B.A.* xvi (1932 for 1930), 327–44; an explanation of the errors made by Gildas, a thoughtful writer, is given in C. E. Stevens, 'Gildas and the civitates of Britain', *E.H.R.* lii (1937), 193–203, and his 'Gildas sapiens', *E.H.R.* lvi (1941), 353–73; on which see M. Deanesly in *Saxl Essays* (No. 1452); P. Grosjean, 'Remarques sur le *De excidio* attribué à Gildas', *Bulletin du Cange* (No. 303), xxv (1955), 155–87; K. Hughes, *Church* (No. 2670), especially pp. 39–44. Other articles are listed in Kenney, *Sources* (No. 23), pp. 150–2 and 176–7; Bonser, *A.-S.C.B.* (No. 12), see index under 'Gildas', *C.B.E.L.* i. 99–100. See also I. Foster and G. Daniel, *Prehistoric . . . Wales* (No. 1984).

2163 INGULF (d. 1109). (*a*) Historia Croylandensis (*c.* 626–1091), with a continuation by Peter de Blois to 1117. Ed. by Fulman, *Scriptores* (No. 1098), pp. 1–132. (*b*) The chronicle of Croyland Abbey. Ed. by W. de Gray Birch. Wisbech. 1883. (This edition closes with the year 1085 and is inferior to Fulman's.) Translated to 1091 by J. Stevenson, *Church historians* (No. 1123), and to 1117 by H. T. Riley in Bohn's Library (No. 1089), pp. 1–270.

This chronicle with its appended charters is a forgery, ascribed to Ingulf, the first Norman abbot of Crowland and a chancery clerk under William the Conqueror. Until it was proved to be a forgery, it was regarded as a work of great historical value. In 1826 Francis Palgrave produced evidence that it was a 'mere monkish invention' (*Quarterly Review*, xxxiv (1826), 289–98) and his view was confirmed by the investigation of Riley (*Archaeol. Jour.* xix (1862), 32–49, 114–33); Hardy, *Catalogue* (No. 21), ii. 58–64, 128–9; Liebermann in *Neues Archiv*, xviii (1893), 225–67; and W. G. Searle, *Ingulf and the Historia Croylandensis* (Cambr. 1894). Liebermann, in his masterly exposition, believed that the fabrication dates from about the middle of the fourteenth century; whereas Riley assigns it to about A.D. 1414.

For the authentic and valuable fifteenth-century *Historia Croylandensis*, see No. 2900.

2164 LIBER ELIENSIS edited for the Royal Historical Society by E. O. Blake. Camden, 3rd Ser. xcii. Lond. 1962. (*b*) Liber Eliensis ad fidem codicum variorum. Ed. by D. J. Stewart. (Books i–ii.) Anglia Christiana Soc. Lond. 1848. (*c*) Bk. ii, in Gale, *Scriptores XV* (No. 1100), pp. 463–523. (*d*) An epitome of the history in bks. i–iii, in Wharton, *Anglia Sacra* (No. 1125), i. 593–630; with continuations to 1554, ibid. i. 631–77. (*e*) Some charters from bks. ii and iii are printed in Bentham, *Hist. . . . Ely* (No. 5708), i, app. 9–21; and (*f*) thirty papal letters from bk. iii in Holtzmann, *Papsturkunden* (No. 1132), ii, *passim*.

Blake's edition is the only critical one; it prints for the first time the whole of Book iii and, in addition to the editor's Introduction, it includes a Foreword by Dorothy Whitelock. The *Liber Eliensis* is a compilation made by a monk of Ely between 1131 and 1174. The name of the compiler is unknown; Blake regards Richard, the known author of other tracts and probably the prior of Ely after 1177, as a stronger claimant than Thomas, to whom the work has sometimes been ascribed. It comprises three books. Book i runs from the foundation of St. Etheldreda to its destruction during the Danish invasions and is basically a life of St. Etheldreda with additions. Book ii from 970 to 1107 'makes much use of vernacular documents' and is 'a source of outstanding value for tenth century history' (Whitelock in her Foreword). Book iii is a chartulary and chronicle from the creation of the bishopric of Ely in 1109 to 1169, and includes papal letters as well as charters. From 'a careful scrutiny for signs of forgery, . . . the documents emerge remarkably well'; but the worth of the narrative chronicle is 'more uneven'.

Commentaries on the work may be found in: E. O. Blake, 'The Historia Eliensis as a source for twelfth-century history', *B.J.R.L.* xli (1959), 304–27; Mary Bateson, 'Thomas of Ely', *D.N.B.* xix. 653–4; W. Holtzmann, *Papsturkunden* (No. 1132), ii. 78–93, analyses bk. iii; Edward Miller, *The abbey and bishopric of Ely* (No. 5711).

2165 LIBER MONASTERII DE HYDA, comprising a chronicle of the affairs of England and a chartulary of the abbey of Hyde, in Hampshire, A.D. 455–1023. Ed. by Edward Edwards. Rolls Series. Lond. 1866. Translated by J. Stevenson, *Church historians* (No. 1123).

Probably compiled late in the fourteenth century. Chaps. i–xi give a brief summary of the history of the heptarchic kingdoms and their union into one state. This is followed by a chronicle of each reign from Ethelwulf to Cnut. The author quotes Bede, Henry of Huntingdon, William of Malmesbury, Roger of Wendover, Higden, and other chronicles, some of which are not now extant. The *Book of Hyde* affords some information not obtainable elsewhere, especially regarding the reign of Alfred. It is a chartulary as well as a chronicle; each reign from Alfred to Ethelred the Unready has an appendix of charters relating directly or indirectly to the monastery of Hyde, some of which are not found elsewhere. Edwards, in his edition, pp. 283–21, also prints the brief *Chronica Monasterii de Hida, A.D. 1035–1120*, compiled in the reign of Henry I.

2166 MONMOUTH, GEOFFREY OF (d. 1154). (*a*) Historia regum Britanniae of Geoffrey of Monmouth, with contributions to the study of its place in early British history by Acton Griscom, together with a literal translation of the Welsh manuscript No. lxi of Jesus College, Oxford, by Robert Ellis Jones. Lond. etc. 1929. (*b*) Edmond Faral. La légende Arthurienne: études et documents. 3 vols. Paris. 1929 (vol. iii contains Geoffrey's text). (*c*) Historia regum Britanniae: A variant version. Ed. by Jacob Hammer. Cambr. (Mass.). 1951. (*d*) Historia Britonum (to 689). Ed. by J. A. Giles. Caxton Soc. Lond. 1844. (*e*) Gottfried von Monmouth Historia regum Britanniae . . . und Brut Tysylio. Ed. by San-Marte (Albert Schulz). Halle. 1854. (*f*) Ystorya brenhined y Brytanyeit (a Welsh translation of the Historia Regum, made in the first half of the fourteenth century). Ed. by John Rhys and J. G. Evans, Red Book of Hergest (No. 2386), vol. ii: The text of the Bruts from the Red Book, 1–256. Oxf. 1890. (*g*) Brut y brenhinedd: Cotton Cleopatra version. Ed. and trans. by John J. Parry. Cambr. (Mass.). 1937. Consult Edmund Reiss, 'The Welsh versions of Geoffrey of Monmouth's *Historia*', *Welsh Hist. Rev.* iv (1968), 97–127. (*h*) Gesta regum Britanniae. Ed. by Francisque Michel. Cambrian Archaeol. Assoc. Lond. 1862. A good translation is by Sebastian Evans. Temple Classics. Lond. 1904. Also Histories of the kings of Britain. Trans. by Sebastian Evans with introduction by L. A. Paton (Everyman's Library. Lond. 1912. Reprinted 1920, 1928, etc.). Translated also by Giles. Bohn Library (No. 1089), and in *Historians* (No. 1101). The translation by Lewis Thorpe (Penguin Classics, 1966) provides a recent bibliography.

Geoffrey of Monmouth, probably of Breton blood and brought up on the Welsh Marches, lived for a considerable period at or near Oxford. He witnessed several charters, dated between 1129 and 1151, dealing with the neighbouring monasteries of Oseney, Godstow and Thame. He enjoyed the patronage of Alexander, bishop of Lincoln, and of Robert, earl of Gloucester. Geoffrey was consecrated bishop of St. Asaph in 1152 and died two years later. About 1135, he wrote a *Little Book of Merlin*, which may not have circulated separately, and between 1136 and 1138 he compiled his

Historia regum, which he dedicated both to King Stephen and to Robert of Gloucester. The history, in 12 books, begins with Brutus and is generally considered to be largely fiction drawn from Celtic legends and Geoffrey's imagination. For the debate on the historical value of Geoffrey's work, see W. M. Flinders Petrie, 'Neglected British History', *P.B.A.* viii (1917), 251–78; R. W. Chambers, 'Geoffrey of Monmouth and the Brut as sources of early British history', Historical Revision in *History*, N.S. iii (1918–19), 225–8, and iv (1919–20), 34–45; F. Liebermann, 'Die angebliche Entdeckung einer brythonischen Geschichte aus Römerzeit: Galfrid von Monmouth und Tysylio' in *Archiv für das Studium der Neueren Sprachen und Literaturen*, cxliv (1922), 31–6; and Griscom, part i, *passim*, who strongly and possibly tendentiously strives to support Geoffrey's historical value.

Geoffrey asserted that he was merely translating a very old Welsh history which his friend Archdeacon Walter had lent him. Virtually all authorities agree that this assertion is false. Roberts and San-Marte believed that Geoffrey's *Historia* is based on a Welsh brut, or chronicle, of Tysilio, a Welsh saint (*fl. c.* A.D. 600), but the *Brut Tysilio* has been shown to be a late translation of Geoffrey's work. The *Brut Tysilio* is printed in Welsh in the *Myvyrian Archaiology*, ii (1801), 81–390 (new edn. Denbigh, 1870, pp. 434–75). Translated into English by Peter Roberts, *The chronicle of the kings of Britain* (Lond. 1811). San-Marte's translation into German is admittedly from Roberts's English translation, not from the Welsh. Edmund Reiss, 'The Welsh versions of Geoffrey of Monmouth's *Historia*', *Welsh History Rev.* iv (1968), 97–127. Geoffrey's work is the basis of Wace's *Roman de Brut* and of Layamon's *Brut* (Nos. 2974, 2914), and is a fountain-head of medieval romances and the principal source of the legends of Merlin and Arthur. The bibliography is very extensive; it may be found in *C.B.E.L.* (No. 14); Voretzsch (No. 299); Bonser (No. 12) and most of the works cited in this item. Current references are found in *Bulletin bibliographique de la société internationale Arthurienne* (Paris, 1949).

Among the scholarly works of most use to the historian, Edmund K. Chambers, *Arthur of Britain* (Lond. 1927); J. S. P. Tatlock, *The legendary history of Britain: Geoffrey of Monmouth's Historia Regum Britanniae and its early vernacular versions* (Berkeley and Los Angeles, 1950); J. D. Bruce, *The evolution of Arthurian romance to A.D. 1300*, 2 vols. (Baltimore, 1923); Roger S. Loomis, *Arthurian literature in the middle ages: a collaborative history* (Oxf. 1959); Stuart Piggott, 'The sources of Geoffrey of Monmouth', *Antiquity*, xv (1941), 269–86; and on his use of sources, see R. Bromwich (No. 2122) and C. Brooke (No. 2665). On Geoffrey's life and influence, some significant pieces are John E. Lloyd, 'Geoffrey of Monmouth', *E.H.R.* lvii (1942), 460–8; H. E. Salter, 'Geoffrey of Monmouth and Oxford', ibid. xxxiv (1919), 382–5; Laura Keeler, *Geoffrey of Monmouth and the late Latin chroniclers (1300–1500)* (Berkeley, Calif. 1946); Thomas D. Kendrick, *British Antiquity* (Lond. 1950). Roger S. Loomis, *Wales and the Arthurian Legends* (Cardiff, 1958). Thomas Jones, 'The early evolution of the legend of Arthur', *Nottingham Mediaeval Stud.* viii (1964), 3–21 (a translation of the Welsh article in *B.B.C.S.* xvii (1958), 237–52). The *Modern Language Quarterly* prints annually 'A Bibliography of Critical Arthurian Literature'.

2167 NENNIUS. (*a*) Nennius et l'historia Brittonum: étude critique, suivie d'une édition des diverses versions de ce texte. Ed. by Ferdinand Lot. Paris. 1934. (*b*) Edmond Faral, La légende Arthurienne: études et documents. 3 vols. Paris. 1929 (vol. iii contains Nennius' text). (*c*) Historia Brittonum cum additamentis Nennii by Theodor Mommsen, in M.G.H. *AA*. (No. 1114), xiii. 111–98. (For emendation, see Ifor Williams, 'Mommsen and the Vatican Nennius', *Bull. Board of Celtic Studies*, xi (1941), 43–8.) (*d*) Nennii Historia Britonum. Ed. by Joseph Stevenson. Eng. Hist. Soc. Lond. 1838. (*e*) Other editions by Gale, *Scriptores XV* (No. 1100); C. J. Bertram, *Britannicarum Gentium Historiae Antiquae Scriptores Tres*. Copenhagen. 1757; Petrie's *Monumenta* (No. 1084), pp. 47–82.

Translations: (*f*) Arthur W. Wade-Evans, Nennius' 'History of the Britons' together with 'The annals of the Britons' and court pedigrees of Hywel the Good, also the story of the loss of Britain. Lond. 1938. (*g*) Translated also by Giles, *Scriptores* (No. 1101). Reprinted, 1908. (*h*) The Irish version of the Historia Britonum of Nennius (compiled by Gilla Coemgin about 1071). Ed. with a translation by J. H. Todd. Irish Archaeol. Soc. Dublin. 1848. (*i*) Lebor Bretnach: The Irish version of the Historia Britonum ascribed to Nennius edited from all the MSS. by Anton Gerard van Hamel. Irish MSS. Commission. Dublin. 1932.

There is much controversy as to the authorship of the work, compiled early in the ninth century. It is a jumble of romantic stories mixed with a few historical notices. It is probably a composite work, based on early annals (Jackson, immediately below). It has great significance for the study of early British mythology, particularly for the story of Arthur. Yet its regnal lists for 796, with notes, may be cautiously used for early Northumbrian history. See *Eng. Hist. Docs.* i. 117–18.

The literature on Nennius may be located through Kenney (No. 23), p. 152; *C.B.E.L.* (No. 14), i. 100; Bonser, *A.-S.C.B.* (No. 12). The most important commentaries are Heinrich Zimmer, *Nennius vindicatus: über Entstehung, Geschichte, und Quellen der Historia Brittonum* (Berlin, 1893). Rudolf Thurneysen, 'Nennius vindicatus' in *Zeitschrift für deutsche Philologie*, xxviii (1895), 80–113; and 'Zu Nennius', ibid. xx (1935), 97–137, 185–91. H. H. Howorth, 'Nennius and the Historia Britonum', *Archaeol. Cambrensis*, 6th Ser. xvii (1917), 87–122, 321–45; xviii (1918), 199–262. F. Liebermann 'Nennius the author of the Historia Brittonum' in *Tout Essays* (No. 1458), pp. 25–44. Kenneth Jackson, 'Nennius and the twenty-eight cities of Britain' in *Antiquity*, xii (1938), 44–55, and his essay in *Celt and Saxon* (No. 2123). Ifor Williams in *B.B.C.S.* vii (1935), 380–9; ix (1939), 342–4. N. Chadwick, *Early British Church* (No. 2665), pp. 37–46. Differing from Todd's edition, Van Hamel's edition of the Irish version shows 'the gradual growth of the Irish text from the eleventh to the sixteenth century.... Of the pre-Nennian Irish version one copy has come down to us in the *Book of Lecan*. It reveals more about the origin and growth of the *Historia Britonum* than any of our Latin texts' (Irish MSS. Comm. *Catalogue of Publications 1928–1962* (Dublin, 1962), p. 13).

2168 NORTHERN ANNALS (THE LOST). See *Eng. Hist. Docs.* i. 118–19. These annals are not extant, but passages based on them are embedded in a few surviving works, especially in Simeon of Durham's *Historia regum*. One set for the period after Bede, 732–802, is printed in Arnold's edition of Simeon (No. 2157), ii. 38–66; and for *c.* 900–57 in Arnold, ii. 93–4. The northern annals were also used by the northern recension of the *Anglo-Saxon Chronicle* (MSS. D and E) and there the first set extends to 806. Other annals presumably from York were used by Roger of Wendover in his thirteenth-century *Flores historiarum*. Florence of Worcester, Roger of Hoveden, and the *Chronicle of Melrose* made use of northern annals. See W. S. Angus, 'The annals for the tenth century in Simeon of Durham's Historia regum', *Durham Univ. Jour.* xxxii, N.S. i (1940), 213–29. Peter Hunter Blair, 'The Moore Memoranda on Northumbrian history', in *Chadwick Mem. Studies* (No. 1429), pp. 243–57; idem, 'Some Observations in, *Celt and Saxon* (No. 2123). Kenneth Harrison, 'The pre-Conquest churches of York with an appendix of eighth century annals', *Yorks. Arch. Jour.* xl (1960), 232–49. See H. H. E. Craster, 'The Red Book of Durham', *E.H.R.* xl (1925), 504–32. Cyril Hart, 'The Ramsey computus' (No. 2366).

2169 RECUEIL DES ACTES DES DUCS DE NORMANDIE, 911–1066. Ed. by Marie Fauroux.

See No. 1097.

2170 TIGERNACH O'BRAEIN (d. 1088). The annals of Tigernach. Ed. with English trans. of the entries in Irish by Whitley Stokes. *Revue Celtique*, xvi (1895), 374–419; xvii (1896), 6–33, 119–263, 337–420; xviii (1897), 9–59, 150–97, 267–303, 374–91. The edition in O'Conor's *Scriptores* (No. 1117), ii. 1–134 is very inaccurate. Extracts A.D. 501–1099 are printed in Skene, *Chronicles of the Picts and Scots* (No. 1120), pp. 66–78, 141. A fragment is edited by Kuno Meyer, *Facsimiles of Irish MSS. Rawlinson B. 502* (No. 2399), pp. 1–24.

See K. Hughes (No. 22), chap. 4. The extant fragments of his *Annals*, written partly in Latin and partly in Irish, extend from the time of the prophets to 1088, with a continuation to 1178; but the years 767–974 are wanting, and there are other gaps. The continuation was in some large measure written contemporaneously. This valuable work seems to be the source from which most of the later annalists of Ireland borrowed their materials for Irish history down to 1088. It also throws some light on the affairs of Scotland and England. O'Curry, *Lectures* (No. 30), pp. 57–70; E. MacNeill, 'The authorship and structure of the Annals of Tigernach', *Ériu*, vii (1914), 30–113; Paul Walsh, 'The annals attributed to Tigernach', *Irish Hist. Stud.* ii (1940), 154–9. See also Nos. 2160, 2780, 2786, 2839.

2171 VITA AEDWARDI REGIS QUI APUD WESTMONASTERIUM REQUIESCIT: The life of King Edward who rests at Westminster attributed to a monk of St. Bertin. Ed. and trans. by Frank Barlow. Medieval Texts. Lond. etc. 1962. Also printed in Henry R. Luard, *Lives of Edward the Confessor*, pp. 387–435. Rolls Series. Lond. 1858.

This remarkable life of Edward the Confessor is dedicated to his wife, Edith. It devotes much space to Godwin and his children as well as to a saint's life of Edward. Marc Bloch held that this biography was composed between 1103 and 1120 and was therefore not a contemporary source. Southern and Heningham, in rejecting Bloch's thesis, produced reasons for dating the composition as between 1066 and 1075, possibly even before 6 January 1067. The anonymous author may have been a monk of St. Bertin's of St. Omer and possibly either Goscelin or Folchard. See Barlow's introduction to his edition; Marc Bloch, *Analecta Bollandiana*, xli (1923); R. W. Southern, 'The first life of Edward the Confessor', *E.H.R.* lvii (1943), 385–400; Eleanor K. Heningham, 'The genuineness of the Vita Aeduuardi regis', *Speculum*, xxi (1946), 419–56; F. Barlow, 'Vita Aedwardi (Book II): The seven sleepers', *Speculum*, xl (1965), 385–97. The purpose of the *Vita Aedwardi Regis* is discussed in Appendix A of F. Barlow, *Edward the Confessor* (Lond. 1970).

Other biographies of Edward are:

(a) Vita beati ac gloriosi regis Anglorum Eadwardi, by Marc Bloch in *Analecta Bollandiana*, xli (1923), introduction pp. 5–63, text pp. 64–123, appendices pp. 124–31. This is the life written about 1138 by Osbert de Clare, prior of Westminster, and presented to the papal legate to promote the canonization of Edward.

(b) Vita Edwardi regis by Ailred of Rievaulx (cf. No. 6634). Ed. in Twysden, *Scriptores* (No. 1124), pp. 369–414. Derived almost entirely from Osbert, it was compiled about 1163 to commemorate the recent (1161) canonization of Edward.

(c) Vita Edwardi regis et confessoris, in Henry R. Luard, *The lives of Edward the Confessor*, pp. 359–77. A latin poem, probably composed between 1440 and 1450, and derived from Ailred of Rievaulx.

(d) La estoire de Seint Ædward le rei. Ed. with a trans. from Cambr. Univ. Lib. Ee. iii. 59, by Luard, ibid. pp. 1–178. Also La estoire de Seint Ædward le rei: The life of St. Edward the confessor. Reproduced in facsimile from the unique manuscript (Cambr. Univ. Lib. Ee. iii. 59) with an introduction by M. R. James. Roxburghe Club. Oxf. 1920. Written about 1245, by Matthew Paris, dedicated to Eleanor of

Provence, wife of Henry III, and derived from Ailred of Rievaulx. See Vaughan, *Matthew Paris* (No. 2941), pp. 168 ff.

(e) La vie d'Édouard le confesseur. Poème Anglo-Normand du 12ᵉ siècle. Ed. by Osten Södergard. Uppsala, 1948. On the complicated relationship of Anglo-Norman lives in prose and verse of Edward, see Paul Meyer, 'Notice du MS. Egerton 745 du Musée Britannique', *Romania*, xl (1911), 41–69; and M. Dominica Legge, 'The Vatican life of Edward the Confessor', *Medium Ævum*, vi (1937), 31–3.

(f) The Middle English verse life of Edward the Confessor. Ed. by Grace E. Moore. Philadelphia, 1942.

(g) Saga Jatvardar Konungs hins helga. Ed. by Charles C. Rafn and John Sigurðsson, in *Annaler for Kongelige Nordiske Oldskriftselskab*. Copenhagen, 1852, pp. 3–43. Also C. C. Rafn and John Sigur sson, eds. The saga of St. Edward the king. Trans. by Thorlief Guðmundson Repp, in *Mémoires de la Société royale des Antiquaires du Nord*. Copenhagen, 1845–9, pp. 265–86. Also in *Icelandic Sagas*. Ed. by Guðbrand Vigfússon and trans. by G. W. Dasent, Rolls Ser. i. 388–400 and trans. iii. 683 ff. See H. L. Rogers, 'An Icelandic Life of St. Edward the Confessor', *Saga Book*, xiv (1956–7), 259–72; and Christine Fell in *Anglo-Saxon England*, i (1972), 147–58.

2172   VITA HAROLDI (II). Ed. with a trans. by Walter de Gray Birch. Lond. 1885. Imperfect edns. in F. Michel, *Chroniques Anglo-Normandes* (No. 1112), ii. 143–221; and in J. A. Giles, *Vitae Quorundam Anglo-Saxonum* (No. 2285), pp. 30–95.

A historical romance, of little value, probably written in 1216. See Hardy, *Catalogue* (No. 21), i. 668–71.

2173   WALLINGFORD, JOHN OF. The chronicle attributed to John of Wallingford. Ed. by Richard Vaughan. *Camden Miscellany*, xxi. Camden Soc. 3rd Ser. xc. Lond. 1958.

An early thirteenth-century (c. 1220) compilation by an anonymous author whose work was incorporated by John of Wallingford into the book which contained John's own chronicle (No. 2975). This anonymous chronicle extends from Brut to Cnut and includes, by insertion, lives of many saints. The historical sections are based largely on *Libellus de Regibus Saxonicis*, on William of Jumièges, and on the 'lost Northumbrian chronicle'; for the last the chronicle is important.

2174   WAR OF THE GAEDHIL WITH THE GAILL, or the invasions of Ireland by the Danes and other Norsemen. The original Irish text, ed. and trans. by James H. Todd. Rolls Series. Lond. 1867.

This Irish saga, which extends from about 800 to the battle of Clontarf in 1014, was compiled about 1160. The first part is merely another version of the *Annals of Ulster*; but the second part, preserved in the *Book of Leinster*, is devoted to the history of the Munster chieftains, especially to the exploits of Brian Boru, the victorious king of Munster, who lost his life at Clontarf. The second part is strongly nationalistic in bias. See Sawyer, *Vikings* (No. 2596), pp. 27–8; A. J. Goedheer, 'Irish and Norse traditions about the battle of Clontarf', *Nederlandsche bijdragen op het gebied von Germansche philologie en linguistie* (Haarlem), ix (1938), 1–45; K. Hughes, *Irish Church* (No. 2670), p. 204. Cf. O'Lochlainn, 'Poets on the battle of Clontarf', *Eigse: A journal of Irish studies*, iii (1942), 208–18, and iv (1943), 33–47. See No. 2605.

B. ADMINISTRATIVE SOURCES

1. *Anglo-Saxon*

The fundamental documentary sources for the study of Anglo-Saxon administration, as well as for social and economic history, may be grouped as (a) the laws issued by kings or privately compiled; (b) Latin law-books, (c) the charters, the writs, the wills, and similar documents; and (d) isolated pieces.

(a) Anglo-Saxon laws

When the Saxons and Angles settled in England, all their law was probably preserved in the form of oral tradition or customs, not dissimilar to the law of other Germanic peoples. The earliest written laws in any Germanic language are those of King Ethelbert of Kent (d. 616), now surviving in a twelfth-century manuscript *Textus Roffensis* (No. 441). These and the laws of later kings come down to us through transcriptions made by the clergy; although the laws of Ine and Alfred are extant in a MS. of the early tenth century, the laws of other kings survive only in copies of the eleventh and twelfth centuries. The two most important codices, made in the reign of Henry I, are *Textus Roffensis* (No. 441) and the St. Paul's MS., now C.C.C.C. 383. The *Quadripartitus* (No. 2189) fills some gaps. The laws relate mainly to crime, to wergilds, and to the enforcement or modification of existing regulations; they are not designed to be complete codifications of law. They are not modelled on Roman or continental collections; they are written in the vernacular language. They were issued by several kings from Æthelbert to Cnut (c. 601–1020), with a long gap of about two centuries (c. 695–890), since the laws of Offa which once existed have not survived. The larger part of the law remained unwritten and customary, but the surviving charters shed considerable light on it.

Although Anglo-Saxon legislation ends with Cnut, the interest in preserving the Anglo-Saxon legal system which, as amended by William I and Henry I, was regarded as still in force, continued well into the twelfth century. Private collections of the eleventh and twelfth centuries provide not only the texts of the laws issued by Anglo-Saxon kings but also fragments or isolated pieces of uncertain date and a series of Latin law-books which reveal the late Anglo-Saxon law. The isolated pieces naturally touch on a variety of subjects; particularly interesting are those which deal with the status of persons and with the management of an estate as described in the extensive *Rectitudines Singularum Personarum* (No. 2212). The Latin law-books of the twelfth century, especially of the time of Henry I, were written mainly by Frenchmen in England to expound the still operative Anglo-Saxon law. They attempt 'to provide a digest of Old English law for those who could not read the original texts'.

The classic edition of Anglo-Saxon laws is by Liebermann (No. 2177); the handiest edition with English translations of the laws of Anglo-Saxon kings are those of Attenborough (No. 2175) and Robertson (No. 2178). Thorpe (No. 2180) printed private and ecclesiastical codes as well as the laws of kings; Haddan and Stubbs, *Councils* (No. 2254), give ecclesiastical laws to 870. Whitelock's *English historical documents* (No. 17), i. 327–439, provides translations of many laws, together with informative introduction and bibliography.

Commentaries are listed in Bonser, *A.-S.C.B.* (No. 12), pp. 113–21; but the glossary in volume ii and the detailed notes in volume iii of Liebermann's great work must form the basis of any study. Pollock and Maitland (No. 1242) and Plucknett's *Concise History*, and *E.E.L.L.* (Nos. 1241; 3674) furnish summary treatments; and Holdsworth (No. 1235) a fuller one. Chadwick (No. 2494) is more detailed on some specific institutions. Important recent contributions on specific codes are Kenneth Sisam's articles on Athelstan's laws, reprinted in his *Studies* (No. 2361), pp. 232–58 from *Mod. Lang. Rev.* xviii (1923), 100–4, and xx (1925), 253–69; Dorothy Whitelock's articles on Wulfstan's connections with the so-called laws of Edward and Guthrum and Cnut in *E.H.R.* lvi (1941), 1–21; lxiii (1948), 433–52; lxx (1955), 72–85; Dorothy Bethurum, 'Six anonymous old English codes', *Jour. Eng. and Germ. Phil.* xlix (1950), 449–63, where these codes are plausibly ascribed to Wulfstan; and Kenneth Sisam's 'The relationship of Æthelred's Codes V and VI' in *Studies* (No. 2361), pp. 278–87. H. G. Richardson and G. O. Sayles, *Law and Legislation from Æthelberht to Magna Carta* (Edin. 1966), Chapters i and ii, pp. 1–53, make their assessments of most of the works which are entered immediately below; and in Appendix I, pp. 157–69, give an excursus on 'Kent under Æthelberht'; but their views have been subjected to severe criticism (see Nos. 1218, 1219).

2175 ATTENBOROUGH (FREDERICK L.). The laws of the earliest English kings, edited and translated. Cambr. 1922. *

2176 ECKHARDT (K. A.), ed. Gesetze der Angelsachsen, 601–925. Göttingen, 1958. An edition and translation of the laws from Æthelberht to Athelstan.

2177 LIEBERMANN (FELIX). Die Gesetze der Angelsachsen, herausgegeben im Auftrage der Savigny-Stiftung. 3 vols. Halle. 1898 (1903)–1916. *

Vol. i contains (a) in columnal form variant Anglo-Saxon texts, Latin texts, and a translation into German of all the known laws issued in a king's name (pp. 1–371); and (b) Anglo-Saxon laws lacking a king's name, fragments or isolated pieces, the laws of William I and Henry I, and Latin law-books of the first half of the twelfth century (pp. 373–675). For some texts of (b) see below, Nos. 2186, 2187. Vol. ii provides a dictionary and detailed glossary. Vol. iii presents an introduction and commentary to each text printed in vol. i.

2178 ROBERTSON (AGNES J.). The laws of the kings of England from Edmund to Henry I. Cambr. 1925.

2179 SCHMID (REINHOLD). Die Gesetze der Angelsachsen. Leipzig. 1832. 2nd edn. much enlarged. 1858.

The best edition prior to Liebermann's.

2180 THORPE (BENJAMIN) and PRICE (R.). Ancient laws and institutes of England, with an English translation of the Saxon; also monumenta ecclesiastica. Record Comm. 2 vols. Lond. 1840. Also published in one folio volume. 1840. See No. 2259.

(b) Latin law-books

For Latin law-books, see Plucknett, *E.E.L.L.* (No. 3674), Chap. ii; Whitelock, *Eng. Hist. Docs.* (No. 17), i. 329–30; Richardson and Sayles (Nos. 1218–19).

2181 CONSILIATIO CNUTI. Ed. by Felix Liebermann. Halle. 1893. Liebermann also prints it in columns in his *Gesetze*, 279–371, with a preface and cross-references in i. 618–19.

So called by the editor because the text begins 'Hec est consiliatio quam Cnutus . . . consiliatus est.' It is a glossed translation of Cnut's laws (based on a lost Anglo-Saxon MS.), made in south England about 1110–30, probably by a cleric of French birth.

2182 HIC INTIMATUR. Ed. by Liebermann. *Gesetze*, i. 486–8. Robertson, pp. 238–42. Stubbs, *Charters*, pp. 97–9. *Eng. Hist. Docs.* ii. 399–400.

Sometimes called 'Laws of William the Conqueror', these ten articles are almost certainly not the Conqueror's legislation. They are discussed at some length in Richardson and Sayles, *Law and Legislation* (No. 1219).

2183 INSTITUTA CNUTI. Ed. by J. L. A. Kolderup-Rosenvinge, under the title, Legum regis Canuti Magni versio antiqua Latina ex codice Colbertino, cum textu Anglo-Saxonico. Copenhagen. 1826. Schmid, pp. 425–32, prints part of the Latin version. Liebermann prints it in columns in his *Gesetze*, i. 279–367, with cross references on pp. 612–17.

This is a translation into Latin of Cnut's laws, with glosses from some earlier kings, including about a dozen enactments of which no Anglo-Saxon text survives. See Liebermann, 'On the instituta Cnuti', *T.R.H.S.* n.s. ix (1893), 77–107.

2184 LEGES ANGLORUM. See Liebermann, Ueber die Leges Anglorum saeculo xiii ineunte Londoniis collectae. Halle, 1894. Also Liebermann, *E.H.R.* xxviii (1913), 732–45.

A large collection of laws, compiled by a citizen of London in the latter part of John's reign. It comprises extracts from part i of the *Quadripartitus* (i.e. many dooms of Ine, Alfred, Athelstan, and Cnut), portions of the *Articuli Willelmi* and of the *Leges Edwardi Confessoris*, together with many of the compiler's own inventions and interpolations. He seems to have been a layman in favour of the baronial movement against John.

2185 LEGES EDWARDI CONFESSORIS. Liebermann, *Gesetze*, i. 627–72. Schmid, pp. 491–519. Thorpe, i. 442–62. Stubbs, in his edition of Hoveden's *Chronica* (No. 2903), ii. 219–41.

This work exists in three recensions, the first dates from the last years of Henry I, the second from about the end of Stephen's reign, and the third from early Henry II. On its value, there is disagreement. Liebermann places some confidence in it in his *Ueber die Leges Edwardi Confessoris* (Halle, 1896). Richardson and Sayles, *Law* (No. 1219), pp. 47–9, while counselling caution, think that 'all in all he seems to be a guide of some worth to the local administration of justice under Henry I'. Whitelock in *Eng. Hist. Docs.* i. 330 regards it as an unreliable compilation 'by a writer ready to romance in favour of ecclesiastical interests, who pretends that he is giving the laws of Edward the Confessor as stated by juries to William I'.

2186 LEGES HENRICI PRIMI. Liebermann, i. 547–611. Schmid, pp. 432–90. Thorpe, i. 497–631. Translated extracts in *Eng. Hist. Docs.* ii. 459–62. Ed. and trans. by L. J. Downer. Oxf. 1972.

This work derives its title from the fact that it includes the coronation charter of Henry I. It was probably written between 1110 and 1118 as a replacement for the contemplated book iii of the *Quadripartitus* (No. 2189). Liebermann thought both *Leges* and *Quadripartitus* were written by the same author, but Richardson and Sayles feel convinced that they were not. A poorly arranged assortment of Anglo-Saxon laws and contemporary customary law, concerned largely with crime, it may have been written for local courts. See Plucknett, *E.E.L.L.* (No. 3674), Chap. ii; and Richardson and Sayles, *Law* (No. 1219), pp. 43–5.

2187 LEGES WILLELMI CONQUESTORIS. Best edition, giving both Latin and Old French texts, by Liebermann, 'Leis Willelme' in his *Gesetze*, i. 492–520. Also in Schmid, pp. 322–51. Thorpe, i. 466–87. Robert Kelham, *The laws of William the Conqueror*. Lond. 1779. Palgrave, *English Commonwealth*, ii. 88–140. John E. Matzke, *Lois de Guillaume le Conquérant*. Paris. 1899. Robertson, pp. 252–75.

The first section professes to contain the laws observed in the time of Edward the Confessor and newly promulgated by the Conqueror. The text, which is preserved in both Latin and Old French, is made up largely of Anglo-Saxon dooms by a compiler who knew some Roman law. Liebermann regards the Old French text as the original and dates it 1090–1135; but Richardson and Sayles (pp. 121–5 and App. ii) hold that the Latin text preceded the French text and assign it to the reign of Henry II.

2188 PSEUDO-CNUTS CONSTITUTIONES DE FORESTA. Liebermann, *Gesetze*, i. 620–6. Schmid, pp. 318–21. Thorpe, i. 426–30.

A forgery, compiled about 1184, by a layman, perhaps a forest official of the baronial party who desired that the king should select forest judges from the feudal aristocracy. It gives an account of the administration and judicature of the forests of Henry II's time. See F. Liebermann, *Ueber Pseudo-Cnuts Constitutiones de Foresta* (Halle, 1894).

2189 QUADRIPARTITUS. Liebermann, *Gesetze*, i. 529–46. First published by Liebermann, as Quadripartitus, ein englisches Rechtsbuch von 1114, nachgewiesen und, soweit bisher ungedruckt, herausgegeben von F. Liebermann. Halle. 1892.

The *Quadripartitus* was compiled about 1114, by an 'anonymous author [who] moved in the service of Archbishop Gerhard of York' (Plucknett, *E.E.L.L.* p. 24), who wished to make known the 'laga Edwardi' as amended by William I and Henry I. The prologue gives some account of English institutions, A.D. 1018–1110. Book i gives a translation into Latin of most of the Anglo-Saxon laws, those of Cnut being given first. Some dooms of Athelstan, Edmund, and Æthelred and a short tenth-century document concerning theft survive only in this Latin version. Several private tracts, including *Rectitudines*, are entered here. Book ii is a collection of documents of the reign of Henry I, his coronation charter, his enactment concerning the hundred and shire courts, and various pieces regarding the investiture struggle. Books iii and iv are not extant and perhaps were never written as planned by the author.

(c) Charters, writs, wills, etc.

A variety of instruments, public and private, which collectively form the most important documentary evidence for the Anglo-Saxon period, may be conveniently classified together, despite their differences in form and structure. They include royal charters or diplomata, private charters, writs, wills, manumissions, guild regulations, and similar documents. For the early history of political and administrative institutions, they supplement the annals and elucidate the laws. They throw light on ecclesiastical history; they are essential for social and economic matters, especially for questions of tenure, topography, and status of persons.

The royal charter or diploma which was derived from Roman sources records by Alfred's time the transfer of bookland which the king grants normally to a church with the right of free alienation and immunity from all services except *trimoda necessitas*. Vague and not stereotyped in its early stages, it is a solemnly phrased document, almost invariably in Latin, and includes an invocation to the deity, a proem of the avowed reason for the grant, the substance of the grant, a curse on infringers, and a date; it is subscribed by witnesses. The earliest authentic survivals come from the second half of the seventh century.

The writ is a succinct order of the executive government, addressed as a letter to the individuals responsible for its execution and authenticated by a wax seal. Before the Norman conquest it is written invariably in Anglo-Saxon. It contains neither invocation nor proem nor punitive clauses. The earliest surviving writs seem to be two from the reign of Æthelred II (978–1016), 'neither of which is free from suspicion'. Miss Harmer (No. 2197) traces the writ by inference back to the reign of Alfred; Geoffrey Barraclough's rejection of the inference in 'The Anglo-Saxon Writ' (*History*, xxxix (1954), 193–215) has itself been generally rejected: Bishop and Chaplais (No. 2191), p. ix. The writ became the basic instrument of administration under the Normans.

Some fifty wills of the Anglo-Saxon period are extant in contemporary form or in later copies. They are usually in Anglo-Saxon and the earliest date from the ninth century. The earliest guild-regulations concern London and survive as the sixth code of Athelstan (924–39). Likewise the earliest known surviving manumission is one by King Athelstan in 925.

Students of the documents classified in this section are confronted with several problems. On the authenticity of extant charters, reference may be made to *Eng. Hist. Docs.* (No. 17), i. 337–43 and 353; Harmer, *Writs* (No. 2197), pp. 105–18; and Frank M. Stenton, *The Latin Charters* (No. 2220). The articles on diplomas by Pierre Chaplais (No. 2215) are of basic importance. The question of the force at law of charters and wills, that is whether they are dispositive or merely records of already completed transactions, has provoked discussion, summarized by T. F. T. Plucknett in *T.R.H.S.* 4th ser. xxxiii (1950), 143–4. On the existence of a royal scriptorium or chancery from which documents issued in Anglo-Saxon times, see Harmer (No. 2197), pp. 57–61; and *Regesta* (No. 3779), vol. i, pp. xi–xv.

The critical study of Anglo-Saxon diplomata was begun by George Hickes and Humphrey Wanley at the beginning of the eighteenth century (see No. 425). The now indispensable guide and bibliography to Anglo-Saxon charters is the work of P. H. Sawyer (No. 2219). The most comprehensive collection is by Kemble (No. 2201), supplemented for the period before 975 by Birch's *Cartularium* (No. 2190). Although these are still the basic collections, neither of them satisfies the modern canons of research. The eight volumes of facsimiles issued by the British Museum and the Ordnance Survey (Nos. 444, 448) are of considerable value. The third volume of Haddan and Stubbs, *Councils* (No. 1129), contains many charters taken from Kemble's *Codex* and Dugdale's *Monasticon* (No. 1147), with valuable notes. Although competent scholars have in recent decades produced new editions of groups of documents, the critical edition of the corpus of Anglo-Saxon diplomata is still a desideratum which is under the consideration of a committee of the British Academy and the Royal Historical Society.

In addition to the general collections, printed chartularies and the publications of local societies contain charters purporting to come from Anglo-Saxon times.

For the chartularies see the index below under 'Charters, Anglo-Saxon'. References to texts or translations thereof and topographical studies of charters in the transactions of local societies can be found in Sawyer (No. 2219; *Eng. Hist. Docs.* i. 352–3; Bonser, *A.-S.C.B.* (No. 12), pp. 15–23; and Milne, *Writings* (1934–45) (No. 39), *passim.* Among them are the studies, published in the 1930's, by George B. Grundy for the south-western counties and by Gordon Ward for Kent. New regional studies are being made, especially at the University of Leicester under the inspiration of H. P. R. Finberg (No. 2196). See also Ker's *Catalogue* (No. 977), and the sections of post-Conquest charters and wills on pp. 636–54 below.

2190 BIRCH (WALTER DE GRAY). Cartularium Saxonicum: a collection of charters relating to Anglo-Saxon history (A.D. 430–975). 3 vols. Lond. 1885 (1883)–93. Reprinted, 1963. Index Saxonicus: an index to the names of persons in Cartularium Saxonicum. 1899. Reprinted. 1963.

Birch's *Cartularium* contains 1,354 documents, many of which are not in Kemble's *Codex.* It deals only with the period before A.D. 975 and includes pieces not of a strictly diplomatic character, such as professions of obedience made by newly elected bishops, papal correspondence, etc. The two documents anterior to A.D. 604 are a charter and a letter of St. Patrick. Birch adheres more closely to the text of the MSS. than Kemble does, but his critical apparatus of notes etc. is very meagre: he does not profess to be 'the critical expositor' of the contents of the charters. See also his paper, 'The Anglo-Saxon Charters of Worcester Cathedral' (a calendar etc. of the charters), *Brit. Archaeol. Assoc. Jour.* xxxviii (1882), 24–54.

2191 BISHOP (TERENCE A. M.) and CHAPLAIS (PIERRE), eds. Facsimiles of English royal writs to A.D. 1100 presented to Vivian Hunter Galbraith. Oxf. 1957.

T. A. M. Bishop, 'A charter of King Edwy', *Bodleian Lib. Rec.* vi (1957), 369–73.

2192 BRUCKNER (ALBERT) and MARICHAL (ROBERT). Chartae antiquiores: A facsimile edition of all Latin charters prior to the ninth century. Lausanne. 1954+.

Vol. iii (Charters from) The British Museum, 1963; vol. iv, other British archives, 1968. After completing vol. iv, Bruckner expects to produce a study on A.-S. diplomatic. See *B.E.C.* cxxviii (1965), 231–6.

2193 CALENDAR OF ROYAL CHARTERS which occur in letters of inspeximus, exemplification, or confirmation, and in cartularies, in the Public Record Office. Pt. i, from Ethelbert of Kent to William II. Deputy Keeper's Reports. xxix. 7–48. Lond. 1868.

Contains an abstract of their contents.

2194 DAVIDSON (JAMES B.). 'On some Anglo-Saxon charters at Exeter.' *Brit. Archaeol. Assoc. Jour.* xxxix (1883), 259–303.

Edits fifteen documents, A.D. 938–1069, five of them never before printed; only four of the fifteen are in Kemble's *Codex.* See also his paper, 'On the Charters of King Ine', *Somerset Archaeol. and Nat. Hist. Soc. Procs.* xxx, pt. ii (1884), 1–31; and Pierre Chaplais, 'The authenticity of the Royal Anglo-Saxon diplomas of Exeter', *B.I.H.R.* xxxix (1966), 1–34.

2195   EARLE (JOHN). A hand-book to the land-charters and other Saxonic documents. Oxf. 1888.

A selection of about 250 well-edited documents, some of which are not printed by Kemble or Birch. An elaborate introduction deals with the structure and language of the charters and with the origin of the manor; much attention is devoted to gesiths and laenland. Earle believed that at the time of the Conquest the military chiefs or captains were placed over the conquered villages, thus becoming manorial lords with police and military functions; he identified them with the gesiths. See W. H. Stevenson's criticism in *E.H.R.* iv (1889), 353–9.

2196   FINBERG (HERBERT P. R.). The early charters of Devon and Cornwall. Dept. of Eng. Local Hist. Leicester, Occasional Papers, No. 2. Leicester. 1953. A supplement, ibid. no. 13. 1960. Second edn. Leicester. 1963. Idem, The early charters of the West Midlands. Leicester. 1961. Idem, The early charters of Wessex. Leicester. 1964.

Each volume constitutes a handbook of charters, writs, wills, and like documents down to 1066. In each volume a series of complementary chapters discusses problems on related subjects. See also Finberg, 'Some Crediton documents re-examined, with some observations on the criticism of Anglo-Saxon charters', *Antiquaries Jour.* xlviii (1968), 59–86.

2197   HARMER (FLORENCE E.). Anglo-Saxon writs. Manchester. 1952.

Also her 'Three Westminster writs of King Edward the Confessor', *E.H.R.* li (1936), 97–103. G. Barraclough, 'The Anglo-Saxon writ', *History*, N.S. xxxix (1954), 193–215.

2198   HARMER (FLORENCE E.). Select English historical documents of the ninth and tenth centuries. Cambr. 1914.

Also her 'Anglo-Saxon charters and the historian', *B.J.R.L.* xxii (1938), 339–67.

2199   HART (CYRIL J. R.). The early charters of Essex. Dept. of Eng. Local Hist. Leicester, Occasional Papers, No. 10: Saxon Period. 1957. No. 11: The Norman Period. 1957. No. 5: The early charters of eastern England. Leicester. 1966. Idem, '*Codex Wintoniensis*', *Agricultural H.R.* xviii (1970), Supp. 7–38.

2200   HEMMING. Hemingi Chartularium ecclesiae Wigorniensis. Ed. by Thomas Hearne. 2 vols. Oxf. 1723.

The Cotton manuscript which Hearne printed consists of two distinct manuscripts. Only the second one, beginning on page 248 of Hearne's edition, can be attributed to Hemming, who was sub-prior of Worcester at the end of the eleventh century. The first part of the Cotton MS. is written in several hands of the early eleventh century. Most of the charters of Hearne's edition are royal grants of the ninth and tenth centuries; they are reprinted in Kemble's *Codex*. See N. R. Ker, 'Hemming's Cartulary' in *Studies . . . to F. M. Powicke* (No. 1450), pp. 49–75; and V. H. Galbraith, 'Samson, bishop of Worcester', *E.H.R.* lxxii (1967), 93–101.

2201   KEMBLE (JOHN M.). Codex diplomaticus aevi Saxonici. Eng. Hist. Soc. 6 vols. Lond. 1839–48. *

The Codex comprises 1,369 documents, from A.D. 604 to about 1061. Some of them are inaccurately printed, either because they were not collated with the originals or with the oldest copies, or because an attempt was made to construct a composite text based upon various MSS. The elaborate introduction in vol. i deals with the origin of charters, their structure, and their contents; see also the prefaces in vols. iii and vi. Cf. Bruce Dickins,

'John Mitchell Kemble and Old English scholarship', *P.B.A.* xxv (1939), 51–84. For criticism of Kemble's *Codex*, see Julius Aronius, *Diplomatische Studien über die älteren angelsächsischen Urkunden* (to A.D. 839) (Königsberg, 1883). Some translations are given in W. H. Stevenson and W. H. Duignan, 'Anglo-Saxon charters relating to Shropshire (A.D. 664–1004)', *Shropshire Archaeol. and Nat. Hist. Soc. Trans.* 4th Ser. i (1911), 1–22. Henry Sweet, *Anglo-Saxon Reader* (No. 286), pp. 423–60, adds a few charters not in Kemble. See also Joan C. Lancaster, 'The Coventry forged charters: a reconsideration', *B.I.H.R.* xxvii (1954), 113–39; and E. S. Lindley, 'The Anglo-Saxon charters of Stoke Bishop', *Trans. Bristol and Glos. Archaeol. Soc.* lxxviii (1959), 96–109.

2201A LOYD (LEWIS C.) and STENTON (DORIS M.), eds. Sir Christopher Hatton's book of seals. Northants Rec. Soc. Pubns. xv. Oxf. 1950.

2202 NAPIER (ARTHUR S.) and STEVENSON (WILLIAM H.). The Crawford collection of early charters and documents now in the Bodleian Library. Oxf. 1895.

Nineteen documents, A.D. 739–1150, eight of them never before published; with elaborate notes. A model edition.

2203 ROBERTSON (AGNES J.). Anglo-Saxon Charters, edited with translations. Cambr. 1939. 2nd edn. 1957.

This basic, convenient edition of charters in Old English contains a few items not previously printed.

2204 THORPE (BENJAMIN). Diplomatarium Anglicum aevi Saxonici: a collection of English charters, from A.D. 605 to William the Conqueror, with a translation of the Anglo-Saxon. Lond. 1865.

About 325 documents, in large part a selection from Kemble's *Codex*, arranged under four heads: (1) miscellaneous charters, excluding simple grants of land; (2) wills; (3) gilds; (4) manumissions and acquittances. About twenty pieces in the *Diplomatarium* (including three of the four collections of gild statutes) were not printed by Kemble.

2205 WHITELOCK (DOROTHY). Anglo-Saxon wills. Ed. with trans. and notes. The introduction is by H. D. Hazeltine. Cambr. Studies in Eng. Legal Hist. Cambr. 1930.

(d) Isolated pieces

Some of the isolated pieces printed in Liebermann or elsewhere are listed separately here. Most of them are written in Anglo-Saxon, are of uncertain date but mainly of the eleventh century, and are private compilations based on custom or authentic legislation. Most of them can also be found in Schmid (No. 2179) and Thorpe (No. 2180). *Eng. Hist. Docs.* (No. 17), i. 431–9, has translations of a few, which are not listed here.

2206 BURGHAL HIDAGE. Robertson's *Charters* (No. 2203), pp. 246–9. R. E. W. Flower, 'The text of the Burghal Hidage'. *London Mediaeval Studies*, i (1937), 60–4.

A brief document, drawn up c. 911–19, concerning the garrisoning of fortresses in southern England, to each of which is assigned a number of hides. See Maitland's *Domesday Book and beyond* (No. 2636), pp. 502–8; Chadwick, *Anglo-Saxon institutions* (No. 2494), pp. 204–27; Robertson, *Charters*, pp. 494–6; Nicholas Brooks, 'The unidentified forts of the Burghal Hidage', *Medieval Archaeology*, viii (1964), 74–90; and David Hill, 'The Burghal Hidage: the establishment of a text', ibid. xiii (1969), 84–92.

2207 DE INSTITUTIS LUNDONIAE. Liebermann, i. 232–7. Schmid, pp. 218–21. Thorpe, i. 300–3. Hohlbaum, Hansisches Urkundenbuch (No. 5336), iii. 378–81.

> According to Schmid, Thorpe, and Liebermann, this belongs to the time of Ethelred II; but Hohlbaum believes that it was compiled after 1066. It contains enactments regarding the tolls collected at the gates of London, foreign merchants, counterfeiting, and house-breaking.

2208 DEMA, OR JUDEX. Liebermann, i. 474–6. Liebermann, *Zeitschrift für Rechtsgeschichte*, xviii (1884), Germ. Abth. 207–13.

> Deals with the duties of a judge about 1000.

2209 GEREFA. Liebermann, i. 453–5. Liebermann in *Anglia*, ix (1886), 251–66. Cunningham, *Growth of English Industry* (No. 1366), i. 571–6.

> Compiled in first half of eleventh century; generally accepted as a continuation of the *Rectitudines* (No. 2212); expounds the duties of a reeve and the management of a large estate.

2210 HUNDRED ORDINANCE. Liebermann, i. 192–5. Schmid, pp. 182–4. Thorpe, i. 258–61. Robertson's *Laws*, pp. 16–19. Stubbs, *Select Charters*, 9th edn. pp. 80–2. *Eng. Hist. Docs.* i. 393–4.

> Anonymous royal ordinance 946–68, sometimes called I Edgar, on how the hundred court shall be held. Commentaries: Stenton, *A.-S. Eng.* (No. 1189), pp. 295–8, and H. M. Cam, 'Manerium cum Hundredo', *E.H.R.* xlvii (1932), 353–76; reprinted in No. 1462, and E. B. Demarest, 'The Hundred Pennies', *E.H.R.* xxxiii (1918), 62–72.

2211 ORDINANCE CONCERNING THE DUNSAETE. Liebermann, i. 374–9. Schmid, pp. 358–63. Thorpe, i. 352–7.

> An ordinance made in the tenth century, perhaps in the reign of Athelstan, by the English witan and Welsh counsellors concerning the inhabitants of the mountains of Wales. See F. Liebermann in *Archiv für das Studium der neueren Sprachen*, cii (1899), 267–96, and F. M. Stenton in *R.C.H.M.* (No. 737), *Herefordshire*, iii, pp. lviii–lix.

2212 RECTITUDINES SINGULARUM PERSONARUM. Liebermann, i. 444–53. Schmid, pp. 370–83. Thorpe, i. 432–41. Heinrich Leo, *Rectitudines singularum personarum*. Halle. 1842. A translation may be found in *Eng. Hist. Docs.* ii. 813–16, to which other statements of services in late Anglo-Saxon times are added. Also translated in Bland, Brown, and Tawney, *Eng. Econ. Docs.* (No. 1362), pp. 5–9.

> Compiled probably between 1000 and 1060, this valuable exposition of the services rendered to a lord by various classes of persons is of prime importance for evidence on the early development of the manor. See Stenton, *A.-S. Eng.* (No. 1189), pp. 465–9.

2213 TRIBAL HIDAGE. Birch (No. 2190), p. 297.

> A list, probably drawn up in Mercia in the eighth century, of territorial divisions in the Midlands under tribal names, giving a number of hides for each. See W. J. Corbett, 'The tribal hidage', *T.R.H.S.* N.S. xiv (1900), 187–230; John Brownbill, 'The tribal hidage', *E.H.R.* xxvii (1912), 625–48; and ibid. xl (1925), 497–503, where the oldest manuscript is reproduced in facsimile as it is in Hodgkin, *Anglo-Saxons* (No. 2496), ii, opposite p. 389; J. C. Russell, 'The tribal hidage', *Traditio*, v (1947), 193–209; and 'Westerna in the tribal hidage', *Notes and Queries*, cxciv (28 May 1949), 228; F. Williamson, 'The tribal hidage', ibid. cxcii (20 Sept. and 4 Oct. 1947), 398–400, 423–26. E. T. Leeds, 'The end of Mid-Anglian paganism and the tribal hidage', *Antiq. Jour.* xxxiv (1954), 195–200. Cyril J. R. Hart, 'Tribal hidage', *T.R.H.S.* 5th Ser. xxi (1971), 133–57.

(e) Studies on Anglo-Saxon charters

For the study of charters, the periodical literature is listed in Bonser, *A.-S.C.B.* (No. 12), especially pp. 13–23. The introductions to Harmer's *Writs* (No. 2197), Bishop and Chaplais (No. 2191), and Whitelock's *Wills* (No. 2205) are very valuable. See also the works on Anglo-Saxon diplomatic above, Nos. 389, 390, 394, 425. The other principal commentaries follow.

2214 BRUNNER (HEINRICH). Zur Rechtsgeschichte der römischen und germanischen Urkunde. Vol. i. Berlin. 1880. *

> *Das angelsächsische Landbuch*, pp. 149–208. Examines the structure of the charters etc.; his conclusions are open to criticism. Bresslau (No. 415) and Giry's *Manuel de diplomatique* (No. 417A) likewise need correction.

2215 CHAPLAIS (PIERRE). 'The origin and authenticity of the royal Anglo-Saxon diploma'. *Jour. Soc. Archivists*, iii (1965–6), 48–61. Idem, 'The Anglo-Saxon Chancery from the diploma to the writ'. Ibid. iii (1965–6), 160–76. Idem, 'Some early diplomas on single sheets: originals or copies'. Ibid. iii, No. 7 (1968), 315–36. Idem, 'Who introduced charters into England? The case for Augustine'. Ibid. iii, No. 10 (1969), 526–42.

2216 CRONNE (HENRY A.). 'Charter scholarship in England'. *Univ. Birmingham Hist. Jour.* viii (1961), 26–61.

2217 GALBRAITH (VIVIAN H.). 'Monastic foundation charters of the 11th and 12th centuries'. *Cambr. Hist. Jour.* iv (1934), 205–22, 296–8.

2218 LEVISON (WILHELM). 'The charters of King Ethelbert I of Kent and the descent of the Anglo-Saxon charters' in his *England and the Continent* (No. 2282), App. i, pp. 174–233.

2219 SAWYER (PETER H.). Anglo-Saxon Charters: an annotated list and bibliography. Royal Historical Society Guides and Handbooks, No. 8. Lond. 1968.

> 'This book lists the charters granting land or secular rights over land . . .' The introductory section comprises an extensive bibliography, concordances with the principal editions, and a long list of manuscripts which contain the charters mentioned in this volume. 'The first section is devoted to the charters of which reasonable full texts have survived' and lists with annotations 1,602 charters. 'The second section lists charters which have been lost or are preserved only partially' and runs to 273 items.

2220 STENTON (FRANK M.). The Latin charters of the Anglo-Saxon period. Oxf. 1955.

> An important summary in 95 pages. Other studies on Anglo-Saxon charters by Stenton are *The Early History of the Abbey of Abingdon* (Oxf. 1913); 'The supremacy of Mercian Kings', in *E.H.R.* xxxiii (1918), 433–52; 'Medeshamstede and its colonies' (above, Nos. 1455, 1496); and 'St. Frideswide and her times', *Oxoniensia*, i (1936), 103–12. Professor Stenton made extensive use of the evidence of charters in his *Anglo-Saxon England* (No. 1186). See also Eric John, 'An alleged Worcester charter of the reign of Edgar', *B.J.R.L.* xli (1958), 54–80; and Eric John, 'Some Latin charters of the tenth century reformation in England', *Rev. Bénédictine*, lxx (1960), 333–59. See also Eric John's *Land tenure* (No. 2632) and *Orbis Britanniae* (No. 1475). For reprints of Stenton's articles, see No. 1496.

2221 STEVENSON (WILLIAM H.). 'An old English charter of William the Conqueror in favour of St. Martin's-le-Grand, London, A.D. 1068'. *E.H.R.* xi (1896), 731–44. Idem, 'Yorkshire surveys and other 11th century documents in the York Gospels'. Ibid. xxvii (1912), 1–25. Idem, 'Trinoda Necessitas'. Ibid. xxix (1914), 689–703.

These are seminal articles on charters and other questions of Anglo-Saxon diplomatic. See also his notes in *Crawford Charters* (No. 2202) and his edition of Asser (No. 2147).

2. *Laws of the Celtic Areas*

(*a*) Wales

The study of old Welsh laws may be begun by reference to Sir Goronwy Edwards' lecture (No. 2232) and Lloyd's *History* (No. 1186), pp. 337–43 and 354–6; and to the *Hywel Dda Millenary Volume* (No. 2230), whose extensive bibliography need not be repeated here. Emanuel's texts (No. 2234) are the best editions of the Latin texts. The MSS. are described in H.M.C. Reports, *Report on MSS. in the Welsh Language*, 2 vols. (1898–1910).

According to the oldest manuscripts of the Welsh laws, Hywel Dda or Howel the Good, who was the ruler of virtually all of Wales from 942 to about 950, summoned an assembly in which each cantref was represented by six men. In this assembly a Welsh law-book is said to have been drawn up and subsequently promulgated by Hywel. No copy of the original code has survived; none of the existing MSS. seems to have been transcribed earlier than the late twelfth century and the extant law-books contain much matter that cannot have been included in a book promulgated by Hywel. Although incorporating much in common, the surviving law-books appear in three recensions in Welsh and in three principal Latin translations. To these recensions, Owen (No. 2222) attached the inappropriate and misleading tags: Venedotian, Dimetian, and Gwentian.

2222 ANCIENT LAWS AND INSTITUTES OF WALES: comprising laws supposed to be enacted by Howel the Good, modified by subsequent regulations under the native princes prior to the conquest by Edward I; and anomalous laws; with an English translation of the Welsh text; to which are added a few Latin transcripts containing digests of the Welsh laws, principally of the Dimetian code. Ed. by Aneurin Owen. Record Comm. 2 vols. Lond. 1841. Also published in one folio volume. 1841. This superseded the imperfect editions of William Wotton's *Leges Wallicae* (Lond. 1730), and in *Myvyrian Archaiology* (No. 1116) vol. iii (of 1st edn.), 361–437, and vol. i (of 1870 edn.), 964–1010.

Of Owen's edition vol. i includes (*a*) pp. 1–335 Venedotian Code from Peniarth MS. 29, (*b*) pp. 338–617 Dimetian Code from Cotton Titus D. IX, and (*c*) pp. 620–797 Gwentian Code from Peniarth MS. 37. Volume ii prints various 'anomalous laws', including the Latin translations.

2223 THE LAWS OF HYWEL DDA: The Black Book of Chirk. Ed. by Timothy Lewis in *Zeitschrift für celtische Philologie*, xx (1935), 30–96. Also Facsimile of the Chirk Codex of the Welsh Laws. Ed. by J. Gwenogvryn Evans. Llanbedrog, 1903. Cf. Morgan Watkin, *Nat. Lib. Wales Jour.* xiv (1966), 351–60; D. Jenkins, ibid. xv (1967), 104–7.

2224 THE LAWS OF HOWEL DDA: a facsimile reprint of Llanstephan MS. 116 in the National Library of Wales, Aberystwyth. Ed. by Timothy Lewis. Lond. 1912.

Part of the Dimetian Code, followed by excerpts and pleadings similar to 'anomalous laws'.

2225 CYFREITHIAU HYWEL DDA yn ôl Llyfr Blegywryd (Dull Dyfed) (The laws of Hywel Dda, according to the Book of Blegywryd (Dyfed version).) Ed. by Stephen J. Williams and J. E. Powell. Cardiff. 1942, and 1961.

2226 CYFREITHIAU HYWEL DDA. Ed. by Melville Richards. Cardiff. 1957. The Laws of Hywel Dda (the Book of Blegywryd). Translated by Melville Richards. Liverpool. 1954.

Mainly a Dimetian text of about 1400. Blegywyrd has been traditionally regarded as an influential member of the assembly at which the Hywel Dda code was presumably drawn up.

2227 LLYFR COLAN. Ed. by Dafydd Jenkins. Cardiff. 1963.

Jenkins edits the texts of a fragment of Cyfraith Hywel (Peniarth MS. 30); it is part of the Venedotian group and is presumably an attempt to improve upon Llyfr Iowerth, the standard law-book of thirteenth-century Gwynedd. See *E.H.R.* lxxx (1965), 380–1, and *History*, l (1965), 347–8.

2228 LLYFR IORWERTH: A critical text of the Venedotian Code . . . mainly from B.M. Cotton MS. Titus D. II. Transcribed and edited by Aled R. Wiliam. Board of Celtic Stud. Hist. and Law Ser. xviii. Cardiff. 1960.

2229 WELSH MEDIEVAL LAW, being a text of the laws of Howel the Good. Ed. with translation by Arthur W. Wade-Evans. Oxf. 1909.

The Gwentian code from B.M. Harley 4353. For the works of Wade-Evans, see H. D. Emanuel, 'The Rev. A. W. Wade-Evans: An appreciation of his contribution to early Welsh history', *Hon. Soc. Cymmrodorion Trans.* (No. 126), (1965), pp. 257–71.

2230 THE HYWEL DDA MILLENARY VOLUME. Aberystwyth Studies by member of the University College of Wales, x (1928).

These six studies by different scholars, including (pp. 151–82) a catalogue of the MSS., editions of published texts, and a bibliography of books and articles relating to Hywel Dda and his laws, are indispensable for this subject.

2231 DAVIES (R. R.). 'Twilight of Welsh laws, 1284–1536'. *History*, li (1966), 143–64. Idem, 'The survival of the blood-feud in medieval Wales'. Ibid. liv (1969), 338–57.

2232 EDWARDS (J. GORONWY). Hywel Dda and the Welsh law books. Bangor. 1929. Idem, 'The historical study of the Welsh law-books'. *T.R.H.S.* 5th ser. xii (1962), 141–55. Idem, 'The royal household and the Welsh law-books', ibid. xiii (1963), 163–76.

2233 ELLIS (THOMAS P.). Welsh tribal law and custom in the middle ages. 2 vols. Oxf. 1926. Idem, 'Hywel Dda: codifier'. *Hon. Soc. Cymmrodorion Trans.* 1928, pp. 1–69; Idem, 'The Catholic Church in the Welsh laws'. *Y Cymmrodor*, xlii (1930), 1–68. Idem, 'Mamwys: Textual references'. Ibid. xl (1929), 230–50.

2234 EMANUEL (HYWEL D.). The Latin texts of the Welsh laws. Board of Celtic Stud. Hist. and Law Ser. xxii (1967). Idem in No. 2410, pp. 73–100.

2235 LEWIS (HUBERT). Ancient laws of Wales, viewed in regard to the light they throw upon the origin of English institutions. Ed. by J. E. Lloyd. Lond. 1889.

> Elaborate but not reliable; marred by the effort to discover everywhere traces of Celtic influence.

2236 LEWIS (TIMOTHY). A glossary of mediaeval Welsh law, based on the Black Book of Chirk. Manchester. 1913.

2237 MAITLAND (FREDERIC W.). 'The laws of Wales: the kindred and the blood feud'. *Law Mag. and Review*, 4th Ser. vi (1881), 344–67. Reprinted in his Collected Papers (No. 1482), i. 202–29.

2238 PIERCE (T. JONES). 'The law of Wales: the last phase'. *Hon. Soc. Cymmrodorion Trans.* (1963), pp. 7–32. Idem, 'The laws of Wales: the hundred and the blood feud', *Univ. Birmingham Hist. Jour.* iii (1952), 119–37.

2239 THE WELSH HISTORY REVIEW. Special number. 1963. The Welsh Laws. Papers of the Colloquium on the study of the Welsh laws, held at Aberystwyth, 9–11 April 1962, and printed there, were given by Sir Goronwy Edwards, Aled R. Wiliam, Hywel D. Emanuel, T. Jones Pierce, Dafydd Jenkins, and Idris Ll. Foster.

(b) Ireland

The study of Irish law tracts should begin with Binchy's lecture (No. 2246). The lawyers who compiled these tracts formed a class of professional jurists, not judges. Written in archaic language, the tracts 'received their final redaction in the eighth century at latest'. Thereafter the texts were heavily glossed and have come down to us in late manuscripts in which it is not easy to distinguish text from gloss. Six volumes of the law tracts were published in the second half of the nineteenth century (No. 2240), but it was not until the work of Thurneysen and Binchy that satisfactory texts were established. A considerable number of tracts still await re-edition. See K. Hughes (No. 22), Chap. 2.

2240 ANCIENT LAWS OF IRELAND, published under the direction of the commissioners for publishing the ancient laws and institutes of Ireland. 6 vols. Dublin, etc. 1865–1901.

> Irish text with an English translation. The *Senchas Mar* is in vols. i–iii, the *Book of Aicill* in vol. iii, and various Brehon law-tracts in vols. iv–v. The first four volumes were edited by W. N. Hancock and A. G. Richey from transcripts made in the 1850s by John O'Donovan and Eugene O'Curry. This edition is very severely criticized and the introduction is held to be worse than useless (Binchy). Vol. v and the glossary in vol. vi were edited by Robert Atkinson; they too are deemed inadequate. See Whitley Stokes, *A criticism of Dr. Atkinson's Glossary of vols. i–v of the Ancient Laws of Ireland* (Lond. 1903). See Sheehy (No. 2261).

2241 SENCHAS MÁR: the oldest fragments of the Senchas Már. Ed. by Richard I. Best and Rudolf Thurneysen. Facsimile in collotype of Irish MSS. i. Dublin. 1931. Addenda and corrigenda in *Analecta Hibernica*, x (1941), 299–303.

From Trinity College, Dublin, MS. H. 2. 15, it is a textbook concerned chiefly with the civil law and contains much that seems to be attributable to early Irish society.

2242 (VARIOUS TEXTS). THURNEYSEN (RUDOLF). 'Aus dem irischen Recht i–v'. *Zeitschrift für celtische Philologie*, xiv–xix (1923–33). Idem, 'Coic Conara Fugill: die fünf Wege zum Urteil'. *Abhandl. Preuss. Akad. Wiss. Phil.-hist. Klasse*, 1925, No. 7. Berlin. 1926. Idem, 'Die Burgschaft im irischen Recht'. Ibid. 1928, No. 2. 1928. Idem, 'Irisches Recht'. Ibid. 1931, No. 2. 1931.

2243 CRÍTH GABLACH. Ed. by Daniel A. Binchy. Medieval and Modern Irish Series, xi. Dublin. 1941.

This work does not include a translation, but it contains a very important glossary of technical terms.

2244 CAIN ADAMNÁIN. An Old Irish treatise on the law of Adamnan. Ed. and trans. by Kuno Meyer. *Anecdota Oxoniensia*, xii. Oxf. 1905.

A composite document, the oldest section going back to the seventh century (Ryan) or eighth century (Binchy). A law of Adamnan was promulgated at the synod of Birr in 697, the first of a series designed to protect non-combatants and church property from violence. See Nos. 2246 and 2251.

2245 BOOK OF RIGHTS. Lebor na Cert: The Book of Rights. Ed. and trans. by Myles Dillon. Irish Texts Soc. xlvi. Dublin. 1962. Leabhar na g-Cert. Ed. with translation by John O'Donovan. Celtic Society. Dublin. 1847.

This work 'gives an account of the monarchs of all Ireland, and the revenues payable to them by the principal kings of the several provinces, and of the stipends paid by the monarchs to the inferior kings for their services', and similar matters. It is a compilation of antiquarian learning, drawn up probably in the eleventh century.

2246 BINCHY (DANIEL A.). 'The linguistic and historical value of the Irish law tracts'. *P.B.A.* xxix (1943), 195–227.

This is the fundamental account. See also his 'Ancient Irish Law', *Irish Jurist* (Dublin), i (1966), 84–92.

2247 BINCHY (DANIEL A.). 'Sick maintenance in Irish law'. *Ériu*, xii (1938), 78–134. Idem, 'Bretha Nemed'. Ibid. xvii (1955), 4–6. Idem, 'Irish law tracts re-edited: I. Coibnes Uisce Thairidne'. Ibid. xvii (1955), 52–85. Idem, 'The date and provenance of Uraicecht Becc'. Ibid. xviii (1958), 44–54.

2248 BINCHY (DANIEL A.). 'Secular institutions', in *Early Irish Society*, ed. by Myles Dillon (Dublin, 1954), pp. 52–65.

2249 MacNEILL (EOIN). 'Ancient Irish law. The law of status or franchise'. *Royal Irish Acad. Procs.* Sect. C. xxxvi (1923), 265–316. Idem, Early Irish laws and institutions. Dublin. 1935.

See also his *Phases of Irish History* (No. 1201) and his *Celtic Ireland* (No. 2128). Consult Eoin MacNeill, 'Ancient Laws of Ireland', ed. by J. M. Kelly with introduction and footnotes by D. A. Binchy, *The Irish Jurist*, New Ser. ii, pt. i (1967), 106–15.

2250 PLUMMER (CHARLES). 'On the fragmentary state of the text of the Brehon laws'. *Zeitschrift für celtische Philologie*, xvii (1928), 157–66.

2251 THURNEYSEN (RUDOLF), ed. Studies in early Irish law. Dublin. 1936.

A series of studies by diverse hands; some on the position of women, and one by John Ryan on the *Cain Adamnáin*.

C. CHURCH SOURCES

The comprehensive collections of ecclesiastical sources are listed on pages 144–51. The sources for the study of the Anglo-Saxon church may be classified as below. The most important collection is that by Haddan and Stubbs (No. 2254); Whitelock, in *Eng. Hist. Docs.* (No. 17), translates a considerable number, pp. 588–859, and provides a bibliography, pp. 581–3. See also Chambers (No. 1209).

The histories, laws, and charters were included on pp. 283–307. Among the histories, Bede's *Historia* is the most important; Elmham and William of Malmesbury and the monastic histories of Abingdon, Ely, Evesham, Hyde, and Ramsey are also useful, because they are based in part on earlier records no longer extant. Among the dooms of the Anglo-Saxon kings are many ecclesiastical laws, and separate collections of these were made by the witan under Edmund, Edgar, Ethelred, and Cnut. Some of the charters are grants of lands to churches: a considerable number of them are grants to thegns, who made grants to churches. The *Liber Vitae* of Winchester is entered at No. 5814 below.

Another type of source material is formed by the various lists of bishops which accompany the royal genealogies. See No. 2161, and R. I. Page, 'Anglo-Saxon episcopal lists', *Nottingham Mediaeval Stud.* ix (1965), 71–95, and x (1966), 2–24.

Four other categories of sources are considered immediately below, namely: (1) canons, penitentials, etc., (2) homilies, (3) monastic rules, and (4) the lives and letters of saints and scholars.

1. *Canons, Penitentials, etc.*

The canons and other records of the transactions of the church councils to A.D. 870 are set forth by Haddan and Stubbs (No. 2254) and those from 870 to 1066 by Wilkins and Thorpe (Nos. 1142, 2259). The penitential books as manuals for confessors are collections of Latin penitential canons issued under the authority of some eminent prelate for the purpose of establishing the uniform administration of discipline in the church; they prescribe specific penances for certain sins. The earliest penitentials, those of Ireland and Wales, belong to the fifth and sixth centuries, and were spread by Celtic and Anglo-Saxon missionaries to the Continent. They are printed in Haddan and Stubbs and in Wasserschleben, who also edits the penitential books ascribed to Theodore of Tarsus, Bede, and Egbert, Archbishop of York (d. 766).

See the works on canon law, pp. 168–70, and especially Fournier and Le Bras (No. 1305), and Kenney (No. 23); and K. Hughes (No. 22), chap. 3.

2252 BIELER (LUDWIG). The Irish penitentials, with appendix by Daniel A. Binchy. *Scriptores Latini Hiberniae*. Dublin. 1963.

2253 FINSTERWALDER (PAUL). Die Canones Theodori Cantuariensis und ihre Ueberlieferungsformen. Weimar. 1929.

2254 HADDAN (ARTHUR W.) and STUBBS (WILLIAM). Councils and ecclesiastical documents relating to Great Britain and Ireland. 3 vols. Oxf. 1869–78. Reprinted. 1965. See No. 1129.

2255 MacNEILL (JOHN T.) and GAMER (HELENA M.). Medieval handbooks of penance. A translation of the principal *libri poenitentiales* and selections from related documents. Columbia Univ. Records of Civilization, xxix. N.Y. 1938.*

> Useful for commentaries and bibliographical references. Critical review in *Speculum*, xiv (1939), 254–6. Cf. Mac Neill, 'The Celtic penitentials', *Revue Celtique*, xxxix (1922), 257–300; and xl (1923), 51–103, 320–41.

2256 NAPIER (ARTHUR S.), ed. The Old English version of the enlarged rule of Chrodegang together with the Latin original. An Old English version of the Capitula of Theodulf together with the Latin original. An interlinear Old English rendering of the Epitome of Benedict of Aniane. E.E.T.S. Old Ser. cl. 1916.

2257 SPINDLER (ROBERT). Das altenglische Bussbuch, sog. Confessionale pseudo-Egberti. Leipzig. 1934.

2258 RAITH (JOSEF), ed. Die altenglische Version des Halitgar'schen Bussbuches. Grein and Wülker, *Biblio. A.-S. Prosa* (No. 2286), xiii. 1933. 2nd edn. Darmstadt. 1964.

2259 THORPE (BENJAMIN). Ancient laws and institutes of England; also monumenta ecclesiastica. Record Comm. 2 vols. Lond. 1840. See No. 2180.

> (*a*) Penitentials of or ascribed to Theodore and Egbert: ii. 1–62, 170–239.
> (*b*) Canons enacted under King Edgar: ii. 244–89.
> (*c*) Institutes of polity: ii. 304–41.
> (*d*) Canons and epistles of Ælfric, A.D. 998–1016: ii. 342–93.
> (*e*) Ecclesiastical institutes: ii. 394–443.

> This collection is valuable, but some of the records are not well edited. Thorpe does not print the genuine texts of the penitentials, and the document called 'Ecclesiastical Institutes' is the translation of a work written by Bishop Theodulf of Orleans, who flourished about A.D. 797. See Walther von Hörmann, 'Ueber die Entstehungsverhältnisse des sogen. Poenitentiale Pseudo-Theodori' in *Mélanges Fitting* (Montpellier, 1908), ii. 1–21; and Liebermann, 'Zu Bussbüchern der lateinischen Kirche', *Zeitschrift für Rechtsgeschichte*, liv: *Kanonistische Abteilung*, x (1920), 292–301.

2260 WASSERSCHLEBEN (F. W. HERMANN). Die Bussordnungen der abendländischen Kirche. Halle. 1851.

> Old British, Irish, and Anglo-Saxon penitentials, pp. 101–352. A valuable collection, well edited. See also H. J. Schmitz, *Die Bussbücher und die Bussdisciplin der Kirche*, 2 vols. (Mainz, etc. 1883–98); 'Die Bussbücher der Angelsachsen', i. 490–587, ii. 645–701.

2261 WASSERSCHLEBEN (F. W. HERMANN), ed. Die irische Kanonen·
sammlung. Giessen. 1874. 2nd edn. Leipzig. 1885. *

> This Latin collection of canons was probably compiled in Ireland early in the eighth
> century. It contains usages of the Irish church intermingled with those of the Roman
> church. See Henry Bradshaw, *The Early Collection of Canons known as the Hibernensis*
> (Cambridge, 1893); Paul Fournier, 'De l'influence de la Collection Irlandaise sur la
> formation des Collections Canoniques', *Nouvelle Revue Historique de Droit Français et
> Étranger*, xxiii (1899), 27–78; and Mac Neill, No. 2255 above, and various articles by
> Thomas P. Oakley, cited in Bonser, *A.-S.C.B.* (No. 12), pp. 265–6. Maurice Sheehy,
> 'Influences of ancient Irish law on the *Collectio Canonum Hibernensis*'. *Procs. Third
> Congress of Canon Law* (Vatican City, 1971), pp. 31–42.

Commentaries:

For commentaries on penitentials, see J. Lahache, in *Dict. du droit canonique*
(p. 168), vi (1957), 1337–43, under 'Pénitentiels'; and G. Le Bras in *Dict. de théol.
cath.* (No. 1267), xii (1933), 1160–79, under 'Pénitentiels', and the following
books:

2262 MORTIMER (ROBERT C.). The origins of private penance in the
western church. Oxf. 1939.

2263 OAKLEY (THOMAS P.). English penitential discipline and Anglo-
Saxon law in their joint influence. N.Y. 1923. *

> Oakley published several articles between 1932 and 1940; they are listed in Bonser,
> *A.-S.C.B.* (No. 12), pp. 265–6; see particularly T. P. Oakley, 'The penitentials as
> sources for mediaeval history', *Speculum*, xv (1940), 210–23.

2264 POSCHMANN (BERNHARD). Die abendländische Kirchenbusse im
Ausgang des christlichen Altertums. Munich. 1928. Idem, Die abendländische
Kirchenbusse im frühen Mittelalter. Breslau. 1930.

2265 WATKINS (OSCAR D.). A history of penance, being a study of the
authorities. 2 vols. Lond. etc. 1920.

> A commentary with printed texts. Vol. i for the whole church to A.D. 450 and vol. ii for
> the western church from A.D. 450 to 1215.

2. *Homilies*

Homilies help to exemplify the doctrines of the church and some of them throw
light upon the social life of England during this period. Besides the Latin sermons
of Bede (No. 2297), there are four main collections written in Anglo-Saxon
during the tenth and early eleventh centuries: the Blickling Homilies, the
Vercelli Homilies, and those of Ælfric (No. 2292) and of Wulfstan (No. 2315).
For this literature, consult Anderson (No. 2349), Chaps. ix and x, to each of
which are subjoined numerous bibliographical notes; Ker's *Catalogue* (No. 977),
pp. 527–36; *C.B.E.L.* i. 63, 89–93; v. 86–8; and Greenfield, *Hist. Old English
Literature* (No. 2355).

2266 ANGELSÄCHSISCHE HOMILIEN UND HEILIGENLEBEN. Ed.
by Bruno Assmann in Grein–Wülker, *Biblio. A.-S. Prosa* (No. 2286), iii. 2nd edn.
with supplementary introduction by Peter Clemoes. Darmstadt. 1964.

2267 THE BLICKLING HOMILIES OF THE TENTH CENTURY. Ed. with a modern English translation by Richard Morris. E.E.T.S. Nos. lviii, lxiii, lxxiii. 1874–80. Reproduced in Early English MSS. in Facsimile (No. 441), x (1960), by Rudolph Willard.

'A motley collection of sermons of various age and quality.' The date of the MS., which was in the library of Blickling Hall, Norfolk, is 971; but many of the homilies seem to belong to the ninth century.

2268 DIE VERCELLI HOMILIEN, zum ersten Male herausgegeben von Max Förster in Grein–Wülker, *Biblio. A.-S. Prosa* (No. 2286), xii. Hamburg. 1932. Reproduced, Darmstadt. 1964.

Twenty-two homilies in Anglo-Saxon from a MS. at Vercelli, Italy. The MS. contains poetry intermingled with the homilies. Some of the homilies were printed earlier; but Förster's is the most complete edition. Förster also published a facsimile edition as *Il codice Vercellese con omelie e poesie in lingua Anglosassone* (Rome, 1913). For the poetry in this MS., see Nos. 2340–1, 2327 below.

3. *Monastic Rules*

By the mid tenth century monasticism had been nearly extinguished in England, possibly as much through the secularization of the church as through Viking depredation. The monastic revival, stemming from the Continent and encouraged by King Edgar, was 'the work of saints [who] made no compromise with interests which were not spiritual': Dunstan, Æthelwold, and Oswald. As the main aim was to secure uniform practice and observance based on the Rule of St. Benedict and continental customs, it was necessary to publish regulations that should secure uniformity of practice in monastic life. Such regulations were drawn up in a synod at Winchester, held about 970, and are known as *Regularis Concordia*, written in Latin. The Anglo-Saxon compilations are described in Ker's *Catalogue* (No. 977) (see his index p. 519 under 'Benedict'). The MSS. which have come down to us contain:

1. An English translation of St. Benedict's rule, probably made by Æthelwold about 970 (Nos. 2272, 2274, 2275).
2. The *Regularis Concordia*, or *De Consuetudine Monachorum* (No. 2274). Latin compilation of regulations, drawn from several sources, it is sometimes ascribed to Æthelwold, on the basis of Ælfric's vague statement; but more probably inspired by Dunstan and executed by Æthelwold and others.
3. A Latin abridgement or digest of the *Regularis Concordia*; this is in the form of a letter written by Ælfric, abbot of Eynsham, for his monastery, about 1005 (No. 2272).
4. Fragments of the *Regularis Concordia* translated into English (No. 2274).
5. The Rule of Chrodegang, bishop of Metz (742–66), based on the Benedictine rule, was designed for priests living a common and regular life. It was sometimes adopted in England (No. 2273).
6. The Benedictine Office (No. 2277) which was 'neither strictly an office nor specifically Benedictine' is entered here as part of the work of the Wulfstan–Ælfric reformers.

For monastic customaries, see *Corpus Consuetudinum Monasticarum* (No. 1146).

2269 BATESON (MARY). 'Rules for monks and secular canons after the revival under king Edgar'. *E.H.R.* ix (1894), 690–708.

An account of the MS. material.

2270 BRECK (EDWARD). Fragment of Ælfric's translation of Æthelwold's *De consuetudine monachorum.* Leipzig. 1887.

2271 EDGAR'S ESTABLISHMENT OF MONASTERIES. Ed. by Oswald Cockayne in *Leechdoms* (No. 2369), iii. 432–45. Rolls Series. Lond. 1866.

An Anglo-Saxon fragment of a postscript to Æthelwold's translation of St. Benedict's rule (No. 2275), containing a contemporary statement of the reform measures. Translated except for first folio on Augustine's mission, in *Eng. Hist. Docs.* i. 846–9.

2272 EXCERPTA EX INSTITUTIONIBUS MONASTICIS ÆTHEL-WOLDI (No. 2274), compilata in usum fratrum Egneshamnensium per Ælfricum abbatem (circa 1005). Ed. by Mary Bateson, in G. W. Kitchin's *Compotus Rolls* (No. 5812), pp. 171–98.

See *E.H.R.* ix (1894), 702–7; C. L. White, *Ælfric* (No. 2292), Chap. xii.

2273 NAPIER (ARTHUR S.), ed. The Old English version of the enlarged rule of Chrodegang together with the Latin original. An Old English version of the Capitula of Theodulf together with the Latin original. An interlinear Old English rendering of the Epitome of Benedict of Aniane. E.E.T.S. Old Ser. cl. 1916.

2274 REGULARIS CONCORDIA ANGLICAE NATIONIS MONA-CHORUM SANCTIMONIALIUMQUE. Edited and translated with introduction and notes by Dom Thomas Symons. Nelson's Medieval Classics. Lond. etc. 1953. Printed also in Reyner, *Apostolatus Benedictinorum in Anglia* (No. 1302), Appendix, 77 ff.; and reprinted therefrom in Dugdale, *Monasticon* (No. 1147), i, pp. xxvii–xlv, and in Migne, *P.L.* (No. 1135), cxxxvii. 475–502. New edition by Willem S. Logeman, 'De consuetudine monachorum', *Anglia*, xiii (1891), 365–414; xv (1893), 20–40. See No. 2272.

Cf. Knowles, *Monastic Order* (No. 1298), Chap. iii; Duckett, *St. Dunstan* (No. 2280), Chap. vii. See also Ælfric (No. 2292); T. Symons, 'The sources of the *Regularis concordia*', *Downside Rev.* lix (1941), 14–36, 143–70, 264–89; idem, 'The *Regularis concordia* and the council of Winchester', ibid. lxxx (1962), 140–56. Symons's edition is the best; Logeman's edition has an interlinear Anglo-Saxon translation.

2275 THE RULE OF ST. BENET, LATIN AND ANGLO-SAXON INTERLINEAR VERSION. Ed. by Henri Logeman. E.E.T.S. Orig. Ser. xc (1888). Also Angelsächsische Prosabearbeitungen der Benedictinerregel. Ed. by Arnold Schröer, in Grein–Wülker, *Biblio. A.-S. Prosa* (No. 2286), vol. ii. 2 pts. Cassel. 1885–8. 2nd edn. with supplementary introduction by Helmut Gneuss. Darmstadt. 1964. Die Winteney-Version der Regula S. Benedicti, lateinisch und englisch (Middle English). Ed. by Arnold Schröer. Halle, 1888.

Various versions of Æthelwold's English translation of St. Benedict's rule. See No. 2271.

2276 TUPPER (FREDERICK). 'History and texts of the Benedictine reform of the tenth century'. *Modern Language Notes*, viii (1893), 344–67.

2277 URE (JAMES), ed. The Benedictine Office: an Old English text. Edin. 1957.

'Neither an office nor specifically Benedictine, but an exposition in English, probably to be used by the secular clergy, of part of a Latin ritual.' See reviews in *Jour. Eng. Germ. Philol.* lvii (1958), 333–4, and *Speculum*, xxxiii (1958), 567–9.

4. *Lives and Letters of Saints and Scholars*
(*a*) Anglo-Saxon

For general works on hagiography, see pp. 148–51 above. Bonser, Hardy, Kenney, Potthast, and Manitius (Nos. 12, 21, 23, 62, and 56) provide references to particular persons. The articles in the French encyclopaedias (Nos. 1265–6) and in *The New Catholic Encyclopedia* (No. 1271) are useful. Some of the most valuable 'epistolae' are found in Haddan–Stubbs (No. 2254), vol. iii.

(i) *General commentaries*

Recent general commentaries, with bibliographical references, are:

2278 COLGRAVE (BERTRAM). 'The earliest saints' lives written in England'. *P.B.A.* xliv (1958), 35–60.

2279 CRAWFORD (SAMUEL J.). Anglo-Saxon influence on western Christendom, 600–800. Lond. 1933. *

2280 DUCKETT (ELEANOR S.). Anglo-Saxon saints and scholars. N.Y. 1947.* Idem, Alcuin, friend of Charlemagne, his world and his work. N.Y. 1951.* Idem, Saint Dunstan of Canterbury: a study of monastic reform in the tenth century. N.Y. 1955. Idem, Wandering saints of the early middle ages. N.Y. 1959. *

Charmingly written studies of several saints in each volume.

2281 JONES (CHARLES W.). Saints' lives and chronicles in early England. Ithaca. 1947. *

Fundamentally an analysis of the method of composition of Bede and other hagiographical writers. Includes translations (pp. 97–160) of the oldest life of Pope Gregory the Great by a monk of Whitby, and of the life of St. Guthlac of Crowland by Felix.

2282 LEVISON (WILHELM). England and the Continent in the eighth century. Oxf. 1946.

To the body of these learned Ford lectures is added (pp. 174–323) an appendix of important studies and texts on ancillary topics, such as early charters and the beginning of the year in Bede's *Historia*.

2283 ROBINSON (JOSEPH ARMITAGE). The times of Saint Dunstan. Oxf. 1923. *

(ii) *Collections of sources*

2284 ALBERTSON (CLINTON), ed. and trans. Anglo-Saxon saints and heroes. N.Y. 1967.

Lives of Cuthbert (anon.); Wilfrid by Eddius Stephanus; Guthlac by Felix; the Abbots by Bede; Ceolfrith (anon.); Willibrord by Alcuin; and Boniface by Willibald.

2285 GILES (JOHN A.), ed. Vita quorundum (Vitae quorundum) Anglo-Saxonum: original lives of Anglo-Saxons and others who lived before the conquest. Caxton Soc. Lond. 1854. *

The contents are: *Vita Waldevi comitis*; *Excerptum de familia Herewardi*; *Vita Haroldi regis*; two lives of Bede; Faricius' *Vita Aldhelmi*; Willibald's *Vita Bonifacii*; Eddi's *Vita Wilfridi*; *De inventione S. Crucis Walthamensis*; two lives of Gildas; Brithwald's *Vita Egwini Wigorniensis episcopi* (d. 717).

2286 GREIN (CHRISTIAN W. M.), ed. Bibliothek der angelsächsischen Prosa. Fortgesetzt . . . von R. P. Wulker. 13 vols. Cassel and Göttingen. 1872–1933. *

All volumes, except i, iv, vi, viii, were reprinted with supplementary introductions in the 1960s and published at Darmstadt.

2287 HORSTMANN (CARL). Nova legenda Angliae as collected by John of Tynemouth, John Capgrave, and others . . . now re-edited with fresh material. Oxf. 1901.

2288 KRUSCH (BRUNO) and LEVISON (WILHELM), eds. Passiones vitaeque sanctorum aevi Merovingici. M.G.H. *Script. Rerum Merov.* (No. 1114), vi (1913), vii (1920).

2289 RAINE (JAMES), ed. Historians of the church of York and its arch-bishops. Rolls Series. 3 vols. Lond. 1879–94. See No. 1130.

This valuable collection contains Alcuin's *Carmen* (No. 2295 below); several lives of bishops Oswald and Wilfrid (Nos. 2311, 2313); lives of Bishop John of Beverley, who died in 721; *Chronica Pontificum Ecclesiae Eboracensis*, A.D. 601–1140, written in the first half of the twelfth century; vol. iii, documents relating to the church of York, only three of them before A.D. 1066.

2290 TALBOT (CHARLES H.), ed. and trans. The Anglo-Saxon missionaries in Germany; being the lives of SS. Willibrord, Boniface, Sturm, Leoba, and Lebuin, together with the Hodoeporicon of St. Willibald, and a selection from the correspondence of St. Boniface. Lond. and N.Y. 1954.

2291 WILLELMI MALMESBIRIENSIS DE GESTIS PONTIFICUM ANGLORUM LIBRI QUINQUE. Ed. by N. E. S. A. Hamilton. Rolls Series. Lond. 1870. Also in Migne's *P.L.* clxxix, 1441–1680. Paris. 1855. An imperfect text of bks. i–iv is printed in Savile's *Scriptores* (No. 1119), 111–68. Lond. 1596. Extracts, ed. by Waitz, in M.G.H. *SS.* (No. 1114), x, 454–7, notes; ed. by Pauli, ibid. xiii, 136–9. Hanover, 1852–81.

Completed A.D. 1125; contains a valuable account of the bishops and abbots of England A.D. 601 to the writer's own time. Bk. v (which is also printed in Gale's *Scriptores XV*, 337–81, and in Wharton's *Anglia Sacra*, ii. 1–49) is devoted to the life of Aldhelm.

(iii) *Individual saints and scholars*

2292 ÆLFRIC (d. *c.* 1020). Pupil of St. Æthelwold and abbot of Eynsham; paramount scholar of the monastic revival. See No. 2293; and *Repert. Font.* ii. For Ælfric's monastic rules, see Nos. 2269–70, 2272.

(a) Homilies.

THORPE (BENJAMIN), ed. The homilies of the Anglo-Saxon church: the homilies of Ælfric, in the original Anglo-Saxon with an English version. Ælfric Soc. 2 vols. Lond. 1844–6.

ASSMANN (BRUNO), ed. Angelsächsische Homilien und Heiligenleben, Grein–Wülker (No. 2286), iii. Cassel. 1899. Reprinted, with supplementary introduction by Peter Clemoes. Darmstadt. 1964.

POPE (JOHN C.), ed. Homilies of Ælfric: A supplementary collection. Vol. i, Homilies i–xii. E.E.T.S. cclix (1967); vol. ii, Homilies xiii–xxx. E.E.T.S. cclx (1968).
Pope provides an excellent commentary.

ELIASON (NORMAN) and CLEMOES (PETER). Ælfric's first series of Catholic homilies. E.E.MSS. F. (No. 441), xiii. Copenhagen. 1966.

SKEAT (WALTER W.). Ælfric's lives of saints: being a set of sermons on saints' days. E.E.T.S. Orig. Ser. lxxvi, lxxxii, xciv, cxiv. 2 vols. in 4 pts. Lond. 1881–1900.

For brief commentary and translated sections, see D. Whitelock, *Eng. Hist. Docs.* i. 850–3. Further commentaries: D. Bethurum in *Stud. in Philol.* xxix (1932), 515–33; J. E. Cross in *Anglia*, lxxxvi (1968), 59–78; M. R. Godden in *Anglia*, lxxxvi (1968), 79–88; and especially Sisam, *Studies* (No. 2361), pp. 140–98, and Cyril L. Smetana, 'Aelfric and the early medieval homiliary', *Traditio*, xv (1959), 163–204; xvii (1961), 457–69. See also N. Ker, *Catalogue A.-S. MSS.* (No. 977), pp. 511–16 and his index under 'Homilies'.

(b) Heptateuch.

CRAWFORD (SAMUEL J.), ed. The Old English version of the Heptateuch: Ælfric's treatise on the Old and New Testament and his preface to Genesis. E.E.T.S. Orig. Ser. clx. Lond. 1922.

GREIN (CHRISTIAN W. M.), ed. Älfrik de Vetere et Novo Testamento, Grein–Wülker (No. 2286), i. Hamburg. 1921.

(c) Pastoral letters.

FEHR (BERNHARD), ed. Die Hirtenbriefe Ælfrics. . . . Grein–Wülker (No. 2286), ix. 1914. Reprinted with a supplement to the introduction by Peter Clemoes. Darmstadt. 1966.

(d) De temporibus anni.

HENEL (HEINRICH), ed. Ælfric's de temporibus anni. E.E.T.S. Orig. Ser. ccxiii. 1942. Translation in Thomas Wright, Popular treatises on science written in the Middle Ages. Lond. 1841.

(e) Hexameron.

CRAWFORD (SAMUEL J.), ed. and trans. Exameron anglice; or the Old English hexameron. Grein–Wülker (No. 2286), x, 1921.

(f) Grammar.

ZUPITZA (JULIUS), ed. Ælfrics Grammatik und Glossar, pp. 297–322. Berlin. 1880.

See also Wright–Wülker (No. 315), i. 304–36.

(g) Colloquies.

GARMONSWAY (GEORGE N.), ed. Ælfric's Colloquy. Methuen's Old English Library. Lond. 1939. 2nd edn. 1947.

THORPE (BENJAMIN), ed. Colloquium Aelfrici, in Analecta Anglo-Saxonica. Lond. 1868. pp. 18–36.

See also Wright–Wülker (No. 315), i. 89–103; and W. H. Stevenson in *Anecdota Oxoniensia, Med. and Mod. Ser.* xv (1929), 75–101.

Modern Commentaries.

(h) CLEMOES (PETER). 'The Old English Benedictine Office (C.C.C.C. MS. 190) and the relation between Ælfric and Wulfstan: a reconsideration'. *Anglia,* lxxviii (1960), 265–83. Idem, 'Chronology of Ælfric's works'. *Dickins essays* (No. 1433 *(m)*.)

(i) DU BOIS (MARGUERITE M.). Ælfric: sermonnaire, docteur et grammairien; contribution à l'étude de la vie et de l'action bénédictines en Angleterre au dixième siècle. Paris. 1943.

This work includes an extensive bibliography.

(j) GEM (SAMUEL H.). An Anglo-Saxon abbot: Ælfric of Eynsham. Edin. 1912.

(k) WHITE (CAROLINE L.). Aelfric: a new study of his life and writings. Yale Stud. in English. Boston. 1898. ★

Cf. Edward Dietrich, 'Abt Ælfric', *Zeitschrift für die historische Theologie,* xxv (1855), 487–594; xxvi (1856), 163–256.

2293 ÆTHELWOLD (d. 984). Bishop of Winchester.

(a) VITA S. ÆTHELWOLDI episcopi Wintoniensis auctore Ælfrico, *Chronicon . . . Abingdon* (No. 2153), ii. 253–66.

Translations in *Eng. Hist. Docs.* i. 832–9, and in S. H. Gem (No. 2292 *(j)*); and Nos. 2271–2).

(b) Another and longer life of Æthelwold is printed in Mabillon (No. 1151) saec. v, pp. 608–24, and in Migne, *P.L.* (No. 1135), cxxxvi, 81–108. Cf. D. J. V. Fisher, 'The early biographers of St. Ethelwold'. *E.H.R.* lxvii (1952), 381–91.

(c) DUCKETT (ELEANOR S.). Saint Dunstan of Canterbury. Lond. 1955. pp. 111–36.

(d) ROBINSON (JOSEPH ARMITAGE). The times of St. Dunstan. Oxf. 1923. pp. 104–22.

(e) KEIM (H. W.). 'Æthelwold und die Mönchreform in England'. *Anglia,* xli (1917), 405–43.

2294 ÆTHELWULF (d. c. 820). De abbatibus. Ed. by Alistair Campbell. Oxford. 1967. Also edited in Migne, *P.L.* xcvi; and in Simeon of Durham, *Opera,* Rolls Series (No. 2157), i. 265–94.

A Latin poem of early ninth century concerning an unidentified monastery subordinate to Lindisfarne. See *Repert. Font.* ii. 139–40.

2295 ALCUIN (d. 804). As historical sources for Anglo-Saxon England, the most valuable of Alcuin's works are *Epistolae, De Pontificibus et Sanctis Ecclesiae Eboracensis Carmen*, and *Vita S. Willibrordi*. The letters which relate to England (the affairs of Northumbria, devastations of the Danes, etc.) are indicated in Hardy's *Catalogue* (No. 21), i. 505 and in Smith and Wace's *Dictionary of Christian Biography* (No. 1268), i. 75. The poem *De Pontificibus* gives an account of the archbishops Wilfrid II, Egbert, and Ethelbert, which throws light upon the history of the church of York, A.D. 718-80, and contains interesting notices of the schools and library of York in the eighth century. For the life of Willibrord, see No. 2314 below. These works are printed in:

(*a*) Alcuini opera, cura Frobenii (Frobenius Forster). 2 vols. in 4. Ratisbon. 1777. (*Epistolae* in vol. i, 4-302 and *De Pontificibus* in vol. ii, 241-58.) Reprinted in Migne, *P.L.* (No. 1135), c-ci.

(*b*) Monumenta Alcuiniana. Ed. by Wilhelm Wattenbach and Ernst Dümmler, in Jaffé's *Bibliotheca Rerum Germanicarum*, vol. vi. Berlin. 1873.
Vita Alcuini auctore anonymo. 1-34.
Alcuini Vita S. Willibrordi. 35-79.
De pontificibus Ebor. carmen. 80-131.
Epistolae. 132-897.

(*c*) Epistolae Karolini Ævi. Ed. by Ernst Dümmler in M.G.H. *Epistolae*, vol. vi (No. 1114). Berlin. 1895. ii. 1-493. See Levison (No. 2282), pp. 245-6; 318-23.

(*d*) De Pontificibus . . . Ed. by Ernst Dümmler, in M.G.H. *Poetae Latini* (No. 1114). Berlin. 1881. i. 169-206. Raine, *Historians . . . York* (No. 1130), i. 349-98. Other poems deal largely with his activities in the Carolingian empire.

Modern commentaries: See Bonser, *A.-S.C.B.* esp. nos. 7057-97; *C.B.E.L.* i. 106-7; v. 93; Levison (No. 2282), pp. 148-73; *Repert. Font.* ii. 178-84.

(*e*) DUCKETT (ELEANOR S.). Alcuin, friend of Charlemagne: his world and his work. Lond. and N.Y. 1951. *

(*f*) ELLARD (G.). Alcuin, liturgist: a partner of our piety. Chicago. 1956.

(*g*) KLEINCLAUSZ (ARTHUR). Alcuin. Annales de l'université de Lyon. 3rd Ser. *Lettres*, xv. Paris. 1948.

(*h*) WALLACH (LUITPOLD). Alcuin and Charlemagne: studies in Carolingian history and literature. Cornell Studies in Classical Philology, xxxii. Ithaca. 1959. Rev. and amended edn. N.Y. and Lond. 1968.
See also Wallach's review-article in *Speculum*, xxix (1954), 820-5.

2296 ALDHELM (d. 709). Abbot of Malmesbury and first bishop of Sherborne, with a reputation for learning.

(*a*) Opera. Ed. by Rudolf Ehwald in M.G.H (No. 1114), *Auctores Antiq.* vol. xv. 1919. By Giles, *Patres* (No. 1102). Reprinted in Migne, *P.L.* (No. 1135), lxxxix. (Includes about fourteen letters and *Vita Aldhelmi* by Faricius, abbot of Abingdon, who died in 1117.)

(b) Vita Aldhelmi by William of Malmesbury in Hamilton's edition of *Gesta Pontificum* (No. 2291), pp. 330–443.

Modern commentaries: Bonser, nos. 3911–34; *C.B.E.L.* i. 103; v. 93; Duckett, *A.-S. Saints* (No. 2280), 3–97. *Repert. Font.* ii. 185.

(c) BÖNHOFF (LEO). Aldhelm von Malmesbury: ein Beitrag zur Kirchengeschichte. Dresden. 1894.

(d) BROWNE (GEORGE F.). St. Aldhelm: his life and times. Lond. 1903.

(e) COOK (ALBERT S.). 'Sources for the biography of Aldhelm'. *Trans. Connecticut Acad. of Arts and Sciences*, xxviii (1927), 273–93.

(f) JAMES (MONTAGUE R.). Two ancient English scholars: St. Aldhelm and William of Malmesbury. Glasgow. 1939.

2297   BEDE (d. 735).

Besides his *Ecclesiastical History* (above, No. 2148), Bede composed manuals on orthography, verse forms, chronology, cosmography and other scientific subjects, homilies, numerous commentaries on the scriptures, lives of saints, biographies of abbots of Wearmouth and Jarrow, and letters. He enumerates his writings at the end of the *Ecclesiastical History*, Chap. xxiv. A modern list of most of the surviving MSS. of Bede's genuine works is given in *A hand-list of Bede's manuscripts* by Max L. W. Laistner in collaboration with Henry H. King (Ithaca and London, 1943); on which see H. S. Prestre in *Scriptorium*, vi (1952), 287–93; ibid. xvii (1963), 110–13; C. H. Beeson in *Classical Philology*, xlii (1947), 73–87, and especially N. R. Ker in *Medium Ævum*, xiii (1944), 35–40. For some spurious attributions, see Charles W. Jones, *Bedae Pseudepigrapha: scientific writings falsely attributed to Bede* (Ithaca, 1939). Consult W. F. Bolton, 'A Bede bibliography 1935–1960', *Traditio*, xviii (1962), 436–45; and *Repert. Font.* ii. 469–73.

Except for his historiographical work, satisfactory critical editions were not produced until the mid twentieth century. Modern critical editions are: *Bedae Venerabilis Expositio Actuum Apostolorum et Retractatio*, ed. by Max L. W. Laistner (Cambridge, Mass. 1939); *Bedae Opera de Temporibus*, ed. by Charles W. Jones (Cambridge, Mass. 1943), the introduction to which provides a notable discussion of the evolution of Easter reckoning; and *Bedae Venerabilis Opera: Opera Homiletica et Rhythmica* (Corpus Christianorum, series Latina, vol. cxxii, pts. iii and iv) (Turnholt, 1955) and *Opera Exegetica* (ibid. cxix (1962)); cxx (1960). Cf. Wilhelm Levison, 'Modern editions of Bede', *Durham Univ. Jour.* xxxvii (1945), 78–85.

The works of particular interest to students of English history are:

1. *Ecclesiastical History* (No. 2148).

2. Biographies, in prose and verse, of St. Cuthbert: Giles, iv. 202–357; Stevenson, pp. 45–137; W. Jaager, *Bedas Metrische Vita Sancti Cuthberti* (Leipzig, 1935). The definitive edition of the prose life is by Colgrave (No. 2302).

3. *Vita Abbatum*, a history of abbots of Wearmouth and Jarrow: Giles, iv. 358–401; Stevenson, pp. 139–62; Plummer, i. 364–87.

4. Letters: Giles, i. 106–216; Migne (No. 1135), xciv. 655–710. The most important of the letters is *Epistola ad Egbertum*, written in 734, a lament over the degenerate condition of the church; Giles, i. 108–43; Stevenson, 207–26; Plummer (2148 (*b*)), i. 405–23; Haddan and Stubbs (No. 1129), iii. 314–25. The letter to Egbert is translated in *Eng. Hist. Docs.* i. 735–45.

(*a*) GILES (JOHN A.), ed. The works of Bede, with a translation of the historical works. Patres Ecclesiae (No. 1102). 12 vols. Lond. 1843–4. See also No. 1101.

vol. i.	Letters, etc.	vol. v.	Homilies.
vol. ii–iii.	*Historia Ecclesiastica.*	vol. vi.	Scientific tracts.
vol. iv	Historical tracts.	vol. vii–viii.	Commentaries on scriptures.

(*b*) STEVENSON (JOSEPH), ed. Venerabilis Bedae Opera historica minora. English Hist. Soc. Lond. 1841.

Contains Bede's metrical and prose lives of Cuthbert, his *Vita Abbatum, Chronicon,* and *Epistola ad Egbertum.* The best editions of Bede's *Chronica Majora ad annum 725* and *Chronica Minora ad annum 703* are by Theodor Mommsen in M.G.H. *Auctores Antiq.* (No. 1114) xiii (1895), 223–354.

(*c*) THOMPSON (ALEXANDER HAMILTON), ed. Bede, his life, times and writings. Oxf. 1935.*

Nine essays by various hands, in commemoration of the twelfth centenary of Bede's death. An older work is still useful: Karl Werner, *Beda der Ehrwürdige und seine Zeit* (Vienna, 1875; new edn. 1881). Numerous books and essays on Bede are listed in Bonser (No. 12); Whitelock (No. 17); *C.B.E.L.* i. 86–7 and v. 83, 93; Manitius (No. 56), i. 70–87. Two excellent essays are Duckett, *Anglo-Saxon Saints* (No. 2280), pp. 217–336; and R. W. Chambers, 'Bede' in *P.B.A.* xxii (1936), 129–56.

2298 BIRINUS (d. 649 or 650). FIELD (JOHN E.). St. Berin, the apostle of Wessex: the history, legends and traditions of the beginning of the West Saxon church. Lond. 1902.

Discusses primary sources. Cf. Hardy, *Catalogue* (No. 21), i. 235–9.

2299 BONIFACE (d. 754) or Winfrid, the apostle of Germany. His letters, some of which are addressed to English kings and prelates, throw much light on the manners and opinions of the eighth century. The most valuable life of Boniface was written by Willibald (d. 786), another Englishman who aided in his missionary work.

(*a*) Monumenta Moguntina, in Jaffe's *Bibliotheca rerum Germanicarum*, vol. iii. Berlin. 1866.

S. Bonifatii et Lulli *Epistolae*, 8–315.
Willibaldi *Vita S. Bonifatii*, 429–71.

(*b*) Sancti Bonifacii opera omnia. Ed. by Giles in *Patres* (No. 1102). 2 vols. Lond. 1844.

Vol. i. *Epistolae.*
Vol. ii. Homilies, Willibald's *Vita*, etc.
Also printed in Migne, *P.L.* (No. 1135), lxxxix, 597–892.

(*c*) S. Bonifatii et Lulli Epistolae. Ed. by Ernst Dümmler in M.G.H. (No. 1114), *Epistolae*, iii, 215–433. Die Briefe der heiligen Bonifatius und Lullus, by

Michael Tangl. *Epistolae selectae in usum scholarum ex M.G.H. separatim editae*, i. Berlin. 1916.

Translations: *The English correspondence of Saint Boniface*, by Edward Kylie (Lond. 1911; reprinted 1924). *The letters of Saint Boniface*. Trans. with an introduction by Ephraim Emerton. Columbia Univ. Records of Civilization, xxxi (N.Y. 1940). C. H. Talbot, *The Anglo-Saxon Missionaries in Germany*. The Makers of Christendom series (Lond. and N.Y. 1954), pp. 65–149, gives a selection of Boniface's letters.

(*d*) Vitae Sancti Bonifatii Archiepiscopi Moguntini. Ed. by Wilhelm Levison. *Scriptores rerum Germanicarum in usum scholarum.* Hanover. 1905.

Translation: see Albertson (No. 2284). George W. Robinson, *The Life of St. Boniface by Willibald* (Cambr. (Mass.), 1916). C. H. Talbot, op. cit., pp. 25–62.

Modern commentaries: Bonser, *A.-S.C.B.*, nos. 5266–5362; Kenney (No. 23), pp. 519–21 and index; Levison, *England and the continent* (No. 2282), pp. 70–93; Duckett, *A.-S. Saints* (No. 2280), pp. 339–459. The bibliography for Boniface is extensive; the older works are cited in Potthast's *Bibliotheca* (No. 62), ii. 1217–20, and the commemoration of his death in 1954 produced a spate of works which are noticed in *R.H.E.* (No. 166) for 1954 and following years. Cf. *Repert. Font.* ii. 558–9.

(*e*) COENS (MAURICE). 'S. Boniface et sa mission historique d'après quelques auteurs récents'. *Analecta Bollandiana*, lxxiii (1955), 462–95.

(*f*) GREENAWAY (GEORGE W.). Saint Boniface. Lond. 1955.

(*g*) HAUCK (ALBERT). Kirchengeschichte Deutschlands. 5 vols. Leipzig. 1906–20. Reprinted, 1922–9. On Boniface, see especially, i (1922), 418–52. Other editions of individual volumes, 1887–1920.

(*h*) Sankt Bonifatius. Gedenkgabe zum zwölfhundertsten Todestag. Herausgegeben von der Stadt Fulda in Verbindung mit den Diözesen Fulda und Mainz. Fulda. 1954.

(*i*) SCHIEFFER (THEODOR). Winfrid-Bonifatius und die christliche Grundlegung Europas. Freiburg. 1954.

2300   BREGWINE (d. 764). 'Eadmer's life of Bregwine, archbishop of Canterbury, 761–764'. Ed. by Bernhard W. Scholz. *Traditio*, xxii (1966), 127–48.

2301   CEOLFRITH (d. 716). Abbot of Wearmouth and Jarrow, who took to the Continent the Codex Amiatinus, the oldest extant MS. of the Vulgate.

(*a*) The Life of Ceolfrith is Historia Abbatum auctore anonymo, printed with Bede's works by Plummer (No. 2148), i. 388–404. It was written by a Wearmouth monk between 717 and 725. See Colgrave, *Earliest Saints' Lives* (No. 2278), pp. 58–9, and a translation in *Eng. Hist. Docs.* i. 697–708; and Albertson (No. 2284).

(*b*) The life of Ceolfrid . . . by an unknown writer of the eighth century. Trans. by Douglas S. Boutflower. (Includes an article on the Codex Amiatinus by J. L. Low.) Sunderland. 1912.

(*c*) HOWORTH (HENRY H.). 'The Codex Amiatinus: its history and importance'. *Archaeol. Jour.* lxxii (1925), 49–68.

2302 CUTHBERT (d. 687). Abbot, then bishop of Lindisfarne. His body was eventually (999) entombed in Durham Cathedral.

Bede's prose *Vita S. Cuthberti* (No. 2297) is one of the best pieces of medieval biography which we possess. It is based in part on an older anonymous life of Cuthbert (*b*) below, 'the earliest of the Saints' Lives to be written in England'. Bede's metrical *Life* has little value as a historical source. The *Historia translationum S. Cuthberti* (*e*) below, probably written in the twelfth century, deals with the translations of his body and with the history of the church of Durham from *c.* 875 to 1080.

The following two works are valuable for the ecclesiastical history of Durham, but contain little information concerning Cuthbert's life:

1. Historia de S. Cuthberto, in J. H. Hinde, *Symeonis Dunelmensis Opera*. Surtees Soc. (1868), i. 138–52. In Thomas Arnold, *Symeonis Monachi Opera*. Rolls Series (1882), i. 196–214. Compiled seemingly about 1050. Cf. No. 2157 (*c*).

2. Reginaldi Monachi Dunelmensis Libellus de Admirandis Beati Cuthberti Virtutibus. Ed. by James Raine. Surtees Soc. (1835). Written in the second half of the twelfth century by Reginald of Coldingham. It contains some interesting notices of manners and public affairs, especially in the time of King Stephen and Henry II.

Three lives of Cuthbert, of little historical value, were published by the Surtees Society: two in *Miscellanea Biographica*, by James Raine (1838), and *The Life of St. Cuthbert in English Verse, circa 1450*, by J. T. Fowler (1891).

(*a*) Two lives of St. Cuthbert: a life by an anonymous monk of Lindisfarne and, Bede's prose life. Texts, translation, and notes by Bertram Colgrave. Cambr. 1940. (The definitive edition.)

(*b*) Vita S. Cuthberti auctore anonymo. Ed. by Stevenson in Bede's *Opera* (No. 2297), 259–84. Trans. by W. Forbes-Leith, *The Life of St. Cuthbert*, written anonymously about A.D. 700. Edin. 1888.

(*c*) Vita S. Cuthberti auctore Beda. Ed. by Giles (No. 2297 (*a*)), iv. 202–357; and by Stevenson (No. 2297 (*b*)), 45–137.

(*d*) Bedas metrische Vita sancti Cuthberti, by Werner Jaager. *Palaestra*, cxcviii. Leipzig. 1935.

(*e*) Historia translationum S. Cuthberti, by J. H. Hinde, *Symeonis Dunelmensis Opera* (No. 2157), i. 158–201. Stevenson's text in Bede's *Opera* (No. 2297), pp. 285–317, is imperfect.

(*f*) The relics of Saint Cuthbert: Studies by various authors collected and edited with a historical introduction by C. F. Battiscombe. Oxf. 1956.

Modern commentaries: Bonser, *A.-S.C.B.* nos. 4280–4325.

(*g*) EYRE (CHARLES). The history of St. Cuthbert, or an account of his life, decease, and miracles; of the wandering of his body at intervals during 124 years, etc. Lond. 1849. 3rd edn. 1887.

(*h*) RAINE (JAMES). Saint Cuthbert, with an account of the state in which his remains were found . . . in 1827. Durham. 1828.

See B. Colgrave in *Chadwick essays* (No. 1429).

2303 DUNSTAN (d. 988). Except for a vernacular letter which is translated in *Eng. Hist. Docs.* i. 822–3, virtually no literary remains of the great archbishop survive. The most valuable biography was written by a contemporary priest who calls himself B. The best modern commentaries are by Stubbs in the introduction to (*a*) below, which is reprinted in No. 4041; by Robinson (No. 2283); and by Duckett (No. 2280).

(*a*) Memorials of St. Dunstan. Ed. by William Stubbs. Rolls Series. Lond. 1874.

This collection of materials contains:

1. Vita S. Dunstani auctore B. Written *c.* 1000 by a Saxon priest, perhaps at Canterbury.
2. Epistola Adelardi ad Elfegum archiepiscopum de Vita S. Dunstani. Written 1006–11 by a monk of Saint Peter's Abbey, Ghent.
3. Vita S. Dunstani auctore Osberno. Written *c.* 1090; relates miracles of Dunstan, with many mistakes and fabrications. The author was precentor of Christ Church, Canterbury.
4. Vita S. Dunstani auctore Eadmero. Written 1109–22, by precentor of Christ Church, Canterbury.
5. Vita S. Dunstani auctore Willelmo Mamlesberiensi. Written *c.* 1126; criticizes Osbern's *Vita*.
6. Vita S. Dunstani. Compiled early in the fifteenth century by John Capgrave; of little value.
7. Epistolae ad Dunstanum, and other letters of his time.
8. Fragmenta Ritualia de Dunstano.

Stubbs in his valuable introduction gives a full account of the various biographers and an excellent sketch of Dunstan's career. This collection is supplemented by the Dunstan Saga, ed. by G. Vigfússon, with a trans. by G. W. Dasent, in *Icelandic Sagas*, Rolls Series (1887–94), ii. 385–408; iv. 397–420. It was written early in the fourteenth century by Arne Lawrence's son, a monk of Thingore. See Lenore Harty, 'The Icelandic life of St. Dunstan', *Saga Book of the Viking Soc.* xv (1961), 263–93. Thomas Symons, 'Notes on the life and work of St. Dunstan', *Downside Rev.* lxxx (1962), 250–61, 355–66.

(*b*) A facsimile of St. Dunstan's class-book from Glastonbury. Ed. by Richard W. Hunt, in Umbrae Codicum Occidentalium, vol. iv. Amsterdam. 1961.

2304 EDITH OF WILTON (d. 984).

(*a*) WILMART (ANDRÉ). 'La légende de Ste Édith en prose et vers par le moine Goscelin'. *Anal. Boll.* lvi (1938), 5–101.

For Goscelin, who wrote *c.* 1080, see Wilmart in *Revue bénédictine*, xlvi (1934), 414–38; and l (1938), 42–83; Frank Barlow, *Life of King Edward* (No. 2171), pp. 91–111; C. H. Talbot, 'The Liber confortatorius of Goscelin of St. Bertin', *Studia Anselmiana* (Rome), xxxvii (1955), 1–117.

(*b*) CHRONICON VILODUNENSE SIVE DE VITA ET MIRACULIS S. EDITHAE, regis Edgari filiae, carmen vetus Anglicum, cura W. H. Black, sumptibus R. C. Hoare. Lond. 1830. S. EDITHA SIVE CHRONICON VILODUNENSE. Ed. by Carl Hortsmann. Heilbronn. 1883.

This work, written *c.* 1430, contains an account of the history of Wilton abbey and of the miracles of St. Edith.

2305 EDMUND (d. 870). King of East Anglia 855–70. The oldest life of Edmund, the martyred king of East Anglia, was written in England by Abbo of

Fleury about 985. The various lives of Edmund are listed in Hardy's *Catalogue*, i. 526–38, and in Loomis; most of them are printed in Arnold's *Memorials*.

(*a*) Memorials of St. Edmund's abbey. Ed. by Thomas Arnold. Rolls Series. 3 vols. Lond. 1890–6.

> Contains the work of Abbo of Fleury, i. 3–25; miracles of St. Edmund, by Herman the archdeacon, i. 26–92, of which there is a good edition in Liebermann (No. 1095), 203–81; lives by Galfridus de Fontibus, and Abbot Samson, i. 93–209; *La Vie Seint Edmund le rey* by Denis Piramus, of which the best edition is by Hilding Kjellman (Göteborg, 1935).
>
> Ælfric's *Lives of the Saints* (No. 2292) includes an Old English life of St. Edmund, based on Abbo. For the French lives, see M. D. Legge, *Anglo-Norman in the Cloisters* (No. 293), pp. 6–9 and *passim*; and M. E. Porter and J. H. Baltzell, 'The Old French lives of Saint Edmund, king of East Anglia', *Romanic Rev.* xlv (1954), 81–8.

(*b*) HERVEY (LORD FRANCIS), ed. Corolla S. Edmundi; the garland of St. Edmund, king and martyr. Lond. 1907 (extracts from chroniclers, lives of Edmund, and other sources, with translations). Idem, The history of King Eadmund the martyr and the early years of his abbey. Lond. 1929. (The A.-S. text of 4 leaves concerning the eleventh-century possessions of the abbey rather than the saint.) See Ker, *Catalogue* (No. 977), pp. 430–1.

(*c*) LOOMIS (GRANT). 'The growth of the Saint Eadmund legend'. *Harvard Studies . . . in Philol. and Lit.* iv (1932), 83–113. (A scholarly summary.)

2306 ELPHEGE or ÆLFHEAH (d. 1012). Vita S. Elphegi archiepiscopi Cantuariensis auctore Osberno monacho Cantuariensi. Ed. by H. Wharton, *Anglia Sacra* (No. 1125), ii (1691), 122–42; by Langebek, *Scriptores* (No. 1106), ii. 439–63; by Migne, *P.L.* (No. 1135), cxlix (1853), 371–94.

> Written about 1080. Contains some particulars regarding the Danes in England.

2307 ÆTHELBERT (d. *c.* 793). King of East Anglia and martyr.

(*a*) JAMES (M. R.). 'Two lives of St. Ethelbert, king and martyr'. *E.H.R.* xxxii (1917), 214–44. (Prints text of life by Giraldus Cambrensis and of *Passio sancti Æthelberhti* in C.C.C.C. MS. 308.)

2308 GREGORY I (Pope 590–604).

(*a*) The earliest life of Gregory the Great by an anonymous monk of Whitby. Ed. and trans. by Bertram Colgrave. Lawrence (Kans.). 1968. Another edition as, A life of Pope St. Gregory the Great, written by a monk of Whitby. Ed. by Francis A. Gasquet. Westminster. 1904.

> The Latin text of the earliest extant life of Gregory. Paul Ewald discovered it in a St. Gall MS. and published extracts in *Historische Aufsätze dem Andenken an Georg Waitz gewidmet* (Hanover, 1866), 17–54. It is translated by C. W. Jones in *Saints' Lives* (No. 2281), pp. 97–121. For other lives of Gregory, see Potthast (No. 62), ii. 1349. Colgrave's edition is the best edition and the best translation.

(*b*) Gregorii Magni Registrum epistolarum. Ed. by Paul Ewald and L. M. Hartmann in M.G.H. *Epistolae* (No. 1114), vols. i–ii. 2 vols. in 3 pts. Berlin. 1887–99. Also in Migne, *P.L.* (No. 1135), lxxvii. 441–1460.

> For older editions, see Potthast (No. 62), i. 539–40. The letters written to Augustine, Mellitus, King Æthelbert, and others are valuable for the study of the introduction of Christianity into England. They are reprinted in Haddan and Stubbs (No. 1129), iii.

5–38, and in Stevenson's *Bedae Opera* (No. 2297), pp. 230–52. The text of those which relate to Augustine's mission is given, with a translation, in Mason's *Mission* (No. 2704). M. Deanesly and P. Grosjean, 'The Canterbury edition of the answers of Pope Gregory I, the Great, to St. Augustine', *J.E.H.* x (1959), 1–49; and the criticism of this article by Paul Meyvaert, 'Les "Responsiones" de St. Grégoire le Grand à St. Augustin de Cantorbéry', *R.H.É.* liv (1959), 879–94. See No. 2704.

(*c*) BRECHTER (HEINRICH SUSO). Die Quellen zur Angelsachsenmission Gregors des Grossen: eine historiographische Studie. *Beiträge z. Gesch. d. alten Mönchtums u. d. Benediktinerordens,* fasc. xxii. Munster. 1941.

2309 GRIMBALD OF ST. BERTIN (d. *c.* 901–3).

(*a*) GRIERSON (PHILIP). 'Grimbald of St. Bertin'. *E.H.R.* lv (1940), 529–61.

Analyses the two lives of, and other references to, St. Grimbald, apart from Asser, the most famous of the scholars who came to England in the reign of Alfred.

(*b*) BATELY (JANET M.). 'Grimbald of St. Bertin's'. *Medium Ævum,* xxxv (1966), 1–10.

2310 GUTHLAC (d. 714). Hermit of Crowland.

(*a*) Felix's life of St. Guthlac. Ed. by Bertram Colgrave. Cambr. 1956 (the critical edn. of text, trans., and introduction). Also Vita S. Guthlaci auctore Felice. Ed. by W. de Gray Birch, *Memorials of St. Guthlac of Crowland.* Wisbech. 1881. pp. 1–64. Trans. in Jones (No. 2281), pp. 123–60; *Eng. Hist. Docs.* i. 708–13; and Albertson (No. 2284). W. F. Bolton, 'The Latin revisions of Felix's Vita Sancti Guthlaci'. *Mediaeval Studies* (Toronto), xxi (1959), 36–52. See also M. Chibnall, *Orderic Vitalis* (No. 2937), ii. 323–39.

(*b*) Das angelsächsische Prosa-Leben des heiligen Guthlacs. Ed. by Paul Gonser. *Anglistische Forschungen,* xxvii. Heidelberg. 1909. Also the Anglo-Saxon version of the life of St. Guthlac, originally written by Felix of Crowland. Ed. with a trans. by C. W. Goodwin. Lond. 1848.

(*c*) The Anglo-Saxon poem on Guthlac is found in the *Exeter Book,* of which a complete photographic facsimile is given in the *Exeter Book of Old English Poetry,* with introductory chapters by R. W. Chambers, Max Förster, and Robin Flower (Lond. 1933). The text is printed in the *Exeter Book.* Ed. by George P. Krapp and Elliott Dobbie. (*The Anglo-Saxon Poetic Records,* iii.) N.Y. 1936; where other editions are cited on page xc. Cf. Ker, *Catalogue* (No. 977), p. 153. For modern commentary, with bibliography, see F. Olivero, 'Sul poemetto anglosassone Guthlac', *Memorie della Reale Accademia delle Scienze di Torino,* Ser. 2, lxx (1942), 223–65.

(*d*) The Guthlac roll: scenes from the life of St. Guthlac of Crowland by a twelfth-century artist reproduced from Harley roll Y. 6 in the British Museum, with introduction by Sir George Warner. Roxburghe Club. Oxf. 1928. Includes 25 plates.

2311 OSWALD (d. 992). Vita Oswaldi archiepiscopi Eboracensis auctore anonymo. Ed. by James Raine, *Historians of the Church of York* (No. 1130), i. 399–475.

Written by a monk of Ramsey between 995 and 1005. By far the best account of Oswald's life; of great value for the reigns of Edgar and Ethelred; contains notices of public affairs, and throws light on the monastic reformation. This work also gives the best account of Odo, archbishop of Canterbury (d. 958). Raine, in his *Historians of the Church of York*, vol. ii, also prints lives of Oswald by Eadmer, by Prior Senatus of Worcester, and by Capgrave. The last two are of little value, and Eadmer derives much of his material from the monk of Ramsey.

(b) ROBINSON (JOSEPH A.). St. Oswald and the church of Worcester. Brit. Acad. Supplemental Papers, v. Lond. 1919. See note in *Eng. Hist. Docs.* i. 839, where a portion is translated on pp. 839–43; and Duckett, *St. Dunstan* (No. 2280), Chap. vi, and pp. 237–8.

2312   SWITHUN (d. 862). Bp. of Winchester.

(a) Sancti Swithuni, episcopi translatio et miracula. Ed. by E. P. Sauvage in *Anal. Boll.* iv (1885), 367–410. (The work of Lantfred, monk of Winchester, written not later than 1006.)

(b) Vita Sancti Swithuni, Wintoniensis episcopi. Ed. by E. P. Sauvage, in *Anal. Boll.* vii (1888), 373–80. Formerly attributed to Goscelin. See Barlow, *Vita Aedwardi* (No. 2171), p. 111.

(c) Wulfstani cantoris. Narratio metrica de Sancto Swithuno. Ed. by Alistair Campbell in *Breviloquium . . . Wilfredi* (No. 2313 (b) below), pp. 63–183. (The work of Wulfstan, monk of St. Swithun's, Winchester, in early eleventh century.)

(d) EARLE, JOHN. Gloucester fragments: facsimiles of some [three] leaves in Saxon writing on St. Swithun . . . Lond. 1861. (Includes an essay on life and times, pp. 21–56; the life attributed to Goscelin and two other lives of St. Swithun, pp. 67–81.) These leaves are fragments of Ælfric's life of St. Swithun in Ælfric's *Lives of Saints*, ed. by Skeat, i. 440–71.

2313   WILFRID (d. 709). Bp. of York.

(a) The life of Bishop Wilfred by Eddius Stephanus; text, trans., and notes by Bertram Colgrave. Cambr. 1927. Vita Wilfridi I episcopi Eboracensis. Ed. by Wilhelm Levison in M.G.H. *Script. Rerum Merov.* (No. 1114), vi. 163–263. Hanover. 1913. Also ed. in Raine, *Historians . . . York* (No. 1130), i. 1–103; and in Gale, *Scriptores XV* (No. 1100), pp. 40–90.

Written at Ripon soon after 710. Displays much partisan zeal in favour of Wilfrid in his appeals to Rome against archbishops of Canterbury, but the work is of considerable interest because it was used by Bede and because it is one of the earliest literary productions of England which includes material not found elsewhere.

(b) Frithegodi monachi Breviloquium vitae beati Wilfredi, et Wulfstani cantoris Narratio metrica de sancto Swithuno. Ed. by Alistair Campbell. Thesaurus Mundi. Zürich. 1950. For criticism of this edition, see D. C. C. Young in *Bull. Du Cange*, xxv (1955), 71–98. Also ed. by Raine, op. cit. i. 105–59. A metrical life by Frithegode of Canterbury, written about the middle of the tenth century and derived mainly from Eddi.

(c) Vita Wilfridi by Eadmer of Canterbury (d. 1124). Ed. in Raine, op. cit. i. 227–37.

Eadmer's Life is based on Eddi and Frithegode. Raine also prints three later Lives of Wilfrid which have little historical value.

Modern Commentaries:

Duckett, *A-S. Saints* (No. 2280), pp. 101–214.

R. L. Poole, 'St. Wilfrid and the see of Ripon', *E.H.R.* xxxiv (1919), 1–24.

2314 WILLIBRORD (d. 739). Apostle of Frisia.

(*a*) Alcuini Vita S. Willibrordi archiepiscopi Traiectensis. Ed. by Wilhelm Levison. M.G.H. *Script. Rerum Merov.* vii (1920), 81–141. Also edited in *Acta Sanctorum* (No. 1152), iii (1910), 435–57. Trans. in Alexander Grieve's *Willibrord, missionary in the Netherlands.* S.P.C.K. Lond. 1923; and in C. H. Talbot (No. 2290), pp. 3–22.

(*b*) Miracula. Ed. by W. Levison. M.G.H. *SS.* xxx, pt. ii (1934), 1368–71.

(*c*) The calendar of St. Willibrord . . . a facsimile and transcription, introduction and notes, by H. A. Wilson. Henry Bradshaw Soc. lv. Lond. 1918.

Modern Commentaries: See Levison (No. 2282), Duckett's *Alcuin* (No. 2295 (*e*)), and Bonser, *A.-S.C.B.* pp. 262–3.

(*d*) LEVISON (WILHELM). St. Willibrord and his place in history. *Durham Univ. Jour.* xxxii (1940), 23–41.

(*e*) VERBIST (GABRIEL H.). Saint Willibrord, apôtre des Pays-Bas et fondateur d'Echternach. Louvain. 1939.

(*f*) WAMPACH (CAMILLE). Sankt Willibrord, sein Leben und Lebenswerk. Luxemburg. 1953.

A popular work without critical apparatus by a recognized authority.

2315 WULFSTAN II, Archbp. of York (d. 1023). The Homilist.

The homilist should not be confused with Wulfstan I, archbp. of York (d. 956), or with Wulfstan III, bp. of Worcester (d. 1095) below. For Wulfstan II's connection with the legislation of Anglo-Saxon kings, see above, p. 301.

(*a*) Wulfstan: Sammlung der ihm zugeschriebenen Homilien nebst Untersuchungen über ihre Echtheit. Ed. by Arthur Napier. *Sammlung englisches Denkmäler,* vol. iv. Berlin. 1883. Dorothy Bethurum. *Homilies of Wulfstan.* Lond. 1957. (The best annotated edition, with a study of his career.)

(*b*) Sermo lupi ad Anglos. Ed. by Dorothy Whitelock. Methuen's Old English Library. Lond. 1939. 2nd edn. 1952. 3rd edn. 1963.

Wulfstan's best-known homily, written about 1014, giving a vivid picture of the wretchedness and corruption due to the ravages of the Danes. Another edn. in Napier's *Sammlung,* pp. 156–67; and other edns. and translations cited in Whitelock's edn. See also *Eng. Hist. Docs.* i. 855–9.

(*c*) Die 'Institutes of polity, civil and ecclesiastical': ein Werk Erzbischof Wulfstans von York. Ed. by Karl Jost. Berne. 1959.

See review by D. Whitelock in *Rev. Eng. Stud.* xii (1961), 61–6.

(*d*) BETHURUM (DOROTHY). 'Archbishop Wulfstan's commonplace book'. *P.M.L.A.* lvii (1942), 916–29.

(*e*) JOST (KARL). Wulfstanstudien. Schweizer anglistische Arbeiten, xxiii. Berne. 1950.

(*f*) WHITBREAD (L.). 'Wulfstan Homilies xxix, xxx and some related texts'. *Anglia*, lxxxi (1963), 347–64.

(*g*) WHITELOCK (DOROTHY). 'Archbishop Wulfstan, homilist and statesman'. *T.R.H.S.* 4th ser. xxiv (1942), 25–45. Idem, 'Wulfstan at York' in *Franciplegius: Medieval and modern studies in honor of Francis Peabody Magoun, Jr.*, ed. by J. B. Bessinger and R. P. Creed. N.Y. 1965. pp. 216–31.

2316   WULFSTAN III (d. 1095). Bp. of Worcester 1062–95. See No. 5843.

(*a*) The Vita Wulfstani of William of Malmesbury: to which are added the extant abridgements of this work and the miracles and translation of St. Wulfstan. Ed. by Reginald R. Darlington. Camden Soc. 3rd ser. xl. Lond. 1928.

> The first complete edn. with a valuable introduction. William of Malmesbury's life is a Latin translation of an A.-S. biography of Wulfstan by his chaplain and chancellor, Coleman. Coleman's life has been lost. For English translation of Malmesbury's life, see *Life of St. Wulfstan* . . . rendered into English by James H. F. Peile (Oxf. 1934).

(*b*) LAMB (JOHN W.). Saint Wulfstan, prelate and patriot: a study of his life and times. Lond. 1933.

2317   WULSIN OF SHERBORNE (*c.* 980–1000).

TALBOT (CHARLES H.). 'The life of St. Wulsin of Sherborne by Goscelin'. *Rev. Bénédictine*, lxix (1959), 68–85.

(*b*) Celtic saints

For the general histories of medieval Ireland, see p. 155; for general works on the Celtic Church, see pp. 379–82; for collections of saints' lives, see pp. 148–51. Père Paul Grosjean has published numerous articles and notes on Celtic hagiography, particularly in *Analecta Bollandiana*: see 'Bibliography of his works', *Anal. Boll.* lxxxii (1964), 307–18. Ludwig Bieler reported 'Recent research in Irish hagiography', *Studies* (No. 239), xxv (1946), 20–36; and 'The Celtic hagiographer', *Studia Patristica*, v (1962), 243–65. Some lives of Celtic saints are translated in the fifth series of *Translations of Christian literature* (London, 1923). Canon Doble's essays on Cornish and Welsh saints are noticed below under No. 2666. Louis H. Gray has written bibliographical essays as 'A survey of studies in Cornish Hagiography', *The Review of Religion*, iv (1940), 431–4; and 'Brythonic Christianity', ibid. vii (1942), 1–31 and ix (1944), 42–4. Kathleen Hughes, 'The historical value of the Lives of St. Finnian of Clonard (d. 549)', *E.H.R.* lxix (1954), 353–72, has wide applicability on the historicity of Irish saints.

2318   BRENDAN (d. 578). NAVIGATIO SANCTI BRENDANI ABBATIS. Ed. by Carl Selmer. Univ. Notre Dame Pubns. in Mediaeval Stud. xvi (1959). Translated by J. F. Webb in *Lives of the Saints*. Penguin Classics. 1965. pp. 33–68.

> St. Brendan, the founder of the monastery of Clonfert in Galway, *c.* 560, visited Iona and elsewhere in Britain. His fame rests largely on a tenth-century adventure story of a saint who with his companions visited far-off, mythical islands in the Atlantic Ocean. The story has been adapted into several languages. Selmer edited a tenth-century Latin text of the voyage, which is called by Nora Chadwick 'The Christian Odyssey of early Ireland' (*Age of Saints* (No. 2664), p. 75).

2319   COLUMBA OF IONA (d. 597).

(a) ADOMNAN'S LIFE OF COLUMBA. Ed. with trans. and notes by Alan O. and Marjorie O. Anderson. Lond. 1961. Vita S. Columbae auctore Adamnano. Ed. by William Reeves. Issued by Irish Archaeol. and Celtic Soc. Dublin. 1857; and by *Bannatyne Club*. Edin. 1857. Reeves's edition was reprinted, somewhat abridged and rearranged, with a translation by Skene in *Historians of Scotland*, vol. vi, Edin. 1874. Adomnan's Life was also edited from Reeves's text by J. T. Fowler. Oxf. 1894. 2nd edn. 1920.

(b) Paul Grosjean, 'The life of St. Columba from the Edinburgh MS.' *Scot. Gaelic Stud.* ii (1928), 111–71, and iii (1931), 84–5. This is a recension of the Irish text of *Betha Coluim Chille* with an English translation.

(c) BULLOUGH (DONALD A.). 'Columba, Adomnan and the achievement of Iona'. *Scot. H. R.* xliii (1964), 111–30; and xliv (1965), 17–33.

(d) ANDERSON (MARJORIE O.). 'Columba and other Irish saints'. *Historical Stud. . . . the Sixth Irish Conference* (1963). Ed. by J. L. McCracken. Lond. 1965. pp. 26–36. BYRNE (FRANCIS J.). 'The Ireland of St. Columba'. ibid. pp. 37–58.

The *Life of St. Columba* by Adomnan, abbot of Iona (d. 704), is a most important source for seventh-century Celtic saints. The best edition is the Anderson edition. Reeves's edition contains much material illustrating early Irish history and the introduction of Christianity into Scotland. Further references can be found in Kenney (No. 23), pp. 422–36; Anderson, *Sources* (No. 1088A), i. 22 ff.; and Bonser, *A.-S.C.B.* (No. 12), pp. 234–8.

2320   COLUMBAN (d. 615). Missionary and founder of Bobbio.

(a) Sancti Columbani Opera. Ed. by G. S. M. Walker. Scriptores Latini Hiberniae, vol. ii. Dublin. 1957. (See K. Hughes (No. 22), p. 196, n. 5).
This edition with an English translation and a full bibliography contains all the known works of St. Columban, preceded by important commentaries by various scholars.

(b) Vitae Columbani abbatis discipulorumque eius libri duo auctore Jona. Ed. by Bruno Krusch in 'Passiones vitaeque sanctorum aevi Merovingici'. M.G.H. *SS. Rerum Merov.* iv (1902), 1–156, and vii (1920), 822–7. 'Ionae vitae Sanctorum Columbani, Vedastis, Johannis'. M.G.H. *Scriptores rerum Germanicarum*, xxv (1905), 1–294. Migne, *P.L.* lxxxvii. 1014–46. Jonas, Vita Columbani et discipulorum eius. Ed. by Michele Tosi; and trans. into Italian by E. Cremona and M. Paramidan. Piacenza. 1965. English trans. by Dana C. Munro, 'The life of St. Columban by the monk Jonas'. *Translations and Reprints from the Original Sources of European History*, ii, No. 7. Philadelphia. 1897.

(c) Miracula Sancti Columbani. Ed. by H. Bresslau. M.G.H. *SS.* xxx, pt. ii (1934), 993–1015.

(d) Columbani abbatis Luxoviensis et Bobbiensis epistulae. Ed. by W. Gundlach. M.G.H. *Epistolae*, iii (1892), 154–90.
See Kenney (No. 23), pp. 189–95.

(e) Ordo S. Columbani abbatis De vita et actione monachorum. Ed. by Otto Seebass. *Zeitschrift für Kirchengeschichte*, xiv (1894), 76–92. Regula monachorum Sancti Columbani abbatis. Ed. by O. Seebass. Ibid. xv (1895), 366–86. Regula coenobialis, etc. Ed. by O. Seebass. Ibid. xvii (1897), 215–34.

(*f*) Das Poenitentiale Columbani. Ed. by O. Seebass. Ibid. xiv (1894), 430–48. Le Pénitentiel de Saint Columban. Ed. by J. Laporte. Tournai. 1960.

Commentaries: For the literature on St. Columban, see Bonser, *A.-S.C.B.*, pp. 257–61; Kenney (No. 23), especially pp. 186–205; Bieler and Binchy, *Irish penitentials* (No. 2252).

(*g*) BLANKE (FRITZ). Columban und Gallus: Urgeschichte des schweizerischen Christentums. Zürich. 1940.

(*h*) LAUX (JOHANN J.). Der heilige Kolumban: sein Leben und seine Schriften. Freiburg i. B. 1919.

(*i*) MARTIN (LÉON E.). St. Columban. Paris. 1905. 3rd edn. 1921.

(*j*) O'CARROLL (JAMES). 'The chronology of St. Columban'. *Irish Theol. Quart.* xxiv (1957), 76–95.

2321   DAVID (d. *c.* 601). Patron saint of Wales.

(*a*) RHIGYFARCH'S LIFE OF ST. DAVID: the basic mid-twelfth-century Latin text. Ed. and trans. by J. W. James. Cardiff. 1967. RHYGYFARCH, Buched Dewi. Ed. by D. S. Evans. Cardiff. 1959.

(*b*) RHYGYFARCH'S LIFE OF ST. DAVID. Ed. and trans. by Arthur W. Wade-Evans. *Y Cymmrodor*, xxiv (1913), 1–73.

This translation was issued in a revised edition in *Translations of Christian Literature*, 5th Ser.: 'Lives of the Celtic Saints' (Lond. etc. 1923). The text is reprinted in *Vitae Sanctorum Britanniae . . .* (Cardiff, 1944). The edition and translation by W. J. Rees in *Lives of the Cambro-British Saints* (Llandovery, 1853) cannot be recommended. This biography, written by Rhygyfarch, son of Bishop Sulien of St. David's, seeks to uphold the claim of Welsh episcopal independence of Canterbury.

(*c*) RHYS (ERNEST). The life of St. David. Gregynog. 1927.

2322   KENTIGERN (d. *c.* 603–12). Missionary to Strathclyde, patron saint of Glasgow Cathedral.

(*a*) Vita Kentegerni auctore Jocelino monacho Furnesensi. Ed. by A. P. Forbes, 'Lives of S. Ninian and S. Kentigern' in *The Historians of Scotland*. Edin. 1874. v. 159–242; translated pp. 29–119.

(*b*) Vita Kentegerni imperfecta, auctore ignoto. Ibid. v. 243–52; translated pp. 123–33.

(*c*) JACKSON (KENNETH H.). 'The sources for the Life of St. Kentigern', in Chadwick, *Studies Brit. Church* (No. 2665), pp. 273–342, with appendix pp. 343–57.

2323   NINIAN (d. *c.* 432). Scottish missionary and founder of Candida Casa.

(*a*) Vita Niniani Pictorum Australium Apostoli auctore Ailredo Rievallensi. Ed. by A. P. Forbes in *The Historians of Scotland*. Edin. 1874. v. 137–57; translated pp. 3–26. Also in Anderson, *Sources* (No. 1088A), i. 9–39.

(*b*) The legends of SS. Ninian and Machor from a unique MS. in the Scottish dialect of the fourteenth century. Ed. by W. M. Metcalfe. Paisley. 1904.

(*c*) LEVISON (WILHELM). 'An eighth century poem on St. Ninian'. *Antiquity*, xiv (1940), 280–91.

Levison calls attention to Karl Strecker's edition and studies on St. Ninian in M.G.H. *Poetae Latini aevi Carolini*, iv. fasc. ii–iii (1923); and *Neues Archiv*, xliii (1920–2), 1–26; and to other works which indicate that the eighth-century poet used an old life which Ailred elaborated.

(*d*) BOYLE (ALEXANDER). 'Saint Ninian: some outstanding problems'. *Innes Rev.* xix (1968), 57–70.

(*e*) CHADWICK (NORA K.). 'St. Ninian: a preliminary study of sources'. *Dumfries. and Galloway Nat. Hist. and Antiq. Soc. Trans.* 3rd ser. xxvii (1950), 9–55. J. D. Mackie. Ibid. xxx (1953), 17–37. P. A. Wilson. 'St. Ninian and Candida Casa'. Ibid. xli (1964), 156–85; xlvi (1970), 40–59.

Nora Chadwick believes that Bede's account rests on traditions not much older than Bede's lifetime and that Ninian probably never went to Rome or founded Candida Casa. See also Chadwick, *Studies Brit. Hist.* (No. 2122).

(*f*) MacQUEEN (JOHN). St. Nynia. Edin. and Lond. 1961.

John MacQueen, 'History and miracle stories in the biography of Nynia', *Innes Rev.* xiii (1962), 115–29.

(*g*) SIMPSON (WILLIAM D.). Saint Ninian and the origins of the Christian Church in Scotland. Edin. 1940.

For differing views, see Alan O. Anderson, 'Ninian and the southern Picts', *Scot. H.R.* xxvii (1948), 25–47; E. A. Thompson, 'The origin of Christianity in Scotland', ibid. xxxv (1958), 17–22; Paul Grosjean, 'Les Pictes apostats dans l'épître de S. Patrice', *Anal. Boll.* lxxvi (1958), fascs. iii and iv; Dermot Fahy, 'The historical reality of St. Ninian', *Innes Rev.* xv (1964), 35–46.

2324 PATRICK (*fl.* fifth century). Apostle of Ireland.

The paucity of records for the fifth century and the entries in Irish annals of 461 and 493 (and possibly 457) as the date of his death lead to controversy on St. Patrick's chronology and indeed on the number of Patricks involved. The traditional account is found in Bury (*j*); it asserts that the missionary Palladius came to Ireland in 431, that Patrick arrived in the following year, 432, and died in 461. MacNeill, Grosjean, Bieler, and Mohrmann follow the general lines of the traditional account. However, O'Rahilly (*r*) holds that there were two Patricks, namely Palladius who died in 461 and the British Patrick who arrived about 461 and died in 493. Carney (*k*) maintains that there was only one Patrick, the British Patrick who laboured in Ireland from about 456 to 493; Carney also holds that the first mission to Ireland was that of St. Secundinus about 439. Esposito (*l*) believes that the British Patrick preceded Palladius and died before the latter's arrival. Binchy's article (*i*) is a most important critique of Patrician controversies.

On matters of chronology, the writings of St. Patrick do not afford precise answers. Among the writings attributed to him are the *Confessio* and the *Epistola ad Coroticum*; together they form the fundamental sources for his biography. The *Lorica*, or religious breast-plate, now not attributed to St. Patrick, is an early hymn written in Irish, but probably not as early as the fifth century. Some information regarding St. Patrick is also found in a Latin hymn, the first St. Patrick hymn, attributed to St. Secundinus (d. *c.* 457). All of these pieces, together with certain canons attributed to St. Patrick and others, were edited in Haddan and Stubbs, *Councils* (No. 1129), vol. ii, pt. ii, and by Stokes, *Tripartite Life* (*g*). Good editions of the *Confessio* and the *Epistola* are by Bieler (*c*) and White (*e*).

The two earliest biographies of St. Patrick are Bishop Tírechán's notes, which purport to have been obtained from Bishop Ultan (d. 657) and were put together in the second half of the seventh century; and the memoirs, or life of St. Patrick, compiled by Muirchú Maccu-Machtheni toward the end of the seventh century. Both works are in Latin; and are found, along with the oldest copy of the *Confessio*, in the *Book of Armagh*, a volume written about 807. The *Book of Armagh* contains most of the important sources for the life of St. Patrick, but not the Letter to Coroticus. The best editions are the diplomatic edition by J. Gwynn (*b*) and the facsimile edition by E. Gwynn (*b*). Some of the documents in the *Book of Armagh* were printed by Hogan (*a*) and by Stokes (*g*). These lives, together with the *Liber Angeli* (*a*) are important sources for the seventh-century development of the see of Armagh.

Seven later lives can be found in Colgan's *Acta Sanctorum* (No. 1160), vol. ii. For these lives see Kenney (No. 23), pp. 399–48.

The bibliography on St. Patrick is very long. Kenney, pp. 319–50 and elsewhere, lists the sources and commentaries to 1928; Bonser, *A.-S.C.B.*, pp. 219–28 and elsewhere, gives about 240 titles. Among the recent Patrician scholars, Père Paul Grosjean, Ludwig Bieler, and Daniel Binchy are perhaps the foremost.

(*a*) Documenta de S. Patricio Hibernorum apostolo ex libro Armachano. Ed. by Edmund Hogan. 2 pts. Brussels. 1882 (1884)–1889.

> The first part of the *Book of Armagh* contains the lives by Muirchu and Tírechán and *Additamenta*; it is also printed in *Anal. Boll.* i (1882), 531–85; ii (1883), 35–68, 213–38. The second part contains *Liber Angeli* and the *Confessio*. The *Liber Angeli* is discussed and translated by Hughes (No. 2670), pp. 275–81. Douglas Powell, 'The textual integrity of St. Patrick's Confession', *Anal. Boll.* lxxxvii (1969), 387–409.

(*b*) Liber Ardmachanus: the Book of Armagh. Ed. with introduction and appendices by John Gwynn. Dublin. 1913. The Book of Armagh: the Patrician documents, with an introduction by Edward Gwynn. *Facsimiles in Collotype of Irish MSS.* iii. Dublin. 1937.

(*c*) Libri epistolarum Sancti Patricii Episcopi: introduction, text, and commentary by Ludwig Bieler. *Classica et Mediaevalia*, xi (1950), 1–150; xii (1951), 79–214. Reprinted by Irish Hist. MSS. Comm. 2 vols. Dublin. 1952. Addenda by Bieler in *Analecta Hibernica*, (1966), 313–15.

(*d*) The works of St. Patrick and St. Secundinus' hymn on St. Patrick. Trans. by Ludwig Bieler. *Ancient Christian Writers in Translation*. Ed. by Johannes Quasten and Joseph C. Plumpe. Vol. xvii. Westminster (Md.). 1953.

(*e*) Liber S. Patricii: the Latin writings of St. Patrick (the *Confessio* and the *Epistola*). Ed. with a translation Newport J. D. White. *Royal Irish Acad. Procs.* C, xxv (1905), 201–326. Revised text and translation in Texts for Students. S.P.C.K. Nos. 4 and 5. Lond. 1918.

(*f*) St. Patrick: his writings and life. By Newport J. D. White. *Translations of Christian Literature*. Ser. 5: 'Lives of the Celtic Saints'. Lond. etc. 1920. Reprinted, 1932.

(*g*) The tripartite life of Patrick, with other documents relating to that saint. Ed. with translations by Whitley Stokes. 2 vols. Lond. 1887.* A more critical edition as Bethu Phátraic: the Tripartite Life of St. Patrick by Kathleen Mulchrone. Dublin. 1939.

The *Tripartite Life* is so called from its division into three parts. Although the manuscripts come from the fifteenth century, the subject-matter of the *Tripartite Life* probably assumed its present form towards the end of the ninth century. Cf. Kenney (No. 23), pp. 342–5.

(*h*) BIELER (LUDWIG). The life and legend of St. Patrick: problems of modern scholarship. Dublin. 1949.

This fundamental study by a Patrician scholar deals critically with the sources. See, for example, the review in *Traditio*, viii (1952), 449–55. Idem, *Codices Patriciani Latini*: a descriptive catalogue of Latin manuscripts relating to St. Patrick. Dublin, 1942. [Addenda to *Codices* in *Anal. Boll.* lxiii (1945), 243–56.] Idem, 'Vindiciae Patricianae: remarks on the present state of Patrician studies'. *Irish Eccles. Rec.* lxxix (1953), 161–85. Idem, 'Patrick and the kings: apropos a new chronology of St. Patrick'. Ibid. lxxxv (1956), 171–89. Idem, 'Patriciology: reflections on the present state of Patrician studies'. *Seanchas Ardmhacha* (1961–2), pp. 9–36. This issue of *Seanchas Ardmhacha: Journal of the Armagh Diocesan Historical Society*, edited by Tomas O'Fiach, is entitled 'The Patrician Year' and includes miscellaneous articles on St. Patrick.

(*i*) BINCHY (DANIEL A.). 'Studia Patriciana: Patrick and his biographers, ancient and modern'. *Studia Hibernica*, ii (1962), 7–173.

This very important study insists that the only reliable sources for Patrick are the *Confessio* and the *Epistola ad Coroticum*.

(*j*) BURY (JOHN B.). Life of St. Patrick and his place in history. Lond. 1905.

This critical study set Patrician studies on firmer foundations than theretofore.

(*k*) CARNEY (JAMES). The problem of St. Patrick. Institute of Advanced Stud. Dublin. 1961.

See also Carney, 'Comments on the present state of the Patrician problem', *Irish Eccles. Rec.* xcii (1962), 1–28; and his 'St. Patrick's *Confessio*', ibid. pp. 148–54. For another problem, see H. P. R. Finberg, 'St. Patrick at Glastonbury', *Irish Eccles. Rec.* 5th Ser. cxii (1967), 345–61, reprinted in *West Country Historical Stud.* (No. 1611).

(*l*) ESPOSITO (MARIO). 'The Patrician problem and a possible solution'. *Irish Hist. Stud.* x (1956), 131–55. Idem, 'St. Patrick's *Confessio* and the Book of Armagh'. Ibid. ix (1954), 1–12.

(*m*) GROSJEAN (PAUL). 'Notes sur les documents anciens concernant S. Patrice'. *Anal. Boll.* lxii (1944), 42–73; and preceding pp. 33–41. Idem, 'S. Patrice d'Irlande et quelques homonymes dans les anciens martyrologes'. *J.E.H.* i (1950), 151–71.

Consult the bibliography of Grosjean's writings (No. 1153).

(*n*) HANSON (RICHARD P. C.). Saint Patrick: his origins and career. Oxf. and N.Y. 1968.

An adverse review by Francis Shaw in *Studies* (No. 239), lvii (1968), 186–91. See (*s*) below.

(*o*) MacNEILL (EOIN). St. Patrick, apostle of Ireland. Lond. 1934. 2nd edn. by John Ryan with a memoir by Michael Tierney and a bibliography of Patrician literature by F. X. Martin. Dublin and Lond. 1964.

(*p*) McNALLY (ROBERT E.). 'Saint Patrick, 461–1961'. *Catholic Hist. Rev.* xlvii (1961–2), 305–24.

(*q*) MOHRMANN (CHRISTINE). The Latin of St. Patrick. Four lectures. Dublin. 1961.

(*r*) O'RAHILLY (THOMAS F.). The two Patricks: a lecture on the history of Christianity in fifth-century Ireland. Dublin. 1942. Reprinted, 1957.

(*s*) O RAIFEARTAIGH (T.). 'The life of St. Patrick: a new approach'. *Irish Hist. Stud.* xvi (1968), 119–37.

A balanced commentary on Hanson ((*n*) above) setting forth the complexity of the problems involved.

D. LITERATURE AND LEARNING

1. *Anglo-Saxon*

A detailed account of Anglo-Saxon literature does not fall within the scope of this bibliography of English history. For retrospective bibliography, consult the *Cambridge Bibliography of English Literature* (No. 14) and Robinson (No. 2360). For current bibliography, *The Years' Work in English Studies* (No. 276), the *Annual Bibliography of English Language and Literature* (No. 272), and the April issue of *Publications of Modern Language Association* (No. 268). The first issue of a projected annual publication, entitled *Anglo-Saxon England*, from the Cambridge University Press under the editorship of Peter Clemoes, appeared in 1972. Devoted solely to Anglo-Saxon studies, it included sixteen articles and a full bibliography for 1971. Reference to Greenfield (No. 2355) is profitable. For MSS. see Ker's *Catalogue* (No. 977).

The sources in prose have been listed in preceding pages; some poems which contribute especially to our knowledge of the political or social life of the period are mentioned below.

In addition to scattered pieces in the *Anglo-Saxon Chronicle*, the bulk of surviving Anglo-Saxon poetry 'is preserved in the Cottonian *Beowulf*, the *Exeter Book*, the Junius MS. of Caedmon and the Vercelli Codex'. The information regarding institutions and social life gleaned from poems like those of Cynewulf is meagre: see No. 2343. The scene of popular epics like *Beowulf*, the *Fight at Finnsburg*, and *Waldhere* lies in foreign lands, and their material is in large part legendary; therefore they add little to our stock of knowledge regarding Britain, although they help to illustrate and illuminate some of the social and governmental principles of our Germanic ancestors. (See Whitelock, No. 2362.) Of much greater value are the purely historical poems of the tenth and eleventh centuries, namely, the *Battle of Maldon* (No. 2344) and the national songs embodied in the *Anglo-Saxon Chronicle*. Of the latter the *Battle of Brunanburh*, A.D. 937, is the most important. Other poetical pieces in the *Chronicle* relate to the reconquest of the Five Boroughs, A.D. 942; Edgar's reign, coronation, and death;

the death of Edward the Martyr; Alfred the Ætheling; the son of Edmund Ironside; and the death of Edward the Confessor.

(a) Sources

The collected editions are Grein and Wülker's *Bibliothek* and Krapp and Dobbie; and in the publications of the Early English Text Society (No. 187). For facsimile editions, see *Early English MSS. in Facsimile* (No. 441).

2325 GREIN (CHRISTIAN W. M.), ed. Bibliothek der angelsächsischen Poesie. 4 vols. Göttingen. 1857–64. New edition by Richard P. Wülker. 3 vols. in 4 parts. Cassel. 1883–98.

> Vol. i is of most interest to students of history; it contains *Beowulf, Battle of Maldon, Battle of Brunanburh*. For *Biblio. A.-S. Prosa*, see No. 2286.

2326 KERSHAW (NORAH). Anglo-Saxon and Norse Poems, edited and translated. Cambr. 1922.

> Texts and translations. Part i, Anglo-Saxon poems, including the *Battle of Brunanburh*. Part ii, Norse poems. For other works by this author, see index under Chadwick, Nora K.

2327 KRAPP (GEORGE P.) and DOBBIE (ELLIOTT). The Anglo-Saxon Poetic Records. 6 vols. N.Y. 1931–53.

> (a) The Junius MS. Ed. by Krapp. 1931.
> (b) The Vercelli Book. Ed. by Krapp. 1932.
> (c) The Exeter Book. Ed. by Krapp and Dobbie. 1936.
> (d) Beowulf and Judith. Ed. by Dobbie. 1953.
> (e) The Paris Psalter and the Meters of Boethius. Ed. by Krapp. 1933.
> (f) The Anglo-Saxon minor poems. Ed. by Dobbie. 1942.

2328 METHUEN'S OLD ENGLISH LIBRARY. Ed. by A. H. Smith, F. Norman, and A. Brown. Lond. 1933 in progress.

> (a) Three Northumbrian Poems: Caedmon's hymn, Bede's Death Song, The Leiden Riddle. Ed. by A. H. Smith.
> (b) Deor. Ed. by Kemp Malone.
> (c) Waldere. Ed. by F. Norman. 2nd edn. 1949.
> (d) The Dream of the Rood. Ed. by Bruce Dickins and Alan S. C. Ross.
> (e) Widsith. Ed. by Kemp Malone. Revised edn. Copenhagen. 1962.
> (f) The Seafarer. Ed. by Ida L. Gordon.
> (g) The Battle of Maldon. Ed. by E. V. Gordon.
> (h) Judith. Ed. by B. J. Timmer.
> (i) Juliana. Ed. by Rosemary Woolf.
>
> (Series B.)
> (j) The Parker Chronicle. Ed. by A. H. Smith.
> (k) Ælfric's Colloquy. Ed. by G. N. Garmonsway. 1939. 2nd edn. 1947.
> (l) Sermo Lupi ad Anglos. Ed. by D. Whitelock. 3rd edn. 1963.
> (m) Ælfric's Lives of Three Saints. Ed. by G. I. Needham. 1966.

2329 SWEET (HENRY), ed. The oldest English Texts. E.E.T.S. Orig. Ser. lxxxiii (1885).

> 'This collection is intended to include all the extant Old English texts up to about 900 that are preserved in contemporary MSS., with the exception of the *Chronicle* and the works of Alfred.'

2330 WILSON (RICHARD M.). The lost literature of medieval England. Lond. 1952. 2nd edn. 1970.

(Beowulf)

2331 BEOWULF. Reproduced in facsimile from the unique manuscript, British Museum MS. Cotton Vittelius A. xv. With a transliteration and notes by Julius Zupitza. 2nd edn. containing a new reproduction of the manuscript, with an introductory note by Norman Davis. E.E.T.S. Orig. Ser. ccxlv (1959/60).

Earlier edition E.E.T.S. Orig. Ser. lxxvii (1882).

2332 THE THORKELIN TRANSCRIPTS OF BEOWULF. Ed. by K. Malone. Early English MSS. in Facsimile, Copenhagen. 1951.

A facsimile of two transcripts made by G. J. Thorkelin in 1787 before the edges of the Cottonian MS. began to crumble. See also K. Sisam, *Studies* (No. 2361), pp. 61–97.

2333 THE NOWELL CODEX: BEOWULF. B.M. Cotton Vitellius A. xv. Ed. by Kemp Malone. Early English MSS. in Facsimile, xii. Copenhagen. 1963.

2334 KLAEBER (FREDERICK). Beowulf and the Fight at Finnsburg. N.Y. 1922. 1928. 1930 (new edn.), 1941. 1950 (with supplements).

2335 WRENN (CHARLES L.), ed. Beowulf and the Finnesburg fragment. Lond. etc. Rev. edn. 1958. Also edited by Dobbie (No. 2327). 1953.

For commentary, see Raymond W. Chambers, *Beowulf, an introduction to the study of the poem with a discussion of the stories of Offa and Finn* (Cambr. 1921; 3rd edn. 1959, with supplement by Charles L. Wrenn); and bibliography in Anderson (No. 2349), pp. 98–103. Arthur G. Brodeur, *The art of Beowulf* (Berkeley, 1959); Kenneth Sisam, *The structure of Beowulf* (Oxf. 1965). For translations, see Farrar and Evans (No. 52), pp. 73–5; and C. W. Kennedy (N.Y. 1940); Burton Raffel (N.Y. 1963); and E. Talbot Donaldson (N.Y. 1966).

2336 WYATT (ALFRED J.) and CHAMBERS (RAYMOND W.), eds. Beowulf with the Finnsburg fragment. Cambr. 1914. New edn. 1935/6.

Exeter Book

2337 THE EXETER BOOK OF OLD ENGLISH POETRY, with introductory chapters by R. W. Chambers, Max Förster, and Robin Flower. Lond. 1933.

A complete photographic facsimile of the MS. See K. Sisam, *Studies* (No. 2361), pp. 97–108.

2338 THE EXETER BOOK, re-edited from the unique manuscript. Pt. i by Israel Gollancz; pt. ii by W. S. Mackie. E.E.T.S. Orig. Ser. civ (1895), and cxciv (1934).

(Junius Manuscript)

2339 GOLLANCZ (ISRAEL). The Caedmon manuscript of Anglo-Saxon Biblical poetry, Junius XI in the Bodleian Library. Oxf. 1927.

A facsimile of the whole MS. For commentary, see Charles W. Kennedy, *The Caedmon poems* (Lond. 1916); and Charles L. Wrenn, 'The poetry of Caedmon', *P.B.A.* xxxii (1946), 277–95. E. B. Irving, Jr., 'On the dating of the Old English poems *Genesis* and *Exodus*', *Anglia*, lxxvii (1959), 1–11.

2340 WÜLKER (RICHARD P.), ed. Codex Vercellensis. Die angelsächsische Handschrift zu Vercelli in getreuer Nachbildung. Leipzig. 1894. (A photographic facsimile of the section of poetry.)

See K. Sisam, *Studies* (No. 2361), pp. 109–18.

2341 FOERSTER (MAX), ed. Il codice vercellese con omelie e poesie in lingua anglosassone. Rome. 1913. (A photographic facsimile of the whole MS.)

(*Brunanburh, Battle of*)

2342 CAMPBELL (ALISTAIR), ed. The battle of Brunanburh. Lond. 1938.

Critical edition of the poem on the battle of 937 in which Athelstan defeated a coalition of Norse from Ireland and Scots. For additional references, see Bonser (No. 12); and J. McN. Dodgson, 'The background of Brunanburh', *Saga Book*, xiv (1956–7), 303–16.

(*Cynewulf*)

2343 KENNEDY (CHARLES W.), ed. The poems of Cynewulf. Lond. 1910.

Cf. the important paper by Kenneth Sisam, 'Cynewulf and his poetry', *P.B.A.* xviii (1932), 303–31; reprinted in his *Studies* (No. 2361). P. O. E. Gradon, ed., *Cynewulf's Elene* (Lond. 1958).

(*Maldon, Battle of*)

2344 GORDON (ERIC V.), ed. The battle of Maldon. Methuen Old English Library. Lond. 1937.

A critical edition of the poem of the battle of 991 in which Byrhtnoth of Essex was slain. Another edition, with translation in Ashdown, *Docs.* (No. 2437), pp. 22–37. See also *Eng. Hist. Docs.* (No. 17), pp. 132 and 293–7. See Nos. 2325, 2588.

N. F. Blake, 'The battle of Maldon', *Neophilologus* (Gröningen), xlix (1965), 332–45. For controversial views and citations, see George Clark, 'The battle of Maldon: a heroic poem', *Speculum*, xliii (1968), 52–71; and Michael J. Swanton, 'The battle of Maldon: a literary caveat', *J.E.G.P.* lxvii (1968), 441–50.

(*Widsith*)

2345 CHAMBERS (RAYMOND W.). Widsith, a study in Old English heroic legend. Cambr. 1912.

Cf. Alfred Anscombe, 'The historical side of the Old English poem of Widsith', *T.R.H.S.* 3rd Ser. ix (1915), 123–65, which includes R. W. Chambers's reply to criticism.

2346 MALONE (KEMP), ed. Widsith. Methuen Old English Library. Lond. 1936. 2nd edn. with extensive bibliography (*Anglistica*, xiii). Copenhagen. 1962.

(*King Alfred's translations*)

2347 WHOLE WORKS OF KING ALFRED THE GREAT, with preliminary essays illustrative of the history, arts and manners of the ninth century. 3 vols. in 2. Oxf. 1852–3. Reprinted, Lond. 1858.

For more modern editions, see *C.B.E.L.* i. 85–8; v. 83–4.

2348 BROWNE (GEORGE F.). King Alfred's books. Lond. and N.Y. 1920.

See Anderson (No. 2349), pp. 256–95, and his notes pp. 295–307; Asser's *Life* (No. 2147); Greenfield (No. 2355), pp. 27–44; and modern biographies (Nos. 2575, 2579, and 2594). Janet M. Bately, 'King Alfred and the Latin MSS. of Orosius' History', *Classica et Mediaevalia*, xxii (1961), 69–105; and D. Whitelock in *Continuations* (No. 2352).

(b) Modern commentaries

For the myriad of studies on Anglo-Saxon literature, the reader should consult the bibliographies noted above, p. 339. Anderson's *Literature* (No. 2349) and Greenfield (No. 2355) are good starting-points. A few recent generalized works of high quality may serve as guides to the historian. Cf. pp. 34–6.

2349 ANDERSON (GEORGE K.). The literature of the Anglo-Saxons. Princeton. 1949.

It includes long bibliographical notes at the end of each chapter.

2350 AN ANTHOLOGY OF BEOWULF CRITICISM. Ed. by L. E. Nicholson. Notre Dame (Ind.). 1963.

2351 CHADWICK (HECTOR M.). The heroic age. Cambr. 1912.

2352 CONTINUATIONS AND BEGINNINGS: Studies in Old English literature. Ed. by Eric G. Stanley. Lond. 1966.

Seven essays by various hands, including D. Whitelock on Alfredian prose, E. G. Stanley on *Beowulf*, P. Clemoes on Ælfric, and D. Bethurum on Wulfstan.

2353 DICKINS (BRUCE). Runic and heroic poems of the Old Teutonic peoples. Cambr. 1915. *

Texts and commentary.

2354 GORDON (ROBERT K.). Anglo-Saxon poetry. Everyman's Library. Lond. etc. 1926. New edn. 1954.

Translations.

2355 GREENFIELD (STANLEY B.). A critical history of Old English literature. N.Y. and Lond. 1965.

This excellent survey of the literary sources is supported by footnotes which constitute a notable bibliography.

2356 KENNEDY (CHARLES W.). The earliest English poetry: a critical survey of the poetry written before the Norman conquest. Lond. etc. 1943.

C. W. Kennedy has also published several books of translations; the latest is *An anthology of Old English poetry* (Lond. 1960). See also the translations of Michael Alexander, *The earliest English poems* (Penguin Classics, 1966); and Burton Raffel, *Poems of the Old English* (2nd edn., Lincoln (Nebr.), 1964).

2357 KER (WILLIAM P.). Epic and romance. Lond. 1896. *

Reprinted, paperback. N.Y. 1957.

2358 LAISTNER (MAX L. W.). Thought and letters in Western Europe A.D. 500 to 900. Lond. and N.Y. 1931. New, revised edn. 1957. Idem, Intellectual heritage of the early middle ages: selected essays (by M. L. W. Laistner). Ed. by C. G. Starr. Ithaca (N.Y.). 1957.

See also Bernhard Bischoff, 'Das griechische Element in der abendländischen Bildung des Mittelalters', *Byzantinische Zeit.* xliv (1951), 27–55.

2359 OGILVY (JACK D. A.). Books known to Anglo-Latin writers from Aldhelm to Alcuin (670–804). Cambr. (Mass.). 1936. Idem, Books known to the English, 597–1066. Cambr. (Mass.). 1967.

Reviewed by Luitpold Wallach in *J.E.G.P.* lxviii (1969), 156–61.

2360 ROBINSON (FRED C.). Old English literature: a select bibliography. Toronto Medieval Bibliographies. Toronto. 1970.

2361 SISAM (KENNETH). Studies in the history of Old English literature. Oxf. 1953.

A collection of important essays and notes, mostly reprinted from journals. Includes studies on Cynewulf, *Beowulf*, *Exeter Book*, Vercelli Book, Ælfric's *Homilies*, Æthelred's *Codes*, and other matters.

2362 WHITELOCK (DOROTHY). The audience of Beowulf. Oxf. 1951. Idem, 'Anglo-Saxon poetry and the history'. *T.R.H.S.* 4th Ser. xxxi (1949), 75–94.

2363 WRENN (CHARLES L.). A study of Old English literature. Lond. 1967.

An admirable survey with a good chapter on Latin writings.

2364 WRIGHT (CYRIL E.). The cultivation of saga in England. Edin. 1939.

(c) Scientific Writings

For general works, see Nos. 1418–24. For Anglo-Saxon period, see Anderson (No. 2349), Bonser (No. 12), *C.B.E.L.* (No. 14), and No. 2378. After Bede (p. 324), the earliest surviving writings on science, lore, charms, etc. come from the tenth and eleventh centuries. The principal writings are:

1. Byrhtferth's *Handbook*. Byrhtferth (*fl.* 1010), a monk of Ramsey, wrote this manual dealing principally with astronomical and astrological lore mixed with much religious material. He drew heavily on Bede, on whose scientific works he also wrote commentaries. The early portions of the *Handbook* are in Latin and Anglo-Saxon; but the later sections are in Anglo-Saxon only.

2. *Herbarium* Apuleii. A miscellany drawn from many authors, but falsely ascribed to Apuleius, on the virtues of herbs as cures. It was written in Anglo-Saxon in the first half of the eleventh century, apparently on the basis of a Latin version.

3. *Medicina de Quadrupedibus*. Folklore in Anglo-Saxon, based on a Latin version.

4. Bald's *Leechbook*. A treatise on medicine followed by a series of prescriptions and recipes. Probably from the later tenth century. The name of the owner, Bald, appears in a colophon.

5. A Herbal or miscellany of plant folklore (B.M. Harley 585). The first part is based on 2 and 3 above; the second part includes the *Lacnunga*, a miscellany of recipes, charms, etc.

6. *Peri Didaxeon* or *Schools of Medicine*. A textbook on medicine.

2365 BALD'S LEECHBOOK. B.M. Royal MS. 12 D ii. Ed. by Cyril E. Wright, with introduction by Bertram Colgrave, and a linguistic appendix by Randolph Quirk. Early Eng. MSS. in Facsimile, v. Copenhagen etc. 1955.

2366 BYRHTFERTH'S MANUAL (A.D. 1011). Ed. by S. J. Crawford. E.E.T.S. clxxvii (1929).

Cf. Charles and Dorothea Singer, 'Byrhtferd's diagram' in *The Bodleian Quarterly Record*, ii (1917), 45–51. N. R. Ker, 'Two notes on MS. Ashmole 328', *Medium Ævum*, iv (1935), 16–19. Cyril Hart, 'The Ramsey computus', *E.H.R.* lxxxv (1970), 29–44.

2367 GRATTAN (JOHN H. G.) and SINGER (CHARLES). Anglo-Saxon magic and medicine, illustrated specifically from the semi-pagan text Lacnunga. Lond. 1952.

The first part is a survey; the second part prints the text, with translation, of *Lacnunga*. The latter is also printed in Cockayne, *Leechdoms*, iii. 2–80.

2368 HERBARIUM APULEII: Cotton MS. Vitellius C iii. Ed. by Aaltje J. G. Hilbelink. Amsterdam. 1930.

2369 LEECHDOMS, WORTCUNNING AND STARCRAFT OF EARLY ENGLAND. Ed. by Oswald Cockayne. Rolls Series. 3 vols. Lond. 1864–6.

A collection of documents illustrating the history of science in England before the Norman Conquest. Volume i contains Nos. 2 and 3 above; Volume ii, No. 4; and Volume iii, No. 5. Volumes i and iii include other material.

2370 WRIGHT (THOMAS). Popular treatises on science written during the middle ages. Lond. 1841.

2371 BONSER (WILFRID). The medical background of Anglo-Saxon England: a study in history, psychology and folklore. Lond. 1963.

2372 THE EARLY HISTORY OF SCIENCE: a short handlist. Helps for Students of History, No. 52. The Historical Assoc. Lond. 1950.

2373 GRENDON (FELIX). 'The Anglo-Saxon Charms'. *Jour. American Folk-lore*, xxii (1909), 105–237.

Cf. Storms (No. 2379). Dobbie's *A.-S. Minor Poems* (No. 2327) contains material on charms.

2374 GUNTHER (ROBERT W. T.). The herbal of Apuleius Barbarus. Oxf. 1925.

2375 HENEL (HEINRICH). 'Altenglischer Mönchsaberglaube'. *Englische Studien*, lxix (1935), 329–49.

2376 PAYNE (JOSEPH F.). English medicine in the Anglo-Saxon times. Lond. 1904.

2377 RIESMAN (David). The story of medicine in the middle ages. N.Y. 1935.

2378 SINGER (CHARLES). From magic to science. Lond. 1928. *

Chaps. iii, iv and v on England. See his 'Early English magic and medicine', *P.B.A.* xviii (1919–20), 341–74.

2379 STORMS (GODFRID). Anglo-Saxon magic. The Hague. 1949.

Commentary and texts and translations, largely on charms. Cf. review in *Speculum* xxviii (1953), 203–12.

2380 TALBOT (CHARLES H.). 'Some notes on Anglo-Saxon medicine', *Medical History* (Lond.), ix (1965), 156–69. See Talbot (No. 1421).

2. *Celtic Literature*
(*a*) Sources

The heroic poetry and sagas which preserve the traditions of the Celtic people may be discreetly used for the purposes of history. They are classified below in two groups, first those deriving from the Celtic fringe of Britain proper and secondly those originating in Ireland. For the first group, the four fundamental surviving manuscripts are *The Black Book of Carmarthen, The Book of Aneirin, The Book of Taliesin,* and *The Red Book of Hergest.* Although Taliesin, who lived around A.D. 600, can be credited with the authorship of some poems, the book bearing his name also contains poems composed at much later dates. For the second group the Old Irish literature has come down to us largely through collections compiled between the twelfth and sixteenth centuries. The seven principal collections are listed below (Nos. 2393 to 2399). Individual texts are published in the series, mentioned below (Nos. 2389–90), in O'Grady (No. 2391), and in Stokes and Strachan (No. 2392). Printed translations of separate pieces in both groups are listed in Farrar and Evans (No. 52). See Hughes (No. 22), chap. 9.

2381 FOUR ANCIENT BOOKS OF WALES, containing the Cymric poems attributed to the bards of the sixth century. Ed. (with translations) by W. F. Skene. 2 vols. Edin. 1868.

Among the Welsh poems here edited from the four MSS. mentioned above, there are seventy containing allusions to historical events. The translations of the Arthurian poems 'cannot be relied upon' (E. K. Chambers, *Arthur*, (No. 2166), p. 286).

2382 THE MYVYRIAN ARCHAIOLOGY OF WALES, collected out of ancient MSS. Ed. by Owen Jones, Edward Williams, and W. O. Pughe. Denbigh. 1870. Earlier edn. 3 vols. Lond. 1801–7. See No. 1116.

2383 THE BLACK BOOK OF CARMARTHEN. Facsimile edition by J. Gwenogvryn Evans. Series of Old Welsh Texts, iii. Oxf. 1888. Reproduced and edited by same. Pwllheli. 1906. Skene, *Anc. Books* (No. 2381), ii. 1–61.

The earliest MS. written entirely in Welsh, compiled about 1200; it is described in *H.M.C. Repts., MSS. in the Welsh language,* i. 297.

2384 THE BOOK OF ANEIRIN. CANU ANEIRIN. Ed. by Ifor Williams. Cardiff. 1938. Skene, *Anc. Books* (No. 2381), text in ii. 62–107; translation by D. S. Evans in i. 374–427. The Text of the Book of Aneirin. Reproduced and edited (with translation) 2 pts. by J. Gwenogvryn Evans. Series of Old Welsh

Texts, viii. Pwllheli. 1908. An English translation with a historical introduction is furnished in Kenneth Jackson, *The Gododdin: the oldest Scottish poem*. Edin. and Chicago. 1969.

The MS. is described in *H.M.C. Repts., MSS. in the Welsh language*, ii. 91. Aneirin wrote the *Gododdin*, a eulogy of a band of 300 warriors from the Edinburgh area who died in a fruitless raid on Catterick in Yorkshire about A.D. 600. For summaries of Williams's edition, see K. Jackson, 'The Gododdin of Aneirin', *Antiquity*, xiii (1939), 25–34; and Colin A. Gresham, 'The book of Aneirin', ibid. xvi (1942), 237–67. See Bromwich in *Studies Early Brit. Hist.* (No. 2122); and P. K. Ford's review of Jackson's translation in *Speculum*, xlv (1970), 140–3.

2385   THE BOOK OF TALIESIN. CANU TALIESIN. Ed. by Ifor Williams. Cardiff. 1960. Reproduced and ed. by J. Gwenogvryn Evans. Series of Old Welsh Texts, ix. Llanbedrog. 1910. An amended text with translation. Ibid. ix B. 1915. Skene, *Anc. Books*, ii. 108–217. Armes Prydein o Lyfr Taliesin, gyda Rhagymadrodd a Nodiadau gan Ifor Williams. Cardiff. 1955. The poems of Taliesin, English version by J. E. Caerwyn Williams. Mediaeval and Modern Welsh Series, No. 3. Dublin. 1968.

The MS. is described in *H.M.C. Repts., MSS. in the Welsh language*, i. 300–12. For criticism of J. G. Evans's editions, see John Morris Jones in *Y Cymmrodor*, xxviii (1918); and the reply by J. G. Evans, ibid. xxxiv (1924). The *Armes Prydein* is concerned with the opposition to Athelstan of the Celtic-Dane coalition between 927 and 937. It is a 'rousing, contemporary, patriotic Welsh poem'. See Roger S. Loomis, *Wales and the Arthurian legend* (Cardiff, 1956), pp. 131–78; and Saunders Lewis, 'The tradition of Taliesin', *Hon. Soc. Cymmrodorion Trans.* ii for 1968 (1969), 293–8.

2386   THE RED BOOK OF HERGEST. CANU LLYWARCH HEN. Ed. by Ifor Williams. Cardiff. 1935. The poetry of the Red Book of Hergest. Reproduced and edited by J. Gwenogvryn Evans. Series of Old Welsh Texts, xi. Llanbedrog. 1911. Skene, *Anc. Books*, ii. 218–308. Cf. Ifor Williams, 'The poems of Llywarch Hen'. *P.B.A.* xviii (1932), 269–302.

The MS. is described in *H.M.C. Repts., MSS. in the Welsh language*, ii. 1–29. The poems, coming from North Wales, are about Llywarch Hen and not by him. They are a lament for the deaths of the 24 sons of Llywaroh, a sixth-century chief. See Patrick K. Ford, 'Llywarch, ancestor of Welsh princes', *Speculum*, xlv (1970), 442–50.

2387   BROMWICH (RACHEL). Trioedd Ynys Prydein. The Welsh triads, edited with introduction, translation, and commentary. Cardiff. 1961. Idem, 'Trioedd Ynys Prydain: the Myvyrian Third Series', *Hon. Soc. Cymmrodorion Trans.* 1968 (1969), 299–338; 1969 (1970), 127–55.

See R. Bromwich, 'Trioedd Ynys Prydain in Welsh literature and scholarship' (c. 1550–c. 1800), G. J. Williams Memorial lecture, 1968 (Cardiff, 1969); and review thereof by Thomas Parry in *Antiquity*, xliv (1970), 242–3.

2388   IRISCHE TEXTE. Ed. by Ernst Windisch and Whitley Stokes. 4 vols. Leipzig. 1880–1909. See No. 351.

2389   IRISH TEXTS SOCIETY, PUBLICATIONS. Lond. and Dublin. 1899+.

Listed in *Repert. Font.* i. 342.

2390 MEDIEVAL AND MODERN IRISH TEXTS. Institute for Advanced Study. Dublin. 1931+.

Listed in *Repert. Font.* i. 412–13.

2391 O'GRADY (STANDISH H.). Silva gadelica . . . a collection of tales in Irish . . . edited and translated. 2 vols. Lond. 1892.

2392 STOKES (WHITLEY) and STRACHAN (JOHN). Thesaurus palaeo-hibernicus: a collections of old Irish glosses, scholia, prose, and verse. 2 vols. Cambr. 1901–3. Supplement. Halle a. S. 1910.

A monumental work which includes most of the oldest Irish documents.

2393 BOOK OF THE DUN COW. Lebor na h-Uidhri. A collection of pieces in prose and verse in the Irish language, compiled and transcribed about A.D. 1100 . . . (A facsimile edition prepared under the auspices of the Royal Irish Academy.) Dublin. 1870. Text also edited by Richard I. Best and Osborn Bergin. R.I.A. Dublin. 1929.

The oldest surviving collection, largely of romantic tales of the Ulster cycle. The MS. is now in the library of R.I.A. See H. P. A. Oskamp, 'Notes on the history of Lebor na h'Uidri', *Royal Irish Acad. Procs.* lxv (1967), Sec. C, vi, pp. 117–37.

2394 BOOK OF LEINSTER. A collection (as above) compiled in part about the middle of the twelfth century. (A facsimile edition prepared by Robert Atkinson under the auspices of R.I.A.) Dublin. 1880. Also The Book of Leinster, ed. by Richard I. Best, Osborn Bergin, and Michael A. O'Brien. Dublin. 1954. In progress.

A very large volume of ancient Irish lore, including some historical and genealogical materials, including *Annals*, among a quantity of romance. The MS. is now at Trinity College, Dublin; the prototype may have been written in the tenth century. See also W. O'Sullivan, 'Notes on the script and make-up of the Book of Leinster', *Celtica*, vii (1966), 1–31. Volume v of the Best–O'Brien edition appeared in 1967. See Cecile O'Rahilly, ed. and trans. *Táin Bo Cúalnge* (Dublin, 1967); and review thereof by R. T. Meyer in *Speculum*, xliv (1969), 486–8.

2395 YELLOW BOOK OF LECAN. A collection (as above) compiled at the end of the fourteenth century. (A facsimile edition prepared by Robert Atkinson under the auspices of R.I.A.) Dublin. 1896.

A quarto volume of about 500 pages, containing some historical and topographical materials among romances. The MS. is now at Trinity College, Dublin.

2396 BOOK OF BALLYMOTE. A collection (as above) compiled about the beginning of the fifteenth century. (A facsimile edition prepared by Robert Atkinson under the auspices of R.I.A.) Dublin. 1887.

The most important for historical purposes of all these collections. It includes genealogies of many Irish families, tales of early Irish kings, the Irish translation of Nennius (see above, No. 2167), the *Book of Rights* (see No. 2245), Flann's *Synchronisms* (No. 2160), and much else. The MS. is now in the Library of R.I.A.

2397 THE SPECKLED BOOK. Leabhar Breac. A collection (as above) compiled about the close of the fourteenth century. (A facsimile edition with a description of the MS. compiled by B. O'Looney and a preface by S. Ferguson under the auspices of R.I.A.) Dublin. 1876.

Almost exclusively religious and ecclesiastical materials. The MS. is now in the Library of R.I.A.

2398 BOOK OF LISMORE. Lives of saints from the Book of Lismore. Ed. with translation by Whitley Stokes. Anecdota Oxoniensia. Mediaeval and Modern Series 5. Oxf. 1890.

A collection, compiled from manuscripts now lost, in the latter half of the fifteenth century. It includes secular materials as well as saints' lives.

2399 BODLEIAN MS. RAWLINSON B 502. A collection of pieces in prose and verse in the Irish language of the eleventh and twelfth centuries, with an introduction by Kuno Meyer. (A facsimile edition.) Oxf. 1909.

2400 THE CIRCUIT OF IRELAND by Muircheartach MacNeill, prince of Aileach: a poem written in the year 942 by Cormacan Eigeas, chief poet of the north of Ireland (Irish text, with a translation). Ed. by John O'Donovan. Irish Archaeol. Soc. Tracts relating to Ireland, vol. i, No. 2. Dublin. 1841.

The poem celebrates the expedition made in 941 by MacNeill, a renowned warrior-prince, to exact hostages to insure his succession to the kingship.

2401 CORMAC'S GLOSSARY, or Sanas Cormaic. Ed. by Whitley Stokes. *Three Irish Glossaries*, 1–46. Lond. 1862. Edited also by Kuno Meyer in *Anecdota from Irish MSS.* iv. Halle, 1912. Cormac's Glossary. Translated by John O'Donovan, edited by Whitley Stokes. Irish Archaeol. and Celtic Soc. Calcutta. 1868.

This glossary is attributed to Cormac, king of Cashel (d. 908); it is the earliest Irish dictionary, and 'the oldest attempt at a comparative vernacular dictionary made in any language of modern Europe'.

2402 GILLA COEMGIN'S CHRONOLOGICAL POEM. Ed. with a translation of the Irish by Whitley Stokes. *Tripartite Life of Patrick*, pp. 530–41. Rolls Series. Lond. 1887.

2403 LEABHAR GABHALA. The book of the conquests of Ireland. The recension of Michael O'Cléirigh. Part i, edited by R. A. Stewart Macalister and John MacNeill. Dublin. 1916.

Irish and English, partly in verse.

2404 LEBOR GABÁLA ÉRENN, the book of the taking of Ireland. Ed. and translated by R. A. Stewart Macalister. Irish Texts Soc. xxxiv, xxxv, xxxix, xli, xliv. 5 vols. Dublin. 1938–56.

A collection of early poems and prose of myth or fiction about early invasions; it is of small value as history. The first complete text of the *Book of invasions* in its earliest recension is that in the *Book of Leinster*, about 1160 (No. 2394). Cf. Myles Dillon, 'Lebor Gabala Erenn', *Jour. Roy. Soc. Antiq. Ireland*, lxxxvi (1956), 62–72; and Liam O'Buachalla, 'The Lebor Gabala or Book of invasions of Ireland: notes on its construction', *Cork Hist. Archaeol. Soc. Jour.* lxvii (1962), 70–9.

(b) Modern studies on Celtic literature

See Chadwick (No. 2119); Celtic Philology (pp. 40–4); The Celts (pp. 279–82); Dillon and Chadwick (No. 2125); and studies by Kenneth Jackson, especially his *Language and History* (No. 2127).

The modern studies on Celtic literature are abundant. For the journals dealing with the Celtic fringe, refer to Nos. 109–11, 126, 134, 141–2; and for retrospective bibliography to Bonser, *A.-S.C.B.* (No. 12), and Nos. 10, 20, 27, 317–18. The contributions of the Welsh scholar, Sir John Rhys, are described in *P.B.A.* xi (1924–5), 187–212. For the journals dealing with the Irish literature, refer to Nos. 230–2, and for articles to Bonser (No. 12). The two most important bibliographical guides are O'Curry's *Materials* (No. 30) and Best's *Bibliography* (No. 2406). For descriptions of the manuscripts see Thurneysen (No. 2424) and the Catalogues (Nos. 1079–83).

2405   ANWYL (EDWARD). 'Prolegomena to the study of Old Welsh poetry', *Hon. Soc. Cymmrodorion Trans.* (1903–4), 59–83.

2406   BEST (RICHARD I.). A bibliography of Irish philology and of printed Irish literature. Dublin. 1913. Idem, Bibliography of Irish philology and manuscript literature, 1913–1941. Dublin. 1942. See No. 9. Cf. G. Dottin, 'La Littérature gaélique de l'Irlande'. *Rev. de synthèse historique*, iii (1901), 60–97. See Charles Donahue, 'Medieval Celtic literature' (a bibliography) on pp. 382–409 of John H. Fisher, ed. *The medieval literature of western Europe: a review of research, mainly 1930–1960* (No. 317); and Davies (No. 2124).

2407   BROMWICH (RACHEL). 'The character of the early Welsh tradition' in Chadwick's *Studies Early Brit. Hist.* (No. 2122), pp. 83–136.

2408   CARNEY (JAMES), ed. Early Irish poetry. Thomas Davis lectures. Lond. 1965.

2409   CARNEY (JAMES). Studies in Irish literature and history. Dublin. 1955. Idem, Mediaeval Irish lyrics, selected and trans. Dublin. 1967.

2410   DILLON (MYLES), ed. The cycles of the kings. Lond. 1946.

2411   DILLON (MYLES). Early Irish literature. Chicago. 1948.

The translations and summaries of sagas form a companion to Flower (No. 2412).

2412   FLOWER (ROBIN). The Irish tradition. Oxford. 1947.

'The best introduction to medieval Irish literature' (Donahue).

2413   GREAT BOOKS OF IRELAND. Thomas Davis lectures. Dublin. 1967.

2414   HAMEL (ANTON G. VON). De oudste keltische en angelsaksische geschiedbronnen. Middleburg. 1911.

2415   HYDE (DOUGLAS). A literary history of Ireland. Lond. 1899. New edn. 1920.

2416 JOYCE (PATRICK W.). A social history of ancient Ireland. 2 vols. Lond. 1903.

2417 JACKSON (KENNETH). Language and history in early Britain. See No. 2127.

> Among other books by Kenneth Jackson are: *Studies in early Celtic nature poetry* (Cambr. 1935); *Early Welsh gnomic poems* (Cardiff, 1935); *A Celtic miscellany* (with excellent translations (Lond. 1951)); *The oldest Irish tradition: a window on the Iron Age* (Cambr. 1964).

2418 MEYER (KUNO). Learning in Ireland in the fifth century and the transmission of learning. Dublin. 1913.

2419 MURPHY (GERARD). Early Irish lyrics. Oxf. 1956. Idem, Saga and myth in ancient Ireland. Dublin. 1955.

2420 O'CONNOR (FRANK) and GREENE (DAVID H.). A golden treasury of Irish poetry, 600–1200. Dublin and Berkeley–Los Angeles. 1967.

2421 O'CURRY (EUGENE). On the manners and customs of the ancient Irish. 3 vols. Dublin. 1873.

2422 O'RAHILLY (THOMAS F.). Early Irish history and mythology. No. 2129.

2423 PARRY (THOMAS). A history of Welsh literature. Translated from the Welsh by H. Idris Bell. Oxf. 1955.

> A translation of *Hanes Llenyddiaeth Gymraeg hyd 1900* (1944).

2424 THURNEYSEN (RUDOLF). Die irische Helden- und Königsage bis zum siebzehnten Jahrhundert. Halle. 1921. Idem, 'Zu irischen Handschriften und Literaturdenkmälern'. *Abhandl. der K. Gesellschaft . . . zu Göttingen. Phil.-hist. Klasse*, N.F. xiv (1912–13).

> Fundamental for the sagas of the Ulster cycle.

2425 WILLIAMS (IFOR). Lectures on early Welsh poetry. Dublin. 1944.

3. *Scandinavian Literature*

The Scandinavian literature bearing on British history during the two centuries before the Norman conquest is chiefly of Icelandic origin or written by Icelanders in Norway. It consists of the sagas and of the poems of the skalds. Skaldic poetry developed in a complicated alliterative verse-form in which were embedded numerous concise metaphors (kennings). The poems were frequently composed in praise of a king or chieftain; indeed skalds were often court poets; and some kings were themselves skalds. The sagas were prose epics, narrating tales of a chieftain's adventures at home or abroad. Some scholars hold that the sagas, passed on by oral tradition, were committed to writing in the second half of the twelfth century or more commonly in the thirteenth century. Others maintain that they were moulded and elaborated by thirteenth-century authors. Similar heroic epics were composed elsewhere. Those sagas which are of particular interest to students of British history may be classified as follows:

1. Icelandic family sagas (*Islendinga sögur*), each containing the life and exploits of an Icelandic chieftain or family, mainly in the period A.D. 900 to 1030; but not written down until *c*. 1200 (Nos. 2439–40, 2445, 2449).
2. Kings' sagas (*Konunga sögur*), memoirs of kings, chiefly of Norway (Nos. 2438, 2447, 2450).
3. Sagas referring to countries other than Iceland and Norway (Nos. 2448, 2451).

The extensive literature on skaldic poems and on sagas must be sought elsewhere. Here we confine ourselves to (i) helpful bibliographical guides, (ii) the principal collective editions, (iii) editions of the sagas most pertinent to British history, and (iv) important commentaries written in English.

For England the texts, with translations, of three skaldic poems and of portions of six sagas are given in Ashdown (No. 2437); and translations of seven poems and a portion of Egil's saga may be found in Whitelock's volume of *Eng. Hist. Docs.* (No. 17), pp. 299–312. For Scotland, a considerable number of translated extracts from sagas are printed in chronological order in Anderson's *Sources* (No. 1088A).

The sagas are valuable for the study of the Northmen in Britain and Ireland, especially in the tenth and eleventh centuries, but since their intent was largely entertainment they must be used cautiously. The kings' sagas throw most light upon the doings of the Northmen in Britain and Ireland, being filled with stories like those concerning the relations of Harold Fair-Hair to Athelstan, the exploits of Eric Blood-Axe in Northumbria, the expeditions of the two Olafs, Cnut, and Harold Hardrada to England, the forays of jarls in the British Isles, and the account of the battle of Stamford Bridge.

The Latin sources coming from Denmark and Norway also contribute to British history. For collections of them, consult Langebek (No. 1106) and Storm (No. 1115). The best edition of Saxo Grammaticus is by Olrik and Raeder (No. 2426).

2426 SAXONIS GESTA DANORUM, primum a C. Knabe et P. Herrmann recensita, recognoverunt et ediderunt J. Olrik et H. Raeder. 2 vols. Copenhagen. 1931–57.

Vol. i (1931) contains the text; vol. ii (1935–57) provides an index, published in fascicules, by Franz Blatt. Of the sixteen books, the first nine are mythological. For other editions, see Potthast, ii. 999–1001. For commentary, Alistair Campbell, 'Saxo Grammaticus and Scandinavian historical tradition', *Saga Book*, xiii, pt. i (1946), 1–22. For facsimile edition, see Corpus Codicum danicorum medii aevi, iv, 44–250 (Copenhagen, 1962).

(*a*) Bibliographical guides

Current bibliographies may be found in *P.M.L.A.* (No. 268), *Year's Work in Modern Language Studies* (No. 269), and the journals cited immediately below (Nos. 2430, 2432, 2434). Among journals in English, *Journal of English and*

Germanic Philology is useful for reviews. For historiographical commentary, consult Halldór Hermannsson, 'Old Icelandic literature', *Islandica*, xxiii (1933).

2427 ACTA PHILOLOGICA SCANDINAVICA. Copenhagen. 1926+.

2428 ARKIV FÖR NORDISK FILOLOGI. (Christiania) Oslo. 1889+.

2429 BEKKER-NIELSEN (HANS). Old Norse-Icelandic studies: a select bibliography. Toronto Medieval Bibliographies. Toronto. 1970.

2430 BIBLIOGRAPHY OF OLD NORSE-ICELANDIC STUDIES. Copenhagen. 1964+.

An annual bibliography.

2431 HOLLANDER (LEE M.). A bibliography of Skaldic studies. Copenhagen. 1958.

2432 HUMANIORA NORVEGICA. Two years' work in Norwegian humanities and social sciences. Oslo. 1950.

For 1954 and after, this bibliographical and critical survey in English is annual as *The year's work in Norwegian humanities.*

2433 KULTURHISTORISK LEKSIKON FOR NORDISK MIDDEL-ALDER FRA VIKINGETID TIL REFORMATIONSTID. Copenhagen. 1956+. Oslo. 1956+.

2434 MEDIAEVAL SCANDINAVIA. Odense. i+. 1968+.

Devoted to the study of medieval civilization in Scandinavia and Iceland, with articles usually in English.

2435 SCANDINAVICA. Lond. and N.Y. 1962+.

(b) Principal collective editions

2436 ALTNORDISCHE SAGA-BIBLIOTHEK. Ed. by Gustav Cederschiöld, Hugo Gering, and Eugen Mogk. Vols. i–xviii. Halle. 1892–1929.

The volumes were edited or re-edited by Finnur Jónsson, Eugen Mogk, and Emil Olson.

2437 ASHDOWN (MARGARET), ed. and trans. English and Norse documents relating to the reign of Ethelred the Unready. Cambr. 1930.

Cf. N. Kershaw (Chadwick) (No. 2326) and *Eng. Hist. Docs.* (No. 17), i. 298–312. Ashdown gives selections from six sagas and three poems. Whitelock in *Eng. Hist. Docs.* gives translations from Egil's saga and eight poems.

2438 FORNMANNA SÖGUR. 12 vols. Copenhagen. 1825–37. Latin translation: Scripta historica Islandorum. 12 vols. Copenhagen. 1828–46.

A series of kings' lives, fuller than those in the Heimskringla. Vols. i–vi, x–xi, include lives of Olaf Tryggvason, St. Olaf, Magnus the Good, and Harold Hardrada (to 1066); also Knytlinga saga (to 1187).

2439 ÍSLENDINGA SÖGUR. 30 vols. Reykjavik. 1942–50.

A new edition of the series which had been printed at Reykjavik, 1891–1907. Some volumes of this series are re-edited.

2440 ÍSLENDINGA SÖGUR. Ed. by Guðni Jónsson. 13 vols. Reykjavik. 1946–9. 2nd edn. Akureyri. 1953.

The popular complete edition of the family sagas, including some as late as the nineteenth century. Vol. xiii contains an important index of personal and place names, and a list of editions of the sagas.

2441 ÍSLENZK FORNRIT. Hið íslenzka fornritafélag. 12 vols. Reykjavik. 1933–54. In progress.

Attractive editions of Old Icelandic literature. See *Medium Ævum*, iv (1935), 209–18.

2442 JÓNSSON (FINNUR). Den norsk–islandske Skjaldedigtning. 4 vols. Copenhagen and Christiania. 1908–15. Revised edn. by Ernst A. Kock. Lund. 1946.

2443 ORIGINES ISLANDICAE: a collection of the more important sagas and other native writings relating to the settlement and early history of Iceland. Edited and translated by Guðbrand Vigfússon and F. York Powell. 2 vols. Oxf. 1905.

2444 SAMFUND TIL UDGIVELSE AF GAMMEL NORDISK LITTE-RATUR. Copenhagen. 1880+. In progress.

(c) Particular sagas

2445 EGILS SAGA SKALLGRIMSSONAR. Ed. by Finnur Jónsson in *Samfund* (No. 2444). Copenhagen. 1886–8. (A critical edition.) Egil's saga. Ed. by Finnur Jónsson in *Altnord. Saga Biblio.* (No. 2436). 1894. New edn. 1924 (an annotated edition). Egil's saga. Ed. by Sigurður Nordal in *Íslenzk fornrit* (No. 2441). 1933. New edn. 1955. Also in *Íslendinga Sögur* (No. 2439), vol. iv. 1937 and 1950; and in popular series (No. 2440), ii. 1–312.

Translation: Egil's saga: done into English out of the Icelandic with an introduction, notes, etc. by Eric R. Eddison. Cambr. 1930. (A literal translation with learned notes and a list of the translations of the sagas.) Also translated by William C. Green. Lond. 1893; and by Gwyn Jones. Syracuse. 1960. Extracts are translated by D. Whitelock in *Eng. Hist. Docs.* vol. i, 298–304.

This most important Icelandic family saga is the story of a feud of that family with Harold Fair-Hair and his descendants, c. A.D. 870–980. Egil was a guest at the court of King Athelstan. It contains interesting notices, particularly on the battle of Brunanburh and on York. Jónsson and other scholars deny its authorship to Snorri; but Nordal presents arguments in Snorri's favour. Gwyn Jones, 'Egill Skallagrimsson in England', *P.B.A.* xxxviii (1952), 127–44. On questions of authorship, see works cited in *J.E.G.P.* lix (1960), 513–15.

2446 GUNNLAUGS SAGA ORMSTUNGU. Ed. by Finnur Jónsson in *Samfund* (No. 2444), vol. xlii (1916). Ed. by Guðni Jónsson in Íslendinga Sögur (No. 2439), vol. ix (1934). Ed. by L. M. Small. (Leeds School of English Language: texts and monographs, No. 1. Kendal. 1935). Ed. by Peter G. Foote and Randolph Quirk. Viking Society's Text Series, No. 1. Lond. 1953.

Translated as 'The Story of Gunnlaug the worm-tongue' in William Morris, *Three northern love-stories*. Lond. 1875 and 1901.

Translated as 'The saga of Gunnlaug the Snake-tongued' in Margaret Schlauch's *Medieval Narrative*. N.Y. 1928. pp. 35–72.

2447   HEIMSKRINGLA. Noregs konunga sögur af Snorri Sturluson. Ed. by Finnur Jónsson. 4 vols. Copenhagen. 1893–1900.

This is the critical edition in *Samfund* (No. 2444). The text is reprinted in one volume (Copenhagen, 1911 and 1936). Another edition is *Islensk fornrit* (No. 2441), xxvi–xxviii, by Bjarni Aðalbjarnarson (Reykjavik, 1941–51). For other editions, see Potthast, *Bibliotheca* (No. 62), ii. 1024–5.

Translations into English: The Heimskringla; or Chronicle of the kings of Norway; translated from the Icelandic of Snorri Sturleson, with a preliminary dissertation by Samuel Laing. 3 vols. Lond. 1844. Laing's translation of the Olaf sagas was reprinted in the Everyman's Library, 1915 and 1930; his translation of the Norse King sagas, other than the Olaf sagas, was reprinted in another volume of the Everyman's Library in 1930. Another translation is Heimskringla; or the lives of the Norse kings, by Snorre Sturlason, edited with notes by Erling Monsen and translated into English with the assistance of A. H. Smith (Cambr. and N.Y. 1932). Heimskringla: history of the kings of Norway by Snorri Sturluson, trans. by Lee M. Hollander. (Austin, 1964).

Snorri Sturlason (1178–1241), the great historian and poet, was an Icelander of good family who was prominent in the public affairs of his country. His Heimskringla—the Earth's Circle, so called from the first words in one of the manuscripts of the work—was written about 1230. It comprises abbreviated kings' sagas, interwoven with facts derived from the Kings' Book of Ari the Historian (d. 1148). The sagas of Harold Fair-Hair, the two great Olafs, Magnus the Good, and Harold Hardrada contain many references to English affairs in the tenth and eleventh centuries. See Potthast, *Bibliotheca*, ii. 1024–6.

2448   KNYTLINGA SAGA. Sögur Danakonunga: i. Sögubrot af fornkonungunum. ii. Kyntlinga saga *in* Samfund til udgivelse af gammel nordisk litteratur av Carl af Petersens och Emil Olson. Copenhagen. 1919–25. (A critical edition.) Also in *Fornmanna Sögur* (No. 2438), xi. 179–402. Copious extracts, with a Latin translation, by Finnur Jónsson in M.G.H. *Scriptores* (No. 1114), xxix (1892), 271–322. Cf. Gustav Albeck, *Knytlenga: Sagærne om Danmarks konger*. Copenhagen. 1946.

Contains the lives of the kings of Denmark from *c.* 930 to *c.* 1190; written down about 1270. Important for reign of King Cnut.

2449   NJAL'S SAGA. Ed. by Guðni Jónsson in *Íslendinga Sögur* (No. 2439), vol. x; and in the popular series (No. 2440), xi. 1–434. Ed. by Einar O. Sveinsson in *Íslenzk fornrit* (No. 2441), vol. xii. 1954. Ed. by Finnur Jónsson in *Altnordische Saga-Bibliothek* (No. 2436), xiii. 1908. Translated by George W. Dasent. The story of Burnt Njal, or life in Iceland at the end of the tenth century. 2 vols. Edin. 1861; and republished in Everyman's Library. Njal's saga: translated from the old Icelandic with introduction and notes by Carl F. Bayerschmidt and Lee M. Hollander. N.Y. 1955; and by Magnús Magnússon and Hermann Pálsson (Penguin Classics, 1960).

One of the most popular of the family sagas; covers approximately the years 970–1014. Contains some valuable details regarding the battle of Clontarf in which the Irish king Brian Boru 'fell, but saved his kingdom' from the Norse (1014). See Goedheer (No. 2583).

2450   OLAFS SAGA TRYGGVASONAR. There are four sagas about Olaf Tryggvason, king of Norway 995–1000. (i) Icelandic translation of a Latin original of *c.* 1190 by the monk Oddr Snorrason; (ii) Snorri's saga in Heimskringla; (iii) The saga about the Faroes islands; and (iv) The longer Olaf saga, probably composed in the fourteenth century. Only (i) and (iv) concern us here.

(i) Saga Ólafs konúngs Tryggvasonar in *Fornmanna Sögur* (No. 2438), x (1835), 216–376. Saga Olafs Tryggvasonar af Oddr Snorrason munk. Ed. by Finnur Jónsson. Copenhagen. 1932. (The critical edition.)

(ii) Saga Ólafs konúngs Tryggvasonar in *Fornmanna Sögur* (No. 2438), vols. i–iii. Copenhagen. 1825–7. Extracts, with a Latin translation by Finnur Jónsson in M.G.H. *Scriptores* (No. 1114), xxix (1892), 381–94. The saga of King Olaf Tryggwason who reigned over Norway A.D. 995 to A.D. 1000. Translated by J. Sephton. Lond. 1895.

Contains notices of English affairs, about 918–1035.

2451 ORKNEYINGA SAGA. Icelandic sagas and other historical documents relating to the settlements and descents of the Northmen on the British Isles. Rolls Series. 4 vols. Lond. 1887–94. Vol. i, texts by Guðbrand Vigfússon of Orkneyinga and Magnus sagas; vol. ii, text of Hakonar saga and a fragment of Magnus saga; vols. iii and iv, translations by George W. Dasent.

Orkneyinga saga. Ed. by Sigurður Nordal in *Samfund* (No. 2444). 2 vols. 1913–16. The Orkneyinga saga: translated from the Icelandic by Jón A. Hjaltalin and Gilbert Goudie, edited with notes and introduction by Joseph Anderson. Edin. 1873. The Orkneyinga saga: a new translation with introduction and notes by Alexander B. Taylor. Edin. 1938.

Gives an account, written about 1200, of the conquest of the Orkneys and their subsequent history under the Norse jarls, c. 872–1170. Cf. A. W. Johnston, 'Orkneyinga saga', *Scot. H.R.* xiii (1916), 393–400; and Alexander B. Taylor, 'The Orkneyinga saga: its relation to other saga literature: its place of composition', *Orkney Antiq. Soc. Procs.* xii (1934), 9–64.

(d) Modern commentaries in English

See above, pp. 351–2; and Nos. 2569, 2587, 2596. For articles, see Bonser (No. 12), pp. 35–8; 62–7; 281–2; 406–8; 417–18; and *C.B.E.L.* (No. 14), v. 42–7. Many articles are to be found in the *Saga Book of the Viking Society* (No. 2466). Here are entered the more important books in English on this subject.

2452 CRAIGIE (WILLIAM A.). Icelandic sagas. Cambr. 1913. *

2453 GORDON (ERIC V.). An introduction to Old Norse. Oxf. 1927. New edn. 1957.

2454 HOLLANDER (LEE M.). The Skalds: a selection of their poems. Princeton and N.Y. 1945.

2455 KOHT (HALVDAN). The Old Norse sagas. N.Y. 1931. *

2456 LIESTØL (KNUT). The origin of the Icelandic family sagas. Translated from the Norwegian by A. G. Jayne. Oslo. 1930.

2457 NORDAL (SIGURÐUR). The historical element in the Icelandic family sagas. Glasgow. 1957.

2458 OLRIK (AXEL). Viking Civilization: revised by Hans Ellekilde. N.Y. 1930. *

  Translated into English by Jacob W. Hartmann and Hanna A. Larsen.

2459 OXENSTIERNA (ERIC C. G.). The Norsemen. Trans. by Catherine Hutter. Greenwich (Conn.). 1965; Lond. 1966.

  This is a translation from the German, *Die Wikinger*, which is a translation from *Sä levde vikingarna*.

2460 PHILLPOTTS (BERTHA S.). Edda and Saga. Home University Library. Lond. 1931.

2461 SVEINSSON (EINAR Ǒ.). Dating the Icelandic sagas: an essay in method. Viking Soc. Text Ser. iii. Lond. 1958.

2462 TURVILLE-PETRE (EDWARD G.). The heroic age of Scandinavia. Hutchinson's University Library. Lond. 1951. Idem, Origins of Icelandic literature. Oxf. 1953. Idem, 'Notes on the intellectual history of the Icelanders'. *History*, xxvii (1942), 111–23.

2463 WILLIAMS (MARY W.). Social Scandinavia in the Viking age. N.Y. 1920. *

E. NON-LITERARY SOURCES

To the framework of the literary sources, the complementary disciplines provide detailed investigations of the non-literary survivals which have enormously advanced our knowledge within the past half-century. Since further discoveries of artifacts can be anticipated while the literary sources remain as they stand, future shifts in our knowledge are most likely to be contributed by the non-literary sources. The scientific scrutiny of place-names indicating the linguistic origins of the dominant settlers; numismatics, particularly in the studies of Sutherland and Dolley; and the manifold and wide-ranging researches in archaeology and art have recast our conceptions of the Anglo-Saxon period, especially in the formative stages. Accordingly reference must be made to the general works on auxiliaries cited in Chapter III above.

  The fountain-heads of the modern current of archaeology and art were Leeds's *Archaeology of the Anglo-Saxon Settlements* (1913) (No. 2481), Baldwin-Brown's *The Arts* (No. 2471), and Reginald Smith's *Guide* (No. 2472). Subsequent contributions by Leeds and Kendrick were especially fruitful. The *Ordnance Survey map of the Dark Ages* (No. 604) marks the sites; and the *V.C.H.* (No. 1529) includes some good surveys, particularly those by Reginald Smith, written between 1900 and 1926. The collections of studies dedicated to Chadwick (No. 1429), Crawford (No. 1432), and Leeds (No. 1442) contain important articles.

  To the principal journals listed on pp. 85–7 must be added Nos. 2465 and 2466 below. For Scandinavian investigations, see Nos. 2483, 2484, and 2568. For current bibliographies, consult especially *Antiq. Jour.* (No. 107) and *Biblio. Brit. Art.* (No. 778). Bonser *A.-S.C.B.* cites over 4,000 titles germane to hits section.

Some remarkable finds have been made in recent years. In 1939 excavators uncovered at Sutton Hoo in Suffolk the remains of a 'royal funeral' ship, buried about A.D. 650 (No. 2487). It proved to contain 'the richest and most brilliant treasure ever found on British soil' (Wilson, p. 45). In 1958 a remarkable hoard of Celtic metalwork was found in Shetland; a preliminary report of this discovery is given in 'The St. Ninian Isle Silver Hoard', *Antiquity*, xxxiii (1959), 241–68, and a fuller account by O'Dell (No. 2482). Further 'recent excavations at Yeavering in Northumberland and at Cheddar in Somerset have revealed the ground-plans of two Saxon royal residences, the one of the seventh, the other of the ninth and later centuries' (Colvin, *The King's Works* (No. 781), vol. i, p. 2); and for Cheddar, see *Medieval Archaeology*, vi (1962), 53–66.

For detailed studies the references in the previous paragraphs must be consulted; here only a few fundamental monographs on sites and finds are noted.

2464   MEANEY (AUDREY). Gazetteer of early Anglo-Saxon burial sites. Lond. 1964.

A valuable inventory for students of Anglo-Saxon archaeology.

2465   MEDIEVAL ARCHAEOLOGY: Journal of the society for medieval archaeology. i+. Lond. 1957+.

2466   SAGA BOOK OF THE VIKING SOCIETY. i+. Lond. 1892/6+.

2467   ABERG (NILS). The Anglo-Saxons in England during the early centuries after the invasion. Uppsala and Cambr. 1926.

A careful description of surviving remains with a view to establishing the chronology of the early A.-S. period. See also his *The Occident and the Orient in the art of the seventh century*, part i: The British Isles (Stockholm, 1943).

2468   AKERMAN (J. Y.). Remains of pagan Saxondom. Lond. (1852)–55. 40 valuable plates.

2469   ALLEN (JOHN R.). Celtic art in pagan and Christian times. Lond. 1904. Idem, Early Christian monuments of Scotland. Edin. 1903.

Allen's *Celtic Art* is superseded by Leeds's *Celtic Ornament* (No. 2481). Cf. C. L. Curle, 'The chronology of early Christian monuments in Scotland', *Procs. Soc. Antiq. Scot.* lxxiv (1939–40), 60–116.

2470   ASHE (GEOFFREY), ed. The quest for Arthur's Britain. Lond. 1968.

This is partly an illustrated report of the Camelot Research Committee, South Cadbury, Somerset. On the controversial surveys of this committee, see *Antiquity*, xliii (1969), 27–30, 52–6, 138–40; and the annual reports by Leslie Alcock in *Antiq. Jour.* 1966 to 1972.

2471   BALDWIN-BROWN (GERARD). The arts in early England. 6 vols. Lond. 1903–37.

vol. i. The life of Saxon England. 1903. New edn. 1926.

vol. ii. A.-S. architecture. 1903. New edn. 1925.

vols. iii and iv. Saxon art and industry in the pagan period. 1915.

vol. v. The Ruthwell and Bewcastle Crosses, the Gospels of Lindisfarne and
   other Christian monuments of Northumbria. 1921.
vol. vi. pt. i. Northumbrian art. 1930.
vol. vi. pt. ii. A.-S. sculpture. 1937.

2472 BRITISH MUSEUM. Guide to Anglo-Saxon and foreign Teutonic
antiquities. (Compiled by Reginald Smith.) Lond. 1923.

2473 BRØNSTED (JOHANNES). Early English ornament: the sources,
development and relation to foreign styles of pre-Norman ornamental art in
England. Trans. by A. F. Major. Lond. and Copenhagen. 1924.

2474 COLLINGWOOD (WILLIAM G.). Northumbrian crosses of the pre-
Norman age. Lond. 1927.
   For the numerous articles and inventories by W. G. Collingwood, see Bonser,
   A.-S.C.B. (No. 12).

2475 DARK AGE BRITAIN. Ed. by D. B. Harden (No. 1442).

2476 DAVIDSON (HILDA R. ELLIS). The sword in Anglo-Saxon England.
Oxf. 1962.

2477 FOX (CYRIL). Offa's Dyke: a field survey of the western frontierworks
of Mercia in the seventh and eighth centuries A.D. Lond. and N.Y. 1955.
   Cf. his 'The boundary line of Cymru', *P.B.A.* xxvi (1940), 275–300.

2478 FOX (CYRIL). 'Anglo-Saxon monumental sculpture in the Cambridge
district'. *Procs. Cambr. Antiq. Soc.* xxiii (1920–1), 15–45.
   Cf. *Archaeology of the Cambridge Region*, 1st edn. 1923 (No. 1985); and *The personality
   of Britain* (No. 613).

2479 JESSUP (RONALD F.). Anglo-Saxon jewellery. Lond. 1950.
   Cf. Joan R. Kirk, *The Alfred and Minster Lovell jewels*. Oxf. 1948. 2nd edn. by J. R.
   Clarke (née Kirk), 1961.

2480 KENDRICK (THOMAS D.). Anglo-Saxon art to A.D. 900. Lond. 1938.
Idem, Late Saxon and Viking Art. Lond. 1949.

2481 LEEDS (EDWARD THURLOW). The archaeology of the Anglo-Saxon
settlements. Oxf. 1913. Reprinted with introduction by J. N. L. Myres. 1970.
Idem, Early Anglo-Saxon art and archaeology. Oxf. 1936. *
Idem, A corpus of early Anglo-Saxon great square-headed brooches. Oxf. 1949.
Idem, 'A Saxon village near Sutton Courtney, Berkshire'. *Archaeologia*, lxxiii
(1922–3), 147–92; lxxvi (1926–7), 59–80; cxii (1947), 79–94. Idem, Celtic
ornament in the British Isles down to A.D. 700. Oxf. 1933.
   For a list of Leeds's writings, see No. 1442. The *Archaeology of the Anglo-Saxon Settlements* was a brilliant seminal treatise from which much subsequent research has sprung.
   Sutton Courtney was the first Saxon village to be excavated. *Celtic Ornament*, besides
   giving the documentation for numerous pieces of Celtic art, presents the essential
   framework for an intricate subject.

2482 O'DELL (ANDREW C.) and CAIN (A.). St. Ninian's Isle treasure.
Aberdeen Univ. Stud. No. 141. 1960.

2483 SHETELIG (HAAKON), ed. Viking antiquities in Great Britain and Ireland. 6 parts. Oslo. 1940+.

Each part written by a separate author.

2484 SHETELIG (HAAKON) and FALK (HJALMAR). Scandinavian archaeology. Trans. by E. V. Gordon. Oxf. 1937.

Invaluable guide combining archaeology and philology for the Scandinavian influence on western Europe, especially on England.

2485 STEENSTRUP (JOHANNES C. H. R.). Normannerne. 4 vols. Copenhagen. 1876–82.

A pioneer work on relations between England and Scandinavia. In Danish. See No. 2598.

2486 STUART (JOHN). Sculptured stones of Scotland. 2 vols. Spalding Club, xxvii, xxv. Aberdeen. 1856–67.

2487 THE SUTTON HOO SHIP-BURIAL: A provisional guide. R. L. S. Bruce-Mitford. The British Museum. Lond. 1947. 5th edition. 1956. New edn. as *A Handbook.* 1968.

Cf. No. 2496. A definitive publication in four volumes is in preparation. For the story of the excavation, see C. W. Phillips in *Recent Archaeol. Excavations* (No. 766), pp. 145–66. For bibliography, see F. P. Magoun, Jr., 'The Sutton Hoo Ship-Burial: A chronological bibliography', *Speculum*, xxix (1954), 116–24; and J. B. Bessinger, Jr., ibid. xxxiii (1958), 515–22. Charles Green, *Sutton Hoo, the excavation of a royal burial ship* (Lond. 1963); C. F. C. Hawkes, 'Sutton Hoo: twenty-five years after', *Antiquity*, xxxviii (1964), 252–6. J. N. L. O'Loughlin, 'Sutton Hoo: the evidence of the documents', *Medieval Archaeology*, viii (1964), 1–19. J. O. Prestwich, 'King Æthelhere and the battle of Winwaed', *E.H.R.* lxxxiii (1968), 89–95. On the lyre, see R. and M. Bruce-Mitford in *Antiquity*, xliv (1970), 7–13; and on the coins, Grierson, ibid. pp. 14–18.

2488 WAINWRIGHT (FREDERICK T.), ed. The problem of the Picts. Studies in History and Archaeology, vol. i. Edin. 1955.

A series of contributions by various scholars on fortifications, houses, graves, art, and language of the Picts from about A.D. 300 to A.D. 850. For earlier studies, see W. J. Watson, 'The Picts: their original position in Scotland', *Gaelic Soc. of Inverness Trans.* xxx (1919–22), 240–61; and J. Fraser, 'The question of the Picts', *Scottish Gaelic Studies*, ii, pt. ii (1927–8), 172–201.

2489 WHEELER (ROBERT E. MORTIMER). London and the Vikings (London Museum Catalogue). Lond. 1927. Idem, London and the Saxons (London Museum Catalogue). Lond. 1935.

2490 WILSON (DAVID M.). The Anglo-Saxons. *Ancient Peoples and Places.* Lond. 1960.

XII. MODERN COMMENTARIES ON THE ANGLO-SAXON PERIOD

A. GENERAL COMPREHENSIVE SURVEYS

Cf. No. 604 (*b*), and *V.C.H.* (No. 1529), esp. Wilts.

2491 THE ANGLO-SAXONS. Ed. by Peter Clemoes (No. 1433).

2492 ASPECTS OF ARCHAEOLOGY. Ed. by W. F. Grimes (No. 1432).

2493 BLAIR (PETER HUNTER). An introduction to Anglo-Saxon England. Cambr. 1956.

Well-written, up-to-date survey of archaeological and literary materials, under a topical rather than a chronological organization. Cf. No. 1430.

2494 CHADWICK (HECTOR M.). Studies on Anglo-Saxon institutions. Cambr. 1905. *

See *Early Cultures*. Ed. by C. Fox and B. Dickins (No. 1429).

2495 DARK AGE BRITAIN. Ed. by D. B. Harden (No. 1442).

2496 HODGKIN (ROBERT H.). A history of the Anglo-Saxons. 2 vols. Oxf. 1935. 3rd edn. 1952. Reprinted, 1967.

This magnificently produced work is based on diverse types of sources, but goes only to the death of Alfred. The third edition (1952) includes an appendix on the Sutton Hoo ship-burial, by R. L. S. Bruce-Mitford.

2497 HODGKIN (THOMAS). The history of England from the earliest times to the Norman conquest. Lond. etc. 1906. *

See No. 1183.

2498 KEMBLE (JOHN M.). The Saxons in England. 2 vols. Lond. 1849. New edn. by W. de Gray Birch. 1876. *

A substantial work based on a broad sweep of sources; it deals especially with institutions. See Bruce Dickins (No. 2201).

2499 LOYN (HENRY R.). Anglo-Saxon England and the Norman conquest. Longmans' Social and economic history of England. Lond. etc. 1962.

Summarizes, with independent judgements, the several facets of recent research, and includes a good, selective bibliography. D. P. Kirby, *The making of early England* (Lond. 1967), contains a long bibliography, in addition to its useful, introductory text.

2500 OMAN (CHARLES W. C.). England before the Norman conquest. Lond. 1910. 8th edn. revised. 1938.

See No. 1188. Oman's work is based on literary sources.

2501 PALGRAVE (FRANCIS). The rise and progress of the English commonwealth: Anglo-Saxon period. 2 pts. Lond. 1832.

Lays stress on the development of legal institutions. Badly arranged and discursive. Palgrave also wrote a popular account of the same subject, entitled *History of England, Anglo-Saxon Period* (Lond. 1831; new editions, *History of Anglo-Saxons*, 1867, 1869, 1876, 1887, etc., and in his *Collected Historical Works*, vol. v, Cambr. 1921). Also an essay on the materials of Anglo-Saxon history, in *Quarterly Review*, xxxiv (1826), 248–98.

2502 SAYLES (GEORGE O.). The medieval foundations of England. Lond. 1948. 2nd edn. 1950.

2503 STENTON (FRANK M.). Anglo-Saxon England. Oxf. 1943. 2nd edn. 1947. 3rd edn. 1970.

See No. 1189. A masterly volume by the foremost modern authority. Indispensable both for its coherent exposition and for its annotated bibliography. See also his summary of the fundamental works in 'Early English history, 1895–1920', *T.R.H.S.* 4th Ser. xxviii (1946), 7–19.

2504 WHITELOCK (DOROTHY). The beginnings of English society. Pelican History of England, vol. i. Harmondsworth. 1952.

A brief summary by an eminent scholar, largely social history. See also her *Changing currents in Anglo-Saxon studies* (Cambr. 1958).

B. ANGLO-SAXON INVASIONS AND SETTLEMENTS

1. *The Anglo-Saxon Invaders in their Continental Homelands*

The fundamental source on the continental homelands of the Anglo-Saxons is archaeological; for which the principal commentaries are listed below. Lacking the archaeological evidence, our knowledge would be very scanty indeed. An illiterate people did not commit their contemporary history to writing. Tacitus' *Germania* gives an account of the Germans some three centuries earlier; yet how far this description is applicable to the particular Germanic groups which invaded England in the fifth century is debatable. The traditions preserved in the *Anglo-Saxon Chronicle*, Bede, Widsith, and other works are fragmentary and recorded long after the events. These morsels are conveniently translated in Chambers (No. 1209), Chap. ii, and listed in Hardy's *Catalogue* (No. 21).

English summaries of research to about 1935 given by Myres in *Roman Britain and the English Settlement* (No. 1189), Chap. xx, and by Hodgkin in *History of the Anglo-Saxons* (No. 2496), chap. i; and to later dates in Loyn (No. 2499) and Hunter-Blair (No. 2493). For recent bibliography see *C.B.E.L.* (No. 14), i. 54–8; v. 42–54; and C. F. C. Hawkes in *Dark Age Britain* (No. 1442), especially pp. 106–7. Several volumes listed above under commentaries on the Anglo-Saxon period (pp. 360–2) have introductory sections germane to the present subject. The modern material dealing rather exclusively with Germanic homelands is listed immediately below; the best authorities are Nos. 2508, 2511, 2515. For Danish historiography, see No. 50 above.

2505 TACITUS (CORNELIUS). De origine et situ Germanorum. Ed. by John G. C. Anderson. Oxf. 1938. Trans. by Harold Mattingly, Tacitus on Britain and Germany. Penguin Classics. Harmondsworth. 1948. Reprinted, 1951 and 1954. Also Germania. Ed. by Rudolf Much. 3rd edn. H. Jankuhn and W. Lange. Heidelberg. 1968.

Anderson's text is based on Henry Furneaux's edition (Oxf. 1894), which provides an English commentary. For German commentary, see Rudolf Much, *Die Germanen des Tacitus* (Heidelberg, 1937), and M. Schuster, *Das Germanentum bei Cäsar und Tacitus* (Vienna, 1939). See No. 2025.

2506 BOELES (PIETER). Friesland tot de elfde Eeuw: Zijn voor en vroege geschiedenis. The Hague. 1927. 2nd edn. 1951. Index by Harmen T. OBreen. Leeuwarden. 1962.

2507 BRUNNER (HEINRICH). Deutsche Rechtsgeschichte. 2 vols. Leipzig. 1887–92. 2nd edn. of vol. i. 1906; of vol. ii, by Claudius Freiherr von Schwerin. 1928.

Early Germans, i. 1–267. Cf. P. Grierson, 'Election and inheritance in early Germanic kingship', *Cambr. Hist. Jour.* vii (1941), 1–22. See 2560A.

2508 DRÖGEREIT (RICHARD). 'Ausbreitung der nordwestdeutschen Küstenvölker über See'. *Neues Archiv für Niedersachsen*, xxiii (1951), 229–51. Idem, 'Die Besiedlung Britanniens durch die Angelsachsen'. *Nachrichten aus Niedersachsens Urgeschichte*, xiii (1939), 47–95. Idem, 'Sachsen und Angelsachsen', *Niedersächsisches Jahrbuch für Landesgeschichte*, xxi (1949), 1–62.

2509 ERDMANN (AXEL). 'Über die Heimat und den Namen der Angeln'. *Skrifter Humanistiska Vetenskaps Samfundet*, II. i, No. i, Uppsala. 1890.

The Angles came from Schleswig.

2510 GUMMERE (FRANCIS B.). Germanic origins: a study in primitive culture. N.Y. 1892. Revised as, Founders of England, with supplementary notes by Francis P. Magoun, Jr. N.Y. 1930.

2511 JANKUHN (HERBERT). 'The continental home of the English'. *Antiquity*, xxvi (1952), 14–24.

See also his *Denkmäler der Vorzeit zwischen Nord- und Ostsee: Kulturströmungen und Völkerbewegungen im alten Norden* (Schleswig, 1957). Idem, 'Siedlungs- und Kultur-geschichte der Angeln vor ihrer Abwanderung nach England', *Jahrbuch des Angeler Heimatsvereins*, xiv (1950), 54–132.

2512 LANGENFELT (GÖSTA). 'Notes on the Anglo-Saxon pioneers'. *Englische Studien*, lxvi (1931), 161–244.

Fundamentally a bibliographical survey on historical and literary questions from continental homelands to Beowulf.

2513 LOT (FERDINAND). 'Les migrations saxonnes en Gaule et en Grande-Bretagne du IIIᵉ au Vᵉ siècle'. *Revue historique*, cxix (1915), 1–40.

See also Mélanges Bémont (No. 1426), pp. 1–19.

2514 MEITZEN (AUGUST). Siedelung und Agrarwesen der Westgermanen und Ostgermanen. 3 vols. and atlas. Berlin. 1895. *

2515 PHILIPPSON (ERNST A.). Germanisches Heidentum bei den Angel-sachsen. *Kölner Anglist. Arbeiten*, iv. Leipzig. 1929. *

An extensive bibliography.

2516 PLETTKE (ALFRED). Ursprung und Ausbreitung der Angeln und Sachsen. *Die Urnenfriedhöfe in Niedersachsen*, III. i. Hildesheim and Leipzig. 1921.

2517 RADFORD (C. A. RALEGH). 'The Saxon house: a review and some parallels'. *Medieval Archaeology*, i (1957–8), 27–38.

2518   ROEDER (FRITZ). Die sächsische Schalenfibel der Völkerwanderungs-zeit. Göttingen. 1927. Reprinted from *Göttinger Beiträge zur deutschen Kultur-geschichte* (1927), 15–52. Idem, 'Neue Funde auf kontinental-sächsischen Friedhöfen der Völkerwanderungszeit'. *Anglia*, lviii, N.F. xlv (1933), 321–60.

2519   SALIN (BERNHARD). Die altgermanische Thierornamentik: typo-logische Studie über germanische Metalgegenstände aus dem IV. bis IX. Jahrhundert. Stockholm and Berlin. 1904. New edn. 1935.

2520   SCHUTTE (GUDMUND). Vor folkergruppe gottjod. Copenhagen. 1926. Trans. by Jean Young: Our forefathers, the Gothonic nations: a manual of the ethnography of the Gothic, German, Dutch, Anglo-Saxon, Frisian, and Scandinavian peoples. 2 vols. Cambr. 1929–33.

> An extraordinary miscellany of data, almost exclusively linguistic. The sections on the Anglo-Saxons were revised by Professor Zachrisson. See also the article 'Die Wohnsitze der Angeln und Kimbern', *Acta Philologica Scandinavica*, xiv (1940), 21–30.

2521   SCHWARZ (ERNST). Germanische Stammeskunde. Heidelberg. 1956. A reprint from Germanische Bibliothek, Reihe 5. Handbücher und Gesamt-darstellungen zur Literatur- und Kulturgeschichte.

> A general survey of all German tribes, including sections on the invaders of England.

2522   STRASSER (KARL). Sachsen und Angelsachsen. Hamburg. 1932. Revised edn. 1941.

2523   THOMPSON (EDWARD A.). The early Germans. Oxf. 1965.

> Thompson holds that by the fourth century 'the people whom Tacitus described have in most cases disappeared from history . . . at any rate under those names'. The institu-tions, however, changed very little.

2524   WADSTEIN (NILS ELIS). Norden och Västeuropa in gammal tid. Stockholm. 1925. See also his 'On the origin of the English'. *Skrifter K. Humanistiska Vetenskaps=Samfundet*, Uppsala, xxiv, No. 14. Uppsala. 1927.

> See Zachrisson (No. 2562).

2525   WAITZ (GEORG). Deutsche Verfassungsgeschichte. Vol. i: Die Ver-fassung des Volkes in ältester Zeit. Kiel. 1844. 3rd edn. Berlin. 1880.

2. *The Anglo-Saxon Invasions and Settlements to* c. A.D. *871*

The narrative sources are Gildas, Bede, Nennius, the *Anglo-Saxon Chronicle*, and a few lines from continental writers. The latter are embedded in the *History of Zosimus*, the chronicle erroneously attributed to Prosper Tiro, the *Bella Gothica* by Procopius, and the *Life of St. Germanus*. All of these gleanings are translated in Chambers (No. 1209), pp. 75–8. The genealogy of kings (No. 2161) must also be considered. The important, if fragmentary, sources are reinforced by archaeological, linguistic, place-name, and agronomic evidence. Through the developments in this complementary evidence our knowledge of the dark fifth and sixth centuries has been substantially increased in the twentieth century. Two seminal works, H. M. Chadwick's *Origins* and E. T. Leeds's *Archaeology*

(Nos. 2529, 2548), provided the starting-points for much later research. For summaries of the trends of research, consult Nos. 2493, 2499. The archaeological evidence is listed in pp. 357–60 above; and in Nos. 604, 2465, 2490. The place-name evidence is given in pp. 75–8, especially in the introductions to the volumes of the Place-Name Society. The articles in *Festschriften* and collected works are listed in Nos. 1426, 1429–30, 1432–3, 1442, 1451, 1454, 1465, 1470, 1496; for other articles, see Bonser (No. 12) and *C.B.E.L.* (No. 14) and the periodic bibliographies in *Antiquaries Journal* (No. 107). A few of the more important of the numerous specialized studies are named immediately below.

In supporting the view of a gradual Germanization of Britain rather than a fifth-century catastrophic invasion, Donald A. White cites the historiography in 'Changing views on the *Adventus Saxonum* in the nineteenth and twentieth century English scholarship', *Jour. Hist. Ideas*, xxxii (1971), 585–94.

2526 ANGLES AND BRITONS. O'Donnell Lectures. Cardiff. 1963.
   (a) K. Jackson, Angles and Britons in Northumbria and Cumbria.
   (b) N. K. Chadwick, The British or Celtic part in the population of England.
   (c) W. Rees, Survivals of ancient Celtic custom in medieval England.

2527 BLAIR (PETER HUNTER). 'The origins of Northumbria'. *Archaeol. Aeliana*, 4th series, xxv (1947), 1–51. Idem, 'The Northumbrians and their southern frontier'. Ibid. xxvi (1948), 98–126. Idem, 'The boundary between Bernicia and Deira'. Ibid. xxvii (1949), 46–59. See No. 2122. Idem, *The World of Bede*. Lond. 1970. N.Y. 1971.

2528 BLUNT (CHRISTOPHER E.). 'The Anglo-Saxon coinage and the historian'. *Medieval Archaeology*, iv (1960), 1–15. See No. 1454.

2529 CHADWICK (HECTOR M.). The origins of the English nation. Cambr. 1907. *

2530 CHADWICK (NORA K.), ed. Studies in early British history. Cambr. 1954. Idem, Studies in the early British church. Cambr. 1958. Idem, Celt and Saxon: studies in the early British border. Cambr. 1963.

In each book of this trilogy, several collaborators present various aspects of early British history. These works are analysed in Nos. 2122, 2665, 2123. See also No. 2664.

2531 CHAMBERS (EDMUND K.). Arthur of Britain. Lond. 1927. Pb. N.Y. 1967. *

2532 CLARK (MARY G.). Sidelights on Teutonic history during the migration period: being studies from Beowulf and other Old English poems. Cambr. 1911.

Analyses historical references in the poems.

2533 COPLEY (GORDON J.). The conquest of Wessex in the sixth century. Lond. 1954. Idem, The archaeology of south-east England: a study in continuity. Lond. 1958.

Supports the general reliability of the narrative sources and questions the Maitland–Vinogradoff thesis of the rapid overthrow of the Roman system.

2534　DEANESLY (MARGARET). 'The court of King Æthelberht of Kent'. *Cambr. Hist. Jour.* vii (1942), 101–14.

2535　DEMOUGEST (ÉMILIENNE). 'Les invasions germaniques et la rupture des relations entre la Bretagne et la Gaule'. *Moyen Âge,* 4th ser. xvii (1962), 1–50.

2536　DRÖGEREIT (RICHARD). 'Sachsen und Angelsachsen'. *Niedersächsisches Jahrbuch für Landesgeschichte,* xxi (1949), 1–62. Cf. No. 2508.

2537　ELTON (CHARLES I.). Origins of English history. Lond. 1882. 2nd edn. 1890.

2538　EVISON (VERA). The fifth-century invasions south of the Thames. Lond. 1965.

> A reinterpretation of the archaeological evidence, presenting theses which are regarded as highly controversial. See, e.g., the review in *Jour. Roman Stud.* lvii (1967), 274–5.

2539　FINBERG (HERBERT P. R.). Roman and Saxon Withington. Leicester. 1955.

> See No. 2099 and Finberg's *Lucerna* (No. 1470).

2540　FOX (SIR CYRIL). Offa's Dyke (No. 2477).

2541　HAWKES (SONIA C.). 'The Jutish style A: a study of German animal art in southern England in the fifth century A.D.'. *Archaeologia,* xcviii (1961), 29–74.

2542　HOMANS (GEORGE C.). 'The Anglo-Saxon invasions reconsidered'. *Procs. Massachusetts Hist. Soc.* lxxi (1959), 37–49. Cf. Nos. 2551–2.

2543　HOSKINS (WILLIAM G.). The westward expansion of Wessex. Leicester. 1960. Idem, 'The Anglian and Scandinavian settlement of Leicestershire'. *Leics. Archaeol. Soc. Trans.* xviii (1934–5), 110–47; xix (1936–7), 94–109.

2544　JACKSON (KENNETH). The Gododdin: the oldest Scottish poem. Edin. 1969.

> Cf. his 'The Gododdin of Aneirin', *Antiquity,* xiii (1939), 25–34. See Jackson, 'The Britons in southern Scotland', *Antiquity,* xxix (1955), 77–88; and Nos. 1433, 2123.

2545　JOLLIFFE (JOHN E. A.). Pre-feudal England: the Jutes. Oxf. 1933.*

2546　JONES (GLANVILLE). 'Settlement patterns in Anglo-Saxon England'. *Antiquity,* xxxv (1961), 221–32. G. R. J. Jones, 'The tribal system in Wales: a re-assessment in the light of settlement studies'. *Welsh Hist. Rev.* ii (1961), 111–32. See No. 2647.

2547　KIRBY (DAVID P.). 'Problems of early West Saxon history'. *E.H.R.* lxxx (1965), 10–29.

> Kirby is concerned with the dating of the early kings.

2548　LEEDS (EDWARD T.). The archaeology of the Anglo-Saxon settlements. Oxf. 1913.* Idem, 'The West Saxon invasion and the Icknield Way'.

History, New Ser. x (1925), 97–109. Idem, 'The early Saxon penetration of the Upper Thames area'. *Antiquaries Jour.* xiii (1933), 229–51. Idem, 'The distribution of Angles and Saxons, archaeologically considered'. *Archaeologia*, xci (1945), 1–107. Idem, 'Jutish art in Kent'. *Medieval Archaeology*, i (1957), 5–26 (cf. Hawkes's article in *Dark Age Britain* (No. 1442)).

2549 LENNARD (REGINALD V.). 'The character of the Anglo-Saxon conquests: a disputed point'. *History*, New Ser. xviii (1933–4), 204–15. Cf. No. 2105.

> Rejects the view, advanced by Lot (No. 2550), that the conquest was rapid and co-ordinated.

2550 LOT (FERDINAND). 'Bretons et Anglais aux Ve et VIe siècles'. *P.B.A.* xvi (1930), 327–44. Cf. No. 2549.

2551 MYRES (JOHN N. L.). Anglo-Saxon pottery and the settlement of England. Rhind Lectures, 1965. Oxf. 1969.

> An archaeological study of some 3,500 pots which helps to unravel the history of the settlement. Cf. Idem, *P.B.A.* lvi (1970), 145–74.

2552 MYRES (JOHN N. L.). 'The Teutonic settlement of Northern England'. *History*, New Ser. xx (1935–6), 250–62. Idem, 'The present state of the archaeological evidence for the Anglo-Saxon conquest'. Ibid. xxi (1936–7), 317–30. Idem, 'Some English parallels to the Anglo-Saxon pottery of Holland and Belgium in the migration period'. *L'Antiquité classique* (Brussels), xvii (1948), 453–72. R. R. Clarke and J. N. L. Myres, 'Norfolk in the Dark Ages A.D. 400–800'. *Norfolk Archaeology*, xxvii (1939–40), 163–249. J. N. L. Myres, 'Archaeology and history: Britons and Saxons in the post Roman centuries'. *Council for British Archaeology: Report ii* (1961). Idem, 'Wansdyke and the origin of Wessex' in *Essays . . . presented to Sir Keith Feiling*, edited by H. R. Trevor-Roper. Lond. 1964. Idem, 'The adventus Saxonum' in *Crawford essays* (No. 1432).

2553 RADFORD (C. H. RALEGH). 'Vortigern'. *Antiquity*, xxxii (1958), 19–24.

> See J. D. Bu'lock, 'Vortigern and the pillar of Eliseg'. *Antiquity*, xxxiv (1960), 49–53; and D. P. Kirby in *B.B.C.S.* xxiii (1968), 37–59.

2554 SMITH (ALBERT H.). 'Place-names and the Anglo-Saxon settlement'. *P.B.A.* xlii (1956), 67–88.

> Cf. J. McN. Dodgson, 'The significance of the distribution of the English place-names in *-ingas, -inga* in south-east England', *Medieval Archaeology*, x (1966); Dodgson, 'The English arrival in Cheshire' (sixth and seventh centuries), *Hist. Soc. Lancs. and Ches. Trans.* ciix (1967/8), 1–37.

2555 STENTON (FRANK M.). 'The supremacy of the Mercian kings'. *E.H.R.* xxxiii (1918), 433–52. Idem, 'The foundations of English history'. *T.R.H.S.* 4th Ser. ix (1926), 159–73. Idem, 'The historical bearing of place-name studies'. Ibid. xxi (1939), 1–19; xxii (1940), 1–22; xxiii (1941), 1–24; xxiv (1942), 1–24; xxv (1943), 1–13. Idem, 'Lindsey and its kings' (No. 1448). Idem, 'East

Anglian kings' (No. 1433). All reprinted in *Preparatory to Anglo-Saxon England* (No. 1496).

The papers in *T.R.H.S.* form a series of presidential addresses given before the Royal Historical Society from 1938 to 1942 dealing with the Anglo-Saxon period. For other works by Stenton, see index below.

2556 STEVENSON (WILLIAM H.). 'The beginnings of Wessex'. *E.H.R.* xiv (1899), 32–46.

2557 STUDIES IN EARLY BRITISH HISTORY. No. 2122.

2558 WADE-EVANS (ARTHUR W.). The emergence of England and Wales. Wetteren (Belgium). 1956.

A learned, if somewhat contentious, discussion, especially of Gildas and Bede, which neglects the non-literary evidence. See the critical reviews in *Jour. Rom. Stud.* xlviii (1958), 217–18; *J.E.G.P.* lvi (1957), 469–70; *R.H.E.* lii (1957), 719–20.

2559 WAINWRIGHT (FREDERICK T.). 'The Anglian settlement in Lancashire'. *Hist. Soc. Lancs. and Ches. Trans.* xciii (1941), 1–44. J. McN. Dodgson, 'The English arrival in Cheshire'. Ibid. cxix (1968), 1–37.

2560 WALKER (H. E.). 'Bede and the Gewissae'. *Cambr. Hist. Jour.* xii (1956), 174–86.

2560A WALLACE-HADRILL (JOHN M.). Early Germanic kingship in England and on the continent (to Alfred). Lond. 1971.

2561 WILLIAMS (IFOR). 'Wales and the North'. *Cumb.-Westm. Antiq. & Archaeol. Soc. Trans.* li (1951–2), 73–88.

Discusses Nennius, Aneirin, and other early sources.

2562 ZACHRISSON (ROBERT E.). Romans, Kelts and Saxons in ancient Britain: an investigation into the two dark centuries (400–600) of English history. Uppsala. 1927.

3. *Alfred to the Norman Invasion*

The *Saga Book* of the Viking Society for Northern Research (formerly the Viking Club, founded 1892) has contained many important studies. The papers of the periodic Viking Congresses should be consulted. See also Nos. 2466, 2581, and Campbell's introduction (No. 2571).

2563 BARLOW (FRANK). Edward the Confessor. English Monarch Series. Lond. and Berkeley. 1970. Also F. Barlow, 'Edward the Confessor's early life, character and attitudes', *E.H.R.* lxxx (1965), 225–51.

2564 BARROW (G. W. S.). 'Northern English society in the early middle ages'. *Northern History*, iv (1969), 1–28.

2565 BERSU (GERHARD). 'The Vikings in the Isle of Man'. *Manx Museum Jour.* vii (1968), 83–8.

2566 BRØGGER (ANTON W.). Ancient emigrants: a history of Norse settlements of Scotland. Oxf. 1929.

2567 BRØNDSTED (JOHANNES). The Vikings. Trans. by Estrid Bannister-Good. Penguin. Harmondsworth. 1960.

2568 BUGGE (ALEXANDER). Vikingerne: billeder fra vore forfaedres liv. 2 pts. Copenhagen and Christiania. 1904; 1906.

Northmen in Ireland: i. 114–69. Northmen in England: ii. 237–342. See his *Contributions to the history of the Norsemen in Ireland* (3 pts. Christiania. 1900).

2569 BUGGE (ALEXANDER) *et al.* Norges historie. 6 vols. Christiania. 1909–17.

Vol. i to A.D. 1030 by A. Bugge; vol. ii, pt. i for A.D. 1030 to 1103 by Ebbe Hertzberg and A. Bugge; pt. ii, A.D. 1103 to 1319 by A. Bugge.

2570 BUGGE (ALEXANDER). 'The Norse settlements in the British islands'. *T.R.H.S.* 4th Ser. iv (1921), 173–210.

See also No. 2150; and Duald MacFirbis, *On the Formorians and the Norsemen*, the original Irish text, edited and trans. by Alexander Bugge. Christiania, 1905.

2571 CAMPBELL (ALISTAIR). The battle of Brunanburh. Lond. 1938.

A critical edition, with scholarly apparatus, of the famous poem.

2572 CAMPBELL (ALISTAIR). 'Two notes on the Norse kingdoms in Northumbria'. *E.H.R.* lvii (1942), 85–97.

2573 CHARLES (BERTIE G.). Old Norse relations with Wales. Cardiff. 1934.

2574 COLLINGWOOD (WILLIAM G.). Scandinavian Britain. Lond. 1908. Idem, Angles, Danes and Norse in the district of Huddersfield. Huddersfield. 1921.

2575 CONYBEARE (JOHN W. E.). Alfred in the chroniclers. (Extracts from the chroniclers.) Lond. 1900. 2nd edn. 1914.

2576 DAVIS (R. H. C.). 'East Anglia and the Danelaw'. *T.R.H.S.* 5th Ser. v (1955), 23–39. G. C. Homans, 'The Frisians in East Anglia'. *Econ. H.R.* 2nd Ser. x (1957), 189–206.

2577 DARLINGTON (REGINALD R.). 'The last phase of Anglo-Saxon history'. *History*, xxii (1937–8), 1–13.

Summary review of various facets of recent investigations. Cf. R. A. Brown, 'The Norman Conquest', *T.R.H.S.* 5th Ser. xvii (1967), 109–30.

2578 DOUGLAS (DAVID). 'Edward the confessor. Duke William of Normandy and the English succession'. *E.H.R.* lxviii (1953), 526–45.

Douglas expresses some doubts concerning the accuracy of the *A.-S. Chronicle*'s account of William's visit to England in 1051; he also finds William of Jumièges more satisfactory than William of Poitiers for the events preceding the Norman conquest. For critique of these suggestions, see T. J. Oleson, 'Edward the Confessor's promise of the throne to Duke William of Normandy', *E.H.R.* lxxii (1957), 221–8. See also B. Wilkinson, 'Freeman and the crisis of 1051', *B.J.R.L.* xxii (1938), 368–87, and 'Northumbrian Separatism in 1065 and 1066', ibid. xxiii (1939), 504–26. Consult Douglas's *William the Conqueror* (No. 3986).

2579 DUCKETT (ELEANOR S.). Alfred the Great and his England. Chicago. 1956.

2580 EKWALL (EILERT). Scandinavians and Celts in the north-west of England. Lunds Universitets Årsskrift. Lund. 1918. Idem, 'The proportion of Scandinavian settlers in the Danelaw'. *Saga Book*, xii (1936–7), 19–34. See No. 1465 (*d*). See No. 579.

2581 THE FOURTH VIKING CONGRESS (Papers read at York, 1961). Ed. by Alan Small. Edin. and Lond. 1965.

Important papers on northern England in the Viking period.

2582 FREEMAN (EDWARD A.). History of the Norman conquest. 6 vols. Oxf. 1867–79.* 2nd edn. of vols. i–iv, 1870–6. 3rd edn. of vols. i–ii, 1877. Revised American edn. vols. i–v. N.Y. 1873–6.

For critique, see H. A. Cronne, 'Edward Augustus Freeman, 1823–1892' (Historical Revision ciii), *History*, xxviii (1943), 78–92.

2583 GOEDHEER (A. J.). 'Irish and Norse traditions about the battle of Clontarf'. *Nederlandsche bijdragen op het gebied van germaansche philologie en linguistiek* (Haarlem), ix (1938), 1–45.

2584 GREEN (JOHN R.). The making of England. Lond. 1881; 1885; 2 vols. 1897. Idem, The conquest of England. Lond. 1883; 1884.

For critical appreciation, citing E. Guest, *Origines Celticae* (Lond. 1883) and W. H. Stevenson, *E.H.R.* xvii (1902), 625–42, see Stenton, *Anglo-Saxon England* (No. 2503), p. 702.

2585 GRIERSON (PHILIP). 'The relations between England and Flanders before the Norman Conquest'. *T.R.H.S.* 4th Ser. xxiii (1941), 71–112. Reprinted in No. 1493. Idem, 'A visit of Earl Harold to Flanders in 1056'. *E.H.R.* li (1936), 90–7.

2585A HALIDAY (CHARLES). The Scandinavian kingdom of Dublin. Ed. by J. P. Prendergast. Dublin, etc. 1881. 2nd edn. 1884. Reissued with new introduction. Shannon. 1970.

2586 JONES (GWYN). A history of the Vikings (to 1066). Lond. 1968.

2587 KENDRICK (THOMAS D.). A history of the Vikings. Lond. 1930. *

Covers with wide learning the whole field of Viking enterprise as a chronicle of events. Of other general histories, G. Turville-Petre, *The Heroic age of Scandinavia* (Lond. etc. 1951), is a closely packed factual volume in the Hutchinson's University Library series; and Peter G. Foote and David M. Wilson, *Viking achievement* (Lond. and N.Y. 1970), provides 'a survey of the society and culture of early medieval Scandinavia'.

2588 LABORDE (EDWARD D.). Byrhtnoth and Maldon. Lond. 1936.

2589 LARSON (LAURENCE M.). Canute the Great 995–1035 and the rise of Danish imperialism during the Viking Age. N.Y. and Lond. 1912. *

Cf. G. N. Garmonsway, *Canute and his empire*, The Dorothea Coke Memorial Lecture for 1963 (Lond. 1964).

2590   LEES (BEATRICE A.). Alfred the Great, the truth-teller, maker of England, 848–99. Lond. and N.Y. 1915.

2591   MAWER (ALLEN). The Vikings. Cambr. 1913.

A. Mawer, 'The Vikings' (A historical revision), *History*, ix (1924–5), 116–20. Idem, 'The Scandinavian kingdom of Northumbria' in *Essays and studies presented to William Ridgeway*, edited by E. C. Quiggin (Cambr. 1913), pp. 306–14. Idem, 'The redemption of the five boroughs (942)', *E.H.R.* xxxviii (1923), 551–7. Idem, 'The Scandinavian settlements in England as reflected in English place-names', *Acta philol. scandinavica*, vii (1932–3), 1–30. Also Nos. 636, 1496, 2602. Rosemary Cramp, *Anglian and Viking York*, Borthwick Papers, No. 33 (York, 1967); and K. Cameron, 'The Scandinavians in Derbyshire: the place-name evidence', *Nottingham Mediaeval Stud.* ii (1958), 86–118.

2592   MUNCH (PETER A.). Det norske folks historie. 6 pts. in 8 vols. Christiania. 1852–63.

Vols. i–iii contain much information concerning the Danes in England and Ireland.

2593   NELSON (JANET L.). 'The problem of King Alfred's royal anointing'. *Jour. Eccles. Hist.* xviii (1967), 145–63.

Deals in part with sources for Alfred.

2594   PLUMMER (CHARLES). The life and times of Alfred the Great. Oxf. 1902. *

The best biography of Alfred.

2595   SABBE (ÉTIENNE). 'Les relations économiques entre l'Angleterre et le continent au haut Moyen Âge'. *Le Moyen Âge*, lvi (1950), 169–93.

Treats the relations down to about 1050.

2596   SAWYER (PETER H.). The age of the Vikings. Lond. 1962. 2nd edn. 1971.

Sawyer covers the age of the Vikings from Byzantium to Iceland and devotes much of the book to the British Isles. Chap. ii presents a critique of the written sources and chap. iii the archaeological evidence. See also the papers on the Vikings by D. Binchy, N. K. Chadwick, F. Henry, P. MacCana, and others in *International Congress of Celtic Studies Procs.* (Dublin, 1959).

2597   SEARLE (WILLIAM G.). Anglo-Saxon bishops, kings and nobles: the succession of the bishops and the pedigrees of the kings and nobles. Cambr. 1899.

M. L. R. Beaven, 'The regnal years of Alfred, Edward the Elder and Athelstan', *E.H.R.* xxxii (1917), 517–31. W. S. Angus, 'The chronology of the reign of Edward the Elder', ibid. liii (1938), 194–210.

2598   STEENSTRUP (JOHANNES C. H. R.). Normannerne. 4 vols. Copenhagen, 1876–82. Vol. i translated by Eugène de Beaurepaire: Études pour servir à l'histoire des Normands. Caen. 1880.

Vol. i. Introduction to Norman times.
Vol. ii. Expeditions of Vikings in the 9th century.
Vol. iii. Their kingdoms in the British Isles in the 10th and 11th centuries.
Vol. iv. 'Danelag': Danish institutions in England and their influence: a study in comparative legal history.
Steenstrup's volumes constitute a fundamental work on which the history of the Vikings rests.

2599 STENTON (FRANK M.). 'The Danes in England'. *P.B.A.* xiii (1927/30), 203–46. Idem, 'The Danes in England' (A historical revision). *History*, v (1920–1), 173–7. Idem, 'Scandinavian colonies in England and Normandy'. *T.R.H.S.* 4th Ser. xxvii (1945), 1–12. See No. 1496.

> See also Nos. 636, 2555 and W. G. Hoskins, 'The Anglian and Scandinavian settlement in Leicestershire', *Leicestershire Archaeol. Soc. Pubns.* xviii (1934–5), 110–47; idem, 'Further notes', ibid. xix (1936–7), 93–109 and P. H. Sawyer, 'The density of the Danish settlement in England', *Univ. Birmingham Hist. Journ.* vi (1957–8), 1–17.

2600 WAINWRIGHT (FREDERICK T.). 'Ingimund's invasion'. *E.H.R.* lxiii (1948), 145–69. (This important study deals with the Norse infiltration into northwest England in the early tenth century). Idem, 'The submission to Edward the Elder (A.D. 920)'. *History*, xxxvii (1952), 114–30; and the articles cited there.

2601 WHEELER (RAYMOND E. MORTIMER). London and the Vikings. London Museum Catalogue, No. i. Lond. 1927.

2602 WHITELOCK (DOROTHY). 'Scandinavian personal names in the Liber Vitae of Thorney'. *Saga Book*, xii (1936–40), 127–53.

2603 WILSON (DAVID M.). 'The Viking relationship with Christianity in northern England'. *Jour. Brit. Archaeol. Assoc.* 3rd Ser. xxx (1967), 37–46.

2604 WILSON (P. A.). 'On the use of the terms "Strathclyde" and "Cumbria"'. *Cumb.-Westm. Antiq. Archaeol. Soc. Trans.* N.S. lxvi (1966), 57–92.

2605 YOUNG (JEAN I.). 'A note on the Norse occupation of Ireland'. *History*, N.S. xxxv (1950), 11–33.

> See A. T. Lucas, 'Irish-Norse relations: time for a reappraisal', *Cork Hist. and Archaeol. Soc. Jour.* lxxi (1966), 62–75; and Lucas (No. 2672); also John Ryan, 'Brian Borumha, king of Ireland', *North Munster Review* (1967), 355–74. See No. 2174.

C. ANGLO-SAXON ADMINISTRATION AND LAW

The works of Round, Maitland, Vinogradoff, Chadwick, and Stenton are fundamental. Good summaries as of their dates of publication can be found in *Cambr. Med. History*, vol. ii, Chap. xvii (1913), and vol. iii, Chap. xv (1922) by W. J. Corbett; but the more recent general studies, Nos. 2493, 2499, 2503, utilize the results of subsequent research. The studies on feudalism, listed on pp. 661–6, often include material on Anglo-Saxon backgrounds. On the origin of the jury, see the comments under Brunner (No. 1248).

2606 BINCHY (DANIEL A.). Celtic and Anglo-Saxon kingship. The O'Donnell Lectures for 1967–8. Oxf. 1970.

2607 BULLOUGH (DONALD A.). 'Anglo-Saxon institutions and early English society'. *Annali della Fondazione Italiana per la Storia Amministrativa*, ii (1965), 647–59. Milan. 1968.

2608   CAM (HELEN M.). 'The evolution of the medieval English franchise'. *Speculum*, xxxii (1957), 427–42. Reprinted (No. 1461).

From Cnut to Edward I. Holds that jurisdictional immunity did not exist before the Norman conquest; but by Edward I's time 'the lords of liberties had learned to exercise governmental functions unimagined by their forerunners, under a control equally inconceivable to them'. Cf. Naomi D. Hurnard, 'The Anglo-Norman franchises', *E.H.R.* lxiv (1949), 289–323, 433–60.

2609   CAM (HELEN M.). Local government in Francia and England: a comparison of the local administration and jurisdiction of the Carolingian empire with that of the West Saxon kingdom. Lond. 1912.

Discusses the comitatus, shire, benefice, immunity, and army.

2610   CHANEY (WILLIAM A.). The cult of kingship in Anglo-Saxon England. Berkeley, 1969, and Manchester, 1970. See No. 2560A.

2611   DRÖGEREIT (RICHARD). 'Kaiseridee and Kaisertitel bei den Angelsachsen'. *Zeitschrift der Savigny-Stiftung, Germanistische Abt.* lxix (1953), 27–73.

Convincingly maintains that the imperial titles in A.-S. charters are merely stylistic flourishes. This article is analysed by H. R. Loyn, 'The imperial style of the tenth century Anglo-Saxon kings', *History*, xl (1955), 111–15. For a more general study, see Fritz Kern, *Kingship and law in the middle ages*, edited and trans. by S. B. Chrimes (Oxf. 1939).

2612   ESSAYS IN ANGLO-SAXON LAW. Boston etc. 1876.

Courts of law, by Henry Adams.   Family law, by Ernest Young.
Land-law, by H. C. Lodge.   Legal procedure, by J. L. Laughlin.

2613   GOEBEL (JULIUS, JR.). Felony and misdemeanor. A study in the history of English criminal procedure. N.Y. 1937.

A learned treatise on the effect of continental, particularly Frankish, criminal procedure on England to the end of the eleventh century. See the reviews by T. F. T. Plucknett in *Law Quar. Rev.* liv (1938), 295–8, and by H. M. Cam in *A.H.R.* xliii (1938), 583–7.

2614   HOLLISTER (C. W. WARREN). Anglo-Saxon military institutions. Oxf. 1962.

2615   LARSON (LAURENCE M.). The king's household in England before the Norman conquest. Madison (Wisc.). 1904. *

The standard work on the household, which also deals with the comitatus, gesiths, thegns, housecarls, etc.

2616   LIEBERMANN (FELIX). 'Kesselfang bei den Westsachsen im siebenten Jahrhundert'. *Akademie der Wissensch. zu Berlin, Sitzungsberichte*, ii (1896), 829–35. Idem, 'Die Friedlosigkeit bei den Angelsachsen', in *Festschrift Heinrich Brunner zum siebzigsten Geburtstag dargebracht*, pp. 17–37. Weimar. 1910.

The Kesselfang shows that 'ceace' (kettle) should be read for 'ceape' in Ine's laws, cc. 37, 62; hence that the ordeal was well known in Ine's time, and was not introduced into England in the ninth or tenth century, as most writers had asserted.

2617   LIEBERMANN (FELIX). The national assembly in the Anglo-Saxon period. Halle. 1913. *

Cf. No. 2620, where Liebermann's views are criticized.

2618 LOYN (HENRY R.). 'The king and the structure of society in late Anglo-Saxon times'. *History*, xlii (1957), 87–100.

An important article which concludes that 'it may be that the contrast between territorial and personal kingship so well drawn by Mr. Jolliffe [*Angevin Kingship*] should be
pushed back before the 11th century'.

2619 MORRIS (WILLIAM A.). The early English county court. An historical
treatise with illustrative documents. Berkeley. 1926. Idem, The frankpledge
system. N.Y. 1910. Idem, 'The office of sheriff in the Anglo-Saxon period'.
E.H.R. xxxi (1916), 20–40. Idem, The medieval English sheriff to 1300. Manchester, Lond. and N.Y. 1927. *

2620 OLESON (TRYGGVI J.). Witenagemot in the reign of Edward the
Confessor: a study in the constitutional history of 11th century England. Lond.
and Toronto. 1955.

2621 STEVENSON (WILLIAM H.). 'Trinoda necessitas'. *E.H.R.* xxix
(1914), 689–703. See also E. J. Davis, 'Trinoda necessitas', *History*, N.S. xiii
(1928), 33–4; 337. E. John, 'The imposition of the common burdens on the lands
of the English Church'. *B.I.H.R.* xxxi (1958), 117–29.

2622 TAYLOR (C. S.). 'The origin of the Mercian shires'. *Bristol and Glouc.
Archaeol. Soc. Trans.* xxi (1898), 32–57. Reprinted in H. P. R. Finberg, *Gloucestershire Studies*. Leicester. 1958.

2623 VINOGRADOFF (PAUL). 'Folkland'. *E.H.R.* viii (1893), 1–17.
Reprinted No. 1501 above.

Sets forth the view that folkland was land held by folklaw or custom, as distinguished
from bookland, which was land held by a charter or 'book'. See also Vinogradoff's
'Transfer of land in Old English Law' in *Harvard Law Rev.* xx (1907), 532–48; his
'Romanistische Einflüsse im angelsächsischen Recht, das Buchland' in *Mélanges Fitting*
(Montpellier, 1908), ii. 499–522; and his *English Society* (No. 2650). Compare, however,
T. F. T. Plucknett, 'Bookland and Folkland', *E.H.R.* vi (1935), 64–72; G. J. Turner,
'Bookland and Folkland' (No. 1455 above); J. E. A. Jolliffe, 'English Book-right',
E.H.R. l (1935), 1–21; and Stenton, *A.-S. England*, pp. 306–8.

2624 ZINKEISEN (FRANK). 'The Anglo-Saxon courts of law'. *Political
Science Quarterly*, x (1895), 132–44.

A criticism of H. Adams's essay in *Essays in Anglo-Saxon Law* (No. 2612).

D. STRUCTURE OF SOCIETY IN ANGLO-SAXON TIMES

The changing structure of Anglo-Saxon society is pieced together by proceeding
from the known details of *Domesday Book* retrospectively to the earlier laws,
charters, place-names, and archaeological remains. The nature and scarcity of
the evidence leads to diverse conclusions and the brevity of the thumb-nail
statements on complicated issues may distort scholarly opinion. Broadly speaking, however, researches of recent decades have tended to modify, and in the
opinion of some scholars to demolish, the emphatic Germanist views of the
nineteenth century. The 'mark theory' of a free peasantry associated in a free
community in early German society is now generally regarded as untenable. The

conditions of migration and settlement probably altered in any case the trans-
planted homeland institutions. The survival of a considerable British population,
but only rarely of Roman institutions, in the area overrun by the German
invaders is generally accepted. The importance of the Humber estuary as a
debarkation point and the dispersion of the invaders from that point have been
recognized. Topography rather than racial differences, as advocated by Meitzen
(No. 1372), may account for the variation of the nucleated village from the hamlet
of scattered homesteads. The origin of the manor and the constitution of the fyrd
are in debate. The extent of the continuity of Anglo-Saxon institutions into
Norman times dovetails with feudalism and the general character of the Norman
conquest. These are some of the major areas of discussion on the structure of
Anglo-Saxon society.

Succinct epitomes of the problems and opinions on the early Anglo-Saxon
period are set forth cautiously in Loyn, *Anglo-Saxon England* (No. 2499),
pp. 1–44; and the positions of Kemble, Seebohm, Maitland, Chadwick, and
Stenton are summarized on pages 289–92. Aston (No. 2626) demonstrates the
complexity of the problem of the origin of the manor. Some of the issues on the
continuity of Anglo-Saxon institutions into Norman times are described in
Hollister's *Military Organization* (No. 4304), pp. 1–13. The starting-point for
the modern study of Anglo-Saxon institutions is Maitland's classic *Domesday
Book and Beyond* (No. 2636), for which Edward Miller's Introduction (1960)
cites some modifications of Maitland's views which subsequent research
suggests or requires.

1. *Rural Society*

Consult Gray (No. 1370), Orwin (No. 1373), and *Agrarian History* (No. 1360).

2625 ANDREWS (CHARLES M.). The old English manor. Baltimore. 1892.

An account of the lands and tenants of the manor, agricultural arrangements, recreations,
etc.

2626 ASTON (T. H.). 'The origins of the manor in England'. *T.R.H.S.* 5th
Ser. viii (1958), 59–83. Reprinted on pp. 9–35 of *Essays in Agrarian History*.
Ed. by W. E. Minchinton. Newton Abbot. 1968.

**2627 BRAUDE (JACOB). Die Familiengemeinschaften der Angelsachsen.
Leipzig. 1932.**

Cf. Fritz Roeder, *Die Familie bei den Angelsachsen*, pt. i, *Mann und Frau* (Halle, 1899).

2628 DOUGLAS (DAVID C.). The social structure of medieval East Anglia.
Oxf. 1927. Idem, 'Fragments of an Anglo-Saxon survey from Bury St. Edmunds'.
E.H.R. xliii (1928), 376–83.

See Barbara Dodwell, 'The free peasantry of East Anglia in Domesday', Norf. and Norwich Archaeol. Soc. *Original Papers*, xxviii, pt. i (1939), 145–57; idem, 'The sokemen
of the southern Danelaw', *B.I.H.R.* xvi (1938), 110–12.

**2629 GOMME (GEORGE L.). The village community, with special reference
to Britain. Lond. 1890.**

Contends that the village community was common to all Aryan peoples, and hence
existed in Celtic as well as in Anglo-Saxon England.

2630 HUDSON (WILLIAM). 'The Anglo-Danish village community of Martham'. *Norfolk Archaeol.* xx (1921), 273–316. Cf. Idem, 'Manorial life'. *History Teachers' Miscellany*, i (1923), 97–100 and 116–20.

2631 JESSEN (KNUD) and HELBAEK (HANS P.). Cereals in Great Britain and Ireland in prehistoric and early historic times. Copenhagen. 1944.

2632 JOHN (ERIC). Land tenure in early England. Leicester. 1958. Idem, 'English feudalism and the structure of Anglo-Saxon society'. *B.J.R.L.* xlvi (1963), 14–41, which is now reprinted in No. 1475.

> These controversial treatises form sharp attacks on the Germanist point of view from Stubbs to Stenton. See reviews of *Land Tenure* by H. R. Loyn in *History*, xlvi (1961), 233–5; and by R. S. Hoyt in *Speculum*, xxxvi (1961), 663–5.

2633 JOLLIFFE (JOHN E. A.). Pre-feudal England: the Jutes. Oxf. 1933. *

> Cf. Jolliffe, 'Northumbrian institutions', *E.H.R.* xli (1926), 1–42; and 'The era of the folk' (No. 1451).

2634 LITTLE (ANDREW G.). 'Gesiths and thegns'. *E.H.R.* iv (1889), 723–9.

2635 LOYN (HENRY R.). 'Gesiths and thegns in Anglo-Saxon England from the 7th to the 10th century'. *E.H.R.* lxx (1955), 529–49. Idem, 'The term *ealdorman* in the translations prepared at the time of King Alfred'. *E.H.R.* lxvii, (1953), 513–25.

2636 MAITLAND (FREDERIC W.). Domesday book and beyond: three essays in the early history of England. Cambr. 1897. Reprinted, 1907. Reprinted as paperback with an Introduction (pp. 15–22) by Edward Miller (1960).

> I. Domesday Book. II. England before the Conquest. III. The hide.
> This indispensable commentary on *Domesday Book* is followed by an inquiry into pre-Norman society in England. It throws much light on the early history of the manor, on the elements of feudalism, classes of society, and land tenures and advances strong arguments against Seebohm's view. It also presents a suggestive but questionable account of the origin of boroughs; and holds that the hide usually contained 120 acres. See James Tait's review in *E.H.R.* xii (1897), 768–77, and J. H. Round, ibid. xv (1900), 293–302. See also Corbett (No. 2213) and C. S. Taylor, 'The pre-Domesday hide of Gloucestershire', *Bristol and Glouc. Arch. Soc. Trans.* xviii (1895), 288–319; Cyril Hart, 'The hidation of Huntingdonshire', *Cambr. Antiq. Soc. Procs.* lxi (1968), 55–66. See Bell's *Maitland* (p. 201), Chaps. ii–iii; and Cyril Hart's forthcoming book.

2637 MAITLAND (FREDERIC W.). 'Surnames of English villages'. *Archaeol. Rev.* iv (1889), 233–40. Idem, 'The survival of archaic communities', *Law Quarterly Rev.* ix (1893), 36–50, 211–28. Both papers are reprinted in his *Collected Papers* (No. 1482), ii. 84–95, 313–65. Cambr. 1911.

> The 'Surnames' tries to show that the township was originally identical with the hundred, and that the latter gradually resolved itself into various townships. The 'Survival' argues against the antiquity of communal ownership of land.

2638 MAURER (KONRAD VON). Über das Wesen des ältesten Adels der deutschen Stämme in seinem Verhältnis zur gemeinen Freiheit. Munich. 1846.

Idem, 'Angelsächsische Rechtsverhältnisse'. *Kritische Überschau der deutschen Gesetzgebung*, i. 47–120, 405–31; ii. 30–68, 388–440; iii. 26–61. Munich. 1853–6.

The second work deals with the family, mark, hundred, tithing, shire, mutual surety-ship, land-laws, classes of society, feud, and wergeld.

2639 PAGE (R. I.). Life in Anglo-Saxon England. Everyday Life Ser. Lond. 1970.

2640 PAYNE (F. G.). 'The plough in ancient Britain'. *Archaeol. Jour.* civ (1947), 82–111. Idem, 'The British plough'. *Agricultural Hist. Rev.* v (1957), 74–84.

2641 PEAKE (HAROLD). The English village: the origin and decay of its community. Lond. 1922.

Cf. William Page, 'Notes on the types of English villages and their distribution', *Antiquity*, i (1927), 447–68.

2642 PHILLPOTTS (BERTHA S.). Kindred and clan in the middle ages and after: a study in the sociology of the Teutonic races. Cambr. 1913.

Cf. Lorraine Lancaster, 'Kinship in Anglo-Saxon society', *Brit. Jour. Sociology*, ix (1958), 230–50, 359–77; and D. A. Bullough, 'Early medieval social groupings: the terminology of kinship', *Past and Present*, No. 45 (1969), 3–18.

2643 REID (RACHEL R.). 'Barony and thanage'. *E.H.R.* xxxv (1920), 161–99.

2644 SANDYS (CHARLES). Consuetudines Kanciae: a history of gavelkind and other customs in Kent. Lond. 1851.

See also Nellie Neilson, 'Custom and the common law in Kent', *Harvard Law Rev.* xxxviii (1924–5), 482–98; Charles I. Elton, *The tenures of Kent* (Lond. 1867); William Somner, *A treatise of gavelkind* (Lond. 1660; 2nd edn. 1726); Silas Taylor, *History of gavelkind* (Lond. 1663). Cf. Thomas Robinson, *The common law of Kent, or customs of gavelkind and borough English* (Lond. 1741); 5th edn. by C. I. Elton and H. J. H. Mackay, *Robinson on gavelkind* (Lond. 1897), which contains many extracts from the assize rolls of the thirteenth and fourteenth centuries. Cf. Jolliffe (No. 2633).

2645 SEEBOHM (FREDERIC). Customary acres and their historical importance: a series of unfinished essays. Lond. 1914.

2646 SEEBOHM (FREDERIC). The English village community: an essay on economic history. Lond. 1883. 4th edn. 1890. Reprinted several times. *

A valuable contribution to agrarian history, which holds that the Roman villa often survived as the modern village and that Anglo-Saxon society began with serfdom and private property. Seebohm rejects the theory of the mark. For one of his main theories, see G. Jones, 'Settlement patterns' (No. 2546), and J. N. L. Myres (No. 2106). For appreciation of his unorthodox views, see Stephenson (No. 1497), arts. i and j.

2647 SEEBOHM (FREDERIC). Tribal custom in Anglo-Saxon law. Lond. etc. 1902. Idem, Tribal system in Wales. Lond. 1895. 2nd edn. 1904.

Devotes much attention to wergelds. See also F. W. Maitland, 'The laws of Wales: the kindred and the blood feud', in *Law Magazine and Rev.* 4th Ser. vi (1881), 344–67; reprinted in his *Collected Papers* (No. 1482), i. 202–29.

2648 STENTON (FRANK M.). Types of manorial structure in the northern Danelaw. Oxf. Stud. in Social and Legal Hist. ii. 3–96. Oxf. 1910. Idem, 'The free peasantry of the northern Danelaw'. *Arsber. K. Human. Vetenskapssamf. Lund* (1926), 73–185. Reprinted, Oxf. 1970. See also his *Danelaw Charters* (No. 4403); and *Preparatory to Anglo-Saxon England* (No. 1496).

2649 STEPHENSON (CARL). 'The origin and significance of feudalism'. *A.H.R.* xlvi (1941), 788–812. Idem, 'Feudalism and its antecedents in England'. Ibid. xlviii (1943), 245–65. Idem, 'The problem of the common man in early mediaeval Europe'. Ibid. li (1946), 419–38. Reprinted in *Mediaeval Institutions*: (No. 1497).

2650 VINOGRADOFF (PAUL). English society in the eleventh century. Oxf. 1908. *

> Deals with military organization, jurisdiction, taxation, land tenure, manors, social classes. Much of the material relates to the periods before and after the eleventh century, centring on *Domesday Book*.

2651 VINOGRADOFF (PAUL). The growth of the manor. Lond. etc. 1905. 3rd edn. 1920. Reprinted, 1932. *

2652 VINOGRADOFF (PAUL). Villainage in England: essays in English mediaeval history. Oxf. 1892. *

> Consists of two essays, one on the peasantry of the feudal age, the other on the manor and the village community. See reviews by I. S. Leadam in *Political Science Rev.* viii (1893), 653–76; and by F. Seebohm in *E.H.R.* vii (1892), 444–65.

2653 WILSON (DAVID M.). 'Anglo-Saxon rural economy: a survey of the archaeological evidence and a suggestion'. *Agricultural Hist. Rev.* x (1962), 65–79.

E. THE CHURCH IN ANGLO-SAXON TIMES

1. *Survivals of Paganism*

See Bonser, *A.-S.C.B.* pp. 168–70. Maps indicating places with heathen names can be found in Ordnance Survey *Map of South England in the Dark Ages* (No. 604), in Myres (No. 1189), and in Stenton's article (No. 2661).

2654 BONSER (WILFRID). 'Survivals of paganism in Anglo-Saxon England'. *Birmingham Arch. Soc. Trans.* lxvi (1934), 37–90.

2655 CHANEY (WILLIAM A.). 'Paganism to Christianity in Anglo-Saxon England'. *Harvard Theological Rev.* liii (1960), 197–217.

2656 DICKINS (BRUCE). 'English names and Old English heathenism'. *Essays and Studies by Members of the English Assoc.* xix (1934), 148–60.

2657 GELLING (MARGARET). 'Place-names and Anglo-Saxon paganism'. *Birmingham Univ. Jour.* viii (1961), 7–25.

2658 MAGOUN (FRANCIS P., Jr.). 'On some survivals of pagan belief in Anglo-Saxon England'. *Harvard Theological Rev.* xl (1947), 34–46.

2659 PHILIPPSON (ERNST A.). Germanisches Heidentum bei den Angelsachsen. Leipzig. 1929. *

2660 STANLEY (ERIC G.). 'The search for Anglo-Saxon paganism'. *Notes and Queries*, N.S. xi (1964), 204–9, 242–50, 282–7, 324–31.

2661 STENTON (FRANK M.). 'The historical bearing of place-name studies: Anglo-Saxon heathenism'. *T.R.H.S.* 4th Ser. xxiii (1941), 1–24. Reprinted in No. 1496.

2. *The Celtic Church*

The chief sources for the history of the Celtic Church are to be found in Patrick's own writings for fifth-century Ireland and in Gildas's admonitory letter for sixth-century Britain; in the ecclesiastical legislation which is particularly important for the sixth, seventh, and eighth centuries; and in the monastic rules. The saints' lives, beginning in the seventh century, form valuable commentaries on the period in which they were written; and the annals from the eighth century onwards provide a detailed and, in the main, contemporary commentary on ecclesiastical affairs. Kenney (No. 23) is an indispensable guide. Hughes (No. 2670) builds up the history of the Irish Church from the contemporary sources. See also Anderson (No. 1088A), Bullough (No. 2319(*c*)), Chadwick (Nos. 2664, 2665), Gougaud (No. 2667), Haddan and Stubbs (No. 1129), Ryan (No. 2676). Norman and St. Joseph, *Early development of Irish society* (No. 756), provides interesting new evidence.

2662 ALLEN (JOHN R.). The monumental history of the early British church (to 1066). Lond. 1889.

2662A BIELER (LUDWIG). St. Patrick and the coming of Christianity. Dublin, 1967.

Bieler's work is vol. i, fasc. i of Corish, *A history of Irish Catholicism* (No. 1274).

2663 BOWEN (EMRYS G.). The settlements of the Celtic saints in Wales. Cardiff. 1954. 2nd edn. 1956.

Historical geography of dedications of Celtic saints and of siting of early churches and spheres of Celtic influence. See also Bowen, *Saints, seaways and settlements in the Celtic lands* (Maps, diagrams, and plates). Cardiff, 1969.

2664 CHADWICK (NORA K.). The age of the saints in the early Celtic church. Riddell Lectures. Lond. 1961.

2665 CHADWICK (NORA K.), ed. Studies in the early British church. Cambr. 1958.

(*a*) N. K. Chadwick, Introduction. 1–28.
(*b*) N. K. Chadwick, Early culture and learning in North Wales. 29–120.
(*c*) N. K. Chadwick, Intellectual life in West Wales in the last days of the Celtic church. 121–82.
(*d*) K. Hughes, British Museum MS. Cotton Vespasian A. XIV (Vitae Sanctorum Wallensium): its purpose and provenance. 183–200.

(*e*) C. Brooke, The archbishops of St. David's, Llandaff and Caerleon-on-Usk. 201–42.
(*f*) K. Hughes, The distribution of Irish scriptoria and centres of learning from 730 to 1111. 243–72.
(*g*) K. H. Jackson, The sources for the life of St. Kentigern. 273–357.

2666 DOBLE (GILBERT H.). Cornish saints series. Ed. by Donald Attwater, 5 pts. Truro. 1960–70.

For a list of Nos. 1–32, see *Writings, 1901–33* (No. 38), ii. 22–3. Also G. H. Doble, *Lives of the Welsh saints*. Ed. by D. Simon Evans (Cardiff, 1971).

2667 GOUGAUD (LOUIS). Les Chrétientés celtiques. Paris. 1911. Revised edn. translated by Maud Joynt: Christianity in Celtic lands: a history of the churches of the Celts, their origin, their development, influence and mutual relations. Lond. 1932. Idem, Les Saints irlandais hors d'Irlande. Louvain and Oxf. 1936.

Cf. *Gaelic pioneers of Christianity*, translated by Victor Collins (Dublin, 1923) which appeared originally in *Rev. Hist. Eccles.* ix (1908), 21–37, 255–77, and in *Revue celtique*, xxxix (1922), 199–226; additional notes, ibid. pp. 355–8.

2668 HADDAN (ARTHUR W.). Remains of the late A. W. Haddan. Ed. by A. P. Forbes. Oxf. etc. 1876.

(*a*) The churches of the British confession. 211–39.
(*b*) Britons on the continent. 258–94.
(*c*) The early English church. 294–329.

2669 HOPKIN-JAMES (LEMUEL J.). The Celtic gospels: their story and their text. Oxf. 1934.

See also Donald MacLean, *The law of the Lord's day in the Celtic church* (Edin. 1926).

2670 HUGHES (KATHLEEN). The church in early Irish Society. Cambr. 1966.

The best general study of the subject. See her chapter in No. 1203.

2671 LOOFS (FRIEDRICH). Antiquae Britonum Scotorumque ecclesiae quales fuerint mores. Leipzig. etc. 1882.

2672 LUCAS (A. T.). 'The plundering and burning of churches in Ireland, 7th to 16th century'. *North Munster Studies*. Ed. by Étienne Rynne. Limerick. 1967. pp. 172–229.

2673 MacNAUGHT (JOHN C.). The Celtic church and the see of Peter. Oxf. 1927.

2674 MEISSNER (JOHN L. G.). The Celtic church in England after the synod of Whitby. Lond. 1929.

2675 NASH-WILLIAMS (VICTOR E.). The early Christian monuments of Wales. Cardiff. 1950.

Authoritative; inventory by counties of 415 monuments; with references.

2675A RADFORD (C. A. RALEGH). 'The Celtic monastery in Britain'. *Archaeol. Cambrensis*, cxi (1962), 1–24.

2676 RYAN (JOHN). Irish monasticism: origins and early development. Lond. 1931.

Detailed account of the Celtic form of monasticism.

2677 STOKES (GEORGE T.). Ireland and the Celtic church (to 1172). Lond. 1886. 6th edn. 1907.

H. J. Lawlor and R. I. Best, 'The ancient list of the coarbs of Patrick', *Royal Irish Acad. Procs.* xxxv, sect. C (1919), 315–62.

2678 TAYLOR (THOMAS). The Celtic Christianity of Cornwall: diverse sketches and studies. Lond. 1916.

2679 WADE-EVANS (ARTHUR W.). Welsh Christian origins. Oxf. 1934.

2680 WARREN (FREDERICK E.). The liturgy and ritual of the Celtic church. Oxf. 1881.

2681 WILLIAMS (HUGH). Christianity in early Britain. Oxf. 1912.

Cf. F. J. Haverfield's review in *Jour. Roman Stud.* ii (1912), 115. See also Williams's paper, 'Some aspects of the Christian church in Wales during the fifth and sixth centuries', *Soc. of Cymmrodorion Trans.* (1893–4), 55–132 (Lond. 1895).

2682 WILLIS-BUND (JOHN W.). The Celtic church of Wales. Lond. 1897.

Use with caution.

2683 WILSON (P. A.). 'Romano-British and Welsh Christianity: Continuity or discontinuity?'. *Welsh Hist. Rev.* iii (1966), 5–21, 103–20.

2684 ZIMMER (HEINRICH). The Celtic church in Britain and Ireland. Translated by A. Meyer (from *Realenzyklopädie für Protestantische Theologie* (1901), x. 204–43). Lond. 1902.

Brief but stimulating and controversial. Contends that St. Patrick was an unimportant missionary in a limited field; but cf. Bury (No. 2324).

2685 DOWDEN (JOHN). The Celtic church in Scotland, being an introduction to the history of the Christian church in Scotland down to the death of St. Margaret. Lond. 1894.

2686 DUKE (JOHN A.). The Columban church. Oxf. 1932. *

Criticizes the theories on the extent of pre-Columban Christianity in northern and central Scotland. See No. 2323 (g) and Edward C. Trenholme, *The story of Iona* (Edin. 1909).

2687 KNIGHT (GEORGE A. F.). Archaeological light on the early Christianizing of Scotland. 2 vols. Lond. 1933.

2688 REEVES (WILLIAM). The Culdees of the British Islands. Dublin. 1864.

See also his contribution to the *Royal Irish Acad. Trans.* xxiv (1867), 'On the Céli-dé, commonly called Culdees'; Donald Mackinnon, 'The Culdees of Scotland', *Book of the Soc. Friends of Dunblane Cathedral*, iii (1939), 58–67; and K. Hughes, *The Church* (No. 2670), chap. 16.

2689 SIMPSON (WILLIAM D.). The Celtic church in Scotland: a study of its penetration lines and art relationships. Aberdeen Univ. Studies, cxi. Aberdeen. 1935.

See also No. 2323 (*g*).

2690 SCOTT (ARCHIBALD B.). The rise and relations of the church of Scotland: early Brittonic period and St. Ninian's period. Edin. 1933.

The author's 'The Brito-Celtic church on the northern mainland and islands', *Gaelic Soc., Inverness, Trans.* xxxiii for 1925–7 (1932), 327–55, discusses the Ninianic foundations in Caithness and the northern isles.

2691 THOMPSON (EDWARD A.). 'The origin of Christianity in Scotland'. *Scot. H.R.* xxxv (1958), 17–22.

3. *Anglo-Saxon Church*
(*a*) From Augustine to Bede

For modern studies, see the general histories, pp. 164–6, the volumes of the *Victoria County History* (No. 1529), the *Cambridge Medieval History* (No. 1176), and the works of E. S. Duckett (No. 2280) and Crawford (No. 2279).

2692 BIRCH (WALTER DE GRAY). Fasti monastici aevi Saxonici, or an alphabetical list of the heads of religious houses in England previous to the Norman conquest. Lond. 1872.

Superseded by Knowles, Brooke and London (No. 5895).

2693 BRIGHT (WILLIAM). Chapters of early English church history. Oxf. 1878. 3rd edn. 1897. *

Chap. i is devoted to the ancient Celtic church; the other chapters deal with the period 597–709. A useful, old work on early English church history.

2694 BROWNE (GEORGE F.). The conversion of the heptarchy. Lond. etc. 1896. New edn. 1906.

Seven popular lectures.

2695 CABROL (FERNAND). L'Angleterre chrétienne avant les Normands. Paris. 1909.

2696 DEANESLY (MARGARET). 'Early English and Gallic minsters'. *T.R.H.S.* 4th Ser. xxiii (1941), 25–69.

An appendix, pp. 53–69, on the Charters of King Æthelberht.

2697 DEANESLY (MARGARET). The pre-Conquest Church in England. Lond. 1961. 2nd edn. 1963.

The best summary treatment. See also her chapter in No. 1281.

2698 DEANESLY (MARGARET). Sidelights on the Anglo-Saxon Church Lond. 1962. Idem, Augustine of Canterbury. Leaders of Religion series. Lond. 1964. Idem, 'The familia at Christ Church, Canterbury' (No. 1458).

2699 DUDDEN (F. HOMES). Gregory the Great. 2 vols. Lond. 1905. *

2700 GODFREY (JOHN). The church in Anglo-Saxon England. Lond. 1962. Idem, The English parish 600–1300 (brief introduction). Lond. 1969.

2701 GROSJEAN (PAUL). 'La date du colloque de Whitby'. *Anal. Boll.* lxxviii (1960), 233–74.

See also Rosalind Hill, 'Christianity and geography in early Northumbria', *Stud. in Church Hist.* iii (1966), 126–39.

2702 HOWORTH (HENRY H.). Saint Gregory the Great. Lond. 1912. Idem, Augustine the Missionary. Lond. 1913.* Idem, The golden days of the early English church from the arrival of Theodore to the death of Bede. 3 vols. Lond. 1917. *

Five volumes of somewhat miscellaneous details, to be used with caution. See reviews in *E.H.R.* xxxiii (1918), 255–9; and *A.H.R.* xxiii (1918), 374–6.

2703 HUNT (WILLIAM). The English church, A.D. 597–1066. Lond. 1899.

There is a useful survey of the authorities at the end of each chapter. See No. 1289.

2704 MASON (ARTHUR J.), ed. The mission of St. Augustine to England, according to the original documents. Cambr. 1897.

(*a*) Letters of Gregory the Great and extracts from Bede, with a translation. 1–160.
(*b*) Political outlook of Europe in 597, by C. W. C. Oman. 161–83.
(*c*) Mission of Augustine, by A. J. Mason. 184–208.
(*d*) Landing-place of Augustine, by T. M. Hughes. 209–34.
(*e*) Liturgical questions, by H. A. Wilson. 235–52.

See also R. A. Markus, 'The chronology of the Gregorian mission to England: Bede's narrative and Gregory's correspondence', *J.E.H.* xlv (1963), 16–27.

2705 PLUMMER (ALFRED). The churches in Britain before A.D. 1000. 2 vols. Lond. 1911–12.

Expanded from papers in *The Churchman*, 1910–11.

2706 THOMPSON (ALEXANDER HAMILTON), ed. Bede, his life, times, and writings. Oxf. 1935.* (No. 2148).

(*b*) From the death of Bede to Norman Conquest

See Levison (No. 2282), Robinson (No. 2283), Knowles (No. 1298), and the works on individual monasteries on pp. 810–46 and on lives of saints, pp. 320–33.

2707 ALLISON (THOMAS). English religious life in the eighth century as illustrated by contemporary letters. Lond. N.Y. and Toronto. 1929.

2708 ANGUS (W. S.). 'Christianity as a political force in Northumbria in the Danish and Norse periods'. *Fourth Viking Congress.* Ed. by A. Small. Edin. and Lond. 1965. pp. 142–65.

2709 BARLOW (FRANK). The English Church 1000–1066: a constitutional history. Lond. 1963.

Barlow 'argues that the work of the tenth century reformers reached its logical fulfilment in the legal codification of Archbishop Wulfstan, and that between Wulfstan and the conquest, the reform movement maintained its full vigour in the diocese of Worcester'.

2710 BOEHMER (HEINRICH). 'Das Eigenkirchentum in England', in *Texte und Forschungen zur englischen Kulturgeschichte: Festgabe für Felix Liebermann.* Halle. 1921. pp. 301–53.

2711 COOPER (JANET). 'The dates of the bishops of Durham in the first half of the eleventh century'. *Durham Univ. Jour.* lx (1968), 131–7.

2712 COTTON (CHARLES). The Saxon cathedral at Canterbury and the Saxon saints buried therein. Manchester. 1929.

2713 CRASTER (HERBERT H. EDMUND). 'The patrimony of St. Cuthbert'. *E.H.R.* lxix (1954), 177–99.

2714 CRASTER (H. H. E.). 'Some Anglo-Saxon records of the see of Durham'. *Archaeol. Aeliana*, 4th Ser. i (1925), 189–98. Idem, 'The Red Book of Durham'. *E.H.R.* xl (1925), 504–52.

2715 DARLINGTON (REGINALD R.). 'Ecclesiastical reform in the late Old English period'. *E.H.R.* li (1936), 385–428. Idem, 'Æthelwig, abbot of Evesham'. Ibid. xlviii (1933), 1–22.

> Darlington convincingly counteracted the older opinion that the Anglo-Saxon church deteriorated in the late Saxon period. For the earlier reform movements, see D. J. V. Fisher (No. 2718). For the tenth-century movement, see Thomas Symons, 'The English monastic reform of the tenth century', *Downside Rev.* lx (1942), 1–22, 196–222, 268–79; D. J. V. Fisher, 'The anti-monastic reaction in the reign of Edward the Martyr', *Cambr. Hist. Jour.* x (1952), 254–70. Consult the articles by Eric John reprinted in *Orbis Britanniae* (No. 1475), to which may be added his 'The church of Winchester and the tenth century reformation', *B.J.R.L.* xlvii (1965), 404–29.

2716 DEANESLY (MARGARET). 'The archdeacons of Canterbury under Archbishop Ceolnoth (833–870)'. *E.H.R.* xlii (1927), 1–11.

2717 FINBERG (HERBERT P. R.). Tavistock abbey. A study in the social and economic history of Devon. Cambr. 1951. Idem, 'Sherborne, Glastonbury and the expansion of Wessex'. *T.R.H.S.* 5th Ser. iii (1953), 101–24, which unites political history with the endowments of monasteries.

2718 FISHER (D. J. V.). 'The church in England between the death of Bede and the Danish invasions'. *T.R.H.S.* 5th Ser. ii (1952), 1–19. Idem, 'The anti-monastic reaction in the reign of Edward the Martyr'. *Cambr. Hist. Jour.* x (1950–2), 254–70.

2719 GRIERSON (PHILIP). 'Grimbald of St. Bertin's'. *E.H.R.* lv (1940), 529–61.

2720 KIRBY (D. P.). 'The Saxon bishops of Leicester, Lindsey (Syddensis), and Dorchester'. *Leicestershire Archaeol. and Hist. Soc. Trans.* xli (1965/6), 1–8.

2721 MILES (GEORGE). The bishops of Lindisfarne, Hexham, Chester-le-Street and Durham. A.D. 635–1020. Lond. 1898.

2722 PAGE (R. I.). 'Anglo-Saxon episcopal lists'. *Nottingham Mediaeval Studies*, ix (1965), 71–95; x (1966), 3–24.

2723 ROBINSON (JOSEPH ARMITAGE). The Saxon bishops of Wells: a historical study in the tenth century. Lond. 1918.

2724 SMITH (REGINALD A. L.). 'The early community of St. Andrews at Rochester, 604–c. 1080'. *E.H.R.* lx (1945), 289–99.

> Holds that the bishop's familia was composed of secular clergy, not of monks. For similar views on Worcester and Canterbury, see Smith's footnotes on p. 292 and M. Deanesly in No. 1458 above.

2725 STENTON (FRANK M.). The early history of the abbey of Abingdon. Oxf. 1913.

> Uses oldest MS. to amend Stevenson's edition of *Chronicon . . . Abingdon* (No. 2153) and charters for a history of the abbey in Anglo-Saxon times. See also his 'Medeshamstede and its colonies' (Nos. 1455, 1496).

2726 WHITELOCK (DOROTHY). 'The conversion of the eastern Danelaw'. *Saga Book of the Viking Society*, xii (1941), 159–76.

2727 WHITING (CHARLES E.). 'The Anglian bishops of Hexham'. *Archaeol. Aeliana*, 4th Ser. xxiv (1946), 119–56.

> Includes a life of Wilfrid and a northern chronicle.

2728 WILLIAMS (LAURENCE F. R.). History of the abbey of St. Alban. Lond. 1917.

2729 WILLIS-BUND (JOHN W.). 'Worcestershire and Westminster'. *Assoc. Archaeol. Soc. Repts.* (No. 171), xxxiv (1918), 329–62.

PART FIVE

FROM NORMANS TO TUDORS

THE chronicles provide narratives and viewpoints or commentaries on the political history of the period; the law tracts throw much light on legal and other institutions. The public records, compiled for current administrative purposes, are valuable for most facets of history; and in the twentieth century have furnished the bases for most historical research. The concentration on public records has tended to submerge the accounts of the chroniclers on which nineteenth-century historians heavily rested. The public records, examined below, are placed under the headings to which they primarily relate; but the contents of each series are often of a miscellaneous character, yielding information on various kinds of institutions and societal developments. For example, 'Domesday Book' and the pipe rolls illustrate many subjects besides finance; and the plea rolls and memoranda rolls exemplify many topics besides the judicial or strictly legal.

For general surveys of the public records, the section concerned with the Public Record Office on pp. 111–18 should be consulted; and for printed collections of sources, pp. 134–51. The volumes of *English historical documents* (No. 17) for the period, with their copious translated extracts and extensive bibliographies, form substantial groundwork; for volume iv, A. R. Myers has translated a considerable number of documents, some hitherto unpublished. As guides, such summaries as Elton's *England, 1200–1640* (No. 256); J. J. Bagley, *Historical interpretation: sources of English medieval history, 1066–1540* (Penguin Books, Harmondsworth, 1965); and Galbraith's *Studies* (No. 949) are helpful. The volumes of the *Oxford history of England* (No. 1189) contain annotated bibliographies.

XIII. CHRONICLES AND ROYAL BIOGRAPHIES

A. INTRODUCTORY COMMENTS

The chronicles of the post-conquest period are generally broader in horizon and more cosmopolitan in outlook than those of Anglo-Saxon times. This development was in part the result of the closer contact of England with the Continent and in part the reflection of the intellectual influence of the twelfth-century Renaissance. The Anglo-Saxon culture of the eleventh century gave way to the Latinized literature of the French-speaking Normans, although one version of the *Anglo-Saxon Chronicle* held its life until 1154 and provides an important narrative to that date.

For the period of the conquest, the French chroniclers, William of Jumièges (No. 2908), and William of Poitiers (No. 2943), are sources of the first importance. They are followed by Ordericus Vitalis (No. 2937), who, although born in

England, spent most of his life in a Norman abbey where he wrote his lively and somewhat diffuse *Historia Ecclesiastica*. Among the English writers, Eadmer (No. 2863) composed a remarkable history mainly for the period 1093–1109; and William of Malmesbury (No. 2921) attempted the first comprehensive history, based on a judicious use of sources, since Bede. Although not 'an exceptionally gifted narrator' (Darlington), Malmesbury was a scholarly historian attempting a synthesis of his sources on the past rather than a mere compilation of dry annals. The relative dearth of contemporary accounts of the later years of Stephen's reign has been somewhat relieved by the recent discovery of the continuation of *Gesta Stephani* to 1154 (No. 2880). For commentaries on the Anglo-Norman historians, consult especially R. R. Darlington's inaugural lecture, entitled *Anglo-Norman historians* (Lond. 1947), and D. C. Douglas and G. W. Greenaway, *English historical documents* (No. 17), vol. ii.

Most of the chronicles were produced in monastic scriptoria and reflect their religious origin. Many begin their compilations with the long-distant past by copying from available accounts, sometimes accounts which are no longer extant; but few attempt a studied synthesis of their sources. For the purposes of the modern historian, chronicles take on most importance when they deal with contemporary events. Sometimes, as in the last quarter of the twelfth century, non-monastic writers among the secular clergy produce the more important chronicles; among them are the author of *Gesta Regis Henrici Secundi* (No. 2879), Hoveden (No. 2903), Diceto (No. 2860), and Giraldus Cambrensis (No. 2881). The first three, who seem to have been in close touch with the courts of Henry II and Richard I, included in their narratives many valuable state papers. However, the best historical writing from the second half of the twelfth century comes from a northern Austin canon, William of Newburgh (No. 2932). In his critical, discriminating history, Newburgh displayed independent, but sound, judgement. Stubbs, in his introduction to his edition of Hoveden (No. 2903, reprinted in No. 4041), gives an account of the northern or Northumbrian school of history; John Taylor carries that account into the thirteenth and fourteenth centuries in his *Medieval historical writing in Yorkshire* (St. Anthony's Hall Pubns. no. 19. York, 1961).

In the thirteenth century the historical literature of England was again almost wholly confined to the monasteries; but in the fourteenth century some of the best accounts were written by secular clerks, like Robert of Avesbury (No. 2790), Geoffrey le Baker (No. 2791), Adam of Murimuth (No. 2931), Adam of Usk (No. 2966), and the author of the *Annales Paulini* (No. 2768). Among the modern surveys of this literature are William Stubbs, *Historical introductions to the Rolls Series*, edited by Arthur Hassall (Lond. 1902); Claude Jenkins, *The Monastic Chronicler and the early school of St. Albans*. S.P.C.K. (Lond. 1922); Vivian H. Galbraith, *Historical research in medieval England* (Creighton Lecture, 1949. Lond. 1951); and John Taylor, *The use of medieval chronicles* (Helps for Students of History, no. 70. Lond. 1965).

The annals composed in the medieval cloisters are of three kinds: those dealing mainly or wholly with the history of the writer's monastery, such as *Gesta Abbatum* of St. Albans (No. 6168), Elmham on St. Augustine, Canterbury (No. 6181), and Hugh Candidus on Peterborough (No. 6270), which are examined below under monastic records; those dealing partly with local monastic history and partly with general history; and those concentrating on general history. The annals of the second kind are strong on the thirteenth century; some of the best of them have been printed in Luard's *Annales Monastici* (No. 2730), and some of the shorter ones in Liebermann's *Geschichtsquellen* (No. 2738). To the third group belong the writers of the St. Albans school, which produced Wendover, Matthew Paris, and Wallingford in the thirteenth century (Nos. 2979, 2941, 2975); the authors of *Annales Regni Scotiae* (No. 2770), Blaneford (No. 2797), and Amundesham (No. 2750); and Rishanger (No. 2948), Trokelow (No. 2964), Walsingham (No. 2976), and Whethamsted (No. 2980). The writers of the St. Albans school included numerous valuable documents in their works; they were also pro-baronial in outlook and bias. The most eminent of this school was the many-sided Matthew Paris; for appreciations of his work, see No. 2941 below. Walsingham was another distinguished historiographer at St. Albans. V. H. Galbraith's studies assemble an assortment of chronicles covering the period 1272–1422 into a series of chronicles ascribed solely to Walsingham; for this, see No. 2976 below.

Many other abbeys, most of them old Benedictine houses of the south of England, were more or less active in the production of chronicles; in addition from the north of England, the *Anonimalle Chronicle* (No. 2787) from St. Mary's, York, must be signalized. In the north also, the Cistercians and the Austin canons composed valuable accounts, as the works of Guisborough (No. 2888), Knighton (No. 2912), Wykes (No. 2983), and Kirkstall and Meaux chronicles (Nos. 2910, 2806) show. From the friars come the works of Eccleston, Trevet (No. 2963), and Capgrave (No. 2808), and the *Lanercost Chronicle* (No. 2836). The most popular chronicle in the late Middle Ages was the comprehensive *Polychronicon* of Ranulf Higden (No. 2895).

In the fifteenth century there was a decline in monastic historiography. Walsingham continued as the most eminent chronicler down to the third decade; but with him the St. Albans series closes. In the second half of the fifteenth century, the most valuable monastic chronicle is the Crowland continuation of 'Ingulf' (No. 2900). For the period of the Hundred Years War, the French chroniclers add perspective to the English accounts; some of the most useful of them for English history are listed in the catalogue below.

In the fourteenth century a layman, Thomas Gray, composed *Scalacronica* (No. 2881); and in the late fifteenth century laymen such as William of Worcester, Hardyng, and Fabyan (Nos. 2982, 2889, 2866) were displacing monks as historians. In the last quarter of the fifteenth century the scriptorium was beginning to make way for the printing-press; the first chronicle printed in England came from the Caxton Press in 1480 (No. 2811). Another development was the production of city histories, a group of mayors' chronicles. Except for Ricart's *Bristol Kalendar* (No. 5083) and the meagre chronicle of Lynn (No. 2742), they relate to London. The oldest are FitzThedmar's *Cronica Majorum* (No. 2870), compiled about 1274; the *Annales Londonienses* (No. 2761), compiled in the first half of the fourteenth century; the French *Croniques de London* (No. 2857); the *English Chronicle of London* (No. 2823), compiled about 1442; and the magnificent *Great Chronicle of London* (No. 2885). These chronicles contain the names of the chief civic officers, together with notices of the municipal and national events which occurred during each mayoralty. Owing to the important part which London played in the history of the kingdom, the civic annalists were not inclined to ignore national affairs. For commentaries on the London chronicles, see Fenley (No. 2742), the introduction to Kingsford's *Chronicles of London* (No. 2732), and especially the introduction to the Thomas-Thornley edition of the *Great Chronicle of London* (No. 2885), and Jacob, *Fifteenth century* (No. 1189), pp. 700–1.

An indispensable guide to fifteenth-century English chronicles is C. L. Kingsford's *English historical literature in the fifteenth century* (Oxf. 1913), which provides not only commentaries on the chroniclers, but also prints many shorter chronicles or extracts therefrom. Further, A. R. Myers, *English historical documents* (No. 17), vol. iv, 1327–1485, supplies translated excerpts and bibliographical comments of prime importance. The work of sixteenth-century scholars, Leland, Bale, Wharton, Stow, and many others, in salvaging manuscripts and publishing some of them is charmingly described in T. D. Kendrick, *British Antiquity* (Lond. 1950), and May McKisack, *Medieval history in the Tudor Age* (Oxf. 1971).

Most of the chronicles are printed in one or both of two series: the Rolls Series and Oxford Medieval Texts (formerly Nelson's Medieval Texts or Classics). The Rolls Series, bearing the official title *Rerum Britannicarum Medii Aevi Scriptores*, was sponsored by the Master of the Rolls from 1858 to 1896 and includes editions of most of the medieval English chronicles; for a description of the enterprise and a criticism of some of the editions, see Knowles, *Great historical enterprises* (No. 262). The series of Medieval Texts, published by Nelson between 1949 and 1966, is being continued as Oxford Medieval Texts, published by the Clarendon Press (No. 1113).

REGNAL TABLE OF CHRONICLERS

WILLIAM I (1066–87)

Amiens, Guy of,	Jumièges, William of
Anglo-Saxon chronicle	Malmesbury
Baudri	Ordericus Vitalis
Brevis relatio	Poitiers, William of
Eadmer	Wace
Gesta Herwardi	Worcester, Florence of

WILLIAM II (1087–1100)

Anglo-Saxon chronicle	Ordericus Vitalis
Eadmer	Worcester, Florence of
Malmesbury	

HENRY I (1100–35)

Anglo-Saxon chronicle	Jumièges, William of
Durham, Simeon of, 1119–29	Malmesbury
Eadmer, to 1109	Ordericus Vitalis
Hexham, John of, 1130–	Worcester, Florence of
Huntingdon, 1127–	

STEPHEN (1135–54)

Anglo-Saxon chronicle
Canterbury, Gervase of
Chronicon Anglo-Scoticum
Gesta Stephani
Hexham, John of
Hexham, Richard of, to 1139
Huntingdon

Malmesbury, to 1142
Newburgh
Ordericus Vitalis, to 1141
Rievaulx, Aelred of, 1138
Salisbury, John of
Torigni, Robert of
Worcester, John of, to 1141

HENRY II (1154–89)

Annals of Winchcombe (No. 2775)
Canterbury, Gervase of
Chronica de Mailros
Chronicon Anglo-Scoticum
Continuatio Beccensis, 1157–60
Diceto, 1173–
Fantosme, 1173–74
Gesta Regis Henrici II (No. 2879)
Giraldus Cambrensis

Histoire de Guillaume le Maréchal
Newburgh
Niger
Rigord, 1179–
Rouen, Etienne de, to 1169
Song of Dermot, to 1175
Torigni, Robert of, to 1186
Vigeois, Geoffrey of, to 1184

RICHARD I (1189–99)

Ambroise
Canterbury, Gervase of
Chronica de Mailros
Coggeshall
Devizes, to 1192
Diceto

Gesta Regis Henrici II
Histoire de Guillaume le Maréchal
Hoveden, 1192–
Itinerarium
Newburgh
Rigord

JOHN (1199–1216)

Annales monastici
Annales S. Edmundi, to 1212
Annales Stanleienses, 1204–14
Annals of Southwark
Canterbury, Gervase of, to 1210
Chronica de Mailros
Coggeshall

Coventry
Diceto, to 1202
Histoire de Guillaume le Maréchal
Histoire des ducs de Normandie
Hoveden, to 1201
Rigord and William the Breton (No. 2947)
Wendover

HENRY III (1216–72)

Annales monastici
Annales S. Pauli, 1250–72
Annals of Southwark
Chronica de Mailros
Chronicon de Lanercost
Coggeshall, to 1223
Cotton, 1264–
Coventry, to 1225
Eccleston (No. 6008)
English Cluniac (No. 2935)
FitzThedmar

Flores historiarum, 1259–
Gloucester, Robert of
Histoire de Guillaume le Maréchal, to 1219
Morins
Paris, 1235–59
Rishanger, 1259–
Silgrave, 1263–67
Tayster, 1258–65
Wallingford, 1201–58
Wendover, to 1235
Wykes

EDWARD I (1272–1307)

Annales Londonienses, 1301–
Annales monastici
Annales regni Scotiae
Barbour
Bury Chronicle
Chronicon de Lanercost
Commendatio lamentabilis
Cotton, to 1298

Flores historiarum
Fordun
Guisborough
Langtoft
Morins
Rishanger
Trevet
Wykes

EDWARD II (1307–27)

Annales Londonienses, to 1316
Annales Paulini
Baker
Barbour
Blaneford, 1323–4
Chronicon de Lanercost
Flores historiarum, to 1326
Fordun

Gesta Edwardi de Carnarvan
Gray's *Scalacronica*
Guisborough
Higden
Pipewell
Trokelowe, to 1323
Tynemouth
Vita Edwardi II

EDWARD III (1327–77)

Annales Paulini, to 1341
Anonimalle Chronicle, 1376–
Avesbury, 1339–56
Baker, to 1356
Chandos, the Herald of
Chronicon Angliae
Chronicon de Lanercost, to 1346
Chronique de Richard Lescot
Chronique des quatre premiers Valois
Chronique normande
Eulogium historiarum, 1356–
Fordun
Froissart
Gesta Edwardi (No. 2876)

Grandes chroniques de France, 1350–77
Gray's *Scalacronica*, to 1362
Grey Friars of Lynn
Guisborough (continuation to 1346)
Higden (Malvern's continuation), 1364–
Klerk, 1337–41
Knighton, 1336–66
Le Bel, to 1361
Murimuth (with continuation), 1337–77
Reading, John of
Speculum Regis (No. 2995)
Tynemouth
Venette, Jean de
Wyntoun

RICHARD II (1377–99)

Annales Ric. II, etc. 1392–
Anonimalle Chronicle
Chronicon Angliae, to 1388
Chronique de la traïson, 1397–9
Chronique du religieux de S. Denys
Creton, 1399
Dieulacres Chronicle
Eulogium historiarum (continuation)
Favent
Froissart
Higden (continuations by Malvern and an

anonymous Westminster chronicler), to 1394
Historia vitae Ric. II by a monk of Evesham
Kirkstall Chronicle
Knighton (continuation), to 1395
Le Beau
Otterbourne
Pipewell Chronicle
Usk, 1397–
Walsingham

HENRY IV (1399–1413)

Annales Ric. II, etc., to 1406
Capgrave
Chronicon Angliae: No. 2833

Chronique du religieux de S. Denys
Eulogium historiarum (continuation)
Froissart, to 1400

Historia vitae Ric. II
Monstrelet
Otterbourne

Usk, to 1404
Walsingham

HENRY V (1413–22)

Capgrave
Chronique du religieux de S. Denys
Elmham
Hardyng
Henrici V gesta, to 1416
Journal d'un bourgeois
Juvenal des Ursins
Le Fevre, 1415

Livy
Monstrelet
Otterbourne, to 1420
Page, 1418
Strecche
Versus rhythmici
Walsingham

HENRY VI (1422–61)

Account of St. Albans battle, 1455
Amundesham, to 1440
Berry the Herald, 1449–50
Blakman
Blondel, 1449–50
Capgrave, to 1446
Chronicle (Short English)
Chronicle of Rich. II, etc.
Fifteenth-Century Chronicle (No. 2869)
Great Chronicle of London

Gregory's Chronicle
Hardyng
Historiae Croylandensis continuatio, 1459–
Journal d'un bourgeois, to 1449
Letters and Papers (No. 3815)
Monstrelet, to 1444
Notes (Brief), 1459– (No. 2934)
Waurin, 1444–
Whethamstede's Register, 1455–61
Worcester, William of

EDWARD IV (1461–83)

Chronicle (Brief Latin), to 1464
Chronicle (Short English), to 1465
Chronicle of the rebellion, 1470
Commynes
Fabyan
Fragment of a chronicle, to 1470
Great Chronicle of London

Gregory's Chronicle, to 1469
Historiae Croylandensis continuatio
Historie of the arrivall of Edw. IV, 1471
Notes (Brief), to 1462 (No. 2934)
Warkworth's Chronicle, to 1474
Waurin, to 1471
Worcester, William of, to 1468

RICHARD III (1483–5)

Fabyan
Hall
Historiae Croylandensis continuatio
Mancinus

More, Sir Thomas
Rous
Vergil, Polydore

B. GENERAL COLLECTIONS OF CHRONICLES

2730 ANNALES MONASTICI (A.D. 1–1432). Ed. by Henry R. Luard. Rolls Ser. 5 vols. Lond. 1864–9.

Vol. i. Annals of Margam (No. 2754), Tewkesbury (No. 2765), and Burton (No. 2763).
Vol. ii. Annals of Winchester (No. 2767) and Waverley (No. 2766).
Vol. iii. Annals of Dunstable (No. 2929) and Bermondsey (No. 2762).
Vol. iv. Annals of Osney (No. 2764) and Worcester (No. 2769); and Wykes' Chronicle (No. 2983).
Vol. v. Index and glossary.

Each work in this important collection contains the annals of a monastery interwoven with general history. The collection is of great value for the political history of the thirteenth century, especially for the relations of the barons to Henry III. Each work is described separately below.

2731 CHRONICA MONASTERII S. ALBANI (A.D. 793–1488). Ed. by Henry T. Riley. Rolls Series. 12 vols. Lond. 1863–76.

This group contains Walsingham's *Historia Anglicana* (No. 2976), his *Ypodigma Neustriae* (No. 2976), his *Gesta Abbatum* (No. 6168); the volume of Trokelowe, Blaneford, the *Opus Chronicorum*, and Walsingham's *Annales Ricardi II et Henrici IV* (No. 2976); Amundesham's *Annales* and an anonymous chronicle (No. 2750); *Registra Abbatum* (No. 6169) and Rishanger and two anonymous chronicles (Nos. 2770, 2752). This collection comprises the principal chronicles of St. Albans, except Wendover (No. 2979), Matthew Paris (No. 2941), Walsingham's *Chronicon Angliae* (No. 2976), and Walsingham's *Chronicle 1406–1420* (No. 2976).

The histories end in 1440 but the registers of abbots continue to 1488. All study of the *St. Albans Chronicles* after Matthew Paris should begin with the introduction and essay on the descent of the *St. Albans Chronicles 1259–1422* which preface V. H. Galbraith, *The St. Albans Chronicle 1406–1420* (Oxf. 1937); and *E.H.R.* xlvii (1932), 12–30.

2732 CHRONICLES OF LONDON. Ed. by Charles L. Kingsford. Oxf. 1905.

Three English chronicles, 1189–1432, 1415–43, 1440–1516. Meagre down to the reign of Richard II. Contains some valuable notices of events in the fifteenth century. See also Kingsford, *Hist. Lit.*, pp. 70–112, 292–8; and his paper in the *E.H.R.* xxix (1914), 505–15. For other London chronicles, see index under 'London, Chronicles'.

2733 CHRONICLES OF THE REIGNS OF EDWARD I AND EDWARD II. Ed. by William Stubbs. Rolls Ser. 2 vols. Lond. 1882–3.

Vol. i. *Annales Londonienses* (No. 2761) and *Annales Paulini* (No. 2768).
Vol. ii. *Commendatio lamentabilis Edwardi I* (No. 2852); *Gesta Edwardi de Carnarvan* (No. 2876); the anonymous *Vita Edwardi II* (No. 2971); and 'More's' *Vita et mors Edwardi II* (No. 2928).

2734 CHRONICLES OF THE REIGNS OF STEPHEN, HENRY II, AND RICHARD I. Ed. by Richard Howlett. Rolls Ser. 4 vols. Lond. 1884–9.

Vol. i. William of Newburgh's history, bks. i–iv (No. 2932).
Vol. ii. The same, bk. v, with a continuation to 1298; and the *Draco Normannicus* of Étienne de Rouen (No. 2949).
Vol. iii. *Gesta Stephani* (No. 2880); the chronicle of Richard of Hexham (No. 2894); Aelred of Rievaulx's *Relatio de standardo* (No. 2946); the chronicles of Jordan Fantosme (No. 2867) and Richard of Devizes (No. 2859).
Vol. iv. Robert of Torigni (No. 2962).

2735 CHRONICLES OF THE WHITE ROSE OF YORK: a series of fragments, proclamations, letters, and other contemporary documents relating to the reign of Edward IV. Ed. by J. A. Giles. Lond. 1845.

Fragment of an old English chronicle, pp. 1–30 (No. 2873). *History of the arrivall of Edward IV*, pp. 31–96 (No. 2901). Warkworth's *Chronicle*, pp. 97–142 (No. 2977). Proclamations, etc., of Richard III, (1483), pp. 269–82.

The three English chronicles in this collection, which are here presented in modern orthography, were written by eye-witnesses of the events narrated. They are not well edited.

2736 HISTORICAL COLLECTIONS OF A CITIZEN OF LONDON IN THE FIFTEENTH CENTURY. Ed. by James Gairdner. Camden Soc. New Ser. xvii. Lond. 1876.

Page's poem on the siege of Rouen, pp. 1–46 (No. 2940).
Lydgate's verses on the kings of England, pp. 47–54 (No. 2818).
Gregory's *Chronicle*, pp. 55–239 (No. 2886).

These three pieces are taken from a fifteenth-century commonplace-book of a citizen of London; perhaps it was made by William Gregory, skinner, who was mayor of London in 1451.

2737 KINGSFORD (CHARLES L.). English historical literature in the fifteenth century, with an appendix of chronicles and historical pieces hitherto for the most part unprinted. Oxf. 1913. Reprinted N.Y. 1962.

Appendices i–xv (pp. 275–388) contain extracts from chronicles and historical pieces. These important sources are a continuation of Higden's *Polychronicon* for 1399–1430 (see No. 2895), and versions of the *Brut* (see No. 2811), and *A Tewkesbury Chronicle* for 1471.

2738 LIEBERMANN, FELIX, ed. Ungedruckte anglo-normannische Geschichtsquellen. Strassburg. 1879.* See No. 1108.

2739 MEMORIALS OF HENRY V. Ed. by C. A. Cole. Rolls Ser. Lond. 1858.

Redman's *Vita*, pp. 1–59 (No. 2945).
Versus in laudem regis, pp. 61–75 (No. 2969).
Elmham's *Liber metricus*, pp. 77–165 (No. 2864).

2740 MONUMENTA GERMANIAE HISTORICA, SCRIPTORES: (Ex Scriptoribus rerum Anglicarum saec. xii et xiii. Ed. by F. Liebermann and R. Pauli). Also xxvii (1885); (Ex rerum Anglicarum scriptoribus saeculi xiii. Ed. by F. Liebermann). xxviii (1888). See No. 1114.

2741 SCRIPTORES RERUM GESTARUM WILLELMI CONQUE-STORIS. Ed. by J. A. Giles. Caxton Soc. Lond. 1845.

Brevis relatio, pp. 1–23 (No. 2801).
Guy of Amiens, pp. 27–51 (No. 2749).
William of Poitiers, pp. 77–159 (No. 2943).
Annalis historia brevis, pp. 161–74 (No. 2776).
Chrestien de Troyes, pp. 179–269.
Le dit de Guillaume, pp. 270–97 (No. 2861).
And ten other brief pieces running from William I to Stephen.

2742 SIX TOWN CHRONICLES OF ENGLAND. Ed. by Ralph Flenley. Oxf. 1911.

Portions of five chronicles of London and one of Lynn, fifteenth century. At pp. 96–8 Flenley prints a list of the London chronicles. Cf. a supplementary note by G. Baskerville, in *E.H.R.* xxviii (1913), 124–7. On Robert Bale, see C. L. Kingsford, 'Robert Bale, the London Chronicler', *E.H.R.* xxxi (1916), 126–8.

2743 THREE FIFTEENTH-CENTURY CHRONICLES, with historical memoranda by John Stowe. Ed. by James Gairdner. Camden Soc. New Ser. xxviii. Lond. 1880.

A short English chronicle, pp. 1–80 (No. 2818).
Historical memoranda (Cade's proclamation, list of lords serving under Edward III,

at the siege of Calais, 1346–7, etc.), pp. 81–147, some in John Stowe's handwriting. Brief notes (a Latin chronicle, 1307–1462), pp. 148–63 (No. 2934).

A brief Latin chronicle, 1429–71, pp. 164–85 (No. 2817).

C. ALPHABETICAL TABLE OF CHRONICLES

2744 ABBREVIATA CHRONICA, 1377–1469. Ed. by J. J. Smith. Cambr. Antiq. Soc. Cambr. 1840.

> Brief historical notes, 'in tabular form', seemingly written by John Harryson (d. 1473) who was not, as is sometimes asserted, the chancellor of the University of Cambridge. See Emden, *Cambridge* (No. 532), p. 290.

2745 ABBREVIATIO CHRONICORUM ANGLIAE (1000–1255). Ed. by Frederic Madden, *Matthaei Parisiensis Historia Anglorum*, iii. 151–348. Rolls Ser. Lond. 1869. Excerpts. Ed. by Liebermann, in M.G.H., SS. xxviii. 443–55.

> Written at St. Albans, and ascribed by Madden to Matthew Paris. Liebermann (pp. 101–2) questioned this ascription; but Vaughan (No. 2941), pp. 38–9, presents evidence in its favour.

2746 ACCOUNT OF THE FIRST BATTLE OF ST. ALBANS (1455), from a contemporary manuscript. Ed. by John Bayley. *Archaeol.* xx (1824), 519–23. Reprinted in James Gairdner, *Paston Letters*, i. 327–31.

> Written in English. On this battle and the sources for its study, see C. A. J. Armstrong, 'Politics and the battle of St. Albans, 1455', *B.I.H.R.* xxxiii (1960), 1–72.

2747 AGNELLUS (THOMAS) (*fl.* 1183). De morte et sepultura Henrici regis junioris (1183). Ed. by Joseph Stevenson, *Radulphi de Coggeshall Chronicon Anglicanum*, pp. 263–73. Rolls Ser. Lond. 1875.

> Stevenson calls it 'a contemporary account of an event which deeply moved the feelings of England and France at the time when it occurred, and exercised no trifling influence upon the history of these two kingdoms'. The tract eulogizes the young king. The author was Archdeacon of Wells.

2748 AMBROISE (*fl.* 1195). L'estoire de la guerre sainte (1190–2) (with a French translation). Ed. by Gaston Paris. *Documents inédits* (Paris, 1897). Extracts. Ed. by Liebermann, in M.G.H., SS. xxvii. 532–46. Translations in: *The crusade of Richard Lion-Heart by Ambroise*, trans. by Merton J. Hubert with notes and documentation by John L. LaMonte. Columbia Univ. Records of Civilization. New York, 1941; and in Edward N. Stone, *Three old French chronicles of the crusades*. Univ. of Washington Pubns. in the Social Sciences. Seattle, 1939.

> This old French poem and the *Itinerarium regis Ricardi* (No. 2906) constitute the best narrative sources for Richard's crusade. They bear some relationship to one another; both of them may be based on an unknown original, written by a participant in the crusade. See J. G. Edwards, 'Itinerarium regis Ricardi and the Estoire de la guerre sainte' in *Tait essays* (No. 1455), pp. 59–77; and LaMonte's introduction, mentioned above; and Hans E. Mayer, *Das Itinerarium Peregrinorum*, which is analysed below under No. 2906.

2749 AMIENS (GUY OF) (d. c. 1075). De bello Hastingensi carmen auctore Widone, in Petrie's *Monumenta*, pp. 856–72. Lond. 1848. Reprinted in app. C to the Report on Rymer's *Foedera* (No. 3765), pp. 73–86. Michel's *Chroniques Anglo-Normandes* (No. 1112), iii. 1–38. Giles's *Scriptores* (No. 2741), 27–51. A critical edition with translation by Catherine Morton and Hope Muntz for the series Oxford Medieval Texts was published in 1972.

> This anonymous poem is traditionally ascribed to Guy, Bishop of Amiens, on the ground that William of Jumièges and Ordericus Vitalis assert that Guy wrote a poem on the battle of Hastings. It affords valuable information concerning the battle of Hastings and events in England for about four months after the battle. On its validity as an independent source, see Douglas, *William the Conqueror* (No. 3986), p. 200 note 2; G. H. White in *Complete peerage* (556 h); and Frank Barlow, 'The Carmen de Hastingae proelio' in *Studies in International History: essays presented to W. N. Medlicott*, ed. by Kenneth Bourne and Donald C. Watt (Lond. 1967), pp. 35–67.

2750 AMUNDESHAM (JOHN). Annales monasterii S. Albani, 1421–40, quibus praefigitur Chronicon rerum gestarum in monasterio S. Albani, 1422–31, a quodam auctore ignoto compilatum. Ed. by H. T. Riley. Rolls Ser. 2 vols. Lond. 1870–1.

> Amundesham was a monk of St. Albans concerning whose life little is known: the assignment of the authorship of these annals to him is very doubtful. These annals 1421–40 are concerned with the affairs of the abbey during the first abbacy of John of Whethamstede (No. 2980). The anonymous Chronicle 1422–31, although devoted mainly to abbey affairs, gives some information concerning the current events of the day; it made some 'use of one of the early versions of the London Chronicles'. See Kingsford, *Hist. Lit.* pp. 150–1.

2750A ANGLO-SAXON CHRONICLE, to 1154. See Nos. 2141–2.

> Valuable for the years 1066–1154.

2751 ANNÁLA CONNACHT: The Annals of Connacht. A.D. 1244–1544. Ed. and trans. by A. Martin Freeman. Dublin. 1944. Freeman's Introduction and the Irish text down to A.D. 1412 were printed in *Revue celtique*, 1930–5.

> *The Annals of Connacht* and *The Annals of Loch Cé* have much in common; the first fills some gaps in the second. They were both compiled by the O'Duigenan family. Father Gwynn shows that the *Annals of Connacht* are in fact the Book of the Duigenans which the Four Masters used. The two *Annales* had a common thirteenth-century source which may have been composed in the abbey of Cong. Aubrey Gwynn, 'The Annals of Connacht and the Abbey of Cong', *Jour. Galway Archaeol. and Hist. Soc.* xxvii (1956–7), 1–9.

2752 ANNALES ANGLIAE ET SCOTIAE (1292–1300). Ed. by Henry T. Riley, *Willelmi Rishanger Chronica* (No. 2948), pp. 371–408. Rolls Ser. Lond. 1865. Brief extract. Ed. by Liebermann, in M.G.H., SS. xxviii (1888), 525–6.

> Bale assigned the annals to Rishanger; and Galbraith in *St. Albans Chronicle* (No. 2731), p. xxxiii, is inclined to accept this attribution. They were written at St. Albans.

2752A ANNALES CAMBRIAE, to 1288. See Nos. 2144 and 3785A.

2753 ANNALES CESTRIENSES, or chronicle of the abbey of S. Werburg at Chester (A.D. 1–1297, with a translation). Ed. by R. C. Christie. *Lancs.-Ches. Record Soc.* xiv (1887).

> Probably written at Chester under the direction of Abbot Simon of Whitchurch (d. 1290) and completed after his death. The work deals mainly with the affairs of the kingdom. Much seems to be derived from Matthew Paris, but most of the entries from 1250

onward are original. The author favours the cause of Simon de Montfort. For a collation of Christie's text with the Lichfield MS., see *Reports of the Historical MSS. Commission*, xiv (1895), pt. viii, 206–11. On St. Werburgh's, see No. 6105.

2754 ANNALES DE MARGAN (*recte* MARGAM) SIVE CHRONICA ABBREVIATA (1066–1232). Ed. by H. R. Luard, *Annales Monastici*, i. 1–40. Rolls Ser. Lond. 1864. Another edition (bad), in Gale's *Scriptores Quinque* (No. 1099), pp. 1–19. Extracts, 1084–1229. Ed. by Liebermann, in M.G.H., *SS.* xxvii. 428–30.

Written in the thirteenth century, the Margam annals contain many notices of public events relating to England and Wales. The portion 1066–1147 is meagre, and is derived mainly from William of Malmesbury. On their value for John's reign, see F. M. Powicke, *Loss of Normandy* (1961 edn.), pp. 316–22.

2755 ANNALES DE MONTE FERNANDI: annals of Multifernan, A.D. 45–1274. Ed. by Aquilla Smith. Irish Archaeol. Soc. *Tracts relating to Ireland*, vol. ii (no. 2), 1–26. Dublin. 1842–3.

Although these annals record few facts relating to the history of Ireland which are not found elsewhere, 'they claim some degree of attention from their antiquity, and are perhaps the most ancient annals of this country written exclusively in the Latin language'. It is not certain that they were compiled in the monastery of Multifernan. J. Ware, *De Scriptoribus Hiberniae* (No. 30), conjectured that the author was Stephen of Exeter (b. 1246).

2756 ANNALES DORENSES (A.D. 1–1283, with a continuation to 1362). Ed. by R. Pauli, in M.G.H., *SS.* xxvii. 514–31.

Pauli edits only extracts, A.D. 687–1362. These annals of the abbey of Dore, Herefordshire, deal with the general history of England. The chief sources of the original work, to 1283, are Robert of Torigni, the *Annals of Margam*, and the *Annals of Tewkesbury*.

2757 ANNALES FURNESIENSES (1199–1298). Ed. by Richard Howlett, *Willelmi de Novoburgo Historia Rerum Anglicarum*, ii. 501–83. Rolls Ser. Lond. 1885. Extracts, 1252–98. Ed. by Liebermann, in M.G.H., *SS.* xxviii. 557–9.

A continuation of William of Newburgh's history, written in Furness abbey late in the thirteenth century. From 1202 to 1271 it is derived mainly from the *Annales Stanleienses* (No. 2774).

2758 ANNALES GANDENSES. Ed. by Frantz Funck-Brentano. *Collection de Textes* (No. 1094), Paris, 1896. Annales Gandenses. Ed. and trans. by Hilda Johnstone. Medieval Classics. Lond. etc. 1951.

Latin chronicle 1296–1310. Professor Johnstone's text is based on that by Funck-Brentano. For other editions and commentaries, see *Repert. Font.* ii. 284.

2759 ANNALES HIBERNIAE, 1162–1370. Ed. by J. T. Gilbert, *Chartularies of St. Mary's Abbey, Dublin*, ii. 303–98. Rolls Ser. Lond. 1884. First printed in Camden's *Britannia*, pp. 794–832. Lond. 1607. For a translation, see Gough's translation of Camden's *Britannia* (No. 609).

This work has been ascribed to Christopher Pembridge of Dublin (*fl.* 1370?), but the author and the time of compilation are unknown. Gilbert calls it 'the chief authority on the affairs of the English settlement in Ireland to the year 1370'. These annals agree in substance with the corresponding years of James Grace's *Annales Hiberniae*, edited, with a translation, by Richard Butler for the Irish Archaeological Society (Dublin,

1842). Both works may have been taken from a common original. Grace compiled his annals between 1537 and 1539; from 1370 to 1536 they consist mainly of obits of the Lacys, Burkes, Butlers, and Fitzgeralds. Valuable fragments for 1308–10, 1316, 1317, are printed in Gilbert, ii. 293–302.

2760 ANNALES HIBERNIAE EX LIBRO ROSSENSI. Ed. by Richard Butler, *The Annals of Ireland, by John Clyn and Thady Dowling*, pp. 41–6. Irish Archaeol. Soc. Dublin. 1849.

This fragment of the *Annals of Ross* contains brief notices relating to the history of Ireland, 1265–1480.

2761 ANNALES LONDONIENSES (1194–1330 with a gap 1293–1301). Ed. by William Stubbs, *Chronicles of the Reigns of Edward I and Edward II*, i. 1–251. Rolls Ser. Lond. 1882. Extracts, 1195–1301. Ed. by Liebermann, in M.G.H., *SS.* xxviii. 552–4.

In large part an abridgement of the *Flores Historiarum* (No. 2871) to 1301, then the account of the general history of England, 1301–16, is valuable. The narrative from 1316 to 1330 relates mainly to the civic history of London. The work was written by a citizen of London who had easy access to the records of the corporation, perhaps by Andrew Horn, chamberlain of the city (d. 1328).

2762 ANNALES MONASTERII DE BERMUNDESEIA, 1042–1432. Ed. by Henry R. Luard, *Annales Monastici*, iii. 421–87. Rolls Ser. Lond. 1866.

This work, compiled *c*. 1433, deals mainly with the affairs of the priory of Bermondsey, but it devotes some attention to general history, and is of some value for the reigns of Henry IV and Henry V. The chief source of the earlier portion is the *Flores Historiarum*. For its inaccuracies, see *Graham papers* (No. 1471), pp. 93 ff. and 121 ff.; and Knowles *et al.* (No. 5895), pp. 6 and 114 ff.

2763 ANNALES MONASTERII DE BURTON, 1004–1263. Ed. by Henry R. Luard, *Annales Monastici*, i. 181–510. Rolls Ser. Lond. 1864. Another edition (bad), in Fulman's *Scriptores* (No. 1098), pp. 246–448. Extracts, 1211–62. Ed. by R. Pauli, in M.G.H., *SS.* xxvii. 473–84.

Written in the thirteenth century, the entries to 1188 are brief, and those from 1189 to 1201 are taken mainly from Hoveden. The part from 1211 to 1263 (chiefly a collection of documents connected by short notices of events concerning Burton and the kingdom) is particularly valuable. Luard calls it 'one of the most valuable collections of materials for the history of the time that we possess'. The most important part is that which relates to the Provisions of Oxford and to the Barons' War, 1258–63.

2764 ANNALES MONASTERII DE OSENEIA, 1016–1347. Ed. by Henry R. Luard, *Annales Monastici*, iv. 1–352. Rolls Ser. Lond. 1869. Another edition of the years 1289–1307, in Gale's *Scriptores Quinque* (No. 1099), pp. 118–28. Oxf. 1687. Extracts, 1133–1293. Ed. by R. Pauli, in M.G.H., *SS.* xxvii. 484–503.

These annals, to 1258, have much in common with those of Thomas Wykes; from that year onward the former favour the barons, while Wykes is a strong royalist. Luard believes that Wykes used the early portion of the Osney annals, that this portion was compiled at Osney about 1233 mainly from Diceto and Florence of Worcester, and that thereafter the events were entered from year to year, as they occurred, until 1277. The bulk of the chronicle is an original authority for the general history of England from 1233 to 1293. The part 1293–1347 is taken from Higden and his continuator. See Wykes (No. 2983).

2765 ANNALES MONASTERII DE THEOKESBERIA, 1066–1263. Ed. by Henry R. Luard, *Annales Monastici*, i. 41–180. Rolls Ser. Lond. 1864. Extracts, 1147–1258. Ed. by R. Pauli, in M.G.H., *SS*. xxvii. 464–70.

Written in the thirteenth century. Meagre to the year 1200. Entries concerning general history are intermingled with notices of monastic affairs. There is a valuable account of the war between Henry III and the barons, pp. 163–80; the chronicler favours the baronial cause. Jottings in a calendar of the abbey which add a few details between 1066 and 1137 are edited by René Poupardin in *Bémont essays* (No. 1426), pp. 99–104. For Thomas of Kidderminster as author of portions of the annals, see Russell, *Writers* (No. 541), pp. 164–5.

2766 ANNALES MONASTERII DE WAVERLEIA, A.D. 1–1291. Ed. by Henry R. Luard, *Annales Monastici*, ii. 127–411. Rolls Ser. Lond. 1865. Another edition of the years 1066–1291 (bad), in Gale's *Scriptores Quinque* (No. 1099), pp. 129–243. Extracts, 1122–1291. Ed. by Pauli, in M.G.H., *SS*. xxvii. 458–64.

These annals are derived largely from a lost Winchester chronicle. They form an important narrative source for the reign of Henry III, especially for the events preceding and following the battle of Evesham. For the complicated relationship of Waverley annals with other monastic annals, see Liebermann, *Geschichtsquellen* (No. 2738), pp. 173–202, and N. Denholm-Young, 'The Winchester-Hyde Chronicle', *E.H.R.* xlix (1934), 85–93; reprinted in his *Collected papers* (No. 1467), pp. 86–95; and M. Tyson, 'The annals of Southwark and Merton', *Surrey Archaeol. Collections*, xxxvi (1925), 24–44 (No. 2785).

2767 ANNALES MONASTERII DE WINTONIA, A.D. 519–1277. Ed. by Henry R. Luard, *Annales Monastici*, ii. 1–125. Rolls Ser. Lond. 1865. Extracts in Wharton's *Anglia Sacra* (No. 1125), i. 288–314; and ed. by Pauli, M.G.H., *SS*. xxvii. 452–58. Trans. by Joseph Stevenson, *Church Historians* (No. 1123), iv, pt. 1, 347–84.

Luard printed the portion A.D. 519–1066 from a MS. at Corpus Christi College, Cambridge, which in fact carried the annals to 1139. This MS. is thought to be the work of Richard of Devizes. Luard printed the portion from 1066 to 1277 from a Cotton MS. in the British Museum, which for the period 1066–1139 differs in several respects from the Cambridge MS. for the same period. The annals in the Cotton MS. for 1139–90 are scanty; but from 1196 to 1202 are again fuller and may well have been written by Richard of Devizes. (John T. Appleby, 'Richard of Devizes and the Annals of Winchester', *B.I.H.R.* xxxvi (1963), 70–7.) Appleby (pp. 75–7) prints a few entries for 1066 to 1138 from the unprinted section of the Cambridge MS.

The portion of the *Annals of Winchester*, 1202 to 1277, was copied in the Cotton MS. from a Hyde chronicle in a Bodley MS. (N. Denholm-Young, 'The Winchester-Hyde Chronicle', *E.H.R.* xliv (1934), 85–93; reprinted in his *Collected papers* (No. 1467). It is valuable for the reign of Henry III and particularly for the full account of the events following the battle of Evesham 1267–77, which appears to be by the hand of a contemporary. See also Waverley annals (No. 2766). The work also contains much information concerning the bishops of Winchester. Extracts from other Winchester annals, continued at Canterbury, 741–1179, are edited by Liebermann, *Geschichtsquellen* (No. 2738), pp. 56–83.

2768 ANNALES PAULINI. Ed. by William Stubbs, *Chronicles of the reigns of Edward I and Edward II*, i. 253–370. Rolls Ser. Lond. 1882.

An abridgement of the *Flores Historiarum* (No. 2871) to 1307; continued from 1307 to 1341 by several authors. Stubbs prints only the portions from 1307 to 1341. Although Stubbs regarded the continuation as the work of a single author, connected with St.

Paul's, Richardson presents evidence of four distinct works and holds that 'large parts of the chronicle are hardly worth the reading'. H. G. Richardson, 'The Annales Paulini', *Speculum*, xxiii (1948), 630–40. See *Repert. Font.* ii. 313.

2769 ANNALES PRIORATUS DE WIGORNIA, A.D. 1–1377. Ed. by Henry R. Luard, *Annales Monastici*, iv. 353–564. Rolls Ser. Lond. 1869. Extracts relating to the years 680–1308, in Wharton's *Anglia Sacra* (No. 1125), i. 467–530, and to 1165–1346, ed. by R. Pauli, in M.G.H., SS. xxvii. 464–73.

Down to 1303 these annals were written by a monk of Worcester early in the fourteenth century, and the work originally ended with the year 1308. The continuation to 1377 comprises only a few meagre entries. The *Annals of Worcester* contain notices of public events, and are also rich in material illustrating the history of the priory and diocese of Worcester. Luard believes that they 'will always rank very high as an authority for the latter years of the thirteenth century'.

For W. de Bradewas as a possible author down to 1228, see Russell, *Writers* (No. 541), p. 174; and for Nicholas of Norton for the part 1280–1303, ibid., pp. 89–90.

2770 ANNALES REGNI SCOTIAE (with a translation). Ed. by Henry T. Riley, *Willelmi Rishanger Chronica* (No. 2948), pp. 233–368. Rolls Ser. Lond. 1865. Extracts. Ed. by Liebermann, in M.G.H., *SS.* xxviii. 521–4.

This account of the 'Great Cause' concerning the succession to the Scottish crown in 1291–2 was given the above title by the editor, Henry Riley. It was composed largely in French at St. Albans, presumably in the early fourteenth century. Its authorship is uncertain. It was attributed to Rishanger by Bale and others; and Galbraith, *St. Albans Chronicle* (No. 2731), p. xxxiii, is disposed to accept this attribution. The suggestion that John of Caen was its compiler is unacceptable. However, the author, whoever he was, seems to have had at hand documents provided by John of Caen, the notary public who compiled 'The Great Roll of Scotland', on proceedings relative to the disputed succession. See E. L. G. Stones, 'The Records of the "Great Cause" of 1291–92', *Scot. H.R.* xxxv (1956), 89–109. For a continuation, see above No. 2752.

2771 ANNALES RICARDI SECUNDI ET HENRICI QUARTI REGUM ANGLIAE. See Walsingham (No. 2976).

2772 ANNALES S. EDMUNDI, A.D. 1–1212. Ed. by Felix Liebermann, *Geschichtsquellen*, pp. 97–155. Extracts, 1065–1212. Ed. by Liebermann, in M.G.H., *SS.* xxvii. 426–7. See also No. 2819.

The part 1200–12 is a contemporary record, valuable for the general history of England.

2773 ANNALES S. PAULI LONDONIENSIS (1064–1274). Ed. by Liebermann, in M.G.H., *SS.* xxviii. 548–51.

These annals, from which Liebermann edits extracts for 1194–1274, give an accurate account of the barons' war in the reign of Henry III. The author, a member of the cathedral chapter, seems to have been an eye-witness of many of the events narrated from 1250 onward.

2774 ANNALES STANLEIENSES (from Brutus to 1271). Ed. by Richard Howlett, *Chronicles of the reigns of Stephen, Henry II, and Richard I*, ii. 506–58. Rolls Ser. Lond. 1885. Extracts, 1207–71. Ed. by Liebermann, in M.G.H., *SS.* xxviii. 555–7.

Howlett edits only the part 1202–71. The work seems to have been begun in Stanley abbey about the middle of the thirteenth century. The author, who sympathizes with the barons in their conflicts with John and Henry III, made use of Geoffrey of Monmouth, Coggeshall, and a lost chronicle of some value for the years 1204–14.

2775   ANNALES WINCHECUMBENSES (1049–1181). Ed. by R. R. Darlington. *Miscellanea D. M. Stenton* (No. 1453), pp. 115–37. Excerpts in M.G.H., *SS.* xvi. 481–2. See Levison (No. 2282), pp. 249–59.

2776   ANNALIS HISTORIA BREVIS SIVE CHRONICA MONASTERII S. STEPHANI CADOMENSIS (A.D. 633–1293). Ed. by André Duchesne, *Historiae Normannorum Scriptores* (No. 1096), pp. 1015–21. Reprinted in Maseres's *Monumenta* (No. 1111), pp. 355–66; and in Giles's *Scriptores* (No. 2741), pp. 161–74.

> The chronicle of Caen contains brief notices of Norman and English affairs, especially from 1066 onward.

2777   ANNALS FROM THE BOOK OF LEINSTER, A.D. 457–1189, with a translation of the Irish. Ed. by Whitley Stokes, *Tripartite life of Patrick*, pp. 512–29. Rolls Ser. Lond. 1887. The book of Leinster, formerly Lebar na Núachongbála. Ed. by R. I. Best, O. Bergin, and M.Á. O'Brien, 5 vols. Dublin. 1954–67.

> These annals, written in the twelfth century, are printed in Irish only in the Best-O'Brien edition, vol. i (1954). See also Aubrey Gwynn, 'Some notes on the history of the Book of Leinster', *Celtica*, v (1960), 8–12.

2778   (ANNALS OF BOYLE) Annales Buelliani (from the creation to 1253 or 1257). Ed. by Charles O'Conor, *Rerum Hibernicarum Scriptores*, ii (pt. iv), 1–48. Buckingham. 1825. The annals of Cotton MS. Titus A XXV transcribed and edited by A. Martin Freeman. Paris. 1929.

> O'Conor edits only the part A.D. 420–1245, which deals mainly with the history of Ireland. The text is Irish interspersed with Latin. The time of compilation is unknown. O'Curry says that, 'as far as the annals themselves can show', there is nothing to indicate that they are annals of Boyle except the words 'Annales Monasterii in Buellio in Hibernia', written in the MS. by a modern hand. See O'Curry, *Lectures on MS. materials* (No. 30), pp. 81, 105–13.

2779   ANNALS OF CLONMACNOISE, being annals of Ireland from the earliest period to A.D. 1408, trans. into English. Ed. by Denis Murphy. Royal Soc. of Antiq. of Ireland. Dublin. 1896.

> This translation (completed in 1627) was made by Conall Mageoghegan of Lismoyne, in Westmeath. No extant copy of the Irish text is known. 'The records contained in it are brief, but they sometimes preserve details of singular interest, not to be found in any of our other annals', O'Curry, *Lectures on MS. materials* (No. 30), p. 131.

2780   ANNALS OF INNISFALLEN: ANNALES INISFALENSES (from the creation to 1321). Ed. with introduction, translation, and notes by Seán Mac Airt. Inst. of Advanced Studies, Dublin. 1951. Facsimile edition of Bodleian MS. Rawlinson B 503 with introduction by R. I. Best and Eoin MacNeill. Royal Irish Academy. Dublin and Lond. 1933. Imperfect edition of the part A.D. 428–1196 in O'Conor, *Scriptores* (No. 1117), ii, part ii, 1–156. Excerpts A.D. 434–1030, in W. F. Skene, *Chronicles of the Picts* (No. 1120), pp. 167–70.

> The text is Irish interspersed with Latin. It is especially valuable for the history of Munster and contains much on King Brian (976–1014). The main portion of the *Annals*, written by a contemporary hand about A.D. 1092, was composed by a scribe of Killaloe, who copied from a then existing composite chronicle. (Aubrey Gwynn, 'Were the

Annals of Innisfallen written at Killaloe?', *North Munster Antiq. Jour.* viii (1958), 20–33.) There are no authentic contemporary Irish annals before 1092. The annals from 1092 to 1244 and from 1258 to 1285 are probably contemporary with the events recorded but those for the intervening years were written later.

O'Conor, *Scriptores*, ii, part iii, 1–76 prints another set of so-called *Annales Innisfallenses*. These run from A.D. 250 to 1061 and were compiled from various sources by John Conry in 1765. See K. Hughes (No. 22), pp. 108–14.

2781 ANNALS OF IRELAND. See No. 2759.

2782 ANNALS OF IRELAND, 1443–68. Trans. from the Irish by Dudley Firbisse, or Duald MacFirbis, for Sir James Ware in 1666. Ed. by John O'Donovan Irish Archaeol. Soc. *Miscellany*, i (1846), 198–302, of which the translation is on pp. 200–63.

It is difficult to ascertain from what compilation MacFirbis made this translation.

2783 ANNALS OF LOCH CÉ: a chronicle of Irish affairs 1014–*c.* 1588. Ed. and trans. by W. M. Hennessy. Rolls Ser. 2 vols. Lond. 1871. Reproduced by Irish MSS. Comm. 2 vols. Dublin. 1939.

The MS. was copied in 1588 from an earlier compilation from various sources. Down to 1220 the *Annals of Loch Cé* and the A-text of the *Annals of Ulster* (No. 2786) are basically a single chronicle. For the later period, the *Annals of Loch Cé* are very close to the *Annals of Connacht* (No. 2751). 'They are much more copious in details of the affairs of Connacht than any of our other annals.' O'Curry, *Lectures on MS. materials* (No. 30), p. 101; cf. ibid., pp. 93–104. See also Gearóid MacNiocaill, 'Annála Uladh agus Annála Locha Cé, 1014–1220', *Galvia*, vi (1959), 18–25.

2784 ANNALS OF THE KINGDOM OF IRELAND, by the four masters, from the earliest period to 1616 (Irish text, with an English translation). Ed. by John O'Donovan. 7 vols. Dublin. 1851. Reissued in 1966. Another edition (inaccurate) of the part to 1171, in O'Conor, *Rerum Hibernicarum Scriptores*, vol. iii. Buckingham. 1824.

This digest or synthesis of various old annals of Ireland, some of which have since been lost, was compiled in 1632–6 by several Franciscan friars in the monastery of Donegal under the direction of Michael O'Clery, O.F.M. The compilers were first called 'The Four Masters' by Colgan in *Acta Sanct. Hibern.* (No. 1160). This compilation is the most important of all the sources for the history of medieval Ireland. See O'Curry, *Lectures on MS. materials* (No. 30), pp. 140–61; and Paul Walsh, *The four masters and their work* (Dublin, 1944).

2785 ANNALS OF SOUTHWARK AND MERTON, described by M. Tyson, *Surrey Archaeol. Collections*, xxxvi (1925), 24–44 with an appendix, pp. 45–57, of passages for selected years from 1209 to 1234. Extracts of Southwark Annals. Ed. by Pauli in M.G.H., *SS.* xxvii. 430–2. Extract from Merton Annals for 1216–17. Ed. by Charles Petit-Dutaillis, in *Étude sur la vie et le règne de Louis VIII* (Paris, 1894), pp. 513–15.

The *Annals of Merton* seem to have been compiled from an earlier copy of the *Annals of Southwark* or from a common prototype. For the period 1219 to 1240 they are in substantial agreement. Down to 1208, they borrow from well-known chronicles, for one part especially from Ralph de Diceto; but from 1208 to 1240 or 1242 the *Southwark Annals* were contemporaneously written and are valuable. They seem to have been used by Matthew Paris, and in *Flores Historiarum* and *Liber de Antiquis Legibus*; and they are related to the annals of Bermondsey, Waverley, and Worcester.

2786   ANNALS OF ULSTER, otherwise Annals of Senat: a chronicle of Irish affairs, A.D. 431–1541 (Irish text, with a translation). Ed. by W. M. Hennessy (vols. ii–iv by B. MacCarthy). Published by the authority of the Lords Commissioners of her Majesty's Treasury. 4 vols. (vol. iv, introduction and index). Dublin. 1887–1901. Another edition of the part to 1131 (very inaccurate), in O'Conor's *Rerum Hibernicarum Scriptores* (No. 1117), vol. iv. An edition by S. MacAirt and Gearóid Mac Niocaill is expected. [See K. Hughes (No. 22), chap. 4.]

> Compiled on the island of Senait Mac Manus, now called Belle Isle, in Loch Erne, by Cathal Maguire, the vicar-general of Clogher, who died in 1498; continued to 1540 by Rory O'Cassidy, and afterwards by an unknown writer to 1604. The work relates more to the history of Ulster than to that of any of the other provinces of Ireland. For a severe criticism of the new edition, see Whitley Stokes, 'The Annals of Ulster', in *Revue celtique*, xviii (1897), 74–86. He says that 'the volumes here noticed are worse than worthless, as their existence will for years, perhaps for ever, preclude the publication of an accurate edition of one of the best documentary sources of the history of Ireland'. See also O'Curry, *Lectures on MS. materials* (No. 30), pp. 83–92. The language of the *Annals* is discussed by Tomás Ó Máille, in the Celtic series of the publications of the University of Manchester, 1910, which shows that the language of an early source (say about A.D. 700) is retained in *The Annals*. Father Aubrey Gwynn, 'Cathal Mac-Maghnusa and the Annales of Ulster', *Clogher Record*, ii (1958), 230–43, 370–84, discusses the careers of the chief compiler and principal scribe of these annals.

2787   THE ANONIMALLE CHRONICLE, 1333–81. Ed. by V. H. Galbraith. Manchester. 1927. Reprinted 1970. Extracts from a sixteenth-century transcript in G. M. Trevelyan, 'An account of the rising of 1381', *E.H.R.* xiii (1898), 509–22. Translation of extract in Charles W. C. Oman, *The Great Revolt of 1381*, pp. 186–205. Oxf. 1906.

> An important chronicle for fourteenth-century history written in French at St. Mary's abbey, York. It is largely a 'patchwork' of translations from the works of others. It is probable that the portion before 1356 was written prior to 1382; and that the rest was written between 1396 and 1399. For the years 1334–46 it seems to be based on a lost contemporary Minorite chronicle which served as a basis of the *Chronicon de Lanercost* (No. 2836). After 1346 it follows unknown sources with additions of its own. The portion from 1376 to 1381 becomes more detailed and supplies 'the most valuable of surviving contemporary accounts' of the Good Parliament and the Peasants' Revolt. That section may have been taken from a lost London chronicle. J. G. Edwards in his review of Galbraith's edition in *E.H.R.* xliii (1928), 103–9, suggests that an unknown Guisborough chronicle may have been a source for the later years of *Anonimalle Chronicle*. A. F. Pollard in 'The authorship and value of the Anonimalle chronicle', *E.H.R.* liii (1938), 577–605, suggests that the author of the portion from 1376 to 1381 may have been John Scardeburgh, clerk of chancery and under-clerk of parliament.

2788   ANONYMOUS. THE CRUSADE AND DEATH OF RICHARD I. Ed. by R. C. Johnston. *Anglo-Norman texts*, xvii. Oxf. 1961.

> An Anglo-Norman prose chronicle written about 1300 which draws on Howden, Matthew Paris, and an unknown source.

2789   ARNOLD (RICHARD) (d. 1521). The customs of London, otherwise called Arnold's Chronicle. Reprinted from the 1st edn. (*c.* 1502), with the additions included in the 2nd (*c.* 1520). Ed. by Francis Douce. Lond. 1811.

> In the two sixteenth-century editions, the work lacked a title, except for the statement: 'In this book is conteyned the names of ye baylifs custos maires a. sherefs of London.' It was first called 'Arnold's Chronicle' by Thomas Hearne; the title 'The Customs of

London' was invented by Douce. The list of mayors and other officials, with brief historical notes, runs from 1189 to 1520. The bulk of the work is a collection of charters, municipal regulations, and other documents relating chiefly to London in the fourteenth and fifteenth centuries. Arnold was a citizen of London.

2790 AVESBURY (ROBERT OF) (d. before 1359). De gestis mirabilibus regis Edwardi Tertii (to 1356). Ed. by E. M. Thompson. Rolls Ser. Lond. 1889. Another edition, by Thomas Hearne, Oxf. 1720.

Deals especially with the military history of Edward III's reign, 1339–56; contains many valuable documents. Avesbury was registrar of the court of the Archbishop of Canterbury. Particulars of his life are not known, save that his will was enrolled in 1359.

2791 BAKER (GEOFFREY LE) (d. 1358–60). Chronicon Galfridi le Baker de Swynebroke (1303–56). Ed. by E. M. Thompson. Oxf. 1889. Another edition, by J. A. Giles. Caxton Soc. Lond. 1847.

Writing after 1341 at the request of his patron Sir Thomas de la More, Baker relied mainly on Adam of Murimuth down to 1341, but gives some valuable information not found elsewhere. The life of Edward II ascribed to Thomas de la More (No. 2928) is an extract from Baker's *Chronicon*. In 1347 Baker also wrote a worthless *Chroniculum*, extending from the creation to 1336, which Thompson edits with the *Chronicon*, pp. 156–75. Swinbrook, Oxfordshire, seems to have been Baker's native place; and he was a secular clerk.

2792 BARBOUR (JOHN) (d. 1395). The Bruce, or the book of Robert de Broyss, king of Scots (1286–1332). Ed. by Walter W. Skeat. Scottish Text Soc. 2 vols. Edinburgh, etc. 1894; and reprint N.Y. 1966. (This is mainly a reprint of the edition prepared by Skeat for the E.E.T.S. 2 vols. 1870–89.) Another edition printed for the Spalding Club. Aberdeen. 1856. The Bruce. Ed. by W. M. Mackenzie. Lond. 1909. For other editions, see Potthast (No. 62), i. 133; *Repert. Font.* ii. 446–7; Skeat's edition of 1894, vol. i, preface; and R. M'Kinlay, 'Barbour's Bruce', *Records of Glasgow Bibliographical Society*, vi (1920), 20–38. A translation into modern English prose is provided by George Eyre-Todd. Lond. and Glasgow. 1907. A rendition in modern English verse is given in *The Bruce: an epic poem . . . By John Barbour*, trans. and ed. by Archibald A. H. Douglas. Glasgow. 1964.

This English poem, completed, as Neilson points out, in 1376, is a national epic which gives an account of the Scottish war of independence and narrates the deeds of King Robert I of Scotland. Barbour was Archdeacon of Aberdeen and an auditor of the exchequer of Scotland. 'Consciously or unconsciously, he emphasized the chivalrous qualities in Bruce and in Douglas, his other hero', and of their age. . . . 'Nevertheless, on the score of general reliability Barbour must be reckoned a biographer, not a romancer' (G. W. S. Barrow, *Robert Bruce* (Lond. 1965), p. 431). See also George Neilson, *John Barbour, poet and translator* (Lond. 1900); and R. Dunlop in *Tout essays* (No. 1458).

2793 BASIN (THOMAS) (d. 1491). Historia Caroli VII et Ludovici XI. Ed. by Jules Quicheret. Société de l'histoire de France. 4 vols. Paris, 1855–9. Histoire de Charles VII (1407–50). Ed. and trans. (into French) by Charles Samaran and Henry de Surirey de Saint-Rémy. Les Classiques de l'histoire de France au moyen âge. 2 vols. Paris. 1934–45. Histoire de Louis XI, vols. i–ii (1461–77). Ed. and trans. (into French) by Charles Samaran. Les Classiques. Paris. 1963–6.

Thomas Basin, a man of affairs and Bishop of Lisieux 1448–74, had been employed by the Duke of York; but in 1449 he took the oath of fealty to Charles VII. For opposition to Louis XI, he fled in 1468 and resigned his bishopric in Rome in 1474.

His history of Charles VII is valuable for Norman matters at the end of English domination. Molinier, *Sources* (No. 57), iv. 4137. His seven books on the reign of Louis XI form a diatribe against that king. For other works and editions, see *Repert. Font.* ii. 463–4.

2794 BERRY (HÉRAULT DU ROY) (d. *c.* 1457). Le recouvrement de Normendie (French text, with a translation). Ed. by Joseph Stevenson, *Narratives of the Expulsion of the English from Normandy, 1449–50*, pp. 239–376. Rolls Ser. Lond. 1863. Translation (by Joseph Stevenson): *The recovery of Normandy from the English in 1449.* Ed. by Edmund Goldsmid, *Collectanea Adamantea*, vol. xx. 2 vols. in 1. Edin. 1887.

Berry's real name was Gilles le Bouvier. He was king-at-arms of Charles VII for the district of Berry. For his other works, see Molinier, *Sources* (No. 57), iv. 4134.

2795 BEVERLEY (ALURED, or ALFRED, OF). Annales sive Historia de gestis regum Britanniae (from Brutus to 1129). Ed. by Thomas Hearne. Oxf. 1716.

A worthless compilation, taken mainly from Geoffrey of Monmouth and Simeon of Durham; written seemingly soon after 1143. The author was sacristan of the church of Beverley. The time of his death is unknown.

2796 BLACMAN (JOHN). De virtutibus et miraculis Henrici VI. Ed. by Thomas Hearne, in his edition of Otterbourne (No. 2938), pp. 285–307. Oxf. 1732. Henry the sixth, a reprint of John Blacman's memoir with translation and notes by Montague R. James. Cambr. 1919.

A laudatory characterization of Henry VI, written by a Carthusian who flourished during that king's reign. The original MS. is not known to exist; but James collated his text with Robert Coplande's text (Lond. *c.* 1510). See also Paul Grosjean, ed., 'Henrici VI, Angliae regis, miracula postuma ex codice Musei Britannici Regio 13 C VIII', *Subsidia Hagiographica* (Brussels, 1935). Grosjean prints for the first time the accounts of 166 miracles from a compilation based on official inquiries in the reign of Henry VII; Grosjean's introduction of 266 pages is an important commentary. The accounts of twenty-three of these miracles are translated in Ronald Knox and Shane Leslie, *The miracles of King Henry VI* (Cambr. 1923). See Emden, *Oxford* (No. 533), pp. 194–5.

2797 BLANEFORD (HENRY OF). Chronica (1323–4). Ed. by Henry T. Riley, *Johannis de Trokelowe et Henrici de Blaneforde Chronica et Annales*, pp. 131–52. Rolls Ser. Lond. 1866. Another edition, with Trokelowe's Annals, by Thomas Hearne, Oxf. 1729.

A fragment of a larger chronicle, written soon after 1330 and probably intended as a continuation of Trokelowe's *Annals*. It is important for the reign of Edward II. The author was either a monk of St. Albans of whose life we have no particulars or Rishanger (No. 2948).

2798 BLONDEL (ROBERT) (d. *c.* 1461). De reductione Normanniae. Ed. by Joseph Stevenson, *Narratives of the Expulsion of the English from Normandy, 1449–50*, pp. 1–238. Rolls Ser. Lond. 1863. Another edition, by Alexandre Héron, *Œuvres de Robert Blondel*, vol. ii. Société de l'Histoire de Normandie. Rouen, 1893.

A trustworthy account of the expulsion of the English from Normandy in 1449–50. The author, a native of Normandy, with an implacable hatred of the English, was an

ardent adherent of Charles VII. See Auguste Vallet de Viriville, 'Notice sur Robert Blondel', in *Mémoires de la Société des Antiquaires de Normandie*, xix (1851), 161–226.
Blondel also wrote *Liber de complanctu bonorum Gallicorum* and *Oratio historialis*, both printed in Héron's *Œuvres*, vol. i, and both diatribes against the English.

2799 BOOK OF HOWTH. Ed. by J. S. Brewer and William Bullen, *Calendar of Carew MSS.* v, pp. 1–260. Rolls Ser. Lond. 1871.

Called the *Book of Howth* because it used to be in the possession of the family of Howth. It was compiled by various unknown writers, one of whom was perhaps Richard Howth (d. 1554). It is a chronicle of Irish affairs, *c.* A.D. 330 to 1579, written in English. The authorities used were Bede, Giraldus Cambrensis, Higden, Fabyan, etc.; the part dealing with the conquest of Ireland seems to be taken mainly from an early translation of the *Expugnatio Hibernica* of Giraldus Cambrensis. The work is chiefly valuable for 'the traditional anecdotes and personal notices contained in it'. See J. H. Round, *Commune of London* (Westminster, 1899), pp. 146–9.

2800 BRAY (THOMAS). The English conquest of Ireland, 1166–85: a parallel text. Ed. by F. J. Furnivall. Pt. i: Text. E.E.T.S. Lond. 1896. Another edition, by J. S. Brewer and William Bullen, *Calendar of Carew MSS.* v, pp. 261–317. Rolls Ser. Lond. 1871.

Probably copied, in large part, from an early English translation of the *Expugnatio Hibernica* of Giraldus Cambrensis. Bray seems to have lived in the fifteenth century: Tanner, *Bibliotheca* (No. 33), p. 122.

2801 BREVIS RELATIO DE ORIGINE WILLELMI. Ed. by J. A. Giles, *Scriptores* (No. 2741), pp. 1–23. Lond. 1845. Another edition, by Silas Taylor, *History of Gavelkind*, pp. 185–209. Lond. 1663.

'This account, though brief, is apparently truthful.' It seems to have been written in the reign of Henry I.

2802 BROMPTON (JOHN) (*fl.* 1437). Chronicon, A.D. 588–1198 (1199). Ed. by Roger Twysden, *Scriptores Decem*, pp. 721–1284. Lond. 1652.

An untrustworthy compendium, made up of extracts from Bede, Henry of Huntingdon, Higden, and other well-known sources. It appears that Brompton was not the author. He was elected abbot of Jervaulx in 1436 and was still abbot in 1464; he secured a copy of this chronicle for his abbey's library. See Hardy, *Catalogue*, ii. 539–41, and Emden, *Oxford* (No. 533), i. 277.

2803 BRUT (THE), OR CHRONICLES OF ENGLAND.

For the important English continuations to the French Brut, see below, Caxton (No. 2811).

2804 BRUT Y SAESON, or Chronicle of the Saxons (A.D. 800–1382). Ed. by John Rhys and J. Gwenogvryn Evans, *The Text of the Bruts from the Red Book of Hergest* (Oxf. 1890), ii. 385–403. Another less satisfactory edition in *Myvyrian Archaiology* (No. 2382).

2805 BRUT Y TYWYSOGION, or the chronicle of the princes (Welsh text in three versions, A.D. 680–1282).

(*a*) Red Book of Hergest version, critical text and translation by Thomas Jones. Board of Celtic Studies, History and Law Series, No. 16. Cardiff. 1955. A good edition also in John Rhys and J. Gwenogvryn Evans, *The Text of the Bruts from the Red Book of Hergest* (Oxf. 1890), ii, 257–384. A less satisfactory text is printed in *Myvyrian Archaiology* (Lond. 1801), ii. 391–467, and in its second edition (Denbigh, 1870), pp. 602–51. Badly edited, with a translation, by John Williams ab Ithel. Rolls Ser. Lond. 1860. The part A.D. 681–1066 is edited, with a translation by Aneurin Evans in Petrie's *Monumenta* (No. 1084), pp. 841–55. Extracts with Latin translation, 681–1282. Ed. by Liebermann, M.G.H., *SS.* xxvii. 444–8.

(*b*) Peniarth MS. 20 version. Ed. by Thomas Jones, B.C.S. Hist. and Law Series, No. 6. Cardiff. 1941. Translation and introduction by Thomas Jones, B.C.S. Hist. and Law Series, No. 11. Cardiff. 1952. This version has a continuation from 1282 to 1332, which is printed in *Hist. MSS. Comm. Reports*, 'Reports on MSS. in the Welsh language' (Lond. 1899), i, pt. ii, 343–6.

(*c*) Brenhinedd y Saeson (Kings of the Saxons, 683–1197). Printed in *Myvyrian Archaiology* (Lond. 1801), ii. 485–532, and in its second edition (Denbigh, 1870), pp. 652–84. See P. C. Bartrum, in *Études celtiques*, xii (1968–9), 157–94.

This *Brut*, which is one of the chief authorities for Welsh history in the Middle Ages, begins where Geoffrey of Monmouth ended. It survives in three distinct versions. Each version, namely *Red Book*, *Peniarth*, and *Brenhinedd*, is deemed to be a translation into Welsh from one Latin archetype, which is no longer extant. The lost archetype had some connection with the Latin *Annales Cambriae* (No. 2752A) and *Cronica de Wallia* (No. 3785A). The missing archetype may have been associated with St. David's to about 1100, then with Llanbadarn Fawr from about 1100 to 1175, and then with Strata Florida to its termination. It seems likely that the Latin text from which the various Welsh translators produced the differing translations was a Strata Florida chronicle of the thirteenth century.

The translators are anonymous. Furthermore the so-called *Gwentian Brut*, which is printed in *Myvyrian Archaiology*, ii (1801), 468–582, is now considered a forgery, fabricated by Edward Williams (Iolo Morganwy 1747–1826), one of the editors of *Myvyrian Archaiology*. Before the forgery was unmasked, it had been reproduced as 'Brut y Tywysogion: The Gwentian chronicle of Caradoc of Llancarvan with a translation (A.D. 660–1196)'. Ed. by Aneurin Owen. Cambrian Archaiol. Assoc. (Lond. 1863).

Version *b* is fuller than version *a*, but not as correct. Version *c* not only stops at 1197, but also makes use of the *Annales de Wintonia* (No. 2767) in addition to the source for *a* and *b*. The MSS. in the *Red Book* and in Peniarth MS. 20 are assigned to the late fourteenth century.

In his review of Jones's edition of Peniarth MS. 20, J. G. Edwards raises some questions and suggests some answers about the continuation from 1282 to 1332. *E.H.R.* lvii (1942), 342–5.

The above summary is made from J. E. Lloyd, 'The Welsh Chroniclers', *P.B.A.* xiv (1928), 369–91, J. G. Edwards, *E.H.R.* lvii (1942), 340–5; I. Ll. Foster, *E.H.R.* lxx (1955), 269–73. Other critiques may be found in Egerton Phillimore's 'Publication of Welsh historical records', *Y Cymmrodor*, xi (1892), 133–75; and the introductions in Thomas Jones's works cited above.

For a different work see immediately above *Brut y Saeson* (No. 2804).

2806 BURTON (THOMAS OF) (d. 1437). Chronica monasterii de Melsa (1150–1396, with a continuation to 1406). Ed. by E. A. Bond. Rolls. Ser. 3 vols. Lond. 1866–8.

'A faithful and often minute record of the establishment of a religious community, its progress . . . and its relations to the governing institutions of the country'; compiled after 1399. In his account of each abbot's rule, Burton treats of the affairs of the Cistercian abbey of Melsa, or Meaux, and then reviews the leading events of English history. Much of this general history is taken from Higden's *Polychronicon*. With the reign of

Edward I, the narrative of public affairs expands; and the portions concerning the relations of England to Scotland are of some value. Burton was abbot of Meaux, 1396–9.

2807 CANTERBURY (GERVASE OF) (d. *c.* 1210). The historical works of Gervase of Canterbury. Ed. by William Stubbs. Rolls Ser. 2 vols. Lond. 1879–80.

Chronica, 1135–99, preceded by a brief account of the years 1100–35; i. 84–594. Another edition, in Twysden's *Scriptores Decem* (No. 1124), pp. 1289–1628; Extracts. Ed. by Pauli, in M.G.H., *SS.* xxvii. 297–308. The author used Florence of Worcester, Henry of Huntingdon, Benedict of Peterborough, the biographies of Becket, etc. The work is of some value for the reigns of Stephen, Henry II, and Richard I. The portion 1170–99 deals mainly with ecclesiastical affairs. The earlier part (ed. Stubbs, i. 29–38) contains the *Imaginationes* (composed *c.* 1188), or statements of the case of each side in the disputes between the Archbishop and the monks of St. Augustine, Canterbury, 1178–91.

Gesta regum, from Brutus to 1210, with a continuation to 1328; ii. 3–324. Extracts. Ed. by Pauli, in M.G.H., *SS.* xxvii. 308–15. Valuable for the reign of John. The part to 1135 is drawn mainly from Geoffrey of Monmouth and William of Malmesbury, and this is followed by an abstract of Gervase's *Chronica*, 1135–99.

Actus pontificum Cantuariensis ecclesiae, A.D. 597–1205; ii. 325–414. Another edition, in Twysden's *Scriptores Decem* (No. 1124), pp. 1629–84. Extract. Ed. by Pauli, in M.G.H., *SS.* xxvii. 315. Trans. by Joseph Stevenson, *Church Historians* (No. 1124); vol. v, pt. i. A standard authority on the history of the archbishopric.

Mappa mundi; ii. 414–49: a survey of the counties of England (lists of bishoprics, religious houses, castles, etc.). This work is now of little value.

In his writings Gervase exhibits much dislike of the Plantagenet kings. Though of some importance, he is not a chronicler of the first rank. He became a monk of Christ Church, Canterbury, in 1163, and he was sacristan of the convent in 1193.

2808 CAPGRAVE (JOHN) (d. 1464). The chronicle of England (from the creation to 1417). Ed. by F. C. Hingeston. Rolls Ser. Lond. 1858. Liber de illustribus Henricis. Ed. by F. C. Hingeston. Rolls Ser. Lond. 1858. Trans. by F. C. Hingeston: The book of the illustrious Henries. Lond. 1858.

Both works are badly edited. *The Chronicle*, written in English, ends abruptly in 1417. Except for an addition concerning Henry IV, it is excerpted from Walsingham. The other work, completed between 1446 and 1453, is a collection of memoirs of German emperors A.D. 918–1198, English kings 1100–1446, and other illustrious men who had borne the name of Henry in various parts of the world from 1031 to 1406. The portion relating to Henry VI is a contemporary record, but it consists namely of 'pious ejaculations' in praise of the king. The chapter on Henry IV is derived from well-known chroniclers, and that on Henry V 'is merely a prose version of the *Liber Metricus* of Thomas Elmham' (Kingsford, p. 39).

Capgrave was an Austin friar at Lynn who also composed saints' lives (Nos. 1158, 2287). For his biography, see Alberic de Meijer, 'John Capgrave O.E.S.A.', in *Augustiniana* (Louvain), v (1955), 400–40; vii (1957), 118–48, 531–75. His works are cited in H. S. Bennett, *Chaucer and the fifteenth century* (Oxf. 1947), pp. 152 and 267. See also Emden, *Cambridge* (No. 532), pp. 121–2; and Peter J. Lucas, 'John Capgrave (O.S.A. 1393–1404): scribe and publisher', *Cambr. Bibliog. Soc. Trans.* v (1969), 1–35.

2809 CASE (THOMAS). Annales monasterii beatae Mariae virginis, juxta Dublin (A.D. 1–1405). Ed. by J. T. Gilbert. *Chartularies of St. Mary's Abbey, Dublin*, ii. 241–92. Rolls Ser. Lond. 1884.

Completed in 1427. Devotes much attention to the history of England and Ireland. The information is drawn from Henry of Huntingdon, Giraldus Cambrensis, and other chroniclers.

2810   CASTELFORD (THOMAS). Chronicum Brittanicum versibus anglicis conscriptum ab antiquissimis temporibus usque ad Edwardum II incl.

This chronicle in English verse, though for the most part unprinted, is described with considerable fullness by M. L. Perrin, *Ueber Thomas Castelford's Chronik von England* (Göttingen and Boston, 1890; reprinted 1891). It follows Geoffrey of Monmouth and Wace, and seems to have been finished about 1327. It is edited only for the period from Arthur to the death of Cadwallader (A.D. 710) by Frank Behre in *Göteborgs högskolas årsskrift*, xlvi, 2, nos. i–ii (Göteborg, 1940). See John Taylor, *Medieval historical writing in Yorkshire* (St. Anthony's Hall, Pubns. no. 19. York, 1961), pp. 18–19. Castelford was a monk of Pontefract. See R. H. Fletcher, 'The Arthurian material in the Chronicles', in *Studies and Notes in Philology and Literature*, x (1906), 202–3.

2811   CAXTON (WILLIAM) (d. 1491). [The chronicles of England]. Lond. 1480. Other editions: Lond. 1482; St. Albans, 1483; Antwerp, 1493; Lond. 1497, 1502, 1504, 1510, 1515, 1520, 1528. Best edition: The Brut, or the Chronicles of England. Ed. by Friedrich W. D. Brie. Pts. i–ii. E.E.T.S. Orig. Ser. cxxxi, cxxxvi. Lond. 1906–8. See No. 2803.

Caxton's edition, printed in 1480, is an English version of the *Brut*, a history of Britain from the days of mythical Brutus to 1461. The *Brut* is preserved in numerous MSS. in French, Latin, and English versions. The basic French versions extend to 1333, and to 1307 have no independent historical value; but for the reign of Edward II a French version contains 'information which is peculiar to itself or fuller and more detailed than in other chronicles' (see below, Taylor; cf. Galbraith). Late in the fourteenth century the French version was translated into English and continued as an independent English chronicle from 1333 to 1377. For the reign of Edward III, it contains some material not found in other surviving chronicles (Kingsford, *Hist. Lit.*, pp. 114–15). From 1377 to 1461, when the chronicle ends, there are two major continuations in English. See Davies's edition (No. 2829).

For the French versions, see Paul Meyer, 'De quelques chroniques anglo-normandes qui ont porté le nom de Brut', *Bulletin de la Société des Anciens Textes Français* (1878), 104–45; V. H. Galbraith, 'Extracts from the Historia Aurea and a French Brut, 1317–47', *E.H.R.* xliii (1928), 203–7, 215–17; and John Taylor, 'The French Brut and the reign of Edward II', ibid. lxxii (1957), 423–37; and *An Anglo-Norman Brut*, ed. by Alexander Bell (Anglo-Norman Texts, xxi–xxii. Oxf. 1969). For all texts, see Friedrich Brie, *Geschichte und Quellen der mittelenglischen Prosakronik: the Brute of England* (Marburg, 1905). For the texts from 1377 to 1461, see Kingsford's *Hist. Lit.*, pp. 113–39, and 299–337. For the continuation 1377–1461 see Davies's edition (No. 2829) and for continuations of the Latin *Brut*, see Kingsford, pp. 158–9, 310–37, 346–9. See *Repert. Font.* iii. 210–11. For Caxton as a printer, see Nos. 7213–21.

2812   CHANDOS, HERALD OF. Life of the Black Prince, by the herald of Sir John Chandos. Ed. (with a prose translation) by Mildred K. Pope and Eleanor C. Lodge. Oxf. 1910. The Black Prince, an historical poem written in French, with a translation. Ed. by Henry O. Coxe. Roxburghe Club. Lond. 1842. Le Prince Noir, poème du heraut d'armes Chandos (with a translation). Ed. by Francisque Michel. Lond. etc. 1883.

This metrical biography written about 1386, in continental French rather than in Anglo-Norman, is of special value for the Black Prince's Castilian expedition. The author appears to have been an eye-witness of many of the events which he narrates. Michel plagiarized the work of Coxe. The Pope-Lodge edition is excellent; it gives two parallel texts, one the only surviving text and the second a hypothetical normalization of that text as well as a translation into English.

See T. F. Tout's review in *E.H.R.* xxvii (1912), 345–9. For the expedition to Castille in 1367, see Pedro López de Ayala, *Crónicas de los Reyes de Castilla* (Madrid, 1779), and the translations thereform in Myers, *Eng. Hist. Docs.* iv. 110–14. See *Repert. Font.* iii. 222.

2813 CHARTIER (JEAN) (d. 1464). Chronique de Charles VII roi de France. Ed. by Auguste Vallet de Viriville. 3 vols. Bibliothèque Elzevirienne. Paris. 1858. Ed. by Denys Godefroy. Histoire de Charles VII. Paris. 1661. La Chronique latine inédite de Jean Chartier (1422–50). Ed. by Charles Samaran. Bibliothèque du xvᵉ siècle. Paris. 1928. Charles Samaran in *Annuaire Bulletin de la Société de l'histoire de France* (Paris), lxiii (1926), 183–273.

> The Vallet de Viriville edition is the French chronicle for the *Grandes Chroniques* series. It has some dependence on the Berry herald (No. 2794) and on La Pucelle (No. 2840). The edition by Samaran is a fragmentary Latin chronicle by Chartier who was the royal historiographer at St. Denis. Consult Charles Samaran, 'La Chronique latine inédite de Jean Chartier (1422–1450) et les derniers livres du Religieux de Saint-Denis', *B.E.C.* lxxxvii (1926), 142–63. See *Repert. Font.* iii. 233–4.

2814 CHASTELLAIN (GEORGES) (d. 1475). Œuvres de Georges Chastellain. Ed. by Kervyn de Lettenhove. 8 vols. Brussels. 1863–6. Buchon, *Chron.* (No. 1091), vols. xli–xliii. Paris. 1825–7.

> Volumes i–v of the Brussels edition print all the surviving fragments of this important chronicle (1420–74), written by a councillor of Philip the Good of Burgundy. For Chastellain, see Kenneth Urwin, *Georges Chastellain: la vie, les œuvres* (Paris, 1937); and Luc Hommel, *Chastellain 1415–1474* (Brussels, 1945). For an edition and translation of Chastellain's *Chronique de Normandie, 1414–22*, see below No. 2877. See *Repert. Font.* iii. 234–5.

2815 CHRISTINE DE PISAN (d. 1431?). Le Livre des fais et bonnes meurs du sage roy Charles V. Ed. by Suzanne Solente. Société de l'histoire de France. 2 vols. Paris. 1936–41.

> A panegyric, written in French in 1404 at the request of Philip the Bold of Burgundy. Compiled from well-known sources, such as *Les Grandes Chroniques* and *La Chronique normande*, it adds some information given orally. The chronology is confused. See the introduction to the edition cited.

2816 CHRONICA MINOR S. BENEDICTI DE HULMO (from the earliest times to 1294, with a continuation to 1503). Ed. by Henry Ellis, *Chronica Johannis de Oxenedes*, pp. 412–39. Rolls Ser. Lond. 1859.

> Brief annals of the monastery of St. Benet Holme, Norfolk; many of the notices relate to general history.

2817 CHRONICLE (A BRIEF LATIN), 1422–71. Ed. by James Gairdner, *Three Fifteenth-Century Chronicles*, pp. 164–85. Camden Soc. Lond. 1880.

> A contemporary record for the reign of Edward IV, especially valuable for the years 1461–71. It is a continuation of the Latin *Brut*, being the concluding portion of 'Compilatio de gestis Britonum et Anglorum' in a College of Arms MS.

2818 CHRONICLE (A SHORT ENGLISH): Cronycullys of Englonde. Ed. by James Gairdner, *Three Fifteenth-Century Chronicles*, pp. 1–80. Camden Soc. Lond. 1880.

> This work comprises three short chronicles which were written or transcribed by the same pen soon after 1465. The first (pp. 1–28) is a brief abridgement of the *Brut* to 1 Henry IV. Then come (pp. 28–31) Lydgate's verses on the kings of England, of which another version is in No. 2736 above. Finally there is one of the regular London city

chronicles, 1189–1465, the latter part of which (i.e. 1450–65) 'has all the value of an original and independent authority for the reigns of Henry VI and Edward IV'.

2819 CHRONICLE OF BURY ST. EDMUNDS 1212–1301. Ed. with introduction, notes, and translation by Antonia Gransden. Nelson's Medieval Texts. Lond. etc. 1964. Cronica abbreviata (1152–1265). Ed. by Benjamin Thorpe, *Florentii Wigorniensis Chronicon*, ii. 136–96. Eng. Hist. Soc. Lond. 1849. Extracts (to 1301). Ed. by Liebermann, M.G.H., *SS*. xxviii (1888), 584–600. The second continuation 1296–1301, by V. H. Galbraith, 'The St. Edmundsbury Chronicle, 1296–1301', *E.H.R.* lviii (1943), 61–78.

> The *Annales Sancti Edmundi* (No. 2772) in the surviving form stop at 1212. The *Chronica Buriensis*, the chronicle here catalogued, is 'original' from 1212 to 1301. It consists of three sections: (*a*) 1212–65 is probably the work of John de Taxter (Tayster) who had begun his chronicle with the creation and carried on to 1265; (*b*) the first continuation 1265–96 by an unknown writer; and (*c*) the second continuation 1296–1301 by a third author. Taxter was a monk of Bury and a partisan of Simon de Montfort. There is no evidence that John de Eversden, the cellarer of Bury who is mentioned in the annal for 1300, was the author of the second continuation. For the above summary and the use of the *Bury Chronicle* by other chronicles see Antonia Gransden's Introduction. Besides Liebermann's preface and Galbraith's article, cited above, one may consult the twenty-six pages of Sir Ernest Clarke, *Bury Chronicles of the thirteenth century* (Bury and Lond. 1905). For other Bury documents, see below, Nos. 2958 and 6335–6.

2820 CHRONICLE OF DIEULACRES ABBEY, 1381–1403. Printed as pp. 164–81 in M. V. Clarke and V. H. Galbraith, 'The deposition of Richard II', *B.J.R.L.* xiv (1930), pp. 125–81. Reprinted in Maude V. Clarke, *Fourteenth century studies* (No. 1464). A portion is printed in No. 2841, pp. 280–5.

> A composite chronicle of two unknown writers of opposing views. Important for Richard's reign and deposition.

2821 CHRONICLE OF HOLYROOD. A Scottish chronicle known as the Chronicle of Holyrood. Ed. by Marjorie O. Anderson. Scottish Historical Soc. 3rd Ser., no. 30. Edin. 1938. Chronicon Anglo-Scoticum (60 B.C.–A.D. 1187 with additions to 1355). Ed. by C. W. Bouterwek. Elberfeld. 1863. Chronicon coenobii S. Crucis Edinburgensis (60 B.C.–A.D. 1163). Ed. by Robert Pitcairn. Bannatyne Club. Edin. 1828. The part A.D. 596–1163, in Wharton, *Anglia Sacra* (No. 1125), i. 152–62. Very brief extracts, 1084–1181. Ed. by Liebermann, M.G.H., *SS.* xxvii. 60. Translated to 1163, Joseph Stevenson, *Church historians* (No. 1123), iv, pt. i. 61–75.

> The Holyrood chronicle consists of three parts: (*a*) 60 B.C.–A.D. 734, derived from Bede and then a gap to 1065; (*b*) 1065–1187, based on Simeon of Durham to 1129 and then on another English chronicle to 1187. The notices from 1129 to 1189, though brief, are valuable, and relate chiefly to Scotland and northern England; (*c*) after a gap for the years 1188–1285, a few scanty notes for the period 1286 to 1355.
>   The introduction to the Anderson edition discusses the interrelationships of various other contemporaneous chronicles.

2822 THE CHRONICLE OF JOHN STRECCHE FOR THE REIGN OF HENRY V (1414–1422). Ed. by Frank Taylor. *B.J.R.L.* xvi (1932), pp. 137–87.

> In the *Historia Regum Anglie* (from Vortigern to 1422) of John Strecche, probably an Augustinian canon of Kenilworth, the portion of Book v dealing with the reign of Henry V has independent value. This portion only has been printed by Taylor. Despite

its inaccuracies and confusion, it provides information on minor events which is not found in other contemporary chronicles.

2823 CHRONICLE OF LONDON, 1089–1483. Lond. 1827.

According to the Catalogue of the Library of the British Museum, this work was edited by Edward Tyrrell and N. H. Nicolas. The chronicle originally ended in 1442, about which time it was compiled; a later hand continued it to 1483. It is a London city chronicle, written in English, but it deals mainly with the history of the kingdom.

A continuation, from 1446 to 1450, is edited by C. L. Kingsford, 'An historical collection of the fifteenth century', in *E.H.R.* xxix (1914), 505–15. He also edits a chronicle from 1416 to 1418 which may have been compiled in London. See also the *Great Chronicle of London* (No. 2885) and the introduction thereto.

2824 THE CHRONICLE OF MELROSE (A.D. 735–1270). A facsimile edition from Cotton MS. Faustina B ix, edited by Alan O. Anderson and Marjorie O. Anderson. Lond. 1936. Chronica de Mailros. Ed. by Joseph Stevenson. Bannatyne Club. Edin. 1835. Another edition, in Fulman, *Scriptores* (No. 1098), pp. 135–244. Extracts, 813–1264. Ed. by Pauli in M.G.H., *SS.* xxvii. 432–42. Trans. by Joseph Stevenson, *Church historians* (No. 1123), iv, pt. i. 79–242.

The part to 1129, derived mainly from Simeon of Durham, was compiled soon after 1236 by a monk of Melrose; and the work was continued in different hands by other monks of that abbey. After the middle of the twelfth century it is an original authority, and much of the information is contemporaneous. Although it is particularly heavy on the ecclesiastical history of the abbey of Melrose, it is also one of the most important sources of Scottish history. Partly founded on English annals, it is useful for English history, especially in the reign of Henry III.

The editions by Fulman and Stevenson are inaccurate; the Anderson facsimile edition is well produced, with an Anderson introduction and a notably complete index by W. C. Dickinson. The facsimile edition provides a means for the palaeographical study of various Scottish hands.

2825 A CHRONICLE OF THE CIVIL WARS OF EDWARD II (1295–1322). Ed. by George L. Haskins. *Speculum*, xiv (1939), 73–81.

This contemporary account was composed about 1327.

2826 CHRONICLE OF THE GREY FRIARS OF LONDON (1189–1556). Ed. by J. G. Nichols. Camden Soc. Lond. 1852. A better edition, by Richard Howlett, *Monumenta Franciscana*, ii. 143–260. Rolls Ser. Lond. 1882.

Forms a part of the register book of the London grey friars; written in English. It is a regular city chronicle, dealing with general and local history, but the names of the mayors of London are omitted in Nichols's edition. The medieval portion is meagre, and was probably compiled early in the sixteenth century.

2827 CHRONICLE OF THE MONASTERY OF ABINGDON, 1218–1304 (Latin text, with a translation). Ed. by J. O. Halliwell. Berkshire Ashmolean Soc. Reading. 1844.

Comprises additions made to a copy of *Hemingburgh's Chronicle* which used to belong to the monastery of Abingdon and which is now in the University library, Cambridge. For a more valuable chronicle of Abingdon, A.D. 201–1189, see No. 2153.

2828 CHRONICLE OF THE REBELLION IN LINCOLNSHIRE, 1470. Ed. by J. G. Nichols. Camden Soc., *Camden Miscellany*, vol. i. Lond. 1847.

Written in English. Nichols says that it 'evidently proceeded from one who wrote under the immediate influence of the royal authority and had consequently the best means of information'. Cf. Kingsford, *Hist. Lit.*, pp. 173-4.

2829   CHRONICLE (AN ENGLISH) OF THE REIGNS OF RICHARD II, HENRY IV, HENRY V, AND HENRY VI (1377-1461). Ed. by J. S. Davies. Camden Soc. Lond. 1856.

This continuation of the *Chronicle of Brut* (No. 2811) was compiled between 1461 and 1471. It is valuable especially for the reign of Henry VI, e.g. for Cade's rebellion. The author was an ardent Yorkist.

2830   CHRONICLE OF THE THIRTEENTH CENTURY (1066-1298). *Archaeol. Camb.* 3rd Ser. viii (1862), 272-83.

Useful as a continuation of the annals of Margam.

2831   CHRONICON ABBATIAE DE PARCO LUDAE: the chronicle of Louth Park abbey (1066-1413). Ed. by Edmund Venables, with a translation by A. R. Maddison. Lincs. Record Soc. Horncastle. 1891.

Probably compiled in the reign of Henry VI, it deals in a meagre fashion with general history. The appendix contains a 'compotus' roll (seemingly of the fifteenth century), charters, and other records, *c.* 1200-1614.

2832   CHRONICON ANGLIAE, 1328-88. See Walsingham (No. 2976).

2833   CHRONICON ANGLIAE (INCERTI SCRIPTORIS) DE REGNIS HENRICI IV, HENRICI V ET HENRICI VI (1399-1455). Ed. by J. A. Giles. (Half-title: Chronicon Angliae temporibus Ricardi II, Henrici IV, Henrici V et Henrici VI.) Lond. 1848.

Poorly edited. Giles omits pt. i on the ground that it is similar to *Vita Ricardi Secundi* (No. 2899); but this statement is not entirely true. For the reign of Henry IV it resembles London chronicles. The part relating to Henry V is identical with *Gesta Henrici Quinti*, sometimes ascribed to Thomas of Elmham (No. 2877). 'The Chronicle of Henry VI has, at all events, the merit of being the most nearly complete Latin history of the reign, coming down to 1455 . . .', with some new material after 1438. Yet 'such value as it possesses is due more to the defect of other authorities than to any merit of its own'. See Kingsford, pp. 24-8 and 155-9.

2834   CHRONICON ANGLIAE PETRIBURGENSE (A.D. 654-1368). Ed. by J. A. Giles. Caxton Soc. Lond. 1845. Another edition, in Sparke's *Scriptores* (No. 1122), pp. 1-137. Lond. 1723.

Compiled in the fourteenth century. Sparke, without good grounds, ascribes the latter part, *c.* 1260-1368, to Robert of Boston; and he prints the rest of the work under the name of John of Peterborough, though he seems inclined to attribute it to Abbot John Deeping, who died in 1439. There was no John, abbot of Peterborough, in the fourteenth century. The author used Hugh Candidus, Swaffham, Huntingdon, 'Ingulf', and other pre-existing chroniclers. The work is of little historical value. See Felix Liebermann, *Geschichtsquellen* (No. 1107), pp. 235-45.
   For Peterborough chroniclers dealing mainly with local history, see Nos. 6265, 6268, 6270.

2835   CHRONICON ANGLO-SCOTICUM. See Chronicle of Holyrood (No. 2821).

2836   CHRONICON DE LANERCOST, 1201-1346. Ed. by Joseph Stevenson. Bannatyne Club. Edin. 1839. Trans. by Sir Herbert Maxwell: 'Chronicle of Lanercost (1272–1346)', *Scot. H.R.* vols. vi–x, *passim*. Glasgow. 1908–13. Published separately, with introduction by James Wilson. 1913.

Deals with the general history of England and Scotland, and favours English interests. This valuable work was written by Franciscans and 'adapted and interpolated by a canon or canons of Lanercost'. The portion of the original chronicle from 1201 to 1297 was compiled by a Franciscan, possibly Friar Richard of Durham, writing between 1280 and 1297; and the portion from 1298 to 1346 by another Franciscan. See A. G. Little, 'The authorship of the Lanercost Chronicle' in *E.H.R.* xxxi (1916), 269–79; xxxii (1917), 48–9. Reprinted in his *Franciscan Papers* (No. 6024), pp. 42–54.

2837 CHRONICON (ANONYMI) GODSTOVIANUM. Ed. by Thomas Hearne, *William Roper's Vita Thomae Mori*, pp. 180–246. Oxf. 1716.

Extends from the creation to 1431. 'It is no more than an imperfect copy of the Latin Brut': Kingsford, *Hist. Lit.*, p. 311. It formerly belonged to the abbey of Godstow, near Oxford; but its contents have nothing to do with Godstow.

2838 CHRONICON MONASTERII DE BELLO. Ed. by J. S. Brewer. Anglia Christiana Soc. Lond. 1846. Trans. by M. A. Lower: The chronicle of Battel abbey, 1066–1176. Lond. etc. 1851.

Appears to have been completed about 1176. Contains a brief account of the Norman conquest, but the bulk of the chronicle relates to the history of the abbey, 1067–1176. See H. W. C. Davis's paper in *E.H.R.* xxix (1914), 426–34. For the fragment of another *Chronicon de Bello*, which is of some value for the Barons' War (1258–65), see Bémont, *Simon de Montfort*, pp. 373–80; and Liebermann, in M.G.H., SS. xxviii. 554.

2839 CHRONICON SCOTORUM: a chronicle of Irish affairs, from the earliest times to 1135, with (a translation of the Irish text and) a supplement, 1141–50. Ed. by W. M. Hennessy. Rolls Ser. Lond. 1866.

This chronicle, which was compiled in the monastery of Clonmacnoise, gives many interesting notices not found in other Irish annals. The earlier portion contains much legendary matter; the later part devotes much attention to the invasions of foreigners and the wars of the Irish among themselves. The unknown compiler and Tigernach (No. 2170) seem to have transcribed many passages from a common original. See O'Curry, *Lectures on MS. materials* (No. 30), pp. 120–30; and MacCarthy (No. 2160).

2840 CHRONIQUE DE LA PUCELLE OU DE COUSINOT, suivie de la Chronique Normande de Pierre Cochon. Ed. by A. Vallet de Viriville. Paris, 1859; new edn. 1892. Better edition by Charles de Beaurepaire, cited below.

Originally published by Denis Godefroy in his *Histoire de Charles VII* (Paris, 1661), Vallet de Viriville assigned the *Chronique de la Pucelle* to Guillaume Cousinot de Montreuil. René Panchenault, 'La Chronique de la Pucelle', *B.E.C.* xciii (1932), 56–104, shows that Cousinot was not the author and by comparisons with other known chroniclers shows that the *Chronique de la Pucelle* is largely a compilation. The evidence of the remaining original sections points to an author whose activities match those of Jean Jouvenel des Ursins (see No. 2909). The chronicle of Pierre Cochon (d. 1456) runs from the end of the twelfth century to 1430 and is important for the conquest of Normandy by Henry V. It is printed in Charles de Beaurepaire, *Chronique normande de Pierre Cochon: notaire apostolique à Rouen* (Rouen, 1870). See *Repert. Font.* iii. 423.

2841 CHRONIQUE DE LA TRAÏSON ET MORT DE RICHARD II, roi d'Engleterre (1397–1400, with an English translation of the French text). Ed. by Benjamin Williams. English Hist. Soc. Lond. 1846.

The author, a Burgundian temporarily in the Duke of Exeter's household, supports

Richard II. His work, written *c.* 1400, is largely independent; it incorporates extracts from Creton and is the basis of Le Beau's *Chronique* (No. 2915). See Molinier, *Sources*, No. 3988; M. Clarke, *Studies* (No. 1464), pp. 53–89; Steel, *Richard II*, pp. 298–300; and the forthcoming edition by J. J. N. Palmer.

2842 CHRONIQUE DE MERTON. (No. 2785).

2843 CHRONIQUE DE RICHARD LESCOT, religieux de Saint-Denis, 1328–44, suivi de la continuation, 1344–64. Ed. by Jean Lemoine. Société de l'histoire de France. Paris. 1896.

Itinéraires d'Édouard III pendant ses expeditions en France, 1329–60, pp. 203–9. The continuation is by another monk of Saint-Denis. For Lescot and his other writings, see Molinier, *Sources*, iv, no. 3097.

2844 CHRONIQUE DES QUATRE PREMIERS VALOIS, 1327–93. Ed. by Siméon Luce. Société de l'histoire de France. Paris. 1862. Repr. 1965.

This chronicle, written by a Norman clerk who favoured the popular cause, is original for the wars of Normandy after 1350 only.

2845 CHRONIQUE DES RÈGNES DE JEAN II ET DE CHARLES V. Ed. by R. Delachanel. Société de l'histoire de France. 4 vols. Paris. 1910–20.

Supplants the edition by Paulin Paris listed under *Les Grandes Chroniques de France* (see No. 2883). Vol. iv prints miniatures. See *Repert. Font.* iii. 358–9.

2846 CHRONIQUE DU MONT-SAINT-MICHEL, 1343–1468. Ed. by Siméon Luce. Société des Anciens Textes Français. 2 vols. Paris. 1879–83. Reprinted 1966.

The chronicle of rather bare annals occupies pp. 1–84. However, Luce printed on pp. 85–322 of vol. i and throughout vol. ii, 300 documents containing acts of Henry VI and his ministers, 1418–63. These documents lend value to this edition.

2847 CHRONIQUE DU RELIGIEUX DE SAINT-DENYS, 1380–1422 (with a French translation of the Latin text). Ed. by Louis Bellaguet. Documents inédits. 6 vols. Paris. 1839–52. Trans. by Jean Le Laboureur: Histoire de Charles VI. Paris. 1663.

Written by a contemporary of the events narrated, a secretary of Charles VI, who was in England in 1381. The work is valuable for the relations of England to France. Perhaps the author derived his information concerning Richard II from Creton's poem (No. 2856). For the literature relating to this chronicle, see Potthast (No. 62), i. 313–14. See also Molinier, *Sources*, iv, no. 3572; and Charles Samaran, 'Les Manuscrits de la chronique latine de Charles VI dite . . . du religieux de Saint Denis', *Le Moyen Âge*, xviii (1963), 657–71. See *Repert. Font.* iii. 432–3.

2848 CHRONIQUE NORMANDE DU XIVe SIÈCLE. Ed. by Auguste and Émile Molinier. Société de l'histoire de France. Paris. 1882.

Valuable for the history of the Anglo-French wars of the fourteenth century, especially for 1337–72. Written in French by a noble Norman some time after 1372. It is incorporated, with numerous additions, in 'Chronique des Pays-Bas, de France, d'Angleterre, et de Tournai', edited by J. J. de Smet, *Corpus Chronicorum Flandriae* (Brussels, 1856), iii. 111–570. See Molinier, *Sources*, iv, nos. 3100, 3949, and *Repert. Font.* iii. 394.

2849 CLYN, JOHN (d. *c.* 1349). Annales Hiberniae ad annum 1349. Ed. by Richard Butler, *Annals of Ireland*, pp. 1–39. Irish Archaeol. Soc. Dublin. 1849.

A contemporary authority for the years 1315–49. The brief notes from the creation to 1315 are of little value. Clyn was a Franciscan friar of Kilkenny.

2850 COGGESHALL, RALPH OF (d. *c.* 1227). Chronicon Anglicanum (1066–1223). Ed. by Joseph Stevenson. Rolls. Ser. Lond. 1875. Other editions: by Edmond Martène and Ursin Durand, *Veterum Scriptorum Collectio* (No. 1109) v. 801–81. Paris. 1729. A. J. Dunkin, Radulphi Abbatis de Coggeshal Opera, pp. 67–285. Noviomago. 1856. Nearly the whole chronicle is also printed in Bouquet's *Recueil* (No. 1090), xviii. 59–120: and there are extracts, edited by Pauli, in M.G.H., *SS.* xxvii. 344–58.

> The entries to 1186 are brief; from 1187 to 1223 they are fuller, and many of them are very valuable, especially for the reigns of John and Henry III. The part 1066–1154 seems to be compiled chiefly from Florence of Worcester or Henry of Huntingdon; the part 1187–95 was used by Roger of Wendover (No. 2979). Ralph was abbot of the Cistercian abbey of Coggeshall, 1207–18, and probably wrote his hostile account of John (1207–16) after about 1220. See F. M. Powicke, 'Roger of Wendover and the Coggeshall Chronicle', *E.H.R.* xxi (1906), 286–96; and *Cat. Royal MSS. in B.M.* (1921), ii. 81–2.

2851 COMMYNES, PHILIPPE DE (d. 1509). Mémoires (1464–98). Ed. by Joseph Calmette and G. Durville. 3 vols. Paris. 1924–5. Mémoires. Ed. by Bernard de Mandrot. *Collection de textes* (No. 1094). 2 vols. Paris. 1901–3. Mémoires. Ed. by L. M. E. Dupont. Société de l'histoire de France. Paris. 1840–7. Mémoires, livres i à vi. Ed. by Noël Coulet. Paris. 1963. Translation: The memoirs of Philip de Commines . . . to which is added The Scandalous Chronicle or the Secret History of Louis XI by Jean de Troyes, edited by Andrew R. Scoble. Bohn's Library. 2 vols. Lond. 1855–6. Reprinted, Lond. 1886; 1894–6.

> The author, one of the greatest medieval historians of France, was a Burgundian who left the service of the duke of Burgundy in 1472 and entered that of Louis XI, and later that of Charles VIII; he was a diplomat who participated in many of the negotiations which he describes. Books iii–iv contain details regarding Edward IV's relations with France. For other editions, translations and commentaries, see Potthast (No. 62), i. 328–40; Molinier (No. 57), v. 4663; Bossuat (No. 43), i. 504–7; and introductions to editions cited above. English translations are listed in Farrar and Evans (No. 52). See *Repert. Font.* iii. 519–22.

2852 COMMENDATIO LAMENTABILIS IN TRANSITU MAGNI REGIS EDWARDI. Ed. by William Stubbs, *Chronicles of the Reigns of Edward I and Edward II*, ii. 3–21. Rolls Ser. Lond. 1883.

> A sort of funeral sermon on the death of Edward I, probably written by John of London soon after 7 July 1307. The author eulogizes the king.

2853 CONTINUATIO BECCENSIS, 1157–60. Ed. by Richard Howlett, *Chronicles of the Reigns of Stephen, Henry II, and Richard I*, iv. 317–27. Rolls Ser. Lond. 1889.

> A contemporary record, dealing mainly with the continental transactions of Henry II. For this and other continuations of Robert of Torigni, see Delisle's edition (No. 2962), ii. 137–80.

2854 COTTON, BARTHOLOMEW (d. *c.* 1298). Historia Anglicana, A.D. 449–1298. necnon ejusdem Liber de archiepiscopis et episcopis Angliae. Ed. by H. R. Luard. Rolls Ser. Lond. 1859. Extracts. 1292–8. Ed. by Liebermann in M.G.H., *SS.* xxviii. 604–21.

The *Historia* is a composite chronicle, compiled by Bartholomew Cotton, a monk of Norwich. It has independent value for 1263–79 and 1285–98. Bk. i (De Regibus Britonum) is copied from Geoffrey of Monmouth and is not printed by Luard. The part A.D. 449–1066 is mainly an abridgement of Henry of Huntingdon; the entries from 1066 to 1291 are transcribed from the *Annals of Norwich*; and the continuation from 1292 to 1298 is original by Cotton.

The above-mentioned *Annals of Norwich*, to 1263, are based mainly upon Matthew Paris, John of Wallingford, and Taxter; and from 1279 to 1285 on Taxter's continuator. The annals are independent from 1263 to 1279 and 1285 to 1291. Extracts from it, 1074–1292, are edited by Liebermann, op. cit., pp. 600–3. A notable feature of this part of the work is the large number of papal bulls, royal letters, and other documents which it contains. The *Liber de Archiepiscopis et Episcopis* is mainly an abridgment of William of Malmesbury's *De Gestis Pontificum*. The portion relating to the bishops of Norwich is also printed in Wharton's *Anglia Sacra* (No. 1125), i. 403–12.

2855   COVENTRY, WALTER OF. Memoriale fratris Walteri de Coventria: the historical collections of Walter of Coventry (from Brutus to 1225). Ed. by William Stubbs. Rolls Ser. 2 vols. Lond. 1872–3. A portion of the work is printed in Bouquet's *Recueil* (No. 1090), xviii. 164–87; and extracts of the part 1202–25 are edited by Liebermann in M.G.H., *SS.* xxvii. 183–90.

Stubbs says that 'the book is one on which its creator has bestowed very, very little more than manual labour'. It was compiled between 1293 and 1307. The part down to the year 1201 is taken chiefly from Geoffrey of Monmouth, Florence of Worcester, Henry of Huntingdon, Benedict of Peterborough, and Hoveden. The entries from 1201 to 1225, which form a continuation of Hoveden and are derived from a chronicle of the monastery of Barnwell, are of great value for the study of John's reign; Stubbs regards them as the best source of information concerning the eventful years 1212–16. The Barnwell annals, of which an edition is projected in the Oxford Medieval Texts series, seem to have been drawn up about the year 1227 (perhaps at Crowland); after the middle of the thirteenth century they were incorporated in a compilation of historians made at Crowland or Peterborough, and from that compilation were transferred into the *Memoriale*. Luard, in his edition of Matthew Paris's *Chronica Majora*, vol. ii, p. xii, plausibly asserts that Walter of Coventry was probably not the author of this work, the title 'Memoriale' meaning simply that he left the book as a memorial to his monastery; but Stubbs believes that 'memoriale' means things worth remembering, or historical collections. Concerning Walter of Coventry almost nothing is known. Perhaps he was a monk of St. Mary's abbey, York, in the reign of Edward I. See John Taylor, *Medieval Historical Writing in Yorkshire*, pp. 15–16.

2856   CRETON, JEAN. Histoire du roy d'Angleterre Richard, Traictant particulièrement la rebellion de ses subiectz et prinse de sa personne: composée par un gentilhomme françois de marque, qui fut à la suite dudict roy, avec permission du roy de France. Ed. by John Webb. *Archaeol.* xx (1824), 295–423; with a translation, ibid., pp. 13–242; and appendices of documents, pp. 243–92. Another edition. J. A. Buchon, *Collection des chroniques* (No. 1091), xxiii. 321–466.

Webb's paper was read on 14 January 1819; hence his edition is sometimes dated 1819. Buchon's edition is based on a better MS. than Webb's. The authorship of the poem is very doubtful. None the less the poem is of high value for the last months of Richard's reign. The author was an eye-witness to many, perhaps most, of the events which he narrates. Some relationship exists between this poem and the prose *Chronique de la traïson* (No. 2841). For commentary see Molinier (No. 57), no. 3987; Bossuat, Supplement (No. 43), p. 105; and especially E. J. Jones, 'An examination of the authorship of the Deposition and Death of Richard II attributed to Creton', *Speculum*, xv (1940), 460–77, with the citations given there. Jones tentatively suggests John Trevor, Bishop of St. Asaph, as a possible author; but Palmer (No. 2841) will sustain Creton.

2857 CRONIQUES DE LONDON. Ed. by G. J. Aungier. Camden Soc.
Lond. 1844. Trans. by H. T. Riley: The French chronicle of London, 1259–1343.
Lond. 1863. Trans. by Edmund Goldsmid: The chronicles of London. 3 vols.
Edin. 1885–6.

> This 'unsophisticated, typical civic chronicle, purely annalistic in method' deals with
> the affairs of the kingdom as seen by London citizens. It seems to have been compiled
> about the middle of the fourteenth century.

2858 DE EXPUGNATIONE LYXBONENSI: The Conquest of Lisbon. Ed.
by William Stubbs in *Chronicles and Memorials in the Reign of Richard I*,
pp. cxlii–clxxii. Rolls Ser. Lond. 1864–5. Ed. from a transcript made by N. E. S. A.
Hamilton in *Portugaliae monumenta historica, Scriptores*, i. 391–405. Lisbon.
1861. Extracts. Ed. by R. Pauli, in M.G.H., SS. xvii. 5–10. Trans. with copious
commentary by Charles W. David. Columbia Univ. Records of Civilization.
New York. 1936. Giles Constable, 'A note on the route of the Anglo-Flemish
crusaders of 1147', *Speculum*, xxviii (1953), 525–6; idem, 'The second crusade
as seen by contemporaries', *Traditio*, ix (1953), 213–79. For a conjecture on
authorship, see J. C. Russell, 'Ranulf de Glanville', *Speculum*, xlv (1970), 69–79.

2859 DEVIZES, RICHARD DE. Chronicon Richardi Divisensis De tempore
regis Richardi primi. Ed. and trans. by John Appleby. Medieval Texts. Lond.
etc. 1963. De rebus gestis Richardi primi (1189–92). Ed. by Richard Howlett,
Chronicle of the reigns of Stephen, Henry II, and Richard I, iii. 379–454. Rolls
Ser. Lond. 1886. Another edition by Joseph Stevenson. Eng. Hist. Soc. Lond.
1838. Extracts. Ed. by Liebermann, M.G.H., SS. xxvii. 75–80. Transl. by
J. A. Giles, Chronicle of Richard of Devizes. Lond. 1841; reprinted, with
emendations, in *Chronicles of the Crusades*, pp. 1–64. Bohn's Antiquarian Library.
Lond. 1848. A better translation by Joseph Stevenson, *Church historians* (No.
1123), v, pt. i. Lond. 1858.

> Probably completed in 1193. Howlett says that it is 'one of the most amusing products
> of the middle ages', and that 'in it classical quotations, bombastic speeches, and keen
> gibes are mixed up with valuable historical facts'. It supplies details to be found in no
> other chronicle regarding the condition of affairs in England during the first years of
> Richard's reign. The author, a monk of St. Swithun's, Winchester, was still alive in
> 1202.

2860 DICETO, RALPH DE (d. *c.* 1201). Opera historica. Ed. by William
Stubbs. Rolls Ser. 2 vols. Lond. 1876.

> *Abbreviationes chronicorum*, from the creation to 1147, *Opera*, i. 3–263; also in Twysden's
> *Scriptores Decem* (No. 1125), pp. 429–524, Lond. 1652. Extracts. Ed. by Pauli, in
> M.G.H., SS. xxvii. 254–60. This work is made up of extracts from pre-existing
> chronicles.
>   *Imagines historiarum*, 1148–1202, *Opera*, i. 267–440, ii. 3–174; also in Twysden's
> *Scriptores*, pp. 525–710. Extracts, Ed. by Pauli, in M.G.H., SS. xxvii. 260–86. These
> 'Outlines of History', down to about 1172, are based on Robert of Torigni; after 1172
> the work is original, and from 1188 onward it is a valuable contemporary record,
> which contains many letters, papal bulls, and other documents. The author's chronology
> is, however, often faulty.
>   Minor works (of little value), *Opera*, ii. 177–285.
>   Ralph de Diceto was elected dean of St. Paul's, London, in 1180, and held that office
> to the time of his death. His birthplace is sometimes identified with the parish of Diss
> in Norfolk. See D. E. Greenway (No. 5581), p. 5, n. 11.

2861   DIT (LE) DE GUILLAUME D'ANGLETERRE. Ed. by Francisque Michel, *Chroniques anglo-normandes* (No. 1112), iii. 173–211. Rouen. 1840. Another edition, in Giles, *Scriptores* (No. 2741), pp. 270–97.

An Anglo-French poem, concerning the authorship of which nothing is known.

2862   DURHAM, SIMEON OF. No. 2157.

2863   EADMER (d. *c.* 1130). Historia novorum in Anglia (*c.* 960–1122). Ed. by Martin Rule. Rolls Ser. Lond. 1884. Other editions: by John Selden. Lond. 1623; Gabriel Gerberon. Paris. 1675, 1721 (reprinted, Venice, 1744); and in Migne's *Patrologia*, clix (1854), 347–588. Extracts, 1051–1121. Ed. by Pauli, in M.G.H., *SS.* xiii. 139–48. Translation of Books i–iv by Geoffrey Bosanquet, Eadmer's History of Recent Events in England. Philadelphia. 1965; translation of parts in *Eng. Hist. Docs.* (No. 17), ii. 651–73.

Eadmer, a monk of Christ Church, Canterbury, was the confidant of Anselm. The first four books give a brief summary of the eleventh century and then a minute contemporary account of Anselm's pontificate 1093–1109. Presumably Eadmer had been making notes and gathering material since 1093 and had assembled them together as his history between 1109 and 1115. For the period 1093–1100 he reported as an eyewitness; for the period 1100–9 he wrote from documents. His *Historia novorum* is the first genuine history with a great theme since Bede (paraphrase of R. W. Southern in preface to Bosanquet's translation). Liebermann believes that as regards unity of plan and of treatment this work has no equal among the great historians of England in the twelfth century. It is a primary authority on the investiture controversy.

Books v and vi are a continuation written by Eadmer after 1119 to rebut the charges made by detractors of Anselm and his successor Archbishop Ralph. It is a passionate defence to 1122 of the Archbishop of Canterbury in the bitter dispute with the Archbishop of York. It includes the documents recently forged to support Canterbury's case. See Liebermann, 'Ueber Eadmer', in *Geschichtsquellen* (No. 2738), pp. 284–302; Richard W. Southern, *Saint Anselm and his biographer* (Cambr. 1963), pp. 229–40 and pp. 298–313; R. W. Southern, 'The Canterbury forgeries', *E.H.R.* lxxiii (1958), 193–226. For Eadmer's *Life of Anselm*, see Nos. 6529–30.

2864   ELMHAM, THOMAS OF (d. *c.* 1428). Liber metricus de Henrico Quinto. Ed. by Charles A. Cole in *Memorials of Henry the Fifth* (No. 2837), pp. 77–166.

Liber metricus, written in 1418–19, supplements the *Gesta Henrici Quinti* (No. 2877), which was formerly attributed to Elmham. Elmham also began a *Chronica regum nobilium Angliae*. Its prologue was printed by Hearne in *Vita et gesta Henrici Quinti* (No. 2919), pp. 377–81; but its surviving chronological table has not been published. On this *Chronica*, see Frank Taylor, 'A note on Rolls Series 8', *B.J.R.L.* xx (1936), 379–82. Rolls Ser. 8 is Elmham's *Historia monasterii S. Augustini* (No. 2158).

Elmham was born in 1364 (see above, Taylor, p. 382), became a monk at St. Augustine's Canterbury, and in 1414 prior of the Cluniac priory of Lenton. For his life and works see Wylie, *The reign of Henry V* (Cambr. 1914–29), ii. 77–88; Kingsford, *Hist. Lit.*, pp. 45–60; Rose Graham, *Eng. Eccl. Studies* (No. 1471), pp. 67–72.

2865   EULOGIUM HISTORIARUM SIVE TEMPORIS: chronicon ab orbe condito usque ad annum domini 1366, a monacho quodam Malmesburiensi exaratum (with a continuation to 1413). Ed. by F. S. Haydon. Rolls Ser. 3 vols. Lond. 1858–63.

The first part of this general survey of English history was probably written by a monk of Malmesbury named Thomas, who completed his work in 1367. It is largely a compilation from Geoffrey of Monmouth and particularly from Higden's *Polychronicon*. However, the part 1356–66 is contemporaneous. The continuation to 1413, printed in vol. iii, pp. 333–421, was written in the first half of the fifteenth century and is valuable, especially for the proceedings of parliament in Richard II's time. Haydon conjectured that the continuation had been written by a Canterbury monk; but Evan J. Jones thinks that it was composed by John Trevor, Bishop of St. Asaph. See *Speculum*, xii (1937), 196–202. J. I. Catto writes on 'An alleged great council of 1374' (for which the continuation of *Eulogium* is the source), *E.H.R.* lxxxii (1967), 764–71.

2866 FABYAN, ROBERT (d. 1513). The new chronicles of England and France (from Brutus to 1485) by Robert Fabyan, named by himself the Concordance of histories, reprinted from Pynson's edition of 1516, the first part collated with the editions of 1533, 1542, and 1559. Ed. by Henry Ellis. Lond. 1811.

The first edition ends in 1485; later editions add continuations. In his attempt to harmonize the accounts of various chroniclers Fabyan shows little critical power. From 1189 onward the *Concordance*, which is written in English, has the form of a regular London chronicle, the record of each year being headed by the names of the mayor and sheriffs for that year. The principal source was a version of 'The Main City Chronicle' and so the work is of some value for the history of London and for the affairs of the Kingdom, especially during the reigns of Edward IV and Richard III. Fabyan was made sheriff of the city in 1493. See Kingsford, *Hist. Lit.*, pp. 103–6.

2867 FANTOSME, JORDAN. La guerre d'Ecosse: 1173–1174. Ed. by Philipp Aug. Becker. *Zeitschrift für romanische Philologie*, lxiv (1944), 478–535. (Introduction pp. 449–78 and notes pp. 536–56.) Chronique de la guerre entre les Anglois et les Ecossais en 1173 et 1174 (with a translation). Ed. by Richard Howlett, *Chronicles of the Reigns of Stephen, Henry II, and Richard I*, iii. 202–377. Rolls Ser. Lond. 1886. Other editions: by Francisque Michel, Surtees Soc. 1840; and in his edition of the chronicle of Benoît de Sainte-Maure (No. 2952), iii. 531–613. Paris. 1844. Extracts. Ed. by Liebermann, in M.G.H., SS. xxvii. 53–9. Trans. by Joseph Stevenson, *Church historians* (No. 1123), iv, pt. i. 246–88: *Jordan Fantosme's Chronicle*. Lond. 1856.

This valuable Anglo-French poem was completed before 1183. Fantosme asserts that he saw many of the events which he narrates. He was chancellor of the diocese of Winchester. See René Herval, 'Deux écrivains-combattants normands du xiie siècle — Raoul de Caen et Jourdain Fantosme', *Acad. des sciences, belles-lettres et arts de Rouen* (1940), pp. 125–48. See also Iain Macdonald, 'The chronicle of Jordan Fantosme: manuscripts, author and versification', *Studies in Medieval French presented to Alfred Ewert* (Oxf. 1961), pp. 242–58; and M. D. Legge, *Anglo-Norman Literature* (No. 294), pp. 75–81.

2868 FAVENT, THOMAS. Historia sive narracio de modo et forma mirabilis parliamenti apud Westmonasterium anno domini millesimo ccclxxxvj, regni vero regis Ricardi Secundi post conquestum anno decimo per Thomam Fauent Clericum indictata. Ed. by May McKisack. Camden 3rd Ser. xxxvii, *Camden Miscellany*, xiv (1926).

A pro-Appellant partisan political pamphlet, describing events in England between October 1386 and June 1388; it gives a good description of the physical setting of the Parliament House.

2869 A FIFTEENTH-CENTURY CHRONICLE AT TRINITY COLLEGE, DUBLIN. Noted by G. L. Harriss. *B.I.H.R.* xxxviii (1965), 212–18.

This notice of the chronicle (creation to 1462) promises an edition of the folios for 1422–62.

2870 FITZ-THEDMAR, ARNOLD (d. 1275). De antiquis legibus liber: cronica majorum et vicecomitum Londoniarum, 1188–1274 (with later additions in French to 20 Edward II). Ed. by Thomas Stapleton. Camden Soc. Lond. 1846. Extracts. Ed. by Pauli and Liebermann, in M.G.H., *SS.* xxviii. 527–47. Trans. by H. T. Riley: Chronicles of the mayors and sheriffs of London. Lond. 1863.

One of the most valuable of the regular London city chronicles. It deals with the history of the city and the kingdom, and seems to have been finished in 1274. Probably it was called *Liber de Antiquis Legibus* because the MS. volume in which the chronicle is found contains various ancient enactments, notably the oldest code of ordinances for the government of the city—the building assize of Henry Fitz-Ailwin, *c.* A.D. 1189. The portion 1236–74, which is devoted mainly to the affairs of London, is fuller and more valuable than the part 1188–1235. The appendix (pp. 197–205) contains a chronicle of the years 1135–1223, in which Louis VIII's expedition to England in 1216–17 is minutely described. Compare *Chronicle of Merton* (No. 2785). Fitz-Thedmar was an alderman of London. See Russell (No. 541), pp. 20–1; and G. A. Williams, *Medieval London* (No. 1748), *passim.*

2871 FLORES HISTORIARUM (FROM THE CREATION TO 1326). Ed. by Henry R. Luard. Rolls Ser. 3 vols. Lond. 1890. Other editions, to the end of 1306, by Matthew Parker. Lond. 1567, 1570; reprinted, Frankfurt, 1601. Extracts. 1154–1307. Ed. by Liebermann, in M.G.H., *SS.* xxviii. 456–504. Trans. by C. D. Yonge: The flowers of history, to 1307. Bohn's Antiquarian Library. 2 vols. Lond. 1853.

This chronicle was for a long time attributed to Matthew of Westminster, but we now know that he is 'an entirely imaginary person' and that the work ascribed to him was written by various persons at various times. The earliest MS. (Chetham MS. 6712 in the John Rylands Library) belonged to St. Albans Abbey to 1265 when it was transferred to Westminster Abbey. Down to 1265 *Flores Historiarum* is a St. Albans chronicle, derived to 1259 from Matthew Paris and up to the annal for 1249 probably written by Matthew Paris. From 1259 to 1265 there is an important detailed continuation thereof. The continuation which favours the barons is of high value. After the MS. had passed to Westminster, it was continued there by various hands to 1306, with which year most of the copies end. This portion is royalist in tone. The chronicle in the Chetham MS. was continued from 1307, and possibly from 1299 or 1302, down to 1326, by a contemporary monk of Westminster, who was probably Robert of Reading. The last entries for 1326 seem to have been added by still another Westminster monk. This portion of the chronicle displays a strong animus against Edward II.

See Luard's prefaces; Liebermann's introduction (loc. cit.); Hardy, *Catalogue* (No. 21), iii. 313–26, 399–445; T. F. Tout, 'The Westminster Chronicle attributed to Robert of Reading', *E.H.R.* xxxi (1916), 450–64; reprinted in his *Collected papers* (No. 1499), ii. 289–304; V. H. Galbraith, 'The St. Albans' Chronicle' (No. 2731), pp. xxviii–xxix; idem, 'Roger Wendover and Matthew Paris' (No. 2941); A. Hollaender, 'The pictorial work in the "Flores historiarum" ', *B.J.R.L.* xxviii (1944), 361–81.

2872 FORDUN, JOHN OF (d. *c.* 1384). Chronica gentis Scotorum (from Noah to 1383, with a translation). Ed. by W. F. Skene, in *Historians of Scotland*, vols. i and iv. Edin. 1871–2. Other editions, with the title 'Scotichronicon', to 1066, in Gale's *Scriptores XV* (No. 1100), pp. 563–699; with Walter Bower's continuation, to 1437, by Thomas Hearne, 5 vols. Oxf. 1722; to 1437, by Walter Goodall, 2 vols. Edin. 1759.

This was the first attempt to write a complete history of Scotland; and the *Scotichronicon*, with Bower's continuation, became the groundwork of Scottish annals. Fordun was probably a chantry priest in the cathedral at Aberdeen. Walter Bower, abbot of Inchcolm (d. 1449), really wrote the part 1153–1437, but he made use of Fordun's notes to 1383. The *Scotichronicon* is valuable for the study of the relations between Scotland and England.

2873 FRAGMENT (A REMARKABLE) OF AN OLD ENGLISH CHRONICLE, OR HISTORY, OF THE AFFAIRS OF EDWARD IV (1459–70). Ed. by Thomas Hearne, *Thomae Sprotti Chronica*, pp. 283–306. Oxf. 1719. The same, with modernized orthography, in *Chronicles of the White Rose of York* (No. 2735), pp. 1–30. Lond. 1845.

This valuable fragment seems to be part of a biography of Edward IV, written between 1517 and 1524. The author, who favours the house of York, is well informed concerning the events which he narrates. See Jakob Engel, *Kritische Bemerkungen über A Remarkable Fragment of an Old English Chronicle* (Berlin, 1875); and Kingsford, *Hist. Lit.*, pp. 176–8.

2874 FROISSART, JEAN (d. *c.* 1410). Chroniques (1307–1400). Ed. by Siméon Luce, Gaston Raynaud, and Léon and Albert Mirot. 14 vols. (to 1388). Société de l'histoire de France. Paris. 1869–1967 and in progress. Older editions to 1400: in Buchon, *Chron.* (No. 1091), vols. x–xxiii and appendices vols. xxiv–xxv. Paris. 1824–6; and excellently edited with many documents by Kervyn de Lettenhove, 25 vols. in 26. Brussels. 1867–77. Reprinted 1967. Trans. by John Bourchier, Lord Berners: Chronicles of England, France, etc. 2 vols. Lond. 1523–5; reprinted, 2 vols. 1812; 4 vols. 1814–16; and again in six volumes for *Tudor Translations*, 1901–3; 8 vols., Stratford-upon-Avon, 1927–8. Trans. also by Thomas Johnes, 5 vols., Hafod, 1803–10; and reprinted in whole, or in part, many times.

Froissart is one of the most celebrated chroniclers of France and provides a principal source for the study of the Hundred Years War in the period 1361 to 1400. Froissart from Valenciennes was in England from 1361 to 1366 as secretary to Queen Philippa; in 1367–8 he spent another sojourn there, and in 1394 he made another visit. The historical value of the chronicle is severely criticized by Molinier, *Sources* (No. 57), iv, 12–14; it concentrates on knightly exploits and chivalrous attitudes; vivid and uncritical, it falls into a considerable number of errors of detail. However, Froissart had access to some documents, avidly gathered reports from participants, and was himself present at some events which he narrates. Used with caution, it is valuable. The part 1307–24 is very brief, and down to 1361 many passages are borrowed from Jean le Bel (No. 2916). Composed periodically, in the earliest redactions its tone is pro-English; but from about 1375 on it takes on a hostile attitude toward England. The chronicle was continued by Monstrelet (No. 2926).

For bibliography, see Potthast, i. 474–5; Molinier, *Sources*, iv, nos. 3094, 3233; Bossuat (No. 43), i. 483–6, and Supplement, p. 104. For Froissart's life, F. S. Shears, *Froissart, Chronicler and poet* (Lond. 1930); George G. Coulton, *The chronicler of European chivalry* (Lond. 1930), which contains reproductions of miniatures; and the introduction to Julia Bastin, *Jean Froissart, chroniqueur, romancier et poète* (Brussels, 1941).

2875 GAIMAR, GEOFFREY (GEFFREI). L'estoire des Engleis. Ed. by Alexander Bell. Anglo-Norman Text Soc. nos. 14–16. Oxf. 1960. L'estoire des Engles solum la translacion maistre Geffrei Gaimar (A.D. 495–1100, with a translation). Ed. by T. D. Hardy and C. T. Martin. Rolls Ser. 2 vols. Lond. 1888–9. Other editions: to 1066, in Petrie's *Monumenta* (No. 1084), pp. 764–829;

A.D. 1066–1100, in Michel's *Chroniques anglo-normandes* (No. 1112), i. 1–64;
A.D. 495–1100, by Thomas Wright. Caxton Soc. Lond. 1850. Reprinted N.Y.
1966. Trans. by Joseph Stevenson, *Church historians* (No. 1123), vol. ii, pt. ii:
Gaimar.

This rhyming French chronicle was written between 1135 and 1147. For the period
before the Norman conquest its chief sources are Geoffrey of Monmouth and the
Anglo-Saxon Chronicle. For the portion after 1066 the author is indebted to Florence
of Worcester or Simeon of Durham. Gaimar was a Norman by birth. Concerning his
life little is known; he seems to have resided in Lincolnshire. For literature, see Bossuat
(No. 43), p. 347, and Supplement, p. 78; and Alexander Bell, 'Maistre Geffrei Gaimar',
Medium Aevum, vii (1938), 184–98; idem, 'Gaimar's early "Danish" kings', *P.M.L.A.*
lxv (1950), 601–40; Tatlock, *Legendary history* (No. 2166), chap. xxi; and the critique
of Bell's edition by Ronald N. Walpole in *Philolog. Quart.* xli (1962), 373–85.

2876 GESTA EDWARDI DE CARNARVAN AUCTORE CANONICO BRIDLINGTONIENSI, CUM CONTINUATIONE (GESTA EDWARDI TERTII) AD A.D. 1377. Ed. by William Stubbs, *Chronicles of the reigns of Edward I and Edward II*, ii. 25–151. Rolls Ser. Lond. 1883.

A brief and important chronicle of the reign of Edward II, it was written by a canon
of the priory of Bridlington. It did not assume its present shape before 1377, although
the earlier portion seems to rest on contemporary material. After 1339 the continuation
comprises incidental jottings of little value. Stubbs ranks the work 'high among the
second-rate authorities for the history of a period which is singularly deficient in first-
rate authorities'. A fourteenth-century memorandum-book at Bridlington known as
Incidentia Chronicorum contained copies of documents, see Galbraith, *Historical
Research*, p. 32, n. 1.

2877 GESTA HENRICI QUINTI (1413–16). Ed. by J. S. Roskell and F. Taylor. Oxford Medieval Texts. (In press.) Also edited by Benjamin Williams. Eng. Hist. Soc. Lond. 1850. Also printed in Giles, *Chronicon Angliae* (No. 2833).

The *Gesta*, often called the *Chronicle of the Chaplain* because it was written by a chaplain
in Henry V's army, is the best narrative authority for the first four years of Henry V's
reign. It should not be confused with *Vita et Gesta* (No. 2972). The author, who
probably wrote in 1416, was an eye-witness to many of the events which he describes;
he gives a detailed account of the siege of Harfleur and the battle of Agincourt. Williams
surmised that the author was Jean de Bordin, who accompanied Henry on his first
campaign; but in 1874 Max Lenz in *König Sigismund und Heinrich V von England*
(Berlin, 1874), p. 14, argued that the chaplain was Thomas of Elmham, a conclusion
accepted by J. H. Wylie, 'The Agincourt Chaplain', *Athenaeum*, 23 August 1902,
p. 254, and by C. L. Kingsford, 'The early biographies of Henry V'. However J. S.
Roskell and F. Taylor, 'The authorship and purpose of the *Gesta Henrici Quinti*',
B.J.R.L. liii (1970–1), 428–64; liv (1971–2), 223–40, reject the ascription of the *Gesta* to
Elmham. They regard it as 'a piece of deliberate propaganda', perhaps directed at the
Council of Constance, proclaiming that Henry wanted only peace with justice. On the
historiography of Henry V, see C. T. Allmand, *Henry V*. Hist. Assoc. Pamphlet, no. 68
(Lond. 1968).

Williams included in the above edition of the *Gesta*, pp. 109–63, an abridgement of
Vita and Gesta 1417–22 (No. 2972), and on pp. 165–262 the *Chronique de Normandie*,
1414–22, by Georges Chastelain (No. 2814) with an English translation. The latter
gives a good account of Henry V's residence in Paris.

2878 GESTA HERWARDI INCLITI EXULIS ET MILITIS. Ed. by Thomas Duffus Hardy and Charles Trice Martin in *Gaimar's L'estorie des Engles*, i. 339–404. Rolls Ser. 1888. Also ed. and trans. by S. H. Miller, *De gestis Herwardi*

Saxonis, which is appended to *Fenland Notes and Queries*, iii (Peterborough, 1895). Other editions, which are badly edited, in Michel's *Chroniques anglo-normandes*, ii. 1–98; and in Thomas Wright, *Chronicle of Gaimar*, app. pp. 46–108. Caxton Soc. 1850.

> This work professes to have been compiled from an English life of Hereward written by his priest Leofric; but Liebermann contends that it was written about 1150 by Richard, a monk of Ely, who died before 1189. Freeman says: 'The early part of the story in the *Gesta* is plainly mere romance; but when we get Hereward in the Isle, we are on somewhat surer ground.' See Freeman, *Norman Conquest*, vol. iv, app. DD; and Liebermann, *Über ostenglische Geschichtsquellen* (No. 1107), pp. 238–43.

2879 GESTA REGIS HENRICI SECUNDI BENEDICTI ABBATIS: the chronicle of the reigns of Henry II and Richard I, 1169–1192, known commonly under the name of Benedict of Peterborough. Ed. by William Stubbs. Rolls Ser. 2 vols. Lond. 1867. Another edition, by Thomas Hearne: *De vita et gestis Henrici II et Ricardi I*. 2 vols. Oxf. 1735. Extracts. Ed. by Liebermann in M.G.H., *SS*. xxvii. 81–132.

> This valuable chronicle has been shown by Lady Stenton to have been Roger of Howden's earlier draft which he revised for his chronicle of the period 732–1201. See No. 2903. Stubbs' introduction to his edition, reprinted in *Historical Introductions* (No. 4041), is a classic survey of the reign of Henry II.

2880 GESTA STEPHANI: the Deeds of Stephen (1135–54). Ed. and trans. from the Latin with introduction and notes by K. R. Potter. Medieval Texts. Lond. Edin. etc. 1955. All of the following editions contain only the portions from 1135–47: Richard Howlett, ed. *Chronicles* (No. 2734), iii. 3–136; Duchesne (No. 1096), pp. 927–75; reprinted by R. C. Sewell. Eng. Hist. Soc. Pubns. Lond. 1846. Brief extracts. Ed. by Liebermann in M.G.H., *SS*. xxvii. 3–4. Trans. by Thomas Forester; the chronicle of Henry of Huntingdon; also the acts of Stephen (No. 1089). Lond. 1853. Trans. by Joseph Stevenson, *Church historians* (No. 1123) v, pt. i (1858).

> The most detailed source for Stephen's reign, written by a contemporary who may have been Robert of Lewes, Bishop of Bath and Wells, 1136–66 (R. H. C. Davis, 'The authorship of the *Gesta Stephani*', *E.H.R.* lxxvii (1962), 209–32). The author was a partisan of Stephen as against Mathilda, but was more impartial between Stephen and Henry II. Whether or not he was an eye-witness of some of the events which he narrates, he had good sources of information.
> The Laon MS. from which Duchesne printed ended in 1147 and subsequently disappeared; hence Duchesne's text became the only known text until R. A. B. Mynors discovered at Valenciennes a MS. of the *Gesta* which runs to 1154. Accordingly Potter's edition, based on both texts, is the only complete edition. The importance of the newly discovered MS. is discussed by A. L. Poole in Potter's edition, pp. xv–xxix; this is supplemented by R. H. C. Davis, 'King Stephen and the Earl of Chester revised', *E.H.R.* lxxv (1960), 654–60; and his *King Stephen* (Lond. 1967), p. 146.

2881 GIRALDUS CAMBRENSIS (GERALD DE BARRI, d. *c.* 1223). *Opera*. Ed. by J. S. Brewer, J. F. Dimock, and G. F. Warner. Rolls Ser. 8 vols. Lond. 1861–91. Extracts. Ed. by Pauli in M.G.H., *SS*. xxvii. 395–421. Gerald's four works commonly called historical are treated here; they are translated in the Bohn Library (No. 1089) as 'The historical works of Giraldus Cambrensis', containing the topography of Ireland and the history of the conquest of Ireland.

Trans. by Thomas Forester. . . . *The itinerary through Wales and the description of Wales.* Trans. by Sir Richard C. Hoare, revised by Thomas Wright. Lond. 1863. Reprinted, N.Y. 1967. For his other writings, see No. 6573.

(a) *Topographia Hibernica.* Ed. by Dimock, *Opera.* Rolls Ser. (1867) v. 1–204. Camden, *Anglica . . . Scripta* (No. 1092), pp. 692–754. John O'Meara, ed. 'Giraldus Cambrensis in Topographia Hibernie: Text of the first recension', in *Roy. Irish Acad. Procs.* lii, sect. C, no. 4 (1949), 113–78. Translations by John J. O'Meara, *The topography of Ireland*, Dundalk, 1951; and by Forester, as above.

The first recension appeared in 1188. Gerald collected material for his description of Ireland and its inhabitants, and for his *Expugnatio*, during his two visits to Ireland in 1183 and 1185–6.

(b) *Expugnatio Hibernica*, 1166–85. Ed. by Dimock, *Opera.* Rolls Ser. v. 205–411; Camden, op. cit., pp. 755–813. Whitley Stokes, 'The Irish abridgment of the *Expugnatio Hibernica*', edited with a translation in *E.H.R.* xx (1905), 77–115. English texts of the fifteenth century are edited by Frederick J. Furnivall, *The English conquest of Ireland, A.D. 1166–1185*, mainly from the *Expugnatio Hibernica* of Giraldus Cambrensis. E.E.T.S. Lond. 1896. Trans. by Forester, as above.

(c) *Itinerarium Cambriae.* Ed. by Dimock, *Opera.* Rolls Ser. vi. 1–152. Camden, op. cit., pp. 815–78. Trans. in 1806 by Hoare, as above; which is reprinted with introduction by W. Llewelyn Williams in Everyman's Library. Lond. etc. 1908. T. Jones, ed., *Gerald the Welshman's Itinerary through Wales and description of Wales.* National Library of Wales. Aberystwyth. 1950.

This itinerary gives an account of Archbishop Baldwin's tour in Wales in 1188 to preach the crusade; it also deals with the topography, natural history, etc., of Wales. The first recension appeared in 1191; the third about 1214.

(d) *Descriptio Cambriae*, in two books. Ed. by Dimock, *Opera.* Rolls Ser. vi. 153–227. Book i in Camden, op. cit., pp. 879–96; Book ii in Wharton's *Anglia Sacra* (No. 1125), ii. 447–55. Trans. by Hoare, as above, which is reprinted by Williams, as above.

The first recension appeared about 1194, the second about 1215. See also J. Conway Davies, 'The Kambriae Mappa of Giraldus Cambrensis', *Jour. Hist. Soc. Church in Wales*, ii (1952), 46–60; and Urban T. Holmes, 'The Kambriae Descriptio of Gerald the Welshman', *Medievalia et Humanistica*, 2nd Ser. i (1970), 217–31.

Giraldus was born in Pembrokeshire in 1146 or 1147; studied at Paris, and in England; held various churches in Wales and England; was Archdeacon of Brecon, c. 1175 to 1203; was twice proposed as Bishop of St. David's, but failed to secure possession; he declined other bishoprics. For details on his life see his autobiography (No. 6573); the *Dictionary of Welsh Biography* (No. 542); Emden, *Oxford* (No. 533), i. 117–118; Lloyd, *Hist. of Wales* (No. 1186), ii. 554–64; J. Conway Davies, 'Giraldus Cambrensis 1146–1946', *Archaeol. Camb.* xcix (1946), 85–108 and 256–80; F. M. Powicke, 'Gerald of Wales', *B.J.R.L.* xii (1928), 389–410, reprinted in *Christian Life* (No. 1486), pp. 107–29; Thomas Jones, *Gerald the Welshman* (Cardiff, 1947); Michael Richter, 'Giraldus Cambrensis: the growth of the Welsh nation', *Nat. Lib. of Wales Jour.* xvi (1970), 293–318; xvii (1971), 1–50; Eileen A. Williams, 'A bibliography of Giraldus Cambrensis', *Nat. Lib. of Wales Jour.* xii (1961), 97–140.

2882 GLOUCESTER, ROBERT OF. The metrical chronicle of Robert of Gloucester (from Brutus to 1270). Ed. by W. A. Wright. Rolls Ser. 2 vols. Lond.

1887. Another edition, by Thomas Hearne, 2 vols. Oxf. 1724; and in *Works of Hearne*, vols. i–ii. Lond. 1810. Extracts, 1192–1270. Ed. by Liebermann, in M.G.H., *SS*. xxviii. 663–9. Translation: J. Stevenson, *Church historians* (No. 1123), v, pt. i.

Much is known of a Robert of Gloucester who died in 1322: Emden, *Oxford* (No. 533), pp. 773–4; but whether this Robert was the author of the metrical chronicle is not certain. In any case the narrative of the Barons' War in the time of Henry III is of some value. See Pafford in *Jenkinson Studies* (No. 1441), pp. 309–19; and for further bibliography, Wells (No. 275) and *C.B.E.L.* (No. 14), i. 165.

2883 GRANDES CHRONIQUES DE FRANCE (or Chroniques de Saint-Denis). Ed. by Jules Viard. Société de l'histoire de France. 10 vols. Paris. 1920–53. Followed by *Chronique des règnes de Jean II et de Charles V*. Ed. by R. Delachenal. Société de l'histoire de France. 3 vols. Paris. 1910–20. Another edition (to 1380). Ed. by Paulin Paris. 6 vols. Paris. 1836–8.

Viard's edition contains the chronicles from the origins to 1350; references to English affairs begin with vol. v. Vol. x contains a French version of the life of St. Louis by Guillaume de Nangis and an index to the first nine volumes. The *Grandes Chroniques* are regarded as official historiography, inspired by St. Louis and compiled from time to time by various monks of St. Denis. The third volume of Delachenal's edition contains an appendix of thirty-two documents (1354–80) drawn from various archives. For description of the chronicles, see the introductions to the editions cited above, and Molinier, *Sources*, especially nos. 2530 and 3099.

2884 GRAY, THOMAS (d. 1369?). Scalacronica: a chronicle of England and Scotland (1066–1362). Ed. by Joseph Stevenson. Maitland Club. Edin. 1836. Scalacronica, the reigns of Edward I, Edward II, and Edward III, as recorded by Sir Thomas Gray. Translated by Sir Herbert Maxwell. Glasgow. 1907. (First printed in *Scot. H.R.* iii–v, Oct. 1905–Oct. 1907, *passim*.)

This large masterpiece, written in French, was begun in 1355 while the author was a prisoner in Edinburgh. Extends from the creation, but Stevenson edits only the part 1066–1362. The title 'Scalacronica' points to the ladder in the Gray arms, on the rungs of which different sources stand. A large portion of the chronicle is based on Bede, Higden, and other well-known writers; but it contains some useful information concerning the reigns of Edward II and Edward III, especially in regard to the wars between England and Scotland. Gray was lord of Heaton manor in Northumberland, and perhaps the first English layman to write a chronicle. See Legge, *A.-N. Lit.* (No. 294), pp. 283–7.

2885 THE GREAT CHRONICLE OF LONDON. Ed. by A. H. Thomas and I. D. Thornley. Lond. and Aylesbury. 1938.

A magnificent, limited edition of a chronicle written in English. The MS., apparently used by Stow and now acquired from private hands by the Guildhall in 1933, consists of two parts; (i) covering 1189 to 1439, written in a mid-fifteenth-century hand, and (ii) covering 1439 to 1512, written in the late fifteenth century or early sixteenth century. The second part is the best surviving London chronicle for the period; it has independent value for the reign of Edward IV and contemporary value from 1485 to 1512.

The editors' long introduction is a model of thorough research and cautious statement. In relating the *Great Chronicle* to other chronicles, the editors revise Kingsford's classification of the manuscripts. The editors, as against Kingsford, conclude that the compiler of part ii was, in all probability, Robert Fabyan, the author of *Fabyan's Chronicle*. See Conyers Read, *Bibliography of Tudor History* (Oxf. 1959), nos. 305 and 310.

2886 GREGORY, WILLIAM (d. 1467). Gregory's Chronicle, 1189–1469. Ed. by James Gairdner, *Historical Collections of a Citizen of London in the Fifteenth Century*, pp. 55–239. Camden Soc. 1876.

A London city chronicle, which devotes much attention to national transactions. For the years 1440–69 it and the *Great Chronicle* (No. 2885) form the best of the London chronicles: Kingsford, *Hist. Lit.*, p. 96. The part 1440–52 seems to have been written by William Gregory, who was mayor of London in 1451, but the portion 1454–69 is the work of another. The work contains one of the best accounts of Cade's rebellion and includes much of value for the first decade of Edward IV's reign. See George Kriehn, *The English Rising in 1450* (Strasburg, 1892), pp. 8–16.

2887 GREY FRIARS OF LYNN. A fourteenth-century chronicle of. Ed. by Antonia Gransden in *E.H.R.* lxxii (1957), 270–8.

Prints brief annals for 1340, 1345–9, 1356–7, and 1360–77.

2888 GUISBOROUGH, WALTER OF. The chronicle of Walter of Guisborough, previously edited as the chronicle of Walter of Hemingford or Hemingburgh. Ed. by Harry Rothwell. Camden Ser. lxxxix. 1957. Chronicon Walteri de Hemingburgh, vulgo Hemingford nuncupati, de gestis regum Angliae (1048–1346). Ed. by H. C. Hamilton. Eng. Hist. Soc. 2 vols. 1848–9. Other editions: The part 1066–1273 in Gale, *Scriptores Quinque* (No. 1099), pp. 453–594; the part 1274–1346 by Thomas Hearne. 2 vols. Oxf. 1731. Extracts, 1129–1307. Ed. by Liebermann in M.G.H., *SS.* xxviii. 627–46.

The Walter to whom this chronicle is attributed was a canon regular of the priory of Guisborough in Yorkshire; he may have been Walter of Hemingburgh who was subprior of that house in the early fourteenth century. Walter's chronicle runs from the Norman invasion and the cause thereof to 1305, and perhaps to 1312. Down to 1198 it is a compilation from Henry of Huntingdon, Simeon of Durham, Peter Langtoft, and especially William of Newburgh. From 1198 to 1291 it is thin. From 1291 to 1312 the period is contemporary with its author, and its accounts of Anglo-Scottish relations are temperate, although Professor Rothwell questions its over-all reliability for this period. It incorporates some valuable documents including the only surviving contemporary copy of 'De Tallagio Non Concedendo' of 1297.

One of the late MSS. of Walter's chronicle appends a chronicle running from 1327 to 1346, an appendage which appears independently elsewhere. V. H. Galbraith in *Poole essays* (No. 1448), pp. 379–98, and in *E.H.R.* xliii (1928), 203–17, has established a strong probability that this appendage is an altered version of John of Tynemouth's *Historia Aurea* (No. 2965).

2889 HALL, EDWARD (d. 1547). Hall's chronicle, containing the history of England during the reigns of Henry IV and the succeeding monarchs to the end of the reign of Henry VIII . . . carefully collated with the editions of 1548 and 1550. (Ed. by Henry Ellis.) Lond. 1809. The union of the two noble and illustre families of Lancastre and Yorke. Lond. 1548, 1550.

This work is a glorification of the house of Tudor, but it gives some useful particulars regarding English history in the fifteenth century. Although Hall followed Polydore Vergil in the main, he utilized other sources, some of which are now lost or unidentified. See Kingsford, pp. 260–4. The fictitiousness of the legend of a printed edition of 1542 is shown by Graham Pollard, 'The bibliographical history of Hall's Chronicle', *B.I.H.R.* x (1932), 12–17. For one of Hall's sources, namely the account of Peter Basset for 1415–29, see Benedicta J. H. Rowe, 'A contemporary account of the Hundred Years' War from 1415 to 1429', *E.H.R.* xli (1926), 504–13.

2890 HARDYNG, JOHN (d. *c.* 1465). Chronicle, from the earliest period of English history (to 1461), together with the continuation by Richard Grafton to 34 Henry VIII. Ed. by Henry Ellis. Lond. 1812. Two separate editions, with the continuation, were printed in 1543. 'Extracts from the first version of Hardyng's Chronicle', by C. L. Kingsford, in *E.H.R.* xxvii (1912), 740–53.

Hardyng's *Chronicle* is in English verse, but Grafton (d. *c.* 1572) wrote his continuation in prose. Hardyng's work, which was completed about 1465, survives in two recensions: one urges 'Henry VI to reform his government; and the second, Yorkist in sympathy, is addressed to Edward IV' (Jacob). It is of some historical value, in that it affords some information regarding the reigns of Henry IV, Henry V, Henry VI, and Edward IV. He took part in the battle of Agincourt, and was employed by Henry V and Henry VI to secure documents supporting the claim of England to the fealty of the Scottish kings. These documents were forgeries. Hardyng was for many years constable of the castle to Kyme, in Lincolnshire. For a sketch of his life and chronicle, see Kingsford in *E.H.R.* xxvii (1912), 462–82, and in his *Historical literature.* ch. vi. See also J. A. Kingdon's *Incidents in the lives of Thomas Poyntz and Richard Grafton* (Lond. 1895); and his *Richard Grafton, citizen and grocer* (Lond. 1901).

2891 HENRICI QUINTI ANGLIAE REGIS GESTA. See **GESTA** (No. 2877).

2892 HERD, JOHN (d. 1588). Historia quattuor regum Angliae (1460–1509). Ed. by Thomas Purnell. Roxburghe Club. Lond. 1868.

A metrical chronicle derived mainly from Hall and Vergil (Nos. 2888, 2968).

2893 HEXHAM, JOHN OF (d. *c.* 1209). Historia Johannis prioris Hagustaldensis ecclesiae xxv annorum (1130–54). Ed. by Thomas Arnold, *Symeonis Monachi Opera*, ii. 284–332. Rolls Ser. Lond. 1885. Other editions: in Twysden's *Scriptores X* (No. 1124), pp. 257–82; by James Raine, *Priory of Hexham*, i. 107–72, Surtees Soc. 1864. Extracts. Ed. by Liebermann, in M.G.H., *SS.* xxvii. 14–16. Trans. by Joseph Stevenson, *Church historians* (No. 1123), iv, pt. i, 3–32: The chronicle of John, prior of Hexham.

This continuation of Simeon's *Historia Regum* (No. 2862) relates mainly to the affairs of northern England, and was probably compiled between 1162 and 1170. It contains some original information. John seems to have succeeded Richard (No. 2894) as prior of Hexham, and to have based his history for the years 1135–9 largely on Richard's work.

2894 HEXHAM, RICHARD OF. Historia de gestis regis Stephani et de bello de standardo (1135–39). Ed. by Richard Howlett, *Chronicles of the reigns of Stephen, Henry II, and Richard I*, iii. 139–78. Rolls Ser. Lond. 1886. Other editions: in Twysden's *Scriptores X* (No. 1125), pp. 309–30; by James Raine, *Priory of Hexham*, i. 63–106. Surtees Soc. 1864. Extract. Ed. by Liebermann, in M.G.H., *SS.* xxvii. 11–14. Trans. by Joseph Stevenson, *Church historians* (No. 1123), iv, pt. i. 35–58: The acts of king Stephen and the battle of the standard.

A valuable detailed contemporary narrative of the period 1135–9, written before 1154, which is occupied mainly with the invasions of the Scots under King David. It gives much information not found elsewhere, including the only known text by which Innocent II recognized Stephen: Davis, *King Stephen*, p. 148. Richard was elected prior of Hexham in 1141, and seems to have died between 1162 and 1174. For his history of the church of Hexham, see No. 6274.

2895 HIGDEN, RANULF (d. *c.* 1363–4). Polychronicon Randulphi Higden monachi Cestrensis (from the creation to 1352); together with the English translations of John Trevisa and of an unknown writer of the fifteenth century. Vols. i–ii. Ed. by Churchill Babington. Vols. iii–ix. Ed. by Joseph R. Lumby. Rolls Ser. 9 vols. Lond. 1865–86. Another edition of the parts relating to Great Britain in Thomas Gale, *Scriptores XV* (No. 1100), pp. 179–287.

A scholarly commentary is provided in John Taylor, *The Universal Chronicle of Ranulf Higden* (Oxf. 1966). Higden was a monk of St. Werburgh's Abbey, Chester; in 1352 he was summoned to come to a *consilium* at Westminster *una cum omnibus cronicis vestris*; J. G. Edwards, 'Ranulph, monk of Chester', *E.H.R.* xlvii (1932), 94. The most popular work of universal history during the fourteenth and fifteenth centuries, *The Universal Chronicle* survives in more than 100 manuscripts. It is a compilation from classical and medieval sources arranged in seven books. It is designed as a history, not as a contemporary chronicle; for the latter purpose it is of little value. Book I is geographical: it describes the countries of the earth. The other six books comprise a universal history from Adam to the fourteenth century. In Lumby's edition vol. vi to vol. viii, p. 338 cover the period 635–1344. It is a 'storybook, a mine of anecdotes and exempla, composed by a literary glutton' (Taylor). In some manuscripts, Higden's compilation, the short version, ends in 1327. Between 1327 and 1340 Higden seems to have made numerous changes in the earlier version, as what may well be his autograph copy indicates: see V. H. Galbraith, 'An autograph MS. of Ranulph Higden's Polychronicon', *Huntington Library Quarterly*, xxiii (1959), 1–18. In a few manuscripts, additions, presumably made by Higden, run on into the 1350s.

The short version of the *Polychronicon* was the main source of *Historia Aurea* (No. 2965) down to 1327; and the *Historia Aurea* from 1327 to 1347 'became in its turn the source of a new version of Higden's chronicle' (Taylor).

Numerous Latin continuations of the *Polychronicon* were made by various hands. These continuations are a major source of English history to about the middle of the fifteenth century. Lumby printed in vol. viii, pp. 355–406 (to 1380) and vol. ix, pp. 1–283 (1381–94) a continuation ascribed to John of Malvern, a monk of Worcester (d. *c.* 1415). It was, however, shown by J. A. Robinson, 'An unrecognized Westminster chronicler', *P.B.A.* iii (1907–8), 61–92, that Malvern wrote only to 1377 and that the rest of this continuation 1381–94 (which is particularly valuable for events 1388–92) is by a monk of Westminster. Both the Malvern and Westminster continuations are good authorities for their periods. For a misleading transposed sentence in Lumby's edition, see L. C. Hector, 'Chronicle of the Monk of Westminster', *E.H.R.* lxviii (1953), 62–5. Another Latin continuation running from 1352 to 1380 is printed in Lumby, viii. 407–28. See also Adam of Usk's chronicle (No. 2966); and the Northern Chronicle printed in Kingsford, *Hist. Lit.*, pp. 279–91. For other fifteenth-century continuations, see Kingsford, pp. 24, 32, 35, 36, 342.

In 1385–7 John Trevisa translated Higden's chronicle into English and carried the story down to 1360 (printed in Lumby's edition). Caxton wrote a continuation to 1460 in English (Lumby's edition, viii. 522–87). Caxton printed Trevisa and his own continuation in 1482; this edition was reprinted in 1495 and 1527: David C. Fowler, 'New Light on John Trevisa', *Traditio*, xvii (1962), 289–317. Another fifteenth-century translation of Higden and a continuation thereof to 1402 is printed from Harley MS. 2261 in Lumby's edition, concurrently with Higden's Latin to 1344 (viii. 339) and then as an appendix (viii. 429–521). Higden also wrote *Ars componendi sermones* and *Speculum Curatorum*, for which see Taylor, op. cit., pp. 3–5.

2896 HISTOIRE DE GUILLAUME LE MARÉCHAL, comte de Striguil et de Pembroke, régent d'Angleterre (*c.* 1140–1219). Ed. by Paul Meyer. 3 vols. Société de l'histoire de France. Paris. 1891–1901.

The author of this valuable Anglo-French poem wrote in England about 1225. Gaston Paris (*La Littérature française*, 4th edn., 1909, p. 149) calls it 'un des documents les plus importants qui nous soient parvenus non seulement sur l'histoire, mais sur les mœurs, etc., du XIIe et du XIIIe siècle'. See also Paul Meyer, 'L'Histoire de Guillaume le Maréchal', *Romania*, xi (1882), 22–74; T. F. Tout, 'The Fair (Battle) of Lincoln and the "Histoire de Guillaume le Maréchal" ', *E.H.R.* xviii (1903), 240–65; Molinier, *Sources*, iii, no. 2271; and Sidney Painter, *William Marshal* (Baltimore, 1933).

2897 HISTOIRE DES DUCS DE NORMANDIE ET DES ROIS D'ANGLETERRE (from the first arrival of the Danes in Gaul to 1220). Ed. by Francisque Michel. Société de l'histoire de France. Paris. 1840. Reprinted 1965. Portions, re-edited by Holder-Egger, in M.G.H., *SS.* xxvi. 699–717. See also 'Extrait d'une chronique française des rois de France par un anonyme de Béthune (to 1217)', edited by Leopold Délisle, in Bouquet's *Historiens de la France* (No. 1090), xxiv. 750–75. Paris. 1904.

To 1199 the *Histoire* is an abridgment of William of Jumièges, with some additions. The part 1199–1220 was probably written by an eye-witness of the events narrated; it has a valuable account of the end of John's reign and of the French invasion of England in 1216. On these two works, which are important sources for the reign of John, see Charles Petit-Dutaillis, 'L'Anonyme de Béthune', in *Revue Historique*, l (1892), 63–71. He shows that they are probably by the same author. Cf. Molinier, *Sources*, iii, nos. 2217–18.

2898 HISTORIA (ANONYMI) EDUARDI TERTII (1326–77). Ed. by Thomas Hearne, *Walteri Hemingford Historia de Rebus Gestis Eduardi I*, etc., pp. 387–452. Oxf. 1731.

This seems to be in large part a compilation from the works of Higden and Murimuth.

2899 HISTORIA VITAE ET REGNI RICARDI II (1377–1402) a monacho quodam de Evesham consignata. Ed. by Thomas Hearne. Oxf. 1729.

Probably written at Evesham soon after 1402. Follows Walsingham to 1390, but then seems to become an independent authority, and gives a valuable account of the parliament of 1397, of the revolution of 1399, and of the early years of Henry IV. The author is hostile to Richard II. See George Kriehn, 'The Monk of Evesham's chronicle', *A.H.R.* vii (1902), 268–74; and Kingsford, *Hist. Lit.*, pp. 23–5 and 342.

2900 HISTORIAE CROYLANDENSIS CONTINUATIO (Three continuations of Ingulf, No. 2163). Ed. by William Fulman, *Scriptores* (No. 1098), pp. 451–593. Trans. by Henry T. Riley, *Ingulf's Chronicle . . .* (No. 1089), pp. 271–533.

The three continuations, as they are printed, concern respectively the periods 1149–1470, 1459–86, October 1485–April 1486. The second continuation, 1459–86, is a valuable contemporary source. In the printed edition, there seems to be some disorder in the sequence of sections. Furthermore, it is by no means certain that the author was one of the king's councillors, a D.C.L., and a member of a diplomatic mission in 1471, as C. L. Kingsford thought, pp. 179–84. The author is generally Yorkist in sympathy, friendly towards Edward IV, but hostile to Richard III. For a critical analysis, see J. G. Edwards, 'The Second Continuation of the Crowland Chronicle: was it written in ten days?', *B.I.H.R.* xxxix (1966), 117–29.

2901 HISTORIE OF THE ARRIVALL OF EDWARD IV IN ENGLAND and the final recoverye of his kingdomes from Henry VI, A.D. 1471. Ed. by John Bruce. Camden Soc. Lond. 1838. Reprinted, with modernized orthography, in *Chronicles of the White Rose of York* (No. 2733), pp. 31–96. Contemporary French abridgement of the English text: *La Révolte du comte de Warwick contre le roi*

Edward IV. Ed. by J. A. Giles. Caxton Soc. Lond. 1849. Another edition of a French text, by L. M. E. Dupont, *Mémoires de Philippe de Commines*, iii. 281–93. Société de l'histoire de France. Paris. 1847. Translation of a French abridgement, by Edward Jerningham: 'Account of Edward IV's second invasion of England, 1471, drawn up by one of his followers', *Archaeologia*, xxi (1827), 11–23.

> The English narrative is official propaganda, 'an authorised relation put forth by the Yorkists themselves'. The writer calls himself 'a servant of the king that presently saw in effect a great part of his exploits'. The facts are presented by an eye-witness, although the writer was a Yorkist partisan. For a critical study of the MSS. and their problems, see J. A. F. Thomson, 'The Arrival of Edward IV: the development of the text', *Speculum*, xlvi (1971), 84–93.

2902 HISTORY OF GRUFFYDD AP CYNAN (1054–1137): the Welsh text, with translation, introduction, and notes. Ed. by Arthur Jones. Manchester. 1910.

> Written, probably in Latin, in the reign of Henry II. Important for the history of Wales and the English border down to 1137. Gruffudd, King of Gwynedd, 'is the only mediaeval Welsh prince whose biography, in the form of pure eulogy, has survived' (*Dict. Welsh Biog.*). For earlier versions, see Jones's introduction; T. F. Tout's article on Gruffydd in the *D.N.B.* xxiii. 301–4; and T. Parry on Gruffudd in *Dict. Welsh Biog.*, pp. 310–11.

2903 HOVEDEN, OR HOWDEN, ROGER OF (d. after 1201). Chronica Rogeri de Houedene (A.D. 732–1201). Ed. by William Stubbs. Rolls Ser. 4 vols. Lond. 1868–71. Another edition, in Savile's *Scriptores* (No. 1119), pp. 230–471. Lond. 1596; reprinted, Frankfort. 1601. Extracts. Ed. by Liebermann, in M.G.H., *SS.* xxvii. 133–83. Trans. by H. T. Riley: *The annals of Roger de Hoveden.* Bohn's Antiquarian Library. 2 vols. Lond. 1853.

> This chronicle written after 1192 and Howden's first draft of the section 1169–92, which was once attributed to Benedict of Peterborough, constitute the most valuable narratives for the reigns of Henry II and Richard I. The first part, A.D. 732–1148, is copied from the *Historia post Bedam*, a compilation (still extant in manuscript) made at Durham between 1148 and 1161, which is based on Simeon of Durham and Henry of Huntingdon. The second part, 1148–69, is a meagre compilation taken from the *Chronicle of Melrose*, the lives and letters of Becket, etc. The third portion, 1169–92, is a revision of Howden's first draft which survives as *Gesta Regis Henrici Secundi* and was once ascribed to Benedict of Peterborough (see No. 2879). The fourth portion, 1192–1201, is Howden's continuation of the third portion. The third and fourth sections are enriched with an abundance of documents: the author had access to the public records and held intercourse with the leading men of the time.
>
> Roger may have been parson of Howden in Yorkshire 1173–76; he was a royal clerk who accompanied Henry II to France in 1174 and was an Itinerant Justice of the Forest on several occasions between 1185 and 1190. F. Barlow, 'Roger of Howden', *E.H.R.* lv (1950), 352–60. He accompanied Richard I on the Third Crusade, but had returned to England by Christmas of 1191. Probably he then settled down at Howden to write this chronicle which included the revision of his earlier *Gesta Regis Henrici II.* See Doris M. Stenton, 'Roger of Howden and Benedict', *E.H.R.* lviii (1953), 574–82.

2904 HUNTINGDON, HENRY OF (d. *c.* 1155). Historia Anglorum, 55 B.C.–A.D. 1154. Ed. by Thomas Arnold. Rolls Ser. Lond. 1879. Other editions: in Savile's *Scriptores* (No. 1119), pp. 169–229. Lond. 1596 (reprinted, Frankfort. 1601); in Migne's *Patrologia*, cxcv. 799–978; to A.D. 1066, in Petrie's *Monumenta* (No. 1084), pp. 689–763. Extracts, 768–1154. Ed. by Liebermann, in M.G.H.,

SS. xiii. 148–54. Trans. by Thomas Forester: *The chronicle of Henry of Hunting-don*. Bohn's Antiquarian Library. Lond. 1853.

Five recensions appeared between 1130 and 1154. The author's main sources of information to about 1126 are Bede and the *Anglo-Saxon Chronicle*. After that date he derives many of his statements from oral report, apparently written year by year, but he does not give us many new facts. It was long believed that his chronicle contained valuable material relating to Anglo-Saxon history based on old folk-songs. Liebermann has shown, however, that this view is untenable, and that some of the details presented in the *Historia Anglorum* which are not found elsewhere are figments of the imagination. He is sympathetic to neither Stephen nor Mathilda. His sketchy contemporary annals (1120–54) form an independent source of only moderate value. Henry became archdeacon of Huntingdon about 1110. See Felix Liebermann, 'Heinrich von Huntingdon', in *Forschungen zur deutschen Geschichte*, xviii (1878), 265–95; and cf. Molinier, *Sources*, ii, no. 1988; R. L. Poole, *Chronicles* (No. 374), pp. 52–4 and R. R. Darlington, *Anglo-Norman Historians* (Lond. 1947), pp. 16–18.

'In his letter to his friend Walter, called the De Contemptu Mundi, the best thing that he wrote, he gives some neatly executed sketches of men of his time, both great and small' (Darlington, p. 18).

2905 'ISLIP, SIMON' see SPECULUM REGIS (No. 2955).

2906 ITINERARIUM PEREGRINORUM ET GESTA REGIS RICARDI (1187–99). Auctore ut videtur Ricardo canonico S. Trinitatis Londoniensis. Ed. by William Stubbs, *Chronicles and memorials of the reign of Richard I*. vol. i. Rolls Ser. Lond. 1864. *Das 'Itinerarium Peregrinorum'*. *Eine zeitgenössische englische Chronik zum dritten Kreuzzug in ursprünglicher Gestalt*. Ed. by (with introduction pp. 1–244 and text 245–357) Hans-Eberhard Mayer. *Schriften der Monumenta Germaniae historica*, xviii. Stuttgart. 1962. Another edition (bad) in Gale's *Scriptores Quinque* (No. 1099), pp. 247–429. Fragments. Ed. by Pauli in M.G.H., *SS.* xxvii. 191–219. Extracts from Stubbs's edition in M. T. Stead, *Itinerarium Regis Ricardi*. Texts for Students, No. 21 (S.P.C.K.). Lond. 1920. Trans. in *Chronicles of the Crusades*, pp. 65–339: 'Itinerary of Richard I'. Bohn's Antiquarian Library. Lond. 1848. The Bohn translation is the basis of Kenneth Fenwick's edition, entitled *The Third Crusade*. Folio Society. Lond. 1958.

This history of the Third Crusade is no longer ascribed to Geoffrey of Vinsauf. It bears a close relationship to Ambroise (No. 2748). Gaston Paris held that it is in large part a later translation of Ambroise (*Romania*, xxvi (1897), 353–93); Kate Norgate maintained that the relationship was more complicated (*E.H.R.* xxv (1910), 523–47); J. G. Edwards adduced reasons for believing that both works were derived from an unknown original in French prose written by a participant in the Crusades, (*Tait essays* (No. 1455), pp. 59–77). After an extensive study of the manuscripts, Mayer affirms that the *Itinerarium* as printed in Stubbs's edition is basically a conflation of two separate works. The first, which Mayer calls IP 1 and runs from 1187 to the death of Archbishop Baldwin in November 1190, was written before September 1192 in the Holy Land by an unknown author, probably a Templar of English birth. This is the text which Mayer prints. The second text, which Mayer calls IP 2, is a compilation probably made between 1216 and 1222 by Richard de Templo who became the prior of the Augustinian priory of Holy Trinity, London. This compilation IP 2 virtually incorporates IP 1 with a translation into Latin of the *Estoire de la Guerre Sainte*, ascribed to Ambroise (No. 2748). The author of IP 2 enriched his account from Howden and from an unknown writer who accompanied the English crusade from Tours to Marseilles. For fuller summaries of Mayer's important book, see reviews in *Bibl. École des Chartes*, cxxi (1963), 273–5; *Historische Zeitschrift*, cxcviii (1964), 380–7; and *Speculum*, xxxix (1964), 185–8; and then H. E. Mayer, 'Zum Itinerarium Peregrinorum; eine Erwiderung', *Deutsches Archiv für Erforschung*, xxi (1964), 210–20; and M. L. Bulst, 'Noch einmal das Itinerarium Peregrinorum', ibid. xxi (1965), 593–606. For a day-by-day itinerary of Richard, see Lionel Landon in Pipe Roll Soc. Pubns. li (1935).

2907   JOURNAL D'UN BOURGEOIS DE PARIS, 1405–49. Ed. by Alexandre Tuetey. Société de l'histoire de Paris. Paris. 1881. For other editions, see Potthast (No. 62), i. 686–7. Trans. as *A Parisian journal . . .* by Janet Shirley. Oxf. 1968.

A contemporary chronicle, written in French; valuable for its exact account of conditions in Paris throughout the period. See Molinier, *Sources*, iv, No. 4149.

2908   JUMIÈGES, GUILLAUME DE (*fl. c.* 1070). Gesta Normannorum ducum. Ed. by Jean Marx. Paris and Rouen. 1914. Other editions: *Willelmi Calculi Gemmeticensis monachi Historiae Normannorum libri viii* (A.D. 851–1137). Ed. by André Duchesne, *Historiae Normannorum Scriptores*, pp. 215–317. Paris. 1619. Reprinted in Migne's *Patrologia*, cxlix. 777–910. Paris 1853. Another edition, in Camden's *Anglica . . . Scripta* (No. 1092), pp. 604–91. Trans. into French in F. P. G. Guizot's *Collection des Mémoires* xxix, 1–316: 'Histoire des Normands'. Paris. 1826. Book viii is trans. in Stevenson, *Church historians* (No. 1123), v, pt. i.

Duchesne's edition includes many later interpolations by Ordericus Vitalis and Robert of Torigny; and gives as Book viii, *Historia Henrici Primi Regis Angliae* (1087–1137) by Robert of Torigny. Marx, who excised the interpolations and thereby distinguished the original from the accretions, prepared the only critical edition. The original stands in close relationship with William of Poitiers's *Gesta Willelmi* (No. 2943).
    William of Jumièges's work is a contemporary source from *c.* 1028 to 1070, and is valuable for its account of the Norman conquest. Of his life, virtually nothing is known. See Molinier: *Sources*, ii, no. 1964; Léopold Delisle, 'Matériaux pour l'édition de Guillaume de Jumièges préparée par Jules Lair', *Bibl. École des Chartes*, lxxi (1910), 481–526; J. Marx, 'Guillaume de Poitiers et Guillaume de Jumièges' in F. Lot, *Mélanges* (No. 1443 above); C. H. Haskins's review of Marx's edition in *E.H.R.* xxxi (1916), 150–3; *Engl. Hist. Docs.* ii. 215–16 and 279–80.

2909   JUVÉNAL (OR JOUVENEL) DES URSINS, JEAN (d. 1473). Histoire de Charles VI, 1380–1422. Ed. by Denis Godefroy. Paris. 1616 and 1653. Also edited in J. A. C. Buchon, *Collection* (No. 1091), vol. iv. Michaud and Poujoulat, *Mémoires pour servir à l'histoire de France*, 1st Ser., vol. ii. Paris. 1836.

Written in French about 1431. Valuable for the relations of Henry V to France. The author was Archbishop of Rheims and councillor of Charles VII; his tone is pro-Armagnac. See Molinier, *Sources*, iv, no. 3574; Bossuat, p. 489; and D. Kirkland, 'Jean Juvénal des Ursins and François de Surienne', *E.H.R.* liii (1938), 263–7.

2910   THE KIRKSTALL ABBEY CHRONICLES. Ed. by John Taylor. Thoresby Society Pubns. xlii (1952). Partial text, ed. by M. V. Clarke and N. Denholm-Young in *B.J.R.L.* xv (1931), 121–37 (reprinted in No. 1464).

Two chronicles, called the short chronicle and the long chronicle. The short chronicle, written sometime between 1400 and 1405, includes scattered sections on 1355–7 and an important account of some of the events of Richard II's reign, especially of its final years. Taylor prints the whole Latin text and an English translation thereof. Clarke and Denholm-Young print the text of the most significant sections.
    The long chronicle, probably written sometime between 1370 and 1376, runs from Vortigern to 1360. Its material is drawn from several other chronicles. Taylor gives a translation only of the section for the years 1328 to *c.* 1355, and that section utilized at length John Erghome's Bridlington prophecies (see No. 7049).

2911 KLERK, JAN DE (d. 1365). Van den Derden Edewaert, Coninc van Engelant: Rymkronyk geschreven circa 1347. Ed. by J. F. Willems. Ghent. 1840. Translated into French by Octave Delepierre: *Édouard III, roi d'Angleterre, en Belgique*. Ghent. 1841.

Valuable for the years 1337–41. The author favours the cause of Edward III. He was a native of Antwerp, and was also called Jan Boendaele. See H. Haerynck, *Jan Boendaele* (Ghent, 1888); and Henry S. Lucas 'Edward III and the poet chronicler John Boendale', *Speculum*, xii (1937), 367–9.

2912 KNIGHTON, HENRY (d. *c.* 1396) Chronicon. Ed. by J. R. Lumby. Rolls Ser. 2 vols. Lond. 1889–95. Another edition, in Twysden's *Scriptores* (No. 1124), pp. 2311–2742.

The chronicle begins with the genealogy of William the Conqueror, and extends from 1066 to 1395, with a gap for 1366–77. It is one of the principal sources for the reign of Richard II, and is partisan towards John of Gaunt, Duke of Lancaster.

Lumby, whose edition is severely criticized by James Tait in *E.H.R.* xi (1896), 568–9, followed Shirley in believing that Knighton's authorship ended in 1366 and that the account of 1377–95 was the work of a continuator. Galbraith has shown that Knighton was the author of the whole chronicle; he adduces strong arguments for believing that Knighton composed the portion from 1377 to 1395 first and then decided to preface it with an account from 1066 on. Down to 1377 the latter account is derived mainly from Higden and Hemingburgh (or Guisborough). Knighton apparently did not complete the chronicle for the period 1366–77. Knighton was a canon regular of St. Mary's in the Meadows, Leicester; of his life we know very little. See V. H. Galbraith, 'The Chronicle of Henry Knighton', in *Saxl Memorial Essays* (No. 1452), pp. 136–45; to which is appended (pp. 146–8) an examination of Cotton MS. Tiberius C VII, apparently the author's autograph, by R. A. B. Mynors.

See also M. V. Clarke, 'Henry Knighton and the library catalogue of Leicester abbey', *E.H.R.* xlv (1930), 103–7; reprinted in her *Fourteenth century studies* (No. 1464).

2913 LANGTOFT, PETER (d. after 1307). The chronicle of Pierre de Langtoft in French verse (from Brutus to 1307, with a translation). Ed. by Thomas Wright. Rolls Ser. 2 vols. Lond. 1866–8. Extracts, 1190–1307. Ed. by Liebermann, in M.G.H., *SS.* xxviii. 647–62.

A large part of this chronicle in rhyming French was translated into English by Robert Mannyng of Brunne (No. 2923). To the end of Henry III's reign it is taken from Geoffrey of Monmouth, Huntingdon, Malmesbury, and other well-known writers. For the years 1272–1307 it is a contemporary record, much of which is devoted to Edward I's Scottish wars, and includes satirical poems. The author's tone is strongly hostile to the Scots. He was a canon of the priory of Bridlington in Yorkshire. See M. D. Legge, 'A list of Langtoft manuscripts, with notes on MS. Laud Misc. 637', *Medium Ævum*, iv (1935), 20–4; and Russell, *Writers* (No. 541), p. 101; and M. D. Legge, *A-N in Cloisters* (No. 293), pp. 70–5 and index.

2914 LAYAMON (*fl.* 1200). Layamon's Brut, or chronicle of Britain, a poetical semi-Saxon paraphrase of the Brut of Wace (with a translation). Ed. by Frederic Madden. Soc. of Antiq. of London. 3 vols. Lond. 1847. G. L. Brook and R. F. Leslie, *Laʒamon: Brut*, vol. i. E.E.T.S. Lond. 1963. Selections with notes edited by John Hall. Oxf. 1924; and edited by G. L. Brook. Oxf. 1963. Translation of portion concerning Arthur in Arthurian Chronicles represented by Wace and Layamon. Ed. by Lucy A. Paton. Everyman's Library (1912), pp. 117–264.

Although Layamon's *Brut* may have been written between 1157 and 1173, the most generally accepted date of composition is A.D. 1203–4. Based on Wace (No. 2974) it contains additions from some Welsh traditions and Layamon's imagination. Layamon was a priest of Areley in Worcestershire. See H. B. Hinckley, 'The date of Layamon's Brut', *Anglia*, vi (1932), 45–57. For a commentary with copious footnotes, see J. S. P. Tatlock, *The legendary history of Britain* (Berkeley, Cal., 1950), pp. 483–531. For bibliography, *C.B.E.L.* i. 163–5; v. 117; and Wells, *Manual* (No. 275).

2915 LE BEAU, JEAN. Chronique de Richard II, 1377–99. Ed. by J. A. (C.) Buchon, *Collection* (No. 1092), vol. xxiv, supplement ii.

Buchon erroneously assigned this work to a Jean Le Beau. It is, however, another redaction of *Chronique de la Traison* (No. 2841), and not the reverse as H. Moranville contended in 'La Chronique du Religieux de St. Denis, . . . et la Chronique de la Mort de Richard II', *Bibl. École des Chartes*, l (1889), 5–40. See Molinier, *Sources*, no. 3988; *Revue Historique*, xl (1889), 403; and the forthcoming edition of *La Traison* (No. 2841).

2916 LE BEL, JEAN (d. 1370). Chronique de Jean le Bel (1272–1361, but no details till 1326). Ed. by Jules Viard and Eugène Déprez. Société de l'histoire de France. 2 vols. Paris. 1904–5. Les Vrayes Chroniques de Jehan le Bel (1326–61). Ed. by M. L. Polain. Académie Royale de Belgique. 2 vols. Brussels. 1863. (A poor edition.)

Written in French about 1356–61, and deals mainly with the wars of England and France. This valuable work is the basis of the early part of Froissart's *Chronicles*, and constitutes one of the most important sources of information regarding the Hundred Years War. The author, a canon of St. Lambert, Liège, took part in Edward III's expedition against the Scots in 1327, and was an admirer of that king. See Henri Pirenne, 'Jean le Bel', in *Biographie nationale de Belgique*, xi (1891), 518–25; A. Coville, 'Jean le Bel, chroniqueur', in *Hist. litt. de la France*, xxxviii (1941), 234–58; and Molinier, *Sources*, iv, no. 3093. The Viard–Déprez edition includes in an appendix 'pièces justificatives' (1342–9) drawn from the Public Record Office.

2917 LE FÈVRE, JEAN (d. 1468). Chronique (1408–35). Ed. by François Morand. Société de l'histoire de France. 2 vols. Paris. 1876–81. For other editions, see Potthast, i. 715.

This chronicle, written in French, borrows much from Monstrelet, but is very valuable for the battle of Agincourt, at which Le Fèvre was present on the English side. He was seigneur of Saint-Rémy and privy councillor of Philip the Good, Duke of Burgundy.

2918 LE LIVERE DE REIS DE BRITTANIE E LE LIVERE DE REIS DE ENGLETERE (from Brutus to 1274, with two continuations to 1326 and a translation). Ed. by John Glover. Rolls Ser. Lond. 1865.

An abridged French prose translation of extracts from Geoffrey of Monmouth, Florence of Worcester, Ralph of Diceto, and other well-known chroniclers; perhaps compiled by Peter of Ickham (*fl. c.* 1290). It consists of two parts, which the editor calls *Le Livere de Reis de Brittanie* and *Le Livere de Reis de Engletere*; and neither part has independent value. On Peter of Ickham, see Russell, *Writers* (No. 541), pp. 99–100. See also Vising, *A-N. Lit.* (No. 299), no. 298; and M. D. Legge, *A-N. Lit.* (No. 294), pp. 247–8, 291.

2919 LIVY, TITUS (FRULOVISI) (*fl.* 1437). Titi Livii Foro-Juliensis Vita Henrici Quinti regis Angliae. Ed. by Thomas Hearne. Oxf. 1716. The first English life of King Henry the Fifth, written in 1513 by an anonymous writer known commonly as the translator of Livius. Ed. by C. L. Kingsford. Oxf. 1911.

The Latin life of Henry V, written in 1437 or 1438 at the behest of Humphrey, Duke of

Gloucester, is a valuable source, particularly for the foreign campaigns of 1414–19, in which Gloucester participated. Its author was Titus Livy Frulovisi (of Forlì) who, having written plays in Venice, came to England, probably in 1436, and entered Gloucester's service. His sources were official records, chronicles (especially a version of the *Brut*), and information supplied by Gloucester. See Kingsford, *Hist. Lit.*, pp. 50–6; idem, 'The early biographies of Henry V', *E.H.R.* xxv (1910), 58–92; C. W. Previté-Orton, 'The earlier career of Titus Livius de Frulovisiis', ibid. xxx (1915), 74–8; idem, *Opera hactenus inedita T. Livii de Frulovisiis de Ferrara* (Cambr. 1932) (introduction); and R. Weiss, *Humanism in England* (No. 6930), pp. 41–5.

Frulovisi's *Vita* is the principal source of *The First English Life*, which also includes excerpts from an important lost life of Henry V, completed soon after 1455 and containing information derived from the Earl of Ormonde (d. 1452). See the introduction of Kingsford's edition of *The First English Life*.

2920　MacCONMIDHE, GILLA-BRIGHDE (*fl.* 1260). Poem on the battle of Dun (1260), Irish text, with English translation. Ed. by John O'Donovan. *Celtic Soc., Miscellany*, iii (1849), 145–83.

'The poem affords curious glimpses into the distracted state of Ireland at the period to which it refers.' The author was chief poet of Ulster and a follower of Brian O'Neill, king of the Irish of the north. At the battle of Dun (Downpatrick), which was fought with the English settlers, Brian was slain.

2921　MALMESBURY, WILLIAM OF (d. *c.* 1142). De gestis regum Anglorum libri quinque (A.D. 449–1127); Historiae novellae libri tres (1125–42). Ed. by William Stubbs. Rolls Ser. 2 vols. Lond. 1887–9. Historia Novella. Ed. with a translation from the Latin with introduction and notes by K. R. Potter. Medieval Texts. Lond., Edin., etc. 1955. Other editions: Savile (No. 1119), pp. 1–110; T. D. Hardy, Eng. Hist. Soc., 2 vols. Lond. 1840, which is reprinted in Migne's *Patrologia Latina*, clxxix (1855), 995–1440; Bks. i–iii of *Gesta Regum*, in Commelin (No. 1095), pp. 281–348. Extracts from *Gesta Regum* and *Historia Novella*. Ed. by Waitz in M.G.H., *SS.* x. 449–85; and ed. by Pauli, ibid. xiii. 134–5. Translated by John Sharpe: *The history of the kings of England* and *The modern history of William of Malmesbury*. Lond. 1815. Other translations: by J. A. Giles in Bohn's Antiquarian Library, Lond. 1847; and by Joseph Stevenson, *Church Historians* (No. 1123), iii, pt. i.

The *Gesta Regum*, whose first composition was finished in 1125, is a scholarly, historical synthesis which is based on the works of previous writers. Malmesbury was 'the first writer after Bede who attempted to give to his details of dates and events such a systematic connexion, in the way of cause and sequence, as entitles them to the name of History'. For the contemporary account, the *Historia Novella* is better than the *Gesta Regum*.

The *Historia Novella*, written 1140–2, 'is a contemporary narrative of first-rate importance'. The author, a monk of Malmesbury, was a partisan of the cause of Mathilda. 'It would not be altogether unfair to describe the *Historia Novella* as a panegyric of the Earl of Gloucester', Mathilda's champion (Potter). Robert B. Patterson, in 'William of Malmesbury's Robert of Gloucester: a re-evaluation of the *Historia Novella*', *A.H.R.* lxx (1965), 983–97, contends that 'The Historia Novella is an unreliable historical source for Stephen's reign'.

For Malmesbury's other works, especially his *Gesta Pontificum*, see Nos. 1143, 2291, 2303, 2316. Brief annals, probably written at Malmesbury, are printed by W. H. Stevenson in the *E.H.R.* xxii (1907), 81–2. See also, besides Stubbs's prefaces, W. de Gray Birch, *Life and Writings of William of Malmesbury*, reprinted from the *Trans. Royal Soc. Literature*, New Ser. vol. x (Lond. 1874); and Kate Norgate, *England under the*

Angevin Kings (Lond. 1887), i. 83–93. Marie Schütt suggests that Malmesbury took Suetonius as his literary model for the reigns of William II and Henry I: 'The literary form of William of Malmesbury's Gesta regum' in *E.H.R.* xlvi (1931), 255–60. For other sidelights see Neil R. Ker, 'William of Malmesbury's handwriting', *E.H.R.* lix (1944), 371–6; Hugh Farmer, 'William of Malmesbury's life and works', *J.E.H.* xiii (1962), 39–54; and R. R. Darlington, *Anglo-Norman Historians*, pp. 3–11.

2922 MANCINI (DOMINICO). Ad Angelum Catonem de occupatione regni Angliae per Riccardum tercium libellus. The usurpation of Richard III. Ed. and trans. by C. A. J. Armstrong. Lond. 1936. 2nd edn. Oxf. 1969.

Mancini, an Italian in England in 1483, wrote this tract for his patron, Angelo Catone, Archbishop of Vienne.

2923 MANNYNG, ROBERT (*fl. c.* 1338). The story of Robert Manning of Brunne (to A.D. 689). Ed. by F. J. Furnivall. Rolls Ser. 2 vols. Lond. 1887. Peter Langtoft's *Chronicle*, as improved by Robert of Brunne (A.D. 689–1307). Ed. by Thomas Hearne. 2 vols. Oxf. 1725; also in Hearne's *Works*, vols. iii–iv. Lond. 1810.

Written in English verse and completed in 1338. The part edited by Furnivall is mythical history derived from Wace and Geoffrey of Monmouth; the second part, edited by Hearne, is a translation of Langtoft's *Chronicle*, with some useful additions. The author, a native of Brunne (Bourne) in Lincolnshire, is often called Robert of Brunne. He was a member of the Gilbertine order. See Ruth Crosby, 'Robert Mannyng of Brunne: a new biography', *P.M.L.A.* lvii (1942), 15–28; and *C.B.E.L.* i. 165, and Wells, *Manual* (No. 275). Robert Stepsis, 'The manuscripts of Robert Manning of Brunne's Chronicle of England', *Manuscripta* (St. Louis), xiii (1969), 131–41.

2924 MARLBOROUGH, HENRY OF (*fl.* 1420). Quae sequuntur descripta sunt e chronicis manuscriptis Henrici de Marleburgh (1372–1421). Ed. by William Camden, *Britannia* (No. 609), pp. 832–6. Trans. by James Ware, *Historie of Ireland*, pt. iii, pp. 207–23; Henry of Marlborough's Chronicle of Ireland (1285–1421). Dublin. 1633. Ware's translation reprinted, in his *Ancient Irish Histories*, vol. ii. Dublin 1809.

The chronicle from which Camden prints this extract is called *Cronica Exerpta de Medulla Diversorum Cronicorum*. It extends from the birth of Christ to 1421, and was begun in 1406. The first part is a mere compilation, and the later part deals mainly with the affairs of the English settlers in Ireland.

2925 MISCELLANEOUS IRISH ANNALS (A.D. 1114–1437). Ed. and trans. by Séamus Ó hInnse. Institute of Advanced Stud. Dublin. 1947.

Fragment i: MacCarthaigh's Book (1114–1437).
Fragment ii: Rawlinson MS. B 488 (1237–1314).
Fragment iii: Rawlinson MS. B 488 (1392–1407).

  Fragment ii is essentially a collection of Connacht annals, comparable with the *Annals of Connacht* (No. 2751) or the *Annals of Loch Cé* (No. 2783).

2926 MONSTRELET, ENGUERRAND DE (d. 1453). La chronique de Monstrelet, 1400–1444. Ed. by Louis Douët d'Arcq. Société de l'histoire de France. 6 vols. Paris. 1857–62. Reprinted 1967. Trans. by Thomas Johnes: *The chronicles of Monstrelet (with continuations) to 1516*. 5 vols. Hafod. 1809. Other editions: 4 vols. Hafod. 1809; 13 vols. Lond. 1810; 2 vols. Lond. 1840 and 1853.

A continuation of Froissart, which contains information concerning the relations of England with France. Monstrelet was a magistrate of Cambrai. For the editions of his chronicle and the modern literature concerning him, see Potthast, i. 792; Molinier, *Sources*, iv, no. 3946; and André Lesort, 'Notes biographiques sur Monstrelet', in *Bulletin historique et philologique du Comité des travaux historiques et scientifiques* (Paris, 1908), pp. 153–7.

2927 MORE, SIR THOMAS (d. 1535). History of King Richard III. Ed. by Richard S. Sylvester, in *The Yale Edition of the Complete Works of St. Thomas More*, vol. ii. New Haven and Lond. 1963.

The English Works of Sir Thomas More volume the first. Ed. with commentaries by W. E. Campbell, A. W. Reed, R. W. Chambers, and W. A. G. Doyle-Davidson. Lond. and N.Y. 1931.

History of king Richard III. Ed. by J. R. Lumby. Cambr. 1883; 2nd edn., reprinted. Cambr. 1911 and 1924.

Historia Ricardi regis Angliae in Thomas Mori Omnia . . . Latina Opera . . . Louvain 1565.

The two versions, English and Latin, are represented by several texts. The generally accepted English text is that printed by Rastell in 1557 and the generally accepted Latin text is the Louvain edition of 1565. The 1931 Campbell edition includes a facsimile of Rastell's edition and a rendition into modern English. The 1963 Yale edition prints the English version of Rastell and the Latin version of Louvain on facing pages. The Yale edition also gives a transcript of an early Latin draft from MS. Arundel 43 in the College of Arms, as well as the collation of various editions.

The work, which was unfinished, is 'not so much a history as a dramatic literary tract, Lancastrian in its partisanship, yet attacking non-moral state-craft of the early sixteenth century'.

The authorship of Sir Thomas More was firmly established by R. W. Chambers in his commentary 'The authorship of the history of Richard III' in the 1931 Campbell edition, pp. 24–42; and on the same subject A. F. Pollard's review of that edition in *History*, xvii (1933), 317–23, may be consulted. See also Pollard in the *Tait essays* (No. 1455), pp. 223–38. The best biography of More is by Robert W. Chambers (Lond. and N.Y. 1935). A bibliography is provided in F. and M. P. Sullivan, *Moreana 1478–1945* (Kansas City, 1946).

2928 'MORE, THOMAS DE LA' (*fl.* 1340). Vita et mors Edwardi regis Angliae (1307–27). Ed. by William Stubbs, *Chronicles of the reigns of Edward I and Edward II*, ii. 297–319. Rolls Ser. Lond. 1883. Another edition, in Camden's *Anglica*, . . ., *Scripta* (No. 1093), pp. 593–603.

Merely an extract from Geoffrey le Baker's *Chronicle*, erroneously ascribed to More. More represented Oxfordshire in parliament in 1340; he was Baker's patron.

2929 MORINS, RICHARD DE (d. 1242). Annales prioratus de Dunstaplia, A.D. 33 to 1297. Ed. by Henry R. Luard, *Annales Monastici*, iii. 1–420. Rolls Ser. 1866. Another edition by Thomas Hearne. 2 vols. Oxf. 1733. Extracts, 1207–97. Ed. by R. Pauli, in M.G.H., SS. xxvii (1885), 504–13.

These annals were begun in 1210 by Richard de Morins, who was prior of Dunstable 1202–42. Down to 1200 he leaned heavily on Ralph de Diceto, and from 1201 to 1210 he used the additions to a Diceto MS., borrowed from the library of St. Albans Abbey. The Annals from 1201 to 1297 contain much original, contemporary material, particularly on the financial and judicial affairs of the abbey. 'Many historical facts', says Luard, 'are known solely from this chronicle.' Cheney endorses Luard's high estimate, and states that 'as they advance through the thirteenth century they give an incomparable view of the ordinary secular proceedings of an English monastery, and at the same time preserve the texts of records and make interesting comments on public events, amplifying our information from other quarters' (C. R. Cheney in *Wilkinson essays*) (No. 1459), pp. 79–98). Russell suggests that Richard de Morins, or de Mores, was Richard Anglicus, the well-known canonist; Kuttner and Rathbone accept this identification and expand the evidence in its favour. (Russell, *Writers* (No. 542), pp. 111–13; Kuttner and Rathbone, *Anglo-Norman canonists* (No. 6435), pp. 329–39.)

2930   MOROSINI, ANTONIO. Chronique. Ed. by Germain Lefèvre-Pontalis and L. Dorez. Société de l'histoire de France. 4 vols. Paris. 1898–1902.

Italian text with a French translation. Vol. iv is a study of the author and his work. Morosini, a citizen of Venice, was still writing in 1434. His chronicle is valuable for the relations of England and France for the period 1405–33. Molinier, *Sources*, iv, no. 4073.

2931   MURIMUTH, ADAM (d. 1347). Continuatio chronicarum (1303–47). Ed. by E. M. Thompson. Rolls Ser. Lond. 1889. Other editions (imperfect), with a continuation to 1380: by Anthony Hall, Oxf. 1721 (appended to his edition of the continuation of Nicholas Trevet's *Annales*, 1722); by Thomas Hog for English Hist. Soc. Lond. 1846.

Begun about 1325; three recensions appeared between 1337 and 1347. The part 1303–37 is meagre; the later portion, 1337–47, is valuable for the history of the English campaigns in France. The author was a canon of St. Paul's, London, precentor of Exeter, and at various times the holder of other benefices. He was employed by Edward II on missions to the papal court, and elsewhere. The continuation, especially the part 1359–77, seems to be the work of a well-informed contemporary writer. See Emden, *Oxford* (No. 533), iii. 1329–30.

2932   NEWBURGH, WILLIAM OF (d. *c.* 1198). Historia rerum Anglicarum (1066–1198, with a continuation to 1298). Ed. by Richard Howlett, *Chronicles of the reigns of Stephen, Henry II, and Richard I*, i. 1–408; ii. 409–583. Rolls Ser. Lond. 1884–5. Other editions: by William Silvius, Antwerp, 1567 (bad); in Commelin's *Scriptores* (No. 1095), pp. 353–496, Heidelberg, 1587 (bad); by John Picard, Paris, 1610, also 1632; by Thomas Hearne, 3 vols. Oxf. 1719; by H. C. Hamilton for English Hist. Soc. 2 vols. Lond. 1856. Extracts. Ed. by Pauli, in M.G.H., *SS*. xxvii. 221–48. Trans. by Joseph Stevenson, *Church historians* (No. 1123), iv, pt. ii, 297–672: The history of William of Newburgh. Lond. 1856. Extracts 1154–89 are translated in *Eng. Hist. Docs.* ii. 322–73.

A valuable authority for reign of Henry II, especially so for 1154–74; the *Historia* 'was begun before 1196 and completed soon after that date'. Although much of the matter was taken from other chroniclers, it was entirely recast. The author displayed considerable judgement and impartiality in dealing with men and events; with his critical attitude, he boldly assailed the fables of Geoffrey of Monmouth. He was the finest historian of his age.

We know little of the chronicler's personal life. It seems unlikely that he was that William of Newburgh, a layman, who married an heiress in the 1160s. In any case, he was by 1182 or 1183 almost certainly an Augustinian canon at Newburgh. See Kate Norgate in *D.N.B.* lxi. 360–3; H. E. Salter in *E.H.R.* xxii (1907), 510–14, and in *Osney Cartulary* (No. 6292), iv. 373; R. Jahncke, *Guilelmus Neubrigensis* (Bonn, 1912); Bruce Dickins, 'A Yorkshire Chronicler, William of Newburgh', in *Trans. Yorks. Dialect Soc.*, v, pt. 35 (1934), 15–76; and *Eng. Hist. Docs.* ii. 99–100 and 322: and the citations in C. N. L. Brooke's review in *E.H.R.* lxxvii (1962), 564, of John C. Gorman, *William of Newburgh's Explanatio Sacri Epithalamii in Matrem Sponsi* (Fribourg, 1960).

2933 NIGER, RALPH (d. *c.* 1205). Radulphi Nigri Chronica; the chronicles of Ralph Niger. Ed. by Robert Anstruther. Caxton Soc. Lond. 1851. Reprinted N.Y. 1967. Extracts. Ed. by Pauli, in M.G.H., *SS.* xxvii. 327–44.

The two Chronicles are:
Chronicon, from the creation to 1199, pp. 1–104; and *Chronicon secundum*, A.D. 1–*c.* 1171, with a continuation, 1162–78, pp. 105–91.

The first chronicle does not contain many notices relating to England; those in the second are taken from Geoffrey of Monmouth, William of Malmesbury, and Henry of Huntingdon. The work is interesting chiefly on account of the bitter invective against Henry II, who obliged Ralph to go into exile. The latter was an ardent supporter of Becket. See Reinhold Pauli, 'Die Chroniken des Radulphus Niger', in *Nachrichten der Gesellschaft der Wissenschaften zu Göttingen*, 1880, pp. 569–89; G. B. Flahiff, 'Ralph Niger, an introduction to his life and works', *Medieval Studies* (Toronto), ii (1940), 104–36; H. Kantorowicz and B. Smalley, 'An English theologian's view of Roman Law: Pepo, Irnerius, Ralph Niger', *Med. and Ren. Studies*, i (1943), 237–52.

2934 NOTES (BRIEF) OF OCCURRENCES UNDER HENRY VI AND EDWARD IV (1422–1462). Ed. by James Gairdner, *Three Fifteenth-Century Chronicles* (No. 2743), pp. 148–63.

Mainly Latin; written in the fifteenth century. Mere jottings till the middle of the fifteenth century, but of some value for the years 1459–62.

2935 NOTES ON AN ENGLISH CLUNIAC CHRONICLE. Ed. by H. M. Cam and E. F. Jacob. *E.H.R.* xliv (1929), 94–104.

Chronicle for priory of St. Andrews, Northampton, which runs A.D. 1–1339 and becomes of general interest about the middle of the thirteenth century. Here the annals 1258–68 are printed.

2936 OPUS CHRONICORUM (1259–96). Ed. by Henry T. Riley, *Johannis de Trokelowe et Henrici de Blaneford Chronica*, etc., pp. 3–59. Rolls Ser. Lond. 1866. Brief extracts. Ed. by Liebermann, in M.G.H., *SS.* xxviii. 520–1.

Written 1301–8, by a monk of St. Albans, it 'becomes more and more meagre in its details as it approaches his own times'. It was used by Rishanger and may have been compiled by him (No. 2948). See St. Albans' Chronicles (Nos. 2964 and 2976).

2937 ORDERICUS VITALIS (d. *c.* 1141). Historia ecclesiastica (A.D. 1–1141). Ed. by Auguste Le Prévost. Société de l'histoire de France. 5 vols. Paris. 1838–55. Other editions: in Duchesne's *Historiae Normannorum Scriptores* (No. 1096), pp. 319–925; Bouquet's *Recueil des Historiens* (No. 1090), ix. 10–18, x. 234–6, xi. 221–48, xii. 585–770. Extracts. Ed. by Pertz and Waitz, in M.G.H., *SS.* xx. 50–80, xxvi. 11–28. Trans. into French (by L. F. Du Bois) in F. P. G. Guizot's *Collection des Mémoires* (vols. xxv–xxviii): Histoire de Normandie. 4 vols. Paris. 1825–7. Trans. into English by Thomas Forester: *The ecclesiastical history of England and Normandy*. Bohn's Antiquarian Library. 4 vols. Lond. 1853–6.

This huge work of thirteen books was compiled during the years 1123–41. Though poorly organized, digressive, and imprecise in chronology, it is a valuable account of English and Norman history, secular and ecclesiastical, from 1066 to 1141. Ordericus's information regarding the period of the Norman conquest was derived from William of Jumièges and William of Poitiers; his account takes on additional value because he seems to have copied the lost section of William of Poitiers. For the subsequent period he depended rather heavily on oral testimony. He was born the son of a French clerk, in Shropshire in 1075; ten years later he went to Normandy, where he became a monk of St. Évroul.

See Hardy's *Catalogue* (No. 21), ii. 217–23; L. Delisle's introduction to the fifth volume of Le Prévost's edition; reprinted, with an additional note, in *Orderic Vital et l'abbaye de Saint-Évroul* (Alençon, 1912), pp. 1–78; Hans Wolters, *Ordericus Vitalis: ein Beitrag zur kluniazensischen Geschichtsschreibung* (Wiesbaden, 1955); *Eng. Hist. Docs.* ii. 98 and 281–9; R. R. Darlington, *Anglo-Norman Historians*, pp. 11–13; Davis, *King Stephen*, p. 147. A new edition with translation is expected in six volumes in Oxford Medieval Texts series, of which vol. ii for Books iii and iv, edited by Marjorie Chibnall, appeared in 1969, and vol. iii for Books v and vi in 1972.

2938 OTTERBOURNE, THOMAS (ascribed to) Chronica regum Angliae (from Brutus to 1420). Ed. by Thomas Hearne, *Duo Rerum Anglicarum Scriptores Veteres*, i. 3–283. Oxf. 1732.

This chronicle is drawn mainly from the St. Albans' Chronicles: it adds a few items from other sources. Hearne, apparently following Stow, attributed the chronicle to Thomas of Otterbourne, a Franciscan friar, but this is doubted by A. G. Little who finds that it 'bears no traces of having been the work of a Franciscan, and goes down to 1420, fully half of it being devoted to the reigns of Richard II, Henry IV and Henry V', whereas Friar Thomas Otterbourne flourished *c.* 1350. Little suggests that Otterbourne might possibly have been the author of the last part of the Lanercost Chronicle. See A. G. Little, 'The authorship of the Lanercost Chronicle', *E.H.R.* xxxi (1916), 269–79, and xxxii (1917), 28–9; reprinted in *Franciscan Papers* (No. 6024), 42–54; exp. pp. 51–2. See also Emden, *Oxford* (No. 533), ii. 1410.

2939 OXENEDES, OR OXNEAD, JOHN DE. Chronica (A.D. 449–1293). Ed. by Henry Ellis. Rolls Ser. Lond. 1859.

Written late in the thirteenth century. The author, a monk of St. Benet, Holme, Norfolk, made use of William of Malmesbury, Roger of Wendover, Matthew Paris, and other chroniclers, adding no new information except some facts of local interest concerning Norfolk, 1280–93.

2940 PAGE, JOHN. Poem on the siege of Rouen (1418). Ed. by James Gairdner, *Historical collections of a citizen of London in the fifteenth century*, pp. 1–46. Camden Soc. 1876. Excerpts in Myers, *E.H.D.* iv, no. 110. Another edition, by J. J. Conybeare and Frederic Madden, *Archaeologia*, xxi (1827), 43–78, and xxii (1829), 350–98. A more recent edition by H. Huscher, in *Kölner anglistische Arbeiten*, i (Leipzig, 1927).

An accurate account, written in English soon after the siege. See Kingsford, *Hist. Lit.*, pp. 116–18.

2941 PARIS, MATTHEW (d. 1259?). (*a*) Chronica majora (from the creation to 1259). Ed. by Henry R. Luard. 7 vols. Rolls Ser. Lond. 1872–83. (Vol. vi is Liber Additamentorum and vol. vii is an index.) Excerpts, A.D. 47–1259. Ed. by F. Liebermann in M.G.H., SS. xxviii. 107–389. Trans. into French by Alphonse Huillard-Bréholles: *La Grande chronique de Matthieu Paris*. 9 vols. Paris. 1840–1. Trans. into English by J. A. Giles, *Matthew Paris' English history (with a continuation) from 1235 to 1273*. Bohn's Antiquarian Library. 3 vols. Lond. 1852–4. For other editions, see Potthast, i. 778–9.

(*b*) Historia Anglorum sive historia minor (1066–1253). Ed. by Frederic Madden. 3 vols. Rolls Ser. Lond. 1866–9. Excerpts. Ed. by Liebermann, in M.G.H., SS. xxviii. 390–434.

Matthew Paris is commonly regarded as England's greatest medieval historian. His *Chronica majora* is essentially a revised copy, with additions especially after 1213, of

Roger of Wendover (No. 2979) to 1235, and an independent continuation thereof from 1235 to 1259. The *Historia Anglorum*, begun in 1250, is an abridgement, concentrating on English history, of the *Chronica Majora*, but it also includes some additional material for the period A.D. 1067–1253. The *Liber Additamentorum*, printed as vol. vi by Luard, is a collection of documents utilized by Matthew and forming a kind of appendix to the *Chronica Majora* and *Gesta Abbatum* (No. 6168). This collection may have reached its present form after Matthew's death.

Matthew Paris became a monk of St. Albans in 1217, and succeeded Roger Wendover as historiographer of that abbey in 1236. He drew his information from many documentary sources including papal bulls and royal letters and from conversations with eye-witnesses of the events narrated. Vaughan (see below) gives a list of his known friends and informants. His style is graphic; his view is broad; and his opinions are expressed with fervour. He condemns what he regarded as abuses of the court and church; he rebukes pope, king, nobles, and clergy, when he deems them worthy of blame. Matthew was a man of many interests and attainments. See his *Gesta Abbatum* (No. 6168); for his maps, Nos. 595, 596. It seems likely that he was also the author of *Abbreviatio Chronicorum* (No. 2745) and *Flores Historiarum* (No. 2871) up to the year 1249. For these ascriptions see Vaughan, pp. 37–41. His hagiographical works are described in Vaughan, chap. ix, and for those on Stephen Langton and on Edmund of Abingdon, see Nos. 5634, 5626.

In addition to Luard's and Liebermann's prefaces, consult Richard Vaughan, *Matthew Paris* (Cambr. 1958); and F. M. Powicke's review thereof in *E.H.R.* lxxiv (1959), 482–5; F. M. Powicke, 'The compilation of the Chronica Majora of Matthew Paris', *P.B.A.* xxx (1944), 147–60; V. H. Galbraith, 'Roger Wendover and Matthew Paris' (The David Murray Lecture), *Glasgow Univ. Pubns.* lxi (Glasgow, 1944).

2942 PETERBOROUGH, BENEDICT OF. See No. 2879.

2943 POITIERS, GUILLAUME DE (*fl. c.* 1075). Histoire de Guillaume le Conquérant. Ed. and trans. (into French) by Raymonde Foreville. Paris. 1952. Gesta Willelmi ducis Normannorum et regis Angliae (1035–67). Ed. by André Duchesne, *Historiae Normannorum Scriptores* (No. 1096), pp. 178–213. Reprinted by Francis Maseres, *Historiae Anglicanae Selecta Monumenta* (No. 1111), pp. 37–167. Other editions: in Giles's *Scriptores* (No. 2741), pp. 77–159; and Migne's *Patrologia*, cxlix. 1217–70. Trans. into French in F. P. G. Guizot's *Collection des Mémoires*, xxix, 319–439: Vie de Guillaume le Conquérant. Paris. 1826.

The unique and incomplete MS. which Duchesne used and published has vanished; but some of the missing conclusion seems to have been copied by Ordericus (No. 2937) and thus preserved. Although the work is a panegyric, 'an epic' as Mlle Foreville calls it, of William the Conqueror, its record of facts is basically accurate and its account of the battle of Hastings the best that a contemporary has given us. Guillaume de Poitiers, a Norman, who had made a long sojourn in Poitiers, was Archdeacon of Lisieux and chaplain of William the Conqueror. He wrote his history about 1073–4; for its relationship with Guillaume de Jumièges's *Gesta*, see No. 2908 above. Consult the introduction and footnotes of Mlle Foreville's edition; and *Eng. Hist. Docs.* ii. 217–31.

2944 READING, JOHN OF (d. 1368–9). Chronica Johannis de Reading et anonymi Cantuariensis 1346–1367. Ed. by James Tait. Manchester. 1914.

Tait's valuable introduction traces the relationship of John of Reading's *Chronicle* to *Flores Historiarum* (No. 2871) and its use as a source for later compilations. John's continuation of the *Flores* for the period 1346–67 lacks literary skill and critical discrimination; although he is credulous and inaccurate for the earlier years, he is more careful and precise for the 1360s. Similarly the *Anonymous Canterbury Chronicle*

1346–67 shows more independence as it approaches its terminus. The latter chronicle used to be wrongly ascribed to Stephen Birchington.

2945 REDMAN, ROBERT. Henrici Quinti historia (1413–22). Ed. by C. A. Cole, *Memorials of Henry V*, pp. 1–59. Rolls Ser. Lond. 1858.

Of no historical value, this history was written in praise of Henry V, probably between 1574 and 1578. On the author see R. R. Reid, 'The date and authorship of Redmayne's "Life of Henry V"', *E.H.R.* xxx (1915), 691–8.

2946 RIEVAULX, AILRED OF. Relatio de standardo (Nos. 2734, 6634–5).

2947 RIGORD (d. *c.* 1209). Gesta Philippi Augusti (1179–1208). Ed. by H. F. Delaborde, Œuvres de Rigord et de Guillaume le Breton, i. 1–167. Société de l'histoire de France. 2 vols. Paris. 1882–5. Extracts. Ed. by Auguste Molinier, in M.G.H., *SS.* xxvi. 288–94. Trans. into French in F. P. G. Guizot's *Collection des Mémoires*, ix. 1–179: Vie de Philippe-Auguste. Paris. 1825.

Rigord, a monk of St. Denis, began his career as a physician of Languedoc. His work was abridged, and continued to 1223, by William of Armorica, or Guillaume le Breton, chaplain of Philip Augustus (d. *c.* 1226), in his *Gesta Philippi Augusti* and in his great poem entitled *Philippide*, both of which are printed in Delaborde's edition and extracts from both are edited by A. Molinier and others in M.G.H., *SS.* xxvi (1882), 295–389, and both of which are translated into French in Guizot's *Collection*, ix (1825), 183–351, and vol. x. The works of Rigord and Guillaume le Breton are valuable for the relations to France of Henry II, Richard I, and John. See Alexander Cartellieri, *Philipp II August* (Leipzig, 1899–1910), i, Beilagen, pp. 31–5. For other editions, etc., see Potthast, i. 552 and ii. 973; and Molinier, *Sources*, iii, nos. 2211–12.

2948 RISHANGER, WILLIAM (d. after 1312). Willelmi Rishanger . . . chronica et annales, regnantibus Henrico tertio et Edwardo primo. Ed. by Henry T. Riley. Rolls Ser. Lond. 1865. Chronicon Willelmi de Rishanger: de duobus bellis apud Lewes et Evesham commissis. Ed. by Henry T. Riley in Walsingham's *Ypodigma Neustriae* (No. 2976), pp. 491–565; another edition by James O. Halliwell, *The chronicle of William de Rishanger of the barons' war*. Camden Soc. Lond. 1840. Extracts from Rishanger's work are edited by Liebermann in M.G.H., *SS.* xxviii. 512–19.

The edition of the *chronica et annales* includes (*a*) pp. 1–230, *Chronica* (1259–1306), a continuation of Matthew Paris, compiled at St. Albans by an unknown author after the middle of the fourteenth century; it is primarily based on the chronicle of Nicholas Trevet interlarded with extracts of works ascribed to Rishanger. For the period 1272 to 1307 the text is almost identical with Walsingham's *Historia Anglicana* (No. 2976). The *Chronica* has no original, independent value. (*b*) pp. 233–368, *Annales regni Scotiae* (1291–2), a collection of material on the succession to Scotland compiled at St. Albans (see No. 2770). (*c*) pp. 371–408, *Annales Angliae et Scotiae* (1292–1300) (see No. 2752). (*d*) pp. 411–33, *Gesta Edwardi Primi* (1297–1307), compiled soon after 1307 probably by Rishanger; (*e*) Three fragments of *Annales regis Edwardi primi*, pp. 437–99. They are probably Rishanger's work.

The *Chronicon de duobus bellis* is largely a copy of *Flores Historiarum* (No. 2871) for the period 1259–65, whose importance is indicated under *Flores*. For other works probably written by Rishanger see *Opus chronicorum* (No. 2936) and John de Trokelowe (No. 2964). The above summary is based on Galbraith, *The St. Albans Chronicle* (No. 2731), pp. xxvii–xxxvi.

2949 ROUEN, ÉTIENNE DE (d. *c.* 1170). Stephani Rothomagensis monachi Beccensis poema cui titulus 'Draco Normannicus'. Ed. by Richard Howlett,

Chronicles of the reigns of Stephen, Henry II, and Richard I, ii. 585–781. Rolls Ser. Lond. 1885. Other editions: by Angelo Mai, in *Appendix ad Opera edita ab Angelo Maio*, pp. 20–65. Rome. 1871; by Henri Omont, *Le Dragon Normand et autres poèmes d'Étienne de Rouen*, pp. 1–167. Société de l'histoire de Normandie. Rouen. 1884. A large part of it is also printed in M.G.H., *SS.* xxvi. 153–94.

Deals with Henry II and his parents, King Stephen, William the Conqueror, Hugh Capet, Charlemagne, the death of the Empress Maud, and other topics, to 1169. Large portions of the work are derived from Dudo of St. Quentin and William of Jumièges; but it furnishes some new facts for the history of the years 1153–69. Draco, in the title of the poem, means 'standard'. See Charles Fierville, 'Étienne de Rouen', in *Bulletin de la Société des Antiquaires de Normandie* (Caen, 1878), viii. 54–78, 421–42.

2950 ROUS, JOHN (d. 1491). Historia regum Angliae (from the creation to 1485). Ed. by Thomas Hearne. Oxf. 1716; 2nd edn. 1745.

Written between 1485 and 1491, the *Historia* was dedicated to Henry VII. Its account down to 1483 is meagre, but becomes somewhat fuller for the reign of Richard III and is censorious of that king. Rous eloquently denounces the decline of Christian charity and the destruction of villages for sheep-folds. He was a native of Warwickshire and a chantry-priest at Guy's Cliff, a foundation of the Earl of Warwick.

Rous was also responsible for the production of two Warwick Rolls of Arms, one in English and one in Latin. These rolls, each about two feet in length, are beautifully illustrated with line-drawn portraits and coats-of-arms of the holders of the earldom of Warwick from time immemorial to 1491. The English version, done before 1485, is Yorkist in outlook and commemorates the Beauchamps and Nevilles; the Latin version, a revision done after 1485, pays tribute to Henry VII. A lithographic facsimile of the English roll with a transcript of the text by Lambert Larking and an introduction by William Courthope was published by H. G. Bohn (Lond. 1859). For the English roll, see C. E. Wright in *Brit. Mus. Quart.* xx (1956), 77–81; for the Latin roll, see A. G. B. Russell in *Burlington Magazine*, xxx (1917), 23–31. For both rolls, see A. R. Wagner, *A Catalogue of English Mediaeval Rolls of Arms* (No. 499), pp. 116–20. For Rous, see T. D. Kendrick, *British Antiquity* (Lond. 1950), pp. 19–29; and Emden, *Oxford* (No. 534), iii. 1596–7. Both Russell and Kendrick print illustrations from the Latin version.

2951 RUDBORNE, THOMAS (*fl.* 1460). Historia major de fundatione et successione ecclesiae Wintoniensis (A.D. 164–1138). Ed. by Henry Wharton, *Anglia Sacra* (No. 1126), i. 177–286. Lond. 1691.

Written about 1454. Deals with the general history of England, as well as with the affairs of the see of Winchester. Rudborne was a monk of St. Swithun's, Winchester. The *Historia Minor*, which seems to have been a summary of the *Historia Major*, is not now extant.

2952 SAINTE-MAURE, BENOÎT DE (d. after 1189). Chronique des ducs de Normandie (from the creation to 1135). Ed. by Carin Fahlin. Bibliotheca Eckmaniana. 2 vols. Uppsala. 1951–4. Vol. iii (Glossary). Ed. by Östen Söder-gård. Uppsala. 1967. Other edition. Ed. by Francisque Michel. *Documents inédits.* 3 vols. Paris. 1836–44.

A French poem, of no great historical value, written about 1180 at the request of Henry II. Its chief authorities are Dudo of St. Quentin and William of Jumièges. Benoît was a Norman who was attached to the court of Henry II. See Bossuat (No. 43), i. 350, and Supplement, p. 79.

2953 SILGRAVE (or SULGRAVE), HENRY DE. Chronicon Henrici de Silegrave: a chronicle of English history, from the earliest period to 1274. Ed. by C. Hook. Caxton Soc. Lond. 1849. Reprinted N.Y. 1966.

> To 1066 it is taken mainly from William of Malmesbury. Some of the brief notices of the barons' war, 1263–5, are useful. Nothing is known concerning the author. Perhaps he was a monk of St. Martin's, Dover. See Russell, *Writers* (No. 541), p. 47.

2954 SONG OF DERMOT AND THE EARL, an old French poem (to about 1175, with a translation). Ed. by G. H. Orpen. Oxf. 1892. Another edition, by Francisque Michel: Anglo-Norman poem of the conquest of Ireland by Henry II. Lond. 1837.

> In its present form, it was probably composed about 1225. Perhaps it was based on a chronicle furnished or written by Morice Regan, an eye-witness of much that the song narrates on his authority; but it is difficult to determine his share in the authorship of the work. Regan was secretary of Dermot MacMurrough, King of Leinster. The poem has much historical value. It is concerned mainly with the adventures of Dermot and his son-in-law Strongbow, Earl of Pembroke (d. 1176). See J. H. Round, *Commune of London* (Westminster, 1899), ch. vii; F. Liebermann, *E.H.R.* viii (1893), 129–33; and J. F. O'Doherty, 'Historical criticism of the Song of Dermot and the Earl', *Irish Hist. Stud.* i (1938), 4–20; 294–6.

2955 SPECULUM REGIS EDWARDI III. Ed. by Joseph Moisant, De Speculo Regis Edwardi III seu tractatu quem de mala regni administratione conscripsit Simon Islip, cum utraque ejusdem recensione manuscripta nunc primum edita. Paris. 1891.

> The two recensions of the *Speculum* are printed in full on pp. 81–169. This tract is an ardent remonstrance addressed to young Edward III against purveyance and spoliation of the church by the king's household. It may have been written between 1330 and 1333, surely not by Simon Islip, but possibly by Simon Meopham, Archbishop of Canterbury. See James Tait, 'On the date and authorship of the *Speculum Regis Edwardi*', *E.H.R.* xvi (1901), 110–15; and Emden, *Oxford* (No. 533), p. 1437. However, Leonard E. Boyle is convinced that the author of the *Speculum* was William of Pagula, who is generally accepted as the author of *Epistola ad Regem Edwardum III*. Refer to L. E. Boyle, 'William of Pagula and the *Speculum Regis Edwardi III*', *Mediaeval Stud.* xxxii (1970), 329–36.

2956 SPROTT, THOMAS (*fl.* 1272). Chronica (from the creation to 1377). Ed. by Thomas Hearne. Oxf. 1719. Thomas Sprott's Chronicle of profane and sacred history (from the creation to 1307). Trans. by William Bell, accompanied by a facsimile of the codex (in a separate roll). Liverpool. 1851.

> These are two distinct chronicles, of little value, which have erroneously been attributed to Sprott. He was a monk of St. Augustine's, Canterbury, who wrote a history of the abbots of that monastery from 596 to 1272. This work, which was used by Thorne has not been edited. See Russell, *Writers* (No. 541), p. 170.

2957 STONE, JOHN. Chronicle (1415–71). Ed. by W. G. Searle. Cambridge Antiq. Soc. Cambr. etc. 1902.

> Stone was a monk of Christ Church, Canterbury, 1415–71. His work, though chiefly concerned with the history of Christ Church, has many notices of battles and political events in the Wars of the Roses.

2957A STOW, JOHN. Annales of England . . . collected out of the most autenticall authors, records and other monuments of antiquitie. . . . Lond. 1605.

> The first edition was published in 1580 as *The chronicles of England from Brute unto the present yeare of Christ 1580.* The several editions are listed in Read's *Tudor bibliography* (No. 32), no. 317. John Stow (1525–1605) was a diligent researcher among public records as well as a reader of chronicles; from both he copied carefully. He wrote a rather dry, stolid prose directly from his sources. His fame rests more on his remarkable topographical *Survey of London* than on his *Annales.* For appreciations of his contributions, turn to the indexes under 'Stow' in Kingsford's *Hist. Lit.* and McKisack's *Medieval History in the Tudor Age.*

2958 TAYSTER, or TAXTER, JOHN DE (d. after 1265). Cronica abbreviata (from the creation to 1265). Ed. by Benjamin Thorpe in *Florentii Wigorniensis Chronicon*, ii. 136–96. Eng. Hist. Soc. Lond. 1849. A better text of the years 1258–62. Ed. by H. R. Luard, *Bartholomaei Cotton Historia Anglicana*, pp. 137–40. Rolls Ser. Lond. 1859. Extracts from Tayster and from two continuations to 1300. Ed. by Liebermann, M.G.H., *SS.* xxviii. 584–98.

> Tayster, a monk of Bury St. Edmunds, was a partisan of Simon de Montfort. Thorpe edits only the part from 1152 to 1265. The entries for the years 1258–65 seem to be original. For the continuations from 1265 to 1295 and from 1296 to 1301, see Bury St. Edmunds (No. 2819).

2959 THORNE, WILLIAM (*fl.* 1397). Chronica de rebus gestis abbatum S. Augustini Cantuariae (A.D. 578–1397). Ed. by Roger Twysden, *Scriptores* (No. 1124), pp. 1753–2202. Lond. 1652. Rendered into English by A. H. Davis. Oxf. 1934.

> Although basically a history of St. Augustine's Abbey, this work deals with the general history of England. To 1228 it is derived mainly from Sprott's *Chronicle* (No. 2956). It includes transcripts of documents. Thorne was a monk of St. Augustine's, Canterbury.

2960 TIGERNACH (d. 1088). Annals of Ireland to 1088, with a continuation to 1178. See No. 2170.

2961 TILBURY, GERVASE OF (d. *c.* 1228). Otia imperialia. Ed. by G. G. Leibnitz. *Scriptores Rerum Brunsvicensium*, 1. 881–1004; ii. 751–84. Hanover. 1707–10. Extracts. Ed. by Joseph Stevenson, *Radulphi de Coggeshall Chronicon*, pp. 419–49, Rolls Ser. Lond. 1875; and by R. Pauli, in M.G.H., *SS.* xxvii. 359–94.

> Written about 1212 for the recreation of the emperor Otto IV, it contains odds and ends about natural history, lore, politics, etc., and an interesting account of the kings of England from 1066 to 1199. Gervase, a native of Tilbury in Essex, entered the service of Otto IV, who made him marshal of the kingdom of Arles. He travelled widely from England to Sicily. See Reinhold Pauli, 'Gervasius von Tilbury', *Nachrichten der Gesellschaft der Wissenschaften zu Göttingen* (1882), pp. 312–32; and especially H. G. Richardson, 'Gervase of Tilbury', *History*, xlvi (1961), 102–14; J. G. Caldwell, 'Gervase of Tilbury's addenda to Otia imperialia', *Mediaeval Stud.* (Toronto), xxiv (1962), 95–126; and Caldwell on Gervase's MSS. in *Scriptorium*, xi (1957), 87–98; xvi (1962), 28–45 and 246–74.

2962 TORIGNI, ROBERT OF, or ROBERT DE MONTE (d. 1186). Chronique (A.D. 94–1186). Ed. by Léopold Delisle. Société de l'histoire de Normandie. 2 vols. Rouen. 1872–3. *The chronicle of Robert of Torigni (Chronica Roberti de Torigneio).* Ed. by Richard Howlett, *Chronicles of the reigns of Stephen,*

Henry II, and Richard I, iv. 3–315. Rolls Ser. Lond. 1889. Ed. by L. C. Beth-mann, in M.G.H., *SS*. vi. 475–535; reprinted in Migne's *Patrologia*, clx. 411–546. Trans. by Joseph Stevenson, *Church historians* (No. 1123), vol. iv, pt. ii: 'The chronicles of Robert de Monte'.

Written from time to time, A.D. 1150–86; the first recension seems to have been completed in 1157. To 1100 the work is borrowed mainly from Sigebert of Gembloux. The author also uses Henry of Huntingdon, Eadmer, William of Jumièges, etc. The chronicle is valuable for the period from 1150 and for the internal affairs of England in 1153–4, and for the foreign policy of Henry II. Robert of Torigni also wrote a history of Henry I (No. 2908). He became prior of Bec about 1149, and was elected abbot of Mont-Saint-Michel in 1154. He visited England in 1157 and 1175. For other editions of his chronicle, besides those named above, see Howlett's preface, pp. lxv–lxix; and Potthast, ii. 977. For the chronicle of Sigebert of Gembloux (d. 1112), which Robert of Torigni continued, see Potthast, ii. 1016–17; Hardy, *Catalogue of Materials* (No. 21), ii. 116–18; and Molinier, *Sources*, ii, no. 2193.

2963 **TREVET, NICHOLAS** (*fl.* 1320). Annales sex regum Angliae, 1135–1307. Ed. by Thomas Hog. Eng. Hist. Soc. Lond. 1845. Other editions: in Luc d'Achery's *Spicilegium*, viii (1668), 411–728 (new edn. iii (1723), 143–231); by Anthony Hall, Oxf. 1719; and *Nicolai Triveti annalium continuatio* (1307–18). Ed. by Anthony Hall. Oxf. 1722.

Trevet was a well-known Dominican theologian who taught at Oxford. In addition to several theological works and commentaries on Seneca, Livy, and possibly other classical writers, Trevet composed three histories: (*a*) the *Annales* mentioned above, (*b*) *Chronicles* in French, and (*c*) a Latin translation of *Chronicles*. Only the *Annales* have been printed; the sources which he used are cited by A. G. Little (see below). The continuation, though brief, is said to contain several notices found nowhere else; with it is printed Adam Murimuth's chronicle (No. 2931). For a summary of Trevet's life and work, with bibliography, see Emden, *Oxford* (No. 533), pp. 1902–4; and for the *Annales*, see A. G. Little, 'Chronicles of the mendicant friars', *Franciscan Papers*, etc. (No. 6024), 38–40; reprinted from his *Franciscan Essays*, vol. ii; also B. Smalley, *Friars and Antiquity* (No. 6924), pp. 58–65, and index.

2964 **TROKELOWE, JOHN OF** (*fl.* 1330). Annales (1307–26). Ed. by Henry T. Riley, Johannis de Trokelowe et Henrici de Blaneforde Chronica et Annales, 61–127. Rolls Ser. Lond. 1866. Another edition, by Thomas Hearne. Oxf. 1729.

Trokelowe may have been the compiler of the *Annales* or he may have been merely the scribe of a work, compiled by Rishanger. See Galbraith, *The St. Albans Chronicle* (No. 2731), pp. xxx–xxxi. In either case, the work is valuable for the reign of Edward II and formed the basis of Walsingham's account of the years 1307–23.

2965 **TYNEMOUTH, JOHN OF** (d. 1348). Historia Aurea, in Hamilton's edition of *Chronicon . . . Hemingburgh* (Guisborough No. 2888), ii. 297–426.

Historia Aurea is an enormous compilation of twenty-three books, drawn in large measure from Higden's *Polychronicon* to 1327. Hamilton prints only a version for the years 1327–46. Galbraith prints extracts for the years 1313, 1317, 1318, 1319, 1326, 1346, and 1347. V. H. Galbraith, 'Extracts from the Historia Aurea and a French Brut (1317–47)', *E.H.R.* xliii (1928), 203–17. Horstman in *Nova Legenda Anglie* (Oxf. 1901), p. xlix, maintained that Tynemouth's *Chronicle* for 1327–47 continued the St. Albans series after Henry of Blaneford. But Galbraith in *Poole essays* (No. 1448) shows that it is highly unlikely. John of Tynemouth was the author of the *Sanctilogium* (Nos. 1158, 2287), much of which he included in *Historia Aurea*.

2966 USK, ADAM OF (d. 1430). Chronicon, 1377–1404. Ed. with trans. by
E. M. Thompson. Royal Soc. of Literature. Lond. 1876. 2nd edn. (1377–1421).
1904.

Adam of Usk appended his chronicle to a copy of Higden's *Polychronicon* (No. 2895).
The last section covering 1404–21 was discovered in 1885 after Thompson had printed
the first edition. It is particularly valuable for the period 1397–1401. The author, a
Welshman, was a distinguished ecclesiastical lawyer. He sat on the commission for the
deposition of Richard II; but losing favour with Henry IV, he went in 1402 to Rome,
where he became an auditor in the Sacra Romana Rota until 1406. Later he returned to
England. For the life see Emden, *Oxford* (No. 533), pp. 1937–8; and *Dict. Welsh Biog.*
(No. 542), pp. 2–3.

2967 VENETTE, JEAN DE (d. *c.* 1370). Chronique, 1340–68. Ed. by H.
Géraud, *Chronique latine de Guillaume de Nangis*, ii. 179–378. Société de l'histoire
de France. Paris. 1843. J. Birdsall and R. A. Newhall, *The Chronicle of Jean de
Venette*. Trans. by J. Birdsall, and edited with an introduction and notes by
R. A. Newhall. Columbia Univ. Records of Civilization. N.Y. 1953.

This anonymous chronicle, continuing Guillaume de Nangis, is the work of Jean de
Venette, prior of the Carmelite convent in Paris. See Newhall's important introduction,
cited above; and Molinier, *Sources*, iv, no. 3098.

2968 VERGIL, POLYDORE (d. 1555). Anglicae historiae libri xxvii (from
earliest times to 1538). Leyden. 1651. Other editions, Basle. 1555, 1556, and
1570. Editions of books i–xxvi to 1509; Basle. 1534, 1546; 2 vols., Ghent. 1556–7;
2 vols., Douai. 1603. *Three books of Polydore Vergil's English history*, comprising
the reigns of Henry VI, Edward IV, and Richard III (1422–85, from a translation
of Henry VIII's time). Ed. by Henry Ellis. Camden Soc. xxix (1844). *Polydore
Vergil's English history*, from an early translation. Vol. i containing the first eight
books, comprising the period prior to the Norman conquest. Ed. by Henry Ellis.
Camden Soc. xxxvi (1846). *The Anglica Historia of Polydore Vergil* A.D. 1485–
1537. Ed. with a translation by Denys Hay. Camden Soc. 3rd Ser. lxxiv (1950).

A long Latin chronicle drawn from many sources, it begins to have considerable
independent importance after about 1450 and is of primary value for the reign of Henry
VII. Vergil weighed the statements of his predecessors, discounted fables, and repudi-
ated some accepted traditions. Vergil, an Italian, came to England in 1502 as deputy-
collector of papal revenues; and save for 'brief intervals abroad, Vergil spent nearly
the whole of his later life in England'. For his life, his works and sources, and his
significance as an historian, see the introduction to Hay's edition; Kingsford, *Hist.
Lit.* 254–9; Denys Hay, *Polydore Vergil: Renaissance historian and man of letters* (Oxf.
1952). Idem, in *Jour. Warburg and Courtauld Institute*, xii (1949), 132–51. F. A. Gasquet,
'Some materials for a new edition of Polydore Vergil's History', *T.R.H.S.*, New Ser.
xvi (1902), 1–17.

2969 VERSUS RHYTHMICI DE HENRICO QUINTO. Ed. by C. A. Cole,
Memorials of Henry V, pp. 61–75. Rolls Ser. Lond. 1858.

A eulogy of the character of Henry V, to whose household the writer may have belonged.

2970 VIGEOIS, GEOFFREY OF (*fl.* 1184). Chronica Gaufridi prioris
Vosiensis coenobii (A.D. 996–1184). Ed. by Philippe Labbe, *Nova Bibliotheca*, ii.
279–342. Paris. 1657. Extracts. Ed. by Holder-Egger, in M.G.H., *SS.* xxvi.
198–203.

Completed in 1184. Valuable for the continental policy of Henry II. The author was prior of the abbey of Vigeois. See François Arbellot, *Étude historique et bibliographique sur Geoffroy de Vigeois* (Limoges, etc., 1888).

2971 VITA EDWARDI II (1307–48). Ed. by William Stubbs, *Chronicles of the reigns of Edward I and Edward II*, ii. 155–294. Rolls Ser. Lond. 1883. Another edition, by Thomas Hearne, *Johannis de Trokelowe Annales*, pp. 93–250. Oxf. 1729. Ed. and trans. from the Latin with introduction and notes by N. Denholm-Young (Nelson's Medieval Texts). Lond., Edin., etc. 1957.

A memoir (1307–26) valuable for the reign of Edward II, strong in the characterizations of the principal political participants and probably written in 1325–6 by a knowledgeable person. It is entirely independent of any known extant chronicle; but it survives in only a transcript made by Hearne from a manuscript now lost. Hearne attributed it on insufficient grounds to a monk of Malmesbury. Its author was almost certainly not a monk. Denholm-Young presents plausible inferences for attributing the work to John Walwyn, canon of Hereford and St. Paul's (d. 1326). See the introduction to his edition and his article, 'The authorship of Vita Edwardi Secundi', *E.H.R.* lxxi (1956), 189–211. Subsequently Denholm-Young suggested that the author 'may well have been a corrodar of the abbey of Malmesbury' (*Country Gentry* (No. 473), p. 39). The continuation in the Hearne transcript from 1326 to 1348 is merely a series of extracts from Higden's *Polychronicon*. For another contemporary account of the last years of Edward II, see *Lettre de Manuel de Fiesque concernant les dernières années d'Édouard II*, ed. by A. C. Germain (Montpellier, 1878). Manuel held several important benefices in England from about 1328, became Bishop of Vercelli in 1343, and died in 1348. The letter, which is addressed to Edward III, is not dated.

2972 VITA ET GESTA HENRICI QUINTI. Ed. by Thomas Hearne. Oxf. 1727.

This work was, without sufficient reason, attributed by Hearne to Elmham; but Wylie and Kingsford hold that it was written by an unknown author, not Elmham. It is divisible into two sections: the first ninety-one chapters closely resemble Titus Livy (No. 2919); and the following thirty-eight chapters are derived for the most part from other sources. Probably written in 1446, it is much longer than the work of Titus Livy; but a few years later, an abbreviated version appeared. It is this abbreviated version which Williams appended to his edition of the *Gesta* (No. 2877). See Kingsford, *Hist. Lit.*, pp. 56–63; and Wylie, *E.H.R.* xxiv (1909), 84–9.

2973 VOYAGE DE NICOLAS DE BOSC évêque de Bayeux pour negocier la paix entre les couronnes de France et d'Angleterre (1381), in *Voyage Littéraire de Deux Religieux Bénédictins* (by Edmond Martène and Ursin Durand), ii. 307–60. Paris. 1724. Also printed in Kervyn de Lettenhove's edition of Froissart's works, xxiii. 354–75. Brussels. 1876.

Written in French. Nicholas was accompanied on his mission by Guillaume de Lestrange, Archbishop of Rouen.

2974 WACE (d. *c.* 1175). (*a*) Le roman de Brut. Ed. by Ivor Arnold. Société des Anciens Textes Français. 2 vols. Paris. 1938–40. Also *La Partie arthurienne du Roman de Wace*. Ed. by Ivor Arnold and M. Pelan. Strasbourg. 1962. Another edition by A. J. V. Le Roux de Lincy. 2 vols. Rouen. 1836–8. Partial translation in Arthurian chronicles represented by Wace and Layamon: introduction by Lucy A. Paton. Everyman's Library. Lond. and N.Y. 1912.

(*b*) *Le Roman de Rou et des ducs de Normandie* (from Rollo to 1106). Ed. by Frédéric Pluquet. 2 vols. and Supplement. Rouen. 1827–9. Another edition (more nearly complete, but not good) by Hugo Andresen. 2 vols. Heilbronn. 1877–9.

Master Wace: his chronicle of the Norman conquest from the Roman de Rou. Trans. by Edgar Taylor. Lond. 1837.

These are two French metrical chronicles. (*a*) The *Roman de Brut*, completed in 1155, is partly a translation and partly a paraphrase of Geoffrey of Monmouth's work, and served as a basis of Layamon's *Brut* (No. 2914). On this see Bossuat (No. 43), i. 348–9, and Supplement, p. 78; Arnold's introduction; and Tatlock's *Legendary History* (No. 2166), chap. xxii; Margaret E. Houck, *Sources of the Roman de Brut of Wace* (Berkeley, 1941); Urban T. Holmes, 'Norman literature and Wace', in *Medieval Secular Literature: four essays*, edited by William Matthews (Berkeley, 1965), pp. 46–67; and Pierre Gallais, 'La variant version de *l'Historia Regum Britanniae* et le *Brut* de Wace', *Romania*, lxxxvii (1966), 1–32.

(*b*) Wace's *Roman de Rou* (Rollo), written 1160–74, is of much more historical value. His chief sources were Dudo of St. Quentin and William of Jumièges; probably he also used Malmesbury's *Gesta regum*. On this see Bossuat, i. 349 and Supplement, pp. 78–9; Hardy, *Catalogue* (No. 21), ii. 428–37; Molinier, *Sources*, ii, no. 1975; J. H. Round, 'Wace and his authorities', in his *Feudal England*, pp. 409–18; C. H. Haskins, 'Materials for the reign of Robert I of Normandy', *E.H.R.* xxxi (1916), 260–3; and A. J. Holden, 'L'Authenticité des premières parties du Roman de Rou', *Romania*, lxxv (1954), 22–53, and the studies cited there.

2975 WALLINGFORD, JOHN OF (d. 1258), the chronicle attributed to John of Wallingford. Ed. by Richard Vaughan. Camden Soc. 3rd Ser. xc: *Camden miscellany*, xxi (1958). Poorly edited in Thomas Gale, *Scriptores Quindecim* (No. 1100), pp. 525–50. Trans. by J. Stevenson, *Church historians* (No. 1123), ii, pt. ii. 521–64: 'The chronicles of John Wallingford A.D. 449–1035'. Lond. 1854. See No. 2173.

In addition to the anonymous chronicle, John of Wallingford's book contains an abridgement of Matthew Paris, which almost certainly was made by John himself. Excerpts 1201–58 of this compilation are edited by Liebermann in M.G.H., *SS.* xxviii. 505–11.

2976 WALSINGHAM, THOMAS (d. *c.* 1422).

(*a*) Historia Anglicana (1272–1422). Ed. by Henry T. Riley. Rolls Ser. 2 vols. Lond. 1863–4. Other editions, with the title *Historia Brevis ab Edwardo I ad Henricum V*: (by Matthew Parker), Lond. 1574; in Camden, *Anglica . . . Scripta* (No. 1092), 37–408.

(*b*) Chronicon Angliae, 1328–88, auctore monacho quodam Sancti Albani. Ed. by E. M. Thompson. Rolls Ser. Lond. 1874. The portion for 1376–7 is translated in *Archaeologia*, xxii (1829), 212–84.

(*c*) Annales Ricardi Secundi et Henrici Quarti regum Angliae (1392–1406). Ed. by H. T. Riley, *Johannis de Trokelowe, Annales* (No. 2964 above), 153–420.

(*d*) The St. Albans chronicle, 1406–20. Edited from Bodley MS. 462, by V. H. Galbraith. Oxf. 1937. (This edition is prefaced by a notable commentary on 'The descent of the St. Albans chronicle, 1259–1422'.)

(*e*) Ypodigma Neustriae. Ed. by H. T. Riley. Rolls Ser. Lond. 1876. Other editions: (by Matthew Parker) Lond. 1574; in Camden's *Anglica . . . Scripta*, 409–592. This is an epitome of English history from 911 to 1419—'the final attempt at compression'—the shortest of short histories (Galbraith).

All of the above works, as well as *Gesta Abbatum S. Albani* (No. 6168) and *Liber Benefactorum*, are now with considerable probability ascribed to Walsingham. Riley believed that the *Annales* were not written by Walsingham, and Thompson ascribed only portions of the *chronicon* to him. However, V. H. Galbraith supplies reasons for accepting the authorship of Walsingham for both in 'Thomas Walsingham and the Saint Albans chronicle 1272–1422', *E.H.R.* xlvii (1932), 12–30, and in his full introduction to (*d*) above. Galbraith holds that Walsingham wrote a series comprising the *Chronica maiora* and an abbreviation thereof, and revisions of both the *Chronica maiora* and the abbreviation. Walsingham's contemporaneous writings begin with 1376; the sections of *chronica majora* are printed for 1376–82 in (*b*) *Chronicon Angliae*, pp. 68–354; for 1382–92 in (*a*) *Historia Anglicana*, ii. 70–211; for 1392–1406 in (*c*) *Annales*, pp. 155–420; and for 1406–20 in (*d*) *St. Albans Chronicle*. The abbreviation is printed 1376–88 in (*b*) *Chronicon*; for 1392–1405 and 1393–1422 in (*a*) *Historia*.

Walsingham was precentor and 'scriptorarius' of the Abbey of St. Albans. In 1394 he became prior of Wymondham but returned to St. Albans in 1397. His contemporary historical writing is original and valuable; indeed in Galbraith's opinion Walsingham wrote 'the only strictly contemporary chronicles for the period 1399–1422'. In the earlier years, he was bitter against John of Gaunt and the Lancastrians; but in the 1390s he modified his views about Gaunt and eventually wrote favourably of the house of Lancaster. In the later years of his life Walsingham became known as a student of the classics.

2977   WARKWORTH, JOHN (d. 1500). A chronicle of the first thirteen years of the reign of Edward IV (1461–74). Ed. by James O. Halliwell. Camden Soc. 1st Ser. x (1839), pp. 1–27. Reprinted, with modernized orthography, in *Chronicles of the White Rose of York* (No. 2735), pp. 97–142. Lond. 1845.

A short but valuable historical fragment, written in English, contemporaneously with the events narrated, in continuation of a copy of Caxton's *Chronicle*. It was bequeathed by Warkworth to Peterhouse, Cambridge, of which he was master, A.D. 1473–1500; its authorship is usually attributed to him, but there is no evidence to prove that he wrote it. The chronicle exhibits a distinct bias in favour of the Lancastrian house, and is fullest for 1469–71. For Warkworth, see Emden, *Oxford* (No. 533), iii. 1992–3. In the notes to Halliwell's edition (pp. 29–71) other contemporary documents are cited.

2978   WAURIN, JEHAN DE (d. *c.* 1474). Recueil des croniques et anchiennes istories de la Grant Bretaigne (from the earliest times to 1471). Ed. by William Hardy and E. L. C. P. Hardy. Vol. i, Albina to A.D. 688; vols. ii–v, 1399–1471. Rolls Ser. 5 vols. Lond. 1864–91. The part 1325–1471 was edited by L. M. E. Dupont. 3 vols. Société de l'histoire de France. Paris. 1858–63. Trans. from the French by William Hardy and E. L. C. P. Hardy: *A collection of chronicles and ancient histories of Great Britain* (from Albina to A.D. 688, and 1399–1431). Rolls Ser. 3 vols. Lond. 1864–91.

A general collection of the then existing materials of English history. The part to 1413 was completed about 1455; the rest was written in the time of Edward IV. The author made much use of the *Chronicle of Brute* (No. 2811), and of Froissart and Monstrelet; but from 1444 to 1471 the work is in large part original and contemporary. Waurin belonged to a noble family of Artois. He fought at the battle of Agincourt on the French side, but later he served against the French under the banner of the Duke of Burgundy, 1419–35. For other fragments of his chronicles, from a MS. at Vienna, see *Bulletin historique et philologique du Comité des travaux historiques et scientifiques*, 1892, pp. 49–56.

2979   WENDOVER, ROGER OF (d. 1236). Flores historiarum (from the creation to 1235). Ed. by H. O. Coxe. Eng. Hist. Soc. 4 vols. and appendix. Lond. 1841–4. (This edition begins with the year A.D. 447.) Another edition, of the part 1154–1235 (badly edited), by H. G. Hewlett. Rolls Ser. 3 vols. 1886–9. Luard's edition of M. Paris, *Chronica Majora* (No. 2941) prints the Wendover text in small type and thus provides the best edition of Wendover. Excerpts,

A.D. 304–1235. Ed. by Liebermann, in M.G.H., *SS.* xxviii. 21–73. Trans. by J. A. Giles: *Roger of Wendover's Flowers of history, A.D. 447–1235.* Bohn's Library (No. 1089). 2 vols. Lond. 1849.

This general chronicle, by the historiographer of the Abbey of St. Albans, relates to the Continent as well as to England. Although it is an original authority of considerable value, it is hostile to King John and not reliable for his reign. 'His signal merit as a contemporary chronicler, which atones for many deficiencies, is his fearless frankness of speech without respect of persons.' The question whether Wendover was the founder of the St. Albans historical school has been much discussed. Madden believed that he was, but Hardy, Luard, Liebermann, Rickert, and Jenkins expressed doubts. Luard suggested Abbot John de Cella (1195–1214) as the author of a compilation to 1188, which Wendover used. But Powicke and Galbraith find no evidence to support Luard's suggestion. Powicke writes, 'I see no reason why he [Wendover] should not be given the credit for the work which goes by his name, at any rate from the year 1065'. For discussion of the problem, see Richard Vaughan, *Matthew Paris* (Cambr. 1958), chap. ii; F. M. Powicke, 'The compilation of the Chronica Majora of Matthew Paris', *P.B.A.* xxx (1944), 148–51; V. H. Galbraith, 'Roger Wendover and Matthew Paris', *Glasgow Univ. Pubns.* lxi (1944); J. C. Holt, 'The St. Albans Chroniclers and Magna Carta', *T.R.H.S.* 5th Ser. xiv (1964), 67–88; Richard Kay, 'Wendover's last annal', *E.H.R.* lxxxiv (1969), 779–85.

2979A THE WESTMINSTER CHRONICLE, 1381–94. See HIGDEN (No. 2895).

2980 WHETHAMSTEDE, JOHN (d. 1465). Registrum abbatiae Johannis Whethamstede Roberto Blakeney cappellano quondam adscriptum (1451–61). Ed. by Henry T. Riley, *Registra Quorundam Abbatum Monasterii S. Albani*, i. 1–433. Rolls Ser. Lond. 1872. Another edition, under the title Johannis de Whethamstede Chronicon, e Registro ejus, by Thomas Hearne, *Duo Rerum Anglicarum Scriptores Veteres*, ii. 311–540. Oxf. 1732.

The *Registrum* is a continuation in form and literary style of the *Annales*, doubtfully, ascribed to Amundesham (No. 2750); whereas the *Annales* dealt with the first abbacy of Whethamstede at St. Albans 1420–40, the *Registrum* (1451–61) dealt with his second abbacy, 1452–65. Both are 'due tct he inspiration, if they are not the authentic work, of a single *dictator*' (Jacob, p. 267). Blakeney formerly owned the manuscript; he was not its author.

For vol. ii of Riley's edition of the *Registra*, which contains some letters of Whethamstede, see No. 6169. Whethamstede is a well-known humanist of the fifteenth century; for his literary work, consult E. F. Jacob, 'Florida verborum venustas', *B.J.R.L.* xvii (1933), 266–78 (reprinted in No. 1473); and Emden, *Oxford* (No. 533), iii. 2032–4.

2981 WORCESTER, FLORENCE OF (d. 1118). Chronicon ex chronicis (A.D. 450–1117) with two continuations, one to 1141 and the other to 1295. Ed. by Benjamin Thorpe. Eng. Hist. Soc. 2 vols. Lond. 1848–9. Other editions: from the creation to 1141 by Lord William Howard. Lond. 1592; from A.D. 450 to 1066 in Petrie's *Monumenta* (No. 1084), pp. 522–615. The continuation from 1118 to 1140 is printed in the Chronicle of John of Worcester. Ed. by J. R. H. Weaver. *Anecdota Oxoniensia, Med. and Mod. Ser.* part xiii. Oxf. 1908. Trans. by J. Stevenson, *Church historians* (No. 1123), vol. ii, pt. 1; and by Thomas Forester; the *Chronicle of Florence of Worcester with two continuations* (to 1295). Bohn's Library (No. 1089). Lond. 1854.

No satisfactory edition of these important annals as yet exists. The nucleus of this composite work is the general chronicle of Marianus Scotus which ends in 1082 and was brought to England by direction of Robert, Bishop of Hereford: see W. H. Stevenson, *E.H.R.* xxii (1907), 72–84. Its authorship is doubtful. It includes many additions, drawn from Bede, Asser, lives of saints, and a version of the *Anglo-Saxon Chronicle* that is no longer extant. They are valuable because the compiler apparently followed his sources. It is this additional material and not the Marianus nucleus which Petrie printed. After 1082 the work becomes a valuable, if somewhat arid, compilation; from 1095 to 1121 its chief source was Eadmer's *Historia Novorum*. The author of the continuation (1118–40), John of Worcester, was a contemporary of the events which he records. The other continuation is extracted (1152–1265) from Henry of Huntingdon (No. 2904), John of Taxter (No. 2958), and from 1265–95 written by an unknown author, but formerly ascribed to John of Eversden. Clarke's *Bury Chroniclers* (No. 2819) has some interesting remarks about the value of Taxter and Eversden, who were monks at Bury St. Edmunds.

On Florence of Worcester, see Weaver's introduction; V. H. Galbraith, *Historical research* (Lond. 1951), 19–22; R. L. Poole, *Chronicles* (Oxf. 1926), pp. 49–50, and R. R. Darlington, *Anglo-Norman historians* (Lond. 1947), pp. 13–16; and Davis, *King Stephen* (Lond. 1967), p. 148.

2982 WORCESTER, WILLIAM OF (d. *c.* 1480). Annales rerum Anglicarum (1324–1468, 1491). Ed. by Thomas Hearne, *Liber niger scaccarii*, ii. 424–521. Oxf. 1728; reprinted, Lond. 1771. Also reprinted in Joseph Stevenson, *Letters and papers illustrative of the wars of the English in France during the reign of Henry VI*, ii. 743–93. Rolls Ser. Lond. 1864. William Worcester's Collections respecting the wars of the English in France and Normandy. Ed. by Joseph Stevenson, ibid. ii. 519–742. *The Boke of Noblesse*. Ed. by J. Gough Nichols. Roxburghe Club, no. 77. Lond. 1860.

William of Worcester was not the author of the *Annales*, which seem to have been 'fabricated' by Hearne 'from a number of separate items' in a College of Arms MS. Stevenson merely reprinted Hearne's improvised text. The *Annales* draw heavily on London chroniclers and contain virtually nothing otherwise unrecorded. The entries from November 1459 to May 1463 and for 1491 were written in 1491, i.e. after Worcester's death.

The *Boke of Noblesse* is an interesting treatise which glorifies knightly military action. A 'vernacular polemic', which was probably originally composed for presentation to Henry VI, it deplored the loss of the English conquests in France. It presents aristocratic reactions to the civil strife in England. Later it was revised and in 1475 presented to Edward IV, presumably with the design of stimulating war against France. McFarlane (p. 213) declares that the *Boke*, 'judged merely as a source, deserves a place besides Fortescue's *Governance of England*'.

The Collections of materials, made by Worcester probably from originals belonging to Fastolf, are documents in French and English for the period 1423–52. William of Worcester also wrote a Latin itinerary which was in part edited by James Nasmith, *Itineraria Symonis Simeonis et Willelmi de Worcestre*, pp. 77–378 (Cambr. 1778). It is a sort of diary of a trip from Norwich to Cornwall containing topographical data, particularly relating to Norfolk and Bristol. The part concerning Bristol is also printed in James Dallaway, *Antiquities of Bristowe* (Bristol, 1834). The whole work, excluding Bristol, is now printed as *William Worcestre, Itineraries*, edited from the unique MS. C.C.C.C. 210 by John H. Harvey (Oxford Medieval Texts, 1969).

William of Worcester, who is also called William Botoner, was a native of Bristol and secretary to John Fastolf, the celebrated Norfolk knight. Kendrick describes him as 'our first practising antiquary who was a layman'. See T. D. Kendrick, *British Antiquity* (No. 1476), pp. 29–33; Emden, *Oxford* (No. 533), iii. 2086–7; and especially K. B. McFarlane, 'William Worcester', in Jenkinson, *Studies* (No. 1441), pp. 196–221.

2983 WYKES, THOMAS (d. *c.* 1291). Chronicon vulgo dictum Chronicon Thomae Wykes (1066–1289). Ed. by Henry R. Luard, *Annales Monastici*, iv.

6–319. Rolls Ser. Lond. 1869. Another edition, in Gale's *Scriptores Quinque* (No. 1099), pp. 21–118. Extracts, 1147–1288. Ed. by Pauli, M.G.H., *SS.* xxvii (1885), 484–502.

> In the Rolls Series edition, Wykes's *Chronicle* is printed, year by year, beneath the *Annals of Osney* (No. 2764); but Wykes's *Chronicle* is divisible into three sections. The first section, 1066–1256, is derived from Florence of Worcester, Diceto, Newburgh, Matthew Paris, and possibly a source which was also used by the Osney annalist. The second section, 1256–78, is entirely independent and can hardly have emanated from Osney. For this period it is of primary importance; and contrasting with most chroniclers, who were partisans of Simon de Montfort, Wykes was an ardent royalist with Richard of Cornwall as his hero. The first two sections down to 1278 may have been written before Wykes became a canon of Osney in 1282. The third section, 1278–89, is almost identical with the *Osney Annals* and is probably the work of Wykes as historiographer of Osney Abbey. There is a continuation from 1289 to 1293, the first two years of which may be the work of Wykes. See N. Denholm-Young, 'Thomas de Wykes and his chronicle', *E.H.R.* lxi (1946), 157–79.

2984 WYNTOUN, ANDREW OF (d. *c.* 1425). The orygynale cronykil of Scotland (from the creation to 1408). Ed. by David Laing, in *Historians of Scotland* (No. 1103 A), vols. i, iii, ix. 3 vols. Edin. 1872–9. Another edition, by David Macpherson, 2 vols. Lond. 1795. *The original chronicle of Andrew of Wyntoun.* Ed. by F. J. Amours. 6 vols. Scottish Text Soc. Edin., etc. 1903–14.

> An English poem, completed about 1420. The author was a canon regular of the priory of St. Andrews, and prior of St. Serf's in Loch Leven. See W. A. Craigie, 'Wyntoun's Original Chronicle', in *Scottish Review*, xxx (1897), 33–54; and his paper, 'The St. Andrew MS. of Wyntoun's Chronicle', *Anglia*, xx (1898), 363–80.

XIV. LAW TRACTS

The *Quadripartitus* and other law-books of the first half of the twelfth century, which are examined above on pages 301–3, are in large part undigested collections of Anglo-Saxon dooms, with some amendments made by William the Conqueror and his sons. The treatise which goes under the name of Glanvill (No. 2989) begins as a somewhat more systematic exposition of English law and becomes a commentary on the writs embodying the reforms introduced by Henry II. In Henry III's reign Bracton, the greatest law writer of medieval England, produced the first comprehensive survey of English Law (No. 2985). Bracton's extensive work evoked abridgements which appeared towards the end of the century in Latin as Hengham, Fleta, and Thornton, and in French as Britton (Nos. 2997, 2986, 2987, 3003). In the second half of the thirteenth century a series of handbooks on procedure, written in law-French, was designed as practical short-cut guides for the busy men in the courts (Nos. 2992–3004). To the reign of Edward I belongs also the enigmatic *Mirror of Justice* (No. 2991). We have then to wait until the fifteenth century before important legal writers appear in the persons of Fortescue and Littleton (Nos. 2988, 2990).

The works on Canon Law in England from the Norman conquest to about 1485 will be found listed below on pages 846–58.

Besides the general histories of law, such as Pollock-Maitland and Holdsworth, two summaries specifically devoted to law-writers are Percy Winfield, *The chief* sources of *English legal history* (Cambridge, Mass., 1925), and Theodore F. T. Plucknett, *Early English legal literature* (Cambr. 1958). For volumes which have appeared in the publications of the Selden Society, the *General guide to the society's publications* compiled by A. K. R. Kiralfy and Gareth H. Jones (Lond. 1960) gives a detailed analysis of the contents of each volume. For the early editions of the treatises listed in this section, see Pollard-Redgrave and Wing (No. 71) and Joseph H. Beale, *A bibliography of early English law-books* (Cambridge, Mass., 1926).

A. PRINCIPAL TREATISES

2985 BRACTON (BRATTON), HENRY DE (d. 1268). De legibus et con-suetudinibus regni Angliae. Ed. by George E. Woodbine. 3 vols. New Haven. 1915–40. Woodbine's edn. is reprinted with revisions and a translation by Samuel E. Thorne. Vols. i–ii (Cambr. Mass.), 1968. Also edited, not well, with a translation by Sir Travers Twiss. Rolls Ser. 6 vols. Lond. 1878–83. Thorne's introduction in the first volume of his monumental edition, to be completed in five volumes, is fundamental for a modern study of Bracton. The review of Thorne's edition by A. A. Schiller in *Speculum*, xlv (1970), 492–8, sets forth some of the problems as does that by G. D. G. Hall in *Amer. Jour. Legal Hist.* xiii (1969), 304–8.

The citations given in Richardson's *Bracton* and in Tierney's article combine to form an excellent bibliography on Bractonian problems; and those given in Emden, *Oxford* (No. 533), i. 240–1, concern his life.

(a) *BRACTON'S NOTE BOOK.* Ed. by F. W. Maitland. 3 vols. Lond. etc. 1887. The introduction, i. 13–61, contains a good account of Bracton's life and law-book. See D. M. Stenton, *Justices in Eyre*, Selden Soc. (No. 3481), where 'This volume (by Lady Stenton) is in the nature of a supplement to Bracton's *Notebook*.'

(b) *SELECT PASSAGES FROM THE WORKS OF BRACTON AND AZO.* Ed. by F. W. Maitland. Selden Soc. viii (1894). Lond. 1895. This volume contains those portions of Bracton in which he follows Azo, a legist of Bologna in the early thirteenth century. It shows the Romanist influences in Bracton. See Kiralfy (No. 195), pp. 12–13. See H. G. Richardson, 'Azo, Drogheda and Bracton', *E.H.R.* lix (1944), 22–47.

(c) *FESEFELDT (WIEBKE), Englische Staatstheorie des 13. Jahrhunderts: Henry de Bracton und sein Werk.* Göttingen, 1962.

(d) GÜTERBOCK (CARL). *Henricus de Bracton und sein Verhältnis zum römischen Recht; ein Beitrag zur Geschichte des römischen Rechts.* Berlin, 1862. Trans. by Brinton Coxe, *Bracton and his relation to the Roman Law.* Philadelphia, 1866.

(e) . . . KANTOROWICZ (HERMANN), *Bractonian problems.* David Murray Lecture. Glasgow, 1941. Kantorowicz holds in this published lecture, not delivered owing to his death, that the text which has survived is a corrupted redaction by Bracton's clerk (see comment below). See C. H. McIlwain in *Harvard Law Review*, lvii (1943), 220–40, and Plucknett, *E.E.L.L.* (No. 3674), pp. 53–77; Woodbine's review in *Yale Law Jour.* lii (1941–2), 428–44. See also Gaillard Lapsley, 'Bracton and the authorship of the "addicio de cartis" ', *E.H.R.* lxii (1947), 1–19.

(f) LEWIS (EWART), 'King above law *Quod principi placuit* in Bracton', *Speculum*, xxxix (1964), 241–69.

(g) MILLER (S. J. T.), 'The position of the king in Bracton and Beaumanoir', *Speculum*, xxxi (1956), 263–96.

(h) POST (GAINES), 'A romano-canonical maxim, *quod omnes tangit*, in Bracton', *Traditio*, iv (1946), 197–251; reprinted in his *Studies in medieval thought: public law and the State 1100–1322* (Princeton, 1964), as are other important articles by Post.

(*i*) RICHARDSON (HENRY G.), *Bracton: the problem of the text*. Selden Soc. Supplementary Ser. no. ii (1965), consists of two parts: i. an expanded lecture on Bracton given to the Selden Society, and ii. parallel texts of Bracton and his Romanist sources.

(*j*) SCHULZ (FRITZ), Articles in *Law Quarterly Rev.* lix (1943), 172–80; ibid. lxi (1945), 286–92; *Traditio*, iii (1945), 265–305; *E.H.R.* lx (1945), 136–76; *Seminar* (Annual Extraordinary Number of the *Jurist*), ii (1944), 41–50.

(*k*) TIERNEY (BRIAN), 'Bracton on government', *Speculum*, xxxviii (1963), 295–317, with good bibliography of recent date.

(*l*) A BRACTON SYMPOSIUM, *Tulane Law Rev.* (New Orleans), xlii (1968), 455–602.

Pp. 455–518: Mitchell Franklin, 'Bracton, Para-Bracton(s) and the vicarage of the Roman law', is a strongly expressed, somewhat contentious, attempt to treat Bracton as a complete Romanist.

Pp. 519–54: Gaines Post, 'Bracton on kingship', is a series of notes, with references to civil and canon laws and the glossators, on the general subject that the king is under no man, but under God and the law. Cf. Idem, *Procs. Third International Congress of Medieval Canon Law* (Vatican City, 1971), pp. 113–30.

Pp. 555–83: J. L. Barton, 'Bracton as a civilian', is a critical review of Richardson's *The Problem* and holds that 'Bracton knew his civilian material tolerably well' (p. 572).

Pp. 584–602: G. D. G. Hall, 'The early history of entry sur disseisin', is only indirectly concerned with Bracton; it cites cases from 1194 to 1235/6 on the situation of the disseisee against the heir of the disseisor.

Bratton, which seems to be the correct spelling of his name, held several ecclesiastical benefices and in 1264 became the chancellor of the cathedral church of Exeter. He was in the king's service, presumably as the law-clerk to Justice William Raleigh, by 1240; he was a justice in eyre from 1244 and served on various commissions until his death. His great work, *De legibus*, is concerned with jurisprudence and the principles of law, not with procedure and the techniques of the court. It is the first comprehensive exposition of English law and by far the most important law-book of medieval England. Its ground-plan has similarities with works on Roman jurisprudence; some of its maxims were borrowed from Roman law, especially from the *Summa* of Azo of Bologna. Its main structure is systematized English law built on the *Note Book* (No. 3481) of about 2,000 cases taken from the plea rolls. In a controversial work of 1941 ((*e*) above) Hermann Kantorowicz revived by textual criticism some Bractonian problems and reached the conclusion that the texts which survive follow a corrupted redaction, made by Bracton's clerk after Bracton's death, of a work which Bracton had written before 1239 when Bracton was a law-clerk of William Raleigh. Thorne accepts the likelihood of an incompetent redactor, but doubts many of the conjectural emendations by Kantorowicz. A learned commentary on the issues and on the diverse positions taken by the critics is given in Plucknett, *E.E.L.L.* (No. 3674), pp. 53–77.

2986 BRITTON. Britton: the French text carefully revised, with an English translation. Ed. by F. M. Nichols. 2 vols. Oxf. 1865. Trans. by Robert Kelham: Book i: *The ancient pleas of the crown*. Lond. 1762. *Britton: an English translation and notes* by F. M. Nichols. Ed. by S. E. Baldwin. Washington. 1901.

The name Britton is applied to a treatise compiled about 1291, which makes the law appear in the king's name and in the form of royal precepts. It is in large part an abridgement of Bracton, but the writer shows some originality in the arrangement of the material. Nothing is known regarding the authorship of the work. It used to be ascribed to John le Breton, Bishop of Hereford; Nichols thought this unlikely, but G. Turner in *Brevia placitata*, p. xxx, sees 'no reason to doubt' the authorship by John le Breton. The best account of Britton will be found in the introduction to Nicholas's excellent edition.

2987 FLETA. Ed. and trans. by H. G. Richardson and G. O. Sayles. Vols. ii,
iii, text only. Selden Soc. lxxii (1953), lxxix (1972). Lond. 1955, 1972. (Vol. i will
contain introduction, notes, and indexes.). *Fleta seu commentarius juris Anglicani*;
accedit tractatulus Fet assavoir dictus; subjungitur etiam Joannis Seldeni Ad
Fletam dissertatio historica. Lond. 1647; 2nd edn. 1685. *Fleta: liber primus*. Ed.
by Sir Thomas Clarke. Lond. 1735. *Ad Fletam dissertatio*, reprinted from the
edition of 1647 with parallel translation by David Ogg. Cambr. 1925. Trans. also
by Robert Kelham. Lond. 1771.

> The Latin Treatise of *c*. 1290 which goes under the name of Fleta has several merits.
> It is an abridgement of Bracton, it comments on the legislation of Edward I, it describes
> the law-courts and the royal household, and it contains a Latin version of the tract on
> estate management which in its French version is ascribed to Walter of Henley. See
> Plucknett, *E.E.L.L.* (No. 3674), p. 78; and D. Oschinsky, *Walter of Henley* (No. 4631).
> For a plausible candidate for the authorship, see N. Denholm-Young, 'Who wrote
> Fleta?', *E.H.R.* lviii (1943), 1–12; and idem, 'Matthew Cheker', ibid. lix (1944), 252–7;
> reprinted in his *Collected papers* (No. 1467). Ernst H. Kantorowicz, 'The prologue to
> Fleta and the school of Petrus de Vinea', *Speculum*, xxxii (1957), 231–49.

2988 FORTESCUE, SIR JOHN (d. 1479 or after). De Laudibus legum
Angliae. Ed. and trans. by Stanley B. Chrimes. Cambr. 1942. *The governance
of England: otherwise called The difference between an absolute and limited monarchy*.
Ed. by Charles Plummer. Oxf. 1926. *The works of Sir John Fortescue*, collected
by Thomas (Fortescue), Lord Clermont. 2 vols. Lond. 1869. From vol. i,
pp. 57–90, William Stubbs reprinted with a translation *De titulo Edwardi comitis
Marchiae*, 1877. *De natura legis naturae*. Ed. by Lord Clermont. Lond. 1864.

> Commentaries: Chrimes's edition of *De Laudibus* includes an introduction on For-
> tescue's life and works and a study of Fortescue's significance in English law by H. D.
> Hazeltine. Plummer's edition of *The governance* contains on pp. 347–51 the 'Articles
> sent from the Prince of Wales to Richard Neville, earl of Warwick (1470–1)'; its intro-
> duction gives a biography of Fortescue.
>
> (*a*) GILBERT (FELIX), 'Sir John Fortescue's Dominium regale et politicum',
>   *Medievalia et Humanistica*, ii (1944), 88–97.
> (*b*) FERGUSON (A. B.), 'Fortescue and the renaissance: a study in transition',
>   *Studies in the Renaissance* (New York), vi(1959), 175–94. This article lists a consider-
>   able bibliography; as do *C.B.E.L.* (No. 14), i. 261; v. 148; and Ewart Lewis,
>   *Mediaeval political ideas* (N.Y. 1954), ii. 648.
> (*c*) CHRIMES (STANLEY B), 'Sir John Fortescue and his theory of dominion',
>   *T.R.H.S.*, 4th Ser. xvii (1934), 117–47. See M. A. Shepard in *McIlwain essays*
>   (No. 1444).
> (*d*) JACOB (ERNEST F.), 'Sir John Fortescue and the law of nature', *B.J.R.L.* xviii
>   (1934), 359–76. Reprinted in No. 1473.
> (*e*) SKEEL (CAROLINE A. J.), 'The influence of the writings of Sir John Fortescue',
>   *T.R.H.S.*, 3rd Ser. x (1916), 77–114.

Sir John Fortescue was chief justice of the king's bench and an ardent adherent of the
house of Lancaster. Having been attainted for treason by Edward IV, he went into exile
with Queen Margaret in 1463, and remained abroad until 1471. He was taken prisoner
at the battle of Tewkesbury, was induced to retract all that he had written against
Edward IV's title, and was pardoned by the king. He wrote several tracts in favour of
the Lancastrian house (*De Natura legis naturae*, etc.). His two principal works, the *De
Laudibus legum Angliae* and the *Governance of England*, though concerned more with
politics than with law, throw light on trial by jury and other legal institutions of
England. In the *De Laudibus*, which was written between 1468 and 1470, in the form
of a dialogue, for the instruction of Edward, son of Henry VI, Fortescue compares the

law of England with that of the Continent (especially with the civil law of France), and commends the advantages of the former. His chief object is to show the superiority of a constitutional over a despotic government and to emphasize the advantages of a limited over an absolute monarchy.

2989 GLANVILL, RANULF DE (d. 1190). Tractatus de legibus et con-suetudinibus regni Anglie qui Glanvill vocatur. Ed. by G. D. G. Hall. Medieval Texts. Lond., Edin., etc. 1965. Also ed. by George E. Woodbine. New Haven. 1932. Trans. by John Beames. Lond. 1812; reprinted, with an introduction by J. H. Beale, Jr. Washington, 1900. Trans. of a portion in *Eng. Hist. Docs.* ii. 937–43.

Woodbine printed what he called the 'beta' text; R. W. Southern in 'A note on the text of Glanville', *E.H.R.* lxv (1950), 81–9, showed the 'alpha' text to be preferable; Hall printed the 'alpha' text.

The date of the *Tractatus* is probably between 1187 and 1189; its authorship is uncertain. Lady Stenton (see below) proposes, as does Southern, Geoffrey fitz Peter as a more suitable candidate than Glanville or Hubert Walter; Hall suggests the pos-sibility of a royal clerk, not necessarily a judge. In any case 'there is no doubt that the treatise presents the work of the royal court in an authoritative way' (Hall). It presents the writs of Henry II's reign, describes the procedure on each of them, and adds a commentary. As the first important handbook on the Common Law, it is the oldest of the legal classics of England. It has accordingly been subjected to much learned com-mentary. R. C. Van Caenegem in *Royal writs* (No. 3503) touched upon Glanville in many places, and especially on pp. 349–59. Lady Stenton deals with Glanville in *Pleas before the king* (No. 3494), i. 9–25. See H. G. Richardson, 'Glanville continued', *Law Quart. Rev.* liv (1938), 381–99. To Van Caenegem's discussion of the influences of Roman and Canon Law (op. cit., pp. 360–90) may be added Horst Kaufmann, 'Causa debendi und causa petendi bei Glanville sowie im romanischen und kanonischen Recht seiner Zeit', *Traditio*, xvii (1961), 107–62, where a large body of literature is cited. See Josiah C. Russell, 'Ranulf de Glanville', *Speculum*, xlv (1970), 69–79.

A large portion of Glanville was transcribed into the manual on Scoto-Norman law which is known from its opening words as *Regiam Majestatem*. According to Lord Cooper in *An introduction to Scottish legal history* (Stair Soc. Edin. 1958), p. 7, this manual was compiled by an unknown ecclesiastic about 1230. It is printed in *Acts of the parliament of Scotland* (Record Comm. 1844), pp. 597–641; and as *Regiam Maje-statem and Quoniam Attachiamenta*, ed. by Thomas M. Cooper (Stair Soc. xi), Edin. 1947. For commentary, see H. G. Richardson, 'Roman Law in the *Regiam Majestatem*', *Juridical Review*, lxvii (1955), 155–87; and A. A. M. Duncan, '*Regiam Majestatem*', ibid. lxxiii (1961), 199–217, and Peter Stein, 'The source of the Romano-canonical part of the *Regiam Maiestatem*', *Scot. H.R.* xlviii (1969), 107–23.

2990 LITTLETON, SIR THOMAS (d. 1481) Lyttleton: his treatise of Tenures, in French and English; a new edition to which are added the ancient treatise of the Olde Tenures and the customs of Kent. Ed. by T. E. Tomlins. Lond. 1841. *The first part of the Institutes of the laws of England* (by Sir Edward Coke), or a commentary upon Littleton. Lond. 1628. 19th edn. by Francis Hargrave and Charles Butler. 2 vols. Lond. 1832; reprinted, Philadelphia. 1853. *Littleton's tenures in English.* Ed. by Eugene Wambaugh. Washington. 1903.

Littleton was appointed one of the judges of the court of common pleas in 1466 and Knight of the Bath in 1475. His treatise, which was probably compiled in 1474–5, contains a lucid account of the various tenures and estates of England. It is the most renowned legal treatise between Bracton and Blackstone. The first part of Coke's *Institutes*, commonly designated 'Coke on Littleton', contains Littleton's text with a translation and an elaborate commentary; in this form the treatise long remained the

chief authority on the English law of real property. For Littleton's life and a full bibliography of the numerous editions of his work, see the introduction to Wambaugh's
translation. For commentary see Winfield, *Sources* (No. 1229), pp. 309–14 and 336–7;
and Holdsworth, *History* (No. 1235), ii. 571–91.

2991 THE MIRROR OF JUSTICES. Ed. (French text with a translation) by
W. J. Whittaker, with an introduction by F. W. Maitland. Selden Soc. vii (1893).
Lond. 1895. Earlier edition: *La somme appelle Mirroir des justices.* Lond. 1642.
Trans. by W(illiam) H(ughes). 1646; other editions, 1649, 1659, 1768, 1840.
Trans. by W. C. Robinson. Washington. 1903.*

This work, which was probably written in the reign of Edward I, perhaps between
1285 and 1290, is usually attributed to Andrew Horn, chamberlain of the city of London, but it is not certain that he was the author. It treats of all branches of the law,
and proposes remedies for various legal abuses. The treatise abounds in conjectures and
myths. 'What then shall we say of this book? and what shall we call its author? Is he
lawyer, antiquary, preacher, agitator, pedant, faddist, lunatic, romancer, liar? A little
of all perhaps, but the romancer seems to predominate.' This quotation is taken from
Maitland's introduction (to Whittaker's edition), where the best account of the *Mirror*
will be found. See also I. S. Leadam, 'The Authorship of the Mirror of Justices', in
Law Quart. Rev. xiii (1897), 85–103; he believes that the work was transcribed under
the direction of Andrew Horn, but that it was probably compiled by an earlier member
of the Horn family. See H. G. Reuschlein, 'Who wrote the Mirror of Justices?', *Law
Quart. Rev.* lviii (1942), 265–79.

B. TRACTS, LARGELY ON PROCEDURE

2992 BREVIA PLACITATA. Ed. by G. J. Turner, and completed by T. F. T.
Plucknett. Selden Soc. lxvi (1947). Lond. 1951.

This important long thirteenth-century treatise in Norman French deals with pleadings
in the king's courts. 'It supplies the writ, count and further pleas, with occasional
illustrative additions, such as speeches of advocates and notes of certain judges' opinions'
(Kiralfy). In this edition there is no translation into English, but the introduction
supplies an extensive commentary on the text and on the writs used therein.

2993 CASUS PLACITORUM, AND REPORTS OF CASES IN THE
KING'S COURTS (1272–8). Ed. by William H. Dunham, Jr. Selden Soc. lxix
(1950). Lond. 1952.

The first tract, the *Casus*, is a book of notes on cases determined about the middle of
the thirteenth century. It is written in Anglo-Norman and survives in many copies.
Two separate collections of Anglo-Norman reports follow and these resemble the Year
Books, but also include Latin extracts from the Plea Rolls.
    In addition to the description of the manuscripts and the contents, Dunham's intro-
duction touches on legal education in the thirteenth century and on the origin of law
reporting. For some identifiable cases, he includes the record from the de Banco rolls.
The appendices print *Casus et Judicia* in Latin, pp. lxxv–lxxxiv, and pages from a
Student's Work Book in law-French, pp. lxxxv–lxxxix.

2994 CONSUETUDINES DIVERSARUM CURIARUM, printed in Ap-
pendix ii, pp. cxci–cciii of Richardson and Sayles, *Procedure without writ*
(No. 3495A).

This 'anonymous tract on procedure in ecclesiastical and secular courts' dates from
about 1250.

2995 COURT BARON (THE), being precedents for use in seignorial and other local courts, together with select pleas from the court of Littleport. Ed. with a translation by F. W. Maitland and W. P. Baildon. Selden Soc. iv (1890). Lond. 1891.

> This collection consists of five tracts:
> La cour de baron, pp. 19–67. Compiled late in the thirteenth century.
> De placitis et curiis tenendis, pp. 68–78. Perhaps written by John of Oxford, a monk of Luffield, toward the end of Henry III's reign or early in Edward I's.
> Modus tenendi curias, pp. 79–92. Compiled about 1307.
> Modus tenendi curias, pp. 93–106. Professes to relate what happened in certain imaginary courts in 14–16 Edward III; written about 1342, partly in French and partly in Latin.
> Pleas at Littleport, pp. 107–47.
> Cf. N. J. Hone, *A Mannor and Court Baron* (No. 4968).
> For Robert Carpenter of Hareslade as the likely compiler, see Denholm-Young, *Collected Papers* (No. 1467).

2996 FOUR THIRTEENTH-CENTURY LAW TRACTS. Ed. (but not well) by G. E. Woodbine. New Haven. 1910.

> Fet asaver, pp. 53–115; also printed in Fleta (No. 2987), edns. of 1647 and 1685. This is an Anglo-Norman tract of good quality on procedure, the date and thoughtful author of which are unknown.
> Judicium essoniorum, pp. 116–42;
> Modus componendi brevia, pp. 143–62;
> Exceptiones ad cassandum brevia, pp. 163–83.
> Woodbine thinks that some of these anonymous tracts may have been written by Hengham (No. 2997), but Dunham (No. 2997) rejects this thesis. For appreciations of Fet asaver and Modus componendi brevia, see Plucknett, *E.E.L.L.* (No. 3674), pp. 94–7.

2997 HENGHAM, RALPH DE (d. 1311). Radulphi de Hengham Summae. Ed. by William H. Dunham, Jr. *Cambridge Studies in English Legal History.* Cambr. 1932. Also printed with Fortescue's *De Laudibus*, edns. of 1616, 1660, 1672, 1737, 1741, 1775.

> Hengham Magna and Hengham Parva are two little treatises on procedure, dealing with essoins, defaults, writs, etc. In Dunham's edition, pp. ix–xxxix, H. D. Hazeltine writes on Hengham's place in legal literature. Hengham, chief justice of the king's bench, was convicted of false judgement in 1289–90; in 1301 he was appointed chief justice of the court of common pleas. See W. H. Dunham, Jr., 'The chronology of Hengham's dismissal', *E.H.R.* xlvii (1932), 88–93.

2998 NOVAE NARRATIONES. Ed. and trans. by the late Elsie Shanks; completed with a legal introduction by S. F. C. Milsom. Selden Soc. lxxx (1963). Lond. 1963. Also printed as *Herein is contiened the booke called Novae narrationes, the booke called Articuli ad Novas Narrationes, and the booke of Diversities of courtes.* Lond. 1561.

> This formulary in Anglo-Norman, which dates from the reign of Edward I and is added to from time to time, is a practical handbook on pleadings on the various writs. 'Each count (narration) is an exact and detailed statement of the plaintiff's case against the defendant, given in the form which the pleader must use in opening the action before the justices.' Milsom's legal introduction is a distinguished commentary on each of the actions: writs of right, advowson, debt, detinue, etc. The tract called *Articuli ad Novas Narrationes* has some similarities and marked differences with both *Novae Narrationes* and *Brevia Placitata.* For editions unsatisfactory) and comment ,see Winfield, *Sources* (No. 1229), pp. 283–5.

2999 OLDE TENERS NEWLY CORRECTED. Lond. 1525. Two earlier editions, without title-page; for other editions, see Pollard-Redgrave (No. 71), Beale (No. 1224), Holdsworth, *History* (No. 1235), ii. 575.

A meagre French tract of uncertain date, ascribed to the end of the reign of Edward III, is called *Old Tenures* to distinguish it from Littleton's work on the same subject.

3000 OXFORD, JOHN OF. 'A conveyancer in the thirteenth century'; F. W. Maitland. *Law Quart. Rev.* vii (1891), 63–9. Reprinted in Maitland's *Collected Papers* (No. 1482), ii. 190–201.

Maitland here gives an account of a collection of precedents or forms of conveyancing, written by John of Oxford, a monk of Luffield priory, early in the reign of Edward I. See Emden, *Oxford*, iii. 1414–15. For a paper giving many examples *in extenso*, see T. F. Kirby, 'Some notes on fourteenth century conveyancing', *Archaeologia*, lix (1904), 255–80. See No. 2995 and D. Oschinsky (Nos. 4631–2).

3001 PLACITA CORONE or LA CORONE PLEDEE DEVANT JUS-TICES. Ed. and trans. by J. M. Kaye. Selden Soc. Supplementary vol. iv. Lond. 1966.

This volume contains two versions of an Anglo-Norman tract on criminal procedure in the late thirteenth century. Its main concern is felony and gaol delivery cases. The volume also contains as an appendix an abbreviation of parts of Bracton entitled *Tractatus Coronae*.

3002 READINGS AND MOOTS AT THE INNS OF COURT IN THE FIFTEENTH CENTURY. Ed. by Samuel E. Thorne. Vol. i. Selden Soc. lxxi (1952). Lond. 1954.

Thorne edits in full and translates five principal readings of about 1450; and in the appendix edits parts of eleven other readings between 1420 and 1437. Each reader gave two readings at his own inn at five-year intervals; he commented on the texts of the principal statutes, apparently in chronological order and evoked discussion from his hearers.

3003 THORNTON, GILBERT DE. Summa de legibus. (Commentary and table of contents.) T. F. T. Plucknett, 'The Harvard manuscript of Thornton's Summa', *Harvard Law Rev.* li (1937–8), 1038–56.

Thornton's *Summa* was thought to have been lost: G. E. Woodbine, 'The *Summa* of Gilbert of Thornton', *Law Quart. Rev.* xxv (1909), 44–52. However, a manuscript which was acquired by the Harvard Law Library in 1924 proved to be a complete copy similar to the one on which Selden had reported. See S. E. Thorne, 'Gilbert of Thornton's Summa de Legibus', *Toronto Law Jour.* vii (1947–8), 1–26.

3004 VACARIUS (d. *c.* 1200). Liber pauperum of Vacarius. Ed. by F. de Zulueta. Selden Soc. xliv (1927). Lond. 1927.

Vacarius, who presumably taught at Oxford *c.* 1150, and at Northampton, prepared this epitome and gloss of the Roman *Corpus Juris* for his poor students.
F. Liebermann, 'Magister Vacarius', *E.H.R.* xi (1896), 305–14; xiii (1898), 297–8. J. de Ghellinck, 'Magister Vacarius, un juriste theologien peu aimable pour les canonistes', *R.H.E.* xliv (1949), 173–8. Emden, *Oxford* (No. 533), iii. 1939.

XV. PUBLIC ADMINISTRATIVE RECORDS

A. EXCHEQUER RECORDS

1. *General Documents: Dialogus and Exchequer Books*

3005   DIALOGUS DE SCACCARIO. The best edition is *De necessariis observantiis scaccarii dialogus commonly called Dialogus de scaccario by Richard, son of Nigel, Treasurer of England and Bishop of London.* Ed. by Arthur Hughes, C. G. Crump, and C. Johnson. Oxf. 1902. This text is reprinted and a translation into English is given by Charles Johnson in the series Medieval Classics (No. 1113). Lond. and N.Y. 1950. The text was edited also by Thomas Madox, in the appendix to his *History of the Exchequer*. Lond. 1711. 2nd edn. 1769. Madox's text was reprinted first wholly and then largely by Stubbs in *Select Charters*. The dialogue is also translated in E. F. Henderson, *Select historical documents in the Middle Ages*, pp. 20–134 (Lond. 1892); and in *Eng. hist. docs.* ii. 491–569.

The author, Richard Fitz-Neal, was treasurer of England from 1158 and Bishop of London from 1189 to his death in 1198. His treatise in two books is in the form of a dialogue between a master and his disciple and describes in detail the origin, organization, and procedure of the upper and lower exchequers. In addition to the introductions in the 1902 and 1950 editions cited above, the following commentaries are indispensable: Felix Liebermann, *Einleitung in den Dialogus de Scaccario* (Göttingen, 1875); Reginald Lane Poole, *The exchequer in the twelfth century* (Oxf. 1912); H. G. Richardson, 'Richard fitz-Neal and the Dialogus de Scaccario', *E.H.R.* xliii (1928), 161–71; 321–40.

3006   LIBER NIGER SCACCARII. Ed. by Thomas Hearne. 2 vols. Oxf. 1728; 2nd edn. Lond. 1771; reprinted 1774.

This is the *Liber Niger Parvus*, which was probably compiled in the early thirteenth century by Alexander de Swereford, archdeacon of Salop and a clerk of the Exchequer. Its contents listed in Giuseppi (No. 951), i. 102–3, include treaties of Henry I and Henry II with the count of Flanders; an agreement between Henry II and William I, King of Scotland; four bulls of Pope Alexander III, all printed in Rymer's *Foedera*; and the 'cartae of 1166' (see Stenton, No. 4679); the *Constitutio Domus Regis* (No. 3116), and various charters. This book should not be confused with the unprinted Liber Niger, a register of official memoranda from the middle of the thirteenth century to 1834 (Giuseppi, i. 210). This unprinted Black Book includes the *Dialogus*, and miscellaneous entries relating to the exchequer from 19 Edward II to 1715. A part of the contents of both Black Books is also found in the *Liber Rubeus* (No. 3007). For papers relating to the Little Black Book, and dealing mainly with the 'cartae' of 1166, see George Wrottesley, 'The Liber Niger Scaccarii', *Wm. Salt Archaeol. Soc. Collections*, i (1881), 145–240; Henry Barkly, 'Remarks on the Liber Niger', *Bristol–Glos. Archaeol. Soc. Trans.* xiv (1890), 285–320; and No. 3174.

3007   LIBER RUBEUS DE SCACCARIO. The red book of the Exchequer. Ed. by Hubert Hall. Rolls Ser. 3 vols. Lond. 1896.

The earlier portion of this work was compiled about A.D. 1230 by Alexander de Swereford; many additions were made from time to time, some of them as late as the sixteenth century. It contains charters, inquisitions, statutes, correspondence, surveys, fiscal accounts, exchequer precedents, papal bulls, etc. Hall prints many of the most important documents and a table of contents of the MS. volume. Among the valuable pieces which he omits are the *Leges Henrici Primi* (No. 2186) and the *Dialogus de Scaccario*. More than two-thirds of the material in his edition consists of records relating to feudal tenures, mainly of the reigns of Henry II, Richard I, and John: for example, the 'cartae' of 1166; lists of persons subject to the payment of scutage, A.D. 1156–1252; lists of knights' fees under the first four Angevin kings; etc. Volume iii contains the *Constitutio Domus Regis* (*c.* 1136); privileges and exemptions of exchequer officers; three royal ordinances of 1323-6 which aims to reform the exchequer administration; a fourteenth-century treatise on the mint, etc. These documents throw light on the fiscal machinery of the thirteenth and fourteenth centuries, and the editor's elaborate preface gives much information regarding scutage, tenures, the exchequer administration, and other topics. For the controversy which resulted from J. H. Round's severe criticism of Hall's edition, in Round's *Studies on the Red Book of the exchequer* (Lond. 1898), see *Family origins* (No. 569), pp. 28-31; and F. W. Maitland, *Letters* (No. 1482). Joseph Hunter's *Three catalogues* (London, 1838), reprinted from the appendix of the Record Commissioners' Report of 1837, pp. 165-77, describes the contents of the Red Book. For the portion relating to the counties of Nottingham and Derby, see Yeatman, *Feudal history of Derby* (No. 1601), i. 265-364. Some documents from the Red Book for the thirteenth and fourteenth centuries are printed and translated in Charles Johnson, *The de moneta of Nicholas Oresme and English mint documents* (Medieval Texts. Lond. etc. 1956).

3008 TABLE OF CONTENTS OF THE RED BOOK (of the Irish exchequer). *Deputy Keeper's Reports, Ireland,* xxiv. 96-9. Dublin. 1892.

The earliest entries are of the time of John and Henry III. See J. F. Ferguson, 'A calendar of the contents of the Red Book of the Irish exchequer', *Kilkenny and Southeast of Ireland Archaeol. Soc. Procs.* iii (1856), 35-52. See also No. 3217.

2. *Domesday Book and its Satellites*

a. Domesday Book

3009 DOMESDAY BOOK SEU LIBER CENSUALIS WILHELMI PRIMI REGIS ANGLIAE. By Abraham Farley. 2 vols. Lond. 1783. Vols. iii-iv by Henry Ellis. Rec. Comm. Lond. 1816. Domesday Book, photozincographed facsimile. 33 (35) pts. Ordnance Survey Office. Southampton. 1861-4.

The best edition is that of 1783-1816. Vol. i contains:

Bedfordshire	Hampshire	Oxfordshire
Berkshire	Herefordshire	Shropshire
Buckinghamshire	Hertfordshire	Somersetshire
Cambridgeshire	Huntingdonshire	Staffordshire
Cheshire	Kent	Surrey
Cornwall	Leicestershire	Sussex
Derbyshire	Lincolnshire	Warwickshire
Devon	Middlesex	Wiltshire
Dorset	Northamptonshire	Worcestershire
Gloucestershire	Nottinghamshire	Yorkshire

Vol. ii. Essex, Norfolk, Suffolk.
Vol. iii. Indexes and general introduction. See No. 3049.
Vol. iv. Additamenta: Exon Domesday, Inquisitio Eliensis, Liber Winton, Boldon Book.

For the last four of these surveys, see Nos. 3011, 3010, 3072, 3076. The *Exon Domesday*, preserved among the muniments of the dean and chapter of Exeter, gives an account of Cornwall, Devon, Somerset, Dorset, and Wilts., derived directly or indirectly from the verdicts of the Domesday jurors; it contains some particulars omitted from the Exchequer Domesday. At the beginning of the MS. (pp. 1-75 of Ellis's edition) we find the *Inquisitio Geldi*, an inquest for the assessment of a Danegeld levied in 1084 on the hundreds of these five counties.

Domesday Book is a unique record, unmatched in any other country at so early a date. The materials from which it was compiled were collected by royal commissioners in the shire courts in 1086. Some information was almost certainly recorded village by village and hundred by hundred; none of these 'original returns', however, is known to have survived. Later, by what procedure and at what date is a matter of debate, this information was rearranged and digested for each county under the borough and under the names of the tenants-in-chiefs; and finally bound in two volumes. For the controversy on the procedure of the redaction of Domesday Book, consult No. 3053.

The first volume, containing 383 folios written in double columns, includes thirty counties south of the Tees and Westmorland; the counties of Northumberland, Durham, Cumberland, and Westmorland are not reported in Domesday Book, although sections of modern Cumberland and Westmorland are contained under Yorkshire. Lancashire is not included, although portions of it appear under the heading 'Land between Ribble and Mersey' at the end of Cheshire, and in the West Riding of Yorkshire. No survey of London appears. The second volume, called 'The Little Domesday', contains 450 smaller folios without columns and comprises fuller reports for Essex, Norfolk, and Suffolk. For this volume, see R. Welldon Finn, *Domesday Studies: The Eastern Counties* (Lond. 1967). For rebinding, see No. 3046. William's intent in projecting the survey is also a matter of controversy. The thesis that it was designed as a record of feudal tenures rather than as a tax-book now has strong support. (See the numbers cited immediately above.) Whatever its purpose, it furnishes a vast mass of details regarding the classes of society, social life, feudal tenures, and legal institutions both before and after the Norman conquest. It is the fundamental source for the social and economic history of the period; accordingly the student should consult particularly Nos. 4973, 4980. Galbraith's study (No. 3053) is fundamental.

The Exchequer Domesday is supplemented by 'satellites' which are directly related to the survey itself (No. 3011), by geld inquests of William I's reign (Nos. 3065–6), and by complementary local surveys of the following century (Nos. 3067–76).

The bibliography on Domesday Book is very extensive; Bonser alone lists well over 400 separate titles. The older works are listed in the British Museum Catalogue *sub* 'Domesday Book'; partial bibliographies are given in Nos. 3039, 3044, 3047, 3051–3. All modern research on Domesday Book begins with Round (No. 3061), followed before 1914 by the writings of Maitland (No. 3058), Vinogradoff (No. 2650), and Stenton (Nos. 2648, 4679). For each county the Victoria County History (No. 1529) provides a translation of the appropriate portion with an introduction.

b. Satellites

3010 INQUISITIO COMITATUS CANTABRIGIENSIS, subjicitur INQUISITIO ELIENSIS. Ed. by Nicholas E. S. A. Hamilton. Lond. 1876. Trans. in V.C.H. *Cambridgeshire*, i (1938), 400–27.

These two inquests are derived, at first or second hand, from the original returns made by the Domesday jurors; they are contained in a Cotton MS. formerly belonging to the Abbey of Ely. Both give the names of the jurors which are omitted in Domesday Book. The Cambridgeshire inquest gives the holdings hundred by hundred in thirteen of the sixteen hundreds of that county. The Ely inquest is a 'private monastic summary . . . of the lands of the Abbey of Ely' in the counties of Cambridge, Hertford, Essex, Norfolk, Suffolk, and Huntingdon. Hamilton's edition is better than Ellis's (No. 3009). For commentaries, see especially Nos. 3017, 3044, 3052, and Edward Miller, 'The Ely land pleas in the reign of William I', *E.H.R.* lxii (1947), 438–56; R. W. Finn, 'The Inquisitio Eliensis re-considered', *E.H.R.* lxxv (1960), 385–409; Finn, 'The Essex entries in the Inquisitio Eliensis', *Essex Archaeol. Soc. Trans.* 3rd Ser. i (1961–5), 190–5; and Galbraith, *Studies* (No. 949), p. 158.

3011 THE EXON DOMESDAY or Liber Exoniensis is printed in vol. iv (Additamenta) of the Record Commission's edition of Domesday Book (No. 3009).

It is still preserved among the MSS. of the dean and chapter of Exeter. It is a draft in single columns in contemporary non-curial hands, and accordingly differs from the double columns in the curial hands of Domesday Book. It comprises reports on Cornwall, Devon, and Somerset, on much of Dorset, and on one manor of Wiltshire. For Cornwall, Devon, and Somerset it includes sections on *terrae occupatae*, lands occupied since 1066, which are not entered in Domesday Book. For *Inquisitio geldi*, see No. 3066. County portions are printed in Nos. 3028, 3034. Translations are provided in the appropriate volumes of V.C.H., see especially Darlington in V.C.H. *Wiltshire*, ii, and Ann Williams in V.C.H. *Dorset*, iii.

Commentaries:

T. W. Whale, 'Analysis of Exon Domesday' (part relating to Devon), *Devon. Assoc. for Advancement of Science, etc, Trans.* xxviiii, 391–463; xxxiv, 289–324; xxxv, 662–712; xxxvi, 156–72 (Plymouth 1896–1904). 'History of the Exon Domesday', ibid. xxxvii (1905), 246–83.

F. H. Baring, 'The Exeter Domesday', *E.H.R.* xxvii (1912), 309–18 (A seminal article).

Reginald Lennard, 'A neglected Domesday satellite', *E.H.R.* lviii (1943), 32–41. This satellite is found in a Bath cartulary (No. 6305), pp. 67–8.

R. W. Finn, *Domesday Studies: the Liber Exoniensis* (Lond. 1964).

R. W. Finn, 'The Exeter Domesday and its construction', *B.J.R.L.* xli (1958–9), 360–87.

R. S. Hoyt, 'The *terrae occupatae* of Cornwall and the Exon Domesday', *Traditio*, ix (1953), 155–75.

3012 THE FEUDAL BOOK OF ABBOT BALDWIN OF BURY ST. EDMUNDS, printed in David C. Douglas, *Feudal Documents from the Abbey of Bury St. Edmunds* (No. 6336 below), pp. 1–44. Extracts are printed in the fourteenth-century *Pinchbeck Register* (No. 6342), i. 410–21.

The prologue connects this document to the Domesday survey. For description see introduction to Douglas's *Feudal Documents*, and *E.H.D.* ii. 889. Cf. Galbraith, *E.H.R.* lvii (1942), 167–8.

3013 The Christ Church, Canterbury survey, printed by Douglas in *Domesday Monachorum* (No. 3070).

3014 St. Augustine's Canterbury inquest printed in Adolphus Ballard's *An eleventh-century inquisition of St. Augustine's, Canterbury.* Brit. Acad. Records of the social and economic history of England and Wales, iv, part ii. Lond. 1920.

A copy made in the thirteenth century, of a copy made between 1100 and 1154 (or possibly 1124) of an independent compilation made in or before 1087, from the original returns of the hundreds from which Domesday Book was compiled.

c. Domesday Book by counties

For local studies of Domesday Book, see the bibliographies in the appropriate volumes of Darby's series (No. 3046) and in Finn's *Introduction to Domesday Book* (No. 3051). The more important ones are listed hereunder.

BEDFORDSHIRE

3015 AIRY (WILLIAM). A digest of the Domesday of Bedfordshire. Bedford. 1881.

3016 FOWLER (GEORGE H.). Bedfordshire in 1086: an analysis and synthesis of Domesday book. Beds. Hist. Rec. Soc., *Quarto Memoirs*, i (1922); idem, Domesday notes. Beds. Hist. Rec. Soc. i (1913); v (1920).

CAMBRIDGESHIRE

3017 DOMESDAY BOOK: or great survey of England of William the Conqueror, A.D. 1086: Cambridgeshire. Ed. C. H. Evelyn White. (Extension of the text by H. G. Evelyn White, with transcript of an unpublished translation made by William Bawdwen in 1867.) *East Anglian*, 3rd Ser. xi–xii, *passim*. Norwich, etc. 1905–8; separately printed, 1910. Cf. *Inquisitio* (No. 3010).

Cf. R. W. Finn, 'Some reflections on the Cambridgeshire Domesday', *Cambr. Antiq. Soc. Procs.* liii (1960), 29–38.

CHESHIRE

3018 TAIT (JAMES). The domesday survey of Cheshire. Chetham Soc. N.S. lxxv (1916). Idem, 'Flintshire in Domesday Book', *Flints. Hist. Soc. Pubns.* xi (1925), 1–37.

DEVONSHIRE

3019 THE DEVONSHIRE DOMESDAY AND GELD INQUEST: extensions, translations, and indices. Ed. by J. B. Rowe and others. Devon. Assoc. for Advancement of Science, etc. 2 vols. Plymouth. 1884–92.

Contains the Devon portions of both the Exchequer Domesday and the Exon Domesday. For various papers on the Devon Domesday by O. J. Reichel, see *Devon. Assoc. for Advancement of Science*, etc., *Trans.* xxvi–xliv (1894–1912), *passim*; and V.C.H. *Devonshire*, i. 375–549. See also Exon Domesday (No. 3011); and R. W. Finn, 'The making of the Devonshire Domesdays', *Devonshire Assoc. Reports and Trans.* lxxxix (1957), 93–113.

DORSET

3020 EYTON (ROBERT W.). A key to Domesday, exemplified by an analysis and digest of the Dorset survey. Lond., etc. 1878.

Cf. Ann Williams in V.C.H. *Dorset*, iii (1968), 1–114; and 115–48.

THE EASTERN COUNTIES

3021 FINN (REX W.). Domesday Studies: the Eastern Counties. Lond. 1967.

See also Barbara Dodwell, 'The free peasantry of East Anglia in Domesday', *Norfolk Archaeol.* xxvii (1941), 145–57.

GLOUCESTERSHIRE

3022 ELLIS (A. S.). 'Some account of the landholders of Gloucestershire named in Domesday'. *Bristol-Glos. Archaeol. Soc. Trans.* iv (1880), 86–198. Reprinted separately.

3023 TAYLOR (C. S.). Analysis of the Domesday survey of Gloucestershire. Bristol-Glos. Archaeol. Soc. Bristol. 1887.

KENT

3024 LARKING (L. B.). The Domesday book of Kent, with translation and appendix. Lond. 1869.

LANCASHIRE

3025 FARRER (WILLIAM). Domesday survey of Lancashire, analysis, etc. *Lancs. and Ches. Antiq. Soc. Trans.* xvi (1899), 1–38; xviii (1901), 88–113. For his later discussion of the subject, see V.C.H. *Lancashire*, i (1906), 269–381.

LINCOLNSHIRE

3026 FOSTER (C. W.) and LONGLEY (THOMAS). The Lincolnshire Domesday and the Lindsey Survey. Lincoln Rec. Soc. xix (1924).

An edition and translation by Foster and Longley, with an introduction by F. M. Stenton.

SHROPSHIRE

3027 EYTON (ROBERT W.). 'Notes on Domesday', reprinted from *Salop. Archaeol. Soc., Trans.* (1877). Lond. 1880. See No. 1801.

SOMERSET

3028 EYTON (R. W.). Domesday studies: analysis and digest of the Somerset survey (according to the Exon. codex) and of the Somerset gheld inquest of A.D. 1084, as collated with Domesday. 2 vols. Lond., etc. 1880.

There is a good Domesday map of Somerset, by Bishop Edmund Hobhouse, in the *Somersetshire Archaeol. and Nat. Hist. Soc. Procs.* xxxv (1890), pt. i. See also E. H. Bates, 'The five-hide-unit in the Somerset Domesday', ibid. xlv (1899), 51–107; and T. W. Whale, *Analysis of Somerset Domesday* (Bath, 1902), to which is appended his *Principles of Domesday*, with an analysis in hundreds. F. W. Morgan, 'The Domesday geography of Somerset', *Somerset Archaeol. and Nat. Hist. Soc. Procs.*, lxxxiv (1939), 139–55. R. W. Finn, 'The making of the Somerset Domesday', ibid. xcix–c (1954–5), 21–37.

STAFFORDSHIRE

3029 EYTON (R. W.). Domesday studies: analysis and digest of the Staffordshire survey. Lond. etc. 1881.

SUFFOLK

3030 SUFFOLK DOMESDAY: the Latin text extended and translated. By John Hervey. 2 vols. Bury St. Edmunds. 1888–91.

Cf. F. Barlow, 'Domesday Book: A letter of Lanfranc', *E.H.R.* lxxviii (1963), 284–9.

SUSSEX

3031 DOMESDAY BOOK IN RELATION TO THE COUNTY OF SUSSEX. Ed. (with a facsimile of the text, a translation, and a map) for the Sussex Archaeol. Soc., by W. D. Parish. Lewes. 1886.

On hides and virgates in Sussex, see James Tait and L. F. Salzmann, *E.H.R.* xviii (1903), 705–8; xix (1904), 92–6, 503–6. J. E. A. Jolliffe, 'The Domesday hidation of Sussex and its rapes', *E.H.R.* xlv (1930), 427–35.

WILTSHIRE

3032 JONES (W. H. R.). Domesday for Wiltshire, with translations. Bath, etc. 1865.

Contains the extended texts of the Exchequer Domesday and Exon Domesday, with an analysis, etc.

3033 FINN (REX W.). 'The making of the Wiltshire Domesday'. *Wilts. Archaeol. and Nat. Hist. Magazine*, lii (1949–50), 318–27.

F. W. Morgan, 'The Doomsday geography of Wiltshire', ibid. xlviii (1938), 68–81; M. W. Hughes, 'The Domesday boroughs of Wiltshire', ibid. liv (1951–2), 257–78.

3034 VICTORIA COUNTY HISTORY OF WILTSHIRE: A history of Wiltshire. Ed. by R. B. Pugh and Elizabeth Crittall.

Vol. ii (1955) is almost exclusively the work of R. R. Darlington and deals with Anglo-Saxon Wiltshire and Domesday Book, Geld Rolls and Exon Domesday so far as they concern Wiltshire.

WORCESTERSHIRE

3035 SAWYER (P. A.). 'Evesham A, a Domesday text'. Worcs. Hist. Soc. *Miscellany*, i (1960), 3–36.

Prints, with an introduction, the Evesham Abbey cartulary section. J. H. Round mentions it in *Feudal England*, p. 178; also in *V.C.H. Worcestershire*, i. 327. Sawyer holds that the Worcestershire Domesday and Evesham A had a common source. Evesham A is interesting for the method of compiling Domesday.

YORKSHIRE

3036 DOMESDAY BOOK FOR YORKSHIRE. Translated by R. H. Skaife. *Yorks. Archaeol. Soc. Jour.* xiii. 321–52, 489–536; xiv. 1–64, 249–312, 347–89. Lond. 1895–8; also printed separately.

Translation only.

3037 ELLIS (A. S.). Some account of the landholders of Yorkshire named in Domesday. (Reprinted from the *Yorks. Archaeol. and Topogr. Assoc. Jour.* iv (1877), 114–57, 214–48, 384–415; v (1879), 289–330).

See No. 3042.

3038 STEVENSON (W. H.). 'Yorkshire surveys and other documents of the eleventh century in the York gospels'. *E.H.R.* xxvii (1912), 1–25.

Anglo-Saxon surveys of three Yorkshire estates, probably of about the year 1030.

d. Modern commentaries on Domesday Book

3039 BALLARD (ADOLPHUS). The Domesday inquest. Lond. 1906; 2nd edn. 1923.

Valuable general analysis. The second edition (pp. 267–71) contains 'A bibliography of matter relating to Domesday Book published between the years 1906 and 1923' by Mrs. Hilary Jenkinson. See also Ballard's *Domesday Boroughs* (No. 5347).

3040 BARING (FRANCIS H.). Domesday tables for the counties of Surrey, Middlesex, Hertford, Buckingham, and Bedford, and for the New Forest. Lond. 1909.

See also his 'The Exeter Domesday', *E.H.R.* xxvii (1912), 309–18. The appendix to Domesday tables contains articles (originally published in *E.H.R.* 1898, 1905, 1907), relating to William's march from Hastings to London, and to the battle of Hastings.

3041 BIRCH (WALTER DE GRAY). Domesday Book. Lond. 1887; 2nd edn. 1908.

A popular account. Bibliography, pp. 315–24.

3042 BROOKS (FRANK W.). 'Domesday Book and the East Riding'. East Yorks. Local Hist. Soc. Ser. no. 21. York. 1966.

3043 CORBETT (WILLIAM J.). 'The development of the Duchy of Normandy and the Norman Conquest of England'. *Cambr. Med. Hist.* v (1926), 505–13; 886–93.

3044 DARBY (HENRY C.). The Domesday geography of eastern England. Cambr. 1952. The Domesday geography of midland England. By H. C. Darby and I. B. Terrett. Cambr. 1954. Domesday geography of South-east England, by H. C. Darby and E. M. J. Campbell. Lond. 1962. Of Northern England, by H. C. Darby and I. S. Maxwell. 1962. South-west England, by H. C. Darby and R. W. Finn (1967).

> The volumes of a series of the whole of Domesday England are a rich quarry of information. Each chapter in each volume provides a bibliographical note. There are numerous excellent maps.

3045 DEMAREST (E. B.). 'The hundred-pennies'. *E.H.R.* xxxiii (1918), 62–72. Idem, 'The firma unius noctis', ibid. xxxv (1920); 78–89. Idem, 'Inter Ripam et Mersham', ibid. xxxviii (1923), 161–70. Idem, 'Consuetudo regis in Essex, Norfolk and Suffolk', ibid. xlii (1927), 161–79.

3046 DOMESDAY RE-BOUND. H.M.S.O. Lond. 1954.

> A brochure on the details of the binding with commentary on the origin and history of Domesday, a list of published editions and much else.

3047 DOMESDAY STUDIES: papers read at the meeting of the Domesday commemoration, 1886. Ed. by P. E. Dove. 2 vols. Lond. 1888–91. Reprinted 1965.

> The study of Domesday, by Stuart A. Moore, i. 1–36. Domesday survivals, by Isaac Taylor, i. 47–66. Danegeld and finance, by J. H. Round, i. 77–142. The ploughland, by Isaac Taylor, i. 143–88. Measures of land, by J. H. Round, i. 189–225. Unit of assessment, by O. C. Pell, i. 227–385, ii. 561–619. The church (episcopal endowments), by James Parker, ii. 399–432.
> Official custody of Domesday, by Hubert Hall, ii. 517–37.
> An early reference to Domesday, by J. H. Round, ii. 539–59.
> Domesday bibliography, by H. B. Wheatley, ii. 663–95.
> Some of these essays, especially those of Round, are very valuable. On the early custody of Domesday, see also the papers by Round and Hall in the *Antiquary*, xv (1887), 246–9; xvi (1887), 8–12, 62–4. Round continued his discussion of measures of land in the *Archaeol. Rev.* i (1888–9), 285–95; iv. 130–40. See also No. 3061.

3048 DOUGLAS (DAVID). 'The Domesday Survey'. *History*, xxi (1936–7), 249–57.

> A 'historical revision' and a bibliographical article.

3049 ELLIS (HENRY). General introduction to Domesday Book. Rec. Comm. 2 vols. Lond. 1833.

> An older edition will be found in vol. iii of Domesday (No. 3009). Ellis gives useful statistics compiled from the survey.

3050 FEILITZEN (OLOF VON). The pre-conquest personal names of Domesday Book. Uppsala. 1937.

3051 FINN (REX WELLDON). An introduction to Domesday Book. N.Y. 1963. Idem, 'The immediate sources of the Exchequer Domesday'. *B.J.R.L.* xl

(1957), 47–78. Idem, 'The evolution of successive versions of Domesday Book'. *E.H.R.* lxvi (1951), 561–4.

An introduction brings together the several studies made by Finn.

3052 FINN (R. W.). Domesday Studies: The Eastern Counties. Lond. and Hamden (Conn.). 1967.

A study of Domesday ii, *Inquisitio Eliensis*, and Feudal Book of Abbot Baldwin.

3053 GALBRAITH (VIVIAN H.). The making of Domesday Book. Lond. 1961.

An important book on the relationship of Domesday with its satellites and on the procedure by which Domesday Book was compiled. The book was preceded by a seminal article of the same title, *E.H.R.* lvii (1942), 160–77. This attack on Round's thesis produced much controversial comment, for which reference may be made to D. C. Douglas, *William the Conqueror* (No. 3986), p. 348. See also Nos. 3062–3 and Galbraith's 'Notes on the career of Samson, bishop of Worcester' (1096–1112)', *E.H.R.* lxxxii (1967), 86–101, where it is asked if Samson was the man behind Domesday Book. Barbara Dodwell, 'The making of Domesday survey in Norfolk: the hundred and a half of Clacklose', *E.H.R.* lxxxiv (1969), 79–84.

3054 HOYT (ROBERT S.). 'Farm of the manor and community of the vill in Domesday Book'. *Speculum*, xxx (1955), 147–69.

3055 INMAN (ALFRED H.). Domesday and feudal statistics, with a chapter on agricultural statistics. Lond. 1900.

Idem, Domesday and feudal statistics exemplified, with some observations on early knight service. Lond. 1901.

3056 KELHAM (ROBERT). Domesday Book illustrated. Lond. 1788. Includes, pp. 135–369, a glossary of difficult words.

3057 LENNARD (REGINALD). 'Domesday plough-teams: the south-western evidence'. *E.H.R.* lx (1945), 217–33.

Idem, 'The economic position of the Domesday *villani*', *Econ. Jour.* lvi (1946), 244–64. Idem, 'The economic position of the Domesday sokemen', *Econ. Jour.* lvii (1947), 179–95. Idem, 'The economic position of the bordars and cottars of Domesday book', *Econ. Jour.* lxi (1951), 342–71. Idem, 'The hidation of "demesne" in some Domesday entries', *Econ. Hist. Rev.* N.S. vii (1954), 67–70. See Lennard's *Rural England* (No. 4973). Idem, 'Composition of the Domesday caruca', *E.H.R.* lxxxi (1966), 770–5.

3058 MAITLAND (FREDERIC W.). Domesday book and beyond. Cambr. 1897. Reprinted, 1907.

A classic consisting of three essays: (i) Domesday Book, pp. 1–219; (ii) England before the conquest, pp. 220–356; (iii) The hide, pp. 357–520.

3059 PAGE (WILLIAM). 'Some remarks on the churches of the Domesday survey'. *Archaeol.* lxvi (1914–15), 61–102.

3060 POLLOCK (FREDERICK). 'A brief survey of Domesday'. *E.H.R.* xi (1896), 209–30.

3061 ROUND (JOHN HORACE). Feudal England; historical studies of the 11th and 12th centuries. Lond. 1895. Reprinted, 1909 and 1964.

Domesday Book, pp. 3–146.
The Northamptonshire Geld-roll, pp. 147–56.
The knights of Peterborough, pp. 157–68.
The Worcestershire survey (Hen. I), pp. 169–80.
The Lindsey survey (1115–18), pp. 181–95.
The Leicestershire survey (1124–9), pp. 196–214.
The Northamptonshire survey (Hen. I–Hen. II), pp. 214–24.
The introduction of knight service into England, pp. 225–314.

Part ii (Historical Studies), covering pp. 317–576, is a miscellaneous series of short studies. Round's studies on Domesday are fundamental; they are scattered in many places but can be traced in the bibliography of his writings in *Family Origins* (No. 569).

3062 SAWYER (PETER H.). 'The "Original Returns" and Domesday Book'. *E.H.R.* lxx (1955), 177–97. Idem, 'The place names of the Domesday manuscripts'. *B.J.R.L.* xxxviii (1955–6), 483–506.

3063 STEPHENSON (CARL). 'Notes on the composition and interpretation of Domesday book'. *Speculum*, xxii (1947), 1–15. Idem, 'Commendation and related problems in Domesday'. *E.H.R.* lix (1944), 289–310. Cf. Barbara Dodwell, 'East Anglian commendation', ibid. lxiii (1948), 289–306.

3064 STEVENSON (WILLIAM H.). 'The hundreds of Domesday'. *E.H.R.* v (1890), 95–100. Idem, 'A contemporary description of the Domesday survey'. *E.H.R.* xxii (1907), 72–84.

3. *Local Inquests and Surveys 1066–1200*

Arranged Chronologically

On these surveys, see R. W. Southern, 'The place of Henry I in English history', *P.B.A.* xlvii (1962), 166–9.

3065 NORTHAMPTONSHIRE GELD ROLLS (1068–1083). Ed., trans., and annotated in Robertson, *Charters* (No. 2203), pp. 230–7; 481–4; printed as a footnote in Ellis (No. 3009), i. 184–7. Trans. in *Eng. hist. docs.* ii. 483–6. For commentaries, see Round, *Feudal England* (No. 3061), pp. 147–56; and V.C.H. *Northamptonshire*, i. 259.

3066 INQUISITIO GELDI. Printed in the Record Commission's edition of Domesday Book (No. 3009), iii. 1–75; and 489–91. Text and translation by R. R. Darlington in V.C.H. *Wiltshire*, ii. 178–217.

Bound up with the Exon Domesday, it records 'the amount of geld which the king obtained from the several hundreds' of the five south-western shires. Eyton (No. 3028) dates it 1084; Galbraith dates it slightly after the 1086 inquest: V. H. Galbraith, 'The date of the Geld Rolls in Exon Domesday', *E.H.R.* lxv (1950), 1–17; J. F. A. Mason, 'The date of the Geld Rolls', ibid. lxix (1954), 283–9. See also Darlington in V.C.H. *Wiltshire*, ii. 169–77; and Ann Williams in V.C.H. *Dorset*, iii. 115–49.

3067 THE NORTHAMPTONSHIRE SURVEY. Ed. by J. H. Round, in *Feudal England* (No. 3061), pp. 214–24. Trans. by J. H. Round, in V.C.H. *Northamptonshire* (No. 1529), i. 357–92.

In his *Feudal England* Round prints only about a fifth of the survey, which is somewhat similar to that of Leicestershire (No. 3074). He believes that it 'was originally made under Henry I, and was subsequently corrected here and there, to bring the entries up to date, down to the days of Henry II'. See also his essay on the 'Hidation of Northamptonshire', *E.H.R.* xv (1900), 78–86; and F. Baring's two papers, 'The Hidation of Northamptonshire in 1086', and 'The Pre-Domesday Hidation of Northamptonshire', ibid. xvii (1902), 76–83, 470–9; and Cyril Hart, *The hidation of Northamptonshire* (Leicester Univ. Dept. Local Hist. 2nd Ser. Leicester, 1970).

3068 ABINGDON. D. C. Douglas. 'Some early surveys of the abbey of Abingdon'. *E.H.R.* xliv (1929), 618–25.

3069 PETERBOROUGH. Descriptio militum de abbatia de Burgo, edited in Thomas Stapleton, *Chronicon Petroburgense.* Camden Soc. Old Ser. xlvii (1849), 168–75. (See No. 6265.)

C. W. Hollister, 'The Knights of Peterborough and the Anglo-Norman fyrd', *E.H.R.* lxxvii (1962), 417–36. Edmund King, 'The Peterborough *Descriptio militum*', ibid. lxxxiv (1969), 84–101.

3070 THE DOMESDAY MONACHORUM OF CHRIST CHURCH, CANTERBURY. Edited with an introduction by David C. Douglas. Lond. 1944.

A facsimile and transcribed text of a manuscript written in three hands of about 1100, 1150, and 1200. It includes four groups of documents, (*a*) ecclesiastical documents relating to Kent in the late eleventh century; (*b*) the Christ Church survey which is a Domesday satellite; (*c*) a list of knights of the Archbishop of Canterbury of about 1095; and (*d*) miscellaneous documents concerning the affairs of Christ Church of the late twelfth century. The printed text is preceded (pp. 3–71) by an important introduction by D. C. Douglas.

3071 THE WORCESTERSHIRE SURVEY. *Temp.* Hen. I, in Thomas Hearne's edition of Heming's *Chartularium Ecclesiae Wigorniensis*, pp. 313–16. Oxf. 1723.

This survey seems to have been made in consequence of a dispute between the sheriff of the shire and the church of Worcester as to the number of hides in the county for which that church should be rated. See Round, *Feudal England* (No. 3061), pp. 169–80; also his translation of 'some early Worcestershire surveys', appended to his edition of the Domesday survey in V.C.H. *Worcestershire* (No. 1529), i. 324–31.

3072 LIBER WINTON. Ed. Henry Ellis, *Domesday Book* (No. 3009), iv. 529–62. Rec. Comm. Lond. 1816.

The *Liber Winton*, which is preserved in the library of the Society of Antiq. of Lond., comprises two distinct records. The first is a survey of royal lands in Winchester, with the landgavel and geld paid in the time of Edward the Confessor and Henry I; it was made between 1103 and 1115, by order of the king, from the verdicts of eighty-six burgesses. The second is an inquest of all lands in Winchester, made in 1148 by command of the Bishop of Winchester. See Round's account of the Winchester survey, in V.C.H. *Hampshire* (No. 1529), i. 527–37.

3073 THE LINDSEY SURVEY (1115–18): The Lincolnshire survey, *temp.* Hen. I (facsimile of the whole text, with a translation). Ed. by James Greenstreet. Lond. 1884. Printed in Hearne's *Liber Niger Scaccarii* (No. 3006). Trans. by R. E. C. Waters, *A roll of the owners of land in the parts of Lindsey in Lincolnshire, compared with the Domesday survey of Lindsey.* Reprinted from *Asso. Arch. Soc. Repts.* (No. 171), xvi, pt. ii (1882). Trans. in C. W. Foster, *et al.*, *The Lincolnshire Domesday and the Lindsey Survey*, Lincoln Rec. Soc. xix (1924), 237–60.

This survey, made in 1115–18 for the assessment of a geld, is drawn up riding by riding and wapentake by wapentake, and gives the names of the tenants. See Round, *Feudal England* (No. 3061), pp. 181–95.

3074 THE LEICESTERSHIRE SURVEY, *c.* A.D. 1130. Ed. by C. F. Slade. Univ. Coll. of Leicester, Dept. of Eng. Loc. Hist., Occasional Papers, No. 7 (1956). The Leicestershire survey, ed. by J. H. Round, *Feudal England* (No. 3061), pp. 196–203. Survey of Leicestershire (with a photographic copy. Trans. by W. K. Boyd.), *Leicestershire Archit. and Archaeol. Soc., Trans.* viii (1896), 179–83. Leicestershire survey (with map). Trans. by F. M. Stenton, in V.C.H. *Leicestershire* (No. 1529), i. 339–54.

This survey deals with the landowners of various hundreds, vill by vill, and was probably compiled in connection with the assessment of a geld.

3075 THE HEREFORDSHIRE DOMESDAY, *c.* 1160–70, reproduced by collotype from facsimile photographs of Balliol College Manuscript 350. Ed. by V. H. Galbraith and James Tait. Pipe Roll Soc. N.S. xxv (1950).

A transcript of the Herefordshire portion of Domesday Book, made in the royal scriptorium about 1160–70, to which the names of some new holders of the properties are added. It appears to be an experimental attempt 'to bring the Domesday of Hereford up-to-date'. It may have been compiled by that Master Thomas Brown who is mentioned in the *Dialogus*.

3076 BOLDON BUKE: a survey of the possessions of the see of Durham made by order of bishop Hugh Pudsey in 1183, with a translation. Ed. by William Greenwell. Surtees Soc. Durham. 1852. Trans. with critical introduction, by G. T. Lapsley, in V.C.H. *Durham* (No. 1529), i. 259–341.

This survey enumerates various services and rents due to the bishop; it is called *Boldon Book* because the services of the village of Boldon are often referred to as a standard. There is another edition, by Ellis (No. 3009). Lapsley's text is based on a collation of the MSS. used by Ellis and Greenwell with the older Stowe MS., which they had not seen. Greenwell, in his appendix, prints extracts from the pipe rolls of Henry I, Richard I, and John, with Bishop Bek's great roll of receipts, A.D. 1309, and several charters.

4. *Pipe Rolls*

These great annual rolls of the Exchequer were so called because of their resemblance, when rolled, to drainage or similar pipes. Originally they contained only, county by county, the audited accounts of sheriffs and other Crown debtors. Details of royal income are to be found not only in the regular revenues from royal demesnes but also in the irregular taxations, judicial amercements, and agreements made with the king for privileges and favours. Details of some expenditure are given in the recurring grants of alms and lands and in the non-recurring expenditure of sheriffs and some others on the king's behalf. To these county accounts there were later added private charters enrolled for safe custody, and other accounts audited in the Exchequer, of customs, army, navy, etc. These foreign accounts became so numerous that ordinances 1323–6 directed their separate enrolment; many remained on the pipe, however, until 42 Edw. III (1368), when the regular series of foreign account rolls began. See the 1963 *Guide to the P.R.O.* (No. 951), i. 76–8.

The extant series of pipe rolls begins in 31 Henry I (1130) and continues, after a long break from 1130 until 2 Henry II (1156), with a few later losses, until 1832. It is one of the most complete series of national records, particularly important in the twelfth century, which lacks most official records.

There is a parallel series of pipe rolls, prepared for the Chancellor and known as Chancellor's rolls. The rolls are generally duplicates, containing a little additional material, particularly enrolled private charters. This imperfect series runs from 9 Henry II (1163) to 1832.

a. General collections

The early pipe rolls are printed in two series: the editions produced by Joseph Hunter for the Record Commission and the editions published by the Pipe Roll Society.

3077 RECORD COMMISSION EDITIONS produced by Joseph Hunter. Magnum Rotulum Scaccarii, vel rotulum pipae, anno tricesimo-primo regni Henrici primi. Lond. 1833. This edition of the earliest surviving pipe roll was reissued in facsimile, with some corrections listed by Charles Johnson, by H.M.S.O. in 1929. The Great Roll of the Pipe for the second, third, and fourth years of the reign of King Henry the Second, A.D. 1155–6, 1156–7, 1157–8. Lond. 1844. Reissued in facsimile by H.M.S.O. in 1931. The Great Roll of the Pipe for the first year of the reign of Richard the First, A.D. 1189–1190. Lond. 1844. Rotulus Cancellarii, vel antigraphum magni rotuli pipae, de tertio anno regni regis Jonannis. Lond. 1833.

3078 THE GREAT ROLL OF THE PIPE (For the fifth year of the reign of King Henry the Second, A.D. 1158–1159 . . . for the thirty-fourth year of the reign of King Henry the Second, A.D. 1187–1188). 30 vols. Pipe Roll Soc. Pubns. 1884–1925.

The volumes from the twenty-second year to the thirty-third year contain introductions by J. H. Round.

3079 THE GREAT ROLL OF THE PIPE (For the second year of the reign of Richard the First, . . . for the seventeenth year of the reign of King John). 24 vols. Pipe Roll Soc. Pubns. 1925–64.

Most of the volumes in this new series have been edited by Doris M. Stenton.

3080 THE GREAT ROLL OF THE PIPE for the fourteenth year of the reign of Henry III, Michaelmas 1230. Ed. by Chalfant Robinson. Pipe Roll Soc. Pubns. New Ser. iv (1927).

3081 THE GREAT ROLL OF THE PIPE for the twenty-sixth year of the reign of King Henry III, A.D. 1241–2. Ed. by H. L. Cannon. Yale Hist. Pubns. New Haven. 1918.

3082 THE CHANCELLOR'S ROLL for the eighth year of the reign of King Richard I, Michaelmas 1196. Ed. by D. M. Stenton. Pipe Roll Soc. Pubns. New Ser. vii (1930).

b. Pipe rolls by counties

BEDFORDSHIRE

3083   A CALENDAR OF THE PIPE ROLLS of the reign of Richard I for
Buckinghamshire and Bedfordshire. Ed. by G. H. Fowler and M. W. Hughes.
Beds. Hist. Rec. Soc. Pubns. vii (1923).

CHESHIRE

3084   CHESHIRE IN THE PIPE ROLLS, 1158–1301. (Transcribed from
1237 by Mabel H. Mills.) Ed. by Ronald Stewart-Brown. Lanc. and Chesh. Rec.
Soc. xcii (1938). See Palatinate of Chester, below, pp. 574–6.

The appendix gives the first account of the chamberlain (1301).

CUMBERLAND, ETC.

3085   THE PIPE ROLLS FOR THE COUNTIES OF CUMBERLAND,
WESTMORLAND, AND DURHAM during the reigns of Henry II, Richard I,
and John. Ed. by J. H. Hinde. Soc. of Antiq. of Newcastle. 1847.

3086   THE PIPE ROLLS OF CUMBERLAND AND WESTMORLAND,
1222–1260. Ed. by F. H. M. Parker. Cumb. and Westm. Antiq. and Archaeol.
Soc. Kendal. 1905.

See also a translation of early Cumberland pipe rolls, 1130–1214, by James Wilson
in V.C.H. *Cumberland* (No. 1529), i. 338–418.

DERBYSHIRE AND NOTTS.

3087   EXTRACTS FROM THE PIPE ROLLS FOR THE COUNTIES OF
NOTTINGHAM AND DERBY, 1131–1307. Ed. by J. P. Yeatman in *Feudal
Hist. of the County of Derby*, i. 89–263. Lond. 1886.

Translation only. Also separately published.

DEVONSHIRE

3088   REICHEL (O. J.). Extracts from the pipe rolls of Henry II relating to
Devon, with an appendix from *Testa de Nevill*. Reprinted from the *Devon. Assoc.
for the Advancement of Science, etc., Trans.* xxix (1897), 453–509.

Contains translations of extracts, 1158–67, and the translation of an account roll of aids
taken from *Testa de Nevill*, A.D. 1236 (No. 4337).

3089   WHALE (T. W.). 'Notes on the pipe rolls of Henry II'. *Devon. Assoc. for
Advancement of Science, etc., Trans.* xxxiii (1901), 363–98.

Contains extracts from the *Red Book* (No. 3007).

DORSET

3090   BARNES (W. M.). 'The pipe rolls, Dorset 1130–1210'. *Dorset Nat. Hist.
and Antiq. Field Club, Procs.* xiv. 119–38; xv. 117–41; xvi. 129–49; xix. 65–81.
Dorchester. 1893–8.

Brief notes and abstracts.

LANCASHIRE

3091 THE LANCASHIRE PIPE ROLLS (1130–1216); also early Lancashire charters (1093–1216). Ed. by William Farrer. Liverpool. 1902.

Valuable. See also No. 3563.

NORTHUMBERLAND

3092 THE PIPE ROLLS FOR NORTHUMBERLAND, 1273–84, in continuation of the series printed in Hodgson's 'History of the county' (No. 1775), with a translation and notes. Ed. by William Dickson. 3 pts. Newcastle. 1854–60.

3093 PIPE ROLLS OF EDWARD I. 'Calendar of Northumberland Pipe Rolls, 1286–98'. By A. J. Lilburn. *Archaeol. Aeliana*, 4th Ser. xxxii (1954), 323–40; xxxiii (1955), 163–75; xxxiv (1956), 176–95; xxxv (1957), 144–62; xxxvi (1958), 271–95; xxxviii (1960), 179–91; xxxix (1961), 327–43; xli (1963), 107–22.

For vol. xxxii, the membrane for 1284–5 is transcribed, for the rest of the volumes, the membranes are calendared.

STAFFORDSHIRE

3094 THE STAFFORDSHIRE PIPE ROLLS, 1130–1216. The Latin text extended and notes added. Ed. by R. W. Eyton. Wm. Salt Archaeol. Soc. *Collections*, i (1881), 1–143; ii (1882), 1–177.

See also C. G. O. Bridgeman's 'Forest Pleas in the Staffordshire Pipe Roll of 13 Hen. II (1166–67)', ibid. vol. for 1923, 291–302. Lond. 1924.

SURREY

3095 THE PIPE ROLL FOR 1295, SURREY MEMBRANE (Pipe Roll 140). Ed. by Mabel Mills. Surrey Rec. Soc. xxi (1924).

The introduction provides an excellent description of exchequer procedure at the end of the thirteenth century.

WILTSHIRE

3096 WILTSHIRE PIPE ROLLS, *temp.* Henrici II, A.D. 1159 ad 1179. Ed. by Thomas Phillipps. Middle Hill Press. 1853.

Zincographed facsimile.

IRELAND

3097 CATALOGUE OF ACCOUNTS ON THE PIPE ROLLS OF (THE) IRISH EXCHEQUER (Hen. III and 1–12 Edw. I). *Deputy Keeper's Reports, Ireland*, xxxv (1903), 29–50; xxxvi (1904), 22–77.

3098 INVENTORY OF THE (IRISH) PIPE ROLLS. 13 Hen. III–Geo. II. *Irish Record Comm.* 8th report (1819), 125–36.

3099 IRISH PIPE ROLL OF 14 JOHN, 1211–12. Ed. by Oliver Davies and David B. Quinn. *Ulster Jour. Archaeology*, 3rd. Ser. iv (1941), *Supplement*.

3100 LYDON (J. F.). 'Survey of the memoranda rolls of the Irish exchequer, 1294–1509'. *Analecta Hibernica*, xxiii (1966), 49–134. Idem, 'Three exchequer documents from the reign of Henry III'. *Royal Irish Acad. Procs.* lxv. *Sect. C*, no. 1 (1966), 1–27.

For fifteenth-century rolls of Irish exchequer, turn to No. 3217. Articles on Irish revenues, by Lydon are noticed in (No. 3248).

3101   QUINN (DAVID B.). 'Guide to English financial records for Irish history, 1461–1558'. *Analecta Hibernica*, x (1941), 1–69.

See No. 3260, and 'The state of the exchequer' in *Cal. Docs. Ireland* (No. 3797).

NORMANDY

3102   MAGNI ROTULI SCACCARII NORMANNIAE SUB REGIBUS ANGLIAE. Ed. by Thomas Stapleton. Soc. Antiq. of London. 2 vols. Lond. 1840–4.

Stapleton's edition contains, besides the editor's learned introduction, a roll of 1180, a fragment of the roll of 1184, two rolls of 1195 and 1198, and detached membranes of the years 1201–3. This edition was reprinted, with an additional fragment of 1184, in *Mémoires de la Société des antiquaires de Normandie*, xv–xvi (Paris, etc. 1846–52). Henry Petrie also edited *Magni rotuli scaccarii Normanniae, 1184* (Lond. 1830). Michel de Boüard, 'La Salle de l'Echiquier au Château de Caen', *Medieval Archaeology*, ix (1965), 64–81.

3103   MISCELLANEOUS RECORDS OF THE NORMAN EXCHEQUER, 1199–1204. Edited with a critical commentary by Sidney R. Packard. Smith College Stud. in Hist. xii (1926–7).

See also G. F. B. de Gruchy, 'The entries relating to Jersey in the great rolls of the exchequer of Normandy of A.D. 1180', Société Jersiaise (Jersey, 1919). Also J. Le Patourel, 'The account of Hugh of St. Philibert, 1226', *Société Jersiaise Bull.* xv (1952), 465–73.

5. *Receipt and Issue Rolls*

See 1963 *Guide to P.R.O.* (No. 951), pp. 95–6; and Steele (No. 3263). These rolls include:

1. Receipt rolls. The earliest receipt rolls are arranged under counties, like the pipe rolls, but from 21 Henry III (1237) they are in chronological order. They cover, with gaps, the period 7 Hen. II (1161)–22 George III (1782), with duplicates and sometimes triplicates prepared for different Exchequer officers.

Separate rolls, Jewish receipt rolls, were kept for receipts from the tallages etc. imposed on the Jews, 14 John (1216)–23 Edward I (1295); others record receipts from taxes on movables, 19 Edward I (1291)–11 Edward II (1317), and renewals of lost tallies (Innovate rolls), 19 Edward I (1291)–27 Charles II (1675).

2. Issues rolls (*a*) Liberate rolls. Warrants for the issue of money from the Exchequer, or allowances to accountants at audit, were first enrolled on the Chancery close rolls, then on the parallel series of Exchequer and Chancery liberate rolls, 2 John (1200)–14 Henry VI (1435). These are important for the thirteenth century but decline in interest thereafter.

(*b*) Issue rolls. These contain entries of all payments made by the Treasurer and Chamberlains in the lower Exchequer, covering the period 25 Henry III

(1241)–19 Edward IV (1479), and 9 Elizabeth I (1567)–37 George III (1797). Duplicates and even triplicates survive, prepared for various Exchequer officers; later gaps can be supplied from Pells Issue Books.

(c) Praestita rolls, John–James I, which record payments made from the Exchequer to royal officers and others as advances or loans and charged to the account of the recipient. See Wardrobe.

(d) Misae rolls, only two survive, 11 and 14 John (Nos. 3104, 3110); they contain a journal of the expenses of the court probably prepared in the Chamber. They are properly household accounts.

Various Irish receipt rolls and treasurers' accounts of Edward I's reign are printed in the *Calendar of Documents relating to Ireland* (No. 3797).

3104 DOCUMENTS ILLUSTRATIVE OF ENGLISH HISTORY IN THE THIRTEENTH AND FOURTEENTH CENTURIES, from the records of the queen's remembrancer. Ed. by Henry Cole. Rec. Comm. Lond. 1844.

Rotulus misae, 14 John, pp. 231–69. *Rotulus de praestito*, 7 John, pp. 270–6. See Nos. 3310 and 3518.

3105 EXTRACTS FROM THE LIBERATE ROLLS RELATIVE TO (THE REPAYMENT OF) LOANS SUPPLIED BY ITALIAN MERCHANTS TO THE KINGS OF ENGLAND IN THE THIRTEENTH AND FOURTEENTH CENTURIES, with an introductory memoir by E. A. Bond. Ed. by C. G. Young. *Archaeologia*, xxviii (1840), 207–326.

3106 ISSUE ROLL OF THOMAS DE BRANTINGHAM, treasurer of England, 44 Edward III, A.D. 1370. Trans. by Frederick Devon. Rec. Comm. 1835.

Translation only.

3107 ISSUES OF THE EXCHEQUER. (Extracts, Hen. III–39 Hen. VI; with an appendix, I Edw. IV–45 Eliz.). Trans. by Frederick Devon. Rec. Comm. 1837.

Translation only. The extracts 10–26 Henry III are from the liberate rolls. Devon also translated extracts from later issue rolls: *Issues of the Exchequer during the Reign of James I* (Lond. 1836). These two volumes and No. 3106 were published under the direction of the comptroller of the receipt of the Exchequer.

3108 JENKINSON (HILARY) and BROOME (DOROTHY). 'An exchequer statement of receipts and issues: 1339–1340'. *E.H.R.* lviii (1943), 210–16.

3109 RECEIPT ROLL OF THE EXCHEQUER FOR MICHAELMAS TERM, 1185: a fragment of a unique record, reproduced in thirty-one plates. Ed. by Hubert Hall. Lond. 1899.

This was apparently one of a series of receipt rolls made up in the lower Exchequer twice a year, at the Easter and Michaelmas sessions; of this series only fragments are now extant. The roll of 1185 seems to have recorded all sums received at the lower Exchequer, while the pipe rolls recorded 'only such as were paid on account or were connected with a permanent liability'. Single payments made in full, such as fines and amercements, were usually entered in the receipt roll.

3110 ROTULI DE LIBERATE AC DE MISIS ET PRAESTITIS
REGNANTE JOHANNE. Ed. by T. D. Hardy. Rec. Comm. Lond. 1844.

Contains liberate rolls, 2, 3, 5 John, the misae roll of 11 John, and the praestita roll
of 12 John. See also 'Liberate Rolls, Henry III, relating to Staffordshire', in *Wm. Salt
Archaeol. Soc. Collections*, xiv (1911), 1–25. Hitherto unprinted fragments of the Liberate
Rolls of 2 John are printed in Memoranda Rolls. Pipe Roll Soc. Pubns. xxi (1943),
88–97. Praestita Roll 14–17 John. Ed. by J. C. Holt. Pipe Roll Soc. Pubns. xxxvii
(1964). See No. 3774.

6. *The Household: Wardrobe and Chamber*

All medieval government departments had their origin in the royal household,
dealing with the business of both kingdom and household. As the business of the
kingdom increased, the departments concentrated on it, settled in a fixed place,
and left the court. Household administration fell to a new office, variously called
the Chamber and the Wardrobe. The Chamber was dominant up to the early
years of the thirteenth century: in Henry III's reign it was replaced by the
Wardrobe, to be revived in the reigns of Edward II and Edward III.

The departments drew money from special assignments or from the Exchequer,
but were exempt from all Exchequer control except audit. As they were com-
paratively small and flexible, they gave the king an independence from the
established governmental machine which provoked opposition from the barons
in 1258 and 1311. Reinforced with privy (Wardrobe) or signet (Chamber) seals,
they were also capable of expansion, e.g. to organize the Scottish wars of
Edward I, while continuing to deal through their sub-departments, e.g. Pantry
and Buttery, Great Wardrobe, with the daily household routine. Lesser wardrobes
dealt with the domestic business of queens, princes, etc. The wardrobe accounts
extend from John's reign to 56 George III. The fullest of those in print can be
found in *Liber quotidianus* of 28 Edward I (No. 3126), and in Myers's study of
the accounts of Edward IV (No. 3128).

The classic volumes on the wardrobe developments are Tout, *Administrative
history* (No. 1223). There is also much for Edward II's reign in Tout's *Edward II*
(No. 4140) and Conway Davies, *Baronial Opposition* (No. 4115). Myers is the
authority for the household of the mid-fifteenth century. The P.R.O. *List of
documents* (No. 3127) 'attempts to bring together on paper as many as possible
of the surviving documents which, now scattered over a number of present-day
record classes, can be recognized as having once formed part of the archives of
a single department of medieval administration' (preface). The list's categories
indicate the diversity of the wardrobe's interests.

Numerous wardrobe documents are printed in Tout's *Administrative history*
(No. 1223) and his *Edward II* and some extracts are given in Bain's *Calendar*
(No. 3789) and in Stevenson's *Documents* (No. 3791).

a. Household ordinances and accounts

3111 ACCOUNTS OF THE EXPENSES OF THE GREAT WARDROBE
OF EDWARD III, 1344–49. Ed. by N. H. Nicolas. *Archaeol.* xxxi (1846), 5–103.

3112 BAILDON (WILLIAM P.). 'A wardrobe account of 16–17 Richard II, 1393–94'. *Archaeol.* lxii, pt. ii (1911), 497–514.

3113 BOOK OF PRESTS OF THE KING'S WARDROBE FOR 1294–95. Presented to John Goronwy Edwards. Ed. by E. B. Fryde. Oxf. 1962.

This Book of Prests records heavy commitments of money and payments made during the Welsh campaign of 1294–5. Related documents are printed in the appendix as well as a list of the writings of Sir Goronwy Edwards. The introduction shows the place of prests in wardrobe administration.

3114 COLLECTION OF ORDINANCES AND REGULATIONS FOR THE GOVERNMENT OF THE ROYAL HOUSEHOLD, EDWARD III– WILLIAM AND MARY. Soc. of Antiq. of London. Lond. 1790.

Regulations of 21 Edward III, 33 Henry VI, Liber Niger Domus Regis (Edward IV), etc.: a valuable collection. Household Ordinance of 1279, printed in Tout, *Administrative history* (No. 1223), ii. 158–63; Household Ordinances of Edward II, 1318 and 1323, in Tout, *Place . . . Edward II* (No. 4115), 1st edn., pp. 267–318; 2nd edn., pp. 244–84. A poor translation into English in *Life-records of Chaucer* (No. 7008), pt. ii. Household Ordinance of 1454, in *Procs. . . . Privy Council* (No. 3294), vi. 220–33. See A. R. Myers (No. 3128).

3115 COMPUTUS MAGISTRI WILLIELMI DE LUDA (10–13 Edward I for the expedition to Wales). Printed by H. Ellis in *Chronica . . . Oxenedes* (No. 2939), pp. 326–36.

Gives receipts from various sources.

3116 CONSTITUTIO DOMUS REGIS (*c.* A.D. 1136), printed in C. Johnson, *Dialogus de Scaccario* (No. 3005), 128–35. Hall, *Red Book* (No. 3007), iii. 807–13. Hearne, *Liber Niger* (No. 3006), i. 341–59.

See also G. H. White, 'The household of the Norman kings', *T.R.H.S.* 4th Ser. xxx (1948), 127–55; and his 'The Constitutio Domus Regis and the king's sport', *Antiquaries Jour.* xxx (1950), 52–63.

3117 COPY OF A ROLL OF PURCHASES MADE FOR THE TOURNA- MENT OF WINDSOR PARK, 6 EDWARD I. Ed. by Samuel Lysons. *Archaeol.* xvii (1814), 297–310.

3118 DAVIES (J. CONWAY). 'The first journal of Edward II's chamber'. *E.H.R.* xxx (1915), 662–80.

3119 DENHOLM-YOUNG (NOEL). 'Edward of Windsor and Bermondsey priory'. *E.H.R.* xlviii (1933), 431–3. Repr. in *Collected Papers* (No. 1465).

Household expenses of Edward of Windsor 1325.

3120 EXTRACTS FROM THE ROTULUS FAMILIAE, 18 EDWARD I. Ed. by Samuel Lysons. *Archaeol.* xv (1806), 350–62.

This roll contains the daily expenses of the royal family for seventeen weeks.

3121 HOUSEHOLD ROLL OF EDWARD PRINCE OF WALES, 1302–3, in Bain, *Calendar* (No. 3789), ii. 364–70. See No. 4604.

3122 INVENTORY OF CROWN JEWELS (in the king's wardrobe), 3 Edward III. Ed. by Craven Ord. *Archaeol.* x (1792), 241–60.

There is another inventory of jewels in Cole's *Documents* (No. 3104), pp. 277–84: 'De jocalibus a thesauro garderobae surreptis', 31 Edward I.

3123 JOHNSTONE (HILDA). 'The wardrobe and household accounts of the sons of Edward I'. *B.I.H.R.* ii (1925), 37–45.

A list of surviving accounts running from 1273 to 1312.

3124 JOHNSTONE (HILDA). 'The wardrobe and household of Henry, son of Edward I'. *B.J.R.L.* vii (1923), 384–420.

3125 LETTERS OF EDWARD, PRINCE OF WALES, 1304–5. Ed. by Hilda Johnstone. Roxburghe Club, cxciv (1931).

For a calendar of some of these letters, see Deputy Keeper's Report, ix (1848), app. ii, 246–9; some extracts are printed in W. H. Blaauw, *Sussex Archaeol. Collections*, ii (1844), 80–98.

3126 LIBER QUOTIDIANUS CONTRAROTULATORIS GARDERO-BAE. 28 Edward I, A.D. 1299–1300. Soc. of Antiq. of London. Lond. 1787.

Contains receipts and payments of the wardrobe; preceded by John Topham's observations regarding the record. This valuable day-book of the Comptroller of the Wardrobe is preserved in the library of the Society of Antiquaries.

3127 LIST OF DOCUMENTS RELATING TO THE HOUSEHOLD AND WARDROBE. John–Edward I. Public Record Office Handbook, no. 7. H.M.S.O. Lond. 1964.

3128 MYERS (ALEC R.). The household of Edward IV: the black book and the ordinance of 1478. Manchester. 1959.

Prints the ordinance of 1445, the Black Book of the household of Edward IV, the ordinance of 1471, and a draft of the ordinance of 1478. See also N. H. Nicolas, ed., *Privy purse expenses of Elizabeth of York*, (and) *wardrobe accounts of Edward IV* (Lond. 1830), where on pp. 112–70 are the wardrobe accounts of 1480. Reprinted, 1972.

3129 MYERS (ALEC R.). 'Some household ordinances of Henry VI'. *B.J.R.L.* xxxvi (1953–4), 449–67. Idem, 'The captivity of a royal witch: the household accounts of Queen Joan of Navarre, 1419–21'. Ibid. xxiv (1940), 263–84; xxvi (1941–42), 82–100. Idem, 'The household of Queen Margaret of Anjou 1452–53'. Ibid. xl (1957–8), 79–113, 391–431. Idem, 'The household of Queen Elizabeth Woodville, 1466–67'. Ibid. l (1967–8), 207–35; 443–81. Idem, 'The jewels of Queen Margaret of Anjou'. Ibid. xlii (1959), 113–31.

3130 PROCEEDINGS OF HIS MAJESTY'S COMMISSIONERS ON THE PUBLIC RECORDS, 1832–33. Ed. by C. P. Cooper. Lond. 1833.

Excerpts from the wardrobe accounts of 18 Edward II, pp. 173–80.

3131 ROLL OF EXPENSES OF EDWARD I AT RHUDDLAN CASTLE IN WALES (A.D. 1281–82). Ed. by Samuel Lysons, with a translation by John Brand. *Archaeol.* xvi (1812), 32–79.

Payments for carpenters, archers, masons, food, timber, etc.

3132 STAPLETON (THOMAS). 'A brief summary of the wardrobe accounts of 10, 11, 14 Edward II'. *Archaeol.* xxvi (1836), 318–45.

Commentary with English translation of documents.

3132A WOLFFE (BERTRAM P.). The Crown Lands, 1461–1536. Historical Problems: studies and documents. Lond. and N.Y. 1970.

The introduction, pp. 15–88, is a critical and meaty study of the revenues and financial organization of the frequently changing king's landed estate. On pp. 91–197 are printed translations of twenty-three documents, largely exchequer records, not previously printed. This study is important in showing the revival, under Edward IV, of the chamber as against the Exchequer as the receiver of revenues from royal estates. See also B. P. Wolffe, 'The management of English royal estates under the Yorkist kings', *E.H.R.* lxxi (1956), 1–27; and his 'Henry VII's land revenues and chamber finance', ibid. lxxix (1964), 225–54.

b. Modern commentaries

3133 EHRLICH (LUDWIG). 'Exchequer and Wardrobe in 1270'. *E.H.R.* xxxvi (1921), 553–4.

3134 HILL (MARY C.). The king's messengers 1199–1377: a contribution to the history of the royal household. Lond. 1961.

This book deals with the organization and life within the royal household especially at the lower levels, as well as the duties of messengers in the transport of letters, etc.

3135 JOHNSON (CHARLES). 'The system of account in the wardrobe of Edward I'. *T.R.H.S.* 4th Ser. vi (1923), 50–72.

3136 JOHNSON (JOHN H.). 'The king's wardrobe and household', in *The English government at work*, 1327–1336 (No. 3836), i. 206–49. Idem, 'The system of account in the wardrobe of Edward II'. *T.R.H.S.* 4th Ser. xii (1929), 75–104.

3137 JOHNSTONE (HILDA). 'The queen's household', in *The English Government at work*, 1327–36 (No. 3836), i. 250–99. Idem, 'Poor-relief in the royal households of thirteenth-century England'. *Speculum*, iv (1929), 149–67. Idem, 'The queen's exchequer under the three Edwards', in *Tait essays* (No. 1455), pp. 143–53. Idem, 'Pascasius Valentini and the Frescobaldi'. *B.I.H.R.* vi (1929), 10–12.

3138 OTWAY-RUTHVEN (JOCELYN). The king's secretary and the signet office in the fifteenth century. Cambr. 1939.

3139 ROUND (JOHN HORACE). The king's serjeants. Lond. 1911. J. H. Round, 'The legend of Eudo dapifer'. *E.H.R.* xxxvii (1922), 1–34. C. T. Clay, 'The keepership of the old palace of Westminster'. Ibid. lix (1944), 1–21.

3140 SAYLES (GEORGE O.). 'A dealer in wardrobe bills (1345)'. *Econ. H.R.* iii (1931), 268–73.

3141 STEEL (ANTHONY). 'The place of the king's household in English constitutional history to 1272'. *History*, xv (1930–1), 289–95. Idem, 'The negotiation of wardrobe debentures in the fourteenth century'. *E.H.R.* xliv (1929), 439–43.

7. *Subsidy Rolls and Taxation*

The subsidy rolls begin in Henry II's reign; they fall into two classifications: lay and clerical. For the clerical group turn to pp. 892–3 below. The lay subsidy rolls contain accounts, assessments, etc., relating to carucages, scutages, tallages, feudal aids, poll taxes, and especially the subsidies of tenths and fifteenths and other fractions on movables. It is generally thought that the tax on movables was introduced as the Saladin Tithe in 1188. It went through an 'experimental stage' (Willard) in the thirteenth century; and then from 1290 to 1332 it was collected on sixteen occasions on individual assessments of named persons. Accordingly for these four decades the reports (*particule compoti*) provide detailed information on individual named holders of movable property. Charges of corruption against the assessors and collectors of the 1332 subsidy led to a new practice in 1334. The levy of 1334 was negotiated with each community, vill, or borough, and assessed on the community as a unit. This type of levy, a tenth on the aggregate movable property in towns and a fifteenth on that in rural areas, became the 'standardized levy' for the rest of the Middle Ages and after. The particulars of account are concerned no longer with the assessments on individual persons.

Scutage and feudal aids were levied on knights' fees. The scutage rolls, 16 John–20 Edward III, as a rule give the names of persons exempted from the payment of scutage because they had performed their military service, or had compounded for it by paying a fine. A calendar of a few scutage rolls for 13 Edward I to 19 Edward II is printed in *Calendar of Chancery Rolls, Various, 1277–1326*, pp. 363–99. Assessments of feudal aids are contained in the Book of Aids (P.R.O. Exch. K.R. Misc. Books iii) which gives details of the aid for the knighting of the Black Prince (1346) and of the aid for the marriage of Henry IV's eldest daughter (1401–2). The Book of Aids is printed, county by county, in *Feudal Aids* (No. 4341), wherein other returns of holders of knight's fees used for assessing feudal dues are also printed. The poll taxes were assessed at a flat rate on nearly all persons above a certain age and were collected in 1377, 1379, and 1381. The printed poll-tax rolls for various counties are given under Nos. 3146, 3152, 3178, 3179, 3182, 3185, 3191, 3204, 3205. For analyses, turn to Oman, *The great revolt* (No. 4151), and Russell, *British medieval population* (No. 1377), chap. vi.

For documents relating to scutage, see Palgrave's *Parliamentary writs* (No. 3316), especially vol. ii, pt. ii; and the *Red Book of the Exchequer* (No. 3007). The best general commentaries on lay subsidies are the introductions by Willard and Johnson (No. 3191), and the various works by Willard (No. 3268). A brief account, with references to record material, is provided by Beresford (No. 3142).

a. General collections

3142 BERESFORD (MAURICE W.). Poll taxes (of 1377, 1379, and 1381) and lay subsidies (1290–1334; after 1334). Canterbury. 1963.

An informative sketch of twenty-nine pages, expanded from articles in *The Amateur Historian* (No. 1502).

3143 BIRD (SAMUEL R. SCARGILL). 'The scutage and marshal's rolls'. *Genealogist*, New Ser. i (1884), 65–76.

It contains lists of these rolls (also printed in his *Guide to the Public Records*, 2nd edn. by Scargill-Bird, pp. 23–4); and the scutage roll of 6 Henry III in full. See also No. 3753; and a single membrane of Scutage Roll, 16 John. Ed. by J. C. Holt. Pipe Roll Soc. xxxvii (1964), 105–8.

3144 INVENTORY OR CALENDAR OF ACCOUNTS, ASSESSMENTS, etc. (4 Hen. III–38 Hen. VIII). *Deputy Keeper's Reports*, ii, app. ii. 136–89; iii, app. ii. 3–104. Lond. 1841–2.

A calendar of tenths, fifteenths, etc., aids, tallages, reliefs, and the like. Continued to 27 Elizabeth, ibid. Reports iv–v (1843–4).

3145 NONARUM INQUISITIONES IN CURIA SCACCARII TEMP. REGIS EDWARDI III. Rec. Comm. Lond. 1807.

The record of a subsidy of a ninth of corn, wool, and lambs in every rural parish, a ninth of movables in boroughs, and a fifteenth of the movables of foreign merchants. These nonae rolls of 14–15 Edward III also specify the value of every benefice, and state how far it exceeded or fell short of the Valuation of Pope Nicholas in 1292 (No. 6783); the ninth of corn, wool, and lambs in 1340 was considered worth as much as the tenth of those commodities in 1292. Not all these rolls of 14–15 Edward III have yet been printed.

3146 SUBSIDY ROLL OF 51 EDWARD III. Ed. by John Topham. *Archaeol.* vii (1785), 337–47.

Contains, besides 'the Great Enrollment' of the poll-tax of 51 Edward III, a tenth and fifteenth, 47 Edward III; but these records give only the total sums of money levied in various counties and boroughs. It is copied in Oman, *The great revolt* (No. 4151), pp. 163–5; and its population figures are given in Russell, *British medieval population* (No. 1377), pp. 132 and 142.

b. Taxation by counties

BEDFORDSHIRE

3147 GAYDON (A. T.). 'The taxation of 1297: a translation of the local rolls of assessment for Barford, Biggleswade and Flitt hundreds, and for Bedford, Dunstable, Leighton Buzzard and Luton.' Bedfordshire Hist. Rec. Soc. Pubns. xxxix (1959).

The detailed local rolls rather than the summary county rolls of a ninth on movables.

3148 HERVEY (S. H. A.). 'Two Bedfordshire subsidy lists, 1309 and 1332'. Suffolk Green Books (Bury St. Edmunds), xviii (1925).

3149 JENKINSON (Mrs. HILARY). 'An early Bedfordshire taxation'. Bedfordshire Hist. Rec. Soc. Pubns. ii (1914), 225–38. Idem, 'Some Bedfordshire assessments for the taxation of a ninth'. Ibid. viii (1924), 119–31.

BUCKINGHAMSHIRE

3149A EARLY TAXATION RETURNS. Ed. by A. C. Chibnall. Bucks. Record Soc. 1967.

English translation of returns for 1332.

CAMBRIDGESHIRE

3150 LAY SUBSIDIES, CAMBRIDGESHIRE, I EDWARD III, 1326 (1327, a twentieth). Ed. by J. J. Muskett. *East Anglian*, 3rd Ser. x–xii, *passim*. Norwich, etc. 1904–8.

3151 LIST OF CAMBRIDGESHIRE SUBSIDY ROLLS, 1250–1695. By W. M. Palmer. *East Anglian*, vii–x, xii–xiii, *passim*. Norwich, etc. 1898–1910.

The appendices (in vols. xii–xiii) contain poll-taxes, 1377–81, including the clerical poll-tax of 1378; land taxes, 1404, 1411; income taxes, 1435, 1450; etc.

CORNWALL

3152 MACLEAN (JOHN). 'Poll-tax account for Cornwall, 51 Edw. III, 1377, with remarks'. *Royal Institution of Cornwall Jour.* iv (1872), 27–41.

For extracts from the subsidy roll of 1 Edward III, see Maclean, *Trigg Minor* (No. 4583), under the names of the various parishes.

3153 SUBSIDY ROLLS . . . of the parish of St. Constantine (Kerrier), Cornwall. Devon and Cornwall Rec. Soc. Pubns. iv (1910).

Transcripts of subsidy rolls 1 Edw. III–12 Chas. II.

CUMBERLAND

3154 KIRBY (J. L.) and KIRBY (A. D.). 'The poll tax of 1377 for Carlisle'. *Cumb.-Westm. Antiq. and Archaeol. Soc., Trans.* New Ser. lviii (1959), 110–17. Idem, 'Some early records of Cumberland lay subsidies' (before 1332). Ibid. New Ser. liii (1954), 63–8.

3154A STEEL (J. P.), ed. Cumberland lay subsidy: being an account of the fifteenth and tenth, 6 Edw. III. *Lancs.-Ches. Record Soc.* xxxi (1912).

See C. M. Fraser, 'Cumberland and Westmorland lay subsidy, 1332', *Cumb.-Westm. Antiq. Soc. Trans.* lxvi (1966), 131–58.

DERBYSHIRE

See also No. 1601.

3155 DERBYSHIRE IN 1327–8: a lay subsidy roll (a twentieth). Ed. by J. C. Cox. *Derbysh. Archaeol. and Nat. Hist. Soc. Jour.* xxx (1908), 23–96.

DEVONSHIRE

3156 AN EXETER MANUSCRIPT. Done into English out of Latin by O. J. Reichel. Exeter. 1907.

Contains a short chronicle of the church of Exeter to 1394 (pp. 9–16), tenths and fifteenths of the hundreds of Devon, 1384 (pp. 16–37), etc. Translation only. Of little value.

3157 WHALE (T. W.). 'The tax roll for Devon, 31 Edward I'. *Devon. Asso. for Advancement of Science, etc. Trans.* xxxi (1899), 376–429.

Abstracts of persons, places, and fees; does not give the amount of tax or the rate. For feudal aids of Devon, see Whale, ibid. xxxii (1900), 521–51. A. M. Erskine (ed.), *The Devonshire Lay Subsidy of 1332*, Devon and Cornwall Rec. Soc., New Ser. XIV, 1969,

ESSEX

For poll-tax returns of part of the hundred of Hinckford, 1381, see Oman's *Great Revolt of 1381* (No. 4151), app. iii. 167–82; and for those of Ongar hundred, V.C.H. *Essex*, iv (1956).

3158 FOWLER (R. C.). 'An early Essex subsidy'. *Essex Archaeol. Soc. Trans.* xix (1927), 27–37.

3159 RICKWORD (GEORGE). 'Taxations of Colchester, 1296 and 1301'. *Essex Archaeol. Soc. Trans.* ix (1906), 126–55.

> Summary of contents, etc. For the texts, see *Rotuli Parliamentorum* (No. 3322), i. 228–38, 243–65.

GLOUCESTERSHIRE

Extracts from subsidy rolls, especially from the roll of 1 Edward III, will be found, under the names of the various parishes, in Ralph Bigland's *Historical collections of the county of Gloucester* (No. 1650). 2 vols. Lond. 1786–92.

3160 AID (THE) LEVIED IN GLOUCESTERSHIRE in 20 Edward III (to knight the Black Prince). Ed. by John Maclean. *Bristol and Glos. Archaeol. Soc. Trans.* x (1886), 278–92.

> Taken from the *Books of Aids*.

3161 GLOUCESTERSHIRE SUBSIDY ROLL, 1 Edward III, 1327. Middle Hill Press, n.d.

> A twentieth of movables.

3162 THE TALLAGE OF 6 Edward II, December 16, 1312, and the Bristol rebellion. Ed. by E. A. Fuller. *Bristol and Glos. Archaeol. Soc. Trans.* xix (1895), 171–278.

> Two subsidy rolls, so far as they relate to Bristol, are here printed. One of them records the levy of a fifteenth of movables and a tenth of rents, 6 Edward II; the other, a twentieth of movables, 1 Edward III.

HAMPSHIRE

3163 TAXATION OF THE TENTH AND FIFTEENTH IN HAMP-SHIRE, 1334. *Collectanea Topog. et Genealogica* (No. 1505), i. (1834), 175–83.

KENT

For extracts from the subsidy roll of 1 Edward III, relating to Blackheath hundred, see H. H. Drake's edition of Hasted's *History of Kent* (No. 1693), p. 286.

3164 ASSESSMENTS IN KENT FOR THE AID TO KNIGHT THE BLACK PRINCE, 20 Edward III. Ed. by James Greenstreet. *Archaeol. Cantiana*, x (1876), 99–162.

> Taken from the *Book of Aids*.

3165 KENT SUBSIDY ROLL OF 1334/5. Ed. by H. A. Hanley and C. W. Chalklin. *Documents illustrative of medieval Kentish society*. Ed. by F. R. H. Du Boulay. Kent Archaeol. Soc. Records Branch, xviii (1964), 58–172.

3166 VALUATION OF THE TOWN OF DARTFORD, 29 Edward I. Ed. by R. P. Coates. *Archaeol. Cantiana*, ix (1874), 285–98.

This is a subsidy roll, a fifteenth.

LANCASHIRE

3167 EXCHEQUER LAY SUBSIDY ROLL OF THE COUNTY OF LANCASTER, 1332 (a tenth and fifteenth). Ed. by J. P. Rylands. Lancs.-Ches. Record Soc. *Miscellanies*, ii (1896).

3168 LANCASHIRE LAY SUBSIDIES: an examination of the lay subsidy rolls, Henry III–Charles II. Ed. by John A. C. Vincent, vol. i, 1216–1307. Lancs.-Ches. Record Soc. (1893).

Contains some valuable documents relating to taxes on movables, scutages, and tallages, and a considerable amount of commentary.

LEICESTERSHIRE

For the aid of 20 Edward III, see Nichols, *History of the County of Leicester* (No. 1714), i, pp. cii–cx; and for 1377 poll-tax, V.C.H. *Leicestershire*, iii.

3169 THE EARLIEST LEICESTERSHIRE LAY SUBSIDY ROLL, 1327 (a twentieth). Ed. by W. G. D. Fletcher. *A.A.S.R.P.* xix (1888), 209–312 and 447–78; xx (1889), 130–78.

3170 HOSKINS (W. G.). 'Wigston Magna lay subsidies'. *Leics. Archaeol. Soc. Trans.* xx, pt. i (1939), 55–64.

LONDON AND MIDDLESEX

3171 LAY SUBSIDY, LONDON, 1411–12. Ed. by J. C. L. Stahlschmidt. *Archaeol. Jour.* xliv (1887), 56–82.

Half a mark on every 20 annual value of lands and rents.

3172 EKWALL (EILERT). Two early London Subsidy Rolls (for 1292 and 1319), with introduction, comment, and indexes of taxpayers. Lond. 1951.

See Margaret Curtis, 'London lay subsidy for 1332' (No. 1469).

NORFOLK

For subsidy rolls of 1, 6, 18 Edward III and 8 Edward IV, so far as they relate to the hundred of North Erpingham, see Walter Rye, *Rough Materials* (No. 3586), pt. ii. 403–31.

3173 ASSESSMENT OF NORFOLK FOR TENTHS AND FIFTEENTHS IN 1334, with the deductions made in 1449. Ed. by William Hudson. Norfolk and Norwich Archaeol. Soc. *Norfolk Archaeol.* xii (1895), 263–97.

See also ibid. xvi (1907), 177–96, for extracts from a subsidy roll of 1332 (a tenth and fifteenth).

3174 EXTRACTS FROM LIBER NIGER SCACCARII, AND THE ACCOUNT OF THE AID TAKEN 20 EDWARD III. Ed. by J. R. Daniel Tyssen. *Norfolk Antiq. Miscellany*, i (1877), 1–106.

Contains the 'cartae' of 1166, extracted from the *Little Black Book of the Exchequer* (above, No. 3006); and the aid 20 Edward III to knight the Black Prince, taken from the *Book of Aids* (No. 4341).

3175 SUBSIDY ROLL IN THE POSSESSION OF LYNN REGIS (a fifteenth, c. 3 Edw. I). Ed. by G. H. Dashwood. Norfolk and Norwich Archaeol. Soc. *Norfolk Archaeol.* i (1847), 334-54.

Contains the record of the levy so far as it relates to Lynn.

NORTHUMBERLAND

3176 BRADSHAW (F.). 'Lay subsidy roll of 1296'. *Archaeol. Aeliana*, 3rd Ser. xiii (1916), 186-302.

A description of the roll. See *History of Northumberland* (No. 1772).

3177 THE NORTHUMBERLAND LAY SUBSIDY ROLL OF 1296. Ed. by C. M. Fraser. Soc. Antiq. Newcastle upon Tyne Record Ser. i (1968).

OXFORDSHIRE

3178 OXFORD CITY DOCUMENTS, 1268-1665. Ed. by J. E. T. Rogers. Oxford Hist. Soc. 1891.

Poll-tax of Oxford (1380-1), pp. 1-45. Other taxes of the fourteenth century, pp. 45-54. Calendar of lay subsidies, 1312-1469, pp. 96-107.

SHROPSHIRE

3179 THE POLL-TAX FOR THE TOWN AND LIBERTIES OF SHREWSBURY, 1380. Ed. by W. G. D. Fletcher. *Shropshire Archaeol. and Nat. Hist. Soc. Trans.* 2nd Ser. ii (1890), 17-28.

3180 THE SHROPSHIRE LAY SUBSIDY ROLL OF 1327 (a twentieth). Ed. by W. G. D. Fletcher. Ibid. (1889-1907), *passim*. Reprinted, Oswestry. 1907.

3181 A SHREWSBURY SUBSIDY ROLL, 1445-46. Ed. by J. L. Hobbs. *Shropshire Archaeol. Soc. Trans.* liii (1949-50), 68-75.

A local subsidy roll with names of the persons assessed in the borough of Shrewsbury.

SOMERSET

3182 A BATH POLL-TAX, 2 Richard II. Ed. by Emanuel Green. *Bath Nat. Hist. and Antiq. Field Club Procs.*, vi (1889), 294-315. 'Bath lay subsidies, Henry IV–Henry VIII'. Ed. by Emanuel Green. Ibid. vi (1889), 379-411.

For Somerset subsidy roll (13 Hen. IV), ed. by C. W. Shickle, ibid. ix (1898-1901), 188-98.

3183 EXCHEQUER LAY SUBSIDIES: tax roll (of a twentieth) for Somerset, 1 Edward III. Ed. by F. H. Dickinson. Somerset Record Soc. Pubns. iii (1889), 79-284.

Pp. 1-52, *Kirkby's quest* for Somerset; pp. 53-78, *Nomina villarum* as in Palgrave, *Parlia. Writs*, ii. 374 ff.

STAFFORDSHIRE

3184 EXCHEQUER SUBSIDY ROLL OF A.D. 1327 (a twentieth). Ed. by George Wrottesley. *Wm. Salt Archaeol. Soc. Collections*, vii, pt. i (1886), 193-255.

3185 POLL-TAX OF A.D. 1379–81 FOR THE HUNDREDS OF OFFLOW AND CUTTLESTONE. Ed. by W. K. Boyd. Ibid. xvii (1896), 155–205.

Cf. L. Margaret Midgley, 'Some Staffordshire poll-tax returns, 1377'. Staffs Record Soc. 4th Ser. vi. (1970), 1–25.

3186 SUBSIDY ROLL OF 6 EDWARD III, 1332–33 (a tenth and fifteenth). Ed. by George Wrottesley. Ibid. x (1890), 79–132.

SUFFOLK

3187 GREAT DOMESDAY BOOK OF IPSWICH, LIBER SEXTUS. Ed. by C. H. E. White. Ipswich. 1885. (Tax roll of Suffolk, 32 Hen. VI, pp. 7–24.) The taxation of Ipswich for the Welsh war in 1282 (a thirtieth). Ed. by Edgar Powell. *Suffolk Institute of Archaeol. Procs.* xii (1906), 127–57.

3188 SUFFOLK HUNDRED (A) IN THE YEAR 1283: the assessment of the hundred of Blackbourne for a tax of one thirtieth, and a return showing the land tenure there. Ed. by Edgar Powell. Cambr. 1910.

Contains tables of the tax-lists of 1283, extents of four manors, 1302, etc.

3189 SUFFOLK SUBSIDY ROLL, I EDWARD III, hundred of Lackford (a twentieth). *East Anglian,* New Ser. v (1893), 51–4, 87–90, 125–7, 169–71. Suffolk in 1327: being a subsidy return (a twentieth). Ed. by S. H. A. Hervey. Suffolk Green Books, no. ix, vol. ii. Woodbridge. 1906.

3190 TRANSCRIPTS OF ALL THE POLL-TAX LISTS [1381] WHICH REMAIN IN THE RECORD OFFICE FOR THE HUNDREDS OF THINGO AND LACKFORD. Ed. by Edgar Powell. *T.R.H.S.* New Ser. viii (1894), 227–49.

These, with other poll-tax lists of Suffolk, are also printed in Powell's *Rising in 1381* (No. 4155).

SURREY

3191 SURREY TAXATION RETURNS: (Part A) fifteenths and tenths, being the 1332 assessment and (Part B) subsequent assessments to 1623. Surrey Record Soc. xviii (1922); xxxiii (1932).

With introductions by James F. Willard and H. C. Johnson. Part A by Willard prints the roll for 1332; Part B by Johnson gives 1336 roll, and lists and calendars.

SUSSEX

3192 ASSESSMENT OF THE HUNDREDS OF SUSSEX TO THE KING'S TAX, 1334 (a tenth and fifteenth). Ed. by William Hudson. *Sussex Archaeol. Collections,* i (1907), 153–75.

3193 ROLL OF A SUBSIDY LEVIED, 13 Henry IV, 1411–12, so far as relates to Sussex. Trans. by T. H. Noyes. Ibid. x (1858), 129–46.

Contains a translation of the record of a levy of 6s. 8d. on every £20 annual value of lands and rents.

3194 SUBSIDY ROLL OF THE RAPE OF LEWES, 1296 (an eleventh). Ed. by W. H. Blaauw. Ibid. ii (1849), 288–306.

3195 THE THREE EARLIEST SUBSIDIES FOR THE COUNTY OF SUSSEX IN THE YEARS 1296, 1327, 1332. Ed. by William Hudson. Sussex Rec. Soc. x (1910).

Subsidy roll of Eastbourne *c.* 1300; *Sussex Archaeol. Collections*, xliii (1900), 194–6. L. F. Salzman, 'Early taxation in Sussex', ibid. xcviii (1960), 29–43; xcix (1961), 1–19.

WARWICKSHIRE

3196 LAY SUBSIDY ROLL OF 1327. *Midland Rec. Soc. Trans.* iii–vi, *passim* (1899–1902) (Birmingham).

3197 THE LAY SUBSIDY ROLL FOR WARWICKSHIRE OF 6 Edward III, 1332. Trans. and ed. with introduction by W. F. Carter. Dugdale Soc. vi (1926). With appendix of 3 Subsidy Rolls (1309, 1313, 1332) for Stratford-upon-Avon. Ed. by F. C. Wellstood.

There is included an extract from an assize roll of 1323.

WILTSHIRE

3198 WILTES. Rotulus Hildebrandi de London' et Johannis de Harnham taxatorum et collectorum quintedecime et decime. Middle Hill Press. n.d.

Levied 7 Edward III. For the lay subsidy assessments of 1334 and for the 1377 poll-tax, see V.C.H. *Wilts.* iv. 294–314.

WORCESTERSHIRE

3199 LAY SUBSIDY ROLL FOR THE COUNTY OF WORCESTER, *c.* 1280. Ed. by J. W. Willis-Bund and John Amphlett. Worcestershire Hist. Soc. Oxf. 1893.

Owing to the mutilated condition of the roll the nature of the tax is not stated.

3200 LAY SUBSIDY ROLL FOR THE COUNTY OF WORCESTER, 1 Edward I [*sic*] [1 Edw. III, a twentieth]. Ed. by F. J. Eld. Worcestershire Hist. Soc. Oxf. 1895.

3201 LAY SUBSIDY ROLL, 1332–33 (a tenth and fifteenth), and *nonarum inquisitiones*, 1340 for the county of Worcester, Oxf. 1899. Lay subsidy rolls, 1346 [a feudal aid] and 1358 [a tenth and fifteenth, with a translation]. Oxf. 1900. Lay subsidy rolls, 1427–29 [a tax on parishes and knights' fees, with a translation]. Oxf. 1902.

These three volumes were edited by John Amphlett for the Worcestershire Hist. Soc.

YORKSHIRE

Kirkby's Quest for Yorkshire (No. 4396), pp. 277–95, contains the record of the aid to marry the king's eldest daughter, 31 Edward I, relating to part of the West Riding.

3202 HONOR AND FOREST OF PICKERING. Ed. by R. B. Turton. North Riding Record Soc. Records, New Ser. iv (1897).

A twentieth, 1 Edw. III, a tenth and fifteenth, 6 Edw. III, pp. 131–62.

3203 LAY SUBSIDY ROLLS, 1 Edward III, N.R. York and the city of York (a transcript). Ed. by John W. R. Parker. Yorks. Archaeol. Soc. Record Ser. lxxiv (*Miscellanea*, ii) (1929), 104–71.

3203A POLL-TAX RETURNS FOR THE EAST RIDING 1379 (The city of York). Ed. by J. N. Bartlett. *East Riding Antiq. Soc. Trans.* xxx (1953), 1–91.

3204 POLL-TAX RETURNS FOR THE EAST RIDING, 4 Ric. II (1381). Ed. by Eleanor Lloyd. *Yorks. Archaeol. Soc. Jour.* xx (1909), 318–52. A poll-tax roll of the East Riding, with some account of the peasant revolt of 1381. Ed. by J. C. Cox, *East Riding Antiq. Soc. Trans.* xv (1909), 1–70. Reprinted separately for private circulation.

3205 ROTULI COLLECTORUM SUBSIDII REGI A LAICIS ANNO SECUNDO CONCESSI IN WESTRYTHYNGO. (Poll-tax, 2 Rich. II.) *Yorks. Archaeol. and Topog. Asso. Jour.* v. 1–51, 241–66, 417–32; vi. 1–44, 129–71, 287–342; vii. 6–31, 145–93. Lond. 1879–82; reprinted separately, 1882. Assessment roll of the poll-tax for Howdenshire, etc. 1379. Ibid. ix (1886), 129–62.

3206 TWO SUBSIDY ROLLS OF SKYRACK [a twentieth, 1 Edw. III, a tenth and fifteenth, *c.* 10 Edw. III]. Ed. by John Stansfeld. Thoresby Soc. *Miscellanea*, i (1891), 85–97.

3207 YORKSHIRE LAY SUBSIDY, being a ninth collected in 25 Edward I, 1297. Ed. by William Brown. *Yorks. Archaeol. Soc. Rec. Ser.* xvi (1894).

3208 YORKSHIRE LAY SUBSIDY, being a fifteenth collected 30 Edward I, 1301. Ed. by William Brown. Ibid. xxi (1897).

8. *Memoranda and Originalia Rolls*

There are two series of Memoranda rolls, kept respectively by the King's and the Lord Treasurer's remembrancers. Before the Exchequer ordinances of 1323 (see H. Hall, *Red Book of the Exchequer* (No. 3007), pp. 863–87), the series are approximate duplicates; thereafter each series has exclusive material. The rolls, which survive 1 John (1199)–1926, contain memoranda and enrolments concerning all aspects of the collection and disbursement of revenue and of ancillary exchequer business. In the course of the thirteenth century, the rolls were subdivided into various sections, e.g. *Communia*, dealing with particular types of business. See James Conway Davies, 'The Memoranda Rolls of the Exchequer to 1307' in *Studies presented to Sir Hilary Jenkinson* (Oxford, 1957); 1963 *Guide to P.R.O.*, pp. 60–2 and 75; and Richardson's introduction to Memoranda Roll for John (3215).

For Irish exchequer memoranda of the reign of Edward I, see Mary Bateson in *E.H.R.* xviii (1903), 497–513; and cf. Round's note on Decies and Desmond, ibid., p. 709; and Nos. 3211 and 3217.

The Originalia rolls were sent from the Chancery to the Exchequer. They contain abstracts, estreats, from the Chancery enrolments of all matter affecting the revenue, and survive 15 John (1213)–1851.

3209 CALENDAR OF MEMORANDA ROLLS (EXCHEQUER) preserved in the Public Record Office. Michaelmas 1326–Michaelmas 1327. H.M.S.O. Lond. 1968.

3210 CATALOGUE OF RECORDS IN THE OFFICE OF THE KING'S REMEMBRANCER OF THE EXCHEQUER, 1066–1272. Rec. Comm. Lond. 1835.

See also *Lists and Indexes* (No. 956), no. xxxv.

3211 A CLASSIFIED SCHEDULE AND INVENTORY OF THE [IRISH] MEMORANDA ROLLS, 6 Edward I–50 George III. Irish Rec. Comm., Eighth Report (No. 1075), pp. 522–58. Lond. 1819.

See also ibid., pp. 622–6: James Hardiman's report on these rolls.

3212 EXTRACTS FROM THE MEMORANDA ROLLS: the negotiations preceding the Confirmatio cartarum, 1297. By Hubert Hall. *T.R.H.S.* New Ser. iii (1886), 281–91.

3213 INDEX LOCORUM ET RERUM TO THE MEMORANDA OF THE EXCHEQUER, Henry III, 1831. Printed by the benchers of the Inner Temple. Lond. 1831.

This title is given in Flaherty's *Annals of England* (Oxf. 1876), p. 591, but no such index seems ever to have been printed.

3214 JONES (EDWARD). Index to records called the originalia [Hen. VIII–Anne] and memoranda of the lord-treasurer's remembrancer's side of the exchequer [Hen. III–Geo. II]. 2 vols. Lond. 1793–5.

3215 THE MEMORANDA ROLL FOR THE MICHAELMAS TERM [1 John], together with fragments of the originalia roll of (1195–6). Ed. with an introduction by H. G. Richardson. Pipe Roll Soc. New Ser. xxi (1943). 'The Memoranda Roll' [10 John]. Ed. by R. Allen Brown. Pipe Roll Soc. New Ser. xxxi for 1955 (1957). The Memoranda Roll of the king's remembrancer for Michaelmas 1230–Trinity 1231. Ed. by Chalfant Robinson. Pipe Roll Soc. New Ser. xi (1933).

Richardson's introduction describes the financial system.

3216 PROCEEDINGS OF HIS MAJESTY'S COMMISSIONERS ON THE PUBLIC RECORDS, 1832–33. Ed. by C. P. Cooper. Rec. Comm. Lond. 1833.

Memoranda roll of 3 Henry III (king's remembrancer's office), pp. 287–97, 382–92, 455–80.

Extracts from 'memoranda in scaccario de tempore regis Edwardi Primi' are appended to vol. i of the *Year Books* (Lond. 1678), pp. 1–43; there are also many extracts from the memoranda rolls in Madox's *History of the Exchequer* (No. 3250). It seems that only twenty-five copies of this volume were printed, for the use of the commissioners.

3217 ROTULI SELECTI AD RES ANGLICAS ET HIBERNICAS SPECTANTES. Ed. by Joseph Hunter. Rec. Comm. Lond. 1834.

Two rolls containing copies of grants of annuities, etc., Hen. V–Hen. VI, taken from the memoranda of the Irish Exchequer, pp. 63–95. See Nos. 3008 and 3780.

3218 ROTULORUM ORIGINALIUM IN CURIA SCACCARII ABBRE-
VIATIO. Rec. Comm. 2 vols. Lond. 1805–10.

An abstract of the originalia, 20 Hen. III–51 Edw. III. They are extracts from chancery
rolls sent to the Exchequer for the collection of certain fines.

9. *Miscellaneous: Various Classes*

Various classes of exchequer documents, which are grouped together here, are
Ministers' Accounts, Escheators' Accounts, Customs Accounts, and others
which are classified in the Public Record Office as Special Collections (Ancient
Correspondence and Ancient Petitions).

The Ministers' Accounts, Henry III to the eighteenth century, comprise the
yearly accounts of bailiffs, farmers, reeves, collectors, receivers, and other
officials appointed to collect the issues of royal manors and lands which did not
form part of the farms of the sheriffs. They include many rentals and surveys,
and the accounts of the English possessions of the Knights Templars which came
into the hands of Edward II. Ministers' Accounts were at first entered in the
pipe rolls, but from 42 Edward III (1368) onward they were embodied within
a distinct series of rolls called Foreign Accounts because they were accounts
foreign to the business of the sheriff. For Ministers' Accounts, see the index
below.

Escheators' Accounts deal with the revenue arising from lands escheated or
forfeited to the crown. The medieval accounts normally contain particulars of
the property with which the account deals. In addition to the Escheators'
Accounts are the Escheators' Files. From the latter the inquisitions post mortem
have been removed to form a separate class, 'Inquisitions post mortem'; for them
see below pp. 627–38.

Customs' Accounts begin with Edward I; general tables drawn from them will
be found in Nos. 3219, 3222, 7222 below. They can be most appropriately dealt
with in the section on Urban Society, since most of the printed studies are concerned with particular ports in England or abroad. See index under 'Customs'.

Ancient Correspondence and Ancient Petitions are modern classifications of
documents of similar character drawn from the records of various departments.
The volumes of Ancient Correspondence enclose 'Royal Letters', official and
private correspondence, and memoranda from the reign of Henry II to that of
Henry VII, mostly of the thirteenth and fourteenth centuries. Many of these
documents have been printed, sometimes inaccurately, in Rymer's *Foedera*
(No. 3765) and in the Rolls Series editions of Royal and Historical Letters
(Nos. 2112–13). The Cely and Stonor Papers (Nos. 5330, 4615) are included in
this class. Ancient Petitions from Henry III to James I make up files of petitions
to the king, to the king and council, to parliament, to the chancellor, and other
officers. Many of them are printed in Rotuli parliamentorum (No. 3322). Documents drawn from Ancient Correspondence and Ancient Petitions have, of
course, been published in various studies; a considerable number can be found
in the introductions to Sayles's *Select Cases in the King's Bench* (No. 3510).

3219 CARUS-WILSON (ELEANORA M.) and COLEMAN (OLIVE). England's export trade, 1275–1547. Oxf. 1963.

This work presents full tables on wool and cloth exports, drawn from Enrolled Accounts in the Exchequer. For customs accounts of particular towns, see index under 'Customs'.

3220 A DESCRIPTIVE CATALOGUE OF ANCIENT DEEDS IN THE PUBLIC RECORD OFFICE. 6 vols. H.M.S.O. 1890–1915.

Ancient deeds (before 1603) comprise several series. This class is made up, in large measure, of documents which originally belonged to private or monastic muniments, they have been assembled from the treasury of receipt, the king's remembrancer's department, the court of augmentations, and the chancery.

3221 A SUMMONS OF THE GREEN WAX TO THE SHERIFF OF SOMERSET AND DORSET. Ed. by T. Bruce Dilks, arranged by T. F. Palmer. Somerset Rec. Soc. Pubns. xxxix, *Collectanea*, i (1924), 175–206.

This article lists fines and amercements which the sheriff was to pay into the Exchequer, 1465–8, drawn from the borough of Bridgewater muniments.

3222 TABLES OF ENROLLED CUSTOMS AND SUBSIDY ACCOUNTS, 1399 to 1482, in Power-Postan, *Studies in English trade* (No. 5393), pp. 321–60.

Pp. 321–30, introduction by Howard L. Gray; pp. 330–60, tables.

3223 YORKSHIRE DEODANDS IN THE REIGNS OF EDWARD II AND EDWARD III. *Yorks. Archaeol. Soc. Jour.* xv (1898), 199–210.

This article lists the object, or its value, which caused a human death, taken from K.R. miscellaneous records.

3224 PUBLIC RECORD OFFICE: Lists and indexes xv: List of ancient correspondence of the chancery and the exchequer. H.M.S.O. 1902; revised edition as Index to ancient correspondence etc. in two vols. 1969.

Royal letters and the Cely and Stonor papers are included in this class, as well as many miscellaneous documents, mostly of the thirteenth and fourteenth centuries.

3225 PUBLIC RECORD OFFICE; Lists and Indexes i: Index of ancient petitions of the chancery and of the exchequer. H.M.S.O. 1892.

See Constance M. Fraser, *Ancient petitions relating to Northumberland* (nearly all from the fourteenth century) (Surtees Soc. 1966). G. O. Sayles prints several from this class in his volumes on King's Bench (No. 3510).

3226 PUBLIC RECORD OFFICE: Lists and indexes. Supplementary ix: Exchequer records. 2 vols. H.M.S.O. 1969.

i. List of accounts, various. See No. 956.
ii. Index of warrants for issues, etc. 1399–1485.

3227 PUBLIC RECORD OFFICE: Lists and indexes, xi: List of foreign accounts enrolled on the great rolls of the exchequer (Henry III–Richard III). H.M.S.O. 1900.

3228 PUBLIC RECORD OFFICE: Lists and indexes v, viii, xxxiv: Lists of original ministers' accounts (to 38 Henry VIII). 3 pts. H.M.S.O. 1894–1910.

Pt. ii is an appendix and index to pt. i.

10. *Selected Commentaries on the Exchequer and Taxation*

The literature about the exchequer and financial developments is naturally voluminous; it is cited for the most part in the works listed below. Some works specifically devoted to surveys of the literature are by Steel (No. 3263) and by Lady Stenton (No. 3264).

The basic study of the exchequer is by Madox (No. 3250). The twelfth-century evolution is described by White (No. 3267), Poole (No. 3257), Round (No. 3261), Richardson and Sayles (No. 1218), Johnson (No. 3005), and Hall (No. 3241). The thirteenth-century procedural changes can be found in Tout (No. 1223), Richardson (No. 3259), Jenkinson (No. 3245), Mabel Mills (No. 3254), and the works on the Household (Nos. 3111–41) and the Memoranda Rolls (Nos. 3209–18). For the first half of the fourteenth century, Tout's *Edward II* (No. 4140), Davies's *Baronial opposition* (No. 4115), and *The English Government at work* (No. 3836) should be consulted.

As the kings of the later Middle Ages sought to meet financial problems with credit operations and assignments of anticipated income, the procedural machinery of the Exchequer and the Wardrobe became more complex. Further, as the law cases entertained by the Court of the Exchequer became more numerous, the importance of the Memoranda Rolls expanded.

For some phases of the late medieval period, see Steel (No. 3263), McFarlane (No. 3253), and Wolffe (Nos. 3132A and 3270): but the Exchequer procedure of the fifteenth century still lacks a full-length study.

Taxation may be studied in Dowell (No. 3234), Mitchell (No. 3255), Ramsay (No. 3258), and Willard (No. 3268). Customs are best treated in Gras (No. 3238); but see also the index under 'Customs'. The Norman exchequer is dealt with by Stapleton (No. 3101) and by Packard (No. 3102). For royal taxation of the clergy, see below, pp. 892–3. For the Exchequer of the Jews, turn to the index under 'Exchequer'.

3229 BAKER (ROBERT L.). The English customs service, 1307–1343: a study of medieval administration. *American Philos. Soc. Trans.* New Ser. li. Philadelphia. 1961.

3230 BROOME (DOROTHY M.). 'Auditors of the foreign accounts of the exchequer (1310–27)'. *E.H.R.* xxxviii (1923), 63–71; xxxix (1924), 482.

3231 BRYANT (W. N.). 'The financial dealings of Edward III with the county communities, 1330–1360'. *E.H.R.* lxxxiii (1968), 760–71.

3232 CARUS-WILSON (ELEANORA M.). 'The aulnage accounts: a criticism'. *Econ. H.R.* ii (1929), 114–23; reprinted in her *Medieval merchant venturers* (No. 5379).

R. A. Pelham, 'The earliest aulnage accounts for Worcestershire', *Worcs. Archaeol. Soc. Trans.* xxix (1952), 50–2.

3233 CAZEL (FRED A. Jr.). 'The tax of 1185 in aid of the Holy Land'. *Speculum*, xxx (1955), 385–92. Idem, 'The fifteenth of 1225'. *B.I.H.R.* xxxiv (1961), 67–81.

3234 DOWELL (STEPHEN). A history of taxation and taxes in England. 4 vols. Lond. 1884; 2nd edn. 1888; 3rd edn. with new introduction, 1965.

3235 THE ENGLISH GOVERNMENT AT WORK 1327–37 (No. 3836). vol. ii: fiscal administration.

3236 FRYDE (EDMUND B.). 'Materials for the study of Edward III's credit operations, 1327–1348'. *B.I.H.R.* xxii (1949), 105–38; xxiii (1950), 1–30. Idem, 'The English farmers of customs, 1343–51'. *T.R.H.S.* 5th Ser. ix (1959), 1–17.

3237 GIBSON (S. T.). 'The escheatries, 1327–1341'. *E.H.R.* xxxvi (1921), 218–25.

See E. R. Stevenson in *English Government at work* (No. 3836), i. 109–67.

3238 GRAS (NORMAN S. B.). The early English customs system: a documentary study . . . thirteenth to sixteenth century. Cambr. (Mass.). 1918.

Gras's book is the standard study of its subject. See also Mabel H. Mills, 'The London customs house during the middle ages', *Archaeologia*, lxxxiii (1933), 307–25.

3239 GROSS (CHARLES). The exchequer of the Jews of England in the middle ages. Lond. 1887.

3240 HALE (MATTHEW). A short treatise touching sheriffs' accounts. Lond. 1683; another edition 1716. Idem, A treatise in three parts: de juris maris; de portibus maris; concerning the custom of goods imported and exported: in Francis Hargrave's *Collection of Tracts*, i. 1–289. Dublin. 1787.

3241 HALL (HUBERT). The antiquities and curiosities of the exchequer. Lond. 1891. Reprinted 1898. Idem, History of the custom-revenue in England. 2 vols. Lond. 1885. New edition 1 vol. 1892. Idem, Introduction to the study of the pipe rolls. Pipe Roll Soc. 1884. Idem, 'The exchequer chess-game'. *Antiquary*, ix (1884), 206–12. Idem, 'The site of the ancient exchequer at Westminster'. *Archaeol. Rev.* ii (1889), 386–96.

3242 HARRISS (G. L.). 'Preference at the medieval exchequer'. *B.I.H.R.* xxx (1957), 17–40. Idem, 'Aids, loans and benevolences'. *The Historical Jour.* vi (1968), 1–19.

3243 HASKINS (CHARLES H.) and GEORGE (M. D.). 'Verses on the exchequer in the fifteenth century'. *E.H.R.* xxxvi (1921), 58–67.

3244 HOYT (ROBERT S.). The royal demesne in English constitutional history 1066 to 1272. Ithaca. 1950. Idem, 'Royal taxation and the growth of the realm in mediaeval England'. *Speculum*, xxv (1950), 36–48.

3245 JENKINSON (HILARY). 'Medieval tallies, public and private'. *Archaeologia*, lxxiv for 1923–4 (1925), 280–351. Idem, 'The financial records of the reign of King John'. *Magna Carta Commemoration Essays* (No. 3290), pp. 244–300.

3246 JOLLIFFE (JOHN E. A.). 'The camera regis under Henry II'. *E.H.R.* lxviii (1953), 1–21.

See also Jolliffe in *Powicke essays* (No. 1450); and H. G. Richardson, 'The chamber under Henry II', *E.H.R.* lxix (1954), 596–611.

3247   KIRBY (JOHN L.). 'Issues of the Lancastrian exchequer and Lord Cromwell's estimates of 1433'. *B.I.H.R.* xxiv (1951), 121–51. Idem, 'The financing of Calais under Henry V'. Ibid. xxiii (1950), 165–77. Idem, 'The rise of the under-treasurer of the exchequer'. *E.H.R.* lxxii (1957), 666–77.

3248   LYDON (J. F.). 'Edward II and the revenues of Ireland in 1311–12', and in appendix 'Calendar of sums of Irish treasure received by the king, 1203–1311'. *Irish Hist. Stud.* xiv (1965), 39–53. See No. 3100; and M. Dolley, 'Anglo-Irish monetary policies, 1172–1637 (with bibliography)'. *Historical Stud.* vii (1969), 45–64.

3249   LYON (BRYCE) and VERHULST (A. E.). Medieval finance: a comparison of financial institutions in northwestern Europe. Providence (R.I.). 1967.

Lyon wrote the sections on English institutions of the twelfth and thirteenth centuries; Verhulst wrote the sections on Flanders, Normandy, and the French Royal Domain.

3250   MADOX (THOMAS). The history and antiquities of the exchequer of England (1066–1327). Lond. 1711; index is appended to Madox's *Baronia Anglica* (No. 4669); 2nd edn. of the *History*, with the index, 2 vols. Lond. 1769.

This 'monument of erudition of which any country might be proud' (R. L. Poole), contains many extracts from the pipe rolls and other public records; its chaps. ii, iii, and xix deal with the officers of the royal household and with the central judicature. Catherine S. Sims prints 'An unpublished fragment of Madox's History of the Exchequer' in *Huntington Library Quart.* xxiii (1959), 61–94. F. S. Thomas, *The ancient exchequer of England* (Lond. 1848), is a useful résumé and continuation of Madox's treatise. For Madox, see H. D. Hazeltine, *Law Quart. Rev.* xxxii (1916), 268–89, 352–72.

3251   MARTIN (ADAM). Index to repertories and other records in the court of exchequer. Lond. 1819.

3252   MATE (MAVIS). 'A mint of trouble, 1279–1307'. *Speculum*, xliv (1969), 201–12.

Michael Prestwich, 'Edward I's monetary policies and their consequences', *Econ. H.R.* 2nd Ser. xxii (1969), 406–16.

3253   McFARLANE (KENNETH B.). 'Loans to the Lancastrian kings: the problem of inducement'. *Cambr. Hist. Jour.* ix (1947), 51–68.

E. J. Davis and M. I. Peake, 'Loans from the city of London to Henry VI, 1431–49', *B.I.H.R.* iv (1927), 165–72.

3254   MILLS (MABEL H.). 'Experiments in exchequer procedure 1200–1232'. *T.R.H.S.* 4th Ser. viii (1925), 151–70. Idem, 'The reforms at the exchequer 1232–1242'. Ibid. x (1927), 111–33. Idem, 'Adventus vicecomitum 1258–72'. *E.H.R.* xxxvi (1921), 481–96. Idem, 'Adventus vicecomitum 1272–1307'. Ibid. xxxviii (1923), 331–54. Idem, 'Exchequer agenda and estimates of revenue, Eastern term, 1284'. Ibid. xl (1925), 229–34. Miss Mills's introduction to the 1295 pipe roll for Surrey (No. 3095) is an excellent description of exchequer procedure at that date.

3255   MITCHELL (SYDNEY K.). Studies in taxation under John and Henry III. New Haven, 1914. Idem, Taxation in medieval England. Ed. by Sidney Painter. New Haven. 1951.

3256 PALGRAVE (FRANCIS). The antient kalendars and inventories of the treasury of his majesty's exchequer, with other documents illustrating the history of that repository. Record Comm. 3 vols. Lond. 1836.

See also William Prynne, *Aurum reginae: or a compendious tractate and chronological collection of records concerning the queen's gold* (Lond. 1668).

3257 POOLE (REGINALD L.). The exchequer in the twelfth century. Oxf. 1912.

See also C. H. Haskins, 'The abacus and the king's curia', *E.H.R.* xxvii (1912), 101–6.

3258 RAMSAY (JAMES H.). A history of the revenues of the kings of England, 1066–1399. 2 vols. Oxf. 1925.

Ramsay tried to estimate the king's revenue year by year; but see M. H. Mills's review in *E.H.R.* xli (1926), 429–31. For the fifteenth century, Ramsay gives a financial summary of each reign in his *Lancaster and York* (No. 1193). He also published abstracts of many issue and receipt rolls in *Antiquary*, vols. i, iv, vi, viii, x, xiv, xvi, xviii (1880–8). He discussed the customs revenues of Edward II in *E.H.R.* xxvi (1911), 97–108. Somewhat similar attempts to estimate revenue and expenditure are R. J. Whitwell, 'Revenue and expenditure under Henry III', *E.H.R.* xviii (1903), 710–11; and T. F. Tout and D. M. Broome, 'A national balance sheet for 1362–3', ibid. xxxix (1924), 404–19.

3259 RICHARDSON (HENRY G.). 'William of Ely, the king's treasurer, 1195–1215'. *T.R.H.S.* 4th Ser. xv (1932), 45–90. Idem, 'The exchequer year'. *T.R.H.S.* 4th Ser. viii (1925), 171–90. See No. 3215.

3260 RICHARDSON (HENRY G.) and SAYLES (GEORGE O.). 'Irish revenue, 1278–1384'. *Royal Irish Acad. Procs.* lxii, *Sect. C*, no. 4 (1962), 87–100.

3261 ROUND (JOHN HORACE). 'The great carucage of 1198'. *E.H.R.* iii (1898), 501–10. Idem, 'The dating of the early pipe rolls'. Ibid. xxxvi (1921), 321–33. Idem, 'The Saladin tithe'. Ibid. xxxi (1916), 447–50.

For the further discussion of carucage, by Kate Norgate, Round, and W. H. Stevenson, see ibid. iii (1898), 702–4; iv (1899), 105–10. See also A. Tomkinson, 'The carucage in an Oxfordshire hundred', *B.I.H.R.* xli (1968), 212–16.

3262 SAINTY (J. C.). 'The tenure of offices in the exchequer'. *E.H.R.* lxxx (1965), 449–75.

Pp. 449–57 for the medieval period.

3263 STEEL (ANTHONY B.). The receipt of the exchequer, 1377–1485. Cambr. 1954. Idem, 'The present state of studies on the English exchequer in the middle ages'. *A.H.R.* xxxiv (1928–9), 485–512. Idem, 'Some aspects of English finance in the fourteenth century'. *History*, xii (1928), 298–309. Idem, 'The practice of assignment in the later fourteenth century'. *E.H.R.* xliii (1928), 172–80.

The book, *The Receipt of the Exchequer*, is a full-length study heavily based on a series of articles published by Steel over nearly three decades. Steel printed a summary of its main conclusions as 'The financial background of the Wars of the Roses' in *History*, N.S. xl (1955), 18–30. The book's introduction is in some measure a critical assessment of modern researches on the Exchequer. The *A.H.R.* article is a bibliographical study in narrative form.

3264 STENTON (DORIS M.). 'The pipe rolls and the historians, 1600–1883'. *Cambr. Hist. Jour.* x (1952), 271–92.

3265 STEVENS (JOHN). The royal treasury of England, or an historical account of all taxes. Lond. 1725; 2nd edn. An historical account of all taxes. Lond. 1733.

> The references to the sources in this work are useful. The first edition was published anonymously.

3266 TURNER (GEORGE J.). 'The sheriff's farm'. *T.R.H.S.* New Ser. xii (1898), 117–49.

> C. H. Walker, 'Sheriffs in the pipe roll of 31 Henry I', *E.H.R.* xxxvii (1922), 67–79. B. E. Harris, 'King John and the sheriff's farm', ibid. lxxix (1964), 532–42.

3267 WHITE (GEOFFREY H.). 'Financial administration under Henry I'. *T.R.H.S.* 4th Ser. viii (1925), 56–78.

3268 WILLARD (JAMES F.). Parliamentary taxes on personal property, 1290 to 1334: A study in mediaeval English financial administration. Cambridge, Mass. 1934.

> In this important treatise, Willard cites *inter alia* his several specialized articles, published largely in *E.H.R.*, *B.I.H.R.* and Tout, *Essays* (No. 1456). Willard's introduction to *Surrey Taxation Assessments* (No. 3191) describes *inter alia* the Exchequer of Receipt. See also I. R. Abbott, 'Taxation of personal property and of clerical incomes, 1399–1402', *Speculum*, xvii (1942), 471–98.

3269 WOLFFE (BERTRAM P.). The royal demesne in English history: the crown estate in the governance of the realm from the conquest to 1509. Lond. and Athens (Ohio). 1971.

> A well-documented, fundamental study of the financial resources of the crown which challenges older interpretations, including the notion that the king was expected in normal circumstances 'to live of his own'. The constantly fluctuating crown estate was used for the endowment of members of the royal family and the dispensation of royal patronage. See No. 3132A.

3270 WOLFFE (BERTRAM P.). 'Henry VII's land revenues and chamber finance'. *E.H.R.* lxxix (1964), 225–54.

> Wolffe argues that the early Tudor exchequer procedures paralleled earlier developments; he also criticizes the general thesis and the figures of Frederick C. Dietz's *English Government finance, 1485–1558* (Univ. Illinois Studies in the Social Sciences, ix (1920)). See also James R. Hooker, 'Some cautionary notes on Henry VII's household and chamber system', *Speculum*, xxxiii (1958), 69–75. For another viewpoint, consult Walter C. Richardson, *Tudor chamber administration 1485–1547* (Baton Rouge, Louisiana, 1952), chaps. i–iv.

B. KING AND COUNCIL

Apart from the *leges*, or private compilations, of the twelfth century which are examined above on pp. 301–3, the principal laws which were issued before parliament was established were the laws of William the Conqueror, the generalized charters of Henry I, Stephen, and Henry II, the assizes and constitutions of Henry II, and Magna Carta.

The best editions of these laws and charters down to 1135 can be found in Liebermann's *Gesetze*, vol. i, in his text of Henry I's coronation charter (No. 3279), and in Robertson's *Laws* (No. 2178). They are conveniently brought together in Stubbs's *Charters* (No. 1208); and they are translated in *English historical documents* (No. 1177), vol. ii, and in Stephenson-Marcham (No. 1207). The charters and assizes from 1135 to 1189 are printed in Stubbs, *Charters*, on which see Richardson-Sayles, *Governance* (No. 1218), especially Appendix iv on the assizes of Henry II. Translations and brief commentaries can be found in *English historical documents*, vol. ii, and in Stephenson-Marcham. For the Constitutions of Clarendon, see Nos. 6487–6510. For the assizes, see such works as D. M. Stenton, *English justice* (No. 3681), and van Caenegem, *Royal writs* (No. 3503), as well as the works on constitutional history on pp. 155–9.

1. Royal Prerogatives

See Nos. 1350–9.

3271 ALLEN (JOHN). Inquiry into the rise and growth of the royal prerogative in England. Lond. 1830. New edn. 1849.

3271A BLOCH (MARC L. B.). Les Rois thaumaturges: étude sur le caractère surnaturel attribué à la puissance royale, particulièrement en France et en Angleterre. Strasbourg, Lond. and N.Y. 1924.

3272 CHRIMES (STANLEY B.). Sir John Fortescue: De laudibus legum Angliae. Cambr. 1942.

See also Chrimes, 'Sir John Fortescue's theory of dominion', *T.R.H.S.* 4th Ser. xvii (1934), 117–47; and Felix Gilbert, 'Sir John Fortescue's Dominium regale et politicum', *Medievalia et Humanistica*, ii (1944), 88–97. See No. 2988.

3273 KANTOROWICZ (ERNST H.). Laudes regiae. Berkeley, Cal. 1946. Idem, The king's two bodies. Lond. and Princeton. 1957.

3274 KERN (FRITZ). Kingship and law in the middle ages. Trans. by S. B. Chrimes. Oxf. 1939. Reprinted, 1968.

3275 MAITLAND (FREDERIC W.). 'The praerogativa regis'. *E.H.R.* vi (1891), 67–72. Reprinted in his *Collected papers* (No. 1482).

The document which passes under the title *Praerogativa regis* seems to have been a tract written by a lawyer in the early part of Edward I's reign. On this subject see Samuel E. Thorne's introduction to *Prerogativa regis: tertia lectura Roberti Constable de Lyncolnis Inne anno 11 H. 7* (New Haven, 1949).

3275A PALMER (C. F. R.). 'The King's confessors (1256–1450)'. *Antiquary*, xxii (1890), 114–20, 159–61, 262–6; xxiii (1891), 24–6.

3276 POST (GAINES). 'Status regis'. *Studies in Medieval and Renaissance history* (Nebraska), i (1964), 1–103. See No. 2985 *l*.

3277 SCHULTZ (FRITZ). 'Bracton on kingship'. *E.H.R.* lx (1945), 136–76.

See also S. J. T. Miller, 'The position of the king in Bracton and Beaumanoir', *Speculum*, xxxi (1956), 263–96.

3278 STAUNFORD (WILLIAM). An exposition of the king's prerogative. Lond. 1567. Other editions 1568, 1573, 1577, 1590, 1607.

See Birdsall on dispensing power in *McIlwain essays* (No. 1444).

2. *Charters of Liberty: Magna Carta, etc.*

Two basic studies of Magna Carta are those by McKechnie (No. 3288) and Holt (No. 3286); its role in constitutional developments in the next four centuries is traced by Faith Thompson (No. 3292). A recent bibliography is provided in Holt, pp. 363–8, where *inter alia* the several important studies of C. R. Cheney, F. M. Powicke, and H. G. Richardson are listed, and not repeated here.

Texts of Magna Carta and its reissues have been frequently printed; they may be found, for example, in Stubbs, *Select Charters*; in Statutes of the Realm (No. 3327), i. 6–44; in Bémont (No. 3280); in McKechnie (No. 3288); and in Holt (No. 3286).

3279 LIEBERMANN (FELIX). 'The text of Henry I's coronation charter'. *T.R.H.S.* New Ser. viii (1894), 21–48.

3280 BÉMONT (CHARLES). Chartes des libertés anglaises, 1100–1305. Paris. 1892.

This work contains critical texts of the charters of Henry I, Stephen, Henry II, and John, the articles of the barons, the forest charter, Henry III's confirmation of 1225, and Edward I's confirmations, Bémont's introduction gives an account of the history of Magna Carta, with the older literature of the subject.

3281 CAM (HELEN M.). Magna Carta, event or document. Selden Soc. Lecture. Lond. 1965.

3282 CHENEY (CHRISTOPHER R.). 'The twenty-five barons of Magna Carta'. *B.J.R.L.* l (1968), 280–307.

3283 COLLINS (ARTHUR J.). 'The documents of the Great Charter of 1215'. *P.B.A.* xxxiv for 1948 (1952), 233–79.

J. C. Fox, 'The originals of the Great Charter of 1215', *E.H.R.* xxxix (1924), 321–36.

3284 GALBRAITH (VIVIAN H.). 'Runnymede revisited'. *Amer. Philos. Soc. Procs.* cx (1966), 307–17. Idem, 'A draft of Magna Carta (1215)'. *P.B.A.* liii (1967), 345–60.

3285 THE GREAT CHARTER: Four essays on Magna Carta and the history of our liberty. New York. 1965.

Essays by Samuel E. Thorne, William H. Dunham, Jr., Philip B. Kurland, and Sir Ivor Jennings.

3286 HOLT (JAMES C.). Magna Carta. Cambr. 1965. Paperback, 1969.

The approach of this excellent commentary 'is different from McKechnie's, for it is the work of a historian not a lawyer. Its object is to present the Charter in a context of the politics, administration and political thought of England and Europe in the twelfth and thirteenth centuries' (p. ix). There are nine appendixes of relevant documents, including the texts of 1215 and 1225, the Charter of the Forest of 1225, the Articles of the Barons of 1215. Holt's work is not an exposition of the terms of Magna Charta, for which McKechnie should be consulted.

3287 HOLT (J. C.). The Northerners: a study in the reign of King John. Oxf. 1961.

3288 McKECHNIE (WILLIAM S.). Magna Carta: a commentary on the Great Charter of King John. Glasgow. 1905; 2nd edn., revised, 1914. Repr. 1960.

After a historical introduction (pp. 1–182), McKechnie analyses Magna Carta chapter by chapter (pp. 185–480). An appendix contains documents relative to, or illustrative of, Magna Carta.

3289 MAGNA CARTA ESSAYS. General editor: A. E. Dick Howard. Magna Carta Commission. Charlottesville, Virginia. 1964+.

Of the several essays, the following may be signalized:
J. C. Holt, 'The making of Magna Carta'.
Lady Stenton, 'After Runnymede: Magna Carta in the middle ages'.
Maurice Ashley, 'Magna Carta in the seventeenth century'.
Arthur Goodhart, 'Law of the land (chap. 39)'.
Gottfried Dietze, 'Property (chaps. 28, 30, 31)'.

3290 MALDEN (HENRY E.), ed. Magna Carta commemoration essays. Lond. 1917.

3291 ROUND (JOHN HORACE). 'An unknown charter of liberties'. *E.H.R.* viii (1893), 288–94.

This charter, found in Paris, seems to date from either November 1213 or the spring of 1215. See Holt, *Magna Carta* (No. 3286), app. ii, pp. 296–303, and index under 'charter the unknown'.

3292 THOMPSON (FAITH). The first century of Magna Carta; why it persisted as a document. Univ. Minnesota Stud. in Social Sciences, no. 16. Minneapolis. 1925. Reprinted N.Y. 1967. Idem, Magna Carta: its role in the making of the English constitution, 1300–1629. Minneapolis. 1948; Lond. 1949.

See J. W. Gray, 'The church and Magna Charta in the century after Runnymede', *Historical Stud.* vi (1968), 23–38; and Herbert Butterfield, 'Magna Carta in the historiography of the sixteenth and seventeenth centuries', Stenton Lecture, no. 2 (1968) (Reading, 1969).

3. *Council Documents*

3293 LEADAM (ISAAC S.) and BALDWIN (JAMES F.), eds. Select cases before the king's council. Selden Soc. xxxv (1918).

See also *Select cases in the Star Chamber* (No. 3506).

3294 PROCEEDINGS AND ORDINANCES OF THE PRIVY COUNCIL OF ENGLAND (1386–1542). Ed. by N. Harris Nicolas. Record Comm. 7 vols. Lond. 1834–7.

A most valuable source for the study of the council. Vols. i–vi comprise records preserved in the British Museum.

4. *Modern works on the King's Council*

3295 ADAMS (GEORGE B.). Councils and courts in Anglo-Norman England. New Haven. 1926; reprinted, N.Y. 1965.

3296 BALDWIN (JAMES F.). The king's council in England during the middle ages. Oxf. 1913. Reprinted, 1969. Idem, 'The King's Council' in *English Government at work* (No. 3836), i. 129–61. Idem, 'Concilium and consilium'. *A.H.R.* xx (1914–15), 330–3.

3297 BROOKS (FRANK W.). The Council of the North. Hist. Asso. Pamphlet. Lond. 1953. Revised edn. 1966.

3298 BROWN (ALFRED L.). 'The king's councillors in fifteenth century England'. *T.R.H.S.* 5th Ser. xix (1969), 95–118. Idem, 'The commons and the council in the reign of Henry IV'. *E.H.R.* lxxix (1964), 1–30; reprinted in Fryde-Miller (No. 3365). Idem, Early history of the clerkship of the council (a pamphlet). Univ. Glasgow Press. 1969.

3299 KIRBY (JOHN L.). 'Councils and councillors of Henry IV, 1399–1413'. *T.R.H.S.* 5th Ser. xiv (1964), 35–65.

3300 LANDER (JACK R.). 'The Yorkist council and administration'. *E.H.R.* lxxiii (1958), 27–46. Idem, 'Council, administration and councillors, 1461–1485'. *B.I.H.R.* xxxii (1959), 138–80.

3301 LEVETT (ADA E.). 'The summons to a great council, 1213'. *E.H.R.* xxi (1916), 85–90.

Edward Jenks, 'The alleged Oxford council of 1213', *A.H.R.* xxii (1916–17), 87–90. A. B. White, 'The Oxford meeting of 1213', ibid. xxii (1916–17), 325–9.

3302 LEWIS (NORMAN B.). 'The Continual Council in the early years of Richard II, 1377–80'. *E.H.R.* xli (1926), 246–51.

3303 MORRIS (WILLIAM A.). 'The lesser *curia regis* under the first two Norman kings of England'. *A.H.R.* xxxiv (1928–9), 772–8.

3304 PALGRAVE (FRANCIS). An essay upon the original authority of the king's council. Record Comm. Lond. 1834.

See M. Hale, *The jurisdiction* (No. 3372).

3305 PLUCKNETT (THEODORE F. T.). 'The place of the council in the fifteenth century'. *T.R.H.S.* 4th ser. i (1918), 157–89.

3306 ROSKELL (JOHN S.). 'The office and dignity of Protector of England'. *E.H.R.* lxviii (1953), 193–233.

3306A VIRGOE (ROGER). 'The composition of the king's council, 1437–61'. *B.I.H.R.* xliii (1970), 134–60.

C. PARLIAMENT

1. *Parliamentary Records*

a. General records

Some parliamentary records are printed or translated in Chrimes and Brown (No. 1205), in Stephenson and Marcham (No. 1207), in Wilkinson (No. 3852), and in *English historical documents* (No. 1177), vol. iv.

3307 CAM (HELEN M.). The relation of English members of parliament to their constituencies in the fourteenth century: a neglected text. Univ. Louvain, Recueil de Travaux, 2nd Ser. no. 50. Louvain. 1939.

This is a report among the *Études présentées à la commission internationale pour l'histoire des assemblées d'états* (No. 3366), iii. 143–53.

3308 COTTON (ROBERT). An exact abridgement of the records in the Tower of London, Edward II–Richard III, of all the parliaments. Revised by William Prynne. Lond. 1657. Reprinted, 1689.

Contains abstracts of the rolls of parliaments.

3309 DE CONCILIO HIBERNIAE PER MAGNATES TOTIUS ILLIUS INSULAE. Irish Archaeol. Soc. *Miscellany*, i (1846), 15–33.

The earliest extant record of an Irish parliament; the session was held in some year between 1289 and 1303. The Latin text, which is here printed, is translated in Betham's *Dignities* (No. 3367), pp. 262–71. M. V. Clarke, 'Irish parliaments in the reign of Edward II', *T.R.H.S.* 4th Ser. ix (1926), 29–62. D. B. Quinn, 'Chronological list of parliaments and great councils in Ireland, 1461–1586', *Irish Hist. Stud.* iii (1942), 60–77. H. G. Richardson, 'The Irish parliament rolls of the fifteenth century', *E.H.R.* lviii (1943), 448–61. H. G. Richardson and G. O. Sayles, *Parliaments and Councils of medieval Ireland* (No. 3392).

3310 DOCUMENTS ILLUSTRATIVE OF ENGLISH HISTORY in the thirteenth and fourteenth centuries. Ed. by Henry Cole. Record Comm. Lond. 1844 [printed, 1835].

Rotulus parliamenti, 12 Edw. II, pp. 1–54.
Petitiones in parliamento, 18 Edward I, pp. 55–82.
Placita parliamentaria, 35 Edw. I, pp. 129–38.
Parliamentary writs of summons, 28 Edw. I, pp. 333–40.

3311 DUGDALE (WILLIAM). A perfect copy of all summons of the nobility to the great councils and parliaments of the realm [49 Hen. III–1 James II]. Lond. 1685.

This valuable work seems to have been reprinted in 1794, with the date 1685 on the title-page.

3312 DUNHAM (WILLIAM H. Jr.), ed. The Fane fragment of the 1461 Lords' Journal. New Haven. 1935.

R. Virgoe, 'A new fragment of the Lords' Journal of 1461', *B.I.H.R.* xxxii (1959), 83–7.

3313 ELSYNGE (HENRY). The ancient method and manner of holding parliaments in England. Ed. by Thomas Tyrwhitt. Lond. 1768. Earlier editions, 1660, 1663, 1675.

Elsynge was clerk of the Commons 1632–48. See Catherine S. Sims, 'Expedicio billarum antiquitus: an unpublished chapter of the second book of the manner of holding parliaments in England', *Études présentées à la commission internationale* (No. 3366), xvi (1951) (Louvain); and C. S. Sims, *A.H.R.* xlii (1937), 225–43.

3313A FRASER (CONSTANCE M.). 'Some Durham documents relating to the Hilary parliament of 1404'. *B.I.H.R.* xxxiv (1961), 192–9.

3314 GALBRAITH (VIVIAN H.). 'Articles laid before the parliament of 1371'. *E.H.R.* xxxiv (1919), 579–82.

3315 HASKINS (GEORGE L.). 'Three early petitions of the commonalty'. *Speculum*, xii (1937), 314–18.

3315A MYERS (ALEC R.). 'A parliamentary debate of the mid-fifteenth century' (1449). *B.J.R.L.* xxii (1938), 389–97.

>   See No. 3423.

3316 PARLIAMENTARY WRITS AND WRITS OF MILITARY SUMMONS [Edw. I–Edw. II]. Ed. by Francis Palgrave. Record Comm. 2 vols. in 4. Lond. 1827–34.

>   Contains writs summoning peers to parliament, writs and returns for the election of members of the House of Commons, writs for levying expenses of representatives of the commons, and writs and other documents relating to military service. It is an elaborate collection of records, of great value for the study of parliamentary history. Palgrave intended that these ponderous volumes should be a mere introduction to many others: 'he looked down long vistas of imperial folios'. See C. P. Cooper, *Account of the Public Records* (Lond. 1832), ii. 33–88; and his *Observations . . . on the parliamentary writs* edited by F. Palgrave (Lond. 1832). Certain writs and returns for the parliament of 1275 have been discovered and printed by Hilary Jenkinson, 'The first parliament of Edward I' (No. 3410).

3317 PRYNNE (WILLIAM). A brief register, kalendar, and survey of the several kinds of all parliamentary writs. 4 pts. Lond. 1659–64.

>   This pioneer work contains much valuable material, especially writs for great councils, parliaments, etc. A.D. 1203–1483; and writs of expenses of knights, citizens, and burgesses, with returns to writs, etc. Edw. I–Edw. IV. It is not always reliable. The third part has a separate title: *Brevia Parliamentaria Rediviva* (1662).

3318 PUBLIC RECORD OFFICE. Lists and indexes, no. 1: Index of ancient petitions of the chancery and the exchequer preserved in the public record office. Lond. 1892. Revised on reissue, 1966.

>   An index of the names of persons and places mentioned in about 16,500 petitions addressed to the king, the council, parliament, the chancellor in his executive capacity, and to other officers of state, Edw. I–Hen. VII. See also 'Index to the petitions to the King in Council', in *Deputy Keeper's Reports*, xxxiv (1873), 1–162.

3319 RECORDS OF THE PARLIAMENT AT WESTMINSTER IN 1305. Ed. by F. W. Maitland. [Half-title: Memoranda de parliamento.] Rolls Ser. Lond. 1893.

>   The best-edited of all the printed parliament rolls. Contains, besides the roll of 1305, thirteen original petitions and a valuable introduction, which throws light on the history of parliament and the privy council and on the nature of the petitions. The introduction is reprinted in his *Collected essays* (No. 1482) and portions of it in Cam's *Selections* (No. 1484) and Hazeltine *et al.* (No. 1483). A missing membrane of this roll as edited by Maitland is printed by R. L. Atkinson, 'The Channel Islands petitions of 1305', *E.H.R.* xxxvi (1921), 554–6.

3320 RICHARDSON (HENRY G.) and SAYLES (GEORGE O.). 'The early records of the English parliaments'. *B.I.H.R.* v (1928), 129–54; vi (1929), 71–88, 129–55. Idem, 'Parliamentary documents from formularies'. Ibid. xi (1934), 147–62. Idem, 'The parliament of Carlisle 1307: some new documents'. *E.H.R.* liii (1938), 425–37.

3321 ROLL OF THE PROCEEDINGS OF THE KING'S COUNCIL IN IRELAND 1392–93 [with a translation]. Ed. by James Graves. Rolls Ser. Lond. 1877.

The MS., the text of which is mainly in French, is preserved among the muniments of the Marquis of Ormonde. The greater part of the record is made up of petitions presented to the council, with the answers thereto. On pp. lv–lxxiv is a translation of the ordinances of a great council of Ireland, 1455. The appendix contains various documents, including a calendar of Irish close rolls, 16 Richard II. See above No. 3392.

3322 ROTULI PARLIAMENTORUM; ut et petitiones et placita in parliamento [1278–1503]. 6 vols. n.p., n.d. Index, 1832.

The most valuable collection of material relating to the history of parliament. It was printed in accordance with an order of the House of Lords, dated 9 March 1767. In 1777 the six volumes were 'in a very short time' to be 'ready to be delivered to the lords': *Lords' Journals*, xxxv. 236. The official copy of the work, formerly in the old record office in the Tower, has a MS. inscription stating that the same was presented in 1783 by the king's command. The text of this edition is inaccurate, having been printed from transcripts which were not collated with the originals. The appendices contain many petitions and extracts from letters patent and close. For rolls not included in these six volumes, see Nos. 3323, 3319. The elaborate Index to the Rolls of Parliament, 1832, was edited by John Strachey, John Pridden, and Edward Upham, by order of a committee of the lords.

3323 ROTULI PARLIAMENTORUM ANGLIE HACTENUS INEDITI, 1279–1373. Ed. by H. G. Richardson and G. O. Sayles. Camden Ser. 3rd Ser. li (1935).

The memoranda of the Easter parliament of 1279, printed by Richardson and Sayles, pp. 1–17, was previously printed by E. F. Jacob in *T.R.H.S.* 4th Ser. x (1927), 48–53.

3324 RYLEY (WILLIAM). Placita parlamentaria [*sic*] [Edw. I–Edw. II]. Lond. 1661.

Contains rolls of parliament; with an appendix comprising extracts from patent and close rolls, Edw. I–Edw. II, and petitions in parliament, Edw. I–Hen. VI. This collection has been superseded by the *Rotuli Parliamentorum* (No. 3322).

3325 SOME PARLIAMENTARY NOTES AND TRANSCRIPTS from plea rolls of the exchequer of pleas (prepared by Isobel D. Thornley and Margery A. Fletcher). *B.I.H.R.* viii (1931), 83–7.

b. Statutes: collections and individual

3326 CHRONOLOGICAL TABLE (AND INDEX) OF THE STATUTES, covering the period from 1235 to (various recent dates). By Authority. Lond. 1877– in progress.

Published by the Statute Law Committee, the edition of 1968 carries the table to the end of 1967. The table refers to all the old, repealed acts, and shows how they were affected by later legislation.

3327 STATUTES OF THE REALM (1101–1713). Ed. by A. Luders, T. E. Tomlins, J. Raithby, and others. 11 vols. Record Comm. 1810–28.

Vols. x and xi are indexes. Although this is the best and most nearly complete collection of the statutes of England to 1713, it does not always satisfy the canons of modern scholarship. (See Plucknett, *Legislation*, No. 3339, p. 19.) The introduction to volume i refers to older editions of the statutes and includes some background material. For extracts from that introduction, consult *Select essays* (No. 1246), ii. 169–205, and Cooper's *Account* (No. 3316), i, chap. 6, pp. 124–206.

3328 THE STATUTES: revised edition (1235–1948). 32 vols. By Authority. Lond. 1950.

This is the third edition of a work which appeared first in eighteen volumes in 1870; the second edition carrying the statutes down to 1920 was completed in 1929. Published under the direction of the Statute Law Committee, these editions include only those statutes which are unrepealed. Consult *Chronological Table* (No. 3326).

3329 THE STATUTES OF WALES (1215–1902). Ed. by Ivor Bowen. Lond. 1908.

3330 STATUTES AND ORDINANCES AND ACTS OF THE PARLIA-MENT OF IRELAND, King John to Henry V (vol. i). Ed. by H. F. Berry. Dublin. 1907.

3331 STATUTE ROLLS OF THE PARLIAMENT OF IRELAND, reign of King Henry VI. Ed. by H. F. Berry. Dublin. 1910.

3332 STATUTE ROLLS OF THE PARLIAMENT OF IRELAND, first to the twelfth years of the reign of King Edward IV. Ed. by H. F. Berry. Dublin. 1914; twelfth and thirteenth to the twenty-first and twenty-second years of the reign of King Edward IV. Ed. by J. F. Morrissey. Dublin. 1939.

3333 STATUTES AT LARGE, PASSED IN THE PARLIAMENTS HELD IN IRELAND, 1310–1761. Published by Authority. 8 vols. Dublin. 1765. Another edition (1310–1800, by J. G. Butler), published by Authority. 20 vols. Dublin. 1786–1801. THE IRISH STATUTES: revised edition (omitting most of the repealed statutes). Published by Authority. Lond. 1885.

Vol. viii of each of the first two editions is an index. There are not many Irish statutes of the fourteenth and fifteenth centuries. An abstract of the statutes will be found in pt. vi of *Liber munerum publicorum Hiberniae*, edited by Rowley Lascelles: an incomplete work, planned by the Irish Record Commission, printed 1822–30, and issued from the Rolls House, London, in 2 vols., 1852. There is an index to the *Liber munerum* in *Deputy Keeper's Reports, Ireland*, ix (1877), 21–58.

3334 WOODBINE (GEORGE E.). 'The misdating of the statute of Merton in Bracton'. *Law Quart. Rev.* xxvi (1910), 251–5.

3335 SAYLES (GEORGE O.). 'The sources of two revisions of the statute of Gloucester, 1278'. *E.H.R.* lii (1937), 467–74.

3336 TURNER (GEORGE J.). 'Some thirteenth century statutes'. *Law Magazine and Review*, 4th Ser. xxi (1896), 300–16; xxii (1897), 240–50.

See also his paper, 'A newly-discovered ordinance' (40 Hen. III, forbidding tenants-in-chief to alienate fiefs without licence), *Law Quart. Rev.* xii (1896), 299–301.

3337 LEES (BEATRICE A.). 'The statute of Winchester (1285) and villa integra'. *E.H.R.* xli (1926), 98–103.

3338 GRAVES (EDGAR B.). 'Circumspecte agatis'. *E.H.R.* xliii (1928), 1–20.

Although not an act of parliament, the writ came to be regarded as a statute.

3339 PLUCKNETT (THEODORE F. T.). Legislation of Edward I. The Ford Lectures, 1947. Oxf. 1949.

3340 PLUCKNETT (T. F. T.). Statutes and their interpretation in the first half of the fourteenth century. Cambr. 1922.

3341 RICHARDSON (HENRY G.) and SAYLES (GEORGE O.). The early statutes. Lond. 1934.

Reprinted from articles in *Law Quart. Rev.* for 1934, pp. 201–23, 540–71. See George Sayles, *King's Bench, Edw. I* (No. 3510), iii, pp. xi–xliii.

3342 HALL (HUBERT). 'Negotiations preceding the Confirmatio Cartarum'. *T.R.H.S.* New Ser. iii (1888), 281–91. J. G. Edwards, 'Confirmatio Cartarum and baronial grievances in 1297'. *E.H.R.* lviii (1943), 147–71, 273–300. Harry Rothwell, 'Confirmation of the Charters, 1297'. Ibid. lx (1945), 16–35, 177–91, 300–15 (prints a new text of De tallagio non concedendo). Rothwell in *Powicke essays* (No. 1450). G. O. Sayles, 'The seizure of wool at Easter, 1297'. *E.H.R.* lxvii (1952), 543–7.

3343 HASKINS (GEORGE L.). The Statute of York and the interest of the Commons. Cambr. (Mass.). 1935.

G. T. Lapsley, 'The interpretation of the Statute of York', *E.H.R.* lvi (1941), 22–49, 411–46. Reprinted in *Crown community and parliament* (No. 1478), pp. 153–230; Clementi in *Album Helen Maud Cam* (No. 3366), vol. xxiii. The extensive literature on this controversial subject is listed in J. H. Trueman, 'The statute of York and the Ordinances of 1311', *Medievalia et Humanistica*, x (1956), 64–81. See No. 3366.

3344 PUTNAM (BERTHA H.). The enforcement of the statute of labourers during the first decade after the Black Death, 1349–1359. (Columbia Univ. Studies in History, Economics and Public Law, 32.) N.Y. 1908.

See Ada E. Levett, 'A note on the statute of labourers', *Econ. H.R.* iv (1932), 77–80. Miss Putnam's Appendix 6*–463* of documents, extracts from documents, lists, and tables is a valuable collection of sources from various classes of records.

3345 WAUGH (WILLIAM T.). 'The great statute of praemunire' (1393). *E.H.R.* xxxvii (1922), 173–205.

See E. B. Graves, 'The legal significance of the statute of praemunire of 1353', in *Haskins essays* (No. 1439).

3345A READINGS AND MOOTS AT THE INNS OF COURT IN THE FIFTEENTH CENTURY. Ed. with an introduction by Samuel E. Thorne. vol. i. Selden Soc. lxxi (1954).

See also Thorne's edition of *A discourse upon the exposicion & understandinge of statutes with Sir Thomas Egerton's additions*, edited from MSS. in the Huntington Library (San Marino, 1942). Cf. T. F. T. Plucknett, 'Ellesmere on statutes', *Law Quart. Rev.* lx (1949), 542–9.

3346 HANBURY (H. G.). 'The legislation of Richard III'. *Amer. Jour. Legal Hist.* vi (1962), 95–113.

2. *Modus Tenendi Parliamentum*

The anonymous tract of twenty-six short paragraphs provides a presumptive account of the composition and proceedings of parliament. Its date, its purpose, and its significance have been sharply debated. Hardy dated in 1294–1327; Bémont placed it in the reign of Richard II. Richardson and Sayles hold that at least the extant copies of the English *Modus* follow the Irish *Modus* and hence cannot precede the late fourteenth century. Morris dated it 1321 and regarded it as a Lancastrian programme. Miss Clarke made the study of the *Modus* the focus of her *Medieval Representation and Consent*; she dated it 1322 as a programme of the moderates. Galbraith placed its composition between 1316 and 1324 and suggested the well-known chancery clerk, William Ayreminne (Airmyn), as a candidate for authorship. Galbraith tends to regard the *Modus* as propaganda of the baronial faction for the subordination of the crown. 'The author is an expert, at a revolutionary moment, sincerely anxious to set out how parliament should actually be conducted' (Galbraith, p. 95). Wilkinson, *Constitutional history, 1216–1399* (Lond. 1958), ii. 323–58, writes a commentary on the *Modus* and translates some portions of it.

3347 MODUS TENENDI PARLIAMENTUM [with a translation]. Ed. by T. D. Hardy. Record Comm. 1846. Excerpts in Stubbs's *Select Charters* (No. 1206).

Hardy contends that it was written between 1294 and 1327.

3347A MODUS TENENDI PARLIAMENTA ET CONCILIA IN HIBERNIA. Ed. by Anthony Dopping, bishop of Meath. Dublin. 1692. New edition, 1772.

A Latin tract, of uncertain date, which used to be ascribed to the reign of Henry II.

3348 BÉMONT (CHARLES). 'La date de la composition du Modus tenendi parliamentum'. In *Mélanges Julien Havet: Recueil de travaux dédiés à la mémoire de Julien Havet*, pp. 465–80. Paris. 1895.

Believes that the tract was written soon after the accession of Richard II.

3349 CLARKE (MAUDE V.). Medieval representation and consent: a study of early parliaments in England and Ireland, with special reference to the Modus tenendi parliamentum. Lond. and N.Y. 1936.

Miss Clarke provides a text and the basic, thorough, if controversial, commentary. Dorothy K. Hodnett and Winifred P. White, 'The manuscripts of the Modus tenendi parliamentum', *E.H.R.* xxxiv (1919), 208–15; E. Jeffries Davis, 'A fifteenth century English version of the Modus', ibid. pp. 216–25. John Taylor, 'The manuscripts of the Modus . . .', *E.H.R.* lxxxiii (1968), 673–88.

3350 CUTTINO (GEORGE). 'A reconsideration of the Modus tenendi parliamentum', in *The forward movement of the fourteenth century*. Ed. by Francis L. Utley. Pp. 31–60. Columbus, Ohio. 1961.

Supports Miss Clarke's analysis and translates her text, pp. 44–56.

3351 GALBRAITH (VIVIAN H.). 'The Modus tenendi parliamentum'. *Warburg and Courtauld Inst. Jour.* xvi (1953), 81–99.

Dates the *Modus* 1316–24 and tentatively suggests William Ayreminne as a plausible author. 'Despite its "misstatements" it remains our earliest systematic treatise on parliament.'

3352 HARDY (THOMAS D.). 'On the Modus tenendi parliamentum, with special reference to the unique French version'. *Archaeol. Jour.* xix (1862), 259–74.

Contains the text of the French version.

3353 MORRIS (WILLIAM A.). 'The date of the Modus tenendi parliamentum'. *E.H.R.* xlix (1934), 407–22.

3354 RICHARDSON (HENRY G.) and SAYLES (GEORGE O.). The Irish parliament in the middle ages. Philadelphia. 1952.

Richardson and Sayles on pp. 137–8 assert that the Irish *Modus* preceded the English *Modus*, which must therefore be assigned to the late fourteenth century. Galbraith in the article cited above (No. 3351), pp. 95–9, presents evidence to controvert this inversion.

3355 ROSKELL (JOHN S.). 'A consideration of certain aspects and problems of the English Modus tenendi parliamentum'. *B.J.R.L.* l (1967–8), 411–42.

3. *Modern Studies on Parliament*

The origins of parliament are a subject of sharp controversy. In the mid-twentieth century, the fundamental issue turns on the connotation of the word 'parliament' as it was used by medieval contemporaries. Richardson and Sayles insist that 'parliament' had a precise connotation. They write 'parliaments are of one kind only and that, when we have stripped every non-essential away, the essence of them is the dispensing of justice by the king or by someone who in a very special sense represents the king' (*B.I.H.R.* v (1928), 133). The judicial character differentiates *parliamentum* from *consilium, tractatus,* and *colloquium.* Many other scholars, notably Plucknett, Powicke, Treharne, Edwards, and Wilkinson see little or no justification for such confining precision.

Summaries of the various positions are provided by Miller (No. 3361) and Templeman (No. 3364) and in the introductions to Fryde-Miller (No. 3365). The fifteenth-century character of parliament is described by Chrimes in *English Constitutional Ideas* (Cambr. 1936), chaps. ii–iii.

Studies on parliamentary institutions of various countries have been, and are being, fostered by the International Commission for the History of Representative and Parliamentary Institutions. Established in 1936 under the title Commission internationale pour l'histoire des Assemblées d'États and as a sub-committee of Comité international des sciences historiques, its English title was added in 1950. Its publications are partly subsidized by UNESCO. A complete list of *Studies presented to the International Commission* is given, down to 1954, in *Mediaeval representation* (No. 3366), vol. xvii, below and, down to 1965, in *Liber Memorialis* (No. 3366), vol. xxvii. Those studies pertaining specifically to English or Irish medieval institutions are mentioned in No. 3366 below.

The project for a full-length, co-operative History of Parliament was discussed by English historians during the inter-war period and received enthusiastic promotion from Colonel (later Lord) Wedgwood. In 1936–8, the latter published two volumes out of a projected three on the personnel of the parliaments from 1439 to 1509. The next important step was the appointment in 1940 of a board of trustees, drawn from both houses of parliament, for over-all supervision of the History. However, the planning and actual composition of the History were committed to an editorial board of distinguished historians. The editorial board decided not to incorporate the Wedgwood volumes into the now projected History, yet none the less to concentrate on the House of Commons by studies of the biographies of the members. The Government provides a substantial annual grant for the organization and completion of the History in about 100 volumes. No volumes on the parliaments of the Middle Ages had appeared in this series by the end of 1970; but the three volumes by Sir Lewis Namier and John Brooke, *The House of Commons, 1754–1790* (H.M.S.O., 1964), may illustrate the form which the History will take.

Some of the problems, accompanied by brief extracts from modern commentaries, are set forth in Gerald P. Bodet, *Early English parliaments* (Problems in European Civilization series, Boston, 1968), and in Peter Spufford, *Origins of the English parliament* (Problems and Perspectives in History series, Lond. 1967). A convenient collection of twenty-three important articles, with valuable introductions summarizing recent research, is edited by E. B. Fryde and Edward Miller as *Historical studies of the English Parliament* (No. 3365).

a. Surveys of recent interpretations

3356 CAM (HELEN M.), et al. 'Recent work and present views on the origins and developments of representative assemblies'. Relazioni del x Congresso Internazionale di scienze Storiche Rome, 1955 (Florence, 1956) pp. 1–101.

3357 CUTTINO (GEORGE P.). 'Mediaeval parliament reinterpreted'. *Speculum*, xli (1966), 681–7.

3358 EDWARDS (JOHN GORONWY). Historians and the medieval English parliament. David Murray Lecture, no. 22 (1955). Glasgow. 1960. ⋆

3359 FRYDE (EDMUND B.) and MILLER (EDWARD). Historical studies of the English parliament. 2 vols. Cambr. 1970. (Analysed as No. 3365.)

3360 HOYT (ROBERT S.). 'Recent publications in the United States and Canada on the history of western representative institutions before the French Revolution'. *Speculum* (a special number), xxix (1954), 356–77. (No. 3366).

3361 MILLER (EDWARD). 'The origins of parliament'. Pamphlet General Series No. 44. The Historical Association. 1960.

3362 POWICKE (FREDERICK MAURICE). 'Recent work on the origins of the English parliament'. *Université de Louvain: Recueil de travaux*, 2nd Ser. No. 50. Louvain. 1939. See No. 3366.

3363 ROSKELL (JOHN S.). 'Perspectives in English parliamentary history'. *B.J.R.L.* xlvi (1964), 448–75. Reprinted in Fryde-Miller (No. 3365).

3364 TEMPLEMAN (GEOFFREY). 'The history of parliament to 1400 in the light of modern research'. *Univ. Birmingham Hist. Jour.* i (1948), 202–31; reprinted in Robert L. Schuyler and Herman Ausubel, *The making of English history* (N.Y. 1952), pp. 109–27.

3365 FRYDE (EDMUND B.) and MILLER (EDWARD). Historical studies of the English parliament. 2 vols. Cambr. 1970. Also paperback edn.

Vol. i:

(*a*) E. Miller, Introduction. 1–30.
(*b*) J. E. A. Jolliffe, Some factors in the beginnings of parliament (*T.R.H.S.* 4th Ser. xxii (1940), 101–39). 31–69
(*c*) R. F. Treharne, The nature of parliament in the reign of Henry III (*E.H.R.* lxxiv (1959), 590–610). 70–90.
(*d*) F. W. Maitland, Introduction to Memoranda de Parliamento, 1305 (No. 3319 above). 91–135.
(*e*) J. G. Edwards, The Plena Potestas of English parliamentary representatives (*Salter essays*). 136–49.
(*f*) J. G. Edwards, The personnel of the commons in parliament under Edward I and Edward II (*Tout essays*). 150–67.
(*g*) H. M. Cam, The legislators of medieval England (*Cam papers, Law-finders*). 168–94.
(*h*) T. F. T. Plucknett, Parliament, 1327–36 (*Eng. Government at work* (No. 3836), i. 82–128). 195–241.
(*i*) E. B. Fryde, Parliament and the French war, 1336–40 (*Wilkinson essays*). 242–61.
(*j*) H. M. Cam, The theory and practice of representation in medieval England (*Cam papers, Law-finders*). 262–78.
(*k*) J. G. Edwards, 'Justice' in early English parliaments (*B.I.H.R.* xxvii (1954), 35–53). 279–97.
(*l*) T. F. Tout, The English parliament and public opinion, 1376–88 (*Tout papers*). 298–315.
(*m*) J. G. Edwards, the parliamentary committee of 1398 (*E.H.R.* xl (1925), 321–33). 316–28.
(*n*) B. Wilkinson, The deposition of Richard II and the accession of Henry IV (*E.H.R.* liv (1939), 215–39). 329–53.
(*o*) Editorial notes and select bibliography. 355–81.

Vol. ii: (1399 to 1603):

(*a*) Edmund Fryde, Introduction. 1–30.
(*b*) A. L. Brown, The commons and the council in the reign of Henry IV (*E.H.R.* lxxix (1964), 1–30). 31–60.
(*c*) B. P. Wolffe, Acts of resumption in the Lancastrian parliaments, 1399–1456 (*E.H.R.* lxxiii (1958), 583–613). 61–91.
(*d*) J. R. Lander, Attainder and forfeiture, 1453–1509 (*Historical Jour.* iv (1961), 119–51). 92–124.
(*e*) H. Miller, London and parliament in the reign of Henry VIII (*B.I.H.R.* xxxv (1962), 129–49). 125–46.
(*f*) J. E. Neale, The commons' privilege of free speech in parliament (*Tudor studies . . . to A. F. Pollard* (1924), 257–86). 147–76.
(*g*) G. R. Elton, Parliamentary drafts, 1529–1540 (*B.I.H.R.* xxv (1952), 117–32). 177–92.
(*h*) G. R. Elton, The political creed of Thomas Cromwell (*T.R.H.S.* 5th Ser. vi (1956), 69–92). 193–216.
(*i*) J. E. Neale, The Elizabethan Acts of Supremacy and Uniformity (*E.H.R.* lxv (1950), 304–32). 217–45.
(*j*) J. E. Neale, Peter Wentworth (*E.H.R.* xxxix (1924), 36–54, 175–205). 246–95.
(*k*) J. S. Roskell, Perspectives in English parliamentary history (*B.J.R.L.* xlvi (1964), 448–75). 296–323.
(*l*) Editorial notes and select bibliography. 324–38.

3366 INTERNATIONAL COMMISSION FOR THE HISTORY OF REPRESENTATIVE AND PARLIAMENTARY INSTITUTIONS, Studies presented to. Louvain, Paris, etc. 1937– in progress.

The studies pertaining to the medieval English and Irish institutions are printed in the following volumes:

- i. H. M. Cam, 'Recent books in English on the parliamentary institutions of the British Isles in the middle ages' (*International Comm. Hist. Sci. Bull.* ix (1937), 413–18).
- iii. F. M. Powicke, 'Recent work on the origin of the English parliament', pp. 131–40. Louvain, 1939. H. M. Cam, 'The relation of English members of parliament to their constituencies in the fourteenth century: a neglected text'. See No. 3307.
- x. H. G. Richardson and G. O. Sayles, *The Irish parliament in the Middle Ages*. Philadelphia. 1952.
- xiv. J. S. Roskell. *The commons in the parliament of 1422: English society and parliamentary representation under the Lancastrians*. Manchester. 1954.
- xvi. Henry Elsynge. *Expeditio billarum antiquitus*. Ed. by Catherine S. Sims. Louvain. 1954. See No. 3313.
- xvii. MEDIAEVAL REPRESENTATION IN THEORY AND PRACTICE: Essays by American members of the International Commission (etc.). Printed in *Speculum*, xxix, pt. ii (1954), 347–476.
  347–55, H. M. Cam, 'Introduction';
  356–77, R. S. Hoyt, 'Recent publications in the United States and Canada on the history of western representative institutions before the French Revolution';
  378–94, W. O. Ault, 'Village by-laws by common consent';
  395–409, G. P. Cuttino, 'King's clerks and the community of the realm';
  410–16, J. R. Strayer and George Rudisill, Jr., 'Taxation and community in Wales and Ireland, 1272–1327';
  417–32, Gaines Post, 'The two laws and the statute of York'.
- xx. JOURNÉES INTERNATIONALES, PARIS 1957. Louvain, Paris, 1959.
  pp. 5–14, H. M. Cam, 'The evolution of the English franchise'.
- xxiii. ALBUM HELEN MAUD CAM. 2 vols. Louvain, Paris, 1960.
  Vol. i. 1–10, C. Robbins, 'Helen Maud Cam, C.B.E.';
  11–35, W. O. Ault, 'Village assemblies in medieval England';
  55–70, J. C. Holt, 'Rights and liberties in Magna Carta';
  Vol. ii. 13–26, R. S. Hoyt, 'Representation in the administrative practice of Anglo-Norman England';
  93–100, D. Clementi, 'That the statute of York of 1322 is no longer ambiguous';
  117–38, J. Otway-Ruthven, 'The mediaeval Irish chancery';
  139–53, A. R. Myers, 'The English parliament and the French estates-general in the middle ages'.

xxv. Antonio Marongiu, IL PARLAMENTO IN ITALIA nel MEDIO EVO e nell'ETÀ MODERNA. Milan, 1962.

This comparative study of parliaments in Europe has been translated into English by Stuart Woolf as *Medieval parliaments: a comparative study* (Lond. and N.Y. 1968).

xxvii. LIBER MEMORIALIS SIR MAURICE POWICKE. Louvain and Paris, 1965. Pp. 7–25, H. M. Cam,'Frederick Maurice Powicke, 1879–1963', and a bibliography of Powicke's writings.

xxviii. J. S. Roskell, THE COMMONS AND THEIR SPEAKERS IN ENGLISH PARLIAMENTS, 1376–1523. Manchester, 1965.

xxix. Paris, 1966. Pp. 47–62, G. I. Langmuir, 'Politics and parliament in the early thirteenth century'.

xxxi. Louvain and Paris, 1966.
1–6, G. L. Harriss, 'Parliament and taxation: the middle ages';
7–12, D. Pennington, 'Parliament and taxation, 1485–1660';
103–11, G. L. Haskins, 'Les fonctions des representants aux parlements du roi Édouard Ier d'Angleterre'.

xxxviii. LIBER MEMORIALIS GEORGES DE LAGARDE. London, 1968, with a preface, etc. 1969. Louvain and Paris, 1970. No. 4147.

b. General descriptions of early development

3367 BETHAM (WILLIAM). Dignities, feudal and parliamentary. Vol. i. Lond. 1830. Ireland, pp. 225–379.

3368 CLARKE (MAUDE V.). Medieval Representation and Consent (No. 3349).

See also *Fourteenth century studies* (No. 1464).

3369 COBBETT (WILLIAM). The parliamentary history of England, 1066–1803. 36 vols. Lond. 1806–20.

3370 EDWARDS (JOHN GORONWY). The commons in medieval English parliaments. The Creighton Lecture for 1957. Lond. 1958.

The Creighton lecture argues that the lords did not dominate the commons. See J. S. Roskell's review in *E.H.R.* lxxiv (1959), 523–4. W. N. Bryant, 'Some earlier examples of intercommuning in parliament, 1340–48', *E.H.R.* lxxxv (1970), 54–8.

3371 GRAY (HOWARD L.). The influence of the Commons on early legislation: a study of the fourteenth and fifteenth centuries. Lond. and Cambr. (Mass.). 1932.

3372 HALE (MATTHEW). The jurisdiction of the lord's house. Lond. 1796.

3373 HASKINS (George L.). The growth of English representative government. Oxf. and Philadelphia. 1948.

G. L. Haskins, 'The king's high court of parliament holden at Westminster', *History*, New Ser. xxiv (1939–40), 295–310. Idem, 'Parliament in the later middle ages', *A.H.R.* lii (1946–7), 667–83. Idem, 'The petitions of representatives in the parliaments of Edward I', *E.H.R.* liii (1938), 1–20.

3374 HOUSE OF LORDS. I: Its origin, by G. L. Gomme. II: Its functions, by James Gairdner. III: Its place of meeting, by H. B. Wheatley. IV: Transition from tenure to writ, by J. H. Round. *Antiquary*, ix–xi, *passim*. Lond. 1884–5.

Round's paper, under the title 'The Origin of the House of Lords', is reprinted in his *Peerage and pedigree* (No. 569), i. 324–62.

3375 McILWAIN (CHARLES H.). The high court of parliament and its supremacy: an historical essay on the boundaries between legislation and adjudication in England. New Haven. 1910.*

An influential study, following in the steps of Maitland's *Memoranda de parliamento* (No. 3319). See also McIlwain, 'Medieval estates', *Cambr. Med. Hist.* vii. 644–715.

3376 PARRY (C. H.). The parliaments and councils of England chronologically arranged, 1066–1688. Lond. 1839.

A list of parliaments, with a brief account of the writs issued and the business transacted. Valuable.

3377 PASQUET (DESIRÉ). Essai sur les origines de la chambre des communes. Paris. 1914. Trans. by R. G. D Laffan: An essay on the origins of the house of commons. Cambr. 1925. Reprinted, 1964.

See also Petit-Dutaillis and Lefebvre (No. 1221), iii. 305–47, and 406–505.

3378 PIKE (LUKE O.). A constitutional history of the house of lords. Lond. etc. 1894. Repr. 1964.

The best work on this subject.

3379 PLUCKNETT (THEODORE F. T.). 'Parliament', in *English Government at work* (No. 3836), i. 82–128. Reprinted in Fryde-Miller (No. 3365).

3380 POLLARD (ALBERT F.). The evolution of parliament. Lond. 1920. 2nd edn. 1926; repr. 1934.

A. F. Pollard, *Parliament in the wars of the roses* (Glasgow, 1936). Idem, 'Two notes on parliamentary history', *B.I.H.R.* xvi (1939), 19–23. Idem, 'Plenum parliamentum', *E.H.R.* xxx (1915), 660–2. Thor Thorgrimsson, 'Plenum parliamentum', *B.I.H.R.* xxxii (1959), 69–82.

3381 POWELL (J. ENOCH) and WALLIS (KEITH). The house of lords in the middle ages: a history of the English house of lords to 1540. Lond. 1968.

3382 REPORTS FROM THE LORDS' COMMITTEES APPOINTED TO SEARCH THE JOURNALS OF THE HOUSE, ROLLS OF PARLIAMENT, AND OTHER RECORDS FOR ALL MATTERS TOUCHING THE DIGNITY OF A PEER. 5 vols. Lond. 1820–9.

Vol. i First report: history of legislative assemblies in England, etc. Vols. ii–iii Appendix i to first report: writs of summons, John–Edw. IV Vol. iv Second report (with appendices ii–iv to the first report); third and fourth reports (dealing mainly with the history of the peerage). Vol. v Fifth report, i.e., appendix v: patents of creation, etc., Stephen–Edw. IV.

The committee was first appointed in 1815, and was often revived between 1816 and 1829. Reports were made in 1816, 1817, and 1818; the first general report was presented to the lords in 1819, the second in 1820, the third in 1822, the fourth in 1825, the fifth in 1829. Vols. i–iv were reprinted for the House of Commons in 1826 (Parl. Papers, vols. vi–ix); and for the lords in 1829 (Sessional Papers, vols. cclii–cclvi). Vols. i–iii, which are very valuable for the study of parliamentary history, will be found also in the *Journals of the House of Lords*, lvi (1824), 470–1104; vol. iv, ibid. liii (1820), 364–6 (2nd report); ibid. iv (1822–3), 348–463 (3rd report); ibid. lvii (1825), 1209–55 (4th report); and vol. v, ibid. lxi (1829), 729–926. For a valuable criticism of this work, see 'History of the English Legislature' (by John Allen), in *Edinburgh Rev.* xxxv (1821), 1–43.

3383 RICHARDSON (HENRY G.) and SAYLES (GEORGE O.). 'Parliament and Great Councils in Medieval England'. *Law Quart. Rev.* lxxvii (1961), 213–36; 401–26; Reprinted separately, Lond. 1961.

These two articles form a strong summary recapitulation of the authors' arguments as well as a rebuttal of criticisms on the early development of parliament. Their principal earlier articles on this subject are in *T.R.H.S.* 4th Ser. xi (1938), 137–83; *B.I.H.R.* v (1928), 129–54; vi (1929), 71–88 and 129–55; ibid. viii (1931), 65–82; ix (1932), 1–18. *E.H.R.* xlvi (1931), 529–50; xlvii (1932), 194–203, 377–97; *T.R.H.S.* 4th Ser. xxviii (1946), 21–45.

3384 RIESS (LUDWIG). Geschichte des Wahlrechts zum englischen Parlament im Mittelalter. Leipzig. 1885.

Trans. by K. L. Wood-Legh as *The history of the English electoral law in the Middle Ages* (Cambr. 1940).

3385 RIESS (LUDWIG). Der Ursprung des englischen Unterhauses. *Hist. Zeitschrift*, lx (1888), 1–33.

Contends that Edward I's object in summoning the commons to parliament was not to obtain pecuniary aid. For a criticism of this and the preceding work, see *E.H.R.* v (1890), 146–56. See also D. Pasquet, *Essai sur les origines* (No. 3377) and White, *Concentration* (No. 3390).

3386 RUSSELL (JOSIAH C.). 'Early parliamentary organization'. *A.H.R.* xliii (1937–8), 1–21.

3387 THOMPSON (FAITH). A short history of parliament 1295–1642. Lond. 1953.

3388 WAGNER (ANTHONY) and SAINTY (J. C.). 'The origin of the introduction of peers in the House of Lords'. *Archaeologia*, ci (1967), 119–50.

Concerned with the antecedents of the present ceremony.

3389 WEDGWOOD (JOSIAH C.) and HOLT (ANNE D.). History of parliament: biographies of the members of the commons house, 1439–1509; register of the ministers and members of both houses, 1439–1509. 2 vols. Lond. 1936–8.

3390 WHITE (ALBERT B.). Self-government by the king's command. Minneapolis. 1933.

A. B. White, 'Was there a common council before parliament', *A.H.R.* xxv (1919–20), 1–17.

3391 WILKINSON (BERTIE). Studies in the constitutional history of the thirteenth and fourteenth centuries. Manchester. 1937.

Ten essays centring on parliament and council. See also Wilkinson, 'English politics and politicians of the thirteenth and fourteenth centuries', *Speculum*, xxx (1955), 37–48.

3392 RICHARDSON (HENRY G.) and SAYLES (GEORGE O.). Parliament and Council of medieval Ireland. vol. i. Irish MSS. Comm. Dublin. 1947. See No. 3366.

> See also their 'The Irish parliaments of Edward I', *Royal Irish Acad. Procs.* xxxviii *Sect. C*, no. 6 (1929), 128–47. Idem, 'Parliament in medieval Ireland', Pamphlet no. 1 in Medieval Irish History Series (Dundalk, 1964). J. F. Lydon, 'William of Windsor and the Irish parliament', *E.H.R.* lxxx (1965), 252–67.

c. Articles on specific developments

3393 BARRACLOUGH (GEOFFREY). 'Law and legislation in (later) medieval England'. *Law Quart. Rev.* lvi (1940), 57–92.

3394 BROWN (ALFRED L.). 'The commons and the council in the reign of Henry IV'. *E.H.R.* lxxix (1964), 1–30. Reprinted in Fryde-Miller (No. 3365). Also No. 3298.

3395 CAM (HELEN M.). 'From witness of the shire to full parliament'. *T.R.H.S.* 4th Ser. xxvi (1944), 13–35. Reprinted in *Lawfinders* (No. 1461). Idem, 'The theory and practice of representation in medieval England'. *History*, New Ser. xxxviii (1953), 11–26. Idem, 'The legislators of medieval England'. *P.B.A.* xxxi (1947), 127–50; reprinted in Fryde-Miller (No. 3365).

3396 CHRIMES (STANLEY B.). 'House of Lords and House of Commons in the fifteenth century'. *E.H.R.* xlix (1934), 494–7.

3397 EDWARDS (JOHN GORONWY). 'Justice in early English parliaments'. *B.I.H.R.* xxvii (1954), 35–53. Reprinted in Fryde-Miller, as are his articles in *Salter essays* (No. 1451) and *Tout essays* (No. 1458).

> Also Edwards, 'Taxation and consent in the court of common pleas', *E.H.R.* lvii (1942), 473–82.

3398 HARRISS (GERALD L.). 'Parliament and taxation: the middle ages'. *Stud. . . . International Comm. . . . Parliamentary Institutions* (No. 3366). Idem, 'Parliamentary taxation and the origins of appropriation of supply in England (1207–1340)'. *Recueils de la Société Jean Bodin*, xxiv: *Gouvernés et gouvernants*, 3rd part (1966), 165–79.

> Alan Rogers, 'Henry IV; the commons and taxation', *Mediaeval Stud.* (Toronto), xxxi (1969), 44–70.

3399 HASKINS (GEORGE L.). 'Petitions of representatives in the parliament of Edward I'. *E.H.R.* liii (1938), 1–20. See No. 3373.

3400 JOLLIFFE (JOHN E. A.). 'Some factors in the beginnings of parliament'. *T.R.H.S.* 4th Ser. xxii (1940), 101–39. Reprinted in Fryde-Miller.

> An influential article.

3401 MEDIAEVAL REPRESENTATION IN THEORY AND PRACTICE: Essays by American members of the International Commission for the History of Representative and Parliamentary Institutions. *Speculum*, xxix (1954), 347–476. See No. 3366, vol. xvii.

3402 McFARLANE (KENNETH B.). 'Parliament and bastard feudalism'. *T.R.H.S.* 4th Ser. xxvi (1944), 53–79.

3403 MORRIS (WILLIAM A.). 'Magnates and the community of the realm in parliament, 1264–1327'. *Medievalia et Humanistica*, i (1943), 58–94.

3404 MYERS (ALEC R.). 'Parliamentary petitions in the fifteenth century'. *E.H.R.* lii (1937), 385–404; 590–613. Idem, 'A parliamentary debate of the mid-fifteenth century (1449)'. *B.J.R.L.* xxii (1938), 388–404. Idem, 'Observations on the procedure of the Commons in dealing with bills in the Lancastrian period'. *Univ. Toronto Law Jour.* iii (1939), 51–73.

  The parliamentary debate is printed from a seventeenth-century transcript.

3405 RAYNER (DORIS). 'Forms and machinery of the commune petition the fourteenth century'. *E.H.R.* lvi (1941), 198–233; 549–70.

  Shows *inter alia* separate procedure of the private petition from that of the common petition by 1339.

3406 STEPHENSON (CARL). 'The beginnings of representative government in England'. In *The Constitution reconsidered*, edited for the Amer. Hist. Asso. by Conyers Read. N.Y. 1938, pp. 25–36.

  See Stephenson in *Haskins essays* (No. 1439).

3407 TREHARNE (REGINALD F.). 'The nature of parliament in the reign of Henry III'. *E.H.R.* lxxiv (1959), 590–610. Reprinted in Fryde-Miller (No. 3365).

  Treharne holds that up to 1272 at least, 'Englishmen thought of parliament as a primarily political assembly' rather than as a law court.

3408 WHITE (ALBERT B.). 'Some early instances of concentration of representatives in England'. *A.H.R.* xix (1913–14), 735–50.

3409 WOLFFE (BERTRAM P.). 'Acts of resumption in the Lancastrian parliaments'. *E.H.R.* lxxiii (1958), 583–613. Reprinted in Fryde-Miller (No. 3365).

d. Articles on specific parliaments

3410 JENKINSON (HILARY). 'The first parliament of Edward I'. *E.H.R.* xxv (1910), 231–42; lviii (1943), 462–3.

3411 ROUND (JOHN HORACE). 'The house of lords and the model parliament'. *E.H.R.* xxx (1915), 385–97.

3412 RICHARDSON (HENRY G.) and SAYLES (GEORGE). 'The parliament of Carlisle. Some new documents'. *E.H.R.* liii (1938), 425–37.

  See W. E. Lunt, 'William Testa and the parliament of Carlisle', *E.H.R.* xli (1926), 332–57.

3413 JOHNSTONE (HILDA). 'The parliament of Lincoln, 1316'. *E.H.R.* xxxvi (1921), 53–7, 480. H. G. Richardson and G. O. Sayles, 'The parliament of Lincoln, 1316'. *B.I.H.R.* xii (1935), 105–7. Arthur Hughes, 'The parliament of Lincoln, 1316'. *T.R.H.S.* x (1896), 41–58.

  Hughes's article deals mainly with chancery and exchequer under Edward I and Edward II.

3414 HARRISS (G. L.). 'The commons petitions of 1340'. *E.H.R.* lxxviii (1963), 625–54.

3415 LAMBRICK (GABRIELLE). 'The impeachment of the abbot of Abingdon in 1368'. *E.H.R.* lxxxii (1967), 250–76.

3416 GOODMAN (ANTHONY). 'Sir Thomas Hoo and the parliament of 1376'. *B.I.H.R.* xli (1968), 139–49.

3417 BELLAMY (J. G.). 'Appeal and impeachment in the Good Parliament'. *B.I.H.R.* xxxix (1966), 35–46.

See *Anonimalle Chronicle* (No. 2787).
M. V. Clarke, *Fourteenth century studies* (No. 1464), or *Salter essays* (No. 1451). B. Wilkinson, *Studies in Const. Hist.* (No. 3391), and Roskell, Peter de la Mare (No. 3427).

3418 PLUCKNETT (THEODORE F. T.). 'The Origin of Impeachment'. *T.R.H.S.* 4th Ser. xxiv (1942), 47–71. Idem, 'The impeachments of 1376'. Ibid. 5th Ser. i (1951), 153–64. Idem, 'Impeachment and attainder'. Ibid. 5th Ser. iii (1953), 145–58. Idem, 'State trials under Richard II'. Ibid. 5th Ser. ii (1952), 159–71. Margaret Aston, 'The impeachment of Bishop Despenser'. *B.I.H.R.* xxxviii (1965), 127–48.

3419 EDWARDS (JOHN G.). 'Some common petitions in Richard II's first parliament'. *B.I.H.R.* xxvi (1953), 200–13.

See Albert F. Pollard, 'The chronology of Richard II's first parliament', *B.I.H.R.* xvi (1939), 19–21.

3419A PALMER (J. J. N.). 'The parliament of 1385 and the constitutional crisis of 1386'. *Speculum*, xlvi (1971), 477–90.

3420 TUCK (J. A.). 'The Cambridge parliament, 1388'. *E.H.R.* lxxxiv (1969), 225–43.

3421 EDWARDS (JOHN G.). 'The parliamentary committee of 1398'. *E.H.R.* xl (1925), 321–33. Reprinted in Fryde-Miller (No. 3365).

See *Tout essays* (No. 1458), *Salter essays* (No. 1451), both reprinted in Fryde-Miller (No. 3365).

3422 RICHARDSON (HENRY G.). 'Richard II's last parliament'. *E.H.R.* lii (1937), 39–47. G. T. Lapsley, 'Richard II's last parliament'. Ibid. liii (1938) 53–78; reprinted in *Crown, community and parliament* (No. 1478), pp. 341–73. H. G. Richardson, 'The elections to the October parliament of 1399'. *B.I.H.R.* xvi (1939), 137–43.

3422 A FRASER (CONSTANCE M.). 'Some Durham documents relating to the Hilary parliament of 1404'. *B.I.H.R.* xxxiv (1961), 192–9.

3423 DUNHAM (WILLIAM H., JR.). 'Notes from the parliament at Winchester, 1449'. *Speculum*, xvii (1942), 402–15.

R. Virgoe, 'A list of members of the parliament of February, 1449', *B.I.H.R.* xxxiv (1961), 200–10. See No. 3315A.

e. Officers and meeting-places

3424 MARSDEN (PHILIP). The officers of the Commons 1363–1965. Lond. 1966.

3425 POLLARD (ALBERT F.). 'Fifteenth-century clerks of parliament'. *B.I.H.R.* xv (1937–8), 137–61. Idem, 'The mediaeval under-clerks of parliament, 1362–1509'. Ibid. xvi (1938–9), 65–87. Idem, 'Receivers of petitions and clerks of parliament'. *E.H.R.* lvii (1942), 202–26. Idem, 'The clerk of the crown'. Ibid. pp. 312–33. Idem, 'The clerical organization of parliament'. Ibid. pp. 31–58.

3426 RICHARDSON (HENRY G.) and SAYLES (GEORGE O.). 'The king's ministers in parliament, 1272–1307'. *E.H.R.* xlvi (1931), 529–50; and for 1307–77, xlvii (1932), 194–203, 377–97.

3427 ROSKELL (JOHN S.). The Commons and their speakers in English parliaments, 1376–1523. Manchester. 1965.

Roskell printed articles on individual speakers in *Nottingham Mediaeval Stud.* iii (1958); v (1961); vii (1963); *Archaeol. Cant.* lxx (1956–7); and in *Cambr. Antiq. Soc. Procs.* lii (1959).

3428 ROSKELL (JOHN S.). 'Medieval speakers for the Commons in parliament'. *B.I.H.R.* xxiii (1950), 31–52.

The speakers were not puppets of aristocratic factions.

3429 ROUND (JOHN H.). 'John Doreward, Speaker (1399, 1413)'. *E.H.R.* xxix (1914), 717–19.

3430 COOPER (IVY M.). 'The meeting-places of parliament in the Ancient Palace of Westminster'. *Brit. Archaeol. Asso. Jour.* 3rd Ser. iii (1939), 97–138.

3431 HASTINGS (MAURICE). Parliament House: the Chambers of the House of Commons and its place in the development of the perpendicular style in England. Lond. 1950. Idem, St. Stephen's chapel. Cambr. 1955.

3432 PELHAM (R. A.). 'The provisioning of the Lincoln parliament of 1301'. *Univ. Birmingham Hist. Jour.* iii (1951), 16–32.

f. Elections and attendance

3433 ALEXANDER (JOHN J.). 'The dates of early county elections'. *E.H.R.* xl (1925), 1–12.

3434 E. J. D. (E. J. DAVIS). 'A parliamentary election in 1298'. *B.I.H.R.* iii (1926), 45–6.

3435 EDWARDS (SIR GORONWY). 'The emergence of majority rule in English parliamentary elections'. *T.R.H.S.* 5th Ser. xiv (1964), 175–96.

See Edwards in *Wilkinson essays* (No. 1459).

3436 ROGERS (ALAN). 'Parliamentary electors in Lincolnshire in the fifteenth century'. *Lincolnshire Hist. Archaeol.* iii (1968), 41–79; iv (1969), 33–53; v (1970), 47–58. Idem, 'Parliamentary elections to Grimsby in the fifteenth century'. *B.I.H.R.* xlii (1969), 41–79.

3437 WEDGWOOD (JOSIAH C.). 'John of Gaunt and the packing of parliament'. *E.H.R.* xlv (1930), 623–5.

3438 WILLIAMS (CHARLES H.). 'A Norfolk parliamentary election, 1461'. *E.H.R.* xl (1925), 79–86.

> Prints a document. For electoral procedure, see K. N. Houghton, 'A document concerning the parliamentary election at Shrewsbury in 1478', *Shropshire Archaeol. Soc. Trans.* lvii (1961–4), 162–5; and No. 3447.

3439 POLLARD (ALBERT F.). 'History, English and Statistics'. *History*, New Ser. xi (1926–7), 15–24. See J. G. Edwards, 'Personnel of the Commons', in *Tout essays* (No. 1456). J. G. Edwards, '"Re-election" and the medieval parliament'. *History*, New Ser. xi (1926–7), 204–10. N. B. Lewis, 'Re-election to parliament in the reign of Richard II'. *E.H.R.* xlviii (1933), 364–94.

3440 ROSKELL (JOHN S.). 'The problem of the attendance of the lords in medieval parliaments (Edw. I–Henry VIII)'. *B.I.H.R.* xxix (1956), 153–204.

3441 WOOD-LEGH (KATHLEEN L.). 'The knights' attendance in the parliaments of Edward III'. *E.H.R.* xlvii (1932), 398–413.

3442 CAM (HELEN M.). 'The parliamentary writs "de expensis" of 1258'. *E.H.R.* xlvi (1931), 630–2. Idem, 'L'Assiette et la perception des indemnités des représentants des comtés dans l'Angleterre médiévale'. *Rev. hist. de droit franç. et étranger*, 4th Ser. xviii (1939), 206–22.

> See her *Liberties and Communities* (No. 1462).

3443 LATHAM (L. C.). 'Collection of the wages of the knights of the shire in the fourteenth and fifteenth centuries'. *E.H.R.* xlviii (1933), 455–64.

g. Representation: general studies and returns

3444 THE INTERIM REPORT OF THE COMMITTEE ON HOUSE OF COMMONS PERSONNEL AND POLITICS, 1264–1832. Cmd. 4130. H.M.S.O. Lond. 1932.

3445 CAM (HELEN M.). See Nos. 1461, 1462, 3395, 3442.

3446 LAPSLEY (GAILLARD T.). 'Knights of the shire in the parliaments of Edward II'. *E.H.R.* xxxiv (1919), 25–42, 152–71. Reprinted in *Crown, Community and Parliament* (No. 1478), pp. 111–52.

3447 McKISACK (MAY). The parliamentary representation of the English boroughs during the middle ages. Lond. 1932.*

> K. N. Houghton, 'Theory and practice in borough elections to parliament during the later fifteenth century', *B.I.H.R.* xxxix (1966), 130–40.

3448 POST (GAINES). 'Plena potestas and consent in medieval assemblies: a study of romano-canonical procedure and the rise of representation, 1150–1325'. *Traditio*, i (1943), 355–408. Reprinted in Post, *Studies in Medieval Legal Thought*. Princeton. 1964. Pp. 91–162.

3449 RETURN OF THE NAME OF EVERY MEMBER OF THE LOWER HOUSE OF THE PARLIAMENTS OF ENGLAND, SCOTLAND AND IRELAND, with name of constituency represented and date of return, 1213–1874. *Parl. Papers, 1878,* vol. lxii, pts. i–iii. 3 vols. Lond. 1878.

> Pt. iii, which is the index to pt. i (1213–1702), though ordered to be printed in 1878, seems not to have been published until 1888. The continuation of the names of members of parliament to 1885, with an index of names from 1705 to 1885, will be found in *Parliamentary papers, 1890–91,* vol. lxii (Lond. 1891).

3450 ROSKELL (JOHN S.). The commons in the parliament of 1422: English society and parliamentary representation under the Lancastrians. Manchester. 1954.

> J. S. Roskell, 'Social composition of the Commons in a fifteenth century (1422) parliament', *B.I.H.R.* xxiv (1951), 152–72.

3451 SAYLES (GEORGE O.). 'Representation of cities and boroughs in 1268'. *E.H.R.* xl (1925), 580–5. Idem, 'Parliamentary representation in 1294, 1295 and 1307'. *B.I.H.R.* iii (1926), 110–15.

3452 WOOD-LEGH (KATHLEEN L.). 'Sheriffs, lawyers, and belted knights in the parliaments of Edward III'. *E.H.R.* xlvi (1931), 372–88.

h. Parliamentary representation by counties, alphabetically

3453 BASSETT (MARGERY). 'Knights of the shire for Bedfordshire during the middle ages'. Beds. Hist. Rec. Soc. xxix (1949).

3454 TAYLOR (MARY M.). 'Parliamentary elections in Cambridgeshire, 1332–38'. *B.I.H.R.* xviii (1940), 21–6.

3455 LAWRANCE (WILLIAM T.). Parliamentary representation of Cornwall, 1295–1885. Truro. 1925. William P. Courtney. The parliamentary representation of Cornwall to 1832. Lond. 1889.

3456 ALEXANDER (JOHN J.), and others. 'Biographies of members of Parliament 1439–1509'. *Devon and Cornwall N. and Q.* xix (1936–7), 219–21, 278–9, 326–7.

> Alexander (John J.). 'Carpet-baggers in the fifteenth century, 1439–1509', *Devon and Cornwall N. Q.* xix (1936–7), 106–12; 272–3; 323–4.

3457 ALEXANDER (JOHN J.), ed. 'Devon County Members of Parliament (1213–1832)'. *Devonshire Asso. Report and Trans.* xliv (1912), 366–81; xlv (1913), 247–69; xlvi (1914), 478–96; xlvii (1915), 357–71; xlviii (1916), 320–40; xlix (1917), 363–75; l (1918), 589–601; lxii (1930), 157–60; lxv (1933), 141–6; lxvi (1934), 93–104; lxvii (1935), 145–8; lxviii (1936), 105–21; lxix (1937), 155–83; lxxi (1939), 145–66; lxxii (1940), 117–25.

3458 DRIVER (J. T.). 'Parliamentary burgesses for Bristol and Gloucester, 1422–1437'. *Bristol–Glos. Archaeol. Soc. Trans.* lxxxiv (1955), 60–127.

3459 WILLIAMS (WILLIAM RETLAW). The parliamentary history of the county of Hereford, 1213–1896. Brecknock. 1896.

He has also written the parliamentary history of Gloucestershire, 1213–1898 (Hereford, 1898); Oxfordshire, 1213–1899 (Brecknock, 1899); Worcestershire, 1213–1897 (Hereford, 1897).

3459A PROBY (GRANVILLE). 'Huntingdonshire members of parliament, 1290–1945'. *Cambr. and Huntingdonshire Archaeol. Soc. Trans.* vi (1947), 215–43.

3460 CAVE-BROWNE (J.). 'Knights of the shire for Kent, 1275–1831'. *Archaeol. Cantiana*, xxi (1895), 198–243. Frederick Francis Smith, *Rochester in parliament, 1295–1933* (Lond. 1933).

3461 McKISACK (MAY). 'The parliamentary representation of King's Lynn before 1500'. *E.H.R.* xlii (1927), 583–9.

3462 HORNYOLD-STRICKLAND (HENRY). 'Biographical sketches of the members of parliament of Lancashire, 1290–1550'. Chetham Soc. New Ser. xciii (1935).

   J. S. Roskell, 'The knights of the shire for the county palatine of Lancaster, 1377–1460', Chetham Soc. New Ser. xcvi (1937). H. G. Richardson, 'John of Gaunt and the parliament representation of Lancashire', *B.J.R.L.* xxii (1938), 175–222. W. D. Pink and A. B. Beaven, *Parliamentary representation of Lancashire, 1258–1885* (Lond. 1889).

3463 ROSKELL (JOHN S.). 'The parliamentary representation of Lincolnshire during the reigns of Richard II, Henry IV and Henry V'. *Nottingham Mediaeval Stud.* iii (1959), 53–77.

3464 BLAIR (C. H. HUNTER). 'Members of parliament for Northumberland'. *Archaeol. Aeliana*, 4th Ser. x (1933), 140–77; xii (1935), 82–132; xiii (1936), 59–94. Idem, 'Members of parliament for Newcastle-on-Tyne, 1377–1588'. Ibid. xiv (1937), 22–66.

3465 OWEN (L. V. D.). 'The representation of Nottingham and Nottinghamshire in the early parliaments'. *Thoroton Soc. Trans.* xlvii (1944), 20–8.

3466 HARBIN (SOPHIA W. BATES). Members of parliament for the county of Somerset. Taunton. 1939. (Originally printed in *Somerset Archaeol. Nat. Hist. Soc. Procs.* (1932–9).)

3467 WEDGWOOD (JOSIAH C.). Staffordshire parliamentary history from the earliest times to the present day. 3 vols. in 4 pts. Wm. Salt Archaeol. Soc. *Collections* for 1917–20.

   Vol. i covers the period from 1213 to 1603.

3468 VIRGOE (ROGER). 'Three Suffolk parliamentary elections of the mid-fifteenth century'. *B.I.H.R.* xxxix (1966), 185–96.

3469 SMITH (JOHN EDWARD). The parliamentary representation of Surrey, 1290–1924. Lond. 1927.

3470 COOPER (WILLIAM D.). The parliamentary history of Sussex. Lewes. 1834. William Albery. *A parliamentary history of the ancient borough of Horsham, 1295–1885.* Lond. 1927.

3471 WHITLEY (T. W.). The parliamentary representation of the city of Coventry (Warwickshire), from the earliest times. Coventry. 1894.

3472 WASHINGTON (GEORGE S. H. L.). 'Early Westmorland M.P.'s, 1258–1327'. *Cumb.-Westm. Antiq. Soc. Tract,* xv (1959).

3473 MANLEY (F. H.). 'A list of the representatives in Parliament from 1295–1832 for the county and boroughs of Wiltshire, as given in the parliamentary return of 1872'. *Wilts. Archaeol. Mag.* xlvii (1935), 177–264.

3474 GOODER (ARTHUR). The parliamentary representation of the county of York, 1258–1832. Yorks. Archaeol. Soc. Rec. Ser. xci (1935), xcvi (1938).

3475 PARK (GODFREY R.). The parliamentary representation of Yorkshire (Edw. I–1886). Hull. 1886.

i. The clergy in parliament

3476 DEIGHTON (H. S.). 'Clerical taxation by consent'. *E.H.R.* lxviii (1953), 161–92.

3477 LOWRY (EDITH C.). 'Clerical proctors in parliament and knights of the shire, 1280–1374'. *E.H.R.* xlviii (1933), 443–55.
Concerned with expenses paid to clerical proctors.

3478 REICH (ALOYSE M.). 'The parliamentary abbots to 1470: a study in English constitutional history'. Univ. California Pubns. in Hist. xvii (1941), 265–402.

3479 RICHARDSON (HENRY G.) and SAYLES (GEORGE O.). 'The clergy in the Easter parliament, 1285'. *E.H.R.* lii (1937), 220–34.

3480 WESKE (DOROTHY B.). 'The attitude of the English clergy in the thirteenth and fourteenth centuries towards the obligation of attendance on convocations and parliaments'. *McIlwain essays* (No. 1444), pp. 77–108. See also her *Convocation* (No. 6820).

D. THE CENTRAL COURTS

1. *Introduction*

A brief but profitable survey of sources is made in John H. Baker, 'Unprinted sources of English legal history', *Law Library Jour.* lxiv (1971), 302–13.

The courts whose printed records are listed here are the *curia regis,* the common bench, the king's bench, court of chancery, exchequer of pleas, the eyres and assizes, the exchequer of the Jews, and the forest courts. The local courts of the king, the county courts, the hundred courts, and other royal local courts are treated subsequently on pp. 555–7. Courts of private or special jurisdiction such as those of the palatinates or particular seignorial franchises are dealt with on pp. 574–88.

The classification of the court records in the Public Record Office is described in its 1963 *Guide* (No. 951). Since it is difficult to distinguish in the records before Edward I's reign between the court *coram rege* and the court of the bench, the early records are classified together as *curia regis* rolls. They extend from 5 Richard I to 56 Henry III; they comprise the minutes of proceedings in the bench and *coram rege* for the whole period and of those of the justices in eyre which survive for the reigns of Richard and John. The printed editions of the rolls of the bench for Richard's reign are listed in Pipe Roll Society publication, New Ser. xxxi (1955), 95; and editions of eyre rolls for the same reign on p. 96.

The rolls of the bench are separated from those of the king's bench or *coram rege* from 1272 on.

Arranged in one class in the Public Record Office (*Guide*, pp. 123–5) are eyre rolls from 1201 to 1348, assize rolls from 1248 to 1482, trailbaston or general oyer and terminer rolls from 1305 to the fifteenth century, records of *ad hoc* courts from 1225 to the fifteenth century, and a few other court records. The earliest surviving eyre roll is for the Wiltshire eyre of 1194 and is printed in *Placitorum abbreviatio* (No. 3493), pp. 10–20, and in Maitland's *Three rolls* (No. 3521), pp. 65–115.

The jurisdiction of the exchequer of pleas was originally confined to matters directly concerning the king's revenue; but by a fiction it was broadly extended to many actions between the king's subjects. Suits on the payment of tithes were often instituted in the exchequer. These plea rolls run from 20 Henry III to 1875. The rolls of the justices of the Jews, which are classed as exchequer records, extend from 3 Henry III to 15 Edward I. The pleadings in the court of chancery are of two kinds, common law and equity. The common law side is represented in *placita in cancellaria* which stretch from Edward I to Richard III. The equity side falls under early chancery proceedings which begin with Richard II. The rolls of the forest eyres which were held in the thirteenth and fourteenth centuries are classified largely among the exchequer records and contain pleas, perambulations, and other transactions.

Feet of fines, *pedes finium*, or final concords (see index below) are records of agreements made by leave of the court between parties to a suit designed to reach agreement for the conveying of land. When such a case came up for trial, the parties secured permission from the court to settle or put an end (*finis*) to the suit, and the land was adjudged to belong to the plaintiff according to a pre-arranged agreement between him and the defendant. A copy or indenture of the judgement was given to each of them, and its counterpart, called the foot, was kept by the court as evidence of the new owner's title. Final concords seem first to have come into use in the second half of Henry II's reign, but only a few fines of that period have survived. The continuous series of *pedes finium*, which begins in 1195, is remarkably complete, and extends to 1834, when fines were abolished by statute. They are particularly valuable to the genealogist, the topographer, and the local historian. See Pollock and Maitland (No. 1242), ii. 94–106; and on the earliest fines, J. H. Round, in *E.H.R.* xii (1897), 293–302, and in his *Feudal England* (No. 3061), pp. 509–18. For a valuable description of feet of fines consult Pugh (No. 3618).

2. *Records of Central Courts*

3481   BRACTON'S NOTEBOOK: a collection of (1990) cases decided in the king's courts during the reign of Henry III, annotated by a lawyer of that time, seemingly Henry of Bratton. Ed. by F. W. Maitland. 3 vols. Lond. etc. 1887.

Vol. i: Apparatus (introduction, including a good account of Bracton's life, etc.); vols. ii–iii: Latin text. This famous work contains transcripts of entries on the *de banco* (1217–34), *coram rege* (1234–9), and eyre rolls (1–24 Henry III). The MS. is in the British Museum. See D. M. Stenton, *Justices in Eyre*, Selden Soc. liii (No. 3629), where 'This volume is in the nature of a supplement to Bracton's Notebook'; and H. G. Richardson in *E.H.R.* lix (1944), 34–7.

For a review of the *Note Book*, see J. B. Thayer's *Legal Essays* (Boston, 1908), pp. 355–66; and for a brief commentary, Bell's *Maitland* (No. 1482), pp. 48–57. For cases in the *Note Book*, see the references in the indexes of *Curia Regis Rolls* (No. 3485) from vol. viii on. For Bracton, in general, see above, No. 2985.

3482 CALENDAR OF THE PLEA ROLLS OF THE EXCHEQUER OF THE JEWS, 1218–75. Ed. by J. M. Rigg. 2 vols. Jewish Hist. Soc. of England. Lond. 1905–10. Vol. iii (1275–7). Ed. by Hilary Jenkinson. J.H.S.E. Lond. 1929.

For the texts see No. 3518. The Justices of the Jews had jurisdiction in all matters between Jews and the Crown or Christians. See C. A. F. Meekings, 'The Justices of the Jews, 1218–68: a provisional list', *B.I.H.R.* xxviii (1955), 173–88.

3483 CALENDAR OF PROCEEDINGS IN CHANCERY IN THE REIGN OF ELIZABETH, WITH EARLIER EXAMPLES. Rec. Comm. 3 vols. 1827–32.

Vol. i, pp. 1–cxxvi contain proceedings of the court of Chancery, Richard II–Henry VII. An analysis of portions of the Record Commissioners' calendar may be found in H. W. Seton's *Early records in equity* (Calcutta, 1842). Cf. 'Calendar of early chancery proceedings' in *Deputy Keeper's Reports*, xlix (1888), 201–8; and 'Some chancery proceedings of the fifteenth century', ed. by C. Trice Martin, *Archaeologia*, lix, or 2nd Ser. ix (1904), 1–24; lx, or 2nd Ser. x, pt. ii (1906), 353–78. Vol. lx concentrates on clerical life in the fifteenth century, as illustrated by proceedings of the Court of Chancery. C. A. Walmisley has compiled *An index of persons named in early chancery proceedings, Richard II (1385) to Edward IV (1467) preserved in the P.R.O.* 2 vols. Harleian Soc. lxxviii–lxxix (1927–8). For other records of Court of Chancery, see No. 3509, and for translations turn to Myers, *Eng. Hist. Docs.* iv, nos. 303, 306, 307, 548, 551, 552, 650, 725, 726, 730. See E. L. Storey in *K. Major essays* (No. 7224), pp. 236–59.

3484 COMPLETE COLLECTION OF STATE TRIALS and proceedings for high treason and other crimes and misdemeanors from the earliest times to 1820. By T. B. Howell and T. J. Howell. 33 vols. Lond. 1809–26. General index. By D. Jardine. Lond. 1828.

The first 12 volumes seem to be by William Cobbett. Vol. i runs from Henry II to Elizabeth I. See also No. 3519.

3485 CURIA REGIS ROLLS, preserved in the P.R.O. H.M.S.O. 15 vols. to 1968 (in progress). 1922+.

The Latin texts of the proceedings in the bench and in the court *coram rege* are transcribed. In some cases charters and other documents which were produced in court are given; these can be located through the subject index of each volume; for the first seven volumes they are gathered together and listed county by county in vol. vii, pp. vii–lvi.

Vols. i–vii include proceedings for the reigns of Richard I and John; they do not reprint the cases given in *Rotuli curiae regis* (No. 3501), or in the Pipe Roll Society Publications (Nos. 3078–9), or in D. M. Stenton's *Pleas* (No. 3494). By using recently recovered membranes for *Curia Regis Roll* 8B (Easter 1198), R. A. Brown completes the printing of that roll in Pipe Roll Soc. New Ser. xxxi for 1955 (1957), 93–118. See also L. H. Biddulph, 'A roll of pleas of the crown of 1199', *Australian Law Jour.* xxx (1956/7), 332–6.

Vols. viii–xv of the *Curia Regis Rolls* run from 1219 to 1237, but the series is to be continued.

Some commentaries may be found in G. E. Woodbine's article, 'Cases in new curia regis rolls affecting old rules of English legal history', *Yale Law Jour.* xxxix (1930), 505–13, and in G. D. G. Hall's reviews of volumes x to xiv in *E.H.R.* from 1958 to 1964. A valuable summary and index for 1199–1230 is provided in Sir Cyril Flower's *Introduction* (No. 3664).

3486   FEET OF FINES, 28 Henry II–10 Richard I (1182–99). Pipe Roll Soc. Pubns. xvii (1894); xx (1896); xxiii (1898, reprinted 1929); xxiv (1900, reprinted 1929). See No. 3487.

3487   FINES SIVE PEDES FINIUM (1195–1214). Ed. by Joseph Hunter. Rec. Comm. 2 vols. 1835–44.

Hunter's edition is arranged alphabetically by counties, but it is incomplete and covers only Bedford to Dorset. There is a manuscript transcript for the remaining counties in the P.R.O. Forty-eight fines Richard I–Henry VIII are printed in Madox's *Formulare Anglicanum* (No. 426), pp. 217–37. Some interesting cases are given in H. G. Richardson, 'The forgery of fines, 1272–1376', *E.H.R.* xxxv (1920), 405–18.

3488   INVENTORY OF THE RECORDS RELATING TO THE ROYAL FORESTS (formerly) in the Wakefield Tower. *Deputy Keeper's Reports*, v (1844), 46–59; xx (1859), 126–7.

Pleas, perambulations, etc., John–Charles I. See below section on forests (Nos. 3885–3928).

3489   ORIGINAL DOCUMENTS ILLUSTRATIVE OF THE ADMINIS-TRATION OF THE CRIMINAL LAW IN THE TIME OF EDWARD I. Ed. by F. M. Nichols. *Archaeol.* xl (1866), 89–105.

Articles of Trailbaston, pp. 102–4.

3490   PLACITA ANGLO-NORMANNICA: law-cases from William I to Richard I, preserved in historical records. Ed. by M. M. Bigelow. Boston. 1879.

This work provides a valuable collection of 'unofficial records of litigation' comprising mainly narrative accounts of cases taken from the chroniclers. See also Francis Palgrave, *Rise and progress of the English Commonwealth* (Lond. 1832), ii. 5–87, for the suit of Richard of Anstey to recover the lands of his uncle, A.D. 1158–63; and for the case of the Abbot of Battle Abbey *v.* Bishop of Chichester, A.D. 1148–57. On the Anstey case see P. M. Barnes in *Miscellany for D. M. Stenton* (No. 1453), pp. 1–24, and *Eng. hist. docs.* ii. 456–7; and H. Hall, *Court life under the Plantagenets* (Lond. 1899), chap. vii. A few other early suits are cited in *Eng. hist. docs.* ii. 449–58. For the Battle Abbey case, see Eleanor Searle, 'Battle Abbey and exemption: the forged charters', *E.H.R.* lxxxiii (1968), 449–80.

3491   PLACITA CORAM DOMINO REGE: pleas of the court of king's bench, Trinity term, 25 Edward I (1297). Ed. by W. P. W. Phillimore. British Record Soc., Index Library, xix. 1898.

3492   PLACITA DE QUO WARRANTO, Edward I–Edward III, in curia receptae scaccarii Westm. asservata. Ed. by William Illingworth. Rec. Comm. 1818.

These are pleadings held before the itinerant justices and based on writs of *quo warranto* requiring certain persons, boroughs, abbeys, and other communities to show by what authority they claimed franchises. These pleadings resulted from the inquiries recorded in the hundred rolls (No. 4245), and from the Statute of Gloucester, 1278. After 10 Edward III, the *quo warranto* proceedings took place in the king's bench or in the exchequer, and are entered on the *coram rege* or memoranda rolls. Some *placita de quo warranto* of Edward III's reign can be found in the *Record of Caernarvon* (No. 4943 A), 133–207. A list for 1292–3 based on the 1818 edition is given by A. Cantle, 'The pleas of Quo Warranto for the County of Lancaster', Chetham Soc. New Ser. xcviii (1937).

See H. M. Cam, *Liberties*, etc. (No. 1462), pp. 173–82; Donald W. Sutherland, *Quo Warranto proceedings in the reign of Edward I, 1278–1294* (Oxf. and N.Y. 1963); Plucknett, *Legislation* (No. 3675), pp. 35–49; and Lapsley, *Crown* (No. 1476).

3493 PLACITORUM IN DOMO CAPITULARI WESTMONASTERII ASSERVATORUM ABBREVIATIO. RICHARD I–EDWARD II. Rec. Comm. 1811.

These abstracts of pleas, held in the *curia regis*, king's bench, common pleas, eyres, king's council, parliament, etc., are said to have been compiled by Arthur Agarde (d. 1615), deputy chamberlain of exchequer, and others in the time of Elizabeth and James I. Many interesting cases are omitted, and the transcripts contain some errors; nevertheless the book is of value and leads the student to the rolls themselves. However, many of the pleas appear in modern editions, cited in this section on central court records, especially by G. O. Sayles.

3494 PLEAS BEFORE THE KING OR HIS JUSTICES, 1198–1212. Ed. by D. M. Stenton. Selden Soc. lxvii (for 1948, 1953), lxviii (for 1949, 1952), lxxxiii (for 1966, 1967), lxxxiv (1967).

The first two volumes, lxvii and lxviii, bear the title 1198–1202; the subsequent volumes bear the title 1198–1212. All volumes print essoins; however, numerous pleas and *veredicta* of the *curia regis* rolls or drawn from assize and eyre rolls form a most valuable collection of proceedings for John's reign. Vol. lxxxiii includes an appendix (pp. xlvii–ccxiv) on the development of the judiciary, 1100–1215.

3495 PROCEEDINGS BEFORE THE JUSTICES OF THE PEACE IN THE FOURTEENTH AND FIFTEENTH CENTURIES, EDWARD III TO RICHARD III. Ed. by Bertha H. Putnam. The Ames Foundation. Cambr. (Mass.) and Lond. 1938.

See also B. H. Putnam, 'Early records of the Justices of the Peace', *E.H.R.* xxviii (1913), 321–30; idem, 'The ancient indictments in the Public Record Office', ibid. xxix (1914), 479–505; idem, 'Records of the courts of common law, especially of the sessions of the justices of the peace', *American Philos. Soc. Procs.* xci, no. 3 (1947), 258–73; idem, *Early treatises on the practice of the justices of the peace in the fifteenth and sixteenth centuries* (Oxford Stud. in Social and Legal History, vii, 1924); idem, 'The transformation of the keepers of the peace into the justices of the peace, 1327–1380', *T.R.H.S.* 4th Ser. xii (1929), 19–48; idem, 'Records of the peace and their supervisors, 1307–27', *E.H.R.* xlv (1930), 435–44; idem, *English Government at Work* (No. 3836), iii. 185–217. Rosamond Sillem, 'Commissions of the Peace, 1380–1485', *B.I.H.R.* x (1932), 81–104.

For other proceedings before the justices of the peace, see index below under 'Justices of the peace', and Elisabeth Kimball, 'Bibliography of printed records of justices of the peace for counties', *Toronto Law Jour.* vi (1945–6). The older work is Charles A. Beard, *The office of the justice of the peace in England in its origin and development* (N.Y. 1904). Besides the justices of the peace, other local officers were the keeper of the peace (*custos pacis*), for which office see Alan Harding, 'The origins and early history of the keeper of the peace', *T.R.H.S.* 5th Ser. x (1960), 85–109; and the serjeants of the peace, for whom see R. Stewart-Brown, *The serjeants of the peace in medieval England and Wales* (Manchester, 1936).

3496 PUBLIC RECORD OFFICE. Lists and Indexes (see No. 956). iv. List of plea rolls of various courts (1894; new and revised edn. 1910).

Includes rolls of the old *curia regis*, king's bench, common pleas, exchequer, eyres, marshalsea, exchequer of the Jews, palatinates of Durham, Lancaster, and Chester, courts of Wales, coroners' inquests.

xii. List of early chancery proceedings. Vol. i. Richard II–Edward IV (1901).

xvi. List of early chancery proceedings. Vol. ii, 1467–85 and undated (1903) [Later volumes continue this series to 1558].

xxxii. Index of placita de banco, 1327–28 (1910). pt. i. Bedford to Norfolk; pt. ii. Northampton to York, diverse counties, and miscellaneous.

Other and supplementary lists for plea and essoin rolls are in preparation, see Sectional List No. 24. H.M.S.O. 1968.

3497 PUBLIC WORKS IN MEDIEVAL LAW. Ed. by Cyril Flower. 2 vols. Selden Soc. xxxii (1915); xl (1925).

The cases are drawn from Ancient Indictments and the *coram rege* rolls on such matters as the maintenance of roads, bridges, rivers, and sewers, arranged by counties. Vol. xxxii goes from Bedford to Lincolnshire; vol. xl from London to Yorks.

3498 RECORDS OF THE TRIAL OF WALTER LANGETON, BISHOP OF COVENTRY AND LICHFIELD, 1307–1312. Ed. by Alice Beardwood. Camden Ser. 4th Ser. vi (1969).

Pp. 9–242 contain a transcript of P.R.O. E 13/31; pp. 247–351 a transcript from Assize Rolls, P.R.O. J.I. i. 1344. A commentary can be found in Alice Beardwood, 'The trial of Walter Langton, bishop of Lichfield, 1307–1312', *Amer. Philos. Soc. Trans.* liv (1964).

3499 REGISTRUM OMNIUM BREVIUM TAM ORIGINALIUM QUAM JUDICIALIUM. 2 pts. Lond. 1531. 4th edn. 4 pts. corrected and amended with appendix. 1687. EARLY REGISTERS OF WRITS. Ed. by Elsa de Haas and G. D. G. Hall. Selden Soc. lxxxvii (1970).

A register of writs gives the various forms of 'original writs current in the English Chancery, that is, writs originating actions'. The learned edition, published by the Selden Society, contains, pp. xi–xxix, a general introduction by Dr. de Haas; and, pp. xxxi–cxli, a commentary by G. D. G. Hall on the five registers whose texts are printed in this volume, on original and judicial writs, and on unusual registers, as well as general thoughts on the growth and nature of registers, on the problem of authority, and on their value. The critical apparatus is extensive and valuable.

The earliest surviving register was thought to have been sent to Ireland in 1227, but Hall (p. xl) concludes that it was not. See F. W. Maitland (No. 1482). The growth of the register is illustrated in Holdsworth, *History* (No. 1235), ii, app. v.

An early register of about 1240 is discussed in A. R. Humphreys, 'A register of writs in roll form', *B.I.H.R.* xviii (1940–1), 1–12; and more fully by C. A. F. Meekings in ibid. xxxii (1959), 209–21.

There is also the anonymous *Natura Brevium*, or *La vieux Natura Brevium*, which seems to have been compiled in Edward III's reign; it contains the principal kinds of writs, with a short commentary explaining their nature and application. For the editions published in the sixteenth century, see Beale (No. 1224), pp. 119–23, and Winfield (No. 1229), pp. 279–80.

A work of similar character by Anthony Fitzherbert is called *La Nouvelle Natura Brevium* (Lond. 1534 and later edns.; translation 1652; 9th edn. 1794). [See Winfield (No. 1227), p. 303.] Many law writs can be found in Glanvill's treatise and in the law books of the thirteenth century. Particular attention is paid to them in the introduction to Turner's *Brevia placitata* (No. 2992) and to Van Caenegem's *Royal Writs* (No. 3503). The register of Roger Martival, Bishop of Salisbury 1315–30, is unusually full of royal writs; they are abstracted to the number of 876 by Susan Reynolds in volume iii of the printed edition (No. 5801). See also Conway Davies's article (No. 3662), and Richardson and Sayles, *Select cases of procedure without writ* (No. 3513).

3500 A ROLL OF THE KING'S COURT IN THE REIGN OF KING RICHARD I (Hilary, 1196). Pipe Roll Soc. xxiv (1900), 214–44. Re-edited ibid. New Ser. xxxi (for 1955, 1957), 69–91.

See J. H. Round, 'A plea roll of Richard I', *E.H.R.* xxii (1907), 290–2.

3501 ROTULI CURIAE REGIS. Rolls and records of the court held before the king's justiciars or justices. Ed. by Francis Palgrave. Rec. Comm. 2 vols. 1835.

Vol. i contains rolls of the bench for Michaelmas 1194, Easter 1198, and Easter 1199–Easter 1200, and eyre rolls for Herts., Essex, and Middlesex, 1198. Vol. ii, a roll of 1 John. See Nos. 3485, 3521.

3502 ROTULI SELECTI AD RES ANGLICAS ET HIBERNICAS SPECTANTES. Ed. by Joseph Hunter. Record Comm. 1834.

This edition comprises (*a*) pp. 1–38: transcripts of patent roll, 7 John; (*b*) pp. 39–103: transcripts of the original writs and returns of all discharges of debts, etc. granted by the Irish exchequer, *temp.* Hen. V and Hen. VI; and (*c*) pp. 105–265: transcripts of six rolls, mainly of pleas, held in pursuance of the Dictum of Kenilworth, relating to lands of rebel barons in the counties of Cambridge, Essex, Northampton, and Suffolk, 52–54 Hen. III.

3503 ROYAL WRITS IN ENGLAND FROM THE CONQUEST TO GLANVILL. Ed. by R. C. van Caenegem. Selden Soc. lxxvii (1959).

This book is fundamentally a study of royal writs between 1066 and 1189; but its introduction of 400 pages provides a learned excursus on many aspects of the early common law. This treatise consists of three parts, dealing with (*a*) the historical setting of the law in the twelfth century, law courts, pleadings, recognitions, the jury, etc.; (*b*) the royal writs and their development; and (*c*) some problems of the twelfth-century law, including the influences of the Roman and Canon Law. The critical apparatus, including a list of the collections of charters quoted and a list of works quoted, is very full and of great value. The texts of a dozen types of writs, drawn from a variety of printed and unprinted sources and dating from *c.* 1072 to *c.* 1188, are printed on pp. 413–515. An English translation is immediately subjoined to each of the 198 Latin originals. See Jean Yver, 'Le bref anglo-normand', *Tijdschrift voor rechtsgeschiedenis*, xxix (1962), 313–30.

3503A SCROPE (THE) AND GROSVENOR CONTROVERSY: De controversia in curia militari inter Ricardum le Scrope et Robertum Grosvenor, 1385–90. Ed. by N. H. Nicolas. 2 vols. Lond. 1832.

Vol. i contains proceedings in the court of chivalry concerning the right to bear certain arms; vol. ii, the history of the family of Scrope. On the case in the court of chivalry (1385–90), see Squibb (No. 3679), p. 16 and index.

Transcripts of documents of at least four other cases in the court of chivalry for the reigns of Richard II and Henry IV have survived. They are the cases of Lovel *v.* Morley (1385), which has not been printed; 'Hoton versus Shakell: a ransom case in the court of chivalry, 1390–5', by Alan Rogers in *Nottingham Mediaeval Stud.* vi (1962), 74–108, and vii (1963), 53–78; and Grey *v.* Hastings, some of the proceedings of which have been printed in *An account of the controversy between Reginald Lord Grey of Ruthyn and Sir Edward Hastings in the court of chivalry in the reign of Henry IV*, ed. by C. G. Young (Lond. 1841). See also A. R. Wagner, 'A fifteenth century description of the brass of Sir Hugh Hastings at Elsing, Norfolk', *Antiquaries Jour.* xix (1939), 421–8.

There is also a tract on the use of the judicial combat in that court, called the *Ordenaunce and Fourme of fightyng within Listes*, written in French about 1390 by Thomas of Woodstock, Duke of Gloucester, son of Edward III, printed with an old translation in the *Black Book of Admiralty* (No. 4286), i. 301–29; there is a Latin version in Henry Spelman's *Glossarium Archailogicum* (Lond. 1687) under 'Campus'. See Squibb (No. 3679), p. 23 n. 2; and Viscount (Harold A.) Dillon, 'On a MS. Collection of ordinances of chivalry of the fifteenth century', *Archaeol.* lvii (1900), 29–70, in which Gloucester's letter to Richard II on judicial duels is transcribed on pp. 61–9. A good description of a judicial duel in 1380 on a case in the court of chivalry is given in J. G. Bellamy, 'Sir John de Annesley and the Chandos inheritance', *Nottingham Mediaeval Stud.* x (1966), 94–105.

3504   SELECT BILLS IN EYRE (1292–1333). Ed. by William C. Bolland. Selden Soc. xxx (1914).

The French texts with English translations of a selection of petitions to judges during eyres for a few counties; some extracts from the original eyre rolls are given. On eyres, see H. M. Cam, 'On the material available in the eyre rolls', *B.I.H.R.* iii (1926), 152–60; idem, 'The general eyres of 1329–30', *E.H.R.* xxxix (1924), 241–52 (reprinted in No. 1462), where are printed speeches by Scrope and Herle, and the text of new articles of the eyre of 1329–30. Consult also R. E. Latham and E. K. Timings, 'Six letters concerning the eyres of 1226–28', *E.H.R.* lxv (1950), 492–504. For commentaries, see No. 3661.

3505   SELECT CASES BEFORE THE KING'S COUNCIL 1243–1482. Ed. by I. S. Leadam and J. F. Baldwin. Selden Soc. xxxv (1918).

These forty cases tried before the council are drawn from various records; the council had no rolls of its own. App. II, pp. 130–1, gives a list of cases printed elsewhere before about 1910.

3506   SELECT CASES BEFORE THE KING'S COUNCIL IN THE STAR CHAMBER. Ed. by I. S. Leadam. 2 vols. Selden Soc. xvi (for 1902, 1903); xxv (for 1910, 1911).

Vol. xvi includes cases from 1477 to 1509; its introduction deals with the origins and procedures of the Star Chamber. On the latter subject, see the articles by A. F. Pollard, 'Council, star chamber and privy council under the Tudors', *E.H.R.* xxxvii (1922), 337–60, 516–39; xxxvii (1923), 42–60.

3507   SELECT CASES CONCERNING THE LAW MERCHANT. Ed. by Charles Gross and Hubert Hall. 3 vols. Selden Soc. xxiii (1908); xlvi (1929); xlix (1932).

Vol. xxiii: Local Courts, 1270–1638, ed. C. Gross, is made up largely of the records of piepowder or fair courts.
Vol. xlvi: Central Courts, including assizes, 1239–1633, ed. by H. Hall, includes much supplementary information.
Vol. xlix: Supplementary volume (1251–1779). Statutory recognizances and special assizes, ed. by H. Hall.

3508   SELECT CASES FROM THE CORONERS' ROLLS, 1265–1413. Ed. by Charles Gross. Selden Soc. ix (1896).

The introduction gives an account of the history of the coroner's office, and deals also with Englishry, the jury, and the duties of neighbouring townships. See Hunnisett (No. 3734).

3509   SELECT CASES IN CHANCERY (1364–1471). Ed. by William P. Baildon. Selden Soc. x (1896).

The first part continues the transcript of Early Chancery Proceedings (1383–1412), of which bundles 1 and 2 were printed in *Calendar of Chancery Proceedings* (No. 3483). The second part contains selected petitions of various dates, some from the later fifteenth century. See also No. 3483.

3510   SELECT CASES IN THE COURT OF KING'S BENCH (1272–1422). Ed. by G. O. Sayles. 7 vols. Selden Soc. lv (1936); xlvii (1938); xlviii (1939); lxxiv (1955); lxxvi (1957); lxxxii (1965); lxxxviii (1971).

The first three volumes produce cases in the reign of Edward I, the fourth volume cases of Edward II's reign, and vols. v and vi cases of Edward III's reign. The seventh and final volume prints cases from the reigns of Richard II, Henry IV, and Henry V. The introductions to each of the volumes constitute important erudite treatises on the evolution and jurisdiction of the king's bench and on the justices and officials of the king's bench and common bench. Many documents drawn from other classes, such as ancient petitions, ancient correspondence, and L.T.R. memoranda rolls, in the P.R.O. are transcribed. A chronological list of these documents is printed in vol. iii (S.S. xlviii), pp. cxxxvii–cxlvi. Vol. v (S.S. lxxvi) deals with equity in the king's bench and chancery on pp. lxvii–xcvii and cxliii–cliv. Vol. vi (S.S. lxxxii) carries the lists of justices and officials down to 1422.

3511   SELECT CASES IN THE EXCHEQUER CHAMBER, before all the Justices of England. Ed. by Mary Hemmant. 2 vols. Selden Soc. li (1933); lxiv (for 1945, 1948).

These cases in which all the justices express their opinions on points of law are drawn from year books. In some instances the original court record is cited. Vol. li runs from 1377 to 1461; vol. lxiv from 1461 to 1509.

3512   SELECT CASES IN THE EXCHEQUER OF PLEAS (1236–1304). Ed. by Hilary Jenkinson and Beryl Formoy. Selden Soc. xlviii (1931).

For a calendar of tithe-suits in the exchequer of pleas from Edward IV to George III, see *Deputy Keeper's Reports*, ii (1841), App. ii, pp. 249–72. See Charles Gross, 'The jurisdiction of the court of the exchequer under Edward I', *Law Quart. Rev.* xxv (1909), 138–44.

3513   SELECT CASES OF PROCEDURE WITHOUT WRIT UNDER HENRY III. Ed. by H. G. Richardson and G. O. Sayles. Selden Soc. lx (1941).

The cases, drawn from the *curia regis* and assize rolls, concern plaints before royal justices which could not be brought under any existing writ. App. ii (pp. cxci–cciii) comments on and prints from Caius College MS. no. 205 'an anonymous tract on procedure in ecclesiastical and secular courts', dating from about 1240 and entitled here *Consuetudines Diversarum Curiarum*. For its compiler see Denholm-Young, 'Robert Carpenter' (No. 1467); and C. A. F. Meekings, 'More about Robert Carpenter of Hareslade', *E.H.R.* lxxii (1957), 260–9.

3514   SELECT CIVIL PLEAS (1200–1203). Ed. by W. P. Baildon. Selden Soc. iii (for 1889, 1890).

These pleas drawn from the *coram rege* rolls and held before the justices of the bench and justices in eyre, relate mainly to real property. The four eyres whose civil pleas are transcribed here have their pleas of the Crown transcribed in Maitland's volume below (No. 3516).

3515   SELECT PLEAS IN THE COURT OF ADMIRALTY. Ed. by R. G. Marsden. 2 vols. Selden Soc. vi (for 1892, 1894); xi (1897).

The introduction to vol. vi contains a good account of the early history of this court. The extant series of records of Admiralty Court begins in 1524, but Marsden prints two cases from the years 1390–1404.

See Marsden, 'Early prize jurisdiction and prize law in England', *E.H.R.* xxiv (1909), 675–97; Charles Johnson, 'An early admiralty case, A.D. 1361', Camden Ser. xli, *Camden Miscellany*, xv, no. 4 (1929). See Schofield in *Jenkinson studies* (No. 1441).

3516 SELECT PLEAS OF THE CROWN (1200–1225). Ed. by F. W. Maitland. Selden Soc. i (for 1887, 1888).

This volume contains pleas before the king, the justices of the bench, and the justices in eyre (1202–3, 1221, and 1225), with a valuable introduction on the early history of the courts of king's bench and common pleas. For an extract from *curia regis* roll, 18–19 Henry III, see Maitland, 'The murder of Henry Clement', *E.H.R.* x (1895), 294–7; and Powicke (No. 1490), and see Baildon above (No. 3514).

3517 SELECT PLEAS OF THE FOREST (1209–1334). Ed. by G. J. Turner. Selden Soc. xiii (for 1899, 1901).

This volume contains extracts for selected years from the rolls of the forest eyre, from forest inquisitions, from forest perambulations, and related documents. The introduction is a valuable essay on the forests of the thirteenth century. See a review of this volume in *Edinburgh Rev.* cxcv (1902), 456–80; and the summary in Kiralfy-Jones, *Guide* (No. 195), pp. 23–6. On forests, refer to Nos. 3885–3928.

3518 SELECT PLEAS, STARRS, AND OTHER RECORDS FROM THE ROLLS OF THE EXCHEQUER OF THE JEWS (1220–1284). Ed. by J. M. Rigg. Selden Soc. xv (for 1901, 1902).

This work was also issued as a special volume (1902) of the publications of the Jewish Historical Society of England. See also the calendar of these rolls (No. 3482) and for pleas 3–4 Henry III, Cole's *Documents* (No. 3104), pp. 285–332. See C. A. F. Meekings, 'Justices of the Jews, 1218–68: a provisional list', *B.I.H.R.* xxviii (1955), 173–88. On Jews, refer to Nos. 3929–73.

3519 STATE TRIALS OF THE REIGN OF EDWARD I (1289–93). Ed. by T. F. Tout and Hilda Johnstone. Camden. 3rd Ser. ix (1906).

The volume contains the official proceedings of the trials of the judges and other royal officers before a special commission from an assize roll and the *Narratio de passione justiciariorum*.

3520 SELECTION OF CASES FROM THE STATE TRIALS. Trials for treason, 1327–1681. 2 vols. in 3 pts. Cambr. 1879–82.

See also, T. F. T. Plucknett, 'State trials under Richard II', *T.R.H.S.* 5th Ser. ii (1952), 159–71; Vernon Harcourt, 'The Baga de secretis', *E.H.R.* xxiii (1908), 508–29.

3521 THREE ROLLS OF THE KING'S COURT IN THE REIGN OF KING RICHARD THE FIRST, 1194–1195. Introduction and ed. by F. W. Maitland. Pipe Roll Soc. xiv (1891).

This volume prints the earliest surviving rolls of the king's court, that of Trinity term, 1194; an eyre roll for Wilts., 1194, and another for Beds. and Bucks., 1195.

3. *Law Records of Particular Counties*

BEDFORDSHIRE

3522 ANCIENT INDICTMENTS, 1341–2. Ed. by G. H. Fowler. Beds. Hist. Rec. Soc. Pubns. iv (1917), 54–9.

3523 BEDFORDSHIRE CORONERS' ROLLS. Ed. by R. F. Hunnisett. Beds. Hist. Rec. Soc. Pubns. xli (1961).

3524 A CALENDAR OF THE FEET OF FINES FOR BEDFORDSHIRE, Richard I–Edward I. Ed. by G. H. Fowler. Beds. Hist. Rec. Soc. Pubns. vi (1919); xii (1928).

3525 THE DISSEISINS BY FALK DE BREAUTÉ AT LUTON. Ed. by G. H. Fowler and M. W. Hughes. Beds. Hist. Rec. Soc. Pubns. ix (1925), 51–60, 183.

Printed from the Rolls of King's Court 1224, pleas before Martin Pattishull.

3526 ROLL OF BEDFORDSHIRE SUPERVISORS OF THE PEACE, 1314. Ed. by Joyce Godber. Beds. Hist. Rec. Soc. Pubns. xxxii (1952), 27–70.

3527 ROLL OF THE JUSTICES IN EYRE AT BEDFORD, 1202. Ed. by G. H. Fowler. Beds. Hist. Rec. Soc. Pubns. i (1913), 134–247. (For) 1227, ibid. iii (1916), 1–206. (For) 1240, ibid. ix (1925), 75–146. (For) 1247, calendar, ibid. xxi (1939).

For 1202, a transcript and translation; for the other years, an English abstract or calendar. See Northamptonshire (No. 3588).

3528 ROLLS FROM THE OFFICE OF THE SHERIFF OF BEDS. AND BUCKS., 1332–1334. Ed. by G. H. Fowler. Beds. Hist. Rec. Soc. Quarto Memoirs, iii (1929).

On these rolls, see C. H. Jenkinson and M. H. Mills in *E.H.R.* xliii (1928), 21–32.

3529 SESSIONS OF THE PEACE FOR BEDFORDSHIRE, 1355–1359, 1363–1364. Ed. by Elisabeth G. Kimball. Beds. Hist. Rec. Soc. Pubns. xlviii (1969); H.M.S.O. Lond. 1970.

BERKSHIRE

3530 BERKSHIRE COURT ROLL. Ed. by N. J. Hone. *Berks., Bucks., and Oxon. Archaeol. Jour.* New Ser. xv–xvii (1909–11).

3531 FEET OF FINES FOR BERKSHIRE. Extracted by L. J. A. Pile. *Berks., Bucks., Oxon. Archaeol. Jour.* New Ser. xiv–xvii (1908–11); xix–xx (1913–14).

BUCKINGHAMSHIRE

3532 CALENDAR OF THE FEET OF FINES FOR THE COUNTY OF BUCKINGHAM: 7 Richard I–44 Henry III. Ed. by M. W. Hughes. Bucks. Archaeol. Rec. Soc. Rec. Ser. iv (1942).

3533 CALENDAR OF THE ROLL OF THE JUSTICES ON EYRE, 1227. Ed. by J. G. Jenkins. Bucks. Archaeol. Rec. Soc. Rec. Ser. vi (1945).

CAMBRIDGESHIRE

3534 PALMER (WILLIAM M.). On the Cambridgeshire assize rolls [with brief extracts, Hen. III–Edw. I]. *Cambr. Antiq. Soc. Procs.* ix (1897), 209–26.

See also No. 3502, and W. M. Palmer, *Feet of Fines* (relating to Cambridgeshire, Richard

I–Richard III; and index to Cambridgeshire entries in De Banco Rolls, Edward IV–Henry VII) (Norwich, n.d.; reprinted from *East Anglian*, 1896). See Palmer's articles on Cambridge eyres in *History teachers' miscellany*, v–vii (1927–9). Also his *The assizes held at Cambridge, 1260* (Linton, 1930).

3535 PEDES FINIUM RELATING TO THE COUNTY OF CAMBRIDGE [calendar, 7 Rich. I–1485]. Ed. by Walter Rye. Cambr. Antiq. Soc. 1891.

3536 TAYLOR (MARY M.). 'Some sessions of peace in Cambridgeshire in the fourteenth century: 1340, 1380–83'. Cambr. Antiq. Soc. Octavo Pubns. lv (1942).

CHESHIRE

3537 CALENDAR OF COUNTY COURT, CITY COURT, AND EYRE ROLLS OF CHESTER, 1259–1297, with an inquest of military service, 1288. Ed. by R. Stewart-Brown. Chetham Soc. New Ser. lxxxiv (1925).

3538 EXTRACTS FROM THE CHESHIRE PLEA ROLLS of the reigns of Edward III, Richard II, and Henry IV. William Salt Archaeol. Soc. xvi (1895).

3539 WELSH RECORDS: calendar of fines (pedes finium), counties of Chester and Flint, Edward I. *Deputy Keeper's Reports*, xxviii (1867), 6–19.

CORNWALL

3540 CORNWALL FEET OF FINES, 1195–1461. Ed. by J. H. Rowe and others. Devon–Cornwall Rec. Soc. 2 vols. Exeter. 1914–50.

CUMBERLAND

3541 A CALENDAR OF FEET OF FINES FOR CUMBERLAND, to Henry VII. Ed. by F. H. M. Parker. *Cumberland–Westm. Antiq.–Archaeol. Soc. Trans.* New Ser. vii (1907).

DERBYSHIRE

3542 A CALENDAR OF THE FINES IN THE COUNTY OF DERBY, 1196–1324. Ed. by W. H. Hart and Charles Kerry. *Derbys. Archaeol.–Nat. Hist. Soc. Jour.* vii (1885), 195–217; viii (1886), 15–64; ix (1887), 84–93; x (1888), 151–8; xi (1889), 93–106; xii (1890), 23–42; xiii (1891), 9–31; xiv (1892), 1–15; xv (1893), 1–19; xvii (1895), 95–113; xviii (1896), 1–17.

See also Yeatman, *Feudal history of Derby* (No. 1601).

3543 GLEANINGS FROM THE ASSIZE ROLLS FOR DERBYSHIRE [Hen. III]. By Charles Kerry. Ibid. xviii (1896), 94–117. Selections from assize roll, Derbyshire, 4 Edward III. By J. C. Cox. Ibid. xxxi (1909), 115–28.

3544 LUGARD (C. E.). Trailbaston (Derbyshire). 3 vols. Privately printed. 1934–5 (The Assize Roll of 1306). Idem, Calendar of cases for Derbyshire 1256–72), 1938; ibid. (1275–81), 1944.

DEVONSHIRE

3545 DEVON FEET OF FINES 1196–1369. Ed. by O. J. Reichel, *et al.* Devon and Cornwall Rec. Soc. 2 vols. Exeter. 1912–39.

DORSET

3546 FULL ABSTRACTS OF THE FEET OF FINES RELATING TO DORSET, 1195–1485. Ed. by E. A. Fry and G. S. Fry. Dorset Records, v (1896); x (1910).

DURHAM

3547 TWO THIRTEENTH CENTURY ASSIZE ROLLS FOR THE COUNTY OF DURHAM [27 and 53 Henry III]. Ed. by K. E. Bayley. Surtees Soc. cxxvii, *Miscellanea*, ii (1916). See No. 3592.

ESSEX

3548 FEET OF FINES FOR ESSEX [abstracts, 1182–1422]. Ed. by R. E. G. Kirk and E. F. Kirk. Essex Archaeol. Soc. 3 vols. Colchester. 1899–1949. Vol. iv (1423–1547). Ed. by P. H. Reaney and Marc Fitch. Ibid. 1964.

3549 ESSEX SESSIONS OF THE PEACE, 1351, 1377–79. Ed. by Elizabeth C. Furber. Essex Archaeol. Soc., Occasional Pubns., no. 3. Colchester. 1953.

GLOUCESTERSHIRE

3550 PEDES FINIUM: or excerpts from the feet of fines for the county of Gloucester, 7 John–57 Henry III. Ed. by John Maclean. *Bristol and Glos. Archaeol. Soc. Trans.* xvi (1892), 183–95.

3551 PLEAS OF THE CROWN FOR THE COUNTY OF GLOUCESTER BEFORE THE JUSTICES ITINERANT, 1221. Ed. by F. W. Maitland. Lond. 1884. Pleas of the crown for the hundred of Swineshead and the township of Bristol, 1221. Ed. by E. J. Watson. Bristol. 1902. 'Pleas of the crown at Bristol in 1287' [translation]. By E. A. Fuller. *Bristol and Glos. Archaeol. Soc. Trans.* xxii (1899), 150–78.

3552 ROLLS OF THE GLOUCESTERSHIRE SESSIONS OF THE PEACE, 1361–98. Ed. by Elisabeth G. Kimball. *Bristol and Glos. Archaeol. Soc. Trans.* lxii (1942).

3553 ROLLS OF THE JUSTICES IN EYRE BEING THE ROLLS OF PLEAS AND ASSIZES FOR GLOUCESTERSHIRE, WARWICKSHIRE AND STAFFORDSHIRE, 1221–2. Ed. by Doris M. Stenton. Selden Soc. lix (1940).

HERTFORDSHIRE

3554 FEET OF FINES FOR HARPENDEN, Henry V–Henry VII . . ., listed by Bernard P. Scattergood. *St. Albans and Herts. Archit. and Archaeol. Soc. Trans.* 1932, 1935.

HUNTINGDONSHIRE

3555 A CALENDAR OF THE FEET OF FINES RELATING TO THE COUNTY OF HUNTINGDON, 1194–1603. Ed. by G. J. Turner. Cambr. Antiq. Soc. Cambr. 1913.

A valuable introduction treats of the diplomatic in the formulae of the fines and of the units of property conveyed.

KENT

For the record of the opening of an eyre in Kent, 6 Edward II, see *Year Book* 30–1 Edward I. Ed. A. J. Horwood, Rolls Ser., 1863, pp. lv–lx; for the year books of the eyre, see No. 3558. For extracts from plea rolls, see Nos. 1692, 3559, 3562.

3556 ABSTRACTS OF THE KENT FINES [Edw. II–7 Edw. III]. Ed. by James Greenstreet. *Archaeol. Cantiana*, xi. 305–58; xii. 289–308; xiii. 289–320; xiv. 241–80; xv. 273–310; xviii. 337–52; xx. 161–86. Lond. 1877–93.

3557 CALENDAR OF KENT FEET OF FINES TO THE END OF HENRY III's REIGN. Ed. by Irene J. Churchill, R. Griffin and F. W. Hardman. Kent Archaeol. Soc.: *Kent Records*, xv (1939–40), 1956.

Valuable introduction on feet of fines by F. W. Jessup.

3558 THE EYRE OF KENT, 6 and 7 Edward II, A.D. 1313–1314. Ed. by F. W. Maitland, L. W. V. Harcourt, and W. C. Bolland. 3 vols. Year Books of Edward II series. Selden Soc. xxiv (1910); xxvii (1912); xxix (1913).

F. J. Pegues, 'A monastic society at law in the Kent eyre of 1313–14', *E.H.R.* lxxxvii (1972), 548–64.

3559 FRAMPTON (T. S.). A glance at the hundred of Wrotham. Maidstone, etc. 1881.

This little book consists mainly of extracts from the assize rolls, 1293–1313.

3560 KENT KEEPERS OF THE PEACE, 1316–1317. Ed. by B. H. Putnam. Kent Archaeol. Soc.: *Kent Records*, xiii (1933).

3561 PEDES FINIUM [Rich. I–John]. Ed. by L. B. Larking. *Archaeol. Cantiana*, i. 217–88; ii. 239–78; iii. 209–40; iv. 273–308; v. 259–90; vi. 225–34. Lond. 1858–66.

3562 SOME ANCIENT INDICTMENTS IN THE KING'S BENCH REFERRING TO KENT, 1450–52. Ed. by R. Virgoe. Documents illustrative of medieval Kentish society. Kent Archaeol. Soc. Records Branch, xviii (1964), 214–65.

LANCASHIRE

3563 A CALENDAR OF LANCASHIRE ASSIZE ROLLS, 1202–85, in the P.R.O. London. Transcribed and calendared by John Parker. 2 pts. Lancs. and Ches. Rec. Soc. xlvii, xlix, [1904–5].

English abstracts 1241–85, with notes on assizes since 1202; abstracts of amercements before the justices in eyre on the pipe rolls 1216–72. Tables of Assize Rolls 1241–1377 and of pleas of the Crown, 1246–1363.

3564 FINAL CONCORDS OF THE COUNTY OF LANCASTER, . . . (or feet of fines) (1196–1558). Transcribed and translated by William Farrer. Lancs. and Ches. Rec. Soc. pt. i: xxxix (1899); pt. ii: xlvi (1903); pt. iii: l (1905); pt. iv: lx (1910).

Vol. xxxix for years 1196–1307; vol. xlvi for years 1307–77; vol. l for years 1377–1509; vol. lx for years 1510–58.

3565 THE PLEAS OF QUO WARRANTO FOR THE COUNTY OF LANCASTER (1292–3). Ed. by A. Cantle. Chetham Soc. New Ser. xcviii (1937).

See *Placita de Quo Warranto* (No. 3492).

3566 PLEA ROLLS OF THE COUNTY PALATINE OF LANCASTER: Roll I (1401–6). Ed. by John Parker. Chetham Soc. 2nd Ser. lxxxvii (1928).

3567 SOUTH LANCASTER IN THE REIGN OF EDWARD II as illustrated by the pleas at Wigan recorded in *coram rege* roll no. 254. Ed. by G. H. Tupling. Chetham Soc. 3rd Ser. i (1949).

LEICESTERSHIRE

3568 SOME UNPUBLISHED DOCUMENTS RELATING TO LEICESTERSHIRE (in P.R.O.). Ed. by W. G. D. Fletcher, A. H. Thompson, and G. F. Farnham. *Asso. Archit. Soc. Reports and Papers*, xxiii (1895), 213–52, 392–436; xxiv (1897), 234–77; xxxiv (1917–18), 153–200, 363–414; xxxv (1919–20), 159–97, 305–22.

These public records comprise feet of fines (1199–1210), inquests post mortem, assize rolls, an inquest concerning knights' fees (1428), *curia regis* rolls for John and Henry III. See also 'The Pipe Roll (for 1199–1200), with selected pleas from the De Banco Rolls (for 1338–63)', *Leicestershire Archaeol. Soc. Trans.* xi (1918), 346–99, introduction by A. H. Thompson.

LINCOLNSHIRE

3569 THE EARLIEST LINCOLNSHIRE ASSIZE ROLLS, A.D. 1202–1209 (Pleas from Assize rolls and Curia Regis rolls). Ed. by Doris M. Stenton. Lincoln Rec. Soc. xxii (1926).

3570 FEET OF FINES FOR THE COUNTY OF LINCOLN, 1199–1216. Ed. by Margaret Walker. Pipe Roll Soc. xxix for 1953 (1954).

3571 FINAL CONCORDS OF THE COUNTY OF LINCOLN, 1244–1722, with additions from various sources 1176–1250. Ed. by C. W. Foster. Lincoln Rec. Soc. xvii (1920).

This volume of English abstracts continues and corrects Massingberd's *Abstracts* (No. 3573). Its introduction described the procedure of final concords.

3572 A LINCOLNSHIRE ASSIZE ROLL FOR 1298. Ed. by Walter S. Thomson. Lincoln Rec. Soc. xxxvi (1944).

The introduction treats rural local government in Lincolnshire 1294–8.

3573 LINCOLNSHIRE RECORDS: abstracts of final concords, Richard I, John, and Henry III (1193–1244). Ed. by W. O. Massingberd. [Transcribed and translated by W. K. Boyd.] Vol. i. Lond. 1896.

The abstracts are said to be 'inadequate and inaccurate', *E.H.R.* lxxi (1956), 139. See the continuation edited by C. W. Foster (No. 3571).

3574 RECORDS OF SOME SESSIONS OF THE PEACE IN LINCOLN-SHIRE, 1360–1375. (From Assize rolls and Ancient Indictments.) Ed. by Rosamond Sillem. Lincoln Rec. Soc. xxx (1936), 1937.

3575 RECORDS OF SOME SESSIONS OF THE PEACE IN LINCOLN-
SHIRE, 1381–1396. Ed. by Elisabeth G. Kimball. 2 pts. Lincoln Rec. Soc. xlix
(1955), and lvi (1962). RECORDS . . . IN THE CITY OF LINCOLN, 1351–
1354, AND THE BOROUGH OF STAMFORD, 1351. Ed. by E. G. Kimball.
Ibid. lxv (1971).

3576 ROLLS OF THE JUSTICES IN EYRE BEING THE ROLLS OF
PLEAS AND ASSIZES FOR LINCOLNSHIRE, 1218–19, and WORCES-
TERSHIRE, 1221. Ed. by Doris M. Stenton. Selden Soc. liii (1934).

London and Middlesex

See Weinbaum in *Tait essays* (No. 1455).

3577 CALENDAR OF CORONERS' ROLLS OF CITY OF LONDON,
1300–1378. Ed. by Reginald R. Sharpe. Lond. 1913.

3578 A CALENDAR OF THE FEET OF FINES FOR LONDON AND
MIDDLESEX, Richard I–12 Elizabeth. Ed. by W. J. Hardy and William Page.
2 vols. Lond. 1892–3.

3579 THE EYRE OF LONDON, 14 EDWARD II, A.D. 1321. Ed. by H. M.
Cam. 2 vols. Year Books of Edward II. Selden Soc. xxvi, pt. i (1968); pt. ii
(1969). E. J. Davis and M. Weinbaum, 'Sources for the London eyre of 1321',
B.I.H.R. vii (1930), 35–8. Ralph V. Rogers, 'Year book, eyre of London,
14 Edward II (1321)', *Amer. Acad. Arts and Sciences, Memoirs*, xix (1941).
H. Cam, *Law-finders* (No. 1461), pp. 95–105.

3579A THE LONDON EYRE OF 1244. Ed. by H. M. Chew and M. Weinbaum. London Rec. Soc. Pubns. vi (1970).

3580 LONDON POSSESSORY ASSIZES: a calendar (1340–1451). Ed. by
Helena Chew and William Kellaway. London Rec. Soc. Pubns. i (1965).

Norfolk

3581 EXTRACTS FROM CORONERS' ROLLS AND OTHER DOCU-
MENTS IN THE RECORD ROOM OF THE CORPORATION OF
NORWICH (Hen. III–Edw. I). By Henry Harrod. Norfolk and Norwich
Archaeol. Soc. *Norfolk Archaeol.* ii (1849), 253–79.

3582 FEET OF FINES FOR THE COUNTY OF NORFOLK (1198–1202).
Ed. by Barbara Dodwell. Pipe Roll Soc. lxv, or New Ser. xxvii (1950).

3583 INDEX LOCORUM TO THE DE BANCO ROLLS, 1307–27, in
Norfolk Records. Ed. by W. D. Selby and Walter Rye. 2 vols. Norfolk and
Norwich Archaeol. Soc. Norwich. 1886–92. Vol. i, pp. 223–65.

3584 NORFOLK SESSIONS OF THE PEACE: Roll of mainpernors and
pledges, 1394–97. Trans. by Lilian J. Redstone. Norfolk Rec. Soc. viii (1936),
1–14.

3585 PEDES FINIUM RESPECTING THE COUNTY OF NORFOLK, 1191–96. Ed. by G. H. Dashwood. Norfolk and Norwich Archaeol. Soc. Norwich. 1863. Pedes finium relating to Norfolk [abstracts], 3 Richard I to the end of the reign of John. Ed. by Walter Rye. Norfolk and Norwich Archaeol. Soc. Norwich. 1881. A short calendar of the feet of fines for Norfolk [Rich. I–Rich. III]. Ed. by Walter Rye. 2 pts. Norwich. 1885–6.

3586 SOME ROUGH MATERIALS FOR A HISTORY OF THE HUNDRED OF NORTH ERPINGHAM. Ed. by Walter Rye. 3 pts. Norwich. 1883–9.

> Pt. i, pp. 218–20 and 228–30, prints extracts from the plea rolls for 34 Henry III and 14 Edw. I.

3587 RYE (WALTER). 'Crime and accident in Norfolk'. *Norfolk Antiq. Miscellany*, ii (1883), 159–93; *Archaeol. Rev.* ii (1889), 20–5.

> The first of these papers contains extracts from plea rolls, 34, 41, 52–3 Henry III, 14 Edward I; the second, extracts from gaol-delivery rolls, 14 Edward I. For an abstract of a roll of crown pleas and gaol-delivery, 1332, see Rye's 'Crime in Norfolk', *East Anglian*, iii (1869), 148–53.

NORTHAMPTONSHIRE

3588 THE EARLIEST NORTHAMPTONSHIRE ASSIZE ROLLS, A.D. 1202 and 1203. Ed. by D. M. Stenton. Northants. Rec. Soc. v (1930).

> Includes some Bedfordshire cases omitted in No. 3527.

3589 ROGERS (RALPH V.). 'MS. of eyre of Northampton, 3 Edw. III (1329)' [with extracts]. *B.J.R.L.* xxxiv (1951–2), 388–431.

3590 ROLLS OF NORTHAMPTONSHIRE SESSIONS OF THE PEACE. Roll of supervisors, 1314–16; roll of keepers of the peace, 1320. Ed. with translations by Marguerite Gollanz. Northants. Rec. Soc. xi (1940).

NORTHUMBERLAND

3591 EXTRACTS FROM THE DE BANCO ROLLS RELATING TO NORTHUMBERLAND, 1308–1558. Ed. by F. W. Dendy. *Archaeol. Aeliana*, 3rd Ser. vi (1910), 41–88.

3592 FEET OF FINES, NORTHUMBERLAND AND DURHAM. Ed. by A. M. Oliver and Charles Johnson. [Abstracts in English, 1196–1228]. Newcastle Upon Tyne Rec. Comm. Pubns. x, for 1931 (1933).

3593 FEET OF FINES, NORTHUMBERLAND (1273–1346). Ed. by Charles Johnson from English abstracts. Ibid. xi, for 1932 (1934).

3594 NORTHUMBERLAND PLEAS FROM THE CURIA REGIS AND ASSIZE ROLLS, 1198–1272. English trans. by A. H. Thompson. Ibid. ii (1922).

3595 NORTHUMBRIAN PLEAS FROM DE BANCO ROLLS 1–37 (1–8 Edw. I). Ed. in English by A. H. Thompson. Surtees Soc. clviii–clix (1950).

3596 THREE EARLY ASSIZE ROLLS FOR NORTHUMBERLAND.
Ed. by William Page. Surtees Soc. lxxxviii (1891).

Contains rolls of 1256, 1269, and 1279; also abstracts of feet of fines for these rolls, pp. 401–26.

OXFORDSHIRE

3597 THE FEET OF FINES FOR OXFORDSHIRE, 1195–1291. Ed. by
H. E. Salter. Oxford. Rec. Soc. Pubns. xli (1930).

3598 OXFORD CITY DOCUMENTS, 1268–1665. Ed. by J. E. T. Rogers.
Oxf. Hist. Soc. Oxf. 1891.

Coroners' inquests, etc. 1297–1520; pp. 150–81, 236–41. Pleas before the justices in eyre at Oxford, 1285; pp. 194–236.

3599 PROCEEDINGS OF OXFORD JUSTICES OF PEACE (1390–4), in
Medieval Archives of University of Oxford, ii. Oxf. Hist. Soc. 1921.

3600 RECORDS OF MEDIEVAL OXFORD: Coroner's inquests, etc. Oxf.
1912.

RUTLAND

3601 MEEKINGS (C. A. F.). 'The Rutland eyre of 1253: a correction'.
E.H.R. lxxi (1956), 615–18.

Deals with a misconception of the eyre in general.

SHROPSHIRE
See No. 1801

3602 RECORDS OF PROCEEDINGS BEFORE THE CORONERS OF
SALOP, 1295–1306: a fragment. Ed. by C. H. Drinkwater. *Shropshire Archaeol.-Nat. Hist. Soc. Trans.* 3rd Ser. v (1905).

3603 SHROPSHIRE ASSIZE ROLLS, 1203. By W. K. Boyd. Ibid. 2nd Ser.
xi (1899), 243–51.

Translation only.

3604 SHROPSHIRE FEET OF FINES, 1196–1211, 1218–48. Transcribed
by W. K. Boyd with introduction by W. G. D. Fletcher. Ibid. 2nd Ser. x. 307–30;
3rd Ser. vi. 167–78, vii. 379–89; 4th Ser. i. 385–401. 1898–1911.

Translation only.

3605 THE SHROPSHIRE PEACE ROLL, 1400–1414. Ed. by Elisabeth G.
Kimball. Shrewsbury. 1959.

SOMERSET

3606 PEDES FINIUM FOR THE COUNTY OF SOMERSET [abstracts,
1196–Henry VI]. Ed. by Emanuel Green. Somerset Rec. Soc. 4 vols. vi for
1196–1307 (1892), xii for 1307–46 (1898), xvii for 1347–99 (1902), xxii for
Hen. IV–Hen. VI (1906).

3607 SOMERSETSHIRE PLEAS, CIVIL AND CRIMINAL, FROM
THE ROLLS OF THE ITINERANT JUSTICES [end of twelfth century

to 8 Edw. I]. Ed. by C. E. H. C. Healey and Lionel Landon. Somerset Rec. Soc. xi (1897); xxxvi (1923); xli (1926); xliv (1929).

These are particularly valuable rolls.

3608 A SUMMONS OF THE GREEN WAX. To the sheriff of Somerset and Dorset. Ed. by T. Bruce Dilks. Somerset Rec. Soc. *Collectanea*, i (1924), 175–206.

Latin transcripts of amercements and distraints, 1465–8.

STAFFORDSHIRE
See Gloucester, No. 3553

3609 EARLY CHANCERY PROCEEDINGS [bills of complaint addressed to the chancellor], Richard II–Henry VII. Ed. by George Wrottesley. Wm. Salt Archaeol. Soc. *Collections*, New Ser. vii (1904), 237–93.

3610 EXTRACTS FROM PLEA ROLLS [Rich. I–Rich. III]. Trans. by George Wrottesley. Ibid. 1st Ser. iii. 1–163; iv. 1–215; v, pt. i. 123–80; vi, pt. i. 37–300; vii. 1–191; ix. 1–118; x. 1–75; xi. 1–123; xii. 1–173; xiii. 1–204; xiv. 1–162; xv. 1–126; xvi. 1–93; xvii. 1–153; New Ser. iii. 121–229; iv. 92–212; vi, pt. i. 89–164 (1882–1903).

Valuable extracts from *coram rege, de banco*, assize rolls, etc. The pleas from 1194 to 1214 are printed in full. Pleas of the forest, 1262–1300, v, pt. i, 123–80. Vol. vi, pt. i, pleas of Henry III taken from B.M. MS. Add. 12269.

3611 FINAL CONCORDS, OR PEDES FINIUM, STAFFORDSHIRE [calendars or abstracts, 1196–1547]. Ed. by George Wrottesley. Ibid. 1st Ser. iii. 165–77; iv. 217–63; xi. 127–292 (1882–91).

Continued in later volumes of the *Collections* for later dates.

SUFFOLK

3612 A CALENDAR OF THE FEET OF FINES FOR SUFFOLK [1 Rich. I–3 Rich. III]. By Walter Rye. Suffolk Institute of Archaeology. Ipswich. 1900.

SURREY

3613 [CALENDAR OF] PEDES FINIUM, OR FINES RELATING TO SURREY, Richard I–Henry VII. Ed. by F. B. Lewis. Surrey Archaeol. Soc. Guildford. 1894.

See also Ralph Nevill, 'Surrey Feet of Fines', *Surrey Archaeol. Collections*, xiii (1897), 130–40.

SUSSEX

3614 AN ABSTRACT OF FEET OF FINES RELATING TO SUSSEX [2 Rich. I–24 Henry VII]. By L. F. Salzmann. Sussex Rec. Soc. ii, vii, xxiii. Lewes. 1903–16.

WARWICKSHIRE
See No. 3553

3615 ROLLS OF THE WARWICKSHIRE AND COVENTRY SESSIONS OF THE PEACE, 1377–1397. Transcribed and ed. by Elisabeth G. Kimball, with an analytical index of indictments by T. F. T. Plucknett. Dugdale Soc. xvi (1939).

3616 WARWICKSHIRE FEET OF FINES [1195–1509]. Ed. by Ethel Stokes, Lucy Drucker, *et al.* Dugdale Soc. xi (1932); xv (1939); xviii (1943).

WESTMORLAND

3617 DISORDERS IN LANCASTRIAN WESTMORLAND: Some early chancery proceedings. Ed. by R. L. Storey. *Cumber.–Westm. Antiq.–Archaeol. Soc. Trans.* New Ser. liii (1954).

3618 NOTES ON WESTMORLAND ASSIZE ROLL, 1256. By A. P. Brydson. Ibid. New Ser. xiii (1913).

WILTSHIRE

3619 ABBREVIATION OF PEDES FINIUM, 7 Richard I–11 Henry III, and inquis[itiones] post mort[em], 27 Henry III–12 Edward I, for Wiltshire. Ed. by Thomas Phillipps. Middle Hill Press, n.d.

3620 ABSTRACTS OF FEET OF FINES RELATING TO WILTSHIRE FOR THE REIGN OF EDWARD I AND EDWARD II. Ed. by R. B. Pugh. Wilts. Archaeol. Soc. Record Branch, New Ser. i (1939).

   The introduction has a valuable description of feet of fines.

3621 CALENDAR OF FEET OF FINES RELATING TO WILTSHIRE REMAINING IN THE P.R.O. 1195–1272. Ed. by Edward A. Fry. Wilts. Archaeol. and Nat. Hist. Soc. 1930.

3622 CROWN PLEAS OF THE WILTSHIRE EYRE, 1249. By C. A. F. Meekings. Wilts. Archaeol. and Nat. Hist. Soc. Record Branch, xvi (1961).

   The introduction gives an important account of the general eyre and its procedure. Also M. T. Clanchy, ed. *Civil Pleas of the Wiltshire Eyre, 1249*, Wilts. Rec. Soc. xxvi for 1970 (1971).

3623 INDEX OF WILTSHIRE FINES, 1 Edward III to Richard III. Middle Hill Press, n.d.

3624 OFFENDERS AGAINST THE STATUTE OF LABOURERS IN WILTSHIRE, 1349 [translation of an assize roll]. By E. M. Thompson. *Wilts. Archaeol. and Nat. Hist. Soc. Magazine*, xxxiii (1904), 384–409.

3625 THE VEREDICTUM OF CHIPPENHAM HUNDRED, 1281. Ed. by R. E. Latham and C. A. F. Meekings. Wilts. Archaeol. Soc. Record Branch, *Collectanea.* Ed. by N. J. Williams, xii (1956).

   The jurors' answers to the articles of the eyre.

WORCESTERSHIRE

3626 INDEX PEDUM FINIUM PRO COM. WIGORN., ab 1 Edw. III ad Hen. VI. Ed. by Thomas Phillipps. Cheltenham. 1865.

3627 ROLLS OF THE JUSTICES IN EYRE, BEING THE ROLLS OF
PLEAS AND ASSIZES [for Lincolnshire 1218–9 and] WORCESTERSHIRE
1221. Ed. by D. M. Stenton. Selden Soc. liii (1934).

YORKSHIRE

3628 EXTRACTS FROM A YORKSHIRE ASSIZE ROLL, 3 Henry III
(1219). Ed. by W. T. Lancaster. Yorks. Archaeol. Soc. Record Ser. lxi, *Miscellanea*, i (1920), 170–85.

3629 FEET OF FINES FOR THE COUNTY OF YORK. Yorks. Archaeol.
Soc. Record Ser.

> 1218–72, ed., by John Parker. lxii for 1218–31 (1921), lxvii for 1232–46 (1925), lxxxii
> for 1246–72 (1932).
> 1272–1300, ed. by F. H. Slingsby. cxxi (1956).
> 1300–14, ed. by M. Roper. cxxvii (1965).
> 1327–77, ed. by W. P Baildon. xlii (1910), lii (1915).

3630 HONOR AND FOREST OF PICKERING. Ed. by R. B. Turton.
North Riding Rec. Soc. Records. New Ser. vols. i–iv. Lond. 1894–7.

> Pleas before the itinerant justices of the forest, 1334–8; ii. 49–200; iii. 1–185; iv. 1–69.
> *Coram rege* rolls, 7–24 Edw. III; iii. 186–220; iv. 167–81. Assize rolls, 15 Henry III:
> iv. 163–4.

3631 PEDES FINIUM EBOR. TEMPORE RICARDI I [1191–99]. Ed. by
William Brown. *Yorks. Archaeol. and Topog. Asso. Jour.* xi (1891), 174–88. 'Pedes
finium Ebor. regnante Johanne' [ed. William Brown]. Surtees Soc. xciv (1897).

3632 ROLLS OF THE JUSTICES IN EYRE BEING THE ROLLS OF
PLEAS AND ASSIZES FOR YORKSHIRE in 3 Henry III (1218–19). Ed. by
Doris M. Stenton. Selden Soc. lvi (1937).

3633 THREE YORKSHIRE ASSIZE ROLLS FOR THE REIGNS OF
JOHN AND HENRY III. Ed. by C. T. Clay. Yorks. Archaeol. Soc. Record
Ser. xliv (1911).

> English translations for which Lady Stenton prints the original Latin for John's reign
> (1208) in Selden Soc. lxxxiv, pp. 94–117.

3634 YORKSHIRE FINAL CONCORDS OF THE REIGN OF HENRY II.
Ed. by Charles Clay. *Yorks. Archaeol. Jour.* xl (1959), 78–89.

3635 YORKSHIRE SESSIONS OF THE PEACE, 1361–1364. Ed. by B. H.
Putnam. Yorks. Archaeol. Soc. Record Ser. c (1939).

WALES

3636 APPEAL OF RICHARD SIWARD TO THE CURIA REGIS from
a decision in the curia comitatus in Glamorgan, 1248. Ed. by G. T. Clark.
Archaeol. Cambrensis. 4th Ser. ix (1878), 241–63.

3637 FLINT PLEAS, 1283–1285. Ed. by J. G. Edwards. Flintshire Hist. Soc.
Pubns. no. 8. Chester. 1922.

> For the body of this edition, Latin original and English translation are on opposite
> pages.

3637A AN INVENTORY OF EARLY CHANCERY PROCEEDINGS CONCERNING WALES. Ed. by E. A. Lewis. Cardiff. 1937.

3638 THE MARCHER LORDSHIPS OF SOUTH WALES, 1415–1536: select documents. Ed. by Thomas B. Pugh. Board of Celtic Stud. Hist.–Law Ser. Cardiff. 1963.

> Prints four assize rolls 1415, 1432, 1476, 1503: and a financial report of the Lordship of Newport.

3639 THE WELSH ASSIZE ROLL 1272–1284. Ed. by James Conway Davies. Board of Celtic Stud. Hist.–Law Ser. no. 7. Cardiff. 1940.

3640 DAVIES (R. REES). 'The law of the March'. *Welsh H.R.* v (1970), 1–30.

> This article concerns 'the law as it was operated in the courts of the lordships themselves'. For the judicial claims of the English crown, see A. J. Otway-Ruthven, 'The constitutional position of the great lordships of south Wales', *T.R.H.S.* 5th Ser. viii (1958), 1–20.

IRELAND

3641 CALENDAR OF THE JUSTICIARY ROLLS OF IRELAND, 23–35 Edward I. (1295–1307). Ed. by James Mills. 2 vols. Dublin. 1905–14; vol. iii (1308–14), prepared by Herbert Wood and Albert E. Langman, and revised by Margaret C. Griffith. Stationery Office. Dublin. 1956.

3641 A CLASSIFIED SCHEDULE AND GENERAL INVENTORY OF THE PLEA ROLLS [36 Henry III–25 Charles II]. *Irish Rec. Comm. Eighth Rept.* 1819 (No. 1076), pp. 79–125.

3642 EARLY ROLLS OF JUDICIAL PROCEEDINGS (lists of Irish plea rolls, 36 Henry III–16 Charles I). *Deputy Keeper's Reports, Ireland*, xxvi (1894), 52–68; xxviii (1896), 39–56.

> See G. J. Hand, *English law* (No. 3666).

CHANNEL ISLANDS

3643 ROLLS OF THE ASSIZES IN THE CHANNEL ISLANDS IN 1309. Ed. and trans. by Gervaise le Gros and E. T. Nicolle. Société Jersiaise. St. Helier. 1903.

4. *Year Books*

The Year Books, 1292–1535, are anonymous law reports, written in Law French, containing the discussions of the judges and counsel on points of law and the grounds of judgment in some cases tried before the royal justices either at Westminster or in eyre. Presumably they report the actual language used in court and the substance of the oral arguments. They are not formal court records, but rather 'professional memoranda . . . intended to give information on points of interest to legal practitioners'; hence they lay emphasis on pleading and technical forms rather than on matters of substance. There are normally several surviving manuscripts for each year book, which are often not identical in content or in order of entry. Their origin is therefore a matter of dispute. They may be 'private notes made in court by young apprentice lawyers' (Maitland) and when the notes were recopied or expanded, variations in texts occurred. Bolland suggested that serjeants-at-law employed apprentices to make notes which were then compiled and collated in a scriptorium. Turner conjectured that for Edward II's reign at least they might be pamphlets for students compiled by a professional organization. Maitland's interest in and promotion of the printing of year books are recounted in Bell's *Maitland* (No. 1482), chap. vii.

The earliest surviving year books for 1292 and for other years of Edward I have been published in the Rolls Series. Similar reports of cases at the beginning of Edward I's reign are printed by Dunham in *Casus Placitorum* (No. 2993). Since 1903 the Selden Society has been publishing the year books of Edward II's reign; by 1964 the twelfth year of that reign had been reached. In addition, the Selden Society provided three volumes on the year book of the 1313–14 eyre of Kent and in 1968–9 two volumes of the year book of the 1321 eyre of London. The year books for 11 to 20 Edward III appear in fifteen volumes of the Rolls Series. The Ames Foundation began the publication of the year books for Richard II's reign with three volumes for the years 1387 to 1390. The Selden Society has published two fifteenth-century year books, one for 1422 and another for 1470.

The commentaries and analyses by L. O. Pike in the Rolls Series editions and by the various authors in the Selden Society editions should be studied for an appreciation of the year books. The Selden Society editions contain the Anglo-Norman of the year books and the Latin record of the plea rolls on the left-hand pages and a translation of both into English on the right-hand pages. Special consideration of the Anglo-Norman language is given by Maitland in vol. xvii, by M. D. Legge in vols. lii and liv, and by J. P. Collas in vol. lxxxi.

A long list of the early printed editions of the year books and abridgements from 7 Edward III to Elizabeth covers pp. 51–110 of Beale's *Bibliography* (No. 1224). A convenient list of editions, in which the printed year book for each regnal year is set forth, may be found in the Maxwell bibliography (No. 1228), i. 312–19. A preliminary list of the surviving manuscripts, compiled about 1935–6 by Jennifer Nicholson and entitled 'Register of Manuscripts of Year Books Extant', was issued in typescript for the Selden Society by the Hist. MSS. Comm. in 1956. On the manuscripts consult the articles by R. V. Rogers (No. 3658). One part of the year books for Edward III (part v of the 1678–80 edition) is called *Le Livre des assises* or *Liber assisarum*; on this, see W. C. Bolland in *Cambridge Law Journal*, ii (1922), 192–211.

There are also valuable digests of the year books, arranged under titles in alphabetical order; the best are by Anthony Fitzherbert (No. 3654) and by Robert Brooke (No. 3653). The value of these digests is assessed in Winfield (No. 1229), pp. 200–38, and in Cowley (No. 3656).

3644 LES REPORTS DES CASES (Edward II–27 Henry VIII). 11 pts. Lond. 1678–80.

This edition, sometimes cited as Maynard's edition, provides reports for each reign over a long period; some of these reports have not been printed elsewhere; but this edition is badly edited and poorly printed.

3645 YEAR BOOKS, 20–22 and 30–35 EDWARD I. Ed. by Alfred J. Horwood. 5 vols. Rolls Ser. Lond. 1866–79.

> For reports of cases in the king's courts *c.* 1272–*c.* 1278, see Dunham, *Casus Placitorum* (No. 2993), pp. 45–141.

3646 YEAR BOOK SERIES for the reign of Edward II. Selden Society. 1903+ (in progress).

> xvii (1903), 1 Edw. II. Ed. by F. W. Maitland.
> xix (1904), 2–3 Edw. II. Ed. by F. W. M.
> xx (1905), 3 Edw. II. Ed. by F. W. M.
> xxii (1907), 3–4 Edw. II. Ed. by F. W. M. and G. J. Turner.
> xxvi (1911), 4 Edw. II. Ed. by G. J. T.
> xlii (1925), 4 Edw. II. Ed. by G. J. T.
> lxiii (1944), 5 Edw. II. Ed. by G. J. T.
> xxxi (1915), 5 Edw. II. Ed. by W. C. Bolland.
> xxxiii (1916), 5 Edw. II. Ed. by W. C. B.
> xxxiv (1917), 6 Edw. II. Ed. by P. Vinogradoff and L. Ehrlich.
> xxxviii (1921), 6 Edw. II (pt. i). Ed. by P. V. and L. E.
> xliii (1926), 6 Edw. II (pt. ii). Ed. by W. C. B.
> xxxvi (1918), 6–7 Edw. II. Ed. by W. C. B.
> xxxix (1922), 7 Edw. II. Ed. by W. C. B.
> xli (1924), 8 Edw. II. Ed. by W. C. B.
> xxxvii (1920), 8 Edw. II. Ed. by W. C. B.
> xlv (1928), 9 Edw. II. Ed. by W. C. B.
> lii (1934), 10 Edw. II. Ed. by M. D. Legge and W. Holdsworth.
> liv (1935), 10 Edw. II. Ed. by M. D. L. and W. H.
> lxi (1942), 11 Edw. II. Ed. by J. P. Collas and W. H.
> lxv (1946), 12 Edw. II. Ed. by J. P. C. and T. F. T. Plucknett.
> lxx (1951), 12 Edw. II. Ed. by J. P. C. and T. F. T. P.
> lxxxi (1964), 12 Edw. II. Ed. by J. P. C.
> xxiv (1909), Eyre of Kent, 6–7 Edw. II. Ed. by F. W. M., L. W. V. Harcourt, and W. C. B.
> xxvii (1912), Eyre of Kent, 6–7 Edw. II. Ed. by F. W. M., L. M. V. Harcourt, and W. C. B.
> xxix (1913), Eyre of Kent, 6–7 Edw. II. Ed. by W. C. B.
> lxxxv (1968), Eyre of London, 14 Edw. II (vol. i). Ed. by H. M. Cam.
> lxxxvi (1969), Eyre of London, 14 Edw. II (vol. ii). Ed. by H. M. C.

3647 YEAR BOOKS, 11–12 Edw. III. Ed. by Alfred J. Horwood. 1 vol. Rolls Ser. Lond. 1883.

> J. G. Edwards printed entries from the common bench roll and assize roll for an interesting case in this volume: 'Taxation and consent in the court of common pleas, 1338', *E.H.R.* lvii (1942), 473–82.

3648 YEAR BOOKS, 12–20 Edw. III. Ed. by L. O. Pike. 14 vols. Rolls Ser. Lond. 1885–1911.

3649 YEAR BOOKS OF RICHARD II. The Ames Foundation. Cambr. (Mass.) and Lond.

11 Rich. II (1387–8). Ed. by Isobel D. Thornley, with commentary by T. F. T. Plucknett (1937).

12 Rich. II (1388–9). Ed. by George F. Dreiser (1914).

13 Rich. II (1389–90). Ed. by Theodore F. T. Plucknett (1929).

> Note that *Select Cases in the Exchequer Chamber* for 1377–1509 (No. 3511) are drawn from year books.

3650 YEAR BOOK 9–10 Hen. V (1421–2). Ed. by Ralph V. Rogers. Privately printed. 1948.

3651 YEAR BOOK 1 Hen. VI (1422). Ed. by C. H. Williams. Selden Soc. 1 for 1933 (1933).

3652 YEAR BOOK 10 Edw. IV and 49 Hen. VI (1470). Ed. by Nellie Neilson. Selden Soc. xlvii for 1930 (1931).

3653 BROOKE (ROBERT). La graunde abridgement. Lond. 1573.

> Other editions were published, all posthumously, in 1568, 1570, 1576, and 1586. Brooke's abridgement of the year books is a more detailed enlargement of Fitzherbert's.

3654 FITZHERBERT (ANTHONY). La graunde abridgement. 3 vols. Lond. 1516. 2 vols. Lond. 1565.

> This work is 'remarkable for its accuracy' (Holdsworth, ii. 544), and useful for its references to cases from the reign of Henry III forward. See S. E. Thorne, 'Fitzherbert's Abridgment', *Law Library Jour.* xxix (1936), 59–63. Ralph V. Rogers, 'A source for Fitzherbert's La graunde abridgment', *E.H.R.* lvi (1941), 605–28.

3655 BOLLAND (WILLIAM C.). The year books. Cambr. 1921. Idem, A manual of year book studies. Cambr. 1925.

3656 COWLEY (JOHN D.). A bibliography of abridgements, digests, dictionaries and indexes of English law to the year 1800. Selden Soc. Lond. 1932.

> W. M. Geldart, 'The year-books of Edward II', *E.H.R.* xxvi (1911), 239–56. F. J. Pegues, 'Medieval origins of modern law reporting', *Cornell Law Quart.* xxxviii (1953), 491–510. Alfred W. B. Simpson, 'The circulation of year books in the fifteenth century', *Law Quart. Rev.* lxxiii (1957), 492–505. Idem, 'Source and function in the later year books', ibid. lxxxvii (1971), 94–118.

3657 NICHOLSON (JENNIFER). Register of manuscripts of year books extant. Published for the Selden Society by the Hist. MSS. Comm. Lond. 1956.

> This preliminary typescript compiled by Miss Nicholson about 1935 was only partly updated when it was published in 1956. A list of the published extracts from year books is given in Maxwell, *Legal Bibliography* (No. 1228), pp. 313–19.

3658 ROGERS (RALPH V.). 'Manuscript year books for 1–10 Edward III (1327–37)', *E.H.R.* lv (1940), 562–97; idem, 'The editing and reporting of the year books of Edward III', *Law Library Jour.* xliv (1951), 71–8; idem, 'Law reporting and the multification of law reports in the fourteenth century', *E.H.R.* lxvi (1951), 481–506; idem, 'The John Rylands Library Manuscript of the eyre of Northampton, 3 Edward III (1329)', *B.J.R.L.* xxxiv (1952), 388–431.

5. Modern Treatises on Law Courts

a. General

The comprehensive treatises on law and law courts, of which the classics are by Pollock and Maitland (No. 1241) and by Holdsworth (No. 1235), are listed above on pp. 159–62. The introductions to the various volumes of the publications of the Selden Society present learned commentaries; they are summarized in Kiralfy-Jones (No. 195). Recent essays descriptive of the courts for the twelfth century are to be found in Van Caenegem (No. 3503) and D. M. Stenton (Nos. 3681–2; 3494), for the early thirteenth century in Flower, *Introduction* (No. 3664), for the thirteenth and fourteenth centuries in Sayles, *King's Bench* (No. 3510), and for 1327–36 in vol. iii of *English Government at work* (No. 3836). On legal procedure the section on law writers on pp. 459–61 above should be consulted.

3659   ADAMS (GEORGE B.). Council and courts in Anglo-Norman England. New Haven. 1926; reprinted N.Y. 1965.

This collection of studies was previously published in such journals as the *Columbia Law Review* and the *Yale Law Journal*.

3660   BIGELOW (MELVILLE M.). History of procedure in England, 1066–1204. Boston and Lond. 1880.

This is a fundamental study; its appendix of hitherto unpublished writs and charters of the eleventh and twelfth centuries forms a complement to the author's *Placita Anglo-Normannica* (No. 3490).

3661   BOLLAND (WILLIAM C.). The general eyre. Cambr. 1922.

A better account of the eyre is given by Meekings in his introduction to No. 3622. See also H. M. Cam, *Liberties* (No. 1462). See William T. Reedy, Jr., 'The origin of the general eyre in the reign of Henry I', *Speculum*, xli (1966), 688–724.

3662   DAVIES (J. CONWAY). 'Common law writs and returns: Richard I to Richard II'. *B.I.H.R.* xxvi (1953), 125–56; xxvii (1954), 1–34.

See M. T. Clanchy, 'The franchise of return of writs', *T.R.H.S.* xvii (1967), 59–79.

3663   EHRLICH (LUDWIK). Proceedings against the crown (1216–1377). Oxford Studies in Social and Legal History. vi. Oxf. 1921. W. S. Holdsworth, 'The history of remedies against the crown', *Law Quart. Rev.* xxxviii (1922), 141–64; 280–96.

3664   FLOWER (CYRIL T.). Introduction to the curia regis rolls, 1199–1230. Selden Soc. lxii for 1943 (1944).

Part i describes the central courts as they appear in the rolls of this period: the *curia regis*, pleas before the king, the bench and other central courts of the exchequer, forests, and Jews. The references in these rolls to proceedings in other courts shed light on the justices in eyre, the county court, the hundred court, and other local courts of the king, the numerous courts of private jurisdiction, and the court christian.
Part ii describes the forms and subjects of actions.
Part iii deals with procedure.

3665   HALE (MATTHEW). Historia placitorum coronae: the history of the pleas of the crown. 2 vols. Lond. 1736; new edns. 1778, 1800, 1847.

This most important work of an eminent justice who died in 1676 is 'regarded as a book of the highest authority' (Holdsworth, *Sources*, pp. 152–3). Only the book on capital offences was completed and this was not printed until sixty years after Hale's death, under the editorship of Solomon Emlyn.

3666   HAND (GEOFFREY J. P.). English law in Ireland: 1290–1324. Cambr. 1967. See J. A. Watt in *Gwynn essays* (No. 1438).

3667   HARCOURT (LEVESON W. VERNON). His grace the steward and trial of peers. Lond. etc. 1907.

This volume contains many extracts from the patent, close, and charter rolls and other records. See also his 'Baga de secretis', *E.H.R.* xxiii (1908), 508–29. For a critical review, consult J. H. Round in *E.H.R.* xxii (1907), 778–82; also Squibb (No. 3679), chap. i.

3667A HARDING (ALAN). A social history of English law. Penguin Books. Baltimore. 1966. Idem, The law courts of medieval England. Lond. and N.Y. 1973.

3668 HASTINGS (MARGARET). The court of common pleas in the fifteenth century: a study of legal administration and procedure. Ithaca. 1947; Lond. 1948.

See also Nellie Neilson in *English Government at work* (No. 3836), iii. 259–85.

3668A HILL (GEORGE F.). Treasure trove in law and practice. Oxf. 1936.

William Martin, 'The law of treasure trove', *Antiquary*, xxxix (1903), 54–7, 142–6, 230–3, 279–82. F. C. Hamil, 'Wreck of the sea in mediaeval England', Univ. Michigan Pubns. Hist. & Pol. Sci. xi (1937), 1–24.

3669 JEUDWINE (JOHN W.). Tort, crime and police in mediaeval Britain: a review of some early law and custom. Lond. 1917.

Cf. George L. Haskins, 'Executive justice and the rule of law: some reflections on thirteenth-century England', *Speculum*, xxx (1955), 529–38.

3670 JONES (W. R.). 'The court of the verge: the jurisdiction of the steward and the marshal of the household in the later middle ages'. *Jour. British Stud.* x (1970), 1–29.

3671 KEETON (GEORGE W.). The Norman Conquest and the common law. Lond. and N.Y. 1966.

3672 MILSOM (STROUD F. C.). Historical foundations of the common law. Lond. 1969.

This fundamental treatise has excellent bibliographical references on pp. 375–429.

3673 NEILSON (NELLIE). 'The early pattern of the common law (1066–1250)'. *A.H.R.* xlix (1943–4), 199–212.

Professor Neilson's presidential address deals with customary law, with franchises, and with special jurisdictions, as well as some other matters. See also her 'Custom and common law in Kent', *Harvard Law Rev.* xxxiii (1925), 482–98.

3674 PLUCKNETT (THEODORE F. T.). Early English legal literature. Cambr. 1958.

3675 PLUCKNETT (T. F. T.). Edward I and criminal law. Cambr. 1959. See No. 3339.

Cf. J. C. Davies, 'Felony in Edwardian Wales', *Hon. Soc. Cymmrodorion Trans.* (1916–17), 145–96.

3676 PUTNAM (BERTHA H.). The enforcement of the statute of labourers during the first decade after the Black Death, 1349–59. N.Y. etc. 1908. See No. 3344.

3677 PUTNAM (B. H.). Records of the courts of common law, especially of the sessions of the justices of peace . . . *American Philosophical Soc. Procs.* xci, no. 3 (1947).

Hilary Jenkinson, 'Some preliminaries to the study of the English common law records',

Cambr. Law Jour. x (1948), 375–91. Henry G. Richardson, 'Year books and the plea rolls as sources of historical information', *T.R.H.S.* 4th Ser. v (1922), 28–70. C. H. Williams, 'Fifteenth century *coram rege* rolls', *B.I.H.R.* i (1925), 69–72.

3678   SIMPSON (ALFRED W. B.). An introduction to the history of the land law. Lond. 1961.

3679   SQUIBB (GEORGE D.). The high court of chivalry: a study of the civil law in England. Oxf. 1959.

The high court of chivalry was the joint court of the constable and the marshal; it had its origin in the middle of the fourteenth century. It was not a court of common law; but it administered 'justice in relation to the military matters which are not governed by the common law'. In its use, it developed particularly into a court of heraldry. None of the original records of this court seem to survive from the Middle Ages; but a few transcripts of cases of the late fourteenth century exist; and further, since appeals were made to the king in chancery, the patent rolls contain commissions of such appeals (Squibb, pp. 16–25). See No. 3503A.

3680   STAUNFORD or STAUNDFORD (WILLIAM). Les plees del coron. Lond. 1557; other edns. 1560, 1567, 1568, 1574, 1583, 1607.

This once popular work, written in law French by a judge of common pleas who died in 1558, rests heavily upon Bracton and the year books.

3681   STENTON (DORIS M.). English justice between the Norman conquest and the great charter 1066–1215. *American Philosophical Society Procs.* Philadelphia. 1964.

3682   STENTON (DORIS M.). 'King John and the courts of justice'. *P.B.A.* xliv (1958), 103–27.

3683   TURNER (RALPH V.). The king and his courts: the role of John and Henry III in the administration of justice, 1199–1240. Ithaca (N.Y.). 1968.

See also R. V. Turner, 'The royal courts treat disseizin by the king: John and Henry III, 1199–1240', *Amer. Jour. Legal Hist.* xii (1969), 1–18.

3684   WEST (FRANCIS). The justiciarship in England, 1066–1232. *Cambridge Stud. in Med. Life and Thought.* New Ser. xii. Cambr. 1966. See No. 3850.

The justiciar was much more than a law officer; he was the king's *alter ego* whose manifold duties placed him at the centre of government from William I to Henry III.

b. Personnel

Consult Powicke and Fryde (No. 371), Sayles, *King's Bench* (No. 3510), and Richardson and Sayles on Ireland (No. 3846), Campbell (No. 529), and Foss (No. 534). For Hengham, see No. 2997. For the reputation of lawyers, see Ives (No. 7152).

3685   BOLLAND (WILLIAM C.). Chief justice Sir William Bereford. Cambr. 1924.

3686   FOSS (EDWARD). Tabulae curiales, or tables of the superior courts of Westminster hall, showing the judges who sat in them, 1066–1864. 2 pts. Lond. 1865.

Refer to Foss's other works (No. 534).

3687 HARDY (THOMAS D.). A catalogue of lords chancellors, keepers of the great seal, masters of the rolls, and officers of the court of chancery. Lond. 1843.

3688 HARGREAVES-MAWDSLEY (W. N.). A history of legal dress in Europe until the end of the 18th century. Oxf. 1963.

3689 MEEKINGS (CECIL A. F.). 'Martin Pateshull and William Raleigh'. *B.I.H.R.* xxvi (1953), 157–80. Idem, 'Robert of Nottingham, justice of the bench, 1244–46'. Ibid. xli (1968), 132–8. Idem, 'Alan de Wassand' (a judge of Henry III's reign). *Yorks. Archaeol. Jour.* xxxiii (1952–5), 465–73.

3690 PEGUES (FRANK J.). 'The *clericus* in the legal administration of thirteenth-century England'. *E.H.R.* lxxi (1956), 529–59.

3691 PUTNAM (BERTHA H.). The place in legal history of Sir William Shareshull, chief justice of the king's bench, 1350–61. Lond. 1950. Idem, 'Chief Justice Shareshull and the economic and legal codes of 1351–1352'. *Univ. Toronto Law Jour.* v (1944), 251–81.

3692 SAYLES (GEORGE O.). 'Medieval judges as legal consultants'. *Law Quart. Rev.* lvi (1940), 247–54.

3693 STONES (EDWARD L. G.). 'Sir Geoffrey le Scrope (*c.* 1285–1340), chief justice of the king's bench'. *E.H.R.* lxix (1954), 1–17.

c. Procedure

Legal procedure is consider in several of the treatises cited on pp. 160–3, and in Nos. 3659–83, especially Fox (No. 1234), and Bigelow (No. 3660). The introductions to law records, especially those in the Selden Society series, often deal at some length with matters of legal procedure; for the latter turn to the index of Kiralfy-Jones, *Guide* (No. 195), under 'Procedure'. Good starting-points are the introductions to *Brevia Placitata* (No. 2992), to *Novae Narrationes* (Nos. 2998 and 3705), to *Procedure without Writ* (No. 3513), and to Van Caenegem's *Royal writs* (No. 3503). A summary can be found in Plucknett's *History* (No. 1241), pp. 353–416. See Bigelow (No. 3660).

3693A BARTON (J. L.). 'The medieval use'. *Law Quart. Rev.* lxxxi (1965), 562–77.

3694 FIFOOT (CECIL H. S.). History and sources of the common law: tort and contract. Lond. 1949.

3695 GABEL (LEONA C.). Benefit of clergy in England in the later middle ages. Northampton (Mass.). 1929.

3696 HAAS (ELSA DE). Antiquities of bail; origin and historical development in criminal cases to the year 1275. N.Y. 1940.

3697 HAMIL (FREDERICK C.). 'The king's approvers: a chapter in the history of English criminal law'. *Speculum*, xi (1936), 238–58. Idem, 'Presentment of Englishry and the murder fine'. Ibid. xii (1937), 285–98.

An approver, *probator regis*, was an accused person who turned king's or state's evidence to inform on his accomplices. For an example, see Margaret Aston, 'A Kent approver of 1440', *B.I.H.R.* xxxvi (1963), 83–90.

3698 HURNARD (NAOMI D.). The king's pardon for homicide. Oxf. 1969.

N. D. Hurnard, 'The jury of presentment and the assize of Clarendon', *E.H.R.* lvi (1941), 374–410.

3699 JOHNSON (CHARLES). 'Notes on thirteenth century judicial procedure'. *E.H.R.* lxii (1947), 508–21.

3700 JOÜON DES LONGRAIS (FRÉDÉRIC). La conception anglaise de la saisine du xiie au xive siècle. *Études de droit anglais*, i (Paris, 1924). Idem, 'Le droit criminel anglais au moyen âge'. *Revue hist. de droit français et étranger.* 4th Ser. iii (1956), 391–435.

3701 KAYE (J. M.). 'Early history of murder and manslaughter'. *Law Quart. Rev.* lxxiii (1967), 365–95; 569–601.

3702 KIRALFY (ALBERT K. R.). The action on the case: a historical survey of the development up to the year 1700. Lond. 1951.

Elizabeth J. Dix, 'Origins of the action of trespass on the case'. *Yale Law Jour.* xlvi (1937), 1142–76. See No. 3706.

3703 MAITLAND (FREDERIC W.). 'The beatitude of seisin'. *Law Quart. Rev.* iv (1888), 24–39, 286–99. Reprinted in No. 1482.

This article deals with the history of possessory actions. See also Maitland's other articles on seisin in his *Collected Papers* (No. 1482).

George D. G. Hall, 'The early history of entry sur disseisin', in *Bracton Symposium* (No. 2985*l*).

Samuel E. Thorne, 'Livery of seisin', *Law Quart. Rev.* lii (1936), 345–64.

3704 MAITLAND (FREDERIC W.). The forms of action at common law; a course of lectures by F. W. Maitland. Ed. by A. H. Chaytor and W. J. Whittaker. Cambr. 1936. Reprinted, 1962. See No. 3725.

3705 MILSOM (STROUD F. C.). 'Commentary on the actions' in *Novae Narrationes* (2998), pp. xxx–ccxiv.

3706 MILSOM (S. F. C.). 'Trespass from Henry III to Edward III'. *Law Quart. Rev.* lxxiv (1958), 195–224, 407–36, 561–90.

George D. G. Hall, 'Some early writs of trespass' [prints 16 writs], *Law Quart. Rev.* lxxiii (1957), 65–73. George E. Woodbine, 'The origin of the action of trespass', *Yale Law Jour.* xxxiii (1924), 799–816; xxxiv (1925), 343–70. See No. 3702.

3707 SUTHERLAND (DONALD W.). 'Mesne process upon personal actions in the early common law'. *Law Quart. Rev.* lxxxii (1966), 482–96.

3708 WINFIELD (PERCY). The history of conspiracy and abuse of legal procedure. Cambr. 1921.

This work is concerned mainly with offences against procedure during the Middle Ages in England.

d. Law of treason

3709 BELLAMY (J. G.). The law of treason in England in the later middle ages. Cambr. Stud. in English Legal Hist. Cambr. and N.Y. 1970.

A comprehensive study, largely from 1300 to 1485. See M. H. Keen, 'Treason trials under the law of arms', *T.R.H.S.* 5th Ser. xii (1962), 85–103.

3710 CHRIMES (STANLEY B.). 'Richard II's questions to the judges, 1387'. *Law Quart. Rev.* lxxii (1956), 365–90. D. Clementi, 'Richard II's ninth question to the judges', *E.H.R.* lxxxvi (1971), 96–113.

3711 HILL (L. M.). 'The two-witness rule in English treason trials: some comments on the emergence of procedural law'. *Amer. Jour. Legal Hist.* xii (1968), 95–111.

3712 LANDER (JACK R.). 'Attainder and forfeiture 1453–1509'. *Hist. Jour.* iv (1961), 119–51.

3713 PLUCKNETT (THEODORE F. T.). 'State trials under Richard II'. *T.R.H.S.* 5th Ser. ii (1952), 159–71.

3714 REZNECK (SAMUEL). 'Constructive treason by words in the fifteenth century'. *A.H.R.* xxxiii (1927–8), 544–52. Idem, 'The early history of parliamentary declaration of treason'. *E.H.R.* xlii (1927), 497–513.

3715 ROGERS (ALAN). 'Parliamentary appeals for treason in the reign of Richard II'. *Amer. Jour. Legal Hist.* viii (1964), 95–124.

3716 ROSS (CHARLES D.). 'Forfeiture for treason in the reign of Richard II'. *E.H.R.* lxxi (1956), 560–75.

> Criticizes Maude Clarke's argument in 'Forfeiture and treason in 1388' (No. 1464).

3717 THORNLEY (ISOBEL D.). 'Treason by words in the fifteenth century'. *E.H.R.* xxxii (1917), 556–61.

e. Equity

Refer to O. W. Holmes and L. O. Pike in *Select essays* (No. 1246), ii. 705–21 and 722–36; to Pike's introduction (pp. xci–cxi) to his edition of the Year Book 12–13 Edw. III (No. 3649); and to introductions to Selden Society series as indexed in Kiralfy-Jones, *Guide* (No. 195); and to G. O. Sayles, *King's Bench* (No. 3510).

3718 ADAMS (GEORGE B.). 'The origin and continuation of English equity' in his *Council and Courts* (No. 3659), pp. 179–213.

3719 AVERY (MARGARET E.). 'The history of the equitable jurisdiction of chancery before 1460'. *B.I.H.R.* xlii (1969), 129–44. Idem, 'An evaluation of the effectiveness of the court of chancery under the Lancastrian kings'. *Law Quart. Rev.* lxxvii (1970), 84–97.

3720 BARBOUR (WILLARD T.). The history of contract in early English equity. Oxford Stud. in Social and Legal Hist. iv. Oxf. 1914.

> Pt. i is on contract in the common law; pt. ii on contract in equity. An appendix of cases, pp. 172–234, cites petitions to the chancellor 1431–81. See also W. T. Barbour 'Some aspects of fifteenth century chancery', *Harvard Law Rev.* xxxi (1918), 834–59.

3721 HARGREAVES (A. D.). 'Equity and the Latin side of chancery'. *Law Quart. Rev.* lxviii (1952), 481–99.

3722 HAZELTINE (HAROLD D.). 'The early history of English equity', in *Essays in Legal History*, edited by Paul Vinogradoff (Oxf. 1913), pp. 261–85.

3723 KEIGWIN (CHARLES A.). 'The origin of equity'. *Georgetown Law Jour.* xviii (1930), 15–35, 92–119, 215–40, 299–326; xix (1931), 48–65, 165–84.

3724 KERLY (DUNCAN M.). An historical sketch of the equitable jurisdiction of the court of chancery. Cambr. 1890.

3725 MAITLAND (FREDERIC W.). Equity: a course of lectures. Ed. by A. H. Chaytor and W. J. Whittaker; revised by John Brunyate. Cambr. 1936.

These lectures, together with those on forms of actions (No. 3704), were first published in a single volume by Chaytor and Whittaker in 1909.

3726 PALGRAVE (FRANCIS). 'Origin of equitable jurisdiction'. *Quarterly Rev.* xxxii (1825), 92–125. Reprinted in his *Collected works* (Cambr. 1922), ix. 243–78.

3727 SPENCE (GEORGE). The equitable jurisdiction of the court of chancery. 2 vols. Lond. 1846–9; Philadelphia. 1846–50.

On the value of this elaborate work on the court of chancery, see Maitland, *Collected Papers* (No. 1482), ii. 6.

3728 TREATISE OF THE MAISTERS OF THE CHAUNCERIE in Francis Hargrave's *Collection of Tracts relative to the Law of England* (Dublin and Lond. 1787), i. 291–319.

6. *The County Court*

The county court comprised a court for civil pleas whose proceedings were enrolled by the sheriff and a court for pleas of the Crown whose proceedings were enrolled by both the sheriff and the coroners. Only the coroners' rolls were considered to be 'of record'. On these subjects see especially Hunnisett (No. 3735) and Plucknett (No. 3741). Some cases from the county court were taken up to the courts at Westminster; hence some transcriptions or extracts from the county court records were entered into the *curia regis* rolls (No. 3485). General works on county or local administration often treat of the county court. A list of sheriffs for England and Wales, from the earliest times to 1831 is provided in *P.R.O. Lists and indexes* (No. 955). For summary, see *V.C.H. Wilts.* (No. 1529), v. 1–43.

3729 CAM (HELEN M.). Studies in the hundred rolls: some aspects of thirteenth century administration. Oxf. Stud. in Soc. and Legal Hist. vi. 1921.

3730 CAM (HELEN M.). The hundred and the hundred rolls: an outline of local government in medieval England. Antiquary Books. Lond. 1930.

3731 CAM (HELEN M.). 'Shire officials: coroners, constables, bailiffs'. *English Government at work* (No. 3836), iii. 143–83.

See also her numerous papers in her *Lawfinders* (No. 1459), her *Liberties and communities* (No. 1460), and her 'An east-Anglian shire-moot of Stephen's reign, 1148–53', *E.H.R.* xxxix (1924), 568–71.

3732 CRONNE (HENRY A.). 'The office of local justiciar in England under the Norman kings'. *Univ. Birmingham Hist. Jour.* vi (1958), 18–38.

3733 DOCUMENTS ILLUSTRATING THE OFFICE OF SACRABAR in D. M. Stenton, *English justice* (No. 3681), pp. 124–37.

See also J. M. Kaye, 'The sacrabar', *E.H.R.* lxxxiii (1968), 744–58.

3734 HENRY (ROBERT L.). Contracts in the local courts of medieval England. Lond. and N.Y. 1926.

3735 HUNNISETT (ROY F.). The medieval coroner. Cambridge Stud. in English Legal Hist. Cambr. 1961.

This exemplary study followed a series of articles by the same author: 'An early coroner's roll (1229)', *B.I.H.R.* xxx (1957), 225–31; 'The origin of the office of coroner', *T.R.H.S.* 5th ser. viii (1958), 85–104; 'Pleas of the crown and the coroner', *B.I.H.R.* xxxii (1959), 117–37; 'The medieval coroners' rolls', *Amer. Jour. Legal Hist.* iii (1959), 95–124, 205–21, 324–59; *Bedfordshire coroners' rolls*, Beds. Hist. Rec. Soc. xli (1961).

3736 JENKINSON (HILARY). 'Plea rolls of the medieval county courts'. *Cambridge Hist. Jour.* i (1923), 103–7.

This article demonstrated that contrary to previous opinion the county court kept records. See No. 3741.

3737 LAPSLEY (GAILLARD T.). 'The court, record and roll of the county in the thirteenth century'. *Law Quart. Rev.* li (1935), 299–325.

Cf. S. E. Thorne, 'Notes on courts of record in England', *West Virginia Law Quart.* xl (1934), 347–59.

3738 MAITLAND (FREDERIC W.). 'The suitors of the county court'. *E.H.R.* iii (1888), 417–21; reprinted in *Collected Papers* (No. 1482), i. 458–66, and in Schuyler's *Selections* (No. 1482), pp. 188–97.

Maitland contended that not all freeholders were bound to attend the court, but only those who owed suit by the terms of their tenure. On this general subject, see Round's paper in *Archaeol. Rev.* ii (1888), 66–9; Lapsley's article on Buzones in *E.H.R.* xlvii (1932), 177–93, 545–67, and in *Crown, community*, etc. (No. 1478); and Cam, 'Suitors and scabini' in No. 1462.

3739 MORRIS (WILLIAM A.). The early English county court: an historical treatise with illustrative documents. Univ. California Pubns. in Hist. xiv, pt. ii. Berkeley. 1926.

See also Morris, *Frankpledge System* (No. 1254). Flower in Introduction to *Curia Regis Rolls* (No. 3664), pp. 61–91, treats county and hundred and other local courts.

3740 MORRIS (WILLIAM A.). The mediaeval English sheriff to 1300. Univ. Manchester Pubns. Hist. Ser. xlvi. Manchester. 1927. Reprinted.

Consult Morris on sheriffs in *English Government at Work* (No. 3836), ii. 41–108.

3741 PLUCKNETT (THEODORE F. T.). 'New light on the old county court'. *Harvard Law Rev.* xlii (1928–9), 639–75.

Plucknett's study stems from Jenkinson's article (No. 3736). For a critical review see G. E. Woodbine, 'County court rolls and county court records', *Harvard Law Rev.* xliii (1929–30), 1083–1110; and Plucknett's rejoinder in ibid., pp. 1111–18.

3472 PUTNAM (BERTHA H.). Early treatises on the practices of the justices of the peace in the fifteenth and sixteenth centuries. Oxf. Stud. in Social-Legal Hist. Oxf. 1924. Idem, 'The transformation of the keepers of the peace into the justices of the peace, 1327–80'. *T.R.H.S.* 4th Ser. xii (1929), 19–48. Idem, 'Shire officials: keepers of the peace and justice of the peace', in *English Government at work* (No. 3836), iii. 185–217. Idem, 'Early records of the justices of the peace, 1359–1414'. *E.H.R.* xxviii (1913), 321–30.

3743   ROGERS (ALAN). 'The Lincolnshire county court in the fifteenth century'. *Lincolnshire Hist.–Archaeol. Soc.* i, no. 3 (1968), 167–79; no. 4 (1969), 33–55.

3744   SIMPSON (H. B.). 'The office of constable'. *E.H.R.* x (1895), 625–41.

3745   STEWART-BROWN (RONALD). The serjeants of the peace in medieval England and Wales. Univ. Manchester Pubns. Hist. Ser. lxxi. Manchester. 1936.

> Deals with police officers in Cheshire, Lancashire, Shropshire and Wales. Prints documents.

3746   TAYLOR (MARY M.). 'Justices of assize', in *English Government at work* (No. 3836), iii. 219–57.

3746A   TEMPLEMAN (GEOFFREY). The sheriffs of Warwickshire in the thirteenth century. Dugdale Soc. Occasional Papers, no. 7. Oxf. 1948.

3747   WELLINGTON (RICHARD H.). The king's coroner, a collection of statutes relating to the office, with a short history of the same. 2 vols. Lond. 1905–6.

3748   WHITE (GEOFFREY H.). 'Constables under Norman kings'. *Genealogist.* New Ser. xxxviii (1922), 113–27.

E. CHANCERY ENROLMENTS AND RECORDS

1. *Introductory Comments*

The records of the chancery fall basically into two groups: files and enrolments. The files are formed from individual documents which have been classified into various collections. The enrolments comprise (*a*) copies of documents as they issued from the chancery in various classifications, such as letters patent, letters close, charters, or (*b*) contemporary accounts of proceedings in the chancery or elsewhere.

The rolls of the chancery were formed by sewing the separate membranes end to end into one continuous strip, which was then rolled up; whereas the membranes of the plea rolls and most of the exchequer records were fastened by stitching together the tops of each membrane. The earliest chancery enrolments come from the reign of John and there is no evidence that the practice of enrolment had been adopted in the chancery before this.

Most of the records examined in this section are chancery enrolments of group (*a*). The enrolments of accounts of legal proceedings are consigned to the section on courts. . . . The enrolled copies of documents relate to a great variety of transactions, falling under the supervision of the Chancellor. That officer 'as

Keeper of the Great Seal supervised the drafting of charters, letters patent, letters close, commissions, treaties and other expressions of the royal will that issued under that seal'. The collections or series of documents considered in this section are:

1. Charters, letters patent, and letters close, which form the most valuable of the chancery enrolments. These three series contain royal grants of lands, offices, privileges, and the like to individuals or communities, mandates to royal officers, etc.; the patent and close rolls also comprise truces, treaties, diplomatic correspondence, and documents concerning the revenue, judicature, and other branches of the English government. Royal charters and letters patent, although they often resemble each other as to their contents, are distinguished from each other as regards their form. The royal charters were the most solemn form of chancery instrument and were addressed 'To the archbishops, bishops, abbots, priors, earls, barons, etc.' and were executed in the presence of various witnesses; whereas letters patent were addressed 'To all to whom these present shall come' and were often witnessed by the king himself (*teste meipso*). Letters patent were so called because they were delivered open, with the Great Seal pendent at the bottom; in this respect they do not differ from charters. Letters close were mainly royal mandates addressed to one individual or more; therefore they were closed and sealed on the outside.

In addition to the charters enrolled on the charter rolls, the charters of confirmation or *inspeximus* of previous grants may be enrolled (*a*) before 1 Richard III on charter or patent rolls; (*b*) on confirmation rolls 1 Richard III–1 Charles I (Nos. 3750, 3758, 3770) which recite in full and confirm older grants, some of them presumably as old as the seventh century, and (*c*) on the rolls of Cartae Antiquae (Nos. 3750, 3759) which comprise chancery transcripts of royal and other charters of various dates from Ethelbert of Kent to Edward I. The entries on Cartae Antiquae rolls are probably copies of charters brought to the chancery in the twelfth and thirteenth centuries for exemplification and enrolment. Many of the charters recorded here can be shown to be spurious (1963 *P.R.O. Guide*, p. 15).

2. The Fine Rolls, 1 John–23 Charles I 'take their name from the enrolment on them of fines or payments made for writs, grants, licences, pardons and exemptions of various kinds'. The payments were made for documents issued under the Great Seal in the form of letters patent and of letters close for grants and confirmations of liberties and franchises of various kinds, for exemptions from tolls, for grants of wardships and marriages, for pardons, for the expedition of justice, and many other matters. As entries of payments made to the king by way of oblation, these rolls were at first called oblate rolls; but the name fell into disuse after the reign of John. The Fine Rolls not only provide a source of large historical and genealogical importance; they also give the impression that the payments, enrolled thereon, constituted a great source of wealth to the Crown (1963 *P.R.O. Guide*, p. 19; Madox (No. 3250), chaps. xi–xiii).

3. Liberate Rolls, 2 John–14 Henry VI, contain copies of writs issued by the chancery under the Great Seal, directing the exchequer to 'deliver' or pay out of the treasury sums of money for salaries and other expenses of the Crown. The use of writs in this class declined, so that 'towards the end of the reign of

Edward III they [the rolls] cease to be made up for each separate year and from Richard II onward there is only one roll for each reign' (1963 *P.R.O. Guide*, p. 20).

4. Ancient Correspondence, Henry II–Henry VII, is a collection of miscellaneous documents mostly of the thirteenth and fourteenth centuries drawn from the files of various offices and dealing with both foreign and domestic business. The former collection of royal letters, 'Litterae Regum', forms the nucleus of this class, in which some private papers, e.g. Cely Papers, can be found. See Nos. 3752, 3782, 5330. Some examples, cited to illustrate particular points, are printed in Sayles, *Select cases in King's Bench* (No. 3510).

5. Diplomatic Correspondence is included in several series of rolls. The Treaty Rolls, 19 Henry III–26 Charles II, among which are now included rolls formerly classified as Almain Rolls and French Rolls, contain much more than texts of treaties. They also comprise 'documents concerning the administration of the possessions of the English kings in France, except Gascony; numerous references to the administration of the Channel Islands; documents of military and commercial importance, etc.' (1963 *P.R.O. Guide*, p. 26). Special series of documents are the Gascon Rolls, 38 Henry III–7 Edward IV; the Norman Rolls, 2–6 John, 5–10 Henry V; the Roman Rolls, 34 Edward I–31 Edward III, chiefly letters to popes and cardinals of which many are printed in Rymer (No. 3765); and Scotch Rolls, 19 Edward I–7 Henry VIII (No. 3791).

An excellent account of the beginnings of the chancery rolls is given by H. G. Richardson in his introduction to the *Memoranda Roll of 1 John*, Pipe Roll Soc. Pubn. (No. 3215).

2. General Rolls, Registers, etc. for England

See Lists and Indexes (No. 955), especially vol. xxvii.

3749 ANCIENT CHARTERS, ROYAL AND PRIVATE, PRIOR TO 1200 (1095–1200). Ed. by J. H. Round. Pipe Roll Soc. x. Lond. 1888.

Taken from the P.R.O., but not from the rolls known as the *cartae antiquae*, for which see Nos. 3750, 3759.

3750 AYLOFFE (JOSEPH). Calendars of the ancient charters (*cartae antiquae*) and of the Welsh and Scottish rolls. Lond. 1774.

For an earlier edition, see No. 946. There is a table of references to charters contained in the *cartae antiquae* and in the confirmation rolls, from Æthelbert of Kent to James I, in the *Deputy keeper's reports*, xxvii (1866), 30–47. See, in general, No. 3759.

3751 BISHOP (TERENCE A. M.). Scriptores regis: facsimiles to identify and illustrate the hands of the royal scribes in original charters of Henry I, Stephen, and Henry II. Oxf. 1961.

A valuable introduction on the twelfth-century chancery is followed by a list of charters and documents, of which originals existed within the past half-century, and by plates of facsimiles.

3752 CALENDAR OF ANCIENT CORRESPONDENCE among the miscellaneous documents of the ancient treasury of the receipt of the exchequer (32 Henry III–17 Edward II). *Deputy Keeper's Reports*, viii (1847), app. ii, 180–4. (A now obsolete class of royal letters. See Nos. 3775, 3784.)

3753 CALENDAR OF CHANCERY ROLLS, VARIOUS, 1277–1326. H.M.S.O. Lond. 1912.

Pp. 1–156, Supplementary Close Rolls, 1277–1326.
Pp. 157–362, Welsh Rolls, 1277–94.
Pp. 363–99, Scutage Rolls, 1285–1324.
The Welsh Rolls 5–9 Edward I (1277–80) were privately printed in full by Sir Thomas Phillipps (No. 3787). For Scutage Rolls, see No. 3143.

3754 CALENDAR OF CHANCERY WARRANTS (Privy seals), 1244–1326. H.M.S.O. Lond. 1927.

See Pierre Chaplais, 'Some private letters of Edward I', *E.H.R.* lxxvii (1962), 79–86.

3755 CALENDAR OF DIPLOMATIC DOCUMENTS formerly in the treasury of the receipt of the exchequer, the chapter house, Westminster (1101–1624). *Deputy Keeper's Reports*, xlv (1885), app. i, 283–380; xlviii (1887), 561–619.

See No. 3763.

3756 CALENDAR OF INQUISITIONS MISCELLANEOUS (Chancery) preserved in the P.R.O. (Henry III–Henry V). 7 vols. H.M.S.O. Lond. 1916–68.

A calendar of the inquests which remain after those of Post mortem and Ad quod damnum had been extracted. Vol. vii is for 1399–1422.

3757 CALENDAR OF ROYAL AND OTHER LETTERS AND WRITS AND SOME FEW PATENTS (formerly) in the Wakefield Tower (Rich. I–Edw. I). *Deputy Keeper's Reports*, iv (1843), app. ii. 140–64; v (1844), app. ii. 60–96; vi (1845), app. ii. 88–115; vii (1846), app. ii. 239–76.

3758 CALENDARIUM ROTULORUM CHARTARUM (1199–1483) ET INQUISITIONUM AD QUOD DAMNUM (1307–1461). Ed. by J. Caley and R. Lemon. Rec. Comm. 1803.

This calendar is printed from a P.R.O. MS. and seems to have been compiled in the time of James I. For a list of inquisitions Ad quod damnum, 1244–85, see P.R.O. *Lists & Indexes* (No. 955), xvii and xxii. 'Inquisitions Ad quod damnum were taken, when the grant of a market, fair or other privilege was solicited, to ascertain whether such a grant would prejudice existing interests.'
For a calendar of royal charters which occur in letters of inspeximus, exemplification, or confirmation, and in chartularies in the P.R.O., see *Deputy Keeper's Reports*, xxix (1868), 7–48; xxx (1869), 197–211.

3759 CARTAE ANTIQUAE, Rolls 1–10. Ed. by Lionel Landon. Pipe Roll Soc. xvii (1939). Rolls 11–20. Ed. by J. Conway Davies. Ibid. New Ser. xxxiii (1960).

3760 (Charter Rolls). ROTULI CHARTARUM IN TURRI LONDINENSI ASSERVATI, 1199–1216. Ed. by T. D. Hardy. Rec. Comm. 1837. CALENDAR OF THE CHARTER ROLLS, 1226–1516. 6 vols. H.M.S.O. Lond. 1903–27.

For the period 1216–25, when the king was a minor, there are no Charter Rolls. Vol. i contains an appendix, pp. 284–304, for the years 1215–88. Each volume contains a list of earlier charters under letters of inspeximus.

3761 (Close Rolls). ROTULI LITTERARUM CLAUSARUM IN TURRI LONDINENSI ASSERVATI, 1204–27. Ed. by T. D. Hardy. 2 vols. Rec. Comm. 1833–44. CLOSE ROLLS OF THE REIGN OF HENRY III (1227–72). [in Latin]. 14 vols. H.M.S.O. Lond. 1902–38. CALENDAR OF THE CLOSE ROLLS (1272–1485). 45 vols. H.M.S.O. Lond. 1892–1954.

The Close Roll for 1238–9 is missing. The calendars for 1374–7, 1392–6, 1409–13, 1422–9 include also Supplementary Rolls. Portions of the Close Roll of 1215 and 1216 are printed in Pipe Roll Soc. New Ser. xxxi (1955), 127–44.

3762 DIPLOMATIC CORRESPONDENCE OF RICHARD II. Ed. by Édouard Perroy. R.H.S. Camden 3rd Ser. xlviii (1933).

3763 DIPLOMATIC DOCUMENTS (Chancery and Exchequer). Ed. by Pierre Chaplais. i (1101–1272). H.M.S.O. Lond. 1964.

Vols. ii (1307–27) and iii (1327–40) are in preparation. 'The Diplomatic Documents of the Exchequer comprise the original treaties and formal instruments delivered to English sovereigns by foreign contracting parties. Those of the Chancery may be briefly described as the extant records of the medieval "Foreign Office" for the period beginning in 1220.'

3764 (Fine Rolls). ROTULI DE OBLATIS (1, 2, 3, 9 John) ET FINIBUS (6, 7, 15, 17, 18 John) in TURRI LONDINENSI ASSERVATI. Ed. by T. D. Hardy. Rec. Comm. 1835. EXCERPTA E ROTULIS FINIUM in Turri Londinensi Asservatis, 1216–72. Ed. by Charles Roberts. 2 vols. Rec. Comm. 1835–6. CALENDAR OF THE FINE ROLLS, i–xxii (1272–1509). H.M.S.O. 1911–62.

Excerpts from the Fine Rolls for Staffordshire 1307–27, translated by George Wrottesley, Wm. Salt Arch. Soc. *Collections*, ix (1888), 119–32. A roll for 27 Henry III of fines attested by the king in Gascony is printed in *Rôles Gascons*, i (No. 3826).

3765 FOEDERA, conventiones, litterae, et cujuscunque generis acta publica inter reges Angliae et alios quosvis imperatores, reges, pontifices, principes, vel communitates (1101–1654). Ed. by Thomas Rymer; vols. xvi–xx, by Robert Sanderson. 20 vols. Lond. 1704–35; 2nd edn. by George Holmes, 17 vols. 1727–9, published by Tonson; 3rd edn. 10 vols. The Hague. 1739–45. New edn. (1069–1383), by Adam Clarke, Frederic Holbrooke, and John Caley. 4 vols. in 7 pts. Rec. Comm. 1816–69 (vol. iv printed 1833, published 1869). Syllabus of documents in Rymer's *Foedera*. By T. D. Hardy. 3 vols. H.M.S.O. Lond. 1869–85.

Vols. i–xvii (Lond. 1704–17), extending to 1625, are often called the first edition. The 'new edition' contains many municipal charters. All the editions are fully described in Hardy's valuable *Syllabus*, which also contains a good index and chronological abstract of the various editions. See also C. P. Cooper, *Account of the Public Records*, (1832), ii. 89–144. A General Introduction to the *Foedera* (pp. 72) was printed by the Record Commission in 1817, but not published; pp. 1–24 of this Introduction correspond to pp. i–xii of vol. i. of the *Foedera*, 1816. This great national work was undertaken at the public expense; Rymer (b. 1641, d. 1713) was appointed editor in 1693.

3766 (Foedera, etc.). ACTA REGIA, or an account of the treaties etc., published in Rymer's Foedera (1101–1625). Translated from the French [of Paul de Rapin de Thoyras, by Stephen Whatley]. 4 vols. Lond. 1726–7. Reprinted, 4 vols. 1731; 1 vol. 1732; 1 vol. 1733.

Rapin's abstract or abridgement of the *Foedera* was originally published in Le Clerc's *Bibliothèque Choisie* (Amsterdam), xvi (1708), 1–61; and later volumes. It is also printed in vol. x of the Hague edition of the *Foedera*, under the title, *Abrégé historique des Actes Publics d'Angleterre*.

3767 (Foedera). [Report on Rymer's Foedera: appendices, A–E. By Charles P. Cooper. Rec. Comm. 3 vols. Lond. 1836?] (Not published).

App. A. Catalogue of various MSS. relating to Great Britain in Continental libraries.
App. B. Fragments of Anglo-Saxon literature found in Continental libraries.
App. C. Documents from the archives of Hamburg, Munich, etc.
App. D. Inventories of documents relating to Great Britain in the national archives of France.
App. E. A chronological catalogue of the materials transcribed for the new edition of the *Foedera*. This valuable work was not completed or published, but copies of the portions in print were distributed by the Master of the Rolls in 1869.

3768 GRANTS, ETC. FROM THE CROWN DURING THE REIGN OF EDWARD V, from the original docket book, MS. Harl. 433. Ed. by J. G. Nichols. Camden Soc. Old Ser. lx. Lond. 1854.

Mainly letters patent and close, and includes two speeches for opening parliament by John Russell, Bishop of Lincoln, Lord Chancellor.

3769 INVENTORY OF THE RECORDS IN THE TOWER. *Deputy Keeper's Reports*, ii (1841), app. ii. 1–65.

Cartae Antiquae. 1–2.
Charter, patent, and close rolls. 2–24.
Treaty Rolls. 37–45.

3770 INVENTORY OF THE RECORDS OF CHANCERY IN THE ROLLS CHAPEL (from 1 Edward V onward). App. ii. *Deputy Keeper's Reports*, iii (1842), app. ii. 135–55; iv (1843), app. ii. 99–112.

French and Scotch rolls, iii. 140–1.
Charter and patent rolls, iii. 142–8.
Close and confirmation rolls, iii. 148–51; iv. 99–107.

3771 LETTERS AND PAPERS ILLUSTRATIVE OF THE REIGNS OF RICHARD III AND HENRY VII. Ed. by James Gairdner. Rolls Ser. 2 vols. Lond. 1861–3.

Most of the documents of Richard III's reign are copies from the Harleian MSS. and deal mainly with England's foreign relations.

3772 LETTERS OF THE KINGS OF ENGLAND (Rich. I–Charles I). Ed. by J. O. Halliwell. 2 vols. Lond. 1846; reprinted, 1848.

Translations only.

3773 LETTERS OF QUEEN MARGARET of Anjou and Bishop Beckington and others, written in the reigns of Henry V and Henry VI. Ed. by Cecil Monro. Camden Soc. Old Ser. lxxxvi. 1863.

For a more valuable collection of Beckington's letters, see No. 3776.

3774 (Liberate Rolls) ROTULI DE LIBERATE AC DE MISIS ET
PRAESTITIS, REGNANTE JOHANNE. Ed. by T. D. Hardy. Rec. Comm.
1844. CALENDAR OF LIBERATE ROLLS (1226–72). 6 vols. H.M.S.O.
Lond. 1917–64.

Vol. vi (1267–72) includes Appendices 1220–67. The Record Commission edition
contains liberate rolls 2, 3, 5 John, the misae roll of 11 John, and the praestita roll of
12 John. The misae and praestita rolls are now placed with Accounts, Various, among the
Exchequer Records. The Liberate Rolls enrolled writs under the Great Seal by which
the officers of the exchequer were ordered to make payments. For the Liberate Rolls for
Staffordshire in the reign of Henry III, see Wm. Salt Arch. Soc. *Coll.* xiv (1911), 1–25.
Fragments for 2 John are printed in Pipe Roll Soc., New Ser. xxi (1943), 88–97.

Rolls for 26 Henry III and for 27 Henry III are printed in *Rôles Gascons* (No. 3826).
Cf. Edward A. Bond and Charles G. Young, 'Extracts from the Liberate rolls relative
to loans supplied by Italian merchants to the kings of England (1200–1400)', *Archaeol.*
xxviii (1840), 207–326.

3775 LIST OF ANCIENT CORRESPONDENCE OF THE CHANCERY
AND EXCHEQUER preserved in the public record office (royal letters, etc.
c. Rich. I–Hen. VII): P.R.O., Lists and indexes, no. xv. Lond. 1902; new edn.
in the press.

See a review of the *List of Ancient Correspondence* by C. V. Langlois, in *Journal des
Savants*, 1904, 380–93, 446–53; and see his paper on 'Nova Curie', in *Revue Historique*,
lxxxvii (1905), 55–79. See also No. 3784.

3776 MEMORIALS OF THE REIGN OF KING HENRY VI: Official
correspondence of Thomas Bekynton, secretary to Henry VI and Bishop of Bath
and Wells. Ed. by George Williams. 2 vols. Rolls Ser. 1872.

Contains many letters of Henry VI to continental potentates, and other documents
throwing light upon the foreign relations of England during the first half of the fifteenth
century. An English translation of the Latin text (ii. 177–248) is provided by N. H.
Nicolas in *A Journal by one of the suite of Thomas Beckington, during an embassy to negotiate a marriage between Henry VI and a daughter of the count of Armagnac, A.D. 1442*
(Lond. 1828). A French translation of the same, with notes, was published by Gustave
Brunet in *Indicateur of Bordeaux* in 1842 under the title 'Journal d'un ambassadeur
anglais à Bordeaux en 1442'.

Beckington also wrote in Latin a journal of his mission to Calais, 1439, which is
printed in *Proceedings of the Privy Council* (No. 3294), v. 334–407.

3777 ORIGINAL LETTERS ILLUSTRATIVE OF ENGLISH HIS-
TORY, including numerous royal letters (1418–1726). Ed. by Henry Ellis.
(1st Ser.) 3 vols. Lond. 1824. 2nd edn. 1825. 2nd Ser. (Henry IV–1795). 4 vols.
1827. 3rd Ser. (1074–1799). 4 vols. 1846.

3778 (Patent Rolls) ROTULI LITTERARUM PATENTIUM IN TURRI
LONDINENSI ASSERVATI (1201–16). Ed. by T. D. Hardy. Rec. Comm.
1835. PATENT ROLLS OF THE REIGN OF HENRY III (1216–32). 2 vols.
H.M.S.O. 1901–3. CALENDAR OF THE PATENT ROLLS preserved in the
P.R.O. (1232–1509). 52 vols. H.M.S.O. Lond. 1891–1916 (not consecutively).

The printed editions to 1232 are Latin transcriptions; the calendars from 1232 are
English summaries. The Patent Rolls for 1238–40 are lost. Hardy's introduction was
also printed separately under the title *A description of the Patent Rolls to which is added
an Itinerary of King John*. 1835. Note that some letters patent for 1242–3 and for 1262

are calendared in *C.P.R. 1266–72*; that some letters, attested abroad for 1286–7, are calendared in *C. Charter R. 1427–1516*; and that some for January–February 1340 and for July 1345 are calendared in *C.P.R. 1374–7*.

The series of calendars supersedes the various calendars in the *Deputy Keeper's reports* for 1865, 1879, and 1881–9, and the *Calendarium rotulorum patentium* (3 John. 23 Edw. IV) Rec. Comm. 1802, which seems to be a seventeenth-century collection which does not cover more than one fifth of the entries.

3779 REGESTA REGUM ANGLO-NORMANNORUM, 1066–1154. (Projected by Henry W. C. Davis.) 4 vols. Oxf. 1913–69.

Vol. i. 1066–1100, edited by H. W. C. Davis with the assistance of R. J. Whitwell (1913). A chronological calendar in English of charters, grants, and privileges of 487 documents; the charters are printed in their original language in the appendix. The learned introduction deals with the early chancery, the household, justices, and administration; it outlines the itinerary of William I. Errata and Addenda in vol. ii, pp. 390–413.

Vol. ii. 1100–35, edited by Charles Johnson and H. A. Cronne from the collections of the late H. W. C. Davis (1956). A continuation of the calendar of documents, numbered 488 to 1991; the charters are printed in the original Latin in the appendix; and the introduction continues the topics of vol. i. (See P. Chaplais, 'The seals and charters of Henry I', *E.H.R.* lxxv (1960), 260–75.)

Vol. iii. 1135–54, edited by H. A. Cronne and R. H. C. Davis (1968). The documents, numbered 1–1009, are printed in the original Latin in alphabetical order by beneficiaries. The introduction deals with the governments of Stephen in England, of the empress Matilda in England, and of the Dukes Geoffrey and Henry in Normandy. The itineraries of Stephen, the empress, and Geoffrey are outlined.

Vol. iv. Facsimiles of original charters and writs of King Stephen, the Empress Matilda, and Dukes Geoffrey and Henry, 1135–54 (1969).

3780 ROTULI SELECTI AD RES ANGLICAS ET HIBERNICAS SPECTANTES. Ed. by Joseph Hunter. Rec. Comm. Lond. 1834.

Contains patent roll 7 John, pp. 1–38; letters patent of discharges of debts and arrears of accounts, and patents of annuities, enrolled in the memoranda of the Irish exchequer Hen. V–12 Hen. VI, pp. 39–103.

3781 ROYAL AND HISTORICAL LETTERS DURING THE REIGN OF HENRY IV. Ed. by F. C. Hingeston. Vol. i, 1399–1404. Rolls Ser. Lond. 1860. Vol. ii, 1405–13 and index to both volumes, printed in 1864, issued with amendments. H.M.S.O. 1965.

These documents, taken mainly from the Cottonian and Harleian MSS., relate to the affairs of Scotland, Wales, Ireland, France, and other countries.

3782 ROYAL AND OTHER HISTORICAL LETTERS ILLUSTRATIVE OF THE REIGN OF HENRY III, from the originals in the public record office. Ed. by W. W. Shirley. Rolls Ser. 2 vols. Lond. 1862–6.

Made up of 'litterae regum', or 'ancient correspondence', together with some letters taken from the patent and close rolls.

3783 TREATY ROLLS, preserved in the P.R.O. vol. i (1235–1325). Ed. by Pierre Chaplais. H.M.S.O. Lond. 1956; vol. ii (1337–9). Ed. by J. Ferguson. 1972.

Documents already printed in Rymer (No. 3765) are here calendared; others are given *in extenso*. Rolls formerly classified as French Rolls in the P.R.O. are now called Treaty Rolls. For some of them see Calendar of French Rolls (1 Henry V–49 Henry VI) in *Deputy Keeper's Reports*, xliv (1883), 545–638; and xlviii (1887), 217–450.

3. *Records for Wales, Scotland, Ireland, Channel Isles*

WALES

The printed sources for the history of Wales are listed in the *Bibliography of the History of Wales* and its supplements; and in R. Ian Jack, *Medieval Wales* (No. 22). Relatively few of the entries there are repeated in the present volume. Current bibliography can be followed in the annual issues of *Bibliotheca Celtica* (No. 110). For the sources which are catalogued in this volume, reference should be made to the index below under 'Wales: records'. Important collections of correspondence, charters, and similar documents are enumerated herewith.

3784 CALENDAR OF ANCIENT CORRESPONDENCE CONCERNING WALES. Ed. by J. Goronwy Edwards. Board of Celtic Stud. Hist.–Law–Ser. no. 2. Cardiff. 1935.

3784A CALENDAR OF THE PUBLIC DOCUMENTS RELATING TO PEMBROKESHIRE. Ed. by Henry Owen. Cymmrodorion Record Ser. 3 vols. Lond. 1914–18.

> George Owen of Henllys, The description of Penbrokshire (*sic*), ed. by Henry Owen. Cymmrodorion Record Ser. 4 vols. Lond. 1902–36.

3785 CARTAE ET ALIA MUNIMENTA QUAE AD DOMINIUM DE GLAMORGAN (new edn., GLAMORGANCIA) PERTINENT. Ed. by George Thomas Clark. 4 vols. Dowlais, etc. 1885–93. New edn. by Godfrey L. Clark. 6 vols. Cardiff. 1910.

> Contains charters, extents, inquests *post mortem*, pleas, etc. A.D. 441–1721; in all there are 1456 documents.

3785A CRONICA DE WALLIA (1190–1266) AND OTHER DOCUMENTS FROM EXETER CATHEDRAL LIBRARY MS. 3514. By Thomas Jones. *B.B.C.S.* xii (1948), 27–44.

> See J. Beverley Smith, ibid. xx (1963), 261–82.

3786 LITTERE WALLIE, preserved in Liber A in the Public Record Office. Ed. by J. Goronwy Edwards. Board of Celtic Stud. Hist.–Law–Ser. no. 5. Cardiff. 1940.

3786A ORIGINAL DOCUMENTS. *Archaeol. Camb.* 4th Ser. viii supplement (1877).

> Accounts relating to Beaumaris castle, Edw. II–Edw. III: pp. xviii–lxxii.
> Glamorganshire charters (relating to the family of Carne of Nash, Edw. I–1558, etc.): pp. lxxiii–lxxxvi and clxxv–cxci.
> Roll of fealty on the accession of the Black Prince to the principality of Wales (ministers' accounts 16–17 Edw. III): pp. cxlviii–clxxv.

3786B ORIGINAL DOCUMENTS. *Archaeol. Camb.* 4th Ser. x supplement (1879).

> Charters relating to Glamorgan county, Hen. I–Hen. VII: pp. xv–xxvi.
> Charters (early town charters of Wales): pp. xxvi–xlvi.
> Charters relating to St. John's priory, Carmarthen: pp. xlvi–li.
> Temporalities of the bishopric of St. Asaph, 19–32 Edw. III: pp. lxiii–lxxii.

3787 ROTULUS WALLIAE, or transactions between Edward I and Llewellyn, the last prince of Wales [5–9 Edw. I. ed. Thomas Phillipps] pt. i. Cheltenham. 1865.

For a calendar of Welsh rolls, 1277–94, see No. 3753.

3787A WELSH RECORDS IN PARIS. Ed. by T. Matthews. Carmarthen. 1910.

Contains letters of Owen Glendower, 1401–6; bulls of Urban IV (translations only), etc.

SCOTLAND
See Nos. 1089 A–B

3788 ANGLO-SCOTTISH RELATIONS 1174–1328: some selected documents. Ed. and trans. by E. L. G. Stones. Medieval Texts. Lond. 1965. Reprinted.

3789 CALENDAR OF DOCUMENTS RELATING TO SCOTLAND preserved in the public record office, London [1108–1509]. Ed. by Joseph Bain. 4 vols. Scottish Record Pubns. H.M. Register House. Edin. 1881–8.

A valuable calendar of documents in the patent, charter, close, and plea rolls, etc.
Cf. E. L. G. Stones, 'Joseph Bain (1826–1911) and the origin of the calendar of documents relating to Scotland', *Archives*, vi, No. 30 (1963), 78–84. The Kraus reprint includes vol. v (Supplementary).

3790 DOCUMENTS AND RECORDS ILLUSTRATING THE HISTORY OF SCOTLAND and the transactions between the crowns of Scotland and England (21 Hen. III–35 Edw. I). Ed. by Francis Palgrave. Vol. i. Rec. Comm. Lond. 1837.

The elaborate introduction deals with the history of the relations of Scotland to England.

3791 DOCUMENTS ILLUSTRATIVE OF THE HISTORY OF SCOTLAND, 1286–1306. Ed. by Joseph Stevenson. 2 vols. Scottish Record Pubns. H.M. Register House. Edin. 1870.

See also *Documents Illustrative of Sir William Wallace, his Life and Times* (temp. Edw. I). Ed. by Joseph Stevenson. Maitland Club. Edin. 1841.

3792 INSTRUMENTA PUBLICA SIVE PROCESSUS SUPER FIDELITATIBUS ET HOMAGIIS SCOTORUM DOMINO REGI ANGLIAE FACTIS, 1291–6. Ed. by Thomas Thomson. Bannatyne Club. Edin. 1834.

Title on the cover, The Ragman Rolls. Contains documents concerning the succession to the Scottish crown and concerning the English claim of feudal superiority over Scotland. Cf. Rymer's *Foedera*, (1816), i. 762–84; H. T. Riley's edition of *Rishanger* (No. 2948), pp. 233–368; and Stones (No. 3788).

3793 LIST OF DIPLOMATIC DOCUMENTS. SCOTTISH DOCUMENTS AND PAPAL BULLS. *P.R.O. Lists and Indexes*, xliv. H.M.S.O. Lond. 1923.

3794 REGESTA REGUM SCOTTORUM, Vol. 1. The Acts of Malcolm IV (1153–65). Ed. by G. W. S. Barrow. Edin. 1960. Vol. 2. The Acts of William I (1165–1214). Ed. by G. W. S. Barrow. Edin. 1971.

3795 ROTULI SCOTIAE in turri Londinensi et in domo Westmonasteriensi asservati, 1291–1516. Ed. by D. Macpherson and others. 2 vols. Rec. Comm. 1814–19. A transcript of documents illustrating political transactions between England and Scotland.

See E. L. G. Stones, 'An addition to the "Rotuli Scotiae" ', *Scot. H.R.* xxlx (1950), 23–51 (A Scottish roll of 2 Edward III).

3796 TRACTS RELATING TO THE ENGLISH CLAIMS, 1301 (extracts), in W. F. Skene's *Chronicles of the Picts and Scots.* Edin. 1867. Pp. 216–84.

IRELAND

See Nos. 1010, 3392; and the index under 'Ireland, Records'. J. Otway-Ruthven, 'The Medieval Irish chancery' in *Album Helen Maud Cam* (No. 3366).

3797 CALENDAR OF DOCUMENTS RELATING TO IRELAND [1171–1307]. Ed. by H. S. Sweetman. 5 vols. H.M.S.O. Lond. 1875–86.

Abstracts of letters patent and close, and of other documents: See G. J. Hand, 'Materials used in Calendar of Documents relating to Ireland', *Irish Hist. Stud.* xii (1960), 99–104.

3798 CHARTAE, PRIVILEGIA, ET IMMUNITATES: TRANSCRIPTS OF CHARTERS AND PRIVILEGES TO CITIES, TOWNS, ABBEYS, etc. 1171–1395. Irish Record Comm. (1829–30). Dublin. 1889.

Particularly valuable for the study of municipal history, it contains letters patent and close, bulls, etc. This work was not completed.

3799 LIBER MUNERUM PUBLICORUM HIBERNIAE. Ed. by Rowley Lascelles. [Not completed: planned by the Irish Record Comm., printed 1822–30: and issued from the Rolls House. 2 vols. Lond. 1852.]

Vol. i, pt. iv, pp. 1–147, contains patents of office, letters patent and close, etc. 1181–1653; taken from Rymer's *Foedera*, Prynne's *Animadversions on Coke's Fourth Institute*, etc. There is an index of the Liber Munerum in *Deputy Keeper's Reports, Ireland* 1877, ix. 21–58.

3800 ROTULORUM PATENTIUM ET CLAUSARUM CANCEL-LARIAE HIBERNIAE CALENDARIUM [Ed. by Edward Tresham] vol. i, pt. i. Hen. II–Hen. VII. Irish Record Comm. Dublin. 1828.

A calendar of charters, letters patent, statutes, inquisitions, etc. See also No. 3321.

3801 UNPUBLISHED LETTERS FROM RICHARD II IN IRELAND 1394–5. *Royal Irish Acad. Procs.* xxxvii (1927), Sect. C. 276–303.

CHANNEL ISLES

3802 ANCIENT PETITIONS OF THE CHANCERY AND THE EX-CHEQUER, ayant trait aux Isles de la Manche. (Henry III–1454.) Trans. by E. T. Nicolle. Société Jersiaise. Saint-Hélier. 1902.

3802A CARTULAIRE DES ÎLES NORMANDES: Recueil de documents concernant l'histoire de ces Îles. Société Jersiaise. Jersey. 1918–24.

4. *Continental Affairs: Chancery and Foreign Documents*

FRANCE

The rolls in the P.R.O. formerly classified as French Rolls are now entitled Treaty Rolls, for which see No. 3783. The Gascon Rolls proper begin at 38 Henry III and extend to 7 Edward IV. The rolls called Gascon Rolls for 26–38 Henry III were drawn from various classes of Chancery Rolls. The Norman Rolls contain documents under the Great Seal when Normandy was under the dominion of the English crown; they cover 2–6 John and 5–10 Henry V. There is a significant group of documents, 1418–63, in the appendix to *Chronique du Mont-Saint-Michel* (No. 2846); and *pièces justificatives* are printed in the Viard-Déprez edition of *Chronique de Jean le Bel* (No. 2916).

3803 ACTES CONCERNANT LES RAPPORTS ENTRE LES PAYS-BAS ET LA GRANDE-BRETAGNE de 1293 à 1468, conservés au château de Mariemont. Ed. by Paul Bonenfant. *Bulletin Comm. Royale d'Histoire*, cix (1944), 51–125.

3803A ACTES DE LA CHANCELLERIE D'HENRI VI concernant la Normandie sous la domination anglaise [1422–35]. Ed. by Paul Le Cacheux. Société de l'histoire de Normandie. 2 vols. Paris. 1907–8.

3804 BOCK (FRIEDRICH). 'Some new documents illustrating the early years of the hundred years war (1353–1356)'. *B.J.R.L.* xv (1931), 60–83.

They relate to negotiations on Brittany and Guienne.

3805 BROOME (DOROTHY M.). The ransom of John II, king of France, 1360–1370. Camden 3rd Ser. xxxvii (1926). *Camden Miscellany*, xiv, no. 4.

See also No. 3809.

3806 CALENDAR OF DOCUMENTS PRESERVED IN FRANCE illustrative of the history of Great Britain and Ireland. Ed. by J. H. Round. Vol. i, A.D. 918–1206. Rolls Ser. Lond. 1899.

A calendar of royal charters, private deeds, etc.; most of them are grants to religious houses. See also a calendar of Richard I's charters, in Cartellieri's *Philipp II, August* (Leipzig, 1899–1910), ii. 288–301; iii. 217–33; a calendar of those issued by John as count of Mortain, 1192–8; ibid. iii. 234–5; and Delisle, *Recueil des actes de Henri II* (No. 3823).

3807 CALENDAR OF FRENCH ROLLS (1 Hen. IV–49 Hen. VI). *Deputy Keeper's Reports*, xliv (1883), 543–638; xlviii (1887), 217–450.

3808 CARTE (THOMAS). Catalogue des rolles gascons, normans et françois. Conservés dans les archives de la Tour de Londres. 2 vols. Paris and Lond. 1743.

3809 CHAPLAIS (PIERRE). Some documents relating to the fulfilment and interpretation of the Treaty of Bretigny (1361–9). Camden 3rd Ser. lxxx (1952), *Camden Miscellany*, xix, no. 1.

E. Perroy, 'Charles V et le traité de Brétigny', *Le Moyen Âge*, xxix (1928), 256–81.

3810 CHAPLAIS (PIERRE). The War of Saint-Sardos (1323–1325). Gascon correspondence and diplomatic documents. Camden 3rd Ser. lxxxvii (1954).

3811 COLLECTION GÉNÉRALE DES DOCUMENTS FRANÇAIS QUI SE TROUVENT EN ANGLETERRE. Ed. by Jules Delpit. Paris. 1847.

3812 CUTTINO (GEORGE P.). The Gascon calendar of 1322, edited from Miscellaneous Books. Exch. T.R. 187. Camden 3rd Ser. lxx (1949).

A calendar of documents relating to Aquitaine going back to 1197 but largely of the reigns of Edward I and II. See also G. P. Cuttino, 'An unidentified gascon register (1319) (from Cotton MS. Julius E i)', *E.H.R.* liv (1939), 293–9; idem, 'A memorandum book of Elias Joneston' (on documents in Joneston's custody in 1317 as keeper as processes relating to Aquitaine), *Speculum*, xvii (1942), 74–85; idem, 'Another memorandum book of Elias Joneston', *E.H.R.* lxiii (1948), 90–103.

3812A DOCUMENTS CONCERNANT L'ANGLETERRE ET L'ÉCOSSE, anciennement conservés à la chambre des comptes de Lille (xii–xiv cent). By Pierre Chaplais. *Revue du Nord*, xxxviii (1956), 185–210.

3813 DOCUMENTS INÉDITS SUR L'INVASION ANGLAISE ET LES ÉTATS AU TEMPS DE PHILIPPE VI ET JEAN LE BON. Ed. by Adolphe A. Guesnon. *Bulletin hist. et phil. du Comité des travaux hist. et scientif.* (1897).

3813A EXTRAIT DU REGISTRE DES DONS, ETC. faits dans le duché de Normandie pendant 1418–20 par Henry V. Ed. by Charles Vautier [i.e. Crescent Guiton]. Paris. 1828.

3814 LES GRANDS TRAITÉS DE LA GUERRE DE CENT ANS (1359–1444). Ed. by E[ugène] Cosneau. Paris. 1889.

3815 LETTERS AND PAPERS ILLUSTRATIVE OF THE WARS OF THE ENGLISH IN FRANCE DURING THE REIGN OF HENRY VI [with a translation]. Ed. by Joseph Stevenson. Rolls Ser. 2 vols. in 3 pts. Lond. 1861–4.

Transcribed from various archives in England and France.

3816 LETTRES DE ROIS, REINES ET AUTRES PERSONNAGES DES COURS DE FRANCE ET D'ANGLETERRE, depuis Louis VII jusqu'à Henri IV, tirées des archives de Londres par Bréquigny. Ed. by J. J. Champollion-Figeac. Documents inédits. 2 vols. Paris. 1839–47.

Contains mandates, letters patent and close, diplomatic correspondence, etc., of English kings relating to their possessions in France, etc.

3817 LE LIVRE D'AGENAIS publié d'après le MS. Bodley 917. Ed. by George P. Cuttino in *Cahiers de l'association Marc Bloch de Toulouse: documents d'histoire méridionale*, no. 1. Toulouse. 1956.

A register of 1283 detailing the rights of the king of England in Agenais as a result of the Treaty of Amiens of 1272. Cf. J. P. Trabut-Cussac, 'Le livre d'Agenais à propos d'une édition récente', *Bib. de l'École des Chartes*, cxv (1957), 179–89.

3818 MIROT (LÉON) and DEPREZ (EUGÈNE). Les ambassades anglaises pendant la guerre de cent ans: catalogue chronologique, 1327–1450. *Bib. de l'École des Chartes*, lix (1898), 550–77; lx (1899), 177–214; lxi (1900), 20–58.

Catalogue of a series of exchequer accounts in the P.R.O., rendered by ambassadors to France.

See Alfred Larson, 'The payment of fourteenth-century English envoys', *E.H.R.* liv (1939), 403–14; and idem, 'English embassies during the Hundred Years' War', ibid. lv (1940), 423–31. Mary C. L. Salt, 'List of English embassies to France, 1272–1307', ibid. xliv (1929), 263–78.

3819 NARRATIVES OF THE EXPULSION OF THE ENGLISH FROM NORMANDY, 1449–50. Ed. by Joseph Stevenson. Rolls Ser. Lond. 1863.

De reductione Normanniae, by Robert Blondel, pp. 1–238. See No. 2798.
Le recouvrement de Normendie, par Berry, hérault du roy, pp. 239–376. See No. 2794.
Negotiations between France and England, pp. 377–514.

3820 ORIGINAL DOCUMENTS RELATING TO THE HOSTAGES OF JOHN KING OF FRANCE AND THE TREATY OF BRÉTIGNY IN 1360. Ed. by Sir George F. Duckett. Lond. 1890.

3821 PERROY (ÉDOUARD). The Anglo-French negotiations at Bruges, 1374–77. Camden Ser. lxxx (1952). *Camden Miscellany*, xix. 2.

3822 RECUEIL D'ACTES RELATIFS À L'ADMINISTRATION DES ROIS D'ANGLETERRE EN GUYENNE AU XIIIe SIÈCLE (recogniciones feodorum in Aquitania). Ed. by Charles Bémont. Documents inédits. Paris. 1914.

3823 RECUEIL DES ACTES DE HENRI II concernant les provinces françaises et les affaires de France: introduction and atlas. By Léopold Delisle. Paris. 1909. Recueil, etc.: œuvre posthume de Léopold Delisle, revue et publiée par Élie Berger. 3 vols. Paris. 1916–27.

Delisle's introduction is an important study of the diplomatic and the chronology of the documents. He contends that in 1172–3 the title Henricus rex Anglorum was replaced in royal documents by Henricus Dei gratia rex Anglorum and hence serves as a turning-point for the dating of undated royal documents. This thesis, advanced by Delisle in *Bib. École des Chartes*, lxvii (1906), 361–401, was attacked by J. H. Round in *Archaeological Jour.* lxiv (1907), 63–79; Delisle replied in *B.E.C.* lxviii (1907), 525–36; and was supported by R. L. Poole in *E.H.R.* xxiii (1908), 79–83.

Berger prints in vols. i and ii about 785 documents, mostly charters and largely drawn from Delisle's unprinted collection; and in vol. iii supplies a chronological table and an index. See also H. E. Salter, 'Two forged charters of Henry II', *E.H.R.* xxxiv (1919), 65–8; V. H. Galbraith, 'Seven charters of Henry II at Lincoln Cathedral', *Antiquaries Jour.* xii (1932), 269–79; T. A. M. Bishop, 'A chancery scribe: Stephen of Fougères', *Cambr. Hist. Jour.* x (1950), 106–7.

3824 RECUEIL DES ACTES DES DUCS DE NORMANDIE (911–1066). Ed. by Marie Fauroux, completed with index by Lucien Musset. *Mémoires de la Société des antiquaires de Normandie*, xxxvi–xxxvii. Caen. 1961–7.

3825 RICHARDSON (HENRY G.). 'Illustrations of English history in the mediaeval registers of the parlement of Paris'. *T.R.H.S.* 4th Ser. x (1927), 55–85.

3826 RÔLES GASCONS, 26–38 Henry III (1242–54). Ed. by Francisque Michel. Documents inédits. Paris. 1885. Supplement for 1254–5. Ed. by Charles Bémont. Documents inédits. 1896.

These are documents attested by Henry III in Gascony and drawn from various chancery rolls, not from rolls specifically designated as Gascon rolls. The roll for 26 Henry

III (1242), which is printed by Michel and by the Record Commission as *Rotulus Vasconiae, Henricus III* (Lond. 1836?), is in reality a Patent Roll and now is so classified, whence it is calendared in *C.P.R. 1232–47*, pp. 306–406. In like manner, the roll for 27 Henry III has been transferred to the Fine Rolls. The first Gascon Roll is for 38 Henry III; the Gascon entries therefrom has been printed by J.-P. Trabut-Cussac in *Recueil de travaux offerts à M. Clovis Brunel* (Paris, 1955), ii. 599–615.

3827 RÔLES GASCONS [39 and 44 Henry III and 2–35 Edward I]. Ed. by Charles Bémont. 3 vols. Documents inédits. Paris. 1896–1906.

Vol. i is supplement mentioned above (1896). Vol. ii gives rolls for 1273–90 (1900). Vol. iii gives rolls for 1290–1307 (1906).

Acts relative to the county of Ponthieu, which were transcribed in the Gascon Rolls, are printed in appendices.

Bémont printed a supplement as 'Un rôle gascon de lettres closes expediées par la chancellerie du Prince Édouard (1254–5)', *Bulletin philologique et historique*, Année 1915 (1916), 92–139. He also described a roll of 1286 as 'Un rôle gascon d'Édouard Ier retrouvé' (which had been misfiled under 14 Edw. II), in *Bib. de l'École des Chartes*, lxxi (1910), 219–22; and printed it in *Archives historiques de la Gironde*, xliv (1909), 31–60. These twenty-seven letters of 1286 are reprinted in the Renouard-Fawtier edition (No. 3828) along with four other letters from the reign of Edward I.

Maitland printed thirteen Gascon petitions as Appendix I to *Memoranda de parliamento* (No. 3319).

3828 RÔLES GASCONS. Rôles d'Édouard II: Ier partie (1307–17). Ed. by Yves Renouard and Robert Fawtier. Documents inédits. Paris. 1962. Published also as Gascon Rolls preserved in the Public Record Office, 1307–17. H.M.S.O. Lond. 1962.

A second volume (1317–27) is anticipated. Acts relative to the county of Ponthieu (1307–17) are printed in an appendix. See also Y. Renouard, 'Édouard II et Clément V d'après les rôles gascons', *Annales du Midi*, lxvii (1955), 119–41.

3829 RÔLES NORMANDS ET FRANÇAIS ET AUTRES PIÈCES, tirées des archives de Londres par Bréquigny. Société des antiquaires de Normandie, *Mémoires*, vol. xxiii, pt. i. Paris. 1858.

An extensive collection of documents, mainly letters patent of Henry V relating to France.

3830 ROTULI NORMANNIAE, 1200–1205, 1417–18. Ed. by T. D. Hardy. Rec. Comm. Lond. 1835. Another edition, 1417–22. Société des antiquaires de Normandie, *Mémoires*, xv. 215–90. Paris, etc. 1846. Also Rotulus Normannie, 1346–7, in *Calendar of Patent Rolls*, 1345–8, pp. 473–503. Lond. 1903. Calendar of Norman Rolls, 6–10 Henry V, in *Deputy Keeper's Reports*, xli (1880), app. i, 671–810; xlii (1881), 313–472. A fragment for 5 John in Pipe Roll Soc. New Ser. xxi (1943), 97–8.

The first roll of the series, 2 John, was misplaced; it is a Liberate or Close Roll. Pipe Roll Soc. New Ser. xxi (1943), 91–7.

3831 SANDERS (I. J.). 'The texts of the peace of Paris, 1259'. *E.H.R.* lxvi (1951), 81–97.

Pierre Chaplais, 'The making of the treaty of Paris (1259) and the royal style', *E.H.R.* lxvii (1952), 235–53; idem, 'Le Traité de Paris de 1259 et l'inféodation de la gascogne allodiale', *Le Moyen Âge*, lxi (1955), 121–38. See M. Gavrilovitch (No. 4098).

3832   TRABUT-CUSSAC (JEAN-PAUL). 'Les cartulairer gascons d'Édouard II, d'Édouard III et de Charles VII'. *Bibl. École des Chartes*, cxi (1953–4), 65–106. Idem, 'Les archives de la Gascogne anglaise (1152–1453)'. *Rev. Hist. Bordeaux*, v (1956), 69–82. Idem, 'Bordeaux dans les rôles gascons d'Édouard II, 1307–17'. *Annales du Midi*, lxxvii (1965), 83–98. Idem, 'Actes gascons dispersés émanant d'Édouard Ier d'Angleterre pendant son séjour en France (1286–9)'. *Bulletin philologique et historique*, année 1962 (1965), 63–139.

ITALY

3833   (Calendar of) STATE PAPERS AND MANUSCRIPTS existing in the archives and collections of Milan. Vol. i. 1385–1618. Ed. by A. B. Hinds. H.M.S.O. Lond. 1912.

3834   (Calendar of) STATE PAPERS AND MANUSCRIPTS relating to English affairs, existing in the archives and collections of Venice, and in other libraries of Northern Italy. Vol. i. 1202–1509. Ed. by Rawdon Brown. H.M.S.O. Lond. 1864.

NORWAY

3835   AKTSTYKKER VEDRORENDE NORGES FORBINDELSE MED DE BRITISKE ØER. Ed. by Alexander Bugge. Vol. i, A.D. 991–1323. [Diplomatarium Norvegicum, 19th Ser. pt. i.] Christiania. 1910.

> Texts (Latin) of English documents, letters, charters, accounts, etc., bearing on the relations between England and Norway.

5. *Specialized Studies on Administrative History*

In broad terms, the chancery was the centre of the royal administration. Important descriptions of the work of the chancery have already been catalogued under Diplomatic (pp. 50–3), under Seals (pp. 57–9), under Constitutional History (Nos. 1212, 1223), and under Anglo-Saxon Charters (pp. 309–10). The section on the Household Administration (pp. 479–82) includes some items germane to general administration. The works on palaeography and diplomatic by Jenkinson and Johnson (Nos. 387–8) provide examples of documents, as does the recent volume by Chaplais on royal documents (No. 3838).

For the history of the chancery the introductions to Bishop's *Scriptores regis* (No. 3751) and to Davis *et al. Regesta regum* (No. 3779), and the full-length studies of Maxwell-Lyte on the great seal (No. 3844) and of Wilkinson on the chancery under Edward III (No. 3851) are the basic works. A modern survey for all departments of government for the decade 1327–36 is entitled *The English Government at work* (No. 3836).

3836   THE ENGLISH GOVERNMENT AT WORK, 1327–1336. 3 vols. Mediaeval Academy of America. Cambr. (Mass.). 1940–50.

> Vol. i: Central and prerogative administration. Ed. by J. F. Willard and W. A. Morris.
> Vol. ii: Fiscal administration. Ed. by W. A. Morris and J. R. Strayer.
> Vol. iii: Local administration and justice. Ed. by J. F. Willard, W. A. Morris, and W. H. Dunham, Jr.

3837 BARRACLOUGH (GEOFFREY). 'The English royal chancery and the papal chancery in the reign of Henry III'. *M.I.Ö.G.* lxii (1954), 365–78.

The subtitle is 'The evidence for influence of formulae of the papal chancery on English chancery practice in the reign of Henry III'.

3838 CHAPLAIS (PIERRE). English royal documents: King John–Henry VI, 1199–1461. Oxf. 1971.

This work provides basic information, with plates, on diplomatic and seals. See also Chaplais, 'Privy seal drafts: rolls and registers, Edw. I–Edw. II', *E.H.R.* lxxiii (1958), 270–3. For English notaries see Chaplais, 'Master John de Branketre and the office of notary in chancery, 1355–1375', *Jour. Soc. Archivists*, iv, no. 3 (1971), 169–99.

3839 CUTTINO (GEORGE P.). English diplomatic administration, 1259–1339. Oxford Hist. Ser. Lond. and Oxf. 1940.*

This study deals, in part, with administrative practices in foreign relations. The appendices include three expense accounts of envoys to foreign parts, namely those of Philip Martel, Elias Joneston, and Roger Staunford, all of whom held the office of Keeper of the Processes touching the duchy of Aquitaine. For a financial account of a mission abroad, consult Cuttino, 'Bishop Langton's mission for Edward I, 1296–7', in *Studies in British history*, edited by C. W. de Kiewiet (Iowa City, 1941), pp. 147–83. See also Cuttino, 'King's clerks and the community of the realm', *Speculum*, xxix (1954), 395–409. See Kingsford in *Poole essays* (No. 1448).

3840 DIBBEN (L. B.). 'Chancellor and keeper of the seal under Henry III'. *E.H.R.* xxvii (1912), 39–51. Idem, 'Secretaries in the thirteenth and fourteenth centuries'. Ibid. xxv (1910), 430–44.

F. M. Powicke, 'The chancery in the minority of Henry III', *E.H.R.* xxiii (1908), 220–35. See A. E. Stamp in *Tait essays* (No. 1455).

3841 DICKINSON (JOYCELYNE G.). 'Blanks and blank charters in the fourteenth and fifteenth centuries'. *E.H.R.* lxvi (1951), 375–87.

3842 HASKINS (GEORGE L.). 'Charter lists in the reign of King John'. *Speculum*, xiii (1938), 319–25.

J. C. Russell, 'Charter lists again', *Speculum*, xiv (1939), 108–9; idem, 'Attestation of charters in the reign of John', ibid. xv (1940), 480–98.

3843 HUGHES (DOROTHY). A study of social and constitutional tendencies in the early years of Edward III. Lond. 1915.

3844 MAXWELL-LYTE (HENRY C.). Historical notes on the use of the great seal. H.M.S.O. Lond. 1926.

A. L. Brown, 'The authorization of letters under the great seal', *B.I.H.R.* xxxvii (1964), 125–56. See Wyon and others (No. 469), and Prescott (No. 3851).

3845 OTWAY-RUTHVEN (JOCELYN). The king's secretary and the signet office in the fifteenth century. Cambr. 1939.

3846 RICHARDSON (HENRY G.) and SAYLES (GEORGE G.). The administration of Ireland, 1172–1377. Dublin. 1963.

3847 SANDERS (GEORGE W.). Orders of the high court of chancery and statutes of the realm relating to chancery from the earliest period. 2 vols. Lond. 1845.

3848 TOUT (THOMAS F.). 'The household of the chancery and its disintegration', in *Poole essays* (No. 1448) and *Collected papers* (No. 1499).

3849 TRUEMAN (JOHN H.). 'The privy seal and the ordinances of 1311'. *Speculum*, xxxi (1956), 611–25.

3850 WEST (FRANCIS J.). Justiciarship in England, 1066–1232. Cambr. 1966. See No. 3684.

> F. J. West, 'The *curia regis* in the late twelfth and early thirteenth centuries', *Historical Stud.* vi, no. 2 (1954). R. W. Southern, 'Ranulf Flambard and the Anglo-Norman administration', *T.R.H.S.* 4th Ser. xvi (1933), 95–128; now revised in Southern, *Medieval Humanism* (Oxf. and N.Y. 1970).

3851 WILKINSON (BERTIE). The chancery under Edward III. Univ. Manchester Pubns. Hist. Ser. Manchester. 1929. Idem, 'The chancery' in *English Government at work* (No. 3836), i. 162–205.

> See Wilkinson, 'The authorization of chancery writs', *B.J.R.L.* viii (1924), 107–39; Hilda Prescott, 'The early use of Teste me ipso', *E.H.R.* xxxv (1920), 211–17; and Crump in *Poole essays* (No. 1448).

3852 WILKINSON (BERTIE). The constitutional history of England, 1216–1399, with select documents. 3 vols. Lond. and N.Y. 1948–58. Idem, The constitutional history of England in the fifteenth century. Lond. and N.Y. 1964.

> Vol. i: Politics and the constitution, 1216–1307;
> Vol. ii: Politics and the constitution, 1307–99;
> Vol. iii: Development of the constitution, 1216–1399.
>
> These volumes are largely commentaries on numerous translated documents relating to specific crises or developments; they often present controversial theses. See also Wilkinson, 'The government of England during Richard's absence on the Third Crusade', *B.J.R.L.* xxviii (1944), 485–509.

3853 WILLARD (JAMES F.). 'The dating and delivery of letters and writs in the fourteenth century'. *B.I.H.R.* x (1933), 1–11.

F. SPECIAL JURISDICTIONS

1. *Palatinate of Chester*

The palatine county of Chester was but a portion of the earldom of Chester which had been established in 1071 and came to extend among many counties in England. In 1237 Henry III purchased the rights of the coheiresses to the county of Chester and annexed it. In 1254 the king transferred the title to the county to his son, Edward. Macclesfield on the east and Overton on the west were included in the grant to Edward. The county retained its privileges and developed into a palatinate in which the king's writ did not run. On the conquest of north Wales in 1284, Edward I added the new county of Flint to the palatinate of Chester and the hundred of Macclesfield. The county-palatinate passed to Edward of Caernarvon in 1301 and to Edward of Woodstock, the Black Prince, in 1333.

The palatinate had its own administration and kept its own records, separate from the royal administration. The exchequer of Chester was a court of justice and equity as well as an office for revenue; and the chamberlain exercised broad powers, secretarial and judicial. The financial, judicial, and administrative records of the exchequer of Chester and the common law records were transferred to the Public Record Office in 1854.

For the geographical area of the palatinate, consult Lysons, *Magna Britannia* (No. 1519), iv, pt. ii. For modern narratives see the section of Local History: Cheshire, Nos. 1562–77; 1698–1702. For records and treatises in addition to those cited immediately below, see the index under 'Cheshire, records'. A full-length history of the county-palatine of Chester sponsored by the Cheshire County Council and edited by John J. Bagley is promised (No. 1570).

3854   ACCOUNTS OF THE CHAMBERLAINS AND OTHER OFFICERS OF THE COUNTY OF CHESTER, 1301–1360. Ed. by Ronald Stewart-Brown. Lancs.–Ches. Rec. Soc. lix (1910).

Besides the chamberlains' accounts, there are accounts of sheriffs, bailiffs, foresters, and escheators. The introduction is informative and scholarly as are the other writings of Stewart-Brown (see No. 1571). For the first account (1301) of the chamberlain of Chester, see No. 3084.

3855   BARRACLOUGH (GEOFFREY). 'The earldom and county palatine of Chester'. *Hist. Soc. Lancs.–Ches. Trans.* ciii (1951) (No. 1571). Reprinted Oxf. 1953.

See James W. Alexander, 'New evidence on the palatinate of Chester', *E.H.R.* lxxxv (1970), 715–29; and R. R. Davies in *McKisack essays* (No. 7223).

3856   DEPUTY KEEPER'S REPORTS (entitled 'Welsh Records').

In the Public Record Office the archives of the county-palatinate were classified as 'Welsh Records'. See R. I. Jack, *Medieval Wales* (No. 22), pp. 73–8.

(*a*) Calendar of deeds, inquisitions, and writs of dower enrolled on the plea rolls of Chester (40 Henry III–38 Henry VIII): xxvi (1865), 36–55; xxvii (1866), 94–123; xxviii (1867), 20–71; xxix (1868), 49–98; xxx (1869), 121–96.

(*b*) Calendar of fines (pedes finium), counties of Chester and Flint, Edward I: xxviii (1867), 6–19.

(*c*) Calendar of recognizance rolls of the palatinate of Chester (*c.* 1309–11 George IV): xxxvi (1875), App. ii. 1–548; xxxvii (1876), App. ii. 1–819; xxxix (1878), 1–306. These are the palatinate's chancery rolls of charters, letters patent, commissions, etc., issued under the seal of the palatinate.

(*d*) Index to inquisitions, etc. (Edward III–Charles I), counties of Chester and Flint: xxv (1864), 32–60.

(*e*) List of officers of the palatinate of Chester in the counties of Chester, Flint, and North Wales: xxxi (1870), App. 169–261.

(*f*) Report on the records of the county palatine of Chester: i (1840), 78–122. This report was compiled by W. H. Black, assistant-keeper of the public records, and is sometimes referred to by his name. For a list of the records, consult *P.R.O. Lists and Indexes* (No. 955), xl (1914).

3857   (DOMESDAY ROLL). Memoir on the Cheshire Domesday Roll. By George Ormerod. Lond. 1851.

See Ronald Stewart-Brown, 'The Domesday Roll of Cheshire', *E.H.R.* xxxvii (1922), 481–500; and *Cheshire Sheaf*, 3rd Ser. xx (1923); and xxxv (1940). This is a roll of judgments in the palatine court and exchequer at Chester from about the year 1195. It has no connection with Domesday Book.

3858 FLINTSHIRE MINISTERS' ACCOUNTS, 1301–1328. Ed. by Arthur Jones. Flintshire Hist. Soc. Pubns. iii (1913).

3859 FLINTSHIRE MINISTERS' ACCOUNTS, 1328–1353. Ed. by D. L. Evans. Flintshire Hist. Soc. Rec. Ser. ii (1929).

3860 MORRIS (RUPERT H.). Chester in the Plantagenet and Tudor periods. Chester. 1893.

Much of this volume is given over to a collection of documents relating to the city of Chester and drawn from the muniment rooms of the city of Chester.

3861 ORMEROD (GEORGE). The history of the county palatine and city of Chester. 3 vols. Lond. 1819. 2nd edn. By Thomas Helsby. 3 vols. (1875)–82.

Built around family history and manors, but contains a valuable collection of charters and other documents.

3862 REGISTER OF EDWARD THE BLACK PRINCE preserved in the Public Record Office. 4 vols. H.M.S.O. Lond. 1930–3.

A calendar of documents as follows:
Vol. i for England, Wales, Cornwall and Chester, 1346–8;
Vol. ii The white book of Cornwall, 1351–65 and 1382;
Vol. iii for the palatinate of Chester and Flint, 1351–67, and for north Wales, 1354–6;
Vol. iv for England 1351–65.
For 'the central administrative system of the Black Prince [and] the diplomatic of the Black Prince's central secretarial department' see Margaret Sharp's sections in Tout, *Administrative history* (No. 1223), v. 289–431; and appendix thereto (pp. 431–40) lists the officers of the Black Prince's household. Refer also to No. 3786A above and to Mrs. Sharp's essay in No. 1458. R. V. H. Burne, 'Cheshire under the Black Prince', *Chester Archaeol.-Hist. Soc. Jour.* xliv (1957), 1–18.

3863 WILSON (K. P.). Chester customs accounts, 1301–1566. Lancs.–Ches. Rec. Soc. cxi (1969).

Deals with the palatine customs organization in the port of Chester.

2. *Palatinate of Durham*

The county-palatine of Durham, which came to extend over much of north-east England, was presided over by the bishop of Durham. Its origin 'is a matter of extreme obscurity', the franchise of the region with extensive immunities stretches back to an unknown time. It is in the thirteenth century, however, that its judicial institutions and administrative system rapidly enlarged; and by the end of that century the title of *palatinus* was first applied to the bishop of Durham. The palatinate had its own chancery which issued writs, its own justices who could hear civil and criminal actions, its own coroners, sheriffs, mint, and market-place. 'The powers of the palatine-bishops were indeed real, yet so geographically circumscribed that any independent action on their part contrary to royal policy was unthinkable or at least impractical' (Fraser).

The chief surviving records of the palatinate are described by Lapsley (No. 3868), pp. 327–37; they were transferred to the Public Record Office in 1868–70. Some of them which were specifically related to the estates of the bishopric were claimed by the Ecclesiastical Commissioners and handed over to their custody in

1876, whence they were deposited in the Prior's Kitchen, Durham, in 1956. Although the bulk of the palatinate records remain in the Public Record Office, documents relative to the palatinate can be found in the registers of the bishops of Durham and among the extensive muniments of the dean and chapter of Durham. For these matters, refer to Davies (No. 1044).

In addition to the works mentioned immediately below, pertinent records will be found in *Boldon Book* (No. 3076), in appendix to *Scriptores Tres* (No. 5685), in *Feodarium* (No. 4738), in Bury's formulary (No. 6561). Consult also the sections on the bishopric of Durham and on Local History: Durham (pp. 226–7).

3864 BISHOP HATFIELD'S SURVEY: a record of the possessions of the see of Durham. Ed. by William Greenwell. Surtees Soc. xxxii (1857).

The survey, pp. 1–199, was compiled 1377–82; it gives a list of the tenants, with the amount of land which they held and the services belonging to each manor. The appendix, pp. 200–75, contains bailiffs' rolls of various palatine manors, *temp.* Edw. III, and a receiver's roll of Bishop Fordham, *temp.* Rich. II.

3865 DEPUTY KEEPER'S REPORTS (Durham records):

(a) Abstracts or transcripts of inquisitions post mortem, 1318–1442: xlv (1884–5), App. i 153–282; (same) 1448–?: xliv (1883), 310–542.

(b) Chancery enrolments (by bishops)
Bury–Hatfield (1333–66): xxxi (1870), App. i. 42–168;
Hatfield–Fordham (1366–88): xxxii (1871), App. i. 265–330;
Skirlaw–Langley (1388–1437): xxxiii (1872), App. i. 43–210; Neville (1438–57): xxxiv (1873), App. i. 163–264; Bothe-Dudley (1457–83): xxxv (1874), App. i. 76–156.

(c) Indexes to places and persons in Kellawe's Register (No. 3867): xxx (1869), 99–120.

(d) Inventory and lists of documents transferred from the county-palatine of Durham pursuant to warrant dated 17 November 1868: xxx (1869), 44–98.

(e) Report of T. D. Hardy on the Durham records: xvi (1855), 44–93; xxix (1868), 104–12.

3866 DURHAM UNIVERSITY. List of rentals and surveys among the records of the palatinate of Durham and bishopric estates deposited by the Church Commission in the Prior's Kitchen. Durham. 1959.

3867 REGISTRUM PALATINUM DUNELMENSE: the register of Richard de Kellawe, Bishop of Durham, 1311–16. Ed. by T. D. Hardy. 4 vols. Rolls Ser. 1873–8.

Vol. iii contains various documents, 1279–1374, including some palatinate records of the thirteenth and fourteenth centuries. For indexes, see No. 3865.

3868 LAPSLEY (GAILLARD T.). The county palatine of Durham: a study in constitutional history. N.Y. etc. 1900.

The best history; but see also the appropriate chapters in C. M. Fraser's *Bek* (No. 5689) and R. L. Storey's *Langley* (No. 5690). Lapsley, 'The problem of the north', *A.H.R.* v (1900), 440–66; reprinted in No. 1476 above. C. M. Fraser, 'Edward I of England and the regalian franchise of Durham', *Speculum*, xxxi (1956), 329–42; idem, 'Prerogative and the bishops of Durham, 1267–1376', *E.H.R.* lxxiv (1959), 467–76. Jean Scammell, 'The origin and limitations of the liberty of Durham', ibid. lxxxi (1966), 449–73. C. M. Fraser and K. Emsley, 'Law and society in Northumberland and Durham, 1290–1350', *Archaeol. Aeliana*, 4th Ser. xlvii (1969), 47–70, which shows that 'the law of England was recognized as much within the franchise of Durham as in Northumberland where the king's officers administered justice'. Idem, 'Justice in north-east England, 1256–1356', *American Jour. Legal Hist.* xv (1971), 163–85.

3. *Duchy of Lancaster*

The duchy of Lancaster was created from the earldom of Lancaster when the earl became duke in 1351. It expanded into a congeries of estates, castles, and jurisdictions in nearly every county in England and Wales. With the accession of Henry IV, the duchy was linked to the throne, but retained its independent, corporate existence as the personal property of the sovereign. It had its own seal, chancellor, justices, and muniments. The duchy of Lancaster is still the private property of the sovereign and its chancellor today is normally a member of the Government. In 1868 Queen Victoria presented the private muniments of the duchy to the nation; they were thereupon transferred to the Public Record Office. An inventory of the duchy's records is given in No. 3871 below.

The county of Lancaster, although part of the duchy, was elevated to the special status of palatinate by Edward III in 1351. It had its own seal, its own chancellor, judges and officials, and its own court with exclusive jurisdiction as the county-palatine. The records of the county-palatine were deposited in the Public Record Office in 1873. Lists of those now preserved there are printed in No. 3878. The standard history of the duchy is by Somerville (No. 3883). Consult the section on Local History: Lancaster (Nos. 1695–1707).

3869 BALDWIN (JAMES F.). 'The chancery of the duchy of Lancaster'. *B.I.H.R.* iv (1927), 129–43. Idem, 'The household administration of Henry Lacy and Thomas of Lancaster'. *E.H.R.* xlii (1927), 180–200.

The latter article includes an account of a keeper of the earl's wardrobe for 8 Edward II.

3870 CHARTERS OF THE DUCHY OF LANCASTER. Trans. and ed. William Hardy. Lond. 1845.

This edition contains the charters granted by the Crown to the earls and dukes of Lancaster, 1342–99, together with the subsequent acts of parliament relating to the management of the Lancastrian possessions as settled upon the king to 1558. For charters from 1093 to 1216, see No. 3091.

3871 DEPUTY KEEPER'S REPORTS (of the duchy of Lancaster records):

(a) Calendar of ancient charters or grants (private deeds, Henry I–5 Edward IV): xxxv (1874), App. i. 1–41; xxxvi (1875), App. i. 161–205.
(b) Calendar of the rolls of the chancery (fines, charters, letters close and patent, etc., 1355–1469): xxxii (1871), App. i. 331–65; xxxiii (1872), App. i. 1–42.
(c) Calendar of royal charters, William II–Richard II: xxxi (1870), 1–41.
(d) Inventory of accounts of ministers and receivers, Edward I–George III: xlv (1885), App. i. 1–152.
(e) Inventory of court rolls (especially rolls of courts leet and baron): xliii (1882), App. i. 206–362.
(f) Inventory and lists of documents transferred from the duchy of Lancaster office to the public record office, 1868: xxx (1869), 1–43.

3872 DEPUTY KEEPER'S REPORTS (of the county-palatine of Lancaster records):

(a) Calendar of inquisitions post mortem: xxxix (1878), 532–49. See No. 3873.

(b) Calendar of patent rolls, 4 Richard II–21 Henry VII: xl (1879), 521–45.
(c) Calendar of privy seals, Richard II: xliii (1882), App. i. 363–70.
(d) Calendar of rolls of the chancery (close rolls): xxxvii (1876), App. i. 172–9.
(e) Inventory and lists of the records transferred from the county-palatine of Lancaster to the public record office: xxxv (1874), 42–75.

3873   DUCATUS LANCASTRIAE. (Ed. by R. J. Harper, J. Caley, and W. Minchin.) 3 vols. Rec. Comm. Lond. 1823–34.

Vol. i, pt. i, Calendarium inquisitionum post mortem, etc. Edw. I–Chas. I.
See also Abstracts of inquisitions post mortem (1297–1637) made by Christopher Towneley and Roger Dodsworth, edited by William Langton. 2 vols. Chetham Soc. Old Ser. xcv (1875); xcix (1876).

3874   FOX (LEVI). The administration of the honour of Leicester in the fourteenth century. Leicester. 1940.

A study of the accounts of one of Lancaster's possessions. For a general survey, consult Levi Fox, 'The honour and earldom of Leicester: origin and descent, 1066–1399' (including a list of the component fees of that honour in the early fourteenth century), *E.H.R.* liv (1939), 385–402. See No. 3880.

3875   JOHN OF GAUNT'S REGISTER (1371–5). Ed. by Sydney Armitage-Smith. 2 vols. Camden 3rd Ser. xx–xxi (1911).

3876   JOHN OF GAUNT'S REGISTER (1379–83). Ed. by Eleanor C. Lodge and Robert Somerville. 2 vols. Camden 3rd Ser. lvi–lvii (1937).

3877   LANCASHIRE AND CHESHIRE RECORDS PRESERVED IN THE PUBLIC RECORD OFFICE. Ed. by Walford D. Selby. 2 pts. Lancs.–Ches. Rec. Soc. vii–viii (1882–3).

Pt. i gives class-lists, etc. of these records; pt. ii prints a portion of the 'Great Ayloffe, 1692': calendars and indexes of charters, inquests post mortem, pleas, feet of fines, etc. Ayloffe was keeper of the records of the duchy court of Lancaster.

3878   LISTS AND INDEXES (of the county-palatine records). No. 956 above. Assize rolls, plea rolls, iv (1910); xl (1914).

3879   LISTS AND INDEXES (of the duchy records). No. 956 above. Court rolls, vi (1896); Records of the duchy of Lancaster, xiv (1914); and Supplementary Lists and Indexes V in 3 vols: supplementary, royal charters and cartae miscellaneae: Rentals and surveys, xxv (1908).

3880   MINISTERS' ACCOUNTS OF THE HONOR OF LEICESTER. Ed. by Levi Fox. *Leics. Archaeol. Soc. Trans.* xix (1936–7), 199–273; xx (1938–9), 77–158.

3881   MYERS (ALEC R.). 'An official progress through Lancaster and Cheshire in 1476'. *Hist. Soc. Lancs.–Ches. Trans.* cxv (1963). Cf. A. R. Myers in *Eng. Hist. Docs.* iv, no. 333.

Some documents relating to the duchy, otherwise unprinted, are translated by Myers in *Eng. Hist. Docs.* iv, nos. 173, 334, 574, 583, 609, 626, 651, 653, 654, 657, 663.

3882   PLEA ROLLS OF THE COUNTY PALATINE OF LANCASTER: Roll 1 (1401–1406). Ed. by John Parker. Chetham Soc. 2nd Ser. lxxxvii (1928).

3883 SOMERVILLE (ROBERT). History of the duchy of Lancaster. Vol. i (1265–1603). Lond. 1953. Vol. ii (1603–1965). 1970.

The best study of the duchy, detailed, scholarly and based on the records of the duchy. Somerville provides a brief account in 'The duchy and county palatine of Lancaster', *Hist. Soc. Lancs.–Ches. Trans.* ciii (1951), 59–67. See also his 'The duchy of Lancaster council and court of duchy chamber', *T.R.H.S.* xxiii (1941), 159–77; and his 'Duchy of Lancaster records', ibid. xxix (1947), 1–17. See Nos. 4127 and 4178.

3884 TURTON (ROBERT B.), ed. The honor and forest of Pickering. 4 vols. North Riding Record Soc. New Ser. 1894–7.

This work contains many transcripts from the coucher book of the duchy of Lancaster and other duchy of Lancaster records in the Public Record Office.

4. *Forests*

The basic studies on the medieval English forests are those of Liebermann (No. 3894), Manwood (No. 3914), Neilson (No. 3916), Petit-Dutaillis (No. 3920), and Turner (No. 3897). Reference should also be made to the Victoria County Histories (No. 1529) and to Darby's series on Domesday geography (No. 3044).

a. Primary sources

3885 BAILLIE-GROHMAN (WILLIAM A. and FLORENCE) eds. The master of the game, by Edward, second duke of York, the oldest English book on hunting (1406–13). Lond. 1904; 1909.

The editors give a history of English hunting laws in the Middle Ages.

3886 BOULTON (HELEN E.). The Sherwood Forest book. Thoroton Soc. Rec. Ser. xxiii (1965).

This book deals with the eyres of the justices of the forest for 15 Edw. I and for 1334.

3887 FEODARIUM PRIORATUS DUNELMENSIS (No. 4738).

Pp. 230–8: an account of the bishop's forest in Durham, *c.* 1228.

3888 GOUGH (JOHN W.). Mendip mining laws and forest bounds. Somerset Rec. Soc. xlv (1931).

Prints the texts of perambulations of Mendip forest in 1219, 1279, 1298, and 1300. For perambulations of Somerset forests in 1298, see Adam de Domerham, *Historia* (No. 6309), i. 184–202.

3889 INVENTORY OF THE RECORDS RELATING TO THE ROYAL FORESTS (formerly) in the Wakefield Tower. *Deputy Keeper's Reports*, v (1844), 46–59.

Pleas, perambulations, etc. John–Charles I. See also ibid. xx (1859), 126–7.

3890 THE HONOR AND FOREST OF PICKERING. Ed. by Robert Turton. North Riding Rec. Soc. New Ser. i–iv (1894–7).

Pleas before the itinerant justices of the forest, 1334–8, are given in ii. 49–200; iii. 1–185; iv. 1–69.

3891 MANWOOD (JOHN). A brefe collection of the lawes of the forest, with an abridgment of cases in the assises of the forests of Pickering and Lancaster. Lond. 1592.

3892 PERAMBULATION OF THE FOREST OF DENE (Glos.) 10 Edward I. Ed. by John Maclean. *Bristol and Glos. Archaeol. Soc. Trans.* xiv (1890), 356–69.

> Another perambulation, *c.* 1340 (translation), by John Maclean: ibid. xv (1891), 304–6. See also below Nos. 3896, 3900, 3908.

3893 THE PLEAS OF THE FOREST, STAFFORDSHIRE, *temp.* Henry III–Edward I. Trans. by G. Wrottesley. Wm. Salt Archaeol. Soc. *Collections*, v, pt. i (1884), 123–80.

> See also 'Forest pleas in the Staffordshire pipe roll of 13 Henry II', by Charles G. O. Bridgeman: ibid. New Ser. 1923 (1924).

3894 PSEUDO-CNUTS CONSTITUTIONES DE FORESTA. Ed. by Schmid (No. 2179), 318–21; by Thorpe (No. 2180), i. 426–30; by Liebermann, *Gesetze* (No. 2177), i. 620–6; and Liebermann, *Ueber Pseudo-Cnuts Constitutiones de Foresta* (No. 2188), pp. 49–55.

> This forgery was compiled about 1184 by a layman, perhaps a forest official of the baronial party who desired that the king should select forest judges from the feudal aristocracy. Liebermann's commentary in No. 2186 is the best account of forest law and administration in the twelfth century.

3895 RAWLE (EDWIN J.). Annals of the ancient royal forest of Exmoor. Taunton, etc. 1893.

> This work contains perambulations of 1279 and 1298; pleas of the forest, 1257–1368, etc.

3896 REPORTS OF THE COMMISSIONERS appointed to inquire into the state and condition of the woods, forests, and land revenues of the crown. Seventeen reports printed in the *Journals of the House of Commons*, xlii–xlviii (1787–93).

> These reports contain perambulations of the forests, *temp.* Edw. I: Dean: xliii (1788), 586–7; New Forest: xliv (1789), 575–6; Aliceholt and Woolmer: xlv (1790), 136–7; Salcey: xlvi (1791), 106; Whittlewood and Bere: xlvii (1792), 153–4 and 1038; Sherwood: xlviii (1793), 476–7.

3897 SELECT PLEAS OF THE FOREST (1209–1334). Ed. by George J. Turner. Selden Soc. xiii (1901).

> Turner's introduction is a valuable contribution on the forests of the thirteenth century. For a review, see 'English forests and forest laws of the thirteenth century', *Edinburgh Rev.* cxcv (1902), 456–80. See also G. J. Turner, 'Justices of the forest south of Trent', *E.H.R.* xviii (1903), 112–16. J. L. Fisher, 'An early forest plea (1246) [Hatfield Forest]', *Essex Archaeol. Soc. Trans.* New Ser. xxiii (1945), 356–8.

3898 TANQUEREY (FRÉDÉRIC J.). 'Lettres de roi Edward I à Robert de Bavent, king's yeoman, sur des questions de vénerie'. *B.J.R.L.* xxiii (1939), 487–503.

b. Secondary works

3899   BARING (FRANCIS H.). 'The making of the New Forest'. *E.H.R.* xvi (1901), 427–38 (reprinted in his *Domesday Tables*, Lond. 1909, pp. 194–205). See also ibid. xxvii (1912), 513–15.

Baring's article is regarded as the most satisfactory account.

3900   BAZELEY (MARGARET L.). 'The extent of the English forest in the thirteenth century'. *T.R.H.S.* 4th Ser. iv (1921), 140–72.

See M. L. Bazeley, 'The forest of Dean in its relation to the crown', *Bristol and Glos. Archaeol. Soc. Trans.* xxxiii (1910), 153–286.

3901   BIRRELL (JEAN). 'Peasant craftsmen in the medieval forest'. *Agric. Hist. Rev.* xvii (1969), 91–107.

3902   BRAINE (A.). The history of Kingswood forest, including all the ancient manors and villages in the neighbourhood. Lond. and Bristol. 1891.

3903   COX (JOHN C.). The royal forests of England. Lond. (1905).

This account is mainly medieval. See also R. Grant, 'Royal forests', in *V.C.H. Wilts.* iv. 391–460.

3904   CRONNE (HENRY A.). 'The royal forest in the reign of Henry I', in *Essays in British and Irish History in honour of James Eadie Todd* (Lond. 1949), pp. 1–23.

3905   FISHER (WILLIAM R.). The forest of Essex: its history, laws, administration, and ancient customs. Lond. 1887.

Perambulation of 1301 on pp. 393–9. Fisher's book is supplemented by J. H. Round's essay on the same subject in *Brit. Archaeol. Asso. Jour.* New Ser. iii (1897), 36–42.

3906   FOX (LEVI) and RUSSELL (PERCY). Leicester forest. Leicester. 1948.

See V.C.H. *Leicestershire*, ii (1955), 265–70.

3907   GRESWELL (WILLIAM H. P.). The forests and deer parks of the county of Somerset. Taunton. 1905.

3908   HART (CYRIL EDWIN). Royal forest: a history of Dean's woods as producers of timber. Oxf. 1966.

C. E. Hart, 'The Herefordshire portion of the ancient forest of Dean', *Woolhope Nat. Field Club Trans.* xxxii (1948). Idem, 'The extent and boundaries of the forest of Dean and hundred of Briavels', *Bristol and Glos. Archaeol. Soc. Trans.* (1947) reprinted; 1947.

3909   HISTORY OF THE FOREST AND CHASE OF SUTTON COLD-FIELD (Warwick). Lond. and Birmingham. 1860.

Contains a translation of the customs of 1309.

3910   HUMPHREYS (JOHN). The forest of Feckenham. *Birmingham Archaeol. Soc. Trans.* xlv (1920).

See Hilton, *Medieval society* (No. 4964), p. 287, n. 48, and pp. 241–8.

3911   HUTCHINSON (HORACE G.). The New Forest. Lond. 1895, 1904; 3rd edn. (1907).

3912 KERRY (CHARLES). 'A history of Peak forest' (Derby). *Derbysh. Archaeol. and Nat. Hist. Soc. Jour.* xv (1893), 67–98.

3913 LENNARD (REGINALD). 'The destruction of woodland in the eastern counties under William the Conqueror'. *Econ. H.R.* xv (1945), 36–43. New Ser. i (1949), 144.

3914 MANWOOD (JOHN). A treatise and discourse of the lawes of the forest. Lond. 1598; 4th edn. 1717; 5th edn. (same as the fourth with a new title page), 1744.

See his collection of forest laws (No. 3891).

3915 MOORE (STUART A.). A short history of the rights of common upon the forest of Dartmoor and the commons of Devon. Report of S. A. Moore to the committee, and appendix of documents. Dartmoor Preservation Assoc. Plymouth. 1890.

3916 NEILSON (NELLIE). 'The forests' in *English Government at work* (No. 3836), i. 394–467.

See N. Neilson, 'Early English woodland and waste', *Jour. Econ. Hist.* ii (1942), 54–62. F. G. Roe, 'Forests and woods in mediaeval England', *Royal Soc. of Canada Trans.* xlix (1955), 67–93.

3917 NEWBIGGING (THOMAS). History of the forest of Rossendale (Lancashire). Lond. 1868; 2nd edn. Rawtenstall. 1893.

3918 PARKER (FRANCIS H. M.). 'The forest laws and the death of William Rufus'. *E.H.R.* xxvii (1912), 26–38. Cf. F. Baring, ibid., pp. 513–15.

Parker argues that the story of William's devastation was fabricated to cover the conspiracy which resulted in William II's death. Baring disagrees.

3919 PARKER (FRANCIS H. M.). 'Inglewood forest'. *Cumb. and Westm. Antiq. and Archaeol. Soc. Trans.* New Ser. v (1905), 35–61; vi (1906), 159–70; vii (1907), 1–30; ix (1909), 24–37; x (1910), 1–28; xi (1911), 1–34; xii (1912), 1–28.

3920 PETIT-DUTAILLIS (CHARLES). Studies and notes supplementary (No. 1221), ii. 147–251 (the forest).

See also Petit Dutaillis in *Bémont essays* (No. 1426), pp. 59–76.

3921 ROWE (SAMUEL). A perambulation of the forest of Dartmoor. Plymouth. (1848); 3rd edn. Exeter. 1896.

Chap. xiii contains historical documents.

3922 SHAW (R. CUNLIFFE). The royal forest of Lancaster. Preston. 1956.

3923 STEWART-BROWN (RONALD). 'Disafforestation of Wirral (1376)'. *Historic Soc. Lancs. and Cheshire Trans.* lix (1908), 165–80.

3924 STRAKER (ERNEST). 'Ashdown forest and its enclosures'. *Sussex Archaeol. Coll.* lxxxi (1940), 121–35.

3925 WEST (J.). 'The forest offenders of medieval Worcestershire'. *Folk Life* (Soc. for Folk Life Studies, Cardiff), ii (1964).

3926 WEST (WILLIAM). A history of Cranborne Chase. Gillingham. 1816.

3927 WISE (JOHN R.). The New Forest (Hants.): its history and scenery. Lond. 1863 (1862); 5th edn. 1895.

The author argues that the chroniclers greatly exaggerate the extent of the desolation wrought by William the Conqueror in the construction of the New Forest. F. Baring, however, disagrees with this view; as he does with Parker's argument (No. 3918).

3928 WRIGHT (ELIZABETH C.). Common law in the thirteenth-century English royal forests. Philadelphia. 1928.

Mrs. Wright incorporates her article in *Speculum*, iii (1928), 166–91, and adds notes.

5. *The Jews*

The best studies are those by Adler (No. 3946), Jacobs (No. 3957), Richardson (No. 3966), and Roth (Nos. 3968–70).

3929 JEWISH HISTORICAL SOCIETY OF ENGLAND, TRANSACTIONS. Lond. 1893–4+. MISCELLANIES. i+. 1925+.

An index to *Transactions*, i–xii, is provided in *Miscellanies*, i (1925); and *Index to Transactions and Miscellanea, 1893–1945*, J.H.S.E. Lond. 1955.

3930 JEWISH QUARTERLY REVIEW. Lond. i–xx. 1888–1908; Philadelphia. New Ser. i+. 1910+.

3931 MAGNA BIBLIOTHECA ANGLO-JUDAICA: a bibliographical guide to Anglo-Jewish history. New edn. by Cecil Roth. Lond. 1937.

Originally published by Joseph Jacobs and Lucien Wolf, Lond. 1888.

3932 NOVA BIBLIOTHECA ANGLO-JUDAICA: A bibliographical guide to Anglo-Jewish history 1937–1960. Ed. by Ruth P. Lehmann. J.H.S.E. Lond. 1961.

3933 CALENDAR OF THE PLEA ROLLS OF THE EXCHEQUER OF THE JEWS, 1218–75. Ed. by James M. Rigg. J.H.S.E. 2 vols. Lond. 1905–10; vol. iii (1275–7). Ed. by Hilary Jenkinson. Lond. 1929.

See Picciotto (No. 3964).

3934 DOCUMENTS RELATING TO THE HISTORY OF THE JEWS IN THE THIRTEENTH CENTURY. Ed. by Charles Trice Martin. *J.H.S.E. Trans.* iii (1899), 187–212.

3935 HEBREW DEEDS OF ENGLISH JEWS (1182–1290). Ed. by Myer D. Davis. Pubns. Anglo-Jewish Hist. Exhibition, no. 2. Lond. 1888.

3936 JENKINSON (HILARY). 'Medieval records of exchequer receipts from the English Jewry'. *J.H.S.E. Trans.* viii (1915–17), 19–54. Idem, 'Some medieval notes'. Ibid. ix (1922), 185–7. Idem, 'Tallies and receipt rolls'. Ibid. ix (1922), 188–92. Idem, 'List of plea rolls of the exchequer of the Jews in the Public Record Office, not yet calendared'. Ibid. xii (1931), p. xv. Idem, 'Jewish entries in the *curia regis* rolls and elsewhere', *J.H.S.E. Miscellanies*, v (1948), 128–34. Idem, 'Medieval sources for Anglo-Jewish history: the problem of publication'. *J.H.S.E. Trans.* xviii (1955), 285–93.

3937   THE LIFE AND MIRACLES of St. William of Norwich. By Thomas of Monmouth; edited, with a translation, by Augustus Jessopp and M. R. James. Cambr. 1896.

> This life, compiled in 1172-3 by a monk of Norwich, is the starting-point of the myth of Jewish ritual murders, and throws some light on the religious life of England in the twelfth century. The Jews were accused of crucifying William in 1144. For a similar legend regarding Hugh of Lincoln (d. 1255), see *D.N.B.* x, 169-71; Child, *Popular ballads* (No. 7045), iii. 233-43; and *Jewish encyclopedia* (1904), vi. 487-8.
>
> The William of Norwich story was refuted by Cardinal Ganganelli (Pope Clement XIV) in 1759, and his work is edited and translated by Cecil Roth, *The ritual murder libel and the Jew* (Lond. 1935). See G. I. Langmuir, *Speculum*, xlvii (1972), 459-82.

3938   THE NORTHAMPTON 'DONUM' OF 1194. Ed. by Israel Abrahams. *J.H.S.E. Miscellanies*, i (1925), lix-lxxxvi.

> Hilary Jenkinson wrote the description of the membranes.

3939   SELECT PLEAS, STARRS AND OTHER RECORDS. Selden Soc. (See No. 3518).

> Cf. Cole, *Documents* (No. 3104), pp. 285-332.

3940   STARRS AND JEWISH CHARTERS PRESERVED IN THE BRITISH MUSEUM, with illustrative documents, translations and notes. By Israel Abrahams, Henry P. Stokes, and Herbert Loewe. 3 vols. J.H.S.E. (1930-2).

3941   RECORDS OF MSS. AND DOCUMENTS POSSESSED BY THE JEWS IN ENGLAND BEFORE EXPULSION. By Henry P. Stokes. *J.H.S.E. Trans.* viii (1918), 78-97.

> See H. P. Stokes, 'Extracts from the close rolls', *J.H.S.E. Miscellanies*, pt. i (1925), pp. vi-xvii.

3942   THE TESTIMONY OF THE LONDON JEWRY AGAINST THE MINISTERS OF HENRY III. Ed. by Michael Adler. *J.H.S.E. Trans.* xv (1941), 141-85.

> The testimony is taken from the *curia regis* roll for 1234. On this subject, consult Rigg, *Select Pleas* (No. 3518), pp. xliv-xlvii.

3943   AN UNPUBLISHED PIPE ROLL OF 1285. Ed. by Michael Adler. *J.H.S.E. Miscellanea*, ii (1935), 56-71.

> This is an inventory of the property of condemned Jews. See also M. Adler, 'Jewish tallies of the thirteenth century', ibid. ii (1935), 8-23.

3944   ABRAHAMS (BARNETT LIONEL). The expulsion of the Jews from England in 1290. (Reprinted from the *Jewish Quart. Rev.* 1894-5.) Oxf. etc. 1895. Idem, 'The condition of the Jews of England at the time of their expulsion in 1290'. *J.H.S.E. Trans.* ii (1896), 76-105. Idem (Sir Lionel), 'The economic and financial position of the Jews in medieval England'. Ibid. viii (1915-17).

3945   ADLER (ELKAN NATHAN). London. Jewish Communities Series. Philadelphia. 1930.

> Pp. 1-76 deal with the Jews in London in the Middle Ages.

3946 ADLER (MICHAEL). Jews in medieval England. J.H.S.E. Lond. 1939.

This work is a collection of articles by M. Adler; it includes: 'The Jewish women in medieval England'; 'The Jews of medieval Canterbury' (*J.H.S.E. Trans.* vii (1911), 19–96); 'Aaron of York and Henry III' (ibid. xiii (1936), 113–55); 'The Jews of Bristol in pre-expulsion days' (ibid. xii (1931), 117–86); 'Medieval Jewish MSS. in the library of St. Paul's cathedral, London' (*J.H.S.E. Misc.* iii (1937), 15–33); 'History of the Domus Conversorum; 1290–1891' (*J.H.S.E. Trans.* iv (1903), 16–75).

3947 ADLER (MICHAEL). 'The Jews of medieval Exeter'. *Trans. Devonshire Asso.* lxiii (1931), 221–40.

3948 BARON (SALO W.). A social and religious history of the Jews. 3 vols. N.Y. 1937. 2nd edn. 12 vols. 1952–67.

The arrangement is generally topical rather than geographical, and the notes to each chapter form an annotated bibliography. For the Jews in England, see especially vol. x (1965), 92–117 and 344–53; vol. xi (1967), *passim*, and pp. 201–11 and 384–8; and vol. xii (1967), *passim*.

3949 CHEW (HELENA M.). 'A Jewish aid to marry, A.D. 1221'. *J.H.S.E. Trans.* xi (1928), 92–111.

This concerns the aid for the marriage of the king's sister Joan to King Alexander of Scotland.

3950 DAVIES (ROBERT). 'The medieval Jews of York'. *Yorks. Archaeol. and Topog. Asso. Jour.* iii (1875), 147–97.

3951 DAVIS (MYER D.). 'Medieval Jews of Ipswich'. *East Anglian*, New Ser. iii (1889–90), 89–127, *passim*. Idem, 'Medieval Jews of Lincoln'. *Archaeol. Jour.* xxxviii (1881), 178–200. Idem, 'An Anglo-Jewish divorce, A.D. 1242'. *Jewish Quart. Rev.* v (1893), 158–65.

3952 ELMAN (PETER). 'The economic causes of the expulsion of the Jews in 1290'. *Econ. H.R.* 1st Ser. vii (1937), 145–54. Idem, 'Jewish trade in thirteenth century England'. *Historia Judaica*, i (1939), 91–104. Idem, 'Jewish finance in thirteenth century England'. *J.H.S.E. Trans.* xvi (1945–51); and his thesis summary in *B.I.H.R.* xv (1937), 112–13.

3953 GOLDSCHMIDT (SALOMON). Geschichte der Juden in England bis zu ihrer Verbannung. Pt. i. xi und xii Jahrhundert. Berlin. 1886.

3954 GRAYZEL (SOLOMON). The church and the Jews in the thirteenth century: a study of their relations during the years 1198–1254, based on the papal letters and conciliar decrees of the period. Philadelphia. 1933; New edn. N.Y. 1966.

For some episodes of malevolence towards the Jews, see St. William of Norwich (No. 3937). I. Abrahams's preface to the reprint of Maitland's 'The deacon and the Jewess', *J.H.S.E. Trans.* vi (1912), 254–9 and 260 ff.; and No. 1482. W. Rye, 'The alleged abduction and circumcision of a boy at Norwich in 1230', The *Norwich Antiquarian Miscellany*, i, pt. 2, 312–44. On Little St. Hugh of Lincoln, see Joseph Jacobs, *J.H.S.E. Trans.* i (1893), 89–135; *D.N.B.* xxvii. 169–71; and *Jewish Encyclopedia* (1904), vi. 487–8.

3955 GROSS (CHARLES). The exchequer of the Jews of England in the middle ages. Papers read at the Anglo-Jewish historical exhibition (1887). Lond. 1887.

> Alice C. Cramer, 'The Jewish exchequer: an inquiry into its fiscal functions', *A.H.R.* xlv (1939–40), 327–37; idem, 'The origins and functions of the Jewish exchequer', *Speculum*, xvi (1941), 226–9.

3956 HYAMSON (ALBERT M.). A history of the Jews in England. J.H.S.E. Lond. 1908; 2nd edn. 1928.

3957 JACOBS (JOSEPH). The Jews of Angevin England: documents and records from Latin and Hebrew sources, printed and manuscript (to 1206). Lond. 1893.

> A valuable supplement to Prynne's *Demurrer* (No. 3965). J. Jacobs, 'Notes on Jews of England under Angevin kings', *Jewish Quart. Rev.* iv (1892), 628–55; idem, 'Further notes on Jews in Angevin England', ibid. v (1893), 51–77. Idem, *The London Jewry, 1290: a lecture* (Lond. 1887).

3958 LANGMUIR (GAVIN I.). 'The Jews and the archives of Angevin England: reflections on medieval anti-Semitism'. *Traditio*, xix (1963), 183–244.

> A somewhat prolix examination of Richardson's *English Jewry* (No. 3966) 'in the light of present work in the social sciences, especially the findings of modern sociology and psychology'.

3959 LEONARD (GEORGE H.). 'The expulsion of the Jews by Edward I'. *T.R.H.S.* New Ser. v (1891), 103–45.

3960 LINCOLN (FREDMAN ASHE). The Starra, their effect on early English law and administration. Oxf. and Lond. 1939.

> See Jacob J. Rabinowitz, 'The influence of Jewish law on the development of the common law', in Louis Finkelstein, ed., *The Jews: their history, culture and religion* (Philadelphia, 1949), pp. 497–527.

3961 LIPMAN (V. D.). The Jews of medieval Norwich. J.H.S.E. Lond. 1967.

3962 NEUBAUER (ADOLF). 'Notes on the Jews in Oxford'. *Oxf. Hist. Soc. Collectanea*, ii (1890), 277–316.

> Consists mainly of extracts from records. See Roth (No. 3970).

3963 PARKES (JAMES). The Jew in the medieval community: a study of his political and economic situation. Lond. 1938.

3964 PICCIOTTO (CYRIL M.). 'The legal position of the Jews in pre-expulsion England, as shown by the plea rolls of the Jewish exchequer'. *J.H.S.E. Trans.* ix (1922), 67–84.

3965 PRYNNE (WILLIAM). A short demurrer to the Jewes long discontinued remitter into England. 2 pts. Lond. 1655–6; 2nd edn. of pt. i. 1656.

> Although it exhibits a marked prejudice against the Jews, the work is of value owing to its numerous extracts from the public records.

3966 RICHARDSON (HENRY G.). The English Jewry under Angevin kings. Lond. 1960.

Documents are given in the Appendix, pp. 237–94. For critique, see Langmuir (No. 3958).

3967 RIGG (JAMES M.). The Jews of England in the thirteenth century. *Jewish Quart. Rev.* xv (1902), 5–22.

Reprinted as the introduction to the second volume of his *Calendar* (No. 3933). See also his introduction to his *Select Pleas* (No. 3518).

3968 ROTH (CECIL). A history of Jews in England. Oxf. 1941; 2nd edn. 1949; 3rd edn. 1964.

C. Roth, *Medieval Lincoln Jewry and its synagogue*, J.H.S.E. 1934. See also Hill, *Medieval Lincoln* (No. 5145), chap. xi.

3969 ROTH (CECIL). The intellectual activities of medieval English Jewry. Brit. Acad. Supplemental Papers, no. 8. Lond. 1949.

C. Roth, 'Elijah of London (1220–84)', *J.H.S.E. Trans.* xv (1943), 29–62. See also, A. Marmorstein, 'New material for the literary history of the English Jews before the expulsion', ibid. xii (1931), 103–15; and the pamphlet by Beryl Smalley, *Hebrew scholarship among Christians in thirteenth century England* (Lond. 1939).

3970 ROTH (CECIL). The Jews of medieval Oxford. Oxf. Hist. Soc. New Ser. ix (1951).

C. Roth, 'Jews in Oxford after 1290', *Oxoniensia*, xv (1950). Sarah Cohen, 'The Oxford Jewry in the thirteenth century', *J.H.S.E. Trans.* xiii (1932–5), 293–322.

3971 SCHECHTER (FRANK I.). 'The rightlessness of mediaeval English Jewry'. *Jewish Quart. Rev.* New Ser. iv (1913–14), 121–51.

3972 STOKES (HENRY P.). Studies in Anglo-Jewish history. J.H.S.E. Edin. 1913.

Contains an appendix of records. See also his 'The relationship between the Jews and the royal family in England in the thirteenth century', *J.H.S.E. Trans.* viii (1918), 153–70.

3973 WEBB (P. C.). The question whether a Jew was a person capable by law to purchase and hold lands. By a gentleman of Lincoln's Inn. Lond. 1753.

The appendix contains valuable documents.

XVI. MODERN POLITICAL NARRATIVES

The modern narratives relating to the political affairs of some portion of the period from the Norman conquest to the accession of the Tudors are far too numerous to be listed completely here. Some are entered under the modern studies of the king's council (pp. 502–3), of parliament (pp. 510–19), and of general administrative history (pp. 572–4).

The comprehensive surveys in series are catalogued in vol. i, Nos. 1174–98. These surveys carry bibliographies. The best of them form the Oxford History of England (No. 1189), in each volume of which will be found footnote citations and an ample annotated bibliography. For British history written in the period from 1901 to 1945 *Writings in British history* (Nos. 38 and 39) should be consulted. The lists below (a) include older standard or classic narratives on which more recent studies depend and (b) concentrate on the publications of recent decades, which for the most part provide footnote citations and selective bibliographies.

For the sake of convenience, the political history of the period 1066–1485 is broken down into five segments. These are followed for the thirteenth, fourteenth, and fifteenth centuries by sections on the relations of England with foreign states.

A. WILLIAM I TO STEPHEN, 1066–1154

Bonser's Anglo-Saxon bibliography (No. 12) runs on to 1087 and thus includes the secondary accounts of the battle of Hastings and of the Conqueror's reign. Sveaas Andersen reviews some of the recent works on the conquest in 'England, Normannerne og Europe: Nyforskning omkringet klassisk problem' (England, the Normans and Europe. New research on a classic problem), *Historisk Tidsskrift* (Oslo), xlvi (1967), 308–22. Altschul (No. 15) cites studies on political history and foreign relations 1066–1154 (and later), many of which are not repeated below. The bibliographical citations in *English historical documents*, vol. ii, 1087–1189, and in A. L. Poole, *From Domesday to Magna Carta*, are extensive and annotated.

In his classic history, Freeman, believing in the continuity of English history, developed the thesis that the Norman conquest modified, but did not destroy, Anglo-Saxon institutions. J. H. Round argued strongly that the conquest brought a sharp revolutionary break with the past; hence that English institutions grew from Norman origins. Following in broad outline Round, Sir Frank Stenton presented in his *Anglo-Saxon England* a viewpoint which came to be widely accepted. In recent years, some scholars, Eric John, and Richardson and Sayles have sought to modify or reject Round's thesis; while others, for example Brown and Holt, have sought to sustain it. One of the bitterest arguments between Freeman and Round developed around the battle of Hastings itself. The current debate on the introduction of feudal tenure is treated below on pp. 661–6. The economic consequences of the Norman period are described in Nos. 2650, 3986, 3989, and 4973. The studies of the Conquest's effects on the Church in England are entered in the chapter relating to the Church.

3974 BAKER (TIMOTHY). The Normans. Lond. and N.Y. 1966. Paperback: N.Y. 1969.

A well-written, popular introductory survey of politics, culture, and art from 911 to c. 1087. Select bibliography.

3975 BARLOW (FRANK). The feudal kingdom of England, 1042–1216. Lond. 1955. 2nd edn. 1961.

3976 BARLOW (FRANK). William I and the Norman Conquest. Teach Yourself History Series. Lond. 1965. Reprinted, 1970. Paperback: Lond. and N.Y. 1967.

For background, see Barlow, *Edward the Confessor* (Lond. and Berkeley, Cal., 1970).

3977 BARROW (GEOFFREY W. S.). Feudal Britain: the completion of the medieval kingdoms, 1066–1314. Lond. 1956.

3978 BOÜARD (MICHEL DE). Guillaume le conquérant. Paris. 1958.

Idem, 'Les études d'histoire Normande de 1928 à 1951', *Annales de Normandie* (Caen), i (1951), 150–92.

3979 BROWN (REGINALD ALLEN). The Normans and the Norman Conquest. Lond. and N.Y. 1969.

R. A. Brown, 'The Norman Conquest', *T.R.H.S.* 5th Ser. xvii (1967), 109–30. Brown gives vigorous support to the thesis that the conquest produced a complete revolution.

3980 CHEVALLIER (CHARLES T.), ed. The Norman Conquest: its setting and impact. Lond. 1966. Paperback: 1966.

Four essays by Dorothy Whitelock, David C. Douglas, Charles H. Lemmon, and Frank Barlow, commemorating the ninth centenary.

3981 CRONNE (HENRY A.). The reign of Stephen, 1135–54: anarchy in England. Stud. in Medieval Hist. Lond. 1970.

Primarily a study on the administrative side of the reign. The volumes of Cronne and Davis (No. 3984) complement one another to form the best studies on the reign. Also H. A. Cronne, 'Ranulf de Gernons, earl of Chester, 1129–1153', *T.R.H.S.* 4th Ser. xx (1937), 103–24; and R. H. C. Davis, 'King Stephen and the earl of Chester revised', *E.H.R.* lxxv (1960), 654–60. See also H. W. C. Davis in *Poole essays* (No. 1448); and in *Davis papers* (No. 1466); and Megaw in *Todd essays* (No. 1457).

3982 DARLINGTON (REGINALD R.). The Norman Conquest. The Creighton Lecture. Lond. 1963.

Brief and excellent.

3983 DAVID (CHARLES W.). Robert Curthose, duke of Normandy. Harvard Hist. Stud. xxv. Cambr. (Mass.). 1920.

3984 DAVIS (RALPH H. C.). King Stephen. Berkeley and Los Angeles (Cal.) and Lond. 1967.

An excellent study of the political aspects of the reign utilizing the new information in the recently discovered final section of *Gesta Stephani* (No. 2880). Appendix 1 on Earls and Earldoms shows the importance of that office in contrast to Round's view. Davis's views are expressed in 'What happened in Stephen's reign', *History*, xlix (1964), 1–12. Cronne (No. 3981) and Davis force revision in the hitherto standard account given in

Round, *Geoffrey de Mandeville* (No. 4006). See R. H. C. Davis, 'Geoffrey de Mandeville reconsidered', *E.H.R.* lxxix (1964), 299–307. John T. Appleby provides a popular summary in *The troubled reign of King Stephen* (Lond. 1969; N.Y. 1970).

3985 DOUGLAS (DAVID C.). The Norman achievement. Lond. 1969.

The comparative history of the Normans throughout Europe, especially in south Italy in the second half of the eleventh century. Cf. D. C. Douglas, 'Les Réussites normandes (1050–1100)' in *Revue Historique,* ccxxxvii (1967), 1–16; and John Le Patourel, 'The Norman colonization of Britain', *I Normanni e la loro espansione in Europa nell'alto medioevo* (Spoleto, 1969), pp. 409–38.

3986 DOUGLAS (DAVID C.). William the Conqueror: the Norman impact upon England. Lond. 1964. Paperback edn.: Berkeley and Los Angeles (Cal.) 1967 and Lond. 1969.

The standard biography of William, strong on the Norman background and on impact on England; for criticism, see D. J. A. Matthew in *E.H.R.* lxxxvi (1971), 561–3. The select bibliography (pp. 427–47) is extensive. The historiography of the conquest is also considered by Douglas in *The Norman Conquest and British historians* (Glasgow, 1946).

3987 EDWARDS (J. GORONWY). 'The Normans and the Welsh March'. *P.B.A.* xlii (1956), 155–77.

A. J. Otway-Ruthven, 'The constitutional position of the great lordships of south Wales', *T.R.H.S.* 5th Ser. viii (1958), 1–20, deals with the whole later Middle Ages.

3988 FARRER (WILLIAM). 'An outline itinerary of King Henry the first'. *E.H.R.* xxxiv (1919), 303–82; 505–79.

Also printed separately with an index added.

3989 FINN (REX WELLDON). The Norman Conquest and its effect on the economy, 1066–86. Lond. 1970 and Hamden (Conn.). 1971.

3990 FREEMAN (EDWARD A.). History of the Norman Conquest. 6 vols. Oxf. 1867–79.* 2nd edn. of vols. i–iv. 1870–6; 3rd edn. of vols. i–ii. 1877; revised American edn. vols. i–v. N.Y. 1873–6.

The longest narrative supplemented by appendixes on the sources.
Vol. i: Anglo-Saxon history (449–1042): and Norman history (tenth century). 77 notes in Appendix.
Vols. ii–iii: Reigns of Edward the Confessor and Harold. 46 notes and 42 notes in Appendices.
Vol. iv: William the Conqueror. 37 notes in Appendix.
Vol. v: The effects of the conquest, with two long chapters on the reigns of Henry I and Stephen, and a brief account of English history, 1154–1272. 52 notes in Appendix.
Vol. vi: Index.
    For a brief critique, see Stenton, *Anglo-Saxon England*, 2nd edn. pp. 702–3, e.g. 'As an introduction to the sources for the political history of the period the book is of great and permanent value. The criticism of the sources is less satisfactory.' For Round's fierce attack on Freeman's account of the battle of Hastings, see Round, *Feudal England* (No. 4005), pp. 332–98 (Round's views were originally set forth in the *Quarterly Rev.* (July 1892) and in *E.H.R.* ix (1894), 209–59). See for a bibliography of the controversy, J. H. Round in *Sussex Archaeol. Collections*, xlii (1899), 54–63, where Freeman's rejoinders are listed. Compare T. A. Archer and Kate Norgate in *E.H.R.* ix (1894), 1–76.

3991 FREEMAN (EDWARD A.). The reign of William Rufus and the accession of Henry I. 2 vols. Oxf. 1882. *

3992 HASKINS (CHARLES H.). Norman institutions. Cambr. (Mass.). 1918. * Idem, The Normans in European History. Cambr. (Mass.) 1915. *

See M. de Boüard, 'Le Duché de Normandie', in F. Lot and R. Fawtier, *Institutions françaises au moyen âge*, i (1957), 1–33, and John Le Patourel, 'The Norman succession, 996–1135', *E.H.R.* lxxxvi (1971), 225–50.

3993 KEETON (GEORGE W.). The Norman Conquest and the common law. Lond. and N.Y. 1966.

3994 KORNER (STEN). The battle of Hastings, England and Europe, 1035–1066. Lund. 1964.

3995 LAPORTE (JEAN). 'Les opérations navales en Manche et Mer du Nord pendant l'année 1066'. *Annales de Normandie* (Caen), xvii (1967), 3–42.

Maurice J. Graindor, 'Le débarquement de Guillaume en 1066: un coup de maître de la marine normande', *Archaeologia*, lxxx (1969), 40–50.

3996 LEYSER (KARL). 'England and the empire in the early twelfth century'. *T.R.H.S.* 5th Ser. x (1960), 61–83.

3997 LOYN (HENRY R.). The Norman Conquest. Hutchinson's University Library. Lond. 1965. Reprinted, 1968. Also paperback.

Bibliographical note, pp. 196–202.

3998 MATTHEW (DONALD J. A.). The Norman Conquest. Lond. 1966.

This introduction solidly based on the sources and broad in scope is concerned with the personalities and achievements of the Normans to the end of Henry I's reign. List of references pp. 303–26.

3999 MILNE (D. GRINNELL). The killing of William Rufus: an investigation in the New Forest. Newton Abbot. 1968. (Lacks critical apparatus.)

4000 NELSON (LYNN H.). The Normans in South Wales, 1070–1171. Austin (Texas). 1966.

A. J. Roderick, 'Marriage and politics in Wales, 1066–1282', *Welsh H.R.* iv (1968), 1–20.

4001 PALGRAVE (FRANCIS). The history of Normandy and England (to 1101). 4 vols. Lond. 1851–64.

4002 RITCHIE (ROBERT L. GRAEME). The Normans in Scotland. Edin. 1954.

4003 RÖSSLER (OSKAR). Kaiserin Mathilde und das Zeitalter der Anarchie in England. Berlin. 1897.

4004 ROUND (JOHN HORACE). THE COMMUNE OF LONDON and other studies. Westminster. 1899. *

Chap. i. Settlement of the Saxons.
Chap. ii. Ingelric the priest and Albert of Lotharingia.
Chap. iii. Anglo-Norman warfare.
Chap. iv. Origin of the exchequer.
Chap. v. London under Stephen.
Chap. vi. The inquest of sheriffs.
Chaps. vii–viii. Conquest of Ireland.

Chap. ix. Coronation of Richard I.
Chap. x. King John and Longchamp.
Chap. xi. The commune of London.
Chap. xii. The great inquest of service (1212).
Chap. xiii. Castle-ward and cornage.
Chap. xiv. Bannockburn.
Chap. xv. The marshalship of England.

4005   ROUND (J. H.). Feudal England: historical studies of the eleventh and
twelfth centuries. Lond. 1895. Reprinted, 1909, 1964.

Domesday Book and other surveys, pp. 3–224. See No. 3061. (See Galbraith's critique,
No. 3053).
Introduction of knight service, pp. 225–314.
Normans under the Confessor, pp. 317–31.
Mr. Freeman and the battle of Hastings, pp. 332–98.
Other essays, dealing with the period 1066–1198, pp. 399–571.
    Round argued tenaciously that the Norman conquest brought a complete and sharp
break from Anglo-Saxondom.

4006   ROUND (J. H.). Geoffrey de Mandeville: a study of the anarchy (reign
of Stephen). Lond. etc. 1892. *

The author regards the career of Geoffrey as 'the most perfect and typical presentment
of the feudal and anarchic spirit that stamps the reign of Stephen'. The book throws
fresh light on the title of the English crown, the origin and character of earldoms, the
development of the fiscal system, the early administration of London, etc. Cf. No. 3984.

4007   SOUTHERN (RICHARD W.). 'The place of Henry I in English
history'. Raleigh lecture. *P.B.A.* xlviii (1962), 127–56. Reprinted with revision
in Southern's *Medieval Humanism* (No. 6911), pp. 206–33.

Southern argues that Henry did not create institutions, he created men; his system was
a social order which survived in Stephen's reign. For Henry's reign see also L. Voss,
Heinrich von Blois (No. 5823), and C. W. David in *Haskins essays* (No. 1439); M.
Dominica Legge, 'L'Influence littéraire de la cour d'Henri Beauclerc', *Mélanges offerts
à Rita Lejeune*, ed. by F. Dethier (Gembloux, 1969), pp. 679–87.

4008   SOUTHERN (R. W.). 'Ranulf Flambard and early Anglo-Norman
administration'. *T.R.H.S.* 4th Ser. xvi (1933), 95–128. Reprinted with revision
in Southern, *Medieval Humanism* (No. 6911), pp. 183–205.

4009   SPATZ (WILHELM). Die Schlacht von Hastings. Berlin. 1896.

Reviewed by J. H. Round in *Revue Historique*, lxv (1897), 61–77. See Charles H.
Lemmon, *The field of Hastings* (3rd edn. St. Leonards-on-Sea, 1965); and No. 3980.

4010   STENTON (FRANK M.). William the Conqueror and the rule of the
Normans. N.Y. and Lond. 1908. * Reprinted, 1912, 1915. *

B. HENRY II TO JOHN, 1154–1216

The bibliographical citations in *English Historical Documents*, ii, continue through
Henry II's reign; they may be supplemented by reference to A. L. Poole,
Domesday Book to Magna Carta; to the *Cambridge Medieval History*, vols. v and
vi; and to Richardson and Sayles, *Governance* (No. 1218), pp. 471–95. Boussard,
Le Gouvernement d'Henri II, pp. xiii–lxviii, gives an extensive list under 'sources
et bibliographie'. For the Becket controversy, refer to pp. 853–8 below.

4011 APPLEBY (JOHN T.). Henry II, the vanquished king. Lond. and N.Y. 1962. Idem, England without Richard, 1189–1199. Lond. and Ithaca (N.Y.). 1965. Idem, John, king of England. Lond. 1960.

Well-written, popular summaries based on wide reading.

4012 BOUSSARD (JACQUES). Le comté d'Anjou sous Henri Plantegenêt et ses fils, 1151–1204. Paris. 1938.

See Josèphe Chartrou, *L'Anjou de 1109 à 1151: Foulque de Jérusalem et Geoffroi Plantegenêt* (Paris, 1928).

4013 BOUSSARD (JACQUES). Le gouvernement d'Henri II Plantegenêt. Paris. 1956. Trans. by Jean Penfold. Lond. 1959.

A bulky work of much detail and extensive documentation. See commentary by H. M. Colvin in *History*, xliii (1958), 85–9; H. G. Richardson, in *E.H.R.* lxxiii (1958), 659–63; and Raymonde Foreville, in *Le Moyen Âge*, lxiv (1958), 351–6.

4014 CARTELLIERI (ALEXANDER). Philipp II August, König von Frankreich. Vols. i–iv, pt. i. Leipzig. 1899–1921. *

Valuable for the relations of Philip II to Henry II, Richard I, and John to 1206.

4015 DELISLE (LEOPOLD). Recueil des actes de Henri II (No. 3823).

4016 DEPT (GASTON G.). Les influences anglaise et française dans le comté de Flandre au début du xiiime siècle. Ghent and Paris. 1928.

4017 EYTON (ROBERT W.). Court, household and itinerary of Henry II. Lond. 1878.

Indispensable. An itinerary of Henry II will also be found in Stubbs's edition of Benedict of Peterborough (No. 2879); vol. ii, pp. cxxix–cxlviii.

4018 HALL (HUBERT). Court life under the Plantagenets (*temp.* Hen. II). Lond. etc. 1890. Reprinted, 1902.

Deals with the royal household, council, court, exchequer, etc.

4019 HARDY (THOMAS D.). 'Itinerarium Johannis regis Angliae'. *Archaeologia*, xxii (1829), 124–60.

Also printed in his edition of the Patent Rolls (No. 3778).

4020 HOLLISTER (C. WARREN). 'King John and the historians'. *Jour. British Stud.* i (1961), 1–19.

4021 HOLT (JAMES C.). The Northerners: a study in the reign of King John. Oxf. 1961.

See Holt's *Magna Carta* (No. 3286); and his booklet on *King John*, Historical Asso. pamphlet G. 53 (Lond. 1963).

4022 JOLLIFFE (JOHN E. A.). Angevin kingship. Lond. 1955. 2nd edn. 1963.

Reviewed by H. G. Richardson in *E.H.R.* lxxi (1956), 447–53; and Sidney Painter in *A.H.R.* lxi (1955–6), 381–2.

4023 KELLY (AMY R.). Eleanor of Aquitaine and the four kings. Cambr. (Mass.). 1950.

Cf. Curtis H. Walker. *Eleanor of Aquitaine* (Chapel Hill, N.C. 1950). See also H. G. Richardson. 'The letters and charters of Eleanor of Aquitaine', *E.H.R.* lxxiv (1959), 193–213.

4024 LANDON (LIONEL). The itinerary of King Richard I, with studies on certain matters of interest connected with his reign. Pipe Roll Soc. Pubns. New Ser. xiii (1935).

4025 LEACH (HENRY B.). Angevin Britain and Scandinavia. Harvard Stud. in Comp. Lit. vi. Cambr. (Mass.). 1921.

4026 LYTTELTON (GEORGE). The history of the life of Henry II. 2 vols. and a volume of notes. Lond. 1767; 3rd edn. 4 vols. 1769. Vol. iii, 1777; 2nd edn. 2 vols. 1772–3.

The most elaborate account of Henry II's reign. Useful, but in large part obsolete.

4027 NORGATE (KATE). England under the Angevin kings (1100–1206). 2 vols. Lond. 1887.*

4028 NORGATE (KATE). John Lackland. Lond. etc. 1902. *

4029 NORGATE (KATE). Richard the Lion Heart. Lond. 1924. *

For Richard's Crusade, see Steven Runciman, *A history of the Crusades*, iii (Cambr. 1954), pp. 34–75; and Sidney Painter, 'The Third Crusade: Richard the Lionhearted and Philip Augustus' in Kenneth M. Setton, ed. *A history of the Crusades*, ii (Philadelphia, Pa., 1962), 45–86. Painter provides a considerable list of references. See also Bertie Wilkinson, 'The government of England during the absence of Richard I on the third crusade', *B.J.R.L.* xxviii (1944), 485–509. See also A. L. Poole in *Powicke essays* (No. 1450), and in *Poole essays* (No. 1448).

4030 ORPEN (GODDARD H.). Ireland under the Normans 1169–1333. 4 vols. Oxf. 1911–20. *

For recent bibliography, see P. W. A. Asplin, *Medieval Ireland, c. 1170–1485: a bibliography of secondary works*. A New History of Ireland, Ancillary Pubns. no. 1. Royal Irish Acad. (Dublin, 1971).

4031 OTWAY-RUTHVEN (A. JOCELYN). 'The character of the Norman settlement in Ireland'. *Historical Stud.* v (1965), 75–84.

See Otway-Ruthven, *History of medieval Ireland* (No. 1203), especially chaps. i and ii, and bibliography.

4032 PAINTER (SIDNEY). The reign of King John. Baltimore. 1949. 3rd printing. 1964. Paperback: 1966.

See Jolliffe in *Powicke essays* (No. 1450).

4033 PAINTER (SIDNEY). William Marshal, knight-errant, baron, and regent of England. Johns Hopkins Historical Pubns. Baltimore. Md. 1933.

Cf. Jessie Crosland, *William the marshal: the last great feudal general* (Lond. 1962).

4034 PETIT-DUTAILLIS (CHARLES E.). Le déshéritement de Jean sans Terre et le meurtre d'Arthur de Bretagne. Paris. 1925.

Reprinted from *Revue Historique*, cxlvii–cxlviii (1924–5). This study resolved the debate concerning the trials of John in the court of France. It argued that John was neither tried nor condemned in 1203 for the murder of Arthur, but that he may well have been condemned in 1202 to forfeiture, perhaps by acclamation rather than formal sentence, on the complaint of the Lusignans of La Marche. The arguments are summarized by Powicke in *Cambridge Medieval History*, vol. vi, pp. 249, 315, 320; in Powicke, *Loss of Normandy* (No. 4035, 1961 edn.), pp. 309 ff.; and in Petit-Dutaillis, *L'Essor des États* (No. 1182), pp. 142–5, and his *Feudal monarchy* (No. 1179), pp. 216–22. The pertinent articles are the following: Charles Bémont, 'De la condamnation de Jean Sans Terre par la cour des pairs de France en 1202', *Revue Historique*, xxxii (1886), 33–72, 290–311; which accepted the condemnation of 1202 but rejected the trial of 1203; P. Guilhiermoz, 'Les Deux condamnations de Jean Sans Terre par la cour de Philippe Auguste', *B.E.C.* lx (1899), 45–85, which holds that John was condemned on both dates; the reply from Bémont and the rejoinder by Guilhiermoz in *B.E.C.* lx (1899), 363–72; articles in *Revue Historique* by C. Petit-Dutaillis, lxxi (1899), 33–41; by Gabriel Monod, lxxii (1900), 96–9, 100–1; by Achille Luchaire, lxxii (1900, 285–90); by Kate Norgate, 'The alleged condemnation of King John in 1202', *T.R.H.S.* xiv (1900), 1–18, which rejects both trials of 1202 and 1203; and F. M. Powicke, 'King John and Arthur of Brittany', *E.H.R.* xxiv (1909), 659–74 (No. 1490), which held, especially on the authority of the Annals of Margam, that John was condemned for the murder of Arthur; subsequently Powicke changed his opinion and agreed with Petit-Dutaillis.

4035 POWICKE (FREDERICK MAURICE). The loss of Normandy, 1189–1204. Manchester. 1913. 2nd edn. revised. 1961.

See Powicke, *Stephen Langton* (No. 5634).

4036 RENOUARD (YVES). 'Essai sur le rôle de l'empire angevin dans la formation de la France et de la civilisation française au xiie et xiiie siècles'. *Revue Historique*, cxcv (1945), 289–304.

4037 RICHARD (ALFRED). Histoire des comtes de Poitou, 778–1204. 2 vols. Paris. 1903.

For Eleanor of Acquitaine, ii. 54–457.

4038 RICHARDSON (HENRY G.). 'The marriage and coronation of Isabelle of Angoulême'. *E.H.R.* lxi (1946), 289–314.

Cf. Fred A. Cazel and Sidney Painter, 'The marriage of Isabella of Angoulême', ibid. lxiii (1948), 83–9; H. G. Richardson, 'King John and Isabelle of Angoulême', ibid. lxv (1950), 360–71; F. A. Cazel and S. Painter, 'The marriage of Isabelle of Angoulême', ibid. lxvii (1952), 233–5 (No. 1486).

For Lusignan genealogy, see Painter in *Speculum*, xxx (1955), pp. 374–84.

4039 RICHARDSON (H. G.). 'The morrow of the Great Charter'. *B.J.R.L.* xxviii (1944), 422–43. Idem, 'The morrow of the Great Charter: an addendum'. Ibid. xxix (1945), 183–99.

4040 SALZMAN (LOUIS F.). Henry II. Boston (Mass.), etc. 1914. Reprinted, 1967.

For Henry II's invasion of Wales in 1157, see D. J. C. King in *Welsh H.R.* ii (1965), 367–73, and J. G. Edwards, ibid. iii (1967), 251–63.

4041 STUBBS (WILLIAM). Historical introductions to the Rolls Series. Lond. N.Y. etc. 1902. ★

The introductions to Stubbs's editions of Benedict of Peterborough (No. 2879) and Roger of Howden (No. 2903) are invaluable for the history of the second half of the twelfth century.

4042 WARREN (WILFRED L.). King John. Lond. 1961.

C. THE THIRTEENTH CENTURY, 1216–1307

1. *Domestic Politics*

Powicke's *The Thirteenth Century* and the *Cambridge Medieval History*, vols. vi and vii, supply bibliographies. Jacob contributed chap. viii, 'England: Henry III' to the *Cambridge Medieval History*, vol. vi; and Hilda Johnstone, chap. xiv, 'England: Edward I and Edward II', to vol. vii. Powicke's *Henry III and the Lord Edward* (No. 4062) is a masterpiece on political history in its social context.

The studies by Jacob (No. 4052) and Treharne (No. 4068) are the best on the baronial movement and Simon de Montfort. Some particular political domestic episodes of the thirteenth century are examined under other headings (Nos. 3252; 3254–5; 3342; 3410–12).

4043 BÉMONT (CHARLES). Simon de Montfort, comte de Leicester. Paris. 1884. New edn. and trans. by E. F. Jacob. Oxf. 1930.

Note that the French edition contains an appendix of documents, omitted in the English translation. See also C. H. Knowles, *Simon de Montfort, 1265–1965*. Historical Asso. Pamphlet G. 60. Lond. 1965.

4044 BLAAUW (WILLIAM H.). The barons' war. Lond. 1844; 2nd edn. Cambr. 1871.

4045 BROOKS (FREDERICK W.) and OAKLEY (F.). 'Campaign and battle of Lincoln (1217)'. *A.A.S.R.P.* xxxvi (1922), 295–312.

See Powicke, *Henry III* (No. 4062), pp. 736–9.

4046 CHENEY (CHRISTOPHER R.). 'The paper constitution preserved by Matthew Paris'. *E.H.R.* lxv (1950), 213–21.

Cf. N. Denholm-Young, 'The paper constitution attributed to 1244' (No. 1467).

4047 CLANCY (M. T.). 'Did Henry III have a policy?' *History*, liii (1968), 203–16.

4048 DENHOLM-YOUNG (NOEL). Documents of the barons' wars. (No. 1467). Idem, 'Robert Carpenter and the provisions of Westminster' (No. 1467).

4049 ELLIS (CLARENCE). Hubert de Burgh: a study in constancy. Lond. 1952.

R. F. Walker, 'Hubert de Burgh and Wales 1218–32', *E.H.R.* lxxxvii (1972), 461–94.

4050 GOUGH (HENRY). Itinerary of Edward I, 1272–1307. 2 vols. Paisley. 1900.

An expanded and corrected version is kept in the Round Room at P.R.O. Cf. C. H. Hartshorne, 'An itinerary of King Edward I', *Collectanea Archaeologica*, ii (1871), 115–36; and J. P. Trabut-Cussac, 'Itinéraire d'Édouard Ier en France, 1286–1289', *B.I.H.R.* xxv (1952), 160–203.

4051 JACOB (ERNEST F.). 'The reign of Henry III: some suggestions'. *T.R.H.S.* 4th Ser. x (1927), 21–53.

See Jacob's chapter on Henry III in *C.M.H.* vi (1929).

4052 JACOB (E. F.). Studies in the period of baronial reform and rebellion, 1258–1267. Oxf. Stud. in Social–Legal Hist. Oxf. 1925.

Peter Walne, 'The barons' argument at Amiens, January, 1264', *E.H.R.* lxix (1954), 418–25; see Treharne in *Powicke essays* (No. 1450).

4053 JOHNSTONE (HILDA). Edward of Carnarvon, 1284–1307. Univ. Manchester Hist. Ser. Manchester. 1947.

See A. J. Taylor, 'The birth of Edward of Caernarvon and the beginnings of Caernarvon castle', Historical Revision. *History,* New Ser. xxxv (1950), 256–61.

4054 KINGSFORD (CHARLES L.). Sir Otho de Grandison (1238–1328). *T.R.H.S.* 3rd Ser. iii (1909), 125–95.

Grandison (or Granson) was secretary and companion of Edward I. His relations with Edward II, etc. are treated on pp. 158–88; with an appendix of documents, pp. 188–95.

4055 LABARGE (MARGARET W.). Simon de Montfort. Lond. 1962.

Reviewed *E.H.R.* lxxix (1964), 582–3.

4056 LEWIS (ALUN). 'Roger Leyburn and the pacification of England, 1265–7'. *E.H.R.* liv (1939), 193–214.

4057 LEWIS (FRANK R.). 'William de Valence' (*c.* 1230–96). *Aberystwyth Stud.* xiii (1934), 11–35; xiv (1936), 69–92.

4058 LUBIMENKO (INNA). Jean de Bretagne, comte de Richmond, sa vie et son activité en Angleterre, en Écosse, et en France, 1266–1334. Lille. 1908.

4059 MORRIS (J. E.). The Welsh wars of Edward I. Oxf. 1901 (No. 4310).

R. A. Griffiths, 'The revolt of Rhys ap Maredudd, 1287–8', *Welsh H.R.* iii (1966), 121–43. M. Prestwich, 'A new account of the Welsh campaign of 1294–5', ibid. vi (1972), 89–94.

4060 McFARLANE (KENNETH B.). 'Had Edward I a policy towards the earls?' *History,* l (1965), 145–59.

The policy of aggrandisement of Edward's family. See also T. F. Tout, 'The earldoms under Edward I', *T.R.H.S.* viii (1894), 129–55.

4061 NORGATE (KATE). The minority of Henry the Third. Lond. 1912.

4062 POWICKE (FREDERICK M.). Henry III and the Lord Edward: the community of the realm in the thirteenth century. 2 vols. with continuous pagination. Oxf. 1947. 1-volume edn. 1966.

This political history in its social context deals primarily with the period 1216–74, but adds a chapter on the English conquest of Wales and an epilogue on Edward I. Its theme is the endeavour of important persons to live in a community, not a mutual antipathy of king and barons. The sense of community increases as the century progresses. Its chapters on Poitou, Gascony, and the Sicilian Adventure form excellent summaries of Henry's foreign relations; and the chapter on the reform of the exchequer clarifies administrative history. Powicke is not sympathetic to Simon de Montfort. For reviews, turn to C. R. Cheney in *E.H.R.* lviii (1948), 110–14; and R. F. Treharne in *History,* xxxiv (1949), 121–3. See index below under 'Powicke'.

4063 RICHARDSON (HENRY G.) and SAYLES (G. O.). 'The provisions of Oxford: a forgotten document and some comments'. *B.J.R.L.* vii (1933), 291–321.

4064 SALZMAN (LOUIS F.). Edward I. Lond. 1968.

E. L. G. Stones, *Edward I*, Clarendon Biographies (Lond. 1968), is an elementary yet scholarly survey in sixty pages. See Lyon in *Wilkinson essays* (No. 1459).

4065 SNELLGROVE (HAROLD S.). The Lusignans in England, 1247–1258. Albuquerque. 1950.

4066 TEMPLEMAN (GEOFFREY). 'Edward I and the historians'. *Cambr. Hist. Jour.* x (1950), 16–35.

See Powicke in *Saxl essays* (No. 1452).

4067 TOUT (THOMAS F.). 'Wales and the March during the barons' wars, 1258–1267', in his *Collected papers* (No. 1499).

4068 TREHARNE (REGINALD F.). The baronial plan of reform, 1258–1263. Univ. Manchester Pubns. Hist. Ser. Manchester. 1932.

R. F. Treharne, 'The personal rule of Henry III and the aims of the baronial reformers of 1258', Historical Revision. *History*, New Ser. xvi (1931–2), 336–40; idem, 'The significance of the baronial reform movement, 1258–1267', *T.R.H.S.* 4th Ser. xxv (1943), 35–72; idem, 'The "mad" parliament of Oxford, 1258', Historical Revision. *History*, New Ser. xxxii (1947). 108–11; idem, 'The personal role of Simon de Montfort in the period of baronial reform and rebellion, 1258–65', *P.B.A.* xl (1954), 75–102; idem, 'Knights in the period of reform and rebellion, 1258–67', *B.I.H.R.* xxi (1948), 1–12; idem, *The battle of Lewes, 1264; its place in English history* (Lewes, 1964)—a collection of essays by Powicke, Lemmon, Beamish, Treharne.

4069 TURNER (GEORGE J.). The minority of Henry III. *T.R.H.S.* New Ser. xviii (1904), 245–95; 3rd Ser. i (1907), 205–62.

4070 WATERS (WILLIAM H.). The Edwardian settlement of north Wales in its administrative and legal aspects, 1284–1343. Cardiff. 1935.

A. D. Carr, 'An aristocracy in decline: the native Welsh lords after the Edwardian conquest', *Welsh Hist. Rev.* v (1970), 103–29.

4071 WILKINSON (BERTIE). The constitutional history of England 1216–1399. i. Politics and the Constitution 1216–1307. Lond. etc. 1948.

B. Wilkinson, 'The council and the crisis of 1233–4', *B.J.R.L.* xxvii (1942–3), 384–93. See No. 3391, or 4144.

2. *Anglo-Scottish Relations*

G. Barrow's *Feudal Britain* (No. 3977) provides a good summary of Anglo-Scottish relations to the early fourteenth century as does Powicke's *The Thirteenth Century*. For some sources about military campaigns, turn to Nos. 4279, 4293–5.

4072 ANGLO-SCOTTISH RELATIONS, 1174–1328. Some selected documents. Ed. and trans. by Edward L. G. Stones. Lond. 1965. Reprinted with corrections. Oxf. 1971.

4073 BALFOUR-MELVILLE (EVAN W. M.). Edward III and David II. Historical Asso. pamphlet G. 27. Lond. 1954.

4074 BALFOUR-MELVILLE (E. W. M.). Papers relating to the captivity and release of David II. Scot. Hist. Soc. Miscellany ix (1958).

4075 BARRON (EVAN M.). The Scottish war of independence: a critical study. Lond. 1914. 2nd edn. Inverness. 1934.

4076 BARROW (GEOFFREY W. S.). 'The Anglo-Scottish border'. *Northern History*, i (1966), 21–42. Idem, 'Northern English society in the twelfth and thirteenth centuries'. Ibid. iv (1969), 1–28.

4077 BARROW (G. W. S.). Robert Bruce and the community of the realm of Scotland. Lond. 1965.

> Reviewed by A. A. M. Duncan in *Scot. H.R.* xlv (1966), 184–201. See also E. L. G. Stones, 'The submission of Robert Bruce to Edward I, *c.* 1301–2', ibid. xxxiv (1955), 122–34. J. Scammell, 'Robert I and the north of England', *E.H.R.* lxxiii (1958), 385–403; R. Nicholson, 'The last campaign of Robert Bruce', ibid. lxxvii (1962), 233–46; A. A. M. Duncan, 'The nation of Scots and the declaration of Arbroath (1320)', Hist. Asso. pamphlet G. 75 (Lond. 1970).

4078 FERGUSSON (JAMES). William Wallace. Guardian of Scotland. Lond. 1938. New edn. Stirling. 1948.

4079 LYDON (JAMES F.). 'An Irish army in Scotland, 1296'. *Irish Sword* (Dublin), v (1963), 184–9. Idem, 'Irish levies in the Scottish wars, 1296–1302'. Ibid. v (1963), 207–17.

> R. Nicholson, 'An Irish expedition to Scotland in 1335', *Irish Hist. Stud.* xiii (1963), 197–211.

4080 MILLER (EDWARD). War in the north: the Anglo-Scottish wars of the middle ages (Lecture, 1960). Univ. of Hull Pubns. 1960.

4081 MORRIS (JOHN E.). Bannockburn. Cambr. 1914.

> See T. F. Tout, 'The battle of Bannockburn'. Historical Revision. *History*, New Ser. v (1920–1), 37–40; and Barrow, *Bruce* (No. 4077), pp. 290–332; *The complete peerage* (No. 556), xi, App. B; and J. D. Mackie, *Scot. H.R.* xxix (1950), 207–10.

4082 NICHOLSON (RANALD). Edward III and the Scots: the formative years of a military career (1327–35). Lond. 1965.

> See also R. Nicholson, 'David II, the historians and the chroniclers', *Scot. H.R.* xlv (1966), 59–78 (with many references to Anglo-Scottish relations).

4083 NICHOLSON (R.). 'Franco-Scottish and Franco-Norwegian treaties of 1295'. *Scot. H.R.* xxxviii (1959), 114–32.

4084 PRESTWICH (MICHAEL). 'Victualling estimates for English garrisons in Scotland during the fourteenth century'. *E.H.R.* lxxxii (1967), 536–43.

4085 REID (W. STANFORD). 'Sea-power in the Anglo-Scottish war 1296–1327'. *Mariner's Mirror*, xlvi (1960), 7–23.

4086   STONES (EDWARD L. G.). 'The records of the Great Cause of 1291-2'. *Scot. H.R.* xxv (1956), 89-109.

Stones, 'The appeal to history in Anglo-Scottish relations between 1291 and 1401', *Archives*, xli (1969), 11-21; xlii (1969), 80-3.

4087   STONES (E. L. G.). 'The English mission to Edinburgh in 1328'. *Scot. H.R.* xxviii (1949), 121-32. Idem, 'The treaty of Northampton, 1328'. Historical Revision. *History*, New Ser. xxxviii (1953), 54-61.

4088   WEBSTER (BRUCE), ed. Handlist of the acts of David II. Regesta Regum Scottorum, 1329-1371. Edin. 1958+.

3. *Relations with the Continent*

See the footnote citations in Powicke, *The Thirteenth Century*, especially chaps. iii, vii, and ix, and the chapters on foreign affairs in Powicke's *King Henry III and the Community of the Realm*.

4089   BÉMONT (CHARLES). 'La campagne de Poitou, 1242-43, Taillebourg et Saintes'. *Annales du Midi* (1893), 289-314.

4090   BÉMONT (CHARLES). La Guyenne pendant la domination anglaise, 1152-1453: esquisse d'une bibliographie méthodique. Helps for Students of History, no. 27. Lond. 1920.

4091   BERGER (ÉLIE). 'Les Préparatifs d'une invasion anglaise et la descente de Henri III en Bretagne (1229-30)'. *B.E.C.* liv (1893), 5-44.

4092   BOCK (FRIEDRICH). 'Englands Beziehungen zum Reich unter Adolf von Nassau'. *M.I.O.G. Erg. Bd.* xii (1932), 199-257. See No. 4109.

4093   BOISSONNADE (PROSPER). Histoire de Poitou: ouvrage illustré de gravures hors texte. Paris. 1915.

4094   BOUTARIC (EDGARD P.). Saint Louis et Alphonse de Poitiers. Étude sur la réunion des provinces du midi et de l'ouest à la couronne et sur les origines de la centralisation administrative, d'après des documents inédits. Paris. 1870.

4095   CUTTINO (GEORGE). English Diplomatic Administration 1259-1339 (No. 3839). 2nd edn. 1971.

4096   DENHOLM-YOUNG (NOEL). Richard of Cornwall. Oxf. 1947.

Cf. F. R. Lewis, 'Beatrice of Falkenburg, the third wife of Richard of Cornwall', *E.H.R.* lii (1937), 279-82; idem, 'The election of Richard of Cornwall as senator of Rome in 1261', ibid. lii (1937), 657-62. C. C. Bayley, 'The diplomatic preliminaries of the double election of 1257 in Germany', ibid. lxii (1947), 457-83. H. S. Lucas, 'John of Avesnes and Richard of Cornwall', *Speculum*, xxiii (1948), 81-101.

4097   FAWTIER (ROBERT). L'Europe occidentale de 1270 à 1380. pt. i (1270-1328) in *Histoire général*, edited by G. Glotz, vol. vi, pt. i. Paris. 1940.

Excellent on Anglo-French relations. See also Fawtier, *The Capetian kings of France: monarchy and nation* (987-1328), trans. by Lionel Butler and R. J. Adams. Lond. 1960.

4098 GAVRILOVITCH (MICHEL). Étude sur le traité de Paris de 1259. Paris. 1899.

Includes pièces justificatives. See also I. J. Sanders, 'The texts of the treaty of Paris, 1259', *E.H.R.* lxvi (1951), 81–97; and Pierre Chaplais, 'Le Traité de Paris de 1259 et l'inféodation de la Gascogne allodiale', *Le Moyen Âge*, lxi (1955), 121–37.

4099 HELLE (KNUT). 'Anglo-Norwegian relations in the reign of Håkon Håkonsson (1217–63)'. *Medieval Scandinavia*, i (1968), 101–14.

4100 JOHNSTONE (HILDA). 'The county of Ponthieu, 1279–1307'. *E.H.R.* xxix (1914), 435–52.

4101 KÖHLER (RUTH). Die Heiratsverhandlungen zwischen Eduard I. von England und Rudolf von Habsburg: ein Beitrag zur englisch-deutschen Bündnispolitik am Ausgang des 13. Jahrhunderts. Meisenheim am Glan. 1969.

4102 LYON (BRYCE D.). 'Un compte de l'echiquier relatif aux relations d'Édouard Iᵉʳ d'Angleterre avec le duc Jean II de Brabant'. *Bull. de la Commission royale d'histoire* (Brussels), cxx (1955), 67–93.

See J. de Sturler, *Deux comptes . . . de Robert de Segre . . .* (1294–6) (Brussels, 1960).

4103 MARSH (FRANK B.). English rule in Gascony, 1199–1259, with special reference to the towns. Univ. Michigan Hist. Stud. Ann Arbor. 1912.

See J. P. Trabut-Cussac, *L'Administration anglaise en Gascogne (1254–1307).* (Paris and Geneva, 1972).

4104 PAINTER (SIDNEY). The scourge of the clergy: Peter of Dreux, duke of Brittany. Johns Hopkins Hist. Pubns. Baltimore. 1937.

4105 PETIT-DUTAILLIS (CHARLES E.). Étude sur la vie et le règne de Louis VIII (1187–1226). Paris. 1894.

Élie Berger, *Histoire de Blanche de Castille, reine de France.* Paris. 1895.

4106 RÖHRICHT (REINHOLD). 'La Croisade du prince Édouard d'Angleterre, 1270–1274'. *Archives de l'Orient latin.* i (1881), 617–32.

4107 ROTHWELL (HARRY). 'Edward I's case against Philip the fair over Gascony in 1298'. *E.H.R.* xlii (1927), 572–82. See Nos. 4098 and 4164.

See J. G. Black, 'Edward I and Gascony in 1300', *E.H.R.* xvii (1902), 518–27.

4108 SALT (MARY C. L.). 'List of English embassies to France 1272–1307'. *E.H.R.* xliv (1929), 263–78.

Cf. *B.I.H.R.* vi (1928), 29–31.

4109 TRAUTZ (FRITZ). Die Könige von England und das Reich 1272–1377, mit einem Rückblick auf ihr Verhältnis zu den Staufen. Heidelberg. 1961.

Trautz's study begins with a summary of the period 1106 to 1272. See also Henry S. Lucas, 'Diplomatic relations of Edward I and Albert of Austria', *Speculum*, ix (1934), 125–34; and Hilda Johnstone, 'John de Cole, envoy of Edward I, and some of his colleagues', *Speculum*, xi (1936), 212–24. Other important studies are Geoffrey Barraclough, 'Edward I and Adolf of Nassau: a chapter of medieval diplomatic history', *Cambr. Hist. Jour.* vi (1940), 225–62. More generally, Walther Kienast, *Die deutschen*

Fürsten im Dienste der Westmächte bis zum tode Philipps des Schönen von Frankreich (2 vols. Utrecht. 1924–31); and Fritz Kern, *Die Anfänge der französischen Ausdehnungspolitik bis zum Jahr 1308* (Tübingen. 1910). See No. 4092.

D. THE FOURTEENTH CENTURY, 1307–1399

1. *Domestic Politics*

May McKisack's *The Fourteenth Century* and the *Cambridge Medieval History*, vol. vii, supply bibliographies. The fourth volume of *English historical documents* begins with 1327. *Chaucer's life records* (No. 7007) includes documents on public affairs. Margaret Hastings's bibliographical essay in Furber's *Changing views* (No. 18), pp. 58–100, reprinted with additions from *Speculum*, xxxvi (1961), 225–53, is a valuable interpretative study of the books and articles on English history for the fourteenth and fifteenth centuries published between 1930 and 1961; it will repay careful reading. Wilkinson's *Constitutional history* (No. 4143) prints recent references at the beginning of each chapter. See the entries under the law of treason (Nos. 3709–17) and under impeachments (No. 3418).

4110 BELLAMY (J. G.). 'The northern rebellions in the last years of Richard II'. *B.J.R.L.* xlvii (1965), 254–74.

Cf. J. A. Tuck, 'Richard II and the border magnates', *Northern History*, iii (1968), 27–52.

4111 BIRD (RUTH). The turbulent London of Richard II. Lond. and N.Y. 1949.

Helen Suggett, 'A letter describing Richard II's reconciliation with the city of London', *E.H.R.* lxii (1947), 209–13.

4112 CLARKE (MAUDE V.). Fourteenth century studies (No. 1464). Idem, Medieval Representation (No. 3349). Idem, 'Committees of estates and the deposition of Edward II' in *Tait essays* (No. 1455).

4113 CLARKE (MAUDE V.) and GALBRAITH (VIVIAN H.). 'The deposition of Edward II'. *B.J.R.L* xiv (1930), 125–81 (No. 1464).

Sir E. Maunde Thompson, 'A contemporary account of the fall of Richard II', *The Burlington Magazine*, v (1904), 160–72, 267–70. H. G. Wright, 'The protestation of Richard II in the tower in September, 1399', *B.J.R.L.* xxiii (1939), 151–65. B. Wilkinson, 'The deposition of Richard II and the accession of Henry IV', *E.H.R.* liv (1939), 215–39; and compare Lapsley (No. 1478). G. E. Caspary, 'The deposition of Richard II and the canon law', *Procs. Second International Congress of Medieval Canon Law* (Boston, 1962) *Procs.* (Vatican City, 1965), pp. 189–201.

4114 CURTIS (EDMUND). Richard II in Ireland 1394–5 and the submission of the Irish chiefs. Oxf. 1927.

Also E. Curtis, 'Unpublished letters from Richard II in Ireland, 1394–5', *Royal Irish Acad. Procs.* xxxvii, Sect. C, no. 14 (1927), 276–303. J. F. Lydon, 'Richard II's expeditions to Ireland', ibid. xciii (1963), 135–49.

4115 DAVIES (JAMES CONWAY). The baronial opposition to Edward II, its character and policy: a study in administrative history. Cambr. 1918. *

This first-class study in administrative history, along with Tout's similar work (No. 4140), maintained the thesis of a rather solid baronial opposition. That thesis is rejected by Maddicott and by Phillips (No. 4127).

4116 DAVIES (J. C.). 'The Despenser war in Glamorgan'. *T.R.H.S.* 3rd Ser. ix (1915), 21–64.

> G. A. Holmes, 'Judgement on the younger Despenser', *E.H.R.* lxx (1955), 261–7. Idem, 'A protest against the Despensers 1326' (by Lady Clare against the loss of inheritance), *Speculum*, xxx (1955), 207–12. B. Wilkinson, 'The Sherburn indenture and the attack on the Despensers, 1321', *E.H.R.* lxiii (1948), 1–28. George L. Haskins, 'The Doncaster petition, 1321', ibid. liii (1938), 478–85. See Maddicott (No. 4127), pp. 259 ff.

4117 DAVIES (RICHARD G.). 'Some notes from the register of Henry de Wakefield, bishop of Worcester, on the political crisis of 1386–1388'. *E.H.R.* lxxxvi (1971), 547–58.

4118 DUNN-PATTISON (RICHARD P.). The Black Prince. Lond. 1910.

> Cf. Peter Shaw, 'The Black Prince', *History*, N.S. xxiv (1939–40), 1–15. David L. Evans, 'Notes on the history of the principality of Wales in the time of the Black Prince', *Hon. Soc. Cymmrodorion Trans.* (1925–6), 25–100. See M. Sharp in *Tout essays* (No. 1458).

4119 EDWARDS (KATHLEEN). 'The political importance of the English bishops during the reign of Edward II'. *E.H.R.* lix (1944), 311–47.

4120 HARTSHORNE (CHARLES H.). 'An itinerary of Edward II'. *Collectanea Archaeologica*, i (1861), 113–44; and privately printed, 1861.

4121 HOLMES (GEORGE A.). 'The rebellion of the earl of Lancaster, 1328–29'. *B.I.H.R.* xxviii (1955), 84–9.

4122 HUGHES (DOROTHY). A study of social and constitutional tendencies in the early years of Edward III, as illustrated more especially by the events connected with the ministerial inquiries of 1340 and the following years. Lond. 1915.

> B. Wilkinson, 'The protest of the earls of Arundel and Surrey in the crisis of 1341', *E.H.R.* xlvi (1931), 177–93.

4123 HUTCHISON (HAROLD F.). The hollow crown: a life of Richard II. Lond. and N.Y. 1961.

> A provocative vindication of the king.

4124 JONES (RICHARD H.). The royal policy of Richard II: absolutism in the later middle ages. Oxf. 1968.

> Caroline M. Barron, 'The tyranny of Richard II', *B.I.H.R.* xli (1968), 1–18. L. C. Hector, 'An alleged historical outburst of Richard II', *E.H.R.* lxviii (1953), 62–5.

4125 LAPSLEY (GAILLARD). Crown, community and parliament. Ed. by Helen M. Cam and Geoffrey Barraclough. Oxf. 1951.

> Analysed under No. 1478.

4126 McKISACK (MAY). 'Edward III and the historians'. *History*, xlv (1960), 1–15.

> A vindication of Edward III rather than a bibliographical study.

4127 MADDICOTT (JOHN R.). Thomas of Lancaster 1307–1322: a study in the reign of Edward II. Oxford Hist. Monographs. Lond. 1970.

Concerned with the politics of the reign viewed 'through the eyes of a great noble rather than those of the king', and maintains that personal interests of barons rather than a solid baronial opposition to the king form the substance of the politics of the reign. Apparently a similar thesis is upheld by J. R. S. Phillips in *Aymer de Valence, earl of Pembroke 1307–1324: baronial politics in the reign of Edward II* (Oxf. 1972). See Davies (No. 4115). For the treaty of Leake (1318), see Edwards in *Poole essays* (No. 1448), and Wilkinson in *Powicke essays* (No. 1450).

4128   MATHEW (GERVASE). The court of Richard II. Lond. 1968.

A broadly based work on cultural history with its final chapters on politics.

4129   MIDDLETON (ARTHUR E.). Sir Gilbert de Middleton and the part he took in the rebellion in the north of England in 1317. Newcastle-upon-Tyne. 1918.

4130   MYRES (JOHN N. L.). 'The campaign of Radcot Bridge in December 1387'. *E.H.R.* xlii (1927), 20–33.

Discussed the value of the sources, namely: Malvern, Knighton, and Walsingham.

4131   POWICKE (MICHAEL R.). 'The English commons in Scotland in 1322 and the deposition of Edward II'. *Speculum*, xxxv (1960), 556–62.

4132   THE REIGN OF RICHARD II. Essays in honour of May McKisack. Ed. by F. R. H. Du Boulay and Caroline M. Barron. Lond. 1971. Analysed in No. 7223.

4133   ROBERTS (RICHARD A.). Edward II, the lord ordainers and Piers Gaveston's jewels and horses, 1312–13. Camden 3rd Ser. xli. *Camden Miscellany*, xv (1929).

Transcript from Vatican archives on Edward's recovery of the jewels.

4134   SAYLES (GEORGE O.). 'The formal judgments on the traitors of 1322'. *Speculum*, xvi (1941), 57–63.

George L. Haskins, 'Judicial proceedings against a traitor after Boroughbridge, 1322', *Speculum*, xii (1937), 509–11.

4135   SAYLES (G. O.). 'King Richard II of England: a fresh look'. *Amer. Philos. Soc. Procs.* cxv (1971), 28–31.

4136   SMITH (SIDNEY ARMITAGE). John of Gaunt. Westminster. 1904. Reprinted, 1964.

4137   STEEL (ANTHONY). Richard II. Cambr. 1941. Reprinted, 1962.

Cf. V. H. Galbraith, 'A new life of Richard II', *History*, New Ser. xxvii (1942), 223–39.

4138   TAIT (JAMES). 'Did Richard II murder the duke of Gloucester?' Historical essays . . . of the Owens College, Manchester. (No. 1472.) Reprinted with an index. Manchester. 1907.

A. E. Stamp, 'Richard II and the death of the duke of Gloucester', *E.H.R.* xxxviii (1923), 249–51; xlvii (1932), 453, and 726. R. Atkinson, ibid. xxxviii (1923), 563–4. H. G. Wright, ibid. xlvii (1932), 276–80.

4139 TOUT (THOMAS F.). 'The captivity and death of Edward of Carnarvon', in his *Collected papers* (No. 1499).

Joseph Hunter, 'Measures taken for the apprehension of Sir Thomas de Gournay, one of the murderers of Edward II', *Archaeologia*, xxvii (1838), 274–97. For some documents relating to the death of Edward II, edited by S. A. Moore, see ibid. l (1887), 215–26. F. J. Tanquerey, 'The conspiracy of Thomas Dunheved, 1327', *E.H.R.* xxi (1916), 119–24. Gabriele Lambrick, 'Abingdon and the riots of 1327', *Oxoniensia*, xxix–xxx (1964–5), 129–41.

4140 TOUT (THOMAS F.). The place of the reign of Edward II in English history. Ford lectures 1913. Manchester. 1914. 2nd edn., revised throughout by Hilda Johnstone. Manchester. 1936.

Appendix contains the household ordinances of York of 1318 and 1323, and lists the officials under Edward II. See Davies (No. 4115) and Maddicott (No. 4127).

4141 TRUEMAN (JOHN H.). 'The privy seal and the ordinances of 1311'. *Speculum*, xxxi (1956), 611–25. Idem, 'The Statute of York and the Ordinances of 1311'. *Medievalia et Humanistica*, x (1956), 64–81. Idem, 'The personnel of mediaeval reform, the English lords ordainers'. *Medieval Stud.* xxi (1959), 247–71.

4142 TUPLING (GEORGE H.), ed. South Lancashire in the reign of Edward II as illustrated by the pleas at Wigan in Coram Rege roll no. 254. Chetham Soc. 3rd Ser. i (1949).

4143 WILKINSON (BERTIE). Constitutional history of medieval England, 1216–1399. Vol. ii: Politics and the constitution, 1307–1399. Lond. etc. 1952.

4144 WILKINSON (BERTIE). Studies in the constitutional history of the thirteenth and fourteenth centuries. Manchester. 1937.

2. *Peasants' Revolt of 1381*

Réville's volume (No. 4156) published posthumously by Petit-Dutaillis, has a valuable introduction by Petit-Dutaillis, reprinted in No. 4153, and an indispensable appendix of records. Of Petrushevsky's study of Wat Tyler (No. 4154), M. M. Postan wrote: 'especially in its earlier editions, one of the most important studies of English rural society in any language' (*Econ. H.R.* 2nd Ser. iii (1950–1), 120, note 2). Oman's book is the best study in English, and its 1969 edition is fortified with an introduction by E. B. Fryde. For its background, see the index below under poll-tax; and for its contemporary chroniclers, see Nos. 2787, 2912, and 2976. Local risings are described in some volumes of the *Victoria County History* (No. 1529). An excellent brief account is given in May McKisack, *The Fourteenth Century*, pp. 406–23; and on the revolt in London, in Ruth Bird, *Turbulent London* (No. 4111), pp. 526–62.

4145 DOBSON (R. B.). The peasants' revolt of 1381. History in Depth series. Lond. 1970. Paperback edn.

Translations into English of extracts from chronicles and records (404 pages) with an introduction and brief, selective bibliography.

4146 FLAHERTY (WILLIAM E.). 'The great rebellion in Kent, 1381, illustrated from the public records'. *Archaeologia Cantiana*, iii (1860), 65–96; iv (1861), 67–86.

4147 FRYDE (EDMUND B.). 'The English parliament and the peasants' revolt of 1381'. *Liber memoralis Georges de Lagarde* (No. 3366), pp. 73–88.

4148 HILTON (RODNEY H.) and FAGAN (HYMAN). The English rising of 1381. Lond. 1950.

A Marxist interpretation. R. H. Hilton, 'Peasant movements in England before 1381', *Econ. H.R.* 2nd Ser. ii (1949), 117–36; reprinted in *Essays in economic history* (No. 1468), ii. 73–90.

4149 KENYON (NORA). 'Labour conditions in Essex in the reign of Richard II'. *Econ. H.R.* iv (1934), 429–51.

Reprinted in *Essays in economic history* (No. 1468), ii. 91–111.

4150 KRIEHN (GEORGE). 'Studies in the sources of the social revolt in 1381'. *A.H.R.* vii (1901–2), 254–85; 458–84.

4151 OMAN (CHARLES). The great revolt of 1381. Oxf. 1906. New edn. with introduction by Edmund B. Fryde. Lond. 1969.

See appendices on the poll-tax rolls in the Record Office, the population in England in 1381, detailed poll-tax returns of a typical hundred (Hinckford, Essex), and other documents.

4152 PALMER (WILLIAM M.). 'Records of the villein insurrection in Cambridgeshire'. *East Anglian* (Ipswich), New Ser. vi (1896), 81–4; 97–102; 135–9; 167–72; 209–12; 234–7.

Prints extracts from plea rolls, 5 Rich. II.

4153 PETIT-DUTAILLIS (CHARLES). 'The causes and general characteristics of the rising of 1381', in *Studies Supplementary to Stubbs* (No. 1221), ii. 252–304.

4154 PETRUSHEVSKY (DMITRI M.). Vosstanie Uota Tailera (the rising of Wat Tyler). 2 vols. Vol. i: St. Petersburg. 1897; vol. ii, Moscow. 1901. Revised edn. in one volume, 1914 and 1927.

A valuable work based on research in the P.R.O. Not translated into English, but summarized in reviews by Alexander Savine, *E.H.R.* xvii (1902), 780–2; and by Vinogradoff, *Deutsche Literaturzeitung*, xxiii (22 February 1902), 487–91.

4155 POWELL (EDGAR). The rising in East Anglia in 1381: with an appendix containing the Suffolk poll-tax lists for that year. Cambr. 1896.

The expansion of a paper on the rising in Suffolk, 1381, in *T.R.H.S.* New Ser. viii (1894), 203–49. See also J. A. Sparvel-Bayly, 'Essex in insurrection, in 1381', *Essex Archael. Soc. Trans.* New Ser. i (1878), 205–19. Reprinted in *Antiquary*, xix (1889), 11–14, 69–73.

4156 RÉVILLE (ANDRÉ). Le Soulèvement des travailleurs d'Angleterre en 1381, par André Réville: études et documents, publiés avec une introduction historique par Charles Petit-Dutaillis. Société de l'École des Chartes, Mémoires et documents, ii. Paris. 1898.

The introduction by Petit-Dutaillis is an excellent general account of the uprising. The body of the work by Réville gives a detailed history of the revolt in the counties of Hertford, Norfolk, and Suffolk. The appendices, pp. 175–294, comprise a valuable collection of documents relating to the rising in most of the counties of England. See also Petit-Dutaillis (No. 4153).

4157 TREVELYAN (GEORGE M.). England in the age of Wycliffe. Lond. etc. 1899. New edn. 1904.

Deals mainly with the early part of Richard II's reign, especially with the rise of Lollardy and the peasants' revolt.

4158 TREVELYAN (G. M.) and POWELL (EDGAR). The peasants' rising and the Lollards (1381–98): a collection of documents forming an appendix to *England in the age of Wycliffe*. Lond. 1899.

4159 WARREN (WILFRED L.). 'The peasants' revolt of 1381'. *History today*, xii (1962), 845–53; xiii (1963), 44–51. Reprinted in Crowder, *English society* (No. 4199), pp. 41–70.

4160 WILKINSON (BERTIE). 'Peasants' revolt in 1381'. *Speculum*, xv (1940), 12–35.

3. *Relations with the Continent*

a. Comprehensive narratives

4161 BOUTRUCHE (ROBERT). La crise d'une société: seigneurs et paysans du Bordelais pendant la guerre de cent ans. Paris. 1947.

4162 BURNE (ALFRED H.). The Crécy war: a military history of the hundred years war from 1337 to the treaty of Bretigny. Lond. 1955. Idem, The Agincourt war: a military history of the latter part of the hundred years war from 1369 to 1453. Lond. 1956.

4163 CARR (A. D.). 'Welshmen and the hundred years war'. *Welsh History Rev.* iv (1968), 21–46.

4164 LODGE (ELEANOR C.). Gascony under English rule. Lond. 1926. *

E. C. Lodge, 'The relations between England and Gascony, 1152–1453', *History*, New Ser. xix (1934–5), 131–9. Idem, 'The constables of Bordeaux in the reign of Edward III', *E.H.R.* i (1935), 225–41, 501. (The constables from 1254 to 1399 are listed in Tout, *Administrative history* (No. 1223), vi. 65–72. G. P. Cuttino, 'The process of Agen', *Speculum*, xix (1944), 161–78 (royal commissioners negotiate on Guienne). P. Chaplais, 'English arguments concerning the feudal status of Aquitaine in the fourteenth century', *B.I.H.R.* xxi (1948), 203–13. Idem, Le duché-pairie de Guienne', *Annales du Midi*, lxix (1957), 5–38. É. Perroy, 'Édouard III d'Angleterre et les seigneurs gascons en 1368', ibid. lxi (1948), 91–6. Yves Renouard, 'Ce que l'Angleterre doit à l'Aquitaine', *Conférences de Lundi*. Univ. Bordeaux Pubns. no. 7 (1945–61), 113–24. B. Guillemain, 'Les Tentatives pontificales de médiation dans le litige franco-anglais de Guyenne au XIVᵉ siècle', *Bull. philol. et hist. du Comité des travaux histor. et scientif.* (Paris) (1957), 423–32. See Déprez and Loviette in *Bémont essays* (No. 1426), and Chaplais in *Jenkinson studies* (No. 1441), in *Le Moyen Âge*, xviii (1963), 448–69.

4165 PAULI (REINHOLD). Bilder aus Alt-England. Gotha. 1860. 2nd edn. 1876. Trans. by E. C. Otté, Pictures of Old England. Cambr. etc. 1861.

  II. Die Politik Wilhelms des Eroberers.
  III. Das Parlament im 14. Jahrhundert.
  IV. Englands älteste Beziehungen zu Oesterreich und Preussen.
  V. Ludwig IV. und Eduard III.
  VIII. John Wiclif.
  IX. Heinrich V und König Sigismund.
  XI. Herzog Humfrid von Gloucester.

4166 PERROY (ÉDOUARD). La guerre de cent ans. Paris. 1946. Trans. by W. B. Wells. Lond. 1951.

  Kenneth Fowler, ed. *The hundred years war* (Lond. 1971), provides original, up-to-date essays, with bibliographies, by eight scholars.

4167 PIRENNE (HENRI). Histoire de Belgique. 7 vols. Brussels. 1900–32.

  Vol. ii: Du commencement du XIVe siècle à la mort de Charles le Téméraire.

4168 RENOUARD (YVES), ed. Bordeaux sous les rois d'Angleterre. Bordeaux. 1965.

  This work of collaboration is vol. iii of *Histoire de Bordeaux*. Ed. by Charles Higounet.

4169 STURLER (JEAN V. de). Les Relations politiques et les échanges commerciaux entre le duché de Brabant et l'Angleterre au moyen âge. Paris. 1936.

4170 VAUGHAN (RICHARD). Philip the Bold: the formation of the Burgundian state. Lond. 1962. Idem, John the Fearless: the growth of Burgundian power. Lond. 1966. Idem, Philip the Good: the apogee of Burgundy. Lond. 1970.

  The best studies in English on Burgundy in the late Middle Ages; useful for relations with England; include exhaustive bibliographies.

b. Hundred Years War—First Phase

The bibliographies in Fowler (No. 4178) and in the Birdsall–Newhall edition of the *Chronicle of Jean de Venette* (No. 2967) are useful.

4171 BOCK (FRIEDRICH). Das deutsch–englische Bündnis von 1335–1342. i: Quellen. Quellen und Erörterungen z. bayer. Geschichte. New Ser. xii. Munich. 1956. See No. 3804.

  H. S. Offler, 'England and Germany at the beginning of the hundred years war', *E.H.R.* liv (1939), 608–31.

4172 BUENO DE MESQUITA (DANIEL M.). 'The foreign policy of Richard II in 1397: some Italian letters'. *E.H.R.* lvi (1941), 628–37.

4173 CAMPBELL (JAMES). 'England, Scotland, and the hundred years war in the fourteenth century', in *Europe in the late Middle Ages*. Ed. by John Hale, J. R. L. Highfield, and B. Smalley. Lond. and Evanston (Ill.). 1965. Pp. 184–216.

  Useful bibliographical citations.

4174 CHAPLAIS (PIERRE). 'Réglement des conflits internationaux franco-anglais au XIVᵉ siècle (1293–1377)'. *Le Moyen Âge*, lvii (1951), 269–302.

Adds five *pièces justificatives*.

4175 DELACHENAL (ROLAND). Histoire de Charles V. 5 vols. Paris. 1909–31.

Vols. ii and iii include *pièces justificatives*.

4176 DENIFLE (HENRI). La Désolation des églises, monastères et hôpitaux en France pendant la guerre de cent ans. i (1337–84). Paris. 1889. *

4177 DÉPREZ (EUGÈNE). Les Préliminaires de la guerre de cent ans. La papauté, la France et l'Angleterre. Paris. 1902.

4178 FOWLER (KENNETH). The king's lieutenant: Henry of Grosmont, first duke of Lancaster, 1310–1361. Lond. and N.Y. 1969.

Almost exclusively concerned with Lancaster's role in the first phases of the hundred years war. Extensive and excellent bibliography and reference-notes; and eight unpublished documents.

4179 FRYDE (EDMUND B.). 'Financial resources of Edward III in the Netherlands, 1337–40'. *Revue belge de philol. et d'hist.* xlv (1967), 1142–1215.

See idem, 'Parliament and the French war, 1336–40', *Wilkinson essays* (No. 1459).

4180 HEWITT (HERBERT J.). The Black Prince's expedition of 1355–1357. Manchester. 1958.

4181 JENKINS (HELEN). Papal efforts for peace under Benedict XII, 1334–42. Lond. and Philadelphia. 1933.

F. Unterkircher, 'Peregrinarius Hugonis von Jahre 1342', *M.I.O.G.* lix (1951), 123–35 (a poem calling for peace between Edward III and Philip VI). See also Déprez in *Tout essays* (No. 1458).

4182 JONES (MICHAEL). Ducal Brittany 1364–1399. Relations with England and France during the reign of Duke John IV. Oxf. 1970.

4182A JONES (M.), ed. Some documents relating to the disputed succession to the duchy of Brittany, 1341. R.H.S. Camden, 4th Ser. lx *Camden Miscellany*, xxiv (1972), 1–78.

4183 LE PATOUREL (JOHN). 'Edward III and the kingdom of France'. *History*, xliii (1958), 173–89. Idem, 'The treaty of Brétigny, 1360'. *T.R.H.S.* 5th Ser. x (1960), 19–39.

4184 LUCAS (HENRY S.). The Low Countries and the hundred years war, 1326–1347'. Univ. Michigan Pubns. Hist. and Pol. Sci. viii. Ann Arbor. 1929. Idem, John III, duke of Brabant, and the French alliance, 1345–1347. Univ. Washington Pubns. iv, no. 1. Seattle. 1927.

H. Lucas, 'Diplomatic relations between England and Flanders from 1329 to 1336', *Speculum*, xi (1936), 59–87. Idem, 'A document relating to the marriage of Philippa of Hainault in 1327', *Pirenne études* (No. 1447).

4185 LUCE (SIMÉON). La France pendant la guerre de cent ans; épisodes historiques et vie privée aux XIVᵉ et XVᵉ siècles. Paris. 1890.

4186 MOLLAT (GUILLAUME). 'Innocent VI et les tentatives de paix entre la France et l'Angleterre (1353–55)'. *R.H.E.* x (1909), 729–43.

G. Mollat, 'La Diplomatie pontificale au XIVᵉ siècle', *Mélanges . . . Louis Halphen* (Paris, 1951), pp. 507–12. É. Perroy, 'Quatre lettres du cardinal Guy de Boulogne (1352–1354)', *Revue du Nord*, xxxvi (1954), 159–64. See B. Guillemain (No. 4164); and Bock (No. 3804).

4187 PALMER (J. J. N.). 'The Anglo-French peace negotiations, 1390–6'. *T.R.H.S.* 5th Ser. xvi (1966), 81–94.

J. Palmer, 'Articles for the final peace between England and France, 16 June 1393', *B.I.H.R.* xxxix (1966), 180–5; idem, 'The background of Richard II's marriage to Isabel of France (1396)', ibid. xliv (1971), 1–17.

4188 PERROY (ÉDOUARD). L'Angleterre et le grand schisme d'Occident: étude sur la politique religieuse de l'Angleterre sous Richard II (1378–1399). Paris. 1933.

An excellent study on England and the Papacy; useful also for the Anglo-Imperial alliance, for Bishop Despenser's crusade to Flanders, and for John of Gaunt's intervention in Spain. See also Perroy, 'France and Navarre from 1359 to 1364', *B.I.H.R.* xiii (1936), 151–4; idem, 'Franco-English relations, 1350–1400', *History*, New Ser. xxi (1936–7), 148–54; idem, 'Louis de Male et les négociations de paix franco-anglaises', *Revue belge de philol. et d'hist.* xxvii (1949), 138–50; idem, 'L'Administration de Calais, 1371–1372', *Revue du Nord*, No. 132 (1951), 218–27; idem, 'Compte de William Gunthorp, trésorier de Calais 1371–1372', *Mémoires de la Commission, Département des monuments historiques du Pas-de-Calais* (Arras) x, fasc. i (1959); idem, 'The Anglo-French negotiations at Bruges, 1374–77', *R.H.S. Camden Miscellany*, xix (1952).

4189 RUSSELL (PETER E.). The English intervention in Spain and Portugal in the time of Edward III and Richard II. Oxf. 1955.

4190 SHERBORNE (J. W.). 'The Hundred Years War, the English navy: shipping and manpower, 1369–1389'. *Past and Present*, xxxvii (1967), 163–75. Idem, 'The battle of La Rochelle and the war at sea, 1372–5'. *B.I.H.R.* xlii (1969), 17–29.

For a list of ships used to transport Henry of Lancaster's troops to Bordeaux in 1345, see Hewitt, *The organization of war* (No. 4303), app. ii. For a description of galleys, see Russell, *English intervention* (No. 4189), pp. 229–33.

4191 TEMPLEMAN (GEOFFREY). 'Edward III and the beginnings of the hundred years war'. *T.R.H.S.* 5th Ser. ii (1952), 69–88.

Cf. Philippe Wolff, 'Un Problème d'origines: la guerre de cent ans', *Éventail de l'histoire vivante: hommage à Lucien Febvre* (Paris, 1953), ii. 141–8. G. P. Cuttino, 'Historical revision: the causes of the hundred years war', *Speculum*, xxxi (1956), 463–77.

4192 TIMBAL (PIERRE-CLÉMENT). La Guerre de cent ans vue à travers les registres du parlement, 1337–1360. Paris. 1962.

4193 WROTTESLEY (GEORGE). Crécy and Calais. Lond. 1898. (No. 4278.)

See Greaves in *Finance and trade* (No. 1469); and Tout's *Collected papers* (No. 1499).

E. THE FIFTEENTH CENTURY, 1399–1485

1. *Domestic Politics*

Until recent decades, the English fifteenth century was often regarded as a dull and sterile age of war and civil strife, sandwiched in between the constructive Middle Ages and modern Tudors. Fifteenth-century England seemed to exemplify 'The Waning of the Middle Ages'. Since the Second World War a generation of scholars has devoted itself to detailed investigations which bring this century to life. That generation is strongly represented in the following list. Further studies find their appropriate places in sections on the exchequer (e.g. Nos. 3253, 3263), on the council and parliament (e.g. Nos. 3298–3300), and on the Church (e.g. Nos. 5627, 5629, 5690). E. F. Jacob's *The Fifteenth Century* and the *Cambridge Medieval History*, vol. viii, provide modern studies and useful retrospective bibliographies.

4194 ARMSTRONG (CHARLES A. J.). 'Politics and the battle of St. Albans, 1455'. *B.I.H.R.* xxxiii (1960), 1–72.

4195 BAGLEY (JOHN J.). Margaret of Anjou, queen of England. Lond. 1948.

A. R. Myers, 'The household of Queen Margaret of Anjou, 1452–3', *B.J.R.L.* xl (1957–8), 79–113; prints the Account Book of William Cotton, Esquire, Receiver-General of Queen Margaret.

4196 CHRIMES (STANLEY B.). Lancastrians, Yorkists and Henry VII. Lond. 1964.

S. B. Chrimes, 'The fifteenth century', *History*, xlviii (1963), 19–27, a review of Jacob *The Fifteenth Century* (No. 1189).

4197 CHRIMES (S. B.). 'Some letters of John of Lancaster as warden of the east marches towards Scotland (1399–1412)'. *Speculum*, xiv (1939), 3–27.

4198 CHRISTIE (MABEL E.). Henry VI. Lond. etc. 1922.

F. A. Gasquet, *The religious life of King Henry VI* (Lond. 1923).

4199 CROWDER (CHRISTOPHER M. D.), ed. English society and government in the fifteenth century: a selection of articles from *History today*. Edin. and Lond. 1967.

4200 DU BOULAY (FRANCIS R. H.). The age of ambition: English society in the late middle ages. Lond. and N.Y. 1970.

4201 ERLANGER (PHILIPPE). Marguerite d'Anjou et la guerre des deux roses. Paris. 1961. English translation. Coral Gables (Florida). 1971.

A popularization of limited use.

4202 EVANS (HOWELL T.). Wales and the wars of the roses. Cambr. 1915.

Ralph A. Griffiths, 'Gruffydd ap Nicholas and the fall of the house of Lancaster', *Welsh History Rev.* ii (1965) 213–31.

4203 GAIRDNER (JAMES). Life and reign of Richard III. Lond. 1878. 2nd edn. 1879. New edn. Cambr. 1898. *

Consult Sylvester's edition of More's *History of Richard III* (No. 2927); J. Gairdner, 'Did Henry VII murder the princes?', *E.H.R.* vi (1891), 444–64, 813–15; an answer to

C. R. Markham, ibid. vi (1891), 250–83, 806–13. In a subsequent book (No. 4222), Markham strove to absolve Richard III of charges against him. Some references concerning the death of the princes are given in *The Complete peerage* (No. 556). Dennis E. Rhodes writes on 'The princes in the Tower and their doctor', *E.H.R.* lxxvii (1962), 304–6; and describes the career of that doctor in 'Provost Argentine of King's and his books', *Cambr. Bibliog. Soc. Trans.* ii (1956), 205–12. The examination of bones of children found in the Tower of London is described by L. E. Tanner and W. Wright, 'Recent investigations regarding the fate of the princes in the Tower', *Archaeologia*, lxxxiv (1934), 1–26. For current opinions, see Jacob, *The Fifteenth Century* (No. 1189), pp. 623–5; Myers (No. 4224); and Kendall, *Richard III* (No. 4210), app. i, pp. 465–95, where Kendall concludes that 'The available evidence admits of no decisive solution'.

4204 GILSON (JULIUS P.). 'A defence of the proscription of the Yorkists'. *E.H.R.* xxvi (1911), 511–23.

4205 GRIFFITHS (RALPH A.). 'Local rivalries and national politics: the Percies, the Nevilles and the Duke of Exeter, 1452–55'. *Speculum*, xliii (1968), 589–632.

4206 HARRISS (G. L.). 'The struggle for Calais: an aspect of the rivalry between Lancaster and York' (1456–60). *E.H.R.* lxxv (1960), 30–53.

4207 HAWARD (WINIFRED I.). 'Economic aspects of the wars of the roses in east Anglia'. *E.H.R.* xli (1926), 170–89.

4208 IVES (E. W.). 'Andrew Dymmock and the papers of Antony, earl Rivers, 1482–3'. *B.I.H.R.* xli (1968), 216–25.

Letters from Rivers to his London lawyer on business and politics. For Earl Rivers's pilgrimage to Rome in 1475, see Curt F. Bühler, 'A letter from Edward IV to Galeazzo Maria Sforza', *Speculum*, xxx (1955), 239–40.

4209 KELLY (H. A.). 'Canonical implications of Richard III's plan to marry his niece'. *Traditio*, xxiii (1967), 269–311.

4210 KENDALL (PAUL M.). Richard the Third. Lond. 1955.

P. M. Kendall, *Warwick the kingmaker*. Lond. 1957.

4211 KINGSFORD (CHARLES L.). Henry V, the typical mediaeval hero. Heroes of the Nations. N.Y. 1901. 2nd edn. 1923.

Idem, 'Two forfeitures in the year of Agincourt', *Archaeologia*, 2nd Ser. xx (1920), 71–100.

4212 KINGSFORD (CHARLES L.). Prejudice and promise in fifteenth-century England. Ford Lectures. Oxf. 1925. *

4213 KIRBY (JOHN L.). Henry IV of England. Lond. and Hamden (Conn.). 1971.

See Kirby on Council (No. 3299); J. M. W. Bean, 'Henry IV and the Percies', *History* xliv (1959), 212–17. Peter McNiven, 'The Cheshire rising of 1400', *B.J.R.L.* lii (1969–70), 375–96. Idem, 'The betrayal of Archbishop Scrope', ibid. liv (1971), 173–213. A. Rogers, 'The political crisis of 1401', *Nottingham Mediaeval Stud.* xii (1968), 85–96. Anthony Goodman, 'The Countess (Joan, the sister of Archbishop Arundel) and the rebels: Essex and a crisis in English society (1400)', *Essex Archaeol. Soc.* New Ser. ii (1970), 267–79.

4214 KRIEHN (GEORGE). The English rising in 1450. Strasburg. 1892.

W. D. Cooper, 'John Cade's followers in Kent', *Archaeologia Cantiana*, vii (1868), 233–71. Idem, 'Participation of Sussex in Cade's rising, 1450', *Sussex Archaeol. Collections*, xviii (1866), 17–36. B. B. Orridge, *Illustrations of Jack Cade's rebellion, to which are added contributions by W. D. Cooper* (Lond. 1869). Helen M. Lyle, 'The rebellion of Jack Cade 1450', Historical Asso. Pamphlet G. 16. (1950).

4215 LANDER (JACK R.). 'Edward IV: the modern legend; and a revision'. *History*, xli (1956), 38–52.

4216 LANDER (J. R.). Conflict and stability in fifteenth century England. Hutchinson University Library. Lond. etc. 1969. Also paperback.

J. R. Lander, 'Henry VI and the Duke of York's second protectorate', *B.J.R.L.* xliii (1960), 46–69. Idem, 'Attainder and forfeiture, 1453–1509', *Historical Jour.* iv (1961), 119–51. Idem, 'Marriage and politics in the fifteenth century: the Nevilles and the Wydevilles', *B.I.H.R.* xxxvi (1963), 129–52.

4217 LANDER (J. R.). The wars of the roses. History in the Making. Lond. 1965.

Basically a series of translations of extracts from records and chronicles.

4218 LAPSLEY (GAILLARD T.). 'The parliamentary title of Henry IV', in *Crown, community and parliament* (No. 1478).

4219 LLOYD (JOHN E.). Owen Glendower: Owen Glyn Dŵr. Oxf. 1931.

Ralph A. Griffiths, 'Some secret supporters of Owain Glyn Dŵr?', *B.I.H.R.* xxxvii (1964), 77–100. Idem, 'Some partisans of Owain Glyndŵr at Oxford', *B.B.C.S.* xx (1963), 282–92; xxii (1967), 152–68. R. Rees Davies, 'Owain Glyn Dŵr and the Welsh squirearchy', *Hon. Soc. Cymmrodorion Trans.* 1967–8 (Lond. 1969), 150–69. Glyn Roberts, 'The Anglesey submissions of 1406', *B.B.C.S.* xv, pt. i (1952), 39–61. J. Beverley Smith, 'The last phase of the Glyndŵr rebellion', ibid. xxii (1968), 250–60. J. E. Messham, 'The county of Flint and the rebellion of Owen Glyndŵr in the records of the earldom of Chester', *Flintshire Hist. Rec. Soc. Pubns.* xxiii (1967–8), 1–34.

4220 MacGIBBON (DAVID). Elizabeth Woodville (1437–1492). Her Life and Times. Lond. 1938.

C. Fahy, 'The marriage of Edward VI and Elizabeth Woodville: a new Italian source', *E.H.R.* lxxvi (1961), 660–72, prints a poem by Antonio Corrazzano, written about 1470: 'a pleasant tale, not an historian's or chronicler's version'.

4221 McFARLANE (KENNETH B.). The wars of the roses. Raleigh lecture. *P.B.A.* l for 1964 (1965), 87–119. Idem, Lancastrian kings and Lollard knights. Ed. by J. R. L. Highfield and G. L. Harriss. Oxf. and N.Y. 1972.

R. J. Knecht, 'The episcopate and the wars of the roses', *Univ. Birmingham Hist. Jour.* vi (1957–8), 108–31; and C. Head, 'Pius II and the wars of the roses', *Archivum Historicum Pontificiae* (Rome), viii (1970), 139–78.

4222 MARKHAM (CLEMENTS R.). Richard III, his life and character reviewed in the light of recent research. Lond. 1906. *

See Gairdner (No. 4203) and the commentary there.

4223 MYERS (ALEC R.). 'Richard III and historical tradition'. *History*, liii (1968), 181–202.

A. R. Myers, 'The character of Richard III', *History today*, iv (1954), 511–21; reprinted in Crowder (No. 4199), pp. 112–32; and correspondence in *History today*, iv (1954), 706–10. M. Levine, 'Richard III, usurper or lawful king?', *Speculum*, xxxiv (1959), 391–401. On Richard and Lord Hastings, see A. Hanham, *E.H.R.* lxxxvii (1972), 233–48.

4224 PUGH (THOMAS B.). The Marcher lordships. (No. 4675.)

4225 RICHARDSON (HENRY G.). 'John Oldcastle in hiding, August–October, 1417'. *E.H.R.* lv (1940), 432–8.

Prints an entry on Coram Rege roll, with precise details.

4226 RICHMOND (C. F.). 'Fauconberg's Kentish rising of May 1471'. *E.H.R.* lxxxv (1970), 673–92.

4227 ROSKELL (JOHN S.). 'William Catesby, counsellor to Richard III'. *B.J.R.L.* xlii (1959–60), 145–74.

4228 SCOFIELD (CORA L.). The life and reign of Edward the fourth, king of England and of France and lord of Ireland. 2 vols. Lond. 1923. *

C. L. Scofield, 'The capture of Lord Rivers and Sir Anthony Woodville, 19 January 1460', *E.H.R.* xxxvii (1922), 253–5, prints document giving names of captors. See A. L. Brown and B. Webster, 'The movements of the earl of Warwick in the summer of 1464: a correction', *E.H.R.* lxxxi (1966), 80–2. See Huizinga in *Pirenne Mélanges* (No. 1446).

4229 STOREY (ROBIN L.). The end of the house of Lancaster. Lond. 1966.

Firmly based on judicial records in the P.R.O., with the thesis that the wars of the roses grew from private feuds fostered by bastard feudalism. See also Storey, 'Lincolnshire and the wars of the roses', *Nottingham Mediaeval Stud.* xiv (1970), 64–83.

4230 STOREY (R. L.). 'The wardens of the marches of England towards Scotland, 1377–1489'. *E.H.R.* lxxii (1957), 593–615.

4231 VICKERS (KENNETH H.). Humphrey, duke of Gloucester: a biography. Lond. 1907.

For the correspondence of Duke Humphrey, see *E.H.R.* x (1895), 99–104; xix (1904), 509–26; xx (1905), 484–98. Ralph A. Griffiths, 'The trial of Eleanor of Cobham: an episode in the fall of Duke Humphrey of Gloucester', *B.J.R.L.* li (1968–9), 381–99.

4232 VIRGOE (ROGER). 'The death of William de la Pole, duke of Suffolk (1450)'. *B.J.R.L.* xlvii (1965), 489–502.

4233 WILKINSON (BERTIE). Constitutional history of England in the fifteenth century, 1399–1485. Lond. 1964.

Chaps. i–iii: politics and the constitution, with citations of recent studies.

4234 WILKINSON (BERTIE). 'Fact and fancy in fifteenth-century English history'. *Speculum*, xlii (1967), 673–92.

See also S. B. Chrimes, C. D. Ross, and R. A. Griffiths, eds. *Fifteenth century England, 1399–1509.* (Manchester, 1972), which includes challenging papers by the editors and A. L. Brown, B. P. Wolffe, T. B. Pugh, and R. L. Storey.

4235 WYLIE (JAMES H.). History of England under Henry the Fourth. 4 vols. Lond. 1884–98. *

4236 WYLIE (J. H.) and WAUGH (WILLIAM T.). The reign of Henry the Fifth. 3 vols. Cambr. 1914–29. *

Cf. C. T. Allmand, *Henry V.* Historical Asso. pamphlet. Lond. 1968.

2. *Relations with the Continent*

See Vaughan's volumes on Burgundy (No. 4170), with exhaustive bibliographies.

4237 ALLMAND (C. T.). Documents relating to the Anglo-French negotiations of 1439. R.H.S. Camden 4th Ser. ix. *Camden Miscellany*, xxiv (1972), 79–149. Idem, 'The Anglo-French negotiations, 1439'. *B.I.H.R.* xl (1967), 1–33, which includes useful citations.

4238 ARMSTRONG (CHARLES A. J.). 'La Double monarchie France-Angleterre et la maison de Bourgogne, 1420–1435: Le Déclin d'une alliance'. *Annales de Bourgogne* (Dijon), xxxvii (1965), 81–112.

4239 BONENFANT (PAUL). Du meurtre de Montereau au traité de Troyes. Mémoires de l'Académie royale de Belgique. Brussels. 1958.

A thorough study of the Anglo-Burgundian alliance in 1419–20.

4240 BONENFANT (P.). Philippe le Bon. 3rd edn. Brussels. 1955.

4241 BOSSUAT (ANDRÉ). Jeanne d'Arc. Paris. 1967.

4242 BOSSUAT (A.). 'Le Parlement de Paris pendant l'occupation anglaise'. *Revue Historique*, ccxxix (1963), 19–40.

4243 BOSSUAT (A.). Perrinet Gressert et François de Surienne, agents de l'Angleterre. Contribution à l'étude de relations de l'Angleterre et de la Bourgogne avec la France sous le règne de Charles VII. Paris. 1936.

A. Bossuat, 'La Littérature de propagande au XVᵉ siècle. Le mémoire de Jean de Rinel, sécretaire du roi d'Angleterre, contre le duc de Bourgogne (1435)', *Cahiers d'Histoire publiés par les Universités Clermont-Ferrand, Grenoble et Lyon* (Grenoble), i (1956), 129–46. P. S. Lewis, 'War-propaganda and historiography in fifteenth-century France and England', *T.R.H.S.* 5th Ser. xv (1965), 1–21.

4244 CALMETTE (JOSEPH L. A.) and PÉRINELLE (GEORGES). Louis XI et l'Angleterre (1461–1483). Paris. 1930.

J. Calmette and E. Déprez, *La France et l'Angleterre en conflit* (No. 1182), vol. vii, pt. i.

4245 CHAMPION (PIERRE). Louis XI. 2 vols. Paris. 1927. 2nd edn. 1928. Trans. and adapted in one volume by W. S. Whale. Lond. N.Y. etc. 1929.

4246 CHAMPION (PIERRE), ed. Procès de condamnation de Jeanne d'Arc. 2 vols. Paris. 1920–1.

Champion provides also a French translation. R. Oursel, *Les Procès de Jeanne d'Arc* (Paris. 1959). See No. 4267.

4247 CHAMPION (P.). Vie de Charles d'Orléans, 1394–1465. Biblio. du XVᵉ siècle. Paris. 1911.

Robert Steele, ed. *The English poems of Charles of Orleans*. E.E.T.S. Orig. Ser. ccxv (1941); ccxx (1946). Norma L. Goodrich, *Charles Duke of Orleans: a literary biography* (N.Y. 1963); and Enid McLeod, *Charles of Orleans, prince and poet* (Lond. 1969).

4248 CHAMPION (P.) and THOISY (P. de). Bourgogne, France, Angleterre au traité de Troyes. Paris. 1943.

4249 DICKINSON (JOYCELYNE G.). The congress of Arras, 1435: a study in medieval diplomacy. Oxf. 1955.

Appendix A prints sixteen unpublished documents. Reginald Brill, 'The English preparations before the treaty of Arras: a new interpretation of Sir John Fastolf's Report, September 1435', *Stud. in medieval and renaissance hist.* vii (1970), 213–47.

4250 DU FRESNE DE BEAUCOURT (GASTON). Histoire de Charles VII. 6 vols. Paris. 1881–91.

4251 HOMMEL (LUC). Marguerite d'York. Paris. 1959.

4252 HUGUET (ADRIEN). Aspects de la guerre de cent ans en Picardie maritime, 1400–1450. 2 vols. Mémoires de la Société des Antiquaires de Picardie (Amiens), xlviii (1941); l (1944).

4253 JACOB (ERNEST F.). Henry V and the invasion of France. Hutchinson Univ. Library. Lond. 1947.

E. F. Jacob, 'The collapse of France in 1419–20', *B.J.R.L.* xxvi (1941–2), 307–26.

4254 KIRBY (JOHN L.). 'Calais sous les Anglais, 1399–1413'. *Revue du Nord*, xxxvii (1955), 19–30.

J. L. Kirby, 'The Council of 1407 and the problem of Calais', *History today*, v (1955), 44–52. V. Fris, 'Documents Gantois concernant la levée du siège de Calais en 1436', *Mélanges Paul Frédéricq* (Brussels, 1904), pp. 245–58.

4255 KNOWLSON (GEORGE A.). Jean V, duc de Bretagne, et l'Angleterre, 1399–1442. Cambr. and Rennes. 1964.

4256 LE CACHEUX (PAUL). Rouen au temps de Jeanne d'Arc et pendant l'occupation anglaise, 1419–1449. Documents publiés avec introduction et notes par P. Le Cacheux. Rouen and Paris. 1931.

See Le Cacheux's *Actes de la chancellerie anglaise* (No. 3803).

4257 LENZ (MAX). König Sigismund und Heinrich V von England, (ein Beitrag zur Geschichte der Zeit des Constanzer Councils). Berlin. 1874.

Friedrich Schoenstedt, 'König Sigismund und die Westmachte, 1414–1415', *Die Welt als Geschichte* (Stuttgart), xiv (1954), 149–64. C. M. D. Crowder, 'Henry V, Sigismund and the Council of Constance: a re-examination', *Historical Stud.* iv (1962), 93–110.

4258 LONGNON (AUGUSTE). Paris pendant la domination anglaise (1420–36): documents extraits des registres de la chancellerie de France. Paris. 1878.

4259 McFARLANE (KENNETH B.). 'War, the economy and social change: England and the hundred years war'. *Past and Present*, xxii (1962), 3–13.

M. M. Postan, 'The costs of the hundred years war', ibid. xxvii (1964), 34–53. Idem, 'Some social consequences of the hundred years war', *Econ. H.R.* xii (1942), 1–12.

4260 McKENNA (J. W.). 'Henry VI of England and the Dual Monarchy: aspects of royal political propaganda, 1422–1432'. *Jour. Warburg and Courtauld Institutes*, xxviii (1965), 145–62.

The propaganda as shown in coinage, posters, and pageantry.

4261 MALDEN (ARTHUR R.). 'An official account of the battle of Agincourt'. *Ancestor*, xi (1904), 26–31.

Philippe Contamine, *Azincourt* (Paris. 1964). See No. 4297.

4262 NEWHALL (RICHARD A.). The English conquest of Normandy, 1416–1424. A study in fifteenth century warfare. Yale Hist. Pubns. Miscellany, 13. New Haven (Conn.). 1924. *

See Newhall, *Muster and review* (No. 4311), and paper in *Haskins essays* (No. 1439). Cf. Jacob (No. 4253), and Waugh, 'The administration of Normandy, 1420–22', in *Tout essays* (No. 1458). C. M. de Robillard de Beaurepaire, 'Les États de Normandie sous la domination anglaise', *Extrait de Recueil de la Société libre de l'Eure* (Évreux. 1859). G. Lèfevre-Pontalis, 'Épisodes de l'invasion anglaise: la guerre de partisans dans la Haute-Normandie (1424–9)', *B.E.C.* xcvii (1936), 102–30. See Rowe (No. 4270).

4263 OWEN (LEONARD V. D.). The connection between England and Burgundy during the first half of the fifteenth century. Oxf. 1909.

L. V. D. Owen, 'England and the Low Countries, 1405–1413', *E.H.R.* xxviii (1913), 13–33.

4264 PERNOUD (RÉGINE M. J.). Jeanne d'Arc, par elle-même et par ses témoins. Paris. 1962. Trans. by Jeanne Unger Duell. N.Y. 1962. Trans. by Edward Hyams. N.Y. 1966.

The records about Jeanne presented in translation.

4265 PEYRÈGNE (A.). Les Émigrés gascons en Angleterre, 1453–1485'. *Annales du Midi*, lxvi (1954), 113–28.

4266 POCQUET DU HAUT-JUSSÉ (BARTHÉLEMY A. M. J.). 'Anne de Bourgogne et le testament de Bedford (1429)'. *B.E.C.* xcv (1934), 284–326. Idem, 'François II, duc de Bretagne, et l'Angleterre'. *Mémoires de la Société d'histoire . . . de Bretagne* (Paris), ix (1928), 171–506.

4267 PROCÈS DE CONDAMNATION DE JEANNE D'ARC . . . Texte établi et publié par Pierre Tissier avec le concours de Yvonne Lanhers. Société de l'histoire de France. Paris. 1960+.

See also *Documents et recherches à Jeanne la Pucelle*. Ed. by Paul Doncoeur and others. (Paris. 1952+.) See Waugh in *Tait essays* (No. 1455).

4268 QUICHERAT (JULES E. J.). Procès de condamnation et de réhabilitation de Jeanne d'Arc dite la Pucelle. 5 vols. Paris. 1841–9. * Vol. i was re-edited 1960.

Wilfred P. Barrett provides a commendable point of departure in *The trial of Joan of Arc: a complete translation of the text of the original documents*. Broadway Medieval Library. Lond. 1931.

4269 RICHMOND (C. F.). English naval power (No. 4334).

4270 ROWE (BENEDICTA J. H.). 'Discipline in the Norman garrisons under Bedford, 1422–35'. *E.H.R.* xlvi (1931), 194–208. Idem, 'The estates of Normandy under the duke of Bedford, 1422–35', ibid. xlvi (1931), 551–78. Idem, 'John, duke of Bedford and the Norman "brigands"', ibid. xlvii (1932), 583–600. Idem, 'The grand conseil under the duke of Bedford, 1422–35', in *Salter essays* (No. 1451).

See also Allmand, 'The Lancastrian land settlement in Normandy, 1417–50', *Econ. H.R.* 2nd Ser. xxi (1968), 461–79; and R. Jouet, 'La Résistance à l'occupation anglaise en Basse-Normandie (1418–53)', *Cahiers des annales de Normandie* (Caen. 1969).

4271 THIELEMANS (MARIE-ROSE). Bourgogne et Angleterre. Relations politiques et économiques entre les Pays-Bas bourguignons et l'Angleterre, 1435–1467. Brussels. 1966.

J. H. Munro, 'An economic aspect of the collapse of the Anglo-Burgundian alliance, 1428–1442', *E.H.R.* lxxv (1970), 225–44. A. R. Myers, 'The outbreak of war between England and Burgundy in February 1471', *B.I.H.R.* xxiii (1960), 114–15. J. H. Munro, 'The costs of Anglo-Burgundian interdependence', *Revue belge de philol. et de l'hist.* xlvi (1968), 1228–38.

4272 VALE (M. G. A.). English Gascony, 1399–1453: a study of the government and politics during the later stages of the hundred years war. Oxf. 1970.

4273 WILLIAMS (ETHEL C.). My Lord of Bedford, 1389–1435. Lond. 1963.

Cf. A. R. Myers, 'John of Lancaster, duke of Bedford, 1389–1435', *History today*, x (1960), 460–8.

XVII. MILITARY AND NAVAL HISTORY

A. SOURCES

The principal sources for the study of the history of the army and navy are:

1. Writs of military summons, most of which are entered on the close and treaty rolls: Nos. 3761, 3783.

2. Muster and marshalsea rolls, and indentures of retinue, giving the names of those who served in various campaigns: Nos. 3143, 4283–4, 4287–8, 4292, 4297. For a muster roll of the army, 1417, see Benjamin Williams's edition of *Gesta Henrici Quinti* (No. 2877), pp. 265–73; for rolls on the army for the Poitou expedition in 1214, see J. C. Holt in Pipe Roll Soc. Pubns. xxxvii (1964), 71–108; for part of a muster roll, 21 Edward III, see Yeatman, *Derby* (No. 1601), i. 479–82.

3. Accounts of payments to men who served in various campaigns: Nos. 4277, 4291, 4293.

4. Ordinances for the army and navy: Nos. 4282, 4286.

5. The Black Book of the Admiralty, the chief source for the study of maritime law: No. 4286.

6. The Bayeux Tapestry, which throws light on the battle of Hastings and events which led to it: No. 4276. Baudri, bishop of Dol, 1107–30, wrote a poem, addressed to Adela, daughter of William the Conqueror, in which he describes a tapestry similar to that of Bayeux; this poem has been edited by Léopold Delisle, in *Mémoires de la Société des Antiquaires de Normandie*, xxviii (1871), 187–224.

7. The scutage rolls and wardrobe accounts: see index.

8. Rolls of arms: refer to Denholm-Young (Nos. 473–4); H. S. London (No. 496); and A. R. Wagner, *Catalogue* (No. 499).

4274 AN ACCOUNT OF THE ARMY WITH WHICH RICHARD II INVADED SCOTLAND IN 1385. Ed. by N. H. Nicolas. *Archaeologia*, xxii (1829), 13–19.

A catalogue naming leaders with the numbers of their men-at-arms and archers, pp. 16–19.

4275 THE ASSESSMENT OF KNIGHT SERVICE IN BEDFORDSHIRE. By John E. Morris. *Beds. Hist. Rec. Soc. Pubns.* ii (1914), 185–218; v (1926), 1–26. Also RECORDS OF KNIGHT SERVICE IN BEDFORDSHIRE. Ed. by G. H. Fowler. Ibid. ii (1914), 245–63.

4276 BAYEUX TAPESTRY, A comprehensive survey. By Sir Frank Stenton (General editor), Simone Bertrand, George Wingfield Digby, Charles H. Gibbs-Smith, Sir James Mann, John L. Nevinson, and Francis Wormald. Lond. and N.Y. 1957.

> In this volume all of the tapestry is reproduced in over a hundred plates with accompanying notes. The historical background, the design, the technique, the armour, the costumes, and the history of the tapestry are described, with selective bibliographies. Numerous editions of the tapestry have been published. It was first engraved for Abbé Montfaucon's *Monuments de la monarchie française* (Paris, 1729–30). Good editions are *The Bayeux tapestry reproduced in autotype, with historic notes*, by Frank R. Fowke (Arundel Soc. Lond. 1875; abridged edns. 1898, 1913); and Eric R. D. Maclagan, *The Bayeux tapestry* (King Penguin Books, Lond. 1943). It is wholly reproduced with other illustrations in *The National Geographic Magazine* (Washington), cxxx (1966), 206–51, with a commentary by Kenneth M. Setton entitled 'The Norman Conquest'. The extensive literature is listed in Marquet de Vasselot, *Bibliographie de la tapisserie* (Paris, 1935); and in Bonser, *A.-S.C.B.* nos. 1431–81. Maclagan's edition includes a selective bibliography.
>
> The tapestry is a strip of linen, two hundred and thirty feet long and twenty inches wide, on which are embroidered scenes on the relations of Harold and William and on the battle of Hastings. The most widely accepted view is that the embroidery was probably designed by an artist of the school of Canterbury at the direction of Bishop Odo of Bayeux for display in the new cathedral at Bayeux; but see C. R. Dodwell in *Burlington Magazine*, cviii (1966), 549–60.

4277 COMPTE (LE) DE L'ARMÉE ANGLAISE AU SIÈGE D'ORLÉANS, 1428–9. Ed. by Louis Jarry. Orleans. 1892.

> The 'compte', pp. 87–204, is a contemporary document which enumerates the English captains, their troops, pay, etc. It is preceded by an account of the organization of the English army.

4278 CRÉCY AND CALAIS (1346–7), from the public records. Ed. by George Wrottesley. William Salt Archaeol. Soc. *Collections*, xviii, pt. ii (1897).

> This important source contains translations of extracts from the following records:
> French rolls, 19–21 Edw. III, pp. 58–136.
> Memoranda rolls, 21–35 Edw. III, pp. 136–90.
> Accounts of the treasurer of the royal household, 18–23 Edw. III, pp. 191–219.
> Norman roll, 20 Edw. III, pp. 219–59.
> Calais roll, 21 Edw. III, pp. 260–79.

4279 DIARY OF THE EXPEDITION OF EDWARD I INTO SCOTLAND, 1296. Ed. by P. F. Tytler. Bannatyne Club, *Bannatyne Miscellany*, i (1827), 265–82.

> Contains a French text, which seems to be contemporary with the date of the expedition, and a sixteenth-century translation. This translation is also edited by N. H. Nicolas, 'A narrative of the progress of Edward I in his invasion of Scotland in 1296', *Archaeologia*, xxi (1827), 478–98.

4280 DOCUMENTS RELATING TO LAW AND CUSTOM OF THE SEA (1205–1767). Ed. by R. G. Marsden. 2 vols. Navy Records Soc. 1915, 1917.

> See *Select Pleas in the Court of Admiralty* (No. 3515).

4281 EDWARD IV'S FRENCH EXPEDITION OF 1475: The leaders and their badges. Ed. by Francis P. Barnard. Oxf. 1925.

A facsimile of a College of Arms MS., with a transcript thereof and extensive notation.

4282 EXCERPTA HISTORICA, or illustrations of English history (1205–1586). Ed. by Samuel Bentley. Lond. 1833.

Contains the ordinances made for the army by Henry V in 1419, and by John Talbot, earl of Shrewsbury, *temp.* Hen. VI, pp. 28–43; a narrative of the tournament between Anthony Woodville, Lord Scales, and the Bastard of Burgundy, pp. 171–222; the marriage of Princess Margaret (to Burgundy, 1468), pp. 223–39.

4283 INDENTURES OF RETINUE UNDER JOHN OF GAUNT, duke of Lancaster, enrolled in chancery, 1367–99. Ed. by Norman B. Lewis. Camden Soc. 4th Ser. i, *Miscellany*, xxii (1964), 77–112.

Here are printed indentures confirmed by the king on John of Gaunt's death; and entered on the Patent Rolls, hence they are calendared in *Cal. Pat. Rolls.* On the importance of these personal contracts between a lord and a retainer who promised to serve his lord for life in peace and war for a fixed fee, see A. E. Prince, 'The indenture system under Edward III' in *Tait essays* (No. 1455); N. B. Lewis, 'An early indenture of military service, 27 July 1287', *B.I.H.R.* xiii (1935), 85–9 (for an earlier example of 1270 see Richardson and Sayles, Governance (No. 1218), pp. 463–5); Lewis, 'An early fourteenth century contract for military service', *B.I.H.R.* xx (1944), 111–18; idem, 'The organization of the indentured retinue in fourteenth century England', *T.R.H.S.* 4th Ser. xxvii (1945), 29–39 (No. 1493); idem, 'The recruitment and organization of a contract army, May to November, 1337', *B.I.H.R.* xxxvii (1964), 1–19. Cf. Dunham on Lord Hastings's retainers (No. 4284), and B. D. Lyon (No. 4308). For a retinue of Henry of Lancaster see A. Tomkinson, 'Retinues at the tournament of Dunstable (1308–9)', *E.H.R.* lxxiv (1959), 70–89. See Nos. 3862, 3875–6.

4284 LORD HASTINGS' INDENTURED RETAINERS, 1461–1483: the lawfulness of livery and retaining under the Yorkists and Tudors. By William H. Dunham, Jr. *Connecticut Academy of Arts and Sciences Trans.* xxxix (1955).

Dunham analyses the services performed by the listed retainers, and contends that the system of retainers who promised loyal service in peace and in war for life in return for 'good and favourable' lordship rather than for a tenurial fief or money fee was a more sophisticated arrangement than feudalism.

4285 MILITARY SERVICE PERFORMED BY STAFFORDSHIRE TENANTS (1230–1392). Ed. by George Wrottesley. William Salt Archaeol. Soc. *Collections*, viii (1888), 1–122; xiv (1894), 221–64.

Translations of extracts (writs of protection) taken mainly from the Scottish and French rolls.

4286 MONUMENTA JURIDICA: the Black Book of the Admiralty (with an English translation of French and Latin texts, and with an elaborate appendix). Ed. by Sir Travers Twiss. 4 vols. Rolls Ser. 1871–6.

Vol. i contains the Black Book, pp. 1–344; documents connected with the admiralty of Sir Thomas Beaufort (9 Hen. IV–4 Hen. VI), pp. 347–94; ordinances of war made in 1385 and 1419, pp. 453–72. Vols. ii–iv contain the Domesday of Ipswich on maritime law, the Coutumes d'Oleron, the Rolls of Oleron, the Spanish Customs of the Sea, and the maritime laws of Gotland, Wisby, Flanders, etc.

The Black Book of the Admiralty is a collection of rules and orders, in French and Latin, relating to the Admiralty, and to the practice in the Court of Admiralty. Twiss's edition is 'printed from an eighteenth-century transcript collated with earlier MSS.'. The original, 'which was discovered while the work [by Twiss] was in progress', seems to have been compiled in Henry VI's reign; but it includes earlier documents.

4287 MUSTER ROLL OF CAVALRY, temp. Edw. III. Ed. by Henry Appleton. *Yorks. Archaeol. Jour.* xiv (1896–8), 239–41.

Translation only, giving the names of horse hobilars and archers charged with the safe-keeping of Perth in Scotland.

4288 MUSTER ROLL OF THE RAPE OF HASTINGS, 13 Edw. III. *Collectanea Topog. et Genealogica* (No. 115), vii (1841), 118–28.

4289 NOMINA ET INSIGNIA GENTILITIA NOBILIUM EQUI-TUMQUE SUB EDOARDO I MILITANTIUM; ACCEDUNT CLASSES EXERCITUS EDOARDI III CALETEM OBSIDENTIS. Ed. by Edward R. Mores. Oxf. 1749.

The second document gives the number of men besieging Calais in 1347. See also John Topham, ed. 'A roll of Edward III's fleet before Calais', *Archaeologia*, vi (1782), 213–15, which is also printed, with another document concerning Edward III's forces at Calais, in Champollion-Figeac's collection of letters (No. 3816), ii. 82–92.

4290 OPPENHEIM (MICHAEL), ed. Naval accounts and inventories in the reign of Henry VII. Navy Rec. Soc. viii. Lond. 1896.

See No. 4330.

4291 ORDINANCE FOR CHARGES OF THE CASTLES (OF) NORTH WALES, 2 Edward III and 5, 6 Henry IV. *Archaeol. Cambrensis*, 3rd Ser. viii (1862), 123–9.

A document giving the number of men for each castle, with their pay.

4292 PARLIAMENTARY WRITS AND WRITS OF MILITARY SUMMONS (Edw. I–Edw. II). Ed. by Francis Palgrave. 2 vols. in 4. Record Comm. 1827–1834.

Contains writs of summons, commissions of array, and other documents relating to military levies; of great value for the history of the army. See especially i. 193–380; and ii, div. ii, 367–763. Many of these records relate to scutage; and among the documents printed are three marshalsea rolls, 5 and 10 Edw. I, i. 197–213 and 228–43.

4293 PROCEEDINGS OF HIS MAJESTY'S COMMISSIONERS ON THE PUBLIC RECORDS, 1832–33. Ed. by C. P. Cooper. Lond. 1833.

'Liber Roberti Hayroun contrarotulatoris Walteri de Amondesham de denariis regis receptis pro expensis exercitus in partibus Scotiae faciendis (1297)', pp. 506–36.

4294 SCOTLAND IN 1298: documents relating to the campaign of Edward I in that year. Ed. by Henry Gough. Lond. etc. 1888.

Contains two rolls of the horses belonging to the royal household, and numerous extracts from the patent and close rolls. On the Falkirk Roll, printed herein, see Denholm-Young, *History and Heraldry* (No. 474), pp. 103–11. Cf. C. H. Hunter Blair, 'Northern knights at Falkirk, 1298', *Archaeol. Aeliana*, 4th Ser. xxv (1947), 68–114.

4295 THE SIEGE OF CAERLAVEROCK, 1300, with the arms of the earls, barons, and knights who were present; with a translation, a history of the castle, etc. Ed. by N. H. Nicolas. Lond. 1828. A better edition by Thomas Wright, The rolls of the princes, barons, and knights who attended Edward I at the siege of Caerlaverock, with a translation. Lond. 1864.

An interesting Northern French poem, giving a catalogue of Edward I's followers, with a description of their coat-armour and persons, and an account of the siege. See Denholm-Young's lecture in *P.B.A.* xlvii (1962), 251–62 (Nos. 474 and 1467). A new edition of the poem, edited by N. Denholm-Young and C. Bullock Davies, is promised.

4296 SUMMONSES TO MILITARY SERVICE EARLY IN THE REIGN OF HENRY III (1228–9). By J. S. Critchley. *E.H.R.* lxxxvi (1971), 79–95.

4297 WYLIE (JAMES H.). 'Notes on the Agincourt Roll', *T.R.H.S.* 3rd Ser. v (1911), 105–40.

Cf. Nicholas Harris Nicolas, *History of the battle of Agincourt* (Lond. 1827). See No. 4261.

B. SECONDARY WORKS

1. *Army*

There is no full-scale military history of English warfare of the Middle Ages. Of the comprehensive histories, Sir James Ramsay's volumes (No. 1193) are the fullest on military aspects. Works on feudalism, scutage, and retainers naturally deal with military obligations. For arms and armour, see pp. 103–6. Consult also *Cambridge Medieval History* (No. 1176), vi. 785–98, and A. L. Poole, *Obligations* (No. 4674). More specialized studies on particular subjects and individual campaigns are entered elsewhere, particularly in Chapter XVI. For bibliographic essay, see Beeler in R. Higham, *A guide to the sources of military history* (Berkeley, 1971), pp. 43–64.

4298 BEELER (JOHN). Warfare in England: 1066–1189. Ithaca (N.Y.). 1966.

A controversial study; compare the review in *E.H.R.* lxxxiii (1968), 818–20, with that in *Speculum*, xliv (1969), 442–4.

4299 BURNE (ALFRED H.). The battlefields of England. Lond. 1950. 2nd edn. 1951. Idem, More battlefields of England. Lond. 1952.

4300 COCKLE (MAURICE J. D.). A bibliography of English military books up to 1642 and of contemporary foreign works. Lond. 1900.

A few additions and corrections appear in the *Papers of the Bibliographical Society of America*, xxxiv (1940), 186.

4301 COWPER (HENRY S.). The art of attack: being a study in the development of weapons and appliances of offence from the earliest time to the age of gunpowder. Ulverston. 1906.

See G. H. Fowler, 'Munitions in 1224', *Beds. Hist. Rec. Soc. Pubns.* v (1920), 17–32; and T. F. Tout, 'Firearms', in Tout's *Collected papers* (No. 1499), i. 233–76. Idem, 'The tactics . . . of Boroughbridge', ibid. i. 221–6.

4302 HAY (DENYS). 'The division of the spoils of war in fourteenth-century England'. *T.R.H.S.* 5th Ser. iv (1954), 91–109.

K. B. McFarlane, 'The investment of Sir John Fastolf's profits of war', ibid. vii (1957), 91–116.

4303 HEWITT (HERBERT J.). The organization of war under Edward III, 1338–62. Manchester. 1966.

4304 HOLLISTER (CHARLES WARREN). Anglo-Saxon military institutions on the eve of the Norman Conquest. Oxf. 1962. Idem, Military organization of Norman England. Oxf. 1965.

> Richard Glover, 'English warfare in 1066', *E.H.R.* lxvii (1952), 1–18. John Schlight, 'Monarchs and mercenaries (1066–1189)', *British Hist. and Culture*, published by the Conference on British Studies, i (N.Y. 1968).

4305 KEEN (MAURICE H.). The laws of war in the late middle ages. Lond. 1965.

> General survey, more French than English in orientation. Cf. F. P. Barnard, *The essential portions of Nicholas Upton's 'De studio militari' before 1446, translated by John Blount, Fellow of All Souls (c. 1500)* (Oxf. 1931). A. B. Ferguson, *The Indian summer of English chivalry* (Durham, N.C. 1960).

4306 LEWIS (NORMAN B.). 'The last medieval summons of the English feudal levy, 13 June 1385'. *E.H.R.* lxxiii (1958), 1–26. Idem, 'The summons of the English feudal levy: 5 April 1327', in *Wilkinson essays* (No. 1459).

> Cf. J. J. N. Palmer, 'The last summons of the feudal army in England (1385)', *E.H.R.* lxxxiii (1968), 771–5.

4307 LOT (FERDINAND). L'art militaire et les armées au moyen âge en Europe et dans le Proche Orient. 2 vols. Paris. 1946.

> Particularly useful for France; but based on Oman for England. For the author's opinion of his own work, see *Hist. institutions françaises*, ii, *Institutions royales*, edited by Ferdinand Lot and Robert Fawtier (Paris, 1958), p. 511.

4308 LYON (BRYCE D.). From fief to indenture: the transition from feudal to non-feudal contract in western Europe. Cambr. (Mass.). 1957.

> A broad, basic study, not confined to England. Chap. v, pp. 182–244, concerns 'The military role of the fief-rente'. Idem, 'The money fief under the English kings 1066–1485', *E.H.R.* lxvi (1951), 161–93; idem, 'The feudal antecedent of the indenture system', *Speculum*, xxix (1954), 503–11.

4309 McFARLANE (KENNETH B.). 'A business-partnership in war and administration, 1421–1445'. *E.H.R.* lxxviii (1963), 290–308.

> Prints and discusses a contract of 1421 between two English esquires as brothers-in-arms. For a broad treatment, see Maurice Keen, 'Brotherhood in arms', *History*, xlvii (1962), 1–17.

4310 MORRIS (JOHN E.). The Welsh wars of Edward I: a contribution to mediaeval military history, based on original documents. Oxf. 1901. *

> Idem, 'Mounted infantry in mediaeval warfare', *T.R.H.S.* 3rd Ser. viii (1914), 77–102.

4311 NEWHALL (RICHARD A.). Muster and review: a problem of English military administration, 1420–1440. Harvard Hist. Monographs. Cambr. (Mass.). 1940.

> Cf. R. A. Newhall, 'The war finances of Henry V and the Duke of Bedford', *E.H.R.* xxxvi (1921), 172–98.

4312   OMAN (CHARLES W. C.). The art of war in the middle ages, A.D. 378–1515. Oxf. etc. 1885. Revised edn. by John H. Beeler. Ithaca (N.Y.). 1953. Idem, A history of the art of war: the middle ages from the fourth to the fourteenth century. Lond. etc. 1898. 2nd edn. (to the end of the fifteenth century), 2 vols. 1924. *

> The latter is an expansion of the former; but the former is the generally better account. Oman's attention is devoted mainly to tactics. See Tout, 'Firearms' (No. 1499), an article reprinted with an introduction by Claude Blair (Lond. 1968).

4313   O'NEIL (BRYAN H. ST. JOHN). Castles and cannon: a story in early artillery fortifications in England. Oxf. 1960.

4314   POWICKE (MICHAEL). Military obligation in medieval England: a study in liberty and duty. Oxf. 1962.

> A scholarly 'connected account of the development of military obligation' from the Anglo-Saxon fyrd to the fifteenth-century militia. For a sidelight, turn to A. Z. Freeman, 'A moat defense: the coast defense scheme of 1295', *Speculum*, xlii (1967), 442–62. See also Barnaby C. Keeney, 'Military service and the development of nationalism in England, 1272–1327', *Speculum*, xxii (1947), 534–49.

4315   PRESTWICH (J. O.). 'War and finance in the Anglo-Norman state'. *T.R.H.S.* 5th Ser. iv (1954), 19–43.

> Jacques Boussard, 'Les mercenaires au xiie siècle: Henri Plantegenêt et les origines de l'armée de métier', *B.E.C.* cvi (1945–6), 189–224.

4316   PRINCE (ALBERT E.). 'The army and the navy', in *The English Government at work* (No. 3836), i. 332–93. Idem, 'The strength of English armies in the reign of Edward III'. *E.H.R.* xlvi (1931), 353–71. Idem, 'The payment of army wages in Edward III's reign'. *Speculum*, xix (1944), 137–60. See *Tait essays* (No. 1455).

> J. H. Ramsay, 'The strength of English armies in the middle ages: estimates of chroniclers and modern writers', *E.H.R.* xxix (1914), 221–7.

4317   SANDERS (IVOR J.). Feudal military service in England: a study of the constitutional and military powers of the barones in medieval England. Lond. 1956.

4318   SHERBORNE (J. W.). 'Indentured retinues and the English expeditions to France (1368–1380)'. *E.H.R.* lxxix (1964), 718–46.

> Drawing on unpublished exchequer documents, this article presents tables for several expeditions.

4319   SMAIL (RAYMOND C.). Crusading warfare, 1097–1193. Cambr. Stud. in Medieval Life and Thought. Cambr. 1956. Idem, 'Art of war', in *Medieval England* (No. 1485), i. 128–67.

4320   WARNER (PHILIP). Sieges of the middle ages (1066–1485). Lond. 1968.

2. *Navy*

4321   ADMIRALTY LIBRARY. Subject catalogue of printed books. Pt. i: Historical section. By W. G. Perrin. Lond. 1912.

4322 CALLENDER (GEOFFREY A. R.). Bibliography of naval history. Historical Asso. Leaflets 58 and 61. Lond. 1924–5.

4323 MANWARING (GEORGE E.). A bibliography of British naval history: a biographical and historical guide to printed and manuscript sources. Lond. 1930. New impression, 1970.

4324 MARINER'S MIRROR. The journal of the Society for Nautical Research. Lond. 1911+. Index for vols. i–xx.

4325 BROOKS (FREDERICK W.). The English naval forces, 1199–1272. Hull, 1932; Lond. 1933. Reprinted 1963.

F. W. Brooks, 'Naval armament in the thirteenth century', *Mariner's Mirror*, xiv (1928), 115–31; idem, 'The king's ships and galleys, mainly under John and Henry III', ibid. xv (1929), 15–48; idem, 'Naval administration and the raising of fleets under John and Henry III', ibid. xv (1929), 351–90; idem, 'William of Wrotham and the office of the keeper of the king's ports and galleys', *E.H.R.* xl (1925), 570–9. For another phase of Wrotham's activities, see W. R. Powell, 'The administration of the navy and the stannaries, 1189–1216', *E.H.R.* lxxi (1956), 177–88.

4326 CLOWES (WILLIAM L.), and others. The royal navy: a history from the earliest times to the present. 7 vols. Lond. 1897–1903; vols. i–ii reprinted, 1911–13.

The part prior to 1422 is based largely on the work of Nicolas (No. 4331).

4327 GOLDINGHAM (C. S.). 'The navy under Henry VII'. *E.H.R.* xxiii (1918), 472–88.

R. C. Anderson, 'The *Grace de Dieu* of 1446–86', *E.H.R.* xxxiv (1919), 584–6.

4328 THE LIBELLE OF ENGLYSHE POLYCYE. Ed. by G. Warner. Oxf. 1926. See No. 5338.

4329 MARCUS (GEOFFREY J.). A naval history of England. Vol. i: the formative centuries. Lond. 1961.

Pp. 1–20 for the medieval period are too brief to be valuable.

4330 MOORE (ALAN). 'Accounts and inventories of John Starlyng, clerk of the king's ships to Henry IV'. *Mariner's Mirror*, iv (1914), 20–6, 167–73.

4331 NICOLAS (NICHOLAS HARRIS). A history of the royal navy . . . 2 vols. Lond. 1847.

Still a standard work; vol. i: to 1327; vol. ii: 1327–1422.

4332 OPPENHEIM (MICHAEL). A history of the administration of the royal navy and of merchant shipping in relation to the navy from MDIX to MDCLX, with an introduction treating of the preceding period. Lond. 1896. *

Pp. 1–44: the navy before 1509. Based on some manuscript research, these pages provide the best brief account.

4333 PRYNNE (M.). 'Henry V's *Grace Dieu*', *Mariner's Mirror*, liv (1968), 115–28.

4334 RICHMOND (C. F.). 'English naval power in the fifteenth century'. *History*, lii (1967), 1–15 (lists the royal ships built from 1461 to 1490). Idem, 'The keeping of the seas during the Hundred Years War, 1422–40'. Ibid. xlix (1964), 283–98 (gives a table of king's ships, 1423–5).

4335 TINNISWOOD (J. T.). 'English galleys, 1272–1377', *Mariner's Mirror*, xxxv (1949), 276–315.

4336 TURNER (MRS. W. J. CARPENTER). 'The building of the *Gracedieu*, *Valentine*, and *Falconer* at Southampton, 1416–20'. *Mariner's Mirror*, xl (1954), 55–72. Idem, 'The building of the *Holy Ghost of the Tower*, 1414–16, and her subsequent history'. Ibid. xl (1954), 270–81. Idem, 'Southampton as a naval centre, 1414–1458', in *Collected essays on Southampton*, edited by J. B. Morgan and Philip Peberdy (Southampton, 1958), pp. 40–6.

More generally on the navy in the early fifteenth century, J. H. Wylie, *Henry V* (No. 4236), ii. 369–90.

XVIII. LAND TENURE AND ESTATES

A. GENERAL PUBLIC RECORDS

Many of the public records mentioned in preceding sections contain material bearing on knights' fees and other feudal tenures. For the period before the thirteenth century, the most important are *The Red Book of the Exchequer* (No. 3007), *Domesday Book* and its satellites (Nos. 3009–38), and the local surveys, 1066–1200 (Nos. 3065–76). Scutage rolls are cited in Nos. 1601, 3007, 3143, 3168, 3290, 3753, 4292, 4645.

The public records subsequent to 1200 which relate primarily to feudal tenures are:

1. Inquisitions *post mortem*, Henry III–Charles II (Nos. 4338–40; 4342; 4346; 4348; etc.). These inquests were held on the death of any of the king's tenants-in-chief, to enable him to exercise his rights of relief, wardship, and escheat. The jury, assembled by the escheator of the county, declared what lands the tenant held at the time of his death, what their annual value was, by what rents or services they were held, who the next heir was, and how old he then was. If he was of age, he appeared in court, performed homage, and paid a feudal relief to the crown; if he was a minor, the king would take wardship of the estate; if there was no heir, the estate would escheat to the crown. Although the regular series of these records does not begin until early in Henry III's reign, similar information regarding reliefs, wardships, and the like is afforded by certain rolls of the year 1185 (No. 4344). The inquests *post mortem* are the favourite hunting-grounds of genealogists; they are also of great value for the study of manorial history, for they often include minute 'extents', or surveys, of manors, which give details regarding the tenants on an estate, their services, and holdings. 'Inquisitions *ad quod damnum* were originally filed with the Inquisitions *post mortem*, but those from Henry III to Richard III inclusive have now been formed into a distinct series.' For Inquisitions *ad quod damnum*, see Nos. 3758 and 955, vols. xvii, xxii.

2. Hundred rolls (No. 4345). In the Record Commission's edition these rolls are 'a collection that has been sorted and rearranged for purposes of publication'. They contain inquisitions by a jury of each hundred concerning infringements of the king's rights, encroachments on the royal demesne, and oppressive measures of the sheriffs and other local officers of the crown. During the disorders of Henry III's reign the magnates and sheriffs had been guilty of many usurpations and exactions. In 1274 and again in 1279 Edward I appointed commissioners who visited the various counties to secure data regarding the nature of these abuses. The jury for each hundred gave information concerning the owners and occupiers of lands, the extent and tenures of their estates, the services rendered by under-tenants, the feudal profits of the king which had been wrongfully withheld, manorial courts and privileges, exactions of the nobility and royal officers, and many other matters. Hence the verdicts or reports of the juries throw much light upon feudal tenures and manorial institutions. The printed edition concentrates on the inquests of 1274–5 and 1279, but contains scattered references to inquiries of about 1251, 1255, and 1285. Thereafter similar inquisitions were held before the itinerant justices, and are entered on the eyre rolls.

3. The Book of Fees or *Liber Feodorum*, commonly called *Testa de Nevill* (No. 4337). It is a register of inquisitions compiled in two volumes for exchequer use in 1302, probably for the assessment of an aid for the marriage of Edward I's eldest daughter. It consists of copies of returns to inquiries made on several occasions between 1198 and 1293 into knights' fees and serjeanties, and also about widows and heiresses whose marriages were in the gift of the king, with the value of their lands, churches in the gift of the king, escheats, and the amount of scutage and aid paid by each tenant. For similar material see *Feudal aids* (No. 4341).

The title *Testa de Nevill* refers only to certain older lists or returns which form a small part of the whole register. It has been suggested that this title was derived from a sketch of a head of Nevill on a receptable which held documents concerning knights' fees and such matters. See the introduction to *The Book of Fees*, pp. xii–xiv.

4. Kirkby's Quest. This is a survey of various counties, made in 1284–5, under the direction of John de Kirkby, the king's treasurer. Originating as an inquiry into debts to the crown, it developed into an inquiry concerning knights' fees. 'The return of knights' fees, which eventually determined the importance of this survey to later exchequer officials, and to modern students, was apparently a subordinate part of the inquiry, not required by the statute, and possibly designed to facilitate the collection of the scutage of 1285'. Few of the original returns have survived; in most cases we have only abridgments of original inquisitions, or extracts from them. A good account of Kirkby's Quest is in *Feudal Aids* (No. 4341), vol. i, pp. viii–xxii.

5. *Nomina Villarum* (No. 4343). These documents are returns by the sheriffs to writs issued in 1316 for the military levies of that year, when each township was to supply one man-at-arms. The sheriffs reported on the number of hundreds and wapentakes within their bailiwicks, on the cities, boroughs, and townships therein, and on their lords. Few of the original returns survive, even the older transcripts have vanished, but copies of a transcript of 1 Henry VII and some

of the original returns formed the basis of the edition in Palgrave's *Parliamentary Writs* (Nos. 3316, 4292).

4337 BOOK OF FEES. *Liber Feodorum*: The Book of Fees commonly called *Testa de Nevill* (1198–1293), reformed from the earliest MSS. by the Deputy Keeper of the Records. 2 vols. in 3. Lond. 1920–31.

This excellent edition supersedes the confused and erroneous transcript published in 1807 by the Record Commission as *Testa de Nevill sive Liber feodorum*. In the new edition the reports are arranged more or less in chronological order and then by county.
For commentaries, see Hubert Hall, 'Testa de Nevill', *Athenaeum*, ii (1898), 353–4, 420–1; Hall's edition of *Red Book of the exchequer*, vol. ii, pp. ccxxi–ccxxx; Henry Barkly, 'Testa de Nevill, with an attempt to determine the dates of the returns pertaining to the county of Gloucester contained therein', *Genealogist*, New Ser. v (1889), 35–40, 75–80; J. H. Round, 'The great inquest of service (1212)' in his *Commune of London* (No. 4004), pp. 261–77.

4338 CALENDAR OF INQUISITIONS POST MORTEM and other analogous documents in the Public Record Office. (Hen. III–7 Rich. II). 15 vols. H.M.S.O. 1904–70.

Second Ser. 1–14 Hen. VII. 3 vols. H.M.S.O. 1898–1956. See also *Calendarium Genealogicum* (Hen. III–Edw. I). Ed. by Charles Roberts. 2 vols. H.M.S.O. 1865. The chief object of this valuable work is to present the genealogical matter contained in the inquests *post mortem* and in similar inquisitions. See Hunnisett in *K. Major essays* (No. 7224).

4339 CALENDARIUM GENEALOGICUM: calendar of heirs extracted from the inquisitions (*post mortem*, etc.) 1–2 Edw. II. *Deputy Keeper's Reports*, xxxii (1871), app. i, pp. 237–63. Continued, 3–4 Edw. II, by J. A. C. Vincent. *Genealogist*, New Ser. i (1884), 190–4, 206–13; ii (1885), 61–4, 88–93; iii (1886), 49–53, 98–100, 179–85, 210–15; iv (1887), 55–9, 119–22, 143–8, 215–17; vi (1890), 158–64, 243–50.

4340 CALENDARIUM INQUISITIONUM POST MORTEM SIVE ESCAETARUM (Hen. III–Rich. III). Ed. by John Caley and John Bayley. 4 vols. Record Comm. 1806–28.

Printed from an inaccurate ms. calendar, which seems to have been compiled in the reign of James I. It contains many inquests which are not inquisitions *post mortem*.

4341 (FEUDAL AIDS). INQUISITIONS AND ASSESSMENTS RELATING TO FEUDAL AIDS, with other analogous documents preserved in the Public Record Office, 1284–1431. 6 vols. H.M.S.O. 1899–1920.

This work, based on various accounts, returns, surveys, etc., illustrates the succession of holders of land during the years from 1284 to 1431, and may be regarded as a supplement to the *Book of Fees* (No. 4337). It covers all the counties in alphabetical order.

4342 HEREDES EX INQUISITIONIBUS POST MORTEM, 1272–1439. Ed. by Thomas Phillipps. Middle Hill Press. 1841.

4343 NOMINA VILLARUM: returns of the names of lords of townships, etc. for the purpose of effecting the military levies ordained in the parliament of England, 9 Edward II. Ed. by Francis Palgrave in *Parliamentary Writs*, ii, div. iii, pp. 301–416. Record Comm. 1834.

4344 ROTULI DE DOMINABUS ET PUERIS ET PUELLIS DE DONATIONE REGIS IN XII COMITATIBUS, 31 Hen. II, 1185. Ed. by John Horace Round. Pipe Roll Soc. Pubns. xxxv (1913).

> Another edition by Stacey Grimaldi (Lond. 1830). Contains abstracts of inquisitions of wardships, reliefs, and other feudal profits due to the king from the widows and children of his tenants-in-chief.

4345 ROTULI HUNDREDORUM TEMP. HEN. III ET EDW. I in turr, Lond. et in curia receptae scaccarii West. asservati. 2 vols. Record Comm. 1812–18.

> Covers all the present counties of England except Cheshire, Cumberland, Durham, Lancashire, Middlesex, Monmouth, Surrey, and Westmorland; the records for the counties of Huntingdon, Oxford, and Cambridge are especially full. For commentaries, see Helen M. Cam, *The Hundred and the Hundred Rolls* (No. 3730); idem, *Studies in the Hundred Rolls* (No. 3729); and E. A. Kosminsky, *Studies* (No. 4971).

B. RECORDS BY COUNTY

BEDFORD

4346 CALENDAR OF INQUISITIONS POST MORTEM. By George Herbert Fowler. 2 pts. Beds. Rec. Soc. Pubns. v (1920) and xix (1937).

> Pt. i: 1250–71; pt. ii: 1272–86.

CHESHIRE AND FLINTSHIRE

4347 WELSH RECORDS: INDEX TO INQUISITIONS, ETC., COUNTIES OF CHESTER AND FLINT (Edw. III–Charles I). *Deputy Keeper's Reports*, xxv (1864), 32–60.

CORNWALL

4348 A CALENDAR OF INQUISITIONES POST MORTEM FOR CORNWALL AND DEVON, 1216–1649. Ed. by Edward A. Fry. Devon and Cornwall Record Soc. 1906.

CUMBERLAND

> A translation of the *Testa de Nevill* for Cumberland, by James Wilson, is printed with an introduction, in the *Victoria History of Cumberland* (No. 1529), i. 304–8, 419–25.

DERBYSHIRE AND NOTTINGHAMSHIRE

4349 A SURVEY OF THE HONOUR OF PEVEREL, 1250. By Charles Kerry. *Derbys. Archaeol. and Nat. Hist. Soc. Journal*, xiv (1892), 40–53.

> Translation only. Contains a list of knights' fees, etc., held of the king.

4350 THE TESTA DE NEVILL FOR NOTTS AND DERBY. Reprinted from the *Feudal History of the County of Derby* (i. 365–456). Ed. by John P. Yeatman. Lond. 1886.

> Translation only. For a translation of *Kirkby's Quest* and the Hundred Rolls, for Derbyshire, and of various documents relating to knights' fees see Yeatman's *Feudal History*, i. 457–511; iii. 36–68.

DEVONSHIRE
See No. 4348

4351 WHALE (THOMAS W.). 'The tax roll of *"Testa de Nevill"* (with index)'. *Devon Assoc. for Advancement of Science, etc. Trans.* xxx (1898), 203–57; xxxiv (1902), 289–324. Idem, 'The tax roll for Devon, 31 Edward I'. (A list of knights' fees.) Ibid. xxxi (1899), 376–429.

See also Oswald J. Reichel, 'The Earlier Sections of *"Testa Nevill"* relating to Devon (with remarks by J. H. Round)', ibid. xxxvii (1905), 410–56; xxxviii (1906), 313–17; his 'The hundred of Budleigh in the time of *Testa de Nevil*, 1244', ibid. xxxv (1903), 279–317; also his 'Hundred of Haytor in the time of *Testa de Nevil*, 1244', ibid. xl (1908), 110–37; his 'Hundred of Stanborough 1243', ibid. xlv (1913), 169–218; and his 'Hundred of Lifton in the time of *Testa de Nevill* (1243)', ibid. xlvi (1914), 185–219. Each article was reprinted in its year of publication.

DORSET
See No. 4379

4352 FRY (EDWARD A.). 'On the inquisitions *post mortem* for Dorset, 1216–1485'. *Dorset Nat. Hist. and Antiq. Field Club, Procs.* xvii (1896), 1–53.

4353 INQUISITIONS POST MORTEM FOR DORSET (1269–1483). *Notes and Queries for Somerset and Dorset,* vols. viii–xiii *passim.* 1903–13.

Abstracts only.

4354 TESTA DE NEVILL AND KIRKBY'S QUEST FOR DORSET, in Hutchins's *History of Dorset* (No. 1620), 3rd edn. vol. iv, pp. lxiv–lxxvi. Westminster. 1870.

DURHAM

4355 DURHAM RECORDS. Cursitors' records: inquisitions *post mortem,* etc. (fourteenth to seventeenth century). *Deputy Keeper's Reports,* xliv (1883), 310–542; xlv (1885), app. i. 153–282.

GLOUCESTERSHIRE

4356 ABSTRACTS OF INQUISITIONS POST MORTEM FOR GLOUCESTERSHIRE. Ed. by Sidney J. Madge and Edward A. Fry. Pts. iv–v. 1236–1358. British Rec. Soc. Index Library, xxx (1903) and xl (1910). Pt. vi, 1359–1413. Abstracted by Ethel Stokes. Ibid. xlvii (1914).

Pts. i–iii are concerned with reign of Charles I. These records are also published in the *Transactions of the Bristol and Gloucestershire Archaeological Society.*

4357 KIRKBY'S QUEST: pt. i: its history; pt. ii: the return for Gloucestershire. Ed. by Henry Barkly. *Bristol and Glos. Archaeol. Soc. Trans.* xi (1887), 130–54.

4358 KNIGHTS' FEES IN GLOUCESTERSHIRE (on which an aid for the marriage of the king's daughter was levied), 3 Henry IV. Ed. by John Maclean. Ibid. xi (1887), 312–30.

4359 TESTA DE NEVILL: RETURNS FOR (THE) COUNTY OF GLOUCESTER. Ed. by Henry Barkly. Ibid. xii (1888), 235–90; xiii (1889), 23–34, 297–358; xiv (1890), 14–47.

Contains a valuable commentary on the Gloucestershire entries. See also No. 4337.

KENT

4360 FRAGMENT OF THE KENT PORTION OF KIRKBY'S INQUEST. Ed. by James Greenstreet. *Archaeologia Cantiana*, xi (1877), 365–9.

4361 HOLDERS OF KNIGHTS' FEES IN KENT AT THE KNIGHTING OF THE KING'S ELDEST SON, 38 Henry III. Ed. by James Greenstreet. Ibid. xii (1878), 197–237.

4362 INQUISITIONES POST MORTEM (1235–71). Ibid. ii (1859), 279–336; iii (1860), 243–74; iv (1861), 311–21; v (1862–3), 292–304; vi (1864–5), 237–50.

Translation only.

LANCASHIRE

4363 ABSTRACTS OF INQUISITIONS POST MORTEM (1297–1637), extracted from MSS. at Towneley. Ed. by William Langton. Chetham Soc. 2 vols. Manchester. 1875–6.

4364 DUCATUS LANCASTRIAE CALENDARIUM INQUISITIONUM POST MORTEM, EDWARD I–CHARLES I. Record Comm. 1823.

Relates to lands in various counties.

4365 GREGSON (MATTHEW). Portfolio of fragments relative to the history, etc., of the county and duchy of Lancaster. 3 pts. Liverpool, 1817. 3rd edn. by John Harland. Lond. etc. 1869.

Testa de Nevill, pp. 307–36.
Tenants of the Duke of Lancaster, 1311 (Birch Feodary), pp. 333–47.

4366 LANCASHIRE: (CALENDAR OF) INQUISITIONS POST MORTEM, RICHARD II–ELIZABETH. *Deputy Keeper's Reports*, xxxix (1878), 532–49.

4367 LANCASHIRE INQUESTS, EXTENTS, AND FEUDAL AIDS (1205–1355). By William Farrer. Lancs.–Ches. Record Soc. Pubns. 3 pts. Vols. xlviii, liv, lxx. 1903–15.

Contains inquests *post mortem*, the great inquest of service of 1212, rentals, extents, etc. Translation only.

4368 LANSDOWNE FEODARY (A LIST OF KNIGHTS' FEES OF THE DUKE OF LANCASTER, 1349), in Baines's *History of the County of Lancaster* (No. 1705) (1836) iv. 756–64; translation, ibid. (1870) ii. 692–6.

4369 STOKES (ETHEL). Calendar of the duchy of Lancaster inquisitions post mortem (Edw. I–Hen. VIII). *Genealogical Magazine*, ii (1899), 427–31, 533–6; iii (1900), 27–9, 64–6, 113–15; iv (1901), 69–70, 220, 258–9, 355–6, 504–6; vi (1903), 395–6.

Relates to lands in various counties.

4370 THREE LANCASHIRE DOCUMENTS OF THE FOURTEENTH
AND FIFTEENTH CENTURIES. Ed. by John Harland. Chetham Soc. 1868.

The great De Lacy *post mortem* inquisition of 1311, pp. 1–27. See No. 4793.

LEICESTERSHIRE

See Nichols, *County of Leicester* (No. 1714) and Fletcher's *Documents* (No. 5739).

LINCOLNSHIRE

4371 EARLY LINCOLNSHIRE INQUISITIONS POST MORTEM
(1241–82; translation only). By William O. Massingberd. *A.A.S.R.P.* xxv
(1899), 1–35.

For extracts from *Testa de Nevill* and Hundred Rolls, see Boyd's *Records of ancient
Horncastle* (No. 5147).

NORFOLK

4372 NORFOLK RECORDS. Ed. by W. D. Selby (vol. ii by Walter Rye).
Norfolk and Norwich Archaeol. Soc. 2 vols. 1886–92.

Vol. ii is an index to four series of Norfolk inquests *post mortem*, Hen. III–Charles I.

4373 BLAKE (W. J.). 'Norfolk manorial lords in 1316'. *Norfolk Archaeology*,
xxx (1952), 234–61, 263–86.

NORTHUMBERLAND

4374 PROOFS OF AGE OF HEIRS TO ESTATES IN NORTHUMBRIA
(1328–40, 1401–72; translation). By J. C. Hodgson. *Archaeologia Aeliana*, xxii
(1900), 116–30; xxiv (1903), 126–7; 3rd series, iii (1907), 297–305. (See also
ibid. iv (1855), 326–30, for proofs of age 21 Edw. III–13 Hen. IV). Idem, 'The
sources of *Testa de Nevill* (the original returns for Northumberland)'. Ed. by
J. C. Hodgson. Ibid. 1st Ser. xxv (1904), 150–67. See also 'An unpublished
Northumberland hundred roll (1274)'. Ed. by H. H. E. Craster. Ibid. 3rd Ser.
iii (1907), 187–90.

NOTTINGHAMSHIRE

4375 ABSTRACTS OF THE INQUISITIONES POST MORTEM relating
to Nottinghamshire. Vol. ii: 1279–1321. Ed. by John Standish. Thoroton Soc.
Rec. Ser. (1914). Vol. iii: 1321–1350 (*post mortem* and other inquisitions). Ibid.
(1939). Vol. iv: 1350–1436. Ed. by K. S. S. Train. Ibid. (1952). Vol. v: 1437–
1485. Transcribed and edited (as English abstracts) by Mary A. Renshaw. Ibid.
(1956).

Vol. i deals with the inquisitions 1485–1546.

OXFORDSHIRE

4376 OXFORDSHIRE HUNDRED ROLLS OF 1279. Ed. by E. Stone and
Patricia Hyde. Oxfordshire Record Soc. xlvi (1968). (The hundred of Bampton by
E. Stone; the hundred of Witney by P. Hyde.)

Cf. Rose Graham, ed., 'A description of Oxford, from the hundred rolls of Oxfordshire,
A.D. 1279'. Oxf. Hist. Soc. xlvii. *Collectanea*, 4th Ser. (1905), 1–98.

4377 SHROPSHIRE INQUISITIONS POST MORTEM (1254–1383). Translated by W. K. Boyd. *Shrops. Archaeol. and Nat. Hist. Soc. Trans.* 2nd Ser. xi (1899), 262–76.

Translation only.

4378 TENANTS-IN-CAPITE AND SUB-TENANTS IN SHROPSHIRE, *circa temp.* Edw. I. From an original roll in the collection of Edward Lloyd. *Collectanea Topog. et Genealogica* (No. 115), i (1834), 111–21.

Gives information similar to that contained in the *Testa de Nevill*.

SOMERSET

4379 ABSTRACT OF INQUISITIONS POST MORTEM, temp. Hen. III, for Somerset and Dorset. *Collectanea Topog. et Genealogica*, ii (1835), 48–56, 168–74.

4380 FEODARY (A) OF GLASTONBURY ABBEY (to 1342). Ed. by F. W. Weaver. Somerset Record Soc. 1910.

4381 FRY (EDWARD A.). 'On the *inquisitiones post mortem* for Somerset (a calendar), 1216–1485'. *Somerset Archaeol. and Nat. Hist. Soc. Procs.* xliv (1898), 79–148.

4382 KIRKBY'S QUEST FOR SOMERSET, NOMINA VILLARUM FOR SOMERSET, etc. Ed. by F. H. Dickinson. (No. 3183).

STAFFORDSHIRE

4383 THE INQUESTS ON THE STAFFORDSHIRE ESTATES OF THE AUDLEYS OF A.D. 1273, 1276, 1283, 1299, 1308. With an introduction and notes by Josiah Wedgwood. Wm. Salt Archaeol. Soc. *Collections.* New Ser. xi (1908), 231–70.

English abstracts of inquisitions *post mortem*.

4384 INQUISITIONS POST MORTEM, AD QUOD DAMNUM, etc. Staffordshire 1223–1366. (English translations.) Ibid. New Ser. xiv (1911), 113–375; and xvi (1913), 1–178.

4385 LIBER NIGER SCACCARII, STAFFORDSCIRA. Ed. by George Wrottesley (No. 3006).

Lists the feudatories in Staffordshire in 1166.

4386 THE STAFFORDSHIRE HUNDRED ROLLS, *temp.* Hen. III and Edw. I. Ed. by George Wrottesley. Wm. Salt Archaeol. Soc. *Collections*, v, pt. i (1884), 105–21.

Contains a translation of the parts relating to Seisdon hundred, 39 Hen. III, and Totmonslow hundred, 3 Edw. I, which are not printed in *Rotuli Hundredorum* (No. 4345). The Latin text of the Offlow hundred roll will be found in Stebbing Shaw's *History of Staffordshire* (1798), appendix to the general history, vol. i, pp. xvi–xix.

4387 TESTA DE NEVILL AND LATER FEUDATORIES, Staffordshire, 1212–1316. By J. C. Wedgwood. Ibid. xiv (1911), 377–414.

Includes *Nomina Villarum* of 1316.

SUFFOLK

4388 HUNDRED ROLLS, 2 EDWARD I (3 EDW. I), county of Suffolk: Lothingland. Edited with a translation by John Hervey. (Suffolk Institute of Archaeology.) Ipswich. 1902.

4389 NOMINA VILLARUM, SUFFOLK, 1316. Ed. by V. B. Redstone. *Suffolk Institute of Archaeology. Procs.* xi (1903), 173–99.

SUSSEX

4390 THE HUNDRED ROLL FOR SUSSEX. By L. F. Salzman. *Sussex Archaeol. Collections,* lxxxii (1942), 20–34; lxxxiii (1943), 35–54; lxxxiv (1945), 60–81.

For some Sussex knights' fees, see L. B. Larking, ibid. xviii (1866), 49–52.

WESTMORLAND

4391 THE FEOFFEES OF THE CLIFFORDS, 1283–1482. By Frederick W. Ragg. *Cumb.–Westm. Antiq.–Archaeol. Soc. Trans.* viii (1908), 253–330, 404–10.

Pp. 268–97, a return of the fiefs and feoffees of the Clifford barony of Westmorland, 1452.

WILTSHIRE

4392 ABSTRACTS OF WILTSHIRE INQUISITIONES POST MORTEM returned into the court of chancery, 1242–1326. Ed. by Edward A. Fry. British Rec. Soc. Index Library, xxxvii (1908). (For) 1327–77. Abstracted by Ethel Stokes. Ibid. xlviii (1914).

Issued also by Wiltshire Archaeol. and Nat. Hist. Soc. See also No. 3619.

4393 NOMINA VILLARUM FOR WILTSHIRE, 1316. Ed. by W. H. (R.) Jones. *Wilts. Archaeol. and Nat. Hist. Soc. Magazine,* xii (1870), 1–43.

Also printed in R. C. Hoare's *Repertorium Wiltunense* (Bath, 1821).

WORCESTERSHIRE

4394 THE INQUISITIONES POST MORTEM FOR THE COUNTY OF WORCESTER. Ed. by J. W. Willis-Bund. Pts. i–ii, 1242–1326. Worcesters. Hist. Soc. Oxford, 1894–1909.

Translations only.

YORKSHIRE

4395 INQUISITIONS POST MORTEM relating to Yorkshire, of the reigns of Henry IV and Henry V. (English translations.) Ed. by W. Paley Baildon and J. W. Clay. Yorks. Archaeol. Soc. Record Ser. lix (1918).

4396 THE SURVEY OF THE COUNTY OF YORK TAKEN BY JOHN DE KIRKBY, CALLED KIRKBY'S INQUEST: also inquisitions of knights' fees, the *Nomina Villarum* for Yorkshire, and an appendix of illustrative documents. Ed. by R. H. Skaife. Surtees Soc. 1867.

The inquisitions of knights' fees were taken 31 Edward I, preparatory to levying an aid for the marriage of the king's eldest daughter. The appendix contains other lists of knights' fees.

4397 YORKSHIRE INQUISITIONS (1241–1316). Ed. by William Brown. Yorks. Archaeol. and Topog. Assoc. Record Ser. vols. xii (1892); xxiii (1898); xxxi (1902); xxxvii (1906).

Translation only. Contains mainly inquisitions *post mortem* (in which there are various manorial extents), with some inquests *ad quod damnum*. Valuable.

C. CHARTERS, DEEDS, AND WILLS

1. *Collections and Catalogues*

The fullest list of cartularies is given in Godfrey Davis's *Medieval cartularies* (No. 4401). For catalogues of individual charters, see *Index to the charters and rolls in the British Museum* (No. 1004), *Calendar of charters and rolls in the Bodleian Library* (No. 1020), and *Handlist of charters . . . (in) John Rylands Library* (No. 1037). *A guide to the Victoria History of the Counties of England* by H. A. Doubleday and W. Page (Lond. 1903) lists MSS. and editions of chartularies, county by county. For charters in chancery enrolments, see Nos. 3749, 3750, 3760, and the index below. For facsimiles, turn to Nos. 444, 451, and 4410. *The Bulletin of the National Register of Archives* (No. 943) and the *Historical MSS. Commission Reports* (No. 945) record numerous charters and cartularies.

The most important printed collections of charters are *Cartae Antiquae* (No. 3759); *Charter rolls* (No. 3758 and 3760); *Christopher Hatton's book of seals* (No. 4410); Davis *et al.*, *Regesta* (No. 3779); Douglas, *Social structure*, appendix (No. 4404); Dugdale's *Monasticon* (No. 1147); Farrer, *Feudal Cambridgeshire* (No. 4420); Farrer, *Honors and knights' fees* (No. 4651); Farrer and Clay, *Early Yorkshire charters* (Nos. 4498–9); Foster and Major, *Registrum Antiquissimum* (No. 5744); Madox, *Formulare* (No. 426); Round, *Ancient charters* (No. 3749); Round, *Calendar of documents in France* (No. 3806); Round, *Geoffrey de Mandeville*, appendix (No. 4006); and Stenton, *Danelaw charters* (No. 4403) and *Gilbertine charters* (No. 5957); and D. M. *Stenton Miscellany* (No. 1453).

A good study of 'Charter scholarship in England' by H. A. Cronne appeared in *Univ. Birmingham Historical Journal*, viii (1961), 26–61.

Charters for churches and religious houses are listed with the documents relating to the church (pp. 755–846); and borough charters are considered on pp. 700–30.

4398 BIRCH (W. DE GRAY). 'A fasciculus of the charters of Mathildis, empress of the Romans'. *Brit. Archaeol. Asso. Jour.* xxi (1875), 376–98.

4399 BISHOP (TERENCE A. M.). *Scriptores regis* (No. 3751).

T. A. M. Bishop, 'Two charters of Stephen at Jesus College'; *Cambr. Antiq. Soc. Procs.* xlv (1951), 1–4; P. Chaplais, 'The seals and original charters of Henry I', *E.H.R.* lxxv (1960), 260–75; V. H. Galbraith, 'Seven charters of Henry II', *Antiquaries Jour.* xii (1932), 269–78; R. L. Poole, 'The dates of Henry II's charters', *E.H.R.* xxiii (1908), 79–83.

4400 CARTAE ANTIQUAE OF LORD WILLOUGHBY OF BROKE. Ed. by J. H. Bloom. 4 pts. i: Cambridgeshire; ii: Hertfordshire; iii: Somersetshire; iv: Wiltshire. Hemsworth. 1900–1.

4401 DAVIS (GODFREY R. C.). Medieval cartularies of Great Britain: a short catalogue. Lond. N.Y. etc. 1958.

> Pt. i: Cartularies of religious houses, England, Wales, and Scotland.
> Pt. ii: Secular cartularies.
> In the introduction, pp. xvi–xvii, are printed Finding-lists of Cartularies. For each cartulary, the repository's reference-number of each manuscript, a date, a brief description of contents, editions (if any), and commentaries (if any) are given; and the indexes list the present owners and former owners. See D. Walker in *K. Major essays* (No. 7224).

4402 DESCRIPTIVE CATALOGUE OF ANCIENT DEEDS IN THE PUBLIC RECORD OFFICE. 6 vols. H.M.S.O. 1890–1915.

> This valuable catalogue comprises, for the most part, conveyances of land; but it also includes agreements, bonds, acquittances, wills, and other documents concerning private persons, from the twelfth to the sixteenth century. Some of them 'seem to have been brought into the courts of law as evidence of title, others to have been deposited in the chancery for enrolment on the close rolls'.

4403 DOCUMENTS ILLUSTRATIVE OF THE SOCIAL AND ECONOMIC HISTORY OF THE DANELAW. Ed. by F. M. Stenton. British Acad. Records of the Social and Economic History of England and Wales, no. 5. 1920.

> Mainly charters of the twelfth century.

4404 DOUGLAS (DAVID C.). The social structure of East Anglia. Oxf. 1927.

> An appendix of charters.

4405 FACSIMILES OF EARLY CHARTERS IN OXFORD MUNIMENT ROOMS. Ed. by Herbert E. Salter. Oxf. 1929.

4406 GALBRAITH (VIVIAN H.). 'Monastic foundation charters of the eleventh and twelfth centuries'. *Cambr. Hist. Jour.* iv (1934), 205–22, 296–8.

4407 INDEX OF PERSONS IN OXFORDSHIRE DEEDS ACQUIRED BY THE BODLEIAN LIBRARY, 1878–1963. Oxfordshire Rec. Soc. xlv (1966).

4408 LÉONARD (E. G.). 'Les plus anciennes chartes originales d'histoire normande ou anglaise à la Bibliothèque Nationale'. *Normannia* (Caen), viii (1935), 427–93.

4409 LIST OF ROYAL CHARTERS OF RICHARD I (1189–99), in Lionel Landon, *Itinerary of King Richard I* (Pipe Roll Soc. New Ser. xiii (1935), 146–72 and 183).

4410 LOYD (LEWIS) and STENTON (DORIS M.), eds. Sir Christopher Hatton's Book of Seals, to which is appended a select list of the works of Frank Merry Stenton. Northamptonshire Record Soc. and Oxf. 1950.

> A book, made c. 1640 for Sir Christopher Hatton, of copies of 529 charters drawn from thirty-two distinct sources and representing most of England. 'Of the 529 charters in

the book, 240 are facsimiles of the original deeds done with painful care.' Nearly all of the charters date from the twelfth and thirteenth centuries and form an important source for feudal history. This well-produced edition includes a scholarly introduction by Lady Stenton and learned notes by Lewis Loyd; it was presented to Sir Frank Stenton on his seventieth birthday. See review by David Douglas in *E.H.R.* lxvi (1951), 260–3.

2. *Charters and Deeds by County*

BEDFORDSHIRE

4411   ANCIENT BEDFORDSHIRE DEEDS. By Frederick A. Page-Turner. Beds. Hist. Rec. Soc. Pubns. ii (1914), 93–110.

4412   EARLY RECORDS OF TURVEY AND ITS NEIGHBOURHOOD. Ed. by George Herbert Fowler. Ibid. xi (1927), 47–107.

Drayton charters, 1138–1403.

4413   THE GOSTWICKS OF WILLINGTON (13th–19th cent.). By Herbert P. R. Finberg. Ibid. xxxvi (1956).

4414   RECORDS OF KNIGHT SERVICE IN BEDFORDSHIRE. Ed. by G. H. Fowler. Ibid. ii (1914), 245–63.

J. E. Morris, 'The assessment of knight service in Bedfordshire', ibid. ii (1914), 185–218; v (1920), 1–26.

4415   THE SHIRE OF BEDFORD AND THE EARLDOM OF HUNTING-DON. By G. H. Fowler. Ibid. ix (1925).

BERKSHIRE

4416   BOARSTALL CARTULARY. Ed. by Herbert E. Salter and A. H. Cooke. Oxf. Hist. Soc. lxxxviii (1930).

A private cartulary of mid-fifteenth century which includes a list of knights' fees of the honour of Wallingford of 1300.

4417   ST. MARY'S, HURLEY, IN THE MIDDLE AGES. By F. T. Wethered. Lond. 1898.

Pp. 89–225: Abstracts of charters and deeds to the parish of Hurley, 1086–1536.
Pp. 227–38: Translation of nine charters and deeds, *c.* 1086–1334.

BUCKINGHAMSHIRE

4418   A CALENDAR OF DEEDS AND OTHER RECORDS IN THE MUNIMENT ROOM AT THE MUSEUM, AYLESBURY. Bucks. Archaeol. Soc. Rec. Branch. v for 1941 (1944).

4419   EARLY BUCKINGHAMSHIRE CHARTERS. Ed. by G. Herbert Fowler and J. G. Jenkins. Bucks. Archaeol. Soc. Rec. Branch iii (1939).

CAMBRIDGESHIRE

4420   FARRER (WILLIAM). Feudal Cambridgeshire. Cambr. 1920.

CHESHIRE

4421   ARLEY CHARTERS: a calendar of ancient family charters preserved at Arley Hall, Cheshire. By William Beamont. Lond. 1866.

4422   BARRACLOUGH (GEOFFREY), ed. Facsimiles of early Cheshire charters, presented to William Fergusson Irvine on his eighty-ninth birthday. Lancs.–Ches. Record Soc. Pubns. (for 1958). Oxf. 1957.

4423   A MIDDLEWICH CHARTULARY. Ed. by Joan Varley and the late Professor Tait. Chetham Soc. New Ser. cv, cviii (1941, 1944).

   Contains transcripts of medieval deeds.

4424   TALBOT DEEDS, 1200–1682. Ed. by Eric E. Barker. Lancs.–Ches. Record Soc. Pubns. ciii (for 1948), 1953.

4425   STEWART-BROWN (RONALD). THE WAPENTAKE OF WIR-RAL: a history of the hundred and hundred court. Liverpool. 1907.

4426   TAYLOR (FRANK). 'Handlist of the Legh of Booth's charters in the John Rylands library'. *B.J.R.L.* xxxii (1949–50), 229–300.

CORNWALL

4427   TREVELYAN PAPERS PRIOR TO A.D. 1558. Ed. by J. Payne Collier. Camden Soc. Old Ser. lxvii. 1857.

   Charters, letters, pardons, wills, etc., relating to the Trevelyans, a Cornish family which supported the Lancastrian cause. Most of the documents belong to the period 1318–1551.

CUMBERLAND

4428   ANCIENT CHARTERS RESPECTING PROPERTY IN CUMBER-LAND AND OTHER COUNTIES IN THE NORTH OF ENGLAND. Ed. by John Hodgson. *Archaeologia Aeliana*, ii (1832), 381–411.

   Contains thirty-three charters.

DERBYSHIRE

4429   CHARTERS CONNECTED WITH THE CHURCH OF ASH-BURNE, DERBYSHIRE. Ed. by Francis Jourdain. *Derbys. Archaeol.–Nat. Hist. Soc. Jour.* xiii (1891), 52–107.

   Most of them are of the thirteenth century. See also, Charles Kerry, 'Early charters of Breadsall (translation), with some notes on the condition of the villani in the thirteenth century', ibid. xvi (1894), 157–82.

4430   THE GLAPWELL CHARTERS. Ed. by Reginald R. Darlington. Derbys. Archaeol.–Nat. Hist. Soc. 1957–9.

   For the holders of Glapwell, see Farrer, *Honors and knights' fees* (No. 4651), vol. i.

4431   JEAYES (ISAAC H.). Descriptive catalogue of the charters and muni-ments in the possession of R. W. Chandos-Pole at Radbourne Hall (*c.* 1170–1558). Lond. 1896. Idem, Descriptive catalogue . . . of the Gresley family (*c.* 1148–1676) in the possession of Sir Robert Gresley at Drakelowe. Lond. 1895.

Idem, Descriptive catalogue of Derbyshire charters in libraries and muniment-rooms. (*c.* 1129–1550.) Lond. 1906.

4432 A SURVEY OF THE HONOUR OF PEVEREL, 1250. By Charles Kerry. *Derbys. Archaeol.–Nat. Hist. Soc. Jour.* xiv (1892), 40–53.

Translation only. Contains a list of knights' fees, etc., held of the king.

DURHAM

4433 NORTH COUNTRY DEEDS. Calendared by William Brown. Surtees Soc. cxxvii, *Miscellanea,* ii (1916), 107–29.

Largely fourteenth century for the counties of Durham, Northumberland, and York.

ESSEX

See Cyril Hart, *Early Charters The Norman period* (No. 2199); and Bury St. Edmunds (Nos. 6336–42).

4434 ASHEN CHARTERS (13 Edw. I–20 Hen. VI). *East Anglian,* New Ser. iii (1889–90), 221–3, 291–4, 305–7, 321–3, 387–90; iv (1891–2), 87–9, 213–15, 290–3, 330–2; v (1893–4), 11–13, 58–61, 82–4, 108–9.

4435 WILLIAMS (J. F.). A collection of Essex deeds at Queens' College, Cambridge. *Essex Archaeol. Soc. Trans.* New Ser. xx (1930–3), 78–85.

Deeds from fourteenth to sixteenth centuries.

GLOUCESTERSHIRE

4436 CALENDAR OF CHARTERS, ROLLS, AND OTHER DOCU-MENTS (from 1182 onward) **IN THE MUNIMENT ROOM AT SHER-BORNE HOUSE.** n.p. 1900.

4437 JEAYES (ISAAC H.). Descriptive catalogue of the charters and muniments in the possession of Lord Fitzhardinge at Berkeley castle. Bristol. 1892.

Contains abstracts of charters, wills, and manorial rolls, etc. See also J. A. Neale, *Charters and records of the Neales of Berkeley, Yale, and Corsham.* (Warrington, 1907). This is a calendar, from about 1100 onward, relating mainly to Wilts. and Glos.; for the period 1100–1500 recourse has been had chiefly to muniments in Berkeley castle.

4438 PATTERSON (ROBERT B.), ed. The charters and scribes of the Earls and Countesses of Gloucester to A.D. 1217. Oxf. 1973.

Useful also as a palaeographical study.

4439 RUDD (M. A.). 'Abstracts of deeds relating to Chalford and Chalcombe'. *Bristol–Glos. Archaeol. Soc. Trans.* li (1930), 211–24.

HEREFORD

4440 CHARTERS OF THE EARLDOM OF HEREFORD, 1095–1201. Ed. by David Walker. Camden 4th Ser. i, *Camden Miscellany,* xxii (1964), 1–75.

Prints 124 documents. See also D. Walker, 'Miles of Gloucester, earl of Hereford' *Bristol–Glos. Archaeol. Soc. Trans.* lxxvii (1958–9), 66–84; and his 'The honours of the earls of Hereford in the twelfth century', ibid. lxxix (1960–1), 174–211.

See Duchy of Lancaster, pp. 578–80.

4441 ANCIENT CHARTERS AT SCARISBRICK HALL (1180–1705). Abstracted by Edward Powell. *Historic Soc. of Lancs. and Ches. Trans.* xlviii (1897), 259–94; xlix (1898), 184–230.

4442 A CALENDAR OF THE DEEDS AND PAPERS IN THE POSSES-SION OF SIR JAMES DE HOGHTON, bart., of Hoghton Tower, Lancashire. Ed. by J. H. Lumby. Lancs.–Ches. Record Soc. lxxxviii (1936).

4443 A CALENDAR OF THE NORRIS DEEDS (Lancashire), 12th to 15th century. Ed. by J. H. Lumby. Lancs.–Ches. Record Soc. xciii (1939).

4444 CHARTERS AND DEEDS RELATIVE TO THE STANDISH FAMILY OF STANDISH AND DUXBURY, co. Lancaster. Ed. by J. P. Earwaker. Manchester. (1898).

A calendar, 1222–1633, but chiefly *temp.* Edw. III, concerning various places.

4445 DUNKENHALGH DEEDS, *c.* 1200–1600. Ed. by G. A. Stocks and James Tait. Chetham Soc. New Ser. lxxx *Chetham Miscellanies,* iv (1921), 1–108.

4446 LANCASHIRE DEEDS. vol. i: Shuttleworth deeds, pt. i. Ed. by John Parker. Chetham Soc. New Ser. xci (1934).

Begins in thirteenth century.

4447 LANSDOWNE FEODARY (a list of knights' fees of the Duke of Lancaster, 1349) in Baines, *History of the county of Lancaster* (No. 1705) iv. 756–64; translation, ibid. (1870), ii. 692–6.

4448 LANCASHIRE PIPE ROLLS AND EARLY LANCASHIRE CHAR-TERS. Ed. by William Farrer. Liverpool. 1902.

4449 SCHEDULE OF DEEDS AND DOCUMENTS PRESERVED IN THE MUNIMENT ROOM AT SHAW HILL, CHORLEY. By R. D. Radcliffe. *Historic Soc. of Lancs. and Ches. Trans.* xli–xlv, *passim.* (1890–4).

4450 TRAPPE-LOMAX (RICHARD). A history of the township and manor of Clayton-le-Moors, co. Lancaster. Chetham Soc. lxxxv (1926).

Extracts from deeds which provide pedigrees.

4451 FOX (LEVI). 'The honor and earldom of Leicester: origin and descent, 1066–1399'. *E.H.R.* liv (1939), 385–402.

4452 EARLY LAND CHARTERS OF RIPPINGALE. Ed. by G. Herbert Fowler. *A.A.S.R.P.* xli, pt. ii for 1933 (1935), 141–8; xliii for 1935 (1937), 153–6.

4453 REGISTRUM ANTIQUISSIMUM OF THE CATHEDRAL CHURCH OF LINCOLN (No. 5744).

NORFOLK

4454 CARTHEW (GEORGE A.). The hundred of Launditch and deanery of Brisley: evidences and notes from public records, etc. 3 pts. Norwich. 1877-9.

Contains the following and many other records illustrating manorial and family history: charters of Castle Acre priory, Wissingsete, and North Elmham, i. 117-34, 253-75, 285-97; inquests *post mortem*, etc. relating to Gressenhall, i. 201-21. A valuable collection of materials, marred by many errors of transcription.

4455 ELEVEN DEEDS OF THE TIMES OF HENRY III AND EDWARD I from among the court rolls of the manor of Keswick in the possession of Hudson Gurney. Lond. 1841.

NORTHAMPTONSHIRE

4456 HENRY OF PYTCHLEY'S BOOK OF FEES. Ed. by W. T. Mellows. Northamptonshire Rec. Soc. Pubns. ii (1927).

Concerns for the most part knights' fees of abbey of Peterborough.
See also Stenton, Facsimiles of early charters (No. 451), and Hatton's Book of Seals (No. 4410).

4457 KERR (WILLIAM J. B.). Higham Ferrers: a history of a medieval lordship. Northampton. 1925.

NORTHUMBERLAND

4458 CALENDAR OF DEEDS IN THE LAING CHARTERS RELATING TO NORTHUMBERLAND. Ed. by A. Macdonald. *Archaeologia Aeliana*, xxviii (1950), 105-31.

Seventy-one deeds, dated *c*. 1253 to 1496, in the Laing Collections at the University of Edinburgh.

4459 HALCROW (ELIZABETH M.). 'Ridley charters'. *Archaeologia Aeliana*, xxxiv (1956), 57-76.

English calendar of 107 charters, many of which were published in Latin in Hodgson, *History of Northumberland* (No. 1775).

4460 OFFLER (HILARY S.). 'A Northumberland charter of King Henry I'. *Archaeologia Aeliana*. 4th Ser. xlv (1967), 181-8.

OXFORDSHIRE

4461 THE BOARSTALL CARTULARY. Ed. by Herbert E. Salter and A. H. Cooke. Oxf. Hist. Soc. lxxxvii (1930).

The appendix concerns the honour of Wallingford. See No. 4416.

4462 A COLLECTION OF CHARTERS RELATING TO GORING, STREATLEY, AND THE NEIGHBOURHOOD, 1181-1546, preserved in the Bodleian Library, with a supplement. Ed. by T. R. Gambier-Parry. 2 pts. Oxfordshire Rec. Soc. Rec. Ser. xiii-xiv (1931-2).

4463 EARLY ROLLS OF MERTON COLLEGE, OXFORD, WITH AN APPENDIX OF THIRTEENTH CENTURY OXFORD CHARTERS. Ed. by J. R. L. Highfield. Oxf. Hist. Soc. New Ser. xviii (1960-4).

Includes the will of Walter de Merton, the accounts of his executors, rolls of college officers, charters, etc.

4464   NEWINGTON LONGEVILLE CHARTERS. Transcribed and edited by H. E. Salter. Oxfordshire Rec. Soc. Rec. Ser. iii (1921). See No. 6094A.

An alien priory acquired by New College, Oxford, in 1441.

4465   THE OXFORD DEEDS OF BALLIOL COLLEGE. Ed. by H. E. Salter. Oxf. Hist. Soc. lxiv (1913).

See Oxford University (Nos. 7061 ff.).

Shropshire

4466   DEEDS RELATING TO LARDEN (1400–1543). Ed. by R. C. Purton. *Shrops. Archaeol. Soc. Trans.* liv (1951–3), 234–9.

4467   MUNIMENTS OF SHAVINGTON: A catalogue of the deeds, etc., in the muniment room of Shavington Hall. By H. D. Harrod. Shrewsbury. 1891.

Somersetshire

4468   DOCUMENTS AND EXTRACTS ILLUSTRATING THE HISTORY OF THE HONOUR OF DUNSTER. Ed. by H. C. Maxwell Lyte. Somerset Record Soc. Pubns. xxxiii (1917–18).

See also H. C. Maxwell Lyte, *Historical notes on some Somerset manors formerly connected with the honour of Dunster.* Ibid. Extra Ser. 1931.

4469   THE HYLLE CARTULARY. Ed. by R. W. Dunning. Somerset Rec. Soc. lxviii (1968).

Compiled by Robert Hylle of Spaxton, shortly after 1408.

4470   TWO REGISTERS FORMERLY BELONGING TO THE FAMILY OF BEAUMONT OF HATCH. Ed. by H. C. Maxwell-Lyte. Lond. 1920.

Staffordshire

4471   ANCIENT DEEDS PRESERVED AT THE WODEHOUSE, WOMBOURNE. Ed. by G. P. Mander. Wm. Salt Archaeol. Soc. *Collections.* 3rd Ser. for 1928 (1930), 3–134.

4472   CALENDAR OF EARLY CHARTERS, ETC., IN THE POSSESSION OF LORD HATHERTON. Ed. by H. L. E. Garbett. Ibid. 3rd Ser. for 1928 (1930), 135–71; for 1931 (1933), 235–54.

4473   CALENDAR OF LONGDON, LICHFIELD, AND OTHER STAFFORDSHIRE CHARTERS . . . Ed. by Isaac H. Jeayes. Ibid. 3rd Ser. for 1939 (1940), 71–158, 238–40.

These are the charters not concerned with the abbey of Burton-on-Trent in the same collections. See No. 6326.

4474   CHETWYND CHARTULARY. Ed. by George Wrottesley. Ibid. xii (1892), 241–336.

Contains documents relating to the family of Chetwynd, c. 1166–1506.

4475 A DOMESTIC CARTULARY, CHIEFLY CONCERNING THE BROMLEY OF BROMLEY, . . . (and other lands). Ed. by C. Swynnerton. Ibid. New Ser. xvi (1913), 221–71.

Abstracts of deeds concerned with Newcastle under Lyme.

4476 HISTORY OF THE BAGOT FAMILY, WITH COPIES OF THE DEEDS AT BLITHFIELD. Ed. by G(eorge) Wrottesley. Ibid. New Ser. xi (1908), 1–224.

Pp. 145–99: Deeds, *c.* 1197–1508.
Pp. 200–15: A rental of Blithfield, etc. 1402.

4477 MANDER (GERALD P.). History of the Wolseley charters. Ibid. 3rd Ser. pt. ii for 1934 (1935), 53–94.

4478 RYDEWARE CHARTULARY. Ed. by Isaac H. Jeayes. Ibid. xvi (1895), 257–302.

Compiled by order of Thomas de Rydeware, *temp.* Edw. II. Contains charters, pleas, etc. relating to the Rydeware family.

4479 SHENSTONE CHARTERS. Ed. by George Grazebrook, with notes by H. S. Grazebrook. Ibid. xvii (1896), 237–98.

They relate to persons and lands in Shenstone, *c.* 1126–1387; and are copied from the Great Coucher Book of the duchy of Lancaster. Additions by H. E. Savage, 'Shenstone Charters' (mainly from an Oseney cartulary) ibid. 3rd Ser. for 1923 (1924), 257–77.

4480 STAFFORDSHIRE CARTULARY, 1200–1327. By Josiah C. Wedgwood. Ibid. 3rd Ser. (1911), 416–48. See No. 6331.

SURREY

4481 FITZNELL'S CARTULARY: a calendar of Bodleian Library MS. Rawlinson B 430. Ed. by C. A. F. Meekings and Philip Shearman. Surrey Rec. Soc. xxvi for 1965–6 (1968).

SUSSEX

4482 ABSTRACTS OF SUSSEX DEEDS AND DOCUMENTS FROM THE MUNIMENTS OF THE LATE H. C. LANE, ESQ. OF MIDDLETON MANOR, WESTMESTON, SUSSEX. Sussex Rec. Soc. xxix (1924).

Only a few deeds from the fourteenth and fifteenth centuries.

4483 THE BOOK OF BARTHOLOMEW BOLNEY. Ed. by Marie Clough. Sussex Rec. Soc. lxiii (1964).

Fifteenth-century charters.

4484 EARLY SUSSEX CHARTERS AND DOCUMENTS. Ed. by H. M. R. Murray. *Sussex Notes and Queries*, viii (1940), 13–15, 73–4, 98–9.

WARWICKSHIRE

4485 RECORDS OF ROWINGTON: extracts from the deeds in the possession of the feoffees of the Rowington charities, with an appendix of MSS. from the Public Record Office. Ed. by J. W. Ryland. Birmingham. (1896).

Pp. 1–83: charters, 1141–1895.
Pp. 119–216: Extracts from public records, 1080–1648.

WESTMORLAND

4486 THE FEOFFEES OF THE CLIFFORDS, 1283–1482. By Frederick W. Ragg. *Cumb.–Westm. Antiq.–Archaeol. Soc. Trans.* New Ser. viii (1908), 253–330, 404–10 (index).

Contains a return, with translation, of the fiefs and feoffees of the Clifford barony of Westmorland, 1452, pp. 268–97.

4487 RECORDS RELATING TO THE BARONY OF KENDALE. By William Farrer. Ed. by John F. Curwen. 2 vols. Cumb.–Westm. Antiq.–Archaeol. Soc. Record Ser. iv (1923), viii (1932).

See Mullins, *Texts*, pp. 301–2.

WILTSHIRE

4488 CALENDAR OF ANTROBUS DEEDS BEFORE 1625. Ed. by Ralph B. Pugh. Wilts. Archaeol.–Nat. Hist Soc. Records Branch. iii (1947).

About 75 of the deeds are of date before 1500, and relate to Amesbury.

4489 RECORDS OF WILTSHIRE PARISHES. By E. M. Thompson. *Wiltshire Notes and Queries*, i–vi (1895–1909), *passim*.

Contains translations of extracts from inquests *post mortem*, feet of fines, assize and subsidy rolls, etc. 1066–1770 for Cholderton and Bratton, Erchfont (or Urchfont) and Stert; those for Bratton are taken mainly from the Edington chartulary.

4490 THE TROPENELL CARTULARY. Ed. by J. Silvester Davies. 2 vols. Wilts. Archaeol.–Nat. Hist. Soc. 1908.

The contents of an old Wiltshire muniment chest: deeds, etc., relating to Salisbury and other places in Wilts., mainly of the fourteenth and fifteenth centuries. The MS. was begun by order of Thomas Tropenell in 1464, and was added to until he died in 1488.

4491 WILTSHIRE DEEDS IN THE BATH PUBLIC LIBRARY, 1437–60. Ed. by J. H. P. Pafford. Wilts. Archaeol. Soc. Records Branch, *Collectanea*, edited by N. J. Williams. 1956.

4492 HODGETT (G. A. J.). 'Feudal Wiltshire'. *V.C.H. Wilts.* v. 44–71.

WORCESTERSHIRE

4493 JEAYES (ISAAC H.). Descriptive catalogue of the charters and muniments of the Lyttelton family at Hagley Hall. Lond. 1893.

4494 THE KYRE PARK CHARTERS. Ed. by John Amphlett. Worcesters. Hist. Soc. 1905.

A calendar, 1301–1758; relates to various places in Worcestershire.

YORKSHIRE

4495 ABSTRACTS OF OLD DEEDS (mainly 14th and 15th cent.). By Charles Jackson. *Yorks. Archaeol. and Topog. Asso. Jour.* vi (1881), 58–72. Also Yorkshire deeds (English abstracts, 1236–1530). By A. S. Ellis. Ibid. xii (1893), 92–115, 230–62, 289–308; xiii (1895), 44–83. Also Yorkshire deeds (1268–1661, abstracts). Ibid. xvi (1902), 84–107; xvii (1903), 96–126. Also Abstracts of deeds in the possession of James Montagu of Melton-on-the-Hill, near Doncaster (of the 13th and 14th cent.). Ed. by Charles Jackson. Ibid. v (1879), 227–40.

4496 CALVERLEY CHARTERS PRESENTED TO THE BRITISH MUSEUM. Edited by William P. Baildon and Samuel Margerison. Vol. i. Thoresby Soc. Pubns. vi (1904).

Contains 400 charters, mainly grants to members of the Calverley family of Calverley, Hen. II–1499.

4497 CATALOGUE OF THE MUNIMENTS AT KIRKLEES (1200–1800) IN THE POSSESSION OF SIR GEORGE J. ARMYTAGE. (Lond. 1900).

Relates to various places in Yorkshire.

4498 EARLY YORKSHIRE CHARTERS, being a collection of documents anterior to the thirteenth century. Ed. by William Farrer. 3 vols. Yorks. Archaeol. Soc. Rec. Ser. Extra Ser. 1914–16.

4499 EARLY YORKSHIRE CHARTERS. Based on the manuscripts of the late William Farrer and edited by Charles Travis Clay.

An outstanding collection.

   i. (vol. iv as continuation of No. 4498). The honour of Richmond, pt. i (1935).
   ii. (vol. v). The honour of Richmond, pt. 2 (1936).
   iii. (vol. vi). The Paynel fee (1939).
   iv. C. T. Clay and Edith M. Clay, Early Yorkshire charters, vols. i–iii; consolidated index of persons and places.
   v. (vol. vii). The honour of Skipton (1947).
   vi. (vol. viii). The honour of Warenne (1949).
   vii. (vol. ix). The Stuteville fee (1952).
   viii. (vol. x). The Trussebut fee (1955).
   ix. (vol. xi). The Percy fee (1963).
   x. (vol. xii). The Tison fee (1965).

4500 HARWOOD EVIDENCES: REDMAN OF HARWOOD AND LEVENS. Ed. by George Duckett. *Yorks. Archaeol. and Topog. Asso. Jour.* iv (1877), 85–113.

Extracts from charters, wills, etc. Hen. II–Hen. VIII.

4501 PERCY CHARTULARY (1167–1377). Ed. by M. T. Martin. Surtees Soc. cxvii for 1909 (1911).

Contains over 1100 grants relating to lands of the Percys in Yorkshire and Northumberland.

4502 PUDSAY DEEDS. Ed. by Ralph P. Littledale. Yorks. Archaeol. Soc. Record Ser. lvi (1916).

4503 REGISTRUM HONORIS DE RICHMOND. Ed. by Roger Gale. Lond. 1722.

Pp. 20–7: Extent of lands in Richmondshire. 30 Hen. II.
Pp. 37–64: *Inquisitiones feodorum*, 15 Edw. I.
Pp. 65–75: *Extenta feodorum*, 11–12 Edw. II.
Pp. 89–106: Charters, pleas, etc.
   App. pp. 28–56. Extenta honoris de Richmond, 8 Edw. I.
   The appendix also contains many charters and other records.

4504 YORKSHIRE DEEDS (12th–17th centuries, abstracts). Ed. by William Brown (i–iii); C. T. Clay (iv–viii), M. J. Hebditch (ix), M. J. Stanley Price (x). 10 vols. *Yorks. Archaeol. Soc. Record Series*, vols. xxxix, l, lxiii, lxv, lxix, lxxvi, lxxxiii, cii, cxi, cxc. 1909–55.

3. *Wills*

Down to 1858 there were in each diocese an episcopal registry or depository of wills, and various minor registries. When the deceased had goods in only one diocese, his will was normally probated in a registry within that diocese. When the deceased had goods in more than one diocese, his will was probated in the prerogative court of the province. The surviving records of the prerogative court at Canterbury begin in 1383; they were preserved at Somerset House, London, until 1970, when many were transferred to the P.R.O. The extant records of the similar archiepiscopal court for the province of York begin in 1389 and are now housed in the Borthwick Institute at York.

Since 1945 the pre-1858 probate records from other registries have, in large measure, been transferred to county record offices and borough record offices. The locations of these records are given county by county in Gardner and Smith (No. 511) and in Camp (No. 4506), as of 1959 and 1963. These two works are fundamental for the study of wills, and the studies listed under Biography and Genealogy on pp. 62–71 are sometimes useful for testaments. Copies of wills are also to be found in episcopal registers, for example Gibbons's *Ely episcopal records* (No. 5704), *Registrum Edmundi Lacy of Exeter*, ed. by G. R. Dunstan (No. 5717), vol. iv, pp. 1–64. The indexes to *Registrum Thome Bourgchier* and to D. Douie's volumes of Pecham's Registers (Nos. 5609–10) should be consulted; and particularly vol. ii of *Registrum Henrici Chichele* (No. 5609), pp. 371–636, where the wills proved before the archbishop are printed in full, and pp. 637–85 where notes on the testators are supplied.

a. Indexes and aids

4505 BOUWENS (BETHELL G.). Wills and their whereabouts. Lond. 1939. 2nd edn. by H. G. Thacker. Soc. Genealogists Lond. 1950.

See Camp, the next entry.

4506 CAMP (ANTHONY J.). Wills and their whereabouts. Being a thorough revision and extension of the previous work of the same name by B. G. Bouwens. Canterbury. 1963.

Gives up-to-date locatio of probate records; the transfer of the majority of pre-1858 wills has occurred since 1945, largely to County Record Offices.

4507 GROSS (CHARLES). 'The medieval law of intestacy'. *Harvard Law Rev.* xviii (1904), 120–31. Reprinted separately, Cambr. (Mass.). 1904; and in *Select essays* (No. 1246) iii. 723–36.

4508 MARSHALL (GEORGE W.). Handbook of the ancient courts of probate and depositories of wills. Lond. 1895.

Superseded by Camp (No. 4506); but for its date it gave an alphabetical list of all known courts of probate, with details as to their records and jurisdiction and with bibliographical notes. For the older repositories, see also N. H. Nicolas, *Notitia Historica* (Lond. 1824), pp. 142–205; and *Report of the Record Commissioners, 1837* (No. 965), pp. 257–81.

4509 SHEEHAN (MICHAEL M.). The will in medieval England. From the conversion of the Anglo-Saxons to the end of the thirteenth century. Studies and Texts, no. 6. Pontifical Inst. of Mediaeval Stud. Toronto. 1963.

A full-length study of the subject, with excellent documentation. Appendix A is a list of citations to fifty-six wills of the thirteenth century. See also M. M. Sheehan, 'A list of (161) thirteenth century wills', *Genealogists' Magazine*, xiii (1961), 259–66.

4510 SKEEL (CAROLINE). 'Medieval Wills'. *History*, x (1926), 300–10.

Bibliographical note on p. 310 gives some citations. See also R. Sharpe France, 'Wills', *History*, l (1965), 36–9.

4511 WALNE (PETER). English wills. Probate records in England and Wales, with a brief note on Scottish and Irish wills. Virginia Colonial Record Project. Richmond (Va.). 1964.

b. Collections of wills

4512 ABSTRACTS OF ANCIENT WILLS (1300–1488). *Collectanea Topog. et Genealogica* (No. 115), iii (1836), 99–106.

4513 A COLLECTION OF THE WILLS OF THE KINGS AND QUEENS OF ENGLAND, from William the Conqueror to Henry VII. (Ed. by John Nichols.) Lond. 1780.

4514 THE FIFTY EARLIEST ENGLISH WILLS IN THE COURT OF PROBATE, LONDON, 1387–1439, 1454. Ed. by Frederick J. Furnivall. E.E.T.S. Orig. Ser. lxxviii. 1882.

4515 INDEX OF WILLS PROVED IN THE PREROGATIVE COURT OF CANTERBURY (1383–1588) and now preserved in . . . Somerset house. John Challenor C. Smith. 2 vols. British Rec. Soc. Index Library. ix (1893); xi (1895).

Other volumes for later periods.

4516 NORTH COUNTRY WILLS, being abstracts of wills relating to the counties of York, Nottingham, Northumberland, Cumberland, and Westmorland at Somerset House and Lambeth Palace 1383–1558. Ed. by John W. Clay. Surtees Soc. cxvi (1908).

A second volume (cxxi, 1912) carries the abstracts to 1604.

4517 TESTAMENTA LAMBETHANA: a complete list of wills and testaments recorded in the archiepiscopal registers at Lambeth, 1312–1636. By Dr. (A. C.) Ducarel. Middle Hill Press. 1854.

There is a calendar of Lambeth wills, 1313–1644, in the *Genealogist*, v (1881), 211–17, 324–9; vi (1882), 23–32, 127–35, 217–28. For a calendar of Lambeth administrations, see ibid. vii (1883), 204–12, 271–84; and New Ser. i (1884), 80–2. These calendars have superseded Ducarel's list. Also John Challenor C. Smith, 'Calendar of Lambeth wills', *Genealogist*, New Ser. xxxiv (1918), 53–64, 149–601, 219–34; xxxv (1919), 45–51, 102–26.

4518   TESTAMENTA VETUSTA: illustrations from wills, of manners, customs, etc. from the reign of Henry II to the accession of Elizabeth. Ed. by Nicholas H. Nicolas. 2 vols. Lond. 1826.

Mainly translations of wills.

c. Wills by county

BEDFORDSHIRE

4519   CALENDAR OF BEDFORDSHIRE WILLS. By F. A. Blaydes. Bedford. 1893.

Most of these wills are of the sixteenth and seventeenth centuries.

4520   SOME BEDFORDSHIRE WILLS AT LAMBETH AND LINCOLN (mostly 14th and 15th centuries). Ed. by Mrs. Hilary Jenkinson and George H. Fowler. *Beds. Hist. Rec. Soc. Pubns.* xiv (1931), 79–130. Also Bedfordshire Wills, 1480–1519. Ed. by P. Bell. Ibid. xlv (1966); and The Bedfordshire wills and administrations proved at Lambeth Palace and in the archdeaconry of Huntingdon. Ed. by Frederick A. Page-Turner. Ibid. ii (1914), 3–59.

BERKSHIRE

4521   EARLY BERKSHIRE WILLS ANTE 1558. By G. F. T. Sherwood. *Berks., Bucks., and Oxon. Archaeol. Jour.* i–vii (*passim*). Reading. 1895–1901.

Abstracts of wills, most of them dated after 1485.

CUMBERLAND

4522   TESTAMENTA KARLEOLENSIA: The series of wills from the prae-Reformation registers of the bishops of Carlisle, 1353–86. Ed. by Richard S. Ferguson. Cumb.–Westm. Antiq.–Archaeol. Soc. 1893.

DORSET

4523   FRY (GEORGE S.). Calendar of Dorset wills in the prerogative court of Canterbury, 1383–1700. Dorset Records: indexes, calendars, and abstracts of records. Ed. by Edward A. and G. S. Fry. Vol. xi. Lond. 1911.

DURHAM, ETC.

4524   WILLS AND INVENTORIES ILLUSTRATIVE OF THE HISTORY, MANNERS, LANGUAGE, ETC. OF THE NORTHERN COUNTIES OF ENGLAND, FROM THE ELEVENTH CENTURY ONWARDS. (Ed. by James Raine. Pt. ii, by William Greenwell. Pt. iii, by J. C. Hodgson. Pt. iv, by H. M. Wood). 4 pts. Surtees Soc. ii (1835), xxxviii (1860), cxii (1906), cxlii (1912).

Those dating before 1500 (i. 1–104) relate mainly to the counties of Durham and Northumberland.

ESSEX

4525   ANCIENT WILLS (Essex 1377–1658). Ed. by H. W. King. *Essex Archaeol. Soc. Trans.* i (1858), 149–60; iii (1865), 53–63, 74–94, 167–97; iv

(1869), 1–24, 147–82; v (1873), 281–93; New Ser. i (1878), 142–52, 165–78; ii (1884), 55–70, 359–76; iii (1889), 230–7, 287–303.

See George S. Fry, 'Abstracts of wills relating to Walthamstow, Co. Essex (1335–1559)'. *Walthamstow Antiq. Soc. Pubn.* ix (1921).

4526 WILLS AT CHELMSFORD (Essex and East Hertfordshire). Vol. i, 1400–1619. Ed. by Frederick G. Emmison. British Record Soc. Index Library, lxxviii (1958).

Later wills in later volumes.

GLOUCESTERSHIRE

4527 NOTES OR ABSTRACTS OF THE WILLS CONTAINED IN THE VOLUME ENTITLED THE GREAT ORPHAN BOOK AND BOOK OF WILLS, IN THE COUNCIL HOUSE AT BRISTOL (1381–1605). By Thomas P. Wadley. Bristol–Glos. Archaeol. Soc. 1886.

4528 A CALENDAR OF WILLS PROVED IN THE COURT OF THE BISHOP OF BRISTOL, 1572–1792, AND A CALENDAR OF WILLS IN THE GREAT ORPHAN BOOKS PRESERVED IN THE COUNCIL HOUSE, BRISTOL, 1379–1674. By Edward A. Fry. British Rec. Soc. Index Library, xvii (1897).

HUNTINGDONSHIRE

4529 CALENDAR OF HUNTINGDONSHIRE WILLS, 1479–1652. Ed. by William M. Noble. British Rec. Soc. Index Library, xlii (1911).

KENT

4530 CALENDAR OF WILLS RELATING TO KENT PROVED IN THE PREROGATIVE COURT OF CANTERBURY, 1384–1559. By Leland L. Duncan. Lewisham Antiq. Soc. Lee. 1890.

4531 EARLY KENTISH WILLS (1442–67). Ed. by James Greenstreet. *Archaeologia Cantiana*, xi (1877), 370–87.

4532 HUSSEY (ARTHUR). (Compiled wills or abstracts for various parishes in Kent). *Archaeologia Cantiana*, xxxi (1916), xxxii (1917), xxxiv–xlvii (1920–35), xlix–li (1937–39).

4533 INDEX OF WILLS AND ADMINISTRATIONS NOW PRESERVED IN THE PROBATE REGISTRY AT CANTERBURY 1396–1558 AND 1640–1650. Transcribed and arranged by Henry R. Plomer. Kent Archaeol. Soc. Kent Records vi and British Rec. Soc. Index Library, l (1920).

4534 INDEX OF WILLS PROVED IN THE ROCHESTER CONSISTORY COURT BETWEEN 1440 AND 1561. Compiled by Leland L. Duncan. Kent Archaeol. Soc. Kent Records. ix (1924).

4535 SEDE VACANTE WILLS: a calendar of wills proved before the commissary of Christ Church, Canterbury, during vacancies in the primacy, with an appendix containing transcripts of archiepiscopal and other wills of importance. Compiled and edited by C. Eveleigh Woodruff. Kent Archaeol. Soc. Kent Records. iii (1914).

Woodruff also printed four wills (1278–1441) in *Archaeologia Cantiana*, xlvi (1934), 27–35.

4536 TESTAMENTA CANTIANA: a series of extracts from fifteenth and sixteenth century wills relating to church building and topography. West Kent, by Leland L. Duncan; East Kent, by Arthur Hussey. 2 pts. in 1 vol. Lond. 1906–7.

LANCASHIRE

4537 COLLECTION OF LANCASHIRE AND CHESHIRE WILLS not now to be found in any probate registry 1301–1752. Ed. by William F. Irvine. Lancs.–Ches. Rec. Soc. xxx (1896).

4538 A LIST OF LANCASHIRE WILLS PROVED WITHIN THE ARCHDEACONRY OF RICHMOND (formerly) PRESERVED IN SOMER-SET HOUSE, LONDON, FROM A.D. 1457 TO 1680. . . . Ed. by Henry Fishwick. Lancs.–Ches. Rec. Soc. x (1884).

Later volumes for wills of later periods.

LINCOLNSHIRE

4539 CALENDARS OF LINCOLN WILLS (1320–1600). Ed. by Charles W. Foster. British Rec. Soc. Index Library xxviii (1902).

Calendars for 1601–52, ibid. xli (1910).

4540 EARLY LINCOLN WILLS: an abstract of all the wills recorded in the episcopal registers of the old diocese of Lincoln, 1280–1547. By Alfred Gibbons. Lincoln. 1888.

See also A. Clark, *Lincoln diocese documents* (No. 5741).

4541 LINCOLNSHIRE WILLS PROVED IN THE PREROGATIVE COURT OF CANTERBURY, 1384–1468 and 1471–90. *Archit.–Archaeol. Soc. Lincoln and Northampton Papers and Reports* (No. 171), lxxxix (1932), 61–114, 179–218.

4542 LINCOLN WILLS REGISTERED IN THE DISTRICT PROBATE REGISTRY AT LINCOLN. Ed. by Charles W. Foster. Vol. i: A.D. 1271 to A.D. 1526. Lincoln Record Soc. v (1914).

Later wills to 1532 in ibid. x (1918) and xxiv (1930).

LONDON

4543 ACCOUNT OF THE EXECUTORS OF RICHARD (de Gravesend), BISHOP OF LONDON, 1303, AND OF THE EXECUTORS OF THOMAS (de Bitton), BISHOP OF EXETER, 1310. Ed. by William H. Hale and Henry T. Ellacombe. Camden Soc. New Ser. x (1874).

4544 CALENDAR OF WILLS PROVED AND ENROLLED IN THE COURT OF HUSTING, LONDON, 1258–1688. Ed. by Reginald R. Sharpe. 2 vols. Lond. 1889–90.

An elaborate work, well edited.

4545 INDEXES TO THE ANCIENT TESTAMENTARY RECORDS OF WESTMINSTER. By Arthur M. Burke. Lond. 1913.

Covers miscellaneous testamentary records, 1228–1700, etc. but little for the period before 1485.

4546 INDEX TO TESTAMENTARY RECORDS OF THE COMMISSARY COURT OF LONDON (London Division), now preserved in the Guildhall Library. Ed. by Marc Fitch. Vol. i: 1374–1488. Hist. MSS. Comm. and H.M.S.O. Lond. 1969.

Also *London consistory court wills, 1492–1547*. Ed. by Ida Darlington. London Record Soc. Pubns. iii (1967).

NORFOLK

4547 EARLY NORWICH WILLS FROM THE NORWICH REGISTRY (1370–83). Ed. by John L'Estrange. *Norfolk Antiq. Miscellany* (Norwich). i (1877), 345–412.

4548 EXTRACTS FROM EARLY WILLS IN THE NORWICH REGISTRIES (1370–1411). By Henry Harrod. *Norfolk Archaeology*, iv (1855), 317–39.

Also H. Harrod, 'Extracts from early Norfolk wills' (five wills before 1485), ibid. i (1847), 111–28.

4549 INDEX OF WILLS PROVED IN THE CONSISTORY COURT OF NORWICH AND NOW PRESERVED IN THE DISTRICT PRIVATE REGISTRY AT NORWICH 1337–1550, AND WILLS AMONG THE NORWICH ENROLLED DEEDS, 1286–1508. Compiled and edited by Margaret A. Farrow. British Rec. Soc. Index Library, lxix (1945), and Norfolk Rec. Soc. xvii, pts. 1–2 (1943–5).

Later wills in vol. lxxiii (1950); and in vol. lxxi (1950).

OXFORDSHIRE

4550 SOME OXFORDSHIRE WILLS PROVED IN THE PREROGATIVE COURT OF CANTERBURY, 1393–1510. Ed. by John R. H. Weaver and Alice Beardwood. Oxfordshire Rec. Soc. xxxix. 1958.

SHROPSHIRE

4551 A CALENDAR OF SHROPSHIRE WILLS, 1321–1591. *Shrops. Archaeol. and Nat. Hist. Soc. Trans.* v (1882), 257–64; vi (1883), 319–32.

SOMERSET

4552 SOMERSET MEDIEVAL WILLS. Ed. by Frederic W. Weaver. (First Ser.). 1383–1500. Somerset Rec. Soc. xvi (1901).

Abstracts from wills registered in Prerogative Court of Canterbury, now deposited at the Public Record Office, London. Later wills in later volumes.

SUFFOLK

4553 CALENDAR OF EARLY SUFFOLK WILLS: Ipswich registry, 1440–1620. *East Anglian* (Ipswich), New Ser. i–iv (1885–94).

See also *Calendar of wills at Ipswich, 1440–1600*. By F. A. Crisp. (Lond. 1895).

4554 CALENDAR OF PRE-REFORMATION WILLS, ETC., REGISTERED AT THE PROBATE OFFICE, BURY ST. EDMUNDS (1354–1535). Ed. by Vincent B. Redstone. *Suffolk Institute Archaeol. Procs.* xii (1904–6).

4555 CALENDAR OF WILLS RELATING TO THE COUNTY OF SUFFOLK, proved in the prerogative court of Canterbury between 1383 and 1604. Compiled by C. W. S. Randall Cloke. Ed. by T. W. Oswald-Hicks. Lond. 1913.

4556 WILLS AND INVENTORIES FROM THE REGISTERS OF THE COMMISSARY OF BURY ST. EDMUNDS AND THE ARCHDEACON OF SUDBURY (1370–1650). Ed. by Samuel Tymms. Camden Soc. Old Ser. xlix (1850).

Surrey

4557 CALENDAR OF WILLS IN THE CONSISTORY COURT OF THE BISHOP OF CHICHESTER, 1482–1800. Ed. by Edward A. Fry. British Record Soc. Index Library. xlix (1915).

4558 SOME SURREY WILLS IN THE PREROGATIVE COURT OF CANTERBURY, 1383–1570. Ed. by H. J. Hooper. *Surrey Archaeol. Collections.* lii (1950–1).

Sussex

4559 TRANSCRIPTS OF SUSSEX WILLS AS FAR AS THEY RELATE TO ECCLESIOLOGICAL AND PAROCHIAL SUBJECTS, UP TO THE YEAR 1560. Transcribed and classified by R. Garraway Rice, ed. by Walter H. Godfrey. 4 vols. Sussex Record Soc. xli (1935), xlii (1938), xliii (1939), xlv (1941).

Wiltshire

4560 For some Wiltshire wills, 1383–1640, see *Wiltshire Notes and Queries* i–ii, v–vii (1894+), *passim.*

Worcestershire

4561 CALENDAR OF WILLS AND ADMINISTRATIONS IN THE CONSISTORY COURT OF THE BISHOP OF WORCESTER, 1451–1600. Ed. by Edward A. Fry. British Rec. Soc. Index Library. xxxi (1904), xxxix (1910); and Worcesters. Hist. Soc. 2 vols. (1904–11).

Yorkshire

4562 INDEX OF WILLS IN THE YORK REGISTRY, 1389–1514. By Francis Collins. Yorks. Archaeol.-Topog. Asso. Record Ser. vi (1889). Index of wills etc. from the dean and chapter's court at York, 1321–1636. Ibid. xxxviii (1907). Index of the wills and administrations entered in the registers of the archbishops at York, being consistory wills, etc. A.D. 1316–1822, known as the archbishops' wills. Ibid. xciii (1937).

4563 SOME EARLY CIVIC WILLS OF YORK (1385–1406, with a translation). Ed. by Robert B. Cook. *A.A.S.R.P.* xxviii (1906), 827–71.
Continued in vols. xxxi–xxxv.

4564 TESTAMENTA EBORACENSIA: a selection of wills from the registry at York (1300–1551). Ed. by James Raine, Sen., James Raine, Jun., and John W. Clay. 6 vols. Surtees Soc. iv (1836); xxx (1855); xlv (1865), liii (1869); lxxix (1884); cvi (1902).

4565 TESTAMENTA LEODIENSIS (1391–1524). Extracted from the probate registry at York by William Brigg. Thoresby Soc. Pubns. ii (1891), 98–110, 205–14; iv (1895), 1–16, 137–47.

Continued for later dates in later volumes.

4566 WILLS AND INVENTORIES FROM THE REGISTRY OF THE ARCHDEACONRY OF RICHMOND, extending over portions of the counties of York, Westmoreland (*sic*), Cumberland, and Lancaster (1442–1579). Ed. by James Raine, Jun. Surtees Soc. xxvi (1853).

4567 WILLS DEPOSITED AT LAMBETH AND RELATING TO YORKSHIRE, 1385–1589. By John Challenor C. Smith. *Yorks. Archaeol. Soc. Jour.* xxiv (1914), 104–5.

D. SOME FAMILIES AND THEIR RECORDS

Consult the section on Biography and Genealogy in vol. i, pp. 62–71.

4568 ALTSCHUL (MICHAEL). A baronial family in medieval England: The Clares, 1217–1314. Johns Hopkins Univ. Stud. lxxxiii. Baltimore. 1965.

Pt. i: the family; pt. ii: the estates. See also Jennifer C. Ward, *B.I.H.R.* xxxvii (1964), 114–17.

4569 AUTHORITIES AND PRECEDENTS IN SUPPORT OF THE CLAIM OF BARON OF BERKELEY AS A PEERAGE BY TENURE. Lond. 1862.

4570 BARCLAY (CHARLES W.) and (HUBERT F.) and WILSON-FOX (ALICE). A history of the Barclay family (1066–1933). 3 vols. Lond. 1924–34.

4571 BEAUMONT PAPERS. Letters relating to the family of Beaumont, of Whitley, Yorkshire, from the fifteenth to the seventeenth centuries. Ed. from the originals in the Bodleian Library by William D. Macray. Roxburghe Club. 1884.

4572 THE BOHUN MSS. A group of five MSS. executed in England about 1370 for members of the Bohun family. Described by Montague R. James, with introduction by Eric G. Millar. Roxburghe Club. 1936.

4573 BURROWS (MONTAGU). The family of Brocas of Beaurepaire and Roche Court, with some account of the English rule in Aquitaine. Lond. 1886.

Contains many charters and other records, including on pp. 296–8 and 401–6 manorial accounts of the time of Edward III.

4574 CLAY (CHARLES T.). 'The family of Longvillers'. *Yorks. Archaeol. Jour.* xlii (1968), 41–51.

4575 COPINGER (WALTER A.). History and records of the Smith-Carington family from the Conquest to the present time. Lond. 1907.

See also Round's *Peerage and Pedigree* (No. 4589), ii. 134–257: The Great Carington Imposture.

4576 DE FONBLANQUE (EDWARD B.). Annals of the house of Percy from the Conquest to the opening of the nineteenth century. 2 vols. Lond. 1887.

See also Gerald Brenan, *History of the House of Percy*. 2 vols. (Lond. 1902).

4577 ELLIS (GEOFFREY). Earldoms in fee: a study in peerage law and history. Lond. 1963.

A scholarly work, providing a medieval background to modern practice.

4578 FINLASON (WILLIAM F.). A dissertation on the history of hereditary dignities, with special reference to the case of the earldom of Wiltes. Lond. 1869.

4579 GRAZEBROOK (HENRY S.). The barons of Dudley. Wm. Salt Archaeol. Soc. *Collections*, vol. ix, pt. ii. Lond. 1889.

Translation of manorial extents, *temp*. Edw. I, pp. 25–38.

4580 GURNEY (DANIEL). The record of the house of Gournay. Lond. 1848. Supplement, 1858.

Contains extracts from the public records, including charters.

4581 INGPEN (ARTHUR R.). An ancient family: a genealogical study showing the Saxon origin of the Ingpen family. Lond. 1916.

Appendix contains charters and extracts from records.

4582 JACK (R. IAN). 'Entail and descent: the Hastings inheritance, 1370–1436'. *B.I.H.R.* xxxviii (1965), 1–19.

4582A LE STRANGE (HAMON). Le Strange records: a chronicle of the early Le Stranges of Norfolk and the March of Wales, A.D. 1100–1310. Lond. 1916.

Scholarly work with documents and charters, useful for history of Welsh March.

4583 MACLEAN (JOHN). The parochial and family history of the deanery of Trigg Minor (Cornwall). 3 vols. Lond. 1873–9.

4584 MADDISON (ARTHUR R.). The Tournays of Caenby. *A.A.S.R.P.* xxix (1907), 1–42.

The appendix contains three rentals in full, 1414–45.

4585 MARSH (JOHN F.). Annals of Chepstow castle, or six centuries of the lords of Striguil, from the conquest to the revolution. Ed. by Sir John Maclean. Exeter. 1883.

4586 MASON (J. F. A.). 'Roger de Montgomery and his sons (1067–1102)'. *T.R.H.S.* 5th Ser. xiii (1963), 1–28. See No. 4628.

4587 MAY (TERESA). 'The Cobham family in the administration of England, 1200–1400'. *Archaeologia Cantiana*, lxxxii (1967), 1–31. Idem, 'The estates of the Cobham family in the later thirteenth century', ibid. lxxiv (1969), 211–29.

4588 PILKINGTON (JOHN). The history of the Lancashire family of Pilkington and its branches, 1066–1600. 2nd edn. Liverpool. 1894.

Extracts from the public records, 1355–1460, pp. 68–85. The first edition seems to have been published in the *Transactions of the Historic Society of Lancashire and Cheshire,* xlv (1894), 159–218.

4589 ROUND (JOHN HORACE). Studies in peerage and family history. Westminster, 1901.* Idem, Peerage and pedigree: studies in peerage law and family history. 2 vols. Lond. 1910.* Idem, Family origins and other studies. Ed. by William Page. Lond. 1930.*

Three important studies by a master in this field. *Family origins* was published posthumously; it includes Round's long bibliography of books and innumerable articles.

4590 SCOTT (JAMES RENAT). Memorials of the family of Scott, of Scott's Hall, Kent, with an appendix of documents. Lond. 1876.

4591 SHIRLEY (EVELYN P.). Stemmata Shirleiana, or the annals of the Shirley family. Lond. 1841; 2nd edn. 1873.

The appendix contains a rent roll of Sir Ralph Shirley, 2 Hen. V, deeds, etc.

4592 SITWELL (GEORGE R.). The barons of Pulford in the eleventh and twelfth centuries, and their descendants. Scarborough. 1889.

Contains many extracts from the public records.

4593 SMYTH (JOHN). The Berkeley MSS. (Vols. i–ii: The lives of the Berkeleys, lords of the manor of Berkeley. Vol. iii: Description of the hundred of Berkeley.) Ed. by John Maclean. Bristol and Glos. Archaeol. Soc. 3 vols. Gloucester. 1883–5.

An important collection which contains abstracts of many records, and much information concerning the social condition of the people. See W. J. Smith, 'The rise of the Berkeleys: an account of the Berkeleys of Berkeley Castle, 1243–1361', *Bristol–Glos. Archaeol. Soc. Trans.* lxxi (1952), 101–21.

4594 WATSON (JOHN). Memoirs of the ancient earls of Warren and Surrey. 2 vols. Warrington, 1782. Earlier edns. 1776, 1779.

4595 WIGHTMAN (WILFRED E.). The Lacy family in England and Normandy, 1066–1194. Oxf. 1966.

4596 WROTTESLEY (GEORGE). History of the family of Wrottesley, co. Stafford. (Reprinted from the *Genealogist,* new ser. vols. xv–xix.) Wm. Salt Archaeol. Soc. *Collections,* New Ser. vol. vi, pt. ii. Lond. 1903.

Contains many charters.

4597 YEATMAN (JOHN P.). The early genealogical history of the house of Arundel. Lond. 1882.

See L. F. Salzman, 'The property of the earl of Arundel', 1397, *Sussex Archaeol. Collections,* xci (1953), 32–52; Mark A. Tierney, *History and antiquities of the castle and town of Arundel including the biography of the earls from the Conquest to the present time* (Lond. 1834). Also *Notes of evidence relating to the earldom of Arundel* (Lond. 1860).

E. HOUSEHOLD BOOKS AND LETTERS

See Tout, *Chapters* (No. 1223), ii. 165–87; iii. 189–200; v, chap. xviii. For the household accounts of kings and members of the royal family, see above Nos. 3111–41. Rogers, *History of Agriculture* (No. 1376), ii. 635–47, prints records of expenses for journeys, etc. in 1331 and 1395; and iv, p. 565 for Fastolf.

4598 ACCOUNT OF THE EXPENSES OF JOHN OF BRABANT AND THOMAS AND HENRY OF LANCASTER, A.D. 1292–3. Ed. by Joseph Burtt. Camden Soc. Old Ser. lv, Miscellany, ii (1853).

The expenses incurred in England where John of Brabant married Margaret, daughter of Edward I.

4599 AMYOT (THOMAS), ed. Transcript of two rolls containing an inventory of effects formerly belonging to Sir John Fastolfe. *Archaeologia*, xxi (1827), 232–80.

Most of these effects were in his house at Caister near Yarmouth.

4600 COMPOTA DOMESTICA FAMILIARUM DE BUKINGHAM ET D'ANGOULÊME [Ed. by W. B. D. D. Turnbull]. Abbotsford Club. Edin. 1836.

Three household books, belonging to Humphrey, duke of Buckingham, 1443–4; the earl of Angoulême, 1452; and Anne, widow of the aforesaid Humphrey, 1463–4. To these are added a few fragments of a roll of expenses incurred by an earl in 1273 in a journey from the county of Durham to the south Welsh march.

4601 EXPEDITIONS TO PRUSSIA AND THE HOLY LAND MADE BY HENRY, EARL OF DERBY (afterwards King Henry IV), in 1390–91 and 1392–93: being the accounts kept by his treasurer. Ed. by L. T. Smith. Camden Soc. New Ser. lii (1894). A German edition, H. G. Prutz, *Rechnungen über Heinrich von Derbys Preussenfahrten*, appeared in Leipzig, 1893.

Contains two accounts from the records of the duchy of Lancaster. See also Grace Stretton, 'Some aspects of medieval travel, etc., with special reference to the wardrobe accounts of Henry, earl of Derby, 1390–93'. *T.R.H.S.* 4th Ser. vii (1924), 77–97.

4602 FOWLER (GEORGE HERBERT). 'A household expense roll, 1328'. *E.H.R.* lv (1940), 630–4.

The week-by-week journal of household expenses of Thomas Bezoun of Woodford.

4603 HOUSEHOLD BOOK OF DAME ALICE DE BRYENE OF ACTON HALL, September 1412–September 1413. Trans. by Marian K. Dale and ed. by V. B. Redstone, Suffolk Institute Archaeol. and Nat. Hist. 1931.

4604 HOUSEHOLD BOOK OF QUEEN ISABELLA OF ENGLAND for the fifth regnal year of Edward II (1311–12). Ed. by F. D. Blackley and G. Hermansen. Univ. Alberta Classical and Hist. Stud. i. Edmonton (Canada). 1971.

4605 HOUSEHOLD BOOKS OF JOHN (HOWARD), DUKE OF NORFOLK, AND THOMAS, EARL OF SURREY, 1481–90. Ed. by J. P. Collier. Roxburghe Club. 1844.

Contains domestic accounts.

4606 HOUSEHOLD ROLL OF BISHOP RALPH OF SHREWSBURY (1337–8). Ed. by J. Armitage Robinson and arranged by T. F. Palmer. Somerset Record Soc. xxxix *Collectanea*, i (1924), 72–174.

Household expenses for pantry, butlery, kitchen, etc.

4607 LABARGE (MARGARET W.). A baronial household of the thirteenth century. Lond. 1965.

Drawn largely from the household accounts of Eleanor of Montfort, countess of Leicester; the oldest such accounts known to survive. See below, No. 4609.

4608 LETTERS OF ROYAL AND ILLUSTRIOUS LADIES OF GREAT BRITAIN (1103–1558). Ed. by M. A. E. Wood (afterwards Green). 3 vols. Lond. 1846.

H. G. Richardson, 'The letters and charters of Eleanor of Aquitaine', *E.H.R.* lxxiv (1959), 193–213.

4609 MANNERS AND HOUSEHOLD EXPENSES OF ENGLAND IN THE THIRTEENTH AND FIFTEENTH CENTURIES. Ed. by T. H. Turner. Roxburghe Club. 1841.

Contains the household roll of Eleanor, countess of Leicester, 1265; accounts of the executors of Queen Eleanor, 1291; accounts, etc. of John Howard, duke of Norfolk, 1462–71.

4610 THE PASTON LETTERS, 1422–1509. Ed. by James Gairdner. 3 vols. Lond. 1872–5; reprinted with corrections. 3 vols. 1896; reprinted with a supplement 4 vols. Westminster. 1900–01. New edn. 6 vols. Lond. 1904.* Another edition in three parts by Norman Davis is in progress; part i was published, Oxf. 1971.

Other edns., by John Fenn. 5 vols. (Lond. 1787–1823); and re-edited by Mrs. Archer-Hind. 2 vols. (Lond. 1924). Abridged editions by A. Ramsay. 2 vols. (Lond. 1840–1), and as *Paston Letters, selected and edited with an introduction, notes and glossary by Norman Davis*. (Clarendon Medieval and Tudor Ser. Oxf. 1958.)

Commentaries by Henry S. Bennett, *The Pastons and their England: studies in an age of transition* (Cambr. 1922; 2nd edn. 1932; reprinted 1968); and by Gairdner in his introductions.

These letters were written by and to members of the family of Paston in Norfolk. Many of them are from Sir John Fastolf and other persons of high rank. They elucidate public affairs and domestic manners.

4611 PLUMPTON CORRESPONDENCE: a series of letters, chiefly domestic, written in the reigns of Edward IV, Richard III, Henry VII, and Henry VIII. Ed. by Thomas Stapleton. Camden Soc. Old Ser. iv. Lond. 1839.

The correspondence of a prominent Yorkshire family, preceded by biographical notices of its members.

4612 ROLL OF THE HOUSEHOLD EXPENSES OF RICHARD DE SWINFIELD, BISHOP OF HEREFORD, 1289–90. Ed. by John Webb. 2 vols. Camden Soc. 1854–5.

Vol. i: Text and appendix. Vol. ii: Abstract and illustrations.

4613 SCOTT (JAMES R.). Receipts and expenditures of Sir John Scott in the reign of Edward IV (1463, 1466). *Archaeologia Cantiana*, x (1876), 250–8.

4614   STEER (F. W.). 'A medieval household: the Urswick inventory'.
Essex Rev. lxiii (1954), 4–20.

4615   THE STONOR LETTERS AND PAPERS, 1290–1483. Ed. by
Charles L. Kingsford. 2 vols. R.H.S. Camden Ser. 3rd Ser. xxix–xxx (1919).
Idem, 'Supplementary Stonor letters and papers, 1314–1482'. R.H.S. Camden
Ser. xxxiv (1924), *Camden Miscellany,* xiii, pt. 2.

4616   STRETTON (GRACE). 'The travelling (noble) household in the middle
ages'. *Brit. Archaeol. Asso. Jour.* xl (1934), 75–103.

F. ESTATE MANAGEMENT

See Denholm-Young, *Seignorial administration* (No. 4619), T. B. Pugh, *Marcher Lordships*
(No. 4675), Somerville, *Lancaster* (No. 3883), Myers, *Household ordinances* (No. 3129).
See also Drew (No. 5815), Stone (No. 5788); and *Flintshire Ministers' Accounts* (Nos.
3858–9).

4617   BLAAUW (W. H.). 'Letters of Ralph de Neville, bishop of Chichester
and chancellor to King Henry III'. *Sussex Archaeol. Collections,* iii (1850), 35–76.

Contains details relating to the management of a landed estate.

4618   DAVIES (ROBERT REES). 'Baronial accounts, incomes and arrears
in the later middle ages'. *Econ. H.R.* 2nd Ser. xxi (1968), 211–19.

4619   DENHOLM-YOUNG (NOËL). Seignorial administration in England.
Oxford Hist. Ser. Oxf. 1937. *

Deals for the later thirteenth century with bailiffs, stewards, baronial courts and liberties,
ministers' accounts, etc. particularly for estates of Isabella de Fortibus, countess of
Devon, and Roger Bigod, earl of Norfolk. In appendix iii, prints a transcript of *Regule
compoti.*

4620   FOX (LEVI). The administration of the honour of Leicester in the
fourteenth century. Leicester. 1940.

A study of the accounts of one of Lancaster's possessions.

4621   GIUSEPPI (MONTAGUE S.). 'Wardrobe and household of Bogo de
Clare'. *Archaeologia,* lxx (1920), 1–56.

For Bogo, see Altschul, *The Clares* (No. 4568), pp. 176–87 and 306–8.

4622   GRAY (HOWARD L.). 'The household administration of Henry Lacy
and Thomas of Lancaster'. *E.H.R.* xlii (1927), 180–200.

See Maddicott (No. 4127), pp. 8–16; and Fowler (No. 4178), pp. 172–86.

4623   GRAY (H. L.). 'Incomes from land in England in 1436'. *E.H.R.* xlix
(1934), 607–39.

Cf. Pugh and Ross, 'The English baronage and the income tax of 1436', *B.I.H.R.* xxvi
(1953), 1–28, who regard Gray's estimates as much too low.

4624   HILTON (RODNEY). Ministers' accounts of the Warwickshire estates
of the Duke of Clarence, 1479–80. Dugdale Soc. Pubns. xxi (1952).

4625   JACK (R. I.). Grey of Ruthin Valor. Sydney. 1965.

Ministers' accounts for 1467–8 from English manors of Edmund Grey, earl of Kent.

4626 JEULIN (P.). 'Un grand honneur anglais. Aperçus sur le comté de Richmond en Angleterre, possession des ducs de Bretagne (1069–1398)'. *Annales de Bretagne*, xlii (1935), 265–302.

4627 KIRBY (JOHN L.). 'An account of Robert Southwell, receiver-general of John Mowbray, earl marshal, 1422–3'. *B.I.H.R.* xxvii (1954), 192–8.

Contains payments for the recent expedition to France.

4628 MASON (J. F. A.). 'The officers and clerks of the Norman earls of Shropshire'. *Shropshire Archaeol. Soc. Trans.* lvi (1957–60), 244–57. Idem. 'The Norman earls of Shrewsbury: miscellaneous notes'. Ibid. lvii (1961–4), 152–61.

4629 MIDGLEY (MARGARET). Ministers' accounts of the earldom of Cornwall, 1296–97. 2 vols. Camden 3rd Ser. lxvi (1942), and lxviii (1945).

These accounts relate to nine estates scattered throughout England.

4629A MINISTERS' ACCOUNTS FOR WEST WALES, 1277–1306. Part i: text and translation. Ed. by Myvanwy Rhys. Cymmrodorion Record Ser. Lond. 1936. ACCOUNTS OF THE MINISTERS FOR THE LANDS OF THE CROWN IN WEST WALES FOR THE FINANCIAL YEAR 1352–3. Ed. by William Rees. *B.B.C.S.* x (1939–41), 60–83, 139–56, 256–71.

4630 MYATT-PRICE (E. M.). 'The Cromwell household accounts, 1417–76', in *Studies in the History of Accounting*. Ed. by A. C. Littleton and B. S. Yamey. Lond. 1956.

4631 OSCHINSKY (DOROTHEA). Walter of Henley and other treatises on estate management and accounting. Oxf. 1971.

This is designed as a critical edition of the four best-known treatises on estate management, formerly edited for the Royal Historical Society by Elizabeth Lamond in 1890. These four French tracts, compiled in the thirteenth century, are the anonymous Senechaucy, the Husbandry of Walter of Henley, the Rules sent by Grosseteste to the Countess of Lincoln, and an anonymous treatise on the audit and on the offices of steward and reeve. To these has been added an appendix of extracts from other treatises. Walter of Henley's Husbandry and the anonymous Husbandry were printed in facsimile of the English translations of 1510 and 1589 by F. H. Cripps-Day in the *Manor Farm* (Lond. 1931).

4632 OSCHINSKY (D.). 'Medieval treatises on estate accounting'. *Econ. H.R.* xvii (1947), 52–61; reprinted in *Studies in the History of Accounting* (No. 4630). Idem, 'Medieval treatises on estate management'. *Econ. H.R.* 2nd Ser. viii (1956), 296–309. Idem. 'Quellen zur Verwaltungs- und Wirtschaftsgeschichte der englischen Gutsherrschaft im Mittelalter'. *M.I.O.G.*, lviii (1950), 228–43. Idem, 'Notes on the editing . . . of estate accounts'. *Archives*, ix (1969), 84–9; 142–52. See No. 3000.

4632A POWELL (A. D.). 'Miscellaneous ministers' accounts, etc. for the Radnorshire area (thirteenth to fifteenth centuries)'. *Radnorshire Record Soc. Trans.* xli (1971), 56–78.

E. J. Cole, 'Account for the lordship of Maelienydd 1356–7', ibid. xxxiv (1964), 31–8. Idem, 'An incomplete account of 10–11 Edward III', ibid. xxxviii (1968), 39–43.

4633   REES (WILLIAM). South Wales and the March, 1284–1415. A study in social and agrarian history. Lond. etc. 1924.

Rees refers to many documents, particularly to unpublished ministers' accounts. See also Arthur J. Roderick and William Rees, eds. 'The lordships of Abergavenny, Grosmont, Skenfrith and White Castle: account of the ministers for the year 1256–7'. South Wales and Monmouthshire Record Soc. Pubns. iii (1954), iv (1957).

4633A   ROBERTS (R. A.). 'Cymru fu: some contemporary statements'. *Hon. Soc. Cymmrodorion Trans.* 1895–6 (1897), 87–137.

Deals with ministers' accounts relating to Wales, and prints those of 6–8 Edward I relating to Cardiganshire.

4634   ROSENTHAL (JOEL T.). 'Fifteenth century incomes and Richard, Duke of York'. *B.I.H.R.* xxxvii (1964), 233–9. Idem, 'The estates and finances of Richard, Duke of York (1411–60)'. *Stud. in Medieval and Renaissance Hist.* (Nebraska), ii (1965), 115–204.

The second article is a study of ministers' accounts, with numerous tables; much material is drawn from P.R.O. Special Collections, Rentals and Surveys. See *Welsh H.R.* iii (1967), 299–302.

4635   ROSS (CHARLES D.). The estates and finances of Richard Beauchamp, earl of Warwick. Dugdale Soc. Occasional Papers. xii (1956).

4636   ROSS (CHARLES D.) and PUGH (THOMAS B.). 'Materials for the study of baronial incomes in fifteenth century England'. *Econ. H.R.* 2nd Ser. vi (1953), 185–94.

See Pugh and Ross above (No. 4623); and R. E. Glasscock, 'The distribution of lay wealth in Kent, Surrey and Sussex in the early fourteenth century', *Archaeologia Cantiana*, lxxx (1965), 61–8.

4637   SAYERS (JANE). Estate documents at Lambeth Palace Library: a short catalogue. Leicester. 1965.

4638   SCHOFIELD (ROGER S.). 'The geographical distribution of wealth in England, 1334–1649'. *Econ. H.R.* 2nd Ser. xviii (1965), 483–510.

Cf. E. J. Buckatzsch, 'The geographical distribution of wealth in England 1086–1843', ibid. iii (1950), 180–202; and Christopher Dyer, 'A redistribution of incomes in fifteenth century England', *Past and Present* (1968), 11–33.

4639   WOOD-LEGH (KATHLEEN L.). A small household of the fifteenth century: being the account-book of Munden's Chantry, Bridport. Manchester. 1950.

G. FEUDAL TENURES

The *Complete Peerage* (No. 556), Dugdale's *Baronage* (No. 559), topographical portions of the *Victoria County History* (No. 1529), and the sections on palatinates (pp. 574–80), especially Somerville's *Duchy of Lancaster* (No. 3883), are useful on this subject. See especially the works on military history, pp. 619–23.

4640   ADAMS (GEORGE B.). Anglo-Saxon feudalism. *A.H.R.* vii (1901), 11–35. Reprinted separately, 1901.

Contends that the feudal system did not exist in England in the Anglo-Saxon period because the benefice and the vassalage were not yet united.

4641　APPS (UNA). 'The muntatores: their relation to other military tenures in the twelfth and thirteenth centuries'. *E.H.R.* lxiii (1948), 528–33.

4642　BEAN (JOHN M. W.). The decline of English feudalism 1215–1540. Manchester. 1967.

4643　BEAN (J. M. W.). The estates of the Percy family, 1416–1537. Oxf. 1958.

Includes an analysis of surviving Percy estate accounts. R. Jeffs, 'The Poynings–Percy dispute: an example of the interplay of open strife and legal action in the fifteenth century', *B.I.H.R.* xxxiv (1961), 148–64.

4644　CHEW (HELENA M.). The English ecclesiastical tenants-in-chief and knight service, especially in the thirteenth and fourteenth centuries. Oxf. 1932.

An important study within the bounds set for itself.

4645　CHEW (HELENA M.). 'Scutage under Edward I'. *E.H.R.* xxxvii (1922), 321–36. Idem, 'Scutage in the fourteenth century'. Ibid. xxxviii (1923), 19–41.

W. A. Morris, 'A mention of scutage in the year 1100', ibid. xxxvi (1921), 45–6. James F. Baldwin, *Scutage and knight service in England.* (Chicago, 1897).

4646　CRONNE (HENRY A.). 'The honour of Lancaster in Stephen's reign'. *E.H.R.* l (1935), 670–80.

G. W. S. Barrow, 'King David I and the honour of Lancaster', ibid. lxx (1955), 85–9.

4647　DALRYMPLE (JOHN). An essay towards a general history of feudal property in Great Britain. Lond. 1757.

Arthur Collins, *Proceedings, precedents and arguments on claims concerning baronies by writ and other honours.* Lond. 1734.

4648　DENHOLM-YOUNG (NOËL). 'Feudal society in the thirteenth century: the knights'. *History*, New Ser. xxix (1944), 107–119. Reprinted in No. 1467. See also his *Seignorial administration* (No. 4619).

4649　DOUGLAS (DAVID C.). 'The Norman Conquest and English feudalism', *Econ. H.R.* ix (1939), 128–43.

4650　DUGDALE (WILLIAM). Baronage of England. 2 vols. Lond. 1675–6.

4651　FARRER (WILLIAM). Honors and knights' fees: an attempt to identify the component parts of certain honors and to trace the descent of the tenants of the same who held by knight's service or serjeanty from the eleventh to the fourteenth century. 3 vols. Lond. and Manchester, 1923–5.

The original feature of Farrer's work is that it treats each feudal honour as a whole, regardless of county or other artificial boundaries. The honour of Wardon is an exception: it is confined to Bedfordshire (Tait). See *The honour of Wardon*, by the late William Farrer, with an introduction by James Tait, *Beds., Hist. Rec. Soc. Pubns.* xi (1927), 1–46.

4652　FOX (LEVI). 'The honor and earldom of Leicester: origin and descent, 1066–1399'. *E.H.R.* liv (1939), 385–402.

4653　HARVEY (SALLY). 'The knight and the knight's fee in England'. *Past and Present*, xlix (1970), 3–43.

4654 HASKINS (CHARLES H.). 'Knight-service in Normandy in the eleventh century'. *E.H.R.* xxii (1907), 636–49.

See Haskins, *Norman Institutions* (Cambr. (Mass.) 1918. 2nd edn. 1925).

4655 HOLLINGS (MARJORY). 'The survival of the five hide unit in the western midlands'. *E.H.R.* lxiii (1948), 453–87.

Miss Hollings argued 'that the Anglo-Saxon five hide unit survived the Norman Conquest to become the basis of knights' fees in parts of the western Midlands' (Hollister).

4656 HOLLISTER (C. WARREN). '1066: The feudal revolution', *A.H.R.* lxxiii (1968), 708–23.

Hollister here summarizes, with bibliographical references, the principal lines of argument in the debate over revolution or continuity of the military force. See also his books (No. 4304).

4657 HOLLISTER (C. WARREN), and HOLT (J. C.). 'Two comments on the problem of continuity in Anglo-Norman feudalism'. *Econ. H.R.* xvi (1963), 104–18.

J. O. Prestwich, 'Anglo-Norman feudalism and the problem of continuity', *Past and Present*, xxvi (1963), 39–57.

4658 HOLMES (GEORGE A.). The estates of the higher nobility in fourteenth century England. Cambr. 1957.

An excellent treatise dealing with the rise and fall of estates, emphasizing the developments in the estates of Mortimer, Bohun, Montague, Vere, Courtenay, and Burgh; with retinues and indentures; and with the trends in the economy of the inheritance. Appendix i prints unpublished documents; appendix ii lists the retinues of Thomas, earl of Lancaster; appendix iii deals with estate profits.

4659 HOLT (JAMES C.). 'Feudalism revisited'. *Econ. H.R.* 2nd Ser. xiv (1961–2), 333–40. Idem, 'The *carta* of Richard de La Haye 1166: a note on the "continuity" in Anglo-Norman feudalism'. *E.H.R.* lxxiv (1969), 289–96.

4660 HOYT (ROBERT S.). The royal demesne in English constitutional history, 1066–1272. Ithaca (N.Y.), 1950; Lond. 1951.

R. S. Hoyt, 'The nature and origins of the ancient demesne', *E.H.R.* lxv (1950), 145–74.

4661 HURNARD (NAOMI). 'The Anglo-Norman franchises'. *E.H.R.* lxiv (1949), 289–327, and 433–60.

Helen M. Cam, 'The evolution of the medieval English franchise' (No. 1461). Cf. Barraclough, *Earldom of Chester* (No. 1571), p. 17, note 2.

4662 JOLLIFFE (JOHN E. R.). 'Northumbrian institutions'. *E.H.R.* xli (1926), 1–42.

J. E. A. Jolliffe, 'Alod and fee', *Cambr. Hist. Jour.* v (1937), 225–34. Idem, 'A survey of fiscal tenements', *Econ. H.R.* vi (1936), 157–71; challenged by R. Lennard, 'The origin of the fiscal carucate', ibid. xiv (1944), 51–73.

4663 KIMBALL (ELISABETH G.). 'The judicial aspects of frank almoign tenure'. *E.H.R.* xlvii (1932), 1–11. Idem, 'Tenure in frank almoign and secular services'. Ibid. xliii (1928), 341–53.

Maitland, *Collected papers* (No. 1482), ii. 205–22.

4664 KIMBALL (E. G.). Serjeanty tenure in medieval England. Yale Hist. Pubns. Miscellany xxx. New Haven and Lond. 1936.*

Timothy Lewis, 'An English serjeanty in a Welsh setting', *History*, New Ser. xxxi (1946), 85–99.

4665 KING (EDMUND). 'Large and small landowners in thirteenth century England: the case of Peterborough abbey'. *Past and Present*, no. 47 (1970), 26–50.

This is concerned with the changing position of the gentry *vis-à-vis* the aristocracy.

4666 LAPSLEY (GAILLARD T.). 'Some castle officers in the twelfth century'. *E.H.R.* xxxiii (1918), 348–59.

J. H. Round, 'Castle guard', *Archaeological Jour.* lix (1902), 144–59; idem, 'Castle guard', *Ancestor*, vi (1903), 72–8; idem, 'The staff of a castle in the twelfth century', *E.H.R.* xxxv (1920), 90–7; idem, 'Castle watchmen', ibid. xxxv (1920), 400–1. Sidney Painter, 'Castle-guard', *A.H.R.* xl (1934–5), 450–9.

4667 LOYD (LEWIS C.). The origins of some Anglo-Norman families. Harleian Soc. ciii (1951).

A learned work on Anglo-Norman feudalism, broader than the title suggests. On a related subject, see F. M. Stenton, 'English families and the Norman conquest' (No. 1496).

4668 McFARLANE (KENNETH B.). 'The English nobility in the later middle ages'. Rapports, Comité international des sciences historiques. xii Congrès international des sciences historiques. Vienna, 1965. Vol. i, pp. 337–45.

K. B. McFarlane, 'Parliament and "bastard feudalism" ', *T.R.H.S.* 4th Ser. xxvi (1944), 53–79 (reprinted No. 1493); idem, 'Bastard feudalism', *B.I.H.R.* xx (1945), 161–80. H. M. Cam, 'The decline and fall of English feudalism' (No. 1462); idem, 'The quality of English feudalism' (No. 1461).

4669 MADOX (THOMAS). Baronia Anglica: history of land-honors and baronies, and of tenure *in capite*. Lond. 1736. Reprinted, 1841.

Contains many extracts from plea rolls and other public records.

4670 MILLER (EDWARD). 'The state and landed interests in thirteenth century France and England'. *T.R.H.S.* 5th Ser. ii (1952), 109–29.

Concerned with the break-up and alienation of feudal tenements.

4671 MOORE (MARGARET F.). The lands of the Scottish kings in England: the honour of Huntingdon, the liberty of Tyndale, and the honour of Penrith. Lond. 1915.

4672 NICHOLS (FRANCIS M.). 'On feudal and obligatory knighthood'. *Archaeologia*, xxxix (1863), 189–244.

4673 PAINTER (SIDNEY). Studies in the history of the English feudal barony. Johns Hopkins Univ. Stud. lxi. Baltimore (Md.). 1943.

S. Painter, 'The family and the feudal system in twelfth-century England', *Speculum*, xxxv (1960), 1–16; reprinted in No. 1486.

4674 POOLE (AUSTIN LANE). Obligations of society in the twelfth and thirteenth centuries. Ford lectures, 1944. Oxf. 1946.

4675 PUGH (THOMAS B.). The marcher lordships of South Wales, 1415–1536. Cardiff. 1963.

Contains law and financial records, a survey, and other documents.

4676 REID (RACHEL R.). 'Barony and thanage', *E.H.R.* xxv (1920), 161–99.

Concerned with the difference between tenure by barony and tenure by knight-service in the thirteenth century.

4677 ROUND (JOHN HORACE). Feudal England: historical studies of the eleventh and twelfth centuries. Lond. 1895. Reprinted, 1909; 1964. See No. 4005.

The author believed that knight service was not gradually evolved after 1066 out of the Anglo-Saxon obligation to provide one armed man for every five hides, but was introduced *de novo* by the Conqueror; that 'the assessment of knight service was based on a five knights unit, irrespective of area or value'; and 'that the feudal element introduced at the Conquest had a greater influence on our national institutions than recent historians admit'. See also J. H. Round, 'The knight-service of Malmesbury abbey', *E.H.R.* xxxii (1917), 249–52.

4678 SANDERS (IVOR J.). English baronies: a study of the origin and descent 1086–1327. Oxf. 1960.

This book traces, concisely but with ample documentation, the descent of some two hundred estates. It is a mine of details.

4679 STENTON (FRANK M.). The first century of English feudalism, 1066–1166. Ford lectures 1929. Oxf. 1932. 2nd edn. 1961.

Appendix of charters.
Stenton's lectures provide the standard account of Anglo-Norman society; they present what may be called 'the orthodox view' on the controversial question of continuity between Norman feudalism and Anglo-Saxon tenure. See J. C. Holt's review in *Econ. H.R.* xiv (1961), 333–40. Also F. M. Stenton, 'The changing feudalism of the middle ages', *History*, New Ser. xix (1934–5), 289–301.

4680 STEPHENSON (CARL). 'Feudalism and its antecedents in England'. *A.H.R.* xlviii (1943), 245–65. Reprinted in his *Mediaeval Institutions* (No. 1497).

See his 'Seignorial tallage' in *Pirenne essays* (No. 1446); and his 'The origin and significance of feudalism', *A.H.R.* xlvi (1941), 788–812; reprinted in No. 1497.

4681 SUTHERLAND (DONALD W.). *Quo Warranto* proceedings in the reign of Edward I, 1278–1294. Lond. and N.Y. 1963.

See T. F. T. Plucknett, *Legislation of Edward I* (No. 3339), pp. 35–50; E. C. Lodge, 'Edward I and his tenants-in-chief', *T.R.H.S.* 4th Ser. vii (1924), 1–26; H. M. Cam, 'The *Quo warranto* proceedings under Edward I' (No. 1462). G. T. Lapsley, 'John de Warenne' (No. 1478). N. D. Hurnard, 'Did Edward I reverse Henry II's policy upon seisin?', *E.H.R.* lxix (1954), 529–53; C. M. Fraser, 'Edward I and the regalian franchise of Durham', *Speculum*, xxxi (1956), 329–42; K. B. McFarlane, 'Had Edward I a "policy" towards the earls?', *History*, l (1965), 145–59.

4682 TAIT (JAMES). 'Knight-service in Cheshire'. *E.H.R.* lvii (1942), 437–59.

Complementary to researches of Round and Stenton, but the peculiarities of Cheshire are shown.

4683 THORNE (SAMUEL E.). 'English feudalism and estates in land'. *Cambr. Law Jour.* (1959), 193–209.

4684 TOUT (THOMAS F.). 'The earldoms under Edward I'. *T.R.H.S.* New Ser. viii (1894), 129–55.

4685 TURTON (ROBERT B.). The honor and forest of Pickering. North Riding Rec. Soc. New Ser. 4 vols. 1894–7.

Important documents, largely from Duchy of Lancaster records.

4686 WHITE (GEOFFREY H.). 'Stephen's earldoms'. *T.R.H.S.* 4th Ser. xiii (1930), 51–82.

See R. H. C. Davis, *King Stephen* (No. 3984), App. i: 'The earldoms in Stephen's reign'; and J. H. Round, *Geoffrey de Mandeville* (No. 4006).

4687 WIGHTMAN (WILFRED E.). 'The palatine earldom of William fitz Osbern in Gloucestershire and Worcestershire (1066–71)'. *E.H.R.* lxxvii (1962), 6–17. Idem, The Lacy family (No. 4595).

4688 WOLFFE (BERTRAM P.). The crown lands, 1461–1536: An aspect of Yorkist and early Tudor government. Historical Problems: Studies and Documents. Lond. and N.Y. 1970.

See also Hubert Hall and S. R. (Scargill) Bird, 'Notes on the history of the crown lands', *Antiquary*, xiii (1886), 1–6, 85–6, 89–95, 159–62, 194–6.

XIX. AGRARIAN SOCIETY

A. SOURCES FOR MANORIAL HISTORY

The principal sources for manorial history are account rolls, court rolls, and surveys. The surveys consist of three kinds, extents, customals, and rentals. The character of the sources is described with cautionary remarks on their use by Titow in *Rural Society* (No. 4701), pp. 24–33. The account rolls of bailiffs and reeves record the manorial income of the lord and the expenditures made in his behalf. 'The earliest surviving series comes from the estates of the bishops of Winchester' and go back to 1208–9. The court rolls, minutes of the proceedings in the manorial courts, throw light on the condition and activities of the peasants and on their relations to their lord. 'The earliest surviving court rolls date from about 1245.' Maitland in his *Court Baron* (No. 4716) edits certain tracts on the method of holding the manorial tribunals. Manorial surveys were drawn up on the information of a sworn verdict returned by a jury of tenants to a set of questions addressed to them by the lord's steward. An extent is a survey which gives valuations of both demesne and tenants' holdings. A custumal is a survey of the tenants' holdings only with a list of the services due from them. A rental is a survey which confines itself to rents only. Many surveys are found in monastic cartularies and registers, for example, Nos. 6042, 6044, and pp. 810–46, *passim*; and the section on charters (pp. 636–47). Some are printed in the Monasticons of Dugdale and Oliver (Nos. 1147, 6109); others are comprised in the inquests *post mortem*. The Hundred Rolls (No. 4345) give valuable extents of manors in Cambridgeshire and some other counties. Many manorial records are preserved in the British Museum and in the Public Record Office. See for examples, *Index to the charters and rolls in the British Museum* (No. 1004) and

P.R.O. *Lists and indexes* (No. 955) nos. vi and xxv. The Manorial Society Publications (No. 4694) provide other lists. The *Historical MSS. Commission Reports* summarize documents pertinent to manorial history (No. 4693). The bulletins and full reports of the National Register of Archives (Nos. 942–3 and pp. 108–9) are indispensable for the surveys of manorial documents in numerous archives. Current bibliographies can be found in the annual lists published in *Agricultural History Review* and *Economic History Review*.

The principal twelfth-century manorial surveys come from the monasteries of Peterborough (No. 6265), Burton (No. 6326), Worcester (No. 5836), Ramsey (No. 6173), Boldon Book of Durham (No. 3076), and Glastonbury (No. 6314). The most important studies of particular manors from the thirteenth century on are those by Davenport on Forncett (No. 4819), by Hilton on Leicestershire estates (No. 4800), by Hoskins on Wigston Manor (No. 4802), by Chibnall on Sherington (No. 4711), by Miller on Ely (No. 5711), by Ault, Neilson, and Raftis on Ramsey (Nos. 6174–6), by Page on Crowland (No. 6213), by Smith and Du Boulay on Canterbury (Nos. 5622, 5619), by Finberg on Tavistock (No. 6126), by Postan and Brooke on Peterborough (No. 6266), by Greenwell on Bishop Hatfield's Survey of Durham (No. 5672).

It must be noted that the collections of manorial documents in the registers or cartularies of ecclesiastical estates are catalogued in the section devoted to Church documents (pp. 755–86); whereas the documents for lay estates and individual manors are listed by county on pp. 669–91.

1. *Bibliographical Aids*

4689 DAVENPORT (FRANCES G.). A classified list of printed original materials for English manorial and agrarian history during the middle ages. Boston. 1894.*

Full references to account rolls, court rolls, rentals, customaries and extents, with a topographical index.

4690 GUTNOVA (EVGENIIA V.). 'Osnovnye istochniki i istoriografiia po istorii krest'ianskoi ideologii v Anglii XIII–XIV vv'. (Principal sources and historiography of the history of the peasant ideology in England in the thirteenth and fourteenth centuries). *Srednie veka* (Moscow), xxix (1966), 70–89. English summary, p. 89.

4691 HALL (HUBERT). A classified list of agrarian surveys in the Public Record Office (London). *Economica*, iv (1922), 28–50. See also his 'Select bibliography' (No. 19).

4692 HILTON (RODNEY H.). 'The content and sources of English agrarian history before 1500'. *Agricultural Hist. Rev.* iii (1955), 3–19.

R. H. Hilton, 'L'Angleterre économique et sociale des xive et xve siècles: théories et monographies', *Annales: économies, sociétés, civilisations*, xiii (1958), 541–63.

4693 HISTORICAL MSS. COMM. Reports. See No. 945.

Samples of calendars of deeds, extents, accounts, etc., may be found in No. 6366 and (*a*) MSS. belonging to the Ewelme Almshouse in the county of Oxford. Eighth Rept. pp. 625–8.

(*b*) Calendar of MSS. of the Dean and Chapter of Wells. 2 vols. (1907).

(*c*) Report of MSS. of Marquess of Lothian at Blickling Hall, Norfolk. (1905), pp. 1–74.

(*d*) Report of MSS. of Lord Middleton at Wollaston Hall, Nottinghamshire. (1911), pp. 1–118 for various counties for the period 1150–1480.

(*e*) MSS. of the Duke of Rutland at Belvoir Castle. Fourth Rept. (1905), pp. 1–187. A vast collection, for several counties but especially strong on charters, rolls, etc. relating to Leicestershire and Devonshire.

(*f*) Report of the Hastings MSS. vol. 1 (1928), pp. 1–353.

4694 MANORIAL SOCIETY PUBLICATIONS

Listed in Mullins, *Guide* (No. 28), p. 250. See especially the following: *Lists of manor court rolls in private hands*, edited by A. L. Hardy. 3 vols. 1907–10. *Descriptive catalogue of manorial rolls belonging to Sir H. F. Burke*, edited by E. Margaret Thompson. 2 vols. 1922–3. *A catalogue of manorial documents preserved in the muniment room of New College, Oxford*, 1929.

4695 MOORE (MARGARET F.). 'Bibliography of manorial and agrarian history' in her *Two Select Bibliographies of Mediaeval Historical Study* (Lond. 1912), * pp. 71–185.

4696 SAYERS (JANE). Estate documents at Lambeth Palace Library: a short catalogue. Leicester. 1965.

Lists court rolls, account rolls, terriers, rentals, largely medieval.

4697 TAYLOR (FRANK). 'Court rolls, rentals, surveys and analogous documents in the John Rylands Library'. *B.J.R.L.* xxi (1948), 345–86.

2. *Collected Sources*

4698 LEGAL AND MANORIAL FORMULARIES EDITED FROM ORIGINALS AT THE BRITISH MUSEUM AND THE PUBLIC RECORD OFFICE IN MEMORY OF JULIUS PARNELL GILSON. Oxf. 1933.

Contains formulary of deeds and accounts written by a John of Oxford, monk of Luffield, after the issuance of *Quia Emptores* (B.M. Add. MSS. 41201); and a *Forma Compoti* (P.R.O. MS.). See Neilson, 'Manorial forms' (No. 4976), and *Regule compoti* in Denholm-Young, *Seignorial Administration* (No. 4619), pp. 169–76.

4699 SELECT DOCUMENTS OF THE ENGLISH LANDS OF THE ABBEY OF BEC. Ed. by Marjorie Chibnall. R.H.S. Camden 3rd Ser. lxxiii (1951).

Charters, custumals, and account rolls. See also Jean Birdsall, 'The English manors of La Trinité at Caen', in *Haskins essays* (No. 1439).

4700 SELECT PLEAS IN MANORIAL COURTS (Hen. III–Edw. I). Ed. by F. W. Maitland. Selden Soc. ii for 1888. (1889.)

See under Huntingdonshire (No. 4777). 'In order to present a cross-section of this jurisdiction the editor selected the rolls of (*a*) an ordinary manor court (Ramsey), (*b*) an honour court (Broughton), (*c*) a court on the ancient desmesne (King's Repton), (*d*) a court of a private hundred (Whorwelsdown)'. See Kiralfy and Jones (No. 195), pp. 2–5.

4701 TITOW (JAN Z.). English rural society 1200–1350. Historical Problems: studies and documents. Ed. by G. R. Elton. Lond. 1969.

The introduction, pp. 15–102, comprises three sections: namely; sources and problems, landlords and tenants, and the standard of living controversy. Pp. 105–205 comprise English translations of twenty documents, i.e. account rolls, surveys, extents, court-rolls, etc. from a variety of sources. Thirteen of the twenty documents have apparently not been printed elsewhere in any form; many of them concern the manors of the bishop of Winchester. See review in *Speculum*, xlv (1970), 330–2.

3. *Manorial Sources by County*

BEDFORDSHIRE

4702 ACCOUNT-ROLL OF THE MANOR OF CLAPHAM BAYEUX, 1333–34. Ed. by Frederick G. Emmison. Beds. Hist. Rec. Soc. Pubns. xiv (1931), 133–45.

4703 COURT ROLL OF CHALGRAVE MANOR, 1278–1313. Ed. by Marian K. Dale. Ibid. xxviii (1950).

4704 THE HONOUR OF OLD WARDON. Ed. by William Farrer. Ibid. xi (1927), 1–46.

4705 A KEMPSTON ESTATE IN 1341. By F. B. Stitt. Ibid. xxxii (1952), 71–91.

4706 TWO CRANFIELD MANORS. By Joyce Godber. Ibid. xxv (1947), 4–9.

BERKSHIRE

4707 BARFIELD (SAMUEL). Thatcham, Berks. and its manors. Ed. by James Parker. 2 vols. Oxf. etc. 1901.

Vol. ii is a collection of wills, deeds, charters, etc. *c.* 975–1899.

4708 BERKS COURT ROLLS. By Nathaniel Horne. *Berks. Archaeol.–Archit. Soc. Quart. Jour.* (Reading). iii (1894), 153–7, 173–8.

Contains a translation of a few membranes relating to various manors, Hen. VI–Hen. VII.

4709 KERRY (CHARLES). History and antiquities of the hundred of Bray. Lond. 1861.

Deals with manorial history.

4710 ST MARY'S HURLEY IN THE MIDDLE AGES. By F. T. Wethered. Lond. 1898.

Pp. 89–225: Abstracts of charters and deeds relating to the parish of Hurley, Berks., 1086–1536; pp. 227–38; translation of nine charters and deeds, *c.* 1086–1334.

BUCKINGHAMSHIRE

See Harris, *Landlords and tenants* (No. 4958).

4711 CHIBNALL (ALBERT C.). Sherington: fiefs and fields of a Buckinghamshire village. Cambr. 1965.

Feudal and agrarian history from Norman conquest to twentieth century with much statistical and genealogical material.

4712 EXTENTS OF THE ROYAL MANORS OF AYLESBURY AND BRILL, *c.* 1155. By G. Herbert Fowler. *Records of Bucks.* xi, no. 7 (1926), 401–5.

One of the earliest documents of its class.

4713 EXTRACTS FROM THE COURT ROLLS OF THE MANOR OF WINSLOW, EDWARD III AND HENRY VI. Ed. by William Cunningham, *Growth of English Industry* (No. 1366), 5th edn. i. 610–15.

4714 MANOR COURT ROLLS OF FENNY STRATFORD AND ETONE (1371–84). By William Bradbrooke. *Records of Bucks.* xi (1922), 289–314.

CAMBRIDGESHIRE

4715 COMPOTUS OF THE MANOR OF NEWTON, 1395. *East Anglian*, iv (1869), 69–80, 85–94.

4716 COURT BARON (THE), together with select pleas from the bishop of Ely's court at Littleport. Ed. by F. W. Maitland and W. P. Baildon. Selden Soc. iv for 1890 (1891).

Pp. 107–47: Pleas in the court at Littleport, A.D. 1285–1327, with a translation.

4717 DARBY (HENRY C.). The draining of the fens. Cambr. 1940. 2nd edn. 1956.

4718 FOWLER (GEORGE HERBERT). 'An early Cambridgeshire feodary'. *E.H.R.* xlvi (1931), 442–3.

Gives surnames of under-tenants at time of Domesday Book. See *Inquisitio comitatus* (No. 3010).

4719 MAITLAND (FREDERIC W.). The history of a Cambridgeshire manor (Wilburton), see *Collected papers* (No. 1482) ii. 366–402. Reprinted in No. 1484.

4720 PAGE (FRANCES M.). 'The customary poor-law of three Cambridge-shire manors'. *Cambr. Hist. Jour.* iii (1930), 125–33.

4721 PALMER (WILLIAM M.). 'Village gilds of Cambridgeshire'. *Cambs. and Hunts. Archaeol. Soc. Trans.* i (1904), 330–402.

4722 PALMER (W. M.) and SAUNDERS (HERBERT W.). Documents relating to Cambridgeshire villages. 2 vols. Cambr. 1926.

Includes *Nomina Villarum*, cases of sanctuary, peasants' revolt.

4723 SPUFFORD (MARGARET). A Cambridgeshire community: Chippenham from settlement to enclosure. Leicester Univ. Occasional Papers, no. 20 (1965).

CHESHIRE

See Lancashire, and Hewitt, *Medieval Cheshire* (No. 1573).

4724 AN ACCOUNT OF THE (MANORIAL) ROLLS OF THE HONOUR OF HALTON. By William Beamont. Warrington. 1879.

4725 STEWART-BROWN (RONALD). 'The royal manor and park of Shotwick'. *Historic Soc. of Lancashire and Cheshire Trans.* lxiv (1912), 82–142.

4726 STEWART-BROWN (R.). The wapentake of Wirral: a history of the hundred and the hundred court. Liverpool. 1907.

CORNWALL

See Hatcher (No. 4960).

4727 MINISTERS' ACCOUNTS OF THE EARLDOM OF CORNWALL, 1296–1297. Ed. by L. Margaret Midgley. 2 vols. R.H.S. Camden Ser. lxvi (1942) and lxviii (corrected from lxvii) (1945).

DERBYSHIRE

4728 ATLOW COURT ROLLS, 19 Edw. III–4 Rich. II. Ed. by R. H. Oakley. *Derbys. Archaeol.–Nat. Hist. Soc. Jour.* lxxiii (1953), 90–101.

4729 COURT ROLLS OF BASLOW (abstracts, 1319–1545). By Charles Kerry. Ibid. xxii (1900), 52–90; xxiii (1901), 1–39.

4730 EGGINTON COURT ROLLS, 1306–7 to 1311–12. Ed. by F. N. Fisher. Ibid. lxxv (1956), 36–61.

4731 TEMPLE NORMANTON COURT ROLLS 1447–1518. Ibid. lxxviii (1959), 40–88.

DEVONSHIRE

See Hoskins and Finberg, *Devonshire Studies* (Nos. 1470, 1611).

4732 WREYLAND DOCUMENTS. Ed. by Cecil Torr. Cambr. 1910.

Contains two fifteenth-century court rolls, and a few other medieval records; but most of the documents are of later date.

4733 ALCOCK (N. W.). 'An East Devon manor (Bishop's Clyst) in the later middle ages'. *Devonshire Asso. Reports and Trans.* cii (1970), 141–87.

4734 UGAWA (KAORU). 'The economic development of some Devon manors in the thirteenth century'. Ibid. xciv (1962), 630–83.

DORSET

4735 DREW (C. D.). 'The manors of the Iwerne Valley, Dorset'. *Dorset. Nat. Hist. and Archaeol. Soc. Procs.* lxix for 1947 (1950), 45–50.

4736 DREW (J. S.). 'Early account rolls of Portland, Wyke and Elwell'. Ibid. pt. 1. lxvi (1944), 31–45; pt. 2. lxvii (1945), 34–54.

4737 JERVOISE (E.). 'The manor of Barton, Shaftesbury'. Ibid. lxxvi (1954), 67–73.

DURHAM

4738 FEODARIUM PRIORATUS DUNELMENSIS. A survey of the estates of the priory and convent of Durham, compiled in the fifteenth century. Ed. by William Greenwell. Surtees Soc. lviii (1872). No. 5682.

4739 HALMOTA PRIORATUS DUNELMENSIS. Extracts from the halmote court or manor rolls of the prior and convent of Durham, 1296–1384. Ed. by W. H. D. Longstaffe and John Booth. Surtees Soc. lxxxii (1889).

ESSEX

See Cyril Hart, *Early Charters: the Norman period* (No. 2199).

4740 CATALOGUE OF ESSEX PARISH RECORDS, 1240–1894. Ed. by F. G. Emmison. Essex Record Office Pubn. no. 7. Chelmsford. 1950. 2nd edn. 1966.

4741 CUSTOMAL, A.D. 1298, OF THE MANOR OF WYKES, HUNDRED OF TENDRING. Ed. by A. J. H(orwood). *Essex Archaeol. Soc. Trans.* New Ser. i (1878), 109–15.

4742 DEMAREST (E. B.). '*Consuetudo regis* in Essex, Norfolk and Suffolk'. *E.H.R.* xlii (1927), 161–79.

Renderings from the land paid by freemen or sokemen to the king.

4743 EMMISON (FREDERICK G.). 'Supplementary list of manorial documents in Essex Record Office'. *Genealogists' Magazine*, ix, no. 15 (1947), 14–18 [578–82, error in pagination].

4744 EXTENTA MANERII DE BORLE (Borley) 1 Edw. II. Ed. by W. Cunningham in *Growth of English Industry* (No. 1366) 5th edn. i. 576–84.

See G. F. Beaumont, 'The manor of Borley, A.D. 1308', *Essex Archaeol. Soc. Trans.* New Ser. xviii, pt. iv (1927), 254–69; and J. F. Nichols, 'The manor of Borley', ibid. xix, pt. 1 (1928), 60–1.

4745 THE HARLOW CARTULARY. By John L. Fisher. *Essex Archaeol. Soc. Trans.* New Ser. xxii (1940), 239–71.

A series of rentals and extents of a manor belonging to the abbey of Bury St. Edmunds, presumably drawn up in 1429 for Abbot William Curteys.

4746 INVENTORY OF GOODS BELONGING TO THOMAS, DUKE OF GLOUCESTER, SEIZED IN THE CASTLE AT PLESHY, ESSEX, 1397, with their values, as shown in the escheators' accounts. Ed. by Viscount Dillon and W. H. St. John Hope. *Archaeol. Jour.* liv (1897), 275–308.

4747 MANOR OF BARRINGTON'S FEE. *East Anglian.* New Ser. v (1894), 186–9, 198–200, 232–3, 261.

The Latin text of a rental, 1446, printed in full.

4747A NEWTON (K. C.). The manor of Writtle: the development of a royal manor in Essex, 1086–1500. Chichester. 1970.

4748 NICHOLS (JOHN F.). 'An early fourteenth century petition from the tenants of Bocking to their manorial lord'. *Econ. H.R.* ii (1930), 300–7. Idem, 'Expenditure on Essex manors', *Essex Archaeol. Soc. Trans.* xix, pt. i (1927), 61–2. Idem, 'The extent of Lawling, A.D. 1310'. Ibid. xx, pt. ii (1930–3), 173–98.

4749 RECORDS RELATING TO HADLEIGH CASTLE. By J. A. Sparvel-Bayly. *Essex Archaeol. Soc. Trans.* New Ser. i (1878), 86–108; 187–91.

Abstracts of letters patent and close, ministers' accounts, etc. 1227–1544. Some of them are also printed in the *East Anglian*, New Ser. iv (1891–2), 36–41, 75–7.

4750 REEVE'S ACCOUNT OF THE MANOR OF BURNHAM, 14–15 Richard II (1390–1). *Essex Archaeol. Soc. Trans.* 3rd Ser. ii (1967), 147–58.

4751 THAXTED IN THE FOURTEENTH CENTURY. An account of the manor and borough with translated texts. By K. C. Newton. Essex Record Office Pubns. xxxiii (1960). Chelmsford. 1960.

4752 TITHINGS LISTS FROM ESSEX, 1329–43. Ed. by Andrew Clark. *E.H.R.* xix (1904), 715–19.

GLOUCESTERSHIRE

4753 COURT ROLLS OF THE MANOR OF STONEHOUSE, KING'S STANLEY, WOODCHESTER AND ACHARDS, 1461–1533. *Bristol–Glos. Archaeol. Soc. Trans.* xlv (1923), 203–51.

Pp. 218–21: a roll for King's Stanley for 1461; all the other rolls are for the period after 1485.

4754 ELLACOMBE (HENRY T.). The history of the parish of Bitton. 2 pts. Exeter. 1881–3.

Contains court rolls, wills, inquests *post mortem*, etc.

4755 HICKS (F. W. P.). 'A Tewkesbury compotus'. *Bristol–Glos. Archaeol. Soc. Trans.* lv (1934), 249–55.

4756 SHREWSBURY (TALBOT) MANUSCRIPTS. Calendared by Edith S. Scroggs. Ibid. lx for 1938 (1939), 260–96.

4757 SMYTH (JOHN). The Berkeley MSS. (No. 4593).

4758 TENURES OF LAND BY THE CUSTOMARY TENANTS IN CIRENCESTER. By E. A. Fuller. *Bristol–Glos. Archaeol. Soc. Trans.* ii (1878), 285–319.

Contains some manorial inquisitions, etc., from 1086 to 1540.

4759 WATSON (C. E.). 'The Minchinhampton custumal and its place in the story of the manor'. Ibid. liv (1933), 203–384.

4760 WICK RISSINGTON TRANSCRIPTS. By A. L. Browne. Ibid. lix for 1937 (1938), 211–19.

4761 BADDELEY (WELBORE ST. CLAIR). A Cotteswold manor: being the manor of Painswick. Gloucester, etc. 1907. 2nd edn. Lond. 1929.

4762 HILTON (RODNEY H.). 'Winchcombe abbey and the manor of Sherborne'. *Univ. Birmingham Hist. Jour.* ii (1949–50), 31–52.

HAMPSHIRE

See Maitland. *Manorial pleas* (No. 4777); Haskins on manor of Portswood in *Bémont essays* (No. 1426). For the bishopric of Winchester, see No. 5815.

4763 COLLECTION OF RECORDS AND DOCUMENTS RELATING TO THE HUNDRED AND MANOR OF CRONDAL. Ed. by F. J. Baigent. Pt. i. Hampshire Rec. Soc. 1891.

> Charters, etc. 1163–1487: pp. 12–50.
> Compotus rolls of the manors of Crondal and Long Sutton, 1248: pp. 51–83, 505–12.
> Customal and rent rolls, Crondal, 1287 and Sutton 1351: pp. 83–141.
> Court roll of the hundred of Crondal, *c.* 1281–2: pp. 142–55.
> Inquests *post mortem*, charters, etc. 1267–1707: pp. 410–80.

4764 GOODMAN (ARTHUR W.). The manor of Goodbegot in the city of Winchester. Winchester. 1923.

4765 GRAS (NORMAN B. S.) and (ETHEL C.). The economic and social history of the English village: Crawley, Hampshire, A.D. 909–1928. Cambr. 1930. *

4766 HERVEY (THOMAS). A history of the united parishes of Colmer and Priors Dean. Colmer. 1880.

> Deals with manorial history.

4767 THE MANOR OF MANYDOWN. Ed. by G. W. Kitchin. Hampshire Rec. Soc. 1895.

> History of the manor: pp. 1–107.
> Compotus and court rolls, 1300–1661: pp. 122–63.
> Rental of Hannington, 1351: pp. 164–7.
> Stock book, 1390: pp. 168–70.

4768 STEVENS (JOSEPH). A parochial history of St. Mary Bourne with an account of the manor of Hurstbourne Priors. Lond. 1888.

HEREFORD

See Duncomb, *Collections* (No. 1670).

4769 THE BAILIFF'S ACCOUNTS FOR THE MANOR OF KINGS-LAND, 1389–90. Trans. by E. J. Cole. *Woolhope Naturalists Field Club Trans.* xxxv (1956).

4770 BANNISTER (ARTHUR T.). 'Manorial customs on the Hereford bishopric estates'. *E.H.R.* xliii (1928), 218–30.

See Colvin, 'Holme Lacy', *Graham essays* (No. 1437).

HERTFORDSHIRE

See Clutterbuck, *Hertford* (No. 1677).

4771 COMPOTUS ROLL OF THE MANOR OF ANSTIE (Anstey), 2–3 Hen. IV. Ed. by William Cunningham in *Growth of English Industry* (No. 1366) 5th edn. i. 591–610.

4772 HINE (REGINALD L.). The history of Hitchin. 2 vols. Lond. 1927-9.

The early chapters are on the manor, the church, and the priory of Hitchin.

4773 MARDEN: Collections concerning the manor of Marden. By Thomas, earl of Coningsby. 2 pts. (Lond. 1722-7).

An elaborate collection of extracts from plea rolls, inquisitions, etc., most of which belong to modern times.

4774 RICKMAN (LYDIA L.). 'Brief studies in the manorial and economic history of Much Hadham'. *East Herts. Archaeol. Soc. Trans.* vii, pt. 3 (1934), 288-312.

HUNTINGDONSHIRE

4775 EARLY RECORDS OF THE DUKE OF MANCHESTER'S ENGLISH MANORIAL ESTATES. By C. G. Boxall. Lond. 1892.

Contains translations of charters, pleadings, inquisitions, etc., relating to St. Ives, Houghton, Stukeley, and other places in Huntingdonshire, 1086-1628.

4776 ELTON MANORIAL RECORDS, 1279-1351. Ed. by S. C. Ratcliff, with a translation by D. M. Gregory and preface by G. Proby. Roxburghe Club. 1946.

A magnificent edition of ministers' accounts and court rolls of this manor which belonged to the abbey of Ramsey.

4777 SELECT PLEAS IN MANORIAL AND OTHER SEIGNORIAL COURTS. Ed. by F. W. Maitland. (Hen. III and Edw. I.). Selden Soc. Pubns. ii for 1888 (1889). See 'Leet and tourn' (No. 1484).

Pp. 3-47: Pleas in manorial courts of the abbot of Bec (various counties) 1246-96.
Pp. 48-85: Pleas in the court of the abbot of Ramsey's honour of Broughton, Hunts., 1258, and 1293-5.
Pp. 86-98: Pleas in the courts of manors of the abbot of Ramsey, Hunts., 1278 and 1290.
Pp. 99-129: Pleas in the court of the abbot of Ramsey's manor of King's Repton, Hunts., 1288-1303.
Pp. 130-60: Pleas in the court of the abbot of Ramsey in the fair of St. Ives, Hunts., 1275.
Pp. 161-75: Pleas in the court of the abbot of Battle's manor of Brightwaltham, Berks., 1293-6.
Pp. 176-83: Pleas in the courts of the abbess of Romsey's hundred of Whorwelsdown and manor of Ashton, Wilts. 1262.

KENT

See *Textus Roffensis* (No. 5794), Pipe Roll Account (No. 4784).

4778 CHURCHILL (IRENE J.). East Kent records: a calendar of some unpublished deeds and court rolls in the library of Lambeth Palace. Kent Arch. Soc. Rec. Branch. 1922.

4779 THE COURT ROLLS AND OTHER RECORDS OF THE MANOR OF IGHTHAM AS A CONTRIBUTION TO LOCAL HISTORY. By Edward Harrison. *Archaeologia Cantiana*, xlviii for 1936 (1937), 169-218; xlix for 1937 (1938), 1-95.

4780 CUSTUMALE ROFFENSE. Ed. by John Thorpe (the younger). Lond. 1788.

Contains many curious particulars regarding the tenures, services, etc., of manors of the cathedral church of Rochester. This custumal is said to have been compiled by John de Westerham, a monk of Rochester, who died about 1320. The greater part of Thorpe's volume is a treatise on the antiquities of Kent.

4781 FABRIC ROLL OF ROCHESTER CASTLE (1367–9). Ed. by L. B. Larking. *Archaeologia Cantiana*, ii (1859), 111–32.

4782 A FARNBOROUGH COURT ROLL OF 1408. Ed. M. F. Bond. Ibid. lvii (1944). 21–5.

4783 A FOURTEENTH-CENTURY COURT ROLL OF THE MANOR OF AMBREE, ROCHESTER, 1316–1363. Ed. by A. A. Arnold. Ibid., xxix (1915), 89–153.

4784 KENT RECORDS: DOCUMENTS ILLUSTRATIVE OF MEDI-EVAL KENTISH SOCIETY. Ed. by Francis R. H. Du Boulay. Kent Archaeol. Soc. Records Pubn. Comm. xviii (1964).

(a) H. M. Colvin, A list of the archbishop of Canterbury's tenants by knight-service in the reign of Henry II. 1–40.
(b) F. R. H. Du Boulay, The pipe roll account of the see of Canterbury during the vacancy after the death of Archbishop Pecham, 1292–5. 41–57.
(c) H. A. Hanley and C. W. Chalklin, The Kent lay subsidy roll of 1334/5. 58–172.
(d) S. L. Thrupp and H. B. Johnson, The earliest Canterbury freemen's rolls, 1298–1363. 173–213.
(e) R. Virgoe, Some ancient indictments in the king's bench referring to Kent, 1450–2. 214–65.
(f) F. R. H. Du Boulay, Calendar of archbishopric demesne leases, 1503–1532. 266–97.
(g) Index to the lay subsidy roll. 299–357.
(h) Map of medieval Kent. Drawn by Miss A. M. Oakley, faces page 172.

4785 KNOCKER (HERBERT W.). 'The valley of Holmesdale: pt. 1: its evolution and development'. *Archaeologia Cantiana* xxxi (1915), 155–77. Pt. 2: 'The village communities'. Ibid. xl (1928), 159–63. Pt. 3: 'The manor of Sundrish'. Ibid. xliv (1932), 189–210.

4786 MUHLFELD (HELEN E.). A survey of the manor of Wye. Columbia Univ. Stud. in Hist. etc. N.Y. 1933. *

4787 RENT ROLL OF ROGER DE SCACCARIO, Lord of the manor of Addington (1257–71). Ed. by Lambert B. Larking, *Domesday Book of Kent* (No. 3024), app. pp. 21–7.

LANCASHIRE

4788 COURT ROLLS OF THE HONOR OF CLITHEROE (1377–1663). Trans. by William Farrer. 3 vols. Manchester, etc. 1897–1913.

4789 FISHWICK (HENRY). The history of the parish of Rochdale. Rochdale, etc. 1889.

Chap. xv contains extracts from manorial court rolls, 1335–6.

4790 LANCASHIRE INQUESTS, EXTENTS AND FEUDAL AIDS.
Ed. by William Farrer. Pt. i 1205–1307. Pt. ii, 1310–1333; Pt. iii, 1313–1355.
Lancs.–Ches. Rec. Soc. xlviii (1903), liv (1907), lxx (1915).

English abstracts. Pt. ii contains the inquisition *post mortem* of Henry de Lacy, earl
of Lincoln. Pt. iii includes, pp. 67–153, an important extent of 1346; and pp. 171–99,
a ministers' account of 1348 derived from Duchy of Lancaster Accounts in P.R.O.

4791 MAMECESTRE: being chapters from the early history of the barony,
the lordship, or manor; the vill, borough, or town of Manchester. Ed. by John
Harland. 3 vols. Chetham Soc. liii, lvi, lviii (1861–2).

Continuous pagination. Pp. 69–84: *Testa de Nevill*. Pp. 140–77: extent of the manor,
1282. Pp. 178–207: town charters of Preston, Clitheroe, Chester, Liverpool, Salford,
and Wigan. Pp. 209–46: charter of Manchester, 1301. Pp. 273–358: survey of the manor
and barony, 1320. Pp. 359–532: extent of the manor, 1322, and rental, 1473.

**4792 SOME COURT ROLLS OF THE LORDSHIPS, WAPENTAKES,
AND MANORS OF THOMAS, EARL OF LANCASTER, IN THE
COUNTY OF LANCASTER,** 1323–4 (translation only). By William Farrer.
Lancs.–Ches. Rec. Soc. xli (1901).

**4793 THREE LANCASHIRE DOCUMENTS OF THE FOURTEENTH
AND FIFTEENTH CENTURIES:** The great De Lacy inquisition (post
mortem), 1311; the survey (of manors), 1320–46; custom roll and rental of the
manor of Ashton-under-Lyne, 1422. Ed. by John Harland. Chetham Soc. lxxiv
(1868).

The custom roll and rental of 1422 is also printed in Samuel Hibbert's (i.e. Hibbert-
Ware's) *Illustration of the customs of a manor of North England* (Edin. 1822), app.
pp. 3–20.

**4794 TWO 'COMPOTI' OF THE LANCASHIRE AND CHESHIRE
MANORS OF HENRY DE LACY, EARL OF LINCOLN,** 24 and 33 Edw. I.
Transcribed and translated by P. A. Lyons. Chetham Soc. cii (1884).

Contains accounts of the earl's stewards, parkers, bailiffs, etc. For a *compotus* of his
Yorkshire estates, 1295–6, see *Yorks Archaeol.–Topog. Asso. Jour.* viii (1884), 351–8.

4795 TWO CUSTUMALS OF THE MANOR OF COCKERHAM, 1326
and 1483. Ed. by R. S. France. *Lancs.–Ches. Antiq. Soc. Trans.* lxiv (1954),
38–54.

**4796 WARRINGTON IN 1465 AS DESCRIBED IN A CONTEM-
PORARY RENT ROLL.** Ed. by William Beamont. Chetham Soc. xvii (1849).

LEICESTERSHIRE

Many records are printed in Nichols's *History of the County of Leicester* (No. 1714).
See R. H. Hilton, 'Medieval agrarian history' in *V.C.H. Leicestershire*, ii (1955), 145–95.

**4797 CUSTOMARY OF THE MANOR AND SOKE OF ROTHLEY, IN
THE COUNTY OF LEICESTER.** Ed. by G. T. Clark, *Archaeologia*, xlvii
(1883), 89–130.

An undated rental, together with the duties of manorial officers, etc.

4798 SOME UNPUBLISHED DOCUMENTS RELATING TO NOSE-LEY, co. Leicester. Ed. by Henry Hartopp. *A.A.S.R.P.* xxv (1900), 431–58; xxvi (1901), 276–320. (Charters, court rolls, etc. 1220–1636).

4799 FARNHAM (GEORGE F.), compiler. Leicestershire medieval village notes. With an introduction by A. Hamilton Thompson. 6 vols. (Privately printed.) Leicester. 1929–33.

4800 HILTON (RODNEY H.). The economic development of some Leicester-shire estates in the 14th and 15th centuries. Oxford Hist. Ser. Lond. 1947.

Estates of Leicester abbey and of Owston abbey.

4801 HOSKINS (WILLIAM G.). Essays in Leicestershire history. Liver-pool. 1950.

4802 HOSKINS (W. G.). The midland peasant. The economic and social history of a Leicestershire village. Lond. 1957.

The village is Wigston Magna, sixth to nineteenth centuries. It serves as a model for at least the midlands. See also Hoskins, 'Studies in Leicestershire agrarian history', *Leicestershire Archaeol. Soc. Trans.* 1949, and 'The population of an English village 1086–1801: a study of Wigston Magna', ibid. xxxiii (1957), 15–35.

4802A PROVISIONAL LIST OF DESERTED MEDIEVAL VILLAGES IN LEICESTERSHIRE. Ibid. xxxix (1963–4), 24–7.

4803 A THIRTEENTH CENTURY POEM ON SOME DISPUTED VILLEIN SERVICES. Ed. by R. H. Hilton. *E.H.R.* lvi (1941), 90–7.

This poem on the disputed services of the people of Stoughton, tenants of the abbot and convent of Leicester, is apparently related to an actual case reported in *coram rege* roll Mich. 4–5 Edw. I. See also G. Farnham, *Leicestershire village notes* (No. 4799), iv. 152 ff.

LINCOLNSHIRE

4804 COLE (ROBERT E. G.). 'The royal burgh of Torksey'. *A.A.S.R.P.* xxviii (1906), 451–530.

Contains an abstract of a custumal, *c.* 1238.

4805 DUDDING (REGINALD C.). History of the parish and manors of Alford with Rigsby and Ailby, with some account of Well in the county of Lincoln. Horncastle. 1930.

See his *History of the manor and parish of Salesby with Thoresthorpe in the county of Lincoln* (Horncastle, 1922).

4806 FOSTER (CHARLES W.). A history of the village of Aisthorpe and Thorpe in the Fallows. Lincoln. 1927.

4807 GIBBONS (ALFRED) and FOSTER (W. E.). '(Lists of) Lincolnshire court rolls'. *Lincs. Notes and Queries*, i (1889), 44–6, 209–10.

4808 HALLAM (HERBERT E.). Settlement and society. A study of the early agrarian history of south Lincolnshire. Cambr. Stud. in Econ. Hist. Cambr. 1965.

A study, with good documentation, of the progress of reclamation of fenland between the eleventh and thirteenth centuries and of the adaptation of farmers to the new conditions, and explains the different social structure. See also Hallam, 'The agrarian economy of south Lincolnshire in the mid-fifteenth century', *Nottingham Mediaeval Stud.* xi (1967), 86–95.

4809 THE HEIGHINGTON TERRIER. Ed. by F. W. East. *Lincolnshire A.A.S.R.P.*, New Ser. iv (1952), 131–63; v (1953), 28–69.

4810 HILL (FRANCIS). 'Manor of Hungate'. *A.A.S.R.P.* xxxviii (1927), 175–208.

4811 HOSFORD (W. H.). 'The manor of Sleaford in the thirteenth century', *Nottingham Mediaeval Stud.* xii (1968), 21–39.

4812 MANOR OF INGOLDMELLS-CUM-ADDLETHORPE COURT ROLLS (extracts, 1292–1503). Ed. by Arthur R. Maddison. *A.A.S.R.P.* xxi (1892), 176–90.

See W. O. Massingberd, *Court roll of the manor of Ingoldmells* (1291–1578, translation only), (Lond. 1902); and his 'Some accounts of the manor of Ingoldmells' (1295–1485, translation only), *Lincolnshire Notes and Queries*, vii (1904), 157–60, 167–78, 203–4.

4813 THE MANOR OF STALLINGBOROUGH (Rental of), 1352. Ed. by A. R. Maddison. *A.A.S.R.P.* xxiii (1896), 274–89.

4814 MASSINGBERD (WILLIAM O.). History of the parish of Ormsby-cum-Ketsby. Lincoln, 1893.

Pp. 244–83: Court rolls of the manor of Ormsby, 1410–1832. The work also contains a translation of many charters, etc.

4815 SOME ANCIENT RECORDS RELATING TO THE MANOR OF LANGTON AND ITS LORDS (1202–1617). By W. O. Massingberd. *A.A.S.R.P.* xxii (1894), 157–73.

4816 SURVEY OF THE MANOR OF STOW, 1283 (translation of). By W. O. Massingberd. Ibid., xxiv (1898), 299–347.

4817 A TERRIER OF FLEET, LINCOLNSHIRE. Ed. by Nellie Neilson. British Acad. Records of Social and Economic History. iv. Lond. 1920.

Concerned with the fenland near the Wash. See Darby (No. 4717), and Hallam (No. 4808).

NORFOLK

4818 CRABBE (GEORGE). Some materials for a history of the parish of Thompson. Ed. by Augustus Jessopp. Norwich. 1892.

Deals with manorial history.

4819 DAVENPORT (FRANCES G.). The economic development of a Norfolk manor (Forncett), 1086–1565. Cambr. 1906. *

The appendix contains account rolls of the manor, 1272–3, 1376–8; court rolls, 1400, etc.

4820 FIVE COURT ROLLS OF GREAT CRESSINGTON (1328–1584, with a translation). Ed. by H. W. Chandler. Lond. 1885.

One of the rolls, dated 1414, is really a rental.

4821 REPORT ON THE MUNIMENTS OF MERTON HALL, NOR-FOLK. By George Crabbe. *Norfolk Antiq. Miscellany*, ii (1883), 553–629; iii (1887), 1–113.

4822 THREE CARROW ACCOUNT ROLLS. By Lilian J. Redstone. *Norfolk Archaeology*, xxix (1947), 41–88. (Accounts of the abbey's cellaress).

4823 THREE MANORIAL EXTENTS OF THE THIRTEENTH CEN-TURY. By William Hudson. Ibid. xiv (1899), 1–56.

Translations only, relating to the manors of Bradcar and Banham in Norfolk and Wykes in Suffolk in the time of Edward I.

4824 HUDSON (WILLIAM). 'Traces of primitive agricultural organization as suggested by the survey of the manor of Martham, Norfolk (1101–1292)'. *T.R.H.S.* 4th Ser. i (1918), 28–58.

4825 LEWIS (P. S.). 'Sir John Fastolf's lawsuit over Twitchwell, 1448–1455'. *The Historical Jour.* i (1958), 1–20.

See K. B. McFarlane, 'The investment of Sir John Fastolf's profits of war', *T.R.H.S.*, 5th Ser. vii (1957), 91–116.

4826 THE PASTON LETTERS (No. 4610).

NORTHAMPTONSHIRE

See *Carte Nativorum* (No. 6266), and Stenton, *Northamptonshire Collections* No. 451.

4827 CHAPTER HOUSE RECORDS. Trans. by John Lister. Thoresby Soc. xxxiii, *Miscellanea*, x (1935), 83–102.

Gives translations of several extents of 1341 for Northamptonshire and Yorkshire.

4828 COMPOTUS OF THE MANOR OF KETTERING, 1292, with translation. Ed. by Charles Wise. Kettering. 1899.

4829 THE COURT ROLLS OF HIGHAM FERRERS. By R. M. Serjeantson. *A.A.S.R.P.* xxxiii (1915), 95–141; xxiv (1917), 326–75.

Part of the duchy of Lancaster. See William J. B. Kerr, *Higham Ferrers and its ducal and royal castle: a history of the mediaeval lordship.* (Northampton. 1925.)

4830 ESTATE BOOK OF HENRY DE BRAY OF HARLESTON, NOR-THANTS, *c.* 1289–1340. Ed. by Dorothy Willis. R.H.S. Camden 3rd Ser. xxvii (1916).

Contains relations of Bray with his overlords, Bray's ecclesiastical holdings, Bray's manorial and agrarian concerns, and Bray family history. See also Joan Wake, 'Communitas villae' *E.H.R.* xxxvii (1922), 406–13, where is printed an agreement between lords and men concerning the cultivation of common fields at Harleston.

4831 EXEMPLIFICATION OF RECORDS AND CHARTERS RE-LATING TO THE MANOR OF MORTON PYNKENY, etc. in the county of Northampton, temp. Edw. II and Edw. III. Ed. by L. B. L(arking). *Collectanea Topog. et Genealogica* (No. 115), iv (1837), 223–31.

4832 A FIFTEENTH CENTURY RENTAL OF ROTHWELL. Ed. by William T. Lancaster. Thoresby Soc. xxiv. *Miscellanea*, vii (1919), 281–303.

4833 KINGSTHORPIANA: a calendar of old documents in the church chest of Kingsthorpe, with a selection of the MSS. Ed. by John H. Glover. Lond. 1883.

Contains extracts from manorial court rolls, Edw. III–James I; etc.

4834 ON THE COMPOTUS ROLLS OF THE MANOR OF OUNDLE (with extracts, 1365–1473). By Isaac H. Jeayes. *Brit. Archaeol. Asso. Jour.* xxxiv (1878), 384–90.

4835 WELLINGBOROUGH MANORIAL ACCOUNTS, A.D. 1258–1323, from the account rolls of Crowland abbey. Ed. by Frances M. Page (with a translation and introduction) Northamptonshire Rec. Soc. Pubns. viii, 1936; reprinted *c*. 1964.

4836 ALLISON (K. J.), BERESFORD (M. W.), and HURST (J. G.). The deserted villages of Northamptonshire. Leicester. 1966.

NORTHUMBERLAND

Hodgson's *History of Northumberland* (No. 1042) contains many documents.

4837 PERCY BAILIFF'S ROLLS OF THE FIFTEENTH CENTURY AT ALNWICK CASTLE. Ed. by John C. Hodgson. Surtees Soc. cxxxiv, 1921.

Texts of manorial accounts for 1471 and 1472; and a household roll for 1563–5.

4838 PERCY CHARTULARY (1167–1377). Ed. by M. T. Martin. Surtees Soc. cxvii for 1909 (1911).

Contains grants relating to lands of the Percys in Northumberland and Yorkshire.

4839 HEDLEY (WILLIAM P.). 'Manor of Simonburn and Warks Park'. *Archaeologia Aeliana*, 4th Ser. xxx (1952), 80–105.

4840 MILLER (E.). 'The tenants of Birting'. *Soc. Antiq. Newcastle-on-Tyne Procs.* 5th Ser. (1952), 117–23.

NOTTINGHAMSHIRE

4841 DOCUMENTS RELATING TO THE MANOR AND SOKE OF NEWARK-ON-TRENT. Ed. by M. W. Barley. Thoroton Soc. Rec. Ser. xvi (1956).

With contributions by the late W. H. Stevenson and by Kenneth Cameron. Contains (*a*) list of inhabitants of Newark, *c*. 1175, (*b*) a survey of 1225–31; and (*c*) a survey of the bishop of Lincoln's demesne, 1348–9.

4842 MISCELLANY OF NOTTS. RECORDS. Ed. by Thomas M. Blagg. Thoroton Soc. Rec. Ser. xi (1945).

Contains *inter alia*, Three items ed. and trans. by L. V. D. Owens,
(*a*) Pp. 147–50: Rental of Robert de Caunton, February 1340;
(*b*) Pp. 151–66: An extent of Langar and Barnstone, *c*. 1340;
(*c*) Pp. 167–75: An annual account roll of the manors of Scarrington, Car-Colston, Screverton, and Orston, 1413–14.

4843 SECOND MISCELLANY OF NOTTINGHAMSHIRE RECORDS. Ed. by K. S. S. Train. Thoroton Soc. Rec. Ser. xiv (1951).

Includes an extent of Upton, 1431. Trans. and ed. by Violet W. Walker.

OXFORDSHIRE

4844 ADDERBURY 'RECTORIA'. The manor at Adderbury belonging to New College, Oxford; the building of the chancel, 1408–18; account rolls, deeds, and court rolls. Ed. by T. F. Hobson. Oxfordshire Rec. Soc. Rec. Ser. viii (1926).

Includes compotus rolls Hen. IV–Hen. VI; court rolls, Rich. II–Hen. VI; and other documents and notes.

4845 CUSTOMAL (1391) and BYE-LAWS (1386–1526) OF THE MANOR OF ISLIP. Ed. by Barbara F. Harvey. Oxfordshire Rec. Soc. Rec. Ser. xl (1959), 79–119.

Latin transcript and English translation are on facing pages.

4846 THE EARLY HISTORY OF MAPLEDURHAM. By Alfred H. Cooke. Oxfordshire Rec. Soc. Rec. Ser. vii (1925).

Includes extracts from court rolls, 1416–93.

4847 GLYMPTON. THE HISTORY OF AN OXFORDSHIRE MANOR. By Herbert Barnett. Oxfordshire Rec. Soc. Rec. Ser. v (1923).

Includes extracts from court rolls, 1351–72.

4848 THE HISTORY OF DEAN AND CHALFORD. By Mary D. Lobel. Oxfordshire Rec. Soc. Rec. Ser. xvii (1935).

Includes transcripts of Oriel College deeds to manors, 1204–1549; subsidy returns for 1316 and 1327.

4849 A MEDIEVAL OXFORDSHIRE VILLAGE: CUXHAM, 1240–1400. By P. D. A. Harvey. Oxford Hist. Ser. 2nd Ser. Lond. 1965.

Prints a remarkable series of account rolls. Some of these rolls were used by Rogers in *History of Agriculture* (No 1376), ii. 617–30, as a bailiff's account for 1316–17; and as rentals of God's House in Southampton *c.* 1245. and of Cuxham and Ibstone (Bucks.), ibid. ii. 648–59.

4850 WHEATLEY RECORDS, 956–1956. Ed. by William O. Hassall. Oxfordshire Rec. Soc. Rec. Ser. xxxvii (1956).

Village records.

4851 COLVIN (HOWARD M.). A history of Deddington, Oxfordshire. Lond. 1963.

4852 DUNKIN (JOHN). The history and antiquities of Bicester. Lond. 1816.

The appendix contains a rental of the manor of Bicester, 1325; priory accounts, 1425; etc.

4853 JORDAN (JOHN). A parochial history of Enstone. Lond. 1857.

Contains charters, extracts from court rolls, etc., fourteenth–sixteenth centuries.

4854 KENNETT (WHITE). Parochial antiquities attempted in the history of Ambrosden, Burcister (Bicester), and other adjacent places in the counties of Oxford and Bucks. Oxf. 1695; new edn. 2 vols. 1818.

Deals mainly with the manorial history; contains many charters.

4855 MARSHALL (EDWARD). The early history of Woodstock manor and its environs. 1 vol. and supplement. Oxf. 1873–4.

> See also Adolphus Ballard, 'Woodstock manor in the thirteenth century', *Viertel-jahrschrift für Social- und Wirtschaftsgeschichte*, vi (1908), 424–59; reprinted separately (Stuttgart, 1908).

4856 PEARMAN (MORGAN T.). History of the manor of Bensington (Benson). Lond. 1896.

4857 UL'IANOV (IU. R.). Oksfordshirskii Manor Uotlington v 1086–1300 gg. (Watlington Manor, Oxfordshire, 1086–1300. Changes in the structure and economic organization of large secular estates in medieval England). *Srednie veka* (Moscow), xxix (1966), 28–68. English summary, pp. 68–9.

SHROPSHIRE

4858 THE CONDOVER EXTENTS, 1283–1580: a study in ancient demesne tenure. By W. J. Slack. *Shrops. Archaeol. Soc. Trans.* l for 1939–40 (1940–1), 105–42.

4859 DOCUMENTS RELATING TO THE MANOR OF CHURCH STRETTON. Ed. by R. C. Purton. Ibid. liv, pt. 1 (1951–2), 36–42.

> R. C. Purton, 'The manor of Okes, in the parish of Pontesbury'. Ibid. liv, pt. 2 (1951–2).

4860 EXTENT OF THE MANOR OF CHESWARDINE AND A MOIETY OF THE MANOR OF CHILDS ERCALL. Translated by W. K. Boyd. *Shrops. Archaeol. and Nat. Hist. Soc. Trans.* 3rd Ser. viii (1908), 361–7. EXTENT OF THE MANOR OF ELLESMERE, 1280. Translated by W. K. Boyd. Ibid. 2nd Ser. xi (1899), 252–9. EXTENT OF THE MANOR OF WELCH HAMPTON. Trans. by W. K. Boyd. Ibid. 2nd Ser. xi (1899), 260–1.

4861 RENTAL OF (the manor of) WROXETER, 1350. Ed. by Thomas Wright. Ibid. xi (1888), 382–6.

4862 HAYWARD (LILLIAN H.). 'Ancient land-tenures, principally of Shropshire and the West Midlands'. Ibid. xlix (1938), 65–84.

4863 KENYON (ROBERT L.). 'Manor (and township) of Ruyton'. Ibid. 3rd Ser. i (1901), 33–106, 213–50; ii (1902), 107–42, 359–406; iv (1904), 297–336.

> Ruyton comprised what are now the two parishes of Ruyton and West Felton. For a list of Kenyon's other papers on the subject, see ibid. iv (1904), 332.

4864 SLACK (W. J.), ed. The lordship of Oswestry, 1393–1607. Shrops. Archaeol. Soc. Pubns. Shrewsbury. 1952.

> A series of extents and rentals. See R. C. Purton, 'Deeds relating to Oswestry', *Shropshire Archaeol. Soc. Trans.* lxiii (1949–50), 94–111.

SOMERSET

4865 ACCOUNT OF THE PROCTORS (OR WARDENS), OF THE CHURCH OF YEOVIL, 1457–8. *Collectanea Topog. et Genealogica* (No. 115). iii (1836), 134–41.

4866 COURT ROLLS OF THE MANOR OF CURRY RIVEL IN THE YEARS OF THE BLACK DEATH, 1348–9 (translation only). By John F. Chanter. *Somerset. Archaeol. and Nat. Hist. Soc. Procs.* lvi, pt. ii for 1910 (1911), 85–135.

4867 DOCUMENTS AND EXTRACTS ILLUSTRATING THE HISTORY OF THE HONOUR OF DUNSTER. Ed. by H. C. Maxwell-Lyte. Somerset Record Soc. xxxiii (1918).

Idem, 'Historical notes on some Somerset manors formerly connected with the honour of Dunster', Somerset Rec. Soc. Extra Ser. 1931. Idem, *Dunster and its lords* (Exeter, 1882), which includes on pp. 114–33 Dunster household accounts, 1401–32.

4868 HANCOCK (FREDERICK). Minehead in the county of Somerset: a history of the parish, the manor, and the port. Taunton. 1903.

Contains extracts from court rolls and other manorial documents, from subsidy rolls 1–6 Edw. III, etc.

4869 HEALEY (CHARLES E. H. CHADWYCK). History of part of west Somerset. Lond. 1901.

Account rolls of the bailiffs of Porlock and Brendon, 1419–29; pp. 422–70.

4870 HOLMES (THOMAS S.). The history of the parish and manor of Wookey. Bristol. 1886.

Contains abstracts of manorial accounts, 1329 and 1462.

4871 HUNT (TIMOTHY J.). The medieval customs of the manors of Taunton and Bradford on Tone. Somerset Rec. Soc. lxvi (1962).

An English translation of a thirteenth-century custumal for Taunton, a manor of the bishop of Winchester, and a fourteenth-century one for Bradford, a lay manor.

4872 ILCHESTER ALMSHOUSE DEEDS, 1200–1625. Ed. by W(illiam) Buckler. Yeovil. 1866.

4873 NOTICE OF THE CUSTUMAL OF BLEADON AND OF AGRICULTURAL TENURES OF THE THIRTEENTH CENTURY. By Edward Smirke. Royal Archaeol. Inst. of Great Britain: *Memoirs of Wiltshire and Salisbury*, pp. 182–210. Lond. 1851.

Redditus, servitia, et consuetudines manerii de Bledone, pp. 201–10.

STAFFORDSHIRE

4874 ALREWAS COURT ROLLS, 1259–61, 1268–9, 1272–3. Ed. by Walter N. Landor. Wm. Salt Archaeol. Soc. *Collections*, New Ser. x (1907), 245–93; 3rd Ser. (1910), 87–137.

4875 CHETWYND (WALTER). Collections for a history of Pirehill hundred Ed. by Frederick Parker. 2 vols. Ibid. New Ser. xii (1909), 1–273; 3rd Ser. (1914), 1–183.

The collections of Walter Chetwynd of Ingestre, *c.* 1679.

4876 COURT ROLLS OF THE MANOR OF TUNSTALL, 1326–1719. North Staffs. Field Club. lix (1924–5), lxvi (1931–2), *passim*.

4877 HARDY (REGINALD). A history of the parish of Tatenhill. 2 vols. Lond. 1907–8.

Contains court rolls, accounts, and other manorial documents.

4878 SALT (EDWARD). The history of Standon parish, manor and church. Birmingham. 1888.

Contains abstracts of court rolls. A.D. 1338–1773, etc.

4879 BRIDGEMAN (CHARLES G. O.). Notes on the manors of Aston and Walton, near Stone, in the thirteenth and fourteenth centuries. Wm. Salt Archaeol. Soc. *Collections,* 3rd Ser. (1913).

4880 BRIDGEMAN (ERNEST R. O.) and **(CHARLES G. O.).** History of the manor of Weston-under-Lizard in the county of Stafford. Ibid. New Ser. ii (1899).

SUFFOLK

4881 BAILIFF'S ROLL OF THE MANOR OF LAWSHALL, 1393–4. By H. W. Saunders. *Suffolk Inst. Archaeol. Procs.* xiv (1910–12), 111–46.

4882 COMMONPLACE BOOK OF THE FIFTEENTH CENTURY. Ed. by Lucy T. Smith. Lond. 1886.

Pt. ii concerns manorial law, manorial dues, and other matters relating to Stuston, Suffolk, including articles of the court baron and leet.

4883 EXTENTA MANERII DE HADLEGHE (1305). Ed. by Hugh Pigot. *Suffolk Inst. Archaeol. Procs.* iii (1863), 229–52. Translation by Lord John Hervey, ibid. xi (1903), 152–72.

4884 SOME FOURTEENTH-CENTURY DOCUMENTS RELATING TO HERRINGSWELL, CO. SUFFOLK. Ed. by R. G. C. Livett. *East Anglian* (Norwich), 3rd Ser. x (1903–4), 121–4, 253–5, 330–2, 386–9; xi (1905–6), 242–4, 269–71, 302–4, 324–7.

Contains a terrier, 1304; and court rolls, 1318–99.

4885 ICKLINGTON PAPERS. By Henry Prigg. Woodbridge, 1901.

Includes accounts of bailiff of Icklington Manor, 1342–3.

4886 LENNARD (REGINALD). 'An unidentified twelfth-century custumal of Lawshall (Suffolk)'. *E.H.R.* li (1936), 104–7.

4887 CALLARD (ERNEST). The manor of Freckenham, an ancient corner of East Anglia. Lond. 1924.

4888 COPINGER (WALTER A.). The manors of Suffolk: notes on their history and devolution. 7 vols. Lond. etc. 1905–11.

4889 PARKER (WILLIAM). The history of Long Melford. Lond. 1873.

Contains a translation of charters, manorial extents, etc.

SURREY

4890 ABSTRACT OF THE COURT ROLLS OF THE MANORIAL RECORDS (county of Surrey). By D(orothy) L. Powell. Records of Ancient Monuments Committee, County of Surrey. Kingston-on-Thames. 1928. Likewise *List of court rolls* (Guide to Archives . . . Surrey). Surrey Rec. Soc. Pubns. No. 28 (1928).

4891 CATALOGUE OF MSS. AND MUNIMENTS OF ALLEYN'S COLLEGE OF GOD'S GIFT, DULWICH. By George F. Warner. Lond. 1881.

Deeds, court rolls, etc. of Dulwich manor, 1323–1626, pp. 272–336.

4892 COURT ROLLS OF THE MANOR OF CARSHALTON (Edw. III–Hen. VII). By Dorothy L. Powell. Surrey Rec. Soc. ii (1916).

4893 COURT ROLLS OF TOOTING BECK MANOR. (Ed. by George L. Gomme). vol. i: 1394–1422. London County Council. Lond. 1909.

Extension and translation, with an appendix of earlier rolls in possession of King's College, Cambridge.

4894 EXTRACTS FROM THE COURT ROLLS OF THE MANOR OF DULWICH, 1333–1693. Ed. by F. B. Bickley in William Young's *History of Dulwich College* (Lond. 1889), ii. 266–320.

4895 EXTRACTS FROM THE COURT ROLLS OF THE MANOR OF WIMBLEDON (1461–1864, with a translation). With prefatory remarks by Philip H. Lawrence. Lond. 1866.

4896 REGISTER OR MEMORIAL OF EWELL (1408–23). Ed. by Cecil Deedes. Lond. 1913.

4897 SURREY MANORIAL ACCOUNTS. A catalogue and index of the earliest surviving rolls down to the year 1300 . . . By Helen M. Briggs. Surrey Rec. Soc. xv (1935).

Transcripts of rolls for manors of Maldon, Farley, Thornycroft, and Chessington.

4898 LAMBERT (HENRY C. M.). History of Banstead. 2 vols. Lond. 1912–13.

Contains many records, manorial accounts, extents, court rolls, etc.

SUSSEX

4899 THE BOOK OF BARTHOLOMEW BOLNEY (a fifteenth-century lawyer). Ed. by Marie Clough. Sussex Rec. Soc. lxiii (1964).

Deals with extents, rentals, etc., of various manors, such as Bolne, Denton.

4900 CUSTUMALS OF THE MANORS OF LAUGHTON, WILLINGDON, AND GORING. Ed. by Arthur E. Wilson. Sussex Rec. Soc. l (1961).

4901 CUSTUMALS OF THE SUSSEX MANORS OF THE ARCHBISHOP OF CANTERBURY. Ed. by Brian C. Redwood and A. E. Wilson. Sussex Rec. Soc. lvii (1958).

See F. R. H. Du Boulay, 'The Pagham estates of the archbishops of Canterbury during the fifteenth century', *History*, New Ser. xxxviii (1953), 201–18.

4902 LATHE COURT ROLLS AND VIEWS OF FRANKPLEDGE IN THE RAPE OF HASTINGS, A.D. 1387 to 1474. Ed. by Elinor J. Courthorpe and Beryl E. R. Formoy. Sussex Rec. Soc. xxxvii (1934).

4903 MINISTERS' ACCOUNTS OF THE MANOR OF PETWORTH, 1347–1353. Ed. by Louis F. Salzman. Sussex Rec. Soc. lv (1955).

Accounts of reeves and bailiffs; five rolls translated into English. The introduction deals with accounts and formulae, and the Black Death.

4904 ON A SERIES OF ROLLS OF THE MANOR OF WISTON (13th–16th centuries). By William Hudson. *Sussex Archaeol. Collections*, liii (1910), 143–82; liv (1911), 130–82.

Contains a translation of the old custumal of Wiston (late thirteenth century), of extents or rentals of Wiston, Chiltington, Heene, etc., and of fragments of account rolls; with a paper on the agriculture of the fourteenth century by P. S. Godman.

4905 RECORDS OF THE BARONY AND HONOUR OF THE RAPE OF LEWES. Ed. by Arnold J. Taylor. Sussex Rec. Soc. xliv (1940).

Various court rolls and account rolls of thirteenth to fifteenth centuries.

4906 SURVEY OF THE CHURCH OF THE COLLEGE OF MALLING, NEAR LEWES. Ed. by J. R. Daniel-Tyssen. *Sussex Archaeol. Collections*, xxi (1869), 159–90.

Two inquests or surveys of the lands of the collegiate church of Malling, 40 Edw. III and 21 Rich. II.

4907 THIRTEEN CUSTUMALS OF THE SUSSEX MANORS OF THE BISHOP OF CHICHESTER, AND OTHER DOCUMENTS, FROM LIBRI P AND C OF THE EPISCOPAL MANUSCRIPTS. Trans. and ed. by W. D. Peckham. Sussex Rec. Soc. xxxi (1925).

4908 TWO ESTATE SURVEYS OF THE FITZALAN EARLS OF ARUNDEL. Ed. by M. Clough. Sussex Rec. Soc. lxvii (1969).

4909 BRENT (J. A.). 'Alceston manor in the later middle ages'. *Sussex Archaeol. Soc. Collections*, cvi (1968), 89–102.

4910 HUDSON (WILLIAM). 'The manor of Eastbourne: its early history'. Ibid. xliii (1900), 166–200.

See also on a single-vill hundred, W. Hudson, 'The hundred of Eastbourne and its six "boroughs" ', ibid. xlii (1899), 180–208.

WARWICKSHIRE

Dugdale, *Antiquities of Warwickshire* (No. 1849) ii, 911–12, gives an interesting inquisition regarding the manorial customs of Sutton Coldfield.

4911 EXTENTA MANERII (ET BURGI) DE VETERI STRATFORD facta quinto-decimo pontificatus domini Walter de Cantilupo (1252). Middle Hill Press. *c.* 1840.

Only eight pages.

4912 MINISTERS' ACCOUNTS OF THE COLLEGIATE CHURCH OF ST. MARY, WARWICK, 1432–85. Ed. by Dorothy Styles. Dugdale Soc. xxvi (1969).

4913 MINISTERS' ACCOUNTS OF THE WARWICKSHIRE ESTATES OF THE DUKE OF CLARENCE, 1479–80. Ed. by Rodney H. Hilton. Dugdale Soc. xxi (1952).

4914 RECORDS OF BEAUDESERT, HENLEY-IN-ARDEN, CO. WARWICK. Ed. by William Cooper. Leeds. 1931.

4915 HILTON (RODNEY H.). The social structure of rural Warwickshire in the middle ages. Dugdale Soc. Occasional Papers. No. 9 (1950).

4916 ROSS (CHARLES D.). The estates and finances of Richard Beauchamp, earl of Warwick. Dugdale Soc. Occasional Papers. No. 12 (1956).

Wiltshire

4917 ACCOUNTS AND SURVEYS OF THE WILTSHIRE LANDS OF ADAM DE STRATTON. Ed. by Michael W. Farr. Wilts. Archaeol. Soc. Rec. Branch. xiv (1959).

> Most of the documents are audited accounts of the manor of Sevenhampton 1269–88. Some are extents, some reeve's accounts, etc.

4918 COURT ROLLS OF THE WILTSHIRE MANORS OF ADAM DE STRATTON. Ed. by Ralph B. Pugh. Wilts. Archaeol. Soc. Rec. Ser. (Wiltshire Rec. Soc.). xxiv for 1968 (1970).

4919 FARMERS' AND COLLECTORS' ACCOUNTS: Alton Barnes, 1455–1531, and Takeley (Essex), 1473–75. Ed. by J. E. T. Rogers, *History of Agriculture* (No. 1376), iii. 705–15.

4920 PLEAS IN THE LIBERTY OF THE ABBOT OF BATTLE AT BROMHAM, 1289. Ed. by Susan Reynolds. Wilts. Archaeol.-Nat. Hist. Soc. Records Branch. xii, *Collectanea*, (1956), 129–41.

4921 THE ROLLS OF HIGHWORTH HUNDRED, 1275–1287. Ed. by Brenda Farr. 2 vols. Wilts. Archaeol. Soc. Rec. Ser. xxi for 1965 (1966); and xxii for 1966 (1968).

> Part of the documents relating to the Wiltshire lands of Adam de Stratton, who later forfeited the hundred as a result of the state trials of 1289–93.

4922 SCROPE (GEORGE P.). History of the manor and barony of Castle Combe, in the county of Wilts. Lond. 1852.

> Contains rental, 1340; extracts from court rolls, 1344–1700; an extent of the manor, 1454; accounts of the bailiff, 1408–60; charters, etc. Idem, 'On the self-government of small manorial communities, as exemplified in the manor of Castle Combe. *Wilts. Archaeol. and Nat. Hist. Soc. Magazine*, iii (1857), 145–63. Castle Combe was in the lordship of Sir John Fastolf.

4923 SURVEY OF THE MANOR AND FOREST OF CLARENDON, in 1272. Ed. by Thomas Phillipps. *Archaeologia*, xxv (1834), 151–8.

4924 TWO ROYAL SURVEYS OF WILTSHIRE DURING THE INTER-DICT. Ed. by W. Raymond Powell, *Interdict Documents* (No. 5809), pp. 3–32.

These are the surveys of the manors of the bishop and canons of Salisbury, and of the black monks in Wiltshire.

4925 PAYNE (RICHENDA C.). 'Agrarian conditions on the Wiltshire estates of the duchy of Lancaster'. *B.I.H.R.* xviii (1940), 116–18.

4926 PUGH (RALPH B.). 'The early history of the manors in Amesbury'. *Wilts. Archaeol.–Nat. Hist. Magazine.* lii, no. 187 (1947), 70–110.

4927 THOMSON (T. R.). 'The customal of Abingdon court, Cricklade'. Ibid. lii, no. 189 (1948), 369–71.

WORCESTERSHIRE

4928 COURT ROLLS OF THE MANOR OF HALES (Halesowen). 1270–1307. Ed. by John Amphlett and Sidney G. Hamilton. 2 pts. Worcestershire Hist. Soc. 1910–12. Pt. iii, containing additional courts of the years 1276–1301, and Romsley courts, 1280–1303. Ed. by Rowland A. Wilson. Ibid. 1933.

4929 MADRESFIELD: EXCERPTA E SCRINIO MANERIALI DE MADRESFIELD, in Com. Vigorn. (Lond.). 1873.

Mainly court rolls, 6 Rich. II–9 Hen. IV.

YORKSHIRE

4930 CHAPTER HOUSE RECORDS. Translated by John Lister. Thoresby Soc. Pubns. xxxiii (1930), 83–102.

Extents (1341) for Leeds, Rothwell, Allerton, Bywater, Kippax, and Ledston.

4931 COMPOTI OF THE YORKSHIRE ESTATES OF HENRY DE LACY. Yorks. Archaeol.-Topog. Jour. viii (1884), 351–8.

See Turton's *Pickering* (No. 3630).

4932 COURT ROLLS OF THE MANOR OF WAKEFIELD. (1274–1331). Ed. by William P. Baildon, John Lister, and J. W. Walker. 5 vols. Yorks. Archaeol. Soc. Rec. Ser. xxix (1901), xxxvi (1906), lvii (1917), lxxviii (1930), cix (1945).

4933 THE EXTENT OF BARTON IN RICHMONDSHIRE, 1309. By T. A. M. Bishop. *Yorks. Archaeol. Jour.* xxxii (1934), 86–97.

4934 EXTENTS OF THE PREBENDS OF YORK (*c.* 1295). Ed. by T. A. M. Bishop. Yorks. Archaeol. Soc. Rec. Ser. xciv *Miscellanea*, iv (1936), 1–38.

See also T. A. M. Bishop, 'The distribution of manorial demesne in the vale of York-shire', *E.H.R.* xlix (1934), 386–406. Idem, 'Monastic granges in Yorkshire', ibid. li (1936), 193–214.

4935 EXTRACTS FROM THE COURT ROLLS OF THE MANOR OF ALDBOROUGH (1338–9). Ed. by Thomas Lawson-Tancred and John W. Walker. Yorks. Archaeol. Soc. Rec. Ser. lxxiv, *Miscellanea*, ii (1929), 40–3.

4936 FOURTEENTH CENTURY COURT ROLLS OF THE MANOR OF THORNER (38–9 Edw. III: translation only). By William T. Lancaster. Thoresby Soc. Pubns. xv, *Miscellanea*, v for 1906 (1909), 153–73.

4937 HISTORY OF METHLEY (West Riding). Appendix: Methley manor rolls (1331–1590). Ed. by Hubert S. Darbyshire and George D. Lumb. Thoresby Soc. Pubns. xxxv for 1934 (1937), 131–244.

A few Methley deeds are calendared, pp. 93–104.

4938 THE MANOR AND PARK OF ROUNDHAY. By J. W. Morkill. Thoresby Soc. Pubns. ii, *Miscellanea*, i (1891), 215–48.

Contains abstracts of manorial extents and other documents of the fourteenth and fifteenth centuries.

4939 REGISTRUM HONORIS DE RICHMOND. (Ed. by Roger Gale.) Lond. 1722. See No. 4503.

4940 BARLEY (MAURICE W.). 'Early Yorkshire manorial by-laws'. *Yorks. Archaeol. Jour.* xxxv (1940), 35–60.

4941 DONKIN (R. A.). 'Settlement and depopulation of Cistercian estates'. See No. 5936 and Waites, No. 6393.

4941A GREEN (W. A.). Historical antiquities of Ackworth. Lond. 1910. Contains an extent, 1311, and manorial accounts.

4942 RUSTON (ARTHUR G.) and WITNEY (DENIS). Hooton Pagnell, the agricultural evolution of a Yorkshire village. Lond. 1934.

An excellent monograph on village history.

4943 UGAWA (KAORU). Lay estates in medieval England. Tokyo, 1966.

The account rolls, etc., of the estates of the De Fortibus family in Holderness. See also Noël Denholm-Young, 'The Yorkshire estates of Isabella de Fortibus', *Yorks. Archaeol. Jour.* xxxi, pt. 4. (1934), 389–420.

WALES

4943A REGISTRUM VULGARITER NUNCUPATUM. 'The record of Caernarvon'. Ed. by Henry Ellis. Record Comm. 1838.

Extents of manors, chiefly 26 Edw. III, in the counties of Caernarvon and Anglesey: pp. 1–91.
　　Other extents of commotes and manors, 1335, pp. 92–116.
　　Quo warranto proceedings relating to the bishop of Bangor, to various boroughs and religious houses, etc. in north Wales, *temp.* Edw. III, pp. 133–207.
　　Parliamentary petitions from communities, etc., of north Wales, 33 Edw. I, pp. 212–25.
　　Taxation of the clergy of the diocese of Bangor (undated), pp. 226–30.
　　Extent of the temporalities of the see of Bangor, 22 Rich. II, pp. 231–7.
　　Survey of the temporalities of Prestoll abbey, 48 Edw. III, pp. 249–51.
　　Extent of Merioneth, 7 Hen. V, pp. 261–92.
　　For the Record of Caernarvon, see R. W. Banks, 'On the Welsh records in the time of the Black Prince', *Archaeologia Cambrensis*, 4th Ser. iv (1873), 157–88; and for various other extents, Seebohm's *Tribal system* (No. 2647).

4943B SURVEY OF THE HONOUR OF DENBIGH, 1334. Ed. by Paul
Vinogradoff and Frank Morgan. British Academy Records (No. 181), vol. i.
Lond. 1914.

> This comprehensive extent presents a society of tribal communities on which a modified
> form of the English manorial system has been superimposed. It also sketches the
> condition of affairs before the Edwardian Conquest. See Jack (No. 22), pp. 120–1.

B. MODERN DESCRIPTIONS OF AGRARIAN SOCIETY

1. *Manor and Village*

For the general commentaries on the structure of society, see vol. i, pp. 174–7,
374–8; and for more specialized treatises on the Anglo-Saxon period and later,
pp. 2645–52. The classics by Maitland, Seebohm, Stenton, and Vinogradoff
are found in items 2636, 2645–52. The most up-to-date account on manorial
history is the notable chapter by M. M. Postan in vol. i of *Cambridge economic
history* (1966 edn.). A selective list of modern studies is given below; for more
complete lists, see the *Cambridge economic history*, the annual bibliographical
lists in *Economic History Review* and in *Agricultural History Review*.

4944 ASTON (TREVOR H.). 'The English manor'. *Past and Present*, x
(1956), 6–13. Idem, 'The origins of the manor in England' (No. 2626).

> 'The English manor' is a review of Kosminsky's *Studies* (No. 4971). See also Sidney O.
> Addy, *Church and manor: a study in English economic history* (Lond. 1913), * and
> Latham in *Social life* (No. 1495).

4945 AULT (WARREN O.). Open field husbandry and the village community:
a study in agrarian by-laws in medieval England. *American Philosophical Soc.
Trans.* iv, pt. 7 (1965).

> Idem, 'Some early village by-laws', *E.H.R.* xlv (1930), 208–31. Idem, 'The self-directing
> activities of village communities in medieval England (a lecture. Boston, 1952). Idem,
> 'Village by-laws by common consent', *Speculum* (special number), xxix (1954), 378–94.
> Idem, 'By-laws of gleaning and the problems of the harvest', *Econ. H.R.* 2nd Ser. xiv
> (1961–2), 210–17. Idem, 'Manor court and parish church in fifteenth-century England:
> a study of village by-laws', *Speculum*, xlii (1967), 53–67. Idem, 'The village church and
> the village community in mediaeval England', *Speculum*, xlv (1970), 197–215. See also
> his paper on local government, 'Village assemblies in medieval England' in *Studies* . . .
> *Hist. Representative and Parliamentary Institutions* (No. 3366), xxiii (1960). Also H. M.
> Cam, 'The community of the vill' (Nos. 1437, 1461).

4946 AULT (W. O.). Private jurisdiction in England. Yale Hist. Pubns.
Miscellany x. New Haven. 1923.

4947 BARG (MIKHAIL A.). Issledovaniia po istorii angliiskogo feodalizma
v XI–XIII vv. (Studies on the history of English feudalism from the eleventh to
the thirteenth centuries). Moscow. 1962.

> The Russian titles of some of Barg's articles are given below in English translation.
> M. A. Barg, 'The question of the growth of English population from the eleventh to the
> thirteenth centuries', *Voprosy istorii*, 1947, fasc. ii, pp. 87–90. Idem, 'The evolution of
> feudal landownership in England from the eleventh to the thirteenth centuries', ibid.
> 1953, fasc. ii, pp. 97–105. Idem, 'The Norman conquest and the formation of serfdom
> in England', ibid. 1957, fasc. vii, pp. 87–103.

4948 BENNETT (HENRY S.). Life on the English manor: a study of peasant conditions, 1150–1400. Cambr. Stud. in Medieval Life and Thought. Cambr. 1938. 3rd edn. 1948. Reprinted, 1965. Also paperback edn.

Useful for the thirteenth century, somewhat out of date for the fifteenth century. See also H. S. Bennett, 'The reeve and the manor in the fourteenth century', *E.H.R.* xli (1926), 358–65. T. F. T. Plucknett, *The Mediaeval bailiff.* Creighton Lecture. 1954.

4949 BERESFORD (MAURICE W.). The lost villages of England. Lond. 1954. 4th impression with corrections. 1963.

4950 BERESFORD (M. W.) and HURST (JOHN G.). Deserted medieval villages: studies edited by Maurice Beresford and John G. Hurst. Lond. 1971.

Part 1: England. Pp. 3–75: A review of historical research (to 1968); pp. 76–144: A review of archaeological research (to 1968); pp. 145–68: Gazetteer of excavations at medieval house and village sites (to 1968); pp. 169–81: An historian's (Beresford's) appraisal of archaeological research; pp. 182–212: County gazetteers of deserted medieval villages (known in 1968); pp. 213–26: Select bibliography, England.
Parts ii–iv: Scotland, Wales and Ireland. The study of deserted villages, etc.
   Beresford's review of historical research (pp. 3–75) is a revision of his 'Villages Désertés: bilan de la recherche anglaise' in *Les Hommes et la Terre* (Paris), xi (1965), 533–80. The useful bibliography for England (pp. 213–26) cites numerous articles on deserted villages and related subjects. Current research may be followed in the annual *Reports of the Deserted Villages Research Group,* 1+ (Lond. 1953+). See also Beresford and St. Joseph, *Medieval England: an aerial survey* (No. 752).

4951 BLOCH (MARC). La société féodale (No. 1363). Idem, Les caractères originaux de l'histoire rurale française. Oslo and Cambr. (Mass.) etc. 1931. Trans. by Janet Sondheimer. Berkeley. 1966. Idem, Seigneurie française et manoir anglais. Préface de Georges Duby. *Cahiers des Annales,* no. 16. Paris, 1960. Idem, Mélanges historiques. Ed. by Charles-Edmond Perrin. Paris, 1965. Extracts translated as *Land and work in medieval Europe: selected papers.* By J. E. Anderson. Berkeley. 1967.

4952 BOUTRUCHE (ROBERT). Seigneurie et féodalité. Vol. i: Le premier âge, des liens d'homme à homme. Paris. 1959. Vol. ii: L'apogée (xi–xiii siècles). Paris. 1970. Vol. iii: in preparation.

A broad European treatise on feudalism and manorialism.

4953 CARUS-WILSON (ELEANORA M). 'Evidences of industrial growth on some fifteenth century manors'. *Econ. H. R.* 2nd Ser. xii (1959), 190–205.

Reprinted in *Essays in economic history* (No. 1468).

4954 DAVENPORT (FRANCES J.). The economic development of a Norfolk manor (No. 4819).

4955 DODWELL (BARBARA). 'Holdings and inheritance in medieval East Anglia'. *Econ. H.R.* 2nd Ser. xx (1967), 53–66.

Deals with diversity in a complex social structure and with the peasant land market. See also A. R. H. Baker, 'Open fields and partible inheritance on a Kent manor', ibid. xvii (1964), 1–23. R. J. Faith, 'Peasant families and inheritance customs in medieval England', *Agricultural H.R.* xiv (1966), 77–95. D. Roden, 'Inheritance customs and succession to land in the Chiltern Hills in the thirteenth and fourteenth centuries', *Jour. British Stud.* vii (1967), 1–11. See No. 4999.

4956 DOUGLAS (DAVID C.). The social structure of medieval East Anglia. Oxford Stud. in Social and Legal Hist. ix. Oxf. 1927. Idem, The medieval fenland. Cambr. 1940.

4957 DU BOULAY (FRANCIS R. H.). 'Who were farming the English demesnes at the end of the middle ages?'. *Econ. H.R.* 2nd Ser. xvii (1964-5), 443-55.

> See idem, Nos. 4784, 5619. Barbara Harvey, 'The leasing of the abbot of Westminster's demesnes in the later middle ages', *Econ. H.R.* 2nd Ser. xxii (1969), 17-27; and idem, Abbot Gervase and fee farms (No. 6237).

4958 DYER (CHRISTOPHER). 'A redistribution of incomes in fifteenth-century England'. *Past and Present*, xxxix (1968), 11-33.

> Deals with peasant resistance to rents charged on the bishop of Worcester's estates, where demesne-cultivation had been largely given up, hence estate documents for demesne set forth leases. On a similar subject, see Barbara J. Harris, 'Landlords and tenants in the later middle ages: the Buckingham estates', ibid. xliii (1969), 146-50.

4959 GRAY (HOWARD L.). 'The commutation of villein services before the Black Death'. *E.H.R.* xxix (1914), 625-56.

> F. J. Davenport, 'The decay of villeinage in East Anglia,' *T.R.H.S.* 2nd Ser. xiv (1900), 123-41. T. W. Page, *The end of villainage in England* (N.Y. 1900). E. P. Cheyney, 'The disappearance of English serfdom', *E.H.R.* xv (1900), 20-37. F. Bradshaw, 'The decline and fall of serfdom in Durham', *Archaeologia Aeliana*, 3rd Ser. iv (1908), 91-105. For a good example from the village of Broughton (Hunts.), see Raftis in *Wilkinson essays* (No. 1459). Consult Hilton, *Decline of serfdom* (No. 4961).

4960 HATCHER (JOHN). Rural economy and society in the duchy of Cornwall 1300-1500. Cambr. 1970.

> Concerned with the seventeen assessionable manors which were demesne in the estates of the earldom of Cornwall when it became the duchy in 1337. The environment fostered individual system of farming, different from the so-called 'classical' manor. There were relatively few villeins, but many tenants by contract and free tenants. Cornwall showed significant deviations from the usual pattern. See Hatcher, 'A diversified economy: later medieval Cornwall', *Econ. H.R.* 2nd Ser. xxii (1969), 208-27, and idem, 'Non-manorialism in medieval Cornwall', *Agricultural Hist. Rev.* xviii (1970), 1-16.

4961 HILTON (RODNEY H.). The decline of serfdom in medieval England. (A pamphlet of 72 pages in the series): Studies in Economic History. Lond. and N.Y. 1969.

> Idem, 'Freedom and villeinage in England', *Past and Present*, xxxi (1965), 3-19.

4962 HILTON (R. H.). The economic development of some Leicestershire estates in the fourteenth and fifteenth centuries. Oxford Hist. Ser. Lond. 1947.

> This examination of the feudal and manorial aspects of Leicester abbey and Owston abbey has broader applicability.

4963 HILTON (R. H.). 'England in the twelfth and thirteenth centuries: an economic contrast'. *Econ. H.R.* xxiv (1971), 1-14.

> See also Edmund King, 'Large and small landowners in thirteenth century England: the case of Peterborough abbey', *Past and Present*, no. 47 (1970), 26-50.

4964 HILTON (R. H.). A medieval society: the west Midlands at the end of the thirteenth century. N.Y. 1967.

A well-presented, documented survey of the various facets of the society of the region, broadly the bishopric of Worcester. Idem, 'Lord and peasant in Staffordshire in the middle ages', *North Staffordshire Jour. of Field Stud.* x (1970), 1–20.

4965 HILTON (R. H.). 'Peasant movements in England before 1381'. *Econ. H.R.* 2nd Ser. ii (1949), 117–36.

4966 HILTON (R. H.). 'Rent and capital formation in feudal society'. *Papers presented to the Second International Conference on Economic History at Aix-en Provence, 1962*: Middle ages and modern times (Paris, 1963), ii, pp. 33–68.

4967 HOMANS (GEORGE C.). English villagers of the thirteenth century. Cambr. (Mass.). 1941. * Paperback: N.Y. 1970.

A fundamental study in social anthropology. Idem, 'The rural sociology of medieval England', *Past and Present*, iv (1953), 32–43. Idem, 'The explanation of English regional differences', ibid. xlii (1969), 18–34. See Powicke in *Dopsch essays* (No. 1434).

4968 HONE (NATHANIEL J.). The manor and manorial records. Lond. 1906. *

See N. J. Hone, ed. *A mannor and court baron.* Manorial Soc. Pubn. no. 3. (Lond. 1909).

4969 HOSKINS (WILLIAM G.). The midland peasant: (No. 4802).

4970 HYAMS (PAUL R.). 'The origins of a peasant land market in England', *Econ. H.R.* 2nd Ser. xxiii (1970), 18–31.

This article develops from Postan's introduction to *Carte Nativorum* (No. 6266). See also Hilton, 'Peasant movements' (No. 4965).

4971 KOSMINSKY (EUGENE A.). Studies in the agrarian history of England in the thirteenth century. Ed. by Rodney H. Hilton. Trans. (slightly abbreviated) from the Russian by Ruth Kisch. Stud. in Medieval History. Oxf. 1956.

Although principally a statistical study of the Hundred Rolls of 1279, this important book becomes a fairly comprehensive account of English rural society in the thirteenth century. It stresses the complexity and diversity of manorial structure even in the midlands, often regarded as the area of the typical manor described by Seebohm and Vinogradoff; it demonstrates that obligations were most often money payments and that profits were mainly money rents; it gives a prominent place to the small landowner in the manorial system.

Kosminsky first dealt with such problems in 'The hundred rolls of 1279–80 as a source of English agrarian history', *Econ. H.R.* iii (1931), 16–44; and 'Services and money rents in the thirteenth century', ibid. v (1935), 24–45 (see No. 1468). He expanded these articles into a book in Russian: *Angliiskaia derevnia v xiii veke* (The English village in the thirteenth century), Moscow and Leningrad, 1935. Its theses were summarized by M. M. Postan in *Econ. H.R.* vi (1935–6), 223–6. A revision of the book was published in 1947 as *Issledovaniia po agrarnoi istorii Anglii xiii veka*; it is this revision which was translated into English by Ruth Kisch. Postan commented upon the Russian edition in *Econ. H.R.* 2nd Ser. iii (1950), 119–125; and Kosminsky replied to some of Postan's criticisms in a foreword to the 1956 translation. The English translation was reviewed by Postan in *E.H.R.* lxxiii (1958), 663–7; by R. Lennard in *History*, xlii (1957), 49–51; by E. Miller in *Econ. H.R.* 2nd Ser. ix (1957), 499–501; and by T. H. Aston in *Past and Present*, x (1956), 6–13.

Other important articles in Russian by Kosminsky deal with 'Labour on English manorial estates in the thirteenth century' (*Voprosy istorii*, 1945, fasc. i, 59–83; and 'Some problems relative to agrarian history of England in the fifteenth century' (*Vopr. ist.* 1948, fasc. i, 59–76).

In addition to the well-known writings of Vinogradoff and of Savine, other Russian scholars have contributed to English manorial history. D. M. Petrushevsky, whose book on Wat Tyler's rebellion is cited above as No. 4154, contributed 'Die Entwicklung der Grundherrschaft in England', *Zeitschrift für die gesamte Staatswissenschaft*, lxxxviii (1930), 114–66; and Ignatii N. Granat's book *K voprosv ob obezzemelenii krest'ianstva v Anglii* (Moscow, 1908) is on the question of the divorce of the peasantry in England from the land.

Some of the articles written in the Russian language on the English manorial system are cited here in English translation. I. S. Zvavich, 'The class nature of manorial justice', *Uchenye zapiski Instituta Istorii* (Moscow), iii (1929), 248–61. Idem, 'The break-up of manorial system in England', *Istoricheskii sbornik*, iii (1934), 5–34. S. A. Tokarev, 'The trade of the English manor in the thirteenth century and the first half of the fourteenth century', *Uchenye zapiski Instituta Istorii* (Moscow), vii (1928), 36–79. I. Polianskii, 'The bourgeois Russian historians of English rural life', *Voprosy istorii*, 1949, fasc. iii, pp. 93–107. E. V. Gutnova, 'Principal sources and historiography of the history of peasant ideology in England in the thirteenth and fourteenth centuries', *Srednie veka* (Moscow), xxix (1966), 70–89; English summary, p. 89. See the works of M. A. Barg (No. 4947); and the article on Watlington manor, Oxfordshire, by Ul'ianov (No. 4857).

4972 LEADAM (ISAAC S.). The inquisition of 1517: inclosures and evictions. Ed. from the Lansdowne MS. I. 153 by I. S. Leadam. *T.R.H.S.* New Ser. vi (1892), 167–314.

The introduction deals with the earlier status of villeins.

4973 LENNARD (REGINALD). Rural England, 1086–1135: a study of social and agrarian conditions. Oxf. 1959.

The most significant study of its subject; Lennard's numerous articles are cited therein. For sources, see Lennard, 'What is a manorial extent?', *E.H.R.* xliv (1929), 256–63. Idem, 'Early manorial juries', ibid. lxxvii (1962), 511–18.

4974 LEVETT (ADA E.). Studies in manorial history. Ed. by H. M. Cam, M. Coate, and L. S. Sutherland. Oxf. 1938. No. 1480 above.

See also F. B. Stitt, 'The medieval minister's account: some points from its form and development', *Soc. Local Archivists Bull.* xi (1953), 2–8.

4975 MAITLAND (FREDERIC W.). Northumbrian tenures (thegnage and drengage in the twelfth and thirteenth centuries). *E.H.R.* v (1890), 625–32. Reprinted in his *Collected Papers* (No. 1482), ii. 96–109.

Cf. G. T. Lapsley, 'Cornage and drengage', *A.H.R.* ix (1904), 670–95. The thegns and drengs, though freemen, had some of the marks of villeins.

4976 NEILSON (NELLIE). Customary rents. Oxford Stud. in Social and Legal History, ii. Oxf. 1910.

Idem, 'Custom and common law in Kent', *Harvard Law Rev.* xxxviii (1924–5), 482–98. Idem, 'English manorial forms', *A.H.R.* xxxiv (1928–9), 725–39.

4977 POSTAN (M. M.). The famulus: the estate labourer in the twelfth and thirteenth centuries. *Econ. H.R.* Supplement, no. 2. Cambr. 1954.

Idem, 'The chronology of labour services', *T.R.H.S.* 4th Ser. xx (1937), 169–93. Idem,

'The manor in the hundred rolls', *Econ. H.R.* 2nd ser. iii (1950), 119–25. For a bibliography of Postan's works turn to No. 5462.

4978 RAFTIS (J. AMBROSE). Tenure and mobility: studies in the social history of a medieval English village. Toronto. 1964.

A detailed sociological study of the villagers, based on manorial court rolls, particularly relating to unfree tenants on the abbey of Ramsey's estates. It is fortified with translations of numerous court records and appendixes of Latin excerpts. See Raftis, 'The concentration of responsibility in five villages', *Mediaeval Stud.* xxviii (1966), 92–118. Idem, 'Changes in an English village after the Black Death' (the village of Upwood, Hunts., belonging to the abbey of Ramsey), ibid. xxlx (1967), 158–77. Idem, 'Court rolls and village social history', *Jour. Soc. Archivists*, iii, no. 8 (1968), 423–4.

4978A REES (WILLIAM). South Wales and the March, 1284–1415: a social and agrarian study. Oxf. 1924.

4979 SAVINE (ALEXANDER). Copyhold cases in the early chancery proceedings (Hen. VI–Ed. IV). *E.H.R.* xvii (1902), 296–303.

4980 STENTON (FRANK M.). Types of manorial structure in the northern Danelaw. Oxford Stud. in Social and Legal Hist. Oxf. 1910.

A classical study of an area characterized by freemen, villages rather than manors, and relatively weak lordship.

4981 TITOW (JAN Z.). 'Some differences between manors and the effects on the conditions of the peasants in the thirteenth century'. *Agricultural H.R.* x (1962), 1–13; and reprinted in *Essays in Agrarian History*, ed. by W. E. Minchinton (Newton Abbot, 1968), pp. 37–51.

4982 VINOGRADOFF (PAUL). 'Agricultural services'. *Econ. Jour.* x (1900), 308–22. Reprinted in *Vinogradoff papers* (No. 1501).

For his *Villainage in England*, see No. 2652.

2. Agriculture and Husbandry

See *Cambridge economic history*, vol. i; and Oschinsky (No. 4631).

4983 FINBERG (HERBERT P. R.). 'Recent progress in English agrarian history'. *Geografiska Annaler* (Stockholm), xlvii (1963), 75–9.

4984 HILTON (RODNEY H.). 'The content and sources of English agrarian history before 1500'. *Agricultural Hist. Rev.* iii (1955), 3–19.

4985 ASHLEY (WILLIAM). 'The place of rye in the history of English food'. *Econ. Jour.* xxxi (1921), 285–308.

Ashley disputes Thorold Rogers's generalization that wheat was the principal grain.

4986 BAKER (ALAN R. H.). Some evidence of a reduction in the acreage of cultivated lands in Sussex during the early fourteenth century. *Sussex Archaeol. Collections*, cix (1966), 1–5.

See also his 'Evidence in the *Nonarum Inquisitiones* of contracting arable lands in England in the early fourteenth century', *Econ. H.R.* 2nd Ser. xix (1966), 518–22. Idem, 'Some fields and farms in medieval Kent', *Archaeologia Cantiana*, lxxx (1965), 152–74. Idem, 'The Kentish jugum and its relationship to soils at Gillingham', *E.H.R.* lxxxi

(1966), 74–9, which gives a table of rental values of 1447, and maintains that 'fiscal assesments were related to soil values'. Idem, 'Cooperative farming in medieval England' *Geographical Magazine* xiii (1970), 496–505.

4987   BARLEY (MAURICE W.). The English farm-house and cottage. Lond. 1961.

Refer to the section above on Domestic architecture, vol. i, pp. 96–7; and R. K. Field, 'Worcestershire peasant buildings, household goods and farm equipment in the later middle ages', *Medieval Archaeol.* ix (1965), 105–45.

4988   BENNETT (RICHARD) and ELTON (JOHN). History of corn milling. 4 vols. Lond. 1898–1904.

4989   BISHOP (TERENCE A. M.). 'The distribution of manorial demesne in the Vale of Yorkshire'. *E.H.R.* xlix (1934), 386–406. Idem, 'Assarting and the open fields', *Econ. H.R.* vi (1935), 13–29; reprinted in *Essays in Economic History* (No. 1468). Idem, 'The rotation of crops at Westerham (Kent), 1297–1350'. *Econ. H.R.* ix (1938–9), 38–44. Idem, 'Monastic granges in Yorkshire'. *E.H.R.* li (1936), 193–214; see No. 4994.

4990   BRITNELL (R. H.). 'Production for the market on a small fourteenth-century estate'. *Econ. H.R.* xix (1966), 380–7.

Account rolls of Langenhoe, Essex.

4991   DARBY (HENRY CLIFFORD). Draining of the fens. Cambr. 2nd edn. 1956. Idem. The medieval fenland. Cambr. 1940.

See H. E. Hallam, 'The new lands of Elloe: a study of early reclamation in Lincoln-shire', Department of English Local History, Occasional Papers. no. 6. Leicester, 1954. Also Hallam, *Settlement and society* (No. 4808).

4992   DONKIN (R. A.). 'Cattle on the estates of medieval Cistercian monas-teries in England and Wales'. *Econ. H.R.* 2nd Ser. xv (1962–3), 31–53.

4993   DONKIN (R. A.). 'Some aspects of Cistercian sheep-farming in England and Wales'. *Cîteaux in de Nederlande*, xiii (1962), 296–310.

See Donkin on disposal of wool (No. 5411).

4994   DONNELLY (JAMES S.). 'Changes in the grange economy of English and Welsh Cistercian abbeys, 1300–1540'. *Traditio*, x (1954), 399–458.

See R. A. Donkin, 'The Cistercian grange in England in the twelfth and thirteenth centuries, with special reference to Yorkshire', *Studia Monastica* (Barcelona), vi (1964), 95–144.

4995   DYER (CHRISTOPHER). 'Population and agriculture on a Warwick-shire manor in the later middle ages'. *Univ. Birmingham Hist. Jour.* ii (1968), 113–27.

4996   ERNLE (LORD). See Prothero (No. 5013).

4997   FISHER (JOHN L.). A medieval farming glossary of Latin and English words, taken mainly from Essex records. Lond. 1968.

4998 FUSSELL (GEORGE E.). Farming technique from pre-historic to modern times. Oxf. 1966.

Idem, 'Social change but static technology: rural England in the fourteenth century', *History Studies* (Oxford), i (1968), 23–32.

4999 GRAY (HOWARD L.). English field systems. Harvard Historical Series. no. 22. Cambr. (Mass.). 1915.

See Orwin, *The open fields* (No. 5007); Joan Thirsk, 'The common fields', *Past and Present*, xxix (1964), 3–25. J. Z. Titow, 'Medieval England and the open field system', ibid. xxxii (1965), 86–102; Joan Thirsk, 'The origin of the open fields', ibid. xxxiii (1966), 412–17; J. L. G. Mowat, ed. *Sixteen old maps of properties in Oxfordshire in the possession of the colleges of Oxford, illustrating the open field system* (Oxf. 1888).
On field systems in Kent, see Alan R. H. Baker in *Archaeologia Cantiana*, lxxviii (1963), 96–118, and lxxx (1965), 152–74. D. Roden and A. R. H. Baker, 'Field systems of the Chiltern Hills and parts of Kent from the late thirteenth to the early seventeenth century', *Inst. British Geographers Trans. and Papers*, xxxviii (1966), 73–88. A. R. H. Baker, 'Some terminological problems in studies of British field systems', *Agricultural Hist. Rev.* xvii (1969), 136–40. Idem, 'Field systems in the Vale of Holmesdale', ibid. xiv (1966), 1–24. See also *Vinogradoff papers* (No. 1501).

5000 HALCROW (E. M.). 'The decline of demesne farming in the estates of Durham Cathedral Priory'. *Econ. H.R.* 2nd Ser. vii (1954–5), 345–56.

5001 HILTON (RODNEY H.). 'A study in the prehistory of English enclosure in the fifteenth century'. *Stud. in onore di A. Sapori*, pp. 673–85.

5002 HOSKINS (WILLIAM G.), ed. The making of the English landscape (No. 617).

Idem, 'Sheep farming in Saxon and medieval England', in Hoskins, *Provincial England; essays in social and economic history* (Lond. 1964), pp. 1–14.

5003 LUCAS (HENRY S.). 'The great European famine of 1315, 1316 and 1317.' *Speculum*, v (1930), 343–77. Reprinted in *Essays in Economic History* (No. 1468).

5004 MOORE (J. S.). 'The Domesday teamland: a reconsideration'. *T.R.H.S.* 5th Ser. xiv (1964), 109–30.

Cf. R. W. Finn, 'The teamland of the Domesday inquest'. *E.H.R.* lxxxiii (1968), 95–101.

5005 MOORE (STUART A.). A short history of the rights of common upon the forest of Dartmoor and the commons of Devon. Report of S. A. Moore to the Committee, and an appendix of documents. Dartmoor Preservation Asso. Plymouth. 1890.

5006 ORWIN (CHARLES S.). History of English farming. Lond. 1949.

5007 ORWIN (CHARLES S. and CHRISTABEL S.). The open fields. Oxf. 1938. 3rd edn. by Joan Thirsk. 1967.

A seminal work based on the open fields of Laxton, Notts. The introduction of the third edition includes a survey of recent studies; on this see J. Thirsk and J. Titow in *Past and Present*, 1964–6 (No. 4999 above).

5008 PAGE (FRANCES M.). 'Bidentes Hoylandie' (a medieval sheep-farm). *Econ. Hist.* i (1929), 603–13.

5009 PARAIN (CHARLES). 'The evolution of agricultural technique'. *Cambr. Econ. Hist.* i (1966 edn.), 125–79.

5010 PAYNE (FRANCIS G.). 'The British plough: some stages in its development'. *Agricultural Hist. Rev.* v (1957), 74–84.

See also John B. Passmore, *The English plough*. Reading Univ. Stud. (Lond. 1930).

5011 PLATT (COLIN). The monastic grange in medieval England: a reassessment. Lond. 1969.

Fundamentally a study of the buildings and investment of the grange, particularly the Cistercian grange in Yorkshire. See J. S. Donnelly, No. 4994.

5012 POSTAN (MICHAEL M.). 'Village livestock in the thirteenth century'. *Econ. H.R.* 2nd Ser. xv (1962), 219–49. Idem, 'Investment in medieval agriculture'. *Jour. Econ. Hist.* xxvii (1967), 576–87.

5013 PROTHERO (ROWLAND E. Baron Ernle). English farming, past and present. Lond. 1912. Reissued, 1917, 1922, 1927. 5th edn. by A. D. Hall, 1936. 6th edn. with introduction by G. E. Fussell and O. R. McGregor, 1961.

5014 RICHARDSON (HENRY G.). 'The medieval plough-team'. *History*, New Ser. xxvi (1942), 287–96.

Cf. Reginald V. Lennard, 'The composition of demesne plough-teams in twelfth century England', *E.H.R.* lxxv (1960), 193–207; and his 'Domesday plough-teams, the southwestern evidence', *E.H.R.* lxxx (1965), 217–33.

5015 SCOTT (RICHARD A.). 'Medieval agriculture'. *V.C.H. Wiltshire*, iv (1959), 7–42.

5016 SCRUTTON (THOMAS E.). Commons and common fields, or the history of the laws relating to commons. Cambr. 1887.

5017 SLICHER VAN BATH (BERNARD H.). The agrarian history of western Europe, A.D. 500–1850. Trans. by Olive Ordish. Lond. 1963. Idem, Yield ratios (of cereal crops), 810–1820. Wageningen. 1963.

Sometimes catalogued under 'Bath'.

5017A SMITH (REGINALD A. L.). 'The Benedictine contribution to mediaeval English agriculture' (No. 1494).

5018 TATE (WILLIAM E.). The enclosure movement. N.Y. 1967.

Summary treatment from Statute of Merton of 1235 to the general enclosure acts of 1836 and 1945. See Harriett Bradley, *The enclosure in England: an economic reconstruction.* Columbia Univ. Stud. in Hist. lxxx (1918). *

5019 TROW-SMITH (ROBERT). A history of the British livestock husbandry. 2 vols. Lond. 1957–9.

Sometimes catalogued as Smith (Robert Trow). Vol. i to 1700; vol. ii, 1700–1900.

5020 WAITES (BRYAN). Moorland and vale-land farming in north-east Yorkshire: the monastic contribution in the 13th and 14th centuries. Borthwick Papers, no. 32. York. 1967. Idem, 'Aspects of thirteenth and fourteenth century arable farming on the Yorkshire wolds'. *Yorks. Archaeol. Jour.* xlii

(1968), 136–42. Idem, 'The monastic grange as a factor in the settlement of north-east Yorkshire'. Ibid. xl (1962), 627–56.

5021 WRETTS-SMITH (MILDRED). 'Organization of farming at Croyland abbey, 1257–1321'. *Jour. Econ. and Business Hist.* iv (1931), 168–92.

> Based on accounts of Croyland Abbey (Lincs.) in the possession of Queens' College, Cambridge.

XX. URBAN SOCIETY

A. URBAN RECORDS

For charters of boroughs, see H. W. C. Davis *et al., Regesta* (No. 3779), R. C. Hoare, *Wiltshire* and other older county histories, such as J. P. Earwaker, *East Cheshire*.

For general histories of boroughs, see Lobel (No. 1386), Maitland (No. 1387), Stephenson (No. 1389), and Tait (No. 1390), Tait's work presents the generally accepted view that the late Saxon borough was mercantile as against Stephenson's contention that it was military in character.

Charles Gross's *A Bibliography of British municipal history* (No. 1511) has served as a standard reference for many decades since its publication in 1897. A full-length supplement for the period from 1897 to the present, edited by Geoffrey H. Martin and Sylvia McIntyre, is now in press. Most of the entries in Gross's original work and in the new supplement are omitted from this chapter. Reference to those bibliographies is recommended. In the selection given below, collections of printed sources are entered in alphabetical order of boroughs and are followed by studies which are primarily modern narratives.

1. Comprehensive Urban Records

5022 BATESON (MARY). 'The laws of Breteuil'. *E.H.R.* xv (1900), 73–8, 302–18, 496–523, 754–7; xvi (1901), 92–110, 332–45.

> A series of papers which show how these laws were adopted as a model by many baronial boroughs in England. In a supplementary paper, 'The creation of boroughs', ibid. xvii (1902), 284–96, Miss Bateson edited charters of Deganwy (Denbighshire), Dunster (Somers.), Higham Ferrers (Northants.), Bolton (Lancs.), Warton (Lancs.), and Roby (Lancs.) in full. The first five of these charters are *temp.* Henry III; that of Roby, 1372. See also A. Ballard, 'The laws of Breteuil', *E.H.R.* xxx (1915), 646–58; and Hemmeon's *Burgage Tenure* (No. 5353).

5023 BRITISH RECORDS ASSOCIATION. Borough charters: Catalogue of an exhibition at the County Hall, Westminster Bridge, 24–25 November 1959.

> A pamphlet which lists charters of some boroughs.

5024 BRITISH BOROUGH CHARTERS, 1042–1216. Ed. by Adolphus Ballard. Cambr. 1913. British Borough Charters, 1216–1307. Ed. by A. Ballard and James Tait. Cambr. 1923. British Borough Charters, 1307–1660. Ed. by Martin Weinbaum. Cambr. 1943.

> See Davis, 'An Oxford charter' (No. 5235). M. Weinbaum, *The incorporation of boroughs* (Manchester, 1937).

5025 BOROUGH CUSTOMS. Ed. by Mary Bateson. 2 vols. Selden Soc. xviii (1904); xxi (1906).

Deals in exemplary fashion and important introductions with the customary laws of boroughs. There is a valuable list of borough custumals, as of the date of publication, in vol. i, pp. xviii–lvi.

5026 MADOX (THOMAS). Firma burgi, or an historical essay concerning the cities and boroughs of England. Lond. 1726.

Contains many extracts from the pipe rolls and other public records, mainly of the thirteenth and fourteenth centuries.

5027 PENSON (EVA). 'Charters to some western boroughs in 1256'. *E.H.R.* xxxv (1920), 558–64.

Concerned with Hereford, Shrewsbury, Gloucester, Bridgnorth, and Worcester.

2. Urban Records by County

BEDFORDSHIRE

5028 SCHEDULE OF THE RECORDS OF THE CORPORATION OF BEDFORD. Bedford. 1883.

5029 EARLY RECORDS OF TURVEY AND ITS NEIGHBOURHOOD. Ed. by G. H. Fowler. Beds. Hist. Rec. Soc. Pubns. xi (1925).

The Drayton charters 1138–1403.

5030 AUSTIN (WILLIAM). The history of Luton and its hamlets. 2 vols. Newport. 1928.

BERKSHIRE

For Reading, see *Historic towns* (No. 1386), vol. i; and for Windsor, ibid. vol. ii.

5031 READING RECORDS: Diary of the corporation, 1431–1654. Ed. by J. M. Guilding. 4 vols. Lond. etc. 1892–96.

Minutes of the official proceedings of the mayor and burgesses; the medieval material is in vol. i.

5032 HEDGES (JOHN K.). The history of Wallingford from the invasion of Caesar to the present time. 2 vols. Lond. 1881.

5033 TIGHE (ROBERT R.). and DAVIS (JAMES E.). Annals of Windsor: a history of the castle and town. 2 vols. London. 1858.

BUCKINGHAMSHIRE

5034 CHARTERS AND GRANTS TO THE BOROUGH OF CHEPPING WYCOMBE, IN THE COUNTY OF BUCKINGHAM (5 John–4 Eliz). Wycombe. 1817.

Translation only.

5035 THE FIRST LEDGER BOOK OF HIGH WYCOMBE. Ed. by Robert W. Greaves. Bucks. Record Soc. xi (1956).

It was begun in 1475, but copied some earlier records back to Edward I; however, the bulk is post-medieval.

5036 PARKER (JOHN). The early history and antiquities of Wycombe. Wycombe. 1878.

CAMBRIDGESHIRE

V.C.H. Cambridgeshire, iii, for the city and university of Cambridge; and *Historic towns* (No. 1386), vol. ii.

5037 CAMBRIDGE BOROUGH DOCUMENTS. Ed. by William M. Palmer. Cambr. 1931.

5038 CAMBRIDGE GILD RECORDS (1298–1389). Ed. by Mary Bateson. Cambr. Antiq. Soc. Pubns. xxxix (1903).

5039 CHARTERS OF THE BOROUGH OF CAMBRIDGE (Hen. I–1685 with a translation). Ed. by Frederic W. Maitland and Mary Bateson. Cambr. 1901.

5040 COOPER (CHARLES H.). Annals of (the borough of) Cambridge. 5 vols. (vol. v. ed. by J. W. Cooper). Cambr. 1842–1908.

5041 CAM (HELEN M.). 'The origin of the borough of Cambridge' (No. 1462).

5042 CLAPHAM (JOHN H.). 'A thirteenth-century market town: Linton, Cambs.' *Cambr. Hist. Jour.* iv (1933), 194–202.

CHESHIRE

5043 CHESTER CUSTOMS ACCOUNTS, 1301–1566. Ed. by K. P. Wilson. Lancs.–Ches. Rec. Soc. Pubns. cxi (1969).

K. P. Wilson, 'The port of Chester in the fifteenth century', *Hist. Soc. Lancs.–Ches. Trans.* cxvii (1966), 1–15.

5044 CHESTER IN THE TWELFTH AND THIRTEENTH CENTURIES. By William F. Irvine. *Archit. Archaeol. and Nat. Hist. Soc. of Chester Jour.* New Ser. x (1904), 13–52.

Translations of seventy-three charters or grants of land, about 1178–1296. See also James Hall, 'Royal charters and grants to the city of Chester', *Chester and North Wales Archaeol. Soc. Jour.* New Ser. xviii (1911), 26–75. For Chester rolls, see 'Rolls of the freemen of the city of Chester (1392–1805)', edited by J. H. E. Bennett. Record Soc. for Lancs. and Ches. (London) li and lv. 2 vols. 1906–8. (Entries for 1392–1485 on pp. 1–9 in vol. li (1906)). See Morris, *Chester* (No. 5047), which contains extracts from town records.

5045 LIBER LUCIANI DE LAUDE CESTRIE, written about 1195 and now in the Bodleian library, Oxford. Ed. by M. V. Taylor. Lancs.–Ches. Rec. Soc. Pubns. lxiv. 1912.

The earliest account of Chester, imbedded in sermons, treatises on saints, nuns, etc.: 'Really but one long sermon disguised as a guide-book'. Appended (pp. 79–103) are printed some obits of abbots and founders of St. Werburgh's abbey, of which Lucian was a monk.

5046 SELECT ROLLS OF THE CHESTER CITY COURTS, LATE THIRTEENTH AND EARLY FOURTEENTH CENTURIES. By Albert W. Hopkins. Chetham Soc. 3rd Ser. ii. 1950.

5047	MORRIS (RUPERT H.). Chester in the Plantagenet and Tudor periods. Chester. 1893.

CUMBERLAND

5048	ROYAL CHARTERS OF THE CITY OF CARLISLE. Ed. by R. S. Ferguson. Cumb.–Westm. Antiq.–Archaeol. Soc. 1894.

Latin charters, with a translation, 21 Edw. I–36 Chas. II.

5049	CHARTERS OF THE BOROUGH OF EGREMONT (thirteenth century). Trans. by the Rev. Canon Knowles. *Cumb.–Westm. Antiq.–Archaeol. Soc. Trans.* i (1874), 282–7.

5050	KIRKBY STEPHEN CHURCHWARDENS' ACCOUNTS. Ed. by J. Breay. Ibid. New Ser. liv (1955), 165–83.

5051	CHIPPINDALL (W. H.). History of the township of Ireby. Chetham Soc. xcv. 1935. *

DERBYSHIRE

5052	RECORDS OF THE BOROUGH OF CHESTERFIELD: extracts from the archives of the corporation, etc. Ed. by (J.) Pym Yeatman. Chester-field, etc. 1884.

Valuable, but not well edited.

5053	COX (JOHN CHARLES) and HOPE (W. H. ST.JOHN). The chronicles of the collegiate church of All Saints, Derby. Lond. 1881.

Pp. 157–73: churchwardens' accounts, 1465–1527.

DEVONSHIRE

5054	BARNSTAPLE RECORDS. By John R. Chanter. *North Devon Jour.* 9 January 1879 to 5 May 1881; *North Devon Herald,* 9 January 1879 to 21 April 1881. Reprinted by J. R. Chanter and Thomas Wainwright. 2 vols. Barnstaple. 1900.

A catalogue of town records. See Susan Reynolds, 'The forged charters of Barnstaple', *E.H.R.* lxxxiv (1969), 699–720.

5055	ANGLO-NORMAN CUSTUMAL OF EXETER. Ed. by Jacob W. Schopp and R. C. Easterling. History of Exeter Research Group, no. 2 (1925).

5056	EXETER CITY MUNIMENTS. *Notes and Gleanings of Devon and Cornwall,* vols. ii–v, *passim.* Exeter. 1889–92.

5057	LETTERS AND PAPERS OF JOHN SHILLINGFORD, MAYOR OF EXETER, 1447–50. Ed. by S. A. Moore. Camden Soc. New Ser. ii (1871).

They relate to a suit brought against the city by Edmund Lacy, bishop of Exeter.

5058	BARLOW (FRANK) and others. Exeter and its region. Exeter. 1969.

5059	OLIVER (GEORGE). History of Exeter. Exeter. 1821. New edition by E. Smirke. 1861. Index by J. S. Attwood, 1884.

5060 WILKINSON (BERTIE). The medieval council of Exeter. Hist. Exeter Research Group. No. 4 (1931).

5061 CALENDAR OF THE PLYMOUTH MUNICIPAL RECORDS. By Richard N. Worth. Plymouth. 1893.

5062 PLYMPTON: The borough and its charters (1242–1790). By Joshua B. Rowe. *Devon. Asso. for Advancement of Science, etc. Trans.* xix (1887), 555–648.

See J. B. Rowe, *A history of the borough of Plympton Erle, the castle and manor of Plympton* (Exeter, 1906).

5063 RECORDS OF THE BOROUGH OF SOUTH MOLTON. Ed. by John Cock. Exeter. 1893.

5064 CALENDAR OF THE TAVISTOCK PARISH RECORDS. By R. N. Worth. Plymouth. 1887.

Contains extracts from churchwardens' accounts, 1385–1725; deeds, 1287–1742, etc. Cf. H. P. R. Finberg, 'The Borough of Tavistock: its origins and early history', in *Devonshire studies* (No. 1611); his *Tavistock Abbey* (No. 6126) and his 'The early history of Werrington' (to *c.* 1200), *E.H.R.* lix (1944), 237–51.

DORSET

5065 THE MUNICIPAL RECORDS OF THE BOROUGH OF DOR-CHESTER. Ed. by Charles Herbert Mayo. Exeter. 1908.

Charters, etc. 1305–78.

5066 THE MUNICIPAL RECORDS OF THE BOROUGH OF SHAFTES-BURY. (Half-title: Shastonian records). By C. H. Mayo. Sherborne. 1889.

A calendar of the records, with extracts.

5067 FOWLER (JOSEPH J.). Mediaeval Sherborne, taken from original Sherborne documents. Dorchester. 1951.

Cf. 'Sherborne almshouse building accounts, 1440–1444', *Dorset Notes and Queries,* xxix (1970), 291 ff.

5068 DESCRIPTIVE CATALOGUE OF THE CHARTERS, MINUTE-BOOKS, AND OTHER DOCUMENTS OF THE BOROUGH OF WEYMOUTH AND MELCOMBE REGIS, 1252–1800, with extracts. By Henry J. Moule. Weymouth. 1883.

DURHAM

See W. Hutchinson, *History of Durham* (No. 1625) for 1179 charter by Hugh Puiset; and also the episcopal see of Durham (pp. 768–72).

5069 CHARTERS GRANTED TO THE BURGESSES OF BARNARD CASTLE. G. Allan's Darlington Press, n.d.

5070 DRINKWATER (G. N.). 'Gateshead charters and companies from the twelfth to the seventeenth centuries and later'. *Archaeol. Aeliana,* 4th Ser. xxxvi (1958), 165–206.

ESSEX

5071 CALENDAR OF THE COURT ROLLS OF THE BOROUGH OF COLCHESTER (4 Edw. II–2 Chas. II). By Henry Harrod. Colchester. (1865). Idem, Repertory of the records and evidences of the borough of Colchester. Colchester. (1865). Idem, Report on the records of the borough of Colchester. Colchester. (1865).

5072 CONSTITUTIONS OF THE BURGH OF COLCHESTER (Rich. II–1808). Ed. by Benjamin Strutt. (Colchester). 1822.

See B. Strutt, History and description of Colchester. 2 vols. Lond. 1803.

5073 COURT ROLLS OF THE BOROUGH OF COLCHESTER, 3 vols. Ed. by Isaac H. Jeayes. Colchester. 1921–41.

vol. i: 1310–1352 (1921) with Introduction, etc. by W. Gurney Benham;
vol. ii: 1353–1367 (1938);
vol. iii: 1372–1379 (1941).

5074 THE RED PAPER BOOK OF COLCHESTER. Ed. by William Gurney Benham. Colchester. 1902.

Ordinances, oaths, etc. Thirteenth–sixteenth centuries, with a translation. See also W. G. Benham, *The charters and letters patent of Colchester* (Colchester, 1904), 1189–1818, translations only. Also W. G. Benham, ed. *The oath book or red parchment book of Colchester* (1327–1564, with a translation) (Colchester, 1907).

5075 MORANT (PHILIP). History and antiquities of . . . Colchester. 3 pts. Lond. 1748.

See [J. H. Round], *History and antiquities of Colchester Castle* (Colchester, 1882).

GLOUCESTER

For Gloucester, see *Historic towns* (No. 1386), vol. i; and for Bristol, ibid., vol. ii.

5076 ANCIENT BRISTOL DOCUMENTS. *Clifton Antiq. Club Procs.* (Exeter).

Scattered throughout the Procs. is a series of ancient Bristol documents; e.g. in vol. v for 1901–3, documents 16–20: five deeds 1370–1408; in vol. vi for 1904–8 (1908), 21: A deed of A.D. 1364; 22: a dispute over a wall in Bristol (1482).

5077 BRISTOL CHARTERS, 1155–1373. Ed. by N. Dermott Harding. Bristol Rec. Soc. Pubns. i (1930). BRISTOL CHARTERS 1378–1499. Ed. by Henry A. Cronne. Ibid. xi (1946).

5078 BRISTOL TOWN DUTIES (customs, tolls, etc.): a collection of documents. Ed. by Henry Bush. Bristol. 1828.

Most of the documents are of the fourteenth, fifteenth, and sixteenth centuries.

5079 CALENDAR OF DEEDS, CHIEFLY RELATING TO BRISTOL (circa 1207–1701). Collected by George W. Braikenridge and edited by Francis B. Bickley. Edin. 1899.

5080 CHARTERS AND LETTERS PATENT GRANTED BY THE KINGS OF ENGLAND TO THE CITY OF BRISTOL. Ed. by Samuel Seyer. Bristol. 1812.

Latin, with a translation. See also John Latimer's *Calendar of the charters* (Bristol, 1909).

5081 THE GREAT RED BOOK OF BRISTOL. Ed. by Edward W. W. Veale. Bristol Rec. Soc. Pubns. 5 vols. 1932–53.

Vol. ii (1932): Introduction, Burgage tenure in mediaeval Bristol. Includes calendar of Bristol feet of fines and of Bristol deeds for thirteenth and fourteenth centuries. Vols. iv (1933), viii (1938), xvi (1951), xviii (1953): Text. See Mullins, *Texts*, p. 332.

5082 LITTLE RED BOOK OF BRISTOL. Ed. by Francis B. Bickley. 2 vols. Bristol, etc. 1900.

Contains town charters, ordinances of the common council, ordinances of trade gilds, etc. fourteenth and fifteenth centuries. Vol. i, pp. 57–85, *Lex Mercatoria*, a valuable treatise on the law merchant, composed about 1300. See Lucy T. Smith, *E.H.R.* xvii (1902), 356; Paul R. Teetor, 'England's earliest treatise on the law merchant: the essay on the *Lex Mercatoria* from the Little Red Book of Bristol', *Amer. Jour. Legal Hist.* vi (1962), 178–210.

5083 MAIRE (THE) OF BRISTOWE IS KALENDAR. By Robert Ricart. Ed. by Lucy T. Smith. Camden Soc. New Ser. v. (1872).

Ricart was elected town clerk of Bristol in 1479, and held the office at least twenty-seven years. The first three parts of the Kalendar contain brief historical notes concerning England and Bristol: the other three parts contain local customs and laws. Extracts are also printed in Smith's *English Gilds* (No. 5369), pp. 413–31. See John Latimer, 'The Maire of Bristowe is kalendar, its list of civic officers collated with contemporary legal MSS.' *Bristol–Glos. Archaeol. Soc. Trans.* xv (1891), 139–82, 254–96.

5084 THE OVERSEAS TRADE OF BRISTOL IN THE LATER MIDDLE AGES. Selected and edited by Eleanora M. Carus-Wilson. Bristol Rec. Soc. Pubns. vii (1937). *

Miscellaneous records 1291–1484, customs accounts, etc. described in Mullins, *Texts*, pp. 332–3.

5085 SOME ACCOUNT OF THE ANCIENT FRATERNITY OF MERCHANT TAILORS OF BRISTOL, WITH TRANSCRIPT OR ORDINANCES AND OTHER DOCUMENTS (1392–1832). By F. F. Fox. Bristol. 1880.

See also John Latimer, *Merchant venturers* (No. 5379).

5086 THE CHURCH BOOK OF ST. EWEN'S, BRISTOL, 1454–1584 Ed. by B. R. Masters and E. Ralph. Bristol–Glos. Archaeol. Soc. Record Section vi (1967).

5087 WAY (LEWIS J. V.). 'The early charters of Saint Nicholas church, Bristol (*c.* 1180–1380)'. *Bristol–Glos. Archaeol Soc. Trans.* xliv (1923), 121–144.

5088 NICHOLLS (JAMES F.) and TAYLOR (JOHN). Bristol, past and present. 3 vols. Bristol. 1881–2.

5089 SHERBORNE (JAMES W.). The port of Bristol in the middle ages . . .
Bristol Univ. 1965.

  A local history pamphlet of the Bristol branch of the Historical Association.

5090 CALENDAR OF RECORDS OF THE CORPORATION OF
GLOUCESTER. By William H. Stevenson. Gloucester. 1893.

  Pp. 3–69, Abstract of royal charters and letters, 1155–1672;
  Pp. 70–454, Abstract of local deeds and charters, 1175–1667;
  Pp. 455–66, Rolls, council books, etc, 1272 to nineteenth century.

5091 RENTAL OF ALL THE HOUSES IN GLOUCESTER, A.D. 1455,
from a roll in the possession of the corporation of Gloucester. Compiled by
Robert Cole; and edited, with a translation, by W. H. Stevenson. Gloucester.
1890.

  Well edited, this rental was compiled to facilitate the collection of the landgavel.

5092 FINBERG (HERBERT P. R.). 'The geneses of Gloucestershire towns',
in *Gloucestershire Studies* (No. 1651).

5093 FULLBROOK-LEGGATT (LAWRENCE E. W.). Anglo-Saxon and
medieval Gloucester. Gloucester. 1952.

  Sometimes catalogued as LEGGATT (L. E. W. F.).

5094 FULLER (ERNEST A.). 'Cirencester: manor and town.' *Bristol–Glos.
Archaeol. Soc. Trans.* ix (1885), 298–344.

  For other interesting papers by the same writer on Medieval Cirencester, on the gild
  merchant in Cirencester, see ibid. xviii (1893–4), 32–74, 175–6; 'Cirencester documents',
  xx (1895–7), 114–26; and on customary tenants (No. 4757).

Hampshire

5095 ARCHIVES OF ANDOVER. Ed. by Charles Collier and R. H. Clutterbuck. 2 pts. Andover. n.d. (1885?).

  Pt. i: Churchwardens' accounts, 1470; pt. ii: charters and grants.

5096 BAIGENT (FRANCIS J.) and MILLARD (JAMES E.). A history of
the town and manor of Basingstoke. Basingstoke, etc. 1889.

  Pp. 247–356: Selections from the court rolls, 1390–1588.

5097 EXTRACTS FROM RECORDS IN THE POSSESSION OF THE
MUNICIPAL CORPORATION OF THE BOROUGH OF PORTSMOUTH.
By Richard J. Murrell and Robert East. Portsmouth. 1884. New edition by
Robert East. 1891.

5098 ANCIENT ORDINANCES OF THE GILD MERCHANT OF
SOUTHAMPTON. Ed. by Edward Smirke. *Archaeol. Jour.* xvi (1859), 283–96,
343–52.

  The fourteenth-century ordinances are also printed in Davies (No. 5103), and in Gross,
  Gild merchant (No. 1385).

5099 BLACK BOOK OF SOUTHAMPTON (*c.* 1388–1620). Ed. with translation by Annie B. Wallis Chapman. 3 vols. Southampton Rec. Soc. Pubns. 1912–15.

5100 BOOK OF REMEMBRANCE OF SOUTHAMPTON (1303–1620). Ed. by Harry W. Gidden. 3 vols. Southampton Rec. Soc. Pubns. 1927–30.

5101 BROKAGE BOOK OF SOUTHAMPTON, from 1439–40. Ed. by Barbara D. M. Bunyard. Southampton Rec. Soc. Pubns. vol. i: 1439–40 (1941). BROKAGE BOOK, 1443–44. 2 vols. Ed. by Olive Coleman. Southampton Rec. Ser. (1960–1).

See O. Coleman, 'Trade and prosperity in the fifteenth century: some aspects of the trade of Southampton', *Econ. H.R.* 2nd Ser. xvi (1963–4), 9–24.

5102 CHARTERS OF THE BOROUGH OF SOUTHAMPTON (1199–1836). Ed. with translation by Harry W. Gidden. 2 vols. Southampton Rec. Soc. Pubns. 1909–10.

Vol. i: 1199–1480; vol. ii: 1484–1836.

5103 DAVIES (JOHN S.). A history of Southampton. Southampton, etc. 1883.

5104 HEARNSHAW (FOSSEY J. C.). Leet jurisdiction in England: illustrated by records of the court leet of Southampton. Southampton Rec. Soc. Pubns. 1908.

5105 LETTERS OF THE FIFTEENTH AND SIXTEENTH CENTURIES FROM THE ARCHIVES OF SOUTHAMPTON. Ed. by Roger C. Anderson. Southampton Rec. Soc. Pubns. 1921.

5106 LOCAL PORT BOOK OF SOUTHAMPTON, 1439–40. Ed. by Henry S. Cobb. Southampton Rec. Ser. 1961.

5107 OAK BOOK OF SOUTHAMPTON, of *c.* A.D. 1300. Ed. with translation by Paul Studer. 3 vols. Southampton Rec. Soc. Pubns. 1910–11.

Vol. i: Anglo-French ordinances of the ancient gild merchant of Southampton.
Vol. ii: Customs, 1300; a fourteenth-century version of the Rolls of Oleron; etc.
Vol. iii: Notes on the Anglo-French dialect of Southampton in the fourteenth century; with glossary.

5108 PORT BOOKS OF SOUTHAMPTON, 1427–30. Ed. with translation by Paul Studer, Southampton Rec. Soc. Pubns. 1913.

Accounts in Anglo-French.

5109 PORT BOOKS OR LOCAL CUSTOMS ACCOUNTS OF SOUTHAMPTON FOR THE REIGN OF EDWARD IV. Ed. by David B. Quinn and Alwyn A. Ruddock. 2 vols. Southampton Rec. Soc. Pubns. 1937–8.

Tables on Southampton trade and on Italian ships: and a list of custom accounts for Mediterranean trade.

5110 RUDDOCK (ALWYN A.). Italian merchants and shipping in Southampton, 1270–1600. Southampton Rec. Ser. 1951.

5111 STEWARDS' BOOKS OF SOUTHAMPTON, from 1428 (to 1439).
Ed. by Harry W. Gidden. 2 vols. Southampton Rec. Soc. Pubns. 1935–9.

5112 BIRD (WILLIAM H. B.). The black book of Winchester. Winchester.
1925.

Some records, not in chronological order, of the city assemblies from 1266 to 1546.

5113 FURLEY (JOHN S.). The city government of Winchester from the
records of the xivth and xvth centuries. Oxf. 1923.

In appendix prints a bailiff's account of 1354–5 and 'The usages of the City'; for the
latter, see J. S. Furley, ed. *The ancient usages of the city of Winchester* (c. 1275), from the
Anglo-French version preserved in Winchester College, with glossary by E. W. Patchett
(Oxf. 1927).

5114 GALBRAITH (VIVIAN H.). 'Royal charters to Winchester'. *E.H.R.*
xxxv (1920), 382–400.

5115 KITCHIN (GEORGE W.). ed. A charter of Edward the third confirming
and enlarging the privileges of St. Giles fair, Winchester, A.D. 1349. Winchester
Cathedral Records, No. 2. 1886.

HEREFORD
For Hereford, see *Historic towns* (No. 1386), vol. i.

5116 HEREFORD MUNICIPAL RECORDS AND CUSTOMS OF
HEREFORD. Ed. by W. H. Black and G. M. Hills. *British Archaeol. Asso.
Jour.* xxvii (1871), 453–88.

The 'customs' are municipal regulations, based on older records (of Edw. I, etc.),
written out and renewed in 1486. Extracts will be found in the works of Duncomb and
Johnson (Nos. 1670, 5117,) and in *Record of Caernarvon* (No. 4943A).

5117 JOHNSON (RICHARD). The ancient customs of the city of Hereford,
with translations of charters; also some account of the trades of the city. Lond.
1868. 2nd edn. 1882.

HUNTINGDONSHIRE
5118 COLLECTION OF ANCIENT RECORDS RELATING TO THE
BOROUGH OF HUNTINGDON. By Edward Griffith. Lond. 1827.

Comprises translations of extracts from the public records and the town archives,
Wm. I–Wm. III.

KENT
See Cinque Ports (pp. 729–30)

5119 THE EARLIEST CANTERBURY FREEMEN'S ROLLS, 12 9–
1363. By Sylvia L. Thrupp and Harold B. Johnson. In *Kent Records* (No. 4784),
pp. 173–213.

Lists the names of newly admitted freemen, and the methods of admission. 'It is to be
noted that the names of Canterbury freemen admitted between 1392 and 1500 were
printed by Joseph Meadows Cowper in a private edition limited to 50 copies in 1903'
(p. 173 note i).

5120 MINUTES, COLLECTED FROM THE ANCIENT RECORDS AND ACCOUNTS IN THE CHAMBER OF CANTERBURY, OF TRANSACTIONS IN THAT CITY. Ed. by Civis. (Canterbury. 1801–2).

A valuable collection of extracts from the city muniments, from 1234 onward, seemingly compiled by C. R. Bunce.

5121 TRANSLATION OF THE CHARTERS, ETC. GRANTED TO THE CITIZENS OF CANTERBURY (Edw. IV–Chas. II). By a citizen (C. R. Bunce). Canterbury. 1791.

5122 PLOMER (HENRY R.). Short accounts of the records of Canterbury. Canterbury. 1892.

5123 SOMNER (WILLIAM). Antiquities of Canterbury. Canterbury. 1640. 2nd ed. 2 pts. 1703.

The most elaborate history of Canterbury.

5124 URRY (WILLIAM J.). Canterbury under the Angevin kings. Lond. 1966; N.Y. 1967.

Based on the rentals of Canterbury property of the monks of Christ Church.

5125 COLLECTION OR ABSTRACT OF LEGAL DOCUMENTS RELATING TO THE CHURCH AND POOR OF THE PARISH OF DARTFORD (1284–1799). Ed. by John Langdale. Lond. 1829.

Most of the documents are later than the fifteenth century.

LANCASHIRE

5126 ANCIENT CHARTERS AND OTHER MUNIMENTS OF THE BOROUGH OF CLITHERO (*c.* 1283–1674, with a translation). Ed. by John Harland. Manchester. 1851.

On these charters, see also *British Archaeol. Asso. Jour.* vi (1851), 425–37. See also Mamecestre (No. 4791).

5127 MATERIALS FOR THE HISTORY OF LANCASTER. By William O. Roper. 2 pts. Chetham Soc. New Ser. lxi–lxii. (1907).

Contains town charters from 1193; and the 'old constitutions' of the town, 36 Edw. III.

5128 CITY OF LIVERPOOL: selections from the municipal archives and records, from the thirteenth to the seventeenth century inclusive. Ed. by James A. Picton. 2 vols. Liverpool. 1883–6.

Picton, 'Notes on the charters of the borough of Liverpool', *Historic Soc. of Lancs. and Ches. Trans.* xxxvi (1887), 53–128. Ramsay Muir and E. M. Platt, *A history of municipal government in Liverpool to 1835.* 2 pts. in one volume (Lond. 1906).

5129 TAIT (JAMES). Mediaeval Manchester and the beginnings of Lancashire. Manchester. 1904.

Contains the parallel charters of Salford, Stockport, and Manchester.

5130 CHARTERS GRANTED TO THE BURGESSES OF PRESTON (Hen. III–Eliz. with a translation). Ed. by John Lingard. Preston. 1821.

5131 EXTRACTS FROM ANCIENT DOCUMENTS IN THE ARCHIVES OF PRESTON (Ed. by John Addison. Preston. 1842).

Contains a facsimile of the charter of King John; an undated custumal of Preston; extracts from the records of the gild merchant, 1397; etc. See also W. A. Abram, ed. 'The rolls of burgesses of the guilds merchant of the borough of Preston, 1397–1682', Lancs.–Ches. Rec. Soc. ix (1884).

5132 RECORDS OF THE PARISH CHURCH OF PRESTON IN AMOUNDERNESS. By Tom C. Smith. Preston. 1892.

5133 CHARTERS OF THE BOROUGH OF WIGAN, in Latin and English. Warrington. 1808.

LEICESTERSHIRE

5134 SKILLINGTON (STEPHEN H.). 'Medieval Cossington'. *Leics. Archaeol. Soc. Trans.* xviii (1934–5), 203–48; xix (1936–7), 1–26, 275–92.

A narrative based on the researches of George Francis Farnham.

5135 CHARTERS OF THE BOROUGH OF LEICESTER. Ed. by John Nichols. *Bibliotheca Topographica Britannica* (No. 1505), viii (1790), 931–68, 1347–8.

A valuable collection of town charters, John–Chas. II.

5136 INDEX TO THE ANCIENT MANUSCRIPTS OF THE BOROUGH OF LEICESTER. By John C. Jeaffreson. Westminster. 1878.

Several charters granted to Leicester in the thirteenth century are printed in full in this index.

5137 RECORDS OF THE BOROUGH OF LEICESTER, 1103–1603. Ed. by Mary Bateson. 3 vols. Cambr. etc. 1899–1905.

Contains town charters, rolls of the gild merchant, mayors' accounts, tallage rolls, court rolls, coroners' rolls, etc. Admirably edited, with a translation and a valuable introduction on the municipal history of Leicester. Vol. i: 1103–1327; vol. ii: 1327–1509; vol. iii: 1509–1603.

5138 RECORDS OF THE CORPORATION OF LEICESTER. Published by the Department of Archives of Leicester. 1956.

A catalogue of charts, court records, gild records, etc., from the earliest period to 1835.

5139 REGISTER OF THE FREEMEN OF LEICESTER, 1196–1930. Abstracted from the borough records by Henry Hartopp. 2 vols. Leicester. 1927–33.

Vol. i: 1196–1770.

5140 THE CITY OF LEICESTER. *Victoria County History of Leicestershire.* Ed. by R. A. McKinley. Vol. iv, pp. 1–54.

5141 HARTOPP (HENRY), ed. Roll of the mayors of the borough and lord mayors of the city of Leicester, 1209 to 1935. Leicester. 1936.

5142 THOMPSON (JAMES). The history of Leicester, to the end of the seventeenth century. Leicester, etc. 1849.

5143 MARKET HARBOROUGH PARISH RECORDS TO 1530. By John E. Stocks and W. B. Bragg. Lond. 1890.

W. G. Hoskins, 'The origin and rise of Market Harborough,' *Leics. Archaeol. Soc. Trans.* xxv (1949), 56–68.

LINCOLNSHIRE

5144. RECORDS OF ANCIENT HORNCASTLE (1086–1328). By William K. Boyd. *Lincolnshire Notes and Queries*, iii (1893), 213–17, 244–7; iv (1895), 16–18, 57–62, 116–20, 185–8, 217–21, 234–8; v (1898), 216–22, 243–50.

Includes translated extracts from Domesday, *Testa de Nevill*, feet of fines, pipe rolls, hundred rolls, etc.; a chancery roll of 1318, a subsidy-roll of 1327–8, etc.

5145 CIVITAS LINCOLNIA; from its municipal and other records. (By John Ross.) Lincoln. 1870.

Pp. 1–53: Abstracts of town charters, Hen. II–Chas. II; and acts of the common council, 1421–1511. See W. de Gray Birch, *The royal charters of the city of Lincoln, Hen. II–Wm. III* (Cambr. 1911).

5146 HILL (JAMES W. F.). Medieval Lincoln. Cambr. 1948. Reprinted, 1965.

One of the best of the histories of English towns.

5147 GILLETT (EDWARD). A history of Grimsby. Lond., N.Y., etc. 1970. (Pp. 1–85 on the medieval period.)

5147A ROGERS (ALAN), ed. The making of Stamford. Leicester. 1965.

LONDON

a. Sources

In addition to the Jones and Smith, *Guide to records* (No. 1728) and the article on the Guildhall Library in *Archives* (No. 1504), a handlist of London records has been compiled by J. M. Sims (No. 5148) under the auspices of the London Record Society. That Society, founded in 1964, had published several volumes by 1971, four of which (Nos. 3579A, 3580, 5201, 6225) are concerned with medieval subjects.

For the general history of London in the Middle Ages, books of first importance are Gwyn Williams, *Medieval London* (No. 5181) and Sylvia Thrupp, *The merchant class in medieval London* (No. 5178). Further, Stenton's *Norman London*, which includes a twelfth-century description of the city (No. 1495), and various studies by Martin Weinbaum (Nos. 5179, 1455, 3579, 3579A), and the introduction to Helen Cam's *Eyre of 1321* (No. 3579) should be consulted. Articles on medieval London are given in the *festschrift* to P. E. Jones, entitled *Studies in London history* (No. 5177). For the numerous studies concerned with London's history, consult the index below under 'London'. An eight-volume history of London is in preparation; volume one will bear the title 'Roman and Dark Age London', volume two the title 'Saxon and Norman London', and volume three the title 'Medieval London'.

5148 LONDON AND MIDDLESEX PUBLISHED RECORDS: A hand-list. Compiled by J. M. Sims. London Rec. Soc. Occasional Paper, no. i (1970).

This handlist is not confined, of course, to medieval records; it gives page references to records printed in books, e.g. by Weinbaum, Tomlins, *et al.* For a general account, see E. J. Davis, 'London and its records', *History*, New Ser. vi (1921–2), 173–82, 240–6.

5149 A BOOK OF LONDON ENGLISH 1384–1425. Ed. by R. W. Chambers and Marjorie Daunt, with an appendix on English documents in the Record Office by M. M. Weale. Oxf. 1931.

5150 BREWER (THOMAS). Memoir of John Carpenter, Town Clerk of London in the reigns of Henry V and VI. Lond. 1836 and 1856. See No. 5161.

5151 CALENDAR OF CORONERS' ROLLS OF THE CITY OF LONDON, 1300–1378. Ed. by Reginald R. Sharpe. Lond. 1914.

5152 CALENDAR OF EARLY MAYORS' COURT ROLLS preserved among the archives of the corporation of the city of London at the Guildhall A.D. 1298–1307. Ed. by Arthur H. Thomas. Cambr. 1924.

5153 A CALENDAR OF THE FEET OF FINES FOR LONDON AND MIDDLESEX. Ed. by William J. Hardy and William Page. 2 vols. Lond. 1892–3.

5154 CALENDAR OF LETTER-BOOKS OF THE CITY OF LONDON. Ed. by Reginald R. Sharpe. Letter-books A–L Edw. I–Hen. VII. 11 vols. Lond. 1899–1912.

They comprise recognizances of debts, civic regulations, coroners' rolls, pleas held before the mayor, etc. Their value is marred by inaccuracies of translation.

5155 CALENDAR OF LETTERS FROM THE MAYOR AND CORPORA-TION OF THE CITY OF LONDON, 1350–70. Ed. by Reginald R. Sharpe. Lond. 1885.

These letters throw light on the intercourse of London with the chief municipalities of Flanders and England.

5156 CALENDAR OF PLEA AND MEMORANDA ROLLS preserved among the archives of the corporation of the city of London at the Guildhall, A.D. 1323–1482. Ed. by Arthur H. Thomas (vols. i–iv); by Philip E. Jones (vols. v–vi). 6 vols. Cambr. 1926–61.

Cf. A. H. Thomas, 'Illustrations of the mediaeval municipal history of London from the Guildhall records', *T.R.H.S.* 4th Ser. iv (1921), 81–102.

5157 EKWALL (EILERT). Two early London subsidy rolls (for 1292 and 1319). Lund. 1951. Cf. Margaret Curtis 'The London lay subsidy of 1332' in Unwin, *Finance and trade* (No. 1469), pp. 35–92; and 'London lay subsidy for 1411–12', edited by J. C. L. Stahlschmidt (No. 3171).

5158 HISTORICAL CHARTERS AND CONSTITUTIONAL DOCU-MENTS OF THE CITY OF LONDON. By Walter de Gray Birch. Revised edition. Lond. 1887. 1st edn. 'by an antiquary', 1884.

Only a translation of the charters is here printed. Other translations are John Evelyn's

Charters of the city of London (Lond. 1745); John Luffman's *Charters of London* (Lond. 1793) and No. 1742.

5159 A LONDON MUNICIPAL COLLECTION OF THE REIGN OF JOHN. By Mary Bateson. *E.H.R.* xvii (1902), 480–511, 707–30.

Important for the early constitutional history of London.

5160 MEMORIALS OF LONDON AND LONDON LIFE, in the XIIIth, XIVth and XVth centuries: being a series of extracts . . . from the . . . archives of the city of London, A.D. 1276–1419. Translated and edited by Henry T. Riley. Lond. 1868.

Contains extracts from the letter-books.

5161 MUNIMENTA GILDHALLAE LONDONIENSIS: Liber albus, Liber custumarum, et Liber Horn. Ed. by H. T. Riley. Rolls Ser. 3 vols. in 4 pts. Lond. 1859–62.

Vol. i: *Liber Albus*, by John Carpenter, 1419. See No. 5150.
Vol. ii (2 pts.): *Liber Custumarum, c.* 1320.
Vol. iii: Translations of the Anglo-Norman passages in *Liber Albus*; glossaries, etc. Liber Horn, 1311, probably compiled by Andrew Horne, not published.

These volumes contain valuable documents illustrating the legal, social, and constitutional history of London, especially during the thirteenth and fourteenth centuries. The *Liber Albus* was translated by H. T. Riley (Lond. 1861). See also N. R. Ker, 'Liber Custumarum and other manuscripts formerly at Guildhall', *Guildhall Miscellany*, i, no. 3 (1954), 37–45.

b. Some secondary works

5162 BAKER (TIMOTHY). Medieval London. N.Y. and Washington. 1970.

A well-illustrated, popular account, strong on topography.

5163 BAYLEY (JOHN). The history and antiquities of the Tower of London. 2 pts. Lond. 1821–25; 2nd edn. 1830.

The record tower, pp. 212–57. See also 'Regulations framed in the reign of Richard II: For the government of the Tower of London'. Ed. by Henry Ellis. *Archaeologia*, xviii (1817), 275–80.

5164 BEAVEN (ALFRED B.). The aldermen of the city of London, *temp.* Henry III–1912. 2 vols. Lond. 1908–13.

A 'practically exhaustive' list of the London aldermen, arranged by wards. See also No. 5192.

5165 BIRD (RUTH). Turbulent London of Richard II. Lond. 1949. See No. 1740.

M. B. Honeybourne, *Sketch map of London under Richard II* (London Topograph. Soc. Pubn. no. 93. Lond. 1960).

5166 CHEW (HELENA M.). 'The office of escheator in the city of London during the middle ages'. *E.H.R.* lviii (1943), 319–30.

5167 EKWALL (EILERT). Studies on the population of medieval London. Stockholm. 1956.

Cf. J. C. Russell, 'Mediaeval Midland and northern migration to London, 1100–1365'

Speculum, xxxiv (1959), 641–5. See also Ekwall, *Early London personal names* (Lund, 1947); and *Street names of the city of London* (Oxf. 1954).

5168 GOMME (GEORGE LAURENCE). The governance of London; studies on the place occupied by London in English institutions. Lond. 1907.

Contends that long after the departure of the main body of the Romans from Britain the constitution of London remained essentially Roman.

5169 KINGSFORD (CHARLES L.). 'Historical notes on mediaeval London houses'. *London Topographical Record*. x (1916) 44–144, xi (1917), 28–81.

'A mine of exact information for the history of London and Westminster'. See also chap. three of Thrupp, *Merchant class* (No. 5178).

5170 MILLS (MABEL H.). 'The London customs house during the middle ages'. *Archaeologia*, lxxxiii (1933), 307–25.

5171 MYERS (ALEX R.). 'The wealth of Richard Lyons'. *Wilkinson essays* (No. 1459), pp. 301–29.

Prints an inventory of Lyons's goods at the time of their seizure on his impeachment in 1376. It comprises 'an inventory of a London merchant's house which lists the contents room by room' as well as 'The contents of his drapery shop and the furnishings of three taverns which he controlled'.

5172 PENDRILL (CHARLES). London life in the 14th century. Lond. 1925. *

Idem, *Wanderings in medieval London* (Lond. 1928) and *Old parish life in London* (Lond. etc. 1937).

5173 PINKS (WILLIAM J.). The history of Clerkenwell. 2nd edn. Lond. 1881.

Also Thomas Cromwell, *History and description of the parish of Clerkenwell*; with . . . engravings by J. and H. S. Storer (Lond. 1828).

5174 PULLING (ALEXANDER). The laws, customs, usages, and regulations of the city and port of London. 2nd edn. Lond. (1854). Earlier editions: A practical treatise on the laws, customs, etc. 1842, 1849.

The edition of 1849, like that of 1854, is called the second.

5175 RICKERT (EDITH). 'Extracts from a fourteenth-century account book'. *Modern Philology*, xxiv (1926–7), 111–19 and 249–56.

Prints some portions of the 1390–5 ledger of Gilbert Maghfeld, ironmonger and merchant. Maghfeld's activities are further discussed in Margery K. James, 'A London merchant of the fourteenth century', *Econ. H.R.* 2nd Ser. viii (1956), 364–76.

5176 ROUND (JOHN HORACE). The commune of London, in his Commune of London and other Studies (No. 4004), chap. xi.

See also ibid. chap. v. (London under Stephen); Round's Geoffrey de Mandeville (No. 4006); and G. B. Adams, 'London and the Commune', in *E.H.R.* xix (1904), 702–6, xxiv (1909), 490–95 (reprinted in his *Origin of the English Constitution* (No. 1211), pp. 355–69).

5177 STUDIES IN LONDON HISTORY, presented to Philip Edmund Jones. Ed. by A. E. J. Hollaender and William Kellaway. Lond. 1969.

(a) Marjorie B. Honeybourne, The pre-Norman bridge of London. 17–59.

(*b*) N. R. Ker, Books at St. Paul's before 1313. 43–72.
(*c*) William Kellaway, The coroner in medieval London. 75–91.
(*d*) Betty R. Masters, The mayor's household before 1600. 95–114.
(*e*) Martin Weinbaum, A fourteenth-century law book of London interest. 117–30.
(*f*) Elspeth M. Veale, Craftsmen and the economy of London in the fourteenth century. 133–51.
(*g*) Jean M. Imray, Les bones gentes de la Mercerye de Londres: a study of the membership of the medieval mercers' company. 155–78.
(*h*) Olive Coleman, The collectors of customs in London under Richard II. 181–94.
(*i*) Caroline M. Barron, Richard Whittington: the man behind the myth. 197–248.
(*j*) Sylvia L. Thrupp, Aliens in and around London in the fifteenth century. 251–72.
The subsequent articles, pp. 275–474 deal with post-medieval subjects. Pages 477–9 give a list of writings by P. E. Jones.

**5178	THRUPP (SYLVIA L.). The merchant class of medieval London, 1300–1500. Chicago. 1948. Paperback edn.: 1962.**

An interesting, well-documented study of the economic, social, and political activities of the dominant class in the city. Appendix A gives thumbnail biographies of about 350 members of 'Aldermanic Families'. Appendix B lists 'London landowners in 1436' from an Exchequer Lay Subsidy Roll. Appendix C, 'Geographical Origins and Social Background of Apprentices' lists occupations and place of residence of the fathers of apprentices. See also G. Unwin in *Finance and trade* (No. 1469), and *Unwin papers* (No. 1500).

**5179	WEINBAUM (MARTIN). Verfassungsgeschichte Londons, 1066–1268. *Beihefte zur Vierteljahrschrift für Sozial- und Wirtschaftsgeschichte*, xv. Stuttgart, 1929. Idem, London unter Eduard I. and II.: Verfassungs- und Wirtschaftsgeschichtliche Studien. 2 vols. Stuttgart. 1933.**

Vol. ii of *London unter Eduard I und II* is devoted to the texts of important records. See also idem, 'Londons Aldermänner und Warde im 12–14 Jahrhundert', in *Aus Sozial- und Wirtschaftsgeschichte: Gedächtnisschrift für Georg von Below* (Stuttgart, 1928), pp. 105–14. Cf. Kurt Knoll, *London im Mittelalter: seine wirtschaftliche, politische und kulturelle Bedeutung für das britische Volk* (Vienna, 1932); Henry G. Richardson 'Henry I's charter to London', *E.H.R.* xlii (1927), 80–7; J. S. P. Tatlock, 'The date of Henry I's charter to London', *Speculum*, xi (1936), 461–9; T. F. Tout, 'The beginnings of a modern capital: London and Westminster in the 14th century', *P.B.A.* x (1923), 487–511 and *Collected papers* (No. 1499).

**5180	WILLIAMS (ELIJAH). Early Holborn and the legal quarter of London. 2 vols. Lond. 1927.**

**5181	WILLIAMS (GWYN A.). Medieval London: from commune to capital. Univ. London Hist. Stud. xi. Lond. 1963.**

The best general history of medieval London. For Saxon and Viking London, see Wheeler, No. 2489. F. M. Stenton, 'Norman London', Nos. 1495, and 1496. A. H. Thomas 'Notes on the history of the Leadenhall, 1195–1488', *London Topographical Record*, xiii (1923), 1–22. The latter prints for the first time two letters of 1393 written by the famous condottiere Sir John Hawkwood and points out that they are 'the earliest known private letters extant in the English language'.

c. London gilds and companies

**5182	CITY OF LONDON LIVERY COMPANIES' COMMISSION. Report and appendix. *Parl. Papers*. 1884. vol. xxxix. 5 pts. Lond. 1884.**

See also the report of 1837 (No. 965).

5183 HERBERT (WILLIAM). The history of the twelve great livery companies of London. 2 vols. Lond. 1836–7. *

Still useful as a general history of the great companies, but Unwin's work is the best.

5184 KAHL (WILLIAM F.). The development of the London livery companies: an historical essay and a select bibliography. Kress Library Pubn. no. 15. Boston (Mass.). 1960.

5185 KELLETT (J. R.). 'The breakdown of gild and corporation control over the handicraft and retail trade in London'. *Econ. H.R.* 2nd Ser. x (1958), 381–94.

5186 UNWIN (GEORGE). The gilds and companies of London. Lond. 1908; * revised edition by F. J. Fisher. 1936.

See Appendix for bibliography of printed company records and of reliable company histories which contain extracts from records.

5187 ALFORD (B. W. E.) and BARKER (T. C.). A history of the **Carpenters'** Company. Hamden (Conn.). 1969.

See review in *A.H.R.* lxxv (1970), 845–7.

5188 **COOPERS'** COMPANY: HISTORICAL MEMORANDA, CHARTERS, DOCUMENTS, etc. 1396–1848. Ed. by James F. Firth. Lond. 1848.

Sir William Foster, *A short history of the worshipful company of coopers of London* (Cambr. 1944).

5189 JOHNSON (ARTHUR H.). The history of the worshipful company of the **drapers** of London, preceded by an introduction on London and her gilds up to the close of the XVth century. 5 vols. Oxf. 1914–22.

Cf. *Roll of the drapers' company of London.* Ed. by Percival Boyd (Croydon, 1934).

5190 PRIDEAUX (WALTER S.). Memorials of the **goldsmiths'** company: being gleanings from their records between the years 1335 and 1815. (Privately printed) 2 vols. Lond. 1896–7.

W. S. Prideaux, *A list of the wardens, members of the court of assistants and liverymen of the worshipful company of goldsmiths* (Lond. 1936).

5191 HEAL (AMBROSE). The London **goldsmiths,** 1200–1800. . . . Cambr. 1935.

Cf. Thomas F. Reddaway, 'The London goldsmiths *c.* 1500', *T.R.H.S.* 5th Ser. xii (1962), 49–62.

5192 FACSIMILE OF THE FIRST VOLUME OF MS. ARCHIVES OF THE WORSHIPFUL COMPANY OF **GROCERS,** A.D. 1345–1463. Ed. by John A. Kingdon. 2 vols. Lond. 1883–6.

See also S. L. Thrupp, 'The grocers of London, a study of distributive trade', in *Studies in English trade in the fifteenth century* (No. 5393), pp. 247–92, and Joseph A. Rees, *The worshipful company of grocers* (Lond. 1923).

5193 ACTS OF COURT OF THE **MERCERS'** COMPANY, 1453–1527. Ed. by Laetitia Lyell and Frank D. Watney. Cambr. 1936.

See also *Charters, ordinances, and bye-laws of the mercers' company* (1393–1808) (Lond. 1881).

5194 IMRAY (JEAN M.). The charity of Richard Whittington: a history of the trust administered by the **mercers'** company, 1424–1966. Lond. 1968.

5195 CHARTERS OF THE **MERCHANT TAYLORS'** COMPANY (1327–1719). Ed. by Frederick M. Fry and R. T. D. Sayle. Lond. 1937.

The royal letters patent are reproduced in facsimile, with translations and notes.

5196 FACSIMILE OF ANCIENT DEEDS OF THE MERCHANT TAYLORS, 1331–1531. Lond. 1889.

5197 WELCH (CHARLES). History of the worshipful company of **paviors** of the city of London. Lond. 1909.

5198 WELCH (CHARLES). History of the worshipful company of **pewterers** of the city of London, based upon their own records. 2 vols. Lond. 1902.

5199 JONES (PHILIP E.). The worshipful company of **poulters** of the city of London: a short history. Lond. 1939. New edn. 1965.

5200 SHERWELL (JOHN W.). History of the guild of **saddlers** of the city of London. Lond. 1889. 3rd edn. revised by Kenneth S. Laurie. Lond. 1956.

5201 **SCRIVENERS'** COMPANY COMMON PAPER 1357–1628, with a continuation to 1678. Ed. by F. W. Steer. London Rec. Soc. iv (1968).

5202 RECORDS OF THE **SKINNERS** OF LONDON, EDWARD I TO JAMES I. Compiled and ed. by John J. Lambert. Lond. 1933.

5203 BLAGDEN (CYPRIAN). The **stationers'** company: a history 1403–1959. Cambr. (Mass.). 1960.

5204 CONSITT (FRANCES). The London **weavers'** company. Vol. i: From the twelfth century to the close of the sixteenth century. Oxf. 1933.

NORFOLK

5205 REPORT ON THE DEEDS AND RECORDS OF THE BOROUGH OF KING'S LYNN. By Henry Harrod. King's Lynn. 1874.

See No. 3175; and G. H. Dashwood, ed. 'Extracts from the Chamberlain's Book of Accounts, 14 Hen. IV', *Norfolk Archaeology*, ii (1849), 183–92; and Hudson Gurney, ed. 'Extracts from the Hall Books 1430–1731,' *Archaeologia*, xxiv (1832), 317–28. Also *'Calendar of the freemen of Lynn, 1292–1836'* (Norfolk and Norwich Archaeol. Soc. 1913).

5206 CALENDAR OF THE FREEMEN OF NORWICH, 1317–1603. By John L'Estrange. Ed. by Walter Rye. Lond. 1888.

5207 CATALOGUE (Revised) OF THE RECORDS OF THE CITY OF NORWICH. By William Hudson and John C. Tingey. Norwich (1898).

See Records (No. 5211).

5208 EVIDENCES RELATING TO THE TOWN CLOSE ESTATE. Norwich. 1886.

Documents admitted in the case of Stanley v. the mayor, etc., of Norwich. Several of the town charters in full, and copious extracts from public records, leet rolls, assembly rolls, etc., 1086–1886, though badly edited, are valuable.

5209 EXTRACTS FROM CORONERS' ROLLS AND OTHER DOCU-MENTS IN THE RECORD-ROOM OF THE CORPORATION OF NORWICH (Hen. III–Edw. I). By Henry Harrod. *Norfolk Archaeology*, ii (1849), 253–79.

Translation only.

5210 LEET JURISDICTION IN THE CITY OF NORWICH DURING THE THIRTEENTH AND FOURTEENTH CENTURIES. Ed. by William Hudson. Selden Soc. v (1892).

Contains a tithing roll, 1311; inquisitions, 1350; and extracts from leet rolls, 1288–1391, selections from which are printed in Hudson–Tingey, *Records* (No. 5211), i. 357–86. See Kiralfy–Jones (No. 195), pp. 6–7. See also Hearnshaw (No. 5104).

5211 RECORDS OF THE CITY OF NORWICH. Ed. by William Hudson and John C. Tingey. 2 vols. Norwich, etc. 1906–10.

Contains documents relating to the government of the city, *c.* 1086–1695, with a valuable sketch of its municipal development. In vol. ii there is a list of the trades and occupations followed in Norwich during the last half of the thirteenth century. Hudson also edited several rolls of array and 'view of arms', 1355–70, in his paper on 'Norwich militia in the fourteenth century', *Norfolk Archaeology*, xiv (1901), 263–320. See Walter Rye, ed. *A short calendar of deeds relating to Norwich enrolled in the court rolls of that city, 1285–1306.* (Norfolk and Norwich Archaeol. Soc. Norwich, 1903); idem, *Calendar of Norwich deeds . . . 1307–1341.* Ibid. 1915.

5212 RECORDS OF THE GILD OF ST. GEORGE IN NORWICH, 1389–1547. Transcribed by Mary Grace. Norfolk Rec. Soc. ix (1937).

5213 SOME NORFOLK GILD CERTIFICATES (12 Rich. II). Ed. by Walter Rye. *Norfolk Archaeology*, xi (1892), 105–36.

5214 REPERTORY OF DEEDS AND DOCUMENTS RELATING TO THE BOROUGH OF GREAT YARMOUTH. (By Henry Harrod.) Great Yarmouth. 1855.

See *Calendar of freemen of Great Yarmouth, 1429–1800* (Norfolk and Norwich Archaeol. Soc. 1910).

NORTHAMPTONSHIRE

5215 RECORDS OF THE BOROUGH OF NORTHAMPTON. Ed. by Christopher A. Markham and John C. Cox. 2 vols. Northampton, etc. 1898.

Contains, although not well edited, charters and letters patent, 1189–1878; the *Liber Custumarum* (with a translation) compiled about 1460. The *Liber Custumarum* is particularly useful; the earlier portion seems to be a translation from an Anglo-French original of the fourteenth century. It is also edited separately by Markham, with a translation: *The Liber Custumarum of Northampton* (Northampton, 1895). See F. Lee, 'The origins of Northampton', *Archaeol. Jour.* xc (1953), 164–74.

5216 PETERBOROUGH LOCAL ADMINISTRATION. Parochial government before the Reformation. Churchwardens' accounts, 1467–1573, with supplementary documents, 1107–1488. Ed. by William T. Mellows. Northamptonshire Rec. Soc. Pubns. ix (1939).

A wide variety of documents relating to the town. Mellows's other volumes on Peterborough local administration relate to the post-medieval period.

NORTHUMBERLAND

5217   THE CARR MANUSCRIPT, 1432–1634. A cathaloge of all the maiores and sherifs of his maiestye towne and countye of Newcastle upon Tyne . . . (since 1432). Ed. by Charles H. Hunter Blair. *Archaeologia Aeliana*, 4th Ser. xviii (1940), 15–63.

See C. H. H. Blair, 'The mayors and lord mayors of Newcastle-upon-Tyne, 1216–1940; and the sheriffs of the county of Newcastle-upon-Tyne, 1399–1940', *Archaeol. Aeliana*, 4th Ser. xviii (1941).

5218   EARLY DEEDS RELATING TO NEWCASTLE-UPON-TYNE. Ed. by Arthur M. Oliver. Surtees Soc. cxxxvii (1924).

5219   EXTRACTS FROM THE RECORDS OF THE MERCHANT ADVENTURERS OF NEWCASTLE-UPON-TYNE (1480–1898). Ed. by Frederick W. Dendy. 2 vols. Surtees Soc. xciii, ci. 1895, 1899.

5220   THE REGISTER OF FREEMEN OF NEWCASTLE-UPON-TYNE, From the corporation guild and admission books, chiefly of the seventeenth century (Ed. by Madeleine H. Dodds). Newcastle-upon-Tyne Records Committee Pubns. iii (1923).

Begins with 1409.

5221   BRAND (JOHN). History and antiquities of Newcastle-upon-Tyne. 2 vols. Lond. 1789. Index by William Dodd. Newcastle. 1881.

5222   STATUTA GILDAE. Ed. by Cosmo Innes in *Ancient Laws of the Burghs of Scotland* (Edin. 1868), pp. 64–96.

Various enactments made by the gild merchant of Berwick-upon-Tweed, from 1249–1294. See Gross, *Gild merchant* (No. 1385), i, 207–13, 227–40.

NOTTINGHAMSHIRE

For Nottingham, see *Historic towns* (No. 1386), vol. i.

5223   ACCOUNT BOOKS OF THE GILDS OF ST. GEORGE AND OF ST. MARY IN THE CHURCH OF ST. PETER, NOTTINGHAM. Trans. by R. F. B. Hodgkinson, with introduction by L. V. D. Owen. Thoroton Soc. 1939.

Covers 1459–1546.

5224   RECORDS OF THE BOROUGH OF NOTTINGHAM, extracts from the archives of the corporation (1155–1702, with a translation). Ed. by William H. Stevenson. 5 vols. Lond. etc. 1882–1900.

Vol. v of the Records was edited by W. T. Baker. The volumes for later periods are vol. vi by Everard L. Guilford and vol. vii by Duncan Gray and Violet W. Walker. Also D. Gray and V. W. Walker, *Nottingham through 500 years* (Nottingham, 1960).

See also *Royal charters granted to the burgesses of Nottingham, 1155–1712*, edited with a translation by W. H. Stevenson (Lond. etc. 1890).

Oxfordshire

For records of the university and colleges, see 916–19 and for Banbury, see *Historic towns* (No. 1386), vol. i.

5225 BEESLEY (ALFRED). History of Banbury, including copious historical and antiquarian notices of the neighbourhood. Lond. 1841.

5226 THE BURFORD RECORDS. A study in minor town government. By Richard H. Gretton. Oxf. 1920.

5227 HENLEY BOROUGH RECORDS: Assembly books, i–iv, 1395–1543. Ed. by Phyllis M. Briers. Oxfordshire Rec. Soc. Rec. Ser. xli, 1960.

5228 DESCRIPTION OF OXFORD, from the hundred rolls of Oxfordshire, A.D. 1279. Ed. by Rose Graham. Oxf. Hist. Soc. xlvii *Collectanea*, iv (1905), 1–98.

5229 MUNIMENTA CIVITATIS OXONIE. Ed. by Herbert E. Salter. Oxf. Hist. Soc. lxxi, 1920.

From seventeenth-century transcripts, including chamberlain's accounts, 1306–1545.

5230 OXFORD CITY DOCUMENTS, FINANCIAL AND JUDICIAL, 1268–1665. Ed. by James E. Thorold Rogers. Oxf. Hist. Soc. xviii, 1891.

5231 OXFORD MARKET (THE). By Octavius Ogle. Oxf. Hist. Soc. xvi, *Collectanea*, ii, (1890), 1–135.

A collection of extracts from documents relating to the history of the market, 1214–1855.

5232 PARLIAMENTARY PETITIONS RELATING TO (the town of) OXFORD (1379–1496). Ed. by Lucy T. Smith. Oxf. Hist. Soc. xxxii, *Collectanea*, iii (1896), 77–161.

5233 ROUGH LIST OF MANUSCRIPT MATERIALS RELATING TO THE HISTORY OF OXFORD (city and university). By Falconer Madan. Oxf. 1887.

5234 ROYAL LETTERS ADDRESSED TO OXFORD AND NOW EXISTING IN THE CITY ARCHIVES. Ed. by Octavius Ogle. Oxf. 1892.

Contains charters, letters patent, inquisitions, writs, orders in council, and letters from the crown, 1136–1684.

5235 DAVIS (RALPH H. C.). 'An Oxford charter of 1191 and the beginnings of municipal freedom'. *Oxoniensia*, xxxiii (1968), 53–65.

5236 LOBEL (MARY D.). 'Some aspects of the crown's influence on the development of the borough of Oxford up to 1307'. In *Beiträge zur Wirtschafts- und Stadtgeschichte. Festschrift für Hektor Ammann*, ed. by Hermann Aubin *et al.* (Wiesbaden, 1965), pp. 65–83. Idem, 'Some Oxford borough customs' in *Miscellanea mediaevalia in memoriam Jan Frederik Niermeyer* (Groningen, 1967), pp. 187–200.

5237 SALTER (HERBERT E.). Medieval Oxford. Oxf. Hist. Soc. 1936.

The best history of the medieval city, including some documents.

5238　SALTER (HERBERT E.). A survey of Oxford. Ed. by William A. Pantin. Oxf. Hist. Soc. New Ser. xiv, 1960. Vol. ii. Ed. by W. A. Pantin and W. T. Mitchell. Ibid. xx, 1969.

SHROPSHIRE

5239　RECORDS OF THE CORPORATION OF OSWESTRY. Ed. by Stanley Leighton. *Shrops. Archaeol. Soc. Trans.* ii–vii (1879–84). Reprinted, Oswestry. 1884.

Contains town charters, 1262–1835.

5240　BAILIFF'S ACCOUNTS OF SHREWSBURY, 1275–77. Ed. by Charles H. Drinkwater. *Shrops. Archaeol. and Nat. Hist. Soc. Trans.* 2nd Ser. iii (1891), 41–92. SHREWSBURY PAVING AND OTHER ACCOUNTS, 1269–70. Ed. by C. H. Drinkwater. Ibid. 3rd Ser. vii (1907), 193–218.

5241　CALENDAR OF THE MUNIMENTS OF THE BOROUGH OF SHREWSBURY. Shrewsbury. 1896.

5242　EARLY CHRONICLES OF SHREWSBURY, 1372–1603. Ed. by William A. Leighton. Shrewsbury, etc. 1880.

The original is a thick folio volume in MS. (preserved at Shrewsbury), of which the editor has printed only such parts as relate to Shrewsbury and Shropshire.

5243　MERCHANTS' GILD OF SHREWSBURY. By Charles H. Drink-water. *Shrops. Archaeol. and Nat. Hist. Soc. Trans.* 2nd Ser. ii (1890), 29–59; viii (1896), 21–43. (Contains gild rolls of the reigns of John, Hen. III, and Edw. I).

Also C. H. Drinkwater, ed. 'The merchant gild of Shrewsbury: seven rolls of the thirteenth century', ibid. xii (1900), 229–82. Idem, 'Shrewsbury gild merchant rolls of the fourteenth century', ibid. 3rd Ser. i (1901), 119–24; ii (1902), 65–106; iii (1903), 47–98, 351–62; iv (1904). 217–36. Idem, 'Shrewsbury gild merchant rolls of the fourteenth and fifteenth centuries', ibid. v (1905), 35–54, 81–100. The two earliest surviving rolls for 1209–10 and 1219–20 were printed by W. Cunningham, 'The gild merchant of Shrewsbury', *T.R.H.S.* ix (1895), 99–117.

For some records of the cordwainers and drapers of Shrewsbury, 1323–4 and 1461–2, see *Shrops. Archaeol. and Nat. Hist. Soc. Trans.* 2nd Ser. vi (1894), 284–90; viii (1896), 175–90; and Michael Peile, 'Medieval deeds of the Shrewsbury Drapers' Company', ibid. lii (1947–8), 212–35.

5244　TRANSLATION OF THE CHARTERS OF THE CORPORATION OF WENLOCK. (Wenlock). 1820.

5245　WENLOCK. Extracts from the records. By Henry F. Vaughan. *Shrops. Archaeol. and Nat. Hist. Soc. Trans.* 2nd Ser. vi (1894), 223–83.

SOMERSET

5246　MUNICIPAL RECORDS OF BATH, 1189–1604. By A. J. King and B. H. Watts. Lond. (1885).

An account of the charters granted to Bath, etc.

5247　BRIDGWATER BOROUGH ARCHIVES. (1200–1468). Ed. by Thomas Bruce Dilks. 4 vols. Somerset Rec. Soc. xlviii (1933), liii (1938), lviii (1945), lx (1948).

Charters, borough accounts, court rolls, wills, leases, churchwardens' accounts, etc.

See also T. B. Dilks, 'A calendar of some medieval MSS. (*c.* 1200–1484) in the custody of the Bridgwater corporation', Somerset Rec. Soc. lvii *Collectanea*, iii (1942), 25–30.

5248 WELLS CITY CHARTERS. Ed. by Dorothy O. Shilton and Richard Holworthy. Somerset Rec. Soc. xlvi (1932).

'English abstracts of charters and patents, 12th–17th centuries, title deeds, 13th–17th centuries; and lists of freemen, 1377–1600' (Mullins, *Texts*, p. 431).

5249 HUMPHREYS (ARTHUR L.). Materials for the history of the town and parish of Wellington. Lond. 1889. New and enlarged edn. Pts. i–iii. Lond. 1908–13.

Contains manorial court rolls, wills, etc.

STAFFORDSHIRE

5250 ANCIENT CHARTERS RELATING TO THE ABBEY AND TOWN OF BURTON-ON-TRENT. Ed. by William H. Black. *British Archaeol. Asso. Jour.* vii (1852), 421–8.

They relate chiefly to burgage tenements in Burton, *c.* 1200–1349.

5251 THE GILD OF ST. MARY, LICHFIELD, being ordinances of the gild of St. Mary, and other documents. Ed. by Frederick J. Furnivall. E.E.T.S. Extra Ser. cxiv (1920).

Includes Ordinances of 1387; Ordinances of Lynn tailors, 1449; etc. See Harry Thorpe, 'Lichfield: A study of its growth and function', Staffs. Rec. Soc. for 1950–1 (1954), 139–211.

5252 ROYAL CHARTERS AND LETTERS PATENT GRANTED TO THE BURGESSES OF STAFFORD, 1206–1828. Ed. by J. W. Bradley. Stafford, 1897.

Latin text and translation.

5253 TAMWORTH BOROUGH RECORDS. Being a catalogue of civic records with appendices. Ed. by Henry Wood. Tamworth. 1952.

5254 MOSLEY (OSWALD). History of castle, priory and town of Tutbury. Lond. 1832.

5255 CALENDAR OF THE DEEDS AND DOCUMENTS BELONGING TO THE CORPORATION OF WALSALL (John–1688). By Richard Sims. Walsall, etc. 1882.

See 'Churchwarden's accounts of All Saints' Church, Walsall, 1462–1531'. Ed. by Gerald P. Mander. Wm. Salt Archaeol. Soc. *Collections* for 1928 (1930), pp. 173–267.

SUFFOLK

5256 LOBEL (MARY D.). The borough of Bury St. Edmunds: a study in the government and development of a monastic town. Oxf. 1935.

5257 YATES (RICHARD). An illustration of the monastic history of the town and abbey of St. Edmund's Bury. 2 pts. Lond. 1805; 2nd edn. 1843.

See also H. W. C. Davis, 'The Commune of Bury St. Edmunds, 1264', in *E.H.R.* xxiv

(1909), 313–15; and 'The Liberties of Bury St. Edmunds' (with an appendix of records, 1066–1154), ibid. 417–31.

5258 THORNTON (GLADYS A.). 'A study in the history of Clare, Suffolk, with special reference to its development as a borough'. *T.R.H.S.*, 4th Ser. xi (1928), 83–115.

5259 BACON (NATHANIEL). The annals of Ipswich. Ed. by William H. Richardson. Ipswich. 1884.

Contains numerous extracts from the town records.

5260 THE DOMESDAY OF IPSWICH, a collection of municipal ordinances, compiled 19 Edw. I, is printed in the *Black Book of the Admiralty* (No. 4286) vol. ii, 16–207.

See Charles H. E. White, 'The Ipswich Domesday books', *Suffolk Institute of Archaeology Procs.* vi (1888), 195–219; and 1089.

5261 THE EARLY COURT ROLLS OF THE BOROUGH OF IPSWICH. By Geoffrey H. Martin. Univ. College of Leicester, Dept of Local History, Occasional papers, No. 5 (1954).

A brief essay (44 pp.) on the custumal of Ipswich and the town courts, with comparisons with other town courts of East Anglia.

5262 MARTIN (GEOFFREY H.). 'The records of the borough of Ipswich to 1422'. *J. Soc. Archivists.* i (1956), 87–93.

An account of the records and the gaps.

5263 PRINCIPAL CHARTERS WHICH HAVE BEEN GRANTED TO THE CORPORATION OF IPSWICH (1199–1688). Ed. by Richard Canning. Lond. 1754.

Translation only.

5264 WODDERSPOON (JOHN). Memorials of Ipswich. Ipswich, etc. 1850.

Lilian J. Redstone, *Ipswich through the ages*. Ipswich. 1948.

SURREY

5265 GUIDE TO ARCHIVES AND OTHER COLLECTIONS OF DOCUMENTS RELATING TO SURREY. (See No. 1827).

Pubn. no. 29 (1929), *Borough records*, by Dorothy L. Powell.

5266 CHARTERS OF THE TOWN OF KINGSTON-UPON-THAMES (1208–1662). Ed. by George Roots. London, 1797.

Translation only.

5267 HEALES (ALFRED C.). 'Early history of the church of Kingston-upon-Thames (with an appendix of records)'. *Surrey Archaeol. Collections*, viii (1883), 13–156 f.

5268 TYSON (M.). 'On Annals of Southwark and Merton.' Ibid. xxvi (1926), 24–57. See No. 2785.

SUSSEX

See Cinque Ports (pp. 729–30).

5269 THE EARLY MUNICIPAL CHARTERS OF THE SUSSEX BOROUGHS. Ed. by Adolphus Ballard. *Sussex Archaeol. Collections.* lv (1912), 35–40.

5270 A DESCRIPTIVE LIST OF THE ARCHIVES OF THE CITY OF CHICHESTER. West Sussex Record Office. 1949.

F. W. Steer, *Chichester city charters.* Chichester Papers No. 3 (Chichester, 1956).

5271 FLEMING (LINDSAY). History of Pagham in Sussex, illustrating the administration of an archiepiscopal hundred, the decay of manorial organization, and the rise of a seaside resort. 3 vols. (Privately printed by Ditchling Press.) 1949–50.

WARWICKSHIRE

For Coventry, see *Historic towns* (No. 1386); and for the city of Coventry and the borough of Warwick, see *V.C.H. Warwickshire,* iii (1969).

5272 ANCIENT RECORDS OF COVENTRY. Ed. by Mary D. Harris. Dugdale Soc. Occasional Papers, no. i (1924).

5273 CHARTERS AND MSS. OF COVENTRY: their story and purport. Ed. by T. W. Whitley. 2 pts. Warwick. 1897–8.

Contains translations of charters granted to the church and the borough of Coventry in the eleventh and twelfth centuries. Joan C. Lancaster, 'The Coventry forged charters: a reconsideration', *B.I.H.R.* xxvii (1954), 113–40. R. H. C. Davis, 'An unknown Coventry charter', *E.H.R.* lxxxvi (1971), 533–45.

5274 COVENTRY LEET BOOK, or mayor's register, 1420–1555. Ed. by M. D. Harris. 4 pts. E.E.T.S. 1907–13.

5275 THE REGISTER OF THE GUILD OF THE HOLY TRINITY, ST. MARY. ST. JOHN THE BAPTIST, AND ST. KATHERINE OF COVENTRY, vol. i. Ed. by M. D. Harris. Dugdale Soc. xiii (1935), vol. ii. Ed. by Geoffrey Templeman. Ibid. xix (1944).

5276 THE STATUTE MERCHANT ROLL OF COVENTRY, 1392–1416. Ed. by Alice Beardwood. Dugdale Soc. xvii (1939).

5277 HARRIS (MARY D.). Life in an old English town: a history of Coventry. Lond. etc. 1898.

See her *Story of Coventry* (Lond. 1911)*; her 'Unpublished documents relating to town life in Coventry', *T.R.H.S.* 4th Ser. iii (1920), 103–14; and Levi Fox, 'The early history of Coventry', *History*, New Ser. xxx (1945), 21–37; and his *Coventry's heritage: an introduction to the history of the city* (Coventry, 1947); and his 'The administration of gild property in Coventry in the fifteenth century', *E.H.R.* lv (1940), 634–47.

5278 REGISTER OF THE GUILD OF KNOWLE, 1451–1535. Ed. by William B. Bickley. Birmingham and Midland Institute. Walsall. 1894.

5279 REGISTER OF THE GILD OF THE HOLY CROSS, THE BLESSED MARY, AND ST. JOHN THE BAPTIST OF STRATFORD-UPON-AVON (1406–1535). Ed. by James H. Bloom. Lond. 1907.

See Levi Fox, *The borough town of Stratford-upon-Avon* (Stratford-upon-Avon, 1953), a short history from the Bronze Age to the nineteenth century.

5280 ANCIENT RECORDS OF WARWICK. Ed. by Edward G. Tibbits. Dugdale Soc. Occasional Papers. no. 5 (1938).

See Henry A. Cronne, 'The borough of Warwick in the middle ages'. Dugdale Soc. Occasional Papers, no. 10 (1951).

WILTSHIRE

For Salisbury see Jones and Macray, *Charters* (No. 5799), and *Historic towns* (No. 1386), vol. I.

5281 LIST OF WILTSHIRE BOROUGH RECORDS EARLIER IN DATE THAN 1836. Ed. by Maurice G. Rathbone. Wiltshire Archaeol.-Nat. Hist. Soc. Records Branch. v (1951)

Introduction by Ralph B. Pugh. For boroughs, see Mullins, *Texts*, p. 467.

5282 CHURCHWARDENS' ACCOUNTS OF S. EDMUND AND S. THOMAS, SARUM, 1443–1702, with other documents. Ed. by Henry J. F. Swayne. Wilts. Rec. Soc. Salisbury. 1896.

5283 GLEANINGS FROM THE ARCHIVES OF SALISBURY. Ed. by H. J. F. S(wayne). *Salisbury and Winchester Jour.* 25 November 1882–27 December 1884. Salisbury. 1882–4.

An important collection of charters, extracts from town accounts, etc., from the thirteenth to the seventeenth century inclusive.

5284 MUNIMENTS OF THE CORPORATION OF THE CITY OF SALISBURY. Hist. MSS. Comm. Reports. Various Collections iv (1907), 191–249.

5285 BENSON (ROBERT) and HATCHER (HENRY). Old and New Sarum, 1443–1702, with other documents. Ed. by Henry J. F. Swayne, Wilts. Rec. Soc. Salisbury. 1896.

WORCESTERSHIRE

5286 ORIGINAL CHARTERS RELATING TO THE CITY OF WORCESTER IN THE POSSESSION OF THE DEAN AND CHAPTER. Ed. by J. Harvey Bloom. Worcestershire Hist. Soc. 1909.

Thirteenth to sixteenth centuries.

5287 SMITH (BRIAN S.). History of Malvern. Leicester. 1964.

YORKSHIRE

5288 BEVERLEY TOWN DOCUMENTS. Ed. by Arthur F. Leach. Selden Soc. xiv. 1900.

Charters, customs and liberties, gild ordinances, etc., fourteenth to sixteenth centuries.

Latin text with translation. See Kiralfy–Jones (No. 195), pp. 27–9. See George Poulson, *Beverlac*, or the antiquities and history of the town of Beverley, 2 vols. Lond. 1829.

5289 NOTES ON DEWSBURY CHURCH (with extracts from assize rolls, Wakefield court rolls, wills, etc. 1225–1567). Ed. by Samuel J. Chadwick. *Yorks. Archaeol. Soc. Jour.* xx (1909), 369–446.

See also *The Dewsbury moot hall* (with account rolls of Dewsbury rectory, 1348–56), edited by S. J. Chadwick. Ibid. xxi (1911), 345–92; xxii (1913), 126.

5290 CALENDAR TO THE RECORDS OF THE BOROUGH OF DON-CASTER. (Ed. by William J. Hardy). 4 vols. Doncaster. 1899–1903.

Charters, court rolls, etc. 1086–1838.

5291 BOYLE (JOHN R.). The early history of the town and port of Hedon. Hull, etc. 1895.

Contains an elaborate appendix of charters, churchwardens' accounts (Rich. II–Edw. IV), bailiffs' accounts etc.

5292 CALENDAR OF ANCIENT DEEDS, LETTERS AND MISCEL-LANEOUS DOCUMENTS IN THE ARCHIVES OF THE CORPORA-TION (OF HULL). Calendared and indexed by L. M. Stanewell. Kingston-upon-Hull. 1951.

5293 CHARTERS AND LETTERS PATENT GRANTED TO KINGSTON-UPON-HULL (1299–1897). Translated by John R. Boyle. (Hull.) 1905.

5294 THE CITY OF KINGSTON-UPON-HULL. Ed. by K. J. Allison. *V.C.H. Yorkshire, East Riding,* i. 1969.

5295 DOCUMENTS RELATING TO THE MANOR AND BOROUGH OF LEEDS (1066–1400). Ed. by John Le Patourel. Thoresby Soc. Pubns. xlv (1957).

George Woledge, 'The medieval borough of Leeds', Thoresby Soc. Pubns. xxxvii, *Miscellanea*, xi (1945), 288–309.

5296 A FIFTEENTH CENTURY RENTAL OF LEEDS (1425). By William T. Lancaster. Ibid. xxiv *Miscellanea*, vii for 1915 (1919), 6–22.

Also, idem, 'A fifteenth century rental of Rothwell', ibid., pp. 281–303. Idem, 'Fifteenth century rentals of Barwick and Scholes', ibid. xxviii for the year 1925 (1928), *Miscellanea*, ix, 238–54.

5297 A FIFTEENTH CENTURY RENTAL OF PONTEFRACT. Ed. by George D. Lumb. Thoresby Soc. Pubns. xxvi (1924), *Miscellanea*, viii, 253–73.

5298 CATALOGUE OF THE ANCIENT CHARTERS OF SHEFFIELD (with abstracts of wills, 1297–1554). Ed. by Thomas W. Hall. Sheffield. 1913.

For the numerous catalogues of the muniments of Sheffield by Thomas W. Hall, see Besterman, *A world bibliography* (No. 1), *sub* Sheffield, iii, cols. 3792–3. W. T. Freemantle, *A bibliography of Sheffield and vicinity, to the end of 1700.* (Sheffield, 1911.)

5299 ATKINSON (JOHN C.). Memorials of old Whitby. Lond. 1894.

5300 THE CITY OF YORK. Ed. by P. M. Tillott. *V.C.H. Yorkshire*: The City of York. 1961.

5301 ACTS AND ORDINANCES OF THE COMPANY OF MER-CHANT TAYLORS IN THE CITY OF YORK. Ed. by Bernard Johnson. York. 1949.

5302 DRAKE (FRANCIS). Eboracum, or the history and antiquities of the city of York, with the history of the cathedral church. Lond. 1736.

The most important of the earlier histories of York.

5303 DISCOVERY OF THE REGISTER AND CHARTULARY OF THE MERCERS' COMPANY, York (with extracts from these records, 1420–1523). By Charles Kerry. *Antiquary*, xxii (1890), 266–70; xxiii (1891), 27–30, 70–3.

5304 EXTRACTS FROM THE MUNICIPAL RECORDS OF THE CITY OF YORK, during the reigns of Edw. IV, Edw. V, and Rich. III. Ed. by Robert Davies. Lond. 1843.

Extracts from the chamberlains' accounts and from the minutes of proceedings of the city council.

5305 RAINE (ANGELO). Mediaeval York: a topographical survey based on original sources. Lond. 1955.

For a study of topographic nomenclature of tenth and eleventh centuries, see H. Lind-kvist, 'A study of early medieval York'. *Anglia, neue folge*, xxxviii (1926), 345–94. A. G. Dickens, 'The "shire" and privileges of the archbishop in eleventh century York'. *Yorks. Arch. Jour.*, xxxviii (1952–4), 131–147.
For a population study, J. N. Bartlett, 'The expansion and decline of York in the later middle ages'. *Econ. H.R.* 2nd Ser. xii (1959), 17–33.
For a plea on political corruption, drawn from the Assize Rolls, see George Sayles 'The dissolution of a gild at York in 1306', *E.H.R.* lv (1940), 83–98.

5306 REGISTER OF THE FREEMEN OF THE CITY OF YORK, 1272–1759 (Ed. by Francis Collins.) 2 vols. Surtees Soc. xcvi (1897); cii (1900).

Vol. i: 1272–1558; vol. ii: 1559–1759.

5307 REGISTER OF THE GUILD OF CORPUS CHRISTI IN THE CITY OF YORK (1408–sixteenth century), with an appendix of illustrative documents. (Ed. by Robert H. Skaife). Surtees Soc. lvii (1872).

5308 A VOLUME OF ENGLISH MISCELLANIES ILLUSTRATING THE HISTORY AND LANGUAGE OF THE NORTHERN COUNTIES OF ENGLAND. (Ed. by James Raine, Jr.). Surtees Soc. lxxxv (1890).

Miscellaneous documents, largely from York city records. For contents, see Mullins, *Texts*, p. 321.

5309 YORK CIVIC RECORDS (1475–1588). Ed. by Angelo Raine. 8 vols. Yorks. Archaeol. Soc. 1939–53.

Vol. i: for 1475–87 is Y.A.S. Rec. Ser. xcviii (1939).
Vol. ii: for 1478–1504 is Y.R.S. Rec. Ser. ciii (1941).

5310 THE YORK MERCERS AND MERCHANT ADVENTURERS
1356–1917. Ed. by Maud Sellers. Surtees Soc. cxxix (1918).

Few records prior to the sixteenth century.

5311 YORK MEMORANDUM BOOK. (Ed. by Maud Sellers). pt. i: 1376–
1419; pt. ii: 1388–1493. Surtees Soc. cxx (1912), cxxv (1915).

'A book of diverse memoranda concerning the city of York'; city ordinances, gild
regulations, etc. Text with translations.

3. Cinque Ports

The name of Cinque Ports was applied in the twelfth century to a cluster of
ports along the south-east coast of England which had the obligation to provide
ships annually for the king's service in return for which the towns received special
rights. The original five were Hastings, Romney, Hythe, Dover, and Sandwich;
but the confederation grew to include about thirty towns.

The history of the Cinque Ports is detailed in Miss Murray's 1935 volume
(No. 5322); and the bibliography of manuscript sources and printed works
attached thereto need not be repeated here. Reference should also be made to
G. H. Martin and Sylvia McIntyre's *Bibliography of British and Irish municipal
history* (No. 1511).

5312 BOYS (WILLIAM). Collections for a history of Sandwich, with notices
of the other Cinque Ports. Canterbury. 1792.

Contains the custumal of Sandwich.

5313 BURROWS (MONTAGU). Historic towns. Cinque Ports. Lond. 1888.

5314 A CALENDAR OF THE WHITE AND BLACK BOOKS OF THE
CINQUE PORTS, 1432–1955. H.M.S.O. 1966.

These are the minute books of the general assembly (Brodhull) of the confederation;
the White Book for the period 1432–1571; the Black Book for the period from 1572
on to the present.

See Felix Hull, 'A calendar (1432–85) of the White and Black Books of the Cinque
Ports', *Kent Records*. Kent Archaeol. Soc. xix (1966), 1–94.

5315 CHARTERS OF THE CINQUE PORTS (Edw. I–Chas. II, with
a translation). Ed. by Samuel Jeake. Lond. 1728.

5316 CUSTUMAL OF PEVENSEY, 1356. Ed. by Lambert B. Larking.
Sussex Archaeol. Collections, iv (1851), 209–18. Trans. by Edward Turner. Ibid.
xviii (1866), 49–52.

5317 GIRAUD (FRANCIS F.), ed. Municipal archives of Faversham, 1304–
24. *Archaeologia Cantiana*, xiv (1882), 185–205.

Contains town accounts, arrears of tallages, etc. See also his other papers on Faversham,
ibid. ix (1874) pp. lxii–lxx, x (1876), 221–41; xxvii (1905), 37–43.

5318 HOLLOWAY (WILLIAM). History and antiquities of the ancient town
and port of Rye, with incidental notices on the Cinque Ports. Lond. 1847.

Contains a sixteenth-century English version of the custumal of Rye.

5319 RECORDS OF LYDD: Lydd Chamberlains' Accounts (1423–35). Translated and transcribed by Arthur Hussey and M. M. Hardy. Ed. by Arthur Finn. Ashford. 1911.

5320 LYON (JOHN). The history of the town and port of Dover, and of Dover castle: with a short account of the Cinque Ports. 2 vols. Dover. 1813–14.

Vol. i, pp. 246–366 deals mainly with the institutions of the Cinque Ports; vol. ii contains an English version of the abbreviated custumals of Dover, Romney, Rye, Sandwich, and Winchelsea. Rose Graham, 'An interdict on Dover, 1298–9' (No. 1471), following opposition to a citation outside the town of citizens during a metropolitical visitation.

5321 MOSS (WILLIAM G). History and antiquities of the town and port of Hastings. Lond. 1824.

5322 MURRAY (KATHARINE M. E.). Constitutional history of the Cinque Ports. Univ. Manchester Hist. Ser. lxviii. Manchester. 1935.

The best book on the subject. See her 'Faversham and the Cinque Ports', *T.R.H.S.* 4th Ser. xviii (1935), 53–84. Also Frederick W. Brooks, 'The Cinque Ports', *The Mariner's Mirror*, xv (1929), 142–91; and No. 4325.

5323 REGISTER OF DANIEL ROUGH, COMMON CLERK OF ROMNEY, 1352–1380. Transcribed and edited, with introduction, by K. M. E. Murray. Kent Archaeol. Soc. Rec. Branch, xvi (1945).

A custumal and register of town records.

5324 STATHAM (SAMUEL P. H.). Dover charters and other documents in the possession of the corporation of Dover. Lond. 1902.

Idem, 'Dover chamberlains' accounts, 1365–1367', *Archaeologia Cantiana*, xxv (1901), 75–87.

4. *Commercial Records*

5325 ACCOUNTS OF JOHN BALSALL, purser of the *Trinity* of Bristol, 1480–1. Ed. by Thomas F. Reddaway and Alwyn A. Ruddock. R. H. S. Camden 4th Ser. vii (1969), 1–28.

5326 ACTS OF COURT OF THE MERCERS' COMPANY 1453–1527. Ed. by Laetitia Lyell and Frank D. Watney. Cambr. 1936.

Important for the London cloth trade.

5327 THE BROKAGE BOOK OF SOUTHAMPTON, from 1439–40. (No. 5101).

5328 CARSON (EDWARD A.). 'The customs, records of the Kent ports', *Jour. Soc. Archivists*, iv (1970), 31–44.

5329 CARTULAIRE DE L'ANCIENNE ESTAPLE DE BRUGES (862–1492): Recueil de documents. . . . Ed. by Louis Gilliodts van Severen. Société d'Émulation de Bruges, Recueil de Chroniques, etc. 4 vols. Bruges. 1904–6.

A calendar; many of the documents throw light on the commercial relations between England and Flanders.

5330 CELY PAPERS (THE). Selections from the correspondence and memoranda of the Cely family, merchants of the staple A.D. 1475–1488. Ed. by Henry E. Malden. R.H.S. Camden. 3rd Ser. i (1900).

George Daumet, *Calais sous la domination anglaise* (Arras. 1902) contains some documents on the staple.

5331 CHESTER CUSTOMS ACCOUNTS, 1301–1566. Ed. by K. P. Wilson. Lancs.–Ches. Rec. Soc. Pubns. cxi (1969).

In the Middle Ages, Chester was a palatine port and its customs are in the accounts of the chamberlain of Chester.

5332 DAVIES (J. CONWAY). 'The wool customs accounts for Newcastle-upon-Tyne for the reign of Edward I'. *Archaeologia Aeliana*, 4th Ser. xxxii (1954), 220–308.

Idem, 'An assembly of wool merchants in 1322', *E.H.R.* xxxi (1916), 596–606, where are printed chancery writs by which merchants are to appear before King and Council as technical advisers or witnesses.

5333 THE EARLY YORKSHIRE WOOLLEN TRADE: extracts from the Hull customs' rolls and complete transcripts of the ulnagers' rolls. Ed. by John Lister. Yorks. Archaeol. Soc. Record Ser. lxiv (1924).

5334 FRYDE (EDMUND B.). The wool accounts of William de la Pole, a study of some aspects of the English wool trade at the start of the Hundred Years War. St. Anthony's Hall Pubns. xxv. York. 1964.

Prints three accounts of the export of wool 1337 and 1339. See also Fryde, 'The last trials of Sir William de la Pole (d. 1366)', *Econ. H.R.* 2nd Ser. xv (1962), 17–30, on charges going back to 1337, including smuggling wool to the Netherlands.

5335 HANSEAKTEN AUS ENGLAND, 1275–1412. Ed. by Karl Kunze. Hansische Geschichtsquellen, vi. Halle. 1891.

The publications of Hansischer Geschichtsverein, founded in 1870, are (*a*) *Hanserecesse und andere Akten der Hansetage* (1256–1535), 25 vols. 1870–1940; (*b*) *Hansisches Urkundenbuch* (975–1500) 11 vols. 1876–1907, and 1938; (*c*) *Hansische Geschichtsquellen* (7 vols. 1875–1894); subsequently (1900+) entitled *Quellen und Darstellungen zur hansischen Geschichte*, 12 vols. 1875+; (*d*) *Hansische Geschichtsblätter*, 1872+; supplemented by *Pfingstblätter*, 1905+.

5336 HANSISCHES URKUNDENBUCH, vols. i–iii (A.D. 975–1358). Ed. by Konstantin Höhlbaum; vols. iv–vi (1361–1453). Ed. by Karl Kunze; vols. viii–x (1451–85). Ed. by Walther Stein. Halle, etc. 1876–1907; vols. vii. pt. 1 (1434–42). Ed. by H. G. von Rundstedt. 1938.

Contains many documents concerning English trade. Vol. ii, pt. 2 has not been published.

5337 LAPPENBERG (JOHANN M.). Urkundliche Geschichte des hansische Stahlhofes zu London. Hamburg. 1851.

5338 THE LIBELLE OF ENGLYSHE POLYCYE: A poem on the use of sea power, 1436. Ed. by Sir George Warner. Oxf. 1926.

This critical edition supersedes those printed in Hakluyt's *Voyages* (1598), i. 187–208; in Thomas Wright, *Political poems and songs* (Edw. III–Rich. III) (Rolls Series 1859–61)

ii. 157–205; and in Wilhelm Hertzberg, *The libell of Englishe policye* (with a metrical translation into German) (Leipzig, 1878). It is printed in modernized English in W. H. Dunham and Stanley Pargellis, *Complaint and reform in England, 1436–1714* (N.Y. 1938), pp. 3–30.

The introduction, pp. vii–lvi, and the copious notes and glossary in Warner's edition are fundamental to a study of the text. See also F. Taylor, 'Some manuscripts of the Libelle of Englysche Polycye', *B.J.R.L.* xxiv (1940), 376–418. An excellent critique is provided by G. A. Holmes, 'The Libel of English polity', *E.H.R.* lxxvi (1961), 193–216.

The poem is intended to point out the political and commercial benefits accruing from command of the sea. It is severely critical of the policy of the Beaufort faction, and was not written by Adam Moleyns, as has been sometimes suggested. It is the best known of a contemporary series of political pamphlets which satirized government policies. See below, pp. 914–16.

5339 THE LOCAL PORT BOOK OF SOUTHAMPTON, 1439–40. (No. 5106).

5340 THE ORDINANCE BOOK OF THE MERCHANTS OF THE STAPLE. Ed. by Edwin E. Rich. Cambr. 1937.

Little on the medieval staple before 1485.

5341 THE OVERSEAS TRADE OF BRISTOL IN THE LATER MIDDLE AGES. Selected and edited by Eleanora M. Carus-Wilson. Bristol Rec. Soc. Pubns. vii (1937). Bristol. 1937. *

Calendar or transcripts of various records 1291–1484, customs accounts, etc.

5342 THE PORT BOOKS OF SOUTHAMPTON, OR ANGLO-FRENCH ACCOUNTS OF ROBERT FLORYS, water-bailiff and receiver of petty customs, A.D. 1427–1430. (No. 5108.)

5343 THE PORT BOOKS OR LOCAL CUSTOMS ACCOUNTS OF SOUTHAMPTON FOR THE REIGN OF EDWARD IV. (No. 5109.)

5344 QUELLEN ZUR GESCHICHTE DES KÖLNER HANDELS UND VERKEHRS IM MITTELALTER. Ed. by Bruno Kuske. Cologne. 1917. Reprinted, Bonn. 1934.

For the interest of these records for English students, see *Econ. H.R.* vi (1935–6), 116. In general, F. R. Salter, 'The Hansa, Cologne, and the crisis of 1468', ibid. iii (1931), 93–101.

5345 SMIT (HOMME J.), ed. Bronnen tot de geschiedenis van den handel met Engeland, Schotland en Ierland. (Vol. i, 1150–1435; vol. ii, 1435–1485.) 2 vols. Rijks Geschiedkundige Pubns. lxv–vi. The Hague. 1928.

5346 STURLER (JEAN V. de), ed. 'Debita mercatorum Brabancie: documents anglais relatifs aux article livrés à la Garde-robe par des negociants Brabançons au paiement tardif de ces fournitures ainsi qu'aux modes de paiement (1296–1321)'. *Bull. de la Comm. Royale d'Histoire* (Brussels), cxxxiv (1968), 285–356. See No. 5401.

B. MODERN STUDIES OF BOROUGHS AND TOWNS

1. *Comprehensive Accounts*

The fundamental treatises are M. D. Lobel, ed. *Historic towns* (No. 1386), Stephenson, *Borough and town* (No. 1389), and Tait, *The medieval English borough* (No. 1390).

5347 BALLARD (ADOLPHUS). The Domesday boroughs. Oxf. 1904.

See also Ballard's articles, 'The walls of Malmesbury', *E.H.R.* xxi (1906), 98–105; and 'The burgesses of Domesday', ibid. xxi (1906), 699–709. For supplementary material, cf. reviews of Ballard's book by Mary Bateson, ibid. xx (1905), 143–51, and xxi (1906), 709–22; and Ballard's rejoinder, 722–3.

5348 BALLARD (ADOLPHUS). 'The English borough in the reign of John'. *E.H.R.* xiv (1899), 93–104.

Analyses the municipal charters granted by John.
See also his lectures on *The English borough in the twelfth century* (Cambr. 1914).

5349 BERESFORD (MAURICE). New towns of the middle ages. Lond. 1967.

Concerned with the deliberate creation of new towns planted by kings, clerics, barons, in England, Wales, and Gascony, largely between 1066 and 1349.
See Tout, 'Mediaeval town planning', in *Collected papers* (No. 1499).

5350 COLBY (CHARLES W.). 'The growth of oligarchy in English towns'. *E.H.R.* v (1890), 633–53.

5351 GREEN (A. S. MRS. JOHN R.). Town life in the fifteenth century. 2 vols. Lond. 1894. Reprinted in 1 vol. 1907. *

Deals with medieval borough history from the Norman conquest to the end of the fifteenth century. Her view that before the fourteenth century the 'communitas' formed a corporate body distinct from the burgesses is untenable.

5352 GROSS (CHARLES). 'Modes of trial in the mediaeval boroughs of England'. *Harvard Law Rev.* xv (1902), 691–706. Idem, 'Mortmain in medieval boroughs'. *A.H.R.* xii (1907), 733–42.

5353 HEMMEON (MORLEY de WOLF). Burgage tenure in mediaeval England. Harvard Historical Studies. Cambr. (Mass.) and Manchester. 1914.

J. Tait, 'Liber burgus' in Tout *essays* (No. 1458).

5354 MAITLAND (FREDERIC W.). Township and Borough. No. 1387.

For extract see No. 1484.

5355 MARTIN (GEOFFREY H.). 'The English borough in the thirteenth century'. *T.R.H.S.* 5th Ser. xiii (1963), 123–44. Idem, 'The origins of borough records', *Jour. Soc. Archivists*, ii (1960–4), 147–53.

5356 PACKARD (SIDNEY R.). 'The Norman communes under Richard and John. 1189–1204' in *Haskins essays* (No. 1439). Idem, 'The Norman communes once more, 1189–1223'. *A.H.R.* xlvi (1940–1), 338–47. Idem, 'A list of the Norman communes, 1189–1223'. *Speculum*, xvi (1941), 297–303.

5357 SALUSBURY (GORONWY T.). Street life in medieval England. Oxf. 1938. 2nd edn. 1948.

Uses municipal records. The author's name is sometimes catalogued as G. T. S. Jones.

5358 TRENHOLME (NORMAN M.). The English monastic boroughs. Univ. Missouri Studies, ii. no. 3. 1927.

5359 YOUNG (CHARLES). The English borough and royal administration, 1130–1307. Durham (North Carolina). 1961.

2. *Gilds and Livery Companies*

See Liebermann (No. 1385) for early gilds. See also individual towns in Index under 'gilds'.

5360 CLEMESHA (H. W.). 'The borough of Preston and its gild merchant'. Historical Essays . . . Owens College (No. 1472).

5361 COORNAERT (ÉMILE). 'Les ghildes mediévales'. *Revue Historique*, cxcix (1948), 22–55, 208–43.

A basic reconsideration of the problems.

5362 CUNNINGHAM (WILLIAM). 'The formation and decay of craft gilds'. *T.R.H.S.* New Ser. iii (1886), 372–92.

5363 FISHER (DOUGLAS J. V.). 'Economic institutions in the towns of medieval England'. *La Ville. Recueils de la Société Jean Bodin*, vii (1955), 531–50.

5364 GROSS (CHARLES). The gild merchant. 2 vols. Lond. 1890.

Vol. ii. contains many records concerning the municipal history of particular towns. See a review by F. W. Maitland, in *Economic Journal*, i (1891), 220–4 (reprinted in his *Collected papers*, No. 1482, ii. 223–31); and cf. C. G. Crump, 'London and the Gild Merchant', in *E.H.R.*, xviii (1903), 315. See also No. 5371.

5365 KRAMER (STELLA). The English craft gilds and the government. N.Y. etc. 1905. *

See also her paper on 'The amalgamation of the English mercantile crafts', *E.H.R.* xxiii (1908), 15–34, 236–51.

5366 KRAMER (STELLA). The English craft gilds: studies in their progress and decline. N.Y. 1927. * Oxf. 1928.

5367 MEYER (ERWIN F.). 'English craft gilds and borough governments in the later middle ages'. *Univ. Colorado Stud.* xvi (1929), 323–78; xvii (1930), 350–426.

5368 PALMER (WILLIAM M.). 'Village gilds of Cambridgeshire'. *Cambs. and Hunts. Archaeol. Soc. Trans.* i (1904), 330–402.

5369 SMITH (TOULMIN) and SMITH (LUCY TOULMIN). English gilds: the original ordinances of more than one hundred English gilds, together with the old usages of the city of Winchester, etc. E.E.T.S. Orig. Ser. xcl (1870).

Prints regulations of gilds merchant, craft gilds, and religious and social gilds; mainly returns, English and Latin, made to the royal council in 1388–9 by the masters and wardens of the gilds.

5370 THRUPP (SYLVIA L.). 'Medieval gilds reconsidered'. *Jour. Econ. Hist.* ii (1942), 164–73.

An important article with bibliographical notes.

5371 UNWIN (GEORGE). The gilds and companies of London. The Antiquary's Books. Lond. 1908. *

Appendix B includes a list of sources for the history of the existing London companies.

5372 WESTLAKE (HERBERT F.). The parish gilds of mediaeval England.
Lond. 1919.

Includes an appendix on gild certificates of 1389.

C. STUDIES ON COMMERCE AND TRADE

1. *General Accounts*

5373 BAKER (JOHN N. L.). Medieval trade routes. Historical Asso. pamphlet, no. 111 Lond. 1938. Reprinted in Barraclough, ed. *Social Life* (No.
1495).

5374 BLAKE (J. B.). 'The medieval coal trade of north-east England: some
fourteenth century evidence'. *Northern History*, ii (1967), 1–26.

Trade with France, Low countries, and Baltic area.

5375 BOURNE (HENRY R. F.). English merchants: memoirs in illustration
of the progress of British commerce. 2 vols. Lond. 1866. * New edns. in one
volume. 1886; 1898.

Deals with early English commerce, the De la Poles of Hull (1311–66), Richard
Whittington of London, the Canynges of Bristol (1360–1475), etc.

5376 BRIDBURY (ANTHONY R.). England and the salt trade in the later
middle ages. Oxf. 1955.

5377 BRODNITZ (GEORG). Englische Wirtschaftsgeschichte. Jena. 1918.

5378 BURWASH (DOROTHY). English merchant shipping, 1460–1540.
Toronto, 1947.

5379 CARUS-WILSON (ELEANORA M.). Medieval merchant venturers:
collected studies. Lond. 1954. Paperback edn.: 1967.

A collection of eight important essays and articles, e.g., 'The origin and early development of the Merchant Adventurers' organization in London as shown in their own
mediaeval records', *Econ. H.R.* iv (1932–3), 147–76. See also John Latimer, *History
of the Society of Merchant Venturers of Bristol* (Bristol, 1903). E. M. Carus-Wilson, 'The
merchant adventurers of Bristol in the fifteenth century', *T.R.H.S.* 4th Ser. xi (1928),
61–82. L. G. Taylor, 'The merchant venturers of Bristol', *Bristol–Glos. Archaeol. Soc.
Trans.* lxxi (1952), 5–12.

5380 CARUS-WILSON (E. M.). 'The medieval trade of the ports of the
Wash', *Medieval Archaeology*, vi–vii (1962–3), 182–201.

For medieval foreign trade in eastern and western ports, see No. 1465.

5381 CUNNINGHAM (WILLIAM). The growth of English industry and
commerce. Vol. i: The middle ages. Cambr. 1882. 4th edn. Cambr. 1905; 5th
edn. 1910. Reprinted 2 vols. Lond. 1915. *

A standard treatise. See No. 1366.

5382 DAVIES (J. CONWAY). 'Shipping and trade in Newcastle-upon-Tyne, 1294–1296'. *Archaeologia Aeliana*, 4th Ser. xxxi (1953), 175–204.

5383 FRASER (CONSTANCE M.). 'The pattern of (internal) trade in the north-east of England, 1265–1350'. *Northern History*, iv (1969), 44–66.

5384 GRAS (NORMAN S. B.). The early English customs system: a documentary study of the institutional and economic history of the customs from the thirteenth to the sixteenth century. Harvard Econ. Stud. xviii. Cambr. (Mass.) and Lond. 1918.

> N. S. B. Gras, 'English customs up to 1275', *Amer. Hist. Asso. Annual Report for 1917* (1920), 293–301. See Rupert C. Jarvis, 'The archival history of the customs records', *Jour. Soc. Archivists*, i, no. 9 (1959), 239–50. See Nos. 3229, 3238, 3241.

5385 GRAS (N. S. B.). The evolution of the English corn market from the twelfth to the eighteenth century. Cambr. (Mass.). 1915. * Lond. 1926.

> For a criticism, see Ernst Kneisel, 'The evolution of the English corn market', *Jour. Econ. Hist.* xiv (1954), 46–52.

5386 JENCKES (ADALINE L.). The origin, the organization, and the location of the staple of England. Philadelphia. 1908.

> Bibliography, pp. 81–3. See Ward (No. 5406) and Brodhurst in *Select Essays* (No. 1246). E. E. Rich 'The mayors of the staple', *Cambr. Hist. Jour.* iv (1933), 120–42; 192–3. Frederic Miller, 'The Middleburgh staple, 1383–88', ibid. ii (1926), 63–5. R. L. Baker, 'The establishment of the wool staple in 1313', *Speculum*, xxxi (1956), 444–53. W. Stanford Reid, 'The Scots and the staple ordinance of 1313', ibid. xxxiv (1959), 598–610. J. H. Munro, 'Bruges and the abortive staple in English cloth: an incident in the shift of commerce from Bruges in the fifteenth century', *Revue belge de phil. et d'hist.* xliv (1966), 1137–59. See No. 5330.

5387 KERLING (NELLIE J. M.). Commercial relations of Holland and Zeeland with England from the late thirteenth century to the close of the middle ages. Leyden. 1954.

5388 LINGELBACH (WILLIAM E.). The merchant adventurers of England, their laws and ordinances, with other documents. Philadelphia. 1902. *

5389 McCUSKER (JOHN J. Jr.). 'The wine prise and mediaeval mercantile shipping'. *Speculum*, xli (1966), 279–96.

> A broad treatment with good documentation.

5390 MACE (FRANCES A.). 'Devonshire ports in the fourteenth and fifteenth centuries'. *T.R.H.S.* 4th Ser. viii (1925), 98–126.

> N. J. G. Pounds, 'The ports of Cornwall in the middle ages', *Devon–Cornwall Notes and Queries*, xxiii (1947–9), 65–73.

5391 MOLLAT (MICHEL). 'Anglo-Norman trade in the fifteenth century'. *Econ. H.R.* xvii (1947), 143–50.

5392 POSTAN (M. MICHAEL). 'Spread of techniques: Italy and the economic development of England in the middle ages'. *Jour. Econ. Hist.* xi (1951), 339–46. Idem, 'Partnership in English medieval commerce', *Studi in onore di A. Sapori* (Milan, 1957), pp. 519–49.

5393 POWER (EILEEN E.) and POSTAN (M. M.), eds. Studies in English trade in the fifteenth century. Lond. 1933. Reissued, 1966.

(*a*) H. L. Gray, English foreign trade from 1446 to 1482. 1–38.
(*b*) E. E. Power, The wool trade in the fifteenth century. 39–90.
(*c*) M. M. Postan, The economic and political relations of England and the Hanse from 1400 to 1475. 91–153.
(*d*) E. M. Carus-Wilson, The Iceland trade. 155–82. (No. 5379).
(*e*) E. M. Carus-Wilson, The overseas trade of Bristol. 183–246. (No. 5379).
(*f*) S. Thrupp, The grocers of London, a study of distributive trade. 247–92.
(*g*) W. I. Haward, The financial transactions between the Lancastrian government and the merchants of the Staple from 1449 to 1461. 293–320.
(*h*) H. L. Gray, Tables of enrolled customs and subsidy accounts, 1399–1482. Introduction, 321–30; tables, 330–60.
(*i*) Notes to the text. 361–99.
(*j*) Appendix A. Variations in English foreign trade, 1446 to 1482. Annual averages by periods. 401.
(*k*) Appendix B. Total English foreign trade, 1446 to 1482. 402–6.
(*l*) Broadcloths exported by the Hanseatic merchants, 1406 to 1480. 407–8.

5394 QUINN (DAVID B.). 'Edward IV and exploration'. *Mariner's Mirror*. xxi (1935), 275–84.

D. B. Quinn, 'The argument for the English discovery of America between 1480 and 1494', *The Geographical Jour.* cxxvii (1961), 277–85, which deals with the voyages to the 'Isle of Brasil' financed by Bristol merchants between 1480 and 1494.

5395 RENOUARD (YVES). 'Le grand commerce des vins de Gascogne au moyen âge'. *Revue historique*, ccxxi (1959), 261–304.

See also his Bordeaux (No. 4168). F. Sargeant, 'The wine trade with Gascony', in *Finance and Trade* (No. 1469), pp. 257–311. André L. Simon, *The history of the wine trade in England.* 3 vols. (Lond. 1906–9). Margery K. James, 'The fluctuations of the Anglo-Gascon wine trade in the fourteenth century', *Econ. H.R.* 2nd Ser. iv (1951), 170–96; reprinted in vol. ii of *Essays in Econ. Hist.* (No. 1468). Idem, 'The medieval wine dealer', *Explorations in Entreprenurial History*, 1st Ser. x (1957), 45–53. J. P. Trabut-Cussac (No. 5403). A volume of the collected papers of Margery K. James appeared as *Studies in the medieval wine trade*, edited by Elspeth M. Veale (Oxf. 1971).

5396 SALZMANN (LOUIS F.). English trade in the middle ages. Oxf. 1931.

5397 SAYLES (GEORGE O.). 'The English Company of 1343 and a merchant's oath'. *Speculum*, vi (1931), 177–205.

Describes the chequered career of the earliest syndicate of English merchants; associated with William de la Pole.

5398 SCAMMELL (GEOFFREY V.). 'English merchant shipping at the end of the middle ages: some east coast evidence'. *Econ. H.R.* 2nd Ser. xiii (1960), 327–41.

J. B. Blake, 'Medieval smuggling in the north-east: some fourteenth century evidence', *Archaeologia Aeliana*, 4th Ser. xliii (1965), 243–60.

5399 SCAMMELL (G. V.). 'Shipowning in England, c. 1450–1550'. *T.R.H.S.* 5th Ser. xii (1962), 105–22.

5400 SCHANZ (GEORG VON). Englische Handelspolitik gegen Ende des Mittelalters mit besonderer Berücksichtigung des Zeitalters der beiden ersten Tudors, Heinrich VII und Heinrich VIII. 2 vols. Leipzig. 1880–1.

5401 STURLER (JEAN V. de). Les relations politiques et les échanges commerciaux entre le duché de Brabant et l'Angleterre au moyen âge. Paris. 1936. See No. 5346.

5402 THIELEMANS (MARIE-ROSE). Bourgogne et l'Angleterre: relations politiques et économiques entre les Pays-Bas bourguignons et l'Angleterre, 1435–67. Brussels. 1966.

5403 TRABUT-CUSSAC (JEAN-PAUL). 'Les coutumes ou droits de douane perçus à Bordeaux sur les vins et les marchandises par l'administration anglaise de 1252 à 1307'. *Annales du Midi*, lxii (1950), 135–50.

5404 UNWIN (GEORGE), ed. Finance and trade under Edward III. Analysed in No. 1469; and extract in No. 1500.

William Cunningham, 'The commercial policy of Edward III', *T.R.H.S.* New Ser. iv (1889), 197–220.

5405 VEALE (ELSPETH M.). The English fur trade in the latter middle ages. Oxf. 1966.

A broad treatment of furs, their place in society, the trade through Europe, based largely on records of the Skinners Company of London.

5406 WARD (GRACE F.). 'The early history of the merchants staplers'. *E.H.R.* xxxiii (1918), 297–319.

The Cely Papers (No. 5330) and the *Stonor Letters* (No. 4615) give information on the staplers.

5407 WEINBAUM (MARTIN). 'Beiträge zur älteren englischen Gewerbe- und Handelsgeschichte'. *Vierteljahrschrift für Sozial- und Wirtschaftsgeschichte*, xviii (1925), 277–311.

2. *Wool and Woollens*

5408 ASHLEY (WILLIAM). The early history of the English woollen industry. Baltimore. 1887.

Howard L. Gray, 'The production and exportation of English woollens in the fourteenth century', *E.H.R.* xxxix (1924), 13–35.

5409 BIGWOOD (GEORGES). Un marché de matières premières: laines d'Angleterre et marchands italiens vers la fin du xiiie siècle. *Annales Hist. écon. et social.* (Paris) ii (1930), 193–209.

Armand De Roisy, 'Les routes terrestres des laines anglaises vers la Lombardie'. *Revue du Nord*, xxv (1939), 40–60. For the embargo on wool, 1270–4, see Berben in No. 1447.

5410 CARUS-WILSON (ELEANORA M.). 'The English cloth industry in the late twelfth and early thirteenth century'. *Econ. H.R.* xiv (1944), 32–50. Idem, 'Trends in the export of English woollens in the fourteenth century'. Ibid. 2nd Ser. iii (1950), 162–79. Idem, 'The (Wiltshire) woollen industry before 1500' *V.C.H. Wilts.* iv. 115–47. For reprints, see No. 5379.

5411 DONKIN (R. A.). 'The disposal of Cistercian wool in England and Wales during the twelfth and thirteenth centuries'. *Cîteaux in de Nederlanden,* viii (1957), 109–31; 181–96. Idem, 'Cistercian sheep-farming and the wool sales in the thirteenth century'. *Agricultural H.R.* vi (1958), 2–8.

> See No. 4994.

5412 FRYDE (EDMUND B.). 'Edward III's wool monopoly of 1337: a fourteenth century trading venture'. *History,* New Ser. xxxvii (1952), 8–24.

5413 HEATON (HERBERT). The Yorkshire woollen and worsted industries. Oxford Hist.-Lit. Stud. x. Oxf. 1920. *

> See Maude Sellars in *V.C.H. Yorks.* ii; and Denholm-Young, *Seignorial administration* (No. 4619), pp. 53–66.

5414 LIPSON (EPHRAIM). The history of the [English] woollen and worsted industries. Lond. 1921.

> Partly revised in his *Economic history* (No. 1371).

5415 McCLENAGHAN (BARBARA). The Springs of Lavenham and the Suffolk cloth trade in the fifteenth and sixteenth centuries. Ipswich. 1924.

> See George Unwin in *V.C.H. Suffolk,* ii; and No. 1500.

5416 MILLER (EDWARD). 'The fortunes of the English textile industry during the thirteenth century'. *Econ. H.R.* 2nd Ser. xviii (1965), 64–82.

5417 PEGOLOTTI (FRANCESCO BALDUCCI), La practica della mercatura. Ed. by Allan Evans. Cambr. (Mass.). 1936.

> Pegolotti was an agent for Bardi, 1310–40, and in England, 1318–21. In this merchant's guide, he supplies information on the wool produced by English monasteries, on weights and measures, etc., throughout fourteenth-century Christendom. See No. 5498.

5418 PELHAM (R. A.). 'Some aspects of the East Kent wool trade in the thirteenth century'. *Archaeologia Cantiana,* xliv (1932), 218–28.

> Idem, 'The cloth markets of Warwickshire during the later middle ages'. *Birmingham Archaeol. Soc. Trans.* lxvi (1950), 131–41.

5419 POWER (EILEEN E.). The wool trade in English medieval history. Oxf. 1941.

> The best book on the subject. Also E. E. Power, *The Paycocks of Coggeshall* (Lond. 1920). Idem, 'The English wool trade in the reign of Edward IV', *Cambr. Hist. Jour.* ii (1926), 17–35. Idem, 'The wool trade in the fifteenth century', in *Stud. in English Trade* (No. 5393).

5420 SAGHER (HENRI E. de). 'L'immigration des tisserands flamands et brabançons en Angleterre sous Édouard III'. *Mélanges Pirenne* (No. 1446).

5421 SMITH (JOHN). Chronicon rusticum-commerciale, or memoirs of wool. 2 vols. Lond. 1747. 2nd edn. 1756–7.

5422 WHITWELL (ROBERT J.). 'English monasteries and the wool trade in the thirteenth century'. *Vierteljahrschrift für Sozial- und Wirtschaftsgeschichte,* ii (1904), 1–33.

3. *Alien Merchants*

5423 ARENS (FRANZ). 'Wilhelm Servat von Cahors als Kaufmann zu London, 1273–1320'. *Vierteljahrschrift für Sozial- und Wirtschaftsgeschichte*, xi (1913), 477–514.

See Renouard (No. 5434).

5424 BEARDWOOD (ALICE). Alien merchants in England: their legal and economic position, 1350–1377. Medieval Academy of America. Cambr. (Mass.) 1931.

M. S. Giuseppi, 'Alien merchants in England in the fifteenth century', *T.R.H.S.* New Ser. ix (1895), 75–98; and R. Flenley, 'London and foreign merchants in the reign of Henry VI', *E.H.R.* xxv (1910), 644–55.

5425 BRANDT (AHASVER von). 'Recent trends in research on Hanseatic history'. *History*, xli (1956), 25–37.

This bibliographical article, showing little on England, continues from A. Weiner's bibliography in *Cambridge medieval history*, vii (1932), 853–7.

5426 DAENELL (ERNST R.). Die Blütezeit des deutschen Hanse. 2 vols. Berlin, 1905–6.

Book i: The Hanse *c.* 1356–1418, including chapter 'Die Hanse und England'.
Book ii: The struggle for the mastery of the North Sea, 1418–74.
Book iii: The organization of the Hanse.
　　See Karl Engel, 'Die Organisation der deutschhansischen Kaufleute in England, im 14. and 15. Jahrhundert (to 1474). *Hansische Geschichtsblätter*, xix (1913), 445–517; xx (1914), 173–225.

5427 DEPT (GASTON G.). 'Les Marchands flamands et le roi d'Angleterre, 1154–1216'. *Revue du Nord*, xii (1926), 303–24.

See also Dept, *Les Influences anglaise et française dans le comté de Flandre au début du xiiie siècle* (to 1226) (Ghent and Paris. 1928). C. Wyffels, 'De Vlaamse Hanze van Londen op het einde van de xiiie eeuw', *Annales de la Société d'émulation de Bruges*, xcvii (1960), 5–30.

5428 DOLLINGER (PHILIPPE). La Hanse (xiie–xviie siècles). Paris. 1964. Translated by D. S. Ault and S. H. Steinberg. Palo Alto (Calif.). 1970.

A synthesis of high quality, selective bibliography, and good documentation. See André Joris, 'La Hanse teutonique au moyen âge à propos d'un ouvrage récent', *Moyen Age*, lxxi (1965), 301–15. See for England, W. Stein, 'Die Hansebruderschaft der Kölner Englandfahrer und ihr Statut vom Jahre 1324', *Hansische Geschichtsblätter*, xiv (1908), 197–240; idem, 'Die Hanse und England beim Ausgang des hundert-jährigen Krieges', ibid. xxvi (1921), 27–126; M. Weinbaum, 'Stahlhof und deutsche Gildhalle zu London', ibid. xxxiii (1928), 45–65; G. A. Löning, 'Deutsche und Gotländer in England im 13. Jahrhundert', ibid. lxvii–viii (1943), 165–91; Erich Weise, 'Die Hanse, England und die merchants adventurers. Das Zusammenwirken von Köln und Danzig', *Jahrbuch des kölnischen Geschichtsvereins*, xxxi–ii (1957), 137–64; Hyman Palais, 'England's first attempt to break the monopoly of the Hanseatic League, 1377–1380', *A.H.R.* lxiv (1959), 852–65.

5429 GROSCH (GEORG). Geldgeschichte hansischer Kaufleute mit englischen Königen im 13. und 14. Jahrhundert. *Archiv für Kulturgeschichte*, ii (1904), 121–71; 265–95.

Joseph Hansen, 'Der englische Staatskredit unter König Eduard III (1327-77) und die hansischen Kaufleute', *Hansische Geschichtsblätter*, xvi (1910), 323-415.

5430 HEERS (JACQUES). 'Les Génois en Angleterre: la crise de 1458-66'. *Studi in onore di Armando Sapori* (Milan, 1957), pp. 807-32.

5431 KEUTGEN (FRIEDRICH). Die Beziehungen der Hanse zu England im letzten Drittel des 14. Jahrhunderts. Giessen. 1890.

5432 MAGNÚSSON (FINNUR). 'Om de Engelskes Handel og Foerd paa Island i det 15de Aarhundrede'. *Nordisk Tidsskrift for Oldkyndighed* (Copenhagen), ii (1833).

5433 PAGEL (KARL). Die Hanse. Oldenburg. 1943. 4th edn. Braunschweig. 1965.

5434 RENOUARD (YVES). 'Les Cahorsins, hommes d'affaires français du xiiie siècle'. *T.R.H.S.* 5th Ser. xi (1961), 43-67.

See Philippe Wolff, 'Le problème des Cahorsins', *Annales du Midi*, lxii (1950), 229-38; See Denholm-Young in his *Collected papers*, 2nd edn. (No. 1467), and Arens (No. 5423).

5435 ROON-BASSERMANN (ELIZABETH von). 'Die ersten Florentiner Handelsgesellschaften in England', *Vierteljahrschrift für Sozial- und Wirtschaftsgeschichte*, xxxix (1952), 97-128.

5436 RUDDOCK (ALWYN A.). Italian merchants and shipping in Southampton, 1270-1600. Southampton Rec. Ser. Southampton, 1951.

5437 SAPORI (ARMANDO). La crisi delle compagnie mercantili dei Bardi e dei Peruzzi. Florence. 1926. Idem, La compagnia dei Frescobaldi in Inghilterra. Florence. 1947.

See Rhodes in *Owens college essays* (No. 5517); Russell in No. 1469; and O'Sullivan for Ireland in No. 1438. Emilio Re, 'La compagnia dei Riccardi in Inghilterra e il suo fallimento alla fine del secolo xiii', *Archivio della Società Romana di Storia patria*, xxxvii (1914), 87-138; G. A. Holmes, 'Florentine merchants in England, 1346-1436', *Econ. H.R.* 2nd Ser. xiii (1960-1), 193-208; M. E. Mallett, 'Anglo-Florentine commercial relations, 1465-1491', ibid. xv (1962-3), 250-65. A. Sapori, 'Italian companies in England (thirteenth to fifteenth centuries)', *Banca Nazionale di Lavoro: Moneta e Credito* (Rome), iii (1950), 219-38.

5438 SCHAEFER (DIETRICH). Die deutsche Hanse. Monographien zur Weltgeschichte, xix (1903). Ed. by E. Heyck. Bielefeld and Leipzig. 4th edn. 1943.

A scholarly monograph designed for the general public.

5439 SCHULZ (FRIEDRICH). Die Hanse und England von Eduards III bis auf Heinrichs VIII Zeit. Abhandlungen zur Verkehrs- und Seegeschichte, v (Ed. by Dietrich Schaefer). Berlin. 1911.

5440 THRUPP (SYLVIA L.). 'A survey of the alien population of England in 1440'. *Speculum*, xxxii (1957), 262-73.

Nelly J. M. Kerling, 'Aliens in the county of Norfolk 1436-1485', *Norfolk Archaeol.* xxxiii (1965), 200-12. Alwyn A. Ruddock, 'Alien merchants in Southampton in the later middle ages', *E.H.R.* lxi (1946), 1-17; idem, 'Alien hosting in Southampton in the fifteenth century', *Econ. H.R.* xvi (1946), 30–7. Martin Weinbaum, 'Zur Stellung des Fremden im mittelalterlichen England', *Zeitschrift für vergleichende Rechtswissenschaft*, xlvi (1931), 360–78.

5441 WATSON (W. B.). 'The structure of Florentine galley trade with Flanders and England in the fifteenth century'. *Revue belge de philol. et d'hist.* xxxix (1961), 1073–91; xl (1962), 317–47.

5442 WINTERFELD (LUISE von). 'Tidemann Lemberg: ein Dortmunder Kaufmansleben aus dem 14. Jahrhundert'. *Hansische Volkshefte*, x (1926). Separately, Bremen. 1927.

D. MISCELLANEOUS STUDIES ON SOCIETY

1. *Comprehensive Studies*

5443 BALDWIN (JOHN W.). Masters, princes and merchants: the social views of Peter the Chanter and his circle. Vol. i: text; vol. ii: notes. Princeton. 1970.

> The circle included, among others, Langton, Chobham, and Gerald of Wales. The text is an analysis of the opinions of the circle on many aspects of urban life, such as Paris and the academic life, the relations of church and state, the merchants and their activities. The notes of volume two present numerous, wide-ranging citations.

5444 BRIDBURY (ANTHONY R.). Economic growth: England in the later middle ages. Lond. 1962.

> A controversial study which argues that the average wealth increased and agriculture benefited during the decline in population and in cost of production, in opposition to Postan's theses.

5445 CAMBRIDGE ECONOMIC HISTORY OF EUROPE (No. 1364), ii (1952), 232–51: M. M. Postan, 'The English challenge' (in trade). Ibid. 355–428: E. Carus-Wilson, 'The (European) woollen industry.' iii (1963), 290–340: E. Miller, 'Economic policies' (France and England). Ibid. 451–72: E. B. and M. M. Fryde, 'Public credit' (England).

5446 CHADWICK (DOROTHY). Social life in the days of Piers Plowman. Cambr. Stud. in Medieval Life and Thought. Cambr. 1922. *

5447 COULTON (GEORGE G.). Life in the middle ages: selected and translated and annotated. 4 vols. Cambr. (2nd edn.) 1928–30. *

> First edn. entitled *A medieval garner* (Lond. 1910).

5448 COULTON (G. G.). Social life in Britain from the Conquest to the Reformation. Cambr. 1918. * Idem, The medieval village. Cambr. 1925. * Idem, The medieval scene: an informal introduction to the middle ages. Cambr. 1930. * Idem, Medieval panorama. Cambr. 1938. Idem, Medieval scene from Conquest to Reformation. Cambr. 1939.

5449 CUTTS (EDWARD L.). Scenes and characters of the middle ages. Lond. 1872. 7th edn. 1930. *

5450 DOUGLAS (DAVID C.). The social structure of medieval East Anglia. Oxford Stud. in Social and Legal History, edited by Paul Vinogradoff. Oxf. 1927.

5451 DU BOULAY (FRANCIS R. H.). An age of ambition: English society in the late middle ages. Lond. and N.Y. 1970.

5452 HILTON (RODNEY H.). A medieval society. The west midlands at the end of the thirteenth century. Lond. and N.Y. 1967.

A broadly based study of lords, estates, peasants, townsmen, and social controls.

5453 HOSKINS (WILLIAM K.). Provincial England: essays in social and economic history. Lond. 1963.

1-14: Sheep farming in Saxon and medieval England.
53-67: Origin and rise of Market Harborough.
115-30: Seven deserted village sites in Leicestershire.
181-208: Population, a study of Wigston.

5454 JUSSERAND (JEAN A. A. J.). English wayfaring life in the middle ages (fourteenth century). Translated (from the French) by Lucy Toulmin Smith. Lond. 1889. Many editions. New edition revised and enlarged by the author. Lond. 1920. Reprinted; also in paperback.

The original French title is: Les Anglais au moyen âge: la vie nomade et les routes d'Angleterre au xive siècle (Paris, 1884).

5455 KEEN (MAURICE H.). The outlaws of medieval legend. Lond. and Toronto. 1961.

See also E. L. G. Stones, 'The Folvilles of Ashby-Folville, Leicestershire, and their associates in crime, 1326-47', *T.R.H.S.* 5th Ser. vii (1957), 117-36; J. G. Bellamy, 'The Coterel gang: an anatomy of a band of fourteenth century criminals', *E.H.R.* lxxix (1964), 698-717; Constance M. Fraser and Kenneth Emsley, 'Law and society in Northumberland and Durham, 1290-1350', *Archaeologia Aeliana*, xlvii (1969), 47-70.

5456 KENDALL (PAUL M.). The Yorkist age: daily life in England during the wars of the Roses. Lond. 1962.

5457 MILLER (EDWARD). 'The English economy in the thirteenth century, implications of recent research'. *Past and Present*, no. 28 (1964), 21-40. Idem, 'England in the twelfth and thirteenth centuries: an economic contrast?' *Econ. H.R.* 2nd Ser. xxiv (1971), 1-14.

5458 O'BRIEN (GEORGE). An essay on medieval economic teaching. Lond. 1920. *

An important study of the economic theories of the thirteenth and fourteenth centuries.

5459 PERROY (ÉDOUARD). 'A l'origine d'une économie contractée: les crises du xive siècle'. *Annales Écon. Soc. Civil.* iv (1949), 167-82.

See H. A. Miskimin, 'Monetary movements and market structure: forces for contraction in fourteenth and fifteenth century England', *Jour. Econ. Hist.* xxiv (1964), 470-90.

5460 POOLE (AUSTIN L.). Obligations of society in the twelfth and thirteenth centuries. Oxf. 1947.

5461 POSTAN (M. MICHAEL). 'The fifteenth century'. *Econ. H.R.* ix (1938–9), 160–7.

In this Revision in Economic History, Postan maintains that the fifteenth century was a period of depression. For a contrary opinion, see Bridbury (No. 5444); E. A. Kosminsky, 'The evolution of feudal rent in England from the eleventh to the fifteenth centuries', *Past and Present*, vii (1955), 12–36; idem, 'Peut-on considérer les xive et xve siècles comme l'époque de la décadence de l'économie européenne', *Studi in onore di Armando Sapori* (Milan, 1957), pp. 551–69; W. I. Haward, 'Economic aspects of the Wars of the Roses in East Anglia', *E.H.R.* xli (1926), 170–89. See also Barbara Harvey, 'Population trend' (No. 5477).

5462 POSTAN (M. M.). 'The rise of a money economy'. *Econ. H.R.* xiv (1944), 123–34; reprinted in *Essays in economic history* (No. 1468). Idem, 'Medieval capitalism: Studies in bibliography'. Ibid. iv (1933), 212–27.

Professor Postan is a prolific scholar of large influence; other works of his can be found in the index under 'Postan'. A bibliography of his writings is given in *Essays in economic history presented to Professor M. M. Postan*, which is the first issue of volume xviii (1965) of *Economic History Review*.

5463 POWER (EILEEN E.), and POSTAN (M. M.), eds. Studies in English trade in the fifteenth century (No. 5393).

5464 POWER (E. E.). Medieval people. Lond. and Boston, 1924. *
111–45: Thomas Betson, a merchant of the staple in the fifteenth century.
146–69: Thomas Paycocke of Coggeshall, an Essex clothier in the reign of Henry VII.

5465 SALZMAN (LOUIS F.). English life in the middle ages. Lond. 1926.

5466 SAWYER (PETER H.). 'The wealth of England in the eleventh century'. *T.R.H.S.* 5th Ser. xv (1965), 145–64.

5467 STENTON (DORIS M.). English society in the early middle ages (1066–1307). Penguin Books. Harmondsworth. 1952.

5468 THRUPP (SYLVIA). 'Economy and society in medieval England'. *Jour. British Stud.* ii (1962–3), 1–13.

2. *Population Problems*

A long bibliography on demography throughout Europe can be found in the wide-ranging *Historical demography* by T. H. Hollingworth (Lond. 1969).

5469 BEAN (J. W. M.). 'Plague, population, and economic decline in the later middle ages'. *Econ. H.R.* 2nd Ser. xv (1963), 423–37.

See John Saltmarsh, 'Plague and economic decline in the later middle ages', *Cambr. Hist. Jour.* vii (1941–3), 23–41. E. Carpentier, 'Autour de la peste noire: famines et épidémies dans l'histoire du xive siècle'. *Annales Écon. Soc. Civil.* xvii (1962), 1062–92.

5470 CAMPBELL (ANNA M.). The black death and men of learning. N.Y. 1931.

5471 COOPER (J. P.). 'The social distribution of land and men in England'. *Econ. H.R.* 2nd Ser. xx (1967), 419–40.

5472 COULTON (GEORGE G.). The black death. N.Y. 1930.

5473 CREIGHTON (CHARLES). History of epidemics in Britain. 2 vols. Cambr. 1891–4. *

See No. 5482.

5474 EKWALL (BROR O. EILERT). Studies in the population of medieval London. Stockholm. 1956.

See Russell, 'Mediaeval midland . . . migration' (No. 5481), Thrupp (No. 5440, 5481, 5484) and Williams, London (No. 5181) App. A.

5475 GASQUET (FRANCIS A.). The great pestilence, 1348–9. Lond. 1893. Idem, The black death of 1348–9. Lond. 1908.

5476 HALLAM (H. E.). 'Some thirteenth century censuses'. *Econ. H.R.* 2nd Ser. x (1958), 340–61. Idem, 'Population density in medieval fenland'. Ibid. xiv (1961), 71–81.

5477 HARVEY (BARBARA F.). 'The population trend in England between 1300 and 1348'. *T.R.H.S.* 5th Ser. xvi (1966), 23–42.

The citations are useful in setting the whole problem of population trends.

5478 HELLEINER (K. F.). 'Population movement and agrarian depression in the later middle ages'. *Canadian Jour. Econ. and Pol. Sci.* xv (1949), 368–77.

5479 LEVETT (ADA E.) and BALLARD (ADOLPHUS). The black death on the estates of the see of Winchester. Oxford Stud. Social and Legal Hist. v. Oxf. 1916.

5480 POSTAN (M. MICHAEL). 'Some economic evidence of declining population in the later middle ages'. *Econ. H.R.* 2nd Ser. ii (1950), 221–46.

See also his 'Fifteenth century' (No. 5461); and D. G. Watts, 'A model for the early fourteenth century' (No. 5495). Christopher Dyer, 'Population and agriculture on a Warwickshire manor in the later middle ages', *Univ. Birmingham Hist. Jour.* xi (1968), 113–27.

5481 RUSSELL (JOSIAH C.). British medieval population. Albuquerque (N. Mex.). 1948.

A pioneer work which broke new ground and provoked controversy. See, for example, Jan Z. Titow, *Eng. Rural Soc.* (No. 4701), pp. 64–93 *passim*; and more favourably, Sylvia Thrupp in *Comparative Stud.* viii (1965–6), 474–83. See Russell, 'Mediaeval midland and northern migration to London, 1100–1365', *Speculum*, xxxiv (1959), 641–5; idem, 'A quantitative approach to medieval population change', *Jour. Econ. Hist.* xxiv (1964), 1–21; idem, 'The pre-plague population of England', *Jour. Brit. Stud.* v (1966), 1–21; idem, 'Recent advances in mediaeval demography', *Speculum*, xl (1965), 84–101. K. C. Newton, 'A source for medieval population statistics', *Jour. Soc. Archivists* iii (1969), 543–6. J. Krause, 'The medieval household, large or small', *Econ. H.R.* 2nd Ser. ix (1956–7), 420–32.

5482 SHREWSBURY (J. F. D.). A history of bubonic plagues in the British Isles (1348–1670). Cambr. 1970.

A scholarly work which replaces Creighton (No. 5473). See review in *Hist. Jour.* xiv (1971), 205–15.

5483 THOMPSON (ALEXANDER HAMILTON). 'The pestilences of the fourteenth century in the diocese of York'. *Archaeol. Jour.* lxxi (1914), 97–154.

George G. Coulton, *The influence of the black death on the English monasteries* (Menasha, Wis. 1916). William Rees, 'The black death in Wales', *T.R.H.S.* 4th Ser. iii (1920), 115–35. E. Robo, 'The black death in the hundred of Farnham' *E.H.R.* xliv (1929), 560–72. C. E. Boucher, 'The black death in Bristol', *Bristol–Glos. Archaeol. Soc. Trans.* lx (1938), 31–46. J. L. Fisher, 'The black death in Essex', *Essex Rev.* lii (1943), 13–20.

5484 THRUPP (SYLVIA L.). 'The problem of replacement-rates in late medieval English population'. *Econ. H.R.* 2nd Ser. xviii (1965), 101–19.

5485 TITOW (JAN Z.). 'Some evidence of the thirteenth century population increase'. *Econ. H.R.* 2nd Ser. xiv (1961), 218–24.

5486 ZIEGLER (PHILIP). The black death. Lond. 1969. Penguin paperback. 1970.

A well-done, popular work, with a good bibliography.

3. *Wages and Prices*

5487 ASHLEY (WILLIAM J.). The bread of our forefathers. Oxf. 1928.

Alan S. C. Ross, 'The assize of bread', *Econ. H.R.* 2nd Ser. ix (1956–7), 332–42.

5488 BENNETT (M. K.). 'British wheat yield per acre for seven centuries'. *Econ. Hist.* iii no. 10 (1935), 12–29. Reprinted in *Essays in Agrarian History*, edited by W. E. Minchinton (Newton Abbot, 1968), pp. 53–72.

5489 BEVERIDGE (WILLIAM H.) *et al.* Prices and wages in England from the twelfth to the nineteenth century. vol. i: price tables. Lond. and N.Y. 1939. *

W. H. Beveridge, 'The yield and price of corn in the middle ages,' *Econ. H.R.* i (1929), 93–113; reprinted in *Essays in Economic Hist* (No. 1468). Idem, 'Wages in the Winchester manors', *Econ. H.R.* vii (1936), 22–43. Idem, 'Westminster wages in the manorial era', ibid. 2nd Ser. viii (1955), 18–35.

5490 FARMER (D. L.). 'Some price fluctuations in Angevin England'. *Econ. H.R.* 2nd Ser. ix (1956), 34–43. Idem, 'Some grain price movements in thirteenth century England'. Ibid. x (1957–8), 207–20. Idem, 'Some livestock movements in thirteenth century England'. Ibid. xxii (1969), 1–16.

See Austin L. Poole, 'Live-stock prices in the twelfth century', *E.H.R.* lv (1940), 284–95.

5491 KNOOP (DOUGLAS) and JONES (G. P.). 'Masons' wages in medieval England'. *Econ. Hist.* ii (1930–3), 473–99.

5492 LENNARD (REGINALD). 'Statistics of corn yields in medieval England'. *Econ. Hist.* iii (1936–7), 173–92, 345–9.

5493 POSTAN (M. MICHAEL). 'Investment in medieval agriculture'. *Jour. Econ. Hist.* xxvii (1967), 576–87.

A generalized summary of Postan's position on production and yields.

5494 PRIOR (W. H.). 'Notes on the weights and measures of medieval England'. *Bulletin Du Cange*, i (1925), 77–97, 141–70.

5495 ROGERS (JAMES E. THOROLD). A history of agriculture and prices in England, 1259–1793. 7 vols. Oxf. 1866–1902. *

The basic study. See also Beveridge (No. 5489); and A. P. Usher, 'Prices of wheat and commodity price indexes for England, 1259–1930', *Rev. Econ. Statistics*, xiii (1931), 103–13.

Etienne Robo, 'Wages and prices in the hundred of Farnham in the thirteenth century', *Econ. Hist.* iii, no. 9 (1934), 24–34. J. Schreiner, 'Wages and prices in England in later middle ages', *Scandinavian Econ. Hist. Rev.* ii (1954), 61–73. S. V. Hopkins, 'Seven centuries of wages and prices: some earlier estimates', *Economica*, xxviii (1961), 30–6. See Phelps-Brown and Hopkins in *Essays in Econ. Hist.* (No. 1468). D. G. Watts, 'A model for the early fourteenth century', *Econ. H.R.* 2nd Ser. xx (1967), 543–7.

5496 SCHOFIELD (R. S.). 'The geographical distribution of wealth in England, 1334–1649'. *Econ. H.R.* 2nd Ser. xviii (1965), 483–510.

5497 SELECT TRACTS AND TABLE BOOKS RELATING TO ENGLISH WEIGHTS AND MEASURES, 1100–1742. Ed. by Hubert Hall and Frieda J. Nicholas. R.H.S. Camden 3rd Ser. xli, *Camden Miscellany*, xv, no. 5 (1929).

J. W. Shilson, 'Weighing wool in the middle ages', *Antiquity*, xviii (1944), 72–7.

5498 ZUPKO (RONALD E.). A dictionary of English weights and measures: from Anglo-Saxon times to the nineteenth century. Madison (Wisconsin). 1968.

See review in *Le Moyen Âge*, lxxvii (1971), 170–4. R. E. Zupko, 'Notes on medieval English weights and measures in Francesco Balducci Pegolotti's "La practica della mercatura"', *Explorations in Economic History*, vii (1969–70), 153–9. See No. 5417.

4. *Money, Banking and Industry*

See section of Numismatics, particularly vol. i, pp. 80–4.

5499 AMES (EDWARD). 'The sterling crisis of 1337–1339'. *Jour. Econ. Hist.* xxv (1965), 496–522.

5500 BUTLER (RODNEY F.). The history of Kirkstall forge through seven centuries, 1200–1954: the story of England's oldest ironworks. Kirkstall. 1945. 2nd edn. York. 1954.

See also Rhys Jenkins, 'The rise and fall of the Sussex iron industry', *Newcomen Soc. Trans.* i (1920–1), 16–33; and Ernest Straker, *Wealden iron* (Lond. 1931). Henry G. Nicholls, *Iron making in olden times, as instanced in the ancient mines, forges and furnaces of the forest of Dean* (Lond. 1866).

5501 CARUS-WILSON (ELEANORA M.). 'An industrial revolution of the thirteenth-century'. *Econ. H.R.* xi (1941), 39–60. Idem, 'Evidences of industrial growth on some fifteenth century manors'. Ibid. 2nd Ser. xii (1959–60), 190–205. Both reprinted in *Essays in Econ. Hist.* (No. 1468).

See R. W. C. Taylor, *Introduction to a history of the factory system* (Lond. 1886), which devotes much attention to the middle ages.

5502 COPY OF AN INDENTURE MADE IN 1469 BETWEEN EDWARD IV AND WILLIAM, LORD HASTINGS, master of the mint, respecting the regulation of the coinage. *Archaeologia*, xv (1806), 164–78.

Some valuable documents of the reigns of Henry III and Edward I concerning the mint, and a fourteenth-century tract on the same subject, will be found in Hubert Hall's edition of the *Red book* (No. 3007), 979–1010, 1072–81. See No. 688.

5503   DAVIS (ELIZA J.) and PEAKE (MARGARET I.), eds. 'Loans from the city of London to Henry VI, 1431–49'. *B.I.H.R.* iv (1926–7), 165–72.

See K. B. McFarlane, 'Loans to Lancastrian kings' (No. 3253).

5504   DOUCET (ROGER). 'Les finances anglaises en France à la fin de la guerre de cent ans, 1413–35'. *Le Moyen Âge*, xxxvi (1926), 265–332.

5505   FRYDE (EDMUND B.). 'Some business transactions of York merchants, John Goldbeter, William Acastre and partners, 1336–49'. Borthwick Papers. York. 1966. See also Fryde (Nos. 3236, 4179).

5506   GOUGH (JOHN W.). The mines of Mendip. Oxf. 1930.

5507   HAMILTON (HENRY). The English brass and copper industries to 1800. Lond. 1926. *

5508   HEATH (PETER). 'North sea fishing in the fifteenth century: the Scarborough fleet'. *Northern Hist.* iii (1968), 53–69.

5509   JENKINSON (C. HILARY) and STEAD (M. T.). 'William Cade, a financier of the twelfth century'. *E.H.R.* xxviii (1913), 209–27, and 731–2.

Contains a roll of the debtors to Cade (d. *c.* 1166), a Christian usurer in close relation to the crown. See also J. H. Round, 'The debtors of William Cade', *E.H.R.* xxviii (1913), 522–7, and C. H. Haskins, ibid. 730–1. See Jenkinson in *Poole essays* (No. 1448).

5510   JOHNSON (CHARLES). London shipbuilding A.D. 1295. *Antiquaries Jour.* vii (1927), 424–37.

5511   LAPSLEY (GAILLARD). 'The account roll of a fifteenth century ironmaster'. *E.H.R.* xiv (1899), 509–29.

An account rendered to the bishop of Durham by a keeper of a forge, 1408–9.

5512   LE PATOUREL (H. E. JEAN). 'Documentary evidence and the medieval pottery industry'. *Medieval Archaeology*, xii (1968), 101–26.

5513   LEWIS (GEORGE R.). The stannaries: a study of the English tin mines. Harvard Economic Stud. Cambr. (Mass.) 1908. Reprinted 1924 and 1966.

See H. P. R. Finberg, 'The stannary of Tavistock', *Devonshire Asso. Trans.* lxxxi (1949), 155–84; and L. F. Salzman in *English Government at work* (No. 3836) iii. 67–104.

5514   ORIGINAL DOCUMENTS (relating to royal silver mines in Devon, *temp.* Edw. I.). Ed. by Edward Smirke. *Archaeol. Jour.* xxvii (1870), 129–33, 314–22.

5515   POSTAN (M. MICHAEL). 'Private financial instruments in medieval England'. *Vierteljahrschrift für Sozial- und Wirtschaftsgeschichte*, xxiii (1930), 26–75. Idem, 'Credit in medieval trade'. *Econ. H.R.* i (1928), 234–61; reprinted in *Essays in Economic Hist.* (No. 1468).

5516   PUGH (RALPH B.). 'Some mediaeval money lenders'. *Speculum*, xliii (1968), 274–89.

5517 RHODES (WALTER E.). Italian bankers in England and their loans to Edward I and Edward II. Historical Essays by Members of Owens College (No. 1472). Manchester. 1902. See Sapori (No. 5437).

5518 SALZMAN (LOUIS F.). English industries in the middle ages. Lond. 1913. 2nd edn. Oxf. 1923.

5519 SCHUBERT (HANS (JOHN) R.). History of the British iron and steel industry (to *c.* 1800). Lond. 1957.

5520 SPUFFORD (PETER). 'Coinage and Currency' in Cambr. Econ. Hist. (No. 1364), iii (1963), 576–602.

5521 UNWIN (GEORGE). Industrial organization in the sixteenth and seventeenth centuries. Oxf. 1904. *

Chaps. i and ii deal mainly with the fourteenth and fifteenth centuries.

5522 WHITWELL (ROBERT J.). 'Italian bankers and the English crown'. *T.R.H.S.* New Ser. xvii (1903), 175–233.

Includes a chart of advances to the court of Rome, 1200–33. Pp. 218–33: appendixes of sources.

5. Fairs, Markets, and Inland Transportation

See Mullins, *Texts*, nos. 35.2, 44.10, 61.59.

5523 CATE (JAMES L.). 'The church and market reform in England during the reign of Henry III', *Medieval and Historiographical Essays in honor of James Westfall Thompson* (Chicago, 1938), pp. 27–65. Idem, 'The English mission of Eustace of Flay' (No. 1447). (Eustace sought to end Sunday markets.)

5524 GROSS (CHARLES). Select cases concerning the law merchant (No. 3507).

Extracts from the records of fair courts, e.g. St. Ives (Hunts.), 1270–1324, staple courts, pie-powder courts, etc.

5525 KITCHIN (GEORGE W.), ed. Charter of Edward III confirming and enlarging the privileges of St. Giles fair, Winchester, 1349. Lond. 1886.

5526 MacCUTCHEON (KENNETH L.). Yorkshire fairs and markets to the end of the eighteenth century. Thoresby Soc. xxxix (1940).

5527 MORLEY (HENRY). Memoirs of Bartholomew fair. Lond. 1859. New edn. 1880. *

5528 OGLE (OCTAVIUS). The Oxford market (13th to 19th cent.). Oxford Hist. Soc. *Collectanea.* 2nd Ser. (1890), 1–135.

5529 ORDNANCE SURVEY MAP: Bodleian map of Great Britain (1325–1350). Chessington.

5530 PASSINGHAM (WILLIAM J.). London's markets: their origin and history. Lond. 1935.

5531 REPORTS OF THE ROYAL COMMISSION ON MARKET RIGHTS AND TOLLS. *Parliamentary Papers*, 1888, vols. liii–lv; 1889, vols. xxxviii; 1890–1, vols. xxxvii–xli. 14 vols. in 17. 1889–91.

5532 RICHARDSON (H.). The medieval fairs and markets of York. St. Anthony's Hall Pubns. no. 20. Borthwick Inst. of Hist. Research. 1961.

5533 RICHARDSON (HENRY G.). 'Law merchant in London in 1292'. *E.H.R.* xxxvii (1922), 242–9.

5534 SALZMAN (LOUIS F.). 'The Legal status of markets'. *Cambr. Hist. Jour.* ii (1928), 205–12.

5535 STENTON (FRANK M.). 'The road system in medieval England'. *Econ. H.R.* vii (1936), 1–21. Reprinted in No. 1496.

  F. M. Stenton, 'The roads of the Gough map' (transparent overlay to map showing modern names) for E. J. S. Parsons, *Map of Great Britain* (No. 602).

5536 TUPLING (GEORGE H.). 'The origin of markets and fairs in mediaeval Lancashire'. *Lancs.–Ches. Antiq. Soc. Trans.* xlix for 1933 (1935), 75–94. Idem, 'Early Lancashire markets and their tolls'. Ibid. l for 1934–5 (1937), 107–37. Idem, 'An alphabetical list of the fairs and markets of Lancashire, recorded before 1701'. Ibid. li for 1936 (1937), 86–110. Idem, 'Markets and fairs in medieval Lancashire' in *Tait essays* (No. 1455), pp. 345–56.

5537 WALFORD (CORNELIUS). Fairs, past and present: a chapter in the history of commerce. Lond. 1883. *

  Deals particularly with Stourbridge fair and Bartholomew fair.

5538 WEDEMEYER (ELLEN). 'Social groupings at the fair of St. Ives (1275–1302)'. *Mediaeval Stud.* xxxii (1970), 27–59.

5539 WILLARD (JAMES F.). 'Inland transportation in England during the fourteenth century'. *Speculum*, i (1926), 361–74.

  Idem, 'The use of carts in the fourteenth century' (Historical Revision), *History*, New Ser. xvii (1932–3), 246–50.

XXI. THE CHURCH, 1066–1485

The principal collections of ecclesiastical sources dealing with the Middle Ages as a whole are to be found on pp. 144–51. Since the quantity of surviving records increases as time passes, the collections are considerably fuller for the period after the Norman conquest. These records which are concerned exclusively with some portion of the period from 1066 to 1485 are entered here. They include papal letters, acts of the General Councils, diocesan records and records of religious orders. There follows a section on Canon Law in England from 1066 to 1485, which includes studies on ecclesiastical courts and on the Becket controversy. Then the 'Lives' and Works of some of the foremost scholars, saints, and mystics are listed. This chapter concludes with a section on modern, secondary writings on church history between 1066 and 1485.

A. PAPAL LETTERS CONCERNING ENGLAND

The papal letters down to 1198, collected from a wide variety of sources from all of western Christendom, are itemized in Jaffé–Löwenfeld (No. 1131). This collection is supplemented, often with full transcripts, in Kehr's *Regesta* (No. 1132), of which Holtzmann's *Papsturkunden* (No. 5550) for England is invaluable. A collection for the thirteenth century similar to Jaffé–Löwenfeld is listed in Potthast's *Regesta* (No. 1138). There is projected as an international enterprise an *Index actorum pontificum* to list all original papal bulls preserved in all archives from 1198 to 1417, on this, see Leo Santifaller, 'Der Censimento der spät-mittelalterlichen Papsturkunden', *M.I.O.G.* lxxii (1964), 122–34.

The letters in the papal registers concerning Great Britain and Ireland for the period from 1198 to 1492 are noted in the Bliss–Twemlow *Calendar* (No. 5547), which calendars entries from *Registra Vaticana*, but not from *Registra Avenionensia*. The editions of registers issued by the French School at Rome (Nos. 5552–3) are often useful for matters touching England; in some cases entries from the Avignonese Registers are included. Papal letters concerning Ireland can be found in Theiner (No. 5554) and in Sheehy (No. 1137). A few registers for individual popes have been published separately; and are entered below in order of papal succession. For a guide, see Boyle (No. 5540).

1. *Vatican Archives*

5540 AMBROSINI (MARIA LUISA). The secret archives of the Vatican. Boston. 1969.

> The general history of the archives intended for the general public should be used with discretion. By far the best guide in English is the convenient, informative handbook by Leonard E. Boyle, entitled *A survey of the Vatican Archives and of its medieval holdings* (Toronto, 1972).

5541 ARCHIVUM HISTORIAE PONTIFICIAE. By the Faculty of Ecclesiastical History at the Gregorian University. Rome. Vol. i+. 1963+.

> *Bibliographia historiae pontificiae* constitutes each year the second part of *Archivum Hist. Pont.*

5542 BAUMGARTEN (P. M.). Aus Kanzlei und Kammer. Freiburg im Breisgau. 1907.

> Geoffrey Barraclough, 'Audientia litterarum contradictarum', *Dictionnaire de droit canonique*, i (1935), cols. 1387–99. See Poole, *Lectures on the papal chancery* (No. 420); and Cheney, *Study of . . . chancery* (No. 420). Peter Herde, *Beiträge zum papstlichen Kanzlei- und Urkundenwesen im 13. Jahrhundert.* Münchener Historische Studien (Kallmünz, 1961, 2nd. edn. 1967). For the fifteenth century, W. von Hofmann, *Forschungen zur Geschichte der kurialen Behörden vom Schisma bis zur Reformation.* 2 vols. (Rome, 1914). See Nos. 3837 and 6452.

5543 BIBLIOGRAFIA DELL'ARCHIVIO VATICANO. Vatican City. 1962+ (in progress).

5544 FINK (KARL A.). Das Vatikanische Archiv: Einführung in die Bestände und ihre Erforschung. Rome. 1943. 2nd edn. 1951.

5545 MacFARLANE (LESLIE J.). The Vatican Archives, with special reference to sources for British medieval history. Lond. 1959.

A useful and convenient essay reprinted from *Archives*, iv, nos. 21–2 (1959), 29–44 and 84–101. There is also a concise outline in Ian B. Cowan, 'The Vatican Archives: a report on pre-reformation Scottish material', *Scot. H.R.* xlviii (1969), 227–42.

2. Papal Letters

5546 BULLARIUM DIPLOMATUM ET PRIVILEGIORUM SS. ROMANORUM PONTIFICUM. Taurinensis editio. 25 vols. Turin. 1857–72.

5547 CALENDAR OF ENTRIES IN THE PAPAL REGISTERS RELATING TO GREAT BRITAIN AND IRELAND: PAPAL LETTERS (1198–1492). Ed. by W. H. Bliss and J. A. Twemlow. 14 vols. H.M.S.O. Lond. 1893–1960.

Vol. 13 consists of two parts. The letters in the paper *Registra Avenionensia*, many of which record provisions and expectancies to English benefices, are not entered into the parchment *Registra Vaticana*; and hence are not found in this *Calendar*. Some full transcripts of the letters in the *Calendar* can be found in the Marini Collection in the British Museum Add. MSS. 15351–15401, entitled *Monumenta Britannica ex Autographia Romanorum Pontificum Regestis ceterisque documentis deprompta*, a few letters before 1216 and then 1216–1758. Add. MS. 15401 is an index.

5548 CALENDAR OF ENTRIES IN THE PAPAL REGISTERS RELATING TO GREAT BRITAIN AND IRELAND: PETITIONS TO THE POPE. Ed. by W. H. Bliss. Vol. i. 1342–1419. H.M.S.O. Lond. 1896.

No more published; and not a continuous series.

5549 CALENDAR OF SCOTTISH SUPPLICATIONS TO ROME (1418–1432). Ed. by E. R. Lindsay and Annie I. Cameron (Dunlop). Scot. Hist. Soc. Pubns. 3 vols. Edin. 1934–70.

See Annie I. Cameron, *The Apostolic camera and Scottish benefices, 1418–1488.* Lond. N.Y., etc. 1934.
'The text is a calendar of all the entries relating to Scotland' for the period.

5550 HOLTZMANN (WALTHER). Papsturkunden in England. 3 vols. Abhandlungen der Gesellschaft der Wissenschaften zu Göttingen, Phil.–Hist. Klasse. Neue Folge, Bd. xxv. 1–2; Dritte Folge, xiv–xv, xxxiii. Berlin and Göttingen. 1930–52.

This English section of Kehr's *Regesta*, which is designed as a collection of papal documents anterior to 1198, prints the documents *in extenso*. The editing and the commentaries are admirable. Also to be consulted are H. I. Bell, 'A list of original bulls and briefs in the department of manuscripts, British Museum', *E.H.R.* xxxvi (1921), 393–419, 556–83; *P.R.O. Lists and Indexes* (No. 955), xlix (1923); Kathleen Major, 'Original papal documents in the Bodleian Library', *Bodleian Lib. Rec.* iii (1951), 242–56; and Jane E. Sayers, 'Original papal documents in the Lambeth Palace Library', *B.I.H.R.* xl (Special Supplement no. 6), 1967. See Johnson in *Tout essays* (No. 1458). C. R. Cheney, 'On the Cheltenham (Phillipps) manuscripts and some others described in *Papsturkunden in England*', *Traditio*, xxiii (1967), 512–16.

5551 RAYNALDUS (ODORICUS). Annales ecclesiastici ab anno quo desinit Card. C. Baronius, 1198 usque ad annum 1534 (–1565). Cologne. 1694–1727; 38 vols. Lucca. 1738–59. 37 vols. Bar-le-Duc. 1864–83. Several other edns.

5552 REGISTRES ET LETTRES DES PAPES DU XIIIe siècle. Ed. for Bibliothèque des écoles françaises d'Athènes et de Rome. 2nd. Ser. Paris. 1883+.

Registers from Gregory IX (1227) to Benedict XI (1303–4). Except for repetitive forms, the letters are printed in full. Listed in *Repert. Font.* i. 93–4.

5553 REGISTRES ET LETTRES DES PAPES DU XIVe SIÈCLE. Ed. for Bibliothèque des écoles françaises d'Athènes et de Rome. 3rd Ser. Paris. 1899+.

Listed in *Repert. Font.* i. 94–5. The letters are retained in their categories: those published in whole or in part by 1970 were

(a) Lettres communes for John XXII, Benedict XII, and Urban V.
(b) Lettres secrètes et curiales relatives à la France for John XXII.
(c) Lettres closes, patentes et curiales rapportant à la France for Benedict XII, Clement VI, Innocent VI, Urban V, and Gregory XI.
(d) Lettres closes, patentes et curiales intéressant les pays autres que la France for Benedict XII, Clement VI, and Gregory XI.
(e) Lettres secrètes et curiales (a new series beginning in 1959 of these letters for all countries) for Innocent VI.
(f) Recueil des bulles for one year (1362–3) for Urban V.
The lettres communes are calendared; the other letters are printed frequently *in extenso*.

5554 THEINER (AUGUSTIN). Vetera monumenta Hibernorum et Scotorum historiam illustrantia . . . 1216–1547. Rome. 1864.

See Sheehy (No. 1137); and A. Gwynn, 'Gregory VII and the Irish church', *Studi Gregoriani* (Rome), iii (1948), 105–28.

5555 CASPAR (ERICH L. E.). Das Register Gregors VII. 2 vols. M.G.H. Epistolae Selectae. Berlin. 1920–3.

Philipp Jaffé, *Monumenta Gregoriana* (Bibliotheca Rerum Germanicarum, ii (1965). Berlin) prints letters not in the register as well as those formally registered.
The correspondence of Pope Gregory VII: selected letters from the registrum, trans. by Ephraim Emerton. Columbia Univ. Records of Civilization. N.Y. 1932. A new edition of *Epistolae Vagantes* of Gregory VII has been published by H. E. J. Cowdrey. Oxf. 1972.

5556 LAUDABILITER, an alleged papal bull. Ed. by M. Sheehy in *Pontificia Hibernica* (No. 1137), pp. 15–16, doc. no. 4. Trans. by G. H. Orpen, *Ireland under the Normans* (No. 4030), i. 294–7; and in *Eng. Hist. Docs.* ii. 776–7.

No original of this alleged grant by Adrian IV to Henry II, approving the proposed conquest of Ireland, has been found; what purports to be a copy is entered in Giraldus Cambrensis, *Expugnatio Hibernica* in Rolls Series edition of his *Opera* (No. 2881), v. 316. The controversy on its authenticity is summarized, up to 1911, by G. H. Orpen, op. cit. i. 287–318; and 399–400. Kate Norgate in *E.H.R.* viii (1893), 18–52 maintained its authenticity; J. H. Round in *Commune of London* (No. 4004), pp. 171–200, denied it. More recent studies are J. F. O'Doherty, 'Rome and the Anglo-Norman invasion of Ireland', *Irish Eccles. Record*, xlii (1933), 131–45; J. Watt, '*Laudabiliter* in medieval diplomacy and propaganda', ibid. 5th Ser. lxxvii (1957), 420–32; M. P. Sheehy, 'The bull *Laudabiliter*: a problem in medieval diplomatical and history', *Jour. Galway Archaeol.-Hist. Soc.* xxix (1961), 45–70. See *Eng. Hist. Docs.* ii. 776–80; Lunt, *Financial relations . . . to 1327*, p. 133 n. 5.

5557 ALEXANDRI III ROMANI PONTIFICIS OPERA OMNIA, id est epistolae et privilegia, in Migne, *Patrologia*, cc (1855).

Cf. Walther Holtzmann, 'Die Register Papst Alexander III in den Handen der Kanonisten', *Quellen und Forschungen aus ital. Archiven und Bibliotheken*, xxx (1940/41), 13–87.

5558 THE LETTERS OF POPE INNOCENT III (1198–1216). Ed. by C. R. Cheney and Mary G. Cheney. Oxf. 1967.

A superbly edited calendar of over 1200 letters, with an appendix of texts, concerning England and Wales. For 'Additions and corrections', see *B.I.H.R.* xliv (1971), 98–115. A new edition of Innocent III's register by the Austrian Institute at Rome is in preparation, the first volume is edited by Othman Hageneden and Anton Haidacher as *Die Register Innocenz III: Pontifikatsjahr 1198–1199* (Graz and Cologne, 1964). It is reviewed in *E.H.R.* lxxxii (1967), 109–11; in *Speculum*, xlii (1967), 153–62; in *Le Moyen Âge*, lxxiii (1967), 295–9; in *Historische Zeitschrift*, cciv (1967), 638–42.

5559 SELECTED LETTERS OF POPE INNOCENT III CONCERNING ENGLAND (1198–1216). Ed. and trans. by C. R. Cheney and W. H. Semple. Medieval Texts. Lond. 1953.

Patrick J. Dunning, 'The letters of Innocent III to Ireland', *Traditio*, xviii (1962), 229–53; and *Studies in Church History*, i (1964), 154–9.

5560 REGESTA HONORII PAPAE III. Ed. by Petrus Pressutti. 2 vols. Rome. 1888–95.

5561 REGESTUM CLEMENTIS PAPAE V. Ed. by Monks of the Order of St. Benedict. 8 vols. Rome. 1885–92. Index as Tables établiés par Yvonne Lanhers et Cyrille Vogel sous la direction de Robert Fawtier et Mgr. G. Mollat. Biblio. des Écoles françaises d'Athènes et de Rome. Paris. 1948–57.

5562 HALLER (JOHANNES). England und Rom unter Martin V (No. 6731).

Prints some papal letters.

B. GENERAL COUNCILS AND ENGLAND

See Hefele–Leclercq (No. 1279).

5563 ACTA CONCILII CONSTANCIENSIS. Ed. by Heinrich Finke, J. Hollnsteiner, and H. Heimpel. 4 vols. Munster i. W. 1896–1928.

A. D. Breck, 'The leadership of the English delegation at Constance', *Univ. Colorado Studies in Humanities*, i. 289–99 (Boulder. 1941). C. M. D. Crowder, 'Correspondence between England and the Council of Constance, 1414–18', *Stud. in Church Hist.* i (1964), 184–206. A. Gwynn, 'Ireland and the English nation at the Council of Constance', *Royal Irish Acad. Procs.* xlv (1940), Sect. C, pp. 183–233. Louise R. Loomis, 'Nationality at the Council of Constance: an Anglo-French dispute', *A.H.R.* xliv (1938/9), 508–27. See No. 5566.

5564 CONCILIUM BASILIENSE: STUDIEN UND QUELLEN ZUR GESCHICHTE DES KONZILS VON BASEL. Ed. by Johannes Haller. 7 vols. Basel. 1896–1926.

See Denys Hay and W. K. Smith, eds. and trans. *Aeneas Sylvius Piccolominus (Pius II): De gestis Concilii Basiliensis commentariorum libri II*. Oxford Medieval Texts (Oxf. 1967).

5565 THE COUNCIL OF CONSTANCE: THE UNIFICATION OF THE CHURCH. Trans. by Louise R. Loomis; and ed. by John H. Mundy and Kennerly M. Woody. Columbia Univ. Records of Civilization. N.Y. 1961.

Translation of Cardinal Fillastre's important *Diary*, of Richental's *Chronicle*, and Cerretano's *Journal*.

5566 CROWDER (CHRISTOPHER M. D.). 'Constance *Acta* in English libraries'. Pp. 477–517 in *Das Konzil von Konstanz: Beiträge zu seiner Geschichte und Theologie*. Ed. by August Franzen and Wolfgang Müller. Freiburg-im-B. 1964.

5567 CUMING (G. T.) and BAKER (DEREK), eds. Councils and assemblies: papers read at the eighth summer and the ninth winter meeting of the Ecclesiastical History Society. *Stud. in Church Hist.* vii. Cambr. 1971.

Includes articles on Pisa, Constance, and Basel.

5568 HUNT (WILLIAM). 'The English bishops at the Lateran Council of 1139'. *E.H.R.* xxxviii (1923), 557–60.

5569 JACOB (ERNEST F.). Essays in the Conciliar epoch (No. 1473). Idem, Essays in later medieval history (No. 1474). Idem, 'Reflections upon the study of the General Councils of the fifteenth century', *Stud. in Church Hist.* i (1964), 80–97. Idem, 'A note on the English concordat of 1418', *Gwynn essays* (No. 1438), pp. 349–58.

5570 MÜLLER (EWALD). Das Konzil von Vienne, 1311–1312; seine Quellen und seine Geschichte. Münster i. W. 1934.

5571 TIERNEY (BRIAN). Foundations of the conciliar theory. The contribution of the medieval canonists from Gratian to the Great Schism. Cambr. 1955.

See also B. Tierney, 'Ockham, the conciliar theory, and the canonists', *Jour. Hist. Ideas*, xv (1954), 40–70; and John B. Morrall, 'Ockham and ecclesiology', in *Gwynn essays* (No. 1438), pp. 481–91.

5572 VALOIS (NOËL). La France et le Grand Schisme d'Occident. 4 vols. Paris. 1896–1902. Idem, La crise religieuse du XVe siècle: le pape et le concile, 1418–50. 2 vols. Paris. 1909.

Valois provides the basic account. A brief summary of the early stages is given in Walter Ullmann, *The origins of the Great Schism* (Lond. 1948).

5573 ZELLFELDER (AUGUST). England und das Basler Konzil. *Historische Studien, edited by E. Ebering.* cxiii. Berlin. 1913.

A. N. E. D. Schofield, 'The first English delegation to the Council of Basel', *J.E.H.* xii (1961), 167–96; idem, 'The second English delegation to the Council of Basel', ibid. xvii (1966), 29–64; idem, 'England, the pope and the Council of Basel 1435–1449,' *Church History*, xxxiii (1964), 248–78, reprinted in *Reunion*, vi (1965), 13–28; idem, 'Ireland and the Council of Basel', *Irish Eccles. Record*, 5th Ser. cvii (1967), 374–87; idem, 'Some aspects of English representation at the Council of Basel', *Stud. in Church Hist.* vii (1971), 219–27. W. Ullmann, 'Eugenius IV, Cardinal Kemp, and Archbishop Chichele', *Gwynn essays* (No. 1438), pp. 359–83.

C. DIOCESAN RECORDS AND HISTORIES

1. *General Introduction*

For most of the period between the Norman conquest and the Tudors, there were seventeen dioceses in England and four in Wales. Eight cathedrals of the

English dioceses were administered by monks, and nine by secular chapters. The monastic cathedrals were Canterbury, Carlisle, Durham, Ely, Norwich, Rochester, Winchester, and Worcester; Carlisle being a house of regular canons.

Lists of archbishops and bishops of England, Wales, Scotland, and Ireland are provided in Eubel, *Hierarchia* (No. 6711), and in Powicke–Fryde, *Handbook* (No. 371). The standard reference works for episcopal and cathedral dignitaries are those by Brady, Godwin, LeNeve, and Stubbs (Nos. 5576, 5579–83). Substantial biographies of prominent ecclesiastics are printed in *Dictionnaire de Théologie Catholique* (No. 1267).

The principal classes of diocesan records are the archiepiscopal and episcopal registers, and the manuscripts of the cathedral administrators, whether dean and chapter or prior and convent. The earliest surviving episcopal register is that of Hugh of Wells, bishop of Lincoln, which begins about the year 1215; it is followed in point of time by that of Walter Gray, archbishop of York, which starts in 1225. The registers surviving in manuscript are listed in Fowler's pamphlet (No. 5578); and the printed editions are mentioned below under each diocese. A survey of archiepiscopal registers is made by E. F. Jacob in St. Anthony's Hall Pubn. no. 4 (1953). Other episcopal *acta*, both earlier and later, have, of course, been found in other manuscripts; see, for example, No. 5577. Reports on cathedral manuscripts are printed in the *Historical MSS. Commission Reports*; and their present location is given in the *Twenty-fifth Report*, 1963–7 (H.M.S.O. 1967), appendix III. Wharton's *Anglia Sacra* (No. 1125) forms a remarkable collection of documents, including numerous biographies of bishops and other ecclesiastical dignitaries. A. R. Myers gives in translation a wide variety of documents, some hitherto unpublished, in *Eng. Hist. Docs.* iv, nos. 376–483.

For the archives of ecclesiastical records, see above, pp. 127–9. The two most useful general surveys are the following.

5574 OWEN (DOROTHY M.). The records of the established church in England excluding parochial records. Archives and the User, no. 1. British Records Asso. 1970.

An informative manual describing, pp. 7–57, the records of diocese, the archdeaconry, the peculiar jurisdictions, the province, the national church, and capitular bodies. Pp. 58–60 provide a list of the location of the records. A supplement is published in *Archives*, x (1971), 53–6, which includes references to the *National Register of Archives* and to H.M.C. Reports.

5575 A SURVEY OF ECCLESIASTICAL ARCHIVES. Compiled under the direction of L. Margaret Midgley (1946–51).

On this survey, see above, p. 109.

5576 BRADY (WILLIAM M.). The episcopal succession in England, Scotland and Ireland. A.D. 1400 to 1875. 3 vols. Rome. 1876–7.

Brady included some appointments to monasteries and some extracts from consistorial acts.

5577 CHENEY (CHRISTOPHER R.). English bishops' chanceries, 1100–1250. Manchester. 1950.

F. M. Stenton, '*Acta episcoporum*', *Cambr. Hist. Jour.* iii (1929), 1–14; Kathleen Major,

'Episcopal *acta* in medieval capitular archives', *B.I.H.R.* ix (1932), 145–53; K. Major, '*Acta Stephani Langton*' (No. 5598); Mayr-Harting (No. 5650); Offler (No. 5679); and acts collected in biographies of archbishops and bishops, such as Theobald, Foliot, Bartholomew of Exeter, du Puiset. See D. Owen in *K. Major Essays* (No. 7224), pp. 189–205.

5578 FOWLER (ROBERT C.). Episcopal registers of England and Wales. Helps for Students of History. Lond. 1918.

E. F. Jacob, *The medieval registers of Canterbury and York. Some points of comparison.* (St. Anthony's Hall Pubn. no. 4. Lond. 1953). Rosalind Hill, *Ecclesiastical letter-books of the thirteenth century* (privately printed, n.d.). Descriptions of the registers of a particular diocese are entered under the appropriate diocese, especially A. H. Thompson on the York registers (No. 5877).

5579 GODWIN (FRANCIS). De praesulibus Angliae commentarius. 2 pts. Lond. 1616. Another edn. by William Richardson. 2 vols. Cambr. 1743.

This is a Latin translation of Godwin's *Catalogue of the bishops of England* (Lond. 1601; another edition 1615). Contains brief biographies of the bishops of England. Richardson's edition is the better.

5580 LE NEVE (JOHN). Fasti ecclesiae anglicanae; or A calendar of the principal ecclesiastical dignitaries in England and Wales, and of the chief officers in the universities of Oxford and Cambridge, from the earliest time to the year MDCCXV. Lond. 1716. Corrected and continued to the present time by T. Duffus Hardy. 3 vols. Oxf. 1854.

5581 LE NEVE (JOHN). Fasti ecclesiae anglicanae, 1066–1300. Institute of Hist. Research. Lond. 1968+. (In progress).

1. St. Paul's, London. Compiled by Diana E. Greenway. 1968.
2. Monastic cathedrals: northern and southern provinces. Compiled by D. E. Greenway. 1971.

5582 LE NEVE (JOHN). Fasti ecclesiae anglicanae, 1300–1541. Institute Hist. Research. Lond. 1962–7.

1. Lincoln diocese, by H. P. F. King.
2. Hereford diocese, by J. M. Horn.
3. Salisbury diocese, by J. M. Horn.
4. Monastic cathedrals (southern province), by B. Jones.
5. St. Paul's, London, by J. M. Horn.
6. Northern province (York, Carlisle, and Durham), by B. Jones.
7. Chichester diocese, by J. M. Horn.
8. Bath and Wells diocese, by B. Jones.
9. Exeter diocese, by J. M. Horn.
10. Coventry and Lichfield diocese, by B. Jones.
11. The Welsh dioceses (Bangor, Llandaff, St. Asaph, St. Davids), by B. Jones.
12. Introduction, errata, index (for all the preceding volumes. This volume should be regularly consulted for *errata* and *addenda*).

5583 STUBBS (WILLIAM). Registrum sacrum Anglicanum: an attempt to exhibit the course of episcopal succession in England. Oxf. 1858. 2nd edn. 1897.

2. *English Dioceses, Bishops and Chapters*

BATH AND WELLS

For annals of the bishops of Bath and Wells, see Wharton, *Anglia Sacra* (No. 1125), i. 591–688. There is an elaborate account of the archives of the dean and chapter of Wells in *Calendar of MSS.* (No. 5584). For a cartulary of Bath priory, see No. 6305. J. Armitage Robinson, *Somerset Historical Essays* (No. 1491) includes important essays on the first deans of Wells, the early Somerset archdeacons, Bishop Jocelin.

5584 CALENDAR OF THE MSS. OF THE DEAN AND CHAPTER OF WELLS. 2 vols. Hist. MSS. Comm. 1907–1914.

5585 ECCLESIASTICAL DOCUMENTS. I: A brief history of the bishopric of Somerset from its foundation to the year 1174 (Historiola de primordiis episcopatus Somersetensis). II: Charters from the library of Dr Cox Macro. Ed. by Joseph Hunter. Camden Soc. 1st Ser. viii. 1840.

> The Historiola is from a copy of an anonymous treatise, compiled in Henry II's reign. The Macro charters are copies of grants to religious houses, papal bulls, etc. in various dioceses, William I–Henry VIII; and are now deposited in the British Museum.

5586 THE HISTORIA MINOR AND THE HISTORIA MAJOR FROM THE WELLS LIBER ALBUS II. Ed. by J. Armitage Robinson. Somerset Rec. Soc. xxxix *Collectanea*, i (1924), 48–71.

> Transcripts of late medieval biographies of the bishops.

5587 HOUSEHOLD ROLL OF BISHOP RALPH OF SHREWSBURY, 1337–8. Ed. by J. Armitage Robinson. Somerset Record Soc. xxxix *Collectanea*, i (arranged by T. F. Palmer), xxxix (1924), 72–174. Also No. 4606.

> On pp. 166–74, A. H. Thompson compares this roll with that of Richard de Swinfield (No. 4612).

5588 INDEXES TO THE RECORD BOOKS OF THE DEAN AND CHAPTER OF THE CATHEDRAL CHURCH OF S. ANDREW, WELLS. Ed. by F. H. Dickinson. Somersetshire Archaeol. and Nat. Hist. Soc. Bristol. 1876.

5589 REGISTERS OF BISHOPS Giffard (1265–6), Drokensford (1309–29), Shrewsbury (1329–63), Bowett (1401–7), Bubwith (1407–24), Stafford (1425–43), Bekynton (1443–65), Stillington (1466–91), calendared or abstracted for the Somerset Record Society. 11 vols. 1887–1937.

5590 WELLS CATHEDRAL: its foundation, constitutional history, and statutes. Ed. by Herbert E. Reynolds. (Leeds). 1881.

> The preface contains Nathaniel Chyle's 'History of Wells Cathedral', *c.* 1680. The body of the work (pp. 1–113) the *Ordinale et Statuta*, transcribed 1634; and (pp. 115–240) excerpts from the Red Book, a register in the possession of the dean and chapter of the cathedral church of Wells, 1198–1515.

5591 BRETT-JAMES (N. G.). 'John de Drokensford, bishop of Bath and Wells'. *London–Middlesex Archaeol. Soc. Trans.* New Ser. x (1951), 281–301.

5592 CHURCH (CHARLES M.). Chapters in the early history of Bath and Wells, 1136–1333. Lond. etc. 1894. Reprinted, 1903.

> The expansion of a series of papers in *Archaeologia*, vols. l–lii (1887–90), and includes four charters granted to the city of Wells, 1174–1201. See also his *Four Somerset bishops, 1136–1242* (Lond. 1909); and his 'The rise and growth of the chapter of Wells from 1242 to 1333', *Archaeologia*, liv (1894), 1–40; and J. A. Robinson, 'Bishop Jocelin and the interdict' (No. 1491) (Jocelin supported King John).

5593 FREEMAN (EDWARD A.). History of the cathedral church of Wells, as illustrating the history of the cathedral churches of the old foundation. Lond. 1870.

5594 HOLMES (THOMAS S.). Wells and Glastonbury: a historical and topographical account. Lond. 1908.

5595 JUDD (ARNOLD F.). The life of Thomas Bekynton, secretary to King Henry VI and Bishop of Bath and Wells, 1443–65. Chichester. 1961. Idem, 'The episcopate of Thomas Bekynton, bishop of Bath and Wells, 1443–65'. *J.E.H.* viii (1957), 153–65.

> See also G. G. Perry, 'Bishop Beckington and Henry VI', *E.H.R.* ix (1894), 261–74; and A. Wilmart, 'Le florilège mixte de Thomas Bekynton', *Mediaeval and Renaissance Stud.* i (1941), 41–84.

5596 VINCENT (JOHN A. C.). The first bishop of Bath and Wells (Roger of Sarum) (with an appendix of records, 1090–1245); reprinted from the Genealogist, New Ser. ii–viii. Exeter. 1899.

> This is a criticism of part of Freeman's *History of the Cathedral Church of Wells*. For John of Tours, bishop of Bath 1088–1122, see R. A. L. Smith (No. 1494).

5597 WEAVER (FREDERIC W.). Somerset incumbents (13th–18th cents.). Bristol. 1889.

> J. A. Robinson, 'Early Somerset archdeacons' (No. 1491).

CANTERBURY

The archiepiscopal records are kept at Lambeth Palace; the dean and chapter records at Canterbury. For the latter, see *Hist. MSS. Comm. Reports*, v. 425–62; viii. 315–54; ix. 72–128; Various i. 205–81; xvi. 99–100.

5598 ACTA STEPHANI LANGTON CANTUARIENSIS ARCHIEPIS-COPI, A.D. 1207–1228. Ed. by Kathleen Major. Cant.–York Soc. l (1950).

5599 CALENDAR OF INSTITUTIONS BY THE CHAPTER OF CANTERBURY SEDE VACANTE. Ed. by C. E. Woodruff. Kent Archaeol. Soc. *Kent Records*. Canterbury. 1924.

5600 CATALOGUE OF LAMBETH MANUSCRIPTS 889 to 910: Carte antique et miscellanee. Compiled by Dorothy M. Owen. Lond. 1968.

5601 CHRIST CHURCH LETTERS: a volume of mediaeval letters relating to the affairs of the priory of Christ Church, Canterbury (1334–c. 1539). Ed. by J. B. Sheppard. Camden Soc. New Ser. xix (1877).

The contents of the Register of Prior Henry Eastry (1284–1321) and of the *sede vacante* registers for the periods after Pecham and Winchelsey are analysed in *Cambr. Univ. Lib. Catalogue of MSS.* (No. 1032), ii. 191–250.

5602 DOMESDAY MONACHORUM OF CHRIST CHURCH, CANTER-BURY. Ed. by David C. Douglas. Lond. 1944.

5603 DOCUMENTS CONCERNING CHRIST CHURCH CATHEDRAL PRIORY, CANTERBURY, 1207–1213. Ed. by Patricia M. Barnes in *Interdict Documents*. Pipe Roll Soc. Pubns. lxxii. New Ser. xxxiv for 1958 (1960), pp. 33–104.

5604 EPISTOLAE CANTUARIENSES. Ed. by William Stubbs in Chronicles and memorials of the reign of Richard I, vol. ii. Rolls Ser. Lond. 1865.

The letters of the prior and convent of Christ Church, Canterbury, A.D. 1187–99; they relate to the dispute which arose from the attempts of archbishops Baldwin and Hubert to found a college of secular canons at Canterbury.

5605 INVENTORIES OF CHRIST CHURCH, CANTERBURY (1294–1780). Ed. by John Wickham Legg and W. H. St. John Hope. Westminster. 1902.

5606 LAMBETH MS. 1212 AND THE WHITE BOOK OF CANTER-BURY. By Rosemary G. Barnes. *B.I.H.R.* xxxii (1959), 57–62.

Shows that this frequently used 'composite cartulary' did in fact belong to the arch-bishop of Canterbury.

5607 LITERAE CANTUARIENSES: the letter-books of the monastery of Christ Church, Canterbury. Ed. by J. B. Sheppard. Rolls Ser. 3 vols. Lond. 1887–9.

T. F. Lindsay, 'The letter books of Christ Church Canterbury, 1296–1536', *Dublin Review*, no. 468 (1955), 127–41.

5608 PIPE ROLL ACCOUNT OF THE SEE OF CANTERBURY (1292–5). By F. R. H. Du Boulay in *Kent records* (No. 4784), pp. 41–57.

A translation of the account of the royal keepers during the vacancy. For a list of such accounts, see M. Howell (No. 6766), pp. 214–15.

5609 REGISTRA (Registers of Archbishops) Pecham (1279–92 (in part, see No. 5610)), Winchelsey (1294–1313), Langham (1366–8), Chichele (1414–43), Bourgchier (1454–86), transcribed for the Cant.–York Soc. 10 vols. 1909–69.

Listed until vol. 1 of Bourgchier's register in Mullins, *Texts* (No. 29). Wilkins, *Concilia*, prints fairly extensively from registers.

5610 REGISTRUM EPISTOLARUM JOHANNIS PECKHAM ARCHI-EPISCOPI CANTUARIENSIS (1279–92). Ed. by Charles Trice Martin. Rolls Ser. 3 vols. Lond. 1882–5.

Since the Rolls Series edition omitted all formal letters, the Canterbury and York Society printed them in two supplementary volumes; the first volume was edited by F. N. Davis and originally printed in two parts in 1908 and 1910; and became Cant.–York Soc. lxiv with a title-page, a brief introduction, and an itinerary in 1969; the second volume was edited by Decima Douie as Cant.–York Soc. lxv (Torquay, 1968).

5611 THE SACRIST'S ROLLS OF CHRIST CHURCH, CANTERBURY.
By C. E. Woodruff. *Archaeol. Cantiana*, xlviii (1936), 38–80.

5612 STEPHANI BIRCHINGTONI HISTORIA DE ARCHIEPISCOPIS CANTUARIENSIBUS A.D. 597–1369. Ed. by Henry Wharton, *Anglia Sacra*, i. 1–48.

It is valuable for the crisis of 1340–1. According to Tait (No. 2944) this history is wrongly attributed to Birchington. For other annals of Canterbury see, Wharton, *Anglia Sacra*, i. 49–176.

5613 TABLE OF CANTERBURY ARCHBISHOPRIC CHARTERS. By Irene Churchill. Camden Soc. 3rd Ser. xli. *Camden Miscellany*, xv (1929).

5614 WOODRUFF (CHARLES E.). 'A monastic chronicle lately discovered at Christ Church, Canterbury (1331–1414)'. *Archaeol. Cantiana*, xxix (1911), 47–84. Idem, 'The chronicle of William Ghastynbury, monk of the priory of Christ Church, Canterbury, 1419–1448'. Ibid. xxxvii (1925), 121–51. See also Chronicle of John Stone (No. 2957).

5615 BÖHMER (HEINRICH). Die Fälschungen Erzbischof Lanfranks. Leipzig. 1902.

These documents were designed to uphold the primacy of Canterbury over York. Lanfranc is no longer generally held responsible for any forgery committed in them. See C. N. L. Brooke, 'The Canterbury forgeries and their author', *Downside Rev.* lxviii (1950), 462–76; lxix (1951), 210–31. R. W. Southern, 'The Canterbury forgeries', *E.H.R.* lxxiii (1958), 193–226. Southern dates the documents about A.D. 1120; in which case they are not attributable to Lanfranc. On the Canterbury–York dispute see Hugh the Chantor (No. 5853); and D. Bethell, 'William of Corbeil (archbishop 1123–36) and the Canterbury–York dispute', *J.E.H.* xix (1968), 145–59; and the biographies of archbishops of Canterbury and York.

5616 CHENEY (CHRISTOPHER R.). 'The so called statutes of John Pecham and Robert Winchelsey for the province of Canterbury'. *J.E.H.* xii (1961), 14–34.

5617 CHURCHILL (IRENE J.). Canterbury administration: the administrative machinery of the archbishopric of Canterbury illustrated from original records. 2 vols. Lond. 1933.

A. Bennett, '*The jurisdiction of the archbishop of Canterbury: a historico-juridical study*' (Rome, 1958). Marjorie M. Morgan, 'Early Canterbury jurisdiction', *E.H.R.* lx (1945), 392–9.

5618 DAHMUS (JOSEPH H.). Metropolitan visitations of William Courteney, archbishop of Canterbury, 1381–1396. Urbana (Illinois). 1950.

5619 DU BOULAY (FRANCIS R. H.). The lordship of Canterbury: an essay on medieval society. Lond. 1966.

Deals with the landed possessions of the see of Canterbury and the archbishop as territorial lord. Based largely on archival material, it is a highly valuable treatise. See also Hubert Hall and F. J. Nicholas, 'Manorial accounts of the priory of Canterbury, 1260–1420', *B.I.H.R.* viii (1931), 137–55; and Jane E. Sayers, 'A record of the archbishop of Canterbury's feudal right', *Jour. Soc. Archivists*, iii, no. 5 (1967), 213–21. E. G. Box, 'Donations of manors to Christ Church, Canterbury, and appropriation of churches',

Archaeol. Cantiana, xliv (1932), 103–19. Irene J. Churchill, ed. 'Table of Canterbury archbishopric charters' (No. 5613). F. R. H. Du Boulay, 'A rentier economy in the later middle ages (on estates of the archbishop of Canterbury)', *Econ. H.R.* 2nd Ser. xvi (1964), 427–38.

5620   KNOWLES (M. DAVID). 'The Canterbury election of 1205–6'. *E.H.R.* liii (1938), 211–20.

Knowles points out that a number of incidents in the narrative in Stubbs's introduction to Walter of Coventry (No. 2855) cannot be accepted as historical facts. For an addendum, see C. R. Cheney in *B.I.H.R.* xxi (1948), 233–8.

5621   MEDIAEVAL RECORDS OF THE ARCHBISHOP OF CANTERBURY. Lond. 1962.

Papers by Irene Churchill on the Archbishop's Registers (pp. 11–20); by E. W. Kemp on the Archbishop in Convocation (pp. 21–34); by E. F. Jacob on the Archbishop's Testamentary Jurisdiction (pp. 35–49); and F. R. H. Du Boulay, on the Archbishop as Territorial Magnate (pp. 50–70). See also Jane E. Sayers, 'The medieval care and custody of the Archbishop of Canterbury's archives', *B.I.H.R.* xxxix (1966), 95–107; and Dorothy M. Owen, 'Canterbury archiepiscopal archives in Lambeth Palace Library', *Jour. Soc. Archivists,* ii (1960–4), 140–7.

5622   SMITH (REGINALD A. L.). Canterbury Cathedral priory: a study in monastic administration. Cambr. 1943. Reprinted, 1969.

See also his 'The central financial system of Christ Church, Canterbury, 1186–1512', *E.H.R.* lv (1940), 353–69, and reprinted in No. 1494. Dorothy Sutcliffe, 'The financial condition of the see of Canterbury, 1279–1292', *Speculum,* x (1935), 53–68. C. E. Woodruff, 'The financial aspect of the cult of St. Thomas of Canterbury as revealed by a study of the monastic records', *Archaeol. Cantiana,* xliv (1932), 13–32. Idem, 'Note on the inner life and domestic economy of the priory of Christ Church in the fifteenth century', ibid. liii (1940), 1–16.

5623   WOODRUFF (CHARLES E.) and DANKS (WILLIAM). Memorials of the cathedral and priory of Christ Church in Canterbury. Lond. and N.Y. 1912.

John Dart, *The history and antiquities of the cathedral church of Canterbury and the once-adjoining monastery* (with an appendix of charters, etc.) (Lond. 1726). Arthur P. Stanley, *Historical memorials of Canterbury* (Lond. 1855; 10th edn. 1904; new edn. 1912), which comprises chapters on the landing of Augustine, the murder of Becket, the Black Prince, and the shrine of Becket. See also W. P. Blore and John H. Harvey, 'Recent discoveries in the archives of Canterbury Cathedral', *Archaeol. Cantiana,* lviii (1945), 28–39.

5624   WOODRUFF (CHARLES E.). 'Some early (sede vacante) visitation rolls preserved in Canterbury (1292–1328)', *Archaeol. Cantiana,* xxxii (1917), 143–80; xxxiii (1918), 71–90. Idem, 'Some early professions of canonical obedience to the see of Canterbury'. *St. Paul's Ecclesiological Soc. Trans.* vii (1911–15), 160–76. Idem, 'Some early professions ... by heads of religious houses'. *Archaeol. Cantiana,* xxxvii (1925), 53–72.

5625   HOOK (WALTER F.). Lives of the archbishops of Canterbury. 12 vols. Lond. 1860–76.

To be used with considerable discretion.

Abingdon, Edmund of (1234-40)

5626 LAWRENCE (CLIFFORD HUGH). St. Edmund of Abingdon: a study in hagiography and history. Lond. 1960.

> This work provides the best biography of St. Edmund; it examines the contemporary 'Lives' and cognate material, and contains an edition of the three following documents:
> (a) The *Quadrilogus*, consisting of depositions by four members of Edmund's *familia* on the sanctity of St. Edmund;
> (b) *Vita S. Edmundi auctore Eustachio*;
> (c) *Vita S. Edmundi auctore Matthaeo Parisiensi*.
>   There is also Wilfrid Wallace's *Life of St. Edmund of Canterbury* (Lond. 1893), a scholarly work of piety, with appendixes containing much manuscript material.
>   See also H. W. C. Davis, 'An unpublished life of Edmund Rich', *E.H.R.* xxii (1907), 84-92; and Emden, *Oxford* (No. 533).

Anselm (1093-1109)

5626A SOUTHERN (RICHARD W.). St. Anselm and his biographer. Cambr. 1962.

> See below, Nos. 6526-35.

Arundel, Thomas (1397 and 1399-1414)

5627 ASTON (MARGARET). Thomas Arundel, a study of church life in the reign of Richard II. Oxf. 1967.

> Arundel was bishop of Ely from 1374 to 1388, archbishop of York from 1388 to 1396, archbishop of Canterbury 1397, bishop of St. Andrews from 1397 to 1399, archbishop of Canterbury from 1399 to 1414. The above cited work is a broad study of church administration and politics set within Arundel's biography. It is based on an examination of numerous manuscript sources as well as on printed works, and ends in 1397.

Boniface of Savoy (1241/5-1270)

5628 STRICKLAND (GIUSEPPE). 'Ricerche storiche sopra il B. Bonifacio di Savoia, arcivescovo di Cantorbery, 1207-70'. *Miscellanea di Storia Italiana* (Turin), xxii (1895), 349-432.

Chichele, Henry (1414-43)

5629 JACOB (ERNEST F.). Archbishop Henry Chichele. Lond. 1967.

> See also Jacob's Creighton Lecture: *Henry Chichele and the ecclesiastical politics of his age* (Lond. 1952), and his introduction to his edition of Chichele's register (No. 5609); Jacob's paper in *Powicke essays* (No. 1450); and documents nos. 366 and 367 in *Eng. Hist. Docs.* iv (Myers).

Courtenay, William (1381-96)

5630 DAHMUS (JOSEPH). William Courtenay, archbishop of Canterbury. University Park (Pennsylvania) and Lond. 1966.

> This solid biography deals with Courtenay as bishop of London (1375-81) and then as archbishop, especially with his opposition to Wyclif and the Lollards, and his metropolitical visitations.

Lanfranc (1070-89)

5631 BEATI LANFRANCI Archiepiscopi Cantuariensis Opera Omnia. Ed. by J. A. Giles, *Patres Ecclesiae* (No. 1102). 2 vols. Oxf. 1844. Also printed in Migne's *Patrologia*, cl. 1854.

Giles's edition is based on Luc d'Achery's edition of 1648. These volumes contain (a) *Vita Lanfranci auctore Milone Crispino*; (b) *Epistolae*; (c) *Statuta pro Ordine S. Benedicti*; etc.

Milo Crispin was a pupil of Lanfranc and precentor of Bec; his 'Life' of Lanfranc is partly based on Gilbert Crispin's account of Lanfranc's early life, which can now be found in J. A. Robinson, *Gilbert Crispin, abbot of Westminster* (Cambr. 1911), pp. 95–102; and is translated in *Eng. Hist. Docs.* ii. 626–31.

Lanfranc's letters are important for ecclesiastical history in the reign of William I; a few are translated in Hook's *Lives* (No. 5625), vol. ii; and a few in *Eng. Hist. Docs.* ii. 636–9 *passim*.

For editions of his monastic constitutions, see Knowles (No. 1146); and for the forgeries once attributed to him see Böhmer (No. 5615).

There is a contemporary outline of Lanfranc's career as archbishop printed in the Earle and Plummer edition of the Anglo-Saxon Chronicle (No. 2141), i. 287–92; and translated in *Eng. Hist. Docs.* ii. 631–5.

5632 MACDONALD (ALLAN J.). Lanfranc: a study of his life, work and writing. Oxf. 1926. 2nd edn. Lond. 1944.

See Frank Barlow, 'A view of Archbishop Lanfranc', *J.E.H.* xvi (1965), 163–77; Southern's important studies in Powicke *Essays* (No. 1450) and under Böhmer (No. 5615) and C. N. L. Brooke in *Collectanea Stephan Kuttner* (No. 6429); Felix Liebermann printed three letters from Pope Clement III inviting Lanfranc to Rome in 'Lanfranc and the antipope', *E.H.R.* xvi (1901), 328–32.

Langton, Stephen (1207/13–1228)

5633 ACTA STEPHANI LANGTON. Ed. by Kathleen Major (No. 5598).

K. Major, 'The *familia* of Archbishop Stephen Langton', *E.H.R.* xlviii (1933), 529–53.

5634 POWICKE (FREDERICK M.). Stephen Langton. Oxf. 1928. Reprinted 1965.

F. M. Powicke, 'Bibliographical note on recent work upon Stephen Langton', *E.H.R.* xlviii (1933), 554–7; and No. 1488. On the Canterbury election of 1205/6 see No. 5620. On Matthew Paris's biography of Langton see Vaughan (No. 2941), chap. ix; it was edited by Liebermann in *Geschichtsquellen* (No. 1108) and extracts in M.G.H. *SS.* xxviii. 441–3.

F. A. Cazel, jr. deals with 'The last years of Stephen Langton' in *E.H.R.* lxxix (1964), 672–97. For Langton's theological works, see Nos. 6594–8.

Morton, John (1486–1500)

5635 WOODHOUSE (REGINALD I.). Life of John Morton, archbishop of Canterbury. Lond. etc. 1895.

Pecham, John (1279–92)

5636 DOUIE (DECIMA L.). Archbishop Pecham. Oxf. 1952.

For editions of Pecham's writings, see D. Douie, p. v, note 1, and footnotes of chap i; and Emden, *Oxford* (No. 533). For Pecham's register see No. 5610. For his sermons, D. Douie in *Powicke essays* (No. 1450); and for his work on optics, (No. 6954).

5637 KNOWLES (M. DAVID). 'Some aspects of the career of Archbishop Pecham'. *E.H.R.* lvii (1942), 1–18; 178–201.

See also Theodore Crowley, 'John Peckham, O.F.M., archbishop of Canterbury, versus new Aristotelianism', *B.J.R.L.* xxxiii (1950/1), 242–55.

Reynolds, Walter (1313-27)

5638 WRIGHT (J. R.). 'The supposed illiteracy of Archbishop Walter Reynolds'. *Stud. in Church Hist.* v (1969), 58-68.

Stafford, John (1443-52)

5639 JACOB (ERNEST F.). 'Archbishop John Stafford'. *T.R.H.S.* 5th Ser. xii (1962), 1-23. Reprinted in No. 1474.

Sudbury, Simon (1375-81)

5640 WARREN (WILFRED L.). 'A reappraisal of Simon Sudbury, bishop of London and archbishop of Canterbury'. *J.E.H.* x (1959), 139-52.

Theobald (1139-61)

5641 SALTMAN (AVROM). Theobald, archbishop of Canterbury. Lond. 1956. *

Especially important for the letters and charters which are printed on pp. 233-549.

Walter, Hubert (1193-1205)

5642 CHENEY (CHRISTOPHER R.). Hubert Walter. Lond. 1967.

A condensation of the ecclesiastical history of Walter's lifetime in about 200 pp.

5643 YOUNG (CHARLES R.). Hubert Walter, lord of Canterbury and lord of England. Durham (North Carolina). 1968.

Winchelsey, Robert (1293/5-1313)

5644 GRAHAM (ROSE). 'Archbishop Winchelsey from his election to his enthronement'. *Church Quart. Rev.* cxlviii (1949), 161-75.

Cuthbert Smith, 'Some aspects of the scholastic career of Archbishop Winchelsey', *Dominican Stud.* vi (1953), 101-26.

CARLISLE

5645 NOTITIA ECCLESIAE CATHEDRALIS CARLIOLENSIS ET NOTITIA PRIORATUS DE WEDDERHAL. By Hugh Todd, D.D. Ed. by R. S. Fergusson. Cumb.-Westm. Antiq.-Archaeol. Soc. Tract Ser. 1891.

Dr. Todd was prebendary of Carlisle, 1685-1728. See Mullins, *Texts*, p. 303.

5646 REGISTER OF JOHN DE HALTON (1292-1324). Cant.-York Soc. and Cumb.-Westm. Antiq.-Archaeol. Soc. 2 vols. 1913.

Tout's introduction is reprinted in No. 1499. Listed in Mullins, *Texts*.
For other fourteenth-century Carlisle registers, consult *Hist. MSS. Comm. Report*, ix, pp. 177-96; and Raine's *Historical papers . . . from Northern registers* (No. 5852). For Bishop Bell, see Dobson (No. 5696).

5647 CHENEY (CHRISTOPHER R.). 'The medieval statutes of the diocese of Carlisle'. *E.H.R.* lxii (1947), 52-7.

5648 DAVEY (C. R.). 'Early diocesan accounts at Carlisle'. *Jour. Soc. Archivists*, iii (1968), 424-5.

5649 STOREY (ROBIN L.). 'Marmaduke Lumley, bishop of Carlisle (1429/ 30–50)'. Cumb.–Westm. Antiq.–Archaeol. Soc. 1955.

CHICHESTER
See *Hist. MSS. Comm. Report*, Various, i. 177–204.

5650 THE ACTS OF THE BISHOPS OF CHICHESTER 1075–1207. Ed. Henry Mayr-Harting. Cant.–York Soc., pt. cxxx (1964).

H. Mayr-Harting, 'Hilary, bishop of Chichester, 1147–69, and Henry II', *E.H.R.* lxxviii (1963), 209–24. Idem, *The bishops of Chichester, 1075–1207* (Chichester, 1963).

5651 THE ACTS OF THE DEAN AND CHAPTER OF THE CATHE-DRAL CHURCH OF CHICHESTER, 1472–1544 (The White Act Book). Ed. by W. D. Peckham. Sussex Rec. Soc. lii (1951/2).

An English abstract.

5652 THE CHARTULARY OF THE HIGH CHURCH OF CHICHES-TER. Ed. by W. D. Peckham. Sussex Rec. Soc. xlvi (1946).

Peckham, 'The vicars choral of Chichester Cathedral', *Sussex Archaeol. Collections,* lxxviii (1937), 126–59.

5653 EARLY STATUTES OF THE CATHEDRAL CHURCH OF THE HOLY TRINITY, CHICHESTER (mainly 1232–51). Ed. by M. E. C. Walcott. *Archaeologia*, xlv (1880), 143–234; also separately printed.

5654 THE EPISCOPAL REGISTER OF ROBERT REDE, BISHOP OF CHICHESTER, 1397–1415. Ed. (with a translation) by Cecil Deedes. Sussex Rec. Soc. viii and xi (1908; 1910).

5655 MEDIEVAL REGISTERS OF THE BISHOPS OF CHICHESTER (an abstract of the contents of four registers, 1396–1502). By M. E. C. Walcott. *Royal Soc. of Literature Trans.* 2nd Ser. ix (1870), 215–44.

5656 MISCELLANEOUS RECORDS: extracts from the episcopal records of Richard Praty, bishop of Chichester, 1438–45. Ed. and trans. by Cecil Deedes. Sussex Rec. Soc. iv (1905), 83–236.

5657 RECORDS OF THE DIOCESE OF CHICHESTER. Compiled by Francis W. Steer and Isabel M. Kirby. West Sussex County Council. Chiches-ter. 1966+.

Vol. i: A catalogue of the records of the bishop, archdeacons, and former exempt jurisdictions. 1966.
Vol. ii: A catalogue of the records of the dean and chapter, vicars choral, St. Mary's Hospital, colleges and school. 1967.

5658 STATUTES AND CONSTITUTIONS OF THE CATHEDRAL CHURCH OF CHICHESTER (1193–1832, with a translation). Ed. by F. G. Bennett, R. H. Codrington, and Cecil Deedes. Chichester. 1904.

5659 SWAINSON (CHARLES A.). The history and constitution of a cathe-dral of the old foundation, illustrated from documents in the registry and muni-ment room of the cathedral of Chichester. Pt. i. Lond. etc. 1880.

Contains a valuable collection of records.

5660 GREEN (VIVIAN H. H.). Bishop Reginald Pecock: a study in ecclesiastical history and thought. Cambr. Univ. Press. 1945.

For Peacock, see Nos. 6628–30.

5661 HENNESSY (GEORGE). Chichester diocese clergy lists. Lond. 1900.

5662 JACOB (ERNEST F.). 'St. Richard of Chichester (bishop 1245–53)'. *J.E.H.* vii (1956), 174–88.

5663 STEPHENS (WILLIAM R. W.). Memorials of the south Saxon see and cathedral church of Chichester. Lond. 1876.

COVENTRY AND LICHFIELD

For statutes of Lichfield Cathedral, see Dugdale, *Monasticon*, vi. 1255–65. For MSS. of dean and chapter, *Hist. MSS. Comm. Reports*, xiv, pt. 8, 205–36.

5664 BENEFACTIONS OF THOMAS HEYWOOD, DEAN (1457–92), to the Cathedral Church of Lichfield. By J. Charles Cox. *Archaeologia*, lii (1890), 617–46.

Consists, in large part, of a collection of documents relating to his benefactions.

5665 CATALOGUE OF THE MUNIMENTS AND MANUSCRIPT BOOKS pertaining to the dean and chapter of Lichfield. Compiled by J. Charles Cox. William Salt Archaeol. Soc. vi, pt. 2 (1886).

An analysis of *Magnum registrum album* (No. 5666); includes pp. 199–224, sacrist's roll for 1345. See Mullins, *Texts*, p. 437.

5666 THE GREAT REGISTER OF LICHFIELD CATHEDRAL KNOWN AS MAGNUM REGISTRUM ALBUM. English abstract by H. E. Savage. Wm. Salt Archaeol. Soc. *Collections*, for 1924. 1926.

The *Registrum Album* was compiled in the fourteenth century. The documents entered in it are mainly of the thirteenth century, and most of them concern the dean and chapter. See No. 1047.

5667 REGISTER OF ROGER DE NORBURY, BISHOP OF LICHFIELD AND COVENTRY, 1322–58; an abstract of its contents and remarks. By Bishop (Edmund) Hobhouse. Wm. Salt Archaeol. Soc. *Collections*, i. 241–88. Birmingham. 1880.

5668 THE REGISTERS OR ACT BOOKS OF THE BISHOPS OF COVENTRY AND LICHFIELD. Book 4, being the register of the guardians of the spiritualities during the vacancy of the see, and the first register of Bishop Robert de Stretton, 1358–1385. An abstract by Rowland A. Wilson. Wm. Salt Archaeol. Soc. *Collections*, New Ser. x, pt. 2 (1907). Idem, Book 5, being the second register of Bishop Robert de Stretton, A.D. 1360–1385. An abstract by R. A. Wilson. Ibid. viii (1905).

5669 THOMAE CHESTERFELD CANONICI LICHFELDENSIS HISTORIA DE EPISCOPIS COVENTRENSIBUS ET LICHFELDENSIBUS (656–1347, with a continuation to 1559). Ed. by Henry Wharton, *Anglia Sacra* (No. 1125), i. 421–59.

See *Repert. Font.* iii. 238–9.

5670 BROWNE (A. L.). Lichfield cathedral chancellors; biographical collections (to 1501) by A. L. Browne. Staffs. Record Soc. lxiii for 1939 (1940).

5671 HARWOOD (THOMAS). The history and antiquities of the church and city of Lichfield. Gloucester. 1806.

DURHAM

For the records of the palatinate of Durham, see vol. i, p. 227; and for the history of the palatinate, see pp. 576–8. The best history of the palatinate is by Lapsley, to which important articles by Fraser and Jean Scammell should be added (No. 1626). For William of St. Carilef, bishop 1081–96, see No. 5675. For MSS. see catalogues, see Conway Davies and Mynors (No. 1044). A. R. Myers translates four unpublished documents from the dean and chapter muniments in *Eng. Hist. Docs.* iv. nos. 389, 438, 460, 718.

5672 BISHOP HATFIELD'S SURVEY: A RECORD OF THE POSSESSIONS OF THE SEE OF DURHAM. Ed. by William Greenwell. Surtees Soc. xxxii (1857).

> The survey, pp. 1–199, was compiled A.D. 1377–82; it gives a list of the tenants, with the amount of land which they held and the services belonging to each manor. The appendix, pp. 200–75, contains reeve or bailiff rolls of various palatine manors 1337–50, and a receiver's roll for 1385–6.

5673 BISHOP HATFIELD'S VISITATION OF DURHAM PRIORY IN 1354. By Barbara Harbottle. *Archaeol. Aeliana*, xxxvi (1958), 81–100.

> Pp. 98–100: Injunctions, 1355.

5674 BOLDON BUKE: A survey of the possessions of the see of Durham, 1183. See No. 3076.

5675 DE INJUSTA VEXATIONE WILLELMI EPISCOPI PRIMI PER WILLELMUM REGEM FILIUM WILLELMI MAGNI in *Symeonis monachi opera omnia*. Ed. by Thomas Arnold. (No. 1767), i. 170–95. Also printed in Dugdale's *Monasticon* (No. 1147), i. 244–50. Trans. in Stevenson's *Church Historians* (No. 1123), iii, pt. 2, pp. 731–50; and in *Eng. Hist. Docs.* ii. 609–24.

> H. S. Offler, 'The tractate *De iniusta vexacione Willelmi episcopi primi*', *E.H.R.* lxvi (1951), 321–41; idem, 'William of St. Calais', *Durham–Northumberland Archit.-Archaeol. Soc. Trans.* x (1950). This valuable historical document, presumably written by a monk of Durham, gives a vivid account of William II's persecution of the bishop of Durham for his complicity in the policy of Odo of Bayeux and of his trial before the king's court at Salisbury in 1088. C. W. David, in *Robert Curthose*, pp. 211–16, holds that the tractate is a composite document; Offler argues that it should be dated in the second quarter of the twelfth century; but Southern in *St. Anselm* (No. 6535), p. 148 n. 1 queries Offler's conclusions.

5676 DEPOSITIONS AND OTHER ECCLESIASTICAL PROCEEDINGS FROM THE COURTS OF DURHAM, 1311 to the reign of Elizabeth. Ed. by James Raine. Surtees Soc. 1845.

> A. H. Thompson, 'William Beverley, archdeacon of Northumberland', *Graham essays* (No. 1437), which deals with the case of accidental homicide against the archdeacon.

5677 DIALOGI LAURENTII DUNELMENSIS MONACHI AC PRIORIS. Ed. by James Raine. Surtees Soc. lxx (1880).

A latin poem, written 1144–49, dealing with William Cumin's attempt to succeed Geoffrey Rufus (d. 1140) as bishop of Durham.

5678 DURHAM ANNALS AND DOCUMENTS OF THE THIR-TEENTH CENTURY. Ed. by Frank Barlow. Surtees Soc. clv for 1940 (1945).

5679 DURHAM EPISCOPAL CHARTERS, 1071–1152. Ed. by H. S. Offler. Surtees Soc. clxxix (1968).

Prints, with annotations, forty-six charters, some of which are regarded as spurious.

5680 DURHAM JURISDICTIONAL PECULIARS. By Frank Barlow. Oxf. Hist. Ser. Lond. 1950.

5681 EXTRACTS FROM THE ACCOUNT ROLLS OF THE ABBEY OF DURHAM. Ed. by J. T. Fowler. 3 vols. Surtees Soc. xcix (1898), c (1899), ciii (1901).

Vol. i contains *rotuli celerariorum*, 1307–1535; *hostillariorum*, 1303–1529; *camerariorum*, 1324–1533; *elemosinariorum*, 1312–1527; *magistrorum infirmariae*, 1352–1535. Vol. ii contains *rotuli communiariorum*, 1416–1535; *terrariorum*, 1401–1513; and the rolls of various other monastic officers, 1278–1538. Vol. iii contains *rotuli bursariorum*, 1371–1541, etc. with a full index and valuable glossary.

5682 FEODARIUM PRIORATUS DUNELMENSIS. A survey of the estates of the priory and convent of Durham, compiled in the fifteenth century. Ed. by William Greenwell. Surtees Soc. lviii (1872).

Feodarium, pp. 1–92: a rental of freehold estates, compiled in 1430.
Inventarium prioratus Dunelmensis, pp. 98–211: an inventory of lands and moveables, 1464.
Le convenit, pp. 212–17: an agreement between the bishop and the prior of Durham in 1229.
Attestaciones testium, pp. 220–301: concerning a dispute between the bishop and the convent, *c.* 1225.
   See Elizabeth M. Halcrow, '*Feodarium prioratus Dunelmensis*', *Jour. Soc. Archivists*, i (1955–9), 228–9.

5683 GESTA DUNELMENSIA, A.D. M° CCC°. Ed. by Robert K. Richardson. *Camden Miscellany*, xiii. Camden Ser. 3rd Ser. xxxiv (1924).

An account, by a partisan of the prior, of the quarrel between Bishop Bek and Prior Hoton about episcopal visitation. See also Robert K. Richardson, 'Bishopric of Durham under Anthony Bek, 1283–1311', *Archaeol. Aeliana*, 3rd Ser. ix (1913), 89–229; and C. M. Fraser, *Records* (No. 5689).

5684 HALMOTA PRIORATUS DUNELMENSIS: extracts from the halmote court or manor rolls of the prior and convent of Durham, 1296–1384. Ed. by W. H. D. Longstaffe and John Booth. Surtees Soc. lxxxii (1889).

Myers translates extracts in *Eng. Hist. Docs.* iv, pp. 997–1001.

5685 HISTORIAE DUNELMENSIS SCRIPTORES TRES, Gaufridus de Coldingham, Robertus de Graystanes, et Willelmus de Chambre. Ed. by James Raine. Surtees Soc. (1839).

Liber Gaufridi de Coldingham de statu ecclesiae Dunelmensis, 1152–1214, pp. 1–31. The author was sacrist of the priory of Coldingham, a cell of the priory of Durham, and seems to have flourished early in the thirteenth century. His chronicle devotes some attention to the public affairs of the kingdom. Graystanes's *Historia de statu ecclesiae Dunelmensis, 1214–1336*, pp. 33–123. The author, a monk of Durham, was elected bishop of Durham in 1333, but was prevented by intrigue from taking possession of the see. His chronicle devotes some attention to public affairs, and is more valuable than the other two.

Chambre's *Continuatio historiae Dunelmensis, 1336–1571*, pp. 125–56, is a somewhat meagre collection of historical notes, the earlier part of which may have been written by a William de Chambre who received a corrody from the prior and convent of Durham in 1365.

These three chronicles are inaccurately printed in Wharton's *Anglia Sacra* (No. 1125), i. 718–84. Raine's edition has an elaborate and valuable appendix of 335 documents: charters, letters, papal bulls, etc. mainly from Durham Cathedral treasury, illustrating the history of the convent and see of Durham, 1082–1556.

5686 HISTORICAL PAPERS AND LETTERS FROM THE NORTHERN REGISTERS. Ed. by James Raine. Rolls Ser. 1873.

Contains some letters of the bishops of Durham, 1265–1415.

5687 LIBER VITAE ECCLESIAE DUNELMENSIS: NEC NON OBITUARIA DUO EJUSDEM ECCLESIAE. Ed. by Joseph Stevenson. Surtees Soc. 1841. Also a collotype facsimile of the original manuscript. Ed. by A. Hamilton Thompson. Surtees Soc. 1923.

5688 OBITUARY ROLL OF WILLIAM EBCHESTER AND JOHN BURNBY, PRIORS OF DURHAM, with notices of similar records preserved at Durham, from the year 1233 downwards, letters of fraternity, etc. Ed. by James Raine. Surtees Soc. xxxi (1856).

Ebchester was prior 1446–56, and Burnby 1456–68.

5689 RECORDS OF ANTONY BEK, BISHOP AND PATRIARCH, 1283–1311. Ed. by C. M. Fraser. Surtees Soc. clxii for 1947 (1953).

Not an official register, but a collection of documents from various sources. See C. M. Fraser, *A history of Antony Bek, bishop of Durham, 1283–1311* (Oxf. 1957); idem, 'Officers of the bishopric of Durham under Antony Bek, 1283–1311', *Archaeol. Aeliana*, xxxv (1957), 22–38; see Nos. 1626, 3868.

5690 THE REGISTER OF THOMAS LANGLEY, BISHOP OF DURHAM, 1406–37. Ed. by Robin L. Storey. Surtees Soc. clxiv for 1949 (1956); clxvi for 1951 (1957); clxix for 1954 (1959); clxx for 1955 (1961); clxxvii for 1962 (1966).

See R. L. Storey, *Thomas Langley and the bishopric of Durham, 1406–1437* (Lond. 1961), where chap. ii, pp. 52–134 deals with the county palatine of Durham, and an appendix, pp. 245–62, prints the report of the inquisition of 1433 in which the jurors criticized and challenged the existence of the franchises of Durham.

5691 REGISTRUM PALATINUM DUNELMENSE. The register of Richard de Kellawe, lord palatine and bishop of Durham, 1311–16. Ed. by Thomas D. Hardy. 4 vols. Rolls Ser. 1873–8. Index in *Deputy Keeper's Report*, xxx (1869), 99–120.

Vol. iii contains various documents, 1279–1374, including some palatinate records, a part of Bishop Bury's register, 1338–43, and part of William Legat's. Vol. iv contains additions from plea rolls, letters patent and close, and other public documents.

5692 RICHARD D'AUNGERVILLE OF BURY. FRAGMENTS OF HIS
REGISTER, AND OTHER DOCUMENTS. Ed. by G. W. Kitchin. Surtees
Soc. cxix (1910).

See also *Registrum Palatinum* (No. 5691) and *Liber Epistolaris* (No. 6561).

5693 SANCTUARIUM DUNELMENSE ET SANCTUARIUM BEVER-
LACENSE. Ed. by James Raine. Surtees Soc. 1837.

Sanctuary registers for Durham, 1464–1524; for Beverley, c. 1478–1539.

5694 CRASTER (H. H. EDMUND). 'A contemporary record of the pontificate of Ranulf Flambard'. *Archaeol. Aeliana*, 4th Ser. vii (1930), 41–50.

R. W. Southern, 'Ranulf Flambard and early Anglo-Norman administration', *T.R.H.S.*
4th Ser. xvi (1933), 95–128; revised in Southern, *Medieval humanism*, pp. 183–205.
H. S. Offler, 'Rannulf Flambard as bishop of Durham (1099–1128)', *Durham Univ.
Jour.* lxiv (1971), 14–25.

5695 CRASTER (H. H. EDMUND). 'The Red Book of Durham'. *E.H.R.* xl
(1925), 504–32. See No. 2168.

The Red Book, now in the library of Lincoln's Inn, comprises two MSS. (*a*) A history
of the church of Durham from 635 to about 1195, compiled from known sources
probably by Prior John Wessington (1416–46) with charters and a fragmentary chronicle.
(*b*) Hagiographical tracts.

5696 DOBSON (R. BARRIE). 'Richard Bell, prior of Durham (1464–78) and
bishop of Carlisle (1478–95)'. *Cumb.–Westm. A.A. Soc. Trans.* New Ser. lxv
(1965), 182–221.

5697 DODDS (M. HOPE). 'The bishop's boroughs (Durham)'. *Archaeol.
Aeliana*, 3rd Ser. xii (1915), 81–185.

5698 FASTI DUNELMENSES: A record of the beneficed clergy of the
diocese of Durham down to the dissolution of the monastic and collegiate
churches. Ed. by D. S. Boutflower. Surtees Soc. cxxix (1926).

H. S. Offler, 'The early archdeacons in the diocese of Durham', *Durham–Northumberland
Archit.–Archaeol. Soc. Trans.* xi (1962), 189–207. R. Donaldson, 'Sponsors, patrons
and presentations to benefices in the gift of the priors of Durham in the late middle
ages', *Archaeol. Aeliana*, 4th Ser. xxxviii (1960), 169–77.

5699 HALCROW (ELIZABETH M.). 'Obedientiaries and counsellors in
monastic administration at Durham'. *Archaeol. Aeliana*, xxxv (1957), 7–21.
Idem, 'The social position and influence of the priors of Durham, as illustrated
by their correspondence' (largely fourteenth and fifteenth centuries, with some
notice to patronage of churches). Ibid. xxxiii (1955), 70–86.

5700 SCAMMELL (GEOFFREY V.). Hugh du Puiset, bishop of Durham.
Cambr. and N.Y. 1956.

An appendix contains a dozen of Hugh's hitherto unpublished *acta*, his itinerary, and
a note on forgeries. G. V. Scammell, 'A note on the chronology of the priors, archdeacons and sheriffs of Durham during the episcopate of Hugh du Puiset', *Archaeol.
Aeliana*, xxxiii (1955), 61–5; idem, 'Seven charters relating to the *familia* of Bishop Hugh
du Puiset', ibid. xxxiv (1956), 77–90; and idem, 'Four early charters (of Hugh de Puiset)
relating to York', *Yorks. Archaeol. Jour.* xxxix (1956–8), 86–90. The Surtees Society
anticipates an edition of *Acta* of Hugh du Puiset, by G. V. Scammell.

5701 SCAMMELL (JEAN). 'Some aspects of medieval English monastic government: the case of Geoffrey Burdon, prior of Durham (1313–21)'. *Rev. Bénédictine*, lxviii (1958), 216–50.

5702 THOMPSON (A. HAMILTON). 'The collegiate churches of the bishopric of Durham'. *Durham Univ. Jour.* xxxvi (1944), 33–42.

ELY

See Liber Eliensis (No. 2164) and *Hist. MSS. Comm. Reports*, vi. 289–300; xii, pt. 9, 375–96.

5703 ELY CHAPTER ORDINANCES AND VISITATION RECORDS, 1241–1515. Ed. by Seiriol A. J. Evans. R.H.S. Camden Ser. lxiv. *Camden Miscellany*, xvii. (1940).

5704 ELY EPISCOPAL RECORDS: a calendar of the episcopal records in the muniment room of the palace of Ely. By Alfred Gibbons. Lincoln. 1891.

> Court rolls, 30 Edw. I–1788, pp. 68–78; bailiffs' rolls, rentals, etc. 9 Edw. I–1807, pp. 92–108; royal plea rolls, 1423–1775, pp. 112–23; wills (in full), 1382–1526, pp. 193–223; extracts from episcopal registers, 1375–1587, pp. 392–420. For a full abstract of the registers 1337–92, see J. H. Crosby, 'Ely episcopal registers', *Ely Diocesan Remembrancer*, Nov. 1889–Jan. 1900, etc. and Dorothy M. Owen, 'Ely diocesan records', *Stud. in Church Hist.* i (1964), 176–83.

5705 SACRIST ROLLS OF ELY (1291–1360). Ed. by Frank R. Chapman. 2 vols. Cambr. 1907.

> Well-edited account-rolls.

5706 VETUS LIBER ARCHIDIACONI ELIENSIS. Ed. by C. L. Feltoe and E. H. Minns. Cambr. Antiq. Soc. Octavo Ser. xlviii (1917).

5707 ASTON (MARGARET). Thomas Arundel: a study of church life in the reign of Richard II. Oxf. 1967.

> Treats at length the diocese of Ely while Arundel was bishop from 1374 to 1388. Chap. 4 describes, with the use of manuscript sources, the long dispute between the bishop and the archdeacon of Ely. For Arundel's archbishoprics, see Nos. 5627, 5861.

5708 BENTHAM (JAMES). The history and antiquities of the cathedral church of Ely. 2 vols. Cambr. 1721. 2nd edn. 1 vol. Norwich. 1812. Supplement by William Stevenson. Norwich. 1817.

5709 BOIVIN-CHAMPEAUX (LOUIS). Notice sur Guillaume de Longchamp, évêque d'Ely, vice-roi d'Angleterre. Evreux, etc. 1885.

5710 GRAHAM (ROSE). 'The administration of the diocese of Ely during the vacancies of the see, 1298–9 and 1302–3'. *T.R.H.S.* 4th Ser. xii (1929), 49–74.

5711 MILLER (EDWARD). The abbey and bishopric of Ely: the social history of an ecclesiastical estate from the tenth to the early fourteenth century. Cambr. Stud. in Medieval Life and Thought. Cambr. 1951.*

> A learned contribution to economic and social history.

5712 PALMER (WILLIAM M.). 'Fifteenth century visitation records of the deanery of Wisbech (Cambs.)'. *Cambr. Antiq. Soc. Procs.* (for 1938–9), xxxix (1940), 69–75.

5713 ULLMANN (WALTER). 'The disputed election of Hugh Balsham, bishop of Ely'. *Cambr. Hist. Jour.* ix (1949), 259–68.

> The appeal to Rome in this dispute in 1257 led Alexander IV to issue the decree *Dilecti filii procuratores* (Friedberg, ii, col. 952). See also G. Barraclough, 'The making of a bishop in the middle ages', *Catholic Hist. Rev.* xix (1933–4), 275–319.

EXETER

Hist. MSS. Comm. Various, iv. 13–95.

5714 ACCOUNT OF THE EXECUTORS OF RICHARD (de Gravesend), BISHOP OF LONDON, 1303, AND OF THE EXECUTORS OF THOMAS (de Bitton), BISHOP OF EXETER, 1310. Ed. by W. H. Hale and H. T. Ellacombe. Camden Soc. 1874.

> Pp. 1–45, *compotus* of Bitton; 47–110, *compotus* of Gravesend; 111–16, will of Gravesend.

5715 EPISCOPAL REGISTERS OF THE DIOCESE OF EXETER. Ed. by Francis C. Hingeston-Randolph. Lond. 1886–1909.

> Nine volumes, mainly indexes of the contents but with copious extracts of the registers of bishops from 1257 to 1455. Register of Bronescombe and Quivil 1257–91 with some records of Bitton 1292–1307 (1889).
> Register of Walter de Stapledon, 1307–26 (1892).
> Register of John de Grandisson, 1327–69. 3 vols. (1894–9).
> Register of Thomas de Brantyngham, 1370–94. 2 vols. (1901–6).
> Register of Edmund Stafford, 1395–1419. (1886).
> Register of Edmund Lacy, 1420–55, pt. i (Institutions) (1909).
>   A full abstract of sixty wills, 1397–1419, is printed in Stafford's register, pp. 379–424. With Grandisson's register, iii. 1563–1610, the editor prints a fragment of the chartulary of Buckfast Abbey. For a life of Grandisson based upon his register, see Adam Hamilton, in *Dublin Rev.* cxxviii (1901), 305–23; and Frances B. Rose-Troup, *Bishop Grandisson, student and art-lover* (Plymouth, 1929).

5716 ORDINALE EXON. Ed. by J. N. Dalton and G. H. Doble. 4 vols. Henry Bradshaw Soc. 1909–40.

5717 REGISTER OF EDMUND LACY, BISHOP OF EXETER, 1420–55. Registrum Commune. Ed. by G. R. Dunstan. Cant.–York Soc. and Devon–Cornwall Record Soc. Torquay. vol. i (1963); ii (1966); iii (1967); iv (1971); v (1972).

> This edition supersedes the work published as Register of Edmund Lacy, pt. ii, the Registrum Commune, transcribed and summarized by C. G. Browne, edited and annotated by O. J. Reichel. Devon–Cornwall Record Soc. (1915). Dunstan's edition begins with the Vicar-General's Register 1420–1 and follows from p. 60 with Bishop Lacy's Register. For some aspects of Lacy's Register, see Dunstan in *J.E.H.* vi (1955), 37–47. For *Liber Pontificalis of Edmund Lacy*, see No. 1317.

5718 THE USE OF EXETER CATHEDRAL ACCORDING TO JOHN DE GRANDISSON (Bishop 1327–67): abstract of chapter acts and other documents illustrating the history of the church and diocese of Exeter, 1380–1660. Ed. by Herbert E. Reynolds. Lond. 1891.

5719 BOGGIS (ROBERT J. E.). A history of the diocese of Exeter. Exeter. 1922.

5720 ERSKINE (AUDREY M.). 'The medieval financial records of the cathedral church of Exeter'. *Jour. Soc. Archivists*, ii (1960–4), 254–66.

5721 MOREY (ADRIAN). Bartholomew of Exeter, bishop and canonist: a study in the twelfth century. Cambr. 1937.

The appendixes list the early archdeacons of Exeter and print some charters and other documents. Part II prints Bartholomew's *Penitential*. For other topics, see Nos. 6456, 6513.

5722 OLIVER (GEORGE). Lives of the bishops of Exeter, and a history of the cathedral. Exeter. 1861. Index by J. S. Attwood. 1887.

Includes a valuable appendix, containing fabric rolls, charters, etc. See also Oliver's *Monasticon* (No. 1147).

5723 REYNOLDS (HERBERT E.). A short history of the ancient diocese of Exeter. Exeter. 1895.

Donald Cawthron, 'The administration of the diocese of Exeter in the fourteenth century', *Devonshire Asso. Reports and Trans.* lxxxvii (1955), 130–64.

HEREFORD
See Bannister's Catalogue (No. 1046).

5724 CALENDAR OF THE EARLIER HEREFORD CATHEDRAL MUNIMENTS. Compiled by B. G. Charles and H. D. Emanuel. 3 vols. Lond. 1955.

5725 CHARTERS AND RECORDS OF HEREFORD CATHEDRAL. Ed. by W. W. Capes. Cantilupe Soc. Hereford. 1908.

Charters, account rolls, etc. *c.* A.D. 840–1421. See also roll of expenses of Bishop Swinfield (No. 4612).

5726 DE S. THOMA DE CANTILUPE episc. Herefordensi in Anglia apud montem Flasconis in Hetruria pontificia commentarius praevius in Bolland's *Acta Sanctorum Octobris* (No. 1152), i. 539–609 (vita), 610–705 (miracula). Antwerp. 1765.

Based on the almost contemporary *Processus Canonisationis* preserved in the Vatican (Vat. MS. 4015). See T. F. Tout's elaborate article in *D.N.B.* viii. 448–52; and No. 5730.

5727 EXTRACTS FROM THE CATHEDRAL REGISTERS OF THE DIOCESE OF HEREFORD, 1275–1535. Trans. by E. N. Dew. Cantilupe Soc. Hereford. 1932.

5728 FOLIOT (GILBERT). See Nos. 5761, 6515–17.

5729 INDEX TO THE REGISTERS OF THE DIOCESE OF HEREFORD, 1275–1535. Compiled by E. N. Dew. Cantilupe Soc. Hereford. 1925.

5730 REGISTERS OF THE BISHOPS OF HEREFORD. 1275–1535/8. Cant.-York Soc. and Cantilupe Soc. 1907–21.

Registers of Thomas de Cantilupe (1275–82), Richard de Swinfield (1283–1317), Adam de Orleton (1317–27), Thomas Charlton (1327–44), John de Trillek (1344–61), Lewis Charlton (1361–70), William Courtenay (1370–5), John Gilbert (1375–89), John Trefnant (1389–1404), Robert Mascall (1404–16), Edmund Lacy (1417–20), Thomas Poltone (1420–2), Thomas Spofford (1422–48), Richard Beauchamp (1449–50), Reginald Boulers (1451–3), John Stanbury (1453–74), Thomas Myllyng (1474–92), Richard Mayew (1504–16), and Charles Bothe (1516–35), with abstracts of register of Edward Fox (1535–8).

5731 A TRANSCRIPT OF THE RED BOOK OF THE BISHOPRIC OF HEREFORD, *c.* 1290. Ed. by A. T. Bannister. R.H.S. Camden Ser. xli (1929), *Camden Miscellany*, xv.

5732 BANNISTER (ARTHUR T.). The cathedral church of Hereford: its history and constitution. Lond. 1924.

5733 BANNISTER (ARTHUR T.). 'Visitation returns of the diocese of Hereford in 1397'. *E.H.R.* xliv (1929), 279–89, 444–53; xlv (1930), 92–101, 444–63.

See Bannister, 'Parish life in the fourteenth century', *The Nineteenth Century*, cii (1927), 399–404. The returns of this parochial visitation are summarized here.

5734 BROOKE (ZACHARY N.) and BROOKE (C. N. L.). 'Hereford Cathedral dignitaries in the twelfth century'. *Cambr. Hist. Jour.* viii, no. 1 (1944), 1–21. Supplement (of corrections). Ibid. viii, no. 3 (1946), 179–85.

5735 HAVERGAL (FRANCIS T.). Fasti Herefordenses and other antiquarian memorials of Hereford. Edinburgh. 1869.

5736 RAWLINSON (RICHARD). The history of the cathedral church of Hereford. Lond. 1717.

The appendix contains seventy-one Latin charters, and a calendar with obits.

5737 WOODRUFF (C. EVELEIGH), ed. 'The will of Peter de Aqua Blanca, bishop of Hereford, 1268'. R.H.S. Camden Series, xxxvii (1926). *Camden Miscellany*, xiv.

François Mugnier, *Les Savoyards en Angleterre au xiiiᵉ siècle et Pierre d'Aigueblanche, évêque d'Hereford* (Chambéry, 1891).

LINCOLN

See *Hist. MSS. Comm. Report*, xii, pt. 9, 553–72 and several catalogues (No. 1048); particularly K. Major's *Handlist* (No. 1049); for St. Hugh of Lincoln, bishop 1186–1200, see No. 5742.

5738 CONSUETUDINARIUM ECCLESIAE LINCOLNIENSIS, tempore Richardi de Gravesend episcopi (1258–79), redactum, with notes by Christopher Wordsworth. Ed. by H. E. Reynolds. Exeter. 1885.

Contains cathedral statutes, etc.

5739 DOCUMENTS FROM REGISTERS RELATING TO LEICESTERSHIRE. Extracts by G. D. Fletcher. *A.A.S.R.P.* xxi (1892), 277–329; xxii (1894), 109–50, 227–365.

On the registers of Bishop John Gynewell, for the years 1347–50, see A. H. Thompson, *Archaeol. Jour.* lxviii (1911), 301–60, which includes tables of institutions that throw light on the conditions produced by the Black Death. On Lincoln episcopal registers, see C. W. Foster 'The Lincolnshire episcopal registers', *Lincoln and Northampton Reports and Papers* for 1933, xli, pt. 2 (1935), 155–68b.

5740 LIBER ANTIQUUS DE ORDINATIONIBUS VICARIARUM TEMPORE HUGONIS WELLS. Ed. by Alfred Gibbons. Lincoln. 1888.

A record of the establishment of nearly 300 vicarages; valuable for the relations of the bishop of Lincoln to the monasteries.

5741 LINCOLN DIOCESE DOCUMENTS, 1450–1544. Ed. by Andrew Clark. E.E.T.S. cxlix (1914).

Documents in English, such as wills, proceedings against the Lollards, and leases, taken from the Lincoln episcopal registers.

5742 MAGNA VITA SANCTI HUGONIS: The life of St. Hugh of Lincoln. Ed. and trans. by Decima L. Douie and Dom Hugh Farmer. 2 vols. Lond. etc. 1961–2. Also edited by James F. Dimock. Rolls Ser. 1864. Extracts were edited by Pauli in M.G.H. *SS.* (No. 1114), xxvii. 316–23.

Hugh of Avalon, a Carthusian monk, was bishop of Lincoln from 1186 to 1200. He was canonized in 1220. This exemplary biography was written before 1220 by Adam, abbot of Evesham and Hugh's chaplain. It includes many notices on public affairs. The introduction to the Douie–Farmer edition (pp. vii–liv) provides a good commentary. There are two other medieval 'Lives' of St. Hugh: (a) *Metrical Life of St. Hugh, bishop of Lincoln*. Ed. by James F. Dimock (Lincoln, 1860). Extracts edited by Pauli in M.G.H. *SS.* xxvii, 323–4. (b) Gerald of Wales's *Vita S. Hugonis* in *Giraldi Cambrensis Opera* (No. 6573), vol. vii, which includes an appendix of documents relating to the bishops and cathedral of Lincoln in the twelfth and thirteenth centuries.

A good modern biography of St. Hugh is Herbert Thurston, *Life of St. Hugh of Lincoln* (Lond. 1898), which is essentially a translation, with large additions and appendixes, of *Vie de Saint Hugues, évêque de Lincoln, 1140–1200*, par un religieux de la Grande Chartreuse (Montreuil, 1890). See also Hugh Farmer, 'St. Hugh of Lincoln and his biographers', *American Benedictine Rev.* xvi (1965), 396–412; idem, 'The canonization of St. Hugh of Lincoln', *Lincs. Archit.-Archaeol. Soc. Papers*, (1956), 86–117.

5743 REGISTER OF BISHOP PHILIP REPINGDON, 1405–19. Ed. by Margaret Archer. Lincoln Record Soc. lvii–lviii. 1960–3.

M. Archer, 'Philip Repingdon, bishop of Lincoln, and his cathedral chapter', *Univ. Birmingham Hist. Jour.* iv (1954), 81–97.

5744 REGISTRUM ANTIQUISSIMUM of the Cathedral Church of Lincoln. Ed. by C. W. Foster and Kathleen Major. Vols. i+. Lincoln Record Soc. 1931 (in progress). 9 vols. to 1968.

This scholarly edition of a remarkable collection of charters and similar documents which have survived either as originals or as copies registered in Lincoln cartularies is indispensable for church history of the twelfth and thirteenth centuries. The *Registrum Antiquissimum* of charters from 1061 to 1235 forms the framework for this edition. Among its documents, which are printed in chronological order, the editors have interpolated similar documents, originals or copies from other sources; accordingly the entries run on into the early fourteenth century. Royal charters, papal bulls, grants to Lincoln cathedral, grants of citizens to parishes, and similar documents are transcribed and properly annotated; they reach the number 2666 at the end of vol. ix. A tall volume of *Facsimiles of Charters for volumes v and vi of the Registrum Antiquissimum* was issued as vol. xlii for 1945 by the Lincoln Record Society; it displays thirty facsimiles of charters from about 1160 to about 1245. From the *Registrum Antiquissimum*, W. O. Massingberd translated 'Lincoln Cathedral charters', (Hen. I–Hen. III, but mainly *temp.* John), *A.A.S.R.P.* xxvi (1901), 18–96, 321–69; xxvii (1903), 1–91. See also Herbert E. Salter, 'Charters of Henry II at Lincoln Cathedral (granted to the church of Lincoln)'. *E.H.R.* xxiv (1909), 303–13. For some Lincoln charters 1101–54, see *E.H.R.* xxi (1906), 505–9; xxiii (1908), 725–8; xxv (1910), 114–16. For documents from 1215 to 1311, Dorothy M. Owen, '*Vetus Repertorium*: an early memorandum book of the diocese of Lincoln', *Cambr. Bibliog. Soc. Trans.* iv (1964–8), 100–6.

5745 THE ROLLS AND REGISTER OF BISHOP OLIVER SUTTON, 1280–99. Ed. by Rosalind M. T. Hill. Lincoln Record Soc. 1948 (in progress, 6 vols. by 1969).

The introduction to vol. i of this edition is fittingly informative on several topics. Relating to the register, see Rosalind Hill, 'Bishop Sutton and his archives: a study in the keeping of records in the thirteenth century', *J.E.H.* ii (1951), 43–53; and *Lincoln Minster Pamphlets* (No. 5752). Idem, 'Bishop Sutton and the institution of heads of religious houses in the diocese of Lincoln', *E.H.R.* lviii (1943), 201–9.

5746 ROTULI HUGONIS DE WELLES, EPISCOPI LINCOLNIENSIS, (1209–35). Ed. by W. P. W. Phillimore and F. N. Davis. 3 vols. Cant.–York Soc. 1907–9, and Lincoln Record Soc. 1912–14.

The date of the earliest entry has not been definitely determined, but between 1215 and 1219.

5747 ROTULI RICARDI GRAVESEND, DIOCESIS LINCOLNIENSIS, 1258–79. Ed. by F. N. Davis, C. W. Foster, and A. H. Thompson. Cant.–York Soc. 1925 and Lincoln Record Soc. xx. 1925.

5748 ROTULI ROBERTI GROSSETESTE, EPISCOPI LINCOLNIEN-SIS, 1235–53. Ed. by F. N. Davis. Cant.–York Soc. 1913, and Lincoln Record Soc. xi. 1914.

Includes a roll of institutions of Bishop Henry of Lexington (1254–8). For Grosseteste, see Nos. 6574–84.

5749 STATUTES OF LINCOLN CATHEDRAL. Arranged by Henry Bradshaw and edited by Christopher Wordsworth. 2 pts. in 3 vols. Cambr. 1892–7.

Liber niger, i. 1–468: a book of customs of Lincoln Cathedral containing statutes, charters, etc. from 1160 onward.
Early cathedral statutes of Salisbury, Lichfield, Hereford, and York, ii. 7–135.
Lincoln customs and awards (lauda). 1214–1439, ii. 136–60; iii. 161–267.
Novum ecclesiae Lincolniensis registrum, iii. 268–363: a collection of statutes, 1440–42.
Lincoln episcopal visitations, 1437–44, iii. 364–465.
Lincoln registers and chapter acts, 1421–48, iii. 468–538.
Chronological table of English uses, iii. 824–59; a bibliography of works relating to English church services.
This collection has superseded the *Statuta Ecclesiae Lincolniae*, printed in 1873.

5750 VISITATIONS OF RELIGIOUS HOUSES IN THE DIOCESE OF LINCOLN (1420–49). Ed. by A. Hamilton Thompson. (No. 6222).

5751 FOSTER (CHARLES W.). Institutions to benefices in the diocese of Lincoln, *sede vacante*, 1200–3; 1234–5. *A.A.S.R.P.* xxxix (1929–30), 179–216.

5752 LINCOLN MINSTER PAMPHLETS. Lincoln.

These short, popular accounts of topics relating to Lincoln Cathedral are generally scholarly. No. 2. J. H. Srawley, *The book of John de Schalby*. 1949. No. 4. Rosalind M. T. Hill, *Oliver Sutton, dean of Lincoln, later bishop of Lincoln (1280–99)*. 1959.

5753 MAJOR (KATHLEEN). 'The finances of the dean and chapter of Lincoln from the twelfth to the fourteenth century: a preliminary survey'. *J.E.H.* v (1954), 149–67.

K. Major, 'The office of chapter clerk at Lincoln', in *Graham essays* (No. 1437). Idem, 'Presentation deeds' in *Powicke essays* (No. 1450).

5754 MORRIS (COLIN). 'The commissary of the bishop of the diocese of Lincoln'. *J.E.H.* x (1959), 50–65.

5755 NOBLE (WILLIAM M.) and LADDS (SIDNEY I.), eds. 'Records of the archdeaconry of Huntingdon (a catalogue)'. *Cambs.–Hunts. Archaeol. Soc. Trans.* iv (1920). Separately printed. Ely. 1921.

5756 THOMPSON (ALEXANDER HAMILTON). Lambeth institutions to benefices: being a calendar of institutions to benefices in the old diocese of Lincoln during vacancies of the episcopal see and during the visitation of the diocese by the archbishop of Canterbury as metropolitan, with collation of benefices made by the archbishops *jure devoluto*, from the archiepiscopal registers in the library of Lambeth Palace, 1279–1532. *A.A.S.R.P.* xl (1930–1), 33–110.

LONDON

Hist. MSS. Comm. Reports, Various, vii. 1–9; and ix. 1–71. See Richard Gravesend (No. 5714).

5757 DICETO (RALPH DE). Opera. See No. 2860.

5758 DOCUMENTS ILLUSTRATING THE HISTORY OF ST. PAUL'S CATHEDRAL (1140–1712). Ed. by William S. Simpson. Camden Soc. New Series, xxvi (1880). For contents, see Milne, *Centenary Guide* (No. 177).

5759 THE DOMESDAY OF ST. PAUL'S OF THE YEAR 1222, or Registrum de visitatione maneriorum per Robertum decanum, and other original documents relating to the manors and churches belonging to the dean and chapter of St. Paul's in the twelfth and thirteenth centuries. Ed. by William H. Hale. Camden Soc. Old Series. 1858.

Contains the survey of 1222; a manorial rental, 1240; a twelfth-century lease of manors; inquisitio maneriorum, 1181; manorial accounts, 1300, etc., with valuable introduction and notes.

5760 EARLY CHARTERS OF THE CATHEDRAL CHURCH OF ST. PAUL, LONDON. Ed. by Marion Gibbs. R.H.S. Camden 3rd Series, lviii (1939).

The charters date almost exclusively from 1066 to 1241. See Davis in *Tout essays* (No. 1458).

5761 FOLIOT (GILBERT). The letters and charters of Gilbert Foliot. Ed. by Dom Adrian Morey and Christopher N. L. Brooke. Cambr. 1967.

See Morey and Brooke, *Gilbert Foliot and his letters* (Cambr. 1965), where Appendix iv gives the names of the chapter's and the bishop's households of Hereford, 1148–63, and London, 1163–87. See Nos. 6515–17.

5762 REGISTRUM ELEEMOSYNARIAE D. PAULI LONDONIENSIS. Ed. by Maria Hackett. Lond. 1827.

Includes most of the benefactions to St. Paul's for eleemosynary purposes prior to Richard II's reign; many deeds of gift are printed in full.

5763 REGISTRUM RADULPHI BALDOCK, GILBERTI SEGRAVE, RICARDI NEWPORT, ET STEPHANI GRAVESEND, EPISCOPORUM LONDONIENSIUM, 1304–38. Ed. by Robert C. Fowler. Cant.–York Soc. 1911.

5764 REGISTRUM SIMONIS DE SUDBIRIA, DIOCESIS LONDONI-ENSIS, 1362–75. Ed. by R. C. Fowler and Claude Jenkins. 2 vols. Cant.–York Soc. 1927–8.

See C. Jenkins, 'Sudbury's London register', *Church Quart. Rev.* cvii (1928), 222–54.

5765 REGISTRUM STATUTORUM ET CONSUETUDINUM ECCLE-SIAE CATHEDRALIS S. PAULI (1294–1855). Ed. by William S. Simpson. Lond. 1873.

Includes on pp. 326–58 'Charter and statutes of the college of the minor canons in St. Paul's cathedral (1394–6)', reprinted from *Archaeologia*, xliii (1871), 165–200, and separately Lond. 1871; 'Constitutions of the Diocese of London, *c.* 1213–22', by R. M. Woolley in *E.H.R.* xxx (1915), 285–302.

5766 TWO INVENTORIES OF THE CATHEDRAL CHURCH OF ST. PAUL, 1245 and 1402. Ed. by W. S. Simpson. *Archaeologia*, l (1887), 439–524.

5767 VISITATIONS OF CHURCHES BELONGING TO ST. PAUL'S CATHEDRAL, 1249–52. Ed. by W. S. Simpson. Camden Soc. New Ser. liii (1895). *Camden Miscellany*, ix. 1–38. Idem, Visitations of churches belonging to St. Paul's cathedral in 1297 and in 1458. Camden Soc. New Ser. lv (1895).

5768 BROOKE (CHRISTOPHER N. L.). 'The composition of the chapter of St. Paul's, 1086–1163'. *Cambr. Hist. Jour.* x (1951), 111–32. Idem, 'The deans of St. Paul's *c.* 1090–1499'. *B.I.H.R.* xxix (1956), 231–44.

See Diana E. Greenway, 'Succession to Ralph de Diceto, dean of St. Paul's', *B.I.H.R.* xxxix (1966), 86–95; and her edition of LeNeve (No. 5581).

5769 DUGDALE (WILLIAM). History of St. Paul's cathedral. Lond. 1658. Another edition, with additions, by Henry Ellis. Lond. 1818.

The body of the work is mainly descriptive; the appendix contains valuable documents.

5770 MATTHEWS (WALTER R.) and ATKINS (WILLIAM M.), eds. A history of St. Paul's cathedral and the men associated with it. Lond. 1957.

Chapters by C. N. L. Brooke, E. F. Carpenter, *et al.*

5771 MILMAN (HENRY H.). Annals of St. Paul's cathedral. Lond. 1868. 2nd edn. 1869.

5772 NEWCOURT (RICHARD). Repertorium ecclesiasticum parochiale Londinense; history of the diocese of London, the parish churches, etc. 2 vols. Lond. 1708–10.

George Hennessy's *Novum Repertorium Parochiale Londinense* (Lond. 1898) is virtually, so far as the present diocese is concerned, a new edition and continuation of Newcourt's work.

5773 SIMPSON (WILLIAM SPARROW). Chapters in the history of old St. Paul's. Lond. 1881. Idem, Gleanings from old St. Paul's. Lond. 1889. Idem, St. Paul's cathedral and old city life, from the thirteenth to the sixteenth centuries. Lond. 1894. Idem, 'Visitations of certain churches in the city of London in the patronage of St. Paul's Cathedral Church between the years 1138 and 1250', *Archaeologia*, lv (1897), 282–300.

NORWICH

5774 ARCHDEACONRY OF NORWICH: inventory of church goods, *temp.* Edward III (1368). Transcribed by Aelred Watkin. 1 vol. in 2. Norfolk Record Soc. xix (1947–8).

5775 THE CAMERA ROLL. Compiled by Bartholomew Cotton. Ed. by William Hudson. *Norfolk and Norwich Archaeol. Soc. Original Papers*, xix (1917), 268–313.

The roll was compiled for the prior of Norwich in 1283.

5776 CUSTOMARY OF THE CATHEDRAL PRIORY CHURCH OF NORWICH. Ed. by J. B. L. Tolhurst. Henry Bradshaw Soc. lxxxii (1948).

5777 EPISTOLAE HERBERTI DE LOSINGA, Osberti de Clara, et Elmeri prioris Cantuariensis, Ed. by Robert Anstruther. (Half-title: Scriptores monastici). Brussels. etc. 1846. Also published by the Caxton Society. Lond. 1846.

Herbert de Losinga, bishop of Norwich (1090/1–1119), was in high favour at the court of Henry I. Osbert de Clare, prior of Westminster (xii cent.), wrote a life of Edward the Confessor (No. 2171). Elmer (d. 1137) was prior of Christ Church, Canterbury. See also *The life, letters and sermons of Bishop Herbert de Losinga*; the letters, as translated by the editors, being incorporated with the life, and the sermons being now first edited, with an English translation and notes, by E. M. Goulburn and Henry Symonds. 2 vols. Lond. etc. 1878.

5778 THE FIRST REGISTER OF NORWICH CATHEDRAL PRIORY. Transcribed and translated by Herbert W. Saunders. Norfolk Rec. Soc. xi (1939).

A chronicle and charters to 1300.

5779 AN INTRODUCTION TO THE OBEDIENTIARY AND MANOR ROLLS OF NORWICH CATHEDRAL PRIORY. By Herbert W. Saunders. Norwich. 1930.

5780 VISITATIONS OF THE DIOCESE OF NORWICH, A.D. 1492–1532. Ed. by Augustus Jessopp. Camden Soc. New Series. xliii (1888).

5781 ALEXANDER (JAMES W.). Herbert of Norwich, 1091–1119: studies in the history of Norman England. *Studies in Medieval and Renaissance History,* vi (1969), 115–232.

5782 BEECHING (H. C.) and JAMES (M. R.). 'The library of the cathedral of Norwich, with an appendix of priory MSS. now in English libraries'. *Norfolk Archaeology,* xix (1917), 67–116; 174.

5783 CARTER (EDWARD H.). Studies in Norwich cathedral history. Norwich. 1935.
   1. Visitation process in 1308 by Bishop John Salmon.
   2. Archbishop Arundel's judgement in controversy between Bishop Alexander Tottington and Prior Robert de Brunham in 1411.

5784 CHENEY (CHRISTOPHER R.). 'Norwich Cathedral Priory in the fourteenth century'. *B.J.R.L.* xx (1936), 93–120.

5785 DODWELL (BARBARA). 'The foundation of Norwich Cathedral'. *T.R.H.S.* 5th Ser. vii (1957), 1–18.

5786 GRASSI (J. L.). 'William Airmyn and the bishopric of Norwich'. *E.H.R.* lxx (1955), 550–61.

5787 JACOB (ERNEST F.). 'Thomas Brouns, bishop of Norwich, 1436–45'. Essays in history presented to Sir Keith Feiling, edited by H. R. Trevor-Roper. Lond. and N.Y. 1965. Pp. 61–83.

5788 STONE (ERIC). 'Profit-and-loss accountancy at Norwich Cathedral priory (thirteenth and fourteenth centuries)'. *T.R.H.S.* 5th Ser. xii (1962), 25–48.

ROCHESTER

5789 ANNALES ECCLESIAE ROFFENSIS (A.D. 604–1307), ex Historia ecclesiastica Edmundi de Hadenham monachi Roffensis. Ed. by Henry Wharton, *Anglia Sacra* (No. 1125), i. 341–55.
   These notes are interpolations which Hadenham (*fl.* 1307) made in a copy of the chronicle *Flores Historiarum.*

5790 CUSTUMALE ROFFENSE (No. 4780).

5791 RECORDS OF ROCHESTER (Diocese). Ed. by C. H. Fielding. Dartford. 1910.
   Contains brief histories of the churches, with lists of clergy, etc. See also *Extracts from the records relating to the rectors of High Halden, 1322–1899.* Ed. by W. B. Grimaldi (Lond. 1900).

5792 REGISTRUM HAMONIS HETHE, DIOCESIS ROFFENSIS (1319–52). Ed. by Charles Johnson. 2 vols. Cant.–York Soc. 1914, 1948.
   Vol. ii, pp. 911–1043; Acts of the Consistory Court, 1347–8.

5793 REGISTRUM ROFFENSE: a collection of antient records, charters, etc. illustrating the history of the diocese and cathedral church of Rochester. Ed. by John Thorpe (the elder). Lond. 1769.

The Registrum contains charters, bulls, ordinations, pleadings, etc., many of them taken from the episcopal registers of Rochester.

5794 TEXTUS ROFFENSIS. Ed. by Thomas Hearne. Oxf. 1720. Facsimile edition by Peter Sawyer in Early English MSS. in facsimile, vii and xi (No. 441).

See Samuel Pegge, *An historical account of the Textus Roffensis* (Lond. 1784); and Felix Liebermann, 'Notes on the Textus Roffensis', *Archaeologia Cantiana*, xxiii (1898), 101–12.

According to Liebermann, this work was written *c.* 1140–50 by an unknown scribe, who was induced to compile it by Ernulf, bishop of Rochester; but Sawyer dates the main hand *c.* 1122–3. The first part is a rich collection of Anglo-Saxon laws; the second is a chartulary of the church of St. Andrew. Hearne does not edit the whole work. Most of the charters are printed in Kemble's *Codex* (No. 2201), and in Thorpe's *Registrum Roffense* (No. 5793).

5795 WILLELMI DE DENE HISTORIA ROFFENSIS (1314–50 with a continuation to 1540). Ed. by Wharton, *Anglia Sacra* (No. 1125), i. 356–83.

The author, a notary public, flourished about 1350; his work is valuable for the end of Edward II's reign. See Reg. Hethe (No. 5792), i, p. vii.

5796 BROWNE (A. L.). 'The medieval officials-principal of Rochester'. *Archaeologia Cantiana*, liii for 1940 (1941), 29–61.

5797 SMITH (REGINALD A. L.). 'The financial system of Rochester cathedral priory'. *E.H.R.* lvi (1941), 586–95. Reprinted in No. 1494.

SALISBURY

Hist. MSS. Comm. Report, i. 90–1; Various, iv. 1–12.

5798 THE CANONIZATION OF SAINT OSMUND, FROM THE MANUSCRIPT RECORDS IN THE MUNIMENT ROOM OF SALIS-BURY CATHEDRAL. Ed. by A. R. Malden. Wilts. Record Soc. 1901.

5799 CHARTERS AND DOCUMENTS ILLUSTRATING THE HIS-TORY OF THE CATHEDRAL, CITY AND DIOCESE OF SALISBURY IN THE TWELFTH AND THIRTEENTH CENTURIES. Selected from the capitular and diocesan registers by W. H. Rich Jones. Ed. by W. D. Macray. Rolls ser. 1891.

Contains charters, papal bulls, cathedral regulations, constitutions of Bishop Poore (*c.* 1223), documents concerning episcopal elections, etc.

5800 HEMINGBY'S REGISTER. Ed. by Helena M. Chew. *Wilts. Archaeol. and Nat. Hist. Soc. Record Branch*, xviii (1963).

This edition of the earliest surviving Chapter Act Book of Salisbury cathedral contains a valuable introduction.

5801 THE REGISTERS OF ROGER MARTIVAL, BISHOP OF SALIS-BURY, 1315–1330. Ed. by Kathleen Edwards, C. R. Elrington, and Susan Reynolds. 4 vols. Cant.–York Soc. 1959–72.

5802 REGISTRUM SIMONIS DE GANDAVO, DIOCESIS SARES-BIRIENSIS, 1297–1315. Ed. by C. T. Flower and M. C. B. Dawes. 2 vols. Cant.–York Soc. 1934.

5803 STATUTA ET CONSUETUDINES ECCLESIAE CATHEDRALIS BEATAE MARIAE VIRGINIS SARISBIRIENSIS. Ed. by C. Wordsworth and D. Macleane. Lond. 1915.

5804 STATUTA ET CONSUETUDINES ECCLESIAE CATHEDRALIS SARISBERIENSIS (1091–1697). Ed. by E. A. Dayman and W. H. R. Jones. Bath. 1883.

See also *Ceremonies and Processions of the Cathedral Church of Salisbury* (from a MS. written *c.* 1445). Ed. by Christopher Wordsworth. (Cambr. 1901).

5805 VETUS REGISTRUM SARISBERIENSE: alias dictum registrum S. Osmundi episcopi: the register of S. Osmund. Ed. by W. H. R. Jones. 2 vols. Rolls Ser. 1883–4.

S. Osmundi consuetudinarium, i. 1–185: divine services. Cf. *Wilts. Archaeol. and Nat. Hist. Soc. Magazine,* xix (1881), 321–41.
Vetus registrum, i. 187–271, 315–93; ii. 3–124: charters, letters, bulls, etc. 1091–*c.* 1276.
Visitatio ecclesiarum, 1220–4, i. 273–314.

5806 DODSWORTH (WILLIAM). An historical account of the episcopal see and cathedral church of Sarum. Salisbury, etc. 1814.

5807 JONES (WILLIAM H. RICH). Fasti ecclesiae Sarisberiensis, or calendar of the bishops, deans, etc. of the cathedral body of Salisbury. Salisbury, etc. 1879.

C. Moor, 'Cardinals beneficed in Sarum Cathedral', *Wilts. Archaeol. Magazine,* l (1943), 136–48.

5808 PHILLIPPS (THOMAS), ed. Institutiones clericorum in comitatu Wiltoniae, 1297–1810. 2 vols. Middle Hill Press. 1825. Index by J. E. Jackson in *Wilts. Archaeol. and Nat. Hist. Soc. Magazine,* xxviii (1896), 210–35.

Gives names of churches, chapels, hospitals, etc., together with the names of the clergy presented to them, and the patrons who presented. The material is derived from episcopal registers.

5809 POWELL (W. RAYMOND). 'Two royal surveys (of church lands) of Wiltshire during the interdict', in *Interdict Documents.* Pipe Roll Soc. lxxii. New Ser. xxxiv for 1958 (1960), pp. 3–32.

WINCHESTER
See Titow, *Rural Society* (No. 4701).

5810 THE BLACK BOOK OF WINCHESTER. Ed. by William H. B. Bird. Winchester. 1925.

From a transcript of B.M. Add. MS. 6063 made by F. J. Baigent.

5811 CHARTULARY OF WINCHESTER CATHEDRAL. Ed. by A. W. Goodman. Winchester. 1927.

5812 COMPOTUS ROLLS OF THE OBEDIENTIARIES OF ST. SWITHUN'S PRIORY, WINCHESTER (1308–1537). Ed. by G. W. Kitchin. Hampshire Record Soc. 1892.

5813 CONSUETUDINARY OF THE FOURTEENTH CENTURY FOR THE REFECTORY OF THE HOUSE OF ST. SWITHUN IN WINCHESTER. Ed. by G. W. Kitchin. Lond. 1886.

5814 LIBER VITAE: REGISTER AND MARTYROLOGY OF NEW MINSTER AND HYDE ABBEY, WINCHESTER. Ed. by Walter de Gray Birch. Hampshire Record Soc. 1892.

Anglo-Saxon and later documents.

5815 THE PIPE ROLL OF THE BISHOPRIC OF WINCHESTER, 1208–9. Ed. by Hubert Hall. Lond. 1903. THE PIPE ROLL OF THE BISHOPRIC OF WINCHESTER, 1210–11. Ed. by N. R. Holt. Manchester. 1964.

These rolls form part of a long series of surviving rent rolls of the bishopric; they run from the early thirteenth to the mid-fifteenth century. Hubert Hall printed a list (1208–1454) in *Economica*, x (1924), 52–61. Holt provides a scholarly introduction on the organization of the bishop's finances, and the administration of his estates and his courts. W. O. Ault reviewed Holt's edition in *Speculum*, xl (1965), 142–3.

See Beveridge on wages and prices (No. 5489). J. S. Drew, 'Manorial accounts of St. Swithin's priory, Winchester', *E.H.R.* lxii (1947), 20–41, reprinted in No. 1468; M. M. Postan and J. Titow, 'Heriots and prices on Winchester manors', *Econ. H.R.* 2nd Ser. xi (1958–9), 383–411. Dom Aelred Watkin deals with 'Fragment from a thirteenth-century receiver's roll from Winchester cathedral priory', *E.H.R.* lxi (1946), 89–105. There are translated extracts in Titow, *Rural Society* (No. 4701).

See now J. Z. Titow, *Winchester yields* (Cambr. 1972).

5816 REGISTERS OF JOHN DE SANDALE AND RIGAUD DE ASSERIO, BISHOPS OF WINCHESTER, 1316–23, with an appendix of illustrative documents. Ed. by Francis J. Baigent. Hampshire Record Soc. 1897.

5817 REGISTRUM HENRICI WOODLOCK, DIOCESIS WINTONIENSIS, 1305–16. Ed. by A. W. Goodman. 2 vols. Cant.–York Soc. 1940–1.

5818 REGISTRUM JOHANNIS DE PONTISSARA, EPISCOPI WYNTONIENSIS, 1282–1304. Ed. by Cecil Deedes. 2 vols. Cant.–York Soc. 1915–24, and Surrey Record Soc. 1913–24.

5819 WYKEHAM'S REGISTER, 1366–1404. Ed. by T. F. Kirby. 2 vols. Hampshire Record Soc. 1896–9.

5820 CHANDLER (RICHARD). The life of William Waynflete, bishop of Winchester (with an appendix of records). Lond. 1811.

5821 COSGROVE (A. J.). 'The elections to the bishopric of Winchester, 1280–2'. *Stud. in Church Hist.* iii (1966), 169–78.

5822 MOBERLY (GEORGE H.). Life of William of Wykeham. Lond. 1887. 2nd edn. 1893.

Moberly includes two brief 'Lives' written shortly after Wykeham's death. See also Robert Lowth, *Life of William of Wykeham, bishop of Winchester* (with an appendix of documents). One vol. and Supplement (Lond. 1758–9; 3rd edn. Oxf. 1777). George C. Heseltine, *William of Wykeham*, a commentary (Lond. 1932). J. R. L. Highfield, 'The promotion of William de Wickham to the see of Winchester', *J.E.H.* iv (1953), 37–54, where some documents are printed.

5823 VOSS (LENA). Heinrich von Blois, Bischof von Winchester, 1129-1171. Berlin. 1932.*

For Henry of Blois's interest in art, see 'Gifts of Bishop Henry of Blois, Abbot of Glastonbury, to Winchester Cathedral' in Edmund Bishop's *Liturgica Historica* (Oxf. 1918), pp. 392-401.

WORCESTER
Hist. MSS. Comm. Report, xiv, pt. 8, pp. 165-205.

5824 AN ANCIENT RENTAL OF WORCESTER PRIORY. Ed. by Cosmo Gordon. Worcestershire Hist. Soc. *Collectanea* (1912), 81-90.

5825 ACCOUNTS OF THE PRIORY OF WORCESTER . . . (1521-2), ed. by James M. Wilson and A CATALOGUE OF THE ROLLS OF THE OBEDIENTIARIES (Edw. I-Hen. VIII), prepared by J. Harvey Bloom and edited by Sidney G. Hamilton. Worcestershire Hist. Soc. 1907.

5826 ANNALES PRIORATUS DE WIGORNIA. No. 2769.

5827 A CALENDAR OF THE REGISTER OF WOLSTAN DE BRANS-FORD, BISHOP OF WORCESTER, 1339-49. Ed. by Roy M. Haines. Worcestershire Hist. Soc. and Hist. MSS. Comm. 1966.

See also R. M. Haines, *The administration of the diocese of Worcester in the first half of the fourteenth century* (Lond. 1965).

5828 CARTULARY OF WORCESTER CATHEDRAL PRIORY. Ed. by R. R. Darlington. Pipe Roll Soc. lxxvi for 1962-3 (1968).

5829 A CATALOGUE OF CERTAIN ROLLS in the archives of the dean and chapter of Worcester. Comp. by J. Harvey Bloom. Worcestershire Hist. Soc. *Collectanea*. 1912.

5830 CORRODIES AT WORCESTER IN THE FOURTEENTH CENTURY: some correspondence between the crown and the priory of Worcester in the reign of Edward II concerning the corrody of Alicia Conan. Ed. by J. M. Wilson and Ethel C. Jones. Worcestershire Hist. Soc. 1917.

5831 EARLY COMPOTUS ROLLS (1278-1352) of the priory of Worcester. Transcribed and edited by J. M. Wilson and C. Gordon. Worcestershire Hist. Soc. 1908. Also COMPOTUS ROLLS . . . of the fourteenth and fifteenth centuries. Ed. by Sidney G. Hamilton. Ibid. 1910.

5832 THE LIBER ALBUS OF THE PRIORY OF WORCESTER, parts 1 and 2, priors John de Wyke, 1301-1317, and Wulstan de Bransford, 1317-1339, folios 1 to 162. A short abstract of all the documents, with indices to the original, and an introduction. By James M. Wilson. Worcestershire Hist. Soc. 1919.

See also James M. Wilson, *The Worcester liber albus: glimpses of life in a great Benedictine monastery in the fourteenth century.* S.P.C.K. Lond. 1920.

5833 LIBER ECCLESIAE WIGORNIENSIS: A LETTER BOOK OF THE PRIORS OF WORCESTER. Ed. by J. Harvey Bloom. Collated with the original MS. by Ethel Stokes. Worcestershire Hist. Soc. 1912.

English abstract with some Latin transcripts; fourteenth century.

5834 LIBER ELEMOSINARII: THE ALMONER'S BOOK OF THE PRIORY OF WORCESTER. Ed. by J. Harvey Bloom. Worcestershire Hist. Soc. 1911.

English abstract of the cartulary and the accounts of the almoner, thirteenth to sixteenth century.

5835 LIBER PENSIONUM PRIORATUS WIGORN: being a collection of documents relating to pensions from appropriated churches and other payments receivable by the prior and convent of Worcester and to the privileges of the monastery. Ed. by Clement Price. Worcestershire Hist. Soc. 1925.

English abstracts.

5836 THE RED BOOK OF WORCESTER, containing surveys of the bishop's manors and other records, chiefly of the twelfth and thirteenth centuries. Ed. by Marjory Hollings. 1 vol. in 4 pts. Worcestershire Hist. Soc. 1934–50.

5837 REGISTER OF BISHOP GODFREY GIFFARD, 1268–1301. Ed. by John W. Willis-Bund. 2 vols. Worcestershire Hist. Soc. 1898–1902.

This is a calendar of the register.

5838 REGISTER OF BISHOP WILLIAM GINSBOROUGH, 1303–7. Ed. by J. W. Willis-Bund. Worcestershire Hist. Soc. 1907. Reprinted with an introduction by Rowland A. Wilson. Lond. 1929.

5839 REGISTER OF THE DIOCESE OF WORCESTER DURING THE VACANCY OF THE SEE, usually called REGISTRUM SEDE VACANTE, 1301–1435. Ed. by John W. Willis-Bund. 1 vol. in 2 pts. Worcestershire Hist. Soc. 1897.

Contains documents relating to the election of a new bishop, and to the general administration of the diocese during the vacancy of the episcopate; letters, writs, institutions, etc.

5840 THE REGISTER OF THOMAS DE COBHAM, BISHOP OF WORCESTER, 1317–27. Ed. by Ernest H. Pearce. Worcestershire Hist. Soc. 1930.

E. H. Pearce, *Thomas de Cobham, bishop of Worcester, 1317–27; some studies drawn from his register* (Lond. etc. 1923).

5841 REGISTER OF WALTER REYNOLDS, BISHOP OF WORCESTER, 1308–13. Ed. by Rowland A. Wilson. Worcestershire Hist. Soc. 1927, and Dugdale Soc. 1928.

5842 REGISTRUM SIVE LIBER IRROTULARIUS ET CONSUETU-DINARIUS PRIORATUS BEATAE MARIAE WIGORNIENSIS. Ed. by William H. Hale. Camden Soc. xci (1865).

A few of the documents are of a public nature (the Provisions of Merton, etc.). There are also royal, episcopal, and private charters relating to the church of Worcester, together with pleadings before the itinerant justices. The larger portion of the volume comprises a valuable rental of the possessions of the monastery in the middle of the thirteenth century.

5843 THE VITA WULFSTANI OF WILLIAM OF MALMESBURY:
to which are added the extant abridgements of this work and the miracles and
translations of St. Wulfstan. Ed. by Reginald R. Darlington. R.H.S. Camden
Soc. 3rd Ser. xl (1928).

> This is the first complete edition, with a valuable introduction, of William of Malmes-
> bury's 'Life' which is a Latin translation of an Anglo-Saxon biography of Wulfstan by
> his chaplain and chancellor, Coleman. Coleman's work has been lost. For an English
> translation of Malmesbury's 'Life', see *Life of St. Wulfstan . . . rendered into English* by
> James H. F. Peile (Oxf. 1934). A modern biography is John W. Lamb, *Saint Wulfstan,
> prelate and patriot: a study of his life and times* (Lond. 1933).

5844 ATKINS (SIR IVOR). 'The church of Worcester from the eighth to the
twelfth century'. *Antiq. Jour.* xx (1940), 1–38.

> See V. H. Galbraith, 'Notes on the career of Samson, bishop of Worcester (1096–1112)'
> *E.H.R.* lxxxii (1967), 86–101; and No. 3053.

5845 GRAHAM (ROSE). 'The metropolitical visitation of the diocese of
Worcester by Archbishop Winchelsey in 1301'. *T.R.H.S.* 4th Ser. ii (1919),
59–93. Reprinted in No. 1471.

5846 HAINES (ROY M.). 'Aspects of the episcopate of John Carpenter,
bishop of Worcester, 1444–1476'. *J.E.H.* xix (1968), 11–40.

5847 PEARCE (ERNEST). 'Worcester institutions six centuries ago'. *Church
Quart. Rev.* xciv (1922), 140–55. Idem, 'Worcester ordinations six centuries ago'.
Ibid. xciii (1922), 249–63. Idem, 'Worcester priory and its bishop'. Ibid. xciv
(1922), 240–58.

5848 THOMAS (WILLIAM). A survey of the cathedral church of Worcester,
with an account of the bishops thereof to 1660. Lond. 1736.

> Includes a valuable appendix of documents.

YORK

5849 DOCUMENTS RELATING TO DIOCESAN AND PROVINCIAL
VISITATIONS from the registers of Henry Bowet (1407–23) and John Kempe
(1425–52). *Miscellanea*, ii. 131–334. Surtees Soc. cxxvii (1916).

> Pp. 291–302: Notes on canons of York and Beverley and other clerks whose names
> appear in the above documents. Pp. 280–90: Composition between Archbishop Melton
> and the Chapter on the manner and form of visitation (1328).

5850 FABRIC ROLLS OF YORK MINSTER (1360–1639, with an appendix,
1165–1704). Ed. by James Raine. Surtees Soc. 1859.

5851 HISTORIANS OF THE CHURCH OF YORK AND ITS ARCH-
BISHOPS. Ed. by James Raine. 3 vols. Rolls Series. 1879–94.

> For details of contents, see above, No. 1130; and *Repert. Font.* iii, pp. 324–5.

5852 HISTORICAL PAPERS AND LETTERS FROM THE NORTHERN
REGISTERS. Ed. by James Raine. Rolls Series. 1873.

> Contains many letters of the archbishops of York, and of the bishops of Durham and
> Carlisle, 1265–1415.

5853 HUGH THE CHANTOR. History of the church of York (1069–1127).
Ed. by Charles Johnson. Medieval classics. Lond. 1961.

Hugh the Chantor (d. *c.* 1139) presents the York case in the dispute with Canterbury over primacy.
See Denis Bithell, 'William of Corbeil and the Canterbury–York dispute', *J.E.H.* xix (1968), 145–59. For an outline of the issues, see A. H. Thompson in York Minster Hist. Tracts (No. 5880); and for more detailed treatment, M. Dueball, *Die Suprematstreit zwischen den Erzdiözesen Canterbury und York, 1070–1126*, in Historische Studien, ed. by E. Ebering, clxxxiv (1929). Cf. No. 5615.

5854 INDEX OF THE ORIGINAL DOCUMENTS OF THE CON-
SISTORY COURT OF YORK, 1427–1658. Yorks. Archaeol. Soc. Record Ser.
lxxiii (1928).

5855 LAWTON (GEORGE). Collections relative to the dioceses of York and
Ripon. 2nd edn. Lond. 1842.

5856 LETTERS OF WILLIAM WICKWANE, CHANCELLOR OF
YORK, 1266–1268. By Christopher R. Cheney. *E.H.R.* xlvii (1932), 636–42.

5857 THE REGISTER OR ROLLS OF WALTER GRAY, ARCH-
BISHOP OF YORK, with appendices of illustrative documents. Ed. by James
Raine, jr. Surtees Soc. lvi. 1872.

The early parts are lost; so covers only the years from 1235 to 1255.

5858 THE REGISTERS OF THE ARCHBISHOPS OF YORK. Surtees
Soc. 1904+.

Registers of Walter Giffard (1266–79); William Wickwane (1279–85); John le Romeyn (1286–96) and Henry of Newark (1296–9) 2 vols.; Thomas of Corbridge (1300–4), 2 vols.; William Greenfield (1306–15), 5 vols.
Listed in Mullins, *Texts* (No. 29).
See Thompson in *Tait essays* (No. 1455) for William Zouche.

5859 REGISTERS OF THE ARCHDEACONRY OF RICHMOND,
1361–1442. Ed. by A. Hamilton Thompson. *Yorks. Archaeol. Jour.* xxv (1919),
129–268; for 1442–65, ibid. xxx (1930), 1–132; xxxii (1935), 111–47.

The first section is edited from the abstract made by Matthew Hutton (B.M. Harleian MS. 6978); and the second section from a John Rylands MS.

5860 THE STATUTES, ETC. OF THE CATHEDRAL CHURCH OF
YORK (*c.* 1221). Ed. by James Raine. Lond. 1879. 2nd edn. Leeds. 1900.

5861 ASTON (MARGARET). Thomas Arundel. See Nos. 5627, 5707.

5862 BRENTANO (ROBERT). 'Late medieval changes in the administration
of vacant suffragan dioceses: Province of York'. *Yorks. Archaeol. Jour.* xxxvii
(1952/5), 496–503.

See for a vindication of Archbishop Romeyn's rights *sede vacante*, Brentano, 'The Whithorn vacancy of 1293–4', *Innes Rev.* iv, no. 2 (1953). See No. 6449, chap. vi.

5863 BUTLER (L. H.). 'Archbishop Melton, his neighbours and his kinsmen,
1317–1340'. *J.E.H.* ii (1951), 54–68.

Butler studies the loans made by Melton.

5864 BROWN (WILLIAM). 'A list of benefices in the diocese of York vacant
between 1316 and 1319'. Yorks. Archaeol. Soc. Record Series, lxi (1920),
Miscellanea, i. 136–48.

5865 BROWNE (JOHN). The history of the church of St. Peter, York. 2 vols.
Lond. etc. 1838–47.

5866 CLAY (CHARLES T.). 'The early treasurers of York'. *Yorks. Archaeol.
Jour.* xxxv (1940), 7–33. Idem, 'The early precentors and chancellors of York'.
Ibid. xxxv (1941), 116–38. Idem, 'Notes on the early archdeacons in the church
of York'. Ibid. xxxvi (1944–7), 269–87; 409–34. Idem, 'Notes on the chronology
of the early deans of York', ibid. xxxiv (1938/9), 361–78. Idem, York Minster
fasti: being notes on the dignitaries, archdeacons and prebendaries in the church
of York prior to the year 1307. Yorks. Archaeol. Soc. Record Ser. cxxiii–iv
(1958–9).

5867 DIXON (WILLIAM H.). Fasti Eboracenses: 'Lives' of the archbishops
of York. Ed. by James Raine. vol. i. Lond. 1863.

> The introduction contains a brief history of the archbishopric; the body of the work
> contains the 'Lives' of the archbishops to 1373.

5868 DRAKE (FRANCIS). Eboracum, or the history and antiquities of the
city of York . . . together with the history of the cathedral church and the 'Lives'
of the archbishops of that see. Lond. 1736.

5869 DOUIE (DECIMA L.). Archbishop Geoffrey Plantagenet and the
chapter of York. *St. Anthony's Hall Pubns.* no. 18 (1960).

5870 NICHOLL (DONALD). Thurstan, archbishop of York 1114–40. York.
1964.

> For the disputed election following Thurstan's death, see Knowles, 'The case of St.
> William of York' (No. 1477).

5871 PURVIS (JOHN S.). A medieval act book (1396–1485) with some account
of ecclesiastical jurisdiction at York. York. 1943.

5872 ST. ANTHONY'S HALL PUBLICATIONS, 1–26 (1952–64).
BORTHWICK PAPERS, 27+ (1965+).

> Booklets, published semi-annually, on subjects relating chiefly to York and the north of
> England: York diocesan archives, registers of York and Canterbury, four pamphlets on
> the parochial system, palaeography and forgery, diocesan administration in fifteenth
> century, Archbishop Geoffrey Plantagenet and the Chapter of York, medieval historical
> writing in Yorkshire, medieval fairs and markets of York, medieval clerical accounts,
> Anglian and Viking York (an archaeological study).

5873 THOMPSON (ALEXANDER HAMILTON). 'The chapel of St. Mary
and the Holy Angels, otherwise known as St. Sepulchre's chapel at York'. *Yorks.
Archaeol. Jour.* xxxvi (1944/7), 63–77; 214–48.

> The second section lists the canons (not canons of the cathedral) of this chapel built
> adjacent to the cathedral as a chantry for Archbishop Roger (d. 1181). See Frederick
> Harrison, *Life in a medieval college: the story of the vicars-choral of York minster* (Lond.
> 1952). Idem, 'The bedern college and chapel', *Yorks. Archit.-Archaeol. Soc. Procs.*
> ii (1936), 19–43.

5874 THOMPSON (A. H.). 'The jurisdiction of the archbishops of York in Gloucestershire, with some notes on the history of the priory of St. Oswald at Gloucester'. *Bristol and Glos. Archaeol. Soc. Trans.* xliii (1922), 85–180.

5875 THOMPSON (A. H.). 'The registers of the archbishops of York'. *Yorks. Archaeol. Soc. Jour.* xxxii (1935), 245–63.

5876 THOMPSON (A. H.) and CLAY (CHARLES T.), eds. Fasti parochiales, being notes on the advowsons and pre-reformation incumbents of the parishes in the deanery of Doncaster. Yorks. Archaeol. Soc. Record Series, lxxxv (1933), cvii (1942/3). C. T. Clay and Norah K. M. Gurney, Fasti . . . in the deanery of Craven. Ibid. cxxxiii for 1970 (1971). N. A. H. Lawrance, Fasti . . . in the deanery of Dickering. Ibid. cxxix for 1966 (1967).

5877 TRAIN (K. S. S.). 'Lists of the clergy of central Nottinghamshire'. Thoroton Soc. Record Ser. xv, pt. i (1953).

See also David Robinson, *Beneficed clergy in Cleveland and the East Riding, 1305–40.* Borthwick Papers, no. 37 (1970).

5878 YORK MINSTER HISTORICAL TRACTS. Ed. by A. Hamilton Thompson (York. 1927).

Thirty pamphlets of sixteen pages each on phases of the history of York Cathedral, written by experts. Two-thirds of the pamphlets deal with the medieval period, of which eight were written by the editor. The subjects are the founding, and the building of the minster, religion in Roman York, St. Chad, St. Wilfrid, Alcuin, St. Oswald and York, York in eleventh century, twelfth century, dispute with Canterbury, Walter de Gray, medieval archbishops, medieval chapter, the fourteenth century, Archbishop Scrope, the fifteenth century, statutes, service books, glass, Vicars choral, etc.

3. Welsh Dioceses

The few surviving medieval records of the four Welsh dioceses are now deposited in the National Library of Wales. They are examined by J. Conway Davies in 'The records of the church in Wales', *National Library of Wales Journal,* iv (1945–6), 1–34. A. Hamilton Thompson describes 'The Welsh medieval dioceses' in *Journal of the Historical Society of the Church in Wales,* i (1948), 91–111. The lists of bishops and dignitaries are given by B. Jones in the 1965 edition of Le-Neve (No. 5582). G. Williams provides the standard history of the Welsh medieval church (No. 5879c). For fuller references, see *Bibliography of the History of Wales* (No. 10); and R. I. Jack, *Medieval Wales* (No. 22), Chap. 5.

5879 EPISCOPAL ACTS AND COGNATE DOCUMENTS RELATING TO WELSH DIOCESES, 1066–1272. Ed. by J. Conway Davies. 2 vols. Hist. Soc. of the Church in Wales Pubns. Cardiff. 1946–8.

Since no Welsh episcopal register exists for this period, the documents calendared by Davies are drawn from records surviving elsewhere and arranged chronologically by diocese. The extensive introductions describe the records of the church in Wales, the sources for the acts printed here, and give details of the more fundamental problems of the Welsh church during this period. These introductions form the best history of the church in Wales from 1066 to 1272.

5879A CHARLES (B. G.). and EMANUEL (H. D.). 'Welsh records in the Hereford capitular archives'. *National Library of Wales Jour.* viii (1953–4), 59–73.

Calendars some of the records, mostly before 1485.

5879B NEWELL (EBENEZER J.). A history of the Welsh church to the dissolution of the monasteries. Lond. 1895.

5879C WILLIAMS (GLANMOUR). The Welsh church from the conquest to the Reformation. Cardiff. 1962.

The introduction, pp. 1–32, summarizes the history of the church in Wales from *c.* 1070 to 1282; then pp. 35–558 treats the subject in detail from 1283 to 1536. For the history from 1066 to 1282, turn to the introductions in Davies, *Episcopal Acts* (No. 5879). See also J. A. Price, 'The ecclesiastical constitution of Wales on the eve of the Edwardine conquest', *Y Cymmrodor*, xxvi (1961), 191–214.

5879D WILLIS (BROWNE). A survey of the cathedral church of Bangor. Lond. 1721. Idem, . . . of Llandaff. Lond. 1719. Idem, . . . of St. Asaph. Lond. 1720, 2nd ed. Wrexham/1801. Idem, . . . of St. Davids. Lond. 1717.

BANGOR

5880 THE REGISTER OF BENEDICT, BISHOP OF BANGOR, 1408–17. Transcribed by Arthur I. Pryce. *Archaeologia Cambrensis*, lxxvii (1922), 80–107.

LLANDAFF

5880A LIBER LANDAVENSIS. The text of the book of Llan Dav. Ed. by John Gwenogvryn Evans and John Rhys. Oxf. 1893.

Completed in the second quarter of the twelfth century, it contains charters, papal bulls, 'Lives' of eminent prelates of Llandaff, purporting to come from the second to the twelfth century, and supporting claims of the bishopric of Llandaff. The documents for the early twelfth century are particularly important. There is an older edition by William J. Rees, *Liber Landavensis*, or the ancient register of the cathedral church of Llandaff, with a translation (Llandovery, 1840). See Arthur W. Haddan, 'The original MS. of the Liber Landavensis; *Archaeologia Cambrensis*, 3rd Ser. xiv (1868), 311–28; Evan D. Jones, 'The Book of Llandaff', *National Library of Wales Jour.* iv (1945–6), 123–57; and C. N. L. Brooke in *Stud. in Early British Church* (No. 2665), pp. 219–33, 236–40. Brooke's theses are discussed or challenged by J. W. James in *Hist. Soc. of Church in Wales Jour.* ix (1959), 5–22; by Ceri Lewis in *Morgannwg*, iv (1960), 50–65; by Ceri Lewis in *Llên Cymru*, vii (1963), 125–71; by Morgan Watkin in *National Library of Wales Jour.* xi (1960), 181–226; by John Morris in *Welsh H. R.* i (1960–4), 230–2; by J. W. James in *Hon Soc. Cymmrodorion Trans.* (1963), 82–95, and in *National Library of Wales Jour.* xvi (1970), 319–52. See Wendy Davies in *E.H.R.* lxxxviii (1973), 335–51.

5880B MEMORIALS OF THE SEE AND CATHEDRAL OF LLANDAFF. Ed. by Walter de Gray Birch. Neath. 1912.

ST. ASAPH

5880C LLYFR COCH ASAPH. By David L. Evans. *National Library of Wales Jour.* iv (1945–6), 177–83.

Not an episcopal register, but a collection of documents from the time of Innocent III to *c.* 1314. Although most of the original has been lost and the surviving portion is largely in tabloid form, the *Llfyr Coch Asaph* is "a major source of information on political and ecclesiatical history" (for north Wales) "for nearly a hundred years" (Davies, *Episcopal Acts*, p. 27). See also D. R. Thomas, 'Index to *Llfyr Coch Asaph*', *Archaeologia*

Cambrensis, 3rd Ser. xiv (1868), 151–66, 329–39, 433–42; and 'Summa libri rubei Asaphensis' *Collectanea Topog. et Geneal.* (No. 115), ii, 255–79.

5880D THOMAS (DAVID R.). History of the diocese of St. Asaph. 3 vols. 2nd edn. Oswestry. 1908–13.

"A series of parochial histories".

ST. DAVID'S

5880E ACTS OF THE BISHOPS OF ST. DAVID'S, 1203–1484. By George E. Evans. Carmarthenshire Antiq. Soc. xxix (1939).

Cf. H. D. Emanuel, 'Early St. David's records', *National Library of Wales Jour.* viii (1954), 258–63, where are printed some records for the vacancy of the see 1388–9 and some consistory records for the fourteenth century.

5880F BLACK BOOK OF ST. DAVID'S: an extent of lands and rents of the lord bishop of St. David's, made by Master David Fraunceys, chancellor of St. David's . . . 1326. Ed. by J. W. Willis-Bund. Hon. Soc. Cymmrodorion Record Ser. v (1902).

A Latin transcript, with English translation, of an extent of lands in Pembrokeshire, Cardiganshire, Carmarthenshire, Gower, and the archdeaconry of Brecon. See J. Conway Davies, 'The Black Book of St. David's', *National Library of Wales Jour.* iv (1945–6), 158–76.

5880G EPISCOPAL REGISTERS OF THE DIOCESE OF ST. DAVID'S, 1397–1518. Ed. by R. F. Isaacson. Hon. Soc. Cymmrodorion Record Ser. vi. 2 vols. in 3 (1917–20).

Vol. i: 1397–1407; vol. ii: 1407–1518; vol. iii: A study of the published registers by R. Arthur Roberts. See Hywel D. Emanuel, 'A fragment (for 1415) of the register of Stephen Patrynton, bishop of St. David's.' *Hist. Soc. of the Church in Wales Jour.* ii (1950) 31–45.

5880H RICHTER (MICHAEL). 'Professions of obedience and the metropolitan claim of St. David's'. *National Library of Wales Jour.* xv (1967), 197–214. Idem, 'Canterbury's primacy in Wales and the first stage of Bishop Bernard's opposition'. *J.E.H.* xxii (1971), 177–89. I. P. Shaw, 'Giraldus Cambrensis and the primacy of Canterbury', *Church Quart. Rev.* cxlviii (1949), 82–101. See Davies, *Episcopal Acts* (No. 5879) 190–233; and No. 2321.

5880I YARDLEY (EDWARD). Menevia Sacra. Ed. by Francis Green. Cambrian Archaeol. Asso. Supplemental volume. Lond. 1927.

For his eighteenth-century history Yardley used some records which are now lost. See also a series of articles on the bishops and clergy of St. David's by W. Greenway in *Hist. Soc. of the Church in Wales Jour.* x (1960), 9–16; *J.E.H.* xi, no. 2 (1960), 152–63; *Church Quart. Rev.* clxi (1960), 436–48, and clxii (1961), 33–49.

D. MONASTIC RECORDS AND HISTORIES

1. *General Introduction*

For monastic history the records and the secondary works are, for convenience, grouped in this section; accordingly the listing of documentary records is followed by modern studies of the religious orders and houses.

The general sources for monastic history are catalogued on pp. 147-8. Dugdale's *Monasticon* (No. 1147), which prints many records, is indispensable; Tanner (No. 1150) includes references which are still useful. *The Map of Monastic Britain* (No. 604) and the *Map of Monastic Ireland*, published by the Ordnance Survey, Dublin, in 1959, are reliable and helpful. Those general chronicles which were written at monasteries naturally contain information about their own houses, e.g. *Annales Monastici*, the St. Albans series, Knighton of Leicester. The chronicles which are fundamentally histories of particular houses are given under the names of the houses, e.g. St. Peter's, Gloucester; Thorne's St. Augustine, Canterbury; and Whethamstede's St. Albans. The monastic cathedrals are considered under English Dioceses, pp. 758-90.

Heimbucher (No. 1296) provides an excellent bibliography, as of the date of publication, for each of the religious orders. The footnotes to Knowles–Hadcock, *Medieval religious houses* (No. 1299), give some references to individual houses as do Gwynn–Hadcock (No. 1295); Colvin's *White canons* treats each Premonstratensian house separately. The current publications on religious orders are conveniently listed in *Revue d'histoire ecclésiastique*.

For the general history of monasticism in England, the fundamental volumes are those by Knowles. Good histories of individual houses are printed, county by county, in the *Victoria County History*, frequently in vol. ii for each county. Some studies overlapping several orders are given immediately below; for others the numerical reference is given to the entry elsewhere.

5881 DICTIONNAIRE DE SPIRITUALITÉ ASCÉTIQUE ET MYSTIQUE. Doctrine et histoire. Ed. by M. Viller *et al*. Paris. 1932+.

Includes an article on each of the religious orders.

5882 CHENEY (CHRISTOPHER R.). Episcopal visitation of monasteries in the thirteenth century. Univ. of Manchester. Hist. Ser. lviii. Manchester. 1931.

5883 CHIBNALL (MARJORIE M.). 'Monks and pastoral work; a problem in Anglo-Norman history'. *J.E.H.* xviii (1967), 165-72.

5884 CLAY (ROTHA M.). The hermits (No. 6683). Idem, 'Further studies on medieval recluses'. *Jour. British Archaeol. Asso.* 3rd Ser. xvi (1953), 74-86.

5885 COULTON (GEORGE C.). Five centuries (No. 1291).

5886 CRANAGE (DAVID H. S.). The home of the monk (No. 1303).

5887 DARWIN (FRANCIS D. S.). The English medieval recluse. S.P.C.K. Lond. 1944.

5888 DICKINSON (JOHN C.). Monastic life (No. 1292).

5889 GALBRAITH (VIVIAN H.). 'Monastic foundation charters of the eleventh and twelfth centuries'. *Cambr. Hist. Jour.* iv (1934), 205-22; 296-8.

5890 GASQUET (FRANCIS A.). English monastic life (No. 1291). Idem, Monastic life (No. 1294).

See Knowles, *The historian and character* (No. 1477).

5891   GRAHAM (ROSE). English ecclesiastical studies (No. 1471).

Also *Medieval studies presented to Rose Graham* (No. 1437). Idem, 'An essay on English monasteries' (No. 1495).

5892   HEIMBUCHER (MAXIMILIAN J.). Die Orden und Kongregationen (No. 1296).

5893   HELYOT (PIERRE). L'Histoire des ordres monastiques, religieux et militaires. Paris. 1714.

5894   KNOWLES (DAVID). The monastic order (No. 1298). Idem, Religious orders (No. 1300). Knowles and Hadcock, Religious houses (No. 1299).

5895   KNOWLES (DAVID), BROOKE (C. N. L.), and LONDON (VERA), eds. The heads of religious houses: England and Wales, 940–1216. Cambr. 1972.

5896   POWER (EILEEN). Medieval nunneries (No. 1301).

5897   PURVIS (JOHN S.). Monastic chancery proceedings. Yorks. Archaeol. Soc. Record Ser. lxxxviii (1934).

Translates Latin and French and modernizes English originals for monasteries and colleges in alphabetical order.

5898   ROBERTS (H. ERNEST). Notes on the medieval monasteries of England and Wales. Lond. 1949.

Notes on monastic buildings. Similar studies are A. H. Thompson, *English monasteries* (Cambr. 1913. 2nd edn. 1923); D. Knowles and J. K. St. Joseph, *Monastic sites from the air* (No. 755); R. Gilyard-Beer, *Abbeys; an introduction to the religious houses of England and Wales* (H.M.S.O. 1958); and Roger L. Palmer, *English monasteries in the Middle Ages* (Lond. 1930). Knowles, 'The monastic buildings of England', (No. 1477).

5899   RUSSELL (JOSIAH C.). 'The clerical population of medieval England'. *Traditio,* ii (1944), 177–212.

5900   SMITH (REGINALD A. L.). 'The *regimen scaccarii* in English monasteries'. *T.R.H.S.* 4th Ser. xxiv (1942), 73–94. Reprinted in No. 1494.

See H. E. Aikens, 'Bishops and monastic finance in fourteenth century England', *Univ. of Colorado Stud.* xxii, no. 4 (1935), 365–80.

5901   SNAPE (ROBERT H.). English monastic finances in the later middle ages. Cambr. Stud. in Mediaeval Life and Thought. Cambr. 1926.

5902   SWEET (ALFRED H.). 'The Apostolic See and the heads of English religious houses'. *Speculum,* xxviii (1953), 468–84. Idem, 'Papal privileges granted to individual religious'. *Speculum,* xxi (1956), 602–10.

5903   THOMPSON (A. HAMILTON). 'A corrody from Leicester Abbey, A.D. 1393–4, with some notes on corrodies'. *Leicestershire Archaeol. Soc. Trans.* xiv (1926), 114–34.

An important study of corrodies.

5904 WAITES (BRYAN). 'The monastic settlement of north-east Yorkshire'. *Yorks. Archaeol. Jour.* xl (1961), 478–95. See No. 5020.

5905 WOOD (SUSAN). English monasteries and their patrons in the thirteenth century. Oxford Hist. Ser. Lond. and N.Y. 1955.

2. *The Monastic Orders*

a. Monks and nuns

Benedictines

5906 KAPSNER (OLIVER L.). A Benedictine bibliography: an author–subject union list. 2 vols. Collegeville (Minn.). Vol. i: authors. 2nd edn. 1962; vol. ii: subject headings and classification schedule. 2nd edn., enlarged 1964.

See *Repert. Font.* iii. 624–32 for various editions of *Consuetudines Benedictinae*.

5907 CONSTITUTIONES CAPITULI GENERALIS CELEBRATI A MONACHIS ORDINIS S. BENEDICTI PROVINCIAE CANTUARIENSIS IN MONASTERIO S. ANDREAE APUD NORTHAMPTON ANNO 1225. Ed. in Dugdale, *Monasticon*, i, pp. xlvi–li.

5908 DOCUMENTS ILLUSTRATING THE ACTIVITIES OF THE GENERAL AND PROVINCIAL CHAPTERS OF THE ENGLISH BLACK MONKS, 1215–1540. Ed. by William A. Pantin. 3 vols. R.H.S. Camden 3rd Ser. xlv (1931), xlvii (1933), lix (1937).

This work is sometimes cited as 'Chapters of the English Black Monks'. See also Pantin, 'General and provincial chapters of the English Black Monks', *T.R.H.S.* 4th Ser. x (1927), 195–263; and his 'English monastic letter-books' in *Tait essays* (No. 1455).

5909 THE MONASTIC CONSTITUTIONS OF LANFRANC. Ed. and trans. by Michael David Knowles. Medieval Classics. Lond. etc. 1951. 2nd edn. in *Corpus Constitutionum Monast.* (No. 1146). 1966.

Lanfranc's constitutions were designed for Christ Church, Canterbury. See J. Armitage Robinson, 'Lanfranc's Monastic Constitutions', *Jour. Theolog. Stud.* x (1909), 375–88.

5910 THE MONASTIC BREVIARY OF HYDE ABBEY. Ed. by J. B. L. Tolhurst. 6 vols. Henry Bradshaw Soc. lix, lxx, lxxi, lxxvi, lxxviii, lxxx. 1930–42.

Vol. lxxx, the sixth volume, gives a detailed account of the services.

5911 THE RULE OF SAINT BENEDICT IN LATIN AND ENGLISH. Ed. and trans. by Abbot Justin McCann. Lond. 1952.

There are many editions and translations in various languages of the rule. A critical edition is that by Rudolf Hanslik in *Corpus Scriptorum Ecclesiasticorum Latinorum*, vol. lxxv (Vienna, 1960). Among the many commentaries, one of the best is Paul Delatte, *Commentaire sur la règle de Saint Benoît* (Paris, 1913), trans. by Justin McCann (Lond. 1921; 2nd edn. 1950). The question of the relationship of the Rule of St. Benedict to the so-called Rule of the Master is summarized by David Knowles in his Birkbeck Lecture, 'The *Regula Magistri* and the *Rule* of St Benedict', *Great historical enterprises* (No. 262), pp. 139–95.

5912 BISHOP (EDMUND). 'The methods and degrees of fasting and abstinence of the Black Monks in England before the Reformation'. *Downside Rev.* xlvi (1925), 184–237.

5913 BUTLER (EDWARD CUTHBERT). Benedictine monachism (p. 167).

See Knowles, *The historian and character* (No. 1477), pp. 264–362.

5914 SWEET (ALFRED H.). 'The English Benedictines and their bishops in the thirteenth century'. *A.H.R.* xxiv (1918–19), 565–77.

Cf. 'Regulars as bishops' in Knowles, *Religious orders*, ii, app. iii, pp. 369–75.

Alien priories; Cluniac houses

5915 CHARTERS AND RECORDS AMONG THE ARCHIVES OF THE ABBEY OF CLUNI, 1077–1534, illustrative of the acts of some of our early kings, and all the abbey's English foundations. Ed. by George F. Duckett. 2 vols. Lewes. 1888.

Before the whole edition was sold, the title was changed to *Monasticon Cluniacense Anglicanum, or Charters and Records* etc.; and this new title-page was sent to subscribers and purchasers of the work. See also *Recueil des chartes de l'Abbaye de Cluny*, edited by Alexandre Bruel, 6 vols. (Paris, 1876–1903).

5916 SELECT DOCUMENTS OF THE ENGLISH LANDS OF THE ABBEY OF BEC. Ed. by Marjorie M. Chibnall. R. H. S. Camden 3rd Ser. lxxiii (1951).

A selection of eleventh- and twelfth-century charters, custumals, account rolls, etc.

5917 VISITATIONS OF ENGLISH CLUNIAC FOUNDATIONS IN 47 Hen. III, 1262; 3 & 4 Edw. I, 1275–6; and 7 Edw. I, 1279. Trans. from the original records . . . to which . . . are added, in part, those of 27 Edw. I, 1298; 13 Rich. II, 1390; 6 Hen. IV, 1405. By George F. Duckett. Lond. 1890.

In Duckett's, *Visitations and chapter-general of the order of Cluni in respect of the province of Germany* . . . (Lond. 1893), are printed visitations of England, 1259–1317 pp. 207–317.

5918 AUVRY (CLAUDE). L'histoire de la congrégation de Savigny. Ed. by Auguste Laveille. 3 vols. Paris. 1896–8.

The standard work on Savigny and her daughter houses. See also Léon Guilloreau, 'Les fondations anglaises de l'abbaye de Savigny', *Rev. Mabillon*, v (1909), 290–335.

5919 CAM (HELEN M.). 'The English lands of the abbey of St. Riquier'. *E.H.R.* xxxi (1916), 443–7. Prints a charter of William I.

5920 CHETTLE (H. F.). 'The English houses of the Order of Fontevaud'. *Downside Rev.* lx (1942), 33–55.

5921 CHIBNALL (MARJORIE MORGAN). The English lands of the abbey of Bec. Oxf. 1946.

See also idem, 'The relations of St. Anselm with the English dependencies of the abbey of Bec, 1079–1093', *Spicilegium Beccense* (Paris), i (1959), 521–30; and Marjorie Morgan, 'The abbey of Bec-Hellouin and its English priories', *Jour. British Archaeol. Asso.* 3rd Ser. v (1940), 33–61; idem, 'The suppression of the alien priories', *History*, xxvi (1941), 204–12.

5922   EVANS (JOAN). Monastic life at Cluny. Lond. 1931.

See Noreen Hunt, ed. *Cluniac monasticism in the central middle ages* (Lond. 1971).

5923   MATTHEW (DONALD J. A.). The Norman monasteries and their English possessions. Lond. 1962.

5924   NEW (CHESTER). History of the alien priories in England to the confiscation of Henry V. Chicago. 1916.

See priory of Burwell (No. 6212).

5925   SMITH (LUCY MARGARET). Cluny in the eleventh and twelfth centuries. Oxf. 1930.

Carthusians

See St. Hugh of Lincoln (No. 5742); and the Charterhouses of London (Nos. 6223–4) and Witham (No. 6324).

5926   LE COUTEULX (CAROLUS). Annales ordinis cartusiensis (1084–1429). 8 vols. Montreuil. 1887–91.

5927   THOMPSON (E. MARGARET). The Carthusian order in England. Lond. 1930.

See also her *Somerset Carthusians* (No. 6304).

Cistercians

For various editions of *Consuetudines Cistercienses*, see *Repert. Font.* iii. 636–9. Consult also the articles on 'Cisterciens' and on individual houses in *Dictionnaire d'histoire et de géographie ecclésiastiques* (No. 1266).

5928   ANALECTA SACRI ORDINIS CISTERCIENSIS. Rome. 1945+.

5929   CISTERCIAN STATUTES. Ed. by J. T. Fowler. *Yorks. Archaeol. Topog. Asso. Jour.* ix (1886), 223–40, 338–61; x (1889), 51–62, 217–33, 388–406, 502–22; xi (1891), 95–127. Also printed separately as Cistercian statutes, 1256–88. Lond. 1890. For statutes of General Chapters, see Canivez (No. 1145).

5930   CÎTEAUX: Commentarii Cistercienses. Westmalle (Belgium). 1950+.

5931   COLLECTANEA ORDINIS CISTERCIENSIUM REFORMATORUM. Westmalle. 1934+. After 1965, COLLECTANEA CISTERCIENSIA.

From 1958 to 1968 a full-length Cistercian bibliography was printed annually in *Collectanea;* since 1968 the annual list has been published separately as *Documentation Cistercienne.* Another offshoot from the *Collectanea* is *Cistercian Studies,* published by St. Joseph's Abbey, Spencer (Mass.) since 1966.

5932   LETTERS FROM THE ENGLISH ABBOTS TO THE CHAPTER AT CITEAUX, 1442–1521. Ed. by Charles H. Talbot. R.H.S. Camden 4th Ser. iv (1967).

Talbot prints 140 letters, of which thirty-eight date before 1485.

5933   MONUMENTS PRIMITIFS (LES) DE LA RÈGLE CISTERCIENNE. Ed. by Ph(ilippe) Guignard. Dijon. 1878.

Recent critical studies, particularly those of J.-A. Lefèvre from 1954 on, have modified opinion on these documents, on which see *R.H.E.* li (1956), 5–41, and Knowles, 'The primitive Cistercian documents' in *Great historical enterprises* (No. 262), pp. 197–224.

5934 BIRCH (WALTER DE GRAY). 'On the date of foundation ascribed to the Cistercian abbeys in Great Britain'. *Brit. Archaeol. Asso. Jour.* xxvi (1870), 281–99, 352–69.

5935 DONKIN (R. A.). Checklist of the printed works relating to the Cistercian Order as a whole and to the houses of the British Isles in particular. *Documentation Cistercienne*, ii. Abbaye N. D. de S. Remy. Rochefort, Belgium. 1969.

For the portion on the British Isles, the organization is by houses, Aberconway to Woburn, then Scotland, and next Ireland; the general secondary works; and then the secondary works by houses alphabetically.

5936 DONKIN (R. A.). 'Settlement and depopulation on Cistercian estates during the twelfth and thirteenth centuries, especially in Yorkshire'. *B.I.H.R.* xxxiii (1960), 141–65. Idem, 'The Cistercian order and the settlement of northern England'. *The Geographical Rev.* lix (1969), 403–16.

Idem, 'The Cistercian order in England: some conclusions', *Inst. British Geographers Trans.* xxxiii (1963), 181–98. Idem, 'The Cistercian settlement and the royal forests', ibid. x (1959)–xi (1960). See nos. 4992–3; 6393.

5937 DONKIN (R. A.). 'The urban property of the Cistercians in medieval England'. *Analecta S.O. Cisterciensis*, xv (1959), 104–31.

5938 FLETCHER (JOSEPH S.). The Cistercians in Yorkshire. Lond. 1919.

5939 GRAVES (COBURN V.). 'The economic activities of the Cistercians in medieval England'. *Analecta S.O. Cisterciensis*, xiii (1957), 3–60.

5940 HILL (BENNETT D.). English Cistercian monasteries and their patrons in the twelfth century. Urbana (Illinois) and Lond. 1968.

A. M. Cooke, 'The settlement of the Cistercians in England', *E.H.R.* viii (1893), 625–76.

5941 HOLDSWORTH (CHRISTOPHER J.). 'John of Ford and early Cistercian writing 1167–1214'. *T.R.H.S.* 5th Ser. xi (1961), 117–36.

5942 JANAUSCHEK (LEOPOLD). Originum (No. 1148).

5943 KNOWLES (DAVID). 'Cistercians and Cluniacs: the controversy between St. Bernard and Peter the Venerable', in *The historian and character* (No. 1477), pp. 50–75.

5944 LEKAI (LOUIS J.). The White Monks. Okauchee (Wisconsin). 1953. French trans. *Les Moines blancs*. Paris. 1957 (includes revisions).

5945 MAHN (J.-B.). L'Ordre cistercien et son gouvernement des origines au milieu du xiiie siècle, 1098–1265. Biblio. des Écoles françaises. Paris. 1945. 2nd edn. 1951.

5946 MANRIQUE (ANGEL). Cisterciensium seu verius ecclesiasticorum annalium tomi i–iv. Lyons. 1642–59.

The most elaborate survey of the general history of the Cistercians throughout Europe in the twelfth and thirteenth centuries. See the index to each volume, under the names of English kings.

5947 MORSON (JOHN). 'The English Cistercians and the bestiary'. *B.J.R.L.* xxxix (1956), 146–70.

5948 MULLIN (FRANCIS A.). The history of the work of the Cistercians in Yorkshire (1131–1300). Washington. 1932.

5949 O'SULLIVAN (JEREMIAH F.). Cistercian settlements in Wales and Monmouthshire, 1140–1540. N.Y. 1947.

5950 WILLIAMS (DAVID H.). The Welsh Cistercians: aspects of their economic history. Pontypool (Wales). 1969.

Rhys W. Hays, 'The Welsh Cistercians: recent research and future prospects,' *Stud. in Medieval Culture*, iii (1970), 70–80.

Grandmontines

5951 GRAHAM (ROSE). 'The order of Grandmont and its houses in England', in *English ecclesiastical studies* (No. 1471).

b. Regular canons

For *Consuetudines canonicorum regularium* (various orders), see *Repert. Font.* iii. 632–6.

Augustinian canons

5952 CHAPTERS OF THE AUGUSTINIAN CANONS. Ed. by Herbert E. Salter. Oxf. Hist. Soc. lxxiv (1920); and Cant.–York Soc. xxix (1921–2).

5953 DICKINSON (JOHN C.). The origins of the Austin canons and their introduction into England. Lond. 1950.

J. C. Dickinson, 'English regular canons and the continent in the twelfth century', *T.R.H.S.* 5th Ser. i (1951), 71–89. Idem, 'St. Anselm and the first regular canons in England', *Spicilegium Beccense* (Paris), i (1959), 541–6. Idem, 'Les Constructions des premiers chanoines réguliers en Angleterre', *Cahiers de Civilisation Médiévale*, x (1967), 179–98. See No. 1437 for suppression.

5954 HOLMES (THOMAS S.). 'The Austin canons in England in the twelfth century'. *Jour. Theol. Stud.* v (1904), 343–56.

Gilbertine canons and nuns

5955 CHENEY (CHRISTOPHER R.). 'Some papal privileges to Gilbertine houses'. *B.I.H.R.* xxi (1948), 39–58.

5956 FOREVILLE (RAYMONDE). Un procès de canonisation à l'aube du xiiie siècle (1201–2): le livre de Saint Gilbert de Sempringham. Paris. 1943.

5957 STENTON (FRANK M.). Transcripts of charters to the Gilbertine houses of Sixle, Ormsby, Catley, Bullington, and Alvingham. Lincoln Record Soc. xviii (1922).

5958 VITA S. GILBERTI CONFESSORIS in Dugdale's *Monasticon*, vi, pp. v–xxix; and an Early English translation in *John Capgrave's Lives*, edited by J. J. Munro, E.E.T.S. cxl (1910).

5959 GRAHAM (ROSE). St. Gilbert of Sempringham and the Gilbertines. Lond. 1901. Reprinted, 1904.

Premonstratensian canons

5960 ANALECTA PRAEMONSTRATENSIA. Tongerloo. 1925+.

Previously *Analectes de l'ordre de Prémontré*. Brussels. 1905–14. See *Repert. Font.* iii, 635.

5961 COLLECTANEA ANGLO-PREMONSTRATENSIA (*c.* 1281–1505). Ed. by Francis A. Gasquet. 3 vols. R.H.S. Camden 3rd Ser. vi (1904), x (1906), xii (1906).

For corrections to this addition, see Colvin, *White Canons* (No. 5964), pp. 389–91. Gasquet has an article 'The English Premonstratensians', *T.R.H.S.* New Ser. xvii (1903), 1–22.

5962 DRYBURGH (ADAM OF). Liber de ordine, habitu et professione ordinis Praemonstratensis, in Migne, *P.L.* cxcviii. 440–610.

See James Bulloch, *Adam of Dryburgh* (Lond. 1958).

5963 BACKMUND (NORBERT). Monasticon Praemonstratense (No. 1144).

5964 COLVIN (HOWARD M.). The White Canons in England. Oxf. 1951.

In addition to a general study of the Premonstratensian Order in England, Colvin deals separately with each of its thirty-three English abbeys; the bibliography gives references to studies about each abbey.

5965 KIRKFLEET (CORNELIUS J.). The White Canons of St. Norbert: a history of the Praemonstratensian Order in the British Isles and America. St. Norbert's Abbey (West De Père, Wisconsin). 1943.

c. Friars

Austin friars

5966 ANALECTA AUGUSTINIANA. Rome. 1905+.

In the volumes from 1907 to 1914, the decrees of the chapters general of the Austin Friars are edited by E. Esteban.

5967 AUGUSTINIANA. Tijdschrift voor die studie van Sint Augustinus en de Augustijnenorde. Louvain. 1951+.

5968 AUGUSTINIANUM. Collegium Internationale Augustinianum. Rome. 1961+.

5969 BULLARIUM ORDINIS EREMITARUM S. AUGUSTINI (Innocent III–Urban VIII). Ed. by Laurentius Empoli. Rome. 1678.

5970 IRISH MATERIALS IN THE AUGUSTINIAN ARCHIVES, ROME, 1354–*c.* 1620. Ed. by F. X. Martin and A. de Meijer, *Archivium Hibernicum* xix (1956), 61–134.

5971 GWYNN (AUBREY). The English Austin Friars in the time of Wyclif. Lond. 1940.

> This is not a general history of the Austin Friars in England; it is rather a series of notable excursions into aspects of that history in the second half of the fourteenth century.

5972 ROTH (FRANCIS). The English Austin Friars, 1249-1538. Vol. i: history; N.Y. 1966. Vol. ii: sources. N.Y. 1961. Originally printed in *Augustiniana*, viii (1958) to xvii (1967).

> See review in *Speculum*, xliii (1968), 537-9.

Carmelite friars

See *Repert. Font.* iii. 620.

5973 ACTA CAPITULORUM GENERALIUM ORDINIS FRATRUM B.V. MARIAE DE MONTE CARMELO. Ed. by Gabriel Wessels. 2 vols. Vol. i: 1318-1593. Rome. 1912-34.

5974 CARMELUS: commentarii ab Instituto Carmelitano editi. Rome. 1954+.

> Includes Bibliographia Carmelitana Annualis.

5975 ÉTUDES CARMÉLITAINES HISTORIQUES ET CRITIQUES sur les traditions, les privilèges et la mystique de l'ordre par les pères Carmes déchaussés de la province de France. Paris. 1911-39; 1946+.

5976 MONUMENTA HISTORICA CARMELITANA. Ed. by Benedictus Zimmerman. Vol. i. Lerins. 1907.

5977 DU BOULAY (FRANCIS R. H.). 'The quarrel between the Carmelite friars and the secular clergy of London, 1464-1468'. *J.E.H.* vi (1955), 156-74.

5978 McCAFFREY (PATRICK R.). The white friars: an outline of Carmelite history with special reference to the English speaking provinces. Dublin. 1926.

5979 SHEPPARD (LANCELOT C.). The English Carmelites. Lond. 1943.

Dominican friars

5980 ANALECTA S. ORDINIS FRATRUM PRAEDICATORUM. Rome. 1893+.

> Includes C. F. R. Palmer, ed. 'Monumenta conventus S. Mariae et S. Joannis Baptistae Londinensis', iii (1897-8), 268-306; idem, 'Monumenta provinciae Angliae sacri ordinis Praedicatorum', iii. 549-66.

5980A ARCHIVUM FRATRUM PRAEDICATORUM. Institutum Historicum FF. Praedicatorum. Rome. 1932+.

5981 BULLARIUM ORDINIS FRATRUM PRAEDICATORUM. Ed. by Tomás Ripoll and A. Bremond. 8 vols. Rome. 1729-40.

5982 IRISH MATERIAL IN THE REGISTERS OF THE DOMINICAN MASTERS GENERAL, 1290-1649. Ed. by Hugh Fenning. *Archivum Fratrum Praedicatorum*, xxxix (1969), 249-336.

5983 LIVES OF THE BRETHREN OF THE ORDER OF PREACHERS, 1206–1259. Ed. by J. Placid Conway and Bede Jarrett. Lond. 1924.

5984 MONUMENTA ORDINIS PRAEDICATORUM HISTORICA, i–xiv. Rome. 1896–1904.

Includes *Acta capitulorum generalium ordinis Praedicatorum*, edited by B. Reichert, vols. iii, iv, viii, and ix.

5985 QUÉTIF (JACQUES) and ECHARD (JACQUES). Scriptores ordinis praedicatorum recensiti. 2 vols. Paris. 1719–21.* New edn., enlarged, by Remi Coulon. pts. i–vi. Paris. 1910–13.

5986 BARKER (ERNEST). The Dominican Order and convocation: a study of the growth of representation in the church during the thirteenth century. Oxf. 1913.

5987 BENNETT (RALPH F.). The early Dominicans. Cambr. 1937.*

Idem, 'Pierre Mandonnet, O.P. and Dominican studies', *History*, New Ser. xxiv (1939/40), 193–205.

5987A DAVIES (J. CONWAY). 'The Dominicans in Wales'. *National Library of Wales Jour.* iii (1945), 50–1.

A commentary on an article by W. A. Hinnebusch.

5988 EMDEN (ALFRED B.). A survey of Dominicans in England, based on the ordination lists in episcopal registers, 1268–1538. Dissertationes Historicae of the Dominican Historical Institute, xviii. Rome. 1967.

5989 FORMOY (BERYL E. R.). The Dominican Order in England before the Reformation. Lond. 1925.

5990 GALBRAITH (GEORGINA R.). The constitution of the Dominican Order 1216 to 1360. Manchester. 1925.

Still a useful work.

5991 GOLDTHORP (L. M.). 'The Franciscans and Dominicans in Yorkshire'. *Yorks. Archaeol. Jour.* xxxii (1935), 365–428.

5992 GUMBLEY (WALTER). The Cambridge Dominicans. Oxf. 1938.

W. Gumbley, 'Provincial priors and vicars of the English Dominicans 1221–1916', *E.H.R.* xxxiii (1918), 243–51, and 496–7.

5993 HINNEBUSCH (WILLIAM A.). The early English friars preachers. Rome. 1951.

The best book on its subject. A more general book is W. A. Hinnebusch, *The history of the Dominican Order: origins and growth to 1500*. Vol. i (Staten Island, N.Y., 1966).

5994 JARRETT (BEDE). The English Dominicans. Lond. 1921. 2nd edn. revised by W. Gumbley. 1937.

5995 KNOWLES (W. H.). 'The Black-Friars of Gloucester'. *Bristol–Glos. Archaeol. Soc. Trans.* liv (1932), 167–201. Idem, 'Monastery of the Black Friars, Newcastle-upon-Tyne'. *Archaeol. Aeliana*, 3rd Ser. xvii (1920), 315–36.

5996   LITTLE (A. G.) and EASTERLING (R. C.). No. 6027.

5997   MARTIN (ALAN R.). 'The Dominican priory at Canterbury', *Archaeol. Jour.* lxxxvi (1930), 152–77.

5998   PALMER (CHARLES F. R.). 'Fasti ordinis fratrum praedicatorum: or the provincials of the Friar Preachers in England'. *Archaeol. Jour.* xxxv (1878), 134–65.

> Some sixty articles in the *Reliquary* and other journals by Father Palmer, O.P., an indefatigable researcher, are listed in Hinnebusch, pp. xxxiv–vi.

5999   RASHDALL (HASTINGS). Friars Preachers v. the University. Oxford Hist. Soc. xvi. *Collectanea*, ii (1890), 193–217.

Franciscan friars

6000   LITTLE (ANDREW G.). A guide to Franciscan studies. Helps for Students of History. Lond. 1920.

> See also A. G. Little's bibliography in *Cambr. Med. Hist.* vi. 960–1. Heimbucher (No. 1296) is useful for Franciscans as well as for other orders. Current bibliographies are provided in the *Chronica* in *Archivum Fran. Hist.* (No. 6002).

6001   ANALECTA FRANCISCANA, sive chronica aliaque varia documenta ad historiam fratrum minorum spectantia. Edita a patribus collegii S. Bonaventurae. Quaracchi. 1885+.

> A valuable collection which includes (i. 215–75) Thomas of Eccleston's *De adventu.* See No. 6008.

6002   ARCHIVUM FRANCISCANUM HISTORICUM. Periodica publicatio trimestris cura PP. Collegii D. Bonaventurae. Quaracchi. 1908+.

6003   BRITISH SOCIETY OF FRANCISCAN STUDIES. (B.S.F.H.) Publications. 1908–37.

> Listed in Mullins, *Texts*, pp. 115–18; and in Mullins, *Guide*, p. 55. Continued as *Franciscan Studies* by the Franciscan Institute of St. Bonaventure University. New Ser. 1941+, which includes theological studies on English Franciscans.

6004   BULLARIUM FRANCISCANUM. Ed. by J. H. Sbaralea, and A. de Latera and C. Eubel. 10 vols. Rome and Quaracchi. 1759–1908.

> Sbaralea published four vols. 1759–68; de Latera added one more, 1780; Eubel edited three more 1898–1904; and calendared the volumes of Sbaralea in 1908. U. Huntemann and J. M. Pou y Martí began a new series with the year 1431 (Quaracchi 1929†)

6005   COLLECTANEA FRANCISCANA. Instituto dei Fr. Minori Cappuccini. Rome 1931†. (Full bibliography).

6006   COLLECTANEA FRANCISCANA. B.S.F.S. 1914+.* Vol. i. Ed. by A. G. Little, M. R. James, and H. M. Bannister. 1914.

> (*a*) A. G. Little, 'Brother William of England, companion of St. Francis, and some Franciscan drawings in the Matthew Paris MSS.'.
> (*b*) A. G. Little, 'Description of a Franciscan MS. formerly in the Phillipps library'.
> (*c*) M. R. James, 'The library of the Grey friars of Hereford'.
> (*d*) H. M. Bannister, 'A short notice of some MSS. of the Cambridge friars, now in the Vatican library'.

(e) A. G. Little, 'Records of the Franciscan province of England' (an early fourteenth-century obituary).
Vol. ii. Ed. by C. L. Kingsford *et al.* 1922.
(f) Charles Cotton, 'Notes on the documents in the cathedral library at Canterbury relating to the Grey friars'.
(g) M. R. James, 'The list of libraries prefixed to the catalogue of John Boston, and the kindred documents'.
(h) C. L. Kingsford, 'Additional material for the history of the Grey friars, London'.
(i) A. G. Little, 'Friar Henry Wodestone and the Jews' (anti-Semitism about 1270).

6007 DOCUMENTA ANTIQUA FRANCISCANA. Ed. by L. Lemmens. Quaracchi. 1901.

6008 ECCLESTON. TRACTATUS FR. THOMAE VULGO DICTI DE ECCLESTON. De adventu fratrum minorum in Angliam. Ed. by Andrew G. Little. Collection d'études . . . du moyen âge, vii. Paris. 1909. Reprinted. Manchester. 1951. Also printed in *Monumenta Franciscana* (No. 6010) and in *Analecta Franciscana* (No. 6001), i (1885), 215–75. Excerpts edited by F. Liebermann in M.G.H. *SS.* xxviii. 560–9.

> The best edition is by Little. Translations: Fr. Cuthbert, *The Friars and how they came to England* (Lond. 1903) and *The chronicle of Thomas of Eccleston* (Lond. 1909); E. G. Salter and H. Böhmer, *The coming of the friars minor to England and Germany, being the chronicles of Brother Thomas of Eccleston and Brother Jordan of Giano* (Lond. 1926); and L. Sherley-Price in *The coming of Franciscans* (Lond. 1964).

6009 GRANSDEN (ANTONIA). 'A fourteenth century chronicle from the Grey Friars at Lynn (1349, 1360–77)'. *E.H.R.* lxxii (1957), 270–8. See No. 2887.

6010 MONUMENTA FRANCISCANA. Ed. by J. S. Brewer and Richard Howlett. 2 vols. Rolls Ser. 1858–82.

> Thomas of Eccleston's *De adventu* (see No. 6008), i. 1–72 and ii. 7–28.
> *Epistolae Adae de Marisco* (d. *c.* 1257), i. 77–489. See No. 6602.
> Primo fundatio fratrum minorum Londoniae (1224–1351), i. 493–543.
> Dispute between the Franciscans and the monks of Westminster (1290), ii. 31–62.
> The rule of St. Francis, ii. 65–78.
> Statutes of Franciscans (1451), ii. 81–119.
> Chronicle of the Grey Friars, London (1189–1556), ii. 143–260. See No. 2826.

6011 WADDING (LUKE). Annales Minorum seu trium ordinum a S. Francisco institutorum. 7 vols. Lyon. 1625–54. 2nd edn. with additions by J. M. Fonseca. 19 vols. Rome. 1731–41. Vols. xviii–xxv by John de Luca and others. Rome. 1740–1886. 3rd edn. Cura et studio sodalium eiusdem Ordinis. Quaracchi. 1931–5.

6012 WADDING (LUKE). Scriptores ordinis minorum. Rome. 1650.* Another edn. with Supplement by J. H. Sbaralea. 2 vols. Rome. 1806–8. Another edn. 1906–8.

6013 BOURDILLON (ANNE F. C.). The Order of Minoresses in England. B.S.F.S. xii. 1926.*

6014 BROOKE (ROSALIND B.). Early Franciscan government. Cambr. 1959.

6015 COTTON (CHARLES). The Grey Friars of Canterbury. B.S.F.S. 1924.*

Alan R. Martin, The Grey Friars of Canterbury. Reprinted from Royal Archaeol. Inst. Great Britain and Ireland (Cambr. 1932, 14 pp.).

6016 DOUIE (DECIMA L.). The nature and effects of the heresy of the Fraticelli. Manchester. 1932.

6017 FITZMAURICE (E. B.) and LITTLE (A. G.), eds. Materials for the history of the Franciscan province of Ireland, 1230–1450. B.S.F.S. ix. Manchester. 1920.*

6018 GREEN (V.G.). The Franciscans in medieval English life (1224–1348). Franciscan Studies (Paterson, N.J.) xx (1939).

6019 HOLZAPFEL (HERIBERT). Handbuch der Geschichte des Franziskanerorder. Freiburg im Breisgau. 1909. Trans. into English by A. Tibesar. Teutopolis (Illinois). 1948.

6020 HUBER (RAPHAEL M.). Documented history of the Franciscan Order, 1182–1517. Milwaukee (Wisconsin). 1944.

6021 HUTTON (EDWARD). The Franciscans in England, 1224–1538. Lond. 1926.

6022 KINGSFORD (CHARLES L.). The Grey Friars of London. B.S.F.S. vi. Aberdeen. 1915.*

Idem, 'Additional material' in *Collect. Franc.* (No. 6006).

6023 LITTLE (ANDREW G.). Franciscan history and legend in English medieval art. B.S.F.S. xix. Manchester. 1937.*

6024 LITTLE (A. G.). Franciscan papers, lists and documents. Manchester. 1943.

(a) The seventh centenary of St. Francis of Assisi (B.S.F.S. *Franciscan Essays*, ii (1932), 1–17). 1–15.
(b) Brother William of England, companion of St. Francis, and some Franciscan drawings in the Matthew Paris manuscripts (No. 6006). 16–24.
(c) Chronicles of the mendicant friars (B.S.F.S. *Franciscan Essays*, ii. 83–103). 25–41.
(d) The authorship of the Lanercost chronicle (*E.H.R.* xxxi (1916), 269–79; xxxii (1917), 48–9). 42–54.
(e) The Franciscan school at Oxford (adapted from *Essays in Commemoration* and *Archivum Fran. Hist.*). 55–71.
(f) Roger Bacon (*P.B.A.* xiv (1928), 265–96). 72–97.
(g) Thomas Docking [*Poole essays* (No. 1448)]. 98–121.
(h) Friars and theology at Cambridge (adapted from *Mélanges Mandonnet* (Paris, 1930), ii. 389–401). 122–43.
(i) Royal inquiry into property held by the mendicant friars in England in 1349 and 1350 [*Tait essays* (No. 1455)]. 144–55.
(j) The constitution of provincial chapters in the minorite order [*Tout essays* (No. 1458)]. 156–78.
(k) Paul Sabatier, historian of St. Francis. 179–88.
(l) List of provincial ministers. 189–207.
(m) List of provincial chapters. 208–16.

(*n*) List of custodies and houses in the Franciscan province of England. 217–229.
(*o*) Licence to hear confessions under the bull *Super Cathedram*. 230–43.
(*p*) A fifteenth-century sermon. 244–56.

6025 LITTLE (A. G.). The Grey Friars in Oxford. Oxford Hist. Soc. xx (1892).

A. G. Little, 'Franciscans at Oxford', *Franciscan Essays*. B.S.F.S. Extra Ser. i. Aberdeen. 1912. Idem, 'The first hundred years of the Franciscan School at Oxford', in *Essays in Commemoration* (No. 6034). Idem, 'The Franciscan school at Oxford in the thirteenth century'. *Archivum Franciscanum Historicum*, xix (1926), 803–74. Idem, Franciscan School at Oxford: Grosseteste and Roger Bacon, *Studies in Eng. Fran. Hist.*, pp. 193–221. Idem, 'Educational organization of the mendicant friars in England', *T.R.H.S.* New Ser. viii (1895), 49–70.

6026 LITTLE (A. G.). Studies in English Franciscan history. Manchester. 1917.

Idem, 'The introduction of the Observant Friars into England', *P.B.A.* x (1922/3), 455–71. Idem, 'The Grey Friars of Aylesbury', *Records of Bucks*, xiv (1942), 77–98.

6027 LITTLE (A. G.) and EASTERLING (RUTH C.). The Franciscans and Dominicans of Exeter. Exeter. 1927.

See also R. C. Easterling, 'The friars in Wales', *Archaeol. Cambrensis*, 6th Ser. xiv (1914), 323–56.

6028 LITTLE (A. G.) and PELSTER (FRANZ). Oxford theology and theologians. Oxford Hist. Soc. xciv (1934).

6029 MARTIN (ALAN R.). Franciscan architecture in England. B.S.F.S. xviii. Manchester. 1937.*

6030 MOORMAN (JOHN R. H.). The Grey Friars in Cambridge. Cambr. 1952.

6031 MOORMAN (J. R. H.). A history of the Franciscan Order from its origins to the year 1517. Oxf. 1968.

The best general history of the order in the English language.

6032 PARKINSON (ANTHONY). Collectanea Anglo-Minoritica: a collection of the antiquities of the English Franciscans. 2 pts. Lond. 1726.

6033 SHARP (DOROTHEA E.). Franciscan philosophy at Oxford in the xiii[th] century. B.S.F.S. xvi. Oxf. 1930.*

6034 SAINT FRANCIS OF ASSISI, 1226–1926: ESSAYS IN COMMEMORATION. Ed. by Walter Seton. Lond. 1926.

6035 SMALLEY (BERYL). English friars and antiquity in the fourteenth century. Oxf. 1960.

Important for intellectual history.

6036 WEARE (GEORGE E.). *Collectanea* relating to the Bristol Friars Minor. Bristol. 1893.

Lesser orders of monks and friars

6037 AUNGIER (GEORGE J.). History and antiquities of Syon monastery. Lond. 1840.

See also Margaret Deanesly, *The Incendium Amoris of Richard Rolle* (No. 6679), pp. 91–144.

6038 BECK (EGERTON). 'The order of the Holy Cross (Crutched Friars) in England'. *T.R.H.S.* 3rd Ser. vii (1913), 191–208.

6039 CHETTLE (H. F.). 'The Friars of the Holy Cross in England'. *History*, xxxiv (1949), 204–20. Idem, 'The "Boni-homines" of Ashridge and Edington'. *Downside Rev.* lxii (1944), 40–55. (Similar to Augustinian canons.) Idem, 'The Trinitarian Friars and Easton Royal'. *Wilts. Archaeol. Mag.* li (1946), 365–75. (The Trinitarians are not a mendicant order, see Knowles–Hadcock, p. 180.)

6040 EMERY (R. W.). 'The Friars of the Sack'. *Speculum*, xviii (1943), 323–4. Idem, 'The Friars of the Blessed Mary and the Pied Friars'. Ibid. xxiv (1949), 228–38.

6041 MAJOR (KATHLEEN). 'An unknown house of Crutched Friars at Whaplode'. *A.A.S.R.P.* lxi (1933), 149–54.

d. Military orders

Hospitallers

6042 CARTULAIRE GÉNÉRAL DE L'ORDRE DES HOSPITALIERS DE S. JEAN DE JÉRUSALEM, 1100–1310. Ed. by Joseph M. A. Delaville Le Roulx. 4 vols. Paris. 1894–1906.

For England and Ireland, see vol. i, pp. clvii–clxvi, and many documents in the body of the work. See also his *Mélanges sur l'Ordre de S. Jean de Jérusalem* (Paris, 1910) for various papers connected with the development of the order.

6043 DOCUMENTS RELATING TO THE LANDS OF THE PRE-CEPTORIES OF THE KNIGHTS HOSPITALLERS. Ed. by E. W. Crossley. Yorks. Archaeol. Soc. Record Ser. xciv. *Miscellanea*, iv (1936), 73–172.

Mostly post-1485, but court rolls of Kirkheaton for 1333 and of Hellifield for 1482.

6044 KNIGHTS HOSPITALLERS IN ENGLAND: being the report of prior Philip de Thame to the grand master Elyan de Villanova for A.D. 1338. Ed. by Lambert B. Larking, with an historical introduction by John M. Kemble. Camden Soc. Old Ser. lxv (1857).

A transcript of *Extenta Terrarum*: 'The work is a balance-sheet for every manor', giving an account of the profit and loss, etc.

6045 THE RULE, STATUTES AND CUSTOMS OF THE HOSPITAL-LERS, 1099–1310. By Edwin J. King. Lond. 1934.

6046 FALKINER (CAESAR L.). 'The hospital of St. John of Jerusalem in Ireland'. *Royal Irish Acad. Procs.* Sect. C. xxvi (1907), 275–317.

6047 KING (EDWIN J.). The grand priory of the order of the Hospital of St. John of Jerusalem in England: a short history. Lond. 1924. Idem, The knights of St. John in the British empire. Lond. 1934.

J. H. Round, 'The order of the Hospital in Essex', *Essex Archaeol. Soc. Trans.* New Ser. viii (1901), 182–6. Clarence Perkins, 'The knights hospitallers in England after the fall of the order of the Temple', *E.H.R.* xlv (1930), 285–9. B. Bromberg, 'The financial and administrative importance of the knights hospitallers to the English crown', *Econ. Hist.* iv (1940), 307–11. See No. 461.

6048 REES (J. R.). 'Slebech commandery and the knights of St. John'. *Archaeol. Cambrensis*, 5th Ser. xiv (1897), 85–107, 197–228, 261–84; xv (1898), 33–53; xvi (1899), 220–34, 283–98.

6049 REES (WILLIAM). The order of St. John in Wales and on the Welsh border. Cardiff. 1947.

Templars

6050 DESSUBRÉ (M. ?). Bibliographie de l'Ordre des Templiers: imprimés et manuscrits. Bibliothèque des initiations modernes, v. Paris. 1928.

6051 AIBON (GUIGES A. M. J. A. MARQUIS d'). Cartulaire général de l'Ordre du Temple, 1119–1150. Paris. 1913. Supplément. 1922.

6052 CHENEY (CHRISTOPHER R.). 'The downfall of the templars and a letter in the defence'. *Medieval Miscellany presented to Eugène Vinaver* . . . Ed. by F. Whitehead, *et al.* Manchester. 1965. Pp. 65–79.

6053 COLE (HENRY), ed. 'Corrodia petita de domibus templariorum, 1307–13', in his *Documents illustrative* (No. 3104), pp. 139–230.

6054 MAC NIOCAILL (GEAROID). 'Documents relating to the suppression of the templars in Ireland'. *Analecta Hibernica*, xxiv (1967), 181–226.

6055 RECORDS OF THE TEMPLARS IN ENGLAND IN THE TWELFTH CENTURY: THE INQUEST OF 1185. Ed. by Beatrice A. Lees. The British Academy Records of Social and Economic Hist. ix. Lond. 1935.

See also 'Original documents relating to the knights templars', *Gentleman's Magazine*, New Ser. iii (1857), 273–80, 519–26.

6056 RIBSTON AND THE KNIGHTS TEMPLARS. Ed. by R. V. Taylor. *Yorks. Archaeol.–Topog. Asso. Jour.* vii (1881–2), 429–52; viii (1883–4), 259–99; ix (1885–6), 71–98.

A collection of documents made up largely of charters granting lands to the templars.

6057 THE SANDFORD CARTULARY. Ed. by Agnes M. Leys. 2 vols. Oxfordshire Record Soc. Record Ser. xix (1938); xxii (1941).

A thirteenth-century cartulary of the templars, containing copies of deeds, charters, etc.

6058 ADDISON (CHARLES G.). The history of the knights templars. Lond. 1842. 3rd edn. 1852. N.Y. 1874.

6059 CAMPBELL (GEORGE A.). The knights templars, their rise and fall. Lond. 1937.

6060 DELISLE (LÉOPOLD). Mémoire sur les opérations financières des templiers (in England and France). Académie des Inscriptions et Belles Lettres, *Mémoires*, xxxiii, pt. ii (1889).

Eleanor Ferris, 'The financial relations of the Knights Templars to the English crown' *A.H.R.* viii (1902), 1–17. See also Agnes Sandys in *Tout essays* (No. 1458).

6061 FINKE (HEINRICH). Papsttum und Untergang des Templerordens. 2 vols. in 1. Münster in W. 1907.

Cf. Georges Lizerand, ed. *Le Dossier de l'affaire des templiers* (Paris, 1923); and Edward J. Martin, The trial of the Templars (Lond. 1928). H. C. Lea, *A history of the inquisition in the Middle Ages* (Philadelphia), iii. 238–334.

6062 PERKINS (CLARENCE). 'The trial of the templars in England'. *E.H.R.* xiv (1909), 432–47. Idem, 'The knights templars in the British Isles'. Ibid. xxv (1910), 209–30. Idem, 'The wealth of the knights templars in England and the disposition of it after their dissolution'. *A.H.R.* xv (1910), 252–63. See also A. M. Leys, 'The forfeiture of the lands' in *Salter essays* (No. 1451).

6063 PARKER (THOMAS W.). The Knights Templars in England. Tucson (Arizona). 1963.

Includes an up-to-date bibliography.

6064 WILLIAMSON (JOHN BRUCE). The history of the temple, London, from the institution of the order of the knights of the temple to the close of the Stuart period: compiled from original records. Lond. 1924. 2nd. edn. 1925.

Largely concerned with the Temple Inn of Court. For London Temple, see M. Reddan in *V.C.H. London*, i. 485–90.

6065 WOOD (HERBERT). The Templars in Ireland. *Royal Irish Acad. Procs.* Sect. C. xxvi (1907), 327–77.

e. Secular colleges

6066 DENTON (JEFFREY H.). English royal free chapels, 1100–1300. Manchester. 1970.

Free chapels are collegiate churches, with a community of canons, exempt from ordinary ecclesiastical jurisdiction. See W. R. Jones (No. 6850).

6067 KEMPE (ALFRED J.). Historical notices of the collegiate church or royal chapel and sanctuary of St. Martin-le-Grand. Also observations on the different kinds of sanctuary formerly recognized by the Common Law. Lond. 1825.

6068 OLLARD (SIDNEY L.), ed. Historical monographs relating to St. George's Chapel, Windsor Castle. Windsor. 1939+.

Includes A. K. B. Roberts, *St. George's Chapel, Windsor Castle, 1348–1416: a study in collegiate administration* (1948). S. L. Ollard, *Fasti Wyndesorienses: the deans and canons of Windsor* (1950). J. N. Dalton and Maurice F. Bond, *The manuscripts of St. George's Chapel, Windsor Castle* (1957), Shelagh Bond, ed. *The chapter acts of the deans and canons of Windsor* (1967). See also M. F. Bond, in *J.E.H.* viii (1957), 166–81.

6069 THOMPSON (ALEXANDER HAMILTON). 'Notes on colleges of secular canons in England'. *Archaeol. Jour.* lxxiv (1917), 139–99.

f. Hospitals

There were some 750 to 800 medieval hospitals in England, which were, of course, ecclesiastical rather than medical institutions. A tabulated list by county is given in Appendix B of R. M. Clay's book (No. 6070); and an alphabetical list by location in Knowles and Hadcock (No. 1299). The most convenient place to find accounts of the history, often with lists of wardens or masters, of individual hospitals is in the sections on 'Religious Houses' in the Victoria County Histories (No. 1529). Some records and histories of hospitals are entered below; see the index under 'hospitals'.

6070 CLAY (ROTHA M.). The mediaeval hospitals of England. Antiquary's Books. Lond. 1909.

3. *Religious Houses, County by County*

The basic general references to the sources for individual religious houses are cited above on pp. 167–8. The *Victoria County History* carries for each county a brief history, with footnote references, of each religious house within the county. The existing cartularies are described by Godfrey Davis (No. 6071).

6071 DAVIS (GODFREY R. C.). Medieval cartularies of Great Britain: a short catalogue. Lond. and N.Y. 1958.

Pt. i: Cartularies of religious houses, England, Wales, and Scotland. Pt. ii: Secular cartularies. In the introduction, pp. xvi–xvii, are printed finding-lists of cartularies.

BEDFORDSHIRE
See No. 6148.

6072 BUSHMEAD CARTULARY. *Beds. Notes and Queries*, iii (1893), 129–45.
Contains extracts, by F. A. Blaydes.

6073 CARTULARY OF BUSHMEAD PRIORY. Ed. by George H. Fowler and Joyce Godber. Beds. Hist. Rec. Soc. Pubns. xxii (1945).

6074 EARLY CHARTERS OF THE PRIORY OF CHICKSAND. Ed. by G. H. Fowler. Ibid. i (1913), 101–28.

6075 A DIGEST OF THE CHARTERS PRESERVED IN THE CARTULARY OF THE PRIORY OF DUNSTAPLE. By G. H. Fowler. Ibid. x (1926).

6076 EXCERPTA E CHARTULARIO PRIORATUS DE DUNSTAPLE [1135–1556]. Ed. by Thomas Hearne, *Annales Prioratus de Dunstaplia*, ii. 676–713. Oxf. 1733.

For the Annals of Dunstable, see No. 2929.

6077 TRACTATUS DE DUNSTAPLE ET DE HOCTON. Ed. by G. H. Fowler. Beds. Hist. Rec. Soc. Pubns. xix (1937), 1–99.

Late thirteenth-century text with English translation of immunities granted to Dunstaple.

6078 RICHMOND (ROBERT). 'Three records of the alien priory of Grove and the manor of Leighton Buzzard'. Ibid. viii (1924), 15–46.

6079 RECORDS OF HARROLD PRIORY. Ed. by G. H. Fowler. Ibid. xvii and xviii (1935).

See G. D. Gilmore, 'Two monastic account rolls', ibid. xlix (1970), 19–55.

6080 HARROLD PRIORY: a twelfth century dispute. Ed. by C. R. Cheney. Ibid. xxxii (1952), 1–26.

6081 THE CARTULARY OF NEWNHAM PRIORY. Ed. by Joyce Godber. Ibid., pts. i and ii, xliii (1963–4).

6082 EARLY RECORDS OF TURVEY AND ITS NEIGHBOURHOOD. Ed. by G. H. Fowler. Ibid. xi (1927), 47–107.

6083 CARTULARY OF THE ABBEY OF OLD WARDON. Ed. by G. H. Fowler. Ibid. xiii (1930).

BERKSHIRE

See Nos. 4777, 6357.

6084 ACCOUNTS OF THE OBEDIENTIARS OF ABINGDON ABBEY. Ed. by Richard E. G. Kirk. Camden Soc. 1892.

Twenty-six accounts of various officers of the abbey, 1322–1479; also abstracts of eleven manorial accounts, together with two rentals and a court roll, 1384–1532. Gabrielle Lambrick, 'Abingdon abbey administration', *J.E.H.* xvii (1966), 159–83.

6085 CHRONICON MONASTERII DE ABINGDON. Ed. by Joseph Stevenson. Rolls Ser. 2 vols. Lond. 1858.

De consuetudinibus Abbendoniae, ii. 296–334: customs affecting the receipts and expenditures of the various monastic officers in the 12th century.
De obedientiariis abbatiae Abbendonensis, ii. 335–417; an account of the privileges and duties of the monastic officers toward the end of the 13th century.
For the chronicle itself, see No. 2153.

6086 DOUGLAS (DAVID C.). 'Some early surveys from the abbey of Abingdon'. *E.H.R.* xliv (1929), 618–25.

G. D. G. Hall, 'The abbot of Abingdon and the tenants of Winkfield', *Medium Ævum*, xxviii (1959), 91–5.

6087 STENTON (F. M.). The early history of the abbey of Abingdon. Oxf. 1913.

See Martin Biddle, 'The early history of Abingdon, Berkshire and its abbey', *Medieval Archaeology*, xii (1968), 26–69.

6088 LANDS AND TYTHES OF HURLEY PRIORY, 1086–1535. Ed. by F. T. Wethered. Reading. 1909.

Cf. F. T. Wethered, *St. Mary's Hurley in the Middle Ages.* (Lond. 1898).

6089 BARFIELD (S.). 'Lord Fingall's cartulary of Reading abbey'. *E.H.R.* iii (1888), 113–25. (A description of the cartulary.)

6090 COPE (S. TREHEARNE). 'St. Bartholomew's hospital at Newbury'. *Newbury District Field Club. Trans.* vii (1937), 287–94.

6091 ORIGINAL DOCUMENTS: A contribution towards the history of Reading abbey. Ed. by Albert Way. *Archaeol. Jour.* xx (1863), 281–96; xxii (1865), 151–61.

> Charters, etc. granted to the abbey, Hen. I–Hen. VI.

6092 HURRY (JAMIESON B.). Reading abbey. Lond. 1901.

BUCKINGHAMSHIRE

See *Early Buckingham Charters* (No. 4419).

6093 CHARTERS RELATING TO THE ABBEY OF BURNHAM, CO. BUCKINGHAM [1266–1512]. Ed. by J. G. N. *Collectanea Topog. et Genealogica* (No. 115), viii (1843), 120–31.

6094 THE CARTULARY OF MISSENDEN ABBEY. Ed. by John G. Jenkins. 3 pts. Bucks. Archaeol. Soc., Rec. Branch, ii for 1938 (1939); x for 1946 (1955). Pt. 3. Joint pubn. of Bucks. Archaeol. Soc. Rec. Branch and Hist. MSS. Comm. 1962.

> G. H. Fowler, 'Bedfordshire charters in the Missenden cartulary.' Beds. Hist. Rec. Soc. ii (1914).

6094A NEWINGTON LONGEVILLE CHARTERS. No. 4464.

6095 THE LOST CARTULARY OF NUTLEY ABBEY. Ed. by J. G. Jenkins. *Huntington Libr. Quart.* xvii (1953–4), 379–96.

6096 THE CARTULARY OF SNELSHALL PRIORY. Ed. by J. G. Jenkins. Bucks. Rec. Soc. ix for 1945 (1952).

6097 THREE LAND CHARTERS OF MONKS OF RISBOROUGH. Ed. by G. H. Fowler. Rec. of Bucks. xi (1924), 343–8.

CAMBRIDGESHIRE

For the cathedral-priory of Ely, see pp. 772–3, especially No. 5711.

6098 LIBER MEMORANDUM ECCLESIE DE BERNEWELLE. Ed. by John W. Clark. Cambr. 1907.

> Compiled in 1296. Contains many charters, extracts from the rolls of the central courts at Westminster, an extent of the lands of the priory, and other records.

6099 OBSERVANCES IN USE AT THE AUGUSTINIAN PRIORY OF ST. GILES AND ST. ANDREW AT BARNWELL, CAMBRIDGESHIRE. Ed. with a translation and glossary by J. W. Clark. Cambr. 1897.

> Compiled in 1295–96. Throws light on monastic life in the thirteenth century. The introduction gives an excellent account of the history of Barnwell priory.

6100 NICHOLS (JOHN). 'The history and antiquities of Barnwell abbey and of Sturbridge fair [with an appendix of records]', in his *Bibliotheca Topographica Britannica* (No. 1505), v, no. 38. Lond. 1786.

6101   PRIORY OF ST. RADEGUND, CAMBRIDGE. Ed. by Arthur Gray. Cambr. Antiq. Soc. Cambr. etc. 1898.

Charters (abstracts), pp. 74–144. Accounts (1449–82), pp. 145–85.

6102   WARNER (RICHARD H.). The history of Thorney abbey. Wisbeck, etc. 1879.

CHESHIRE

6103   BOOK OF THE ABBOT OF COMBERMERE, 1289–1529. By James Hall. Lancs. and Ches. Rec. Soc. *Miscellanies,* ii (1896), 1–74.

Contains translations of charters and rentals.

6104   FOUNDATION CHARTER OF RUNCORN PRIORY. Ed. by James Tait. Chetham Soc. c (1939), *Chetham Miscellanies,* vii.

6105   THE CHARTULARY OR REGISTER OF THE ABBEY OF ST. WERBURGH, CHESTER. 2 pts. Ed. with introduction and notes by James Tait. Chetham Soc. lxxix and lxxxii (1920–3).

R. V. H. Burne, *The Monks of Chester* (Lond. 1962).

6106   THE LEDGER-BOOK OF VALE ROYAL ABBEY. Ed. by John Brownbill. Lancs. and Ches. Rec. Soc. lxviii (1914).

CORNWALL

For other monastic records of Cornwall, see Oliver, *Monasticon* (No. 6109).

6107   ABSTRACT OF THE GLASNEY CARTULARY. Trans. by John A. C. Vincent. *Royal Institution of Cornwall Jour.* vi (1881), 216–63.

6108   HULL (PETER L.). The cartulary of St. Michael's Mount. Devon and Cornwall Record Soc. New Ser. v for 1958 (1962).

6109   OLIVER (GEORGE). Monasticon dioecesis Exoniensis: records illustrating the ancient foundations in Cornwall and Devon. Exeter. 1846. Additional supplement. 1854. See No. 1147.

CUMBERLAND

For the cathedral-priory of Carlisle, see pp. 765–6.

6109A   REGISTER AND RECORDS OF HOLM CULTRAM (c. 1236). Ed. by Francis Grainger and William G. Collingwood. Cumb.–Westm. Antiq.–Archaeol. Soc. Record Ser. vii (1929).

George E. Gilbanks, *Some records of a Cistercian abbey: Holm Cultram.* (Lond. 1899).

6110   WALCOTT (MACKENZIE E. C.). 'Breviate of the cartulary of Lanercost'. *Royal Soc. Lit. Trans.* 2nd Ser. viii (1866), 434–524.

6111   MOORMAN (JOHN R. H.). 'The estates of the Lanercost canons'. *Cumb.–Westm. Antiq.–Archaeol. Soc. Trans.* New Ser. xlviii (1949), 77–107.

6112 THE REGISTER OF THE PRIORY OF ST. BEES. Ed. by James Wilson. Surtees Soc. cxxvi (1915).

6113 REGISTER OF THE PRIORY OF WETHERHAL. Ed. by John E. Prescott. Cumb.–Westm. Antiq.–Archaeol. Soc. Record Ser. 1897.

Contains many charters.

DERBYSHIRE

See Jeayes, *Derbyshire charters* (No. 4431), and No. 6326.

6114 PEGGE (SAMUEL). An historical account of Beauchief abbey. Lond. 1801.

Consists mainly of an abstract of its chartulary. G. R. Potter, 'The cartulary of Beauchief abbey', *Derbys. Archaeol. Jour.*, New Ser. xii (1938), 160–62. Sidney O. Addy, *Historical memorials of Beauchief abbey* (Oxf. etc. 1878). (Visitations of the abbey, 1278–1501, pp. 73–114.)

6115 THE CARTULARY OF DALE ABBEY. Ed. by Avrom Saltman. Derbys. Archaeol. Soc. and Hist. MSS. Comm. 1966.

Of particular interest on peasant life in the Danelaw. See A. Saltman, 'The history of the foundation of Dale Abbey or the so-called Chronicle of Dale', *Derbysh. Archaeol. Jour.* lxxxvii (1967), 18–38. Also John C. Cox, 'Chartulary of the abbey of Dale (an abstract)', *Derbys. Archaeol.–Nat. Hist. Soc. Jour.* xxiv (1902), 82–150.

6116 CHRONICLE OF THE ABBEY OF ST. MARY DE PARCO STANLEY, OR DALE, DERBYSHIRE. Ed. by W. H. St.John Hope. *Derbys. Archaeol.–Nat. Hist. Soc. Jour.* v (1883), 1–29.

See A. Saltman above (No. 6115).

6117 THOMAE DE MUSCA CHRONICON. Ed. by Francis Peck, *Desiderata Curiosa*, vol. ii, bk. xv. Lond. 1735. New edn. 1779. Idem, 'Historia monasterii de Parco Stanley' printed in Dugdale, *Monasticon*, vi. 892–5. Trans. by Stephen Glover in *History and gazetteer of the County of Derby*, ii. 371–8. Derby. 1833.

The author entered the abbey of Stanley Park, or Dale, in the time of Abbot Grauncorth, 1235–54.

6118 THE CARTULARY OF DARLEY ABBEY. Ed. by Reginald R. Darlington. Derbys. Archaeol. and Nat. Hist. Soc. 2 vols. 1945.

Darlington's introduction is excellent. A calendar of the cartulary is included in John C. Cox, 'History and chartulary of the abbey of Darley', *Derbys. Archaeol.–Nat. Hist. Soc. Jour.* xxii (1904), 82–140.

DEVONSHIRE

See Oliver's Monasticon (No. 6109); and for a fragment of a Buckfast cartulary, see Bishop Grandisson's Register (No. 5715).

6119 ROWE (JOSHUA B.). Contributions to a history of Cistercian houses of Devon. Plymouth. 1878.

6120 STEPHAN (JOHN). The ancient religious houses of Devon. Exeter. 1935.

6121 REYNOLDS (SUSAN). 'The forged charters of Barnstaple'. *E.H.R.* lxxxiv (1969), 699–720.

6122 THE CARTULARY OF CANONSLEIGH ABBEY: a calendar. Ed. by Vera C. M. London. Devon and Cornwall Record Soc. New Ser. viii. 1965.
  A calendar of charters; a description of a survey of 1323.

6123 REMARKS ON SOME EARLY CHARTERS AND DOCUMENTS RELATING TO THE PRIORY OF AUSTIN CANONS AT CANONS-LEIGH [with an appendix of charters, etc.]. By C. S. Perceval. *Archaeologia*, xl (1871), 417–50.

6124 LIST OF CHARTERS IN THE CARTULARY OF ST. NICHOLAS PRIORY, AT EXETER. *Collectanea Topog. et Genealogica* (No. 115), i. (1834), 60–5, 184–9, 250–4, 374–88.
  They cover the period William I–Henry VI.

6125 THE COLLEGIATE CHURCH OF OTTERY ST. MARY: being the ordinacio et statuta ecclesie sancte Marie de Otery, Exon. diocesis, A.D. 1338, 1339. Ed. by John N. Dalton. Cambr. 1917.

6126 FINBERG (HERBERT R. P.). Tavistock Abbey: a study in the social and economic history of Devon. Cambr. 1951. Idem, 'Some early Tavistock charters'. *E.H.R.* lxii (1947), 352–77.

6127 WATKIN (HUGH R.). History of Totnes priory and medieval town, Devonshire. 3 vols. Torquay. 1914–17.

DORSET

6128 CARTULARY (THE) OF CERNE ABBEY, known as the red book of Cerne [text and translation, the latter by B. Fossett Lock]. *Dorset Nat. Hist. and Antiq. Field Club Procs.* xxviii (1907), 65–95; xxix (1908), 195–224.
  Mainly records of lawsuits affecting the abbey, Henry III–Edward III.

6129 CARTULAIRE DE LODERS, PRIEURÉ DÉPENDANT DE L'ABBAYE DE MONTEBOURG [twelfth–fourteenth centuries]. Ed. by Léon Guilloreau. *Revue Catholique de Normandie*, xvii (1907), 267–74; xviii (1908), 18–35, 72–87, 119–35, 165–73, 230–9; xix (1909), 13–23, 61–73. Evreux. 1907–9.

6130 COURT ROLL OF SHAFTESBURY ABBEY, 1453. Ed. by Charles H. Mayo. *Notes and Queries for Somerset and Dorset*, i (1890), 201–3, ii (1891), 34–6, 116–19, 244–6. Sherborne. 1890–1.
  See also the charters relating to Mary, abbess of Shaftesbury (who is identified with Marie de France), printed by J. C. Fox in the *E.H.R.* xxvi (1911), 317–26. Arthur J. Collins, 'A chartulary of Shaftesbury abbey', *Brit. Museum Quart.* x (1935), 66–8.

6131 THE SHERBORNE CHARTULARY. See F. Wormald in *Saxl Memorial essays* (No. 1452).

DURHAM

For Durham cathedral-priory, see pp. 768–72.

6132 CORRESPONDENCE, INVENTORIES, ACCOUNT ROLLS, AND LAW PROCEEDINGS OF THE PRIORY OF COLDINGHAM (1214–1478). Ed. by James Raine. Surtees Soc. 1841.

Until the latter part of the fifteenth century this Scottish priory was subordinate to the church of Durham. These records are taken largely from Durham registers, and date mostly before 1399. See also the appendix to Raine's *North Durham* (No. 6276); and Barrie Dobson, 'The last English monks on Scottish soil: the severance of Coldingham priory from the monastery of Durham, 1461–78', *Scot. H.R.* xlvi (1967), 1–25.

6133 MEMORIALS OF ST. GILES'S, DURHAM, with documents relating to the hospitals of Kepier and St. Mary Magdalene. Ed. by James Barmby. Surtees Soc. 1896.

Documents relating to the two hospitals, 1112–1554, pp. 192–247.

6134 CHARTERS OF ENDOWMENT, INVENTORIES, AND ACCOUNT ROLLS OF THE PRIORY OF FINCHALE [c. 1143–1535]. Ed. by James Raine. Surtees Soc. 1837.

6135 COLLECTIONS RELATING TO ST. EDMUND'S HOSPITAL AT GATESHEVED, with several charters, etc., concerning the town and church [1247–1610]. G. Allan's *Darlington Press*. 1769.

6136 COLLECTIONS RELATING TO THE HOSPITAL AT GRETHAM. *Darlington Press*. 1770.

Statutes, charters, etc., A.D. 1272–1610.

6137 COLLECTIONS RESPECTING THE MONASTERY OF JARROW. Ed. by John Hodgson. *Collectanea Topog. et Genealogica* (No. 115), i (1834), 66–73.

Accounts of the manor of Wardley, A.D. 1376–79, etc.

6138 INVENTORIES AND ACCOUNT ROLLS OF THE BENEDICTINE HOUSES OR CELLS OF JARROW AND MONK-WEARMOUTH [1303–1537]. Ed. by James Raine. Surtees Soc. 1854.

6139 COLLECTIONS RELATING TO SHERBURN HOSPITAL. *Darlington Press*. 1771.

Statutes, charters, etc., A.D. 1181–1748.

ESSEX

See No. 6357.

6140 EARLY CHARTERS OF BARKING ABBEY. Ed. by Cyril Hart. Colchester. 1953.

6141 CARTULARIUM MONASTERII S. JOHANNIS BAPTISTE DE COLECESTRIA. Ed. by Stuart A. Moore. Roxburghe Club. 2 vols. Lond. 1897.

Valuable. See also J. H. Round, 'The early charters of St. John's Abbey, Colchester',

E.H.R. xvi (1901), 721–30; and an appendix to J. A. Robinson's *Gilbert Crispin* (No. 6246).

6142 THE LEDGER BOOK OF ST. JOHN'S ABBEY, COLCHESTER. Ed. by John L. Fisher. *Essex Archaeol. Soc. Trans.* New Ser. xxiv (1951), 77–127.

A calendar of a memorandum book of manorial extents, leases, royal letters, etc., esp. fourteenth–fifteenth centuries. See also J. L. Fisher, 'Customs and services on an Essex manor in the thirteenth century', ibid. Old Ser. xix, pt. ii (1928), 111–16.

6143 CARTULARIUM PRIORATUS DE COLNE. Ed. by J. L. Fisher. Essex Archaeol. Soc., Occasional Pubns. No. 1 (1946).

6144 HORNCHURCH PRIORY. A kalendar of documents in the possession of the wardens and fellows of New College, Oxford. Ed. by Herbert F. Westlake. Lond. 1923.

Charters, quit-claims, etc. from Henry II to the early fifteenth century.

6145 FOWLER (ROBERT C.). 'A balance sheet of St. Osyth's Abbey' (1491). *Essex Archaeol. Soc. Trans.* Old Ser. xix, pt. iii (1929), 186–92.

6146 THE BOOK OF THE FOUNDATION OF WALDEN ABBEY. Transcribed and translated by C. H. Emson. *Essex Rev.* xlv–xlvi (1936–7). Printed separately, Colchester. 1938.

H. G. Richardson prints a short extract of the Latin text in *Gwynn essays* (No. 1438), and criticizes the above translation.

6147 FOUNDATION OF WALTHAM ABBEY: the tract De inventione sanctae crucis nostrae in Monte Acuto [Montacute, Somerset] et de ductione ejusdem apud Waltham. Ed. by William Stubbs. Oxf., etc., 1861. Imperfect editions, by Francisque Michel, 1836, and J. A. Giles, 1854: Nos. 1112, 2285.

This anonymous tract was written in the last quarter of the twelfth century. It devotes some attention to the career of King Harold and to public events, but it deals mainly with the history of the collegiate church of Waltham, from the time of its foundation by Harold to the year 1177, when the secular canons were replaced by regulars. Stubbs, pp. 50–6, adds some charters, 1096–1144.

6148 HISTORICAL NOTES ON SOME OF THE ANCIENT MANU-SCRIPTS [cartularies, etc.] FORMERLY BELONGING TO THE MON-ASTIC LIBRARY OF WALTHAM HOLY CROSS. By William Winters. *T.R.H.S.* vi (1877), 203–66.

For some charters relating to the estates of Waltham at Arlesey, Bedfordshire, see *Collectanea Topogr. et Genealog.* (No. 115) vi (1840), 196–236.

6149 BROOKE (C. N. L.). 'Episcopal charters for Wix priory (Essex)'. *D. M. Stenton Miscellany* (No. 1453).

GLOUCESTER

6150 SOME MANORIAL ACCOUNTS OF ST. AUGUSTINE'S ABBEY, BRISTOL, being the *computa* of the manors for 1491–2 and 1496–7 and other documents of the fifteenth and sixteenth centuries. Ed. by Arthur Sabin. Bristol Record Soc. Pubns. xxii (1960).

6151 TWO COMPOTUS ROLLS OF SAINT AUGUSTINE'S ABBEY, BRISTOL, for 1491–2 and 1511–12. Ed. by Gwen Beachcroft and Arthur Sabin. Ibid. ix (1938).

6152 CARTULARY OF ST. MARK'S HOSPITAL, BRISTOL. Ed. by Charles D. Ross. Ibid. xxi (1959).

A calendar of 445 charters, deeds, and records of lawsuits.

6153 THE CARTULARY OF CIRENCESTER ABBEY. Ed. by Charles D. Ross. 2 vols. Oxf. 1964.

A third volume of a later cartulary will be published. This one was probably made in time of Abbot Hugh of Brampton (1230–50), with additions to c. A.D. 1450. It has an admirable introduction.

6154 CARTULARY AND HISTORICAL NOTES OF THE CISTER-CIAN ABBEY OF FLAXLEY. Ed. by Arthur W. Crawley-Boevey. Exeter. 1887.

Valuable. This edition has superseded the *Cartularium de Flaxley*. Ed. by Thomas Phillipps, Middle Hill Press, 1866.

6155 LANGSTON (J. N.). 'Priors of Lanthony in Gloucester'. *Bristol–Glos. Archaeol. Soc. Trans.* lxiii (1942), 1–144.

6156 EARLY DEEDS RELATING TO ST. PETER'S ABBEY, GLOU-CESTER. Ed. Welbore Baddeley. Ibid. xxxvii (1915), 221–34; xxxviii (1916), 19–68.

For charters of St. Peter's abbey, see Walker in *D. M. Stenton Miscellany* (No. 1453); and for Gloucester forgeries, see Morey-Brooke, *Gilbert Foliot* (No. 6517), chap. viii.

6157 HISTORIA ET CARTULARIUM MONASTERII S. PETRI GLOUCESTRIAE. Ed. by William H. Hart. Rolls Ser. 3 vols. Lond. 1863–7.

The short chronicle which precedes the chartulary gives an account of the monastery from its foundation, A.D. 681, to the time of Abbot Froucester (d. 1412). (See *Celt and Saxon* (No. 2123), pp. 258–322.) Vols. i–ii contain numerous charters of the twelfth and thirteenth centuries. There are some valuable manorial extents, 1265–67: iii. 35–213; and rules of unknown date concerning the management of manors: iii. 213–21. Vol. iii also contains various judicial records. See F. Baring, 'Domesday and some Thirteenth-Century Surveys', in *E.H.R.* xii (1897), 285–90; and R. H. Hilton, 'Gloucester abbey leases in the late thirteenth century', *Univ. Birmingham Hist. Jour.* iv (1953–4), 1–17.

6158 DOCUMENTS RELATING TO THE CISTERCIAN MONAS-TERY OF ST. MARY, KINGSWOOD. By V. R. Perkins. *Bristol and Glos. Archaeol. Soc. Trans.* xxii (1899), 179–256.

Contains charters, account rolls, etc., c. 1230–1415 in translation only. E. S. Lindley, 'Kingswood abbey, its lands and mills', ibid. lxxiii (1954), 115–191.

6159 TEWKESBURY COMPOTUS. Ed. by F. W. P. Hicks. (No. 4755).

An account of the abbey's chamberlain for 1351–2.

6160 LANDBOC SIVE REGISTRUM MONASTERII BEATAE MARIAE VIRGINIS ET SANCTI CENHELMI DE WINCHELCUMBA. Ed. by David Royce. 2 vols. Exeter. 1892–1903.

A well-edited chartulary, extending to 1477; containing many charters of the thirteenth and fourteenth centuries, but only three anterior to 1175. The introduction to vol. i contains a good account of the history of the town, that to vol. ii an account of the monastery. Vol. ii comprises the register of Abbot John of Cheltenham, compiled 1422. See also *Cartularium Monasterii de Winchcombe, abbreviatum per Joh. Prynne* (*Middle Hill Press*, 1854). List of Charters in the Winchcomb Cartularies, in *Collectanea Topogr. et Genealog.* (No. 115), ii (1835), 16–39; and R. H. Hilton, 'Winchcombe abbey and the manor of Sherborne', *Gloucestershire Studies*. Ed. by H. R. P. Finberg (Leicester, 1957).

6161 WINCHOMBE ANNALS, 1049–1181. By Reginald R. Darlington in *D. M. Stenton Miscellany* (No. 1453).

Gordon Haigh, *History of Winchcombe abbey* (from the ninth century to the dissolution). (Lond. 1950).

6162 THOMPSON (ALEXANDER HAMILTON). 'The jurisdiction of the archbishop of York in Gloucestershire, with some notes on the history of the priory of St. Oswald, Gloucester'. *Bristol–Glos. Archaeol. Soc. Trans.* xliii (1922), 85–180.

HAMPSHIRE
See No. 6357.

6163 HOCKEY (FREDERICK). Quarr abbey (Isle of Wight) and its lands, 1132–1631. Leicester and N.Y. 1970.

6164 LIVEING (HENRY G. D.). Records of Romsey abbey: an account of the Benedictine house of nuns. Winchester. 1906.

6165 CALENDAR OF CHARTERS AND DOCUMENTS RELATING TO SELBORNE AND ITS PRIORY, preserved in the muniment rooms of Magdalen College. Ed. by William Dunn Macray. 2 vols. Hampshire Record Soc. 1891, 1894.

The 1894 volume relates 'to property in places other than Selborne' (Mullins, *Texts*).

HEREFORD
6166 BANNISTER (ARTHUR T.). History of Ewias Harold. Hereford. 1902.

6167 KEMP (BRIAN R.). 'The monastic dean of Leominster'. *E.H.R.* lxxxiii (1968), 505–15.

HERTFORD
6168 GESTA ABBATUM MONASTERII S. ALBANI A THOMA WALSINGHAM (A.D. 793–1401). Ed. by Henry T. Riley. 3 vols. Rolls Ser. Lond. 1867–9.

To 1255 it is derived mainly from Matthew Paris's *Gesta Abbatum*; the part 1255–1307 is by an anonymous writer; the part 1308–81 is Walsingham's work; and there is a continuation to 1401. This chronicle contains much documentary material relating to the abbey. The peasants' rising in Herts. is dealt with in vol. iii, pp. 285–372. The appendix to vol. ii contains synodal constitutions, A.D. 1326–49, for the clergy of St. Albans and for the neighbouring hospital of St. Julian; also the customs of the nuns of St. Mary at Sopwell, A.D. 1338. For Walsingham's other works, see No. 2976.

6169 REGISTRA JOHANNIS WHETHAMSTEDE, WILLELMI AL-
BON, ET WILLELMI WALINGFORDE, ABBATUM MONASTERII
S. ALBANI [1459–88]. Ed. by Henry T. Riley, *Registra Quorundam Abbatum*,
ii. 1–291. Rolls Ser. Lond. 1873.

See No. 2980.

6170 NEWCOME (PETER). The history of the abbey of St. Alban. Lond.
1793; reprinted, 1795.

James A. Froude, 'Annals of an English abbey', *Short Studies* (3rd ser. Lond. 1877).
Vivian H. Galbraith, *The abbey of St. Albans from 1300 to the dissolution of the monasteries* (Oxf. 1911). L. F. Rushbrook Williams, *History of the abbey of St. Alban* (Lond.
1917). Richard Vaughan, 'The election of abbots of St. Albans in the thirteenth and
fourteenth centuries', *Cambr. Antiq. Soc. Procs.* xlvii (1953), 1–12. M. D. Knowles,
'The case of St. Albans abbey in 1490', *J.E.H.* iii (1952), 144–58.

6171 STUDIES IN THE MANORIAL ORGANIZATION OF ST.
ALBANS ABBEY in A. E. Levett, *Studies* (No. 1480), pp. 69–299.

In appendix, pp. 300–68, are printed the court book and the extent of Codicote for 1332.
Idem, 'The courts and the court rolls of St. Albans abbey', *T.R.H.S.* 4th Ser. vii (1924),
52–76. See Maitland and Baildon, *The Court Baron* (No. 4716).

HUNTINGDON

6172 GORHAM (GEORGE C.). The history and antiquities of Eynesbury
and St. Neots, 2 vols. and Supplement. Lond. 1824.

The Supplement contains an abstract of two chartularies of the priory of St. Neots;
and vol. ii contains extracts from these chartularies, together with various other records.

6173 CARTULARIUM MONASTERII DE RAMESEIA. Ed. by William
H. Hart and P. A. Lyons. Rolls Ser., 3 vols. Lond. 1884–93.

Contains charters, inquisitions, manorial extents, surveys of knights' fees, final concords,
pleas in royal courts, etc. A.D. 974–1436. The material relating to manorial history is
particularly valuable. See F. Baring, 'Domesday and some thirteenth-century surveys',
in *E.H.R.* xii (1897), 285–90.

6174 COURT ROLLS OF THE ABBEY OF RAMSEY AND OF THE
HONOR OF CLARE. Ed. by Warren O. Ault. *Yale Hist. Pubns.* (New Haven,
Conn.). ix (1928).

See Maitland, *Select pleas in manorial courts* (No. 4777).

6175 NEILSON (NELLIE). Economic conditions on the manors of Ramsey
abbey. Philadelphia. 1899.

Compotus rolls of Wistowe, Hunts., 1297; app. 1–103. Rental of Wistowe, 1381; app.
104–16. Compotus roll of the banlieu of Ramsey, 1312; app. 119–20. Miss Neilson
believed that from about A.D. 1150 to 1250 there was an increase of villein obligations
on the Ramsey manors.

6176 RAFTIS (J. A.). The estates of Ramsey abbey: a study in economic
growth and organization. Toronto. 1957.

6177 TRIKINGHAM, ELIAS OF (*fl.* 1320). Annales (A.D. 626–1268). Ed.
by Samuel Pegge. Lond. 1789.

This meagre collection of historical notes gleaned from various chroniclers is of no value, apart from a few details regarding the abbeys of Peterborough and Ramsey. The author was probably a monk of Ramsey.

KENT

For the cathedral-priory of Christ Church, Canterbury, see pp. 759–65; and for the cathedral-priory of Rochester, see pp. 781–2. Also No. 6357.

6178 THE CARTULARY AND TERRIER OF THE PRIORY OF BIL-SINGTON, KENT. Ed. by Nellie Neilson. Brit. Acad. Records Social and Economic Hist. vii (1928).

Cartulary is largely thirteenth century and the terrier fifteenth century.

6179 CUSTOMARY OF THE MONASTERIES OF ST. AUGUSTINE, CANTERBURY, AND ST. PETER, WESTMINSTER. Ed. by E. M. Thompson. Henry Bradshaw Soc. 2 vols. Lond. 1902–4.

The customary of St. Augustine's comes from the early fourteenth century. The Westminster customary, compiled 1259–83, is a version of that of Canterbury. See also E. L. Taunton, *The English black monks* (Lond. 1897), vol. i, appendix.

6180 AN ELEVENTH-CENTURY INQUISITION OF ST. AUGUSTINE'S, CANTERBURY. Ed. by Adolphus Ballard. Brit. Acad. Records Social and Economic Hist. iv (1920).

6181 ELMHAM (THOMAS). Historia monasterii S. Augustini Cantuariensis (No. 2158); and Frank Taylor, 'A note on Rolls Series no. 8 (Elmham's Historia)', *B.J.R.L.* xx (1936), 379–82.

6182 THE REGISTER OF ST. AUGUSTINE'S ABBEY, CANTERBURY, commonly called the Black Book. Ed. by George J. Turner and Herbert E. Salter. Brit. Acad. Records Social and Economic Hist., 2 pts. (1915–24).

A rental, a collection of charters, and much else. Pt. 2 documents of thirteenth and fourteenth centuries. For a summary in translation of the account of the treasurer of St. Augustine's for 1446–7, see *Eng. Hist. Docs.* iv, no. 477. Also Charles Cotton, 'St. Austin's abbey, Canterbury: treasurers' accounts, 1468–9, and others', *Archaeol. Cantiana*, li for 1939 (1940), 66–107.

6183 THORNE (WILLIAM). (*fl.* 1397). Chronica de rebus gestis abbatum S. Augustini Cantuariae [A.D. 578–1397]. Ed. by Roger Twysden in *Scriptores X*, cols. 1753–2202. Lond. 1652. Trans. as William Thorne's Chronicle of St. Augustine's Abbey Canterbury by A. H. Davis. Oxf. 1934. See No. 2959.

Although it touches on the general history of England, it deals largely with the affairs of the abbey. Many documents on lawsuits, donations of land, accounts, etc. To 1228 the work is derived mainly from Sprott's Chronicle. Thorne was a monk of St. Augustine's, Canterbury. See Eric John, 'The litigation of an exempt house, St. Augustine's, Canterbury, 1182–1237', *B.J.R.L.* xxxix (1956–7), 390–415. For a fourteenth-century dispute between St. Augustine's abbey and the archbishop of Canterbury, see W. A. Pantin, 'The letters of John Mason', *Wilkinson essays* (No. 1459).

6184 BOGGIS (ROBERT J. E.). A history of St. Augustine's monastery, Canterbury. Canterbury. 1901.

6185 CARTULARY OF THE PRIORY OF ST. GREGORY, CANTER-
BURY. Ed. by Audrey M. Woodcock. R.H.S. Camden Soc. 3rd ser. lxxxviii
(1956).

6186 THE REGISTER AND CHARTULARY OF THE HOSPITAL OF
ST. LAURENCE, CANTERBURY. Ed. by Charles E. Woodruff. *Archaeol.
Cantiana*, l (1938), 33–49.

6187 DUNCOMBE (JOHN) and BATTELY (NICHOLAS). The history
and antiquities of the three episcopal hospitals at and near Canterbury: viz.
St. Nicholas, at Harbledown; St. John's, Northgate; and St. Thomas, of Eastbridge. *Bibliotheca Topog. Brit.* (No. 1505), i. no. 30 (1785).

6188 CHARTERS OF CUMBWELL PRIORY (1160–1270). *Archaeol.
Cantiana*, v (1863), 194–222; vi (1866), 190–222; viii (1872), 271–93.

6189 HAINES (CHARLES R.). Dover Priory: a history of the priory of St.
Mary the Virgin, and St. Martin of the new work. Cambr. 1930.

6190 ARMSTRONG (C. A. J.). 'Thirteenth century notes on the rights of the
abbey of Faversham in London from a manuscript of Grenoble'. *E.H.R.* liv
(1939), 677–85.

6191 A KENTISH CARTULARY OF THE ORDER OF ST. JOHN OF
JERUSALEM. Ed. by Charles Cotton. *Kent Archaeol. Soc. Kent Records.* 1930.

6192 WADMORE (JOHN F.). 'The knight hospitallers in Kent'. *Archaeol.
Cantiana*, xxii (1897), 232–74; xxiv (1900), 128–38.

6193 THE CARTULARY OF LEEDS PRIORY [abstracts]. Ed. by L.
Sherwood. *Archaeol. Cantiana*, lxiv (1951), 24–34.

6194 CHARTULARY OF THE MONASTERY OF LYMINGE. Translated and illustrated by Robert C. Jenkins. Folkestone. 1886.

6195 CHARTERS OF MONKS HORTON PRIORY, 1140–1311. Ed. by
J. R. Scott. *Archaeol. Cantiana*, x (1876), 269–81.

6196 GRIFFIN (RALPH). 'The leper's hospital at Swainestrey'. *Archaeol.
Cantiana*, xxxiv (1920), 63–78.

Lancaster

6197 AN EDITION OF THE CARTULARY OF BURSCOUGH PRIORY.
Ed. by A. N. Webb. Chetham Soc. Manchester. 1970.

6198 THE CHARTULARY OF COCKERSAND ABBEY, of the Premonstratensian order. Ed. by William Farrer. Chetham Soc. 3 vols. in 7 pts.
Manchester. 1898–1909.

Contains mainly charters of the thirteenth century.

6199 THE COUCHER BOOK OF FURNESS ABBEY. Ed. by John C.
Atkinson and John Brownbill. Chetham Soc. 2 vols. in 6 pts. New Ser. ix, xi,

xiv, lxxiv, lxxvi, lxxviii (1886–1919). For transcript of the lost folio 70, see Cyril T. Flower in *Chetham Miscellanies*, New Ser. vi (1935), 1–4.

6200 BECK (THOMAS A.). Annales Furnesienses: history and antiquities of the abbey of Furness. Lond. etc. 1844.

Chap. ii The Cistercian monks. Chap. iii History of the abbey. App. Table of contents of the chartulary, and other records.

6201 MATERIALS FOR THE HISTORY OF THE CHURCH OF LANCASTER. Ed. by William O. Roper. Chetham Soc. 4 vols. Manchester. 1892–1906.

Vols. i–ii comprise mainly charters of the thirteenth and fourteenth centuries, from the chartulary of the priory of St. Mary, Lancaster, with a translation; vols. iii–iv, extracts from church books and registers, etc.

6202 DOCUMENTS RELATING TO THE PRIORY OF PENWOR-THAM AND OTHER POSSESSIONS IN LANCASHIRE OF THE ABBEY OF EVESHAM (Wm. I–Hen. VIII). Ed. by William A. Hulton. Chetham Soc. xxx (1853).

6203 THE COUCHER BOOK, OR CHARTULARY, OF WHALLEY ABBEY. Ed. by W. A. Hulton. Chetham Soc. 4 vols. Manchester. 1847–9.

Contains charters, etc., of the thirteenth, fourteenth, and fifteenth centuries.

6204 WHITAKER (THOMAS D.). The history of the original parish of Whalley and the honour of Clitheroe. Blackburn. 1801. 4th edn. By J. G. Nichols and P. A. Lyons. 2 vols. Lond. 1872–6.

Vol. i contains many records relating to the abbey of Whalley.

6205 EARLY CHARTERS OF THE KNIGHTS HOSPITALLERS RELATING TO MUCH WOOLTON, NEAR LIVERPOOL [*c.* 1180–1230, with a translation]. Ed. by Robert Gladstone. *Hist. Soc. of Lancs. and Ches. Trans.* liv (1904), 173–96.

6206 FRANCE (R. S.). 'A rental of the Lancashire lands of the hospital of St. John of Jerusalem.' *Lancs. and Ches. Antiq. Soc. Trans.*, lviii (1947), 57–70.

LEICESTER

See Nichols, *County of Leicester* (No. 1714).

6207 JACK (SYBIL). 'Monastic lands in Leicestershire and their administration on the eve of the dissolution'. *Leics. Archaeol. Soc. Trans.* xli (1965–6), 9–40.

6208 THOMPSON (ALEXANDER HAMILTON). The abbey of St. Mary of the Meadows. Leics. Archaeol. Soc. 1949.

6209 THOMPSON (A. H.). A calendar of charters and other documents belonging to the hospital of William Wyggeston at Leicester. Leicester. 1933.

6210 THOMPSON (A. H.). The history of the hospital and college of the Annunciation of St. Mary in the Newarke, Leicester. Leicester. 1937.

A revised and enlarged edition of articles which had appeared in *A.A.S.R.P.*, xxxii (1913–14), 245–92, 351–402; xxxiii (1915–16), 178–215, 412–72.

6211 THOMPSON (A. H.). 'The monasteries of Leicestershire in the fifteenth century'. *Leics. Archaeol. Soc. Trans.* xi (1913), 99–108.

LINCOLNSHIRE

6212 (BURWELL). 'Les Possessions anglaises de l'abbaye de la Sauve-Majeure: le prieuré de Burwell (Lincolnshire)'. By J. P. Trabut-Cussac. *Bull. philol.-hist. du Comité des Travaux historiques et scientifiques.* Année 1957 (1958), 137–83.

6213 THE ESTATES OF CROWLAND ABBEY: A study in manorial organization. By Frances M. Page. Cambr. 1934.

App. i, pp. 159–72: Charters and extracts.
App. ii, pp. 174–330: Account Rolls.
App. iii, pp. 331–448: Court Rolls.

6214 HISTORY AND ANTIQUITIES OF CROYLAND ABBEY in (Richard Gough) *Bibliotheca Topographica Britannica* (No. 1505) iii, no. xi (1783).

The appendix contains charters, extracts from the abbey registers, etc. See also Nos. 2310, 2900.

6215 ENGLISH (HENRY S.). Crowland and Burgh: a light on the historians and on the history of Crowland abbey and the monastery at Peterborough, to 1193. 3 vols. Lond. 1871.

6216 TRANSCRIPTS OF CHARTERS RELATING TO GILBERTINE HOUSES OF SIXLE, ORMSBY, CATLEY, BULLINGTON AND AL-VINGHAM. Ed. and trans. (from K. R. Memo Rolls) by Frank M. Stenton. Lincoln Rec. Soc. xviii (1922).

6217 BROOKS (FREDERICK W.). 'The hospital of the Holy Innocents without Lincoln'. *Asso. Archit. Socs. Lincs.–Northants. Reports and Papers*, xlii for 1935 (1937), 157–88.

6218 CHRONICLE OF LOUTH PARK ABBEY (No. 2831).

6219 ABSTRACTS OF THE DEEDS AND CHARTERS RELATING TO REVESBY ABBEY, 1142–1539. By Edward Stanhope. Horncastle. 1889.

6220 CHARTERS RELATING TO THE PRIORY OF SEMPRINGHAM. Ed. by E. M. Poynton. *Genealogist*, New Ser. xv (1899), 158–61, 221–7; xvi (1900), 76–83, 153–8, 223–8; xvii (1901), 29–35, 164–8, 232–9.

Mainly of the twelfth century. M. D. Knowles, 'The revolt of the lay brothers of Sempringham', *E.H.R.* l (1935), 465–87.

6221 THE THORNTON CHRONICLE (extracts from a compilation made in 1532). By Kathleen Major. *Archaeol. Jour.* ciii (1946), 174–8.

6222 VISITATIONS OF RELIGIOUS HOUSES IN THE DIOCESE OF LINCOLN from the registers of Richard Flemyng and William Gray (1420–49). Ed. by A. Hamilton Thompson. Cant.–York Soc. xvii (1915); xxiv (1919); xxxiii (1927); and Lincoln Record Soc. 1914, 1918, 1929.

The first volume contains an important introduction on visitations in general, on monastic houses in Lincoln diocese, and on the Lincoln chapter of 1432. See also A. H. Thompson, 'Visitations of religious houses by William Alnwick, bishop of Lincoln, 1436–49', *Soc. Antiq. Procs.* 2nd Ser. xxvi (1914), 89–103.

LONDON AND MIDDLESEX

6223 HOPE (WILLIAM ST. J.). The history of the London Charterhouse from its foundation until the suppression of the monastery. Lond. 1925.

6224 KNOWLES (DAVID) and GRIMES (WILLIAM F.). Charterhouse: the medieval foundation in the light of recent discoveries. Lond. 1954.

The architectural foundations and a brief history of the medieval Charterhouse.

6225 CARTULARY OF HOLY TRINITY, ALDGATE. Ed. by Gerald A. J. Hodgett. London Record Soc. Pubns. vii (1971).

A calendar in English of charters, wills, pleas in the husting, etc. (1042–1426).

6226 BOOK (THE) OF THE FOUNDATION OF ST. BARTHOLO-MEW'S IN LONDON, the church belonging to the priory of the same in West Smithfield. Ed. by Norman Moore in *St. Bartholomew's Hospital Reports*, ed. by W. S. Church and John Langton, xxi (1885), pp. xxxix–cix. Also in E.E.T.S., Orig. Ser. clxiii (1923).

An old English translation (*c.* 1400) of the *Liber Fundacionis Ecclesiae S. Bartholomei*, 1123–43, which was written about 1180. It deals mainly with the life and miracles of Rahere, the first prior of St. Bartholomew.

6227 MOORE (NORMAN). The history of St. Bartholomew's hospital. 2 vols. Lond. 1918.

Moore quotes many documents.

6228 WEBB (EDWARD A.). The records of St. Bartholomew's priory and the church and parish of St. Bartholomew the Great, West Smithfield. 2 vols. Lond. 1921.

6229 CARTULARY OF ST. MARY CLERKENWELL. Ed. by William O. Hassall. R.H.S. Camden Ser. 3rd Ser. lxxi (1949).

The charters run almost exclusively from the mid twelfth to the mid thirteenth century. See W. O. Hassall, 'Two papal bulls for St. Mary, Clerkenwell', *E.H.R.* lvii (1942), 97–101; and idem, 'The Dorset properties of the nunnery of St. Mary, Clerkenwell', *Dorset Nat. Hist. and Archaeol. Soc. Procs.* lxviii for 1946 (1947), 43–51; idem, 'The Cambridgeshire properties . . . Clerkenwell', *Cambr. Antiq. Soc. Procs.* xlii (1948), 30–40. J. H. Round, 'The foundation of the priories of St. Mary and of St. John, Clerkenwell', *Archaeologia*, lvi (1899), 233–8.

6230 (DUCAREL, A. C.). History of the royal hospital and collegiate church of St. Katharine near the Tower of London. *Bibliotheca Topog. Britannica* (No. 1505), ii, no. v.

LONDON: WESTMINSTER ABBEY

Hist. MSS. Comm. Report, i. 94–7; iv. 171–99. See also No. 6838, churchwardens' accounts; No. 6345, papal visitation; No. 4545, testamentary records.

6231 ABSTRACT OF CHARTERS AND OTHER DOCUMENTS CONTAINED IN A CARTULARY OF THE ABBEY OF ST. PETER, WESTMINSTER, in the possession of Samuel Bentley. Lond. 1836.

For a customary of St. Peter's, see No. 6179.

6232 DOCUMENTS ILLUSTRATING THE RULE OF WALTER DE WENLOK, abbot of Westminster, 1283–1307. Ed. by Barbara F. Harvey. R.H.S. Camden 4th Ser. ii (1965).

Ernest H. Pearce, *Walter de Wenlock*. (Lond. 1920).

6233 FLETE (JOHN). History of Westminster abbey (to 1386). Notes and documents relating to Westminster Abbey. Ed. by J. Armitage Robinson. Cambr. 1909.

Flete was a Westminster monk from 1420 to 1465. Robinson's edition contains an appendix of charters.

6234 CHAPLAIS (PIERRE). 'Original charters of Herbert and Gervase, abbots of Westminster, 1121–57'. *D. M. Stenton Miscellany* (No. 1453), pp. 89–110.

6235 GALBRAITH (VIVIAN H.). 'A visitation of Westminster in 1444'. *E.H.R.* xxxvii (1922), 83–8.

This was a special visitation ordered by the General Chapter and the pope.

6236 HARMER (FLORENCE E.). 'Three Westminster writs of Edward the Confessor'. *E.H.R.* li (1936), 97–103.

6237 HARVEY (BARBARA F.). 'Abbot Gervase de Blois and the fee farms of Westminster abbey (1138–58)'. *B.I.H.R.* xl (1967), 127–42. Idem, 'The leasing of the abbot of Westminster's demesnes in the later Middle Ages'. *Econ. H.R.* 2nd Ser. xxii (1969), 17–27.

6238 INVENTORY OF THE VESTRY IN WESTMINSTER ABBEY IN 1388. Ed. by John Wickham Legg. *Archaeologia*, lii (1890), 195–286.

6239 THE LETTERS OF OSBERT OF CLARE, PRIOR OF WESTMINSTER. Ed. by Edward W. Williamson, with a biography by J. Armitage Robinson. Oxf. 1929.

6240 SCHOLZ (BERNHARD W.). 'Two forged charters from Westminster abbey'. *E.H.R.* lxxvi (1961), 466–78.

6241 SULCARD OF WESTMINSTER. 'Prologus de construccione Westmonasterii', ed. by B. W. Scholz. *Traditio*, xx (1964), 59–80; text, 80–91.

A brief history of the abbey, written between c. 1076 and 1085. See No. 2171.

6242   CARPENTER (EDWARD), ed. A house of kings. The official history of Westminster abbey. Lond. and N.Y. 1966.

Pp. 3–*c.* 92 of this handsomely illustrated volume deal with the medieval period.

6243   PEARCE (ERNEST H.). The monks of Westminster: being a register of brethren of the convent from the time of the Confessor to the dissolution. Cambr. 1916.

6244   PEARCE (E. H.). William of Colchester, abbot of Westminster. (d. 1420) Lond. 1915. Idem, Walter de Wenlock, abbot of Westminster (d. 1307). Lond. 1920.

6245   ROBINSON (J. ARMITAGE). The abbot's house at Westminster (with illustrative documents and notes). Cambr. 1912.

6246   ROBINSON (J. A.). Gilbert Crispin, abbot of Westminster. Cambr. 1911.

Pp. 85–110 contains the text of Crispin's Life of Herluin, abbot of Le Bec. See *Eng. Hist. Docs.* ii. 626–31.

6247   ROBINSON (J. A.). 'Simon Langham, abbot of Westminster'. *Church Quart. Rev.* lxvi (1908), 339–66.

6248   ROBINSON (J. A.) and JAMES (MONTAGUE R.). Manuscripts of Westminster Abbey. Cambr. 1909. Cf. Tanner (No. 6250).

6249   STANLEY (ARTHUR P.). Historical memorials of Westminster abbey. Lond. 1868; 5th edn. 1882; Amer. edn. from the 6th Lond. edn. 3 vols. N.Y. 1888–9.

Ch. i: Foundation of the abbey. Ch. ii: The coronations.
Ch. iii: The abbey before the Reformation.

6250   TANNER (LAWRENCE E.). 'The nature and use of the Westminster abbey muniments'. *T.R.H.S.* xix (1936), 43–80.

Joseph Burtt, 'Some account of the muniments of the abbey of Westminster', *Archaeol. Jour.* xxix (1872), 135–50.

6251   WESTLAKE (HERBERT F.). Westminster Abbey. 2 vols. Lond. 1923.

MONMOUTHSHIRE

6252   CHARTES ANCIENNES du prieuré de Monmouth au diocèse d'Hereford. Ed. by Paul Marchegay. Les Roches-Baritaud. 1879 (25 charters 1069–1160). 'Les Prieurés anglais de Saint-Florent près Saumur, notice et documents inédits.' Ed. by Paul Marchegay. *B.E.C.* xl (1879), 154–94. (33 charters, papal bulls, etc. 1069–1488, relating mainly to the priory of Monmouth.)

Rose Graham, 'Four alien priories of Monmouthshire', *Brit. Archaeol. Assoc. Jour.* xxxv, pt. i (1929–30), 102–21.

NORFOLK

For the cathedral-priory of Norwich, see pp. 780–1.

6253   CELLARER'S ROLL, Bromholm priory, 1415–1416. Ed. Lilian J. Redstone. Norfolk Rec. Soc. xvii *Miscellany* for 1944 (1947), 45–91.

6254　CARROW ABBEY, its foundation, etc. (with appendices containing charters, extracts from wills, etc.). By Walter Rye. Norwich. 1889. See No. 4822.

6255　THE REGISTER OF CRABHOUSE NUNNERY. Ed. by Mary Bateson. *Norfolk Archaeology*, xi (1892), 1–71.

Contains an enumeration of donations to the house, a rental, etc. The material is mainly of the fifteenth century.

6256　A CARTULARY OF CREAKE ABBEY. Ed. by Arthur L. Bedingfield. Norfolk Record Soc. xxxv. 1966.

6257　A CELLARER'S ACCOUNT ROLL OF CREAK ABBEY, 5–6 Edward III. Ed. by George A. Carthew. *Norfolk Archaeology*, vi (1864), 314–59.

6258　ACCOUNT ROLLS OF CERTAIN OF THE OBEDIENTIARIES OF THE ABBEY OF ST. BENEDICT AT HOLME (19 Hen. VI and 16–17 Hen. VIII). By Richard Howlett. *Norfolk Antiq. Miscellany*, ii (1883), 530–49.

Translation only.

6259　REGISTER OF ABBEY OF ST. BENET OF HOLME, 1020–1210. Transcribed by J. R. West. Norfolk Rec. Soc. ii, iii (1932).

Vol. ii: Latin and English abstracts; vol. iii: introduction. See *Chronica minor Sancti Benedicti de Hulmo*, in appendix to *Chronica Johannis de Oxenedes* (No. 2816); and F. M. Stenton, 'St. Benet of Holme and the Norman Conquest', *E.H.R.* xxxvii (1922), 225–35.

6260　CARTER (EDWARD H.). 'The constitutions of the hospital of St. Paul (Normanspital) in Norwich'. *Norfolk Archaeology*, xxv (1935), 342–53.

6261　DICKINSON (JOHN C.). The shrine of Our Lady of Walsingham. Cambr. and N.Y. 1956.

NORTHAMPTONSHIRE

See Stenton, *Northamptonshire charters* (No. 451).

6262　DENHOLM-YOUNG (NOËL). 'An early thirteenth century Anglo-Norman MS.' (Chronicle of the nuns of Delapré). *Bodleian Quart. Rec.* vi (1931), 225–30.

6263　LUFFIELD PRIORY CHARTERS, pt. 1. Ed. by G. R. Elvey. Northamptonshire Record Soc. xxii (1968).

6264　THE BOOK OF WILLIAM MORTON, almoner of Peterborough monastery, 1448–1467. Transcribed by the late William T. Mellows. Ed. by P. I. King, with introduction by C. N. L. Brooke. Northamptonshire Rec. Soc. xvi (1954).

For translations of documents in the register of Abbot Richard Ashton, the contemporary abbot, see *Eng. Hist. Docs.* iv, nos. 418, 480, 482, 575, 678.

6265　CHRONICON PETROBURGENSE. Ed. by Thomas Stapleton. Camden Soc. 1849.

Fairly detailed financial and estate records. Compiled in the reign of Edward I by an unknown monk of the abbey of Peterborough. The chronicle begins in 1122, and for 150 years comprises brief entries relating principally to public affairs. The greater part of the work, A.D. 1273–95, pp. 20–155, relates mainly to lawsuits in which the abbey was involved. The appendix, pp. 157–83, contains a valuable survey of the manors of the abbey, 1125–8; together with a list of knights' fees held of the abbey, 1100–20. For these knights' fees, see J. H. Round, *Feudal England*, (No. 4005), pp. 157–68. For other chronicles of Peterborough, see Nos. 2834, 6268.

6266 CARTE NATIVORUM: A Peterborough Abbey cartulary of the fourteenth century. Ed. by Christopher N. L. Brooke and M. M. Postan. Northamptonshire Rec. Soc. xx (1960).

This cartulary is mainly a collection (of abstracts) of charters, compiled in the 1340s, from early thirteenth century to the 1330s. It is important for agrarian history, partly because it records sales of land by and to peasants of both free and villein status.

6267 HENRY OF PYTCHLEY'S BOOK OF FEES. Ed. by William T. Mellows. Northamptonshire Rec. Soc. ii (1927).

Deals with knights' fees of Peterborough abbey, c. 1400. See A. H. Thompson, 'A Peterborough cartulary', *E.H.R.* xxxiv (1919), 582–4. Mellows's introduction describes the cartularies of the abbey.

6268 HISTORIAE COENOBII BURGENSIS SCRIPTORES VARII. Ed. by Joseph Sparke, *Historiae Anglicanae Scriptores*, pt. iii, pp. 1–256. Lond. 1723.

Hugonis Candidi coenobii Burgensis Historia, A.D. 655–1177, pp. 1–94. Contains some passages relating to general history, most of which were taken from the A-glo-Saxon Chronicle. Hugh was a monk of Peterborough (d. c. 1175). His work was continued by Robert Swapham.

Roberti Swaphami Historia coenobii Burgensis, 1177–1245, pp. 97–122. Written between 1250 and 1262. Swapham or Swafham (d. c. 1273) was cellarer of the abbey of Peterborough. Continued by Walter de Whitlesey.

Walteri de Whitlesey Historia coenobii Burgensis, 1246–1321, pp. 125–216. Contains an extent of the manors of the abbey and escheators' accounts, 15 Edw. II, pp. 175–216.

Historiae coenobii Burgensis continuatio, per anonymum, 1321–38, pp. 217–37.

Historia vetus coenobii Petriburgensis, pp. 241–56: an abridged Anglo-French poetical version of the work of Hugh Candidus, to 1132, written about the end of the 12th century.

On the chronicles of Peterborough, see Felix Liebermann, 'Ueber Ostenglische Geschichtsquellen des 12. 13. 14. Jahrhunderts', in *Neues Archiv der Gesellschaft für ältere deutsche Geschichtskunde*, xviii (1892), 225–67. See also Mary Bateson, 'The English and the Latin Versions of a Peterborough Court Leet, 1461', in *E.H.R.* xix (1904), 526–8.

6269 THE HISTORY OF THE CHURCH OF PETERBOROUGH (with an appendix of charters). By Simon Gunton. Lond. 1686.

See H. S. English, *Crowland and Burgh* (No. 6215).

6270 THE PETERBOROUGH CHRONICLE OF HUGH CANDIDUS WITH LA GESTE DE BURCH. Ed. by William T. Mellows and A. Bell. Lond. 1949.

Mellows edited the chronicle; Bell edited *La Geste*. The chronicle of the abbey's history was compiled in the late twelfth century; *La Geste*, drawn up in the early fourteenth century, is a résumé in French of the Latin chronicle. W. T. Mellows and C. Mellows had translated the Chronicle for Peterborough Nat. Hist. Soc. 1941; 2nd edn. Peterborough, 1966.

6271 (PIPEWELL CHRONICLE). A short French chronicle of the reign of Edward II, followed by extracts from a register of Pipewell is described in M. V. Clarke, *Medieval Representation* (No. 3349), pp. 193–5.

NORTHUMBERLAND

Hodgson's *History of Northumberland* (No. 1775) contains many documents.

6272 CHRONICA MONASTERII DE ALNEWYKE (1066–1377, with a translation). Ed. by William Dickson. *Archaeol. Aeliana*, iii (1844), 33–44.

A brief chronicle of the lords of the barony of Alnwick and of the abbots of the monastery.

6273 CHARTULARY OF BRINKBURN PRIORY. Ed. by William Page. Surtees Soc. xc (1893).

Mainly grants to the priory, Hen. I–Rich. II.

6274 PRIORY (THE) OF HEXHAM, its chroniclers, endowments and annals. Vol. ii: The priory of Hexham, its title-deeds, black book, etc. 2 vols. Ed. by James Raine. Surtees Soc. xliv, xlvi (1864–5).

Annals of Hexham, etc.: vol. i, pp. i–cxci. Prior Richard's History of the church of Hexham, A.D. 674–1138: i. 1–62. Another edition in Twysden's *Scriptores* (No. 1124), pp. 285–308. In large part derived from Bede, Eddi, and Simeon of Durham.
Prior Richard's account of the Battle of the Standard: i. 63–106. See No. 2894.
Prior John's Continuation of the chronicle of Simeon, 1130–54: i. 107–72. See No. 2893.
Ailred of Rievaulx on the saints of the church of Hexham; i. 173–203.
Appendix of charters, letters, etc.: vol. ii, pp. i–clxviii.
The black book of Hexham: ii. 1–82: a rental of the lands of the priory, completed in 1479. Charters and other documents: ii. 83–169.

6275 CHARTULARIUM ABBATHIAE DE NOVO MONASTERIO ORDINIS CISTERCIENSIS. Ed. by J. T. Fowler. Surtees Soc. lxvi (1878).

Consists mainly of charters granted to the abbey of Newminster, 1137–1547.

6276 RAINE (JAMES). The history and antiquities of north Durham. Lond. 1852.

Contains copious extracts from account rolls and inventories relating to the religious houses of Holy Island and Farne, and to the parish and castle of Norham. There is an elaborate appendix of 1404 documents, mainly charters concerning the priories of Coldingham, Holy Island, Farne, etc. Until 1844 this section of Northumberland formed part of the county palatine of Durham (Nos. 1625–6).

6277 GIBSON (WILLIAM S.). The history of the monastery of Tynemouth. 2 vols. Lond. 1846–7.

Contains a valuable appendix of charters, etc.

NOTTINGHAMSHIRE

6278 THE BLYTH PRIORY CARTULARY. Summarized by R. T. Timson. *B.I.H.R.* xxxviii (1965), 223–4.

6279 THE DUKERY RECORDS: notes illustrative of Nottinghamshire history. By Robert White. Worksop. 1904.

Contains abstracts of chartularies of Newstead priory and Welbeck abbey, translations of records concerning Rufford abbey, Worksop, etc.

6280 LENTON PRIORY, ESTATE ACCOUNTS 1296–98. Ed. by F. B. Stitt. Thoroton Soc. Record Ser. xix (1959).

The accounts of the king's agents for 21 months when the priory was in the king's hands; they form a Minister's Account. John T. Godfrey, *The history of the parish and priory of Lenton* (Lond., 1884).

6281 NEWSTEAD PRIORY CARTULARY, 1344 and other archives. Trans. by Violet W. Walker. Ed. by Duncan Gray. Thoroton Soc. Record Ser. viii (1940).

See A. Hamilton Thompson, 'The priory of St. Mary of Newstead in Sherwood forest, with some notes on houses of regular canons', *Thoroton Soc. Trans.* xxiii (1920), 33–139.

6282 REGISTRUM CARTARUM PRIORATUS DE NOVO LOCO (Newstead). Ed. by Charles G. Young. Lond. 1831.

Gives only the titles of the instruments contained in the chartulary.

6283 VISITATIONS AND MEMORIALS OF SOUTHWELL MINSTER. Ed. by Arthur F. Leach. Camden Soc. xlviii (1891).

Latin transcripts from the *Liber Albus* and the chapter register.
Visitations of the Southwell collegiate church. 1469–1542: pp. 1–95.
Wills proved before the chapter of Southwell, 1470–1541: pp. 96–145.
Statutes of Southwell collegiate church, 1221–1335: pp. 201–16.

6284 RASTALL (WILLIAM D.). A history of the antiquities of the town and church of Southwell. Lond. 1787.

See A. H. Thompson, 'The cathedral church of the Blessed Mary, Southwell', *Thoroton Soc. Trans.* xv (1912), 15–62.

6285 THOMPSON (ALEXANDER HAMILTON). The Premonstratensian abbey of Welbeck. Lond. 1938.

OXFORDSHIRE

See Oxford colleges, Nos. 7061–82; also No. 6357.

6286 CARTULARY OF THE MEDIEVAL ARCHIVES OF CHRIST CHURCH (Oxford). Ed. by Noël Denholm-Young. Oxf. Hist. Soc. xcii (1931).

A calendar of deeds from various monasteries, especially valuable for the priories of Daventry (Northants.) and Wallingford (Berks.).

6287 BLOMFIELD (JAMES C.). History of the present deanery of Bicester. 8 pts. Lond. 1882–94.

Accounts of bursars, etc., of Bicester priory (1296–1481): ii. 136–205.

6288 THE CUSTOMARY OF THE BENEDICTINE ABBEY OF EYNSHAM in Oxfordshire. Ed. by Antonia Gransden. Corpus Consuetudinum Monasticarum. Siegburg (W. Germany), 1963.

A thirteenth-century MS. on the regulations of the monastery and the function of monks.

6289 EYNSHAM CARTULARY. Ed. by Herbert E. Salter. Oxf. Hist. Soc. xlix (1909); li (1908).

Vol. i contains charters, some Anglo-Saxon but mostly twelfth–fourteenth centuries; vol. ii mainly a series of inquisitions, c. 1360, concerning the manors farmed by the abbey. Vol. ii, pp. 255–371: Vision of the monk of Eynsham (a vision of the next world by a monk in a trance about 1200) written down by Adam the author of *Magna Vita Hugonis* (No. 5742). See Edmund K. Chambers, *Eynsham under the monks* (Oxf. 1936).

6290 ENGLISH REGISTER (THE) OF GODSTOW NUNNERY NEAR OXFORD, written about 1450 [containing many charters, mainly of the thirteenth and fourteenth centuries]. Ed. by Andrew Clark. 3 pts. E.E.T.S. Orig. Ser. cxxix, cxxx, cxlii. (1905–11).

6291 A COLLECTION OF CHARTERS RELATING TO GORING (PRIORY). Ed. by Thomas R. Gambier-Parry. Oxfordshire Rec. Soc. xiii–xiv (1931–2).

6292 CARTULARY OF OSENEY ABBEY. Ed. by Herbert E. Salter. 6 vols. Oxf. Hist. Soc. lxxxix, xc, xci, xcvii, xcviii, ci (1929–36). See No. 4479.

A valuable collection of charters.

6293 THE ENGLISH REGISTER OF OSENEY ABBEY, by Oxford, written about 1460. Ed. by Andrew Clark. 2 pts. E.E.T.S. Orig. Ser. cxxxiii, cxliv (1907–13).

6294 'ANNALS OF THE ABBOTS OF OSENEY'. Ed. by Herbert E. Salter. *E.H.R.* xxxiii (1918), 498–500.

6295 CARTULARY OF THE MONASTERY OF ST. FRIDESWIDE AT OXFORD. Ed. by Spencer R. Wigram. Oxf. Hist. Soc. xxviii, xxxi. 2 vols. (1895–6).

A collection of charters, 1004–1537.

6296 A CARTULARY OF THE HOSPITAL OF ST. JOHN THE BAPTIST. Ed. by Herbert E. Salter. 3 vols. Oxf. Hist. Soc. lxvi (1914), lxviii (1915), lxix (1920).

6297 THE SANDFORD CARTULARY. Ed. by Agnes M. Leys. Oxfordshire Rec. Soc. xix (1938), xxii (1941).

Latin Transcript 'of the only surviving cartulary of the English Templars, 12th and 13th centuries' (Mullins).

6298 THE THAME CARTULARY. Ed. by Herbert E. Salter. Oxfordshire Rec. Soc. xxv–xxvi. 2 vols. 1947–8.

The documents come largely from twelfth and thirteenth centuries (Mullins). A cartulary of Thame abbey is given on pp. 342–79 of Frederick G. Lee, *History, description and antiquities of the prebendal church of the Blessed Virgin Mary of Thame* (Lond. 1883), which also includes, pp. 15–87, extracts from churchwardens' accounts, 1443–1648.

SHROPSHIRE

See David H. S. Cranage, *Churches of Shropshire*, 4 vols. Wellington. 1901, 1912; and the documents in Eyton's *Antiquities of Shropshire* (No. 1801).

6299 THE COLLEGE OF ST. MARY MAGDALENE, BRIDGNORTH, with some account of the deans and prebendaries. By W. G. Clark-Maxwell and A. Hamilton Thompson. *Archaeol. Jour.* lxxxiv (1927), 1–87.

Lists the deans and canons from *c.* 1161 to 1545.

6300 EXTRACTS FROM THE CARTULARY OF HAGHMON [Haughmond abbey, Hen. II–Hen. VI]. *Collectanea Topog. et Genealogica* (No. 115), i (1834), 362–74.

R. A. Leighton, 'Extracts from the cartulary of Haghmon abbey, co. Salop', *Shropshire Archaeol. Soc. Trans.* i (1877), 173–216.

6301 EXTRACTS FROM THE CARTULARY OF ST. PETER'S ABBEY AT SHEWSBURY, comprising an index of the charters. *Collectanea Topog. et Genealogica* (No. 115), i (1834), 23–8, 190–6.

6302 ABSTRACT OF THE GRANTS AND CHARTERS CONTAINED IN THE CHARTULARY OF WOMBRIDGE PRIORY. By George Morris. *Salop. Archaeol. and Nat. Hist. Soc. Trans.* ix. 305–80; xi. 325–48; 2nd ser., i. 294–310; ix. 96–106; x. 180–92; xi. 331–46; xii. 205–28 (1886–1900).

SOMERSET

6303 HUGO (THOMAS). The medieval nunneries of the county of Somerset. Lond. etc. 1867.

6304 THOMPSON (E. MARGARET). A history of the Somerset Carthusians. Lond. 1895.

6305 TWO CHARTULARIES OF THE PRIORY OF ST. PETER AT BATH. Ed. by William Hunt. Somerset Rec. Soc. vii. 1893.

The documents extend from A.D. 672 to 1520, but most of them fall within the period 1066–1377. See a review by F. W. Maitland, in *E.H.R.* x (1895), 558–60; reprinted in his *Collected Papers* (No. 1482), iii. 17–20.

6306 TWO CARTULARIES OF THE AUGUSTINIAN PRIORY OF BRUTON AND THE CLUNIAC PRIORY OF MONTACUTE. Ed. by H. C. Maxwell Lyte and others. Somerset Rec. Soc. viii. (1894).

Contains an English abstract of the charters, which are mainly of the twelfth, thirteenth, and fourteenth centuries; and notes on the priors.

6307 A CARTULARY OF BUCKLAND PRIORY, 1152–1423. Ed. by Frederick W. Weaver. Somerset Rec. Soc. xxv. (1909).

English abstracts.

6308 ON THE CHARTERS AND OTHER ARCHIVES OF CLEEVE ABBEY. By Thomas Hugo. *Somerset. Archaeol. and Nat. Hist. Soc. Procs.* vi, pt. ii (1856), 17–73.

6309 ADAMI DE DOMERHAM HISTORIA DE REBUS GESTIS GLASTONIENSIBUS. Ed. by Thomas Hearne. 2 vols. Oxf. 1727.

William of Malmesbury's *De antiquitate Glastoniensis ecclesiae*: i. 1–122. (See No. 6316.)
De electione Walteri More abbatis Glastoniensis, (1456): i. 123–83.
Perambulations of Somerset forests (1298): i. 184–202.
Charters, etc., relating to Glastonbury (1173–1385): i. 228–77.
Adam of Domerham's *Historia* (1126–1290): ii. 303–596, made up largely of papal bulls, charters, pleas in eyre, etc. Adam was sacristan of Glastonbury abbey, *temp.* Edward I.

Appendix of documents: ii. 597–675.
See C. H. Slover 'William of Malmesbury and the Irish', *Speculum*, ii (1927), 268–83, for the twelfth-century self-advertising campaign at Glastonbury. H. P. R. Finberg, 'Sherborne, Glastonbury and the expansion of Wessex', *T.R.H.S.* 5th Ser. iii (1953), 101–24.

6310 FEODARY (A.) OF GLASTONBURY ABBEY [to 1342]. Ed. by F. W. Weaver. Somerset Rec. Soc. xxvi. (1910).

6311 GLASTONBURY ABBEY IN 1322. Ed. by Henry C. Maxwell-Lyte and Robin Flower. Somerset Rec. Soc. Collectanea, xxxix (1924), 1–34.

Translation of an account of inquest made by the king's agent while the temporalities were in the king's hands. The account is taken from the Exchequer Memoranda Rolls and Pipe Rolls.

6312 THE GREAT CHARTULARY OF GLASTONBURY. Ed. by Aelred Watkin. 3 vols. Somerset Rec. Soc. lix (1947), lxiii (1952), lxiv (1956).

Miscellaneous subject-matter from Anglo-Saxon period to about 1340 in this important chartulary. For brief analysis, see Mullins, *Texts*, pp. 433–4. Refer to Postan (No. 6318). See also Ian Keil, 'The chamberer of Glastonbury abbey in the fourteenth century', *Somerset Archaeol. & Nat.-Hist. Soc. Procs.* cvii (1963), 179–92.

6313 JOHANNIS GLASTONIENSIS CHRONICA SIVE HISTORIA DE REBUS GLASTONIENSIBUS. Ed. by Thomas Hearne. 2 vols. Oxf. 1726.

Extends from the earliest times to 1493; the part from 1320 to 1493 is very brief. The work contains many charters granted to Glastonbury, and some meagre notices of public affairs. The author, John, a monk of Glastonbury (*fl.* 1400), abridged Adam of Domerham's history of the abbey, 1126–1290, and continued it to about 1400. The work seems to have been carried on to 1493 by another monk of Glastonbury late in the fifteenth century.

6314 LIBER HENRICI DE SOLIACO ABBATIS GLASTON[IENSIS]: an inquisition of the manors of Glastonbury abbey, 1189. Ed. by John E. Jackson. Roxburghe Club. Lond. 1882.

A valuable rental.

6315 RENTALIA ET CUSTUMARIA MICHAELIS DE AMBRESBURY, 1235–52, et Rogeri de Ford, 1252–61, abbatum monasterii beatae Mariae Glastoniae. Ed. by Edmund Hobhouse and Thomas S. Holmes. Somerset Rec. Soc. v (1891).

This includes an excursus on manorial land tenures by C. J. Elton.

6316 WILLIELMI MALMESBURIENSIS DE ANTIQUITATE GLASTONIENSIS ECCLESIAE [A.D. 63–1126]. Ed. by Thomas Gale, *Scriptores XV* (No. 1100), pp. 289–335. Also ed. by Hearne (No. 6309); and in Migne's *Patrologia*, clxxix, 1681–1734.

Cf. W. W. Newell, in *P.M.L.A.* xviii (1903), 459–512. J. Armitage Robinson, *Somerset historical essays* (No. 1491), chaps. i and ii.

6317 ASHE (GEOFFREY). King Arthur's Avalon: the story of Glastonbury. Lond. 1957. N.Y. 1958.

6318 POSTAN (M. M.). 'Glastonbury estates in the twelfth century'. *Econ. H.R.* v (1953), 356–67. Reginald Lennard, 'The demesnes of Glastonbury abbey in the eleventh and twelfth centuries'. Ibid. viii (1956), 355–63. M. M. Postan, 'Glastonbury estates in the twelfth century: a reply'. Ibid. ix (1956), 106–18.

6319 ROBINSON (JOSEPH ARMITAGE). Two Glastonbury legends: King Arthur and St. Joseph of Arimathea. Cambr. 1926.

6320 WATKIN (AELRED). The story of Glastonbury. Lond. 1960.

A brief introduction by an authority.

6321 TWO CARTULARIES OF THE BENEDICTINE ABBEYS OF MUCHELNEY AND ATHELNEY. Ed. by Edward H. Bates. Somerset Rec. Soc. xiv (1899).

Mainly English abstracts of charters, etc., A.D. 725–1445.

6322 MUCHELNEY MEMORANDA, edited from a breviary of the abbey by Bertram Schofield, with an essay on Somerset medieval calendars by the dean of Wells (J. Armitage Robinson). Somerset Rec. Soc. xlii (1927).

'Miscellaneous items from the early 14th century to the dissolution.'

6323 STOGURSEY CHARTERS: Charters and other documents relating to the property of the alien priory of Stogursey. Ed. by T. D. Tremlett and Noel Blakiston. Somerset Rec. Soc. lxi (1949).

6324 THOMPSON (E. MARGARET). 'A fragment of a Witham Charterhouse chronicle and Adam of Dryburgh, Premonstratensian, and Carthusian of Witham'. *B.J.R.L.* xvi (1932), 482–506.

Pp. 496–506: *De vita et conversatione magistri Ade Cartusiensis secundum quod habetur in cronica domus de Witham*. A better text of the chronicle is found in Dom A. Wilmart, 'Maître Adam, chanoine Prémontré devenue Chartreux à Witham', *Analecta Praemonstratensia*, ix (1933), 207–32. On Witham, see Douie–Farmer edition of *Magna Vita S. Hugonis* (No. 5742), bk. 2, pp. 45–89; and E. M. Thompson, *Somerset Carthusians* (No. 6304). For Adam of Dryburgh, see No. 5962.

STAFFORDSHIRE
For the annals of Burton monastery, see No. 2763.

6325 THE PRIORY OF THE BLACK LADIES OF BREWOOD, co. Stafford: some charters, records, etc. assembled by Gerald P. Mander. Staffs. Rec. Soc. *Collections*, lxiii (1939).

6326 THE BURTON ABBEY TWELFTH CENTURY SURVEYS. Ed. by Charles G. O. Bridgeman. Wm. Salt Archaeol. Soc. *Collections*. 3rd Ser. xli for 1916 (1918), 209–300. Abstract of the contents of the Burton chartulary. By George Wrottesley. Ibid. 1st ser. v, pt. 1 (1884), 1–101.

Contains a survey or extent of the lands of the abbey, *temp.* Henry I, pleas in the royal courts, charters, etc., 1004–1437. For the Derbyshire portion, see *Derbyshire Archaeol. and Nat. Hist. Soc. Jour.* vii (1885), 97–153. Cf. Francis H. Baring. 'Domesday Book and the Burton Cartulary', in *E.H.R.* xi (1896), 98–102; and J. H. Round, 'The Burton Abbey Surveys', ibid. xx (1905), 275–89 (reprinted, Wm. Salt Archaeol. Soc. *Collections*, New Ser. ix (1906), 269–89).

6327 DESCRIPTIVE CATALOGUE OF THE CHARTERS AND MUNI-MENTS belonging to the Marquis of Anglesey, compiled by I. H. Jeayes. Staffs. Rec. Soc. *Collections*, lxi (1937), 1–195.

Deeds, etc., of the abbey of Burton-on-Trent with preface by Margaret Deanesly.

6328 CHARTULARY OF DIEULACRES ABBEY. Ed. by George Wrottesley. Wm. Salt Archaeol. Soc. *Collections*, New Ser. ix (1906), 293–365.

Contains charters, mainly *temp*. Henry III, from late copies. See J. M. Wagstaff, 'The economy of Dieulacres Abbey, 1214–1539', *North Staffs. Jour. of Field Stud.* x (1970), 83–101.

6329 CHARTULARY OF RONTON PRIORY. Abstracted by George Wrottesley. Wm. Salt. Archaeol. Soc. *Collections*, 1st ser. iv (1884), 264–95.

Contains mainly charters of the thirteenth century.

6330 CHARTULARY OF THE PRIORY OF S. THOMAS THE MARTYR, near Stafford. Ed. by F. P. Parker. Ibid. viii (1888), 125–201.

Extends from 1174 to 1416.

6331 STAFFORDSHIRE CHARTULARY. Ed. by Robert W. Eyton and George Wrottesley. Ibid. ii (1882), 178–276; iii (1883), 178–231.

A collection of charters relating to religious houses, etc. in Staffordshire, 1072–*c*. 1237., See also a chartulary of deeds, etc., relating mainly to North Staffordshire, 1200–1327. Ed. by Josiah C. Wedgwood. Ibid. xxxvi (1911), 416–48.

6332 STONE CHARTULARY: an abstract of its contents. By George Wrottesley. Ibid. vi, pt. i (1885), 1–28.

Mainly charters of the thirteenth century concerning Stone priory.

6333 CHARTULARY OF THE AUSTIN PRIORY OF TRENTHAM. Ed. by F. P. Parker. Ibid. xi (1891), 295–336.

Contains charters, *c*. 1100–1526.

6334 THE CARTULARY OF TUTBURY PRIORY. Ed. by Avrom Saltman. (Joint publication of) Staffs. Rec. Soc. and Hist. MSS. Comm. H.M.S.O. Lond. 1962.

The Tutbury cartulary, compiled under Prior Thomas Gedney (1433–58) contains about 340 documents, of which about sixty come from the twelfth century. A brief register is to be found in *Registrum cartarum prioratus Tutteburiensis*. By C. G. Young (Lond. 1831).

SUFFOLK

6335 THE CHRONICLE OF JOCELIN OF BRAKELOND, concerning the acts of Samson, abbot of the monastery of St. Edmund. Ed. and trans. by Harold E. Butler. Medieval Classics. Lond. and N.Y. 1949.

The well-known account of the history of the abbey for the late twelfth and early thirteenth centuries, centring on Abbot Samson. On the identity of Jocelin, see Davis (No. 6338), pp. li–lvii. The chronicle was also edited by John Gage (Rokewode) for the Camden Soc., Ser. i, vol. xiii (1840), and in Arnold's *Memorials* (No. 6341), i. 209–336. For other translations see Farrer and Evans (No. 52). The translation (1907) by L. C. Jane has been reprinted several times.

6336 FEUDAL DOCUMENTS FROM THE ABBEY OF BURY ST. EDMUNDS. Ed. by David C. Douglas. British Academy Records of Social and Economic History. viii (1932).

Prints the Feudal Book of Abbot Baldwin (1065–98) and charters and miscellaneous documents (1066–*c.* 1188). Prefaced with an important introduction, pp. xv–clxxi. See also D. C. Douglas, 'A charter of enfeoffment under William the Conqueror', *E.H.R.* xlii (1927), 245–7.

6337 THE HARLOW CARTULARY. By John L. Fisher. *Essex Archaeol. Soc. Trans.* New Ser. xxii (1940), 239–71.

A series of rentals and extents from the twelfth to fifteenth centuries, presumably compiled for the abbot of Bury St. Edmunds in 1429.

6338 THE KALENDAR OF ABBOT SAMSON OF BURY ST. ED-MUNDS and related documents. Ed. by Ralph H. C. Davis. R.H.S. Camden, 3rd Ser. lxxxiv (1954).

The kalendar, continuing Douglas (No. 6336) from 1182 to 1211, is 'a general inventory of revenues due from the hundreds of the Liberty of St. Edmund's on the basis of regalian rights'. It was drawn up between about 1186 and 1191. In this edition the kalendar is followed by 165 charters of Abbot Samson's time (1182–1211). Part of the kalendar is printed in John Gage (Rokewode), *History of Thingoe Hundred*, Introduction, pp. xii–xvii.

6339 LETTER-BOOK OF WILLIAM OF HOO, sacrist of Bury St. Edmunds 1280–94. Ed. by Antonia Gransden. Suffolk Rec. Soc. 1963.

6340 LIBER DE CONSUETUDINIBUS MONASTERII S. EDMUNDI. n.p. (1838).

6341 MEMORIALS OF ST. EDMUND'S ABBEY. Ed. by Thomas Arnold. 3 vols. Rolls Ser. 1890–6.

Various works on the life and miracles of St. Edmund: i. 3–208; ii. 137–250.
Annales S. Edmundi: 1032–1212, ii. 3–25. Also edited by Liebermann (Nos. 1108, 2772).
Three accounts of elections of abbots, 1213–1302: ii. 29–130; 253–9; 299–323.
Expulsion of Franciscans from Bury, 1257–63: ii. 263–85.
Conflicts between the abbot and the burgesses of Bury, 1327–31: ii. 327–61. See M. D. Lobel, 'A detailed account of the 1327 rising at Bury St. Edmund's and the subsequent trial'. *Suffolk Inst. Archaeol., Procs.* xxi (1933), 215–31.
Chronica Buriensis 1020–1346: iii. 1–73. See Antonia Gransden, 'The *Chronica Buriensis* and the abbey of St. Benet of Hulme', *B.I.H.R.* xxxvi (1963), 77–82; and her edition of the Bury chronicle (No. 2819). Fifteenth-century letters: iii. 241–79.
By-laws of the weavers of Bury, 1477: iii. 358–68.

6342 THE PINCHBECK REGISTER relating to the Abbey of Bury St. Edmund's. Ed. by Lord Francis Hervey. 2 vols. Brighton, Lond., etc. 1925.

Drawn up by Walter Pyncebeke, a monk of Bury St. Edmunds about 1333. Contains papal bulls, pleas before royal justices, charters, accounts, tenures, table of contents of first register of Abbot William Curteys, and miscellaneous materials. Cf. Douglas (No. 6336) and Davis (No. 6338).

6343 BATTELY (JOHN). Antiquitates Rutupinae et antiquitates S. Edmundi Burgi ad annum 1272 perductae. Oxf. 1745.

6344 ROWE (JOY). 'The medieval hospitals of Bury St. Edmunds'. *Medical Hist.* (London), ii (1958), 253–63.

6345 GOODWIN (ALBERT). The abbey of St. Edmundsbury. Oxf. 1931.

V. H. Galbraith, 'The East Anglian see and the abbey of Bury St. Edmund's', *E.H.R.* xl (1925), 222–8; R. H. C. Davis, 'The monks of St. Edmund 1021–1148', *History*, xl (1955), 227–39. M. R. James, 'On the abbey of S. Edmund at Bury' (the library and the church). Cambr. Antiq. Soc. Octavo Ser. xxviii (1895), 150–212. Rose Graham, 'A papal visitation of Bury St. Edmunds and Westminster in 1234', *E.H.R.* xxvii (1912), 728–39. For Bury's library, R. M. Thomson, *Speculum*, xlvii (1972), 617–45.

6346 THE REGISTER OR CHRONICLE OF BUTLEY PRIORY, SUFFOLK, 1510–1535. Ed. by Arthur G. Dickens. Winchester. 1951.

See 'Notes on Butley priory' in *Salter essays* (No. 1451).

6347 TWO RENTALS OF THE PRIORY OF THE HOLY TRINITY IN IPSWICH. *Temp.* Hen. III and Edw. I. Ed. by William P. Hunt. Ipswich. 1847.

6348 'A VISITATION OF ST. PETER'S PRIORY' (Ipswich) (between 1327 and 1336), by C. R. Cheney. *E.H.R.* xlvii (1932), 268–72.

6349 THE SIBTON ABBEY ESTATES: select documents, 1325–1509. Ed. by Anthony H. Denney. Suffolk Rec. Soc. ii (1960).

The management of the estates of a small Cistercian house. See also Brown in *D. M. Stenton Miscellany* (No. 1453).

SURREY
See No. 6357.

For the annals of Bermondsey and Waverley, see Nos. 2762, 2766; and for Bermondsey monastery, see Nos. 1467, 1471.

6350 CHERTSEY (ABBEY) CARTULARIES. Ed. by Montague S. Giuseppi and Patricia M. Barnes. 2 vols. in 3 pts. Surrey Rec. Soc. (Vol. i), 1933; (Vol. ii, pt. 1), 1958; (Vol. ii, pt. 2), 1963.

Sidney Painter, 'A synthetic charter of Chertsey abbey', *Medievalia et Humanistica*, iii (1945), 81–5. Reprinted in No. 1486.

6351 CHERTSEY ABBEY COURT ROLLS ABSTRACT: being a calendar of Lansdowne MS. 434 in the British Museum. Ed. by Elsie Toms; note by Hilary Jenkinson. Surrey Rec. Soc. (Nos. 38 and 48), xxi (1937–54).

The court rolls for 1–21 Edward III when John de Rutherwyk was abbot.

6352 HEALES (ALFRED). Records of Merton Priory. Lond. 1898.

See M. L. Colker, 'Latin texts concerning Gilbert, founder of Merton Priory', *Studia Monastica*, xii (1970), 241–71.

6353 CHARTULARY OF THE HOSPITAL OF ST. THOMAS THE MARTYR, SOUTHWARK, 1213–1525. Privately printed. 1932.

6354 HEALES (ALFRED). Tan(d)ridge priory and the Austin canons (with an appendix of records). *Surrey Archaeol. Collections*, ix (1885/8), 19–156.

6355 BRAKSPEAR (HAROLD). Waverley abbey. Surrey Archaeol. Soc. Lond. 1905.

SUSSEX

See Chronicon monasterii de Bello (No. 2838).

6356 CUSTUMALS OF THE SUSSEX MANORS OF THE ARCH-BISHOP OF CANTERBURY. Ed. by Brian C. Redwood and Arthur E. Wilson. Sussex Rec. Soc. lvii (1960).

6357 CUSTUMALS OF BATTLE ABBEY, 1283–1312. Ed. by Samuel R. Scargill-Bird. Camden Soc. 1887.

Contains extents and rentals of various manors in Sussex, Berks., Essex, Hants, Kent Oxfordshire, Surrey, and Wilts. Valuable.

6358 DESCRIPTIVE CATALOGUE OF THE ORIGINAL CHARTERS, MONASTIC CHARTULARY, MANORIAL ROLLS, ETC., constituting the muniments of Battle abbey. On sale by Thomas Thorpe. Lond. 1835.

This collection was bought by Sir Thomas Phillipps, for which see Munby (No. 973). See also Rose Graham, 'The monastery of Battle (Wm. I)', in No. 1481; V. H. Galbraith, 'A new charter of Henry II to Battle Abbey', *E.H.R.* lii (1937), 67–73; and Eleanor Searle, 'Battle abbey and exemption: the forged charters', *E.H.R.* lxxxiii (1968), 449–80.

6359 TRANSLATION OF A LATIN ROLL, dated 31 Edward III, relating to the liberties of Battle abbey. By John R. Daniel-Tyssen and Mark A. Lower. *Sussex Archaeol. Collections*, xxvi (1875), 152–92.

6360 THE OBEDIENTIARY ROLLS OF BATTLE ABBEY. Ed. by Eleanor Swift. *Sussex Archaeol. Collections*, lxxviii (1938). Eleanor Swift, 'Obedientiary and other accounts of Battle Abbey in the Huntington Library', *B.I.H.R.* xii (1935), 83–101. Eleanor Searle and Barbara Ross, trans. *Accounts of the cellarers of Battle abbey, 1275–1513* (Sydney. 1967).

6361 THE CHARTULARY OF BOXGROVE PRIORY. Ed. and trans. by Lindsay Fleming. Sussex Rec. Soc. lix (1960).

6362 CHARTULARY OF ST. MARY'S HOSPITAL, CHICHESTER [a calendar of its contents, mainly deeds, *temp.* Henry III]. By Adolphus Ballard. *Sussex Archaeol. Collections*, li (1908), 37–64.

6363 THE CHARTULARY OF THE PRIORY OF ST. PANCRAS OF LEWES (Sussex portion). Ed. by Louis F. Salzman. 2 parts. Sussex Rec. Soc. xxxviii (1933); xl (1935).

6364 THE CHARTULARY OF LEWES PRIORY: the portions relating to counties other than Sussex. Sussex Rec. Soc. 1943.

In this volume are included portions, printed by other societies, for Cambridgeshire, Norfolk, Surrey, Yorks., and (by the Sussex Rec. Soc.) for Wilts., Devon., and Dorset. See Mullins, *Texts* (No. 29), p. 461. V. H. Galbraith prints a dozen charters, which are also calendared elsewhere, in his 'Osbert, dean of Lewes', *E.H.R.* lxix (1954) 289–302. B. M. Crook, 'General history of Lewes priory in the twelfth and thirteenth centuries', *Sussex Archaeol. Collections*, lxxxi (1940), 68–96.

6365 DOCUMENTS RELATING TO LEWES PRIORY [fourteenth century], with translations. Ed. by J. R. Daniel-Tyssen. *Sussex Archaeol. Collections*, xxv (1873), 136–51.

6366 DOCUMENTS RELATING TO ROBERTSBRIDGE ABBEY. Ed. by C. L. Kingsford. Report on *the MSS.* of *Lord de L'Isle . . . at Penhurst Palace*, vol. i, pp. xii–xix and 33–171, H.M.C. Reports. lxvii (1925).

> G. M. Cooper, 'Notices of the abbey of Robertsbridge', *Sussex Archaeol. Collections*, viii (1856), 141–76.

6367 THE CHARTULARY OF THE PRIORY OF ST. PETER AT SELE. Ed. by L. F. Salzman. Cambr. 1923.

WARWICKSHIRE

6368 THE COVENTRY FORGED CHARTERS: a reconsideration (1100–1140). By Joan Lancaster. *B.I.H.R.* xxvii (1954), 113–40.

> See J. Tait in *Poole essays* (No. 1448).

6369 THE STONELEIGH LEGER BOOK. Ed. by Rodney H. Hilton. Dugdale Soc. Pubns. xxiv (1960).

> The Leger Book was compiled about 1393 by Abbot Thomas Pype; it consists of two parts: (*a*) The early history of the house, and (*b*) estate survey of about 1393 of peasant tenures, customs of the manor, court rolls, a rental, etc.

6370 MINISTERS' ACCOUNTS OF THE COLLEGIATE CHURCH OF ST. MARY, WARWICK, 1432–85. Ed. by Dorothy Styles. Dugdale Soc. xxvi (Oxf.). 1969.

6371 RECORDS OF WROXALL ABBEY AND MANOR. By John W. Ryland. Lond. 1903.

> The records, given a translation, are charters, rentals, surveys, court rolls, etc., c. 1150–1900.

WILTSHIRE
See Nos. 4777, 6357.

6372 BOWLES (WILLIAM L.) and NICHOLS (JOHN G.). Annals and antiquities of Lacock abbey. Lond. 1835.

> The appendix contains an abstract of the abbey chartulary, and other documents.

6373 CUSTOMS OF FOUR MANORS OF THE ABBEY OF LACOCK (Bishopstrow, Heddington, Hatherop, Lacock, *circa* 1260–80). Ed. by William G. Clark-Maxwell. *Wilts. Archaeol. and Nat. Hist. Soc. Magazine*, xxxii (1902), 311–46.

6374 REGISTRUM MALMESBURIENSE: the register of Malmesbury abbey. Ed. by J. S. Brewer and Charles T. Martin. 2 vols. Rolls Ser. 1879–80.

> Begins with public documents: Magna Carta, the forest charter, and statutes of the thirteenth century. Then follows a detailed account of the property of the abbey in Malmesbury and the neighbourhood: dues of the inhabitants of Malmesbury and a rent roll of the manors outside the town. Then come charters, A.D. 685 to the end of the thirteenth century.

6375 RENT ROLL OF THE ABBEY OF MALMESBURY, 12 Edward II. Ed. by J. Y. Akerman. *Archaeologia*, xxxvii (1857), 273–303.

6376 COLLECTIONS TOWARDS THE HISTORY OF THE CISTER-
CIAN ABBEY OF STANLEY. Ed. by Walter de Gray Birch. *Wilts. Archaeol.
and Nat. Hist. Soc. Magazine*, xv (1875), 239–307.

A small collection of charters, 1186–1363, and a calendar of documents of the abbey.

6377 REGISTRUM EPISTOLARUM STEPHANI DE LEXINGTON,
abbatis de Stanlegia et de Savigniaco. Ed. by Bruno Griesser. 2 pts. *Analecta
S.O. Cisterciensis* (No. 5928), ii for 1946 (1951), 1–118; viii (1952), 181–378.

6378 FIFTEENTH CENTURY CARTULARY OF ST. NICHOLAS'
HOSPITAL, SALISBURY, with other records. Ed. by Christopher Wordsworth. Wilts. Rec. Soc. 1902.

Charters, etc., 1214–1899.

6379 CRITTALL (ELIZABETH). 'Fragment of an account of the cellaress
of Wilton abbey, 1299'. Wilts. Archaeol. and Nat. Hist. Soc. Records Branch,
Collectanea, xii (1956), 142–56.

WORCESTERSHIRE

For the cathedral-priory of Worcester, see pp. 785–7.

6380 CHRONICON ABBATIAE DE EVESHAM AD ANNUM 1418.
Ed. by William D. Macray. Rolls Ser. 1863. Extracts, 1035–1236, ed. by Liebermann, in M.G.H. *SS.* xxvii. 422–5.

Bks. i–ii contain the life and miracles of St. Egwin, bishop of Worcester (d. 717). Bk. iii,
which sets forth the actual history of the abbey from 714 to 1418, was probably compiled
by Thomas of Marlborough, abbot of Evesham (1230–6), as far as the year 1214, and
from 1214 to 1418 by an unknown continuator. On its date and authorship, see
Knowles, *Monastic Order*, pp. 704–5. The work furnishes us with a vivid picture of the
inner life of a great monastery. Much attention is devoted to the struggle of the abbey
to secure exemption from the visitations of the bishop of Worcester, 1202–6; pp. 109–
200; and the constitutions of the abbey, 1214, are given in full on pp. 205–22.

6381 THE CHRONICLE OF EVESHAM ABBEY. Trans. by David C. Cox.
Vale of Evesham Hist. Soc. 1965.

This chronicle deals exclusively with monastic affairs from the twelfth to the fifteenth
century, then continued to 1539.

6382 DOCUMENTS RELATING TO THE PRIORY OF PENWORT-
HAM AND OTHER POSSESSIONS IN LANCASHIRE OF THE ABBEY
OF EVESHAM [Wm. I–Hen. VIII]. Ed. by William A. Hulton. Chetham Soc.
xxx. (1853). See No. 6202.

Includes papal and royal charters, and annals of the abbots of Evesham.

6383 ST. EGWIN AND THE ABBEY OF EVESHAM. By the Benedictines
of Stanbrook [Stanbrook abbey, Worcester]. Lond., etc. 1904.

See also R. R. Darlington, 'Aethelwig, abbot of Evesham', *E.H.R.* xlviii (1933), 1–22;
177–98. J. C. Jennings, 'The writings of Prior Dominic of Evesham', ibid. lxxvii (1962),
298–304.

6384 ANTIQUITATES PRIORATUS MAJORIS MALVERNE CUM CHARTIS ORIGINALIBUS EASDEM ILLUSTRANTIBUS EX REGISTRIS SEDIS EPISCOPALIS WIGORNIENSIS (1279–1314). Ed. by William Thomas. Lond. 1725.

Most of the documents here printed, app. 1–204, are taken from the register of Godfrey Giffard (No. 5837). James Nott, *Some of the antiquities of 'Moche Malverne'* [Great Malvern]. (Malvern, 1885).

6385 CHARTERS FROM ST. SWITHUN'S, WORCESTER. Ed. by J. Harvey Bloom. Worcestershire Hist. Soc. *Collectanea* (1912), 1–67.

6386 ANNALS OF THE HOSPITAL OF S. WULSTAN, or the commandery of the city of Worcester: with a chartulary of the said hospital (*c.* 1230–1513). By Frederick T. Marsh. Worcester, etc. 1890.

YORKSHIRE

See Farrer and Clay, *Early Yorkshire charters* (Nos. 4498–9).

6387 BURTON (JOHN). Monasticon Eboracense. York 1758. Idem. Appendix of charters, 1759.

Contains a detailed account of the lands of each religious house.

6388 CLAY (CHARLES T.). 'The early abbots of Yorkshire Cistercian houses', *Yorks. Archaeol. Jour.* xxxviii (1952–5), 8–43.

6389 DENHOLM-YOUNG (NOEL). 'Yorkshire monastic archives', *Bodleian Quart. Rec.* viii (1935), 95–100.

6390 DOCUMENTS RELATING TO DIOCESAN AND PROVINCIAL VISITATIONS (1407–52). No. 5849.

6391 MONASTIC CHANCERY PROCEEDINGS (Yorkshire), late fourteenth century to 1540. Ed. by John S. Purvis. Yorks. Archaeol. Soc. Record Ser. lxxxviii (1934).

6392 NOTES ON THE RELIGIOUS AND SECULAR HOUSES OF YORKSHIRE, extracts from the public records. By William P. Baildon. Yorks. Archaeol. Soc. Record Ser. xvii (1895); lxxxi (1931).

These notes are mainly abstracts of cases in the plea rolls relating to abbeys and priories from the time of Henry III to that of Henry VIII.

6393 WAITES (BRYAN). 'The monastic settlement of north-east Yorkshire'. *Yorks. Archaeol. Jour.* xl (1959–62), 478–95.

See also No. 5020 on the monastic grange as a factor of settlement.

6394 FOUR EARLY CHARTERS OF ARTHINGTON NUNNERY. Ed. by William T. Lancaster. Thoresby Soc. xxii. *Miscellanea* (vi) (1915), 118–28.

6395 MEMORIALS OF BEVERLEY MINSTER: the chapter act book of the collegiate church of S. John of Beverley, 1286–1347 (with extracts from registers of the archbishops of York). Ed. by Arthur F. Leach. Surtees Soc. xcviii (1898); cviii (1903). 'A fifteenth century fabric roll of Beverley minster'

(1445–46, with a translation). Ed. by A. F. Leach. *East Riding Antiq. Soc. Trans.* vi (1898), 56–103; vii (1899), 50–83. 'Sanctuarium Dunelmense (1464–1524) et sanctuarium Beverlacense (1478–1539)'. Ed. by James Raine. Surtees Soc. v (1837).

> On rearrangement of entries, see I. D. Thornley, 'The sanctuary register of Beverley', *E.H.R.* xxxiv (1919), 393–7. On the conflict between the archbishop of York and the canons of Beverley, 1381–89, see A. F. Leach, 'A clerical strike at Beverley in the fourteenth century', *Archaeologia*, lv (1896), 1–20.

6396 BOLTON PRIORY RENTALS AND MINISTERS' ACCOUNTS, 1473–1539. Ed. by Ian Kershaw. Yorks. Archaeol. Soc. Record Ser. cxxxii for 1969 (1970).

> The rental of 1473 gives rents with acreage; also a *compotus* for 1286–1325.

6397 EXTRACTS FROM THE ACCOUNTS OF THE PRIORY OF BOLTON, 1290–1325. Pp. 448–67 of Thomas D. Whitaker, *History and antiquities of the deanery of Craven*, edited by Alfred W. W. Morant. Leeds, etc. 1878.

6398 THOMPSON (ALEXANDER HAMILTON). 'History and architectural description of the priory of St. Mary, Bolton-in-Wharfedale', with some account of the canons regular of the order of St. Augustine and their houses in Yorkshire. Thoresby Soc. xxx (1928).

6399 ABSTRACTS OF THE CHARTERS AND OTHER DOCUMENTS contained in the chartulary of the priory of Bridlington in the East Riding of the county of York. Ed. by William T. Lancaster. Leeds. 1912.

> John S. Purvis, 'A foundation charter of Bridlington Priory', *Yorks. Archaeol. Jour.* xxix (1929), 395. W. Ullmann, 'A forgotten dispute of Bridlington priory: its canonistic setting', ibid. xxxvii (1951), 456–73.

6400 MEMORIALS OF THE ABBEY OF ST. MARY OF FOUNTAINS. Ed. by John R. Walbran and Joseph T. Fowler. 3 vols. Surtees Soc. xlii, lxvii, cxxx (1863–1918). Abstracts of the charters and other documents contained in the chartulary of the Cistercian abbey of Fountains. . . . Ed. by William T. Lancaster. 2 vols. Leeds. 1915.

> In the Memorials, vol. i contains two brief chronicles to about 1442, one of which was written about 1207; and documents relating to the history of the abbey 1132–1574. The chronicle (i, pp. 1–128) is entitled 'Hugo de Kirkstall, monachus Fontanensis, postea Kirkstallensis, narratio fundationis de fundatione Fontanis monasterii'. It is partly edited in Dugdale, *Monasticon*, v. 292–306. Vol. ii contains royal charters, papal privileges, etc. Vol. iii consists of bursar's books 1456–9 and memorandum book of Thomas Swynton 1446–58. Lancaster's Abstracts are from a fifteenth-century chartulary and include royal, papal, and episcopal charters. (Davis.) For architectural history, see W. H. St.John Hope, 'Fountains abbey', *Yorks. Archaeol. Soc. Jour.* xv (1900), 269–402. See also 'The disputed election 1410–16', in *Rose Graham essays* (No. 1437 and 1474); and Denis Bethell, 'The foundation of Fountains abbey and the state of St. Mary's, York in 1132', *J.E.H.* xvii (1966), 11–27; and L. G. D. Baker, 'The genesis of English Cistercian chronicles: the foundation history of Fountains abbey', *Analecta S. O. Cisterciensis* (No. 5928), xxv (1969–70), 14–41 (to be continued).

6401 CARTULARIUM PRIORATUS DE GYSEBURNE [Guisborough].
Ebor. dioeceseos ordinis S. Augustini. Ed. by William Brown. 2 vols. Surtees
Soc., lxxxvi (1889), lxxxix (1894).

Contains mainly grants to the priory; extracts from the registers of the archbishops of
York; ii. 358–411; and a rent roll of the priory, c. 1300; ii. 412–50.

6402 THOMPSON (ALEXANDER HAMILTON). 'The monastic settle-
ment at Hackness and its relation to the abbey of Whitby'. *Yorks. Archaeol. Jour.*
xxvii (1924), 388–407.

6403 THE CHARTULARY OF THE AUGUSTINIAN PRIORY OF ST.
JOHN THE EVANGELIST OF THE PARK OF HEALAUGH. Ed. by John
S. Purvis. Yorks. Archaeol. Soc. Record Ser. xcii (1936).

6404 TWO CHARTERS ISSUED TO KIRKLEES PRIORY. Ed. by
Charles T. Clay. *Yorks. Archaeol. Jour.* xxxviii (1952–5), 335–8.

6405 CHARTERS RELATING TO POSSESSIONS OF KIRKSTALL
ABBEY IN ALLERTON. Ed. by F. R. Kitson and others. Thoresby Soc.
Miscellanea, ii (1895), 42–59, 81–116. [sixty-four charters 1210–1525]. 'Foundation of Kirkstall abbey'. Ed. by E. K. Clark. Ibid. ii. 169–208. 'The coucher
book of the Cistercian abbey of Kirkstall in the West Riding of the county of
York'. Ed. by W. T. Lancaster and W. P. Baildon. Thoresby Soc. Pubns. viii
(1904) (charters, final concords, pleas, papal bulls, etc., c. 1150–1368). 'A rent
roll of Kirkstall abbey (1459)'. Ed. by John Stansfeld. Thoresby Soc. *Miscellanea*,
i (1891), 1–21. 'The Kirkstall abbey chronicles'. Ed. by John Taylor. Thoresby
Soc., Pubns. xlii (1952).

The Kirkstall chronicles are (*a*) a long chronicle from Vortigern to 1360, of part of
which Taylor gives only an English translation; and (*b*) a short chronicle mainly of
Richard II's reign, of which M. V. Clarke and N. Denholm-Young printed about two-
thirds in *B.J.R.L.* xv (1931), 100–37; and of which Taylor gives the complete text
with a translation. For the architecture, see W. H. St. John Hope and John Bilson,
'Architectural description of Kirkstall abbey', Thoresby Soc. Pubns. xvi (1907); and
T. A. Hume and D. E. Owen, 'Kirkstall abbey excavations, 1950–1954', ibid. xliii
(1955), 1–82.

6406 GRAHAM (ROSE). 'The finance of Malton priory 1244–57'. *T.R.H.S.*,
New Ser. xviii (1904), 131–56. Reprinted in No. 1471.

6407 CHARTERS OF ST. ANDREW'S PRIORY IN THE PARISH OF
MARRIGG ((Marrick), Hen. II–Hen. VIII). *Collectanea Topog. et Genealogica*
(No. 115), v. 100–124, 221–59.

6408 DOCUMENTS RELATING TO THE FOUNDATION AND
ANTIQUITIES OF THE COLLEGIATE CHURCH OF MIDDLEHAM
(1477–1786). Ed. by William Atthill. Camden Soc. xxxviii (1847).

For the statutes of this secular house, 1478, see the *Archaeol. Jour.* xiv (1857), 160–70.

6409 ABSTRACTS OF THE CHARTULARIES OF THE PRIORY OF
MONKBRETTON. By John W. Walker. Yorks. Archaeol. Soc. Record Ser.
lxvi (1924).

J. S. Purvis, 'New light on the chartularies of Monkbretton priory', *Yorks. Archaeol.*

Jour. xxxvii (1951), 67–71. J. W. Walker, *An historical and architectural description of the priory of St. Mary Magdalene of Monk Bretton*, Yorks. Archaeol. Soc. Extra vol. v (1926).

6410 EXTENT OF MONK FRISTON, 1320. Ed. by Terence A. M. Bishop. Yorks. Archaeol. Soc. Record Ser. xcix. *Miscellanea*, iv (1937), 39–72.

6411 A FIFTEENTH CENTURY RENTAL OF NOSTELL PRIORY. Ed. by William T. Lancaster. Yorks. Archaeol. Soc. Record Ser. lxi. *Miscellanea*, i (1920), 108–35. The chartulary of Tockwith alias Scokirk, a cell to the priory of Nostell. Ibid. lxxx. *Miscellanea*, iii (1931), 149–206; 223–27.

6412 CHARTULARY OF ST. JOHN OF PONTEFRACT (*c.* 1090–1258). Ed. by Richard Holmes. 2 vols. Yorks. Archaeol. Soc. Record Ser. xxv (1899), xxx (1902).

C. T. Clay, 'The early priors of Pontefract', *Yorks. Archaeol. Jour.* xxxvi (1944–7), 269–87; 409–34; and xxxviii (1952–5), 456–64.

6413 CARTULARIUM ABBATHIAE DE RIEVALLE ORDINIS CISTERCIENSIS. Ed. by John C. Atkinson. Surtees Soc. lxxxiii (1889).

Contains charters of Rievaulx abbey, 1132–1539. Valuable.

6414 ACTS OF CHAPTER OF THE COLLEGIATE CHURCH OF SS. PETER AND WILFRID, RIPON, 1452–1506. Ed. by Joseph T. Fowler. Surtees Soc. lxiv (1875).

6415 MEMORIALS OF THE CHURCH OF SS. PETER AND WILFRID, RIPON. Ed. by J. T. Fowler. Surtees Soc. lxxiv, lxxviii, lxxxi, cxv (1882–1908). 4 vols.

Excerpts from chronicles, etc., grants to the church, papal bulls, etc., A.D. 657–1571, i. 1–332.
Extracts from the archbishops' registers at York, (1230–1538): ii. 1–182.
Fasti Riponienses, (1272–1885): ii. 184–354. Fabric rolls, (1354–1542): iii. 88–206.
Treasurers' and chamberlains' rolls, (1401–1560): iii. 207–330.
Cartulary (charters, 1114–1322): iv. 36–98.

6416 CARTAE XVI ad abbatiam Rupensem spectantes: xvi charters of Roche abbey (most of them seem to belong to the fourteenth century). Ed. by Sidney O. Addy. Sheffield. 1878. Roche abbey charters: transcripts by S. O. Addy, ed. by T. Walter Hall. *Hunter Archaeol. Soc. Trans.* iv, pt. 3 (1935), 226–48.

James H. Aveling, *The History of Roche abbey* (Lond. etc. 1870).

6417 THE CHARTULARY OF THE CISTERCIAN ABBEY of St. Mary of Sallay (Sawley) in Craven. Ed. by Joseph McNulty. 2 vols. Yorks. Archaeol. Soc. Record Ser. lxxxvii (1933); xc (1934).

J. McNulty, 'Salley abbey (1148–1536)', *Lancs.–Ches. Antiq. Soc. Trans.* liv for 1939 (1940), 194–204.

6418 COUCHER BOOK OF SELBY. Ed. by Joseph T. Fowler. Vol. 1, to which is prefixed (pp. 1–54) *Historia Selebiensis monasterii*, reprinted from

Labbe, *Nova bibliotheca* (i. 594–626); vol. ii, ed. by Charles C. Hodges. Yorks. Archaeol. and Topogr. Asso., Record Ser. x (1891), xiii (1893).

The *Coucher Book* is a chartulary 1070–1445.
The *Historia*, written about 1184, is anonymous.
　Cf. William Farrer, *Early Yorks. Charters* (No. 4498) i. 359–63; Barrie Dobson, 'The election of John Ousthorp as abbot of Selby in 1436', *Yorks Archaeol. Jour.* xlii (1967), 31–40.

6419 ACCOUNT ROLL OF SELBY ABBEY, 1397–8. *Yorks Archaeol. Soc. Jour.* xv (1900), 408–18.

6420 PRESENTMENTS OF THE JURIES AT THE COURTS OF THE ABBOT OF SELBY [1472–1533]. Ed. by James Raine. *English Miscellanies*, pp. 22–34. Surtees Soc. lxxxv (1890), 22–34.

6421 CHARTERS OF THE PRIORY OF SWINE IN HOLDERNESS. Ed. by George Duckett. *Yorks. Archaeol. and Topog. Asso. Jour.* vi (1881), 113–24.

They are of the twelfth and thirteenth centuries.

6422 CARTULARIUM ABBATHIAE DE WHITEBY ORDINIS S. BENEDICTI [1078–1547]. Ed. by John C. Atkinson. 2 vols. Surtees Soc. lxix (1879); lxxii (1881).

Lionel Charlton, *History of Whitby and of Whitby abbey* (York, 1779), which contains a translation of many charters relating to the abbey.

6423 STAPLETON (THOMAS). 'The ancient religious community of secular canons in York' [the church of the Holy Trinity], with biographical notices of the founder Ralph Paynell and of his descendants. *Royal Archaeol. Inst. of Great Britain, Memoirs of York*, pp. 1–230. Lond. 1848.

6424 THE CHRONICLE OF ST. MARY'S ABBEY, YORK. Ed. by Herbert H. Edmund Craster and M. E. Thornton. Surtees Soc. cxlviii (1934).

Pp. 3–74: Latin transcript of annals of the house with a few references to national affairs, for the period 1258 to 1326. The annals 1258–1312 seem to have been written after 1312; those 1312–26 seem to have been written currently.
Pp. 74–80: Lists of priors, etc.
Pp. 80–109: Custumal of St. Mary's.

6425 CHARTERS TO ST. PETER'S (ST. LEONARD'S HOSPITAL), YORK, AND TO BYLAND ABBEY. Ed. by Frederick W. Ragg. *Cumb.–Westm. Antiq.–Archaeol. Soc. Trans.* ix (1909), 236–51; 252–70.

E. CANON LAW IN ENGLAND, 1066–1485

1. *General Studies on Canon Law in England*

The general studies on canon law are reviewed in vol., i, pp. 168–70. Below the reception and application of the canon law in England from the eleventh to the fifteenth century are considered.

6426 BULLETIN OF MEDIEVAL CANON LAW. The Institute of Medieval Canon Law. New Ser. i+. Berkeley (Calif.). 1971+.

From 1955 to 1970 the *Bulletin* of the Institute was printed annually in *Traditio*; owing to its increased size, it has now become a separate annual publication. The *Bulletin* includes the annual report of the president of the Institute, some articles, and a highly useful select bibliography.

6427 ANONYMUS 'EBORACENSIS'. Ed. by Karl Pellens as Die Texte des Normannischen Anonymus. Wiesbaden. 1966. Also partly edited by George H. Williams, 'The Norman Anonymous of 1100 A.D.', *Harvard Theological Stud.* xviii (1951), 208–36. * Six of the tracts were printed by Heinrich Böhmer in M.G.H. *Libelli de Lite* (No. 1114), iii (1897), 645–87; and eighteen more of them in idem, *Kirche und Staat* (No. 6785), * pp. 436–97.

Böhmer attributed the authorship of these tracts to Archbishop Gerard of York; but Williams and most recent writers ascribe them to a Norman of Rouen about 1100, or perhaps to several authors. They comprise some thirty tractates which vigorously attack the hierocratic theories based on the Petrine doctrine. They form part and parcel of the numerous polemical literature which the contest between church and state under Gregory VII evoked.

Pellens's edition is the first edition of the full text of the Cambridge MS.; it is critically reviewed by Walter Ullmann in *Historische Zeitschrift*, ccvi (1968), 696–703. Among the recent commentaries are Cantor (No. 6728), pp. 174–97; Ruth Nineham, 'The so-called Anonymous of York', *J.E.H.* xiv (1963), 31–45; K. Pellens, 'The tract of the Norman Anonymous', *Cambr. Bibliog. Soc. Trans.* iv (1965), 155–65; and Ruth Nineham, 'K. Pellens' edition of the tract of Norman Anonymous', ibid. iv (1965), 302–9. Other commentaries can be found in *Repert. Font.*, ii. 359–60; and in *Eng. Hist. Docs.* ii. 675–8. Roger E. Reynolds, 'The unidentified sources of the Norman Anonymous, C.C.C.C. MS. 415', *Cambr. Bibliog. Soc. Trans.* v (1970), 122–31.

6428 THE CANON LAW OF THE CHURCH OF ENGLAND. Being the report of the archbishops' commission on canon law, together with proposals for a revised body of canons. Lond. 1947.

6429 COLLECTANEA STEPHAN KUTTNER. *Studia Gratiana*, post octava decreti saecularia. Collectanea historiae iuris canonici. Ed. by G. Forchielli and A. M. Stickler. Vols. xi–xiv. Bologna, 1967.

The papers specifically relating to England are:
(a) C. R. Cheney, 'An annotation of Durham Cathedral MS. C III 3 and unpublished decretals of Innocent III': xi. 37–68.
(b) J. W. Baldwin, 'A debate at Paris over Thomas Becket between Master Roger and Master Peter the Chanter': xi. 119–32.
(c) L. E. Boyle, 'Three English pastoral summae and a "Magister Galienus"': xi. 133–44.
(d) E. Rathbone, 'Roman law in the Anglo-Norman realm': xi. 253–71.
(e) C. N. L. Brooke, 'Archbishop Lanfranc, the English bishops and the council of London of 1075': xii. 39–59.
(f) H. G. Richardson, 'The marriage of Isabella of Angoulême: a problem of canon law': xii. 397–423.
(g) W. Ullmann, 'A decision of the Roman Rota on the benefit of clergy in England': xiii. 455–89.
(h) Charles Duggan, 'English decretals in continental primitive collections': xiv. 51–71.
(i) F. D. Logan, 'An early thirteenth century papal judge-delegate formulary of English origin': xiv. 73–87.

6430 DUGGAN (CHARLES). Twelfth century decretal collections and their importance in English history. Lond. 1963.

Charles Duggan, 'The reception of canon law in England in the later twelfth century'

Boston Proceedings (No. 1313) 359–90; C. Duggan, 'A Durham canonical MS. of the later twelfth century', *Stud. in Church Hist.* ii (1965), 179–85; C. N. L. Brooke, 'The canons of the English church councils in the early decretal collections', *Traditio*, xiii (1957), 471–9: C. Duggan, 'Primitive decretal collections in the British Museum', *Stud. in Church Hist.* i (1964), 132–44. For a critical review of Duggan's book, see P. Landau in *Zeitschrift für Kirchengeschichte*, lxxvi (1965), 362–75. Cf. Jacoba J. H. M. Hanenburg, 'Decretals and decretal collections in the second half of the twelfth century', *Tijdschrift voor Rechtsgeschiedenis*, xxxiv (1966), 522–99.

6431 GIBSON (EDMUND). Codex juris ecclesiastici Anglicani, or the statutes, constitutions, etc., of the Church of England. 2 vols. Lond. 1713; 2nd edn. Oxf. 1761. *

Deals mainly with church law since the Reformation, but also includes many medieval documents.

6432 HOLTZMANN (WALTHER) and KEMP (ERIC W.). Papal decretals relating to the diocese of Lincoln in the twelfth century. Lincoln Rec. Soc., Pbns. xlvii (1954).

Edited with an introduction on the sources by Holtzmann and with translations of the texts and an introduction on the canon law and its administration in the twelfth century by Kemp.

6433 JOHNSON (JOHN). Collection of ecclesiastical laws (translation only). 2 pts. Lond. 1720. New Edn. by John Baron. 2 vols. Oxf. 1805–51. *

6434 KEMP (ERIC W.). An introduction to canon law in the church of England. Lond. 1957.

Three lectures: the first on the Middle Ages, the second on famous canonists and writers on canon law, and the third of the nineteenth century.

6435 KUTTNER (STEPHAN) and RATHBONE (ELEANOR). 'Anglo-Norman canonists of the twelfth century: an introductory study'. *Traditio*, vii (1949–51), 279–358.

This masterly study forms a firm foundation for further detailed research. See also Kuttner's Wimmer lecture, *Harmony from dissonance: an interpretation of medieval canon law* (Latrobe, Pa. 1961).

6436 LYNDWOOD (WILLIAM). Provinciale, seu constitutiones Angliae, continens constitutiones provinciales archiepiscoporum Cant' a Stephano Langtono ad Henricum Chichleium, cum annotationibus J. de Athona. 2 pts. Oxf. 1679. *

The most authoritative digest of the medieval canon law of England, Lyndwood's work was completed in 1430 and was first printed at Oxford, without title, in the late fifteenth century. This edition was soon followed by others, for which see *D.N.B.* (No. 531), xxxiv (1893), 341. The best edition is that of 1679. On the contents and value of the work, see Maitland in *E.H.R.* xi (1896), 446–78 and his *Roman canon law* (No. 6437), pp. 1–50. J. V. Bullard and H. C. Bell, *Lyndwood's Provinciale*, (Lond. 1929), is a translation of a portion of that work. For commentary see C. R. Cheney, 'William Lyndwood's Provinciale', *Jurist* (Washington, D.C.), xxi (1961), 405–34; Emden, *Reg. Oxford* (No. 533) and *Reg. Cambridge* (No. 532). John of Acton's annotations or commentary on the constitutions of Otho and Ottoboni, papal legates in England in the thirteenth century, was compiled between 1333 and 1348. On Acton, see Emden, *Oxford* and Leonard Boyle, 'The *Summa Summarum* and some other English works of canon law', *Boston Proceedings* (No. 1313), 415–56, which is mainly concerned with Acton's contemporary, William of Pagula. For Pagula see Emden, *Reg. Oxford* and L. E. Boyle, 'The *Oculis Sacerdotis* and some other works of William of Pagula', *T.R.H.S.* 5th Ser. v (1955), 81–110.

6437 MAITLAND (FREDERIC W.). Roman canon law in the church of England: six essays (reprinted from the *E.H.R.* and the *Law Quart. Rev.*). Lond. 1898. *

I.   William Lyndwood.
II. Church, state, and decretals.
III. William of Drogheda.
IV. Henry II and criminous clerks.
V.   *Execrabilis* in the common pleas.
VI. The deacon and the Jewess.

Essays iv–vi are printed in his *Collected Papers* (No. 1482). The author contends, largely after a study of Lyndwood's *Provinciale*, that the canon law of Rome was binding on the ecclesiastical courts of England, a refutation of Stubbs's view (Nos. 6442, 6445). See also his *History of English law*, bk. i, ch. v; and his paper, 'Canon law in England, a reply to Dr. MacColl' (who opposed his views), in *E.H.R.* xvi (1901), 35–45; reprinted in *Collected Papers*, iii. 137–56; and see ibid. 65–77. Cf. J. H. Round, in *Contemporary Review*, lxxv (1899), 814–22; Arthur Ogle, *The canon law in mediaeval England* (Lond. 1912); L. T. Dibdin, in *Quarterly Rev.* ccxvii (1912), 413–36; H. W. C. Davis, 'The canon law in England', *Zeitschrift der Savigny-Stiftung, Kanonistische Abteilung*, iii. xxxiv (1913), 344–63, reprinted in (No. 1466), pp. 123–43; C. P. Sherman, 'A brief history of medieval Roman canon law in England', *Univ. of Pennsylvania Law Rev.* lxviii (1920), 233–58; S. E. Thorne, 'Le droit canonique en Angleterre', *Revue historique de droit français et étranger*, xiii (1934), 499–513; J. W. Gray, 'Canon law in England: some reflections on the Stubbs–Maitland controversy', *Stud. Church Hist.* iii (1966), 48–68. R. J. Schoeck, 'Canon law in England on the eve of the Reformation', *Mediaeval Stud.* xxv (1963), 125–47.

6438 NOONAN (JOHN T. S.). The scholastic analysis of usury. Cambr. (Mass.). 1957.

T. P. McLaughlin, 'The teaching of the canonists on usury (twelfth to fourteenth centuries)', *Mediaeval Stud.* i (1939), 81–147; ii (1940), 1–22.

6439 PHILLIMORE (ROBERT). The ecclesiastical law of the church of England. 2 vols. and supplement. Lond. 1873–6; 2nd edn. 2 vols. 1895.

Deals mainly with modern times.

6440 POWICKE (FREDERICK M.) and CHENEY (CHRISTOPHER R.). Councils and synods (see No. 6816).

6441 REICHEL (OSWALD J.). The canon law of church institutions. Vol. i. Lond. 1922.

6442 REPORT OF THE COMMISSIONERS APPOINTED TO INQUIRE INTO THE CONSTITUTION AND WORKING OF THE ECCLESIAS-TICAL COURTS. 2 vols. in 1. *Parl. Papers*, 1883, vol. xxiv. Lond. 1883.

Contains a good short account of the history of church courts to 1832, by William Stubbs, i. 21–51 (for his later views see No. 6445, especially the last edition), and cf. Maitland's refutation, No. 6437; and trials for heresy in England prior to 1533, also by Stubbs, i. 52–70.

6443 SELDEN (JOHN). The original of ecclesiastical jurisdiction of testaments, in his *Works*, iii. 1664–74. Lond. 1726.

See also his 'Disposition of intestates' goods', ibid. iii. 1676–85.

6444 SHEEHAN (MICHAEL M.). 'Canon law and English institutions; some notes on recent research'. *Boston Proceedings* (No. 1313), pp. 391–8.

6445 STUBBS (WILLIAM). Seventeen lectures on the study of mediaeval and modern history. Oxf. 1886; * reprinted, 1887; 3rd edition, with a new preface, 1900.

Chap. xiii–xiv: History of the canon law in England, with a prefatory note (in the 3rd edition) discussing Maitland's views.

6446 TIERNEY (BRIAN). Medieval poor law: a sketch of canonical theory and its application to England. Berkeley (Calif.). 1959.

6447 DER TRAKTAT DES LAURENTIUS DE SOMERCOTE KANONIKUS VON CHICHESTER ÜBER DIE VORNAHME VON BISCHOFSWAHLEN, 1254. Ed. by Alfred von Wretschko. Weimar. 1907.

6448 WAHRMUND (LUDWIG), ed. William of Drogheda, Summa aurea. *Quellen zur Geschichte des römisch-kanonischen Prozesses im Mittelalter*, vol. ii, pt. ii. Innsbruck. 1914. Richard Anglicus. Summa de ordine judiciario. Ibid. Vol. ii, pt. iii. Innsbruck. 1915.

For Drogheda, see the citations in Emden, *Reg. Oxford*. For Richard Anglicus, now identified as Richard de Mores, see the citations in *New Catholic encyclopedia* (No. 1271), xii. 482; and C. E. Lewis, 'Richard Anglicus: a *familiaris* of Archbishop Hubert Walter', *Traditio*, xxii (1966), 469–71. William H. Bryson, 'Witnesses: a canonist's view (Ricardus Anglicus)', *Amer. Jour. Legal Hist.* xiii (1969), 57–67.

2. *Judicial Relations with the Papacy*

6449 BRENTANO (ROBERT). York metropolitan jurisdiction and papal judge delegate (1279–96). Univ. California Pubns. in Hist. no. 58. Berkeley and Los Angeles. 1959.

6450 GRAVES (EDGAR B.). 'The judicial relations of the papacy with England in the Middle Ages'. Year Book of the American Philosophical Soc. (1954), 261–4.

Gives a brief report on surviving records of English cases tried in the *Sacra Romana Rota* 1464–1534.

6451 HELMHOLZ (RICHARD). 'Canonists and standard of impartiality for papal judges delegate'. *Traditio*, xxv (1969), 386–404.

6452 HERDE (PETER). Audientia litterarum contradictarum: Untersuchungen über die päpstlichen Justizbriefe und die päpstliche Delegationsgerichtsbarkeit vom 13. bis Beginn des 16. Jahrhunderts. 2 vols. Bibliothek des deutschen historischen Instituts in Rom. Tübingen. 1969–70.

See Barraclough (No. 5542). P. Herde, 'Papal formularies for letters of justice (13th to 16th centuries): their development and significance for medieval canon law'. *Boston Proceedings* (No. 1313), pp. 321–45.

6453 KELLY (H. A.). 'Canonical implications of Richard III's plan to marry his niece'. *Traditio*, xxiii (1967), 269–311.

6454 LA DUE (WILLIAM J.). Papal rescripts of justice and English royal procedural writs, 1150–1250. Pontificia Universitas Lateranensis Institutum Utriusque Juris, Theses ad Lauream, no. 155. Rome. 1960.

6455 McNULTY (JOSEPH), ed. Thomas Sotheron *v.* Cockersand Abbey: a suit as to the advowson of Mitton church, 1369–70. *Chetham Miscellanies,* vii. Chetham Soc. New Ser. c (1939).

> A transcript, in over 100 pages, of documents in Vatican Archives, Collectorie 417A, for a suit brought before the auditors of the Apostolic Palace. It provides an example of procedure in the Roman curia.

6456 MOREY (DOM ADRIAN). Bartholomew of Exeter, bishop and canonist: a study in the twelfth century. Cambr. 1937.

> Treats Bartholomew as papal judge-delegate, pp. 44–78; and prints some documents concerning cases, pp. 128–43.

6457 SAYERS (JANE). 'Canterbury proctors at the court of audientia litterarum contradictarum'. *Traditio*, xxii (1966), 311–45.

> The appendix, pp. 332–45, of this important article contains documents from the dean and chapter archives at Canterbury. See her paper 'Proctors representing British interests at the papal court, 1198–1415' in *Proceedings of the Third International Congress of Medieval Canon Law*. Strasbourg, 1968 (Vatican City, 1971), 143–63.

3. *Ecclesiastical Courts in England*

6458 BISHOP ALNWICK'S COURT BOOK (1446–52) in Thompson, *English Clergy* (No. 6804), pp. 206–46.

> See also the acts of the consistory court of Rochester (No. 4534).

6459 DEPOSITIONS AND OTHER ECCLESIASTICAL PROCEEDINGS FROM THE COURTS OF DURHAM, 1311 to the reign of Elizabeth. Ed. by James Raine. Surtees Soc. 1845. See No. 5676.

6460 DIDIER (NOËL). 'Henri de Suse en Angleterre (1236?–1244)'. *Studi in onore di Vincenzo Arangio-Ruiz* (Naples. 1952), ii. 333–51.

> See Southern, *Western Society* (No. 6722), pp. 128–9.

6461 ERSKINE (AUDREY M.). 'Ecclesiastical courts and their records in the province of Canterbury'. *Archives*, iii, no. 17 (1957), 8–17. J. S. Purvis, 'Ecclesiastical courts of York'. Ibid., pp. 18–27.

6462 FLAHIFF (GEORGE B.). 'The use of prohibitions by clerics against ecclesiastical courts in England'. *Mediaeval Stud.* iii (1941), 101–16. Idem, 'The writ of prohibition to court christian in the thirteenth century'. Ibid. vi (1944), 261–313; and vii (1945), 229–90.

> See also Norma Adams, 'The writ of prohibition to court christian', *Minnesota Law Rev.* xx (1936), 272–93.

6463 FOWLER (R. C.). 'Secular aid for excommunication'. *T.R.H.S.* 3rd Ser. viii (1914), 113–17.

The writ significavit in Chancery files in P.R.O. See No. 6473.

6464 GABEL (LEONA C.). Benefit of clergy in England in the later middle ages. Smith College Stud. in Hist. xiv. Northampton (Mass.). 1928–9. *

C. B. Firth, 'Benefit of clergy in the time of Edward IV', *E.H.R.* xxxii (1917), 175–91.
A. L. Poole, 'Outlawry as a punishment of criminous clerks', in *Tait essays* (No. 1455).
R. Génestal, Le *Privilegium fori* en France du décret de Gratien à la fin du xiv⁰ siècle. Paris. 1921. 1924. See also Cheney (No. 6504).

6465 GOTWALD (WILLIAM K.). Ecclesiastical censure at the end of the fifteenth century. Johns Hopkins Univ. Stud. Baltimore. 1927.

6466 GRANSDEN (ANTONIA). 'Some late thirteenth-century records of an ecclesiastical court in the archdeaconry of Sudbury'. *B.I.H.R.* xxxii (1959), 62–9.

6467 GRAVES (EDGAR B.). 'Circumspecte agatis'. *E.H.R.* xliii (1929), 1–20.

Deals with Edward I's writ to define jurisdiction between royal and ecclesiastical courts.

6468 HELMHOLZ (R. H.). 'Bastardy litigation in medieval England'. *Amer. Jour. Legal Hist.* xiii (1969), 360–83.

6469 HILL (ROSALIND). 'Public penance: some problems of a thirteenth century bishop (O. Sutton)'. *History*, New Ser. xxxvi (1951), 213–26. Idem, 'The theory and practice of excommunication in medieval England'. Ibid. xlii (1957), 1–11.

6470 HODGE (C. E.). 'Cases from a fifteenth century archdeacon's book'. *Law Quart. Rev.* xlix (1933), 268–74.

6471 HUNT (R. W.). 'A tuitorial appeal in the fourteenth century before the Court of Arches'. *Hist. Soc. Lancs.–Ches. Trans.* ci (1949), 47–61.

6472 JONES (WILLIAM R.). 'Bishops, politics and the two laws: the *gravamina* of the English clergy, 1237–1399'. *Speculum*, xli (1966), 209–45. Idem, 'The two laws in England: the later middle ages'. *A Jour. of Church and State* (Waco, Texas), xi (1969), 111–31. Idem, 'The relations of the two jurisdictions: conflict and cooperation in England during the thirteenth and fourteenth centuries'. *Stud. in Medieval and Renaissance Hist.* vii (1970–1), 79–210.

6473 LOGAN (F. DONALD). Excommunication and the secular arm in medieval England: a study of legal procedure from the thirteenth to the sixteenth century. Pontifical Inst. Stud. and Texts, no. 15. Toronto. 1968.

6474 MORGAN (MARJORIE M.). 'Early Canterbury jurisdiction'. *E.H.R.* lx (1945), 392–9.

6475 MORRIS (COLIN). 'A consistory court in the Middle ages' (Lincoln). *J.E.H.* xiv (1963), 150–9. Idem, 'From synod to consistory: the bishops' courts in England, 1150–1250'. Ibid. xxii (1971), 115–23.

R. W. Dunning, 'The Wells consistory court in the fifteenth century', *Somerset Archaeol. Nat. Hist. Soc. Procs.* cvi (1962), 46–61.

6476 MORRIS (COLIN). 'William I and the church courts'. *E.H.R.* lxxxii (1967), 449–63.

C. H. Walker, 'The date of the Conqueror's ordinance separating ecclesiastical and lay courts', *E.H.R.* xxxix (1924), 399–400.

6477 THE REGISTERS OF ROGER MARTIVAL, BISHOP OF SALIS-BURY (No. 5801), iii (1965): Royal writs. Cant. and York Soc. vol. lix.

6478 RICHARDSON (HENRY G.). 'Heresy and the lay power under Richard II'. *E.H.R.* li (1936), 1–28.

6479 RICHIE (C. I. A.). The ecclesiastical courts of York. Arbroath. 1957.

6480 SAYERS (JANE E.). 'A judge delegate formulary from Canterbury'. *B.I.H.R.* xxxv (1962), 198–211. Idem, 'The judicial activities of the general chapters'. *J.E.H.* xv (1964), 18–31, 168–85.

See Haas and Hall, *Early registers of writs* (No. 3499), pp. xxxiii–xl.

6481 SAYERS (JANE E.). Papal judges delegate in the province of Canterbury, 1198–1254: a study in ecclesiastical jurisdiction and administration. Oxford. Hist. Monographs. Lond. and N.Y. 1971.

See Morey, *Bartholomew of Exeter* (No. 6456).

6482 A SERIES OF PRECEDENTS AND PROCEEDINGS IN CRIMI-NAL CAUSES, 1475–1640, extracted from act books of ecclesiastical courts in the diocese of London. By William H. Hale. Lond. 1847.

6483 SHEEHAN (MICHAEL M.). Ius matrimoniale in Anglia in saeculo quartodecimo: exemplum diocesis Eliensis. Acta Conventus Internationalis Canonistarum Romae (1968). Vatican City. 1970, pp. 674–8.

'A brief survey of the seventy-five marriage cases in the *Registrum Primum* (1374–9) of the consistorial court of Ely'. See M. M. Sheehan, 'The formation and stability of marriage in fourteenth century England: evidence of an Ely register', *Mediaeval Stud.* xxxiii (1971), 228–63.

6484 SLATTER (M. D.). 'The records of the Court of Arches'. *J.E.H.* iv (1953), 139–53.

6485 WOODCOCK (BRIAN L.). Medieval ecclesiastical courts in the diocese of Canterbury. Oxford Hist. Ser. Lond. 1952.

6486 WOODRUFF (CHARLES E.). 'Notes from a fourteenth century act-book of the consistory court of Canterbury'. *Archaeol. Cantiana*, xl (1928), 53–64.

4. *Becket and his Contemporaries*

a. The Becket controversy

The quarrel between Henry II and Becket gave focus to the relationships between the crown and the papacy as well as between church and state in England. It resulted, of course, not only in the archbishop's dramatic murder but also in long-term consequences which produced numerous contemporary texts and volumes of modern commentaries.

Garnier's *Vie* and the nine biographies printed in Robertson's *Materials* (No. 6487) are contemporary works, written soon after Becket's death. Several of the biographers were intimate friends of Becket, or had been in close touch with him. Herbert of Bosham was a member of Becket's household; John of Salisbury was a loyal friend, and Gilbert Foliot an adversary of the archbishop. Grim, a secular clerk, happened to be visiting Canterbury at the time of the murder and wrote his account of Becket almost immediately thereafter. William Fitzstephen's 'Life' is regarded as the best of the contemporary biographies. Among the modern commentaries the most satisfactory biographical approach to Becket is to be found in the studies by Dom David Knowles (Nos. 6498-9).

6487 MATERIALS FOR THE HISTORY OF THOMAS BECKET. Ed. by James C. Robertson; and for vol. vii J. C. Robertson and J. B. Sheppard. 7 vols. Rolls Ser. 1875-85. Extracts from the various 'Lives' noted below were edited by Pauli in M.G.H., *SS.* xxvii. 17-42.

Vol. i. *Vita S. Thomae auctore Willelmo monacho Cantuariensi.*
Vol. ii. 'Lives' of Becket, by Benedict of Peterborough, John of Salisbury, Alan of Tewkesbury, and Edward Grim.
Vol. iii. 'Lives' of Becket, by William Fitzstephen and Herbert of Bosham. See No. 6518.
Vol. iv. Two contemporary anonymous 'Lives' of Becket, and the *Quadrilogus.* One of the anonymous lives was formerly ascribed to Roger of Pontigny. The *Quadrilogus* is a composite 'Life' drawn from earlier biographers. It exists in two forms: one was written in 1198-9 by a monk of Evesham; the other is of later date.
Vols. v-vii. Letters written to or by Becket, or relating to him. Among these are letters from Henry II, Alexander III, John of Salisbury, Gilbert Foliot, Arnulf of Lisieux, Herbert of Bosham, and Peter of Blois.

This collection of 'Lives' and letters, whose shortcomings are noted by Knowles (*Episcopal Colleagues*, pp. 1-3), has superseded the older one by J. A. Giles in his *Patres Ecclesiae* (No. 1102), which followed *editio princeps* of the letters by C. Lupus, 'Epistolae et Vita' (of Becket) (Brussels, 1682; and new edns. 1724 and 1728).

For contemporaries involved in the Becket quarrel, see John of Salisbury (pp. 872-3), and Arnulf of Lisieux, Bartholomew of Exeter, David of London, Gilbert Foliot, Herbert of Bosham, Peter of Blois, and Richard of Ilchester (pp. 856-8).

6488 THOMAS SAGA ERKIBYSKUPS: a life of Becket in Icelandic, with English translation. Ed. by Eirikr Magnússon. Rolls Ser. 2 vols. Lond. 1875-83.

There was a Thomas Saga in Iceland in the thirteenth century, but the saga as it has come down to us was probably written by Arngrim, abbot of Thingeyrar, who died in 1362. It was compiled mainly from Benedict's work (No. 6487) and from a contemporary, but now lost, 'Life' of Becket by Robert of Cricklade. It contains some details which are not found in the other extant biographies. Magnússon, in vol. ii, has carefully investigated the chronological order of the contemporary lives of Becket. On a 'reconstruction' of Cricklade's *Vita*, see Margaret Orme, *Anal. Boll.* lxxxiv (1966), 379-98.

6489 LA VIE DE SAINT THOMAS, by Guernes (or Garnier) de Pont Sainte Maxence. Ed. by Emmanuel Walberg. Lund. 1922. Reprinted in *Les Classiques françaises.* Paris. 1936. Also edited by Célestin Hippeau in *Collection de poètes français du moyen âge.* Paris. 1859.

A French poem of 5,833 lines, completed by 1176 after Guernes had visited Canterbury.

6490 HUTTON (WILLIAM H.). S. Thomas of Canterbury. Lond. 1889. Reprinted 1899, 1910, and enlarged 1926.

A collection of extracts from contemporary writers.

6491 THE LIFE AND DEATH OF THOMAS BECKET, chancellor of England and Archbishop of Canterbury, based on the account of William fitz-Stephen his clerk with additions from other contemporary sources translated and edited by George Greenaway. Lond. 1961.

6492 POOLE (REGINALD L.). 'Two documents concerning Archbishop Roger of York'. *Speculum*, iii (1928), 81–4. Reprinted in No. 1487.

6493 SALTMAN (AVROM). 'Two early collections of the Becket correspondence and other contemporary documents'. *B.I.H.R.* xxii (1949), 152–7.

6494 ABBOTT (EDWIN A.). St. Thomas of Canterbury, his death and miracles. 2 vols. Lond. 1898.

Translations of various accounts arranged by episodes.

6495 ALEXANDER (JAMES W.). 'The Becket controversy in recent historiography'. *Jour. British Stud.* ix (1970), 1–26.

6496 BORENIUS (TANCRED). St. Thomas Becket in Art. Lond. 1932.

T. Borenius, 'The iconography of St. Thomas of Canterbury', *Archaeologia*, lxxix (1929), 29–54; lxxxi (1932), 19–32; lxxxiii (1933), 171–86.

6497 FOREVILLE (RAYMONDE). Le Jubilé de Saint Thomas Becket du xiiie au xve siècle (1220–1470). Études et documents. Paris. 1959.

See Sandquist in *Wilkinson essays* (No. 1459).

6498 KNOWLES (DAVID). 'Archbishop Thomas Becket: a character study'. *P.B.A.* for 1949, xxxv (1952), 177–205. Reprinted in *The Historian and Character* (No. 1477), pp. 98–128. Idem, Thomas Becket. Leaders of Religion Ser. Lond. 1970.

T. F. Tout, 'The place of St. Thomas of Canterbury in history', *B.J.R.L.* vi (1921–2), 235–65. Reprinted in No. 1499.

6499 KNOWLES (DAVID). The episcopal colleagues of Archbishop Thomas Becket. Ford Lectures for 1949. Cambr. 1951.

6500 RADFORD (LEWIS B.). Thomas of London before his consecration. Cambr. 1894.

A scholarly work with many references to sources.

6501 SALTMAN (AVROM). Theobald, archbishop of Canterbury. Lond. 1956.

Becket was a member of Theobald's *familia*.

6502 WALBERG (EMMANUEL). La Tradition hagiographique de Saint Thomas Becket avant la fin du XIIe siècle: études critiques. Paris. 1929.

Walberg's work is said to contain 'the best discussion of the dates of composition and mutual relationships' of the contemporary biographies.

On Becket's dispute with Henry II and its results, the following studies in addition to Knowles (Nos. 6498–9), are particularly valuable.

6503 BROOKE (ZACHARY N.). 'The effect of Becket's murder on papal authority in England'. *Cambr. Hist. Jour.* ii (1926/8), 213–28. See also his English Church and the papacy (No. 6727).

In the seminal article Brooke holds that a considerable increase in appeals to Rome and the spread of canon law in England resulted directly from Henry's submission in the Compromise of Avranches. It seems rather that the increase resulted from the general developments in canon law and was common to much of Europe, rather than peculiar to England. From a different angle, see Kuttner–Rathbone, *Anglo-Norman canonists* (No. 6435). See also M. Cheney (No. 6505), Morey (No. 6513), Duggan (No. 6506), Gray (No. 6508), Mayr-Harting (No. 6510).

6504 CHENEY (CHRISTOPHER). 'The punishment of felonious clerks'. *E.H.R.* li (1936), 215–36.

6505 CHENEY (MARY). 'The Compromise of Avranches of 1172 and the spread of Canon Law in England'. *E.H.R.* lvi (1941), 177–97.

See also Charles Johnson, 'The reconciliation of Henry II with the papacy: a missing document', *E.H.R.* lii (1937), 465–7. F. W. Maitland, 'An unpublished "Revocation" of Henry II', *Collected papers* (No. 1482), iii. 115–18.

6506 DUGGAN (CHARLES). 'The Becket dispute and criminous clerks'. *B.I.H.R.* xxxv (1962), 1–28. Cf. No. 6503.

6507 FOREVILLE (RAYMONDE). L'Église et la royauté en Angleterre sous Henri II Plantagenet (1154–89). Paris. 1942.

See review by A. L. Poole in *E.H.R.* lxii (1947), 89–92, which holds that this large volume, displaying much industry, should be used with some caution.

6508 GRAY (J. W.). 'The *ius praesentandi* in England from the Constitutions of Clarendon to Bracton'. *E.H.R.* lxvii (1952), 481–509.

6509 MAITLAND (FREDERIC W.). 'Henry II and the criminous clerks'. *E.H.R.* vii (1892), 224–34. Also printed in his *Roman Canon Law* (No. 6437) and in his *Collected papers* (No. 1482), ii. 232–50.

6510 MAYR-HARTING (HENRY). 'Hilary, bishop of Chichester (1147–69) and Henry II'. *E.H.R.* lxxviii (1963), 209–24. Idem, 'Henry II and the papacy, 1170–1189'. *J.E.H.* xvi (1965), 39–53.

b. Some participants in the Becket controversy

See Knowles, *Episcopal Colleagues* (No. 6499).

Arnulf of Lisieux (d. c. 1182).

6511 ARNULFI LEXOVIENSIS EPISCOPI Epistolae. Ed. by J. A. Giles, *Patres Ecclesiae* (No. 1102). Also in Migne, *Patrologia*, cci. 17–152.

6512 THE LETTERS OF Arnulf of Lisieux. Ed. by Frank Barlow. R.H.S. Camden Soc. lxi (1939).

Many of these letters are addressed to Henry II, Becket, and other English prelates. They touch several facets of ecclesiastical history from about 1150 to 1181, including the Becket quarrel. Some letters of Arnulf and his English contemporaries can be found in *Spicilegium Liberianum* (ed. by Francesco Liverani, Florence, 1863), pt. i, 551–3,

573–92, 603–28; and in R. Poupardin, 'Dix-huit lettres inédites', *B.E.C.* lxiii (1902), 352–73. See also No. 6487. Arnulf was bishop of Lisieux 1141–81, went on the Second Crusade, and was caught up in the politics of his age.

Bartholomew of Exeter (d. 1184).

6513 MOREY (ADRIAN). Bartholomew of Exeter, bishop and canonist: a study in the twelfth century. Cambr. 1937.

In addition to the sections on Bartholomew's support of Becket, there is a good chapter on the papal judge delegate. For other topics, see Nos. 5721; 6456.

David of London

6514 DAVID OF LONDON, Register of letters. Ed. by Francesco Liverani, *Spicilegium Liberianum*. Florence. 1863.

Z. N. Brooke, 'The register of Master David of London and the part he played in the Becket crisis', in R. L. Poole *essays* (No. 1448), with references and corrections needed to elucidate Liverani's text. See F. Barlow, *Edward the Confessor* (No. 3976), App. D.

Gilbert Foliot (d. 1187).

6515 THE LETTERS AND CHARTERS OF GILBERT FOLIOT. Ed. by Dom Adrian Morey and Christopher N. L. Brooke. Lond. and N.Y. 1967.

This critical edition of the valuable collection of letters written by Foliot, bishop of Hereford and London, supersedes the edition by Giles. Foliot was a bitter opponent of Becket.

6516 GILBERTI EPISCOPI primum Herefordensis deinde Londoniensis epistolae. Ed. by J. A. Giles, *Patres* (No. 1102). 2 vols. Oxf. 1845. Also in Migne's *Patrologia*, cxc, 739–1068. Paris. 1854.

6517 MOREY (DOM ADRIAN) and BROOKE (CHRISTOPHER N. L.). Gilbert Foliot and his letters. Cambr. 1965.

This work comprises commentaries on various subjects related to Foliot; it deals with his career, the case for Empress Mathilda, the Gloucester forgeries, and much else.

Herbert of Bosham (*fl.* 1162–86).

6518 HERBERTI DE BOSEHAM S. Thomae Cant. clerici a secretis Opera omnia. Ed. by J. A. Giles, *Patres Ecclesiae* (No. 1102). 2 vols. Oxf. 1845–6. Also in Migne's *Patrologia*, cxc, 1070–1474. Paris. 1854.

Contains *Vita S. Thomae* (valuable), *Liber Melorum*, *Epistolae*, etc. The *Liber Melorum*, which is mainly a comparison between the sufferings of Becket and Christ, is of little historical value. For the *Vita S. Thomae*, written 1184–6, see No. 6487, and Theodore Craib, 'The Arras MS. of Herbert of Bosham', *E.H.R.* xxxv (1920), 218–24. Herbert was a member of Becket's household.

Peter of Blois (d. *c.* 1212).

He was secretary of the archbishop of Canterbury, and was in great favour at the court of Henry II.

6519 PETRI BLESENSIS Bathoniensis archidiaconi Opera omnia. Ed. by J. A. Giles, *Patres Ecclesiae* (No. 1102). 4 vols. Oxf. 1846–7. Also in Migne's *Patrologia*, vol. ccvii. Paris. 1855.

Vols. i–ii: *Epistolae*. Written mainly 1169–1202; many of them relate to English affairs. See No. 6487.

Vol. iii: *Opuscula: Dialogus inter Henricum II et abbatem Bonaevallensem*, etc.

Vol. iv. *Sermones*, etc.

E. S. Cohn, 'The manuscript evidence for the letters of Peter of Blois', *E.H.R.* xli (1926), 43–60. R. W. Southern, 'Some new letters of Peter of Blois', ibid. liii (1938), 412–24. J. Armitage Robinson, *Somerset Hist. Essays* (No. 1491), pp. 100–40.

The *Dialogus inter Henricum II et abbatem Bonaevallis* is also edited by R. B. C. Huygens in *Revue Bénédictine* lxviii (1958), 87–113. See Southern, *Medieval Humanism* (No. 6911), pp. 105–32.

Richard of Ilchester (d. 1188).

He was a royal clerk who supported Henry's case and became bishop of Winchester.

6520   DUGGAN (CHARLES). 'Richard of Ilchester, royal servant and bishop'. *T.R.H.S.* 5th Ser. xvi (1966), 1–21.

F. SCHOLARS, MYSTICS, AND THEIR WORKS

1. *Individual Scholars*

The general collections of lives of prelates and saints, such as those of Wharton, Mabillon, and the Bollandists, are entered above on pp. 144–51. See also William of Malmesbury, *Gesta Pontificum* (No. 1143). The printed episcopal registers and the biographies of bishops are listed diocese by diocese on pp. 758–92. Writings, appearing between 1901 and 1933, of biographies of medieval Englishmen of ecclesiastical, cultural, or scientific distinction are listed in *Writings* (No. 38), ii. 277–99.

Since it is clearly impractical to list all the English saints and scholars here, the selection below is limited to persons, writings, and modern appraisals of major significance or to works which refer to significant studies. Recent publications have generally been given preference since they make reference to important earlier studies. A large proportion of the persons included below can be found named in Emden's registers (Nos. 532–3). Biographies of some are included in *Dictionnaire de Théologie Catholique* (No. 1267) and in *Dictionnaire de Droit Canonique* (p. 168). Bibliographical details on the theologians and philosophers can be discovered in de Brie (No. 49), Gilson (No. 6884), and other general works mentioned under Intellectual Interests, pp. 898–907 below. Current references are given in *Bibliographie de la Philosophie* (No. 6876), *Répertoire bibliographique de la Philosophie* (No. 6877), and *Archives d'Histoire doctrinale et littéraire du Moyen Âge* (Paris, 1926+). Perceptive sketches of several saints and scholars are made by David Knowles, *Saints and scholars* (Cambr. 1962), drawn from Nos. 1298 and 1300 above. A new series entitled Auctores Britannici Medii Aevi is being sponsored by the British Academy; for the first volume, see No. 6532.

ADELARD OF BATH (*fl.* 1130)

See *C.B.E.L.* i. 284.

6521   BLIEMETZRIEDER (FRANZ P.). Adelhard von Bath. Munich. 1935.

6522 CLAGETT (MARSHALL). 'The medieval translations from the Arabic of the Elements of Euclid with special emphasis on the versions of Adelard of Bath'. *Isis*, xliv (1953), 16–42.

6523 GOLLANCZ (HERMANN). Dodi Ve-Nechdi (the work of Berachya Hanakhan) to which is added the first English translation from the Latin of Adelard of Bath's *Quaestiones naturales*. Lond. 1920.

6524 HASKINS (CHARLES H.). 'Adelard of Bath'. *E.H.R.* xxvi (1911), 491–8; xxviii (1913), 515–16, 831. Idem, Studies in the history of mediaeval science. Cambr. (Mass.). 1927, pp. 20–42.

6525 WILLNER (HANS). Des Adelard von Bath Traktat *De eodem et diverso* . . . *Beiträge zur Geschichte der Philosophie des Mittelalters*, iv. Münster. 1903.

ANSELM (d. 1109)

See E. R. Fairweather, *A Scholastic Miscellany: Anselm to Ockham*. The Library of Christian Classics (Philadelphia, 1956), vol. x, pp. 47–215; *Eng. Hist. Docs.* (No. 17), ii. 651–75; and the biographies in *Dict. Théol. Cath.* (No. 1267), and *Dict. Hist. Géog. Ecclés.* (No. 1266).

6526 S. ANSELMI CANTUARIENSIS ARCHIEPISCOPI Opera omnia. Ed. by Franciscus S. Schmitt. i+. Seckau. 1938. 6 vols. Edin. and Lond. 1940–61. Cur Deus homo, ed. by F. S. Schmitt, in *Florilegium Patristicum*. . . . Ed. by B. Geyer and J. Zellinger, fasc. xviii (Bonn. 1929). Liber monologion, ibid. xx (1929). Epistola de incarnatione verbi, ibid. xxviii (1931). Liber proslogion, ibid. xxix (1931).

Schmitt's edition is now standard and replaces that of G. Gerberon. F. S. Schmitt, 'Die echten und unechten Stücke der Korrespondenz des hl. Anselm von Canterbury', *Rev. Bénédictine*, lxv (1955), 218–27. Idem, 'Die Chronologie der Briefe des hl. Anselm von Canterbury', *Rev. Bénédictine*, lxiv (1954), 176–207. Idem, 'Die unter Anselm veranstaltete Ausgabe seiner Werke und Briefe, die Codices Bodley 271 und Lambeth 50', *Scriptorium*, ix (1955), 64–75.

6527 S. ANSELMI OPERA OMNIA. Ed. by Gabriel Gerberon. Paris. 1675. 2nd edn. 1721; reprinted in 2 vols. Venice, 1744. Also in Migne's *Patrologia*, vols. clviii–clix.

Eadmer's *Vita S. Anselmi*, clviii. 49–118; *Epistolae Anselmi* (concerning the investiture struggle, etc.), clix. 9–272.

6528 ST. ANSELM'S PROSLOGION (and Gaunilo's reply on behalf of the fool and St. Anselm's rejoinder). Trans. by M. J. Charlesworth and printed in parallel columns with Dom Franciscus Schmitt's Latin text. Oxf. 1965.

6529 EADMERI HISTORIA NOVORUM IN ANGLIA; et Opuscula duo de vita S. Anselmi. Ed. by Martin Rule. Rolls Ser. Lond. 1884. Extracts. Ed. by R. Pauli, in M.G.H. *SS*. xiii. 139–48.

Eadmer's *De vita et conversatione Anselmi*, pp. 305–424. This is the best life of Anselm, but there is also much information concerning him in Eadmer's *Historia Novorum*. Both works are valuable for the study of the investiture struggle. Eadmer was Anselm's confidential adviser. See No. 2863; and Pauli's introduction in M.G.H. *SS*. xiii. 97–101.

6530 EADMER. The Life of St. Anselm, archbishop of Canterbury. Ed. and trans. by Richard W. Southern. *Medieval Texts*. Lond. etc. 1962. Oxf. 1972.

6531 FIDES QUAERENS INTELLECTUM: Anselm's proof of the existence of God. By Karl Barth. Trans. by Ian W. Robertson. Lond. 1960.

6532 MEMORIALS OF SAINT ANSELM. Ed. by Richard W. Southern and F. S. Schmitt. Auctores Britannici Medii Aevi. Oxf. 1969.

6533 THEOLOGICAL TREATISES. Ed. by Jasper Hoskins and Herbert Richardson. 3 vols. Cambr. (Mass.). 1965–7.

6534 CHURCH (RICHARD W.). Saint Anselm. Lond. 1870.

Reprinted many times.

6535 SOUTHERN (RICHARD W.). St. Anselm and his biographer. Cambr. 1963.

See C. J. Holdsworth, 'Saint Anselm reconsidered', *History*, 1 (1965), 60–5. R. W. Southern, 'St. Anselm and his pupils', *Mediaeval and Renaissance Studies*, i (1941), 3–34. Idem, 'St. Anselm and Gilbert Crispin', ibid. iii (1954), 78–115. Idem, 'St. Anselm', in his *Medieval Humanism* (No. 6911), pp. 9–18.

BACON, ROGER (d. 1292–4)

Franciscan philosopher and scientist

See Isis Bibliography (No. 6934), i. 91–9.

6536 FRATRIS ROGERI BACON COMPENDIUM STUDII THEO-LOGIAE. Ed. by Hastings Rashdall. British Soc. Franciscan Stud. iii. Aberdeen. 1911.

At pp. 71–112 there is a full list of Bacon's writings compiled by A. G. Little.

6537 FR. ROGERI BACON OPERA QUAEDEM HACTENUS INEDITA. Ed. by John S. Brewer. Vol. i contains *Opus Tertium, Opus Minus*, and *Compendium Philosophiae*. Rolls Ser. Lond. 1859.

6538 OPERA HACTENUS INEDITA ROGERI BACONI. Ed. by Robert Steele, Ferdinand Delorme, *et al.* 16 vols. Oxf. 1909–40.

Part ix: *De retardatione accidentium senectutis, cum aliis opusculis de rebus medicinalibus*, edited by Andrew G. Little and E. Withington, appears also in British Soc. Franciscan Stud. xiv (1928).

6539 THE OPUS MAJUS OF ROGER BACON. Ed. by John H. Bridges. 3 vols. Oxf. 1897–1900. * Trans. by Robert B. Burke. 2 vols. Philadelphia and Lond. 1928. *

Bridges's introduction was enlarged and printed separately as *The life and work of Roger Bacon*, edited by H. Gordon Jones. (Lond. 1914).

6540 ROGERI BACONIS MORALIS PHILOSOPHIA. Ed. by Ferdinand Delorme and Eugenio Massa. Thesaurus Mundi. Zurich. 1953.

6541 ALESSIO (FRANCO). 'Un secolo di studi su Ruggero Bacone (1848–1957)'. *Rivista critica di storia della filosofia* (Milan), xiv (1959), 81–102.

6542   CROWLEY (THEODORE). 'Roger Bacon: the problem of universals in his philosophical commentaries'. *B.J.R.L.* xxxiv (1951–2), 264–75.

6543   EASTON (STEWART C). Roger Bacon and his search for a universal science. Oxf. and N.Y. 1952.

Includes a good bibliography.

6544   MANLY (JOHN M.). 'Roger Bacon and the Voynich MS.'. *Speculum*, vi (1931), 345–91.

Manly disproves the validity of the deciphering by William R. Newbold of a mysterious (Voynich) MS. attributed perhaps falsely to Roger Bacon.

6545   MASSA (EUGENIO). Ruggero Bacone: Etica e poetica nella storia dell' *Opus Maius*. Rome. 1955.

6546   ROGER BACON ESSAYS, contributed by various writers on the occasion of the commemoration of the seventh centenary of his birth. Ed. by Andrew G. Little. Oxf. 1914.

See also A. G. Little, *Grey friars of Oxford* (No. 6025), pp. 195–211; and idem, 'Roger Bacon', *P.B.A.* xiv (1928), 265–96. See also *Poole essays* (No. 1448).

6547   THORNDIKE (LYNN). 'The true Roger Bacon'. *A.H.R.* xxi (1915–16), 237–57, 468–80.

BARTHOLOMAEUS ANGLICUS (d. *c*. 1250)
English Franciscan, taught at Paris and Magdeburg

6548   DE PROPRIETATIBUS RERUM. Selections are translated in Mediaeval Lore from Bartholomaeus Anglicus. By Robert Steele. Lond. and Boston. 1907. *

This Latin compilation from the natural sciences, as found in Isidore of Seville, Robert Grosseteste and others, was translated into several vernaculars. John de Trevisa translated it into English in 1397. Modern translation with introduction by James J. Walsh in *Medical Life* (American Soc. of Medical Hist.), xl (1933), 449–602.

6549   BOYAR (GERALD E. SE). 'Bartholomaeus Anglicus and his encyclopedia'. *J.E.G.P.* xix (1920), 168–89.

6550   HANFORD (JAMES H.). 'De proprietatibus rerum of Bartholomaeus Anglicus'. *Princeton Univ. Library Chron.* xxiii (1962), 126–30.

6551   MACNIOCAILL (GEAROID). 'Bartholomaei Anglici de Proprietatibus Rerum liber octavus'. *Celtica*, viii (1968), 201–42.

BOCFIELD, ADAM DE (d. 1278–94)
See de Brie (No. 49), 7331–5, and Russell, *Writers* (No. 541), pp. 2–3.

6552   ADAM OF BUCKFIELD. Sententia super secundum metaphysicae, ed. by Armand Maurer in *Nine Mediaeval Thinkers*. Ed. by J. R. O'Donnell (Toronto, 1955), pp. 91–144.

6553   GRABMANN (MARTIN). 'Die Aristoteles Kommentatoren Adam von Bocfeld und Adam von Bouchermefort: Die Anfänge der Erklärung des neuen

Aristotelis in England', in *Mittelalterliches Geistesleben Abhandlungen zur Geschichte der Scholastik und Mystik*. (Munich. 1936), ii. 138–92, 614–16.

6554 THOMSON (S. HARRISON), 'A note on the works of Master Adam de Bocfield'. *Medievalia et Humanistica*, ii (1944), 55–87. Idem, 'An unnoticed MS. . . . of Magister Adam of Bocfield'. Ibid. iii (1945), 132–3. Idem, 'A further note on Master Adam of Bocfeld'. Ibid. xii (1958), 21–32. Louis Bataillon, 'Adam of Bocfield: further manuscripts'. *Ibid.* xiii (1960), 35–9.

BOLDON, UTHRED of (d. 1397)

6555 THE MEDITACIO DEVOTA of Uthred of Boldon. Ed. by Hugh Farmer in *Analecta monastica* (Studia Anselmiana, Rome), xliii (1958), 187–206.

6556 KNOWLES (DAVID). 'The censured opinions of Uthred of Boldon'. *P.B.A.* xxxvii (1951/53), 305–42. Reprinted in No. 1477.

See W. A. Pantin in *Powicke essays* (No. 1450), and *The English Church* (No. 6799), pp. 166–75; and D. Knowles, *Religious Orders* (No. 1300), ii. 65–89.

BRADWARDINE, THOMAS (d. 1349)
Archbishop of Canterbury, mathematician
See Emden, *Oxford*, pp. 244–6.

6557 THE SERMO EPINICIUS ascribed to Thomas Bradwardine (1346). Ed. with introduction by H. A. Oberman and J. A. Weisheipl in *Archives d'Hist. doct. et litt. du Moyen Âge*, xxv (1958), 295–329.

6558 THOMAS BRADWARDINE: HIS TRACTATUS DE PROPORTIONIBUS, its significance for the development of mathematical physics. By H. L. Crosby. Madison (Wisconsin). 1955.

6559 LEFF (GORDON). Bradwardine and the Pelagians: a study of his De Causa Dei and its opponents. Cambr. 1957.

6560 OBERMAN (HEIKO). Archbishop Thomas Bradwardine. A fourteenth century Augustinian: A study of his theology in its historical context. Utrecht. 1957. Idem, ed. Forerunners of the Reformation: the shape of late medieval thought, illustrated by key documents. N.Y. 1966.

Of the English forerunners, Holcot and Bradwardine are discussed on pp. 123–64.

BURY, RICHARD DE (d. 1345)
See Emden, *Oxford*, i. 323–6; and Nos. 5691–2 above.

6561 THE LIBER EPISTOLARIS OF RICHARD DE BURY. Ed. by Noël Denholm-Young. Roxburghe Club. Lond. 1950. Portions printed in *Formularies . . . of Oxford* (No. 7063); and calendared in *Hist. MSS. Comm. Reports: Fourth Report*, pp. 379–97.

The *Liber epistolaris* is a formulary compiled about 1324, containing some 1,500 documents. Many documents are from Roman Rolls or Gascon Rolls, now in the P.R.O.

6562 RICHARD DE BURY, The Philobiblon. Ed. by E. C. Thomas. Lond.
1888, reprinted 1903, 1909, 1925; and reprinted by Michael Maclagan:
Oxf. 1962. Philobiblon oder über die Liebe zu den Büchern. Ed. with German
translation by A. Hartmann. Burgdorf. 1955. The Philobiblon of Richard de
Bury. Ed. and trans. into English by Andrew F. West. N.Y. 1889. The love of
books, the philobiblon of Richard de Bury, trans. by E. C. Thomas. Lond. 1909.
Also trans. by A. Campbell. Berkeley, Calif. 1948.

> There have been several other editions of the Philobiblon; but the three above are pro-
> bably the best. 'Thomas ascribed the authorship to Robert Holcot.'

6563 DENHOLM-YOUNG (NOËL). 'Richard de Bury, 1287-1345'.
T.R.H.S. 4th Ser. xx (1937), 135-68. Reprinted in No. 1467.

6564 GHELLINCK (JOSEPH DE). 'Un évêque bibliophile au XIVᵉ siècle:
Richard Aungerville de Bury'. *R.H.E.* xviii (1922), 271-312, 482-508; xix (1923),
157-200.

DUNS SCOTUS (d. 1308)

6565 OPERA OMNIA. Ed. by Karl Balić. Vatican City. 1950+ Ed. by Luke
Wadding *et al.* 12 vols. Lyon. 1639; and 26 vols. Paris. 1891-5. The De primo
principio of John Duns Scotus. Ed. and trans. by Evan Roche. St. Bonaventure
(N.Y.). 1949. Philosophical writings. Ed. and trans. by Allan B. Wolter. N.Y.
1962.

> Commentary in Emden, *Oxford*, pp. 607-10; and in Encyclopedias (Nos. 1266-71);
> John K. Ryan and Bernardine M. Bonansea, eds. *John Duns Scotus, 1265-1965.*
> (Washington, 1965.)

6566 CONGRESSUS SCHOLASTICUS INTERNATIONALIS (Oxf. and
Edin. 1966). De doctrina Ioannis Duns Scoti. Acta Congressus . . . 11-17
September 1966. 4 vols. Studia Scholastico-scotistica, i-iv. Rome. 1968.

6567 GILSON (ÉTIENNE). Jean Duns Scot: introduction à ses positions
fondamentales. Paris. 1952.

> Cf. Charles Harris, *Duns Scotus.* 2 vols. Oxf. 1927. 2nd edn. Lond. 1960; and C. K.
> Brampton in *Studies*, New Ser. xxiv (1964), 5-20.

FITZRALPH, RICHARD (d. 1360)
See Pantin, *The English Church* (No. 6799), pp. 151-65.

6568 GWYNN (AUBREY). The sermon diary of Richard Fitzralph, archbishop of Armagh. *Royal Irish Acad. Procs.* xliv Sect. C (1937), 1-57. Idem,
'Two sermons of Primate Richard Fitzralph'. *Archivium Hibernicum*, xiv (1949),
50-65.

> See A. Gwynn, *Austin friars* (No. 5971); and A. Gwynn, 'Richard Fitzralph, archbishop
> of Armagh', *Studies*, xxii (1933), 389-405, 591-607; xxiii (1934), 395-411; xxiv (1935),
> 29-42, 528-72; xxv (1936), 81-96; xxvi (1937), 50-67. R. R. Betts, 'Richard FitzRalph
> . . . and the doctrine of dominion', in *Todd essays* (No. 1457); and Gwynn's criticism in
> *Irish Hist. Studies.* vii (1950-1), 131-3.

6569 LEFF (GORDON). Richard Fitzralph: Commentator of the Sentences.
Manchester. 1964.

6570   PERRY (A. J.), ed. John Trevisa's translation of Fitzralph's sermon 'Defensio curatorum'. E.E.T.S. Orig. Ser. clxvii (1925).

GASCOIGNE, THOMAS (d. 1458)

6571   LOCI E LIBRO VERITATUM: passages selected from Gascoigne's Theological Dictionary illustrating the condition of church and state, 1403–58. Ed. by J. E. Thorold Rogers. Oxf. 1881.

Combats evils in the church, assailing the clergy for neglecting their duties; and gives information regarding the University of Oxford. A valuable work, badly edited. On Gascoigne's *Theological Dictionary*, see James Gairdner, *Lollardy* (No. 6870), i. 243–64.

6572   PRONGER (WINIFRED A.). 'Thomas Gascoigne'. *E.H.R.* liii (1938), 606–26; liv (1939), 20–37.

GIRALDUS CAMBRENSIS (d. c. 1223)
For his chronicles, see No. 2881.

6573   GIRALDI CAMBRENSIS OPERA. Ed. by J. S. Brewer, J. F. Dimock, and G. F. Warner. 8 vols. Rolls Ser. Lond. 1861–91.

Vol. i: *De Rebus a se Gestis; Invectionum Libellus; Symbolum Electorum.* These works give many details regarding the author's life. The *Symbolum Electorum* is made up chiefly of his letters and poems. Passages from *De rebus* and from *De iure et statu Menevensis ecclesiae* and briefer extracts from other works are translated as *The autobiography of Giraldus Cambrensis* by Harold E. Butler: (Lond. 1937).
Vol. ii: *Gemma Ecclesiastica.* Interprets disputed points of doctrine; gives regulations regarding services, etc., throwing light on the manners of the age and on the condition of morality and religion in certain districts of England and Wales.
Vol. iii: *De Invectionibus; De Menevensi Ecclesia Dialogus; Vita S. David.* The first two works contain various details regarding Gerald's life. 'De invectionibus partes sex', ed. by W. S. Davies, *Y Cymmrodor*, xxx (1920), 1–238 is a better edition than that in the Rolls Series.
Vol. iv: *Speculum Ecclesiae* (mainly an attack on the monastic bodies); *De Vita Galfridi Archiepiscopi Ebor'*, d. 1212 (containing some useful details regarding the reigns of Henry II and Richard I).
Vol. v: *Topographia Hibernica; Expugnatio Hibernica.* See No. 2881.
Vol. vi: *Itinerarium Kambriae; Descriptio Kambriae.* See No. 2881.
Vol. vii: *Vita S. Remigii* (an untrustworthy history of the bishops of Lincoln, 1067–1200); *Vita S. Hugonis.* This life of Hugh, bishop of Lincoln, 1186–1200, is trustworthy, but contains little that is new.
Vol. viii: *De Principis Instructione Liber.* Trans. by Joseph Stevenson, *Church Historians* (Lond. 1858), vol. v, pt. i. Completed about 1217. It is directed against the princes of Gerald's own time, especially against Henry II and his sons, and contains many references to the affairs of Henry II's reign. *De instructione principum libri iii*, ed. by J. S. Brewer (Anglia Christiana Soc. Lond. 1846).

GROSSETESTE, ROBERT (d. 1253)
Scholastic and bishop of Lincoln

See Emden, *Oxford*, ii. 830–3; Rashdall, No. 7090; Russell, *Writers* (No. 541), pp. 135–8; *Isis Bibliography* (No. 6934), i. 156.

6574   DIE PHILOSOPHISCHEN WERKE DES ROBERT GROSSE-TESTE, Bischofs von Lincoln. Ed. by Ludwig Baur. *Beiträge zur Geschichte der Philosophie und Theologie des Mittelalters*, ix. Münster. 1912.

6575 ROBERTI GROSSETESTE Episcopi Lincolniensis (1235–53) Epistolae. Ed. by Henry R. Luard. Rolls Ser. Lond. 1861.

6576 CALLUS (DANIEL A. P.), ed. Robert Grosseteste, scholar and bishop. Essays in commemoration of the seventh centenary of his death. Oxf. 1955. *
    See Callus in *Powicke essays* (No. 1450).

6577 CROMBIE (ALISTAIR C.). Robert Grosseteste and the origins of experimental science 1100–1700. Oxf. 1953.

6578 DALES (RICHARD C.), ed. Robert Grosseteste Commentarius in octo libros physicorum Aristotelis. Boulder (Colorado). 1963.
    Idem, 'Commentarius . . . Aristotelis', *Medievalia et Humanistica*, xi (1957), 10–33.

6579 DALES (RICHARD C.), 'Robert Grosseteste's Scientific Works'. *Isis*, lii (1961), 381–402.

6580 HUNT (RICHARD W.). 'MSS. containing the indexing symbols of Robert Grosseteste'. *Bodleian Library Record*, iv (1953), 241–55.

6581 MORGAN (MARJORIE M.). 'The excommunication of Grosseteste in 1243'. *E.H.R.* lvii (1942), 244–50.

6582 POWICKE (FREDERICK MAURICE). 'Robert Grosseteste and the *Nicomachean Ethics*'. *P.B.A.* xvi (1930), 85–104. Idem, 'Robert Grosseteste, bishop of Lincoln'. *B.J.R.L.* xxxv (1952–3), 482–507.

6583 RUSSELL (JOSIAH C.). 'Richard of Bardney's account of Robert Grosseteste's early and middle life'. *Medievalia et Humanistica*, ii (1944), 45–54. Idem, 'Phases of Grosseteste's intellectual life'. *Harvard Theological Rev.* xliii (1950), 93–116. Idem, 'Some notes upon the career of Robert Grosseteste', ibid. xlviii (1955), 197–211.

6584 STEVENSON (FRANCIS S.). Robert Grosseteste. Lond. 1899.

6585 THOMSON (S. HARRISON). The writings of Robert Grosseteste. Cambr. and N.Y. 1940. Idem, 'The "notule" of Grosseteste on the *Nicomachean Ethics*'. *P.B.A.* xix (1933), 195–218. Idem, 'Two early portraits of Robert Grosseteste', *Medievalia et Humanistica*, viii (1954), 20–21. Idem, 'Grosseteste's concordantial signs'. Ibid. ix (1955), 39–53. Idem, 'Grosseteste's Questio de calore de cometis and de operacionibus solis'. Ibid. xi (1957), 10–33.

6586 TIERNEY (BRIAN). 'Grosseteste and the theory of papal sovereignty'. *J.E.H.* vi (1955), 1–17.

HALES, ALEXANDER OF (d. 1245)
Franciscan theologian of major proportions

6587 HERSCHER (IRENAEUS). 'A bibliography of Alexander of Hales'. *Franciscan Studies* (St. Bonaventure, N.Y.), v. (1945), 434–54.

6588 EXPOSITIO QUATUOR MAGISTRORUM (i.e. Alexander of Hales and three others) SUPER REGULAM FRATRUM MINORUM, 1241–1242. Accedit eiusdem regulae textus cum fontibus et locis parallelis. Ed. by Livarius Oliger. Storia et Letteratura, xxx. Rome. 1950.

6589 PROLEGOMENA to Alexander of Hales, *Summa Theologica*. 4 vols. Bibliotheca Franciscana Scholastica Medii Aevi. Quaracchi-Florence. 1948.

HOLCOT, ROBERT (d. *c.* 1349)
Dominican scientist
Emden, *Oxford*, ii. 946–7.

6590 GILLESPIE (RICHARD E.). 'Robert Holcot's Quolibeta'. *Traditio*, xxvii (1971), 480–90.
A list of Quolibeta, with citations of recent studies.

6590A HOLCOT (ROBERT). 'Utrum theologia sit scientia: a quodlibet question'. Ed. by J. T. Muckle, *Mediaeval Stud.* (Toronto) xx (1958), 127–53.

6591 SMALLEY (BERYL). 'Robert Holcot, O.P.'. *Archivum Fratrum Praedicatorum*, xxvi (1956), 5–97.

6592 THORNDIKE (LYNN). 'A new work by Robert Holcot'. *Archives Internationales d'Histoire des Sciences* (Paris), x (1957), 227–35.

KILWARDBY, ROBERT (d. 1279)
Dominican philosopher, archbishop of Canterbury.
Emden, *Oxford*, ii. 1051–2; Russell, *Writers* (No. 541), pp. 138–9.

6593 SOMMER-SECKENDORFF (ELLEN M. F.). Studies in the life of Robert Kilwardby, O.P. Rome, 1937.
These studies include the text of a sermon and some correspondence.

LANGTON, STEPHEN (d. 1228)
Archbishop of Canterbury
See Nos. 5633–4.

6594 ANTL (L.). 'An introduction to the *Quaestiones Theologicae* of Stephen Langton'. *Franciscan Stud.* xiii (1952), 151–75.

6595 LACOMBE (GEORGE) and LANDGRAF (ARTUR M.). 'The *Quaestiones* of Cardinal Stephen Langton'. *New Scholasticism*, iii (1929), 1–8; 113–58; iv (1930), 115–64.

6596 LACOMBE (GEORGE) and SMALLEY (BERYL). 'Studies on the Commentaries of Cardinal Stephen Langton'. *Archives d'Hist. doct. et litt. du Moyen Âge*, v (1930), 5–266.
Lacombe, pp. 5–151; Smalley, pp. 152–266.

6597 LANDGRAF (ARTUR M.). 'Der Sentenzenkommentar des Kardinals Stephan Langton'. Beiträge zur Geschichte der Philosophie und Theologie des Mittelalters, xxxvii, pt. i (1952).

> B. Smalley, 'Stephen Langton and the four senses of scripture', *Speculum*, vi (1931), 60–76; idem, 'Exempla in the Commentaries of Stephen Langton', *B.J.R.L.* xvii (1933), 121–9. See also her *Bible in the Middle Ages* (No. 6895).

6598 ROBERTS (PHYLLIS B.). Studies in the sermons of Stephen Langton. Pontifical Inst. Stud. and Texts, no. 16. Toronto. 1968.

MAP, WALTER (d. *c.* 1210)
Archdeacon and satirist

See Emden, *Oxford*, ii. 1219; *Eng. Hist. Docs.* ii. 389; *C.E.E.B.* (No. 14).

6599 GUALTERI MAPES De nugis curialium distinctiones quinque. Ed. by Montague R. James. Anecdota Oxoniensia, Med. and Mod. Ser. Oxf. 1914. Trans. by Montague R. James, with historical notes by John E. Lloyd, ed. by E. Sidney Hartland. Cymmrodorion Record Ser. 1923. Also trans. by Frederick Tupper and Marbury B. Ogle, as Courtiers' Trifles. Lond. 1924.

> Henry Bradley, 'Notes on Walter Map's *De nugis curialium*', *E.H.R.* xxxii (1917), 393–400; reprinted in his *Collected papers* (Lond. 1928). R. E. Bennett, 'Walter Map's Sadius and Galo', *Speculum*, xvi (1941), 34–56. See Manitius, *Geschichte der Lateinischen Literatur* (No. 56), iii. 264–74.

6600 GUALTERI MAPES De nugis curialium distinctiones quinque. Ed. by Thomas Wright. Camden Soc. l (1850). Extracts, ed. by Pauli, in M.G.H., *SS*. xxvii. 61–74.

> This 'book of court table-talk', completed between 1181 and 1193, is a collection of notes on the life of his day made at different times. See J. Hinton, 'Walter Map's *De Nugis Curialium*: its plan and composition', *PMLA*, xxxii (1917), 81–132.

6601 THE LATIN POEMS COMMONLY ATTRIBUTED TO WALTER MAPES. Ed. by Thomas Wright. Camden Soc. 1841.

> Although some of these poems are of English origin, it is unlikely that any were written by Walter Map. They are mainly satires on the clergy, especially on the monks.

MARSH, ADAM OF (d. 1258)

Franciscan theologian at Oxford and royal adviser. Emden, *Oxford*, ii. 1225–6.

6602 EPISTOLAE Adae de Marisco. *Monumenta Franciscana* (No. 6010), i. 77–489.

> He was an intimate friend of Simon de Montfort.

6603 CANTINI (G.). 'Adam de Marisco, O.F.M., auctor spiritualis'. *Antonianum*, xxiii (1948), 441–74.

6604 DOUIE (DECIMA), 'A. de Marisco'. *Durham Univ. Jour.* xxxii (1940), 81–97.

MELUN, ROBERT DE (d. 1167)

Bishop of Hereford

6605 ŒUVRES (Robert de Melun). Ed. by Raymond M. Martin and R. M. Gallet. Spicilegium Sacrum Lovaniense. 3 vols. Louvain. 1932–52.

See Knowles, *Episcopal colleagues* (No. 6499).

6606 MARTIN (RAYMOND M.). 'L'Œuvre théologique de Robert de Melun'. *R.H.E.* xv (1914), 456–89.

NECKHAM, ALEXANDER (d. 1217)

Augustinian theologian, scientist

See Emden, *Oxford*, ii. 1342–3.

6607 NECKHAM, ALEXANDER. De naturis rerum libri duo. Ed. by Thomas Wright. Rolls Ser. Lond. 1863.

P. W. Damon, 'A note on the Neckham canon', *Speculum*, xxxii (1957), 99–102.

6608 ESPOSITO (MARIO). 'On some unpublished poems attributed to Alexander Neckam'. *E.H.R.* xxx (1915), 450–71.

6609 HOLMES (URBAN T. Jr.). Daily living in the twelfth century, based on the observations of Alexander Neckham in London and Paris. Madison (Wisconsin). 1952.

J. C. Russell, 'Alexander Neckham in England', *E.H.R.* xlvii (1932), 260–8. Powicke in *Poole Essays* (No. 1448).

6610 KANTOROWICZ (HERMANN). 'A medieval grammarian on the sources of law'. *Tijdschrift voor rechtsgeschiedenis* (Haarlem), xv (1937), 25–47.

NETTER, THOMAS (d. 1430)

See Emden, *Oxford*, ii. 1343–4, and Dict. Théol. Cath. (No. 1267). Knowles, *Religious Orders* (No. 1300), ii. 145–8.

6611 EPISTOLAE WALDENSIS. Ed. by Benedictus Zimmermann, in *Monumenta historica Carmelitana*, i. 444–82.

6612 FASCICULI ZIZANIORUM magistri Johannis Wyclif cum tritico, ascribed to Thomas Netter of Walden. Ed. W. W. Shirley. Rolls Ser. Lond. 1858.

A series of documents extending to 1428, connected by a narrative. In this work we have the only contemporary account of the rise of the Lollards. Shirley, in his valuable introduction, states that a large part of the work was probably compiled in 1392–4 by Stephen Patryngton, who gave his papers to Netter, and that the latter made additions during the years 1414–28. In 1426 Netter also completed his *Doctrinale Antiquitatum Fidei Ecclesiae Catholicae contra Wiclevistas et Hussitas*, 3 vols. (Paris, 1521–32; other editions, Venice, 1571 and 1757–9). Netter, who is better known as Walden, was the confessor of Henry V, prior provincial of the Carmelites; and one of the ablest opponents of the Lollards. J. Crompton in *J.E.H.* xii (1961), 35–45, 155–66, argues that the *Fasciculi* was not written until 1439 and that Thomas Netter was not the author.

OCKHAM, WILLIAM OF (d. 1347)

Emden, *Oxford*, ii. 1384–7; A. G. Little, *Grey Friars of Oxford*, pp. 224–34. De Brie (No. 49) nos. 7290–7330. See No. 5571.

6613 BREVILOQUIUM DE POTESTATE PAPAE. Ed. by L. Baudry, in *Études de philosophie médiévale* (Paris), xxiv (1937).

6614 BREVILOQUIUM DE PRINCIPATU TYRANNICO. Ed. by Richard Scholz. Schriften des Reichsinstituts für ältere deutsche Geschichtskunde. viii (1944).

6615 DE IMPERATORUM ET PONTIFICUM POTESTATE of William of Ockham. Hitherto unpublished, now ed. by C. Kenneth Brampton. Oxf. 1927.

See Richard McKeon, 'A note on William of Ockham', *Speculum*, ii (1927), 455–6, where earlier editions are revealed.

6616 EPISTOLA AD FRATRES MINORES. Ed. by C. Kenneth Brampton. Oxf. 1929.

6617 GUILLELMI DE OCKHAM Opera politica. Vol. i. Ed. by J. G. Sikes, B. L. Manning, R. F. Bennett. Vols. ii and iii. Ed. by H. S. Offler. Manchester. 1940–56.

6618 OCKHAM (WILLIAM). Philosophical writings: a selection. Ed. and trans. by Philotheus Boehner. Nelson Philosophical Texts. Lond. 1957.

6619 OCKHAM (WILLIAM). Summa logica. Ed. by Philatheus Boehner. Franciscan Institute Pubns. St. Bonaventure (N.Y.), 1951.

The Franciscan Institute has published several studies on Ockham.

6620 BAUDRY (LÉON). Guillaume d'Occam: sa vie, ses œuvres, ses idées sociales et politiques. Vol. i. Paris. 1949.

See review by Ph. Boehner in *Franciscan Studies* (St. Bonaventure, N.Y.), xii (1952) 305–16. L. Baudry, *Lexique philosophique de Guillaume d'Ockham: études des notions fondamentales* (Paris. 1958).

6621 BOEHNER (PHILOTHEUS). Collected articles on Ockham. Ed. by E. M. Buytaert. St. Bonaventure (N.Y.). 1958.

6622 HEYNCK (VALENS B.). 'Ockham Literatur 1919–1949'. *Franziskanische Studien* (Münster), xxxii (1950), 164–183. Continued by James P. Reilly, Jr. 'Ockham bibliography, 1950–67'. *Franciscan Stud.* (St. Bonaventure, N.Y.), xxviii (1969), 197–214.

6623 JACOB (ERNEST F.). 'Ockham as a political thinker', in *Essays in the Conciliar Epoch* (No. 1473). 2nd edn., pp. 85–105, 245–7. Revised from *B.J.R.L.* xx (1936), 332–53.

J. B. Morrall, 'Some notes on a recent interpretation of William of Ockham's political philosophy'. *Franciscan Stud.* (St. Bonaventure, N.Y.), lx, New Ser. ix (1949), 335–69. A. C. Pegis, 'Some recent interpretations of Ockham', *Speculum*, xxiii (1948), 452–63.

6624 LAGARDE (GEORGES de). La Naissance de l'esprit laïque au declin du moyen âge. Saint-Paul-Trois-Chateaux. 1934+.

Vols. iv–vi: L'Individualisme Ockhamiste.

6625 PELZER (AUGUSTE). 'Les 51 articles de Guillaume d'Occam censurés en Avignon en 1326'. *R.H.E.* xviii (1922), 240–71.

See David Burr, 'Ockham, Scotus, and the censure at Avignon', *Church Hist.* xxxvii (1968), 144–59.

6626 TIERNEY (BRIAN). 'Ockham, conciliar theory and the canonists'. *Jour. Hist. Ideas*, xv (1954), 40–70.

6627 WEISHEIPL (JAMES A.). 'Ockham and some Mertonians'. *Mediaeval Stud.* xxx (1968), 163–213.

The Mertonians here are Bradwardine, Heytesbury, Dumbleton, and Swinehead.

PECOCK, REGINALD (d. *c.* 1460)
Philosopher, bishop of St. Asaph and of Chichester
Emden, *Oxford*, iii. 1447–9 and p. xxxviii; and *C.B.E.L.* i, 260–1; v. 148.

6628 REGINALD PECOCK'S BOOK OF FAITH. Ed. by J. L. Morison. Glasgow. 1909.

6629 THE REPRESSOR OF OVERMUCH BLAMING OF THE CLERGY. By Reginald Pecock. Ed. by Churchill Babington. Rolls Ser. 2 vols. Lond. 1860.

Cf. Thomas Gascoigne, *Loci e Libro Veritatum*, (No. 6571). Gascoigne, Chancellor of Oxford, was one of Pecock's enemies who brought him to trial in 1457. Pecock's Repressor, written about 1449 but published about 1455, defends the clergy against the attacks of the Lollards.

6630 GREEN (VIVIAN H. H.). Bishop Reginald Pecock. Cambr. 1945. Green lists Pecock's works in Appendix ii.

E. F. Jacob, 'Reynold Pecock, bishop of Chichester', *P.B.A.* xxxvii (1951), 121–53. Reprinted in No. 1474. Everett H. Emerson, 'Reginald Pecock: Christian rationalist,' *Speculum*, xxxi (1956), 235–42, which is critical of portions of Green's book. See Nos. 6870–1.

PULLEN, ROBERT (d. 1146)
Theologian, cardinal
Emden, *Oxford*, iii. 1525.

6631 COURTNEY (FRANCIS). Cardinal Robert Pullen: an English theologian of the twelfth century. *Analecta Gregoriana*, lxiv. Rome. 1954.

See R. L. Poole in *Tout essays* (No. 1458); reprinted in Poole, *Studies* (No. 1487).

PURVEY, JOHN (d. early fifteenth century)
Emden, *Oxford*, iii. 1526–7.

6632 REMONSTRANCES AGAINST ROMISH CORRUPTIONS IN THE CHURCH, addressed to the people and parliament of England in 1395. By John Purvey. Ed. by Josiah Forshall. Lond. 1851.

These Remonstrances assail the clergy and the pope. During the later years of Wyclif's life, Purvey was his companion and secretary. He became a leading Lollard and probably had a hand in making the Wyclif translations of the Vulgate (see Emden). We lose sight of Purvey about 1407.

RIEVAULX, AILRED OF (d. 1167)
Abbot, saint and writer

6633   AELREDI RIEVALLENSIS. Opera Omnia. Ed. by Anselm Hoste and C. H. Talbot. Corpus Christianorum. Continuatio Mediaevalis, i: Opera Ascetica. Turnholt. 1971.

Brief introduction and short preface to each work. Includes *Speculum Caritatis*, *De Spiritali Amicitia*, *De Institutione Inclusarum*, *De anima*, and other works. See also The Mirror of Charity, Trans. by Geoffrey Webb and Adrian Walker. (Lond. 1962).

6634   BEATI AELREDI ABBATUS RIEVALLENSIS Opera omnia, in Migne's *Patrologia*, vol. cxcv. Paris. 1855.

Sermones, cols. 209–500.
De bello Standardii, cols. 701–12. See No. 6635.
Vita S. Edwardi regis, cols. 739–90. See No. 2171. See B. W. Scholz, 'The canonization of Edward the Confessor,' *Speculum*, xxxvi (1961), 38–60.

6635   RELATIO DE STANDARDO. Ed. by Richard Howlett, in *Chronicles of the reigns of Stephen, Henry II and Richard I*, iii. 179–99. Rolls Ser. Other editions, in Twysden, *Scriptores* (No. 1124), pp. 337–46; and Migne, *Patrologia*, vol. cxcv. 701–12.

This account of the Battle of the Standard, 1138, is less important than that by Richard of Hexham (No. 2894). Ailred spent his youth at the court of David I of Scotland. He entered the Cistercian abbey of Rievaulx about 1134 and became abbot there in 1147. See Ritchie, *The Normans in Scotland* (No. 4002), pp. 246–57, and *Eng. Hist. Docs.* ii. 314–21.

6636   SERMONES INEDITI B. AELREDI ABBATIS RIEVALLENSIS. Ed. by Charles H. Talbot. Rome. 1952.

Talbot has also edited *De Anima* (Lond. 1952), and *De Institutis Inclusarum* (*Analecta S.O. Cisterciensis* (No. 5928), vii (1951)). For Ailred's sermons, see C. H. Talbot, in *Sacris erudiri* (Steenbrugge, Belgium), no. 13 (1962), 153–93.

6637   WALTER DANIEL, The life of Ailred of Rievaulx. Ed. and trans., by Frederick M. Powicke. Medieval Classics. Lond. N.Y. etc. 1950.

Walter Daniel was a monk at Rievaulx for many years under the abbacy of Ailred. His biography of Ailred is an important contemporary document. See F. M. Powicke, 'Ailred of Rievaulx and his biographer, Walter Daniel', *B.J.R.L.* vi (1921), 310–51, 452–521; revised reprint (Manchester, 1922). Reprinted in No. 1490.

6638   HOSTE (ANSELM). Bibliotheca Aelrediana. A survey of the manuscripts, old catalogues, editions and studies concerning St. Aelred of Rievaulx. Instrumenta Patristica, ii. The Hague. 1962. Supplement in *Cîteaux*, xviii (1967), 402–7; and xvii (1967), fasc. 4 is devoted entirely to Aelred.

C. M. Sage, 'The MSS. of St. Aelred', *Catholic Hist. Rev.* xxxiv (1949), 437–45. Aelred Squire, *Aelred of Rievaulx*. (Lond. 1969).

SALISBURY, JOHN OF (d. 1180)

Twelfth-century humanist, bishop

6639 JOANNIS SARESBERIENSIS Opera omnia. Ed. by J. A. Giles, *Patres Ecclesiae* (No. 1103). 5 vols. Oxf. 1848. Also in Migne's *Patrologia*, vol. cxcix. Extracts (chiefly from the Policraticus), ed. by Pauli in M.G.H. *SS.* xxvii. 43–52.

> Vols. i–ii: Epistolae, 1155–80. Valuable, especially for the conflict between Henry II and Becket. Many of them are also printed in *Recueil des Historiens de la France* (No. 1090), xvi, 488–625; and in No. 6487.
> Vols. iii–iv: *Policraticus sive De nugis curialium et vestigiis philosophorum*. This Statesman's Book, or Trifles of Courtiers, dedicated to Becket in 1159, is John's most important work. It deals with the principles of government, with philosophy, learning, and the vices of the age, particularly those of the court, giving vivid glimpses of the corruption in church and state.
> Vol. v: *Opuscula: Metalogicus*, etc.

6640 JOANNIS SARESBERIENSIS HISTORIAE PONTIFICALIS quae supersunt. Ed. by Reginald Lane Poole. Oxf. 1927. Historia pontificalis of John of Salisbury. Ed. and trans. by Marjorie Chibnall. Medieval Texts. Edin. etc. 1956. Also edited by Wilhelm Arndt in M.G.H., *SS.* xx, 515–45.

> This history of the papal court covers the years 1148–1152, and is full of interesting and important details. See R. L. Poole, 'John of Salisbury at the papal court', *E.H.R.* xxxviii (1923), 321–30; reprinted in No. 1487.

6641 LETTERS. The letters of John of Salisbury, vol. i. The early letters (1153–1161). Ed. by W. J. Millor, H. E. Butler, and C. N. L. Brooke. Medieval Texts. Edin. etc. 1955.

> R. L. Poole, 'The early correspondence of John of Salisbury', *P.B.A.* (1924–25), 27–53; H. G. Richardson, 'The early correspondence of John of Salisbury', *E.H.R.* liv (1939), 471–3. Giles Constable, 'The alleged disgrace of John of Salisbury in 1159', *E.H.R.* lxix (1954), 67–76. For John of Salisbury's life of Becket, see No. 6487.

6642 METALOGICON. Ed. by Clement C. J. Webb. Oxf. 1929. The Metalogicon of John of Salisbury: a twelfth-century defense of the verbal and logical arts of the trivium. Translated with an introduction, critical notes and bibliography by Daniel D. McGarry. Berkeley (Calif.), 1955. *

> D. D. McGarry, 'Educational theory in the *Metalogicon* of John of Salisbury', *Speculum*, xxiii (1948), 659–75. Sister Mary B. Ryan, *John of Salisbury on the Arts of Language in the Trivium* (Washington, D.C. 1958). R. L. Poole, 'The masters of the schools at Paris and Chartres in John of Salisbury's time (1136–46)', *E.H.R.* xxxv (1920), 321–42.

6643 POLICRATICUS. Ed. by Clement C. J. Webb. 2 vols. Oxf. 1909. Books iv–vi and pts. of vii–viii translated as The Statesman's Book of John of Salisbury, by John Dickinson, N.Y. 1927; * The rest is translated as Frivolities of Courtiers and Footprints of Philosophers, by Joseph B. Pike. Minneapolis 1938. *

> John Dickinson, 'The medieval conception of kingship as developed in the *Policraticus*', *Speculum*, i (1926), 308–37. On magic in Books i and ii, see Barbara Helbling-Gloor, 'Natur und Aberglauben im Policraticus des Johannes von Salisbury', Geist und Werk der Zeiten, Heft. 1 (Zurich, 1956).

6644 HOHENLEUTNER (H.). 'Johannes von Salisbury in der Literatur der letzten zehn Jahre'. *Historisches Jahrb uchder Görres-Gesellschaft* (Munich), lxxvii (1958), 493–500.

6645 LIEBESCHÜTZ (HANS). Mediaeval humanism in the life and writings of John of Salisbury. Studies of the Warburg Inst. xvii. Lond. 1950.

Idem, 'Chartres und Bologna', *Archiv für Kulturgeschichte*, l (1968), 3–32.

6646 SCHAARSCHMIDT (CARL). Johannes Sarisberiensis nach Leben und Studien. Leipzig. 1862.

6647 WEBB (CLEMENT C. J.). John of Salisbury. Lond. 1932. *

See Poole, *Illustrations* (No. 1416), and *Poole papers* (No. 1487).

WYCLIF, JOHN (d. 1384)
Philosopher and theologian

The best biography of Wyclif is by Workman (No. 6664), but it should be checked through McFarlane (No. 6657). *The Library of Christian Classics* (No. 1133), vol. 14, gives a few translations and a brief bibliography; the *C.B.E.L.* i. 203–5 and v. 129 provide some references. I. H. Stein and S. H. Thomson dealt with several of Wyclif's MSS. in *Speculum* between 1928 and 1933. The Wyclif society printed thirty-six volumes of Wyclif's works. Its work has been discussed by J. P. Whitney in *Poole essays* (No. 1448). The *Cambridge Medieval History*, vol. viii, has a sizeable bibliography, pp. 900–7. See also *Fasciculi Zizaniorum* (No. 6612) and the Lollards (pp. 896–8). *Shirley's Catalogue* (No. 6648), and E. W. Talbert and S. H. Thomson 'Wycliffe and his followers' in Severs, *Manual* (No. 275), ii (1970), 354–77, 517–33.

6648 (WYCLIF LATIN WORKS) Wyclif Soc. 36 vols. Lond. 1883–1922. * Cf. Whitney's article cited above.

W. W. Shirley, A catalogue of the original works of John Wyclif. Oxf. 1865. Revised by Johann Loserth for the Wyclif Society. Lond. 1924.
When the Wyclif Society discontinued publication, S. Harrison Thomson began a project to continue the printing of Wyclif's writings. By 1963, four books had appeared in *Studies and texts in medieval thought*, published in Boulder, Colorado. They were:
(a) John Wycliffe, Summa de ente. Ed. by S. Harrison Thomson. Boulder. 1956.
(b) Jan Hus, Tractatus de ecclesia. Ed. by S. H. Thomson. Boulder and Cambr. 1956. Prague. 1958.
(c) Johannis Wyclif, Tractatus de Trinitate. Ed. by Allen duPont Breck. Boulder. 1962.
(d) R. C. Dales, Robert Grosseteste (No. 6578).

6649 THE HOLY BIBLE . . . in the earliest versions made by J. Wycliffe and his followers. Ed. by Rev. Josiah Forshall and Frederic Madden. Lond. 1950. Also THE NEW TESTAMENT in English, according to the version of John Wycliffe, and revised by John Purvey. Formerly edited by Josiah Forshall and Sir Frederic Madden. Lond. 1879.

S. L. Fristedt, 'The Wycliffe Bible; pt. i: The principal problems connected with Forshall and Madden's edition', *Stockholm Stud. in English*, iv (1953). Idem, 'New light on John Wycliffe and the first full English Bible', *Stockholm Stud. in Modern Philology*, New Ser. iii (1968), 61–86. See Deanesly, *The Lollard Bible* (No. 6653).

6650 SELECT ENGLISH WORKS OF JOHN WYCLIF (Sermons, treatises, controversial tracts, etc.). Ed. by Thomas Arnold. 3 vols. Oxf. 1869–71. English works of Wyclif hitherto unprinted. Ed. by F. D. Matthew. E.E.T.S. Lond. 1880. Select English writings. Ed. by H. E. Winn. Oxf. 1929.

E. W. Talbert, 'The date of the composition of the English Wyclifite collection of sermons', *Speculum*, xii (1937), 464–74.

6651 CROMPTON (JAMES). 'John Wyclif: a study in mythology'. *Leics. Archaeol. Soc. Trans.* xlii (1966–7), 6–34.

See the useful references here.

6652 DAHMUS (JOSEPH H.). The prosecution of John Wyclif. New Haven and Lond. 1952.

6653 DEANESLY (MARGARET). The Lollard Bible and other medieval Biblical versions. Cambr. 1920.

See No. 6895.

6654 LECHLER (GOTTHARD V.). Johann von Wiclif und der Vorgeschichte der Reformation. 2 vols. Leipzig. 1873. Trans. (and abridged) by Peter Lorimer: John Wiclif and his English precursors. 2 vols. Lond. 1878; new edns. in 1 vol. 1881 (1884).

6655 LEFF (GORDON). 'John Wyclif, the path to dissent'. *P.B.A.* lii (1966), 143–80.

See also Leff, *Heresy* (No. 6871), pp. 494–558.

6656 LOSERTH (JOHANN). Hus und Wiclif. Prague. 1884. 2nd edn. Munich. 1925. Trans. by M. J. Evans, Wiclif and Hus. Lond. 1884.

J. Loserth, 'The beginnings of Wyclif's activity in ecclesiastical politics', *E.H.R.* xi (1896), 319–28. R. R. Betts, 'English and Čech influence on the Hussite movement', *T.R.H.S.* 4th Ser. xxi (1939), 71–102. S. Harrison Thomson, ed. *Magistri Johannis Hus, Tractatus de ecclesia* (Boulder and Cambr. 1956). Otakar Odložilík, 'Wycliffe's influence upon Central and Eastern Europe', *Slavonic Rev.* vii (1928–9), 634–48. Gordon Leff, 'Wyclif and Hus: a doctrinal comparison', *B.J.R.L.* l (1968), 387–410. See Šmahel (No. 6661).

6657 McFARLANE (KENNETH B). John Wycliffe and the beginnings of English non-conformity. Teach Yourself History. Lond. 1952.

A brief but capital book. See also Margaret Aston, 'John Wycliffe's reformation reputation', *Past and Present*, xxx (1965), 23–51; and E. C. Tatnall, 'John Wyclif and *Ecclesia Anglicana*', *J.E.H.* xx (1969), 19–44).

6658 POOLE (REGINALD L.). Wycliffe and movements for reform. Lond. 1889. Reissued, 1911.

6659 RICHARDSON (HENRY G.). 'Heresy and the lay power under Richard II'. *E.H.R.* li (1936), 1–28.

6660 ROBSON (JOHN A). Wyclif and the Oxford schools: the relation of the *Summa De Ente* to scholastic debates at Oxford in the later fourteenth century. Cambr. 1961.

Treats Thomas Buckingham, Richard FitzRalph, Walter Burley, Uthred Boldon, Thomas Netter, and others; and includes good references. See also *Callus essays* (No. 1428).

6661 ŠMAHEL (FRANTIŠEK). 'Doctor Evangelicus super omnes evangelistas. Wyclif's fortune in Hussite Bohemia'. *B.I.H.R.* xliii (1970), 16-34.

6662 THOMSON (S. HARRISON), 'The philosophical basis of Wyclif's theology'. *Jour. of Religion*, xi (1931), 86-116.

6663 VOOGHT (PAUL DE). Les Sources de la doctrine chrétienne d'après les théologiens du XIVᵉ siècle et début du XVᵉ (1317-1414). Bruges, 1954.

De Vooght offers, *inter alia*, a 'reappraisal of Wyclif'. See Michael Hurley, 'Scriptura sola: Wyclif and his critics', *Traditio*, xvi (1960), 275-352, which argues that Wyclif did not invent the thesis that Scripture was the sole source of relevation.

6664 WORKMAN (HERBERT B.). John Wyclif. 2 vols. Oxf. 1926. *

For 'Wyclif on English and Roman law', see F. W. Maitland, *Collected papers* (No. 1482), iii. 50-3.

2. *Mystics, Anchorites, and their Writings*

6665 COLLEDGE (ERIC), ed. The mediae valmystics of England. N.Y. 1961. *

Introduction, pp. 3-90: Some bibliographical information on several mystics, pp. 91-102; excerpts from St. Edmund Rich, Rolle, Hilton, Julian, Margery Kempe, and the Cloud of Unknowing, pp. 103-304.

6666 DAUPHIN (HENRI). 'L'Érémitisme en Angleterre aux xiᵉ et xiiᵉ siècles', in *L'eremitismo in Occident nei secoli xi e xii*. Milan. 1965.

6667 GARDNER (J. EDMUND G.), ed. The cell of self knowledge: seven early English mystical treatises printed by Henry Pepwell in 1521. New Mediaeval Library, Lond. 1910.

6668 YORKSHIRE WRITERS: Richard Rolle of Hampole and his followers. Ed. by Carl Horstmann. 2 vols. Lond. 1895-6.

The Middle English texts of several religious treatises and other documents, chiefly of a mystical character.

6669 (Christina) THE LIFE OF CHRISTINA OF MARKYATE: a twelfth century recluse. Ed. and trans. by Charles H. Talbot. Oxf. 1959.

Latin text with English translation on opposite page.

6670 THE CLOUD OF UNKNOWING AND THE BOOK OF PRIVY COUNSELLING. Ed. with introduction etc. by Phyllis Hodgson. E.E.T.S. Orig. Ser. ccxviii. Lond. 1944.

See also (Dionysius Areopagita) Deonise Hid divinite and other treatises on contemplative prayer related to the Cloud of Unknowing . . . ed. Phyllis Hodgson. E.E.T.S. Orig. Ser. ccxxxi Lond. 1955.

6671 THE CLOUD OF UNKNOWING. Ed. by Evelyn Underhill. Lond. 1912. Other editions by Justin McCann, Lond. 1924; by Howard H. Brinton, N.Y. 1948; by Ira Progoff, N.Y. 1957; and by Clifton Wolters, Lond. 1961.

These are all modernized versions.

6672 (Hilton, Walter) THE SCALE OF PERFECTION. Ed. by Evelyn Underhill. Lond. 1923. Other editions by Gerard Sitwell, Lond. 1953; and by Leo Sherley-Price (Penguin), 1957.

THE MINOR WORKS OF WALTER HILTON. Ed. by Dorothy Jones. Lond. 1929.

These are all modernized versions. For studies, see Helen L. Gardner, 'The text of the Scale of Perfection', *Medium Ævum*, v (1936), 11–29; idem, 'Walter Hilton and the mystical tradition in England', *E.S.M.E.A.* (*Essays and Studies*), xxii (1937), 103–27; and Phyllis Hodgson, 'Walter Hilton and The Cloud of Unknowing: a problem of authorship reconsidered', *Modern Language Rev.* l (1955), 395–406.

6673 (Julian of Norwich) REVELATIONS OF DIVINE LOVE, recorded by Julian, anchoress at Norwich, anno domini 1373. Ed. by Grace Warrack. Lond. 1901, 13th edn. Lond. 1950. Another edition by Roger Hudleston, Lond. 1927; 2nd edn. 1952. Also Comfortable works for Christ's lovers. Ed. by Dundas Harford. Lond. (1911), 3rd edn. Chicago, 1925. Earlier editions R. F. S. Cressy, 1670; G. H. Parker, 1843; H. Collins, 1872.

Robert H. Thouless, *The lady Julian; a psychological study* (Lond. and N.Y. 1924). P. Franklin Chambers, *Julian of Norwich: an introductory appreciation and an interpretative anthology* (Lond. 1955). Paul Molinari, *Julian of Norwich; the teaching of a fourteenth century English mystic* (Lond. 1958).

6674 (Kempe, Margery) THE BOOK OF MARGERY KEMPE: The text from the unique MS. owned by Colonel W. Butler-Bowdon (vol. i). Ed. by Sanford B. Meech and introduction by Hope E. Allen. E.E.T.S. Orig. Ser. ccxii. Lond. 1940.

Modern version by W. Butler-Bowdon (Lond. 1936).

6675 LIBELLUS DE VITA ET MIRACULIS S. GODRICI, HEREMI-TAE DE FINCHALE, auctore Reginaldo monacho Dunelmensi. Ed. by Joseph Stevenson. Surtees Soc. xx (1847).

6676 MEDITACIONES CUIUSDAM MONACHI APUD FARNELAND QUONDAM SOLITARII. Ed. by Hugh Farmer. *Studia Anselmiana*, (Analecta monastica. Textes et études sur la vie des moines du moyen âge. 4th Ser. Rome, 1957), xli (1957), 141–245. Trans. by a Benedictine of Stanbrook. Lond. 1961.

See W. A. Pantin, 'The Monk-solitary of Farne: a fourteenth century English mystic', *E.H.R.* lix (1944), 162–186.

6677 (Rolle, Richard. d. 1349) ALLEN (HOPE EMILY). Writings ascribed to Richard Rolle, hermit of Hampole, and materials for his biography. Mod. Lang. Asso. Amer. Monograph iii N.Y. and Lond. 1927.

6678 ENGLISH WRITINGS OF RICHARD ROLLE, HERMIT OF HAMPOLE. Ed. by Hope Emily Allen. Oxf. 1931.

The Middle English texts of the lyrics, prose treatises, and four commentaries on the psalms. Cf. *English prose treatises of Richard Rolle of Hampole*. Ed. by George G. Perry. E.E.T.S. Orig. Ser. xx (1866). Reprinted 1920. See also Horstmann (No. 6668).

6679 THE INCENDIUM AMORIS OF RICHARD ROLLE OF HAMPOLE. Ed. by Margaret Deanesly. Manchester, etc. 1915.

The latin text. The Middle English translation made by Richard Misyn in 1434 was edited by Ralph Harvey in E.E.T.S. Orig. Ser. cvi (1896) and was modernized as *The Fire of love or melody of love and the mending of life or rule of living*, by F. M. M. Comper with introduction by E. Underhill (Lond. 1914). A modern translation is given in Roy C. Petrie, *Late medieval mysticism*. Library of Christian Classics, xiii (Philadelphia, 1957).

6680 THE MELOS AMORIS OF RICHARD ROLLE OF HAMPOLE. Ed. by E. J. Arnould. Oxf. 1957.

The Latin text.

6681 SPECULUM INCLUSORUM, auctore anonymo anglico saeculi xiv. Ed. by S. Livario Oliger, *Lateranum*, New Ser. iv (1938).

6682 (Wulfric) LIFE OF WULFRIC OF HASELBURY BY JOHN, ABBOT OF FORD. Ed. by Dom Maurice Bell. Somerset Rec. Soc. xlvii (1933).

6683 CLAY (ROTHA M.). The hermits and anchorites of England. Antiquary Books. Lond. 1914. *

6684 COLEMAN (THOMAS W.). English mystics of the fourteenth century. Lond. 1938. *

6685 HODGSON (GERALDINE E.). The English Mystics. Lond. and Oxf. 1922.

6686 HODGSON (PHYLLIS). Three fourteenth century mystics. Lond. 1967.

The three are Rolle, the author of the Cloud of Unknowing, and Hilton.

6687 JONES (RUFUS M.). The flowering of mysticism. N.Y. 1939.

6688 KNOWLES (DAVID). The English mystical tradition. Lond. and N.Y. 1961.

Chapters on background, Rolle, Hilton, Julian, Margery Kempe, and the Cloud of Unknowing, with interspersed translated excerpts.

3. *Devotional Writings and Sermons*

From the mass of devotional and homiletic literature, a few important or popular examples, drawn in part from Pantin's *English Church*, follow. For the social content of sermons, see Baldwin, *Masters, Princes* etc. (No. 5443).

6689 AZENBITE OF INWIT, *c.* 1340. Ed. by Richard Morris. E.E.T.S. Orig. Ser. xxiii (1866). Reprinted 1895.

6690 CHOBHAM, THOMA DE. Summa confessorum. Ed. by F. Broomfield. Analecta mediaevalia Namurcensia, xxv. Louvain and Paris. 1968.

A guide for confessors written *c.* 1215 by Thomas of Chobham, sub-dean of Salisbury. See Thomas Kaeppeli, 'Un recueil de sermons prêchés à Paris et en Angleterre', *Archivum fratrum praedicatorum* (No. 5980A), xxvi (1956), 186–91. For Thomas of Chobham, see Baldwin '*Masters, Princes*', etc. (No. 5443) index.

6691 LAY FOLKS' CATECHISM. Ed. by Thomas F. Simmons and Henry E. Nolloth. E.E.T.S. Orig. Ser. cxviii (1901).

The English and Latin versions of Archbishop Thoresby's instructions for the people; together with a Wycliffite adaptation of the same, and the corresponding canons of the council of Lambeth (1281).

6692 LES CONTES MORALISÉS DE NICOLE BOZON, FRÈRE MINEUR. Ed. by Lucy T. Smith and Paul Meyer. Société des Anciens Textes Français. Paris. 1889.

A collection of stories used in sermons, written in Anglo-Norman about 1320. Bozon, a prolific writer, was attached probably to a Nottingham friary. He assails prelates and others in high places, and exhibits sympathy for the lower classes. Meyer in the introduction, p. xxviii, writes: 'Il n'y a pas, dans toute la littérature anglo-normande, un second ouvrage qui puisse nous donner une idée aussi complète de ce qu'était en Angleterre et au commencement du xive siècle la prédiction populaire.' See M. D. Legge, *Anglo-Norman literature* (No. 294), pp. 229–32 and index; Antoine Thomas in *Histoire littéraire de la France* (Paris), xxxvi, 400–24, especially 403–12. M. Amelia Klenke published *Three saints' lives by Nicholas Bozon* (N.Y. 1947); and *Seven more poems by Nicholas Bozon* (Louvain, 1951).

6693 THE LIVRE DE SEYNTZ MEDICINES. Ed. by Émile J. F. Arnould. Anglo-Norman Text Soc. 1940.

Written in Anglo-Norman in 1354 by Henry, duke of Lancaster. See also Arnould, 'Henry of Lancaster and his *Livre des Saintes Medicines*', *B.J.R.L.* xxi (1937), 352–86; and Fowler, *King's Lieutenant* (No. 4178), chap. xv, esp. pp. 193–6. See also M. B. Hackett, 'William Flete and the *De Remediis contra temptaciones*', in *Gwynn essays* (No. 1438).

6694 LE MANUEL DES PÉCHÉS. Études de littérature religieuse anglo-normande (xiiie siècle). Paris. 1940.

This study is not an edition of the *Manuel*; it is rather a study of the problems facing an editor and the significance of this confessional treatise addressed to laymen. The *Manuel* is the immediate source of Brunne's *Handlyng Synne*; both are printed in the Roxburghe Club 1862 edition (No. 6699). See Hope E. Allen, 'The Manuel des Pechiez and the scholastic prologue', *Romanic Rev.* viii (1917), 434–63; idem, 'The mystical lyrics of the Manuel des Pechiez', ibid. ix (1918), 154–93; Charlton Laird, 'Manuscripts of the Manuel des Pechiez', *Stanford Stud. in Language and Literature* (1941), 99–123; idem, 'The character and growth of the Manuel des Pechiez', *Traditio*, iv (1946), 253–306; D. W. Robertson, Jr., 'The Manuel des Péchés and an English episcopal decree', *Modern Language Notes*, lx (1945), 439–47.

6695 LE MERURE DE SEINTE EGLISE, by Saint Edmund (Rich) and Richard Rolle's Devout Meditacioun. Ed. by Harry W. Robbins. Lewisburg (Pa.). 1925.

See also Carl Horstmann, *Yorkshire Writers* (No. 6668), pp. 240–61. Idem, *Minor poems of the Vernon MS.* pt. i, E.E.T.S. xcviii (1892), pp. 221–51; F. J. Furnivall, *Minor poems*, pt. ii, E.E.T.S. cxvii (1901), 268–97. H. W. Robbins, 'An English version of St. Edmund's *Speculum* ascribed to Richard Rolle', *P.M.L.A.* xl (1925), 241–51. *The Mirror of St. Edmund*, done into modern English by Francesca M. Steele (Lond. 1905).

6696 MIRK (MYRC) (JOHN). Instructions for parish priests. Ed. by Edward Peacock. E.E.T.S. Orig. Ser. xxxi (1868). Revised by F. J. Furnivall. 1902.

A poem in English written by the prior of Lilleshall (Salop.), in the early fifteenth century. See Karl Young, 'Instructions for parish priests', *Speculum*, xi (1936), 225–30.

6697 MIRK'S FESTIAL: a collection of homilies. Ed. by Theodor Erbe. E.E.T.S. Extra Ser. xcvi (1905).

See Martyn F. Wakelin, 'The MSS. of John Mirk's "Festial",' *Leeds Stud. in English*, i (1967), 93–118.

6698 PRICK OF CONSCIENCE. A Northumbrian poem. Ed. by Richard Morris. Published for the Philological Society. Berlin. 1863.

Sometimes falsely ascribed to Richard Rolle; see H. E. Allen, *Writings* (No. 6677), pp. 372–97.

6699 ROBERT OF BRUNNE'S HANDLYNG SYNNE (1303), and its French original. Ed. by Frederick J. Furnivall. E.E.T.S. Orig. Ser. cxix (1901), cxxiii (1903). Also edited by Furnivall for Roxburghe Club (1862).

See D. W. Robertson, 'The cultural tradition of Handlyng Synne', *Speculum*, xxii (1947), 162–85. See Robert Mannyng of Brunne (No. 2923).

6700 ROSS (WOODBURN O.), ed. Middle English sermons edited from B.M. MS. Royal 18 B xxiii. E.E.T.S. Orig. Ser. ccix (1940).

6701 SERMONS OF THOMAS BRINTON, bishop of Rochester, 1373–89. Ed. by Sister Mary Aquinas Devlin. 2 vols. R.H.S. Camden. 3rd Ser. lxxxv–vi (1954).

6702 BLENCH (JOHN W.). Preaching in England in the late fifteenth and sixteenth centuries: a study of English sermons 1450–c. 1600. Oxf. and N.Y. 1964.

An analytical study dealing with the spiritual interpretation, form, style, classical allusions, themes, and influence on poetry and drama.

6703 CAPLAN (HARRY). Mediaeval artes praedicandi. Ithaca (N.Y.). 1934. Supplementary Handlist. Ithaca. 1936.

6704 CHARLAND (THOMAS M.). Artes praedicandi: contribution à l'histoire de la rhétorique au moyen âge. Paris and Ottawa. 1936.

6705 LECOY DE LA MARCHE (ALBERT). La Chaire française au moyen âge, specialement au xiii\ siècle. Paris. 1868. 2nd edn. 1886.

See also Étienne Gilson, 'Michel Menot et la technique du sermon medieval', in his *Les Idées et les lettres* (2nd edn. Paris, 1955), pp. 93–154.

6706 MOSHER (JOSEPH A.). Exemplum in the early religious and didactic literature of England. N.Y. 1911. *

6707 OWST (GERARD R.). Preaching in medieval England. Cambr. 1926. * Idem, Literature and pulpit in medieval England. Cambr. 1933.

See Hinnebusch, *Dominicans* (No. 5993) chaps. xv–xix (on preaching and learning); D. W. Robertson, Jr., 'Frequency of preaching in thirteenth century England', *Speculum*, xxiv (1949), 376–88; Jennifer Sweet, 'Some thirteenth-century sermons and their authors', *J.E.H.* iv (1953), 27–36.

6708 PFANDER (HOMER G.). The popular sermon of the medieval friar in England. N.Y. 1937.

6709 SCHNEYER (JOHANNES B.). Wegweiser zu lateinischen Predigtreihen des Mittelalters. Bayerische Akademie der Wissenschaften. Munich. 1965.

Schneyer is preparing a valuable *repertorium* including English material; the first volume is *Repertorium der lateinischen Sermones des Mittelalters für die Zeit von 1150–1350*: Autoren A-D. (Münster, 1969).

6709A WELTER (J. Th.). L'Exemplum dans la littérature religieuse et didactique du moyen âge. Paris. 1927.

Beryl Smalley, '*Exempla* in the Commentaries of Stephen Langton', *B.J.R.L.* xviii (1933), 121–9. A. C. Friend, 'Master Odo of Cheriton', *Speculum*, xxiii (1948), 641–58 (Odo of Cheriton, who died 1246–7, composed Latin *exempla* for peachers).

XXII. MODERN STUDIES OF THE MEDIEVAL ENGLISH CHURCH

A. THE PAPACY AND PAPAL ADMINISTRATION

1. *General Histories of the Papacy*

For bibliographical information refer to *Revue d'histoire ecclésiastique* and *Traditio*; and for narratives Nos. 1274–89 above.

6710 CREIGHTON (MANDELL). A history of the papacy from the Great Schism to the sack of Rome. 6 vols. Lond. 1897. * Reprinted 1901.

The first edition was entitled *A history of the papacy during the period of the reformation* (1378–1527). 5 vols. (Lond. 1882–94.)

6711 EUBEL (CONRAD). Hierarchia catholica medii aevi, sive summorum pontificum, S.R.E. cardinalium, ecclesiarum antistitum series ab anno 1198 usque ad annum 1605 perducta e documentis tabularii praesertim Vaticani collecta, digesta, edita per Conradum Eubel. 3 vols. Münster i. W. 1898–1910. New edn. of vols. i and ii (1198–1503). Regensburg. 1913/4; of vol. iii (from 1503–c. 1605), by L. Schmitz-Kallenberg. Regensburg. 1923.

The standard listing of the hierarchy, popes, cardinals, and bishops.

6712 FOLZ (ROBERT). 'La Papauté médiévale vue par quelques uns des historiens récents'. *Rev. Historique*, ccxviii (1957), 32–63.

R. E. McNally, 'The history of the medieval papacy: a survey of research, 1954–59', *Theological Stud.* (Woodstock, Md.) xxi (1960), 92–132. Augustin Fliche, 'Orientations et méthodes de l'histoire ecclésiastique médiévale', *B.I.H.R.* xxi (1946/8), 13–22. See periodic summaries in *Rev. Historique*, e.g. ccxxxvi (1966), 135–78.

6713 GABEL (LEONA C.), ed. Memoirs of a renaissance pope: the commentaries of Pius II. Smith College Stud. in Hist. xxii, xxv, xxxv, xliii (1937–57). Reprinted N.Y. 1959.

6714 GUILLEMAIN (BERNARD). La Cour pontificale d'Avignon (1309–1376); étude d'une société. Bibliothèque des Écoles françaises d'Athènes et de Rome. Paris. 1962.

6715 HALLER (JOHANNES). Das Papsttum: Idee und Wirklichkeit. 3 pts. Stuttgart. 1934–9. Better edition. 5 vols. Basel. 1951–3.

Geoffrey Barraclough, *The Medieval Papacy*, History of European Civilization Library (Lond. and N.Y. 1968), is a summary in 200 pages, with numerous illustrations, of papal history to the Reformation, and concludes with brief, critical bibliographical notes.

6716 JEDIN (HUBERT). A history of the Council of Trent. Trans. from the German by Dom Ernest Graf. Lond. 1957+.

Vol. i, pp. 5–75, deals with the conciliar theory and the papal reaction thereto down to Alexander VI.

6717 LE BRAS (GABRIEL). Institutions ecclésiastiques de la chrétienté médiévale. Pt. i, books ii to vi. Paris. 1964.

This is vol. xii in the Fliche–Martin series; *Histoire de l'église depuis les origines jusqu'à nos jours* (No. 1277).

6718 LEMARIGNIER (J-F.), GAUDEMET (J.), and MOLLAT (G.). Institutions ecclésiastiques. Paris. 1962.

This is vol. iii of Ferdinand Lot, ed. *Histoire des institutions françaises au moyen âge.*

6719 MOLLAT (GUILLAUME). Les Papes d'Avignon. Paris. 1912. 9th edn. Rev. and expanded. 1949. 10th edn. 1965. Trans. by Janet Love. Lond. 1963 and N.Y. 1965.

The classic work on the subject. The translation includes the footnotes but not the extensive bibliographies. See Mollat's critical edition of Étienne Baluze, *Vitae paparum avenionensium*, 4 vols. (Paris. 1914–27). See also Yves Renouard, *La Papauté à Avignon 1305–1403* (Paris. 1954); trans. by Denis Bethell (Lond. 1970). G. Mollat, 'Le Sacré collège', *R.H.E.* xlvi (1951), 22–112.

6720 PASTOR (LUDWIG). The history of the popes from the close of the middle ages (1305–1799). Trans. by F. I. Antrobus, R. F. Kerr, Ernest Graf and E. F. Peeler. 40 vols. Lond. 1891–1953. *

A standard history of the papacy. Vol. i surveys briefly the Avignonese popes and the popes and councils to 1447; vols. ii–v deal in detail with the period from the election of Nicholas V (1447) to the pontificate of Alexander VI.

6721 SEPPELT (FRANCIS X.). Geschichte der Päpste. 5 vols. Munich. 1954–9.

6722 SOUTHERN (RICHARD W.). Western society and the church in the middle ages. The Pelican History of the Church, ii. Harmondsworth. 1970.

6723 TELLENBACH (GERD). Church, state and Christian society at the time of the Investiture Contest. Stud. in Mediaeval Hist. no. 3. Oxf. 1945.

6724 ULLMANN (WALTER). The growth of papal government in the middle ages. Lond. 1955. 2nd edn. 1963. Idem, 'The papacy as an institution of government in the middle ages'. *Stud. in Church Hist.* ii (1965), 78–101. Idem, Medieval papalism. Lond. 1949.

6725 WATT (JOHN A.). The theory of papal monarchy in the thirteenth century: the contribution of the canonists. N.Y. 1966.

Originally published in *Traditio,* xx (1964), 179–317.

6726 WHITNEY (JAMES P.). Hildebrandine essays. Cambr. 1932.

2. England and the Papacy 1066–1485

a. General studies

6727 BROOKE (ZACHARY N.). The English church and the papacy, from the Conquest to the reign of John. Cambr. 1931. Reprinted 1969.

Brooke's volume is the standard treatment of the subject; but Charles Duggan's chapter in *English Church and Papacy* (No. 6734) should also be consulted. See R. L. Poole in *Poole papers* (No. 1487), or *Tout essays* (No. 1458); and H. W. C. Davis in *Davis papers* (No. 1466). H. E. J. Cowdrey, 'Pope Gregory VII and the Anglo-Norman church and kingdom'. *Studi Gregoriani* (Rome), ix (1972), 77–114.

6728 CANTOR (NORMAN F.). Church, kingship, and lay investiture in England 1089–1135. Princeton. 1958. *

See review by C. R. Cheney in *Speculum,* xxxiv (1959), 653–6.

6729 CHENEY (CHRISTOPHER R.). 'England and the Roman curia under Innocent III'. *J.E.H.* xviii (1967), 173–86.

C. R. Cheney, 'King John and the papal interdict', *B.J.R.L.* xxxi (1948), 295–317; idem, 'King John's reaction to the interdict in England', *T.R.H.S.* 4th Ser. xxxi (1949), 129–50; idem, 'A recent view (that of Richardson and Sayles in *Governance*) on the general interdict on England, 1208–14', *Stud. in Church Hist.* iii (1966), 159–68. See also P. Barnes and W. R. Powell in *Interdict documents* (Nos. 5603, 5809); and T. M. Parker, 'The terms of the interdict of Innocent III', *Speculum,* xi (1936), 258–60. For the whole pontificate of Innocent III, consult Achille Luchaire, *Innocent III.* 6 vols. (Paris, 1905–8).

6730 DEHIO (LUDWIG). Innocenz IV und England: ein Beitrag zur Kirchengeschichte des 13. Jahrhunderts. Berlin. 1914.

6731 HALLER (JOHANNES). Papsttum und Kirchenreform. Vier Kapitel zur Geschichte des ausgehenden Mittelalters. vol. i. Berlin. 1903. *

An important study of England and the papacy in the fourteenth century, pp. 375–465. See also Haller, *England und Rom unter Martin V* (Rome, 1905), reprinted from *Quellen und Forschungen aus Italienischen Archiven,* viii (1905), 249–304.

6732 JUNGHANNS (HERMANN). Zur Geschichte der englischen Kirchenpolitik von 1399–1413. Freiburg im Breisgau. 1914.

6733 LACOMBE (GEORGE). 'An unpublished document on the great interdict'. *Catholic H.R.* New Ser. ix (1930), 408–20.

Prints a sermon preached by Langton in London, 25 August 1213.

6734 LAWRENCE (CLIFFORD H.), ed. The English church and the papacy in the middle ages. Lond. 1965.

The chapters by C. Duggan, 'From the Conquest to the death of John'; by C. H. Lawrence, 'The thirteenth century'; by W. A. Pantin, 'The fourteenth century'; and by F. R. H. Du Boulay, 'The fifteenth century', constitute the best survey of up-to-date research on this subject.

6735 LUARD (HENRY R.). On the relations between England and Rome during the early portion of the reign of Henry III. Cambr. etc. 1877.

See Noël Denholm-Young, 'A letter from the council to Pope Honorius III, 1220–1', *E.H.R.* lx (1945), 88–96, in which nine councillors petition the pope against the recall of certain people who had been banished. F. A. Gasquet, *Henry III and the church* (Lond. 1905). Arthur L. Smith, *Church and state in the middle ages* (Oxf. 1913). MacKenzie in *Haskins essays* (No. 1439).

6736 McFARLANE (KENNETH B.). 'Henry V, Bishop Beaufort and the Red Hat, 1417–21'. *E.H.R.* lx (1945), 316–48.

See McFarlane in *Powicke essays* (No. 1450); and G. L. Harriss, 'Cardinal Beaufort, patriot or usurer?', *T.R.H.S.* 5th Ser. xx (1970), 129–48.

6737 PANTIN (WILLIAM A.). 'Grosseteste's relations with the papacy and the crown', in *Robert Grosseteste*, ed. by D. Callus (No. 6576), pp. 178–215.

6738 PERROY (ÉDOUARD). L'Angleterre et le grand schisme d'occident, i: étude sur la politique religieuse de l'Angleterre sous Richard II (1378–1399). Paris. 1933.

J. J. N. Palmer, 'England and the great western schism, 1388–1399', *E.H.R.* lxxxiii (1968), 516–22. Rose Graham, 'The great schism and the English monasteries of the Cistercian order', *E.H.R.* xliv (1929), 373–87; for a similar article on the order of Cluny, see above, *Graham papers* (No. 1471).

6739 RENOUARD (YVES). 'Édouard II et Clement V d'après les rôles gascons'. *Annales du Midi*, lxvii (1955), 119–41.

H. G. Richardson, 'Clement V and the see of Canterbury (1313)', *E.H.R.* lvi (1941), 97–103.

6740 ULLMANN (WALTER). The origins of the Great Schism. A study in fourteenth century ecclesiastical history. Lond. 1948.

See Ullmann, 'Cambridge and the Great Schism', *Jour. Theological Stud.* New Ser. ix (1958), 53–77. Leslie Macfarlane, 'An English account of the election of Urban VI, 1378', *B.I.H.R.* xxvi (1953), 75–85.

6741 ULLMANN (WALTER). 'The pontificate of Adrian IV', *Cambr. Hist. Jour.* xi (1953–5), 233–52.

b. Legates and envoys

See papal collectors (No. 6778–80); Brentano, *Two Churches* (No. 6787), chap. i; Gibbs and Lang, *Bishops* (No. 6793), index under 'Legates'.

6742 CHENEY (CHRISTOPHER R.). 'The papal legate and English monasteries in 1206'. *E.H.R.* xlvi (1931), 443–52. Idem, 'Cardinal John of Ferentino, papal legate in England in 1206'. Ibid. lxxvi (1961), 654–60.

6743 GRAHAM (ROSE). 'Letters of Cardinal Ottoboni' (1265–68). *E.H.R.* xv (1900), 87–120. Idem, 'Cardinal Ottoboni and the monastery of Stratford Langthorne'. *E.H.R.* xxxiii (1918), 213–25.

6744 HEIDEMANN (JOSEPH). Die englische Legation des Cardinals Guido Fulcodi, des späteren P. Clemens IV. Münster i. W. 1904. Idem, Papst Clemens IV: Pt. i: das Vorleben des Papstes und sein Legationsregister. Münster i. W. 1903.

6745 HALLER (JOHANNES). Piero da Monte, ein gelehrter und päpstlicher Beamter des 15. Jahrhunderts. Bibliothek des deutschen historischen Instituts in Rom, xix. Rome. 1941.

Prints the envoy's letters to the papacy in the 1430s.

6746 MERCATI (ANGELO). 'La prima relazione del Cardinale Nicolò de Romanis sulla sua legazione in Inghilterra (1213)', in *Poole essays* (No. 1448).

6747 TILLMANN (HELENE). Die päpstlichen Legaten in England bis zur Beendigung der Legation Gualas (1218). Bonn. 1926.

H. G. Richardson 'Letters of the legate Guala' [3 letters 1217–18], *E.H.R.* xlviii (1933), 250–9.

6748 WILLIAMSON (DOROTHY M.). 'Some aspects of the legation of Cardinal Otto in England, 1237–41'. *E.H.R.* lxiv (1949), 145–73. Idem, 'The legate Otto in Scotland and Ireland'. *Scot.H.R.* xxviii (1949), 14–30.

6749 ZIMMERMANN (HEINRICH). Die päpstliche Legation in der ersten Hälfte des 13. Jahrhunderts. Paderborn. 1913.

6750 BEHRENS (B.). 'Origins of the office of English resident ambassador in Rome'. *E.H.R.* xlix (1934), 640–56.

6751 HASKINS (GEORGE L.) and KANTOROWICZ (ERNST H.). 'A diplomatic mission of Francis Accursius and his oration before Pope Nicholas III (in 1278)'. *E.H.R.* lviii (1943), 424–47.

Prints pp. 440–7 the oration which is important for the study of medieval rhetoric and was given to support the election of Burnell to the see of Canterbury in 1278. For Accursius as Edward I's secretary 1273–81, see G. L. Haskins in *Law Quart. Rev.* liv (1938), 87–94.

6752 HECKEL (RUDOLF von). 'Das Aufkommen der ständigen Prokuratoren an der päpstlichen Kurie im 13. Jahrhundert'. *Miscellanea Francesco Ehrle* (Studi et Testi, nos. 37–42. Rome, 1924), ii. 290–321.

6753 HILL (MARY C.). 'Jack Faulkes, king's messenger, and his journey to Avignon in 1343'. *E.H.R.* lvii (1942), 19–30.

6754 JACOB (ERNEST F.). 'To and from the court of Rome in the early fifteenth century'. (William Swan as English proctor in papal curia 1409–30.) *Jacob papers* (No. 1474).

See also Jacob in No. 1437.

6755   JUDD (ARNOLD). 'A Wells archdeacon (Andrew Holes) at the Roman curia 1429–44'. *Church Quart. Rev.* clxi (1960), 293–307.

6756   KIRSCH (J. P.). 'Andreas Sapiti, englischer Prokurator an der Kurie im 14. Jahrhundert'. *Historisches Jahrbuch*, xiv (1893), 582–603.

6757   PARKS (GEORGE B.). The English traveler to Italy. Vol. i: the middle ages (to 1525). Stanford (Calif.), 1954. See No. 6922.

6758   THE ENGLISH HOSPICE IN ROME. The Venerabile, sexcentenary issue, vol. xxi (May 1962). Exeter.

Essays by various hands on the history of the hospice since 1362, with valuable lists of Englishmen in Rome from 1333 to 1514. See also Francis A. Gasquet, *A history of the Venerable English College in Rome* (Lond. 1920); and V. J. Flynn, 'Englishmen in Rome during the renaissance', *Modern Philology*, xxxvi (1938), 121–38.

c. Nominations to benefices

6759   BARRACLOUGH (GEOFFREY). Papal provisions: aspects of church history, constitutional, legal and administrative, in the later middle ages. Oxf. 1935. *

See also H. Baier, *Päpstliche provisionen für niedere Pfrunden bis zum Jahre 1304* (Münster, 1911).

6760   CHEYETTE (FREDERIC). 'Kings, courts, cures, and sinecures: the statute of provisors and the common law'. *Traditio*, xix (1963), 295–349.

6761   DAVIES (CECILY). 'The statute of provisors of 1351'. *History*, xxxviii (1953), 116–33.

6762   DEELEY (ANN). 'Papal provision and royal rights of patronage in the fourteenth century'. *E.H.R.* xliii (1928), 497–527.

See F. W. Maitland, '*Execrabilis* in the Common Pleas', in *Collected papers* (No. 1482), iii. 54–64. For one of the numerous disputes, see T. F. T. Plucknett, 'The case of the miscreant cardinal (1382–3)', *A.H.R.* xxx (1925), 1–15, where the cardinal is Robert of Geneva, who became Avignonese Pope, Clement VII. Also W. Pantin, *English church* (No. 6799), chaps. iii and iv.

6763   DRIVER (J. T.). 'The papacy and the diocese of Hereford, 1307–77'. *Church Quart. Rev.* clxv (1947), 31–47.

6764   GAUDEMET (JEAN). La Collation par le roi de France des bénéfices vacants en régale. Paris. 1935.

6765   HARTRIDGE (R. A. R.). 'Edward I's exercise of the right of presentation to benefices as shown by the patent rolls'. *Cambr. Hist. Jour.* ii (1927), 171–7.

6766   HOWELL (MARGARET). Regalian right in medieval England. Lond. 1962.

Arnold Pöschl, *Die Regalien der mittelalterichen Kirche* (Graz, 1928).

6767 LLOYD (MRS. A. H.). 'Notes on Cambridge clerks petitioning for benefices 1370–1399'. *B.I.H.R.* xx (1944–5), 75–96, 192–211.

See E. F. Jacob, 'Petitions for benefices' (No. 1473) and his 'On the promotion of English clerks during the later Middle Ages', *J.E.H.* i (1950), 172–86. For the subject in general, and especially for Paris and Orleans, see Donald E. R. Watt, 'University clerks and rolls of petitions for benefices', *Speculum*, xxiv (1959), 213–29.

6768 LUNT (WILLIAM E.). Financial relations . . . 1327–1534 (No. 6779), pp. 307–445.

Some essential documents on the development of provisions are translated in Lunt, *Papal revenues*, (No. 6780), ii. 217–33, 315–72. For numerous provisors from whom annates were due, see Lunt, *Collectors' accounts* (No. 6778).

6769 MOLLAT (GUILLAUME). La Collation des bénéfices ecclésiastiques à l'époque des papes d'Avignon (1305–1378). Paris. 1921.

This is also the introduction to Mollat's edition of *Lettres communes de Jean XXII* (No. 5553). See also Mollat, '*Le Roi de France et la collation plénière pleno jure des bénéfices ecclésiastiques*'. *Mémoires présentés . . . à l'Académie des Inscriptions et Belles-Lettres,* xiv, 2nd partie (1951). Also separately, Paris, 1951.

6770 SMITH (WALDO E. L.). Episcopal appointments and patronage in the reign of Edward II; a study in the relations of church and state. Chicago. 1938.

6771 SOMERVILLE (ROBERT). 'Duchy of Lancaster presentations, 1399–1485 (to churches, abbeys, etc. in various dioceses)'. *B.I.H.R.* xviii (1941), 52–76.

6772 THOMPSON (A. HAMILTON). 'Pluralism in the medieval church'. *A.A.S.R.P.* xxxiii (1915), 35–73; xxxiv (1917), 1–26; xxxv (1919), 87–108; xxxvi (1921), 1–41.

For returns of pluralists in province of Canterbury in 1366, see Langham's register (No. 5609) and Sudbury's London Register (No. 5764). C. J. Godfrey, 'Pluralists in the province of Canterbury in 1366', *J.E.H.* ii (1960), 23–40. W. T. Waugh, 'Archbishop Peckham and pluralities', *E.H.R.* xxviii (1913), 625–35. For a cardinal with numerous provisions in England, see Norman P. Zacour, 'Talleyrand, the Cardinal of Périgord (1301–1364)', *Amer. Phil. Soc. Trans.* (Philadelphia. 1960).

6773 WAUGH (WILLIAM T.). 'The great statute of praemunire (1393)'. *E.H.R.* xxxvii (1922), 173–205.

For the background and implementation of the statute of praemunire of 1353 see E. B. Graves in *Haskins essays* (No. 1439).

d. Papal taxation of the clergy

The outstanding studies on papal taxation in England are the works of William E. Lunt (Nos. 6778–80).

6774 COSTELLO (MICHAEL A.). De annatis Hiberniae: a calendar of the first fruits' fees levied on papal appointments to benefices in Ireland, A.D. 1400 to 1535, extracted from the Vatican and other Roman archives. With introduction by Ambrose Coleman, and supplementary notes by W. H. Grattan Flood. Vol. i. for Ulster. Dundalk. 1909; and Catholic Record Soc. Maynooth. 1912.

6775   FABRE (PAUL). Étude sur le liber censuum de l'église romaine. Biblio. Écoles françaises d'Athènes et de Rome. Paris. 1892.

P. Fabre, 'Recherches sur le denier de Saint Pierre en Angleterre au moyen-âge', in Mélanges G. B. de Rossi. Supplément aux *Mélanges d'Archéologie et d'Histoire*, xii (1892), 159–82.

6776   FAVIER (JEAN). Les Finances pontificales à l'époque du grand schisme d'occident. Bibliothèque des Écoles françaises etc. Paris. 1966.

Covers western Europe, with some attention to England.

6777   JENSEN (O.). 'The denarius sancti Petri in England'. *T.R.H.S.*, New Ser. xv (1901), 171–247; xix (1905), 209–77. Idem, Der englische Peterspfennig. Heidelberg. 1903.

The two papers are practically the same, except that in the latter Jensen treats the royal tribute more fully.

6778   LUNT (WILLIAM E.). Accounts rendered by papal collectors in England 1317–1378. Edited with additions and corrections by Edgar B. Graves. Philadelphia. 1968.

A large volume of Latin transcriptions of the accounts in *Collectorie* and *Introitus et Exitus* registers in the Vatican archives, preceded by an introduction on the collectors and the revenues.

6779   LUNT (WILLIAM E.). Financial relations of the papacy with England to 1327. Cambr. (Mass). 1939. Idem, Financial relations of the papacy with England 1327–1534. Cambr. (Mass.). 1962.

In these stout volumes each tax and each levy thereof is treated separately. The first volume includes several appendices, a full list of sources cited and an index. The second volume includes a long appendix on Obligations for and Payments of Services (Servitia) by England's archbishops and bishops from 1327 to 1534; but it does not include a bibliography or an index. It would be a boon to scholars if someone with time and resources compiled an index for the second volume. Lunt's numerous printed papers preparatory to these volumes are listed in the first volume. To that bibliography may be added C. R. Cheney, 'Master Philip the notary and the fortieth of 1199', *E.H.R.* lxiii (1948), 342–50; and F. A. Cazel, Jr., 'The tax of 1185 in aid of the Holy Land', *Speculum*, xxx (1955), 385–92; John A. Yunck, 'Economic conservatism, papal finance and medieval satires on Rome', *Mediaeval Stud.* xxiii(1961), 334–51; and Rose Graham, 'A petition to Boniface VIII' (No. 1471).

6780   LUNT (WILLIAM E.). Papal revenues in the middle ages. 2 vols. Columbia Univ. Records of Civilization. N.Y. 1934. *

Vol. i (pp. 3–136) describes the fiscal administration and the various types of revenues; then from pp. 137 to 341 provides English translations of documents on the fiscal administration. Vol. ii is devoted to translations of documents on the various revenues. Neither volume is specifically English in orientation. The work deals with the papal financial system as a whole. Compare Peter D. Partner, 'Camera papae: problems of papal finance in the later Middle Ages', *J.E.H.* iv (1953), 55–68.

6781   LUNT (WILLIAM E.), ed. The valuation of Norwich. Oxf. 1926.

This assessment compiled in 1254 for a tax 'imposed on the English clergy by Innocent IV, at the instance of Henry III, with the consent of the English prelates' was generally superseded by the valuation of 1291 by Nicholas IV (see No. 6783). Lunt's edition prints the returns in whole or in part from the dioceses of Bangor, Durham, Ely,

Lincoln, Llandaff, London, Norwich, and St. Asaph; fragments from some twenty religious houses; and portions of other valuations of 1217, 1229, 1268, and 1276. A portion of the valuation was edited by William Hudson, 'Norwich taxation of 1254, so far as it relates to the diocese of Norwich, collated with the taxation of Pope Nicholas in 1291', *Norfolk Archaeology*, xvii (1908), 46–157.

6782 MÉLY (FERNAND DE) and BISHOP (EDMUND). Bibliographie générale des inventaires imprimés. 2 vols. in 3 pts. Paris. 1892–5.

England: i. 136–335; ii. 335–70. These lists contain chiefly inventories of moveables belonging to churches, printed in county histories and elsewhere.

6783 TAXATIO ECCLESIASTICA ANGLIAE ET WALLIAE AUC-TORITATE P. NICHOLAI IV CIRCA A.D. 1291. Record Comm. Lond. 1802.

In 1288 Pope Nicholas IV granted the tenth of the revenue of the clergy to Edward I for six years, to defray the expenses of a crusade; and the king ordered a new valuation of all ecclesiastical benefices in the provinces of Canterbury and York, which was completed in 1291–2. A revised valuation for the province of York was made in 1317 and following years, and is printed with that of 1291–2 in the volume published by the Record Commission.

See Rose Graham, 'The taxation of Pope Nicholas IV', *Graham papers* (No. 1471); and Lunt, *Financial relations . . . to 1327* (No. 6779), pp. 346–65. This valuation was used for the remainder of the Middle Ages. For a partial list of unprinted medieval copies, and of portions of the assessment, consult Lunt, *Financial relations . . . to 1327*, pp. 666–75.

B. ADMINISTRATION OF THE CHURCH IN ENGLAND

1. *General Histories*

6784 BARLOW (FRANK). The English church 1000–1066. A constitutional history. Lond. 1963.

Barlow 'argues that the work of the tenth-century reformers reached its logical fulfilment in the legal codification of Archbishop Wulfstan; and that between Wulfstan's death in 1023 and the conquest, the reform movement maintained its full vigour only in the diocese of Worcester'.

6785 BÖHMER (HEINRICH). Kirche und Staat in England und in der Normandie im xi. und xii. Jahrhundert. Leipzig. 1899. *

Devotes particular attention to the period 1066–1154. In pt. ii, 163–269, Böhmer deals with the contemporary literature concerning church and state in England, especially 'der Yorker Anonymous' for which see No. 6427 above. Some of these tracts are printed in his appendix, pp. 433–97.

6786 BÖHMER (HEINRICH). 'Das Eigenkirchentum im England', in *Texte und Forschungen zur englischen Kulturgeschichte. Festgabe für Felix Liebermann*. Pp. 310–53. Halle. 1921.

6787 BRENTANO (ROBERT). Two churches: England and Italy in the thirteenth century. Princeton. 1968.

A comparison of the two churches, written with grace and learning; but not intended as a general history of either church.

6788 CAPES (WILLIAM W.). The English church in the fourteenth and fifteenth centuries. Lond. 1900. *

6789   CHENEY (CHRISTOPHER R.). From Becket to Langton: English church government 1170–1213. Manchester. 1956. See No. 5577.

6790   DIOCESAN HISTORIES. S.P.C.K. (21 vols.). Lond. etc. 1880–1902.

Bath and Wells, by William Hunt, 1885.
Canterbury by R. C. Jenkins, 1880.
Carlisle, by R. S. Ferguson, 1889.
Chester, by R. H. Morris, 1895.
Chichester, by W. R. W. Stephens, 1881.
Durham, by J. L. Low, 1881.
Hereford, by H. W. Phillott, 1888.
Lichfield, by William Beresford (1889).
Lincoln, by Edmund Venables and G. G. Perry, 1897.
Llandaff, by E. J. Newell, 1902.
Norwich, by Augustus Jessopp, 1884.
Oxford, by Edward Marshall, 1882.
Peterborough, by G. A. Poole (1881).
Rochester, by A. J. Pearman, 1897.
St. Asaph, by D. R. Thomas, 1888.
St. David's, by W. L. Bevan, 1888.
Salisbury, by W. H. Jones, 1880.
Sodor and Man, by A. W. Moore, 1893.
Winchester, by William Benham, 1884.
Worcester, by I. G. Smith and Phipps Onslow, 1883.
York, by George Ornsby (1882).

Short but useful accounts, each accompanied by a map of the diocese; some of the volumes having original value.

6791   EDWARDS (KATHLEEN). The English secular cathedrals in the middle ages: a constitutional study with special reference to the fourteenth century. Manchester. 1949. *

6792   FUETER (EDUARD). Religion und Kirche in England im funfzehnten Jahrhundert. Tübingen, etc. 1904. *

A valuable little treatise.

6793   GIBBS (MARION) and LANG (JANE). Bishops and reform, 1215–1272, with special reference to the Lateran Council of 1215. Lond. 1934. *

6794   HILL (GEOFFRY). English dioceses: a history of their limits. Lond. 1900.

6795   LOSERTH (JOHANN). Studien zur Kirchenpolitik Englands im 14. Jahrhundert. (to 1378.) Wien. *Akademie der Wissenschaften Phil.–Hist. Classe, Sitzungsberichte*, cxxxvi, no. i (1897). See No. 6799.

6796   MAKOWER (FELIX). Die Verfassung der Kirche von England. Berlin. 1894. Translated as The constitutional history and the constitution of the church of England. Lond. etc. 1895. *

6797   MOORMAN (JOHN R. H.). Church life in England in the thirteenth century. Cambr. 1945. Reprinted 1946.

Strong on the day-by-day activities of the lesser clergy and the religious. See also Moorman (No. 1283).

6798 OWEN (DOROTHY M.). Church and society in medieval Lincolnshire. *History of Lincolnshire*, v. Lincolnshire Local Hist. Soc. Lincoln, 1971.

6799 PANTIN (WILLIAM A.). The English church in the fourteenth century. Cambr. 1955.

> Kathleen Edwards, 'The political importance of the English bishops in the reign of Edward II', *E.H.R.* lix (1944), 311–47. Idem, 'The social origins and provenance of the English bishops during the reign of Edward II', *T.R.H.S.* 5th Ser. ix (1959), 51–79. J. R. L. Highfield, 'The English hierarchy in the reign of Edward III', *T.R.H.S.* 5th Ser. vi (1956), 115–38. Roy M. Haines, 'The education of the English clergy in the later Middle Ages: some observations on the operation of Pope Boniface VIII's constitution *Cum ex eo* (1298)', *Canadian Jour. Hist.* iv (1969), 1–22; on which see L. E. Boyle, 'The constitution *Cum ex eo* of Boniface VIII', *Mediaeval Stud.* xxiv (1962). 263–302.

6800 REPORT (FIRST) OF HER MAJESTY'S COMMISSIONERS APPOINTED TO INQUIRE INTO THE CONDITION OF THE CATHEDRAL AND COLLEGIATE CHURCHES OF ENGLAND AND WALES. 2 vols. Parl. Papers (1854), vol. xxv.

> The first report contains much historical information. The second and third reports are, from this point of view, less valuable.

6801 SMITH (H. MAYNARD). Pre-reformation England. Lond. 1938. *

6802 STEPHENS (WILLIAM R. W.). The English Church, 1066–1272. Lond. 1901. *

> J. Taylor, 'The Norman Conquest and the church in Yorkshire', *Univ. Leeds Rev.* x (1967), 231–55. Everett U. Crosby, 'The organization of the English episcopate under Henry I', *Stud. in Medieval and Renaissance Hist.* iv (1967), 1–88. D. L. Bethell, 'English Black Monks and episcopal elections in the 1120's' (elections to Canterbury in 1123 and to Worcester in 1125), *E.H.R.* lxxxiv (1969), 673–98.

6803 STOREY (ROBIN L.). Diocesan administration in the fifteenth century. St. Anthony's Hall Pubn. no. 16. York. 1959.

6804 THOMPSON (ALEXANDER HAMILTON). The English clergy and their organization in the later middle ages. Oxf. 1947.

> For ecclesiastical organizations, see M. Aston, Arundel (No. 5627) and R. Haines, *Worcester* (No. 5827). R. J. Knecht, 'The episcopate and the Wars of the Roses', *Univ. Birmingham Hist. Jour.* vi (1958), 108–31. Joel T. Rosenthal, 'The training of an elite group: English bishops in the fifteenth century', *American Philos. Soc. Trans.* New Ser. lx, pt. 5 (Philadelphia, 1970). Idem, 'Richard, duke of York: a xvth century layman and the church', *Church Hist. Rev.* l (1964/5), 171–87. Lita-Rose Betcherman, 'The making of bishops in the Lancastrian period', *Speculum*, xli (1966), 397–419.

6805 WATT (JOHN A.). The church and the two nations in medieval Ireland. Cambr. Stud. in Medieval Life and Thought 3rd Ser. Lond. 1970.

> For the church in Ireland, see Corish (No. 1274).

6806 WILLIAMS (GLANMOR). The Welsh church from the Conquest to the Reformation. Cardiff. 1962.

6807 WOOD-LEGH (K. L.). Studies in church life in England under Edward III. Cambr. 1934.

Chapters on royal administration of religious houses, on royal visitations of hospitals and free chapels, on alienation in mortmain, on chantries, and on the appropriation of parish churches, etc. See also No. 6862.

2. *Convocation and Synod*

See Wilkins's *Concilia* (No. 1142) and Powicke–Cheney (No. 6816).

6808 BARKER (ERNEST). The Dominican Order and convocation. Oxf. 1913.

6809 BARLOW (FRANK). 'The English, Norman, and French councils called to deal with the papal schism of 1159'. *E.H.R.* li (1936), 264–8.

6810 BOLTON (BRENDA). 'The council of London of 1342'. *Stud. in Church Hist.* vii (1971), 147–60.

6811 CHENEY (CHRISTOPHER R.). English synodalia of the thirteenth century. Oxf. 1941. Reprinted 1968.

C. R. Cheney, 'Legislation of the medieval English church', *E.H.R.* l (1935), 193–224, 385–417; idem, 'The earliest English diocesan statutes', *E.H.R.* lxxv (1960), 1–29; idem, 'Statute-making in the English church in the thirteenth century', *Boston Proceedings* (No. 1313), pp. 399–414; idem, 'The so-called statutes of John Pecham and Robert Winchelsey for the province of Canterbury', *J.E.H.* xii (1961), 14–34. See Cheney in *Gwynn essays* (No. 1438). See also D. M. Owen, 'Synods in the diocese of Ely in the latter Middle Ages and sixteenth century', *Stud. in Church Hist.* iii (1966), 217–22. H. Johnstone, 'Archbishop Pecham and the Council of Lambeth of 1281', *Tout essays* (No. 1458).

6812 JOYCE (JAMES W.). England's sacred synods: a constitutional history of the convocations of the clergy. Lond. 1855.

J. W. Joyce, *Handbook of the convocations or provincial synods of the church of England.* Lond. 1887.

6813 KEMP (ERIC W.). Counsel and consent. Aspects of the government of the church as exemplified in the history of the English provincial synods. S.P.C.K. Lond. 1961.

See also E. W. Kemp, 'The origins of the Canterbury convocation', *J.E.H.* iii (1952), 132–43.

6814 KENNETT (WHITE). Ecclesiastical synods and parliamentary convocations. Pt. i. Lond. 1701.

6815 LATHBURY (THOMAS). History of the convocation of the church of England. Lond. 1842. 2nd edn. 1853.

6816 POWICKE (SIR FREDERICK MAURICE) and CHENEY (CHRISTOPHER R.). Councils and synods, with other documents relating to the English church. Oxf. 1964.

Vol. ii, pt. i, 1205–65; pt. ii, 1265–1313. This estimable edition of fully annotated documents is essential: it is a long portion of the revision of Wilkins's *Concilia* (No. 1142).

6817 RECORDS OF THE NORTHERN CONVOCATION (1279–1714). Ed. by G. W. Kitchin. Surtees Soc. cxiii (1907).

Some miscellaneous documents go back to 1207 (Mullins). Kitchin's edition should be used with considerable discretion.

6818 ROBINSON (J. ARMITAGE). 'Convocation of Canterbury: its earliest history'. *Church Quarterly Rev.* lxxxi (1915), 81–137.

6819 WAKE (WILLIAM). The state of the church and clergy of England in their councils, synods, convocations, etc. Lond. 1703. ★

The appendix to this valuable work contains many records.

6820 WESKE (DOROTHY B.). Convocation of the clergy: a study of its antecedents and its rise with special emphasis upon its growth and activities in the thirteenth and fourteenth centuries. Lond. 1937.

See also E. F. Jacob, 'The Canterbury convocation of 1406', in *Wilkinson essays* (No. 1459). D. B. Weske, 'The attitude of the English clergy . . . toward the obligation of attendance on convocations and parliaments', *McIlwain essays* (No. 1444).

3. *Clerical Subsidies*
See *Eng. Hist. Docs.* (Myers) iv, nos. 405, 471.

6821 BROWN (J. E.). 'Clerical subsidies in the archdeaconry of Bedford, 1390–2, 1400–1'. *Beds. Hist. Rec. Soc. Pubns.* i (1913), 27–61.

6822 CHARTULARY OF . . . SALLAY (No. 6417). Vol. ii includes a return of a late fourteenth-century clerical taxation of Yorkshire.

6823 DEIGHTON (H. S.). 'Clerical taxation by consent, 1279–1301'. *E.H.R.* lxviii (1953), 161–92.

6824 DU BOULAY (FRANCIS R. H.). 'Charitable subsidies granted to the Archbishop of Canterbury, 1300–1489'. *B.I.H.R.* xxiii (1950), 147–64.

6825 GRAHAM (ROSE). 'An ecclesiastical tenth for national defense 1298'. *E.H.R.* xxxiv (1919), 200–5.

6826 KIRBY (JOHN L.). 'Two tax accounts of the diocese of Carlisle, 1379–80'. *Cumb.–Westm. Antiq.–Archaeol. Soc. Trans.* lii (1952), 70–84. Idem, 'Clerical poll taxes in the diocese of Salisbury, 1377–81'. Wilts. Archaeol.–Nat. Hist. Soc. Records Branch, xli *Collectanea* (1956), 157–67.

6827 LUNT (WILLIAM E.). 'The collectors of clerical subsidies granted to the king by the English clergy'. *The English Government at work* (No. 3836), ii. 227–80. Idem, 'The consent of the English lower clergy to taxation, 1166–1216', in *Gay essays* (No. 1436). Idem, 'The consent . . . during the reign of Henry III', in *Persecution and liberty*: essays in honor of George Lincoln Burr (N.Y. 1931), pp. 117–69. Idem, 'Clerical tenths . . . Edward II', *Haskins essays* (No. 1439).

6828 REGISTRUM VULGARITER NUNCUPATUM 'The Record of Caernarvon'. Record Comm. 1838.

Taxation of the diocese of Bangor (undated), together with a survey of the temporalities of that see, 22 Rich. II, pp. 226–37.

6829 SUBSIDY COLLECTED FROM THE CLERGY OF SUSSEX, 3 Richard II, 1380. By W. H. Blaauw. *Sussex Archaeol. Collections*, v (1852), 229–43.

Translation only.

6830 WILLARD (JAMES F.). 'The English church and the lay taxes of the fourteenth century'. *Univ. Colorado Stud.* iv, no. 4 (1907), 217–25.

4. *Church Life and the Lower Clergy*

Lists of benefices and their holders are often provided, although incomplete and deficient, in the older county histories, such as Nos. 1549, 1572, 1594, 1764, 1832, and 1847.

6831 ADAMS (NORMA). 'The judicial conflict over tithes'. *E.H.R.* lii (1937), 1–22.

J. A. F. Thomson, 'Tithes disputes in later medieval London', *E.H.R.* lxxviii (1963), 1–17.

6832 ANDRIEU-GUITRANCOURT (PIERRE). Essai sur l'évolution du décanat rural en Angleterre d'après les conciles des xiie, xiiie, et xive siècles. Paris. 1935.

6833 ARROWSMITH (RICHARD S.). The prelude to reformation: a study of English church life from the age of Wycliffe to the breach with Rome. Lond. 1923.

6834 AULT (WARREN O.). 'The village church and the village community in mediaeval England'. *Speculum*, xlv (1970), 197–215.

6835 BILL (P. A.). 'Five aspects of the medieval parochial clergy of Warwickshire'. *Univ. Birmingham Hist. Jour.* x (1966), 95–116.

6836 BROOKE (CHRISTOPHER N. L.). 'Gregorian reform in action: clerical marriage in England, 1050–1200'. *Cambr. Hist. Jour.* xii (1956), 1–21.

B. R. Kemp, 'Hereditary benefices in the medieval English church: a Herefordshire example', *B.I.H.R.* xliii (1970), 1–15.

6837 CHENEY (CHRISTOPHER R.), 'Rules for the observance of feast days in medieval England'. *B.I.H.R.* xxxiv (1961), 117–47.

6838 COX (JOHN C.). Churchwardens' accounts from the fourteenth century to the close of the seventeenth century. The Antiquary's Books. Lond. 1913.

Cox discusses forty-eight accounts for the period before 1485. Elsbeth Philipps, 'A list of printed churchwardens' accounts', *E.H.R.* xv (1900), 335–41, where the list for the period before 1485 names 40 accounts. A good list is *A list of churchwardens' accounts* by Lawrence Blair (reproduced from typewritten copy by Edwards Brothers. Ann Arbor (Mich.), 1939). See Drew (No. 6841).

From the earlier accounts Cox (p. x) selects as valuable printed transcripts: *Churchwardens' accounts of Croscombe, Pilton, Yatton, Tintinhull, Morebath, and St. Michael's,*

Bath (1349–1560) ed. by Edmund Hobhouse (Somerset Record Soc. 1890); Charles Kerry, *A history of the municipal church of St. Lawrence, Reading* (1410) (Reading, 1883); *The medieval records of a London city church, St. Mary at Hill, 1420–1559* (churchwardens' accounts, 1420–95, printed *in extenso*), edited by Henry Littlehales, E.E.T.S. Orig. Ser. nos. 125, 128 (1904–5). The Guildhall Library (London) has published *Churchwardens' accounts of parishes within the city of London: a handlist* (2nd edn. Lond. 1968).

Extracts from medieval churchwardens' accounts are printed for the following places:

(a) Andover (Hants): No. 5095.

(b) Arlington (Sussex), 1455–79: L. F. Salzmann, 'Early churchwardens' accounts', *Sussex Archaeol. Collections*, liv (1911), 85–112.

(c) Ashburton (Devon.), 1470–1580: J. H. Butcher, *The parish of Ashburton in the fifteenth and sixteenth centuries* (Lond. 1870). Newly edited by Alison Hanham, in Devon. and Cornwall Record Soc. Pubns. New Ser. xv (1970).

(d) Bishop's Stortford (Herts.), 1431–1847: J. L. Glasscock, *Records of St. Michael's church, Bishop's Stortford* (Lond. 1882), pp. 1–109.

(e) Bridgwater (Somers.) to 1468: No. 5247.

(f) Bristol, St. Ewen (Glos.), 1455–1553: John Maclean, *Bristol–Glos. Archaeol. Soc. Trans.* xv (1891), 139–82, 254–96. Also *The Church Book of St. Ewen's, Bristol, 1454–1584.* Ed. by Betty R. Masters and Elizabeth Ralph. Bristol–Glos. Archaeol. Soc. Records Sect. vi (1967).

(g) Cowfold (Sussex), 1460–85: W. B. Otter, *Sussex Archaeol. Collections*, ii (1849), 316–25.

(h) Derby, All Saints (Derbyshire), 1465–1527: No. 5053.

(i) Exeter, St. Petrock (Devon.), 1425–1692: Robert Dymond, *Devon Asso. for Advancement of Science, etc. Trans.* xiv (1882), 402–92. Published separately (Exeter, 1889).

(j) Hedon (Yorks.), Rich. II–Edw. IV: No. 5291.

(k) Hythe (Kent), 1412–13: W. A. Scott Robertson, *Archaeol. Cantiana*, x (1876), 242–9.

(l) Kirkby Stephen (Cumb.): No. 5050.

(m) London, All Hallows, 1455–1536: Charles Welch, *Churchwardens' accounts* (Lond. 1912).

(n) London, St. Margaret's, Westminster, 1460–1692: John Nichols, *Illustrations of the manners and expences of antient times in England, deduced from the accompts of churchwardens* (Lond. 1797), pp. 1–76.

(o) London, St. Mary Hill, 1427–1557: John Nichols, op. cit. pp. 85–129.

(p) London, St. Michael, Cornhill, 1456–1608: Ed. by W. H. Overall (Lond. 1871).

(q) London, St. Peter, Cheapside, 1392–1633: *British Archaeol. Asso. Jour.* xxiv (1868), 248–68.

(r) Ludlow (Salop), 1469–1749: Ed. by Llewellyn Jones, *Shropsh. Archaeol.-Nat. Hist. Soc. Trans.* 2nd Ser. i–ii, iv–v (1889–93), *passim*.

(s) Melton Mowbray (Leics.), Edw. IV–1612: Ed. by Thomas North. *Leics. Archit.-Archaeol. Soc. Trans.* iii (1874), 180–206.

(t) Oxford, St. Peter-in-the-East (Oxon.), 1444. Ed. by R. S. Mylne. *Soc. Antiq. of London Procs.* 2nd Ser. (1884), 25–8.

(u) Peterborough (Northants.), 1467–1573: Nos. 5216.

(v) Saffron Walden (Essex), 1439–85: Richard (Griffin), Lord Braybrooke, *History of Audley End and Saffron Walden* (Lond. 1836).

(w) Salisbury, St. Edmund and St. Thomas (Wilts.), 1443–1702: No. 5282.

(x) Tavistock (Devon.), 1385–1725: No. 5064.

(y) Thame (Oxon.), 1443–1648: No. 6298.

(z) Walberswick (Suffolk), 1451–?: Ed. by Robert W. Lewis, *Walberswick churchwardens' accounts* (Lond. 1947). Also in Nichols, *Illustrations of the manners*, pp. 183–93.

(aa) Walsall, All Saints (Staffs.), 1462–1531: No 5255.

(bb) Wigtoft (Lincs.), 1484–7: Nichols, *Illustrations of the manners*, pp. 74–84.

(cc) Yeovil (Somers.), 1457–8: No. 4865.

6839 CUTTS (EDWARD L.). Parish priests and their people in the middle ages in England. Lond. etc. 1898.* 5th edn. 1925. Idem, Scenes and characters of the middle ages. Lond. 1911.* 6th edn. 1926.

For the examination of candidates for the clergy, see Bennett in *Jenkinson Studies* (No. 1441).

6840 DANSEY (WILLIAM). Horae decanicae rurales: the origin, etc. of rural deans. 2 vols. Lond. 1835. 2nd edn. 1844.

6841 DREW (CHARLES). Early parochial organization in England: the origins of the office of churchwarden. St. Anthony's Hall Pubns. no. 7. York. 1954.

6842 GARLICK (VERA F. M.). 'The provision of vicars in the early fourteenth century'. *History*, xxiv (1949), 15–27.

Deals with the substitution of vicars for absentee rectors.

6843 GASQUET (FRANCIS A.). Parish life in medieval England. Lond. 1936.

6844 GODFREY (JOHN). The English parish, 600–1300. Church History Outlines. Lond. 1969.

6845 HALE (WILLIAM). The antiquity of the church-rate system. Lond. 1837.

Reginald Lennard, 'Two peasant contributions to church endowment', *E.H.R.* lxvii (1952), 230–3. Idem, 'Peasant tithe-collectors in Norman England, ibid. lxix (1954), 580–96; Andrew Little, 'Personal tithes', ibid. lx (1945), 67–88.

6846 HALL (DONALD J.). English mediaeval pilgrimage. Lond. 1966.

6847 HARTRIDGE (REGINALD A. R.). A history of vicarages in the middle ages. Cambr. 1930.

6848 HEATH (PETER). The English clergy on the eve of the reformation. Lond. 1969.

Broadly based on printed and MSS. materials, with a good bibliography. Idem, 'Medieval clerical accounts', St. Anthony's Hall Pubns. (York), no. 26 (1964). See *Eng. Hist. Docs.* (Myers), iv, no. 449.

6849 JESSOPP (AUGUSTUS). Before the great pillage. Lond. 1901.

Deals with parish life, pp. 3–72, and with the parish priest, pp. 73–120.

6850 JONES (W. R.). 'Patronage and administration: the king's free chapels in medieval England'. *Jour. British Stud.* ix (1969), 1–23. See No. 6066.

6851 MANNING (BERNARD L.). The people's faith in the time of Wyclif. Cambr. 1919.

6852 MOORMAN (JOHN R. H.). 'The medieval parsonage and its occupants'. *B.J.R.L.* xxvii (1944), 137–53.

Moorman's *Church life* (No. 6797) is valuable for the lesser clergy.

6853 PENDRILL (CHARLES). Old parish life in London. Lond. and N.Y. 1937.

6854 REICHEL (OSWALD J.). The origin and growth of the English parish. Lond. 1921.

> G. W. O. Addleshaw, 'The beginnings of the parochial system', St. Anthony's Hall Pubns. no. 3 (2nd edn. 1959). Idem, The development of the parochial system (768–1099), ibid. no. 6 (1954). Idem, 'Rectors, vicars and patrons', ibid. no. 9 (1956). See also Drew (No. 6841).

6855 RICHARDSON (HENRY G.). 'The parish clergy in the thirteenth and fourteenth centuries'. *T.R.H.S.* 3rd Ser. vi (1912), 89–128.

6856 ROBINSON (DAVID). 'Beneficed clergy in Cleveland and the East Riding, 1306–1340'. Borthwick Papers, no. 37. York. 1970.

6857 SELDEN (JOHN). The history of tithes. Lond. 1618. * Also printed in Works of Selden, iii. 1069–1298. Lond. 1726.

> Still the most exhaustive authority on the history of tithes. Selden held that the practices of the early church are inconsistent with the view that tithes are payable by divine right, though Selden nowhere expressly denies the doctrine of divine right. The work gave great offence to the clergy, and was suppressed by the Court of High Commission. Cf. H. W. Clarke, *A history of tithes* (Lond. 1891; 2nd edn. 1894).

6858 THOMPSON (ALEXANDER HAMILTON). 'Colleges of chantry priests' in his *The English clergy* (No. 6804), pp. 247–91.

> Prints *Ordinacio Cantariarum in Capella de Sibthorp.*

6859 THOMPSON (A. H.). 'Diocesan organization in the Middle Ages: archdeacons and rural deans'. *P.B.A.* xxix (1943), 153–94.

> Jean Scammell, 'The rural chapter in England from the eleventh to the fourteenth century', *E.H.R.* lxxxvi (1971), 1–21.

6860 WATKIN (AELRED), ed. Archdeaconry of Norwich; inventory of church goods, *temp.* Edward III. Norfolk Rec. Soc. xix. i vol. in 2. 1947–8.

6861 WOOD-LEGH (KATHLEEN L.). 'The appropriation of parish churches during the reign of Edward III'. *Cambr. Hist. Jour.* iii (1929), 15–22. See No. 6807.

6862 WOOD-LEGH (KATHLEEN L.). Perpetual chantries in Britain. Cambr. 1965.

> These Birkbeck Lectures are the basic study on chantries in England and Scotland. See also her 'Some aspects of the history of the chantries during the reign of Edward III', *Cambr. Hist. Jour.* iv (1932), 26–50; and 'Some aspects of the history of chantries in the later Middle Ages', *T.R.H.S.* 4th Ser. xxviii (1946), 47–60. See No. 6807.

5. *Heresy and the Lollards*

For documents, see *Fasciculus rerum* (No. 6864); Netter (No. 6612); Pecock (No. 6629–30); Purvey (No. 6632); Wyclif (pp. 873–5); and the translations in *E.H.D.* iv. 837–78. For the early stages of Lollardy, K. B. McFarland's *Wyclif* (No. 6657) provides a good account; for the later stages, J. A. F. Thomson (No. 6873).

6863   THE EXAMINATION OF MASTER WILLIAM THORPE, PRIEST, OF HERESY . . . (1407). THE EXAMINATION OF THE HONOURABLE KNIGHT, SIR JOHN OLDCASTLE . . . Ed. by Alfred W. Pollard in *Fifteenth century prose and verse* (Lond. and N.Y. 1903), pp. 97–189. Also printed in *Select Works of John Bale*, edited by Henry Christmas (Parker Soc. Cambr. 1849), pp. 5–59 for Oldcastle, and pp. 60–133 for Thorpe. See *E.H.D.* iv. 851–3 and 859–64.

> W. T. Waugh, 'Sir John Oldcastle', *E.H.R.* xx (1905), 434–56, 637–58. Idem, 'The Lollard knights', *Scot. H. R.* xi (1914), 55–92. H. G. Richardson, 'John Oldcastle in hiding, August–October 1417', *E.H.R.* lv (1942), 432–8.

6864   FASCICULUS RERUM EXPETENDARUM ET FUGIENDARUM, prout Orthuino Gratio editus est Coloniae A.D. 1535 in concilii tunc indicendi usum et admonitionem; una cum appendice sive tomo ii scriptorum veterum qui ecclesiae Romanae errores et abusus detegunt et damnant. Ed. by Edward Brown. 2 vols. Lond. 1690.

> *Wilhelmus Wodfordus adversus Johannem Wiclefum*: i. 190–265.
> *Articuli Johannis Wiclefi in concilio Constantiensi damnati*: i. 266–95.
> Sermons, letters, etc. of Robert Grosseteste: ii. 250–415. *Defensorium Wilhelmi Ockam contra Johannem XXII*: ii. 436–65.
> *Defensorium curatorum* (of Richard Fitzralph, archbishop of Armagh, directed against the friars, A.D. 1357): ii. 466–87. A much briefer work than his *De Pauperie Salvatoris*, written 1350–3 in seven books, the first four of which are printed by R. L. Poole as an appendix to his edition of Wyclif's *De Dominio Divino* (Wyclif Soc. Lond. 1890). Proceedings against English heretics, etc. 1428: ii. 618–30.

6865   FOXE (JOHN). Actes and monuments. Popularly known as The Book of Martyrs. Lond. 1563. Ed. by S. R. Cattley and George Townsend. 8 vols. Lond. 1837–41. Also edited by Joseph Pratt. 8 vols. Lond. 1870.

> See Conyers Read, *Bibliography* (No. 32), nos. 1726 and 1826; and *E.H.D.* (Myers), iv, 646.

6866   LANTERNE OF LIZT. Ed. by L. M. Swinburn. E.E.T.S. Old Ser. cli (1917).

6867   ASTON (MARGARET E.). 'Lollardy and sedition'. *Past and Present*, xvii (1960), 1–44. Idem, 'Lollardy and the reformation, survival or revival'. *History*, xlix (1964), 149–70.

6868   DAVIS (J. F.). 'Lollard survival and the textile industry in the south-east of England'. *Stud. in Church hist.* iii (1966), 191–201.

6869   DICKENS (ARTHUR G.). 'Heresy and the origins of English protestantism', in *Britain and the Netherlands*. Ed. by J. S. Bromley and E. H. Kossmann (papers delivered to the Anglo-Dutch Historical Conference, 1962), ii. 47–66. Lond. 1964. Idem, Lollards and the protestants in the diocese of York, 1509–58. Lond. 1959.

6870   GAIRDNER (JAMES). Lollardy and the reformation in England; an historical survey. 4 vols. Lond. 1908–13. *

6871 LEFF (GORDON). Heresy in the later middle ages. 2 vols. Manchester and N.Y. 1967.

Vol. iii, 494–558, John Wyclif; 559–605, The Lollards.

6872 RICHARDSON (HENRY G.). 'Heresy and the lay power under Richard II'. *E.H.R.* li (1936), 1–28.

J. H. Dahmus, 'John Wyclif and the English government', *Speculum*, xxxv (1960), 51–68. Henry G. Russell, 'Lollard opposition to oaths by creatures', *A.H.R.* li (1945–6), 668–84.

6873 THOMSON (JOHN A. F.). The later Lollards, 1414–1520. Oxf. Hist. Ser. Lond. 1965.

R. Foreville, 'Manifestations de lollardisme à Exeter en 1421', *Le Moyen Âge*, lxix (1963), 691–706. Eleanor J. B. Reid, 'Lollards at Colchester in 1414', *E.H.R.* xxix (1914), 101–4. M. G. Snape, 'Some evidence of Lollard activity in the diocese of Durham in the early 15th century', *Archaeol. Aeliana*, 4th Ser. xxxix (1961), 355–61. Edwin Welch, 'Some Suffolk Lollards', *Suffolk Institute of Archaeol. Procs.* xxix (1962), 154–65. James Crompton, 'Leicestershire Lollards', *Leics. Archaeol. Soc. Trans.* xliv (1968–9), 11–44. F. D. Logan, 'Another cry of heresy at Oxford: the case of Dr. John Holand', *Stud. in Church Hist.* v (1969), 99–113.

6874 WAUGH (WILLIAM T.). 'The Lollard knights'. *Scot.H.R.* xi (1913–14), 55–92.

See K, McFarlane, *Lancastrian kings and Lollard knights* (No. 4221); and his *John Wycliffe* (No. 6657).

XXIII. INTELLECTUAL INTERESTS 1066–1485

A. LEARNING: PHILOSOPHY AND SCIENCE

The works of Rashdall (No. 7090), Knowles (Nos. 1298, 1300), and the Oxford histories of England provide general guides. The studies listed on pp. 179–83 above give more detailed information. For learning in the English Dominican province and for early English Dominican writers, see Hinnebusch (No. 5993), pp. 332–419. For controversies and personalities of the fourteenth century, including the Merton scholars of natural science, turn to Pantin (No. 6799), pp. 105–85. For the works and modern accounts of individual scholars, refer to pp. 858–75.

1. *General References*

6875 ARCHIVES D'HISTOIRE DOCTRINALE ET LITTÉRAIRE DU MOYEN ÂGE. i+. Paris. 1926–7+.

6876 BIBLIOGRAPHIE DE LA PHILOSOPHIE. (A quarterly published by) l'Institut international de philosophie. Paris. 1+ (1954+).

Selective and annotated. Successor to *Bibliographie de la philosophie* under the same auspices. i–x (1937–53).

6877 RÉPERTOIRE BIBLIOGRAPHIQUE DE LA PHILOSOPHIE. Publié sous les auspices de l'Institut supérieur de philosophie. Louvain. 1+ (1949+).

A quarterly of detailed listings without annotations. Continues Répertoire biblio-graphique in *Revue néoscolastique de philosophie,* 1934+.

6878   BALDWIN (JOHN W.). Masters, princes and merchants (No. 5443).

6879   CURTIUS (ERNST R.). Europäische Literatur und lateinisches Mittelalter. Bern. 1948. Trans. as European literature and the Latin middle ages, by Willard R. Trash. N.Y. 1953.

6880   FOREST (ANDRÉ (i.e. AIMÉ)), VAN STEENBERGHEN (FER-NAND) and GANDILLAC (MAURICE DE). Le mouvement doctrinal du xie au xive siècle, in Fliche and Martin, *Histoire de l'église,* xiii. Paris. 1951.

See Fernand van Steenberghen, *The philosophical movement in the thirteenth century* (Lectures . . . at Belfast). Trans. from the French by J. J. Gaine. (Lond. 1955). Idem, *Aristotle in the west; the origins of Latin Aristotelianism.* Trans. by Leonard Johnston (Louvain, 1955).

6881   GEYER–UEBERWEG: Friedrich Ueberwegs Grundriss der Geschichte der Philosophie. Zweiter Teil: die patristische und scholastische Philosophie, herausgegeben von Dr. Bernhard Geyer. 12th edn. Basel. 1951.

6882   GEWIRTH (ALAN). 'Philosophy and political thought in the fourteenth century', in *The forward movement of the fourteenth century.* Ed. by Francis L. Utley. Columbus (Ohio). 1961. Pp. 125–64.

6883   GHELLINCK (JOSEPH de). L'essor de la littérature latine au xiie siècle. 2 vols. Paris. 1946. Idem, Le mouvement théologique de xiie siècle: Sa prépara-tion lointaine avant et autour de Pierre Lombard, ses rapports avec les initiatives des canonistes. Paris. 1914. * 2nd edn. Bruges. 1948.

6884   GILSON (ÉTIENNE H.). History of christian philosophy in the middle ages. N.Y. 1955.

Pp. 551–804 devoted to exhaustive bibliographical notes.

6885   GLORIEUX (PALÉMON). Répertoire des maîtres en théologie de Paris au xiiie siècle. 2 vols. Paris. 1933–4.

Bio-bibliographical dictionary of 425 theologians and philosophers with lists of MSS. Table of incipits: ii. 375–459.

6886   GRABMANN (MARTIN). Die Geschichte der scholastischen Methode, nach den gedruckten und ungedruckten Quellen dargestellt. 2 vols. Freiburg-im-Breisgau. 1909–11.

6887   HASKINS (CHARLES H.). The renaissance of the twelfth century. Cambr. (Mass.). 1928. * (Reprinted as a paperback.) Idem, Studies in medieval culture. Oxf. 1929.

Cf. William A. Nitze, 'The so-called twelfth century renaissance', *Speculum,* xxiii (1948), 464–71; Urban T. Holmes, 'The idea of a twelfth century renaissance', ibid. xxvi (1951), 643–51; Eva M. Sanford, 'The twelfth century renaissance or proto-renaissance', ibid. xxvi (1951), 635–42.

6888   KNOWLES (MICHAEL DAVID). The evolution of medieval thought. Lond. 1962. Idem, 'Some recent advance in the history of medieval thought'.

Cambr. Hist. Jour. vii (1943), 146–59; ix (1947), 22–50; x (1952), 354–8. Idem, 'A characteristic of the mental climate of the fourteenth century'. *Mélanges offerts à Étienne Gilson* (Toronto and Paris. 1959). Pp. 315–25.

6889   LUBAC (HENRI de). Exégèse médiévale. Les quatre sens de l'Écriture. 2 pts. Paris. 1959–64.

6890   MACDONALD (ALLAN J.). Authority and reason in the early middle ages. Lond. 1933.

6891   O'DONNELL (J. REGINALD), ed. Nine medieval thinkers; a collection of hitherto unedited texts. Toronto. 1955.

Texts of Adam of Bocfield (Nos. 6552–4), Richard of Campsall, Walter Catton, Thomas Sutton, and five non-English writers. All the English are listed in Emden, *Oxford.*

6892   PARÉ (GERARD M.), BRUNET (ADRIEN), and TREMBLAY (PIERRE). La renaissance du xiie siècle: les écoles et l'enseignement. Paris. 1933.

Refonte complète de l'ouvrage de G. Robert *Les Écoles et l'enseignement de la théologie pendant la première moitié du xiie siècle* (Paris, 1909).

6893   POOLE (REGINALD L.). Illustrations of the history of medieval thought (and learning). Lond. 1884; 2nd edn. 1920. *

6894   RABY (FREDERIC J. E.). A history of secular Latin poetry in the middle ages. Oxf. 1934; 2nd edn. 1957. Idem, A history of Christian Latin poetry from the beginnings to the close of the middle ages. Oxf. 1927; 2nd edn. 1953.

6895   SMALLEY (BERYL). The study of the Bible in the middle ages. Oxf. 1941; 2nd edn. 1952. Also paperback reprint.

The index below lists some of the numerous articles by Beryl Smalley to be found in various journals. Consult also H. Glunz, The Vulgate (No. 1335), and *Cambridge History of the Bible* (No. 1327A).

6896   SOUTHERN (RICHARD W.). The making of the middle ages. New Haven. 1953. (Paperback reprint.)

6897   THOMPSON (JAMES W.). The literacy of the laity in the middle ages. Berkeley (Calif.). 1939.

6898   WRIGHT (FREDERICK A.) and SINCLAIR (THOMAS A.). A history of later Latin literature from the middle of the fourth to the end of the seventeenth century. Lond. 1931. *

6899   WULF (MAURICE M. C. J. de). Histoire de la philosophie médiévale. 6th edn. Louvain and Paris. 1947. English trans. as History of medieval philosophy by Ernest C. Messenger (vol. i from the beginnings to the end of the twelfth century). Lond. and N.Y. 1952. Earlier editions were translated by P. Coffey (Lond. 1909) and E. C. Messenger (Lond. 1926, 1935–8).

2. Studies on English Learning, 1066–1300

6900   CALLUS (DANIEL A.). 'Introduction of Aristotelian learning to Oxford'. *P.B.A.* xxix (1943), 229–81. Idem, 'The contribution to the study of the Fathers made by the thirteenth century Oxford schools'. *J.E.H.* v (1954), 139–48.

6901 CARRÉ (MEYRICK H.). Phases of thought in England. Oxf. 1949.

Pp. 1–177 on the Middle Ages.

6902 COULTON (GEORGE G.). Medieval panorama: The English scene from the Conquest to the Reformation. Cambr. (Mass.). 1938; Cambr. 1939.

6903 GALBRAITH (VIVIAN H.). 'The literacy of the medieval English kings'. *P.B.A.* xxi (1937), 201–38. Reprinted in *Studies in history*. Selected by Lucy S. Sutherland. Lond. 1966.

6904 GRAHAM (ROSE). 'The intellectual influence of English monasticism between the tenth and the twelfth centuries'. *T.R.H.S.* New Ser. xvii (1903), 23–65. Reprinted in No. 1471.

6905 HUNT (RICHARD W.). 'English learning in the late twelfth century'. *T.R.H.S.* 4th Ser. xix (1936), 19–42. Reprinted in No. 1493.

See Haskins in *Tout essays* (No. 1458); MacKinnon in *Wilkinson essays* (No. 1459).

6906 KNOWLES (DAVID). 'The cultural influences of English medieval monasticism'. *Cambr. Hist. Jour.* vii (1943), 146–59. See also his four vols. on monastic history (Nos. 1298, 1300) and his excerpts therefrom in *Saints and scholars*. Cambr. 1962. Idem, 'Humanism of the twelfth century' (No. 1477).

6907 LAWRENCE (CLIFFORD H.). 'Stephen of Lexington and Cistercian university studies in the thirteenth century'. *J.E.H.* xi (1960), 164–78.

6908 LITTLE (ANDREW G.) and PELSTER (FRANZ). Oxford theology and theologians, *c.* A.D. 1282–1302. Oxf. Hist. Soc. xcvi (1934). Also A. G. Little, 'Theological schools in medieval England'. *E.H.R.* lv (1940), 624–30. Idem, The Grey friars in Oxford. Oxf. Hist. Soc. xx (1892). Idem, 'The Franciscan school at Oxford in the thirteenth century'. *Archivum Franciscanum Historicum*, xix (1926), 803–74 (adaptation in *Franciscan Papers* (No. 6023), pp. 55–71). Beryl Smalley, 'Robert Bacon and the early Dominican school at Oxford'. *T.R.H.S.* xxx (1948), 1–19.

6909 RUSSELL (JOSIAH C.). Dictionary of writers of thirteenth century England. *B.I.H.R.* Special Supplement, 3 (1936). * Additions and corrections *B.I.H.R.* xvi (1938), 48–50; xviii (1940), 940–2; and xix (1942–3), 99–100, 212–14.

6910 SHARP (DOROTHEA E.). Franciscan philosophy at Oxford in the thirteenth century. British Soc. Franciscan Stud. xvi. Oxf. 1930. *

Deals with Grosseteste, Thomas of York, Roger Bacon, Pecham, Richard of Middleton, and Duns Scotus.

6911 SOUTHERN (RICHARD W.). Medieval humanism and other studies. Oxf. and N.Y. 1970.

Includes essays on Bede, St. Anselm, England's first entry into Europe (*c.* 1066–1200), The place of England in the twelfth century Renaissance (revised from *History*, xlv

(1960), 201–16), Ranulf Flambard, King Henry I, Pope Adrian IV, and various aspects of humanism. See also W. Pantin in *Gwynn essays* (No. 1438).

6912 STUBBS (WILLIAM). Seventeen lectures on medieval and modern history. Oxf. 1886. * 3rd edn. 1900.

Chaps. vi–vii: Learning and literature at the court of Henry II.

3. *Studies on English Learning, 1300–1485*

6913 BENNETT (JOSEPHINE W.). 'Andrew Holes, a neglected harbinger of the English renaissance'. *Speculum*, xix (1944), 314–35.

See Emden, *Oxford* (No. 533), pp. 949–50.

6914 EINSTEIN (LEWIS). The Italian renaissance in England. N.Y. 1902. *

6915 GALBRAITH (VIVIAN H.). 'John Seward and his circle: some London scholars of the early fifteenth century'. *Mediaeval and Renaissance Stud.* i (1941), 85–104.

6916 GRAY (HOWARD L.). 'Greek visitors to England in 1455–1456'. *Haskins essays* (No. 1439), 81–116.

6917 LEFF (GORDON). 'Changing patterns of thought in the earlier fourteenth century'. *B.J.R.L.* xliii (1960–1), 354–72.

This is an amplification and modification of idem, 'The fourteenth century and the decline of scholasticism', *Past and Present*, ix (1956), 30–41. See also Knowles (No. 6888).

6918 MEISSNER (PAUL). England im Zeitalter von Humanismus, Renaissance and Reformation. Heidelberg. 1952.

6919 MITCHELL (ROSAMOND J.). John Free: from Bristol to Rome in the fifteenth century. Lond. 1955. Idem, John Tiptoft, 1427–70. Lond. 1938. Idem, 'English law students at Bologna in the fifteenth century'. *E.H.R.* li (1936), 270–87. Idem, 'English students at Padua, 1460–75'. *T.R.H.S.* 4th Ser. xix (1936), 101–17. Idem, 'English students at Ferrara in the fifteenth century', *Italian Stud.* (Manchester), i (1937–8), 75–82.

6920 PALGRAVE (FRANCIS T.). The Oxford movement of the fifteenth century. *Nineteenth Century*, xxviii (1890), 812–30.

Deals with the revival of studies at Oxford.

6921 PANTIN (WILLIAM A.). The English church in the fourteenth century. Cambr. 1955.

Pt. ii: Intellectual life and controversy.

6922 PARKS (GEORGE B.). The English traveler to Italy: i: the middle ages (to 1525). Stanford (Calif.). 1954. See Nos. 6757–8.

6923 SCHIRMER (WALTER F.). Der englische Frühhumanismus: ein Beitrag zur englischen Literaturgeschichte des 15. Jahrhunderts. Leipzig. 1931. 2nd edn. Tübingen. 1963.

6924 SMALLEY (BERYL). English friars and antiquity in the early fourteenth century. Oxf. 1960.

Includes, *inter alia*, the friars as teachers and preachers, the patronage of letters, and the interest in the classics (*c.* 1320-1350). The principal scholars considered are John Ridevall, John Lathbury, Thomas Waleys, Robert Holcot, William d'Eyncourt, Thomas Hopeman, and Thomas Ringstead.

6925 STEPHENS (GEORGE R.). The knowledge of Greek in England in the middle ages. Philadelphia. 1933.

6926 TAIT (JAMES). 'Letters of John Tiptoft, earl of Worcester, and Archbishop Neville to the university of Oxford'. *E.H.R.* xxxv (1920), 570-4.

6927 TOUT (THOMAS F.). 'Literature and learning in the English civil service in the fourteenth century'. *Speculum*, iv (1929), 365-89. Reprinted in his *Collected papers* (No. 1499).

6928 ULLMAN (BERTHOLD L.). 'Manuscripts of Duke Humphrey of Gloucester'. *E.H.R.* lii (1937), 670-2. M. Creighton, 'Some literary correspondence of Humphrey, duke of Gloucester'. Ibid. x (1895), 99-104. Mario Borsa, 'Correspondence of Humphrey, duke of Gloucester and Pier Candido Decembrio'. Ibid. xix (1904), 509-26. W. L. Newman, 'Correspondence... Decembrio'. Ibid. xx (1905), 484-98. See Vickers (No. 4231) and Bennett, *Six medieval men* (No. 6977).

6929 WEISHEIPL (JAMES A.). 'Developments in the arts curriculum at Oxford in the early fourteenth century'. *Mediaeval Stud.* xxviii (1966), 151-75.

R. J. Schoeck, 'On rhetoric in fourteenth century Oxford', ibid. xxx (1968), 214-25.

6930 WEISS (ROBERTO). Humanism in England during the fifteenth century. Oxf. 1941; revised edn. 1957; 3rd edn. 1967.

The best book on the subject. It cites Weiss's several articles in diverse journals. For 'The Latin classics known to Boston of Bury', see Mynors in *Saxl essays* (No. 1452).

6931 WEISS (R.). The renaissance discovery of classical antiquity. Oxf. 1969.

4. *Science in the Late Middle Ages*

See Crombie (No. 1418), Haskins (No. 1419), Sarton (No. 1420), Talbot (No. 1421), Talbot and Hammond (No. 1422), Thorndike (No. 1423), and White (No. 1424).

The lore, myths, and traditions of the science of the early Middle Ages were countered by the twelfth-century translations of Arabic science and of Aristotle. By the fourteenth century Aristotelian concepts were themselves being rejected. In England the Merton School of mathematical physicists made particularly important developments of doctrines of dynamics. The studies of Bradwardine, Heytesbury, Swineshead, and Dumbleton form a background to modern principles of mechanics; they are forerunners of Galileo in theorems concerning bodies in motion.

A useful bibliography is given chapter by chapter in the second edition of Crombie, *Augustine to Galileo* (No. 1418); and much retrospective bibliography is found in *Isis Cumulative Bibliography* (No. 6934). For current bibliography of science and related subjects see the issues of *Isis* (No. 6933); and for individuals, such as Roger Bacon, Grosseteste, and others, see pp. 858–75.

6932 BRITISH JOURNAL FOR THE HISTORY OF SCIENCE. i+. Leeds. 1962+.

6933 ISIS. International review devoted to the history of science and civilization. Brussels, Bruges, etc., and then Washington. i+ (1913+).

6934 ISIS CUMULATIVE BIBLIOGRAPHY. A bibliography of the history of science formed from Isis critical bibliographies 1–90 (1913–65). Ed. by Magda Whitrow. 2 vols. Lond. 1971.

Vol. i and part of vol. ii: personalities; the rest of vol. ii: institutions.

6935 BULLOUGH (VERN L.). 'Medical study at mediaeval Oxford'. *Speculum*, xxxvi (1961), 601–12. Idem, 'The mediaeval medical school at Cambridge'. *Mediaeval Stud.* xxiv (1962), 161–8. Idem, 'A note on medical care in medieval English hospitals'. *Bulletin of the History of Medicine* (Baltimore), xxxv (1961), 74–7.

6936 CARMODY (FRANCIS J.). Arabic astronomical and astrological sciences in Latin translation. A critical bibliography. Berkeley (Calif.). 1956.

A. E. Roy and E. L. G. Stones, 'The record of eclipses in the Bury Chronicle', *B.I.H.R.* xliii (1970), 125–33.

6937 CATALOGUE OF WESTERN MANUSCRIPTS ON MEDICINE AND SCIENCE IN THE WELLCOME HISTORICAL MEDICAL LIBRARY. i: *MSS.* written before 1650 A.D. Ed. by S. A. J. Moorat. Lond. 1962.

6938 CHOLMELEY (HENRY P.). John of Gaddesden and the *Rosa medicinae*. Oxf. 1912.

6939 CLAGETT (MARSHALL). Archimedes in the middle ages. Vol. i: The Arabo-Latin tradition. Madison (Wisc.). 1964.

6940 CLAGETT (M.). The science of mechanics in the middle ages. Madison (Wisc.). 1959.

A scholarly work of prime importance, interlarded with Latin documents, with English translation and commentary. Important for the Merton School.

6941 CLAGETT (M.). 'Some novel trends in the science of the fourteenth century', in *Art, Science and History in the Renaissance*. Ed. by Charles S. Singleton. Baltimore (Md.). 1967. Pp. 275–303.

6942 CROMBIE (ALISTAIR C.). Robert Grosseteste and the origins of experimental science, 1100–1700. Oxf. 1953.

Includes a full bibliography.

6943 CROMBIE (A. C.) and HOSKIN (MICHAEL A.), eds. History of Science. Vol. i (1962); vol. ii (1963). An annual review of literature, research, and teaching. Cambr. 1962.

Crombie has a summary in *Medieval England* (No. 1485), chap. xviii.

6944 CROMBIE (A. C.), ed. Scientific Change: historical studies in the intellectual, social and technical conditions for scientific discovery and technical invention from antiquity to the present. *Symposium on the History of Science, Univ. Oxford, 9-15 July 1961.* N.Y. 1963.

Part iii, pp. 181-343: Medieval Science and Technology.

6945 DALES (RICHARD C.). 'Anonymi De Elementis: from a twelfth-century collection of scientific works in B.M. MS. Cotton Galba E IV'. *Isis,* lvi (1965), 174-89.

Prints a *Tractatus De Elementis.*

6946 DAWSON (WARREN R.), ed. A leechbook or collection of medical recipes of the fifteenth century. Lond. 1934.

6947 THE EARLIEST ARITHMETICS IN ENGLISH. Ed. by Robert R. Steele. E.E.T.S. Extra Ser. cxviii (1922).

6948 EVANS (JOAN) and SERJEANTSON (MARY S.). English mediaeval lapidaries. E.E.T.S. Orig. Ser. cxc (1933). P. Studer and Joan Evans, Anglo-Norman lapidaries. (Texts of Marbodus, bishop of Rennes.) Paris. 1924.

6949 GRANT (EDWARD). Physical science in the middle ages. N.Y., Lond., etc. 1971.

Severely criticized in *Speculum,* xlviii (1973), 364-5.

6950 GUNTHER (ROBERT W. T.). Early science in Oxford. 14 vols. Oxf. 1920-45.

Vols. 1, 2, 3, 5, and 11 contain material on the Middle Ages. Vols. 1 and 2 appear also in Oxf. Hist. Soc. Pubns., lxxvii-lxxviii (1923). See also his *Early science in Cambridge* (Oxf. 1937). *

6951 HAMMOND (E. A.). 'Incomes of medieval English doctors'. *Journal Hist. Medicine and Allied Sciences* (New Haven), xv (1960), 154-69.

6952 HASKINS (CHARLES H.). Studies in the history of medieval science. Cambr. (Mass.). 1928.* Idem, 'The reception of Arabic science in England'. *E.H.R.* xxx (1915), 56-69.

6953 KARPINSKI (LOUIS C.). Robert of Chester's Latin translation of the algebra of al-Khowarizmi. Univ. Michigan Stud. N.Y. 1915. Idem, 'The algorism of John Killingworth'. *E.H.R.* xxix (1914), 707-17.

6954 LINDBERG (DAVID C.), ed. John Pecham and the science of optics. *Perspectiva communis,* ed. with an English translation. Madison (Wisc.).

Idem, 'Lines of influence in thirteenth century optics: Bacon, Witelo, Pecham', *Speculum,* lxvi (1971), 66-83.

6955 MAIER (ANNELIESE). Die Vorläufer Galileis im 14. Jahrhunderts: Studien zur Naturphilosophie der Spätscholastik. 5 vols. Rome. 1949-58. 2nd edn. 1966.

6956 MacKINNEY (LOREN C.). 'A half-century of medieval medical historiography in America'. *Medievalia et Humanistica*, vii (1952), 18–42.

For current bibliography, 'Current Work in the history of medicine', Wellcome Hist. Medical Library. Lond. 1954+ (appears in parts: i.e. parts 13–28 for 1957–60). See also *Bulletin of the History of Medicine*. (Baltimore. 1933+).

6957 MOLLAND (A. G.). 'The geometrical background to the Merton school'. *Brit. Jour. Hist. Science* (No. 6932), iv (1968), 108–25.

6958 MOODY (ERNEST A.) and CLAGETT (MARSHALL). Medieval science of weights. Madison. (Wisc.). 1952.

A group of Latin treatises, ascribed to various authors, with English translations.

6959 O'BRIEN (JAMES F.). 'Some medieval anticipations of inertia'. *The New Scholasticism* (Washington, D.C.), xliv (1970), 345–71.

6960 PRICE (DEREK J.), ed. The equatorie of the planets. Cambr. 1955.

A photographic reproduction of a Peterhouse MS., sometimes ascribed to Chaucer, with a linguistic analysis of R. M. Wilson, and a transcript and notes.

6961 RUSSELL (JOSIAH C.). 'Hereford and Arabic Science in England'. *Isis*, xviii (1932), 14–25.

Theodore Silverstein, 'Daniel Morley: English cosmogonist and student of Arabic science', *Mediaeval Stud.*, x (1948), 179–96.

6962 SINGER (CHARLES J.). Early English magic and medicine. Lond. 1920.

6963 SINGER (CHARLES). Short History of Medicine. 2dn edn. (thoroughly revised). By E. Ashworth Underwood. Oxf. 1962.

6964 SINGER (DOROTHEA) and ANDERSON (ANNIE). Catalogue of Latin and vernacular plague texts in Great Britain and Eire in manuscripts written before the sixteenth century. Collection de travaux de l'Académie internationale d'histoire des sciences, no. 5. Lond. 1950.

6965 SINGER (DOROTHEA) and ANDERSON (ANNIE). Vernacular alchemical manuscripts in Great Britain and Ireland dating from before the sixteenth century. 3 vols. Brussels. 1928–31.

For an interest in chemistry and the occult, see 'John of Roquetaillade' (No. 1474).

6966 TALBOT (CHARLES H.). 'Mediaeval physician's Vade mecum'. *Jour. Hist. Medicine* (New York), xv (1961), 213–33. D. M. Dunlop, 'Arabic medicine in England', ibid. xi (1956), 166–82.

6967 THORNDIKE (LYNN) and KIBRE (PEARL). Catalogue of incipits of mediaeval scientific writings. in Latin. Cambr. (Mass.). 1937. Revised and augmented edn. Cambr. (Mass.). 1962.

Supplements in *Speculum*, xiv (1939), 93–105; xvii (1942), 342–6. L. Thorndike, 'Notes on medical texts in manuscripts at London and Oxford', *Janus* (Amsterdam, etc., 1896+), xlviii (1959), 141–202; idem, 'Notes on some less familiar British astronomical and astrological manuscripts', *Jour. Warburg Inst.* xxii (1959), 157–171; idem, 'Daniel of Morley', *E.H.R.* xxxvii (1922), 540–4.

6968   WALLACE (WILLIAM A.). 'Mechanics from Bradwardine to Galileo'. *Jour. Hist. of Ideas*, xxxii (1971), 15–28.

A brief summary of recent research.

6969   WEDEL (THEODORE O.). The mediaeval attitude towards astrology, particularly in England. New Haven. 1920.

6970   WEISHEIPL (JAMES A.). The development of physical theory in the middle ages. Newman history and philosophy of science series. Lond. 1959.

6971   WEISHEIPL (J. A.). 'The place of John Dumbleton in the Merton School'. *Isis*, l (1959), 439–54.

6972   WEISHEIPL (J. A.). 'Repertorium Mertonense'. *Mediaeval Stud.* xxxi (1969), 174–224.

A preliminary list of Merton College masters (1300–50).

6973   WILSON (CURTIS). William Heytesbury: medieval logic and the rise of mathematical physics. Madison (Wisc.). 1956.

B. LITERATURE

1. *Middle English Literature*

The writings in Middle English literature and the modern commentaries thereon are catalogued in bibliographies devoted specifically to them. The *Cambridge bibliography of English literature* (No. 14), and Wells's *Manual* with its several supplements (No. 275) form the basic tools for all aspects of Middle English literature. The modern surveys listed below normally include good reference-citations. For current bibliography, which is regularly very extensive, one should consult the annual bibliographies produced by the English Association, by the Modern Humanities Research Association, and by the Modern Language Association of America (Nos. 276; 272; 268).

The considerable literature on sermons, manuals for priests, and writings for moral and religious instruction can be located in the bibliographies mentioned above. Some of it is excellently summarized in Pantin's *English Church* (No. 6799), chapters nine and ten. The Early English Text Society has published many writings germane to these topics. Their titles are given in *List of publications* printed periodically for E.E.T.S. in London; in *B.M. general catalogue* (No. 78) vol. 142 (1964), under London III; 'Early English Text Society', cols. 850–82; and idem, Ten-Year Supplement (1956–1965), vol. 28, cols. 117–20, and in Eleanora A. Baer's *Titles in series: a handbook for librarians and students* (N.Y. 2nd edn. 1964). Examples of devotional literature are also given in *E.H.D.* iv (Myers), pp. 811–37.

Below are listed a few of the most important or widely read of the writings in Middle English in prose and verse, particularly where they impinge on the formal discipline of political and social history. A selection from the numerous modern surveys includes some collections of medieval writings (e.g. Nos. 6978, 6985–6), as well as modern descriptive commentaries.

6974 ACKERMAN (ROBERT W.). Backgrounds to medieval English literature. N.Y. 1967.

6975 ANDERSON (MARY D.). Drama and imagery in English medieval churches. Lond. 1963 (1964).

6976 BAUGH (ALBERT C.). The Middle English period, 1100–1500 in *A literary history of England*. Ed. by A. C. Baugh. N.Y. 1948.

6977 BENNETT (HENRY S.). Chaucer and the fifteenth century. Oxford Hist. of Eng. Lit. ii, pt. 1. Oxf. 1947.

> Deals with Chaucer, the author and his public, and fifteenth century verse and prose. Idem, *Six medieval men and women* (Cambr. 1955), for essays on Humphrey, duke of Gloucester; Sir John Fastolf; Thomas Hoccleve; Margaret Paston; Margery Kemp; and Richard Bradwater.

6978 BROWN (CARLETON F.), ed. English lyrics of the thirteenth century. Oxf. 1924.

6979 BROWN (C. F.) and ROBBINS (ROSSELL H.). Index to Middle English Verse. N.Y. 1943. See No. 7044.

6980 BROWN (C. F.), ed. Religious lyrics of the fourteenth century. Oxf. 1924. 2nd edn. revised by G. V. Smithers, 1952. Idem, Religious lyrics of the fifteenth century. Oxf. 1939.

6981 CHAMBERS (EDMUND K.). English literature at the close of the middle ages. Oxford Hist. of Eng. Lit. ii, pt. 2. Oxf. 1945. Reprinted 1947.

> Deals with drama, lyric, narrative verse, ballad, and Malory.

6982 CHAMBERS (E. K.). The mediaeval stage. 2 vols. Oxf. 1903. Idem, The English folk-play. Oxf. 1933. *

6983 CHAMBERS (RAYMOND W.). 'On the continuity of English prose from Alfred to More and his school', in the introduction to *Nicholas Harpsfield, the life and death of Sir Thomas More*. E.E.T.S. Orig. Ser. clxxxvi (1932).

6984 CHAMBERS (R. W.) and DAUNT (MARJORIE), eds. A book of London English 1384–1425, with an appendix on English documents in the Record Office by M. M. Weale. Oxf. 1931.

6985 CRAIG (HARDIN). English religious drama of the middle ages. Oxf. 1955.

6986 DICKINS (BRUCE) and WILSON (RICHARD M.), eds. Early Middle English texts. Cambr. 1951. 2nd revised impression. 1952.

6987 KANE (GEORGE). Middle English literature. Lond. 1951.

6988 KER (WILLIAM P.). English literature: medieval. Home University Library. N.Y. 1912. Idem, Essays on medieval literature. Lond. and N.Y. 1905.

6989   LEWIS (C. S.). The allegory of love. Oxf. 1936. Reprinted several times.

Although centring in the Romance of the Rose, this perceptive study becomes a critical introduction to the allegory of love in medieval literature.

6990   MATHEW (GERVASE). The court of Richard II. Lond. 1968.

Strong on cultural history, with chapters on Chaucer, Gower, Piers Plowman, and others.

6991   POLLARD (ALFRED W.). Fifteenth century prose and verse. Lond. and N.Y. 1903. *

Includes Lydgate's Battle of Agincourt; the Examination of Master William Thorpe (Lollard), 1407; the Examination of Sir John Oldcastle; etc. See No. 6863.

6992   ROBBINS (ROSSELL H.), ed. Historical poems of the fourteenth and fifteenth centuries. N.Y. 1959. Idem, ed. Secular lyrics of the fourteenth and fifteenth centuries. Oxf. 1952. 2nd edn. 1955. See No. 7046.

6993   STRATMAN (CARL J.). Bibliography of medieval drama. Berkeley and Los Angeles (Calif.). 1954.

6994   TUCKER (LENA L.) and BENHAM (ALLEN R.). A bibliography of fifteenth century literature with special reference to the history of English culture. Univ. Washington Pubns. in Lang. and Lit. ii, no. 3, pp. 113–274. Seattle (Wash.). 1928.

6995   WICKHAM (GLYNNE). Early English stages, 1300 to 1660. 2 vols. Lond. 1959–63.

6996   WILSON (RICHARD M.). The lost literature of medieval England. Lond. 1952. *

6997   WOOLF (ROSEMARY). The English religious lyric in the middle ages. Oxf. 1968.

6998   YOUNG (KARL). The drama of the medieval church. 2 vols. Oxf. 1933.

Includes some important texts.

2. History and Literature
a. Particular writers

See Mathew, *The court of Richard II* (No. 6990), and Tout, *Civil Service* (No. 1499).

Chaucer, Geoffrey (d. 1400)

6999   COMPLETE WORKS OF GEOFFREY CHAUCER. Ed. by Fred N. Robinson. Boston. 1933. 2nd edn. Oxf. 1957.

Albert C. Baugh, *Chaucer's major poetry* (N.Y. 1963) gives well-edited and annotated texts of Chaucer's principal works.

7000   COMPLETE WORKS OF GEOFFREY CHAUCER. Ed. by Walter W. Skeat. 7 vols. Oxf. 1894–7. Idem, ed. The student's Chaucer, being a complete edition of his works. Oxf. 1894. Reprinted 1929.

Various works of Chaucer, and treatises illustrating his works, were published by the Chaucer Society between 1868 and about 1924.

7001 (CHAUCER). The text of the Canterbury tales studied on the basis of all known manuscripts. By John M. Manly and Edith Rickert. 8 vols. Chicago (Ill.). 1940.

> Carleton F. Brown and others. *Sources and analogues of Chaucer's Canterbury tales.* Ed. by W. F. Bryan and G. Dempster. (Chicago. 1941).

7002 HAMMOND (ELEANOR P.). Chaucer: a bibliographical manual. N.Y. 1908. * Reprinted 1933. Continued by Dudley D. Griffith, Bibliography of Chaucer, 1908–53. Univ. Washington Pubns. in Language and Literature. xiii. Seattle. 1955. Continued by William R. Crawford, Bibliography of Chaucer, 1954–63. Seattle. 1967.

> Albert C. Baugh, Chaucer bibliography. (N.Y. 1968). Idem, 'Fifty years of Chaucer scholarship', *Speculum*, xxv (1950), 659–725. R. R. Purdy, 'Chaucer scholarship in England and America: a review of recent trends', *Anglia*, lxx (1951), 345–81. See also *C.B.E.L.* (No. 14).
>
> For current bibliography, see *Annual bibliography of English language and literature* (No. 272), *PMLA* (No. 268), *Year's work in English studies* (No. 276), and especially 'Chaucer research' annually in *The Chaucer review* (Pennsylvania State Univ.), i+ (1966+).

7003 BAUGH (ALBERT C.). 'Kirk's Life Records of Thomas Chaucer'. *PMLA*, xlvii (1932), 461–515.

7004 BOWDEN (MURIEL). A commentary on the general prologue to the Canterbury Tales. N.Y. 1949.

7005 BREWER (DEREK S.). Chaucer and his time. Lond. 1963.

7006 COULTON (GEORGE G.). Chaucer and his England. Lond. 1908; and later editions. Reprinted, with a new bibliography by T. W. Craik. Lond. 1963.

7007 CROW (MARTIN M.) and OLSON (CLAIR C.). Chaucer life records. From materials compiled by John M. Manly and Edith Rickert with the assistance of Lilian J. Redstone and others. Oxf. 1966.

> This collection of 493 documents, drawn from a wide variety of sources and gathered into thirty-one chapters, excellently annotated, is a valuable tool for the history of the second half of the fourteenth century. It provides information on Chaucer's civil service employments, on his journeys, on his legal suits, on the Scrope-Grosvenor controversy, on the port of London, etc.
>
> Some particular studies related to the studies of historians are: Margaret Galway, 'Geoffrey Chaucer, J.P. and M.P.', *Modern Language Rev.* xxxvi (1941), 1–36; E. P. Kuhl, 'Why was Chaucer sent to Milan in 1378?', *Modern Language Notes*, lxii (1947), 42–4; George B. Parks, 'The route of Chaucer's first journey to Italy', *Jour. English Literary Hist.* xvi (1949), 174–87; R. A. Pratt, 'Geoffrey Chaucer, Esq. and Sir John Hawkwood', ibid. xvi (1949), 188–93; D. S. Bland, 'Chaucer and the inns of court: a reexamination', *English Studies*, xxxiii (1952), 145–55. A. C. Baugh, 'The background of Chaucer's mission to Spain', pp. 55–69 in *Chaucer und seine Zeit, Symposium für Walter F. Schirmer. Anglia, Buchreihe*, xiv (Tübingen. 1968).

7008 LIFE RECORDS OF CHAUCER. Chaucer Soc. Pubns. 2nd Ser. xii, xiv, xxi, xxxii. Lond. 1875–1900. Index of Life Records of Chaucer. By Ernest P. Kuhl. Chicago. 1913.

> Superseded by the Crow–Olson edition.

7009 LOOMIS (ROGER S.). A mirror of Chaucer's world. Princeton. 1965.

7010 LOWES (JOHN L.). Geoffrey Chaucer and the development of his genius. Boston. 1934.

7011 MANLY (JOHN M.). Some new light on Chaucer. N.Y. 1926.*

7012 RICKERT (EDITH). Chaucer's world. Ed. by C. C. Olson and M. M. Crow. N.Y. and Lond. 1948.

See also Dorothy Hughes, *Illustrations of Chaucer's England* (No. 1209).

7013 ROWLAND (BERYL), ed. Companion to Chaucer studies. Lond., N.Y. and Toronto. 1968.

Summary-studies by twenty-two specialists. John Speirs, *Chaucer the Maker* (Lond. 1951) provides a critical reading of Chaucer.

7014 SPURGEON (CAROLINE F. E.). Five hundred years of Chaucer criticism and allusion, 1357–1900. 7 pts. Lond. 1914–24. Reprinted in 3 vols. Cambr. 1925.*

Gower, John (d. 1408)

7015 COMPLETE WORKS OF JOHN GOWER. Ed. by George C. Macaulay. 4 vols. Oxf. 1899–1902.*

The standard edition.

7016 GOWER (JOHN). Confessio amantis (The lover's shrift). Trans. by Terence Tiller. Penguin Classics. 1963.

7017 GOWER (JOHN). Poema quod dicitur *Vox Clamantis* necnon Chronica tripartita auctore Johanne Gower. Ed. by Henry Coxe. Roxburghe Club. Lond. 1850.

Eric W. Stockton, trans. *The major Latin works of John Gower: The voice of one crying and the tripartite chronicle* (Seattle, 1962).

The Vox Clamantis is an important Latin poem, begun in 1381, which deals with the causes of the Peasants' Revolt. It gives a vivid picture of the condition of society, denouncing the vices of the clergy, knights, peasants, merchants, and lawyers. The Tripartite Chronicle inveighs against Richard II's public policy from 1396 to 1399, and defends Henry IV's usurpation of the throne. For some of Gower's other historical poems, see No. 7049.

7018 BENNETT (JACK A. W.). Selections from John Gower. Clarendon Medieval and Tudor Ser. Oxf. 1968.

7019 FISHER (JOHN H.). John Gower: moral philosopher and friend of Chaucer. N.Y. 1964.

Karl Meyer, *John Gowers Beziehungen zu Chaucer und König Richard II* (Bonn. 1889). Gardiner Stillwell, 'John Gower and the last years of Edward III', *Stud. in Philology*, xlv (1948), 454–71. George R. Coffman, 'John Gower, mentor for royalty: Richard II', *PMLA*, lxix (1954), 953–64.

Hoccleve, Thomas (d. c. 1437)

7020 HOCCLEVE. Works: i: Minor poems. Ed. by Frederick J. Furnivall. E.E.T.S. Extra Ser. lxi (1892); ii: Minor poems. Ed. by Israel Gollancz. Ibid.

lxxiii (1925); iii: The regiment of princes, A.D. 1411–1412. Ed. by F. J. Furnivall. Ibid. lxxii (1897).

Langland, William (d. c. 1400)

7021 THE VISION OF WILLIAM CONCERNING PIERS PLOWMAN together with VITA DE DOWEL, DOBET, ET DOBEST (together with Richard the Redeless). By William Langland. Ed. by Walter W. Skeat. 4 pts in 5 vols. E.E.T.S. Orig. Ser. xxviii, xxxviii, liv, lxvii, lxxxi. 1867–85. Another edition, 2 vols. Oxf. 1886. 10th edn. Oxf. 1924. Reprinted 1932.

7022 PIERS PLOWMAN: The A version. Will's visions of Piers Plowman and Do-Well. Ed. by George Kane. Lond. 1960. (The first of four planned volumes to include B version, C version, and Glossary.) Translations by Arthur Burrell, Lond. 1912 and later; by Donald Attwater, Lond. 1930 and 1957; by H. W. Wells, N.Y. 1930; by Nevill Coghill, Lond. 1949.

7023 PIERS PLOWMAN: The Huntington library manuscript (HM 143) reproduced in photostat. By R. W. Chambers, R. B. Haselden, and H. C. Schulz. San Marino (Calif.), 1936.

> The Vision of Piers Plowman, begun about 1362, throws much light on the social con-
> ditions of England, especially on the life of the lower classes. It defines the political role
> of the commons, with whom the author exhibits sympathy, and attacks abuses in the
> church.
> For the extensive bibliography, consult *C.B.E.L.* i. 195–200 and v. 126–8; M. W.
> Bloomfield, 'Present state of Piers Plowman Studies', *Speculum*, xiv (1939), 215–32;
> and the general histories of English literature.

7024 BLOOMFIELD (MORTON W.). Piers Plowman as a fourteenth century apocalypse. New Brunswick (New Jersey). 1961.

> This work is designed to relate Piers Plowman to its fourteenth-century milieu; its
> extensive notes cite many recent commentaries.

7025 CHADWICK (DOROTHY). Social life in the days of Piers Plowman. Cambridge Stud. in Medieval Life and Thought. Cambr. 1922. *

7026 DAWSON (CHRISTOPHER H.). Medieval religion. Lond. 1934, pt. iii: The vision of Piers Plowman. Reprinted in idem, *Medieval essays*, chap. xii. Lond. 1953 and N.Y. 1954.

7027 HUSSEY (S. S.), ed. Piers Plowman: critical approaches. Lond. 1969.

7028 KANE (GEORGE). Piers Plowman, the evidence for authorship. Lond. 1965.

7029 SALTER (ELIZABETH). Piers Plowman: an introduction. Oxf. 1962.

Lewis, Glyn Cothi (fl. 1447–86)

7030 THE POETICAL WORKS OF LEWIS GLYN COTHI, A celebrated bard who flourished in the reigns of Henry VI, Edward IV, Richard III, and Henry VII. Ed. by John Jones and Walter Davies. The Honourable Cymmro-dorion, or Royal Cambrian Institution. 2 vols. Oxf. 1837.

Welsh poems throwing light on the Wars of the Roses, by a partisan of the Lancastrians and of Jasper Tudor, with an introductory essay on those wars. The author, a native of Glyn Cothi in Carmarthenshire, was also called Lewis y Glyn.

See Evan David Jones, *Gwaith Lewis Glyn Cothi*. Cyf. i (only volume published) (Caerdydd ac Aberystwyth, 1953). For Welsh literary history 1282–1500, see *Bibliog. Hist. Wales* (No. 10), pp. 114–15.

Lydgate, John (d. c. 1451)

7031 LYDGATE'S FALL OF PRINCES. Ed. by H. Bergen. E.E.T.S. Extra Ser. cxxi–cxxiv. Lond. 1924–7.

7032 THE MINOR POEMS OF JOHN LYDGATE. Ed. by Henry N. MacCracken. E.E.T.S. 2 vols. Lond. 1911–34.

Vol. 1: religious poems; vol. 2: secular poems.

7033 NORTON-SMITH (JOHN), ed. John Lydgate, poems. Clarendon Medieval and Tudor Ser. Oxf. 1966.

Strongest on 'social and polite verse'.

7034 PEARSALL (DEREK). John Lydgate. Lond. and Charlottesville (Virginia). 1970.

7035 RENOIR (ALAIN). The poetry of John Lydgate. Lond. 1967.

7036 SCHIRMER (WALTER F.). Lydgate: ein Kulturbild aus dem 15. Jahrhundert. Tübingen. 1952. Trans. as John Lydgate: a study in the culture of the fifteenth century by Ann E. Keep. Berkeley and Los Angeles, and Lond. 1961.

Cf. Emden, *Oxford* (No. 533), 1185–6; and Anthony S. G. Edwards, 'A Lydgate bibliography, 1928–1968', *Bulletin of Bibliography and Magazine Notes* (Westwood, Mass.), xxvii (1970), 95–8.

Malory, Sir Thomas

7037 THE WORKS OF SIR THOMAS MALORY. Ed. by Eugène Vinaver. 3 vols. Oxf. 1947; second edn. 1968.

Vinaver's edition was based on 'the unique and long-lost manuscript' of *Le Morte Darthur*, identified at Winchester in 1934. See Bennett, *Essays* (No. 7038).

7038 BENNETT (JACK A. W.), ed. Essays on Malory. Lond. 1963.

Seven essays by seven scholars.

7039 MATTHEWS (WILLIAM). The ill-framed knight: a skeptical inquiry into the identity of Sir Thomas Malory. Berkeley and Los Angeles. 1966.

After rejecting various candidates for the authorship of Le Morte Darthur, including the frequently favoured candidate, Sir Thomas Malory of Newbold Revel (Warwickshire), Matthews suggests Sir Thomas Malory of Hutton and Studley (Yorks.) as the most suitable candidate. Matthews is sceptical about the criminality of the author.

7040 VINAVER (EUGÈNE). Malory. Oxf. 1929. Reprinted 1970.

Bibliography in Chambers, *Close of Middle Ages* (No. 6981).

Minot, Laurence (d. *c.* 1352)

7041 THE POEMS OF LAURENCE MINOT. Ed. by Joseph Hall. Oxf. 1887; 3rd edn. 1914. Other editions by Joseph Ritson, 1795 and 1825; by Wilhelm Scholle, 1884; and in Wright's *Political poems* (No. 7049), i. 58–91.

Minot's poems are war-songs dealing with Edward III's victories over the French and Scots, A.D. 1333–52. For bibliography, see *C.B.E.L.* i. 270–1.

b. Political poems; literature of dissent

See Walter Map (Nos. 6599–6601), and Neckham (Nos. 6607–10).

For the English Latin poets of the twelfth century, turn to Raby (No. 6894) chap. xi; for those of the thirteenth century, Russell (No. 6909); for poetry and ballads of the fifteenth century, Kingsford's *Eng. Hist. Lit.* (No. 2737) chap. ix. For Anglo-Norman writers, refer to Vising (No. 298) and for Middle English writers to Brown and Robbins, *Index* (No. 6979). A recent commentary concentrating on this subject is V. J. Scattergood, *Politics and poetry in the fifteenth century* (Lond. 1971; N.Y. 1972).

7042 ANGLO-LATIN SATIRICAL POETS AND EPIGRAMMATISTS OF THE TWELFTH CENTURY. Ed. by Thomas Wright. Rolls Ser. 2 vols. Lond. 1872.

Nigelli Speculum stultorum, i. 3–145. Modern Edition: *Nigel de Longchamp, Speculum stultorum*, Ed. with introduction and notes by John H. Mozley and Robert R. Raymo (Berkeley and Los Angeles, 1960). Trans. by Graydon W. Regenos, The Book of Daun Burnel the Ass: Nigellus Wireker's *Speculum stultorum* (Austin, Texas, 1959).
Tractatus Nigelli contra curiales et officiales clericos, i. 146–230. Modern edition: *Nigellus de Longchamp, dit Wireker*, (*Oeuvres* i). Introduction: *Tractatus contra curiales et officiales clericos*. Ed. by A. Boutemy (Paris, 1959).
Nigel was precentor of Canterbury; both of the above works are dedicated to William Longchamp, bishop of Ely, and satirize the follies of the age, especially the corruptions of the church. See also J. H. Mozley, 'The unprinted poems of Nigel Wireker', *Speculum*, vii (1932), 398–423.
Johannis de Altavilla Architrenius, i. 240–292. Written about 1184; The 'Archweeper' laments over the vices of mankind; the author, John de Hauteville, is said to have been a monk of St. Albans.
Alexandri Neckham (?). *De vita monachorum*, ii. 175–200.

7043 ANGLO-NORMAN POLITICAL SONGS. Ed. by Isabel S. T. Aspin. Anglo-Norman Text Soc. No. 11. Oxf. 1953.

Original texts, with English translations, of sixteen songs. All except one have been published before, ten in Thomas Wright's *Political Songs* (No. 7048), pp. 27–55. Included are 'Trailbaston' and 'Lament for Simon de Montfort', which had been edited by Francis Palgrave in 1818; as well as Thomas Turberville (cf. Edwards in No. 1450), 'Elegy on the death of Edward I and Lament of Edward II'.
There is another song in Latin on the death of Simon, edited by F. W. Maitland, in *E.H.R.* xi (1896), 314–18; and reprinted in his *Collected papers* (No. 1482), iii. 43–9.

7044 BROWN (CARLETON F.) and ROBBINS (ROSSELL H.). Index of Middle English verse. N.Y. 1943. Supplement by R. H. Robbins and John L. Cutler, Lexington (Kentucky). 1965.

A register of secular, religious, and didactic verse, it largely supersedes C. F. Brown *A register of Middle English religious and didactic verse.* 2 vols. (Oxf. 1916–20).

7045   ENGLISH AND SCOTTISH POPULAR BALLADS. Ed. by Francis J. Child. 5 vols. Boston, etc. 1882–98. *

The best collection of ballads; admirably edited. Supersedes Child's older collection in eight vols. (Boston, 1857–8 and 1864). There is a much abbreviated edition by Helen Child Sargent and G. L. Kittredge (Boston, etc. 1904).
For other editions, see *C.B.E.L.* (No. 14), i. 272–3; v. 153.

7046   HISTORICAL POEMS OF THE XIVTH AND XVTH CENTURIES. Ed. by Rossell H. Robbins. N.Y. 1959.

An edition of about 100 Middle English poems, with introduction and notes. See also, R. H. Robbins, 'Middle English poems of protest', *Anglia*, lxxviii (1960), 193–203. For poems on Death of Edward III and Peasants' Revolt, see *Archaeologia*, xviii (1817), 21–8; John Page's poem on the Siege of Rouen, *temp.* Hen. V, is printed ibid. xxi (1827), 43–78.
   For two poems on the siege of 'Harflet' (Harfleur) and the battle of Agincourt, which have been wrongly ascribed to Lydgate, see Hearne's edition of *Vita et Gesta Henrici V* (No. 2972), pp. 359–75; and N. H. Nicolas, *History of the Battle of Agincourt* (Lond. 1827), pp. ccxlix–cclxii; or N. H. Nicolas and E. Tyrrell, *Chronicle of London* (No. 2823), pp. 216–33. See also Oskar Emmerig, 'The Bataile of Agyncourte' *im Lichte geschichtlicher Quellenwerke* (Nuremberg, 1906); and in *Englische Studien*, xxxix (1908), 362–401. Cf. Kingsford, *Eng. Hist. Lit.* (No. 2737), pp. 238–40.

7047   POLITICAL POEMS OF THE REIGNS OF HENRY VI AND EDWARD IV. Ed. by Frederic Madden. *Archaeologia*, xxix (1842), 318–47.

7048   POLITICAL SONGS OF ENGLAND, from the reign of John to that of Edward II. Ed. and trans. by Thomas Wright. Camden Soc. Old Ser. 1839. Another edition, 'revised' by Edmund Goldsmid, in his *Bibliotheca Curiosa*. 4 vols. in 1. Edin. 1884.

Goldsmid omits some of the longer poems printed by Wright. The most valuable song in Wright's volume is that on the battle of Lewes (pp. 72–121), which was written soon after the battle. It is a remarkably bold and complete statement of the baronial programme of constitutional reform. The author was a Franciscan friar. There is an excellent edition of this Latin tract by C. L. Kingsford: *The Song of Lewes*, Oxf. 1890.
   On pp. 323–45 Wright prints a song on the times of Edward II, written about 1320, of which we have a better edition by C. Hardwick: *A Poem on the Times of Edward II.* Percy Society, 1849; and by Thomas W. Ross, 'On the evil times of Edward II. A new version from MS. Bodley 48', *Anglia*, lxxxv (1957), 173–93. Cf. Brown and Robbins, Index (No. 7044), no. 4165.

7049   POLITICAL POEMS AND SONGS RELATING TO ENGLISH HISTORY, from the accession of Edward III to that of Richard II. Ed. by Thomas Wright. Rolls Ser. 2 vols. Lond. 1859–61.

(a) Les voeus du héron (with an English translation): i. 1–25. Purports to relate how Robert of Artois incited Edward III to declare war against Philip of Valois in 1338. Whiting considers it a bitter burlesque on knights, anti-English, anti-war, and not written by one of Artois' partisans (B. J. Whiting, 'The vows of the heron', *Speculum* xx (1945), 261–78). For other editions, see Whiting, p. 261.
(b) John of Bridlington: i. 123–215. It is a satire on the political acts of Edward III, especially from 1327 to 1346, in Latin verse with a prose commentary. For discussions of its authorship, see Montague R. James in *Fasciculus J. W. Clark dicatus* (Cambr. 1909), pp. 9–13; A. Gwynn, *Austin Friars* (No. 5971), pp. 129–38; Emden, *Oxford* (No. 533), p. 644; and Paul Meyvaert, 'John Erghome and the *Vaticinium Roberti Bridlington*', *Speculum*, xli (1966), 656–64.

(c) The reconciliation of Richard II with the city of London (1392) by Richard de Maidstone (d. 1396), an admirer of Richard II: i. 282–300. There is an earlier edition by Thomas Wright, Camden Soc. iii (1838). For Maidstone, see Emden, *Oxford*, p. 1204; and Arnold Williams, 'Protectorium pauperis, a defence of the begging friars by Richard Maidstone', *Carmelus*, v (1958), 132–80. See also Helen Suggett (No. 4111).

(d) The complaint of the plowman, also called the Plowman's Tale: i. 304–46. This work, written about 1394, assails the clergy. There is a better edition in Skeat's *Complete Works of Chaucer* (No. 7000), vii. 147–90.

Another Middle English poem by this unknown author is *Pierce the Plowman's Crede*, edited by Walter W. Skeat. E.E.T.S. xxx (1867); revised edition, Oxf. 1906. This is a Wycliffite satire, written about 1394 and directed particularly against the friars. For references, see *C.B.E.L.* (No. 14).

(e) John Gower's Corruptions of the age, vices of the different orders of society, King Richard II, Tripartite Chronicle, verses on Henry IV, etc.: i. 346–63, 417–54; ii. 1–15. These poems of Gower attack the government of Richard II and denounce the Lollards. They are all included in Macaulay's edition (No. 7015).

(f) On the deposition of Richard II, also known as Richard the Redeless, and now usually entitled *Mum and the Sothsegger*: i. 368–417. Best edition is *Mum and the Sothsegger*. Ed. by Mabel Day and Robert Steele, E.E.T.S., cxcix (1936), pp. 1–26; to which is added on pp. 27–78 FRAGMENT M recovered in 1928, which the editors regard as a continuation of the first part. Modernized version in Allen R. Benham, *English literature from Widsith to the death of Chaucer* (Lond. and New Haven, 1916), pp. 185–200. R. Mohl 'Theories of monarchy in Mum and the Sothsegger', *PMLA*, lix (1944), 26–44.

(g) Jack Upland, ii. 16–39; also printed in Skeat's *Complete Works of Chaucer* (No. 7000), vii. 191–203. A popular indictment of the corruption of the friars, written in 1402.

(h) The Libel of English policy, ii. 157–205. See No. 5338.

7050 TWENTY-SIX POLITICAL AND OTHER POEMS. Ed. by Josef Kail. Pt. i. E.E.T.S. cxxiv. Lond. 1904.

C. EDUCATIONAL INSTITUTIONS

1. *Universities and Colleges*

a. Sources

For catalogues of MSS. in libraries of Oxford and Cambridge, consult pp. 124–6; for medieval libraries, pp. 927–9; for modern literature concerning the universities, pp. 919–24. The cartularies of the religious houses in university towns contain information pertinent to the universities. A selection of documents is given, in translation, in *Engl. Hist. Docs.* iv (Myers), pp. 878–922.

7051 ENACTMENTS IN PARLIAMENT concerning the universities of Oxford and Cambridge, the colleges and halls therein, and the colleges of Winchester, Eton and Westminster (37 Edw. III to 2 Geo. V). Ed. by Lionel L. Shadwell. 4 vols. Oxf. Hist. Soc. lviii–lxi. 1911–12.

For medieval period, i. 1–73 and a few documents for 1366, 1382, 1384 in iv, appendix.

7052 LEACH (ARTHUR F.). Educational charters and documents. Cambr. 1911.

i. *Cambridge*

7053 ANCIENT LAWS OF THE FIFTEENTH CENTURY FOR KING'S COLLEGE, CAMBRIDGE, AND FOR THE PUBLIC SCHOOL OF ETON COLLEGE. Ed. by James Heywood and Thomas Wright. Lond. 1850.

7054 DOCUMENTS RELATING TO ST. CATHERINE'S COLLEGE (Cambridge) (1473-1860). Ed. by Henry Philpott. Cambr. 1861.

7055 DOCUMENTS RELATING TO THE UNIVERSITY AND COL-LEGES OF CAMBRIDGE. Published by direction of the commissioners appointed to inquire into the state, etc., of the university and colleges. 3 vols. Lond. 1852.

> Abstracts of public records i. 1–104. *Statuta antiqua*: i. 308–453.
> Charters and statutes of colleges: vols. ii–iii.

7056 EARLY CAMBRIDGE UNIVERSITY AND COLLEGE STATUTES IN THE ENGLISH LANGUAGE. Ed. by James Heywood. 2 vols. Lond. 1855.

> This superseded his *Collection of Statutes for the University and the Colleges of Cambridge* (Lond. 1840).

7057 EARLY STATUTES OF CHRIST'S COLLEGE, CAMBRIDGE, with the statutes of the prior foundation of God's House. Ed. with translation by H. Rackham. Cambr. 1927.

7058 GRACE BOOK A, containing the proctors' accounts and other records of the university of Cambridge, 1454-88. Ed. by Stanley M. Leathes. Cambr. Antiq. Soc. Luard Memorial Series, vol. i. Cambr. 1897.

> Three more grace books, *B, Γ, Δ*, edited respectively by Mary Bateson (2 vols.), W. G. Searle, and John Venn, carry the records to 1589 (1903–10).

7059 THE ORIGINAL STATUTES OF CAMBRIDGE UNIVERSITY. Ed. and trans. by M. B. Hackett. Cambr. and N.Y. 1970.

> A critical edition of the text of a unique MS. discovered in Rome by M. B. Hackett, who provides a full commentary to the earliest statutes.

7060 THE PRIVILEGES OF THE UNIVERSITY OF CAMBRIDGE. Ed. by George Dyer. 2 vols. Lond. 1824.

> Vol. i consists, in large part, of charters and statutes.

ii. *Oxford*

7061 COLLECTANEA. Ed. by C. R. L. Fletcher, Montagu Burrows, and others. 4 vols. Oxf. Hist. Soc. v, xvi, xxxii, xlvii (1885–1905).

> (a) Letters to king, pope, and others on Stamford schism, on Cardinal de Mota, etc. in 14th century. Ed. by H. H. Henson, v (1885), 1–56. For these letters, see also *Oxford Formularies* (No. 7063), pp. 84–107. On 'The Stamford schism', H. E. Salter in *E.H.R.* xxxvii (1922), 249–53.
> (b) The university of Oxford in the 12th century. Ed. by T. E. Holland, xvi (1890), 137–92. The friars preachers *v.* the university. Ed. by Hastings Rashdall, ibid. 193–273.
> (c) Some Durham college rolls 1315–1542. Ed. by H. E. D. Blakiston, xxxii (1896), 1–76. Poems relating to the riot between town and gown, 1354–55. Ed. by Henry

Furneaux, ibid. 163–87, Tryvytlam's *De laude universitatis Oxoniae*. Ed. by Henry Furneaux, ibid. 188–209, which is 'a 14th century poem by a Franciscan complaining, *inter alia*, against statutes restricting the ability of friars to graduate in theology' (Mullins).

(*d*) Description of Oxford, from the hundred rolls of Oxfordshire, 1279. Ed. by Rose Graham, xlvii (1905), 1–98.

7062 EPISTOLAE ACADEMICAE OXON.: a collection of letters and other documents illustrative of academical life and studies at Oxford in the fifteenth century. Ed. by Henry Anstey. 2 vols. Oxf. Hist. Soc. xxxv–xxxvi (1898).

See C. E. Woodruff, 'Letters to the prior of Christ Church, Canterbury, from university students', *Archaeol. Cantiana*, xxxix (1927). 1–33.

7063 FORMULARIES WHICH BEAR ON THE HISTORY OF OXFORD, *c.* 1204–1420. Ed. by Herbert E. Salter, William A. Pantin, Henry G. Richardson. 2 vols. Oxf. Hist. Soc. New Ser. iv–v for 1939–40 (1942).

Letters as specimens of *ars dictaminis*: documents from Richard of Bury's *Liber Epistolaris* (cf. No. 6561); from Royal ms. 12 D xi including a better edition of letters printed in Collectanea (No. 7061), v (1885); and a university formulary of *c.* 1340–4, from Cotton Vitell. E. X.; and similar specimens. Includes a catalogue of books of Durham College, Oxford, *c.* 1390–1400. In vol. v, *inter alia*, letters of the Oxford dictatores, pp. 329–450.

7064 MEDIAEVAL ARCHIVES OF THE UNIVERSITY OF OXFORD. Ed. by H. E. Salter. 2 vols. Oxf. Hist. Soc. lxx, lxxiii for 1917 and 1919 (1920–1).

Vol. lxx: Privileges and property of university; vol. lxxiii: Proceedings of Justices of Peace 1390–4, by Bertha H. Putnam; assizes of bread and ale 1309–51; proctors' accounts, 1464–97.

7065 MUNIMENTA ACADEMICA, or documents illustrative of academical life and studies at Oxford. Ed. by Henry Anstey. Rolls Ser. 2 vols. Lond. 1868.

Contains chancellors' and proctors' books (statutes, etc., A.D. 1214–1504); acts of the chancellor's court, 1434–67; register of the convocation of the university, 1449–63.

7066 REGISTER OF THE UNIVERSITY OF OXFORD. By C. W. Boase and Andrew Clark. 3 vols. Oxf. Hist. Soc. i, x, xiv (1885–9).

Vol. i (1885) for period 1449–63.

7067 REGISTRUM CANCELLARII OXONIENSIS, 1434–1469. Ed. by H. E. Salter. 2 vols. Oxf. Hist. Soc. xciii, xciv (1932).

7068 SHADWELL (CHARLES L.). Catalogue of Muniments of Oriel College. 10 fascicles. Privately printed, 1893–1905.

7069 SNAPPE'S FORMULARY AND OTHER RECORDS. Ed. by H. E. Salter. Oxf. Hist. Soc. lxxx (1924). For details, see Mullins, *Texts*, p. 421.

7070 STATUTA ANTIQUA UNIVERSITATIS OXONIENSIS. Ed. by Strickland Gibson. Oxf. 1931.

Cf. Graham Pollard, 'The oldest statute book of the university', *The Bodleian Library Record*, viii (1968), 69–92.

7071 STATUTES OF THE COLLEGES OF OXFORD, with royal patents of foundation, etc. Printed by desire of her majesty's commissioners for inquiring into the state of the university of Oxford. 3 vols. Oxf. 1853.

7072 CATALOGUE OF THE ARCHIVES IN THE MUNIMENT ROOMS OF ALL SOULS COLLEGE. Ed. by Charles T. Martin. Lond. 1877.

7073 OXFORD DEEDS OF BALLIOL COLLEGE. Ed. by H. E. Salter. Oxf. Hist. Soc. New Ser. lxiv (1913).

7074 CANTERBURY COLLEGE, OXFORD. By W. A. Pantin. 3 vols. Oxf. Hist. Soc. New Ser. vi–viii (1947–50).

Miscellaneous documents from fourteenth to sixteenth centuries, including proceedings at Rome *c.* 1368–70.

7075 NOTES FROM THE MUNIMENTS OF MAGDALEN COLLEGE, 12th to 17th century. By William D. Macray. Oxf. 1882.

See No. 6165.

7076 REGISTER OF THE PRESIDENTS . . . AND OTHER MEMBERS OF MAGDALEN COLLEGE, OXFORD, FROM THE FOUNDATION OF THE COLLEGE. By John R. Bloxam. 7 vols. and index. Oxf. 1853–85. New series (fellows, 1458–1915). By W. D. Macray. 8 vols. Lond. 1894–1915.

Macray, i. 3–79, prints extracts from registers and rolls, 1454–1520.

7077 FOUNDATION STATUTES OF MERTON COLLEGE, 1270, with subsequent ordinances, from the Latin. Ed. by Edward F. Percival. Lond. 1847.

7078 MERTON MUNIMENTS. Selected and ed. by Percy S. Allen and H. W. Garrod. Oxf. Hist. Soc. lxxxvi for 1926 (1928).

7079 REGISTRUM ANNALIUM COLLEGII MERTONENSIS, 1483–1521. Ed. by H. E. Salter. Oxf. Hist. Soc. lxxvi for 1921 (1923).

7080 THE EARLY ROLLS OF MERTON COLLEGE, OXFORD, with an appendix of thirteenth century Oxford charters. Ed. by John R. L. Highfield. Oxf. Hist. Soc. New Ser. xviii for 1963 (1964).

7081 THE DEAN'S REGISTER OF ORIEL, 1446–1661. Ed. by George C. Richards and H. E. Salter. Oxf. Hist. Soc. lxxxiv for 1925 (1926).

Records of college meetings and a catalogue of MSS. in the library.

7082 ORIEL COLLEGE RECORDS. Ed. by Charles L. Shadwell and H. E. Salter. Oxf. Hist. Soc. lxxxv (1926).

b. Modern accounts

The best general work on English universities is in the Powicke–Emden edition of Rashdall (No. 7090). Detailed accounts of Oxford are presented by Maxwell-Lyte (No. 7123) and Mallet (No. 7125), and of Cambridge by Mullinger (No. 7102). The volume for each university in Victoria County History (No. 1529) is valuable. Emden's registers for Oxford and Cambridge (Nos. 7119, 7095) are essential for the study of individuals; and Venn's biographical list for Cambridge (No. 7110) is helpful for the same purpose. For learning in general, see pp. 898–907 and for individual scholars, pp. 858–75. For a general account, see Emden in *Medieval England* (No. 1485) ii, chap. xv. For bibliography, see E. H. Cordeaux and D. H. Merry. *A bibliography of printed works relating to the University of Oxford* (Oxf. 1968). For rolls of petitions for benefices, No. 6767.

i. *General references*

7083 BOYCE (GRAY C.). 'American studies in medieval education'. *Progress of mediaeval and renaissance studies*, xix (1947), 6–30.

7084 BOYCE (GRAY C.). The English-German nation in the university of Paris during the middle ages. Bruges. 1927.

A. Gabriel, 'English masters and students in Paris during the twelfth century', *Analecta Praemonstratensia*, xxv (1949), 38–40. Reprinted in his *Garlandia: Studies in the history of medieval universities* (Frankfurt. 1969), where also is found 'The English-German nation at the University of Paris from 1425 to 1494'.

7085 DESTREZ (JEAN). La Pecia dans les manuscrits universitaires du xiiie et du xive siècle. Paris. 1935.

A *pecia* (piece) was a quire of a MS. which a stationer in a university town rented, under the supervision of university masters, to a scribe for copying; it was part of an organized system for book production in the thirteenth century. See Karl Christ in *Zentralblatt für Bibliothekswesen*, lv (1938), 1–44; a translated example is given in Lynn Thorndike, *University Records* (N.Y. 1949), pp. 112–17, 166–8, 259. See also *Scriptorium*, xi (1957), 264–80; R. Steele, 'The Pecia', *The Library*, 4th Ser. xi (1931), 230–4. For pledges given on MSS., see Graham Pollard, 'Medieval loan chests at Cambridge', *B.I.H.R.* xvii (1940), 264–80.

7086 HARGREAVES-MAWDSLEY (W. N.). A history of academical dress in Europe until the end of the 18th Century. Oxf. 1963.

7087 HAINES (ROY M.). 'Education in English ecclesiastical legislation of the later middle ages'. *Stud. in church hist.* vii (1971), 161–75.

7088 KIBRE (PEARL). Scholarly privileges in the middle ages. Cambr. (Mass.). 1962.

Pp. 269–324 are devoted to Oxford, with bibliography including some MSS. on pp. 421–4.

7089 LEFF (GORDON). Paris and Oxford universities in the thirteenth and fourteenth centuries: an institutional and intellectual history. N.Y. 1968.

7090 RASHDALL (HASTINGS). The universities of Europe in the middle ages. 3 vols. Oxf. 1895. New edition by F. M. Powicke and A. B. Emden. 3 vols. Oxf. 1936.

Most of vol. 3 is devoted to the origin, organization, and development of the English universities to 1500. The copious footnotes, especially in the 1936 edition, form valuable guides to the intellectual as well as the institutional concerns of the universities. For opposition to Rashdall's theory of origin, see T. E. Holland, 'The origin of the university of Oxford', *E.H.R.* vi (1891), 238–49. For Powicke's articles on universities, see No. 1490.

7091 WILLARD (JAMES F.). The royal authority and the early English universities. Philadelphia. 1902.

ii. *Cambridge*

7092 BALL (WALTER W. R.) and VENN (JOHN A.). Admissions to Trinity College, Cambridge. 5 vols. Lond. 1911–16.

7093 CHIBNALL (A. C.). Master Richard de Badew and the university of Cambridge 1315–1340. Cambr. 1963.

An account of a crisis in the life of the founder of University Hall (now Clare College), shedding light on contemporary Cambridge.

7094 COBBAN (ALAN B.). The King's Hall within the University of Cambridge in the later middle ages. Cambr. Stud. in Medieval Life. 3rd Ser. i. Lond. 1969.

The King's Hall, founded in the early fourteenth century, was dissolved in 1546; it left, however, a remarkable series of accounts used at length by Cobban in this excellent history of an English college.

7095 EMDEN (ALFRED B.). A biographical register of the university of Cambridge to 1500. Cambr. 1963.

R. W. Hays, 'Welsh students at Oxford and Cambridge universities in the middle ages', *Welsh Hist. Rev.* iv (1969), 325–61.

7096 FORBES (MANSFIELD D.). Clare College 1326–1926; University Hall 1326–1346; Clare Hall 1346–1856. 2 vols. Cambr. 1928–30.

7097 FULLER (THOMAS). The history of the university of Cambridge. Lond. 1655.

Two new editions appeared in 1840. This was formerly the standard work on the history of Cambridge university. It is now in large part superseded by Mullinger's book (No. 7102).

7098 THE HISTORICAL REGISTER OF THE UNIVERSITY OF CAMBRIDGE . . . to 1910. Ed. by Joseph R. Tanner. Cambr. 1917.

7099 JONES (WILLIAM H. S.). History of St. Catherine's College, once Catherine Hall, Cambridge. Cambr. 1936.

7100 MASTERS (ROBERT). The history of the college of Corpus Christi, Cambridge (with an appendix of documents). 2 pts. Cambr. 1753. With additional matter, by John Lamb. 1831. Henry P. Stokes. Corpus Christi. Lond. 1898.

7101 MOORMAN (JOHN R. H.). Grey friars in Cambridge. Cambr. 1952.

See also Andrew G. Little, 'The friars and the foundation of the faculty of theology in the university of Cambridge', *Mélanges Mandonnet* (Paris. 1930), ii. 389–401.

7102 MULLINGER (JAMES B.). The university of Cambridge to 1535. Cambr. 1873. (Vol. ii to 1625 (1884) and vol. iii to 1667 (1911).)*

The best history of Cambridge university. Note H. E. Salter, 'The beginning of Cambridge University', *E.H.R.* xxxvi (1921), 419–20; and W. R. Ball, *Cambridge papers* (Lond. 1918).

7103 PEEK (HEATHER E.) and HALL (CATHERINE P.). The archives of the university of Cambridge: an historical introduction. Cambr. 1962.

7104 PEILE (JOHN). Biographical register of Christ's College 1505–1905 and of the earlier foundation, God's House, 1448–1505. Ed. by John A. Venn. 2 vols. Cambr. 1910.

> Albert H. Lloyd. *The early history of Christ's College, Cambridge, derived from contemporary documents* (Cambr. 1934).

7105 ROACH (J. P. C.), ed. The city and university of Cambridge. Being vol. iii of the *V.C.H.* for Cambridgeshire. Lond. 1959.

7106 SALTMARSH (JOHN). 'The office of receiver-general on the estates of King's College'. *Cambr. Hist. Jour.* iii (1930), 206–11. Idem, 'Handlist of the estates of King's College, Cambridge'. *B.I.H.R.* xii (1935), 32–8. Idem, 'A college home-farm in the fifteenth century'. *Econ. Hist.* iii, no. ii (1936), 155–72.

7107 SEARLE (WILLIAM G.). The history of the Queens' College, Cambridge (1446–1662). Cambr. Antiq. Soc. octavo pubns. ix and xiii. 2 pts. Cambr. 1867–71.

7108 STOKES (HENRY P.). The chaplains and the chapel of the university of Cambridge, 1256–1568. Cambr. 1906. Idem, The esquire bedells of the university of Cambridge from the thirteenth to the twentieth century. Cambr. 1911. Idem, Mediaeval hostels of the university of Cambridge. Cambr. 1924.

7109 ULLMANN (WALTER). 'The decline of the chancellor's authority in medieval Cambridge, a rediscovered statute'. *Historical Jour.* i (1958), 176–82.

7110 VENN (JOHN and JOHN ARCHIBALD). Alumni Cantabrigiensis: a biographical list of all known students, graduates and holders of office at the university of Cambridge from the earliest times to 1900. 5 vols. Cambr. 1922–53.

7111 VENN (JOHN). Biographical history of Gonville and Caius College 1349–1897, containing a list of all known members of the college. 4 vols. Cambr. 1897–1912.

> Vol. i: 1349–1713.

7112 WALKER (THOMAS A.). Biographical register of Peterhouse men and some of their neighbours from the earliest days, 1284 to . . . 1616. Cambr. 1927.

7113 WILLIS (ROBERT) and CLARK (J. W.). The architectural history of the colleges of Cambridge and Eton. 4 vols. Cambr. 1886.

> This great work is not restricted to architecture; it contains also much material relating to the life and institutions of the past. For a study based upon it, see W. D. Caröe, 'King's Hostel, Trinity College', Camb. Antiq. Soc. (Cambr. 1909).

iii. *Oxford*

7114 BOASE (CHARLES W.). Registrum Collegii Exoniensis: Register of the rectors, fellows, and members of Exeter College, Oxford (1318–1893), with a history of the college. First printed, with illustrative documents, Oxf. 1879; 2nd edn. 1893–4. New edn. Oxf. Hist. Soc. Oxf. 1894.

A history of Exeter College followed by a register of members in chronological order. The new edition did not reprint the Latin documents of the earlier edition.

7115 BRODRICK (GEORGE C.). Memorials of Merton College. Oxf. Hist. Soc. Oxf. 1885.

7116 CLARK (ANDREW), ed. The colleges of Oxford: their history and traditions. Lond. 1891.

Twenty-one chapters, contributed by members of the colleges; displays much original research.

7117 DAVIS (HENRY W. CARLESS). A history of Balliol College. Revised by R. H. C. Davis, Richard Hunt (and others). Oxf. 1963.

7118 EMDEN (ALFRED B.). 'Accounts (financial) relating to an early Oxford house of scholars'. *Oxoniensia*, xxxi (1966), 77–81.

7119 EMDEN (A. B.). A biographical register of the university of Oxford to A.D. 1500. 3 vols. Oxf. 1957–9.

A mine of information about approximately 15,000 persons. Invaluable. Additions and Corrections in *Bodleian Lib. Record*, vi (1961), 668–88; vii (1963–4), 149–64. See Hays, *Welsh students* (No. 7095).

7120 EMDEN (A. B.). An Oxford hall in medieval times: the early history of St. Edmund Hall. Oxf. 1927. H. E. Salter 'An Oxford hall in 1424', in *Poole essays* (No. 1448), pp. 421–35.

7121 HIGHFIELD (JOHN R. L.). The early rolls of Merton College (No. 7080). Pp. 5–78: Walter de Merton, and His college in Oxford.

7122 JACOB (ERNEST F.). 'The building of All Souls College', in *Tait essays* (No. 1455), pp. 121–35. Idem, 'The Warden's text of the foundation statutes of All Souls College, Oxford'. *Antiq. Jour.* xv (1935), 420–31.

7123 LYTE (HENRY C. MAXWELL). A history of the university of Oxford to 1530. Lond. 1886.

See W. A. Pantin, *Oxford life in Oxford archives* (Oxf. 1972).

7124 MAGRATH (JOHN R.). The Queen's College, Oxford. 2 vols. Oxf. 1921. Robert H. Hodgkin. Six centuries of an Oxford college: a history of the Queen's College, 1340–1940. Oxf. 1949.

7125 MALLET (CHARLES E.). A history of the university of Oxford. 3 vols. Lond. 1924–8.

Vol. 1 is devoted to the medieval university. See H. E. Salter, 'The medieval university of Oxford' (Historical Revision). *History*, New Ser. xiv (1929–30), 57–61; S. Gibson, 'Confirmation of Oxford chancellors in the Lincoln episcopal registers', *E.H.R.* xxvi (1911), 501–12; R. M. T. Hill, 'Oliver Sutton, bishop of Lincoln, and the university of Oxford', *T.R.H.S.* 4th Ser. xxxi (1949), 1–16; George L. Haskins, 'The University of Oxford and the *ius ubique docendi*', *E.H.R.* lvi (1941), 281–92. See six articles in *Oxford Studies presented to Daniel Callus* (No. 1428).

7126 RICHARDS (GEORGE C.) and SHADWELL (CHARLES L.). The provosts and fellows of Oriel College, Oxford. Oxf. 1922.

7127 RICHARDSON (HENRY G.). 'The Oxford law school under John'. *Law. Quart. Rev.* lvii (1941), 319–38. Idem, 'Business training in medieval Oxford'. *A.H.R.* xlvi (1940–1), 259–80. Idem, 'An Oxford teacher of the fifteenth century'. *B.J.R.L.* xxiii (1939), 436–57. Idem, 'The schools of Northampton in the twelfth century'. *E.H.R.* lvi (1941), 595–605.

7128 SALTER (HERBERT E.). Map of Medieval Oxford. Lond. 1934.

7129 SALTER (HERBERT E.). Medieval Oxford. Oxf. Hist. Soc. vol. c (1936). Survey of Oxford by the late Revd. H. E. Salter. Ed. by W. A. Pantin. 2 vols. Oxf. Hist. Soc. New Ser. xiv (1960), and xx (1969).

These two works, and Anthony À. Wood's *Survey* (No. 7134) on the city of Oxford, naturally touch the university at many points, especially topographically.

7130 SALTER (H. E.) and LOBEL (MARY D.). The university of Oxford Being vol. iii of the *V.C.H.* of Oxford. Lond. 1954.

7131 SMITH (WILLIAM). The annals of University College (Oxford). Newcastle. 1728. William Carr. University College. Lond. 1902.

7132 WALCOTT (MACKENZIE E. C.). William of Wykeham and his colleges. Lond. 1852.

Deals with the life of Wykeham and the annals of New College, Oxford, and of Winchester College. See also Moberley (No. 5822).

7132A WILSON (HENRY A.). Magdalen College (Oxford). Lond. 1899.

7133 WOOD (ANTHONY À.). The history and antiquities of the university of Oxford. Ed. by John Gutch. 2 vols. Oxf. 1792–6.

This used to be the standard work on the history of the university. It has been superseded by the treatises of Lyte, Rashdall, and Mallet.

7134 WOOD (ANTHONY À). Survey of the city of Oxford. Ed. by Andrew Clark. 3 vols. Oxf. Hist. Soc. 1889–99.

Vol. i: The city and suburbs;
Vol. ii: Churches and religious houses;
Vol. iii: Addenda and indexes.

2. Schools

For general account and bibliography, consult Margaret Deanesly's chapter 'Medieval Schools to *c.* 1300' in *Cambr. Mediaeval Hist.* vol. v; and G. R. Potter's chapter 'Education in the fourteenth and fifteenth centuries', ibid. vol. viii. See also P. Delhaye, 'L'Organisation scolaire au xiie siècle', *Traditio*, v (1947), 211–68; and Knowles's volumes on monasteries (Nos. 1298, 1300).

7135 ADAMS (HENRY C.). Wykehamica: a history of Winchester College. Oxf. 1878.

7136   ADAMSON (JOHN W.). The illiterate Anglo-Saxon and other essays. Cambr. 1946.

Idem, 'The extent of literacy in England in the fifteenth and sixteenth centuries', *Library*, 4th Ser. x (1930), 173–93.

7137   JONES (EVAN J.). Education in Wales during the middle ages. (Inaugural lecture). Swansea. 1947. Oxf. 1949.

For others, see Bibliography of Wales (No. 10), pp. 15–16.

7138   KIRBY (THOMAS F.). Annals of Winchester College, from 1382 to the present time. Lond. 1892.

Herbert Chitty and E. F. Jacob, 'Some Winchester College muniments' (four documents of 1389–90 touching petitions to pope on behalf of Winchester and New colleges), *E.H.R.* xlix (1934), 1–13. Arthur F. Leach, *History of Winchester College* (Lond. 1899). J. d'E. Firth, *Winchester College* (Winchester, 1949). John H. Harvey, 'Winchester College Muniments', *Archives*, v. (1962–3), 201–16.

7139   LEACH (ARTHUR F.). Educational charters and documents, 598 to 1909. Cambr. 1911.* Idem, Documents illustrating early education in Worcester, 685–1700. Worcestershire Hist. Soc. Lond. 1913. Idem, Early Yorkshire Schools. 2 vols. Yorks. Archaeol. Soc. Record Ser. xxvii (1899), xxxiii (1903).

7140   LEACH (A. F.). The schools of mediaeval England. Antiquary's Books. Lond. 1915.* 2nd edn. 1916.

Idem, articles on schools in several volumes of the Victoria County Histories, e.g. *V.C.H. Hampshire*, ii. 251–366. Idem, 'Some results of research in the history of education in England', *P.B.A.* vi (1913–14), 433–80.

7141   McMAHON (CLARA P.). Education in fifteenth century England. Johns Hopkins Univ. Stud. in Educ. no. 35. Baltimore. 1947.

7142   LYTE (HENRY C. MAXWELL). A history of Eton college, 1440–1875. Lond. 1875. 3rd edn. (1440–1898). 1899.

The best history of Eton. See also Nos. 7113.

7143   PARRY (ALBERT W.). Education in England in the middle ages. Lond. 1920.

Cf. John Lawson, *Medieval education and the Reformation* (Lond. 1967).

3. *Inns of Court*

To each of the four great Inns of Court, Gray's, Inner Temple, Middle Temple, and Lincoln's, were attached two or more Inns of Chancery. The works listed below include some documents from the fifteenth century. For later records, see Read (No. 32), 2nd edn., pp. 142–3. The bibliography of MSS. and printed works is provided by Bland (No. 7144).

Of modern histories, Holdsworth (No. 1235) ii. 484–512 is the best general account. Dugdale's *Origines* (No. 1249) has much material. Chrimes's introduction to *Fortescue's De Laudibus* (No. 2988) and E. Waterhouse, *Fortescutus illustratus* (Lond. 1663), help to elucidate Fortescue's own comments, and the latter includes a report on the Inns of Court made in Henry VIII's reign. See also T. F. Tout, 'Household of the chancery, etc.', in *Collected papers* (No. 1499). The introduction to Sir Cecil Carr's edition of *Pension book of Clement's Inn* (Selden Soc. lxxviii, 1960) discusses the early Inns of Court and of Chancery.

7144 BLAND (DESMOND S.). A bibliography of the Inns of Court and Chancery. Selden Soc. Supplementary Ser. iii. Lond. 1965.

7145 A CALENDAR OF THE INNER TEMPLE RECORDS. Ed. by F. A. Inderwick and R. A. Roberts. 5 vols. Lond. 1896–1937.

7146 MASTERS OF THE BENCH OF THE INNER TEMPLE, 1450–1900 AND OF THE TEMPLE, 1540–1900. 2 vols. Lond. 1883–1901.

Rees J. Lloyd, 'Welsh masters of the bench of the Inner Temple from the earliest times to the end of the eighteenth century', *Hon. Soc. Cymmrodorion Trans.* 1938, pp. 145–200.

7147 READINGS AND MOOTS OF THE INNS OF COURT IN THE FIFTEENTH CENTURY. Ed. by Samuel E. Thorne. Selden Soc. lxxi (1955).

The earliest reading in this edition is for 1420; the first long reading is for 1452.

7148 RECORDS OF THE HONOURABLE SOCIETY OF LINCOLN'S INN: admissions, 1420–1893, and chapel registers. Compiled by William P. Baildon, with introduction by J. Douglas Walker. 2 vols. Lond. 1896.

Vol. i: 1420–1799. See Maitland, *Collected papers* (No. 1482), iii. 78–86.

7149 RECORDS OF THE HONOURABLE SOCIETY OF LINCOLN'S INN: the Black Books. Compiled by W. P. Baildon, with introduction by J. D. Walker. 4 vols. Lond. 1897–1902.

Vol. i: 1422–1586.

7150 DOUTHWAITE (W. R.). Gray's Inn, its history and associations. Lond. 1886.

7151 HERBERT (WILLIAM). Antiquities of the Inns of Court and Chancery. Lond. 1804.

See also H. H. L. Bellot, *The Inner and Middle Temple* (Lond. 1902), with a good bibliography and C. E. A. Bedwell, *A brief history of the Middle Temple* (Lond. 1909).

7152 IVES (E. W.). 'The reputation of common lawyers in English society, 1450–1550'. *Univ. Birmingham Hist. Jour.* vii (1960), 130–61. Idem, 'The common lawyer in pre-Reformation England'. *T.R.H.S.* xviii (1968), 145–73.

7153 MASTER WORSLEY'S BOOK on the history and constitution of the honourable society of the Middle Temple. Ed. by Arthur R. Ingpen. Lond. 1910.

Written 1733. Ingpen's introduction on the origins of the Inns of Court is valuable.

7154 PULLING (ALEXANDER). The order of the coif. Lond. 1884. New edn. 1897.

7155 ROXBURGH (RONALD). The origins of Lincoln's Inn. Cambr. and N.Y. 1963.

See R. J. Schoeck's review in *Speculum*, xxxix (1964), 746–9. Gerald Hurst, *A short history of Lincoln's Inn* (Lond. 1946). For a study of the documents relating to its site, G. J. Turner, *Lincoln's Inn*. (Lond. 1903).

7156 SIMPSON (A. W. B.). 'The early constitution of the Inns of Court'. *Cambr. Law Jour*. xxviii (1970), 241–56.

7157 THORNE (SAMUEL E.). 'The early history of the Inns of Court, with specific reference to Gray's Inn'. *Graya: a magazine for members of Gray's Inn*. (Lond. 1927+), 1 (1959), 79–98.

Phyllis A. Richmond, 'Early English law schools: the Inns of Court.' *Amer. Bar Assoc. Jour*. xlviii (1962), 254–9.

7158 WILLIAMS (ELIJAH). Staple Inn: customs house, wool court, and inn of chancery, its mediaeval surroundings and associations. Lond. 1906.

See also T. C. Worsfold, *Staple Inn and its story* (Lond. 1903).

7159 WILLIAMSON (JOHN BRUCE). A history of the Temple, London, from the earliest institution of the order of the knights of the Temple to the close of the Stuart period: compiled from the original records of the two learned and honourable societies of the Temple (Lond. 1924. 2nd edn. 1925).

4. *Medieval Libraries*

Consult the section on modern catalogues of manuscripts on pp. 118–34 in vol. i. Emden's biographies for Cambridge and Oxford (Nos. 7095, 7119) list books which had belonged to individuals and were bequeathed to institutions, whenever such information has come to his hand. Wormald and Wright (No. 7181) provide the most satisfactory general account. Knowles in *Religious Orders* (No. 1300), vol. ii, chap. xxvi, deals especially with the contents of the libraries of religious houses, and lists some of the catalogues. Ker's *Medieval libraries* (No. 7168) is a superb guide to the surviving books, by geographical location, and to the medieval and modern catalogues. Accordingly the catalogues are not listed here.

7160 ALLEN (PERCY S.). 'Bishop Shirwood (d. 1494) of Durham and his library'. *E.H.R.* xxv (1910), 445–56.

See Emden, *Oxford*, pp. 1692–3.

7161 BECKER (GUSTAV H.). Catalogi bibliothecarum antiqui. Bonn. 1885.

7162 CLARK (JOHN W.). The care of books, an essay on the development of libraries from the earliest times. Cambr. 1901. New edn. 1909.

7163 EMDEN (ALFRED B.). 'Donors of books to S. Augustine's abbey, Canterbury'. Oxford Bibliog. Soc. Occas. Papers, iv (1968).

7164 GARROD (HEATHCOTE W.). 'The library regulations of a medieval college'. *The Library: Transactions of the Bibliographical Society*, viii (1927), 312–35. (Merton College Library).

7165 GNEUSS (HELMUT). 'Englands Bibliotheken im Mittelalter und ihr Untergang'. *Festschrift für Walter Hübner*. Ed. by D. Riesner and H. Gneuss. Berlin. 1964. Pp. 91–121.

7166 GOTTLIEB (THEODOR). Über mittelalterliche Bibliotheken. Leipzig. 1890.

7167 GOUGAUD (LOUIS). 'Inventaires de manuscrits provenant d'anciennes bibliothèques monastiques de Grande-Bretagne'. *R.H.E.* xxxiii (1937), 789–91.

7168 KER (NEIL R.). Medieval libraries of Great Britain: a list of surviving books. R.H.S. Guides and Handbooks, no. 3. Lond. 1941. 2nd edn. 1964.

A fundamental study, in the second edition of which about 6,000 manuscripts are assigned to about 500 medieval libraries of monasteries, friaries, collegiate churches, colleges, etc. Cartularies, rentals, letter-books, and similar materials are excluded. 'It is intended as a guide to medieval books and book-catalogues, and to the modern catalogues in which they are described' (p. viii).

7169 KER (N. R.). 'Records of All Souls College Library, 1437–1600'. Oxford Bibliog. Soc. Pubns. xvi. Oxf. 1971.

7170 MADAN (FALCONER). Books in manuscript. Lond. 1893. 2nd edn. 1920.

7171 MANITIUS (MAX). Handschriften antiker Autoren in mittelalterlichen Bibliothekskatalogen. Leipzig. 1935.

A standard work on the survival of the 'classics'; on which see also Bolgar (No. 1397), Sandys (No. 1397), and Wormald and Wright (No. 7181).

7172 MERRYWEATHER (FREDERICK S.). Bibliomania in the middle ages. Lond. 1849. Revised edn. by H. B. Copinger. 1933.

7173 MILKAU (FRITZ), ed. Handbuch der Bibliothekswissenschaft. 3 vols. (Volume iii is edited by Milkau and G. Leyh.) Leipzig. 1931–40. Register, compiled by Friedrich Bräuninger. Leipzig. 1942. 2nd edn. by Georg Leyh. Stuttgart. 1950+.

A monumental work on the subject, written co-operatively by experts. Vol. i: Shrift und Buch (1,068 pp.) deals *inter alia* with the development of writing, with manuscripts, and with illuminated manuscripts; see the review in *B.E.C.* cxiii (1955), 297–305. Vol. ii: Bibliotheksverwaltung has not appeared. Vol. iii: Geschichte der Bibliotheken is published in fascicles; a section by Carl Christ, revised by Anton Kern, is said to be an excellent treatise on medieval libraries. Christ has a series of articles 'Bibliotheksgeschichte des Mittelalters: zur Methode und zur neuesten Literatur' in *Zentralblatt für Bibliothekswesen*, lxi (1947), 38–56, 149–60, 233–52.

7174 NICOLSON (WILLIAM). The English historical library. 2 vols. Lond. 1696–99. New and corrected edition in The English, Scotch and Irish historical libraries giving a short view and character of most of our historians either in print or manuscript with an account of our records, law-books, coins, etc. by W. Nicolson, late bishop of Carlisle. Lond. 1776.

7175 POWICKE (FREDERICK M.). The medieval books of Merton College. Oxf. 1931.

7176 SAVAGE (ERNEST A.). Old English libraries: the making, collection and the use of books in the middle ages. Lond. 1911 (1912). *

7177 STREETER (BURNETT H.). The chained library: a survey of four centuries on the evolution of the English library. Lond. 1931. *

7178 THOMPSON (JAMES W.). The medieval library. Chicago. 1939. Reprinted with supplement by Blanche B. Boyer. 1957.

7179 WEISS (ROBERTO). 'Henry VI and the library of All Souls College, Oxford'. *E.H.R.* lxii (1942), 102–5.

7180 WEISS (R.). 'Piero del Monte, John Whethamsted and the library of St. Albans' abbey'. *E.H.R.* lx (1945), 399–406.

For library catalogue of Leicester abbey, see Maude Clarke (No. 1464).

7181 WORMALD (FRANCIS) and WRIGHT (CYRIL E.). The English library: studies in its history before 1700. Lond. 1958.

The basic book on the subject, consisting of eleven studies by ten scholars, including the monastic library, the bibliography of the manuscript book, the universities and the medieval library, the contents of the medieval library, the private collector and the revival of Greek learning, the preservation of the classics, the dispersal of the libraries in the sixteenth century, the Elizabethan Society of Antiquaries and the formation of the Cottonian library, the libraries of Cambridge 1570–1700, and the Oxford libraries in the seventeenth and eighteenth centuries. Each chapter carries its own bibliography.

5. *Music of the Later Middle Ages*

One of the most notable periods in English musical history is the later Middle Ages, when for a brief time English composers such as Dunstable, Frye, and Power were in the forefront of stylistic development, strongly influencing musical style on the Continent.

Good selective bibliographies can be found in the volumes of the *New Oxford history of music* (Nos. 7203, 7204), in Harrison, *Music in medieval Britain* (No. 7202), in Friedrich Blume, ed. *Die Musik in Geschichte und Gegenwart* (16 vols. Kassel 1949+), iii (1954), col. 1414; and in Wyn K. Ford, *Music in England before 1800: a select bibliography* (Lond. 1967). Individual musicians and composers are listed in Harrison, in Grove's *Dictionary* (No. 7201), and in *Die Musik in Geschichte und Gegenwart*. Current studies are given in *RILM Abstracts* (Répertoire international de Littérature Musicale. N.Y. 1967+). Since sacred music was in large measure liturgical, the entries for the liturgy (Nos. 1315–49), as well as the manuscripts cited immediately below, should be consulted. In addition to the sources (Nos. 7182–95), most of the secondary books and articles carry samples of the music.

Useful journals are the *Journal of the American Musicological Society* (Boston, Princeton, Philadelphia, 1948+), *Music and Letters* (Lond. 1920+), and *Musica Disciplina* (Cambr. (Mass.), New Haven (Conn.), and Rome. 1946+).

7182 BUKOFZER (MANFRED F.), ed. John Dunstable: complete works. Musica Britannica, viii. Lond. 1953.

7183 DITTMER (LUTHER), ed. The Worcester fragments. Musicological Studies and Documents, ii. American Institute of Musicology. Rome. 1957.

7184 FRERE (WALTER H.), ed. Antiphonale Sarisburiense. 3 vols. Plainsong and Mediaeval Music Soc. Lond. 1901–25.

7185 FRERE (W. H.), ed. Graduale Sarisburiense. Plainsong and Mediaeval Music Soc. Lond. 1894.

7186 FRERE (W. H.), ed. The Winchester Troper. Henry Bradshaw Soc. viii. Lond. 1894.

> Armand Machabey, 'Remarques sur le Winchester Troper', in *Festschrift für Heinrich Besseler* (Leipzig, 1961), pp. 67–90. Andreas Holschneider, *Die Organa von Winchester: Studien zum ältesten Repertoire polyphoner Musik* (Hildesheim, 1968).

7187 HARRISON (FRANK Ll.), ed. The Eton choirbook. 3 vols. Musica Britannica, x–xii. Lond. 1956–8.

> 'The finest surviving English musical manuscript' of the period; it was written between *c.* 1490 and 1502.

7188 HUGHES (DOM ANSELM), ed. Worcester mediaeval harmony of the thirteenth and fourteenth centuries. Plainsong and Mediaeval Music Soc. Lond. 1928.

7189 KENNEY (SYLVIA W.), ed. Walter Frye: collected works. Corpus Mensurabilis Musicae, xix. American Institute of Musicology. Rome. 1960.

7190 MAITLAND (JOHN A. FULLER), ed. English carols of the fifteenth century. Lond. 1891.

7191 McPEEK (GWYNN S.), ed. The British Museum manuscript Egerton 3307 : the music except for the carols. Texts edited and transcribed by Robert W. Linker. Lond. and Chapel Hill (N.C.). 1963.

> See the review by Willi Apel in *Speculum,* xxxix (1964), 728–9.

7192 RAMSBOTHAM (A.), COLLINS (H. B.), and HUGHES (DOM ANSELM), eds. The Old Hall manuscript. 3 vols. Plainsong and Mediaeval Music Soc. Lond. 1933–8.

> The most important surviving English manuscript of pieces of the early fifteenth century. See Margaret Bent, 'Sources of the Old Hall music', *The Royal Musical Asso. Procs.* xciv (1967–8), 19–35; Andrew Hughes and Margaret Bent, 'Old Hall: the inventory', *Musica Disciplina,* xxi (1967), 130–47; Andrew Hughes, 'The Old Hall manuscript: a re-appraisal', ibid. xxi (1967), 97–129. There is a valuable discussion of the Old Hall manuscript in Edgar H. Sparks, *Cantus firmus in mass and motet, 1420–1450* (Berkeley, Calif. 1963).

7193 STAINER (JOHN F. R. and E. CECILIA), eds. Early Bodleian music: Dufay and his contemporaries, fifty compositions (*c.* 1400–1440). 3 vols. Lond. 1898–1913.

7194 STEVENS (JOHN), ed. Medieval carols. Musica Britannica, iv. Lond. 1942.

7195 WOOLDRIDGE (HARRY E.), ed. Early English harmony from the tenth to the fifteenth century. 2 vols. Plainsong and Mediaeval Music Soc. Lond. 1897–1913.

> Vol. ii (1913): Transcriptions by H. V. Hughes.

7196 BUKOFZER (MANFRED F.). Studies in medieval and renaissance music. Lond. and N.Y. 1950.

For Bukofzer's study of the music of *Laudes Regiae*, see No. 1353.

7197 CARTER (HENRY H.). A dictionary of Middle English musical terms. Indiana Univ. Humanities Ser. xlv. Bloomington. 1961. Reprinted N.Y. 1968.

7198 CHAILLEY (JACQUES). Histoire musicale du moyen âge. Paris. 1950. 2nd edn. 1969.

7199 CROCKER (RICHARD L.). A history of musical style. N.Y. 1966.

An excellent, recent general study that includes a section on medieval music, placing developments in England in the context of the general development of western music.

7200 GREENE (RICHARD L.), ed. The early English carol. Oxf. 1935. Idem, A selection of English carols. 1962.

7201 GROVE (SIR GEORGE). Dictionary of music and musicians. 4 vols. Lond. 1879–89. 5th edn. by Eric Blom. 10 vols. 1954–61. 6th edn. in preparation.

7202 HARRISON (FRANK Ll.). Music in medieval Britain (1066 to *c.* 1550). Lond. and N.Y. 1958.

The best book on sacred music, studying it within the context of both liturgy and musical institutions, for these subjects it is a fundamental treatise. Bibliography, pp. 440–53; and Register and index of musicians, pp. 454–65. Samples of music throughout. See also Harrison, 'Ars nova in England: a new source', *Musica Disciplina*, xxi (1967), 67–85.

7203 HUGHES (DOM ANSELM), ed. Early medieval music up to 1300. New Oxford History of Music, ii. Lond. 1954.

A co-operative volume covering all of Christian Europe. Bibliography, pp. 405–17.

7204 HUGHES (DOM ANSELM) and ABRAHAM (GERALD), eds. Ars nova and the renaissance, 1300–1540. New Oxford History of Music, iii. Lond. 1960.

Chap. iii: F. Ll. Harrison, English church music in the fourteenth century.
Chap. iv: M. F. Bukofzer, Popular and secular music in England (to *c.* 1470).
Chap. vi: M. F. Bukofzer, English church music in the fifteenth century.
Chap. ix: F. Ll. Harrison, English polyphony (*c.* 1470–1540).

7205 KENNEY (SYLVIA W.). Walter Frye and the *contenance angloise*. Yale Studies in the History of Music, iii. New Haven (Conn.). 1964.

A study of a controversial subject on the fifteenth-century influence of English music on the Burgundian school of composers, largely through the circulation of the works of Walter Frye (d. 1487).

7206 MEECH (SANFORD B.). 'Three musical treatises in English from a fifteenth-century manuscript'. *Speculum*, x (1935), 235–69.

7207 OXFORD BOOK OF CAROLS. Ed. by P. Deamer, R. Vaughan Williams, and M. Shaw. Lond. 1928.

7208 OXFORD COMPANION TO MUSIC. Ed. by Percy A. Scholes. 10th edn. revised and edited by John O. Ward. Lond. 1970.

7209 REESE (GUSTAVE). Music in the middle ages, with an introduction on the music of ancient times. N.Y. 1940.

7210 WALL (CAROLYN). 'York pageant xlvi and its music', with notes on the transcriptions by Ruth Steiner. *Speculum*, xlvi (1971), 689–712.

> See Lucy T. Smith, *York plays: the plays performed by the crafts and mysteries of York on the day of Corpus Christi in the fourteenth, fifteenth and sixteenth centuries*. Oxf. 1885. Also Matthew L. Spencer, *Corpus Christi pageants in England*. (N.Y. 1911).

7211 WESTRUP (JACK). 'England: Mittelalter', in *Die Musik in Geschichte und Gegenwart*, iii (1954), cols. 1361–5.

6. *Printing*

Consult the publications of the Bibliographical Society of London, its Transactions in its journal, *The Library* (Lond. 1889+). The annotated bibliography by Heilbronner (No. 7218) presents a careful listing of collections of English incunabula and of the modern literature on fifteenth-century English printing.

7212 AMES (JOSEPH). Typographical antiquities: being an historical account of printing in England, with some memoirs of our antient printers, and a register of the books printed by them (1471 to 1600) . . . Lond. 1749. Considerably augmented by William Herbert. 3 vols. 1785–90. Greatly enlarged with copious, notes and engravings by Thomas F. Dibdin. Vols. 1–4 (never completed). 1810–19. Index by Bibliographical Society of London. 1899.

7213 AURNER (NELLIE S.). Caxton, mirrour of fifteenth-century letters: a study of the literature of the first English press. Lond. and Boston. 1926.

> A cultural history stemming from Caxton's works, rather than a survey of printing.

7214 BENNETT (HENRY S.). English books and readers, being a history of the book trade, 1475–1557. Cambr. 1952. 2nd edn. 1969.

> A notable, broadly based study of the culture of the world of early printed books.

7215 BLADES (WILLIAM). The life and typography of William Caxton. 2 vols. Lond. 1861–3.

> Blades is a standard authority on Caxton. He published a condensation of the above as *The biography and typography of William Caxton* (Lond. 1877; reprinted, 1882). See also Henry R. Plomer, *William Caxton* (Lond. 1925); and William W. Roberts, 'William Caxton, writer and critic', *B.J.R.L.* xiv (1930), 410–22. For Caxton's editions of *The chronicles of England*, see No. 2811.

7216 CROTCH (WALTER J. B.), ed. The prologues and epilogues of William Caxton. E.E.T.S. Old Ser. clxxvi (1928).

> The introduction presents an excellent full biography of Caxton. Idem, 'An Englishman of the fifteenth century' (William Caxton), *Economica*, no. 28 (1930), 56–73.

7217 DUFF (EDWARD GORDON). A century of the English book trade, 1457–1557. (London) Bibliographical Society. Lond. 1905. Idem, Early English printing: a series of facsimiles of all the types used in England in the fifteenth century. Lond. 1896. Idem, The printers, stationers and bookbinders of Westminster and London from 1476 to 1535. Lond. 1906.

The first-mentioned work gives short biographical sketches of printers, stationers, and bookbinders.

7218 HEILBRONNER (WALTER L.). Printing and the book in fifteenth century England: a bibliographical survey. Bibliographical Society of the University of Virginia. Charlottesville. 1967.

A basic tool for this subject.

7219 MADAN (FALCONER). The early Oxford press; a bibliography of printing and publishing at Oxford, 1468–1640. Oxf. 1895. (Vol. i of Oxford books: a bibliography).

A detailed fundamental source for Oxford printing.

7220 POLLARD (ALFRED W.) and REDGRAVE (GILBERT R.). A short-title catalogue of books printed in England, Scotland and Ireland and of English books printed abroad, 1475–1640. (London) Bibliographical Society. Lond. 1926; reprinted, 1946; 1970. Index by Paul G. Morrison. Charlottesville (Va.). 1950; reprinted 1961.

The standard bibliography of all known copies.

7221 WINSHIP (GEORGE P.). William Caxton and the first English press. A bio-bibliographical essay. N.Y. 1938.

APPENDIX

7222 The LIST AND INDEX SOCIETY, formed in 1965, supplies, to members only, bound copies of unpublished Public Record Office search room lists and indexes. Currently information regarding subscriptions may be obtained from The Secretary, c/o The Public Record Office, Chancery Lane, London. The following lists and indexes bearing upon medieval history had been distributed by early 1973:

1. Select catalogue of unpublished search room lists in the P.R.O. (1965).
2. Exchequer K.R. Ecclesiastical documents (1965).
3. Exchequer K.R. and T.R. Memoranda rolls (1965).
7. Chancery Miscellanea, vol. i (Bundles 1–14) (1966).
15. Chancery Miscellanea, vol. ii (Bundles 15–21) (1966).
16. Augmentation Office. Miscellaneous Books (E315) (1966).
17. Exchequer of Receipt. Receipt and Issue rolls (1966).
26. Chancery Miscellanea, vol. iii (Bundles 33–57) (1967).
31. Class Lists of Records of the Exchequer of Receipt (1968).
32. Class List of Records of the Treasury of Receipt (1968).
34. List of the Records of Parliament and Council, etc. (1968).
38. Chancery Miscellanea, part iv (1968).
43. Exchequer K.R. Customs Accounts (E122), vol. i: Aldeburgh–Lyme Regis (1969).
44. Exchequer K.R. Lay Subsidy rolls (E179), part i, Bedford–Essex (1969).
49. Chancery Miscellanea, part v (1970).
54. Exchequer K.R. Lay Subsidy rolls (E179), part ii, Gloucester–Lincoln (1970).
63. Exchequer K.R. Lay Subsidy rolls (E179), part iii, London–Somerset (1971).
67. Chancery Common Law Pleadings (C43, C44) (1971).
72. List of Escheators for England and Wales (1971).
75. Exchequer K.R. Lay Subsidy rolls (E179), part iv, Staffs.–Yorks. (1972).
81. Chancery Miscellanea (C47), part vi, Northumberland–Suffolk (1972).
82. Exchequer L.T.R. Class List (1972).
87. Exchequer K.R. Lay Subsidy rolls (E179), part v, Wales, Cinque Ports, Royal Household etc. (1973).
88. Chancery Miscellanea (C47), part vii, Surrey to Worcester, transcripts (1973).

7223 (McKisack) THE REIGN OF RICHARD II. Essays in honour of MAY McKISACK. Ed. by F. R. H. Du Boulay and C. M. Barron. Lond. 1971.

(a) J. N. L. Myres, May McKisack.
(b) J. A. Tuck, Richard II's systems of patronage. 1–20.
(c) P. Chaplais, English diplomatic documents 1377–99. 21–45.
(d) V. H. Galbraith, Thoughts about the Peasants' Revolt. 46–57.
(e) B. White, Poet and peasant. 58–74.
(f) J. J. N. Palmer, English foreign policy, 1388–99. 75–107.
(g) B. F. Harvey, The monks of Westminster and the University of Oxford. 108–30.
(h) R. L. Storey, Liveries and commissions of the peace, 1388–90. 131–52.
(i) F. R. H. Du Boulay, Henry of Derby's expeditions to Prussia 1390–1 and 1392. 153–72.
(j) C. M. Barron, The quarrel of Richard II with London, 1392–7. 173–201.
(k) J. H. Harvey, Richard II and York. 202–17.
(l) R. Virgoe, The Crown and local government: East Anglia under Richard II. 218–41.
(m) R. Hill, 'A chaunterie for Soules': London chantries in the reign of Richard II. 242–55.

(n) R. R. Davies, Richard II and the principality of Chester 1397–9. 256–79.
(o) M. Aston, Richard II and the Wars of the Roses. 280–317.

7224 (Major) THE STUDY OF MEDIEVAL RECORDS. Essays in honour of KATHLEEN MAJOR. Ed. by D. A. Bullough and R. L. Storey. Oxf. 1971.

(a) D. A. Bullough, The writing-office of the Dukes of Spoleto in the eighth century. 1–21.
(b) Pierre Chaplais, English diplomatic documents to the end of Edward III's reign. 22–56.
(c) Jane E. Sayers, Papal privileges for St. Albans abbey and its dependencies. 57–84.
(d) J. C. Holt, The assizes of Henry II: the texts. 85–106.
(e) G. W. S. Barrow, The early charters of the family of Kinninmonth of that Ilk. 107–31.
(f) David Walker, The organization of material in medieval cartularies. 132–50.
(g) G. H. Martin, The registration of deeds of title in the medieval boroughs. 151–73.
(h) A. A. M. Duncan, The making of the Declaration of Arbroath. 174–88.
(i) Dorothy Owen, The records of the bishop's official at Ely: specialization in the English episcopal chancery of the later middle ages. 189–205.
(j) R. F. Hunnisett, The reliability of inquisitions as historical evidence. 206–35.
(k) R. L. Storey, Ecclesiastical causes in chancery. 236–59.
(l) A. L. Brown, The privy seal clerks in the early fifteenth century. 260–81.
(m) Margaret Bowker, Some archdeacons' court books and the Commons' Supplication against the Ordinaries of 1532. 282–316.
(n) List of manuscripts cited. 317–21.
(o) A. E. B. Owen, A bibliography of the writings of Kathleen Major. 322–7.

7225 (Whitelock) ENGLAND BEFORE THE CONQUEST. Studies in primary sources presented to DOROTHY WHITELOCK. Ed. by Peter Clemoes and Kathleen Hughes. Cambr. 1971.

(a) The writings of Dorothy Whitelock. 1–4.
(b) Peter Hunter Blair, The letters of Pope Boniface V and the mission of Paulinus to Northumbria. 5–13.
(c) Paul Meyvaert, Bede's text of the *Libellus Responsionum* of Gregory the Great to Augustine of Canterbury. 15–33.
(d) J. M. Wallace-Hadrill, A background to St. Boniface's mission. 35–48.
(e) Kathleen Hughes, Evidence for contacts between the churches of the Irish and English from the Synod of Whitby to the Viking age. 49–67.
(f) Nicholas Brooks, The development of military obligations in eighth-and ninth-century England. 69–84.
(g) John Pope, Ælfric and the Old English version of the Ely privilege. 85–113.
(h) Henry Loyn, Towns in late Anglo-Saxon England; the evidence and some possible lines of enquiry. 115–28.
(i) Dorothy Bethurum Loomis, *Regnum* and *sacerdotium* in the early eleventh century. 129–45.
(j) Kenneth Cameron, Scandinavian settlement in the territory of the Five Boroughs: the place-name evidence. Part III, the Grimston-hybrids. 147–63.
(k) R. I. Page, How long did the Scandinavian language survive in England? The epigraphical evidence. 165–81.
(l) Olof von Feilitzen and Christopher Blunt, Personal names on the coinage of Edgar. 183–214.
(m) Cecily Clark, The narrative mode of *The Anglo-Saxon Chronicle* before the Conquest. 215–35.
(n) Janet Batley, The classical additions in the Old English Orosius. 237–51.
(o) René Derolez, The orientation system in the Old English Orosius. 253–68.
(p) J. E. Cross, The ethic of war in Old English. 269–82.
(q) Alistair Campbell, The use in *Beowulf* of earlier heroic verse. 283–92.

(r) Peter Clemoes, Cynewulf's image of the Ascension. 293–304.
(s) Francis Wormald, The 'Winchester School' before St. Æthelwold. 305–13.
(t) Neil Ker, The handwriting of Archbishop Wulfstan. 315–31.
(u) Michael Dolley, The nummular brooch from Sulgrave. 333–49.
(v) H. M. Taylor, Repton reconsidered: a study in structural criticism. 351–89.
(w) Martin Biddle, Archaeology and the beginning of English society. 391–408.

INDEX

Page citations are printed in bold type; other references are to numbered entries

Aaron of York, 3946
Abacus, 3257
Abbeys. *See* Monasticism
Abbo of Fleury, 2305
Abbots, 3478. *See* Monasticism
Abbotsford Club, 205
Abbott, Edwin A.: St. Thomas, 6494
— Isabel R.: Taxation, 3268
— Thomas K.: Catalogue, 1083
Abbreviata chronica, 2744
Abbreviatio chronicorum, 1114, 2745
— placitorum, 3493
Abbreviations, MSS., 402–5, 407, 409, 411
Aberafan and Margam District Historical Society (Glam.), 1920
Abercrombie, Nigel: Edmund Bishop, 1325
Abercromby, Hon. John: Bronze-age pottery, 1967
Aberdeen University: Library MSS., 1063
— Review (journal), 104
— Studies, 206
Åberg, Nils F.: Pre-history, 1968; Anglo-Saxons, 2467
Abergavenny (Wales), 1934, 4633
Aberystwyth Studies, 105
Abingdon abbey (Berks.): Accounts, 6084; Anglo-Saxon Chronicle, 2142; Chronicon, 2153, 2725, 2827, 6085; Court rolls, 6084; History, 2725, 6084–7; Riots, 4139; Surveys, 3068, 6086
— abbot of: Impeachment of, 3415
Abingdon Court (Wilts.), 4927
Abinger (Surrey), 766
Abjuratio regni, 1261
Abraham, Gerald: Ars nova, 7204
Abrahams, Barnett Lionel: Condition of Jews, 3944; Expulsion of Jews, 3944
— Israel: Northants. Donum, 3938; Starrs and charters, 3940; The deacon and Jewess, 3954
Abram, William A.: Guilds merchant of Preston, 5131
Acastre, William, York merchant, 5505
Accounts: general; **493**; 790, 955, 955A, 2366, 3144, 3219, 3230, 3231, 3240, 3835, 3854, 3864, 4102, 4543, 4609, 4631, 4701, 4746, 4794, 4931, 5714, 6268, 6848, 7058, 7064, 7118

— Forms and rules, 4698
— Manorial, and village:
Abingdon abbey, 6084
Adderbury, 4844
Alton Barnes, 4919
Anstey, 4771
Banstead, 4898
Beaumaris castle, 3786A
Beaurepaire and Roche court, 4573
Bec, 5916
Brendon, 4869
Burnham, 4750
Car-Colston, 4842
Castle Combe, 4922
Cheshire, 3084, 3854
Chessington, 4897
Clapham Bayeux, 4702
Crondal, 4763
Crowland, 5021
Cuxham, 4849
Dunster, 4867
Durham abbey, 3864, 5681
Elwell, 4736
Farley, 4897
Forncett, 4819
Halton, 4724
Icklington, 4885
Ingoldmells, 4812
Kettering, 4828
Lancashire, 4794
Lewes, 4905
London, St. Paul's, 5759
Long Sutton, 4763
Malden, 4897
Manydown, 4767
Newton, 4715
Norham, 6276
Orston, 4842
Oundle, 4834
Petworth, 4903
Porlock, 4869
Portland, 4736
Ramsey abbey, 6175
St. Mary des Prés, 1480
Scarrington, 4842
Screverton, 4842
Takeley, 4919
Tatenhill, 4877
Tewkesbury, 4755
Thornycroft, 4897

Accounts: Manorial, and village (*cont.*):
Wardley, 6137
Warwick, St. Mary, 4912
Warwickshire, 4913
Wellingborough, 4835
Winchester, 4815–16
Wiston, 4904
Wistowe, 6175
Wookey, 4870
Wyke, 4736
Yeovil, 4865
Yorkshire, 4931
— Monastic, cathedral, etc.
Abingdon, 6084–5
Battle, 6360
Bec, 4699, 5916
Bicester, 4852, 6287
Bolton, 1893, 6396–7
Bristol, St. Augustine's, 6150–1
Bromholm, 6253
Bury St. Edmund's, 6342
Cambridge University, 7058
Canterbury, Christ Church, 4696, 5608, 5611, 5619, 5622
Canterbury, St. Augustine's, 6182–3
Carlisle, 5648
Carrow, 4822
Coldingham, 6132
Creake, 6257
Crowland, 4835, 5021, 6213
Dewsbury, 5289
Durham, 5681
Ely, 5705
Exeter, 5720
Farne, 6276
Finchale, 6134
Glastonbury, 6311
Harrold, 6079
Hereford, 5725
Holme, St. Benedict's, 6258
Holy Island, 6276
Jarrow, 6137–8
Kingswood, St. Mary's, 6158
Lenton, 6280
Lincoln, 5753
Louth Park, 2831, 6218
Malton, 6406
Monk-Wearmouth, 6138
Newnham, 6079
Norwich, 5775, 5788
Oxford, 7118
Peterborough, 6265, 6268
Ripon, SS. Peter and Wilfrid, 6415
Rochester, 5797
Selby, 6419
Tewkesbury, 4755, 6159
Warwick, St. Mary's, 6370
Wilton, 6379

Winchester, St. Swithun's, 1468, 5812, 5815
Worcester, 5825, 5831
Yeovil, 4865
York, 5872
— Municipal:
Bridgwater, 5247
Dewsbury, 5289
Faversham, 5317
King's Lynn, 5205
London merchant, 5175
Salisbury, 5283
Shrewsbury, 5240
— Papal: 6774–83
— *See* 'Bailiffs', 'Churchwarden accounts'; 'Household' (accounts); 'Ministers' accounts'; 'Ship's accounts'; 'Wardrobe' (accounts)
Accursius, Francis, 6751
Achards (Glos.), 4753
Achery, Luc d': Acta Sanctorum, 1151; Lanfranc, 5631; Spicilegium, 1088; Trevet, 2963
Ackerman, Robert W.: Backgrounds, 6974
Ackworth (Yorks.), 4941A
Acquittances, 2204, 4402
Acta episcoporum, 1496, 5577
— Philologica Scandinavica, 2427
— regia, 3766
— Sanctorum, **148–51.** *See* Saints
Actes de Normandie, 3824
Actions, forms of, **552–3**
Acton, John of: Annotations, 6436
Acts of resumption, 3365, 3409
Adalbjarnarson, Bjarni: Heimskringla, 2447
Adam: abbot of Evesham, 5742
— of Bremen, 2149
— of Bocfield, 6552–4, 6891
— of Domerham, 1103, 6309, 6313
— of Eynsham, 6289
— of Marsh, 6010, 6602–4
— of Murimuth, **387**; 2931
— of Orleton, 5730
— of Usk, **387**; 2966
— of Witham, 6324
— Frank: Scottish clans, 506
Adamnan: Law of, 2244; Life of Columba, 2319
Adams, George B.: Anglo-Saxon feudalism, 4640; Constitutional history, 1210; Councils, 3295, 3659; Equity, 3718; London and the commune, 5176; Origin of the constitution, 1211; Political history, 1183; Select documents, 1204
— Henry: A.-S. courts, 2612, 2624
— Henry C.: Wykehamica, 7135
— Norma: Writ of prohibition, 6462; Tithes, 6831

Adamson, John W.: The illiterate Anglo-Saxon, 7136

Adcock, Sir Frank E.: ed., Cambridge Ancient History, 2034

Adderbury (Oxon.), 4844

Addington (Kent), 4787

Addis, Robina: Alchemical MSS., 985

Addison, Charles G.: Templars, 6058

— John: Archives of Preston, 5131

Addleshaw, George W. O.: Parochial system, 6854

Addy, Sidney O.: Beauchief abbey, 6114; Cartae, 6416; Church and manor, 4944; English house, 814

Adela, daughter of William I, 619

Adelard of Bath, 6521-5

— monk of Ghent: Letter to Ælfheah, 2303

Adler, Elkan Nathan: London Jewish communities, 3945

— Michael: Jews in England, 3946; Jews in Exeter, 3947; London Jewry, 3942; Pipe roll (1285), 3943

Administration: county, 555-7; 1529 (Wilts.), 1626

— diocesan, 755-92, 888-91. See Registers, episcopal

Administrative history. See Constitutional history

Admiralty, 955, 1246, 4286, 4321; Pleas, 3515

Adolf of Nassau, 4092, 4109

Adomnan. See Adamnan

Adrian IV, pope, 1459, 1487, 5556, 6741, 6911. See Laudabiliter

Adventus Saxonum, 1432. See also A.-S. invasion

Advocates, faculty of, 131; 1062

Aegidius Tschudi's maps, 596

Ælfheah, archbishop: Adelard's letter on St. Dunstan, 2303; Vita, 1106, 2306

Ælfric: Canons, 2259; Colloquies, 2292, 2328; Concordia, 1347, 2270, 2272; De temporibus anni, 2292; Glossary, 2292; Heptateuch, 2292; Hexameron, 2292; Homilies, 441, 2292, 2361; Lives of saints, 2292, 2305, 2312; Pastoral letters, 2292; Vita S. Æthelwoldi, 2153, 2293; Commentaries, 1433(m), 2292(h-k), 2352, 7225

Aelred (Ailred) of Rievaulx. See Rievaulx

Æthelbert, king of East Anglia, 2307

— king of Kent, 2176; Charters, 2218, 2307-8, 2534, 2696

Æthelflaed, Lady of the Mercians, 1433

Æthelhere, king, 2487

Æthelred, I, 2140

— II, 2189, 2311, 2315, 2361

Æthelweard: Chronicle of, 1084, 1496, 2140, 2142

Æthelwig, abbot of Evesham, 2715, 6383

Æthelwold: 317; Life of, 2153, 2293; Benedictine rule, 2270-2, 2274-5; Benedictional, 880

Æthelwulf, king of West Saxons, 1454

— De abbatis, 2294

Agarde, Arthur: Placitorum abbreviatio, 3493; Repertorie, 960

Agincourt, Battle of, 2877, 2890, 2917, 2978, 4162, 4261, 4297, 6991, 7046, 7049

Agnellus, Thomas: Death of Henry, son of Henry II, 2747

Agrarian history, 174-7, 374-8 and 666-700; 1849, 4808, 6266; Roman, 2039, 2074. See Agriculture

Agricola (Tacitus), 2025, 2071-2, 2081, 2088

Agricultural History Review, 106

Agricultural History (journal), 143

Agriculture, 696-700; 1494, 1501, 1529, 4802, 4904, 4925, 4982

Aicill, Book of, 2240

Aids, feudal, 1601, 2540, 3174, 3242, 3949, 4337, 4341, 630 (Cumb.), 4350-1, 4354, 4358-9, 4365, 4367, 4387, 4396, 4790. See Book of Aids

Aigrain, René, 148

Aikens, H. E.: Bishops and monastic finance, 5900

Ailby (Lincs.), 4805

Ailred of Rievaulx. See Rievaulx

Airmyn, William, bishop, 509; 3151, 5786

Air-photography, 89-90; 766, 1432

Airy, William: Beds. Domesday, 3015

Aisthorpe (Lincs.), 4806

Aitken, A. J.: Dictionary, 332

— Patrick H.: Catalogue, 1065

Akerman, John Y.: Saxon remains, 2468; Rent roll, 6375

Alan of Tewkesbury: Life of Becket, 6487

Aland, Kurt: ed. Mirbt's Quellen, 1136

Alban, St., Illustrations, 890

Albeck, Gustav: Saga, 2448

Albert of Austria, 4109

— of Lotharingia, 4004

Albertson, Clinton A.: A.-S. Saints, 2284

Albery, William: Parliamentary history, 3470

Albion (journal), 158

Albon, William, abbot: Register, 6169

Album Paléographique, 433

Alchemy, MSS., 985, 6965

Alcock, Leslie: Camelot, 2470; Dinas Powys, 1969; Roman Britons, 2095; Settlement in Wales, 1435

— N. W.: Devon manor, 4733

Alcuin: Works by, 1100, 1114, 2284, 2289, 2295, 2314; Commentaries, 1396, 2280, 2359, 5878

Aldborough (Yorks.), 2045, 2052, 4935

Aldermen (Lond.), 5164, 5178

Aldhelm, 1102, 1396, 2285, 2291, 2296, 2359

Aldis, Harry G.: Cambridge Univ. Library, 1031

Alessio, Franco: Roger Bacon, 6541

Alexander, III, pope: Bulls, 3006; Opera, 5557, 6487

— de Swereford, 3006–7

— of Hales, 6587–91

— of St. Albans, 1448

Alexander, James W.: Becket, 6495; Chester palatinate, 3855; Herbert of Norwich, 5781

— John J.: Biographies, 3456; County elections, 3433; Devon members, 3457

— Jonathan J. G.: Illuminated MSS., 878

— Michael, 2356

— William M.: Inscriptions, 355; Scottish place-names, 641

Alföldi, Maria R.: Coins, 647

Alford (Lincs.), 4805

Alford, Bernard W. E.: Carpenters' company, 5187

Alfred, king: Asser, 2147; Coins, 1454; Reign of, 1496, 2142, 2165, 2575, 2579, 2590, 2593–4, 2597; Works of, 2184, 2347–8, 2352. *See* Anglo-Saxon law

Aliceholt (Hants), forest, 3896

Alien merchants, **740–2**; 5177

Alien priories, 1519–21, 5916, 5921, 5923–4, 6078, 6129, 6252, 6323

Allan, G.: Darlington press, 5069, 6135–6, 6139

Allcroft, Arthur H.: Earthwork, 765

Allen, Derek F.: Coins, 652, 668, 704

— Edward: Baron Brotherton, 1038

— Hope Emily: 6674, 6677–8, 6694

— John (M. D.): English legislature, 3382; Prerogative, 3271

— John (of Hereford): Bibliotheca, 1665

— John Romilly: Celtic art, 2469; Early church, 2662

— Percy S.: Bishop Shirwood, 7160

— Thomas: Lincoln, 1723; York, 1889

Allerton (Yorks.), 4930, 6405

Allison, K. J.: 4836; Kingston-Hull, 5294

— Thomas: Religious life, 2707

Allmand, Christopher T.: Henry V, 2877, 4236; Land settlement, 4270; Negotiations (1439), 4237

Allsop, Peter: Index, 132

Alms, 5762, 5834, 6264

Almshouse, 5067

Alnwick abbey (Northumb.), 4837, 6272

Alnwick, William, bishop, 6222, 6458

Alod and fee, 4662

Alphonse of Poitiers, 1448

Alrewas (Staffs.), 4874

Alsace, 1426

Altnordische Saga-Bibliothek, 2436

Altavilla, John de, 7042

Alton, Ernest H.: Book of Kells, 881

Alton Barnes (Wilts.), 4919

Altschul, Michael: Anglo-Norman bibliography, 15; The Clares, 4568

Alured of Beverley, 1103, 2795

Alvingham (Gilbertine house) (Lincs.), 5957, 6216

Amanieu, A.: Dictionnaire, **168**

— Arnaud, sire d'Albret, 1426

Amann, Émile, 1267

Amateur Historian (journal), 1502

Ambree (Kent), 4783

Ambresbury, Michael of, abbot, 6315

Ambroise: L'estoire, 1114, 2748, 2906

Ambrosden (Oxon.), 4854

Ambrosini, Maria L.: Vatican archives, 5540

Amercements (Green Wax), 3608

America, discovery of, 5394

American Archivist (journal), 929

— Historical Association, Guide, 40

— Historical Review, 144

— Law Schools, Association of, 1246

— Musicological Society Journal, **929**

— School of Prehistoric Research, 1960

Ames Foundation, 3649

Ames, Edward: Sterling crisis (1337–9), 5499

— James B.: Assumpsit, parol contracts, trover, 1246

— Joseph: Typographical antiquities, 7212

Amesbury (Wilts.), 4926

Amiens, Mise of, 1450

Amiens, Guy of: De bello Hastingensi, 2749

Ammann, Hektor: Festschrift für, 5236

Ammianus Marcellinus, 2025

Amondesham, Walter de, 4293

Amounderness (Lancs.), 5132, 5360

Amours, François J.: Chronicle of Wyntoun, 2984

Amphlett, John: Court rolls of Hales, 4928; Habington's survey, 1866; Index to Nash's Worcestershire, 1867; Kyre Park charters, 4494; Lay subsidy, 3199, 3201; Worcestershire, 1866–7

Amundesham, John: Annales, 2750

Amyot, Thomas: Sir John Fastolf, 4599

Analecta Augustiana, 5966

— Bollandiana, 145, 1153

— S.O. Cisterciensis, 5928

— Franciscana, 6001
— Hibernica, 221, 1067
— Praedicatorum, 5980
— Praemonstratensia, 5960
Ancaster (Lincs.), Roman, 2061
Ancestor, the (journal), 501
Anchorites, **875-7**
Ancient authors, 2024-5
— Britain, map of, 604
— correspondence, **559**; 2752, 3224, 3775, 3782
— deeds in P.R.O., 3220, 4402
— laws of Ireland, 2240
— monuments guides, **85-7**; 718, 736-8
— peoples and places, 761
— petitions, **493**; 3225
Andersen, Sveaas: Norman Conquest, **589**
Anderson, Alan O.: Annals, 1088; Chronicle of Melrose, 2824; Columba, 2319; Ninian, 2323; Sources, 1088A
— Annie: Science MSS., 985, 6964-5
— George K.: Literature, 2349
— J. E.: M. Bloch's Land and work, 252, 4951
— James: Skene, 2135; Thesaurus, 4341
— John: Laing charters, 1064
— John C.: Shropshire, 1800
— John G. C.: Agricola, 2025, 2081; Germania, 2505
— John P.: Topography, 6, 1503
— Joseph: Orkney saga, 2451
— Marjorie O.: Chronicle of Holyrood, 2821; Chronicle of Melrose, 2824; Columba, 2319; Early kings, 2114; Early Scotland, 1120
— Mary D.: Carving, 842, 851; Drama, 6975
— (Anderson-Arngart), Olaf S.: Hundred names, 628; Leningrad Bede, 441, 2148
— Robert B.: Supplement to Beale, 1224
— Roger C.: The 'Grace de Dieu', 4327; Archives of Southampton, 5105
— William J.: MSS., 985
Anderton, Basil: Catalogue, 1767
Andover (Hants), 5095, 6838
André, J.: Pliny, 2025
Andresen, Hugo: Wace's Roman de Rou, 2974
Andrew of Wyntoun: Chronicle, 2984
Andrews, Charles M.: The manor, 2625
Andrieu, Michel: Le pontifical, 1323
Andrieu-Guitrancourt, Pierre: Décanat rural, 6832
Anecdota Oxoniensia, 1017
Aneirin, Book of, 2384
Anesty, Richard de. See Anstey
Angles, 362-4, 2509, 2526, 2559
Anglesey, 1895-6, 4943A, 6828

— Marquis of: Charters, 6327
Anglia (Zeitschrift), 270
— Christiana Society, 180
— sacra, map of, 605
Anglicus, Bartholomaeus: De proprietatibus rerum, 6548
Anglistische Forschungen, 271
Anglo-Latin satirical poets, 7042
Anglo-Norman: Brut, 2811; Custumal, 5055; Families, 564, 4667; Historians, **387**; Language and literature, **37-8**; 6692-5, 6699, 7043; Text Society, 289; Warfare, 4004
Anglo-Saxon:
— archaeology, **84-92**, and **357-60**
— art and architecture, 788, 802, 809, 811, 872, 880, 882, 889, 904, 912, 924, 1433, 1485, 2123
— burials, 1442
— charters, **303-10**
— Chronicle, **285-6**; 441, 1084, 1089, 1114, 1123, 1458, 1496, 7225
— church, **314-33** and **382-5**
— coins, **80-4**
— courts, 2612, 2624. See A.-S. law
— dictionaries, 277, 279, 283, 286
— England (journal), **339**; 881, 2171
— Germanic background, **362-4**
— invasion and settlement, **364-8**; 1426, 1432, 1433, 1442, 1454, 1465, 2098, 2103, 2467, 2475, 2481, 2490
— law, **300-1** and **372-4**; 1246, 1482, 5794
— MSS., 389, 394, 404, 425, 441, 444, 447-8, 452-3, 469
— period, commentaries on, **360-85**
— poetry, **339-44**
— proper names, **75-8**; 589, 623
— royal genealogies, 547, 2161
— rural economy, 2647A, 2653
— scholars, **319-33**
— science, **344-6**
Anglo-Scottish relations, **599-601**; 1113. See Scotland
Angoulême, earl of: Compotus, 4600
— Isabella of, 1486, 4038, 6429
Angus, W. S.: A.-S. Chronicle, 2142; Edward the Elder, 2597; Northern annals, 2168; Northumbrian Christianity, 2708; Simeon of Durham, 2157
— William: Records, 1059
Anjou, county of, 4012
— Margaret of, 3129, 3773, 4195, 4201
Annales, 146-7, 249, 1108, 1113-14, 2143-5, 2730, 2751-75, 5789, 6341
Annalis Domitiani Latini, 2142
— historia brevis, 1096, 2776
Annalium Angliae Excerpta, 1108

Annals, 1018, 1098–9, 2146, 2754, 2762–6, 2775, 2777–86, 2854, 2969, 2982, 5259, 6161, 6274, 6294, 6382

Annates, Ireland, 6774. *See* Lunt, W. E.

Anne, de Bourgogne, 4266

— widow of Humphrey of Buckingham, 4600

Année Philologique, L', 266, 2014

Annesley, Sir John de, 3503A

Annual Bibliography of English Language and Literature, 272

— Bulletin of Historical Literature, 7, 175

Anonimalle chronicle, 2787

Anonyme de Bethune, 2897

Anonymus Eboracensis, 6427

Anscombe, Alfred: Welsh genealogy, 507, 2115; Widsith, 2345

Anselm, St.: Lives and works, 1088, 1108, 1113, 2863, 6526–33; Modern commentaries, 5626A, 5921, 6534–5, 6911

Anstey (Herts.), Manor, 4771

Anstey, Henry: Epistolae, 7062; Monumenta, 7065

— Richard of: Case of, 1453, 3490

Anstis, John: Register, 550

Anstruther, Robert: Chronica of Ralph Niger, 2933; Epistolae Herberti de Losinga, 5777

Antiquarian Magazine and Bibliographer, 719

Antiquaries Journal, 107

Antiquary (journal), 720

Antiquity, a quarterly review, 721

Antl, L.: Quaestiones theologicae, 6594

Antonine itinerary, 2029, 2044

— wall, 2087

Antony, earl Rivers, 4208, 4228

Antrobus deeds (Wilts.), 4488

Antrobus, Frederick I.: Ludwig Pastor's Popes, 6720

Anwyl, Edward: Dictionary, 342; Welsh poetry, 2405

Apel, Willi, 7191

Apocalypse in art, 891–2

Applebaum, S.: Pattern of settlement, 2037

Appleby, barony of (Westm.), 1851

Appleby, John T.: Devizes chronicle, 2767, 2859; England without Richard, 4011; Henry II, 4011; John, 4011; Stephen, 3984

Appleton, Henry: Muster roll, 4287

Apprentices (London), 5178

Appropriations of churches, 5835, 6807, 6861

Approver, king's, 3697

Apps, Una: Muntatores, 4641

Apthorp, George F.: Library, 1048

Apuleius Barbarus: Herbal, 2374

Aqua Blanca, Peter de, bishop, 5737

Aquitaine, **568–72**; 4023, 4037, 4090, 4103, 4164, 4168, 4180, 4272, 4573

Arabic science, 6936, 6939, 6952–3, 6961, 6966

Arbellot, François: Geoffrey de Vigeois, 2970

Arbman, Eric Holger: Vikings, 761

Arbroath, Declaration of, 4077, 7224

Arc, Jeanne d', 1455, 2840, 4241, 4246, 4256, 4264, 4267–8

Archaeologia (journal), 108

— Aeliana (journal), 722

— Cambrensis (journal), 109

— Scotia (journal), 216

Archaeological Journal, 724

— Review, 725

Archaeology, **84–92**, **256–61**, **268–79**, and **357–60**; 1432, 1961, 2037, 2492, 7225

Archbishops. *See* Canterbury and York

Archbold, William A. J., 1482 (iiiw)

Archer, Margaret: Bishop Repingdon, 5743

— Thomas A.: Battle of Hastings, 3990

Archer-Hind, Mrs.: Paston letters, 4610

Arches, Court of, 6471, 6484

Archimedes, 6939

Architects, Dictionary of, 797

Architecture, **92–8**; 1325, 1433, 1435, 1485, 1495, 2077–80, 2517, 4987, 6029

Archiv für Diplomatik, Schriftgeschichte, Siegel- und Wappenkunde, 412

Archiv für das Studium der neueren Sprachen und Literaturen, 148

Archives: **107–34**; 1039, 1504, 1507, 1509, 1513, 1523

— continental, 1441, 3803, 3806, 3812A, 3833–4

— county, **219–55**

— diocesan, **758–90**; 5574–5, 5872

— local:
  Andover, 5095
  Arley hall, 4421
  Aylesbury, 4418
  Bath, 4491
  Battle abbey, 6358
  Berkeley castle, 4437
  Blithfield, 4476
  Cambridge University, 7103
  Canterbury, cathedral, 5621, 5623
  Chelmsford, 4526
  Chichester, city, 5270
  Cleeve abbey, 6308
  Derbyshire, 4431
  Dulwich, Alleyn's college, 4891
  Durham cathedral, **113**, 1043–4, 1622

Ely, 5704
Hagley hall, 4493
Hoghton tower, 4442
Kirklees, 4497
Lambeth palace. *See* Lambeth palace library
Lichfield, dean and chapter, 1047, 5665
London, 1504, 1728, 5148
Merton hall, 4821
Middleton manor, 4482
Oxford, colleges, 7072
Rome, Augustinian, 5970
Salisbury, city, 5283
Scarisbrick Hall, 4441
Shavington Hall, 4467
Shaw hill, Chorley, 4449
Sherborne House, 4436
Surrey, 5265
Waltham Holy Cross, 1648
Wells, dean and chapter, 5584
Westminster abbey, 1016, 6238
Wombourne, 4471
Worcester, town and cathedral, 1868, 5829
— Vatican, 5540–5
Archives (journal), 930, 1504
— d'histoire doctrinale et littéraire, 858; 6875
Archivist, Irish, Records, 1068
Archivium Hibernicum, 222
Archivum, 931
— Franciscanum Historicum, 6002
— Historiae Pontificiae, 5541
— Praedicatorum, 5980A
Areley (Worcs.), 2914
Arens, Franz: Wilhelm Servat, 5423
Ari: Kings' Book, 2447
Aristotle, 6554, 6900
Arithmetics in English, 6947
Arkiv for Nordisk Filologi, 2428
Arlesey (Beds.), 6148
Arley charters, 4421
Arlington (Sussex), 6838
Armagh, archbishop of, 6568; Book of, 2324; Library of, 1079. *See* Fitz-Ralph
Armitage, Ella S.: Norman castles, 824
Armitage-Smith, Sydney: John of Gaunt's register, 3875
Armorial bearings, 487–500
Armorica, 327. *See* Brittany
— William of: Gesta, 2947
Arms and armour, 103–6; 742, 768, 1982, 4276
Armstrong, Charles A. J.: Anglo-Burgundian alliance, 4238; Battle of St. Albans, 2746, 4194; Communication, 1450; Faversham, 6190; Usurpation of Richard III, 2922; Yorkist kings, 1350

Army, **619–25**; 836, 1455, 1459, 1485, 1495, 1774, 2075–6, 2476, 2650, 2790, 3316, 3538, 4004, 4059, 4162, 4274, 5211
Armytage, Sir George J.: Catalogue, 4497
Arndt, Wilhelm: John of Salisbury, 6640; Shrifttafeln, 413
Arne Lawrence's son, monk of Thingore, 2303
Arngart, O. *See* Anderson
Arngrim, monk of Thingeyrar, 6488
Arnold, A. A.: Court roll, 4783
— Hugh: Stained glass, 861
— Ivor: Le roman de Brut, 2974
— John H.: ed. Frere's papers, 1333
— Richard: Customs of London, 2789
— Thomas: Bury St. Edmunds; 2305, 6341; Cuthbert, 2302; Henry of Huntingdon chronicle, 2904; John of Hexham chronicle, 2893; Simeon of Durham, 2157; Wyclif, 6650
Arnold-Foster, Frances: Dedications, 1154
Arnould, Emile J. F.: Richard Rolle, 6680; Henry of Lancaster, 6693
Arntz, Helmut: Runes, 44; 352
Arnulf of Lisieux, 1102, 6487, 6511–12
Aronius, Julius: Diplomatische Studien, 2201
Arras, Congress of (1435), 4249
Array, rolls of, 5211
Arrivall of Edward IV, 2901
Arrowsmith, Richard S.: Prelude to reformation, 6833
Ars dictaminis, 7063
Art, **92–103** and **358–60**; 1449, 1485, 2541, 2548, 6023, 6496
Arthington nunnery (Yorks.), 6394
Arthur, king, 2166–7, 2470, 2531, 6317, 6319
— duke of Brittany, 1490, 4034
Articuli ad Novas Narrationes, 2998
— Willelmi, 2182
Artois, Robert of, 7049
Arundel: Castle and town, 4597; Earldom of, 4908; House of, 4597; MSS., 993, 1007; Rape of, 1840
Arundel, Joan of, 4213
— Thomas, archbishop, 5627, 5707, 5861
Ashbridge (Wilts.), 6039
Ashburne (Derby), Charters, 4429
Ashburton (Devon), 6838
Ashby-Folville (Leics.), 5455
Ashdown (Sussex) forest, 3924
Ashdown, Charles H.: Arms and armour, 905
— Margaret: Harold, 1433; Norse documents, 2437
Ashe, Geoffrey: Avalon, 2470, 6317

Ashen charters, 4434
Ashley, Maurice: Magna Carta, 3289
— Sir William J.: Bread, 1361, 5487;
  Economic history, 1361; Rye, 4985;
  Surveys, 1361; Woollen industry, 5408
Ashmole, Elias: Berkshire, 1546; MSS.,
  1023
Ashmolean Museum, Oxford, 704
Ashton (Wilts.), 4777
Ashton, Richard, abbot: Register, 6264
Ashton-under-Lyne (Lancs.), 4793
Ashworth, Philip A.: ed. Gneist, 1213
Aspects of Archaeology, 1432, 2492
Aspin, Isabel S. T.: Anglo-Norman songs,
  7043
Asplin, P. W. A.: Medieval Ireland, 16,
  4030
Assarting, 1468, 4989
Asser: Life of Alfred, 2147
Asserio, Rigaud de: Register, 5816
Assize of bread and ale, 5487, 7064
Assize rolls. *See* Plea rolls
Assizes of Henry II, 7224
Assmann, Bruno: Homilies, 2266, 2292
Associated Architectural Societies, 171
Assumpsit, 1246
Astle, Thomas: Ayloffe, 946; Palaeo-
  graphy, 382
Astley, Hugh J. D.: Norfolk, 1755
Aston (Staffs.), 4879
Aston, Margaret: Archbishop Arundel,
  5627, 5707, 5861; Bishop Despenser,
  3418; Kent approver, 3697; Lollardy,
  6867; Richard II, 7223; Wyclif, 6657
— Trevor H.: Kosminsky review, 4971;
  Manor, 2626, 4944
Athelney abbey (Som.), 6321
Athelstan, king, 352; 2184, 2189, 2342,
  2445, 2597
Athona, Johannes de. *See* Acton, John of
Atkins, Sir Ivor: A.-S. chronicle, 2142;
  Worcester, 1052, 5844
— William M.: St. Paul's cathedral, 5770
Atkinson, Donald: Roman governors,
  2071; Roman navy, 1455
— John C.: Furness abbey, 6199; Rievaulx
  abbey, 6413; Whitby, 5299, 6422
— R. L.: Channel Islands petitions, 3319;
  French Bible, 1330; Richard II and
  Gloucester, 4138
— Richard J. C.: Archaeology, 745;
  Stonehenge, 1970
— Robert: Book of Ballymote, 2396; Book
  of Lecan, 2395; Book of Leinster, 2394;
  Flann, 2160; Irish laws, 2240
— Thomas D.: Glossary, 784
Atkyns, Sir Robert: Gloucestershire, 1649
Atlas, historical, 592, 605

Atlow court rolls (Derby), 4728
Attainder, 3365, 3712, 3716, 4216
Attenborough, Frederick L.: Laws, 2175
Atthill, William: Documents, 6408
Attorneys, 1230
Attwater, Donald: Piers plowman, 7022;
  Saints, 148; 1155, 1161, 2666
Attwood, J. S.: Index, 5722
Aubert, R.: 148; Dictionnaire, 593
Aubrey, John: Wiltshire, 1860
Auctores Britannici Medii Aevi, 136
Audientia litterarum contradictarum, 5542,
  6452, 6457
Audley family, 4383
Augustiana (journal), 5967
Augustianum (journal), 5968
Augustine, St.: Gregory's letter, 2308,
  7225; Mission, 2698, 2702, 2704, 5623
Aulnage accounts, 3232
Ault, D. S.: trans. La Hanse, 5428
— Warren O., Husbandry, 4945; Private
  jurisdiction, 4946; Ramsey court rolls,
  6174; Village community, 3366, 4945,
  6834; Winchester pipe rolls, 5815
Aungerville, Richard d'. *See* Bury, Richard
  of
Aungier, George J.: Croniques, 2857;
  Syon, 6037
Aurelius Victor, 2025
Aurner, Nellie S.: Caxton, 7213
Austin canons, 5952–4, 6398
— friars, 5966–72
— priories, 2932, 5952, 6099, 6123, 6306,
  6333, 6354, 6401
Austin, Roland: Gloucestershire, 1641–2
— William: Luton, 5030
Austria, 4101, 4109, 4257
Ausubel, Herman: ed., 1221, 3364
Auvry, Claude: La congrégation, 5918
Avalon, King Arthur's, 2470, 6317
Aveling, James H.: Roche abbey, 6416
— Stephen T.: Heraldry, 471
Avery, Margaret E.: Equitable jurisdiction,
  3719
Avery Library of Columbia University, 92
Avesbury, Robert of: De gestis, 1103, 2790
Avesnes, John of, 4096
Avezac-Macaya, Marie A. P. d': Ravennatis
  Cosmographia, 2031
Avignon, Papacy at, 751; 6714, 6719–20,
  6734, 6756, 6762
Avranches, Compromise of, 6505
Aylesbury (Bucks.), 4418, 4712, 6026
Ayloffe, Joseph: Calendars, 946, 3750, 3877
Ayreminne, William, 509; 3351, 5786
Ayscough, Samuel: B.M. MSS. 992, 1000
Azenbite of Inwit, 6689
Azo, Bracton and, 2985

Babington, Churchill: Higden's poly-chronicon, 2895; Pecock's repressor, 6629

Backer, Joseph de: Acta Sanctorum, 1170; Analecta Bollandiana, 1153

Backmund, Norbert: Monasticon Prae-monstratense, 1144

Bacon, Nathaniel: Ipswich, 5259

— Robert, 6908

— Roger: Commentaries on, 1448, 6024–5, 6910, 6954; Works of, 1114, 6536–47

Bacton (Suffolk), Honour of, 1453

Baddeley, Welbore St. Clair: Cotteswold manor, 4761; St. Peter's, Gloucester, 6156

Badew, Richard de, 7093

Baehrens, Emil: ed. Panegyrici, 2025

— G.: ed. Panegyrici, 2025

Baethgen, Friedrich: Monumenta Ger-maniae Historica, 1114

Baga de secretis, 3520, 3667

Bagley, John J.: Chester, 1570, 2053; Historical interpretation, **386**; Margaret of Anjou, 4195

Bagot family, 4476

Baier, Hermann: Päpstliche Provisionen, 6759

Baigent, Francis J.: Basingstoke, 5096; Black book, 5810; Crondal, 4763; Registers, 5816

Bail, 3696. *See* Procedure

Baildon, William P.: Calverley charters, 4496; Cases in chancery, 3509; Civil pleas, 3514; Coucher book, 6405; Court baron, 2995, 4716; Court rolls, 4932; Feet of fines, 3629; Inquests, 4395; Notes on Yorks. houses, 6392; Records of Lincoln Inn, 7148–9; Wardrobe account, 3112

Bailiffs: 3731, 4619, 4948; Accounts, 3854, 3864, 4769, 4794, 4837, 4849, 4869, 4881, 4885, 4922, 5240, 5291, 5672, 5704

Baillie, John: ed. Library of Christian classics, 1133

Baillie-Grohman, Florence: Master of the game, 3885

— William A.: Master of the game, 3885

Bain, Joseph: Scotland, documents, 3789

Baines, Edward: Lancaster, 1705; Lans-downe feudary, 4367, 4447

Bains, Doris: Notae latinae, 404

Baker, Alan R. H.: Field systems, 1370, 4999; Open fields, 4955; Reduced acreage, 4986

— Blanch M.: The theatre, **103–4**

— Derek: Councils and assemblies, 5567

— Geoffrey le: Chronicon Galfridi, 2791, 2928

— George: Northampton, 1765

— John H.: Sources of legal history, **524**

— John N. L.: Trade routes, 1495, 5373

— L. G. D.: Cistercian chronicles, 6400

— Robert L.: Customs service, 3229; Wool staple, 5386

— Timothy: London, 5162; Normans, 3974

— W. T.: Records of borough of Notting-ham, 5224

— William H.: ed. Guide to Monmouth records, 1930

Bakers' company, 5186A

Balchin, William G. V.: Cornwall, 1517

Bald's Leechbook, **344**; 441, 2365

Baldock, Ralph, bishop, 5763

Baldwin, archbishop, 2881, 5604

— abbot of Bury St. Edmunds, 3012, 6336

— James F.: Cases before king's council, 3293, 3505; King's council, 3296; Lan-caster chancery, 3869; Scutage, 4645

— John W.: Debate, 6429; Masters, princes, 5443, 6878; Ordeals, 1253

— S. E.: Nichols' Britton, 2986

Baldwin-Brown, Gerard: Arts, 2471

Bale, John: 263A, 987; Works, 8, 33, 6863

— Robert: Annals, 2752; London chronicler, 2742

Balfour-Melville, Evan W. M.: David II of Scotland, 4073–4

Balić, Karl: Duns Scotus, 6565

Ball, Walter W. R.: Cambridge papers, 7102; Trinity College, Cambridge, 7092

Ballads, 7045

Ballard, Adolphus: Black death, 5479; Borough charters, 5024; Boroughs, 5348; Chartulary, 6362; Domesday boroughs, 5347; Domesday inquest, 3039; Inquisition, 3014, 6180; Laws of Breteuil, 5022; Municipal charters, 5269; Walls of Malmesbury, 5347; Woodstock manor, 4855

Ballymote, Book of, 2160, 2396

Balsall, John: Accounts, 5325

Balsham, Hugh, bishop, 5713

Baltzell, James H.: St. and King Edmund, 2305

Baluze, Étienne: Vitae paparum, 6719

Banbury (Oxon.), 1386, 5225

Bandinel, Bulkeley: ed. Dugdale's Mon-asticon, 1147

Bangor, diocese of, 4943A, 5879, 5879D, 5880, 6781, 6828

Banham (Norfolk), 4823

Bankers, **747–9**; 5516–17, 5522

Banks, Richard W.: Welsh records, 4943A

— Thomas C.: Baronage, 551; Stemmata anglicana, 551

Banleuca, 1451
Bannatyne Club, 207
Bannerman, John: Senchus Fer nAlban, 2116
Bannister, Arthur T.: Ewias Harold, 6166; Hereford cathedral, 5732; Hereford MSS., 1046, 5731; Manorial customs, 4770; Visitation returns, 5733
— Henry M.: Collectanea Franciscana, 6006; Worcester books, 1052
Bannister-Good, Estrid: trans. The Vikings, 2567
Bannockburn, battle of, 4004, 4081
Banstead (Surrey), 4898
Barber, Henry: Family names, 575
Barbour, John: The Bruce, 1458, 2792
— Willard T.: Contract and equity, 3720
Barclay, Charles W.: Barclay family, 4570
— Hubert F.: Barclay family, 4570
Bardi bankers, 1469, 5417, 5437
Bardney, Richard of: Grosseteste, 6583
Barfield, Samuel: Cartulary of Reading, 6089; Thatcham, 4707
Barford (Beds.), 3147
Barg, Mikhail: Feudalism, 4947
Barger, Evert: Field systems, 1370
Baring, Hon. Francis H.: Burton cartulary, 6326; Domesday, 6157, 6173; Domesday tables, 3040; Exeter Domesday, 3011; New Forest, 3899, 3927; Northants hidation, 3067; William II, 3918
Baring-Gould, Sabine: Saints' lives, 1155
Barker, Eric E.: Æthelweard, 2140; Talbot deeds, 4424
— Sir Ernest: Dominican order, 5986, 6808
— Theodore C.: Carpenters' company, 5187
Barking abbey (Essex), 6140
Barkly, Sir Henry: Kirkby's quest, 4357; Liber niger scaccarii, 3006; Testa de Nevill, 4337, 4359
Barley, Maurice W.: Christianity, 2083; Farm-house, 4987; Manorial by-laws, 4940; Newark-on-Trent, 4841
Barlow, Frank: Arnulf of Lisieux, 6512; Carmen de Hastingae proelio, 2749; Cnut and Emma, 2159; Durham annals, 5678; Durham peculiars, 5680; Edward the Confessor, 2171, 2563; English church, 2709, 6784; Exeter, 5058; Lanfranc, 3030, 5632; Norman conquest, 3980; Papal schism, 6809; Roger of Howden, 2903; William I, 3976
Barmby, James: Memorials of St. Giles, Durham, 6133
Barnard Castle (Durham), 5069

Barnard, Francis P.: Edward IV's expedition, 4281; Medieval England, 1192; Upton's De studio, 4305
Barnes, Frederic R.: Tax of wool, 1469
— Patricia M.: Anstey case, 1453, 3490; Chertsey cartularies, 6350; D. M. Stenton essays, 1453; Interdict documents, 5603
— Ralph: ed. Lacy's pontifical, 1317
— Rosemary G.: Lambeth MS., 5606
— W. M.: Pipe rolls, 3090
Barnett, Herbert: Glympton, 4847
Barnstaple (Devon.), 5054, 6121
Barnstone (Notts.), 4842
Barnwell priory (Cambr.), 6098–100; Chronicle, 2855
Baron, John: Ecclesiastical laws, 6433
— Salo W.: Jews, 3948
Baronage, Anglo-Saxon, **67–70**
Baronial council, 1458, 1480
— incomes, 4623, 4636. *See* Estate management
Baronies, 570
Baronius, Caesar: Annales ecclesiastici, 1126, 5551
Barons' war, 1467, 1472, 2753, 2763–6, 2773–4, 2838, 2871, 2882, 2948, 2953, 2983, 3502, 4043–4, 4048, 4052, 4055–6, 4062–3, 4067–8
Barony and thanage, 2643
Barraclough, Geoffrey: Adolf of Nassau, 4109; Anglo-Saxon writ, **304**; 2197; Audientia, 5542; Cheshire charters, 4422; Chester, 1571; D. M. Stenton essays, 1453; Earldom of Chester, 3855; Lapsley essays, 1478; Law and legislation, 3393; Making of a bishop, 5713; Papacy, 6715; Papal provisions, 6759; Royal and papal chanceries, 3837; Social life, 1495
Barrett, Wilfred P.: Trial of Joan of Arc, 4268
Barri, Gerald de. *See* Giraldus Cambrensis
Barrington's fee, 4747
Barron, A. Oswald: Heraldry, 470; The Ancestor, 501
— Caroline M.: McKisack essays, ed., 4132, 7223; Richard II, 4124, 7223; Richard Whittington, 5177
— Evan M.: Scottish war, 4075
Barrow, Geoffrey W. S.: Anglo-Scottish border, 4076; Charters, 7224; David I and Lancaster, 4646; Feudal Britain, 3977; Northern England, 2564; Regesta regum, 3794; Robert Bruce, 2792
Barth, Karl: Anselm, 6531
Bartholomew fair, 5527, 5537
Bartholomew, Augustus T.: Catalogue of MSS., 1552

— Bolney, Book of, 4483
— John, and J. G.: Gazetteer, 592
— of Exeter, 5721, 6456, 6513
— the Englishman, 6548–51
Bartlett, J. N.: Poll-tax, 3203A; York, 5305
Barton in Richmondshire (Yorks.), 4933
Barton, J. L.: Bracton as a civilian, 2985; Medieval use, 3693A
Bartrum, Peter C.: Brenhinedd y Saeson, 2805; Welsh genealogy, 508; Welsh kings, 544
Basel, Council of, 5564, 5567, 5573
Basin, Thomas: Historia Caroli VII, 2793
Basingstoke (Hants), 1455
Basingwerk abbey (Flint.), 1455
Baskerville, Geoffrey, 2742
Baslow (Derby.), Court rolls, 4729
Basset, Peter, 2889
Bassett, Margery: Knights of shire, 3453
Bastardy, 6468
Bastin, Julia: Froissart, 2874
Bataillon, Louis: Adam of Bocfield, 6554
Bately, Janet M.: Alfred and Orosius, 2348, 7225; Grimbald, 2309
Bates, Cadwallader J.: Border holds, 1773; Northumberland, 1559
— Edward H.: Cartularies, 6321; Five-hide-unit, 3028
Bateson, Frank W.: Cambridge bibliography, 14
— Mary: Æthelwold's rules, excerpta, 2272; Appreciation of, 1482(iii), 1484; Bale, 8; Ballard, reviews of, 5347; Bibliographical reports, 157; Borough customs, 5025; Cambridge gild records, 5038; Charters of Cambridge, 5039; Creation of boroughs, 5022; Grace book, 7058; Irish exchequer memoranda, 491; Laws of Breteuil, 5022; London collection, 5159; Peterborough court leet, 6268; Records of Leicester, 5137; Register of Crabhouse, 6255; Rules for monks, 2269; Thomas of Ely, 2164
Bath (Som.), 5246; Public Library, 4491; Records, 3182; Roman, 2052A; St. Peter's priory, 6305; St. Michael's accounts, 6838
— Natural History and Antiquarian Field Club, 1805
Bath, Adelard of, 6521–5
— Bernard H. Slicher van: Agrarian history, 5017
— and Wells, diocese of, 758–9; 1494, 4606, 4693, 6790
Baths, Romano-British, 2069
Battelli, Giulio: Palaeography, 383
Battely, John: Antiquitates Rutupinae, 6343

— Nicholas: Three hospitals, 6187
Battle abbey (Sussex), 1471, 3490, 4777, 4920; annals, 1108, 1114, 2838; records, 6357–60; roll, 555, 1096, 1111
Baudri, bishop of Dol: Poem, **619**
Baudrillart, Alfred: Dictionnaire, 593, 1266
Baudry, Léon: Breviloquium, 6613; Occam, 6620
Bauer, Wilhelm: German sources, 251
Baugh, Albert C.: Chaucer, Geoffrey, 6999, 7002, 7007; Chaucer, Thomas, 7003; Literary history, **34**; 1399, 6976
Baumgarten, Paul M.: Aus Kanzlei und Kammer, 5542
Baumstark, Anton: Liturgy, 1324
Baur, Ludwig: Grosseteste, 6574
Bautier, Robert-Henri: Archives, 932
Bavent, Robert de: Letters of Edward I on hunting, 3898
Bawdwen, William: Domesday, 3017
Baxter, James H.: Index to writers, 8; Latin word-list, 301; Souter's glossary, 313
Bayerschmidt, Carl F.: trans. Njal's Saga, 2449
Bayeux, Odo of, 2157, 4276, 5675
— Tapestry, 556, 4276
Bayley, Charles C.: German double election, 4096
— John: Battle of St. Albans, 2746; Calendarium inquisitionum, 4340; Tower of London, 5163
— K. E. (Kennett C.?): Assize rolls (Durham), 3547
Baynes, Norman H.: ed. Cambridge Ancient History, 2034
Bazeley, Margaret L.: Forests, 3900
— William: Bibliography, 1642
Beachcroft, Gwen: Compotus rolls, 6151
Beaker pottery, 1979
Beale, Joseph H.: Law books bibliography, 1224; Beames's Glanvill, 2989
Beames, John: Glanvill, 2989
Beamish, Sir Tufton: Battle of Lewes, 4068
Beamont, William: Arley charters, 4421; Halton manor rolls, 4724; Warrington, 4796
Bean, John M. W.: Feudalism in decline, 4642; Henry IV and Percies, 4213; Percy estates, 4643; Plague and population, 5469
Beard, Charles A.: Justice of the peace, 3495
Beardwood, Alice: Alien merchants, 5424; Oxon. wills, 4550; Royal mint, 670; Statute merchant roll, 5276; Trial of Langeton, 3498
Beauchamp, Richard, bishop, 5730

Beauchamp, Richard, earl of Warwick, 4916
Beauchief abbey (Derby), 6114
Beaucourt, Gaston du Fresne de. *See* Du Fresne
Beaudesert (Warw.), 4914
Beaufort, Henry, bishop and cardinal, 1450, 6737
— Thomas, 4286
Beaumanoir: Kingship, 3277
Beaumaris Castle, 3786A
Beaumont of Hatch family, 4470
— Papers, 4571
— George F.: Manor of Borley, 4744
Beaurepaire, Brocas of family, 4573
— Charles de: Chronique normande, 2840
— Eugène de: Normannerne, 2598
Beaven, Alfred B.: Aldermen of London, 5164; Representation of Lancashire, 3462
— Murray, L. R.: Regnal years, 2597
Bec, abbey of: Continuatio Beccensis, 2853; English lands, 4699, 5916, 5921; Manorial courts, 4777
Bec-Hellouin, abbey of, 5921
Beck, Egerton: Order of the Holy Cross, 6038
— Thomas A.: Annales Furnesienses, 6200
Becker, Gustav: Catalogi bibliothecarum, 7161
— Peter: Monastic custumary, 1146
— Philipp A.: Fantosme, 2867
Becket, St. Thomas, archbishop, 853–8; 1102, 1114, 1426, 1459, 1477, 1482, 1499, 5622–3, 6429, 6639
Beckington, Thomas, bishop: Correspondence, 3776; Journal, 3776; Letters, 3773
Beddie, James S.: Libraries, 1439
Bede, the Venerable: Commentaries on, 587, 2123, 2148, 2281–2, 2323, 2558, 2560
— Lives, 1396, 2285, 2706
— Works, 2148, 2297; Chronica, 1114, 2297; Death Song, 2328; Epistolae, 2297; Historia ecclesiastica, 1089, 1095, 1113, 1487, 2148, 2297; [Leningrad Bede, 441, 2148; Moore Bede, 441, 1429]; Historical tracts, 2297; Homilies, 2297; MSS., 2148; Opera, 1084, 1101–2, 1123, 2297, 2704; Scientific tracts, 2297; Vita abbatum, 2284; Vita S. Cuthberti, 2302
Bedford, archdeaconry of, 6821
— Records, 5028
Bedford, John, duke of, 1451, 4266, 4270, 4273
— William K. R.: Episcopal heraldry, 487
Bedfordshire: Charters, 4412, 5029;

Church, 1529; County history, 1529, 1531–9, 4415; County journals and societies, 1533–4; County records, 1504, 1532; Deeds, 4411; Domesday, 1529, 3015–16, 3040; Eyres, 3521, 3527; Feet of fines, 3487, 3524; Feudal tenures, 4275, 4414; Inquests, 4346; Justices of peace, 3526, 3529; Manors and villages, 4702–6; Parliament, 3453; Pedigrees, families, 4413; pleas, 3522; Pipe rolls, 3083; Religious houses, 6072–83; Sheriffs, coroners, etc., 3523, 3528, 3735; Taxation-subsidy rolls, 3147–9; Topography, 1529; Urban history, 5028–30; Wills, 4519–20
Bedingfield, Arthur L.: Creake Abbey, 6256
Bedwell, Cyril E. A.: Middle Temple, 1014, 7151
Beeching, Henry C.: Library of cathedral of Norwich, 5782
Beeler, John: Bibliography, 623; Castle and strategy, 823; Oman's Art of war, 4312; Warfare, 4298
Beer, Roy Gilyard. *See* Gilyard-Beer
Beesley, Alfred: Banbury, 5225
Beeson, Charles H.: Bede, 2297
Behre, Frank: Castelford's chronicle, 2810
Behrens, B.: Resident ambassador in Rome, 6750
Bek, Antony, bishop, 3076, 5683, 5689
Bekker-Nielsen, Hans: Norse Icelandic bibliography, 2429
Bekynton, Thomas, bishop: 5589, 5595; Correspondence of Henry VI, 3776. *See* Beckington
Belfast, Ulster Museum coins, 704
Belgae, 1994
Belgium, 61, 4167
Bell, Alexander: Anglo-Norman Brut, 2811; Gaimar's L'estoire, 2875; Peterborough chronicle, 6270
— Harold Chalmer: Lyndwood's Provinciale, 6436
— Sir Harold Idris: British Museum papal bulls, 5550; Welsh literature, 339, 2423; Welsh MSS., 1003
— Henry E.: Italian archives, 1441; on Maitland, 1482
— Maurice: Wulfric of Haselbury, 6682
— William: Sprott's chronicle, 2956
Bellaguet, Louis: Chronique de Saint-Denys, 2847
Bellamy, John G.: Chandos inheritance, 3503A; Coterel gang, 5455; Good parliament, 3417; Law of treason, 3709; Northern rebellion, 4110
Belloc, Hilaire: Lingard's history, 1185

Bellot, Hugh Hale: Inner and Middle Temple, 7151; Writings (1901–33), 38

Beltz, George F.: Order of the Garter, 552

Belvoir abbey (Lincs.), Charters, 1714

— castle, MSS., 4693

Bémont, Charles: Actes, 3822; Bémont essays, 1426; Chartes des libertés anglaises, 3280; Chronicon de Bello, 2838; Guienne, 4090; John Sans-Terre, 4034; Modus tenendi parliamentum, 3348; Poitou, 4089; Rageman, 1458; Revue historique bibliography, 167; Rôles gascons, 3826–7; Simon de Montfort, 2838, 4043

Benedict, St., Rule of, **317**; 441, 2274–5, 5911

— bishop of Bangor, 5880

— of Aniane, 2256

— of Peterborough, chronicle of, 1103, 1114. *See* Peterborough, Benedict of

Benedictine monks, 5906–14, 6802; Benedictine bibliography, 1297; Contributions to agriculture, 1494; Manors of, 4924; Office, 2277, 2292; **317**; Reformation of tenth century, 2276

Benedictional of St. Ethelwold, 880. *See* Liturgy

Benefices, **885–6**; 1441, 2609, 3145, 5698, 5751, 5756, 5772

Benefit of clergy, 3695, 6429, 6464

Benevolence, the first, 1436, 3242

Benham, Allen R.: Bibliography, 6994; Widsith to Chaucer, 7049

— William: Winchester, 6790

— Sir William Gurney: Colchester, 5073–4

Bennett, Austin P.: Jurisdiction of archbishop of Canterbury, 5617

— Frederick G.: Statutes of cathedral, Chichester, 5658

— Henry S.: Books and readers, 7214; Chaucer and fifteenth century, 1402, 2808, 6977; Life on the manor, 4948; Ordination lists, 1441; Pastons, 4610

— Jack A. W.: Hickes's Thesaurus, 425; John Gower, 7018; Malory, 7038

— John H. E.: Rolls of freemen, 5044

— Josephine W.: Andrew Holes, 6913

— Merrill K.: British wheat yield, 5488

— R. E.: Walter Map's Sadius and Galo, 6599

— Ralph F.: Dominicans, 5987; Ockham's opera, 6617

— Richard: Corn milling, 4988

Benoît de Sainte-Maure, 1112, 2952

Bensington (Benson) (Oxon.), 4856

Benson, Robert: Old and new Sarum, 5285

Benstede, Sir John de, 1448

Bent, Margaret: Old Hall music, 7192

Bentham, James: Church of Ely, 2164, 5708

Bentley, Samuel: Charters of Westminster, 6231; Excerpta historica, 4282

Beowulf: Audience of, 2362; Commentaries, 2350, 2632; Editions, 2325, 2327; Facsimile of Cotton MS., 2331; Nowell codex, 2333; N. K. Chadwick's monsters, 1433k; Thorkelin transcript, 441, 2332

Berben, Henri: Wool embargo, 1447

Berchem, Denis van: Notitia dignitatum, 2030

Bere forest (Hants), 3896

Bereford, Sir William, 3685

Berengar of Tours, 1450

Beresford, Maurice W.: Aerial survey, 752; Deserted villages, 4836, 4950; Lost villages, 607, 1383, 4949; New towns, 1384, 5349; Open fields, 1373; Poll taxes, 3142

— William: Lichfield, 6790

Berg, Knut: Gosforth Cross, 353

Bergen, Henry: Lydgate's Fall of princes, 7031

Berger, Élie: Actes de Henri II, 3823; Blanche de Castille, 4105; Henry III's invasion, 4091

Berghaus, Peter: Coins, 706

Bergin, Osborn J.: ed. Anecdota from Irish MSS., 2148; Book of Leinster, 2394, 2777; Dun Cow, 2393; ed. Irish grammar, 349

Berin, St., 2298

Berkeley, baron of, 4569

— castle of, 4437

— hundred of, 4593

— MSS., 4593, 4757

— family, 4593

Berkshire: Antiquities, 762; Charters, 4416–17, 4704, 4710; Church, 1529; County history, 1529, 1546; County journals and societies, 1543–5, 1732; County records, 1504, 1540–2; Court rolls, 4708; Deeds, 4417, 4704, 4710; Domesday, 1529; Feet of fines, 3487, 3531; Feudal tenures, 4416; Manors and villages, 4704–10, 6357; Pleas, 3530; Religious houses, 6084–92; Topography, 1529; Urban history, 5031–3; Wills, 4521, 4707

Berlière, Ursmer: L'ordre monastique, **167**

Bermondsey priory (Surrey): Annals of, 2762; Charité-sur-Loire and, 1471; Edward of Windsor and, 1467, 3119

Bernard, St., 1477

— Edward: Catalogues, 972

Bernheim, Ernst: Lehrbuch, 251
Bernicia, 2122, 2157, 2527
Berr, Henri: ed. L'évolution de l'humanité, 1179
Berry, C. A. F.: Roman buildings, 2080
— George G.: Langlois-Seignobos, 263
— Henry F.: Statutes of Parliament of Ireland, 3330–2
— Hérault du Roy: Le recouvrement de Normendie, 2794, 3819
Bersu, Gerhard: Vikings, 2565
Bertram, Charles J.: Nennius, 2167; Richard of Cirencester, 2026
Bertrand, Simone: Bayeux tapestry, 4276
Bessinger, J. B.: Magoun festschrift, 2315; Sutton Hoo, 2487
Best, Richard I., 9, 2241; Annals of Innisfallen, 2780; Bibliography of Irish philology, 2406; Book of Leinster, 2394; Coarbs of St. Patrick, 2677; Dun Cow, 2393
Besterman, Theodore: Bibliography, 1
Bestiary, 893, 5947
Betcherman, Lita-Rose: Lancastrian bishops, 6804
Betham, William: Dignities, 3367
Bethell, Denis L.: Black monks, 6802; Fountains abbey, 6400; Papacy, 6719; William of Corbeil, 5615
Bethmann, Ludwig C.: Torigni's Chronica, 2962
Béthune, Anonyme de, 2897
Bethurum, Dorothy: Aelfric, 2292; Six codes, 301; 2212; Wulfstan, 2315, 2352. *See* Loomis, Dorothy B.
Betjeman, Sir John: Guide to parish churches, 789
Betson, Thomas (merchant), 5464
Betts, Reginald R.: Hussite movement, 6656; Richard FitzRalph, 1457, 6568
Bevan, William L.: St. David's, 6790
Bevan-Evans, Myrddyn J.: Flintshire record office, 1916
Beveridge, Sir William H.: Corn yield, 1468; Prices and wages, 5489
Beverley (Yorks.), History of, 1892, 5288
— Minster, 5849, 6395; Sanctuary register, 1262, 5693
— town, 5288
Beverley, Alured (Alfred): Annales, 1103, 2795
— John of, 2289
— William, 1437, 5676
Bewcastle Cross, 44; 353, 2471
Bezoun, Thomas: Household roll, 4602
Bible, The, 1327A, 1330, 1335, 1337, 1344, 6895
Bibliographie de la philosophie, 6876

Bibliography, 1–13; for each subject, consult this index under the appropriate heading
Bibliotheca Britannica, 37
— Britannico-Hibernica, 33
— Celtica, 110
— Hagiographica Latina, 1156
— Latina (Fabricius), 51
— Topographica Britannica, 1505
Bibliothèque de l'école des chartes, 149
— Nationale, Catalogue, 74
Bicester (Oxon.), 4852, 4854, 6287
Bickley, Francis B.: Calendar of deeds, 5079; Court rolls of Dulwich, 4894; H.M.C. index, 945; Index to charters, 1004; Kirklees muniments, 1868; Little Red Book, 5082
— William B.: Register of guild of Knowle, 5278
Biddle, Martin: Abingdon abbey, 2153, 6087
Biddulph, L. H.: Pleas of crown, 3485
Bidentes Hoylandie, 5008
Bidez, Joseph: Science MSS., 985
Biek, Leo: Archaeology and the microscope, 744
Bieler, Ludwig: Christianization of Celts, 2117; Colgan's Lives, 1160; Irish bibliography, 36; Irish catholicism, 1274; Irish penitentials, 2252; Kenney, 23; Lowe's papers, 394; Recent research, 149; 333; St. Patrick, 1160, 2324, 2662A
Bigelow, Melville M.: English will, 1246; Placita Anglo-Normannica, 3490; Procedure, 3660
Biggleswade (Beds.), assessment roll, 3147
Bigland, Ralph: Gloucestershire, 1650
Bignov (Sussex), Roman, 2080
Bigod, Roger, earl of Norfolk: Estate accounts, 4619
Bigwood, Georges: Un marché de matières première: laines, 5409
Bill, Edward G. W.: Lambeth MSS., 1008
— Peter A.: Parochial clergy, 6835
Bilsington priory (Kent), 6178
Bilson, John: Cistercian architecture, 785; Durham vaults, 785; Kirkstall abbey, 6405
Binchy, Daniel A.: Celtic kingship, 2606; Críth Gablach, 2243; Irish law tracts, 2246; Irish sick maintenance, 2247; St. Patrick, 2324; Secular institutions, 2248–9, 2252; Thurneysen's Grammar, 349; Vikings, 2596
Binns, Norman E.: Historical bibliography, 2
Biographia Britannica Literaria, 543

Biography, **62–6, 148–51, 319–39, 858–75.** For biography of an individual, *see* the personal name

Birch feodary, 4365

Birch, Thomas: MSS., 1000

— Walter de Gray: Cartularium, 2190; Charters of Lincoln, 5145; Charters of London, 5158; Charters of Worcester, 2190; Chronicle of Croyland, 2163; Cistercian abbeys, 5934; Collections for Stanley abbey, 6376; Domesday book, 3041; Drawings, 873; Fasti monastici, 2692; Index of styles, 1351; Kemble's Saxons, 2498; Liber vitae, 5814; Life of Malmesbury, 2921; Margam abbey, 1122; Mathilda's charters, 4398; Memorials of Llandaff, 1122; Memorials of St. Guthlac, 2310; Neath abbey, 1122; Seals, 454–5, 459, 469; Vita Haroldi, 2172

Birchington, Stephen: Anonymous chronicle, 2944; Historia de archiepiscopis, 5612

Bird, Ruth: London Richard II, 1740, 4111, 5165

— Samuel R. Scargill: Crown lands, 4688; Custumals, 6357; Guide, 951; Scutage and Marshal's rolls, 3143

— William H. B.: Black book of Winchester, 5112, 5810

Birdsall, Jean: Chronicle of Jean de Venette, 2967; Manors of La Trinité, 1439, 4699

— Paul: Royal dispensing power, 1444, 3278

Birinus, St., 2298. *See* Berin

Birley, Anthony R.: Birley essays, 2045

— Eric: Agricola, 2071; Birley essays, 2045, 2075; Hadrian frontier, 2072; Roman army, 1460, 2075; Roman Scotland, 2087–8; Roman Wales, 2089

Birmingham (Warw.), 1529; Reference library, 1504

— and Midland Institute, 1844

Birrell, Jean: Forest craftsmen, 3901

Birt, Henry N.: Lingard's History, 1185

Birting (Northumb.), 4840

Bischoff, Bernhard: Palaeography, **47;** 384; Greek element, 2358

Bishop, Edmund: Bibliographie générale, 6782; Fasting and abstinence, 5912; Liturgy, 1325, 5823

— Terence A. M.: Assarting, 1468; Cambridge MSS., 1033; Caroline minuscule, 384A; Chancery scribe, 3823; Extents, 4933–4, 6410; Facsimiles, 436, 2191; King Edwy charter, 2191; Manorial demesne, 4989; Normans in

Yorks., 1450, 1468; Scriptores regis, 437, 3751; Stephen's charters, 4399

Bishop's Clyst (Devon.), Manor, 4733

Bishop's Stortford (Herts.), Churchwardens' accounts, 6838

Bishops: General, 1125, 1143, 1438, 2290–1, 4119, 4221, 6447, 6799, 6804, 7224; Anglo-Saxon, 1316, 2597; Arms (heraldry), 487; Chanceries, 422; Lists of, 371, 375, 2597, 5576, 5579–83, 5814, 6711. *See* Dioceses

Bishopstrow (Wilts.), Manor, 6373

Bithell, Denis: Canterbury–York dispute, 5853

Bitton (Glos.), 4754

Bitton, Thomas de, bishop, 4543, 5714–15

Blaauw, William W.: Barons' war, 4044; Clerical subsidy, 6829; Letters of Prince Edward, 3125; Lewes subsidy, 3194; Ralph de Neville's Letters, 4617

Blache, P. Vidal de la: Geography, 611

Black Book of: Admiralty, 4286; Chirk, 2223, 2236; Exchequer, 3006; Household, 3128; St. David's, 5880F; Southampton, 5099; Winchester, 5810

— Death, 1252, 1493, 4903, 5469–70, 5472–3, 5475, 5479, 5482–3, 5486, 5739

— Friars. *See* Dominicans

— Monks. *See* Benedictines

— Prince. *See* Edward, the Black Prince

Black, George F.: Scottish surnames, 576; Scottish books, 11

— J. G.: Edward I and Gascony, 4107

— William H.: Arundel MSS., 1007; Ashmole MSS., 1023; Charters of Burton, 5250; Chronicon Vilodunense, 2304; Hereford records, 5116; Palatine of Chester records, 3856

Blackbourne (Suffolk), Tax, 3188

Blackheath (Kent), Subsidy roll (1327), **486**

Blackley, F. D.: Household book, 4604; Isabella and bishop of Exeter, 1459

Blackwell, Basil H.: Nairn's Handlist, 2016

Blacman (or Blakman) John: Henry VI, 1103, 2796

Blades, William: Life and typography of William Caxton, 7215

Blagden, Cyprian: The stationers' company, 5203

Blagg, Thomas M.: Notts. records, 4842

Blair, Charles Hunter: Armorials on seals, 488; Carr MS., 5217; Castles, 823; Durham seals, 458; Knights at Falkirk, 4294; Northumberland M.P.s, 3464

— Claude: European armour, 906; Firearms, 4312

— Lawrence: Churchwardens' accounts, 6838

Blair, Peter Hunter: A.-S. England, 2493; Bernicians, 2122; Moore Bede, 441, 2148; Moore memoranda, 1429, 2168; Origins of Northumbria, 2527; Paulinus, 7225; Roman Britain, etc., 1174, 1430, 2033; Symeon of Durham, 2123, 2157

Blake, Ernest O.: Liber Eliensis, 2164

— J. B.: Coal trade, 5374; Smuggling, 5398

— Norman F.: Battle of Maldon, 2344

— W. J.: Norfolk manorial lords, 4373

Blakiston, H. E. D.: Durham College rolls, 7061

— Noël: Stogursey charters, 6323

Blakman, John: Henry VI, 1103, 2796

Bland, Alfred E.: Documents, 1362

— Desmond S.: Bibliography of Inns of Court, 7144; Chaucer and the Inns, 7007

Blaneford, Henry of: Chronica, 2797

Blanke, Fritz: St. Columban, 2320

Blatt, Franz: Latin glossary, 311; Saxo Grammaticus, 2426

Blaydes, Frederic A.: Beds. Notes and Queries, 1536; Bushmead cartulary, 6072; Wills, 4519

Bleadon (Som.), 4871

Blegywryd, Book of, 2225–6

Blench, John W.: Preaching in England, 6702

Blickling Hall (Norfolk), MSS., 4693

— homilies, 441, 2267

Bliemetzrieder, Franz P.: Adelhard von Bath, 6521

Bliss, William H.: Papal registers, 5547–8

Blithfield (Staffs.), Deeds, 4476

Bloch, Marc L. B., **30**; Apologie, 252; Les caractères, 4951; Mélanges, 4951; Les rois thaumaturges, 3271A; Seigneurie et manoir, 4951; La société féodale, 1179, 1363, 4951; Vita Edwardi, 2171

— Oscar: French dictionary, 290

Blois, Henry of, 5823

— Peter of, 2163, 6487, 6519

Blom, Eric: Dictionary of music, 7201

Blomefield, Francis: Collectanea Cantabrigiensia, 1557; Norfolk, 1756

Blomfield, James C.: Bicester, 6287

— Joan: Runes, 354

Blondel, Robert: De reductione Normanniae, 2798, 3819

Blood-feud, 2231, 2238

Bloom, James Harvey: Cartae antiquae, 4400; Charters of St. Swithun's, 6385; Charters of Worcester, 5286; Gild of Holy Cross, Stratford, 5279; Priory of Worcester, 5825, 5829, 5833–4

Bloomfield, Morton W.: Incipits, 430; Piers Plowman, 7023–4

Blore, William P.: Recent discoveries in Canterbury archives, 5623

Blount, John: Translator, 4350

Bloxman, John: Magdalen College, Oxford, 7076

Blume, Friedrich: Die Musik, **959**

Blunt, Christopher E.: A.-S. coinage, 671, 2528; Coinage, 1454; Coinage of Edward IV, 707; Reading University coins, 704

Blyborough (Lincs.), 1453

Blyth priory (Notts.), 6278

Board of Celtic Studies, 10, 111, 197

Boarstall (Oxon.): Cartulary, 4416, 4461

Boas, Frederick S.: Sir Thomas Bodley, 1018

Boase, Charles W.: Registers, 7066, 7114

— George C.: Bibliotheca, 1578; Cornwall, 1584; Devon bibliography, 1602

— Thomas S. R.: Art, 1485; Oxford History of Art, 782

Bober, Harry: Astrological MSS., 983

Bocfield, Adam of, 6552–4, 6891

Bock, Friedrich: Documents on Hundred Years War, 3804; German alliance (1335–42), 4171; Relations with Adolf of Nassau, 4092

Bocking (Essex), Manor, 4748

Böcking, Eduard: Notitia dignitatum, 2030

Bodenham, Frederick: Hereford bibliography, 1666

Bodleian Library, **124–5**; 75, 984, 4407, 5550

Bodley, Sir Thomas, 1018

Boehm, Eric H.: Historical periodicals, 88

Boehn, Max Ulrich von: Die Mode, 907

Boehner, Philatheus: Ockham, 6618–19, 6621

Boeles, Pieter: Friesland, 2506

Boendaele, Jan (Chronicler), 2911

Boggis, Robert J. E.: St. Augustine's monastery, 6184; Exeter, 5719

Böhmer, Heinrich: Anonymous Eboracensis, 6427; Coming of the friars, 6008; Das Eigenkirchentum, 2710, 6786; Die Falschungen, 5615; Kirche und Staat, 6785

Bohn's Antiquarian Library, 1089

Bohun, estates of, 4658

— MSS., 895, 4572

Boissevain, Ursulus P.: Cassius Dio, 2025

Boissonnade, Prosper: Histoire de Poitou, 4093; Life and work, 1371

Boivin-Champeaux, Louis: Guillaume de Longchamp, evêque d'Ely, 5709

Boke of Noblesse, 2982

Boldon Buke, 1529, 3076, 5674

Boldon, Uthred of, 6555–6, 6660
Bolgar, Robert R.: Classical heritage, 1397
Bolingbroke, soke of, 1453
Bolland, Jean: Acta Sanctorum, 1152
— William C.: Bills in eyre, 3504; Eyre of Kent (1313–14), 3558; General eyre, 3661; Justice Bereford, 3685; Year books, 3646, 3655
Bollandists, the, **148–9**; 145, 262
Bolney (Sussex), 4899
Bolney, Bartholomew, 4899
Bologna, school of, 6645, 6919
Bolton (Lancs.), 5022
— priory (Yorks.), 1893, 6396–8
Bolton, Brenda: Council of London, 6810
— Whitney F.: A.-S. literature, 1403, 2162; Bede, 2297; Bede bibliography, 2148; St. Guthlac, 2310
Bonansea, Bernardine M.: Duns Scotus, 6565
Bond, Sir Edward A.: Chronica de Melsa, 2806; Facsimiles of MSS., 444–5; Liberate rolls, 3105
— Francis: Gothic architecture, 786; Patron saints, 1157
— John J.: Handbook of dates, 365
— Maurice F.: British Records Association, 1440; Dictionary, 1272; Farmborough court roll, 4782; Record offices, **109**; Windsor MSS., 6068
— Shelagh: Chapter acts, 6068
Bonenfant, Paul: Actes (Low Countries and England), 3803; Montereau à Troyes, 4239; Philippe le Bon, 4240
Bönhoff, Leo: Aldhelm, 2296
Boniface, St., 1102, 1114, 1396, 1471, 2284, 2285, 2290, 2298(a), 2299
— V, pope, 7225
— of Savoy, archbishop, 5628
Boni-homines, 6039
Bonser, Wilfrid: A.-S. and Celtic bibliography, 12; Medical background, 2371; Survival of paganism, 2654; Romano-British bibliography, 13, 2013
Bony, Jean: English gothic, 787
Book of: Aicill, 2240; Aids, **483**; 4341; Aneirin, 2384; Armagh, **337**; 2324; Ballymote, 2160, 2396; Blegywryd, 2225–6; Chirk, **42**; Dun Cow, 2393; Ely, 2164; Fees, **628**; 4337, 6267; Howth, 2799; Hyde abbey, 1123; Kells, 881, 1449; Lecan, 2395; Leinster, 2394, 2777; Lismore, 1171; Merchants of the Staple, 5340; Prests, 3113; Privy counselling, 6670; Rights, 2245, 2396; St. Albans, 1474; Southampton, 5100; Taking of Ireland, 2404
Bookland, 1455, 1501, 2214, 2623

Boon, George C.: Roman Silchester, 2066
Booth, John: Halmota Dunelmensis, 4739, 5684
Bordars, 3057
Bordeaux, 4168, 4190, 5403
Bordin, Jean de: Gesta Henrici V, 2877
Borenius, Tancred: Painting, 856; Becket in art, 6496
Borland, Catherine R.: Edinburgh Univ. MSS., 1064
Borlase, William: Cornwall, 1585
Borley (Essex), Manor, 4744
Born, Lester K.: Microfilms, 438
Boroughs: **177–9** and **700–35**
— bibliography, 1511
— courts, 3507, 3537
— customs, 2789, 3909, 5025
— deeds, 7224
— Domesday, 3033, 5347
— episcopal, 5697
— incorporation of, 5024
— origins of, 1387, 1482, 2636, 5235, 7225
— parliamentary representation, 3451
— seals, 465. For individual boroughs, *see* each under its name
— taxation, 1455
Boroughbridge, battle of, 556, 1499(ii), 4301; roll, 499
Borsa, Mario: Humphrey of Gloucester, 6928
Borthwick Institute of Historical Research, 1873
Bosanquet, Geoffrey: Eadmer, 2863
Bosc, Nicolas de: Voyage of, 2973
Bosham, Herbert of, 6487, 6518
Bossuat, André: Gressert and Surienne, 4243; Jeanne d'Arc, 4241; La littérature de propagande, 4243; Parlement de Paris, 4242
— Robert: Manuel, 43
Boston (Lincs.): Extent, 1723
Boston Proceedings: Canon law, 1313
Boston, John, 6006
— Robert of: Chronicon Petriburgense, 2834
Boston of Bury, 1452, 6930
Bosworth, Joseph: A.-S. dictionary, 277
Botfield, Beriah: Durham Cathedral library, 1043
Bothe, Charles: Hereford register, 5730
Botoner, William. *See* William of Worcester
Botte, Bernard: ed. Baumstark's Liturgy, 1324
Boüard, Alain de: Diplomatic, 414; Palaeography, 396
— Michel de: Duchy of Normandy, 3992; Norman exchequer, 3102; William I, 3978

Boucher, C. E.: Black Death, 5483
Boulers, Reginald: Hereford register, 5730
Boulton, Helen E.: Sherwood Forest Book, 3886
Bouman, Cornelius A.: Sacring and Crowning, 1352
Bouquet, Martin: Recueil, 1090
Bourchier, John: Froissart, 2874
— Thomas, archbishop, 5609
Bourdillon, Anne F. C.: Minoresses, 6013
Bourne, Henry R. F.: Merchants, 5375
— Kenneth: ed., 2749
Boussard, Jacques: Henry II's government, 4013; Le Comté d'Anjou, 4012; Mercenaries, 4315
Boutaric, Edgard P.: St. Louis et Alphonse de Poitiers, 4094
Boutell, Charles: Heraldry, 471
Boutemy, A.: Nigellus de Longchamp, 7042
Bouterwerk, Carl W.: Chronicle of Holyrood, 2821
Boutflower, Douglas S.: Ceolfrith, 2301; Fasti Dunelmenses, 5698
Boutruche, Robert: La crise, 4161; Nouvelle Clio, 45; Seigneurie et féodalité, 4952
Bouvier, Gilles le, 2794
Bouwens, Bethell G.: Wills, 4505, 4506
Bowden, Muriel: Canterbury Tales, 7004
Bowdon, William E. I. Butler, 6674
Bowen, Emrys G.: Celtic saints, 2663; Hist. Merioneth, 1929; Prehistoric geography, 1465; Wales, geography, 608
— H. C.: Celtic background, 2050
— Ivor: Statutes of Wales, 3329
Bower, Walter: Scotichronicon, 2872
Bowet, Henry, archbishop, 5849
Bowker, Margaret: Court books, 7224
Bowles, William L.: Lacock abbey, 6372
Box, Edward G.: Donations of manors, 5619
Boxall, C. G.: Manchester's estates, 4775
Boxgrove priory (Sussex), 6361
Boyar, Gerald E. Se: Bartholomaeus Anglicus, 6549
Boyce, Gray C.: Guide, 59; Universities, 7083-4
Boyd, Percival: Drapers' company, 5189
— William K.: Extents, 4860; Leics. survey, 3074; Lincs. records, 3573; Poll-tax, 3185; Records of Horncastle, 5144; Salop assize rolls, 3603; Salop feet of fines, 3604; Salop inquisitions, 4377
Boyer, Blanche J.: A.-S. MSS., 979
Boyle, Annals of, 1117, 2778
Boyle, Alexander: St. Ninian, 2323
— John R.: Hedon, 5291; Kingston-upon-Hull, 5293

— Leonard E.: Canon law, 1428, 6429, 6436; Constitution *Cum ex eo*, 6799; Vatican archives, 5540; William of Pagula, 2955
Boyne, William: Yorkshire library, 1869
Boys, William: Sandwich, 5312
Bozon, Nicole: Contes, 6692
Brabant trade, 5346, 5401
Brabant, John of, 4598; Expenses, 1492
Brabner, John H. F.: Gazetteer, 594
Brackmann, Albert: Germania pontificia, 1132
Bracton, Henry de: 2985; Bracton and Azo, 2985; De Legibus et Consuetudinibus, 2985; Note-book, 1501, 2985, 3481; on kingship, 3277; Tractatus Coronae, 3001
Bradbrooke, William: Manor court rolls, 4714
Bradcar (Norf.), 4823
Bradewas, W. de, 2769
Bradfield, Nancy M.: Costumes, 908
Bradford Hist. and Antiq. Society (Yorks.), 1874
Bradford on Tone (Som.), 4871
Bradley, Harriett: Enclosure, 5018
— Henry: Dictionary, 287; Ptolemy, 2025(h); Walter Map, 6599
— John W.: Stafford charters, 5252
Bradney, Sir Joseph A.: Monmouthshire, 1934
Bradshaw, Frederick: Lay subsidy roll (1296), 3176; Serfdom, 4959
— Henry: Hibernensis, 2261; Statutes, 170; 5749
Bradwardine, Thomas, archbishop, 6557-60, 6627, 6968
Bradwater, Richard, 6977
Brady, William: Episcopal succession, 5576
Bragg, W. B.: Market Harborough, 5143
Braikenridge, George W.: Bristol deeds, 5079
Brailes, W. de, 884
Brailsford, J. W.: Hod Hill excavations, 2059
Braine, A.: Kingswood forest, 3902
Braithwaite, A. W.: Suetonius, 2025
Brakelond, Jocelin of: Chronica, 1113-14, 6335
Brakspear, Harold: Waverley abbey, 6355
Bramber (Sussex), Rape of, 1840
Brampton, Hugh, abbot: Cirencester cartulary, 6153
— C. Kenneth: Duns Scotus, 6567; Epistola ad Fratres Minores, 6616; Ockham's De Potestate, 6615
Brand, John: Edward's expenses in Wales, 3131; Newcastle-on-Tyne, 5221

Brandenburg, Erich: ed. Dahlmann-Waitz, 48
Brandt, Ahasver von: Hanseatic history, 5425
Branketre, John de, 3838
Bransford, Wulstan de, bishop, 5827, 5832
Brantingham, Thomas de, bishop and treasurer, 3106, 5715
Brass industry, 5507
Brasses, monumental, 869
Bratton (Wilts.), 4489
— Henry of. *See* Bracton, Henry de
Braude, Jacob: A.-S. family, 2627
Braun, Hugh: Castles, 825
— Joseph: Vestments, 922
Bräuninger, Friedrich: Handbuch, 7173
Bray (Berks.), 4709
Bray, Thomas: Conquest of Ireland, 2800
— William: Surrey, 1834
— of Harleston, Henry de, 4830
Braybrooke, Lord Richard: Audley End, 6838
Brayley, Edward W.: Surrey, 1833
Bread of our forefathers, 1361
Breadsall (Derby), 4429
Breakspear, Nicholas (Pope Adrian IV), 1458, 1487, 5556, 6741, 6911
Breauté, Falk (Fawkes) de, 3525
Breay, J.: Churchwardens' accounts, 5050
Brechter, Heinrich Suso: Gregory I, 2308
Breck, Allen Du Pont: English delegation, 5563; Wyclif's De Trinitate, 6648
— Edward: Fragment of Ælfric's Translation, 2270
Brecknockshire, 1897–9
Brecon, archdeaconry of, 5880F
— lordship of, 1899
Bregwine, St., 2300
Brehon law-tracts, 2240, 2250
Bremen, Adam of: Gesta Pontificum, 2149
Bremond, Antoninus: Bullarium, 5981
Brenan, Gerald: House of Percy, 4576
Brendan, St.: Navigatio, 2318
Brendon (Som.), 4869
Brenhinedd y Saeson, 2805
Brent, J. A.: Alceston manor, 4909
Brentano, Robert: Administration of dioceses, 5862; Two churches, 6787; Whithorn vacancy, 5862; York jurisdiction, 6449
Bréquigny, Louis G. O. F. de: Lettres de rois, 3816; Rôles normands, 3829
Bresslau, Harry: St. Columban, 2320; Urkundenlehre, 415
Breteuil, Laws of, 5022
Brétigny, Treaty of, 3809, 3820, 4183
Breton, Guillaume le: Gesta, 2947
— John le, bishop, 2986

Brett, Edwin J.: Armour, 909
Brett-James, N. G.: Bishop Drokensford, 5591
Brevia. *See* Writs
Breviary, 1319, 5910
Brewer, Derek S.: Chaucer, 7005
— John: Book of Howth, 2799; Bray's Conquest, 2800; Carew MSS., 1010; Chronicon de Bello, 2838; Fuller's Church Hist., 1278; Giraldus Cambrensis, 2881, 6573; Monumenta Franciscana, 6010; Registrum Malmesburiense, 6374; Report on Carte-Carew papers, 1026; Rogeri Bacon Opera, 6537
— Thomas: Memoir of John Carpenter, 5150
Brewood priory (Staffs.), 6325
Brian Boru, 2174, 2449, 2605
Briavels (Glos.), 3908
Bridbury, Anthony R.: Economic growth, 5444; Salt trade, 5376
Bridge, London, pre-Norman, 5177
Bridgeman, Charles G. O.: Burton Abbey surveys, 6326; Forest pleas, 3094, 3893; Notes on manors, 4879; Weston-under-Lizard, 4880
— Ernest R. O.: Weston-under-Lizard, 4880
Bridger, Charles: pedigrees, 518
Bridges, John: Northants, 1766
— John H.: Bacon's Opus Majus, 6539
Bridgnorth (Salop), 5027, 6299
Bridgwater (Som.), 5247, 6838
Bridlington, canon of: Gesta Edwardi de Carnarvan, 2876
— priory (Yorks.), 6399
— John (Robert) of: Prophecies, 7049
Bridport (Dorset): Munden's chantry, 4639
Brie, Friedrich W. D.: The Brut, 2811
— G. A. de: Bibliographia, 49
Brief Latin Chronicle, 2817
Brief notes of occurrences, 2934
Brieger, Peter H.: Art (1216–1307), 782; Henry of Almain, 1459
Briers, Phyllis M.: Henley records, 5227
Brigg, William: Testamenta Leodiensis, 4565
Briggs, Helen M.: Surrey manorial accounts, 4897
Bright, William: Church history, 2693
Brightman, Frank E.: English rite, 1326
Brightwaltham (Berks.), 4777
Brigit, St., 1160
Brill (Bucks.), 4712
Brill, Reginald: Fastolf's report, 4249
Brink, Bernhard Ten: Chronicles, 21
Brinkburn priory (Northumb.), 6273

Brinton, Howard H.: Cloud of Unknowing, 6671
— Thomas, bishop: Sermons, 6701
Briscoe, John P.: Nottinghamshire, 1777
Brisley, deanery of (Norfolk), 4454
Bristol (Glos.), 1386, 5076–89, 5341; Black death, 5483; Grey friars, 6036; Jews, 3946; MSS., 1643; Members of parliament, 3458; Merchant venturers, 5379; Pleas, 3551; Rebellion, 3162; Record office, 1504, 1646; St. Augustine's, 6150–1; St. Ewen, 5086, 6838; St. Mark's hospital, 6152; St. Nicholas, 5086; Subsidy rolls, 3162; Trade, 5341, 5393; Wills, 4527–8
Britain, Regional cultures, 1435
Britannia (Camden), 609
Brithwald: Vita Egwini, 2285
British Academy: Proceedings, 172; Records, 181
— Archaeological Association, Journal, 173
— Government: Lists of publications, 134–6; 959
— Humanities Index, 93
— Journal for History of Science, 6932
— Museum: Catalogue of books, 76–8; Catalogue of MSS., 120–2; 874–5, 5547, 5550
— National Archives: Lists, 950
— National Bibliography, 68
— Numismatic Journal, 644
— Record Society: Index Library, 182
— Records Association: 1440; Journal, 1504; Record repositories, 944
— Society of Franciscan Studies, 183, 6003
— Studies Monitor, 148A
— Union Catalogue of periodicals, 89
Britnell, R. H.: Production, 4990
Brittany, duke of, Arthur, 1490, 4034
— Jean de, Comte de Richmond, 4058, 4626
Britton (law tract), 2986
Britton, Charles E.: Meteorological chronology, 607A
— John: Aubrey's Wiltshire, 1860
Brittonic languages, 2127
Broadcloths, 5393
Brocas family, 4573
Brodeur, Arthur G.: Beowulf, 2335
Brodhurst, Spencer: Merchants of the Staple, 1246
Brodnitz, Georg: Wirtschaftsgeschichte, 5377
Brodrick, George C.: Merton College, 7115
Brøgger (Broegger), Anton W.: Norse in Scotland, 2566
Brokage Book, 5101, 5327
Broke, Willoughby of, 4400

Bromberg, B.: Hospitallers, 6047
Bromham (Wilts.), 4920
Bromholm priory (Norf.), 6253
Bromley of Bromley: Cartulary, 4475
Bromley, John: Gilds' armorials, 489
— John Selwyn: Heresy, 6869
Brompton, John: Chronicon, 1124, 2802
Bromwich, John: Paris Psalter, 441
— Rachel: Trioedd, 2387; Welsh genealogy, 508; Welsh tradition, 2122, 2407, 2557
Bronescombe: Walter, bishop, 5715
Brønsted (Broensted), Johannes: Ornament, 2473; Vikings, 2567
Brooches, 2481
Brook, George L.: Laȝamon, 2914; Linguistics, 1433
Brooke, Christopher N. L.: Alfred to Henry III, 1174; Archbishops of St. Davids, 2665; Book of Llandaff, 5880A; Book of William Morton, 6264; Canons of church councils, 6430; Canterbury forgeries, 5615; Carte nativorum, 6266; Church design, 1325; Clerical marriage, 6836; Gloucester and Llancarfan, 2123; Gregorian reform, 6836; Gilbert Foliot, 5761, 6515, 6517; Heads of religious houses, 5895; Hereford dignitaries, 5734; John of Salisbury, 6641; Lanfranc, 6429; Medieval texts, ed., 1113; St. Paul's chapter, 5768; St. Paul's history, 5770; Teaching of diplomatic, 47; Twelfth-century renaissance, 1391; William of Newburgh, 2932; Wix priory charters, 1453, 6149
— George C.: Coins, 653, 672–3, 689
— John: The House of Commons, 511
— Robert: Abridgement, 3653
— Rosalind B.: Franciscan government, 6014
— Zachary N.: Cambridge Medieval History, 1176; David of London, 1448, 6514; Powicke's appreciation of, 1489; Effect of Becket's murder, 6503; English Church, 6727; Hereford dignitaries, 5734
Brooke-Little, J. P.: Boutell's Heraldry, 471
Brooks, Eric St. John: Irish bibliography, 23
— Frederick W.: Battle of Lincoln, 4045; Cinque Ports, 5322; Council of the North, 3297; Domesday and East Riding, 3042; Hospital of Holy Innocents, 6217; Naval forces (1199–1272), 4325; William of Wrotham, 4325
— Nicholas: Burghal hidage, 2206; A.-S. military, 7225

Broome, Dorothy M.: Auditors of foreign accounts, 3230; Exchequer migrations, 1458; Exchequer receipts, 3108; National balance sheet, 3258; Ransom of John II, 3805

Broomfield, F.: Chobham's Summa, 6690

Brotherhood, Jean: Index, 119

Brotherton Library, 1038

Brothwell, Don R.: Archaeology, **85**

Broughton (Hunts.), 4777, 4959

Brouns, Thomas, bishop, 5787

Brown, Alfred L.: Authorization of letters, 3844; Clerkship of council, 3298; Commons and council of Henry IV, 3298, 3365, 3394; Constitutional documents, 1205; Earl of Warwick, 4228; Henry IV, 4234; King's councillors, 3298; Privy seal clerks, 7224

— Carleton F.: English lyrics, 6979; Religious lyrics, 6980; Sources of Chaucer, 7001

— Edward: Fasciculus, 6864

— Gerard Baldwin. *See* Baldwin-Brown

— James Edward: Clerical subsidies, 6821

— Philip A.: Economic documents, 1362

— Rawdon: Archives of Venice, 3834

— Reginald Allen: Castles, 823, 826; Curia regis roll (1198), 3485; King's Works, 781; Memoranda roll, 3215; Norman Conquest, 2577, 3979; Sibton charters, 1453; Treasury, 1441

— T. J.: Book of Kells, 881; Palaeography since Traube, 400

— Thomas: Hereford Domesday, 3075

— William: Cartularium, 6401; North County deeds, 4433; Vacant benefices, 5864; Yorks. deeds, 4504; Yorks. feet of fines, 3631; Yorks. inquisitions, 4397; Yorks. lay subsidy, 3207–8

Brownbill, John: Coucher book of Furness, 6199; Ledger book of Vale Royal, 6106; Tribal hidage, 2213

Browne, A. L.: Lichfield chancellors, 5670; Rochester officials, 5796; Wick Rissington, 4760

— C. G.: Registrum, 5717

— George F.: Aldhelm, 2296; Alfred's books, 2348; Conversion, 2694

— John: St. Peter's, York, 5865

— Richard A.: Latin selections, 302

Bruce, Barbour's, 1458, 2792

— James D(ouglas): Arthurian romance, 2166

— John: Arrivall of Edward IV, 2901

— John C.: Lapidarium, 2021; Roman wall, 2085–6

— John Ronald: Isle of Man, 1946

— Robert, 2792, 4077

Bruce-Mitford, Rupert L. S.: Disc brooches, 1442; Recent excavations, 766; Sutton Hoo, 2487, 2496

Brückmann, J.: Coronation orders, 1459

Bruckner, Albert: Latin charters, 2192

Bruel, Alexandre: Cluny charters, 5915

Bruges, 3821, 4188, 5329, 5386

Brunanburh, battle of, 2325–6, 2342, 2445, 2571

Brunet, Adrien: La renaissance (xii century), 1394, 6892

— Gustave: Journal, 3776

— Jacques-Charles: Manuel, 44

Brunham, Robert de, prior of Norwich, 5783

Brunne, Robert of, 2923, 6694, 6699. *See* Mannying, Robert (of Brunne)

Brunner, Francis A.: Jungmann's Mass, 1338

— Heinrich: Forschungen, 1230; Rechtsgeschichte, 2507; Schwurgerichte, 1248; Sources of English law, 1246; Urkunde, 2214

Brunyate, John: Maitland's lectures, 3725

Brut, the (chronicle), 2803, 2811

— Tysylio, 2166

— y Saeson, 2804

— y Tywysogion, 1084, 1114, 2144, 2805

Bruton priory (Som.), 6306

Bruun, Henry: Danish bibliography, 50

Bryan, Patrick W.: Geography, 621

— William F.: Canterbury Tales, 7001

Bryant, W. N.: Financial dealings of Edward III, 3231; Intercommuning in parliament, 3370

Bryce: Handbook of records, 1059

Brydges, Samuel E.: Collins' peerage, 557

Brydson, Arthur P.: Westmorland assize roll, 3618

Bryene, Alice de: Household book, 4603

Brynmor-Jones, David. *See* Jones, D. B.

Bryson, William H.: Witnesses, 6448

Bubwith, Nicholas, bishop, 5589

Buchanan, James J.: Zosimus, 2025

Buchberger, Michael: Lexikon, 1270

Buchner, Rudolf: Rechtsquellen, 66

Buchon, Jean A. C.: Collection des chroniques, 1091; Creton's Richard II, 2856; Froissart's Chroniques, 2874; Juvénal des Ursins, 2909; Le Beau's Chronique, 2915

Buckatzsch, E. J.: Distribution of wealth, 4638

Buckfast abbey (Devon), Cartulary, 5715

Buckingham, Estates of, 4958

Buckingham, Humphrey, duke of, 4600

— Thomas: Scholastic debates, 6660

Buckinghamshire: Antiquities, 737; Charters, 4419, 4854; Church, 1529; County history, 1529, 1550–1; County journals and societies, 1549, 1732; County records, 1547–8; Deeds, 1547, 4418; Domesday, 1529, 3040; Eyres, 3521, 3533; Feet of fines, 3487, 3532; Manors and villages, 4711–14, 4854; Pleas, 4713–14; Pipe rolls, 3083; Religious houses, 6093–7; Sheriffs, coroners, etc., 3528; Taxation, 3149A; Topography, 1529; Urban history, 5034–6

Buckland priory (Som.), 6307

Buckland, William W.: Roman and common law, 1231

Buckler, William: Ilchester deeds, 4872

Budleigh (Devon), 4351

Bueno de Mesquita, Daniel M.: Foreign policy, 4172

Bugge, Alexander: Akstykker, 3835; Caithreim-Caisil, 2150; Norges historie, 2569; Norse settlements, 2568, 2570; Vikingerne, 2568

Bühler, Curt F.: Edward IV to Sforza, 4208

Building documents, 790, 809, 5067

Bukofzer, Manfred F.: John Dunstable, 7182; Kantorowicz's Laudes, 1353; Popular music, 7204; Studies, 7196

Bullard, John V.: Lyndwood's Provinciale, 6436

Bullarium Franciscanum, 6004
— Praedicatorum, 5981
— S.S. Romanorum Pontificum, 5546

Bullen, William: Book of Howth, 2799; Bray's Conquest, 2800; Carew MSS., 1010

Bulletin Codicologique, 47
— de Théologie ancienne et médiévale, 150
— Du Cange, 303
— of the Board of Celtic Studies, 111
— of the Institute of Historical Research, 112
— of medieval canon law, 6426

Bullington (Lincs.), 5957, 6216

Bulloch, James: Adam of Dryburgh, 5962

Bullough, Donald A.: A.-S. kinship, 2642; A.-S. institutions, 2607; St. Columba, 2319; Spoleto writing-office, 7224
— Vern L.: Medical study, 6935

Bu' Lock, J. D.: Vortigern, 2553

Bulst, Marie Luise: Itinerarium Ricardi, 2906

Bunce, Cyprian R.: Canterbury city, 5120–1

Bund, John W. Willis. *See* Willis-Bund

Bunyard, Barbara D. M.: Brokage book, 5101

Burdon, Geoffrey, prior of Durham, 5701

Burford (Oxon.), 5226

Burgage tenure, 5081, 5353

Burgh, family of, Estates, 4658
— Hubert de, 4049

Burghal hidage, 2206

Burglary, 1499

Burgundy: **616–19**; 1448, 4170, 5402; Anne of, 4266; Bastard of, 4282; Margaret of, 4282

Burials, prehistoric, 1981

Burke, Arthur M.: Indexes, 4545
— Ashworth Peter: Peerage, 553
— Sir Bernard: Armory, 490; Peerage, 553
— Sir Henry F.: Catalogue, 192, 4694
— John: Armory, 490; Peerage, 553; Royal families, 545
— Sir John Bernard: Armory, 490; Royal families, 545
— Robert B.: Roger Bacon, 6539

Burley, Walter, 1428, 1459, 6660

Burlington Magazine, 779

Burn, Andrew R.: Agricola, 2071; Roman inscriptions, 2028
— Richard: Westmorland and Cumberland, 1597, 1851

Burnby, John: Obituary roll, 5688

Burne, Alfred H.: Agincourt war, 4162; Battlefields, 4299; Crécy war, 4162
— Richard V. H.: Cheshire, 3862; Monks of Chester, 6105

Burnell, Robert, bishop, 6751

Burnett, George: Heraldry, 486

Burnham (Essex), Reeve's account, 4750
— abbey (Bucks.), 6093

Burns, Edward: Scots coinage, 674

Burr, David: Ockham, Scotus and censure, 6625
— George Lincoln: Powicke's appreciation of, 1490

Burrell, Arthur: Piers Plowman, 7022

Burrows, Montagu: Cinque Ports, 5313; Collectanea, 7061; Family of Brocas, 4573

Burscough priory (Lancs.), 6197

Burton, John: Monasticon Eboracense, 6387
— John R.: Worcester bibliography, 1862
— Thomas of: Chronica de Melsa, 2806
— William: Antonine itinerary, 2029

Burton-on-Trent, abbey (Staffs.), 4473, 5250, 6326–7; Annals, 1098, 1114, 2763

Burtt, Joseph: Expenses, 4598; Westminster abbey, 6250

Burwash, Dorothy: Merchant shipping, 5378

Burwell priory (Lincs.), 6212

Bury, Boston of: Latin classics, 1452, 6930

— John B.: ed. Cambridge Medieval History, 1176; ed. Freeman's Geography, 614; Notitia dignitatum, 2030; St. Patrick, 2324

— Richard of, 6563–4; Liber epistolaris, 427, 1467, 6561, 7063; Philobiblon, 6562; Register, 5691–2

Bury St. Edmunds (Suffolk), 5256–7, 6335–45; Chronicles, 1108, 1113–14, 2305, 2772, 2819, 6341, 6936; Surveys and rentals, 2628, 3012, 4745; Wills, 4554, 4556

Bush, Henry: Bristol town duties, 5078

Bushe-Fox, Joscelyn P.: Roman excavations, 2070

Bushmead priory (Beds.), 6072–3

Butcher, J. H.: Parish of Ashburton, 6838

Butler, Alban: Saints, 1155

— Charles: Littleton, 2990

— Edward Cuthbert, 167; 1477, 5913

— George Slade: Sussex bibliography, 1835

— Harold E.: Fitzstephen's London, 1746; Giraldus Cambrensis, 6573; Jocelin of Brakelond, 6335; John of Salisbury, 6641; Suetonius, 2025

— James G.: Statutes of Ireland, 3333

— L. H.: Archbishop Melton, 5863

— Richard: Annals of Ireland, 2760, 2849

— Rodney F.: Kirkstall forge, 5500

— V. J.: A.-S. coinage, 1454

Butler-Bowdon, William. *See* Bowdon, William E. I. Butler

Butley priory (Suffolk), 1451, 6346

Butterfield, Sir Herbert: Historical scholarship, 253; Magna Carta, 3292

Büttner, Heinrich: Archiv, 412

Buytaert, Éloi M.: Ockham, 6621

Buzones, 1478, 3738

Byland abbey (Yorks.), 6425

By-laws, 4845, 4940, 4945

Bynames, 590

Byrhtferth's Manual, 2366

Byrhtnoth of Essex, 2344, 2584, 2588

Byrne, Francis J.: Columba, 2319; Irish bibliography, 35

Bywater (Yorks.), 4930

Cabrol, Fernand: Angleterre chrétienne, 2695; Dictionnaire, 763, 1265; Liturgy, 1327

Cade, John, 2743, 2829, 2886, 4214

— William, 5509

Cadoc, St., of Llancarfan, 2123

Caedmon: A.-S. poetry, 882, 2328, 2339

Caen, La Trinité, English manors of, 1439, 4699

— St. Stephen's, 2776

— John of, notary public, 2770

Caenby, Tournays of, 4584

Caenegem, Raoul C. van: Royal writs, 1245, 3503

Caerleon-on-Usk, 2665

Caernarvon: History, 1386; Record of, 4943A, 6828

— Edward of. *See* Edward II

Caernarvonshire, 198, 1504, 1900–3

Caerwent (Roman), 2072

Caesar, Julius, 266; 2025, 2043

Cahiers de civilisation médiévale, 151

Cahors, merchants of, 1467, 5423, 5434

Caillemer, Robert: Executor in law, 1246

Cain, A.: St. Ninian's Isle Treasure, 2482

Cain Adamnain, 2244, 2251

Caister (Norfolk), 4599

Caistor (Lincs.) (Roman), 2061

Caithreim Cellachain Caisil, 2150

Calais, 1469, 2743, 3247, 4188, 4278, 5330

Calder, George: Gaelic grammar, 331

Caldwell, J. G.: Gervase of Tilbury, 2961

Calendar, 2292, 6322. *See* Chronology

Calendarium Genealogicum, 528, 4338–9

Caley, John: Calendarium inquisitionum, 4340; Calendarium rotulorum chartarum, 3758; Duchy of Lancaster, 3873; Dugdale's Monasticon, 1147; Foedera, 3765

Callard, Ernest: Freckenham, 4887

Callender, Geoffrey A. R.: Naval history, 4322

Callmer, Christian: Bibliography, 727

Callus, Daniel: Aristotelian learning, 6900; Essays to, 1428; Grosseteste, 1450, 6576

Calmette, Joseph L. A.: Commynes, 2851; Histoire (xiv–xv centuries), 1182; Le monde féodal, 45; Louis XI, 4244

Calthorp, Dion D.: Costume, 910

Calverley charters, 4496

Cam, Helen Maude: Album to, 3366; Cambridge, 1434, 1462, 1529, 5041; Community of the vill, 1437, 1461; Cluniac chronicle, 2935; Custodes pacis, 1462; Eyre, 1438, 1461–2, 3504, 3579; Feudalism, 1461–2; Franchise, 1461, 2608, 3366; Hundred rolls, 3729–30, 4345; Hundreds, 1441, 1455, 1461–2, 2210; Lands of St. Riquier, 5919; Lapsley's Studies, 1478; Law-finders, 1461; Legislators, 1461, 3365; Levett's Studies, 1480, 4974; Liberties and Communities, 1462; Local government, 1462, 2609; London eyre, 3579; London law courts, 1461; Maitland, 1461, 1482, 1484; Magna Carta, 3281; Manerium, 1462, 2210; Parliament, 1462, 3307,

Cam, Helen Maude (*cont.*):
3356, 3366, 3395, 3442; Quo warranto, 1462; Reviews, 1389–90, 2613; Shire officials, 3721; Stubbs, 1221, 1461; Study of medieval history, 1461; Suitors and scabini, 1462; Villeins and freemen, 1462; Writs de expensis, 3442; Yearbooks, 3646

Cambrensis, Giraldus. *See* Giraldus

Cambridge: Antiquarian Society, 2034
— Bibliographical Society, 1555
— borough, 1386, 1434, 1462, 1529, 5037–42
— early science at, 6950
— Fitzwilliam Museum, 704, 1033
— Great schism and, 6740
— medical school, 6935
— parliament at, 3420
— religious houses, friars, 5992, 6024, 6030; St. Radegund, 6101
— University, 1529, 7053–60, 7090, 7092–113; Bibliography, 1557; Biographical lists, 532, 7095, 7110; College libraries, 446, 972, 974, 1033; Petitions for benefices, 6767; University library, 1031–2

Cambridge: Ancient History, 2034; Bibliography of English Literature, 14; Economic History, 1175, 1364, 5445; Historical Journal, 113; History of the Bible, 1372A; History of English Literature, 1400; Medieval History, 1176

Cambridgeshire: Antiquities, 737, 1985; Charters, 4400, 4420, 6364; County history, 1505, 1529, 1552–61, 3502, 4152; County journals and societies, 1552–61, 1818; County records, 3010, 3150–1, 3534–6; Domesday, 1529, 3009–10, 3017, 3061; Feet of fines, 3487, 3535; Feudal tenures, 4345, 4400, 4404; Gilds, 5368; Manors and villages, 1482, 1484, 4715–23, 5368; Monuments, 737, 761; Parliament, 3454; Place-names, 737, 761; Pleas, 3502, 3534, 3536; Religious houses, 6098–102; Sheriffs, coroners, etc., 1462; Subsidy rolls, 3150–1; Topography, 1505; Urban history, 737, 5037–42

Camden Society Pubns., 184
— William: Anglica Scripta, 1092; Britannia, 609; Marlborough's Chronicle, 2924

Camelot, 2470

Cameron, Alan D.: Historia Augusta, 2025
— Annie I. (Dunlop): Supplications to Rome, 5549
— Kenneth: Manor of Newark, 4841; Mercian boundary, 1433; Place-names,

629, 1433, 2591; Scandinavian settlement, 7225

Camp, Anthony J.: Wills and their whereabouts, **109**; 524, 4506

Campbell, A.: Philobiblon, 6562
— Alistair: Æthelweard, 2140; Æthelwulf, 2294; Battle of Brunanburgh, 2342, 2571; Beowulf, 7225; Breviloquium, 2313; Encomium Emmae, 2159; Norse kings, 2572; Orosius, 441; St. Swithun, 2313; Wilfrid, 2313
— Anna M.: Black death, 5470
— Eila M. J.: Domesday geography, 3044
— George A.: Knights Templars, 6059
— James: Hundred years' war, 4173
— John: Chancellors, 530; Chief justices, 529
— William E.: Works of Sir Thomas More, 2927

Campsall, Richard of, 6891

Candida Casa, 2323

Candidus, Hugh: Peterborough historia, 1122, 6268, 6270

Canivez, Joseph M.: Statuta ordinis Cisterciensis, 1145

Canning, Richard: Charters to Ipswich, 5263

Cannon, Henry L.: Pipe roll, 3081

Canon law, **168–70**, and **846–50**; 1246, 1466, 1482, 3503, 4209, 5557, 5571, 6399, 6883

Canonization, 5726, 5742, 5798, 5956, 6634

Canons, **314–16**; 1129, 1140, 1142, 2254
— regular, **799–800**; 6281

Canonsleigh abbey (Devon), 6122–3

Canterbury: Christ Church: Administration, 5622; Archdeacons (A.-S.), 2716; Architecture, 813, 2712, 2724; Archives, 5621, 5623; Chronicles, 2157, 2807, 2863, 2944, 2957, 5612, 5614, 6529; Commissary court, 4535; Deans, 1040; Domesday monachorum, 3070, 5602; Familia, 1458, 2697; Financial system, 1494, 5622; Inventories, 5605, 5619; Letters and documents, 5601–4, 5607; Library, 1040–1, 6006; Memorials, 5623; Officials, 1040, 1458, 2698, 2716, 5777; Oxford and, 7062, 7074; Sacrist's roll, 5611; Survey, 3013; Visitations, 5618, 5624
— city: **709–10**; Archaeology of, 173; Freemen's rolls, 4784, 5119; Jews of, 3946
— diocese and province: **759–65**; Administration, 5617, 5620–1; Archbishops, 1130, 2807, 5598, 5612, 5625–44, 5851; Archiepiscopal elections, 5620, 6802; Archiepiscopal registers, 5578, 5609–10,

5621; Archives, 1040–1, 5600, 5621, and *see* 'Lambeth Palace Library'; Charters, 5600, 5606, 5613, 5621; Chronicles, 1123, 2141–2, 2157, 2807, 2863, 2944, 5612, 5614, 6529; Clerical subsidies, 6824; Convocation, 6818, 6820; Ecclesiastical courts, 6471, 6480, 6484–6; History, 5623, 6790; Hospitals, 6186–7; Manors and tenants, 4784, 4901, 5619, 5621, 6356; Petition to Pope, 1471; Pipe roll accounts, 4784, 5608; Proctors at Rome, 6457; Pluralists, 6772; Prerogative court, **647**; 4515, 4523, 4530, 4533, 4536, 4541, 4550, 4552, 4555, 4558, 5621; Sede vacante, 4535, 5599, 5601, 5608, 5624; Taxation, 6783; Visitations, metro-political, 5618; Wales, primacy in, 5880H; York, dispute with, 5615, 5853, 5878
— forgeries, 2863, 5615
— psalter, 894
— religious houses: Dominicans, 5997; Franciscans, 6015
St. Augustine's abbey, Black Book, 6182; Customary, 6179; Dispute with archbishop, 2807, 6183; Formulary, 1459; History, 2158, 2807, 2864, 2956, 2959, 6181, 6183–4; Inquests, 3014, 6180; Library, 1041, 7163
St. Gregory, 6185
St. Laurence, hospital of, 6186
— school of illumination, 885
— and York Society, 185
— Gervase of, 1114, 1123–4, 2807
Cantilupe Society (Hereford.), 1668
— Thomas de, bishop, 5726, 5730
— Walter de, bishop, 4911
Cantini, G.: Adam de Marisco, 6603
Cantle, Albert: Quo Warranto, 3492, 3565
Cantor, Norman F.: Lay investiture, 6728
Canute. *See* Cnut
Canynges of Bristol, 5375
Capel, Roger: ed. Dalmais' Liturgy, 1329
Capes, William W.: English church, 1289, 6788; Hereford charters, 5725
Capgrave, John: Chronicle, 2808; Nova Legenda, 1158, 2287; St. Dunstan, 2303; St. Oswald, 2311
Capital formation, 4966
Caplan, Harry: Artes praedicandi, 6703
Cappelli, Adriano: Cronologia, 367; Lexicon, 402
Caradoc of Llancarvan, 2805
Car-Colston (Notts.), 4842
Cardiff Public Library (Glam.), 1919
Cardiganshire, 1904–7, 4633A
Cardinals, benefices of, 5807
Cards, 928A

Carew MSS., 1010, 1026
Carew, Richard: Cornwall, 1586
Carilef, William de, bishop, 2157, 5675
Carlaverock, Song of, 474, 1467, 4295
Carlisle: city of, 1504, 1595, 5048
— parliament of, 3412
— see of, 1499, 1592, 4522, 5645–9, 6790, 6826
Carlyle, Alexander J.: Political theory, 1411
— Robert W.: Political theory, 1411
Carmarthen: Black Book, 2383; St. John's, 3785B
Carmarthenshire, 1905, 1908–11, 5880F
Carmelite friars, 5973–9; Missal, 901
Carmelus (journal), 5974
Carmody, Francis J.: Arabic sciences, 6936
Carne of Nash, Family of, 3786A
Carney, James: Irish literature, 2408–9; St. Patrick, 2324
Carnuntina, 2072
Caröe, William D.: King's hostel, Cambridge, 7113
Carols, 7190, 7194, 7207
Caron, Pierre: Periodicals, 90; Répertoire, 63
Carpenter, Edward F.: House of kings, 6242; St. Paul's cathedral, 5770
— John, bishop, 5846
— John: Liber Albus, 5161; Memoir, 5150
— Robert: Provisions of Westminster, 1467, 2995, 3513, 4048
Carpenters' Company, 5187
Carpentier, Élisabeth C.: La peste noire, 5469
— Pierre: ed., 305
Carr manuscript, 5217
Carr, A. D.: Welsh aristocracy, 4070; Welshmen and Hundred Years War, 4163
— Sir Cecil T.: Clement's Inn, **926**; Corporateness, 1246
— Edward H.: History, 240
— William: University College, Oxford, 7131
Carrawburgh (Northumb.), 766
Carré, Meyrick H.: Phases of thought, 6901
Carrow abbey (Norfolk), 4822, 6254
Carshalton (Surrey), 4892
Carson, Edward A.: Customs records, 5328
Cartae antiquae, 3750, 3769, 4400
— of 1166, 3006–7, 3174
Carte Nativorum, 6266
Carte, Thomas: MSS., 1026; Rolles Gascons, 3808
Cartellieri, Alexander: Philipp II August, 2947, 3806, 4014

Carter, Edmund: Cambridgeshire, 1558
— Edward H.: Hospital, 6260; Norwich cathedral, 5783
— Henry H.: Dictionary of musical terms, 7197
— William F.: Lay subsidy roll, 3197
Carthew, George A.: Hundred of Launditch, 4454; Roll of Creake abbey, 6257
Carthusians, 5926–7, 6304
Carts, 5539
Cartularium Saxonicum, 2190
Caruca, in Domesday, 3057
Carucage, 3261, 4662
Carus-Wilson, Eleanora M.: Aulnage accounts, 3232; Bristol trade, 5084, 5341; Cloth industry, 5410; Export trade, 3219; Iceland trade, 5393; Industrial growth (fifteenth century), 1468, 4953; Industrial revolution (thirteenth century), 1468, 5501; Merchant venturers, 5379; Ports of the Wash, 5380; Towns and trade, 1485
Carving, 842, 851
Cary, Ernest: Cassius Dio, 2025
— Max (Caspari): Roman Britain, **264**; 1209; Suetonius, 2025
Case, Thomas: Annales, 2809
Cash, Caleb G.: Scottish bibliography, 27
Cashel, Cellachan of, 2150
— Cormac, king of, 2401
Cashmore, Herbert M.: Birmingham books, 1842
Casley, David: King's library MSS., 1002
Caspar, Erich L. E.: Das Register Gregors VII, 5555
Caspary, G. E.: Deposition of Richard II, 4113
Cassius Dio, 2025
Castelford, Thomas: Chronicum Brittanicum, 2810
Castille, Blanche of, 4105
Castle Acre priory (Norfolk), 4454
Castle Combe (Wilts.), 4922
Castle guard, 823, 1486, 4004, 4666
Castles, **97–8**; 742–3, 766, 781, 1485–6, 1495, 4291, 4437, 4597, 4746, 4749, 4781, 5033, 6276
Castorius, 2032
Casus placitorum, 2993
Catalogues of:
— books, 67–87, 512, 518–19, 1041, 1087, 1542, 1641, 1665, 1667, 1672, 1679, 1695, 1697, 1724–5, 1730, 1749, 1767, 1828, 1842, 1853, 1862–3, 1871, 4483, 4497, 4891, 4897, 6358, 7072
— deeds, 4402

— manuscripts, 21, 439, 972–1052, 1062–6, 1082–3, 1643, 3767, 4431, 4437, 5207, 5233, 5270, 5665
— seals, 454, 463
Cate, James L.: Church and market reform, 5523; Eustace of Flay, 1447, 5523
Catesby, William, 4227
Cathedral libraries, **127–9**; 972, 974
Cathedrals. *See* under the name of particular cathedrals
Catholic Dictionary of Theology, 1263
Catholicon Anglicum, 304
Catley (Lincs.), Gilbertine house, 5957, 6216
Cattle, 4992
Cattley, Stephen R.: Actes and monuments, 6865
Catto, J. I.: Alleged council, 2865
Catton, Walter, 6891
Caunton, Robert de, 4842
Cauwenbergh, Étienne van: Dictionnaire, 593
Cavalry, 4287
Cave, William, 33, 987
Cave-Browne, John: Knights of shire, 3460
Cawthron, Donald: Diocese of Exeter, 5723
Caxton Society, 186
— William, 2811, 2895, 7213, 7215–16, 7221
Cayzer, Thomas S.: Britannia, **264**
Cazel, Fred A., Jr.: Fifteenth (of 1225), 3233; Isabella of Angoulême, 1486, 4038; Roumare charters, 1453; Stephen Langton, 5634; Tax (of 1185), 3233, 6779
Cederschiöld, Gustav: Saga-Bibliothek, 2436
Celibacy, sacerdotal, 1282
Cella, John de, abbot, 2979
Cellachan of Cashel, king of Munster, 2150
Cellarers' accounts: Battle abbey, 6360; Carrow abbey, 4822; Creake abbey, 6257; Wilton abbey, 6379
Celoria, Francis: Local history, 1516
Celt and Saxon, 2123
Celtic:
— art, 1442, 1987, 1998, 2003
— Britain, **279–82**
— church, **149–51**, **333–9**, and **379–82**; 239, 1137, 1141
— languages and literature, **40–4** and **346–51**; 2122, 2125, 2127
— laws, **310–14**
— Review, 316
— saints, **333–9**
— Society, Publs., 223
Celtica (journal), 230

Celts, **279–82**; 761, 1429–30, 1470, 1997, 2050, 2526, 2537, 2584
Cely Papers, 3224, 5330
Cemeteries, Anglo-Saxon, 2464; Roman, 2070
Census (tax), 6775
Censuses, 5476. *See* Population
Ceolfrith, abbot of Jarrow, 2284, 2301
Ceolnoth, archbishop, 2716
Ceorls, 1470, 1496
Cereals, 2631
Cerne abbey (Dorset), 6128
Cerretano, Jacob: Journal, 5565
Chad, St., 5878
Chadwick, Dorothy: Social life, 5446, 7025
— Hector M.: A.-S. institutions, 2494; Early kingdoms, 2122; Early Scotland, 2118; End of Roman Britain, 2122; Essays to, 1429, 1989; Heroic Age, 2351; Origin of the English nation, 2529; Vortigern, 2122
— John N.: Blomefield's Norfolk, 1756
— Nora Kershaw: Age of the saints, 2664; Anglo-Saxon and Norse poems, 2326; Bede, 2123; Beowulf, 1433; British–Celtic population, 2526; Brittany, colonization of, 2120; Celt and Saxon, 2123, 2530; Celtic background, 2123; Celtic Britain, 761, 2119; Celtic realms, 2125; Celtic West, 1430; Chester, battle of, 2123; Constantine, prince of Devon, 2122; Early culture, 2665; Intellectual contacts, 2122; Intellectual life, 2665; Ninian, 2323; Northumbria, conversion of, 2123; Studies in early British church, 2121, 2530, 2665; Studies in early British history, 2122, 2530, 2557; Vikings, 2596
— Samuel J.: Dewsbury Church, 5289
— William Owen: Victorian church, 1276; Welsh dedications, 2122
Chailley, Jacques: Histoire musicale, 7198
Chalcombe (Glos.), 4439
Chalford (Glos.), 4439
Chalford (Oxon.), 4848
Chalgrave Manor (Beds.), 4703
Chalklin, Christopher W.: Kent subsidy roll, 3165, 4784
Chamber, the, **479–82**; 1450, 3246, 3270
Chamberlain, Office of, 556
Chamberlains' accounts, 1356, 3084, 3854, 5205, 5229, 5304, 5319, 5324, 5331, 6159, 6415
Chambers, Sir Edmund K.: Arthur, 2166, 2531; English literature, 1402, 6981; Eynsham, 6289; Medieval stage, 6982
— John D.: Divine worship, 1328
— Percy Franklin: Julian of Norwich, 6673

— Raymond W.: Bede, 2297; Beowulf, 2335–6; Book of London English, 5149, 6984; Continuity of English prose, 6983; England before Norman Conquest, 1209; Geoffrey of Monmouth, 2166; Piers Plowman, 7023; St. Guthlac, 2310, 2337; Sir Thomas More, 2927; Widsith, 2345
Chambre, Willelmus de: Scriptores Tres, 5685
Champion, Pierre: Burgundy, France and England, 4248; Charles d'Orléans, 4247; Jeanne d'Arc, 4246; Louis XI, 4245
Champollion-Figeac, Jacques J.: Lettres de Rois, etc., 3816
Chancellors, 530, 539, 3687
— Oxford University, 7065, 7069
Chancery: Anglo-Saxon, **304**; 2215
— court of, 1246, 3483, 3509, 3617, 3719–20, 7224
— episcopal, 421, 5577, 7224
— equitable jurisdiction of, **554–5**
— household of, 1448, 1499
— Inns of, **925–7**
— monastic, 6391
— Palatinate of Chester, 3856
— records of, **557–67**; 955, 3082, 3105, 3318, 3483, 3609, 3637A, 3807–8, 3810, 3816, 3823, 3826–30, 3838, 3865, 4979, 5144, 5897, 6391, 7222
— specialized studies on, **572–4**; 460, 469
Chandler, Henry W.: Court rolls, 4820
— Richard: William Waynflete, 5819
Chandos, Herald of: Le Prince Noir, 2812
— Sir John, 2812
— Inheritance, 3503A
Chandos-Pole, R. W., 4431
Chaney, William A.: A.-S. kingship, 2610; A.-S. paganism, 2655
Changing Views of British History, 254
Channel Islands, 1952–9, 2000, 3103, 3319, 3643, 3802, 3802A
Chanter, John F.: Court rolls, 4866
— John R.: Barnstaple records, 5054
Chantries, 6807, 6858, 6862, 7223
Chaplain, Chronicle of the, 2877
Chaplais, Pierre: Anglo-Saxon chancery, 2215; Anglo-Saxon charters, 2215; A.-S. diplomas, 2194, 2215; Chancery of Guyenne, 1441; Charters of Ine, 2194; Diplomatic Documents, 3763, 7223–4; England and Scotland, 3812; Facsimiles, 436, 2191; Feudal status Aquitaine, 4164; Letters of Edward I, 3754; Réglement des conflits, 4174; Royal documents, 3838; Seals, 469; Seals and charters of Henry I, 3779, 4399; Study of palaeography, **47**, 1440;

Chaplais, Pierre (*cont.*):
Treaty of Brétigny, 3809; Treaty of Paris, 3831, 4098; Treaty rolls, 3783; War of Saint-Sardos, 3810; Westminster charters, 1453, 6234
Chapman, Annie B. Wallis: Black book of Southampton, 5099
— Frank R.: Sacrist rolls, 5705
Chapter acts, 5651, 5718, 5800, 5973, 6414
— clerk, 5753
— House Records (York), 4930
Chapters, general, 5907–8, 5952, 5973, 6235, 6480
— provincial, 6024
Charité-sur-Loire, priory, 1471
Charland, Thomas M.: Artes praedicandi, 6704
Charles V (of France), 2845, 4175
Charles VII (of France), 2793, 2813, 4250
Charles, Bertie G.: Angles and Britons, 340; Hereford muniments, 5724; Norse in Wales, 2573; Welsh records, 5879A
Charlesworth, Maxwell J.: St. Anselm's Proslogion, 6528
— Martin P.: Cambridge Ancient History, 2034; Essays to, 771, 1430; Lost province, 2035; Roman stamped ware, 2045
Charlton, Lewis, bishop: Register, 5730
— Lionel: Whitby, 6422
— Thomas, bishop: Register, 5730
Charms, A.-S., 2373
Chart, David A.: North Ireland monuments, 736; North Ireland, P.R.O., 1077
Charterhouses, 6223–4, 6324
Charters and deeds: **636–8**; 370, 426, 437, 444, 946, 992, 1000, 1004, 1020, 1037, 1064, 1139, 1426, 1429, 1453, 1455, 1482, 1487, 2193, 3660, 3749–51, 3758–60, 3769–70, 3779, 3806, 3823, 3841–2, 3877, 4460, 7224
— Anglo-Saxon: **303–7** and **309–10**; 444, 452, 1475, 2151, 2164–5, 2282, 2611, 2696, 6289
— Family:
Antrobus, 4488
Arley, 4421
Bagot, 4476
Bartholomew Bolney, 4483
Beaumont of Hatch, 4470
Brocas of Beaurepaire, 4573
Bromley of Bromley, 4475
Calverley, 4496
Carne of Nash, 3786A
Chandos-Pole, 4431
Chetwynd, 4474
Clayton-le-Moors, 4450
Fitzhardinge, 4437
Fitznell, 4481

Gloucester, earl of, 4438
Gostwick, 4413
Gournay, 4580
Gresley, 4431
Hatherton, 4472
Hoghton, James de, 4442
Hylle, 4469
Ingpen, 4581
Laing, 4458
Legh of Booth, 4426
L'Isle, 6366
Lyttelton, 4493
Neales of Berkeley, 4437
Norris, 4443
Percy, 4501, 4838
Redman, 4500
Rydeware, 4478
Standish, 4444
Talbot, 4424
Trevelyan, 4427
Tropenell, 4490
Wolseley, 4477
Wrottesley, 4596
— Gascon: 1426, 3832
— Gilds: 5303
— Hospitallers: 6042, 6191
— Jewish: 3940
— Manorial, including castles, parishes, etc.:
Arlesley, 6148
Ashen, 4434
Bedfordshire, 4411–12, 5029
Blithfield, 4476
Boarstall, 4416, 4461
Breadsall, 4429
Buckinghamshire, 4418–19, 4854
Castle Combe, 4922
Chalcombe, 4439
Chalford, 4439
Cheshire, 3856, 3877, 4422
Crondal, 4763
Cumberland, 1597, 4428
Derbyshire, 1601, 4431
Dunkenhalgh, 4445
Durham, 4433
Enstone, 4853
Essex, 4435
Glamorganshire, 3785, 3786A
Glapwell, 4430
Harlow, 4745
Hereford, earldom of, 4440
Huntingdonshire, 4775
Hurley, 4417
Ilchester, 4872
Keswick, 4455
Kyre Park, 4494
Lancashire, 3870–2, 3877, 4442–3, 4446
Larden, 4466

Long Melford, 4889
Middlewich, 4423
Morton Pynkney, 4831
Much Woolton, 6205
Newcastle-under-Lyme, 4475
Northamptonshire, 4456
North Elmham, 4454
Northumberland, 1775, 4433, 4458–60
Noseley, 4798
Ormsby-cum-Ketsby, 4814
Oxfordshire, 4462–3, 4465, 4854
Pickering, 4685
Ribston, 6056
Richmond, 4503
Rippingale, 4452
Rowington, 4485
Scarisbrick, 4441
Segrave, 1714
Shenstone, 4479
Sherborne House, 4436
Simonburne, 1775
Staffordshire, 4471–3, 4480
Sussex, 4482, 4484
Tavistock, 5064
Thatcham, 4707
Turvey, 4412
Wallingford, 4416
Westmorland, 1597, 1851
Wiltshire, 1861, 4490–1
Wissingsete, 4454
Worcestershire, 4494
Yorkshire, 4433, 4495, 4498–9, 4504
— Monastic, cathedral, collegiate churches, etc.:
Abingdon, 2725
Alvingham, 5957, 6216
Arthington, 6394
Athelney, 6321
Barking, 6140
Barnstaple, 6121
Barnwell, 6098
Bath, St. Peter's priory, 6305
Battle abbey, 6358
Beauchief, 6114
Bec, 4699, 5916, 5921
Belvoir, 1714
Beverley, 6395
Bilsington, 6178
Blyth, 6278
Boxgrove, 6361
Brewood, 6325
Brinkburn, 6273
Bristol, St. Mark's, 6152
Bruton, 6306
Buckfast, 5715
Buckland, 6307
Bullington, 5957, 6216
Burnham, 6093

Burscough, 6197
Burton, 6326–7
Bury St. Edmunds, 4745, 6336–7, 6342
Bushmead, 6072–3
Byland, 6425
Cambridge, St. Radegund, 6101
— University, 6122, 7053, 7060
Canonsleigh, 6123
Canterbury, archbishopric, 1009, 5606, 5613, 5641
— St. Augustine, 2158, 6182
— St. Gregory, 6185
— St. Lawrence, 6186
Carmarthen, St. John's, 3786B
Carrow, 6254
Castle Acre, 4454
Catley, 5957, 6216
Cerne, 6128
Chertsey, 1486, 6350
Chester, St. Werburgh, 6105
Chichester, cathedral, 5652
— St. Mary's Hospital, 6362
Chicksands, 6074
Cirencester, 6153
Cleeve, 6308
Cluny, 5915
Cockersand, 6198
Colchester, St. John's, 6141
Coldingham, 6276
Colne, 6143
Combermere, 6103
Combwell (Cumbwell), 6188
Crabhouse, 6255
Creake, 6256
Crowland, 2163, 6213–14
Dale, 6115
Darley, 6118
Daventry, 6286
Dieulacres, 6328
Dunstable, 6075–6
Durham, see of, 5679, 5685, 5700
Edington, 4489
Ely, 1475, 2164
Evesham, 6202, 6382
Exeter, cathedral, 5721–2
— St. Nicholas, 6124
Eynsham, 6289
Farne, 6276
Finchale, 6134
Flaxley, 6154
Fountains, 6400
Furness, 6199, 6200
Garendon, 1714
Gateshead, 6135
Glasney, 6107
Glastonbury, 6309, 6312
Gloucester, St. Peter's, 1453, 6156–7
Godstow, 6290

Charters and Deeds, Monastic, etc. (*cont.*):
  Goring, 6291
  Gretham, 6136
  Guisborough, 6401
  Haughmond, 6300
  Healaugh Park, 6403
  Hereford, 5725, 5736
  Hexham, 6274
  Holy Island, 6276
  Hornchurch, 6144
  Hyde, 2165
  Kingswood, 6158
  Kirklees, 6404
  Kirkstall, 6405
  Lacock, 6272
  Lancaster, St. Mary, 6201
  Lanercost, 6110
  Leeds, 6193
  Leicester hospital, 6209
  Lewes, 6363–4
  Lichfield, 5665–6
  Lincoln, 5744, 5749
  Lindisfarne, 6276
  Llandaff, 5880A
  Loders, 6129
  London, Holy Trinity, Aldgate, 6225
  — St. Mary's, Clerkenwell, 6229
  — St. Paul's, 5760
  Louth Park, 2831
  Luffield, 6263
  Lyminge, 6194
  Malmesbury, 6374
  Marrick, St. Andrew's, 6407
  Merton priory, 6352
  Missenden, 6094
  Monk Bretton, 6409
  Monks Horton, 6195
  Monmouth, 6252
  Montacute, 6306
  Muchelney, 6321
  Much Woolton, 6205
  Newminster (Hants), 5814
  — (Northumb.), 6275
  Newstead, 6279, 6281–2
  Newnham, 6081
  Newton Longeville, 6094A
  Norwich cathedral, 5778
  Ormsby, 5957, 6216
  Osney, 4479, 6292
  Oxford, St. Frideswide, 6295
  — St. John Baptist, 6296
  Penwortham, 6382
  Peterborough, 6266–7, 6269
  Pontefract, 6412
  Ramsey, 2151, 6173
  Reading, 6089, 6091
  Revesby, 6219
  Rievaulx, 6413

Ripon, SS. Peter and Wilfrid, 6415
Risborough, 6097
Robertsbridge, 6366
Roche, 6416
Rochester cathedral, 5793
— St. Andrew, 5794
Ronton, 6329
Runcorn, 6104
St. Michael's Mount, 6108
St. Neots, 6172
St. Riquier, 5919
Salisbury cathedral, 5799, 5805
— St. Nicholas hospital, 6378
Sallay (Sawley), 6417
Sanford, 6297
Selborne, 6165
Selby, 6418
Sele, 6367
Sempringham, 6220
Shaftesbury, 6130
Sherborne, 6131
Sherburn hospital, 6139
Shrewsbury, St. Peter's, 6301
Sibton, 1453
Sixle (Sixhills), 6216
Snelshall, 6096
Somerset houses, 5584–5
Southwark hospital, 6353
Stafford, St. Thomas, 6330
Staffordshire houses, 6331
Stanley, 6376
Stogursey, 6323
Stone, 6332
Swine, 6421
Tavistock, 6126
Thame, 6298
Trentham, 6333
Tutbury, 6334
Tynemouth, 6277
Wallingford, 6286
Waltham, 6148
Wardon, 6083
Welbeck, 6279
Wells, 5590
Westminster, 1453, 6231, 6233–4, 6240
Wetheral, 6113
Whalley, 6203
Whitby, 6422
Winchcomb, 6160–1
Winchester cathedral, 5811
— Hyde abbey, 2165
Wix, 1453, 6149
Wombridge, 6302
Worcester cathedral, 452, 1450, 2190, 5834, 5842
— St. Mary, 5842
— St. Swithun's, 6385
— St. Wulstan, 6386

Wroxall, 6311

York, Byland abbey, 6425

— St. Peter's hospital, 6387

Yorkshire houses, 6387

See also Coucher books

— Municipal, town and borough: **700–29**; 4791, 5315, 5329, 5324. Consult individual towns

Charters of liberty, **501–2**

Chartier, Jean: Chronique, 2813

Chartres, school of, 1487, 6642, 6645

Chartrou, Josèphe: L'Anjou, 4012

Chassant, Alphonse: Abréviations, 403

Chastellain, Georges: Chronique, 2814

Châtellerault, lords of, 1486

Chaucer, Geoffrey, **603**; 6960, 6990, 6999–7014

Chauncy, Henry: Hereford, 1676

Chaytor, Alfred H.: Maitland's Equity, 3725; Maitland's Forms of action, 3704

Cheddar (Som.), **358**

Cheker, Matthew, 1467, 2987

Chelmsford (Essex), 4526

Cheltenham, Abbot John of: Register, 6160

Cheney, Christopher R.: Becket to Langton, 6789; Bishop's chanceries, 421, 5577; Canterbury election, 5620; Canterbury statutes, 5616; Carlisle, 5647; Councils, 6440, 6816; Decretals of Innocent III, 6429; Deposition of John, 1450; Dunstable annals, 1459; England and Roman curia, 6729; Episcopal visitation, 5882, 6348; Feasts, 6837; Gilbertine houses, 5955; Handbook, 372; Harrold priory, 6080; Hubert Walter, 5642; Interdict, 1218, 6729; Legislation of church, 1142; Letters of Innocent III, 5558–9; Letters of William Wickwane, 5856; Lyndwood, 6436; Magna Carta, 3282; Norwich cathedral, 5784; Notaries public, 421; Papal chancery, 420; Papal legate, 6742; Paper constitution, 4046; Philip the notary, 6779; Phillipps library, 973, 5550; Punishment of clerks, 6504; Records of medieval England, 937; Synodal statutes, 1438, 6811

— Mary: Compromise of Avranches, 6505

Chepstow castle (Mon.), 4585

Cheriton, Odo of, 6709A

Chertsey abbey (Surrey), 1486, 6350–1

Chess, History of, 928A

Chessington (Surrey), 4897

Chester: battle of, 2123; charter, 4791; city of, 5044–7; customs accounts, 3863, 5043, 5331; earl of, 1453, 3981; exchequer of, 1571; Grosvenor Museum, 704; St. Werburgh abbey, 2753, 2895, 6105

— County and palatinate: **574–6**; Accounts, 3084, 3854; Antiquities, 1577, 2053; Bibliography, 1562; Charters, 3877, 4421–6; Church, **767–8**; 6103–6; County history, 1570–7, 2259, 4213, 7223; County journals and societies, 1563–9; County records, **111**; 1575, 1627, 3537, 3877, 4219, 4347, 4794; Domesday Book, 3009, 3018; Domesday Roll, 3857; Eyres, 3537; Feet of fines, 3487, 3539, 3856; Feudal tenures, 4682; Inquests, 3856, 4347; Justices of peace, 3745; Manors and villages, 4724–6; Pleas, 3496, 3538, 3856; Pipe rolls, 3084; Urban history, 5043–7; Wills, 4537

Chester, Robert of: Algebra, 6953

Chester-le-Street bishops (A.-S.), 2721

Chesterfield (Derby.), 5052

Chesterfield, Thomas: Historia, 5669

Cheswardine (Salop), 4860

Chetham Society, 1698

Chettle, Henry F.: Friars of Holy Cross, 6039; Houses of Fontevault, 5920

Chetwynd family, Chartulary, 4474

Chetwynd, Walter: Pirehill hundred, 4875

Chevalier, Cyr Ulysse J.: Répertoire, 46–7

Chevallier, Charles T.: Norman Conquest, 3980

Chew, Helena M.: Ecclesiastical tenants, 4644; Escheator in London, 5166; Hemingby's Register, 5800; Jewish aid (1221), 3949; London eyre (1244), 3579A; London possessory assizes, 3580; Scutage, 4645

Cheyette, Frederic: Kings, courts, etc., 6760

Cheyney, Edward P.: Serfdom, 4959

Chibnall, Albert C.: Richard de Badew, 7093; Sherington, 4711; Taxation returns, 3149A

— Marjorie Morgan: Anselm and Bec, 5921; John of Salisbury, 6640; Lands of Bec, 4699, 5916, 5921; Monks and pastoral work, 5883; Ordericus Vitalis, 2310, 2937. *See* Morgan, Marjorie

Chichele, Henry, archbishop, 1438, 1450, 5573, 5609, 5629

Chichester (Sussex): City of, 1529, 5270

— rape of, 1840

— see of, 1042, 1108, 3490, 4557, 4617, 4907, 5650–63, 6790

— St. Mary's hospital, 6362

Chicksands, priory (Beds.), 6074

Child, Francis J.: Ballads, 7045

Childe, Vere Gordon: Dawn, 1971; Essays, 1974; Piecing the past, 746; Prehistoric communities, 1972; Prehistoric Scotland, 1973

Childs Ercall (Salop), 4860
Chiltern Hills, 4955, 4999
Chiltington (Sussex), 4904
Chippenham (Cambs.), 4723
— (Wilts.), 3625
Chippindall, William H.: Township of Ireby, 5051
Chipping and Market, 1429
Chirk, Black Book of, 2223
Chitty, Mrs. A. M. H.: Isurium, 2052
— Herbert: Winchester College muniments, 7138
— Lily: Index to Archaeologia Cambrensis, 109
Chivalry, 1450, 2982, 3503A, 4305
Chobham, Thomas de, 5443, 6690
Cholderton (Wilts.), 4489
Cholmeley, Henry P.: Rosa medicinae, 6937
Chorley (Lancs.), 4449
Chrimes, Stanley B.: Administrative history, 1212; Constitutional documents, 1205; Fifteenth-century England (Henry VII), 4234; Fortescue's De Laudibus, 2988, 3372; Introduction to Holdsworth, 1235; John of Lancaster's letters, 4197; Kern's Kingship, 1413, 2611; Lancastrians, Yorkists, 4196; Lords and Commons, 3396; Review of Jacob's Fifteenth Century, 4196; Richard II's questions to judges, 3710
Christ, Carl: Bibliotheksgeschichte, 7173; Zentralblatt, 7085
Christensen, C. A.: Adam of Bremen, 2149
Christie, A. Grace I.: Embroidery, 866
— Mabel E.: Henry VI, 4198
— Richard C.: Annales Cestrienses, 2753
Christina of Markyate, 6669
Christine de Pisan, 2815
Christmas, Henry: ed., 6863
Christopher, Henry G. T.: Palaeography, 941
Chrodegang: Regula canonicorum, 317; 1088, 2256
Chronicle of the Chaplain, 2877
Chronicles: 136–44, 283–99, and 386–454. See Chronicon
— chronological list: 389–92
— commentaries on: 283–4 and 384–9; 21, 374, 1499
— mainly intramural:
Alnwick, 6272
Brakelond, Jocelin of, 6335
Bury St. Edmund's, 6335, 6341
Butley, 6346
Candidus, Hugh, 1122, 6268, 6270
Canterbury, St. Augustine, 2158, 2956, 6181, 6183

Cistercian, 6400
Dale, 6116
Delapré, 6262
Elmham, Thomas, 6181
Evesham, 2899, 6380–1
Exeter, 3156
Fountains, 6400
Franciscan, 6009, 6024
Glastonbury, 6313
Gloucester, St. Peter's, 6157
Hexham, 6274
Kirkstall, 6400, 6405
Louth Park, 2831, 6218
Lynn, Grey friars, 6009
Meaux, 2806
Musca, Thomas de, 6117
Park-Stanley, 6116
Peterborough, 6265, 6268, 6270
Pipewell, 6271
Ripon, 6415
St. Benet of Holme, 6259
Swapham, Robert, 6268
Thorne, William, 6183
Thornton, 6221
Westminster, 6233
Whitlesey, Walter, 6268
Winchcomb, 1453, 2775, 6161
Witham, 6324
York, Chronica Pontificum, 1130, 2289
— St. Mary's, 6424
Chronicon, 1106, 1130, 2151–3, 2304, 2725, 2831–9, 6085, 6265, 6380
Chroniques, 2840–8, 2883
Chronologia brevissima, 1084
Chronologica Anglo-Saxonica, 2142G
Chronology, 45–6; 607A, 621A, 1487, 2045
Church: Bibliography, 164–5, 858; 97; Biography, 319–33 and 858–75; Canon law, 319–33 and 846–53; Canons, penitentials, etc. 314–16; Journals, 114, 116–17, 123, 127, 130, 145, 150, 166, 169, 6875; Legislation, 1140, 1142, and see Cheney, C. R.; Libraries, cathedral, 127–9; 1008–9, 1016, 7168, 7181; Records, 108–9, 144–51, 314–19, and 750–846; Service books, 170–3; 871; Sermons, 316–17 and 877–80; Societies, 170, 183, 185, 191; Treatises, modern, 165–6, 382–5, and 880–98; 7225. See also Courts
Church Quarterly Review (journal), 114
Church, Charles M.: Bath and Wells, 5592; Four Somerset bishops, 5592
— Richard W.: St. Anselm, 6534
— William S.: Hospital reports, 6226
Churchill, Irene J.: Archbishops' registers, 5621; Canterbury administration, 5617; East Kent records, 4778; Feet of fines,

3557; Handbook, 1683; Table of charters, 5613

Church Stretton (Salop), 4859

Churchwarden, 6841

— accounts, **893–4**

Chyle, Nathaniel: History of Wells Cathedral (1680), 5590

Cinque ports, **729–30**; 7222

Circuit of Ireland, 2400

Circumspecte agatis, Writ of, 3328

Cirencester (Glos.), 4758, 5094, 6153

— Richard of, 1089; De situ Britanniae, 1101, 2026; Speculum historiale, 2155

— Roman, 2054

Cistercians: **388** and **797–9**; 785, 986, 1145, 1148, 1343, 1427, 1477, 6400

— economy, 4992–4, 5011, 5411

— particular houses, 2806, 2820, 2850, 2910, 6109A, 6119, 6154, 6158, 6200, 6275–6, 6349, 6388, 6400, 6405, 6413, 6417

— settlement, 4941, 5936, 5940, 6393

Cistercian Studies (journal), 5931

Cîteaux (journal), 5930

Civil service and literature, 1499, 6927

Clagett, Marshall: Archimedes, 6939; Novel trends, 6941; Science of mechanics, 6940; Science of weights, 6958; Translations from Arabic, 6522

Clain-Stefanelli, Elvira E.: Numismatic bibliography, 645

Clanchy, Michael T.: Eyre of Wiltshire, 3622; Henry III's policy, 4047; Return of writs, 3662

Clapham, Alfred W.: Romanesque architecture, 788

— Sir John H.: ed. Cambridge Economic History, 1175, 1364; Concise Economic History, 1365; Linton, 5042

Clapham Bayeux (Beds.), 4702

Clare (Suffolk), 5258, 6174

Clare, family, 4568

Clare, Bogo de, 4621

— Osbert of, 2171, 5777

— Richard of, earl of Hertford, 1486. *See also* Strongbow

Clarence, duke of (1479–80), 4624, 4913

Clarendon (Wilts.), 4923

Clark, Albert C.: Latin cursus, 416

— Andrew: Lincoln diocese documents, 5741; Oxford, city, 7134; Oxford, colleges, 7116; Register of Godstow, 6290; Register of Oseney, 6293; Register of Oxford University, 7066; Tithings lists, 4752

— Arthur: Monmouthshire, 1935

— Cecily: A.-S. chronicle, 2142, 7225

— Charles U.: Ammianus, 2025

Edwin Kitson: Kirkstall abbey, 6405

— George: Battle of Maldon, 2344

— Sir George Norman: Oxford History, 31, 1189

— George S. R. Kitson: University research facilities, 938

— George Thomas: Appeal of Siward, 3636; Architecture, 827; Cartae, 3785; Customary of Rothley, 4797

— Godfrey L.: Cartae, 3785

— John Grahame D.: Archaeology and society, 747; Earliest people, 1430; Excavations, 1975; Flint mines, 2008; Gordon Childe's essays, 1974; Prehistoric England, 1976; Prehistoric Europe, 1977; Prehistoric Societies, 1978; Recent archaeology, 766; Study of prehistory, **85**

— John Willis: Architectural history of colleges, 7113; Barnwell, 6099; Care of books, 7162; Liber memorandum, 6098; Library of, 1552

— Mary G.: Sidelights, 2532

— Mary Kitson: Roman Yorks., 2069

Clark-Maxwell, William G.: Manors of Lacock abbey, 6373; St. Mary Magdalene, Bridgnorth, 6299

Clarke, Adam: Foedera, 3765

— David L.: Beaker pottery, 1979

— Sir Ernest: Bury Chronicles, 2819

— Henry W.: Tithes, 6857

— John, 2090–1

— Maude V.: Committee of estates, 1455, 4112; Deposition of Richard II, 4113; Dieulacres chronicle, 2820; Edward II's deposition, 1455; Fourteenth-century studies, 1464, 4112; Henry Knighton, 2912; Her bibliography, 1464; Impeachment, 1451; Irish parliaments, 3309; Kirkstall chronicle, 2910, 6405; Medieval representation, 3349, 4112; Papers, 1464

— Roy Rainbird: East Anglia, 761; Norfolk, 2552; Recent archaeology, 766

— Sir Thomas: Fleta, 2987

Classen, Ernest: A.-S. Chronicle, 2142

Classica et Mediaevalia (journal), 152

Classical Studies (journal), 2018

Classis Britannica, 1455

Clay, Sir Charles T.: Abbots of Yorkshire, 6388; Charters to Kirklees priory, 6404; Fasti, 5876; Keepership of Westminster, 3139; Longvillers family, 4574; Loyd's A.-N. families, 564; Priors of Pontefract, 6412; Treasurers of York, 5866; Yorks. assize rolls, 3633; Yorks. charters, 4499; Yorks. deeds, 4504; Yorks. final concords, 3634; Yorks. monastic seals, 465

Clay, Edith M.: Yorks. charters, 4499
— John W.: North Country wills, 4516; Peerages, 554; Testamenta Eboracensia, 4564; Yorks. inquests, 4395
— Richard C. C.: Wessex from the air, 753
— Rotha M.: Hermits and anchorites, 1303, 6683; Hospitals, 6070; Recluses, 5884
Clayton-le-Moors (Lancs.), 4450
Cleeve abbey (Som.), 6308
Clegg, I. E.: trans., 1371
Clement III, pope, 5632
— IV, pope, 6744
— V, pope, 3828, 5561, 6739
— VII, Avignonese pope, 6762
Clement, Henry, 1482, 1490, 3516
Clement's Inn, **926**
Clementi, D. R.: Richard II's to judges, 3710; Statute of York (1322), 3366
Clemesha, Henry W.: Preston, 1472, 5360
Clemoes, Peter: Ælfric, 441, 1433, 2292, 2352; Anglo-Saxons ed., 1433, 2491; Assmann's Homilien, 2266, 2292; Benedictine office, 1347, 2292h; Cynewulf, 7225; Journal, A.-S. England, ed., **339**
Clergy, benefit of, 3695
— in parliament, 3477–80
— lists of, **314**; 5580–2, 5661, 5734, 5791, 5807–8, 5847, 5864, 5876–7, 5895, 5998, 6299, 6856
— taxation of, **892–3**; 1436, 1439, 1471, 3268, 3476, 4943A, 6828
Clerical strike, 6395
Clerkenwell (London), 5173
Clerks, royal king's secretary, 3138, 3751, 3839–40
Clermont, Lord: Fortescue's Works, 2988
Cleveland (Yorks.), clergy, 6856
— duchess of: Battle Abbey roll, 555
Clifford, barony, 4391, 4486
Clifton Antiquarian Club (Glos.), 1647
Clio, introduction aux études historiques, 45
Clitheroe (Lancs.), 4788, 4791, 6204
Cloke, C. W. S. Randall: Wills, 4555
Clonfert (Ireland) monastery, 2318
Clonmacnoise, abbot of (Tigernach), 1268, 2779
Clontarf, battle of (1014), 2174, 2449, 2583
Close, letters and rolls, 1139, 1233, 3667, 3753, 3761, 3768–70, 3789, 3797–9, 3830, 3867, 3872, 4294, 4749, 5691
Cloth industry, 1500, 5418. *See* Wool
Cloud of Unknowing, the, 6665, 6670–1, 6686, 6688
Clough, Marie: Book of Bolney, 4483, 4899; Fitzalan surveys, 4908

Clowes, Sir William L.: Royal navy, 4326
Cluniac chronicle, 2935
Cluny, abbey of, 1471, 1477, 5915, 5922, 5925
Clutterbuck, R. H.: Archives of Andover, 5095
— Robert: Hertford, 1677
Clyn, John: Annales Hiberniae, 2760, 2849
Cnut, History of: 2159, 2448, 2589; Laws, 2181, 2183–4
Coamhánach, Séamus: Irish dictionary, 344
Coarbs of St. Patrick, 2677
Coat of Arms (journal), 502
Coate, Mary: ed., 1480, 4974
Coates, R. P.: Valuation of Dartford, 3166
Cobb, Henry S.: Port book of Southampton, 5106
Cobban, Alan B.: King's Hall, Cambridge, 7094
Cobbett, William: Parliamentary history, 3369; State trials, 3484
Cobham family, 4587
Cobham, Eleanor of, 4231
— Thomas de, 5840
Cochon, Pierre: Chronique de la Pucelle, 2840
Cochran, Patrick R. W.: Scottish coinage, 675
Cock, John: Records, 5063
Cockayne, Oswald: Leechdoms, 2271, 2369
Cockerell, Sydney C.: Gorleston Psalter, 883; East Anglian psalters, 903; Work of Brailes, 884
Cockerham (Lancs.), 4795
Cockersand abbey (Lancs.), 6198
Cockle, Maurice J. D.: Military bibliography, 4300
Codex Amiatinus, 2301
— Theodosianus, **266**
— Wintoniensis, 2199
Codicology, **50–3**
Codicote, Manor of, 1480, 6171
Codrington, Robert H.: Statutes of Chichester, 5658
— Thomas: Antonine itinerary, 2029; Roman roads, 2084
Coemgin, Gilla: Irish Nennius, 2167
Coens, Maurice: St. Boniface, 2299
Coffey, Peter: trans., 1410, 6899
Coffman, George R.: John Gower, 7019
Coggeshall, Ralph of: Chronicon, 2850
Coghill, Nevill: Piers Plowman, 7022
Cohen, Gustave: trans., 1182, 1371
— Henry: Roman coins, 657
— Hermann J.: Bar and attornatus, 1232
— Sarah: Oxford Jewry, 3970
Cohn, E. S.: Peter of Blois, 6519

Coins. *See* Numismatics

C[okayne], George Edward: Complete peerage, 556

Coke, Sir Edward: Institutes, 1233

Colby, Charles W.: Oligarchy, 5350

Colchester (Essex): Annals, 1108; History, 5075; Lollards, 6873; Records, 5071–4; Roman, 2055, 2070; Taxation, 3159

— castle, 5075

— St. John's abbey, 6141–2

Coldingham priory (Scotland), 5685, 6132, 6276

Coldingham, Gaufridus de: Scriptores tres, 5685

Cole, Charles A.: Elmham, 2864; Henry V Memorials, 2739, 2945, 2969

— E. J.: Bailiff's accounts, 4769; Ministers' accounts, 4632A

— Henry: Documents, 3104, 3310, 6053

— John de (envoy), 4109

— Robert: Rental in Gloucester, 5091

— Robert E. G.: Torksey, 4804

Coleman: Life of Wulfstan, 2316, 5843

Coleman, Ambrose: De annatis Hiberniae, 6774

— Olive: Brokage book, 5101; Collectors of customs, 5177; Export trade, 3219

— Thomas W.: English mystics of the fourteenth century, 6684

Colgan, John: Acta Sanctorum, 1160, 2784

Colgrave, Bertram: Bald's Leechbook, 2365; Bede, 2148, 2297; Gregory I, 2123, 2308; MSS. in facsimile, 441; St. Cuthbert, 1429, 2302; St. Guthlac, 2310; St. Wilfrid, 2313; Saints' lives, 2278

Colker, M. L.: Merton priory, 6352

Collas, John P.: French language, 291; Year Books, 3646

Collectanea Anglo-Praemonstratensia, 5961

— Cantabrigiensia, 1557

— Cisterciensia, 5931

— Franciscana (Rome), 6005

— Franciscana, ed. A. G. Little, *et al.*, 6006

— Genealogica (Foster), 561

— Ordinis Cisterciensium, 5931

— Topographica et Genealogica, 115

Collected Works, **194–211**

Collectio Canonum Hibernensis, 2261

Collection de documents inédits, 1093

Collection de textes, 1094

Colledge, Eric: Mystics, 6665

College of Arms, MSS., 1007

Collegiate churches, 1147, 4906, 5053, 5702, 6087, 6125, 6147, 6230, 6283–4, 6299, 6370, 6395, 6408, 6414–15, 6800

Collier, Charles: Archives of Andover, 5095

— John Payne: Household books, 4605; Trevelyan Papers, 4427

Collingwood, Robin G.: Archaeology of Roman Britain, 2037; Cambridge Ancient History, 2034; Economic Survey, 2039; Hadrian's Wall, 2085; Idea of history, 241; Inscriptions, 2015, 2027; Roman Britain, 1189, 2036; Writings, **261**; 2037

— William G.: Holm Cultram, 6109A; Hudderfield, 2574; Lake district history, 1594; Northumbrian crosses, 353, 2474; Scandinavian Britain, 2574

Collins, Arthur: Baronies, 4647; Peerage, 557

— Arthur J.: Magna Carta, 3283; Shaftesbury Abbey, 6131

— Francis: Register of freemen, 5306; Wills (York Registry), 4562

— Henry: Comfortable works, 6673

— Henry B.: The Old Hall manuscript, 7192

— S. M.: Continental rolls, 490

— Victor: Gaelic pioneers, 2667

Collinson, John: Somerset, 1810

Colloquies (Ælfric's), 2292(g)

Colloquy, development of, 1433

Colman, St., 2123

Colman, Jeremiah J.: Norfolk library, 1749

Colmer (Hants), 4766

Colne, priory (Essex), 6143

Cologne trade, 5344

Columba, St., 2319

Columban, St., 2320

Columbia University: Avery Library, Catalogue, 92

Colvin, Howard M.: Archbishop's tenants, 4784; Building accounts, 790; Deddington, 4851; Domestic architecture, 815, 1485; Guide to architectural history, 778; Holme Lacy, 1437, 4770; Kings' works, 781; Town planning, 815; White canons, 5964

Combermere (Ches.), abbot of, 6103

Combwell priory (Kent), 6188

Comitatus, 2609, 2615

Commelin, Jerome: Scriptores, 1095

Commendatio Lamentabilis, 2852

Commendation, 3063

Commerce, 730–2 and **735–42**; 1364, 1442, 1455, 1465, 1468–9, 1495

Commercial policies, 5400–4

Commissary of bishop, 5753

Commissions of the peace, 7223. *See* Justices of the Peace

Common law records (P.R.O.), **524–48**; 955, 955A, 7222

— lawyers, reputation of, 3688

— man, problem of, 1497, 2649

Commonplace Book, 2736, 2982, 4882
Communications, **735–8**; 1450, 1485, 1495–6, 2084, 5373, 5534, 5539
Communitas bacheleriae, 1499
— villae, 1437, 4830, 4945, 6834
Communities, survival of, 2637
Commutation, 1459, 4959
Community of the realm, 3366, 3403, 3839
Commynes, Philippe de: Mémoires, 2851
Companions of the Conqueror, 556, 564, 1493, 1496
Comper, Frances M. M.: Fire of love, 6679
Complete peerage, 556
Computus rolls. *See* Accounts
Conan, Alicia: corrody, 5830
Conciliar theory, 5571, 6626
Concordat (1418), 1438, 5569
Concordia regularis, 2272, 2274
Concords, final. *See* Feet of fines
Condover (Salop), 4858
Conference on British Studies, Handbooks, 15; Journal, 158
Confessio (St. Patrick), 2324
Confession, auricular, 1283, 1286–7
Confessors, king's, 3275A
Confirmatio Cartarum, 3212, 3342
Confirmation rolls, 3750, 3758, 3770
Congrès de droit canonique médiéval, **168–9**; 1313
Congress, library of, 85–7
Congress of Prehistoric Sciences, 1963
Coningsby, Thomas, earl of: Marden, 4773
Conisbee, Lewis R.: Beds. bibliography, 1531
Connacht annals, 2751, 2925
Connolly, Richard H.: Edmund Bishop's liturgy, 1325
Conry, John: Annals of Innisfallen, 2780
Cons, George J., **71**
Consiliatio Cnuti, 2181
Consitt, Frances: Weavers' company, 5204
Constable, Giles: Alleged disgrace, 6641; Anglo-Flemish Crusaders (1147), 2858; Hubert Walter, 1459; Monastic tithes, 6857
— Robert: Prerogativa regis, 3275
Constables, 3731, 3744, 3748
Constance, Council of, 4257, 5563, 5565–7, 6864
Constantine, Prince of Devon, 2122
Constantius: Life of St. Germanus, 1114, 2108
Constitutio Domus Regis, 3116
Constitutional history, **155–9**; 1459, 1478, 1498, 3269, 4071, 4115, 4143–4, 4234
Constitutions, church, 1129, 1140, 1142,

5658, 5765, 5799, 5803–4, 6380, 6436, 6811, 6816. *See* Canons
— of Clarendon. *See* Becket controversy, **853–6**
Consuetudinaries, 1146, 4797, 5113, 5738, 5749, 5765, 5776, 5803–5, 5813, 5842, 5906–7, 5909, 6045, 6085, 6099, 6168, 6179, 6288, 6340, 6373
Consuetudines Diversarum Curiarum, 2994, 3513
Contamine, Philippe: Azincourt, 4261
Contempt of court, 1234
Continuatio Beccensis, 2853
— Bedae, 2156
Continuations and Beginnings, 2352
Contract, law of, **552**; 1244, 1246, 3720, 3734
Conveyancing, 1482, 3000, 4402, 4632
Convocation, **891–2**; 1444, 1459, 1482, 3480, 5621, 5986
Conway, John Placid: Lives of Preachers, 5983
Conybeare, John J.: Page's poem, 2940
— John W. Edward: Alfred, 2147, 2575; Cambridgeshire, 1559
Cook, Albert: Asser, 2147; St. Aldhelm, 2296
— Dorothy E.: Costume index, **104**
— George H.: Parish church, 791
— Robert B.: Wills of York, 4563
— Stanley A.: ed. Cambridge Ancient History, 2034
Cooke, Alice M.: Anglia monastica, 605; Settlement of Cistercians, 5940
— Alfred H.: Boarstall cartulary, 4416, 4461; Mapledurham, 4846
— John H.: Bibliotheca Cestriensis, 1562
— William: Ordinale Sarum, 1321
— William H.: Duncumb's Collections, 1670; Grimsworth hundred, 1670
Cooper, Charles Henry: Cambridge, 5040
— Charles Purton: Account of Public Records, 3316, 3765; Observations, 3316; Proposal for record office, 947, 965; Public records, 965, 3130, 3216, 4293; Records, 947; Rymer's Foedera, 3767
— George M.: Robertsbridge abbey, 6366
— Ivy M.: Meeting places, 3430
— J. P.: Social distribution, 5471
— Janet: Bishops of Durham, 2711
— John William: Cambridge, 5040
— Thomas M.: Scottish legal history, 2989
— William: Records of Beaudesert, 4914
— William D.: Cade's followers (Kent), 4214; Parliamentary history of Sussex, 3470; Sussex proofs of age, 4390
Coopers' Company, 5188

Coornaert, Émile: Les ghildes, 5361
Cope, Stanley Trehearne: Heraldry, **59**; S. Bartholomew's hospital, 6090
Copenhagen, coins, 704
Copinger, Harold B.: Bibliomania, 7172; Index, 1824
— Walter A.: County of Suffolk, 1824; Manors of Suffolk, 4888; Smith-Carington family, 4575
Coplande, Robert: Henry VI, 2796
Copley, Gordon J.: Place-names, 630; Wessex, 2533
Copper industry, 5507
Copyhold, 4979
Coram rege rolls, **524–5**; 3481, 3491, 3493, 3496, 3510, 3514, 3677, 4803
Corbeil, William of, 5615, 5853
Corbett, William J.: Duchy of Normandy, 3043; Tribal hidage, 2213
Corbridge (Northumb.): Battle of, 2157; Celtic sculpture, 1442; Roman Corbridge, 2080
Corbridge, Thomas of: Register, 5858
Cordeaux, Edward H.: Oxfordshire bibliography, 1786; Oxford University bibliography, **920**
Corder, Philip: Roman defences, 2069; Roman excavations, 2070; Roman pottery, 2069
Corish, Patrick J.: Irish catholicism, 1274, 2662A
Cormac, king of Cashel: Glossary, 2401
Cormacan Eigeas: Circuit of Ireland, 2400
Corn, 1468, 3145, 4988, 5385
Cornage, 4975
Cornish language, 328–30
— Notes and Queries, 1579
— Saints, 1161, 2666
Cornovii, the, 1435, 2089
Corns, Albert R.: Lincoln bibliography, 1715
Cornwall: Antiquities, 761–2; Bibliography, 1578, 2196; Charters, 4427; Church, **773–4**; 2678, 6107–9; County history, 1529, 1584–91; County journals and societies, 1578–83; County records, **112**; 4629, 4727; Domesday, 3009; Extents, 3487; Feet of fines, 3487, 3540; Inquests, 4348; Language, 328–30; Manors and villages, 4727–31, 4960; Parliament, 3455; Ports, 5390; Rural economy, 4960; Topography, 1470, 1517
— Richard of, 4096
Coronation service, **173–4**; 1459, 2593, 6249
Coroners and their rolls, 3496, 3508, 3523, 3577, 3581, 3598, 3600, 3602, 3731, 3735, 3747, 5137, 5151, 5154, 5177, 5209

Coroticus, Letter to, 2324i
Corpus Christianorum, 1127
— Consuetudinum Monasticarum, 1146
Corrazzano, Antonio: Elizabeth Woodville, 4220
Corrodies, 5830, 5903, 6053
Cosgrove, A. J.: Elections to Winchester, 5821
Cosneau, Eugène: Les grans traités, 3814
Cossington (Leics.), 5134
Costello, Michael A.: De annatis Hiberniae, 6774
Costume, **103–6**; 1485
Coterel gang, 5455
Cottars, 3057
Cottineau, Lawrence H.: Répertoire, 47, 1290
Cotton, Bartholomew: Historia, 1114, 2854, 5775
— Charles: Grey friars, 6006, 6015; Kentish cartulary, 6191; St. Austin's abbey, 6182; Saxon cathedral, 2712
— Robert: Abridgment of Records, 3308
— William: Account book, 4195
Cottonian Library, 962, 7181
Coucher books: Duchy of Lancaster, 3884, 4479; Furness abbey, 6199; Kirkstall abbey, 6405; Selby abbey, 6418; Whalley abbey, 6203
Coulet, Noël: Commynes, 2851
Coulon, Remi: Scriptores, 5985; Steffens' palaeography, 397
Coulter, Edith M.: Historical bibliographies, 2
Coulton, George G.: Black Death, 5472, 5483; Chaucer and his England, 7006; Chronicler of European chivalry, 2874; Five centuries, 1291; Life in the middle ages, 5447; Medieval moneys, 1495; Medieval panorama, 6902; Powicke's estimate, 1489; Social life, 5448
Council for British Archaeology, 1961
— King's: Documents, 3293–4, 3311, 3318, 3365, 3505–6, 7222; Modern works, 2865, 3295–3306A, 3376, 3390, 3659, 4254
— in Ireland, 3309, 3321
Councils, ecclesiastical, **754–5** and **891–2**; 1129, 1140, 1142, 1279, 1473–4, 2254, 6430
Counterfeiting, 2207
County court, 1482, 2619, 3737–9, 3741, 3743
County record offices, **109**; 944, 1504, 1513, 1523, 1532, 1540, 1614, 1631, 1671, 1680, 1684, 1696, 1716, 1726, 1728, 1759, 1779, 1796, 1827
Court baron, 192, 2995, 3871, 4619, 4716, 4882, 4968

Court hand, 387–8, 411
— rolls, Manorial: 1037, 1252, 1443, 1480,
    1484, 2995, 4455, 4689, 4696–7,
    4700–1, 4778, 4882, 4945–6, 4978;
  Abingdon abbey, 6084
  Achards, 4753
  Adderbury, 4844
  Aldborough, 4935
  Alrewas, 4874
  Ambree, 4783
  Ashton, 4777
  Atlow, 4728
  Banstead, 4898
  Basingstoke, 5096
  Baslow, 4729
  Battle abbey, 4777, 4920
  Bec abbey, 4777
  Berkshire, 4708
  Bitton, 4754
  Brightwaltham, 4777
  Broughton, 4777
  Carshalton, 4892
  Castle Combe, 4922
  Chalgrave, 4703
  Chertsey, 6350
  Clare, 6174
  Clitheroe, 4788
  Codicote, 6171
  Crondal, 4763
  Crowland, 6213
  Curry Rivel, 4866
  Dulwich, 4891, 4894
  Durham, 4739, 5684
  Egginton, 4730
  Elton, 4776
  Ely, 4716, 5704
  Enstone, 4853
  Eton, 4714
  Farnborough, 4782
  Fenny Stratford, 4714
  Forncett, 4819
  Glympton, 4847
  Great Cressingham, 4819
  Halesowen, 4928
  Halton, 4724
  Hastings, 4902
  Hellifield, 6043
  Herringswell, 4884
  Higham Ferrers, 4829
  Houghton, 4775
  Huntingdonshire, 4775
  Ightham, 4779
  Ingoldmells, 4812
  Keswick, 4455
  King's Repton, 4777
  Kingsthorpe, 4833
  King's Stanley, 4753
  Kirkheaton, 6043
  Lancaster, duchy of, 3877, 4792
  Lewes, 4905
  Lincolnshire, 4807
  Littleport, 4716
  Madresfield, 4929
  Manydown, 4767
  Mapledurham, 4846
  Marden, 4773
  Minehead, 4868
  Noseley, 4798
  Ormsby, 4814
  Peterborough, 6268
  Ramsey abbey, 4777, 6174
  Rochdale, 4789
  Romsey abbey, 4777
  St. Albans, 6171
  St. Ives, 4775, 4777
  Shaftesbury abbey, 6130
  Standon, 4878
  Stonehouse, 4753
  Stoneleigh, 6369
  Stukeley, 4775
  Surrey, 4890
  Tatenhill, 4877
  Temple Normanton, 4731
  Thorner, 4936
  Tooting Beck, 4893
  Tunstall, 4876
  Wakefield, 4932
  Wellington, 5249
  Whorwelsdown, 4777
  Wiltshire, 4918
  Wimbledon, 4895
  Winslow, 4713
  Woodchester, 4753
  Wreyland, 4732
  Wroxall, 6371
— — Municipal:
  Bridgwater, 5247
  Chester, 5046
  Colchester, 5071, 5073
  Coventry, 5274
  Doncaster, 5290
  Ipswich, 5290
  Leicester, 5137
  London, 5152, 5156
  — Mercers' Company, 5326
  Norwich, 5208–11
  Oxford, 5230
  Southampton, 5104
  Wakefield, 5289
Courtauld Institute of Art, 778
Courtenay, William: bishop, 5618, 5630,
  5730
— family, estates, 4658
Courthorpe, Elinor J.: Lathe court rolls
  4902
— William: Rous' English roll, 2950

Courtney, Charles J.: Surrey bibliography, 1828
— Francis: Cardinal Robert Pullen, 6631
— William P.: Cornwall bibliography, 1578; Cornwall representation, 3455
Courts of law, **301–3, 459–61,** and **524–48;** 955, 955A, 3251, 3591, 4508, 5842, 6098, 6342, 7222
— commentaries, **159–64** and **548–57;** 2612–13, 2619, 2624
— ecclesiastical, **851–3;** 1444, 2994, 4515, 4561–4, 5676, 5713, 5754, 5792, 5854, 6442, 6486. *See* Canon law
— of Chester, 3857
— of Chivalry, 3503A, 3679
— of forests, 3891, 3893, 3897
— of Great Sessions, **113**
— of Ireland, 3641
— of Lancaster, 3871, 3879, 3882
— of the Verge, 3670
— of Wales, 3636
Cousinot: Chronique, 2840
Coveney, Dorothy K.: Catalogue, 1015
Coventry (Warw.), 1386, 1529, 2201, 3471, 3615, 5272–7, 6368
— and Lichfield, see of, 5664–71
Coventry, Walter of: Memoriale, 2855, 5620
Coville, Alfred: Jean le Bel, 2916; L'Europe occidentale, 1182
COWA (journal), 726
Cowan, Ian B.: Vatican archives, 5545
Cowdrey, Herbert E. J.: A.-N. church, 6727; Epistolae Vagantes of Gregory VII, 5555
Cowfold (Sussex), 6838
Cowley, John D.: Bibliography of abridgements, 3656
Cowper, Henry S.: The art of attack, 4301
— Joseph: Canterbury freemen, 5119
Cox, A. C.: Dorsetshire index, 1614
— David C.: Evesham abbey, 6381
— Edward G.: Irish fragment of Bede, 2148
— John Charles: All Saints (Derby), 5053; Benefactions, 5664; Chartularies, 6115, 6118; Churchwardens' accounts, 6838; Derbyshire, 3155, 3543; Muniments of Lichfield, 1047, 5665; Parish, 792, 1521; Pastimes, 928A; Poll tax, 3204; Records of Northampton, 5215; Royal forests, 3903; Sacrist's roll, 5665; Sanctuaries, 1259; Selections, 3543
Coxe, Brinton: Bracton and Roman Law, 2985
— Henry O.: Catalogus, 1020, 1022; Gower's Vox Clamantis, 7017; Poème de Chandos, 2812; Wendover's Flores, 2979

Crabbe, George: Materials, 4818; Merton Hall, 4821
Crabhouse nunnery (Norfolk), 6255
Crafts, 1361, 1381, 5177, 5365, 5369. *See* Gilds
Craib, Theodore: Herbert of Bosham, 6518
Craig, Hardin: Religious drama, 6985
— Sir John: The mint, 676
Craigie, Sir William A.: Icelandic sagas, 2452; Scottish dictionary, 332; Supplement to *O.E.D.*, 282; Wyntoun's Chronicle, 2984
Craik, Thomas W.: Chaucer, 7006
Crambeck, Castle Howard (Yorks.), 2069
Cramer, Alice C.: Jewish exchequer, 3955
Cramp, Rosemary: Anglian-Viking York, 2591
Cranage, David H. S.: Home of the monk, 1303; Shropshire churches, **832**
Cranborne Chase (Hants), 2010, 2100, 3926
Crandall, Ruth: Festschriften, 1425
Cranfield Manors (Beds.), 4706
Craster, Sir Herbert H. E.: Anglo-Saxon records, 2714; Chronicle of St. Mary's Abbey (York), 6424; History of Bodleian, 1019; Northumberland hundred roll, 4374; Record of Flambard, 5694; Red Book, 2157, 2168, 5695; St. Cuthbert, 2713; Summary catalogue, 1027; Western MSS., 1019
Craven, deanery of, 1893, 5876
Crawford charters, 2202
Crawford, Osbert Guy S.: Antiquity, ed., 721; Antonine iter, 2029; Archaeology, 767; Century of air photography, **89;** Essays for, 1432; Long barrows, 1965; Our debt to Rome, 2096; Pictish inscriptions, 359; Ravenna Cosmography, 2031; Roman Scotland, 2088; Wessex from the air, 753
— Samuel J.: Ælfric, 2292; Anglo-Saxon influence, 2279; Byrhtferth's Manual, 2366
— Virginia M.: Legends of Saints, **148**
— William R.: Bibliography of Chaucer, 7002
Crawley (Hants), 4765
Crawley-Boevey, Arthur W.: Cartulary of Flaxley, 6154
Creake Abbey (Norfolk), 6256–7
Crécy, 4162, 4193, 4278. *See* Hundred Years War
Credit, 3236, 5429, 5445, 5515
Crediton (Devon), 2196
Creighton, Charles: Epidemics in Britain, 5473

Creighton, Mandell: Correspondence of Humphrey, 6928; Papacy, 6710
Cremona, E.: St. Columban, 2320
Cressington, Great (Norfolk), 4820
Cressy, Serenus: Juliana of Norwich, 6673
Creton, Jean: Richard II, 2856
Cricklade (Wilts.), 4927
Cricklade, Robert of: Life of Becket, 6488
Crime, **300–3** and **525–44**; 1255, 1257, 3489, 3664–5, 3669, 3675, 6482
Criminous clerks, 1455, 1482, 6464, 6504, 6506, 6509
Cripps-Day, Francis H.: Manor farm, 4631
Crisis (1340–1), 1478, 5612
Crisp, Frederick A.: Suffolk wills, 4553
Crispin, Gilbert, 5631, 6246, 6535
— Milo, 5631
Critchley, John S.: Summonses, 4296
Críth Gablach, 2243
Crittall, Elizabeth: Account of cellaress, 6379; V.C.H. Wilts., 3034
Crocker, Richard L.: Musical style, 7199
Crombie, Alistair C.: Grosseteste and science, 6942; Science, 1418, 1485, 6943; Scientific change, 6944
Crompton, James: Fasciculi, 6612; Leicestershire Lollards, 6873; Wyclif, 6651
Cromwell accounts, 3247, 4630
Cromwell, Thomas: Clerkenwell, 5173
Crondal (Hants), 4763
Crondall hoard (coins), 703
Crone, Gerald R.: Early maps, 595; Haldingham's map, 606
Cronica de Wallia, 2144
Croniques de London, 2857
Cronne, Henry A.: Bristol charters, 5077; Charter scholarship, **636**; 2216; E. A. Freeman, 2582; Earl of Chester, 3981; Forest, 1457, 3904; Honour of Lancaster, 4646; Local justiciar, 3732; Regesta, 3779; Reign of Stephen, 3981; Warwick, 1849, 5280
Crook, B. M.: Lewes priory, 6364
Crookes, M. E. B.: Public arms, 492
Crops, 1980, 4989, 5488–9, 5492–3
Crosby, Everett U.: Episcopate, 6802
— Henry L.: Thomas Bradwardine, 6558
— J. H.: Ely registers, 5704
— Ruth: Robert Mannyng, 2923
Croscombe (Som.), 6838
Crosland, Jessie: William the marshal, 4033
Cross, Frank L.: trans. Baumstark's liturgy, 1324; Oxford dictionary, 1264
— James E.: Ælfric, 2292; Ethic of war, 7225

Crosse, Gordon: Dictionary of church history, 1272
Crosses, **44–5**; 2471, 2474
Crossley, Ely W.: Hospitallers, 6043
— Fred H.: English abbey, 1303; English church monuments, 867
Croston, James: Baines' Lancashire, 1705
Crotch, Walter J. B.: Caxton, 7216
Crow, Martin M.: Chaucer's life records, 7007; Chaucer's world, 7012
Crowder, Christopher M. D.: Constance acta, 5566; Correspondence to Council of Constance, 5563; Sigismund, Council of Constance, 4257; Society and government, 4199
Crowland abbey (Leics.), 2163, 2310, 2900, 5021, 6213–15, 6269
Crowley, Theodore: John Peckham, 5637; Roger Bacon, 6542
Crown lands, 3132A, 4688
Croxton abbey (Leics.), 1714
Cruden, Stewart: Scottish castle, 828
Crump, Charles G.: Chancery, 1448, 1458; Dialogus de Scaccario, 3005; History, 255; Legacy, 1479; London gild merchant, 5364; Public Record Office, 949; Tables of bullion, 708
Crusades, 2788, 2906, 4106
Crutched friars, 6038–9, 6041
Cubbon, William: Isle of Man bibliography, 1944
Cuerdale hoard (coins), 1454
Culdees, 2688
Cum ex eo (papal constitution), 6799
Cumberland: Antiquities, 2021, 2085; Bibliography, 1591A–2; Charters, 1597, 4428; Church, **765–6**; 6109A–13; County history, 1529, 1594–8; County journals and societies, 1593; County records, 1504; Feet of fines, 3541; Inquests, **630**; Pipe rolls, 3085–6; Urban history, 1597, 5048–53; Wills, 4516, 4522, 4566
Cumbria, 2604
Cumin, William, 5677
Cuming, Geoffrey J.: Councils, 5567
Cunliffe, Barry: Fishbourne, 2057; Pre-Roman iron age, 2011; Roman Bath, 2052A
Cunningham, William: Cambridgeshire, 1560; Commercial policy, 5404; Craft gilds, 5362; Gild merchant, 5243; Growth of industry, 1366, 2208, 5381
Cunnington, Augustus: Catalogue, 1630
— Cecil W.: Costume, 911
— Maud E.: Belgic invasion, 1994
— Phyllis: Costume, 911
Cuntz, Otto: Antonine itinerary, 2029
Curia regis. *See* Courts of law *and* Plea rolls

Curle, Cecil L.: Christian monuments, 2469
— James: Roman drift, 2020; Scottish Roman sites, 2020
Curry Rivel (Som.), 4866
Cursitors' records, 3865, 4355
Cursus in Latin, 416, 1451, 1467
Curteys, Abbot William: Register, 6342
Curtis, Edmund R.: Charters, 1445; Ireland, 1199; Richard II, 4114
— Margaret: London lay subsidy, 1469, 3172, 5157
Curtius, Ernst R.: Europäische Literatur, 6879
Curwen, Eliot C.: Air photography, 754; Archaeology of Sussex, 762; Plough and pasture, 1980
— John F.: Kendale, 4487; Westmorland records, 1851
Cussans, John E.: Hertfordshire, 1678
Custodes pacis, 1462
Customary tenants, 4758
Customs of London (Arnold's Chronicle), 2789
Customs of the sea, 4286
— house, 5170, 7158
— revenue, **493**; 1441, 3219, 3222, 3229, 3236, 3238, 3241, 3863, 5043, 5078, 5084, 5177, 5328, 5331–3, 5341–3, 5384, 5393, 5403, 7222
Custumale Roffense, 4780
Custumals or Custumaries, 4689;
    Ambresbury, 6315
    Ashton-under-Lyne, 4793
    Battle abbey, 6357
    Bec, 4699, 5916
    Beverley, 5288
    Bishopstrow, 6373
    Bleadon, 4873
    Bradford on Tone, 4871
    Canterbury archbishopric, 4901, 6356
    — St. Augustine, 6179
    Cinque ports, 5320
    Cockerham, 4795
    Crondal, 4763
    Glastonbury, 6315
    Goring, 4900
    Hatherop, 6373
    Heddington, 6373
    Ipswich, 5261
    Islip, 4845
    Kent, 1694
    Lacock, 6373
    Laughton, 4900
    Lawshall, 4886
    Minchinhampton, 4759
    Pevensey, 5316
    Preston, 5131

Rochester, 4780, 5790
Romney, 5323
Rotheley, 4797
Rye, 5318
Sandwich, 5312
Sussex manors, 4907, 6356
Sutton, 4763
Taunton, 4871
Torksey, 4804
Wellingdon, 4900
Westminster, St. Peter's, 6179
Wiston, 4904
Wykes, 4741
York, St. Mary's, 6424
Cuthbert, St.: Lives of, 2148, 2157, 2284, 2297, 2302; relics of, 1429, 2302
— abbot of Wearmouth and Jarrow: Letter on Bede's death, 2148
— Friar: The friars, 6008
Cutler, John L.: Middle English verse, 7044
Cuttino, George P.: Causes of Hundred Years War, 4191; Diplomatic administration, 3839; Gascon calendar, 3812; King's clerks, 3366; Medieval parliament reinterpreted, 3357; Modus tenendi parliamentum, 3350; Process of Agen, 3817, 4164
Cuttlestone (Staffs.), Poll-tax, 3185
Cutts, Edward L.: Parish priests, 6839; Scenes and characters, 5449, 6839
Cuxham (Oxon.), 4849
Cymmrodorion Society, 126, 202
Cymru fu, 4633A
Cynewulf: Poems of, 2343, 2361, 7225

Daenell, Ernst R.: Hanse, 5426
Dahlmann, Friedrich C.: Quellenkunde, 48
Dahmus, Joseph H.: John Wyclif, 6652, 6872; Metropolitan visitations, 5618; William Courtenay, archbishop, 5630
Daily living, 6609
Dale abbey (Derby.), 6115–17
Dale, Marion K.: Court roll, 4703; Household book, 4603
Dales, Richard C.: Anonymi De Elementis, 6945; Grosseteste, 6578–9
Dallaway, James: Antiquities of Bristowe, 2982; Heraldry, 472; Sussex, 1840
Dalmais, Irénée: Liturgy, 1329
Dalrymple, John: Feudal property, 4647
Dalton, John N.: Ordinale, 5716; Ottery St. Mary, 6125; Windsor MSS., 6068
Daly, Lowrie J.: Walter Burley, 1459
Damon, Phillip W.: A note on the Neckham canon, 6607
Danegeld, **463**; 3047. *See* Inquisitio geldi
Danelaw, 2726, 4403, 4980, 6115

Danes, 1106, 1496, 2315, 2485, 2576, 2580, 2592, 2599

Daniel, Glyn E.: ed. Ancient peoples and places, 761; ed. Antiquity, 721; Chamber-tombs, 1981; Hundred years, 85; Personality of Wales, 1435; Prehistoric people, 1430; Prehistoric Wales, 1984
— Walter: Ailred, 1490, 6637

Daniell, Walter V.: Manual of topography, 1506

Daniel-Rops, Henry (pseud. of Petiot, Jules C. H.): Le miracle irlandais, 1166

Daniel-Tyssen, John R.: Aid for Black Prince, 3174, 3279; Battle abbey liberties, 6359; Lewes priory, 6365; Liber niger, 3174; Malling, 4906

Dansey, William: Horae decanicae, 6840

Danto, Arthur C.: Philosophy of history, 242

Darby, Henry C.: Cambridge region, 1561; Cambridgeshire (V.C.H.), 1529; Domesday geography, 3044; Draining of the fens, 4717, 4991; Historical geography, 610, 1465

Darbyshire, Hubert S.: Methley, 4937

Dark Age Britain, 1442, 2475; Map, 604

Darley abbey (Derby.), 6118

Darlington, Ida: London consistory court, 4546; London record office, 1726
— Reginald R.: Æthelwig, abbot of Evesham, 6383; Annales Winchecumbensis, 1453, 2775, 6161; Anglo-Norman historians, 387; 2904, 2921, 2937, 2981; Darley abbey cartulary, 6118; Ecclesiastical reform, 2715; Exon Domesday, 3011; Glapwell charters, 4430; History of towns, 178; Inquisitio geldi, 1529, 3066; Last phase, 2577; Norman Conquest, 3982; V.C.H. Wilts., 1529, 3034; Vita Wulfstani, 2316, 5843; Worcester cartulary, 5828

Dart, John: Canterbury, 5623

Dartford (Kent), 3166, 5125

Dartmoor forest, 3915, 3921, 5005

Darwin, Francis D. S.: Recluse, 5887
— Kenneth: Irish records, 1078

Dasent, Sir George W.: Sagas, 2171, 2303, 2449, 2451

Dashwood, George H.: Chamberlain's accounts, 5205; Norfolk feet of fines, 3585; Subsidy roll, 3175

Daumet, George: Calais, 5330

Daunt, Marjorie: London English, 5149, 6984

Dauphin, Henri: L'Érémitisme, 6666

Davenport, Frances G.: Decay of villeinage, 1468, 4959; Manorial history, 4689; Norfolk manor, 4819, 4954

Daventry, priory (Northants.), 6286

Davey, C. R.: Diocesan accounts, 5648

David, St., 2123, 2321. See St. David's
— I, king of Scotland, 4646
— II, Acts of, 4088
— of London, 1448, 6514

David, Charles W.: Conquest of Lisbon, 2858; Henry I, 1439; Robert Curthose, 3983, 5675; Simeon of Durham, 2157

Davidson, Hilda R. E.: The sword, 912, 2476
— James: Devonshire bibliography, 1603
— James Bridge: A.-S. charters, 2194
— James Milne: Roman Scotland, 2091

Davies, Constance Bullock: Caerlaverock, 4295
— Cecily: Provisors, 6761
— Ellis: Roman Walls, 2089
— Elwyn: Celtic studies, 317, 2124; Welsh place-names, 640
— James Conway: Black book of St. David's, 5880F; Baronial opposition, 4115; Cartae antiquae, 3759; Common law writs, 3662; Despenser war, 4116; Dominicans in Wales, 5987A; Edward II's chamber, 3118; Episcopal acts, 5879; Felony in Wales, 3675; Giraldus Cambrensis, 2881; Memoranda rolls, 491; 1441; Newcastle shipping, 5382; Prior's kitchen, 113; 1044; Records of church in Wales, 790; Welsh assize roll, 3639; Wool customs accounts, 5332
— John Silvester: An English Chronicle, 2829; Southampton, 5103; Tropnell cartulary, 4490
— Oliver: Roman mines, 2081; Irish pipe roll, 3099
— Richard G.: Notes on crisis (1386–8), 4117
— Robert: Jews of York, 3950; Records of York, 5304
— Robert Rees: Baronial accounts, 4618; Chester, 7223; Law of the March, 3640; Marc Bloch, 252; Owain Glyn Dŵr, 4219; Twilight of Welsh laws, 2231
— Walter: Lewis Glyn Cothi, 7030
— William Llewelyn: National Library, 1053
— William Samuel: De invectionibus, 6573
— William Twiston: John Bale, 8

Davis, Alfred H.: Thorne's chronicle, 2158, 2959, 6183
— Eliza Jeffries: Guide, 90, 716; London eyre (1321), 3579; London loans, 3253, 5503; Modus tenendi parliamentum, 3349; Norman London, 1746; Parliamentary election (1298), 3434; Trimoda, 2621

— Francis N.: Registrum Johannis Peckham, 5610; Rotuli Hugonis de Welles, 5746; Rotuli Ricardi de Gravesend, 5747; Rotuli Roberti Grosseteste, 5748
— Godfrey R. C.: Cartularies, 4401, 6071
— Harold T.: Zosimus, 2025
— Henry W. Carless: Anarchy documents, 1448; Appreciation of, 1489; Balliol College, 7117; Battle abbey, 2838; Bury St. Edmunds, 5257; Canon law, 6437; Companion to English history, 1192; Davis papers, 1466; Edmund Rich, 5626; Normans and Angevins, 1188; Regesta, 3779; St. Paul's lands, 1458; Stubbs, 1208
— J. F.: Lollards and textiles, 6868
— James E.: Windsor, 5033
— Myer D.: Anglo-Jewish divorce, 3951; Hebrew deeds, 3935; Jews of Ipswich, 3951; Jews of Lincoln, 3951
— Norman: Beowulf, 2331; Paston letters, 4610
— Ralph H. C.: Balliol College, 7117; Coventry charter, 5273; Earl Gloucester, 1453; East Anglia, 2576; Geoffrey de Mandeville, 3984; Gesta Stephani, 2880; Kalendar of Abbot Samson, 6338; King Stephen, 2894, 3984; King Stephen and the Earl of Chester, 2880, 3981; Monks of St. Edmund, 6345; Oxford charters, 5235; Regesta, 3779
Davison, Brian K.: Castle, 823
Dawes, Michael C. B.: Registrum, 5802
Dawson, Christopher H.: Piers Plowman, 7026
— Warren R.: A leechbook, 6946
Day, Mabel: Mum and the Sothsegger, 7049
Dayman, Edward A.: Statuta Sarisberiensis, 5804
Deacon and Jewess, 1482, 3954
Deamer, Percy: Carols, 7207
Dean (Oxon.), 4848
— Forest of, 3892, 3896, 3900, 3908, 5500
Dean, James, Armagh MSS.: 1079
— Ruth J.: Anglo-Norman studies, 37; Vising, 298
Deanesly, Margaret: Æthelberht, 2534; Archdeacons, 2716; Early minsters, 2696; Familia of Canterbury, 1458; Pope Gregory, 2308; Gildas, 1452, 2162; History of the church, 1275; Lollard Bible, 1330, 6653; Pre-conquest church, 1276, 2697; Rolle's Incendium, 6679; Roman influences, 2097; Schools, 924; Sidelights, 2698; St. Augustine, 2698
De Banco rolls (Northumb.), 3591. *See* Plea rolls

Debts, London, 5154
Decembrio, Pier Candido: Correspondence, 6928
Decretal collections in England, 6430
Decretals, English, 6429–30
— of Innocent III, 6429
Deddington (Oxon.), 4851
Dedications of churches, 1154
Deedes, Cecil: Miscellaneous records, 5656; Register of Ewell, 4896; Register of Robert Rede, 5654; Registrum de Pontissara, 5818; Statutes of Chichester, 5658
Deeds. *See* Charters, 57 and **636–47**; 422, 3220, 4402, 7224;
    Adderbury, 4844
    Buckinghamshire, 1547
    Cambridge, Queens' College, 4435
    Clayton-le-Moors, 4450
    Dulwich, 4891
    Gloucester, 5090
    Great Yarmouth, 5214
    Hull, 5292
    John Rylands Library, 1037
    Kent, 4778
    King's Lynn, 5205
    Lambeth Palace Library, 4778
    Newcastle-upon-Tyne, 5218
    North County, 4433
    North Staffordshire, 6331
    Norwich, 5211
    Oswestry, 4864
    Oxford, Balliol College, 4465, 7073
    — Bodleian Library, 4407
    — Christ Church College, 6286
    — New College, 4844
    — Oriel College, 4848
    Shaw Hill, 4449
    Walsall, 5255
    Westmeston, 4482
    Wombourne, 4471
Deeley, Ann: Papal provision, 6762
Deeping, Abbot John: Chronicon Petriburgense, 2834
De excidio et conquestu Britanniae, 2162
Defamation, law of, 1246
Defarrari, Roy J.: Orosius, 2025
De Fonblanque, Edward B.: House of Percy, 4576
Deganwy (Denbighs.), 5022
De Gruchy, Guy F. B.: Exchequer entries, 3103
Dehio, Ludwig: Innocenz IV, 6730
Deighton, Herbert S.: Clerical taxation, 3476, 6823
De injusta vexatione Willelmi, 2157, 5675
De inventione S. Crucis, 1112
Deira, 2527

Delaborde, Henri F.: Oeuvres de Rigord, 2947

Delachenal, Roland: Charles V, 4175; Chroniques de Jean II et Charles V, 2845, 2883

Delany, Vincent T. H.: Maitland, 1482

De la Poles of Hull, 5375

Delapré (Northants.), nuns of, 6262

Delatte, Paul: Règle de S. Benôit, 5911

Delaville le Roulx, Joseph M. A.: Hospitaliers, 6042

Delehaye, Hippolyte: Les légendes, 148

Delepierre, Octave: Edward III, 2911

Delisle, Leopold V.: Actes de Henri II, 51; 3823; Album, 433; Baudri's poem, 619; Extrait d'une chronique française, 2897; Guillaume de Jumièges, 2908; Ordericus Vitalis, 2937; Powicke on, 1489; Templar finances, 6060; Torigni's chronicle, 2962; William Marshall's seal, 459

Dell, Richard F.: Archives, 130

Delorme, Ferdinand: Opera Rogeri Bacon, 6538, 6540

Delpit, Jules: Collection générale, 3811

Dema or Judex, 2208

Demangeon, Albert: Géographie, 611

Demarest, E. B.: Consuetudo regis, 4742; The firma unius noctis, 3045; The hundred pennies, 2210, 3045; Inter Ripam et Mersham, 3045

Demense farming, 4957–8, 4989, 5000

Demougest, Émilienne: German invasions, 2535

Dempster, Germaine: Canterbury Tales, 7001

De Navarro, José M.: Bronze age, 4429; Celts, 1430

Denbigh, Honour of, 4943B

Denbighshire, 1912–15

Dendy, Frederick W.: Adventurers of Newcastle, 5219; De banco rolls, 3591

Dene, Forest of. See Dean

— William de: Historia Roffensis, 5795

Denholm-Young, Noël N.: Archives of Christ Church, 6286; Barons' war, 1467; Bodleian catalogue, 1027; Bury's Liber epistolaris, 427, 1467, 6561; Carlaverock, 474, 1467, 4295; County gentry, 473; Cursus, 1451, 1467; Delapré chronicle, 6262; Edward of Windsor, 1467, 3119; Eudo Dapifer, 1467; Fleta, 1467, 2987; Feudal society, 1467, 4648; Handwriting, 385; Hereford map, 606, 1467; History and heraldry, 474; Isabella de Fortibus estates, 4943; Kirkstall chronicle, 1464, 2910, 6405; Letter from Council to pope, 6735; Merchants of Cahors, 1467; Matthew Cheker, 1467; Paper constitution, 1467, 4046; Richard de Bury, 1467, 6563; Richard of Cornwall, 4096; Robert Carpenter, 1467, 4048; Seignorial administration, 4619; Thomas de Wykes, 2983; Tournament, 1450, 1467; Vita Edwardi, 1467, 2971; Walter of Henley, 1467; Winchester-Hyde chronicle, 1467, 2767; Yorks. monastic archives, 6389

Denifle, Henri: La désolation des églises, 4176

Denmark, Bibliography, 50

Denney, Anthony H.: Sibton abbey estates, 6349

Denton (Sussex), 4899

— Jeffrey H.: Royal free chapels, 6066

Deodands, 3223

De officiis ecclesiasticis, 1343

Deor, 2328

De Paor, Liam: Ireland, 761

— Maire: Ireland, 761

Depopulation, 4941

Déprez, Eugène: Charters, 1426; Chronique de Jean le Bel, 2916; La conférence d'Avignon, 1458; La France et l'Angleterre, 4244; Les ambassades anglaises, 3818; Les préliminaires, 4177; L'Europe occidentale, 1182; Seals, 417

Dept, Gaston G.: Les influences anglaise, 4016; Les marchands flamands, 5427

Deputy Keeper of Public Records: 112; Reports of, 967, 3144, 3752, 3755, 3757, 3769–70, 3807, 3830, 3856, 3863, 3865, 3871–2, 3889

— (Ireland), 1076

— (Northern Ireland), 1077

Derby, All Saints, 5053, 6838

Derby, Henry, earl of (Henry IV), 4601

Derbyshire: Archives, 4431; Bibliography, 1599; Charters 1601, 4429–32; Church, 1529; County history, 1433, 1529, 1601, 6117; County journals and societies, 1600, 1782; Domesday, 1529, 1601; Feet of fines, 3487, 3542; Feudal tenures, 4349–50, 4431; Inquests, 4350; Manors and villages, 4728–31; Pleas, 3543–4; Pipe rolls, 3087; Religious houses, 6114–18; Subsidy rolls, 3155; Urban history, 5052–3

Dering, Sir Edward, antiquary, 1429

Dermot, Song of, 2954

De Roisy, Armand: Les routes des laines, 5409

Derolez, René: Orosius, 7225; Runes, 354

Descriptio Cambriae, 2881

Deserted villages, 766, 4802A, 4836, 4950, 5453. See Lost villages

Desiderata Curiosa, 6117

Desjardins, Ernest: Peutinger's Tabula, 2032

Des Marez, Guillaume: (Étude), Maitland's review, 1482

Desmond, first earl of, 1438

Despenser, family, 4116

— Henry, bishop, 3418, 4188

Dessubré: Bibliographie des Templiers, 6050

Destrez, Jean: La Pecia, 7085

Dethier, F.: Mélanges à Rita Lejeune, 4007

Detsicas, A. P.: Samian bowl, 2045

Deutsche Zeitschrift für Geschichtswissenschaft, 153

Deutsches Archiv für Erforschung des Mittelalters, 154

Devizes, Richard de: Annals of Winchester, 2767; Chronicon, 1089, 1101, 1113–14, 1123, 2859

Devlin, Sister Mary Aquinas: Brinton's sermons, 6701

Devon, countess of: Accounts, 4519

— earl of, Seals, 459

Devon, Frederick: Issues of exchequer, 3107; Thomas de Brantingham roll, 3106

Devonshire: Antiquities, 1470; Bibliography, 1602–4; Charters, 2196, 4693; Church, 5714–23; County history, 1522, 1529, 1611–13; County journals and societies, 1605–10; Domesday, **465**; 1529, 3011, 3019; Feet of fines, 3487, 3545; Feudal tenures, 4351; Inquests, 4348; Manors and villages, 4732–4; Parliament, 3456–7; Pipe rolls, 3088–9; Ports, 5390; Religious houses, 6119–27; Silver mines, 5514; Taxation, 3156–7; Urban history, 5054–64

Devotional writings, **677–80**

Dew, Edward N.: Hereford registers, 5727, 5729

Dewsbury Church (Yorks.), 5289

Diack, Francis C.: Pict inscriptions, 355

Dialogus de Scaccario, 1113, 1498, 3005, 3007

Diaz, Albert J.: Microforms, 4

Dibben, L. B.: Chancellor, 3840

Dibdin, Sir Lewis T.: Canon law, 6437

— Thomas F.: Typographical antiquities, 7212

Diceto, Ralph de. 1114, 1124, 2860, 5768

Dickens, Arthur G.: East Riding and Hull, 1870; Heresy and protestantism, 6869; Register of Butley priory, 6346; Shire and archbishop's privileges, 5305

Dickering, deanery of (Yorks.), 5876

Dickins, Bruce: Bibliography of, 1433;

Dream of the Rood, 2328; Early Middle English texts, 6986; ed. Early Cultures, 1429, 1989; Essays for (Anglo-Saxon England), 1433; Heathenism, 2656; J. M. Kemble, 2201; Place-names, 623, 631, 638; Runes, 356, 2353; St. David, 2123; William of Newburgh, 2932

Dickinson, Francis H.: Indexes, 5588; Kirkby's Quest, 3183, 4382; Lay subsidies, 3183; Nomina villarum, 3183, 4382

— John: Statesman's Book, 6643

— John C.: Austin canons, 1437, 5953; ed. Ecclesiastical history, 1276; Monastic life, 1292; Shrine of Walsingham, 6261

— Joycelyne G.: Blank charters, 3841; Congress of Arras (1435), 4249

— William C.: Chronicle of Melrose, 2824

Dickson, Marie P.: Consuetudines Beccenses, 1146

— William: Chronica de Alnewyke, 6272; Pipe rolls, 3092

— William Purdie: Mommsen, 2048

Dictionaries of:

— abbreviations, 402–3, 409

— Anglo-Saxon, 277, 279, 283

— archaeology and art, 763–4, 784, 845

— architects, 797

— biography, **65–6**; 797, 987, 1268, 1422

— Celtic languages, **42–4**

— church history, **164–5**, **168**, and **858**; 593, 5881

— English history, 1187, 1195

— English language, 282, 286–8

— French language, **37–8**

— genealogy and heraldry, 493, 497

— geography, 593, 1266

— heraldry, 493

— Irish language, 344, 346, 348, 350

— Latin language, **38–40**

— liturgy, 1265

— Middle English, 281

— place-names, 632

— theology, **164–5**

— topography, 600

Dictionary of National Biography, 531

Didier, Noël: Henri de Suse, 6460

Dietrich, Edward: Aelfric, 2292

Dietz, Frederick C.: Government finance, 3270

Dietze, Gottfried: Property in Magna Carta, 3289

Dieulacres abbey (Staffs.), 2820, 6328

Digby, George W.: Bayeux Tapestry, 4276

Dilecti filii procuratores (papal decree), 5713

Dilks, Thomas Bruce: Bridgwater archives, 5247; Summons, 3221, 3608

Dillon, Harold A.: Costume, 914; Goods of Thomas, Duke of Gloucester, 4746; Ordinances of chivalry, 3503A
— Myles: Book of Rights, 2245; Catalogue of Irish MSS., 997; Celtic realms, 2125; Cycles of kings, 2410; Early Irish literature, 2411; Early Irish society, 2248; Irish language, 349; Lebor Gabála Érenn, 2404
Dimetian code, 2222, 2224, 2226
Dimock, James F.: Giraldus Cambrensis, 2881, 6573; St. Hugh, 5742
Dinas Powys (Glam.), 1969
Dinnseanchas (journal), 622
Dioceses: Administration, 6803; Histories, 6790; Limits of, 6794; Records, **755–92**
Diodorus Siculus, 2025 (k)
Diplomatic, **50–3**; 304, 1451, 1487, 2215, 3823, 3837–8
— documents, 955, 3762, 3793, 7223–4
Dispensing power, royal, 1444, 3278
Dit (Le) de Guillaume, 1112, 2861
Dittmer, Luther: Worcester fragments, 7183
Dix, Elizabeth J., Action of trespass, 3702
— Gregory: Liturgy, 1331
Dixon, William H.: Fasti Eboracenses, 5867
Dobbie, Elliott: A.-S. poetic records, 2327; St. Guthlac, 2310
Dobie, Marryat R.: National Library, 1062; Hubert's Celts, 1997
Doble, Gilbert H.: Cornish saints, 1161, 2666; Ordinale, 5716
Dobson, Brian: ed. Birley essays, 2045
— Dina P.: Somerset archaeology, 762
— Richard Barrie: Abbot John Ousthorp, 6418; Last monks, 6132; Peasants' revolt, 4145; Richard Bell, prior, 5696
Docking, Thomas, 1448, 6024
Doctors' incomes, 6951
Documenta Antiqua Franciscana, 6007
Documentation Cistercienne, 5931
Documents français, 3811
— inédits, 1093
Dodd, Arthur H.: Caernarvonshire, 1902A
— William: Newcastle-upon-Tyne, 5221
Dodds, Madeleine Hope: Bishop's boroughs, 5697; Freemen of Newcastle, 5220
Dodgson, John McN.: Brunanburh, 2342; English in Cheshire, 2559; Place-names, 636, 2554
Dodsworth MSS. (Bodleian), 1024
Dodsworth, Roger: Inquisitions, 3873
— William: See of Sarum, 5806
Dodwell, Barbara: Bacton charters, 1453; Commendation, 3063; Free peasantry,

2628, 3021; Holdings, 4955; Norfolk Domesday, 3053; Norfolk feet of fines, 3582; Norwich cathedral, 5785
— Charles R.: Bayeux Tapestry, 4276; Illuminations, 885; St. Albans psalter, 902
Dol, Baudri, bishop of, **619**
Dolley, Reginald H. Michael: Anglo-Irish coinage, 679; Anglo-Irish monetary policies, 3248; Carolingian coins, 678; Coinage and coins, 677; General article on coinage, 1485; Numismatic research, 646; Reading University collection, 704; Rome Congress, coins, 647; Stenton essays, 669, 1454; Sulgrave brooch, 7225; Ulster Museum coins, 704
Dollinger, Philippe: La Hanse, 5428
Domerham, Adam of: Historia, 6309, 6313
Domesday Book, **463–71**; 448, 579, 1455, 1470, 1497–8, 1529, 1576, 1601, 1653, 1800, 2636, 4718, 5004, 5014, 5144, 5347, 6157, 6173, 6326
— Monachorum, 1529, 3070, 5602
— of Ipswich, 5260
— Roll (Chester), 3857
Domestic architecture, 814–22, 1435, 1485, 1495
— manners, 1382
Dominic, prior of Evesham, 6383
Dominican friars, 1428, 5980–99, 6590–3
Dominion, doctrine of, 1457, 6568. *See also* Wyclif
Domus Conversorum, 3946
Donagan, Alan: Collingwood's Philosophy, 241
Donahue, Charles: Celtic literature bibliography, 317, 2406
Donaldson, Ethelburt Talbot: Beowulf, 2335
— Gordon: Scotland, 1178
— R.: Sponsors to Durham benefices, 5698
Doncaster (Yorks.), borough of, 5290
— deanery of, 5876
— petition (1321), 4116
Donkin, Robert A.: Cattle on Cistercian estates, 4992; Checklist of works, 5935; Cistercian grange, 4994; Cistercian sheep-farming, 4993; Cistercian wool, 5411; Settlement of Cistercian estates, 4941, 5936; Urban property of Cistercians, 5937
— William C.: Northumberland bibliography, 1514, 1768
Donnelly, James S.: Grange economy, 4994
Dopping, Anthony: Modus tenendi in Hibernia, 3347A

Dopsch, Alfons: Essays, 1434; Wirtschaftliche Grundlagen, 1367

Dorchester, A.-S. bishop of, 2720

— (Dorset), Records, 5065

Dore abbey (Herts.), Annals, 1114, 2756

Doreward, John (Speaker), 3429

Dorez, Léon: Morosini Chronicle, 2930

Dorsch, Theodor S.: Leland and Stow, 134

Dorset: Antiquities, 737; Bibliography, 1614–16; Charters, 6364; Church, 1529; County history, 1517, 1529, 1620–1; County journals and societies, 1617–18, 1806; County records, 1504, 1619; Domesday, 1529, 3020; Feet of fines, 3487, 3546; Feudal tenures, 4354; Inquests, 4352–3, 4379; Manors and villages, 4735–7; Monuments, 737; Pleas, 3608; Pipe rolls, 3090; Religious houses, 6128–31; Urban history, 5065–8; Wills, 4523

Dottin, Georges: ed. Revue Celtique, 324; Littérature gaélique, 2406; Manuel, 318

Doubleday, Herbert A.: ed. Complete peerage, 556; V.C.H., 1197, 1529

Douce Catalogue (Bodleian), 1021

— Francis: Customs of London, 2789

Doucet, Roger: Les Finances anglaises, 5504

Douch, Robert: Dorset, 1615

Douët d'Arcq, Louis: Chronique, 2926; Seals, 457

Douglas, Archibald A. H.: The Bruce, 2792

— David C.: Abingdon surveys, 3068, 6086; A.-S. Chronicle, 2142; Conqueror's companions, 564; Domesday monachorum, 3070, 5602; Domesday survey, 3048; Dugdale, 1147; Edward Confessor and William, 2578; English historical documents, 17, 1177; English scholars, 134; Feudal documents, 6336; Hatton's seals, 4410; Lanfranc and Domesday, 1455; Norman achievement, 3985; Norman Conquest, 3980, 3986, 4649; Réussites normandes, 3985; Social structure, 1825, 2628, 4404, 4956, 5450; William the Conqueror, 3986

Douie, Decima L.: Adam de Marisco, 6604; Archbishop and Chapter of York, 5869; Heresy of Fraticelli, 6016; Pecham, 1450, 5636; Registrum Johannis Peckham, 5610; St. Hugh, 5742

Douthwaite, William R.: Gray's Inn, 7149

Dove, Patrick E.: ed. Domesday studies, 3047

Dover (Kent), 5320, 5324

— interdict on, 1471

— priory, 6189

— St. Martin's library, 1041

Dowden, John: Scottish church, 2685

Dowell, Stephen: Taxation, 3234

Dowle, Anthony: Irish coins, 679

Down (Dun), battle of, 2924

Downer, L. J.: Leges Henrici, 2186

Downside Review (journal), 116

Doyle, James E.: Baronage, 558

Doyle-Davidson, Walter A. G.: Works of More, 2927

Drake, Francis: Eboracum, 5302, 5868

— Henry H.: Blackheath (Kent), 1693

Drakelowe (Derby), 4431

Drama in churches, 842, 6975, 6985, 6993, 6998

Drapers, 5189

Dray, William H.: Philosophy of history, 243

Drayton charters, 5029

Dream of the Rood, 2328

Dreiser, George F.: Year Book, 3649

Drengage, 4975

Dress, Academic, 7086; Legal, 3688. See Costume

Dreux, Peter of, 4104

Drew, Charles: Early parochial organization, 6841

— Charles D.: Manors of Iwerne Valley, 4735

— Joseph S.: Account rolls, 4736; St. Swithun's manorial accounts, 1468, 5815

Drinkwater, Charles H.: Bailiff's accounts, 5240; Coroners, 3602; Merchant gild, 5243

— G. N.: Gateshead charters, 5070

Driver, John T.: Papacy and Hereford, 6763; Parliamentary burgesses, 3458

Drögereit, Richard: Anglo-Saxon expansion, 2508; Saxon and Anglo-Saxon, 2536; Style in A.-S. charters, 2611

Drogheda, William of, 6437, 6448

Drokensford, John de, bishop, 5589, 5591

Drucker, Lucy: Feet of fines, 3616

Druids, the, 761, 1999

Druitt, Herbert: Costume, 913

Dryburgh, Adam of, 5962, 6324

Duan Albanach (Irish poem), 1120

Dublin, Trinity College MSS., 1083

— Fifteenth-Century Chronicle, 2869

— Scandinavian Kingdom of, 2585A

Dublin Review (journal), 117

DuBois, Louis F.: Ordericus Vitalis, 2937

— Marguerite M.: Ælfric, 2292

Du Boulay, Francis R. H.: Age of ambition, 4200, 5451; Archbishop as territorial magnate, 5621; Canterbury piperoll, 5608; Charitable subsidies, 6824;

Du Boulay, Francis R. H. (*cont*.):
Demesne farming, 4957; English church and papacy, 6734; Friars *v.* Seculars, 5977; Henry of Derby's expeditions, 7223; Kent documents, 3165, 4784; Lordship of Canterbury, 5619; McKisack essays, 4132; Pagham estates, 4901

Duby, Georges: Seigneurie, 1368, 4951

Du Cange, Charles Dufresne: Glossarium, 305

Ducarel, Andrew C.: Church of St. Katharine, 6230; Testamenta Lambethana, 4517

Duchesne, André: Scriptores, 1096; Guillaume de Jumièges, 2908

Duckett, Eleanor S.: Alcuin, 2280, 2295; Alfred, 2579; A.-S. saints, 2280; Bede, 2297; St. Dunstan, 2280, 2293; Wandering Saints, 2280

— Sir George F.: Charters, 5915, 6421; Harwood evidences, 4500; Hostages, 3820; Visitations, 5917

Dudden, Frederick Homes: Pope Gregory I, 2699

Dudding, Reginald C.: Manors of Alford, 4805

Dudley, barons of, 4579

— Donald R.: Roman conquest, 2038; Tacitus' Annals, 2025

Dudo of St. Quentin, 1096, 2949

Dueball, Margarete: Die Suprematstreit, 5853

Duell, Jeanne Unger: Jeanne d'Arc, 4264

Dufay, Guillaume (Early music), 7193

Duff, Edward Gordon: Book trade, 7217; John Rylands library catalogue, 1035

Du Fresne de Beaucourt, Gaston: Histoire Charles VII, 4250

Dugdale Society (Warw.), 1845

Dugdale, Sir William: Baronage, 559, 4650; Biography, 1147; Monasticon, 1147; Origines, 1249; St. Paul's cathedral, 5769; Summons to great councils, 3311; Warwickshire, 134; 1849

Duggan, Charles: Becket dispute, 6506; Decretals, 6429–30; English church and papacy, 6734; Richard of Ilchester, 6520

Duhem, Pierre: Système du monde, 1420

Duignan, William H.: A.-S. charters, 2201

Duke, John A.: Columban Church, 2686

Dukery Records, 6279

Dulwich (Surrey), 4891, 4894

Dumbleton, John, 6627, 6971

Dumfries and Galloway Natural History and Antiquarian Society, 208

Dümmler, Ernst: Alcuin, 2295; Geschichtsquellen, 66; St. Boniface, 2299

Du Mont, Francis M.: trans. Voretzsch, 299

Dun, battle of, 2924

Duncan, Archibald A. M.: Declaration of Arbroath (1320), 4077, 7224; Regiam Majestatem, 2989

— Leland L.: Kent wills, 4530; Rochester wills, 4534; Testamenta Cantiana (W. Kent), 4536

Duncan-Jones, Arthur S.: Frere's Liturgy, 1333

Duncombe, John: Three hospitals, 6187

Dun Cow, book of, 2393

Duncumb, John: Hereford, 1670

Dunham, William H., Jr.: Casus placitorum, 2993; Complaint and reform, 5338; English government at work, 3836; Fane fragment, 3312; Hengham, 2997; Lord Hastings' retainers, 4284; Magna Carta, 3285; Winchester parliament (1449), 3423

Dunheved, Thomas (1327), 4139

Dunkenhalgh (Lancs.), 4445

Dunkin, Alfred J.: Coggeshall's Works, 2850

— John: Bicester, 4852

Dunlop, Douglas M.: Arabic medicine in England, 6966

— R.: The Bruce, 1458, 2792

Dunning, Gerald C.: A.-S. trade, 1442; Belgae, 1994; Soldiers and settlers, 2101

— Patrick: Letters of Innocent III, 5559

— Robert W.: Consistory court, 6475; Hylle cartulary, 4469

Dunn-Pattison, Richard P.: The Black Prince, 4118

Dunsaete Ordinance, 2211

Dunstable (Beds.), 3147

— Priory of, Annals, 1103, 1114, 1459, 2929; Charters of, 6075–7

Dunstable, John: Complete works, 7182

Duns Scotus, 6565–7, 6625

Dunstan, St., 317; 2280, 2283, 2303

Dunstan, Gordon R.: Bishop Lacy's Register, 5717

Dunster (Som.), 4468, 4867, 5022

Dupont, Gustave: Channel Isles, 1954

— L. M. Emilie: Commynes' Mémoires, 2851; Révolte de Warwick, 2901; Waurin's chronicle, 2978

Durand, Ursin: Collectio, 1110; Thesaurus, 1109; Voyage littéraire, 2973

Durham: Cathedral and diocese: 768–72; 1529; Annales, 2145; Architecture of cathedral, 785; Archives, 113; 1043–4, 1622; Bishops, 1625–6, 2157, 2711, 2721, 7160; Chronicles and records, 2157, 2714, 3865, 5510; Courts, 6459; Farm-

ing, 5000; History of, 2157, 2302, 6790; Halmote, 4739, 5684; Library, 1622, 7160; Lollards, 6873; Monasteries, 6132–9; Patrimony, 2723, 3864, 3866, 5672; Rituale, 1320; Seals, 458; Siege of, 2157; Valuation, 6781
— college rolls, 7061
— County and palatinate: Boldon Book, 3076; Church, **768–72**; 1529; County history, 1529, 1625–9, 2157, 4681; County journals and societies, 118, 135, 1623–4; County records, 196, 1044; Deeds, 4433; Feet of fines, 3592; Inquests, 4355; Law and society, 5455; Manors and villages, 4738–9; Palatinate, **576–8**; 1044, 1625–7, 1629, 1776, 5672; Pleas, 3547; Pipe rolls, 3085; Religious houses, 6132–9; Serfdom, 4959; Urban history, 5069–70; Wills, 4524
— St. Giles of, 6133
— University Journal, 118
Durham, Richard of, 2836
— Simeon of, 2123, 2157
Durkan, John: Scottish libraries, **131**
Duroselle, Jean B.: Fliche-Martin histoire, 1277
Durville, Georges: Commynes, 2851
Dutcher, George M.: Guide, 40
Duxbury (Lancs.), 4444
Dvornik, Franciscus, 1493
Dyer, Christopher: Population and agriculture, 4995, 5480; Redistribution of incomes, 4638, 4958
— George: Privileges of Cambridge, 7060
Dymmock, Andrew, 4208
Dymond, David P.: Archaeology, 716
— Robert: Churchwardens' accounts, 6838

Eadmer: Historia novorum, 2863, 6529; Life of Bregwine, 2300; Life of St. Odo, 1106; M.G.H., 1114; Miracles of St. Anselm, 1108; St. Dunstan, 2303; St. Oswald, 2311; St. Wilfrid, 2313; Vita Anselmi, 6527, 6529–30, 6535
Eager, Alan R.: Irish bibliography, 16
Ealdorman, 2634
Earldoms, 556, 3984, 4006, 4060, 4684, 4686
Earle, John: A.-S. charters, 2915; A.-S. Chronicle, 2141; St. Swithun, 2312
Early English MSS. in Facsimile, 441
Early English Text Society, Publs., 187; Facsimiles, 442
Early maps, 596
Earwaker, John P.: East Cheshire, 1572; Standish charters, 4444
Easson, David E.: North Sheet of Ordnance Survey, 604; Scottish monasteries, 1299

East, F. W.: The Heighington terrier, 4809
— Robert: Records of Portsmouth, 5097
East Anglia, 761, 1825, 4207, 4404, 4956, 7223
— Anglian (journal), 1818
— Anglian kings, 1433, 1496
— Anglian psalter, 903
Eastbourne (Sussex), manor of, 4910; Subsidy, 3195
Eastbridge, St. Thomas, hospital, 6187
Easter tables, 372, 376
Easterling, R. C.: Anglo-Norman custumal, 5055; Franciscans and Dominicans, 6027; Friars in Wales, 6027
Easton, Stewart C.: Roger Bacon, 6543
Eastry, Prior Henry: Register, 5601
Ebchester, William: Obituary roll, 5688
Ebel, Herman: Grammatica Celtica, 327
Ebert, Max: Reallexikon, 1962
Eccles (Kent), 2045
Ecclesiastical, courts. *See* Courts of Law
— History of England, 1276
— History Society, 174
— Reform (A.-S.), 2715
— Tenants-in-chiefs, 4644
— Terms, 1273
Eccleston, Thomas of, 1114, 6001, 6008, 6010
Echard, Jacques: Scriptores, 5985
Echols, Edward C.: Herodian, 2025
Eckhardt, Karl A.: A.-S. Gesetze, 2176
Eclipses, 6936
Economic history, **174–9** and **742–50**; 19, 95, 1465, 1500, 2039, 3691
— History Review, 119
— Journal, 120
Eddison, Eric R.: Egil's saga, 2445
Eddius Stephanus, 1100; Life of St. Wilfrid, 1100, 2284–5, 2313
Edgar, king, 2311; Canons, 2259; Charters, 1475; Coins, 1454, 7225; Coronation, 1475; Monasteries, 2271
Edinburgh, 1386, 1433, 2821
— Libraries, 79, 509, 1064
— National Museum (coins), 704
Edington (Wilts.), 4489, 6039
Edith of Wilton, 2304
Edmund, St. and king, 2189, 2305
Edmund (Rich) of Abingdon, St., 5626, 6665, 6695
Education, **916–25**; 1392–5, 6025
Edward the Elder, 1496, 2597, 2600
— the Martyr, 2715, 2718
— the Confessor: Arms of, 1454; Biography of, 2563, 2578, 2582, 3976; Canonization of, 6634; Laws of, 2185; Lives of, 1112–13, 2171; Seal of, 469; Writs of, 1433, 6236

Edward I: Biography of, 1452, 4062, 4064, 4066; Brabant, 4102; Chronicles of, **391**, 2733; Coinage, 709; Crusade, 4106; Elegy on, 7043; Funeral oration, 2852; Gascony, 4107; Hunting, 3898; Itinerary, 4050; King's Bench, 3510; Knights, 566, 4289; Legislation, 2987, 3339; Missions for, 1448; Monetary policies, 3252; Parliament, 3410; Policy towards earls, 4060, 4681; Private letters, 3754; Quo warranto, 1462, 3492; Relations with H.R.E., 4101, 4109; Relations with papacy, 6765; Scotland, 4072, 4086, 4279; State trials, 1482, 3519; Statutes, 1459; Welsh castles, 823; Welsh wars, 3131, 3787, 4059

— II: Baronial opposition, 4115–16, 4127, 4133–4, 4141; Bishops, 4119; Chronicles, **391**; 2733, 2825; Church and, 4119, 6739, 6770, 6799, 6827; Coinage, 709; Death, 1499, 4139; Deposition, 1455, 5795, 6341; Gesta, 2876; Guyenne, 1426; Itinerary, 4120; Lament of, 7043; Oath, 1455; Prince of Wales, 2876, 3121, 3125, 4053; Place in history, 4140; Scotland, 4075, 4077, 4081, 4085; Seal, 469; Vita, 1103, 1113, 2971

— III: Biographies, 4126; Chronicles, **391**; Count of Toulouse, 1448; Documents, 2882; Economic policy, 1500; Finance, 1469, 3231, 3236; Historia, 1103, 2898; Indenture system, 1455; Itineraries, 2843; John Gower and, 7019; Poems on reign, 7041, 7046, 7049; The Scots, 4082. *See* Hundred Years War

— IV: Arrivall, 2901; Biographies, 4215, 4228; Black Book, 3128; Chronicles, **392**; 2873, 2934; Coinage, 707; French expedition, 4281; In exile, 1446; Lord Hastings and, 5502

— V: Murder of, 4203

— the Black Prince, 1458, 2812, 3160, 3164, 3174, 3786A, 3862, 4118, 4180, 4943A, 5623

— Duke of York: Author of book on hunting, 3885

— of Windsor, 1467, 3119

Edwards, Anthony S. G.: A Lydgate bibliography, 7036

— B. J. N.: Roman Lancashire, 2045

— Edward: British Museum, 988; Hyde Abbey, 2165; Libraries, 974

— Elizabeth: Index, 109

— Henry J.: Caesar, 2025

— Sir John Goronwy: Ancient correspondence concerning Wales, 3784; Anonimalle Chronicle, 2787; Book of Prests, 3113; Brut, the, 2805; Carmarthen and

Cardigan, 1905; Common petitions, 3419; Commons in parliament, 3370; Confirmatio Cartarum, 3342; Crowland chronicle, 2900; Election (1450), 1459; Essays to, 3113; Flint pleas, 3637; Henry II and Wales, 4040; Higden, 2895; Historians and parliament, 3358; Huntingdonshire election, 3435; Itinerarium Ricardi, 1455; Justice in parliament, 3397; Littere Wallie, 3786; Majority rule in elections, 3435; Normans in Welsh March, 3987; Parliament, 1451; Parliamentary Committee (1398), 3421; Parliamentary personnel, 1459; Personnel of Commons, 3365; Plena potestas, 3365; Re-election to parliament, 3439; Taxation in common pleas, 3647; Third Crusade, 2906; Treaty of Leake (1318), 1448; Turberville treason, 1450; Welsh castles, 823; Welsh law books, 2232, 2239; William Stubbs, 1221

— Kathleen: Political importance of bishops, 4119, 6799; Register of R. Martival, 5801; Secular cathedrals, 6791; Social origins of bishops, 6799

— R. Dudley: Ireland, Papal provisions, 1438; Magna Carta Hibernica, 1445

Edwy, king, charter, 2191

Effigies, monumental, 917, 927

Egbert, archbishop of York, **323**; 2156, 2259, 2297

Egbert, Donald D.: Tickhill psalter, 886

Egerton, Sir Thomas: Exposicion of statutes, 3345A

Egginton (Derby.), 4730

Egil's Saga, 2445

Egremont (Cumb.), 5049

Egwin, St., 2285, 6380, 6383

Ehrlich, Ludwig: Exchequer and wardrobe (1270), 3133; Proceedings against crown, 3663; Year books, 3646

Ehwald, Rudolf: Aldhelm, 2296; Monumenta, 1114

Eigeas, Cormacan. *See* Cormacan

Eigenkirchentum (Das), 2710, 6786

Éigse (a journal of Irish studies), 231

Einstein, Lewis: Italian renaissance, 6914

Ekwall, Eilert: Bibliography of, 632; London population, 5167, 5474; London street names, 632, 5167; London subsidy rolls, 3172, 5157; Old English dialects, 278; Personal names, 577; Place-names, 632, 637, 1455; River names, 632; Scandinavians, 1465, 2580

Eld, John F.: Subsidy roll, 3200

Eleanor of Aquitaine, 4023, 4608

— of Castile, 4609

— of Provence, 2171

— Countess of Leicester, 4609

Elections, episcopal, 5799, 5821, 6400, 6447

Elfege, archbishop. *See* Ælfheah

Elfstrand, Percy: Swedish bibliography, 165

Elgee, Frank W.: Yorkshire, 762

— Harriet W.: Yorkshire, 762

Eliason, Norman: Ælfric, 441, 2292

Elijah of London, 3969

Ellacombe, Henry T.: Bitton parish, 4754; Executors of Richard de Gravesend, 4543, 5714

Ellard, Gerald: Alcuin, 2295

Ellekilde, Hans: Olrik's Vikings, 2458

Ellesmere (Salop), 4860

Ellesmere, Thomas Egerton: Statutes, 3345A

Elliott, Ralph W. V.: Runes, 357

Elliott-Binns, Leonard: Medieval Cornwall, 1587

Ellis, Alfred S.: Domesday landholders, 3032; Yorks. deeds, 4495; Yorks. landholders, 3037

— Clarence: Hubert de Burgh, 4049

— Sir Geoffrey. *See* Ellis, Sir Robert Geoffrey

— Sir Henry: Chronicle of Hulme, 2816; Dugdale, 1147; Domesday Book, 3009, 3049; Fabyan's Chronicle, 2866; Hall's Chronicle, 2889; Hardyng's Chronicle, 2890; John of Oxenedes Chronicle, 2939; Original letters, 3777; Polydore Vergil, 2968; Record of Caernarvon, 4943A; St. Paul's cathedral, 5769; Tower of London, 5163

— Henry John: B.M. charters, 1004; Facsimiles, charters, 444

— Sir Robert Geoffrey: Earldoms, 560, 4577

— Roger H.: ed. Jenkinson essays, 941; H.M.C., 111; 945; P.R.O., 953, 1440

— Thomas P.: Welsh law, 2233

Elloe (Lincs.), 4991

Elman, Peter: Expulsion of Jews, 3952

Elmer, prior of Canterbury, Epistolae, 5777

Elmham North (Norf.), 4454

Elmham, Thomas: Gesta Henrici V, 1103, 2877; Historia S. Augustini Cant., 2158, 6181; Liber Metricus, 2808, 2864; Vita Henrici V, 2972

Elrington, Christopher R.: Register of Roger Martival, 5801; V.C.H. handbook, 1530

Elsynge, Henry: Ancient method, 3313; Expeditio billarum, 3366

Elton (Hunts.), 4776

Elton, Charles Isaac: Kent tenures, 2644; Origins, 2537

— Charles J.: Manorial tenures, 6315; Origins, 2537

— Geoffrey R.: Parliamentary drafts, 3365; Practice of history, 257; Research facilities, 938; Sources, 256

— John: Corn milling, 4988

Elvey, G. R.: Luffield priory charters, 6263

Elwell (Dorset.), Account rolls, 4736

Ely, Church and diocese: 772–3; Bishop's official, 7224; Charters, 1475, 2164; Consistorial court, 6483; Inquisitio Eliensis, 3010; Liber Eliensis, 2164; Library, 1045; Manorial court, 4716, 5704; Privilege of abbey, 7225; Valuation, 6781

— Isle of, 1529

— Palatinate records, 112

Ely, Richard of, 2164; Gesta Herwardi, 2878

— Thomas of, 2164

Emanuel, Hywel D.: Hereford muniments, 5724; Patrynton register, 5880G; Records, 5879A, 5880E; Wade-Evans, 2229; Welsh laws, 2234, 2239

Embassies, 4108–9

Emden, Alfred B.: Cambridge register, 532, 7095; Dominicans, 5988; Donors of books, 7163; Learning, 1485; Oxford accounts, 7118; Oxford Hall, 7120; Oxford register, 533, 7119; Oxford University, 1428; Rashdall's Universities, 7090

Emerson, Everett H.: Reginald Pecock, 6630

Emerton, Ephraim: Correspondence of Gregory VII, 5555; St. Boniface, 2299

Emery, Richard W.: Friars of the sack, 6040; Latin translations, 52; Surnames, 578

Emlyn, Solomon: Historia placitorum coronae, 3665

Emma, Queen: Encomium, 1096, 1106, 1111, 2159

Emmerig, Oskar: Bataile of Agyncourte, 7046

Emmison, Frederick G.: Archives, 1507; Clapham Bayeux manor, 4702; Essex manorial documents, 4743; Essex parish records, 1632, 4740; Essex record office, 1631; Local history handlist, 1514; New sources, 109; Wills at Chelmsford, 4526

Empoli, Laurentius: Bullarium, 5969

Emsley, Kenneth: Justice in north-east England, 3868; Law and society, 3868, 5455

Emson, C. H.: Walden abbey, 6146
Enciclopedia Cattolica, 1269
Enclosures, 5001, 5018
Encomium Emmae, 1096, 1106, 1111, 2159
Engelmann, Wilhelm: Roman bibliography, 2014
Engle, Arthur: Numismatics, 680
— Jakob: Bemerkungen, 2873
— Karl: Die Organisation der Kaufleute, 5426
English Apocalypse, the, 888
— Dialect Society, 288
— Government at work, 3836
— Historical Documents, 17, 1177
— Historical Review, 121
— Historical Society, 188
— Place-Name Society, 189, 272, 623
English, Henry S.: Crowland and Burgh, 6215
Enstone (Oxon.), 4853
Entrèves, Alessandro Passerin d': Political theory, 1415
Epistolae Academicae, Oxon., 7062
— Cantuarienses, 5604
— Waldensis (Netter), 6611
Equity, 554–5; 3483, 3720
Erbe, Theodor: Mirk's Festial, 6697
Erchfont (Urchfont) (Wilts.), 4489
Erdeswicke, Sampson: Staffordshire, 1815
Erdmann, Axel: Home of Angles, 2509
— Carl: Papsturkunden, 1132
Erghome, John, 7049
Erichsen, Balder V. A.: Danish bibliography, 50
Erith, E. J.: Essex parish records, 1632
Eriu (journal), 232
Erlanger, Philippe: Marguerite d'Anjou, 4201
Ernout, Alfred: Latin dictionary, 306; Pliny, 2025
Ernulf, bishop of Rochester, 5794
Erpingham, North (Norf.), 487; 3586
Erskine, Audrey M.: Ecclesiastical courts, 6461; Financial records (Exeter), 5720; Lay subsidy, 3157
Escheators, 493; 3237, 4746, 5166, 7222
Esdaile, Arundell J. K., 131; B.M. Library, 989
Esposito, Mario: Alexander Neckham, 6608; St. Patrick, 2324
Essays in Agrarian History, 2626, 4981, 5488
— in Anglo-Saxon Law, 2612
— in Commemoration (St. Francis), 6034
— in Economic History, 1468
Essex: Antiquities, 737; 1529; Archives, 1504; Bibliography, 1529, 1630–4; Black Death, 5483; Charters, 2199, 4434–5;

Church, 1529, 4740; Consuetudo regis, 3045, 4742; County history, 1529, 1639–40, 4213; County journals and societies, 1635–8, 1732, 1818; County records, 4740, 4997; Domesday, 1529; Feet of fines, 3548; Feudal tenures, 3502; Forests, 3905; Freemen, 4742; Justices of peace, 3549; Labour conditions, 1468, 4149, 4155; Manors and villages, 4740–52, 4919, 6357; Parish records, 1632; Pleas, 3502; Religious houses, 6140–9; Taxation, 3158–9; Tithing lists, 4752; Topography, 1529; Urban history, 5071–5; Wills, 4525–6
Estate management, 659–61; 1008, 2209, 3127, 4519, 4830, 4943, 6349, 7106
Esteban, Eustasio: Analecta Augustiniana, 5966
Estoire de la guerre sainte, 1455
Ethelbert, archbishop of York, 323. See Æthelbert
Étienne de Rouen, 2949
Eton (Bucks.), Court roll, 4714
— Choirbook, 7187
— College, 7142
Études Carmélitaines, 5975
Eubel, Conrad: Bullarium, 6004; Hierarchia, 6711
Eudo Dapifer, 1467
Eugenius IV, pope, 1438, 5573
Eulogium historiarum, 2865
Eustace of Flay, mission of, 1447, 5523
Eustachius, 5626
Eutropius, 2025
Evans, Allan: Pegolotti, 5417
— Aneurin: Brut y Tywysogion, 2805
— Sir Arthur J.: Roman coinage, 658
— Austin P.: Translations, 52
— Cyril J. O.: Glamorgan, 1924; Monmouthshire, 1936
— Daniel: Welsh dictionary, 337
— Daniel Simon: St. David, 2321; Welsh saints, 2666
— Sir David L.: Flintshire ministers' accounts, 3859, 4620; Red Book of St. Asaph, 5880C; Wales of Black Prince, 4118
— Estyn: Prehistoric Ireland, 732
— George E.: Acts of bishops of St. David's, 5880E
— Howell T.: Wales and wars of roses, 4202
— J.: St. Germanus, 2108
— Joan: Art (1307–1461), 782; Jewels, 868; Lapidaries, 6948; Monastic life, 5922
— Sir John: Ancient British coins, 654; Bronze and stone implements, 768, 1982

— John Gwenogvryn: Aneirin, 2384; Black Book (Carmarthen), 2383; Geoffrey of Monmouth, 2166; Liber Landavensis, 5880A; Red Book of Hergest, 2386; Talisien, 2385; Texts of the Bruts, 2804; Welsh laws, 2223; Welsh MSS., 1054
— Maurice J.: Wiclif and Hus, 6656
— Myrddyn J. Bevan: Flintshire record office, 1916
— Sebastian: Geoffrey of Monmouth, 2166
— Seiriol A. J.: Ely chapter ordinances and visitation records, 5703
Eve, George W.: Heraldry, 478
Evelyn, John: Charters of London, 5158
Eversden, John de: Chronicon Buriensis, 2819; Florence of Worcester's Chronicle, 2981
Evesham (Worcs.), abbey, 465, 1114, 2899, 3035, 6202, 6380–3
— Adam, abbot of, 5742
— Æthelwig, abbot of, 2715, 6383
Evison, Vera: Fifth-century invasions, 2538
Ewald, Alexander C.: Public records, 948
— Paul: ed. Jaffé, 1131; Gregory I, 2308
Ewell (Surrey), 4896
Ewelme almshouse (Oxon.), 4693
Ewen, Cecil H. L.: Surnames, 578
Ewert, Alfred: Anglo-Norman, 37
Ewias Harold (Hereford), 6166
Ewing, William C.: ed. Woodward, 1751
Exceptiones ad cassandum brevia, 2996
Excerpta historica, 4282
Exchequer: 462–99; Records, 955, 955A, 956, 959–60, 3318, 3775, 4102, 7224; Red Book, 975, 1601; Memoranda rolls, 491–2; 956, 1441, 1458, 6216, 6311; History, 692, 952, 1458, 1493, 4004
— Chamber cases, 3511, 3649
— of the Jews, Plea rolls, 3482, 3496, 3518, 3933, 3939, 3955, 3964
— of pleas, 525; 3325, 3512
— Queen's, 1455, 3137
Excommunication, 6463, 6469, 6473, 6581
Execrabilis (papal decretal), 1482, 6437, 6762
Executive justice, 3669
Exempla, 6597, 6706. *See* Sermons
Exemption monastic, 6358
Exeter Book of Old English, 2310, 2327, 2337–8
— Cathedral and diocese: 773–4; 1459, 3156, 3785A, 4543, 6027, 6456, 6513
— City: Bibliography, 1604; Charters, 2194; Council of, 5060; Records of, 5055–6
— Jews of, 3947

— Lollards of, 6873
— Religious houses, 1147, 1442, 6124
— Research Group, 1608
— Roman, 2056
— St. Patrick's church, 6838
Exeter, Duke of, 4205
— Bartholomew of, 5721, 6456, 6513
— Stephen of: Annales de Monte Fernandi, 2755
Exmoor forest, 3895
Exon Domesday, 3009, 3011, 3019, 3028, 3032, 3034, 3040
Expeditio billarum, 3366
Exploration, 5394
Exposition of statutes, 3345A
Expugnatio Hibernica, 2881
Extents, or surveys: 471–3 and 666–7; 955, 955A, 4689, 4691, 4693, 4697, 4701, 4899, 4917, 4973;
Abingdon abbey, 3068, 6086
Allerton, 4930
Anglesey, 4943A, 6828
Arundel, 4908
Aylesbury, 4712
Bangor, 4943A, 6828
Banham, 4823
Banstead, 4898
Barnstone, 4842
Barnwell, 6098
Barton, 4933
Battle abbey, 6357
Blackbourne, 3188
Borley, 4744
Boston, 1723
Bradcar, 4823
Brecon, 5880F
Brill, 4712
Burton, 6326
Bywater, 4930
Caernarvon, 4943A, 6828
Canterbury, Christ Church, 3013
Cardiganshire, 5880F
Carmarthenshire, 5880F
Castle Combe, 4922
Cheswardine, 4860
Childs Ercall, 4860
Chiltington, 4904
Clarendon, 4923
Codicote, 6171
Colchester, St. John's, 6142
Condover, 4858
De Lacy, 4793
Denbigh, 181, 4943B
Dudley, 4579
Durham, 3864, 3866, 5672, 5682
Ellesmere, 4860
Eynsham, 6289
Glamorgan, 3785

Extents, or surveys (*cont.*):
  Gloucester, St. Peter's, 6157
  Gower, 5880F
  Guernsey, 1953
  Hadleigh, 4883
  Harlow, 4745
  Hatfield, 1677
  Heene, 4904
  Hertford, borough of, 1677
  Hospitallers, 6044
  Jersey, 1953
  Kelshall, 1677
  Kippax, 4930
  Lancashire, 4367, 4790
  Langar, 4842
  Lawling, 4748
  Ledston, 4930
  Leeds, 4930
  Little Hadham, 1677
  London, St. Paul's, 5759
  Long Melford, 4889
  Malling, 4906
  Manchester, 4791
  Merioneth, 4943A, 6828
  Monk Friston, 6410
  Newark-on-Trent, 4841
  Northamptonshire, 4827
  Oswestry, 4864
  Pembrokeshire, 5880F
  Peterborough abbey, 6265, 6268
  Prestoll, 4943A, 6828
  Ramsey, 6173
  Richmond, 4503
  Rothwell, 4930
  Roundhay, 4938
  St. David's, 5880F
  Salisbury, 4924
  Stevenage, 1677
  Stoneleigh, 6369
  Stow, 4816
  Stratford, 4911
  Stratton, Adam de, 4917
  Totteridge, 1677
  Upton, 4843
  Warwickshire, 4911, 6369, 6371
  Welch Hampton, 4860
  Wiltshire, 4917, 4924
  Winchester, St. Swithun, 4701
  Wiston, 4904
  Wroxall, 6371
  Wye manor, 4786
  Wykes, 4823
  York prebends, 4934
  Yorkshire, 2221, 3038, 4396, 4827
Eyncourt, William d', friar, 6924
Eynesbury (Hunts.), 6172
Eynsham abbey (Oxon.), 6288–9
— Adam of, 6289

Eyre, Charles: St. Cuthbert, 2302
Eyre-Todd, George: The Bruce, 2792
Eyres, **524–5**; 1438, 1445, 1462, 3481,
  3504, 3514, 3521, 3527, 3533–4, 3537,
  3551, 3553, 3558, 3563, 3576, 3579,
  3579A, 3589, 3598, 3601, 3607, 3622,
  3625, 3627, 3632, 3661, 6309
Eyton, Robert W.: Dorset Domesday,
  3020; Henry II's court, 4017; Notes on
  Domesday, 3027; Shropshire, 1801;
  Somerset Domesday, 3028; Staffs.
  chartulary, 6331; Staffs. Domesday,
  3029; Staffs. pipe rolls, 3094

Fabre, Paul: Liber censuum, 6775; Peter's
  pence, 6775
Fabric rolls, 4781, 5722, 5850, 6395, 6415
Fabricius, Johann A.: Bibliotheca, 51
Fabyan, Robert: Concordance, 2866;
  Great Chronicle, 2885
Facsimiles, **53–6**; 3751, 5744
Fagan, Hyman: Peasants' revolt, 4148
Fahlin, Carin: Chronique, 2952
Fahy, Conor: Woodville marriage, 4220
— Dermot: St. Ninian, 2323
Fairbairn, James: Crests, 491
Fairholt, Frederick W.: Costume, 914
Fairhurst, Horace: Roman roads, 2084
Fairley, William: trans. Notitia, 2030
Fairs, 1455, 3507, 5524–7, 5532, 5536–8,
  5872, 6100
Fairweather, Eugene R.: Library of classics,
  1133
Faith, people's, 6851
Faith, R. J.: Peasant families, 4955
Falconer (ship), 4336
Falk de Breauté, 3525. *See* Breauté
Falk, Hjalmar: Scandinavian archaeology,
  2484
Falkenburg, Beatrice of, 4096
Falkiner, Caesar L.: Hospital, 6046
Falkirk, battle and roll, 4294
Falley, Margaret D.: Genealogical guide,
  510
Family, **62–70** and **654–6**; 569, 1492,
  1529, 2612, 2638, 4610–11, 4615, 5330
Famines, 1468, 5003
Famulus, 4977
Fane fragment, 3312
Fane, A. G. C.: Index, 545
Fantosme, Jordan: Chronique, 1114, 1123,
  2867
Faral, Edmond: Geoffrey of Monmouth,
  2166; Nennius, 2167
Faricius: Vita Aldhelmi, 2285, 2296
Farley (Surrey), 4897
Farley, Abraham: Domesday Book, 3009
Farmer, David F. H.: Benedictine rule, 441

— D. L.: Price fluctuations, 5490
— Hugh: Analecta monastica, 6555; Life of St. Hugh, 5742; Meditaciones, 6676; William of Malmesbury, 2921
Farmers' accounts, 4919
Farmhouse, 4987
Farming, 1369, 1375, 4986, 4997–8, 5006, 5013, 5020–1. *See* Demesne farming
Farnborough (Kent), 4782
Farne, monk, solitary of, 6676
Farnham, hundred (Surrey), 5483, 5495
Farnham, George F.: Cossington, 5134; Leicestershire, 3568, 4799
Farr, Brenda: Highworth hundred, 4921
— Michael W.: Accounts, 4917
Farrar, Clarissa P.: Translations, 52
Farrer, William: Chartulary of Cockersand, 6198; Court rolls of Clitheroe, 4788; Court rolls of earl of Lancaster, 4792; Domesday Lancs., 3025; Domesday Yorks., 1529; Feudal Cambridgeshire, 4420; Henry I's itinerary, 3988; Honors and knights' fees, 4651; Honour of Old Wardon, 4704; Kendale records, 4487; Lancs. final concords, 3564; Lancs. inquests etc., 4367, 4790; Lancs. pipe rolls, 3091, 4448; Yorks. charters, 4498–9
Farrow, Margaret A.: Wills, 4549
Fasciculi Zizaniorum, 6612
Fasciculus Rerum, 6864
Fasti, 2692, 5580–2, 5698, 5735, 6415
Fasting, 5912
Fastolf, Sir John, 4249, 4302, 4599, 4610, 4825, 6977
Fauconberg's rising (1471), 4226
Faulkes, Jack, 6753
Fauroux, Marie: Actes, 1097, 2169, 3824
Favent, Thomas: Historia, 2868
Faversham (Kent), 5317, 5322
— abbey, 6190
Favier, Jean: Les Finances pontificales, 6776
Favre, Léopold: ed. Du Cange, 305
Fawtier, Robert: L'Europe occidentale, 4097; Histoire générale, 1182; Index of Register of Clement V, 5561; Institutions françaises, 3992, 4307; John Rylands MSS., 103, 1036; Rôles Gascons, 3828
Feachem, Richard: North Britons, 1983; Prehistoric Scotland, 733
Feast days, 6837
Feavearyear, Sir Albert E.: Pound sterling, 681
Febvre, Lucien: Annales, 30
Feckenham (Warw.), forest, 3910
Fee farms, 6237

Feet of fines, **534–44**; 426, 965, 3486–7, 3764, 3856, 3871, 3877, 4489, 5081, 5144, 5153, 5739, 6173, 6254, 6405
Fehr, Bernhard: Ælfric, 2292
Feiling, Sir Keith: Essays to, 2552, 5787
Feilitzen, Olof von: Ekwall bibliography, 632; Personal names, 579, 3050, 7225
Feine, Hans E.: Canon law, 1304
Felix of Crowland: St. Guthlac, 2281, 2284, 2310
Fell, Bishop John, 1098
Fell, Christine, 2171
Fellowes, Edmund H.: Knights of the garter, 552
Feltoe, Charles L.: Vetus Liber, 5706
Fenland, 4717, 4808, 4956, 4991
Fenn, John: Paston letters, 4610
Fenning, Hugh: Irish material, 5982
Fenny Stratford (Bucks.), Court rolls, 4714
Fenwick, Kenneth: Itinerarium, 2906
Ferentino, John of, cardinal, 6742
Ferguson, Arthur B.: Chivalry, 4305; Fortescue, 2988
— J(ames?) F.: Red Book of Irish exchequer, 3008
— John: Treaty rolls, 3783
— Richard S.: Carlisle, 5048, 5645, 6790; Carlisle wills, 4522; Cumberland, 1595
— Sir Samuel: Speckled book, 2397
— William: Scotland, 1178
Fergusson, Sir James: Edinburgh MSS., 1059; William Wallace, 4078
Ferrara, Englishmen at, 6919
Ferris, Eleanor: Financial relations, 6060
Fesefeldt, Wiebke: Bracton, 2985
Festivals, 370
Festschriften, **183–94** and **934–6**; 5177, 5462
Fet asaver, 2996
Feudal Book of Abbot Baldwin, 3012
Feudalism, 1363, 1459, 1461–2, 1475, 1486, 1493, 1496–8, 1529 (Wilts.), 2632, 2649, 2990, 3007, 3052, 3402, 4306, 4308, 4317, 4344, 4640–88, 4947, 4951, 5619
Feudary, 4337, 4368, 4380, 4391, 4456, 4486, 4503, 4738, 4790, 5682, 6310
Ffoulkes, Charles J.: Armourer, 915; Arms and armour, 1495
Ficker, Johannes: Studien, 889
Field-names, 1455
Field systems, 1370, 4999
Field, John E.: St. Berin, 2298
— R. K.: Peasant buildings, 4987
Fielding, C. H.: Records of Rochester, 5791
Fields, open, 1370, 1373, 1379, 4995, 4999
Fierville, Charles: Étienne de Rouen, 2949
Fiesque, Manuel de: Lettre concernant Édouard II, 2971

Fifoot, Cecil H. S.: Common law, 3694; Maitland, 1482
Filby, Percy William: Genealogy, 517
Fillastre, Guillaume: Diary, 5565
Final concords. *See* Feet of fines
Finance, 1193, 1441, 2153, 3231, 3236, 3252, 5515, 5622, 5797, 5900–1, 6047, 6060, 6145, 6406. *See* Accounts, Exchequer
Finance and Trade (essays), 1469
Finberg, Herbert R. P., 1611; Agrarian history, 1360, 4983; Approaches to history, 250; Devonshire studies, 1611; Early charters, 2196; Glos. landscape, 1517; Glos. studies, 1651, 2622; Glos. towns, 5092; Gostwicks of Willington, 4413; Local history, 1508; Lucerna, 1470; Recent progress, 4983; St. Patrick, 2324; Sherborne, Glastonbury, 6309; Stannary, 5513; Tavistock, 2717, 5513, 6126; Werrington, 5064; West country studies, 1611; Winchcombe abbey, 6160
Finchale, priory (Dur.), 6134
— St. Godric of, 6675
Findlay, George H.: Hunts. record office, 1680
Fines. *See* Feet of fines
Fines, John: Handlist of MSS., 1033
Fingall, Lord: Cartulary, 6089
Fink, Karl A.: Das Vatikanische Archiv, 5544
Finke, Heinrich: Acta Concilii, 5563; Papsttum, 6061
Finkestein, Louis: Jews, 3960
Finlason, William F.: Hereditary dignities, 4578; Reeves' law, 1243
Finn, Arthur: Records of Lydd, 5319
— Patrick: Coins, 679
— Rex Welldon: Cambs. Domesday, 3017; Devon Domesday, 3019; Domesday geography of SW. England, 3044; Domesday studies: the Eastern Counties, 3009, 3021, 3052; Evolution of Domesday, 3051; Introduction to Domesday, 3051; Inquisitio Eliensis, 3010; Liber Exon, 3011; Making of Wilts. Domesday, 3033; Norman Conquest, 3989; Som. Domesday, 3028; Sources of Domesday, 3051; Teamland, 5004
Finnsburg, fight of, 2334–5
Finsterwalder, Paul: Theodore's canons, 2253
Firbisse, Dudley: Annals of Ireland, 2782
Firearms, 1499, 4301, 4312
Firma burgi, 5026
Firma noctis, 1497

Firth, Catherine B.: Benefit of clergy, 6464
— Sir Charles: Powicke on, 1489
— James F.: Coopers' company, 5188
— John d'Ewes: Winchester college, 7138
Fischer, Curtius T.: Diodorus, 2025; Ptolemy, 2025
Fishbourne (Roman), 2057
Fisher, Douglas J. V.: A.-S. church, 2278, 2715; Economic institutions, 5363; St. Æthelwold, 2293
— Ernest A.: A.-S. churches, 793
— F. N.: Egginton court rolls, 4730
— Frederick J.: ed. Gilds of London, 5186
— Herbert A. L.: ed. Maitland, 1240; on Maitland, 1482; ed. Vinogradoff, 1501
— J. L.: Forest plea, 3897
— John: Saints, 1155
— John H.: John Gower, 7019; Medieval literature, 317, 2406
— John Lionel: Black Death, 5483; Cartularium de Colne, 6143; Farming glossary, 4997; Harlow cartulary, 4745, 6337; Ledger Book, 6142
— Thomas: Bedfordshire, 1537
— William R.: Forest of Essex, 3905
Fishing industry, 5508
Fishwick, Henry: Lancashire, 1706; Lancs. library, 1695; Lancs. wills, 4538; Rochdale, 4789
Fitch, Marc: Essex feet of fines, 3548; London commissary wills, 4546
Fitzalan, earls of Arundel, 4908
Fitz-Eylwin, Henry: London building assize, 2870
Fitzhardinge, Lord: Muniments of, 4437
Fitzherbert, Anthony: La graunde abridgement, 3654; La novelle natura brevium, 3499
— William, archbishop, 1130
Fitzmaurice, Edward B.: Franciscan province of Ireland, 6017
Fitz-Neal, Richard: Dialogus de scaccario, 3005
Fitznell's cartulary, 4481
Fitzpatrick, Elizabeth: Irish MSS., 1081
Fitz-Ralph, Richard, archbishop, 1457, 6568–70, 6660, 6864
Fitzstephen, William: Becket, 1122, 6487, 6491; London, 1746
Fitz-Thedmar, Arnold: De antiquis legibus liber, 2870
Fitzwilliam Museum, Cambridge, 704, 1033
Five-hide unit, 3028, 4655, 4677
Flaherty, William E.: Annals of England, 3213; Kent rebellion, 4146
Flahiff, George B.: Ralph Niger, 2933; Use of prohibitions, 6462

Flambard, Ranulf, bishop, 3850, 4008, 5694, 6911
Flanders, 1446–7, 1450, 1493, 2585, 2848, 3006, 4016, 4286, 5155, 5329, 5427, 5441
Flann Mainistreach: Synchronisms, 2160
Flaxley abbey (Glos.), 6154
Flay, Eustace of, 1447, 5523
Fleet (Lincs.), Terrier, 4817
Fleming, Lindsay: Boxgrove cartulary, 6361; Pagham (Sussex), 5271
Flemming, Jessie H.: Sourcebook, 1209
Flemyng, Richard, bishop, 6222
Flenley, Ralph: London and foreign merchants, 5424; Town chronicles, 2742
Fleta, 1467, 2987
Fletcher, Sir Banister F.: Architecture, 794
— Charles R. L.: Collectanea (Oxford), 7061
— G. D.: Registers, 5739
— Joseph S.: Cistercians, 5938
— Margery A.: Parliamentary notes, 3325
— Robert H.: Arthurian material, 2810
— William G. D.: Lay subsidy, 3169; Leics. documents, 3568; Salop feet of fines, 3604; Salop lay subsidy, 3180; Shrewsbury poll-tax, 3179
Flete, John: Westminster abbey, 6233
— William: De remediis, 1438, 6693
Fleure, Herbert J.: Natural history, 612
Fleury, Abbo of: Life of King Edmund, 2305
Fliche, Augustin: Histoire de l'église, 1277; Histoire générale, 1182; Orientations, 6712
Flint mines, 2008
Flintshire, 199, 1504, 1916–18, 3018, 3637, 3858–9
Flitt (Beds.), Assessment roll, 3147
Flood, William H. Grattan: De annatis Hiberniae, 6774
Florence of Worcester, 1084, 1089, 1114, 1123, 2142, 2157
Florentine merchants, 5435, 5441
Flores historiarum, 1114, 2871, 2944
Florys, Robert, 5342
Flower, Sir Cyril: Curia regis rolls, 3664; Furness Coucher Book, 6199; Public Works, 3497; Registrum Simonis de Gandavo, 5802
— Robin: Burghal hidage, 2206; Exeter book, 2337; Glastonbury abbey, 6311; Irish MSS., 997; Irish tradition, 2412; L. Nowell, 283; Parker chronicle, 2142; St. Guthlac, 2310
Floyer, John K.: Worcester MSS., 1052
Flynn, Vincent J.: Englishmen in Rome, 6758

Focillon, Henri: Histoire générale, 1182, 1371
Foedera, 3765–7
Folchard, 2171
Foliot, Gilbert, 1102, 5761, 6487, 6516–17
Folk, the, 1451
Folkland, 1455, 1475, 1501, 2623
Folvilles of Ashby-Folville, 5455
Folz, Robert: La Papauté, 6712
Fonseca, José Maria da: Wadding's Annales, 6011
Fontevault, order of, 5920
Fontibus, Galfridus: St. Edmund's life, 2305
Foote, Peter G.: Gunnlaugs Saga, 2446; Viking achievement, 2587
Forbes, Alexander P.: ed. Haddan, 2668; Vita Niniani, 2323; Vita Kentegerni, 2322
— Mansfield D.: Clare College and University Hall, 7096
— Robert J.: Metallurgy, 2081
Forbes-Leith, W.: St. Cuthbert, 2302
Forchielli, Guiseppi: Studia Gratiana, 6429
Ford, Charles B.: Parish churches, 792
— John of, 5941; Wulfric, 6682
— Patrick K.: Aneirin, 2384; Llywarch, 2386
— Roger de: Rentalia et Custumaria, 6315
— Wyn K., 929
Fordham, John, bishop, 3864
Fordun, John of: Scotichronicon, 1100, 1103, 2872
Foreign accounts, exchequer, 3227, 3230
— merchants, 740–2; 1438, 1467, 2207, 3105, 5409
— policy, beginnings of, 1498
— trade, averages, 5393. *See* Customs, revenue
Forest, André: Le mouvement doctrinale, 6880
Forester, Thomas: Florence of Worcester, 2981; Gesta Stephani, 2880; Giraldus Cambrensis, 2881; Henry of Huntingdon, 2904; Ordericus Vitalis, 2937
Forests, 580–4; 1426, 1457, 1529, 1601, 2188, 3094, 3202, 3286, 3488, 3517, 3610, 3630, 3854, 4923, 5005, 5936, 6349, 6374
Foreville, Raymonde: Canonisation, 5956; Guillaume de Poitiers, 2943; L'Église et la royauté, 6507; Le Jubilé de Becket, 6497; Lollardisme, 6873
Forfeiture, 3365, 3712, 3716, 4216
Forge, 5500
Forgeries, 1499, 2863, 5273, 5615, 5872, 6121, 6156, 6240, 6358, 6368, 6517

Formoy, Beryl E. R.: Dominican order, 5989; Exchequer of pleas, 3512; Lathe court rolls, 4902

Formularies, 423, 427–9, 4698, 4976, 6429, 6452, 6480, 7063

Forncett (Norfolk), 4819

Fornmanna Sögur, 2438

Forshall, Josiah: Holy Bible, 6649; Remonstrances, 6632

Forssner, Thorvald: Personal names, 580

Förster, Max: Exeter Book, 2337; St. Guthlac, 2310; Vercelli Codex, 2268, 2341

Forsyth, William, 1258

Fortescue, Adrian: The Mass, 1332

— George K.: B.M. Subject index, 77

— Sir John: De Laudibus, 2988; De Natura legis naturae, 2988; Political theory, 1444, 1473; Works of, 2988

— Thomas, Lord Clermont, 2988

Fortibus, Isabella de, 4619, 4943

Fortifications, 765, 2069–70, 2089. *See* Castles

Fosbroke, Thomas D.: Gloucestershire, 1652

Foss, Edward: Judges, 534; Tabulae curiales, 3686

Foster, Charles W.: Aisthorpe, 4806; Institutions to benefices, 5751; Lincoln episcopal registers, 5739; Lincs. Domesday, 3026; Lincs. final concords, 357; Lincs. survey, 3073; Lincs. wills, 4539, 4542; Registrum Antiquissimum, 5744; Rotuli Ricardi de Gravesend, 5747

— Idris Ll.: ed. Fox essays, 1435; Prehistoric Wales, 1984; Three fragments, 2146; Welsh chroniclers, 2805; Welsh laws, 2239

— Joseph: Peerage, 561

— W. E.: Lincs. court rolls, 4807

— William: Company of coopers, 5188

Fougères, Stephen of, 3823

Fouke Fitz Warin, 1486

Founders and foundations, 1474

Fountains Abbey (Yorks.), 1437, 1474

Four Masters: Annals, 1117, 2784

Fournier, Paul: Collections canoniques, 1305; Irish canons, 2261

Fowke, Frank R.: Bayeux Tapestry, 4276

Fowler, David C.: Trevisa, 2895

— George Herbert: Aylesbury manor, 4712; Beds. (in 1086), 3016; Beds. and Bucks. sheriffs, 3528; Beds. feet of fines, 3524; Beds. indictments, 3522; Beds. inquests post mortem, 4346; Beds. justices, 3527; Beds. knights' service, 4275, 4414; Beds. pipe roll, 3083; Beds. wills, 3524; Bucks. charters, 4419; Bushmead cartulary, 6073; Cambs.

feodary, 4718; Chicksand charters, 6074; Dunstable charters, 6075; Earldom of Huntingdon, 1538, 4415; Falk de Breauté, 3525; Harrold priory records, 6079; Household roll, 4602; Missenden cartulary, 6094; Munitions, 4301; Old Wardon cartulary, 6083; Rippingale charters, 4452; Risborough charters, 6097; Tractatus de Dunstaple, 6077; Turvey records, 4412, 5029, 6082

— Joseph J.: Medieval Sherborne, 5067

— Joseph T.: Account rolls, 5681; Acts of chapter, 6414; Cartularium, 6275; Coucher book, 6418; Cistercian statutes, 5929; Memorials, 6400, 6415; St. Columba, 2319; St. Cuthbert, 2302

— Kenneth: Henry Grosmont, 4178; Hundred Years War, 4166

— Robert C.: Balance sheet, 1491; Episcopal registers, 5578, 5763–4; Essex subsidy, 3158; Seals, 460; Secular aid, 6463

Fox, Lady Aileen M.: Roman Exeter, 2056; SW. England, 761

— Sir Cyril: Boundary line, 2477; Bronze age burial, 1429; Cambridge region, 1985; Early cultures, 1989; Essays to, 1435; Exeter monastery, 1442; Life and death, 1986; Monmouthshire houses, 816; Monumental sculpture, 2478; Offa's dyke, 2477, 2540; Pattern and purpose, 1987; Personality, 613, 1988

— Earle: Numismatics, 709

— Edward, bishop, 5730

— Francis F.: Merchant taylors, 5085

— Sir John C.: Contempt of court, 1234; Magna Carta originals, 3283; Mary, abbess of Shaftesbury, 6130

— Kenneth O.: Courts, 113

— Levi: Coventry, 5277; Historical scholarship, 134; Honour of Leicester, 1712, 3874, 3880, 4451, 4621, 4652; Leicester forest, 3906; Stratford-upon-Avon, 5279

Fox-Davies, Arthur C.: ed. Boutell, 471; Family crests, 491; Heraldry, art of, 475; Public arms, 492

Foxe, John: Actes and monuments, 6865

Frampton, Thomas S.: Wrotham, 3559

France, Marie de, 6130

— Reginald Sharpe: Custumals, 4795; Lancs. record office, 1696; Rental, 6206; Wills, 4510

Franchises, 574–80; 1461, 2608, 4661. *See* Immunities, Liberties, and Marches

Francis II of Brittany, 4266

Francis, Frank C.: British Museum catalogue, 77

Franciscan friars, 805, 847, 1458, 6000–36, 6341, 6588, 6616, 7049, 7101
— Studies (journal), 6003
Frank, Tenney: Economic history, 2039
Frankalmoign, 1482, 4663
Franklin, Mitchell: Bracton, 2985
Franklyn, Julian: Heraldry dictionary, 493
Frankpledge, 1252, 1254, 2619, 4902
Franks Casket, **44**
Fransson, Gustav: Surnames, 581
Franzen, August: Das Konzil von Konstanz, 5566
Fraprie, Frank R.: Scottish castles, 829
Fraser, Constance M.: Ancient petitions, 3225; Antony Bek, 5689; Justice, 3868; Law and society, 3868, 5455; Lay subsidy, 3154, 3177; Parliament (1404), 3313A, 3422A; Pattern of trade, 5383; Prerogative, 3868
— John: Picts, 2488
Fraticelli, 6016
Fraunceys, Master David: Black book of St. David's, 5880F
Freckenham (Suffolk), 4887
Free chapels, 6850
Free, John, 6919
Freeholder, 1434
Freeman, A. Z.: A moat defence, 4314
— Alexander Martin: Annals of Boyle, 2778; Annals of Connacht, 2750
— Edward A.: Battle of Hastings, 4005; Norman Conquest, 614, 2582, 3990; Wells cathedral, 5593, 5596; William Rufus, 3991
Freemantle, William T., Bibliography, 5298
Freemen, 1462, 2628, 2648, 4742, 4784, 5044, 5120, 5139
French language, **37–8**; 43, 1437, 1493
French rolls, **568**; 3770, 3807, 3829, 4278, 4285
Frere, Sheppard S.: Britannia, 2040; Iron age problems, 2011; St. Albans, 2067
— Walter H.: Antiphonale, 7184; Collected papers, 1333; Graduale, 7185; Troper, 7186; Use of Sarum, 1334
Frescobaldi, 3137, 5437
Frewer, Louis B.: Bibliography, 53
Friars, **800–7**; 7049, 7061
Frideswide, St., 1496, 2220, 6295
Friedberg, Emil: Corpus iuris canonici, 1306
Friend, Albert C.: Master Odo of Cheriton, 6709A
— Albert M., Jr.: Book of Kells, 1449
Fris, V.: Documents, 4254
Frisians, 2506, 2576
Fristedt, S. L.: Wycliffe Bible, 6649

Frithegode of Canterbury, 2313
Froissart, Jean: Chroniques, 1095, 2874
Frontiers (Roman), 2088–94
Froucester, abbot, 6157
Froude, James A.: Annals of an abbey, 6170
Fry, Sir Edward A.: Almanacks, 368; Bristol orphan book, 4528; Chichester wills, 4557; Dorset records, 1619, 3546, 4523; Inquisitions for Cornwall and Devon, 4348; for Dorset, 4352; for Gloucestershire, 4356; for Somerset, 4381; for Wiltshire, 4392; Wiltshire feet of fines, 3621; Worcester wills, 4561
— Frederick M.: Charters of merchant taylors, 5195
— George S.: Dorset records, 1619, 3546, 4523; Walthamstow wills, 4525
Fryde, Edmund B.: ed. Book of Prests, 3113; Business transactions, 5505; Edward III's credit operations, 3236; Edward III's finances in Netherlands, 4179; English Parliament, 3359, 3365; Handbook, 371, 537; Parliament and war, 1459; Peasants' revolt, **606**; 3366, 4147, 4151; Wool accounts, 5334; Wool monopoly, 5412
Frye, Walter: Collected works, 7189; Contenance, 7205
Fueter, Eduard: Religion und Kirche, 6792
Fulcodi, Guido, legate, 6744
Fullbrook-Leggatt, Lawrence E. W.: Gloucester, 2058, 5093
Fuller, C.: Bibliography of Social Sciences, 81
— Ernest A.: Cirencester, 5094; Cirencester tenures, 4758; Pleas of crown, 3551; Tallage, 3162
— Thomas: Cambridge university, 7097; Church history, 1278
Fulman, William, 1098, 1100
Funck-Brentano, Frantz: Annales Gandenses, 2758
Fur trade, 5405
Furber, Elizabeth C.: Changing views, 18, 254; Essex sessions, 3549
Furley, John S.: Winchester, 5113
— Robert: Kent, weald of, 1692
Furneaux, Henry: Poems, 7061; Tacitus' Agricola, 2025
Furness abbey (Lancs.), 1114, 2757, 6199, 6200
Furniture, Roman, 2050, 2080
Furnivall, Frederick J.: Bray's Conquest of Ireland, 2800, 2881; Hoccleve, 7020; Lichfield gild, 5251; Minor poems, 6695; Mirk's Parish priests, 6696; Robert Manning of Brunne, 2923, 6699; Wills, 4514

Fur trade, 5405

Fussell, George E.: English farming, 5013; Farming techniques, 1369, 4998

Fyrd, Anglo-Norman, 3069

Gabel, Leona C.: Benefit of clergy, 3695; Pius II, 6713

Gabriel, Astrik L.: Masters and students, 7084

Gaddesden, John of, 6938

Gaelic literature, 324

Gage, John: Brakelond's chronicle, 6335; Thingoe hundred, 6338

Gage of land, 1246

Gaimar, Geoffrey: L'estoire, 1084, 1112–13, 2875

Gaine, J. J.: trans. Van Steenberghen, 6880

Gairdner, James: Chronicles, 21; Historical collections, 2736, 2940; House of Lords, 3374; Letters of Richard III, 3771; Lollardy, 6870; Paston Letters, 2746, 4610; Princes in the Tower, 4203; Richard III, 4203; Three chronicles, 2743, 2817–18, 2934

Galbraith, Georgina R.: Constitution of Dominican order, 5990

— Vivian H.: 436; Anonimalle chronicle, 2787; Asser, 258, 2147; Battle abbey, 6358; Bury Feudal Book, 3012; Death of a champion, 1450; Deposition of Richard II, 1464; Dieulacres chronicle, 2820; Domesday Book, 3053; East Anglian see, 6345; Geld rolls, 3066; Guisborough's Chronicle, 2888; Handwriting, 1485; Henry II's charters, 3823, 4399, 6358; Herefordshire Domesday, 3075; Higden's Chronicle, 2895; Historia aurea, 1448, 2811, 2965; Historical research, 387; 2876, 2981; John Seward, 6915; Knighton's Chronicle, 1452, 2912; Literacy of kings, 6903; London scholars, 6915; Matthew Paris, 2941, 2979; Modus tenendi parliamentum, 3351; Monastic charters, 2217, 4406, 5889; Osbert of Lewes, 6364; Parliament (1371), 3314; Peasants' revolt, 7223; Public records, 422, 949; Richard II, 4137; Roger Wendover, 2941, 2979; Runnymede revisited, 3284; St. Alban's abbey, 6170; St. Alban's chronicle, 388; 2976; St. Edmundsbury chronicle, 2819; Samson, bishop of Worcester, 2200, 5844; Statutes of Edward I, 1459; Study of history, 258; Tower as exchequer office, 1458; Westminster visitation, 6235; Winchester charters, 5114; Writs, 2191

Galbreath, Donald L.: Manuel, 476

Gale, Robert C.: Powell's roll, 494

— Roger: Registrum, 4503, 4939

— Thomas: Antonine itinerary, 2029, Scriptores XV, 1100; Scriptores quinque, 1099

Galfridus de Fontibus, 2305

Gallais, Pierre: Historia regum, 2974

Gallet, R. M.: Oeuvres de Robert de Melun, 6605

Gallois, Lucien: ed. Géographie, 611

Galloway roll (of arms), 1467

Galster, Georg: Coins, 704

Galway, Margaret: Chaucer, 7007

Gambier-Parry, Thomas R.: Charters, 4462, 6291

Gamer, Helena M.: Penance, 2255

Gandavo, Simon de, bishop, 5802

Gandilhon, René: Bibliography, 42

Gandillac, Maurice de: Le mouvement doctrinale, 6880

Ganganelli, Cardinal (Pope Clement XIV), 3937

Ganshof, François L.: Les destinées, 1182

Garbett, H. L. E.: Charters, 4472

Gardiner, Patrick: Historical explanation, 244

— Samuel R.: Introduction, 21

Gardner, Arthur: Figure-Sculpture, 849

— David E.: Genealogy, 511

— Eric: Air-photography, 753

— Helen L.: Scale of Perfection, 6672

— John Edmund G.: The cell of self-knowledge, 6667

— Samuel: Architecture, 795; Sculpture, 844

Garendon abbey (Leics.), 1714

Garlick, Vera F. M.: Provision of vicars, 6842

Garmonsway, George N.: Ælfric, 2292, 2328; A.-S. Chronicle, 2142; Cnut, 2589; Colloquy, 1433

Garnier de Pont-Sainte-Maxence: La vie de Saint Thomas, 6489

Garrod, Dorothy A. E.: Palaeolithic age, 1990

— Heathcote W.: Library regulations, 7164; Merton muniments, 7078

Garter, Order of, 550, 552

Gascoigne, Thomas, 6571–2, 6629

Gascon rolls, 568; 3826–8, 6561

Gascony, 1426, 1468–9, 3810, 3812, 3822, 3832, 4090, 4103, 4107, 4163, 4265, 4272

Gasquet, Francis A.: Black Death, 5475; English Bible, 1337; Collectanea Anglo-Premonstratensia, 5961; Gregory I, 2308; Henry III and church, 6735; Henry VI religious life, 4198; Knowles on, 1477; Monastic life, 1293–4; Parish

life, 6843; Polydore Vergil, 2968; Venerable College in Rome, 6758
Gateshead (Durham), 5070, 6135
Gatfield, George: Guide, 512
Gaudement, Jean: Institutions ecclésiastiques, 6718; La collation des bénéfices, 6764
Gaunilo, 6528
Gaunt. *See* John of Gaunt
Gautier, Pierre, 1426
Gavelkind, 1378, 2644
Gaveston, Piers, 4133
Gavrilovitch, Michel: La traité de Paris, 4098
Gay, Edwin F., Essays to, 1436
— Victor: Glossaire, 764
Gaydon, Alexander T.: Taxation, 3147
Gazetteer of the British Isles, 592
Gedney, Thomas, prior: Tutbury cartulary, 6334
Gee, Henry: Documents, 1128
Geiriadur Prifysgol Cymru, 337
Geld inquests. *See* Inquisitio geldi
Geldart, William M.: Year-books, 3656
Gelling, Margaret: Place-names, 2657
Gem, Samuel H.: Ælfric, 2292
Gembloux, Sigebert of: Chronicle, 2962
Genealogia regum, 1084, 1106, 2161
Genealogist (journal), 503
Genealogists' Magazine (journal), 504
Genealogy, 62–70 and 654–6; 115, 1106, 1650, 1701, 2161, 4338–9
General Register House, Edinburgh, 130; 1059
Génestal, Robert: Le Privilegium fori, 6464
Genoese, 5430
Gentleman's Magazine (journal), 122
— Magazine Library, 615, 769
Gentry, Thomas G.: Family names, 582
Geoffrey, archbishop of York, 5869, 5872, 6573
— duke of Normandy, 3779
— de Mandeville, 3984
— le Baker, 2791, 2928
— of Coldingham, 5685
— of Monmouth. *See* Monmouth
— of Vigeois, 2970
— of Vinsauf, 2906
Geographical Journal, 71
Geography, 71–5; 1465, 1485
George, Hereford B.: Genealogical tables, 535
— Mary D.: Verses on exchequer, 3243
Gerald of Wales. *See* Giraldus Cambrensis
Gerard, archbishop, 2189, 6427
Gerberon, Gabriel: Eadmer's historia, 2863; St. Anselm, 6526–7
Gerefa, 2209

Gering, Hugo: Saga-Bibliothek, 2436
Germain, Alexandre C.: Fisque's lettre, 2971
Germania (Tacitus), 2505
Germania pontificia, 1132
Germans, early, 362–4
Germanus, St., Life of, 2108
Gernons, Ranulf de, earl of Chester, 3981
Gerould, Gordon Hall: Saints' legends, 1162
Gerstenfeld, Melanie: Bibliographies, 2
Gertz, Martinus Cl.: Encomium Emmae, 2159
Gervase of Canterbury, 1114, 1123–4, 2807
— of Tilbury, 1114, 2961
— of Westminster, 1453, 4957, 6234, 6237
Gesiths, 2615, 2634–5
Gesta abbatum, 6168
— Cnutonis, 2159
— Dunelmensia, 5683
— Edwardi de Carnarvan, 2876
— Henrici Quinti, 2877
— Herwardi, 1112, 2878
— Regis Henrici Secundi, 2879
— Regum, 2166
— Siwardi, 1106
— Stephani, 1114, 2880
Geste du Burgh, La, 6270
Geuss, Herbert: ed. Dahlmann-Waitz, 48
Gewirth, Alan: Political thought, 6882
Gewissae, the, 2560
Geyer, Bernhard: ed. Überweg's Grundriss, 1409, 6881; Liber monologion, 6526
Ghastynbury, William: Chronicle of, 5614
Ghellinck, Joseph de: La Littérature latine, 1404; L'essor, 6883; Le mouvement, 6883; Richard de Bury, 6564; Vacarius, 3004
Ghent, Annals of, 1113, 2758
— Simon of, bishop of Salisbury, 5802
Gibbons, Alfred: Court rolls, 4807; Ely records, 5704; Liber antiquus, 5740; Wills, 4540
Gibbs, Marion: Bishops and reform, 6793; St. Paul's charters, 5760
— Robert: Buckinghamshire, 1550
— Vicary: Cokayne's Peerage, 556
Gibbs-Smith, Charles H.: Bayeux Tapestry, 4276
Gibson, Edmund: Codex juris, 6431; Camden's Britannia, 609
— S. T.: Escheatries, 3237
— Strickland: Libraries, 1018, 1485; Oxford chancellors, 7125; Statuta, 7070
— William S.: Tynemouth monastery, 6277

Gidden, Harry W.: Book of remembrance, 5100; Charters, 5102; Steward's book, 5111
Gierke, Otto von: Genossenschaftsrecht, 1412
Giffard, Godfrey, bishop, 5837, 6384
— Walter, archbishop, 5589, 5858
Gifford, Philip R.: Cambridgeshire, 1553
Gilbanks, George E.: Holm Cultram, 6109A
Gilbert, founder of Merton abbey, 6352
— Edmund W.: Roman Britain, 1465
— Felix: John Fortescue, 2988, 3272
— Henry M.: Hampshire, 1654
— John, bishop, 5730
— Sir John Thomas: Annales Hiberniae, 2759; Archivist, 1068; Chartularies of St. Mary's, 2809; Facsimiles, 448
Gilbertines, 5955
Gildas, 1084, 1089, 1095, 1100–1, 1114, 1452, 2026, 2102, 2162, 2285, 2558
Gilds, 734–5; 489, 1381, 1385, 1472, 1482, 1500, 1511; Berwick-upon-Tweed, 5222; Beverley, 5288; Bristol, 5082, 5085; Cambridge, 4721, 5038, 5368; Cirencester, 5094; Coventry, 5275; Knowle, 5278; Leicester, 5137–8; Lichfield, 5251; London, 489, 5182–204; Newcastle-upon-Tyne, 5219–21; Norfolk, 5213; Norwich, 5212; Nottingham, 5223; Preston, 5131, 5360; Shrewsbury, 5243; Southampton, 5098, 5108; Stratford-upon-Avon, 5279; York, 5301, 5303, 5305, 5307, 5310–11
Giles of Rome, 1459
— John A.: Alan of Tewkesbury, 6487; Baker's Chronicon, 2791; Bede, 2297; Brevis relatio, 2810; Caxton Society, 2166; Chronicon Angliae, 2833; Chronicles, Bohn's library, 1089; Chronicon Petriburgense, 2834; Chronicles of White Rose, 2735; Devizes Chronicle, 2859; Herbert of Bosham, 6518; Malmesbury's history of kings, 2921; Matthew Paris, English History, 2941; Monkish historians, 1101; Patres ecclesiae, 1102; Revolte de Warwick, 2901; Scriptores, 2741; Vitae Anglo-Saxonum, 2285; Wendover's Flowers of history, 2979
— Phyllis M.: Fitzwilliam MSS., 1033
Gill, Conrad: Studies, 1816
Gilla Coemgin: Irish Nennius, 2167; Poem, 2402
Gillam, John P.: Picts, 2090; Roman buildings, 2080; Roman frontier, 2094; Roman pottery, 2072, 2082
Gillespie, Richard E.: Holcot, 6590
Gillett, Edward: Grimsby, 5147

Gillies, Hugh Cameron: Grammar, 336
Gillingham (Kent), 4986
Gilliodts-Van Severen, Louis: L'estaple de Bruges, 5329
Gilmore, G. D.: Account roll, 6079
Gilson, Étienne: Christian philosophy, 1407, 6884; Duns Scot, 6567; Michel Menot, 6705
— Julius P.: Defence of proscription, 4204; Student's guide, 990; Western MSS., 1002
Gilyard-Beer, Roy: Abbeys, 5898; Roman baths, 2069
Ginsborough, William, bishop, 5838
Giraldus Cambrensis: Commentaries on, 1488, 2881, 5443; Opera, 2881, 6573; Other editions, 1089, 1092, 1114, 1123, 1125, 2307, 5742
Giraud, Francis F.: Faversham, 5317
Giry, Arthur: Manuel, 417A
Giuseppi, Montague S.: Alien merchants, 5424; Bogo de Clare, 4621A; Chertsey cartularies, 6350; Guide to P.R.O., 951; Surrey archives, 1827
Gladstone, Robert: Charters of Much Woolton, 6205
Glamorgan, 1919–27, 3636, 3785–6B
Glanville, Ranulf de, 1482; Law writs, 3499; Tractatus de legibus, 1113, 2989
Glapwell charters, 4430
Glasgow, town history, 1386
— Hunterian and Coats Collections (coins), 704
Glass vessels (Anglo-Saxon times), 1442
Glasscock, J. L.: Bishop's Stortford, 6838
— Robin E.: Lay wealth, 4636
Glastonbury abbey (Som.), 813, 1470, 1491, 2303, 2717, 4380, 5594, 6309–20
Glastonbury, John of: Chronica, 6313
Glendower, Owen, 3787A, 4219
Glorieux, Palémon: Migne, 1135; Répertoire, 6885
Glotz, Gustave: Histoire générale, 1182
Gloucester: Dominicans, 5995; History, 1386, 5093; Library, 1504; Members of parliament, 3458; Records, 5027, 5090–1; Roman, 2058; St. Oswald's, 6162; St. Peter's, 1453, 6156–7
— forgeries, 6517
— Statute of, 3492
— Studies, 1651
Gloucester, earls of, 4438, 4687
— Humphrey of, 4165, 4231, 6928, 6977
— Miles of, earl of Hereford, 4440
— Robert of: Chronicle, 2882
— Thomas of Woodstock, duke of, 1472 3503A, 4138, 4746

Gloucestershire: Bibliography, 1641-2, 1644; Charters, 4436-9; Church, 5874; County history, 1448, 1529, 1650-3; County journals and societies, 1645-8; County records, 1504, 1517, 1529, 1643, 5092; Earldom of, 4687; Eyres, 3551, 3553; Feet of fines, 3550; Feudal tenures, 4337, 4356-9; Hide, 2636; Inquests, 4337, 4356; Justices of peace, 3552; Manors and villages, 4753-62; Parliament, 3459; Religious houses, 6150-62; Subsidy rolls, 3161; Taxation, 3160; Topography, 2636; Urban history, 705-7; Wills, 4527-8

Glover, John: Les Reis de Brittanie, 2918
— John H.: Kingsthorpiana, 4833
— Richard: Warfare, 4304
— Stephen: County of Derby, 6117
Glover's roll, 496
Glunz, Hans H.: Vulgate, 1335
Glympton, manor (Oxon.), 4847
Gneist, Rudolf von: Verfassungsgeschichte, 1213
Gneuss, Helmut: Bibliotheken, 7165; Grein-Wülker, 2275
Goadby, Frederic M.: ed. Lévy-Ullman, 1238
Godber, Joyce, 1538; Beds. supervisors, 3526; Bushmead cartulary, 6073; Cranfield manors, 4706; Newnham cartulary, 6081
Goddard, Edward H.: Wiltshire, 1853
Godden, M. R.: Aelfric, 2292
Godefroy, Denys (Denis): Chartier's Charles VII, 2813; Chronique de la Pucelle, 2840; Juvénal's Charles VI, 2909
— Frédéric: Dictionnaire, 292
Godfrey, Cuthbert J.: Pluralists, 6772
— John: A.-S. church, 2700; Parish, 6844
— John T.: Parish and priory of Lenton, 6280
— Walter H.: Sussex wills, 4559
Godman, Percy S.: Agriculture, 4904
Godmundeslaech (Gumley, Leics.), 1496
Gododdin of Aneirin, 2384, 2544
Godric, St., hermit of Finchale, 6675
Godstow Abbey (Oxon.), 2837, 6290
Godwin, Francis: Catalogue, 5579; De praesulibus, 5579
— George N.: Bibliotheca, 1654
Goebel, Julius, Jr.: Felony, 2613
Goedheer, Albertus J.: Battle of Clontarf, 2174, 2583
Goetz, Georg: Glossary, 307
Goldbeter, John, merchant, 5505
Goldingham, Cecil S.: The navy, 4327

Goldschmidt, Adolph: English influence, 1449
— Salomon: Geschichte der Juden, 3953
Goldsmid, Edmund: Bibliotheca Curiosa, 7048; Chronicles of London, 2857; Recovery of Normandy, 2794
Goldsmiths' Company, 5190-1
Goldstein, Leon J.: Collingwood's philosophy, 241
Goldthorp, L. M.: Friars, 5991
Gollancz, Hermann: Adelard of Bath's Quaestiones, 6523
— Sir Israel: Caedmon MS., 882; Exeter book, 2338; Hoccleve, 7020; Junius MS., 2339
Gollanz, Marguerite: Northampton sessions, 3590
Gomme, Allan: Archaeological papers, 717
— Bernard: Archaeological papers, 717
— Sir George L., 769; Archaeological papers, 717; Court rolls, 4893; Folkmoots, 1250; Gentleman's Magazine Library, 122, 615, 769; House of Lords, 3374; Local institutions, 1510; London governance, 5168; Village community, 2627
Gonser, Paul: St. Guthlac, 2310
Goodall, Walter: Scotichronicon, 2872
Goodbegot, manor (Hants), 4764
Gooder, Arthur: Representation, 3474
Goodhart, Arthur L.: Law of land, 1235, 3289
Goodman, Anthony: Countess Joan, 4213; Manor of Goodbegot, 4764; Thomas Hoo, 3416; Winchester cartulary, 5811; Woodlock register, 5817
Goodrich, Norma L.: Charles of Orleans, 4247
Goodwin, Albert: St. Edmundsbury abbey, 6345
— Charles W.: St. Guthlac, 2310
Goodyear, F. R. D.: Tacitus, 2025
Gordian, Origins of, 2045
Gordon, Alexander, 2044
— Cosmo: Worcester compotus rolls, 5831; Worcester rental, 5824
— Donald J.: Saxl essays, 1452
— Eric V.: Battle of Maldon, 2328, 2344; Norse, 2453
— Ida L.: Seafarer, 2328
— Robert K.: A.-S. poetry, 2354
Gorham, George C.: Eynesbury and St. Neots, 6172
Goring priory (Oxon.), 4462, 6291
— (Sussex), 4900
Gorleston psalter, 883
Gorman, John C.: Newburgh's Explanatio, 2932

Goscelin of St. Bertin, 2171, 2303; Life of Swithun, 2312; Life of Wulsin, 2317

Gosforth cross, 353

Gostwicks of Willington, 4413

Gotch, John A.: House, 817

Gottlieb, Theodor: Bibliotheken, 7166

Gotwald, William K.: Ecclesiastical censure, 6465

Goudie, Gilbert: Orkneyinga saga, 2451

Gougaud, Louis: Celtic saints, 2667; Inventaires, 7167; Irish libraries, 1445; Irish scribes, 400

Gough, Henry: Bibliotheca, 1548; Itinerary of Edward I, 4050; Scotland (1298), 4294

— John W.: Mines of Mendip, 2081, 3888, 5506

— Richard: Camden's Britannia, 609; Topography, 616

Gough map, 596, 602, 5535

Goulburn, Edward M.: Bishop Losinga, 5777

Gouldesbrough, Peter: Handlist, 23; 933; Record Commissions of Scotland, 130

Gournay, house of, 4580; Sir Thomas de, 4139

Gower (Wales), 5880F

Gower, John, 6990, 7015–19, 7049

Grabmann, Martin: Die Aristoteles Kommentatoren, 6553; Die Geschichte, 6886

Grace, James: Annales Hiberniae, 2759

— Mary: Gild records, 5212

Grace de Dieu (ship), 4327, 4332, 4336

Gradon, Pamela: Cynewulf, 2343

Graf, Ernest: Council of Trent, 6716; Popes, 6720

Graffiti, 850

Grafton, Richard: Chronicle, 2890

Graham, Rose, 1471; Administration of Ely, 5710; Alien priories, 6252; Archbishop Winchelsey, 5644; Battle abbey, 1471, 6358; Cluny, 1471; Description of Oxford, 4376, 5228, 7061; Ecclesiastical tenth, 1471, 6825; Essays to, 1437; Great schism, 1471, 6738; Intellectual influence, 1471; Interdict, 1471, 5320; Letters of Ottoboni, 6743; Malton finance, 1471, 6406; Metropolitan visitation, 1471, 5845; Monasteries, 1495; Order of Grandmont, 1471, 5951; Papal visitation, 6345; Papers, 1471; St. Gilbert of Sempringham, 5959

Graindor, Maurice J.: Le débarquement, 3995

Grainger, Francis: Holm Cultram, 6109A

Grammar (Aelfric's), 2292(f)

Grampian Club, 209

Granat, Ignatii N.: K voprosu ob obezze-melenii, 4971

Grandes Chroniques, 2883

Grandison, Sir Otho de, 4054

Grandisson, John de, bishop, 5715, 5718

Grandmontines, order of, 1471, 5951

Grange, monastic, 4989, 5011, 5020

Gransden, Antonia: Book of William of Hoo, 6339; Chronicle of Bury, 2819, 6341; Ecclesiastical court, 6466; Eynsham customary, 1146, 6288; Grey friars of Lynn, 2877, 6009

Grant, Edward: Physical science, 6949

— Francis J.: Court, 536

— Maurice H.: Sculpture, 845

— Michael: Tacitus' Annals, 2025

— R.: Royal forests, 3903

Gras, Norman S. B.: Corn market, 5385; Crawley, 4765; Customs system, 3238

Grassi, J. L.: William Airmyn, 5786

Gratius, Orthwin, 6864

Grattan, John H. G.: Magic, 2367

Grauncorth, abbot, 6117

Graves, Coburn V.: Cistercian economic activities, 5939

— Edgar B.: Circumspecte agatis, 3338, 6467; Judicial relations, 6450; Papal accounts, 6778; Praemunire, 1439, 3345

— James: King's Council (Ireland), 3321

Gravesend, Richard de, bishop, 4543, 5714, 5747

— Stephen, bishop, 5763

Gray, Arthur: St. Radegund priory, 6101

— Duncan: Newstead priory cartulary, 6281; Nottingham records, 5224

— George J.: Cole MSS., 1005

— Howard L.: Commutation, 4959; Customs, 3222; Field systems, 1370, 4999; First benevolence, 1436; Foreign trade, 5393; Greek visitors, 1439, 6916; Household administration, 4622; Incomes from land, 4623; Woollens, 5408

— J. W.: Canon law in England, 6437; Church and Magna Carta, 3292; Ius praesentandi, 6508

— Louis H.: Cornish hagiography, 333

— Sir Thomas: Scalacronica, 388; 2884

— Walter de, archbishop, 756; 5857, 5878

— William, bishop, 6222

Graystones, Robert de: Historia, 1125, 5685

Grayzel, Solomon: Church and Jews, 3954

Grazebrook, George: Shenstone charters, 4479

— Henry S.: Barons of Dudley, 4579; Shenstone charters, 4479

Great Cause (1291–2), Documents of the, 4086
— Cressingham (Norfolk), 4820
— Malvern, priory (Worcs.), 6384
— Schism, 1473, 6710, 6738, 6740
— seal, 469, 3687, 3844
Greaves, Dorothy: Calais, 1469
— Robert W.: Ledger book, 5035
Greeks in England, 1439, 6916, 6925
Green, Alice S. (Mrs. John R.): Town life, 5351
— Charles: Sutton Hoo, 2487
— Emanuel: Bath poll-tax, 3182; Bibliotheca, 1802; Somerset feet of fines, 3606
— Francis: Menevia Sacra, 5880 1
— John R.: Conquest of England, 2584; English people, 1180; Making of England, 2584
— Mary A. E.: Princesses, 546. See Wood, M. A. E.
— Victor G.: Franciscans, 6018
— Vivian H. H.: Reginald Pecock, 5660, 6630
— W. A.: Ackworth, 4941A
— William C.: Egil saga, 2445
Greenaway, George W.: English Historical Documents, 17; St. Boniface, 2299; Thomas Becket, 6491
Greene, David H.: Irish poetry, 2420
— Richard L.: Carols, 7200
Greenfield, Stanley B.: Old English Literature, 1401, 2355
— William, bishop, 5858
Greenslade, Stanley L.: Durham library, 1622
Greenstreet, James: Assessments in Kent, 3164; Kent fines, 3556; Kent's Kirkby's inquest, 4360; Kent's Knights fees, 4361; Kent wills, 4531; Lincs. survey, 3073
Greenway, Diana E.: Succession to Diceto, 5768; St. Paul's, London, 5581
— W.: Clergy of St. David's, 5880 1
Greenwell, William: Barrows, 1981; Boldon Buke, 3076; Feodarium Dunelmensis, 5682; Hatfield's survey, 3864, 5672; Northern counties wills, 4524; Pontifical, 1316; Seals, 458
Greg, Sir Walter W.: Facsimiles, 446
Gregory I, pope: Libellus Responsionum, 2308, 7225; Life of, 2123, 2281, 2308; Letters of, 2308, 2699, 2702, 2704; Register of, 1114, 2308
— VII, pope, 5555, 6727, 6836
— Dorothy M.: Elton records, 4776
— William: Chronicle, 2886; Mayor of London, 2736
— Winifred: Union list, 92

Gregson, Matthew: Fragments, 4365
Greimas, Algirdas Julien: Dictionnaire, 292
Grein, Christian W. M.: A.-S. Poesie, 2325; A.-S. Prosa, 2286; Ælfric, 2292
Grendon, Felix: A.-S. charms, 2373
Gresham, Colin A.: Aneirin, 2384; Merioneth, 1929; Settlement patterns, 1435
Gresley family, Charters, 4431
Gressenhall (Norfolk), 4454
Gresset, Perrinet, 4243
Greswell, William H. P.: Forests, 3907
Gretham, hospital (Durham), 6136
Gretton, Richard H.: Burford records, 5226
Grey v. Hastings, 3503A
— of Ruthin: Valor, 4625
— Reginald Lord of Ruthyn, 3503A
— friars at Lynn, 6009
— friars of London, 2826
Grierson, Philip, 647; A.-S. coinage, 682–3, 704, 1454; Bibliographie, 647; England and Flanders, 1493, 2585; Germanic kingship, 2507; Grimbald, 2309, 2719; Oboli de Musc, 710; Sutton Hoo, 2487
Griesser, Bruno: Registrum Stephani de Lexington, 6377
Grieve, Alexander: Willibrord, 2314
— Hilda: Handwriting, 401
Griffin, Ralph: Kent feet of fines, 3557; Swainestrey hospital, 6196
Griffith, Dudley D.: Bibliography of Chaucer, 7002
— Edward: Huntingdon records, 5118
— John E.: Pedigrees, 562
— Margaret C.: Justiciary rolls, Ireland, 3641; P.R.O. Ireland, 1078
Griffiths, Ralph A.: Eleanor of Cobham, 4231; Fifteenth century, 4234; Gruffydd ap Nicholas, 4202; Local rivalries, 4205; Owain Glyn Dŵr, 4219; Rhys ap Maredudd, 4059; Wales and the Marches, 4234
Grigg, Sir James: Parliamentary report, 112
Grim, Edward: Becket, 6487
Grimaldi, Stacey: Rotuli de Dominabus, 4344
— Wynford B.: High Halden, 5791
Grimbald of St. Bertin's, 2309, 2719
Grimes, William F.: Aspects, 1432, 2492; Charterhouse, 6224; Guide, 1991; Holt, 2089; London excavation, 770, 2062; Megalithic Wales, 1965; Recent archaeology, 766
Grimsby (Lincs.), Parliamentary elections, 3436

Grinsell, Leslie V.: Burial mounds, 1981; Wessex, 762

Griscom, Acton: Geoffrey of Monmouth, 2166

Grocers of London, 5192, 5393

Groome, Francis H.: Gazetteer, 597

Gros, Gervaise le: Rolls of assizes, 3643

Grosch, Georg: Geldgeschichte, 5429

Grosjean, Paul: Bibliography of, **149**; 1153; Columba, 2319; Gildas, 2162; Gregory's letter, 2308; Henry VI, 2796; Irish saints, 1159, 1445; Notes d'hagiographie, 1163; Patrick, 2324; Picts, 2323; Whitby, 2701

Grosmont (Wales), 4633

— Henry of. *See* Lancaster, duke of, 4178

Gross, the Revd. Dr.: Chronicle, 1951

— Charles: Bibliography of municipal history, 1511; Coroners rolls, 3508; Court of exchequer, 3512; Exchequer of Jews, 3239, 3955; Gild merchant, 1385, 5364; Intestacy, 1246, 4507; Law merchant, 3507; Modes of trial, 5352

Grosseteste, Robert, **864–5**; 1450, 6025, 6910, 6942; Rolls, 5748; Rules, 4631; Sermons, 6864

Grosvenor, Robert, Scrope controversy, 3503A

Grotefend, Hermann: Taschenbuch, 369

Grove, priory (Beds.), 6078

— George: Dictionary of music, 7201

Grueber, Herbert A.: Coins, 684, 689

Gruffydd ap Cynan, 2902

— ap Nicholas, 4202

Grundmann, Herbert: Monumenta, 1114

Grundy, George B.: Charters, **305**

Guala, legate, 6747

Gudmundson, Thorlief: Icelandic life, 2171

Guesmon, Adolphe A.: Documents, 3813

Guest, Edwin: Origines, 2584

Guienne, 1426, 1441, 4090. *See* Aquitaine

Guignard, Philippe: Monuments primitifs, 5933

Guild of Coventry, 5275

— of Knowle, 5278

— of York, 5307

Guildford (Surrey), Public Library, 1830

Guilding, John M.: Reading records, 5031

Guilford, Everard L.: Nottingham, 5224

Guilhiermoz, Paul: Condamnations de Jean, 4034

Guillaume de Jumièges. *See* Jumièges

— de Longchamp, 4004, 5709, 7042

— de Poitiers. *See* Poitiers

— le Breton, 2947

— le Maréchal, 1499, 2896

Guillemain, Bernard: La Cour pontificale, 6714; Les tentatives, 4164

Guilloreau, Léon: Cartulaire de Loders, 6129; Les fondations anglaises, 5918

Guisborough priory (Yorks.), 6401

— Walter of: Chronicle, 2888

Guizot, François P. G.: Guillaume de Poitiers, 2943; Vie de Philippe-Auguste, 2947; Guillaume de Jumièges, 2908

Gumbley, Walter: Cambridge Dominicans, 5992

Gummere, Francis B.: Germanic origins, 2510

Gundlach, Wilhelm: St. Columban, 2320

Gundulf and A.-N. church, 1494

Gunnlaugs Saga Ormstungu, 2446

Gunther, Robert W. T.: Early science, 6950; Herbal, 2373

Gunthorp, William, 4188

Gunton, Simon: Church of Peterborough, 6269

Guppy, Henry: Rylands library, 1034

Gurney, Daniel: House of Gournay, 4580

— Hudson: Deeds, 4455; Hall book, 5205

— Norah K. M.: Borthwick Institute, 1873; Fasti, 5876

Gutch, John: Oxford University, 7133

Güterbock, Bruno: Bracton, 2985; Index, 327

Guthlac, St., 2281, 2284, 2310

— roll (art), 2310

Gutnova, Eugeniia V.: Sources of peasant ideology, 4971

Guy of Amiens, 1084, 1112, 2749

Guy de Boulogne, Cardinal, 4186

— de Montfort, 1490

Guyenne. *See* Guienne

Gwatkin, H. M.: Cambridge Medieval History, 1176

Gwentian code, 2222, 2229

Gwynn, Arthur ap: Index, 103

— Aubrey: Annals of Connacht, 2751; Annals of Innisfallen, 2780; Annals of Ulster, 2786; Archbishop Nicholas of Armagh, 1445; Austin friars, 5971; Book of Leinster, 2777; Council of Constance, 5563; Essays to, 1438; Gregory VII and Irish church, 5554; Irish bibliography, 23; Irish church, 1274; Irish monasteries, 1295; Otway-Ruthven's History, 1203; Richard Fitzralph, 6568

— Edward J.: Catalogue, 1083; Book of Armagh, 2324

— John: Book of Armagh, 2324

Gynewell, John, bishop, 5739

Haas, Elsa de: Antiquities of bail, 3696; Registers of writs, 3499

Habakkuk, Hrothgar J.: ed. Cambridge Economic History, 1175

Habington, Thomas: Worcestershire, 1866

Habsburg, Rudolf von, 4101

Hackett, M. Benedict: Cambridge University statutes, 7059; William Flete, 1438, 6693

— Maria: Registrum Eleemosynariae, 5762

Hackman, Alfred: Tanner MSS., 1022

Hackness (Yorks.), 6402

Hadcock, Richard N.: English monasteries, 1299; Irish monasteries, 1295; Monastic map, 604

Haddan, Arthur W., 1129; Church councils, 2254; Liber Landavensis, 5880A; Papers, 2668

Hadenham, Edmund de: Notes, 5789

Hadleghe (Suffolk), 4883

— Castle (Essex), Records, 4749

Hadrian's Wall, 766, 2045, 2085–6

Haenel, Gustav: Codex Theodosianus, 266

Haerynck, Hippoliet: Jan Boendaele, 2911

Hageneden, Othman: Die Register Innocenz III, 5558

Hahn, Heinrich: Die Continuatio Bedae, 2156

Haidacher, Anton: Die Register Innocenz III, 5558

Haigh, Gordon: Winchcombe Abbey, 6161

Haines, Charles R.: Dover Priory, 6189

— Herbert: Brasses, 869

— Roy M.: Bishop Bransford, 5827; Bishop Carpenter, 5846; Ecclesiastical legislation, 7087; Education of clergy, 6799

Håkon Håkonsson, king, 4099

Halcrow, Elizabeth M.: Decline of demesne farming, 5000; Feodarium, 5682; Obedientiaries, 5699; Ridley charters, 4459

Haldingham, Richard of: Map, 606, 1467

Hale, John: Europe, 4173

— Matthew: Gravesend's executors, 4543; Jurisdiction of Lord's House, 3372; Placita coronae, 3665; Sheriffs' accounts, 3240

— William H.: Account of executors, 5714; Church-rate system, 6845; Domesday of St. Paul's, 5759; Registrum, 5842; Series of precedents, 6482

Hales (Worcs.), 4928

— Alexander of, 6587–9

Haliday, Charles: Scandinavian kingdom, 2585A

Halifax Antiquarian Society (Yorks.), 1878

Hall, A. C. S.: Guide to H.M.C. reports, 945, 1509

— Alfred D.: ed., English farming, 1375, 5013

— Anthony: Commentarii, 8; Murimuth, 2931; Nicholas Trevet, 2963

— Arthur R.: Technology, 408

— Catherine P.: Archives of Cambridge, 7103

— Donald J.: Pilgrimage, 6846

— Edward: Chronicle, 2889

— George D. G., 1219; Abbot of Abingdon, 6086; Curia regis rolls, 3485; Entry sur disseisin, 2985; Glanvill's tractatus, 2989; Registers of writs, 3499; Thorne's Bracton, 455; Writs of trespass, 3706

— Hubert: Bibliography, 19; Confirmatio cartarum, 3342; Court life under Plantagenets, 3490, 4018; Crown lands, 4688; Custody of Domesday, 3047; Exchequer antiquities, 952, 3241; Exchequer memoranda rolls, 3212; Exchequer receipt roll, 3109; Exchequer red book, 3007; Index to T.R.H.S., 177, 184; Law Merchant cases, 3507; List of agrarian surveys, 4691; Manorial accounts of Canterbury, 5619; Pipe roll of Winchester, 5815; Repertory, 939; Studies, 423; Testa de Nevill, 4337; Weights and measures, 5497; World War archives, 961

— James: Book of Combermere, 6103; Charters of Chester, 5044

— John: Laȝamon, 2914

— John R. C.: A.-S. dictionary, 279

— Joseph: Lawrence Minot, 7041

— Thomas Walter: Cartae (Roche abbey), 6416; Sheffield charters, 5298

Hallam, Herbert E.: Censuses, 5476; New lands of Elloe, 4991; Settlement and society, 4808

Haller, Johannes: Concilium Basiliense, 5564; Das Papsttum, 6715; England und Rom, 5562; Papsttum und Kirchenreform, 6731; Piero da Monte, 6745

Halliday, Frank E.: Cornwall, 1586, 1588

Hallinger, Kassius: ed., Corpus, 1146

Halliwell, James O.: Abingdon chronicle, 2827; Letters of kings, 3772; Rishanger chronicle, 2948; Warkworth's chronicle, 2977

Halliwell-Phillips, James O.: Dictionary, 280

Halmote, 1480, 4739, 5684

Halphen, Louis: Initiation, 55, 259; Louis VII et Henri II, 1426; Peuples et civilisations, 1191

Halton (Ches.), 4724

— John de, bishop, 1499, 5646

Hamel, Anton Gerard van: De geschied-bronnen, 2414; Nennius, 2167

Hamell, Patrick J.: Index, 233

Hamil, Frederick C.: The king's approvers, 3697; Wreck of sea, 3668A

Hamilton, Adam: Life of Grandisson, 5715

— Hans C.: John of Tynemouth, 2965; Walter de Hemingburgh, 2888; William of Newburgh, 2932

— Henry: Brass and copper industries, 5507

— John R. C.: Jarlshof, 1992; Recent archaeology, 766

— Nicholas E. S. A.: Conquest of Lisbon, 2858; Inquisitio comitatus Cantabrigiensis, 3010; William of Malmesbury, 1143, 2291

— Sidney G.: Compotus rolls, 5831; Court rolls, 4928; Obedientiaries, 5825

Hamman, Adalbert: Supplementum to Migne, 1135

Hammer, Jacob: Geoffrey of Monmouth, 2166

Hammond, Eleanor P.: Chaucer, 7002

— Eugene A.: Doctors' incomes, 6951; Medical practitioners, 1422

— Muriel E.: Union Catalogue, 89

Hampshire: Church, 1529; County history, 1663–4; County journals and societies, 1656–62; County records, 1654–5; Domesday, 1529; Manors and villages, 4763–8; Religious houses, 6163–5; Taxation, 3163; Topography, 1529; Urban history, 5095–115

Hampson, Robert T.: Kalendarium, 370

Hanbury, Harold G.: ed. Holdsworth, 1235; Legislation of Richard III, 3346

Hancock, Frederick: Minehead, 4868

— Philip D.: Bibliography, 20

— William N.: Irish laws, 2240

Hand, Geoffrey J. P.: English law in Ireland, 3666; Irish church, 1274; Materials relating to Ireland, 3797

Handelsmann, Marceli: La fin du moyen âge, 1191

Hands, M. S. G.: Cathedral libraries, 127

Hanenburg, Jacoba J. H. M.: Decretals, 6430

Hanford, James H.: De proprietatibus rerum, 6550

Hanham, Alison: Lord Hastings, 4223; Parish of Ashburton, 6838

Hanley, H. A.: Subsidy roll, 3165, 4784

Hannay, Robert: Scottish seals, 455

Hannington (Hants), Rental, 4767

Hansa, 5335–7, 5393, 5425–6, 5428–9, 5433, 5438–9

Hanseakten, 5335

Hansen, Joseph: Der englische Staatskredit, 5429

Hansisches Urkundenbuch, 5336

Hanslik, Rudolf: Corpus Scriptorum, 5911

Hanson, Richard P. C.: Christianity, 2083; St. Patrick, 2324

Harben, Henry A.: London, 1741

Harbin, Sophia W. Bates: Somerset M.P.s, 3466

Harbledown (Kent), 6187

Harbottle, Barbara: Hatfield's Visitation, 5673

Harcourt, Leveson W. Vernon: Baga de secretis, 3520; Eyre of Kent, 3558; Trial of peers, 3667; Year books, 3646

Harcup, Sara E.: Societies, 1512

Hardacre, Paul H.: County record offices, 109; 1513

Hardeman, James: Irish memoranda rolls, 3211

Harden, Donald B.: ed. Dark Age Britain, 1442, 2475, 2495; Glass vessels, 1442

Harding, Alan: Keeper of the peace, 3495; Law courts, 3667A; Social history of law, 3667A

— Norah Dermott: Bristol charters, 5077

Hardman, Frederic W.: Feet of fines, 3557

Hardrada, Harold, 352 and 355; 2438

Hardwick, Charles (of Ely): Elmham's Historia, 2158; Poem on Edward II, 7048

Hardy, Alfred L.: Manor court rolls, 192, 4694

— Edward L. C. P.: Waurin's Recueil, 2978

— M. M.: Records of Lydd, 5319

— Reginald: Tatenhill, 4877

— Sir Thomas Duffus: Catalogue, 21; Durham records, 3865; L'estoire des Engles, 2875; Gesta Herwardi, 2878; John's itinerary, 4019; Le Neve's Fasti, 5580; Liberate rolls, 3110, 3774; Lord chancellors, 3687; Lord Langdale, 953; Malmesbury's De Gestis, 2921; Modus tenendi parliamentum, 3347, 3352; Patent Rolls, 3778; Petrie's Monumenta, 1084; Registrum Palatinum, 3867, 5691; Report, 1026; Rotuli Chartarum, 3760; Rotuli de oblatis et finibus, 3764; Rotuli Litterarum Clausarum, 3761; Rotuli Normanniae, 3830; Syllabus of Foedera, 3765

— Sir William: Duchy of Lancaster charters, 3870; Waurin's Chronicle, 2978

— William J.: Documents, 1128; Doncaster, 5290; London feet of fines, 3578, 5153; Rolls house, 957

Hardyng, John: Chronicle, 2890

Hareslade, Robert Carpenter of, 1467, 2995, 3513, 4048

Harfleur, siege of, 2877, 7046

Harford, Dundas: Comfortable works, 6673

Hargrave, C. P.: Playing cards, 928A

— Francis: Collection of tracts, 3240; Law tracts, 3728; Littleton's treatise, 2990

Hargreaves, Anthony D.: Equity, 3721

Hargreaves-Mawdsley, William N.: Academical dress, 7086; Legal dress, 3688

Häring, Hermann: ed. Dahlmann-Waitz, 48

Harland, John: Charters of Clitheroe, 5126; Fragments on Lancaster, 4365; Lancs. documents, 4370, 4793; Mamecestre, 4791

Harleian MSS., 996, 3771

— Society, Publs., 190

Harleston (Northants.), 4830

Harley, John B.: Ordnance maps, 604

Harlow (Essex), 4745, 6337

Harmer, Florence E.: A.-S. chronicle, 2142; A.-S. writs, 2197; Chipping and Market, 1429; Edward the Confessor writ, 1433, 6236; Documents, 2198

Harnham, John de: Tax rolls, 3198

Harold II, 556, 1433, 2172, 2285, 2585, 3990, 6147

— Fair-Hair, 2445, 2447

— Hardrada, 2438, 2447

— earl, 2585

Harpenden (Herts.), 3554

Harper, R. J.: Ducatus Lancastriae, 3873

Harpsfield, Nicholas: Sir Thomas More, 6983

Harris, Barbara J.: Landlords and tenants, 4958

— Brian E.: Sheriff's farm, 3266

— Charles: Duns Scotus, 6567

— E.: Coins, 644, 648

— Jesse W.: John Bale, 8

— Mary D.: Coventry leet book, 5274; Coventry records, 5272; History of Coventry, 5277; Register of guilds, 5275

— Silas M.: Welsh saints, 1173

— Walter: Irish writers, 30

Harrison, Edward: Court rolls, 4779

— Frank Ll.: Church music, 7204; Eton choirbook, 7187; Music, 1336, 7202

— Frederick: Life in a college, 5873; Stained glass, 862

— Howard G.: Bibliography, 513

— Kenneth: Pre-Conquest churches, 2168

Harriss, Gerald L.: Cardinal Beaufort, 6737; Chronicle, 2869; Common petitions, 3414; Parliament and taxation, 3366, 3398; Preference at exchequer, 3242; Struggle for Calais, 4206

Harrod, Henry: Colchester court rolls, 5071; Great Yarmouth deeds, 5214; King's Lynn deeds, 5205; Norwich coroners' rolls, 3581, 5209; Norwich wills, 4548

— Henry D.: Shavington muniments, 4467

— Leonard M.: London library, 1006

Harrold priory (Beds.), 6079–80

Harryson, John: Chronicle, 2744

Hart, Cyril Edwin: Forest of Dean, 3908

— Cyril James R.: Codex Wintoniensis, 2199; Early charters, 2199, 6140; Hides, 2636; Hunts. hidation, 2636; Northants. hidation, 3067; Ramsey Computus, 2168, 2366; Tribal hidage, 2213

— James M.: Studies for, 2148

— Richard: Records, 1142

— William H.: Cartularium de Rameseia, 6173; Derby fines, 3542; Historia S. Petri, 6157

Harte, Walter J.: Exeter, 1604; Handbook, 371

Hartland, Edwin Sidney: Walter Map, 6599

Hartley, Brian R.: Roman army, 2075; Samian ware, 2037

Hartmann, Alfred: Philobiblon, 6562

— Jacob W.: trans., 2458

— Ludo M.: Gregory I, 2308

Hartopp, Henry: Leicester freemen, 5139; Leicester mayors, 5141; Noseley documents, 4798

Hartridge, Reginald A. R.: Right of presentation, 6765; Vicarages, 6847

Hartshorne, Charles H.: Feudal antiquities, 1774; Itinerary of Edward I, 4050; Itinerary of Edward II, 4120

Hartwell, Ronald M.: Index, 119

Harty, Lenore: St. Dunstan, 2303

Harvard Law Review, 155

Harvey, Alfred: Castles, 830

— Barbara F.: Gervase de Blois, 6237; Islip custumal, 4845; Leasing of demesnes, 4957; Population trend, 5477; Walter de Wenlok, 6232; Westminster and Oxford, 7223

— John H.: Architects, 797; Canterbury archives, 5623; Cathedrals, 796; Perpendicular style, 798; Richard II and York, 7223; William Worcestre's Itineraries, 2982; Wilton diptych, 858; Winchester College muniments, 7138

— Paul D. A.: Cuxham, 4849

Harvey, Ralph: Rolle's Incendarium, 6679
— Sally: Knight's fee, 4653
Harwood Evidences, 4500
— Thomas: ed. Erdeswick's Staffordshire, 1815; Lichfield, 5671
Haselbury, Wulfric of, 6682
Haselden, Reginald B.: Piers Plowman, 7023; Scientific aids, 378
Haseloff, Günther: Die Psalterillustration, 887
Haskell, Daniel C.: Checklist, 94
Haskins, Charles H.: Abacus, 3257; Adelard of Bath, 6524; Essays to, 1439; Henry II as patron, 1458; Norman institutions, 1248, 3992; Norman knight-service, 4654; Portswood manor, 1426; Powicke's appreciation of, 1489; Renaissance (twelfth century), 1391, 6887; Robert of Normandy, 2974; Studies in science, 1419, 6952; Verses on exchequer, 3243; William Cade, 5509; William of Jumièges, 2908
— George L.: Charter lists, 3842; Chronicle of Edward II, 2825; Doncaster petition, 4116; Executive justice, 3669; Fonctions des representants, 3366; Francis Accursius, 6751; King's high court, 3373; Parliament, 3373; Petitions of commonalty, 3315; Petitions of representatives, 3373, 3399; Representative government, 3373; Statute of York, 3343; Traitor (1322), 4134; University of Oxford, 7125
Hassall, Arthur: Editor, 1498
— William O.: Cartulary of Clerkenwell, 6229; Wheatley records, 4850
Hasted, Edward: Kent, 1693
Hastings, battle of, 556, 2749, 3040, 3990, 3994, 4005
— (Sussex): Cinque port, 5321; Rape of, 4288, 4902
— inheritance, 4582
Hastings, Sir Edward, 3503A
— Sir Hugh, 3503A
— Margaret: Changing views, **603**; 18; Court of common pleas, 3668
— Manuscripts, H.M.C. report of, 4693
— Maurice: Parliament house, 3431; St. Stephen's chapel, 798
— Lord William: Master of the mint, 5502; Retainers, 4284
— Lord, and Richard III, 4223
Hatcher, Henry (I), 2026; Cirencester's De situ, 2026
— Henry (II): Sarum, 5285
— John: Rural economy, 4960
Hatfield (Herts.): Manorial survey, 1677

Hatfield, Thomas of, bishop of Durham, 3864, 5672, 5673
Hatherop (Wilts.), 6373
Hatherton, Lord, Charters, 4472
Hatschek, Julius: Constitutional history, 1213
Hatt, Gudmund: Plough and pasture, 1980
Hatton, Sir Christopher, Book of seals 464, 2201A, 4410
Hauck, Albert: St. Boniface, 2299
Haughmond abbey (Salop), 6300
Hauteville, John de: The Archweeper, 7042
Haverfield, Francis J.: **261**; Agricola, 2025; Bibliography (1913-14), 2017; Inscriptions, 2028; Map of Roman Britain, 605; Mining, 2081; Mommsen's Provinces, 2048; Roman Cirencester, 2054; Romanization, 2041; Roman Leicester, 2060; Roman occupation, 2042; Sculpture, 2080; Wales, 2089
Havergal, Francis T.: Fasti Herefordenses, 5735
Havet, Julien: Mélanges, 3348
Haward, Winifred I.: Economic aspects, 4207, 5461; Financial transactions, 5393
Hawkes, Charles F. Christopher: Ancaster, 2061; Archaeology, 774; Belgae, 1994; Britons, Romans, Saxons, 2010, 2100; Excavations, 2070; Hill forts, 1995; Jutes, 1442; Prehistoric Britain, 1996; Prehistoric foundations, 1993; St. Catherine's Hill, 1995; Sutton Hoo, 2487
— Jacquetta: Channel Islands, 2000; Guide, 734; History in earth and stone, 734; Prehistoric Britain, 1996
— Sonia C.: Jutish style, 2541; Soldiers and settlers, 2101
Hawkins, Edward: Silver coins, 685
— Gerald S.: Stonehenge, 1970
Hawkwood, Sir John, 5181, 7007
Hawley, William: Roman Excavations, 2070
Haworth, Peter: Lexicon, 312
Hay, Denys: Aeneas Sylvius, 5564; Polydore Vergil, 2968; Spoils of war, 4302
Haydn, Joseph: Dignities, 538
Haydon, Frank S.: Eulogium, 2865
Hayes, Raymond H.: Roman pottery, 2069
— Richard J.: MSS. for Ireland, 1073
Hayroun, Robert: Tenths for Scottish campaign, 4293
Hays, Rhys W.: Welsh Cistercians, 5950; Welsh students, 7095
Haytor (Devon), 4351
Hayward, Lillian H.: Land tenures, 4862
Hazeltine, Harold D.: A.-S. wills, 2205; Equity, 3722; Fortescue, 2988; Gage of

land, 1246; Hengham's Summae, 2997; Maitland's essays, 1483; Pfandrecht, 1251; Thomas Madox, 3250

Head, C.: Pius II and wars of the roses, 4221

Headicar, Bertie M.: London Bibliography of Social Sciences, 81

Heads of religious houses, 5895

Heal, Ambrose: London goldsmiths, 5191

Heales, Alfred C.: Church of Kingston-upon-Thames, 5267; Merton priory, 6352; Tandridge priory, 6354

Healey, Charles E. H. C.: Somersetshire itinerant justices, 3607; West Somerset, 4869

Healaugh Park, priory (Yorks.), 6403

Hearne, Thomas: Adam de Domerham, Historia, 6309; Alured Beverley's annals, 2795; Arnold's chronicle, 2789; Brunne's Langtoft, 2923; Chronicles, 1103; De gestis mirabilibus, 2790; Dunstable annals, 2929, 6076; Gloucester's Chronicle, 2882; Godstow's Chronicle, 2837; Guisborough's Chronicle, 2888; Hemming's Cartulary, 2200; Historia Edwardi III, 2898; Historia Ricardi II, 2899; Liber Niger Scaccarii, 3006; Livy's Vita Henrici V, 2919, 2972; Otterbourne's Scriptores, 2938; Rous' Historia, 2950; Scotichronicon, 2872; Sprott's Chronicle, 2873, 2956; Trokelow, 2797, 2964, 2971; Vita Henrici II, 2879; Whethamstede's Register, 2980; William of Newburgh, 2932; William of Worcester's Annals, 2982; Worcestershire survey, 3071

Hearnshaw, Fossey J. C.: Leet jurisdiction, 5104; Social and political ideas, 1415

Heath, Hamo, bishop, 5792

— Peter: Clergy on eve of reformation, 6848; North sea fishing, 5508

Heaton, Herbert: Economic history, 1371; Yorkshire woollens, 5413

Heawood, Edward: Tschudi's maps, 596

Hebditch, Margot J.: Yorks. deeds, 4504

Hecht, Joseph Jean: ed. Handbooks, 15

Heckel, Rudolf von: Das Aufkommen der ständigen Prokuratoren, 6752

Hector, Leonard C.: Chronicle of Westminster, 2895; Handwriting, 386; Palaeography, 424; Richard II's outburst, 4124

Heddington (Wilts.), 6373

Hedges, John K.: Wallingford, 5032

Hedley, William P.: Manor of Simonburn, 4839

Hedon (Yorks.), 5291, 6838

Heene (Sussex), 4904

Heers, Jacques: Les Genois en Angleterre: la crise de 1458–66, 5430

Hefele, Carl Joseph von: Conciliengeschichte, 1279

Heidemann, Joseph: Die englische Legation, 6744

Heighington terrier (Lincs.), 4809

Heilbronner, Walter L.: Printing, 7218

Heimbucher, Maximilian J.: Die Orden, 1296

Heimpel, Hermann: ed. Acta Constanciensis, 5563; ed. Dahlmann-Waitz, 48

Heimskringla, 2447

Heirs, 4339, 4374

Heist, William W.: Vitae sanctorum, 1164

Helbaek, Hans P.: Cereals, 2631; Early crops, 1980

Helbling-Gloor, Barbara: Johannes von Salisbury, 6643

Helle, Knut: Anglo-Norwegian relations, 4099

Helleiner, Karl F. M.: Population movement, 5478

Hellifield (Yorks.), 6043

Helmholz, Richard: Bastardy litigation, 6468; Canonists and impartiality, 6451

Helps for Students of History, 177, 260

Helsby, Thomas: Chester, 1574

Helyot, Pierre: Les ordres monastiques, 5893

Hemingburgh, Walter of: Guisborough chronicle, 2827, 2888

Hemmant, Mary: Exchequer chamber cases, 3511

Hemmeon, Morley de Wolf: Burgage tenure, 5353

Hemmings Cartulary, 1103, 1450, 2200, 5800

Hencken, Hugh O'Neill: Cornwall, 762

Henderson, Charles G.: Cornish history, 1589

— Ernest F.: Historical documents, 3005

— George: Illumination, 888

— Isabel: The Picts, 761

— Mary I: Cornish history, 1589

Henel, Heinrich: Ælfric, 2292; Mönchsaberglaube, 2375

Hengham, Ralph de, 1458, 1501, 2996–7

Hengistbury Head (Hants), Roman, 2070

Hening, Crawford D.: Assumpsit, 1246

Heningham, Eleanor K.: Vita Aeduuardi, 2171

Henley (Oxon.), 5227

Henley-in-Arden (Warw.), 4914

Henley, Walter of: Husbandry, 1467, 2987, 4631

Hennessy, George: Chichester clergy lists, 5661; Novum repertorium, 5772
— William M.: Annals of Loch Cé, 2783; Annals of Ulster, 2786; Chronicon Scotorum, 2839
Hennings, Margaret A.: Source book, 1209
Henry I: Charters and laws of, 437, 1455, 1498, 2186, 2189, 3279–80, 3779, 4399, 4460, 5179, 5744; Children, illegitimate, 556; Chroniclers of reign of, **389**; Church, 6785, 6802; Forests, 1457; History of, **590–3**; 3006, 3988, 6802; Learning, 1439; London charter, 5179; Records of, 3067–74, 3779; Revenues, 3267; Seals, 469, 4399
— II: Charters, 437, 1487, 3006–7, 3823, 4399, 5744; Chroniclers of reign of, **390**; 2734; Church, 5550, 5556, 6727, 6789; Conflict with Becket, **853–8**; 1426, 1482, 6437, 6487; History, **593–6**; 3006, 4017, 4315, 6573, 6911; Literature, 1458, 6912; Records, 2989, 3075–6, 3078, 3109, 3823, 7224; Wales and, 4040
— III: Administration, 1455, 3007–8; Anti-foreign movement, 1439; Building accounts, 790; Chroniclers of reign of, **390**; Church and, **882–4**; 1139, 5737, 6793, 6816, 6827; History of, **597–9** and **601–3**; 2897, 4062, 5737; Jews and, 3942; Letters of, 3782; Liber Niger Scaccarii, 3006; Parliament, 3407; Records of, **455–6**; 2994–5, 3006–7, 3080–1, 3107, 3254, 3664, 3754, 3758, 3778, 3782–3, 3826–7, 4296; Revenues, 3258; Rolls of arms, 496
— IV: Accession and title of, 1478, 3365, 4218; Banquet, 1356; Chronicles, **391–2**; Church, 6732; Council, 3298–9, 3365; History, **612–19**; Letters, 3781; Records, 7017, 7049; Taxation, 3398
— V: Chroniclers, **392**; Church, 5566, 5569, 6736; Gesta, 2877; History, **612–19**; 2877; Normandy, 1439; Seal, 469; Vita et Gesta, 2972
— VI: Chroniclers, **392**; Church, 1103, 2796, 5573, 6755; History, **612–19**; 3776; Letters, 3815; Library of All Souls College, 7179; Miracles, 2796; Records, 3803A
Henry:
— earl of Derby, 4601, 7223
— Lord Langdale, 953
— son of Henry II, 2747
— of Almain, 1459
— of Blaneford, 1103, 2797
— of Blois, bishop, 5823
— of Huntingdon, 1084, 1089, 1114, 1119, 2904

— of Marlborough, 2924
— of Pytchley, 6267
— of Silgrave, 2953
Henry Bradshaw Society, 191
Henry, Françoise: Irish art, 846; Irish enamels, 1442; Vikings, 2956
— Robert L.: Contracts, 3734
— Symeonis, 1487
Henschel, G. A. Louis: Du Cange's Glossarium, 305
Henschenius, Godefridus: Acta sanctorum, 1152
Henson, Herbert H.: Stamford schism, 7061
Heptateuch, Old English, 2292(b)
Hepworth, Philip: Archives, 940
Heraldry, **59–62**; 556, 1485, 3679, 4281
Herbal, 2374
Herbarium Apuleii, 2368
Herbert of Bosham, 1102, 6518
— of Norwich, 5781
— of Westminster, 1453, 6234
Herbert, George: Roman villa, 2080
— John A.: Catalogue of romances, 999; Illuminated MSS., 876
— William: Inns of court, 7151; Livery companies, 5183; Typographical antiquities, 7212
Herd, John: Historia, 2892
Herde, Peter: Audientia, 6452; Papal chancery, 5542
Hereford: city of, 1386, 5027, 5116–17
— diocese of, **774–5**; 6763, 6790; Benefices, 6836; Bishop's household, 4612, 5761; Estates of bishopric, 4770; Library, 1046; Statutes of, 5749
— Earldom of, Charters of, 4440
— Grey friars of, Library, 6006
— Mappa Mundi, 606, 1467
— and science, 6961
Hereford, Philip: Bede, 2148
Herefordshire: Antiquities, 737; Charters, 4440; Church, 5724–37, 6836; County history, 1496, 1670; County journals and societies, 1668–9; County records, 1046, 1665–7; Domesday, 1529, 3075; Feudal tenures, 4769–70; Parliament, 3459; Religious houses, 6166–7; Urban history, 5116–17
Heresy, **896–8**; 6016, 6442, 6478, 6659
Hereward, 2285, 2878
Hergenröther, Joseph: Conciliengeschichte, 1279
Hergest, Red Book of, 2166, 2386, 2804
Heriots, 5815
Heritage of Early Britain, 771
Herle, William de (Justice), 3504
Herluin of Bec, Life of, 6246

Herman, the archdeacon, 2305

Hermansen, G.: Household book, 4604

Hermits, 1303, 5884, 5887, 6666, 6669, 6675–83

Herodian, 2025(1)

Héron, Alexandre: Robert Blondel, 2798

Herre, Paul: ed. Dahlmann-Waitz, 48

Herringswell (Suffolk), 4884

Herrmann, Paul: Saxonis Gesta, 2426

Herrtage, Sidney J. H.: Catholicon, 304

Herscher, Irenaeus: Alexander of Hales, 6587

Hertford, borough of, 1677

— earl of, 1486

Hertfordshire: Antiquities, 737; Archives, 1504, 1671; Charters, 4400; Church, 1529; County history, 1529, 1676–8; County journals and societies, 1673–5, 1732; County records, 1504, 1671–2; Domesday, 1529, 3040; Feet of fines, 3554; Manors and villages, 4771–4; Religious houses, 6168–71; Topography, 1529, 1732; Urban history, 1677; Wills, 4526

Hertz, Rudolf: Irish Lexicon, 344

Hertzberg, Ebbe: Norwegian history, 2569

— Wilhelm: Libell of Englishe policye, 5338

Herval, Réne: Deux écrivains (Fantosme), 2867

Hervey, Lord Francis: King Edmund, 2305; Pinchbeck register, 6342

— Lord John: Extent of Hadleigh, 4883; Suffolk Domesday, 3030; Suffolk hundred rolls, 4388

— Sydenham H. A.: Beds. subsidy, 3148; Suffolk, 1820, 3189

— Thomas: Colmer and Priors Dean, 4766

Herward. *See* Hereward

Heseltine, George C.: William of Wykeham, 5822

Hessen's Irish Lexicon, 344

Heubner, Heinz: Tacitus, 2025

Hewitt, Charles R.: Index for Cornwall, 1582

— Herbert J.: Black Prince's expedition, 4180; Medieval Cheshire, 1573; Organization of war, 4303

— John: Armour, 916; Monumental effigies, 927

Hewlett, Henry G.: Wendover's Flores, 2979

— Lionel M.: Coins, 686

Hexameron (Aelfric), 2292

Hexham, bishops of, 2721, 2727

— Honour of, 1776

— John of: Historia, 2893, 6274

— Priory of, 2893–4, 6274

— Richard of: Historia, 1114, 1123–4, 2894, 6274

Heyck, Eduard: Die deutsche Hanse, 5438

Heynck, Valens B.: Ockham Literatur, 6622

Heytesbury, William, 6627, 6973

Heywood, B.: The vallum, 2045

— James: Ancient laws, 7053; Cambridge statutes, 7056

— Thomas: Benefactions, 5664

Hibbert, Samuel: Customs of a manor, 4793

Hibernensis, Collectio canonum, 2261

Hiberno-Norse coins, 704

Hic intimatur, 2182

Hickes, George: **47** and **304**; Thesaurus, 425

Hicks, Frederick W. Potts: Tewkesbury compotus, 4755, 6159

Hides and hidation, 2206, 2213, 2636, 3028, 3031, 3057–8, 3067, 3071, 4655

Higden, Ranulf: Polychronicon, 1100, 2895

Higgs, Eric: Science in archaeology, **85**

Higham Ferrers (Northants), 4457, 4829, 5022

Highfield, John Roger L.: Late Middle Ages, 4173; Hierarchy, 6799; Rolls of Merton College, 4463, 7080, 7121; William of Wickham, 5822

High Halden (Kent), 5791

Highworth Hundred (Wilts.), 4921

High Wycombe (Bucks.), 5035–6

Higounet, Charles: Histoire de Bordeaux, 4168

Hilary, bishop of Chichester, 5650, 6510

Hilbelink, Aaltje J. G.: Herbarium, 2368

Hildebrand of London, 3198

— Bror E.: Catalogue of coins, 687, 1454

Hiler, Hilaire: Costume, **104**

— Meyer: Costume, **104**

Hill, Bennett D.: Cistercian monasteries, 5940

— David: Burghal hidage, 2206

— Francis: Hungate, 4810

— Francis J.: ed. National libraries, **131**

— Geoffry: English dioceses, 6794

— George F.: Treasure trove, 3668A

— Sir James W. Francis: Lincoln, 5146

— L. M.: Treason trials, 3711

— Mary C.: Jack Faulkes, 6753; King's messengers, 3134; Shropshire records, 1796

— Rosalind M. T.: Christianity in Northumbria, 2701; Ecclesiastical letter-books, 5578; London chantries, 7223; Oliver Sutton, 5745, 5752, 7125; Public penance, 6469

Hill-forts, early, 1995

Hills, Gordon M.: Hereford records, 5116

Hilton, Rodney H.: Agrarian history's sources, 4692, 4971, 4984; Clarence accounts, 4913; Decline of serfdom, 4961; Enclosure, 5001; England in twelfth and thirteenth centuries, 4963; English rising (1381), 4148; Gloucester abbey leases, 6157; Leicestershire estates, 4800, 4962; Medieval society, 4964, 5452; Peasant movements, 1468, 4148, 4965; Poem on services, 4803; Rent and capital, 4966; Sherborne manor, 4762, 6160; Stoneleigh leger book, 6369; Warwickshire, 1849, 4624, 4913, 4915; Winchcombe abbey, 4762, 6160

— Walter, 6665, 6672, 6686, 6688

Hinckley, Henry B.: Layamon's Brut, 2914

Hinde, John Hodgson: Northumberland, 1775; Pipe rolls, 3085; St. Cuthbert, 2302; Simeon of Durham, 2157

Hinds, Allen B.: State papers (Milan), 3833

Hine, Reginald L.: Hitchin, 4772

Hingeston, or Hingeston-Randolph: Francis C., Capgrave, 2808; Exeter registers, 5715; Royal letters, 3781

Hingham, (Mrs.) Florence M. G. (*née* Evans): Pre-Tudor secretary, 1458

Hinnebusch, William A.: Friars preachers, 1428, 5987A, 5993

Hinschius, Paul: Das Kirchenrecht, 1307

Hinton, James: Walter Map, 6600

Hippeau, Célestin: Collection de poètes, 6489

Histoire de Guillaume le Maréchal, 1499, 2896

— des ducs de Normandie, 2897

Historia Augusta, 2025

— Aurea, 2895, 2965

— Brittonum, 2167

— Edwardi III, 2898

— Eliensis, 1100, 2164

— Norwegiae, 1115

— Novella, 2921

— Placitorum coronae, 3665

— Pontificalis, 6640

— Rameseiensis, 1100

— Regum (Monmouth), 2166

— Regum (Simeon), 2157

— Ricardi II, 1103, 2899

— Selebiensis Monasterii, 6418

Historiae Croylandensis Continuatio, 1098, 2163

— Dunelmensis, 2157, 5685

Historic towns, 1386

Historical Abstracts, **31**

— Association, 7, 175, 1514

— literature, Guide to, 40

— MSS. Comm. reports, **108–9; 310** 756; 766; 772; 773; 775; 778; 782; 785; 826; 945, 1060, 1509, 4693, 5284, 5646, 6366

— Monuments Comm. reports, 737–9, 1852

— poems, 7046

— research, methods of, 240–65, 1489

— studies (journal), 124, 261

Historische Zeitschrift, 156

History (journal), 125

— and Theory (journal), 245

— in series, 1174–9, 1181–4, 1188–91, 1196–7

— philosophy and practice of, **30–4**

— Studies (journal), 124

Hitchin (Herts.), 4772

Hjaltalin, Jón A.: Orkney saga, 2451

Hoare, Henry W.: Bible, 1337

— Sir Richard C.: Ancient Wiltshire, 772; Giraldus' Wales, 2881; Repertorium Wiltunense, 4393; South Wiltshire, 1861

Hobbs, John L.: Local history, 1515; Shrewsbury subsidy, 3181

Hobhouse, Edmund: Churchwardens' accounts, 6838; Domesday map, 3028; Register of Norbury, 5667; Rentalia, 6315

Hobson, Thomas F.: Adderbury rectoria, 4844; manors, 192

Hoccleve, Thomas, 6977, 7020

Hockey, Stanley Frederick: Quarr abbey, 6163

Hocton (Beds.), 6077

Hodge, C. E.: Archdeacon's book, 6470

Hodges, Charles C.: Coucher book, 6418

Hodgett, Gerald A. J.: Cartulary, 6225; Wiltshire, 4492

Hodgkin, Robert H.: Anglo-Saxons, 2496; Queen's College, 7124

— Thomas: Hadrian's Wall, 2085; History of England, 1183, 2497; Roman army, 2075

Hodgkinson, Robert F. B.: Account books, 5223

Hodgson, Geraldine E.: Mystics, 6685

— Henry W.: Bibliography, 1591A

— John Crawford: Charters, 4428; Collections, 6137; Northumberland, 1775; Percy bailiff's rolls, 4837; Proofs of age, 4374; Testa de Nevill, 4374; Wills, 4524

— Phyllis: Cloud of Unknowing, 6670, 6672, 6686; Mystics, 6686

— Walter Edward: Archbishop Thomas of York, 1130

Hod Hill (Roman), 2059

Hodnett, Dorothy K.: Modus MSS., 3349
Hodson, James W.: Dorset, 1620
Höfer, Josef: Lexikon, 1270
Hofmann, M.: Domesday names, 579
— Walther A. C. von: Forschungen, 5542
Hog, Thomas: Murimuth, 2931; Trevet, 2963
Hogan, Edmund: St. Patrick, 2324
— James: Ui Briain kingship, 1445
Hogg, A. H. A.: Castles, 831
Hoghton, Sir James de: Papers, 4442
Hohenleutner, Heinrich: Johannes von Salisbury, 6644
Hohl, Ernst: Historia Augusta, 2025
Hohlbaum, Konstantin: Urkundenbuch, 2207, 5336
Holand, Dr. John (Lollard), 6873
Holborn (London), 5180
Holbrooke, Frederic: Foedera, 3765
Holcot, Robert, 6560, 6562, 6590–2, 6924
Holden, A. J.: Roman de Rou, 2974
Holder, Alfred T.: Bede, 2148; Sprachschatz, 319
Holder-Egger, Oswald: Ducs de Normandie, 2897; M.G.H., 1114; Vigeois' Chronica, 2970
Holderness (Yorks.), 1776, 1892, 4943, 6421
Holdsworth, Christopher J.: John of Ford, 5941; St. Anselm, 6535
— Sir William Searle: History of Law, 1235; Remedies against crown, 3663; Sources, 1226, 3665; Year Books, 1246, 3646
Hole, Christiana: Shrines, 1157
Holes, Andrew, 6755, 6913
Hollaender, Albert E. J.: editor, 1440, 1747, 5177; Flores historiarum, 2871
Holland, Sir Thomas Erskine: University of Oxford, 7061, 7090
Hollander, Lee M.: Bibliography, 2431; Heimskringla, 2447; Njal's saga, 2449; Skalds, 2454
Hollings, Marjory: Five-hide unit, 4655; Red Book of Worcester, 5836
Hollingworth, Thomas H.: Demography, **744**
Hollis, George: Effigies, 917
— Thomas: Effigies, 917
Hollister, Charles Warren: A.-S. Five-hide unit, 4655; A.-S. military institutions, 2614, 4304; Continuity in feudalism, 4657; Feudal revolution, 4656; Military organization, 4304; King John, 4020; Knights of Peterborough, 3069
Hollnsteiner, Johannes: Acta concilii, 5563

Hollond, Henry A.: Maitland, 1482
Holloway, William: Rye, 5318
Holm Cultram Abbey (Cumb.), 6109A
Holman, William, 1639
Holme Lacy (Hereford), 1437, 4770
Holmes, George: Foedera, 3765
— George A.: Estate of nobility, 4658; Florentine merchants, 5437; Judgement on Despenser, 4116; Lancaster rebellion (1328), 4121; Later Middle Ages, 1174; Libel of English polity, 5338
— Oliver W.: Common law, 1236; Equity, 1246
— Richard: Chartulary, 6412
— Thomas Rice E.: Ancient Britain, 2043; Caesar, 2025
— Thomas S.: Austin canons, 5954; Rentalia et custumaria, 6315; Wells and Glastonbury, 5594; Wookey, 4870
— Urban T.: Daily living, 6609; Giraldus Cambrensis, 2881; Twelfth century renaissance, 6887; Wace, 2974
Holmesdale (Kent), 4785, 4999
Holmquist, Wilhelm: editor, 727
Holmyard, Eric J.: Technology, 408
Holschneider, Andreas: Die Organa, 7186
Holt, Anne D.: Parliament, 3389
— James C.: Army rolls, **619**; Continuity on feudalism, 4657; Feudalism revisited, 4659; F. M. Stenton's lecture, 4679; Henry II's assizes, 7224; Magna Carta, 3286, 3366; Making of Magna Carta, 3289; Northerners, 3287, 4021; Praestita roll, 3110; Review, 1219; Richard de la Haye's carta, 4659; Scutage roll, 3143; St. Albans chroniclers and Magna Carta, 2979; Willoughby deeds, 1453
— Neville R.: Pipe roll, 5815
Holtby, Robert T.: Carlisle library, 1592
Holtzmann, Walther: Die Register Alexander III, 5557; Papal decretals, 6432; Papsturkunden, 1132, 2164, 5550; Wattenbach, 66
Holworthy, Richard: Wells city charters, 5248
Holy Cross, Order of, 6038–9
Holy Ghost of the Tower (Ship), 4336
Holy Land, tax for, 6779
Holyrood, Chronicle of, 2821
Holzapfel, Heribert: Franziskanerorder, 6019
Homans, George C.: A.-S. invasions, 2542; Frisians, 2576; Villagers, 4967
Homburger, Otto: Die Malerschule, 889
Homicide, 5676
Homilies, **878–80**; 441, 2266–8, 2292, 2297, 2315, 2361. *See* Sermon

Hommel, Luc: Chastellain, 2814; Marguerite d'York, 4251

Hone, Nathaniel J.: Berks. court roll, 3530; Manorial records, 4968

Honeybourne, Marjorie B.: London bridge, 5177; London (Henry II), map, 1746; London (Richard II), map, 598, 1740, 5165

Honorius III, pope: Letter to, 6735; Regesta, 5560

Honourable Society of Cymmrodorion, 126, 202

Hoo, Sir Thomas, 3416

— William of, 6339

Hook, Charles: Silgrave's Chronicon, 2953

— Walter F.: Archbishops, 5625

Hooker, James R.: Notes on household, 3270

Hooper, H. J.: Surrey wills, 4558

Hooton Pagnell (Yorks.), 4942

Hope, Sir William H. St. John: All Saints, Derby, 5053; Charterhouse, 6223; Fortresses, 823; Fountains abbey, 6400; Heraldry, 478; Inventories of Christ Church, Canterbury, 5605; Inventory of Thomas of Gloucester, 4746; Kirkstall abbey, 6405; St. Mary de Parco Stanley, 6116

Hope-Taylor, Brian: Archaeology, 766

Hopeman, Thomas, 6924

Hopkin-James, Lemuel J.: Gospels, 2669

Hopkins, Albert W.: Chester city courts, 5046

— S. V.: Wages and prices, 1468, 5495

Hörmann, Walther von: Poenitentiale, 2259

Horn, Andrew: Annals of London, 2761; Liber Horn, 5161; Mirror of justices, 2991

— Joyce M.: Le Neve's Fasti, 5582

Horncastle (Lincs.), 5144

Horncastle (Roman), 2061

Hornchurch Priory (Essex), 6144

Horne, Nathaniel: Court rolls, 4708

Hornyold-Strickland, Henry: Index, 1597, 1851; Lancs. M.P.s, 3462

Horsfield, Thomas W.: Sussex, 1841

Horsham (Sussex): Parliamentary history, 3470

Horsley, John: Britannia Romana, 2044

Horstmann, Carl: Capgrave's Nova legenda, 1158, 2287; Minor poems, 6695; St. Edith, 2304; Women saints, 1165; Yorkshire writers, 6668

Horwood, Alfred J.: Year books, 3645, 3647; Wykes custumal, 4741

Hosford, W. H.: Manor of Sleaford, 4811

Hoskin, Michael A.: Science, 6943

Hoskins, Jasper: Theological treatises, 6533

— William G.: Boundary, 1470; Devon, 1522; Devonshire studies, 1611; Landscape, 617, 1485, 1517; Leicestershire history, 1713, 4801; Leicestershire settlement, 2599; Local history, 1516; Market Harborough, 5143, 5453; Midland peasant, 4802, 4969; Provincial England, 5002, 5453; Westward expansion, 2543; Wigston Magna, 3170, 4802, 5453

Hospitallers, 461, 6042-9, 6191-2, 6205-6

Hospitals, **810**; 4176, 5808, 6070, 6090, 6133, 6135-6, 6139, 6152, 6168, 6186-7, 6196, 6209-10, 6217, 6226-7, 6230, 6260, 6344, 6353, 6362, 6378, 6386, 6425, 6935

Hoste, Anselm: Aelred of Rievaulx, 6633; Bibliotheca, 6638

Hoton, prior of Durham, 5683

Hoton v. Shakell, 3503A

Houck, Margaret E.: Roman de Brut, 2974

Houghton (Hunts.), 4775

Houghton, K. N.: Borough elections, 3447; Shrewsbury election, 3438

House of Kings, 6242

Housecarls, 2615

Household, private, **657-9**; 4601, 5177, 5481, 5587

— royal, **479-82**; 2615, 2987, 3006-7, 3045, 3250, 3670, 4017, 4140, 4195, 4278, 4294, 4604, 4609, 7222

Houses, medieval, 814-22, 1435, 1485, 1495, 2517, 4987, 5169, 5171

Houston, Mary G.: Costume, 918

Hove, Alphonse van: Canon law, 1308

Hoveden, Roger of. *See* Howden

Howard, A. E. Dick: Magna Carta essays, 3289

— John: Accounts, 4609

— Joseph J.: Miscellanea, 505

— William: Florence of Worcester's Chronicon, 2981

— de Walden (Thomas E. Scott-Ellis): Feudal lords, 459

Howden, Roger of: Chronica, 1089, 1114, 1119, 2903; Gesta Henrici II, 2879

Howdenshire (Yorks.), Poll-tax, 3205

Howe, George F.: ed., Guide, 40

Howel Dda, **310**; 2167, 2222-6, 2230

Howell, Margaret: Regalian right, 5608, 6766

— Thomas Bayly: State trials, 3484

— Thomas Jones: State trials, 3484

Howlett, Richard: Accounts rolls, 6258; Annales Furnesienses, 2757; Annales Stanleienses, 2774; Chronicles of Stephen, 2734, 2859, 2867, 2894, 2932,

2949, 2962, 6635; Continuatio Beccensis, 2853; Grey Friars' Chronicle, 2826; Monumenta Franciscana, 6010

Howorth, Sir Henry H.: Codex Amiatinus, 2301; Gregory I, 2702; Nennius, 2167

Howse, William H.: Radnorshire, 1942

Howth, Richard: Book of Howth, 2799

Hoyt, Robert S.: Bibliography, 54; Coronation oath, **173**; Farm of the manor, 3054; Kent assessment, 1453; Publications on representative institutions, 3360, 3366; Royal demesne, 3244, 4660; Terrae occupatae, 3011

Huber, Raphael M.: Franciscan Order, 6020

Hubert de Burgh, 4049

Hubert, Henri: Celts, 1997

— Merton J.: Ambroise, 2748

Hübner, Emil: Inscriptiones, 2028; Romische Heer, 2075

Hudleston, Roger: Revelations, 6673

Hudson, William: 2630; Camera roll, 5775; Leet jurisdiction, 5210; Manor of Eastbourne, 4910; Manor of Wiston, 4904; Manorial extents, 4823; Norfolk assessment, 3173; Norwich militia, 5211; Norwich records, 5207, 5211; Norwich taxation, 6781; Primitive agriculture, 4824; Sussex assessment, 3192; Sussex subsidies, 3195

Hugh (St.), bishop of Lincoln, 1113–14, 5742, 6573

— II, abbot of Reading, 1459

— Candidus, **387**; 6268, 6270

— the Chantor: History of York, 1113, 1130, 5853

— of Kirkstall: Chronicle, 6400

— of Lincoln (alleged Jewish murder), 3937, 3954

— of Wells, bishop, **756**; 5740, 5746

Hughes, Andrew: Old Hall: the inventory, 7192

— Anselm: Ars nova, 7204; Early medieval music, 7203; Old Hall MS., 7192; Worcester harmony, 7188. *See* Hughes, Humphrey

— Arthur: Dialogus de Scaccario, 3005; Lincoln parliament, 3413

— Dorothy: Chaucer's England, 1209

— Hubert D.: Durham Library, 1043

— Humphrey V. (in religion Anselm): Early harmony, 7195

— Kathleen: Culdees, 2688; History of Ireland, 1203; Irish and English churches, 7225; Irish church, 2670; Irish sources, 22; Irish scriptoria, 400, 2665; St. Finnian, **333**; Vitae Sanctorum Wallensium, 2665

— Michael W.: Bucks. feet of fines, 3532; Falk de Breauté, 3525; Gildas, 2102; Pipe rolls, 3083

— Philip: History of church, 1280

— T. M.: St. Augustine, 2704

— William: Mirroir des justices, 2991

Hugo, Thomas: Cleeve abbey charters, 6308; Somerset nunneries, 6303

Huguet, Adrien: Aspects de la guerre, 4252

Huillard-Bréholles, Alphonse: Matthew Paris, 2941

Huizinga, Johan, 1446, 1474

Hull (Yorks.), 1529, 5292–4, 5375

Hull, Felix: Berks. guide, 1540; Cinque ports, 5314; Kent guide, 1684; Local archives, 1440

— Mark R.: Roman Colchester, 2055; Roman excavations, 2070; Roman Malton, 2069; Roman pottery, 2082

— Peter L.: Cartulary, 6108

— Vernam E.: Hessen's Irish lexicon, 344

Hulme, St. Benet of (Norfolk), 2816, 2939, 6258–9, 6341

Hulne abbey (Northumb.), 1043

Hulton, William A.: Coucher book of Whalley, 6203; Penwortham documents, 6202, 6382

Humaniora Norvegica (journal), 2432

Humanism, medieval, 1438, 1477, 6911, 6923, 6930

Hume, T. A.: Kirkstall abbey excavations, 6405

Humphrey, Duke of Buckingham, 4600

— Duke of Gloucester, 1452, 4165, 4231, 6928

Humphreys, A. R.: Register of writs, 3499

— Arthur L.: Berks. parishes, 1541; Handbook, 1518; Somerset parishes, 1803; Wellington, 5249

— John: Bibliography, 1862

— John: Forest of Feckenham, 3910

— Robin A.: Royal Historical Society, 177

Humphrey-Smith, Cecil R.: Heraldry, 481

Hundred: General history, 628, 1237, 1441, 1455, 1461–2, 2210, 2637–8, 3045; court, 1482(i), 1498, 2189, 2210, 3625; Particular hundreds, 1572, 1670, 1800, 3156, 3185, 3188–90, 3551, 3559, 3586, 3625, 4351, 4454, 4593, 4709, 4726, 4741, 4763, 4777, 4875, 4910, 4921

— names, 628

— rolls: **628**; 1601, 2187, 3729–30, 4345, 4350, 4376, 4386, 4388, 4390, 4971, 4977, 5144, 5228, 7061

Hundred Years War: 568–72; 608–11; 616–27; 1499, 2790, 2793–4, 2798, 2840, 2844–8, 2874, 2916–17, 2926, 5334, 5428, 7041
Hungate (Lincs.), 4810
Hunnisett, Roy F.: Beds. coroners' rolls, 3523; Inquisitions, 7224; The medieval coroner, 3735
Hunt, E. D.: trans., 1179
— Noreen: Cluny, 5922
— Richard W.: Balliol College, 7117; Bodleian library, 1027; Clare College MSS., 1033; Cuthbert, 2303; Grammar masters, 1428; Grosseteste's symbols, 6580; Learning (twelfth century), 1493, 6905; Peter of Cornwall, 1450; Phillipps Library, 973; Tuitorial appeal, 6471
— Timothy J.: Taunton and Bradford on Tone, 4871
— William: Bath and Wells, 6790; Bishops at 1139 Council, 5567; English church, 1289, 2703; Political history, 1183; Two chartularies, 6305
— William P.: Two rentals, 6347
Hüntemann, Ulric: Bullarium Franciscanum, 6004
Hunter Archaeological Society (Yorks.), 1878
Hunter, Joseph: Catalogue, 1011; Ecclesiastical documents, 5585; Feet of fines, 3487; Familiae, 563; Pipe rolls, 3077; Rotuli selecti, 3217, 3502, 3780; South Yorkshire, 1890; Thomas de Gournay, 4139; Three catalogues, 975, 3007
Hunter-Blair. See Blair, Charles and Blair, Peter
Hunterian Museum (Glasgow), 704, 1065
Hunting, Letters on, 3898
Huntingdon, archdeacon of, 5755
— borough of, 5118
— earldom of, 1538, 4415, 4671
Huntingdon, Henry of: Historia, 2904
Huntingdonshire: Antiquities, 737; Church 1529, 5755; County history, 1529; County journals and societies, 1682–1682A; County records, 1679–81, 1682A; Domesday, 1529; Feet of fines, 3555; Hidation, 2636; Manors and villages, 4775–7; Parliament, 1459, 3435, 3459A; Religious houses, 6172–7; Topography, 1529; Urban history, 5118; Wills, 4529
Hurley (Berks.), 4417, 4710, 6088
Hurley, Michael: Scriptura sola, 6663
Hurnard, Naomi D.: A.-N. franchises, 2608, 4661; Edward I and seisin, 4681; King's pardon, 3698; Magna Carta, 1450
Hurry, Jamieson B.: Reading abbey, 6092
Hurst, Sir Gerald: Lincoln's Inn, 7155
— John G.: Deserted villages, 4836, 4950; Recent archaeology, 766

Hurstbourne, 1470
— Priors (Hants), 4768
Husbandry, 696–700
Hussey, Arthur: Kent wills, 4532, 4536; Records of Lydd, 5319
— Robert: Bede, 2148
— Stanley S.: Piers Plowman, 7027
Hussite movement, 6656
Husting, court of, 4544
Hutchins, John: Dorset, 1620
Hutchinson, Harold F.: The Hollow Crown, 4123
— Horace G.: New Forest, 3911
— William: Cumberland, 1596; Durham, 1625
Hutter, Catherine: trans., 2459
Hutton, Edward: Franciscans in England, 6021
— Matthew: Registers of Richmond, 5859
— William H.: St. Thomas of Canterbury, 6490
Huygens, Robert B. C.: Henry II, 6519
Hyams, Edward: Jeanne d'Arc, 4264
— Paul R.: Peasant land market, 4970
Hyamson, Albert M.: Jews, 3956
Hyde abbey, Winchester, 1123, 1319, 2165, 5814, 5910
Hyde, Douglas: Literary History, 2415
— Patricia: Hundred rolls, 4376
Hyett, Sir Francis A.: Bibliography, 1642; Catalogue, 1641; MSS. Glos., 1643
Hylle Cartulary, 4469
Hylle, Robert of Spaxton, 4469
Hythe (Kent), 6838
Hywel Dda. See Howel Dda

Ibstone (Bucks.), 4849
Iceland, 1433, 5393, 5432
Ickham, Peter of, 2918
Icklington (Suffolk), 4885
Icknield Way, 2548
Ightham (Kent), 4779
Ihm, Maximilian: Suetonius, 2025
Ilchester (Som.), 4872
Ilchester, Richard of, bishop, 6520
Illingworth, William: Placita, 3492; Public records, 965
Illuminated MSS., 101–3; 7225
Immunities, 2608–9, 6077. See Franchises
Impeachment, origin of, 1451, 1464, 1491, 3415, 3417–18
Imray, Jean M.: Les bones gentes, 5177; Richard Whittington, 5194
Imrie, John: Scottish archives, 130
Incerti Scriptoris Chronicon, 2833
Incipits, 53; 6885, 6967
Inclosures, 4972
Incomes, 4958, 6951

Incorporation, doctrine of, 1246, 1412, 1482, 5024
Indentures of retinue, **619**; 1455, 4283–4, 4308, 5502
Inderwick, Frederick A.: Inner Temple records, 7145
Index actorum pontificum, **751**
— Library, 182
— of Archaeological Papers (Gomme), 717
— Society, 182
— to Legal Periodicals, 1227
Indictments (K.B.), (Kent), 4784
Indulgences, 1283, 1286–7
Industrial revolution (thirteenth century), 1468
Industry, **747–9**; 4953
Ine, king, 2184; laws, 1426, 2616
Ingelric the priest, 4004
Ingimund's invasion, 2146, 2600
Ingleby, Clement: Blomefield's Norfolk, 1756
Inglewood forest, 3919
Inglis, Harry R. G.: Maps, 599
Ingold, J.: Coinage, 1454
Ingoldmells-cum-Addlethorpe (Lincs.), 4812
Ingpen family, 4581
Ingpen, Arthur R.: An ancient family, 4581; Master Worsley's Book, 7153
Ingulf: Historia Croylandensis, 1098, 1119, 1123, 2163
Inheritance, 4955
Inman, Alfred H.: Feudal statistics, 3055
Inner Temple, **925**; 1013, 7145–6, 7159
Innes Review (journal), 127
Innes of Learney, Sir Thomas, 479, 506
— Cosmo: Facsimiles, 448; Statuta gildae, 5222
Innisfallen, Annals of, 1117, 2779–80
Innocent III, pope: Letters, 1113, 5558–9
— IV, pope, 6781
Inns of Chancery, 7144, 7151, 7158
— of Court, **925–7**; 963, 965, 974, 1011, 1013–14, 1249, 6064, 7007
Inquest of Cambridgeshire, 3010
— of Ely, 3010, 3052
— of service, 4004, 4367, 4385. *See* Testa de Nevill
— of Sheriffs, 4004
Inquests post mortem: **627**; 4338–40, 4342;
　Bedfordshire, 4346
　Cheshire, 3856, 4347
　Cornwall, 4348
　Devon, 4348
　Dorset, 4352–3
　Durham, 3865, 4355
　Flint, 3856, 4347

Glamorgan, 3785
Gloucestershire, 4356, 4754
Hampshire, 4763
Hertfordshire, 4773
Huntingdonshire, 4775, 6173
Kent, 4362
Lancashire, 3872–3, 3877, 4363–4, 4366–7, 4369–70, 4790, 4793
Leicestershire, 3568
Lincolnshire, 4371
Norfolk, 4372, 4454
Nottinghamshire, 4375
Shropshire, 4377
Somerset, 4379, 4381
Staffordshire, 4383–4
Wiltshire, 1861, 3617, 4392, 4489
Worcestershire, 4394
Yorkshire, 4395, 4397
Inquisitio geldi, **463**; 3009, 3019, 3066
Inquisitions: 1482(iii), 3756, 7224
— manorial:
　Canterbury, St. Augustine's, 6180
　Cirencester, 4758
　Eynsham, 6289
　Glastonbury, 6311
　Gloucestershire, 4758
　Hertfordshire, 4773
　London, St. Paul's, 5759
　Norwich, 5210
　Oxfordshire, 5234
　Richmond, 4503
　Templars, 6055
Inquisitions ad quod damnum, **627**; 955, 3758, 4384, 4397
Inscriptions, 363, 445, 1650
— Roman, 1084, 2015, 2021, 2027–8, 2044
— Runic, **44–5**
Institut de Recherche et d'Histoire de Textes, 379
Instituta Cnuti, 2183
Institute of Advanced Studies of Dublin, 224
— of Historical Research, London, 112
Institutis Lundoniae, De, 2207
Interdict, 1491, 4924, 5592, 5603, 5809, 6729, 6733
International Bibliography, 53
— Commission on Assemblies, **510**; 3307, 3313
— Congress of Numismatics, 647
— Medieval Bibliography, 54
Intestacy, 1246
Intestates, 6443
Invasions, Britain between (Roman) invasions, 1432, 1994, 2034
Inventaria Archaeologica, 735
Inventione, De: S. Crucis, 2285

Inventories: 1075, 3256, 3488, 3871–2, 4746, 6782;
Bury St. Edmunds, 4556
Canterbury, Christ Church, 5605
Coldingham, 6132
Cumberland, 4566
Durham, 3865, 4524, 5682
Farne, 6276
Finchale, 6134
Holy Island, 6276
Jarrow, 6138
Lancashire, 4566; duchy, 3871
London, Rolls Chapel, 3770
— St. Paul's, 5766
— Tower, 2101
Monk-Wearmouth, 6138
Norham, 6276
Northumberland, 4524
Salisbury, 1343
Westmorland, 4566
Yorkshire, 4566
Inventory of:
— crown jewels, 3122
— Fastolf's effects, 4599
— forest records, 3889
— royal accounts, 3144
Investiture struggle, 2189, 6527, 6529, 6534–5, 6728
Investment in agriculture, 5012
Inwara and Utwara, 1496
Iona, 2319, 2686
Ipswich (Suffolk), 1504, 3187, 4286, 4553, 5259–64
— Holy Trinity priory, 6347
— Jews of, 3951
— St. Peter's priory, 6348
Ireby, township (Cumb.), 5051
Ireland: 1199–203, 1429, 1445, 1464, 2125, 2128–9, 2133, 2174, 2416, 2449, 2605, 2920, 4004, 4030–1, 4079, 4114
— Administration, 539, 3321, 3366, 3846
— Antiquities, 732, 736, 743, 2004–5, 2007
— Archaeology and art, 732, 736, 743, 756, 761, 775, 801, 832, 843, 846, 848, 1979
— Archives, **131–4**
— Bibliographies, 12, 13, 16, 22–3, 30, 35, 68, 128, 2406, 4030
— Chronicles, 2146, 2150, 2160, 2170, 2174, 2403–4, 2751, 2755, 2759–60, 2777–80, 2782–4, 2786, 2799, 2800, 2809, 2839, 2849, 2881, 2920, 2924–5, 2954, 6309, 6573
— Church, 1274, 2662A, 2670–2, 2677, 2684, 6805; Canons and penitentials, 1166, 1438, 2252, 2255, 2260–1; Celtic church, 761, 2670, 2684, 7225 (see Saints); Council of Basel and, 5573; Council of Constance and, 5563; Records,

1129, 1141–2, 2254, 5547, 5554, 5556, 5559; Relations with Rome, 1438, 2673, 5554, 5556, 5559, 6774; Religious houses, **793**; 1295, 1302A, 1438, 1445, 2123, 2676, 2688, 5970–1, 5982, 6017, 6042, 6046, 6054, 6065; Saints, **148–51**; 1445, 2319, 2324, 2667
— Coinage, 679, 684, 693, 701, 1454
— Exchequer and revenue, **491**; 3008, 3097–101, 3211, 3217–18, 3248, 3260, 3366, 3780
— Genealogy, 510, 520, 539, 545, 556, 565, 567, 582
— Geography and place-names, 600, 622
— Heraldry, 490–1, 497
— Journals and societies, **28–9**; 124, 128, 724, 1072, 1081, 2389
— Language and literature, **43–4** and **346–51**; 359, 361, 2954
— Laws, **312–14**; and English law, 1438, 1482, 3666
— Manuscripts, 30, 45, 226, 440, 443, 448, 453, 972, 997, 1010, 1069, 1073, 1076, 1079–83
— Parliament, 1464, 3309, 3329–33, 3347A, 3354, 3366, 3392
— Plea rolls, 3641A–3642
— Records, **131–4**; 21–3, 955, 968, 1010, 1104–5, 3008, 3097–8, 3211, 3217, 3309, 3321, 3330–3, 3502, 3641–2, 3780–1, 3797–800, 3806
— Schools, 1396
— Scriptoria, 391, 400, 1445, 2665
— Society, 1217, 2135, 2248, 2416, 2421
— Vikings, 2150, 2174, 2483, 2585A, 2605
Irish Academy (Royal), 1081
— Archaeological Society, 225
— Ecclesiastical Record, 233
— Historical Studies, 128, 234
— Record Commissioners, 227, 1070
— Record Office, 228
— Text Society, 2389
— Theological Quarterly, 235
Iron Age, problems, 2011
— industry, 5500, 5511, 5519
Irvine, William Fergusson: Cheshire charters, 4422; Chester, 5044; Lancs.-Ches. wills, 4537
Irving, Edward B. Jr.: Genesis and Exodus, 2339
Irwin, Raymond: London libraries, 1006
Isaacson, Robert F.: Registers of St. David's, 5880G
Isabel of France (Richard II's queen), 4187
Isabella (Edward II's queen), 1459, 4604
— of Angoulême, 1486, 4038
Isis (journal), **179**; 6933–4
Isle of Man. *See* Man

Islendinga Sögur, 2439–40
Íslenzk Fornrit, 2441
Islip manor (Oxon.), 4845
Islip, Simon: Speculum, Edward III, 2955
Issue rolls, **477–9**; 3258
Isurium Brigantum. *See* Aldborough
Italia pontificia, 1132
Italian bankers and merchants, 1438, 1469, 1472, 3105, 3774, 5409, 5435–7, 5517, 5522
Italy, Archives, 1441, 3833–4
— Englishmen in, 6750, 6754–8, 6767, 6919, 6922
Itinerant Justices, 5842
Itineraria Romana, 2029
Itineraries, 1089, 1099, 1114, 1455, 2026, 2029, 2843, 2881, 2906, 2982, 3778, 3998, 4017, 4019, 4024, 4050, 4120, 4235
Itinerarium Peregrinorum, 1089, 1099, 1114, 1455, 2906
Ives, E. W.: Andrew Dymmock, 4208; Reputation of lawyers, **551**; 7152
Ivories, 870
Ivy, G. S.: Bibliography, 410
Iwerne Valley (Dorset), 4735

Jaager, Werner: Bede, 2297; Cuthbert, 2302
Jack, R. Ian: Entail and descent, 4582; Grey of Ruthin valor, 4625; Medieval Wales, 22
— Sybil: Monastic lands, 6207
Jackson, Charles: Deeds, 4495
— John: Tacitus, 2025
— John E.: Aubrey's Collections, 1860; Index, 5808; Liber Henrici de Soliaco, 6314
— Kenneth: Aneirin, 2384; Angles and Britons, 2526; Angles in Lothian, 1433; British language, 2122; Britons in South Scotland, 2126; Duan Albanach, 1120; Gododdin, 2384, 2544; Kentigern, 2665; Language and history, 320, 2127, 2417; Nennius, 2123, 2167; Ogam inscriptions, 1429; Place-names, 319
Jacob, Ernest F.: All Souls College, 1455, 7122; Baronial reform, 4052; Book of St. Albans, 1474; Brouns, Thomas, 5787; Canterbury and York registers, **756**; 5578; Canterbury convocation, 1459, 6820; Chichele, 1450, 5629; Cluniac chronicle, 2935; Collapse of France, 4253; Concordat (of 1418), 1438; Councils, 1473, 1474, 5569; Court of Rome, 1474, 6754; Essays, 1473–4; Fortescue, John, 1473, 2988; Founders and foundations, 1474; Fountains abbey election, 1437, 1474; Henry III, **597**;

4051; Henry V, 4253; Huizinga, 1474; John de Roquetaillade, 1474; Legacy, ed., 1479; Life of St. Alban, 890; Ockham, 1473, 6623; Parliament (1279), 3323; Pecock, 1474, 6630; Petitions for benefices, 1473; Promotion of clerks, 6767; St. Richard of Chichester, 5662; Simon de Montfort, 4043; Stafford (John), archbishop, 1474, 5639; Swan, William, 1437, 1474, 6754; Testamentary jurisdiction, 5621; University clerks, 1473; Verborum florida venustas, 1473, 2980; Wilkins, David, 1142; Winchester College, muniments, 7138
Jacobs, Joseph: Bibliotheca, 3931, 3954; Jews of Angevin England, 3957; Little St. Hugh, 3954
Jacobsthal, Paul: Celtic art, 1998
Jaffé, Philipp: Bibliotheca rerum Germanicarum, 2295; Monumenta Gregoriana, 5555; Regesta, 1131
Jahncke, Rudolf: William of Newburgh, 2932
Jahresberichte der deutschen Geschichte, 157
— der Geschichtswissenschaft, 157
James, John W.: Liber Landavensis, 5880A; Rhigyfarch's St. David, 1173, 2321
— Margery K.: Anglo-Gascon wine trade, 5395; London merchant, 5175
— Montague R.: Aberdeen Library, 1063; Aldhelm, 2296; Bohun MSS., 4572; B.M. Royal MSS., 1002; Cambridge catalogues, 1033; Canterbury and Dover libraries, 1041; Collectanea Franciscana, 6006; East Anglian psalters, 903; Ethelbert, 2307; Estoire de Seint Ædward, 2171; Fasciculus J. W. Clark, 7049; Gualteri Mapes, 6599; Henry VI, 2796; Illuminated MSS., 890–5; John Rylands library, 1036; Lambeth catalogue, 1009; Norwich cathedral library, 5782; St. Edmund at Bury, 6345; St. William of Norwich, 3937; Wandering of MSS., 976; Westminster MSS., 1016, 6248
— Thomas: Bodleian librarian, 1018
Jamieson, Alan: Glos. handlist, 1644
Janauschek, Leopold: Origines, 1148
Jane, L. Cecil: Asser, 2147; Bede's History, 2148; Brakelond's Chronicle, 6335
Jankuhn, Herbert: Continental home, 2511; Tacitus, 2505
Janson, Sverker: Bibliography, 727
Jansson, Sven F. B.: Vikings, 357
Jardine, D.: State trials, 3484
Jarlshof, Shetland, 766, 1992

Jarrett, Bede: Dominicans, 5983, 5994
— Michael G.: Birley essays, 1427; Roman army, 2075; Roman Maryport, 2045; Roman Wales, 2089
Jarrow, monastery (Durham), 2297, 6137–8
Jarry, Eugène: Histoire, 1277
— Louis, Armée anglaise, 4277
Jarvis, Rupert C.: Customs records, 5384
Jaryc, Marc: Periodicals, 90
Jayne, Arthur G.: trans. Sagas, 2456
Jeaffreson, John C.: Leicester MSS., 5136; Middlesex records, 1727
Jeake, Samuel: Charters of Cinque Ports, 5315
Jean II, roi de France, 3805, 3820
Jean II et de Charles V, Chronique, 2845
— de Venette: Chronicle, 2967
— le Bel: Chronique, 2916
— le Bon, 3813
Jeanne d'Arc, 1455, 2840, 4241, 4246, 4256, 4264, 4267–8
Jeayes, Isaac H.: Anglesey charters, 6326; Chandos-Pole charters (Radbourne), 4431; Compotus rolls, 4834; Court rolls, 5073; Derbyshire charters, 4431; Fitzhardinge charters (Berkeley), 4437; Gresley charters (Drakelowe), 4431; Lyttleton charters (Hagley), 4493; Rydeware chartulary, 4478; Staffordshire charters, 4473
Jedin, Hubert: Council of Trent, 6716
Jeffs, Robin: The Poynings–Percy dispute, 4643
Jekyll, Thomas: Researches of, 1639
Jenckes, Adaline L.: The staple, 5386
Jenkins, Claude: Chronicles, 387; Lambeth MSS., 1009; Registrum Sudbury, 5764
— Dafydd: Llyfr Colan, 2227; Welsh laws, 2223, 2239
— Helen: Papal efforts for peace, 4181
— John G.: Bucks. charters, 4419; Bucks. eyre roll, 3533; Cartularies, 6094–6
— Rhys: Sussex iron industry, 5500
— Robert C.: Canterbury, 6790; Chartulary, 6194
— Robert T.: Bibliography, 10; Cymmrodorion Society, 126
Jenkinson, Sir Hilary: Archives, 932, 941, 1827; Beds. wills, 4520; Chertsey court rolls, 6351; Common law records, 3677; Essays to, 1440; Exchequer of Jews pleas, 3482, 3933; Exchequer of pleas, 3512; Exchequer receipts, 3108; Introduction to P.R.O. guide, 951; Medieval tallies, 3245; Moneylender, 1448, 5509; Northampton Donum, 3938; Palaeography, 387–8; Parliament (Edward I), 3410; Plea rolls of county courts, 3736;

P.R.O., 949; Receipts from Jewry, 3936; seals, 460, 469; Sheriff, 3528; Studies for, 1441; William Cade, 5509
Jenkinson, Mrs. Hilary (Alice V.): Beds. taxation, 3149; Domesday bibliography, 3039
Jenks, Edward: Doctrine of consideration, 1237; Law and politics, 1237; Negotiable instruments, 1246; Oxford council, 3301; Short history, 1237
Jenner, Henry: Cornish language, 328; Drawings, 873
Jennings, Sir Ivor: Magna Carta, 3285
— J. C.: Dominic of Evesham, 6383
Jensen, Gillian F.: Personal names, 579
— O.: Denarius sancti Petri, 6777
Jerningham, Edward: Edward IV's invasion, 2901
Jersey, 1953, 1956, 2000, 3103. See Channel Islands
Jervoise, E.: Manor of Barton, 4737
Jesperson, Otto: English language, 34
Jessen, Knud: Cereals, 2631
Jessopp, Augustus: Before the great pillage, 6849; Crabbe's Materials, 4818; Life of St. William, 3937; Norwich, 6790; Visitations, 5780
Jessup, Frank W.: Kent, 1685; Twysden, 1124
— Ronald F.: Archaeology, 85; A.-S. jewellery, 2479; Kent, 762; SE. England, 761
Jeudwine, John W.: Tort, crime and police, 3669
Jeulin, Paul: Un grand honneur anglais: Richmond, 4626
Jewels, 868, 1433, 2479, 3122, 3129
Jewish Historical Society, Transactions, 176, 3929
— Quarterly Review, 3930
Jews, 584–8; 6006. See Exchequer of the Jews
Joan of Arundel, 4213
— of Navarre, queen, 3129
Jocelin, bishop of Wells, 1491, 5592
— of Brakelond, 1113–14, 6335
— monk of Furness: Kentigern, 2321
Jocelyn, Arthur: Awards, 495
John XXII, pope, 5553, 6864
John, king of England, 594–6; Boroughs, 5348; Chroniclers of his reign, 390; Church and, 1139, 6729, 6733–4, 6742; Courts and, 3682–3; Deposition alleged (1212–13), 1450; Financial records, 3245; Leges Anglorum, 2184; London, 5159; Magna Carta, 501–2; Seal, 469; Treasure, 1450
— king of France, 2845, 3805, 3820
— count of Mortain, 3806

— duke of Bedford, 1451, 4266, 4270, 4273
— duke of Norfolk, 4605
— of Altavilla, 7042
— of Avesnes, 4096
— of Ayton (Acton), 6436
— of Benstede, 1448
— of Beverley, 2289
— of Bridlington, 7049
— of Brittany, 4058
— of Burgundy, 4170
— of Cella, 2979
— of Cheltenham, 6160
— of Drokensford, 5589
— of Eversden, 2819, 2981
— of Ford, 5941, 6682
— of Fordun, 2872
— of Gaunt, 3437, 3462, 3875–6, 4136, 4283
— of Glastonbury, 1103, 6313
— of Grandisson, 5715
— of Halton, 1499, 5646
— of Hauteville (Altavilla), 7042
— of Hexham, 1114, 1123–4, 2157, 2893, 6274
— of Kirkby, 4396
— of London, 2852
— of Oxford, 2995, 3000
— of Oxnead (Oxenedes), 2939
— of Peterborough, 1122, 2834
— of Pontissara, 5818
— of Reading, 2944
— of Salisbury. *See* Salisbury, John of
— of Sandale, 5816
— of Sautre, 2151
— of Stanbury, 5730
— of Tayster, 2819, 2958, 2981
— of Trefnant, 5730
— of Trillek, 5730
— of Tours, 1494
— of Trokelowe, 1103, 2964
— of Tynemouth, 1158, 1448, 2287, 2888, 2965
— of Wallingford, 1114, 1123, 2975
— of Warenne, 1478
— of Worcester, 2981
John, Eric: A.-S. land tenure, 2632; Common burdens, 2621; Litigation, 6183; Studies, 1475; Worcester charter, 2220
John Rylands Library: Bulletin, 129; Catalogue, 80; MSS., 1034–7
Johnes, Thomas: Froissart, 2874; Monstrelet, 2926
Johnson, Arthur H.: Drapers, 5189
— Bernard: Merchant taylors, 5301
— Charles: Admiralty case, 3515; Bullion coined, 708; Care of documents, 941;

Court hand, 388; De Moneta, 3007; Dialogus, 3005; Domesday (Norfolk), 1529; Edward III as Count of Toulouse, 1448; Feet of fines, 3592–3; Handbook, 371; Helps for Students, 260; Henry I's charter, 1455; Henry II and papacy, 6505; Hugh the Chantor, 5853; Index of writers, 8; Judicial procedure, 3699; Latin wordlist, 301; Papal bulls, 1458; Pipe roll, 3077; Public Record Office, 949, 1441; Regesta, 3779; Registrum Hethe, 5792; Shipbuilding, 5510
— Harold B.: Canterbury freemen's rolls, 4784, 5119
— Harold C.: Surrey taxation, 3191
— John: Ecclesiastical laws, 6433
— John H.: King's wardrobe, 3136
— Richard: Customs of Hereford, 5117
Johnson-Ferguson, Edward A. J.: Placenames, 642
Johnston, Alfred W.: Orkney saga, 2451
— George H.: Heraldry, 479
— Graham: Heraldry, 475
— Leonard: Aristotle in the west, 6880
— Ronald C.: Richard I's Crusade, 2788
Johnstone, Hilda: Accounts of Edward I's sons, 3123–4; Annales Gandenses, 2758; Council of Lambeth, 1458, 6811; County of Ponthieu, 4100; Edward I and II, **597**; Edward of Carnarvon, 4053; John de Cole, 4109; Parliament of Lincoln (1316), 3413; Prince Edward's letters, 3125; Queen's exchequer, 1455; Queen's household, 1223, 3137; State trials, 3519
Jolliffe, John E. A.: Angevin kingship, 4022; Beginnings of parliament, 3365, 3400; Book-right, 2623; Camera regis Henrici II, 3246; Chamber and castle treasury, 1450; Constitutional history, 1214; Era of folk, 1451; Hundred in Kent, 1455; Northumbrian institutions, 4662; Pre-feudal England, 2545, 2633; Sussex hidation, 3031
Jonas, monk of Bobbio: Columban, 2320
Jones, A.: Basingwerk abbey, 1455
— Arnold, H. M.: Roman empire, 2030, 2046
— Arthur: Flint ministers' accounts, 3858, 4620; Gruffydd ap Cynan, 2902
— Arthur G. Prys: Carmarthenshire, 1910
— B.: Le Neve's Fasti, 5582
— Charles W.: Bede, 2297; Saints' lives, 2281
— David Brynmor: Welsh people, 1194
— David W.: (Dafydd Morganwg), 1925
— Dorothy: Walter Hilton, 6672
— Edward: Exchequer index, 3214

Jones, Ethel C.: Corrodies, 5830
— Evan David: Book of Llandaff, 5880A; Glyn Cothi Lewis, 7030; National Library, 1055
— Evan J.: Creton's Richard II, 2856; Eulogium, 2865
— Evan John: Education in Wales, 7137; Heraldry, 480
— F. E.: Coinage, 1454
— Francis: Genealogy, 514
— G. D. B.: Romans, 2093
— Gareth H.: Guide to Selden Society Publs., **455**; 195
— Glanville: Settlement, 2103, 2546, 2646; Tribal system, 2103
— Goronwy T. S. *See* Salusbury, G. T.
— Gwilym P.: Mason's wages, 5491; Mason, 800
— Gwyn: Egil's saga, 2445; Vikings, 2586
— H. Gordon: Bridges's R. Bacon, 6539
— Sir Henry Stuart: Roman sculpture, 2080
— Horace L.: Strabo, 2025
— J. R.: Journal of Roman Studies, 2015
— John: Glyn Cothi Lewis, 7030
— John Morris: Old Irish grammar, 345; Taliesin, 2385; Welsh grammar, 338
— Llewellyn: Churchwarden's accounts, 6838
— Michael: Ducal Brittany, 4182, 4182A
— Owen: Myvyrian Archaiology, 1116, 2382
— Philip E.: Essays to, 1747, 5177; London records, 1728; Plea rolls, 5156; Poulters' company, 5199
— Putnam F.: Bede concordance, 2148
— Richard H.: Royal policy, 4124
— Robert Ellis: Geoffrey of Monmouth, 2166
— Rufus M.: Mysticism, 6687
— Theophilus: Brecknock, 1898
— Thomas: Brut y Tywysogion, 2805; Cronica de Wallia, 2144, 3785A; Giraldus Cambrensis, 2881; King Arthur, 2166
— William H. Rich: Charters of Salisbury, 5799; Domesday for Wiltshire, 3032; Fasti, 5807; Nomina villarum, 4393; Salisbury diocese, 5799, 6790; Statuta, 5804; Vetus registrum, 5805
— William H. Samuel: St. Catherine's college, 7099
— William R.: Court of the verge, 3670; Free chapels, 6850; The two laws, 6472
Joneston, Elias, 3812, 3839
Jónsson, Finnur: Sagas, 2436, 2442, 2445-6, 2448-50
— Guoni: Sagas, 2440, 2446, 2449

Jope, Edward M.: Origin of perpendicular, 798; Regional cultures, 1435; Saxon building, 809; Saxon Oxford, 1442
Jordan, John: Enstone, 4853
— Karl: Archiv für Diplomatik, 412
Joris, André: La Hanse, 5428
Joseph of Arimathea, St., 6319
Joshua, Joan: Modes and manners, 907
Jost, Karl: Wulfstan, 2315
Jouet, Roger: La Resistance, 4270
Joüon des Longrais, Frédéric: La conception de la saisine, 3700
Jourdain, Francis: Charters of Ashburne, 4429
Journal d'un Bourgeois de Paris, 2907
— of British Studies, 158
— of Celtic Studies, 321
— of Documentation, 934
— of Ecclesiastical History, 130
— of Economic History, 159
— of Roman Studies, 2015
Journals, **13-29**
Joyce, James W.: Sacred synods, 6812
— Patrick W.: Social history of Ireland, 2416
Joynt, Maud, 2667
Judd, Arnold F.: Life of Thomas Bekynton, 5595; Wells archdeacon, 6755
Judith, 2328
Julian of Norwich, 6665, 6673, 6688
Juliana, 2328
Jumièges, Guillaume de, 1092, 1096, 1443; Ducs de Normandie, 2897; Gesta, 2908; Guy of Amiens's De bello Hastingense, 2749
Junghanns, Hermann: Kirchenpolitik, 6732
Jungmann, Josef A.: The Mass, 1338
Junius MS., 2327, 2339
Jurisdiction, ecclesiastical, **853-6**; 5617, 5871, 6449, 6456, 6467, 6472, 6476
— private, 4946
Jury, 1248, 1252, 1258, 2988, 3625, 4973, 6420
Jusserand, Jean A. A. J.: Wayfaring life, 5454
Justice, manorial, 4971
— in north-east, 3868
Justices, 529, 534, 1481, 3685-93
— in eyre, **525**; 3492, 3504, 3527, 3533-4, 3553, 3558, 3576, 3579, 3579A, 3589, 3601, 3622, 3625, 3627, 3632, 3661
— of the Jews, 3482
— (keepers) of the peace, 3495, 3526, 3529, 3536, 3549, 3560, 3574-5, 3584, 3590, 3599, 3615, 3635, 3677, 3742, 3745, 7007, 7064, 7223
Justiciars, 3684, 3732, 3850

Jutes, the, 1442, 2541, 2633
Juvénal des Ursins, Jean: Histoire, 2840, 2909

Kaeppeli, Thomas: Un recueil de sermons, 6690
Kahl, William F.: Livery companies, 5184
Kail, Josef: Political poems, 7050
Kalendar of Abbot Samson, 6338
Kaltenbrunner, Ferdinand: ed. Jaffé's Regesta, 1131
Kaminkow, Marion J.: Bibliography, 516; Genealogy, MSS., 515
Kane, George: Middle English literature, 6987; Piers Plowman, 7022, 7028
Kantorowicz, Ernst H.: Fleta, 2987; Francis Accursius, 6751; King's two bodies, 3273; Laudes regiae, 1353, 3273; Petrus de Vinea, 425A
— Hermann: Bractonian problems, 2985; Grammarian, 6610; Ralph Niger, 2933
Kapsner, Oliver L.: Benedictine bibliography, 1297, 5906
Karpinski, Louis C.: Robert of Chester, 6953
Kaufmann, Horst: Glanvill, 2989
Kay, Richard: Wendover's last annal, 2979
Kaye, John M.: Murder and manslaughter, 3701; Placita Corone, 3001; Sacrabar, 3733
Keary, Charles F.: Catalogue, 689
Keeler, Laura: Geoffrey of Monmouth, 2166
Keen, Maurice H.: Brotherhood in arms, 4309; Laws of war, 4305; Outlaws, 5455; Treason trials, 3709
Keeney, Barnaby C.: Military service, 4314
Keep, Ann E.: John Lydgate, 7036
Keeton, George W.: Norman conquest, 3671, 3993
Kehr, Paul F.: Regesta, 1132, 5550
Keigwin, Charles A.: Equity, 3723
Keil, Ian: Chamberer of Glastonbury Abbey, 6312
Keiller, Alexander: Wessex, 753
Keim, H. W.: Æthelwold, 2293
Kelham, Robert: Britton, 2986; Domesday Book, 3056; Fleta, 2987; Laws of William, 2187
Kellaway, William: Bibliography, 24; London possessory assizes, 3580; Studies in London history, 1747, 5177
Kellawe, Richard de, bishop, 3865, 3867, 5691
Kelleher, John V.: Irish genealogies, 567
Keller, Wolfgang: A.-S. palaeographie, 389

Kellett, J. R.: Gild, 5185
Kells, Book of, 881, 1449
Kelly, Amy R.: Eleanor of Aquitaine, 4023
— Francis M.: Costume, 919
— Henry A.: Canonical implications, 4209, 6453
— J. M.: ed. MacNeill's Ancient laws, 2249
Kelshall (Herts.), Manorial survey, 1677
Kemble, John M.: Codex, 2201; Hospitallers, 6044; Names, 589; Saxons, 2498
Kemp, Brian R.: Hereditary benefices, 6836; Monastic dean, 6167
— Eric W.: Canon law, 6434; Convocation, 5621; Counsel and consent, 6813; Papal decretals, 6432
— John, archbishop and cardinal, 1438, 5573, 5849
Kempe, Alfred J.: St. Martin-le-Grand, 6067
— Margery, 6665, 6688, 6977
Kempston (Beds.), 4705
Kendale (Westm.), 4487
Kendall, Paul M.: Richard III, 4210; Warwick, 4210; Yorkist age, 5456
Kendon, Frank: Mural paintings, 857
Kendrick, Sir Thomas D.: Archaeology, 774; A.-S. art, 2480; British antiquity, 1476, 2166, 2950; Channel Islands, 2000; County archaeologies, 762; Druids, 1999; Lindisfarne gospels, 896; Saxon and Viking art, 799; Vikings, 2587
Kenilworth, Dictum of, 3502
Kennedy, Arthur G.: Bibliography, 273
— Charles W.: Beowulf, 2335; Caedmon, 2339; Cynewulf, 2343; Poetry, 2356
— Peter A.: Guide, 1779
Kennett, White: Parochial antiquities, 4854; Synods, 6814
Kenney, James F.: Sources, 23
— Sylvia W.: Walter Frye, 7189, 7205
Kent: Antiquities, 762, 1529; Archives, 1504, 1683-7; Church, **759-65**; 1529; County history, 1529, 1692-4, 4214, 4226; County journals and societies, 1688-91, 1732; County records, 2644, 3164, 4784, 4976; Distribution of wealth, 4636; Domesday, 1529; Eyres, 3558; Farms, 4986; Feet of fines, 3556-7, 3561; Feudal tenures, 3164, 4360-1; Gavelkind, 2644; Inquests, 4360-2; Justices of peace, 3560; Map, 4784; Parliament, 3460; Pleas, 1692, 3562; Religious houses, **821-2**; Subsidy rolls, 3165; Tenures, 2644; Topography, 1505, 4986, 4999; Wills, 4530-6; Wool trade, 5418

Kent, John P. C.: Notitia Dignitatum, 2030, 2104; Roman Britain to Saxon England, 1454; Roman coins, 647, 2072
— Sherman: Writing history, 257
Kentigern, St., 2322, 2665
Kenyon, Sir Frederic G.: British Museum, 989; Facsimiles, 445
— Kathleen: Excavations, 2070
— Nora (Mrs. Nora Ritchie): Labour conditions, 1468, 4149
— Robert L.: Gold coins, 690; Manor of Ruyton, 4863; Silver coins, 685
Kepier, hospital (Durham), 6133
Ker, Neil R.: All Souls' library, 7169; A.-S. MSS., 977, 2292; Bede MSS., 2297; Books at St. Paul's, 5177; B.M. MSS., 978; Byrhtferd, 2366; English MSS., 390; Hemming's Cartulary, 1450, 2200; Liber Custumarum, 5161; Lichfield MSS., 1047; Malmesbury's handwriting, 2921; Medieval libraries, 7168; Norwich MSS., 1050; Pastoral Care, 441; Salisbury MSS., 1051; Salisbury Pontifical, 1433; Worcester MSS., 1052; Wulfstan's handwriting, 7225
— William P.: Epic and romance, 2357; Medieval literature, 6988
Kerling, Nellie J. M.: Aliens, 5440; Commercial relations, 5387
Kerly, Duncan M.: Equitable jurisdiction, 3724
Kermode, Philip M. C.: Isle of Man, 1946; Manx crosses, 358
Kern, Anton: Medieval libraries, 7173
— Fritz: Die fränzosischen Ausdehungspolitik, 4109; Gottesgnadentum, 1413; Kingship and law, 2611, 3274
Kerr, Ralph F.: L. Pastor's Popes, 6720
— William J. B.: Higham Ferrers, 4457, 4829
Kerrier (Cornw.), 3153
Kerry, Charles: Assize rolls, 3543; Baslow court rolls, 4729; Bray hundred, 4709; Breadsall charters, 4429; Calendar of fines, 3542; Church of Reading, 6838; Peak forest, 3912; Peverell survey, 4349, 4432; Register of mercers, 5303
Kershaw, Ian: Bolton priory, 6396
— Norah, 2326. See Chadwick, Nora K.
Keswick, manor of (Norfolk), Court rolls, 4455
Kettering (Northants), 4828
Keutgen, Friedrich: Hanse, 5431
Keynsham (Worcs.), 1052
Kibre, Pearl: Incipits, 432, 6967; Scholarly privileges, 7088
Kidderminster, Thomas of: Annals, 2765

Kienast, Walther: Die deutschen Fürsten, 4109
Kilkenny Archaeological Society, 237, 1072
Killingworth, John: Algorism, 6953
Kilwardby, Robert, archbishop, 6593
Kimball, Elisabeth G.: Beds. sessions of peace, 3529; Frankalmoign tenure, 4663; Glos. sessions of peace, 3552; Lincs. sessions of peace, 3575; Records of J.P.s, 3495; Salop peace roll, 3605; Serjeanty tenure, 4664; Warwick–Coventry sessions of peace, 3615
Kindred, 2237, 2642, 2647
King, Archdale A.: Liturgy, 1339
— Austin J.: Records of Bath, 5246
— D. J. C.: Castles, 831; Henry II and Wales, 4040
— Edmund: Large and small landowners, 4665, 4963; Peterborough knights, 3069
— Edwin J.: Hospitallers, 6045, 6047; Seals, 461
— H. W.: Essex wills, 4525
— Heinz P. F.: Lincoln diocese, 5582
— Henry H.: Bede, 2297; Bede MSS., 2148
— John E.: Bede, 2148
— Patrick I.: Book of William Morton, 6264; Guide to records, 1759
Kingdon, John A.: Archives of grocers, 5192; Incidents, 2890; Richard Grafton, 2890
King's Bench, 3491, 3493, 3510, 4784
— Council, **502–3**; 3505–6, 6735
— Courts, **524–57**
— Household. See Household
— Lynn (Norfolk), 3461, 5205
— Peace, 1246
— Repton (Hunts.), 4777
— Serjeants, 3139
— Stanley (Glos.), 4753
— Works, 781
Kingsbury (Herts.), 1480
Kingsford, Charles L.: Benstede's mission, 1448; Biographies of Henry V, 2877; Chronicles of London, 2732; Franciscan MSS., 6006; Grey friars, 6006, 6022; Hardyng's Chronicle, 2890; Henry V, 4211; Historiae Croylandensis, 2900; Historical collection, 2823; Historical literature, 2737; Historical notes, 5169; Livy's Vita, 2929; Otho de Grandison, 4054; Prejudice and promise, 4212; Robert Bale, 2742; Robertsbridge documents, 6366; Song of Lewes, 7048; Stonor papers, 4615; Stow's Survey, 1746A; Two forfeitures (1415), 4211
— Hugh S.: Seals, 462, 465

Kingship, 1350–9, 2507, 2560A, 2606, 2610–11, 2618, 2985, 2988, 3271–8
Kingsland (Hereford), 4769
Kingsthorpe (Northants.), 4833
Kingston-upon-Hull (Yorks.), 5293–4, 5375
Kingston-upon-Thames (Surrey), 5266–7
Kingswood (Glos.): Forest, 3902; St. Mary's abbey, 6158
Kinninmouth family, 7224
Kinship, Anglo-Saxon, 2642
Kinvig, Robert H.: Isle of Man, 1948
Kippax (Yorks.), 4930
Kiralfy, Albert K. R.: Action on the case, 3702; Selden Society Guide, 195
Kirby, A. D.: Poll tax, 3154
— David P.: Bede sources, 2148; Making of England, 2499; Problems, 2547; Saxon bishops, 2720; Vortigern, 2553
— Isabel M.: Records of Chichester, 5657
— John L.: Calais, 3247, 4254; Councils of Henry IV, 3299, 4254; Guide to periodicals, 91; Henry IV, 4213; Lancastrian exchequer, 3247; Poll tax, 3154, 6826; Robert Southwell's account, 4627
— Thomas F.: Conveyancing, 3000; Winchester College, 7138; Wykeham's register, 5819
Kirk, Ernest F.: Essex fines, 3548
— George E.: Catalogue, 1871
— Jean R.: A.-S. cremations, 1442; A.-S. jewels, 2479
— John L.: Villa, 2069
— Richard E. G.: Accounts of Abingdon, 6084; Essex fines, 3548; Life records of Chaucer, 7003
Kirkby, John de, 4396
Kirkby's Quest, **628**; 1601, 4350, 4354, 4357, 4360, 4396
Kirkby Stephen (Cumb.), 5050, 6838
Kirkfleet, Cornelius J.: White canons, 5965
Kirkheaton (Yorks.), Court rolls, 6043
Kirkland, D.: Jean Juvénal, 2909
Kirklees (Yorks.), Muniments, 1868, 4497
— priory, 6404
Kirkstall (Yorks.), abbey, 1464, 2910, 6400, 6405
— forge, 5500
Kirkstall, Hugo de: Chronicle, 6400
Kirsch, Johann P.: Andreas Sapiti, 6756
Kisch, Ruth: trans. of Kosminsky, 4971
Kitchin, George W.: Catalogus, 1028; Compotus rolls, 5812; Consuetudinary, 5813; Manor of Manydown, 4767; Northern Convocation, 6817; Richard of Bury's register, 5692; St. Giles fair, 5115, 5525
Kitson, F. R.: Charters, 6405

Kittredge, George L.: Ballads, 7045
Kitzinger, Ernst: Art, 852
Kjellman, Hilding: Life of St. Edmund, 2305
Klaeber, Frederick: Beowulf, 2334
Kleinclausz, Arthur: Alcuin, 2295
Klenke, M. Amelia: Saints' lives, 6692
Klerk, Jan de: Rymkronyk, 2911
Klewitz, Hans W.: ed. Bresslau, 415
Klussmann, Rudolf: Roman bibliography, 2014
Knabe, Carl: Gesta Danorum, 2426
Knecht, Robert J.: Episcopate and wars, 4221, 6804
Kneen, John J.: Isle of Man, 583
Kneisel, Ernst: Corn market, 5385
Knight, George A. F.: Christianity in Scotland, 2687
Knighton, Henry: Chronicon, 1124, 1452, 1464, 2912, 4130
Knights, 566, 572, 1467
Knights' fees, 1714, 3007, 3061, 3201, 3568, 4349, 4431, 4447, 4653, 6173, 6265, 6267
Knights' service, 1576, 3061, 4005, 4644–5, 4648, 4654, 4682, 4684
Knocker, Herbert: Holmesdale, 4785
Knoll, Kurt: London, 5179
Knoop, Douglas: Masons' wages, 5491; Medieval mason, 800, 5491
Knowle (Warw.), 5278
Knowles, Canon: Charters, 5049
— Clive H.: Simon de Montfort, 4043
— (Dom) David: Abbot of Wigmore, 1437, 1477; Becket, 1477, 6498–9; Bede, 2148; Black friars, 5995; Canterbury election, 5620; Case of St. Albans, 6170; Case of St. William of York, 1477, 5870; Charterhouse, 6224; Christian centuries, 1280; Cistercians and Cluniacs, 1477, 5943; Cultural influences, 6906; Decreta Lanfranci, 1146; English bishops, 1438; Episcopal colleagues, 6499; Evolution of thought, 6888; Gasquet, 1477; Heads of religious houses, 5895; Heritage, 771, 1430; Historian and character, 1477; Historical enterprises, 262; Lay brothers of Sempringham, 6220; Mabillon, 1149, 1477; Medieval thought, 1408; M.G.H., 262, 1114; Monastic constitutions, 5909; Monastic orders, 1298; Monastic sites, 755; Mystical tradition, 6688; Papers, 1477; Pecham, 5637; R. A. L. Smith, 1494; Religious houses, 1299; Religious life, 1485; Religious orders, 1300; Regula magistri, 5911; Saints and Scholars, **858**; Uthred of Boldon, 1477, 6556

Knowles, John A.: Glass painting, 863
Knowlson, George A.: Jean V, duc de Bretagne, 4255
Knox, Ronald: Miracles, 2796
— T. M.: ed. Collingwood's Idea of history, 241
Knytlinga Saga, 2448
Kock, Ernst A.: Saga, 2442
Koehler, William R. W.: ed. Porter essays, 1449
Koestermann, Erich: Tacitus's Annals, 2025
Köhler, Ruth: Die Heiratsverhandlungen, 4101
Koht, Halvdan: Norse sagas, 2455
Kolderup-Rosenvinge, Jens L. A.: Instituta Cnuti, 2183
Korner, Sten: Battle of Hastings, 3994
Kosminsky, Evgeny A.: Feudal rent, 5461; Russian bibliography, 19; Service and rents, 1468; Studies in agrarian history, 4944, 4971
Kossmann, Ernst H.: ed. 6869
Kovalevsky, Maxime M.: Police administration, 1252
Kramer, Stella: Craft gilds, 5365–6
Kramm, Heinrich: Bibliographie, 99
Krapp, George P.: A.-S. poetic records, 2327; St. Guthlac, 2310
Krarup, Alfred: Dansk bibliografi, 50
Krause, J.: Household, 5481
Kriehn, George: English Rising (1450), 2886, 4214; Evesham Chronicle, 2899; Sources of peasants' rebellion, 4150
Kristeller, Paul O.: Latin MSS. catalogue, 979
Krusch, Bruno: Columban, 2320; M.G.H., 1114; Passiones, 2288
Kuhl, Ernest P.: Chaucer, 7007–8
Kuhlicke, Frederick W.: Local history, 1514
Kuhn, Sherman M.: Middle English dictionary, 281
Kunze, Karl: Hanseakten, 5335; Urkundenbuch, 5336
Kup, Alexander P.: Scottish records, 23; 933
Kurath, Hans: Middle English dictionary, 281
Kurland, Philip B.: Magna Carta, 3285
Kuske, Bruno: Quellen, 5344
Kuttner, Stephen: **168**; Anglo-Norman canonists, 6435; Collectanea, 6429; Friedberg, 1306; Proceedings of Congresses, 1313; Repertorium, 1309; Subsidia, 1313
Kylie, Edward: St. Boniface, 2299
Kyre Park (Worcs.), Charters, 4494

Labarge, Margaret W.: Baronial household, 4607; Simon de Montfort, 4055
Labbe, Philippe: Vigeois Chronica, 2970
Laborde, Edward D.: British Isles, 611; Maldon, 2588
Labour conditions, 1468, 4149, 4155
Labourer (the famulus), 4977
Labourers, Statute of, 3344, 3624, 3676
Laboureur, Jean Le: Charles VI, 2847
Lacaille, Armand D.: Stone age, 2001
Lacey, Arthur D.: Catalogue, 377
Lackford (Suffolk), 3189–90
Lacnunga, 2367
Lacock abbey (Wilts.), 6372–3
Lacombe, George: Interdict document, 6733; Langton's Commentaries, 6596; Langton's Quaestiones, 6595
Lacy family, 4595
— inquisition, 4370, 4793
Lacy, Edmund, bishop of Exeter: Liber pontificalis, 1317; Register, 5715, 5717, 5730; Suit, 5057
— Henry de, 4370, 4622, 4790, 4793–4, 4931
Ladds, Sidney I.: Archdeaconry of Huntingdon, 5755
La Due, William J.: Papal rescripts, 6454
Laet, Siegfried Jan de: Low countries, 761
Laffan, Robert G. D.: trans. Pasquet, 3377
Lagarde, Georges de: L'esprit laïque, 6624
Lahache, J.: Pénitentiels, **316**
La Haye, Richard de: Feudalism, 4659
Laing charters, 1064, 4458
— David: Wyntoun's Chronicle, 2984
— Henry de: Catalogue, 463
— Samuel: Heimskringla, 2447
Laird, Charlton: Manuel des Péchiez, 6694
Laistner, Max L. W.: Bede MSS., 2148; Handlist Bede MSS., 2297; Thought and letters, 2358
Lakin, Storer M.: Salisbury books, 1051
Laking, Guy F.: Armour, 920
Lalit, Adolphus: Periodicals, 88
Lamb, George: trans. Marrou, 1393
— Hubert H.: Climate, 621A
— John: Corpus Christi College, 7100
— John W.: St. Wulfstan, 2316, 5843
Lambarde, William: Perambulation, 1694
Lambert, Henry C. M.: Banstead, 4898
— John J.: London skinners, 5202
Lambeth Bible, 885
— council of, 1458, 6691, 6811
— Palace, library, 963, 965, 974, 1008–10, 1026, 4637, 4696, 4778, 5550, 5600, 5606, 5621, 5756
— Palace, wills, 4516–17, 4520, 4567

Lambrick, Gabrielle: Abingdon abbey, 6084; Abingdon and riots (1327), 4139; Early history of Abingdon, 2153; Impeachment of abbot of Abingdon, 3415

Lambrino, Scarlat: Bibliography, 2014

Lamond, Elizabeth: Estate management, 4631

La Monte, John L.: Ambroise, 2748

Lampe, Geoffrey W. H.: Bible, 1327A

Lancashire: Antiquities, 2045; Bibliography, 1695, 1697; Charters, 4441–50; Church, 6201–2, 6771; County history, 1459, 1517, 1529, 1705–7, 2559, 3567, 4142; County journals and societies, 1698–1704; County records, 1504, 1627, 1696, 3872, 3877, 4793; Deeds, 4441–50; Domesday, 1529, 3025; Extents, 4367; Feet of fines, 3564; Feudal tenures, 4365, 4367–8, 4447; Forests, 3922; Inquests, 4363, 4365–70, 4790; Manors and villages, 4794; Markets, 5536; Parliament, 3462; Pedigrees, families, 561; Pleas, 3492, 3563, 3565–6; Pipe rolls, 3091, 4448; Religious houses, 6197–206; Roman, 2045; Serjeants of the peace, 3745; Subsidy rolls, 3167–8; Wills, 4537–8, 4566

Lancaster, Duchy (and palatinate), 955, 955A, 1441, 1627, 1705–7, 1712, 1776, 3869–84, 4364, 4368, 4479, 4601, 4646, 4685, 4925, 6771
— forest, 3922
— house of, 612–19; 605, 1193
— Henry, earl of, 4598
— Henry, earl and duke of, 4121, 4178, 4283, 6693
— John of (letters), 4197
— John of (Bedford), 4273
— John of. *See* John of Gaunt
— Thomas earl of, 4127, 4598, 4622, 4792

Lancaster, Joan C.: Bibliography, 24; Coventry charters, 5273, 6368
— Lorraine: Kinship A.-S., 2642
— William T.: Arthington charters, 6394; Assize roll, 3628; Bridlington charters, 6399; Fountains chartulary, 6400; Kirkstall, 6405; Leeds rental, 5296; Nostell rental, 6411; Rothwell rental, 4832; Thorner court rolls, 4936

Land, the gage of, 1246

Land, law, 159–62; 2612, 2638, 3339, 3678, 3693A
— market, peasant, 4970
— tenures of, 627–66; 2623, 2632, 2636–7, 2650, 2990, 2999, 3188, 3514, 3700, 3703, 4758, 4780, 4862
— transfer of, 1501

Landboc de Winchelcumba, 6160

Lander, Jack R.: Attainder and forfeiture, 3365, 3712, 4216; Conflict and stability, 4216; Edward IV, legend, 4215; Henry IV and Duke of York, 4216; Marriage and politics, 4216; Wars of the Roses, 4217; Yorkist council, 3300

Landgavel, 5091

Landgraf, Artur M.: Langton's Commentaries, 6597; Langton's Quaestiones, 6595

Landon, Lionel: Cartae antiquae, 3759; Richard I's itinerary, 2906, 4024, 4409; Somerset pleas, 3607

Landor, Walter N.: Alrewas court rolls, 4874

Lane, Henry C.: Deeds, 4482
— Timothy O'N.: Dictionary, 346

Lanercost (Cumb.), 2836, 6110–11, 6024

Lanfranc: Articles on, 1450, 1455, 6429; Forgeries, 5615; Letter, 3030; Lives of, 2863, 5632, 6529; Opera, 1102, 5631; Statutes, 1113, 1302, 5909

Lang, Jane: Bishops and reform, 6793

Langar (Notts.), 4842

Langdale, Lord Henry, Life of, 953
— John: Legal documents, 5125
— Thomas: Yorkshire, 1891

Lange, Wolfgang: Tacitus, 2505

Langebek, Jacob: Danish historians, 1106; Scriptores, 1106, 2306

Langenfelt, Gösta: A.-S. pioneers, 2512

Langenhoe (Essex), 4990

Langham, Simon, abbot and archbishop, 5609, 6247

Langland, William: Piers Plowman, 7021–9

Langley, Thomas, bishop, 5690

Langlois, Charles V.: Ancient correspondence, 3775; Archives, 954; Introduction, 263; Manuel, 55; Nova Curie, 3775

Langman, Albert E.: Justiciary rolls, 3641

Langmuir, Gavin I.: Jews, 3937, 3958; Politics and parliament, 3366

Langston, J. N.: Priors of Lanthony, 6155

Langtoft, Peter: Chronicle, 1103, 1112, 2913, 2923

Langton (Lincs.), manor of, 4815
— (Yorks.), 2069

Langton, John: Reports, 6226
— Stephen, archbishop, 1114, 1488, 5443, 5598, 5633–4, 6594–8, 6709A, 6733
— Walter, bishop, 3498, 3839
— William: Lancs. inquisitions, 3873, 4363

Language and history in early Britain, 320. *See* Philology
— in northern counties, 5308

Lanhers, Yvonne: Jeanne d'Arc, 4246, 4267; Regestum Clementis V, 5561

Lansdowne Feodary, 4368, 4447
— MSS., 998

Lanterne of Lizt, 6866

Lantfred, monk of Winchester: St. Swithun, 2312

Lanthony priory (Glos.), 6155

Lapidaries, 868, 6948

Lapidarium Septentrionale, 2021
— Walliae, 363

Laporte, Jean (Moine): St. Columban, 2320
— Jean: Les opérations navales, 3995

Lappenberg, Johann M.: Adam of Bremen, 2149; Geschichte, 1184; Urkundliche Geschichte, 5337

Lapsley, Gaillard T.: Account roll, 5511; Archbishop Stratford, 1478; Boldon Book, 3076; Bracton's 'addicio', 2985; Buzones, 1478, 3738; Castle officers, 4666; Cornage and drengage, 4975; County court, 3737; Crown, community, and parliament, 1478, 4125; Henry IV's title, 1478, 4218; John de Warenne, 1478; Knights of the shire, 3446; Maitland's essays, 1483; Palatine of Durham, 1626, 3868; Problem of the north, 1478, 1626, 3868; Richard II's last parliament, 1478, 3422; Some recent advance, 1221, 1478; Statute of York, 1478, 3343; V.C.H. Durham, 1529

Larden (Salop), Deeds, 4466

Larking, Lambert B.: Custumal, 5316; Fabric roll, 4781; Hospitallers, 6044; Kent Domesday, 3024; Kent feet of fines, 3561; Knights' fees, 4390; Manor of Morton Pynkeny, 4831; Rent roll, 4787; Warwick roll of arms, 2950

La Rochelle, battle of, 4190

Larsen, Hanna A.: trans. Viking civilization, 2458

Larson, Alfred: Payment of envoys, 3818
— Lawrence M.: Canute, 2589; King's household, 2615

Lascelles, Rowley: Liber munerum, 3333, 3799

Latera, Annibali de: Bullarium Franciscanum, 6004

Lateran Council (1139), 5568; (1215), 6793

Latham, Lucy C.: Manor and village, 1495; Wages of knights of shire, 3443
— Ronald E.: Chippenham veredictum, 3625; Latin wordlist, 301, 308; Letters concerning eyre, 3504; Revised translation of Bede, 2148

Lathbury, John, 6924
— Thomas: Convocation, 6815

Lathe court rolls, 4902

Latimer, John: Calendar of charters, 5080; Maire of Bristowe, 5083; Merchant venturers, 5379

Latin language and literature, **38–40**; 56, 1397, 1403–6, 6894, 6898
— writers, lists of, 8, 33, 37, 56, 6909

Laudabiliter (Papal bull), 5556

Laudes regiae, 1353

Laughlin, James L.: Legal procedure (A.-S.), 2612

Laughton (Sussex), 4900

Launditch (Norfolk), 4454

Laux, Johann J.: St. Columban, 2320

Laveille, Auguste: Congrégation de Savigny, 5918

Lavenham (Suffolk), 5415

Laver, James: Costumes, 921
— Philip G.: Roman Colchester, 2055

Lavisse, Ernest: Histoire, 1181

Law, **159–64** and **524–57**; 1482–4, 1501, 3339–40, 3345A, 3675
— Anglo-Saxon, **300–3** and **372–4**
— canon, **168–70**, **314–16**, and **346–53**; 169, 1245, 1466
— forest, **580–4**
— of Ireland, **312–14**
— language of, **37**
— manorial, 1484, 4698–700, 4700, 4716, 4777, 4882
— maritime, 3240, 5108
— merchant, 3507, 4286, 5082, 5161, 5524, 5533
— of Scotland, 219, 2989
— school at Oxford, 7127
— societies and journals, 96, 132, 155, 169, 195, 219, 1227
— suits, **526–44**; 1450, 1461, 1474, 4777, 5783, 6128, 6132, 6152, 6183
— tracts, **454–61**
— of Wales, **310–12**; 2647

Lawling (Essex), 4748

Lawlor, Hugh J.: St. Patrick, 2677

Lawrance, Henry: Heraldry, 490
— N. A. H.: Fasti, 5876
— William T.: Parliamentary representation, 3455

Lawrence, Arne: St. Dunstan, 2303
— Clifford Hugh: Cistercian university studies, 6907; English church and papacy, 1281, 6734; St. Edmund of Abingdon, 5626
— Laurie A.: Coinage, 691
— Philip H.: Court rolls, 4895
— of Durham: Dialogi, 5677
— of Somercote: 6447

Lawshall (Suffolk), 4881, 4886

Lawson, John: Medieval education, 7143

Lawson-Tancred, Thomas: Court rolls, 4935

Lawton, George: Collections for York, 5855

Lawyers, **551–2**; 7144–59
Laxton (Notts.), 5007
Lay Folk's Catechism, 6691
— investiture, 6727–8
Laȝamon: Brut, 2914
Lea, Henry C.: Celibacy, 1282; Confessions, 1283; Inquisition, 6061; Superstition, 1253
Leabhar Breac, 2397
Leach, Arthur F.: Beverley documents, 5288; Clerical strike, 6395; Educational charters, 7052, 7139; Fabric roll, 6395; Memorials of Beverley, 6395; Schools, 7140; Visitations, 6283; Winchester College, 7138; Yorkshire schools, 7139
— Henry B.: Angevin Britain and Scandinavia, 4025
Leadam, Isaac S.: Cases before king's council, 3293, 3505; Cases in Star Chamber, 3506; Inquisition of 1517, 4972; Mirror of justices, 2991
Leadenhall (London), 5181
Leake, treaty of, 1448, 1450, 4127
Leakey, Louis S. B.: Adam's ancestors, 2002
Learning and literature, **179–83, 339–57,** and **898–907**; 1428, 1473, 1477, 1485, 1490, 1493
Leases, 4784, 5247, 5741, 5759, 6142, 6157
Leask, Harold G.: Irish castles, 832; Irish churches, 801
Leathes, Stanley M.: Grace Book A, 7058
Le Beau, Jean: Chronique, 2915
Le Bel, Jean: Chronique, 2916
Le Bras, Gabriel: Collections, 1305; Histoire du droit, 1310–11; Institutions, 6717; Irish penitentials, 1166; Penitentials, **316**
Lebor Bretnach, 2167
— Gabála Érenn, Book of Taking of Ireland, 2404
— na Cert, 2245
Lebuin, St., 2290
Lecan, Book of, 2395
Le Cacheux, Paul: Rouen, 4256
Lechler, Gotthard V.: Wiclif, 6654
Le Clerc, Jean (d. 1736): Bibliothèque choisie, 3766
Leclercq, Henri: Dictionnaire, 763, 1265; Hefele's Conciles, 1279
Leclère, L.: Magna Carta, 1446
Le Couteulx, Carolus: Annales, 5926
Lecoy de la Marche, Albert: La Chaire, 6705
Ledger book, 6106, 6142
Ledston (Yorks.), 4930
Lee, Frank: Northampton, 5215
— Frederick G.: Church of Thame, 6298; Glossary, 1273

— John M.: Leicestershire, 1708
— Sir Sidney: *D.N.B.*, 531
Leechbook, **344**; 441, 2365, 6946
Leechdoms, 2369
Leeds (Kent), priory, 6193
— (Yorks.), 4565, 4930, 5295–6
— Studies, 1880
— University Library, 1038
Leeds, Edward T.: A.-S. archaeology, 2481, 2548; Celtic ornament, 2003, 2481; Corpus of brooches, 2481; Distribution, 2548; Essays, 1442; Icknield Way, 2548; Jutish art, 2548; Roman coins, 659; Saxon penetration, 2548; Saxon village, 2481; Tribal hidage, 2213
Lees, Beatrice A.: Alfred, 2590; Statute of Westminster, 3337; Templars, 6055; V.C.H., 1529
Leet, 1484, 3871, 4882, 5104, 5208, 5210, 5274, 6268
Lefebvre, Charles: Histoire du droit, 1311
— Georges: Stubbs' History, 1221
Le Fèvre, Jean: Chronique, 2917
Lefèvre, Jean A.: Cistercian documents, 5933
Lefèvre-Pontalis, Germain: L'invasion anglaise, 4262; Morosini's Chronique, 2930
Leff, Gordon: Bradwardine, 6559; Fitzralph, 6569; Heresy, 6871; Paris and Oxford universities, 7089; Patterns of thought, 6917; Wyclif, 6655; Wyclif and Hus, 6656
Legacy of Middle Ages, 1479
Legal formularies, 428
— History. *See* Law
Legat, William, bishop, 5691
Legates, **883–5**; 1448, 6436
Legends, 1454, 6319
Leges Anglorum, 2184
— Edwardi Confessoris, 2184–5
— Henrici Primi, 2186, 3007
— Wallicae, 2222
— Willelmi Conquestoris, 2187
Legg, John Wickham: Coronation orders, 1354; Essays, 1340; Inventories, 5605, 6238
— Leopold G. Wickham: Coronation orders, 1354; *D.N.B.*, 531; Schramm's Geschichte, 358
Leggatt, Lawrence E. O. Fullbrook. *See* Fullbrook-Leggatt
Legge, Mary Dominica: Anglo-Norman, **37**; 293–4; French language, 1437; Langtoft's MSS., 2913; L'influence littéraire, 4007; Vatican Edward the Confessor, 2171; Yearbooks, 3646

Legh, Kathleen L. Wood-. *See* Wood-Legh

Legh of Booth's charters, 4426

Legislation, **300–3** and **506–8**. *See* Law

Legislators, **520–4**; 1461, 3395

Le Hardy, William: Guide, 1671

Lehmacher, Gustav: Hessen's Lexicon, 344

Lehmann, Ruth P.: Anglo-Jewish history, 3932

Lehmann-Brockhaus, Otto: Schriftquellen, 802

Leibnitz, Gottfried G.: Gervase of Tilbury, 2961

Leicester, Abbey of St. Mary, 1464, 1714, 2912, 4800, 4803, 4962, 5903, 6208
— bishop of, 2720
— borough of, 1529, 2070, 5135–42
— College of Annunciation, 6210
— countess of, 4609
— forest of, 3906
— honor of, 3880, 4451, 4620, 4652
— Roman, 2060

Leicestershire: Bibliography, 1708; Charters, 4693; Church, 5739, 6873; County history, 1505, 1529, 1712–14, 2543, 2599; County journals and societies, 1709–11; County records, 3061, 3074, 3568; Domesday, 1529, 3061, 3074; Feet of fines, 3568; Feudal tenures, 1714, 4451, 4620, 4652; Inquests, 3568; Manors and villages, 4797–803, 4962; Pleas, 3568; Pipe rolls, 3568; Religious houses, 6207–11; Subsidy rolls, 3169; Topography, 1505, 1517; Urban history, 5134–43

Leiden riddle, 2328

Leighton, R. A.: Haghmon cartulary, 6300
— Stanley: Records of Oswestry, 5239
— William A.: Shrewsbury chronicle, 5242

Leighton Buzzard (Beds.), 3147, 6078

Leinster, Book of, 2394, 2777

Leiston abbey (Suffolk), 1441

Lekai, Louis J.: White monks, 5944

Leland, John: **134**; 263A, 1476, 2044; Commentarii, 8

Le Livere de Reis, 2918

Lemarignier, Jean-Francois: Institutions ecclésiastiques, 6718

Lemberg, Tidemann, 5442

Lemerle, Paul: Nouvelle Clio., 45

Lemmens, Leonhard: Documenta Franciscana, 6007

Lemmon, Charles H.: Battle of Lewes, 4068; Hastings, 4009; Norman conquest, 3980

Lemoine, Jean: Richard Lescot's Chronique, 2843

Lemon, Robert: Calendarium rotulorum chartarum, 3758

Lene, land of, 1435

Le Nestour, P.: Revue Celtique, 324

Le Neve, John: Fasti, 5580–2

Leningrad Bede, 441, 2148

Lennard, Reginald V.: A.-S. conquest, 2549; Corn yields, 5492; Custumal, 4886; Domesday satellite, 3011; Fiscal carucate, 4662; Glastonbury demesnes, 6318; Peasant contributions, 6845; Review of Kosminsky, 4971; Roman to A.-S., 1434, 2105; Rural England, 4973; William I's destruction, 3913

Lenton Priory (Notts.), 6280

Lenz, Max: König Sigismund, 2877, 4257

Leo, Heinrich: Rectitudines, 2212

Leoba, St., 2290

Leofric, bishop of Exeter, 2147
— priest, Gesta Herwardi, 2878

Leominster, monastic dean (Hereford), 6167

Leon, Mariette: trans., 1179
— Philip: trans., 1179

Léonard, Émile G.: Les plus anciennes chartes, 4408

Leonard, George H.: Jews, 3959

Le Patourel, H. E. Jean: Pottery industry, 5512
— John: Channel Islands, 1955; Edward III and France, 4183; Hugh of St. Philibert, 3103; Manor of Leeds, 5295; Norman colonization, 3985; Norman succession, 3992; Treaty of Brétigny, 4183

Le Quesne, Charles: Jersey, 1956

Le Roulx, Joseph M. Delaville: Les Hospitaliers, 461, 6042

Le Roux de Lincy, A. J. V.: Le roman de Brut, 2974

Lescot, Richard: Chronique, 2843

Leslie, Roy F.: Laȝamon, 2914
— Shane; Miracles of Henry VI, 2796

Lesne, Émile: Les écoles, 1392

Lesort, André: Monstrelet, 2926

Le Strange family, 4582A

Le Strange, Hamon: Le Strange records, 4582A

L'Estrange, John: Freemen of Norwich, 5206; Norwich wills, 4547

Lethaby, William R.: Art, 803; Painting, 860

Lethbridge, Thomas C.: A.-S. settlement, 1442

Lettenhove, Kervyn de: Chastellain, 2814; Froissart, 2874; Nicolas Bosc, 2973

Letter-books, 427, 1455, 2151, 5154, 5160, 5691, 5833, 6561

Letters, historical, 1141, 3224, 3757, 3771, 3775-7, 3781-2, 3787A, 3815-16, 4427, 4608, 4610-11, 4615, 5057, 5090, 5105, 5154-5, 5234, 5330, 5685, 5691, 5932, 6132, 6341, 7061-2. *See* Close letters, Patent letters, Papacy letters

Levett, Ada E.: Accounts, 1480; Baronial councils and manors, 1443, 1480; Black Death, 5479; Court books, 1480; Manorial organization, 1480, 6171; Redditus, 1480; Statute of labourers, 3344; Studies, 1480; Summons to council (1213), 3301

Levine, Mortimer: Richard III, 4223

Levison, Wilhelm: Annales Lindisfarnenses, 2145; Bede, 2297; Charters, 2218; England and the Continent, 2282; M.G.H., 1114; Ninian, 2323; Passiones, 2288; St. Boniface, 2299; St. Germanus, 2108; Wattenbach's Geschichtsquellen, 66; Wilfrid, 2313; Willibrord, 2314

Levy, Fred J.: Tudor thought, 263A

Lévy-Ullman, Henri: Éléments, 1238

Lewes, battle of, 4068, 7048
— rape of, 3194, 4905
— St. Pancras priory, 1108, 6363-5
— Robert of, bishop of Bath and Wells, 2880

Lewis, Alun: Roger Leyburn, 4056
— Ceri: Liber Landavensis, 5880A
— Charles E.: Richard Anglicus, 6448
— Clive S.: Allegory of love, 6989
— Edward A.: Chancery proceedings, 3637A
— Ewart: Bracton, 2985; Political ideas, 1414, 2988
— Frank B.: Surrey feet of fines, 3613
— Frank R.: Beatrice of Falkenburg, 4096; Richard of Cornwall, 4096; William de Valence, 4057
— George R.: Stannaries, 5513
— Henry: Celtic grammar, 323
— Hubert: Ancient laws, 2235
— Idwal: Handlist, 23; 933; Subject index, 103
— Michael J. T.: Temples, 2077
— Norman B.: English in Flanders, 1450; Feudal levies, 1459, 4306; Indentures, 1493, 4283; John of Gaunt, 4283; Re-elections, 3439; Richard II's Council, 3302
— Peter S.: Fastolf's lawsuit, 4825; War propaganda, 4243
— Robert W.: Churchwardens' accounts, 6838
— Samuel: Dictionary, 600
— Saunders: Taliesin, 2385

— Timothy: Glossary, 42; 2236; Laws of Howel Dda, 2223-4; Serjeanty, 4664
— of Glyn Cothi: Poetical works, 7030

Lewisham Antiquarian Society, 1691

Lexikon für Theologie, 1270

Lexington, Stephen of, 6377, 6907

Libelle of Englyshe Polycye, 4328, 5338, 7049

Libellus de primo Saxonum adventu, 2157
— Responsionum of Gregory the Great, 2308, 7225

Liber albus (London), 5161
— albus (Wells), 5586
— albus (Worcester), 5832
— Angeli (Armagh), 2324
— Assisarum, **546**
— Burgus, 1458
— Custumarum (London), 5161
— Custumarum (Northampton), 5215
— de antiquis legibus, 2870
— de illustribus Henricis, 2808
— Elemosinarii, 5834
— Eliensis, 2164
— Epistolaris, 6561
— Feodorum. *See* Testa de Nevill
— Garderobae, 3126
— Horn (London), 5161
— Landavensis, 5880A
— Luciani, 5045
— Melorum, 6518
— Memorandum, 6098
— Memorialis, 3366
— Munerum, 3333, 3799
— Niger Scaccarii, 1103, 3006, 3174
— Pauperum, 1482, 3004
— Pensionum, 5835
— Pontificalis, 1317
— Regalis, 1355
— Regie Capelle, 1318
— Rubeus de Scaccario, 3007
— Vitae, 5814
— Winton, 1012, 3072

Liberati rolls, **477**; 3105, 3774

Liberties (franchises), 1461, 2608, 4652, 5257, 6338, 6359. *See* Franchises, Immunities, and Marches

Libraries, **11-13, 118-34,** and **927-9**; 1033, 1439, 1450, 1464, 2295, 2912, 3767, 4321, 5782, 6345

Library, the (journal), **932**
— of Christian Classics, 1133

Lichfield (Staffs.), Charters, 4473; Gild, 5251
— dean and chapter, 1047, 5664-71, 5749, 6790

Liebermann, Felix: Abbreviatio chronicorum, 2745; Annales Anglosaxonici, 2143; Annales Meneviae, 2144; Annales

Liebermann, Felix (*cont.*):
S. Edmundi, 2772; Annales S. Pauli, 2773; Bury chronicle, 2819; Consiliatio Cnuti, 2181; Consuetutiones de foresta, 2188; Coronation charter, 3279; Dema, 2208; Dialogus de scaccario, 3005; Dunsaete, 2211; Englische Gilde, 1385; Evesham chronicon, 6380; Flores historiarum, 2871; Friedensgilde, 1385; Friedlosigkeit, 2616; Geoffrey of Monmouth, 2166; Gerefa, 2209; Geschichtsquellen, 1108, 2738; Gesetze, 1482, 2177; Gesta Herwardi, 2878; Heinrich von Huntingdon, 2904; Hic intimatur, 2182; Ingulf, 2163; Instituta Cnuti, 2183; Kesselfang, 2616; Lanfranc, 5632; Leges Anglorum, 2184; Leges Edwardi, 2185; Leges Henrici, 2186; Leis Willelme, 2187; Lewes priory, 1108; Literatur, 153; London collection, 5159; Magister Vacarius, 3004; National assembly, 2617; Nennius, 1458, 2167; Ostenglische Geschichtsquellen, 1107, 2878, 6268; Quadripartitus, 2184, 2189; Rectitudines, 2212; Scriptores (M.G.H.), 1114, 2740; Song of Dermot, 2954; Textus Roffensis, 5794; Ueber Eadmer, 1108, 2863; Ueber die Gesetze Ines, 1426

Liebeschütz, Hans: Humanism of John of Salisbury, 6645

Liestøl, Knut: Sagas, 2456

Lifton (Devon), 4351

Lilburn, A. J.: Pipe rolls, 3093

Lilleshall (Salop), prior of, Instructions, 6696

Lincoln Architectural and Archaeological Society, 171

Lincoln, battle of, 2896, 4045
— city of, 2061, 3574–3575A, 5145–6
— diocese of, 1048–9, 1437, 4841, 5738–56, 6432, 6475, 6573, 6575, 6781, 6790, 7125
— fair of, 1499
— hospital of Holy Innocents, 6217
— Jews of, 3951, 3960
— parliament of, 3413, 3432

Lincoln, countess of, 4631
— earl of, 4794
— Fredman Ashe, 3960
— Hugh of, bishop. *See* Hugh (St.)
— Hugh of, 3954

Lincoln's Inn, 975, 1011, 1482, 7148–9

Lincolnshire: Bibliography, 1504, 1715; Charters, 4452–3; Church, 5738–56; County history, 579, 1529, 1723, 2061, 2828, 4229; County journals and societies, 1716–22; County records, 1482, 3569, 3572–3, 5144; Domesday,

3026, 3073, 5144; Eyres, 3576; Feet of fines, 3570–1, 3573, 5144; Feudal tenures, 4371, 5144; Inquests, 4371; Jews, 3968; Justices of peace, 3574–5; Manors and villages, 4804–17; Parliament, 3436, 3463; Pedigrees, families, 563; Personal names, 579; Pleas, 3574, 3743; Pipe rolls, 5144; Religious houses, 1529, 6212–22; Subsidy rolls, 3170A, 5144; Topography, 1505; Urban history, 5144–5147A; Wills, 4539–42

Lincy, A. J. V. *See* Le Roux de

Lindberg, David C.: John Pecham, 6954

Lindelöf, Uno: Rituale, 1320

Lindisfarne (Northumb.), 2145, 2302, 2721, 6276
— Gospels, 896, 2471

Lindkvist, Erik Harald: Place-names, 633; York, 5305

Lindley, E. S.: Charters, 2201; Kingswood Abbey, 6158

Lindsay, Edward R.: Scottish supplications, 5549
— T. F.: Letter books, 5607
— Wallace M.: Early Irish script, 391; Early Welsh script, 392; Glossaria, 307; Notae Latinae, 404; Palaeographia, 393

Lindsey, 1448, 1496, 2555, 2720
— Survey, 3061, 3073

Lingard, John: History, 1185; Preston charters, 5130

Lingelbach, William E.: Merchant adventurers, 5388

Linker, Robert W.: B.M. Egerton MS., 7191

Linton (Cambs.), 5042

Lipman, Vivian D.: Jews of Norwich, 3961

Lipscomb, George: Buckingham, 1551

Lipson, Ephraim: Economic history, 1371; Woollen industries, 5414

Lisbon, Conquest of, 2858

Lisieux, Arnulf of: Epistolae, 1102, 6487, 6511–12

L'Isle MSS., 6366

Lismore, book of, 2398

List and Index Society, 956, 7222

Lister, John: Chapter house records, 4827, 4930; Court rolls, 4932; Woollen trade, 5333

Lists and Indexes, 955–955A

Literacy, 7136

Literae Cantuarienses, 5607

Literature, **179–83**
— Anglo-Saxon, **339–46**
— Celtic, **346–51**
— Lost, 2330, 6996
— Middle English, **907–16**
— Scandinavian, **351–7**

Littere Wallie, 3786
Little Black Book of the Exchequer, 3006
— Hadham (Herts.), 1677
Little, Andrew G.: Collectanea Franciscana, 6006; Eccleston's Chronicle, 6008; Franciscan guide, 6000; Franciscan history, 6023; Franciscan lists, 847; Franciscan papers, 6024; Franciscan studies, 6026; Gesiths, 2634; Grey friars in Cambridge, 7101; in Exeter, 6027; in Ireland, 6017; in Oxford, 6025; Initia operum, 430; Lanercost chronicle, 2836, 2938; Oxford theology, 6028, 6908; Personal tithes, 6845; Roger Bacon, 1448, 6536, 6538, 6546
Littledale, Ralph P.: Deeds, 4502
Littlehales, Henry; Old Service-books, 1315, 1348; St. Mary at Hill, 6838
Littleport (Cambs.), 2995, 4716
Littleton, Ananias Charles: Accounting, 4630
— Sir Thomas: Tenures, 2990
Liturgy, **170-3**; 191, 763, 1066, 2680, 2704, 5718, 5749, 5805, 5910, 7184-7
Liveing, Henry G. D.: Romsey abbey, 6164
Liverani, Francesco: Spicelegium Liberianum, 6512, 6514
Livere de Reis, 2918
Liveries, 7223
Liverpool (Lancs.), 1703-4, 5128
Liversidge, Joan: Furniture, Roman, 2047, 2050, 2080
Livery Companies (London), **716-18**
Livestock, 5012, 5019, 5490
Livett, R. G. C.: Herringswell documents, 4884
Livingstone, Matthew: Guide, 1059
Livre d'Agenais, 3817
— de seyntz medicines, 6693
Livy, Titus: Vita Henrici V, 1103, 2877, 2919, 2972
Lizerand, Georges: Templiers, 6061
Llan Stephan, 2224
Llancarvan, Caradoc of, 2805
Llandaff, 2665, 5880A–B, 6781, 6790
Llewellyn of Wales, 3787
Lloyd, Albert H.: Christ's College, Cambridge, 7104
— Mrs. A. H.: Cambridge clerks, 6767
— Edward, Tenants-in-capite, 4378
— Eleanor: Poll tax, 3204
— John of Brecon, the younger: Breconshire, 1899
— Sir John Edward: Ancient laws, 2235; Carmarthenshire, 1911; Ceredigion, 1906; Coming of Normans, 2144; Geoffrey of Monmouth, 2166; History of Wales, 1186; Owen Glendower, 4219; Walter Map, 6599; Welsh chroniclers, 2805
— L. J.: Fox bibliography, 1435
— Nathaniel: English house, 818
— Rees J.: Welsh masters, 7146
Llwyd, Angharad: Anglesey, 1896
Llyfr Coch Asaph, 5880C
— Colan, 2227
— Iorwerth, 2228
Llywarch Hen: Canu, 2386
Loans, 3253, 3774
Lobel, Mary D.: Banleuca, 1451; Borough of Oxford, 5236; Bury St. Edmunds, 5256, 6341; Historic towns, 1386; History of Dean and Chalford, 4848; University of Oxford, 7130
Local archives, **108–11**; 112, 1440
— history, general, **211–19**
— by county, **219–55**
— special studies, **555–7**; 2609, 7223
Localization of MSS., 419
Loch Cé, annals, 2783
Lock, Benjamin Fossett: Cerne cartulary, 6128
Lockhart, Charles: Hampshire, 1664
Loders (Dorset), priory, 6129
Lodge, Eleanor C.: Black Prince, 2812; Documents, 1206; Edward I's tenants, 4681; Gascony, 4164; John of Gaunt's Register, 3876
— Henry C.: Land-law, 2612
Loewe, Heinz: ed. Wattenbach, 66
Loewenfeld, S.: Jaffé's Regesta, 1131
Löfvenberg, Mattias T.: Surnames, 584
Logan, F. Donald: Excommunication, 6473; Heresy at Oxford, 6873; Judgedelegate formulary, 6429
Logeman, Henri: Rule of St. Benet, 2275
— Willem S.: De consuetudine monachorum, 2274
Loirette, Gabriel: Gascony, 1426
Lollard Bible, 1330, 6653
Lollards, **896-8**; 4157-8, 4221, 5741, 6612, 6629, 6632
Lommatzsch, Erhard: ed. Tobler's Wörterbuch, 297
London, **712-18**; 1469; Aliens, 5177; Antiquities, 737, 762, 766, 770, 2062-4; Apprentices, 5178; Assizes, 3580; Bibliography, 1728-9; Bishop and diocese, 4530, 5630, 5640, 5757-73, 6516-17, 6223-51, 6772, 6781; Charters, 1742-3, 5158, 5179; chroniclers, 1114, 2732, 2742, 2761, 2768, 2773, 2789, 2818, 2823, 2826, 2857, 2866, 2870, 2885-6, 2889; Church councils, 6429, 6810; Companies, **716-19**; 5177; Coroner,

London (*cont.*):
5177; Craftsmen, 5177; Customs, 5170, 5177; De institutis Lundoniae, 2207; Ecclesiastical court, 6482; English language of, 6984; Eyres, 1455, 1461, 3579–3579A, 3646; Feet of fines, 3578, 5153; Frithgild, 1385; History, 1450, 1469, 1495–6, 1499, 1500, 1529, 1740–8, 2489, 2601, 3365, 4004, 4006, 4111, 5162–81, 5503, 6609, 7049, 7223; Jewry, 3942; Journals and societies, 1731–9; Landowners, 5178; Law-courts, 1461, 5177; Libraries, 81–3, 377, 978, 1006–16, 1724–5, 5177; Merchants, 1500, 5175, 5178, 5330, 5379, 5424, 5427; Migration to, 5167, 5481; Officials, 5177; Personal and street names, 577, 632, 5167; Population, 5167, 5474; Records, **712–14**; 1504, 1725–8, 3577–80, 3769, 5175; Steelyard, 5428; Subsidies, 1469, 3171–2, 5157; Tithes, 6831; Topography, 598, 1740, 1746, 5165, 5181; Wills, 4543–6
— Allhallows, London wall, 6838
— Bartholomew fair, 5527, 5537
— British Museum: Books, 6, 76–8; Coins, 668, 672, 678, 684, 689; Franks' casket, **44**; Guides, 1964, 2019, 2472; MSS., **120–3**; 425, 438–9, 444, 499, 874–5, 896, 963, 965, 974, 1643, 3940, 5547, 7191; Seals, 454, 456
— Charterhouse, 6223–4
— College of Arms, 477, 483, 1007
— Dominicans, 5980
— Grey friars, 2826, 6006, 6010, 6022
— Holy Trinity, priory, 6225
— Inns of chancery, 7151
— Inns of court, **925–7**; 1011, 1013–14
— Jewry, 3942
— Library, 82–3
— Religious houses, 6223–51
— St. Bartholomew, 6226–8
— St. Katharine, 6230
— St. Margaret, Westminster, 6838
— St. Martin-le-Grand, 2221, 6067
— St. Mary at Hill, 6838
— St. Michael, Cornhill, 6838
— St. Paul's, Annals, 2768, 2773; Books at, 5177; History of, 5758–60, 5762, 5765–71, 5773; Ordinal, 1343
— Society of Antiquaries, 107–8, 178, 499, 717, 742, 1012, 3072
— Studies in London History, 5177
— Templars, 6064
— Tower of, 960, 3308, 3488, 3769, 5163
— Westminster abbey, 1016, 6179, 6231–51, 7223
London, David of, 6514
— Hildebrand of, 3198

— Hugh Stanford, 469, 481, 496
— John of, 2852
— Vera: Cartulary, 6122; Heads of houses, 5895
Long Melford (Suffolk), 4889
Long Sutton (Hants), 4763
Longchamp, Nigel de. *See* Wireker
— William, 4004, 5709, 7042
Longdon (Staffs.), 4473
Longhurst, Margaret H.: Ivories, 870
Longley, Thomas: Lincs. Domesday, 3026
Longnon, Auguste: Atlas, 601; Paris, 4258
Longstaffe, William H. D.: Halmota, 4739, 5684
Longvillers, family, 4574
Löning, G. A.: Deutsche und Gotländer, 5428
Loofs, Friedrich: Celtic church, 2671
Loomis, Dorothy Bethurum; Regnum and sacerdotium, 7225. *See* Bethurum, Dorothy
— Grant: King St. Edmund, 2305
— Louise R.: Council of Constance, 5563, 5565
— Roger S.: Chaucer's world, 7009; King Arthur, 2166, 2385
López, Pedro de Ayala: Cronicas de los Reyes, 2812
Lords, House of, 961, 3372, 3374, 3378, 3381–2, 3411
Lorenz, Ottokar: Geschichtsquellen, 66
Loretta, countess of Leicester, 1455, 1488
Lorica, **336**
Lorimer, Peter: Lechler's Wiclif, 6654
Loserth, Johann: Beginnings, 6656; Catalogue, 6648; Hus and Wiclif, 6656; Studien, 6795
Losinga, Herbert de: Epistolae, 5777
Lost literature, 2330
— villages, 607, 1383, 4949–50. *See* Deserted villages
Lot, Ferdinand: L'art militaire, 4307; Bretons, 2162, 2550; Essays, 1443; La fin du monde antique, 1179; Gildas, 2162; Hengist, Horsa, 1426; Histoire générale, 1182; Les institutions, 3992, 6718; Les migrations, 2513; Nennius, 2167
Loth, Bernard: Tables, 1267
— Joseph: Cornish, 330; Welsh Dictionary, 337
Lotharingia, Albert of, 4004
Lothian, Anglian occupation, 1433
— Marquess of, MSS., 4693
Lothingland (Suffolk), 4388
Louis VII (France), 1426
— VIII (France), 4105
— IX (France), 2880, 4094

— XI (France), 2793, 4245
Louth Park Abbey, Chronicle, 2831
Love, Janet, trans.: Les Papes d'Avignon, 6719
Lovel *v.* Morley, 3503A
Low, John L.: Codex Amiatinus, 2301; Durham, 6790
— Sidney: Dictionary, 1187
Lowe, Elias A.: 47; Bede, 2148; Codices, 394; Handwriting, 47; Palaeographical papers, 394; Uncial, 394, 447
— W. R. L.: Life of St. Alban, 890
Lower, Mark A.: Chronicle of Battel, 2838; Latin roll, 6359; Patronimica, 585; Surnames, 585
Lowes, John L.: Chaucer, 7010
Lowry, Edith C.: Clerical proctors, 3477
Lowth, Robert: William of Wykeham, 5822
Loyd, Lewis C.: A.-N. families, 564, 4667; Hatton seals, 464, 2701A, 4410
Loyn, Henry R.: A.-S. coinage, 1454; A.-S. England, 2499; A.-S. towns, 7225; Gesiths, 2635; Imperial title, 2611; King and structure, 2618; Norman conquest, 589; 3997
Luard, Henry R.: Annales Monastici, 2730; Cotton's Historia, 2854; England and Rome, 6735; Flores Historiarum, 2871; Grosseteste Epistolae, 6575; Lives of Edward the Confessor, 2171; Matthew Paris's Chronica, 2941; Tayster's Chronica, 2958
Lubac, Henri de: Exégèse médiévale, 6889
Lubbock, John (Lord Avebury): Prehistoric times, 1993
Lubimenko, Inna: Jean de Bretagne, 4058
Luca, John de: Annales, 6011
Lucas, A. T.: Ireland, 2672; Irish–Norse relations, 2605
— Henry S.: Edward I and Albert of Austria, 4109; Diplomatic relations, 4184; Famine, 1468, 5003; John Boendale, 2911; John of Avesnes, 4096; John of Brabant, 4184; Low countries, 4184; Philippa of Hainault, 1447
— Peter J.: John Capgrave, 1158, 2808
Luce, Siméon: Chronique des premiers Valois, 2844; Chroniques du Mont-Saint-Michel, 2846; La France pendant la guerre, 4185; Froissart, 2874
Luchaire, Achille: Innocent III, 6729; Jean Sans Terre, 4034
Luda, William de: Computus, 3115
Luders, Alexander: Statutes, 3327
Ludlow (Salop), 6838
Ludwig IV (emperor), 4165
Luffield Priory (Northants.), Charters, 6263

Luffman, John: Charters of London, 5158
Lugard, Cecil E.: Trailbaston, 3544
Lull, archbishop of Mainz, 2299
Lullingstone (Roman), 766, 2065
Lumb, George D.: Methley, 4937; Rental of Pontefract, 5297
Lumby, John H.: James de Hoghton deeds, 4442; Norris deeds, 4443
— Joseph R.: Bede, 2148; Higden, 2895; Knighton, 2912; Richard III, 2927
Lumley, Marmaduke, bishop, 5649
Lunt, William E.: Accounts rendered, 6778; Clerical subsidies, 6827; Clerical tenths, 1439; Consent of clergy, 1436; Financial relations, 6768, 6779; Papal revenues, 1134, 6780; Valuation of Norwich, 6781; William Testa, 3412
Lupus, Christianus: Epistolae, 6487
Lusignans, 1486, 4034, 4038
Luton (Beds.), 3147, 5030
Luttrell psalter, 897
Lydd (Kent), 5319
Lydgate, John, 6991, 7031–6, 7046
Lydney Park (Glos.), Roman, 2070
Lydon, James F.: Irish army, 4079; Irish exchequer, 3100; Revenues, 3248; Richard II in Ireland, 4114; William of Windsor, 3392
Lyell, Laetitia: Mercers' company, 5193, 5326
Lyle, Helen M.: Jack Cade, 4214
Lyminge (Kent), 6194
Lyndwood, William: Provinciale, 6436–7
Lynn, chronicle, 2742, 6009
— grey friars, 2887
— subsidy, 3175
— tailors, 5251
Lyon, Bryce D.: Constitutional history, 1215; Constitutional king, 1459; Editor of Stephenson papers, 1497; Feudal antecedent, 4308; From fief to indenture, 4308; From Hengist to Edward, 18; Jean II de Brabant, 4102; Medieval finance, 3249; Money fief, 4308
— C. S. S.: Coinage, 1454
— John: Dover, 5320
— William T.: Arms of bishops, 487
Lyons, Ponsonby A.: Cartularium, 6173; Compoti, 4794; Whitaker's Whalley, 6204
— Richard, 1459, 5171
Lysons, Daniel: Magna Britannia, 618, 1519
— Samuel: Edward I's expenses in Wales, 3131; Magna Britannia, 618, 1519, 2044; Rotulus familiae, 3120; Windsor Park, 3117

Lyte, Sir Henry C. Maxwell: Beaumont registers, 4470; Cartularies, 6306; Eton college, 7142; Glastonbury Abbey, 6311; Great seal, 3844; Rolls chapel, 957; Somerset manors, 4468, 4867; University of Oxford, 7123

Lyttelton family, 4493

— George: Henry II, 4026

Lyubimenko, Inna I. *See* Lubimenko

Mabillon, Jean: 47; 1477; Acta sanctorum, 1151; Annales, 1149; De re diplomatica, 418

MacAirt, Seán: Annals of Innisfallen, 2780; Annals of Ulster, 2786

Macalister, Robert A. Stewart: Archaeology, 775; Book of Conquests, 2403; Corpus inscriptionum, 359; Ecclesiastical vestments, 922; Lebor Gabála, 2404; Picts, 355; Stones of Wales, 1449

Macaulay, George C.: John Gower, 7015

McCaffrey, Patrick R.: White friars, 5978

MacCana, Proinnsias: Vikings, 2596

McCann, Justin: Cloud of Unknowing, 6671; Rule of St. Benedict, 5911

MacCarthaigh's Book, Irish annals, 2925

MacCarthy, Bartholomew: Annals of Ulster, 2786; Synchronisms, 2160

McCaul, John: Inscriptions, 2028

McClenaghan, Barbara: Springs of Lavenham, 5415

Macclesfield (Ches.), **574**; 1572

MacColl, Dr. (Malcolm): Canon law, 1482, 6437

Mac Conmidhe, Gilla-Brighde: Battle of Down, 2920

MacCracken, Henry N.: John Lydgate, 7032

McCracken, John L.: ed. Irish historical studies, 2319

McCulloch, Florence: Bestiaries, 893

McCusker, John J., Jr.: Wine prise, 4389

MacCutcheon, Kenneth L.: Yorks. fairs, 5526

MacDermott, Maire: trans. F. Henry's Irish art, 846

Macdonald, A.: Deeds, 4458

— Allan J.: Authority and reason, 6890; Lanfranc, 5632

— Sir George: **261**; Agricola, 2071, 2088; ed. Haverfield, 2042; Roman Britain, 2017; Roman coins, 660; Roman wall, 2087; Romanization of Roman Britain, 2041

— Iain: Fantosme, 2867

— John: Inscriptions, 355

— William R.: Seals, 467

Mace, Frances A.: Devon ports, 5390

McFarlane, Kenneth Bruce: Bastard feudalism, 1493, 3402; Beaufort, 1450, 6737; Boke of Noblesse, 2982; Business partnership, 4309; Edward I and earls, 4060, 4681; Fastolf's profits, 4302, 4825; Lancastrian kings, 4221; Loans to Lancastrians, 3253; Nobility, 4668; War economy, 4259; Wars of Roses, 4221; William of Worcester, 1441, 2982; Wycliffe, 6657

Macfarlane, Leslie J.: Election of Urban VI, 6740; Vatican archives, 5545

MacFirbis, Duald: Annals, 2146; Formorians, 2570

McGarry, Daniel D.: Metalogicon, 6642

MacGibbon, David: Architecture, 804

MacGeoghegan, Conall: Annals of Clonmacnoise, 2779

MacGibbon, David: Domestic architecture, 819; Elizabeth Woodville, 4220

McGregor, Oliver R.: Farming, 5013

Machabey, Armand: Remarques, 7186

Machor, St., Legends of, 2323

McIlwain, Charles H.: Bractonian problems, 2985; Constitutionalism, 1481; Essays, 1444; High Court of Parliament, 3375; Medieval estates, 3375; Political thought, 1415

McIntosh, Angus: Prolegomena, 347

Mack, Richard P.: Coinage, 655

Mackay, Herbert J. H.: Gavelkind, 2644

— Macintosh: Dictionarium, 333

McKechnie, William S.: Magna Carta, 3286, 3288

McKenna, John W.: Coronation oil, 1350; Henry V, 4260

MacKenzie, Hugh: Anti-foreign movement, 1439

Mackenzie, James D.: Castles, 833

Mackenzie, William Mackay; Castles, 834; The Bruce, 2792

McKeon, Richard: William of Ockham, 6615

Mackie, John D.: Bannockburn, 4081; Ninian, 2323

— William S.: Exeter Book, 2338

Mackinder, Sir Halford J.: Britain, **72**; 619

McKinlay, R.: Barbour's Bruce, 2792

McKinley, Richard A.: City of Leicester, 5140

Mackinney, Loren C.: Manuscript reproduction, **54**; Medical historiography, 6956

Mackinnon, Donald: Culdees, 2688; Gaelic MSS., 1062

— H.: William de Montibus, 1459

McKisack, May: Borough representation, 3447; ed. M. V. Clarke, 1464; Edward

III and historians, 4126; Essays in honour of, 4132, 7223; Favent's Historia, 2868; Fourteenth century, **603** and **606**; 1189; King's Lynn representatives, 3461; London and succession, 1450; Medieval history, **389**; 263A

Maclagan, Sir Eric R. D.: Bayeux Tapestry, 4276

— Michael: Bury's Philobiblon, 6562

McLaughlin, Terence P.: Teaching of canonists, 6438

MacLean, Donald: Celtic Church, 2669

Maclean, Sir John: Aid, 3160; Annals of Chepstow, 4585; Berkeley MSS., 4593; Cornwall poll tax, 3152; Forest of Dene, 3892; Glos. feet of fines, 3550; Glos. knights' fees, 4358; St. Ewen, Bristol, 6838; Trigg Minor, 4583

Macleane, Douglas: Statuta (of Salisbury), 5803

McLeod, Enid: Charles of Orleans, 4247

MacLeod, M. S. G.: **127**. *See* Hands, M. S. G.

Maclysaght, Edward: Irish families, 565

McMahon, Clara P.: Education, 7141

MacMahon, Kenneth A.: Guide, 1870

MacMurrough, Dermot: King of Leinster, 2954

McNair, Arnold D.: Roman law, 1231

McNally, Robert E.: Old Ireland, 1200; Papacy, survey of research, 6712; St. Patrick, 2324

MacNaught, John C.: Celtic church, 2673

MacNeill (warrior), 2400

— Eoin: Ancient Irish law, 2249; Annals of Innisfallen, 2780; Book of Conquests, 2403; Celtic Ireland, 2128; Essays to, 1445; Irish MSS. Commission, **132**; Phases, 1201, 2128; St. Patrick, 2324; Tigernach annals, 2170

— John T.: Library of Christian Classics, 1133; Penitentials, 2255

— Muircheartach, 2400

MacNiocaill, Gearóid: Annals of Loch Cé, 2783; Bartholomaeus Anglicus, 6551; Documents on Templars, 6054

McNiven, Peter: Archbishop Scrope, 4213; Cheshire rising (1400), 4213

McNulty, Joseph: Chartulary of St. Mary of Sallay, 6417; Thomas Sotheron *v.* Cockersand abbey, 6455

Macphail, James R. N.: Records, 1059

McPeek, Gwynn S.: British Museum MS., 7191

Macpherson, David: Andrew of Wyntoun, 2984; Rotuli Scotiae, 3795

MacQueen, John: Ninian, 2323

Macray, William D.: Annals, 1018; Ashmole bequest, 1023; Beaumont papers, 4571; Calendar of charters, 6165; Catalogus, 1022; Chronicon abbatiae de Evesham, 6380; Chronicon abbatiae Rameseiensis, 2151; Notes on muniments, 7075; Register, 7076; Salisbury cathedral, 5799

Macro, Cox: Library, 5585

McRoberts, David: Catalogue, 1066

Madan, Falconer: Books in manuscript, 419, 7170; Localization of MSS., 1448; Oxford books, 1787; Oxford press, 7219; Rough list, 5233; Summary Catalogue, 1027

Madden, Sir Frederic: Abbreviatio Chronicorum, 2745; Laȝamon's Brut, 2914; Page's poem, 2940; Paris's Historia Minor, 2941; Political poems, 7047; Wycliffe's Bibles, 6649

Maddicott, John R.: Thomas of Lancaster, 4127

Maddison, Arthur R.: Chronicle of Louth Park, 2831; Court rolls, 4812; Lincolnshire pedigrees, 563; Rental, 4813; Tournays of Caenby, 4584

— Francis: Sir William Dugdale, 1147

Madge, Sidney J.: Inquisitions, 4356

Madox, Thomas: Baronia Anglica, 3250, 4669; Dialogus, 3005; Firma burgi, 5026; Formulare, 426; History of exchequer, 3250

Madresfield (Wilts.), 4929

Maelienydd (Radnorshire), 4632A

Mageoghegan, Conall: Annals of Clonmacnoise, 2779

Maghfeld, Gilbert: Account book, 5175

Magic, A.-S., 2378–9

Magie, David: Historia Augusta, 2025

Magna Bibliotheca Anglo-Judica, 3931

Magna Carta, **501–2**; 1446, 1450, 1481, 1486–7, 1501, 3366, 4039, 6374

Magnin, Étienne: Dictionnaire, **168**

Magnum Registrum Album (Lichfield), 1047, 5666

Magnus the Good, 2438, 2447

Magnússon, Eirikr: Thomas saga, 6488

— Finnur: Om de Engelskes Handel, 5432

— Magnús: Njal Saga, 2449

Magoun, Francis P., Jr.: A.-S. Chronicle, 2142F; Gummere's Origins, 2510; Pagan survivals, 2658; Papers, 2315; Sutton Hoo, 2487

Magrath, John R.: Queen's College, 7124

Maguire, Cathal: Annals of Ulster, 2786

— Mary H.: Oath ex officio, 1444

Mahn, Jean B.: L'Ordre Cistercien, 5945

Mahr, Adolf: Christian art, 843

Mai, Angelo: Appendix ad opera, 2949
Maiden Castle (Dorset), 2070
Maidment, James: Spottiswoode Society, 218
Maidstone, Richard de: Reconciliation of Richard II, 7049; Protectorium pauperis, 7049
Maier, Anneliese: Die Vorlaufer Galileis, 6955
Maigne d' Arnis, W. H.: Lexicon, 305
Maine, Sir Henry J. S.: Ancient law, 1239
Maire of Bristowe, Kalendar, 5083
Maitland Club, 210
Maitland, Frederic W.: **201–3**; 1385, 1461, 1470, 1482–4, 1501, 2177, 2533, 5364, 6305; Anglo-French language, **37**; Archaic communities, 1482, 2637; Beatitude of seisin, 1482, 3703; Body politic, 1482–3; Bracton and Azo, 2985; Bracton's Note Book, 2985, 3481; Cambridgeshire manor, 1482, 1484, 4719; Canon law, 6437, 6445; Charter roll, 1482; Charters of Cambridge, 5039; Church, state, and decretals, 6437; Collected papers, 1240, 1482; Constitutional history, 1216; Conveyancer, 1482, 3000; Corporation sole, 1482–3; Court baron, 2995, 4716; Crown as corporation, 1482–3; Deacon and Jewess, 1482, 3954, 6437; Death of Montfort, 7043; Domesday Book, 2636, 3058; English law, 1242 (P. and M.), 1482, 1484; Equity, 3725; Execrabilis, 1482, 6437, 6762; Eyre of Kent, 3558; Forms of action, 3704; Frankalmoign, 1482; Gierke's Das Genossenschaftsrecht, 1412; Glanvill revised, 1482; Gross's Gild merchant, 1482; Henry II and clerks, 1482, 6437, 6509; Henry II's revocation, 1482, 6505; Horn's Mirror, 2991; Inaugural lecture, 1482; Laws of Anglo-Saxons (Liebermann), 1482; Laws of Wales, 1482, 2237, 2647; Leet and tourn, 1484; Materials for legal history, 1246, 1482; Memoranda de parliamento, 1483–4, 3319, 3365; Mirror of Justices, 2991; Moral personality, 1482–3; Murder of Clement, 1482, 3516; Mystery of seisin, 1246, 1482; Northumbrian tenures, 1482, 4975; Origin of the borough, 1387, 1482; Outlines of legal history, 1482; Pleas in manorial courts, 1484, 4700, 4777; Pleas of the crown, 3516, 3551; Praerogativa regis, 1482, 3275; Prologue, 1242; Records of Lincoln's Inn, 1482, 7148; Records of parliament, 1483–4, 3319, 3365; Register of writs, 1246, 1482;

Seebohm, 1482; Selected essays, 1483–4; Seisin of chattels, 1482; Suitors, 1482, 3738; Surnames, 1482, 2637; Teaching of History, 1482; Three rolls, 3521; Township and borough, 1387, 1484; Trust und Korporation, 1482–3; Vacarii summa, 1482; Why the history of English law is not written, 1482; William Lyndwood, 6436–7; William of Drogheda, 6437; Wyclif on law, 1482, 6664; Year books, 3646
— John A. Fuller: Carols, 7190
Maître, Léon A.: Les écoles, 1392
Major, Albany F.: trans. Brønsted, 2473
— Kathleen: Acta Stephani Langton, 5598; Blyborough charters, 1453; Crutched friars, 6041; Episcopal acta, 5577; Essays to, 7224; Finances of Lincoln, 5753; Handlist, 1049; Langton's familia, 5633; Lincoln chapter-clerk, 1437; Lincoln presentations, 1450; Papal documents, 5550; Registrum Antiquissimum, 5744; Teaching of diplomatic, **47**; Thornton chronicle, 6221
Makower, Felix: Die Verfassung der Kirche, 1284, 6796
Malcolm IV (Scotland), 3794
Malden, Arthur R.: Battle of Agincourt, 4261; Canonization of St. Osmund, 5798
— Henry E.: Cely papers, 5330; Magna Carta, 3290
Maldon (Surrey), 4897
— battle of, 1475, 2325, 2328, 2344, 2588
Male, Louis de, 4188
Mallaber, Kenneth A.: Union list, 89
Mallet, Charles E.: University of Oxford, 7125
Mallett, Michael E.: Anglo-Florentine relations, 5437
Malling (Sussex), church of College of, 4906
Malmesbury abbey (Wilts.), 2296, 2865, 4677, 6374–5
— walls, 5347
Malmesbury, Thomas of: Eulogium, 2865
— William of: 1491; De gestis pontificum, 1100, 1114, 1119, 1143, 2291; De gestis regum, 1089, 1119, 1123, 2921; Glastoniensis ecclesia, 1100, 6309, 6316; Historia novella, 1113, 1119, 1123, 2921; Own times, 1123; Vita Aldhelmi, 2296; Vita S. Dunstani, 2303; Vita S. Wulstani, 2316, 5843
Malone, Kemp: Beowulf, 441, 2332–3; Deor, 2328; Widsith, 2328, 2346
Malory, Sir Thomas, 6981, 7037–40

Malton priory (Yorks.), 1471, 6406
— (Yorks.) (Roman), 2069
Malvern (Worcs.), History of, 5287
— priory, Antiquitates, 6384
Malvern, John of: Higden's Polychronicon, 2895, 4130
Mamecestre. *See* Manchester
Man, Isle of, 583, 1106, 1429, 1944–51, 2132, 2565, 6790
Manchester (Lancs.), 4791, 5129. *See* John Rylands Library
— duke of, 4775
Mancini, Dominico: Usurpation of Richard III, 2922
Mander, Gerald P.: Accounts of Walsall, 5255; Priory of Brewood, 6325; Wodehouse deeds, 4471; Wolseley charters, 4477
Mandeville, Geoffrey de, 3984
Mandonnet, Pierre: Dominican studies, 5987
Mandrot, Bernard de: Commynes Mémoires, 2851
Mangenot, Eugène: Dictionnaire, 1267
Manitius, Max: Handschriften, 7171; Lateinische Literatur, 56, 1404
Manley, F. H.: Parliamentary representatives, 3473
Manly, John M.: Chaucer, 7001, 7007, 7011; Roger Bacon, 6544
Mann, John C.: City foundations (Roman), 2045; Northern frontier, 2094; Tribes of Roman Wales, 2089
— Sir James G.: Arms and armour, 1485; Bayeux Tapestry, 4276
— James S.: Social England, 1196
Manners and household expenses, 4609
Mannert, Conrad: Tabula, 2032
Manning, Bernard L.: Ockham's Opera, 6617; People's faith, 6851
— Owen: Surrey, 1834
Mannyng, Robert: Chronicle, 1103, 2913, 2923, 6694, 6699
Manorial records, **666–91**; 192, 428, 1505, 1677, 3864, 5672, 5674, 5682, 5759, 5779, 5836, 6171. *See* Accounts, Charters and deeds, Court rolls, Custumals, Extents, and Rentals
Manors, **374–8** and **666–700**; 192, 1361, 1437, 1439, 1480, 1495, 2195, 2209, 2212, 2625–6, 2636, 2650–2, 3054, 5619, 5621, 6315. *See* Manorial records
Manrique, Angel: Annales, 5946
Mansi, J. (Giovanni) D.: Baronius Annales, 1126; Concilia, 1142; Fabricius' Bibliotheca, 51
Manuel des Péchés, Le, 6694
Manuel du libraire (Brunet), 44

Manuscripts, **53–4**; 101–3, 515, 523. *See* Archives, Catalogues, Facsimiles, Illuminated MSS
— and Men, 945
Manwaring, George E.: Naval history, 4323
Manwood, John: Collection, 3891; Treatise, 3914
Manx crosses, 358
Manydown (Hants), 4767
Manyon, L. A.: trans. Bloch, 1179, 1363
Map, Walter, 1114, 6599–601
Maps, **71–4**; 1467; diocesan, 6790; London, 1740, 1746, 5165; monastic, **793**; 604; Oxford, 7128; Oxon., 4998; Roman, 2032; Towns, 1386
Mapledurham (Oxon.), 4846
Marcham, Frederick G.: Sources, 1207
Marchegay, Paul: Chartes, 6252; Les prieurés anglais, 6252
Marches of Scotland, 1774, 4076, 4197, 4230
— of Wales, 3638, 4633, 4675, 4978A
Marckwardt, Albert H.: Nowell's Vocabularium, 283
Marcus, Geoffrey J.: Naval history, 4329
Marden (Herts.), 4773
Mare, Peter de la, 3417
Maredudd, Rhys ap, revolt of, 4059
Margam, Annals, 1099, 1114, 2754, 4034
Margaret I, daughter of Edward I, 4598
— of Anjou, 3129, 3773, 4195, 4201
— of Burgundy, 4282
Margary, Ivan D.: Antonine iter, 2029; Roman roads, 2084
Margerison, Samuel: Calverley charters, 4496
Margery Kempe. *See* Kempe
Marichal, Robert: Chartae, 2192
Mariën, Marcel E.: Inventaria, 735
Mariner's Mirror (journal), 4324
Marini Collection, Papal letters, 5547
Maritime law, 4286
Mark, the, 1367, 2638, 2646
Marke, Julius J.: Catalogue, 84, 1225
Markets, **749–50**; 1455, 5872
Market Harborough (Leics.), 5143, 5453
Markham, Christopher A.: Liber Custumarum, 5215; Records of Northampton, 5215
— Sir Clements R.: Murder of princes, 4203; Richard III, 4222
Markus, Robert A.: Gregorian mission, 2704
Marlborough, Henry of: Chronica, 2924
— Thomas of: Chronicle of Evesham, 6380
Marmorstein, Arthur: Jews, 3969
Marongui, Antonio: Il Parlamento, 3366

Marouzeau, Jules: L'année philologique, 2014

Marquardt, Hertha: Runes, 360

Marriage law, 6453, 6483
— of clergy, 6836

Marrick, priory (Yorks.), 6407

Marrou, Henri-Irénée: Histoire de l'éducation, 1393; La méthodologie, 264

Marsden, Philip: Officers of Commons, 3424
— Reginald G.: Admiralty pleas, 3515; Law of the sea, 4280

Marsh, Adam of, 6010, 6602–4
— Frank B.: Gascony, 4103
— Frederick T.: Annals of St. Wulstan, 6386
— John F.: Annals of Chepstow, 4585

Marshal, the, office of, 556, 3143, 4004
— William, 1499, 2896, 4033

Marshall, Edward: Oxford, 6790; Woodstock manor, 4855
— George W.: Genealogist, 503; Guide, 517; Handbook, 4508; Parish registers, 1521

Martel, Philip, 3839

Martène, Edmond: Coggeshall's Chronicon, 2850; Collectio, 1110; Thesaurus, 1109; Voyage littéraire, 2973

Martham (Norfolk), 2630, 4824

Martin V, pope, 5562

Martin, Adam: Exchequer records, 959; Index to repertories, 3251
— Alan R.: Dominican priory, 5997; Franciscan architecture, 805, 6029; Grey friars, 6015
— C.: Walter Burley, 1428
— Charles Trice: Catalogue, 7072; Chancery proceedings, 3483; Gaimar's L'estoire, 2875; Gesta Herwardi, 2878; Jews, 3934; Record interpreter, 405; Registrum Johannis Peckham, 5610; Registrum Malmesburiense, 6374; ed. Wright's Court-hand, 411
— Edward J.: Trial of Templars, 6061
— Francis X: Course of Irish history, 1202; Irish materials, 5970; St. Patrick, 2324
— Geoffrey H.: Bibliography, 1511, 1729; Borough deeds, 7224; Court rolls, 5261; English borough, 5355; Records of Ipswich, 5262
— Jean Baptiste: ed., Mansi, 1142
— Joan S.: Coinage, 1454
— Léon Eugène: St. Columban, 2320
— M. T.: Percy Chartulary, 4501, 4838
— Raymond M.: Robert de Melun, 6605–6
— Victor: Histoire de l'église, 1277

— William: Index, 717; Treasure trove, 3668A

Martival, Roger, bishop, 5801

Martyrology, 5814

Marwick, William H.: Bibliography, 26

Marx, Jean: Guillaume de Jumièges, 1443, 2908; Guillaume de Poitiers, 1443

Mary, abbess of Shaftesbury, 6130

Maryport, garrison of, 2045

Masai, François: Irish miniatures, 391, 881

Mascall, Robert, bishop, 5730

Maseres, Francis: Monumenta, 1111

Maskell, William: Liturgy, 1341

Mas Latrie, Jacques M. J. L. de: Trésor de chronologie, 373

Mason, the medieval, 800, 5491
— Arthur J.: Mission of Augustine, 2704
— John: Letters of, 1459, 6183
— John Frederick A.: Companions of the Conqueror, 564; Geld rolls, 3066; Norman earls, 4627; Roger of Shrewsbury, 4586

Massa, Eugenio: Roger Bacon, 6540, 6545

Massingberd, William O.: Court roll of Ingoldmells, 4812; Lincoln Cathedral charters, 5744; Lincs. inquisitions, 4371; Lincs. records, 3573; Ormsby-cum-Ketsby, 4814; Records of Langton, 4815; Survey of manor of Stow, 4816

Master of the game, 3885

Master Worsley's Book, 7153

Masters, Betty R.: Mayor's household, 5177; St. Ewen's, Bristol, 5086, 6838
— Robert: Corpus Christi College, 7100

Mate, Mavis: Mint of trouble, 676, 3252

Matheson, Cyril: Bibliography, 34

Mathew, Gervase: Court of Richard II, 4128, 6990; Knighthood, 1450

Mathew, Theobald: Law French, **37**

Mathieson, John: Maps, 599

Mathilda, empress and queen, 3779, 4003, 4398, 6517

Matthew of Westminster, 1089, 1118, 2871
— Paris, 596, 1089, 1114, 1459, 2871, 2941

Matthew, Donald J. A.: Norman conquest, 3998; Norman monasteries, 5923
— Frederic D.: Works of Wyclif, 6650

Matthews, Gordon F.: Isles of Scilly, 1590
— John H.: Hundred of Wormslow, 1670
— Thomas: Welsh records, 3787A
— Walter R.: St. Paul's cathedral, 5770
— William: Malory, 7039; Secular literature, 2974

Mattingly, Harold: Fort at Malton, 2069; Roman coins in B.M., 647, 661; Roman imperial coins, 662; trans. Tacitus, 2025, 2505

Matzke, John E.: Lois de Guillaume, 2187

Maurer, Armand: ed. Buckfield's Sententia, 6552
— Konrad von: Rechtsverhältnisse, 2638; Wesen des Adels, 2638
Maurists, 262
Mawdsley, William N. Hargreaves. *See* Hargreaves-Mawdsley
Mawer, Sir Allen: Field names, 1455; Place-names, 623, 634; Vikings, 2591
Mawgan Porth (Cornw.), 766
Maxwell, Sir Herbert: Chronicle of Lanercost, 2836; Scalacronica, 2884
— Ian S.: Domesday geography, 3044
— Leslie F.: Bibliography of law, 1228
— William Harold: Bibliography of law, 1228
Maxwell-Lyte, Sir Henry C. *See* Lyte
May, Teresa: Cobham family, 4587
— Thomas: Roman cemetery, 2070
Mayer, Hans-Eberhard: Itinerarium Peregrinorum, 2906
Mayew, Richard: Hereford register, 5730
Mayhew, Anthony L.: Promptorium, 312
Mayhoff, Carolus: Pliny, 2025
Maynard's Year Books, 3644
Mayo, Irish abbey, 2123
Mayo, Charles H.: Bibliotheca, 1616; Court roll, 6130; Records of Dorchester, 5065; Records of Shaftesbury, 5066
Mayor, John E. B.: Bede, 2148; Richard of Cirencester, 2026, 2155
Mayor's accounts, 5137
— register, 5274
Mayr-Harting, Henry: Acts of bishops of Chichester, 5650; Hilary of Chichester, 6510
Meads, Dorothy M.: Searching records, 1520
Meaney, Audrey: Gazetteer, 2464
Mears, Thomas L.: Admiralty jurisdiction, 1246
Meates, Geoffrey W.: Lullingstone villa, 2065; Recent archaeology, 766
Meaux abbey (Yorks.), Chronicle, 2806
Mechanics, 6940, 6959, 6968
Medeshamstede and its colonies, 1455, 1496, 2220
Mediaeval and Renaissance Studies (journal), 133
— archives of Oxford, 7064
— Scandinavia (journal), 160, 2434
— Studies (journal), 162
Medicine, 1421–2, 2371, 2376, 2380, 6935, 6951, 6956, 6962–4, 6966–7
Medieval and Modern Irish Texts, 2390
— Archaeology (journal), 2465
— England, 1485
— Latin Word List, 301, 308

— Texts (series), 1113
Medievalia et Humanistica (journal), 161
Medium Aevum (journal), 267
Medlicott, William N.: editor, 1183
Meech, Sanford B.: Book of Margery Kempe, 6674; Musical treatises, 7206
Meekings, Cecil A. F.: Alan de Wassand, 3689; Chippenham veredictum, 3625; Fitznell's Cartulary, 4481; Justices of the Jews, 3482, 3518; Pateshull and Raleigh, 3689; Pipe roll, 1441; Register of writs, 3499; Robert of Nottingham, 3689; Rutland eyre (1253), 3601; Wilts. eyre (1249), 3622
Meer, G. van der: Coinage, 687, 1454
Megaw, Basil R. S.: Norse heritage, 1429
— I.: Stephen's policy, 1457
Meier, Hans: Catalogue, 983
Meijer, Alberic de: Irish materials, 5970; John Capgrave, 2808
Meikle, Henry W.: MS. Catalogues, **131**
Meillet, Antoine: Dictionnaire, 306
Meineke, Johann Albrecht: Strabo, 2025
Meinert, Hermann: Papsturkunden, 1132
Meissner, John L. G.: Celtic church, 2674
— Paul: Zeitalter von Humanismus, 6918
Meitzen, August: Siedelung, 1372, 2514
Mélanges d'Archéologie et d'Histoire (journal), 163
Melcombe Regis (Dorset), 5068
Mellitus: Letter of Gregory I, 2308
Mellows, Charles: Peterborough Chronicle, 6270
— William T.: Book of William Morton, 6264; Henry of Pytchley's Book of Fees, 4456, 6267; Peterborough chronicle, 6270; Peterborough local administration, 5216
Melos Amoris of Richard Rolle, 6680
Melrose, Chronicle of, 1098, 1114, 2824
Melton, William, archbishop, 5849, 5863
Melton Mowbray (Leics.), 6838
Melun, Robert de, 6605–6
Melville, Evan W. M. Balfour-. *See* Balfour-Melville
Mély, Fernand de: Bibliographie, 6782
Memoranda rolls, **491–3**; 965, 1075, 4278, 7222; for Ireland, 3211, 3217; for London, 5156. *See* Exchequer
— de parliamento, 1483–4, 3319, 3365
Memorial of Llandaff, 5880B
Memorials of London, 5160
— of St. Edmund's Abbey, 2305, 6341
Mendelssohn, Ludovicus: Zosimus, 2025
Mendip, 2081, 3888, 5506
Menevia. *See* St. David's
Menger, Louis E.: Anglo-Norman dialect 295

Menot, Michel, 6705

Meopham, Simon: Speculum Edwardi III, 2955

Mercati, Angelo: Cardinal Nicolò de Romanis (legate), 1448, 6746

Mercenaries, 4315

Mercer, Eric: Ruthwell cross, 353

Mercer's Company, London, 5177, 5193-4, 5326; York, 5303, 5310

Merchant adventurers, 5219, 5379, 5388, 5428

— law, 3507, 5082, 5524

— shipping, 5378

— tailors, Bristol, 5085; London, 5195-6; York, 5301

Merchants, 1469, 5334-5, 5346, 5375, 5397, 5415, 5419, 5443, 5464, 5505. *See* Gilds *and* Hansa

— alien, 1467, 3105, 5423-42

— of the staple, 1246, 5340, 5386, 5406, 5464

Mercia, 1470, 1496, 2142, 2213, 2220, 2555, 2622

Mercian annals, 2142

Merewether, Henry A.: Boroughs, 1388

Merioneth, 1928-9, 4943A

Meritt, Herbert D.: ed. A.-S. dictionary, 279

Merrifield, Ralph: Roman London, 2063

Merry, Denis H.: Oxford University bibliography, 920; Oxon. bibliography, 1786

Merryweather, Frederick S.: Bibliomania, 7172

Merton, annals of, 2785, 2842, 5268

— College, 7077-80, 7121, 7164-5

— Hall (Norfolk), 4821

— Priory (Surrey), 6352

— provisions of, 5842

— School, 903; 6627, 6940, 6957, 6971-2

— Statute of, 3334

— Walter de, 4463, 7121

Merure de Seinte Eglise, 6695

Messenger, Ernest C.: trans. de Wulfs' History, 1410, 6899

Messham, J. E.: Owen Glyndwr, 4219

Metalwork, Anglo-Saxon, 872

Metcalfe, David M.: A.-S. coinage, 704, 1454

— William M.: ed. Pinkerton's Lives, 1168; Ninian, 2323

Methley (Yorks.), 4937

Methodology, 240-65

Meyer, A.: trans., Celtic church, 2684

— Albert de: Dictionnaire, 593

— Erwin F.: Craft gilds, 5367

— Karl: John Gowers Beziehungen, 7019

— Kuno: Anecdota, 2148; Cain Adam-náin, 2244; Cormac, 2401; Irish lexicography, 348; Learning in Ireland, 2418; Rawlinson MS. (B 502), 440, 2399; Tigernach, 2170

— Paul: De quelques chroniques, 2811; La vie d'Édouard, 2171c; Les contes de Bozon, 6692; L'histoire de Guillaume, 2896

— Paul M.: Codex Theodosianus, 266

— Peter: Book of Kells, 881

— Robert T.: Review, 2394

Meyerhoff, Hans: Philosophy of history, 244

Meyrick, Sir Samuel R.: Cardigan, 1907

Meyvaert, Paul: Gregory's Responsiones, 2308, 7225; John Erghome, 7049

Michael of Ambresbury, 6315

Michaud, Joseph F.: Jean Juvénal des Ursins, 2909

Michel, Albert: Tables, 1267

— Francisque: Chroniques Anglo-Normandes, 1112, 2172, 2861; Fantosme's Chronicle, 2867; Gesta Herwardi, 2878; Gesta regum, 2166; Histoire des ducs, 2897; Le Prince Noir, 2812; Rôles Gascons, 3826; Sainte-Maure's Chronique, 2952; Song of Dermot, 2954

Microfilms, 4, 438

Microforms, 4

Middleburgh staple, 5386

Middle English Dictionary, 281

Middle English literature, 907-16

Middle English names, 580-1, 584

Middleham, collegiate church (Yorks.), 6408

Middlesex, 762, 1504-5, 1522, 1529, 1727, 1732-4, 1738

Middle Temple, 1014, 7153

Middleton, Lord: MSS., 4693

— Sir Arthur E.: Sir Gilbert de Middleton, 4129

— Sir Gilbert de (1317), 4129

— Richard of: Franciscan philosophy, 6910

Middlewich (Ches.), 4423

Midgley, Margaret: Ministers' accounts of Cornwall, 4629, 4727; Staffs. poll-tax, 3185; Survey of archives, 109; 5575

Migne, Jacques Paul: Patrologia, 1135

Milan, State Papers, 3833

Miles, G. C.: editor, 646

— George: A.-S. bishops, 2721

Military history, 619-25

— obligation, A.-S., 7225

— orders, 807-9

Milkau, Fritz: Bibliothekswissenschaft, 7173

Millar, Eric G.: Bohun MSS., 895, 4572; Illuminated MSS., 875, 877; Lindisfarne Gospels, 896; Luttrell Psalter, 897; York Psalter, 898
— and Bryce: Handbook of Edinburgh records, 1059
— Fergus: Cassius Dio, 2025i
Millard, James E.: Basingstoke, 5096
Miller, Edward: Economy in thirteenth century, 5457; Ely abbey, 2164, 5711; Ely land pleas, 3010; Maitland, ed. 2636; Norman Conquest, 1430; Origins of parliament, 3361; Review of Kosminsky, 4971; State and landed interests, 4670; Studies of parliament, 3359, 3365; Tenants of Birting, 4840; Textile industry, 5416; V.C.H., 1529; War in the North, 4080
— Frederic: The Middleburgh staple, 5386
— Helen: London and parliament, 3365
— Konrad: Antonine iter, 2029; Mappaemundi, 603; Peutinger Table, 2032
— Samuel H.: De gestis Herwardi, 2878
— Samuel J. T.: Bracton, 2985, 3277
— Steuart N.: Imperial crisis, 2034; Roman occupation, 2091
— Thomas: Bede's history, 2148
Milling of corn, 4988
Millor, W. J.: Letters of John of Salisbury, 6641
Mills, James: Justiciary rolls of Ireland, 3641
— Mabel H.: Beds. and Bucks. sheriff rolls, 3528; Cheshire in pipe rolls, 3084; Exchequer experiments, 1493; Exchequer procedure, 3254; London custom house, 3238, 5170; Review of Ramsay's Revenues, 3258; Shirehouse, 1441; Surrey pipe roll, 3095
Millward, Roy: Lancashire, 1517
Milman, Henry H.: St. Paul's cathedral, 5771
Milne, Alexander Taylor: Centenary guide, 177; Historical study, 261; Writings, 39
— Duncan Grinnell: Killing of William Rufus, 3999
— Joseph G.: Greek coins, 1656
Milsom, Stroud F. C.: Commentary on the actions, 3705; Foundations of common law, 3672; Novae Narrationes, 2998; Pollock and Maitland, 1242; Trespass from Henry III to Edward III, 3706
Minchin, W.: Ducatus Lancastriae, 3873
Minchinhampton (Glos.), 4759
Minchinton, Walter E.: Agrarian history, 2626, 4981, 5488
Minehead (Som.), 4868

Mines, 2081, 5506, 5513-14
Minet, William: Surrey, 1828
Miniatures, 453, 881
Ministers' accounts: **493**; 955, 955A, 3228, 3871, 4619, 4974; Black Prince, 3786A; Bolton priory, 6396; Chester, 3854; Earldom of Cornwall, 4629, 4727; Elton, 4776; Flintshire, 3858-9; Hadleigh castle, 4749; Honour of Leicester, 3874, 3880, 4620; Lancashire, 4790; Lenton priory, 6280; Percy family, 4643; Petworth manor, 4903; St. Mary's, Warwick, 4912-13, 6370; Wales, 4629A, 4632A, 4633, 4633A; Warwickshire, 4913. See Estate management
Mink, Louis O.: History and theory, 241
Minns, Ellis H.: Vetus liber Eliensis, 5706
Minor Arts, 861-72
Minot, Laurence, 7041
Mints, 670, 676, 679, 687, 698, 1454 (A.-S.), 3007, 5502
Miracles, 1108, 6380
Mirbt, Carl: Quellen, 1136
Mirk, John: Festial, 6697; Parish priests, 6696
Mirot, Léon: Ambassades, 3818; Froissart, 2874
Mirror of justices, 2991
Misae rolls, 3774
Miscellanea Genealogica et Heraldica, 505
Misericords, 851
Miskimin, Harry A.: Monetary movements, 5459
Missenden abbey (Bucks.), 945, 6094
Missions, 2290, 2299, 2320, 2667-8, 2698, 2702, 2704, 5623
Misyn, Richard: Rolle's Incendium, 6679
Mitchell, Sir Arthur: Bibliography, 27
— J. B.: Early maps, 596
— M.: trans. Levy-Ullman's Elements, 1238
— Rosamond J.: Englishmen in Italy, 6919
— Sydney K.: Taxation, 3255; Towns, **178**
— W. T.: Survey of Oxford, 5238
— William: Partnership, 1246
Mithras, cult of, 766
Moberly, George H.: Bede's Historia, 2148; William of Wykeham, 5822
Modern Language Association of America Publs., 268
Modus componendi brevia, 2996
— tenendi curias, 2995
— tenendi parliamentum, **509-10**
Mogk, Eugen: Saga, 2436
Mohl, Ruth: Theories of monarchy, 7049
Mohrmann, Christine: St. Patrick, 2324
Moir, Esther A. L.: Gloucestershire, **1651**

Moisant, Joseph: Speculum, 2955
Moleyns, Adam: Libelle of Englyshe Polycye, 5338
Molinari, Paul: Julian of Norwich, 6673
Molinier, Auguste: Chronique Normande, 2848; Gesta Philippi, 2947; Sources, 57
— Émile: Chronique Normande, 2848
Molland, Andrew G.: Geometrical background, 6957
Mollat, Guillaume: Collation des bénéfices, 6769; Diplomatie pontificale, 4186; Innocent VI et les tentatives de paix, 4186; Institutions ecclésiastiques, 6718; Papes d'Avignon, 6719; Regestum Clementis, 5561
— Michel: Anglo-Norman trade, 5391
Moloney, Michael: Essays to, 679
Molton, South (Devon), 5063
Mommsen, Theodor: Bede's Chronica, 2148; Codex Theodosianus, **266**; Gildas, 2162; M.G.H., 1114; Nennius, 2167; Notitia, 2030; Provinzen, 2048; Römische Geschichte, 2048
Monasticism: Bibliography, 1290; Heads of houses, 2692, 5745, 5895; History, **167–8**; 262, 742, 1426, 1437, 1450, 1453, 1455, 1475, 1477, 1485, 1494–5, 1505, 1529, 2217, 2220, 2292g, 2293e, 2311, 2675A, 2718, 4406, 5257, 5417, 5422; Libraries, **134** and **927–9**; 1439, 1445; Lists, 1295, 1299; Maps, 604–5; Orders, **795–810**; Particular houses, **810–46**; Records, **147–8** and **792–846**; Rules, **317–19**; 2320e, 5909; Seals, 465; Settlements, 5904, 5936, 5938. See Accounts, monastic, Charters, monastic, *and* Knowles, David
Monasticon Anglicanum, 1147
— Eboracense, 6387
— Exoniensis, 1147, 6109
— Praemonstratense, 1144
Monetary policies, 3236, 3248, 3252, 3263, 4179, 5445
Money economy, **747–9**; 1468, 5462
— lenders, 1448, 5503, 5509, 5516–17, 5522
— rents, 4308, 4971
Moneys, meaning of, 1495
Monk Bretton priory (Yorks.), 6409
Monk Friston (Yorks.), 6410
Monk-Wearmouth, abbey (Durham), 2297, 2301, 6138
Monks Horton, priory (Kent), 6195
Monmouth, priory (Mon.), 6252
— Geoffrey of, 999, 1089, 1095, 1101, 1486, 2166
— Thomas of: Life of St. William, 3937
Monmouthshire, 816, 1435, 1930–6

Monod, Gabriel: Bibliographie, 58; Condamnation de Jean, 4034
Monro, Cecil: Letters of Margaret of Anjou, 3773
Monsen, Erling: Heimskringla, 2447
Monstrelet, Enguerrand de: Chronique 2926
Montacute priory (Som.), 6147, 6306
Montagu, James: Deeds, 4495
Montague family, estates, 4658
Monte, Piero da (papal envoy), 6745, 7180
— Robert de: Chronique, 1123, 2962
Montebourg, abbey of, 6129
Montfaucon, Bernard de: Monuments, 4276
Montfort, Eleanor of, household, 4607, 4609
— Guy de, 1490
— Simon de, 1482, 2753, 2838, 2983, 4043, 4055, 4062, 4068, 6602, 7043
Montgomery, Roger de, 4586
Montgomeryshire, 1937
Montifernan, Annals of, 2755
Mont-Saint-Michel, Chronique, 2846
Monumenta Franciscana, 6010
— Germaniae Historica, 262, 1114
— Historica Britannica, 1084
— Historica Carmelitana, 5976
— Historica Norvegiae, 1115
— Juridica, 4286
— Ordinis Praedicatorum, 5984
Monuments de la règle cistercienne, 5933
Moody, Ernest A.: Weights, 6958
— Theodore W.: Irish history, 1202
Mooney, Canice: Irish church, 1274
Moor, Charles: Cardinals beneficed, 5807; Knights, 566
Moorat, Samuel A. J.: Catalogue of Wellcome Library, 6937
Moore, Alan: Accounts of John Starlyng, 4330
— Arthur W.: Isle of Man, 1949; Isle of Man names, 583; Sodor and Man, 6790; Surnames, 639
— Clifford H.: Tacitus' History, 2025
— Grace E.: Edward the Confessor, 2171
— J. S.: Domesday teamland, 5004
— Margaret F.: Bibliography, 19, 4695; Lands of Scottish kings, 4671
— Norman: St. Bartholomew's Hospital, 6226–7
— Ralph W.: Romans in Britain, **264**
— Stuart A.: Cartularium, 6141; Death of Edward II, 4139; Dartmoor forest, 3915; Domesday, 3047; Letters of Shillingford, 5057; Rights of common, 5005
— Thomas: Devon, 1612
Moore manuscript of Bede, 441, 2148

Moorland, farming, 5020

Moorman, John R. H.: Church life, 6797; Estates of Lanercost, 6111; Franciscan order, 6031; Grey friars, 6030, 7101; History of the church, 1285; Parsonage, 6852

Moot hall, 5289

Morand, François: Le Fèvre's Chronique, 2917

Morant, Alfred W.: Whitaker's Craven, 1893, 6397

— Philip: Colchester, 5075; Essex, 1639

Moranville, Henri: Chronique du Religieux, 2915

More, Sir Thomas: Richard III, 1455, 2927

— Thomas de la: Vita Edwardi (II), 1092, 2928

— Walter, abbot, 6309

Morebath (Som.), 6838

Mores, Edward R.: Nomina et insignia, 4289

— Richard de (Richard Anglicus), 6448

Morey, Adrian: Bartholomew of Exeter, 5721, 6456, 6513; Gilbert Foliot, 6517; Letters of Foliot, 5761, 6515

Morgan, E. Victor: Feaveryear's Pound Sterling, 681

— F. W.: Domesday geography of Somerset, 3028; Domesday geography of Wiltshire, 3033

— Frank: Survey of Denbigh, 4943B

— Frederick C.: Hereford Library, 1046

— J. B.: Southampton, 4336

— James A.: Forsyth's Trial by jury, 1258

— Marjorie: Abbey of Bec-Hellouin, 5921; Alien priories, 5921; Canterbury jurisdiction, 5617, 6474; Excommunication of Grosseteste, 6581. *See* Chibnall, M. M.

— Penelope E.: Hereford Library, 1046

— Thomas: Roman mosaic, 2080

Morgannwg (journal), 1923

— Dafydd (pseudonym), 1925

Morins, Richard de: Annals of Dunstable, 2929

Morison, John Lyle: Pecock's Book of faith, 6628

Morkill, John W.: Roundhay, 4938

Morlaix, battle of, 1499(ii)

Morley, Lovel v. Morley, 3503A

Morley, Daniel of, 6961, 6967

— Henry: Bartholomew fair, 5527

Morosini, Antonio: Chronique, 2930

Morrall, John B.: Ockham, 5571, 6623

Morrin, James: Calendar, 1068

Morris, Colin: Bishop's commissary, 5754; Consistory court, 6475; William I and church courts, 6476

— George: Chartulary of Wombridge, 6302

— J.: Dark Age dates, 2045

— John: Liber Landavensis, 5880A

— John E.: Bannockburn, 4081; Beds. knight service, 4275, 4414; Mounted infantry, 4210; Welsh wars, 4059, 4310

— R. B.: Index of Devon books, 1604

— Richard: Azenbite of Inwit, 6689; Blickling homilies, 2267; Prick of conscience, 6698

— Rupert H.: Chester, 3860, 5047; Diocesan history, 6790

— William: Saga, 2446

— William A.: Constitutional history, 1217; County court, 2619, 3739; English government at work, 3836; Frankpledge, 1254; Lesser curia regis, 3303; Magnates and community, 3403; Modus tenendi parliamentum, 3353; Sheriff, 3740; Scutage, 4645

Morrison, Karl F.: Carolingian coins, 678

— Paul G.: Short-title catalogue, 7220

Morrissey, James F.: Statutes of Ireland, 3332

Morson, John: Cistercians and the bestiary, 5947

Mortain, count of, 3806

Mortimer, estates, 4658

Mortimer, Robert C.: Penance, 2262

Mortmain, 5352, 6807

Morton, Catherine: De Bello Hastingensi, 2749

— John, archbishop, 5635

— William, almoner, 6264

Morton Pynkeny (Northants.), 4831

Mosher, Joseph A.: Exemplum, 6706

Mosley, Oswald: Tutbury, 5254

Moss, William G.: Hastings, 5321

Mota, Cardinal de, 7061

Moule, Henry J.: Catalogue, 5068

— Thomas: Bibliotheca, 518

Movius, Hallam L., Jr.: ed. Old World bibliography, 1960; Irish iron age, 2004

Mowat, John L. G.: Maps, 4999

Mowbray, John (earl marshal), 4627

Moyen Âge, Le (journal), 164

Mozley, John H.: Nigel Wireker, 7042

Much, Rudolf: Tacitus, 2505

Much Hadham (Herts.), 4774

— Woolton, Hospitallers, 6205

Muchelney abbey (Som.), 6321–2

Muckle, J. T.: Holcot, 6590A

Muirchú: St. Patrick, 2324

Müller, C.: Ptolemy, 2025

— Ewald: Das Konzil von Vienne, 5570

— Wolfgang: Das Konzil von Konstanz, 5566

Mugnier, François: Les Savoyards, 5737

Muhlfeld, Helen E.: Survey of Wye, 4786

Muir, Ramsey: Municipal government, 5128

Muirchú Maccu-Mactheni: St. Patrick, 337; 337, 2324

Mulchrone, Kathleen: Catalogue, 1081; St. Patrick, 2324

Mullin, Francis A.: Cistercians, 5948

Mullinger, James B.: Bibliography, 21; University of Cambridge, 7102

Mullins, Edward L. C.: Guide, 28; Texts and calendars, 29

Multifernan Annales, 2755

Mum and the Sothsegger, 7049

Munby, Alan N. L.: Phillipps Library, 973

Muncey, Raymond W. L.: Parish registers, 1521

Munch, Peter A.: Chronicle of Man, 1951; Norse, 2592

Munden's chantry, Bridport, 4639

Mundy, John H.: Council of Constance, 5565

Munimenta Academica (Oxford), 7065
— Civitatis Oxonie, 5229
— Gildhallae Londoniensis, 5161

Munro, Dana C.: St. Columban, 2320
— Isabel S.: Bibliography of costume, 104
— J. H.: Anglo-Burgundian interdependence, 4271; Bruges and staple, 5386
— John James: Capgrave's Lives, 5958
— Kate M.: Bibliography of costume, 104

Muntatores, 4641

Muntz, Hope: De Bello Hastingensi, 2749

Murders, ritual, 3937

Murimuth, Adam: 387; Continuatio chronicarum, 2931

Murphy, Denis: Annals of Clonmacnoise, 2779
— Gerard: Irish lyrics, 2419

Murray, H. M. R.: Sussex charters, 4484
— Harold J. R.: Chess, 928A
— Sir James A. H.: Dictionary, 282
— Katharine M. E.: Cinque Ports, 5322; Register of David Rough, 5323; Shipping, 1485
— Robert H.: Guide to P.R.O. Dublin, 1074

Murrell, Richard J.: Records of Portsmouth, 5097

Musca, Thomas de, Chronicon, 6117

Music, 929–32; 1025, 1336

Muskett, Joseph J.: Lay subsidies, 3150

Musset, Lucien: Actes de Ducs de Normandie, 3824

Muster and review, 4311

Muster rolls, 4287–8

Myatt-Price, E. M.: Household accounts, 4630

Myers, Alec R.: Captivity of a royal witch, 3129; Duke of Bedford, 4273; English Historical Documents, 386; 17; Household of Edward IV, 3128; Household of Elizabeth Woodville, 3129; Household of Margaret of Anjou, 3129, 4195; Household ordinances, 3129; Jewels of Margaret of Anjou, 3129; Official progress, 3881; Outbreak of war (1471), 4271; Parliament and Estates General, 3366; Parliamentary debate, 3315A; Parliamentary petitions, 3404; Richard III, 4223; Richard Lyons's wealth, 1459, 5171

Myllyng, Thomas, bishop, 5730

Mylne, Robert S.: Churchwardens' accounts, 6838

Mynors, Sir Roger A. B.: Balliol MSS., 1030; Bede's Historia, 2148; Bookmarkers, 1450; Boston of Bury, 1452, 6930; Durham MSS., 1044; ed. Medieval texts, 1113; Gesta Stephani, 2880; Knighton's Chronicle, 2912; Panegyrici, 2025

Myres, John N. L.: Abingdon abbey, 2153; Adventus Saxonum, 1432; A.-S. pottery, 2551–2; A.-S. settlement, 2552; Butley priory, 1451; Dark Age Norfolk, 2552; Dark Age pottery, 1442; English settlement, 2036; Isurium Brigantum (Aldborough), 2052; Leeds' Archaeology, 2481; Oxford History, 1189, 2036; Pelagius, 2107; Radcot Bridge, 4130; Roman Britain, 1495; St. Catherine's Hill, 1995; Survival of villa, 2106

Mystery of seisin, 1246, 1482

Mystics, 875–7

Myvyrian Archaiology of Wales, 1116, 2382

Nairn, John A.: Handlist, 2016

Names, personal, 70–1; 5167
— place, 75–8; 2656

Namier, Sir Lewis: House of Commons, 511

Namn Och Bygd (journal), 624

Nance, Robert Morton: Dictionary, 329

Nangis, Guillaume de: St. Louis, 2883

Napier, Arthur S.: Crawford charters, 2202; Old English versions, 2256, 2273; Wulfstan, 2315

Narratives of Expulsion from Normandy, 3819

Nash, Treadway R.: Worcestershire, 1867

Nash-Williams, Victor E.: Caerwent, 2072; Christian Wales, 2675; Roman frontier, 2089; Welsh archaeology, 773

Nasmith, James: Itineraria, 2982; Tanner's Notitia, 987, 1150

National Library of Wales Journal, 134
— Register of Archives Bulletin, 108–9; 943, 5574
Natura brevium, 3499
Navarre, 4188
Navarro, José M. de. *See* De Navarro
Navigatio Sancti Brendani Abbatis, 2318
Navy: **625–7**; 2075, 3240, 3995, 4085, 4190, 4269, 4280, 4286, 4289–90, 4316; Roman, 1455
Naz, Raoul: Dictionnaire, **168**
Neale, John A.: Neales of Berkeley, 4437
— Sir John E.: Commons' privilege, 3365; Elizabethan Acts of Supremacy, 3365; Peter Wentworth, 3365
Neath abbey (Glam.), 1122
Neckham, Alexander, 6607–10, 7042
Needham, Geoffrey I.: Ælfric, 2328
Neilson, George: John Barbour, 2792; Motes, 823; Trial by combat, 1253
— Nellie: Agrarian society, 1364; Cartulary and terrier of priory of Bilsington, Kent, 6178; Custom in Kent, 2644; Customary rents, 4976; Domesday in Kent, 1529; Early pattern of common law, 3673; Forests, 3916; Manorial forms, 4698, 4976; Ramsey abbey, 6175; Terrier of Fleet, 4817; Year Book, 3652
Nelson, Janet L.: Alfred, 2593
— Lynn H.: Normans in Wales, 4000
Nennius: Historia Brittonum, 1084, 1089, 1100–1, 1114, 1458, 2026, 2123, 2144, 2162, 2167, 2396
Netherlands, 61, 2509, 2848, 3803, 4184, 4263. *See* Burgundy
Netter, Thomas: Fasciculi Zizaniorum, 6611–12, 6660
Neubauer, Adolf: Jews in Oxford, 3962
Neve, Peter de, 1756
Nevill, Ralph: Surrey feet of fines, 3613
Neville, George, archbishop, 6926
— Ralph de, bishop, 4617
Nevilles, the, 4205, 4216
Nevinson, John L.: Bayeux Tapestry, 4276; Civil costume, 1485
New Catholic Encyclopedia, 1271
— English Dictionary, 282
— Forest (Hants), 3040, 3896, 3899, 3911, 3927
— Survey of England, 1522
— Testament (Wyclif's), 6649
— towns, 1384, 5349
New, Chester: Alien priories, 5924
Newark, Henry of, archbishop, 5858
Newark-on-Trent (Notts.), 4841
Newbigging, Thomas: Forest of Rossendale, 3917
Newbold, William R.: Voynich MS., 6544

Newburgh, William of: **387**; Annals of Furness, 2757; Historia, 2932
Newbury (Berks.), 6090
— District Field Club, 1545
Newcastle under Lyme (Staffs.), deeds, 4475
Newcastle-upon-Tyne (Northumb.), 458, 1441, 1504, 3464, 5217–20, 5222, 5332, 5382, 5995
Newcombe, Luxmoore: Libraries, **124**
Newcome, Peter: Abbey of St. Alban, 6170
Newcourt, Richard: Repertorium, 5772
Newell, Ebenezer J.: Llandaff, 6790; Welsh church, 5879B
— William W.: William of Malmesbury on Glastonbury, 6316
Newhall, Richard A.: Chronique de Jean de Venette, 2967; Conquest of Normandy, 4262; Henry V and Normandy, 1439; Muster and review, 4311
Newington Longeville (Oxon.), 4464, 6094A
Newman, John H.: Saints, 1155
— W. L.: Correspondence . . . Decembrio, 6928
Newminster (Hants), 1475, 5814
— abbey (Northumb.), 6275
Newnham priory (Beds.), 6081
Newstead priory (Notts.), 6279, 6281
Newton (Cambs.), Compotus, 4715
Newton, Kenneth C.: Population statistics, 5481; Thaxted in fourteenth century, 4751; Writtel (Essex), 4747A
New York Public Library, Genealogy, 519
New York University, Law collection catalogue, 84, 1225
Nicholas III, pope, 6751
— IV, pope, Valuation, 1471, 3145, 6781, 6783
— di Romanis, legate, 1448
Nicholas, Frieda J.: Manorial accounts, 5619; Weights and measures, 5497
— Thomas: Glamorgan, 1926
Nicholl, Donald: Archbishop Thurstan, 5870
Nicholls, Henry G.: Iron making, 5500
— James F.: Bristol, past and present, 5088
Nichols, Francis M.: Britton, 2986; Criminal law, 3489; Knighthood, 4672
— John: Barnwell Abbey, 6100; Bibliotheca, 1505, 1714; Charters of Leicester, 5135; County of Leicester, 1714; Manners and expences, 6838; Wills, 4513
— John F.: The manor of Borley, 4744; Tenants of Bocking, 4748

Nichols, John Gough: Boke of Noblesse, 2982; Charters of Abbey of Burnham, 6093; Chronicle of Grey Friars, 2826; Chronicle of Rebellion, 2828; Collectanea, 115; Descriptive catalogue, 184; Grants from crown, 3768; Lacock abbey, 6372; Whitaker's Whalley, 6204

Nicholson, Edward W. B.: Musical MSS., 1025

— Frank C.: Edinburgh Library, 79

— Jennifer, Year Books MSS., **546**; 3657

— Lewis E.: Beowulf, 2350

— Ranald: Bruce's last campaign, 4077; David II, the historians, 4082; Edward III and Scots, 4082; Irish expedition, 4079; Treaties (1295), 4083

Nicolas, Sir Nicholas Harris: Account of the army, 4274; Battle of Agincourt, 4297, 7046; Chronicle of London, 2823; Expenses of wardrobe, 3111; Journal . . . Beckington, 3776; Notitia historica, 4508; Observations, 965; Privy purse expenses, 3128; Proceedings of council, 3294; Progress of Edward I, 4279; Public records, 958; Record Commission, 965; Refutation, 965; Royal navy, 4331; Scrope controversy, 3503A; Siege of Caerlaverock, 4295; Testamenta vetusta, 4518

Nicolle, Edmund T.: Channel Isles petitions, 3802; Rolls of assizes, 3643

Nicolson, Joseph: Westmorland, 1597, 1851

— William: English historical library, 7174; Irish historical library, 30

Nield, Frederick J.: Topography, 1506

Niermeyer, Jan F.: Lexicon, 310

Nigel, Richard, son of: Dialogus, 3005

Niger, Ralph: Chronica, 1114, 2933

Nijhoff, Martinus: Dutch bibliography, 61

Nine medieval thinkers, 6552

Nineham, Ruth: Anonymous of York, 6427

Ninian, St., 2323, 2690

Nitze, William A.: Renaissance, 6887

Njal's Saga, 2449

Nobility, **67–70**; 375, 2597, 2634–5, 2638, 2643, 3311, 4644, 4648, 4650, 4668–9, 4676, 4678

Noble, William M.: Archdeaconry of Huntingdon, 5755; Hunts. wills, 4529

Nolan, Patrick: Monetary history, 693

Nolloth, Henry E.: Lay folks' catechism, 6691

Nomina villarum, **628–9**; 3182, 4343, 4382, 4389, 4396

Nonae rolls, 3145, 3201, 4986

Noonan, John T. S.: Usury, 6438

Noorthouck, John: London, 1742

Norbury, Roger de, bishop, 5667

Nordal, Sigurður: Egil saga, 2445; Icelandic sagas, 2457; Orkney Saga, 2451

Nordman, Carl A.: A.-S. coins, 694

Norfolk: Aliens, 5440; Bibliography, 1749–51; Charters, 4454–5, 6364; Church, 1529, 5774–88; County history, 1529, 2552, 3045, 4742; County journals and societies, 1752–4, 1818; County records, 1504, 1755–8; Domesday, 1529; Feet of fines, 3582, 3585; Feudal tenures, 4373; Freemen, 4742; Inquests, 4372; Justices of peace, 3584; Manors and villages, 4373, 4818–26, 4954; Parliament, 3438; Pleas, 3581, 3583–4, 3586–7; Religious houses, 6253–61; Subsidy rolls, 3175; Taxation, 3173–4; Urban history, 5205–14; Wills, 4547–9

Norfolk, John, duke of, 4605, 4609

— earl of (Roger Bigod), 4519

Norgate, Kate: Angevin Kings, 2921, 4027; Battle of Hastings, 3990; Bull Laudabiliter, 5556; Carucage, 3261; Condemnation of John, 4034; Itinerarium peregrinorum, 2906; John Lackland, 4028; Minority of Henry III, 4061; Richard Lion-Hearted, 4029; William of Newburgh, 2932

Norham castle (Northumb.), 6276

Norman Anonymous, 6427

— Church, 2853, 4699, 4777, 5916, 5921, 6129, 6212, 6252, 6785

— Conquest, **589–93**; 1430, 1450, 1468, 2582, 3990, 4005, 6259, 6802

— rolls, **568**; 3808

Norman, Edward R.: Irish society, 756

— Frederick: ed. Waldere, 2328

Normandy, chroniclers, 1096, 2776, 2794, 2798, 2840, 2846, 2848, 2877, 2897, 2908, 2937, 2943, 2949, 2962, 2976, 2982, 3819

— history, 1439, 1458, 1498, 2582, 3990, 4001, 4035, 4256, 4262, 4654, 5256, 5391. *See* Hundred Years War *and* Norman Conquest

— records, 1097, 2169, 3802A, 3803A, 3808, 3811, 3813A, 3819, 3824, 3829, 4278

Normannerne, 2598

Norris deeds, 4443

Norris, Herbert: Costume, 923

— Herbert E.: Catalogue, 1681

Norse, battles, 2583, 2588

— coins, 704

— literature, **351–7**; 1429, 2326

— personal names, 2602

— place names, 624, 633, 636

— settlements, 2566, 2568, 2570, 2572–4, 2600, 2605

Norsemen. *See* Danes

North Country Wills, 4516

— problem of, 1478

— Jeffrey J.: Coinage, 695

— Thomas: Churchwardens' accounts, 6838

Northampton, 5215; Treaty of, 4087

Northamptonshire: Bibliography, 1759–60; Charters, 451, 4456–7; Church, 1529, 5877; County history, 1529, 1765–6, 3502, 4087; County journals and societies, 1761–4; County records, 2935; Domesday, 1529, 3061, 3067; Jews, 3938; Justices of peace, 3590; Manors and villages, 4827–36; Pleas, 3588–90; Religious houses, 6262–71; Schools, 7127; Subsidy rolls, 3177; Taxation, 3065, 3938; Topography, 1529; Urban history, 5215–16

North Munster Studies, 679

Northern annals, the lost, 2157, 2168

— Convocation, 6817

— History (journal), 135

— Ireland-Belfast, Record office, **132**; 1077

— registers, 5686, 5852

Northgate, Canterbury, hospital, 6187

Northumberland: Antiquities, 823; Bibliography, 1767–8; Charters, 1775, 4458–60, 4501, 4838; Church, 1437; County history, 1772–6, 4662, 5455; County journals and societies, 1769–71; County records, 1775, 2154, 2168, 6272–7; Deeds, 4433, 4458; Domesday, 3061; Feet of fines, 3592–3; Feudal tenures, 4374; Inquests, 4374; Manors and villages, 4837–40; Parliament, 3464; Pedigrees, families, 4374; Pleas, 3591, 3594–6; Pipe rolls, 1775, 3092–3; Religious houses, 6272–7; Subsidy rolls, 3176–7; Taxation, 3061; Urban history, 5217–22; Wills, 4516, 4524

Northumbria, 196, 1114, 1433, 1482, 1776, 2123, 2145, 2154, 2156–7, 2168, 2295, 2526–7, 2578, 2591, 2633, 2701, 2708, 4374, 4975, 7225

Northumbrian chronicle, 1114

Northumbrian tenures, 1482, 4975

Norton (Yorks.), Roman, 2069

— George: Commentaries, 1743

— Nicholas of: Annales de Wigornia, 2769

Norton-Smith, John: Lydgate's poems, 7033

Norway, history, 60, 1115, 2569, 2592, 3835. *See* Norse

Norwich: Annals, 1114, 2854; city, 1504, 3961, 5206–12; Diocese of, 1050, 4549, 5774–88, 6260, 6253–61, 6335–49, 6781, 6790, 6860; Herbert of, 5781; Julian of,

6665, 6673, 6688; St. William of, 3937; Valuation of, 6781

Noseley (Leics.), 4798

Nostell priory (Yorks.), 6411

Notaries public, 421, 2770, 3838

Notes and Queries (journal), 136

Notitia dignitatum, 2030, 2044

— monastica, 987

Nott, James: Great Malvern, 6384

Nottarp, Hermann, 1253

Nottingham, city, 1386, 3465, 5223–4

— Medieval Studies (journal), 137

Nottingham, Robert of (justice), 3689

Nottinghamshire: Bibliography, 1777–81; Church, 1529, 5877; County history, 1784–5; County journals and societies, 137, 1782–3; County records, 4842–3; Domesday, 1529; Feudal tenures, 4350; Inquests, 4375; Manors and villages, 4841–3; Parliament, 3465; Pipe rolls, 3087; Religious houses, 6278–85; Rental, 4842; Urban history, 1386, 5223–4; Wills, 4516

Nova legenda Angliae, 1158, 2287

Novae narrationes, 2998

Novel disseisin, 1461

Nowé, Henri: Bibliographie, 61

Nowell Codex of Beowulf, 441

— Lawrence: A.-S. Chron., 2142G; Vocabularium, 283

Nowicki, M.: Bibliography, 246

Noyes, Thomas H.: Subsidy, 3193

Numismatic Chronicle and Journal, 648

— Circular (journal), 649

— Literature (journal), 650

Numismatics, 78–84; 434, 1084, 1442, 1454, 1485, 1496, 2085, 2111, 2528, 5502, 5520, 7225

Nunneries, 1301, 2837, 6164, 6255, 6290, 6325, 6394. *See* Monasticism

Nutley Abbey (Bucks.), 6095

Oakeshott, Ronald Ewart: Weapons, 924

— Walter F.: Winchester Bible, 899

Oakley, A. M.: Map of Kent, 4784

— F.: Battle of Lincoln, 4045

— Kenneth P.: ed. V. G. Childe's essays, 1974

— R. H.: Atlow court rolls, 4728

— Thomas P.: Articles, 2261; Penitentials, 2263

Oath ex officio, 1444

Obedientiaries, 5699, 5779, 5812, 5825, 6084–5, 6258, 6360

Oberman, Heiko A.: Archbishop Thomas Bradwardine, 6557, 6560

Obituaries of Durham, 5687–8

Obligationes (papal), 6779

Obolensky, Dimitri: Christian centuries, 1280
Oboli de Musc (coins), 710
O Breen, Harmen T.: Index, 2506
Obreen, Henri: Bibliographie, 61
O'Brien, George: Economic teaching, 5458
— James: Anticipations of inertia, 6959
— Michael A.: Book of Leinster, 2394, 2777; Corpus genealogiarum, 567
Observant friars, 6026
Obsessione Dunelmi, (De), 2157
O'Buachalla, Liam: Lebor Gabálá Érenn, 2404
O'Carroll, James: Columban, 2320
O'Cassidy, Rory, Annals of Ulster, 2786
Occupations, 581
Ockham, William of, 1133, 1473, 5571, 6613–27, 6864
O'Clery, Michael: Annals of Four Masters, 2784; Book of Conquest, 2403
O'Connor, Frank: Irish poetry, 2420
O'Conor, Charles: Annals of Boyle, 2778; Annals of Innisfallen, 2780; Annals of Ulster, 2786; Scriptores, 1117, 2784; Stowe Library, 1082
Ó'Cróinín, Donncha: Irish language, 349
Ó Cuív, Brian: Cellachan of Cashel, 2150
Oculis sacerdotis, 6436
O'Curry, Eugene: Irish laws, 2240; Irish manners, 2421; Manuscript materials, 30
O'Dell, Andrew C.: St. Ninian's Isle treasure, 2482
Odlozilik, Otakar: Wycliffe's influence, 6656
Odo, bishop of Bayeux, 2157, 4276, 5675
O'Doherty, John F.: Anglo-Norman invasion, 5556; Song of Dermot, 2954
O'Donnell, J. Reginald: Giles of Rome, 1459; Nine medieval thinkers, 6552, 6891
O'Donovan, John: Annals of Four Masters, 2784; Annals of Ireland, 2146, 2782; Battle of Dun (Down), 2920; Book of Rights, 2245; Circuit of Ireland, 2400; Cormac, 2401; Irish laws, 2240
Offa, of Mercia, 1454, 1496, 2477
Official-principal, 5796
Offler, Hilary S.: De iniusta vexatione, 2157, 5675; Durham archdeacons, 5698; Durham charters, 5679; England and Germany, 4171; Flambard, 5694; Historians of Durham, 2157; Northumb. charter, 4460; Ockham's Opera, 6617
Offlow (Staffs.), 3185, 4386
O'Fiach, Tomás: editor, 2324
O'Flanagan, James R.: Chancellors, 539
Ogam (journal), 322; inscriptions, 1429
Ogden, Charles K.: editor, 1371

Ogg, David: Fleta, 2987
Ogilvie, Robert M.: Tacitus Agricola, 2025
Ogilvy, Jack D. A.: Books known, 2359
Ogle, Arthur: Canon law, 6437
— Marbury B.: Walter Map's Courtiers' Trifles, 6599
— Octavius: Oxford market, 5231, 5528; Royal letters, 5234
O'Grady, Standish H.: Catalogue of Irish MSS., 997; Irish tales, 2391
O'Hanlon, John: Lives of Saints, 1167
O'Hart, John: Irish pedigrees, 520
O hInnse, Séamus: Irish annals, 2925
Okes (Salop), manor, 4859
Olaf, St., 2438, 2447
Olaf Tryggvason, 2438, 2447, 2450
Old Wardon, abbey (Beds.), 6083
—— Honour of (Beds.), 4704
Old World bibliography, 1960
Oldcastle, Sir John, 4225, 6863, 6991
Olde Teners, 2999
Oldfather, Charles H.: Diodorus, 2025
Oleron, Coutumes d', 4286
Oleson, Tryggvi J.: Edward Confessor and William, 2578; Witan, 2620
Oliger, Livario: Expositio, 6588; Speculum, 6681
Oliver, Sir Arthur M.: Feet of fines of Northumb. and Durham, 3592; Newcastle deeds, 5218
— George: Bishops of Exeter, 5722; History of Exeter, 5059; Monasticon, 1147, 6109
Olivero, Federico: St. Guthlac, 2310
Ollard, Sidney L.: Dictionary of Church history, 1272; St. George's Chapel, Windsor, 552, 6068
O'Lochlainn, Gearóid: Battle of Clontarf, 2174
O'Looney, Brian: Speckled Book, 2397
O'Loughlin, John L. N.: Sutton Hoo, 2487
Olrik, Axel: Viking civilization, 2458
— Jørgen: Gesta Danorum, 2426
Olsen, Magnus: Runes, 361
Olsen, Clair C.: Chaucer life records, 7007; Chaucer's world, 7012
— Emil: Editor of Sagas, 2436, 2448
Ó'Maille, Tomás: Annals of Ulster, 2786
Oman, Charles Chicele: Church plate, 871
— Sir Charles W. C.: Anglia Sacra (map), 605; Anonimalle chronicle (trans.), 2787; Art of War, 4312; Castles, 835; Coinage, 696; England (1377–1485), 1183; England before Conquest, 1188, 2500; Glos. boundaries, 1448; Political outlook, 2704; Revolt (1381), 4151
O'Meara, John J.: Giraldus Cambrensis, 2881

Omont, Henri: Poèmes d'Étienne de Rouen, 2949
O'Neil, Bryan H. St.John: Castles, 839; Castles and cannon, 836, 4313; Essays to, 809; Roman coins, 663
O'Neill, Brian, Irish king, 2920
Onions, Charles T.: Dictionaries, 282, 284
Onoma (journal), 75
Onomasticon Anglo-Saxonicum, 589
Onslow, Phipps: Worcester (diocesan history), 6790
Open fields, 1373, 1468, 1501, 4945, 4955, 4989, 4999, 5007
Oppenheim, Michael: Administration of navy, 4332; Naval accounts, 4290
Opus Chronicorum, 1114, 2936
O'Rahilly, Aloysius: ed. Studies, 239
— Cecile: Táin Bó Cualnge, 2394
— Thomas F.: Catalogue MSS., 1081; Early Irish history, 2129, 2422; Goidels, 2129; St. Patrick, 2324
O'Raifeartaigh, T.: St. Patrick, 2324
Orbis Britanniae (Anglo-Saxon), 1475
Ord, Craven: Crown jewels, 3122
Ordeals, 1253, 2616
Ordericus Vitalis, **386–7**; 1111, 2937
Orders in council, 5234
Ordinale Exon., 5716
Ordinances (of 1311), 3343, 3849, 4141
Ordinations, 1441, 5793
Ordish, Olive: Agrarian history, 5017
Ordnance Survey, **89**; 448, 604, 1965, 2022, 5529
O'Reilly, Edward: Irish writers, 30
Oresme, Nicolas: De moneta, 688, 1113
Organ, 7186
Originalia rolls, **491–3**
Origines Celticae, 2584
— Islandicae, 2443
O'Ríordáin, Séan Pádraig: Antiquities, 2005
Orkneyinga Saga, 2451
Orleans, Seige of, 4277
— Charles d', 4247
— Theodulf of: Capitula, 2256, 2259
Orleton, Adam de, bishop, 5730
Orme, Margaret: Cricklade's Vita, 6488
Ormerod, George: Cheshire Domesday roll, 3857; Chester palatinate, 3861; County of Chester, 1574
— James: Derby catalogue, 1599
Ormsby, Gilbertine house (Lincs.), 5957, 6216
Ormsby-cum-Ketsby (Lincs.), 4814
Ornament, early English, 2473, 2479, 2481
Ornsby, George: York, 6790
Orosius, 441, 2025, 2348, 7225
Orpen, Goddard H.: Ireland, map of, 605;
Ireland under Normans, 4030; Laudabiliter, 5556; Song of Dermot, 2954
Orridge, Benjamin B.: Jack Cade's rebellion, 4214
Orston (Notts.), 4842
Orwin, Charles S.: Farming, 5006; Open fields, 1373, 5007
— Christabel S.: Open fields, 1373, 5007
Osbern, monk of Canterbury: Elphege, 2306; St. Dunstan, 2303
Osbert of Clare, prior, 2171, 6239
Osbert, dean of Lewes, 6364
Osborn, William fitz, 4687
Oschinsky, Dorothea: Treatises, 4632; Walter of Henley, 4631
Oskamp, H. P. A.: Dun Cow, 2393
Osmund, St., 1343, 5798, 5805
Osney abbey (Oxon.), 6292–4; Annals 1114, 2764; Cartulary, 4479
Ospringe (Kent), Roman, 2070
O'Sullivan, Mary Donovan: Italian bankers, 1438
— Jeremiah F.: Cistercian settlement, 5949
— W.: Book of Leinster, 2394
— William: Anglo-Irish coinage, 679, 701
Oswald, St., archbishop of York, 1475, 2151, 2289, 2311, 5878
Oswald, Arthur: Architects, 797
— Felix: Roman pottery, 2082
Oswald-Hicks, T. W.: Wills, 4555
Oswestry (Salop), 4864, 5239
Otho de Grandison, 4054
Otté, Elise C.: Pauli's Pictures, 4165
Otter, William B.: Churchwardens' accounts, 6838
Otterbourne, Thomas: Chronica, 1103, 2938
Ottery St. Mary (Devon), 6125
Otto, cardinal and legate, 6436, 6748
Ottoboni, cardinal and legate, 6436, 6743
Otway-Ruthven, Annette Jocelyn: Constitutional position of Wales, 3987; Guide to Irish history, 35; Irish bibliography, 23; Irish chancery, 567; 3366; King's secretary, 3138, 3845; Lordships, 3640; Medieval Ireland, 1203; Norman settlement in Ireland, 4031
Oundle (Northants.), 4834
Oursel, Raymond: Jeanne d'Arc, 4246
Ousthorp, John, abbot, 6418
Outlawry, 1261, 1455, 5455, 6464
Overall, William H.: Churchwardens' accounts, 6838
Overseas trade, 5084
Overton (Cheshire), **574**
Owen, Aneurin: Gwentian chronicle, 2805; Laws of Wales, 2222

Owen, David E.: Kirkstall abbey, 6405
— Dorothy M.: Ely chancery, 7224; Ely records, 5704; Ely synods, 6811; Lambeth MSS., 1009, 5600, 5621; Lincolnshire church, 6798; Records of the church, **109**; 5574; Revesby charters, 1453; Vetus repertorium, 5744
— Edward: Catalogue, 1003
— de Henllys, George: Penbrokeshire, 3784A
— Glendower. *See* Glendower
— Henry: Pembrokeshire, 3784A; Records of Pembrokeshire, 1938
— Leonard V. D.: England and Burgundy, 4263; England and Low Countries, 4263; Notts. account books, 5223; Notts. records, 4842; Notts. representatives, 3465
— Nicholas: Caernarvonshire, 1903
— William: Cambrian biography, 540
Owens College Essays, 1472
Owst, Gerard R.: Literature and pulpit, 6707; Preaching, 6707
Owston abbey (Leics.), 4800, 4962
Oxenedes, John de: Chronica, 2939
Oxenstierna, Eric C. G.: The Norsemen, 2459
Oxford: Ashmolean Museum, 704
— Bodleian Library, 75, 440, 972, 975, 984, 1017-27, 2202, 2399
— City of: Bibliography, 1787; History, 1442, 4376, 5228, 5236-8, 7128-9, 7134; Records, 450, 3178, 3598, 3600, 5230-5
— Dominicans, 6908, 7061
— Franciscans, 6024-5, 6908, 6910
— Hospital of St. John, 6296
— Jews, 3962, 3965, 3970
— Lollard, 6873
— market, 5231, 5528
— mural mansion, 1455
— St. Frideswide, 6295
— St. Peter in the East, 6838
— University: Archives, 1018, 7064; Bibliography, **920**; 1787; Biographies, 533, 7066, 7119; Curriculum, etc., 6567, 6660, 6900, 6908, 6910, 6920, 6929, 6935, 6950, 6957, 6971, 7127; History, 1529, 6571, 7114-34; 7223; Petitions for benefices, 6767; Records, 945, 963-5, 974, 984, 1018-29, 1169, 5233, 6571, 6926, 7061-82
— [Colleges]:
— All Souls, 1455, 7072, 7121, 7169, 7179
— Balliol, 1030, 4465, 7073, 7117
— Canterbury, 7074
— Christ Church, 1028, 6286
— Durham, 7061

— Exeter, 7114
— Magdalen, 6165, 7075-6, 7132A
— Merton, 1029, 4463, 7077-80, 7115, 7121, 7164-5
— New, 192, 4844, 6144, 7132
— Oriel, 4848, 7068, 7081-2, 7126
— Queen's, 7124
— St. Edmund's Hall, 7120
— University, 7131
Oxford Companion to Music, 7208
— Dictionary of English Etymology, 284
— Dictionary of Place-names, 632
— History of England, 31, 1189
— History of English Art, 782
— History of English Literature, 1402
Oxford, Provisions of, 2763, 4063, 4068
Oxford, John of, Conveyancer: 3000; Formulary, 4698; De placitis, 2995
Oxfordshire: Bibliography, 1786-7; Charters, 4461-5; County history, 1529, 4999; County journals and societies, 1788-93; Deeds, 4407; Domesday, 1529; Feet of fines, 3597; Feudal tenures, 4345, 4376; Inquests, 4376; Justices of peace, 3598-9; Manors and villages, 4844-57; Parliament, 3459; Pleas, 3598; Religious houses, 6286-98; Sheriffs, coroners, etc., 3598, 3600; Subsidy rolls, 3178; Taxation, 3178; Urban history, 1386, 3178, 3598, 5225-38; Wills, 4550
Oxoniensia (journal), 1790

Pächt, Otto: Illuminated MSS., 878; St. Albans Psalter, 902
Packard, Sidney R.: Norman communes, 1439, 5356; Norman exchequer, 3103
Padua, English at, 6919
Paetow, Louis J.: Guide, 59
Pafford, John H. P.: Robert of Gloucester's Chronicle, 1441; Wilts. deeds, 4491
Pagan, H.: Numismatic survey, 646
Paganism, **378-9**; 2213, 2468-9
Page, Frances M.: Bidentes Hoylandie, 5008; Crowland abbey, 6213; Customary poor law, 4720; Wellingborough accounts, 4835
— John: Siege of Rouen (1418), 2940, 7046
— Raymond I.: A.-S. episcopal lists, **314**; 2722; A.-S. life, 2639; Bewcastle Cross, 353; Scandinavian language, 7225
— Thomas W.: End of villeinage, 1501, 4959
— William: Chartulary of Brinkburn, 6273; Churches of Domesday, 3059; English village, 1374, 2641; London, 1744; London feet of fines, 3578, 5153;

Northumb. assize rolls, 3596; Northumbrian palatinates, 1776; Round's Studies, 569, 1492, 4589; V.C.H., 1197, 1529

Page-Turner, Frederick A.: Beds. deeds, 4411; Beds. wills, 4520

Pagel, Karl: Die Hanse, 5433

Pagham (Sussex), 4901, 5271

Pagula, William of: Speculum, 2955; Summa, 6436

Painswick (Glos.), 4761

Painter, Kenneth S.: Roman villa, 2064

— Sidney: Castles, 823; Castle-guard, 4666; Charter of Chertsey, 6350; Isabella of Angoulême, 4038; Papers of, 1486; Peter of Dreux, 4104; Reign of John, 4032; Studies on barony, 4673; Third Crusade, 4029; William Marshal, 2896, 4033

Painting, 856–60

Palaeography, 47–50; 423, 445, 941, 977, 1440, 1485, 4438, 5872

Palais, Hyman: Hanseatic League, 5428

Palatinates, 112–13 and 574–80; 1574, 1776, 4687

Palgrave, Sir Francis: Antient kalendars, 959, 3256; Documents on Scotland, 3790; English commonwealth, 2187, 2501, 3490; Equitable jurisdiction, 3726; History of Normandy, 4001; Ingulf, 2163; King's council, 3304; Lament for de Montfort, 7043; Nomina villarum, 4343; Records, 965; Remarks, 965; Rotuli curiae regis, 3501; Writs, 3316, 4292

— Francis T.: Oxford movement of fifteenth century, 6920

Palladius, 336

Palmer, Charles F. R.: Articles on friars, 5998; Fasti, 5998; King's confessors, 3275A; Monumenta, 5980

— John J. N.: Creton, 2856; Chronique de la Traïson, 2841; Foreign policy, 7223; Great schism, 6738; Last summons, 4306; Negotiations (1390–6), 4187; Parliament (1385), 3419A; Richard II's marriage, 4187

— Robert B.: trans. Strecker, 314

— Roger L.: Monasteries, 5898

— Thomas F.: Household roll, 4606; Summons of Green Wax, 3221

— William: Origines liturgicae, 1342

— William M.: Cambridge documents, 5037; Cambs. assizes, 3534; Cambs. eyres, 3534; Cambs. fines, 3534; Cambs. subsidies, 3151; Insurrection, 4152; Village gilds, 4721, 5368; Villages, 4722; Visitation records, 5712

Pálsson, Hermann: Njal Saga, 2449

Panchenault, René: Chronique de la Pucelle, 2840

Panegyrici latini, 2025

Pantin, William A.: Black monks documents, 5908; Canterbury College, 7074; Durham MSS., 1044; English church, 6734, 6799, 6921; Formularies, 7063; Grosseteste, 6736; John Mason, 1459, 6183; John of Wales, 1438; Monastic letter-books, 427, 1455; Monk-solitary, 6676; Oxford halls, 1428; Oxford life, 7123; Powicke's essays (editor), 1450; Survey of Oxford, 5238, 7129; Town houses, 1435; Treatises on monasticism, 1437; Uthred of Boldon, 1450

Paor, Liam de: Ireland, 761

— Maire de: Ireland, 761

Papacy, 880–3; 1281, 1466, 1471, 1487, 5902, 6586

— appeals to, 6429, 6449–50, 6455–7, 6480–1

— archives of, 751–2

— arbitration by, 4158, 4164

— Avignonese, 751; 6714, 6719–20, 6734, 6756

— chancery of, 420, 3837, 5542

— decretals, 1482, 5556, 6024, 6437, 6762, 6799. See Canon Law

— Englishmen at, 1458, 1474, 1487, 6457, 6440, 6750–8, 6919

— legates of, 1448, 6436, 6742–9

— Letters of, 751–4 and 880–8; 420, 955, 1009, 1132, 1137, 1458, 1487, 2158, 2164, 5550, 5585, 5685, 5744, 5793, 5799, 5805, 5966, 5969, 5981, 6229, 6252, 6309, 6342, 6405, 6415

— monasteries and, 5902, 5955

— petitions to, 1471, 5548–9

— proctors to, 1474, 6457, 6750–8

— provisions by, 1438, 1473, 6759–73

— schism (1159), 6809; The great, 5572, 6738, 6740

— taxation by, 886–8; 1134, 1471

Paper and parchment, 948

Paper constitution (1244), 1467, 4046

Papworth, John W.: Dictionary, 497

Parain, Charles: Agricultural techniques, 5009

Paramidan, M.: St. Columban, 2320

Pardon, King's, 3698, 4427

Paré, Gérard M.: La renaissance, 1394, 6892

Pargellis, Stanley: ed., Complaint and reform, 5338

Paris, masters at, 1487, 5443, 6878

— Psalter, 441, 2327

— school of, 6642

— treaty (1259), 3831, 4098

Paris, Gaston: Ambroise, 2748, 2906; Guillaume le Maréchal, 2896; Third Crusade, 2906
— Matthew: Abbreviatio, 2745; Additamenta, 2941; Chronica majora, 1089, 1114, 1118, 2941; Gesta abbatum, 6168; Historia minor, 2941; Life of Langton, 1108; Shields, 496; Vita S. Edmundi, 5626; Commentaries on 1459, 2941, 2979, 4046
— Paulin: Chronique, 2883
— Philip M. de: Periodicals, 89
Parish life and records, **893–6**; 789, 1505, 1521, 1527, 1632, 2700, 3201, 4740, 5733, 5872, 6696, 6861
Parish, William D.: Domesday of Sussex, 3031
Park, halimote of, 1480
— Godfrey R.: Representation, 3475
Parker Chronicle (A.-S. Chronicle), 2142A, 2328
Parker, Francis H. M.: Feet of fines, 3541; Inglewood forest, 3919; New forest and William II, 3918; Pipe rolls, 3086
— Frederick P.: Chartulary of St. Thomas, 6330; Chartulary of Trentham, 6333; Chetwynd's Pirehill hundred, 4875
— George H.: Comfortable works, 6673
— James: Barfield's Thatcham, 4707; Church in Domesday, 3047
— James H.: Domestic architecture, 821; Glossary, 493
— John (of Clitheroe): Assize rolls, 3563; Deeds, 4446; Feet of fines, 3629; Plea rolls, 3566, 3882
— John (of Wycombe): Wycombe, 5036
— John W. R.: Lay subsidy rolls, 3203
— Matthew: 263A; Asser, 1118; Flores Historiarum, 2871; Walsingham, 2976
— Thomas M.: The interdict, 6729
— Thomas W.: Knights Templars, 6063
— William: Long Melford, 4889
Parkes, James: Jews, 3963
— Malcolm B.: Cursive hands, 395
Parkin, Charles: Norfolk, 1756
Parkinson, Anthony: Collectanea, 6032
Parks, George B.: Chaucer's journey to Italy, 7007; English traveler, 6757, 6922; Translations, 52
Parlement de Paris, 3825, 4242
Parliament: Bibliography, 1489, 3356–64, 7222; Clergy in, **524**. *See* Convocation; Committee on local records, 1525; History of, **510–18**; 1221, 1446, 1459, 1464, 1493, 1499, 3301, 4165; Meeting-place, 2868, 3430–1; Modus tenendi, **509–10**; Personnel, **520–4**; 1451,

1458–9, 1461–2, 1478, 1529, 3307; Petitions, 3399, 3404–5, 3414, 4943A, 5232; Records, **503–8**; 4292, 7051; Specific parliaments, **518–19**; 1464, 3312, 3313A, 3342–3, 3401. For Irish parliaments, *see* Ireland
Parol contracts, 1246
Parry, Albert W.: Education, 1395, 7143
— Charles H.: Parliaments and councils, 3376
— John D.: Bedfordshire, 1539
— John J.: Brut, 2166
— Thomas: Gruffydd ap Cynan, 2902; Welsh Literature, 339, 2423
Parry-Williams, Thomas: English loan-words, 340
Parsons, Edward J. S.: Gough map, 602
Parthey, Gustav: Antonine iter, 2029; Ravenna cosmography, 2031
Partner, Peter D.: Camera papae, 6780
Partnership, commercial, 5392
Pascasius Valentini, 3137
Pasquet, Desiré: Chambre des communes, 3377
Passingham, William J.: Coronation, 1356; London markets, 5530
Passmore, John B.: The plough, 5010
Past and Present (journal), 138
Pastimes, 928A, 3885, 3898
Paston letters, 4610
Paston, Margaret, 6977
Pastor, Ludwig: History of popes, 6720
Pastoral Care (Gregory's), 441
Patchett, Ernest W.: Winchester, 1275
Patent letters, **358** and **563**; 1139, 1233, 1252, 3667, 3768, 3778, 3871–2, 4294, 4749, 5080, 5215, 5234, 5252, 5293, 5691
Patetta, Federico: Ordeals, 1253
Paton, Lucy A.: trans., 2166, 2914
Patourel, John Le: Account of Hugh of St. Philibert, 3103; Penenden Heath, 1450; Richardson and Sayles, 1218
Patrick, St., 1160, 2190, 2324, 2662A, 2677, 2684
Patronage, **885–6**, 5698–9, 5905, 7223. *See* Provisions
Patryngton, Stephen: Fasciculi Zizaniorum, 6612; Register, 5880G
Patterson, Edwin F.: Northumberland, 1768
— Robert B.: Charters of earls, 4438; Malmesbury's Gloucester, 2921
Patteshull, Martin (justice), 3525, 3689
Patton, Edward: Index to Holdsworth's History, 1235
Patzelf, Erna: trans. of Dopsch, 1367
Paul, Sir James B.: Scottish families, 525; Scots peerage, 568

Pauli, Reinhold: Bilder, 4165; Gervasius von Tilbury, 2961; Geschichte von England, 1184; M.G.H., 1114; Malmesbury's Gesta, 1143; Radulphus Niger, 2933; Scriptores, 2740
Paulinus, mission of, 7225
Paulus, Nikolaus: Geschichte des Ablasses, 1286
Pavements, mosaic, 2050, 2069, 2080
Paviors' company, 5197
Paycocks of Coggeshall, 5419, 5464
Payne, Francis G.: The plough, 1980, 2640, 5010
— Joseph F.: Medicine, 2376
— Richenda C.: Agrarian conditions, 4925
Paynel fee, Charters, 4499
Paynell, Ralph, 6423
Peace of God, 1483
Peacock, Edward: Myrc's Parish priests, 6696
Peak forest (Derby.), 1601, 3912
Peake, Harold J. E.: Berkshire, 762; English village, 1374; Village, 2641
— Margaret I.: London loans, 3253, 5503
Pearce, Ernest H.: Monks of Westminster, 6243; Register of Thomas de Cobham, 5840; Walter de Wenlock, 6232; William of Colchester, 6244; Worcester institutions, 5847
Pearman, Augustus J.: Rochester, 6790
— Morgan T.: Bensington, 4856
Pearsall, Derek: John Lydgate, 7034
Pearson, Frank S.: Bibliography, 1862
Peasantry, 691–6; 1468, 2652, 3021, 6115, 6266
Peasants' revolt (1381), 606–8; 1468, 3204, 3366, 4965, 4971, 6168, 7017, 7046, 7223
Peate, Iorwerth C.: Celts in Britain, 2119; Long house, 1435; Welsh house, 816
Peberdy, Philip: Southampton, 4336
Pecham, John, archbishop, 1450, 1458, 5609–10, 5616, 5636–7, 6811, 6910, 6954
Pecia, la, 7085
Peck, Francis: Desiderata Curiosa, 6117
Peckham, Walter D.: Acts of Chichester Cathedral, 5651; Chartulary of Chichester, 5652; Custumals of Sussex manors, 4907
Pecock, Reginald, bishop, 1474, 5660, 6628–30
Peculiars, jurisdictional, 5680
Peddie, Robert A.: Subject index, 70
Pedersen, Holger: Grammatik, 323
Pedes finium. See Feet of fines
Pedrick, Gale: Seals, 465
Peek, Heather E.: Cambridge archives, 7103
Peeler, E. F.: trans. Pastor's popes, 6720

Peerages, 67–70; 3382, 4569, 4577–8
Peers, introduction of, 3388
— trial of, 3667
Peers' reports, 3382
Pegge, Samuel: Beauchief abbey, 6114; Sanctuary, 1260; Textus Roffensis, 5794; Trikingham's Annales, 6177
Pegis, Anton C.: Ockham, 6623
Pegolotti, Francesco Balducci: La practica della mercatura, 5417, 5498
Pegues, Franklin J.: Clericus, 3690; Kent eyre, 3558; Law reporting, 3656
Peile, James H. F.: St. Wulfstan, 2316, 5843
— John: Biographical register, 7104
— Michael: Deeds of Shrewsbury drapers, 5243
Pelagians, 2107, 6559
Pelan, Margaret: Wace, 2974
Pelham, Reginald A.: Aulnage accounts, 3232; Eastern ports, 1465; Gough map, 596; Provisioning parliament, 3432; Wool trade, 5418
Pelican History of Art, 783
— History of England, 1190
Pell, O. C.: Unit of assessment, 3047
Pellens, Karl: Texte des Normanischen Anonymus, 6427
Pelster, Franz: Oxford theology, 6028, 6908
Pelzer, Auguste: Abbreviations, 402; Articles d'Occam, 6625; Incipits, 431
Pembridge, Christopher: Annales Hiberniae, 2759
Pembroke, earl of, 459, 2954, 4127. See Marshal, William
Pembrokeshire, 1938–40, 3784A
Penance, 6469. See Penitentials
Pendrill, Charles: London, 5172, 6853
Penenden Heath, trial of, 1450
Penitentials, 314–16; 1166, 2320, 5721
Pennington D.: Parliament and taxation, 3366
Penrith, honour of, 4671
Pensions, 5835
Penson, Eva: Charters to boroughs, 5027
Penwortham, priory of (Lancs.), 6202, 6382
Pepwell, Henry: Cell of self-knowledge, 6667
Pepys, Samuel: Library MSS., 1033
Perceval, Charles S.: Remarks on charters, 6123
Percival, Edward F.: Merton statutes, 7077
Percy, Bailiffs' rolls, 4837
— Chartulary, 4501, 4838
— Family, 4205, 4213, 4499, 4501, 4576, 4643, 4837
Perinelle, Georges: Louis XI, 4244

Periodicals, guides to, 14-16
Perkins, Clarence: Knights hospitallers, 6047; Templars, 6062
— Vincent R.: Kingswood documents, 6158
Pernoud, Régine M. J.: Jeanne d'Arc, 4264
Perrat, Charles: Report by, 47
Perrin, Charles-Edmond: Marc Bloch, 252, 4951
— Marshall L.: Ueber Thomas Castleford, 2810
— William G.: Admiralty Library, 4321
Perroy, Édouard: Administration de Calais, 4188; Compte de Gunthorp, 4188; Current publications, 167; Diplomatic correspondence, 3762; France and Navarre, 4188; Franco–English relations, 4188; Grand schisme, 4188, 6738; Hundred Years War, 4166; Les crises, 5459; Les seigneurs gascons, 4164; Lettres du cardinal, 4186; Louis de Male, 4188; Negotiations at Bruges, 3821, 4188; Peuples et civilisations, 1191; Treaty of Brétigny, 3809
Perry, Aaron J.: Trevisa's translation, 6570
— George G.: Bishop Beckington, 5595; Lincoln, 6790; Treatises of Richard Rolle, 6678
Personal names, 70-1; 1496, 7225
Perth (Scotland), 4287
Pertz, Georg H.: M.G.H., 1114, 2143, 2145
Peruzzi bankers, 1469. See Italian bankers
Peter of Blois, 1102, 1491, 2163, 6519
— of Cornwall, 1450
— of Langtoft, 1114, 2913
— the Chanter, 5443, 6429
— the Venerable (Cluny), 1477
Peter, Geoffrey fitz: Glanville, 2989
Peterborough abbey (Northants.), 441, 1012, 1108, 2142, 2834, 4665, 4963, 6177, 6215, 6264-70; Knights' fees, 3061, 3069, 4456
— Churchwardens' accounts, 5216, 6838
— Local administration, 5216
Peterborough, Benedict of, Gesta, 2879, 2903; Life of Becket, 6487
— John of, Chronicon, 2834
Peter's pence, 6775, 6777
Petersens, Carl af: Knýtlinga saga, 2448
Petersson, H. Bertil A.: A.-S. currency, 697
Petit, Louis: Mansi's Collectio, 1142
Petit-Dutaillis, Charles E.: Anonyme de Béthune, 2897; Désheritement de Jean, 4034; Essor, 1182; Feudal monarchy, 1179; Forests, 1426; Louis VIII, 4105; Merton annals, 2785; Querimoniae, 1458; Rising (of 1381), 4153; Supplement to Stubbs, 1221, 3920

Petrie, Henry: Magni rotuli, 3102; Monumenta, 1084
— Roy C.: Mysticism, 6679
— Sir William M. Flinders: Geoffrey of Monmouth, 2166
Petrushevsky, Dmitry M.: Die Entwicklung der Grundherrschaft, 4971; Vozstanie Uota Tailera, 606; 4154
Petterson, Jhalmar: Bibliotheca, 60
Petworth (Sussex), 4903
Petyt, William, 1013
Peutinger, Konrad, 2032
Peutinger's Table, 2044
Pevensey, Cinque port, 5316
Peverel (Derby.), Records, 1627; Survey, 4349, 4432
Pevsner, Sir Nikolaus: Buildings, 783
Pewterers company, 5198
Peyrègne, A.: Les émigrés gascons, 4265
Pfander, Homer G.: The popular sermon, 6708
Pfister, Chr.: Histoire générale, 1182
Phelps, William: Somersetshire, 1811
Phelps-Brown, Ernest H.: Wages and prices, 1468
Philip the Bold of Burgundy, 4170
— the Good of Burgundy, 4170, 4240
— the notary, 6779
Philippa of Hainault, Marriage of, 1447
Philippe Auguste, 2947, 4014, 4034
Philippe VI, 3813
Philipps, Elsbeth: Churchwardens' accounts, 6838
Philippson, Ernst A.: Heidentum, 2525, 2659
Phillimore, Egerton: Annales Cambriae, 2144; Brut y Tywysogion, 2805; Welsh records, 2144, 2805
— Robert: Ecclesiastical law, 6439
— William P. W.: How to write history, 521; Placita, 3491; Rotuli Hugonis de Welles, 5746
Phillips, Charles W.: Ordnance maps, 604; Recent archaeology, 766; Sutton Hoo, 2487
— James D.: Pembrokeshire, 1940
— John R. S.: Aymer de Valence, 4127
Phillipps, Sir Thomas: Aubrey's Collections, 1860; Cartularium de Flaxley, 6154; Catalogus librorum, 973; Catalogus MSS., 972, 5550; Heredes, 4342; Index finium Wigorn, 3626; Institutiones, 5807-8; Library, 973; Rotulus Walliae, 3787; Survey of Clarendon, 4923; Wilts. fines, 3619; Wilts. pipe rolls, 3096; Wilts. topography, 1860
Phillott, Henry W.: Hereford, 6790

Phillpotts, Dame Bertha S.: Edda, 2460; Kindred, 2642
Philobiblon, 6562
Philology, Celtic, **40–4**
— English, **34–6**
— French, **37–8**
— Latin, **38–40**
Philosophy, **898–903**; 49, 1407–10, 1416, 6033, 6035
— of history, **30–4**
Philpott, Henry: Documents, 7054
Physics, 6940, 6949, 6968, 6970, 6973
Picard, John: Newburgh's Historia, 2932
Picciotto, Cyril M.: Position of Jews, 3964
Pichlmayr, Franz: Aurelius Victor, 2025
Pickering (Yorks.), Honor and forest, 3202, 3630, 3884, 3890–1, 4685
Picton, Sir James A.: Liverpool, 5128
Picts, 761, 1120, 2170, 2488
Piepowder courts, 3507
Pierce, Thomas Jones: Laws of Wales, 2238–9
— the Plowman's Crede, 7049
Piercy, William C.: Dictionary, 1268
Piero da Monte, 6745
Piers plowman, 5446, 6990, 7021–9
Piggott, Stuart: **85**; Ancient Europe, 2006; Archaeology, 749; Camden's Britannia, 609; Celts, Saxons, 2130; Childe essays, 1974; Druids, 761; Flint mines, 2008; Geoffrey of Monmouth, 2166; Ireland and Britain in prehistory, 2007; Picts, 2090; Prehistoric peoples, 776; Prehistoric societies, 1978; Stonehenge, 1432; Scotland before history, 2009
Pigot, Hugh: Extenta, 4883
Pike, Joseph B.: trans., Policraticus, 6643
— Luke Owen: Common law, 1246; History of Crime, 1255; House of lords, 3378; Year Books, 3648
Pile, L. J. A.: Feet of fines, 3531
Pilgrim Trust, **109**
Pilgrimage, 6846
Pilkington family, 4588
Pilkington, John, 4588
Pilton (Som.), Churchwardens' accounts, 6838
Pinchbeck register, 6342
Pinder, Moritz: Antonine iter, 2029; Ravenna cosmographia, 2031
Pine, Leslie G.: Genealogy, 521, 553
Pink, William D.: Representation, 3462
Pinkerton, John: Vitae sanctorum, 1168
Pinks, William J.: Clerkenwell, 5173
Pipe rolls, **473–6**; 193, 955, 1075, 1441, 1529, 1775, 3076, 3241, 3254, 3261, 3264, 3568, 3943, 4448, 4784, 5026, 5144, 5608, 5815, 6311

Pipe Roll Society, 193
Pipewell Chronicle (Northants.), 6271
Piramus, Denis: Life of St. Edmund, 2305
Pirehill hundred (Staffs.), 4875
Pirenne, Henri: Bibliographie de Belgique, 61; Civilisation occidentale, 1182; Economic history, 1371; Études, 1447; Histoire de Belgique, 4167; Jean le Bel, 2916; Mélanges, 1446; Peuples et civilisations, 1191
Pirie, Elizabeth J. E.: Sylloge of coins, 704
Pisa, council of, 5567
Pisan, Christine de: Charles V, 2815
Pitcairn, Robert: Chronicle of Holyrood, 2821
Pits, John: Bibliography, 33
Pitt-Rivers, Augustus Henry L. F.: Cranborne chase, 2010
Pius II, pope, 5564, 6713
Place-names, **75–8**; 777, 1429, 1433, 1455, 1496, 2554–5, 2591, 2657, 2661
Place-name Society, 189, 272, 623
Placita Anglo-Normannica, 3490
— Corone, 3001
— De Quo Warranto, 3492, 3565
Plague, 5469
Planché, James R.: Cyclopaedia, 925; Strutt's Dress, 928
Planets, equatorie of, 6960
Planta, Joseph: Cotton catalogue, 994
Platnauer, Maurice: Classical scholarship, 2025
Platt, Colin: Archaeology, 729; Monastic grange, 5011
— Edith M.: Liverpool, 5128
— Elizabeth T.: Geographical research, **71**
Pleas and plea rolls: **459–61** and **524–33**; 955, 965, 3496, 3665, 3680, 6392, 6405
— Assize, 1601, 1692, 2644, 3498, 3507, 3513, 3534, 3543–4, 3547, 3553, 3559, 3563, 3568–9, 3572, 3576, 3588, 3594, 3596, 3603, 3618, 3620, 3628, 3633, 3639, 3643, 3746, 5289, 5305
— Chancery, 3483, 3509, 3609, 3617, 7224
— Coram rege (King's Bench), 2993, 3491, 3497, 3510, 3562, 3567, 3586–7, 3620, 3637A
— Council, 3505
— County by county, **533–44**; Beds., 3521; Bucks., 3521; Cambs., 4152, 5704; Ches., 3496, 3856, 3877; Durham, 3496, 5691; Hunts., 6173; Kent, 1692, 2644; Lancs., 3496, 3877, 3882; London, 5154, 5156; Staffs., 6326; Suffolk, 6342; Wilts., 3521, 4489; Yorks., 5289, 5305, 6392, 6405
— Court of chivalry, 3503A
— Curia regis, 3481, 3485, 3494, 3500–1,

Pleas and plea rolls: Curia regis (*cont.*):
3513–14, 3516, 3521, 3525, 3568, 3594,
3610
— De banco, 3534, 3568, 3583, 3591, 3595.
See also Coroners, Forests, Exchequer
of the Jews *and* Justices of the peace
Pleshy Castle (Essex), 4746
Plettke, Alfred: Ursprung der Angeln, 2516
Pliny the elder, 2025(c)
Plöchl, Willibald M.: Kirchenrecht, 1312
Plomer, Henry R.: Caxton, 7215; Records
of Canterbury, 5122; Wills, 4533
Plough, 2640, 5010
— and Pasture, 1980
Plough-team, 3057, 5014
Plucknett, Theodore F. T.: Anglo-Norman, 37; Bailiff, 4948; Bookland, 2623;
Brevia placitata, 2992; Charters, 304;
Concise history, 1241; County court,
3741; Deeds and seals, 422; Early legal
literature, 455; 3674; Edward I and
criminal law, 3675; Ellesmere on statutes,
3345A; Impeachment, 3418; Legisla-
tion of Edward I, 3339; Maitland, 1482;
Miscreant cardinal, 6762; Place of
council, 3305; Parliament, 3365; Roman
and common law, 1245; Sessions of
peace, 3615; State trials, 3520, 3713;
Statutes and interpretation, 3340; Tas-
well-Langmead, 1222; Thornton's
Summa, 3003; Year-books, 3646, 3649
Plummer, Alfred: Churches, 2705
— Charles: Alfred the Great, 2594; Bede's
Historia, 2148; Bede's Opera, 2148;
Fortescue's Governance, 2988; Saxon
chronicles, 2141; Vitae Sanctorum,
1169
— Charles: Brehon laws, 2250
Plumpe, Joseph C.: St. Patrick, 2324
Plumpton correspondence, 4611
Pluquet, Frédéric: Le Roman de Rou, 2974
Pluralism, 6772
Plymouth (Devon), 1504, 5061
Plympton (Devon), 5062
— Annals, 1108
PMLA (journal), 268
Pocquet du Haut-Jussé, Barthélemy
A. M. J.: Testament de Bedford, 4266
Poetry, Anglo-Saxon, 339–44
Poitiers, Alphonse of, 1448, 4094
— Guillaume de: Gesta Willelmi, 386;
1443, 2578, 2943
Poitou, county of, 4037, 4093
Polain, Mathieu L.: Le Bel's chroniques,
2916
Pole, William de la, 4232, 5334, 5397
Polianskii, I.: Rural life, 4971
Policraticus, 6639, 6643

Political poems, 7047–50
Political theory, 1411–17, 1490
Pollard, Albert F.: Anonimalle chronicle,
2787; Clerks of crown, 3425; Clerks
of parliament, 3425; Council, Star
Chamber, 3506; Evolution of parlia-
ment, 3380; History and statistics, 3439;
More's Richard III, 1455, 2927; Parlia-
ment and Wars of Roses, 3380; Plenum
parliamentum, 3380; Receivers of peti-
tions, 3425; Richard II's first parlia-
ment, 3420; Under-clerks, 3425
— Alfred W.: Prose and verse, 6863, 6991;
Short-title catalogue, 71, 7220
— Graham: Hall's Chronicle, 2889; Loan
chests, 7085; University statute book,
7070
Pollock, Sir Frederick: Domesday, 3060;
English law, 1242; King's peace, 1246;
Maine's Ancient law, 1239
Poll-taxes, 486–7; 3142, 3146, 3151, 3154,
3178–9, 3182, 3185, 3190, 3203A,
3204–5, 6826
Poltone, Thomas, bishop, 5730
Polwhele, Richard: Cornwall, 1591; Devon-
shire, 1613
Pont-Sainte-Maxence, Garnier de: Vie de
S. Thomas, 6489
Pontefract (Yorks.), 5297
— St. John, priory, 6412
Pontesbury, parish (Salop), 4859
Ponthieu, county of, 4100
Pontificals, 1316–17, 1323
Pontificia Hibernica, 1137
Pontigny, Roger of: Life of Becket, 6487
Pontissara, John de, bishop, 5818
Poole, Austin Lane: Davis essays, ed.
1466; Domesday to Magna Carta, 593;
1189; England and Burgundy, 1448;
Gesta Stephani, 2880; Livestock prices,
5490; Medieval England, ed., 1192;
Obligations of society, 4674, 5460;
Outlawry of clerks, 1455, 6464; R. L.
Poole essays, ed., 374, 1487; Recreations,
1485; Richard I and Germans, 1450
— George A.: Peterborough, 6790
— Reginald Lane: Atlas, 605; Bale's Index,
8; Chronicles and annals, 283; Chronology and history, 374, 1487; Dates of
charters, 3823, 4399; Englishmen at
papal court, 1458; Essays to, 1448;
Exchequer, 3005, 3250, 3257; Fitzralph,
De pauperie, 6864; Illustrations, 1416,
6893; John of Salisbury, 6640–2;
Masters of schools, 6642; Oxford
archives, 1018; Papal chancery, 420,
5542; Political history, 1183; Powicke's
appreciation of, 1489; Roger of York,

6492; Seals and documents, 466; Wilfrid, 2313; Wycliffe, 6658, 6864

Poole's Index, 100

Poor law, 4720, 6446

Poor-relief, 1361, 3137

Poore, Richard, bishop, 5799

Pope, John C.: Ælfric, 2292, 7225

— Mildred K.: Anglo-Norman, **37**; From Latin to French, 295; Life of Black Prince, 2812

Population, **744–6**; 1377, 1381, 4947, 4995, 5167, 5305, 5899

Porlock (Som.), 4869

Port books of Southampton, 5108–9, 5342

Porter, Arthur Kingsley: Crosses of Ireland, 848; Essays to, 1449

— M. E.: St. Edmund, 2305

Portland (Dorset), account rolls, 4736

Portsmouth records (Hants), 5097

Portswood (Hants), manor of, 1426

Pöschl, Arnold: Die Regalien, 6766

Poschmann, Bernhard: Der Ablass, 1287; Die Kirchenbusse, 2264

Post, Gaines: Bracton, 2985; Plena potestas, 3448; Report on MSS., **47**; Review, 1219; Status regis, 3276; Statute of York, 3366

Postan, Cynthia: trans. Duby, 1368

— M. Michael: **691**; Bibliography of, 5462; Cambridge economic history, ed. 1175, 1364; Carte nativorum, 6266; Chronology of labour services, 4977; Costs of Hundred Years War, 4259; Credit in trade, 1468, 5515; Declining population, 5480; England and Hanse, 5393; English village, 1471; Famulus, 4977; Fifteenth century, 5461; Glastonbury estates, 6318; Heriots and prices, 5815; Investment in agriculture, 5012, 5493; Kosminsky, review of, 4971; Manor, 4977; Partnerships, 5392; Private financial instruments, 5515; Rise of money economy, 1468, 5462; Some social consequences, 4259; Spread of techniques, 5392; Studies in English trade, ed. 5393; Village livestock, 5012

Potestate Papae (Ockham), 6613

Potter, George R.: Beauchief cartulary, 6114; Education, **924**

— Kenneth R.: Deeds of Stephen, 2880; Historia Novella, 2921

— W. J. W.: Coinage, 711

Pottery, 1442, 1967, 2069–70, 2072, 2082, 2088, 2551–2, 5512

Potthast, August: Bibliotheca, 62; Regesta, 1138

Pou y Martí, José M.: Bullarium Franciscanum, 6004

Poujoulat, Jean J. F.: Jean Juvénal des Ursins, 2909

Poulson, George: Beverlac, 5288; Holderness, 1892

Poulters' Company, 5199

Pounds, Norman J. G.: Ports of Cornwall, 5390

Poupardin, René: Dix-huit lettres inédites, 6512; Tewkesbury calendar, 2765

Powell, A. D.: Ministers' accounts, 4632A

— Dorothy L.: Borough records, 5265; Court rolls, 4890, 4892; Surrey archives, 1827

— Edgar: Poll-tax lists, 3190; Rising (1381), 4155, 4158; Suffolk hundred, 3188; Taxation of Ipswich, 3187

— Edward: Charters at Scarisbrick, 4441

— Frederick York: Origines Islandicae, 2443

— John Enoch: House of lords, 3381; Laws of Hywel Dda, 2225

— Thomas: Repertorie, 960

— Thomas G. E.: Celts, 761, 1429

— Walter: Catalogue, 1842

— William Raymond: Essex bibliography, 1529, 1633; Navy and stannaries, 4325; Surveys during interdict, 4924, 5809

Powell's roll (of arms), 494, 499

Power, Eileen E.: Boissonnade, 1371; Cambridge Economic History, 1175, 1364; Medieval nunneries, 1301; Medieval people, 5464; Studies in trade, 5393, 5463; Wool trade, 5419

Powicke, Sir Frederick Maurice: Ailred of Rievaulx, 1490, 6637; Alexander of St. Albans, 1448; Arthur of Brittany, 1490, 4034; Battle of Lewes, 4068; Camden, William, 609; Chancery, 3840; Christian life, 1488; Councils and synods, 6440, 6816; Edward I, 1452; England and Europe, 1490; Essays to, 1450, 3366; Freeholder, 1434; Gerald of Wales, 1488, 2881; Grosseteste, 6582; Handbook, 371, 537; Henry III, **597**; 4062; Langton, Stephen, 1488, 5634; Liber memorialis, 3366; Loretta of Leicester, 1455, 1488; Loss of Normandy, 2754, 4035; Medieval state, 1490; Merton books, 1029, 7175; Methods of research, 1490; Modern historians, 1489; Montfort, Guy de, 1490; Murder of Henry Clement, 1490; Paris, Matthew, 2941, 2979; Parliament, origins of, 1489, 3362, 3366; Provisions of Westminster, 1458; Simon of Faversham, 1443, 1490; Thirteenth century, **597**; 1189; Universities, 1490, 7090; Ways of life, 1490; Wendover, Roger, 2850, 2979

Powicke, Michael: Commons in Scotland, 4131; Lancastrian captains, 1459; Military obligation, 4314

Powysland Club, 1937

Poynings–Percy dispute, 4643

Poynton, Edward M.: Charters, 6220

Praemunire, statutes of, 1439, 3345, 6773

Praerogativa Regis, 1482, 3275

Praestita roll, 3110, 3774

Pratt, Joseph: Foxe's Martyrs, 6865

— Robert A.: Chaucer and Hawkwood, 7007

Praty, Richard, bishop: Records, 5656

Prehistoric Archaeology. See Archaeology

Prehistoric people, 761, 776, 1430

— Society (of East Anglia), 1966

Premonstratensians, 1144, 5960–5, 6198, 6285

Prendergast, John P.: Haliday's Dublin, 2585A

Prerogative, royal, 500–1; 1444, 1482, 3868

Prescott, Hilda: Teste me ipso, 3851

— John E.: Register of Wetherhal, 6113

Pressutti, Petrus: Regesta Honorii III, 5560

Prestoll abbey (Wales), 4943A

Preston (Lancs.), 1472, 4791, 5130–2, 5360

Prestre, H. S.: Bede, 2297

Prests, Book of, 3113

Prestwich, J. O.: Battle of Winwaed, 2487; Feudalism and continuity, 4657; War and finance, 4315

— Michael: Monetary policies, 3252; Victualling estimates, 4084; Welsh campaign, 4059

Preuss, Friedrich R. Edward: Bibliotheca, 2014

Previté-Orton, Charles W.: Annales Radingenses, 1108; Chronicon Aquileiensium, 1455; Powicke on, 1489; Titus Livius, 2919

Prévost, Auguste le: Ordericus Vitalis, 2937

Price, Clement: Liber Pensionum, 5835

— Derek J.: The equatorie, 6960

— Frederick G. H.: Roman buildings, 2080

— J. A.: Welsh church, 5879C

— Jacob M.: What is history? 240

— John E.: Roman buildings, 2080

— M. J. Stanley: Yorkshire deeds, 4504

— R.: Ancient laws, 2180

Prices, 1376, 1468, 5489–90, 5495, 5815

Prick of conscience, 6698

Pridden, John: Index, 3322

Prideaux, Walter S.: Goldsmiths' company, 5190

Prigg, Henry: Icklington papers, 4885

Prince, Albert E.: Army and navy, 4316; Army wages, 4316; Indenture system, 1455, 4283; Strength of armies, 4316

Princes in the Tower, 556, 4203

— of Wales, 549

Princesses, 546

Principatu tyrannico, De (Ockham), 6614

Printing, **932–3**; 1485, 5203

Prior, Edward S.: Art, 806–7, 849

— William H.: Weights and measures, 5494

Priories, alien, **796–7**

Priors Dean (Hants), 4766

Prisons, 1256

Pritchard, Violet: Graffiti, 850

Privy seal, 417, 3754, 3838, 3849, 3872, 4141, 7224

Prize jurisdiction, 3515

Proby, Granville: Elton records, 4776; Huntingdonshire members, 3459A

Procedure, legal, **160–3**, **459–61**, and **552–3**; 3503, 3660, 3664. See Equity *and* Impeachment

Proctors, **883–5**

Professions of obedience, 5624

Progoff, Ira: Cloud of unknowing, 6671

Prohibition, writ of, 6462

Promptorium parvulorum, 312

Pronger, Winifred A.: Thomas Gascoigne, 6572

Propaganda, 4243, 4260

Protector of England, 3306

Prothero, George W.: Map, 605

— Rowland E. (Baron Ernle): English farming, 1375, 5013

Prou, Maurice: Manuel, 396

Provisions, papal, **885–6**; 1438–9, 1473

— of Oxford, 2763, 4063, 4068

— of Westminster, 1458

Prussia, expedition to, 4601, 7223

Prutz, Hans G.: Rechnungen, 4601

Pryce, Arthur I.: Register of Benedict, bishop, 5880

— Frederick N.: Diplomas, 2028

— Thomas D.: Roman occupation, 2071; Romans in Scotland, 2088

Prynne, John: Cartularium, 6160

— M.: Henry V's Grace Dieu, 4333

— William: **111–12**; Animadversions, 1233; Aurum reginae, 3256; Brevia, 3317; Cotton's Abridgement, 3308; Demurrer, 3965; Parliamentary writs, 3317; Records, 1139; Vindication, 1139

Prys-Jones, Arthur G.: Carmarthenshire, 1910

Psalters, **102–3**; 441

Pseudo-Cnuts Constitutiones, 3894

Ptolemy's Geography, 2025, 2044
Public Works, 3497
— Record Office, **108–18**; 1086, 1440–1, 3224–8, 3318, 7222
— Records Act (1958), **112**
— Records, history of, 974
— Records, reports on:
 (1719), 961
 (1732), 962
 (1800), 963
 (1819), 964
 (1837), 965
 (1919), 966
Pudsay Deeds, 4502
Pugh, Ralph B.: Adam de Stratton, 4918; Amesbury manors, 4926; Antrobus deeds, 4488; Borough records, 5281; Court rolls, 4918; Feet of fines, Wilts., 3620; Moneylenders, 5516; Parish history, 1521; Prisons, 1256; V.C.H., 1197, 1529–30; V.C.H. Wilts., 3034
— Thomas B.: Baronial incomes, 4636; Glamorgan history, 1927; Income from land, 4623; Magnates, 4234; Marcher lordships, 3638, 4675
Pughe, William Owen: Dictionary, 341; Myvyrian archaiology, 2382
Puiset, Hugh du: bishop, **704**; 3076, 5700
Pullen, Robert, cardinal, Lives of, 1458, 1487, 6631
Pulling, Alexander: Laws of London, 5174; Order of the coif, 7154
— Frederick S.: Dictionary, 1187
Purdy, Rob Roy: Chaucer scholarship, 7002
Purnell, Christopher J.: London library, 82–3
— Thomas: Historia, 2892
Purton, Ralph C.: Deeds for Larden, 4466; Deeds for Oswestry, 4864; Documents of Church Stretton, 4859
Purvey, John: New Testament, 6649; Remonstrances, 6632
Purvis, John S.: Act book, 5871; Archives of York, 1873; Charter of Bridlington, 6399; Chartularies of Monkbretton, 6409; Chartulary of priory of St. John, 6403; Dictionary, 1273; Ecclesiastical courts, 6461; Monastic chancery proceedings, 5897, 6391
Putnam, Bertha H.: Common law records, 3677; Early records of J.P.s, 3742; Keepers of the peace to J.P.s, 3742; Kent keepers of peace, 3560; Oxford proceedings, 7064; Proceedings before J.P.s, 3495; Sessions of peace (Yorks.), 3635; Sir Wm. Shareshull, 3691; Statute of labourers, 3344, 3676; Treatises on J.P.s, 3742

— Peter: trans. Bloch, 252
Pyddoke, Edward: Archaeology, 85
Pyncebeke, Walter: Pinchbeck register, 6342
Pype, Thomas, abbot: Stoneleigh leger book, 6369
Pytchley, Henry of: Book of fees, 4456, 6267

Quadrilogus, 6487
Quadripartitus, 2184, 2189
Quarr abbey (Isle of Wight), 6163
Quasten, Johannes: St. Patrick, 2324
Queen Mary's Psalter, 900
Queen's Beasts, 481
Quency, lords of, 1486
Quentel, Paul: Channel Islands, 1957
Querimoniae Normannorum, 1458
Quétif, Jacques: Scriptores, 5985
Quicheret, Jules: Historia Caroli VII, 2793; Procés de Jeanne d'Arc, 4268
Quiggin, Edmund C.: ed. Ridgeway studies, 2591
Quinn, David B.: Edward IV and exploration, 5394; Irish financial records, 3101; Irish pipe roll, 3099; Irish records, 1078; List of Irish parliaments, 3309; Port books, 5109
Quinton, John: Bibliotheca, 1749
Quirk, Randolph: Bald's Leechbook, 2365; Grammar, 285; Saga, ed., 2446
Quit-claims, 6144. *See also* Pugh, Antrobus deeds
Quivil, Peter, bishop, 5715
Quo warranto, 1462, 1478, 3492, 3565, 4943A

Rabinowitz, Jacob J.: Jewish law, 3960
Raby, Frederic J. E.: Christian poetry, 1405; Secular poetry, 1406, 6894
Rack, Edmund: Somerset, 1810
Rackham, Bernard: Canterbury glass, 864
— Harris: Pliny, 2025; Statutes of Christ's College, 7057
Radbourne Hall (Derby.), 4431
Radcliffe, Richard D.: Deeds and documents, 4449
Radcot Bridge, battle of, 4130
Radford, Courtenay H. Ralegh: Celtic monasteries, 2675A; Pottery, 1442; Saxon house, 2517; Vortigern, 2553; Welsh architecture, 1435
— Lewis B.: Thomas of London, 6500
Radlow (Hereford.), Hundred, 1670
Radnorshire, 1941–3
Raeder, Hans H.: Gesta, 2426
Raffel, Burton: Beowulf, 2335; trans. English poems, 2356

Rafn, Charles: Icelandic life, 2171

Raftery, Joseph: Celts, 2131

Raftis, J. Ambrose: Commutation in village, 1459; Court rolls and village history, 4978; Estates of Ramsey, 6176; M. Bloch, 252; Responsibility in villages, 4978; Tenure and mobility, 4978; Village after Black Death, 4978

Rag, Robert, 1458

Ragg, Frederick W.: Charters, 6425; Feoffees of Cliffords, 4391, 4486

Raglan, Baron. *See* Somerset, Fitz-Roy Richard

Ragman rolls, 1458, 3792

Rahner, Karl: Lexikon, 1270

Raine, Angelo: Medieval York, 5305; York civic records, 5309

— James (the elder): Depositions, 5676, 6459; Miscellanea, 5308; North Durham, 1628, 6276; Obituary roll, 5688; Priory of Coldingham, 6132; Priory of Finchale, 6134; Reginaldi libellus, 2302; Rud's Catalogus, ed. 1043; St. Cuthbert, 2302; Sanctuarium, 5693, 6395; Scriptores tres, 5685; Wills, 4524, 4564

— (the younger): Dialogi, 5677; Dixon's Fasti, 5867; Fabric rolls, 5850; Historians of York, 1130, 2289, 2311, 5851; Historical papers, 5686, 5852; Inventories of Jarrow, 6138; John of Hexham's Historia, 2893; Presentments, 6420; Priory of Hexham, 6274; Register of archbishop Gray, 5857; Richard of Hexham's Historia, 2894; Statutes of York, 5860; Wills, 4564, 4566

Raistrick, Arthur: West Riding, 1517

Raith, Josef: Bussbuch, 2258

Raithby, John: Statutes, 3327

Raleigh, William (justice), 3689

Ralph, archbishop of York, 1130

— of Coggeshall: Chronicon, 1114, 2850

— de Diceto: Opera, 1100, 1124, 2860; Successors, 5768

— Fitz Hubert, Lands of, 1486

— of Hengham, 1458, 1501, 2996–7

— Niger: Chronica, 1114, 2933

— of Shrewsbury, bishop, 5589

Ralph, Elizabeth: Local archives, 1440; St. Ewen's, Bristol, 5086, 6838

Ramackers, Johannes: Papsturkunden, 1132

Ramage, Helen: Cymmrodorion Society, 126

Rambaud, Jacqueline: L'âge classique, 1311

Ramsay, Alexander: Paston Letters, 4610

— Sir James H.: History of revenues, 3258; Series of histories, **623**; 1193 Strength of armies, 4316

Ramsbotham, Alexander: Old Hall manuscript, 7192

Ramsey abbey, 2151, 2311, 2366, 4776–7, 4978, 6173–7

Rand, Edward K.: Notae, 404

Randall, H. J.: Richard of Cirencester, 2026; Welsh place-names, 640

Ranulf de Gernons, earl of Chester, 3981

Rapes of Sussex, 1840, 4288, 4902, 4905

Rapin de Thoyras, Paul de: Acta regia, 3766

Rashdall, Hastings: Bacon's Compendium, 6536; Friars Preachers *v.* University, 5999, 7061; Universities, 7090

Rastall, William D.: Southwell, 6284

Ratcliff, Sidney C.: Elton records, 4776

Rathbone, Eleanor: Anglo-Norman canonists, 6435; Roman law, 6429

— Maurice G.: Wilts. records, 1854–5, 5281

Raven, J. J.: Antonine iter, 2029

Ravennatis Cosmographia, 2031, 2044

Rawle, Edwin J.: Forest of Exmoor, 3895

Rawlinson, Richard: Cathedral of Hereford, 5736

Raymo, Robert R.: Nigel de Longchamp, 7042

Raymond, Irving W.: Orosius, 2025

Raynaldus, Odoricus: Annales, 5551

Raynaud, Gaston: Froissart's Chroniques, 2874

Rayner, Doris: Commune petition, 3405

Re, Emilio: La compagnia dei Riccardi, 5437

Read, Conyers: Bibliography, 32; Constitution, ed., 3406

— E. Anne: Cathedral libraries, 1039

Reading, Abbey, 6089, 6091–2; Annals, 1108; History, 1386; Libraries, 1542; Records, 5031, 6838; University (coins), 704

Reading, John of: Chronica, 2944

— Robert of: Flores, 2871

Readings and moots of Inns, 3002, 3345A, 7147

Reaney, Percy H.: Feet of fines, 3548; Place-names, 635; Surnames, 586

Rebellion in Lincolnshire, 2828

Receipt rolls, **477–9**; 3258

Reclamation of fens, 4717, 4808, 4956, 4991

Record commissions, **112**; 435, 961–8, 1085

— interpreter, 405

— of Caernarvon, 4943A, 6828

— publications, Handlist, 933

— repositories, **108–9**; 944, 1523
Record, Peter D.: Bodleian Library, 1027; Palaeography, 380
Records and record searching, 522, 969
— of social and economic history, 181
Recreations, 928A, 1485
Rectitudines, 2189, 2209, 2212
Recueil des historiens, 1090
Red Book of Durham, 2168, 5695
— of the Exchequer, 3006–7
— of Hereford, 5731
— of Hergest, 2166, 2386, 2805
— of Worcester, 5836
Reddan, Minnie: London Temple, 6064
Reddaway, Thomas F.: Accounts of John Balsall, 5325; Goldsmiths, 5191; King's mint, 676
Rede, Robert, bishop, 5654
Redgrave, Gilbert R.: Short-title, 71, 7220
Redin, Mats A.: Personal names, 587
Redman, Robert: Henrici Quinti historia, 2945
— of Harwood, 4500
Redstone, Lilian J.: Carrow account rolls, 4822; Cellarer's roll, 6253; Chaucer life records, 7007; East Anglian heritage, 1757; Ipswich, 5264; Local records, 1524; Norfolk sessions, 3584
— Vincent B.: Household Book of Alice de Bryene, 4603; Nomina Villarum of Suffolk, 4389; Wills of Bury St. Edmunds, 4554
Redwood, Brian C.: Custumals of manors, 4901, 6356
Reed, Arthur W.: Works of Sir Thomas More, 2927
Reedy, William T., Jr.: General eyre, 3661
Rees, J. R.: Slebech commandery, 6048
— Joseph: Company of grocers, 5192
— William: Black Death in Wales, 1493, 5483; Celtic Saints, 2321; Hospitallers, 6049; Liber Landavensis, 5880A; Lordship of Brecon, 1899; Ministers' accounts, 4629A; South Wales, 4633, 4978; Survivals, 2526; Welsh bibliography, 10; Welsh place-names, 640
Reese, Gustave: Music in middle ages, 7209
Reeves, 4750, 4903, 4917, 4948
— John: English law, 1243
— William: Culdees, 2688; St. Columba, 2319
Reform, Benedictine, 1475
Regalian rights, **885–6**; 6338
Regan, Morice: Song of Dermot, 2954
Regenos, Graydon W.: Daun Burnel, 7042
Regesta Regum Anglo-Normannorum, 3779

Regesta Regum Scottorum, 3794, 4646
Regiam Majestatem, 219, 2989
Reginald of Coldingham: St. Cuthbert, 2302
— of Durham: St. Godric of Finchale, 6675
Reginaldi libellus, 2302
Register of brieves, 219
— of writs, 1246, 1482, 3499, 3662, 5801
Registers: Episcopal
  Bangor, 5880
  Bath and Wells, 5587, 5589
  Canterbury, 5598, 5609–10, 5621
  Carlisle, 5646
  Chichester, 5650, 5654–6
  Coventry and Lichfield, 5667–8
  Durham, 5686, 5689–92
  Ely, 5704
  English dioceses, 5577–8, 5621
  Exeter, 5715, 5717
  Hereford, 5727–30
  Lincoln, 5743, 5745–8
  London, 5761, 5763–4
  Rochester, 5792
  St. Asaph, 5879
  St. Davids, 5880E, 5880G
  Salisbury, 5801–2
  Welsh dioceses, **790–2**
  Winchester, 5816–19
  Worcester, 5827, 5837–41
  York, 5686, 5852, 5857–8
— Manorial, gild, college, etc.:
  Caernarvon, 4943A, 6828
  Coventry, 5275
  Ewell, 4896
  Knowle, 5278
  Lancaster, duchy of, 3875
  Leicester, 5139
  Oxford, 7065–7, 7076, 7079, 7081, 7087–8, 7095, 7098, 7114, 7119
  Richmond, 4503, 4939
  Romney, 5323
  Stratford, 5279
  York, 5303, 5306–7
— Papal, **752–4**; 1114, 2308
Registrum Antiquissimum (Lincoln), 5744
— Cancellarii Oxoniensis, 7067
— Collegii Exoniensis, 7114
— Eleemosynariae, 5762
— Epistolarum Stephani de Lexington, 6377
— Honoris de Richmond, 4503, 4939
— Malmesburiensis, 6374
— Mertonensis, 7079
— Palatinum Dunelmense, 3867, 5691
— Prioratus Wigorniensis, 5842
— Roffense, 5793
— Statutorum S. Pauli, 5765

Registrum Vulgariter nuncupatum (Caernarvon), 4943A, 6828
Regula magistri, 5911
Regularis Concordia, **317**; 1113, 1302, 2274
Regule compoti, 4619, 4698
Reich, Aloyse M.: Parliamentary abbots, 3478
Reichel, Oswald J.: Bishop Lacy's Register, 5717; Canon law, 6441; Devon Domesday, 1529, 3019; Devon feet of fines, 3545; Devon pipe rolls, 3088; Devon Testa de Neville, 4351; Exeter MS., 3156; Origin of parish, 6854
Reichert, Benedictus M.: Acta Praedicatorum, 5984
Reid, Eleanor J. B., 6873
— Rachel R.: Barony and thanage, 2643, 4676; Redmayne's Henry V, 2945
— William Stanford: Scots and staple, 5386; Sea power, 4085
Reidy, John: Dictionary, 281
Reilly, James P.: Ockham bibliography, 6622
Reisner, D.: ed., Festschrift für Walter Hübner, 7165
Reiss, Edmund: Geoffrey of Monmouth, 2166
Relatio de Standardo, 2734, 2894, 6274, 6634–5
Religieux de Saint-Denys: Chronique, 2847
Religious houses. *See* Monasticism
— periodicals, index, 97
Reliquary (journal), 730
Remediis (De) contra temptaciones, 1438, 6693
Remembrancers, **491–2**; 3104, 3215, 3223, 7222
Remigius, bishop of Lincoln, 6573
Remnant, George L.: Misericords, 851
Remonstrances against Romish corruptions, 6632
Renaudet, Augustin: Peuples et civilisations, 1191
Renn, Derek: Castles, 837
Rennell of Rodd, Lord: Lene (Wales), 1435
Renoir, Alain: John Lydgate, 7035
Renouard, Yves: Aquitaine, 4164; Bibliography, 55; Bordeaux, 4168; Cahorsins, 5434; Commerce des vins, 5395; Édouard II et Clément V, 6739; Halphen's Initiation, 259; L'empire angevin, 4036; Papauté à Avignon, 6719; Rôles gascons, 3828, 6739
Renshaw, Mary A.: Inquisitiones, 4375
Rentals, 955, 955A, 1037, 4689, 4696–7;

Abingdon, 6084
Addington, 4787
Ambresbury, 6315
Ashton-under-Lyne, 4793
Barrington's fee, 4747
Battle abbey, 6357
Bicester, 4852
Blithfield, 4476
Bolney, 4899
Bolton, 6396
Caenby, Tournays of, 4584
Canterbury, St. Augustine's, 6182
Castle Combe, 4922
Chiltington, 4904
Combermere, 6103
Crabhouse, 6255
Crondal, 4763
Cuxham, 4849
Denton, 4899
Durham, 5682
Ely, 5704
Gillingham, 4986
Glastonbury, 6314
Gloucester, 5091
Great Cressingham, 4820
Guisborough, 6401
Harlow, 4745, 6337
Heene, 4904
Hexham, 6274
Ibstone, 4849
Ipswich, Holy Trinity, 6347
Kirkstall, 6405
Lancashire, 4367, 6206
Leeds, 5296
Leicester, 1714
London, St. Paul's, 5759
Malmesbury, 6374–5
Manchester, 4791
Manydown, 4767
Nostell, 6411
Nottinghamshire, 4842
Oswestry, 4864
Pontefract, 5297
Rothley, 4797
Rothwell, 4832
Southampton, God's House, 4849
Stallingborough, 4813
Stoneleigh, 6369
Sutton, 4763
Warrington, 4796
Winchester, 5815
Wiston, 4904
Wistowe, 6175
Worcester priory, 5824, 5842
Wroxall, 6371
Wroxeter, 4861
Rents, Customary, 4976
— Money, 1468, 4308, 4966

Répertoire bibliographique de l'histoire de France, 63
— bibliographique de la Philosophie, **30**; 6877
— des sources (Chevalier), 46, 47
Repertorium Fontium Historiae medii aevi, 64
— Novum, 235A
Repingdon, Philip, bishop, 5743
Reports of commissions: Cathedrals, 6800; Dignity of a peer, 3382; Ecclesiastical courts, 6442; Forests, 3896; Historical MSS., 945, 1509; Historical monuments, 737–9; Local records, 1525–6; London livery companies, 5182; Market rights and tolls, 5531; Names of members of parliament, 3444; Public records, **112**; 961–8, 1526, 3130, 3216, 4293; Royal mint, 698
Reports of the deputy keeper, 967
Repositories, Accessions to, 942
Representation in parliament, **521–4**
— Theory of, 1461, 3366, 3401, 3447–8
Representative government, 1497
Repressor of Overmuch blaming, 6629
Reprints, Guide to, 5
Repton (Hunts.), Manor, 4777; Structure, 7225
Rerum Britannicarum Scriptores, 1087
Research facilities in universities, 938
Resident proctors, 6751–2, 6754–6
Retinue, indentures of, **619–23**; 1493, 4283
Reuschlein, Harold G.: Mirror of justices, 2991
Reuss, Rodolphe (Rudolf): Alsace, 1426
Revelations of Divine Love, 6673
Revesby abbey (Leics.), 1453, 6219
Review of English Studies (journal), 274
Réville, André: L'Abjuratio regni, 1261; Le Soulèvement des travailleurs, 4156
Revue celtique, 324
— de droit canonique, **168**
— d'histoire ecclésiastique, 166
— des questions historiques, 165
— de synthèse historique, 252
— historique, 167
Reyner, Clement: Apostolatus, 1302
Reynolds, Herbert E.: Consuetudinarium, 5738; Diocese of Exeter, 5723; Use of Exeter, 5718; Wells Cathedral, 5590
— Paul: Roman walls, 2089
— Roger E.: Norman Anonymous, 6427
— Susan: Charters of Barnstaple, 5054, 6121; Forged charters, 5054; Pleas of Abbot of Battle, 4920; Register of Roger Martival, 3499, 5801
— Thomas: Antonine iter, 2029
— Walter, bishop, 5638, 5841

Rezneck, Samuel: Treason by words, 3714
Rhetoric, 6929
Rhodes, Dennis E.: The princes in the tower, 4203
— Walter E.: Italian bankers, 1472, 5517; trans. Petit-Dutaillis, 1221
Rhuddlan Castle, expenses at, 3131
Rhygyfarch's Life of St. David, 1173, 2321
Rhys, Ernest: St. David, 2321
— Sir John: Celtic Britain, 2132; Facsimiles, **54**; Liber Landavensis, 5880A; Red Book of Hergest, 2166, 2804; Text of the Bruts, 2804; Welsh people, 1194; Welsh philology, **42**; Ystorya brenhined, 2166
— ap Maredudd, Revolt of, 4059
— Myvanwy: Ministers' accounts, 4629A
Ribston (Yorks.), 6056
Ricardus Corinensis, 2026
Ricart, Robert: Kalendar, 5083
Riccardi, Compagnia dei, 5437
Ricci, Seymour de: Census, 980; Collectors of Books, 981
Rice, David Talbot: Art, 782, 803
— Robert Garraway: Sussex wills, 4559
Rich, Edmund. See Edmund of Abingdon
— Edwin E.: Cambridge Economic History, 1364; Mayors of the Staple, 5386; Ordinance book of Staplers, 5340
Richard, Alfred: Comtes de Poitou, 4037
Richard I: Charters, 4409; Chroniclers of, **390**; 2734, 2788; Government of, 3852, 4029; History of, 1450, 4004, 4024, 4029; Seals, 458
— II: Chroniclers of, **391**; 2771, 2829, 2833, 2856, 2899, 2906, 2976; Council, 3302; Deposition, 1464, 2820, 2840, 3365, 4113; History of, **603–8**; 1464, 1468, 1472, 1478, 2820, 2840, 3302, 3365, 3418–22, 3710, 4113, 5177, 5627, 6478, 6990, 7223; Ireland, 3801, 4114; Peasants' revolt, **606–8**; Poems on, 2856, 7017, 7019, 7049; Records of, 3418–19, 3713, 3715–16, 3763, 3801, 4274
— III: Chroniclers, **392**; 2866, 2885, 2900, 2922, 2927, 2950, 2968; History, **612–15**; 4203, 4209–10, 4222–3, 4227; Legislation, 2735, 3346; Letters, 3771; Murder of princes, 556, 4203; Niece and, 4209, 6453
— Anglicus, 2929, 6448
— Bishop of Chichester, 5662
— Canon of Holy Trinity, London, 2906
— Duke of York, 4634, 6804
— of Anstey, 1453, 3490
— of Bardney, 6583
— of Bury, see 'Bury'
— of Cirencester, 1089, 1101, 2026, 2155

Richard of Clare, earl of Hertford, 1486
— of Clare. *See* Strongbow
— of Cornwall, 4096
— of Devizes, 1089, 1101, 1113–14, 1123, 2767, 2859
— of Gravesend, 4543, 5714, 5747
— of Haldingham, 606, 1467
— of Hexham, 1114, 1123–4, 2894, 6274
— of Ilchester, 6520
— of Kellawe, 3865, 3867, 5691
— of Maidstone, 7049
— of Morins, 2929
— of Swinfield, 4612, 5730
— son of Nigel. *See* Fitz-Neal
Richards, George C.: Oriel provosts, 7126; Oriel register, 7081
— Melville: Irish settlements, 2133; Laws of Hywel Dda, 2226; Welsh place-names, 640
Richardson, Ernest C.: Catalogue, 982
— Henry G.: Administration of Ireland, 3846; Annales Paulini, 2768; Azo, Drogheda, and Bracton, 2985; Boussard review, 4013; Bracton, 2985, 3481; Business training, 7127; Chamber under Henry II, 3246; Clement V and Canterbury, 6739; Clergy in parliament, 3479; Commons and politics, 1221; Coronation, 1357; Early statutes, 3341; Eleanor of Aquitaine's letters, 4023, 4608; Exchequer memoranda rolls, 3215; Exchequer year, 3259; Fairs, 5532; Fleta, 2987; Forgery of fines, 3487; Formularies, 427, 7063; Gervase of Tilbury, 2961; Glanville, 2989; Governance, 1218; Guala's letters, 6747; Henry I's charter, 5179; Heresy, 6478, 6659, 6872; Interdict, 6729; Irish administration, 3846; Irish monasteries, 1438; Irish parliament, 3309, 3354, 3366, 3392; Irish revenue, 3260; Isabella of Angoulême, 4038, 6429; Jewry under Angevins, 3966; John of Gaunt, 3462; John of Salisbury, 6641; Jolliffe review, 4022; King's ministers, 3426; Law and legislation, 1219; Law merchant, 5533; Morrow of the charter, 4039; Northampton schools, 7127; Oldcastle in hiding, 4225, 6863; Oxford law school, 7127; Oxford teacher, 7127; Parlement of Paris, register, 3825; Parish clergy, 6855; Parliament and great councils, 3383; Parliament, clergy in, 3479; Parliament documents, 3320; Parliament, King's ministers in, 3426; Parliament, Lancs. representation, 3462; Parliament of Carlisle, 3320, 3412; Parliament of Lincoln, 3413; Parliament,

origins, 1493; Parliament, records, 3320; Parliament, Richard II's last, 3422; Parliament, Rotuli, 3323; Plea rolls, 3677; Plough teams, 5014; Procedure without writ, 3513; Provisions of Oxford, 4063; Regiam majestatem, 2989; Richard II, 3422; Richard fitz-Neal, 3005; Rotuli parliamentorum, 3323; Walden abbey, 6146; William of Ely, 3259; Year books, 3677
— Herbert: Theological treatises, 6533
— Katherine M.: Excavations, 2070
— Robert K.: Gesta Dunelmensia, 5683
— Walter C.: Tudor chamber administration, 3270
— William: Godwin's De praesulibus, 5579
— William H.: Bacon's Annals, 5259
Richborough (Kent), Roman, 2070, 2109
Richental, Ulrich: Chronicle, 5565
Richey, Alexander G.: Irish laws, 2240
Richie, C. I. A.: Ecclesiastical courts, 6479
Richmond (Yorks.), Archdeaconry, 4566, 5859; Comte de, 4058; Honour of, 1529, 1776, 4499, 4502–3, 4626, 4939
Richmond, C. F.: Fauconberg's rising, 4226; Keeping of the seas, 4334; Naval power, 4334
— Sir Ian A.: **261**; Agricola, 2025, 2071–2; Antonine Wall, 2087; Archaeology, 2037; Bruce's Handbook, 2086; Celtic stone-carving, 1442; Cornovii, 1435, 2089; Excavations, 2070; Hadrian's Wall, 2085; Hod Hill, 2059; Pelican Roman Britain, 1190, 2049A; Picts, 2090; Ptolemy, 2025; Ravenna Cosmographia, 2031; Recent archaeology, 766; Recent discoveries, 757; Roman architecture and art, 2049; Roman army, 2076; Roman Britain, 2017; Roman building, 2080; Roman Lincoln, 2061; Roman pavements, 2069; Roman villa, 2050; Tacitus, 2025
— Phyllis A.: Inns of Court, 7157
— Robert: Records of alien priory, 6078
Richmondshire, Extent, 4503
Richter, Michael: Giraldus Cambrensis, 2881; St. David's claim, 5880H
Rickard, Thomas A.: Men and metals, 2081
Rickert, Edith: Account book, 5175; Canterbury Tales, 7001; Chaucer life records, 7007; Chaucer's world, 7012
— Margaret J.: Missal, 901; Painting, 783, 858
Rickman, Lydia L.: Much Hadham, 4774
Rickword, George: Taxations, 3159
Ridevall, John (friar), 6924

Ridgeway, Sir William: Festschrift, 2591
Ridley charters, 4459
Riesenberg, Peter N.: Political theory, 1415
Riesman, David: Medicine, 2377
Riess, Ludwig: Unterhaus, 3385; Wahlrecht, 3384
Rievaulx, abbey (Yorks.), 6413
— Ailred of: Bibliotheca, 6638; Opera, 1124, 6633; Relatio de Standardo, 6634–5; St. Ninian, 2323; Saints of Hexham, 6274; Sermons, 6634, 6636; Vita Edwardi, 2171, 6634; Walter Daniel's Life of, 1113, 1490, 6639
Rigg, James M.: Jews, 3967; Plea rolls of Jews, 3482, 3518
Rigold, Stuart E.: Easterlings, 712
Rigord: Gesta Philippi, 2947
Rigsby (Lincs.), 4805
Riley, D. N.: Aerial reconnaissance, 759
— Henry T.: Amundesham's Annales, 2750; Annales Angliae, 2752; Annales Ricardi II, 2771; Annales Scotiae, 2770; Blaneford's Chronica, 2797; Chronica S. Albani, 2731; Chronicle of London, 2857; Fitz-Thedmar's Chronicles, 2870; Hoveden's Annals, 2903; Ingulf, 2163; Memorials of London, 5160; Munimenta gildhallae, 5161; Opus chronicorum, 2936; Registra S. Albani, 2980; Rishanger's Chronica, 2948; Trokelowe's Annales, 2964; Walsingham's Gesta abbatum, 6168; Walsingham's Historia and Ypodigma, 2976; Whethamstede's Registrum, 6169
RILM Abstracts, **929**
Rinel, Jean de: Le Mémoire, 4243
Ringstead, Thomas (friar), 6924
Riots, 4139, 6341
Ripoll, Tomás: Bullarium, 5981
Ripon (Yorks.), 1487, 5855, 6614–15
Rippingale (Lincs.), 4452
Risborough (Bucks.), 6097
Rishanger, William: Annales Angliae, 2752; Chronica et annales, 1114, 2948; Gesta Edwardi I, 2948
Ritchie, Nora (*née* Kenyon): Labour conditions, 1468
— Robert L. Graeme: Normans in Scotland, 4002
Ritson, Joseph: Minot's poems, 7041
River-names, 632, 640
Rivers, Maintenance of, 3497
— Lord, 4208, 4228
Rivet, Albert L. F.: Roman villa, 2050; Roman town and country, 2051
Roach, John P. C.: Cambridge, 1529, 7105
Roads, 2032, 2084, 3497, 5535

Robbins, Caroline: Album H. M. Cam, 3366
— Harry W.: St. Edmund's Merure, 6695
— Richard M.: Middlesex, 1522
— Rossell H.: Historical poems, 6992, 7046; Index of middle English verse, 6979, 7044
Robert I of Scotland, 2792
— bishop of Hereford, 2981
— dean of St. Paul's, 5759
— of Avesbury, 1103, 2790
— of Boston, 2834
— of Brunne, 2923. *See* Mannyng
— of Cricklade, 6488
— of Gloucester, 1103, 1114, 1123, 1441, 2882
— of Graystanes, 5685
— of Monte, or Torigni, 2962
— of Normandy (Curthose), 3983, 5675
— of Reading, 1499, 2871
— of Stretton, 5668
— Gaston: Les écoles, 6892
Roberts, Anne K. B.: St. George's chapel, 6068
— Charles: Calendarium Genealogicum, 528, 4338; Rotuli Finium, 3764
— Glyn: Anglesey submissions, 4219
— H. Ernest: Notes on monasteries, 808, 5898
— Peter: Monmouth's Chronicle, 2166
— Phyllis B.: Stephen Langton's Sermons, 6598
— Richard A.: Edward II, Lord Ordainers and Piers Gaveston's jewels, 4133
— Richard Arthur; Cymru fu, 4633A; Episcopal registers, 5880G; Inner Temple records, 7145; Public records, 1058
— Richard Julian: Bibliography of place-names, 625
— William W.: William Caxton, 7215
Robertsbridge abbey (Sussex), documents, 6366
Robertson, Agnes J.: A.-S. charters, 2203; Laws to Henry I, 2178, 2182, 2210
— Anne Strachan: Antonine Wall, 2087; Roman coins, 647, 664, 704, 1496; Roman excavations, 2091
— Durante W.: Handlyng Synne, 6699; Manuel des Péchés, 6694; Preaching, 6707
— Ian W.: Fides quaerens intellectum, 6531
— James C.: Materials for Becket, 6487
— M. I. E. (Mysie E. I.): trans. Petit-Dutaillis's Stubbs, 1221
— William A. Scott: Churchwardens' accounts 6838

Robillard de Beaurepaire, Charles Marie de: Les états de Normandie, 4262

Robinson, Chalfant: Memoranda roll, 3215; Pipe Roll (1230), 3080

— David: Beneficed clergy, 5877, 6856

— Fred C.: Old English Bibliography, 2360; Old English names, 588

— Fred N.: Geoffrey Chaucer, 6999

— George W.: Haskins' bibliography, 1439; St. Boniface, 2299

— Joseph Armitage: Abbot's house, 6245; Bishop Jocelin, 5592; Convocation of Canterbury, 6818; Flete's Westminster Abbey, 6233; Gilbert Crispin, 5631, 6246; Glastonbury legends, 6319; Historia minor and Historia major, 5586; Household roll, 4606, 5587; Lanfranc's constitutions, 5909; Osbert of Clare, 6239; St. Dunstan, 2283, 2293; St. Oswald, 2311; Saxon bishops of Wells, 2723; Simon Langham, 6247; Somerset calendars, 6322; Somerset essays, 1491; Westminster Chronicle, 2895; Westminster MSS., 1016, 6248

— Thomas: Gavelkind, 2644

— William C.: Mirror of justices, 2991

Robo, Etienne: Black death, 5483; Wages and prices, 5495

Robson, John A.: Wyclif and the Oxford schools, 6660

Roby (Lancs.), 5022

Rochdale (Lancs.), 4789

Roche abbey (Yorks.), 6416

Roche, Evan: Duns Scotus, 6565

Rochester (Kent), 3460, 4781

— see of, 1494, 2724, 4534, 4780, 5789–97, 6790

Rock, Daniel: Church of our fathers, 1343

Roden, David: Field systems, 4999; Inheritance customs, 4955

Roderick, Arthur J.: Welsh lordships, 4633

Roe, F. G.: Forests, 3916

Roeder, Fritz: Die Familie, 2627; Die sachsische Schalenfibel, 2518

Röhricht, Reinhold: La Croisade du prince Édouard, 4106

Roger, archbishop of York, 1487, 6492

— bishop of Worcester, 1052

— de Scaccario, 4787

— earl of Hereford, 1452

— of Hoveden, 1089, 1114, 1119, 2903

— of Norbury, 5667

— of Pontigny, 6487

— of Wendover, 1089, 1114, 2979

Roger, Maurice: Lettres classiques, 1396

Rogers, Alan: Appeals for treason, 3715; Henry IV and taxation, 3398; Hoton v. Shakell, 3503A; Lincs. county court,

3743; Parliamentary electors, 3436; Political crisis, 4213; Stamford, 5147A

— H. L.: Icelandic life of Edward, 2171

— James E. Thorold: Agriculture, 1376, 5495; Economic interpretation, 1376; Gascoigne's Dictionary, 6571; Oxford City documents, 3178, 3598, 5230; Six centuries, 1376; Wheat, 4985

— Ralph V.: Fitzherbert's Abridgement, 3654; London eyre, 3579; MSS. of year books, 3658; Northampton eyre (1329), 3589; Year book of Henry V, 3650

Rokewode. See Gage, John

Rôles gascons, 3826–8, 6739

— normands, 3829

Rolfe, John C.: Ammianus, 2025; Suetonius, 2025

Rolle, Richard, 6665, 6668, 6677–80, 6686, 6688, 6695, 6698

Rolleston, George: Barrows, 1981

Rolls Chapel, 957, 3770

— Master of, 112–13 and 135

— of arms, 619–23; 473–4, 487–500, 1467, 2950

— of obedientiaries (Worcester), 5825

— of Oleron, 5107

— Series, 135 and 389; 262, 1087; Stubbs's Introductions, 387

Roman Britain, 261–79; 1430, 1432, 1495, 1994; Army, 2045, 2075–6; Art, 2049, 2077–80; Bibliography, etc., 2013–23; Christianity, 2083, 2683; Comprehensive accounts, 2033–51; Coins, 657–67, 1084, 2072, 2111; Frontiers, 2088–94; Inscriptions, 2027–8, 2044; Literary sources, 263–6; 1084; Maps, 604–5, 1465, 2022, 2031–2; Mining, 2081; Pottery, 2045, 2069–70, 2082; Religion, 2083; Roads, 2032, 2084; Sites, 2052–84; Survivals, 618, 1434, 1454, 2069, 2095–113, 2122, 2533; Villas, 766, 2050, 2057, 2065, 2069, 2080, 2106; Walls, 2044–5, 2085–7

— Curia, 1474, 5522, 5713, 6429, 6450, 6455–7, 6714, 6729, 6750–8, 6774–83, 6919, 7074. See Papacy

— Law, 1231, 1239, 1245, 1247, 2623, 3503, 6429, 6664

— Rolls, 559, 6561

Roman de Brut, 2974

— de Rou, 2974

Romances, MSS. of, 999

Romanis, Nicolò de, legate, 1448, 6746

Romeyn, John le, archbishop, 5858, 5862

Romney (Hants), 5320, 5323

Romsey abbey (Hants), 4777, 6184

Romsley (Worcs.), 4928

Ronton priory (Staffs.), 6328

Roon-Bassermann, Elizabeth von: Florentiner Handelsgesellschaften, 5435

Roots, George: Charters, 5266

Roper, M.: Feet of fines, 3629

— William: Vita Thomae Mori, 2837

— William O.: Materials for church of Lancaster, 6201; Materials for (town of) Lancaster, 5127

Roquetaillade, John of (friar), 1474

Rose-Troup, Frances B.: Bishop Grandisson, 5715

Rosenthal, Joel T.: Elite group: bishops, 6804; Incomes and duke of York, 4634; Richard, duke of York, 6804

Rositzke, Harry: A.-S. chronicle, 2142

Roskell, John S.: Attendance of lords, 3440; Commons and speakers, 3366, 3427–8; Commons in parliament (1442), 3366, 3450; Edwards' Commons, 3370; Gesta Henrici V, 2877; Knights of shire (Lancs.), 3462; Lincs. parliamentary representation, 3463; Modus tenendi parliamentum, 3355; Office of Protector, 3306; Perspectives on parliament, 3363, 3365; Social composition, 3450; William Catesby, 4227

Ross, Book of, Annales Hiberniae, 2760

— Alan S. C.: Assize of bread, 5487; Dream of the Rood, 2328

— Anne: Pagan Celts, 2134

— Anthony: Libraries, 48

— Barbara: Accounts of cellarers, 6360

— Charles D.: Baronial incomes, 4636; Beauchamp estates, 4635, 4916; Bristol Cartulary, 6152; Cirencester Cartulary, 6153; Edward IV, 4234; Estates and finances, 4635, 4916; Fifteenth-century England, 4234; Forfeiture for treason, 3716; Income tax, 4623

— John (of Lincoln): Civitas Lincolnia, 5145

— or Rous, John (of Warwick): Historia regum, 1103, 1476, 2950

— Thomas: Architecture, 804, 819

— Thomas W.: On evil times, 7048

— Woodburn O.: Sermons, 6700

Rossendale forest (Lancs.), 3917

Rossi, Giovanni B. de: Mélanges, 6775

Rössler, Oskar: Kaiserin Mathilde, 4003

Rota, Roman, 6429, 6450

Roth, Cecil: Bibliography, 3931; Intellectual activity, 3969; Jews, 3968; Jews of Oxford, 3970; Magna Bibliotheca, 3931; Ritual murder libel, 3937

— Francis: Austin Friars, 5972

Rothley (Leics.), 4797

Rothwell (Northants.), 4832

— (Yorks.), 4930

Rothwell, Harry: Confirmation of charters, 3342; Edward I and charters, 1450; Edward I's case over Gascony, 4107; Guisborough's Chronicle, 2888

Rotuli Scotiae, 3795

Rouen, siege of, 7046

Rouen, Étienne de: Draco Normannicus, 2949

Rough, Daniel: Romney clerk, 5323

Roumare family, 1453

Round, John Horace: Ancient charters, 3749; Anglo-Norman warfare, 4004; Bannockburn, 4004; Battle of Hastings, **589**; 3990, 4009; Bibliography of his writings, 1492, 3061; Burton abbey surveys, 6326; Cade, William, 5509; Calendar of documents, 3806; Canon law, 6437; Carucage, 3261; Castle guard, 4004, 4666; Castles, 823; Charters of St. John's, Colchester, 6141; Chronology of Henry II, 3823; Clerkenwell priories, 6229; Colchester castle, 5075; Commune of London, 1484, 4004, 5176; Conquest of Ireland, 4004; Coronation of Richard I, 4004; Danegeld, 3047; Domesday (twelve counties in V.C.H.), 1529, 2636; Domesday studies, 3047, 3061, 4005; Family origins, 569, 1492, 4589; Feet of fines, **525**; Feudal England, 3035, 3061, 3067, 4005, 4677, 6265; Forest of Essex, 3905; Freeman, Edward A., **589**; 3990, 4005; Geoffrey de Mandeville, 4006; Hall, Hubert, **463**; Hidation, 2636, 3067; Hospitallers in Essex, 6047; House of Lords, 3374, 3411; Ingelric, 4004; Inquest of service, 4004, 4337; Inquest of sheriffs, 4004; Introduction of knight service, 4005; King John and Longchamp, 4004; King's serjeants, 3139; Knights of Peterborough, 3061; Lindsey survey, 3061; Leicester survey, 3061; London under Stephen, 4004; Marshalship, 4004; Normans under the Confessor, 4005; Northamptonshire geld roll, 3061; Northamptonshire survey, 3061, 3067; Origin of exchequer, 4004; Peerage and pedigree, 569, 4589; Plea roll, 3500; Pipe rolls, 3078, 3261; Red Book of exchequer, 3007; Rotuli de dominabus, 4344; Saladin tithe, 3261; Settlement of Saxons, 4004; Suitors, 3738; Testa de Nevill, 4351; Unknown charter, 3291; Winchester survey, 1529, 3072; Worcester survey, 3061, 3071

Roundhay (Yorks.), 4938

Roupell, Marion G.: Catalogue, 89

Rous, John. *See* Ross, John

Rouse, Richard H.: Serial bibliographies, 101

— William H. D.: Years work, 2018

Rowe, Benedicta J. H.: Bedford's council, 1451, 4270; Contemporary account, 2889; Estates of Normandy, 4270; Garrisons under Bedford, 4270; Norman brigands, 4270

— J. G.: Hadrian IV, 1459

— Joseph H.: Cornwall feet of fines, 3540

— Joshua B.: Cistercian houses, 6119; Devon Domesday, 3019; Plympton, 5062

— Joy: Hospitals, 6344

— Samuel: Perambulation, 3921

Rowington charities (Warw.), 4485

Rowland, Beryl: Chaucer studies, 7013

Rowse, Alfred L.: editor, 1589

Roxburgh, Ronald: Lincoln's Inn, 7155

Roxburghe Club, 194

Roy, A. E.: Record of eclipses, 6936

— William: Military antiquities, 2076

Royal Commission Reports on:
— Historical Manuscripts. *See* Historical MSS. Comm. Reports
— Historical Monuments, 737–9, 1832
— Public Records, 112; 961–8
— Public Records (Scotland), 130; 34

Royal demesne, 3244, 3269, 4660, 4688
— domain, 3132A
— families, 545, 547–9
— free chapels, 6066–8
— Historical Society, 177, 1493
— Irish Academy, 229, 236, 348, 1081
— letters, 3772, 3773, 4608, 5234
— prerogative, 3271, 3275, 3278
— Society of Antiquaries of Ireland, 237
— touch, 3271
— wills, 4513

Royce, David: Landboc, 6160

Rubicam, Milton: Genealogy, 521

Rud, Thomas: Catalogus, 1043

Rudborne, Thomas: Historia major, 1125, 2951

Rudd, Mary A.: Deeds of Chalford, 4439

Rudder, Samuel: Gloucestershire, 1653

Ruddimann, Thomas: Thesaurus, 434

Ruddock, Alwyn A.: Accounts of J. Balsall, 5325; Alien merchants, 5440; Italian merchants, 5110, 5436; Port books, 5109

Ruding, Rogers: Coinage, 699

Rudisill, George, Jr.: Taxation, 3366

Rudston (Yorks.), Roman, 2069

Ruehl, Franz: Eutropius, 2025

Ruffer, Veronica: ed., Graham essays, 1437

Rufford abbey (Notts.), 6279

Rufus, Geoffrey, bishop, 5677

Rule of St. Benedict, 317; 441, 2271, 2274–5, 5911
— of law, 1461

Rule, John C.: Bibliography, 30; 246

— Martin: Eadmeri Historia novorum, 2863, 6529

Runciman, Sir Steven: Crusades, 4029

Runcorn abbey (Ches.), 6104

Rundstedt, Hans G. von: Hansisches Urkundenbuch, 5336

Runes, 44–5; 2353, 7225

Rural deans, 6832

Rushforth, Gordon McN.: Inscriptions, 2028

Russell, Archibald G. B.: Rous's Latin roll, 2950

— Ephraim: Bardi and Peruzzi, 1469

— Henry G.: Lollard opposition to oaths, 6872

— John, bishop: Speeches, 3768

— Josiah C.: Alexander Neckham, 6609; British population (and articles), 1377, 5481; Canonization of opposition, 1439; Charter lists, 3842; Clerical population, 5899; Dictionary of writers, 541, 6909; Grosseteste, 6583; Hereford and Arabic science, 6961; Migration to London, 5167, 5481; Parliamentary organization, 3386; Ranulf de Glanville, 2858, 2989; Richard of Bardney, 6583; Tribal hidage, 2213

— Percy: Leicester Forest, 3906

— Peter E.: Intervention in Spain, 4189

Ruston, Arthur G.: Hooton Pagnell, 4942

Rutherwyk, John de, abbot, 6351

Ruthwell Cross (Dumfries), 44, 353, 360, 2471

Rutland, Duke of, MSS., 4693

Rutlandshire, 1529, 1794–5

Rutupina, 1090

Ruyton (Salop), 4863

Ryan, J. Joseph: Congress of Canon Law, 1313

— John: Brian Borumba, 2605; Cain Adamnáin, 2244, 2251; Early church, 1438; Irish monasticism, 1302A, 2676; St. Patrick, 2324

— John K.: John Duns Scotus, 6565

— Sister Mary B.: John of Salisbury, 6642

Rydeware Chartulary, 4478

Rydeware, Thomas de, 4478

Rye (Sussex), 5318, 5320

— Reginald A.: Catalogue, 1015; London libraries, 1006

— Walter: Abduction of Norwich boy, 3954; Cambridge feet of fines, 3535;

Carrow abbey, 6254; Crime in Norfolk, 3587; De Banco rolls, 3583; Gild certificates, 5213; History of Norfolk, 1758; L'Estrange's Calendar, 5206; Norfolk Antiquarian Miscellany, 1753; Norfolk antiquities, 1750; Norfolk feet of fines, 3585; Norfolk records, 1750, 1752, 4372; North Erpingham, 3586; Norwich deeds, 5211; Records and record searching, 522, 969; Suffolk feet of fines, 3612

Ryland, John W.: Records of Rowington, 4485; Records of Wroxall, 6371

Rylands, John P.: Lancs. subsidy roll, 3167

Ryley, William: Placita, 3324

Rymer, Thomas: Foedera, 3765

Rynne, Étienne: ed. North Munster Studies, 679

Sabatier, Paul: St. Francis, 6024

Sabbe, Étienne: Les relations économiques, 2595

Sabin, Arthur: Compotus rolls, 6151; Manorial accounts, 6150

Sabine, George H.: Political theory, 1415

Sacra Romana Rota, 6429, 6450

Sacrabar, 3733

Sacrist's rolls, 5611, 5705

Saddlers company, 5200

Sadius and Galo, 6599

Saenger, Erwin: Catalogue, 89

Saffron Walden (Essex), 6838

Saga Book of Viking Society, 220, 2466

Sagas, Icelandic and Norse, 351–7

Sage, Carleton M.: St. Ailred MSS., 6638

Sagher, Henri E. de: L'immigration des tisserands, 1446, 5420

Sagnac, Philippe: Histoire générale, 1191

St. Albans, abbey, Book of, 1474
— Chroniclers of, 388; 1108, 1448, 2728, 2731, 2750, 2770, 2797, 2871, 2941, 2948, 2964, 2975–6, 2979–80, 6168–9
— History, 171, 1480, 1675, 6170–1, 7180, 7224
— Library, 7180
— Psalter, 902
— Alexander of, 1448
— battle of, 2746, 4194
— Roman, 2067, 2070

St. Andrews, 2688

St. Anthony's Hall (York), 5872

St. Asaph, see of, 5879D, 5880C–D, 6781, 6790

St. Augustine's abbey, Bristol, 6151

St. Augustine's abbey, Canterbury. *See* Canterbury, religious houses

St. Bees, priory (Cumb.), 6112

St. Benet of Hulme, abbey (Norfolk), 2816, 2939, 6258–9, 6341

St. Calais, William of, 2157e, 5675

St. Catherine's Hill, Winchester, 1995

St. David's, see of, 792; 1114, 2144, 2665, 5879D, 6573, 6790

St. Edmund's abbey. *See* Bury St. Edmunds

St. Frideswide, priory (Oxon.), 6295

St. George, James of, Master-builder, 823

St. Giles, Durham, 6133

St. Ives (Hunts.), 4774–5, 5524, 5538

St. John the Baptist, hospital (Oxford), 6296

St. Joseph, John K., Air photography, 89; 752, 755–6, 758–60, 766, 1432, 2091

St. Julian hospital (Herts.), 6168

St. Martin-le-Grand (London), 6067

St. Mary Bourne (Hants), 4768

St. Mary de Parco Stanley. *See* Dale abbey

St. Mary des Prés, priory (Herts.), 1480

St. Mary Magdalen, hospital (Durham), 6133

St. Mary Magdalene, Bridgnorth, college (Salop), 6299

St. Michael's Mount, priory (Cornw.), 6108

St. Neot's, priory (Hunts.), 1100, 2147, 2152, 6172

St. Ninian's Isle, 2482

St. Oswald's priory (Glos.), 5874, 6162

St. Osyth's abbey (Essex), 6145

St. Peter at Bath, priory (Som.), 1482, 6305

St. Peter at Sele, priory (Sussex), 6367

St. Peter of Gloucester, abbey (Glos.), 2123, 6156–7

St. Peter's priory (Ipswich), 6348

St. Radegund priory (Cambs.), 6101

St. Werburgh's abbey (Chester), 5045, 6105

St. Wulstan's, Worcester, 6386

Saint, Lawrence B.: Stained glass, 861

Saint-Allais, Nicolas V. de: L'art de vérifier, 364

Saint-Denis, Chroniques de, 2883
— Religeux, 2843, 2847

Saint-Florent près Saumur, 6252

Saint-Maure, Benoît de, 1112, 2952

Saint-Riquier, 5919

Saint-Sardos, wars of, 3810

Saints, Acta sanctorum, 148–51; Anglo-Saxon, 319–33; Book of, 366; Calendar, 1172; Celtic, 333–9

Sainty, J. C.: Introduction of peers, 3388; Tenure of offices, 3262

Saladin tithe, 3233, 3261, 6779

Salcey forest, 3896

Salesby (Lincs.), 4805

Salford (Lancs.), charters, 4791

Salin, Bernhard, Thierornamentik, 2519
Salisbury (Wilts.):
— city of, 1386, 1861, 4490, 5282–5, 5799
— diocese of, 1051, 1343, 1861, 4924, 5749, 5798–809, 6790
— Pontifical of, 1433
— St. Edmund and St. Thomas, church, 5282, 6838
— St. Nicholas' hospital, 6378
Salisbury, Frederick S.: Notitia Dignitatum, 2030; Richborough coins, 2109
— John of, **872–3**; 1102, 1113, 1114, 1487, 6487
Sallay, or Sawley, abbey (Yorks.), 6417
Salmon, John, bishop, 5783
Salmond, John W.: Contract, 1246; Jurisprudence, 1244
Salt trade, 5376
Salt, Edward: Standon, 4878
— Mary C. L.: Embassies, 3818, 4108
— (William): Archaeological Society (Staffs.), 1814
Salter, Emma Gurney: Coming of friars, 6008
— Elizabeth: Piers Plowman, 7029
— F. R.: The Hansa, 5344
— Herbert E.: Augustinian chapters, 5952; Balliol College deeds, 4465, 7073; Borstall cartulary, 4416, 4461; Cambridge University, 7102; Charters at Oxford, 4405; Charters of Henry II, 5744; Essays to, 1451; Eynsham cartulary, 6289; Feet of fines, 3597; Formularies on Oxford, 427, 7063; Geoffrey of Monmouth, 2166; Munimenta civitatis, 5229; Newington Longeville, 4464, (6094A); Oriel College records, 7081–2, Oseney annals, 6294; Oseney cartulary, 6292; Oxford, city of, 450, 1455, 5229, 5237–8, 7128–9; Oxford, cartulary of hospital of St. John, 6296; Oxford, university of, 1448, 7064, 7067, 7120, 7125, 7130; Registrum Cancellarii Oxon., 7067; Registrum Mertonensis, 7079; St. Augustine's, Canterbury, register, 6182; Snappe's formulary, 429, 7069; Stamford schism, 7061; Thame cartulary, 6298; William of Newburgh, 2932
Saltman, Avrom: Becket correspondence, 6493; Dale cartulary, 6115; Theobald, archbishop of Canterbury, 5641, 6501; Tutbury cartulary, 6334
Saltmarsh, John: King's College estates, 7106; Plague, 5469; Receiver-general, 7106
Salusbury (Jones), Goronwy T.: Street life, 5357

Salway, Peter: ed. Richmond papers, 2049; Roman frontier, 2085, 2092
Salzman, Louis F.: Arundel property, 4597; Building, 809; Chartulary of St. Pancras, 6363; Chartulary of Sele, 6367; Churchwardens' accounts, 6838; Edward I, 4064; English life, 5465; English industries, 5518; English trade, 5396; Feet of fines, 3614; Henry II, 4040; Hides and virgates, 3031; Hundred roll, 4390; Ministers' accounts, 4903; Status of markets, 5534; Taxation in Sussex, 3195; V.C.H., 1197, 1529
Samaran, Charles: Bibliographie, 42; Charles VI, 2847; Charles VII, 2793; Chartier, 2813; L'histoire, 265
Samian ware, 2037
Samson, abbot, 2305, 6335, 6338
— bishop of Worcester, 2200, 3053, 5844
Samuels, M. L.: Prolegomena, 347
San Marte, Albert Schulz: Geoffrey of Monmouth, 2166
Sanctuary, **163–4**; 5693, 6067, 6395
Sandale, John de, bishop: Register, 5816
Sanders, George W.: Court of Chancery, 3847
— Ivor J.: English baronies, 570, 4678; Feudal military service, 4317; Peace of Paris, 3831, 4098
— William B.: Domesday Book, 448; Facsimiles, 448
Sanderson, Robert: Foedera, 3765
Sandford House (Templar) (Oxon.), 6057, 6297
Sandquist, T. A.: Becket, 1459
Sands, Donald B.: Bibliography, 273
Sandwich (Kent), 5312, 5320
Sandys, Agnes: London Temple, 1458
— Charles: Gavelkind, 1378, 2644
— Sir John E.: Classical scholarship, 1397
Sanford, Eva M.: Twelfth-century renaissance, 6887
Santifaller, Leo: Der Censimento, **751**; Geschichte der Beschriebstoffe, 406
Sapiti, Andreas, proctor, 6756
Sapori, Armando: Italian companies, 5437; La crisi delle compagnie, 5437; Studi, 5430, 5461
Sargeant, Frank: Wine trade, 1469, 5395
Sargent, Helen Child: Ballads, 7045
Sarton, George, **179**; Introduction, 1420
Sarum Missal, 1321; Ordinale, 1321
Sarum, Roger of, bishop, 5596
Satire on friars, 7049
Saunders, Herbert W.: Bailiff's roll, 4881; Cambridgeshire villages, 4722; Norwich cathedral records, 5778–9
— J. J.: Matthew Paris, 1459

— O. Elfrida: Art, 852; Illumination, 879

Sautre, John de: Letter-book, 2151

Sauvage, Eugene P. M.: St. Swithun, 2312

Savage, Ernest A.: Old libraries, 7176

— Henry E.: Lichfield register, 5666; Shenstone charters, 4479

— Sir William: Towns, **178**

Savigny, congregation of, 5918

Savile, Henry: Scriptores, 1119

Savine, Alexander, 4971; Copyhold cases, 4979; Wat Tyler, 4154

Savory, Hubert N.: Brooches, 1442; Wales, 1435

Savoy, Boniface of, archbishop, 5628

Savoyards, 5737

Sawyer, Frederick E.: Topographica Sussexiana, 1835

— Peter H.: A.-S. charters, 2219; Bibliography, 54; Danish settlement, 2599; Domesday Book, 3062; Evesham Domesday, 3035; Textus Roffensis, 441, 5794; Vikings, 2596; Wealth, 5466

Saxl, Fritz: British art, 810; Catalogue, 983; Essays, 1452; Parchment, 408; Ruthwell Cross, 353; Sculpture, 853

Saxo Grammaticus: Gesta Danorum, 2426

Saxon shore, 2113

Saxons, settlement of, 4004. *See* Anglo-Saxons

Sayers, Jane E.: Archbishop's archives, 5621; Archbishop's feudal right, 5619; Canterbury proctors, 6457; Estate documents, 4637, 4696; General chapters, 6480; Judge delegate formulary, 6480; Lambeth documents, 1008, 4637, 4696, 5550; Papal documents, 112, 1009, 5550; Papal judges delegate, 6481; St. Albans' privileges, 7224

Sayle, Charles: Cambridge University Library, 1031

— Robert T. D.: Charters of merchant taylors, 5195

Sayles, George O.: **589**; Administration of Ireland, 3846; Clergy in parliament, 3479; Coronation, 1357; Dissolution of a gild, 5305; Earl of Desmond, 1438; Early statutes, 3341; English company, 5397; Fleta, 2987; Governance, 1218; Interdict, 6729; Irish administration, 3846; Irish parliament, 3309, 3354, 3366, 3392; Irish revenue, 3260; Judges as consultants, 3692; King's Bench, 3510; King's ministers, 3426; Law and legislation, 1219; Medieval foundations, 1220, 2502; Parliament and Council in Ireland, 3392; Parliament and Great Councils, 3383; Parliament of Carlisle,

3320, 3412; Parliament, records, 3320; Parliament of Lincoln, 3413; Parliamentary documents, 3320; Procedure without writ, 3513; Provisions of Oxford, 4063; Representation, 3451; Richard II, 4135; Rotuli Parliamentorum, 3323; Seizure of wool, 3342; Statute of Gloucester, 3335; Stubbs, 1221; Traitors (1322), 4134; Wardrobe bills, 3140

Sbaralea, Joannes H.: Bullarium, 6004; Wadding's Scriptores, 6012

Scabini, 1462

Scaccario, Roger de: Rent roll, 4787

Scale of Perfection, 6672

Scales, Lord, 4282

Scammell, Geoffrey V.: Hugh du Puiset, bishop of Durham, 5700; Merchant shipping, 5398; Shipowning, 5399

— Jean: Aspects of monastic government, 5701; Origins and limitations, 1626, 3868; Robert I and north, 4077; Rural chapter, 6859

Scandinavia, 362, 2149

Scandinavian language, 7225

— literature, **351–7**

— personal names, 2602

— settlement, **368–72**; 1465, 1496, 7225. *See* Danes *and* Vikings

Scandinavica (journal), 2435

Scarborough fishing fleet, 5508

Scardeburgh, John of: Anonimalle Chronicle, 2787

Scargill-Bird, Samuel R. *See* Bird

Scarisbrick (Lancs.), 4441

Scarrington (Notts.), 4842

Scattergood, Bernard P.: Feet of fines, 3554

— V. J.: Politics and poetry, **914**

Schaarschmidt, Carl: Johannes Sarisberiensis, 6646

Schaefer, Dietrich: Die Hanse, 5438–9

Schalby, John de, Book of, 5752

Schanz, Georg von: Handelspolitik, 5400

Schechter, Frank I.: Rightlessness of Jewry, 3971

Schenkl, Heinrich: Bibliotheca, 984

Schiaparelli, Luigi: Abbreviature, 407

Schieffer, Theodor: St. Boniface, 2299

Schiller, A. A.: Bracton, **455**; 2985

Schipper, Jacob: Beda's Kirchengeschichte, 2148

Schirmer, Walter F.: Der Frühhumanismus, 6923; Lydgate, 7036

Schism, the Great, 5572, 6738, 6740

— of 1159, 6809

Schlauch, Margaret: Medieval Narrative, 2446

Schleiffer, Hedwig: Index to Festschriften, 1425

Schlight, John: Monarchs and mercenaries, 4304
Schmale, Franz-Joseph: ed. Wattenbach's Geschichtsquellen, 66
Schmeidler, Bernhard: Adam of Bremen, 2149
Schmid, Reinhold: Die Gesetze, 2179
Schmidt, Charles: Petit supplément, 305
Schmitt, Franciscus S.: S. Anselm, 6526, 6528, 6532
Schmitz, Hermann J.: Penitentials, 2260
Schmitz-Kallenberg, Ludwig: Eubel's Hierarchia, 6711
Schnetz, Joseph: Cosmographia, 2031
Schneyer, Johannes B.: Wegweiser zu Predigtreihen, 6709; Repertorium, 6709
Schnürer, Gustav: Kirche und Kultur, 1288
Schoeck, Richard J.: Canon law, 6437; Law French, 37; Rhetoric, 6929; Roxburgh's Lincoln's Inn, 7155; Vising, 298
Schoenstadt, Friedrich: König Sigismund, 4257
Schofield, A. N. E. D.: English delegation, 5573
— B.: Wreck rolls, 1441
— Bertram: Muchelney memoranda, 6322
— Roger S.: Distribution of wealth, 4638, 5496
Scholars, 134; 319–33; 858–75
Scholes, Percy A.: Music, 7208
Scholle, Wilhelm: Minot's poems, 7041
Scholz, Bernhard W.: Canonization, 6634; Forged charters, 6240; St. Bregwine, 2300; Sulcard's Prologus, 6241
— Richard: Breviloquium, 6614
Schools, 924–5; 7127, 7135–43
Schopp, Jacob W.: Anglo-Norman custumal, 5055
Schottus, Andreas: Antonine Iter, 2029
Schram, O. K., 1429
Schramm, Percy E.: Coronation, 1358
Schreiner, J.: Wages and prices, 5495
Schröer, Arnold: Benedictinerregel, 2275
Schubert, Hans (John) R.: Iron and steel industry, 5519
Schulz, Friedrich: Die Hanse, 5439
— Fritz: Bracton, 2985, 3277
— Herbert C.: Piers Plowman, 7023
Schuster, Mauriz: Tacitus, 2505
Schutte, Gudmund: Gothonic nations,
Schütt, Marie: Asser's Vita Alfredi, 2147, 2520
Schuyler, Robert L.: Adams's history, 1210; Making of English history, 1221, 3364; Maitland, 1482; Richardson and Sayles, 1218

Schwabe, Randolph: Costume, 919
Schwartz, Jacques: Historia Augusta, 2025
Schwarz, Ernst: Stammeskunde, 2521
Schwerin, Claudius Freiherrn von: Rechtsgeschichte, 2507
Science, 179; 903–7; 985, 1418–24, 1485, 2297, 6577–9, 6585
Scilly Isles: Archaeology, 762; Survey of, 1590
Scoble, Andrew R.: Memoirs of Commines, 2851
Scofield, Cora L.: Edward IV, 4228
Scokirk, cell of Nostell, 6411
Scotichronicon, 2872
Scotland: 1178;
— Antiquities, 731, 733, 739, 761, 776, 1973, 1992, 2001, 2009, 2482
— Architecture and art, 804, 819, 828–9, 834
— Archives, 130–1
— Bibliographies, 11–13, 20, 25–7, 34, 68, 139
— Castles, 823, 828–9, 834
— Celtic, 1120, 2114, 2116, 2118, 2126, 2135, 2137, 2488
— Chronicles, 1088A, 1088B, 1103A, 1114, 1120, 2157, 2170, 2752, 2770, 2792, 2806, 2821, 2824, 2867, 2872, 2884, 2890, 2894, 2913, 2916, 2984
— Church history, 1129, 1142, 2319, 2322–3, 2671, 2685–91, 5549, 5554
— Clans, 506
— Coinage, 674, 702
— Genealogy, 506, 509–10, 525, 536, 545, 556, 568
— Geography, 72; 597, 599, 600, 604
— Heraldry, 479, 490, 536
— Journals and societies, 23; 34, 127, 139, 151, 205–20, 731
— Language, 331–6, 355, 2544
— Legal history, 219, 2989
— Manuscripts, 34, 434, 448
— Names, 576, 582
— Normans in, 4002
— Norse in, 2566
— Place-names, 627, 641–3
— Records, 566–7; 25, 212, 335, 955, 1059, 1061, 1504, 3750, 3770, 3781, 3812A
— Regesta regum, 3794, 4088
— Relations with England, 566–7; 599–601; 1120, 1774, 4131, 4173, 4197, 4230, 4274, 4279, 4285, 4293–4, 4646, 4671
— Roman, 2020, 2084, 2087–8, 2090, 2094
— Seals, 455, 467
Scott, Archibald B.: Scotland's Church, 2690
— Edward J. L.: Sloane MSS., 1000
— family (Kent), 4590

— Franklin: Guide to A.H.R., 144
— James R.: Charters of Monks Horton, 6195; Receipts and expenditures, 4613; Scott family, 4590
— John: Finances, 4613
— Richard: Agriculture, 5015
Scott-Giles, Charles Wilfrid: Civic heraldry, 498; Heraldry, 471; Romance of heraldry, 482
Scotus, Duns, 6910
— Marianus: Chronicle, 2981
Screverton (Notts.), 4842
Scriptores latini Hiberniae, 224
— praedicatorum, 5985
— regis, 437, 3751
Scriptorium (journal), 381
Scripture, four senses of, 6597
Scriptures, Bede's commentaries on, 2297
Scriveners' company, 5201
Scroggs, Edith S.: Shrewsbury MSS., 4756
Scrope, George P.: Castle Combe, 4922
— Sir Geoffrey le, 3504, 3693
— Sir Richard: Grosvenor controversy, 3503A, 7007
— Richard, archbishop, 1130, 4213, 5878
Scrutton, Thomas E.: Commons and common fields, 5016; Roman law, 1245
Scudder, Vida D.: Bede, 2148
Sculpture, **98–101**; 1449, 2478
Scutage, **627**; 1601, 3007, 3143, 3168, 3290, 3753, 4292, 4645
Sea, law of, 4280
Seaby, Peter: Coinage, 700
— Wilfred: Coinage, 704
Seafarer, the, 1429, 2328
Seals, **57–9**; 422, 488, 742, 1440, 1487, 3838; Great, 458, 469, 3844; Privy, 417, 1223, 3838, 3872
Searle, Eleanor: Battle Abbey, 3490, 6358; Cellarers' accounts, 6360
— William G.: A.-S. bishops, 375, 2597; Grace Book, 7058; Ingulf, 2163; Onomasticon, 589; Queens' College, 7107; Stone's Chronicle, 2957
Seaver, E. I.: Viking figures, 1449
Sechnall, St. See Secundinus, St.
Secretary, king's, 1458. See Seals, Privy
Sectional lists (H.M.S.O.), No. 17: 945; No. 24: 950
Secular colleges, **809–10**
Secundinus, St., 2324
Sede vacante registers, 5624, 5668, 5710, 5756, 5839, 5862
Seebass, Otto: St. Columban, 2320
Seebohm, Frederic: A.-S. Tribal custom, 2647; Customary acres, 2645; Stenton on, 1496; Tribal system (Wales), 2647; Village community, 2646, 4971

— Mabel E.: English farm, 1379
Seeck, Otto: Notitia Dignitatum, 2030
Segrave, honour of, Chartulary, 1714
— Gilbert, bishop, 5763
Segre, Robert de: Accounts, 4102
Seignobos, Charles, 263
Seignorial courts. See Courts, manorial
Seisdon (Staffs.), 4385
Seisin, 1246, 1482, 3703, 4681
Selborne priory (Hants), 6165
Selby abbey (Yorks.), 6418–20
— Walford D.: Index locorum, 3583; Lancs. and Ches. records, 3877; Norfolk records, 1752, 4372
Selden, John: Dissertatio, 2987; Eadmer's Historia novorum, 2863; Intestates' goods, 6443; Testaments, 6443; Tithes, 6857; Titles of honour, 571; Works of, 6857
Selden Society, 195
Sele, St. Peter priory (Sussex), 6367
Select Essays in Anglo-American Legal History, 1246
Self-government, manorial, 4922
Sellar, A. M.: trans. Bede, 2148
Sellers, Maud: Woollens and worsteds, 5413; York Memorandum Book, 5311; York mercers, 5310
Selmer, Carl: St. Brendan's Navigatio, 2318
Semple, William H.: Letters of Innocent III, 5559
Sempringham, Gilbert of, St., 5956, 5958–9
— priory of (Leics.), 6220
Senat, annals of, 2786
Senatus, prior of Worcester: Life of Oswald, 2311
Senchas Már, 2240–1
Senchus Fer nAlban, 2116
Senechauncy, Treatise, 4631
Senior, William: Roman law, 1245
Sephton, John: Saga, 2450
Seppelt, Francis X: Geschichte der Päpste, 6721
Serfdom, **691–6**; Decline of, 4959, 4961
Serjeants, king's, 3139
Serjeantson, Mary S.: Lapidaries, 868, 6948; Loan words, **34**
— Robert M.: Court rolls, 4829
Serjeanty tenure, 4663
Sermo Epinicius, 6557
Sermo Lupi ad Anglos, 1106, 2328
Sermons, **877–80**; 6024, 6568, 6570, 6598, 6634, 6636, 6650, 6733, 6751. See Homilies
Serrure, Raymond: Traité de numismatique, 680

Servat, Wilhelm, alien merchant, 5423
Service books, **170-3**; 5749
Services, labour, 2212, 4803, 4977
Servitia (papal), 6779
Sessions of peace. *See* Justices of peace
Seton, George: Heraldry, 479
— Henry W.: Equity, 3483
Setterwall, Nils Kristian: Bibliografi, 65
Setton, Kenneth M.: Crusades, 4029; Norman Conquest, 4276
Sevenhampton (Wilts.), 4917
Severs, Jonathan Burke: Wells' Manual, 275
Seward, John, 6915
Sewell, Richard C.: Gesta Stephani, 2880
— William H., Jr.: Marc Bloch, 252
Sewers, maintenance of, 3497
Seyer, Samuel: Bristol charters, 5080
Sforza, Galeazzo Maria, 4208
Shadwell, Charles L.: Oriel College Muniments, 7068; Provosts, 7126; Records, 7082
— Lionel L.: Enactments concerning Oxford and Cambridge, 7051
Shafer, Boyd C.: Collingwood's Idea, 240; Historical study, 261
Shaftesbury (Dorset), 4737, 5066
— abbey, 6130
Shakell, Hoton *v.* Shakell, 3503A
Shanks, Elsie: Anglo-Norman, **37**; Novae Narrationes, 2998
Shareshull, Sir William (justice), 3691
Sharp, Dorothea: Franciscan philosophy, 6033, 6910
— Margaret: Black Prince, 1223, 1458, 3862
Sharpe, John: Monumenta, 1084; Malmesbury's History of kings, 2921
— Reginald R.: Coroners' rolls, 3577, 5151; Letters, from mayor, 5155; London, 1745; London letterbooks, 5154; Wills, 4544
Shavington (Salop), 4467
Shaw, Francis: Hanson's St. Patrick, 2324
— Henry: Dresses, 926
— I. P.: Giraldus Cambrensis, 5880H
— Martin: Oxford book of carols, 7207
— Peter: Black Prince, 4118
— Ronald Cunliffe: Lancaster forest, 3922
— Stebbing: Staffordshire, 1816, 4386
— William A.: Knights, 572
Shearman, Philip: Fitznell's Cartulary, 4481
Shears, Frederick S.: Froissart, 2874
Sheehan, Michael M.: Canon law, 6444; Ius matrimoniale, 6483; The will, 4509
Sheehy, Maurice: Collectio Hibernensis, 2261; Laudabiliter, 5556; Pontificia Hibernica, 1137

Sheep farming, 3145, 4993, 5002, 5008, 5453
Sheffield (Yorks.), 5298
Shelby, Lon Royce: Master-mason, 800
Sheldon, Gilbert: Transition, 2110
Shenstone Charters, 4479
Shepard, Max A.: Fortescue, 1444
Sheppard, Joseph B.: Christ Church Letters, 5601; Literae Cantuarienses, 5607; Materials for Becket, 6487
— Lancelot C.: The Carmelites, 5979
Sherborne, bishop of, 2147, 2296
— (Dorset), 1470, 2717, 5066, 6309
— Chartulary, 1452, 6131
— House (Glos.), 4436
— manor of (Glos.), 4762, 6160
Sherborne, James W.: Battle of La Rochelle, 4190; Bristol, 5089; Indentured retinues, 4318; Navy, 4190
Sherburn hospital (Durham), 6139
Sheriffs, 955, 1462, 2619, 2789, 3254, 3395, 3452, 3608, 3740, 3746A, 4004; Accounts of, 3221, 3240, 3248, 3266, 3854
Sherington (Bucks.), 4711
Sherley-Price, Leo: Bede, 2148; Franciscans, 6008; Scale of Perfection, 6672
Sherman, Charles P.: Canon law, 6437
Sherwell, John W.: Guild of saddlers, 5200
Sherwood forest, 3886, 3896
Sherwood, George F. T.: Berkshire wills, 4521
— L.: Cartulary of Leeds Priory, 6193
Shetelig, Haakon: Archaeology, 2484; Viking antiquities, 2483
Shillingford, John: Letters, 5057
Shilson, J. W.: Weighing wool, 5497
Shilton, Dorothy O.: Wells City Charters, 5248
Shipp, William: Hutchins' Dorset, 1620
Ships and shipping, 1485, 4190, 4290, 4333-6, 5325, 5378, 5398-9, 5510; Accounts, 5325
Shire, 555-7; 1237, 1462, 1499, 2638; Court, 2189, 3636, 3738; House, 1441
Shirley family, 4591
Shirley, Evelyn P.: Noble and gentlemen, 573; Stemmata Shirleiana, 4591
— Janet: Parisian journal, 2907
— Walter W.: Catalogue, 6648; Netter's Fasciculi, 6612; Royal letters, 3782
Shirley-Fox, John: Numismatic, 709
Shirwood, John, bishop, 7160
Short-title catalogue, 71, 7220
Shotwick (Ches.), manor, 4725
Shrewsbury (Salop), borough, 3179, 3181, 3438, 5027, 5240-3
— St. Peter's abbey, 6301

— earls of, 4586
— (Talbot) MSS., 4756
Shrewsbury, John F. D.: Bubonic plagues, 5482
— Ralph of, bishop, 4606, 5587, 5589
Shropshire: Charters, 2201, 4466–7; Church, **832**; 6299–302; County history, 1529, 1796, 1800–1; County journals and societies, 1797–9; Deeds, 4466–7, 4864; Domesday, 1529, 1800; Extents, 4858, 4860; Feet of fines, 3604; Feudal tenures, 4377–8; Inquests, 4377; Justices of peace, 3605; Manors and villages, 4858–64; Pleas, 3603; Sheriffs, coroners, etc., 3602; Subsidy rolls, 3180–1; Taxation, 3179; Urban history, 5239–45; Wills, 4551
Shuttleworth deeds (Lancs.), 4446
Shyrack (Yorks.), 3206
Sibton Abbey (Suffolk), 1453, 6349
Sidgwick, Henry: Maitland's lecture, 1482
Sieges, 2157f, 2877, 2940, 4295, 4320, 7046
Sigebert of Gembloux: Chronicle, 2962
Sigismund, king, 4165, 4257
Signet office, 3138, 3845
Sigurðsson, John: Saga of St. Edward, 2171
Sikes, Jeffrey G.: Ockham's Opera, 6617
Silchester (Roman), 2066
Silgrave, Henry de: Chronicon, 2953
Sillem, Rosamond: Commissions of the Peace, 3495; J.P.s Lincs., 3574
Silver mines, 5514
Silverstein, Theodore: Daniel Morley, 6961
Silvius, William: Newburgh's Historia, 2932
Simeon of Durham, **291–2**; 1084, 1114, 1123–4, 2168
Simeonis Symonis Itinerarium, 2982
Simmons, Thomas F.: Lay Folk's Catechism, 6691
Simms, Rupert: Bibliotheca, 1812
Simon, André L.: Wine trade, 5395
— James: Irish coins, 701
Simon de Eye (abbot of Eye): Letters, 2151
— of Faversham, 1443, 1490
— of Hinton, 1450
— of Montfort. *See* Montfort
— of Whitechurch, abbot of Chester, 2753
Simonburne parish (Northumb.), 1775, 4839
Simpson, Alfred W. B.: Inns of Court, 7156; Land law, 3678; Year-books, 3656
— Frank G.: Hadrian's wall, 2085
— Grace: Roman army, 2093
— Grant: Scottish archives, **130**
— H. B.: Constable, 3744

— William Douglas: Castles, 838; St. Ninian, 2323; Scotland, 2689
— William J. Sparrow: St. Paul's cathedral, 5758, 5765–7, 5773
Sims, Catherine S.: Elsynge's Expedicio, 3313; Unpublished fragment of Madox, 3250
— John M.: London records, 5148
— Richard: Calendar of deeds, 5255; Manual, 523
Sinclair, Keith Val: Anglo-Norman, **37**
— Thomas A.: Later Latin Literature, 1404, 6898
Singer, Charles: Byrhtferd, 2366; History of medicine, 6963; Magic, 2367; Magic and medicine, 6962; Magic to science, 2378; Technology, 408
— Dorothea Waley: Alchemical MSS., 985, 6965; Byrhtferd, 2366; Plague texts, 6964
Singleton, Charles S.: Trends in science, 6941
Sisam, Kenneth: Aelfric, 2292; Æthelred's laws, **301**; Æthelweard, 2140; A.-S. royal genealogies, 547, 2161; Beowulf, 2335; Bishop's Liturgica, 1325; Cynewulf, 2343; Old English literature, 2361
Sitwell, George R.: Barons of Pulford, 4592
— Gerard: The Scale of Perfection, 6672
Siward, Richard, Appeal of, 3636
Sixle (Sixhills) (Lincs.), 5957, 6216
Sjörgren, Paul: Skrifter, 65
Skaare, Kolbjørn: Coinage, 646, 1454
Skaife, Robert H.: Domesday Book, 3036; Kirkby's Inquest (Yorks.), 4396; Register of guild, 5307
Skeat, Theodore C.: Catalogues, 991
— Walter W.: Ælfric's Lives of Saints, 2292; Dictionary, 286; Etymology, **37**; Piers the Plowman, 7021; Plowman's Crede, 7049; The Bruce, 2792; Works of Chaucer, 7000
Skeel, Caroline A. J.: Fortescue, 2938; Wills, 4510
Skene, William F.: Adamnan's Vita S. Columbae, 2319; Celtic Scotland, 2135; Chronicles of Picts, 1120, 3796; Flann, 2160; Fordun's Chronica, 2872; Four Books, 2381; Memoir of, 2135
Skenfrith (Wales), 4633
Skillington, Stephen H.: Cossington, 5134
Skinners of London, 5202, 5405
Skipp, Victor: Local history, 1508
Skipton, honour of, 4499
Skyrack (Yorks.), 3206
Slack, W. J.: Condover extents, 4858; Lordship of Oswestry, 4864

Slade, Cecil F.: Leicestershire survey, 3074; Staffs. Domesday, 1529; Whitley deeds, 1453

Slatter, M. Doreen: Court of Arches, 6484

Sleaford (Lincs.), 4811

Slicher van Bath, Bernard H.: Agrarian history, 1380, 5017; Yield ratios, 5017

Slingsby, F. H.: Feet of fines, 3629

Slover, Clark H.: William of Malmesbury, 6309

Šmahel, František: Wyclif, 6661

Smail, Raymond C.: Art of war, 1485; Crusading warfare, 4319

Small, Alan: ed. Viking Congress, 2581, 2708

— L. M.: Gunnlaugs Saga, 2446

Smalley, Beryl: Dominican school at Oxford, 6908; English friars and antiquity, 6035, 6924; Europe, ed., 4173; Exempla, 6597, 6709A; Hebrew scholarship, 3969; Langton and four senses, 6597; Langton's Commentaries, 6596; Ralph Niger, 2933; Robert Holcot, 6591; Simon of Hinton, 1450; Study of Bible, 1344, 6895; Wyclif, 1428

Smedt, Charles de: Acta Sanctorum, 1170; Analecta, 1153; Introductio, 148

Smet, Joseph J. de: Chronica Flandriae, 2848

Smetana, Cyril L.: Ælfric, 2292

Smettisham treasure, 766

Smirke, Edward: Custumal of Bleadon, 4873; Documents on silver mines, 5514; Oliver's Exeter, 5059; Ordinances of gild merchant, 5098

Smit, Homme J.: Bronnen, 5345

Smith, Albert H.: Heimskringla, 2447; Place-names, 623, 637, 1433, 2554; Parker chronicle, 2142, 2328

— Aquilla: Annales Fernandi, 2755

— Arthur L.: Church and state, 6735; Maitland, 1482

— Brian S.: Handlist, 1644; Malvern, 5287

— Cecil R. Humphrey. *See* Humphrey-Smith

— Charles R.: Collectanea, 740

— Cuthbert: Archbishop Winchelsey, 5644

— D. J.: Mosaic pavements, 2050

— Denis Mack: Nelson's History of England, 1174

— Frank A.: Genealogical research, 511

— Frederick Francis: Rochester in parliament, 3460

— Herbert Maynard: Pre-reformation England, 6801

— Isaac Gregory: Worcester, 6790

— J. T.: Longhouse, 1435

— Jenkyn Beverley: Documents, 3785A; Glyndŵr rebellion, 4219

— John (LL.B.): Chronicon rusticum-commerciale, 5421

— John (prebendary of Durham) (d. 1715): Bede's Historia ecclesiastica, 2148

— John Challenor C.: Wills, 4515, 4517, 4567

— John Edward: Parliamentary representation, 3469; Westminster records, 1730

— John James: Chronica, 2744

— John Russell: Bibliotheca, 1687

— Lucy Margaret: Cluny, 5925

— Lucy Toulmin: Bozon's Contes, 6692; Commonplace book, 4882; English gilds, 5369; Expeditions to Prussia, 4601; Jusserand's Wayfaring life, 5454; Little Red Book, 5082; Petitions, 5232; Ricart's Kalendar, 5083; York plays, 7210

— Margaret S.: Cathedral libraries, 127

— P.: Long house, 1435

— Raymond: London, 1728–9

— Reginald Allender: B.M. Guide, 2019, 2472

— Reginald Anthony Lendon: Benedictine contribution, 1494, 5017A; Canterbury Cathedral priory, 1494, 5622; Financial system of Rochester cathedral priory, 1494, 5797; John of Tours, bishop, 1494; Place of Gundulf, 1494; Regimen scaccarii, 1494, 5900; Rochester church, 2724

— Robert Henry Soden: Books on seals, 468

— Robert Trow: Livestock husbandry, 5019

— Sidney Armitage: John of Gaunt, 4136

— Thomas (1638–1710): Catalogus . . . Cotton MSS., 994

— Tom C.: Preston church, 5132

— Toulmin: English gilds, 5369

— W. J.: The Berkeleys, 4593

— Waldo E. L.: Episcopal appointments, 6770

— Wilfrid Kirk: Aeneas Sylvius, 5564

— Sir William (LL.D. 1813–93): Dictionary of Biography, 1268

— William (rector of Melsonby) (d. 1735): University College, 7131

Smith-Carington family, 4575

Smithers, Geoffrey V.: Religious lyrics, 6980

Smuggling, 5334, 5398

Smyth, John: Berkeley MSS., 4593, 4757

Snape, Robert H.: Monastic finances, 5901

— M. G.: Lollard activity, 6873

Snappe's formulary, 429, 7069

Snellgrove, Harold S.: The Lusignans, 4065

Snelshall priory (Bucks.), 6096

Snorrason, Oddr (*c.* 1190): Olaf Tryggvason Saga, 2450

Snorri Sturlason, 2445, 2447, 2450

Social history, 174–7, **374–8**, **606–8**, and 742–6; 181, 1180, 1196, 1495, 1529, 4593, 4610, 4948, 5454, 5711

— Sciences and Humanities Index, 98

Société de l'histoire de France, 1121

Societies, **22–30** and **211–55**; 28–9, 442, 623, 718, 728–9, 731, 930, 935, 956, 1512, 1966, 3078

Society for Medieval Archaeology, **85**; 729

— for Publication of Ancient Welsh MSS., 203

— of Antiquaries, 178, 1012, 2070

— of Antiquaries of Scotland, 216

— of Archaeological historians, **85**

— of Genealogists, 524

Södergård, Östen: La vie d'Édouard, 2171; Sainte-Maure chronique, 2952

Sokemen, 3057, 4742

Sölch, Johann: Die Landschaften, 620

Solente, Suzanne: Christine de Pisan's Le Livre, 2815

Soliaco, Henry de, abbot, 6314

Somercote, Lawrence of: Traktat, 6447

Somerset, Fitz-Roy Richard, Baron Raglan, 816, 1435

Somersetshire: Antiquities, 762; Bibliography, 1802; Charters, 4400, 4468–70, 5246–8, 6305–9, 6312, 6321, 6323; Church, 1529, 1802–3, 5584, 5597; County history, 1529, 1810–11; County journals and societies, 1805–9; Deeds, 4872, 5248; Domesday, 1529; Extents, 4873; Eyres, 3607; Feet of fines, 3606; Feudal tenures, 4380, 4382, 4470; Forests, 3888, 3907; Inquests, 3183, 4379, 4381–2, 6311; Manors and villages, 4468, 4865–73, 6310; Parliament, 1383, 3466; Pleas, 3607–8; Religious houses, 5927, 6303–24; Sheriffs, coroners, etc., 3221, 3608; Subsidy rolls, 3182–3, 4868; Taxation, 3182; Urban history, 5246–9; Wills, 4552, 5247, 5249

Somerville, Sir Robert: Duchy of Lancaster, **113**; 1441, 1707, 3883, 6771; Gaunt's Register, 3876; Handlist, **23**; 933

Sommerfeldt, Wilhelm P.: Norse Bibliography, 60

Sommer-Seckendorff, Ellen M. F.: Robert Kilwardby, 6593

Somner, William: Canterbury, 5123; Gavelkind, 2644

Sondheimer, Janet: trans. M. Bloch, 4951

Song of Carlaverock, 474, 1467, 4295

— of Dermot, 2954

Sopwell, nunnery (Herts.), 6168

Sottovagina, Hugh (the Chantor), 1130

Souter, Alexander: Glossary, 313

South Wales and Monmouth Record Society, 204

Southampton (Hants), 4336, 4849, 5098–III, 5339, 5342–3, 5436, 5440

South-east England, Prehistory and Anglo-Saxon, 761

South-eastern Union of Scientific Societies, 179

Southern, Richard W.: Adrian IV, 6911; Bede, 6911; Canterbury forgeries, 2863, 5615; Eadmer's Life of Anselm, 6530; England's entry, 6911; Glanville's text, 2989; Lanfranc, 1450; Letters of Peter of Blois, 6519, 6911; Making of the middle ages, 1398, 6896; Medieval Humanism, 6911; Place of Henry I, 4007, 6911; Ranulf Flambard, 3850, 4008, 5694, 6911; Royal Historical Society essays, 296, 1493; St. Anselm, 2863, 5626A, 6530, 6532, 6535, 6911; School of Chartres, 6911; Twelfth-century renaissance, 6911; Vita Edwardi (Confessor), 2171; Western society and church, 6722

Southwark, 1114, 2785, 5268, 6353

Southwell minster (Notts.), 6283–4

Southwell, Robert, receiver-general, 4627

South-west England, prehistory, 761

Spalding Club, 217

Sparke, Joseph: Scriptores, 1122, 6268

Sparks, Edgar H.: Cantus firmus, 7192

Sparvel-Bayly, John A.: Essex insurrection, 4155; Hadleigh castle, 4749

Spatz, Wilhelm: Schlacht von Hastings, 4009

Speckled Book, 2397

Speculum (journal), 168

— inclusorum, 6681

— Regis Edwardi III, 2955

— sacerdotale, 1322

— stultorum, 7042

Speirs, John: Chaucer the maker, 7014

Spelman, Sir Henry: Concilia, 1140; Glossarium 3503A

Spence, George: Equitable jurisdiction, 3727

Spencer, Matthew L.: Corpus Christi pageants, 7210

Spicilegium, Achery's, 1088

Spindler, Robert: Das Bussbuch, 2257

Spink's Numismatic Circular, 649

1078 *Index*

Spofford, Thomas, bishop, 5730
Sports. *See* Pastimes
Spottiswoode Society, Miscellany, 218
Springs (family) of Lavenham, 5415
Sprott, Thomas: Chronica, 1103, 2956, 6183
Spufford, Margaret: A Cambridgeshire community, 4723
— Peter: Coinage, 5520; Genealogists' handbook, 524
Spurgeon, Caroline F. E.: Chaucer criticism, 7014
Spurrell, William: Dictionary, 342
Squibb, George D.: Court of chivalry, 3679; Papworth's Dictionary, 497
Squire, Aelred: Aelred of Rievaulx, 6638
Srawley, James H.: Liturgy, 1345; Schaky's Book, 5752
Stafford, St. Thomas the Martyr, priory, 6330
Stafford, Edmund, bishop, 5715
— John, bishop and archbishop, 1474, 5589, 5639
Staffordshire: Bibliography, 1812; Charters, 4472-5, 4477-80, 5252, 6325, 6327-34; Coats of arms, 499, 1529; County history, 1529, 1815-17; County journals and societies, 1812A-1814; County records, 1504; Deeds, 4471, 4475-6, 5255, 6327, 6331; Domesday, 1529, 6326; Extents, 6326; Eyres, 3553; Feet of fines, 3611; Feudal tenures, 4385-7; Forests, 3610, 3893; Inquests, 4383-4; Manors and villages, 4874-80, 4964; Military service, 4285; Parliament, 3467; Pleas, 3094, 3609-10, 3893; Pipe rolls, 3094; Religious houses, 6325-34; Subsidy rolls, 3184, 3186; Taxation, 3185; Topography, 1529; Urban history, 5250-5
Stahlschmidt, John C. L.: London lay subsidy, 3171, 5157
Stained glass, 861-5
Stainer, E.: Cecilia, Bodleian music, 7193
— John F. R.: Bodleian music, 7193
Stair Society, 219
Stallingborough (Lincs.), 4813
Stamford (Lincs.), 3575, 3575A, 5147A
— schism, 7061
Stamp, Alfred E.: Henry III, court and chancery, 1455; Public Record Office, 949; Richard II, 4138
— Sir Laurence D.: Man and the land, 621
Stanborough (Devon), 4351
Stanbrook abbey, Worcester, 6383
Stanbury, John, bishop, 5730
Standard, battle of the, 2734, 2894, 6274, 6634-5

Standish family, deeds, 4444
— John: Inquisitiones post mortem, 4375; Subsidy rolls, 3206
Standon (Staffs.), 4878
Stanewell, L. M.: Deeds, 5292
Stanhope, Edward: Abstracts of deeds, 6219
Stanley abbey (Wilts.), 1114, 2774, 6376-7
Stanley, Arthur P.: Canterbury, 5623; Westminster, 6249
— Eric G.: Beowulf, 2352; ed. Continuations, 2352; Paganism, 2660
Stanley *v.* mayor of Norwich, 5208
Stanley Park. *See* Dale abbey
Stanley-Price (Mrs. Hebditch) M. J.: Deeds, 4504
Stannaries, 4325, 5513
Stansfeld, John: Rent roll, 6405; Subsidy rolls, 3206
Stanwick (Yorks.), 766, 2070
Stapelton, Thomas: trans. Bede, 2148
Staple, 5329-30, 5386
— Inn, 7158
— merchants of, 5340, 5393, 5406, 5464
Stapledon, Walter de, bishop, 5715
Stapleton, Thomas: Canons in York, 6423; Chronicon Petroburgense, 6265; Descriptio militum, 3069; Fitz-Thedmar's Chronicle, 2870; Norman exchequer rolls, 3102; Plumpton correspondence, 4611; Wardrobe accounts, 3132
Star Carr (Yorks.), 766, 1975
Star Chamber, 3506
Starlyng, John, 4330
Starr, Chester G., Jr.: ed. Laistner, 2358; Roman navy, 2075
Starrs, 3518, 3939-40
State Paper Office, 974
— papers, 3833-4
— trials, 3484, 3519-20
Statham, Samuel P. H.: Dover charters, 5324
Stationers' company, 5203, 7217
Statuta Gildae (Berwick-upon-Tweed), 5221
Statute of Gloucester, 3335, 3492
— of labourers, 3344, 3676
— Merchant roll, 5276
— of Merton, 3334
— of praemunire, 1439, 3345
— Quia emptores, 4698
— Rageman, 1458
— of Winchester, 3337
— of York, 1478, 3366, 4141
Statutes: **506-8**; 1233, 2690, 3691, 6374, 7051
— Ecclesiastical, 1129, 1142, 6811, 6816; Canterbury, 5616; Carlisle, 5647;

Chichester, 5653, 5658; Lincoln, 170; 5738, 5749; Middleham church, 6408; St. Paul's, 5765; Salisbury, 5803–4; Southwell, 6283; Wells, 5590; York, 5860
— Religious orders, 1147; Benedictine, 1146, 5631; Cistercian, 1145, 5929; Dominican, 5984; Franciscan, 6010; Hospitals, 6136, 6139; Hospitallers, 6045
— University and college, Cambridge, 7053, 7055–7, 7059–60; Oxford, 7061, 7065, 7070–1, 7077
Staunford, Roger, 3839
— William: Exposition of prerogative, 3278; Les plees del coron, 3680
Stavenhagen, Kurt: Herodian, 2025
Stead, M. T.: Itinerarium, 2906; William Cade, 5509
Steel, Anthony B.: Collector of customs, 1441; King's household, 3141; Receipt of exchequer, 3263; Richard II, 4137
— J. P.: Currel subsidy, 3154A
Steele, Francesca M.: Mirror of St. Edmund, 6695
— Robert Reynolds: Bacon's Opera, 6538; Charles of Orleans, 4247; Earliest arithmetics, 6947; Mum and the Sothsegger, 7049; De proprietatibus rerum, 6548; The Pecia, 7085
Steelyard (London), 5337, 5428
Steenstrup, Johannes C. H. R.: Normannerne, 2485, 2598
Steer, Francis W.: Chichester city charters, 5270; Local records, 1524; Medieval household, 4614; Records of Chichester, 5657; Scrivener's company, 5201; Seals, 1440
— Kenneth A.: Antonine Wall, 2087; Defences, 2052; Picts, 2090; Roman Scotland, 2088
Steffens, Franz: Paläographie, 397
Stein, Henri: Archives, 954; Bibliographie, 63
— I. H.: Wyclif, 873
— Peter: Regiam Maiestatem, 2989
— Walther: Die Hansebruderschaft, 5428; Hanse und England, 5428; Hansisches Urkundenbuch, 5336
Steinberg, Sigfrid H.: Adam of Bremen, 2149; La Hanse, 5428; New dictionary, 1195
Steindorff, Ernst: ed. Dahlmann-Waitz, 48
Steiner, Ruth: York pageant, 7210
Stemmata Anglicana, 551
— Shirleiana, 4591
Stengel, Edmund E.: Archiv für Diplomatik, 412

Stenton, Lady Doris M.: After Runnymede, 3289; Assize rolls, 3569, 3588, 3633; Bibliography of, 1453; Bracton's Note-book, 3481; Chancellor's Roll, 3082; Communications, 1485; English justice, 3681; English society, 1190, 5467; Eyres, 3481, 3553, 3576, 3627, 3632; F. M. Stenton papers, 1496; Hatton's seals, 464, 2201A, 4410; Gesta Henrici II, 2879; King John and courts, 3682; Medieval miscellany for, 1453; Pleas before king, 3494; Pipe rolls, 3079, 3264; Richardson and Sayles (review), 1219; Roger of Howden, 2903; William Dugdale, 1147
— Sir Frank M.: Collected essays: Preparatory to Anglo-Saxon England, 1496; Abingdon abbey, 2153, 2220, 2725, 6087; Acta episcoporum, 1496, 5577; A.-S. ceorl, 1496; Anglo-Saxon chronicle, 1458, 1496; Anglo-Saxon coins (essays to), 669, 1454, 1496; Anglo-Saxon England, 1189, 2503, 3990; Bayeux Tapestry, 4276; Castle, 839, 1495; Danelaw, 4403; Danes, 1496, 2599; Derby Domesday, 1529; Dunsaete ordinance, 2211; Early English history, 1221, 1496; East Anglian kings, 1433, 1496, 2555; Eric John's criticism, 2632; Essays to, 669, 1454; Facsimiles of charters, 451; Families and the Conquest, 1493, 1496, 4667; Feudalism, 1496; First century of feudalism, 4679; Foundations, 1496, 2555; Gilbertine charters, 5957, 6216; Herefordshire, 1496; Huntingdon Domesday, 1529; Knight service, 4682; Latin charters, 2220; Leicestershire Domesday, 1529; Lincolnshire Domesday, 3026; Lindsey and its kings, 1448, 1496, 2555; Manorial structure, 2648, 4980; Medeshamstede, 1455, 1496, 2220; Mercian kings, 1496, 2555; Norman London, 1495–6, 1746; Nottinghamshire Domesday, 1529; Oxfordshire Domesday, 1529; Place-names, 623, 636, 1449, 1496, 2555, 2661; R.H.S. presidential addresses, 2555; Road system, 1496, 5535; Rutland Domesday, 1529; St. Benet of Holme, 6259; St. Frideswide, 1496, 2220; Scandinavian colonies, 1496, 2599; Southwell, 1496; Westmorland, 1496, 1852; William the Conqueror, 4010
Stephan, John: Religious houses of Devon, 6120
Stephanus, Eddius: Bishop Wilfrid, 1114, 2284, 2313
Stephen, king: Charters, 437, 1498, 3779,

Stephen, king: Charters (*cont.*):
4399; Chroniclers, **390**; 1096, 1113, 2734, 2880; History, 1457, 1466, 3981, 3984, 4004; Records, 469, 1123, 1448, 3779

Stephen, George: Norfolk archaeology, 1750

— James Fitzjames: Criminal law, 1257

— Leslie: *D.N.B.*, 531, 1482

Stephens, Archibald J.: Boroughs, 1388

— George: Runic monuments, 362

— George R.: Greek in England, 6925

— Henry M.: Documents, 1204

— William R. W.: Chichester, 5663, 6790; English church, 1289, 6802; Memorials, 5663

Stephenson, Carl: Bibliography of, 1497; Borough and town, 1389; Domesday, 1497, 3063; Feudalism, 1497, 2649, 4680; Firma noctis, 1497; H. Cam on theories, 1462; Papers, 1497; Problem of common man, 1367, 1497; Representative government, 1497, 3406; Seignorial tallage, 1446; Sources, 1207; Taxation and representation, 1439, 1497

— Mill: Surrey Catalogue, 1829

Stepsis, Robert, 2923

Sterling coinage, 706, 712, 1454

— crisis, 5499

Stern, Fritz: Varieties of history, 244

Sterrett, John R. S.: Strabo, 2025

Stert (Wilts.), 4489

Stevenage (Herts.), Manorial survey, 1677

Stevens, Charles Guy: St. Catherine's Hill, 1995

— Courtenay E.: Agriculture, 2039; Between invasions, 1432, 1994, 2034; Gildas, 2162; Hadrian's Wall, 2085; Notitia dignitatum, 2030; Roman conquest, 2043

— John: Dugdale's Monasticon, 1147; Royal treasury, 3265

— John: Carols, 7194

— Joseph: St. Mary Bourne, 4768

Stevenson, Edward L.: Ptolemy, 2025

— Francis S.: Robert Grosseteste, 6584

— George H.: Roman administration, 2071

— John H.: Scottish heraldry, 479; Seals, 467

— Joseph: Bedae Opera, 2297; Bede's Historia ecclesiastica, 2148; Berry's Recouvrement, 2794; Blondel's De reductione Normanniae, 2798; Chronica de Mailros (Melrose), 2824; Chronicle of Isle of Man, 1950; Chronicon de Abingdon, 2153, 6085; Chronicon de Lanercost, 2836; Church historians, 1123, 1950, 2147, 2880, 2962, 2981;

Coggeshall's Chronicon, 2747, 2850; Devizes's De rebus Ricardi I, 2859; Documents, 3791; Gesta Stephani, 2880; Gildas, 2162; Giraldus, De instructione, 6573; Gray's Scalacronica, 2884; Letters and papers, 3815; Liber Vitae, 5687; Narratives, 3819; Nennius, 2167; Public Records, 1059; St. Godric, 6675; Simeon of Durham, 2157; Tilbury's Otia, 2961; Torigni's Chronique, 2962; William of Worcester's Annals, 2982

— Robert Barron K.: Sylloge of coins, 704

— William Henry: Aelfric's Colloquies, 2292; Anglo-Saxon charters, 2201; Annals of Malmesbury, 2921; Annals of St. Neots, 2152; Asser's Alfred, 2147; Beginnings of Wessex, 2556; Bentham's Ely, 5708; Carucage, 3261; Crawford charters, 2202; Domesday, 3064; Earle's Handbook, 2195; Florence of Worcester's Chronicon, 2981; Green's England, 2584; Hundreds, 3064; Map of England, 605; Newark documents, 4841; Records of Gloucester, 5090; Records of Nottingham, 5224; Rental of Gloucester, 5091; Royal charters, 5224; St. Martin's-le-Grand charter, 2221; Trinoda necessitas, 2221, 2621; Yorkshire surveys, 2221, 3038

Steward, the, 3670, 4619, 4631, 4794

Steward's books, 5111

Stewart, Alexander: Grammar, 336

— David J.: Liber Eliensis, 2164

— Ian H.: Scottish coinage, 702; Viking coins, 1454

— James D.: Union-catalogue, 89

Stewart-Brown, Ronald: Accounts of chamberlains, 3854; Avowries, 1571; Cheshire pipe rolls, 3084; Chester rolls, 3537; Disafforestation of Wirral, 3923; Domesday roll (Cheshire), 3857; Earldom of Chester, 1571; Exchequer of Chester, 1571; Serjeants of the peace, 3495, 3745; Shotwick, 4725; Wapentake of Wirral, 4425

Stickler, Alphonsus M.: Collectanea S. Kuttner, 6429; Historia iuris canonici, 1314

Stillington, Robert, bishop, 5589

Stillwell, Gardiner: John Gower, 7019

Stitt, Frederick B.: Kempston estate, 4705; Lenton priory accounts, 6280; Ministers' accounts, 4974

Stock accounts, 4767, 5815–16

Stockport (Lancs.), Charters, 5129

Stocks, George A.: Dunkenhalgh deeds, 4445

— John E.: Market Harborough, 5143

Stockton, Eric W.: John Gower, 7017
Stodart, Robert: Heraldry, 479
Stogursey (Som.), Charters, 6323
Stoke Bishop, Charters, 2201
Stokes, E(thel?): Tables of bullion, 713
— Ethel: Feet of fines (Warwicks.), 3616; Inquests, Glos., 4356; Inquests, Lancs., 4369; Inquests, Wilts., 4392; Liber Wigorniensis, 5833
— George T.: Celtic church, 2677
— Henry P.: Anglo-Jewish history, 3972; Chaplains of Cambridge, 7108; Corpus Christi College, 7100; Records of MSS., 3941
— Whitley: Annals from Book of Leinster, 2777; Annals of Ulster, 2786; Cormac Glossary, 2401; Expugnatio, 2881; Gilla Coemgin, 2402; Glossary of Irish laws, 2240; Irische Texte, 351, 2388; Lismore book, 2398; Lives of Saints, 1171; St. Patrick, 2324; Thesaurus palaeo-hibernicus, 2392; Tigernach, 2170
Stoljar, Samuel J.: Law French, 37
Stone priory (Staffs.), 6332
Stone, Edward N.: French Chronicles, 2748
— Eric: Hundred rolls, Oxon., 4376; Profit and loss accountancy, 5788
— John Frederic S.: Wessex, 761
— John: Chronicle, 2957
— Lawrence: Denholm-Young's gentry, 473
— Lawrence: Sculpture, 783, 854
Stonehenge (Hants), 1432, 1970
Stoneleigh abbey (Warw.), 6369
Stones, Edward Lionel G.: Anglo-Scottish relations, 3788, 4072; Appeal to history, 4086; Eclipses, 6936; Edward I, 4064; Folvilles, 5455; Joseph Bain, 3789; Mission to Edinburgh, 4087; Records of Great Cause, 2770, 4086; Rotuli Scotiae, 3795; Sir Geoffrey le Scrope, 3693; Submission of Bruce, 4077; Treaty of Northampton, 4087
Stonor Papers and Letters, 3224, 4615
Storer, Henry S.: Clerkenwell, 5173
— James S.: Clerkenwell, 5173
Storey, Robin L.: Chancery causes, 7224; Commissions of peace, 7223; Diocesan administration, 6803; Disorders, 3617; End of Lancaster, 4229; Langley's Register, 5690; Marmaduke Lumley, 5649; North of England, 4234; Warden of the Marches, 4230
Storm, Gustav: Monumenta, 1115
Storms, Godfrid: Magic, 2379
Stothard, Charles A.: Monumental effigies, 927

Stoughton (Leics.), 4803
Stourbridge fair, 5537
Stow (Lincs.), 4816
Stow, John: Annals, 2957A; Memoranda, 2743; Otterbourne, 2938; Survey, 1746A
Stowe Library MSS., Irish MSS., 1082
Strabo, 2025
Strachan, John: Thesaurus, 2392; Welsh grammar, 343
Strachey, John: Index to rolls, 3322
Straker, Ernest: Ashdown forest, 3924; Wealden iron, 5500
Strasser, Karl: Sachsen, 2522
Strata Florida, Annales, 1114, 2144
Stratford, John, archbishop, 1478
Stratford-Langthorne, abbey (Essex), 6743
Stratford-upon-Avon (Warw.), 1504, 3197, 4911, 5278–9
Strathclyde, 2322, 2604
Stratman, Carl J.: Bibliography of drama, 6993
Stratmann, Franz H.: Dictionary, 287
Stratton, Adam de, 4917–18, 4921
Strayer, Joseph R.: English government at work, 3836; Taxation and community, 3366
Streatley (Oxon.), 4462
Strecche, John: Chronicle, 2822
Strecker, Karl: Einführung, 314; St. Ninian, 2323
Streeter, Burnett H.: Chained library, 7177
Stretton, Robert de, bishop, 5668
— Grace: Aspects of travel, 4601; Travelling household, 4616
Strickland, Agnes: Queens, 548
— Giuseppe: Boniface of Savoy, 5628
— Henry Hornyold. *See* Hornyold-Strickland
Striguil, lords of, 4585
Strittmatter, Anselm: Corpus consuetudinum, 1146
Ströhl, Hugo G.: Heraldry, 475
Ström, Hilmer: Names in Bede, 587
Strongbow, earl of Pembroke, 459, 2954
Strutt, Benjamin: Constitutions of Colchester, 5072
— Joseph: Dress, 928; Sports, 928A
Stuart, John: Stones, 2486
— Margaret: Scottish families, 525
Stubbs, Thomas: Chronica pontificum, 1124, 1130
— William: 1218, 1221, 1461, 1482, 1484, 2632, 3920; Annales Londonienses, 2761; Annales Paulini, 2768; Benedict of Peterborough's Gesta, 2879; Canon law, 1246, 6445; Chronicles of Edward I and Edward II, 2733, 2768, 2852, 2876,

Stubbs, William (*cont.*):
2928, 2971; Chronicles of Richard I,
2858, 5604; Church courts, 6442;
Constitutional history, 1221; Councils,
1129, 2254; De expugnatione, 2858; De
inventione Crucis, 6147; Diceto's Opera,
2860; Epistolae Cantuarienses, 5604;
Fortescue's De titulo Edwardi, 2988;
Gervase of Canterbury works, 2807;
Gesta Edwardi de Carnarvan, 2876;
Gesta Henrici Secundi, 2879; Hoveden's
Chronica, 2903; Introductions to Rolls
Series, **387**; 4041; Itinerarium, 2906;
Lectures on early history, 1498; Lec-
tures on medieval history, 6445, 6912;
Malmesbury's De gestis regum, 2921;
Memorials of St. Dunstan, 2303;
Registrum Sacrum, 5583; Select charters,
1208, 2210, 3005; Walter of Coventry's
Memoriale, 2855; Waltham abbey, 6147
Studer, Paul: Anglo-Norman lapidaries,
868, 6948; Oak book, 5107; Port books,
5108
Studia Gratiana, **168**
— Hibernica, 238
— Neophilologica (journal), 626
Studies: An Irish quarterly, 239
— in British history, 2557
— in Church history, 174
— in London history, 5177
— in the early British church, 2122
— in peerage, 569
Study of history, 1466
Stukeley (Hunts.), 4775
Stukeley, William: Works of, 2044
Sturbridge fair, 6100
Sturgess, Herbert A. C.: Middle Temple
catalogue, 1014
Sturler, Jean de: Debita mercatorum
Brabancie, 5346; Deux comptes, 4102;
Les relations politiques, 4169, 5401
Sturleson, Snorri: Heimskringla, 2447
Sturm, St., 2290
Stuston (Suffolk), 4882
Stuteville fee (Yorks.), 4499
Styles, Dorothy: Ministers' accounts, 4912,
6370; William Dugdale, 1147
Subsidies, clerical, **892–3**
Subsidy rolls, **483–91**; 1601, 3222, 4489,
4848, 4868, 4784, 5144, 5157, 5393, 7222
Succession, royal, 1450
Suckling, Alfred: Suffolk, 1826
Sudbury, archdeaconry of, 4556, 6466
— Simon of, 5640, 5764
Suetonius: De vita Caesarum, 2025(g)
Suffolk: Charters, 4889, 6337, 6342;
Cloth industry, 1500; Church, 1529,
6345, 6873; Consuetudo regis, 3045;

County history, 1529, 1824–6; County
journals and societies, 1818–23; County
records, 1504; Domesday, 1529, 3030;
Extents, 4889; Feet of fines, 3612;
Feudal tenures, 4388–9, 6342; Freemen,
4742; Manors and villages, 4881–9,
6336; Parliament, 3468; Pleas, 6342;
Rebels, 3502; Religious houses, 6335–
49; Subsidy rolls, 3189; Taxation,
3187–8, 3190, 4155; Topography, 1505;
Urban history, 5256–64; Wills, 4553–6
Suffolk, duke of, 4232
Suggett, Helen: Richard II and London,
4111; Use of French, 296, 1493
Sulcard of Westminster: Westminster
abbey, 6241
Sulgrave brooch, 7225
Sulien, Bishop of St. Davids, 2321
Sullivan, Edward: Book of Kells, 881
— Frank: Moreana, 2927
— Majie P.: Moreana, 2927
Summa Libri Rubei Asaphensis, 5880c
— Logica, 6619
Summerson, Sir John: Addy's English
house, 814
Sumner, Heywood: Local papers, 1663
Sundreys, the, 1951
Sundrish (Kent), 4785
Super Cathedram (papal bull), 6024
Supplications to Rome (Scottish), 5549
Surienne, François de, 2909, 4243
Surirey de Saint-Remy, Henry de: His-
toire de Charles VII, 2793
Surnames, 578, 586
Surrey: Antiquities, 762; Bibliography,
1827–30; Charters, 4481, 5266, 6350–1,
6353, 6364; Church, 1529; County
history, 1529, 1833–4; County journals
and societies, 1732, 1831–2; County
records, 5265; Deeds, 4891; Domesday,
1529, 1834, 3040; Extents, 4898; Feet
of fines, 3613; Manors and villages,
4890–8; Parliament, 3469; Pipe rolls,
3095; Religious houses, 6350–5; Taxation, 3191; Topography, 1505, 1529;
Urban history, 5265–8; Wealth, 4636;
Wills, 4557–8
— earls of, 4594, 4605
— Thomas, earl of, 4605
Surtees Society, 196
Surtees, Robert: Palatine of Durham, 1629
Survey of ecclesiastical archives, **109**; 5575
Surveys, **471–3**. *See* Extents
Survival of Roman villa, 2646
Susa, Henry of (in England), 6460
Sussex: Antiquities, 762; Bibliography,
1835–6; Charters, 4483–4, 6358, 6361–4,
6367; Church, 1529, 6829; County

history, 1529, 1840–1, 4214; County journals and societies, 1837–9; County records, 3031, 4390; Deeds, 4482; Domesday, 1529, 3031; Extents, 4899, 4904; Feet of fines, 3614; Feudal tenures, 4390; Hundred roll, 4390; Inquests, 4906; Iron industry, 5500; Manors and villages, 4899–910, 4986; Parliament, 3470; Religious houses, 6356–67; Subsidy rolls, 3193–5, 6829; Taxation, 3192, 3195; Topography, 1505, 1529; Urban history, 1529, 5269–71; Wealth, 4636; Wills, 4559

Sutcliffe, Dorothy: Financial condition of Canterbury, 5622

Sutherland, Carol Humphrey V.: A.-S. gold coinage, 703, 2111; Coinage (V–VI), 1442; Coin-currency, 665; ed. Mattingly essays, 664; Romano-British imitations, 666

— Donald W.: Mesne process, 3707; Quo Warranto, 3492, 4681

— Dame Lucy S.: Ada Levett's Studies, 1480, 4974; Maude Clarke's Studies, 1464; Studies in History, 6903

Sutton (Hants), 4763

— Coldfield (Warw.), **687**, 3909

— Courtney (Berks.), 2481

Sutton, Albert: Bibliotheca, 1697

— Oliver, bishop, 5745, 5752, 6469, 7125

— Thomas, 6891

Sutton-Hoo, 766, 2487

Sveinsson, Einar O.: Dating sagas, 2461; Njal's Saga, 2449

Svenis Aggonis Historia, 1106

Swainestrey, hospital (Kent), 6196

Swainson, Charles A.: Chichester, 5659

Swan, William (proctor), 1474, 6754

Swanton, Michael J.: Battle of Maldon, 2344

Swapham, Robert: Historia, 1122, 6268

Swarling (Kent), Celtic, 2070

Swarzenski, Hanns: Saxl's Sculptures, 853

Swayne, Henry J. F.: Churchwardens' accounts, 5289; Gleanings from Salisbury, 5283; Sarum, 5285

Swedish archaeological bibliography, 727

Sweet, Alfred H.: Apostolic See and religious houses, 5902; Benedictines and bishops, 5914

— Henry: A.-S. reader, 286; Oldest texts, 2329

— Jennifer: Sermons, 6707

— and Maxwell: Law bibliography, 1228

Sweetman, Henry S.: Documents, 3797

Swereford, Alexander de: Liber niger scaccarii, 3006; Liber rubeus, 3007

Swete, Henry B.: Church services, 1328

Swift, Eleanor: Obedientiary rolls, 6360

Swinburn, Lilian M.: Lanterne of Lizt, 6866

Swine priory (Yorks.), 6421

Swineshead (Glos.), pleas, 3551

Swinfield, Richard de, bishop, 4612, 5730

Swithun, St., 2312

Swoboda, Erich: ed. Carnuntina, 2072

Sword, Anglo-Saxon, 912

Swyneshed, Roger, 1428, 6627

Swynnerton, Charles: Domestic cartulary, 4475

Swynton, Thomas: Memorandum book, 6400

Sydenham, Edward A.: Roman coinage, 662

Sylloge of coins, 704

Sylvester, Richard S.: Richard III, 2927

Syme, Sir Ronald: Ammianus, 2025; Cambridge Ancient History, 2034; Tacitus, 2025

Symington, John A.: Brotherton Library, 1038

Symon the Jew, 1450

Symonds, Henry: Herbert de Losinga, 5777

Symons, Thomas: Regularis concordia, 2274; St. Dunstan, 2303; Tenth-century monasticism, 2715

Synodalia, 6168, 6811

Synods, **891–2**; 1438

Syon monastery, 6037

Tables of bullion, 708, 713

Tabula Peutingeriana, 2032

Tacitus, Cornelius: Agricola, 2025(d), 2071–2, 2081, 2088; Annals, 2025, Historiae, 2025, Germania, 2505

Tailors, 5251

Táin Bó Cualnge, 2394

Tait, James: Borough charters, 5024; Charter of William I, 1448; Cheshire Domesday, 1576, 3018; Chronicon anonymi Cantuariensis, 2944; Dunkenhalgh deeds, 4445; Essays to, 1455; Herefordshire Domesday, 3075; Hides and virgates, 3031; Honour of Wardon, 4651; John of Reading's Chronicon, 2944; Knighton's Chronicon, 2912; Knights' service, 1575, 4682; Letters to Oxford, 6926; Liber burgus, 1458, 5353; Maitland's Domesday Book, 2636; Manchester, 5129; Maps, 605; Medieval borough, 1390; Middlechurch chartulary, 4423; Murder of Gloucester, 1472, 4138; Owens College essays, 1632; Powicke's appreciation of, 1489; Runcorn charter, 6104; St. Werburgh

Tait, James (*cont.*):
chartulary, 6105; Shropshire Domesday, 1529; Speculum Edwardi, 2955; Stephenson's Borough, 1389

Takeley (Essex), 4919

Talbert, Ernest W.: Wycliffe, **873**; 6650

Talbot Deeds, 4424

Talbot, Charles H.: Aelredi Rievallensis, 6633, 6636; A.-S. missionaries, 2290, 2299; Christina of Markyate, 6669; Cistercian MSS., 986; Goscelin, 2304; Letters from abbots to Citeaux, 5932; Medical practitioners, 1422; Medicine, 1421; Notes on medicine, 2380; Physician's Vade mecum, 6966; Sermones Aelredi, 6636; Wulsin, 2317

— John, earl of Shrewsbury, 4282

Taliesin, Book of, 2385

Tallage, 3144, 3162, 3168, 5137, 5317

— Seignorial, 1446

Talleyrand, cardinal of Périgord, 6772

Tallies, 3245

Tamworth (Staffs.), 5253

Tandridge, priory (Surrey), 6354

Tangl, Michael: Schrifttafeln, 413; St. Boniface, 2299

Tanner, John: Heraldry, 493

— Joseph R.: Cambridge Medieval History, 1176; Register of Cambridge, 7098

— Lawrence E.: Fate of the princes, 4203; Westminster muniments, 1016, 6250

— Thomas: Bibliotheca, 33, 987; Notitia, 987, 1150

Tanquerey, Frédéric J.: Conspiracy of T. Dunheved, 4139; Lettres à Robert de Bavent, 3898

Taswell-Langmead, Thomas P.: Constitutional history, 1222

Tate, William E.: Enclosure movement, 5018; Parish chest, 1521

Tatenhill (Staffs.), 4877

Tatlock, John S. P.: Henry I's charter, 5179; Legendary history, 2166, 2914

Tatnall, Edith C.: Wyclif, 6657

Tattersall, Walter M., Glamorgan, 1927

Taunton (Som.), 4871

Taunton, Ethelred L.: Black monks, 6179

Tavistock (Devon), 5064, 5513, 6868

— abbey (Devon), 1470, 2717, 6126

Tawney, Richard H.: Documents, 1362; Unwin papers, 1500

Taxatio ecclesiastica, 6783

Taxation, **483–91** and **495–9**; 1439, 1469, 1497, 2650, 3398. *See* Clergy

Taylor, Alexander B.: Orkneyinga Saga, 2451

— Alfred John: Caernarvon castle, 4053; James of St. George, 823; King's works, 781; Military architecture, 823, 1485; Rose Graham's essays, 1437

— Arnold J.: Barony of Lewes, 4905

— Arthur: Glory of regality, 1359

— C.: Dorset, 1517

— Charles Holt: ed. Haskins essays, 1439

— Charles Samuel: Analysis of Domesday, 3023; Pre-Domesday hides, 2636

— Edgar: Wace's Chronicle, 2974

— Edward B.: Primitive culture, 1993

— Eva G. R.: Guide to periodicals, 90, 716

— Frank: Court rolls and rentals, 4697; Gesta Henrici V, 2877; John Rylands Library MSS., 1034, 1036–7; John Strecche Chronicle, 2822; Legh of Booth's charters, 4426; Libelle of Englysche Polycye, 5338; Note on Rolls Series (8), 2864, 6181; Seals, 465; Westminster palace records, 959

— Harold M.: A.-S. architecture, 811; A.-S. churches, 2123; Pre-conquest churches, 1433; Pre-Norman sculpture, 811; Repton architecture, 7225

— Isaac: Domesday survivals, 3047; The ploughland, 3047

— Joan: A.-S. architecture, 811; A.-S. churches, 2123

— John (of Bristol): Bristol, 5088

— John (of Leeds University): French Brut, 2811; Higden's Chronicle, 2895; Kirkstall chronicles, 2910, 6405; Medieval historical writing, 2810, 2855; Modus tenendi MSS., 3349; Norman Conquest and church in Yorks., 6802; Use of chronicles, **387**

— John (of Northampton): Bibliotheca, 1760

— L. G.: Merchant venturers, 5379

— Margerie V.: Liber Luciani, 5045; Obits, 5045; Roman sites, 2015

— Mary M.: Elections Cambs., 3454; Sessions of the peace, Cambs., 3536

— Richard V.: Ribston, 6056

— Richard W. E.: Factory system, 5501

— Silas: Brevis relatio, 2801; Gavelkind, 2644

— Thomas: Celtic Christianity, 2678

Tayster, John de: Chronica, 1114, 2819, 2958

Techniques, economic, 5392

Teetor, Paul R.: Treatise on law merchant, 5082

Teigler, Elaine: Guide, 144

Tellenbach, Gerd: Church, state, etc., 6723

Templars, **808–9**; 1451, 6297, 7159

Temple Normanton (Derby), Court rolls, 4731

Temple, London, 1458

Temple, Ruth Z.: Greek and Latin translations, 52

Templeman, Geoffrey: Edward I and historians, 4066; Hundred Years War, 4191; Parliament, 1221, 3364; Register of Gilds, 5275; Sheriffs of Warwickshire, 3746A

Templo, Richard de: Third Crusade, 2906

Temporalities, Bangor, 4943A

Tendring (Essex), hundred of, 4741

Tengvik, Gösta: By-names, 590

Tenures of land, **637–54**, **661–6**, and **691–6**; 1242, 1482, 2636, 2644, 2650, 2990, 2999, 3007, 3188, 4758, 4780, 5353, 6242, 6266, 6369

Terrett, Ian B.: Domesday geography, 3044

Terriers, 4696, 4817, 4884, 6178

Terry, Charles S.: Catalogue, 34; Index, 1060

Testa de Nevill, **628**; 1529, 1601, 3088, 4337, 4350–1, 4354, 4359, 4365, 4371, 4374, 4378, 4387, 4791, 5144. *See* Book of Fees

Testa, William, 3412

Testamenta Cantiana, 4536

— Eboracensia, 4564

— Karleolensia, 4522

— Lambethana, 4517

— Leodiensia, 4565

— Vetusta, 4518

Tewkesbury abbey (Glos.), 1114, 2737, 2765, 4755, 6159

— Alan of: Life of Becket, 6487

Textile industry, 5416, 6868

Texts and calendars, 29

Textus Roffensis, 441, 1103, 5794

Thacker, Helen G.: Bouwens' Wills, 4505

Thame (Oxon.), 6298, 6838

— Philip de: Knights hospitallers, 6044

Thanage, 2643

Thatcham (Berks.), manors, 4707

Thaxted (Essex), 4751

Thayer, James B.: Legal essays, 3481; Trial by jury, 1258

Thegns, 2615, 2634–5, 4975

Theiner, Augustin: Baronius' Annales, 1126; Monumenta, 5554

Theobald, archbishop, 5641, 6501

Theodore, archbishop, 2253, 2259, 2702

Theodoric: Historia, 1115

Theodulf, bishop of Orleans, 2256, 2259

Theopold, Ludwig: Untersuchungen, 2145

Thielemans, Marie-Rose: Bourgogne et l'Angleterre, 4271, 5402

Thingeyrar, Arngrim of: Thomas saga, 6488

Thingoe (Suffolk), 3190, 6338

Thirsk, Joan: Agrarian history, 1360; Common fields, 4999; Lincolnshire, 1723; Orwin's Open fields, 1373

Thoisy, Paul de: Bourgogne au traité de Troyes, 4248

Thom, Alexander: Megalithic sites, 2012

Thomae de Musca: Chronicon, 6117

Thomas, I, archbishop of York, 1130

— II, archbishop of York, 1130

— duke of Gloucester, 1472, 3503A, 4138, 4746

— earl of Coningsby, 4773

— earl of Lancaster, 4792

— earl of Surrey, 4605

— of Eccleston: De adventu Fratrum, 1114, 6001, 6008, 6010

— of Ely: Liber, 2164

— of York (Franciscan), 6910

Thomas, Antoine: Bozon's Contes, 6692

— Arthur H.: Calendar of mayors' court rolls, 5152; Calendar of plea rolls, 5156; Great Chronicle, 2885; Leadenhall, 5181

— Charles: Rural settlement, 2074

— David R.: St. Asaph, 5880C, 5880D, 6790

— Elliott C.: Bury's Philobiblon, 6562

— Francis S.: Exchequer, 3250; Handbook, 951; Notes, 970

— I.: Logic, 1428

— Nicholas: Guide, 741

— Richard J.: Welsh place-names, 640

— William: Antiquitates, 6384; Church of Worcester, 5848; Dugdale's Antiquities, 1849

Thompson, parish (Norfolk), 4818

Thompson, Alexander Hamilton: Archbishop Zouche, 1455; Assize rolls, 3594; Bede, 2148, 2297, 2706; Bishop Gynewell's registers, 5739; Chapel of St. Mary and Holy Angels, 5873; Charters of hospital, 6209; Church of Southwell, 6284; Colleges of chantry priests, 6858; Collegiate churches, 5702; Corrody, 5903; Curia regis rolls, 3594; De banco rolls, 3595; English clergy and organization, 6804; English house, 814, 1495; English monasteries, 1303, 5898; Essays, 1456; Fasti parochiales, 5876; Growth of parish church, 812; Hospital of the Annunciation, 6210; Household roll, 5587; Jurisdiction of York in Gloucestershire, 5874, 6162; Lambeth institutions, 5756; Leicestershire documents, 3568; Leicestershire village notes, 4799; Liber vitae, 5687; Local history, 1514; Military architecture, 840; Monasteries of Leicestershire, 6211; Parish history, 1527; Pestilences, 5483; Peterborough

Thompson, Alexander Hamilton (*cont.*): cartulary, 6267; Pluralism, 6772; Registers of archbishops, 5875; Registers of Richmond, 5859; Rotuli R. Gravesend, 5747; St. Mary, Bolton, 6398; St. Mary Magdalene, Bridgnorth, 6299; St. Mary of Newstead, 6281; St. Mary of the Meadows, 6208; Secular canons, 6069; Settlement at Hackness, 6402; Visitations, 5750, 6222; Welbeck abbey, 6285; Welsh dioceses, 790; William Beverley, archdeacon, 1437, 5676; York Minster Tracts, 5878
— E. Margaret: Burke's manor rolls, 192, 4694; Carthusian order, 5927; Customary, 6179; Somerset Carthusians, 6304; Statute of Labourers, 3624; Wilts. parishes, 4489; Witham chronicle, 6324
— Edward A.: Ammianus, 2025; Christianity in Scotland, 2691, 2323; The early Germans, 2523; Zosimus, 2112
— Sir Edward Maunde: Avesbury's De gestis, 2790; B.M. Catalogue, 439; Baker's Chronicon, 2791; Chronicon Angliae, 2976; Facsimiles, 445; Fall of Richard II, 4113; Murimuth's continuation, 2931; Palaeography, 398; Salisbury catalogue, 1051; Usk's Chronicon, 2966
— Frederick H.: Roman Cheshire, 1570, 1577, 2053
— Faith: First century of Magna Carta, 3292; History of parliament, 3387; Magna Carta, its role, 3292
— James: History of Leicester, 5142
— James D. A.: Inventory, 705; Rose noble, 714; Sylloge, 704
— James Westfall: Literacy of laity, 6897; Medieval library, 7178
— John A. F.: Arrival of Edward IV, 2901; Later Lollards, 6873; Tithes disputes, 6831
— Ronald: Historiography, 30
Thomson, R. M.: Bury library, 6345
— Samuel Harrison: Adam de Bocfield, 6554; Hus, 6656; Latin bookbands, 399; Writings of Grosseteste, 6585; Wyclif, 873; 6648, 6662
— Theodore R.: Catalogue, 526; Customal of Cricklade, 4927
— Thomas: Instrumenta: Ragman Rolls, 3792
— Walter S.: Assize Roll, 3572
Thoresby Society (Yorks.), 1883
Thoresby, John, archbishop, Instructions for the people, 6691
Thoresthorpe (Lincs.), 4805
Thorgrimsson, Thor: Plenum parliamentum, 3380

Thorkelin transcripts of Beowulf, 441, 2332
Thorndike, Lynn: Incipits, 432, 6967; Magic and Science, 1423; Robert Holcot, 6592; Roger Bacon, 6547; University records, 7085
Thorne, Samuel E.: Bracton, 2985; Courts of record, 3737; Feudalism, 4683; Fitzherbert, 3654; Inns of court, 7147, 7157; Le Droit canonique, 6437; Livery of seisin, 3703; Magna Carta, 3285; Prerogativa regis, 3275; Readings and moots, 3002, 3345A, 7147; Thornton's Summa, 3003
— William: Chronicle, 1124, 2158, 2959, 6183
Thorner (Yorks.), 4936
Thorney abbey (Cambs.), 2603, 6102
— Island, 1496
Thornley, Isobel D.: Beverley sanctuary register, 1262, 6395; Great chronicle of London, 2885; Parliamentary notes, 3325; Treason by words, 3717; Year Book, 3649; Yorkists, 1209
Thornton chronicle, 6221
Thornton, Gladys A.: Clare (Suffolk), 5258; Documents, 1206
— Gilbert de: Summa de legibus, 3003
— Mary E.: Chronicle of St. Mary's Abbey, York, 6424
Thornycroft (Surrey), 4897
Thoroton Society (Notts.), 1783
Thoroton, Robert: Nottinghamshire, 1784
Thorpe, Benjamin: Ælfric's Homilies, 2292; Ancient laws, 2180, 2259; A.-S. chronicle, 2141; A.-S. kings, 1184; Bury chronicle, 2819; Diplomatarium, 2204; Florence of Worcester, 2981; Norman kings, 1184; Tayster's Chronicle, 2958
— Harry: Lichfield, 5251
— John (the elder): Registrum Roffense, 5793
— John (the younger): Custumale Roffense, 4780
— Lewis: Geoffrey of Monmouth, 2166
— Thomas: Charters of Battle Abbey, 6358
— William (Lollard), 6863, 6991
Thorpe in the Fallows (Lincs.), 4806
Thouless, Robert H.: The lady Julian, 6673
Three Fragments (Annals of Ireland), 2146
Throlam (Yorks.), Roman, 2069
Throsby, John: Thoroton's Nottinghamshire, 1784
Thrupp, Sylvia L.: Aliens, 5177, 5440; Change in medieval society, 175; Canterbury freemen's rolls, 4784, 5119; Early medieval society, 175; Economy and society, 5468; Gilds reconsidered,

5370; Grocers of London, 5192, 5393; Merchant class, 5178; Population, 5481; Problems of replacement-rates, 5484

Thurneysen, Rudolf: Handbook, 349; Irish law, 2251; Irish sagas, 2424; Irish texts, 2242; Nennius, 2167; Senchas Mār, 2241; Zeuss's Grammatica, 327

Thurston, archbishop of York, 1130, 5870

Thurston, Herbert: Life of St. Hugh, 5742; Saints, 1155

Tibbits, Edward G.: Records of Warwick, 5280

Tibesar, Antonine: Handbuch des Franziskanerorder, 6019

Tickhill psalter, 886

Tierney, Brian: Bracton, 2985; Foundations of conciliar theory, 5571; Grosseteste and papal sovereignty, 6586; Ockham, conciliar theory, etc., 5571, 6626; Poor law, 6446; Theological interpretation, 1459

— Mark A.: Arundel, 4597

— Michael: St. Patrick, 2324

Tigernach, Annals, 1117, 2160, 2170

Tighe, Robert R.: Windsor, 5033

Tilbury, Gervase of: Otia imperialia, 2961

Tiller, Terence: Gower's Confessio, 7016

Tillmann, Helene: Die päpstlichen Legaten, 6747

Tillott, P. M.: City of York, 5300

Timbal, Pierre-Clément: La Guerre de cent ans, 4192

Timings, Edward K.: Letters concerning eyre, 3504

Timmer, Benno J.: Judith, 2328

Timson, R. T.: Blyth priory cartulary, 6278

Tingey, John C.: Catalogue, 1750, 5207; Records of city of Norwich, 5211

Tin mines, 4325, 5513

Tinniswood, J. T.: English galleys, 4335

Tintinhull (Som.), 6838

Tipping, Henry A.: English homes, 820

Tiptoft, John, 6919, 6926

Tirechán, bishop: St. Patrick, 2324

Tison fee (Yorks.), 4499

Tissier, Pierre: Jeanne D'Arc, 4267

Tithes, 6088, 6831, 6845, 6857

Tithing, 2638, 5210

Titow, Jan Z.: Differences between manors, 4981; Evidence of population increase, 5485; Heriots and prices, 5815; Open field system, 4999; Rural society, 4701; Weather, 621A; Winchester manors, 5815

Titus, Edna B.: Union list, 92

Titus Livius Frulovisi, 1452, 2919, 2972

Tobler, Adolf: Wörterbuch, 297

Tockwith, cell of Nostell, 6411

Todd, Henry J.: Canterbury MSS., 1040; Lambeth MSS., 1008

— Hugh: Notitia Carliolensis, 5645

— James Eadie (essays), 1457

— James H.: Gaedhil and Gaill, 2174; Nennius, 2167

Tokarev, Sergei A.: Trade of the manor, 4971

Tolhurst, John B. L.: Breviary Hyde Abbey, 1319, 5910; Customary of Norwich, 5776

Tolkien, John R. R.: Angles and Britons, 340

Toller, Thomas N.: Bosworth's Dictionary, 277

Tolls, 2207, 5078, 5531

Tombs, 742, 867

Tomkinson, A.: Carucage, 3261; Retinues, 4283

Tomlins, Sir Thomas E. (d. 1841): Statutes, 3327

— Thomas E. (d. 1872): Olde tenures, 2990

Toms, Elsie: Chertsey Abbey Court rolls, 6351

Tonkin, Thomas: Carew's Cornwall, 1586

Tonnochy, A. B.: Seal-dies, 456

Tooting Beck (Surrey), 4893

Topham, John: Liber Garderobae, 3126; Roll of Edward III's fleet, 4289; Subsidy roll, 3146

Topographica Hibernica, 2881

Topography, 6, 615–16, 618, 1503, 1505–6, 1519, 1528–9. *See* each county by name

Torigni, Robert of: Chronique, 1123, 2962; Continuations of, 2853

Torksey (Lincs.), 4804

Torr, Cecil: Wreyland documents, 4732

Tosi, Michele: St. Columban, 2320

Totmonslow (Staffs.), 4386

Totnes, priory and town (Devon), 6127

Totteridge (Herts.), manorial survey, 1677

Tottington, Alexander, bishop, 5783

Toulouse, count of (Edward III), 1448

Tournaments, 484, 1450, 1467, 3117, 4282–3

Tournays of Caenby, family, 4584

Tourneur, Victor: Celts, 318

Tours, John of, bishop of Wells, 5596

Tout, Mary: Bibliography of T. F. Tout, 1458; St. Ursula, 1472

— Thomas F.: Administrative history, 1223, 1499; Bannockburn, 4081; Beginnings of a capital, 1499, 5179; Black Prince, 2812; Burglary, 1499; Chapters in administrative history, 1223; Civil service, 1499; Collected papers, 1499;

Tout, Thomas F. (*cont.*):
Communitas bacheleriae, 1499; Death of Edward II, 1499, 4139; Earldoms, 4060, 4684; Essays to, 1458; Fair (battle) of Lincoln, 1499, 2896; Firearms, 1499, 4301; Flintshire, 1499, 1918; Forgers, 1499; Gruffydd ap Cynan, 2902; Halton's register, 1499, 5646; History of England (1216–1377), 1183; Household of chancery, 1448, 1499, 3848; Literature and learning, 6927; London (as capital), 1499, 5179; Map under Edward I, 605; National balance sheet, 3258; Owens College essays, 1472; Parliament, 1446, 1499, 3365; Place of Edward II, 4140; Place of St. Thomas, 1499, 6498; Powicke's appreciation of, 1489; Some neglected fights, 1499; State trials, 3519 (review of, 1482); Study of chronicles, 1499; Tactics of Boroughbridge, 1499, 4301; Thomas de Cantilupe, 5726; Town planning, 1499; Wales and the March, 1492, 1499, 4067; Welsh shires, 1499; Westminster Chronicle, 1499, 2871
Town Houses, 96–7; 1435
— Planning, 815, 1384, 1485, 1499, 5349
Towneley, Christopher: Inquisitions, 3873
Towns, Roman, 271–3; 1361, 2045, 2051, 2073. *See* Boroughs
Townsend, George: Foxe's Actes and monuments, 6865
Township, 1387, 1484, 2637, 4450, 4863
Toy, Sidney: Castles, 841
Toynbee, Jocelyn M. C.: Art, 2078; Coins, 667
Tozer, Henry F.: Ancient geography, **266**
Trabut-Cussac, Jean P.: Cartulaires gascons, 3832; Gascony, 4103; Itineraire d'Édouard I, 4050; Le livre d'Agenais, 3817; Les coutumes sur les vins, 5403; Les possessions anglaises, 6212
Trade, manorial, 4971. *See* Commerce
Traditio (journal), 169
Trailbaston, articles of, 3489, 3544, 7043
Traill, Henry D.: Social England, 1196
Train, Keith S. S.: Inquisitiones, 4375; Lists of clergy, 5877; Nottinghamshire records, 4843
Traïson et Mort de Richard II, 2841
Traitors (1322), 4134
Transition Roman to Anglo-Saxon, 1470, 2104–5, 2110
Translations, bibliography of, 52
Transportation, inland, **749–50**
Trappe-Lomax, Richard: Clayton-le-Moors, 4450
Trash, Willard R.: Curtius's Literatur, 6879

Traube, Ludwig: Nomina sacra, 404; Vorlesungen, 400
Trautz, Fritz: England und das Reich, 4109; Literaturbericht, 36
Treason, 1464, 3484, 3519–20, 3709–17, 4211
Treasure trove, 766, 3668A
Treaties, Franco-Norwegian (1295), 4083
— Franco-Scottish (1295), 4083
— Hundred Years War, 3814
Treaty of Arras (1435), 4249
— of Brétigny, 3809, 3820, 4183
— of Northampton (1328), 4087
— of Paris (1259), 3831, 4098
— of Troyes (1420), 4239, 4248
Trefnant, John, bishop, 5730
Treharne, Reginald F.: Baronial plan, 4068; Battle of Lewes, 4068; Constitution, 1459; Knights, 4068; Mad parliament, 4068; Mise of Amiens, 1450; Nature of Parliament, 3365, 3407; Personal role of de Montfort, 4080; Studies supplementary to Stubbs, 1221
Tremblay, Pierre: La renaissance, 1394, 6892
Tremlett, Thomas D.: Rolls of Arms, 496; Stogursey charters, 6323
Trenholme, Edward C.: Iona, 2686
— Norman M.: Monastic boroughs, 5358; Right of sanctuary, 1262
Trentham priory (Staffs.), Chartulary, 6333
Tresham, Edward: Calendarium, 3800
Trespass, 3706
Trevelyan, George M.: Age of Wycliffe, 4157; Anonimalle Chronicle, 2787; Peasants' rising, 4158
— Papers, 4427
Trevet, Nicholas: Annales 1088, 2931, 2963
Trevisa, John de: trans. De proprietatibus, 6548; Fitzralph's Sermon, 6570; Higden's Polychronicon, 2895
Trevor, John, bishop of St. Asaph (possible author), 2856, 2865
Triads, 2387
Trial, by jury, 1248, 1252, 1258, 2988, 3503, 3625
— modes of, 3503, 5352
Trials, by battle, 1253, 1450, 3503A
— for heresy, 6442, 6863
— for treason, 3484, 3519–20, 3709, 3711, 4134
— of judges, 3519–20
— of peers, 3667
— of Templars, 6061–2
— state, 3484, 3519–20, 3713
Tribal custom, 2647
— hidage, 2213. *See* Hides
Trigg Minor (Cornwall), 4583

Trikingham, Elias of: Annales, 6177
Trillek, John de, bishop, 5730
Trinitarian friars, 6039
Trinoda necessitas, 2221, 2621
Tripartite Chronicle, 7017, 7049
— Life of Patrick, 2324
Tristram, Ernest W.: English painting, 856; Wall painting, 859
Trivium, 6642
Trokelowe, John of: Annales, 2964
Tropenell (Wilts.), Cartulary, 4490
Trover, 1246
Trow-Smith, Robert: Livestock husbandry, 5019
Troyes, Jean de: Louis XI, 2851
Trueman, John H.: Statute of York, 3343; Privy seal, 3849, 4141
Trussebut fee (Yorks.), 4499
Tryggvason, Olaf, 2438, 2450
Tschan, Francis: Adam of Bremen, 2149
Tuck, J. A.: Cambridge Parliament, 3420; Richard II and border magnates, 4110; Richard II's patronage, 7223
Tucker, Lena L.: Bibliography, 6994
— Susie I.: Anglo-Saxon Chronicle, 2142
Tudor cult of history, 1476
— historical thought, 263A
Tudor, Jasper, 7030
Tuetey, Alexandre: Journal d'un bourgeois, 2907
Tulane Symposium on Bracton, 2985
Tunstall (Staffs.), 4876
Tupling, George H.: Markets and fairs, 1455, 5536; South Lancashire, 3567, 4142
Tupper, Ferdinand B.: Guernsey, 1958
— Frederick: Benedictine reform, 2276; Map's Courtiers' Trifles, 6599
Turberville, Thomas: Elegy on Edward I, 1450, 7043
Turnbull, William B.: Advocates Library, 1062; Compota, 4600
Turner, Cuthbert H.: Worcester MSS., 452, 1052
— Derek H.: B.M. MSS., 875
— Edward: Custumal of Pevensey, 5316
— George James: Bookland and Folkland, 1455, 2623; Brevia placitata, 2992; Feet of fines (Hunts.), 3555; Forest pleas, 3517, 3897; Lincoln's Inn, 7155; Minority of Henry III, 4069; Register of St. Augustine's abbey, 6182; Statutes, 3336; Sheriff's farm, 3266; Year Books, 3646
— Ralph V.: Jury, 1248; King and his courts, 3683
— Thomas H.: Domestic architecture, 821; Manners and expenses, 4609

— William H.: Bodleian charters, 1020
— Mrs. W. J. Carpenter: Building of the Gracedieu, etc., 4336; Southampton as naval centre, 4336
Turton, Robert B.: Honour of Pickering, 3202, 3630, 3884, 3890
Turvey (Beds.), 4412, 5029, 6079, 6082
Turville-Petre, Edward O. Gabriel: Heroic age, 2462, 2587; Intellectual history, 2462; Legends in Icelandic MSS., 1433; Origins, 2462
Tutbury (Staffs.), 5253, 6334
Twemlow, Jesse A.: Liturgical credentials, 1426; Papal registers, 5547
Twiss, Sir Travers: Bracton, 2985; Monumenta juridica, 4286
Twitchwell, law suit, 4825
Twysden, Roger: Scriptores, 1124, 2802, 6183; Thorne's Chronica, 6183
Tyler, Wat, 4154. *See* Peasants' revolt
Tymms, Samuel: Wills, 4556
Tyndale (Northumb.), liberty of, 4671
Tynemouth (monastery) (Northumb.), 6277
— John of: Historia aurea, 1448, 2888, 2965; Nova legenda, 1158, 2287
Tyrrell, Edward: Chronicle of London, 2823, 7046
Tyrwhitt, Thomas: Ancient method, 3313
Tysilio, Brut, 2166
Tyson, Moses: Annals of Southwark and Merton, 2785, 5268; J. Rylands Library, 1036–7; Powicke's bibliography, 1450; Wilkinson's bibliography, 1459
Tyssen, John R. Daniel. *See* Daniel-Tyssen
Tytler, Patrick F.: Diary (1296), 4279

Überweg, Friedrich: Philosophie, 1409
Ugawa, Kaoru: Economic development, 4734; Lay estates, 4943
Ul'ianov, Iu. R.: Oksfordshirksii Manor, 4857
Ullman, Berthold L.: Duke Humphrey's MSS., 6928
Ullmann, Walter: Adrian IV, 6741; Cambridge chancellor's authority, 7109; Decision of the Roman Rota, 6429; Disputed election of Hugh Balsham, 5713; Eugenius IV, *et al.*, 1438, 5573; Forgotten dispute, 6399; Growth of papal government, 6724; Liber Regie Capelle, 1318; Medieval papalism, 6724; Origins of the Great Schism, 5572, 6740; Pellens's Die Texte, 6427; Principles of government, 1417
Ulnagers' rolls, 5333
Ulrich, Th.: Grotefend's Taschenbuch, 369

Ulrich's Directory, 90

Ulster, annals of, 1117, 2786

Ultan, bishop: St. Patrick, **337**; 2324

Uncial, English, 438

Underhill, Evelyn: Cloud of Unknowing, 6671; Fire of love, 6679; Scale of perfection, 6672

Underwood, Edgar Ashworth: History of medicine, 6963

Undreiner, George J.: Schnürer's Kirche, 1288

Universities, **916–24**; 1490

University clerks, petitions for benefices, 1473

— of Birmingham Historical Journal, 140

Union Catalogue of Periodicals, British, 89

— List of Serials U.S. and Canada, 92

United States, Census of manuscripts, 980

U.S. Library of Congress, Catalogues, 85–7

Unterkircher, Franz: Peregrinarius Hugonis, 4181

Unwin, George: Cloth industry, 1500; Cloth trade, 5415; Economic policy, 1500; Estate of merchants, 1469; Finance and trade, 1469, 5404; Gilds, 1500, 5186, 5371; Industrial organization, 5521; London tradesmen, 1469, 1500; Papers, 1500; Social evolution, 1469, 1500

Upcott, William: Carter's Cambridge, 1558; Topography, 1528

Upham, Edward: Index, 3322

Upland, Jack, 7049

Upton (Notts.), 4843

Upton, Nicholas: De studio militari, 4305

Upwood (Hunts.), 4978

Urban records and studies, **700–35**

Urban IV, pope, 3787A

— VI, pope, 6740

Urchfont (Wilts.), 4489

Ure, James M.: Benedictine office, 1347, 2277

Urry, William J.: Canterbury, 5124

Ursula, St., legend of, 1472

Urswick inventory, 4614

Urwin, Kenneth: Georges Chastellain, 2814

Uses and trusts, 1482

— ecclesiastical, 1334, 5718, 5749. *See* Liturgy

Usher, Abbott P.: Introduction, 1381; Prices of wheat, 5495

Usk, Adam of: Chronicon, **387**; 2966

Ussher, James: Sylloge, 1141

Ustick, W. Lee: Parchment, 408

Usury, 6438

Uthred of Boldon, 1450, 1477, 6555–6, 6660

Utley, Francis L.: Forward movement, 3350, 6882

Uttley, John: Channel Islands, 1959

Vacant, Jean M. Alfred: Dictionnaire, 1267

Vacarius: Liber pauperum, 1482, 3004

Vale Royal abbey (Ches.), 6106

Vale, M. G. A.: English Gascony, 4272

Valence, Aymer de (1307–24), 4127

— William de, 4057

Valentine (ship), 4336

Vallet de Viriville, Auguste: Chronique de Charles VII, 2813; Chronique de la Pucelle, 2840; Robert Blondel, 2798

Vallum, Roman, 2045

Valois, Chronique des, 2844

Valois, Noël: Le grand schisme, 5572

Valuation of Norwich, 6781

— of pope Nicholas, 1471, 3145, 6781, 6783

Van Caenegem, Raoul C.: Influences Roman and Canon Law, 2989; Royal writs, **51**; 3503

Van Dijk, Stephen J. P.: Liturgy, 1346

Van Dusen, Henry P.: Christian classics, 1133

Van Kersen, Lionel W.: National Register, **108**

Van Steenberghen, Fernand: Le mouvement doctrinale, 6880

Varley, Joan: Lincs. archives, 1716; Middlewich chartulary, 4423

— William J.: Hill forts, 1995

Vasselot, Marquet de: Bayeux Tapestry, 4276

Vatican archives, 5540–5

— MSS.: Exempla scriptuarum, **54**

Vaufrey, Raymond: Bibliographie annuelle, 1960

Vaughan, Henry F.: Wenlock, 5245

— Richard: Corpus Christi College MSS., 1033; Dukes of Burgundy, 4170; Election of abbots, 6170; Matthew Paris, 2941, 2979; Parker A.-S. Chronicle, 2142; Wallingford's Chronicle, 2173, 2975

Vautier, Charles: Registre des dons, 3813A

Veale, Edward W. W.: Bristol red book, 5081

— Elspeth M.: Craftsmen, 5177; Fur trade, 5405; Wine trade, 5395

Veeder, Van Vechten: Defamation, 1246

Venables, Edmund: Chronicle of Louth Park, 2831; Lincoln, 6790

Vendryes, Joseph: Lexique, 350; O'Rahilly's Irish history, 2129; Revue Celtique, 324

Venedotian code, 2222–3, 2227–8
Venette, Jean de: Chronique, 2967
Venice, Archives, 3834
Venn, John Archibald: Alumni Cantabrigiensis, 7110; Grace Book, 7058; Register of Christ's College, 7104; Register of Gonville and Caius College, 7111
Venta Silurum (Caerwent), 2072
Verbist, Gabriel H.: Willibrord, 2314
Verborum florida venustas, 1473
Vercauteren-de-Smet, Lina: Chatelains, 1447
Vercelli Book, 2268, 2327, 2340, 2361
Vere estates, 4658
Verge, court of the, 3670
Vergil, Polydore: English history, 2968
Verhulst, Adriaan E.: Finance, 3249
Versus rhythmici, 2969
Vespasian psalter, 1433
Vessberg, Olof: Swedish bibliography, 727
Vestments, ecclesiastical, 922
Vetus Liber Archidiaconi Eliensis, 5706
— Repertorium, 5744
— Registrum Sarisberiense, 5805
Vetusta Monumenta, 178, 742
Viard, Jules: Chronique de Jean le Bel, 2916; Grandes chroniques, 2883
Vicar-general register, 5717
Vicarages, 5740, 6847
Vicars choral, 5652, 5657, 5873, 5878
Vickers, Kenneth H.: England in later middle ages, 1188; Humphrey, duke of Gloucester, 4231
Victoria History of Counties, 1197, 1529–30
Vienne, Council of, 5570
Vierteljahrshrift für Sozial-und Wirtschaftsgeschichte, 170
Vigeois, Geoffrey of: Chronica, 2970
Vigfússon, Guðbrand: Dunstan Saga, 2303; Origines Islandicae, 2443; Orkney Saga, 2451; Saga of St. Edward, 2171
Viking Congress, 2581
— Society for Northern Research, 220
Vikings, **351–7** and **368–72**; 677, 761, 799, 1449, 1454, 2483–5, 2489
Villa (Roman), 2050, 2065, 2069, 2080, 2106
Village community, 1435, 1437, 1461, 2629–30, 2641, 2646, 2652, 3054, 4945
Villages, 1381, 1482, 2481, 2637, 3366, 4849–50, 4949, 6834. *See* Deserted villages *and* Lost villages
Villeins, 1462, 1468, 1501, 2652, 3057, 4429, 4803, 4959, 4972
Viller, Marcel: Dictionnaire, 5881
Villien, Antoine: Dictionnaire, **168**
Vinaver, Eugène: Malory, 7037, 7040; Miscellany to, 6052

Vincent, John A. C.: Calendar of heirs, 4339; First bishop of Bath, 5596; Glasney cartulary, 6107; Lay subsidies, (Lancs.), 3168
Vinea, Peter de, 425A
Vinogradoff, Sir Paul, 1489, 2533, 4971; Agricultural services, 4982; English society, 2650; Folkland, 2623; Growth of the Manor, 2651; Honour of Denbigh, 4943B; Justice Hengham, 1458; Oxford studies, 5450; Papers, 1501; Records, 4943B; Roman law, 1247; Villainage, 2652; Wat Tyler, 4154; Year-books, 3646
Vinsauf, Geoffrey: Third Crusade, 2906
Virginia Colonial Records Project, 971
Virgoe, Roger: Crown and local government, 7223; Elections of Suffolk, 3468; Indictments, Kent, 3562, 4784; King's council, 3306A; Lords' Journal, 3312; Members of parliament (1449), 3423; William de la Pole, 4232
Vising, Johan: Anglo-Norman language, 298
Vision, monk's, 6289
Visitations, 5320, 5618, 5624, 5673, 5703, 5712, 5733, 5750, 5756, 5767, 5780, 5783, 5805, 5845, 5849, 5882, 5917, 6114, 6222, 6235, 6283, 6345, 6348, 6380, 6390, 6807
Vitae. *See* Biography
Vitalis, Ordericus, 2908; Historia ecclesiastica, 1089, 1096, 1111, 1113, 2937
Vocabularium Saxonicum, 283
Voeus du Héron, 7049
Vogel, Cyrille: Regestum Clementis V, 5561
— Fridericus: Diodorus, 2025
Vooght, Paul de: Les Sources, 6663
Voretzsch, Karl: Einführung, 299
Vortigern, 2122, 2553
Voss, Lena: Heinrich von Blois, 5823
Voynich MS., 6544
Vulliamy, Colwyn E.: Middlesex and London, 762

Wace: Le Roman de Brut, 2974; Le Roman de Rou, 2974
Wace, Henry, Dictionary, 1268
Wacher, John S.: Cirencester, 2054; Civitas capitals, 2073
Wadding, Luke: Annales, 6011; Duns Scotus's Opera, 6565; Scriptores, 6012
Wade, Carol: Guide to reprints, 5
Wade-Evans, Arthur Wade: Annales Cambriae, 2144; Celtic Christianity, 2679; Emergence, 2136, 2558; Gildas, 2162; Nennius, 2144, 2162, 2167; St. David, 2321; Vitae, 1173; Welsh law, 2229

Wadley, Thomas P.: Wills, 4527

Wadmore, John F.: Hospitallers, 6192

Wadstein, Nils Elis: Norden och Vast-europa, 2524

Wages, **746–7**; 1376, 1468, 3443

Wagner, Sir Anthony R.: **59**; Catalogue of roll of arms, 499; College of arms records, 483, 1007; English ancestry, 527; English genealogy, 527; Heralds and heraldry, 483, 1485; Heralds of England, 484; Historic heraldry, 483; Hope's Grammar, 478; Introduction of peers, 3388; Kaminkow's Bibliography, 516; Kaminkow's Genealogical MSS., 515; Papworth's Dictionary, 497; Seal of Strongbow, 459; Sir Hugh Hastings' brass, 3503A

Wagstaff, J. M.: Dieulacres' economy, 6328

Wahrmund, Ludwig: William of Drogheda, 6448

Wainwright, Frederick T.: Æthelflaed, 1433; Anglian settlement, 2559; Archaeology, etc., 777; Battles of Corbridge, 2157; Ingimund's invasion, 2146, 2600; Problem of Picts, 2137, 2488

— Thomas: Barnstaple records, 5054

Waites, Bryan: Monastic settlement, 5904, 6393; Moorland farming, 5020

Waitz, Georg: Monumenta, 1114; Quellen-kunde, 48; Verfassungsgeschichte, 2525

Wake, Joan: Communitas villae, 4830

— William: State of church, 6819

Wakefield (Yorks.), 4932

— Tower (London), records in, 3488

Wakefield, Henry de, bishop, 4117

Wakelin, Martyn F.: Mirk's Festial, 6697

Walberg, Emmanuel: Anglo-Norman aspects, 300; Tradition hagiographique de Becket, 6502; Vie de St. Thomas, 6489

Walberwick (Suffolk), 6838

Walbran, John R.: Memorials of Fountains abbey, 6400

Walbrook, honour of, 1467

Walcott, Mackenzie E. C.: Cartulary of Lanercost, 6110; Registers of Chichester, 5655; Statutes of Holy Trinity, Chichester, 5653; William of Wykeham, 7132

Walden abbey (Essex), 6146

Walden, Lord Howard de, 556

— Thomas Netter of, 6611–12, 6660

Waldere, 2328

Wales:

— Administration, **129**; 1499, 2606, 3329, 3366, 3745, 3987

— Agrarian history, 1360

— Archaeology, 363, 385, 734, 738, 759, 773–4, 816, 1435, 1442, 1449, 1965–6, 1969, 1981, 1984, 1986, 1991, 1995, 2675

Wales: Archives, **129–30**; 1504. *See* Records, *below*

— Armorial bearings, 485

— Bibliography, 10, 12–13, 22, 38–9, 103, 110–11, 134, 516, 1627

— Biography and pedigrees, 507–8, 511, 513–14, 516, 540, 542, 544, 549, 562, 574, 2115, 2144

— Castles, 823, 831, 838–9, 1495, 1995, 4053, 4291

— Chroniclers, Annales Cambriae, 1084, 1089, 2144, 3785A; Brut y Twysogion, 2805; Gildas, 2162; Giraldus, 2881; Gruffydd, 2902; Margam annals, 2754; Monmouth, Geoffrey of, 1089, 1095, 2166; Nennius, 2167

— Church history, **379–81** and **790–2**; 200, 1129, 1142, 1147–8, 1150, 2122, 2254, 2321, 2665, 3786B, 5580, 5582, 5942, 5949–50, 5987A, 6027, 6048–9, 6573, 6711, 6783, 6790, 6800, 6806, 6828

— Education, 7095, 7136, 7146

— Geography, 592, 594, 600, 608, 1386, 1505, 2321

— Heraldry, 480, 485, 487, 490, 498

— History, 1186, 1194, 1198, 1435 Celtic, **279–82**; 544, 1360, 2211, 2477, 2546, 2573; Norman to Tudor, 549, 1472, 1493, 1499, 2144, 3187, 3987, 4000, 4040, 4049, 4053, 4059, 4067, 4070, 4116, 4118, 4163, 4202, 4219, 4234, 4310, 4675, 4978A, 5483; Roman, 2089, 2093

— Journals and societies, 28–9, 103, 105, 109–11, 123, 126, 141–2, 197–204, 316, 321, 326, 1563, 2239

— Language, 337–43, 363, 392, 1054, 2401

— Laws, **310–12**; 1194, 1482, 2244, 2647, 3675

— Literature, **346–7** and **350–1**; 339, 2119, 2125, 2127, 2132, 2423, 2665, 7030

— Local history, **26–7** and **250–3**; 1499 (Flintshire), 1499 (Shires), 4978A, 1505, 1512–13, 5022

— Lordships, 3638, 4633, 4675, 4978A

— Manors, 1505, 4675, 4943A, 4943B, 4978A

— Manuscripts and seals, **129**; 203, 423, 454, 1003, 2166, 2222, 2224

— Place-names, 638, 640

— Princes of, 544–5, 549

— Records, **26–7**, **129–30**, and **690–1**; 181, 423, 955, 1003, 1054, 1056, 1116, 1627; Charters, letters, etc., 3750,

3753, 3781, 3784–7, 4347, 4582A, 4633, 4633A, 4675; Church, **790–2**; 6783; Courts, 3496, 3539, 3567, 3636–40, 3675, 4675; Household accounts, 3113, 3115, 3125, 3131; Ministers' accounts, 3858–9, 4629A, 4632A, 4633, 4633A; Palatinate of Chester, 3856, 3859, 3862; Statutes, 3329
— Religious houses, 1299, 5895, 5898, 5949–50, 6048–9, 6252
— Roman, 1991, 2089, 2093
— Saints, **333**; 1155, 1173, 2321, 2665–6
— Sculpture, 1449
— Tribal system, 1482, 2546, 2647
Wales, John of, humanist, 1438
Waleys, Thomas, friar, 6924
Walford, Albert J.: Guide, 3
— Cornelius: Fairs, 5537
— Edward: Brayley's Surrey, 1833; County families, 574
Walford's Roll (c. 1273), 496
Walker, Adrian: Mirror of charity, 6633
— Curtis H.: Date of the Conqueror's ordinance, 6476; Eleanor of Aquitaine, 4023; Sheriffs, 3266
— David: Charters of Earldom of Hereford, 4440; Charters St. Peter's Abbey, Gloucester, 1453, 6156; Material in cartularies, 7224
— G. S. M.: ed. S. Columbani Opera, 2320
— H. E.: Bede, 2560
— James Douglas: Records of Lincoln's Inn, 7148–9
— Joan Hazelden: Liturgy, 1346
— John W.: Chartularies of Monk Bretton, 6409; Court rolls of Aldborough, 4935; Court rolls of Wakefield, 4932; History of Monk Bretton, 6409; Hunter's pedigrees, 563
— Margaret: Feet of fines, 3570
— R. F.: Hubert de Burgh, 4049
— Thomas A.: Biographical register, 7112
— Violet W.: Extent of Upton, 4843; Newstead priory cartulary, 6281; Records of Nottingham, 5224
Wall, Carolyn: York pageant, 7210
Wallace, Wilfred: St. Edmund of Canterbury, 5626
— William, biography of, 4078
— William A.: Mechanics, 6968
Wallace-Hadrill, John M.: Kingship, 2560A; St. Boniface, 7225
Wallach, Luitpold: Alcuin, 2295; Ogilvy's Books, 2359; Wattenbach, 66
Waller, Alfred R.: editor, 1400
Wallingford (Berks.), 4416, 5032, 6286
Wallingford, John of: Chronica, 1100, 2173, 2975

— William: Registrum, 6169
Wallis, John E. W.: Regnal years, 376
— Keith: House of Lords, 3381
Walls, Roman, 2085–7
Walmisley, Claude A.: Index, 3483
Walne, Peter: Barons' argument, 4052; Record Commissions, 963; Wills, **109**; 4511
Walpole, Ronald: Bell's Gaimar, 2875
Walsall (Staffs.), 5255, 6838
Walsh, James J.: De proprietatibus rerum, 6548
— Paul: The Four Masters, 2784; Tigernach annals, 2170
— William H.: Introduction, 247
Walsingham, Our Lady of (Norfolk), 6261
Walsingham, Thomas, 1092, 1118, 4130; see Galbraith, **388**; Annales Ricardi Secundi et Henrici Quarti, 2976; Chronicon Angliae, 2832, 2976; Gesta abbatum, 6168; Historia Anglicana, 2976; St. Albans Chronicle, 2976; Ypodigma Neustriæ, 2976
Walter, of Cantilupe, bishop, 4911
— of Coventry, Memoriale, 1114, 2855
— of Guisborough, Chronicle, 1099, 1103, 1114, 2827, 2888
— of Hemingburgh, or Hemingford. See Walter of Guisborough
— of Henley, Husbandry, 2987, 4631
— of Merton, 7121
— of Stapledon, bishop, 5715
— of Whitlesey, 1122, 6268
Walter, Hubert, archbishop, 1459, 2989, 5604, 5642–3
Walters, Henry B.: Antiquaries, **134**
Waltham Abbey (Essex), 2285, 6147–8
Walthamstow (Essex), 4525
— Antiquarian Society (Essex), 1638
Walther, Johann L.: Lexicon, 409
Walton (Staffs.), 4879
Walwyn, John: Vita Edwardi II, 2971
Wambaugh, Eugene: Littleton's Tenures, 2990
Wampach, Camille: Willibrord, 2314
Wanley, Humphrey, **47** and **304**; 425, 996
Wansdyke, 2552
Wapentakes, 4726, 4792
War, art of, **619–27**; 1485, 7225
— finance, 4259, 4293, 4311, 4315
— law of, 4305
— propaganda, 4243, 4260
Warburg and Courtauld Institute (journal), 780
Warburg, Harold D.: Caesar's expedition, 2043
Ward, Sir Adolphus W.: Cambridge History of English Literature, 1400

Ward, Gladys A.: Essex, 1634. *See* Thornton, Gladys A.
— Grace F.: Merchants staplers, 5406
— Gordon: Kent charters, **305**
— Harry L. D.: Catalogue of romances, 999
— James: Notts. books, 1780–1
— Jennifer C.: 4568
— John: Romano-British buildings, 2079
— John O.: Companion to music, 7208
— Paul L.: Coronation, 1358
Wardley, manor of, 6137
Wardon, honour of (Beds.), 4651
Wardrobe, **479–82**; 965, 1012, 4621, 5346
Wardships, 4344
Ware, Sir James: 33, 987; Annals of Ireland, 2782; Ancient Irish histories, 2924; De scriptoribus, 30; Historie of Ireland, 2924
Warenne, honour of, 4499. *See* Warren
Warenne, John de, 1478, 4681
Warin, Fouke Fitz, Sources of, 1486
Warks Park (Northumb.), 4839
Warkworth, John: Chronicle, 2977
Warner, Sir George F.: Benedictional, 880; Catalogue of B.M. MSS., 439; Catalogue of Dulwich muniments, 4891; Facsimiles, 444–5; Guthlac roll, 2310; Illuminated MSS., 874; Libelle of Polycye, 4328, 5338; Opera Cambrensis, 2881, 6573; Queen Mary's Psalter, 900
— Philip: Sieges, 4320
— Richard H.: Thorney abbey, 6102
Warrack, Grace: Revelations of Divine Love, 6673
Warrand, Duncan: Cokayne's Peerage, 556
Warren and Surrey, earls of, 4594. *See* Warenne
Warren, Frederick E.: Celtic church, 2680; Sarum missal, 1321
— Wilfred L.: King John, 4042; Peasants' Revolt, 4159; Simon Sudbury, 5640
Warrington (Devon), 5064
— (Lancs.), 4796
Wars of the Roses, 4202, 4207, 4221, 6804, 7030, 7223
Wartburg, Walther von: Dictionnaire, 290
Warton (Lancs.), 5022
Warwick (Warw.), 1849, 4210, 5280
— St. Mary's Church, 4912, 6370
— earl of, 2950, 4228, 4635, 4916
— rolls of arms, 2950
Warwickshire: Bibliography, 1842–3; Charters, 4485, 5273, 6371; Church, 1529, 6835; Cloth markets, 5418; County history, 1529, 1849, 4915; County journals and societies, 1844–

1848A; County records, 1504; Deeds, 4485; Domesday, 1529; Extents, 4911, 6369, 6371; Eyres, 3553; Feet of fines, 3616; Feudal tenures, 4624; Justices of peace, 3615; Manors and villages, 1849, 4624, 4911–16, 4995, 5480; Ministers' accounts, 4912–13; Parliament, 3471; Pleas, 3197; Religious houses, 6369–71; Sheriffs, coroners, etc., 3746A; Subsidy rolls, 3196–7; Topography, 1529; Urban history, 1529, 1849, 5272–80, 6368
Washington, George S. H. L.: Westmorland M.P.s, 3472
Wassand, Alande, judge, 3689
Wasserschleben, F. W. Hermann: Bussordnung, 2260; Kanonensammlung, 2261
Waterhouse, Edward: Fortescue, **925**
Waters, William H.: Edwardian settlement, 4070
— Robert E. C.: Roll of Lindsey, 3073
Watkin, Aelred: Archdeaconry of Norwich, 5774, 6860; Glastonbury, 6312, 6320; Receiver's roll, 5815
— Hugh R.: Totnes priory, 6127
— Morgan: Liber Landavensis, 5880A; Welsh laws, 2223
Watkins, Morgan G.: Huntington hundred, 1670; Radlow hundred, 1670
— Oscar D.: Penance, 2265
Watlington manor (Oxon.), 4857
Watney, Frank D.: Mercers' company, 5193, 5326
Watson, Charles B. B.: Maps, 599
— Charles Ernest: Minchinhampton custumal, 4759
— Edward J.: Pleas for Swineshead, 3551
— George: Bibliography, 14
— John: Memoirs, 4594
— W. B.: Florentine galley trade, 5441
— William J.: Celtic place-names, 643; Picts, 2488
Watt, Donald E. R.: University clerks, 6767
— John A.: Church in Ireland, 6805; English law and Irish church, 1438; Laudabiliter, 5556; Theory of papal monarchy, 6725
— Robert: Bibliotheca, 37
Wattenbach, Wilhelm: Alcuin, 2295; Geschichtsquellen, 66; Jaffé's Regesta, 1131; Schriftwesen, 410
Watts, B. H.: Records of Bath, 5246
— D. G.: A model, 5495
Waugh, William T.: Archbishop Peckham, 6772; Henry V, 4236; Joan of Arc, 1455; Lollard knights, 6874; Normandy (1420–2), 1458, 4262; Praemunire, 3345,

6773; Sir John Oldcastle, 6863; Stubbs's Studies, 1221

Waurin, Jehan de: Croniques, 2978

Waverley abbey (Surrey), 1099, 1114, 2766, 6355

Way, Albert, Promptorium, 312; Reading abbey documents, 6091

— Lewis J. V.: Charters of St. Nicholas church, 5087

Waynflete, William, bishop, Life of, 5820

Weale, Magdalene M.: English documents, 5149, 6984

Weapons, **103–6**

Weare, George E.: Collectanea, 6036

Wearmouth, abbey of, 2297, 2301, 6138. *See* Monk Wearmouth

Weatherly, Edward H.: Speculum, 1322

Weaver, Frederick W.: Cartulary of Buckland Priory, 6307; Feodary of Glastonbury, 4380, 6310; Somerset incumbents, 5597; Somerset index, 1810; Somerset wills, 4552

— John R. H.: *D.N.B.*, 531; George's Tables, 535; H. W. C. Davis memoir, 1466; John of Worcester's Chronicle, 2981; Wills, 4550

Weavers, 5204, 5420, 6341

Webb, A. N.: Cartulary of Burscough, 6197

— Clement C. J.: John of Salisbury, 6642–3, 6647; Roger Bacon, 1448

— Edward A.: Records of St. Bartholomew's, 6228

— Geoffrey: Ailred's Mirror of charity, 6633

— Geoffrey: Architecture, 783, 1485

— James F.: Lives of Saints, 2318

— John: Creton, 2856; Household expenses of Swinfield, 4612

— Philip C.: Jew: a legal person, 3973

Webster, Bruce: Acts of David II, 4088; Movements of Warwick, 4228

— Graham: Roman conquest, 2038; Roman mining, 2081; Roman villa, 2050

Wedderhal, priory of, 5645. *See* Wetheral

Wedel, Theodore D.: Attitude towards astrology, 6969

Wedemeyer, Ellen: Social groupings at fair, 5538

Wedgwood, Josiah C.: Audley's estates, 4383; Coats of arms, 499; History of parliament, **510–11**; 3389; John of Gaunt and parliament, 3437; North Staffs. deeds, 6331; Staffs. cartulary, 4480; Staffs. history, 1817; Staffs. parliamentary history, 3467; Testa de Nevill, 4387

Weights and measures, 5417, 5494, 5497–8, 6958

Weinbaum, Martin: Borough charters, 5024; Gewerbe-und Handelsgeschichte, 5407; Incorporation of boroughs, 5024; Law book, 5177; London eyre (1244), 3579A; London eyre (1321), 3579; London eyre (1341), 1455; London unter Eduard I, 1748; Stahlhof zu London, 5428; Verfassungsgeschichte, 5179; Zur Stellung des Fremden, 5440

Weiner, Abraham: Bibliography of Hansa, 5425

Weingarter, Rudolph H.: M. White's historical knowledge, 248

Weinstock, Maureen: Dorset history, 1621

Weise, Erich: Die Hanse, 5428

Weisgerber, Leo: Die Sprache, 325

Weisheipl, James A.: Arts curriculum at Oxford, 6929; John Dumbleton, 6971; Ockham and some Mertonians, 6627; Physical theory, 6970; Repertorium Mertonense, 6972; Roger Swyneshed, 1428; Sermo Epinicius, 6557

Weiss, Roberto: Henry VI and library of All Souls, 7179; Humanism, 6930; Humphrey of Gloucester, 1452; Piero del Monte, etc., 7180; Renaissance discovery, 6931

Welbeck abbey (Notts.), 6279, 6285

Welch, C. E.: Ecclesiastical records, **109**

— Charles: Churchwardens' accounts, 6838; Paviors, 5197; Pewterers, 5198

— Edwin: Suffolk Lollards, 6873

Welch Hampton (Salop), 4860

Well (Lincs.), 4805

Wellcome Historical Medical Library, 6937

Wellesley, Kenneth: Tacitus, 2025

Wellingborough (Northants.), 4935

Wellington (Som.), 5249

Wellington, Richard H.: Coroner, 3747

Wells City (Som.), 2069, 5248, 5592

Wells, cathedral and diocese, **758–9**; 1491, 2723, 6475

— Hugh of, bishop of Lincoln, 5740, 5746

Wells, Henry W.: Piers Plowman, 7022

— John E.: Manual, 275

— Warre B.: trans. Perroy, 4166

Wellstood, Frederick C.: Subsidy rolls, 3197

Welsh laws, **310–12**. *See* Wales

Welter, J. Th.: L'Exemplum, 6709A

Wendover, Roger of: Flores historiarum, 2168, 2979

Wenham, Leslie P.: Eboracum defences, 2045

Wenlock (Salop), Records, 5244–5

— Walter de, abbot, 6232

Were, Francis: Index, 1650

Wergeld, 2638, 2647

Werner, Karl: Bede, 2297

Weske, Dorothy B.: Clergy in parliament, 3480; Convocation, 1444, 6820

Wessels, Gabriel: Acta, 5973

Wessex, 761–2, 1453, 1470, 2298, 2533, 2543, 2547, 2552, 2556, 2616, 6309

Wessington, Prior John: Red book of Durham, 5695

West, Andrew F.: Philobiblon, 6562

— Francis J.: Justiciarship, 3684, 3850

— J.: Forest offenders, 3925

— James R.: Register St. Benet of Holme, 6259

— William: Cranborne Chase, 3926

West Felton (Salop), 4863

West Midlands, A.-S. charters, 2496

West Wales historical records, 201

Westerham (Kent), 4989

Westerham, John de: Custumale Roffense, 4780

Westlake, Herbert F.: Hornchurch priory, 6144; Parish gilds, 5372; Westminster abbey, 6251

Westmeston (Sussex), 4482

Westminster abbey, chronicles of, 2871, 2895

— History, 781, 2729, 5489, 5777, 6010, 6242–51, 7273

— Records, 1016, 1355, 1453, 4957, 6179, 6231–41, 6250

Westminster, area of, 965, 1499, 1742, 1746A, 3241

— palace, 781, 1356, 3139

— provisions of, 1467

— wills, 4545

— Matthew of: Flores Historiarum, 2871, 5789

Westmorland: Antiquities, 737; Bibliography, 1591A; Charters, 1851, 4486–7; County history, 1496, 1597–8, 1851–2; County journals and societies, 1850; County records, 1504; Feudal tenures, 4391, 4486–7; Parliament, 3472; Pleas, 3617–18; Pipe rolls, 3085–6; subsidy, 3154A; Wills, 4516, 4566

Weston-under-Lizard (Staffs.), 4880

Westrup, Sir Jack: England: Mittelalter, 7211

Westwood, John O.: Facsimiles, 453; Lapidarium, 363

Wetheral, priory (Cumb.), 5645, 6113

Wethered, Florence T.: Lands and tythes, 6088; St. Mary's Hurley, 4417, 4710

Weymouth (Dorset), 5068

Whale, Thomas W.: Exon Domesday, 3011; Pipe rolls (Devon), 3089; Somerset Domesday, 3028; Tax Roll (Devon), 3157; Testa de Nevill, 4351

— Winifred S.: Champion's Louis XI, 4245

Whalley abbey (Lancs.), 6203

Whalley, Peter, Bridges's Northamptonshire, 1766

Whaplode (Lincs.), 6041

Wharram Percy (Yorks.), 766

Wharton, Henry: Anglia sacra, 1125, 2164, 5612, 5669

Whatley, Stephen: Rapin's Acta, 3766

Wheat, 5488

Wheatley (Oxon.), 4850

Wheatley, Henry B.: Domesday bibliography, 3047; Lords' meeting place, 3374

— Joseph L.: Armorial bearings, 485

Wheeler, G. H.: Antonine iter, 2029; Asser, 2147; West Saxon kings, 547

— George W.: T. Bodley's letters, 1018

— Harold F. B.: History (a journal), 125

— Sir (Robert E.) Mortimer: Archaeology, 750; Colchester, 2055; Editor, 2057; Homage to C. Fox, 1435; London and Saxons, 2489; London and Vikings, 2489, 2601; Prehistoric and Roman Wales, 1991; Recent archaeology, 766; Roman building, 2080; Roman excavations, 2070; Roman London, 2064

— Tessa V.: Caerleon, 2089; Roman excavations, 2070

Whellan, William: Cumberland and Westmorland, 1598

Whelock, Abraham: Anglo-Saxon Chronicle, 2142

Whethamstede, John: Registrum, 1103, 2980, 6169, 7180

Whimster, Donald C.: Surrey, 762

Whitaker, Thomas D.: Craven, 1893, 6397; Richmondshire, 1894; Whalley, 6204

Whitbread, L.: Æthelweard, 2140; Wulfstan, 2315

Whitby abbey (Yorks.), 6402, 6422

— monk of, 2123, 2281, 2308

— synod of, 2701

— town (Yorks.), 5299

White Book (Cinque Ports), 5314

— Castle (Wales), 4633

— Rose, Chronicles of, 1101, 2735

White, Albert B.: Common council, 3390; Early instances, 3408; Oxford meeting, 3301; Self-government by king's command, 3390

— Beatrice: Poet and peasant, 7223

— Charles H. Evelyn: Domesday Cambs., 3017; Domesday of Ipswich, 3187, 5260

— Caroline L.: Ælfric, 2272, 2292

— Donald A.: Litus Saxonicum, **365**; 2113

— Geoffrey H.: Cokayne's Peerage, 556; Constables, 3748; Financial administration, 3267; Household, 3116; Stephen's earldoms, 4686

— Lynn J.: Technology, 1424

— Morton: Foundations, 248

— Newport J. D.: St. Patrick, 2324

— Peter: Historia Augusta, 2025

— Robert: Dukery Records, 6279

— Winifred P.: Manuscripts of Modus, 3349

Whitehead, F.: ed. Vinaver essays, 6052

Whitelock, Dorothy: After Bede, 2148; Alfredian prose, 2352; Anglo-Saxon Chronicle, 2141–2; Anglo-Saxon coinage, 1454; Anglo-Saxon reader, 286; Asser, 2147; Beginnings, 1190, 2504; Beowulf, 2362; Blake's Liber Eliensis, 2164; Changing currents, 2504; Chevallier's Norman Conquest, 3980; Conversion of Danelaw, 2726; Egil's Saga, 2445; English Historical Documents, 17; Essays to, 7225; Leges Edwardi, 2185; Northumbria, 1433; Pelican history, 1190, 2504; Peterborough Chronicle, 441, 2142; Scandinavian names, 2602; Seafarer, 1429; Sermo Lupi, 2328; Wills, 2205; Wulfstan, 301; 1493, 2315

Whitewell, J. B.: Lincolnshire, 2061

Whithorn (Scottish monastery), 5862

Whiting, Bartlett J.: Vows of the heron, 7049

— Charles E.: A.-S. bishops, 2727

— William: Excavations, 2070

Whitlesey, Walter de: Historia, 6268

Whitley deeds, 1453

Whitley, Edward: Pottery, Roman, 2069

— Thomas W.: Charters of Coventry, 5273; Representation of Coventry, 3471

Whitmore, John B.: Genealogy, 517

Whitney, James P.: Cambridge Medieval History, ed., 1176; Helps for Students, 260; Hildebrandine essays, 6726; Wyclif Society, 1448

Whitrow, Magda: Isis bibliography, 6934

Whittaker, William J.: Horn's Mirror, 2991; Maitland's Equity, 3725; Forms of action, 3704

Whittick, G. Clement: Roman mining, 2081

Whitting, Philip D.: Coinage, 1454

Whittington, Richard, 5177, 5194, 5375

Whittlewood forest, 3896

Whitton, C. A.: Brooke's Coins, 673; Coinages of later Middle Ages, 707, 715

Whitwell, Robert J.: Monasteries and wool trade, 5422; Italian bankers, 5522; Regesta, 3779; Revenue and expenditure, 3258

Whorwelsdown, hundred of, 4777

Wickham, Glynne: Early stages, 6995

Wick Rissington (Glos.), 4760

Wickwane, William, archbishop, 5856, 5858

Wiclif, John. *See* Wyclif, John

Widsith, 2328, 2345–6

Wigan (Lancs.), 3567, 4142, 4791, 5133

Wight, Isle of, 1529, 1659, 1664

Wightman, Wilfred E.: Earldom of fitz Osbern, 4687; Lacy family, 4595

Wigmore (Hereford), last abbot, 1437, 1477

Wigmore, John H.: Tortious acts, 1246

Wigram, Spencer R.: Cartulary, 6295

Wigston Magna (Leics.), 3170, 4802, 5453

Wigtoft (Lincs.), 6838

Wilburton (Cambs.), manor, 4719

Wilfrid, St., 1487, 2284–5, 2289, 2313, 2727, 5878

Wiliam, Aled R.: Welsh laws, 2228, 2239

Wilkes, J. J.: Hadrian wall forts, 2045

Wilkins, David: Concilia, 1142; Tanner's Bibliotheca, 33, 987

Wilkinson, Bertie: Chancery under Edward III, 3851; Constitutional history, 3852, 4071, 4143, 4233; Coronation oath, 1455; Coronation records, 173; Council of Exeter, 5060; Crisis (of 1051), 2578; (of 1233–4), 4071, 4113; Deposition of Richard II, 3365, 4113; Essays to, 1459; Fact and fancy, 4234; Government during Richard's absence, 4029; Later middle ages, 1183; Northumbrian separatism, 2578; Peasants' revolt, 4160; Politics and politicians, 3391; Protest of Arundel and Surrey, 4122; Sherburn indenture, 4116; Studies in constitutional history, 3391, 4144; Treaty of Leake, 1450

Wilks, John: Catalogue of palaeography, 377

— Theodore C.: Hampshire, 1664

Willard, James F.: Church and lay taxes, 6830; Delivery of letters, 3853; English government at work, 3836; Index to writers, 8; Inland transportation, 5539; Memoranda rolls, 1458; Powicke on, 1489; Royal authority and universities, 7091; Surrey taxation returns, 3191; Taxation of boroughs, 1455; Taxes on personal property, 3268

— Rudolph: Blickling homilies, 441, 2267

Willems, Jan Frans: Klerk's Rymkronyk, 2911

William I: Chroniclers of reign, 389; 2741; History of, 589–93; 2578, 3040, 3913, 3918, 4165, 6476; Records of, 436, 469, 555, 1448, 2182, 2187, 2191, 3779, 5631

William II: Chroniclers of reign, **389**; History of, **589–93**; 3918; Records of, 436, 2157, 2191, 3779
— Marshal, earl of Pembroke, 1499, 2896, 4033
— earl of Gloucester, 1453
— king of Scotland, 3794
— Lord Hastings, 5502
— Monk of Canterbury: Vita S. Thomae, 6487
— St., of Norwich, 3937
— St., of York, 1477, 5870
— de Montibus, 1459
— of Amorica, 2947
— of Beverley, 1437, 5676
— of Chambre, 5685
— of Colchester, 6244
— of Dene, 5795
— of Drogheda, 6437, 6448
— of Jumièges, 1092, 1096. *See* Jumièges
— of Longchamp. *See* Longchamp
— of Malmesbury. *See* Malmesbury
— of Newburgh, 1095, 1103, 1114, 1123
— of Pagula. *See* Pagula
— of Poitiers, 1096, 1111
— of St. Calais, 2157, 5675
— of Windsor, 1464, 3392
— of Worcester, 1103, 1113, 1441, 1476, 2982
— of Wykeham. *See* Wykeham
— Salt Archaeological Society (Staffs.), 1814
Williams, Albert H.: Denbighshire, 1914; History of Wales, 1198
— Ann: Dorset Domesday, 3020; Exon Domesday, 3011; Inquisitio geldi, 3066; V.C.H. Dorset, 1529
— Arnold: Protectorium pauperis, 7049
— Benjamin: Gesta Henrici V, 2877; Traïson et Mort, 2841
— Charles H.: Coram rege rolls, 3677; Norfolk election, 3438; Year Book, 3651
— Cyril R.: Flintshire, 1918
— D. T.: Trade, 1465
— David H.: Welsh Cistercians, 5950
— E. T.: *D.N.B.*, 531
— Edward (Iolo Morganwy): Gwentian Brut, 2805; Myvyrian Archiology, 1116, 2382
— Eileen A.: Bibliography of Giraldus, 2881
— Elijah: Early Holborn, 5180; Staple Inn, 7158
— Ethel C.: Lord of Bedford, 4273
— George: Bekynton's Correspondence, 3776
— George H.: Norman Anonymous, 6427

— Glanmor: Welsh church, 5879C, 6806; Welsh local history, **250**
— Gwyn A.: London: commune to capital, 1748, 5181
— Harry F.: Index to Festschriften, 1425
— Hugh: Christianity in early Britain, 2681; Gildas, 2162
— Sir Ifor: Aneirin, 2384; Nennius, 2167; Red Book of Hergest, 2386; Taliesin, 2385; Wales and the North, 2139, 2561; Welsh place-names, 640; Welsh poetry, 2425; When did British become Welsh? 2139
— John: Denbighshire, 1915
— John ab Ithel: Annales Cambriae, 2144; Brut y Tywysogion, 2805
— John E. Caerwyn: Taliesin, 2385
— John F.: Essex deeds, 4435
— Jonathan: County of Radnor, 1943
— Laurence F. Rushbrook: St. Alban's abbey, 2728, 6170
— Mary W.: Social Scandinavia, 2463
— Neville J.: editor, 4491
— Owen: Denbighshire bibliography, 1912
— Ralph Vaughan: Book of carols, 7207
— Robert: Lexicon, 330
— Robert F.: Princes of Wales, 549
— S.: ed., Glamorgan Historian, 1922
— Stephen J.: Laws of Hywel Dda, 2225
— William Llewelyn: Itinerarium Cambriae, 2881
— William O.: Caernarvonshire, 1900
— William Retlaw: Parliamentary history, 3459
Williamson, Dorothy M.: Legation of Cardinal Otto, 6748; Lincoln MSS., 1048. *See* Owen, Dorothy M.
— Edward W.: Letters of Osbert of Clare, 6239
— F.: Tribal hidage, 2213
— John Bruce: The Temple, London, 6064, 7159
Willibald, St.: Hodoeporicon, 2290; Life of St. Boniface, 2284–5, 2290, 2299
Willibrord, St., Life of, 2284, 2290, 2295, 2314
Willingdon (Sussex), 4900
Willis, Browne: Cathedrals of Wales, 5879D
— Dorothy: Estate Book, 4830
— Robert: Architectural history of Canterbury, 813; of colleges of Cambridge, 7113
Willis-Bund, John W.: Black book of St. David's, 5880F; Celtic church, 2682; Inquisitions, 4394; Register of Godfrey Giffard, 5837; Register of William Ginsborough, 5838; Sede vacante

register, 5839; Subsidy roll of Worcestershire, 3199; Worcestershire and Westminster, 2729

Willner, Hans: Adelard von Bath, 6525

Wills, **647–54**; 426, 1246, 2205, 5247, 5249, 5298, 5621, 5704, 5714–15, 5717, 5737, 5741, 6283, 6443

Wilmart, André: Bekynton's Florilège, 5595; Edith of Wilton, 2304; Maître Adam, 6324

Wilmhurst, Thomas B.: Catalogus, 1042

Wilson, Arthur E.: Custumals, 4900–1, 6356

— Curtis: William Heytesbury, 6973

— David M.: A.-S. metalwork, 872; A.-S. rings, 1433; A.-S. rural economy, 2647A, 2653; Anglo-Saxons, 761, 2490; Vikings, 2603; Viking achievement, 2587

— David R.: Roman frontiers, 2094; Roman sites, 2015

— Frank P.: Oxford History of English Literature, 1402

— Henry Austin: Benedictional, 880; Liturgy, 2704; Magdalen College, 7132A; Willibrord, 2314

— James: Chronicon de Lanercost, 2836; Register of St. Bees, 6112; V.C.H. Cumberland, 1529

— James Maurice: Accounts of Worcester, 5825; Compotus rolls, 5831; Corrodies at Worcester, 5830; Liber albus, 5832

— K. P.: Chester customs accounts, 3863, 5043, 5331

— P. A.: Ninian, 2323; Roman and Welsh Christianity, 2683; Use of terms, 2604

— Richard M.: English and French, 296; Equatorie of planets, 6960; Lost literature, 2330, 6996; Middle English texts, 6986; Vespasian Psalter, 1433

— Roger B.: Handlist, 1843

— Rowland A.: Romsley courts, 4928; Register of Walter Reynolds, 5841; Register of William Ginsborough, 5838; Registers of bishops of Coventry, 5668

— William J.: Census of MSS., 980

Wilson-Fox, Alice: Barclay family, 4570

Wilton abbey (Wilts.), 2304, 6379

— diptych, 858, 1464

Wiltshire: Antiquities, 1529; Bibliography, 1853–5; Charters, 1861, 4400, 4437, 4489–90, 5283, 6364, 6372, 6376, 6378; Church, 1529, 1861, 4489, 4924; County history, 772, 1529, 1860–1, 3034, 4492; County journals and societies, 1856–9; Deeds, 4488, 4490–1; Domesday, 1529; Extents, 4917, 4922; Eyres, 3521, 3622, 3625; Feet of fines, 3619–21, 3623, 4489; Feudal tenures, 4393, 4492;

Forests, 1529; Inquests, 1861, 4392–3, 4489; Manors and villages, 4917–27; Parliament, 1529, 3473; Pleas, 1861, 3624, 4489; Pipe rolls, 3096; Religious houses, 6372–9; Subsidy rolls, 3198, 4489; Taxation, 3198; Topography, 1529; Urban history, 5281–5; Wills, 4560; Woollen industry, 1529

— earldom of, 4578

Wimbledon (Surrey), 4895

Winbolt, Samuel E.: Roman villa, 2080

Winchcombe abbey (Glos.), 1453, 2775, 4762, 6160–1

Winchell, Constance M.: Bibliography, 3

Winchelsea (Sussex), 5320

Winchelsey, Robert, archbishop, 1471, 5609, 5616, 5644, 5845, 6811

Winchester, city of, 1386, 5112–15, 5369

— church and see of, chronicles, 1108, 1114, 1123, 1125, 1467, 2142, 2767, 2951; history of, **783–5**; 2312, 2715, 6520, 6790; manors of, 3072, 5479, 5489, 5815

— Hyde abbey, 2165, 5814

— St. Giles fair, 5525

— St. Swithun priory, 1468, 5812–13

— Bible, 899

— College, 7135, 7138

— parliament (1449), 3423

— rout of, 1486

— school of painting, 889

— Lantfred, monk of, 2312

Windisch, Ernst: Irische Texte, 351, 2388

Windsor (Berks.), 1386, 1546, 3117, 5033

— St. George's Chapel, 6068

Windsor, William of, Irish parliament, 3392

Wine trade, 5389, 5395

Winfield, Sir Percy H.: Chief sources, **454–5**; 1229; History of conspiracy, 3708; Maitland's essays, 1483

Wing, Donald G.: Short-title catalogue, 71

Winkfield (Berks.), tenants of, 6086

Winn, Herbert E.: Wyclif's English writings, 6650

Winship, George P.: William Caxton, 7221

Winslow (Bucks.), 4713

Winterbottom, Michael: Æthelweard, 2140

Winterfield, Luise von: Tidemann Lemberg, 5442

Winters, William: Waltham Holy Cross MSS., 6148

Winwaed, battle of, 2487

Wireker, Nigel: Speculum stultorum, 7042

Wirral (Ches.), 3923, 4726

— Notes and Queries, 1568

Wisbeck, deanery (Ely diocese), 5712

Wisby (Gotland), 4286

Wise, Charles: Compotus of Kettering, 4828
— Francis: Asser's Annales, 2147
— John R.: New Forest, 3927
Wissingsete (Norfolk), Charters, 4454
Wiston (Sussex), 4904
Wistowe (Hunts.), 6175
Witan, 2617, 2620
Witelo: Optics, 6954
Witham Charterhouse (Som.), 6324
Withington, Roman and Saxon, 2099, 2539
Withington, Edward T.: Bacon's De retardatione, 6538
Withycombe, Elizabeth G.: Christian names, 591
Witney, Denis: Hooton Pagnell, 4942
Wittkower, Rudolf: Art, 810
Wix priory (Essex), 1453, 6149
Wodderspoon, John: Ipswich, 5264
Woderstone, Henry (friar), 6006
Woledge, George: Borough of Leeds, 5295
Wolf, Lucien: Jewish bibliography, 3931
Wolff, Philippe: Les Cahorsins, 5434; Un Problème d'origines, 4191
Wolffe, Bertram P.: Acts of resumption, 3365, 3409; Crown lands, 3132A, 4688; Henry VI, 4234; Henry VII land revenues, 3132A, 3270; Management of royal estates, 3132A; Royal demesne, 3269
Wollaston Hall (Notts.), MSS., 4693
Wolseley charters, 4477
Wolter, Allan B.: Duns Scotus, 6565
Wolters, Clifton: Cloud of Unknowing, 6671
— Hans: Ordericus Vitalis, 2937
Wombourne (Staffs.), 4471
Wombridge priory (Salop), 6301
Women, ownership of lands, 1496
Wood, Alfred C.: Nottinghamshire, 1785
— Anthony: William Dugdale, 1147
— Anthony À.: Survey of Oxford, 7134; University of Oxford, 7133
— Ethel M. (Lecture), 1330
— Henry: Tamworth records, 5253
— Herbert: Justiciary rolls, 3641; Public Records of Ireland, 1078; Templars in Ireland, 6065
— Herbert Maxwell: Wills, 4524
— Margaret E.: Domestic architecture, 822; Medieval house, 822; Norman domestic architecture, 822; Seals, 467
— Mary A. E. (Green): Letters of royal ladies, 4608
— Susan: Monasteries and patrons, 5905
Woodbine, George E.: Bracton, 2985; County courts, 3741; Glanvill, 2989; Law French, 37; Law tracts, 2996;

New curia regis rolls, 3485; Statute of Merton, 3334; Thornton's Summa, 3003; Trespass, 3706
Woodcock, Audrey M.: Cartulary of St. Gregory, Canterbury, 6185
— Brian L.: Ecclesiastical courts, 6485
Woodford, William: Wyclif, 6864
Woodforde, Christopher: Stained glass, 865
Woodhouse, Reginald I.: John Morton, archbishop, 5635
Wood-Legh, Kathleen L.: Appropriation of parish churches, 6861; Knights' attendance, 3441; Perpetual chantries, 6862; Riess' Electoral law, 3384; Sheriffs, etc. in parliament, 3452; Small household, 4639; Studies in church life, 6807
Woodlock, Henry, bishop, 5817
Woodruff, Charles Eveleigh: Act book of consistory court, 6486; Canterbury Library, 1041; Chartulary of hospital of St. Laurence, 6186; Financial aspect, 5622; Letters to prior of Christ Church, 7062; Memorials of Christ Church, Canterbury, 5623; Monastic chronicle at Canterbury, 5614; Sacrists' rolls, 5611; Sede vacante institutions, 5599; Sede vacante wills, 4535; Visitation rolls, 5624; Will of Peter de Aqua Blanca, 5737
Woodstock (Oxon.), 4855
— Thomas of (Gloucester): Ordenaunce and Fourme of fightyng within Listes, 3503A
Woodville, Anthony (Lord Scales), 4228, 4282
— Elizabeth, 3129, 4216, 4220
Woodward, Bernard B.: Hampshire, 1664; Richard of Cirencester's Tractate, 2026
— John: Ecclesiastical heraldry, 500; Heraldry, 486
— Samuel: Manual, 1751
Woody, Kennerly M.: Council of Constance, 5565
Woof, Richard: Catalogue, 1863
Wookey (Som.), 4870
Wool and woollens, 1381, 1446-7, 1469, 1529 (Wilts.), 3145, 3231, 3342, 5333-4, 5393, 5408-22, 5445
Wooldridge, Harry E.: Harmony, 7195
— Sidney W.: A.-S. settlement, 1465
Woolf, Stuart: trans., Marongiu's Parliament, 3366
— Rosemary: Juliana, 2328; Religious lyric, 6997
Woolhope Naturalists' Field Club (Herefordshire), 1669
Woolley, John S.: Bibliography, 627

— Reginald M.: Catalogue of Lincoln MSS., 1048; Constitutions of diocese of London, 5765

Woolmer forest, 3896

Worcester Chronicle (Anglo-Saxon Chronicle), 2142

— Church and diocese, chronicles of, 1114, 2168, 2769, 2969; history of, 1471, 1475, 2709, 2724, 4958, 4964, 4987, 5844-8, 6784, 6790, 6802; library of, 1052; records of, 452, 2200, 2220, 3071, 4117, 5824-43, 6384

— City, 1863, 5027, 5286, 5369

— St. Swithun's, 6385

— St. Wulstan, 6386

Worcester, Florence of, 2981

— John of, 2981

— Samson, bishop of, 2200, 3053

— Senatus, prior, 2311

— William of. *See* William

Worcestershire: Bibliography, 1862-3; Charters, 1867, 4493-4, 6382, 6385-6; Church, 1529, 1867; County history, 1529, 1866-7; County journals and societies, 1864-5; County records, 1504; Domesday, 1529, 3061, 3071; Eyres, 3576, 3627; Feet of fines, 3626; Feudal tenures, 4687; Inquests, 4394; Manors and villages, 4928-9; Religious houses, 6380-6; Subsidy rolls, 3199-201; Surveys, 1529; Topography, 1529; Urban history, 5286-7; Wills, 4561

Worde, Wynkyn de, 1158

Wordsworth, Christopher: Cartulary of St. Nicholas hospital, 6378; Church services, 1328; Consuetudinarium Lincolniensis, 5738; Old Service-books, 1348; Ordinale Sarum, 1321; Statuta Sarisbiriensis, 5803; Statutes of Lincoln, **170**; 5749

Workman, Herbert B.: John Wyclif, 6664

Worksop (Notts.), 6279

World Map by Richard of Haldingham, 606

Wormald, Francis: A.-S. illumination, 904; Bayeux Tapestry, 4276; Drawings, 904; Fitzwilliam MSS., 1033; Kalendars, 1349; Library before 1700, 7181; St. Albans Psalter, 902; St. Ethelwold's Benedictional, 880; Seals, 465; Sherborne cartulary, 1452, 6131; Westminster paintings, 860; Winchester illumination, 7225

Worsfold, Thomas C.: Staple Inn, 7158

Worth, Richard N.: Records, 5061; Tavistock records, 5064

Wotton, William: Leges Wallicae, 2222

Wreck rolls, 1441

Wrenn, Charles L.: Beowulf, 2335;

Caedmon, 2339; Old English grammar, 285; Old English literature, 2363; Saxons and Celts, 2138

Wretschko, Alfred von: Somercote's Traktat, 6447

Wretts-Smith, Mildred: Farming, 5021

Wreyland (Devon), Documents, 4732

Wright, Andrew: Court-hand, 411

— Charles H.: London Library, 82-3

— Cyril E.: Bald's Leechbook, 441, 2365; Sir Edward Dering, 1429; Disposal of libraries, **134**; Library before 1700, 7181; Rous's English roll, 2950; Saga in England, 2364; Vernacular hands, 401; Wanley, 425, 996

— David H.: Vespasian Psalter, 441; Uncial, 447

— Elizabeth C.: Common law in forests, 3928

— Frederick A.: Later Latin literature, 1404, 6898

— Herbert G.: Protestation of Richard II, 4113; Richard II and Gloucester, 4138

— James: Rutland, 1795

— John K.: Aids to geographical research, 71

— John Robert: Archbishop Walter Reynolds, 5638

— Joseph: Dictionary, 288; Grammar, 288

— Richard P.: Roman inscriptions, 2015, 2027

— Ruth C.: Wanley, 425, 996

— Thomas (F.S.A.): Ancient laws, 7053; Anglo-Latin poets, 7042; Biographia, 543; Celt, Roman, *et al.*, 743; Domestic manners, 1382; Gaimar, 2875; Gesta Herwardi, 2878; Giraldus Cambrensis, 2881; History and topography, 1640; Langtoft, 2913; Maidstone's Richard II, 7049; Map's poems, 6600-1; Neckham's De naturis, 6607; Political songs, 5337, 7048-9; Popular treatises, 2292, 2370; Rental of Wroxeter, 4861; Roll of arms, 4295; Vocabularies, 315

— Thomas of Durham: Louthiana, 743

— William: Investigations of princes in tower, 4203

— William Aldis: Robert of Gloucester's Chronicle, 2882

Writing, 406, 408, 410, 7173

Writings on British History, 38-9

Writs, **51**; 2992, 2996, 3503, 3660, 3662, 3851, 3853, 6454, 6467, 6477

— Anglo-Saxon, **304**; 1433, 2197, 6236

— Facsimiles of, 413, 2191

— Parliamentary, 3317

— Procedure without, 3513

— Register of, 1482, 3499

Writtle, manor of (Essex), 4747A
Wrotham (Kent), Assize rolls, 3559
Wrotham, William of, 4325
Wrottesley, Hon. George: Bagot family, 4476; Burton chartulary, 6326; Chetwynd chartulary, 4474; Crécy and Calais, 4193, 4278; Dieulacres chartulary, 6328; Early chancery proceedings, 3609; Final concords, 3611; Fine rolls, 3764; Forest pleas, 3893; Hundred rolls, 4386; Liber Niger, 3006; Military service, 4285; Plea rolls, 3610; Ronton chartulary, 6329; Staffordshire chartulary, 6331; Stone chartulary, 6332; Subsidy rolls, 3184, 3186; Wrottesley family, 4596
Wroxall Abbey (Warw.) and manor, 6371
Wroxeter (Salop), 2070, 4861
Wulf, Maurice M. C. J. de: Histoire de la philosophie, 1410, 6899; Philosophy and civilization, 1410
Wulfric of Haselbury, 6682
Wulfstan, archbishop (d. 1023), 301; 1347, 1493, 2315, 2352, 2709, 6784, 7225
— bishop of Worcester (d. 1095), 2316–17, 5843
— cantor of Winchester: St. Swithun, 2312
Wülker, Richard P.: Bibliotheca A.-S. poesie, 2325; Bibliotheca A.-S. prosa, 2286; Codex Vercelli, 2340; Vocabularies, 315
Wulsin of Sherborne, 2317
Wurgaft, Lewis D.: Bibliography, 246
Wyatt, Alfred J.: Beowulf, 2336
— Edward G. P.: Walter Frere's Papers, 1333
Wyclif, John, 873–5; 1428, 1448, 1482, 4157, 4165, 6612, 6632, 6691, 6864, 6871–2
Wydevilles, 4216. See Woodville
Wye (Kent), 4786
Wyffels, Carlos: De Vlaamse Hanze, 5427
Wyggeston, William, Hospital of, 6209
Wyke (Dorset), 4736
Wyke, John de: Liber Albus, of Worcester, 5832
Wykeham, William of, bishop, 5819, 5822, 7132, 7135
Wykes (Essex), customal, 4741
— (Suffolk), 4823
Wykes, Thomas: Chronicon, 1114, 2983
Wylie, James H.: Agincourt Chaplain, 2877; Agincourt roll, 4297; Henry IV, 4235; Henry V, 4236; Vita Henrici V, 2972
Wyntoun, Andrew of, Orygynale cronykel, 2984
Wyon, Alfred B.: Seals, 469
— Allan: Seals, 469

Yamey, Basil S.: History of accounting, 4630
Yardley, Edward: Menevia Sacra, 5580 (1)
Yarmouth (Great) (Norfolk), 5214
Yates, Richard: St. Edmunds Bury, 5257
Yatton (Som.), 6838
Year, beginning of the, 1487
Year books, 545–8; 1233, 1246, 1501, 3677
Year's Work in English Studies, 276
— in Modern Language Studies, 269
Yeatman, John Pym: Arundel genealogy, 4597; Feudal history of Derby, 1601, 4350; Records of Chesterfield, 5052
Yeavering (Northumberland), 358
Yellow Book of Lecan, 2395
Yeovil (Som.), 4865, 6838
Yields of farms, 5815
Yonge, Charles D.: Flowers of history, 2871
— Charlotte M.: Christian names, 591
York Anonymous, 6427, 6785
— Archbishops and cathedral, 787–90; 813, 1487, 2157, 2295, 4934, 5302, 5305, 5615, 5749, 5862, 5866, 6395, 6783, 6790; Archiepiscopal registers, 4562, 5686, 5858, 5872, 5875, 6395, 6401, 6415; Historians of church, 1130, 2289, 5851; Lists of clergy, 5864, 5876, 6856. *See* names of individual archbishops
— archives, 1873
— City of, 2787; history of, Roman, 2045, 2067, 2075; Anglo-Saxon, 2295, 2445, 2591; Post Conquest, 1529, 3205, 4563, 5300–11, 5505, 5532, 5749, 7223
— Chapel of Holy Angels, 5873
— Corpus Christi gild, 5307
— Exchequer at, 1458
— Holy Trinity, 6423
— Jews, 3950
— Mercers' company, 5303
— St. Mary's abbey, 2787, 6424
— St. Peter's church, 5865
— St. Peter's (St. Leonard's) hospital, 6425
— plays, 7210
— psalter, 898
— statute of (1322), 3343, 3366, 4141
York, Margaret of, 4251
— Thomas of (Franciscan), 6910
Yorke, Alexander C.: Antonine iter, 2029
Yorkist age, 612–15; 3300, 5451, 5456
Yorkshire: Antiquities, 762, 2069; Bibliography, 1868–72, 4497; Charters, 4496–501, 4503, 5288, 6364, 6399–401, 6403–5, 6407, 6409, 6412–13, 6415–18, 6421–2, 6425; Church, 1529, 1893–4, 2168; County history, 579, 1450, 1468, 1517, 1529, 1889–94, 6668; County journals and societies, 1873–88, 2069;

Deeds, 4433, 4495, 4502, 4504, 4937; Domesday, 1529, 3036–8; Extents, 4503, 4930, 4933–4, 4938, 6410; Eyres, 3632; Farming, 4989, 5020; Feet of fines, 3629, 3631, 3634; Feudal tenures, 4396, 4794; Forest, 3630; Inquests, **490**; 1482, 4395–7, 4503; Justices of peace, 3635; Manors and villages, 4930–43; Medieval historical writing, **387**; 6668; Parliament, 3474–5; Pedigrees, families, 561, 563; Personal names, 579; Pleas, 3628, 3632–3, 4503, 6392; Religious houses, 5904, 5936, 5938, 5948, 6387–425; Subsidy rolls, 3203, 3205–8; Surveys, 2221; Taxation, 3202, 3203A–3205; Topography, 1529, 5305; Urban history, 1529, 3203–4, 5288–311; Wills, 4516, 4562–7

Young, Charles G.: Grey *v.* Hastings, 3503A; Liberate rolls, 3105, 3774; Registrum, 6282, 6334
— Charles R.: Borough and royal administration, 5359; Hubert Walter, 5643
— Douglas: Roman Scotland, 2088
— Douglas C. C.: Wilfrid, 2313
— Ernest: Family Law, 2612
— Jean I.: Latin Genesis, 1433; Norse in Ireland, 2605; Schutte's Vor folkergruppe gottjod, 2520
— John: Hunterian Museum, 1065
— Karl: Drama of church, 6998; Instructions, 6696
— Patrick: Lichfield catalogue, 1047; Worcester catalogue, 1052
— William: Dulwich College, 4894
Ystorya brenhined, 2166
Yunck, John A.: Economic conservatism, 6779
Yver, Jean: Le bref anglo-normand, 3503

Zachrisson, Robert E.: Place-names, 638; Roman, Kelts, 2562; Schutte's Vor folkergruppe, gottjod, 2520
Zacour, Norman P.: Talleyrand, cardinal, 6772
Zane, John M.: Bench and bar, 1246
Zangemeister, Carl Fr. W.: Orosius, 2025
Zarnecki, George: Romanesque sculpture, 855
Zeitschrift für keltische Philologie und Volksforschung, 326
Zeitschrift der Savigny-Stiftung für Rechtsgeschichte: Kanonistische Abteilung, **168**
Zellfelder, August: Das Basler Konzil, 5573
Zellinger, Johannes: Anselm's Liber monologion, 6526
Zeumer, Karl: M.G.H. indices, 1114
Zeuner, Friedrich E.: Dating the past, 751
Zeuss, Johann Kaspar: Grammatica Celtica, 327
Ziegler, Philip: Black death, 5486
Zimmer, Heinrich: Celtic church, 2684; Nennius, 2167
Zimmermann, Benedictus: Epistolae Waldensis, 6611; Monumenta Carmelitana, 5976
— (Benedikt) Ernst Heinrich, Miniatures, 453
— Heinrich: Die päpstliche Legation, 6749
Zinkeisen, Frank: A.-S. courts, 2624
Zosimus, 2025, 2112
Zouche, William, archbishop, 1455
Zulueta, Francis de: Vacarius's Liber pauperum, 3004; Vinogradoff's Roman law, 1247
Zupitza, Julius: Ælfric's Grammatik, 2292; Beowulf, 2331; Fragment, 2142
Zupko, Ronald E.: Weights and measures, 5498
Zvavich, Isaak S.: Manorial justice, 4971